D1482242

The

Population

of the

United

States

STUDIES IN POPULATION DISTRIBUTION

(Numbers 1 through 13 published by Scripps Foundation, Oxford, Ohio)

Number 1. An Exploratory Study of Migration and Labor Mobility Using Social Security Data, by Donald J. Bogue, 1950. Pp. 14. (Supply exhausted.)

Number 2. Metropolitan Decentralization: A Study of Differential Growth, by Donald J. Bogue, 1950. Pp. 17. (Supply exhausted.)

Number 3. Migration Within Ohio, 1935-40: A Study in the Re-Distribution of Population, by Warren S. Thompson, 1951. Pp. ix + 227. $2.00.

Number 4. A Methodological Study of Migration and Labor Mobility in Michigan and Ohio in 1947, by Donald J. Bogue, 1952. Pp. vi + 100. $1.00.

Number 5. Subregional Migration in the United States, 1935-40, Volume I, Streams of Migration, by Donald J. Bogue, Henry S. Shryock, Jr., and Siegfried A. Hoermann, 1957. Pp. vi + 333. $5.25.

Number 6. Subregional Migration in the United States, 1935-40, Volume II, Differential Migration in the Corn and Cotton Belts, by Donald J. Bogue and Margaret Jarman Hagood, 1953. Pp. vi + 248. $2.25.

Number 7. Needed Urban and Metropolitan Research, edited by Donald J. Bogue, 1953. Pp. x + 88. $1.25. (Supply exhausted.)

Number 8. Comparative Population and Urban Research Via Multiple Regression and Covariance Analysis, by Donald J. Bogue and Dorothy L. Harris, 1954. Pp. vii+75. $0.90. (Supply exhausted.)

Number 9. Suburbanization of Manufacturing Activity Within Standard Metropolitan Areas, by Evelyn M. Kitagawa and Donald J. Bogue, 1955. Pp. vi + 162. $1.80. (Supply exhausted.)

Number 10. Suburbanization of Service Industries Within Standard Metropolitan Areas, by Raymond P. Cuzzort, 1955. $1.05. (Supply exhausted.)

Number 11. Metropolitan Growth and the Conversion of Land to Nonagricultural Uses, by Donald J. Bogue. Pp. 33. $0.60.

Number 12. Components of Population Change in Standard Metropolitan Areas, by Donald J. Bogue, 1957. Pp. v + 145. $3.75.

Number 13. Applications of Demography; The Population Situation in the U. S. in 1975, edited by Donald J. Bogue, 1957. Pp. vi + 96. $2.10.

Number 14. The Population of the United States, by Donald J. Bogue, 1959. Pp. xix + 873. $17.50.

The
Population
of the
United States

By DONALD J. BOGUE

Professor of Sociology, The University of Chicago
and Associate Director, Scripps Foundation, Miami University (Ohio)

WITH A SPECIAL CHAPTER ON FERTILITY
By WILSON H. GRABILL
Bureau of the Census

The Free Press of Glencoe, Illinois

WITHDRAWN

LAMBUTH COLLEGE LIBRARY
JACKSON, TENNESSEE

27271

Copyright © 1959 by The Free Press, a corporation

Printed in the United States of America

Library of Congress Card No. 59-12184

LITHOGRAPHED FOR THE PUBLISHERS BY
NOBLE OFFSET PRINTERS, INC., NEW YORK

HB3505
. B62

Preface

It has often been said that researchers become so engrossed in their field of study as to consider it critically important for the whole world to learn what they have learned. The author of this book is no exception. He is unable to comprehend how economists, businessmen, world statesmen, and many others who are experts in varied fields related to our economy and society can make decisions, analyze changes, or interpret happenings that interest them without knowing more than the bare outlines of population events and changes. Even the social psychologist and the psychiatrist (reported to be the least interested in demography) respect the categories of sex, age, marital status, occupation, etc., as being significant differentiators of their subject matter and, therefore, should know how these traits are distributed among the nation and how they are changing. Moreover, an exciting and dramatic "population story" is being enacted daily; this story has such multitudinous implications for our lives only a few short years from now that even the average intelligent lay reader should find it at least as entertaining as much of today's TV drama.

This book is a product of the belief that a considerable number of people need and want, within the covers of a single book, a comprehensive statement of population events, together with an explanation of how and why they are taking place. Although such a book should not be over-simplified by the omission of fundamental information, it should spare the interested but statistically untrained reader elaborate explanations of many technical details that have little effect on his understanding of the results.

Eleven years ago the writer set out to write such a book. The intention was to up-date and expand Warren S. Thompson's and P. K. Whelpton's classic work, Population Trends in the United States. A major goal was to place greater emphasis on population distribution--to point out the great population diversity between regions, between urban and rural areas, and between metropolitan and nonmetropolitan areas, and to explain this diversity. On the premise that previous treatises on population written for the general reader were strong on description and lacked sufficient explanation, a series of researches were launched into the lesser-known and uninterpreted "Detailed Characteristics" and "Special Reports" publications of the U. S. Census Bureau, and into the reports of other agencies that generate population statistics. Years have passed, and the original ambition to interpret the 1950 census in terms of historical and recent events lost its freshness. Gradually, it gave way to the more audacious idea of analyzing and interpreting the results of the 1960 census before it was taken, linking the changes of the 1950 to 1960 decade with the results of the intensive and varied research studies being made of the materials from the 1950 and earlier censuses. The population story for the 1950 to 1960 decade was extracted from the many Current Population Reports, based upon the results of sample surveys and estimates, published by the Bureau of the Census, as well as numerous other researches and surveys made by other organizations. Hence, this book has two major objectives: (1) to describe and interpret the population changes of the 1950 to 1960 decade, insofar as it

iii

is possible to do so in advance of the 1960 census, and (2) to summarize available population knowledge about recent changes and historical trends in each of the leading fields of population analysis, synthesizing the work of others with the special researches carried out as a part of this project. The materials have been organized according to the outline followed by the writer teaching a course, with this same title, at the University of Chicago.

Unfortunately, the American population story is of epic proportions. It became necessary at times to compromise between devoting space to writing and using space to present important analytical tables. Hence, much of the information that is packed into the statistical tables receives only passing notice in the comments. For fullest benefit, the reader should study the tables as well as read the text.

The book is intended primarily for reference use, and has been written and indexed with this in mind. Such a plan makes for some unavoidable repetition between chapters, or even between different sections of the same chapter. The reader who undertakes to read it through systematically should skip or only skim very rapidly Chapters 2 through 5, unless he is especially interested in the topic of population distribution.

So many different people have assisted in this project that, for the sake of honesty as well as gratitude, lengthy acknowledgements are made in a separate statement.

I would like to dedicate this effort to the four professors who taught me demography and research methods: E. B. Reuter, Amos H. Hawley, R. Clark Tibbitts, and Warren S. Thompson, named in the chronological order of their influence.

Chicago, Illinois   Donald J. Bogue
March 25, 1959

Acknowledgements

This study was carried out as a part of a program of research in population distribution under a grant from the Rockefeller Foundation. It has been sponsored jointly by the Scripps Foundation, Miami University, and the Population Research and Training Center, the University of Chicago. The generosity of the Rockefeller Foundation in contributing the major portion of funds for the study, and of the Social Science Division of the University of Chicago for a supplementary grant are gratefully acknowledged.

The index to this volume does not carry an entry for the U. S. Bureau of the Census or for the National Office of Vital Statistics. The reason, of course, is that the entire volume has been constructed of materials provided by these two great statistical institutions, and one or both ought to be footnoted on almost every page. Thanks are due to Robert W. Burgess, Director of the Bureau of the Census and to Halbert W. Dunn, Chief of the National Office of Vital Statistics, and to their professional staffs, who for several years have patiently answered inquiries about materials contained in their reports. The insight and foresight of these experts led them to make special tabulations, equalled by no other nation in the world, which often spelled the difference between ambiguous and unambiguous conclusions concerning particular questions.

Margaret Martin (Office of Statistical Standards, Bureau of the Budget); Wayne Daugherty, Chief of the Housing Division; David Kaplan, Chief of Occupational Statistics; Paul C. Glick, Chief of Social Statistics (Bureau of the Census), and Hugh Carter (National Office of Vital Statistics) gave direct help in preparing the chapters on labor force, housing, occupation, and marriage, respectively. Chapter 23 on religious affiliation owes its wide scope entirely to the generous help of Jacob J. Feldman, of the National Opinion Research Center, in preparing special tabulations of NORC materials on the socio-economic characteristics of vari-religious groups.

My greatest professional indebtedness, however, is owed Wilson Grabill, Chief of Fertility Statistics, Bureau of the Census, for kindly consenting to contribute his chapter.

Responsibility for supervising the assembly of data and making computations was borne by a most competent group of research assistants, some of whom are members of the Scripps Foundation staff and some were advanced graduate students at the University of Chicago. To their initiative, perseverence, and skills must go the full credit for overseeing the operation of distilling mountains of statistics into a more succinct form that would show fundamental changes and trends. Gracie Van Winkle, Elizabeth Bogue, Dorothy Harris, Charlotte Ellis, Jane Schusky, Alma Ficks, and Alma Kuby supervised one or more phases of this statistical work. In addition K. N. Mitra, O. C. Francis, Jane Hartley, Melvin Bloom, and David Lewis carried major responsibilities for making computations. Jeannette Lewis edited the manuscript and greatly improved its readability and clarity. Annice Cottrell and Nettie Ulreich were in charge of the preparation of the book for litho-printing. Mrs. Cottrell typed the manuscript in its various drafts and prepared the final textual materials. Mrs. Ulreich typed statistical tables, composed the pages, and supervised the final steps in preparing copy. Virginia Buckley and Irene Schreyer typed tables and assisted in copy preparation. Elizabeth Switzer prepared all but a few of the maps and charts.

Several generations of students, both upperclassmen at Miami University and graduate students at the University of Chicago, were employed as part-time statistical clerks, typists, or research assistants for this study. Making computations for this project was a part of the Sociology Department's "on the job" research training program at the University of Chicago for three years. The following listing of students' names, in alphabetical order, is a most inadequate way of acknowledging the very large amounts of efforts many of them contributed, and fails almost completely to express the sincere thanks that are felt for their labors in furthering this project.

Theodore Anderson
Aline Andraud
Thomas Aquaviva
James Atwood
David Barr
Annie O. Blair
Mary C. Booth
Mary Botsford
Virginia Buckley
Betty Caldwell
Pongsun Choi
Maria Cohn
Levy Cruz
Ray Cuzzort
S. Del Campo
Charlotte Ellis
Meredith Farmer
Alma Kuby
Lydia Kulchyka
Jean Lawson
Stanley Lieberson
Sue Lorentzen
Shirley Lucas
Lillian Manwell
Prakish Mathur
Julia Matlaw
Ismail Maung
Carol Mertz
Fred Mosher
Ann E. Morton
Dorothy Ombres
Robert Potter
Doris Portner
Inge Powell

Alma Ficks
Ruth Foss
Sarah Fry
Anne Galey
Jeane Geiger
Constantina Gioka
Peggy Glover
Sibyl Hale
Mary Ann Harris
Sultan Hashmi
Nancy Jamison
Carolyn Jeffries
M. S. Jillani
Nathan Kantrowitz
Howard Kaufman
James Kenney
Mella Kessler
Nancy Kirker
Ferdinand Kolegar
Shigemi Kono
Dorothy Pownall
Rosemary Preissler
Margaret Preston
Wallace Reed
Carol Ryne
Marie Rohrer
Emerson Seim
David Stottlemyer
Irene Schreyer
Donald Stansinic
Sue Stickel
Gail Switzer
Mary J. Tunnell
Tomoio Ueda
Richard Weber
Jane Weiler
Agnes Whittington
S. Winsborough
Melvin Zelnick

.An apology should be made to all who have recently analyzed some aspect of United States population for not footnoting and indexing their work. Reference is made almost exclusively to authors who were producers of primary data. A comprehensive bibliography of books and articles was planned for the end of each chapter, but the project had to be abandoned because the bibliographies alone, dealing with 26 very large topics, would have become a book.

If this work should happen to achieve its ambition to help general readers obtain a deeper insight into population developments, in the United States, it will be due largely to the availability of adequate financial resources, to the work of a first-rate research and publications staff, to a job that allows time for research, and to generous aid by fellow demographers.

CONTENTS

PART I

x

xv

Chapter 1

THE SIZE AND GROWTH OF THE UNITED STATES POPULATION

THE SIZE OF THE UNITED STATES POPULATION

It is estimated that, as of July 1, 1960, the population residing in the United States will be about 180 million persons.[1] It has been growing at the rate of 3.1 million persons (1.8 percent) per year. These figures represent a comparatively small share of the earth's inhabitants and of the earth's population growth. Only about 6.1 percent (one-sixteenth) of the world's people live in the United States (Table 1-1). In relation to the area of the world, the area of the United States is even smaller than its population; the United States comprises 5.8 percent of the land area of the world. Although it is the largest nation in the Western Hemisphere, it contains less than half (45 percent) of the population of North, Central, and South America combined, and less than one-fifth of their combined land area.

Three nations--China, India, and the U.S.S.R.-- have populations which are larger than that of the United States: India's by more than 2 1/4 times, China's by about 3 1/4 times, and Russia's by slightly less than one-third.[2] (See Table 1-2 and Figure 1-1 for statistics concerning the present size of the largest nations of the world.) Together, these four largest nations contain almost exactly one-half of the estimated number of people in the world. The estimated population of the major continents and regions of the world, for selected dates from 1920 to 1956, are reported in Table 1-1.

Table 1-2 gives the estimated population in 1956 of the 37 nations which have 10 million or more inhabitants, ranked in order of size.[3] As a supplement to this table, Figure 1-1 illustrates the size of the population of the United States in comparison with the populations of other nations and of the world. Three nations--Japan, Indonesia, and Pakistan--are roughly one-half as large as the

---

[1] Several times each year the Bureau of the Census issues a report entitled "Provisional Estimates of the Population of the United States." These estimates are highly accurate (within a small fraction of one percent). They appear in a publication called Current Population Reports; Population Estimates, Series P-25. Annual estimates of the sex, age, and color composition of the current national population, and estimates as to the size of the current population of states and regions also appear in this series. Each report costs 10 cents. By obtaining the most recent copy, either directly from the Census or from his library, the reader can supplement the materials in this chapter and gain an "up-to-the-minute" picture of present population size and recent growth.

[2] These comparisons are only approximate, for precise data concerning the size of the Chinese and Russian populations are not available. A recent census was taken in China, but the accuracy of the published results is still in doubt. There has not been a census in Russia since 1939, and until the results of the census which the U.S.S.R. plans to take in 1959 are available, reliance must be placed upon estimates.

[3] The United Nations, through its annual publication Demographic Yearbook, and its quarterly publication Population and Vital Statistics Reports, Series E, (both prepared in the Statistical Office of the United Nations) has become an invaluable source of information about world population trends. The U. S. Bureau of the Census, which maintains a research unit in international demography, published a series entitled International Population Reports, Series P-91, which reports estimates of past, present, and future populations of nations for which even crude data are available. By consulting the most recent issues of these publications, the reader can quickly bring up to date the materials concerning the populations of other nations which are presented in this volume.

Table 1-1.—ESTIMATED POPULATION, AREA, AND DENSITY OF THE WORLD BY CONTINENTS AND REGIONS: 1920 TO 1956

| Continent and region | Estimates of midyear populations (millions) | | | | | | Land area (million square miles) | Percent distribution | | Population per square mile 1954 | Population percent change 1920 to 1954 |
	1956	1954	1950	1940	1930	1920		Population 1954	Land area		
WORLD TOTAL...............	2,734	2,652	2,504	2,250	2,013	1,810	52.19	100.0	100.0	51	46.5
UNITED STATES............	168	162	152	132	123	106	3.02	6.1	5.8	54	52.8
AFRICA........................	220	210	198	172	155	140	11.69	7.9	22.4	18	50.0
Northern Africa............	72	68	65	57	51	46	3.95	2.6	7.6	17	47.8
Tropical and Southern Africa.	148	142	134	115	104	94	7.75	5.4	14.8	18	51.1
AMERICA......................	374	357	330	277	244	208	16.25	13.5	31.1	22	71.6
North America..............	186	179	168	146	135	117	8.29	6.7	15.9	22	53.0
Central America............	60	56	51	41	34	30	1.06	2.1	2.0	53	86.7
South America.............	129	122	111	90	75	61	6.89	4.6	13.2	18	100.0
ASIA..........................	1,512	1,451	1,368	1,213	1,073	967	10.44	54.7	20.0	139	50.1
South West Asia............	73	67	62	54	48	44	2.14	2.5	4.1	313	52.3
South Central Asia..........	506	489	466	410	362	326	1.99	18.4	3.8	246	50.0
South East Asia............	190	183	171	155	128	110	1.73	6.9	3.3	106	66.4
East Asia....................	745	712	670	594	535	487	4.58	26.8	8.8	155	46.2
EUROPE........................	412	404	393	380	355	328	1.90	15.2	3.6	213	23.2
Northern and Western Europe..	138	136	133	128	122	115	0.87	5.1	1.7	156	18.3
Central Europe..............	135	132	128	127	120	112	0.39	5.0	0.7	338	17.9
Southern Europe............	139	136	131	125	113	101	0.64	5.1	1.2	212	34.7
OCEANIA.......................	15.1	14.4	13.0	11.3	10.4	8.8	3.30	0.5	6.3	4	63.6
U.S.S.R.......................	...	214	202	196	176	158	8.60	8.1	16.5	25	35.4

Source: United Nations Demographic Yearbook, 1955, Table 2 and 1957, Table A; United Nations Population and Vital Statistics Reports, Series A, Vol. IX, No. 4.

Note: Each of these estimates is subject to a considerable range of error, and should be considered as an approximation. See technical notes in the sources.

United States, and four others--Germany, Brazil, the United Kingdom, and Italy--are about one-third as large. Together, the 37 largest nations listed in Table 1-2 contain 89 percent of the world's population. This means that only 11 percent (one-ninth) of the world's people live in the several hundred small nations, trust territories, possessions, and protectorates that have populations of less than 10 million.

The density of settlement (population per square mile) in the United States--60 per square mile in 1960--is slightly higher than the world average. However, the United States is less densely settled than the other 10 largest nations, with the exception of the U.S.S.R. and Brazil. Because of adverse climatic and topographic conditions and lack of resources, much of the world's land is virtually uninhabited; densities computed in terms of total land area, therefore, are only very crude measures of the relation of population to natural resources.[4] In terms of population per square mile of arable land (even crudely defined), the United

[4]Also, the degree of technological development is a factor in determining the extent to which high or low population density connotes great economic hardship or a high level of living. A better measure of a nation's ability to support its people would be the ratio of population to an index comprised of a weighted average of the total volume of farm products, the volume of manufactured goods, and the volume of personal, business, and professional services. As a measure of the extent to which a nation has the physical resources to feed its people, the ratio of population to a weighted average of cropland and pastureland (with each type of land weighted according to its average comparative food-providing capacity) would be superior to the crude density per square mile.

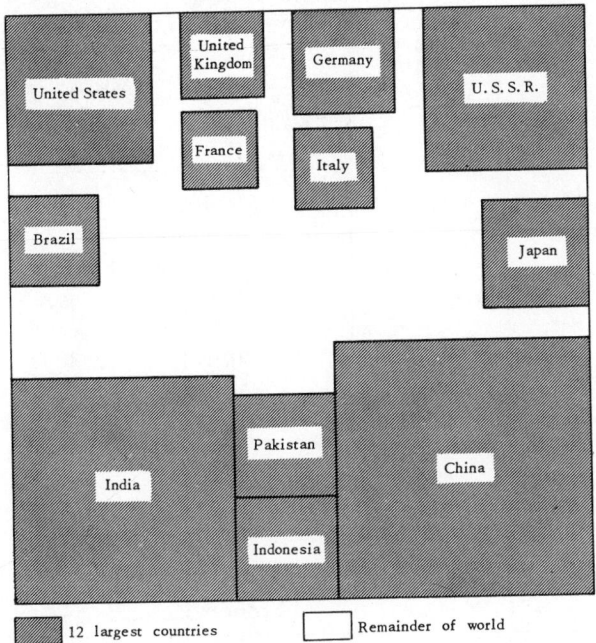

▨ 12 largest countries   ☐ Remainder of world

FIGURE 1 - 1. THE UNITED STATES IN WORLD
POPULATION : 1950

Table 1-2.—ESTIMATED POPULATION, LAND AREA AND
DENSITY OF MAJOR NATIONS OF THE WORLD,
RANKED IN ORDER OF SIZE: 1956

Nation	Population (millions)	Area (000 sq. miles)	Population (per sq. mile)
1. China.............	621.2	3,745	166
2. India.............	387.4	1,270	305
3. U.S.S.R...........	214.5	8,598	25
4. United States.....	168.2	3,022	56
5. Japan.............	90.0	143	629
6. Indonesia.........	84.0	576	146
7. Pakistan..........	83.6	364	230
8. Germany...........	70.7	137	516
9. Brazil............	59.8	3,287	18
10. United Kingdom....	51.4	94	547
11. Italy.............	48.3	116	416
12. France............	43.6	213	205
13. Nigeria...........	31.8	339	94
14. Korea.............	31.4	85	369
15. Mexico............	30.5	760	40
16. Spain.............	29.2	194	151
17. Poland............	27.8	120	232
18. Viet-Nam..........	26.6	127	209
19. Turkey............	24.8	300	83
20. Egypt.............	23.5	386	61
21. Philippines.......	22.3	116	192
22. Thailand..........	20.7	198	105
23. Ethiopia..........	20.0	409	49
24. Burma.............	19.9	262	76
25. Argentina.........	19.5	1,084	18
26. French W. Africa..	18.9	1,835	10
27. Iran..............	18.9	629	30
28. Yugoslavia........	17.9	99	181
29. Romania...........	17.6	92	191
30. Canada............	16.1	3,846	4
31. Union of S. Africa	13.9	472	29
32. Czechoslavakia....	13.2	49	269
33. Afghanistan.......	13.0	251	52
34. Colombia..........	12.9	440	29
35. Belgian Congo.....	12.8	905	14
36. Netherlands.......	10.9	13	838
37. Sudan.............	10.3	965	11

Source: United Nations Demographic Yearbook, 1957.

States has a very low population density in comparison with most of the world, and its food producing capacity in relation to its population size is extremely favorable at the present time.

Despite their limited usefulness, population densities are reported in Tables 1-1 and 1-2 for each continent and world region, and for each of the 37 largest nations. These tables also note, in terms of square miles, the estimated land area of each continent, region, and country.

RECENT GROWTH OF THE U. S. POPULATION

Between the census taken April 1, 1940 and the census taken exactly 10 years later in 1950, the population increased by 19.0 million persons (Table 1-3). This was the largest numerical increase to take place during any one decade in the nation's history. It represented an increase of 14.5 percent over the 131.7 million inhabitants of 1940.

But the population growth in the 1950 to 1960 decade has been even greater; the estimated population of 180 million persons for July 1, 1960, cited above, implies an intercensal growth of 29 million persons, which is more than 50 percent greater than the record gain between 1940 and 1950. Moreover, the rate of growth has been higher between 1950 and 1960 than during the preceding decade. The 1950 to 1960 percent increase is about 19 percent, which is more than 30 percent higher than the growth rate between 1940 and 1950.

In comparison with the rates of growth that were typical of the nation between 1790 and 1890, these

Table 1-3.—POPULATION, POPULATION INCREASE, LAND AREA, AND POPULATION DENSITY
CONTINENTAL UNITED STATES: 1790 TO 1950

Census date	Population (thousands)	Increase over preceding census		Land area (thousand square miles)	Population per square mile
		Number (thousands)	Percent		
1950 (April 1)................	150,697	19,028	14.5	2,975	50.7
1940 (April 1)................	131,669	8,894	7.2	2,977	44.2
1930 (April 1)................	122,775	17,064	16.1	2,977	41.2
1920 (January 1)..............	105,711	13,738	14.9	2,974	35.5
1910 (April 15)...............	91,972	15,978	21.0	2,974	30.9
1900 (June 1).................	75,995	13,047	20.7	2,974	25.6
1890 (June 1).................	62,948	12,792	25.5	2,974	21.2
1880 (June 1).................	50,156	11,597	30.1	2,974	16.9
1870 (June 1).................	38,558	7,115	22.6	2,974	13.0
1860 (June 1).................	31,443	8,251	35.6	2,974	10.6
1850 (June 1).................	23,192	6,122	35.9	2,944	7.9
1840 (June 1).................	17,069	4,203	32.7	1,754	9.7
1830 (June 1).................	12,866	3,228	33.5	1,754	7.3
1820 (August 7)..............	9,638	2,399	33.1	1,754	5.5
1810 (August 6)..............	7,240	1,931	36.4	1,686	4.3
1800 (August 4)..............	5,308	1,379	35.1	868	6.1
1790 (August 2)..............	3,929	...	...	868	4.5

Source: U.S. Bureau of the Census, 1950 Census of Population, Vol. I, U.S. Summary, Table 2.

rates of growth (between 1940 to 1950 and 1950 to 1960) are not extraordinarily high. In fact, the 1940 to 1950 percentage change represented a slower rate of growth than had been exhibited previously during any decade except one--the 1930 to 1940 depression decade, during which the low was 7. 2 percent. (See Table 1-3 and "History of Population Growth in the U. S.," below.) The 1950 to 1960 decade is witnessing an intercensal numerical increase that far outstrips that of any numerical increase during any previous decade, and a rate of growth that has not been exceeded since the 1900 to 1910 decade.

A convenient way to summarize recent population growth is to say that the number of new inhabitants added between 1950 and 1960 was almost exactly equal to the total population growth in the United States from 1790 until 1863. The population increase between 1940 and 1960 is equal to 80 percent of the nation's total population gain during its first century.

Because of World War II, the postwar occupation, and the need for military preparedness, all of which necessitated the sending of many men overseas, there is no single best way to define the total population of the United States. The way in which the population is defined, however, affects the statistics of growth. For most purposes the population living within the continental limits, including military personnel stationed there, is satisfactory; this is the definition which was used in the preceding paragraphs and it is the official census count. For some other purposes, however, it is well to define the total population as including armed forces overseas. Overseas military forces are a part of the nation's economy and of its manpower, and many statistical computations require that they be included. In still other instances it may be preferable to deal with the civilian population only. Estimates of each of these three types of population have been made by the Census Bureau for each six months of the 1940 to 1950 decade and for the years 1950 to 1958, as reported in Tables 1-4 and 1-5. The understanding of recent population changes requires a clear picture of the fluctuating size of the military population.

At the peak of mobilization in mid-1945 there were about 12. 4 million in the armed forces, and almost 7. 5 million of these were overseas. At this time the civilian population was considerably

Table 1-4.—ESTIMATES OF THE TOTAL POPULATION OF THE UNITED STATES AND OF POPULATION IN THE ARMED FORCES AT 6-MONTH INTERVALS: 1940 TO 1950

(Figures in thousands)

Date	Total population including armed forces overseas[1]	Total population residing in the United States[2]	Civilian population[3]	Population in the armed forces	
				Total	Overseas
April 1, 1940......................	131,820	131,669	131,391	429	151
July 1, 1940......................	132,122	131,954	131,658	464	168
January 1, 1941....................	132,794	132,571	131,899	895	223
July 1, 1941......................	133,402	133,121	131,595	1,807	281
January 1, 1942....................	134,161	133,756	132,000	2,161	405
July 1, 1942......................	134,860	133,920	130,942	3,918	940
January 1, 1943....................	135,865	134,244	128,803	7,062	1,621
July 1, 1943......................	136,739	134,245	127,499	9,240	2,494
January 1, 1944....................	137,656	133,872	127,166	10,490	3,784
July 1, 1944......................	138,397	132,885	126,708	11,689	5,512
January 1, 1945....................	139,237	132,175	127,227	12,010	7,062
July 1, 1945......................	139,928	132,481	127,573	12,355	7,447
January 1, 1946....................	140,689	137,227	133,782	6,907	3,462
July 1, 1946......................	141,389	140,054	138,385	3,004	1,335
January 1, 1947....................	142,833	141,982	140,930	1,903	851
July 1, 1947......................	144,126	143,446	142,566	1,560	680
January 1, 1948....................	145,471	144,918	144,052	1,419	553
July 1, 1948......................	146,631	146,093	145,168	1,463	538
January 1, 1949....................	148,001	147,442	146,357	1,644	559
July 1, 1949......................	149,188	148,665	147,578	1,610	523
January 1, 1950....................	150,552	150,085	148,980	1,572	467
April 1, 1950......................	151,132	150,697	149,634	1,498	435

[1]Census count plus estimate of armed forces overseas, including those stationed in the territories and possessions.

[2]Census count.

[3]Census count minus estimate of armed forces in continental United States.

Source: U.S. Bureau of the Census, Current Population Reports, Series P-25, No. 71, April 1, 1953.

smaller than it had been in 1940. Even including armed forces, the total population residing in the United States had grown only slightly since the beginning of the decade. (Figure 1-2.) Only after demobilization began, in late 1945, did the total resident population start to grow. During the twelve months from July 1, 1945 to July 1, 1946, 7.6 million were added to the resident population, and 10.8 million were added to the civilian population. Because of this combination of events, growth was not spread evenly during the decade. One-half of the total increase to the resident population was added during the 18 months from July 1, 1945 to January 1, 1947. Housing and many other items of civilian consumption, the production of which had been drastically curtailed by the war, became acutely scarce when the equivalent of half a decade's growth suddenly descended on communities all over the nation. Figure 1-3 provides a clear picture of how the civilian population grew during these years.

At the time of the 1950 census the demobilization which followed World War II had been completed, and the Korean War had not yet begun. The armed forces overseas had shrunk to a little less than half a million; this was still 284,000 more than had been overseas in 1940, however, which means that the growth of the total population residing in the United States was smaller by about 284,000 than it would have been if the total popu-

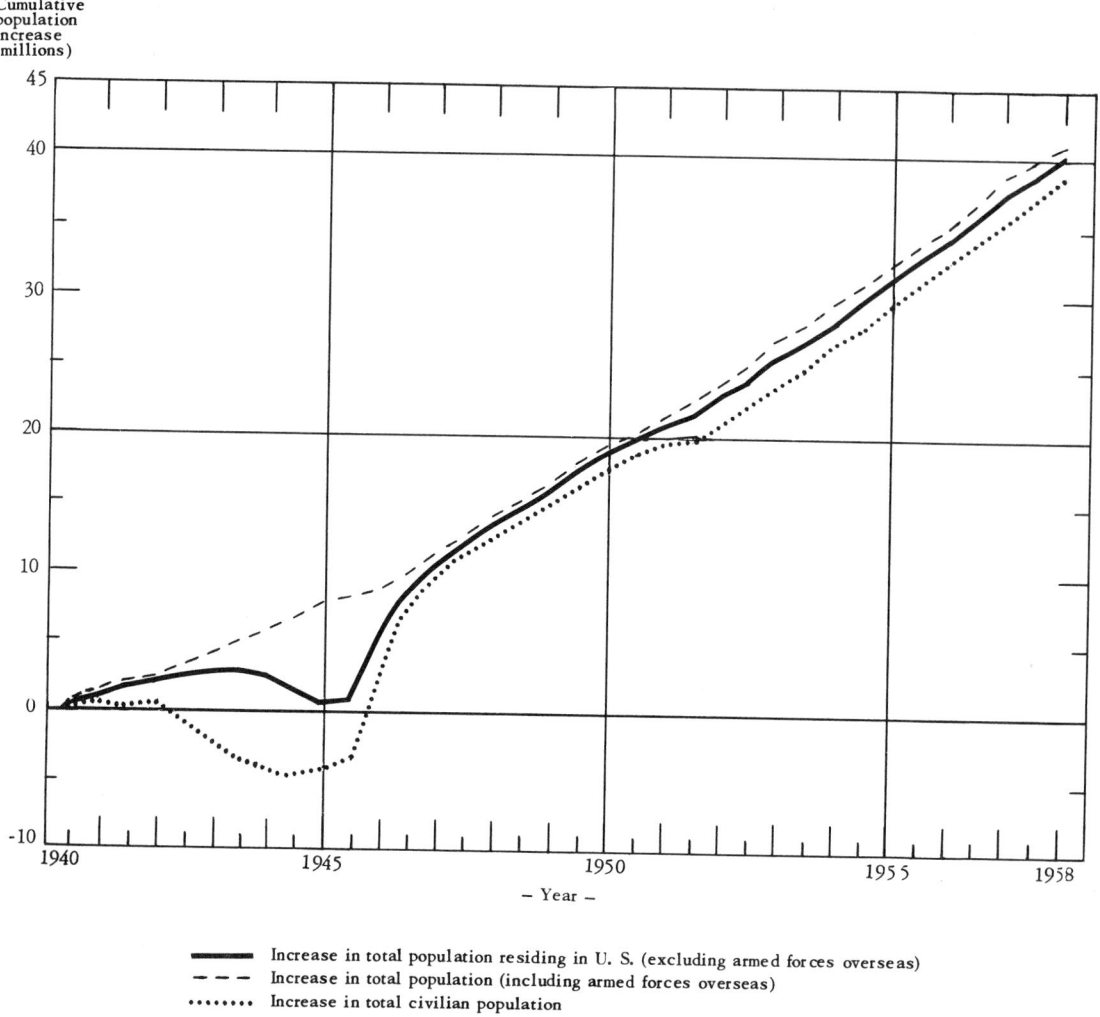

FIGURE 1-2. CUMULATIVE INCREASE IN THE POPULATION OF THE UNITED STATES, BY SIX
MONTH INTERVALS: 1940 TO 1958

lation had been defined as including armed forces overseas. This problem does not greatly affect the over-all rate of growth, although it has a substantial effect on selected age groups. If overseas forces were included in both 1940 and 1950, the percent increase for the decade would be 14.7 instead of 14.5.

Demobilization after World War II decreased the armed forces to 1.4 million (January, 1948). The outbreak of hostilities in Korea caused the nation to start remobilizing in the last half of 1950. Table 1-5, which provides data for the 1950

to 1958 period corresponding to that in Table 1-4, shows that the size of the military forces doubled in the 12 months between July, 1950 and July, 1951. The strength of the armed forces reached its peak about July, 1952, with a total of 4,662,000 persons in military service and 1,267,000 stationed overseas. At the height of the Korean conflict the armed forces were about 40 percent as large as they had been at the time of maximum mobilization for World War II, but the number overseas never exceeded 18 percent of the peak number who were overseas during 1945. The mobilization for the

Table 1-5.—ESTIMATES OF THE TOTAL POPULATION OF THE UNITED STATES AND OF POPULATION IN THE ARMED FORCES AT 6-MONTH INTERVALS: 1950 TO 1958 (THOUSANDS)

Date	Total population including armed forces overseas	Total population residing in the United States	Civilian population	Population in the armed forces	
				Total	Overseas
July 1, 1950.................	151,683	151,234	150,202	1,481	449
January 1, 1951..............	153,072	152,361	150,689	2,383	711
July 1, 1951.................	154,360	153,384	151,082	3,278	976
January 1, 1952..............	155,790	154,649	152,292	3,498	1,141
July 1, 1952.................	157,028	155,761	153,366	3,662	1,267
January 1, 1953..............	158,434	157,177	154,891	3,543	1,257
July 1, 1953.................	159,636	158,313	156,046	3,590	1,323
January 1, 1954..............	161,115	159,825	157,679	3,436	1,290
July 1, 1954.................	162,417	161,191	159,086	3,331	1,226
January 1, 1955..............	163,956	162,927	160,748	3,208	1,029
July 1, 1955.................	165,270	164,303	162,307	2,963	967
January 1, 1956..............	166,805	165,918	163,889	2,916	887
July 1, 1956.................	168,174	167,259	165,339	2,835	915
January 1, 1957..............	169,800	168,914	166,983	2,817	886
July 1, 1957.................	171,196	170,293	168,368	2,828	903
January 1, 1958..............	172,738	171,922	170,087	2,651	816
January 1, 1959..............	175,602	174,844	173,005	2,597	758

Source: U.S. Bureau of the Census, Current Population Reports, Series P-25, Nos. 175, 191 and 195.

Korean conflict, unlike that of World War II, did not cause the civilian population to shrink in size, although civilian growth was slowed down somewhat. (The civilian population grew very rapidly in the six months between July 1, 1952 and January 1, 1953, when demobilization was underway.) Also, demobilization after the Korean hostilities was not as complete nor as rapid as it had been after World War II--instead, the strength of the armed forces has been kept between 2.6 and 3.0 million.

The military situation which has existed during the years since 1950 should be kept in mind in evaluating the population changes that have taken place. For example, the count of the population residing within the country in January, 1958, fails to include 816,000 persons stationed overseas. It should also be remembered that, of the population counted as residing within the nation, about 1,828,000 (a little more than 1 percent) is military, and that most of it lives on military posts.

COMPONENTS OF POPULATION CHANGE

Changes in the size of an area's population involve two components: reproductive change (frequently called natural increase) and net migration.

(a) During any period, a nation or community increases its population by means of live births. During the same period, however, it loses population by the death of some of its members. Repro-

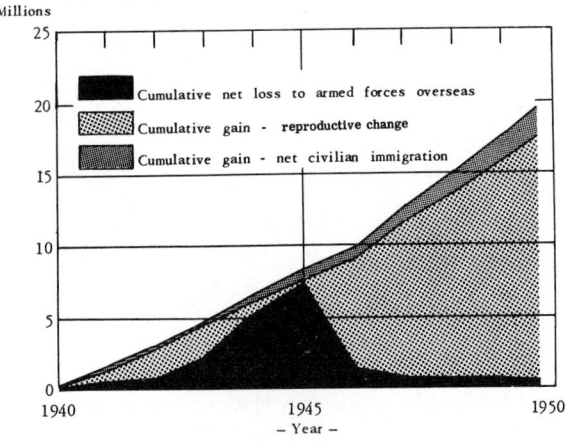

FIGURE 1-3. ESTIMATED COMPONENTS OF POPULATION CHANGE, CUMULATED BY SINGLE YEARS: 1940 TO 1950

ductive change is the net resultant of the two vital processes of birth and death.

(b) During any period, a community increases its population by receiving immigrants or in-migrants from other nations or other areas.[5] During the same time, however, it loses population when emigrants or out-migrants go to other nations or other areas. Net migration is the net resultant of the redistributional processes of immigration or in-migration and emigration or out-migration. When a nation is the unit of study, its growth is affected by international migration but not by internal migration.

Before a change in population size can be fully understood, it must be subdivided into its components and explained in terms of its parts. In addition, where possible, each component should be studied in terms of the processes of which it consists. Thus, the total increase of 19.0 million persons between 1940 and 1950 needs to be split into its reproductive change and net migration components. Although only incidental attention can be given here to the details of recent trends in birth and death rates, each of the vital processes is treated in fuller detail in later chapters.

Table 1-6 presents the components of change in the total population, 1940 to 1950, by geographic divisions, as estimated by the U. S. Census Bureau and the National Office of Vital Statistics. Of the total net increase, 17.7 millions, or 93 percent, was contributed by vital increase. The remaining 1.4 millions, or only 7 percent, was contributed by net migration from abroad. Hence, the recent growth of the population is largely a result of reproductive change, and is caused by an excess of births over deaths. If there had been no growth from this source, and if immigration from abroad had been the only answer, the population would have grown by only 1.0 percent.

It should be pointed out that in Table 1-6 the overseas casualties of World War II have been charged off against immigration; the war losses are treated as emigration. Even if there had been no war losses, however, net immigration would have accounted for only about ten percent of the total population change.

DISTRIBUTION OF GROWTH BY SINGLE YEARS: 1940 TO 1959

It was noted above, and illustrated in Figure 1-2, that during the first half of the decade 1940 to 1950 the total population was being depleted by the shipping of armed forces overseas, whereas during the last half it was being increased by their return. Shortly after the return and demobilization

Table 1-6.—ESTIMATES OF THE COMPONENTS OF CHANGE IN THE TOTAL POPULATION OF THE UNITED STATES, BY GEOGRAPHIC DIVISIONS: APRIL 1, 1940 TO APRIL 1, 1950

Geographic division	Total population		Total net change 1940 to 1950	Reproduction components		Net reproductive change 1940 to 1950	Net migration 1940 to 1950	Percent change 1940 to 1950		
	April 1, 1950 (1950 Census)	April 1, 1940 (1940 Census)		Births 1940 to 1950	Deaths 1940 to 1950			Total	Vital change	Net migration
United States...	150,697,361	131,669,275	19,028,086	31,913,013	14,246,928	17,666,085	1,362,001	14.5	13.4	1.0
New England........	9,314,453	8,437,290	877,163	1,768,636	992,256	776,380	100,783	10.4	9.2	1.2
Middle Atlantic....	30,163,533	27,539,487	2,624,046	5,531,699	3,116,634	2,415,065	208,981	9.5	8.8	0.8
East North Central.	30,399,368	26,626,342	3,773,026	6,075,127	2,970,490	3,104,637	668,389	14.2	11.7	2.5
West North Central.	14,061,394	13,516,990	544,404	2,909,309	1,380,492	1,528,817	-984,413	4.0	11.3	-7.3
South Atlantic.....	21,182,335	17,823,151	3,359,184	5,115,209	1,829,360	3,285,849	73,335	18.8	18.4	0.4
East South Central.	11,477,181	10,778,225	698,956	3,033,699	1,050,075	1,983,624	-1,284,668	6.5	18.4	-11.9
West South Central.	14,537,572	13,064,525	1,473,047	3,607,632	1,210,718	2,396,914	-923,867	11.3	18.3	-7.1
Mountain..........	5,074,998	4,150,003	924,995	1,190,917	433,825	757,092	167,903	22.3	18.2	4.0
Pacific............	14,486,527	9,733,262	4,753,265	2,680,785	1,263,078	1,417,707	3,335,558	48.8	14.5	34.3

Source: U.S. Bureau of the Census, Current Population Report, Series P-25, No. 72, July 1953, Table 3.

---

[5]The terms "immigration" and "emigration" are usually employed to designate movement into or out of a nation. The terms "in-migration" and "out-migration" are employed to designate internal movement within a nation.

of veterans got underway, the number of births increased rapidly, so that birth rates were much higher in the last half of the decade than they had been during the first half. As a consequence, when the population increase 1940 to 1950 is examined by single years in terms of its components an unusual pattern of concentration emerges. Figure 1-3 and Table 1-7 show that from April 1, 1940 to July 1, 1945 the population had increased in size very little (812,000 people), despite the fact that reproductive change had added 7.6 million people and net civilian migration had added 0.7 million people to the population. The military drain on the population ceased in 1945, and births rose shortly thereafter; the result was a sudden growth spurt, followed by yearly population increases that were unmatched in the nation's history. Figure 1-3 illustrates how the components of change caused almost all of the decade's growth to take place within the last half of the decade.

Between January 1, 1950 and January 1, 1958, the components of population change for the nation were as follows:

Total population increase.............. 24,781

Reproductive change................ 22,003

Births............35,670
Deaths 13,667

Net civilian immigration............ 2,778

Of the total increase of 14.3 percent that occurred during these years, 12.7 percent may be attributed to reproductive change and 1.6 percent to net immigration from abroad.

Recently the Bureau of the Census summarized the components of population change for each calendar year from 1940 to 1959, including the population overseas. These components are reported in Table 1-8, together with separate summaries for the 1940 to 1950 and 1950 to 1959 periods. Since 1950, net immigration per year has averaged about 102,000 persons more than it did during the preceding decade, and the reproductive change has been greater by about 784,000 persons per year than it was during the 1940's. The speed of our present population growth may be more readily appreciated if it is noted that during the calendar year 1957 to 1958 the volume of reproductive change was 2 1/2 times as great, and the volume of net immigration was 4 times as great, as during the year 1940 to 1941. As has been noted, more than 3 million persons are being added to the population each year. And nine-tenths of this increase is due to reproductive change. In spite of the additional refugees and other immigrants admitted under the liberalized program which has been in effect since 1946, native fertility rather than foreign immigration is presently the major source of rapid growth.

Table 1-7.—ESTIMATED COMPONENTS OF POPULATION CHANGE, BY SINGLE YEARS: 1940 TO 1950
(Figures in thousands)

| Date | Total population change | Change to succeeding date | | | | |
| | | Reproduction components | | Components of change | | |
		Births	Deaths	Reproductive change	Net civilian migration	Net movement of armed forces
April 1, 1940..................	285	621	345	276	25	-16
July 1, 1940...................	1,167	2,619	1,421	1,198	74	-105
July 1, 1941...................	799	2,776	1,378	1,398	52	-651
July 1, 1942...................	325	3,154	1,430	1,724	141	-1,540
July 1, 1943...................	-1,359	2,975	1,461	1,514	179	-3,053
July 1, 1944...................	-405	2,922	1,385	1,537	237	-2,179
July 1, 1945...................	7,574	2,859	1,422	1,437	100	6,037
July 1, 1946...................	3,392	3,931	1,423	2,508	241	643
July 1, 1947...................	2,646	3,640	1,452	2,188	309	149
July 1, 1948...................	2,572	3,642	1,434	2,208	350	15
July 1, 1949...................	2,033	2,774	1,095	1,679	268	86
April 1, 1950.................	...	...	...	...	...	...
Total change, 1940 to 1950....	19,028	31,913	14,247	17,666	1,976	-614

Source: U.S. Bureau of the Census, Current Population Reports, Series P-25, No. 71, April 1, 1953.

Table 1-8.—ESTIMATES OF CHANGE AND OF COMPONENTS OF CHANGE OF THE UNITED STATES POPULATION INCLUDING ARMED FORCES OVERSEAS: 1940 TO 1959

January 1 of calendar year	Change over preceding date (000)				Percent reproductive change is of total net change
	Total net change		Reproductive change (births minus deaths)	Net civilian immigration	
	Number	Percent			
TOTAL CHANGE					
1950 to 1959......................	25,050	16.6	22,412	2,625	89.5
1940 to 1949......................	18,969	14.4	17,056	1,898	89.9
AVERAGE ANNUAL CHANGE					
1950 to 1958......................	2,783	1.73	2,490	292	...
1940 to 1949......................	1,897	1.36	1,706	190	...
YEARLY CHANGE					
1959..............................	2,864	1.66	2,601	264	90.8
1958..............................	2,936	1.73	2,663	275	90.7
1957..............................	2,984	1.79	2,650	335	88.8
1956..............................	2,862	1.75	2,572	295	89.9
1955..............................	2,841	1.76	2,593	249	91.3
1954..............................	2,681	1.69	2,438	239	90.9
1953..............................	2,644	1.70	2,404	240	90.9
1952..............................	2,718	1.78	2,329	379	85.7
1951..............................	2,520	1.67	2,163	350	85.8
1950..............................	2,551	1.72	2,201	354	86.3
1949..............................	2,530	1.74	2,188	329	86.5
1948..............................	2,638	1.85	2,366	275	89.7
1947..............................	2,145	1.52	2,007	171	93.6
1946..............................	1,452	1.04	1,313	169	90.4
1945..............................	1,581	1.15	1,362	208	86.1
1944..............................	1,791	1.32	1,606	160	89.7
1943..............................	1,704	1.27	1,587	96	93.1
1942..............................	1,367	1.03	1,295	63	94.7
1941..............................	1,210	0.92	1,131	73	93.5
1940..............................	...	...	...	...	...

Source: Bureau of the Census, Current Population Reports, Series P-25, No.195, Feb. 18, 1959, Table 1.

U.S. GROWTH IN COMPARISON WITH THE WORLD AND WITH OTHER NATIONS

Population trends in the United States can be better appreciated if they are viewed from the perspective of population growth throughout the world. Tables 1-1 and 1-9 provide data for making international comparisons of recent population change. It is estimated that as of July 1, 1958 the world contained slightly more than 2.8 billion inhabitants. Both the rate at which world population is growing and the amounts by which it is increasing are simply amazing. The world has acquired one-third of its total present population in the last 30 years; 1.0 billion of the 2.8 billion has been added since 1920. At current rates of growth, world population will double within 50 years or less. Some nations have been growing at this rate or faster for a century or more, but now the whole world is involved; the increases which may be expected are so large that the mind can barely grasp their implications. What are the implications of a world population of 5 to 7 billion persons in the year 2000, or of 10 to 12 billions in 2050? This increase is in sharp contrast to the many thousands of years that elapsed between the origin of man and the middle of the 17th century, before the human species numbered even 500 millions.

In the 300 years since 1660 the population of the earth has increased by more than 2 billions, or until it is almost 6 times the size it was at the earlier date. This great "population explosion," with each decade witnessing an ever-growing increase in the number of people, has resulted from the fact that death rates have declined faster, and by greater amounts, than birth rates. Nations all over the world are benefiting from modern knowl-

Table 1-9.—ESTIMATED POPULATION GROWTH FROM 1938 TO 1958 FOR SELECTED COUNTRIES OF THE WORLD

Country	Estimated population (000)			Estimated change, July 1, 1938 to January 1, 1958		Ratio to United States	
	Projected January 1, 1958	January 1, 1950	July 1, 1938	Number (000)	Percent change	Ratio to numerical increase	Ratio to rate of increase
AFRICA							
Algeria....................	10,010	8,841	7,235	2,775	38.4	.065	1.2
Egypt......................	24,085	20,110	16,295	7,790	47.8	.182	1.5
Union of South Africa.........	14,286	12,251	9,988	4,298	43.0	.101	1.3
ASIA							
Ceylon.....................	9,260	7,401	5,810	3,450	59.4	.081	1.8
China: Taiwan (Formosa).......	9,717	7,397	5,678	4,039	71.1	.094	2.2
Cyprus.....................	539	480	376	163	43.4	.004	1.3
India......................	388,797	351,696	304,878	83,919	27.5	1.963	0.8
Indonesia..................	...	75,400	68,409	...	...	...	...
Israel.....................	1,950	1,174	1,418	532	37.5	.012	1.1
Jews....................	1,738	1,014	401	1,337	333.4	.031	10.1
Non-Jews................	212	160	1,017	-805	-79.2	...	...
Japan......................	91,466	82,049	70,400	21,066	29.9	.493	0.9
Malaya and Singapore..........	7,899	6,159	5,029	2,870	57.1	.067	1.7
Pakistan...................	80,089	75,143	68,594	11,495	16.8	.269	0.5
Philippines................	22,904	19,694	15,814	7,090	44.8	.166	1.4
Thailand...................	21,276	18,316	14,755	6,521	44.2	.153	1.3
Turkey.....................	25,592	20,676	17,173	8,419	49.0	.197	1.5
EUROPE							
Albania....................	1,477	1,196	1,048	429	40.9	.010	1.2
Austria....................	6,992	6,939	6,753	239	3.5	.006	0.1
Belgium....................	8,987	8,625	8,374	613	7.2	.014	0.2
Bulgaria...................	7,716	7,245	6,671	1,045	15.7	.024	0.5
Czechoslovakia.............	13,425	12,333	14,606	-1,181	-8.1	...	...
Denmark....................	4,533	4,252	3,767	766	20.3	.018	0.6
Finland....................	4,361	3,988	3,656	705	19.3	.016	0.6
France.....................	44,123	41,652	41,894	2,229	5.3	.052	0.2
Germany....................	72,005	68,669	59,171	12,834	21.7	.300	0.7
Federal Republic...........	52,207	48,130	39,867	12,340	31.0	.289	0.9
West Berlin..............	2,213	2,121	2,735	-522	-19.1	...	...
Soviet Zone and East Berlin	17,585	18,418	16,569	1,016	6.1	.024	0.2
Greece.....................	8,124	7,517	7,202	922	12.8	.022	0.4
Hungary....................	9,837	9,289	9,166	671	7.3	.016	0.2
Iceland....................	167	141	118	49	41.5	.001	1.3
Ireland....................	2,863	2,975	2,937	-74	-2.5	...	...
Italy......................	48,462	46,712	42,976	5,486	12.8	.128	0.4
Luxembourg.................	317	296	301	16	5.3	.000	0.2
Netherlands................	11,089	10,027	8,684	2,405	27.7	.056	0.8
Norway.....................	3,513	3,250	2,936	577	19.7	.013	0.6
Poland.....................	28,599	24,613	32,100	-3,501	-10.9	...	...
Portugal...................	8,915	8,360	7,506	1,409	18.8	.033	0.6
Rumania....................	18,024	16,216	15,682	2,342	14.9	.055	0.5
Spain......................	29,840	27,769	25,279	4,561	18.0	.107	0.5
Sweden.....................	7,390	6,986	6,297	1,093	17.4	.026	0.5
Switzerland................	5,092	4,670	4,192	900	21.5	.021	0.7
United Kingdom.............	51,736	50,329	47,494	4,242	8.9	.099	0.3
Yugoslavia.................	18,392	16,259	15,922	2,470	15.5	.058	0.5
NORTH AMERICA							
Alaska.....................	162	105	71	91	128.2	.002	3.9
Canada.....................	16,748	13,602	11,448	5,300	46.3	.124	1.4
Costa Rica.................	1,054	789	590	464	78.6	.011	2.4
Cuba.......................	6,462	5,466	4,428	2,034	45.9	,048	1.4
El Salvador................	2,375	1,847	1,591	784	49.3	.018	1.5
Guatemala..................	3,508	2,764	2,133	1,375	64.5	.032	2.0
Honduras...................	1,790	1,408	1,098	692	63.0	.016	1.9

Table 1-9.—ESTIMATED POPULATION GROWTH FROM 1938 TO 1958 FOR SELECTED COUNTRIES OF THE WORLD—Continued

Country	Estimated population (000)			Estimated change, July 1, 1938 to January 1, 1958		Ratio to United States	
	Projected January 1, 1958	January 1, 1950	July 1, 1938	Number (000)	Percent change	Ratio to numerical increase	Ratio to rate of increase
NORTH AMERICA-Con.							
Mexico.........................	32,510	25,466	19,071	13,439	70.5	.314	2.1
Nicaragua......................	1,341	1,043	948	393	41.5	.009	1.3
Panama.........................	962	787	590	372	63.0	.009	1.9
Puerto Rico....................	2,308	2,199	1,810	498	27.5	.012	0.8
United States.................	172,722	150,552	129,969	42,753	32.9	...	...
SOUTH AMERICA							
Argentina......................	19,961	16,961	13,725	6,236	45.4	.146	1.4
Brazil.........................	62,004	51,369	39,480	22,524	57.1	.527	1.6
Chile..........................	6,966	6,017	4,830	2,136	44.2	.050	1.3
Colombia.......................	13,371	11,209	8,702	4,669	53.7	.109	1.6
Venezuela......................	6,223	4,901	3,513	2,710	77.1	.063	2.3
OCEANIA							
Australia......................	9,754	8,046	6,899	2,855	41.4	.067	1.3
Hawaii.........................	550	478	410	140	34.1	.003	1.0
New Zealand....................	2,254	1,892	1,604	650	40.5	.015	1.2
U.S.S.R.............	205,989	180,024	192,294	13,695	7.1	.320	0.2

Source: U.S. Bureau of the Census, International Population Reports, Series P-91, No. 1, March 1953.

edge of medicine and public health. The incidence of those infectious diseases which once removed infants, youth, and young adults before they had a chance to marry and reproduce has been greatly reduced. As a result, a much greater proportion of the infants who are born survive, to age 40 or older, to marry and to have children. Meanwhile, birth rates have declined much more slowly than death rates, and are still high enough to produce a substantial increase. Later chapters on fertility and mortality will describe this phenomenon in detail.

The rate of growth in the United States from 1920 to 1954 (52.8 percent) was slightly higher than the world average of 45.6. The highest growth rates are found in Central and South America. Asia, Africa, and Oceania have growth rates that are about equal to those of the world and of the United States. Only Europe and the U.S.S.R. have grown considerably more slowly than the United States.[6]

Reliable estimates of the rates at which other nations are growing can be secured only for those nations where two or more reasonably accurate censuses have been taken, one of them since World War II. In 1957 the United States Bureau of the Census prepared estimates concerning those nations for which an estimate could be made with reasonable accuracy. These estimates cover a 19 1/2 year period, from July 1, 1938 to January 1, 1958, and make it possible to compare the present rate of growth of the United States with that of other nations. Table 1-9 reports the estimated rates of growth of these nations during this period. Although the estimates differ somewhat from figures given in other sources, they provide a useful basis for computing growth rates.

Of the 65 nations reported in Table 1-9 only one nation, India, gained as much population as did the United States. India's estimated gain was 84

---

[6] The low rates for the U.S.S.R. are not necessarily due to low fertility or high mortality of the normal type; partially, at least, they are a result of mass exodus, famine, and population transfers. At the present time, the components of growth in the U.S.S.R. are unknown. A reasonably good guess might be that, under present conditions and in the absence of internal disorder, its annual rate of increase is approximately the same as, or slightly higher than, that of the United States.

million, or almost twice that of the United States. Roughly one-sixth of the world's population increase in recent years has occurred in India alone. Yet India's rate of increase has been slightly lower than that of the United States. It is such a populous nation that even small rates of growth yield large increases in the number of inhabitants.

Since reliable growth measures cannot be computed for China, and since the rate shown in Table 1-9 for the U.S.S.R. is little more than conjecture, it is impossible to compare precisely the largest nations of the world. From the fragmentary evidence which is available, however, it is reasonable to guess that between 1938 and 1958 the U.S.S.R. gained roughly one-third as many people as did the United States. It is plausible that China did not gain as much population as did the U.S.S.R., although any judgment on this subject is purely speculative. In terms of size increase, it appears that the United States is the second or third fastest growing nation in the world.

In terms of rate of increase, a little more than one-half of the nations for which estimates are reported grew as fast as, or faster than, the United States between 1938 and 1958. The United States grew faster than all the European countries which are reported, except the tiny nations of Albania and Iceland. Its nearest competitor among the larger European nations was the German Federal Republic (whose growth is due largely to the transfer of population). Three European nations—Poland, Czechoslovakia, and Ireland—had substantial population losses, while several others showed only very small gains. The nations which were reported to be growing faster than the United States are, in general, the less industrialized and more rural nations of the world. Rates of growth larger than that of the United States by 50 percent or more are reported for the following nations:

	Ratio		Ratio
Costa Rica	2.4	Ceylon	1.8
Venezuela	2.3	Malaya and Singapore	1.7
Formosa	2.2	Brazil	1.6
Mexico	2.1	Columbia	1.6
Guatemala	2.0	Egypt	1.5
Honduras	1.9	El Salvador	1.5
Panama	1.9	Turkey	1.5

Until recently most of these nations had struck a balance between population and resources by means of high birth rates and high death rates. In recent years various modern technologies and skills, as well as medicine and public health, have been employed in sufficient measure to cause the death rates to fall precipitously in these areas, leaving the birth rates comparatively unaffected. This situation has resulted in rapid rates of population growth that have alarmed and worried statesmen throughout the world. In much of Oceania and the Americas there are enough resources and arable land to absorb population growth for the immediate future, but in many parts of Asia these favorable conditions do not exist. The governments of some of these nations are struggling to reduce birth rates quickly, in order to prevent their populations from multiplying faster than technological and other advances can make possible their support.

It may be of interest to note that the nations which adjoin the United States are also among the more rapidly growing nations of the world, although both of them still have comparatively small populations. Canada was expected to have 16.7 million people in 1958, and has grown 40 percent faster than the United States since 1938; Mexico, with 33 million people expected in 1958, has grown more than twice as fast as the United States. Brazil, the largest of the South American nations, was expected to have 62.0 million persons in 1958 and grew by 57 percent between 1938 and 1958.

HISTORY OF POPULATION GROWTH IN THE UNITED STATES

Some of the implications of the recent population growth in the United States can be more readily appreciated when the components of this increase are viewed in light of the nation's growth from 3.9 million in 1790, and even in relation to the growth of the original settlements and colonies. Only three and one-half centuries ago, there were almost no people of European descent living within the borders of the territory that is now the United States. Almost one and one-half centuries passed before the first million people accumulated (1610 to about 1745). Thereafter the population doubled and redoubled, causing an increase in numbers that astounded all who reflected upon it. The history of the world records no other population as having grown to such a size, and at such a rate, over a comparable span of time. Unfortunately, the available statistics are not detailed enough to give a complete account of the nation's early demographic events. The first census, taken in 1790, must be the starting point for formal analysis, and even the data provided by the first several censuses are much too sparse and incomplete to answer all of the significant questions that could be asked. By considering the conditions that must have given rise to the events and trends which emerged, however, it is possible to build up a fairly complete and reliable history of population growth in terms of the components of this growth. Figure 1-4 allows us to compare the rates and sizes of the major components of growth from 1800 to 1950.

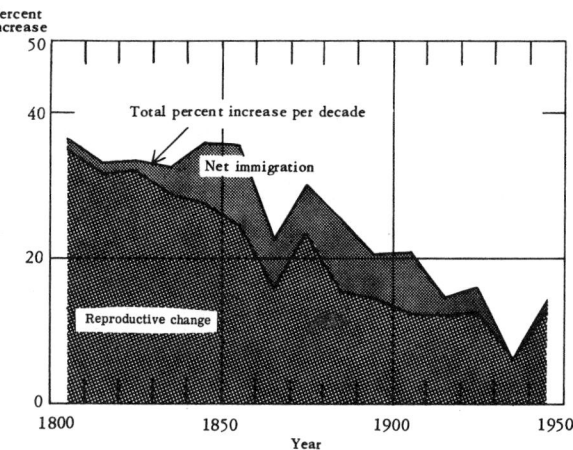

FIGURE 1-4. DECENNIAL PERCENT INCREASE IN POPULATION DUE TO REPRODUCTIVE CHANGE AND NET IMMIGRATION: 1800 TO 1950

In general, the nation has passed through four distinct phases of growth, and is now in a fifth. Each phase has grown out of the one that preceded it, and each represents a distinctive combination of the components of reproductive change and net immigration.

(a) Colonial and Early National Phase: 1620-1830. This stage was characterized by high rates of reproductive change and high rates of net immigration.

Since the first official census of the United States was not taken until 1790, inferences about the earlier part of this period must rest upon fragmentary and incomplete data. In this earlier part of the period, birth rates were extremely high, and approached the average maximum of which the human race is biologically capable. Migrants to the New World appear to have considered children an economic asset in conquering the wilderness. Marriage probably occurred at an earlier age in America than in Europe, which meant that each married couple was exposed for a longer time to the likelihood of bearing children. In much of Europe, deaths were almost as numerous as births; death rates in America were only moderately high, however, and permitted a rapid population growth. As Warren S. Thompson has pointed out, plenty of food and a low density of settlement (conditions which help prevent epidemics) undoubtedly caused death rates in the New World to be lower than they were in Europe and, at the same time, encouraged the rearing of large families. The high fertility of this population enabled the colonies to grow at an almost unprecedented rate for more than two centuries. Meanwhile, immigrants from Europe continued to stream into the colonies. Rapid reproductive growth and immigration combined to produce a great population increase. While America was in this phase, her population grew by 35 percent or more during most decades.

During the last portion of this phase, 1770 to 1830, the rate of immigration from abroad appears to have declined. The insecurity and uncertainty created by the Revolutionary War, the establishment of the Republic, and the War of 1812, tended to reduce temporarily the flow of migrants from abroad. Meanwhile, the rate of reproductive growth continued to be very high.

Thompson and Whelpton estimate that at the beginning of the 19th century there were about 55 births and 25 deaths per thousand residents annually, which means that the United States had a net annual reproductive gain of 30 per thousand, or 3 percent, per year.[7] Such a high rate of growth, phenomenal for any people at any stage of the world's history, attracted world-wide attention even before the Revolutionary War. When Robert Malthus looked around for proof that the human species, like other species, tended to grow by a geometric ratio, he found in the population of the newly established United States the evidence he sought. Thus, even though the net immigration from abroad had declined to a comparatively low point toward the end of the period, the decline had no seriously depressing effect upon population growth. This rapid growth in total numbers is illustrated in Figure 1-5.

Millions

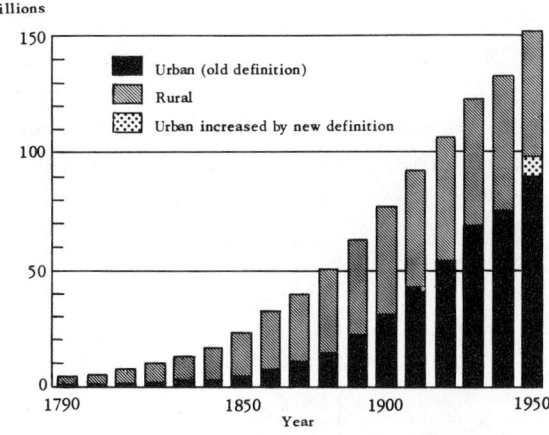

FIGURE 1-5. URBAN AND RURAL POPULATION OF THE UNITED STATES: 1790 TO 1950

(b) Frontier and Early Urbanization Phase: 1830 to 1900. Large but rapidly declining rates of reproductive increase and a very large volume of immigration from abroad characterize this phase. The rapid growth of commerce and industry following the War of 1812 created almost unlimited opportunities for incoming migrants. Land was plentiful and easily obtained. During each decade except one (the first, 1830 to 1840), the nation grew by about 5 percent as a result of immigration

alone. In four of the decades the decennial rate due to net immigration was 8.3 percent or more. Meanwhile, the rate of reproductive change was declining steadily and rapidly from the high point which it had reached about 1800. It fell from about 29 percent in the 1830 to 1840 decade to about 13 percent in the 1900 to 1910 decade. This was a decline of 16 points, or 56 percent, in the short span of 80 years. Since reproductive increase results from the occurrence of more births than deaths, this precipitous drop could have come about only through a narrowing of the gap between birth rates and death rates. Yet it was during this period that great medical discoveries began to be made. The germ theory of disease, epidemic control, antiseptic surgery, regulation of the water supply and of waste disposal, and care of the sick in the interest of public health all began to exercise a measurable influence upon mortality during this era. Their combined effect was to lower the death rate considerably. In order for the rate of natural increase to fall while death rates were declining, birth rates had to fall much more rapidly than death rates. Such a drop in birth rates could have resulted only from lowered fertility. Thus, although the evidence is only crude and approximate, there is no mistaking the fact that the really sharp reduction in American fertility took place in the nineteenth century rather than in the twentieth century. Because the population is known to have halved its rate of reproductive increase, and also to have enjoyed lower death rates, during the 60 years between 1830 and 1890, the inference that birth rates were reduced drastically during this period is inescapable. If, during this period, the crude birth rate dropped from about 50 per thousand residents to about 28 per thousand, and the death rate dropped from about 25 to 15 per thousand, the annual rate of reproductive increase dropped from about 25 per thousand to about 13 per thousand. Although the rates given above for the beginning of the period are only guesses, they are probably accurate enough to illustrate the magnitude of the change.

Demographers who are concerned with the problems involved in reducing fertility in underde-

---

[7] Warren S. Thompson and P. K. Whelpton, Population Trends in the United States, New York: McGraw-Hill, 1933, Ch. 1.

veloped and overpopulated countries might find interesting the fact that their own grandparents and great-grandparents reduced their fertility within a remarkably short time and without the expensive devices which many experts today consider necessary. They seem to have lowered their birth rates by means of later marriages and the use of simple techniques which avoided, or at least postponed, pregnancy.

The period during which this drastic reduction in fertility took place was also the period during which the population became industrialized and urbanized. It has been generally assumed that birth control practices began in the cities and slowly diffused throughout the whole population, and hence, that urbanization and industrialization have been the factors underlying this fertility decline. However, there is evidence that birth rates fell as rapidly in early American rural communities as they did in the cities; even today, many very rural sections of the nation have lower birth rates than many large cities. The specific aspects of urban living to which declining fertility might be related are not clearly established--in fact, the association between city living and declining fertility has not been adequately demonstrated. The exact motivation which was responsible for family limitation in the 19th century is not yet known.

(c) Early Twentieth Century Phase: 1900 to 1925. Moderate and almost unchanging stable rates of reproductive increase, declining immigration. (This phase overlaps the one preceding it, in that the rate of reproductive increase began to be steady at the turn of the century, whereas immigration did not begin to decline until after 1910.)

During this period, both birth and death rates appear to have been declining moderately and at about the same rate. Consequently, between 1900 and 1925 the decennial rate of reproductive change remained steady at about 13.0 percent. (Much more factual data is available for evaluating the trends of this period than for previous periods. Figure 1-6 presents estimates of the actual birth and death rates, from which more exact measure-

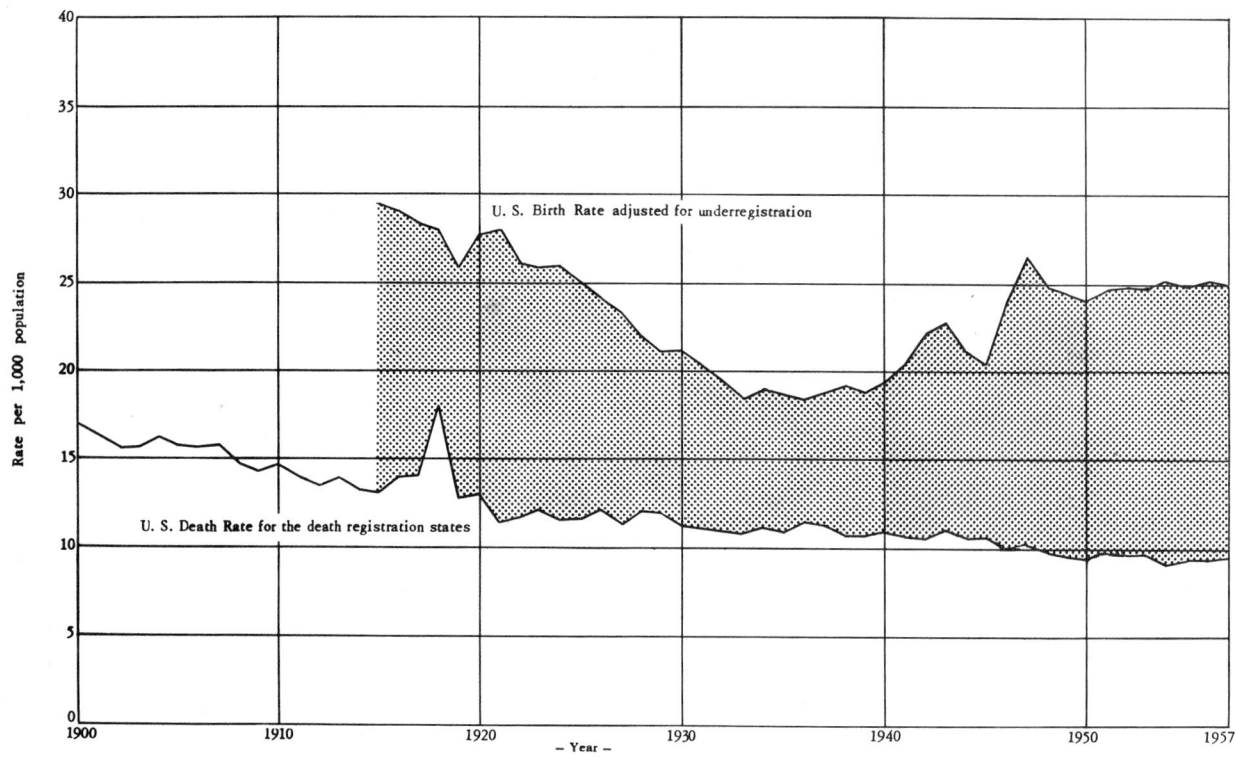

FIGURE 1-6. CRUDE DEATH AND BIRTH RATES FOR THE UNITED STATES: 1900 AND 1915 TO 1957

ments of annual and decennial growth can be made.) With the exception of a temporary fluctuation during and after World War I, the birth rate appears to have leveled off from its previous steep decline, and to have paralleled the more gradual decline of the death rate. Except during 1918, when the influenza epidemic caused a high death rate, deaths continued to decline. During this phase, immigration from abroad declined until it was about a third of what it had been, on the average, during the preceding period. In 1921 Congress passed a bill restricting immigration to a small quota per nation. This combination of growth components resulted in national growth rates that were very moderate in comparison with those of the past; they were still very rapid in comparison with the rates in much of the world, however, and would be considered excessive if they were to apply to a large population for any prolonged period of time.

(d) Post World War I Phase: 1925 to 1940. Precipitous decline in birth rates, very low immigration. In 1919, birth rates had suffered a sharp but temporary decline because of the number of men who were overseas with the armed forces. In 1920 and 1921, birth rates increased as the armed forces were demobilized. Shortly thereafter, about 1925, birth rates began to decline again very rapidly--as rapidly, in fact, as they had at any time during the 1800's. In less than 10 years the birth rate fell by more than 10 points (see Figure 1-6), and then leveled off. It reached its low point in 1933 and remained there until 1939, at which time it made a moderate upswing. The behavior of the birth rate during this 15-year period--particularly during the first five years of it--is an enigma which has not yet been clarified by research. It can hardly be attributed to the economic depression alone, since the decline preceded the economic collapse of 1929. Was it a reaction to the wave of births immediately following World War I--a reaction which, through coincidence, was strengthened and prolonged by the depression and its attendant economic hardships? Or was it a resumption of the sharp downward trend which characterized the years 1830 to 1900; in other words, was the third phase (1900 to 1925) merely an interlude in the rapid descent of fertility rates? Until recently, American demographers believed that this phase was such an interlude, and they forecasted a fairly steep decline for the future.

(e) World War II and Postwar Phase. 1940 to the present (1960). Moderate rates of reproductive increase, limited migration. The upsurge in population growth that has been taking place since 1940 already has been described in an earlier section of this chapter. Just how complete and dramatic it was, as a reversal of the direction of trends in fertility and reproduction that had prevailed for at least a century and a quarter, may now be more fully appreciated when it is viewed from the perspective of the nation's growth history. The following aspects of this upsurge, in comparison with previous trends, are especially significant.

a. The rates of growth for both reproductive change and immigration were small in comparison with earlier decades, especially with decades before 1880.

b. The rate of reproductive increase between 1940 and 1960 was very similar to the rates that prevailed in the decades between 1890 and 1930. However, these earlier rates were based upon a downward trend of birth and death rates, whereas the 1940 to 1960 rate of reproductive change was based upon very low death rates and moderate birth rates.

c. The reproductive change between 1940 and 1960 contrasts sharply with the very small rate of growth that prevailed during the period 1925 to 1940. It is evident that the nation has not returned in recent years to a level of really rapid population growth, either by means of immigration or reproductive change. It is also evident, however, that the expectations of many experts that the nation would soon cease to grow altogether have failed to materialize. Why has the nation continued to grow? Merely because it resumed the moderate trend of the 1900 to 1925 period? Merely because of a temporary inflation of births, resulting from the unprecedented level of prosperity which was associated with World War II and which continued during the years immediately following the war? Does this growth represent, at least in part, a compensation for the births which did not take place during the depression? No final answer to these questions can be made at this time; at least five, and perhaps as many as fifteen, years must elapse before the necessary statistics will be available for correct analysis and interpretation of these recent developments. If sufficiently complete and detailed tabulations are made in the 1960 census, it will begin to yield the data necessary for this assessment. But not until the 1970 census will it be possible to review these events in historical perspective and to place upon them a valid interpretation.

Meanwhile, the demographer is left with the task of trying to make sense out of what appears to be a reversal of an historic trend. It is probably true that large scale immigration from abroad is a thing of the past, and will not again be a major factor in growth except as a result of some unforeseen world emergency. Crude death rates for the total population appear to be approaching a lower limit. (See chapter on mortality.) The course of future growth, therefore, will depend largely upon the course of the birth rate. We do not yet know enough about the factors associated with fluctuations in fertility to hazard a long-range prediction. The birth rate and human fertility have been subjected to prolonged and intensive research, and a great deal more is known about the decline in births than has been indicated in this brief account. For example, a very high proportion (perhaps more than 90 percent) of the adult married population is aware of how to limit family size and probably would be willing to do so if conditions made such limitation desirable. This sug-

gests that recognition of certain possible changes-- economic conditions, in attitudes toward children, and in programs which ease the cost of rearing and educating children--may be of more help in estimating future growth than the extrapolation of past "trends;" such trends may represent only the fact that people are becoming more educated with respect to birth control. A careful reading of the chapter on fertility will provide additional insights that will help in the interpretation of recent trends and in the calculation of the possible future course of population growth.

In many ways, the recent upsurge in fertility has been overdramatized. In terms of fertility rates, it represents merely a return to the fertility level of the middle 1920's. Because of such changes in the population composition (to be described in later chapters) as the unprecedentedly large proportion of persons in their early twenties who are married, the birth rates of the late 1940's and early 1950's may be regarded as maximal, and are almost certain to decline somewhat. The big unanswered questions, however, are "How much decline?," and "Over what period of time?," and "When will it occur?" From the data now available it is impossible to determine whether, in the next decade or two, the population of the United States will continue to increase at its present rate, whether it will almost stop increasing, or whether it will follow a course between these two extremes. Whatever rates prevail in the future will apply to a large population; therefore, unless these rates are nearly zero they will inevitably produce large numerical changes. For example, even a rate of reproductive increase as low as 6 percent per decade (to which the nation has not yet declined) would add 1 million persons to the population annually.

---

*Note. The reader whose principal interest is in the changing size of the population may develop a comprehensive view of this subject by supplementing the materials of this chapter with a reading of Chapters 9 (mortality), 12 (fertility), 14 (international migration), and 26 (future population growth), omitting the intervening chapters

Chapter 2

POPULATION DISTRIBUTION: URBAN-RURAL RESIDENCE

INTRODUCTION TO THE FIELD OF
POPULATION DISTRIBUTION*

Research concerning the spatial arrangement of the earth's people has come to be known as the study of population distribution. This chapter, and the three chapters that follow it, will discuss selected distributional aspects of the United States population. Before discussion of the first of these aspects, time-out should be taken to state a few basic definitions and principles that apply to the study of population distribution generally.

A consideration of population distribution necessarily involves two sets of facts: (a) facts about people and (b) facts about the space they occupy. Explanation of the observed relationships between these two sets of facts is the goal of research in this field. On the most elementary level, population may be considered as undifferentiated units: that is, simply as numbers of living human bodies without regard to differences in their characteristics. On this elementary level land may be treated simply as quantities of surface (number of square miles) without regard to differences in characteristics of the land or the different uses to which it is put. Knowledge arrived at on this basis can be only very general and incomplete. A more sophisticated treatment of population distribution requires the introduction of facts about the population composition within each area. It also requires

a consideration of facts about environmental differences. This calls for a subdivision of space into parcels of territory that have meaning and relevance for the study of a population, and for specifying those characteristics of each parcel which may be a factor in the study of population distribution. Thus, a detailed distributional comparison of two or more populations involves a study of the interrelationships between their compositional traits and their environmental conditions, with both the population and the land classified into types.

From the foregoing, it is evident that the study of population trends has a distributional as well as a compositional aspect. The number and proportion of residents occupying a given type of area may change over a period of time. Also, the nature of the area itself may change, or its use may be altered as a result of technological development or other human effort, with the result that new classes of area are created or that areas shift from one classification to another over a period of time. For example, as it increases or decreases in size, a population may remain widely dispersed on farms and in small agricultural villages, or it may tend to become concentrated in a few giant metropolises.

The total field of population distribution may be subdivided into two major subfields, each of which may be further subdivided, as follows:

1. Regional demography: The study of the broader arrangement of various compositional groups of the population, in terms of major regions or classes of land or of residence. Two major subdivisions of regional demography may be recognized:

---

*The reader who is interested primarily in reading a description of the population may wish to skip this section and proceed directly to the study of urban and rural populations. The reader who is already familiar with the definition of urban and rural populations should skip pages 3-9. Readers who are interested primarily in population composition may want to skip Chapters 2 thru 5 entirely.

(a) The study of types of communities or places. This classification of population has reference to the type of place in which the population resides, irrespective of whether or not the parcels of territory falling in a particular category are contiguous to each other. Examples of this type of analysis are studies of urban-rural or metropolitan-nonmetropolitan residence, and of population distribution in relation to land-use.

(b) The study of broad contiguous territories. (1) This classification concerns areas within which similar environmental conditions exist. Examples: Geographic regions and socio-economic regions and subregions. (2) Areas within which a significant degree of economic and social interdependence exists. Example: Metropolitan regions (a metropolis and its broad hinterland).

2. Micro-demography: The study of population within neighborhoods, communities, and other small local areas. This comprises the internal arrangement and composition of the people of individual metropolitan areas, census tracts, villages, neighborhoods, or city blocks. Its distinguishing feature is that whole communities or other local areas are studied in terms of their constituent subareas.

In this book, only the regional aspects of population distribution are considered. Micro-demography is a very large and specialized field, and is closely allied to the study of the spatial, economic, and social structure of communities. Although it has many very important uses--especially for city planning, urban renewal, housing programs, marketing, and business location--it is of only indirect relevance to this general overview of the American population. The present chapter is devoted to the first of the principal subtopics of regional population distribution--the study of residence in urban and rural places. Chapter 3 deals with residence in metropolitan and nonmetropolitan areas, while Chapters 4 and 5 discuss the broader regional and subregional arrangement of the total population--first with respect to geographic groupings of states, and then with respect to more precisely delimited socio-economic regions, subregions, and subdivisions of subregions.

The facts of population distribution considered in this and the next three chapters fall half-way between the more sophisticated and the most elementary approaches described above. In these presentations, the differentiated aspect of the environment will be recognized; but population will be treated only as numbers of inhabitants of particular types of areas. This oversimplification is resorted to in order that each of the environmental categories may be introduced as units of analysis. Distributional aspects of each of the major population characteristics will be discussed in the several chapters on population composition, of which Chapter 6 is the first.

THE URBAN POPULATION: THE "OLD" DEFINITION

A basic type-of-community classification of population, one which has proved highly useful in a wide variety of research studies, is one that separates urban population (city-dwellers) from rural population (country-dwellers). This separation has been achieved by setting up a definition of the populations that are to be considered urban, and classifying the remainder of the population as rural. Until the 1950 census, the urban population was defined almost entirely on the basis of municipal incorporation and size of place. Places that were incorporated as municipalities and that also had a population of 2,500 people at a decennial census were defined as urban. All remaining places (places that were unincorporated as municipalities, or that were so incorporated but had a population of less than 2,500) were classed as rural. Certain minor civil divisions (townships, etc.) that were populous and very densely settled, but were not incorporated, were defined as urban under special rules. These special rules specified minimum sizes and densities which townships must exhibit before they could qualify as urban, even though they were not incorporated as municipalities. The special rules were applied most frequently in New England, New Jersey, and Pennsylvania, although they were invoked in several other states. The special rules were established to correct inequalities that arose because the constitutions of some states prevented places from being incorporated as a municipality until they had attained 5,000 or even, in some cases, 10,000 inhabitants.

This definition of the urban population was simple and easy to apply. Whether or not a place is incorporated as a municipality is a matter of public record. The Census Bureau could enumerate each incorporated place as a separate entity, make a count of the population in each place, and arbitrarily declare that those with 2,500 or more inhabitants were urban. This definition of the urban population was adopted by the census of 1910 and was used, with minor modifications of the special rules, for the censuses of 1920, 1930, and 1940. Because of its simplicity, the definition could be extended backward through earlier censuses. A special project which reclassed the populations of earlier censuses by application of the urban definition employed from 1910 through 1940, was carried out by the Census Bureau in connection with the 1940 census. This project permitted demographers to chart the growth of urban population with ease, using a single definition that made the results of all censuses directly comparable with each other.

Unfortunately, during the very time this definition of the urban population was being perfected and applied to earlier enumerations, conditions were developing that made its continued use impossible. The validity of the definition depended upon the ability of city boundaries to encompass all of the population that actually lived under conditions such as those that were found in genuinely urban places. It is well known that within recent years cities have developed extensive suburbs outside their city limits. Parts of these suburbs are themselves incorporated places of 2,500 or more which would be classified as urban, but many large areas of dense urban-like suburban settlements remain unincorporated. These areas would be classified as rural under the definition used in 1940. Although suburbanization is a very old phenomenon (even before the Civil War some workers commuted to the city from far-out peripheral residences, using railroad facilities), in this century it has been progressively accelerated. For the

most part, city growth in the 19th century took the form of fairly compact and dense settlement at the periphery, which was rather promptly annexed. Since 1910, new settlement has become more diffuse at the outer periphery, and annexation has failed to absorb the new urban-like subdivisions and housing developments which have spread over extensive areas.

Large suburban areas were developing around New York City, Philadelphia, Boston, Chicago, and a few other very large cities as early as 1910.[1] By 1930, suburbs were forming rapidly around medium-size as well as large cities. The advent of the motor car and its common use for commuting to work supplemented the commuters' train, street car, and bus. As a consequence, within the past three decades the commuting radius has been extended many miles into the hinterland. Large subdivisions and housing developments have sprung up in open country several miles outside the city. A high proportion of these urban-like agglomerations are in unincorporated territory, and hence would be classified as rural under the definition of 1940. By 1940, a few of these suburbs had become so large and densely settled that they caused whole townships to be classed as urban under the special rules.

This trend not only continued uninterrupted during the depression years 1930-40, but even seemed to be accelerated at a time when central cities were making almost no growth. After the results of the 1940 census were known, it was apparent that a change much more extensive than one associated with normal growth of the city was underway. As the suburban trend continued into the 1940's, despite strict gasoline rationing and curtailed automobile manufacture, and became a suburban building boom in 1946 after peace was declared, it became evident to census experts that the official definition of urban population should be modified to more nearly coincide with the facts of population distribution. Were the old definition to

---

[1]For statistical evidence of this see Warren S. Thompson, The Growth of Metropolitan Districts in the United States: 1900-1940. (Washington, D.C. Government Printing Office, 1948.)

be retained, it would result in a large segment of genuinely urban population being classed with the rural. This misclassification would have the unfortunate effects of understating the rate of growth of the urban population and giving to the rural population a more urban character than it actually possessed. Since the trend was expected to continue at a rapid rate, it was apparent that even if the old definition were "patched up" with additional special rules in 1950, by 1960 the suburbanization process would have progressed so far that a new definition would be required anyway. Extensive urban-like suburbs of solidly built-up area were to be found around cities of all sizes, and they were growing at a very rapid rate. In the face of this situation, the Bureau of the Census devised a new definition of urban population for use in the 1950 Census of Population.

THE NEW DEFINITION OF THE URBAN POPULATION

According to the new definition that was adopted for use in the 1950 census, the urban population comprises all persons living in:

(a) Places of 2,500 inhabitants or more incorporated as cities, boroughs, villages, or towns. (In New England, New York, and Wisconsin, where the term "town" refers to units called "townships" in other states, incorporated towns of 2,500 or more are not necessarily defined as urban.)

(b) The densely settled urban fringe around cities of 50,000 or more inhabitants. Although census officials recognized that smaller but similar fringes existed about cities of less than 50,000, limitations of time and budget prevented their delimitation.

(c) Unincorporated villages or other compact settlements of 2,500 or more outside any urban fringe.

The remaining population is classified as rural.

The first part of the above definition is the principal component of the old definition. The establishment of a new concept of urban fringe, and the definition of all areas of this type as urban, irrespective of whether they are incorporated as cities, boroughs, villages, or towns, is the most important additional component of the new definition.

An urban fringe is regarded by the census as the thickly settled territory, characterized by a closely spaced street pattern, that surrounds most medium-size and large cities. The entire urban agglomeration, comprising the central city and its fringe, is termed an urbanized area.

The urban fringe is formally defined as follows: Proceeding outward in each direction from the boundaries of a city of 50,000 or more inhabitants, all territory is included in the urban fringe if it falls in one of the following four types and lies contiguous to an area already included in the fringe:

"1. Incorporated places with 2,500 inhabitants or more in 1940 or at a subsequent special census conducted prior to 1950.

2. Incorporated places with fewer than 2,500 inhabitants containing an area with a concentration of 100 dwelling units or more with a density in this concentration of 500 units or more per square mile. This density represents approximately 2,000 persons per square mile and normally is the minimum found associated with a closely spaced street pattern.

3. Unincorporated territory with at least 500 dwelling units per square mile.

4. Territory devoted to commercial, industrial, transportational, recreational, and other purposes functionally related to the central city.

"Also included are outlying noncontiguous areas with the required dwelling unit density located within 1 1/2 miles of the main contiguous urbanized part, measured along the shortest connecting highway, and other outlying areas within one-half mile of such noncontiguous areas which meet the minimum residential density rule."[2] Figure 2-1 illustrates how the new urban boundaries look in actual practice. Urban fringes were established for 157 cities with 50,000 or more population. Because the fringe delimitation must be made in advance of the census, several cities which first attained 50,000 inhabitants in 1950 did not have their

---

[2]Quoted from "Introduction," U.S. Bureau of the Census, U.S. Census of Population: 1950, Vol. II, Characteristics of the Population, final volumes for individual states.

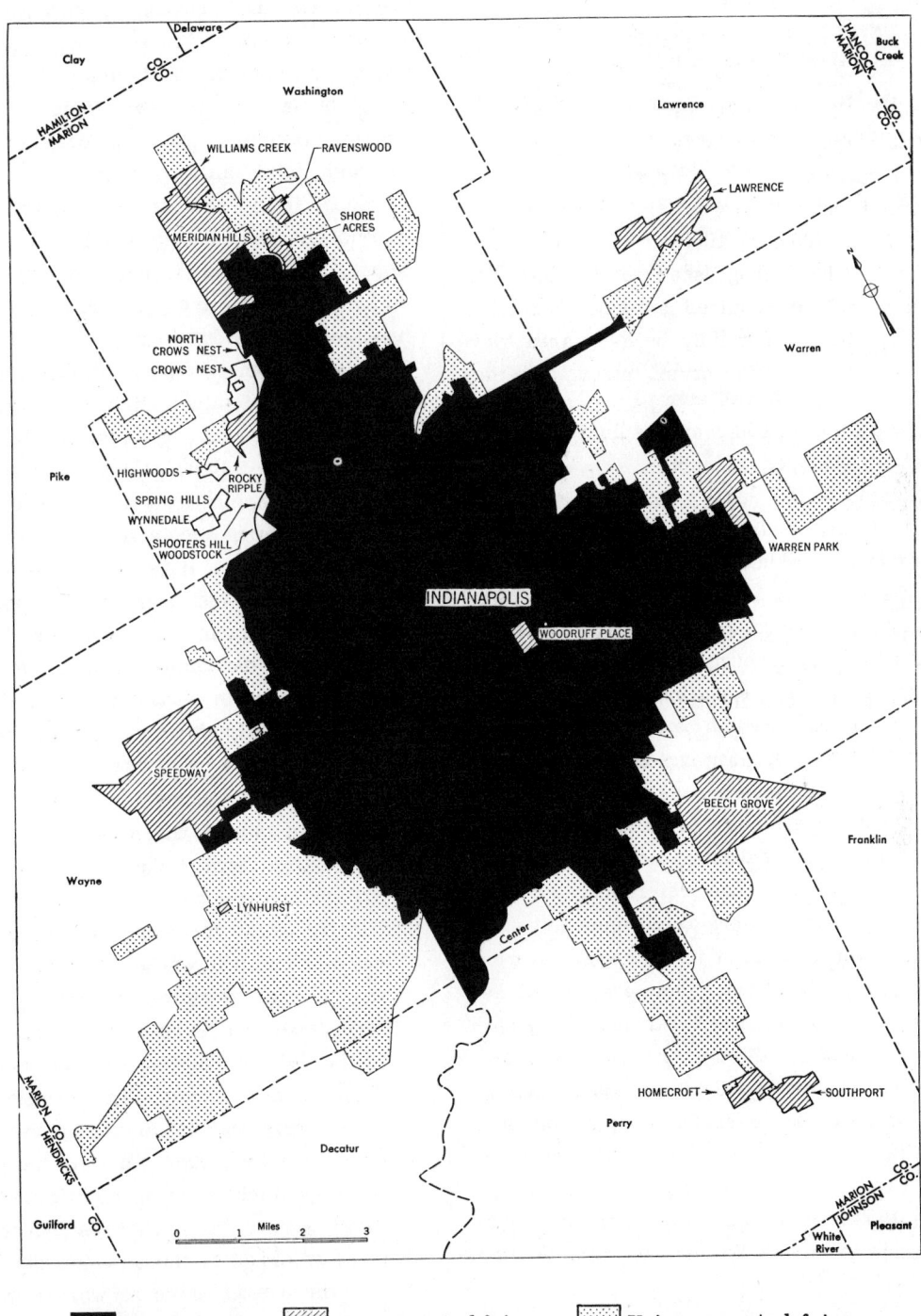

FIGURE 2-1.   INDIANAPOLIS URBANIZED AREA

fringes delimited, and hence are not yet considered to be centers of urbanized areas.

DEFINITION OF THE RURAL-FARM AND RURAL-NONFARM POPULATION

In 1920 the Bureau of the Census experimented with subdividing the rural population into rural-farm and rural-nonfarm residents. For the 1930 census this division was made an integral part of the urban-rural classification.[3] On a type-of-community-of-residence basis, then, the population could be classified as

Urban

Rural nonfarm

Rural farm

Both the 1950 and the 1950 censuses employed this classification developed by Leon E. Truesdell.

This division of the rural population was obtained in 1930 and 1940 by asking every respondent, "Does this household (or person) live on a farm?" The object of the division is to separate the segment of the rural population that earns its livelihood primarily through agriculture from the segment of the rural population which lives in trading centers too small to be classed as cities, in scattered residences along major highways, and in other rural sites that are nonagricultural. Yet it must be remembered that the concept "rural-farm" population is residential rather than occupational or industrial in its reference. In both 1930 and 1940, enumerators were instructed to classify as a farm resident any person who reported himself as living on a farm, even though he did not work on a farm. The rural-nonfarm population was defined as all rural population not living on farms. These are the "old" definitions of the rural-farm and rural-nonfarm population employed in 1940. Both were modified for the 1950 census.

For the 1950 census, the rural-farm population was redefined to exclude households which did not operate farms but which lived on farms and paid cash rent for their homes and yards only. Over the years, the process of consolidating small farms to create fewer but larger farms has left many thousands of old farmsteads free for occupancy by families that have little, if any, connection with farming. These places tend to be rented for cash, as is an apartment or house in a city. Persons living in institutions, summer camps, motels, and tourist camps were classified as nonfarm residents even though they may have reported themselves as living on farms. This procedure has the effect of more nearly limiting the rural-farm population to those who obtain their livelihood from agriculture. But even this change in definition succeeds only in making an approximate division. The following quotation from the "Definitions and explanations" of the 1950 census summarizes the facts succinctly:

"The population living on farms has never, of course, been identical with the population dependent on agriculture; but there is some evidence that the number of persons dependent on agriculture has been decreasing more rapidly than the total number of farm residents. Some workers living on farms have both an agricultural and a nonagricultural job; others shift from agriculture to nonagricultural work with the season. Some farm households contain both an agricultural and a nonagricultural worker. Finally, some farm households do not contain any agricultural workers and conversely some agricultural workers, including farmers and farm laborers, do not live on farms. According to the 1950 Population Census, approximately 27 percent of employed workers living on rural farms were working in nonagricultural industries. On the other hand, 18 percent of the workers employed in agriculture did not live on rural farms. These data on industrial attachment referred to the only job the worker held (or, the one at which he worked the greatest number of hours) during the week preceding his enumeration.... Further evidence on this point is provided by data on major source of earnings over the period of a year. According to the

---

[3]At the same time the census introduced a new category "urban farm." This category, as Table 2-1 shows, has been too small to warrant detailed tabulation. Few people in urban areas report that they live on a farm.

Current Population Survey, about 35 percent of the families living on rural farms in April, 1951, reported that nonfarm work was the major source of their earnings in 1950. Apparently the distinctions between the farm and nonfarm populations have become somewhat blurred, but large differences in way of life still persist and the majority of farm residents are dependent on agriculture for their livelihood." [4]

However, this situation is not necessarily damaging to the usefulness of the concept. In a recent paper entitled "Farm Population As a Useful Demographic Concept," [5] Beale demonstrates that this concept discriminates effectively between the population traits commonly associated with the farm and nonfarm populations.

From the foregoing, it is evident that for the 1950 census the actual definition of the rural-nonfarm population has changed considerably from that of 1940, although the nominal definition remains unchanged. Since this population is a residual--what is left over after the urban and the rural-farm populations have been defined--the new definitions of urban and rural-farm populations have a direct effect upon the rural-nonfarm population. In general, most of the population added to the urban population by the new urban definition would have been classified as rural nonfarm by the 1940 definitions. Hence, the new urban definition decreases the rural-nonfarm group. On the other hand, this loss was partially compensated for by the new definition of rural-farm population, which classifies as rural-nonfarm those people who pay cash rent for homes located on farms, and those who are residents of institutions, summer camps, motels, and tourist camps even though these residences are located on farms. Although the rural-nonfarm population produced by the new definition is more homogeneous than the old population, it still fails to satis-

fy the ambition of some demographers, who would like it to be synonymous with rural village population. At present, incorporated places of all sizes, from 50,000 down to a few hundred, have suburban fringes that were classed as rural nonfarm in 1950. In addition, around the larger cities there are many hundred or thousands of nonfarm dwellings that house workers who live along main highways and commute to work in the city. Although these residences are not sufficiently clustered and close to each other to be a part of an urban fringe, many of the people who occupy them are undoubtedly more urban than rural in their characteristics. As will be shown in Chapter 3, subdivision of the rural population into metropolitan and nonmetropolitan creates more homogeneous classes of rural population. A very strong argument could be made for a four-fold urban-rural classification.

a. Urban
b. Suburban
c. Village and open country nonfarm
d. Rural farm

The suburban population could be defined as rural-nonfarm residents of enumeration districts lying within 5 miles of a city limit or urban fringe boundary.

In order to "bridge the gap" between the 1940 and the 1950 definitions of the urban population, the Bureau of the Census prepared a few basic tabulations of data by both the old and the new definitions. With these data it is possible to arrive at fairly accurate estimates of the detailed changes that occurred in urban and rural areas between 1940 and 1950. In fact, the later discussion of changes in urban and rural composition will rest upon estimates derived from these dual tabulations.

THE URBAN-RURAL COMPOSITION OF THE UNITED STATES POPULATION IN 1950, AND EFFECT OF CHANGING DEFINITIONS [6]

In 1950, almost two-thirds (64.0 percent) of the United States population was urban and one-third

[4] U.S. Bureau of the Census. U.S. Census of Population: 1950. Vol. II, Characteristics of the Population, Part 5, U.S. Summary, Chapter C., page ix.

[5] Calvin L. Beale, "Farm Population as a Useful Demographic Concept," in Donald J. Bogue's, editor, Applications of Demography; Population Situation in the U.S. in 1975, Chapter VII, page 39.

[6] For a more detailed treatment of this subject the reader is referred to Chapter 3 of The Growth of Standard Metropolitan Areas, 1900-1950, With an Explanatory Analysis of Urbanized Areas, by Donald J. Bogue, U.S. Government Printing Office, 1953.

Table 2-1.—URBAN-RURAL COMPOSITION OF THE POPULATION BY OLD AND NEW DEFINITIONS AND PERCENT CHANGE: 1930-40 AND 1940-50

| Urban-rural residence | Number of inhabitants in 1950 (New definition) | Percent distribution | | | | Percent change | | |
| | | 1950 | | 1940 | 1930 | 1940-50 | | 1930-40 |
		New urban definition	Old urban definition			New urban definition[1]	Old urban definition	
Total...............	150,697,361	100.0	100.0	100.0	100.0	14.5	14.5	7.2
Urban.............	96,467,686	64.0	59.0	56.5	56.2	21.8	19.5	7.9
Urban farm......	283,388	0.2	0.2	0.3	0.2	...	-22.8	14.9
Rural.............	54,229,675	36.0	41.0	43.5	43.8	3.4	7.9	6.4
Rural nonfarm...	31,181,325	20.7	25.7	20.5	19.3	32.4	43.2	13.2
Rural farm......	23,048,350	15.3	15.3	22.9	24.6	-18.0	-23.6	0.2
Total farm.........	23,331,358	15.5	15.5	23.2	24.8	....	-23.6	0.3

[1]Estimated. For procedure of estimating, see text.

Source: U.S. Bureau of the Census, U.S. Census of Population: 1950, Vol. II, U.S. Summary, Table 34.

was rural, by the new definition (Table 2-1). Only fifteen percent of the total population was living on farms in rural areas. The balance of the population, about one-fifth, resided in rural-nonfarm areas.

The effect of changing the urban definitions may be observed through comparison of columns 2 and 3 of Table 2-1, and through study of Table 2-3. The change in definitions had the net effect of adding 7,540,222 persons to the urban population, and removing them from the rural. Had the old definition been retained, 5.0 percent more of the total population would have been classed as rural (almost all of it rural-nonfarm) instead of urban. For the urban population this represented a gain of 8.5 percent and for the rural population it represented a loss of 12.2 percent, in comparison with the results that would have been achieved had the old definitions been used. By far the greater share of this change came from establishing the urban fringes, rather than from recognizing outlying unincorporated places as urban, although both changes did much to improve the definition of urban population. A net total of 6,203,569 persons were added to the urban category as a result of introducing the fringe definition, while a net of 1,336,626 persons were added by recognizing outlying unincorporated places. Thus, 82.3 percent of the total increase to the urban population which resulted from change in definition may be attributed to the fringe delimitation.

There is no reliable way to judge the net effect of changing the definition of the rural-farm population. The urban definition is a so-called "office" definition - it is imposed upon places in the census office. For this reason, no particular difficulty is encountered in retaining both the old and the new urban definitions and making a few tabulations for each of them. The rural-farm definition, on the other hand, is a "field" definition. Enumerators were trained to ask the question in one particular way as to whether the person lived on a farm. To have asked the question by using both the old and the new definitions would have led to confusion and great additional cost. Thus, in the 1950 census the statistics for rural-farm population are tabulated by the new definition only.

In addition, there is evidence that at the 1950 census there was a rather serious tendency to misclassify rural-farm population as rural-nonfarm. The Census Bureau, which takes a monthly sample survey of the population using highly trained enumerators, has compared the results of its April, 1950 sample survey with the results of the 1950 census, also taken in April, and reports that the sample survey would have estimated more than 1 1/2 million more rural-farm residents than the 1950 census actually showed. Since this is a greater difference than would be expected from sampling error alone, it is generally agreed that the 1950 census underenumerated the farm population.

The Agricultural Marketing Service, U. S. Department of Agriculture, prepares annual estimates of the farm population. Its series dates back to 1910. Working cooperatively, the AMS and the Census Bureau have arrived at a revised set of estimates for the farm population, making corrections for change in definition, misclassification by 1950 census enumerators, and change in weights, to be applied to the current population survey sample data. Estimates prepared by the two Bureaus indicate that the farm population in 1950 (using the new definition) should have been about 25,058,000, and that this is roughly 957,000 fewer than it would have been had the old definition been used. Accepting these estimates as approximately correct, and assuming that they apply with equal validity to the rural-farm population, the conclusion may be reached that the change in definition of farm residence decreased the rural-farm population by about 3.7 percent and increased the rural-nonfarm by about 3.4 percent.[7] Throughout this monograph it should be kept in mind that the total size of any category of the rural-farm population is probably somewhat greater than indicated by the census figures, and that its rate of decline in the 1940-50 decade is slightly exaggerated.

CHANGES IN URBAN-RURAL COMPOSITION 1940-50

Because of the extensive changes in definition, the rate of change in the urban and rural populations during the past decade can be inferred only roughly. By tabulating the 1950 population on the basis of the old definition it is possible to obtain comparable data from which rates of change for the urban and rural population can be established. But these rates refer to the old rather than to the new definition of the urban population. There is no exact way in which the 1940 data can be corrected to match 1950 definitions; hence all rates of

change must be computed as if the new definitions had not been made at all. (Valid rates of change, by new definitions, will be available at the 1960 census.) Moreover, it will be recalled that no data by the old definition can be made available for the rural-farm population. However, an approximate measurement of change - by old definitions - can be obtained by computing the 1940-50 rates as if the 1940 and 1950 definitions of rural-nonfarm and rural-farm population were approximately correct (after adjustment to the old urban definition), while remembering that such rates are between 5 and 6 percentage points too low for the rural-farm population, and correspondingly too high for the rural-nonfarm population.

Table 2-1 provides measures of the rate of change, computed on the above basis. Whereas the total population increased by 14.5 percent, the urban population increased by 19.5 percent-- a considerably above-average increase. Including the population added by the change in definition, the urban population increased by 29.6 percent. The rural-farm population declined precipitously during the decade, by an indicated 23.6 percent. By the old definition, the rural-nonfarm population grew by 43.2 percent, or at a rate more than twice that of the urban population. This reflects the very rapid growth of suburbs around cities of all sizes. When it is recognized that much of this phenomenal growth refers to areas that are urban in all their conditions of life, little further evidence is needed to argue that the new definition of urban areas was necessary.

A crude guess as to what the amounts and rates of change in 1940-50 were, according to the new definitions of urban, rural nonfarm and rural farm, may be made as follows: [8]

---

[7]Bureau of the Census and Bureau of Agricultural Economics, "Revised Estimates of the Farm Population of the United States 1910 to 1950," Farm Population, Series Census-BAE, No. 16, March, 1953. This release contains a technical appendix describing the history of the farm population estimates, and methods used in revising them to conform to the new definition.

[8]These quantities were estimated on the basis of the following assumptions.

a. Assume that 60 percent of the 6.2 million people added to the urban population by the new urban fringe definition would also have been urban fringe population in 1940, had the new definitions been in effect then. This seems reasonable in the light of general evidence that commuting by automobile and the settlement of unincorporated suburbs has been underway at an accelerating rate for at least three decades. For the 1940 census this assumption has the effect of removing

(continued on following page)

To the extent the assumptions are reasonable, it may be concluded that between 1940 and 1950 the urban populations as defined in 1950 grew by about 22 percent, the rural-nonfarm population increased by about 32 percent, while the rural-farm population declined by roughly 18 percent. Although these estimates are based on very impressionistic assumptions, they do serve to illustrate that the old definitions tend to minimize slightly the growth of the urban population, to mildly exaggerate the decline in the farm population, and to greatly exaggerate the growth of the rural-nonfarm population, as these populations are now defined.

CHANGES IN THE URBAN AND RURAL POPULATION SINCE 1950

The exact degree of urbanization of the population and the average annual rates of urban and rural growth cannot be known exactly until the

---

[8](continued)

4,791,000 inhabitants from the rural-nonfarm category and adding them to the urban population, and allows a 1940-50 growth of 2,749,000 in the fringe areas which were added by the new definition:

b. Assume that 80 percent of the 1,674,223 net addition to the urban population which was made by recognizing outlying unincorporated places of 2,500 or more as urban would also have been urban in 1940 had this definition been in effect. This is reasonable on the grounds that this aspect of the definition of the urban population had been deficient for several censuses. The actual growth of the places that would have been urban in 1940 if the definition had been in effect, plus the population of a comparatively few unincorporated places outside urbanized areas which grew into the minimum size class, is all that should be allowed for in the estimate.

c. Assume that the 337,597 net 1950 population which changed its definition from urban to rural, as a consequence of abandoning the urban under special rule definition in favor of the urban fringe definition, grew by 19 percent between 1940 and 1950.

d. Assume that revised estimates for the total farm population 1940-50, by the new rural-farm definition prepared by the Bureau of Census and of Agricultural Economics, are correct after removal of the 1940 and 1950 counts for the urban-farm population. Adjusting the 1940 and 1950 populations to match these assumptions yields the following estimated rates of change, 1940-50:

Area	Population		Change 1940-50 (000)	Percent distribution 1950	Percent change, 1940-50	
	1950 (000)	1940 (000)			New definitions	Old definitions
U.S. Total....	150,697	131,669	19,028	100.0	14.5	14.5
Urban..........	96,468	79,202	17,266	64.0	21.8	19.5
Rural, total....	54,230	52,468	1,762	36.0	3.4	7.9
Rural nonfarm.	29,487	22,277	7,210	19.6	32.4	43.2
Rural farm....	24,743	30,191	-5,448	16.4	-18.0	-23.6
Total farm......	25,058	30,547	-5,489	16.6	-18.0	...
Urban farm....	315	356	-41	0.2	...	...

1960 census. At that time, new boundaries will have been delimited around the cities, enclosing the new urbanized area that has been built up since 1950. (There is a good possibility that in 1960 the urbanized areas will be delimited around all cities of 25,000 or more inhabitants; this inclusion of urbanized areas around cities of 25,000 to 49,999 will greatly improve the definition.) However, an approximate picture of current urban-rural change can be obtained by estimating the change that has occurred within the urban and rural areas as delimited in 1950.

In March, 1956, and again in March, 1958, the Bureau of the Census conducted a sample survey, from which estimates were obtained of the civilian population living in urban, rural-nonfarm, and rural-farm places as defined in 1950. The results of these surveys were as follows:[9]

Residence	Percent distribution of civilian population		Changes in number of persons 1950-1958 (000)	Percent change 1950-58
	1958	1956		
Total.........	100.0	100.0	21,836	14.6
Urban...........	61.2	63.1	9,000	9.4
Rural...........	38.8	36.9	12,836	23.9
Rural nonfarm...	27.0	23.8	16,772	56.1[1]
Rural farm......	11.8	13.1	-3,935	-16.7[1]

[1]Estimated by the author, using estimates of change in the total farm population prepared by the Bureau of Census and Agricultural Marketing Service.

Source: Current Population Reports, Series, P-20, No. 88,

During the first eight years after the 1950 census, the farm population declined by an additional 3.9 million, or by about 17 percent. This is an average annual rate decline of almost 2.1 percent a year, which corresponds well with the similar average of 1.8 percent estimated above for the 1940-50 decade.

Although the urban population (1950 areas) gained 9.0 million persons and captured slightly more than 1/2 of the total population growth, its

[9]U.S. Bureau of the Census, Current Population Reports, Series P-20, No. 71, December, 1956; also report on Mobility, Series P-20, No. 85, October, 1958, which refers to population 1 year of age and older.

rate of growth was 9.4 percent, which was almost 35 percent below the average for the nation. It has been the rural-nonfarm population that has made the most rapid growth. This category increased by roughly one-half, or 8 percent per year, which represents a great acceleration over the rapid rate of the 1940-50 decade. As was described above, this is not the growth of small villages and open country nonfarm population, but the growth of suburbs around cities of all sizes, and especially around the larger cities. The 1950-60 decade is proving to be a period of unprecedented suburbanization, or settlement of territory that not only lies outside any city but outside any urban fringe (as defined in 1950) as well.

The importance of having a flexible definition of the urban population, one which keeps up with the outward march of urban-like settlement, is illustrated by these statistics. The first column of statistics in the above table reports the percent distribution of the civilian population in 1958, by urban-rural residence. In 1958, 61 percent of this population was living in urban areas, as defined in 1950. But in 1950, 64 percent of the total population was living in these same areas. Thus, unless the flexible-boundary principle is used, successive censuses would show that the population is becoming progressively less urban! Actually, urbanization is continuing at a rapid pace. Rough estimates indicate that when the 1960 census is taken, between 71 and 74 percent of the population will be found living in urban places.

HISTORY OF URBAN AND RURAL GROWTH IN THE UNITED STATES

In the comparatively short space of a century and a half, the United States has been transformed from a very rural and primarily agricultural nation into a highly urbanized and industrial one.[10]

------

[10]A clear distinction must be maintained between "urbanization," or increase in the proportion of population living in urban places, and "urban growth," or percent change in urban population. In order to become more urbanized during any period, the urban population must grow faster than the rural. It is possible for an area to have high but equal rates of urban and rural growth. During such periods there is no increase in urbanization.

Figure 2-4 and Table 2-2 show that at the first census in 1790 only a small share (5.1 percent) of the population was urban; 94.9 percent was rural. During each decade since then (except 1810-20), the urban population has grown faster than the rural, with the result that the population classified as urban has increased almost uninterruptedly. During most decades from 1790 to 1840, the urban population grew roughly twice as fast as the rural. The Civil War period was one of extraordinary urbanization. Between 1860 and 1870 the proportion of the population classed as urban increased 7.7 percentage points; urban areas grew more than four times as fast as rural areas. (The census of 1870 is known to have been a weak one, especially in the South. Perhaps many rural areas there were greatly underenumerated. The above statistics may exaggerate somewhat the urbanization associated with the Civil War, but that war did give an unmistakable impetus to urban development, especially in the North.) From 1880 to 1930 urbanization proceeded at an even more rapid pace than it had earlier. The stream of immigrants from abroad caused cities on the eastern seaboard to grow rapidly. New cities sprang up in the interior as land was homesteaded and brought into production. The events immediately preceding, as well as participation in, World War I further accelerated urbanization. Urban areas increased 9 times as fast as rural areas in the 1910-20 decade. By 1920, the nation had passed the 50-50 mark and was predominantly urban.

Urban growth slackened somewhat in the 1930-40 decade, even in comparison with the lowered rate of national growth. This may have been a result of depressed economic conditions, or the failure of the old urban definition to encompass areas of new urban growth, or both. If it were the latter, it would be permissible to share between the 1930-40 and 1940-50 periods the 7.8 percentage point gain in urbanism made between 1930 and 1950. It is probably true that a very large percentage of the great unincorporated urban fringes, which contributed so heavily to the new definition of urban population, were settled largely in the 1930-50 period.

Table 2-2.—URBAN AND RURAL COMPOSITION, AND RATE OF URBAN AND RURAL GROWTH: 1790 TO 1950

Year	Percent of total population		Percentage point urban gain over preceding decade	Percent change over preceding decade		
	Urban	Rural		Urban	Rural	Ratio urban to rural
New urban definition 1950...............	64.0	36.0	7.5	21.8[1]	3.4[1]	...
Old urban definition 1950...............	59.0	41.0	2.5	19.5	7.9	2.5
1940...............	56.5	43.5	0.3	7.9	6.4	1.2
1930...............	56.2	43.8	5.0	27.3	4.4	6.2
1920...............	51.2	48.8	5.5	29.0	3.2	9.1
1910...............	45.7	54.3	6.0	39.3	9.0	4.4
1900...............	39.7	60.3	4.6	36.4	12.2	3.0
1890...............	35.1	64.9	6.9	56.5	13.4	4.2
1880...............	28.2	71.8	0.7	42.7	25.7	1.7
1870...............	27.5	74.3	7.7	59.3	13.6	4.4
1860...............	19.8	80.2	4.5	75.4	28.4	2.7
1850...............	15.3	84.7	4.5	92.1	29.1	3.2
1840...............	10,8	89,2	2.0	63.7	29,7	2.1
1830...............	8.8	91.2	1.6	62.6	31.2	2.0
1820...............	7.2	92.8	-0.1	31,9	33.2	1.0
1810...............	7.3	92.7	1.2	63.0	34.7	1.8
1800...............	6.1	93.9	1.0	59.9	33.8	1.8
1790...............	5.1	94.9	...	...	...	...

[1]Estimates. For procedure of estimating, see text.

Thus seen in the long perspective of more than a century and a half, the rapid growth of urban population between 1940 and 1950, and its continuation during the 1950's, is only a resumption of a long trend that was temporarily slackened by a combination of business depression and inadequate census definitions. It is quite reasonable to assume that if absolutely comparable definitions could be obtained for the entire span of time, the urban and rural growths of the past 15 years are not unique in terms of their rates of change. Their really unique aspects are the more dispersed pattern of growth, the tremendous number of persons who have been involved, and the broad

Table 2-3.—SUBDIVISIONS OF THE URBAN POPULATION ACCORDING TO NEW AND OLD DEFINITIONS: 1950

Area as classified by new definition	New definition	Old definition	Difference
United States, total...........................	150,697,361	150,697,361	...
Urban, total................................	96,467,686	88,927,464	7,540,222
Urban, within urbanized areas....................	69,249,148	63,045,552	6,203,596
Incorporated places of 2,500 or more...........	61,327,130	61,327,130	...
Incorporated places under 2,500................	577,992	...	577,992
Unincorporated territory......................	7,344,026	1,718,422[1]	5,625,604
Urban, outside urbanized areas......	27,218,538	25,881,912	1,336,626
Incorporated places of 2,500, or more..........	25,223,811	25,223,811	...
Unincorporated places of 2,500 or more..........	1,994,727	320,504[2]	1,674,223
Rural, formerly urban [3].........................	...	337,597	-337,597

[1]Places that were urban under special rule in 1940, urban fringe in 1950.
[2]Places that were urban under special rule in 1940, urban outside urbanized areas in 1950.
[3]Places that were urban under special rule in 1940, rural in 1950.

Source: U.S. Bureau of the Census, U.S. Census of Population: 1950, Vol. I, U.S. Summary, Table B.

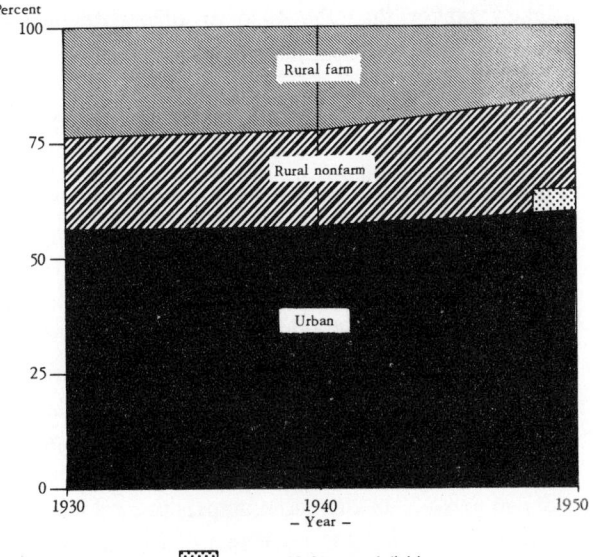

FIGURE 2 - 2. PERCENT OF UNITED STATES POPULATION
IN URBAN, RURAL-NONFARM AND RURAL-FARM
PLACES : 1930 TO 1950

zone of territory around cities of all sizes which
have been affected.

RECENT TRENDS IN THE FARM POPULATION

The sharp downward trend in the farm population which was manifest during the 1940-50 decade represents an acceleration of a trend that has
been underway since World War I. As described
above, the Bureaus of Agricultural Economics and
the Census maintain an annual estimate of the
farm population of the nation which extends back
to 1910. From this series, which recently has
been revised to correspond to the new definition of
farm population, it is possible to trace the recent
pattern of changes.

"In 1916, just prior to the entry of the United
States into World War I, farm population was
estimated at approximately 32 1/2 million. Following a decline during World War I and a
slight increase in the first two postwar years,
farm population moved downward during the
decade of the 1920's. By 1930, it had fallen to
a level of about 30 1/2 million. The depression
of the early 1930's reversed temporarily the
previous pattern of net migration from farms to
urban centers, and the farm population began
to rise again. By 1933 and 1934, it had practically regained the pre-World-War-I level. As
economic conditions improved in the latter part
of the 1930's, however, heavy migration from
farms was resumed. By 1940, the farm population was reduced to about the same size it had
been in 1930.

Farm population dropped at an especially sharp
rate during World War II. From a level of
30 1/2 million at the time of the 1940 Census, it
was reduced to approximately 25 1/2 million by
1944 and 1945. Following V-J Day, farm population increased in the next two years--mainly
because of the return of veterans--and reached
its post-World-War-II peak of some 27 million
in April 1947. After that date, there was a general resumption of the long-term downward
trend in the number of persons living on
farms."[11]

Several factors probably are jointly responsible
for this significant lowering of farm population.
Rapid industrial and commercial development of
the nation, accompanied by rapid urbanization, has
exerted a strong pull upon the younger generations
of farm youth. During the 1930-40 decade, when
this pull was greatly lessened by low employment
opportunities in cities, the farm population managed to grow a little. During both World War I and
World War II this pull was intensified by manpower shortages, plus the need for military recruits. In both wars, farming was considered a
critical and essential occupation, and was grounds
for exemption from military duty for a large proportion of the farm population. Yet many farm
youth, especially those from areas where farming
yielded a meager living, did migrate to urban centers or were inducted into military service. From
Figure 2-3 it appears that a high proportion of
these out-migrants temporarily returned to farms
after the end of the war, but promptly thereafter

---

[11]Bureau of the Census and Bureau of Agricultural Economics,
"Revised Estimates of the Farm Population of the United States, 1910
to 1950," Farm Population, Series Census-BAE, No. 16, March 9,
1953.

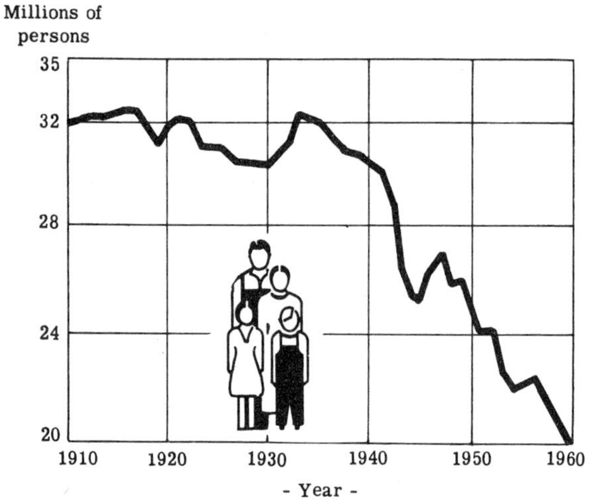

FIGURE 2 - 3. ESTIMATED TOTAL FARM POPULATION OF THE UNITED STATES: 1910 TO 1960

departed for urban areas. During the most recent war-time period of manpower shortages, long-time trends toward farm consolidation and farm mechanization were greatly accelerated. The demand for agricultural labor was greatly reduced. For these reasons, the opportunities to become an operator of a profit-yielding farm were greatly restricted. Wartime inflation and mechanization increased the amount of capital investment required for farm operation. Rationalization and industrialization of farming increased the amount of training necessary to insure successful operation. As a result of these factors, and possibly others, agricultural production has become concentrated in fewer, larger, more highly mechanized, and more scientifically operated farms. The number of small hand-operated or for-home-use farms has tended to decline, except in the vicinity of large cities where farming is combined with non-agricultural employment.

As reported earlier, the farm population has declined further since 1950. In March, 1958, it was down to about 20.3 million persons, which represents a loss of 4.7 million (19 percent) since 1950. It is difficult to know what the immediate future change will be. At the 1960 census it may number only 18 or 19 million persons, and comprise only about 10 or 11 percent of the total population instead of 15.5 percent as in 1950. The percent decline for 1950 to 1960 will be slightly larger than the 1940 to 1950 rate of decline.

URBAN-RURAL COMPOSITION IN COMPARISON WITH OTHER NATIONS

The comparative degree of urbanization in the nations of the world is difficult to determine, for the definitions of "urban" and "rural" vary from one country to another. There is no uniformity in the minimum size of the place that is defined as urban; some nations place it higher, and others lower, than the 2,500 point used in the United States. In the Netherlands, for example, a place must contain 20,000 inhabitants before it is considered urban. In Denmark, separate agglomerations as small as 250 inhabitants are considered urban. Moreover, the legal status of dense agglomerations, and the legal boundaries that delimit them, vary among nations, so that the American concepts of incorporated place and city limits do not find exact counterparts in the legal definitions of other countries. As a consequence, in some countries large urban fringes (as defined in the United States) are excluded from the urban category. In other places, much rural population (by U. S. standards) is included within the legal boundaries of urban places. Thus, a ranking of nations according to the percent of their total population which is urban can be only approximate. Table 2-4 presents such data for 64 nations; it should be interpreted with the reservations described. The following conclusions seem to be warranted from this table:

a. The United States is one of the most urbanized countries in the world. Of the major nations, only Great Britain, the Federal Republic of Germany, and Australia are clearly more urban. Although the United States has only 1/16 of the world's total population, it may have as much as 1/10 or more of the world's urban population.

b. By far the greatest proportion of the nations of the world are rural, and the world's population is predominantly rural. In 1950, less than 1/5 of India's population was urban. China is undoubtedly no less rural than India. Most of the nations in South America, Africa, and Asia have only small proportions of their population residing in urban centers.

c. The more urbanized nations are those of Western Europe and North America.

After surveying the process of world urbanization, the editors of the United Nations Demographic Yearbook conclude that:[12]

a. Urbanization is a necessary aspect of industrialization, and the most urbanized nations are the more industrialized ones.

b. The more industrial nations have a larger proportion of their urban population concentrated in large cities than have the less industrial nations. Hence, the appearance of numerous large metropolitan centers is an aspect of advanced industrialization.

c. At the present time, the nations that are least industrialized and least urbanized are having the most rapid rates of urbanization. Nations whose population is nearing the "saturation point" (almost fully urbanized) are having the smallest increases in urbanization.

d. The rate of urbanization throughout the world appears to be less rapid now than at the beginning of the 20th century, although it is more rapid than during the 1930-40 depression decade. This may result, however, from many western nations nearing the saturation point, while the industrialization of the more rural nations is progressing less rapidly than it did in the nations first to undergo the industrial revolution.

Thus, at the present time, no other large world power has an industrial urban population as large as that of the United States. Because it too is approaching the saturation point, where further urbanization can be achieved only by encroaching upon a small and essential agricultural population, an equilibrium between its urban and rural populations undoubtedly will be reached within the next few decades. It is impossible to predict at what proportions this will occur. Meanwhile, numerous rural nations of the world, both large and small, are urbanizing rapidly.

SIZE OF PLACE AND URBAN-RURAL RESIDENCE

Implicit in the definition of rural and urban population is the proposition that population characteristics, ways of gaining a livelihood, and other important aspects of life vary with the size of the community of residence. Selecting the value 2,500, and declaring every place this large or larger to be urban, is merely an arbitrary division of a continuum. The value 2,500 was selected by the U. S. Bureau of the Census because this is about the average minimum size at which well-defined streets, lots, systematically plotted house numbers, sidewalks, and other characteristics of city-like settlement are found. If there is a systematic variation with size of place, the differences between urban and rural populations could be made to assume any of several values simply by establishing a different lower limit to the size of place to be treated as urban. To comprehend basic rural-urban differences, it is useful to know how those differences vary with size of place.

It is now fully documented that populations do tend to vary in a great many ways according to the size of the place they occupy. Factors such as concentration, density, and variety of economic opportunities vary with size of city, and apparently exert a selective and modifying effect upon community residents. Hence, the concentration of population into larger agglomerations has an effect of its own, in addition to the simple fact that people are living in an urban place. What these effects and conditions are can be learned only by examining the population characteristics in terms of the size-of-place continuum. For these reasons it becomes important to know not only what proportion of a population is urban, but also what proportion of the urban population is living in cities of each of several size classes. Several of the later chapters on population composition will contain a brief presentation of data by size of place in regard to the characteristic which is under discussion. In this chapter, Tables 2-4 and 2-5, together with Figure 2-2, show how the total population is

---

[12]Chapter 1. "Urban trends and characteristics." This issue of the Demographic Yearbook features world urbanization. Table 6 gives the urban and rural populations of each of more than 100 nations, together with the national definitions of urban area, and Table 7 of this Yearbook gives the population of more than 65 nations classified by size of place. Table 8 gives the populations of capitals and of cities of 100,000 or more. All figures are those of a recent census or recent estimate.

Table 2-4.—PERCENTAGE URBAN (BY NATIONAL DEFINITION) AND PERCENTAGE OF THE TOTAL POPULATION IN CITIES OF 100,000 OR MORE INHABITANTS

Country and year	Urban	Cities of 100,000 or more	Country and year	Urban	Cities of 100,000 or more
Scotland, 1951	82.9	50.7	Paraguay, 1950	35.9	14.6
England and Wales, 1951	80.7	51.9	Panama, 1950	35.9	15.9
Israel, 1951	77.5	39.9	Poland, 1949	35.8	15.6
Federal Republic of Germany, 1950	71.1	27.1	Mexico, 1940	35.1	15.2
Hawaii, 1950	69.0	70.6	Malaya and Singapore, 1947	35.1	17.9
Australia, 1947	68.9	51.4	Nicaragua, 1950	34.6	10.2
Denmark, 1950	67.3	33.5	Hungary, 1949	34.5	20.9
Democratic Republic of Germany, 1946	67.6	19.0	Bolivia, 1950	33.6	11.9
United States, 1950	63.7	43.7	Costa Rica, 1950	33.5	17.5
Belgium, 1947	62.7	25.8	USSR, 1939	32.8	17.1
Argentina, 1947	62.5	40.6	Finland, 1950	32.3	14.2
Canada, 1951	62.1	36.7	Tunisia, 1946	32.0	18.7
New Zealand, 1951	61.3	32.8	Guatemala, 1950	31.6	10.2
Spain, 1950	60.5	23.3	Portugal, 1940	31.1	20.0
Sweden, 1950	56.3	22.7	Ecuador, 1950	30.3	14.8
Netherlands, 1947	54.6	35.2	Egypt, 1947	30.1	19.2
Northern Ireland, 1951	53.1	32.4	Colombia, 1938	29.1	8.3
France, 1946	52.9	21.7	Turkey, 1950	25.2	8.3
Chile, 1940	52.4	24.1	Bulgaria, 1946	24.6	8.0
Norway, 1950	50.5	16.7	French Morocco, 1947	24.2	15.9
Venezuela, 1950	49.8	20.7	Philippines, 1948	24.1	9.3
Austria, 1951	49.1	32.8	Dominican Republic, 1950	23.8	11.4
Czechoslovakia, 1947	48.8	13.7	Algeria, 1948	23.6	11.3
Greece, 1940	47.2	19.1	Romania, 1948	23.4	8.0
Italy, 1936	44.6	17.8	Iran, 1950	20.0	9.3
Union of South Africa, 1951	42.4	22.0	Korea, 1949	19.6	14.7
Ireland, Republic of, 1951	40.5	17.6	Jamaica, 1943	18.2	16.3
Puerto Rico, 1950	40.5	16.2	India, 1951	17.3	6.8
Japan, 1950	37.5	25.6	Yugoslavia, 1948	16.2	6.3
Brazil, 1950	36.5	13.9	Ceylon, 1946	15.4	5.4
El Salvador, 1950	36.5	8.6	Haiti, 1950	12.5	4.6
Switzerland, 1950	36.5	20.6	Burma, 1931	10.4	3.9

Source: United Nations Demographic Yearbook, 1952, Table B, page 11.

distributed by size of place and how that distribution has changed over the decade.

By the new urban definition, a total of 4,284 incorporated and unincorporated places of 2,500 or more were defined as urban, while 13,807 smaller places were defined as rural. As table 2-5 shows, big cities contain a large proportion of the population. For example, the 106 cities with 100,000 or more residents were only 2.5 percent of the total number of cities, but they contained 29.4 percent of the total population of the nation. Although the 3,022 places of 2,500 to 10,000 inhabitants were 70.5 percent of the total number of cities, together they comprised only 9.7 percent of the total population.

This picture of intense concentration is in sharp contrast to the situation at the time of the first census of 1790, when there were only 24 urban places. At that time, the two largest cities (New York and Philadelphia) had only 33,131 and 28,522 residents respectively. Three additional cities, Boston, Baltimore, and Charleston, S.C. had between 10,000 and 25,000 inhabitants. All of the remaining 19 cities had less than 10,000 inhabitants. Since 1790 there has been a steady increase

in the number of urban places, and a steady rise in the number of existing urban places moving into larger and larger size classes. The following tabulation provides a general picture of the rapid increase in the number of large and medium size, as well as small, places. Urbanization apparently

Year	Total number of urban places	Places of 50,000 or more	Places of 500,000 or more
1950 (New definition)	4,284	232	18
1950 (Old definition)	4,023	235	18
1940	3,464	199	14
1930	3,165	191	13
1920	2,722	144	12
1910	2,262	109	8
1900	1,737	78	6
1890	1,348	58	4
1880	939	35	4
1870	663	25	2
1860	392	16	2
1850	236	10	1
1840	131	5	..
1830	90	4	..
1820	61	3	..
1810	46	2	..
1800	33	1	..
1790	24	..	..

Source: U.S. Census of Population: 1950 Vol. II, Characteristics of the Population, Part I, United States Summary, Table 5b.

Table 2-5.—PERCENTAGE DISTRIBUTION OF URBAN AND RURAL POPULATION BY SIZE OF PLACE: 1790 TO 1950

Urban and rural territory by size of place	Year																		
	1950		1940	1930	1920	1910	1900	1890	1880	1870	1860	1850	1840	1830	1820	1810	1800	1790
	New urban definition	Old urban definition																
PERCENT OF TOTAL POPULATION																		
United States..............	100.0	100.0	100.0	100.0	100.0	100.0	100.0	100.0	100.0	100.0	100.0	100.0	100.0	100.0	100.0	100.0	100.0	100.0
Urban territory..............	64.0	59.0	56.5	56.2	51.2	45.7	39.7	35.1	28.2	25.7	19.8	15.3	10.8	8.8	7.2	7.3	6.1	5.1
Places of 1,000,000 or more.....	11.5	11.5	12.1	12.3	9.6	9.2	8.5	5.8	2.4	...	...	...	...	...	...	...	...	...
Places of 500,000 to 1,000,000..	6.1	6.1	4.9	4.7	5.9	3.3	2.2	1.3	3.8	4.2	4.4	2.2	...	...	...	...	...	...
Places of 250,000 to 500,000....	5.5	5.5	5.9	6.5	4.3	4.3	3.8	3.9	2.6	4.0	0.8	...	1.8	...	...	...	...	...
Places of 100,000 to 250,000....	6.3	6.4	5.9	6.1	6.2	5.3	4.3	4.4	3.6	2.6	3.2	2.8	1.2	1.6	1.3	...	...	...
Places of 50,000 to 100,000.....	5.9	6.0	5.6	5.3	5.0	4.5	3.6	3.2	1.9	2.0	1.4	1.2	1.1	1.7	1.3	2.1	1.1	...
Places of 25,000 to 50,000.....	5.8	6.3	5.6	5.2	4.8	4.4	3.7	3.6	2.9	2.4	2.1	2.6	1.4	0.8	0.7	1.1	1.3	1.6
Places of 10,000 to 25,000.....	7.9	8.3	7.6	7.4	6.7	6.0	5.7	5.5	4.4	4.4	2.8	2.4	2.4	1.9	1.3	1.5	1.0	1.2
Places of 5,000 to 10,000.......	5.4	5.2	5.1	4.8	4.7	4.6	4.2	3.8	3.4	3.3	3.1	2.6	1.9	1.8	1.6	1.6	1.8	1.2
Places of 2,500 to 5,000........	4.3	3.7	3.8	3.8	4.1	4.1	3.8	3.6	3.2	2.8	1.9	1.4	1.0	1.0	1.0	1.0	0.9	1.1
Places under 2,500..............	0.4	...	...	...	...	...	...	...	...	...	...	...	...	...	...	...	...	...
Unincorporated parts of urbanized areas...................	4.9	...	...	...	...	...	...	...	...	...	...	...	...	...	...	...	...	...
Rural territory..............	36.0	41.0	43.5	43.8	48.8	54.3	60.3	64.9	71.8	74.3	80.2	84.7	89.2	91.2	92.8	92.7	93.9	94.9
Places of 1,000 to 2,500........	4.3	3.6	3.8	3.9	4.5	4.6	4.3	4.0	...	...	...	...	...	...	...	...	...	...
Places under 1,000.............	2.7	2.7	3.3	3.6	4.0	4.3	4.0	3.6	...	...	...	...	...	...	...	...	...	...
Other rural territory...........	29.0	34.7	36.4	36.4	40.3	45.5	52.0	57.3	...	...	...	...	...	...	...	...	...	...

Source: U.S. Bureau of the Census, U.S. Census of Population: 1950, Vol. I, U.S. Summary, Table 5b.

was accelerated by the Civil War, which hastened the growth of large cities. By 1900 there were 38 places of 100,000 or more inhabitants, and a total of 1,737 urban places. World War I appeared also to intensify the growth of urban places at the expense of the rural.

Industrial and commercial development in the United States has led to intensive urbanization in two ways: It has greatly multiplied the number of cities, and it has caused many of those cities to attain such large sizes that together they contain a very important share of the total population. Figure 2-4 illustrates the rapid concentration of population in large centers. From this chart it may be seen that the rise of large metropolitan centers has occurred largely within the past century. The building of railroad networks, and many other technological advances, encouraged this development.

Table 2-5 fails to show the full extent of urban agglomeration, for the medium-size and smaller cities are reported without reference to the fact that many of them are satellite cities within the suburbs of larger metropolitan centers. This table also fails to include in the large agglomeration the unincorporated fringe population around larger cities which was added to the urban classification in 1950. An adequate picture of present concentration should include this satellite and rural fringe population as a part of the large urban agglomerations. A more accurate and complete picture of urban agglomeration at the present time is presented by Table 2-6, where the proportion of the total population contained in each of several size classes of urbanized areas (central cities and their urban fringes) is shown.

This table shows that almost one-half of the population of the United States (46.0 percent) was living within one of the 157 urbanized areas. This is equivalent to 71.8 percent of the total urban population of the nation. 13.9 percent of the total population (21.6 percent of the urban population) lives in urban fringes.

The 3,253 urban places outside the urbanized areas contain less than 1/5 of the total population, and 28.2 percent of the urban population. From this it may be seen that the population of the United States is not only urbanized, but is heavily concentrated in larger urban agglomerations as well. Figure 2-5 shows this fact cartographically.

In the lower portion of Table 2-6, the extent of this concentration in urbanized areas is summarized by size of urbanized area. One-fourth of the total population (55 percent of the urban population) is contained in the 12 urbanized areas with one million or more inhabitants.

The rural population, on the other hand, shows a picture of dispersion. Together, the rural-

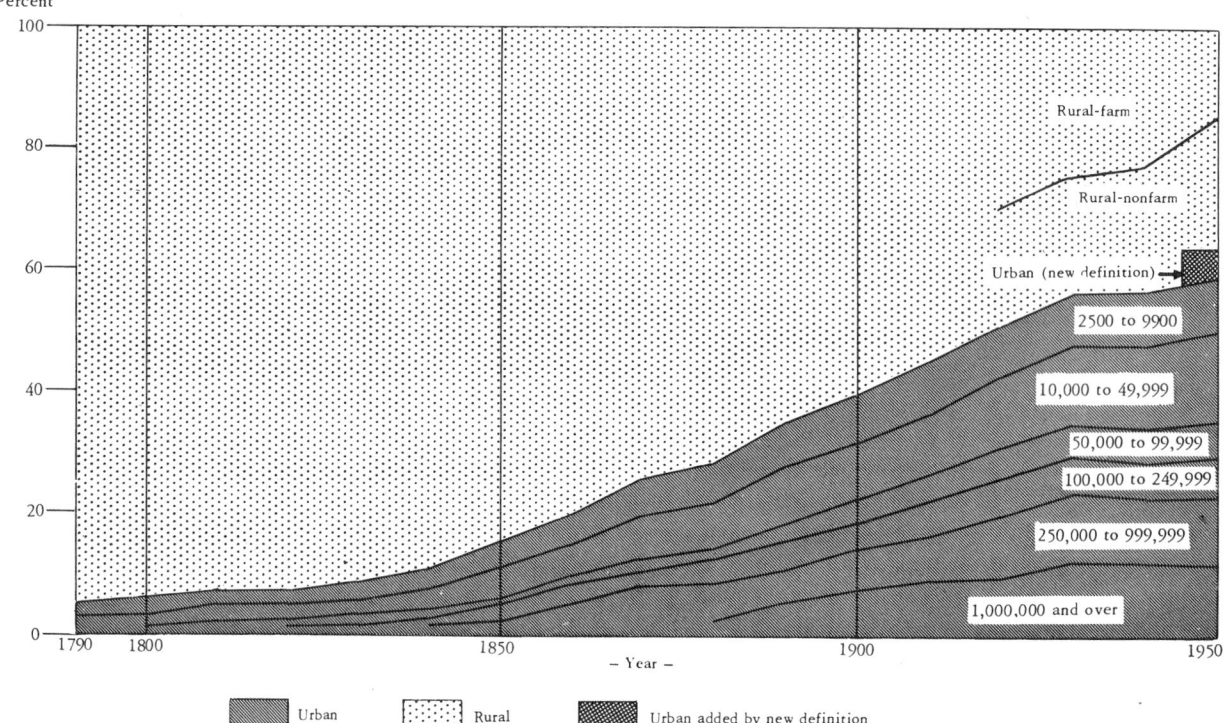

FIGURE 2 - 4. POPULATION OF THE UNITED STATES BY SIZE OF PLACE OF HABITATION, 1790 TO 1950

nonfarm and rural-farm populations comprise 36.0 percent of the total population. The rural-farm population is highly dispersed, as would be expected; 98.4 percent of it lives in unincorporated rural territory. Only a small fraction of the population of small incorporated places is rural farm.

In 1950 it was possible, for the first time, to learn how the rural-nonfarm population is distributed by size of place (Table 2-6). Contrary to what might have been expected, this is not predominantly a population of small incorporated villages and hamlets. Instead, more than two-thirds (69.1 percent) of it lives in rural territory outside incorporated places. Although it is almost certainly true that a significant proportion of this population lives in unincorporated country villages, it is entirely possible that as much as 1/2 to 2/3 of the entire rural-nonfarm population is clustered around the boundaries of smaller cities and villages or around the urbanized areas of larger cities, or is strung out along major highways and all-weather roads. The rural-farm population has

shrunk to a size that makes it only slightly more than 1/8 of the nation's population. With numerous small cities scattered throughout farming areas, and automobile transportation available, this farm population is now able to travel to nearby cities to shop and to satisfy its service needs. Under such circumstances, it is only to be expected that the rural shopping center for farmers should shrink to a very small part of the total United States population. Even after having 7.5 million people removed from it by the new urban definition, as a whole the rural-nonfarm population is, beyond a doubt, a city-oriented rather than a farm-oriented population, as O. D. Duncan has pointed out.

THE SOURCES OF URBAN GROWTH

A proper interpretation of growth rates for urban and rural populations requires familiarity with the sources of that growth. During a given period such as a decade, the urban population can gain population in two ways: (a) places that were urban at the last census can gain additional residents, either through migration or natural increase, and

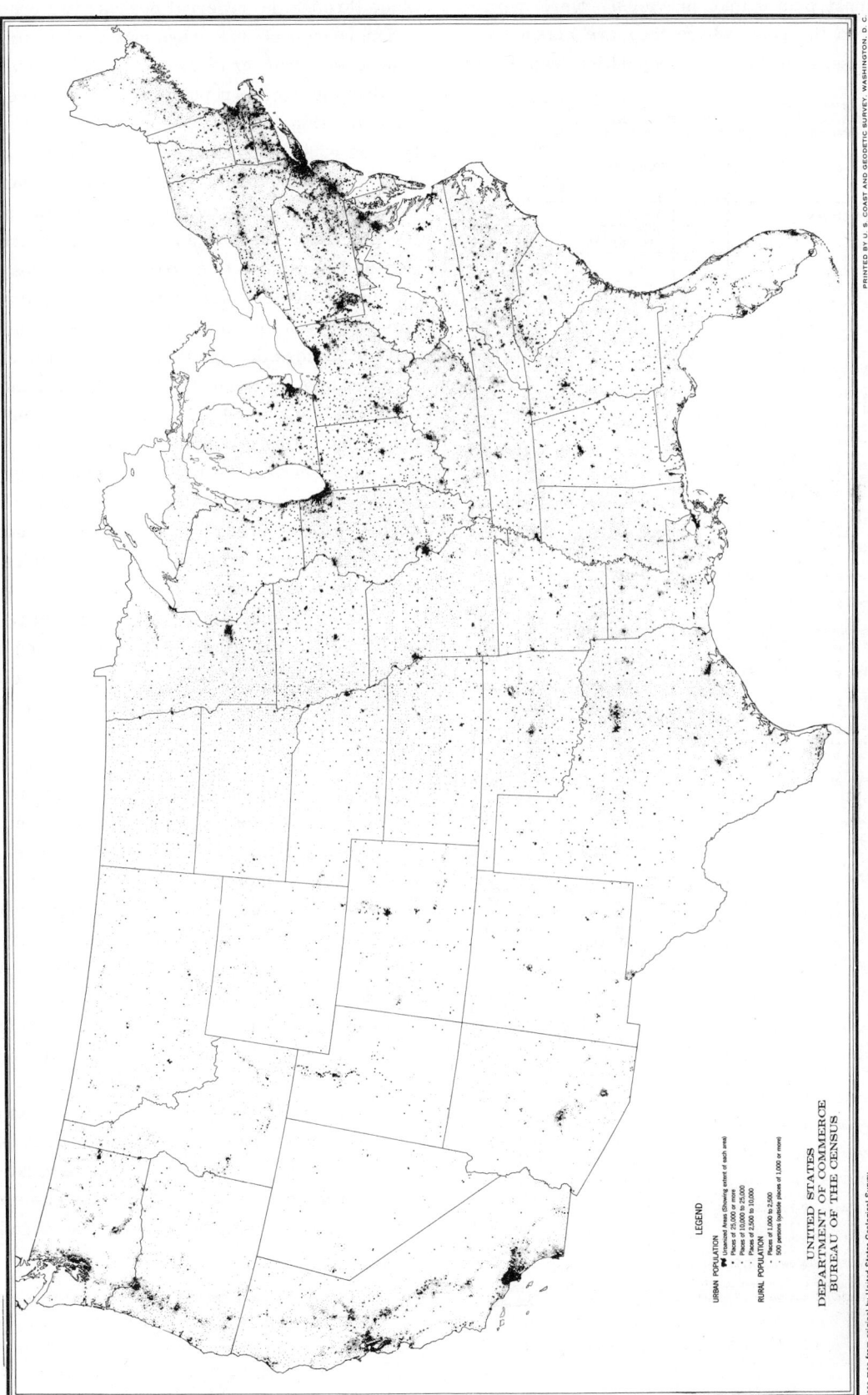

Base map from original by United States Geological Survey
Subject data from 1950 Census of Population

PRINTED BY U. S. COAST AND GEODETIC SURVEY, WASHINGTON, D. C.

LEGEND

URBAN POPULATION
Urbanized Areas (Showing extent of each area)
• Places of 25,000 or more
• Places of 10,000 to 25,000
• Places of 2,500 to 10,000

RURAL POPULATION
• Places of 1,000 to 2,500
• 500 persons (outside places of 1,000 or more)

UNITED STATES
DEPARTMENT OF COMMERCE
BUREAU OF THE CENSUS

FIGURE 2–5. POPULATION DISTRIBUTION, URBAN AND RURAL: 1950

(b) additional places that previously were rural can grow to the point where they are classed as urban. Losses to the urban population can take

Table 2-6.—URBAN AND RURAL POPULATION OF URBANIZED AREAS, OTHER URBAN AREAS, AND RURAL AREAS, BY SIZE OF PLACE: 1950

Type of area and size of place	Number of places	Population	Percent of total population	Percent of total
United States...........	...	150,697,361	100.0	...
URBAN, TOTAL.................	(1)	96,467,686	64.0	100.0
WITHIN URBANIZED AREAS.............	...	69,249,148	46.0	71.8
Central cities, total............	172	48,377,240	32.1	50.1
Cities of 1,000,000 or more.....	5	17,404,450	11.5	18.0
Cities of 500,000 to 1,000,000..	13	9,186,945	6.1	9.5
Cities of 250,000 to 500,000....	22	7,990,793	5.3	8.3
Cities of 100,000 to 250,000....	55	8,244,219	5.5	8.5
Cities of 50,000 to 100,000.....	68	5,172,381	3.4	5.4
Cities under 50,000.............	9	378,452	0.3	0.4
Urban fringes, total............	...	20,871,908	13.9	21.6
Incorporated places of 2,500 more......................	859	12,949,890	8.6	13.4
Incorporated places of 250,000 or more..................	1	250,767	0.2	0.3
Incorporated places of 100,000 to 250,000..............	10	1,234,443	0.8	1.3
Incorporated places of 50,000 to 100,000..............	37	2,562,230	1.7	2.7
Incorporated places of 25,000 to 50,000..............	71	2,494,662	1.7	2.6
Incorporated places of 10,000 to 25,000..............	231	3,629,308	2.4	3.8
Incorporated places of 5,000 to 10,000:.............	268	1,892,680	1.3	2.0
Incorporated places of 2,500 to 5,000....	241	885,800	0.6	0.9
Incorporated places under 2,500.	457	577,992	0.4	0.6
Incorporated places of 2,000 to 2,500..................	80	180,587	0.1	0.2
Incorporated places of 1,500 to 2,000..................	106	183,844	0.1	0.2
Incorporated places of 1,000 to 1,500..................	93	115,660	0.1	0.1
Incorporated places under 1,000......................	178	97,901	0.1	0.1
Unincorporated territory.......	...	7,344,026	4.9	7.6
OUTSIDE URBANIZED AREAS...........	3,253	27,218,538	18.1	28.2
Places of 50,000 or more........	21	1,196,212	0.8	1.2
Places of 25,000 to 50,000......	172	5,934,607	3.9	6.2
Places of 10,000 to 25,000......	547	8,237,197	5.5	8.5
Places of 5,000 to 10,000.......	908	6,245,916	4.1	6.5
Places of 2,500 to 5,000........	1,605	5,604,606	3.7	5.8
RURAL, TOTAL.................	...	54,229,675	36.0	100.0
Places under 2,500.............	13,807	10,504,463	7.0	19.4
Places of 2,500 to 2,500........	758	1,685,599	1.1	3.1
Places of 1,500 to 2,000........	1,272	2,186,571	1.5	4.0
Places of 1,000 to 1,500........	2,128	2,601,145	1.7	4.8
Places under 1,000.............	9,649	4,031,148	2.7	7.4
Other rural territory..........	...	43,725,212	29.0	80.6
URBANIZED AREAS, TOTAL.......	157	69,249,148	46.0	100.0
Areas of 1,000,000 or more......	12	37,817,068	25.1	54.6
Areas of 500,000 to 1,000,000...	13	8,751,241	5.8	12.6
Areas of 250,000 to 500,000.....	24	8,676,270	5.8	12.5
Areas of 100,000 to 250,000.....	70	10,888,119	7.2	15.7
Areas of 50,000 to 100,000......	38	3,116,450	2.1	4.5
RURAL-NONFARM POPULATION.........	...	31,181,325	21.7	100.0
Places 1,000 to 2,500..........	...	6,017,996	4.2	19.3
Incorporated places of less than 1,000......................	...	3,617,034	2.5	11.6
Other rural territory...........	...	1,546,295	15.0	69.1
RURAL-FARM POPULATION............	...	23,331,738	14.2	100.0
Places 1,000 to 2,500...........	...	139,991	0.1	0.6
Incorporated places of less than 1,000......................	...	233,317	0.1	1.0
Other rural territory...........	...	22,958,430	13.9	98.4

[1]There were 4,284 places of 2,500 or more.

Source: U.S. Bureau of the Census, U.S. Census of Population: 1950, U.S. Summary, Table 5a and Vol. IV, Part 5, Characteristics By Size of Place, Table A.

place through the reversal of these two processes.

Emergence of new urban places is an important source of urban growth. To the urban population it adds the entire population of the place whose classification is being changed from rural to urban. In most instances, several decades were required to accumulate this population, yet it is credited as a lump addition to the decade in which the place becomes urban. Thus, rapid urbanization and a rapid rate of growth in the urban population do not necessarily require a rapid average rate of growth for cities already in existence.

This process of reclassification has the effect of continuously depleting the rural population. The more rapidly a rural place grows, the greater are the probabilities that it will be classed as urban at the next census. When reclassification does occur, the entire population of the place as recorded at the preceding census is treated as a loss to the rural population. By the rules of the game, the rural population can grow only by limited amounts and in a dispersed pattern. Rapid growth of a rural village or a suburb leads quickly to its reclassification as urban. This reclassification will be even more frequent under the new urban definition.

After the 1940 census was completed, Howard G. Brunsman of the Census Bureau made a detailed study of the sources of urban and rural growth during the 1930-40 decade. Some of his results are summarized in Table 2-7.[13] As reported in the 1940 census, the urban population grew by 7.9 percent and the rural population by only 6.4 percent in the 1930-40 decade. However, Mr. Brunsman's breakdown of the sources of growth shows that 343 places switched from a rural to an urban classification, while only 44 made the reverse change. The net effect was to transfer, by definition, more than 1 million people from rural to urban. This was almost 20 percent of the total urban growth during the decade. If the growths of areas which retained the same urban-rural classification throughout the decade are

---

[13]Mr. Brunsman kindly gave permission to publish these data; they have not been reported elsewhere.

Table 2-7.—SOURCES OF GROWTH TO THE URBAN AND RURAL POPULATION: 1930 TO 1940

Urban and rural population	Number of places	Number of inhabitants			Percent change, 1930-40
		1940	1930	Change in population 1930-40	
Urban population, 1940...............	3,464	74,423,702	68,954,823	5,468,879	7.9
Places urban in both 1940 and 1930.	3,121	73,280,864	68,837,752	4,443,112	6.5
Places urban in 1940, rural, 1930..	343	1,142,838	781,392	1,142,838	46.3
Places urban in 1930, rural, 1940..	44	105,579	117,071	-117,071	-9.8
Rural population, 1940...............	...	57,245,573	53,820,223	3,425,350	6.4
Places rural in both 1940 and 1930.	...	57,139,994	53,038,831	4,101,163	7.7
Places rural in 1940, urban, 1930..	...	105,579	117,071	105,579	-9.8
Places rural in 1930, urban, 1940..	...	1,142,838	781,392	-781,392	46.3
Urban areas, as defined in 1930....	...	72,243,605	68,173,431	4,070,174	6.0
Rural areas, as defined in 1930....	...	58,177,253	53,703,152	4,474,101	8.3

Source: Unpublished tabulation, prepared under the supervision of Howard G. Brunsman, Bureau of the Census.

compared, it may be seen that rural areas actually grew faster than urban areas between 1930 and 1940. If the factor of annexation is considered, the rural growth would be considerably more rapid than would the urban. This comparison excludes the reclassified areas--those that gained or lost the urban status. The most valid comparison is one by which urban and rural areas, as classified as of the beginning of the decade, are compared. In this case the difference is even greater--rural areas grew more than 1/3 faster than urban areas. Thus, it is valid to say that rural areas grew faster than urban areas during the 1930-40 decade, although the urban population gained at the greater rate.

Although a complete reversal of findings, such as took place for 1930-40, is exceptional, this example serves as a reminder that it is improper to regard the intercensal urban or rural growth rates as an average weighted rate of growth for a fixed set of areas. During any decade, a large proportion of the urban growth is contributed by places whose classification has been changed at the last census, and the low rate of rural growth is due in part to the depletion of rural population, which was caused by whole villages being arbitrarily removed from the rural category and added to the urban.

In studying growth of urban and rural areas during the 1950-60 decade, it will be even more essential to trace the growth to its source. As has already been pointed out, there will be a completely new delineation of the urbanized areas, and much suburban territory will be transferred from the rural to the urban category. In 1950, much of this territory was partially developed and moderately densely settled. Changing its classification will transfer several million persons from the rural to the urban category. A sizable proportion of this population will have been present in these areas in 1950.

THE COMPONENTS OF URBAN GROWTH

This discussion of rapid urban growth should not end without an attempt to answer the question, "Where do these new city dwellers come from?" There is a natural temptation to presume that migration causes all of this growth. Deeper reflection will demonstrate that this is impossible, however. During the 1940-50 decade, for example, cities were gaining population at the rate of about 1.73 million persons per year. None of this was being gained from rural-nonfarm areas, for they were growing faster than cities. If migration were the sole source of urban growth, all of this migration drain of 1.73 million persons per year perforce must come from the rural-farm population. But if this had been the case, the rural-farm population would decline to zero in a few short years; farm families are now so few that they are incapable of exporting that many persons to the cities.

The answer to the question is, "About 70 percent of the increase in city dwellers comes from reproductive change (natural increase) and about 30 percent from rural-urban migration." In 1950, infants were being born into urban populations at the rate of about 22.9 births per year per 1000 residents. At the same time, deaths were occurring at the rate of about 10 per thousand. This means that in the single year 1950 there was a net increase of about 12.9 persons per thousand inhabitants (1.3 percent) due simply to this favorable balance of births and deaths. In a recent article, the author estimated that the ratio of growth from reproductive change to net migration was of the general magnitude of 7 to 3, as suggested above.[14] This is a very approximate estimate, based on a manipulation of populations according to old rather than new definitions. However, it is precise enough to validate the claim that the future course of city growth depends largely upon the future course of city birth rates.

Urbanization, however, is largely a function of migration from farms. If no migration occurred, rural places would grow faster than urban, because rural birth rates are higher than urban birth rates. Under these circumstances, rural population would become an increasingly larger proportion of all population. Even under these conditions, however, much rural growth would be transferred to the urban category by the process of reclassifying communities, as described above in the section on "Sources of Growth." A stream of migration from rural to urban areas, even if moderately small, hastens this process directly, for each city-ward migrant is a loss on the rural side of the ledger and a gain on the urban side. Hence, a very large share of the changes in the proportion of the population that is urban or rural (urbanization) must be attributed directly to migration, and this migration is drawn from the farm population.

The long-time role that migration from farms has played in the process of urbanization may be appreciated from estimates of net migration from the rural-farm population during each of the last three intercensal periods, reported by Gladys Bowles.[15]

Decade	Net migration (000)	Rate of migration
1940-50	-8,610	-30.9
1930-40	-3,498	-12.7
1920-30	-6,085	-19.3

[14] Donald J. Bogue, "Urbanism in the United States, 1950," *American Journal of Sociology*, March, 1955.

[15] Gladys K. Bowles, *Net Migration from the Farm Population, 1940-50*, Washington D.C.: Agriculture Marketing Service Statistical Bulletin 176, 1956.

The above estimates refer to the movement of persons who were both alive at the beginning of the decade, and who lived on farms at the beginning of the decade. Almost one farm resident in three who was living on a farm in 1940 had moved to a nonfarm residence (rural-nonfarm or urban) by 1950. A similar though less intense pattern was in effect during each of the two preceding decades. Between 1940-50, a total of almost 9 million farm residents were removed from farms and deposited in metropolitan areas, suburbs, hinterland cities, and other nonfarm areas. All of these migrants flowed either to urban or to rural-nonfarm areas. Although 9 million migrants is a very large number, it is still small when compared with the total growth of the urban and nonfarm areas.

CHANGES IN DEFINITIONS FOR THE 1960 CENSUS

Since the above materials were written, the Bureau of the Census has been planning, with the consent of interested government agencies, to make certain changes in the definitions of both the urban and farm populations for the 1960 census. The revised boundaries of urbanized areas probably will be delimited in terms of entire enumeration districts (purposely kept small in size) surrounding the old boundaries of urbanized areas. If an enumeration district meets certain criteria of "urban-ness" it will be included with the urban population. This avoids the expensive map and field work of establishing urbanized area boundaries prior to the census enumeration, and produces a definition that reflects population distribution at the time of census enumeration. Also there probably will be a revival of the "urban under special rule" definitions to permit the separate recognition of individual unincorporated city-like places for which separate statistics of population characteristics are not now published.

The rural-farm population will no longer be identified in terms of the single question "Is this place on a farm?," but in terms of questions concerning value of produce grown and size of place. This approach yields a rural-farm population that more nearly corresponds to the residents of places enumerated as farms by the Census of Agriculture. It is estimated that this will transfer 3 to 5 million persons from the rural-farm to the rural-nonfarm category. Thus, there will be a major discontin-uity in the statistics for the rural-farm population between 1960 and earlier censuses.

Note: The probable future trends in urban-rural residence are discussed in Chapter 26.

Chapter 3

POPULATION DISTRIBUTION: RESIDENCE IN METROPOLITAN AND NONMETROPOLITAN AREAS

METROPOLITAN AREAS AS FOCAL POINTS IN THE NATION

An aspect of urban development which was treated briefly in the preceding chapter is the tendency for cities to grow to very large size. Even after they have passed the 100,000 or even the million mark, urban places have been able in the past to enjoy rapid rates of growth. Big cities have been able to get even bigger, and the number of big cities has increased. In order to continue to grow rapidly, these large cities must attract migrants from other areas by providing them with good jobs and other advantages which the migrants are unable to acquire in their smaller hometowns or on their fathers' farms. Big cities are able to offer these advantages, in competition with smaller places, only if the economic and social structure. of the nation favors and fosters the rise of large metropolises. The materials presented in this chapter demonstrate that very strong forces are at work tending toward an ever-greater concentration of population and economic activities in, or within the immediate environs of, big cities. Without an appreciation of this trend toward metropolitan concentration, and a general knowledge of the events that are taking place, it is difficult to understand many of the population changes to be described in later chapters.

One could imagine two alternative courses for the urban development of a nation. (a) It is conceivable that places could grow until they reached an optimum or maximum size, and that thereafter they would grow no more. If great size were a serious economic and social handicap to cities, they would tend, as they approached the optimum or maximum size, to attain an equilibrium with other cities in the area, because they would gain little benefit from added growth. Under these circumstances, the impetus to economic expansion and additional population growth in larger places would be drained off competitively into the growth of smaller urban places. (b) One can also imagine that, after a certain equilibrium were reached, in-migration to a city might slacken to the point where it would exactly balance out-migration, and that thereafter the city would grow only by vital increase. Neither of these developments has occurred consistently in the past. Instead, the largest centers have continued to attract migrants to their environs in excess of their migration losses and to retain their vital increases. This process has been obscured, in part, because much of the growth has taken place in suburbs immediately outside the city limits.

The number of these larger places has increased steadily and rapidly. This observation, coupled with other information as to how the American economy operates, led such scholars as N. S. B. Gras and R. D. McKenzie to regard the big city, or metropolitan center, as the focal point of the industrialized American economy.[1] This theory has been examined in some detail, with the finding that population and economic activities are distributed around large cities in a pattern that does support the theory.[2] In short, it appears that as a nation becomes highly industrialized and

---

[1]N. S. B. Gras, An Introduction to Economic History (New York: Harper and Brothers, 1922). R. D. McKenzie, The Metropolitan Community (New York: McGraw-Hill, 1933).

[2]Donald J. Bogue, The Structure of the Metropolitan Community (Ann Arbor: University of Michigan Press, 1950).

commercialized it also tends to become metropolitanized. Its economic activities tend to be located with reference to large centers, as well as with reference to resources and sources of raw materials. Many factors conspire to produce this tendency toward a concentration of population and economic activities in large metropolitan agglomerations, and to cause the population and economic activities in the hinterlands to be arrayed about the metropolis in an orderly way. Lower total transportation costs, the advantages to wholesalers and retailers of a concentrated market, the advantages of joint location to several industries, the advantages of a large and varied labor supply to employers, the advantages to workers of a large and varied supply of employment opportunities, and the advantages to manufacturers of the economies of large-scale production and distribution--all these factors are said to be among the causes of this tendency toward metropolitan concentration. The term "dominance" has been used as a class name to refer to the phenomenon. A significant aspect of the dominant role of metropolitan centers is the fact that medium-size and smaller cities (as well as dispersed rural populations) appear to perform their functions with reference to the larger centers, even while they are exerting an organizing and integrating influence upon their immediate "trade territory." Thus, it has been said that large metropolitan centers are dominant in the modern industrial economy, while the smaller urban places are "subdominant."

At the present time this hypothesis is only a very general one, however. The exact number of metropolitan regions have not been determined nor their boundaries established. The exact nature of the competition between neighboring metropolitan centers for the privilege of serving the populations near their outer boundaries is not known. How the various components of dominance are affected by differences in resources, climate, and other environmental factors has not been studied. How new metropolitan areas emerge and carve out a hinterland for themselves from the area previously dominated by other metropolitan cities, and the extent to which there is joint or multiple domi-

nance of outlying areas, is little understood. As yet, the internal structure of the metropolitan hinterland is known only in its broadest outline.

An aspect of metropolitan dominance that is much more familiar, and which presents many problems of considerable practical as well as theoretical concern, is the tendency for areas located very near the metropolis to be closely integrated with the metropolis--both economically and socially. The effect of the metropolis upon this close-in area is so direct and so strong that, for many purposes, it is highly important to delimit this area for separate treatment.

There are many practical, as well as theoretical, reasons for separating the metropolises and their immediate environs from the rest of the nation, and for treating them as major units in studying the distribution of population and economic activities. Labor force experts, transportation and traffic specialists, students of industrial location, city planners, and businessmen interested in outlying shopping centers are only a few of those who are interested in these metropolitan areas. The area that should be included in this delimitation is considerably larger than the closely built-up urban fringe, described in Chapter 2. It more nearly corresponds to what one would regard as the labor market area of the metropolis. Automobile transportation now makes it possible for one to live several miles distant from one's place of work. Many office and factory workers in the central business district now choose to live in the more remote suburbs. Since the early 1940's, suburban areas surrounding large metropolises have been the sites of a tremendous building boom--industrial as well as residential and commercial. It is known that even in the areas just beyond the urban fringe, but adjacent to it, there is a ring of rapid population growth several miles across. (A recent popular exposition termed this zone "Exurbia.") A high proportion of the population in this ring is rural-nonfarm. Scattered dwellings are built in long strings and on large lots along main highways leading into the metropolis. Even the rural-farm population in this outer zone of direct metropolitan influence tends to have

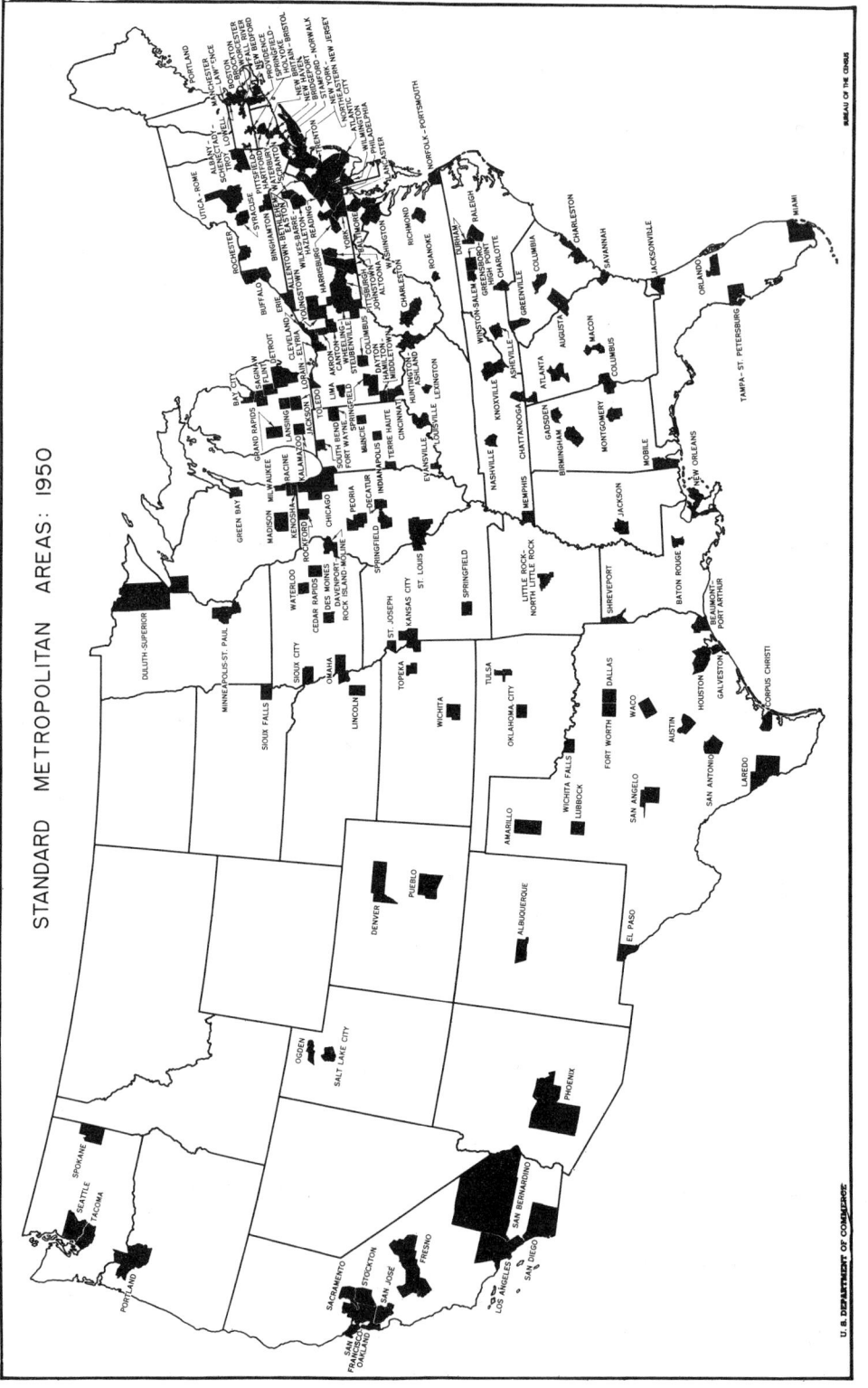

STANDARD METROPOLITAN AREAS: 1950

FIGURE 3-1. STANDARD METROPOLITAN AREAS: 1950

characteristics that differ from those of the rural-farm population in adjacent areas outside the orbit of direct metropolitan dominance. Farms in this outer zone of direct metropolitan influence tend to be much more varied and specialized in their operations and their products. They produce for sale in the nearby metropolitan market. Many farms are operated as a part-time venture, with one or more breadwinners in the family having employment within the metropolis.

When considered in all of these aspects, it is evident that the economic and social entity that may be termed "the metropolis and its immediate environs," or "metropolitan area," is much greater in scope than the central city or even the urbanized area. While it would be a mistake to think that metropolitan areas are not compact, dense, and oriented toward one or more centers, the opposite error would be to assume that the direct and powerful influence of the metropolis ceases at the point where the pattern of urban settlement stops.

THE CENSUS DELIMITATION
OF STANDARD METROPOLITAN AREAS

In order to acknowledge this metropolitanized aspect of the economy, and to provide separate statistics for areas under direct metropolitan dominance, at the time of the 1950 census, the Bureau of the Census recognized 168 large population clusters which it termed "standard metropolitan areas." The official definition of standard metropolitan areas is as follows:

"Except in New England, a standard metropolitan area is a county or group of contiguous counties which contains at least one city of 50,000 inhabitants or more. In addition to the county, or counties, containing such a city, or cities, contiguous counties are included in a standard metropolitan area if according to certain criteria they are essentially metropolitan in character and socially and economically integrated with the central city.

The criteria of metropolitan character relate primarily to the character of the county as a place of work or as a home for concentrations of nonagricultural workers and their dependents. Specifically, these criteria are:

1. The county must (a) contain 10,000 nonagricultural workers, or (b) contain 10 percent of the nonagricultural workers working in the standard metropolitan area, or (c) have at least one-half of its population residing in minor civil divisions with a population density of 150 or more per square mile and contiguous to the central city.

2. Nonagricultural workers must constitute at least two-thirds of the total number of employed persons of the county...

The criteria of integration relate primarily to the extent of economic and social communication between the outlying counties and the central county as indicated by such items as the following:

1. Fifteen percent or more of the workers residing in the contiguous county work in the county containing the largest city in the standard metropolitan area, or

2. Twenty-five percent or more of the persons working in the contiguous county reside in the county containing the largest city in the standard metropolitan area, or

3. The number of telephone calls per month to the county containing the largest city of the standard metropolitan area from the contiguous county is four or more times the number of subscribers in the contiguous county.

In New England, the city and town are administratively more important than the county, and data are compiled locally for such minor civil divisions. Here towns and cities were the units used in defining standard metropolitan areas, and most of the criteria relating to the number and proportion of nonagricultural workers set forth above could not be applied. In their place, a population density criterion of 150 persons or more per square mile, or 100 persons or more per square mile where strong integration was evident, has been used.

Central cities.--Although there may be several cities of 50,000 or more in a standard metropolitan area, not all are necessarily central cities. The largest city in a standard metropolitan area is the principal central city. Any other city of 25,000 or more within a standard metropolitan area, and having a population amounting to one-third or more of the population of the principal city, is also a central city. However, no more than three cities have been defined as central cities of any standard metropolitan area. The name of every central city is included in the name of the area, with the exception that in the case of the New York-Northeastern New Jersey Standard Metropolitan Area, "Jersey City" and "Newark" are not part of the name." [3]

The standard metropolitan area delimitation was made with the co-operation of several agencies of the federal government, the work being co-ordinated by the Bureau of the Budget. The word "standard" in the term "standard metropolitan area" indicates that this delimitation shall be officially binding upon all federal agencies that publish statistics for large cities and their environs. Hence, standard metropolitan areas replace metropolitan districts, industrialized areas, and other units that had been devised to recognize that metropolitan areas are larger than just the central cities.

The delimitation is based upon a great deal of research, inquiry, and consultation with local authorities in each area. The field staff of the Census Bureau was used to gather much of the information necessary for decisions upon the boundaries. Every effort was made to reconcile the available statistical evidence with the views of local experts concerning the areas which could be considered closely integrated with the central city.

Like the new urban and rural definitions, the standard metropolitan area delimitation was introduced in the 1950 census and is an innovation that greatly enhances the usefulness of the census tabulations. Figure 3-1 is a map indicating the names and locations of the standard metropolitan areas.

THE DISTRIBUTION OF POPULATION BETWEEN METROPOLITAN AND NONMETROPOLITAN AREAS

By combining county statistics from each census since 1900, a recent monograph applies the new standard metropolitan area definition to the results of each census since 1900. This permits a study of the growth of population in metropolitan and nonmetropolitan areas over the last half-century, especially as these trends relate to the growth of economic activity. [4] To make this study of trends, it was necessary to redelimit the 16 standard metropolitan areas of New England along county boundaries rather than town lines, because data for the town units were not available in all cases. Since in some instances two or more New England standard metropolitan areas fall in the same county, in order to form a few of the county-equivalent areas it was necessary to combine two or more S.M.A.'s. This reduced the total number of S.M.A.'s from 168 to 162. The S.M.A. definition was extended to earlier censuses only for "principal standard metropolitan areas," that is, S.M.A.'s with a total population of 100,000 or more at any census. [5] (In 1950 this eliminated 15 small S.M.A.'s that had less than 100,000 population, and for the 1940 and earlier censuses required that areas have 100,000 population at the census date before they could be defined as metropolitan.) There were 147 principal S.M.A.'s at the 1950 census.

In 1950, 56.8 percent of the population of the United States lived in the 162 S.M.A.'s. These areas covered only 7.1 percent of the total land area of the nation. Thus, considerably more than 1/2 of the total population was concentrated in 1/14 of the land area.

---

[3] U.S. Bureau of the Census, U.S. Census of Population: 1950. Vol. I, Number of Inhabitants, Chapter 1: U.S. Summary, p. xxxiii.

[4] Donald J. Bogue, The Growth of Standard Metropolitan Areas: 1900-1950, With an Explanatory Analysis of Urbanized Areas (U.S. Government Printing Office, 1953). This monograph presents statistics for each standard metropolitan area, its central city, and the urban and rural parts of its ring for each decade from 1900 to 1950.

[5] All data in the present chapter will present statistics with the New England standard metropolitan areas delimited along county lines. The abbreviation "S.M.A." will be substituted for the term "standard metropolitan area."

Table 3-1.—GROWTH DATA FOR STANDARD METROPOLITAN AREAS, RETROJECTED TO EARLIER CENSUSES: 1900-50

Census year	Number of SMA's	Population (millions)	Percent of U.S. population	Rate of growth (percent change) during preceding decade			Percent of total U.S. population growth claimed by SMA's during preceding decade
				U.S. total	Standard metropolitan areas	Nonmetropolitan areas	
All SMA's, 1950...	162	85.6	56.8	14.5	21.8	6.0	80.6
Principal SMA's							
1950.............	147	84.3	56.0	14.5	21.8	6.3	79.3
1940.............	125	67.1	51.1	7.2	8.3	6.2	57.7
1930.............	115	61.0	49.8	16.1	27.0	7.1	76.2
1920.............	94	46.1	43.7	14.9	25.2	8.1	67.6
1910.............	71	34.5	37.6	21.0	32.6	15.0	53.1
1900.............	52	24.1	31.9	20 7	...	...	...

Source: The Growth of Standard Metropolitan Areas: 1900-50.

In the past half-century, there has been a steady trend toward an increase in the number of standard metropolitan areas, and toward a rise in the proportion of the total population residing in such areas. (See Figure 3-2.) The record of this trend is contained in Table 3-1. Had the S.M.A. delimitation been in effect in 1900, there would have been an estimated 52 areas, and these areas would have contained less than one-third of the total population. At each succeeding census, from 10 to 23 new S.M.A.'s would have been added as a result of additional areas attaining 100,000 population and qualifying as S.M.A.'s under the definition. This, with the higher than average growth rate of S.M.A.'s already defined for earlier censuses, results in a steady rise in the proportion of the total U.S. population living in metropolitan areas.

The extent to which metropolitan centers have tended to agglomerate population about themselves may be appreciated by comparing the growth rates of metropolitan and nonmetropolitan areas, and by noting what proportion of the nation's total population increase for each decade was claimed by the standard metropolitan areas. The right-hand column of Table 3-1 reports this information. During every decade except one, the S.M.A.'s have grown 50 percent faster than the nonmetropolitan areas, and have claimed a disproportionately large share of the total national growth. For example, between 1940 and 1950, the 147 principal S.M.A.'s increased by 21.8 percent, while the nonmetropolitan areas grew by only 6.3 percent. Although they constituted only 51.1 percent of the population in 1940, at the end of the decade they had claimed 79.3 percent of the total population increase during the decade. This growth differential between metropolitan and nonmetropolitan areas narrowed temporarily, both in absolute and relative amounts, during the economically depressed 1930-40 decade. Rapid metropolitan growth during the 1940-50 decade was merely a return to a trend that had dated back to the turn of the century or earlier.

There has been no slackening of this trend since 1950. At one of its period surveys, taken in March, 1956, the Bureau of the Census obtained information concerning the civilian population living inside and outside the 168 standard metropoli-

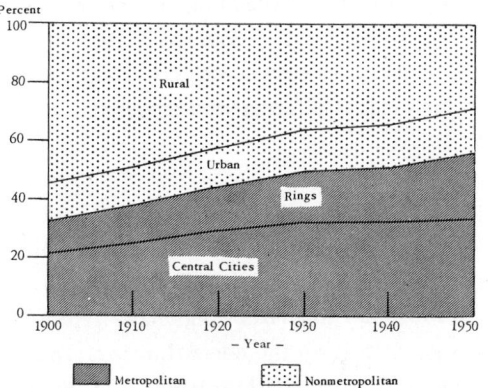

FIGURE 3-2. PERCENT OF THE TOTAL POPULATION OF THE UNITED STATES IN METROPOLITAN AND NONMETROPOLITAN AREAS: 1900 TO 1950

tan areas as defined for the 1950 census.[6] It was found that since the 1950 census the civilian population had increased by 14.7 million persons and that, of this increase, 85 percent (12.4 million persons) had taken place in the standard metropolitan areas. By contrast, the nonmetropolitan areas had managed to attract only 15 percent of the total growth--despite the fact that in 1950 they comprised 43 percent of the nation's population. The rates of growth for metropolitan and nonmetropolitan areas were as follows:

Area	Percent increase 1950-56
Civilian population, U.S. total ..	9.8
Standard metropolitan areas ...	14.8
Nonmetropolitan areas	3.4

Thus, during the current decade the standard metropolitan areas are growing at a rate approximately 4 times that of the nonmetropolitan areas, and are claiming an even higher proportion of the total population increase of the nation than they have claimed in any previous decade.

THE DISTRIBUTION OF POPULATION BETWEEN CENTRAL CITIES AND METROPOLITAN RINGS

The preceding section analyzed the growth of the standard metropolitan areas as units, without reference to the pattern of distribution or growth within the areas. In view of the facts discussed above and in the preceding chapter, it is evident that there is an extraordinary amount of interest in the comparative development of central cities and their suburban areas or "metropolitan rings," as that part of the standard metropolitan area outside the central cities has come to be called. Table 3-2 provides data which, in comparison with Table 3-1, permits the study of trends within metropolitan areas in comparison with trends in the nonmetropolitan areas and the nation as a whole.

Since 1900 there has been a remarkable reversal in the pattern of growth within metropolitan areas. During the 1900-10 and the 1910-20 decades, central cities were growing faster than their

---

[6]Current Population Reports, Population Characteristics, Series P-20, No. 71, December 7, 1956.

rings. In each decade since 1920, rings have been growing faster than central cities. Table 3-2 and Figure 3-3 document this shift. Early in the century rings had only about 1/9 of the population of the nation; now they have about 1/4. Between 1900-10 the rings claimed only about 1/6 of the national

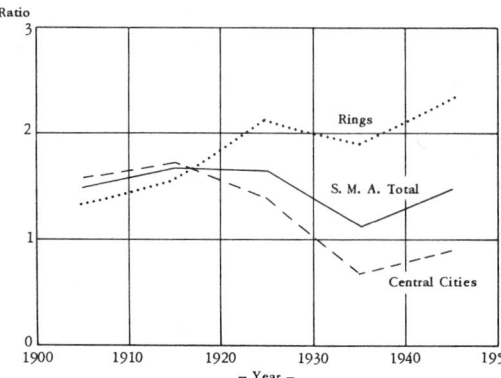

FIGURE 3-3. RATIO OF CENTRAL CITY AND RING RATES OF GROWTH TO THE NATIONAL RATE: 1900 TO 1950

population growth; in 1940-50 they claimed almost 1/2. The relative gap between the growth rate of central cities and rings has become very large; in 1940-50 rings grew almost 2 1/2 times as fast as central cities. In making these comparisons it should be noted also that in both the 1930-40 and 1940-50 decades the growth rates for central cities were below the national average, while the growth rates for rings were well above it. A great acceleration in suburbanization has taken place since the 1950 census. According to the March, 1956 survey of the Census Bureau, cited above,[7] the rates of increase between April, 1950 and March, 1956 for central cities and rings was as follows:

Area	Percent increase 1950-56
Civilian population, S.M.A. total.	14.8
Central cities	4.7
Metropolitan rings	29.3

Since 1950, the suburban rings have grown about 6 times as rapidly as the central cities. Of the 12.4 million civilian population gained by S.M.A.'s between 1950 and 1956, 10.1 million, or 81 percent,

---

[7]Current Population Reports, op. cit.

Table 3-2.—GROWTH DATA FOR CENTRAL CITIES AND RINGS OF STANDARD METROPOLITAN AREAS, RETROJECTED TO EARLIER CENSUSES: 1900-1950

Census year	Number of SMA's	Percent of U.S. population		Rate of growth (percent change) during preceding decade			Percent of total U.S. population growth claimed by SMA's during preceding decade	
		Central cities	Rings	Metropolitan areas, total	Central cities	Rings	Central cities	Rings
All SMA's, 1950...	162	32.8	24.0	21.8	13.9	34.7	31.6	49.0
Principal SMA's								
1950..............	147	32.3	23.8	21.8	13.7	34.8	30.7	48.6
1940..............	125	31.6	19.5	8.3	5.1	13.8	22.8	34.9
1930..............	115	31.8	18.0	27.0	23.3	34.2	43.3	32.9
1920..............	94	28.9	14.8	25.2	26.7	22.4	46.8	20.8
1910..............	71	25.0	12.7	32.6	35.3	27.6	37.4	15.7
1900..............	52	21.2	10.7	...	...	...	...	...

Source: The Growth of Standard Metropolitan Areas: 1900-50.

was claimed by the suburban rings of standard metropolitan areas. It is here that new residential construction has been concentrated. Also, it is informative to note that this suburban increase is equal to 70 percent of the total population increase of the nation.

In 1950, central cities contained about 1/3 of the nation's population. Because central cities have grown much more slowly than the total population (in 1950-56 they grew only 1/3 as rapidly) they are becoming a progressively smaller proportion of the total, while suburbia's relative weight is climbing rapidly.

TRENDS IN THE DISTRIBUTION OF POPULATION ✗ BETWEEN THE URBAN AND RURAL PARTS OF METROPOLITAN RINGS

Within the rings of standard metropolitan areas there has been a reversal in the pattern of growth similar to that which occurred between central cities and rings. Before 1930, urban places in the rings were growing much more rapidly than the rural areas. In fact, in comparison with the national rates of growth, it appears from Table 3-3 that metropolitan areas were building up their central cities, and a constellation of satellite cities, almost to the neglect of rural areas. This growth came from two sources: the growth of already established cities, and the growth of smaller incorporated places to 2,500 or more inhabitants, which automatically caused them to be transferred from the rural to the urban classification. Prior to 1930, both of these processes were operating at

a rapid pace. Because they lost population steadily through the reclassification of incorporated places as urban, the rural areas of rings grew less rapidly than either central cities or satellite urban places. During the 1930-40 decade, however, this situation was completely reversed, and this reversal continued through the 1940-50 decade.[8] Figure 3-4 illustrates this trend. During the last 20 years, the growth in metropolitan rings of incorporated places to a size which put them in the urban class has slackened noticeably, while the suburbanization of unincorporated territory adjacent to metropolitan centers has been accelerated greatly. Thus, the great surge of population into the periphery of standard metropolitan areas has not gone predominantly to outlying urban centers, as in 1900-1930. Instead, it has gone primarily to the unincorporated and less densely settled parts of the ring. The 1940-50 decade merely continued this tendency, which had been the predominant pattern during the depression years.

Since 1950, the urban and rural parts of metropolitan rings have grown in a pattern very similar to that prevailing between 1930 and 1950. This is shown by the following rates of growth, 1950-56:

Area	Percent increase 1950-56
Civilian population, S.M.A. rings	29.3
Urban areas (1950 definition)....	17.0
Rural areas..................	55.8

[8]The old (1940) urban definition has been employed in making these comparisons.

Table 3-3.—GROWTH DATA FOR THE URBAN AND RURAL PORTIONS OF RINGS OF STANDARD METROPOLITAN AREAS, RETROJECTED TO EARLIER CENSUSES: 1900-1950

Census year	Number of SMA's	Percent of U.S. population		Rate of growth (percent change) during preceding decade[1]			Percent of total U.S. population growth claimed by rings during preceding decade	
		Ring-urban	Ring-rural	Ring-total	Ring-urban	Ring-rural	Ring-urban	Ring-rural
All SMA's, 1950...	162	12.0	12.0	34.7	29.2	40.8	21.5	27.4
Principal SMA's								
1950..............	147	12.0	11.7	34.8	29.1	41.3	21.4	27.2
1940..............	125	10.5	8.9	13.8	9.1	19.8	13.1	21.8
1930..............	115	10.3	7.6	34.2	48.4	18.8	24.2	8.7
1920..............	94	8.0	6.8	22.4	38.4	7.6	17.1	3.7
1910..............	71	6.5	6.2	27.6	50.7	9.8	12.6	3.1
1900..............	52	4.9	5.7	...	...	...	...	...

[1]The old (1940) definitions of urban and rural are employed in this table.
Source: The Growth of Standard Metropolitan Areas: 1900-50.

The rural population of S.M.A.'s more than doubled in the six years between 1950 and 1956, and grew at a rate more than 3 times that of the urban areas in metropolitan rings. This is all the more impressive when it is appreciated that the new 1950 definition of urban population, rather than the old 1940 definition, was used in compiling the above figures.

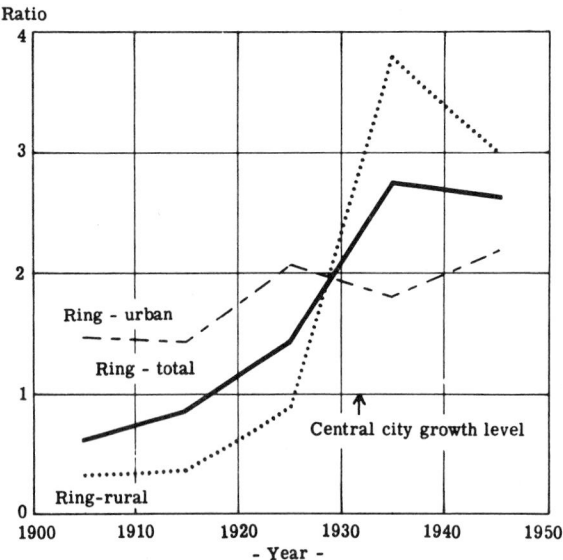

FIGURE 3-4. RATIO TO THE CENTRAL CITY GROWTH RATES OF METROPOLITAN RINGS, URBAN AND RURAL: 1900 TO 1950

When viewed in the light of the discussion of urbanized areas in Chapter 2, it would seem from the above results that the areas of most rapid suburban growth are the areas settled by rural-nonfarm population living outside urbanized areas, as defined in 1950, but within the metropolitan ring.

SIZE OF S. M. A. AND PATTERN OF GROWTH

There are, of course, a few very large S.M.A.'s and numerous smaller ones. The size distribution in 1950 was as follows:

Size (000)	Number of areas	Percent distribution
1,000-over	14	8.6
500-999	23	14.2
250-499	41	25.3
100-249	69	42.6
Under 100	15	9.2
Total	162	100.0

As Table 3-4 (which refers to the 125 areas that would have qualified as S.M.A.'s in 1940) shows, the large S.M.A.'s had a somewhat different internal pattern of growth than the smaller ones. Except for places of 3 million or more, which did appear to have a slower total rate of growth in recent decades than S.M.A.'s generally, there was no consistent relationship between size of S.M.A. and over-all growth rate.

Within S.M.A.'s of all sizes, central cities tended to grow more slowly than their rings, in both the 1930-40 and the 1940-50 decades. Moreover, the relative difference between central city and ring growth tended to be greater for larger than for smaller S.M.A.'s. Since the census of

Table 3-4.—PERCENT INCREASE PER DECADE IN POPULATION OF SMA'S, CENTRAL CITIES, AND RINGS, 1900-50 FOR 125 SMA'S OF 1940

Parts of SMA's and decade	Size of standard metropolitan area in 1940 (in thousands)							
	Total	3,000-over	1,000-2,999	500-999	350-499	250-349	150-249	100-149
Number of areas	125	3	8	13	18	18	34	31
SMA's total								
1940-50.............	21.3	12.2	25.7	25.3	17.9	28.7	28.2	26.9
1930-40.............	8.3	5.4	8.5	11.8	6.1	10.6	11.3	10.9
1920-30.............	27.1	26.8	36.0	23.6	20.0	21.9	29.1	24.1
1910-20.............	25.5	22.0	32.6	20.8	23.3	32.5	28.0	23.0
1900-10.............	32.3	33.6	33.9	32.2	29.9	32.9	36.6	22.8
1900-50.............	177.2	144.4	229.3	176.4	140.6	205.8	221.9	163.8
Central cities								
1940-50.............	13.0	6.0	13.5	14.6	14.5	21.9	18.3	24.6
1930-40.............	5.1	3.8	4.5	7.5	3.7	7.3	6.9	6.5
1920-30.............	23.6	19.9	28.5	20.2	19.1	25.6	34.0	29.3
1910-20.............	27.4	19.1	34.8	22.4	29.4	44.0	39.0	34.3
1900-10.............	36.2	32.5	32.6	37.1	40.8	42.1	55.8	37.2
1900-50.............	154.8	108.1	172.5	148.4	157.7	236.1	264.5	216.3
Rings, total								
1940-50.............	34.7	25.7	40.0	45.2	23.0	39.2	42.4	30.5
1930-40.............	13.8	9.1	13.7	20.7	10.0	16.1	18.1	18.9
1920-30.............	33.9	46.2	46.9	31.4	21.6	16.4	22.0	15.6
1910-20.............	22.0	31.0	29.5	17.3	14.6	18.1	15.9	8.4
1900-10.............	25.8	37.3	35.7	22.6	16.9	23.0	18.8	7.9
1900-50.............	214.9	260.4	310.6	231.3	120.1	173.1	182.6	109.8
Rings, urban								
1940-50.............	28.8	19.3	33.9	40.0	17.0	34.5	42.2	50.6
1930-40.............	9.1	6.6	10.8	14.4	3.0	10.0	14.3	13.8
1920-30.............	48.4	58.1	54.8	36.1	33.7	23.5	36.4	36.7
1910-20.............	38.8	46.2	43.7	23.4	23.2	31.2	64.4	26.4
1900-10.............	51.3	60.0	53.3	41.5	38.5	50.8	57.7	45.7
1900-50.............	338.0	370.8	405.9	280.5	174.8	261.8	474.8	331.6
Rings, rural								
1940-50.............	41.8	44.1	54.1	50.9	27.5	41.3	42.4	27.1
1930-40.............	19.8	17.2	20.8	28.5	15.9	19.0	19.1	19.8
1920-30.............	18.9	17.8	30.0	26.0	12.8	13.1	18.6	12.6
1910-20.............	8.4	4.9	7.1	11.1	9.0	12.9	8.4	6.2
1900-10.............	10.6	10.4	15.0	7.9	6.2	14.8	14.5	4.7
1900-50.............	142.1	130.4	198.0	192.9	93.0	146.7	149.7	90.5

Source: The Growth of Standard Metropolitan Areas: 1940-50.

1900, and probably before, the central cities of the very largest metropolitan areas have been growing more slowly than their rings, while the smaller sizes of S. M. A.'s began this pattern only after 1930. From this it may be inferred that suburbanization began with the largest centers and spread to the smaller ones.

No such diffusion of pattern can be observed in the recent tendency of the rural parts of rings to grow more rapidly than the urban parts, however. In all sizes of S. M. A.'s this aspect of metropolitan growth is the same: before 1930 the urban parts grew faster than the rural parts; after 1930 the rural parts grew faster than the urban parts. The change-over took place in all sizes of S. M. A.'s at about the same time. It appears that the mass ownership of automobiles introduced a new pattern of residential settlement in all metropolitan areas simultaneously.

There is no simple relationship between the size of S. M. A.'s and the rates of growth of their rings. Some of the highest rates of ring growth are found among the larger as well as among the smaller size groups of areas. Generalizations that can be made for the 1940-50 decade on this subject do not hold for the 1930-40 decade. From the limited data presented here, it would appear that the factors responsible for the absolute rate of growth of an S.M.A. and for its suburban ring have only a secondary relationship to the size of the S.M.A.

DISTRIBUTION OF POPULATION WITHIN S.M.A.'S OF VARIOUS SIZES, WITH NEW URBAN DEFINITION

The preceding analysis has left two major questions unanswered. How does the distribution of population within standard metropolitan areas vary with the size of the S.M.A.? What is the urban-rural composition of the ring of S.M.A.'s according to the new urban-rural definitions? Information with which to answer both of these questions is contained in Table 3-5. If suburbanization may be measured by the proportion of the total S.M.A. population that is contained in the ring, then there appears to be no very close relationship between size of S.M.A. and extent of suburbanization. Although there does seem to be a very general tendency for the larger S.M.A.'s to have a higher proportion of their population in the ring, some of the largest size classes of cities are less suburbanized than average, and some of the smaller size classes are more suburbanized than average.

Within the ring, however, there is a distinctive change in rural-urban composition in relation to size of S.M.A. The largest S.M.A.'s have a high proportion of urban population (new definition) in their rings, while the rings of the smaller

S.M.A.'s are predominantly rural. This difference is due primarily to presence or absence of satellite cities in the ring, as shown by the last two lines of Table 3-5. By the old 1940 definition, a high proportion of the total population in the rings of large S.M.A.'s is urban. Smaller S.M.A.'s have few satellite cities.

As of 1950, standard metropolitan areas were about 86 percent urban and 14 percent rural, but this varied considerably with the size of the place. The very largest classes of principal S.M.A.'s were 94 percent urban, while the smallest classes were 73-76 percent urban. This urban population consisted of the urbanized area and any other outlying urban places in the ring. The new urban fringe definition affects the urban-rural composition of S.M.A.'s of all sizes. It increases the urban component of the rings of small S.M.A.'s by about the same proportions as it does that of the rings of the larger S.M.A.'s.

It should be noted, in this connection, that in several instances the urbanized area for a city of 50,000 or more extends beyond the boundaries of the standard metropolitan area. Because the standard metropolitan area delineation must include or exclude an entire county according to whether or not it is integrated into the metropolitan area, it sometimes fails to include small tips or long ribbons of continuously dense settlement that extend along main highways into adjacent non-metropolitan counties.

Table 3-5.—DISTRIBUTION OF POPULATION IN STANDARD METROPOLITAN AREAS, BY NEW DEFINITION, BY SIZE OF SMA: 1950

Area	Size of SMA in 1940 (thousands)								
	All areas	3,000-over	1,000-2,999	500-999	350-499	250-349	150-249	100-149	Under 100
Total......................	100.0	100.0	100.0	100.0	100.0	100.0	100.0	100.0	100.0
Central cities....................	57.7	61.6	50.1	60.7	58.4	48.1	58.4	60.8	69.7
Ring............................	42.3	38.4	49.9	39.3	41.6	51.9	41.6	39.2	30.3
Urban areas in the ring, total...	28.6	32.8	38.7	25.3	24.9	24.4	16.4	12.4	6.4
Urban fringe..................	24.0	29.4	33.7	20.6	19.6	17.3	12.0	7.0	1.6
Other urban..................	4.6	3.4	5.0	4.7	5.3	7.1	4.4	5.4	4.8
Rural areas in the ring, total...	13.6	5.6	11.3	14.0	16.6	27.4	25.2	26.7	23.9
Components of the urban fringe:									
Urban by 1940 definition.......	16.9	23.2	27.3	12.4	11.7	6.5	4.1	2.4	...
Added by 1950 definition.......	7.1	6.1	6.3	8.3	7.9	10.8	7.9	4.7	1.6

Source: The Growth of Standard Metropolitan Areas: 1900-50.

GROWTH OF URBAN AND RURAL PARTS OF NONMETROPOLITAN AREAS

Lower than average growth rates for nonmetropolitan areas, noted above, must be attributed entirely to the rural parts of these areas. As a whole, cities in the more remote hinterland have grown very rapidly at each decade since 1900. Between 1940 and 1950, for example, the urban part of the nonmetropolitan areas grew by 25.8 percent, or almost twice the national rate (see Table 3-6). Moreover, these hinterland cities grew faster than metropolitan areas as a whole, faster than central cities, and almost as fast as urban places in metropolitan rings. A similar pattern has been in effect during each decade since 1900.

The urban places in nonmetropolitan areas grew at 2 times the rate of the rural parts, and 35 percent faster than the central cities of standard metropolitan areas. But they grew at considerably less than the average national rate of growth, and only about 1/3 as fast as urban places in metropolitan areas. These data are only roughly comparable with Table 3-6, because they make use of the new (1950) definition of urban places, while Table 3-6 is based upon the old (1940) definition. The years since 1950, apparently, have been less conducive to the continued growth of hinterland cities than were the previous five decades. Nevertheless, the viability and continued vitality of the more distant hinterland city is still in evidence, and this fact should be kept in mind when

Table 3-6.—GROWTH DATA FOR THE URBAN AND RURAL PORTION OF THE AREA OUTSIDE SMA'S RETROJECTED TO EARLIER CENSUSES: 1900-1950

Census year	Percent of U.S. population			Rate of growth during preceding decade[1]			Percent of total U.S. population growth claimed by area outside SMA's during preceding decade		
	Total	Urban	Rural	Total	Urban	Rural	Total	Urban	Rural
Area outside all SMA's.........	43.2	14.2	29.0	6.0	25.8	-1.6	19.4	23.0	-3.7
Area outside principal SMA's									
1950.........................	44.0	14.7	29.3	6.3	26.0	-1.4	20.7	24.1	-3.4
1940.........................	48.9	14.4	34.5	6.2	13.7	3.4	42.2	25.6	16.7
1930.........................	50.2	14.0	36.2	7.1	23.5	1.8	23.8	19.2	4.6
1920.........................	56.3	14.3	42.0	8.1	28.7	2.5	32.4	24.6	7.8
1910.........................	62.4	14.2	48.2	15.0	41.5	8.9	46.9	24.1	22.8
1900.........................	68.1	13.5	54.6	...	...	...	...	...	...

[1]The old (1940) definitions of urban and rural are employed in this table.

Source: The Growth of Standard Metropolitan Areas: 1900-50.

Apparently this picture has changed somewhat since 1950. The Census Bureau reported the following rates of growth for the urban and rural parts of nonmetropolitan areas during the period April, 1950, to March, 1956:[9]

Area	Percent increase 1950-56
Civilian population, nonmetropolitan areas, total...................	3.4
Urban places in nonmetropolitan areas	6.0
Rural parts of nonmetropolitan areas..	3.0

data are observed which describe the progressive agglomeration of people in larger places. It is from the ranks of these growing hinterland cities that the new metropolitan areas of future decades will emerge.

In contrast, the rural parts of the nonmetropolitan area suffered a small decline between 1940 and 1950. Thus, the growth of the rural population, reported in Table 2-2, Chapter 2, is due entirely to the growth of rural population in metropolitan areas. The rural "wide open spaces" of the United States, which comprises more than 90 percent of the land area, have had a growth rate near zero for forty years. One explanation for this low

[9]Current Population Reports, op. cit.

growth rate, of course, is the long-time decline of the farm population. Another reason is the constant depletion of the village population by the emergence of new cities, described at the end of Chapter 2. By definition, the nonmetropolitan rural population is one source for the growth of all other types of population. If a particular rural village in the hinterland is fortunate enough to have an important factory or some other major economic development located there, the place promptly grows to more than 2,500 people and becomes urban. If it continues to grow until it contains 50,000 people it becomes eligible to become a standard metropolitan area. Thus, the steady agglomeration of people in metropolitan areas, and the rapid increase of nonmetropolitan urban population, is merely another example of the progressive urbanization of the American people at the expense of the nonmetropolitan rural population. In spite of the fact that many of these differences appear to result simply from the way units are defined, they are important realities whose significance it would be difficult to overestimate in any consideration of the problems of urban concentration. Nothing inherent in the definitions would require the medium-size cities to grow to large cities and become S.M.A.'s. Nor does anything inherent in the definitions require country villages in nonmetropolitan areas to become cities or, if they are cities, to grow rapidly. In fact, the fertility pattern of the nation is such that none of these growth differences would take place unless strong social and economic forces stimulated and maintained them. Rural-farm birth rates tend to be higher than rural birth rates generally, and nonmetropolitan birth rates tend to be higher than metropolitan birth rates. Hence, if the vital processes alone were to determine the pattern of population growth, the pattern would be almost the exact reverse of that presented in this and the preceding chapter.

Because of the combination of growth rates in the rural and urban parts of nonmetropolitan areas over the past 50 years, the hinterland has slowly become urbanized. During almost every decade of this span, the urban nonmetropolitan areas have

captured about 1/4 of the nation's total increase. Since much of the new metropolitan population which is added each decade must be deducted from this growth, the nonmetropolitan urban areas have been able only to maintain a constant proportion of the nation's population (about 1.7 percent). Meanwhile, by growing at the rate of almost zero, the rural nonmetropolitan areas have become a progressively smaller part of the total national population.

An obvious but important implication of the foregoing is that the low over-all growth rates for nonmetropolitan areas should not deceive us into concluding that the entire nonmetropolitan area is one of economic stagnation and incipient decline. There are numerous areas of extraordinarily large growth. Some segments of the remote hinterland are very active, and have spurts of growth that cause even small cities to become standard metropolitan areas in a very few years.

COMPONENTS OF GROWTH IN METROPOLITAN AND NONMETROPOLITAN AREAS

A gigantic reshuffling and redistribution of people has been, and is still, required to produce the trends and changes described above. The magnitude of the change can be more fully appreciated when it is expressed in terms of the components of population change: reproductive change (natural increase) and migration.[10] In Table 3-7 the total change in the civilian population between 1940 and 1950 has been subdivided into these components. The 147 principal standard metropolitan areas (those having a total population of 100,000 or more in 1950) gained 6.4 million persons through migration. The nonmetropolitan part of the nation lost 5.8 million persons through net migration. This means that during the 10-year interval, one of each 9 persons changed his residence from a nonmetropolitan to a metropolitan location. If migration had not carried off the lion's share of their rather large reproductive change, the nonmetro-

[10]The data of this section are based upon a recent monograph by Donald J. Bogue, Components of Population Change--Estimates of Net Migration and Natural Increase for Each Standard Metropolitan Area and State Economic Area: 1940-50, Oxford: Scripps Foundation, 1957.

Table 3-7.—COMPONENTS OF POPULATION CHANGE IN METROPOLITAN AND NONMETROPOLITAN AREAS: 1940-50

Population change, 1940-50	U.S. Total	147 Standard metropolitan areas			Nonmetropolitan areas
		Total	Central cities	Metropolitan rings	
Civilian population, total change (millions).	18.3	14.8	4.2	10.6	3.5
Reproductive change (natural increase).....	17.7	8.4	4.9	3.5	9.3
Net migration...........................	0.6	6.4	-0.7	7.1	-5.8
Rate of reproductive change.................	12.6	11.0	10.9	11.1	14.6
Rate of net migration......................	0.4	9.2	-1.6	26.7	-9.3

Source: Components of Population Change: 1940-50, Tables II-A and III-A.

politan areas would have gained 9.3 million persons instead of only 3.5 million. Due to high fertility rates, these nonmetropolitan areas had a rate of reproductive change of 14.6, while the metropolitan areas had a corresponding rate of 11.0, which is only 75 percent as great. Yet the over-all rate of growth of the metropolitan population was more than 3 1/2 times that of the non-metropolitan. Thus, an above-average rate of reproductive change, counterbalanced by a high rate of net out-migration, permitted nonmetropolitan areas to grow at only less than one-half the national rate.

An important insight (that may not be sufficiently appreciated) is provided by Table 3-6: within metropolitan areas fertility rates (even though lower than in nonmetropolitan areas) are sufficiently greater than mortality rates to permit a rather large growth from reproductive change. In the 1940-50 decade, for example, S.M.A.'s gained 14.8 million civilian persons, and 8.4 million, or 57 percent of this was generated within the S.M.A.'s themselves through an excess of births over deaths.

When the components of change for central cities and rings are examined, the volume of change due to migration is also seen to be very great. During the ten year period, suburbs gained 7.1 million persons through net migration. This was equal to 27 percent of the suburban population in 1940. Surprisingly, central cities suffered a net loss of population (0.7 million persons) during the decade. Therefore, the central city growth between 1940 and 1950 (13.5 percent) was produced entirely by the reproductive change (excess of births over deaths) of the central city population. In fact, central cities grew in spite of migration, not because of it. Moreover, the recent growth of central cities may be purely temporary, for it consists entirely of infants and children who may move to the suburbs when they attain adulthood.

If Table 3-7 is examined more closely it will show that, since nonmetropolitan areas lost 5.8 million persons through migration and suburbs gained 7.1 million, the entire migration gain which metropolitan areas enjoyed at the expense of nonmetropolitan areas accrued to the suburbs. In other words, the frequently-made claim that suburbs are "draining the central cities" of their population is not strictly correct--the really heavy net drain appears to be upon the nonmetropolitan areas. Nevertheless, as will be shown in later chapters, central cities appear to be losing long-term residents to the suburbs and replacing them partially with migrants from nonmetropolitan areas. Thus, central cities at the present time have a very high rate of migration turnover, which may alter the composition but which results in a small net loss. Central city populations are still growing because their residents are fertile enough to make up migration losses, not because they are gaining through migration.

Chapter 4

POPULATION DISTRIBUTION: STATES, REGIONS, AND GEOGRAPHIC DIVISIONS

The preceding two chapters have shown that population distribution and growth vary with type of community of residence; the present chapter shows that they vary widely among the broad regions and geographic divisions of the nation. Whereas the urban-rural and the metropolitan-nonmetropolitan distinction classifies people by their community of residence, the present classification undertakes to classify them according to the type of general environmental setting within which their particular community is located. Some major sections of the country (both rural and urban areas, covering a large territory) may be growing at a very rapid rate while other sections may be standing still, or even losing population. Differences of this kind are due to intersectional differences in the components of population growth: Rapidly growing sections may have higher birth rates and lower death rates than the rest of the nation, or they may be centers of rapid in-migration, with low rates of out-migration; slowly growing sections may have low birth rates and high death rates, and/or high rates of out-migration with low rates of in-migration.

Later chapters will also show that population composition (age, occupation, etc.) may differ from one region to another quite independently of urban-rural and other residence classifications. An important part of the study of population distribution consists of investigating these intersectional differences in growth, distribution, and composition, describing them in terms of their components, and explaining them by relating them to various local, social, and economic conditions associated with regions and parts of regions. The task is similar to that involved in the study of urban and rural residence, except that the regional studies make use of area units which are large. Such analysis often uses the 48 states as units, but usually the states are not too satisfactory for this purpose. They vary a great deal in size and, although they are more numerous, they are not a great deal more homogeneous than groupings of states. Two sets of areas--the census regions (four areas), and the census geographic divisions (nine areas)--have traditionally been used for this purpose. A six-region set of areas, delineated by Howard W. Odum, has been widely used, especially in studies of the South. In all three of these sets the areas consist of clusters of similar states. The census delimitations, both for geographic divisions and for regions, are widely used and are generally familiar. They are illustrated in the map, Figure 4-1. Table 4-1 lists the states that are contained in each geographic division, and the geographic divisions that comprise each census region.

In this treatise on population it would be inappropriate to present a detailed description of each state, geographic division, and census region. Yet many users of population statistics may lack precise knowledge about the regional variations within the nation. Unless they acquire such knowledge they will find it difficult to interpret correctly the many large interregional differences, and the changes in interregional differences, that can be observed in the population data. For the aid of the reader who desires a minimum fund of information, a supplementary section entitled

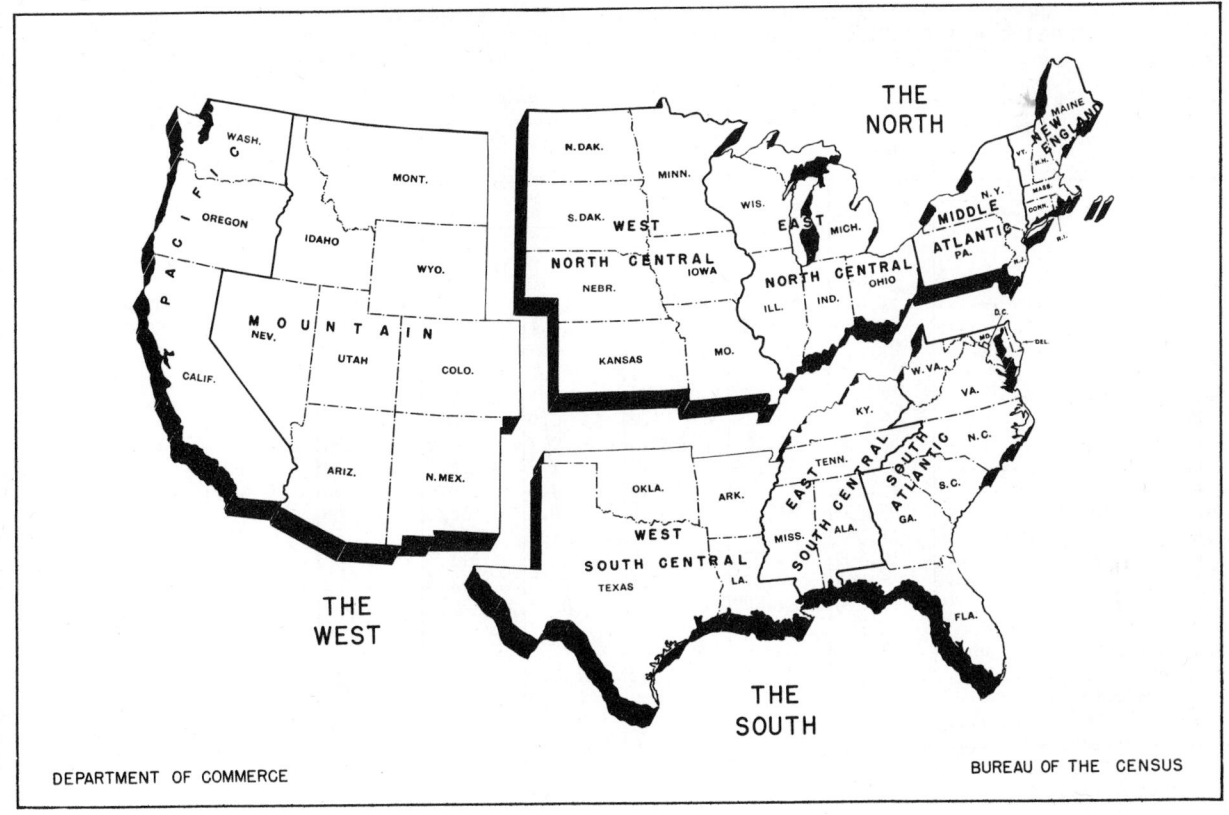

FIGURE 4-1.—CENSUS GEOGRAPHIC REGIONS AND DIVISIONS OF THE UNITED STATES

"A Brief Description of the Socio-Economic Characteristics of the Geographic Divisions" has been appended to this chapter. It consists primarily of a set of statistical tables containing selected indexes, which make it possible to determine readily the traits which each of these areas exhibits to an unusually strong degree (or lacks) in comparison with the nation. The brief text accompanying these tables is intended merely to summarize the high points and to introduce certain additional information not contained in the tables.

RECENT CHANGES IN THE REGIONAL
DISTRIBUTION OF POPULATION

Each year the Bureau of the Census prepares estimates of the current population of each state, geographic division, and region as of July 1 of the preceding year.[1] Table 4-1 reports the official 1950 census count for each of these areas, and the most recent estimate of current population available at the time of writing (1958). This table also contains rates of population change from 1940 to 1950 and from 1950 to 1958, population densities per square mile, and a percentage distribution of the population among the areas. Together, these statistics tell the story of the recent redistribution of the population, and of its present distribution among regions, divisions, and states.

---

[1]These estimates are published in Current Population Reports, Population Estimates, Series P-25. By obtaining a copy of the most recent set of estimates for states, the reader can extend many of the materials of this chapter to include changes that have taken place since the present analysis was made.

Table 4-1.—NUMBER OF INHABITANTS, LAND AREA, PERCENT CHANGE, POPULATION PER SQUARE MILE, AND PERCENT DISTRIBUTION OF POPULATION BY CENSUS REGIONS, GEOGRAPHIC DIVISIONS, AND STATES: 1950 AND 1958

Region, division, and state	Number of inhabitants (000)		Land area (000 sq. miles)	Percent change		Population per square mile		Percent of total population	
	1958	1950		1950 to 1958	1940 to 1950	1958	1950	1958	1950
United States, total...	173,260	150,697	2,974.7	15.0	14.5	58	51	100.0	100.0
REGIONS									
Northeast..............	43,041	39,478	163.7	9.0	9.7	263	241	24.8	26.2
North Central..........	51,009	44,461	755.5	14.7	10.8	68	59	29.4	29.5
South..................	53,838	47,197	878.4	14.1	13.3	61	54	31.1	31.3
West..................	25,373	19,562	1,177.1	29.7	40.9	22	17	14.6	13.0
GEOGRAPHIC DIVISIONS									
New England...........	9,961	9,314	63.2	6.9	10.4	158	148	5.7	6.2
Middle Atlantic........	33,080	30,164	100.5	9.7	9.5	329	300	19.1	20.0
East North Central......	35,618	30,399	244.9	17.2	14.2	145	124	20.6	20.2
West North Central.....	15,391	14,061	510.6	9.5	4.0	30	28	8.9	9.3
South Atlantic.........	25,352	21,182	268.0	19.7	18.8	95	79	14.6	14.1
East South Central.....	11,947	11,477	180.0	4.1	6.5	66	64	6.9	7.6
West South Central.....	16,539	14,538	430.4	13.8	11.3	38	34	9.5	9.6
Mountain..............	6,494	5,075	857.3	28.0	22.3	8	6	3.7	3.4
Pacific...............	18,879	14,487	319.8	30.3	48.8	59	45	10.9	9.6
NEW ENGLAND									
Maine.................	952	914	31.0	4.1	7.9	31	29	0.5	0.6
New Hampshire..........	584	533	9.0	9.6	8.5	65	59	0.3	0.4
Vermont...............	372	378	9.3	-1.4	5.2	40	41	0.2	0.3
Massachusetts..........	4,862	4,691	7.9	3.6	8.7	615	596	2.8	3.1
Rhode Island...........	875	792	1.1	10.5	11.0	795	748	0.5	0.5
Connecticut...........	2,316	2,007	4.9	15.4	17.4	473	410	1.3	1.3
MIDDLE ATLANTIC									
New York..............	16,229	14,830	47.9	9.4	10.0	339	309	9.4	9.8
New Jersey............	5,749	4,835	7.5	18.9	16.2	767	643	3.3	3.2
Pennsylvania..........	11,101	10,498	45.0	5.7	6.0	247	233	6.4	7.0
EAST NORTH CENTRAL									
Ohio..................	9,345	7,947	41.0	17.6	15.0	228	194	5.4	5.3
Indiana...............	4,581	3,934	36.2	16.4	14.8	127	109	2.6	2.6
Illinois..............	9,889	8,712	55.9	13.5	10.3	177	156	5.7	5.8
Michigan..............	7,866	6,372	57.0	23.4	21.2	138	112	4.5	4.2
Wisconsin.............	3,938	3,435	54.7	14.6	9.5	72	63	2.3	2.3
WEST NORTH CENTRAL									
Minnesota.............	3,375	2,982	80.0	13.2	6.8	42	37	1.9	2.0
Iowa..................	2,822	2,621	56.0	7.7	3.3	50	47	1.6	1.7
Missouri..............	4,271	3,955	69.2	8.0	4.5	62	57	2.5	2.6
North Dakota..........	650	620	70.1	5.0	-3.5	9	9	0.4	0.4
South Dakota..........	699	653	76.5	7.1	1.5	9	8	0.4	0.4
Nebraska..............	1,457	1,326	76.7	9.9	0.7	19	17	0.8	0.9
Kansas................	2,116	1,905	82.1	11.0	5.8	26	23	1.2	1.3
SOUTH ATLANTIC									
Delaware..............	454	318	2.0	42.7	19.4	227	161	0.3	0.2
Maryland..............	2,956	2,343	9.9	26.2	28.6	299	237	1.7	1.6
District of Columbia....	825	802	0.1	2.8	21.0		13,151	0.5	0.5
Virginia..............	3,935	3,319	39.9	18.6	23.9	99	83	2.3	2.2
West Virginia..........	1,969	2,006	24.1	-1.8	5.4	82	83	1.1	1.3
North Carolina........	4,549	4,062	49.1	12.0	13.7	93	83	2.6	2.7
South Carolina........	2,404	2,117	30.3	13.6	11.4	79	70	1.4	1.4
Georgia...............	3,818	3,445	58.5	10.8	10.3	65	59	2.2	2.3
Florida...............	4,442	2,771	54.3	60.3	46.1	82	51	2.6	1.8

Table 4-1.—NUMBER OF INHABITANTS, LAND AREA, PERCENT CHANGE, POPULATION PER SQUARE MILE, AND PERCENT DISTRIBUTION OF POPULATION BY CENSUS REGIONS, GEOGRAPHIC DIVISIONS, AND STATES: 1950 AND 1958—Con.

Region, division, and state	Number of inhabitants (000)		Land area (000 sq. miles)	Percent change		Population per square mile		Percent of total population	
	1958	1950		1950 to 1958	1940 to 1950	1958	1950	1958	1950
EAST SOUTH CENTRAL									
Kentucky................	3,080	2,945	39.9	4.6	3.5	77	74	1.8	2.0
Tennessee...............	3,469	3,292	41.8	5.4	12.9	83	79	2.0	2.2
Alabama.................	3,211	3,062	51.1	4.9	8.1	63	60	1.9	2.0
Mississippi.............	2,186	2,179	47.2	0.3	-0.2	46	46	1.3	1.4
WEST SOUTH CENTRAL.									
Arkansas................	1,766	1,910	52.7	-7.5	-2.0	34	36	1.0	1.3
Louisiana...............	3,110	2,684	45.2	15.9	13.5	69	59	1.8	1.8
Oklahoma................	2,285	2,233	69.0	2.3	-4.4	33	32	1.3	1.5
Texas...................	9,377	7,711	263.5	21.6	20.2	36	29	5.4	5.1
MOUNTAIN									
Montana.................	688	591	145.9	16.4	5.6	5	4	0.4	0.4
Idaho...................	662	589	82.8	12.5	12.1	8	7	0.4	0.4
Wyoming.................	320	291	97.5	10.1	15.9	3	3	0.2	0.2
Colorado................	1,711	1,325	103.9	29.1	18.0	16	13	1.0	0.9
New Mexico..............	842	681	121.5	23.6	28.1	7	6	0.5	0.5
Arizona.................	1,140	750	113.6	52.1	50.1	10	7	0.7	0.5
Utah....................	865	689	82.3	25.5	25.2	11	8	0.5	0.5
Nevada..................	267	160	109.8	66.7	45.2	2	2	0.2	0.1
PACIFIC									
Washington..............	2,769	2,379	66.8	16.4	37.0	41	36	1.6	1.6
Oregon..................	1,773	1,521	96.3	16.6	39.6	18	16	1.0	1.0
California..............	14,337	10,586	156.7	35.4	53.3	91	68	8.3	7.0

Source: Current Population Survey, P-25, No. 189, November 13, 1958, and U.S. Census of Population: 1950, Vol. I, Number of Inhabitants, Tables 6, 7, 8, and 9.

The Middle Atlantic and the East North Central Divisions are the most populous and the most densely settled geographic divisions. At the other extreme, the 8 states of the Mountain Division are the most sparsely inhabited. The 7 most populous states are, in order of size:

State	Estimated population, 1958	
	Million persons	Percent of total U. S. population
New York..........	16.2	9.4
California........	14.3	8.3
Pennsylvania......	11.1	6.4
Illinois..........	9.9	5.7
Ohio..............	9.3	5.4
Texas.............	9.4	5.4
Michigan..........	7.9	4.5

The fastest growing states are:

State	Percent change in:	
	1950 to 1958	1940 to 1950
Nevada.............	66.7	45.2
Arizona............	52.1	50.1
Florida............	60.3	46.1
Delaware...........	42.7	19.4
California.........	35.4	53.3
Colorado...........	29.1	18.0
Utah...............	25.5	25.2
Maryland...........	26.2	28.6

California, which was the fastest growing state from 1940 to 1950, now appears to have fallen to fifth place and to be trailing its major competitor, Florida. Phenomenal rates of growth have occurred in several of the Mountain states, both from 1940 to 1950 and from 1950 to 1958. Delaware and Maryland, eastern states in the fast-growing group, have benefited from new industrial installations. All of these fast-growing states were growing at above-average rates between 1940 and 1950. The slowest growing states were:

State	Percent change in:	
	1950 to 1958	1940 to 1950
Arkansas.............	-7.5	-2.0
West Virginia........	-1.8	5.4
Vermont.............	-1.4	5.2
Mississippi..........	0.3	-0.2
Oklahoma............	2.3	-4.4

In general, the states that have been losing population, or gaining only a very small amount, are states in which conditions are comparatively unfavorable for intensive agriculture and which have not been chosen as sites for new industrial expansion.

The regional pattern of growth since 1950 is similar to the 1940 to 1950 decade, with the following modifications:

(a) The New England and Middle Atlantic states are lagging in growth even more than they did in the decades preceding 1950. Despite heavy migration from Puerto Rico and the South, states like New York and Pennsylvania are growing only about one-half as fast as the nation as a whole. Maine and Vermont have had almost no growth since 1950. The only two states in this region which are growing at average rates are Connecticut and New Jersey. Both are benefiting from the suburbanization of New York City and Philadelphia, as well as from the growth of their own metropolitan centers.

(b) The West North Central states, which were growing only very slowly before 1950, appear to have made a surprising recovery; although they are still growing less rapidly than the nation as a whole, the disparity is much smaller than it was in the decade 1940 to 1950. Apparently this new growth is due to the westward diffusion of industry, and to the growth of urban centers in these West North Central states. Although Minnesota, Nebraska, and Kansas are leading this recovery, the increase seems to be distributed among all states of the division. For example, North Dakota, which declined by 3.5 percent between 1940 and 1950, is reported to have gained by about 4 1/2 percent from 1950 to 1958.

(c) The East North Central states (especially Michigan) have grown somewhat more rapidly than the nation as a whole. This differential growth appears to be linked with the fact that this division has been increasingly favored as a site for new manufacturing plants.

(d) In the West South Central Division, two Gulf states, Louisiana and Texas, are growing at rates slightly faster than that of the nation, while Arkansas and Oklahoma are among the slowest growing states.

(e) Although the Mountain states have grown at rapid rates for several decades, they have accelerated their growth since 1950. Before 1950 they grew less than one-half as fast as the Pacific Division, but now they are growing at about the same rate as the Pacific Division.

(f) The growth of the Pacific Division, as a whole, has slackened noticeably. Washington and Oregon have grown at about average rates since 1950, although before that date they were growing almost 3 times as fast as the nation. California grew almost 4 times as fast as the nation between 1940 and 1950; since 1950 it has grown only about 2 1/2 times as fast as the nation--a rate of growth which is still impressively rapid, of course.

Most of these regional variations in growth are caused by streams of migration. For details of recent migration trends, the reader is referred to subsequent chapters (14 and 15) on this subject.

REGIONAL DISTRIBUTION OF POPULATION IN COMPARISON WITH LAND AREA

If the population of the United States were distributed evenly among the regions, each region would be populated in proportion to its land area. Never in the history of the United States has the population been distributed among the geographic divisions in this way, a fact which Table 4-2 establishes. That part of the nation lying east of the Mississippi River (the New England, Middle Atlantic, South Atlantic, East North Central, and East South Central Divisions) comprises 28.8 percent of the total land area, but at the time of the 1950 census it contained 68.1 percent of the total population. Each geographic division in this east-

Table 4-2.—PERCENT DISTRIBUTION OF POPULATION AND LAND AREA BY GEOGRAPHIC DIVISIONS: 1790 TO 1958

| Year | United States total | Northeast | | North Central | | South | | | West | |
		New England	Middle Atlantic	East North Central	West North Central	South Atlantic	East South Central	West South Central	Mountain	Pacific
Land area (1950)....	100.0	2.1	3.4	8.2	17.2	9.0	6.1	14.5	28.8	10.8
Population:										
1958..............	100.0	5.6	19.1	20.5	8.8	14.7	7.0	9.5	3.9	10.9
1950..............	100.0	6.2	20.0	20.2	9.3	14.1	7.6	9.6	3.4	9.6
1940..............	100.0	6.4	20.9	20.2	10.3	13.5	8.2	9.9	3.2	7.4
1930..............	100.0	6.7	21.4	20.6	10.8	12.9	8.1	9.9	3.0	6.7
1920..............	100.0	7.0	21.1	20.3	11.9	13.2	8.4	9.7	3.2	5.3
1910..............	100.0	7.1	21.0	19.8	12.7	13.3	9.1	9.6	2.9	4.6
1900..............	100.0	7.4	20.3	21.0	13.6	13.7	9.9	8.6	2.2	3.2
1880..............	100.0	8.0	20.9	22.3	12.3	15.1	11.1	6.6	1.3	2.2
1860..............	100.0	10.0	23.7	22.0	6.9	17.1	12.8	5.6	0.6	1.4
1840..............	100.0	13.1	26.5	17.1	2.5	23.0	15.1	2.6	...	...
1820..............	100.0	17.2	28.0	8.2	0.7	31.8	12.4	1.7	...	...
1800..............	100.0	23.2	26.4	1.0	...	43.1	6.3	...	...	...
1790..............	100.0	25.7	24.4	...	...	47.1	2.8	...	...	...

Source: 1950 Census of Population, Volume I, U.S. Summary, Table 8, and Current Population Survey, Series P,25, No. 189, November 13, 1958.

ern part of the nation contains a larger proportion of the total population than it does of the total land area. The exact reverse of this situation exists to the west of the Mississippi, which in 1950 contained 71.2 percent of the total land area but only 31.9 percent of the total population.

The greatest concentration of population, in relation to land area, occurs in the Middle Atlantic states of New York, New Jersey, and Pennsylvania, where 1/5 of the nation's population lives on 1/30 of the nation's land. This is a consequence, of course, of the fact that many large industrial and commercial seaports, and other metropolitan and urban centers, are located in the division. The New England and East North Central Divisions, also highly industrial and commercial, have 2 to 3 times the share of the total population one would expect them to have on the basis of size alone. The other two geographic divisions with greater-than-expected concentrations of population are in the South (the South Atlantic and East South Central states). Their excess of population in relation to land area is comparatively small.

Of the four geographic divisions with a deficit of population in relation to land, the Mountain Division is the most sparsely settled. Although more than 1/4 of the nation's total land area lies

in this one division, only 1/25 of the total population lives there. In the Pacific Division the proportions of land area and population are very nearly equal, while the two West Central Divisions have only 1/2 to 2/3 of the population one would expect on the basis of land area.

At least four different sets of factors must be considered in explaining this pattern of population distribution:

a. The east-to-west settlement of the nation.

b. The development of seaports, water transportation, and channels of foreign trade.

c. The location of coal, iron, and other power and mineral resources.

d. The distribution of land suitable for agricultural use, and the differences in rainfall, climate, and other factors affecting agriculture.

A large proportion of the immigrant population landed on the Atlantic coast, rather than on the Pacific or Gulf coast, and slowly pushed westward; this process has been responsible for many of the characteristics of the nation's pattern of population distribution. The cities and towns along the east coast were the first to be made secure against frontier dangers, and were thus able to develop as industrial and commercial centers which served the frontier areas. For more than

200 years they have grown by means of reproductive increase, and at the same time attracted migrants coming from abroad. These cities have been able to offer opportunities which held their own children, and have thus retained a large proportion of their reproductive increase. While pioneers in the West were still clearing land, easterners were able to farm intensively on land which had already been brought under human control.

An even distribution of the population according to land area would have required immigrants from abroad to disperse evenly over all parts of the nation, and would have required the vital increase of already-settled areas to drain itself off completely into less settled areas. Social and economic forces would obviously prevent such a distribution. In addition, the very fact that these eastern cities were the first to be developed meant that they endowed the region with economic and social characteristics which gave it a dominant role in the national life.

Throughout most of the history of the United States, this region has found a ready market for its goods. This market (which has also been the nation's major source of imported goods) has been Europe, and the other parts of the world which are most easily accessible to the United States via the Atlantic Ocean. Thus, the original settlement pattern has been reinforced by the development of large industrial and commercial centers on the Atlantic coast. Internal transportation was made easy and cheap early in the nation's history by navigation on the Mississippi and Ohio Rivers and, later, on the Great Lakes. The seaports, lake ports, and river ports which sprang up in the eastern part of the nation were assembly points and market centers for the increasing flow of agricultural products from the middle and western regions, and were shipping points for the materials needed by hinterland communities. Until the opening of the Panama Canal, transportation and market factors strongly favored the concentration of an urban and commercial population in the northeastern and eastern sections of the nation.

The presence of coal in Pennsylvania, Virginia, Kentucky, and West Virginia, and of iron ore which is easily transportable from Minnesota via ore barges on the Great Lakes, have been tremendous stimuli to manufacturing, and, consequently, to the concentration of population in the East. The nation's growing industries settled where they could obtain, cheaply and easily, coal for power and steel for fabricating. Until recently, the western half of the United States has lacked the combination of power, fuel, and mineral resources that would lead to great industrial concentrations. The development of such nonferrous metals industries as aluminum, magnesium, and copper, which can use electric power generated by water, is partially offsetting the initial advantage of the Middle Atlantic and East North Central Divisions. Modest developments in steel also have been made recently in the West.

Except for the tier of states immediately west of the Mississippi River, and scattered areas in the Pacific Northwest, most of the western states lack sufficient rainfall for intensive crop farming. Moreover, much of the land in the western 1/3 of the country is too mountainous or rough for crop farming. Consequently, the agriculture of the divisions in this section tends to be either very extensive or very intensive. Large cattle ranches, large-scale wheat farming, and dry-land farming characterize much of the area. Fruit or vegetable farms, based on irrigation, are found where water can be made available on suitable land. The agricultural resources of even the eastern part of the West North Central Division, which is the richest agricultural division, favor large farms and a sparse farm population because the prairie land is suitable for highly mechanized farming. Farms in the East tend to be small and numerous; in the West they tend to be large and few. This is due to natural resources, and also to the competitive position of the two areas with respect to markets. Eastern farms specialize in producing vegetables, fruits, poultry, and dairy products for the nearby industrial and commercial centers. The western states specialize in producing meat, basic cereals, and specialty crops of fruit and vegetables.

LONG-RUN TRENDS IN THE REGIONAL DISTRIBUTION AND GROWTH OF POPULATION

Figure 4-2 and Tables 4-2, 4-3, and 4-4 show how the population has redistributed itself among the regions and geographic divisions since 1790. At the time of the first census all the population was concentrated in the Northeast and the South. Almost one-half of the population lived in the South Atlantic states. The New England and the Middle Atlantic states each had about one-fourth of the population. Since then these divisions have had a progressively smaller proportion of the total. First, the North Central region developed. Beginning in 1800 the East North Central states, which border the Great Lakes, enjoyed a very rapid growth that led to their containing 20 percent of the total population. About 1820 the entire middle section of the nation began to grow. In 1820 the West North Central and the West South Central states together contained 2.4 percent of the population. They now contain 18.9 percent. These are the prairie states immediately west of

the Mississippi River. Their steady and rapid growth during the half century from 1850 to 1900 represented the development of the nation's finest agricultural and grazing lands.

As each territory was opened up for settlement it became a part of the decennial census. Column 1 of Table 4-5 reports the data from the decennial census at which each state was first included, and thereby portrays clearly the sequence and the approximate dates of settlement.

From 1940 to 1950, and from 1950 to 1958, the four regions grew at the following rates:

	1950 to 1958	1940 to 1950
Northeast	9.0	9.7
North Central	14.7	10.8
South	14.1	13.3
West	29.7	40.9
U.S. total	15.0	14.5

Table 4-3 provides the growth rate for each geographic division for each decade, 1790 to 1957. Just as Chapter 3 demonstrated that the national growth rate of 14.5 percent from 1940 to 1950 was an average of two sets of very unlike rates for

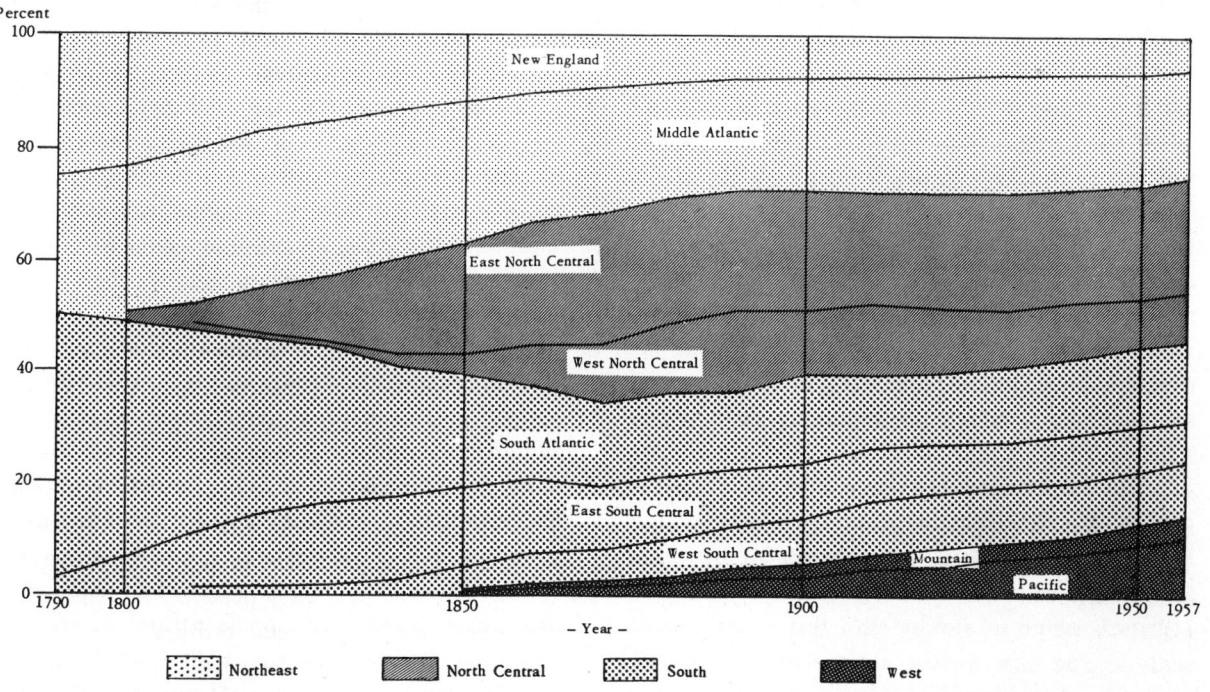

FIGURE 4-2. **PERCENT OF THE UNITED STATES POPULATION IN EACH GEOGRAPHIC DIVISION: 1790 TO 1957**

Table 4-3.—RATES OF INCREASE IN POPULATION FOR GEOGRAPHIC DIVISIONS: 1790 TO 1957

Year	United States total	Northeast		North Central		South			West	
		New England	Middle Atlantic	East North Central	West North Central	South Atlantic	East South Central	West South Central	Mountain	Pacific
1950 to 1957........	13.0	6.0	7.9	15.2	8.9	16.5	3.1	11.8	25.7	27.1
1940 to 1950........	14.5	10.4	9.5	14.2	4.0	18.8	6.5	11.3	22.3	48.8
1930 to 1940........	7.2	3.3	4.9	5.3	1.7	12.9	9.0	7.3	12.1	18.8
1920 to 1930........	16.1	10.3	18.0	17.8	6.0	12.9	11.2	18.9	11.0	47.2
1910 to 1920........	14.9	12.9	15.2	17.7	7.8	14.7	5.7	16.6	26.7	32.8
1900 to 1910........	21.0	17.2	25.0	14.2	12.5	16.8	11.4	34.5	57.3	73.5
1890 to 1900........	20.7	19.0	21.6	18.6	15.8	17.9	17.4	37.8	38.0	28.0
1880 to 1890........	25.5	17.2	21.0	20.3	45.1	16.6	15.1	42.2	85.9	69.4
1870 to 1880........	30.1	15.0	19.1	22.8	59.7	29.8	26.8	64.3	107.1	65.1
1860 to 1850........	22.6	11.2	18.1	31.7	77.7	9.1	9.5	16.2	80.3	52.0
1850 to 1860........	35.6	14.9	26.5	53.1	146.5	14.7	19.6	85.9	139.9	319.3
1840 to 1850........	35.9	22.1	30.3	54.7	106.3	19.2	30.6	109.0	...	...
1830 to 1840........	32.7	14.3	26.2	99.0	203.9	7.7	41.8	82.8	...	...
1820 to 1830........	33.5	17.7	32.9	85.4	110.9	19.1	52.5	46.8	...	...
1810 to 1820........	33.1	12.8	34.0	191.1	236.6	14.4	68.0	116.0	...	...
1800 to 1810........	36.4	19.4	43.6	433.9	...	17.0	111.3	...	...	...
1790 to 1800........	35.1	22.2	46.3	...	...	23.5	206.7	...	...	...

Source: 1950 Census of Population, Vol. I, U.S. Summary, Table 7, and Current Population Survey, Series P,25, No. 189, November 13, 1958.

metropolitan and nonmetropolitan areas, these data show that the national growth rate is an average of very unlike growth rates for the various regions and geographic divisions. From 1940 to 1950 all the regions of the nation grew at below-average rates except one--the West--which grew more than 2 1/2 times as fast as the nation. Even more diversity is evident when growth is examined in terms of geographic divisions or states (Tables 4-3 and 4-4). Two of the divisions (West North Central and East South Central) grew less than half as fast as the nation, and the Pacific grew almost 4 times as fast.

A comparison of the growth rates of each division and state with the growth rates for the nation, for each period from 1790 to 1957, reveals the sequence in which the population has redistributed itself. Table 4-4 makes this comparison easy, by expressing the difference between the growth rate of each state, geographic division, or region, and the national average rate as a ratio of the national rate. A minus sign in this table means a growth which is slower than that of the nation, while a plus sign means above-average growth. The size of the figure indicates, by states, how much faster than the nation each area was growing

in each period since 1790. A negative value of 100 or more denotes that population was lost during the decade, while a positive value of 100 means that the area grew twice as fast as (100 percent faster than) the nation. For example, in no decade from 1790 to the present has the New England Division, as a whole, grown as rapidly as the nation (although between 1890 and 1930 one or more of the states did grow faster than the nation). These first-settled states have been subjected to steady out-migration as the other divisions developed. Until 1820 the Middle Atlantic states of New Jersey and Pennsylvania were growing faster than the nation, but from 1820 to 1890 (a period of rapid westward movement) the national growth was faster than the growth of these states. From 1890 until 1930 (a time of rapid immigration from abroad and of great industrial expansion) the Middle Atlantic Division and the states of Massachusetts and Rhode Island in the New England Division again grew faster than the nation as a whole. In the 1930 to 1940 period the Middle Atlantic Division grew only about 2/3 as fast as the nation. It retained this rate of growth in the 1940 to 1950 period (as has been noted), but has not even done this well since 1950. Thus, the Northeast has had a lower-

Table 4-4.—INDEX OF RELATIVE DIFFERENTIAL GROWTH IN STATES, GEOGRAPHIC DIVISIONS, AND CENSUS REGIONS: 1790 TO 1957

Region, division, and state	Area rate minus national rate divided by the national rate x 100																
	1950 to 1957	1940 to 1950	1930 to 1940	1920 to 1930	1910 to 1920	1900 to 1910	1890 to 1900	1880 to 1890	1870 to 1880	1860 to 1870	1850 to 1860	1840 to 1850	1830 to 1840	1820 to 1830	1810 to 1820	1800 to 1810	1790 to 1800
National rate of growth	13	14	7	16	15	21	21	26	30	23	36	36	33	34	33	36	35
REGIONS																	
Northeast	-42	-33	-38	...	-1	9	1	-22	-40	-29	-36	-23	-33	-19	-24	-11	-3
North Central	2	-26	-44	-17	-7	-36	-16	14	12	89	92	70	231	161	487	1,199	...
South	-9	-8	40	-11	-15	-6	8	-16	14	-54	-33	-19	-33	-13	-16	-12	-4
West	105	182	132	109	104	218	54	196	161	166	591	...	...	...	...	...	...
GEOGRAPHIC DIVISIONS																	
New England	-54	-28	-54	-36	-13	-18	-8	-33	-50	-50	-58	-38	-56	-47	-61	-47	-37
Middle Atlantic	-39	-34	-32	12	2	19	4	-18	-36	-20	-26	-16	-20	-2	3	20	32
East North Central	17	-2	-26	11	19	-32	-10	-20	-24	40	49	52	203	155	477	1,092	...
West North Central	-32	-72	-76	-63	-48	-40	-24	77	98	244	312	196	524	231	615	...	...
South Atlantic	27	30	79	-20	-1	-20	-14	-35	-1	-60	-59	-46	-76	-43	-57	-53	-33
East South Central	-76	-55	25	-30	-62	-46	-16	-41	-11	-58	-45	-15	28	57	105	206	489
West South Central	-9	-22	1	17	11	64	83	66	114	-28	141	204	153	40	250	...	...
Mountain	98	54	68	-32	79	173	84	237	256	255	293	...	...	...	...	...	...
Pacific	108	237	161	193	120	250	35	172	116	130	797	...	...	...	...	...	...
NEW ENGLAND																	
Maine	-75	-46	-14	-76	-76	-67	-76	-93	-88	-101	-78	-55	-22	1	-8	39	63
New Hampshire	-45	-41	-22	-69	-80	-78	-55	-67	-70	-111	-93	-67	-83	-69	-58	-54	-16
Vermont	-105	-64	-101	-88	-107	-83	-84	...	-98	-78	-99	-79	-88	-44	-75	13	130
Massachusetts	-72	-40	-78	-36	-3	-5	22	...	-26	-19	-33	-3	-36	-50	-67	-68	-67
Rhode Island	-32	-24	-47	-15	-24	27	16	-2	-10	8	-48	-1	-63	-49	-76	-69	-99
Connecticut	-6	20	-11	2	60	8	5	-22	-47	-26	-32	-45	-88	-76	-85	-88	-84
MIDDLE ATLANTIC																	
New York	-45	-31	-1	32	-6	21	2	-29	-47	-43	-29	-23	-19	19	30	72	108
New Jersey	26	12	-60	74	64	65	47	9	-18	54	5	-13	-50	-53	-61	-55	-58
Pennsylvania	-60	-59	-61	-35	-7	3	-4	-11	-28	-6	-28	-5	-15	-15	-11	-5	10
EAST NORTH CENTRAL																	
Ohio	22	3	-46	-4	40	-30	-36	-42	-34	-38	-49	-16	90	83	359	1,023	...
Indiana	17	2	-19	-35	-43	-65	-28	-58	-41	8	3	23	206	297	1,411	820	...
Illinois	-18	-29	-51	10	1	-20	26	-5	-30	114	184	120	519	453	956	...	...
Michigan	73	46	18	99	105	-23	-25	9	27	157	148	143	1,646	663	162	...	...
Wisconsin	-4	-34	-6	-27	-14	-39	7	12	-18	59	333	2,370	...	...	...	...	...
WEST NORTH CENTRAL																	
Minnesota	-13	-53	24	-54	1	-12	63	166	158	588	7,570	...	...	...	...	...	...
Iowa	-48	-77	-62	-83	-46	-101	-19	-31	20	240	605	863	...	...	...	...	...
Missouri	-42	-69	-40	-59	-77	-71	-23	--7	-14	102	106	117	430	231	615	...	...
North Dakota	-69	-124	-179	-67	-19	285	224	1,537	4,666	755	...	...	...	...	...	...	...
South Dakota	-42	-90	-200	-45	-40	116	-27	899	2,340	755	...	...	...	...	...	...	...
Nebraska	-27	-95	-162	-61	-42	-44	-98	429	790	1,345	...	...	...	...	...	...	...
Kansas	-7	-60	-160	-61	-69	-29	-86	70	476	962	...	...	...	...	...	...	...
SOUTH ATLANTIC																	
Delaware	190	34	64	-57	-32	-55	-54	-42	-42	-50	-36	-52	-95	-84	-100	-64	-75
Maryland	81	97	61	-22	-20	-57	-32	-55	-35	-39	-50	-33	-84	-71	-79	-69	-81
District of Columbia	-72	45	403	-30	116	-20	1	16	16	234	27	48	-65	-11	54	147	...
Virginia	11	65	47	-70	-20	-47	-42	-63	-22	-98	-75	-74	-106	-66	-79	-76	-52
West Virginia	-112	-63	39	12	34	30	24	-9	33	-24	-31	-4	-18	-12	-10	-6	16
North Carolina	-18	-6	76	48	7	-21	-17	-39	2	-65	-60	-57	-94	-54	-55	-56	-39
South Carolina	-8	-21	29	-80	-26	-38	-21	-39	36	-99	-85	-65	-93	-53	-36	-45	10
Georgia	-25	-29	3	-98	-26	-16	-1	-25	...	-47	-53	-13	3	54	6	52	177
Florida	268	218	306	220	93	102	69	77	44	49	70	68	74	...	...	...	...
EAST SOUTH CENTRAL																	
Kentucky	-75	-76	22	-49	-63	-69	-25	-50	-18	-37	-51	-28	-60	-35	17	131	470
Tennessee	-60	-11	58	-26	-53	-61	-31	-43	-25	-41	-70	-42	-34	83	86	306	458
Alabama	-78	-44	-1	-21	-34	-20	...	-22	-12	-85	-30	-15	178	324	3,870	1,614	...
Mississippi	-98	-101	21	-24	-103	-25	-2	-45	22	-80	-14	71	435	142	326	757	...
WEST SOUTH CENTRAL																	
Arkansas	157	-114	-29	-64	-24	-5	-21	59	118	-50	202	221	576	237	3,658	...	...
Louisiana	10	-7	74	5	-42	-5	14	-26	-3	-88	31	31	94	21	203	...	...
Oklahoma	-85	-130	-135	12	50	422	893	...	...	...	...	...	...	...	...	...	...
Texas	42	39	40	55	32	32	76	58	214	57	617	...	...	...	...	...	...
MOUNTAIN																	
Montana	-3	-61	-43	-113	209	160	240	939	199	...	...	...	...	...	...	...	...
Idaho	-33	-17	149	-81	119	382	300	572	290	...	...	...	...	...	...	...	...
Wyoming	-32	10	56	-1	123	175	131	688	325	...	...	...	...	...	...	...	...
Colorado	102	24	17	-37	18	129	48	342	1,187	-28	...	...	...	...	...	...	...
New Mexico	68	94	256	9	-32	222	6	34	....	-108	-46	...	...	...	...	...	...
Arizona	296	246	103	88	326	215	90	364	959	...	...	...	...	...	...	...	...
Utah	81	74	17	-19	37	66	51	82	119	411	613	...	...	...	...	...	...
Nevada	412	212	193	9	-137	345	-151	-194	54	2,200	...	...	...	...	...	...	...
PACIFIC																	
Washington	11	155	54	-6	26	473	117	1,373	610	372	2,331	...	...	...	...	...	...
Oregon	25	173	97	35	10	199	46	221	206	244	838	...	...	...	...	...	...
California	142	268	201	308	196	186	8	58	80	110	772	...	...	...	...	...	...

than-average growth for a long time; this trend was reversed only slightly, and apparently temporarily, during the last decade or so of the nineteenth century and the first quarter of this century.

The North Central Region was just being opened up during the first few decades after the nation was founded, and its rates of growth were phenomenally high from 1800 to 1840-1870 as settlers rushed in. The settlement of the East North Central Division preceded the settlement of the West North Central states by about 2 or 3 decades, so that growth slackened in Ohio, Illinois, and Indiana before it did in Iowa, Kansas, and Nebraska and the other West North Central states. However, once the East North Central states were settled agriculturally, they proceeded to develop industrially, especially around the shores of the Great Lakes and along the Ohio and Mississippi Rivers. Consequently, these states grew at about the national rate until 1920. In the 1930 to 1940 period their growth slackened to a point well below national averages. During the 1940's a great manufacturing expansion in Detroit, Chicago, Cleveland, and other industrial areas caused the growth of these states to return to about the national rate. This trend appears to have accelerated even more since 1950, especially in Michigan, Indiana, and Ohio. Whether it will persist for several more years, or whether this division will follow the pattern of slower growth that has characterized the Northeast, is a question that cannot be answered easily. Completion of the St. Lawrence Seaway is expected to stimulate additional industrial and commercial growth in this area. The settlement of the West, long a drain on the remainder of the country's population, could slacken and cause a larger proportion of population growth to remain in these East North Central states.

The West North Central states have undergone a much more moderate industrial expansion than the East North Central states. Therefore, when the phase of agricultural settlement was completed, between 1890 and 1900, the growth rates of this division sank to less than half the national rate, and they have remained there. Recent declines in farm population have tended to keep population growth small in this division.

In the South, the South Atlantic Division is one of the areas of original settlement. Like New England, it had below-average growth rates throughout the nineteenth century and the early twentieth century. Unlike New England, however, it had above-average growth rates between 1930 and 1940 and again between 1940 and 1950. This revival of growth was due, in part, to the expansion of Florida, but much of it is also a result of growth in other parts of the division. Recent industrial development in the South has helped to retain population in this area.

The East South Central Division had above-average growth trends only until 1840, but since then they have been below average (except during the 1930 to 1940 decade). Thus, the comparatively low rates of growth between 1940 and 1950 were a resumption of a trend which began more than a century ago.

The development of the West South Central states began later than it did in other regions, and lasted until 1910; since 1940 the growth there has been below average.

The West, the last of the regions to be settled, has been a region of above-average growth during the past century. Since 1850, the Pacific Division has grown at twice the national rate in every decade except one (1890 to 1900), during which it grew 1/3 faster than the nation. Hence, the rapid growth of this division in the 1940 to 1950 decade, and again in the period since 1950, represents a long-time trend. Exactly how long this great westward movement of population can continue is debatable. Undoubtedly, in the not-too-distant future, the rates of growth will follow the pattern set by the older divisions and will sink to a level near the national average. Before 1950 there seemed to be evidence that this had already begun to happen in the Mountain Division, but industrial expansion in the Mountain states during and since the war have given population growth there a new impetus, and it is now one of the fastest growing of the divisions.

Thus, the zone of above-average growth rates

has traveled across the continent from East to West. A secondary set of above-average growth rates has appeared in areas of industrial expansion, first in the Northeast and the East North Central Divisions, and later in the South and the West. The first phase of growth--the settlement of land and the development of agricultural, mineral, and forest resources--has now been completed. It appears that, in the future, a region's growth or lack of growth will depend upon the comparative growth of commerce and industry there. The revolutionary effects of new technologies should not be overlooked. The harnessing of solar energy, the chemical synthesis of foodstuffs, or the direct conversion of nuclear energy to power may create more radical changes upon the future regional distribution of population than might now be envisaged.

URBAN-RURAL COMPOSITION AND GROWTH

New York, New Jersey, Massachusetts, Rhode Island, and California are the most urban of the states; in 1950, 80 percent or more of their population was living in urban places. The most rural states are Mississippi, Arkansas, North Dakota, South Dakota, North Carolina, and West Virginia-- all of these states were only 35 percent urban, or less, in 1950. Table 4-5 shows the urban-rural composition of each state in 1950 (by the new urban definition), while Table 4-6 reports this information for geographic divisions, together with the estimated percent change, 1940 to 1950, of urban-rural areas (old definition). The New England, Middle Atlantic, East North Central, and Pacific Divisions are highly urbanized, while the five remaining divisions are below average. It should be noted that although the two West Central Divisions and the Mountain Division are the three most sparsely inhabited, each of them is more than 50 percent urban. The farm population is a sizable proportion of the total in only a few states and divisions. Only in the South and West North Central Divisions does the rural-farm population comprise 20 percent or more of the total population. The rural-nonfarm population is proportionately larger in these more agricultural states.

The growth rate of a geographic division as a whole is a very poor indication of how its urban and rural parts are changing. For example, in the 1940 to 1950 period the farm population suffered a decline in all divisions--even in the rapidly growing Pacific Division. (Note that the westward movement between 1940 and 1950 was preponderantly to urban and rural-nonfarm areas, and was not a movement of people who intended to settle rural lands.) Losses of farm population were greater, however, in the South than in most other divisions. (The large loss in New England undoubtedly reflects, at least in part, the changed definition of the farm population.) Extraordinarily large increases in the urban population (1940 to 1950) occurred in the South and West. This urbanization of the South has brought, and is still bringing, revolutionary changes in the traditional "way of life," and is one of the major population phenomena of the post-World War II years. In the Northeast, the urban population grew at a rate which was only about one-half as fast as the national rate, and in the North Central it grew at about the national rate.

Rural-nonfarm population grew rapidly in the geographic divisions where there was already a high degree of urban development, or where the urban population was also growing. This tends to confirm the hypothesis advanced in Chapter 2, that the growth of this population is associated largely with cities.

Long-term trends in the urbanization of each geographic division are shown in Table 4-7. (Also, one column of Table 4-5 reports the date of the decennial census at which the population of each state became 50 percent or more urban. This is a further aid to understanding the history of urbanization.) These statistics make it possible to trace the steps by which each division attained its present state of urbanization. For example, by the close of the Civil War the South was only about 10 percent urban, while the Northeast and East North Central states were 40 percent urban. These latter divisions are not a great deal more urban now than they were 40 years ago (1910). It is the states in the South, West North Central, and West that have been making the transition from

Table 4-5.—DATE OF FIRST DECENNIAL CENSUS, PERCENT URBAN, AND PERCENT OF TOTAL POPULATION LIVING IN PLACES OF SPECIFIED SIZE, FOR EACH STATE: 1950

State	Date of first decennial census	Percent of total population in places of:							Census date state became 50 percent urban	Percent urban, 1950
		100,000 or more	50,000 to 100,000	25,000 to 50,000	10,000 to 25,000	Other urban	Agglom-erated rural	Other rural		
UNITED STATES.....	...	29.4	5.9	5.8	7.9	15.0	7.0	29.0	...	...
NEW ENGLAND										
Maine................	1790	...	8.5	7.9	16.3	18.9	7.3	41.0	1950	51.7
New Hampshire........	1790	...	15.5	11.8	20.3	10.0	10.0	32.5	1910	57.5
Vermont..............	1790	...	...	8.8	7.6	20.1	16.0	47.6	...	36.4
Massachusetts........	1790	34.4	15.8	10.7	5.9	17.7	2.2	13.4	1850	84.4
Rhode Island........	1790	31.4	23.6	10.2	4.3	14.8	2.5	13.2	1850	84.3
Connecticut..........	1790	30.1	7.4	10.8	6.5	22.8	3.5	18.9	1890	77.6
MIDDLE ATLANTIC										
New York............	1790	63.5	3.2	3.5	5.1	10.3	2.8	11.6	1870	85.5
New Jersey..........	1790	25.7	10.5	10.5	13.2	26.8	3.0	10.4	1880	86.6
Pennsylvania........	1790	30.7	5.9	3.5	9.9	20.6	6.3	23.2	1900	70.5
EAST NORTH CENTRAL										
Ohio................	1800	36.5	4.6	8.2	8.1	12.7	6.6	23.2	1910	70.2
Indiana.............	1800	23.9	6.7	8.8	7.3	13.3	8.1	32.0	1920	59.9
Illinois............	1810	42.8	7.8	5.8	7.9	13.3	7.2	15.3	1900	77.6
Michigan............	1810	34.4	8.1	6.5	9.1	12.7	5.7	23.7	1920	70.7
Wisconsin...........	1840	18.6	8.0	12.5	7.0	11.8	9.8	32.3	1930	57.9
WEST NORTH CENTRAL										
Minnesota...........	1850	31.4	...	2.8	8.0	12.2	13.5	32.0	1950	54.5
Iowa................	1840	6.8	11.3	10.3	5.8	13.5	17.7	34.6	...	47.7
Missouri............	1810	33.2	3.7	4.4	7.2	13.0	9.0	29.5	1930	61.5
North Dakota........	1860	...	...	10.5	8.3	7.8	25.7	47.7	...	26.6
South Dakota........	1860	...	8.1	3.9	9.0	12.3	20.5	46.3	...	33.2
Nebraska............	1860	18.9	7.5	...	9.1	11.4	19.0	34.1	...	46.9
Kansas..............	1860	15.6	4.1	3.1	14.6	14.6	15.5	32.4	1950	52.1
SOUTH ATLANTIC										
Delaware............	1790	34.7	...	...	...	27.9	8.7	28.7	1920	62.6
Maryland............	1790	40.5	...	3.2	4.3	20.9	4.0	27.1	1910	69.0
District of Columbia.	1800	100.0	...	...	...	...	...	...	1800	100.0
Virginia............	1790	13.4	7.0	5.6	5.0	16.0	5.3	47.7	...	47.0
West Virginia.......	1790	...	10.9	5.8	6.1	11.8	13.0	52.4	...	34.6
North Carolina......	1790	3.3	8.7	4.3	7.8	9.5	8.2	58.1	...	33.7
South Carolina......	1790	...	10.2	1.7	6.0	18.8	8.6	54.7	...	36.7
Georgia.............	1790	13.1	6.4	3.3	6.9	15.5	8.9	45.8	...	45.3
Florida.............	1830	20.9	5.4	12.1	8.0	19.0	6.9	27.6	1930	65.5
EAST SOUTH CENTRAL										
Kentucky............	1790	12.5	4.1	4.4	3.6	12.2	7.8	55.3	...	36.8
Tennessee...........	1790	25.1	...	2.7	3.8	12.6	5.1	50.8	...	44.1
Alabama.............	1800	18.3	1.8	3.5	7.3	12.9	6.7	49.5	...	43.8
Mississippi.........	1800	...	4.5	8.8	6.0	8.6	8.6	63.5	...	27.9
WEST SOUTH CENTRAL										
Arkansas............	1810	5.4	...	8.3	5.8	13.5	10.9	56.1	...	33.0
Louisiana...........	1810	30.7	...	5.5	5.0	13.7	6.7	38.4	1950	54.8
Oklahoma............	1890	19.1	...	6.0	11.7	14.1	11.5	37.5	1950	51.0
Texas...............	1850	27.1	8.1	2.3	10.5	14.9	6.5	30.8	1950	62.7
MOUNTAIN										
Montana.............	1870	...	...	17.6	10.6	15.4	15.8	40.5	...	43.7
Idaho...............	1870	...	...	10.3	16.9	15.8	15.4	41.7	...	42.9
Wyoming.............	1870	...	...	10.8	21.2	17.6	13.8	36.4	...	49.8
Colorado............	1860	31.4	4.8	3.4	8.3	14.8	10.0	27.3	1930	62.7
New Mexico..........	1850	...	14.2	7.9	9.0	19.1	9.4	40.4	1950	50.2
Arizona.............	1870	14.3	...	6.1	3.9	31.3	5.6	38.9	1950	55.5
Utah................	1850	26.4	8.3	4.2	2.4	23.9	18.1	16.6	1930	65.3
Nevada..............	1860	...	...	20.3	15.4	21.6	14.1	28.7	1950	57.2
PACIFIC										
Washington..........	1850	32.5	...	7.4	8.2	15.1	6.8	30.0	1910	63.7
Oregon..............	1850	24.6	...	5.2	7.0	17.1	8.9	37.2	1930	53.9
California..........	1850	38.5	7.9	5.6	10.7	18.0	2.5	16.9	1900	80.7

Source: U.S. Census of Population: 1950, Vol. I, Number of Inhabitants, U.S. Summary, Tables 6 and 15; Vol. II Characteristics of the Population, Table 58.

Table 4-6.—PERCENT DISTRIBUTION IN 1950 AND PERCENT CHANGE, 1940 TO 1950 OF POPULATION OF GEOGRAPHIC DIVISIONS BY URBAN-RURAL RESIDENCE

Residence	United States total	Northeast		North Central		South			West	
		New England	Middle Atlantic	East North Central	West North Central	South Atlantic	East South Central	West South Central	Mountain	Pacific
Percent distribution in 1950:										
U.S. total...............	100.0	100.0	100.0	100.0	100.0	100.0	100.0	100.0	100.0	100.0
Urban (new definition)........	64.0	76.2	80.5	69.7	52.0	49.1	39.1	55.6	54.9	75.0
Rural nonfarm.................	20.7	19.4	14.9	18.1	21.5	29.1	25.7	22.3	28.2	17.6
Rural farm...................	15.3	4.3	4.6	12.2	26.5	21.9	35.3	22.1	16.9	7.4
Percent change, 1940 to 1950:										
U.S. Total...............	14.5	10.4	9.5	14.2	4.0	18.8	6.5	11.3	22.3	48.8
Urban (old definition)........	19.5	7.8	7.1	14.6	17.1	30.0	28.9	48.0	39.8	43.3
Rural nonfarm.................	43.2	35.5	32.0	45.8	16.3	55.2	42.8	28.2	35.9	99.5
Rural farm...................	-23.6	-28.7	-20.3	-19.0	-20.2	-23.2	-23.1	-36.1	-21.7	-11.1

rural to urban in this century. As of 1950, 30 of the 48 states contained more urban people than rural people. It is entirely possible that by 1960 all but 8 or 10 of the states will have become predominantly urban--and the remaining ones will be approaching this condition.

A somewhat surprising finding is the fact that the states of the West became urban very quickly. The Pacific states were more than 30 percent urban by 1870, and more than 50 percent urban by

1910; the Mountain states were 1/3 urban by 1900.

One interesting observation shows how urgent was the need to change the old urban and rural definitions that had been in use: if the old definitions had been used at the 1950 census, the New England, Middle Atlantic, and Pacific Divisions would each have been reported as being proportionately less urban in 1950 than in 1940.

The East South Central Division was the least urbanized in 1950; in 1810 it was the least urban-

Table 4-7.—PERCENT OF TOTAL POPULATION CLASSIFIED AS URBAN BY GEOGRAPHIC DIVISIONS: 1790 TO 1950

Year	United States total	Northeast		North Central		South			West	
		New England	Middle Atlantic	East North Central	West North Central	South Atlantic	East South Central	West South Central	Mountain	Pacific
1950(new definition)	64.0	76.2	80.5	69.7	52.0	49.1	39.1	55.6	54.9	75.0
1950(old definition)	59.0	74.3	75.1	65.7	49.9	42.5	35.5	53.0	48.8	62.9
1940................	56.5	76.1	76.8	65.5	44.3	38.8	29.4	39.8	42.7	65.3
1930................	56.2	77.3	77.7	66.4	41.8	36.1	28.1	36.4	39.4	67.5
1920................	51.2	75.9	75.4	60.8	37.7	31.0	22.4	29.0	36.5	62.2
1910................	45.7	73.3	71.2	52.7	33.2	25.4	18.7	22.3	35.9	56.8
1900................	39.7	68.6	65.2	45.2	28.5	21.4	15.0	16.2	32.3	46.4
1890................	35.1	61.6	58.0	37.9	25.8	19.5	12.7	15.1	29.3	42.6
1880................	28.2	52.4	50.2	27.5	18.2	14.9	8.4	12.5	21.6	36.2
1870................	25.7	44.4	44.2	21.6	18.9	14.4	8.8	13.3	12.3	32.1
1860................	19.8	36.6	35.4	14.1	13.4	11.5	5.9	12.3	10.1	18.4
1850................	15.3	28.8	25.5	9.0	10.3	9.8	4.2	15.1	6.2	6.4
1840................	10.8	19.4	18.1	3.9	3.9	7.7	2.1	23.4	...	...
1830................	8.8	14.0	14.2	2.5	3.5	6.2	1.5	18.7	...	...
1820................	7.2	10.5	11.3	1.2	...	5.5	0.8	16.2	...	...
1810................	7.3	10.1	11.5	0.9	...	4.5	0.6	22.2	...	...
1800................	6.1	8.2	10.2	...	...	3.4	...	...	...	...
1790................	5.1	7.5	8.7	...	...	2.3	...	...	...	...

Source: 1950 Census of Population, Volume I, U.S. Summary, Table 15.

ized of the divisions then in existence, and has retained this position continuously since that time.

SIZE OF PLACE

The degree to which the population is concentrated in large places varies widely among the states, geographic divisions, and regions. Almost one-half of the population of the Middle Atlantic Division, and one-third of the population of the East North Central and Pacific Divisions, lives in places of 100,000 or more. The states in which the largest proportion of the population resides in places of 50,000 or more are:

	Percent
New York.................	66.7
Rhode Island.............	55.0
Illinois.................	50.6
Massachusetts...........	50.2
California..............	46.4
Michigan................	42.5

This does not indicate fully the extent of concentration in these states, for the urbanized area population is not included. (A very large proportion of the category "other urban territory" in Table 4-8 should be included with this group, because it is comprised largely of the fringe population of these larger places.) A larger proportion of the urban population in the South lives in smaller cities than is the case elsewhere in the nation. Some observers consider that this less concentrated pattern of urbanization is the result of the increased use of the automobile and the truck.

Small rural incorporated places (of less than 2,500 population) differ greatly in relative importance among the divisions. In the West North Central Division, the three southern divisions, and the Mountain states they contain from 7 to 15 percent of the population, but in the other areas they contain only 4 percent or less.

Roughly one-half of the population reported as "other rural territory" in Table 4-8 is rural nonfarm, and one-half is rural farm. In the more urbanized divisions, however, this category consists predominantly of rural-nonfarm population, while in the more agricultural states it is predominantly rural farm (compare with Table 4-5).

CONCLUSION

The intent of this chapter has been to illustrate that much of the internal variation in population trends within the nation appears to be associated with environment or location. This variation, here called regional, exists in addition to and independ-

Table 4-8.—PERCENT OF POPULATION IN GROUPS OF PLACES CLASSIFIED ACCORDING TO SIZE, BY GEOGRAPHIC DIVISIONS: 1950

Size of place	United States total	Northeast		North Central		South			West	
		New England	Middle Atlantic	East North Central	West North Central	South Atlantic	East South Central	West South Central	Mountain	Pacific
Total................	100.0	100.0	100.0	100.0	100.0	100.0	100.0	100.0	100.0	100.0
Urban territory........	64.0	76.2	80.5	69.7	52.0	49.1	39.1	55.6	54.9	75.0
Places 100,000 or more....	29.4	26.5	46.0	34.2	21.2	16.4	15.3	23.7	13.9	36.0
Places of 50,000 to 99,999	5.9	13.3	5.3	6.9	4.8	6.6	2.4	4.3	4.3	5.8
Places 25,000 to 49,999...	5.8	10.4	4.6	7.7	4.8	4.9	4.5	4.2	7.9	5.9
Places 10,000 to 24,999...	7.9	7.8	8.1	8.0	8.4	6.1	5.1	9.0	9.2	9.9
Places 5,000 to 9,999...	5.4	3.3	5.9	5.5	5.7	4.7	5.3	7.0	8.5	3.6
Places 2,500 to 4,999.....	4.3	3.0	3.9	3.9	5.0	4.7	4.1	5.3	7.8	3.6
Other urban territory.....	5.3	12.0	6.8	3.5	2.0	5.7	2.4	2.0	3.3	10.2
Rural territory........	36.0	23.8	19.5	30.3	48.0	50.9	60.9	44.4	45.1	25.0
Places 1,000 to 2,499.....	4.3	3.8	2.9	4.0	6.5	5.0	4.5	5.0	7.2	2.9
Places under 1,000........	2.7	0.2	1.1	3.1	8.1	2.4	2.4	2.9	4.8	0.9
Other rural territory.....	29.0	19.7	15.5	23.2	33.4	43.5	54.0	36.5	33.1	21.2

Source: 1950 Census of Population, Volume I, U.S. Summary, Table 16.

ent of the urban-rural and metropolitan-nonmetropolitan classifications discussed in the two preceding chapters. No simple explanation can be found to explain regional variation. Basic physical and climatic characteristics, natural resources, history, market conditions, transportation facilities, location with respect to other similar and competing areas, birth rates, death rates, and migration streams are all simultaneous forces which tend to cause one area to grow faster than another.

BUT AS IMPRESSIVE AS THE AMOUNT OF THIS INTERNAL VARIATION HAS BEEN SHOWN TO BE, IT ACTUALLY IS ONLY A COMPARATIVELY SMALL FRACTION OF THE INTERNAL VARIATION OF THIS TYPE THAT ACTUALLY EXISTS IN THE NATION. Statistics tabulated by states, geographic divisions, and regions fail to reveal the full scope of the existing variation. Also, the available data for state, divisional, and census regions prove to be less than adequate to explain it. The reason for this is that states, geographic divisions, or regions, are themselves clusters of areas that have great internal variation; they are too heterogeneous. Progress in the study of population distribution requires the development of a system of area classification that can reveal this diversity and yet permits urban-rural and metropolitan-nonmetropolitan distinctions. Such a system, invented to serve this very purpose, was created in conjunction with the 1950 census. It is the system of "economic areas," which is the subject of the next chapter.

SUPPLEMENT: A BRIEF DESCRIPTION OF THE
SOCIO-ECONOMIC CHARACTERISTICS OF
THE GEOGRAPHIC DIVISIONS

An excellent, yet simple and direct, way of differentiating among areas is to describe how their residents earn their living; i.e., to describe the differences which exist among areas with respect to the industrial affiliation of workers. Table 4-9 contains the data necessary for such a differentiation. Column 1 of this table reports the industrial

composition for the United States economy as a whole as a percentage distribution. The remainder of the table is a set of percentage-point differences, showing how the composition of each division differs from that of the nation. (For example, in New England, 4.0 percent of the employed population is in the agricultural industries, whereas, in the nation as a whole, 12.5 percent of the employed population is in these industries. The entry of -8.5 in Table 4-9 for agriculture in New England was obtained by subtracting 12.5 from 4.0 percent. Each of the other entries was obtained by this procedure.) A minus sign denotes that an area has a deficit of a particular activity in comparison with the nation, and a plus sign (no sign) shows that an area has an unusual degree of specialization in that particular activity.

Table 4-10 is a simple percent distribution, according to the geographic divisions, of the dollar value of each of 8 different types of economic activity. For example, this table shows that 39.3 percent of all minerals (including petroleum) are extracted in the West South Central Division, that about one-quarter of all agricultural production comes from one division--the West North Central, and that the Middle Atlantic and the East North Central Divisions together contain 57 percent of all manufacturing. This table can best be interpreted by comparing the proportions shown for each economic activity with the proportion of the total population located in the division (Table 4-2).

The footnotes to these tables indicate the sources from which they were compiled. These sources also provide data for each of the 48 states.

The Northeast Region, comprising the New England and Middle Atlantic Divisions, is the most highly industrialized and commercialized part of the nation. Since much of it is mountainous or forested, comparatively little agriculture is found there; with 26 percent of the nation's population, these divisions account for only 8 percent of the value of farm products sold. But they account for a disproportionately large share of manufacturing, wholesale sales, and services (especially professional services).

Table 4-9.—INDUSTRIAL COMPOSITION OF THE GEOGRAPHIC DIVISIONS IN COMPARISON WITH THE NATION: 1950

Industry	United States total	Northeast		North Central		South			West	
		New England	Middle Atlantic	East North Central	West North Central	South Atlantic	East South Central	West South Central	Mountain	Pacific
Total employed............	100.0	14.3	10.4	9.5	14.2	9.5	17.6	13.7	17.0	10.8
Agriculture, forestry and fisheries...................	12.5	-8.5	-9.2	-3.6	12.3	4.2	14.9	7.1	5.6	-3.9
Mining......................	1.7	-1.6	...	-0.8	-0.8	0.7	1.3	1.5	2.3	-1.0
Construction................	6.1	-0.5	-0.6	-1.1	-0.3	0.5	-0.2	1.8	2.1	1.6
Manufacturing..............	25.9	12.6	7.1	9.3	-10.5	-4.2	-7.5	-12.6	-16.4	-5.7
Durable goods............	13.8	4.4	2.2	10.7	-6.9	-6.1	-5.2	-8.0	-9.0	-1.8
Nondurable goods..........	11.9	8.2	4.9	-1.6	-3.6	2.0	-2.3	-4.5	-7.3	-3.8
Transportation, communication, and other public utilities...	7.8	-1.4	0.8	...	0.5	-1.1	-1.6	...	1.8	0.6
Wholesale and retail trade....	18.8	-0.7	0.5	-0.5	0.6	-1.9	-3.4	1.3	1.3	3.1
Finance, insurance, and real estate......................	3.4	0.5	1.3	-0.4	-0.4	-0.8	-1.4	-0.5	-0.5	0.9
Business and repair service...	2.5	-0.1	0.2	-0.1	0.2	-0.5	-0.6	...	0.5	0.7
Personal services...........	6.2	-0.9	-0.3	-1.4	-1.4	2.2	1.2	1.7	-0.1	0.2
Entertainment and recreation services....................	1.0	-0.2	....	-0.1	-0.1	-0.2	-0.3	-0.1	0.3	0.7
Professional and related services...................	8.3	1.1	0.4	-0.5	0.3	-0.8	-1.4	-0.3	1.4	1.3
Public Administration........	4.4	-0.1	-0.2	-0.9	-0.7	1.7	-1.2	-0.2	1.5	1.6
Industry not reported........	1.5	-0.3	-0.1	-0.1	0.4	...	0.2	0.1	0.2	-0.2

Source: U.S. Census of Population: 1950, Characteristics of the Population, U.S. Summary, Table 83.

The North Central Region, which contains the East North Central and West North Central geographic divisions, is a mixed agricultural and industrial region. The East North Central Division, bordering on the Great Lakes, has many large and important industrial cities, yet contains a high proportion of the more fertile, level, and tillable land in the United States. The West North Central Division has a very different economic base; it is much more specialized in agriculture, and less specialized in manufacturing, than the East North Central.

The Southern Region, comprising the South Atlantic, East South Central, and West South Central Divisions is the more rural and generally less industrialized region of the nation. Until recent years it specialized in the production of cash crops--cotton, tobacco, sugar cane, citrus fruits, winter vegetables, peanuts, and various specialty crops. In the past two decades much manufacturing has moved southward, which has resulted in the establishment of many new textile, petroleum, and chemical industries, among others. Mean-

while, the agriculture has become more diversified, and now includes much more dairying and cattle raising. Since World War II, economists have frequently referred to the South as "the New South," in recognition of the great changes that have been made, and which are still taking place. The phenomenal growth of cities and the abandonment of farming, described earlier in this chapter, indicate the industrial transformation which is taking place there. Although this region still contains a disproportionately large share of the lower level-of-living groups of the nation, this concentration has lessened considerably in recent decades.

The region of the West consists of the Mountain and Pacific Divisions. Most of this area is either semi-arid or mountainous, and much of it is both. The really outstanding characteristic of the Pacific Division is the string of major seaports extending from San Diego to Seattle, and the large amount of commercial activity that takes place in them. There are several rich agricultural valleys where large acreages of irrigated crops and fruits are

REGIONS AND DIVISIONS 73

Table 4-10.—PERCENT DISTRIBUTION OF DOLLAR VALUE OF SELECTED TYPES OF ECONOMIC ACTIVITY BY GEOGRAPHIC DIVISIONS: 1954

Type of economic activity	United States total	Northeast		North Central		South			West	
		New England	Middle Atlantic	East North Central	West North Central	South Atlantic	East South Central	West South Central	Mountain	Pacific
PERCENT DISTRIBUTION										
Value of farm products sold...	100.0	2.2	6.1	18.6	24.6	10.7	6.3	11.6	7.3	12.6
Value of minerals extracted...	100.0	0.5	8.3	9.0	7.8	7.3	5.0	39.3	12.1	10.8
Value added by manufacture....	100.0	7.8	26.0	31.2	6.1	9.1	4.0	4.9	1.3	9.6
Value of retail sales.........	100.0	6.4	20.6	21.9	9.5	12.1	4.9	8.7	3.7	12.0
Value of merchant wholesalers sales.....................	100.0	5.5	30.1	19.1	8.9	9.0	4.7	8.8	2.5	11.3
Value of business services....	100.0	3.5	43.9	24.3	5.3	5.1	1.8	4.0	1.4	10.7
Value of auto, hotel, and amusement services.........	100.0	5.4	25.4	18.5	7.5	12.3	3.5	7.4	5.6	14.5
Value of personal services....	100.0	6.2	24.6	22.1	7.6	12.0	4.6	7.9	3.1	11.9

Source: Statistical Abstract of the United States, 1957, Tables 794, 1016, 1084, 1094, and 1101.

grown. There is also much "dry farming" for wheat, peas, beans, and other crops. Cattle and sheep grazing are also major agricultural activities. There are mining and lumbering settlements in many parts of the division. In addition to long-exploited deposits of copper, lead, silver, gold, and other metals, recent discoveries of uranium ore have created a mining boom.

Note: The probable future population trends in states, regions, and geographic divisions are discussed in Chapter 26.

Chapter 5

POPULATION DISTRIBUTION: THE SYSTEM OF ECONOMIC AREAS

Chapter 4 advanced two arguments in favor of subdividing the nation into regions and geographic divisions for the purpose of analyzing population distribution and redistribution. These were:

a. The physical environment (including natural resources), the mode of gaining a livelihood, and the characteristics of the inhabitants vary from one region to another. These differences cannot be explained solely by the fact that the proportions of the population living in urban and rural areas vary in size; they appear also to be related to geographic, climatic, and historic factors, and to other locational aspects of the areas.

b. The administrative functions of government, business, and certain other activities make it useful to recognize specific sections of the nation separately, and to identify major intersectional differences.

The first of the above arguments contains implications which are extremely important in connection with scientific research, and recognition of the validity of the second argument should be a cornerstone in any realistic and effective administrative structure. Seldom can economists and sociologists take group phenomena, as such, into the laboratory; they cannot manipulate at will each of the possibly relevant factors in order to observe what relationship each factor has to the phenomenon under study. So far, the most effective substitute is the collection of as much data as possible concerning whatever type of behavior is the subject of research, and the observation of this behavior, in the form of such data, under a wide variety of conditions. If the behavior tends to change systematically in conjunction with the observable presence of varying amounts or intensities of other specific factors, the investigator, by using appropriate statistical methods, can abstract the degree of interrelationship existing between the conditions and the behavior. For example, if changes in the rate of population growth were found to vary significantly with changes in particular aspects of the environment, this discovery would be an important step toward a scientific explanation of growth. Another example illustrates the "practical" application of data based on regional distinctions: if there are marked differences in population, economy, and environment between one part of his jurisdiction and another, it would be foolish for an administrator to assume that all parts of the territory for which he is responsible are alike and have the same problems. An action or a policy that is realistic, appropriate, and effective for one part of his jurisdiction may be a complete failure in another part, simply because the parts vary with respect to certain conditions. Hence, for an organization which is selling a product, establishing a business, or setting up some specific program which concerns the citizenry of a particular area, it is not enough to recognize national trends with respect to the size, the distribution, and the composition of the population. Any organization, government or business, must be familiar with the current trends in the particular area, with how they have differed in recent years from the national trends, and, insofar as is possible, with the reasons for these differences.

Both of the arguments listed and illustrated above would appear to carry extremely important implications; in fact, they have the appearance of being fundamental principles. If so, they should be utilized to the maximum practicable extent in the preparation of population data and other statistics which are compiled for analytical or administrative use. Ideally, the total land area of the nation should be subdivided in such a way that:

a. Each area would have a high degree of homogeneity

b. Each area would represent a unique combination of people, environment, and resources

c. Not only the major differences, but also the smaller but still important variations in environment and population among the areas would be recognized

d. Each area would represent a meaningful combination of economy and population

e. Each area would have boundaries that are generally recognized, and for each area a map would be universally available

The listing of these criteria leads to the question, "How well do the four census regions and the nine geographic divisions meet them?" The answer, with respect to every criterion listed except the last, must be that the four census regions and the nine geographic divisions are satisfactory only in a very crude and approximate way. None of the census regions or divisions are homogeneous. State boundaries delimit large parcels of territory, but most of them have been laid down with little reference to the realities of geography or economics and tend, therefore, to combine within one state several unlike territories. Missouri illustrates well the inadequacy of this kind of arbitrary division. The northern half of the state is Corn Belt land, where mechanized and scientific farming yields a moderately high level of living. The southern half, which lies in the Ozark hills, has hilly terrain and thin soil, and yields a much more meager living to a population whose characteristics differ greatly from those of the population in the northern part of the state. In spite of these obvious variations, the state and regional statistics concerning the farm population of Missouri combine these two unlike populations and treat them as one. If they are based on such statistics, any trends relating to population and economics in Missouri are only agglomerations or averages of what is happening in the state's two divergent areas; for practical purposes, such trends reflect actual conditions in no specific part of the state, except possibly a few transition areas. Missouri is not unique in this respect--in fact, most of the 48 states are in the same situation. Only a few of them may be said to have boundaries that enclose a homogeneous area, even when one considers their urban and rural parts separately.

An equally important reason for the inadequacy of these arbitrary divisions is the great internal diversity which exists even within those regions whose boundaries are defined precisely. The regions are very large, and each contains highly distinctive subareas in which both the economic activity and the population composition are unique. Certain familiar examples come to mind readily. The South contains such disparate sections as the Mississippi Delta, the Brightleaf Tobacco Belt, and the Piedmont, each of which lies in two or more states; each of these has distinctive characteristics, and they all vary with respect to the conditions and trends which are supposed to typify the region generally known as "The South." Even in the North Central Region, where the physical features which divide it internally are less distinctive, one finds the northern wooded areas (called, until recently, the "cutover" area), the Winter Wheat Belt, the Spring Wheat Belt, the Red River Valley, the Corn Belt, the Dairy Belt, etc. (Each of these sections also lies in two or more states.) In the Northeast Region there are also distinctive subareas, such as the fruit and vegetable areas of the Fingerlakes and the lake shore areas in upstate New York, the Bituminous and Anthracite areas of coal mining, the fishing and resort strip along the upper New England coast, the Green Mountain and White Mountain areas, and the potato-growing area of Maine. In the West, the Rocky Mountains, the various deserts, the central valleys of California, the "Inland Empire" of wheat and lumber around Spokane, and the Willamette Valley are only a few of the subsections in which distinctive population situations have developed in response to unique combinations of factors.

A more detailed study of these variations between sections of the country makes it possible to build up convincing evidence for the argument that each of the major regions should be delimited more accurately, that state boundaries should be abandoned in favor of some type of boundary which would permit distinctive areas to be delimited more realistically, and that each region should then be subdivided into its most distinctive parts, or subregions. Because they divide the nation only at the broad regional level, and because the only smaller units within them are the states, the geographic divisions fail to catch the full range of variation, a variation that is meaningful in terms of economics, population, and other factors. The relative variation within each region is often as great as the range of variation between regions, and for this reason is worthy of recognition.

The above considerations suggest that the system of dividing the country according to four census regions and nine geographic divisions, delimited along state boundaries, stops far short of recognizing the nation's distinctive clusters of population, land area, and human activities. Statistics tabulated in terms of states and geographic divisions fail to provide the full range of information that would be available if another system of division were used. Many improvements, both in research and in administrative activities, would seem to depend upon supplementing this traditional classification with a system of area classification which would correct the above-mentioned defects, at least insofar as such correction is possible within the context in which statistics are assembled and tabulated.

THE SYSTEM OF ECONOMIC AREAS

A system of area classification has been designed especially to fill the needs described in the preceding section, and has been used in compiling population and agricultural statistics for the nation. This particular delimitation is known as the "system of economic areas." Each parcel of land designated by the system comprises a cluster of counties which have similar economic, demographic, physical, and social characteristics. These groupings were arrived at by means of cooperative research which was sponsored jointly by the Bureau of the Census and the Bureau of Agricultural Economics.

The system of economic areas subdivides the entire United States into:

    5 Economic provinces
  13 Economic regions (subdivisions of provinces)
119 Economic subregions (subdivisions of regions)
501 State economic areas (subdivisions of subregions which also recognize state boundaries and, hence, are also subdivisions of states)

Within this system, each standard metropolitan area having 100,000 or more inhabitants is also recognized separately as a state economic area. (If the standard metropolitan area lies in two or more states, the part which lies in each state is treated as a separate state economic area, thereby permitting the pieces of any S.M.A. to be assembled from economic area statistics.) The boundaries of the 5 provinces and the 13 regions in this system are shown on a map (Figure 5-1), while the boundaries of the subregions and the state economic areas, as well as the boundaries of the regions, are shown on another map (Figure 5-2).

A monograph which describes each area in full detail is now in press.[1] The balance of the present

---

[1]The System of Economic Areas, by Donald J. Bogue and Calvin L. Beale, The Free Press, 1959 (2 volumes). Other reports, released after each stage of work was completed, are: U.S. Bureau of the Census, State Economic Areas, by Donald J. Bogue, U.S. Government Printing Office, 1951; and Economic Subregions of the United States, by Donald J. Bogue and Calvin L. Beale, Series Census-BAE, No. 19, U.S. Government Printing Office, 1953.

chapter is devoted to a brief description and explanation of the system.

The system of economic areas is based on the premise that unique areas, from the point of view of the statistician, are units that present unique combinations of traits. Since no two places on the surface of the earth are exactly alike, an infinite number of different areas could be delimited. Thus, any attempt to correct the shortcomings of the census regions and geographic divisions must involve, at the outset, the acknowledgement that it is impossible to recognize individually every distinctive aspect of the environment, and that the units as finally delimited will represent only one of several possible kinds of delimitation. The number of areas delimited will depend on the amount of internal variation that is allowed to remain in each area. Moreover, since combinations of traits are involved, the various users of such statistics would want different combinations of traits, depending on their purposes, and each user would attribute more weight to certain factors than to others in arriving at the boundaries. For this reason, neither this system of economic areas nor any other such system can be considered as providing either the "ideal" or the "best possible" set of statistics. Yet the economic areas do have certain characteristics that earlier delimitations have lacked, and which recommend them for general use. First, and most importantly, they attempt to recognize separately each of the nation's outstanding socio-economic areas which contains 100,000 inhabitants or more and the existence of which (as a separate area) is generally recognized by geographers, economists, and local residents.[2] Second, it is believed that this system does sub-

divide the whole United States into a set of regions that are meaningful in a wide variety of applications, and that the boundaries of these regions are much more accurate than the nine geographic divisions or the four census regions. Each of these regions is already recognized, implicitly or explicitly, in various current works concerning regional variations in climate, economy, and population. Third, it is believed that the subdivision of each region into major subareas has recognized each of the nation's outstanding socio-economic areas. Finally, since the factors that constitute each area have been weighted roughly according to the proportion which they represent of the nation's total population and total economic activity, each area may be regarded, in terms of its usefulness for statistical analysis, as a significant unit.

In other words, each area as it is now delimited tends to be fairly homogeneous internally, and to differ significantly from the areas that adjoin it. Further subdivision of the areas would tend to increase only very moderately the internal homogeneity of each one; decreasing the number of areas would tend to decrease homogeneity greatly. Thus, the system of economic areas has followed the two principles stated at the beginning of this chapter, and has applied the recommendations implicit in these principles almost to the point of diminishing returns.

The system of economic areas must face a second problem, posed by the following question: Are these areas practical units which can be used in research, in the carrying out of marketing surveys and other business activities, and in the planning and administration of various kinds of programs? A preliminary version of the economic areas delimitation, arrived at through a consideration of certain published statistics and reports concerning the economic activities of the nation's various areas, was submitted for review and criticism to geographers, agricultural economists, planners, and others. Sometimes these specialists (who were selected for their familiarity with particular areas) advised that a certain area, as delimited, did not represent a functional entity which

[2]Such areas actually exist, a fact that has been overlooked by some recent writers. These widely-recognized subareas are created by rather sharp discontinuities in the physical environment which require different modes of population adjustment. The view that environmental conditions occur in all combinations and are widely diffused is incorrect. For an example of this naivete concerning the facts of geography and their influence upon human activities, see Rutledge Vining, Journal of the American Statistical Association, 1953.

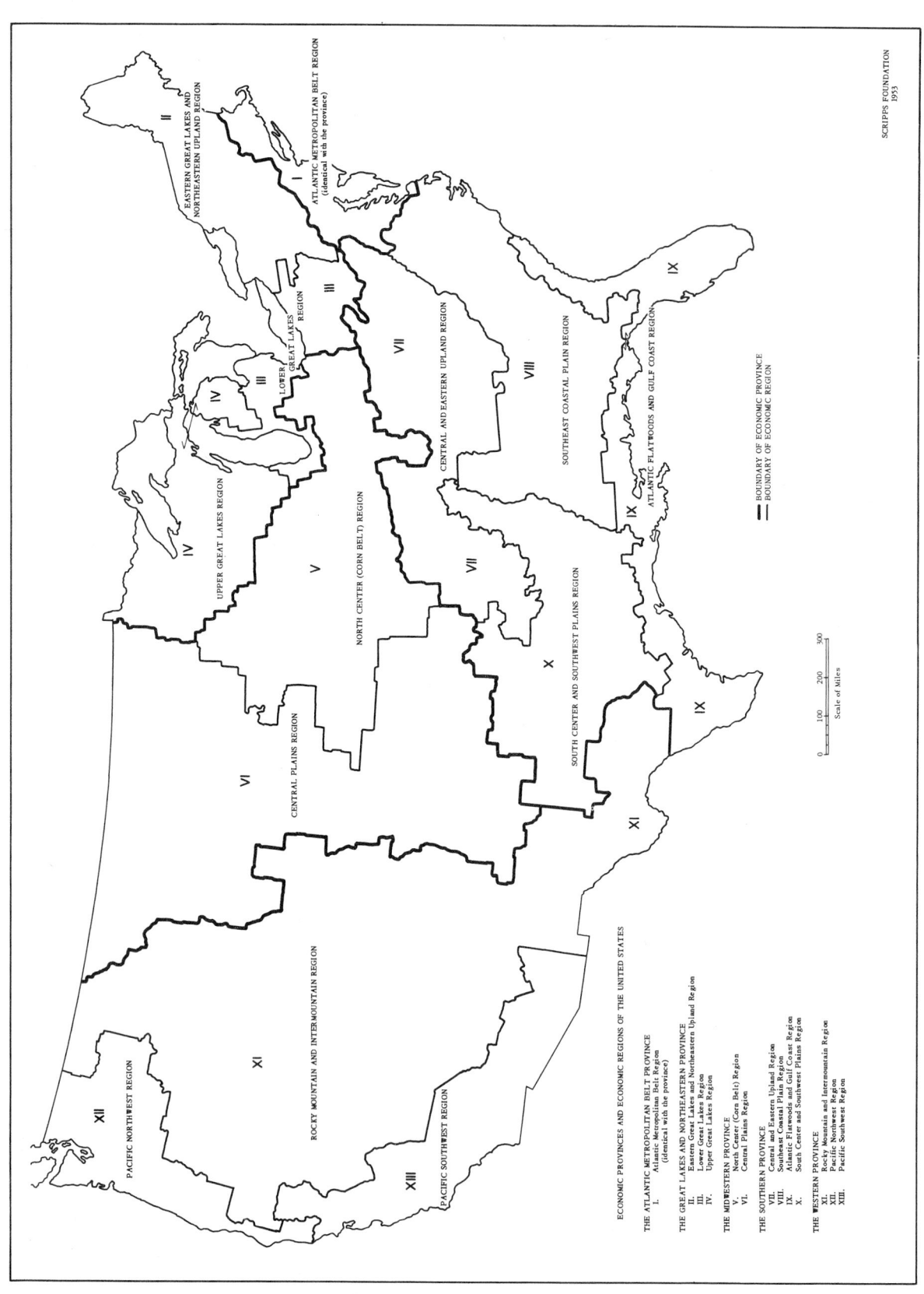

FIGURE 5-1. ECONOMIC PROVINCES AND ECONOMIC REGIONS OF THE UNITED STATES

ECONOMIC PROVINCES AND ECONOMIC REGIONS OF THE UNITED STATES

THE ATLANTIC METROPOLITAN BELT PROVINCE
    I.   Atlantic Metropolitan Belt Region
            (identical with the province)

THE GREAT LAKES AND NORTHEASTERN PROVINCE
    II.   Eastern Great Lakes and Northeastern Upland Region
    III.   Lower Great Lakes Region
    IV.   Upper Great Lakes Region

THE MIDWESTERN PROVINCE
    V.   North Center (Corn Belt) Region
    VI.   Central Plains Region

THE SOUTHERN PROVINCE
    VII.   Central and Eastern Upland Region
    VIII.   Southeast Coastal Plain Region
    IX.   Atlantic Flatwoods and Gulf Coast Region
    X.   South Center and Southwest Plains Region

THE WESTERN PROVINCE
    XI.   Rocky Mountain and Intermountain Region
    XII.   Pacific Northwest Region
    XIII.   Pacific Southwest Region

SCRIPPS FOUNDATION
1953

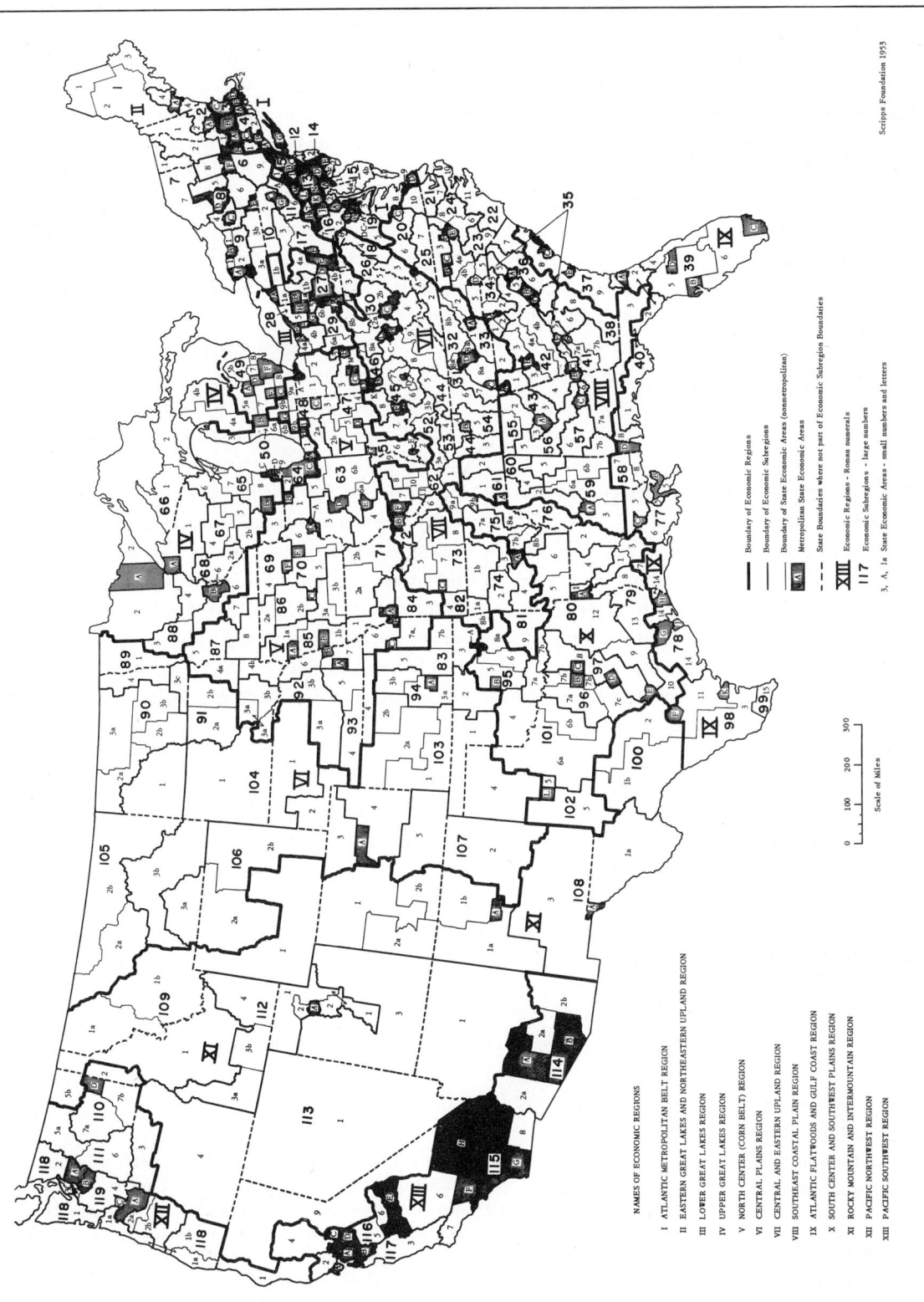

FIGURE 5-2. ECONOMIC REGIONS, ECONOMIC SUBREGIONS, AND STATE ECONOMIC AREAS OF THE UNITED STATES: 1950

Scripps Foundation 1953

NAMES OF ECONOMIC REGIONS

I   ATLANTIC METROPOLITAN BELT REGION
II EASTERN GREAT LAKES AND NORTHEASTERN UPLAND REGION
III LOWER GREAT LAKES REGION
IV UPPER GREAT LAKES REGION
V   NORTH CENTER (CORN BELT) REGION
VI CENTRAL PLAINS REGION
VII CENTRAL AND EASTERN UPLAND REGION
VIII SOUTHEAST COASTAL PLAIN REGION
IX ATLANTIC FLATWOODS AND GULF COAST REGION
X   SOUTH CENTER AND SOUTHWEST PLAINS REGION
XI ROCKY MOUNTAIN AND INTERMOUNTAIN REGION
XII PACIFIC NORTHWEST REGION
XIII PACIFIC SOUTHWEST REGION

Boundary of Economic Regions

Boundary of Economic Subregions

Boundary of State Economic Areas (nonmetropolitan)

Metropolitan State Economic Areas

State Boundaries where not part of Economic Subregion Boundaries

XIII Economic Regions - Roman numerals

117 Economic Subregions - large numbers

3, A, 1a   State Economic Areas - small numbers and letters

Scale of Miles

0   100   200   300

could provide meaningful data for use in practical administration; in such cases, the delimitation was reviewed in the light of the evidence presented by these advisors, as well as the statistics and other information upon which it had been based. Whenever the homogeneity of the area was not seriously impaired by the adoption of these suggestions, or whenever the changes involved in these suggestions helped to improve the preliminary delimitation, the suggestions of the advisors were adopted. As finally established, the boundaries represented what was thought to be the best possible compromise between the abstract requirements of statistical homogeneity and the practical requirements of trained specialists who had observed and lived in the areas whose boundaries were being established.

Thus, the system of economic areas has the following assets:

a. It refines the principle of regionalism, and extends it to include subregions and even smaller local areas. In doing so, it attempts to preserve maximum homogeneity within areas and maximum heterogeneity between areas.

b. The areas adhere to county boundaries in a way that permits statistical data for each area to be collected easily, and to be consolidated from earlier censuses for the purpose of establishing trends.

c. As delimited in this system, the areas have had the review and the approval of local authorities.

d. The system integrates the two other most important area classifications--the rural-urban and the metropolitan-nonmetropolitan.

e. It provides four different levels of homogeneity and detail, to fit the needs of the investigator.[3]

f. A wide variety of data--population, social, and economic--can be assembled for each area, and can then be interpreted in the light of the geographical and other facts connected with the area.

g. The system is flexible, and can be applied to any single state. This procedure, which is often a useful one, is possible because the system recognizes state boundaries in delimiting the most detailed (smallest) units--the state economic areas.

The system has the following disadvantages:

a. Since it is still fairly new, it is unfamiliar to many who might find it useful.

b. Because it is based on county boundaries, in many cases the delimitation is much less exact than would be desirable, even though it is superior to a delimitation based on state boundaries.

c. In certain sparsely populated regions such as the Rocky Mountains and the Great Basin, both the population and the economic activity are insufficient to warrant a recognition of many unique areas as separate economic areas, since to do so would tend to upset the system of approximately equal statistical weighting upon which the whole delimitation is based. In these regions of the western province, several subregions and state economic areas that do not have the minimum desired amount of people or of economic activity are recognized (in violation of the basic principles), but even so the delimitation still fails to show the full range of diversity within the regions.

d. The system is such a detailed one that it is vulnerable to change. Technological advances can cause areas to change markedly in a comparatively short time. For example, such developments as the Grand Coulee Dam or the Savannah River atomic energy plants can bring about rapid changes in the social and economic characteristics of a broad region. Hence, it may prove necessary to revise the economic area delimitation after two or three decades.

---

[3]The 5-area delimitation of economic provinces is not recommended, except in cases where the use of the 13 economic regions is out of the question. Although the 5 economic provinces are far more homogeneous than the 4 census regions, the former, of necessity, still combine entities that are sufficiently unique to be termed regions.

THE ECONOMIC REGIONS

Tables 5-1 to 5-7 present basic population and economic data that show the major characteristics of each economic region. A brief descriptive note about each region is presented here in order to familiarize the reader with the major units. For a detailed description of each region, each sub-region, and each state economic area (together with a variety of statistical data assembled for each area) the reader is referred to the basic monograph cited above.

Region I. Atlantic Metropolitan Belt Region. This region consists of the cluster of seaport cities and the associated nearby urban centers and their environs which, together, form an industrial and commercial concentration along the mid-Atlantic coast. Within this belt lie the great commercial and industrial seaports of Boston, Providence, New York City, Philadelphia, Baltimore, and Norfolk. In addition, the region contains many smaller metropolitan areas such as Hartford, Springfield, Harrisburg, and Wilmington. More than one-half of the total land area lies in metropolitan state economic areas; 93 percent of the population lives in metropolitan areas and only 7 percent is nonmetropolitan. Actually, much of this region's nonmetropolitan area consists of suburbs associated with large centers. Manufacturing in some form provides the chief source of livelihood in this region. In 1950, almost one-third of the employed labor force was in manufacturing industries. Wholesale enterprises that are located here supply manufacturers and distributors throughout the nation with a variety of products assembled from abroad, or from one or another of the areas within the belt.

More than 31 million persons were residing in the region in 1950. The average population density is very high (605 persons per square mile in 1950) and the population is highly urbanized (86 percent urban in 1940). Although the region contains only about 1/60 of the land area of the nation, it contains more than 1/5 of the nation's population. For the past 20 years this region has tended to grow at about the same rate as the nation. It is the only region in the United States whose nonmetropolitan population, taken as a whole, grew at a more rapid pace than its metropolitan population from 1940 to 1950.

The agriculture of this region is quite varied, but it is also specialized, its principal characteristic being its orientation to the immediate metropolitan markets. Dairy farms, vegetable and special crop farms, and poultry farms are the principal types. Because of their proximity to metropolitan centers, many "farms" are merely residences or part-time farms for families whose chief earner works in the city.

Table 5-1.—POPULATION AND URBAN-RURAL AND METROPOLITAN-NONMETROPOLITAN COMPOSITION OF THE POPULATION OF ECONOMIC REGIONS: 1950

Economic region	Region number	Population, 1950	Percent of population				
			Urban	Rural nonfarm	Rural farm	In metropolitan areas	In nonmetropolitan areas
U.S. Total......................	...	150,697,361	64.0	20.7	15.3	56.2	43.8
Atlantic Metropolitan Belt...................	I	31,057,942	85.8	11.5	2.7	92.6	7.4
Eastern Great Lakes and Northeastern Upland..	II	9,220,735	60.9	27.9	11.2	45.0	55.0
Lower Great Lakes............................	III	21,255,544	78.4	15.5	6.1	80.0	20.0
Upper Great Lakes............................	IV	5,020,355	52.0	24.3	23.5	30.6	69.4
North Center (Corn Belt).....................	V	15,250,088	52.7	23.9	23.4	33.2	66.8
Central Plains...............................	VI	5,166,782	49.3	25.7	25.0	20.1	79.9
Central and Eastern Upland...................	VII	14,160,136	43.6	29.4	27.0	37.4	62.6
Southeast Coastal Plain......................	VIII	14,952,020	39.4	26.8	33.8	25.9	74.1
Gulf Coast and Atlantic Flatwoods...........	IX	7,973,759	68.9	21.5	9.6	56.4	43.6
South Center and Southwest Plains...........	X	8,300,506	46.5	23.6	29.9	22.5	77.5
Rocky Mountain and Intermountain.............	XI	3,605,665	49.1	33.3	17.7	17.1	82.9
Pacific Northwest............................	XII	3,911,309	59.5	28.2	12.3	49.5	50.5
Pacific Southwest............................	XIII	10,822,520	81.5	13.2	5.3	84.4	15.6

Table 5-2.—PERCENT CHANGE IN POPULATION OF ECONOMIC REGIONS, BY DECADES: 1900 TO 1950

Economic region	Region number	Percent change, 1900 to 1950	Intercensal percent change:				
			1940 to 1950	1930 to 1940	1920 to 1930	1910 to 1920	1900 to 1910
U.S. Total..........................	...	98.3	14.5	7.2	16.1	14.9	21.0
Atlantic Metropolitan Belt....................	I	114.6	14.5	6.5	18.8	17.9	25.6
Eastern Great Lakes and Northeastern Upland..	II	39.4	6.2	3.0	8.5	6.2	10.5
Lower Great Lakes............................	III	146.0	14.4	4.6	25.8	29.0	26.7
Upper Great Lakes............................	IV	58.1	7.3	8.1	5.5	10.1	17.3
North Center (Corn Belt)....................	V	27.7	7.9	2.4	4.9	6.0	4.0
Central Plains..............................	VI	123.2	7.7	-1.1	11.4	19.0	58.2
Central and Eastern Upland..................	VII	51.1	6.5	9.2	9.0	7.3	11.1
Southeast Coastal Plain.....................	VIII	63.2	9.0	8.7	10.0	8.8	15.1
Gulf Coast and Atlantic Flatwoods...........	IX	261.5	37.0	21.7	35.1	23.1	30.5
South Center and Southwest Plains...........	X	89.1	3.2	4.5	14.6	15.6	32.3
Rocky Mountain and Intermountain............	XI	159.5	19.6	15.6	15.1	15.8	40.7
Pacific Northwest...........................	XII	313.1	39.6	11.8	17.1	17.0	93.3
Pacific Southwest...........................	XIII	695.7	54.8	21.2	66.0	50.5	69.7

Because it is so favorably located with respect to metropolitan markets, the agricultural economy of this region is almost universally prosperous. A very high percent of farm residents are engaged in nonfarm work. Almost one-half of the employed labor force residing on farms in 1950 reported nonfarm occupations. Almost two-fifths of the farm operators reported that they had worked 100 days or more off their farms in 1954.

Region II. Eastern Great Lakes and Northeastern Uplands Region. To the north of the great industrial and commercial belt that spreads along the Atlantic Coast, and to the east of the coal-steel industrial area clustered around Lake Michigan and Lake Erie, lies this inland segment of the manufacturing belt. A high percentage of the region's territory is mountainous or hilly country, or wasteland in the form of cutover forest area. Consequently, many of its subregions are poorly suited to large scale crop farming. Manufacturing is the principal economic base, and is characterized by the fact that it is not only clustered in metropolitan areas, but is also distributed rather widely among the region's numerous small and medium-sized cities. Textiles, leather goods, machinery, lumber, pulp, and paper are among the leading products. The resort and vacation service industries are also important economic activities throughout this region. The result of these traits is that the nonagricultural activities are more dispersed here than they are in most other regions.

During the past 50 years, the rate of population growth in this region has been only two-fifths as high as the national rate of growth, and between 1940 and 1950 its growth was less than one-half that of the nation. The rural areas as a whole have remained almost stationary. Urban and metropolitan areas have grown, but much less rapidly than similar areas in several of the other regions. These population trends are a consequence of the fact that the region's agricultural and other resources were exploited early in the nation's history, and that recent industrial growth has been less rapid and less intense here than in other regions. Proximity to the eastern markets can be listed as one of the region's major resources, as can the high quality of its labor force.

Because so large a proportion of the region's terrain is unsuitable for crops or for pasture, only a few areas are devoted to intensive farming. Nevertheless, the region has a highly developed dairy industry that serves the adjacent eastern metropolitan markets. Specialized crops of fruits and vegetables are grown on much of the land that is suitable for tilling. Since industry is so dispersed, many rural-farm residences are, in reality, the homes of workers whose primary employment is nonagricultural but who live on places classified as farms. In 1954, for example, 36 per-

Table 5-3.—PERCENT CHANGE IN POPULATION OF ECONOMIC REGIONS, BY URBAN AND RURAL AND
METROPOLITAN AND NONMETROPOLITAN AREAS: 1940 TO 1950

Economic region	Region	Total - all areas			Urban and rural nonfarm			Rural farm		
		Total	Metro-politan	Non-metro-politan	Total	Metro-politan	Non-metro-politan	Total	Metro-politan	Non-metro-politan
U.S. Total......................	...	14.5	22.0	6.0	25.8	24.5	28.3	-23.6	-25.8	-23.4
Atlantic Metropolitan Belt.................	I	14.5	14.2	18.6	16.3	15.2	35.9	-24.9	-24.6	-25.3
Eastern Great Lakes and Northeastern Upland.	II	6.2	6.9	5.7	10.8	8.6	12.9	-20.0	-21.6	-19.6
Lower Great Lakes...........................	III	14.4	15.2	11.3	17.6	16.8	22.1	-19.6	-23.5	-17.5
Upper Great Lakes..........................	IV	7.3	16.1	3.9	19.5	20.0	19.2	-19.3	-28.2	-18.6
North Center (Corn Belt)..................	V	7.9	20.3	2.6	19.8	24.3	16.9	-18.6	-25.2	-18.1
Central Plains..............................	VI	7.7	39.4	1.9	25.8	44.4	20.4	-24.8	-29.3	-24.7
Central and Eastern Upland..................	VII	6.5	19.4	...	23.9	23.7	24.0	-22.3	-26.0	-22.0
Southeast Coastal Plain....................	VIII	9.0	27.6	3.7	40.1	36.9	42.2	-24.1	-31.2	-23.6
Gulf Coast and Atlantic Flatwoods..........	IX	37.0	48.5	24.6	52.6	53.7	51.0	-30.3	-44.5	-27.8
South Center and Southwest Plains..........	X	3.2	45.7	-4.9	39.1	56.1	32.7	-35.7	-41.0	-35.5
Rocky Mountain and Intermountain...........	XI	19.6	49.4	14.9	34.9	55.7	30.6	-21.8	-27.7	-21.6
Pacific Northwest..........................	XII	39.6	43.0	36.3	54.1	49.5	59.7	-16.5	-18.0	-16.1
Pacific Southwest..........................	XIII	54.8	56.1	48.3	61.5	60.2	70.2	-10.5	13.8	-7.2

cent of the farm operators were employed off their farms for more than 100 days.

Region III. Lower Great Lakes Region. Manufacturing dominates, and dwarfs, almost every other activity in this region (40 percent of the total labor force was employed in manufacturing in 1950). The region's industrial specialties are the production of steel and the manufacture of machinery and automotive equipment. Iron ore is transported by water from the northwest to various ports along the southern shores of Lake Michigan and Lake Erie. Bituminous coal of good coking quality is mined in the southeastern part of the region, and, via river and rail, is brought together with the ore. Coal also comes into the region from mines in southern Illinois, Indiana, and Kentucky. The furnaces where the coal and the ore are finally brought together are located at various points between the coal mines and the lake ports. A favorable location for steel manufacture may be either at the point where the transportation of ore shifts from lake boat to rails, or at the point where coal transportation shifts from river barge to rails. Consequently, there are important steel mills at all the principal lake ports where the ore must be unloaded from boats for land transportation, and at all points where the coal must be transferred from water to rail carriers. A few steel mills are also located at intermediate points between the coal mines and the lake ports. Pittsburgh, Cleveland, Detroit, Toledo,

and Chicago are steel producing centers because their locations involve comparatively low total transport costs for the merging of coal and ore. Because of its locational advantages, this is the second most populous region, with a population of 21 million. Until 1930 it grew faster than the nation as a whole, but in recent years it has been growing at about the national rate. Most of its population, of course, is either urban or suburban.

Many and varied manufacturing enterprises have been drawn to this region because of its proximity to the supply of steel and coal. The region specializes in the manufacture of heavy machinery and durable goods, and its automobile production is an outstanding example of the rapid and extensive industrial growth which has taken place here.

This region is a part of the Great Lakes dairy area. Like the dairying in Regions I and II, this region's dairying consists largely of the production of fluid milk which supplies the large urban and metropolitan market. However, as a border area lying along the northern edge of the Corn Belt, the region also contains quite a few livestock farms. Except in a very few isolated areas, the agricultural industries are prosperous and provide a good livelihood.

Region IV. Upper Great Lakes Region. The Wisconsin and Minnesota segments of this region contain the "heart" of the Great Lakes dairying industry. In addition, the upper (northern) portions of Michigan, Wisconsin, and Minnesota pro-

Table 5-4.—MEDIAN INCOME BY ECONOMIC REGION, AND URBAN-RURAL COMPOSITION OF NONMETROPOLITAN
PORTION OF EACH ECONOMIC REGION: 1950

Economic region	Region	Median income of families in 1949 (dollars)			Urban-rural composition of nonmetropolitan areas		
		Total	Metro-politan	Non-metro-politan	Percent urban	Percent rural nonfarm	Percent rural farm
U.S. Total......................	...	3,073	3,494	2,364	35.2	33.7	31.1
Atlantic Metropolitan Belt.................	I	3,482	3,543	2,733	35.5	46.7	17.8
Eastern Great Lakes and Northeastern Upland.	II	3,045	3,341	2,763	43.9	39.1	17.0
Lower Great Lakes...........................	III	3,614	3,794	2,972	42.3	37.3	20.4
Upper Great Lakes..........................	IV	3,034	3,660	2,708	37.8	30.5	31.7
North Center (Corn Belt)...................	V	3,051	3,521	2,771	37.5	30.0	32.5
Central Plains.............................	VI	2,984	3,395	2,843	39.6	29.9	30.4
Central and Eastern Upland.................	VII	2,278	3,135	1,795	22.2	37.8	40.0
Southeast Coastal Plain....................	VIII	1,904	2,806	1,589	26.8	30.0	43.1
Gulf Coast and Atlantic Flatwoods..........	IX	2,506	2,951	1,975	44.7	35.9	19.4
South Center and Southwest Plains..........	X	2,121	3,203	1,808	35.2	29.7	35.2
Rocky Mountain and Intermountain...........	XI	3,073	3,369	3,009	42.8	36.7	20.5
Pacific Northwest..........................	XII	3,451	3,640	3,273	40.2	40.8	18.9
Pacific Southwest..........................	XIII	3,557	3,625	3,172	46.7	35.6	17.7

vide some of the raw materials--iron ore, lumber, and wood pulp--that are used in the manufacturing centers of the Lower Great Lakes Region.

Although this region is much more rural and much less metropolitan in character than Regions I, II, and III, its manufacturing is as important a source of livelihood as its farming. Scattered among the region's many smaller cities and towns are factories producing a great variety of products, among the most important of which are wood and paper products derived from the raw materials of the forests. However, there is also much diversified general manufacturing, including machinery and other equipment.

Over the past fifty years the region has grown only about one-half as rapidly as the nation as a whole. In recent years its growth has been slow because of the depletion of its forests, a decline in the reserves of its best iron ores, and the out-migration of its farm population. Along the northern "cutover" margin, vast areas are almost uninhabited; the soil in these areas is unproductive, the forests have been removed, and there is little possibility of earning a livelihood.

Minneapolis, by far the largest metropolis, is the region's major manufacturing, commercial, and financial capital.

Almost two-thirds of the farms are dairy farms, producing fluid milk, condensed milk, cream, butter, and cheese. Although both the soil and the climate are poorly suited to the extensive growing of corn needed to fatten cattle and hogs, they are very favorable for the growing of hay and forage crops required by dairy animals. Potatoes are an important secondary cash crop in many sections.

Because the vast amount of deforested but grown-over land in the north and the innumerable lakes scattered throughout the region attract vacationers in summer and sportsmen the year around, serving tourists and summer residents is one of the region's significant economic activities.

Region V. Corn Belt Region. A rich agricultural development and a moderate amount of industry and commerce are the outstanding traits of this region. It comprises the flat or gently rolling central lowlands of the United States. Almost 95 percent of the total land area is in farms, and more than one-half of the land area is in harvested crops. In most years there is adequate moisture for the growing of crops. The soil is fertile and the growing season is long enough to permit a variety of crops to be raised. Because this combination of resources makes agricultural production so profitable, land values are high.

Table 5-5.—INDUSTRIAL COMPOSITION OF THE EMPLOYED LABOR FORCE OF ECONOMIC REGIONS: 1950

| Economic region | Region | Percent of employed workers in: | | | | | Metropolitan: Percent in manufacturing | Nonmetropolitan: Percent in agriculture |
		Agriculture	Mining	Manufacturing	Wholesale and retail trade	Other		
U.S. Total......................	...	12.4	1.7	25.9	18.8	41.2	30.7	26.6
Atlantic Metropolitan Belt..................	I	2.5	0.1	32.2	19.5	45.7	32.6	14.6
Eastern Great Lakes and Northeastern Upland.	II	8.3	2.7	33.8	17.0	38.2	37.1	12.7
Lower Great Lakes...........................	III	3.4	1.9	39.5	18.4	36.8	41.1	12.4
Upper Great Lakes..........................	IV	20.8	1.6	21.7	18.6	37.3	22.8	28.9
North Center (Corn Belt)....................	V	20.7	0.8	22.0	18.6	37.9	30.4	29.8
Central Plains.............................	VI	25.7	2.5	9.3	19.8	42.7	19.3	31.8
Central and Eastern Upland.................	VII	18.7	5.5	21.9	16.6	37.3	29.4	30.0
Southeast Coastal Plain....................	VIII	26.1	0.7	23.3	14.9	35.0	23.4	34.2
Gulf Coast and Atlantic Flatwoods...........	IX	12.1	1.7	15.1	22.1	49.0	16.7	23.3
South Center and Southwest Plains...........	X	25.1	3.1	11.7	19.1	41.0	16.2	32.6
Rocky Mountain and Intermountain...........	XI	19.0	5.0	10.1	19.0	46.9	11.9	21.6
Pacific Northwest...........................	XII	10.6	0.3	22.3	20.7	46.1	19.8	15.5
Pacific Southwest...........................	XIII	7.7	0.9	18.8	22.6	50.0	20.5	24.7

Farms are highly mechanized; they are also of large average size, as they must be if the fixed costs of equipment are to be spread over the maximum number of acres.

In addition to its profitable agricultural activities, the region has a manufacturing and commercial development of substantial size and importance. Some of the favorable locational factors found in Region III also characterize this region, especially its eastern and central portions. More than one-half of the population of the region as a whole is urban. (The proportion which is urban varies from much more than one-half in the eastern subregions to less than one-fourth in the subregions on the western fringe.) Although there are few of the huge concentrations of industry that characterize Regions II and III, there are many medium and small-sized cities which, together, provide a solid manufacturing base. Metropolitan places such as Dayton, Indianapolis, Fort Wayne, Peoria, St. Louis, Davenport, Des Moines, Kansas City, Omaha, Lincoln, and Sioux City are important manufacturing and wholesaling centers.

In the agricultural sector, corn is the principal crop, and about 45 percent of the total cropland is devoted to it. Such secondary crops as oats, wheat, soybeans, hay, and pasture crops are rotated between crops of corn in order to preserve and replenish the fertility of the soil. In most Corn Belt areas, a high percentage of the corn and other grains thus produced are not sold for cash, but are used to fatten hogs, beef cattle, and sheep for meat production.

Three types of farming enterprises dominate the agricultural economy of the region: livestock farms, cash grain farms, and general farms. More than a third of all farms are livestock farms, specializing in the production of beef animals or hogs for meat. About 30 percent of all farms are cash crop farms, most of which specialize in the growing of corn and feed grains for cash sale. About one-eighth of all farms are classed as general farms, or farms which derive less than one-half of their gross cash income from any one type of farming. Variations in soil, topography, climate, and marketing conditions cause some subregions of the Corn Belt to specialize more heavily in one than in another of these three principal types of farming, or to combine the activities in different proportions.

In general, the limits of the Corn Belt are fixed to the west by lack of sufficient moisture for a cropping pattern dominated by corn, on the north by less fertile soils and short growing seasons, and to the east and the south by rough, hilly land of generally low fertility.

Table 5-6.—ECONOMIC REGIONS: COLOR COMPOSITION IN 1950, AND CHANGE IN COLOR COMPOSITION: 1940 TO 1950

Economic region	Region	Percent nonwhite: 1950						Percent change in nonwhite population: 1940 to 1950		
		Region, urban-rural residence				Metro-politan areas, total	Non-metro-politan areas, total	Total	Metro-politan areas	Non-metro-politan areas
		Total	Urban	Rural nonfarm	Rural farm					
U.S. Total......................	...	10.5	10.1	8.7	14.5	9.8	11.3	17.1	44.4	-3.1
Atlantic Metropolitan Belt..................	I	9.1	9.2	7.7	10.7	8.9	11.9	42.5	47.9	6.5
Eastern Great Lakes and Northeastern Upland..	II	1.3	1.7	0.8	0.4	1.9	0.8	57.9	88.2	21.0
Lower Great Lakes...........................	III	7.3	8.9	1.8	0.6	8.6	2.0	75.3	77.7	43.0
Upper Great Lakes...........................	IV	1.0	0.8	2.0	0.3	1.2	0.9	18.4	55.2	4.4
North Center (Corn Belt)....................	V	3.2	5.4	1.2	0.4	6.9	1.4	25.7	35.7	6.5
Central Plains..............................	VI	3.0	3.5	3.0	2.1	5.1	2.5	14.2	52.0	1.2
Central and Eastern Upland..................	VII	7.6	12.3	5.3	2.5	12.3	4.8	7.3	24.4	-11.2
Southeast Coastal Plain.....................	VIII	33.4	31.3	27.6	40.4	31.2	34.2	-0.1	13.3	-3.8
Gulf Coast and Atlantic Flatwoods...........	IX	21.5	21.1	22.2	22.5	21.0	22.0	19.5	30.5	8.2
South Center and Southwest Plains...........	X	22.2	17.9	19.3	31.2	14.5	24.4	-8.2	23.3	-12.0
Rocky Mountain and Intermountain............	XI	4.5	2.2	6.6	6.9	2.1	5.0	27.2	74.0	24.3
Pacific Northwest...........................	XII	2.2	2.5	1.8	1.7	3.0	1.5	63.7	90.0	28.4
Pacific Southwest...........................	XIII	6.5	6.7	4.3	8.5	6.9	4.5	112.6	128.8	34.7

Region VI. Central Plains Region. The nearly flat, semi-arid prairie stretching from the Corn Belt to the Rocky Mountains makes up this region. The territory is very sparsely settled, having only 9.9 persons per square mile in 1940 (the average for the nation is 50 per square mile). It is predominantly rural, and agriculture is the basic industry. In 1950, only 9 percent of the employed labor force was engaged in manufacturing. Over much of the region, lack of enough moisture for tilled crops precludes the development of the kind of intensive feed grain and livestock economy that characterizes the Corn Belt. The mineral and power resources necessary for an intensive manufacturing development are, in general, either absent or unexploited at the present time. The economy of the region is based largely on the growing of wheat and on livestock ranching. Through a process of farm consolidation and farm abandonment, the average size of farm has increased to the point where most of the farms are large enough (about 850 acres in 1954) to provide a very good livelihood.

About one-quarter of the total area is in harvested cropland, more than 40 percent of which is in wheat. Sorghums and wild hay are, on the average, crops of secondary importance, and provide winter feed for livestock. In certain isolated areas irrigation permits a variety of tilled crops to be grown.

Not only is the moisture supply in this region low, it is also quite variable. Seasons of adequate rainfall are sometimes followed by seasons of more or less severe drought. Consequently, some sectors of the region's economy are often carried on under the shadow of insecurity and hardship, and certain parts have even become known as "The Dust Bowl" because of this variability in rainfall.

The region's rate of growth for the past three decades has been below that of the nation. Between 1930 and 1940 the population here declined by 1.1 percent, while in the nation it increased by 7.2 percent; and although this region's population increased by 7.7 percent between 1940 and 1950, that of the nation grew about twice as rapidly during that period.

In general, the region has not had any significant manufacturing development, although there are isolated exceptions in Wichita, Denver, and Tulsa. The other cities are largely shopping, marketing, and service centers where meat packing and flour milling are almost the only manufacturing activities.

Region VII. Central and Eastern Upland Region. Between the Corn Belt and the Cotton Belt lies a large butterfly-shaped region where most of the land is either rough, hilly, or semi-mountainous. There is good soil on moderate slopes only in the valleys between the mountains or hills, and in a

Table 5-7.—TYPE-OF-FARMING CLASSIFICATION OF FARMS IN ECONOMIC REGIONS: 1954

Economic region	Region	Percent of farms, by type								
		Vegetable, fruit, and nut	Cash-grain	Cotton	Other field-crop	Dairy	Poultry	Livestock, other than dairy and poultry	General	Misc. and unclassified
Atlantic Metropolitan Belt...................	I	4.6	6.0	...	5.4	17.6	14.5	6.4	6.3	39.2
Eastern Great Lakes and Northeastern Upland..	II	3.9	3.1	...	2.2	41.9	7.9	3.2	4.7	33.1
Lower Great Lakes............................	III	3.6	13.0	...	0.6	23.6	4.1	9.1	8.4	37.6
Upper Great Lakes............................	IV	0.9	3.4	...	0.6	61.3	2.2	7.0	7.7	16.9
North Center (Corn Belt).....................	V	0.3	28.8	...	0.3	6.9	2.0	36.3	12.2	13.2
Central Plains...............................	VI	0.3	43.0	1.5	1.5	5.8	1.0	23.8	11.1	12.0
Central and Eastern Upland...................	VII	0.8	4.1	1.3	16.6	9.0	3.1	11.7	6.6	46.8
Southeast Coastal Plain......................	VIII	0.5	1.2	28.7	20.6	2.2	2.2	4.4	4.4	35.8
Gulf Coast and Atlantic Flatwoods............	IX	10.4	3.8	14.9	4.5	3.1	2.6	8.7	3.2	48.8
South Center and Southwest Plains............	X	0.5	3.9	40.7	1.0	2.4	1.8	10.1	4.7	34.9
Rocky Mountain and Intermountain.............	XI	3.2	8.7	3.1	4.7	10.7	2.5	26.9	10.8	29.4
Pacific Northwest............................	XII	11.8	10.0	...	1.2	12.3	5.2	7.0	5.4	47.1
Pacific Southwest............................	XIII	28.8	3.7	7.5	0.9	10.0	9.7	7.3	4.4	27.7

few other exceptional areas. A high percentage of the soil is seriously eroded and low in fertility. The upland areas which form this region reach from the Piedmont to eastern Oklahoma; from east to west, its physiographic areas are the Great Smoky Mountains, the Blue Ridge Mountains, the Appalachian Ridge and Valley area, the Cumberland Plateau, the Kentucky-Tennessee Highland Rim, the Ozark Plateau, and the Ouachita Mountains. Although there are sizable differences between the economic subregions into which the region has been divided, the following characteristics tend to represent the economy of the region as a whole:

For a high proportion of the nonmetropolitan population (and more than 60 percent of the population is nonmetropolitan) a state of near-poverty has become a "normal" circumstance. The lack of good farming land is not compensated for by industrial opportunities, as tends to be the case in Region II. Although there are moderately large concentrations of manufactures in the region, they are small in comparison to the total population, and in many areas they are only beginning to develop. Birth rates are high. The population has grown beyond the point where the area can support it without further declines in the level of living, and this situation has resulted in a steady outmigration to other regions.

In spite of the fact that the agricultural resources of the region are meager, farming is a leading industry. Thirty percent of the total land is made up of forests, wasteland, and other nonagricultural types of terrain. Only one-sixth of the land is in harvested crops. In 1954 less than 40 percent of the farms had tractors, and very little hired help is used in farm operations. The average value of products sold or used per farm is very low; more than one-half of the farms produced less than $2,500 worth of farm products for sale in 1954.

Farming is principally of the "own use," or self-sufficing, type; in this kind of farming the operator's household consumes more than fifty percent of what the farm produces. About forty percent of the farms in the subregion are of this type. Of the commercial farms, the most important type is the cash crop farm; many of these are tobacco farms in Kentucky and Tennessee, and fruit farms in the Great Valley. General farming and livestock farming are also important activities in most of the subregions, and in certain subregions the general farm is the leading type of commercial farm. Coal mining is an important source of employment in the region; one worker in twenty is in the mining industry.

One outstanding characteristic of this region, in view of its location within the territory usually thought of as the South, is the fact that the rural-farm Negro population is a very small share of the total rural-farm population. The nonwhite population constituted only 7.6 percent of the total population in 1950, and most of it was concentrated in the cities. Only 2.5 percent of the rural-farm population was nonwhite in 1950.

Very little cotton is grown in this region. Those upland areas of Arkansas, Alabama, and Georgia which are specialized in cotton growing have been placed in the Cotton Belt Region.

As a whole, this region has several serious social and economic problems, although the conditions which have been described as general characteristics do not apply equally to all of its subregions. The Shenandoah Valley, the Kentucky Bluegrass country, the Nashville Basin, and the Indiana-Ohio Flatland, for example, are subregions that cannot be considered acutely distressed areas.

Region VIII. Southeast Coastal Plain Region. The Southeast Coastal Plain Region consists largely of area which has been known, historically, as the Old South. About 26 percent of its labor force was engaged in agriculture in 1950 (a proportion twice as large as that of the nation); an almost equal share (23 percent) was engaged in manufacturing. In comparison with the nation as a whole, this region has had a deficit of commercial and service industries for many decades.

The region comprises the more intensively cultivated part of the coastal plain east of the Mississippi River, the Piedmont, and the hills bordering Region V. The economy has revolved primarily around cotton, textiles, and tobacco.

Although birth rates have been high here, the rate of population growth during the past half century has only been about three-fifths as high as that of the nation; there has been a large and steady out-migration to the North. Although it is the least urbanized of the regions, its urban growth has been rapid and steady. Its rural-farm population has declined at a very rapid rate, but between 1950 and 1960 its cities grew faster than the more industrialized regions of the Northeast. In 1950, 33 percent of the population was nonwhite, a higher percentage of nonwhite than was found in any other region. Level of living indexes for the rural

population indicate that the rural economy of this region is the least prosperous in the nation.

The growing of crops for cash sale is the predominant agricultural activity, and cotton and tobacco are the chief crops. On many of the farms the land is seriously eroded, or many have soils of generally low fertility. More than one-third of the farm operators are share tenants or share croppers. There is less farm mechanization here than in any other region (only 35 percent of the farms had tractors in 1954). Unpaid family workers constitute a large proportion of the farm labor force.

In an average year, about 20 percent of the harvested land is planted in cotton, 3 percent in tobacco, 8 percent in peanuts, and 41 percent in corn. Although corn is the largest crop in terms of acreage, in most areas it is secondary either to cotton or to tobacco both in terms of labor expended and of farm income.

There are several small and medium-sized metropolitan areas in the region, and they have grown rapidly and steadily. The textile industry has established scattered plants in various villages and small cities in some of the subregions.

Region IX. Gulf Coast and Atlantic Flatwoods Region. In recent decades this region's population has grown more rapidly than that of any except the Pacific Coast Regions. During the decade 1940 to 1950, its population increased by 38 percent, or at a rate more than two and one-half times as high as the national rate. Metropolitan areas have been developing rapidly not only as commercial seaports, but as general metropolitan centers as well. The winter resort industry and the winter vegetable industry have both expanded greatly in recent decades. Economic trends along the Gulf Coast contrast sharply with those found in a large part of the area lying immediately inland, where the economy tends to be developing much more slowly or, in some sections, even remaining stationary.

In 1950, more than two-thirds (69 percent) of the population was urban. Only 12 percent of the employed labor force was working in agriculture (compared with 26 percent for the inland part of the South). One-fifth of the population was non-white.

More than one-half of the region is not enclosed in farms; much of the land consists of swampy, forested flatwoods (or everglades) or sandy coast line. Only about 9 percent of the total land is in cultivated crops. The agriculture of this region is quite varied, including the large citrus fruit industry of Florida and south Texas, the winter vegetable industry that is carried on in Florida and much of the winter vegetable industry of Texas, and the sugar and rice industries along the Gulf Coast. Although cotton farming is not important throughout most of this region, in certain isolated areas it is a leading type of farming. The share-cropping system of farm tenancy which is in Regions VIII and X is rarely found in this region. Interspersed with the areas devoted to specialized farming are areas of self-sufficing, subsistence farming. About one-third of all farms are self-sufficing farms. The forest industries and the fishing industry are also significant elements of the economy.

Region X. South Center and Southwest Plains Region. Region X is a part of the Cotton Belt; much of its land favors the growing of cotton on a large scale with the aid of more mechanized methods. Cattle ranching is a far more important type of farming here than it is in the Southeast. In the western part of the region where rainfall is not plentiful, dry-land methods of farming and irrigation are used.

Although this region has undergone a very rapid urbanization in the last 50 years, its total population has grown at only about the same rate as that of the nation. The area's economy still contains a comparatively small element of manufacturing; in 1950 only 12 percent of the employed labor force worked in the manufacturing industries, and 25 percent were employed in agriculture.

Almost one-fourth (22 percent) of the population was nonwhite in 1950. Although the average level of living of the rural population was below the national average, it was considerably higher in every respect than that of the Southeast Region.

In 1954, one-half of all farm operators were tenants, and 43 percent were classed as share tenants or sharecroppers. More than one-half of the farms were primarily cash crop farms, a majority of which were cotton farms. About 60 percent of the total farm income was derived from the sale of crops for cash, and about 15 percent was derived from the sale of livestock and livestock products. Unlike Region VIII, this region uses large quantities of hired farm labor, much of which is supplied by migratory seasonal workers from Mexico. The use of mechanical tilling equipment combined with hired farm labor has replaced the sharecropper system in several subregions.

The metropolitan areas of this region are less specialized in manufacturing and more specialized in the distributing, wholesaling, and processing functions than are the metropolitan centers to the east and north. During the 1940 to 1950 period, the metropolitan areas grew rapidly, and several small and medium-sized cities grew to metropolitan status.

The petroleum industry is also an important element in this region's economy.

Region XI. Western Mountain and Basin Region. Mountains and semi-arid deserts constitute a large share of this region. Although it is the largest of the regions in terms of area, it has the smallest population. Since it comprises almost one-fourth of the nation's total land area but contains only 3 percent of the total population, it is very sparsely inhabited (5.5 persons per square mile in 1950). Unlike the Central Plains, which is also sparsely inhabited, its rate of population growth during the past half century has been about 50 percent greater than that of the nation. It enjoyed above-average growth during the 1940 to 1950 period, as well as during earlier decades.

Because the region is so large, encompasses such a wide latitude, and has such a variety of physiographic conditions, it is not as homogeneous as the other regions. However, the thinly scattered population and the lack of large and numerous industrial concentrations make it impractical to subdivide the region. Its agriculture is very diverse, because the availability of water in particular spots has transformed them from semi-desert into rich farming land. Although agriculture provides more employment than any other single type of industry, a very large proportion of the land is unsuited for farming or ranching. Mining and transportation are comparatively more important here than in other regions.

The agriculture of the region is balanced about equally between livestock farming and cash crop farming. In the northern part of the region the cash crops consist primarily of wheat and fruit. In the central areas the leading crops are irrigated vegetables, sugar beets and other row crops, winter vegetables, and citrus and other fruits; in these central areas there is also some general farming. In the southern section, agriculture is devoted largely to irrigated cotton. The region's farms are of large average size, and its farm incomes tend to be substantial. However, farm prosperity is not universal; there are isolated areas, especially in the territory assigned to Indians, where the level of living is extremely low.

Region XII. Pacific Northwest Region. Both the strip of Pacific Coast and the inland valleys that lie north of San Francisco lack the warm climate needed to support the citrus and vegetable industries, and are also much less urbanized than other regions. Since this region was one of the last frontier areas, its population has continued to grow rapidly as a result of continued new settlement and economic expansion. The metropolitan areas of Seattle-Tacoma and Portland are major Pacific ports and manufacturing centers, and Tacoma itself is a service center for the "inland empire" east of the mountains. Seattle and Tacoma are important shipbuilding and ship repair centers, as well as supply and marketing outposts for the coastwise trade with Alaska and western Canada. Dams along the Columbia and other rivers provide hydroelectric power for industry and water for irrigation. Recently expansion has been stimulated by atomic energy installations.

As in Region XIII, the farming here is very diversified. Dairying is the leading single type of commercial farming, but the growing of apples, hops, and other vegetable and fruit crops is almost as important. Wheat and dried peas are grown for cash in the non-irrigated dry-farming areas lying south and east of Spokane. Livestock farming is the primary agricultural activity in the semi-arid section east of the mountains, where crop farming is not feasible.

Lumbering is still an important industry here; in fact, much of the nation's small remaining stock of virgin timber is found in this region.

Region XIII. Pacific Southwest Coast Region. This region, lying on the western slopes of the Sierra Nevada and along the Pacific Coast, has grown more than five and one-half times as rapidly as the nation during the past half century. During no decade of this period has it failed to grow less than two and one-half times as rapidly as the nation. Between 1940 and 1950 its population increased by 55 percent. A large share of this growth, particularly in recent years, has taken place in the metropolitan areas of San Francisco, Los Angeles, and San Diego. Because of the region's greatly expanded agriculture industry, its nonmetropolitan populations have also grown more rapidly than those of any other region.

This is perhaps the most diversified region in the United States. Although it provides proportionately less employment in agriculture and manufacturing, and proportionately more employment in trade and services than does the United States as a whole, the region is less specialized in any single branch of industry than most of the other regions, and contains a wide variety of different types of economic activity. In spite of the fact that it contains large areas of wasteland, the region's average density was roughly the same as that of the United States in 1940. Recent economic growth increased the manufacturing element in the region.

As of 1950, about 82 percent of the population was urban. The population is predominantly white; since 1930, however, the nonwhite population has been growing, and it more than doubled in the 1940 to 1950 decade.

The leading type of farming is the production of fruits, vegetables, cotton, and other cash crops;

livestock production and dairying are important in many of the areas not suited for tilling. Although this region's farm operator level of living index is higher than that of any other region in the nation, a larger share of the farm labor force here is composed of wage workers than in any other region. Many of these workers, whose level of living is very low, are perpetual migrants, and others are Mexicans who migrate seasonally to work as harvesters.

THE ECONOMIC SUBREGIONS AND STATE ECONOMIC AREAS

It would be folly to say that any one of the 13 economic regions is completely homogeneous; the reverse is true. Although all the parcels of land enclosed within one region share certain fundamental traits which the parcels in other regions lack (or possess to a lesser degree), the units enclosed within one region vary greatly with respect to certain other important elements. Dividing a region into subregions makes it possible to assemble data which is relevant, in a practical and useful sense, to each of these major internal segments. Accordingly, the 119 subregions have been so established as to reveal the most outstanding aspects of the diversity existing among the various parts of each region.

Just as there is internal diversity within the regions, so there is territorial variation within the subregions. The traits which make parts of each subregion distinctive can be isolated by a division of the subregions into smaller units. This kind of subdivision is accomplished by the establishment of state economic areas. The fact that state boundaries are the limits within which the state economic areas are set up makes the entire system of economic areas more useful to workers in particular states; this adherence to established state boundaries also makes it possible to subdivide a single state into its major socio-economic units, and to comprehend how the particular state fits into the subregional and regional picture with respect to the nation as a whole.

Chapter 6

AGE COMPOSITION OF THE POPULATION

AGING AS A PROCESS *

Like other species, human beings have a distinctive life cycle. In some aspects this cycle is purely physiological; it reflects the process of bodily growth, maturation to adulthood, slow decline in vigor, and eventual death. In other aspects it refers to the definitions of expected behavior and to the social and economic status assigned to members of the society at each of a series of chronological stages. These statuses and definitions are specified in the culture and are not based on physiological considerations alone. Every society places its own interpretations and prescriptions upon the biological process of aging. The age at which it is appropriate to enter the labor force or to perform gainful work, to end formal schooling, to marry, or to retire from the labor force, is determined only in part by the biological aspects of age. Physiological capacity may limit the range of expectations which are placed upon the individuals in each age grade of the society, but it does not specify the full content or mode of expressing these expectations.

Because of this dual significance, the phenomenon of age has a fundamental and universal importance for all branches of social science. Almost any aspect of human behavior, from states of subjective feeling and attitudes to objective characteristics such as income, home ownership, occupation, or group membership, may be expected to vary with age. For this reason, age is one of the first factors that must be controlled in all branches of research which involve the behavior of human beings before the effects or relationships between other less obvious factors can be assessed. These considerations suggest that the age composition of a society has much to do with its form and functioning. A society with a high proportion of young members may be expected to differ in its outlook and mode of life from a society that has a high proportion of older members. Moreover, extensive changes in the age composition of a society may be expected to produce adaptive changes in many areas of its behavior. The age structure of populations, therefore, is a basic aspect of population composition, and should be widely appreciated.

The present chapter is devoted to study of the age composition, and changes in the age composition, of the United States population. Some of the basic cultural definitions which are made with respect to age will be treated in the succeeding chapters by data showing how various of the other compositional aspects differ with age. In this chapter the emphasis will be upon chronological age and stages in the life cycle, the processes which determine how the population is distributed among the age grades, and the types of change which cause age distribution to be altered.

THE DEMOGRAPHIC STUDY OF AGE COMPOSITION

A basic procedure in analyzing age structure is to learn what proportion of the total population is in each stage of the life cycle, how these proportions have been changing, how they differ from place to place, and what factors are responsible

---

*A tabulation presenting age statistics by sex and color for the total, urban, rural-nonfarm, and rural-farm areas of each geographic division for both 1950 and 1940 is contained in Appendix Tables 17 to 20.

for a given age composition or for a change in age composition. A full comprehension of how a population has arrived at its present age structure, or exactly why its age composition is changing as it is requires a study of the components of growth-- births, deaths, and migration for the past century. Each of these components is studied in considerable detail in later chapters. The present chapter states certain basic principles about these components, without complete proof, in order to develop a systematic treatment of age composition.

All three components of population growth tend to be heavily concentrated at particular stages of the life cycle. Every person must enter a population at age zero. He may die at any phase of the life cycle--from a moment after birth to more than a century after birth--but the probability of his death is much greater when he is a very young infant, or after he has reached 50 years of age. The span of life over which he does live affects the age compositon. If he lives to reproduce, both the age at which he does so and the number of offspring he bears have an important effect upon maintaining or changing the age composition. If he migrates, he removes one person from his age group in one place and adds one to his age group in another place; this too can alter age structure. Thus, both short-term and long-term fluctuations in birth, death, and migration rates are reflected in the age composition.

A sudden rise or fall in the birth rate produces an extraordinarily large or small crop of children in particular years. This group ages with the passing of time, and constitutes a wave or a trough in the age structure. At the first census after its occurrence, this rise or fall will appear as an unusually large or small complement of children. At the succeeding census it will constitute a disproportionately large or small youth group. At a third census it will have passed into the adult category, and at succeeding censuses it will reappear at successively later phases of the life cycle until it has died out at the oldest ages. Consequently, unusually large or small birth cohorts of several decades ago may be represented in the present age structure as a disproportionately large or small age group. As an unusually large or unusually small generation passes through adulthood, it tends to produce a correspondingly large or small crop of children, thereby creating a secondary wave or trough in the age structure, with a lag of 20-35 years behind the original one.

Any catastrophe that kills off large numbers of a particular age group, such as military losses among young men in a war, leaves a trough in the age structure that persists until that generation has died. A sudden improvement in methods of prolonging life, such as the use of antibiotics, has the opposite effect: instead of dying, an increased proportion of persons live on into the next age group.

The arrival of a group of migrants has the same effect as would have been produced by an unusually large birth cohort from two to three decades earlier (because migrants tend to be concentrated at young adult ages), and the children of these migrants can constitute a secondary wave. The departure of migrants has the reverse effect. Thus, the age structure of a population at any given time is a composite resulting from all the factors that have influenced fertility, mortality, and migration over the past century or more preceding the date of the census to which the data refer.

The following principles will prove helpful in interpreting age statistics.

(a) If birth rates fall, children tend to comprise a smaller proportion of the total population, and this necessarily increases the proportion of people in the adult and older ages. A rise in birth rates has the opposite effect: the proportion of people in the younger ages tends to increase, and the proportion of adults tends to decrease.

(b) A decline in death rates at any age has the effect of passing on to the next age class a larger proportion of the individuals of the given age than was the case in preceding years. Since death rates have an age pattern (the rates are different at different ages), the nature of the pattern has much to do with the age composition, and changes in this pattern lead to changes in age composition. In comparison with the past, therefore, a differential decline in death rates has the direct effect of

increasing the proportion of people in the particular ages where the decline in death rates was
greatest, and also of increasing it in all later
ages. A rise in death rates for any particular age
group has the opposite result.

(c) Changes in the death rates for persons who
are younger than 40-50 years of age also has an
indirect effect upon age composition, for it influences the number of persons who will be eligible
to marry and bear children.

(d) Most migration streams tend to decrease
the size of the young adult age groups in the areas
from which these streams depart, and tend to augment the young adult age groups of the population
to which they migrate. Where migrants have an
older age composition, they exert their additive
and subtractive effect upon the age groups in
which they fall; young migrants affect all ages.

(e) Since all age groups, especially those above
40 years, are steadily depleted by mortality, the
waves and troughs created at birth tend to become
progressively less important, in relation   to
the total population, as they pass into the upper
ages. If the population is growing rapidly, this
phenomenon of declining importance is even more
pronounced, for the differences are expressed as
percentages of a progressively larger base population.

Note on age statistics.

At its decennial enumeration, the Bureau of the Census asks
the question, "How old was he on his last birthday?" concerning each person enumerated. The last birthday at the date of
enumeration, rather than the nearest birthday, is taken as the
reference point in collecting age data because this procedure
makes easier the computing and interpreting of the rates and
indexes that are associated with demographic work. One important advantage is that it permits the population age group
in a particular year to be matched more precisely with the
births from which this age group originated. Moreover, when
age data are enumerated in terms of age at last birthday, the
class limits for age groups are unambiguous, and the midclass
intervals are either whole numbers or simple fractions.

Although age is one of the most easily enumerated characteristics, the age returns are not complete when they arrive
at the Bureau of the Census after the field enumeration. When
the information about a person is provided by another member
of the household (such as a landlady reporting for a lodger),
the age may be left unstated. In the censuses of 1930 and be-

fore, the age statistics frequently included an "age unknown"
category. However, a special procedure for supplying ages
where they were missing was introduced at the 1940 census
and repeated in 1950. By using other information on the census schedule (marital status, school attendance, employment
status, age of other members of the family, and type of household), it is possible to assign an age which results in less
error than would occur if the persons of unknown age were
distributed proportionately throughout the known categories
(which is usually the only course open to the analyst).

Just as age data are not complete, they are not fully accurate. Inaccuracies arise from two principal sources, which
are (a) differential underenumeration and (b) misstatements of
age.

Differential Underenumeration. Failure of the census enumerators to count all inhabitants results in a distinct age bias.
Children under 5 years of age are thought to be seriously
undercounted in comparison with all ages. Since there is no
really complete source against which to check underenumeration, it is impossible to learn exactly how accurate the age
data are. Several ingenious methods have been devised for
making approximate measurements of underenumeration.

Misstatement of Age. In most statistics from the United
States Census, misstatements of age are of minor importance
if one is dealing only with 5-year age groups. However, if the
analyst wishes to deal with single years of age, as in the construction of detailed life tables or the computing of fertility
rates by single age groups, he quickly discovers that there
have been errors and approximations in reporting age. There
is a tendency for ages to concentrate at years ending in 0 and
5. Various other patterns also emerge, such as a preference
for ages ending in 2 and 8 as well as 0 and 5. These patterns
may differ somewhat from nation to nation, or from one population group to another within the same country. A technique
for estimating this tendency toward misstatement of age, a
tendency to "heap" the statistics on certain digits, has been
developed by R. J. Myers.

Older persons tend to overstate, while a certain number of
mature adults may tend to understate, their true age. In the
censuses of 1940 and 1950, there was an excessive number of
persons 65 years of age and beyond, and a deficit of persons
in the age range 55 to 64 years. It is commonly suspected that
this apparent misstatement is not unrelated to the Social Security program and the eligibility for benefits at age 65. Also,
as persons attain advanced old age, they seem to have a tendency to add a few years in reporting their age to the census
taker; more persons claim to have passed their 85th, 90th, or
100th birthday, for example, than seems possible on the basis
of other evidence.

A new source of error in U. S. census statistics is sampling
error. In earlier censuses, age tabulations were prepared as
100 percent sample counts. In 1950, the basic single-year-of-
age counts and many other detailed counts, in which age is
cross-classified with other characteristics, were based on a
20 percent sample. A 100 percent count is available for 5-
year age groups for certain broad population and residence
groups in 1950. Many of the cross-tabulations cannot be
reconciled to this count. Age statistics for the entire U. S.

MEDIAN AGE OF THE UNITED STATES POPULATION

In order to give a quick and approximate answer to the question, "Is the population old or young in its age composition?" demographers sometimes report the median age of a population. This is the age above which 50 percent of the population fall, and below which 50 percent fall. The median age of the United States population in 1960 and at each census since 1820, is as follows:

Year	Median age	Change since preceding date
1960	29.2	-0.6
1958	29.5	-0.3
1956	29.9	-0.2
1955	30.1	-0.1
1950	30.2	1.2
1940	29.0	2.5
1930	26.5	1.2
1920	25.3	1.2
1910	24.1	1.2
1900	22.9	0.9
1890	22.0	1.1
1880	20.9	0.7
1870	20.2	0.8
1860	19.4	0.5
1850	18.9	1.1
1840	17.8	0.6
1830	17.2	0.5
1820	16.7	...

Source: U.S. Bureau of the Census, Statistical Abstract of the United States, 1953, Table 15, p. 25. Figures for 1955 computed from U.S. Bureau of the Census, Current Population Reports, Population Estimates, Series P-25, Nos. 121 and 146.

Note on age statistics (continued)

have a comparatively small sampling error. However, the tabulations for single years of age or the cross-tabulations of other characteristics by age tend to have a large percentage error, especially for single states, cities, and metropolitan areas.

Because of the deficiencies enumerated above, the user of population statistics should exercise caution in attributing meaning to small differences between the age composition of two populations. However, knowledge of these limitations should not lead to disparagement of the data. Census statistics of age are undoubtedly more accurate than those collected as a part of local surveys and field studies. The sources of inaccuracy can be traced, for the most part, to the two basic problems of census enumeration (a) problems involved in assembling and training a temporary field crew of workers and enumerating a highly mobile population within a comparatively short time without seriously inconveniencing or disrupting the routine of the inhabitants, and (b) problems caused by having to resort to sampling and other approximations because the funds appropriated for the census usually are insufficient to permit a complete and highly precise inventory.

The figures in the above table show that the median age of the population was only 16.7 years in 1820, and rose to 30.2 years in 1950. Thus, within a period of thirteen decades the median age increased by 13.5 years, or by about one year per decade, which resulted in an over-all increase of nearly 81 percent. The rise in the age level was more rapid after 1900. The median may have been even somewhat below 16.7 years in 1800 and 1810, but no adequate age data are available for these earlier years. Between 1950 and 1960 this trend of 130 to 150 years duration was interrupted; the median age in 1960 is 1.0 years lower than it was in 1950. This sudden reversal must be attributed to the reversal of the long-term downward trend in fertility that took place starting about 1944-46. This leveling off was preceded by an unusually large rise in the median age between 1930 and 1940, which resulted from the lower birth rates in these years as well as from the cumulative effects of lower death rates and birth rates in earlier years. The median age of the population must remain at about its present level, or even decline further, if fertility rates remain at their present moderately high level. (See the section on age composition of the future population, in Chapter 26.)

From the perspective of a nation with low birth and low death rates, it may be somewhat surprising to discover that at the time of the Revolutionary War and immediately after it one-half of the population of the United States was 16 years of age or younger. This median age was produced by an unusual combination of high fertility rates, high rates of immigration, and high rates of mortality at the adult as well as infant ages. Certain nations of the world which have this combination of birth and death rates have a median age at the present time that is nearly as low as that of the United States at the time of the Revolution. For example, compare the following two sets of median ages:

Median age of selected nations

Mexico, 1950	19.0	Denmark, 1953*	32.1
India, 1951	21.4	France, 1953*	33.1
South Korea, 1953*	21.7	Germany, 1952*	34.2
Brazil, 1950	18.9	England and Wales, 1953*	35.3

Source: United Nations, Demographic Yearbook,

1954 and 1953. Asterisked items are based on current estimates; other items computed from the latest published census count.

AGE COMPOSITION OF THE UNITED STATES POPULATION IN TERMS OF THE LIFE CYCLE

Despite the fact that the median age is a useful device for giving a general indication of the age level of the population, it cannot give detailed information about age structure or the distribution of the population among the various stages of the life cycle. A more informative procedure is to study the proportions of the population in each of a set of age groupings. These age groupings may be single years of age, five-year age groups (0-4, 5-9, 10-14, etc.) or age intervals that refer to major transitions and status changes in the life cycle. Although the process of aging is continuous, some qualitative differences may be associated with it. These qualitative aspects may be designated as phases or stages of the life cycle, and they represent cultural definitions of the physiological processes. The number of stages,

their length, and the ages to which they refer are not constant from population to population. They change with both time and place. Hence, if two populations have very dissimilar cultures, it is possible to make only approximate comparisons of their age compositions in terms of their life cycles.

In Table 6-1, the entire life span of the United States population has been subdivided into eleven stages of the life cycle. The age span of each stage is intended to represent present cultural definitions in the United States. Although these definitions are imposed on the population data for each census since 1880, their applicability to the earlier years is only approximate. For example, in 1880 a high proportion of the "late adolescence" and the "early old age" groups were active participants in the labor force, whereas today only a comparatively small fraction of these age groups are gainfully employed. In comparing, over a period of time, the changing proportions in each stage of the life cycle, the changing connotation of the life cycle classification itself must be kept in mind. For purposes of broad and general compar-

Table 6-1.—AGE COMPOSITION OF THE UNITED STATES POPULATION IN TERMS OF THE LIFE CYCLE: 1950
(Statistics for 1950 based on a 20 percent sample)

Stages in the life cycle	Age span (years)	Percent distribution								
		1960	1950	1940	1930	1920	1910	1900	1890	1880
All ages............	...	100.0	100.0	100.0	100.0	100.0	100.0	100.0	100.0	100.0
Childhood...............	0-8	19.9	18.0	14.4	17.5	19.7	20.2	21.6	22.1	24.4
Infancy...............	Under 1	2.3	2.1	1.5	1.8	2.1	2.4	2.5	2.5	2.9
Early childhood.......	1-5	11.2	10.5	8.1	9.6	11.0	11.4	11.9	12.2	13.6
Late childhood........	6-8	6.4	5.4	4.8	6.2	6.5	6.4	7.1	7.4	7.9
Youth...................	9-17	16.4	13.2	16.1	17.5	17.5	17.7	18.8	19.7	19.4
Preadolescence........	9-11	6.0	4.6	5.1	6.0	6.1	5.9	6.6	6.6	7.0
Early adolescence.....	12-14	5.5	4.4	5.5	5.8	6.0	6.0	6.2	6.8	6.7
Late adolescence......	15-17	4.9	4.2	5.6	5.7	5.4	5.8	6.0	6.3	5.7
Adulthood..............	18-64	55.0	60.6	62.5	59.5	58.0	57.6	55.3	54.1	52.8
Early maturity........	18-24	8.9	10.5	12.6	12.6	12.3	13.9	13.6	14.1	14.4
Maturity..............	25-44	25.9	29.9	30.1	29.4	29.6	29.2	28.0	26.9	25.8
Middle age............	45-64	20.2	20.2	19.8	17.4	16.1	14.6	13.7	13.1	12.6
Old age................	65-over	8.7	8.2	6.8	5.4	4.7	4.3	4.1	3.8	3.4
Early old age.........	65-74	5.7	5.6	4.8	3.9	3.3	3.0	2.9	2.7	2.4
Advanced old age......	75-over	3.0	2.6	2.0	1.5	1.4	1.2	1.2	1.1	1.0
Not reported............	...	...	...	...	0.1	0.1	0.2	0.3	0.3	...

Source: Compiled from U.S. Census of Population: 1950, Vol. II, Part 1, Table 98. Data for 1960 estimated.

ison, the eleven stages have been grouped into four major categories: childhood, youth, adulthood, and old age.

A comparison of the age composition of the United States population in 1960 and 1940 with the age composition in 1880 may be made as follows:

Major stages of the life cycle	1960	1940	1880
Childhood......	19.9	14.4	24.4
Youth.........	16.4	16.1	19.4
Adulthood......	55.0	62.5	52.8
Old age........	8.7	6.8	3.4
Total.....	100.0	100.0	100.0

Figure 6-1 illustrates the change in each stage of the life cycle over this interval of time. At the present time about 11/20 of the population is adult, about 4/11 are children or youths, and about 1/12 are oldsters. In 1880, eighty years earlier, the adult population was proportionately smaller than now, whereas children and youth were a much larger part of the total population than today. Old folks were a very small part (about 1/30) of the population. Since 1880 the proportion of children and youth has declined by about 20 percent, while the old age component is now about 2 1/2 times what it was then. This difference in age composition, at the younger ages, is due largely to the historic decline in the birth rate. At the older ages the difference is a result of lowered death rates combined with lowered birth rates. Note the effect of the baby boom in altering age composition since 1940.

A look at the more detailed stages within each major stage of the life cycle, reported in Table 6-1, makes it apparent that steady reductions took place in the proportion of infants and children, in both early and late childhood, from 1880 until 1940. Between 1930 and 1940, birth rates fell so low that in 1940 the age groups 0-5 and 5-9 were smaller, by 2,826,000 children, than they had been at the preceding census! While birth rates were falling, the intercensal increase in children was also declining for many decades. During the 1930-40 decade the nation experienced its first negative increase in children. This development was not entirely a result of the economic de-

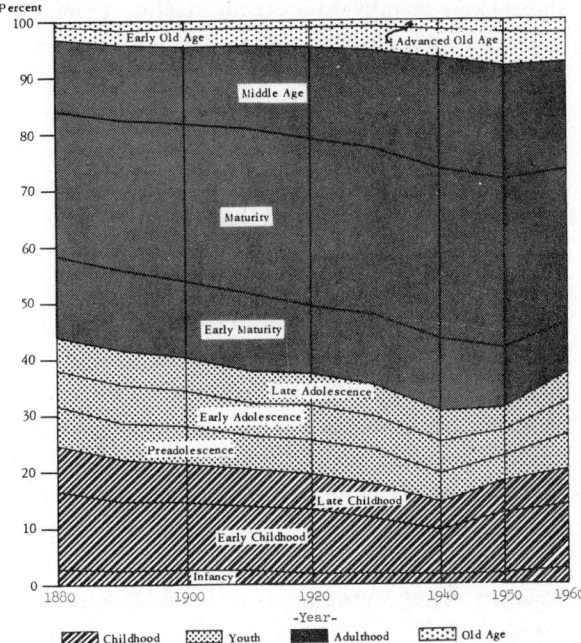

FIGURE 6-1. PERCENT OF THE UNITED STATES POPULATION AT EACH PHASE OF THE LIFE CYCLE; 1880 TO 1960

pression. The number of children born between 1925-29 was slightly smaller, by about 970,000, than the number who had been born in 1920-24. This decline introduced a trough into the age composition of the population, a trough that is now passing successively through the age groups. In 1960, this unusually small crop of children is in the early maturity and maturity groups. During the 1940-60 period, however, the proportions in all three childhood groups increased, and were larger in 1960 than in 1940. Whereas children were only 14.4 percent of the total population in 1940, they are 19.9 percent in 1960. This is a result of the recent increase in fertility rates. Thus, in the data for childhood one may observe the wave effect created by a rise in birth rates. As time passes, this wave of the 1940-60 period will follow through the successive age groups immediately behind the trough of the 1930-40 decade. This combination of events will cause the United States to have an unusual age composition for many decades.

For the three youth phases, and for adults in

their early maturity, a steady decline from 1890 carried over into the 1950 decade. This uninterrupted downward sweep also reflects the long-term decline in fertility. Since all persons in these phases were born before the onset of the current wave of higher fertility, the recent fertility change has not yet had time to affect these age groups. Youth have increased during 1950-60.

The eighty-year span covered by Table 6-1 was also a period of great progress in the reduction of death rates. Infant mortality rates were being lowered greatly. Mortality rates were being reduced substantially for several infectious diseases which had formerly killed both adults and children. Although progress in reducing the toll of mortality at ages above 50 has not yet been as spectacular as the reductions of mortality in the younger ages, substantial reductions have been made. During each decade almost every age group suffered less proportional loss through mortality than it had during the preceding decade. This means that each decade in this period saw a larger total proportion of the population passing into the old-age phase. Whereas in 1880 deaths had claimed almost all of a generation by the time it reached age 75, this was no longer the case in 1960. Thus, the long-run decline in death rates has increased the proportion of population in the upper age brackets. Simultaneously, the lessened proportion of children and youth has caused older persons to constitute a larger proportion of the total population.

During the years of heavy migration from abroad, the age structure of the population was kept low by the stream of young immigrants. Because this flow was curtailed sharply in the early 1920's, the migrants who were already in this country have continued to age without being replaced by new immigrants in the younger age groups. At the present time, this additional factor tends to increase the concentration of population at the older phases of the life cycle. Together, the three factors--declining birth rates, lowered death rates, and reduction of immigration--have caused almost spectacular increases in the proportion of older persons in the population. This is an in-

crease not only in persons of retirement age (65 years and over) but also in persons of middle age. In 1880 middle-aged persons (45-64) were 12.6 percent of the total population; in 1960 they are 20.2 percent. This is an increase of 60 percent. Hence, for many decades before 1940 the components of population growth conspired to decrease the proportion of young people, to increase the proportion of adults in the prime of life, and to increase even more the proportion of middle-aged and older persons. The 1940-60 period partially broke this chain of events.

CHANGE IN AGE COMPOSITION SINCE 1950

Continuation of the higher birth rates since 1950 brought substantial changes in age composition during the 1950-60 decade. Meanwhile, death rates and immigration rates have remained low. As a consequence, children are a larger proportion of the total population now than they were in 1950. Unfortunately, we must wait for another census before we can learn many of the details of those changes in age structure which are taking place during the 1950-60 decade. However, each year the United States Bureau of the Census prepares an estimate of the population of the United States by age, color, and sex. The estimate for July 1, 1957, summarized in Table 6-2, shows that the childhood and youth age groups have grown very rapidly, and that they were a larger percentage of the total population in 1957 than in 1950. The young adult population (18-24 years) has declined. This represents the passing into an older age class of the generation born during the period of low birth rates in the 1930's. (Compare with the age groups 15-17 in Table 6-1.) The number of adults in their prime of maturity (25-44 years) increased only about one-fourth as rapidly as did the general population. The population of middle age grew at about the national average rate. The population 65 years of age and over has continued to grow rapidly, as a result of low death rates and of the lowering of the birth rates for a long time prior to 1940. Thus, at the present time we are witnessing a rapid growth of population at the ex-

Table 6-2.—AGE COMPOSITION OF THE UNITED STATES POPULATION IN TERMS OF THE LIFE CYCLE: 1950
PERCENT CHANGE 1950-57
(Statistics include armed forces overseas and have been adjusted for net census undercount)

Stages in the life cycle	Age span (years)	Number of persons (millions)	Percent distribution 1957			Change in percent 1950-1957			Percent change 1950-1957		
			Total	White	Non-white	Total	White	Non-white	Total	White	Non-white
All ages........	...	172.0	100.0	100.0	100.0	...	...	...	13.2	12.6	18.6
Childhood.........	0.8	34.4	20.0	19.3	25.5	1.7	1.4	3.6	23.7	21.5	38.6
Infancy..........	Under 1[1]	4.2	2.4	2.3	3.2	0.1	0.1	0.2	18.2	17.1	25.4
Early childhood...	1-5[1]	19.5	11.3	10.9	14.6	0.7	0.5	1.9	20.8	18.7	35.7
Late childhood....	6-8	10.7	6.2	6.0	7.8	0.8	0.7	1.7	31.7	29.0	51.3
Youth.............	9-17	25.8	15.0	14.8	16.6	2.0	2.1	1.0	30.6	31.2	26.5
Preadolescence....	9-11	10.1	5.9	5.8	6.6	1.3	1.4	1.1	45.9	46.8	40.2
Early adolescence.	12-14	8.4	4.9	4.8	5.3	0.6	0.6	0.1	28.7	30.0	19.8
Late adolescence..	15-17	7.3	4.2	4.1	4.8	0.1	0.1	...	15.7	15.5	17.9
Adulthood.........	18-64	97.1	56.4	56.9	52.6	-4.3	-4.2	-4.8	5.3	5.0	8.6
Early maturity....	18-24	15.3	8.9	8.8	10.0	-1.7	-1.7	-1.5	-4.7	-5.7	3.2
Maturity..........	25-44	47.1	27.4	27.5	26.1	-2.5	-2.4	-3.2	3.8	3.6	5.6
Middle age.......	45-64	34.7	20.2	20.6	16.5	...	...	-0.1	12.8	12.4	17.6
Old age...........	65-over	14.8	8.6	9.0	5.3	0.6	0.6	0.2	21.0	20.8	22.5
Early old age.....	65-74	9.7	5.7	5.9	3.4	0.2	0.2	-0.2	16.8	17.1	11.9
Advanced old age..	75-over	5.0	2.9	3.0	1.9	0.4	0.3	0.4	30.0	28.8	47.6

[1]Adjusted for net Census undercount.

Source: U.S. Bureau of the Census, Current Population Report. Population Estimates, Series P-25, 1958.

treme ends of the age cycle, with low rates of increase and some actual decreases in the intermediate ages. Between 1950-57 the total population increased by 13.2 percent, but during this time the number of children and youth (0-17 years) increased by about 27 percent and the old age population by 21 percent.

If the present high birth rates continue for another decade, the tendency of the population of 65 and over to be an increasing proportion of the total population will be completely arrested. The median age has already fallen to 29.2 years in 1960, and will decline further unless birth rates fall. The reader should note that Table 6-2 contains age information by color, and that the growth of the nonwhite childhood group is much higher than that of the white.

RURAL-URBAN AGE COMPOSITION
IN TERMS OF THE LIFE CYCLE

The median age of the urban and rural populations in 1950 was as follows:

Urban........... 31.6
Rural nonfarm.... 27.9
Rural farm....... 26.3

A variety of factors contribute to this older median age among urban populations. Urban residents have tended to have lower birth rates than rural residents. Rural-farm residents have tended to have higher birth rates than rural-nonfarm residents. Consequently, in rural areas a higher proportion of the population consists of children and adolescents than in urban areas. Table 6-3 provides information to show that this proved to be the case both in 1950 and in 1940.

Although urban areas have a disproportionately small number of persons in late adolescence, they have a comparative excess of persons in early maturity, as well as in all other adult ages. Because more and more people have been moving from rural to urban areas, however, urban places traditionally have had a higher proportion of their population in the adult age groups than would be expected solely from rates of urban fertility and mortality. This also was true in 1950.

Apparently there is a tendency for people to retire to suburbs and villages (rural-nonfarm areas) in their old age, since the proportion of persons above 65 tended to be higher for the rural-nonfarm population than for either the urban or the rural-farm, both in 1950 and in 1940.

Figure 6-2 shows the rate at which each five-year age group in the nation increased between 1940 and 1950. The more rapid growth of the extremely young and the older age groups is very evident in the urban and the rural-nonfarm populations. The rural-farm population suffered an over-all decline in numbers, but the decrease was smallest in the youngest and the oldest age groups; the rate of decrease was very severe (more than 40 percent) in the 20-24 age group, which has high migration rates.

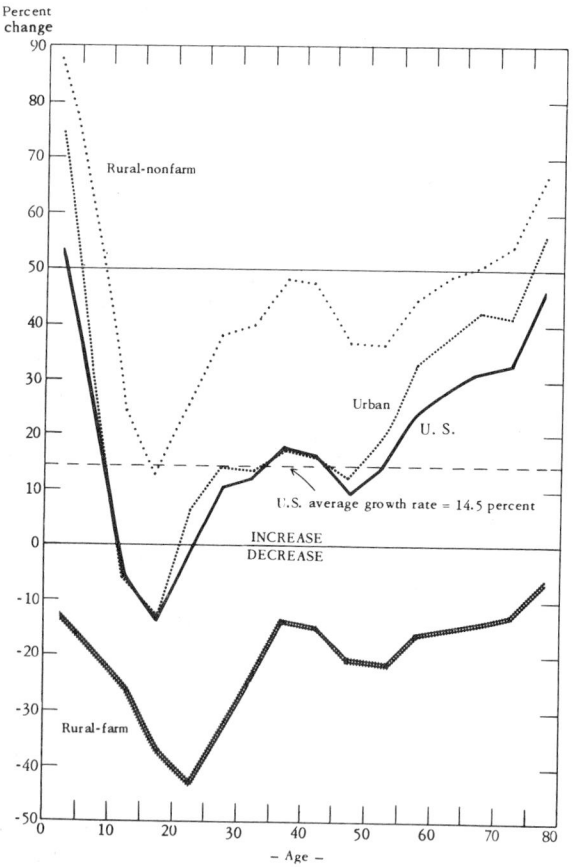

FIGURE 6 - 2. PERCENT CHANGE OF EACH 5 - YEAR AGE
GROUP OF THE POPULATION OF THE UNITED
STATES, 1940 TO 1950

The percentage-point changes, shown at the extreme right of Table 6-3, reveal the relative change in the age structure of the urban and rural populations between 1940 and 1950. The increase in the proportion of children was greater in urban areas than in rural, and greater in rural-nonfarm areas than in rural-farm. This pattern of differential change holds in all three of the first phases of the life cycle. Thus, the current upsurge in fertility appears to have had its greatest incidence among the nonagricultural populations, which previously had lower birth rates. Among the youth phases of the life cycle, the comparative loss was greater in the urban population than in the rural, and greater in the rural-nonfarm than in the rural-farm population. This is a manifestation of the extraordinarily low fertility that characterized urban areas in the 1930's, and of the passing into older ages of the small generations which were born during the depression years. Births were curtailed more sharply in urban than in rural areas, and more in rural-nonfarm than in rural-farm areas, during those years.

Another informative aspect of table 6-3 is its revelation that the cities experienced a slightly higher comparative increase in the proportion of aged than did either the rural-nonfarm or the rural-farm areas. Even though cities had large amounts of in-migration and an increase in birth rates between 1940 and 1950, the age composition of the urban population shifted toward the older ages more rapidly than did the age composition of either of the rural populations. The reasons for this appear to be as follows: Earlier in the century several of the major cities of the nation underwent cycles of very rapid growth. Of the last waves of immigrants which were admitted, large numbers settled in the cities. Growth in these cities has since slackened, and the immigrant and migrant populations have passed into the upper age groups. In addition, family limitation has been practiced more in cities than in rural areas. As a consequence, cities now have a considerably larger middle-aged population than do the rural areas, and they have as high a proportion of older persons as do the rural areas. Thus, the day is

Table 6-3.—AGE COMPOSITION OF THE UNITED STATES POPULATION, BY URBAN AND RURAL RESIDENCE,
IN TERMS OF THE LIFE CYCLE: 1940 AND 1950

Stages in the life cycle	Age span (years)	Percent distribution 1950			Percent distribution 1940			Percent-point change 1940-50			
		Urban	Rural non-farm	Rural farm	Urban	Rural non-farm	Rural farm	Total	Urban	Rural non-farm	Rural farm
All ages........	...	100.0	100.0	100.0	100.0	100.0	100.0	...	...	...	...
Childhood.........	0-8	16.7	20.5	20.4	12.1	16.6	18.3	3.6	4.6	3.9	2.1
Infancy..........	Under 1	2.0	2.3	2.1	1.3	1.8	1.8	0.6	0.7	0.5	0.3
Early childhood...	1-5	9.8	11.9	11.6	6.7	9.4	10.2	2.4	3.1	2.5	1.4
Late childhood....	6-8	4.9	6.2	6.8	4.0	5.4	6.3	0.6	0.9	0.8	0.5
Youth............	9-17	11.4	14.6	19.0	14.4	16.6	20.1	-2.9	-3.0	-2.0	-1.1
Preadolescence....	9-11	4.0	5.2	6.4	4.5	5.5	6.4	-0.5	-0.5	-0.3	...
Early adolescence.	12-14	3.8	4.9	6.5	4.9	5.6	6.9	-1.1	-1.1	-0.7	-0.4
Late adolescence..	15-17	3.6	4.5	6.1	5.1	5.5	6.8	-1.4	-1.5	-1.0	-0.7
Adulthood.........	18-64	63.8	56.3	53.0	66.7	59.6	55.0	-2.0	-2.9	-3.3	-2.0
Early maturity....	18-24	10.8	10.6	9.3	12.7	12.3	12.6	-2.1	-1.9	-1.7	-3.3
Maturity.........	25-44	31.7	28.3	24.5	32.8	29.5	24.1	-0.2	-1.1	-1.2	0.4
Middle age........	45-64	21.3	17.4	19.3	21.2	17.9	18.3	0.4	0.1	-0.5	1.0
Old age...........	65-over	8.2	8.6	7.6	6.8	7.3	6.6	1.4	1.4	1.3	1.0
Early old age.....	65-74	5.6	5.7	5.3	4.8	5.0	4.7	0.8	0.8	0.7	0.6
Advanced old age..	75-over	2.5	2.9	2.3	2.0	2.3	1.9	0.6	0.5	0.6	0.4

Source: Compiled from U.S. Census of Population: 1950, Vol. II, Part 1, Table 94; and Sixteenth Census of the United States; 1940, Vol. IV, Part 1, Table 2.

passing when the urban population of the United States was highly concentrated in the stages of "early maturity" and "maturity."

The changes in age composition for the youngest and oldest ages in urban and rural areas are illustrated in Figures 6-3 and 6-4.

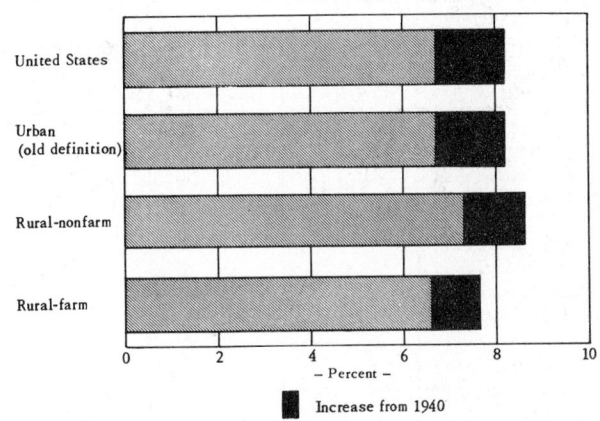

FIGURE 6 - 4. PERCENT OF THE POPULATION OF THE UNITED STATES 65 YEARS OF AGE AND OVER, BY URBAN AND RURAL RESIDENCE, 1940 AND 1950

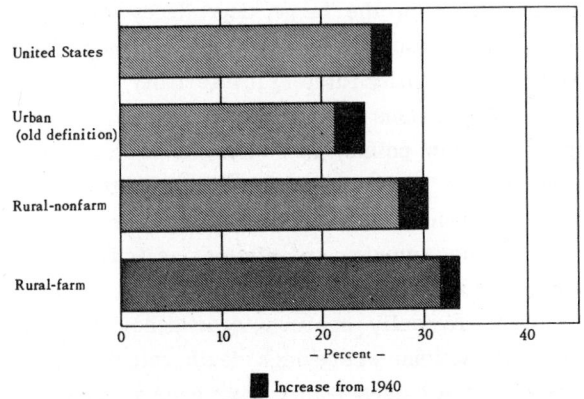

FIGURE 6 - 3. PERCENT OF THE POPULATION OF THE UNITED STATES 0 - 15 YEARS OF AGE, BY URBAN AND RURAL RESIDENCE, 1940 AND 1950

THE DEPENDENCY RATIO

Age statistics are used frequently to compute a measure of the dependency load which the population of working age must carry. This dependency load, composed of children, youth, and people of retirement age, is measured approximately by the "dependency ratio," which is defined as the ratio of the number of persons under 20 or over 65 years of age to the number of persons in the age group 20-64 years, multiplied by 100. This is not a measure of the number of persons each worker must support in addition to himself. However, it is a rough indication of the average number of dependents which each 100 adult persons would be required to support and care for if the load were equally divided among the adult population, and if all persons under 20 and over 65 were dependent. Neither of these conditions is met completely, and the degree to which they are approximated varies from one population to another and, over a period of time, changes for the same population. Nevertheless, in the absence of more detailed information with which to estimate actual dependence, this ratio is very useful for making general comparisons.

The dependency ratios for the United States, for selected dates since 1820, are as follows:

Year	Dependency ratio, 1950		
	Total	Youth	Aged
1960 (est.)	90.9	74.2	16.7
1955..........	81.3	65.8	15.5
1950..........	72.7	58.5	14.2
1940..........	70.4	58.6	11.8
1930..........	79.1	69.4	9.7
1920..........	83.5	74.9	8.6
1910..........	86.2	78.2	8.0
1900..........	94.2	86.2	8.0
1890..........	100.0	92.2	7.8
1880..........	106.2	99.2	7.0
1870..........	111.4	105.1	6.3
1860..........	117.2	111.3	5.9
1850..........	122.4	116.7	5.8
1840..........	133.1	127.3	5.8
1820..........	153.4	146.6	6.8

Note that there was a steady decline in the total dependency ratio from 1820 until 1940. Taken literally, the dependency load in 1940 (70.4) was only 46 percent as large as in 1820. Since 1940 the dependency rate has risen, and in 1960 it is 29 percent greater than in 1940. Because a higher proportion of persons under 20 and over 65 were economically active in the nineteenth and early twentieth centuries, the decline of the actual de-

pendency load was not as great as indicated by the index. Nevertheless, these statistics may be used to illustrate the general magnitude of the decline in dependency, and the time-pattern of that decline. The decline over a 120-year period, from 1820 to 1940, consisted of a net balance between two opposing trends: a fall in the dependency load for the youth, and a rise in the dependency load for the aged. The youth dependency ratio has always been 80 percent or more of the total. Since it fell by 88 points while the old-age dependency ratio increased by only 5 points, the net result was a large decline in the total dependency ratio. One direct result of fertility control is an almost immediate lessening of the over-all burden of dependency, since such control lowers the large burden of youth dependency. In fact, the result is a temporary situation in which the dependency load is unusually light. There are fewer children and many adults, and there is no increase in the ratio of older persons to adults in the 20-64 age groups. Later, when the aging process passes the bonus of adult workers into the older ages, the dependency ratio will tend to rise somewhat, provided the fertility level remains low. The statistical series for the United States shown above illustrates the important principle that the dependency ratio in a low fertility-low mortality population is far lower than the dependency ratio in a high fertility-high mortality population, because of the reduction in the large dependency load for children. Although the transition from high fertility and mortality rates to low fertility and mortality rates raises the dependency load for the aged by a few points, this increase is more than offset by the much greater reduction in the youth dependency load. The recent discussion of the aging of the American population, as if it were a grave social problem, is somewhat out of perspective. A really onerous dependency load is borne by nations where high death rates remove children of all ages before they have a chance to make a productive contribution. From the dependency point of view, the death of a 10-year-old boy and a 75-year-old man are not identical events. One has consumed for ten years as a dependent

without contributing any return; the other has consumed for thirty years as a dependent, but has
also produced for 45 years. As a result of demographic processes the American people, for more
than a century, have borne a smaller dependency
load than most populations of the world have been
carrying. Between 1940 and 1960, three-fourths of
the increase of 20.5 points in the total dependency
ratio was created by the resurgence of fertility
and the increased youth dependency load, and only
one-fourth of the increase was due to the growing
number of persons past 65. Thus, not only is our
old-age dependency still a small part of the total
dependency; it is also the kind of dependency that
signifies the accomplishment of one of the socio-
medical gains for which many peoples of the world
are still only hoping. Considering the present and
proposed schemes of social security and retirement, in which workers invest a portion of their
wages against their retirement, it is doubtful that
the population of the United States will ever become a heavy economic burden in its old age.

At the present time, the urban population of the
United States carries a much smaller dependency
load than the rural population, and the burden of
the rural-nonfarm population is smaller than that
of the rural-farm. These differences are due
largely to variations in the youth dependency ratio
rather than to the dependency ratio for aged persons, as may be seen from the following summary:

Dependency ratio, 1950

Area	Total	Youth	Aged
Urban (new definition)	63.3	50.0	13.2
Rural nonfarm	86.6	70.5	16.1
Rural farm	99.9	84.7	15.2

CHANGES IN THE AGE COMPOSITION OF URBAN AND RURAL AREAS: 1910-50

Since at least 1910, and undoubtedly before, urban populations have had smaller proportions of
youth and children, and much larger concentrations of young adults, than have the rural population. Table 6-4 summarizes the data which are
available for tracing the changing age composition
of urban and rural areas. (Although data are
shown for 1890 also, the 1890 information refers
only to cities of 25,000 and over, and undoubtedly

Table 6-4.—AGE COMPOSITION OF URBAN AND RURAL AREAS: 1890 TO 1950

Area and year	Median age	Dependency ratio			Percent distribution by age							
		Total	Youth	Old age	Total	0-4	5-19	20-29	30-44	45-64	65-over	Age unknown
Urban (new definition)												
1950...................	31.6	63.3	50.0	13.2	100.0	10.1	20.5	16.7	23.0	21.4	8.2	...
1940...................	31.0	58.7	47.8	11.0	100.0	6.7	23.4	18.1	23.7	21.2	6.9	...
1930...................	28.4	65.5	57.0	8.4	100.0	8.2	26.3	18.3	24.0	18.2	5.1	0.1
1920...................	27.4	67.0	60.0	7.0	100.0	9.7	26.1	19.2	23.5	17.0	4.2	0.2
1910...................	26.3	68.8	62.0	6.8	100.0	9.9	26.8	20.9	23.1	15.2	4.0	...
1890...................	24.6	74.8	69.6	5.2	100.0	10.7	29.1	22.1	21.7	13.4	3.0	...
Rural nonfarm												
1950...................	27.9	86.6	70.5	16.1	100.0	12.1	25.7	15.5	20.5	17.5	8.6	...
1940...................	27.7	78.9	65.9	13.0	100.0	9.3	27.6	17.1	21.0	17.9	7.3	...
1930...................	25.8	88.1	75.9	12.2	100.0	10.5	29.8	16.3	20.1	16.7	6.5	0.1
1920...................	25.1	90.1	78.7	11.4	100.0	11.6	29.8	16.6	20.1	15.9	6.0	0.2
Rural farm												
1950...................	26.3	99.9	84.7	15.2	100.0	11.4	30.9	12.0	18.6	19.4	7.5	...
1940...................	24.4	97.2	84.2	13.0	100.0	10.0	32.7	15.2	17.3	18.2	6.6	...
1930...................	21.6	110.5	99.8	10.8	100.0	11.1	36.2	14.2	16.9	16.4	5.1	...
1920...................	20.7	114.4	104.9	9.4	100.0	12.7	36.2	14.7	17.2	14.7	4.4	0.1
Rural												
1910...................	22.1	104.7	95.3	9.4	100.0	13.0	33.5	16.9	17.8	14.1	4.6	...

Source: U.S. Census of Population: 1950, Vol. II, Part 1, Table 38; Sixteenth Census of the United States: 1940, Vol. II, Part 1, Table 7; Thirteenth Census of the United States: 1910, Vol. I, Table 38, p. 332. Data for 1890 are for cities of 25,000 and over only and were computed from W. S. Thompson and P. K. Whelpton, Population Trends in the United States, Table 34, p. 128.

understates the proportion of children in the urban population at that date.)

In 1910, rural areas had a considerably larger proportion of middle-aged and older population than cities. For this reason cities have often been referred to as having "young" populations, even though the median age of the urban population has been higher than that of the rural population since 1910 and, undoubtedly, even before that date. Many of the cities themselves were young and were comprised almost entirely of migrants.

Although fertility rates in urban areas were below those of rural areas in 1910, they were much higher at this time than they were later. Their rapid decline in the next three decades caused cities to have exceptionally small proportions of children and youth. The proportion of the urban population 0-4 years of age fell from 9.7 percent in 1920 to 8.2 percent in 1930 and to 6.7 percent in 1940--a decrease of 30.9 percent in twenty years! The proportion of children in the rural-nonfarm population underwent a similar though somewhat milder decline, and the corresponding change in rural-farm population was a decrease of 21.3 percent. Between 1940 and 1950 urban fertility appears to have rebounded most vigorously. The age structure of urban populations was affected immediately. In 1950, 10.1 percent of the total urban population was 0-4 years of age. This is greater than the percentage for 1910, and is a rise of a little more than 50 percent in ten years. Neither the rural-nonfarm nor the rural-farm populations responded as much as the urban, proportionately, in the 1940-50 decade; the increase in the proportion 0-4 years was 30 percent in rural-nonfarm areas, and 14 percent in rural-farm areas.

Over the years since 1890 and 1910, cities have lost most of their concentration (in comparison with rural areas) of persons in the 20-29 age group, and in 1950 cities actually had a proportion of persons in this migration age group which was little greater than that of the rural-nonfarm population. Cities now show a large concentration of persons in the 45-64 age group, in comparison with rural areas. This is a result of the fact that

earlier waves of migrants to cities have passed into the upper age brackets. Meanwhile, the rural population has been so depleted by migration and by lowered birth rates that it cannot possibly maintain the large streams of migration which are required to maintain a young age composition in the cities, especially with the low birth rates that prevailed in cities between 1920 and 1940.

Instead of having a shortage of persons 65 years of age and over in comparison with rural areas (as had been the case in previous decades), in 1950 urban places had a higher proportion of these older persons than rural areas (the proportion of older persons in rural-nonfarm areas was slightly higher than it was in urban areas). Since there is every indication that this aging process will continue because of the concentration in 1950 of persons in the 45-64 group, it is quite likely that by 1960 or 1970 cities will contain considerably larger proportions of persons 65 years of age and over than will either the rural-nonfarm or rural-farm areas. This difference will be even more marked if birth rates in urban areas again fall to their prewar level.

It should be noted, in passing, that between 1930 and 1940 both rural-nonfarm and rural-farm areas experienced a small increase in the proportion of persons 20-29 years of age. This is indirect evidence that the economic depression temporarily kept young persons in rural areas. By 1950 this situation had changed, for the age group 20-29 was smaller proportionately in the rural populations than it had been at any previous date.

AGE COMPOSITION IN COMPARISON WITH OTHER NATIONS

The preceding discussion makes it evident that each nation in the world has its demographic history impressed upon its age structure. An overall comparison of the age structure of the United States population with the age structures of other countries may be made, using the information provided in Table 6-5, and Figure 6-5. Figure 6-5 consists of four population pyramids. (A population pyramid is constructed by computing a per-

Table 6-5.—AGE COMPOSITION OF SELECTED NATIONS OF THE WORLD: NATIONS OF FIVE MILLION OR MORE INHABITANTS FOR WHICH AGE DATA ARE AVAILABLE

Country	Date of census or estimate	Median age	Dependency ratio			Percent distribution by age						
			Total	Youth	Aged	Total	0-4	5-19	20-29	30-34	45-64	65-over
AFRICA												
Algeria...............	E-1953	18.4	132.3	125.1	7.2	100.0	16.4	37.5	14.5	15.9	12.7	3.1
Egypt.................	C-1947	21.2	105.1	98.8	6.4	100.0	13.7	34.5	15.1	19.9	13.8	3.1
Morocco...............	E-1947	20,0	115.5	107.5	8.0	100.0	16.9	33.1	16.6	20.0	9.9	3.7
Mozambique............	C-1940	19.9	109.9	105.2	4.6	100.0	20.9	29.3	18.8	20.1	8.8	2.2
Nigeria...............	C-1952-3	19.0	121.2	115.0	6.2	100.0	22.5	29.5	15.1	19.1	11.0	2.8
Union of South Africa..	C-1936	19.6	119.5	111.8	7.7	100.0	14.7	36.3	16.7	18.0	10.9	3.5
NORTH AMERICA												
Canada................	E-1953	27.5	86.1	71.6	14.5	100.0	12.4	26.1	15.4	20.8	17.6	7.8
Cuba..................	C-1943	22.1	97.2	90.7	6.5	100.0	13.2	32.8	18.7	19.4	12.6	3.3
Mexico................	C-1950	19.2	123.9	116.3	7.6	100.0	15.4	36.6	36.8	16.3	11.6	3.4
United States.........	E-1953	30.2	77.0	62.3	14.7	100.0	10.9	24.3	14.5	21.7	20.3	8.3
SOUTH AMERICA												
Argentina.............	C-1947	25.3	80.8	73.8	7.1	100.0	11.3	29.5	17.5	21.6	16.2	3.9
Brazil................	C-1950	19.0	122.0	116.7	5.3	100.0	16.2	36.3	17.6	16.7	10.7	2.4
Chile.................	C-1940	21.5	103.5	96.3	7.1	100.0	12.4	35.0	17.6	18.8	12.8	3.5
Colombia..............	C-1938	19.1	122.9	116.5	6.5	100.0	15.4	36.9	17.4	16.9	10.6	2.9
Peru..................	C-1940	19.3	126.8	117.0	9.8	100.0	15.5	36.1	16.3	16.7	11.1	4.3
ASIA												
Burma.................	E-1954	21.6	99.6	94.0	5.6	100.0	13.8	33.3	18.5	19.1	12.5	2.8
Ceylon................	C-1946	21.4	103.5	96.5	6.9	100.0	12.9	34.5	18.3	18.6	12.2	3.4
Taiwan................	E-1953	18.7	124.7	119.1	5.6	100.0	19.0	34.0	16.9	17.0	10.6	2.5
India.................	C-1951	21.4	104.5	97.1	7.3	100.0	13.4	34.2	17.1	18.9	13.0	3.6
Japan.................	E-1952	23.0	99.2	89.2	10.0	100.0	13.1	31.7	17.4	17.7	15.1	5.0
Korea.................	C-1944	18.9	129.4	120.4	8.9	100.0	17.0	35.5	14.1	16.2	13.3	3.9
South Korea...........	E-1953	21.7	102.4	95.7	6.7	100.0	11.8	35.5	15.6	21.3	12.5	3.3
Philippines...........	C-1948	18.1	138.3	130.7	7.6	100.0	15.6	39.3	17.0	15.6	9.4	3.2
Thailand..............	C-1947	18.6	127.8	121.9	5.9	100.0	15.2	38.3	16.0	17.1	10.8	2.6
Turkey................	C-1950	20.1	113.0	106.0	7.0	100.0	14.8	35.0	16.4	17.0	13.6	3.3
EUROPE												
Austria...............	E-1952	35.1	66.7	48.7	18.0	100.0	7.4	21.8	14.2	19.6	26.2	10.8
Belgium...............	E-1952	35.0	64.5	45.9	18.6	100.0	7.9	20.0	15.3	20.2	25.3	11.3
Bulgaria..............	E-1945	27.2	78.1	67.6	10.5	100.0	9.4	28.5	16.8	22.3	17.0	5.9
Czechoslovakia........	C-1947	31.0	67.4	54.7	12.7	100.0	9.4	23.3	15.7	22.9	21.2	7.6
France................	E-1953	33.6	71.4	51.8	19.6	100.0	9.2	21.0	15.2	19.0	24.1	11.4
Germany...............	E-1951	33.2	67.1	51.4	15.7	100.0	7.3	23.5	14.8	20.7	24.4	9.4
Greece................	E-1949	25.7	84.3	73.2	11.1	100.0	11.1	28.6	18.1	19.6	16.5	6.0
Hungary...............	C-1941	29.9	73.9	61.7	12.2	100.0	8.4	27.1	14.6	23.7	19.2	7.0
Italy.................	E-1951	28.9	75.3	61.1	14.2	100.0	9.3	25.5	17.1	20.3	19.6	8.1
Netherlands...........	E-1953	28.5	83.3	68.4	14.9	100.0	10.7	26.6	15.0	19.9	19.6	8.1
Poland................	E-1949	26.4	77.2	68.1	9.0	100.0	10.2	28.3	17.9	21.0	17.6	5.1
Portugal..............	E-1951	26.5	84.8	71.9	12.9	100.0	10.4	28.5	17.2	19.3	17.6	7.0
Romania...............	C-1948	25.5	83.5	73.8	9.7	100.0	9.9	30.3	17.9	17.8	18.8	5.3
Spain.................	C-1950	28.0	77.8	64.9	12.8	100.0	9.2	27.3	16.8	20.7	18.7	7.2
Sweden................	E-1952	34.6	66.5	49.2	17.3	100.0	8.1	21.4	13.5	23.0	23.5	10.4
England and Wales......	E-1953	35.4	66.1	47.5	18.6	100.0	7.7	20.9	13.4	22.1	24.7	11.2
Scotland..............	E-1953	33.0	72.1	54.7	17.4	100.0	8.5	23.2	14.1	21.0	22.9	10.1
Yugoslavia............	E-1953	24.7	88.0	77.4	10.5	100.0	12.3	28.9	18.6	17.2	17.4	5.6
OCEANIA												
Australia.............	E-1953	30.3	74.5	60.2	14.3	100.0	10.8	23.7	15.0	22.1	20.2	8.2

Source: Compiled from United Nations Demographic Yearbook, 1948, 1949-51, 1952, 1953, and 1954.

centage distribution of a population simultaneously cross-classified by age and sex. The percent which each male age group is of the total is plotted on the left, as in the figure, while the corresponding percents for females are plotted on the right. Sometimes numbers, rather than percents, are used in constructing population age pyramids.) Figure 6-5 illustrates the four panels of age composition by sex of (1) a nation with high birth and death rates (Egypt), (2) a nation with low birth and death rates (United Kingdom), (3) a nation which has suffered severe war losses and population transfers in conjunction with low birth rates (Federal Republic of Germany), and (4) the United States. All of the principles concerning the forces that affect age composition are illustrated in this figure. Several noteworthy findings may be derived from this figure and from Table 6-5.

(a) There is great variation in age composition among the nations. This variation applies to all phases of the age cycle and is illustrated in the age pyramids. Where birth and death rates are high, as in Egypt, the age pyramid is broad at the base and rises rapidly to a peak. Where birth and death rates are low, as in the nations in the two lower panels, the age pyramid is narrow at the bottom and rises almost vertically before narrowing at the older ages. Where there has been an upsurge in fertility, as in the United States (evidences are also present in the United Kingdom), a previously constricted base is again broadened and gives the age pyramid a narrow section in the center. Military losses and population transfers are revealed by a great shortage of particular age groups (especially males), as in the age group 30-34 for Germany.

(b) Most nations of Western Europe have an age composition roughly similar to that of the United States: lower proportions of children and youth, and higher proportions of old age, than are found in most other parts of the world. Germany, Austria, France, England and Wales, and Sweden all have lower proportions of population under 20 years of age and a larger proportion over 65 years of age than does the United States, in spite of the fact that the loss of men of military age during World War II tends to reduce these particular differences. These differences between the age composition of the United States and most nations of Western Europe result from lower birth rates and a longer period of declining births in Western Europe than in the United States. The total dependency load for the countries of Europe, and for populations of European descent, tends to be low in comparison with other nations; the median age of these European peoples tends to be high. Although Bulgaria, Greece, Hungary, the Netherlands, Poland, Portugal, Romania, and Yugoslavia have somewhat higher proportions of population under 20 than does the United States, the extent of this difference is not great. The age composition of the United States population is about "average" in this European group.

(c) The less industrialized and more rural nations for which data are available tend to have a much higher proportion of children and youth and a smaller proportion of "old-age" population than does the United States. Their median age is lower, and their dependency ratios higher than those of the United States or of European nations. These differences reflect higher rates of fertility and higher death rates. About one-half, or less, of the native populations of Asia, Africa, and South America for which age statistics are available are less than 20-22 years of age (two major exceptions are Japan and Argentina). Not more than one-third of the United States population is this young. Only 2-4 percent of the people of these less industrialized nations are 65 years of age or over. This amount is less than one-half the proportion of the population which is in these ages in the United States and in the nations of Western Europe.

(d) The proportion of population in the most vigorous working ages, 20-44 years, is roughly the same for all nations--between 30 and 35 percent of the total population. A major difference between the nations with low vital rates and those with high vital rates, however, is that the former contain a much greater proportion of middle-aged persons. Whereas about 20 percent of the United States population (and of most nations of European descent) is in the group 45-64, only about 10-15 percent of the population of many other nations is in this category. In these other nations, high death rates at adult ages have prevented this age group from becoming a larger part of the total population. Undoubtedly, this extra component of seasoned, experienced workers makes for a major

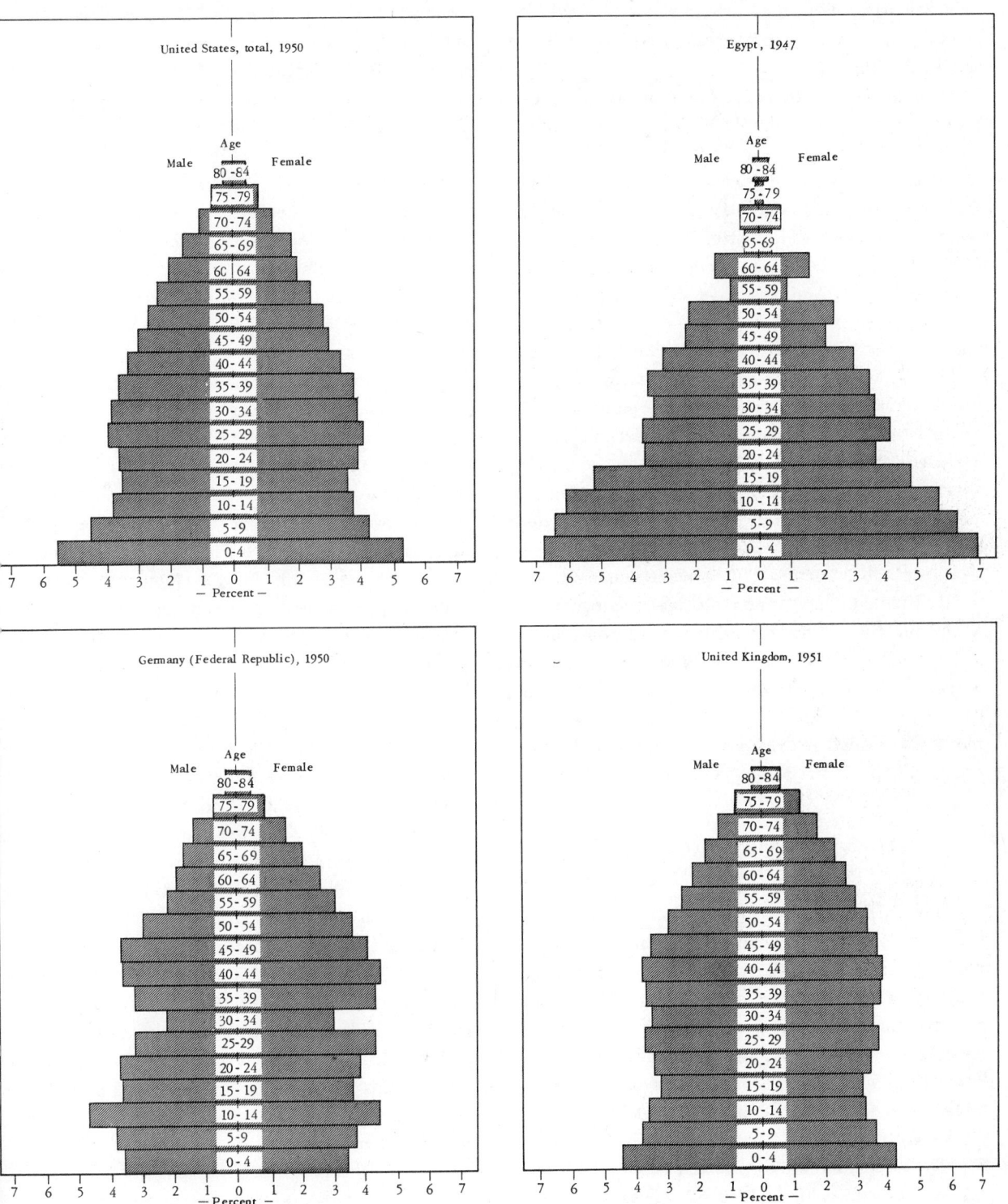

FIGURE 6-5. POPULATION PYRAMIDS FOR FOUR NATIONS OF THE WORLD

difference between the labor forces of the industrialized nations (which have low death rates at adult ages) and the labor forces of the less industrialized nations.

(e) None of the nations for which the age composition is shown now has a dependency ratio as high as the United States had in 1820. The nations with the highest ratios--Algeria, Nigeria, and the Philippine Islands--currently have a dependency index corresponding to that of the United States in 1840. Many of the other populations of Africa, Asia, and South America have age compositions that correspond roughly to those of the United States in the years between 1850 and 1870, although the comparison is complicated by the factor of immigration. Thus, from the point of view of its general age structure and dependency load, the population of the United States is in a more or less intermediate position among the industrialized nations of the world. In comparison with the less industrialized nations, the United States exhibits an age structure that is more concentrated in the "middle age" and "old age" categories. About one-fifth of the dependency load is made up of persons who have produced and retired. Dedendents in the United States are less of a burden than they are in many other nations, and child mortality--which prevents young dependents from ever being productive--has been greatly reduced.

AGE COMPOSITION OF THE POPULATION,
BY GEOGRAPHIC DIVISIONS, 1950

Tables 17, 18, 19, and 20 in the Appendix show the age composition (percent distribution) by 5-year age intervals, of the total population of each geographic division, and also of the urban, rural-nonfarm, and rural-farm populations of each of these geographic divisions, by sex and color. Table 6-6, which is a consolidation of all these tables, provides a broad summary of the interdivisional differences in age structure. Tables 21, 22, 23, and 24 in the Appendix report the estimated percent change, 1940-50, of each 5-year age group of the total, urban, rural-nonfarm, and rural-farm population of each geographic division.

That there are fairly large and important differences between the divisions is evident from Table 6-6. These differences arise, for the most part, from the following factors:

(a) Interdivisional differences in birth rates, both at the present time and during past decades

(b) Interdivisional differences in death rates during past decades

(c) Interdivisional differences in urban-rural composition

(d) Migration history of the divisions

(e) Interdivisional differences in racial composition

(f) Recency of settlement of the divisions

Children and Youth. In general, the geographic divisions that have higher birth rates and a more rural composition tend to have a higher proportion of children and youth in their population than have the geographic divisions which are more urban and which have lower birth rates. The three divisions of the South, and the Mountain Division, which are less industrialized and less urbanized and have had higher birth rates, have proportions of children which are considerably larger than is the average for the total population. The median ages in these divisions are low, and their dependency ratios for youth are well above those of the other divisions. This situation underlies the frequently heard complaint that the areas which are wealthiest, which have the greatest per capita tax base, and which find a highly trained labor force to be most essential for their industries are the very areas which bear the smallest per capita burden of educating the nation's oncoming generations. The New England, Middle Atlantic, and East North Central Divisions, which are the most highly urbanized and metropolitanized areas in the country and which traditionally have had lower birth rates, have comparatively small proportions of children and youth. In the East South Central states, where the total dependency ratio was highest (90.1), 40.2 percent of the population was under 20 years of age in 1950. In the Middle Atlantic states, where the dependency ratio was lowest (62.3), only 29.9 percent of the population was in this age interval.

Table 6-6.-AGE COMPOSITION OF GEOGRAPHIC DIVISIONS, BY URBAN AND RURAL RESIDENCE: 1950

Geographic division	Median age	Dependency ratio (per 100)			Percent distribution by age						
		Total	Youth	Aged	Total	0-4	5-19	20-29	30-44	45-64	65-over
U.S. TOTAL............	30.2	72.7	58.5	14.2	100.0	10.7	23.2	15.7	21.9	20.3	8.2
New England............	32.4	68.8	52.4	16.4	100.0	9.8	21.2	15.5	21.7	22.0	9.7
Middle Atlantic.........	32.9	62.3	48.5	13.8	100.0	9.4	20.5	15.6	23.2	22.8	8.5
East North Central......	31.3	69.2	54.8	14.4	100.0	10.5	21.9	15.7	22.0	21.4	8.5
West North Central......	31.1	76.9	59.5	17.3	100.0	10.6	23.1	14.8	20.4	21.4	9.8
South Atlantic..........	27.2	80.2	68.3	11.9	100.0	11.7	26.2	16.8	21.5	17.2	6.6
East South Central......	26.3	90.1	76.4	13.7	100.0	12.1	28.1	15.5	20.0	17.1	7.2
West South Central......	27.7	81.7	68.6	13.1	100.0	11.7	26.1	15.9	21.1	18.1	7.2
Mountain................	27.5	83.0	70.0	13.0	100.0	12.2	26.0	15.7	21.0	17.9	7.1
Pacific.................	31.9	65.9	51.8	14.1	100.0	10.5	20.7	15.8	23.3	21.1	8.5
U.S. URBAN............	31.6	63.3	50.0	13.2	100.0	10.1	20.5	16.7	23.0	21.4	8.2
New England............	32.9	65.5	49.4	16.0	100.0	9.5	20.4	15.8	22.0	22.7	9.7
Middle Atlantic.........	33.4	58.3	45.3	13.0	100.0	9.1	19.5	16.0	23.8	23.3	8.2
East North Central......	31.9	62.8	49.6	13.2	100.0	10.2	20.3	16.6	22.9	22.0	8.1
West North Central......	31.9	67.2	51.3	15.9	100.0	10.2	20.4	16.7	21.2	21.8	9.5
South Atlantic..........	29.8	63.3	52.2	11.1	100.0	10.6	21.4	18.3	24.0	19.0	6.8
East South Central......	29.0	68.6	56.8	11.8	100.0	11.1	22.6	18.1	22.7	18.5	7.0
West South Central......	28.6	69.9	58.7	11.2	100.0	11.6	22.9	18.1	22.5	18.2	6.6
Mountain................	29.0	74.1	60.7	13.4	100.0	11.7	23.2	16.8	21.9	18.8	7.7
Pacific.................	32.7	62.0	47.6	14.4	100.0	10.3	19.1	16.2	24.0	21.6	8.9
U.S. RURAL NONFARM.....	27.9	86.6	70.5	16.1	100.0	12.1	25.7	15.5	20.5	17.5	8.6
New England............	30.8	79.2	61.5	17.7	100.0	11.2	23.1	14.6	21.5	19.7	9.9
Middle Atlantic.........	30.4	77.6	61.1	16.5	100.0	10.9	23.5	15.0	21.6	19.7	9.3
East North Central......	29.5	85.5	66.9	18.6	100.0	11.8	24.2	14.8	20.5	18.5	10.0
West North Central......	32.5	89.4	63.8	25.6	100.0	10.7	23.0	13.2	18.7	20.9	13.5
South Atlantic..........	25.0	89.6	78.2	11.4	100.0	13.2	28.0	17.5	20.5	14.7	6.0
East South Central......	25.0	96.3	82.1	14.2	100.0	13.4	28.3	16.5	19.5	14.8	7.2
West South Central......	26.7	94.0	77.9	16.1	100.0	12.4	27.7	14.8	19.7	17.0	6.3
Mountain................	25.6	92.9	80.1	12.7	100.0	13.3	28.2	15.3	20.3	16.2	6.6
Pacific.................	28.4	78.6	65.2	13.4	100.0	11.9	24.6	16.0	21.9	18.1	7.5
U.S. RURAL FARM........	26.3	99.9	84.7	15.2	100.0	11.4	31.0	12.0	18.6	19.4	7.6
New England............	31.5	89.7	69.0	20.7	100.0	9.7	26.6	11.9	18.6	22.1	10.9
Middle Atlantic.........	29.6	88.5	70.8	17.7	100.0	10.2	27.4	12.9	18.8	21.4	9.4
East North Central......	30.2	89.7	72.6	17.1	100.0	10.3	27.9	11.6	19.1	21.9	9.0
West North Central......	28.4	88.7	74.9	13.8	100.0	11.2	28.5	12.2	19.9	20.9	7.3
South Atlantic..........	22.7	114.8	100.2	14.6	100.0	12.1	34.5	12.4	17.5	16.6	6.8
East South Central......	23.2	114.8	99.1	15.7	100.0	12.2	34.0	11.9	17.6	17.1	7.3
West South Central......	25.6	103.0	88.6	14.4	100.0	11.5	32.2	11.3	18.7	19.3	7.1
Mountain................	24.9	97.2	86.2	11.0	100.0	12.3	31.4	12.8	19.5	18.4	5.6
Pacific.................	31.2	79.9	66.2	13.6	100.0	10.0	26.9	11.5	20.8	23.4	7.6

Source: Compiled for this study from U.S. Census of Population: 1950, individual volumes for each state, Table 15.

These regional differences are not merely a result of the different proportions of urban and rural among the various divisions. From Table 6-6 it may be noted that children and youth comprise a higher than average proportion of the urban, the rural-nonfarm, and the rural-farm populations in the Southern and Mountain Divisions. The urbanized Northeastern and Pacific Divisions have lower than average proportions of children and youth in their urban, rural-nonfarm, and rural-farm populations. Within each of the geographic divisions, the median age was higher, and the dependency ratio for children lower, in the urban than in the rural areas. This same difference tended to distinguish the rural-nonfarm from the rural-farm areas of each geographic division.

Adults. In 1950 the more urbanized and industrialized divisions had a somewhat higher proportion of their population in the working ages than did the more rural divisions. Migration during the past four decades is responsible for this situation. Apparently, divisions with higher birth rates but less industrialization have tended to be areas of out-migration, and the areas of low birth rates but greater industrialization have tended to be areas of in-migration. Consequently, the rural divisions show a comparative deficit of population in the adult ages, while the urbanized divisions show no deficit, and sometimes even show an excess, in comparison with the nation. The East South Central Division may be cited as an example of an area that has contributed migrants to more urbanized divisions for many decades and consequently it has a comparatively small proportion of adults. The Middle Atlantic Division is an example of an area with low birth rates but a large complement of adults resulting from extensive in-migration. The Pacific Division (especially California) has maintained an unusually large proportion of adult population as a result of in-migration. Although the over-all age pattern of this division is similar to that of the Northeastern states, it differs in the fact that in the West the net in-migration, until a very recent date, was to rural as well as to urban areas.

As a consequence of the prolonged flow of internal migration, the differences in urban-rural composition among the geographic divisions are considerably less now than they were in earlier decades. The interregional differences in the proportion of adults in the population now tend also to be of only moderate size. A comparison of the two divisions which have the largest and the smallest proportion of persons in the 20-64 range shows that the Middle Atlantic Division has 61.6 percent while the East South Central Division has 52.6 percent. The proportion of adults in all the other divisions lie within this range. However, the urban population of each division contains a larger proportion of adults than does the rural population. In addition, the rural-nonfarm population of each division contains a higher proportion of adults 20-44 years of age than does the rural-farm population. The rural populations of the South have smaller proportions of population 20-64 than have the rural populations of other divisions.

The loss which the farm population sustained between 1940 and 1950 seems to have been concentrated in the young adult ages. In each division, the proportion of the population that is 20-29 is considerably less among the rural-farm population than among the rural-nonfarm population. For the age group 30-44 there is a similar, though smaller, deficit among the rural-farm population. In each division the proportion of middle-aged people (45-64 years) is as great among the rural-farm population as it is among the rural-nonfarm, or even greater.

Old Age. The divisions of the United States which have been settled longest tend to have higher proportions of older persons than do other divisions. This is explained, at least in part, by the fact that divisions which have been sources of out-migration for a prolonged time tend to have a higher proportion of oldsters. The West North Central Division, which lost much population between 1930 and 1940, and which lost a great deal of farm population between 1940 and 1950, is an example of this situation. At first thought, one would expect higher proportions of older persons in the South Atlantic Division also, for the same reasons. But death rates at adult ages tend to be higher in these areas than in other divisions, and high fertility maintains a large youth element in the population. Consequently, the proportion of population which is older is not extraordinarily high in the South. The divisions where levels of living are high, and where a large proportion of the population can afford medical attention, also have higher proportions of aged people.

A special aspect of this pattern is the movement of older people to places of retirement. Florida and California (and other suitable spots in southern states) have become favored locations to which older people retire. In Florida, for example, 8.6 percent of the population was 65 and over in 1950, while the average for this age group in the South Atlantic Division, which contains Florida, was only 6.6 percent. Although the Pacific Division has almost the same proportion of oldsters as has the United States as a whole, a large part of this complement has been gained through migration. This division has grown at such a rapid rate for many decades that a normal complement of aged could not possibly have resulted solely from the normal aging of the population residing there in earlier decades. It could arise only from in-migration.

Another interesting example of the same phenomenon is the very high proportion of aged people in the rural-nonfarm population of the West North Central Division. This apparently reflects the tendency of farmers to live in nearby villages after they retire. In the Pacific Division and the northeastern divisions there is a tendency toward higher than average proportions of middle-aged people among the rural-farm and the rural-nonfarm populations. This may mean that people in these areas tend to go into semi-retirement on small farms, as well as in villages, during advancing age; or it may reflect somewhat greater longevity in these areas.

In the New England and Middle Atlantic states, a large proportion of the rural population (both farm and nonfarm) is suburban. For this reason, rural populations tend to resemble the urban population more closely in these divisions than in other divisions.

AGE COMPOSITION OF THE POPULATION OF STATES, 1950

Table 6-7 reports measures of the age composition of each state for 1950. The following states have the "oldest" age composition.

State	Old age de-pendency ratio	Percent over-65	Median age
Vermont............	19.5	10.5	30.0
New Hampshire......	19.0	10.8	32.3
Maine..............	18.8	10.2	30.0
Iowa...............	18.7	10.4	31.0
Kansas.............	18.1	10.2	31.1
Missouri...........	18.0	10.4	32.6
Nebraska...........	17.6	9.9	31.0
Massachusetts......	16.8	10.0	32.8
Indiana............	16.1	9.2	30.4
Minnesota..........	16.0	9.0	30.6

The youngest states are the following:

State	Percent youth dependency ratio	Percent under 20 years of age	Median age
South Carolina...	86.8	43.9	23.6
Mississippi......	86.0	43.0	24.6

Continued.	Percent youth dependency ratio	Percent under 20 years of age	Median age
New Mexico.......	83.2	43.2	24.0
Utah.............	79.9	41.7	25.1
Alabama..........	79.5	41.4	25.5
North Carolina...	77.8	41.3	25.0
West Virginia....	75.2	40.0	26.3
Georgia..........	75.0	40.1	26.2
North Dakota.....	74.6	39.4	27.1
Kentucky.........	74.6	39.3	27.0
Arizona..........	72.3	39.5	26.8
Tennessee........	70.0	38.2	27.3

A few states have unusually low total dependency loads by virtue of having lower birth rates and fewer older people. They are:

| | Dependency ratio: | | |
State	Total	Youth	Old age
District of Columbia......	49.0	38.4	10.6
Delaware..................	52.9	40.2	12.7
New York..................	59.2	45.7	13.5
New Jersey................	60.0	46.9	13.1
Connecticut...............	62.9	48.7	14.2
California................	63.9	50.0	13.9

Median age of the urban, rural-nonfarm, and rural-farm population, and of the white and nonwhite population of each state, is shown in Table 6-8 also. It may be seen that a part, but not all, of the younger age composition of the southern states is due to the nonwhite population. Certain population groups have exceptionally young age composition, such as the following:

State	Median age
North Dakota, nonwhite..................	17.0
South Dakota, nonwhite..................	18.9
Montana, nonwhite.......................	19.2
New Mexico, nonwhite....................	19.3
South Carolina, rural farm.............	19.5
South Carolina, nonwhite...............	19.6

Some unusually high median ages were recorded for the following:

State	Median age
New Hampshire, rural farm...............	34.0
Connecticut, rural farm.................	34.9
New York, white.........................	34.0
Iowa, rural nonfarm.....................	34.2
Nebraska, rural nonfarm.................	34.6
New York, urban.........................	33.9
Massachusetts, rural farm...............	33.5
New Jersey, rural farm..................	33.5

In general, these are places of very slow growth or of in-migration by families with an older age composition.

Table 6-7.--AGE COMPOSITION OF THE STATES POPULATION, BY GEOGRAPHIC DIVISIONS; 1950

Geographic division and state	Percent in age			Dependency ratio (per 100)			Median age					
	Under 20	20-64	65-over	Total	Youth	Old age	Total	White	Non-white	Urban	Rural non-farm	Rural farm
U.S. TOTAL........	33.9	58.0	8.1	72.7	58.5	14.2	30.3	30.8	26.1	31.6	27.9	26.3
NEW ENGLAND.........	31.0	59.3	9.7	68.7	52.3	16.4	32.3	32.4	28.3	32.8	30.7	31.4
Maine.................	35.4	54.4	10 2	83.9	65.1	18.8	30.0	30.0	23.6	30.9	28.9	29.2
New Hampshire.........	32.4	56.8	10.8	76.0	57.0	19.0	32.3	32.3	26.4	32.1	32.1	34.0
Vermont..............	35.6	53.9	10.5	85.5	66.0	19.5	30.0	30.0	32.6	31.4	29.8	27.7
Massachusetts.........	30.3	59.7	10.0	67.6	50.8	16.8	32.8	32.9	29.1	33.1	31.4	33.5
Rhode Island.........	30.3	60.8	8.9	64.4	49.8	14.6	31.7	31.8	25.8	32.3	28.4	32.3
Connecticut..........	29.9	61.4	8.7	62.9	48.7	14.2	32.7	32.8	28.0	32.9	31.5	34.9
MIDDLE ATLANTIC......	29.9	61.7	8.4	62.1	48.5	13.6	32.7	33.0	29.4	33.3	30.4	29.7
New York.............	28.7	62.8	8.5	59.2	45.7	13.5	33.7	34.0	29.9	33.9	32.5	31.0
New Jersey...........	29.3	62.5	8.2	60.0	46.9	13.1	32.9	33.3	28.6	33.1	31.3	33.5
Pennsylvania.........	32.0	59.9	8.5	68.1	53.8	14.3	31.3	31.5	28.9	32.3	28.9	28.2
EAST NORTH CENTRAL...	32.4	59.1	8.5	69.2	54.8	14.4	31.2	31.4	29.0	31.8	29.4	30.1
Ohio.................	32.2	58.9	8.9	69.8	54.7	15.1	31.2	31.4	29.1	32.0	28.8	30.4
Indiana..............	33.5	57.3	9.2	74.6	58.5	16.1	30.4	30.4	29.1	30.8	28.8	31.4
Illinois.............	30.5	61.0	8.7	64.0	49.7	14.3	32.7	33.0	29.5	33.1	31.1	30.8
Michigan.............	34.1	58.7	7.2	70.4	58.1	12.3	29.8	30.0	28.4	30.2	28.2	30.0
Wisconsin............	34.0	57.0	9.0	75.4	59.6	15.8	31.0	31.1	25.9	32.0	31.1	27.7
WEST NORTH CENTRAL...	33.8	56.4	9.8	77.3	59.9	17.4	31.1	31.2	29.1	31.8	32.3	28.4
Minnesota............	34.6	56.4	9.0	77.3	61.3	16.0	30.6	30.7	25.4	31.7	31.1	27.3
Iowa.................	34.0	55.6	10.4	79.9	61.2	18.7	31.0	31.1	28.3	31.8	34.2	27.6
Missouri.............	31.8	57.8	10.4	73.0	55.0	18.0	32.6	32.7	30.7	33.1	32.2	31.0
North Dakota.........	39.4	52.8	7.8	89.4	74.6	14.8	27.1	27.3	17.0	27.8	29.4	24.7
South Dakota.........	37.0	54.5	8.5	83.5	67.9	15.6	28.6	28.9	18.9	29.0	31.1	26.4
Nebraska.............	33.7	56.4	9.9	77.4	59.8	17.6	31.0	31.1	28.3	31.3	34.6	28.2
Kansas...............	33.4	56.4	10.2	77.3	59.2	18.1	31.1	31.1	29.7	30.5	32.3	31.1
SOUTH ATLANTIC.......	37.9	55.5	6.6	80.2	68.3	11.9	27.3	28.3	23.9	29.9	25.0	22.6
Delaware.............	26.3	65.4	8.3	52.9	40.2	12.7	31.2	31.5	29.0	31.9	29.5	30.7
Maryland.............	33.3	59.8	6.9	67.2	55.7	11.5	29.7	30.3	27.2	30.5	27.8	27.6
District of Columbia...	25.8	67.1	7.1	49.0	38.4	10.6	32.6	34.4	29.6	32.6	...	...
Virginia.............	37.1	56.5	6.4	77.0	65.7	11.3	27.3	27.8	25.3	29.1	25.1	25.5
West Virginia.........	40.0	53.2	6.8	88.0	75.2	12.8	26.3	26.2	26.9	30.2	23.6	24.4
North Carolina........	41.3	53.1	5.6	88.3	77.8	10.5	25.0	26.2	21.6	27.9	24.4	21.6
South Carolina........	43.9	50.6	5.5	97.7	86.8	10.9	23.6	26.1	19.6	26.8	23.2	19.5
Georgia..............	40.1	53.5	6.4	87.0	75.0	12.0	26.2	27.4	23.1	28.7	24.7	21.8
Florida..............	32.8	58.7	8.5	70.4	55.9	14.5	30.9	32.0	27.2	32.8	27.3	25.6
EAST SOUTH CENTRAL...	40.2	52.6	7.2	90.1	76.4	13.7	26.2	27.0	23.7	29.0	24.9	23.0
Kentucky.............	39.3	52.7	8.0	89.8	74.6	15.2	27.0	26.7	30.9	30.7	24.3	24.5
Tennessee............	38.2	54.6	7.2	83.2	70.0	13.2	27.3	27.2	27.4	29.3	25.2	25.2
Alabama..............	41.4	52.1	6.5	92.0	79.5	12.5	25.5	26.7	22.7	27.8	24.7	21.5
Mississippi..........	43.0	50.0	7.0	100.0	86.0	14.0	24.6	27.3	21.3	28.2	26.2	20.9
WEST SOUTH CENTRAL...	37.8	55.1	7.1	81.5	68.6	12.9	27.7	28.2	25.2	28.6	26.7	25.5
Arkansas.............	40.4	51.7	7.9	93.4	78.1	15.3	26.9	27.6	24.1	29.9	27.0	23.4
Louisiana............	39.4	54.1	6.5	84.8	72.8	12.0	26.7	28.0	23.9	28.7	24.9	21.6
Oklahoma.............	36.7	54.6	8.7	83.1	67.2	15.9	28.9	29.2	25.4	29.7	28.6	26.5
Texas................	36.9	56.5	6.6	77.0	65.3	11.7	27.9	28.1	26.7	28.1	26.7	28.4
MOUNTAIN.............	38.2	54.7	7.1	82.8	69.8	13.0	27.5	27.8	21.9	29.0	25.6	25.0
Montana..............	35.7	55.7	8.6	79.5	64.1	15.4	29.9	30.2	19.2	31.3	28.8	28.2
Idaho................	39.9	53.3	7.4	87.6	73.7	13.9	27.4	27.5	25.3	28.5	27.2	25.4
Wyoming..............	36.8	57.0	6.2	75.5	64.6	10.9	27.9	28.0	23.0	29.2	26.0	27.1
Colorado.............	34.8	56.5	8.7	77.0	61.6	15.4	29.5	29.6	28.8	31.1	27.0	25.6
New Mexico...........	43.2	51.9	4.9	92.6	83.2	9.4	24.0	24.4	19.3	25.9	22.2	21.3
Arizona..............	39.5	54.6	5.9	83.1	72.3	10.8	26.8	27.8	20.3	28.6	24.8	23.5
Utah.................	41.7	52.2	6.1	91.6	79.9	11.7	25.1	25.0	25.7	26.1	22.8	21.9
Nevada...............	31.7	61.4	6.9	62.8	51.6	11.2	31.7	32.1	25.6	33.0	29.4	31.8
PACIFIC..............	31.2	60.2	8.6	66.1	51.8	14.3	31.8	32.0	28.8	32.6	28.5	31.3
Washington...........	33.0	58.2	8.8	71.8	56.7	15.1	30.9	31.0	27.5	31.8	28.6	30.7
Oregon...............	33.0	58.3	8.7	71.5	56.6	14.9	31.6	31.7	27.2	33.3	28.5	32.3
California...........	30.5	61.0	8.5	63.9	50.0	13.9	32.1	32.3	29.0	32.7	28.4	31.2

Source: 1950 Census of Population, Vol.II, General Characteristics, Tables 63 and 64.

TRENDS IN AGE COMPOSITION OF THE POPULATION,
BY GEOGRAPHIC REGIONS: 1820-1950

Table 6-8 permits a study of the age composition of the entire nation over a period of 130 years, and a comparison of the age structures of the various regions over a period of a century or more. This table shows that the trend toward a declining proportion of children had started by 1840, if not before; the trend toward an increase in the proportion of older people also dates back to this time. This table also shows that although the

Table 6-8.--AGE COMPOSITION OF THE UNITED STATES POPULATION, BY REGIONS, 1820 TO 1950

Age and region	Year												
	1950	1940	1930	1920	1910	1900	1890[1]	1880	1870	1860	1850	1840[2]	1820[2]
UNITED STATES...	100.0	100.0	100.0	100.0	100.0	100.0	100.0	100.0	100.0	100.0	100.0	100.0	100.0
0-4 years.........	10,7	8.0	9.3	11.0	11.6	12.1	12.2	13.8	14.3	15.4	15.1	17.4[3]	18.5[3]
5-19 years........	23.2	26.4	29.5	29.8	30.4	32.3	33.9	34.3	35.4	35.8	37.4	37.2	39.4[3]
20-29 years......	15.7	17.2	16.9	17.4	18.8	18.3	18.3	18.3	17.7	18.2	18.5	18.2	} 30.0[3]
30-44 years......	21.9	21.7	21.5	21.0	20.3	19.5	18.6	17.6	17.7	17.4[4]	16.6[4]	15.7[4]	
45-64 years......	20,3	19.8	17.5	16.1	14.6	13.7	13.1	12.6	11.9	10.4[4]	9.9[4]	9.0[4]	} 12.2
65 years and over.	8.2	6.9	5.4	4.7	4.3	4.1	3.9	3.4	3.0	2.7[4]	2.6[4]	2.5[4]	
NORTHEAST.......	100.0	100.0	100.0	100.0	100.0		100.0		100.0		100.0	100.0	100.0
0-4 years.........	9.5	6.6	8.4	10.5	10.4		10.3		12.2		13.2	15.4	16.9[3]
5-19 years........	20.6	24.4	27.7	27.1	27.4		29.5		32.3		34.4	35.7	39.1[3]
20-29 years......	15.6	17.2	16.7	17.5	19.2		19.4		17.8		19.3	18.6	} 30.7[3]
30-44 years......	22.9	22.9	22.9	22.4	22.4		20.4		19.3		18.1[4]	16.9	
45-64 years......	22.6	21.6	18.6	17.5	15.9		15.3		14.2		11.6[4]	10.2	} 13.3
65 years and over.	8.7	7.2	5.6	4.9	4.8		5.1		4.2		3.4[4]	3.3	
NORTH CENTRAL...	100.0	100.0	100.0	100.0	100.0		100.0		100.0		100.0	100.0	100.0
0-4 years.........	10.5	7.7	8.9	10.5	10.8		12.3		15.1		16.3	19.3	21.6[3]
5-19 years........	22.3	25.1	28.1	28.1	29.6		33.6		36.5		39.2	38.7	40.9[3]
20-29 years......	15.4	16.7	16.5	17.5	18.7		18.5		17.5		17.8	18.2	} 29.2[3]
30-44 years......	21.5	21.7	22.1	21.5	20.5		18.7		17.4		16.1[4]	14.7	
45-64 years......	21.4	21.2	18.2	17.0	15.6		13.1		11.1		8.8[4]	7.5	} 9.2
65 years and over.	8.9	7.7	6.2	5.3	4.9		3.8		2.4		1.8[4]	1.6	
SOUTH..........	100.0	100.0	100.0	100.0	100.0		100.0		100.0		100.0	100.0	100.0
0-4 years.........	11.8	9.6	11.0	12.2	13.8		14.1		15.6		16.3	19.2	19.8[3]
5-19 years........	26.6	30.3	33.6	34.8	35.0		38.9		37.8		39.4	38.4	39.9[3]
20-29 years......	16.2	17.8	17.5	17.3	18.1		16.6		17.7		17.7	17.5	} 29.0[3]
30-44 years......	21.0	20.5	18.9	18.5	17.5		16.3		15.6		15.4[4]	14.6	
45-64 years......	17.5	16.3	14.9	13.4	12.1		11.0		10.7		8.9[4]	8.3	} 11.3
65 years and over.	6.9	5.5	4.2	3.8	3.4		3.1		2.6		2.4[4]	2.2	
WEST...........	100..	100.0	100.0	100.0	100.0		100.0		100.0		100.0		
0-4 years.........	11.0	7.6	8.2	9.8	9.8		10.6		13.0		8.4		
5-19 years........	22.0	23.6	26.3	26.3	25.9		28.2		28.7		23.0		
20-29 years......	15.8	17.1	16.6	17.1	20.7		21.5		19.8		36.4		
30-44 years......	22.7	22.4	23.2	24.0	23.8		23.3		27.0		23.4[4]		
45-64 years......	20.3	21.8	19.7	18.1	15.9		13.8		10.3		7.5[4]		
65 years and over.	8.2	7.5	6.0	4.8	3.9		2.6		1.2		1.2[4]		

[1]Excluding 325,464 persons specially enumerated in 1890 in Indian Territory and on Indian Reservations, for whom statistics of age are not available.

[2]Free whites only. Since they constituted over four-fifths of the total population, their percentages have been used here. The effect of this procedure is undoubtedly to understate the proportion in the younger ages in these years since the Negroes were a younger group than the whites. However, the percentage difference cannot be large so that no significant error is involved in using them for the total population except possibly in the South.

[3]Estimated from the age groups shown by the Census.

[4]Number of persons 40 to 44 and 60 to 64 is estimated from those 40 to 49 and 60 to 69.

Source: U.S. Census of Population: 1950, Vol. II, Part 1, Tables 38 and 61. Sixteenth Census of the United States: 1940, Vol. IV, Table 26. Data for 1820 to 1930 from W. S. Thompson and P. K. Whelpton, Population Trends in the United States, Tables 31 and 33, pp. 110 and 120.

decline has been taking place in each individual region, each region has shown unique deviations from the general trend.

The Northeast. The age composition of the various regions has been influenced by immigration from abroad, by the fertility of immigrant women, and by internal interregional migration--as well as by the vital rates of the residents. Because the Northeast received the major share of immigrants, until 1910 it tended to have above-average proportions of young adults 20-29 years of age. Also, it has had a lower than average proportion of children and a higher than average proportion of adults since 1820. This latter fact is the basis for the general assumption that the tendency toward family limitation began in the Northeast and spread westward and southward. The small proportion of children may not be due entirely to low birth rates, however. The steady inflow of young adult migrants and immigrants, who tend to arrive without children, would have helped to keep the proportion of children fairly low. On the other hand, once they were married, immigrant women may have tended to raise the low fertility rates of this most urbanized area. The precipitous drop of the birth rate of the Northeast between 1920 and 1930 (reflected in Table 6-8 in the decreased proportion of children) may have resulted partly from the restriction of immigration.

As early as 1840 the proportion of aged in the Northeast was higher than the average for the nation; the Northeast has showed this characteristic at each census up to the present. This concentration of older people seems to have been created by at least two factors: rapidly falling birth rates, and the slowing down of migration. In the earliest decades, the regions to the west were frontier areas, and their populations were young; they drew young adults from areas to their east. The aging of the population, therefore, began in the Northeast before it could start in the western regions. When immigration from abroad was curtailed, it was not fully replaced in the Northeast by increased internal migration. While the former immigrants grew old, the somewhat small crop of young native-born children was attracted westward.

The North Central. In 1950, the North Central Region's age composition was very similar to that of the nation. Its most noteworthy trait was its somewhat higher proportion of persons in the age groups 45-64 and 65 years and over, with a counterbalancing smaller proportion of persons less than 30 years of age. A high level of living which has promoted longevity, a migration drainage to the Mountain and Pacific states, and an aging of the generation of settlers and city-builders that poured into the region around the turn of the century appear to underlie this older age composition. Just as the Northeast received many immigrants and then aged rapidly when immigration was restricted, so this region received many in-migrants as it became urbanized and then aged rapidly as the interregional flow turned westward. Fertility appears to have been higher in this region than it was in the Northeast, as indicated by the proportion of children under five years of age. Its fertility was extraordinarily high in 1870 and before, but in this century seems to have declined to a point near the national average.

The West. In the stages of early settlement, the West had a very small proportion of children. This was a rather unusual circumstance, for it was not a characteristic of other frontier areas for any great length of time. From the time of its earliest censuses, the North Central Region had a very high proportion of children. As Chapter 8 will show, the proportion of women was unusually small in the West at these early dates. Apparently the ranching and mining segments of the economy encouraged a rapid influx of men, but produced an age-sex composition in which children were comparatively few. The age structure of the West in 1850 is noteworthy for another characteristic-- the virtual absence of persons 65 years of age and over. All of the inhabitants had arrived so recently that the process of aging had not really had time to pass many residents into the upper age brackets. As the West was settled by successive waves of in-migrants, the bearing of children and aging of earlier arrivals generated a more "normal" age structure. By 1910 its age structure had gradually become more like that of the nation. However, because of continued heavy in-migration and the unusual age structure of its migrants (see below), the West has had a deficit of children and a disproportionately large adult population 30-64 years of age at each recent census until 1950.

By 1930 the West had a higher proportion of people 65 years of age or over than had the nation as a whole. This fact is quite remarkable, in view of the comparative lack of oldsters in the nineteenth century. The West has retained this characteristic in the face of prolonged and rapid growth. Two factors seem to account for this concentration of older persons in the West since 1900. First, the successive waves of migrants who have remained, have aged and passed into the upper age groups. Secondly, since about 1900 or 1910, the migrants to the West appear to have had a rather unusual age composition. Instead of being heavily concentrated in the 20-29 year age group, as migrants to the West were during the nineteenth century, a larger share of the westward migrants since 1900 have been in the age groups 30-44 and 45-64. Although large numbers of persons of retirement age may not have moved West, many mature adults and middle-aged persons have made this move. Such persons pass into the retirement ages in a shorter time than do younger migrants. Also, middle-aged migrants are less likely to be accompanied by children when they move, and do not produce children after they arrive. Undoubtedly this is one reason why the proportion of children in the West has been low in the decades immediately prior to 1950.

The fact that in 1950 the West had an age composition very similar to that of the nation suggests that the economic expansion of the 1940-50 decade attracted a large number of younger migrants as well as older migrants, and that the resurgence of fertility rates was greater there than in many other areas.

The South. The South was exhibiting a higher proportion of children and a lower proportion of adults than the other divisions as early as 1870, and has retained this characteristic during each decade since 1870. From 1820 to 1870 both the North Central states and the South showed high proportions of children and youth, but after 1870

the North Central Region fell behind in this characteristic. Even before the Civil War the South appears to have begun playing its current role of exporting migrants to other regions, for even at this early date the proportion of persons 20-29 was lower than in the Northeast, North Central, and West. The exact date at which this exportation began cannot be determined from Table 6-8, however, because all of the other regions were receiving shipments of migrants of these same ages from Europe, or from other regions, and had inflated proportions of people in this age group.

From the first date at which data for age are available, the South has had unusually small proportions of older persons. Undoubtedly this is due in part to higher death rates and poorer health conditions, especially among Negroes (see Chapter 9), as well as to high fertility rates. Since 1930 the proportion of children has fallen, and the proportion of oldsters has risen rapidly. This implies that in the South the process of reducing fertility and mortality rates has been accelerated, in comparison with that of the nation.

Median age and dependency ratios are shown in Table 6-9 for each of the four regions, in each year for which data are available since 1820. From these data it may be seen that the Northeast Region has experienced a very favorable dependency ratio in comparison with the other regions from a very early date, and that the median age of its population has risen higher than has that of the other regions. Because of its concentration of persons in the years of maturity and middle age, its dependency burden for the aged has been, as yet, no greater than average, while its dependency ratios for youth have been considerably below average, even since 1820. The comparative absence of children in the West during the frontier period is emphasized by the high median age and by the much lower than average dependency ratio for youth at the censuses of 1850, 1870, 1890, and even 1910. By 1950 the dependency ratios of the West were about the same as the average for the nation.

The unusually heavy youth dependency load of the South may be traced as far back as 1820, although at that date it was below that of the North

POPULATION OF THE UNITED STATES

Table 6-9.--MEDIAN AGE AND DEPENDENCY RATIO OF THE UNITED STATES POPULATION, BY REGIONS, 1820 TO 1950

Median age and dependency ratio, by region	Year									
	1950	1940	1930	1920	1910	1890	1870	1850	1840	1820
MEDIAN AGE										
United States...............	30.3	29.1	26.6	25.3	24.3	22.1	20.2	19.0	18.1	17.0
Northeast....................	32.8	31.2	28.3	27.1	26.4	25.3	23.1	21.2	19.5	17.7
North Central...............	31.3	30.3	27.9	26.5	25.1	22.2	19.3	17.9	16.9	15.6
South.......................	27.2	25.7	23.1	21.7	20.7	18.8	18.7	17.8	17.0	16.4
West........................	30.8	31.1	29.3	28.1	26.9	25.2	24.2	25.1	...	...
DEPENDENCY RATIO, TOTAL										
United States...............	72.7	70.4	79.1	83.5	86.2	100 0	111.4	122.4	133.1	153.4[1]
Northeast....................	63.5	61.9	71.6	74.0	74.1	81.5	94.9	104.1	119.0	145.7[1]
North Central...............	71.5	68.0	76.1	78.6	82.7	98.8	117.4	134.2	147.5	171.7[1]
South.......................	82.8	83.2	95.1	103.3	109.2	127.8	127.3	138.3	148.0	163.9[1]
West........................	70.1	63.1	68.1	69.1	65.6	70.6	75.1	48.4	...	...
DEPENDENCY RATIO, YOUTH										
United States...............	58.5	58.6	69.4	74.9	78.2	92.2	105.1	116.7	127.3	146.6[1]
Northeast....................	49.3	50.2	62.0	65.5	65.7	72.2	86.7	97.1	111.8	137.6[1]
North Central...............	56.3	55.0	65.1	69.1	73.7	91.3	112.2	130.0	143.6	167.4[1]
South.......................	70.2	73.1	86.9	95.5	102.1	120.7	121.4	132.6	142.6	157.5[1]
West........................	56.1	50.9	58.0	61.0	59.1	66.2	73.0	46.7	...	...
DEPENDENCY RATIO, OLD AGE										
United States...............	14.2	11.8	9.7	8.6	8.0	7.8	6.3	5.8	5.8	6.8[1]
Northeast....................	14.2	11.7	9.6	8.5	8.3	9.3	8.2	6.9	7.2	8.1[1]
North Central...............	15.3	12.9	10.9	9.5	8.9	7.6	5.2	4.2	4.0	4.3[1]
South.......................	12.6	10.1	8.2	7.7	7.1	7.1	5.9	5.7	5.4	6.3[1]
West........................	13.9	12.2	10.1	8.1	6.5	4.4	2.1	1.8	...	...

[1]Dependency ratios for 1820 were computed by estimating age groups 45-64 years and over by the distribution of 1840.

Source: U.S.Census of Population: 1950, Vol. II, Part 1, Tables 38 and 61. Sixteenth Census of the United States: 1940, Vol. IV, Table 26. Data for 1820 to 1930 from W. S. Thompson and P. K. Whelpton, Population Trends in the United States, Tables 31 and 33, pp. 110 and 120.

Central states. In spite of the fact that dependency ratios for the South have declined over the years, they are considerably greater now, in proportion to the national average than they were in the nineteenth century. The South appears to have begun its demographic transition at a later date than did other areas, and the process seems to be less advanced than it is in other areas. However, it seems to be continuing; the South is the only region whose dependency ratio for youth was considerably lower in 1950 than in 1940.

AGE COMPOSITION AND SIZE OF PLACE

Like many other demographic traits, age composition appears to vary in a somewhat systematic way with size of place. Larger cities may tend to have birth rates and migration rates which differ from those of smaller cities. The larger cities also may have unique histories of immigration. These factors unite to give distinctive age compositions to cities of various sizes. Data showing the age compositions in 1950 of places of various sizes are given in Table 6-11. The following generalizations seem to be warranted by this table:

1. The larger the size of place, the smaller is the proportion in the younger ages. In urbanized areas of 3 million or more inhabitants, 28.0 percent of the population was less than 20 years of age in 1950. With decreasing size of place, this proportion increased fairly steadily, to 35.3 percent in incorporated places of 1,000 to 2,500.

Table 6-10.--AGE COMPOSITION OF THE UNITED STATES POPULATION, BY SIZE OF PLACE: 1950

Size of place	All ages	Age					
		0-4	5-19	20-34	35-44	45-64	65-over
Total United States.................	100.0	10.7	23.2	23.3	14.3	20.3	8.2
Urbanized areas							
3,000,000 or more..............	100.0	9.2	18.8	24.2	16.3	23.6	7.8
1,000,000 to 3,000,000.........	100.0	10.0	20.0	25.2	15.3	21.9	7.6
250,000 to 1,000,000...........	100.0	10.5	20.1	25.4	14.8	21.3	7.8
Less than 250,000..............	100.0	10.6	21.3	25.0	14.6	20.5	8.0
Outside urbanized areas							
25,000 or more.................	100.0	10.5	21.7	25.4	13.8	20.2	8.4
10,000 to 25,000...............	100.0	10.5	22.3	24.7	14.0	19.7	8.8
2,500 to 10,000................	100.0	11.0	23.4	23.5	13.6	19.2	9.2
1,000 to 2,500.................	100.0	11.0	24.3	21.8	13.3	19.4	10.3
Incorporated places less than 1,000....................	100.0	10.3	24.3	19.0	12.4	20.7	13.5
Other rural....................	100.0	12.2	29.1	20.8	12.8	17.9	7.4
Nonfarm.......................	100.0	12.9	26.8	23.8	12.9	16.3	7.2
Farm..........................	100.0	11.5	31.2	17.9	12.6	19.3	7.5

Source: U.S. Census of Population: 1950, Vol. IV, Part 5, Chapter C, Characteristics by Size of Place, Table 1.

Among the open country rural-nonfarm population ("other rural-nonfarm") it was even higher--39.7 percent--and in rural-farm areas outside urbanized areas it was 42.7 percent. The indirect meaning of this progression is that crude fertility rates tend to be inversely related to size of place.

2. The population of retirement age tends to comprise a smaller proportion of the population in the largest places, and to be a progressively larger part of the total within each smaller size-of-place grouping. For example, in 1950 people 65 years of age and over were 13.5 percent of the total population in incorporated places of less than 1,000 outside urbanized areas, but were only 7.8 percent in urbanized areas of 3 million or more inhabitants. Between these two extremes the proportion of older persons increased fairly steadily with decreasing size of place. This is the reverse of the situation that might be expected, in view of the inverse relationship between proportion of children and size of place. It would seem that a high rate of fertility in the smaller places would tend to mean that older adults would be a smaller than average part of the population. That the exact opposite occurs means that other strong factors exist. This size relationship does not extend to the open country population, however. Both the rural-nonfarm and the rural-farm population outside urbanized areas had a smaller proportion of persons 65 and over than did any of the size groups. From this fact one might infer that rural folks living in the open country tend, as they retire, to move into nearby villages or into urban places, rather than to spend their retirement in comparative isolation.

At least three hypotheses may be advanced to explain the general inverse relationship between size of place and percent of "old-age" population. First, a high proportion of the smaller places are areas of out-migration. Many young adults move away from small towns to cities, and from small cities to larger ones. This leaves a concentration of children and old folks in the smaller places. Second, the larger places have become large because they have grown rapidly as a result of receiving in-migrants over a period of several years. This has tended to increase the size of their population 20-44 years and to decrease the proportion of their youth and aged population. Third, there may be a tendency for the older populations of larger metropolitan areas to retire to smaller communities--either to the community where they were reared, to a suburban community, or to other communities in Florida, the Gulf

Coast, the Southwest, or California. This last reason, however, is purely speculative. It has been said by some that as the children of suburban families mature and leave home, the parents tend to give up the suburban home and move back into the city. As yet, data with which to test fully this hypothesis are not available.

3. Since the large places have smaller proportions of both the very young and the oldest age groups, it is evident that they should have a higher proportion of adults aged 20-64 years. However, in the largest places there is a tendency for these adults to be concentrated in the 45-64 year categories, and for this concentration to decrease with size of place. This pattern is quite uniform and pronounced. It is probably due to the fact that most of these places experienced very rapid growth between 1890 and 1930, and that the people who were attracted to them during those years have remained and are now approaching old age. If this is the explanation, and unless there is extensive out-migration of these populations to other areas within the next few years, ten or twenty

years from now these places may contain a much larger proportion of older adults than they do at present. If this happens, the present inverse relationship between the percent of the population that is 65 years of age or more and size of place will disappear.

TWENTY-FIVE LARGEST STANDARD METROPOLITAN AREAS

The 1950 age composition of the twenty-five largest standard metropolitan areas (and of their central cities and suburban rings) is reported in Table 6-11. This table shows that the S.M.A.'s vary a great deal in their age composition. For example, Dallas, Atlanta, Houston, Washington, D.C., and Detroit have extraordinarily small proportions of aged persons in their population. Boston, Providence, Portland (Oregon), Cincinnati, Los Angeles, and Seattle, on the other hand, have a proportion of aged that is 50 percent, or more, greater than that of the "younger" S.M.A.'s. Similar differences may be noted for the youngest age

Table 6-11.—AGE COMPOSITION OF THE TWENTY-FIVE LARGEST STANDARD METROPOLITAN AREAS IN 1950

S.M.A.	S.M.A. Percent of population in each age group						Central city Percent of population in each age group						Suburban ring Percent of population in each age group					
	0-4	5-19	20-29	30-44	45-64	65-over	0-4	5-19	20-29	30-44	45-64	65-over	0-4	5-19	20-29	30-44	45-64	65-over
New York-Northeastern N.J.....	8.9	18.8	15.7	24.6	24.2	7.7	8.5	18.4	16.1	24.7	24.7	7.6	9.8	19.6	14.9	24.6	23.2	7.8
Chicago, Ill..................	9.5	19.4	16.1	24.3	23.3	7.4	9.0	18.3	16.5	24.5	24.0	7.6	10.5	21.5	15.3	23.8	21.9	7.0
Los Angeles, Calif...........	9.7	18.7	15.5	24.5	22.4	9.1	8.8	16.8	15.9	24.9	24.0	9.6	10.5	20.2	15.2	24.3	21.0	8.7
Philadelphia, Pa.............	9.4	20.7	16.2	23.4	22.1	8.1	8.9	19.9	16.5	23.6	22.9	8.3	10.1	21.8	15.9	23.1	21.2	7.9
Detroit, Mich................	10.8	21.5	17.1	23.8	21.4	5.4	9.9	19.9	17.4	24.1	23.0	5.7	12.2	23.9	16.5	23.4	18.9	5.1
Boston-Lowell-Lawrence, Mass..	9.5	20.6	15.7	21.6	22.7	9.9	9.0	20.1	15.5	21.6	22.7	9.9	9.7	20.9	15.5	21.6	22.7	9.9
San Francisco-Oakland, Calif..	10.3	18.0	17.4	24.7	21.7	7.9	8.5	15.5	16.5	24.8	25.1	9.5	12.4	20.6	18.3	24.7	18.0	6.1
Pittsburgh, Pa...............	9.9	21.6	16.5	23.2	21.0	7.8	9.2	20.1	17.0	22.9	22.5	8.3	10.2	22.3	16.2	23.3	20.4	7.5
St. Louis, Mo................	9.9	20.1	16.2	23.1	22.4	8.5	9.0	18.1	16.7	22.9	23.9	9.4	10.7	22.0	15.7	23.3	20.8	7.5
Cleveland, Ohio..............	10.2	18.9	16.0	24.2	23.0	7.7	10.0	18.2	17.4	24.0	22.7	7.8	10.5	20.0	13.8	24.7	23.5	7.6
Washington, D.C..............	10.9	19.0	19.0	26.5	18.8	5.9	8.9	16.8	19.5	26.1	21.6	7.1	13.4	21.6	18.4	26.9	15.2	4.4
Baltimore, Md................	10.4	21.2	17.5	24.0	20.2	6.8	9.7	20.3	17.2	23.9	21.5	7.4	12.1	23.3	18.2	24.2	16.8	5.4
Minneapolis-St. Paul, Minn....	10.9	20.1	16.8	21.4	22.3	8.4	9.8	18.9	17.5	20.7	23.8	9.3	14.2	23.6	15.0	23.2	18.1	5.9
Buffalo, N.Y.................	10.0	20.9	15.7	23.0	22.5	7.9	9.0	19.6	16.2	22.7	24.1	8.4	11.1	22.4	15.1	23.4	20.6	7.5
Cincinnati, Ohio.............	10.1	20.2	15.7	22.5	22.4	9.1	9.6	18.9	16.3	22.0	23.3	10.0	10.8	21.9	15.0	23.1	21.3	7.9
Milwaukee, Wis...............	9.9	19.9	16.2	22.9	23.4	7.7	9.6	19.0	17.0	22.6	23.7	8.1	10.6	22.6	14.1	23.6	22.5	6.7
Kansas City, Mo..............	10.1	19.2	16.7	23.1	22.2	8.7	8.9	17.3	17.4	23.3	23.9	9.2	11.6	21.7	15.9	22.8	20.0	8.0
Houston, Tex.................	11.6	22.0	18.8	25.4	17.4	4.7	11.0	20.7	19.5	25.4	18.4	5.0	13.4	25.8	16.9	25.3	14.7	3.9
Seattle, Wash.........'......	10.8	18.8	16.2	23.4	21.7	9.1	9.2	16.9	16.8	23.2	23.8	10.2	13.6	22.1	15.1	23.9	18.0	7.2
Portland, Oreg...............	10.4	20.1	14.2	22.8	22.8	9.7	9.2	17.3	14.6	22.9	25.0	11.0	11.7	23.2	13.8	22.6	20.4	8.3
New Orleans, La..............	11.1	21.3	17.6	23.3	20.1	6.7	10.5	20.5	17.5	23.3	21.0	7.1	14.1	24.9	18.1	23.2	15.5	4.3
Providence, R.I..............	9.5	20.4	16.2	22.3	22.5	9.1	8.9	19.8	17.3	21.7	22.6	9.8	9.9	20.8	15.6	22.6	22.4	8.7
Atlanta, Ga..................	11.1	22.1	18.3	24.1	18.2	6.0	9.8	20.3	18.9	24.3	19.9	6.7	12.4	23.9	17.7	23.9	16.6	5.4
Dallas, Tex..................	11.1	20.5	18.4	24.8	19.3	5.9	10.8	18.7	19.0	25.6	20.0	6.1	12.2	24.7	17.0	23.1	17.6	5.3
Louisville, Ky...............	11.2	21.3	16.8	22.7	20.1	7.9	10.6	19.9	17.6	22.7	21.0	8.3	12.2	23.8	15.4	22.7	18.7	7.3
Mean......................	10.3	20.2	16.7	23.6	21.5	7.7	9.4	18.8	17.2	23.5	22.8	8.3	11.6	22.4	15.9	23.7	19.6	6.8

Source: Compiled for this study from U.S. Census of Population: 1950, individual volumes for each state, Tables 33 and 41.

groups. The proportion of the population that is 0-4 years of age is considerably higher in the southern S.M.A.'s than in the northern. The dependency load for children is lowest in New York, San Francisco, Chicago, and Los Angeles.

In general, the suburban rings of S.M.A.'s have a considerably higher proportion of their population in the youngest age classes, and a considerably smaller proportion of their population in the upper age groups, than do the central cities. Since the ring areas have been growing rapidly in recent decades, it must be concluded that they have been attracting a large segment of young adults who are in the childbearing years. Apparently, older people (including persons 45-64 years of age) have not settled in the suburban areas as rapidly as have those 30-44 years of age. However, in most central cities the proportion of persons who are 20-29 years of age is higher than it is in the sub-urban ring. This leads to the supposition that the movement to the suburban ring is not a movement of the very youngest adults, but of those who are over 30 but less than 45 years of age. It appears to be a movement of well-established families with young children, rather than a movement of newly married couples.

Dependency ratios, by type of dependency, are reported in Table 6-12 for each S.M.A., by central city and ring. In general, the central cities carry a considerably smaller total dependency load than do the suburban rings, because of their lower proportion of infants, children, and youth. In most cases, the dependency load for older persons is somewhat higher in the central city than in the suburban area; thus the total dependency load varies less between the center and the periphery than does either type of dependency taken by itself.

Table 6-12.--MEDIAN AGE AND DEPENDENCY RATIOS OF THE TWENTY-FIVE LARGEST STANDARD METROPOLITAN AREAS IN 1950

S.M.A.	S.M.A.				Central city				Suburban ring			
	Median age	Dependency ratio			Median age	Dependency ratio			Median age	Dependency ratio		
		Total	Youth	Old age		Total	Youth	Old age		Total	Youth	Old age
New York-Northeastern N.J....	34.0	54.9	43.0	11.9	34.3	52.8	41.1	11.7	33.5	59.4	46.9	12.5
Chicago, Ill.................	32.9	57.1	45.5	11.6	33.6	53.7	42.1	11.6	31.7	64.1	52.6	11.4
Los Angeles, Calif..........	33.5	60.1	45.5	14.6	35.0	54.4	39.5	14.9	32.5	65.1	50.7	14.4
Philadelphia, Pa............	32.2	61.9	48.8	13.1	32.9	58.8	45.7	13.1	31.4	66.0	52.9	13.1
Detroit, Mich...............	30.4	60.5	51.8	8.7	31.6	55.0	46.2	8.8	28.4	70.2	61.5	8.6
Boston-Lowell-Lawrence, Mass.	32.8	66.7	50.2	16.5	32.7	63.7	47.6	16.1	33.0	68.2	51.5	16.7
San Francisco-Oakland, Calif.	32.4	56.7	44.4	12.3	35.7	50.5	36.1	14.3	29.3	64.0	54.0	10.0
Pittsburgh, Pa..............	31.2	64.7	51.9	12.8	32.3	60.2	46.9	13.3	30.8	66.8	54.2	12.6
St. Louis, Mo...............	32.5	62.2	48.5	13.7	34.1	57.6	42.8	14.8	31.0	67.4	54.8	12.5
Cleveland, Ohio.............	32.8	58.2	46.0	12.2	32.5	56.2	44.1	12.1	33.5	61.6	49.3	12.3
Washington, D.C.............	30.6	55.7	46.6	9.1	32.6	48.8	38.3	10.5	28.2	65.0	57.7	7.3
Baltimore, Md...............	30.6	62.2	51.2	11.0	31.7	59.6	47.9	11.8	28.0	69.0	59.8	9.2
Minneapolis-St. Paul, Minn...	31.4	65.2	51.3	13.9	32.6	61.3	46.3	15.0	28.1	77.9	67.4	10.5
Buffalo, N.Y................	32.0	63.4	50.5	12.9	33.2	58.8	45.5	13.3	30.9	69.0	56.7	12.3
Cincinnati, Ohio............	32.6	65.0	50.1	14.9	33.6	62.3	46.2	16.2	31.5	68.5	55.2	13.3
Milwaukee, Wis..............	32.5	60.1	47.7	12.4	32.8	58.1	45.2	12.9	31.7	66.1	55.1	11.1
Kansas City, Mo.............	32.4	61.5	47.4	14.0	34.0	55.1	40.7	14.3	30.5	70.5	56.8	13.7
Houston, Tex................	28.8	62.2	54.6	7.6	29.4	57.9	50.0	7.9	26.4	75.8	69.0	6.8
Seattle, Wash...............	32.5	63.0	48.2	14.8	34.4	56.8	40.8	16.0	29.5	75.2	62.6	12.6
Portland, Oreg..............	33.4	67.2	50.9	16.3	35.8	60.1	42.5	17.6	30.9	76.0	61.4	14.5
New Orleans, La.............	30.0	64.1	53.2	10.9	30.9	61.8	50.3	11.5	26.1	76.4	68.8	7.6
Providence, R.I.............	32.5	64.0	49.1	14.9	32.6	62.5	46.6	15.9	32.5	64.9	50.6	14.3
Atlanta, Ga.................	29.2	64.8	54.8	10.0	30.6	58.2	47.6	10.5	27.7	71.8	62.4	9.3
Dallas, Tex.................	30.0	59.8	50.4	9.4	30.9	54.9	45.4	9.5	27.7	73.1	64.0	9.1
Louisville, Ky..............	30.4	67.7	54.5	13.3	31.2	63.3	49.8	13.5	29.1	76.3	63.4	12.9
Mean.......................	31.7	62.0	49.4	12.5	32.8	57.7	44.6	13.1	30.2	69.1	57.6	11.5

Source: Compiled for this study from U.S. Census of Population: 1950, individual volumes for each state, Tables 33 and 41.

There are large differences among the dependency loads which various S. M. A. populations carry. The lowest dependency loads are carried by New York, Washington, D. C., Chicago, and Cleveland. The highest dependency loads are carried by Louisville, Ky., Portland, Oreg., Boston-Lowell-Lawrence, Minneapolis-St. Paul, and Cincinnati; high ratios of older persons to adults, combined with moderately large proportions of children, create these large dependency ratios. There are also great differences among central cities and among rings in dependency loads, and in the types of dependency loads which they carry. A detailed research study of past migration history and of recent trends in fertility and mortality rates would be necessary to account for these variations.

CONCLUSION

The present chapter has explained the processes which create the age composition of a population and which cause age composition to change. It has also shown how those processes have actually caused the populations of the geographic divisions, the urban and rural areas, and the major metropolitan areas of the United States to differ from each other and to change over a period of time. However, equally important aspects of age composition have been left unstudied. Among these is the analysis of how age composition varies with sex, race, education, occupation, income, marital status, and many other population traits. Also undiscussed is the fact that the changing numbers of persons in each age group imply an increased need for schools, houses, and employment, and a future demand for a great variety of commodities and services. The chapters that follow consider each of the various population characteristics, and the major population problems related to them. Each of these chapters has a separate section pertaining to age composition and the implications of the aging process with respect to the subject of the chapter. In demography, age analysis is a very pervasive consideration. It is impossible to assemble all of the age information in one place. Instead, it is necessary to establish the basic principles of age analysis, to describe the broad trends, and then to allow age to become a variable which is considered in the discussion of almost every other population topic.

Note: The future age composition of the population is discussed in Chapter 26.

Chapter 7

COLOR-NATIVITY-RACE COMPOSITION[*]

Like the characteristic of age, the population characteristics of color, nativity, and race have a social significance that reaches into almost every sphere of inquiry. Innate biological differences between races and nationality groups in regard to their physical health, longevity, and mental abilities are commonly thought to be far smaller than are the observed differences. Nevertheless, the fact should not be overlooked or minimized that actual differences of considerable magnitude are known to exist in the population of the United States at the present time. The course of history and culture-building has created systems involving attitudes toward and prescriptions for the behavior of various minority groups, and the behavior of these groups with respect to each other. These culture forces, and the limiting effect they have upon living conditions and access to income and social position, probably account for a very large share of the observable differences in behavior and capacities between racial and ethnic groups. Because parentage is one of the few traits which a human being cannot change, except by subterfuge, these cultural definitions tend to prescribe class (and even caste) lines which help to determine several other demographic, economic, and social characteristics. For these reasons, the color, nativity, and race composition of a population, and the social and economic characteristics of each race and ethnic group, are matters of rather universal interest. Population statistics provide much of the factual information which is available concerning the conditions under which each group lives and the ways in which the relative positions of the groups are changing. For much of the

demographic analysis in the United States, ethnic and racial origin are basic variables that must be controlled before the effect of other factors can be considered.

THE CENSUS INQUIRY CONCERNING COLOR, NATIVITY, AND RACE

As a part of each decennial enumeration, the Bureau of the Census is asked to perform the difficult task of classifying the population by race, nativity, and national origin. The cultural definitions of these classifications vary throughout the nation. A scientifically accurate and completely reliable system for classifying individuals into race and ethnic types, either on a physical or a cultural basis (or a combination of both), is something that anthropologists have not yet succeeded in developing. Even when highly elaborate measurements have been made of skeletal dimensions and proportions, of facial features, and of degree of pigmentation, and when place of residence of ancestors has been determined, a completely unambiguous classification has not yet been achieved. It is easy to see that anthropologically untrained census enumerators, whose biases on and attitudes toward the subject run the same gamut as do those of the general population, cannot even hope to make a refined and completely reliable classification when such a classification has

---

[*]A tabulation presenting statistics for color by age and sex, and for nativity, for the total, urban, rural-nonfarm, and rural-farm areas of each geographic division, for both 1950 and 1940, is contained in the Statistical Appendix.

thus far proved to be impossible under laboratory conditions. Many people would be offended, sensitive, or evasive about direct questions pertaining to this subject. The enumeration of Indians, for example, may be performed rather poorly unless the enumerators are extraordinarily conscientious and obtain full cooperation of the local officials at reservations. As a consequence, the census inquiry must be limited to aspects of race (a) that cannot be hidden from the enumerator, (b) about which the census enumerator can make assumptions without serious error, and (c) about which people will be willing to furnish information.

The Bureau of the Census must take into account other considerations in making its racial and ethnic classifications. It cannot afford to enumerate and tabulate data for racial or ethnic groups that are so small as to constitute an infinitesimal fraction of the whole population. In addition, many laws and governmental programs involve racial and ethnic considerations, and have their own special definitions of the persons to whom they apply. Legislatures and courts need statistics about the number of persons who are subject to these laws, and where these persons are located. The Census must make its inquiry in such a way that these groups, defined by law or administrative practice, are matched by official counts.

For these reasons, the present census classifications of nativity and race in the United States consist of a set of categories which combine color and place of origin of ancestors; Negroes are identified as a separate race. When given in full detail, the classifications are as follows:

White races
  a. Native-born
  b. Foreign-born
Nonwhite races
  a. Negro
  b. Indian
  c. Chinese
  d. Japanese
  e. Other nonwhite races
    Filipino
    Hindu
    Korean
    Other

In this chapter, the above categories (or combinations of them) will be referred to as the color-nativity-race classification. Enumerators are instructed to obtain much of the racial information by observation and to ask a question when they are in doubt.[1] It is presumed that all members of the household are of the same racial grouping as is the informant, if the informant is related to the other members. Mexicans are enumerated as white (in the 1930 census publications they are included with the group "other races."). A special coding step was introduced in 1950 to permit their separate tabulation in four southwestern states as "persons of Spanish surname." Persons of mixed white and nonwhite parentage are classed according to the classification of the nonwhite parent. Persons of mixed white and Indian parentage are classed as Indians if they are living on a reservation, if they claim major Indian ancestry, or if they report being of one-fourth Indian ancestry or more. Persons of mixed Negro and Indian parentage are classified as Negro unless the Indian blood very definitely predominates or unless the individual is accepted in the community as an Indian. In 1950, for the first time, an attempt was made to identify persons of mixed white, Negro, and Indian ancestry living in certain communities in the eastern United States in a special category so that they might be included in the category "other races." Mixtures of nonwhite races are reported according to the race of the father.

The classification given above is used in making basic counts of population characteristics. The counts for the foreign-born are supplemented by tabulations according to country of birth, both for the foreign-born white and for the total foreign-born (including nonwhite). Statistics for the foreign-born who are classified by country of birth are considered in Chapter 14, as a part of the study of international migration. For cross-tabulating race and nativity with other population

---

[1]This paragraph is paraphrased from U. S. Bureau of the Census. U. S. Census of Population: 1950. Vol. II, Characteristics of the Population, Part I, U. S. Summary, Chapter C, pp. XII-XIII.

characteristics, various combinations of the basic categories are made. Sometimes a four-fold division is made: Native white, foreign-born white, Negro, and other nonwhite.

COLOR-NATIVITY-RACE COMPOSITION
FROM 1790 TO 1960

The color composition of the population in 1960 is estimated to be:

	White	Nonwhite
Population (millions)..........	159.8	20.3
Percent of total...............	88.7	11.3
Percent change (1950 to 1960)..	18.4	28.8

Table 7-1 reports the number of persons who were in each of the major color, nativity, and race categories at each census from 1790 to 1950. Table 7-2 expresses these figures as percent distributions, and Table 7-3 presents percent changes between censuses. In 1950, roughly 90 percent of the total population was classed as white, and 10 percent as nonwhite (see Table 7-2). These proportions had remained almost unchanged for thirty years. Before 1920, the nonwhite population comprised a larger proportion of the total population, as Figure 7-1 indicates. In 1790, Negroes were 19.3 percent of the total population, or about twice the proportion they constituted in 1950. All but a very small part of the Negro population arrived as slaves. At the time of the Civil War, about 90 percent of the Negroes still had that status. The landing of additional slaves was prohibited by law after 1808. Between the Census of 1810 and the Census of 1930, the proportion of Negroes declined. During much of this time large numbers of white immigrants were pouring in from Europe to swell the size of the white population (see statistics for foreign-born in Tables 7-1 to 7-3). Hence, the white population was growing both by natural increase and by migration, while the Negro population could grow only by natural increase. Because of high death rates (see chapter on Mortality for details), the Negro population was able to grow only at a pace considerably slower than that of the white population, until recent years. This fact may be observed by comparing the rates of intercensal change, shown in Table 7-3, for native whites and Negroes.

Table 7-1.—COLOR, NATIVITY, AND RACE COMPOSITION OF THE POPULATION OF THE UNITED STATES: 1790 TO 1950

Year	White			Nonwhite							
	Total	Native	Foreign born	Total nonwhite	Negro		Other nonwhite races				
					Total	Slave	Total	Indian	Japanese	Chinese	All other
1950........	134,942,028	124,780,860	10,161,168	15,755,333	15,042,286	...	713,047	343,410	141,768	117,629	110,240
1940........	118,214,870	106,795,732	11,419,138	13,454,405	12,865,518	...	588,887	333,969	126,947	77,504	50,467
1930........	110,286,740	96,303,335	13,983,405	12,488,306	11,891,143	...	597,163	332,397	138,834	74,954	50,978
1920........	94,820,915	81,108,161	13,712,754	10,889,705	10,463,131	...	426,574	244,437	111,010	61,639	9,488
1910........	81,731,957	68,386,412	13,345,545	10,240,309	9,827,763	...	412,546	265,683	72,157	71,531	3,175
1900........	66,809,196	56,595,379	10,213,817	9,185,379	8,833,994	...	351,385	237,196	24,326	89,863	...
1890........	55,101,258	45,979,391	9,121,867	7,846,456	7,488,676	...	357,780	248,253	2,039	107,488	...
1880........	43,402,970	36,843,291	6,559,679	6,752,813	6,580,793	...	172,020	66,407	148	105,465	...
1870........	33,589,377	28,095,665	5,493,712	4,968,994	4,880,009	...	88,985	25,731	55	63,199	...
1860........	26,922,537	22,825,784	4,096,753	4,520,784	4,441,830	3,953,760	78,954	44,021	...	34,933	...
1850........	19,553,068	17,312,533	2,240,535	3,638,808	3,638,808	3,204,313	...	...	...	...	...
1840........	14,195,805	...	...	2,873,648	2,873,648	2,487,355	...	...	...	...	...
1830........	10,537,378	...	...	2,328,642	2,328,642	2,009,043	...	...	...	...	...
1820........	7,866,797	...	...	1,771,656	1,771,656	1,538,022	...	...	...	...	...
1810........	5,862,073	...	...	1,377,808	1,377,808	1,191,362	...	...	...	...	...
1800........	4,306,446	...	...	1,002,037	1,002,037	893,602	...	...	...	...	...
1790........	3,172,006	...	...	757,208	757,208	697,681	...	...	...	...	...

Source: U.S. Bureau of the Census, Historical Statistics of the United States, 1789-1945, Washington, D.C., 1949, Tables B 13-23, and B 40-47; U.S. Census of Population: 1950, Volume II, Part 1, Table 36.

(a) Persons of Mexican ancestry are classed as white. In 1930, Mexicans were enumerated separately; the census count was 1,422,533. In 1950, an approximation of the Mexican population was made by identifying persons of Spanish surname in the census returns for 5 states known to have a concentration of Mexican population. The census count was 2,289,550.

(b) Counts of some individual groups, enumerated separately in several censuses and included in this group was as follows: Filipinos (1950), 47,272; Filipinos (1940), 45,563; Hindu (1940), 2,405; Korean (1940), 1,711; Filipinos (1930) 45,208; Hindu (1930), 3,130; Korean (1930), 1,860.

Table 7-2.—COLOR, NATIVITY, AND RACE COMPOSITION OF THE POPULATION OF THE UNITED STATES: 1790 TO 1950

Color, nativity, and race	Year																
	1950	1940	1930	1920	1910	1900	1890	1880	1870	1860	1850	1840	1830	1820	1810	1800	1790
All races....	100.0	100.0	100.0	100.0	100.0	100.0	100.0	100.0	100.0	100.0	100.0	100.0	100.0	100.0	100.0	100.0	100.0
White, total......	89.5	89.8	89.8	89.7	88.9	87.9	87.5	86.5	87.1	85.6	84.3	83.2	81.9	81.6	81.0	81.1	80.7
Native.........	82.8	81.1	78.4	76.7	74.4	74.5	73.0	73.4	72.9	72.6	74.6	...	...	...	...	...	...
Foreign born....	6.7	8.7	11.4	13.0	14.5	13.4	14.5	13.1	14.2	13.0	9.7	...	...	...	...	...	...
Nonwhite, total...	10.5	10.2	10.2	10.3	11.1	12.1	12.5	13.5	12.9	14.4	15.7	16.8	18.1	18.4	19.0	18.9	19.3
Negro..........	10.0	9.8	9.7	9.9	10.7	11.6	11.9	13.1	12.7	14.1	15.7	16.8	18.1	18.4	19.0	18.9	19.3
Other races.....	0.5	0.4	0.5	0.4	0.4	0.5	0.6	0.4	0.2	0.3	...	...	...	...	...	...	...
Indian........	0.2	0.3	0.3	0.2	0.3	0.3	0.4	0.1	0.1	0.1	...	...	...	...	...	...	...
Japanese......	0.1	0.1	0.1	0.1	0.1	...	...	...	...	...	...	...	...	...	...	...	...
Chinese.......	0.1	0.1	0.1	0.1	0.1	0.1	0.2	0.2	0.2	0.1	...	...	...	...	...	...	...
All other.....	0.1	...	...	...	...	...	...	...	...	...	...	...	...	...	...	...	...

Source: Data for 1850 to 1950 from U.S. Census of Population: 1950, Volume II, Part 1, Table 36; data for 1790 to 1840 from W. S. Thompson and P. K. Whelpton, Population Trends in the United States, Table 3, p. 6.

The last half of the nineteenth century witnessed the immigration of Chinese populations, and during the early decades of the twentieth century there was an influx of Japanese. In 1950, each of these two oriental populations comprised 0.1 percent of the total population. American Indians comprised 0.2 percent. The census counts of the Indian, Japanese, and Chinese groups, at each census from 1860 to 1950, are shown in Table 7-1, and are illustrated graphically in Figure 7-2. Other nonwhite races combined (Korean, Filipino, Asiatic Indian, etc.) were 0.1 percent of the total population. Thus, in 1950 there were slightly less than three-fourths of a million persons of nonwhite races other than Negro; and only about one

person in 475 was classed as a member of a nonwhite race other than Negro. When statistics for the entire United States are considered, the category "nonwhite" is almost equivalent to the category "Negro," because the Negro population in 1950 was 95.5 percent of the nonwhite population. In particular regions and subregions, such as the West, which have concentrations of American Indians and Japanese populations but a comparatively small Negro population, it would not be correct to consider "nonwhite" nearly equivalent to Negro (see the discussion of regional distribution below).

Beginning in 1850 the white population was subclassified by nativity--that is, into native- and foreign-born. At that time, 9.7 percent of the to-

Table 7-3.—DECENNIAL PERCENT CHANGE IN UNITED STATES POPULATION, BY COLOR, NATIVITY, AND RACE: 1800 TO 1950

Color, nativity, and race	Rate of decennial change during decade ending in:															
	1950	1940	1930	1920	1910	1900	1890	1880	1870	1860	1850	1840	1830	1820	1810	1800
Total.........	14.5	7.2	16.1	14.9	21.0	20.7	25.5	30.1	22.6	35.6	35.9	32.7	33.5	33.1	36.4	35.1
White, total........	14.1	7.2	16.3	16.0	22.3	21.2	27.0	29.2	24.8	37.7	37.7	34.7	33.9	34.2	36.1	35.8
Native...........	16.8	10.9	18.7	18.6	20.8	23.1	24.8	31.1	23.1	31.8	...	...	...	...	...	...
Foreign born......	-11.0	-18.3	2.0	2.8	30.7	12.0	39.0	19.4	34.1	82.8	...	...	...	...	...	...
Nonwhite, total.....	17.1	7.7	14.7	6.3	11.5	17.1	16.2	35.9	9.9	24.2	...	...	...	...	...	...
Negro...........	16.9	8.2	13.6	6.5	11.2	18.0	13.8	34.9	9.9	22.1	26.6	23.4	31.4	28.6	37.5	32.3
Other races......	21.1	-1.4	40.0	3.4	17.4	-1.8	108.0	93.3	12.7	...	...	...	...	...	...	...
Indian..........	2.8	0.5	36.0	-8.0	12.0	-4.5	273.8	158.1	-41.5	...	...	...	...	...	...	...
Japanese........	11.7	-8.6	25.1	53.8	196.6	1093.0	1277.7	169.1	...	...	...	...	...	...	...	...
Chinese.........	51.8	3.4	21.6	-13.8	-20.4	-16.4	1.9	66.9	80.9	...	...	...	...	...	...	...
All other.......	118.4	-1.0	437.3	198.8	...	...	...	...	...	...	...	...	...	...	...	...

Source: U.S. Census of Population: 1950, Volume II, Table 36; data prior to 1860 from W. S. Thompson and P. K. Whelpton, Population Trends in the United States, Table 4.

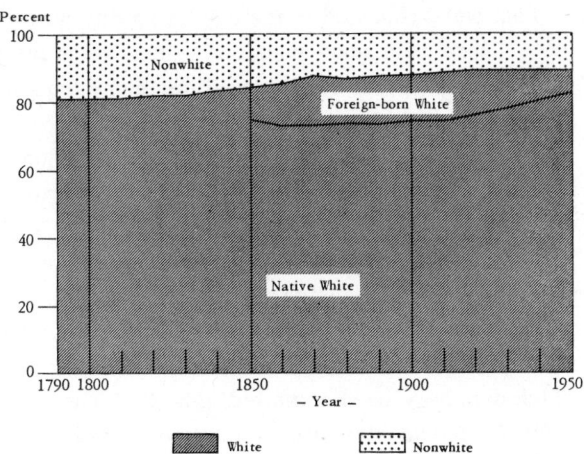

FIGURE 7 - 1. COLOR AND NATIVITY COMPOSITION OF THE UNITED STATES POPULATION, 1790 TO 1950

tal population consisted of foreign-born whites. During the following decades of heavy immigration, this proportion rose to a high of 14.5 percent both in 1890 and 1910. As the immigrants who arrived in the nineteenth century aged and began to die, a larger influx of immigrants would have been required to maintain the same proportion of foreign-born in the population. But restrictions upon immigration began to be imposed; they became increasingly severe during the second decade of the twentieth century. Finally, the "quota system," which has restricted immigration severely, was established in the early 1920's (see

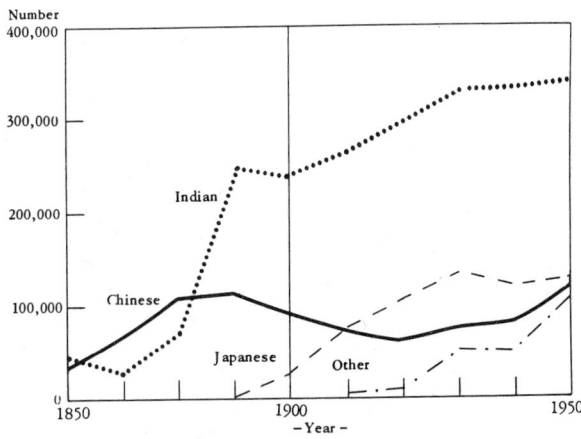

FIGURE 7 - 2. POPULATION OF THE MINOR NONWHITE RACES, UNITED STATES, 1850 TO 1950

Chapter 14). As a result, the proportion of foreign-born has fallen very rapidly during the past three decades. On the one hand, the foreign-born population already residing in the nation has passed into the upper ages where death rates are high, and thus is dying out. The number of foreign-born white persons has declined rapidly from the peak of almost 14 million which was reached in 1930 to about 10 million in 1950. In 1950 the foreign-born white population was 6.7 percent of the total population; this was less than half of what it had been in 1910. If the foreign-born population remains at a constant number, while the rest of the population continues to grow, it is destined to become an even smaller proportion of the total than it was in 1950.

Table 7-3 provides several interesting insights concerning the decennial rates of growth of the race and nativity groups, from 1790 to 1950. First, it shows the rapid rate of growth and then the equally rapid rate of decline of the foreign-born population. Second, it shows that the Negro population grew at a slower rate than did the native white population during almost all decades prior to 1940-50. During the two decades 1940 to 1960, however, the Negro population grew slightly faster than the white. This represents a new development, which will be explained in more detail below. The growth rates of the "Other races" (sometimes called "minor nonwhite races") have been erratic. The irregularities in the statistics are due in part to the difficulties of enumerating precisely small and sometimes dispersed populations to the changing content of the group (especially the inclusion of special communities of mixed white-Indian-Negro parentage in 1950), and in part to the fact that (except for Indians) each minor nonwhite race entered the population within a span of a few years, and the growth of each has been dependent upon natural increase.

URBAN-RURAL RESIDENCE, BY COLOR, NATIVITY, AND RACE

Native white populations and Negro populations, the two largest color-nativity groups, were distributed between urban and rural territories in almost identical proportions in 1950; about 62-63 percent of each was in urban areas (see Table 7-4). Within rural areas their distribution was less similar: proportionately more Negroes than native whites were residing on farms, and proportionately fewer Negroes were residing in rural-nonfarm areas. This difference arises, in large part, from the relative concentration of Negroes in southern agricultural areas and from the relative scarcity of Negroes in suburban areas of northern cities.

Foreign-born white populations have tended to be heavily concentrated in urban areas; in 1950, 83.5 percent were residents of urban places. Table 7-5 shows that this has been an outstanding characteristic of the foreign-born white population since 1870 and probably for several decades before, judging from the fact that the proportion of the foreign-born white population that was urban in 1870 was more than twice that of the native white urban population. Japanese and Chinese populations also are more urbanized than is the population at large.

The American Indian population has had an outstandingly different urban-rural distribution. More than one-half of this group was living in rural villages (primarily on reservations) in 1950, and almost one-third was living on farms. Only 16.3

percent were reported in the census as city dwellers. There is a good possibility that, when they are enumerated off the reservation, many Indians are misjudged to be Negro or white.

The 1950 distribution, described above, is only a cross-section of a rapidly changing urban-rural distribution of the various color, nativity, and race groups. The fact that Negroes were imported as slave labor for plantations dictated that they would have a more rural distribution than the white population. Since 1820, the earliest date for which data have been compiled, this difference has existed. It had almost completely disappeared by 1950. From Table 7-5 it may be inferred that the Negro population has been urbanizing since 1820, but that its cityward movement has proceeded at an extraordinarily rapid pace since 1920, and especially during the 1940-50 decade. The large percentage changes in the nonwhite composition of urban and rural areas during the 1940-50 decade are shown in Figure 7-3.

From 1820 to 1910, as the urbanization movement gained momentum, the urbanization of the white population proceeded at a more rapid pace than did that of the Negro population. (Rate of urbanization is defined in terms of intercensal change in the proportion of population residing in urban places, and is obtained from Table 7-5 by subtracting the percent urban at the beginning of

Table 7-4.—URBAN-RURAL DISTRIBUTION OF THE UNITED STATES POPULATION, BY COLOR, NATIVITY, AND RACE, 1950 AND PERCENT-CHANGE DIFFERENCE: 1940 TO 1950

Urban-rural residence	All races	White			Nonwhite						
		Total	Native	Foreign born	Total	Negro	Other races				
							Total	Indian	Japanese	Chinese	All other
PERCENT DISTRIBUTION, 1950											
U.S. total...........	100.0	100.0	100.0	100.0	100.0	100.0	100.0	100.0	100.0	100.0	100.0
Urban (new definition)....	64.0	64.3	62.7	83.5	61.6	62.4	44.7	16.3	71.1	93.0	47.5
Rural nonfarm.............	20.7	21.1	21.9	11.0	17.2	16.6	30.8	52.0	10.1	5.0	18.9
Rural farm...............	15.3	14.6	15.4	5.4	21.2	21.0	24.5	31.6	18.9	2.0	33.6
PERCENT CHANGE, 1940-50											
U.S. total...........	14.5	14.1	16.8	-11.0	17.1	16.9	21.1	2.8	11.7	51.8	118.4
Urban (old definition)....	19.5	17.2	22.6	-7.1	43.5	43.2	61.5	108.7	44.6	55.8	71.7
Rural nonfarm.............	43.2	43.4	45.3	-18.3	40.4	38.0	55.6	-6.4	-28.4	12.6	189.9
Rural farm...............	-23.6	-22.5	-21.8	-39.5	-29.8	-29.8	-30.2	...	...	...	...

Source: U.S. Census of Population: 1950, Volume II, Part 1, Table 36 and estimates prepared for this study.

Table 7-5.—PERCENT OF THE POPULATION CLASSED AS URBAN, BY COLOR, NATIVITY, AND RACE: 1820 TO 1950

Year	Total	White			Nonwhite	
		Total white	Native	Foreign born	Total nonwhite	Negro
1950 (new definition)..........	64.0	64.3	62.7	83.7	61.6	62.4
1950 (old definition)..........	59.0	59.0	...	...	58.8	...
1940..........................	56.5	57.5	55.1	80.0	47.9	48.6
1930..........................	56.2	57.6	54.5	79.2	43.2	43.7
1920..........................	51.4	53.4	49.6	75.5	33.8	34.0
1910..........................	45.8	48.2	43.6	71.4	27.2	27.3
1900..........................	40.0	42.4	38.1	66.0	22.6	22.7
1890..........................	35.1	37.5	32.9	60.7	...	19.8
1870..........................	25.7	28.0	23.1	53.4	...	13.5
1850..........................	15.3	...	...	...	...	7.8
1840..........................	10.8	12.4	...	...	...	7.6
1820..........................	7.2	7.3	...	...	...	5.9

Source: U.S. Census of Population: 1950, Volume II, Part 1, Tables 34 and 97; Sixteenth Census of the United States: 1940, Volume II, Part 1, Tables 4 and 5; Data for 1900 to 1920 from Fourteenth Census of the United States: 1920, Volume II, Table 23, p. 90-3. Data for years prior to 1900 from W. S. Thompson and P. K. Whelpton, Population Trends in the United States, Tables 13, 14, and 25 in Chapter II.

the decade from the percent urban at the end.) After the Civil War the urbanization of the Negro population began to accelerate, but not until the World War I era (1910-20 decade) was the rate of Negro urbanization able to surpass the urbanization rate of native whites. During the 1910-20 decade the point-change in the percent urban was 6.0 for native whites and 6.7 for Negroes. The boom in employment that accompanied World War I drew many thousands of Negroes from the South into northern cities. This movement continued during the 1920-30 decade. While the 1920-30 point-change in percent urban was 4.9 for native whites, it was 9.7 for Negroes. Again, during the 1930-40 decade, when urbanization was almost at a standstill for whites (point-change in percent urban was 0.6 for native whites) the point-change for Negroes was 4.9. It is clear that the depression of the 1930's slackened the pace at which Negroes were drifting urbanward faster than whites, but did not stop it.

The 1940-50 decade witnessed a greater urbanization of the Negro population than had any preceding decade. By the old urban definition, the point-change in percent urban was 10.9 for nonwhite populations and only 1.5 for the white population. (In 1950 the Census did not tabulate the urban-rural residence of Negroes by the old urban-rural definitions.) Comparing the old defi-

nition for 1940 with the new definition for 1950, the point-change was 13.8 for Negroes and 7.6 for native whites. The magnitude of this extraordinarily large urbanward migration of the nonwhite population during the 1940-50 decade may be more readily appreciated after a look at the lower section of Table 7-4, which presents estimated intercensal change figures. [2] Whereas the native white urban population increased by 22.6 percent (old urban-rural definitions), the Negro urban population increased by 43.2 percent, or at a rate almost twice as fast! A change of this magnitude could arise only from a large-scale migration of Negroes from rural to urban areas. This migration originated primarily from farms. Evidence of this is the fact that the Negro rural-farm population declined by 29.8 percent in the 1940-50 decade. This was a considerably larger rate of decrease than that of the native white farm population.

---

[2] Because of a change in the census definitions of urban populations for the 1950 census, it is impossible to compute exact rates of change, 1940-50, for subgroups of the population (such as the color-nativity-race groups being considered here) separately for urban and rural areas. By an estimating procedure which is described in the Appendix, these rates have been computed for this study. Since they are only estimates and not direct calculations, they must be interpreted with caution. The rates are based on the old, rather than the new, urban definitions.

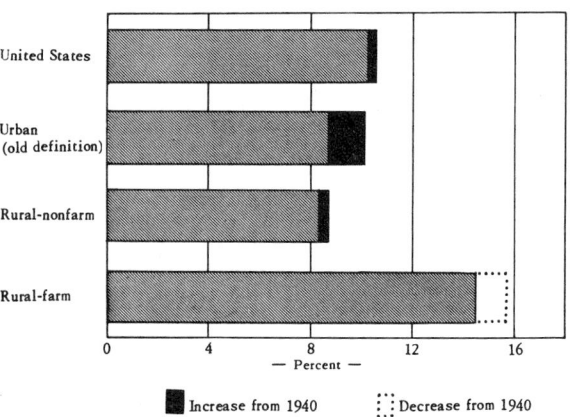

FIGURE 7 - 3. PERCENT OF POPULATION NONWHITE, BY
URBAN AND RURAL RESIDENCE, 1940 AND 1950

Thus, one of the outstanding population shifts of the 1940-50 decade was the removal of many thousands of Negroes from rural-farm areas and their movement to urban places. These and other aspects of internal migration as they affect the various color, nativity, and race groups are discussed more fully later in the chapter on migration.

Although the numbers upon which the rates are based are comparatively small, it appears that the American Indian, Japanese, and Chinese populations also urbanized rapidly during the decade. The wartime removal of persons of Japanese ancestry from West Coast areas, frequently accompanied by loss of their agricultural holdings, undoubtedly accounts in part for the high rate of urbanization of this group.

CHANGE IN THE WHITE AND NONWHITE POPULATIONS: 1950 TO 1958

The following table summarizes the changes in nativity-color composition that occurred between April, 1950 and July 1, 1958.

Color and nativity	Population July 1, 1958 (000)	Change 1950-58 (000)	Percent change 1950-58	Percent distribution 1958
Population, total	174,064	22,932	15.2	100.0
White.........	154,795	19,452	14.4	88.9
Native........	146,895	21,704	17.3	84.4
Foreign born..	7,900	-2,252	-22.4	4.5
Nonwhite......	19,269	3,480	22.0	11.1

In the above table, the statistics for the white and nonwhite populations are official estimates by the Bureau of the Census, but the statistics for native-born and foreign-born whites are only the very crudest of estimates, and must be taken only as approximate indications of the changes that have taken place.

The increases of 19.5 million and 3.5 million in the white and nonwhite populations, respectively, represent growth rates of 14.4 and 22.0 percent. Thus, during the present decade the nonwhite population appears to be growing at a rate which is almost 50 percent greater than that of the white population. A part of this differential, however, is due to a very rapid decline of the foreign-born population (about 22 percent in eight years!) At the present time, the population of the nation is increased by about 300,000 immigrants per year. This is much too small a number to replace the deaths among the foreign-born, who are now at such an advanced age that they are being decimated rapidly. Consequently, there has been a net loss of more than 2 1/4 million foreign-born in the seven years since the last census.

When the dying out of the elderly foreign born is taken into consideration, the differential between the growth of the native white and the nonwhite population becomes much smaller. At the present time the rate of growth for nonwhites is roughly 25 to 27 percent greater than the rate for native whites. This is due, in large part, to the great improvement in the health status of the nonwhite population since 1950 and to their higher birth rates.

The percent distribution of the population by color and nativity in 1958 is shown in the right-hand column of the above table. The 1958 nonwhite population comprises 11.1 percent of the total population, instead of 10.5 percent as in 1950. This is a comparatively small change; unless it continues for several decades or becomes greatly accelerated, it betokens no great change in color composition. The most striking change has been the decline in the proportion of foreign-born whites. In 1950 they were 6.7 percent of the total population, but by 1957 only 4.5 percent. This **rapid shift will continue during the next decade,** with the result that by 1965 the population will be preponderantly native white and Negro. If immigration rates were to continue at about the present level, the number of foreign-born whites would level off at about 12 million, and would become a progressively smaller percentage of the population as the total number of inhabitants tended to increase.

REGIONAL DISTRIBUTION AND COLOR-NATIVITY-RACE COMPOSITION: 1790 TO 1958

The various regions of the United States differ considerably in their color-nativity-race composition, and each color-nativity-race group has its own unique distribution among the regions. Table 7-6 shows the regional distribution by geographic divisions for each of the census color-nativity-race groups as they were in 1950 and in 1880. The regional distribution for the total population (the "all classes" column) may be used as a basis for determining what would be the "expected" proportion in each geographic division if all groups were distributed in the same proportions.

Foreign-born white population. The white immigrants to the United States did not spread out evenly over the land. Instead, they concentrated heavily in the Middle Atlantic and East North Central states, and to a lesser extent in the New England and Pacific states. This tendency to concentrate in the Northeast was characteristic of their distribution both in 1880 and 1950. However, at the earlier date the West North Central Division also contained an important share because of the flow of population to new land. This distribution caused the northeastern states to have a high percentage of foreign-born population (see Table 7-7).

In 1920, 1/4 of the population of New England was foreign-born white, and in the Middle Atlantic states a little more than 1/5 was foreign-born

Table 7-6.—PERCENT DISTRIBUTION AMONG GEOGRAPHIC DIVISIONS OF COLOR, NATIVITY, AND RACE CLASSES: 1950 AND 1880

Geographic division	All classes	White			Nonwhite						
		Total	Native	Foreign born	Total	Negro	Other races				
							Total	Indian	Japanese	Chinese	All other
Census of 1950											
United States......	100.0	100.0	100.0	100.0	100.0	100.0	100.0	100.0	100.0	100.0	100.0
New England..........	6.2	6.8	6.3	12.7	1.0	1.0	1.5	1.0	0.5	4.0	1.3
Middle Atlantic.......	20.0	20.9	19.5	38.5	12.2	12.5	7.1	3.6	4.7	20.6	6.7
East North Central....	20.2	21.2	21.2	21.1	11.8	12.0	7.3	6.5	11.3	7.2	5.2
West North Central....	9.3	10.1	10.4	5.5	3.1	2.8	8.6	15.9	1.9	1.9	1.5
South Atlantic........	14.1	11.9	12.6	3.6	32.6	33.9	6.4	2.2	1.0	4.0	29.2
East South Central....	7.6	6.5	7.0	0.5	17.2	17.9	1.1	1.2	0.2	1.5	1.7
West South Central....	9.6	8.9	9.4	3.3	15.9	16.2	9.6	16.7	0.9	3.4	5.0
Mountain.............	3.4	3.6	3.7	2.3	1.5	0.4	22.9	41.4	10.0	3.2	2.6
Pacific..............	9.6	10.2	10.0	12.4	4.8	3.4	35.5	11.5	69.3	54.3	46.8
Census of 1880											
United States......	100.0	100.0	100.0	100.0	100.0	100.0	100.0	100.0[1]	...	100.0	...
New England..........	8.0	9.1	8.6	12.1	0.6	0.6	1.1	0.6	...	0.4	...
Middle Atlantic.......	20.9	23.7	22.5	30.8	2.8	2.9	1.4	2.9	...	1.2	...
East North Central....	22.3	25.4	24.7	29.2	2.9	2.8	6.6	6.5	...	0.4	...
West North Central....	12.3	13.7	13.4	15.2	3.1	3.1	3.3	18.9	...	0.4	...
South Atlantic........	15.1	10.7	12.2	2.6	43.6	44.7	1.1	1.0	...	0.1	...
East South Central....	11.1	8.4	9.7	1.4	28.5	29.3	1.5	1.4	...	0.1	...
West South Central....	6.6	5.2	5.6	2.7	16.1	16.5	1.6	26.6	...	0.7	...
Mountain.............	1.3	1.4	1.3	2.2	0.6	0.1	19.3	29.0	...	13.5	...
Pacific..............	2.2	2.3	2.0	3.8	1.7	0.1	64.1	13.2	...	83.3	...

[1]Distribution is for 1890 instead of 1880, but 1880 totals for Indians are used in "total other races" column.

Source: U.S. Census of Population: 1950, Volume II, Part 1, Table 59; Thirteenth Census of the United States: 1910, Volume I, Table 21, p. 146 and Table 31, p. 170.

Table 7-7.—COLOR, NATIVITY, AND RACE COMPOSITION OF THE UNITED STATES POPULATION BY GEOGRAPHIC DIVISION: 1850 TO 1950

Color, nativity, race, and year	United States total	Geographic division								
		New England	Middle Atlantic	East North Central	West North Central	South Atlantic	East South Central	West South Central	Mountain	Pacific
Percent native white										
1950......................	82.8	84.5	80.7	86.8	92.5	74.0	76.0	80.5	90.8	86.1
1940......................	81.1	81.0	78.9	86.2	91.2	71.8	73.7	78.7	89.6	84.3
1920......................	76.7	73.6	75.1	82.5	86.5	66.7	70.8	74.8	82.7	77.6
1900......................	74.5	73.2	76.3	81.9	82.5	62.2	65.6	69.0	77.2	75.3
1870......................	72.9	80.5	77.1	80.3	78.8	59.3	64.4	57.2	71.3	64.5
1850......................	74.6	87.9	80.6	86.8	78.4	58.0	65.1	51.6	94.1	77.5
Percent foreign-born white										
1950......................	6.7	13.8	13.0	7.1	4.0	1.7	0.5	2.3	4.7	8.7
1940......................	8.7	17.8	16.4	9.7	5.8	1.6	0.4	2.2	6.3	11.9
1920......................	13.0	25.3	22.1	15.0	10.9	2.3	0.8	4.5	13.6	18.6
1900......................	13.4	25.7	21.4	16.4	14.8	2.0	1.2	4.0	17.2	19.6
1870......................	14.2	18.7	21.2	18.2	17.4	2.9	2.3	6.3	24.4	25.6
1850......................	9.7	11.2	17.3	12.2	11.3	2.2	1.5	9.2	5.8	21.4
Percent Negro										
1950......................	10.0	1.5	6.2	5.9	3.0	24.1	23.5	16.7	1.3	3.5
1940......................	9.8	1.2	4.6	4.0	2.6	26.4	25.8	18.6	0.9	1.4
1920......................	9.9	1.1	2.7	2.4	2.2	30.9	28.4	20.1	0.9	0.9
1900......................	11.6	1.1	2.1	1.6	2.3	35.7	33.1	25.9	0.9	0.6
1870......................	12.7	0.9	1.7	1.4	3.7	37.9	33.2	36.4	0.5	0.7
1850......................	15.7	0.8	2.1	1.0	10.3	39.8	33.4	39.2	0.1	1.1
Percent other races										
1950......................	0.5	0.1	0.2	0.2	0.4	0.2	0.1	0.5	3.2	1.7
1940......................	0.4	0.1	0.1	0.1	0.4	0.2	...	0.5	3.2	2.3
1920......................	1.1	0.1	0.1	0.1	0.5	0.1	...	4.5	7.0	5.2
1900......................	0.5	0.1	0.1	0.1	0.4	0.1	...	1.0	4.7	4.5
1870......................	0.2	...	...	0.1	0.1	...	...	0.1	3.8	9.1
1850......................	...	...	...	...	...	...	...	...	...	...

Source: U.S. Census of Population: 1950, data for 1950 compiled from state reports for this study; Sixteenth Census of the United States: 1940, Volume II, Part 1, Table 24; Data for 1850 to 1920 from W. S. Thompson and P. K. Whelpton, Population Trends in the United States, Table 12, pp. 42-3.

white. Even in 1950, more than 1/8 of the population of these two divisions was foreign-born white. The South provides a sharp contrast; less than 1/30 of the population of the southern divisions was foreign-born white.

This concentration of the foreign-born in the Northeast was fostered by the rapidly growing industrial and commercial cities which provided ready employment for immigrants arriving from Europe. The South offered much less attraction of this kind. During the period of their settlement, the West North Central states also had greater-than-average proportions of foreign-born population. With the complete settlement of the agricultural lands in this area, the inflow to the division from abroad declined. A similar cycle occurred in the Mountain Division, with a lag of two or three decades. Since a very large proportion of these pioneer and frontier immigrants arrived before

the turn of the century, by 1950 they had aged and were beginning to die off; also, native white migrants were beginning to pour in from other parts of the United States. Consequently, they had declined to a smaller-than-average proportion of the total.

Although the Pacific states contained a very small population in 1880, 1/4 of their white members were foreign-born. As the division grew it continued to attract persons from abroad, and in 1950 it contained 12 percent of the nation's foreign-born white residents. From 1850 to 1950, the Pacific Division has had a higher proportion of foreign-born than the national average.

Negro population. The Negro population is highly concentrated in the South Atlantic states; as of 1950 more than 1/3 of all Negroes resided in this area. Together, the other two divisions of the South--the East South Central and West South Central--contained another 1/3. The remaining 1/3 was distributed among the other six divisions. In spite of a large and prolonged migration to northern metropolitan areas, Negroes still have a distribution that is unlike that of the general population. The New England, Mountain, and West North Central Divisions have had very small proportions of the Negro population. Outside the South, only the Middle Atlantic and the East North Central states (which contain large manufacturing centers providing employment for in-migrating Negroes) contain sizable shares of the Negro population.

Figure 7-4 and Table 7-8 furnish the full picture of the geographic distribution and redistribution of Negroes from 1790 to 1950. The picture is one of a gradual deconcentration from the South Atlantic Division. In 1790, 88.9 percent of the Negroes were living in this division. As southern agriculture moved westward, the Negroes spread gradually into the East South Central and West South Central Divisions. Together the four northern divisions contained only 8.9 percent--which is about the same share they had a century later. The Civil War did comparatively little to move this population to the North or Far West. Only the East North Central Division appeared to gain a substantial number of Negroes between 1860 and 1870. The Negro population was growing steadily, and the

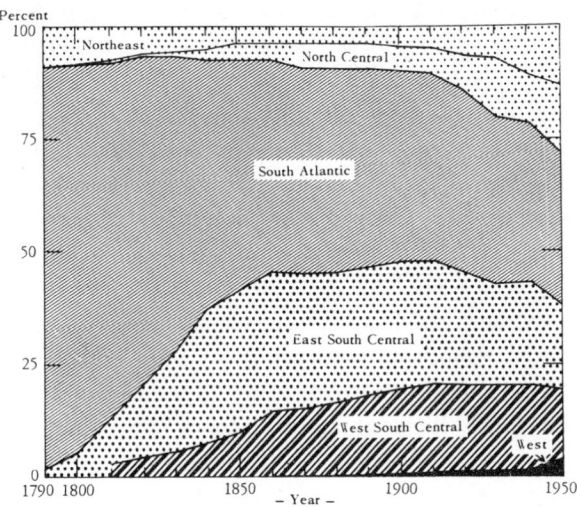

FIGURE 7 - 4. DISTRIBUTION OF NEGROES AMONG THE GEOGRAPHIC DIVISIONS, 1790 TO 1950

North was, to be sure, absorbing its proportionate share--but little more. Between 1890 and 1900 the Middle Atlantic states began to receive a somewhat larger share of the Negro population. This gain continued in the 1900-10 decade. Then, during the decade from 1910 to 1920, the Middle Atlantic and East North Central states increased their proportions of Negroes more than they had in the previous sixty years. The economic expansion associated with World War I drew many Negroes

Table 7-8.—PERCENT DISTRIBUTION OF NEGROES AMONG GEOGRAPHIC DIVISIONS: 1790 TO 1950

Year	United States total	Geographic division								
		New England	Middle Atlantic	East North Central	West North Central	South Atlantic	East South Central	West South Central	Mountain	Pacific
1950....................	100.0	1.0	12.5	12.0	2.8	33.9	17.9	16.2	0.4	3.4
1940....................	100.0	0.8	9.9	8.3	2.7	36.5	21.6	18.8	0.3	1.0
1930....................	100.0	8.8	8.9	7.8	2.8	37.2	22.4	19.2	0.3	0.8
1920....................	100.0	0.8	5.7	4.9	2.7	41.3	24.1	19.7	0.3	0.5
1910....................	100.0	0.7	4.3	3.1	2.5	41.8	27.0	20.2	0.2	0.3
1900....................	100.0	0.7	3.7	2.9	2.7	42.2	28.3	19.2	0.2	0.2
1890....................	100.0	0.6	3.0	2.8	3.0	43.6	28.3	18.4	0.2	0.2
1880....................	100.0	0.6	2.9	2.8	3.1	44.7	29.3	16.5	0.1	0.1
1870....................	100.0	0.6	3.0	2.7	2.9	45.4	30.0	15.2	...	0.1
1860....................	100.0	0.6	3.0	1.4	2.7	46.3	31.4	14.5	...	0.1
1850....................	100.0	0.6	3.5	1.2	2.5	51.1	30.9	10.1	...	...
1840....................	100.0	0.8	4.2	1.0	2.1	55.6	28.9	7.5	...	...
1830....................	100.0	0.9	4.5	0.7	1.1	65.7	21.5	5.6	...	...
1820....................	100.0	1.2	5.1	0.4	0.6	71.9	16.3	4.6	...	...
1810....................	100.0	1.4	6.0	0.3	0.3	78.4	10.6	3.1	...	...
1800....................	100.0	1.9	6.4	0.1	...	85.8	5.9	...	...	...
1790....................	100.0	2.2	6.7	...	...	88.9	2.2	...	...	...

Source: U.S. Census of Population: 1950, and Sixteenth Census of the United States: 1940; Data for 1950 and 1940 computed from compilations of data for individual states, made for this study: Thirteenth Census of the United States: 1910, Volume I, Table 22, p. 154; U. S. Bureau of the Census, Negroes in the United States, 1920-32, Table 3, p. 5.

northward. In the 1920-30 decade this movement was accelerated even more, thus almost doubling the proportionate gains of the 1910-20 period. Substantial but smaller gains were also made in the northeastern divisions between 1930 and 1940. Between 1940 and 1950 the northward movement of Negroes was renewed and speeded up. It effected a redistribution much greater in number than, and equal in proportion to, that of the 1920-30 decade. Simultaneously the Pacific states received a very large influx of Negroes. Thus, even though the Negro population is still heavily concentrated in the South, it shows much evidence of accomplishing a more even distribution among all the divisions.

The effect of this development upon the color-nativity-race composition of the population of each division is shown in Table 7-7. In the Middle Atlantic, East North Central, and Pacific states the proportion of the population that is Negro has more than doubled since 1920. By 1950 Negroes comprised about 6 percent or more of each of the two northeastern divisions, and 3.5 percent of the Pacific states. Since 1850 the proportion of the population that is Negro has declined by 40 percent in the South Atlantic states, by 30 percent in the East South Central states, and by 57 percent in the West South Central states. Even with these marked changes, in 1950 Negroes comprised 24 percent of the population of the South Atlantic and East South Central states and 17 percent of the West South Central states.

At no time has more than a very small fraction of the New England population consisted of Negroes. The Mountain states and the West North Central states likewise contain a very small Negro population. The latter division contained about the same share in 1950 as it had in 1870.

Other nonwhite races. During the seventy years from 1880 to 1950 the minor nonwhite races underwent a very great redistribution. In 1880 they were highly concentrated in the Pacific states (Chinese and Indians) and the Mountain states (Indians and Chinese). By 1950 the Chinese had become a little more evenly distributed among all divisions, although they were especially concentrated in the Middle Atlantic as well as the Pacific

Division. Indians had become much more heavily concentrated in the Mountain Division than they had been previously, and less concentrated in the Great Plains (West South Central and West North Central). The Japanese and other minor nonwhite races did not arrive in any significant numbers until 1880.

Native white population. The proportion of the population defined as native white has increased in those areas where the foreign-born population has decreased. It also has tended to decrease in areas where the proportion of Negroes has increased. In all divisions, the native white population was a larger proportion of the total population in 1950 than in 1940. This increase has tended to be smallest, however, in the three divisions where the proportion of Negroes increased most--the Middle Atlantic, the East North Central, and the Pacific. It tended to increase more where the proportion of Negroes declined--South Atlantic, East South Central, and West South Central states. Whereas 58 percent of the population of the South Atlantic states had been native white in 1850, in 1950 74.0 percent was native white. Similar though smaller changes have taken place in the other two divisions of the South. Undoubtedly, this change in proportions will be reflected in many other social changes in the South, just as the rapid increase in the proportion of Negroes among the population is being accompanied by rapid social change in the North. [3]

COLOR-NATIVITY-RACE COMPOSITION OF THE STATES

Within each of the geographic divisions, there is a certain amount of variation among the states in color-nativity-race composition. For example, in the East South Central Division the population of the state of Mississippi in 1950 was 45 percent Negro, whereas the population of Kentucky was only 6.9 percent Negro. Knowledge of this state-to-state variation can be useful in explaining many aspects of social and economic life, as well as demographic trends. Table 7-9 specifies the color-nativity-race composition of each state:

[3] For an analysis of regional trends, 1950 to 1958 see the next to last paragraph of this chapter.

Table 7-9.—COLOR, NATIVITY, AND RACE COMPOSITION OF THE STATES: 1950

States	Total		White		Nonwhite	
	White	Nonwhite	Native	Foreign born	Negro	Other races
New England.................	98.4	1.6	84.5	13.8	1.5	0.1
Maine.......................	99.7	0.3	91.5	8.1	0.1	0.2
New Hampshire...............	99.8	0.2	88.9	10.9	0.1	0.1
Vermont.....................	99.9	0.1	92.2	7.6	0.1	...
Massachusetts...............	98.3	1.7	83.1	15.2	1.6	0.1
Rhode Island...............	98.1	1.9	83.8	14.3	1.8	0.1
Connecticut.................	97.3	2.7	82.4	14.8	2.6	0.1
Middle Atlantic.............	93.6	6.4	80.7	12.9	6.2	0.2
New York....................	93.5	6.5	76.7	16.8	6.2	0.3
New Jersey..................	93.3	6.7	80.3	13.0	6.6	0.1
Pennsylvania................	93.9	6.1	86.5	7.4	6.1	...
East North Central..........	93.9	6.1	86.8	7.1	5.9	0.2
Ohio........................	93.5	6.5	87.9	5.6	6.5	...
Indiana.....................	95.5	4.4	93.0	2.5	4.4	...
Illinois....................	92.4	7.6	83.4	9.0	7.4	0.2
Michigan....................	92.9	7.1	83.4	9.5	6.9	0.2
Wisconsin...................	98.8	1.2	92.4	6.4	0.8	0.4
West North Central..........	96.5	3.4	92.5	4.0	3.0	0.4
Minnesota...................	99.0	1.0	92.0	7.0	0.5	0.5
Iowa........................	99.2	0.8	96.0	3.2	0.7	0.1
Missouri....................	92.4	7.6	90.1	2.3	7.5	...
North Dakota................	98.2	1.8	90.3	7.9	...	1.8
South Dakota................	96.3	3.7	91.6	4.7	0.1	3.6
Nebraska....................	98.2	1.8	93.9	4.3	1.4	0.4
Kansas......................	96.0	4.0	94.0	2.0	3.8	0.2
South Atlantic..............	75.7	24.3	74.0	1.7	24.1	0.2
Delaware....................	86.1	13.9	81.7	4.4	13.7	0.2
Maryland....................	83.4	16.6	79.8	3.6	16.5	0.1
District of Columbia........	64.5	35.4	59.6	4.9	35.0	0.4
Virginia....................	77.8	22.2	76.7	1.1	22.1	0.1
West Virginia...............	94.2	5.7	92.5	1.7	5.7	...
North Carolina..............	73.4	26.6	73.0	0.4	25.8	0.8
South Carolina..............	61.1	38.9	60.7	0.4	38.8	0.1
Georgia.....................	69.1	30.9	68.6	0.5	30.9	...
Florida.....................	78.1	21.8	73.7	4.4	21.7	0.1
East South Central..........	76.4	23.6	75.9	0.5	23.5	0.1
Kentucky....................	93.1	6.9	92.6	0.5	6.9	...
Tennessee...................	83.9	16.1	83.4	0.5	16.1	...
Alabama.....................	67.9	32.1	67.5	0.4	32.0	0.1
Mississippi.................	54.6	45.4	54.2	0.4	45.3	0.1
West South Central..........	82.8	17.2	80.5	2.3	16.7	0.5
Arkansas....................	77.6	22.4	77.1	0.5	22.3	0.1
Louisiana...................	67.0	33.0	65.9	1.1	32.9	0.1
Oklahoma....................	91.0	9.0	90.2	0.8	6.5	2.5
Texas.......................	87.2	12.8	83.6	3.6	12.7	0.1
Mountain....................	95.5	4.5	90.8	4.7	1.3	3.2
Montana.....................	96.8	3.2	89.5	7.3	0.2	3.0
Idaho.......................	98.8	1.2	95.5	3.3	0.2	1.0
Wyoming.....................	97.8	2.2	93.2	4.6	0.9	1.3

Table 7-9.—COLOR, NATIVITY, AND RACE COMPOSITION OF THE STATES: 1950 Continued

States	Total		White		Nonwhite	
	White	Nonwhite	Native	Foreign born	Negro	Other races
Mountain—Con.						
Colorado	97.9	2.1	93.4	4.5	1.5	0.6
New Mexico	92.5	7.5	90.0	2.5	1.2	6.3
Arizona	87.3	12.7	81.2	6.1	3.5	9.2
Utah	98.2	1.7	93.9	4.3	0.4	1.3
Nevada	93.6	6.4	87.0	6.6	2.7	3.7
Pacific	94.8	5.2	86.1	8.7	3.5	1.7
Washington	97.3	2.6	89.1	8.0	1.3	1.3
Oregon	98.4	1.6	92.9	5.5	0.8	0.8
California	93.7	6.3	84.4	9.3	4.4	1.9

Source: U.S. Census of Population: 1950, Volume II, Part I, Table 59.

Examination of this table shows that the states with the highest proportion of foreign-born white population are:

	Percent
New York	16.8
Massachusetts	15.2
Connecticut	14.8
Rhode Island	14.3
New Jersey	13.0
Michigan	9.5
California	9.3
Illinois	9.0
Washington	8.0

while the states with the smallest proportion of foreign-born white population are:

	Percent
Alabama	0.4
Mississippi	0.4
North Carolina	0.4
South Carolina	0.4
Georgia	0.5
Kentucky	0.5
Tennessee	0.5
Arkansas	0.5

The states with an above-average proportion of Negro population are:

	Percent
Mississippi	45.3
South Carolina	38.8
District of Columbia	35.0
Louisiana	32.9
Alabama	32.0
Georgia	30.9
North Carolina	25.8
Arkansas	22.3
Virginia	22.1
Florida	21.7
Maryland	16.5
Tennessee	16.1
Delaware	13.7
Texas	12.7

The states with sizable proportions of "other nonwhite" races are:

	Percent
Arizona	9.2
New Mexico	6.3
Nevada	3.7
South Dakota	3.6
Montana	3.0
Oklahoma	2.5
California	1.9
North Dakota	1.8

The states with the greatest proportion of native white population are:

	Percent
Iowa	96.0
Idaho	95.5
Kansas	94.0
Utah	93.9
Nebraska	93.9
Colorado	93.4
Wyoming	93.2
Indiana	93.0

CHANGE IN COLOR-NATIVITY-RACE COMPOSITION IN THE URBAN AND RURAL AREAS OF EACH GEOGRAPHIC DIVISION, 1940 TO 1950

More detail can be added to the general picture of change between 1940 and 1950 which is presented above if we consider the rate of change of each color-nativity-race group in the urban and rural areas of each geographic division. Tables 1, 2, 3, and 4 of the Appendix report the color-nativity-race composition in terms of percentage distribution within each group. Tables 5, 6, 7, and 8 in the Appendix present estimated rates of intercensal change, 1940-50, for each of these places.

The content of these tables is summarized below. Table 7-10 specifies the urban-rural composition of color-nativity-race groups in each geographic division in 1950, and Table 7-11 summarizes percent change, 1940-50, from Appendix Tables 5-8, inclusive. Since the discussion is based on estimates, the limitations stated in footnote 1 apply throughout this section.

New England States. Between 1940 and 1950, the native white population of New England grew about as rapidly as did the native white population of the nation generally. The considerably below-average growth rates of the New England total population may be traced in large part to greater-than-average declines in the foreign-born white population. Because New England had attracted a large number of foreign-born in earlier decades, it was being affected by the current decline of this group. Since 84 percent of the foreign-born white population of New England was residing in cities, this sequence of events acted to hinder urban growth. Whereas the rural-nonfarm and rural-farm populations grew at about the average national rate (the rural-farm population declined somewhat more in New England than in the nation), the urban population grew only at about one-half the national rate.

New England's small Negro population grew at above-average rates. This growth was confined to the urban areas. The minor nonwhite races also grew rapidly, both in urban and rural-nonfarm areas.

Middle Atlantic States. The below-average fertility rates of the native white population and a sharp decline in the relatively large foreign-born white population (-13.6 percent) caused this group of states to have an even lower over-all rate of growth than New England. Even the very large influx of Negroes into the division (an increase of 47.8 percent for the decade) was unable to offset the effects of the loss of foreign-born white population and the comparatively low fertility of the native white population.

East North Central States. These states grew at almost exactly the national average between 1940 and 1950, because of a combination of factors: a severe loss of foreign-born population, near-average fertility, and a very large influx of Negroes. The foreign-born white population, which was an important share of the population of this division (especially of its cities), declined by 16.4 percent. The decline was largest in rural-farm areas (-43.5 percent), but was sufficiently large in urban areas (-13.8 percent) to retard growth, es-

Table 7-10.—URBAN-RURAL COMPOSITION OF COLOR-NATIVITY-RACE GROUPS IN EACH GEOGRAPHIC DIVISION: 1950

Color, nativity, race	United States total	Geographic division								
		New England	Middle Atlantic	East North Central	West North Central	South Atlantic	East South Central	West South Central	Mountain	Pacific
Native white, total........	100.0	100.0	100.0	100.0	100.0	100.0	100.0	100.0	100.0	100.0
Urban......................	62.7	74.7	77.8	66.7	50.6	48.7	37.8	55.9	55.8	73.9
Rural nonfarm...............	21.9	20.8	16.9	19.8	21.8	30.8	28.1	22.8	27.7	18.6
Rural farm..................	15.4	4.6	5.3	13.5	27.5	20.4	34.2	21.3	16.6	7.5
Foreign-born white, total..	100.0	100.0	100.0	100.0	100.0	100.0	100.0	100.0	100.0	100.0
Urban......................	83.5	84.3	90.6	84.8	58.3	80.4	67.5	66.9	60.1	80.3
Rural nonfarm...............	11.0	12.5	7.3	9.6	22.8	15.1	19.7	17.1	25.8	12.4
Rural farm..................	5.4	3.2	2.1	5.6	18.9	4.6	12.8	16.1	14.1	7.3
Negro, total...............	100.0	100.0	100.0	100.0	100.0	100.0	100.0	100.0	100,0	100.0
Urban......................	62.4	91.3	94.2	95.0	88.5	48.0	42.7	53.1	76.6	91.9
Rural nonfarm...............	16.6	7.9	5.1	4.1	6.2	24.7	18.0	20.3	17.9	6.7
Rural farm..................	21.0	0.7	0.6	0.9	5.3	27.3	39.3	26.6	5.5	1.3
Other nonwhite races, total	100.0	100.0	100.0	100.0	100.0	100.0	100.0	100.0	100.0	100.0
Urban......................	44.7	72.4	80.4	65.1	21.7	20.5	21.5	28.9	13.8	66.9
Rural nonfarm...............	30.8	25.0	16.5	28.8	52.2	21.7	38.4	34.6	50.9	16.6
Rural farm..................	24.5	2.6	3.1	6.1	26.1	57.8	40.1	36.5	35.3	16.5

Source: Compiled from Appendix tables 9, 10, 11, and 12 of this study.

Table 7-11.—PERCENT CHANGE IN THE COLOR-NATIVITY-RACE GROUPS OF EACH GEOGRAPHIC DIVISION, BY URBAN-RURAL RESIDENCE (OLD DEFINITION): 1940 TO 1950

Color, nativity, race	United States total	Geographic division								
		New England	Middle Atlantic	East North Central	West North Central	South Atlantic	East South Central	West South Central	Mountain	Pacific
Native white, total........	16.8	15.3	12.0	15.0	5.5	22.4	9.7	13.8	24.0	51.9
Urban (old definition).......	22.6	13.2	10.4	15.7	19.1	31.7	31.8	52.5	42.5	46.7
Rural nonfarm...............	45.3	39.9	34.9	47.6	17.9	60.0	46.5	26.6	34.6	101.2
Rural farm..................	-21.8	-27.4	-19.2	-17.8	-18.3	-22.3	-21.7	-35.2	-19.6	-6.7
Foreign-born white, total..	-11.0	-14.2	-13.6	-16.4	-27.7	27.3	18.6	15.2	-9.1	8.5
Urban (old definition).......	-7.1	-14.0	-11.1	-13.8	-16.9	36.6	12.0	26.1	11.7	22.3
Rural nonfarm...............	-18.3	-8.7	-31.6	-15.6	-17.3	-2.1	37.8	24.3	-18.0	-20.2
Rural farm..................	-39.5	-32.8	-34.7	-43.5	-53.4	5.3	31.6	-19.9	-43.0	-33.9
Negro, total...............	16.9	40.8	47.8	68.7	20.9	8.4	-2.9	0.3	82.4	275.6
Urban (old definition).......	43.2	47.5	50.2	70.7	30.3	27.2	22.9	33.0	61.7	273.4
Rural nonfarm...............	38.0	15.3	31.6	58.3	-11.4	38.1	25.3	35.1	69.0	285.2
Rural farm..................	-29.8	-68.1	-24.7	-21.0	-33.6	-25.8	-27.2	-40.7	53.8	45.1
Other nonwhite races,total.	2.8	42.8	33.3	12.6	5.8	-70.1	45.2	-13.4	16.4	14.2
Urban (old definition).......	61.5	58.0	55.9	189.2	171.8	138.3	166.1	87.8	198.0	33.5
Rural nonfarm...............	55.6	57.0	71.7	22.6	26.7	197.3	187.3	31.4	96.5	29.3
Rural farm..................	-30.2	12.1	-36.1	-28.7	-34.7	21.8	50.6	-39.7	-32.3	-39.3

Source: Appendix tables 5, 6, 7, and 8 of this study.

pecially urban growth. The Negro population increased by 68.7 percent; this increase represented primarily a movement to urban places.

The division as a whole gained 734,000 Negroes during the decade. In urban areas the Negro population increased by 735,000, which was a gain of 70.7 percent.

West North Central States. The very low rate of over-all growth (4.0 percent) of this division resulted from its rather large net out-migration of white population and a very large loss of foreign-born population, counterbalanced by moderately high fertility and a moderate increase in the Negro population. In earlier years the foreign-born population in many parts of these midwestern states had been a large part of the total population, for much of the territory had been settled by immigrant groups. The foreign-born white population decreased from 778,000 to 563,000 during the decade, and in the rural-farm areas the decline was 53.4 percent!

Only the urban part of this division had a rate of growth approaching the national average. This gain was created by an increase of 19.1 percent in the native white population. Apparently, much of the large-scale movement from farms was a transfer to cities in the same division. The small urban Negro population grew by 30.3 percent.

The rural-nonfarm growth in this region was small in comparison with rural-nonfarm growth in other divisions. It appears that the agricultural villages were also being depopulated by urbanward migration.

South Atlantic States. The native white population grew rapidly, as a consequence of high fertility, with no net migration drain. (The states of Florida, Maryland, and Virginia and the District of Columbia enjoyed such large net in-migration during this decade that it offset the net migration losses in the other states of this division.) The Negro population, which has an even higher fertility, increased by only 8.4 percent. This was a consequence of the fact that migration removed from this and the other two divisions of the South the many thousands of Negroes who entered urban areas in the Northeast and West. The net movement appears to have been very largely, if not entirely, from farms; a decline of 25.8 percent was registered for the very large Negro rural-farm population of the division. Meanwhile, the Negro population grew quite rapidly in rural-nonfarm (38.1 percent) and urban (27.2 percent) areas. Thus, the Negro population, as well as the white, participated in the rapid urbanization of the Southeast that took place between 1940 and 1950. Oddly enough, this division (which has had only an infinitesimal foreign-born population element) had a rather large percentage increase in this group during the decade (in contrast to the losses in other divisions). Much of this growth resulted from the movement of peoples from Mexico and Central and South America, and from the migration to Florida, Washington, D.C., and other areas of foreign-born persons.

East South Central States. This division underwent a very great change in its color-nativity-race composition during the decade. It grew at only 1/2 the rate of the nation, because of a very heavy net out-migration. It lost Negroes through out-migration at such a rate that in spite of high fertility there were fewer Negroes living in the division in 1950 than there had been in 1940 (a change of -2.9 percent). The native white population grew comparatively more slowly, by only 9.7 percent--also in spite of above-average fertility. Both white and Negro residents were migrating elsewhere.

As in the South Atlantic Division, the net losses due to migration were confined mainly to the rural-farm areas. The population of farms declined very heavily (-21.7 percent for native white and -27.2 percent for the Negro population). Each of these groups comprised a large part of the total divisional population. Both the urban and rural-nonfarm populations of the division experienced a rapid growth of Negro as well as native white population. Hence, a significant part of the exodus from farms was absorbed by the growing cities in the same division.

As in the South Atlantic Division, there was a large percentage increase in the small foreign-born white population, due in large part to the influx of people from Mexico.

West South Central States. In these states the pattern of growth was one of internal urbanization and out-migration of Negroes, and was similar to that of the East South Central states except that the out-migration appears to have been less severe. The Negro population remained almost

stationary for the decade. It declined 40.7 percent in rural-farm areas, but grew rapidly in rural-nonfarm (35.1 percent) and urban areas (33.0 percent). The native white population declined by 35.2 percent in rural-farm areas, but grew by 52.5 percent in urban areas. Thus, the exodus from farms was even more drastic here than in the other southern divisions; but the urbanization movement within the division absorbed enough of the native white population to create a moderate over-all growth, and enough of the Negro population to counterbalance the losses in rural areas. The foreign-born white population (a high proportion of which was born in Mexico) grew by 15.2 percent during the decade.

Mountain States. High fertility, high rates of in-migration, and a comparative absence of foreign-born conspired to make this division grow very rapidly. The rate of growth for the native white was 24.0 percent and for Negroes 82.4 percent. Although the Mountain states had contained few Negroes prior to 1940, they received a fairly large number during this decade, considering the comparatively small size of the total population in the division. These gains were all confined to urban and rural-nonfarm areas, however; the rural-farm population lost heavily. The small foreign-born farm population declined by 43 percent and the native white by 19.6 percent.

Pacific States. In California, Oregon, and Washington the inflow of migrants included all major color-nativity-race groups. The native white population increased by 51.9 percent and the Negro population by 275.6 percent! (The numerical increase in Negro population for the decade was 370,000 persons.) Even the foreign-born white (mostly Mexican) population increased by 8.5 percent. Only the Japanese population declined (by 12.5 percent) as a consequence of the inability of some of its members to return after their concentration in camps during World War II, and because some chose to settle in one of the larger metropolitan cities in the Northeast.

As in the case of Mountain states, this growth was almost entirely urban and rural-nonfarm (much of it suburban). The native white farm population declined by 6.7 percent. The emergence of Negroes as agricultural laborers during this decade led to an increase of 45.1 percent in the Negro rural-farm population of the division.

SIZE-OF-PLACE DIFFERENCES IN COLOR-NATIVITY-RACE COMPOSITION

The color-nativity-race composition in 1950 of each of the various size-of-place categories is presented in Table 7-12. From this table it may be seen that there is a definite tendency for the foreign-born white population to be concentrated in the larger places and to be comparatively more scarce in the smaller places. Table 7-13, reproduced from Thompson and Whelpton, Population Trends in the United States, shows that this has been a characteristic of the foreign-born white population since 1870, and probably before, judging from the clear-cut size-of-place pattern already in existence as of that date.

The decline of the foreign-born whites also has had a size-of-place pattern. In 1870 and 1890, only the rural areas had a lower than average proportion of foreign-born white. By 1910 the smallest size group of cities was also included in this category. In 1930 the next size group of cities, those 10,000 to 25,000, had almost reached the

point of having a relative deficiency. By 1950 all places having less than one million inhabitants had below-average proportions of foreign-born whites. Hence, as the foreign-born population has shrunk, it has declined first and fastest in the rural and smallest places. The decline has spread from the smaller to the larger places.

On the national scene, the Negro population tends to show no uniform size-of-place pattern such as that of the foreign-born white. Table 7-12 shows a concentration in rural-farm areas and in places having 250,000 to 3 million inhabitants. At an earlier time there was an inverse size-of-place pattern for Negroes. Table 7-13 shows that in 1870 the Negro population was concentrated in the rural areas and the cities of less than 250,000. Since then, larger places have had a steady rise in the proportion of their population that is Negro. (The rise in the proportion of Negroes in larger places has been relatively greater than that of whites.) Meanwhile, from 1870 to 1930 the proportion of Negroes in rural territories and in cities of less than 10,000 declined. The recent urbanization of Negroes has included the small and medium-size cities; the proportion of the population that is Negro in these places was clearly higher in 1950 (Table 7-12) than in 1930 (Table 7-13).

The size-of-place comparisons for Negroes can

Table 7-12.—COLOR, NATIVITY, AND RACE COMPOSITION OF THE UNITED STATES POPULATION, BY SIZE OF PLACE: 1950

Size of place	Total	White			Nonwhite		
		Total white	Native	Foreign born	Total nonwhite	Negro	Other
United States, total.........	100.0	89.5	82.8	6.7	10.5	10.0	0.5
Urbanized areas							
3,000,000 or more..............	100.0	91.1	74.7	16.4	8.9	8.4	0.5
1,000,000 to 3,000,000..........	100.0	87.6	76.9	10.7	12.4	12.0	0.5
250,000 to 1,000,000............	100.0	88.6	82.4	6.3	11.4	11.1	0.2
Less than 250,000..............	100.0	90.0	83.5	6.6	10.0	9.7	0.2
Outside urbanized areas							
25,000 or more.................	100.0	90.8	85.7	5.1	9.2	9.0	0.2
10,000 to 25,000...............	100,0	91.2	86.7	4.5	8.8	8.6	0.2
2,500 to 10,000................	100.0	91.5	87.5	3.9	8.5	8.3	0.2
1,000 to 2,500.................	100.0	92.7	88.9	3.8	7.3	7.0	0.3
Inc. places less than 1,000.....	100.0	94.5	91.6	3.0	5.5	5.2	0.2
Other rural....................	100.0	87.7	84.8	2.9	12.3	11.5	0.8
Nonfarm....................	100.0	90.2	86.6	3.6	9.8	8.9	0.9
Farm.......................	100.0	85.4	83.1	2.3	14.6	13.8	0.8

Source: U.S. Census of Population: 1950, Volume IV, Part 5, Chapter A, Characteristics by Size of Place, Table 1.

Table 7-13.—NATIVITY AND RACE COMPOSITION OF THE UNITED STATES POPULATION BY SIZE OF PLACE: 1870 TO 1930

Size of place and color, nativity, and race	Year				
	1930	1920	1910	1890	1870
Percent, native white					
Total............................	77.8	76.5	74.2	73.0	72.9
1,000,000 and over...................	65.4	64.4	60.8	60.8	...
500,000 to 1,000,000.................	73.1	70.9	68.1	66.3	60.5
250,000 to 500,000...................	75.8	75.1	69.1	65.5	61.5
100,000 to 250,000...................	76.2	73.0	71.2	65.3	54.4
25,000 to 100,000....................	78.0	75.9	72.4	68.2	62.4
10,000 to 25,000.....................	80.9	78.7	75.1	70.8	67.2
2,500 to 10,000......................	83.2	81.5	78.2	75.1	71.9
Rural................................	80.6	79.4	77.4	75.7	75.9
Rural nonfarm......................	82.8	80.8	...	...	...
Rural farm.........................	79.0	78.6	...	...	...
Percent, foreign-born white					
Total............................	10.9	12.5	14.3	14.5	14.2
1,000,000 and over...................	27.1	31.5	36.4	37.0	...
500,000 to 1,000,000.................	19.1	23.3	25.9	32.3	37.3
250,000 to 500,000...................	11.3	16.8	24.3	28.5	32.8
100,000 to 250,000...................	14.0	17.5	20.3	26.3	35.8
25,000 to 100,000....................	13.2	16.9	20.1	22.9	29.7
10,000 to 25,000.....................	11.2	14.2	17.3	21.1	25.2
2,500 to 10,000......................	8.1	11.3	13.6	16.3	20.9
Rural................................	4.9	6.5	7.7	8.8	9.0
Rural nonfarm......................	6.6	9.6	...	...	...
Rural farm.........................	3.6	4.6	...	...	...
Percent, Negro					
Total............................	9.7	9.9	10.7	11.9	12.7
1,000,000 and over...................	6.2	3.9	2.6	2.1	...
500,000 to 1,000,000.................	7.1	5.3	5.9	1.3	2.2
250,000 to 500,000...................	11.7	7.7	6.1	4.9	5.7
100,000 to 250,000...................	8.0	9.3	8.0	8.2	8.9
25,000 to 100,000....................	7.4	7.0	7.3	8.6	7.8
10,000 to 25,000.....................	6.9	6.9	7.4	7.9	7.4
2,500 to 10,000......................	6.8	7.0	8.0	8.4	7.1
Rural................................	12.4	13.4	14.3	14.8	14.8
Rural nonfarm......................	8.5	9.0	...	...	...
Rural farm.........................	15.5	16.3	...	...	...

Source: Reproduced from W. S. Thompson and P. K. Whelpton, Population Trends in the United States, Table 15, p. 49.

be made more meaningful by controlling the regional factor. Since Negroes are concentrated in the South, and since the South has many smaller cities, grouping regions (as has been done in Tables 6-12 and 6-13) may hide patterns that otherwise might be observable. That this is true is made clear by Table 7-14, for which the color-nativity-race composition has been computed for each size-of-place in each region. In 1950, the Negro population followed a size-of-place pattern similar to that of the foreign-born in every region except the South. In the Northeast, North Central,

and West the size-of-place pattern is almost perfectly regular, with a high degree of concentration in places of 1 million or more. In these regions, Negroes comprise less than 2 percent of the population in small cities and rural-nonfarm areas. Open country farm populations in the East and North Central are less than 1 percent Negro. Hence, in migrating from the South to other regions, Negroes have been attracted to particular communities with a strength that varies directly with the size of those communities. In the South, where Negroes initially had a highly rural distri-

Table 7-14.—SIZE-OF-PLACE COMPOSITION OF THE MAJOR COLOR-NATIVITY-RACE GROUPS, BY REGIONS: 1950

Size of place	Total	White		Nonwhite		Total	White		Nonwhite	
		Native	Foreign born	Negro	Other		Native	Foreign born	Negro	Other
		NORTHEAST					NORTH CENTRAL				
Urbanized areas										
3,000,000 or more............	100.0	72.0	19.7	8.0	0.3	100.0	74.5	13.3	11.8	0.4
1,000,000 to 3,000,000.......	100.0	78.7	12.1	9.1	0.1	100.0	75.7	11.4	12.8	0.1
250,000 to 1,000,000........	100.0	84.5	12.6	2.8	0.1	100.0	86.2	5.9	7.8	0.1
Less than 250,000...........	100.0	84.8	12.3	2.9	0.1	100.0	90.6	5.1	4.2	0.1
Outside urbanized areas										
25,000 or more..............	100.0	87.0	11.0	2.0	0.1	100.0	91.9	4.5	3.4	0.1
10,000 to 25,000............	100.0	88.0	9.5	2.5	...	100.0	93.8	3.4	2.6	0.1
2,500 to 10,000.............	100.0	90.0	8.4	1.6	...	100.0	94.8	3.7	1.3	0.1
1,000 to 2,500..............	100.0	90.8	7.6	1.4	0.1	100.0	95.1	3.9	0.8	0.2
Inc. places less than 1,000..	100.0	94.6	4.6	0.7	...	100.0	95.5	3.9	0.4	0.2
Other rural.................	100.0	91.3	7.0	1.5	0.2	100.0	95.2	3.3	0.9	0.5
Nonfarm.................	100.0	90.9	7.1	1.8	0.2	100.0	93.6	3.9	0.6	0.9
Farm....................	100.0	92.5	6.7	0.7	0.1	100.0	96.2	3.0	0.5	0.3
		SOUTH					WEST				
Urbanized areas										
3,000,000 or more............	...	...	...	...	...	100.0	83.0	10.3	5.4	1.3
1,000,000 to 3,000,000.......	100.0	72.8	4.8	22.2	0.2	100.0	79.2	11.1	6.8	2.9
250,000 to 1,000,000........	100.0	75.8	2.7	21.4	0.1	100.0	88.2	7.8	2.8	1.1
Less than 250,000...........	100.0	74.9	2.5	22.6	0.1	100.0	88.2	7.7	2.7	1.5
Outside urbanized areas										
25,000 or more..............	100.0	76.3	2.0	21.6	0.1	100.0	90.9	6.2	2.2	0.7
10,000 to 25,000............	100.0	77.4	1.6	20.8	0.2	100.0	91.6	6.2	1.5	0.7
2,500 to 10,000.............	100.0	78.9	1.3	19.6	0.2	100.0	92.6	5.6	0.8	0.9
1,000 to 2,500..............	100.0	80.9	1.0	18.0	0.1	100.0	92.2	6.0	0.5	1.2
Inc. places less than 1,000..	100.0	82.9	0.6	16.2	0.3	100.0	94.9	4.1	0.5	0.4
Other rural.................	100.0	75.9	0.8	22.9	0.4	100.0	88.7	5.8	1.1	4.5
Nonfarm.................	100.0	80.0	1.0	18.6	0.3	100.0	89.3	5.4	1.4	3.9
Farm....................	100.0	72.8	0.6	26.1	0.5	100.0	87.7	6.5	0.5	5.3

Source: U.S. Census of Population: 1950, Volume IV, Part 5, Chapter A, Characteristics by Size of Place, Table 6.

bution, all sizes of communities now have about equal proportions of Negroes, with a slight tendency toward concentration in the largest places and the rural-farm and unincorporated rural-nonfarm areas.

When the regional control is introduced, as in Table 7-14, the proportion of the population that is native white tends to vary inversely with the size of the community. This pattern is very pronounced in the Northeast, North Central, and West; it is moderately strong in the South, except for the rural areas.

Table 7-15 shows how each race-nativity-color group is distributed among the various sizes of places within each of the four census regions. It is useful for showing just how intensely concentrated in larger places the foreign-born and the Negro populations are in areas outside the South. In every region, a much higher proportion of the foreign-born than of the native white population lives in urbanized areas, and especially the largest urbanized areas. More than 80 percent of the Negro population of every region except the South lives in urbanized areas; this is even greater than the percentage of the foreign-born who are in cities. In all regions except the Northeast, more than one-half of the "other races" live in rural areas, and of those in rural areas, about one-half or more are rural-farm.

THE ROLE OF COLOR-NATIVITY-RACE IN URBANIZATION

Each of the color-nativity-race groups has re-

Table 7-15.—SIZE-OF-PLACE DISTRIBUTION OF THE RACE-NATIVITY-COLOR GROUPS IN EACH REGION: 1950

Size of place	Total	White		Nonwhite		Total	White		Nonwhite	
		Native	Foreign born	Negro	Other		Native	Foreign born	Negro	Other
		NORTHEAST					NORTH CENTRAL			
Total..................	100.0	100.0	100.0	100.0	100.0	100.0	100.0	100.0	100.0	100.0
Urbanized areas..............	66.4	62.9	79.8	89.1	73.7	45.1	41.4	67.4	85.0	31.4
3,000,000 or more...........	31.3	27.6	46.9	49.0	52.2	11.1	9.3	24.3	25.9	16.2
1,000,000 to 3,000,000.......	16.8	16.2	15.5	29.8	13.0	12.4	10.6	23.2	31.5	6.0
250,000 to 1,000,000.........	8.3	8.6	8.0	4.6	5.1	13.1	12.8	12.7	20.4	5.6
Less than 250,000..........	10.0	10.4	9.3	5.6	3.4	8.5	8.7	7.2	7.1	3.6
Outside urbanized areas........	17.2	18.8	11.5	6.0	7.7	28.5	30.3	18.1	10.0	17.9
25,000 or more..............	3.2	3.5	2.7	1.2	1.9	5.6	5.8	4.1	3.8	2.9
10,000 to 25,000............	4.3	4.6	3.1	2.1	1.4	5.7	6.0	3.2	3.0	3.3
2,500 to 10,000.............	5.6	6.2	3.6	1.7	1.5	7.8	8.3	4.8	2.0	4.5
1,000 to 2,500..............	3.1	3.5	1.8	0.9	2.9	4.8	5.1	3.1	0.8	4.0
Inc. places less than 1,000..	0.9	1.1	0.3	0.1	0.1	4.7	5.0	3.0	0.4	3.1
Other rural...................	16.4	18.4	8.7	4.9	18.6	26.4	28.4	14.5	5.0	50.8
Nonfarm..................	12.0	13.3	6.4	4.3	15.9	10.0	10.5	6.3	3.3	33.9
Farm....................	4.4	5.0	2.3	0.6	2.8	16.5	17.9	8.1	1.7	16.8
		SOUTH					WEST			
Total..................	100.0	100.0	100.0	100.0	100.0	100.0	100.0	100.0	100.0	100.0
Urbanized areas..............	28.2	27.6	53.5	28.5	14.2	49.8	48.0	61.8	80.5	38.8
3,000,000 or more...........	...	...	...	...	...	20.4	19.4	27.4	38.0	12.9
1,000,000 to 3,000,000.......	5.2	4.9	15.6	5.3	4.5	10.6	9.6	15.3	24.7	14.4
250,000 to 1,000,000.........	13.2	13.1	22.7	13.0	6.1	10.6	10.7	10.7	10.3	5.6
Less than 250,000..........	9.8	9.6	15.2	10.2	3.6	8.3	8.4	8.3	7.6	5.9
Outside urbanized areas........	27.8	28.7	24.3	25.2	17.5	26.1	27.5	19.9	10.7	10.4
25,000 or more..............	5.0	5.0	6.4	5.0	1.7	5.2	5.4	4.2	3.9	1.7
10,000 to 25,000............	5.9	6.0	6.1	5.6	4.6	6.3	6.6	5.1	3.3	2.2
2,500 to 10,000.............	9.6	9.9	7.9	8.6	6.0	8.6	9.1	6.3	2.5	3.8
1,000 to 2,500..............	4.9	5.1	3.0	4.0	2.7	4.1	4.3	3.2	0.7	2.4
Inc. places less than 1,000..	2.6	2.8	1.0	1.9	2.5	1.9	2.1	1.0	0.4	0.4
Other rural...................	44.0	43.7	22.2	46.4	68.2	24.1	24.5	18.3	8.7	50.8
Nonfarm..................	19.0	19.9	12.2	16.3	24.8	14.6	14.9	10.2	7.0	27.1
Farm....................	25.0	23.8	10.0	30.1	43.4	9.5	9.6	8.1	1.8	23.7

Source: U.S. Census of Population: 1950, Volume IV, Part 5, Chapter A, Characteristics by Size of Place, Table 6.

acted differently in its choice of urban and rural residence in the various geographic divisions. Table 7-16 shows what percent of each color-nativity-race group was living in urban places at various censuses from 1820 to 1950, by geographic divisions.

Foreign-born whites settling in the New England and Middle Atlantic Divisions have chosen to live in cities. In 1870, when only 40 percent of the native white population of these two divisions (com-bined) was urban, 70 percent of the foreign-born white population living there was urban. An even greater disparity existed in the South, where 11 percent of the native-born whites, but 59 percent of the small foreign-born white population, lived in cities. Although this same difference character-ized the North Central Region and the West, it was smaller because of the pioneering and land-settling activities of many foreign-born white groups. However, the trend over a period of time in almost

POPULATION OF THE UNITED STATES

Table 7-16.—PERCENT OF POPULATION LIVING IN URBAN AREAS, BY GEOGRAPHIC DIVISIONS: 1820 TO 1950

Color, nativity, race	United States total	Geographic division								
		New England	Middle Atlantic	East North Central	West North Central	South Atlantic	East South Central	West South Central	Mountain	Pacific
Native white										
1950 (new definition)	62.7	74.7	77.8	66.7	50.6	48.7	37.8	55.9	55.8	73.9
1940 (old definition)	55.1	74.2	73.6	62.5	43.1	38.2	28.2	39.9	43.3	64.4
1930	54.5	74.8	74.2	62.8	40.4	36.3	27.6	36.6	39.8	67.2
1920	49.6	76.2	71.1	56.9	36.0	31.8	21.8	28.8	36.6	61.8
1910	43.6	72.1	66.3	48.4	31.6	25.6	17.8	21.6	36.0	55.8
1900	38.1	67.9	60.3	41.1	27.0	21.4	13.9	15.1	32.4	44.4
1890	32.9	54.1		29.5		15.3			35.4	
1870	23.1	39.9		16.6		10.8			18.2	
Foreign-born white										
1950 (new definition)	83.5	84.3	90.6	84.8	58.3	80.5	67.5	66.9	60.1	80.3
1940 (old definition)	80.0	84.2	88.1	82.2	50.7	74.9	71.5	61.1	48.9	71.2
1930	79.2	85.3	88.5	82.8	47.6	73.2	71.8	55.0	43.5	70.7
1920	75.5	87.8	86.3	77.9	44.3	70.4	67.3	48.0	40.0	66.1
1910	71.4	86.7	83.9	71.4	39.2	66.0	66.7	39.2	39.7	61.3
1900	66.0	85.1	81.7	63.0	32.7	69.9	63.9	35.3	37.4	54.8
1890	60.7	78.1		47.0		56.6			46.1	
1870	53.4	69.5		36.8		59.3			36.7	
Negro										
1950 (new definition)	62.4	91.3	94.2	95.0	88.5	48.0	42.7	53.1	76.6	91.9
1940 (old definition)	48.6	86.3	90.4	91.6	80.4	38.4	32.1	37.9	71.1	86.3
1930	43.7	86.6	89.2	91.2	78.1	33.1	28.6	32.6	69.6	86.8
1920	34.0	90.3	86.2	87.2	76.3	26.5	22.6	25.9	54.1	86.9
1910	27.3	85.1	81.2	76.6	67.7	22.1	19.2	22.0	72.0	83.4
1900	22.7	83.9	76.0	69.9	58.6	18.7	15.5	16.7	63.1	72.0
1890	19.8	70.2		55.8		15.3			54.0	
1870	13.6	54.6		37.1		10.4			42.2	
1850	7.8	44.9		12.3		5.9			15.4	
1840	7.6	41.2		8.0		5.8			...	
1830	6.8	34.6		4.6		5.2			...	
1820	5.9	28.5		2.7		4.4			...	
Other races										
1950 (new definition)	44.7	72.4	80.4	65.1	21.7	20.5	21.5	28.9	13.8	66.9
1940 (old definition)	33.5	71.5	78.2	41.3	9.0	13.6	16.8	15.1	5.6	55.6
1930	33.6	75.8	78.0	46.5	12.1	13.6	17.1	17.6	6.8	52.3
1920	29.3	81.3	70.6	35.5	10.4	14.4	14.9	11.0	8.0	47.0
1910	24.7	73.2	58.1	22.9	7.6	15.2	12.8	7.5	8.5	45.6
1900	20.8	73.4	60.4	18.5	2.9	20.4	9.4	3.2	5.9	41.1
1890	...	...		...		...			...	
1870	...	...		...		...			...	

Source: U.S. Census of Population: 1950, Sixteenth Census of the United States: 1940, and Fifteenth Census of the United States: 1930. Data for 1950, 1940, and 1930 computed from compilation of data for individual states, made for this study; Fourteenth Census of the United States: 1920, Volume II, Table 2, p. 88, and Table 23, p. 90; Data for 1870 and 1890 from W. S. Thompson and P. K. Whelpton, Population Trends in the United States, Tables 4, 9, 13, 14, and 25.

every division has been toward a progressive concentration of the foreign-born whites in cities.

Negroes began their residence in the United States as rural residents. Their movement to cities, by regions, is charted in Figure 7-5. In the South (where more than 90 percent were located), only 4.4 percent of Negroes were living in cities in 1820. But at the same time, only 4.6 percent of the total population of the South was urban. As the South has become urbanized, the Negro population has become urbanized proportionately, so that in 1950 the South as a whole had about equal proportions of native whites and Negroes living in cities. Outside the South, however, Negroes have been

highly concentrated in urban areas. In 1820, when only 11 percent of the population of the New England and Middle Atlantic states (combined) was urban, 28.5 percent of the Negroes living in this region were in urban places. Later a similar situation existed in the North Central Region and (still later) in the West. In leaving the South, the Negro has changed his economic role; from farming he has turned to industrial, commercial, and service work in the city.

In 1950 the native white population was the least urbanized of the populations (excluding the small "other races" group, in which Indians are predominantly rural).

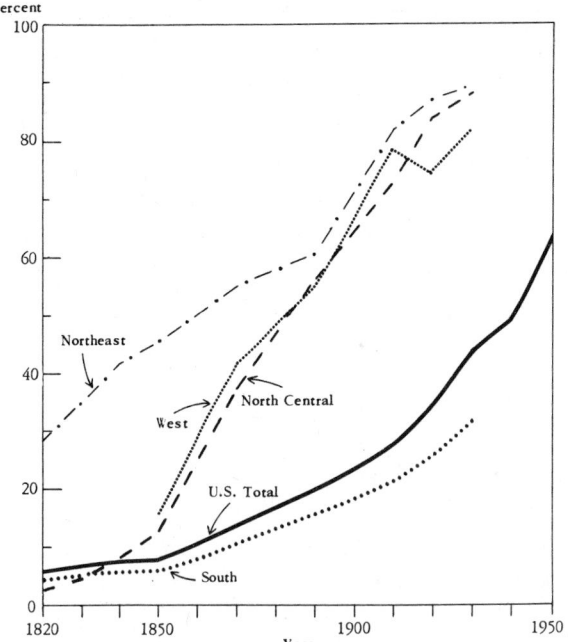

FIGURE 7 - 5. PERCENT OF THE NEGRO POPULATION
OF THE UNITED STATES OF EACH REGION LIVING
IN URBAN AREAS: 1820 TO 1950

Undoubtedly many variables are involved in this tendency of minority groups to congregate in cities. In the case of foreign-born whites, one factor is obvious: a rural foreign-born white father who leaves his farm or establishment to his native-born son is increasing the native white complement of his community. Because economic expansion has occurred chiefly in urban areas, cities have been more attractive to newly arrived immigrants than small towns and rural areas. Thus, the foreign-born population of small towns and rural areas has not been replaced as it has aged. The factors leading to the concentration of Negroes in urban areas may be similar in several ways to those leading to the concentration of foreign-born whites in cities.

AGE COMPOSITION OF COLOR-NATIVITY-RACE GROUPS

The Negro population is considerably younger, and the foreign-born population much older, than the native white population. This is shown in Table

7-17. Higher rates of fertility and mortality tend to keep the Negro population concentrated in the younger ages. Immigrants tend to arrive as adults; restrictions on immigration prevent the full replenishment at the younger ages of the present foreign-born white population. As a result, in 1950 the median age of this group was 56.1 years, and 75 percent of its members were 45 years of age or over.

The foreign-born population in rural-farm and rural-nonfarm areas is somewhat older than it is in urban areas. This is because the foreign-born in rural-farm areas were drawn largely from the immigration of the late nineteenth century; these immigrants were attracted to the settling of new lands as well as to employment in cities.

Both the native white and the Negro populations have a somewhat lower dependency ratio, for youth as well as for aged, in urban areas than in rural areas. Moreover, these ratios are lower in rural-nonfarm than in rural-farm areas. When the factor of color-nativity-race is controlled, however, the age composition of the cities does not show a great deal more concentration in the young adult ages than do the rural-nonfarm areas.

Within cities the 1950 age composition of Negroes and native whites was strikingly similar, and their median age and dependency ratios differed from each other by very little. Only in the rural-farm areas was the contrast in age structure between Negroes and whites still quite large. Among rural-farm Negroes, the proportion of children was much higher; the proportion of adults above 30 years of age was much lower; the median age was much lower; and the dependency ratio for youth was much higher than for native whites. Although similar differences existed between the native white and Negro populations of rural-nonfarm areas, they are much smaller.

Changes in the age composition of each color-nativity-race group over the past several decades may be traced from the data in Table 7-18. In 1850 the dependency ratio for Negroes was 139, and by 1950 it had dropped to 84. The dependency ratio for native whites declined from 128 in 1880 to 75 in 1950. There has been a rapid rise in the median

Table 7-17.—AGE COMPOSITION OF THE COLOR-NATIVITY-RACE GROUPS, BY URBAN AND RURAL RESIDENCE: 1950

Age	Total	White			Nonwhite						
		All classes	Native	Foreign born	All classes	Negro	American Indian	Japanese	Chinese	Fili-pino	Other
U.S.-1950											
Median age.............	30.1	30.8	28.6	56.1	26.0	26.1	19.7	27.8	29.2	33.9	20.2
Dependency ratio, total..	73.3	71.3	75.2	41.8	84.2	84.3	127.5	61.5	53.8	42.9	113.4
Youth................	59.2	56.8	62.9	3.8	73.7	73.7	115.5	49.2	46.8	41.2	105.8
Old age.............	14.1	14.5	12.2	38.0	10.5	10.7	12.1	12.3	7.1	1.7	7.7
Percent distribution.....	100.0	100.0	100.0	100.0	100.0	100.0	100.0	100.0	100.0	100.0	100.0
0 to 4 years..........	10.8	10.5	11.4	0.6	12.6	12.6	15.2	10.3	11.6	11.6	15.7
5 to 19 years........	23.3	22.7	24.6	2.1	27.4	27.4	35.6	20.2	18.8	17.2	33.9
20 to 29 years.......	15.7	15.6	16.5	5.6	16.6	16.5	15.7	25.0	21.4	13.0	19.6
30 to 44 years.......	21.7	22.0	22.3	16.2	21.3	21.4	15.8	19.0	22.9	31.3	16.1
45 to 64 years.......	20.2	20.9	18.4	48.7	16.4	16.4	12.5	18.0	20.7	25.6	11.2
65 years and over.....	8.1	8.5	7.0	26.8	5.7	5.8	5.3	7.6	4.6	1.2	3.6
URBAN-1950											
Median age.............	31.5	32.0	29.3	55.8	28.6	28.6	23.2	28.1	29.2	32.6	25.9
Dependency ratio, total..	64.1	63.1	66.7	39.3	65.7	66.2	88.7	55.5	53.1	45.1	54.1
Youth................	50.7	49.3	55.7	3.6	56.9	57.4	81.3	44.5	46.2	43.4	48.5
Old age.............	13.4	13.9	11.0	35.7	8.8	8.8	7.4	11.0	6.9	1.7	5.5
Percent distribution.....	100.0	100.0	100.0	100.0	100.0	100.0	100.0	100.0	100.0	100.0	100.0
0 to 4 years..........	10.2	10.0	11.1	0.6	11.4	11.5	12.6	10.1	11.7	11.3	9.7
5 to 19 years........	20.7	20.2	22.4	2.0	23.0	23.0	30.5	18.5	18.5	18.6	21.8
20 to 29 years.......	16.7	16.5	17.8	5.5	18.2	18.0	21.4	26.5	21.5	15.0	31.4
30 to 44 years.......	23.0	23.0	23.6	16.5	24.4	24.3	18.4	19.9	23.1	29.6	19.1
45 to 64 years.......	21.3	21.8	18.7	49.8	17.8	17.8	13.2	17.9	20.7	24.3	14.4
65 years and over.....	8.2	8.5	6.6	25.6	5.3	5.3	3.9	7.1	4.5	1.2	5.5
RURAL NONFARM-1950											
Median age.............	27.7	28.3	27.1	58.1	23.8	23.9	18.7	27.8	29.5	34.1	19.8
Dependency ratio, total..	87.3	84.7	87.5	57.8	104.5	102.6	141.0	75.0	57.0	43.3	120.3
Youth................	71.2	68.5	72.8	6.0	89.8	87.8	128.0	58.0	47.3	41.5	111.2
Old age.............	16.1	16.2	14.6	51.8	14.7	14.8	13.0	17.0	9.7	1.9	9.0
Percent distribution.....	100.0	100.0	100.0	100.0	100.0	100.0	100.0	100.0	100.0	100.0	100.0
0 to 4 years..........	12.2	11.9	12.5	1.0	13.8	13.6	16.1	9.5	9.8	12.9	17.6
5 to 19 years........	25.8	25.2	26.4	2.8	30.1	29.7	37.0	23.7	20.3	16.0	32.9
20 to 29 years.......	15.5	15.5	15.8	6.2	16.2	16.2	14.9	21.6	20.9	12.1	19.6
30 to 44 years.......	20.4	20.8	20.9	14.8	18.2	18.4	15.2	16.6	20.3	33.1	16.0
45 to 64 years.......	17.5	17.9	16.7	42.3	14.5	14.7	11.4	19.0	22.5	24.5	9.8
65 years and over.....	8.6	8.8	7.8	32.8	7.2	7.3	5.4	9.7	6.2	1.3	4.1
RURAL FARM-1950											
Median age.............	26.1	27.9	26.7	57.6	18.8	18.6	19.6	26.5	22.5	37.8	17.4
Dependency ratio, total..	100.2	93.6	96.3	55.5	142.6	143.6	130.9	79.7	100.4	35.5	151.6
Youth................	85.0	78.5	82.1	7.8	128.3	129.2	117.6	65.3	91.2	33.9	143.3
Old age.............	15.2	15.1	14.1	47.7	14.3	14.4	13.4	14.4	9.2	1.6	8.3
Percent distribution.....	100.0	100.0	100.0	100.0	100.0	100.0	100.0	100.0	100.0	100.0	100.0
0 to 4 years..........	11.4	10.7	11.1	1.1	15.0	15.0	15.0	11.4	11.7	11.7	17.4
5 to 19 years........	31.1	29.8	30.7	3.9	38.0	38.1	35.9	24.9	33.8	13.3	39.5
20 to 29 years.......	12.0	12.0	12.1	6.0	12.4	12.3	13.9	21.1	17.9	6.4	14.5
30 to 44 years.......	18.6	19.2	19.3	13.7	15.2	15.1	15.4	16.9	18.1	35.9	14.9
45 to 64 years.......	19.4	20.4	19.5	44.6	13.7	13.7	14.0	17.6	13.9	31.5	10.3
65 years and over.....	7.6	7.8	7.2	30.7	5.9	5.9	5.8	8.0	4.6	1.2	3.3

Source: U. S. Census of Population: 1950, Vol. II Part 1, Tables 38 and 97, Special Report on Nonwhite Races Tables 2, 3, 4, 5, and 6.

age of each color-nativity-race group. These changes have resulted from declines both in fertility and in mortality. Thus, the white population seems to have changed its age structure to a greater extent and more rapidly, by lowering its birth and death rates, than has the Negro population.

The foreign-born white population has had an increasing dependency ratio. This is a result, as might be suspected, of the rapid aging of this group since 1920. Before that time the median age was relatively constant at about 37-39, with a dependency ratio of about 25 per hundred. The rapid aging of this group is shown in the last column of Table 7-18. In 1920 the proportion of the foreign-born white population that was 65 years of age and over was 9.7 percent; in 1950 it was 26.7 percent.

CHANGE IN AGE COMPOSITION OF WHITES AND NONWHITES

The more rapid growth of the nonwhite popula-

tion since 1950, noted above, is having a marked effect upon the age composition of this group. The nature of this recent change may be more readily observed from Table 7-19 when the amount and rates of change, 1950-57, are shown separately for each age group, by color. The high rates of growth for ages under 20 reflect the recent rise in fertility. The more rapid growth of the white than of the nonwhite group 10-19 years old implies that the fertility upswing affected the white population first. For ages under 10, however, the rate of increase of the nonwhite population has been well

Table 7-18.—AGE COMPOSITION OF THE MAJOR COLOR, NATIVITY, AND RACE GROUPS: 1880 TO 1950

Color, nativity, and race by year	Median age	Dependency ratio			Percent distribution						
		Total	Youth	Aged	Total	0-4 years	5-19 years	20-29 years	30-44 years	45-64 years	65 years and over
Native white											
1950............	28.5	75.4	63.2	12.3	100.0	11.4	24.6	16.4	22.3	18.3	7.0
1940............	27.0	75.4	65.1	10.4	100.0	8.6	28.5	18.4	21.2	17.4	5.9
1930............	24.0	91.6	82.6	9.0	100.0	10.5	32.6	17.1	19.8	15.3	4.7
1920............	22.5	98.8	90.9	8.0	100.0	12.7	33.0	17.2	18.9	14.2	4.0
1910............	21.6	103.3	95.9	7.3	100.0	13.5	33.7	17.7	18.5	13.0	3.6
1900............	20.3	111.9	104.9	7.0	100.0	13.9	35.6	17.8	17.8	11.6	3.3
1890............	19.5	119.8	112.5	7.3	100.0	14.2	37.0	17.6	17.2	10.7	3.3
1880............	18.7	128.1	123.0	5.1	100.0	15.6	37.8	18.3	15.0	10.1	3.1
Foreign-born white											
1950............	55.4	41.8	4.0	37.9	100.0	0.6	2.2	5.5	16.2	48.8	26.7
1940............	51.6	25.3	2.8	22.6	100.0	0.1	2.1	5.5	26.5	47.8	18.0
1930............	44.3	20.6	5.7	15.0	100.0	0.2	4.5	12.6	34.2	36.1	12.4
1920............	40.6	21.2	9.5	11.8	100.0	0.3	7.5	17.4	35.2	29.9	9.7
1910............	37.6	24.5	13.4	11.1	100.0	0.8	10.0	23.2	31.6	25.5	8.9
1900............	39.1	24.7	13.1	11.6	100.0	0.5	10.0	19.8	32.6	27.8	9.3
1890............	37.3	27.1	17.5	9.5	100.0	1.0	12.8	21.8	29.4	27.5	7.5
1880............	38.4	20.6	15.1	5.5	100.0	1.0	11.3	18.3	34.5	28.8	6.0
Nonwhite											
1950............	26.0	84.2	73.7	10.5	100.0	12.6	27.4	16.6	21.3	16.4	5.7
1940............	25.3	82.3	73.6	8.7	100.0	9.8	30.6	18.1	21.7	15.1	4.8
1930............	23.7	85.5	79.6	5.9	100.0	10.4	32.5	19.1	20.6	14.2	3.2
1920............	22.7	93.4	87.2	6.2	100.0	11.0	34.0	18.7	19.6	13.3	3.2
1910............	21.1	103.5	97.4	6.1	100.0	12.8	35.0	19.5	18.1	11.5	3.0
1900............	19.8	115.5	109.1	6.5	100.0	13.7	36.9	19.3	15.9	11.2	3.0
1890............	18.6	130.2	123.7	6.5	100.0	13.9	39.8	17.5	15.5	10.4	2.8
1880............	18.4	130.9	124.7	6.2	100.0	16.5	37.5	18.1	15.1	10.1	2.7
Negro											
1950............	26.1	84.3	73.7	10.7	100.0	12.6	27.4	16.5	21.4	16.4	5.8
1940............	25.4	81.8	73.1	8.7	100.0	9.7	30.5	18.2	21.7	15.1	4.8
1930............	23.6	85.4	79.6	5.7	100.0	10.4	32.6	19.2	20.6	14.2	3.1
1920............	22.4	94.4	88.2	6.2	100.0	11.0	34.4	18.8	19.5	13.2	3.2
1910............	20.9	105.1	99.0	6.2	100.0	12.9	35.3	19.5	17.9	11.3	3.0
1900............	19.6	117.9	111.3	6.5	100.0	13.8	37.3	19.4	15.6	10.9	3.0
1890............	18.4	134.0	127.4	6.6	100.0	14.1	40.3	17.4	15.0	10.3	2.8
1870............	18.6	127.8	122.1	5.7	100.0	16.2	37.4	18.0	15.6	10.3	2.5
1850............	17.8	139.2	133.5	5.7	100.0	16.5	39.3	17.9	15.2	8.7	2.4

Source: U.S. Census of Population: 1950, Volume II, Part 1, Tables 39 and 100; U.S. Census of Population: 1930, Detailed Characteristics, Table 10; U.S. Census of Population: 1910, Detailed Characteristics, Table 33. Data for Negroes 1850 and 1870 taken from W. S. Thompson and P. K. Whelpton, Population Trends in the United States, Table 42.

Table 7-19.—INCREASE IN THE WHITE AND NONWHITE POPULATION FOR THE TOTAL POPULATION OF THE UNITED STATES, BY AGE: APRIL 1, 1950 TO JULY 1, 1957

Age	Increase, 1950 to 1957 (thousands)			Percent change, 1950 to 1957		
	All classes	White	Nonwhite	All classes	White	Nonwhite
All ages................	20,098	17,121	2,976	13.2	12.6	18.6
0 to 4 years[1]...............	2,981	2,307	673	17.6	15.6	30.7
5 to 9 years................	4,793	3,966	827	36.3	34.2	51.6
10 to 14 years..............	3,869	3,501	367	34.8	36.1	25.8
15 to 19 years..............	1,130	936	194	10.6	10.0	15.0
20 to 24 years..............	-898	-901	3	-7.7	-8.7	0.2
25 to 29 years..............	-849	-830	-18	-6.9	-7.5	-1.4
30 to 34 years..............	723	568	154	6.2	5.5	13.2
35 to 39 years..............	726	717	8	6.4	7.1	0.7
40 to 44 years..............	1,124	1,007	117	11.0	10.9	11.5
45 to 49 years..............	1,466	1,332	134	16.2	16.3	14.9
50 to 54 years..............	896	771	125	10.8	10.2	17.0
55 to 59 years..............	761	633	129	10.5	9.5	22.4
60 to 64 years..............	822	742	79	13.5	13.1	17.7
65 to 69 years..............	614	581	33	12.5	12.7	9.6
70 to 74 years..............	784	748	35	23.0	23.5	15.2
75 to 79 years..............	645	580	65	30.3	29.0	51.6
80 to 84 years..............	257	241	15	22.4	22.5	19.5
85 years and over...........	256	218	38	44.4	41.0	84.4

[1]Adjusted for net Census undercount.

Source: Current Population Reports, Population Estimates "Estimates of the Population of the United States by Age, Color, and Sex: July 1, 1950 to 1957."

above that of the white, and for the ages 0-4 the rate is about twice that of the whites. Also significant are the higher rates of growth of the nonwhite than of the white population at most adult ages. If the former process of higher nonwhite death rates was fully counterbalancing the higher nonwhite fertility, these nonwhite rates of growth should be about equal to those of the whites, or below them. Although the data in Table 7-19 refer to only a short time span, they do forecast that there will be a more rapid growth of the nonwhite population until its fertility comes closer to its lowered mortality. If present differentials in fertility persist, the differences in growth rates shown here for the first 10 years of the life span will spread to older ages.

THE COLOR-NATIVITY-RACE COMPOSITION OF STANDARD METROPOLITAN AREAS

The color-nativity-race composition of the 25 largest S. M. A.'s and their central cities and rings is shown in Table 7-20. This table shows clearly that there is much variation among the S. M. A.'s,

even more than would be expected from regional location. All of the major ports of entry on both the Atlantic and Pacific Coasts have high proportions of foreign-born white; New York and Boston-Lowell-Lawrence have the highest proportions, but they are followed closely by Providence, Seattle, and San Francisco. Those major cities which are so located that they can serve as "ports of entry" for immigrants by land also have high proportions of foreign born: Detroit and Buffalo. Hence, it is evident that immigrants have tended to concentrate in and about major ports of passenger entry. This undoubtedly explains, at least in part, their concentration in the larger cities.

The above-noted tendency does not explain all of the variations, however. Baltimore is a major Atlantic seaport with an extraordinarily low proportion of foreign born, and the proportion of foreign born in Philadelphia could have been expected to be higher than it has been. In addition, Chicago, Cleveland, Milwaukee, and Pittsburgh have high proportions of foreign born and are not major passenger seaports. Presumably immigrants were attracted to these latter places be-

Table 7-20.—COLOR-NATIVITY-RACE COMPOSITION OF THE TWENTY-FIVE LARGEST STANDARD METROPOLITAN AREAS: 1950

S.M.A.	S.M.A. population					Central city population					Suburban ring population				
	All classes	White		Nonwhite		All classes	White		Nonwhite		All classes	White		Nonwhite	
		Native	Foreign born	Negro	Other races		Native	Foreign born	Negro	Other races		Native	Foreign born	Negro	Other races
New York-Northeastern New Jersey..........	100.0	72.4	19.5	7.8	0.3	100.0	67.9	22.0	9.8	0.3	100.0	81.4	14.5	4.0	0.1
Chicago...............	100.0	76.2	12.8	10.7	0.3	100.0	71.4	14.5	13.6	0.5	100.0	85.4	9.5	5.0	0.1
Los Angeles...........	100.0	83.8	9.8	5.0	1.3	100.0	76.7	12.5	8.7	2.0	100.0	89.7	7.6	2.0	0.7
Philadelphia..........	100.0	77.6	9.2	13.1	0.1	100.0	70.5	11.2	18.2	0.1	100.0	86.9	6.6	6.5	0.1
Detroit...............	100.0	74.7	13.3	11.9	0.1	100.0	68.6	14.9	16.2	0.2	100.0	84.4	10.7	4.9	0.1
Boston-Lowell-Lawrence	100.0	82.0	16.0	1.8	0.2	100.0	77.6	17.9	4.1	0.3	100.0	84.3	15.0	0.7	0.1
San Francisco-Oakland.	100.0	79.6	11.0	6.6	2.8	100.0	74.5	13.7	7.9	4.0	100.0	85.0	8.2	5.2	1.6
Pittsburgh............	100.0	84.3	9.5	6.2	...	100.0	78.1	9.6	12.2	0.1	100.0	87.1	9.4	3.5	...
St. Louis.............	100.0	82.9	4.2	12.8	0.1	100.0	77.1	4.9	17.9	0.1	100.0	89.0	3.5	7.5	...
Cleveland.............	100.0	76.5	13.0	10.4	0.1	100.0	69.1	14.5	16.2	0.2	100.0	88.6	10.6	0.8	0.1
Washington............	100.0	72.5	4.1	23.1	0.3	100.0	59.6	4.9	35.0	0.4	100.0	88.2	3.1	8.6	0.1
Baltimore.............	100.0	75.3	4.7	19.8	0.1	100.0	70.8	5.4	23.7	0.1	100.0	86.5	3.0	10.4	0.1
Minneapolis-St. Paul..	100.0	90.8	7.9	1.1	0.2	100.0	89.5	8.8	1.5	0.3	100.0	94.7	5.1	0.1	0.1
Buffalo...............	100.0	84.2	11.4	4.1	0.3	100.0	81.4	12.1	6.3	0.2	100.0	87.4	10.6	1.5	0.5
Cincinnati............	100.0	86.3	3.2	10.5	0.1	100.0	80.3	4.1	15.5	0.1	100.0	93.8	2.0	4.2	...
Milwaukee.............	100.0	87.8	9.6	2.5	0.1	100.0	86.5	10.0	3.4	0.2	100.0	91.3	8.5	0.2	0.1
Kansas City...........	100.0	86.2	3.0	10.7	0.1	100.0	84.3	3.5	12.2	0.1	100.0	88.6	2.5	8.9	0.1
Houston...............	100.0	78.8	2.5	18.5	0.1	100.0	76.0	2.9	20.9	0.1	100.0	86.8	1.5	11.6	0.1
Seattle...............	100.0	85.3	10.6	2.3	1.9	100.0	82.3	11.9	3.4	2.5	100.0	90.4	8.3	0.4	0.9
Portland..............	100.0	90.2	7.5	1.5	0 7	100.0	87.3	9.2	2.6	1.0	100.0	93.5	5.7	0.4	0.4
New Orleans...........	100.0	68.4	2.4	29.1	0.1	100.0	65.5	2.5	31.9	0.2	100.0	82.8	1.7	15.4	0.1
Providence............	100.0	83.1	15.3	1.5	0.1	100.0	80.9	15.6	3.3	0.2	100.0	84.4	15.1	0.5	...
Atlanta...............	100.0	74.3	1.0	24.6	...	100.0	62.1	1.3	36.6	...	100.0	86.2	0.7	13.0	...
Dallas................	100.0	84.7	1.8	13.5	0.1	100.0	84.9	1.9	13.1	0.1	100.0	84.1	1.4	14.4	0.1
Louisville............	100.0	87.3	1.2	11.5	...	100.0	83.0	1.3	15.6	...	100.0	94.9	0.9	4.1	...

Source: Compiled from the U.S. Census of Population: 1950, State Reports.

cause of employment opportunities in industry. St. Louis, Cincinnati, and Minneapolis are industrial cities in which one might have expected to find high proportions of foreign born. Perhaps inland cities such as these, which were able to draw on a broad hinterland for internal migrants and which had no nearby competitors, were less attractive to immigrants than other places. Also, many of the immigrants who went to cities in the interior were purposefully guided there.

Almost without exception, the proportion of foreign-born white is higher in the central city than in the ring. Although the extent of this difference is sizable, averaging about 40 percent, there are great variations in it. The Boston, Providence, Pittsburgh, Milwaukee, and Buffalo areas have almost equal proportions in the central city and ring, while the New York, Philadelphia, Chicago, and San Francisco areas have a large concentration in the central cities. In general, where there are old industrial satellite cities that can attract immigrant labor in their own right the proportion of foreign born in the suburban ring seems to be higher. Otherwise, the foreign-born

population appears to have been attracted into ethnic neighborhoods inside the central city.

S. M. A.'s vary by regions in the proportion of their population that is Negro. However, it is difficult to interpret some of the regional differences without resorting to a theory of competition between foreign-born whites and Negroes. Why, for example, is the proportion of Negroes so low in the industrial and commercial cities of Boston, Providence, Pittsburgh, and Milwaukee, if not because these places had prior concentrations of foreign-born? And is the proportion of foreign-born lower than one might expect in Philadelphia, St. Louis, Baltimore, Cincinnati, and Kansas City (and all southern metropolises) because of the large Negro population already there? It appears that there was a reciprocal influence. In fact, the current rush of Negroes from the South into northern industrial centers dates from the shutting off of immigration. As the foreign-born populations die out, the void left by a social strata willing to live at well below-average levels and to perform the more onerous tasks is being filled by Negroes, Puerto Ricans, and Mexicans.

There is a much greater concentration of Negroes in the central city, and a greater comparative absence of Negroes in the suburban ring, than of the foreign-born white. This is characteristic of southern as well as northern cities. At the present time, movement to the suburbs is one way of maintaining residential segregation. However, the S.M.A.'s vary widely in the proportion of their ring population that is nonwhite. Some have satellite cities (usually industrial) that contain large Negro populations, while others do not.

Paul F. Coe of the Federal Housing Administration recently assembled the data showing the distribution and growth of nonwhite populations in the 168 S.M.A.'s, as defined for the 1950 census. Tables 7-21 and 7-22 summarize the results of this tabulation. From these tables it may be observed that:

(1) S.M.A.'s absorbed more than 2 1/2 million nonwhite residents during the 1940-50 decade. This was more than the total nonwhite increase in the nation during this time. As a result, the nonwhite population actually declined in nonmetropolitan areas as a whole. The 1940-50 rate of increase for the nonwhite population in metropolitan areas was 44.3 percent, and for central cities it was 48.3 percent. Considering the fact that the rate of increase in the nation was 17 percent, this represents a most drastic redistribution.

(2) About 4/5 of the nonwhite increase went to central cities. Although the nonwhite population was only 10 percent of the central city population at the beginning of the decade, fully 1/3 of the central city's total population growth was comprised of nonwhite population. The rate of growth of the nonwhite population in central cities was al-

Table 7-21.—PERCENT CHANGE OF WHITE AND NONWHITE POPULATION OF THE TWENTY-FIVE LARGEST STANDARD METROPOLITAN AREAS: 1930 TO 1940 AND 1940 TO 1950

Standard metropolitan area	S.M.A. population				Central city population				Suburban ring population			
	1940 to 1950		1930 to 1940		1940 to 1950		1930 to 1940		1940 to 1950		1930 to 1940	
	White	Nonwhite	White	Nonwhite	White	Nonwhite	White	Nonwhite	White	Nonwhite	White	Nonwhite
New York-Northeastern New Jersey	8.0	56.4	6.1	33.1	1.4	62.3	4.8	36.5	22.9	32.2	9.2	20.6
Chicago	8.9	80.7	2.3	17.7	-0.1	80.5	-0.7	17.9	29.2	82.1	9.7	16.8
Los Angeles	46.7	115.8	24.9	36.3	25.1	116.2	20.1	45.3	68.8	114.4	30.1	13.6
Philadelphia	11.3	43.7	1.0	11.6	0.8	49.9	-2.9	13.8	26.2	24.8	7.0	5.4
Detroit	20.4	109.5	8.2	23.5	5.0	101.4	1.8	23.6	51.4	164.7	23.9	22.7
Boston-Lowell-Lawrence	7.7	48.8	1.7	4.6	0.6	68.6	-1.4	12.4	11.6	9.8	3.4	-8.1
San Francisco-Oakland	45.3	225.3	8.7	3.3	14.8	198.0	2.0	2.6	98.9	292.6	23.1	4.9
Pittsburgh	5.4	21.6	2.8	5.2	-2.5	32.9	-0.8	12.8	8.9	7.6	4.5	-2.8
St. Louis	14.4	42.9	3.9	18.9	-0.6	41.4	-2.9	15.9	32.9	47.0	13.8	27.4
Cleveland	11.2	74.7	1.0	15.7	-3.5	76.1	-4.2	17.0	41.6	38.2	13.7	-10.2
Washington	52.2	48.2	46.3	37.2	9.2	50.6	34.0	42.0	129.8	37.5	75.3	18.8
Baltimore	20.5	36.9	9.0	14.8	4.5	35.9	4.6	16.6	77.2	43.1	28.1	5.5
Minneapolis-St. Paul	18.3	54.9	9.8	5.2	6.2	52.9	6.0	6.1	76.1	130.5	32.5	-19.6
Buffalo	11.4	100.1	4.8	20.2	-2.7	106.2	-0.2	29.3	32.4	80.2	13.2	-2.4
Cincinnati	12.6	38.6	3.2	13.6	6.4	41.1	-0.8	16.1	20.5	28.0	8.8	4.2
Milwaukee	12.0	141.6	5.6	16.3	6.3	144.7	1.4	16.7	30.2	54.5	22.1	5.6
Kansas City	17.3	30.0	2.9	6.0	12.1	33.9	-0.9	7.2	24.5	23.7	8.5	4.0
Houston	54.5	44.5	48.3	42.9	57.9	45.2	30.2	36.3	46.4	41.0	120.1	88.1
Seattle	44.3	69.4	9.6	-6.9	24.4	91.3	1.0	-5.0	97.2	-12.1	42.1	-13.6
Portland	39.5	113.7	10.3	2.1	20.2	132.8	1.1	3.8	69.2	52.4	28.2	-2.7
New Orleans	23.5	25.5	7.4	14.3	12.5	21.9	5.0	14.9	103.5	78.6	28.8	5.3
Providence	7.3	26.0	2.7	12.2	-2.8	31.5	-0.2	15.8	13.8	8.8	4.7	2.6
Atlanta	35.0	15.6	16.8	19.3	6.2	16.1	9.6	16.1	67.3	14.5	26.1	28.7
Dallas	57.8	35.1	21.3	28.6	54.4	13.4	10.2	29.9	66.6	132.4	65.2	22.6
Louisville	28.5	22.2	8.4	-0.2	14.5	22.4	4.4	-0.4	59.0	20.9	18.2	0.8

Source: Compiled from the U.S. Census of Population: 1950, State Reports.

Table 7-22.—GROWTH TRENDS OF WHITE AND NONWHITE POPULATIONS IN 168 STANDARD METROPOLITAN AREAS: 1930 TO 1950

Color and year	S.M.A.'s			Outside S.M.A.'s
	Total	Central cities	Metropolitan rings	
Population increase, 1940 to 1950 (thousands)................	15,225	6,022	9,203	3,804
White........................	12,691	3,934	8,757	4,037
Nonwhite.....................	2,534	2,088	446	-233
Population increase, 1930 to 1940 (thousands)................	5,445	2,207	3,238	3,449
White........................	4,642	1,508	3,134	3,286
Nonwhite.....................	803	699	104	163
Percent of increase that was nonwhite				
1940 to 1950..................	16.6	34.7	4.8	...
1930 to 1940..................	14.7	31.7	3.2	4.7
Percent of total population that was nonwhite				
1950.........................	9.8	13.0	5.2	11.3
1940.........................	8.3	10.0	5.4	12.4
1930.........................	7.7	8.8	5.7	12.9
Percent change, 1940 to 1950				
White........................	20.0	10.1	35.8	7.4
Nonwhite.....................	44.3	48.3	32.0	-3.0
Percent change, 1930 to 1940				
White........................	7.9	4.0	14.7	6.4
Nonwhite.....................	16.3	19.3	8.0	2.2

Source: Paul F. Coe, "Nonwhite Population Increases in Metropolitan Areas," Journal of the American Statistical Association, June, 1955, Table 2, p. 288.

most five times that of the white population, both in 1930-40 and 1940-50.

(3) During the 1930-40 decade, only 13 percent of the total nonwhite increase went to the ring, while 68 percent of the white population increase went to the ring. During 1940-50, 18 percent of the nonwhite and 69 percent of the white increase went to the ring. In view of the fact that only 5-6 percent of the population of suburban rings were nonwhite during this period, it must be concluded that suburbs were attracting 2-3 times their proportionate share of nonwhite population. Thus, the nonwhite population showed unmistakable though still embryonic tendencies toward a suburbanward movement, although it was masked by an even larger suburbanization of the white population. Note that for the white population the rate of suburban growth in 1940-50 was 1 1/2 times larger than it was in 1930-40. This rate for the nonwhite population is 3 times greater than in 1930-40. As a larger Negro middle-income class develops, this movement may be accelerated in future years.

(4) During the depression years, when metropolitan areas (especially central cities) were proving to be comparatively unattractive to white populations, the nonwhite population continued to flow in, to the extent of 802,000 for the decade and at a rate of 16.3 percent, which was 2 times that of the white population.

Finally, from Table 7-21 it may be noted that the percent change in nonwhite population, 1940-50 and 1930-40, has been extremely high in many of the larger S.M.A.'s. In others, the "invasion" of nonwhites has been less marked. There is every likelihood that these movements will continue, though possibly at a slower pace and in modified form. They have, as one consequence, a more even distribution of the nonwhite population among the white, at least on a regional, metropolitan-nonmetropolitan, and rural-urban basis, even if not on a neighborhood-by-neighborhood basis.

GROWTH OF THE WHITE AND NONWHITE POPULATIONS BY GEOGRAPHIC DIVISIONS: 1950 TO 1958

Rough estimates of the white and nonwhite populations of geographic divisions for the year 1958 are reported in Table 7-23. These data indicate that during the 1950 to 1960 decade there has been a substantial redistribution of both the white and nonwhite populations. But Table 7-23 also shows that the pattern of this distribution is substantially the same as that already described for the 1940 to 1950 decade. Very high rates of growth for the nonwhite population are shown for all geographic divisions outside the South, and below-average rates of growth of nonwhite population for all divisions of the South. (The East South Central Division has had especially low rates of growth among its nonwhite population.) As Chapter 15 demonstrates, this large interregional differential is due largely to a continuation of the flood-stage out-migration of Negroes, departing from the southern states and arriving in the metropolitan centers of the Northeast and West. (See also the illustrative example of the next section in this chapter.) A consequence of this exchange is that in 1958 the South contained 6 percent less of the nation's nonwhite population than it did in 1950. Nevertheless, this out-migration has not caused an actual decline in the nonwhite population of any southern division; it has succeeded only in draining off a substantial part of the large reproductive increase created by high birth rates and lowered death rates.

The white population has also continued the pattern of differential growth of the 1940 to 1950 decade; California and the other states of the Pacific and Mountain Divisions have acquired white population (as well as nonwhite) at rates roughly twice those of the nation.

The southern states (especially the East South Central and West South Central) have been losing many thousands of white persons through out-migration. Large numbers of these have settled in the industrial areas around the Great Lakes (East North Central Division). This has more than compensated for the westward movement of the white populations already resident in these states, and hence has created an above-average rate of growth for white population in the states of Ohio, Indiana, Michigan, and Illinois as a group. This out-migration of white population has been sufficiently large to cause the white population of the East South Central Division to grow only about one-third as fast as the nation, and to cause the West South Central Division to grow only at about the average rate, despite its high fertility rates.

Table 7-23.—ESTIMATED POPULATION OF GEOGRAPHIC DIVISIONS IN 1958, BY COLOR, AND MEASURES OF CHANGE: 1950 TO 1958

Geographic division	Estimated population 1958 (000)			Percent distribution			Change in percent distribution, 1950 to 1958			Percent change 1950 to 1958		
	Total	White	Non-white	Total	White	Non-white	Total	White	Non-white	Total	White	Non-white
U.S. total.......	173,260	154,055	19,205	100.0	100.0	100.0	...	...	...	15.0	14.2	21.9
New England.........	9,961	9,732	229	5.7	6.3	1.2	-0.5	-0.5	0.2	6.9	6.2	49.7
Middle Atlantic.....	33,080	30,418	2,662	19.1	19.7	13.9	-0.9	-1.2	1.7	9.7	7.7	38.2
East North Central..	35,618	32,878	2,740	20.6	21.4	14.3	0.4	0.2	2.5	17.2	15.2	47.6
West North Central..	15,391	14,766	625	8.9	9.6	3.2	-0.4	-0.5	0.1	9.5	8.8	28.9
South Atlantic......	25,352	19,511	5,841	14.6	12.7	30.4	0.5	0.8	-2.2	19.7	21.6	13.6
East South Central..	11,947	9,107	2,840	6.9	5.9	14.8	-0.7	-0.6	-2.4	4.1	3.8	4.9
West South Central..	16,539	13,735	2,804	9.5	8.9	14.6	-0.1	0.0	-1.3	13.8	14.1	12.2
Mountain............	6,494	6,192	302	3.7	4.0	1.6	0.3	0.4	0.1	28.0	27.8	31.9
Pacific.............	18,879	17,717	1,162	10.9	11.5	6.0	1.3	1.3	1.2	30.3	29.0	53.3

Source: Estimated by the author, using "Vital Statistics Method" to obtain estimate for 1956, than extrapolating to 1958, forcing results to equal Census Bureau estimated totals for white and nonwhite population and total population of geographic divisions.

Florida has continued to attract residents by the thousands from other parts of the country, and for this reason the South Atlantic Division shows substantial rates of growth for its white population. Urbanization is also tending to retain a larger proportion of the increase in the white population of these states than in former decades, and this has helped to boost the growth rates of the white population.

CHANGES SINCE 1950 IN COLOR-NATIVITY-RACE COMPOSITION OF METROPOLITAN AND NONMETROPOLITAN AREAS

There is scattered but nevertheless convincing evidence that since 1950 the trends of 1940-50 in color-nativity-race have continued and perhaps even accelerated. The movement of Negroes from rural to urban and metropolitan areas, has been maintaining its pace since 1950. Statistics which document this movement fully will not be available before the 1960 census. However, work by demographers in each of several of the larger metropolitan areas makes it quite clear that in these particular areas the trends have continued. For example, using a new technique of estimating current populations by age, sex, and color for years in which no census is taken, the Population Research and Training Center at the University of Chicago estimated the following population changes for Chicago, 1950-56, on an average per-annum basis, in comparison with the 1940-50 decade:[4]

| | Average change per year: | |
Change	1950-57	1940-50
Total population change..	98,000	66,000
White................	60,000	39,000
Nonwhite.............	38,000	27,000
Net migration...........	17,000	17,000
White................	-4,000	-4,000
Nonwhite.............	21,000	21,000
Reproductive change......	81,000	49,000
White................	64,000	43,000
Nonwhite.............	17,000	6,000

It is expected that the foreign-born white population will continue to decline. By 1960 the foreign-born population of the towns, small hinterland cities, and open country will have almost disappeared, leaving the few million remaining foreign-born whites as residents of the largest places. Also, a rather large-scale movement of Indians from reservations to urban centers is said to be taking place in this decade. Since 1950, the movement of citizens of Puerto Rican ancestry to Chicago and other metropolitan centers has also assumed large proportions. Information concerning this aspect of ethnic change must await the results of the 1960 census.

CONCLUSION

This chapter has shown that the 1940-50 decade was one of almost unprecedented change in color-nativity-race composition and distribution. The decline in the foreign-born population and the urbanization of Negroes through intraregional and interregional migration have brought many social and economic changes, are necessitating large-scale readjustments, and are creating many social problems. There is evidence that these trends have been continued and accelerated in the 1950-60 decade.

Note: The future growth of color-nativity-race groups is discussed in Chapter 26.

---

[4] See Donald J. Bogue and Beverly Duncan, "A Composite Method for Estimating Postcensal Populations of Small Areas, by Age, Sex, and Color," published in Vital Statistics Special Reports, 1958, and Beverly Duncan, "Population Growth in the Chicago Standard Metropolitan Area: 1950-56," Population Research and Training Center, June, 1957.

Chapter 8

SEX COMPOSITION OF THE POPULATION[*]

In 1950, for the first time in its history of census enumeration, the United States had a preponderance of women; until 1950 males had outnumbered females. The extent of the imbalance is only slight. Instead of being divided 50-50, males were 49.7 percent and females were 50.3 percent of the total population. At the time of the fourth census in 1820 these proportions were 50.8 percent male and 49.2 percent female.

It is conventional to describe a population's sex composition in terms of the sex ratio, or the number of males per 100 females. Figure 8-1 (data of Table 8-1) shows that from 1820 to 1910 the sex ratio of the population of the continental United States fluctuated between 102 and 106. From 1910 to the present it has declined steadily, and at the 1950 census it was 98.6.

A part of the decline from 1940 to 1950 was due to the absence of a sizable number of men who were in the armed forces overseas. If the armed forces overseas are combined with the population within the borders of the nation, the sex ratio for 1950 is 99.2. Since 1950 the decline has continued. It is estimated that as of July 1, 1960, the sex ratio of the population and the change in sex ratios since 1950 are as follows: [1]

	Sex ratio, 1960	Change since 1950
Total population.........	97.9	-1.3
White population........	98.2	-1.4
Nonwhite population....	95.5	-0.6

Thus, the 1940-50 change and the change since 1950 are an extension of a long-time downward trend that has been underway for at least 45 years.

Each of the four major color-nativity-race groups has had a distinctive sex ratio history, as graphed in Figure 8-1. The native white population had a sex ratio near 100 between 1870 and 1940, and was always below the general sex ratio for the nation. In 1950 its sex ratio was exactly the same (98.6) as the national average.

The sex ratios of the "foreign-born white" and the "other nonwhite" races show a preponderance of males. During the years of heavy immigration

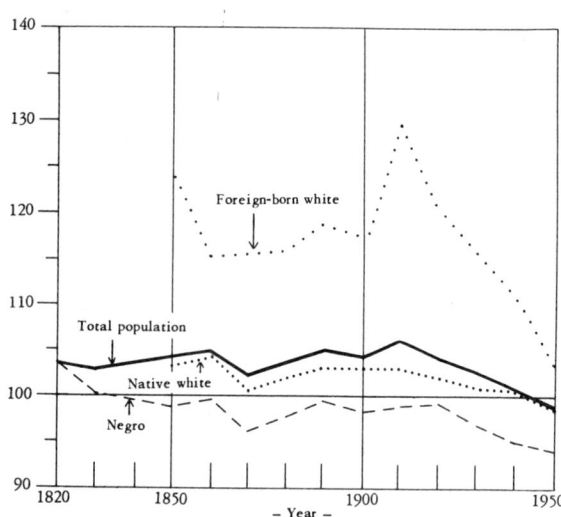

FIGURE 8 - 1. TREND OF THE SEX RATIO OF THE MAJOR RACE, COLOR, AND NATIVITY GROUPS OF THE UNITED STATES POPULATION, 1820 TO 1950

---

*A tabulation presenting statistics for sex by age and color, for the total, urban, rural-nonfarm, and rural-farm areas of each geographic division, for both 1950 and 1940, is contained in Appendix Tables 17 to 20.

[1]These estimates include armed forces overseas and include an adjustment for the underenumeration of young children. See Current Population Reports, Population Estimates, Series P-25, No.146 and corresponding data for later years.

Table 8-1.—SEX RATIO OF THE UNITED STATES POPULATION, BY COLOR-NATIVITY-RACE: 1790 TO 1950

Color, nativity and race	1950	1940	1930	1920	1910	1900	1890	1880	1870	1860	1850	1840	1830	1820	1810	1800	1790
Total population	98.6	100.7	102.5	104.0	106.0	104.4	105.0	103.6	102.2	104.7	104.3	103.7	103.1	103.3	...	...	...
White, total	99.0	101.2	102.9	104.4	106.6	104.9	105.4	104.0	102.8	105.3	105.2	104.5	103.8	103.2	104.0	104.0	103.8
Native	98.6	100.1	101.1	101.7	102.7	102.8	102.9	102.8	102.1	100.6	103.7	103.1	...	...	...	...	...
Foreign born	103.8	111.1	115.8	121.7	129.2	117.4	118.7	115.9	115.3	115.1	123.8	...	...	...	...	...	...
Nonwhite, total	95.7	96.7	99.1	100.9	101.3	101.0	102.2	100.7	98.4	101.2	99.1	...	...	...	...	...	...
Negro	94.3	95.0	97.0	99.2	98.9	98.6	99.5	97.8	96.2	99.6	99.1	99.5	100.3	103.4	...	...	...
Other races	131.7	140.5	150.6	156.6	185.7	185.2	182.5	362.2	400.7	260.8	...	...	...	...	...	...	...
Indian	108.7	105.5	105.1	104.8	103.5	101.5	102.6	104.8	95.0	119.0	...	...	...	...	...	...	...
Japanese	117.7	130.9	143.3	189.8	694.1	2,369.6	687.3	...	...	...	...	...	...	...	...	...	...
Chinese	189.6	285.3	394.7	695.5	1,430.1	1,887.2	2,678.9	2,106.8	1,284.1	1,858.1	...	...	...	...	...	...	...
All other	194.8	596.7	1,168.7	1,065.6	...	...	...	...	...	...	...	...	...	...	...	...	...

Source: Data for 1880-1950 from U.S. Census of Population: 1950, U.S. Summary, Table 36, Statistics for earlier years from W. S. Thompson and P. K. Whelpton, Population Trends in the United States, Table 46.

of white population to the United States, immigrants were predominantly male. Consequently, the sex ratio for the foreign-born white population during that time was extraordinarily high. In 1850, for example, the foreign-born population had a sex ratio of 123.8. In 1910 it was 129.2. In recent years, as the volume of immigration has been curtailed, the number of women immigrants has come to equal, and finally to surpass, that of men. By 1950 the sex ratio for foreign-born whites had declined to 103.8.

The Negro sex ratio has been considerably below the national average. It has been below 100 at each census since 1830. The reasons for this long-time preponderance of women among the Negro population are not fully understood. The sex ratio of Negroes at birth is somewhat lower than that of whites. On the other hand, the sex differential in mortality would tend to keep the Negro sex ratio higher than that of the white population. This would tend to counterbalance the lower sex ratios at birth. It is generally presumed that there is serious underenumeration of males at particular age groups (see below). Both the native white and the Negro sex ratios have declined since 1910, following the pattern for the total population but to a lesser extent.

Other nonwhite races have extraordinarily high sex ratios. In 1950 and in 1940, the sex ratios for each of these groups were as follows:

	1950	1940
Indian	108.6	105.5
Japanese	117.8	130.9
Chinese	189.8	285.3
Filipino	296.8	680.2
Con.	1950	1940
All other	122.7	249.3
Hindu	...	392.8
Other	...	172.8

These high sex ratios may be due, in part, to incomplete enumeration of women; this possibility is especially likely in regard to the Indian population. At the dates when their immigration was just beginning, the Chinese (1860 to 1910) and the Japanese (1900) had sex ratios that were as high as 1,200 to 2,600 or more, indicating that among these groups there were from 12 to 26 men per one woman. Once the men had secured a foothold in this country, Chinese and Japanese women followed, and the sex ratios were lowered. Once their immigration was stopped, natural increase was the only possible source of growth. Thereafter an increasing number of persons of Japanese and Chinese ancestry were born in the United States as American citizens, and the sex ratio for persons of Oriental ancestry declined even more. At each census an increasing proportion of these persons are native born, and as a consequence the sex ratio declines to a point which is closer to 100. For this reason, between 1940 and 1950 the sex ratios of the Chinese, Japanese, and Filipinos registered a large decline.

Implications of sex composition. One should not be too eager to attach profound philosophical, moral, or social meanings to the sex ratio and to small changes in it. The relative proportions of the sexes do influence social, economic, and community activity in many ways, to be sure, but it is doubtful whether small deviations from equality in the number of men and women, or small changes in their ratio, require any detectable adjustment or readjustment. When a whole region is inhabited almost entirely by men, as was the American West in its early days, or when whole generations of one sex have been decimated by war, as men of military age have been in Western Europe (the German Federal Republic had a sex ratio of 73 for persons age 30-34, for example, in 1950), sex composition becomes a factor of first importance. It also becomes significant in studying the distribution of population for local areas that show a great predominance of population of one sex. Although it may be emotionally satisfying to characterize nations with sex ratios above 100 as virile, ambitious, and vigorous, and to describe nations with sex ratios below 100 as decadent, passive, and submissive, it is difficult to support such theories with facts. For example, Germany has had a sex ratio below 100 for almost a century, if not longer. Many other nations, just now entering a stage of rapid growth or just now emerging as major world powers, have low sex ratios. The sex ratio of a nation or of any area within a nation is determined by a number of different factors, several of which could have only a very indirect relationship to the morale qualities of the population. Hence, the relationship between sex composition and other aspects of human life is a subject for research rather than for speculation. One primary step in such research is to comprehend the forces which worked toward the maintenance of a high sex ratio in the United States during earlier decades and those forces which have produced lower sex ratios during recent decades.

FACTORS DETERMINING THE SEX RATIO

At any instant, the sex ratio of a population is only the result of several factors which affect one sex more than the other. A meaning cannot justifiably be attributed to a particular ratio or to changes in a ratio over a period of time until the operation of each of these factors is known and understood.

Sex ratio at birth. Accurate records concerning the sex of liveborn infants show that at birth there are more males than females. In the United States this ratio is about 105.8 among the white population and 102.4 among the nonwhite (see Table 8-2). The rise and fall of the sex ratio at birth shows no discernible trend, although a reduction in stillbirths through improvements in health could cause the sex ratio to rise somewhat. It has often been observed that male babies constitute considerably

Table 8-2.—SEX RATIO AT BIRTH: MALE BIRTHS PER 100 FEMALE BIRTHS, BY COLOR, UNITED STATES: 1935 TO 1955
(Based on live births adjusted for underregistration)

Year	All births	White	Nonwhite
1955	105.1	105.6	102.0
1954	105.1	105.7	102.1
1953	105.3	105.8	102.3
1952	105.1	105.7	101.1
1951	105.2	105.8	101.8
1950	105.4	105.8	102.5
1949	105.4	105.9	102.2
1948	105.4	105.8	102.8
1947	105.5	106.0	102.5
1946	105.8	106.3	102.4
1945	105.5	106.1	102.0
1944	105.5	106.0	102.3
1943	105.5	105.9	102.8
1942	105.8	106.2	103.3
1941	105.3	105.8	102.7
1940	105.4	106.0	101.9
1939	105.4	105.7	103.0
1938	105.2	105.6	102.4
1937	105.3	105.8	102.7
1936	105.1	105.5	102.6
1935	105.3	105.6	103.1
Average	105.4	105.8	102.4

Source: Vital Statistics of the United States, Table 6.07 in reports for 1950, 1951, and 1952, and later years.

more than one-half of all stillborn infants and of all miscarriages. Thus, the sex ratio of conceptions probably is even higher than the sex ratio at birth. It is not known whether there are differences among various ethnic or racial groups in the sex ratio at conception (which must be estimated or approximated if racial or ethnic differences are to be established.) Neither is it known whether environmental conditions affect the sex ratio at conception. Differences in rates of stillbirths and miscarriages among groups, which influence the number of male and female infants reported in the published statistics, are due to differences in adequacy of diet, prenatal and postnatal care, care at birth, and also to the incompleteness and inaccuracy with which deaths occurring during the first few hours or days of life are registered. Undoubtedly some of these factors help to account for the differential in the white and nonwhite sex ratios at birth.

Because of the initial preponderance of males at birth, the sex ratio of the population would inevitably be above 100 if it were not for other factors.

Those who have heard the theory that during wartime a higher proportion of male infants are born may be interested in noting the slight increase in the sex ratio between 1942 and 1947 (Table 8-2). These differences could be random fluctuations in the series. Certainly, if this is a self-preservation response of the human species, it is very inadequate as a means of fulfilling the need for more fighting men.

Differential mortality between the sexes. From the first moment of life, death takes a greater toll of males than of females. Thus the initially high sex ratio is gradually reduced by death rates which are higher for men than for women, until eventually it reaches 100. A fairly precise way of observing the effect of differential mortality upon the sexes, with other disturbing influences held constant, is to compute the sex ratio for a life table cohort. This method requires that a representative group of live births, such as 100,000, be successively exposed at specified ages to the probabilities of dying which are in effect at a given time. The survivors of one age group are exposed to the mortality rates of the next age group, and so on, until all of the original 100,000 are deceased (see Chapter 9, "Mortality"). This technique conveniently summarizes the effect which current death rates would have upon a generation if they were allowed to operate through the life of the cohort. The number who survive to any given age are a measure of the ability of that cohort to withstand death to that age. If the number of females (from a female life table cohort) who live to begin a given year of age is greater than the number of males (from a male life table cohort) who live to begin the same year of age, then there is differential mortality between the sexes in favor of females. Two useful measures of sex differences in mortality may be computed from the life table cohort. (a) A ratio of male survivors to female survivors to any age in the life table is a measure of the cumulative differential effect of mortality upon the sexes to that age. (b) A ratio of male to female death rates within any one interval is a measure of the differential effect of mortality upon the sexes at that age interval, without reference to differences cumulated from earlier ages. Each of these types of sex ratios, computed from the 1949-51 life tables, is shown in Table 8-3 for white and nonwhite populations. Since the life table cohorts for both males and females begin with an equal number at age zero, the preponderance of males at birth in the population has been eliminated from the comparison, and only the effect of death only upon the two sexes is reflected in the ratios. For both the white and the nonwhite

Table 8-3.—SEX RATIO OF THE LIFE TABLE COHORTS LIVING AT EACH AGE, AND OF MORTALITY RATES AT EACH AGE: 1949 TO 1951

Age interval x to x + 5	Living at end of age interval		Mortality rates in age interval	
	White	Nonwhite	White	Nonwhite
0...........	100.0	100.0	100.0	100.0
0 to 5.........	99.2	98.8	128.6	123.1
5 to 10........	99.1	98.7	141.5	125.8
10 to 15.......	98.9	98.5	168.2	147.6
15 to 20.......	98.6	98.3	209.6	130.2
20 to 25.......	98.1	97.8	216.5	139.7
25 to 30.......	97.8	97.3	176.1	130.4
30 to 35.......	97.4	96.8	154.6	123.3
35 to 40.......	96.9	96.3	157.1	116.8
40 to 45.......	96.0	95.7	166.0	113.8
45 to 50.......	94.4	94.7	174.8	115.9
50 to 55.......	91.8	92.8	183.1	121.4
55 to 60.......	87.9	89.9	183.7	123.9
60 to 65.......	82.8	86.3	172.5	124.2
65 to 70.......	76.6	82.2	159.3	123.3
70 to 75.......	70.0	77.2	140.0	123.5
75 to 80.......	63.1	71.3	127.7	123.3
80 to 85.......	56.3	63.7	118.5	125.4
85 to 90.......	48.6	54.0	114.7	125.6
90 to 95.......	42.8	46.7	107.9	111.9
95 to 100......	40.1	43.1	102.6	103.5
100 to 105.....	38.9	42.9	100.1	100.2

Source: Sixteenth Census of the United States: 1950, United States Life Tables: 1949 to 1951.

populations, the number of females in the life table population surviving to begin any age (columns 1 and 2 in the table) is greater than the number of males, and the disproportion increases steadily with advancing age. At the younger ages the sex differential in mortality is not great, but after age 35 it increases rapidly. Among those surviving to age 85, the sex ratio of white males was only 56.3; at 105 years it was only 38.9. From birth to about age 45, the differential is approximately equal for whites and nonwhites, but at ages older than this the differential is considerably greater among the white population than among the nonwhite.

Columns 3 and 4 of Table 8-3 show that the death rates for males are greater than those for females at each age. These two columns show the percent by which the male mortality rates for each age group are greater than those for females. For white persons the differences are greatest at ages 15-25 and 50-65, but they are high at all ages from birth to age 80. For nonwhite persons the greatest differences occur at ages 0 to 35 and 55 to 90. Only at the most advanced years do the age-specific death rates for men and women approach equality, and perhaps it is true then only because both are approaching 100 percent. Thus, at almost all ages women appear to be more viable than men, with white women excelling in this respect more than nonwhite women.

The cumulative effect of such a large mortality differential upon population sex composition is necessarily quite marked. Under the conditions of the life table of 1949-51, if 100 females and 106 males (matching the sex ratios at birth) were to begin life at the same time, by the time the group had attained age 45-50 the number of females would about equal the number of males. As the group passed on into older ages, the sex ratio would fall below 100. Thus, under the present schedule of death rates, the initial masculine sex ratio at birth is only able to counterbalance the differential mortality for about 50 years of life. Since in 1950 the average life expectancy at birth was 68 for males and 72 for females, it is certain that a sex ratio of less than 100 is inevitable, un-

less other factors are present to counteract differential mortality between the sexes. Thus, the present differential mortality between the sexes accounts for much of the tendency for the sex ratio to be less than 100.

Aging of the population. Because of the pattern of differential death rates described above, there tend to be progressively more women than men in each age group of the population which is older than age 50. Hence, as the population as a whole ages (because of earlier declines in the birth rate) these older age groups tend to constitute a larger proportion of the population. Since they are predominately feminine in composition, the process of fertility decline and population aging tends to depress the sex ratio. Conversely, an upsurge in births, such as that which has occurred since 1945, tends to raise the sex ratio.

Immigration. Until 1910, immigrants from abroad were predominantly male. This was noted in Table 8-1, where sex ratios for foreign-born whites are shown to have varied between 115 and 129 from 1850 to 1910. After 1910, sex ratios of immigrants have declined steadily. For example, the sex ratios of immigrant aliens admitted to the United States during the period 1936 to 1953 are as follows:[2]

Years	Sex ratio
1936 to 1940	82.4
1941 to 1945	69.6
1946 to 1950	67.4
1951 to 1955	86.2
1951	93.4
1952	87.1
1953	75.1
1954	84.9
1955	89.1
1956	94.7
1957	90.4

The low ratios for the period since 1941-50 reflect in part the entry of war refugees and "war brides" as alien wives of citizen members of the armed forces. (An act of Congress on December 28, 1945, facilitated the entry of alien wives, husbands, and children of citizen members of the armed forces.) Of all aliens admitted between 1946 and 1950, about

[2]Bureau of the Census, Statistical Abstract of the United States.

1/8 (114, 691) were war brides. When war brides and war grooms (there were 333 war grooms in the 5-year period) are excluded, the sex ratio is still low--86.5. Similar low sex ratios have characterized the years 1950-53.

In summary, the unusually high sex ratio which was found in the United States until recently is seen to have been largely a product of immigration. However, in the decades of declining immigration, it has come to have a feminine balance. Unless there is a radical change in the composition of populations applying for admission, or in the policy governing their admittance, immigration cannot be counted upon to bolster the falling sex ratio; it probably will help to depress it further.

Losses to armed forces overseas and war losses. The sending of armed forces overseas during World War II reduced the sex ratio of the population residing in the United States. Loss of armed forces in combat makes a part of this a permanent rather than a temporary reduction. In 1950 the number of armed forces overseas was much greater than in 1940 (see Chapter 1); hence, a part of the decline in the sex ratio between 1940 and 1950 can be traced to this cause. If armed forces overseas are included when the sex ratios for 1950 are computed, the following results are obtained:

	Excluding armed forces overseas, 1950	Including armed forces overseas, 1950
TOTAL.......	98.6	99.2
White..........	99.0	99.6
Nonwhite.......	95.7	96.1

Thus, between 1940 and 1950 in the United States the sex ratio was 0.6 points below what it would have been if the nation had not had some of its men overseas.

During World War II the United States lost an estimated 325,000 men in combat. If it is assumed that under peacetime conditions these men would have lived to be enumerated in 1950, the sex ratio would have been 0.4 points higher. Thus, the combined effect of combat losses and of having armed forces overseas in 1950 was a decrease in the sex ratio of about 1.0 points. This circumstance alone, therefore, accounts for about one-half of the drop of 2.1 points which took place in the sex ratio between 1940 and 1950.

Underenumeration of young males. A peculiarity of the United States Census enumeration is that it seems to undercount, to some extent, young men between the ages of 20 and 35. One would expect that if the count were complete, the sex ratio for native born young men would, like that shown above for the life table population, show a gradual decline with increasing age. Instead, there is a marked fluctuation between the ages of 15 and 40, with the sex ratio declining and then rising again before it starts to fall because of the greater mortality among males at the older ages. As Table 8-4 shows, this trough is present at each census since 1910. One of the most plausible explanations for this phenomenon is that young men are undercounted and reappear in the censuses of later years to be counted at older ages. The effect of underenumeration upon any one census is to produce a lower over-all sex ratio than would otherwise exist. Some demographers attribute a part of this discrepancy to the misreporting of age at the older and the younger ages, rather than to underenumeration. Since there is no estimate as to the extent of the undercount, or as to whether it has increased or decreased with time, there is no way to find out whether this factor has played any part in the downward trend of the sex ratio. Possibly it has had the effect of lowering all sex ratios below what they would have been otherwise.

Thus, the recent and current lowering of the sex ratio can be attributed to the lower mortality among females than among males, to the aging of the population, to war losses, to the stationing of armed forces overseas, to the reduction of immigration, to a change in the sex composition of immigrants, and possibly to an increase in the tendency to underenumerate young males. This drop in the sex ratio would have been even greater if there had not been a rise in fertility during the 1940-50 decade. If progress in medicine manages to reduce the sex differential in mortality, the sex

Table 8-4.—SEX RATIO OF THE ENUMERATED NATIVE WHITE POPULATION, BY AGE,
FOR THE UNITED STATES: 1900 TO 1950

Age	1900	1910	1920	1930	1940	1950
All ages......................	102.8	102.7	101.7	101.1	100.1	97.6
Under 5 years....................	102.6	102.9	102.9	103.5	103.8	104.4
5 to 9 years.....................	102.3	102.3	102.2	103.0	103.5	104.0
10 to 14 years...................	102.3	102.4	102.2	102.6	103.3	104.1
15 to 19 years...................	99.7	100.0	99.5	100.5	101.3	100.9
20 to 24 years...................	98.6	98.1	96.3	97.6	98.0	96.4
25 to 29 years...................	101.8	100.3	97.6	97.7	98.3	95.4
30 to 34 years...................	104.6	102.4	99.0	98.7	99.1	95.5
35 to 39 years...................	105.8	104.7	103.3	100.2	99.5	96.4
40 to 44 years...................	107.9	105.6	101.9	101.5	100.1	97.3
45 to 49 years...................	109.4	106.8	109.8	102.9	100.7	97.0
50 to 54 years...................	109.3	112.0	108.9	104.8	100.9	95.9
55 to 59 years...................	101.7	110.9	106.6	104.9	100.0	94.6
60 to 64 years...................	100.6	106.9	108.3	103.6	98.3	92.2
65 to 69 years...................	101.5	102.3	106.1	100.8	95.8	87.4
70 to 74 years...................	100.5	99.5	101.1	100.4	94.4	84.9
75 years and over................	93.1	91.5	87.3	90.1	84.5	77.6

Source: Data for 1950 from U.S. Census of Population: 1950, U.S. Summary, Table 97. Statistics for earlier years from Hope T. Eldridge and Jacob S. Seigl, "The Changing Sex Ratio in the United States," American Journal of Sociology, November, 1946, pp. 224-234, Table 1.

ratios of the future may rise. Otherwise, they have every prospect of falling to about 95-97 and remaining there.

SEX COMPOSITION OF URBAN AND RURAL POPULATIONS

Urban populations have had a preponderance of women since 1920, whereas both rural-nonfarm and rural-farm populations have had a preponderance of men (see Figure 8-2). In rural-farm areas the sex ratio was 110.1 in 1950, while in rural-nonfarm areas it was 103.6 (see Table 8-5). The recent decline in the sex ratio has left the sex composition of farm areas almost unchanged; in fact, the sex ratio was higher in these areas in 1950 than in 1920. The national decline has also left the rural-nonfarm areas comparatively unchanged. (The small change that has occurred in rural-nonfarm areas can be traced to the decline in the foreign-born population.) The major decline in sex ratios has taken place in urban areas; the sex ratio of the urban native white population as well as of the urban foreign-born white population has declined over recent decades. Apparently

the economies of the rural areas demand an excess of males: as the sex ratio has declined, the increased number of women have been drawn into cities. Both the native white urban and Negro populations in the urban areas had low sex ratios as far back as 1910.

The sex ratio of the Negro population in rural areas has long remained near 100, which means that there is a disproportion of women in the ur-

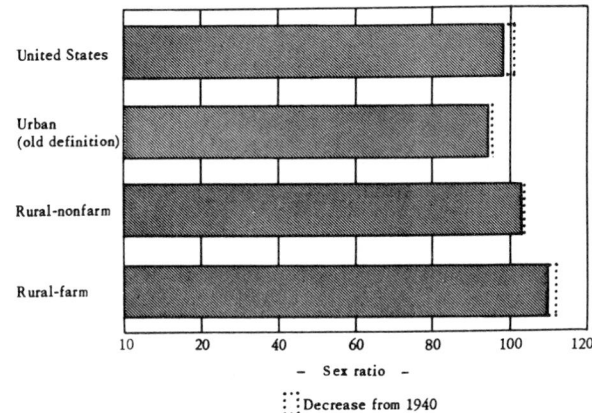

FIGURE 8 - 2. SEX RATIO, BY URBAN AND RURAL RESIDENCE, 1940 AND 1950

Table 8-5.—SEX RATIO OF COLOR-NATIVITY-RACE GROUPS IN URBAN AND RURAL AREAS, BY AGE: 1910 TO 1950

Residence and year	All classes	White			Nonwhite		
		Total	Native	Foreign born	Total	Negro	Other races
Urban							
1950 (new definition)	94.6	94.9	94.3	100.5	91.6	90.0	151.8
1940..................	95.5	96.1	94.5	106.8	90.2	88.1	191.4
1930..................	98.1	98.5	96.0	111.2	94.2	91.3	216.0
1920..................	100.4	100.5	96.9	115.9	98.6	95.4	276.9
1910..................	101.7	102.2	97.3	118.9	95.9	90.8	571.6
Rural nonfarm							
1950 (new definition)	103.6	103.6	103.1	116.3	102.7	101.7	115.0
1940..................	103.7	103.9	102.8	124.4	100.9	99.8	118.6
1930..................	105.0	105.0	102.9	132.6	104.5	102.8	133.0
1920..................	106.5	106.6	102.7	146.2	105.4	103.7	134.7
Rural farm							
1950 (new definition)	110.1	111.4	110.8	136.5	102.7	101.7	121.1
1940..................	111.7	113.1	112.2	140.3	104.1	103.1	122.4
1930..................	111.0	113.0	111.6	139.3	102.2	101.2	123.4
1920..................	109.1	110.8	109.5	136.2	100.9	100.3	121.9

Source: U.S. Census of Population: 1950, Vol. II, U.S. Summary, Table 36; Sixteenth Census of Population: 1940, Vol. II, U.S. Summary, Table 5.

ban areas. A sex ratio of 91 or below for urban Negroes has been registered at four of the last five censuses.

The urban segment of the minor nonwhite races--Indians, Japanese, Chinese, etc., has had much higher sex ratios than the rural segments, but the sex ratio of the rural population of the minor races is also quite high. The fact that American Indians, who have a more "normal" sex ratio, are concentrated in rural areas, whereas the other minor races are primarily urban dwellers, accounts for most of this difference.

SEX COMPOSITION AND AGE

In discussing the significance of differential mortality between the sexes, the changing pattern of sex ratios with age was introduced. The ways in which the sex ratios of color-nativity-race groups of the urban and rural population actually varied with age in 1950 are reported in Table 8-6. Figure 8-3 presents this information as it concerns the native white population. The general pattern, in which males are predominant at the younger ages because of the sex ratio at birth, is present for all groups. Because of their lower sex ratio at birth, the two nonwhite groups have lower sex ratios at the younger ages. For native whites,

the sex ratio decreases rather uniformly with advancing ages. In urban areas there is a sharp dip in the sex ratio between 15 and 24, which presumably is caused by the migration of women from rural areas at a younger age than men. A glance at the rural-farm sex ratios shows that this group has a preponderance of men at these same ages.

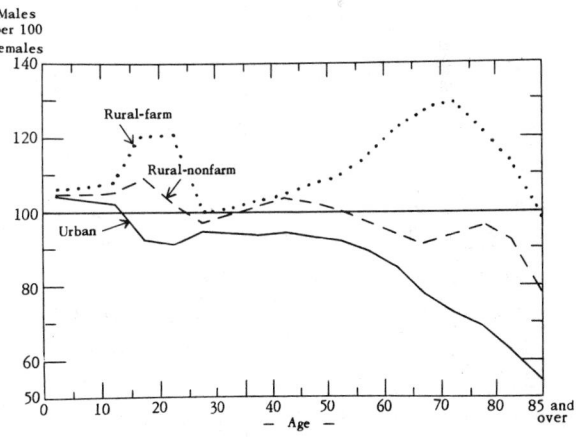

FIGURE 8-3. SEX RATIOS FOR 5-YEAR AGE GROUPS OF THE NATIVE WHITE, URBAN, RURAL-NONFARM AND RURAL-FARM POPULATION, 1950

The masculine balance of the rural-nonfarm population is shown to be derived from the preponderance of young men in all ages under 24, and a near equality of the sexes in the adult ages 35-

Table 8-6.—SEX RATIO OF COLOR-NATIVITY-RACE GROUPS IN URBAN AND RURAL AREAS, BY AGE: 1950

Age	United States					Urban				
	Total	White		Nonwhite		Total	White		Nonwhite	
		Native	Foreign born	Negro	Other races		Native	Foreign born	Negro	Other races
Total.........	98.6	97.6	103.8	94.3	131.7	94.6	94.3	100.5	90.0	151.8
0 to 4 years........	103.9	104.4	99.7	100.5	101.8	103.6	104.1	198.3	100.4	104.2
5 to 9 years........	103.5	104.0	102.7	99.1	100.8	102.6	103.1	102.5	97.8	103.7
10 to 14 years......	103.7	104.1	108.6	99.5	116.6	101.6	102.3	105.5	96.6	127.6
15 to 19 years......	100.1	100.9	106.8	93.2	106.0	91.8	92.6	99.6	84.6	109.9
20 to 24 years......	95.4	96.4	71.0	84.4	112.5	89.6	91.0	66.5	76.6	116.1
25 to 29 years......	95.2	95.4	78.0	86.6	119.0	93.3	94.2	76.4	82.8	128.0
30 to 34 years......	95.4	95.5	84.2	86.2	119.1	93.3	93.8	81.9	83.5	138.9
35 to 39 years......	96.3	96.4	86.5	87.1	154.4	92.9	93.6	84.2	84.2	176.8
40 to 44 years......	98.8	97.3	94.9	93.0	201.0	95.0	93.9	92.7	89.8	267.1
45 to 49 years......	99.6	97.0	102.2	94.3	200.6	96.0	93.2	99.8	92.3	260.5
50 to 54 years......	99.6	95.9	104.9	99.5	177.7	96.1	91.5	103.6	98.8	225.0
55 to 59 years......	100.7	94.6	113.2	105.1	165.5	96.6	89.0	111.7	101.8	202.2
60 to 64 years......	100.5	92.2	119.3	102.9	221.5	95.2	84.7	116.4	97.1	311.1
65 to 69 years......	94.0	87.4	109.9	88.8	209.1	86.2	77.5	105.1	80.6	305.7
70 to 74 years......	91.3	84.9	101.7	96.6	203.5	81.1	72.8	96.3	84.3	309.2
75 to 79 years......	} 85.1	81.6	96.6	98.7	182.7	} 73.5	68.8	89.8	83.5	351.6
80 to 84 years......		76.2	90.8	89.3	137.6		63.0	82.5	76.2	239.1
85 years and over...	69.6	65.3	78.4	64.2	129.2	60.1	54.1	71.3	55.0	274.2

Age	Rural nonfarm					Rural farm				
	Total	White		Nonwhite		Total	White		Nonwhite	
		Native	Foreign born	Negro	Other races		Native	Foreign born	Negro	Other races
Total.........	103.6	103.1	116.3	101.7	115.0	110.1	110.8	136.5	101.7	121.1
0 to 4 years........	104.3	104.2	106.6	101.0	100.2	104.3	105.6	99.5	100.3	100.7
5 to 9 years........	104.3	104.4	100.8	100.7	100.9	105.4	106.3	106.8	100.5	97.7
10 to 14 years......	104.8	104.9	118.4	100.0	111.5	107.9	108.0	118.7	104.2	111.7
15 to 19 years......	108.4	108.8	122.1	101.1	103.6	118.2	120.5	168.3	106.3	103.9
20 to 24 years......	103.6	102.0	71.1	108.2	106.5	117.1	120.7	149.4	94.0	110.8
25 to 29 years......	98.9	97.0	71.9	104.3	108.6	101.2	100.8	130.1	89.1	107.1
30 to 34 years......	101.2	99.2	89.0	98.3	96.8	98.5	98.7	117.3	88.7	104.9
35 to 39 years......	104.3	101.6	95.7	98.9	121.6	103.0	102.8	115.2	90.6	154.4
40 to 44 years......	106.8	103.3	105.7	99.6	143.0	107.7	105.3	118.9	101.9	163.0
45 to 49 years......	106.6	102.1	116.0	97.4	144.2	109.3	107.5	125.6	100.4	162.2
50 to 54 years......	105.0	100.2	111.6	99.5	139.6	110.9	109.6	118.3	102.3	134.1
55 to 59 years......	103.3	96.8	118.4	102.5	139.2	118.1	115.3	130.5	119.8	128.2
60 to 64 years......	101.8	93.6	128.0	101.1	147.6	126.5	122.3	150.2	125.8	176.5
65 to 69 years......	97.8	90.7	125.6	84.6	142.0	130.5	127.3	161.2	121.2	176.1
70 to 74 years......	100.2	93.5	117.9	98.0	116.9	134.6	128.8	154.0	135.3	203.4
75 to 79 years......	} 99.8	95.5	121.6	109.3	115.5	} 125.8	121.6	139.1	136.4	152.8
80 to 84 years......		92.7	119.5	101.9	89.0		113.9	135.6	115.6	162.3
85 years and over...	84.5	78.2	100.1	73.1	99.0	94.8	98.8	111.3	80.0	105.0

Source: U.S. Census of Population: 1950, Vol. II, U.S. Summary, Table 38.

54. Beyond these age groups females predominate by an increasing margin. Several hypotheses may be advanced to explain this distribution, all of which may be simultaneously valid:

(a) Families with young boys are more inclined to live in suburban and small town areas in preference to cities than are families with young girls. Scattered evidence from other sources sup-

ports the contention that this is a factor in determining residence.

(b) Young women begin to migrate to urban
places from rural-nonfarm areas at an earlier age
than young men. There also is evidence that this
is true.

(c) A high proportion of adults in rural areas
are married. This requires a sex ratio of nearly
100 at these ages. Presumably rural women who
do not marry move to cities. This hypothesis also
is supported by evidence.

(d) There are comparatively few opportunities
in rural areas for an unmarried woman to support
herself at the level of living to which she generally
aspires.

The masculine balance of the rural-farm population appears to be based on the three hypotheses
advanced above, plus two more:

(e) Hired hands, foremen, and other agricultural workers who are not farm operators are
usually men. There are few women farm laborers
in the labor force.

(f) When a farmer loses his wife, he generally
remains with the land and lives in the same household, with a son or daughter. When a farmer's
wife loses her husband, she usually migrates to
the city.

Negroes tend to have an age pattern similar to
that of whites, except (a) the ratios of Negroes are
somewhat lower, and (b) their age changes are
somewhat erratic because of misstatement of age.
The existence of this pattern may be verified by
comparing Figure 8-3 with Figure 8-4.

The sex ratios for foreign-born whites reflect
the male predominance among older migrants and
the female balance among more recent immigrants. The great majority of young immigrants
to rural-farm areas are men, despite the net balance in favor of women. The result is that the sex
ratio among young immigrants to cities is extremely low.

By 1950 the immigration of most of the categories in the "other nonwhite races" group had been
curtailed for about 35 years. Hence, in 1950 most
persons younger than 35 were native born, and the
sex ratio was only slightly above 100. At ages 35

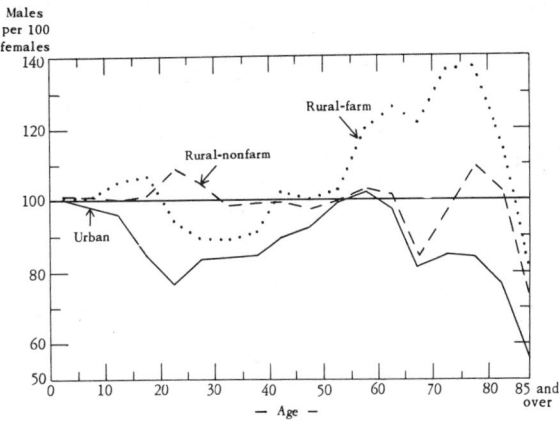

FIGURE 8 - 4. SEX RATIO FOR 5 - YEAR AGE GROUPS OF THE
NEGRO URBAN, RURAL-NONFARM AND RURAL FARM
POPULATION, 1950

and above the sex ratios are exceptionally high,
however, reflecting the sex disproportion which
existed among those who migrated from abroad
before stringent immigration controls were imposed.

Since 1950 the sex composition of the various
age groups has continued to change. Table 8-7 reports that the sex ratios for ages under 5 have remained almost constant, those for ages 5-30 have
increased, and those for ages 30 and over have decreased. The substantial increase in sex ratios at
ages 15-30 reflects the replacement of war losses
and, possibly, a correction (through the procedure
used to estimate the 1957 data) for some errors of
underenumeration and misstatement of age in the
census. The continued fall of the sex ratio at ages
above 30 is a reflection of the dying out of the elderly foreign-born populations and a widening of
the gap between male and female mortality.

SEX COMPOSITION OF THE UNITED STATES
POPULATION IN COMPARISON WITH OTHER NATIONS

The sex ratio of the United States is neither unusually high nor unusually low in comparison with
those of other nations. This may be verified from
Table 8-8. In general, the ratio of the United
States is about the same as the ratios of such nations of Western Europe as Sweden and Belgium,
which have reduced their death rates and lowered

Table 8-7.—SEX RATIO OF THE POPULATION OF THE UNITED STATES, 1957, AND CHANGE IN SEX RATIO SINCE 1950

(Including population overseas; data adjusted for underenumeration of children)

Age	Sex ratio, 1957			Change in sex ratio, 1950-1957		
	Total	White	Nonwhite	Total	White	Nonwhite
Total......................	98.3	98.7	95.7	-1.0	-1.0	-0.6
0 to 5 years....................	104.4	105.0	100.9	-0.2	-0.1	-0.4
Under 1 year...................	104.4	105.0	101.2	-0.2	-0.1	-0.5
1 and 2 years..................	104.4	105.1	100.6	-0.1	0.1	-0.7
3 and 4 years..................	104.4	105.0	101.0	-0.2	-0.2	0.2
5 to 9 years....................	104.4	104.9	101.1	0.9	0.8	1.7
10 to 14 years..................	104.1	104.6	100.2	0.4	0.5	-0.8
15 to 19 years..................	103.1	103.5	99.9	1.4	1.0	4.3
20 to 24 years..................	100.8	101.4	96.5	2.5	1.8	8.2
25 to 29 years..................	99.2	100.4	90.3	2.8	3.2	-0.1
30 to 34 years..................	95.9	97.0	87.7	-0.5	-0.3	-1.1
35 to 39 years..................	96.1	96.9	89.3	-0.7	-0.7	-0.8
40 to 44 years..................	95.8	96.7	88.0	-3.2	-2.6	-8.3
45 to 49 years..................	96.6	97.1	91.9	-3.1	-2.8	-6.3
50 to 54 years..................	96.9	97.0	95.7	-2.8	-2.4	-6.8
55 to 59 years..................	95.0	94.9	96.5	-5.3	-5.3	-5.3
60 to 64 years..................	93.0	92.6	96.9	-7.5	-7.6	-6.8
65 to 69 years..................	91.2	90.8	95.6	-3.4	-3.3	-5.6
70 to 74 years..................	86.0	85.5	93.4	-5.4	-5.2	-7.5
75 to 79 years..................	79.8	79.1	88.7	-7.5	-7.3	-14.5
80 to 84 years..................	76.2	75.2	91.6	-4.7	-5.1	-0.9
85 years and over..............	71.9	71.2	78.2	2.2	1.8	5.1

their fertility. Some nations of Europe have exceptionally low sex ratios: France, Germany, England, Spain, Poland, Austria, Czechoslovakia, Yugoslavia, and Romania. Among the factors responsible for this differential are wars, outmigration to other nations, aging of the population as a result of falling birth rates, and differential mortality in favor of women. Some nations, such as France, Germany, Austria, and Poland have encountered a combination of all or most of these factors and, as a result, have very severe sex imbalances.

Although Table 8-8 does not represent all of the nations of the world, it does represent most of those with 5 million or more inhabitants for which recent sex data are available. Because of the uncertain quality of some of the statistics, unusually high or low sex ratios in Africa, Asia, and South America must be interpreted cautiously. (High sex ratios may result from an underenumeration of women or other defects in the data.) It may be noted, however, that in all three continents a sex ratio of less than 100 is common.

REGIONAL VARIATIONS IN SEX COMPOSITION

Regional variations in sex composition were present in 1950, but were comparatively minor in comparison with those of earlier decades. The over-all trend for several decades has been toward a reduction of regional differences in sex composition. The degree to which these ratios have been converging is illustrated in Figure 8-5. The northeastern and southern states have had low sex ratios, while those in the West (especially the Mountain states) have been considerably higher. Variations in urban-rural composition and in color-nativity-race composition appear to account for most of these differences. Tables 8-9 and 8-10 provide current as well as historical data on regional trends for these major groups.

Figure 8-5 and Table 8-9 show that in 1820 sex ratios were not extraordinarily high in any of the three regions then settled. The native white population in the North has been below 100 during the entire century 1850 to 1950, while the North Central and the South have had rates only moderately

Table 8-8.—SEX RATIO OF THE POPULATION OF SELECTED
NATIONS OF THE WORLD AT RECENT DATES

Country	Date of Census or estimate	Sex ratio
AFRICA		
Algeria.............	E-1953	98.4
Egypt...............	C-1947	98.1
Morocco.............	E-1947	95.2
Mozambique..........	C-1940	90.5
Nigeria.............	C-1953	95.8
Union of South Africa.	C-1936	101.4
NORTH AMERICA		
Canada..............	E-1953	102.7
Cuba................	C-1943	109.6
Mexico..............	C-1950	97.0
United States.......	E-1953	98.9
SOUTH AMERICA		
Argentina...........	C-1947	105.1
Brazil..............	C-1950	99.3
Chile...............	C-1940	98.3
Columbia............	C-1938	98.3
Peru................	C-1940	97.7
Venezuela...........	E-1945	102.8
ASIA		
Burma...............	E-1954	104.4
Ceylon..............	C-1946	113.0
Taiwan..............	E-1953	105.0
India...............	C-1951	105.6
Japan...............	E-1952	96.2
Korea...............	C-1944	99.4
South Korea.........	E-1953	97.6
Philippines.........	C-1948	100.7
Thailand............	C-1947	100.0
Turkey..............	C-1950	101.0
EUROPE		
Austria.............	E-1952	86.6
Belgium.............	E-1952	97.1
Bulgaria............	E-1945	100.5
Czechoslovakia......	C-1947	94.5
France..............	E-1953	93.5
Germany.............	E-1951	88.3
Greece..............	E-1949	98.0
Hungary.............	C-1941	95.9
Italy...............	E-1951	95.0
Netherlands.........	E-1953	99.3
Poland..............	E-1949	90.9
Portugal............	E-1951	92.7
Romania.............	C-1948	93.5
Spain...............	C-1950	92.8
Sweden..............	E-1952	99.3
England and Wales....	E-1953	92.7
Scotland............	E-1953	91.4
Yugoslavia..........	E-1953	94.3
OCEANIA		
Australia...........	E-1953	102.6

Source: United Nations, <u>Demographic Yearbook</u>,
annual volumes, 1948 to 1954.

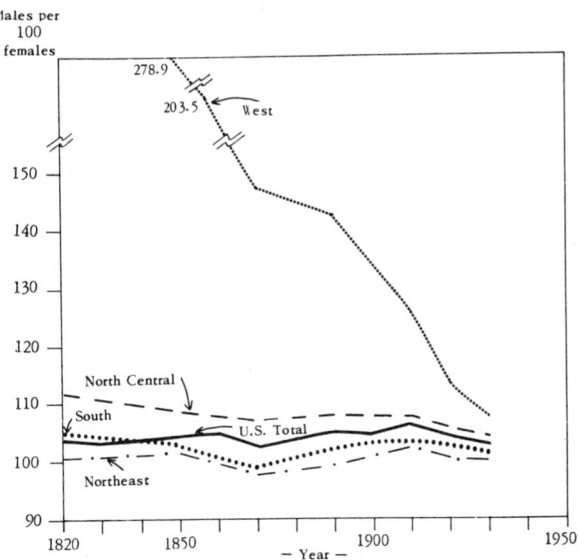

FIGURE 8 - 5. SEX RATIOS OF THE POPULATION OF THE
UNITED STATES, BY REGIONS, 1820 TO 1950

The foreign-born white population of the urbanizing Northeast also has had sex ratios not greatly in excess of 100 for a century or more, except for the short period of very heavy immigration between 1900 and 1910. In the Middle West, the South, and the West the sex ratios for foreign-born whites were much higher. In fact, it appears that the greater the distance from the Atlantic and Pacific ports the greater were the proportions of males in the streams of immigrants. The peak sex ratios were reached in the Mountain states. The native settlers who flowed into the central areas of the nation as these areas were settled appear to have come as families, or at least in nearly equal sex proportions. Among immigrants, on the other hand, the families (or at least a high proportion of the women) seem to have settled in the East, while those who pushed on West and South were usually unattached males.

Since 1820 Negroes have had low sex ratios in all regions except the West and Middle West. For the minor nonwhite races, the sex ratios have been high in all divisions in all years.

In the West, the sex ratios of all groups reached very high levels in the decades of early settlement. In 1850 the sex ratio for the region as a

in excess of 100. It is entirely possible that even these ratios are inflated somewhat by the tendency of persons who were born abroad to claim native birth.

Table 8-9.—SEX RATIO OF THE POPULATION OF GEOGRAPHIC DIVISIONS, BY COLOR-NATIVITY-RACE GROUPS: 1820 TO 1950

Color, nativity, and race by year	Geographic division								
	New England	Middle Atlantic	East North Central	West North Central	South Atlantic	East South Central	West South Central	Mountain	Pacific
All classes									
1950.....................	95.7	96.2	99.3	100.1	98.2	97.9	99.5	104.4	101.4
1940.....................	97.0	99.1	101.9	102.1	99.1	99.1	100.8	107.4	105.0
1930.....................	97.2	100.9	104.1	104.2	99.6	100.2	103.3	111.3	108.7
1920.....................	98.5	101.4	105.7	106.1	101.2	101.1	105.8	115.7	113.9
1910.....................	99.3	103.3	106.0	109.9	101.2	101.9	107.2	127.9	129.5
1900.....................	97.7	100.9	104.7	109.7	100.0	101.9	106.7	128.0	128.2
1890.....................	96.9	100.4	105.4	111.2	99.5	101.7	107.6	141.7	142.0
1880.....................	95.5	98.2	105.5	112.7	97.9	99.9	106.9	160.6	149.3
1870.....................	97.7		107.1			98.3		147.0	
1850.....................	101.2		108.7			102.8		278.9	
1820.....................	100.8		111.4			104.4		...	
Native white									
1950.....................	96.4	95.9	98.5	99.6	99.2	99.3	100.3	103.5	99.9
1940.....................	97.2	98.0	100.5	101.0	100.0	100.6	101.7	105.9	101.6
1930.....................	97.0	98.6	101.5	102.4	100.7	101.5	104.1	108.1	102.5
1920.....................	97.1	97.8	101.8	103.3	101.8	102.4	106.2	110.1	104.9
1910.....................	97.1	98.0	101.4	105.5	101.8	103.1	107.9	117.6	113.8
1900.....................	97.7	98.5	102.1	106.5	101.1	103.0	108.0	120.0	113.6
1890.....................	97.4	98.3	102.2	107.7	99.8	102.2	108.6	132.3	120.2
1880.....................	96.6	97.6	102.4	119.2	97.9	100.7	108.3	146.5	120.3
1870.....................	96.9		103.9			98.4		132.7	
1850.....................	99.4		105.7			103.1		241.7	
Foreign-born white									
1950.....................	90.7	100.6	110.3	114.5	103.0	104.9	111.1	118.7	108.9
1940.....................	95.8	107.0	117.4	123.7	120.8	135.6	112.9	130.1	120.5
1930.....................	97.3	110.1	121.2	126.3	127.1	137.2	133.5	144.2	131.5
1920.....................	102.3	114.1	128.0	131.4	141.6	141.0	131.3	149.2	148.2
1910.....................	104.8	120.9	131.3	141.3	146.9	139.2	138.8	189.6	181.9
1900.....................	97.5	109.8	118.4	130.5	123.3	130.1	134.3	166.1	162.9
1890.....................	95.2	108.3	119.9	130.5	122.7	136.0	139.3	184.5	181.5
1880.....................	91.2	101.4	121.2	134.6	116.1	130.7	141.2	198.8	178.7
1870.....................	101.5		123.8			125.0		194.2	
1850.....................	112.0		132.9			154.1		770.1	
Negro									
1950.....................	98.9	90.0	96.8	95.2	94.7	93.3	93.9	109.8	100.3
1940.....................	96.3	90.2	97.1	97.3	95.4	94.6	95.7	111.4	99.3
1930.....................	99.7	97.9	104.5	102.0	95.2	95.9	97.3	117.2	100.0
1920.....................	103.2	100.7	113.0	106.7	97.3	97.2	99.5	178.1	109.6
1910.....................	97.8	94.9	108.3	107.8	97.5	98.4	100.4	121.3	120.4
1900.....................	93.6	96.1	109.0	104.0	96.9	98.9	99.9	140.4	121.1
1890.....................	94.3	98.2	109.3	104.1	97.9	99.3	101.2	182.0	138.5
1880.....................	92.9	92.2	107.8	101.5	96.8	97.3	99.7	148.0	136.8
1870.....................	93.0		101.6			96.0		157.4	
1850.....................	92.7		100.6			99.3		502.4	
1820.....................	94.9		111.4			104.0		...	
Other races									
1950.....................	184.5	191.2	143.9	110.6	121.7	124.4	107.8	108.6	151.0
1940.....................	223.8	279.2	154.8	110.6	115.3	129.6	107.4	110.1	171.9
1930.....................	273.3	309.7	185.2	123.4	123.3	139.9	105.9	114.9	142.4
1920.....................	360.8	343.5	171.1	114.8	130.4	163.7	106.8	127.9	201.4
1910.....................	415.9	326.7	148.6	112.5	135.6	137.9	105.7	144.3	395.4
1900.....................	640.2	413.0	143.3	104.9	154.4	136.6	103.5	142.1	441.3
1890.....................	328.5	254.7	123.3	100.7	156.7	109.2	110.8	131.6	502.7
1880.....................	156.4	342.3	110.3	111.7	106.2	110.5	180.7	248.6	625.0

Source: U.S. Census of Population: 1950, data for 1950 compiled from state reports. Statistics for 1870-1940 obtained from summaries of censuses of 1940, 1930, 1920, and 1910. Data for 1820 and 1850 from Thompson and Whelpton, Recent Population Trends in the United States, Table 50, p. 183.

Table 8-10.—SEX RATIO OF THE URBAN AND RURAL POPULATION OF EACH GEOGRAPHIC DIVISION,
BY COLOR-NATIVITY-RACE: 1950 AND 1920

Urban-rural residence, color-nativity-race, and year	United States	Geographic division								
		New England	Middle Atlantic	East North Central	West North Central	South Atlantic	East South Central	West South Central	Mountain	Pacific
URBAN										
Native white										
1950....................	94.3	94.0	93.8	95.0	92.4	93.3	91.9	95.9	97.5	95.6
1920....................	96.9	95.2	95.7	98.5	95.7	95.4	94.7	101.2	101.5	97.9
Foreign-born white										
1950....................	100.5	89.3	99.6	108.1	106.0	100.5	103.9	96.9	103.9	101.7
1920....................	115.9	100.8	111.3	126.4	124.5	125.2	125.7	122.0	126.2	133.2
Negro										
1950....................	90.0	96.7	88.0	94.9	92.6	88.3	86.6	88.9	100.6	96.2
1920....................	95.4	102.2	99.1	111.5	103.5	90.4	89.2	92.4	104.8	105.0
Other nonwhite races										
1950....................	151.8	208.6	212.3	160.5	126.1	191.7	151.7	111.7	123.6	146.6
1920....................	276.9	513.4	655.5	471.4	253.9	670.0	...	136.2	291.9	239.9
RURAL NONFARM										
Native white										
1950....................	103.1	101.2	101.5	102.0	99.0	104.1	100.7	102.9	108.8	113.5
1920....................	102.7	99.0	99.8	100.9	99.5	103.7	101.2	106.2	113.6	116.9
Foreign-born white										
1950....................	116.3	95.4	109.4	121.6	116.8	115.1	110.3	128.1	137.2	136.5
1920....................	146.2	114.1	135.5	139.9	134.2	209.5	199.2	156.8	178.6	197.1
Negro										
1950....................	101.7	125.1	129.0	149.5	123.9	99.6	95.6	96.8	154.0	172.4
1920....................	103.7	109.5	109.7	126.8	116.8	100.7	101.9	103.1	450.3	155.9
Other nonwhite races										
1950....................	115.0	137.9	127.2	117.4	102.9	122.2	135.9	105.6	104.5	149.0
1920....................	134.7	120.4	127.8	110.5	104.6	125.5	230.6	102.7	133.5	186.6
RURAL FARM										
Native white										
1950....................	110.8	114.3	111.4	112.0	114.9	107.0	106.9	109.9	116.5	112.0
1920....................	109.5	111.5	109.5	110.4	112.2	105.7	105.8	109.2	117.0	118.0
Foreign-born white										
1950....................	136.5	109.7	117.2	126.8	142.5	110.3	102.0	170.3	162.2	159.9
1920....................	136.2	110.7	122.7	127.2	139.0	137.1	151.2	130.1	152.1	168.6
Negro										
1950....................	101.7	137.8	123.5	113.5	111.2	102.1	100.0	102.5	126.3	122.5
1920....................	100.3	134.3	119.9	120.0	118.8	99.7	99.0	101.9	151.4	129.2
Other nonwhite races										
1950....................	121.1	120.5	130.1	120.5	114.7	104.1	103.0	106.9	109.1	173.2
1920....................	121.9	....	113.7	109.8	106.2	102.6	114.1	104.1	112.5	166.2

Source: U.S. Census of Population: 1950 (Compiled from state reports). U.S. Census of Population: 1930,
Vol. II, Table II, P. 108.

whole was 279. Among the foreign-born it was 770, and among the small Negro population it was 502. A sex ratio of 279 means that only about one person in four was female. This characteristic persisted in the West for many decades. As late as 1940, when all the other divisions had sex ratios near 100 or below, the Mountain and Pacific Divisions still had ratios of 107 and 105, respectively. During the 1940-50 decade, the decline in the foreign-born population and a heavy westward migration appear to have reduced these differences a great deal, although even in 1950 the highest sex ratios were to be found in the two western divisions.

This tendency in the West toward a preponderance of males over many decades has been sustained by selective internal migration as well as by selection among immigrants. From 1850 to 1950 the West has had a higher proportion of males in its native white population than any other division. If there had not been a continued male balance among in-migrants, at least until 1910, this differential would have been reduced much more quickly.

Table 8-10 permits a comparison between the urban and rural sex ratios of each color-nativity-race group for each geographic division, in 1920 as well as 1950. It furnishes evidence that the tendency toward lower urban than rural sex ratios was present in each geographic division, for each color-nativity-race group (except minor nonwhite races), in 1920 as well as in 1950--and probably even before 1920.

The native white urban population is predominantly female in all divisions, and the interdivisional variations in this respect are comparatively small. This situation existed even in 1920. A low sex ratio (near 100) was also shown by the urban foreign-born white population in 1950, although in 1920 this group had high sex ratios in all

divisions except New England. In the past it was the rural areas, and especially the rural territories which were first being settled that showed unusually high sex ratios, both for native and foreign-born whites. With increasing urbanization, these unique concentrations of males have largely disappeared. It is entirely possible that by 1960 the vestiges of this unusual trait of the West will have disappeared, except perhaps in the local statistics of a few remote areas.

SEX RATIOS AND SIZE OF PLACE

Table 8-11 contains sex ratios for the major color-nativity-race groups in 1950, classified according to size of place. Except for the urban-rural and farm-nonfarm differences already mentioned, there is no discernible pattern of changing sex ratios with increase or decrease in size of place. In each size of place the foreign-born white tends to have a higher sex ratio than the native white, and the Negro has a lower sex ratio than the native white. Cities of all sizes tend to have a predominance of women; the extent of this predominance is about as great in small cities as in large cities.

Table 8-11.—SEX RATIO OF THE POPULATION CLASSIFIED BY SIZE OF PLACE, BY COLOR-NATIVITY-RACE: 1950

Size of place	Total	White			Nonwhite		
		Total	Native	Foreign born	Total	Negro	Other races
U.S. total.........	98.6	99.0	98.6	103.8	95.7	94.3	131.7
Urbanized areas							
3,000,000 or more.......	94.0	94.4	93.4	98.8	90.4	87.7	153.9
1,000,000 to 3,000,000..	94.3	94.3	93.7	98.6	94.1	92.1	159.8
250,000 to 1,000,000....	94.0	94.2	93.8	100.0	91.9	91.0	142.1
Less than 250,000.......	93.5	94.1	93.7	100.1	88.5	87.7	121.6
Outside urbanized areas							
25,000 or more..........	93.7	94.0	93.8	97.4	90.5	89.7	138.8
10,000 to 25,000........	93.0	93.4	92.9	102.9	89.5	88.3	142.6
2,500 to 10,000........	93.1	93.4	93.1	100.7	89.4	88.7	117.1
1,000 to 2,500..........	94.3	94.5	94.3	100.6	91.2	90.4	110.7
Incorporated places less than 1,000............	93.8	94.1	93.6	110.6	90.0	88.3	132.4
Other rural.............	107.6	108.2	107.8	123.4	103.5	102.7	115.2
Nonfarm.............	105.7	105.8	105.4	115.2	104.9	104.2	112.9
Farm................	109.5	110.7	110.1	136.1	102.6	101.8	117.9

Source: U.S. Census of Population: 1950, Special Reports, Characteristics by Size of Place, Table 1; U.S. Total, Vol. II, U.S. Summary, Table 36, p. 1-88.

Table 8-12.—SEX RATIOS OF THE TWENTY-FIVE LARGEST STANDARD METROPOLITAN CENTRAL CITIES,
AND SUBURBAN RINGS, BY COLOR: 1950

Twenty-five largest S.M.A.'s	All classes			White population			Nonwhite population		
	S.M.A. total	Central city	Ring	S.M.A. total	Central city	Ring	S.M.A. total	Central city	Ring
New York-Northeastern N.J....	94.4	94.1	95.2	95.1	95.0	95.5	86.9	86.6	88.6
Chicago, Ill................	97.8	96.4	100.4	98.3	97.1	100.3	93.9	92.4	102.4
Los Angeles, Calif..........	93.5	91.9	94.8	93.1	91.3	94.6	98.8	97.6	103.0
Philadelphia, Pa............	96.1	93.7	99.3	96.5	94.5	98.9	93.0	89.9	105.2
Detroit, Mich...............	101.3	100.4	102.6	101.6	100.8	102.7	98.6	98.2	100.8
Boston-Lowell-Lawrence, Mass.	93.0	93.5	92.7	92.8	93.2	92.6	100.9	100.4	102.5
San Francisco-Oakland, Calif.	102.3	99.3	105.5	100.9	97.2	104.8	116.6	116.7	116.4
Pittsburgh, Pa..............	98.1	94.3	99.9	98.1	94.1	99.8	98.3	95.1	103.4
St. Louis, Mo...............	93.9	90.1	98.1	94.4	90.3	98.3	90.7	88.9	95.4
Cleveland, Ohio.............	95.5	96.1	94.5	95.7	96.5	94.5	93.9	94.1	86.4
Washington, D.C.............	94.3	89.1	101.0	94.5	88.2	100.2	93.6	90.6	109.6
Baltimore, Md...............	97.5	94.5	105.2	97.4	94.2	104.5	97.7	95.3	111.9
Minneapolis-St. Paul, Minn...	94.1	91.2	103.0	93.9	90.9	102.9	109.3	107.9	149.8
Buffalo, N. Y...............	97.2	94.6	100.2	97.1	94.4	100.1	100.3	98.7	106.5
Cincinnati, Ohio............	91.7	90.1	93.8	91.9	90.2	93.8	90.2	89.6	93.3
Milwaukee, Wis..............	96.5	95.7	98.6	96.2	95.3	98.6	106.5	106.2	123.8
Kansas City, Mo.............	93.4	90.3	97.4	93.5	90.1	97.8	92.3	92.1	92.8
Houston, Tex................	97.7	95.9	103.2	98.9	97.0	104.0	92.7	92.0	96.8
Seattle, Wash...............	100.9	99.9	102.7	99.8	98.3	102.4	129.9	129.9	130.0
Portland, Oreg..............	97.7	93.3	103.0	97.4	92.6	102.9	114.6	113.0	123.0
New Orleans, La.............	91.8	90.4	99.0	93.5	92.0	99.6	87.7	87.0	95.8
Providence, R. I............	93.9	92.1	94.9	93.8	91.9	94.8	101.7	98.1	116.2
Atlanta, Ga.................	91.9	86.3	97.6	93.9	88.4	98.0	85.9	82.8	95.1
Dallas, Tex.................	93.2	91.0	98.7	93.5	91.2	99.5	91.2	89.9	94.0
Louisville, Ky..............	93.3	90.8	97.9	93.7	91.0	98.0	90.4	89.8	94.6

SEX COMPOSITION IN METROPOLITAN AREAS

Table 8-12 reports the sex composition, in 1950, of the central city and the metropolitan ring of the 25 largest standard metropolitan areas. The most "feminized" places are:

	Sex ratio
Cincinnati..............	91.7
New Orleans.............	91.8
Atlanta.................	91.9
Boston-Lowell-Lawrence...	93.0
Dallas..................	93.2
Louisville.............	93.3
Kansas City.............	93.4
Los Angeles.............	93.5

The most masculine places are:

	Sex ratio
San Francisco...........	102.3
Detroit.................	101.3
Seattle.................	100.9

Within each metropolitan area, the sex ratio of the central city tends to be considerably lower than that of the ring. This is not always true as regards the nonwhite population. The number of female domestic servants living in suburban households appears to cause this irregularity.

IMPLICATIONS OF SEX COMPOSITION

Like age and color-nativity-race, sex composition has cultural as well as biological implications, and therefore it is of basic significance for social science. Women differ from men with respect to the age at which they marry, the period of time they remain in the labor force, the kinds of jobs they hold, the incomes they earn, and the attitudes they have toward many social and economic issues. For this reason, in the chapters that follow, sex is taken into account whenever analysis seems to warrant it.

Note: The future sex composition of the population is discussed in Chapter 26.

Chapter 9

MORTALITY AND CAUSES OF DEATH*

TRENDS IN THE CRUDE DEATH RATE, IN THE UNITED STATES: 1900 TO 1957

It has already been shown that three basic demographic processes--fertility, mortality, and migration--determine the course of population growth, and have a strong influence upon population composition and distribution. With this chapter we begin a systematic and more intensive study of each of these processes, and of how they have functioned in the population of the United States. A detailed study of each process is necessary before past and current changes in population can be evaluated, and before future changes can be predicted. Mortality is discussed first, since the mortality experience of a population should be considered in the study of both fertility and migration. [1]

THE DEATH RATES

The annual death toll among the population as a whole is conveniently expressed as the "general death rate" (sometimes called the "crude death rate"), which is the number of deaths per year per 1,000 residents. [2] One of the nation's great accomplishments, made possible by the application of scientific knowledge and by the raising of the standard of living, has been the lowering of crude death rates from a very high level (estimated at about 25 to 28 in 1800) to 9.6 in 1957--a decline of 60 to 65 percent. In fact, the level of a community's death rates (especially the infant death rate and the death rates connected with certain communicable diseases) is usually a rough but adequate measure of that community's level of living and the state of its technological advancement.

---

[1] Statistics concerning death and its causes are obtained by tabulating the information reported on death certificates. A death certificate contains facts pertinent to the deceased and to the cause of his death, as attested by a physician or other medical authority; it must be filled out according to state regulations, and deposited with the registrar of vital statistics in the city and/or county where death occurred, before a burial permit will be issued to the funeral director. It is known that the registration of deaths is not one hundred percent complete in the United States, especially in the case of infants who die during the first few hours or days of life and whose births have not been attended by a physician; nevertheless, deaths are believed to be among the most accurately and completely counted classes of events that occur among the nation's population. Death certificates are forwarded in each state to the Office of Vital Statistics (a part of the State Department of Health), where annual reports are compiled concerning births and deaths in the state. The state offices send copies of the death certificates to the National Office of Vital Statistics (a part of the United States Department of Health, Education, and Welfare), which tabulates and publishes an integrated report for the nation as a whole, and for each state and county. This annual report is entitled Vital Statistics of the United States.

[2] Ideally, the numerator of such a rate is the number of deaths that occur among a population during a calendar year and the denominator is the population that is exposed to the possibility of dying during the same interval of time. Since this ideal is extremely difficult to achieve in actual practice, it

---

*The National Office of Vital Statistics published an excellent analysis of recent mortality trends, in Volume I of its report, Vital Statistics of the United States: 1950. Much of the present chapter is abstracted or quoted from this source.

Footnote 2 continued.

must be approximated. Death can occur while a person is away from home--in a nearby hospital, on a highway, in a distant sanitarium, in a penitentiary, or visiting in another state. If death statistics are tabulated by place of occurrence, and if rates are computed by relating deaths to the populations residing in the communities where the deaths occurred, the rates may be very misleading. Communities with good hospital facilities will tend to show high death rates because people who are seriously ill travel to these communities for treatment, and a certain proportion of them die there. Towns where sanitaria, penitentiaries, mental hospitals, and homes for the aged are located will also have unusually large death rates. Communities with poor medical facilities may show extraordinarily low mortality rates simply because many of the residents who become seriously ill are taken elsewhere for treatment. Death rates will more accurately reflect the force of mortality upon a population if the mortality data from which they are computed allocate each death to the residence of the deceased. This task must be done with extreme care if the results are to be accurate. For example, maps and coding guides must be up-to-date if one is to determine whether the deaths that are allocated to street addresses in a partially built-up part of a metropolitan area are to be charged to the residents of the central city, to the residents of a particular suburban incorporated city, or to the residents of an unincorporated suburban territory that may be defined by the Census either as urban or rural, depending upon its size, density, and location.

Another difficulty is provided by the underregistration of deaths. If the death of a newborn infant, for instance, is not reported to the local registrar of vital statistics, the statistics are incomplete and the rates reported for the community are too low. Careless and incompetent officials may not register all the deaths that are reported to them, which also results in a reported rate that is too low.

In the United States, the death statistics collected by the 48 states are coordinated by the National Office of Vital Statistics (NOVS). The NOVS works continuously and cooperatively with the various State Offices of Vital Statistics, to reduce the errors resulting from underregistration and to improve in other ways the accuracy of the information reported.

Arriving at a reasonably valid denominator for a death rate also involves technical difficulties. The population that is "exposed" to death in a given community cannot be easily identified: births and deaths are continuously taking place, and people are constantly moving in and moving out. Between January 1 and December 31 of a given year, there may be a large change in a particular community's resident population. In order to compute mortality rates, the demographer must arbitrarily choose a population which he thinks represents the average number of persons "exposed" to the possibility of dying at a certain time. If he assumes that all changes occur uniformly throughout the 12 months of the year, then the midyear population is the most accurate estimate he can make of this average exposed population. The midyear population is equal to the total number of persons who lived one year of

Footnote 2 continued.

their lives in the community during a given calendar year, plus the combined fractions of that calendar year during which migrants, newborn infants, and persons who died during the year lived in the community (provided birth, death, and migration are assumed to have occurred uniformly throughout the year). Therefore, unless he has reason to make other assumptions, the demographer assumes that the population as of July 1 of any year is the correct denominator for computing mortality rates, since it represents the total life-years of exposure for a given year.

The difficulties connected with computing death rates do not end with the finding of an adequate denominator, however. In the United States a census is taken only once every 10 years, on April 1. Death statistics are tabulated for each year. Before the death rate of a community can be computed, the mid-year population of that community must be estimated. If the rate to be computed is for a year after a census has been taken and no new census is yet available, the estimate is termed a postcensal population estimate. If a census is available both for a year before and for a year after the year for which a rate is being computed, an intercensal estimate of the mid-year population may be established. For example, in order to compute a death rate for the year 1945 it would be not only possible, but also wise, to use both the Census of 1940 and the Census of 1950 in making the estimate. Intercensal estimates are more accurate than postcensal estimates, because more information is available. For this reason, vital statisticians sometimes compute preliminary postcensal death rates, which they later revise as intercensal death rates after the next census has been taken.

Accurate estimates of the postcensal or intercensal populations of states, cities, and other small populations are extremely difficult to make, and are frequently impossible unless a sample count is taken. Many methods of making postcensal estimates have been devised, but none is really satisfactory except at the national level. Since it is possible to maintain an accurate estimate of the entire population of the United States (by sex, age, and color), the annual death rates for the nation (by sex, age, and color) are quite reliable. The rates for most of the individual states are moderately accurate, while those for individual standard metropolitan areas, cities, and counties may be very inaccurate.

The one time at which all vital rates for all areas are quite precise is, of course, the year during which a census has been taken. Hence, in studying the historic trends of mortality in the various regions, states, cities, and other local areas, greatest reliance must be placed on the rates for census years.

Another difficulty encountered in computing valid death rates is the need for census data and vital statistics data that are fully comparable. If the definition of place of residence, age, or race that is used by those who collect and tabulate vital statistics is not identical with that used by the Census, then the deaths are not being related exactly to the exposed populations--especially when rates are computed separately for each age, race, sex, and residence group. Both the census data

The conquest of disease and death has been a dramatic part of the history of the United States, involving crusades for pure food, water, and milk, for sanitation in public dining places, for safe disposal of waste, and for immunization against those diseases for which vaccines were available; it has also included attempts to educate the public with respect to certain basic principles of diet, rest, and cleanliness, and the early recognition of the symptons of dangerous ailments; finally, there has been an ever-increasing encouragement of, and interest in, medical research and a drive toward increased knowledge and skill in medicine, surgery, and various other types of therapy.

Unfortunately, the full history of this conquest cannot be traced by means of the official statistics. In the United States, dependable death statistics were not available for all of the states until the year 1933, and almost no official registration statistics are available for years before 1900. Before 1933, the registration systems of some states did not produce death statistics that were sufficiently accurate and complete to permit these states to belong to the "registration area." The registration area consisted of a group of states and major cities that met certain specifications concerning completeness of registration and accuracy of detail of information; these specifications

were set by the United States Bureau of the Census (which collected the nation's vital statistics prior to 1944). [3] In the year 1900 the first of a series of annual data were collected and published for the death registration area. Table 9-1 reports the number of deaths and the crude death rate (deaths per 1,000 total population) for the states included in the death registration area, for each year since 1900. [4]

---

[3] The registration area for deaths was formed in 1880, and comprised two states, the District of Columbia, and several large cities. Statistics for the registration area published prior to 1940 referred to the entire registration area, including the large cities located in states that were not in the registration area. Beginning in 1940, the national tabulations for earlier years excluded these large cities located in non-registration-area states, because good population estimates with which to compute rates were not available for these places. In using vital statistics reports for various years one should distinguish carefully between summaries for the death registration area and for the death registration states. Whereas the death registration area contained 40.5 percent of the nation's population in 1900, the death registration states contained 26.2 percent. (Source: National Office of Vital Statistics, Vital Statistics of the United States, 1950, Vol. I, p. 13.)

[4] Column 3 of this table reports the proportion of the total population that was included in the death registration states. As more states entered the death registration area, the coverage was extended. By 1910 more than one-half of the population was represented. More than 80 percent of the population was in the death registration states in 1920; in 1930 this proportion was 95 percent.

Death rates for the registration area during the early years may not be exactly representative of death rates for the entire United States during those same years, because the registration area did not include certain states in which death rates at each age were thought to be high due to poorer health conditions. On the other hand, many of the states admitted more recently (including states with poorer health conditions) have populations that are comparatively young and comparatively rural, traits which would tend to give them a low crude death rate. The death rates for the expanding registration area (shown in Table 9-1) are somewhat lower than the death rates for the same years computed for the death registration area as it was comprised in 1900. This means that differences in age composition acted to offset any differences in health conditions that may have prevailed in the states more recently admitted to the death registration area. (It also may mean that registration was less complete in the states newly admitted to the registration area.)

Footnote 2 continued.

and the vital statistics data contain errors resulting from misreporting. If those errors are not identical in relative size and distribution, the rates are affected. For example, it is noted in Chapter 6, on Age Composition, that in a census enumeration there is a tendency for persons just under 65 years of age to report themselves as being 65 or older. Unless there is a corresponding tendency toward misreporting when the age of the deceased is stated on the death certificate, the death rates for ages 60 to 64 will be too high and those for age 65 and older will be too low.

Thus, computing accurate death rates requires that the staffs of the offices of vital statistics, at the county, municipal, state, and national levels, be highly trained and conscientious. Even under the best conditions, there are minor flaws in the data. Actuaries have devised special procedures by means of which the basic data can be adjusted before computation of the rates to be used in constructing life tables and the more complex measures of the force of mortality.

The trend indicated by the statistics shown in Table 9-1 (see also Figure 9-1) is thought to be a good approximation of the changes that were taking place in the United States. It is evident that the crude death rate declined rapidly and fairly steadily from 1900 to 1957. From 17.2 per thousand in 1900, it declined to 9.6 in 1950, a fall of 45 percent in a half-century. Since 1950 the rate has hovered around 9.6, except for the year 1954, when it reached an all-time low of 9.2

Epidemics and other variations have caused temporary reversals of the general downward trend. The influenza epidemic of 1918 is the outstanding example; during this year the rate was 18.1 per thousand, almost 50 percent above the average rate for the years preceding or following. If the rates in the states included in the death registration area for the years 1917, 1918, and 1919 are assumed to be representative of the national rates for those years (these states included 68 to 80 percent of the population), it can be estimated that there were about 424,000 more deaths in the United States in 1918 than in 1917, and about 520,000 more than in the year 1919. This widespread infection removed an estimated 450,000 to 475,000 persons (a number approximately equal to the combined population, in 1950, of Nevada and Wyoming) in excess of the number which the normal force of death could be expected to have removed at that time. Other years when death rates were significantly higher than the trend would lead one to expect were 1904, 1923, 1926, 1928, 1936-37, 1943, and 1957. (In 1957 the nation experienced a mild epidemic of "Asian flu.") The decline in death rates seems to have been distributed somewhat unevenly over the years. From 1900 to 1950 the crude death rate dropped 7.6 points. A uniform decline during this period would have amounted to a fall of .15 points per year, or 1.5 points per decade. From 1900 to 1902 the crude death rate dropped by 1.7 points, a decrease accounting in two years for one-fifth of the total decline that took place during the half-century. Between 1902 and 1915 it declined by another 2.3 points, which was above the average rate of .15 points per year. Another one-fifth of the decline occurred in the period 1915 to 1921, in spite of the

Table 9-1.—NUMBER OF DEATHS AND CRUDE DEATH RATES FOR THE DEATH REGISTRATION STATES

Year	Number of deaths	Percent of U.S. pop. registered	General death rate	Change from preceding year
1957......	1,636,000	100.0	9.6	0.2
1956......	1,564,476	100.0	9.4	0.1
1955......	1,528,717	100.0	9.3	0.1
1954......	1,481,091	100.0	9.2	-0.4
1953......	1,517,541	100.0	9.6	...
1952......	1,496,838	100.0	9.6	-0.1
1951......	1,482,099	100.0	9.7	0.1
1950......	1,452,454	100.0	9.6	-0.1
1949......	1,443,607	100.0	9.7	-0.2
1948......	1,444,337	100.0	9.9	-0.2
1947......	1,445,370	100.0	10.1	0.1
1946......	1,395,617	100.0	10.0	-0.6
1945......	1,401,719	100.0	10.6	...
1944......	1,411,338	100.0	10.6	-0.3
1943......	1,459,544	100.0	10.9	0.6
1942......	1,385,187	100.0	10.3	-0.2
1941......	1,397,642	100.0	10.5	-0.3
1940......	1,417,269	100.0	10.8	0.2
1939......	1,387,897	100.0	10.6	...
1938......	1,381,391	100.0	10.6	-0.7
1937......	1,450,427	100.0	11.3	-0.3
1936......	1,479,228	100.0	11.6	0.7
1935......	1,392,752	100.0	10.9	-0.2
1934......	1,396,903	100.0	11.1	0.4
1933......	1,342,106	100.0	10.7	-0.2
1932......	1,293,269	95.2	10.9	-0.2
1931......	1,307,273	95.3	11.1	-0.2
1930......	1,327,240	95.3	11.3	-0.6
1929......	1,369,757	94.7	11.9	-0.1
1928......	1,361,987	94.3	12.0	0.7
1927......	1,211,627	90.1	11.3	-0.8
1926......	1,257,256	88.4	12.1	0.4
1925......	1,191,809	88.1	11.7	0.1
1924......	1,151,076	87.0	11.6	-0.5
1923......	1,174,065	86.5	12.1	0.4
1922......	1,083,952	84.2	11.7	0.2
1921......	1,009,673	80.9	11.5	-1.5
1920......	1,118,070	80.9	13.0	0.1
1919......	1,072,263	79.6	12.9	-5.2
1918......	1,430,079	76.6	18.1	4.1
1917......	981,239	68.0	14.0	0.2
1916......	924,971	65.7	13.8	0.6
1915......	815,500	61.6	13.2	-0.1
1914......	810,914	61.5	13.3	-0.5
1913......	802,909	59.8	13.8	0.2
1912......	745,771	57.5	13.6	-0.3
1911......	749,918	57.5	13.9	-0.8
1910......	696,856	51.4	14.7	0.5
1909......	630,057	48.9	14.2	-0.5
1908......	567,245	43.6	14.7	-1.2
1907......	550,245	39.7	15.9	0.2
1906......	531,005	39.5	15.7	-0.2
1905......	345,863	26.0	15.9	-0.5
1904......	349,855	26.0	16.4	0.8
1903......	327,295	26.0	15.6	0.1
1902......	318,636	26.0	15.5	-0.9
1901......	332,203	26.1	16.4	-0.8
1900......	343,217	26.2	17.2	...

Source: National Office of Vital Statistics, Vital Statistics of the United States, Vol. I, 1950, Table 8.02, and subsequent reports.

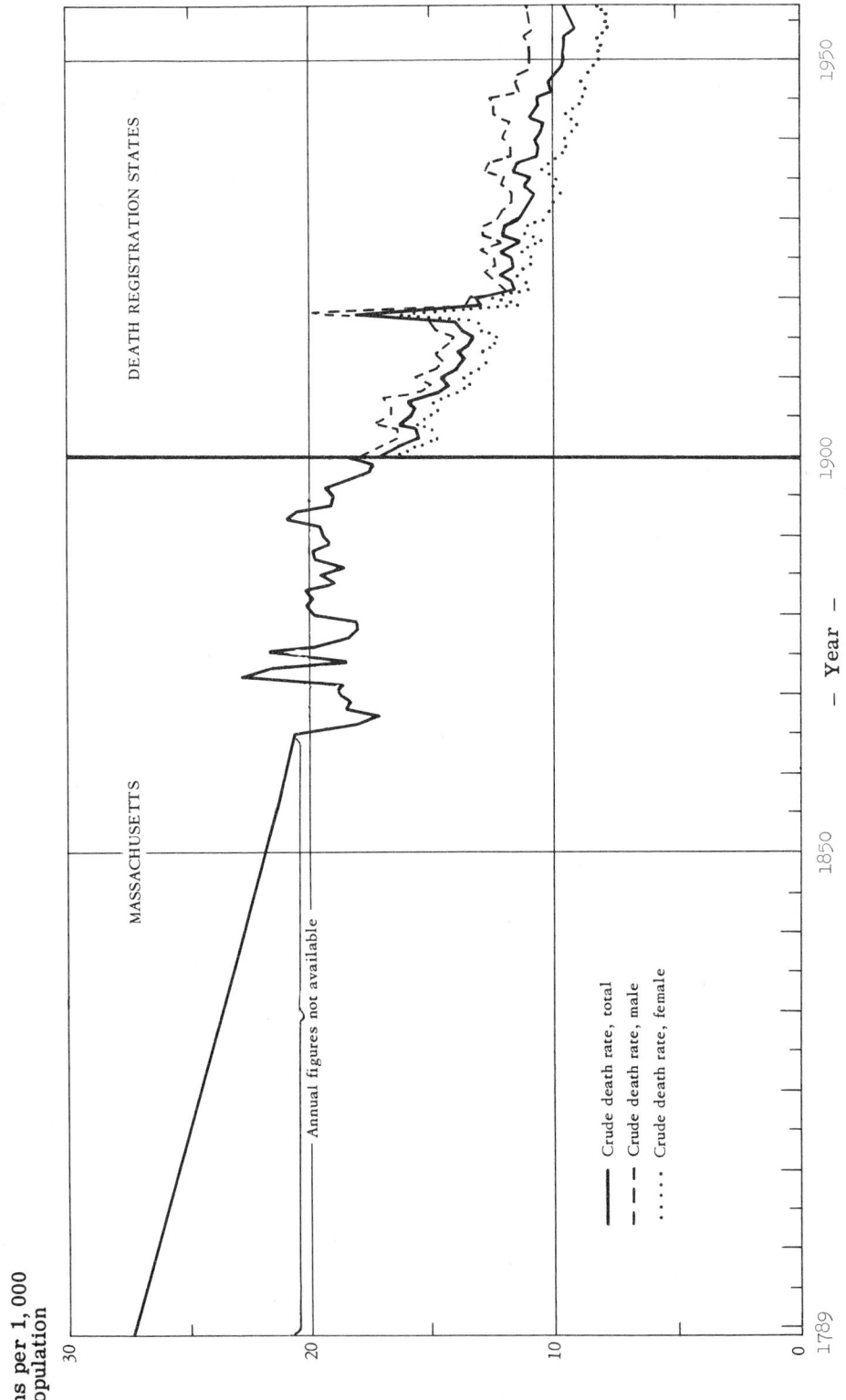

Deaths per 1,000 population

FIGURE 9-1. CRUDE DEATH RATE FOR MASSACHUSETTS, 1789 TO 1900; AND BY SEX FOR THE UNITED STATES, 1900 TO 1957

Source: Massachusetts: For 1789 from Edward Wigglesworth, Memoirs of the American Academy of Arts and Sciences, Vol. 2, old series, Pt. 1 (1793). For 1855 from E. B. Elliott, Proceedings of the American Association for the Advancement of Science, eleventh meeting, 1857. Both of the above sources cited by Warren S. Thompson and P. K. Whelpton, Population Trends in the United States, Table 62, p. 231, from which these two figures are taken. For 1865 to 1900 from Historical Statistics of the United States, 1789-1945, Series C 45-55, p. 46. For 1900 to 1950 from Vital Statistics of the United States, 1950, Vol. 1, Table 8.40, p. 191. For 1950 to 1957, see Table 9-1.

epidemic of 1918. The low rates prevailing during the years 1919 to 1921 may not be as significant as they seem, since medical opinion considers that an epidemic sweeps away many lives already impaired by the weaknesses of old age and by other diseases and disorders. After an epidemic, therefore, death rates may be unusually low. The point to be observed here is that after 1921 the death rate remained on a new low level. Almost exactly 75 percent of the total decline took place in the first 20 years (40 percent) of the 50 year period. Between 1921 and 1937 mortality rates, although fluctuating, went slowly downward and reflected a small but gradual improvement. From 1937 (when sulfa and some of the other "wonder drugs" first came into widespread use) to 1954 the downward trend again became more consistent. Thus, the mortality experience of the twentieth century seems to fall into three periods: A period of fairly rapid decline from 1900 to 1921, a period of moderate decline from 1921 to 1937, and a period of renewed rapid decline from 1937 to 1954. Between 1954 and 1957 the crude death rate remained for the most part on a plateau, rising slightly at times.

Care must be taken in interpreting the rates shown in Table 9-1 for the years 1941 to 1950, since they exclude the armed forces overseas. Because large numbers of young men were withdrawn from the population during these years, the rates as computed are more heavily weighted with older population. Hence, the rates shown in the table are undoubtedly higher than they would have been if the nation had remained at peace. For comparison purposes, the mortality experience of armed forces overseas from 1941 to 1953, and of the United States population including the armed forces overseas, are summarized in Table 9-2. Deaths among members of the armed forces overseas, as reported in column 2 of this table, are deaths from all causes, including combat. Computing the crude death rate of the United States for these years to include deaths among the armed forces overseas lowers it, in years of no combat, by about 0.1 point.

One might inquire, in passing, what effect World War II had on mortality. As Table 9-2 shows, although losses became quite high for a short time, the over-all effect upon the crude death rate in the total population of the nation was quite small. Only in 1944 did war losses cause the crude death rate to rise appreciably. Taking a rate of 10.4 as an estimate of what the crude rate would have been in 1944 if there had been no armed forces overseas, it can be inferred that deaths related to World War II raised the crude death rate by 0.8 points in 1944, or by about 9.6 percent in this peak year of war casualties.

Table 9-2.—ARMED FORCES OVERSEAS AND CRUDE DEATH RATES OF THE UNITED STATES POPULATION, INCLUDING AND EXCLUDING ARMED FORCES OVERSEAS: 1941 TO 1950

Year	Armed forces overseas (000) (1)	Deaths to armed forces overseas (2)	Crude death rate of U.S. including armed forces overseas (3)	Crude death rate of U.S. excluding armed forces overseas (4)	Difference, column 3 minus column 4 (5)
1950	435	11,458	9.7	9.6	0.1
1949	523	1,286	9.7	9.7	...
1948	538	1,317	9.9	9.9	...
1947	680	1,854	10.0	10.1	-0.1
1946	1,335	7,459	9.9	10.0	-0.1
1945	7,447	112,317	10.8	10.6	0.2
1944	5,512	160,959	11.4	10.6	0.8
1943	2,494	40,802	11.0	10.9	0.1
1942	940	25,977	10.5	10.3	0.2
1941	281	3,072	10.5	10.5	...

Source: National Office of Vital Statistics, Vital Statistics of the United States, 1952, Vol. I, Tables L and AF.

THE CRUDE DEATH RATE: 1789 TO 1900

For a knowledge of mortality conditions prior to 1900, it is necessary to piece together a general picture from the vital statistics reports prepared by individual states and cities. Records of births and deaths have been kept by several of the states since the early days of the nation's history, but their completeness and accuracy is not known. Massachusetts appears to have had a fairly good system of registration throughout much of the nineteenth century. The first report concerning vital statistics for an entire state was published by Massachusetts in 1841. Shortly thereafter, several other New England states (Rhode Island, Vermont, Connecticut) began preparing state-wide reports of births and deaths.

At the time when the thirteen colonies became the United States of America, the crude death rate in Massachusetts is estimated to be in the neighborhood of 27 to 28 per thousand. By 1855 it had declined about 6 points (about 20 percent), to a level of 21 to 22 deaths per thousand population. From 1865 to 1897 there was little discernible change in the trend. The crude death rate for the period as a whole was around 18 to 19, although in some years epidemics pushed it above this level and thus caused considerable fluctuation from year to year. From 1900 to the present, the rates for Massachusetts have followed a course very similar to those of the states included in the death registration area, the rates for Massachusetts being a little higher than those of the death registration states. Figure 9-1 attempts to illustrate, using the scanty data that is available, the general source of the crude death rate over the past 170 years. It is this evidence that provides the basis for the rough estimate, given above, that the crude death rate has fallen by about 60 to 65 percent in the last 150 years.

SPECIFIC DEATH RATES

With respect to intensive studies of the effect of mortality on the population of a nation, a region, or a smaller area, general (crude) rates are in-

adequate for many purposes. Demographers wish to learn what types of populations are most subject to death and what types are least subject. For example, in Chapter 8 it was stated that mortality is greater among men than among women. The procedure for demonstrating this fact is to compute a set of sex-specific death rates, or death rates computed separately for males and females. Establishing the age patterns associated with mortality involves computing age-specific death rates, or rates for each age. In other words, if a demographer wants to learn the comparative force with which mortality operates among groups of population that are distinguished by particular traits or combinations of traits, it is necessary to compute a schedule of trait-specific death rates, or a rate for each subgroup that has been classified according to some trait which, in the opinion of the demographer, separates high-mortality groups from low-mortality groups.[5]

Another line of analysis in mortality research is the study of the causes of death, and this work requires the use of cause-specific rates. The numerator of such a rate is the number of deaths from a particular cause, and the denominator is the number of life-years of exposure (midyear population) to the cause, either among the population at large or among the members of a particular subgroup of the population. If the midyear population as a whole is used as the denominator of cause-specific rates, the sum of all the cause-

---

[5] This raises all of the problems discussed above with respect to general rates, plus some additional ones. Both those members of the population who have died, and those who are exposed to the likelihood of death, must be stratified into the classes for which rates are desired. Theoretically, these strata could be set up according to income, education, occupation, and many other socio-economic characteristics. Actually, the strata are limited to the traits that are listed on death certificates and for which the Census collects comparable information. In the United States, sex, age, and color-nativity-race are the only characteristics concerning which the raw information for computing trait-specific rates are generally available. All inferences concerning the relationship between mortality and other population characteristics must be obtained indirectly, by other methods.

pecific rates for a given year is equal to the rude death rate for that year.[6]

Mortality analysis, then, consists largely of the tudy of differences between rates. Mortality differentials may be established by comparing death ates that are trait-specific or cause-specific, or rait-cause-specific. At the present time, the maximum detail afforded by the statistics for the United States is provided by specific death rates according to age, sex, color, and cause, for the nation and for each of its principal parts.

MORTALITY AND AGE

Age-specific death rates have a characteristic curve, of the type graphed in Figure 9-2. The rate is high for the first year of life, then falls to a very low level for ages 1 to about 35 years. Thereafter, the rate rises with increasing age until it becomes very high at the oldest ages. This general shape is characteristic of the age-curves of the death rates of all nations, and of all "normal" times, for which they are recorded. However, there can be great variation among nations as to the height of the curve at each age. There can also be a similar variation among communities within the same nation, and between the schedules of age rates for the same community at different dates. Table 9-3 shows the schedule of average age-specific rates in the United States for 1956, and for a three-year average period around each of the census years since 1900. To establish this table, the rates for the individual years, as computed by NOVS, were simply averaged. This procedure helps to remove the more or less accidental year-to-year variations, and to reveal the long-run trends.

From observation of this table and of Figure 9-3, it is easy to see that the decline in mortality rates has not been evenly distributed among the

age groups. There has been a most remarkable reduction in the death rate for infants under 1 year of age. The average rate for this group from 1901 to 1902 was 147.6; it had declined to 33.6 from 1949 to 1951, or by 77 percent. (Since 1949 to 1956 it has declined even further--to 29.6, or by 12 percent. Although the rate of no other age group declined by this many points during the period 1900 to 1950, there was an equal, or even greater, percentage decline for the ages 1 to 34, as the following tabulation shows:

Decline and percent decline in average age-specific death rates, between 1900-02 and 1949-51

Age	Decline in rate (points)		Percent decline in rate	
	1900-50	1950-56	1900-50	1950-56
All ages....	6.7	0.3	41	3
Under 1 year...	114.0	4.0	77	12
1 to 4 years...	16.4	0.3	92	21
5 to 14 years..	3.0	0.1	83	17
15 to 24 years.	4.2	0.2	76	15
25 to 34 years.	6.1	0.3	77	17
35 to 44 years.	6.4	0.6	64	17
45 to 54 years.	6.1	1.2	41	14
55 to 64 years.	7.9	1.6	29	8
65 to 74 years.	14.7	0.6	27	2
75 to 84 years.	27.7	4.0	23	4
85 years-over..	54.4	8.3	22	4

One often hears the fallacious statement that comparatively little progress has been made in reducing mortality at the upper ages. The above summary shows that an average decline of 25 percent in death rates at the intervals of 65 and over has been effected, and that the point decline is larger than for any other age group except those under 5. However, it is true that the percentage declines for the older ages have not been as spectacular as those for the ages 0 to 44 years. To date, the greatest relative progress in lowering the death rate has been made by saving the lives of infants, of children, and of adults under age 50. Since 1950, substantial declines have taken place in all age groups. The greatest reductions, in terms of points, have come at the infant ages and at the older ages. A 4 percent reduction in death rates for age groups 65 and above, within 6 years, represent substantial progress. The conquest of

---

[6] Establishing cause-specific rates requires that deaths be categorized according to cause. This is a difficult task, involving many problems. The cause-of-death classification, and the limitations on its use, will be discussed in more detail later in this chapter.

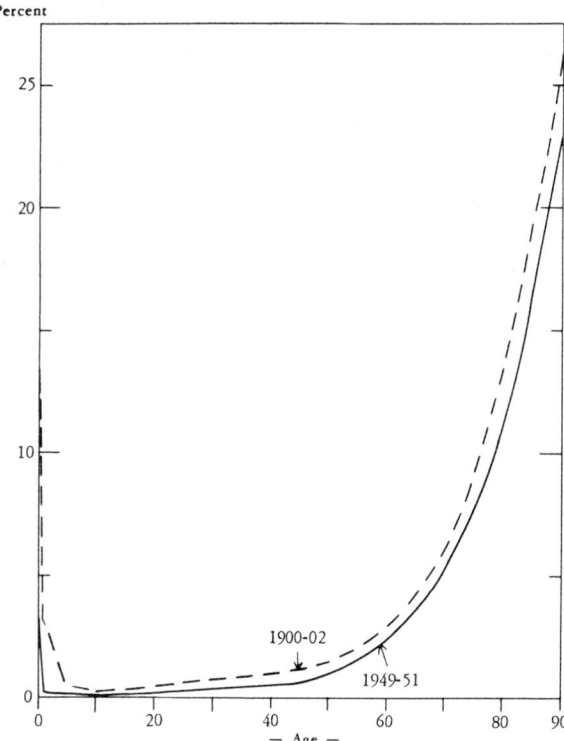

Percent

FIGURE 9-2.   PROBABILITY OF DYING AT EACH
YEAR OF AGE, WHITE MALES,
1900-1902 AND 1949-1951

death is not over; further progress may be expected.

A careful study of Table 9-3 will show that there have been variations among the age groups as regards the time when the decline took place. For example, the large decline in child and youth mortality occurred at a fairly even rate throughout the entire period. The declines at the older ages, on the other hand, have come since the late 1930's. After a rather large decline between 1900 and 1910, the death rates for the ages of mature adulthood (35 to 44 and 45 to 54) were reduced comparatively little during the 1910 to 1920 decade. The rates for these ages resumed their decline after 1920, and decreased by an extraordinary amount in the 1940 to 1950 decade.

CRUDE COLOR, NATIVITY, AND SEX
DIFFERENCES IN MORTALITY

For most of its basic tabulations the National Office of Vital Statistics does not make use of the full color-nativity-race classification set up by the Census, described in Chapter 7. Instead, it tabulates deaths according to whether the deceased was white or nonwhite. Table 9-3 reports the age-specific rates according to this dichotomous classification, by sex, for 1956 and for the 3-year average period surrounding each census since 1900. However, summaries for 1940 and 1950 were prepared according to the Census color-nativity-race classification; the crude rates for each category, by sex, are shown in Table 9-4.

These tables show that the crude death rate for males is considerably higher than it is for females. Figure 9-1 provides evidence that this difference is of long standing, going back at least as far as 1865. The rates for nonwhites (both males and females) are higher than the corresponding rates for whites. Foreign-born white populations have very high crude death rates; this is largely a result of their concentration in the older ages, as will be shown below. Among the nonwhite populations, American Indians have a higher death rate than any other group, while the Japanese and the "other nonwhite races" have rates that are unbelievably low. The high rate for Indians is due partly to the fact that certain groups of mixed Indian-Negro ancestry tend to be classed by the Census as "other nonwhite," while the deaths occurring in these same groups are often reported as Indian deaths. This has the tendency of inflating the rates for Indians and deflating the rates for other nonwhite races. Nevertheless, the National Office of Vital Statistics is of the opinion that "...Even with this limitation, age-specific rates for Indians under 45 years of age are considerably higher than those in any other race group."[7] The Chinese, the Japanese, and other

---

[7] Vital Statistics of the United States: 1950, Vol. I, p. 159.

Table 9-3.—AGE-SPECIFIC DEATH RATES BY COLOR AND SEX: DEATH-REGISTRATION STATES, 1900 TO 1956

Color, sex, and year	All ages (crude rate)	Age										
		Under 1 year	1-4 years	5-14 years	15-24 years	25-34 years	35-44 years	45-54 years	55-64 years	65-74 years	75-84 years	85 years and over
ALL RACES, BOTH SEXES												
1956.................	9.4	29.6	1.1	0.5	1.1	1.5	3.0	7.4	17.5	39.9	89.0	189.7
1949 to 1951........	9.7	33.6	1.4	0.6	1.3	1.8	3.6	8.6	19.1	40.5	93.0	198.0
1939 to 1941........	10.6	53.7	3.0	1.0	2.0	3.1	5.2	10.6	22.0	47.0	109.5	225.0
1929 to 1931........	11.4	68.3	5.7	1.8	3.4	4.7	6.9	12.3	24.0	51.8	115.1	235.0
1919 to 1921........	12.5	88.0	9.1	2.6	4.7	6.4	7.8	11.9	22.9	50.5	112.6	236.5
1909 to 1911........	14.3	124.2	13.1	2.8	4.5	6.4	8.9	13.5	25.9	54.8	120.2	247.2
1900 to 1902........	16.4	147.6	17.8	3.6	5.5	7.9	10.0	14.7	27.0	55.2	120.7	252.4
WHITE MALES												
1956.................	10.8	29.8	1.1	0.5	1.6	1.7	3.3	9.0	22.2	48.9	103.8	203.7
1949 to 1951........	11.0	34.5	1.4	0.7	1.6	1.9	3.8	9.9	23.1	48.4	105.0	216.5
1939 to 1941........	11.4	55.1	2.9	1.1	2.0	2.8	5.1	11.3	24.8	52.9	119.4	242.4
1929 to 1931........	11.8	70.8	5.6	1.9	3.0	4.1	6.7	12.5	25.5	55.6	121.9	245.0
1919 to 1921........	12.5	93.7	9.0	2.7	4.1	5.7	7.5	11.8	23.7	52.3	116.1	242.6
1909 to 1911........	14.9	134.6	13.2	2.9	4.5	6.5	9.5	14.7	27.9	57.7	125.7	253.6
1900 to 1902........	7.0	159.7	18.1	3.6	5.5	7.9	10.5	15.4	28.5	58.2	126.1	262.4
WHITE FEMALES												
1956.................	7.8	22.4	0.9	0.3	0.6	0.9	1.9	4.5	11.1	29.8	79.5	195.9
1949 to 1951........	8.0	26.2	1.1	0.5	0.7	1.1	2.4	5.5	13.0	32.3	84.4	194.3
1939 to 1941........	9.1	42.7	2.4	0.8	1.4	2.2	3.6	7.5	16.8	40.7	102.8	223.8
1929 to 1931........	9.9	55.4	4.9	1.5	2.6	3.7	5.3	9.4	20.0	46.5	109.9	233.5
1919 to 1921........	11.5	73.0	8.2	2.3	4.1	5.9	6.9	10.5	20.9	47.9	110.2	233.5
1909 to 1911........	13.2	108.5	12.1	2.6	4.0	5.8	7.6	11.6	23.1	51.5	115.8	245.1
1900 to 1902........	15.4	129.1	16.7	3.4	5.2	7.6	9.2	13.4	25.0	52.0	115.9	246.7
NONWHITE MALES												
1956.................	11.4	57.1	2.0	0.7	2.3	4.1	7.5	15.3	33.0	62.2	82.4	106.2
1949 to 1951........	12.5	61.5	2.7	1.0	2.9	4.9	8.7	18.7	36.4	51.9	88.1	150.4
1939 to 1941........	14.9	99.5	5.4	1.7	5.0	8.5	13.1	24.0	38.3	54.8	103.4	182.7
1929 to 1931........	17.3	124.2	9.8	2.7	7.8	12.2	17.2	26.0	39.6	65.8	120.6	229.8
1919 to 1921........	17.2	152.1	14.3	3.6	9.8	11.9	14.3	19.5	30.2	56.6	110.6	227.6
1909 to 1911........	22.2	241.4	28.8	5.5	10.4	12.7	17.1	24.8	38.8	68.1	112.7	202.4
1900 to 1902........	25.4	349.1	39.3	7.4	11.6	13.0	15.8	25.1	42.7	69.5	127.1	231.4
NONWHITE FEMALES												
1956.................	8.8	44.1	1.8	0.5	1.2	2.7	5.9	12.2	25.4	47.9	62.9	92.7
1949 to 1951........	9.9	48.4	2.3	0.7	2.2	3.9	7.5	15.6	30.0	39.7	71.3	124.5
1939 to 1941........	12.4	77.3	4.7	1.4	5.0	7.3	11.5	20.7	35.2	45.0	79.9	147.4
1929 to 1931........	15.2	97.6	8.6	2.5	8.2	11.3	15.4	24.9	40.5	59.1	93.3	184.7
1919 to 1921........	16.9	120.7	13.3	3.9	10.7	13.1	15.5	22.6	34.9	57.5	99.9	206.4
1909 to 1911........	20.9	207.5	26.3	6.2	10.9	11.7	16.0	23.8	38.9	61.5	95.4	190.5
1900 to 1902........	23.3	286.6	37.9	8.3	11.3	11.7	15.4	23.8	39.0	63.5	104.6	205.4

Source: National Office of Vital Statistics, annual reports Vital Statistics of the United States, Vol. I, 1950, Table 8.40; and 1956.

nonwhite races also have unusual age compositions; since they are an extremely small proportion of the total population, there are so many opportunities for errors and misclassifications that precise rates cannot be established for them. For example, only 865 of the 1,452,454 deaths that occurred in 1950 were reported to be deaths of Japanese persons. The statistics indicate that both the Chinese and the Japanese groups have crude death rates below those of Negroes.

Inadequacy of the Crude Death Rate. The facts that mortality is so highly concentrated at the two extremes of the age range, and that populations differ with respect to age composition, make it readily apparent that the crude death rate is not a very exact measure of the force of mortality upon

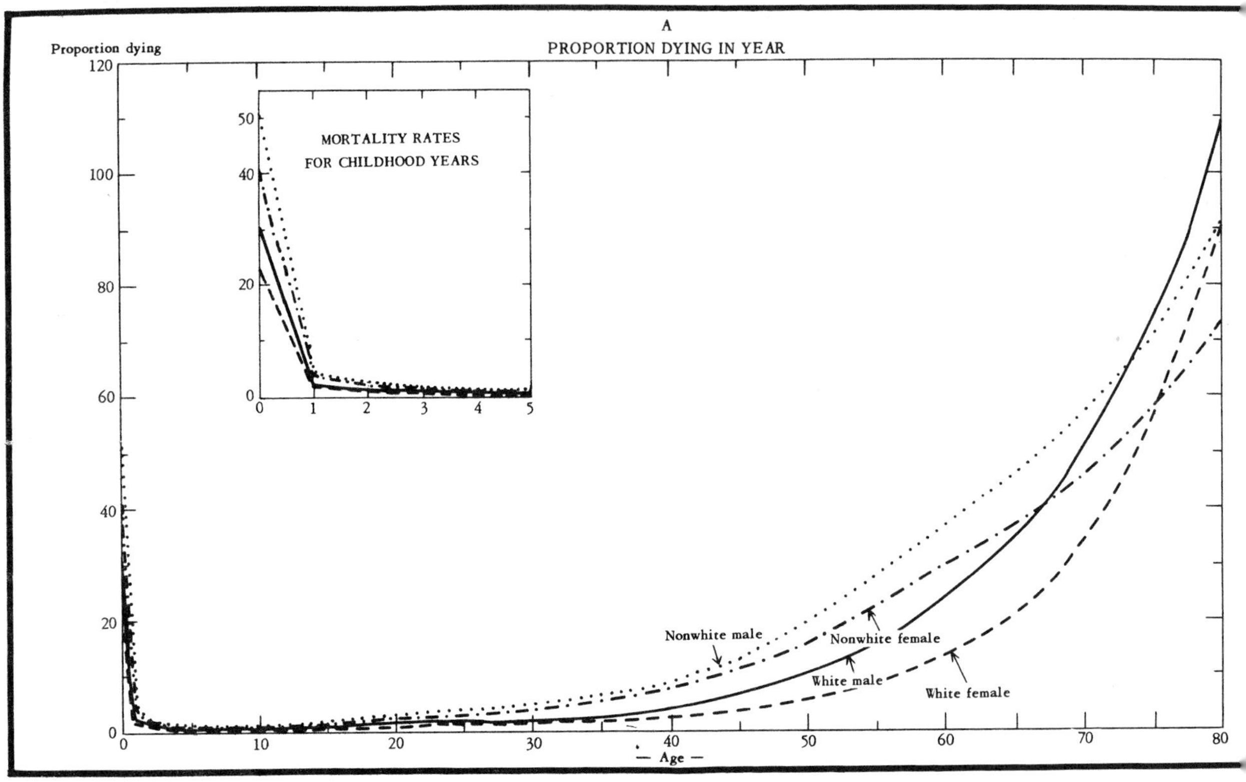

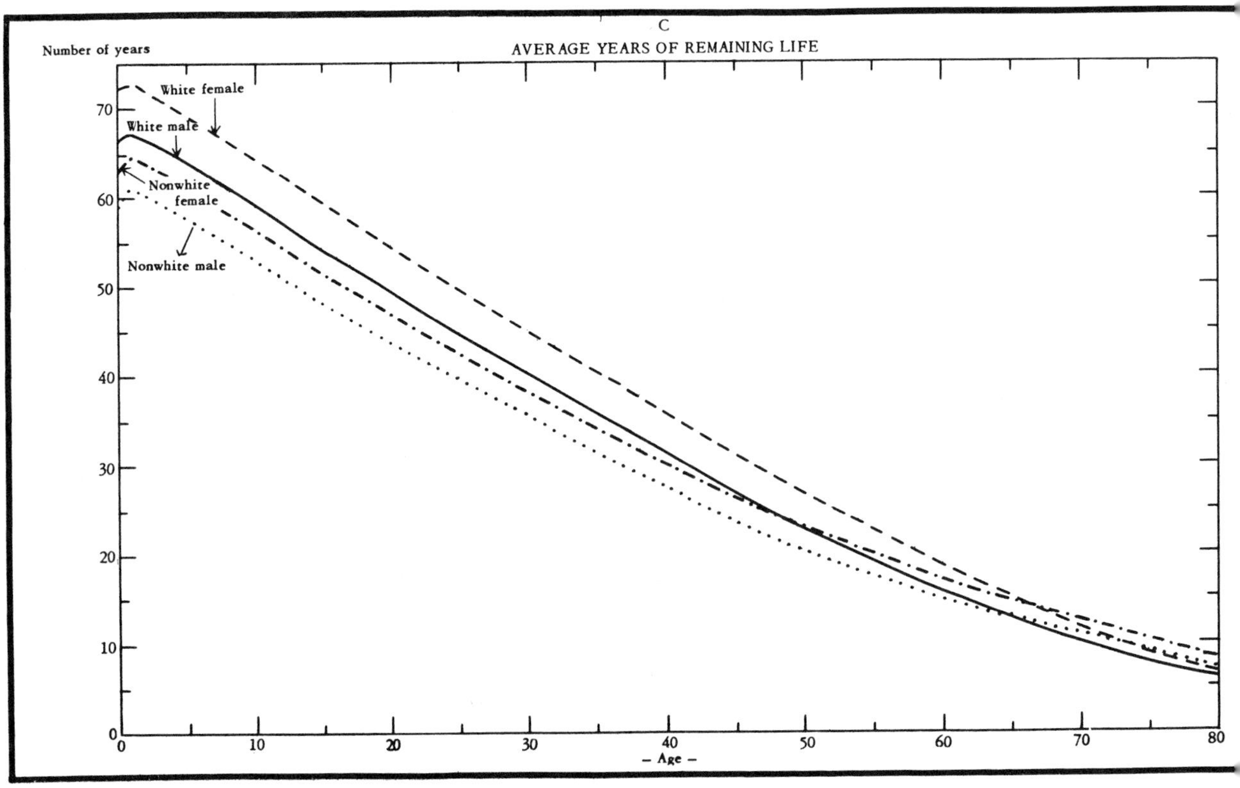

FIGURE 9-3. GRAPHS OF LIFE TABLE FUNCTIONS: UNITED STATES LIFE TABLE, 1949 TO 1951

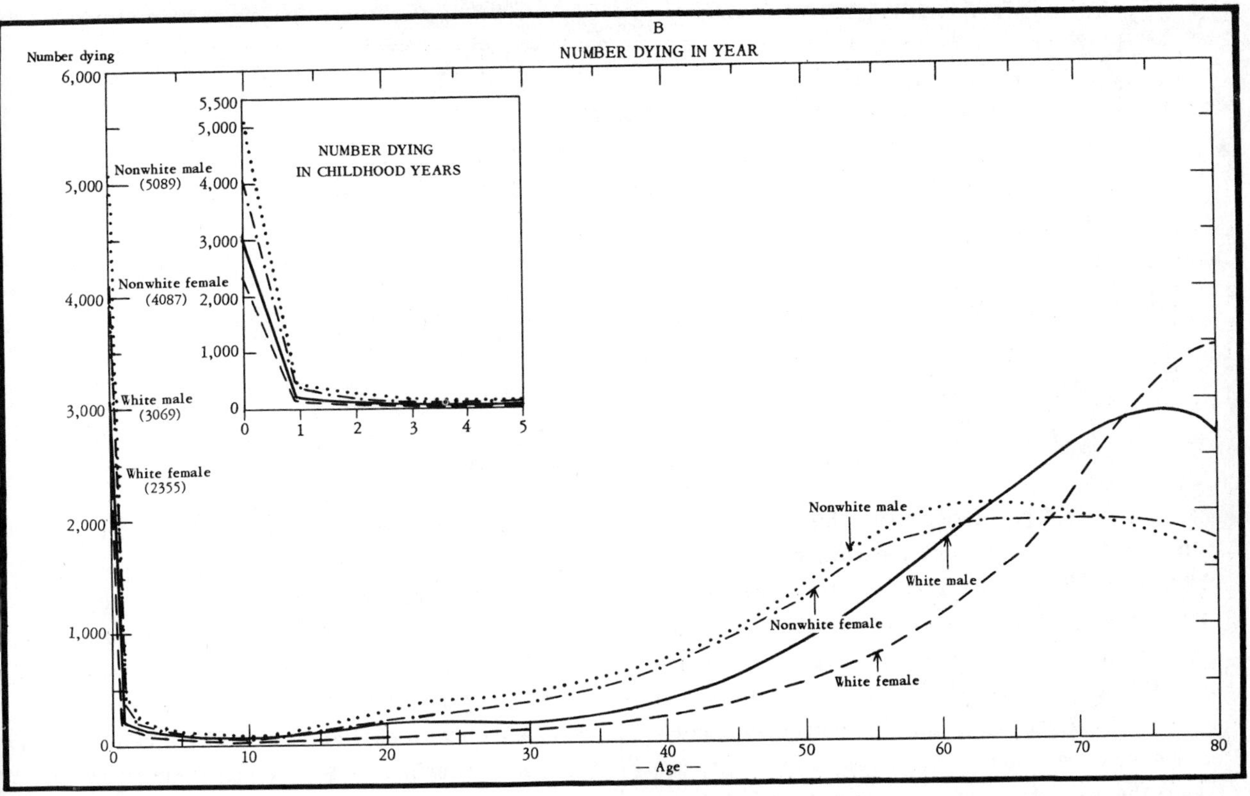

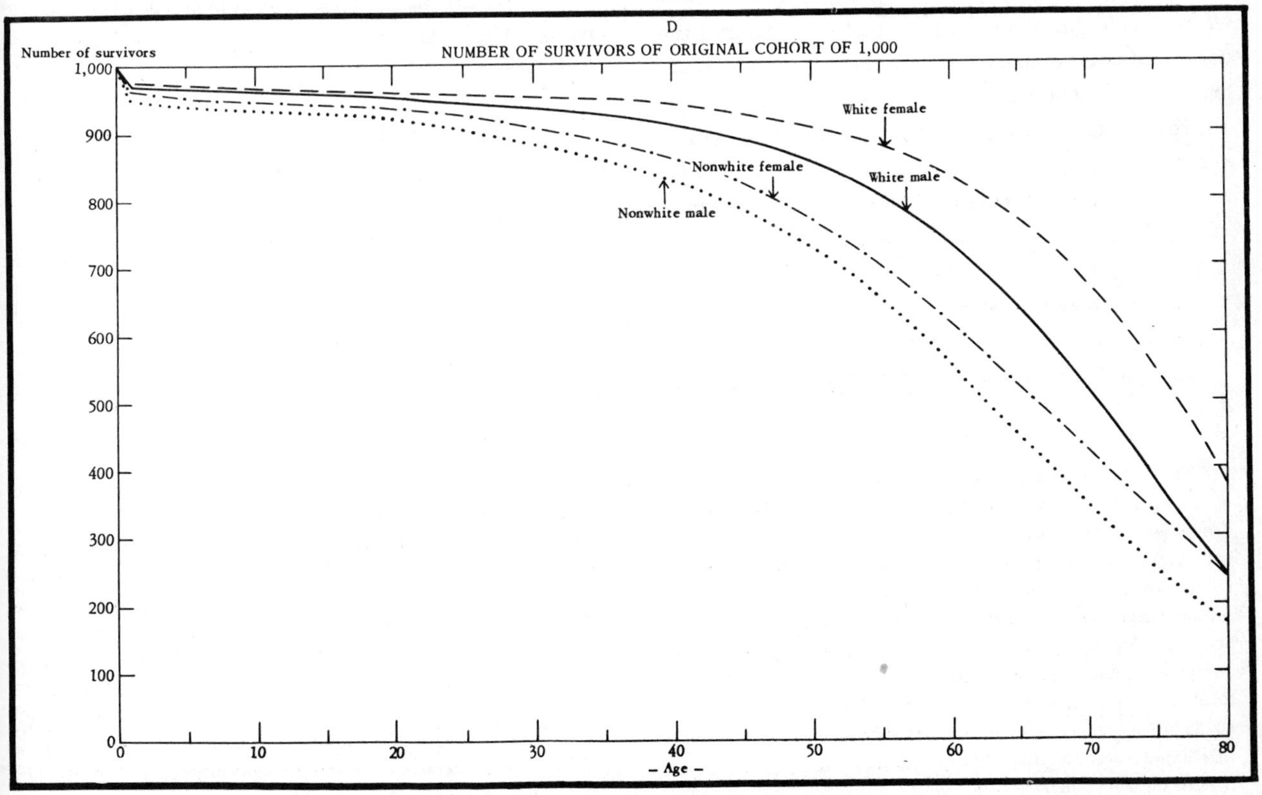

FIGURE 9-3. GRAPHS OF LIFE TABLE FUNCTIONS: UNITED STATES LIFE TABLE, 1949 TO 1951–Con.

Table 9-4.–CRUDE DEATH RATES FOR THE COLOR-NATIVITY-RACE GROUPINGS OF THE UNITED STATES POPULATION, BY SEX: 1940 AND 1950

Color, nativity, and race	1950			1940		
	Both sexes	Male	Female	Both sexes	Male	Female
Total...............	9.6	11.1	8.2	10.8	12.0	9.5
White..................	9.5	10.9	8.0	10.4	11.6	9.2
Native..............	8.1	9.3	6.8	9.1	10.1	8.0
Foreign born..........	25.8	29.5	22.0	23.1	25.0	21.0
Nonwhite...............	11.2	12.5	9.9	13.8	15.1	12.6
Negro...............	11.3	12.6	10.0	13.9	15.2	12.6
Indian..............	13.0	14.0	11.8	14.3	14.7	13.9
Chinese.............	9.0	11.6	4.2	15.3	18.3	6.7
Japanese............	6.1	8.6	3.2	6.7	8.8	4.1
Other...............	3.6	4.6	1.7	9.4	8.7	13.3

Source: National Office of Vital Statistics, Vital Statistics of the United States, Vol. I, Table 8.16, Vol. III, Table 48; Vital Statistics of the United States, 1900-40, Table 9.

a population. A population with a high concentration of older persons and a deficit of youth and children tends to have a higher crude death rate than a population with a concentration of younger persons and a comparative shortage of persons over 50 years of age. Therefore, in order to make a refined analysis of change in mortality experience over time, and of differences in mortality between the various population groups, it is necessary to introduce techniques that will control the factor of age composition. There are two principal ways to control age composition and to show the implications of a given schedule of age-specific mortality rates. These are (a) life tables, and (b) standardized death rates. The available information is sometimes reported in one of these forms and sometimes in the other, since each has its unique advantages. Hence, it is necessary to consider the results of both techniques. [8]

General Death Rate Standardized for Age. As

Chapter 6 described, the age composition of the population has changed considerably in recent years. After reviewing the above evidence concerning the intimate tie between death rates and age, it is only natural to inquire, "What would the general (crude) death rate for the nation be, in comparison with earlier years, if age composition were held constant." By "standardizing" the general rate for each of certain recent years, on the basis of the nation's age composition in 1940, the following result is obtained: [9]

Year	Standardized death rates
1957......	7.9
1956......	7.7
1955......	7.7
1954......	7.7
1953......	8.1
1952......	8.2
1951......	8.3
1950......	8.4
1949......	8.5
1945......	9.5
1940......	10.8

[8] These techniques are a part of the standard methodology of demography. It is outside the scope of the present work to describe and explain them here. If the reader is not familiar with them, he may quickly acquire the basic principles involved from two readily-available sources: "Life Tables," National Office of Vital Statistics, Vital Statistics of the United States, 1950, Vol. I, pp. 148-150, and "Adjusted Death Rates and Other Indices of Mortality," National Office of Vital Statistics, Vital Statistics of the United States, 1900-1940, pp. 60-86. The reader who is not familiar with these techniques will experience no difficulty in understanding the factual findings of the remainder of this chapter, provided he is content to read the text without attempting to study the tables.

[9] For each year, multiply the schedule of age-specific rates by the proportion of the population in each age group in 1940, and sum the results for all age groups (age-standardized rates are also called "age-adjusted rates"). Death rates in the United States now stand at a low level, a level which only a few years ago was regarded by experts as either impossible to achieve or as something that would materialize only after many decades of medical progress--perhaps toward the end of this century. Have we reached the lower limit? Can no further progress be anticipated? This topic will be discussed after a more detailed review of the death rates of particular population groups and the trends in each of the major causes of death.

The above series shows that recent progress in lowering death rates has been even more dramatic than the crude rates of Table 9-1 suggest. Between 1940 and 1950 the age-adjusted death rate declined by 20 percent (the crude rates show a decrease only of 11 percent). Between 1950 and 1954 the standardized rate declined by an additional 8 percent. No apparent progress was made in either 1955 or 1956, and preliminary figures indicate that, because of small epidemics, the rate for 1957 was slightly higher than the rates in the preceding 3 years.

A DETAILED ANALYSIS OF MORTALITY TRENDS
IN THE UNITED STATES SINCE 1900,
BY AGE, SEX, AND COLOR

The technique of standardization and the calculation of life tables (together with the schedules of age-sex-color-specific death rates) provide the means for extracting from death statistics the full details concerning the remarkable transition that has taken place since 1900. The wealth of information provided by the use of these techniques is summarized in the following tables:

Table 9-3. Age-specific death rates, for white and nonwhite populations, 1900 to 1956.

Table 9-5. Age-specific death rates for native white and foreign-born white populations, 1900 to 1950.

Table 9-6. Probability of dying at selected ages, 1949 to 1951, and change in probability of death for each decade, 1900 to 1950, for white and nonwhite populations, by sex.

Table 9-7. Age-standardized death rates for white and nonwhite populations, 1900 to 1953.

Table 9-8. Estimated average length of life at birth for white and nonwhite populations 1900 to 1953.

Table 9-9. Average remaining lifetime at specified ages, for white and nonwhite populations, 1900 to 1953.

In each of the above tables, the information is given separately for males and females. Instead of interpreting these tables seriatum, and thereby finding it necessary to repeat certain findings as they are rediscovered in different forms in successive tables, the following paragraphs attempt to make a single, integrated, and detailed analysis of the fall in mortality rates since 1900. Information will be drawn simultaneously from all of the tables listed above. [10]

The fall of 41 percent in the crude death rate between 1900 and 1950, reported in the discussion of Table 9-1, seriously understates the decline in mortality that actually occurred. The very process of reducing the death rate tends to alter the age structure, by permitting larger numbers of people to pass into the older age groups--a phenomenon described in some detail in Chapter 6. (During this same period, the fall in the birth rate, by advancing the average age, was having an even greater effect on the age composition of the population.) Because the population had a much older age composition in 1950 than in 1900, the crude death rates of the United States for current years have tended to be higher than they would have been if the age composition had remained the same. Table 9-7 presents age-standardized death rates for each five-year period from 1900 to 1950. By using the age composition of 1940 as a standard, the effect of aging is controlled. The following reduction in age-standardized death rates occurred over the half-century:

	Amount of change (point-decline in rate)	Percent decline
Total.........	9.4	53
Male........	8.6	46
Female......	10.1	59
White.........	9.6	55
Male........	8.8	48
Female......	10.3	61
Nonwhite......	15.6	56
Male........	15.2	53
Female......	16.2	59

[10] Before reading this section of the chapter, the reader may find it helpful to look over these tables in order that he may refer to them with ease as he proceeds.

Sex Differences in Mortality. Females made a much greater gain than males, showing a greater decline both in rate points and in percent. The more rapid fall in the rates of females than in those of males was characteristic of both white and nonwhite populations, but the sex difference was considerably greater among the white population. Table 9-7 shows that this sex differential in mortality was present in 1900, among both white and nonwhite populations. The trend over the years has been toward an increase in the magnitude of the differential. In 1900 the sex differential was greater among the white population, and it has increased more in the last half-century among the white than among the nonwhite population. Table 9-7 also indicates that this sex differential may have been relatively stable, or may have been increasing only slowly, prior to 1925. Since that time it has risen in a rather spectacular way.

Color Differences in Mortality. The death rate for the white population fell by 9.6 rate-points, or 55 percent, during the period. The nonwhite population enjoyed a much greater point-decline in age-standardized death rates than the white population, but the percent decline in the nonwhite rate was only a little greater than it was in the rate for whites. It is estimated that a crude death rate of 25 characterized the general population of Massa-

Table 9-5.—AGE-SPECIFIC DEATH RATES OF THE WHITE POPULATION, BY SEX AND NATIVITY: DEATH REGISTRATION, 1900 TO 1950

Sex, nativity, and year	All ages (crude rate)	Age										
		Under 1 year	1-4 years	5-14 years	15-24 years	25-34 years	35-44 years	45-54 years	55-64 years	65-74 years	75-84 years	85 years and over
1950 WHITE												
Native male........	9.3	33.6	1.3	0.7	1.5	1.9	3.8	9.9	22.7	47.6	103.9	220.6
Foreign-born male...	29.5	31.1	2.0	0.9	2.1	1.8	3.8	10.2	24.9	51.5	108.3	220.1
Native female.......	6.8	25.4	1.1	0.4	0.7	1.1	2.3	5.3	12.1	30.5	81.2	193.7
Foreign-born female.	22.0	32.6	1.7	0.7	0.9	1.2	2.5	6.2	15.7	36.9	92.1	194.7
1940 WHITE												
Native male........	10.1	56.7	2.8	1,1	2.0	2.8	5.0	11.0	24.6	53.0	122.2	266.2
Foreign-born male...	25.0	123.0	5.5	1.6	2.4	2.9	5.2	12,6	26.9	57.1	122.1	212.6
Native female.......	8.0	43.6	2.4	0.8	1.4	2.2	3.6	7.2	15.9	39.5	104.3	230.0
Foreign-born female.	21.0	91.6	5.5	1.5	1.9	2.3	3.9	8.7	20.2	48.3	109.8	210.7
1930 WHITE												
Native male........	10.5	71.8	5.5	1.8	3.0	4.0	6.2	11.8	24.7	55.4	120.5	237.1
Foreign-born male...	19.3	72.3	6.5	2.5	3.6	4.4	7.5	13.9	28.5	55.9	119.7	245.7
Native female.......	8.8	56.2	4.7	1.4	2.5	3.6	5.1	9.0	18.9	45.3	107.1	228.0
Foreign-born female.	17.1	50.1	6.2	1.9	3.0	3.6	5.5	10.4	23.6	49.7	112.3	225.5
1920 WHITE												
Native male........	12.1	103.7	9.7	2.7	4.2	5.8	7.5	11.1	23.3	52.9	119.7	247.8
Foreign-born male...	17.6	127.5	17.4	3.4	5.3	6.7	8.6	13.9	27.2	58.0	125.0	251.6
Native female.......	11.3	80.3	8.9	2.3	4.3	6.6	7.4	10.6	21.0	47.6	112.1	238.6
Foreign-born female.	17.6	79.9	17.5	2.9	4.9	6.6	7.3	12.0	24.8	56.5	120.3	246.2
1910 WHITE												
Native male........	14.9	143.5	14.2	3.0	4.4	6.9	9.6	14.2	26.5	56.2	128.2	259.0
Foreign-born male...	17.1	122.4	20.1	3.2	5.7	6.6	10 1	16.8	32.8	63.8	129.4	262.1
Native female.......	12.8	115.5	13.0	2.8	4.1	6.0	7.5	11.2	21.2	48.4	115.5	250.3
Foreign-born female.	16.8	130.7	18.7	3.0	4.1	6.0	8.3	13.4	28.2	59.8	124.2	250.1
1900 WHITE												
Native male........	17.4	175.7	20.0	3.8	5.8	8.4	10.3	13.4	24.5	55.6	126.7	269.4
Foreign-born male...	18.9	191.0	30.5	4.0	5.8	7.6	11.4	19.2	35.2	65.6	132.9	272.0
Native female.......	15.7	142.6	18.5	3.8	5.8	8.1	9.1	12.4	21.5	46.8	113.8	254.9
Foreign-born female.	18.4	142.7	28.8	3.6	5.2	8.0	10.9	17.0	32.4	65.0	131.2	263.1

Source: National Office of Vital Statistics, Vital Statistics of the United States, 1900-40, Table 9.

chusetts (which was mostly white) in about 1800 to 1810, but it was characteristic of the nonwhite (Negro) population until 1905 (see Table 9-3). This lag of about one century in mortality progress among nonwhite populations has been greatly reduced in the past 50 years. Using the standardized rates of Table 9-9 again, the following history of this transition may be derived:

Year	Difference (in points) between white and nonwhite rates[1]	Percent nonwhite is of white
1900	10.2	158
1905	11.8	172
1910	8.5	154
1915	9.0	164
1920	6.9	150
1925	8.6	170
1930	8.4	171
1935	5.2	156
1940	6.0	159
1945	4.1	146
1950	4.2	145
1956	3.5	147

[1]Nonwhite rate minus white rate.

That the rates for whites and nonwhites have been converging since 1905 is readily evident. The difference in their standardized rates was only 3.5 rate points in 1956, whereas it had been almost 3 times as much in 1900. Details concerning the timing of this convergence cannot be learned precisely, because some of the census data for nonwhites appear to contain rather large discrepancies. There is a difference in the completeness with which deaths are registered among the two color groups, although the amount of the difference is not known. Both of these difficulties--the discrepancies in census data and the incompleteness of registration--are more serious for the years prior to 1930 than for the years since. Also, for the years before 1935 the above series refers to only a part of the total United States, i.e., the death registration area. If one can dismiss the data for the year 1920 as having been affected by census error, or as representing an atypical year, it appears that progress in reducing the differential between white and nonwhite death rates was proceeding slowly and irregularly until about 1925. After 1925, the differential de-

clined rapidly and fairly steadily until 1945. Since 1945, white and nonwhite death rates have followed parallel downward courses. Thus, the quarter-century 1925 to 1950 saw rapid progress toward giving the nonwhite population the same low death rates that were beginning to characterize the white population. In 1956, the nonwhite population had the same age-standardized death rate that the white population had had in about 1936. Hence, the lag between the rates of these two groups has been cut from a century to about 20 years. [11]

Nativity Differences in Mortality. Several years ago, considerable attention was given to the death rates for foreign-born white persons. The fact that the crude death rate for this group was much higher than the rate for native-born whites alarmed some of those who believed that the immigrants from southern and eastern Europe were biologically inferior to the native stock. Sufficient evidence has now accumulated to indicate that social and economic differences between these immigrants and the native stock were responsible for

[11] Not infrequently, demographers are inclined to measure differentials in mortality in terms of their relative size, that is, in terms of how much greater, proportionately, one is than another. This kind of measure does not always yield the same picture as the point-change-in-rate method, employed above. For example, throughout the time that nonwhite death rates were falling faster (by more points) than death rates among the white population, the rate for the nonwhite population did not become a great deal smaller, in proportion to the white rate, than it had been in 1900 (see the right-hand column of the above tabulation). For example, the course of death rates for the nonwhite population has been such that by 1950 an estimated 8 of each 1,000 nonwhite persons were alive, instead of dead, at the end of each year thanks to the fact that since 1900 the age-standardized death rates for their group had declined by more points than had the rates for the white population. Yet, in 1950, the age-standardized death rate of the nonwhite population was still almost 50 percent greater than that of the white. This is a good illustration of the principle that two quantities can both approach a limiting value of zero in such a way that they maintain an unchanging ratio to each other. Since zero is the theoretical lower limit for all mortality rates, the ratio method of measuring differentials is not, by itself, a trustworthy indicator of what has happened. The point-change in rate should also be indicated, and it frequently is the more meaningful measure.

much of the former group's higher rate of mortality. Table 9-5 provides age-specific rates for the native-born white population and for foreign-born immigrants, for each census year since 1900. In most of these years, the death rate for infants, young children, and youth are higher among the foreign born than is the rate for these ages among the native white population. When examined age-by-age, however, the differences are not very large. Moreover, the rates for foreign-born whites at these younger ages are based on very small numbers of deaths and refer to a small fraction of the total immigrant population, since most foreign-born persons arrive as young adults. At the adult ages, 24 to 44, death rates for the foreign born and the native born are about equal in most of the years. However, at the ages beyond 45, the foreign-born population has rates that are above those of the native-born population for almost all years. The size of this differential varies between 1 and 10 rate points, and averages about 3 rate points. The foreign-born population is known to be concentrated around the middle and the lower end of the socio-economic scale. A difference of this size (the average of 3 rate points mentioned above) could be accounted for plausibly by differences in income, in knowledge concerning health practices and good diet, and in medical care received. It could also be a result of hardship and various kinds of deprivation experienced by many of the foreign born before their immigration, or during the period when they had just arrived and were trying to adjust to their new environment and gain secure employment. At most ages, the age-specific differences in death rates between native-born and foreign-born whites are smaller than the differences between native white males and native white females. The age-specific rates for the foreign-born white population have shown a decline parallel to the decline in those for the native white population. Finally, some of the greatest differentials between foreign-born and native white populations are found at ages 55 to 64 and 65 to 74, in 1910, and at ages 65 to 74 and 75 to 84 in 1920. Deaths in these groups represent deaths of migrants who entered the United States between 1855

and 1875, well before the transition from the "old" (northwestern European) to the "new" (eastern and southern European) migration. The death rates of the later arrivals have been no higher in comparison with those of the native-born population than the rates of the migrants who arrived earlier.

Age Differences in Mortality. The question arises, "What has been the trend of the decline at each age?" A rough answer to this question could be obtained by comparing the schedules of age-specific rates in Table 9-3 with each other. More precise results can be gained, however, by comparing the probabilities of death that are established for the life tables prepared after each census. These probabilities for selected ages, 1949-51, are reported in Table 9-6. The amount of change in these probabilities since the period 1900 to 1902, and the percent change, are shown in this table. The percent of the total change in these probabilities that occurred in each intercensal period is also shown. [12] A study of this percent change, and of the percent distribution of change, will show when the gains were made in reducing the force of mortality at each age, and how much gain was made in each decade. This information may be obtained for each color-sex group. In general, infant mortality has been reduced in each decade since 1900, and very substantial progress in reducing adult mortality between the ages of 15 and 45 years was made in the decades 1900 to 1910 and 1920 to 1930. Not until 1930 did a steady reduction of mortality rates for ages above 50 begin, and it has continued since. The nonwhite population has made its greatest progress in this direction since 1930.

---

[12] A retrogression, or rise in mortality rate, is shown as a plus quantity. Since the percentage distributions when summed must add to 100 percent, this means that the sum of the percentages of the decrease will add to more than 100 percent if there has been a temporary rise in mortality at any age. It is generally considered bad statistical practice to make a percentage distribution of a distribution that contains both minus and plus qualities. However, no difficulty will be experienced in the present context if each plus quantity is regarded as nullifying an equivalent amount of negative change in another decade.

CHANGE IN MORTALITY CONDITION SINCE 1950

Tables 9-3, 9-7, and 9-8 provide information about changes which have occurred in mortality between 1950 and 1956, by sex and color. It is readily apparent that the years since 1950 have continued the general trend that was already in existence. The infant mortality rate has declined still further (among the white population only). Comparatively large gains (for such a short time) have been made in reducing adult mortality between the ages of 25 and 65, but there has been little improvement in mortality at most ages above 65. In terms of rate points, the mortality experi-

Table 9-6.—THE CHANGING PATTERN OF MORTALITY AS SHOWN BY CHANGES IN LIFE TABLE MORTALITY RATES (q_x)

(Probability of dying (q_x) at selected ages, 1949-51, change in probability of death, 1900-02 to 1949-51, and percent change in probability of death, for each decade, 1900-50.)

Color, sex, and age	Proportion of persons dying at specified age who were alive at beginning of year of age (q_x)	Change in q_x, 1900-02 to 1949-51		Percent of 50-year change that occurred in each decade				
		Amount	Percent	1939-41 to 1949-51	1929-31 to 1939-41	1919-21 to 1929-31	1909-11 to 1919-21	1900-02 to 1909-11
WHITE MALE								
0..............	.0307	-.1028	-.77	-16.9	-13.8	-17.4	-41.9	-9.9
1..............	.0021	-.0324	-.94	-8.6	-15.7	-19.4	-37.0	-19.4
5..............	.0008	-.0052	-.86	-11.5	-23.1	-23.1	-15.4	-26.9
10.............	.0006	-.0021	-.77	-19.0	-23.8	-23.8	-14.3	-19.0
15.............	.0010	-.0023	-.69	-17.4	-26.1	-30.4	4.3	-21.7
20.............	.0016	-.0043	-.72	-11.6	-25.6	-25.6	-14.0	-23.3
25.............	.0017	-.0053	r.75	-13.2	-24.5	-24.5	-9.4	-28.3
30.............	.0018	-.0062	-.78	-16.1	-21.0	-25.8	-14.5	-22.6
35.............	.0025	-.0068	-.73	-17.6	-22.1	-23.5	-25.0	-11.8
40.............	.0039	-.0067	-.63	-17.9	-25.4	-10.4	-40.3	-6.0
45.............	.0064	-.0063	-.50	-20.6	-25.4	...	-54.0	...
50.............	.0101	-.0052	-.34	-26.9	-23.0	19.2	-73.0	3.8
55.............	.0159	-.0053	-.25	-28.3	-15.1	32.1	-94.3	5.7
60.............	.0238	-.0048	-.17	-35.4	-20.8	37.5	-127.1	45.8
65.............	.0344	-.0072	-.17	-33.3	-25.0	51.4	-122.2	29.2
70.............	.0503	-.0087	-.15	-49.4	-39.1	37.9	-86.2	36.8
75.............	.0750	-.0134	-.15	-60.4	-15.7	25.4	-79.9	30.6
80.............	.1099	-.0236	-.18	-62.7	-22.5	43.2	-67.4	9.3
85.............	.1630	-.0287	-.15	-63.1	-12.5	8.4	-30.7	-2.1
90.............	.2289	-.0339	-.13	-59.0	10.0	21.5	-50.1	-22.4
WHITE FEMALE								
0..............	.0236	-.0871	-.79	-16.4	-13.4	-16.4	-44.2	-9.6
1..............	.0019	-.0293	-.94	-8.2	-15.4	-19.8	-38.5	-18.1
5..............	.0006	-.0053	-.90	-9.4	-20.8	-24.5	-18.9	-26.4
10.............	.0004	-.0021	-.85	-14.3	-19.0	-33.3	-14.3	-19.0
15.............	.0005	-.0029	-.86	-13.8	-24.1	-31.0	-6.9	-24.1
20.............	.0007	-.0048	-.87	-14.6	-27.1	-33.3	2.1	-27.1
25.............	.0009	-.0059	-.87	-15.3	-27.1	-35.6	5.1	-27.1
30.............	.0012	-.0066	-.85	-15.2	-22.7	-36.4	...	-25.8
35.............	.0016	-.0068	-.81	-17.6	-23.5	-29.4	-10.3	-19.1
40.............	.0024	-.0069	-.74	-18.8	-23.2	-20.3	-18.8	-18.8
45.............	.0037	-.0069	-.65	-21.7	-26.1	-15.9	-26.1	-10.1
50.............	.0056	-.0078	-.58	-25.6	-25.6	-14.1	-24.4	10.3
55.............	.0085	-.0102	-.55	-27.5	-24.5	-8.8	-31.4	-7.8
60.............	.0154	-.0117	-.47	-31.6	-29.9	-9.4	-35.9	6.8
65.............	.0206	-.0158	-.43	-36.7	-30.4	-2.5	-39.2	8.9
70.............	.0341	-.0196	-.37	-41.8	-32.1	-8.2	-32.7	14.8
75.............	.0565	-.0239	-.30	-51.5	-23.8	-5.9	-27.6	8.8
80.............	.0906	-.0306	-.25	-57.5	-30.1	13.1	-40.5	15.0
85.............	.1396	-.0350	-.20	-66.6	-22.6	1.1	-22.6	10.6
90.............	.2066	-.0388	-.16	-64.2	-0.3	2.3	-43.8	5.9

Table 9-6.—THE CHANGING PATTERN OF MORTALITY AS SHOWN BY CHANGES IN LIFE TABLE MORTALITY RATES (q_x)-Con.

(Probability of dying (q_x) at selected ages, 1949-51, change in probability of death, 1900-02 to 1949-51, and percent change in probability of death, for each decade, 1900-50.)

Color, sex, and age	Proportion of persons dying at specified age who were alive at beginning of year of age (q_x)	Change in q_x 1900-02 to 1949-51		Percent of 50-year change that occurred in each decade				
		Amount	Percent	1939-41 to 1949-51	1929-31 to 1939-41	1919-21 to 1929-31	1909-11 to 1919-21	1900-02 to 1909-11
NONWHITE MALE								
0	.0509	-.2024	-.80	-15.5	-2.5	-8.7	-56.5	-16.7
1	.0047	-.0726	-.94	-6.5	-9.9	-12.3	-56.9	-14.5
5	.0012	-.0096	-.88	-6.2	-11.5	-13.5	-44.8	-24.0
10	.0008	-.0054	-.86	-9.3	-13.0	-11.1	-42.6	-24.1
15	.0016	-.0069	-.81	-15.9	-23.2	-20.3	-31.9	-8.7
20	.0031	-.0088	-.74	-26.1	-36.4	-26.1	-12.5	1.1
25	.0041	-.0090	-.69	-35.6	-41.1	-8.9	-5.6	-8.9
30	.0049	-.0082	-.62	-46.3	-48.8	8.5	-35.4	21.9
35	.0065	-.0086	-.57	-50.0	-47.7	8.1	-36.1	25.6
40	.0088	-.0078	-.47	-61.5	-57.7	44.9	-82.1	56.4
45	.0128	-.0090	-.41	-63.3	-42.2	58.9	-76.7	23.2
50	.0191	-.0064	-.25	-98.4	-32.8	131.2	-192.2	92.2
55	.0276	-.0106	-.28	-46.2	-13.2	85.8	-138.7	12.3
60	.0368	-.0072	-.16	-31.9	-31.9	134.7	-265.3	94.4
65	.0458	-.0084	-.16	-13.1	-46.4	140.5	-302.4	121.4
70	.0562	-.0191	-.25	-9.4	-63.9	58.1	-130.4	45.5
75	.0711	-.0284	-.29	-24.6	-52.1	38.0	-108.1	46.8
80	.0909	-.0497	-.35	-33.0	-45.5	32.6	-35.4	-18.7
85	.1194	-.0680	-.36	-27.0	-58.5	15.9	-19.1	-11.2
90	.1826	-.0566	-.24	14.8	-81.4	23.1	11.0	-67.5
NONWHITE FEMALE								
0	.0409	-.1739	-.81	-14.4	-3.6	-8.9	-56.1	-17.1
1	.0039	-.0664	-.95	-6.2	-9.6	-13.1	-53.9	-17.2
5	.0011	-.0095	-.90	-7.4	-11.6	-17.9	-41.1	-22.1
10	.0006	-.0072	-.93	-6.9	-8.3	-16.7	-31.9	-36.1
15	.0012	-.0090	-.88	-20.0	-22.2	-18.9	-30.0	-8.9
20	.0023	-.0091	-.80	-33.0	-38.5	-30.8	8.8	-6.6
25	.0030	-.0079	-.72	-41.8	-51.9	-30.4	35.4	-11.4
30	.0039	-.0079	-.67	-43.0	-54.4	-21.5	16.5	2.5
35	.0054	-.0080	-.60	-47.5	-51.3	-17.5	7.5	8.8
40	.0077	-.0079	-.25	-51.9	-57.0	11.4	-26.6	24.1
45	.0113	-.0100	-.47	-47.0	-42.0	15.0	-26.0	...
50	.0160	-.0072	-.31	-81.9	-66.7	54.2	-37.5	31.9
55	.0224	-.0099	-.31	-62.6	-64.6	62.6	-61.6	26.3
60	.0295	-.0100	-.25	-52.0	-75.0	48.0	-82.0	61.0
65	.0370	-.0170	-.31	-22.9	-49.4	35.3	-100.0	37.1
70	.0455	-.0205	-.31	-17.6	-61.5	10.7	-57.1	25.9
75	.0577	-.0291	-.34	-17.9	-36.1	0.7	-48.8	2.1
80	.0733	-.0338	-.32	-23.7	-49.1	-15.7	-48.8	37.3
85	.0927	-.0486	-.34	-25.9	-47.3	-17.5	-49.8	40.5
90	.1554	-.0324	-.17	43.2	-94.4	-42.6	41.7	-47.8

Source: National Office of Vital Statistics, U.S. Life Tables 1949-51, Table 10.

ence of the nonwhite population has been one showing a very great improvement. The gains have been greater among nonwhite females than among males, and have thereby widened the sex differential with respect to longevity, which was already large in 1950. The percentage decline which occurred in the rates for nonwhite females in this short period is especially impressive. If changes of this magnitude were to continue for as long as a decade, and if they came to apply to males as well as to females, the color difference in age-specific mortality rates could shrink to a very small amount by 1965 or 1970.

Caution must be used in interpreting the figures for 1956. The data are based on provisional abridged life tables, and there may be discrepancies in the estimates of the base population that were used to compute these figures. The irregularities at the upper ages, for both the white and the nonwhite populations, indicate that such discrepancy does exist. In addition, the year 1956 may have exhibited unusual and unexplained fluctuations.

Expectation of Life at Birth. One of the valuable insights provided by the life table arises from the fact that it shows the average number of years each member of a cohort of infants born in a given year would live, if the group were exposed throughout its life to the schedule of age-specific mortality rates in force in a given year. This is not a prediction of how long the infants born in a current year will live. It seems reasonable to believe that there will be further discoveries in the fields of medicine, surgery, and general health protection. Infants born now will benefit from these advances as they occur, and as a result their lives will be lengthened beyond the present expectations of the persons at each older age level. However, as a summary of what a current year's rates mean in terms of over-all longevity, the expectation of life at birth is a good standard measure. Such data are presented in Table 9-8, for the year 1956 and for each census year since 1900.

The extension of the life span that has taken place since 1900 is one of the greatest accomplishments of this century. Whereas in 1900 the new-born infant had a life table expectancy of 47.3 years, in 1956 he had one of 69.6 years. This means that an average of 22.3 years have been added to the life expectancy at birth of every new-born infant. It is an impressive fact that one year of life expectancy was added during the 6 years between 1950 and 1956.

The material already presented concerning differential mortality has indicated that the life expectancy of women (72.9 years) is greater than that of men (66.7 years), and that the expectancy of the white population is greater than that of the nonwhite.

The nonwhite population has gained about 10 years more of life expectancy than the white population since 1900. From the low level of only 33 years in 1900, nonwhite expectancy rose to 63.3

Table 9-7.—AGE-STANDARDIZED DEATH RATES BY COLOR AND SEX, AND RATIO OF MALE RATE TO FEMALE RATE: DEATH-REGISTRATION STATES 1900 TO 1956

(Computed by the direct method using as the standard population the age distribution of the population of the United States as enumerated in 1940.)

Race and year	Both sexes	Male	Female	Ratio of male rate to female rate
ALL RACES				
1956.........	7.7	9.5	6.1	1.56
1950.........	8.4	10.0	6.9	1.45
1945.........	9.4	11.1	7.9	1.41
1940.........	10.7	12.1	9.4	1.29
1935.........	11.6	12.9	10.4	1.24
1930.........	12.5	13.5	11.3	1.19
1925.........	13.0	13.8	12.2	1.13
1920.........	14.2	14.7	13.8	1.07
1915.........	14.4	15.4	13.4	1.15
1910.........	15.8	16.9	14.6	1.16
1905.........	16.7	17.8	15.7	1.13
1900.........	17.8	18.6	17.0	1.09
WHITE				
1956.........	7.4	9.2	5.8	1.59
1950.........	8.0	9.6	6.5	1.48
1945.........	9.0	10.7	7.5	1.43
1940.........	10.2	11.6	8.8	1.32
1935.........	11.1	12.3	9.8	1.26
1930.........	11.7	12.8	10.6	1.21
1925.........	12.3	13.2	11.4	1.16
1920.........	13.7	14.2	13.1	1.08
1915.........	14.1	15.1	13.0	1.16
1910.........	15.6	16.7	14.4	1.16
1905.........	16.5	17.6	15.4	1.14
1900.........	17.6	18.4	16.8	1.10
NONWHITE				
1956.........	10.9	12.4	9.5	1.31
1950.........	12.2	13.5	10.9	1.24
1945.........	13.1	14.4	11.9	1.21
1940.........	16.2	17.5	14.9	1.17
1935.........	17.3	18.5	16.1	1.15
1930.........	20.1	21.0	19.2	1.09
1925.........	20.9	21.4	20.4	1.05
1920.........	20.6	20.4	21.0	.97
1915.........	23.1	23.5	22.6	1.04
1910.........	24.1	24.8	23.2	1.07
1905.........	28.3	29.7	26.9	1.10
1900.........	27.8	28.7	27.1	1.06

Source: National Office of Vital Statistics, Vital Statistics of the United States, 1950, Vol. I, Table 8.39.

Table 9-8.—ESTIMATED AVERAGE EXPECTATION OF LIFE AT BIRTH IN YEARS: DEATH-REGISTRATION STATES 1900 TO 1956

Race and year	Both sexes	Male	Female	Ratio of male rate to female rate	Difference between male and female (years)
ALL RACES					
1956....	69.6	66.7	72.9	.91	6.2
1950....	68.4	65.8	71.5	.92	5.7
1945....	65.9	63.6	67.9	.94	4.3
1940....	62.9	60.8	65.2	.93	4.4
1935....	61.7	59.9	63.9	.94	4.0
1930....	59.7	58.1	61.6	.94	3.5
1925....	59.0	57.6	60.6	.95	3.0
1920....	54.1	53.6	54.6	.98	1.0
1915....	54.5	52.5	56.8	.92	4.3
1910....	50.0	48.4	51.8	.93	3.4
1905....	48.7	47.3	50.2	.94	2.9
1900....	47.3	46.3	48.3	.96	2.0
WHITE					
1956....	70.2	67.3	73.7	.91	6.4
1950....	69.2	66.6	72.4	.92	5.8
1945....	66.8	64.4	69.5	.93	5.1
1940....	64.2	62.1	66.6	.93	4.5
1935....	62.9	61.0	65.0	.94	4.0
1930....	61.4	59.7	63.5	.94	3.8
1925....	60.7	59.3	62.4	.95	3.1
1920....	54.9	54.4	55.6	.98	1.2
1915....	55.1	53.1	57.5	.92	4.4
1910....	50.3	48.6	52.0	.93	3.4
1905....	49.1	47.6	50.6	.94	3.0
1900....	47.6	46.6	48.7	.96	2.1
NONWHITE					
1956....	63.3	61.1	65.9	.92	4.8
1950....	61.0	59.2	63.2	.94	4.0
1945....	57.7	56.1	59.6	.94	3.5
1940....	53.1	51.5	54.9	.94	3.4
1935....	53.1	51.3	55.2	.93	3.9
1930....	48.1	47.3	49.2	.96	1.9
1925....	45.7	44.9	46.7	.96	1.8
1920....	45.3	45.5	45.2	1.01	-0.3
1915....	38.9	37.5	40.5	.93	3.0
1910....	35.6	33.8	37.5	.90	3.7
1905....	31.3	29.6	33.1	.89	3.5
1900....	33.0	32.5	33.5	.97	1.0

Source: National Office of Vital Statistics, Abridged Life Tables, United States, 1953, Table 5.

in 1953. The life span of the female nonwhite population has so increased that it is almost double its 1900 length. Although the nonwhite male has not quite matched this record, he has also made remarkable progress. Even between 1950 and 1956, nonwhite females added 2.7 years to their life expectancy, and males added 2.3 years to theirs. These increases are more than twice the amount by which the whites increased their expectancy during this same period.

Because of marked irregularities in the data concerning the nonwhite population, mentioned previously, the exact timing of this increase in longevity among nonwhites cannot be specified; however, a very large share of it is known to have taken place since 1925, and especially since 1940. This pattern contrasts sharply with the one according to which the white population increased its longevity. A calculation as to what proportion of the 1900 to 1950 increase in life expectancy fell in the first 25 years, and what proportion in the second 25 years of the period, by color and sex, reveals the following:

	Increase in first 25 years	Increase in second 25 years
White..........	13.1	8.9
Male.........	12.7	7.5
Female.......	13.7	10.5
Nonwhite.......	12.1	16.4
Male.........	12.4	14.8
Female.......	12.2	17.7

Table 9-8 also furnishes additional information about the sex differential in mortality. In 1956, the life expectancy at birth of a female infant was 6.2 years greater than that of a male infant.

In 1956 the expectation of life at birth was greater for women than for men by 6.4 years among the white population, and by 4.8 years nonwhites. For both groups of women, these differences represent large gains over the situation that prevailed in 1930.

AVERAGE REMAINING LIFETIME AT SELECTED AGES

The "average expectation of life" is sometimes criticized on the ground that life expectancy is strongly affected by the hazards connected with birth and the first year of life. Once a person has survived this period, his life expectancy rises. Also, there is great general interest in learning how many years, on an average, persons may expect to live when they have attained a given age, information which the "average expectation of life" does not provide. Table 9-9 reports this informa-

Table 9-9.—AVERAGE REMAINING LIFETIME IN YEARS AT SPECIFIED AGES, BY COLOR AND SEX: DEATH-REGISTRATION STATES, FOR SELECTED YEARS

Color, sex, and year	Average remaining lifetime (years) at age:							
	0	1	5	25	45	55	65	75
WHITE MALE								
1956...................	67.3	68.2	64.4	45.5	27.3	19.3	12.9	7.9
1949 to 1951..........	66.3	67.4	63.8	44.9	26.9	19.1	12.8	7.8
1939 to 1941..........	62.8	65.0	61.7	43.3	25.9	18.3	12.1	7.2
1929 to 1931..........	59.1	62.0	59.4	41.8	25.3	18.0	11.8	7.0
1919 to 1921..........	56.3	60.2	58.3	41.6	26.0	18.6	12.2	7.3
1909 to 1911..........	50.2	56.3	55.4	38.8	23.9	17.0	11.2	6.8
1900 to 1902..........	48.2	54.6	54.4	38.5	24.2	17.4	11.5	6.8
Gain, 1900 to 1953								
Years.................	18.6	13.1	9.6	6.7	2.8	1.8	1.4	1.1
Percent...............	38.6	24.0	17.6	17.4	11.6	10.3	12.2	16.2
WHITE FEMALE								
1956...................	73.7	74.2	70.5	51.1	32.1	23.4	15.5	9.2
1949 to 1951..........	72.0	72.8	69.1	49.8	31.1	22.6	15.0	8.9
1939 to 1941..........	67.3	68.9	65.6	46.8	28.9	20.7	13.6	7.9
1929 to 1931..........	62.7	64.9	62.2	44.2	27.4	19.6	12.8	7.6
1919 to 1921..........	58.5	61.5	59.4	42.6	27.0	19.4	12.8	7.6
1909 to 1911..........	53.6	58.7	57.7	40.9	25.4	18.2	12.0	7.2
1900 to 1902..........	51.1	56.4	56.0	40.0	25.5	18.4	12.2	7.3
Gain, 1900 to 1953								
Years.................	21.8	17.2	13.8	10.5	6.2	4.6	3.1	1.8
Percent...............	42.7	30.5	24.6	26.2	24.3	25.0	25.4	24.7
NONWHITE MALE								
1956...................	61.1	63.1	59.6	41.0	24.6	17.8	12.9	10.2
1949 to 1951..........	58.9	61.1	57.7	39.5	23.6	17.4	12.8	8.8
1939 to 1941..........	52.3	56.0	53.1	35.9	22.0	16.7	12.2	8.1
1929 to 1931..........	47.6	51.1	48.7	32.7	20.6	15.5	10.9	7.0
1919 to 1921..........	47.1	51.6	50.2	35.5	23.6	17.5	12.1	7.6
1909 to 1911..........	34.0	42.5	44.2	30.4	18.8	13.8	9.7	6.6
1900 to 1902..........	32.5	42.5	45.1	32.2	20.1	14.7	10.4	6.6
Gain, 1900 to 1953								
Years.................	27.2	19.2	13.2	7.7	3.7	2.8	2.3	2.9
Percent...............	83.7	45.2	29.3	23.9	18.4	19.0	22.1	43.9
NONWHITE FEMALE								
1956...................	65.9	67.4	63.9	44.8	27.8	20.7	15.3	11.9
1949 to 1951..........	62.7	64.4	60.9	42.4	26.1	19.6	14.5	10.2
1939 to 1941..........	55.5	58.5	55.5	38.3	24.0	18.4	14.0	9.8
1929 to 1931..........	49.5	52.3	49.8	33.9	21.4	16.3	12.2	8.6
1919 to 1921..........	46.9	50.4	48.7	34.4	22.6	17.1	12.4	8.4
1909 to 1911..........	37.7	45.2	46.4	33.0	20.4	15.0	10.8	7.6
1900 to 1902..........	35.0	43.5	46.0	33.9	21.4	15.9	11.4	7.9
Gain, 1900 to 1953								
Years.................	29.4	22.6	16.6	9.8	5.5	4.4	3.3	2.9
Percent...............	84.0	52.0	36.1	28.9	25.7	27.7	28.9	36.7

Source: National Office of Vital Statistics, Abridged Life Tables, United States, 1953, Table 4.

tion, for selected ages, for the year 1956 and for census dates since 1900. The gain at each age, and the percent gain, from 1900 to 1956, are also shown.

If a white female infant survives the first year of life, the life table for 1956 estimates her average remaining lifetime at 74.2 years. In other words, her average expected age at death is 75 years. Surviving the first year of life adds a little less than 1 year to the average remaining lifetime of members of the white population, and almost 2 years to that of members of the nonwhite population.

At age 25, the white male population had an average life expectancy of 45 years in 1956, and females had a life expectancy of 50 years. This means that the average expected age at death, for young adults, is 70 to 75 years. In 1900 and in 1910, life expectancy at age 25 was 38 to 40 years, and the average expected age at death was 63 to 65 years. In other words, the average young worker of 1900 had roughly a 50-50 chance of reaching retirement age, whereas young white men now may look forward to an average retirement age lasting 5 years, and women to one lasting 10 years. Nonwhite men at age 25 now are in the position that white men 25 years old were in about 1910; nonwhite women fare somewhat better in comparison with white women.

It may be noted parenthetically that young white women at age 25 have 5.6 more years, and young nonwhite women at age 25 have 3.7 more years, of life expectancy than young men of their own age and color. The current cultural pattern, according to which men marry women who are about two years their junior, makes it inevitable that a large proportion of married women must expect to be widowed, in many cases for a rather prolonged period, toward the end of their life span. If spouses are to die at about the same time, and thus avoid the loneliness of widowhood in old age, women must marry men 4 to 5 years their junior. Since a large proportion of girls marry between their 20th and 22nd birthdays, this procedure would require them to marry boys between the ages of 15 and 18 years!

It is interesting to note that the figures given above concerning average age at death do not indicate that life expectancy among the white population is greatly increased by survival from age 25 to age 45. This illustrates the fact, noted earlier, that there has been less reduction in mortality at the older ages, a fact which is reflected directly in the statistics of Table 9-9 for ages 65 and 75.

The average remaining lifetime of white men who have reached their 65th birthday has been increased by only 1.4 years in the past half-century. About 60 percent of this gain has taken place since 1940. Even the dramatic increase in the longevity of women has been accomplished by reducing death at the younger ages: only 3.1 years of life have been added for white women, and 3.3 years for nonwhite women, who reach age 65. Although the number of months and years added to the life span has been comparatively small, the proportional increase among the white population is impressive. White males who attain 65 years of age may look forward to an average remaining lifetime that is 12 percent longer than it would have been in 1900; the corresponding proportional increase for women is 25 percent.

SURVIVORS TO EACH AGE

A final and most important insight concerning the effects of reduced mortality on the population is furnished by Table 9-10, since this table shows the number of persons surviving to specified ages from the original hypothetical cohort with which the life table begins. Under conditions of high mortality, fewer of the cohort will survive to enter the labor force, to marry, to have children, to complete the childbearing period, and to retire. The proportion of newborn infants who do reach each of the ages in the life span is of considerable importance as regards the behavior of fertility rates, labor force phenomena, and other aspects of population study. The life table for the year 1953 (which differs only comparatively little from 1956) is used to demonstrate this fact.

The following comparison, taken from this table, will illustrate the use of survivorship statistics. If a group of 1,000 white women, born in 1953, were subjected to the death rate of that year throughout their lives, and if another group, born in 1900, were exposed to the 1900 death rates, the estimated number of each group that would survive to take part in each of the major events and stages in the life cycle are as follows:

	Cohort of 1953	Cohort of 1900	Difference
Birth......................	1,000	1,000	...
Survive to enter kindergarten (5 years)..........	978	834	144
Survive to enter labor force (14 years)..........	970	807	173
Survive to age of marriage (20 years)................	968	790	178
Survive entire childbearing period (45 years).........	935	647	288
Survive to retire (65 years)................	785	438	347
Survive to age 75..........	389	214	175

According to these estimates, only 65 (about 1/15) of the women born in 1953 would die between birth and the completion of the childbearing period, whereas 353 (more than 1/3) of the women born in 1900 would have died by this age.

The story is even more impressive with respect to nonwhites, as indicated by the following comparison for nonwhite males:

	Cohort of 1953	Cohort of 1900	Difference
Birth......................	1,000	1,000	...
Survive to enter kindergarten....................	951	747	204
Survive to enter labor force (15 years)................	934	597	337
Survive to age of marriage (25) years)................	909	533	376
Survive to age 45...........	799	392	407
Survive to retire...........	467	190	277
Survive to age 75..........	252	89	163

The reduction of mortality now permits nine out of ten white persons who are born alive to live at least to age 45, and permits nine out of ten nonwhite persons born alive to survive to age 25. Inasmuch as death rates rise rapidly as the upper ages are reached, the proportion surviving falls quickly after age 50. But even at these ages, sufficient gains have been made to permit a much larger proportion of the population to enter early old age, and even advanced old age, than previously was the case.

In assessing the data in Table 9-10, it should be remembered that all medical advances postpone death for a few years only; they do not completely remove the risk of dying until any certain age is reached. After an illness, the likelihood of death may be greater for some persons in each year that follows, because their health has been impaired, although their lives have been saved temporarily. Persons who would have died at age 25 or 30 in 1900 now may have their life prolonged for 5 or 10 years. Although this has the effect of reducing deaths at the younger ages, it may tend to bring into the older ages a group of impaired lives, as well as the larger group of healthy and vigorous lives, and thereby make it increasingly difficult to lower the mortality rates at advanced ages. Indeed, the progress in the conquest of death at the upper ages may have been much greater than is indicated by official statistics because of this factor of postponement of death at the younger ages.

The postponement aspect of mortality reduction has misled some to rather mystical conclusions. They have said that high infant mortality rates are selective of the more vigorous and healthy, and that lowering these rates tends to save infants whose lives are impaired and who will only die at later ages and hence make it more difficult to reduce the rates at the older ages. The extremely low rates prevailing between age 1 and age 35 indicate that the infants saved are not sufficiently impaired in health to cause death within a short time. If there is a valid basis for the argument, it must consist in showing that a much higher-than-average proportion of the infants thus saved survive as semi-invalids who are unable to participate fully in the life of their generation, who "wear out" at a younger age as adults, and who contribute disproportionately to the death rates between the ages of 45 and 65. No one knows the amount of bodily damage caused by childhood diseases. Actually, the moderate increases in life expectancy at the upper ages may be greatly enlarged when the present generation, which has been spared many of the ravages of serious illness in infancy, passes into the upper ages.

THE LIFE TABLE DEATH RATE

There is a rather widespread desire for a single summary death rate, one that can be used to ex-

Table 9-10.—NUMBER SURVIVING TO SPECIFIED AGES OUT OF 1,000 BORN ALIVE, BY SELECTED YEARS: 1900 TO 1953

Race, sex, and age	Number surviving to specified age	Change, 1902 to 1953		Percent of total change that occurred in each interval					
		Amount	Percent	1949-51 to 1953	1939-41 to 1949-51	1929-31 to 1939-41	1919-21 to 1929-31	1909-11 to 1919-21	1900-02 to 1909-11
WHITE MALE									
0......................	1,000	...	...	...	...	...	...	...	...
1......................	972	105	12.1	2.9	16.2	13.3	17.1	41.0	9.5
5......................	967	158	19.5	1.9	13.9	15.2	18.4	37.3	13.3
10.....................	964	173	21.9	1.7	14.4	16.2	19.1	34.7	13.9
15.....................	961	180	23.1	1.7	14.4	16.7	19.4	33.9	13.9
20.....................	954	191	25.0	1.6	14.7	17.8	20.4	31.4	14.1
25.....................	945	206	27.9	1.0	15.0	18.9	20.9	29.1	15.0
30.....................	938	225	31.6	1.3	15.1	19.6	21.3	26.7	16.0
35.....................	929	246	36.1	1.2	15.4	19.9	22.0	25.6	15.9
40.....................	916	267	41.1	1.5	16.1	20.2	21.3	26.2	14.6
45.....................	895	282	45.9	1.8	16.7	21.3	19.9	27.2	13.1
50.....................	862	290	50.6	2.1	17.6	21.4	17.9	29.0	12.1
55.....................	812	287	54.7	2.4	18.5	21.6	15.3	31.4	10.8
60.....................	740	276	59.4	3.3	19.6	21.4	12.3	34.4	9.1
65.....................	642	250	63.8	2.8	20.8	21.2	9.2	39.6	6.4
70.....................	520	214	69.9	1.4	23.4	22.9	4.7	43.5	4.2
75.....................	389	175	81.8	4.6	26.9	22.3	1.7	43.4	1.1
WHITE FEMALE									
0......................	1,000	...	...	...	...	...	...	...	...
1......................	978	89	10.0	2.2	15.7	13.5	15.7	43.8	9.0
5......................	974	140	16.8	1.4	13.6	15.0	17.9	38.6	13.6
10.....................	972	155	19.0	1.9	13.5	15.5	18.7	35.6	14.8
15.....................	971	164	20.3	1.8	13.4	15.9	19.5	34.1	14.6
20.....................	968	178	22.5	1.7	14.0	16.8	20.8	30.9	15.7
25.....................	964	199	26.0	2.0	14.1	18.6	22.1	26.6	16.6
30.....................	960	222	30.0	1.8	14.9	19.4	23.9	23.0	17.1
35.....................	955	245	34.5	2.0	15.5	20.4	24.5	20.4	17.1
40.....................	947	268	39.5	2.2	16.0	20.5	25.0	19.4	16.8
45.....................	935	288	44.5	2.8	16.7	21.2	24.0	19.1	16.3
50.....................	916	306	50.2	2.9	17.6	21.9	23.2	19.3	15.0
55.....................	888	323	57.2	3.4	19.2	22.3	21.7	19.5	13.9
60.....................	846	339	66.7	4.1	20.9	22.7	20.1	20.1	12.1
65.....................	785	347	79.2	4.9	23.3	23.6	17.9	20.7	9.5
70.....................	691	339	96.3	4.7	26.8	24.8	15.6	21.2	6.8
75.....................	568	314	123.6	7.6	30.9	24.5	13.4	19.7	3.8
NONWHITE MALE									
0......................	1,000	...	...	...	...	...	...	...	...
1......................	951	204	27.3	1.0	15.7	2.0	8.8	55.9	16.7
5......................	942	298	46.3	1.0	13.4	5.0	10.7	55.7	14.1
10.....................	938	321	52.0	1.2	13.1	5.9	10.9	54.5	14.3
15.....................	934	337	56.4	1.2	13.4	6.8	11.3	53.1	14.2
20.....................	925	357	63.0	1.4	14.6	8.7	12.9	49.3	13.2
25.....................	909	376	70.5	1.6	16.5	12.0	13.3	44.7	12.0
30.....................	890	392	78.6	1.8	19.1	14.8	12.0	41.6	10.7
35.....................	869	403	86.7	2.2	21.8	17.6	10.4	39.7	8.2
40.....................	838	408	94.9	2.2	24.5	19.9	8.3	39.0	5.9
45.....................	799	406	103.6	3.0	27.6	22.4	4.4	39.4	3.2
50.....................	745	398	114.4	4.0	30.4	22.6	-0.3	41.5	1.8
55.....................	665	365	121.7	3.8	33.7	23.0	-5.8	45.8	-0.5
60.....................	574	332	137.2	5.7	33.7	22.9	-11.1	50.0	-1.2
65.....................	467	277	145.8	5.4	33.6	23.8	-17.0	58.5	-4.3
70.....................	348	210	152.2	-1.0	34.8	28.1	-24.8	70.0	-7.1
75.....................	252	163	183.1	-1.2	35.0	32.5	-27.0	69.3	-8.6

Table 9-10.—NUMBER SURVIVING TO SPECIFIED AGES OUT OF 1,000 BORN ALIVE, BY SELECTED YEARS: 1900 TO 1953—Con.

Race, sex, and age	Number surviving to specified age	Change, 1902 to 1953		Percent of total change that occurred in each interval					
		Amount	Percent	1949-51 to 1953	1939-41 to 1949-51	1929-31 to 1939-41	1919-21 to 1929-31	1909-11 to 1919-21	1900-02 to 1909-11
NONWHITE FEMALE									
0....................	1,000	...	...	...	...	...	...	...	...
1....................	959	174	22.2	...	14.9	2.9	8.6	56.3	17.2
5....................	951	271	39.8	0.4	12.2	5.5	11.1	53.5	17.3
10....................	948	297	45.6	0.7	12.1	6.4	12.1	50.5	18.2
15....................	946	322	51.6	0.6	12.4	7.1	12.7	49.1	18.0
20....................	940	349	59.0	1.1	14.3	9.7	14.0	44.4	16.3
25....................	931	373	66.8	1.9	17.2	13.1	15.3	37.5	15.0
30....................	919	391	74.0	2.8	19.7	16.1	15.9	31.5	14.1
35....................	902	406	81.8	3.4	21.9	19.0	15.5	27.8	12.3
40....................	877	4416	90.2	4.1	24.3	20.7	14.7	25.5	10.6
45....................	845	422	99.8	5.5	26.3	23.0	12.1	24.4	8.8
50....................	798	421	111.7	6.7	28.7	23.8	9.7	23.5	7.6
55....................	730	399	120.5	7.0	32.1	25.8	5.8	23.3	5.8
60....................	654	379	137.8	9.5	33.8	27.2	2.1	23.7	3.7
65....................	564	344	156.4	11.6	34.0	28.8	-0.6	25.3	0.9
70....................	448	286	177.6	7.7	35.0	32.2	-2.8	28.7	-1.0
75....................	351	241	217.1	9.1	34.0	33.6	-2.5	27.4	-1.7

Source: National Office of Vital Statistics, _Abridged Life Tables, United States, 1953_, Table 3.

press the force of mortality and, at the same time, is independent of the present age composition of the population. The age-standardized death rate is not entirely satisfactory for this purpose, because the rate is dependent on the age composition of the particular population chosen as a standard.

There are two summary rates, both independent of the present age composition, that may be used for this purpose--the life table death rate, and the intrinsic death rate. The life table death rate is the crude death rate that would be characteristic of a life table stationary population (number of births exactly equal to number of deaths each year, with a current schedule of mortality in effect). It may be computed by dividing the expectation of life at birth into 1,000.

One additional idea contributed to this section by the life table death rate is that present crude death rates are artificially low because the population is growing. If fertility were to decline until it equalled mortality, an older age structure would emerge which would cause the crude death rate to rise, even with the present schedule of age-specific death rates. The life table death rate shows what this crude rate would be if the stationary population situation (equal births and deaths)

were to persist long enough to allow this older age distribution to emerge and stabilize.

The intrinsic death rate estimates what the crude death rate would be if the present schedule of fertility, as well as of mortality, were to continue indefinitely. Under such conditions, a stable age structure (not necessarily a stationary one) would emerge. The intrinsic death rate is the crude death rate that would result if the schedule of age-specific rates were to apply to this stable age composition. Usually the standardized death rate extracts most of the information about trends that exists in the data. Table 12-7 reports these rates by color, for the years 1905 to 1952.

MORTALITY IN RELATION TO RESIDENCE AND OCCUPATION

Urban-rural Residence. Persons living in urban areas have death rates that are roughly 20 to 25 percent higher, on an average, than the rates of those living in rural areas. This is true for both the white and the nonwhite populations (see Table 9-11). The exact significance of this differential is not clear, however. In a recent study "Occupa-

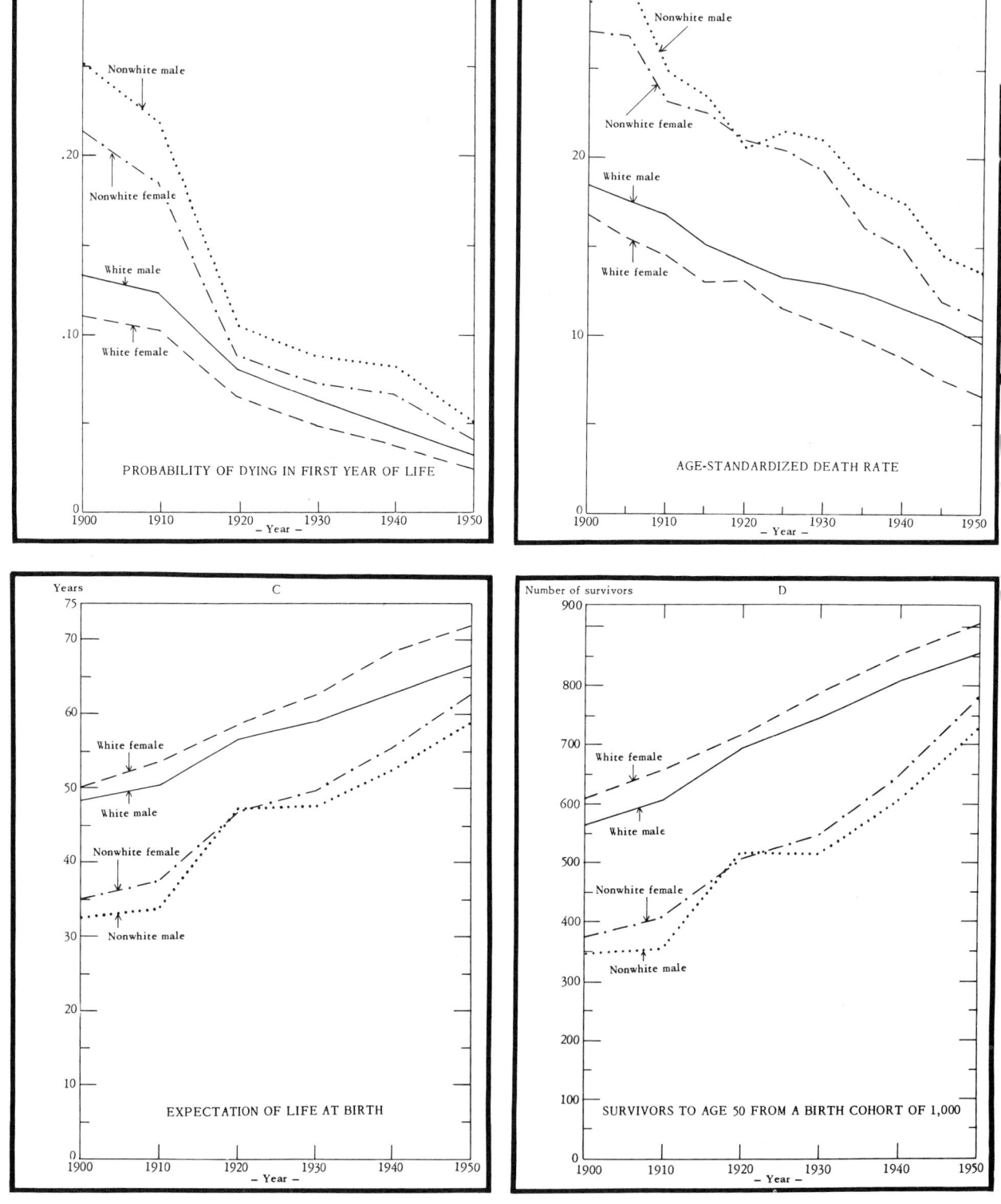

FIGURE 9-4. TREND OF SELECTED MEASURES OF MORTALITY, BY SEX AND COLOR, 1900 TO 1950

Table 9-11.—DEATH RATES BY COLOR AND SEX FOR URBAN AND RURAL AREAS IN METROPOLITAN AND NONMETROPOLITAN COUNTIES, UNITED STATES: 1950

Color and area	All counties			Metropolitan counties			Nonmetropolitan counties		
	Both sexes	Male	Female	Both sexes	Male	Female	Both sexes	Male	Female
All races..................	9.6	11.1	8.2	9.7	11.1	8.3	9.6	11.0	8.1
Urban....................	10.5	12.2	9.0	10.4	11.9	8.9	11.1	13.0	9.4
Rural....................	8.3	9.5	7.1	7.2	8.3	6.2	8.8	10.0	7.4
White.....................	9.5	10.9	8.0	9.5	11.0	8.2	9.3	10.8	7.8
Urban....................	10.4	12.0	8.8	10.2	11.8	8.7	10.8	12.7	9.1
Rural....................	8.1	9.4	6.8	7.1	8.1	6.0	8.6	9.9	7.2
Nonwhite..................	11.2	12.5	9.9	11.2	12.6	9.8	11.2	12.4	10.1
Urban....................	12.0	13.6	10.6	11.5	13.0	10.0	13.9	15.8	12.3
Rural....................	10.0	11.0	9.0	9.2	10.2	8.2	10.2	11.2	9.2
Ratio urban to rural, total.	1.26	1.28	1.27	1.44	1.43	1.44	1.26	1.30	1.27
White....................	1.28	1.28	1.29	1.44	1.46	1.45	1.26	1.28	1.26
Nonwhite.................	1.20	1.24	1.18	1.25	1.27	1.22	1.36	1.41	1.34

Source: National Office of Vital Statistics, Vital Statistics of the United States, 1950, Vol. I, Table 8.11.

tional and Social Class Differences in Mortality" I. M. Moriyama and Lillian Guralnick of NOVS conclude that persons with low socio-economic status have higher death rates than persons with high status, but that the gap probably is narrowing.

Regional Differentials. As reported in Table 9-12, there are marked differences among the geographic divisions in their mortality rates, even after differences in age have been controlled. The lowest death rates are found in the New England, the West North Central, and the Pacific states. The highest rates are found in the South-

Table 9-12.—AGE-ADJUSTED DEATH RATES BY RACE AND SEX, BY GEOGRAPHIC DIVISION, 1950 AND 1940

Color, sex, and year	United States	Geographic division								
		New England	Middle Atlantic	East North Central	West North Central	South Atlantic	East South Central	West South Central	Mountain	Pacific
Total population, 1950.	8.4	7.9	8.8	8.4	7.6	9.1	8.9	8.1	8.2	7.9
Total population, 1940.	10.7	10.2	11.1	10.4	9.1	12.0	11.6	10.8	10.7	10.2
White, total, 1950.......	8.0	7.8	8.5	8.1	7.4	8.0	7.9	7.5	8.0	7.8
Male.................	9.6	9.4	10.1	9.7	8.8	9.8	9.5	9.2	9.6	9.7
Female..............	6.5	6.4	7.1	6.6	6.0	6.2	6.4	5.8	6.2	5.9
Nonwhite, total, 1950....	12.2	10.8	12.6	12.4	13.4	13.0	12.4	11.0	11.7	9.2
Male.................	13.5	11.8	14.3	13.8	15.0	14.6	13.5	12.0	12.5	10.3
Female..............	10.9	9.9	11.0	11.1	11.8	11.4	11.4	10.0	10.8	7.8
Ratio nonwhite to white, 1950...................	1.5	1.4	1.5	1.5	1.8	1.6	1.6	1.5	1.5	1.2
Ratio male to female, white, 1950............	1.5	1.5	1.4	1.5	1.5	1.6	1.5	1.6	1.5	1.6
Ratio male to female, nonwhite, 1950..........	1.2	1.2	1.3	1.2	1.3	1.3	1.2	1.2	1.2	1.3
Percent change, total population, 1940 to 1950	-21.5	-22.5	-20.7	-19.2	-16.5	-24.2	-23.3	-25.0	-23.4	-22.5
Percent change, nonwhite population, 1940 to 1950	-24.7	...	...	...	...	...	...	...	...	...

Source: National Office of Vital Statistics, Vital Statistics of the United States, 1950, Vol. I, Tables 8.14 and 8.41.

ern, the Middle Atlantic, and the East North Central states. However, much of this difference is due to differences in race composition. Among the divisions which have large proportions of Negro or Indian residents, death rates tend to be higher. When the calculations for each region are made separately for the white and the nonwhite populations, most of the interregional differentials become quite small, although the Middle Atlantic Division still stands out as having above-average death rates, and the West North Central and the West South Central Divisions have unusually low death rates among their white populations.

CAUSES OF DEATH

The preceding discussion has treated mortality as a total unitary force, the intensity of which varies with age, color-nativity-race, sex, and other variables, and which has undergone a historic decline over time. From another point of view, mortality is not a single unitary force, but an agglomeration of semi-independent forces, each force being represented by death from a particular cause. According to this view, the fall in the general death rate is simply an indirect consequence of the virtual elimination of those deaths due to certain specific causes, and a great decrease in the deaths due to certain other diseases and disorders. The death rates for some types of illness have resisted the conquests of medical science and the application of public health measures. Only a careful inventory showing the present state of progress with respect to each of the major causes of death makes it possible to appreciate the nature of the accomplishments to date, to understand the problems involved, and to estimate prospects for further reductions.[13] If good data concerning cause of death are available, then death rates by cause (cause-specific rates) can also be calculated for each sex, age, and color group. These rates are usually expressed as number of deaths from a particular cause per 10,000, or per 100,000, population. Demographers are interested in learning the comparative force of each cause of death, how it varies with age, sex, and color, the communities among which

this force is greatest, and how it has changed over time.

The medical information reported on death certificates is classified into cause-of-death categories according to the International Statistical Classification of Diseases, Injuries, and Causes of Death, which is a sixth revision of an international system of classification, complete with a body of definitions and a set of procedures for classification. It was prepared under the sponsorship of the World Health Organization and adopted for use by the member nations at the World Health Assembly in 1948.[14]

Deaths may be classified, by cause, into three major groups:

> Chronic disorders
> Infectious and acute diseases
> Deaths from external causes (accidents, homicides, suicides)

At the present time, the chronic or organic dis-

[13] On each death certificate, the attending physician or other medical authority must attest the cause of death. These reports supply the information from which statistics of death by cause can be tabulated. Although the diseases and disorders that can result in death are very numerous and can occur in many permutations, they are finite in number. Moreover, it is possible to group them into classes or categories that have meaning, both from the standpoint of medical research and from the standpoint of public health and medical efforts to control mortality. Theoretically, it is possible to compute a separate death rate for each of these classes of cause of death. Actually, the extent to which this can be accomplished is determined by the success, accuracy, and consistency with which cause of death can be determined and is reported. Cause-age-specific rates can be standardized for age, or for other characteristics for which there is information concerning both the deceased and the general population.

[14] This list was revised for the seventh time in 1955, and statistics for 1957 and subsequent years will be tabulated in terms of the revised classification. Earlier versions of the international classification had been used in the United States for all data since 1900. The lists have been revised periodically, in order that they may be kept abreast of new discoveries and of the progress being made toward more accuracy and precision in the diagnosis and classification of diseases. Although each change in the lists tends to create a partial discontinuity in the statistical time series, this inconvenience must be accepted as one of the prices of refinement.

eases are the overwhelmingly outstanding causes of death, while the other two kinds of disease have been reduced to secondary (but nevertheless significant) sources of mortality (see Table 9-13). Two groups of organic killers--heart disease and cancer--cause more than one-half of all deaths in the population (54 percent in 1956). If one includes with heart disease other diseases of the circulatory system, this percentage rises to 70 percent. In other words, all causes of death other than those in the cardiovascular renal group and those involving malignant neoplasms together accounted for only 30 percent of all deaths. This 30 percent includes deaths resulting from accidents, homicide, and diseases of early infancy. As the following summary shows, more than 90 percent of all deaths are caused by one of 15 leading causes.

Rank order	Cause of death	Rate[1]	Percent of total deaths
	ALL CAUSES............	935.4	100.0
1	Diseases of heart..........	360.5	38.5
2	Malignant neoplasms, includ. neoplasms of lymphatic and hematopoietic tissues......	147.9	15.8
3	Vascular lesions affecting central nervous system.....	106.3	11.4
4	Accidents.................	56.7	6.1
	Motor-vehicle accidents....	23.7	2.5
	All other accidents........	33.0	3.5
5	Certain diseases of infancy.	38.6	4.1
6	Influenza and pneumonia, except pneumonia of newborn..	28.2	3.0
7	General arteriosclerosis....	19.1	2.0
8	Diabetes mellitus..........	15.7	1.7
9	Congenital malformations....	12.6	1.3
10	Cirrhosis of liver..........	10.7	1.1
11	Suicide....................	10.0	1.1
12	Chronic and unspecified nephritis and other renal sclerosis.................	9.1	1.0
13	Tuberculosis, all forms.....	8.4	0.9
14	Other diseases of circulatory system...............	8.4	0.9
15	Hypertension without mention of heart.................	6.5	0.7
	All other causes...........	96.6	10.3

[1] Per 100,000.
Source: Table BM, pg. XCIX of the 1956 Vol. I of National Office of Vital Statistics Annual Report.

More detailed information about the causes of death is given in Table 9-13. An examination of this table will show that a long list of diseases once dreaded as major threats to health are now only very minor contributors to mortality. Such diseases as typhoid fever, smallpox, scarlet fever, pneumonia, enteritis, and syphilis now have rates so low that they are scarcely a threat to life.[15] The major killers, now and for the foreseeable future, are the chronic diseases, especially the heart and circulatory disorders and cancer.

Sex Differences. Although most of the causes of death have a much more severe incidence among males than among females, the following disorders and causes are extraordinarily more destructive of males than of females:

Arteriosclerotic heart disease, including coronary disease
Malignant neoplasms
    of buccal cavity and pharynx
    of respiratory system
    of urinary organs
Accidents--both motor vehicle and other
Tuberculosis--all forms
Suicide
Homicide
Syphilis and its sequelae
Cirrhosis of liver
Ulcer of stomach and duodenum
Bronchitis
Meningitis

In Table 9-13, the second column from the right margin reports the ratio of male to female death rates for each of 64 groups of diseases. Men have lower death rates than women for only a few disorders. Among them are:

Malignant neoplasms of genital organs
Malignant neoplasms of the breast
Diabetes mellitus
Hypertension with heart disease

[15] A clear distinction must be maintained between the incidence of morbidity and the incidence of mortality from various diseases. For example, although the new case rate for tuberculosis is still quite high, since the introduction of chemotherapy a high proportion of cases are now arrested; in 1956 the death rate from tuberculosis had been reduced to a low of only 8.4 deaths per 100,000 population.

Table 9-13.—DEATH RATES FOR 64 SELECTED CAUSES OF DEATH, BY COLOR AND SEX: UNITED STATES, 1956[1]

Cause of death	Total	White			Nonwhite			Ratio male to female	Ratio nonwhite to white
		Both sexes	Male	Female	Both sexes	Male	Female		
TOTAL									
Major cardiovascular-renal diseases.....	510.7	516.5	591.2	443.6	463.0	492.3	435.2	1.31	0.90
Diseases of cardiovascular system...........	501.5	508.4	582.3	436.2	445.4	473.9	418.3	1.31	0.88
Diseases of the heart...................	360.5	369.0	443.0	296.7	291.4	321.4	263.0	1.47	0.79
Chronic rheumatic heart disease........	11.4	11.7	11.6	11.8	8.7	8.9	8.5	0.99	0.74
Arteriosclerotic heart disease, incl. coronary disease......................	255.6	269.2	344.2	196.0	144.4	171.1	119.0	1.74	0.54
Nonrheumatic chronic endocarditis and other myocardial degeneration........	37.7	37.7	38.4	37.1	37.5	40.5	34.6	1.05	0.99
Other diseases of heart...............	12.6	11.7	14.3	9.2	19.5	22.8	16.4	1.52	1.67
Hypertension with heart disease........	43.3	38.6	34.6	42.6	81.4	78.1	84.5	0.83	2.11
Vascular lesions affecting central nervous system...................................	106.3	104.7	102.3	107.0	119.8	116.3	123.2	0.95	1.14
Rheumatic fever.........................	0.6	0.6	0.6	0.5	1.2	1.1	1.3	1.17	2.00
Hypertension without mention of heart.....	6.5	5.8	6.0	5.7	12.5	13.2	11.7	1.05	2.16
General arteriosclerosis................	19.1	20.0	19.6	20.4	12.4	13.0	11.8	0.97	0.62
Other diseases of circulatory system......	8.4	8.4	10.9	6.0	8.1	8.9	7.4	1.73	0.96
Chronic and unspecified nephritis and other renal sclerosis............................	9.1	8.1	8.9	7.4	17.6	18.4	16.9	1.18	2.17
Malignant neoplasms..........................	147.9	151.5	162.5	140.7	118.3	125.3	111.7	1.15	0.78
of buccal cavity and pharynx..............	3.3	3.4	5.5	1.4	2.6	3.9	1.4	3.79	0.76
of digestive organs and peritoneum........	52.5	53.9	59.5	48.4	41.0	51.1	31.5	1.26	0.76
of respiratory system......................	19.2	20.0	34.4	5.9	13.3	23.0	4.1	5.82	0.67
of breast.................................	13.3	13.8	0.2	27.0	9.3	0.3	17.8	0.01	0.67
of genital organs.........................	22.6	22.0	18.1	25.9	26.8	18.3	34.8	0.67	1.22
of urinary organs.........................	7.0	7.3	9.9	4.8	4.3	5.3	3.4	2.04	0.59
of other unspecified sites...............	16.3	16.8	18.2	15.5	12.2	12.5	11.8	1.17	0.73
Leukemia and aleukemia....................	6.8	7.1	8.3	6.0	4.1	4.8	3.4	1.39	0.58
Lymphosarcoma and other neoplasms of lymphatic and hematopoietic tissues......	6.8	7.1	8.4	5.8	4.7	6.0	3.5	1.49	0.66
Benign neoplasms of unspecified nature.......	2.9	2.8	2.6	3.0	3.9	2.5	5.2	0.81	1.39
Accidents....................................	56.7	55.0	76.9	33.5	70.7	103.5	39.5	2.33	1.29
Motor vehicle accidents...................	23.7	23.3	35.4	11.6	26.8	42.5	11.9	3.11	1.15
All other accidents......................	33.0	31.6	41.6	21.9	43.9	61.0	27.6	1.93	1.39
Influenza and pneumonia, except pneumonia of newborn....................................	28.2	25.6	29.5	21.9	48.7	56.3	41.6	1.34	1.90
Influenza...............................	1.4	1.2	1.2	1.1	3.1	3.1	3.1	1.00	2.58
Pneumonia...............................	26.8	24.5	28.3	20.8	45.6	53.1	38.5	1.36	1.86
Diabetes mellitus............................	15.7	15.8	12.8	18.6	14.7	10.0	19.2	0.67	0.93
Tuberculosis.................................	8.4	7.0	10.5	3.7	19.5	25.9	13.5	2.52	2.79
of respiratory system....................	7.8	6.6	9.9	3.4	17.1	23.3	11.3	2.63	2.59
other forms..............................	0.6	0.4	0.6	0.3	2.4	2.6	2.2	1.60	6.00
Suicide......................................	10.0	10.8	16.9	4.8	3.8	6.1	1.6	3.57	0.35
Homicide.....................................	4.6	2.3	3.3	1.3	23.3	37.0	10.3	3.00	10.13
Syphilis and its sequelae....................	2.3	1.7	2.6	0.9	7.1	10.1	4.2	2.83	4.18
Typhoid fever................................	0.0	0.0	0.0	0.0	0.1	0.1	0.1	0.00	0.00
Dysentery, all forms.........................	0.3	0.2	0.2	0.2	0.9	1.1	0.8	1.00	4.50
Scarlet fever and streptococcal sore throat..	0.1	0.1	0.1	0.1	0.2	0.3	0.2	1.00	2.00
Diptheria....................................	0.1	0.0	0.0	0.0	0.2	0.3	0.1	0.00	0.00
Whooping cough...............................	0.2	0.1	0.1	0.1	0.9	0.9	0.9	1.00	9.00
Meningococcal infections.....................	0.5	0.4	0.5	0.4	0.7	0.8	0.6	1.25	1.75
Acute poliomyelitis..........................	0.3	0.3	0.4	0.3	0.5	0.5	0.4	1.33	1.67
Smallpox.....................................	0.0	0.0	0.0	0.0	0.0	0.0	0.0	0.00	0.00
Measles......................................	0.3	0.3	0.3	0.3	0.6	0.7	0.6	1.00	2.00
Typhus and other rickettsial diseases........	0.0	0.0	0.0	0.0	0.0	0.0	0.0	0.00	0.00
Malaria......................................	0.0	0.0	0.0	0.0	0.0	0.0	0.0	0.00	0.00
Other infective and parasitic diseases.......	2.6	2.3	2.6	2.1	5.1	5.5	4.7	1.21	2.22

[1]Rates per 100,000 population in each specified group.

Table 9-13.—DEATH RATES FOR 64 SELECTED CAUSES OF DEATH, BY COLOR AND SEX: UNITED STATES, 1956—Con.

Cause of death	Total	White			Nonwhite			Ratio male to fe- male	Ratio non- white to white
		Both sexes	Male	Female	Both sexes	Male	Female		
Cirrhosis of liver...........................	10.7	11.0	14.7	7.4	8.5	10.2	6.9	1.95	0.77
Ulcer of stomach and duodenum................	6.0	6.2	9.8	2.8	4.0	5.9	2.2	3.48	0.65
Hernia and intestinal obstruction...........	5.1	5.0	5.1	4.9	5.7	6.5	4.9	1.08	1.14
Gastritis, duodenitis, enteritis, and colitis, except diarrhea of newborn.........	4.5	3.9	4.1	3.7	9.5	10.6	8.4	1.14	2.44
Hyperplasia of prostate.....................	3.2	3.2	6.4	...	3.4	7.1	...	...	1.06
Anemias....................................	1.9	1.8	1.7	1.8	2.8	3.0	2.7	1.00	1.56
Bronchitis.................................	1.9	1.9	2.5	1.3	2.2	2.6	1.7	1.92	1.16
Acute nephritis............................	1.4	1.2	1.4	1.1	3.0	3.3	2.7	1.23	2.50
Meningitis,except meningococcal and tuberculous................................	1.2	0.9	1.1	0.7	3.1	3.6	2.7	1.56	3.44
Deliveries and complications of pregnancy, childbirth, and the puerperium.............	1.0	0.7	...	1.3	3.8	...	7.3	...	5.43
Abortion..................................	0.1	0.1	...	0.2	0.5	...	0.9	...	5.00
All other complications...................	0.9	0.6	...	1.2	3.3	...	6.4	...	5.50
Congenital malformations....................	12.6	12.5	13.7	11.3	13.5	15.3	11.7	1.23	1.08
Certain diseases of early infancy...........	38.6	33.5	40.1	27.1	80.0	94.0	66.7	1.46	2.39
Symptoms, senility, and ill-defined conditions.................................	11.3	8.3	10.3	6.4	35.6	40.3	31.2	1.47	4.29
All other diseases (residual)...............	43.0	42.4	50.6	34.3	48.3	55.5	41.6	1.46	1.14

Source: National Office of Vital Statistics, Vital Statistics of the United States, 1956, Vol. I, Introduction: Table BQ.

Much of the greater longevity among women is due to their very much lower rates of death from most of the diseases of the cardiovascular system, and also to their lower death rates from several other important sources of mortality.

Color Differences. Although the nonwhite population has a higher rate of mortality with respect to most causes of death, in 1956 the following causes were unusually more destructive of nonwhite than of white lives:

Rheumatic fever

Hypertension with heart disease

Chronic and unspecified nephritis

Influenza

Tuberculosis--all forms

Homicide

Syphilis and its sequelae

Scarlet fever and streptococcal sore throat

Whooping cough

Measles

Enteritis, gastritis, duodenitis, and colitis

Acute nephritis

Meningitis

Deliveries and the complications of pregnancy and childbirth

Certain diseases of early infancy

CHANGES IN CAUSE OF DEATH: 1947 TO 1956

Reasonably strict comparability in cause-of-death information can be had for the period 1947 to 1956, because during this period the Sixth Revision of the International List was used to classify deaths by cause. The changes which took place in the crude death rate, with respect to each of several leading causes, are given in the following table:

Cause of death	Rate		Change
	1947	1956	1947- 1956
Tuberculosis, all forms.......	32.1	8.4	-23.7
Malignant neoplasms, total....	133.5	147.9	14.4
of digestive organs and peritoneum................	55.2	52.5	-2.7
of respiratory system.......	11.4	19.2	7.8
of breast..................	11.8	13.3	1.5
of genital organs..........	22.8	22.6	-0.2

Text table—Continued

| Cause of death | Rate | | Change |
	1947	1956	1947-1956
Diabetes mellitus.............	14.9	15.7	0.8
Major cardiovascular-renal disease.....................	507.2	510.7	3.5
Diseases of the heart.......	348.7	360.5	11.8
Vascular lesion affecting central nervous system.....	103.6	106.3	2.7
General arteriosclerosis....	20.2	19.1	-1.1
Chronic rheumatic heart disease....................	15.1	11.4	-3.7
Chronic and unspecific nephritis and other renal disease....................	19.3	9.1	-10.2
Influenza and pneumonia.......	38.7	28.2	-10.5
Congenital malformations......	13.8	12.6	-1.2
Certain diseases of early infancy....................	48.0	38.6	-9.4
Accidents: motor vehicle......	22.8	23.7	0.9
other.............	43.0	33.0	-10.0
Suicide.....................	11.6	10.0	-1.6

Source: Vital Statistics of the United States: 1956, Table BP, page C.

Thus, it appears that the crude death rates for the major killers--heart disease, other circulatory diseases, and cancer--have risen in the last 9 years. As was described above, impaired lives that were spared from other causes of death at the younger ages may fall victim to these diseases at a later age. Outstanding progress has been made in combating tuberculosis, nephritis, influenza, many diseases of early infancy, and accidents other than those involving motor vehicles.

TRENDS IN CAUSE OF DEATH: 1900 TO 1956

The story of the decline in mortality and the increase in longevity would not be complete without a discussion of the long-range trends with respect to specific causes of death. Because of changes in medical theory, and revisions in the system of classifying deaths by cause, a time series cannot be constructed for many causes of death; for other causes, the statistics for earlier years are very unreliable. However, by reviewing the long-term trends connected with a few specific causes for which usable data are available, in each of the three major categories of death (infectious diseases, chronic diseases, and deaths from external causes), one can form a good picture of what has happened.

Trends in Infectious Diseases. Table 9-14 contains death rates for each of seven infectious diseases, reported in terms of 5-year averages, for the period 1900 to 1954, with data for the single years 1955 and 1956. These rates are standardized for age, and are reported separately for the male and the female populations and the white and the nonwhite populations, as well as for the total population. Thus, for each of these selected causes of death it is possible to trace the trend in:

(a) Level of incidence

(b) Sex differential

(c) Color differential

For each of these seven infectious diseases the story is essentially the same: virulence has been reduced to a very small fraction, compared with past years. Following is the percent decline in the age-standardized rate for each disease between 1900 and 1956:

	Percent change, 1900 to 1956
Diphtheria	-99.6
Dysentery	-98.0
Influenza	-88.5
Gastritis, etc.	-96.2
Syphilis, etc.	-87.9
Tuberculosis	-95.9
Typhoid Fever	-100.0

In terms of level, there are almost no deaths nowadays from such diseases as diphtheria, dysentery, and typhoid fever. Death rates from enteritis and syphilis are so low as to be almost insignificant. Only influenza and tuberculosis show rates as high as 5 per 100,000 inhabitants, and the rates for both of these diseases have continued to decline precipitously right to the present time. The prospect is very bright that they will decline much more, and that their rates will suffer the same fate as that of diphtheria. Until very recently, the color differential for the infectious diseases was extremely high, and even at present there is a great deal of "surplus mortality" from these diseases among the nonwhite population.[16]

---

[16] If it can be shown that medical science and public health care are able to reduce the mortality of a particular group to a certain low rate, then, from a strictly demographic point of view, all deaths occurring in excess of that rate among other groups may be defined as "excess mortality."

Table 9-14.—TREND IN AGE-ADJUSTED (STANDARDIZED) DEATH RATES FOR SELECTED INFECTIOUS DISEASES,
BY SEX AND COLOR: 1900 TO 1956

(Rates per 100,000 population, standardized on age composition of the nation in 1940.)

Cause of death and year	Total	Sex		Color	
		Male	Female	White	Nonwhite
DIPTHERIA:					
1956..	0.1	0.1	...	...	0.1
1955..	0.1	0.1	0.1	0.1	0.2
1950 to 1954..................................	0.1	0.1	0.1	0.1	0.3
1945 to 1949..................................	0.6	0.7	0.6	0.6	0.7
1940 to 1944..................................	0.9	1.0	0.8	0.9	1.1
1935 to 1939..................................	2.1	2.2	2.1	2.1	2.4
1930 to 1934..................................	3.9	4.0	3.8	3.9	3.7
1925 to 1929..................................	6.1	6.2	6.0	6.2	4.9
1920 to 1924..................................	11.2	11.3	11.1	11.7	6.5
1915 to 1919..................................	11.9	12.1	11.7	12.1	6.5
1910 to 1914..................................	15.3	15.6	15.0	14.4	8.3
1905 to 1909..................................	19.4	19.8	19.0	...	...
1900 to 1904..................................	27.3	27.3	27.3	...	...
DYSENTERY-ALL FORMS:					
1956..	0.2	0.2	0.2	0.2	0.7
1955..	0.3	0.3	0.2	0.2	0.8
1950 to 1954..................................	0.4	0.5	0.4	0.4	1.2
1945 to 1949..................................	0.7	0.7	0.6	0.6	1.4
1940 to 1944..................................	1.5	1.6	1.4	1.2	3.4
1935 to 1939..................................	2.2	2.3	2.1	1.9	4.9
1930 to 1934..................................	2.3	2.4	2.2	1.9	6.5
1925 to 1929..................................	2.7	2.6	2.6	2.1	8.0
1920 to 1924..................................	3.3	3.3	3.3	2.7	10.1
1915 to 1919..................................	4.8	4.7	4.9	3.9	14.0
1910 to 1914..................................	5.2	5.0	5.4	4.3	10.2
1905 to 1909..................................	7.4	6.9	7.9	...	...
1900 to 1904..................................	10.2	9.6	10.8	...	....
GASTRITIS, DUODENITIS, ENTERITIS, AND COLITIS, except diarrhea of newborn:					
1956..	3.5	3.8	3.2	3.1	6.3
1955..	3.7	3.9	3.4	3.1	7.1
1950 to 1954..................................	4.1	4.4	3.8	3.5	8.4
1945 to 1949..................................	5.3	5.7	4.9	4.8	9.2
1940 to 1944..................................	8.9	9.5	8.3	7.8	17.4
1935 to 1939..................................	14.3	15.2	13.3	13.0	24.8
1930 to 1934..................................	18.7	20.0	17.4	16.7	35.3
1925 to 1929..................................	25.0	26.7	23.3	23.2	42.9
1920 to 1924..................................	34.0	36.2	31.7	32.5	50.6
1915 to 1919..................................	54.3	57.9	50.5	51.9	71.8
1910 to 1914..................................	69.7	73.4	65.9	58.4	79.8
1905 to 1909..................................	89.1	93.4	84.6	...	...
1900 to 1904..................................	91.6	95.3	87.8	...	...
INFLUENZA AND PNEUMONIA:					
1956..	21.9	26.7	17.6	19.4	43.3
1955..	21.3	25.6	17.3	18.7	43.7
1950 to 1954..................................	24.5	29.2	20.3	21.4	53.6
1945 to 1949..................................	36.1	42.0	30.3	32.3	69.8
1940 to 1944..................................	60.3	69.0	51.8	54.1	117.4
1935 to 1939..................................	102.2	115.0	89.0	92.6	191.2
1930 to 1934..................................	108.0	118.3	97.2	98.4	196.6
1925 to 1929..................................	138.9	149.7	127.4	128.3	245.5
1920 to 1924..................................	147.3	154.0	139.9	139.4	231.1
1915 to 1919..................................	263.1	288.8	236.6	275.7	414.8
1910 to 1914..................................	149.0	157.7	139.1	133.3	235.0
1905 to 1909..................................	167.5	175.3	158.5	...	...
1900 to 1904..................................	190.9	197.3	183.7	...	...

Table 9-14.—TREND IN AGE-ADJUSTED (STANDARDIZED) DEATH RATES FOR SELECTED INFECTIOUS DISEASES, BY SEX AND COLOR: 1900 TO 1956—Con.

(Rates per 100,000 population, standardized on age composition of the nation in 1940.)

Cause of death and year	Total	Sex		Color	
		Male	Female	White	Nonwhite
SYPHILIS AND ITS SEQUELAE:					
1956....................................	2.0	3.1	1.0	1.4	8.6
1955....................................	2.0	3.2	1.0	1.4	9.4
1950 to 1954............................	3.5	5.3	1.8	2.4	14.2
1945 to 1949............................	7.9	11.7	4.1	5.5	32.0
1940 to 1944............................	12.3	17.9	6.7	8.4	50.9
1935 to 1939............................	16.1	22.8	9.3	11.2	64.7
1930 to 1934............................	16.4	23.0	9.6	11.8	62.6
1925 to 1929............................	17.9	25.2	10.2	14.1	59.1
1920 to 1924............................	19.1	26.8	10.9	16.3	50.9
1915 to 1919............................	19.4	26.7	11.6	17.4	46.5
1910 to 1914............................	16.6	22.6	10.2	17.0	44.5
TYPHOID FEVER:					
1956....................................	...	...	...	...	0.1
1955....................................	...	...	...	...	...
1950 to 1954............................	...	0.1	...	...	0.2
1945 to 1949............................	0.2	0.3	0.2	0.2	0.6
1940 to 1944............................	0.7	0.7	0.5	0.5	2.0
1935 to 1939............................	2.1	2.4	1.7	1.6	6.0
1930 to 1934............................	3.9	4.5	3.3	3.0	11.7
1925 to 1929............................	5.7	6.4	5.0	4.5	17.2
1920 to 1924............................	7.5	8.4	6.6	6.3	20.1
1915 to 1919............................	12.0	13.8	10.1	10.5	27.7
1910 to 1914............................	18.2	21.2	14.9	14.1	30.6
1905 to 1909............................	24.9	29.0	20.5	...	...
1900 to 1904............................	26.8	31.1	22.3	...	...
TUBERCULOSIS-ALL FORMS:					
1956....................................	7.7	11.3	4.4	6.2	22.5
1955....................................	8.4	12.2	4.9	6.7	24.6
1950 to 1954............................	15.4	21.1	9.9	12.0	46.9
1945 to 1949............................	32.4	41.7	23.3	25.5	92.4
1940 to 1944............................	43.0	52.0	33.8	33.9	122.9
1935 to 1939............................	53.1	60.3	45.3	42.4	147.3
1930 to 1934............................	66.1	72.2	59.4	52.4	188.6
1925 to 1929............................	84.9	89.1	80.0	71.2	217.1
1920 to 1924............................	102.4	106.7	97.4	89.0	241.3
1915 to 1919............................	145.6	160.8	128.5	130.6	347.6
1910 to 1914............................	152.4	167.8	135.3	135.4	395.7
1905 to 1909............................	173.4	187.7	157.8	...	...
1900 to 1904............................	188.5	199.1	177.4	...	...

Source: National Office of Vital Statistics, Special Reports, and annual reports Vital Statistics of the United States, 1955 and 1956.

Since 1950, however, tremendous strides have been made in reducing deaths resulting from infectious diseases among the nonwhite population. This reduction has been due, in no small part, to the rapid urbanization and the northward migration of Negroes, and to the greatly improved economic status of the nonwhite population. The decline which has occurred since 1940 (and even since 1950) among the nonwhite population in mortality resulting from tuberculosis, syphilis, and influenza is very impressive.

Trends in Deaths from Chronic Diseases. A much more discouraging picture is presented by the death rates for chronic diseases.[17] There appears to have been a small but encouraging decline in the major cardiovascular-renal diseases, especially since 1950. (There has been a small

---

[17] Statistics concerning many of the disorders in this group are only approximate, because of changes in medical diagnosis and changes in the classification system.

increase in the crude rate, but when one takes account of the change in age composition, there is indication of a small decrease.) Deaths from malignant neoplasms, on the other hand, seem to be steadily on the rise among males, although

among females such deaths have declined slowly but rather steadily since 1935. (There has been an interesting inversion of the sex differential with respect to death from cancer since 1925; at that time, the death rate for this disease was more

Table 9-15.—TRENDS IN AGE-ADJUSTED (STANDARDIZED) DEATH RATES FOR SELECTED CHRONIC DISEASES, BY SEX AND COLOR: 1900 TO 1956 [1]

Cause of death and year	Total	Sex		Color	
		Male	Female	White	Nonwhite
MAJOR CARDIOVASCULAR-RENAL DISEASES:					
1956	410.7	504.7	324.5	397.3	555.1
1955	410.0	502.0	325.1	396.9	548.6
1950 to 1954	427.2	514.4	345.3	412.0	584.5
1945 to 1949	436.7	513.7	362.4	423.2	569.7
1940 to 1944	469.1	536.7	402.6	453.5	629.8
1935 to 1939	479.1	531.9	425.9	463.3	647.4
1930 to 1934	479.5	520.8	437.4	461.5	678.0
1925 to 1929	502.2	534.9	468.8	484.4	714.7
1920 to 1924	473.9	491.7	456.4	462.8	611.7
1915 to 1919	485.5	513.6	457.7	470.1	656.6
1910 to 1914	477.6	511.4	444.0	469.7	695.0
1905 to 1909	467.2	502.1	433.5	...	...
1900 to 1904	437.1	471.5	405.2	...	...
DISEASES OF HEART:					
1956	292.7	376.6	215.6	287.1	350.6
1955	290.9	372.9	215.0	285.6	343.4
1950 to 1954	299.8	378.5	225.5	293.2	363.7
1945 to 1949	287.5	355.1	221.8	283.7	314.9
1940 to 1944	288.9	345.6	232.7	285.1	316.7
1935 to 1939	280.2	322.7	236.7	275.5	320.9
1930 to 1934	256.8	286.9	225.6	250.5	317.8
1925 to 1929	243.9	263.1	223.9	237.2	318.4
1920 to 1924	210.4	219.9	200.7	206.2	259.8
1915 to 1919	206.6	216.7	196.3	200.4	275.7
1910 to 1914	199.8	211.6	187.9	195.9	293.2
1905 to 1909	199.1	213.1	185.7	...	...
1900 to 1904	180.8	194.5	168.1	...	...
VASCULAR LESIONS AFFECTING CENTRAL NERVOUS SYSTEM:					
1956	83.6	88.2	79.5	78.5	144.1
1955	84.2	88.7	80.1	78.8	144.3
1950 to 1954	87.7	91.1	84.5	82.1	148.7
1945 to 1949	82.6	84.2	81.1	77.7	135.2
1940 to 1944	87.6	88.6	86.7	82.5	144.3
1935 to 1939	92.7	93.4	92.1	87.5	151.0
1930 to 1934	100.4	101.4	99.4	95.4	156.5
1925 to 1929	112.8	113.8	111.7	108.4	165.0
1920 to 1924	122.2	119.8	124.6	119.6	153.9
1915 to 1919	122.4	122.1	122.8	119.7	156.2
1910 to 1914	122.5	124.3	120.8	121.1	163.7
1905 to 1909	131.3	133.4	129.4	...	...
1900 to 1904	134.2	137.1	131.5	...	...
GENERAL ARTERIOSCLEROSIS:					
1956	13.4	14.9	12.1	13.4	16.1
1955	14.1	15.8	12.5	14.0	14.7
1950 to 1954	15.3	17.1	13.7	15.3	15.4
1945 to 1949	15.7	17.7	13.9	15.7	15.3
1940 to 1944	17.4	19.8	15.2	17.4	16.8
1935 to 1939	18.3	20.7	16.0	18.4	17.3
1930 to 1934	20.9	23.9	18.1	21.0	20.2

[1] Rates per 100,000 population, standardized on age composition of the population in 1940.

Table 9-15.—TRENDS IN AGE-ADJUSTED (STANDARDIZED) DEATH RATES FOR SELECTED CHRONIC DISEASES, BY SEX AND COLOR: 1900 TO 1956—Con.

Cause of death and year	Total	Sex		Color	
		Male	Female	White	Nonwhite
MALIGNANT NEOPLASMS:					
1956..	128.1	142.1	116.1	126.6	142.6
1955..	127.4	139.7	116.6	126.2	137.1
1950 to 1954.................................	126.1	134.3	119.0	125.2	131.7
1945 to 1949.................................	121.5	122.7	120.9	121.7	112.8
1940 to 1944.................................	118.4	114.6	122.8	119.5	100.1
1935 to 1939.................................	118.6	110.4	127.5	120.2	93.2
1930 to 1934.................................	115.0	104.0	126.8	116.5	88.4
1925 to 1929.................................	113.8	100.4	128.2	115.4	85.0
1920 to 1924.................................	108.2	93.4	124.3	110.1	76.4
1915 to 1919.................................	101.1	83.0	120.9	102.3	74.9
1910 to 1914.................................	97.6	78.0	118.8	99.7	76.7
1905 to 1909.................................	91.2	70.5	112.9	...	...
1900 to 1904.................................	83.9	63.3	104.7	...	...
DIABETES MELLITUS:					
1956..	13.3	11.0	15.4	12.9	16.9
1955..	13.2	11.1	15.0	12.8	17.3
1950 to 1954.................................	14.0	11.3	16.5	13.6	17.1
1945 to 1949.................................	21.7	16.6	26.7	21.7	20.2
1940 to 1944.................................	25.1	19.1	31.2	25.2	22.2
1935 to 1939.................................	25.1	19.1	31.3	25.3	20.6
1930 to 1934.................................	23.9	18.7	29.2	24.0	19.5
1925 to 1929.................................	21.5	17.3	25.8	21.6	17.3
1920 to 1924.................................	20.8	17.8	24.0	21.3	13.3
1915 to 1919.................................	20.1	18.0	22.5	20.5	11.9
1910 to 1914.................................	19.0	17.3	20.9	20.2	12.4
1905 to 1909.................................	17.2	15.8	18.6	....	...
1900 to 1904.................................	14.6	14.4	14.8	...	...

than 25 percent higher among women than among men. Since 1925, the rate for females has declined slowly but, nevertheless, rather steadily, and has increased steadily and rather rapidly for males. The net result is that the cancer death rate for men is now almost 25 percent higher than it is for women.) Over-all mortality from diabetes, another important member of the chronic cause-of-death group, appears not to have changed a great deal in the past decade, after having undergone a marked decline between 1940 and 1950.

Trends in Deaths from External Causes. Both suicide and homicide have declined rather steadily since 1930. Since men are victims of death from these sources much more frequently than are women, the greater reduction has taken place in the rate for males. Among the nonwhite population, the homicide rate is still discouragingly high--11 times that of the white population. Since

1950 there has been a moderate decline in the homicide rate among the nonwhite population.

As a cause of death, motor vehicles rank above all the infectious diseases, and above all the chronic diseases except diseases of the heart and circulatory system, and cancer. As automobiles increase in number, and as more millions of highway miles are traveled annually, the toll of death from motor vehicle accidents rises. Males are killed in auto accidents much more frequently than females, and the accident death rate is much higher among the nonwhite than among the white population.

The trend of deaths caused by accidents other than motor vehicles has been downward, and to an impressive extent. Safety programs in industry are responsible for much of this improvement. In such accidents, there are about 3 male deaths to each female death, and nonwhite persons are victims of industrial and other non-automobile acci-

Table 9-16.—TRENDS IN AGE-ADJUSTED (STANDARDIZED) DEATH RATES FOR SELECTED EXTERNAL CAUSES,
BY SEX AND COLOR: 1900 TO 1956

(Rates per 100,000 population, standardized on age composition of the nation in 1940.)

Cause of death and year	Total	Sex		Color	
		Male	Female	White	Nonwhite
SUICIDE:					
1956...................................	9.8	15.6	4.4	10.3	4.4
1955...................................	9.9	15.7	4.5	10.5	4.4
1950 to 1954...........................	10.1	16.0	4.4	10.6	4.5
1945 to 1949...........................	10.9	16.8	5.3	11.6	4.3
1940 to 1944...........................	11.7	17.6	5.9	12.4	4.1
1935 to 1939...........................	15.0	22.8	7.0	15.9	5.3
1930 to 1934...........................	17.3	26.9	7.3	18.3	6.1
1925 to 1929...........................	14.5	21.8	6.7	15.2	5.3
1920 to 1924...........................	13.0	19.3	6.3	13.7	4.8
1915 to 1919...........................	14.9	22.0	7.3	15.4	6.6
1910 to 1914...........................	17.3	26.0	7.9	18.1	10.2
1905 to 1909...........................	16.3	24.8	7.4	...	...
1900 to 1904...........................	12.1	18.5	5.7	...	...
HOMICIDE:					
1956...................................	4.9	7.6	2.4	2.4	26.5
1955...................................	4.8	7.5	2.3	2.4	25.7
1950 to 1954...........................	5.2	8.1	2.4	2.5	28.3
1945 to 1949...........................	6.0	9.7	2.5	3.0	31.6
1940 to 1944...........................	5.7	9.2	2.3	2.8	30.9
1935 to 1939...........................	7.6	12.1	3.1	4.2	38.2
1930 to 1934...........................	9.6	15.4	3.6	5.9	42.5
1925 to 1929...........................	8.7	13.7	3.4	5.3	40.9
1920 to 1924...........................	7.9	12.6	3.1	5.4	34.4
1915 to 1919...........................	6.7	10.6	2.6	5.0	28.8
1910 to 1914...........................	5.6	8.5	2.3	5.1	29.1
1905 to 1909...........................	4.0	6.0	1.9	...	...
1900 to 1904...........................	1.2	1.7	0.7	...	...
MOTOR VEHICLE ACCIDENTS:					
1956...................................	25.1	39.3	11.7	24.7	29.7
1955...................................	24.6	38.3	11.6	24.2	28.3
1950 to 1954...........................	24.1	37.7	11.2	23.8	27.8
1945 to 1949...........................	22.2	35.6	9.8	22.4	21.6
1940 to 1944...........................	22.6	35.9	9.7	22.5	23.0
1935 to 1939...........................	28.2	43.2	13.1	28.2	27.9
1930 to 1934...........................	27.2	40.9	13.2	27.3	25.9
1925 to 1929...........................	22.4	32.9	11.7	22.7	19.6
1920 to 1924...........................	13.3	19.6	6.9	13.7	8.8
1915 to 1919...........................	8.3	12.6	3.8	8.4	4.8
1910 to 1914...........................	3.1	4.7	1.3	4.4	2.2
1906 to 1909...........................	0.9	1.3	0.4	...	....
ACCIDENTS EXCEPT MOTOR VEHICLES:					
1956...................................	29.4	42.0	17.2	27.6	43.3
1955...................................	29.8	42.4	17.5	28.1	43.6
1950 to 1954...........................	33.1	46.7	19.8	31.3	47.2
1945 to 1949...........................	42.2	58.4	26.6	41.0	49.7
1940 to 1944...........................	49.0	68.4	30.2	48.2	54.0
1935 to 1939...........................	50.9	67.4	33.6	49.7	58.3
1930 to 1934...........................	52.6	71.4	33.0	51.2	63.0
1925 to 1929...........................	60.5	84.9	34.7	58.8	76.1
1920 to 1924...........................	61.9	86.9	35.5	60.8	72.1
1915 to 1919...........................	74.6	109.8	37.9	72.1	83.8
1910 to 1914...........................	83.1	123.5	39.3	75.6	91.9
1905 to 1909...........................	90.3	136.7	41.3	...	...
1900 to 1904...........................	83.1	124.3	41.1	...	...

dents much more frequently than are white persons.

INFANT MORTALITY

The infant mortality rate is defined as the number of infants, among each 1,000 infants born alive during a calendar year, who die before reaching their first birthday. For most years and for most analytical purposes (except for life table construction) an acceptably precise approximation of the infant mortality rate may be obtained by dividing the number of infants who die in a given calendar year by the total number of infants born alive during the same year.[18] In 1956 there were 26.0 deaths of infants under 1 year of age per 1,000 births (preliminary data show that during 1957 the rate probably was somewhat higher-- 26.4). The 1956 rate was the lowest on record. In 1915, the first year for which birth figures were available from the registration states, the infant mortality rate was 99.9. Within 40 years, the rate declined by 74 percent. Yet even the very high rates for the year 1915 were considerably below the levels that had prevailed throughout the eighteenth century, and, indeed, throughout human history until recent decades. (Only fragmentary data are available to support this assertion). In the state of Massachusetts, the infant mortality rate stood at about 167 in 1880 and at about 145 in 1900.[19] The decline in infant mortality, therefore, appears to have begun in the latter part of the nineteenth century, and to have picked up great momentum by the time the first reliable rates for the registration states were available, in 1915. The full meaning of this remarkable reduction in infant mortality may be more fully appreciated if the above statistics are restated as follows: In 1880, about 1 infant in 6 died before its first birthday; in 1956, only 1 infant in 38 died during the first year of life. These statistics illustrate the important fact that, throughout most of human history, the human race has had to be very fertile in order to counteract the heavy toll of death among infants. Since science and modern technology have focused on the infant mortality problem from a great many angles, one measure of a nation's well-being and technological advancement is its infant mortality rate.

Age of Infant at Death. The rate of infant mortality is highest during the first few hours and days of life. In 1956, considerably more than 1/3 of all infant deaths occurred during the first day of life, and more than 2/3 occurred during the first 28 days (see Table 9-17). (The first 28 days are usually referred to as the "neonatal period," and the mortality rate for these days is referred to as the "neonatal mortality rate.") The greatest proportionate reductions have been made in the later months of the first year. Table 9-17 shows a decline of 80 percent since 1915 in the infant death rate for the third to the twelfth month. As will be shown below, this reduction has been a result of the control of infectious diseases, which had been primarily responsible for the high rate of infant mortality. Less progress has been made in preventing the death, shortly after birth, of immature infants and infants with congenital deficiencies. The death rate for the first day of life remained almost unchanged until about 1936; since then it

---

[18] An exact calculation of this rate requires that the infants who die be allocated to the proper year's cohort of infants with which they were born. Death statistics do not provide the information necessary for such an allocation. Actually, many of the infants who die during a given year were born during the previous year, and some of those born in the later months of a given year die, at less than 12 months of age, in the succeeding year. The approximation to the infant mortality rate assumes a relatively constant number of births from year to year. If the birth rate is fluctuating from one year to the next, the infant mortality rate as calculated above should be adjusted to take account of this fact. If the birth rate is declining rapidly, the infant mortality rate will be too high, whereas if it is rising rapidly, the infant mortality rate will be too low. For most years, this adjustment changes the rate by only about 1 or 2 deaths per 10,000 births. Even the very erratic fluctuations in births between 1945 and 1948 caused the adjusted rate to differ from the approximate rate by only 8 deaths, or less, per 10,000 births.

---

[19] W. S. Thompson and P. K. Whelpton, Population Trends in the United States, Table 65, p. 237.

Table 9-17.—INFANT MORTALITY RATES BY DETAILED AGE: BIRTH-REGISTRATION STATES FOR SELECTED YEARS, 1915 TO 1956

(Exclusive of fetal deaths. Rates per 1,000 live births.)

Age	1956	1950	1940	1930	1920	1915	Percent change, 1915 to 1956
Under 1 year.............	26.0	29.2	47.0	64.6	85.8	99.9	-74.0
Under 1 day..............	9.9	10.2	13.9	15.0	14.8	15.0	-34.0
1 day....................	2.8	3.1	3.5	4.2	4.6	4.9	-42.9
2 days...................	1.7	2.0	2.2	2.9	3.4	3.5	-51.4
3 to 6 days..............	2.1	2.6	3.6	5.1	6.4	6.7	-68.7
7 to 13 days.............	1.2	1.3	2.4	3.9	5.4	6.0	-80.0
14 to 20 days............	0.6	0.7	1.6	2.5	3.8	4.6	-87.0
21 to 27 days............	0.5	0.6	1.4	2.1	3.1	3.7	-86.5
Under 28 days............	18.9	20.5	28.8	35.7	41.5	44.4	-57.4
28 to 59 days............	1.6	1.8	3.5	5.3	7.3	9.0	-82.2
2 months................	1.2	1.4	2.9	4.2	5.7	7.6	-84.2
3 to 5 months...........	2.2	2.8	5.9	8.7	13.1	16.9	-87.0
6 to 8 months...........	1.2	1.7	3.6	6.1	10.0	12.5	-90.4
9 to 11 months..........	0.7	1.0	2.4	4.6	8.3	9.5	-92.6

Source: National Office of Vital Statistics, Special Reports, National Summaries, "Infant Mortality Statistics, United States."

has dropped by about one-third. Although the rates for the various days (after the first day) of the first week of life have declined rather steadily since 1915, the decline has been smaller than for the later periods. The declines for the third to the sixth day have been proportionately greater than those for the first and second days. Thus, the problem of reducing infant mortality has almost become one of assisting the newborn infant to survive birth and the first few days after birth. In 1956, 8 percent of all infant deaths, and 10 percent of neonatal deaths, occurred within the first hour of life.

Sex and Color of Infants Who Die. Table 9-18 presents the infant mortality rates for selected years since 1915, by sex and color. In 1956, mortality among male infants was 29 percent greater than among female infants (29.2 versus 22.6). The relative difference is greater during the first few days and months of life than at later ages.

In 1956, the mortality rate of nonwhite infants was 81 percent greater than that of white infants.

Table 9-18.—INFANT MORTALITY BY COLOR AND SEX FOR SELECTED YEARS: UNITED STATES, 1915 TO 1956

Year	All races			White			Nonwhite		
	Both sexes	Male	Female	Both sexes	Male	Female	Both sexes	Male	Female
1956.....................	26.0	29.2	22.6	23.2	26.2	20.0	42.1	46.7	37.3
1949 to 1951.............	29.6	33.3	25.8	27.2	30.6	23.5	45.5	50.5	40.5
1944 to 1946.............	37.3	41.5	32.8	34.8	39.0	30.3	55.6	60.9	50.2
1939 to 1941.............	46.8	52.1	41.3	42.9	47.8	37.7	74.3	82.2	66.2
1934 to 1936.............	57.6	64.0	50.9	53.1	59.2	46.6	88.4	97.0	79.6
1929 to 1931.............	64.6	71.4	57.4	60.2	66.8	53.3	98.4	107.4	89.2
1924 to 1926.............	71.9	79.8	63.6	68.4	76.0	60.3	111.8	122.6	100.7
1919 to 1921.............	82.6	91.4	73.5	79.2	87.8	70.1	123.6	135.4	111.4
1915 to 1917.............	98.2	108.3	87.7	96.0	106.0	85.6	172.3	188.0	154.8
Percent change:									
1915-17 to 1949-51.......	-69.9	-63.9	-70.6	-71.7	-71.1	-72.6	-73.6	-73.1	-73.8
1949-51 to 1956..........	-12.2	-12.3	-12.4	-14.7	-14.4	-14.9	-7.5	-7.5	-7.9

Source: National Office of Vital Statistics, Vital Statistics of the United States, 1950, Vol I, Table 8.49. Also annual report for 1956, Table BV.

This very large differential has existed, and has been of approximately this proportion, since the first statistics with which to measure it became available in 1915. The differential between the white and nonwhite rates is relatively greater after the first week of life than it is before the end of the first week. In 1956, the neonatal rate for whites was about 1.5 times that for nonwhites, while the rate for the remaining 11 months of the year was 2.7 times as great.

Cause of Infant Deaths. The greatest hazards to infant survival used to be (a) immaturity at birth, injury at birth, congenital debility, asphyxia, and other diseases peculiar to the first year of life; (b) pneumonia and influenza; (c) diarrhea and enteritis; and (d) certain communicable diseases such as whooping cough, measles, and diphtheria. Between 1921 (the first year for which data comparable with those of later years are published) and 1948 (the year preceding the introduction of the Sixth Revision of the International List of Causes of Death) considerable and substantial progress was made in reducing each of these four types of causes. But the greatest reduction, by

far, was made among the enteric, the respiratory, and the communicable diseases. This progress may be attributed to public health education and practices; enforcement of regulations to prevent contamination of water, milk, and other foods; widespread use of refrigeration; improved prenatal care; decline in the practice of employing a midwife as a substitute for an attending physician at birth; and the increase in the number of physicians specializing in childhood ailments. In 1948, the rates for the specific diseases falling in each of these classes (enteric, respiratory, and communicable) were only a small fraction of what they had been in 1929. Much less progress was made in reducing deaths resulting from diseases peculiar to the first year of life. The death rate for immaturity has fallen, but the extent to which this decline has been due to the avoidance of premature birth by better prenatal care, to improved care of the immature infant after birth, and to better medical reporting is not known. By 1950, the infant death rate had been lowered to the point where 70 percent of the deaths occurring in the first month of life were associated with immaturity at birth.

Table 9-19.—INFANT MORTALITY RATES FOR SELECTED CAUSES OF DEATH AND PERCENT CHANGE: 1921 AND 1948

Cause of death	1948	1921	Percent change, 1921 to 1948
Diseases peculiar to first year of life	17.4	29.2	...
Congenital debility	0.5	4.4	-88.6
Immaturity at birth	11.1	17.9	-38.0
Injury at birth	3.4	4.2	-19.0
Other diseases peculiar to the first year of life, including asphyxia	2.4	2.6	-7.7
Congenital malformations	4.5	6.1	-26.2
Pneumonia (all forms) and influenza	3.7	9.3	-60.2
Diarrhea, enteritis, and ulceration of the intestines	1.8	13.6	-86.8
Intestinal obstruction and other diseases of digestive system	0.2	1.8	-88.9
Accidental deaths	1.0	0.9	11.1
Whooping cough	0.2	2.2	-90.9
Diptheria	0.0	0.4	...
Syphilis	0.1	0.9	-88.9
Measles	0.1	0.5	-80.0
Meningitis (not due to meningococcus)	0.2	0.5	-60.0
Convulsions	0.1	0.9	-88.9
Diseases of the heart	0.0	0.4	...
Ill-defined and unknown causes	1.1	2.6	-57.7
Other	1.6	6.3	-74.6
Total	32.0	75.6	-57.7

Source: National Office of Vital Statistics, Vital Statistics of the United States, 1950, Vol. I, Table 8.53.

Immaturity at birth, with mention of no other cause, now accounts for more than 1/3 of all neonatal deaths and 1/5 of all infant deaths.

Cause of Infant Deaths by Race and Sex. Table 9-20 provides the information with which to deter-

the various causes. Similarly, the higher rate of mortality among nonwhite infants is reflected in each of the individual major causes. The high infant mortality rates for the nonwhite population can be traced to immaturity, to influenza and pneu-

Table 9-20.—INFANT MORTALITY RATES FOR SELECTED CAUSES OF DEATH, BY RACE AND SEX: UNITED STATES, 1950

Cause of death	All races both sexes	White		Nonwhite		Ratio of male to female	Ratio of nonwhite to white
		Male	Female	Male	Female		
Total............................	29.2	30.2	23.1	48.9	39.9	1.3	1.7
Certain diseases of early infancy.......	17.2	18.6	13.5	26.1	21.0	1.4	1.5
Immaturity unqualified..............	6.3	6.4	5.0	10.7	9.1	1.2	1.7
Postnatal asphyxia and atelectasis...	3.7	4.3	2.9	4.7	3.7	1.5	1.2
Birth injuries.....................	3.3	4.0	2.6	4.0	2.8	1.5	1.0
Pneumonia of newborn................	0.8	0.8	0.6	1.5	1.4	1.3	2.1
Ill-defined diseases of early infancy	1.1	1.0	0.7	2.4	2.0	1.3	2.4
Other diseases of early infancy......	2.0	2.1	1.7	2.8	2.0	1.3	1.3
Congenital malformations..............	4.0	4.4	3.9	3.0	2.6	1.1	0.7
Influenza and pneumonia (exc. newborn)..	2.4	2.1	1.7	5.8	5.0	1.2	2.8
Gastritis, duodenitis, enteritis, and colitis, exc. diarrhea of newborn......	1.1	1.0	0.8	2.5	2.0	1.3	2.4
Accidents.............................	1.0	1.0	0.7	2.0	1.7	1.2	2.1
Symptons and ill-defined conditions.....	1.0	0.6	0.5	4.5	3.5	1.2	8.0
Other causes..........................	2.5	2.5	2.0	5.0	4.1	1.2	1.9

Source: National Office of Vital Statistics, Vital Statistics of the United States, 1950, Vol. I, Table 8.52.

mine which diseases are responsible for the greater mortality among male than among female infants, and the greater mortality among nonwhite than among white infants. Male infants have higher rates of mortality than female infants with respect to every major cause of death. Although the differential appears to be especially great for birth injuries, it does not vary a great deal among

monia, to digestive ailments, and to "ill-defined conditions" and "other causes."

Regional Variations in Infant Mortality Rates. Table 9-21 demonstrates that there is a considerable amount of region-to-region variation in infant mortality rates. Much of this variation is due to the distribution of the nonwhite population. In all divisions where there are large concentrations of

Table 9-21.—INFANT MORTALITY RATES BY AGE AND COLOR, BY GEOGRAPHIC DIVISIONS: 1950

Geographic division	Under 1 year			Under 28 days			28 days to 11 months		
	All races	White	Nonwhite	All races	White	Nonwhite	All races	White	Nonwhite
United States....	29.2	26.8	44.5	20.5	19.4	27.5	8.7	7.4	16.9
New England.........	24.3	24.0	39.2	18.6	18.4	28.6	5.7	5.6	10.6
Middle Atlantic.....	25.8	24.2	43.2	19.6	18.5	31.7	6.2	5.7	11.5
East North Central..	26.3	25.3	37.7	19.1	18.6	25.7	7.1	6.7	12.0
West North Central..	26.3	25.3	49.8	19.5	19.1	28.9	6.8	6.2	20.9
South Atlantic......	33.7	28.1	46.5	22.5	20.1	27.8	11.2	7.9	18.7
East South Central..	36.2	32.5	44.8	23.3	21.9	26.4	12.9	10.6	18.4
West South Central..	34.6	32.4	43.1	22.3	21.1	26.9	12.3	11.3	16.2
Mountain............	36.2	33.0	90.6	22.5	21.9	32.7	13.7	11.1	58.0
Pacific.............	25.1	24.4	34.6	18.6	18.2	23.8	6.5	6.2	10.8

Source: National Office of Vital Statistics, Vital Statistics of the United States, 1950, Vol. I, Table 8.51.

Negroes or American Indians, the nonwhite infant mortality rates for population are high. The South and the Southwest have above-average infant mortality rates for the white population. (The high rate for the white population in the Mountain Division is probably created by the presence of the Mexican and other Spanish-speaking populations.) Most of these regional differences are associated with deaths which occur after the first month of life.

MATERNAL MORTALITY

The risk of dying during, or as a result of, childbirth has been reduced almost to the level of insignificance (Table 9-22). The provisional statistics for 1957 report only 3.9 maternal deaths for each 10,000 births.[20] The maternal mortality rate has fallen precipitously since 1930, and in 1957 it was less than 1/15 as high as it had been 25 years earlier. The decline in this source of mortality has removed one of the major causes of death among women. Throughout the history of the human race, until the last century, a substantial proportion of women were unable to survive the risks associated with repeated childbirth.

Table 9-22.—MATERNAL MORTALITY RATES BY COLOR: BIRTH-REGISTRATION STATES, 1915 TO 1957

(Maternal deaths per 10,000 live births.)

Year	Total	White	Nonwhite	Ratio, nonwhite to white
1957 (Pro.)....	3.9	2.6	11.3	4.4
1950..........	8.3	6.1	22.2	3.6
1945..........	20.7	17.2	45.5	2.6
1940..........	37.6	32.0	77.3	2.4
1935..........	58.2	53.1	94.6	1.8
1930..........	67.3	60.9	117.4	1.9
1925..........	64.7	60.3	116.2	1.9
1920..........	79.9	76.0	128.1	1.7
1915..........	60.8	60.1	105.6	1.8
Percent change, 1915 to 1957..	-93.6	-95.7	-89.3	...

Source: National Office of Vital Statistics, Vital Statistics of the United States, 1950, Table 8.35 and Statistical Abstract of the United States, 1958, Table 69.

---

[20] These are deaths from deliveries and complications of pregnancy, childbirth, and the puerperium.

The maternal mortality rate still remains much higher among the nonwhite than among the white population. However, the recent declines have reduced the rate for nonwhites by many more points than for whites. Whereas in 1930, 117 nonwhite mothers died for each 10,000 children born, by 1957 this had been reduced to a rate of 11, or by more than 100 points. During the same interval, the rate for white mothers fell by 57 points. Nevertheless, the rate for the nonwhite mother still is 4.4 times that for the white mother.

CONCLUSION

After exploring the story of falling death rates, it is only natural to ask, "Are further reductions possible and probable?" As things now stand, a very high percentage of infants who survive the first day of life live to be 50 years of age. After age 50, the annual probabilities of death are only moderately less grim than they were a half-century ago. Can something be done to increase survival at these later years? Experts agree that further substantial reductions are theoretically possible. The nation's physicians tell us that the average American is overweight, that he smokes too much, drinks too much alcoholic beverage, exercises too little, and neglects many of the general preventive measures that help to maintain health. We still tolerate air pollution, and still permit large numbers of people to live under unhealthful conditions in substandard housing. A very large segment of our population needs medical care which it cannot afford. In comparison with several of the European nations, the death rates among our middle-aged population are excessive. Thus, substantial reductions could be effected if we only made use of all we know now. In addition, there are hopes that research will develop ways to lower the death rates from cancer and heart disease, especially among persons of less than 70 years of age. The reduction of automobile accidents is another means by which lives could be saved.

The extent to which longevity actually increases in the future will depend not only on progress in the fields of medicine and public health, but also on the health conservation activities of the population. Longevity, or even good health itself, is only one of several items valued by human beings. Often they are willing to risk earlier death in order to live heartily, sedentarily, or at a certain socio-economic level.

Although the future may bring impressive proportional reductions in death rates, the point-declines will be rather small in comparison with those of the past. It will not be possible to repeat the impressive feat of reducing the death rate from 28 to 30 per thousand to 10 per thousand.

Chapter 10

MARRIAGE AND MARITAL STATUS

Each of the marital statuses--bachelorhood, marriage, widowhood, separation, and divorce--represents a major type of culturally-prescribed role, and certain appropriate modes of behavior are expected of the individuals who occupy each status. The extent to which a given age group in the population is married or single is closely related to where its members live; what they purchase; whether or not the women work; the kinds of social organizations to which the members of the age group belong; and the extent to which they are interested in certain community activities. Thus, marital status is similar to such personal characteristics as age, color-nativity-race, and sex in that it conditions a great many aspects of life. It differs from these other characteristics in at least two important ways, however. First, each marital status is an acquired trait; and second, one marital status can be exchanged for another. The other characteristics mentioned above are fixed at birth and persist throughout life (except for age, which changes irreversibly); but the marital statuses (as well as other characteristics which are considered in succeeding chapters) can be altered at any time during a socially-specified span of the life cycle.

Few events in the life cycle require more extensive changes in activities, responsibilities, and living habits (or cause greater alterations in attitudes, reranking of values, and alteration of outlook on life) than does a change from one marital status to another. Such changes are considered so important that they are made the occasion for specified social or legal ceremonies. From the viewpoint of the community, marriage is the proc-ess by which a family is formed--it establishes another unit in a basic social institution, and is a mechanism of social control. The disruption of marriage by widowhood, separation, or divorce very often has strong repercussions for the community as well as for individuals, especially if young children are involved.

Demographically speaking, marriage is an event that marks the beginning of exposure to childbearing. To be sure, a small proportion of children are born out of wedlock, and a much greater proportion are conceived out of wedlock. Nevertheless, since the married population is considered exclusively responsible for the bearing of children in the United States, the childbearing of single, widowed, and divorced women is either regarded as negligible by the demographer or is taken account of by means of special corrections to his data; these data are tabulated on the assumption that all fertility is attributable to married women. Thus the total number of married couples, the rate at which marriages are being contracted by persons of each age, and the proportions of the population in each marital status are important variables in fertility analysis.

The demographic study of marriage must rely upon two main bodies of information: (a) enumerations of the marital status of the population at a given instant of time--the numbers and proportions of persons who are single, married, widowed, separated, or divorced, and (b) counts of marriages contracted and of divorces, separations, or deaths of a spouse that occur during a given interval of time. The first type of information involves individual attributes, and is obtained by census procedures.[1] Information of the second type involves events, or changes in marital status; in the United States it is collected annually by the National Office of Vital Statistics and published in its yearly reports. As will be discussed later, census data on marital status may be used to estimate indirectly the net number of marriages that occur, the ages at which they occur, and marriage rates for particular years. But these estimates are designed to supplement, rather than to replace, the statistics concerning events which cause changes in marital status.

This chapter will discuss marital status as one of the population characteristics, and will also study marriage, divorce and widowhood as demographic events.

PART I: MARITAL STATUS*

Information concerning the marital status of the population has been collected and reported for each decennial census since 1890. Annual estimates for years since 1947 are available from the Current Population Survey of the Census Bureau. A question which asks, "Is he now married, widowed, divorced, separated, or has he never been married?" evokes the response which the census tabulates.

"The classification refers to the status at the time of enumeration. Persons classified as married comprise, therefore, both those who have been married only once and those who remarried after having been widowed or divorced. Persons reported as separated or in common-law marriages are classified as married. Those reported as never married or with annulled marriages are classified as single. Since it is probable that some divorced persons are reported as single, married, or widowed, the census returns doubtless understate somewhat the actual number of divorced persons who have not remarried."[2] Demographers frequently refer to the "ever married" population. This is the population that has been married at some time in its life. It is equal to the sum of the married, separated, widowed, and divorced, or to the total population minus the single population.

Table 10-1 summarizes the census data since 1890 for marital status, and Figure 10-1 illustrates the change that has occurred. The third column of this table shows that there was a steady decrease during the 60 years from 1890 to 1950 in the proportion of the population single, and a corresponding increase in the proportions married and ever married. In 1890, only 52.1 percent of the males 14 years of age or over were married, but by 1950 this percentage had increased to 68.2 percent. A similar change occurred among the female population. During the same time the proportion divorced increased more than six-fold. The following statistics summarize the change that has taken place:

Percent divorced:	1890	1950
Male............	0.2	1.8
Female.........	0.4	2.3

Together, these two changes indicate that there has been a very large decline in the never-married population. Whereas in 1890 43.6 percent of the population 14 years of age and over had never married, in 1950 only 24.1 percent of the adult population had never married.

Paralleling this long-time trend has been a progressive lowering of the average age at which persons first marry. (The median age at first marriage is regarded as being a very useful average in this connection. It can be estimated from census data, and is computed by taking one-half of the proportion expected to ever marry and calcu-

---

[1] In recent years the U. S. Census Bureau has used its monthly sample Population Surveys to make special inquiries in this field, and thereby has greatly enriched our knowledge about the processes of family formation and dissolution, and about the social and economic differences associated with variations in these processes. Much of the information in this chapter is derived from the Census Bureau's Current Population Survey, Series P-20, which reports the results of these surveys insofar as they pertain to marital status.

---

*Attention of the reader is invited to the supplementary section "Marital Status in 1958" at the end of this chapter.

[2] U. S. Census of Population: 1950, Vol. II, Characteristics of the Population, Part I, United States Summary, Page 41.

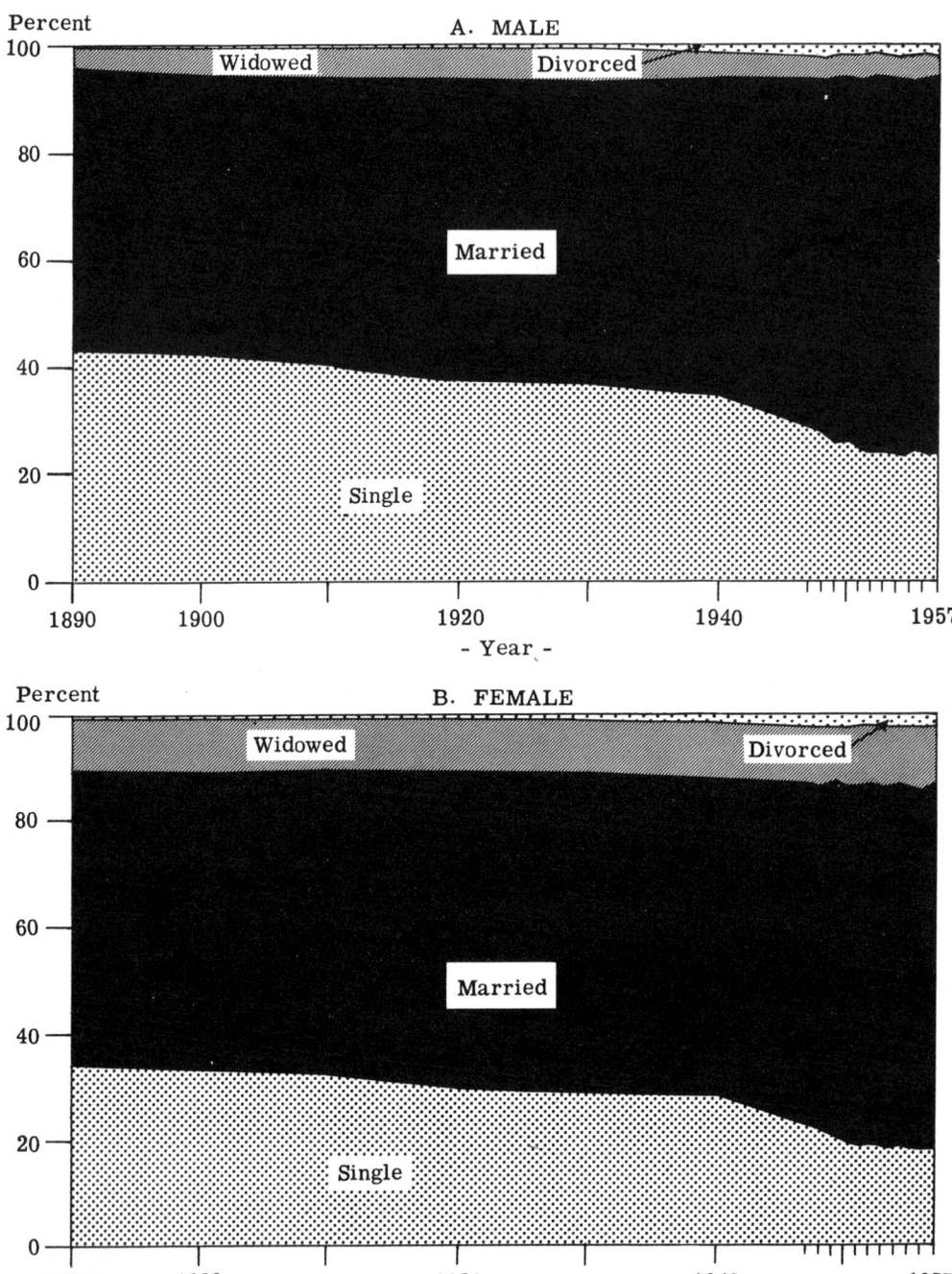

FIGURE 10-1. MARITAL STATUS OF THE UNITED STATES POPULATION 14 YEARS OF AGE
AND OVER: 1890 TO 1957

Table 10-1.—MARITAL STATUS OF THE POPULATION AND ESTIMATED MEDIAN AGE AT FIRST MARRIAGE, UNITED STATES: 1890 TO 1957

Sex and year	Median age at first marriage	Percent distribution by marital status				
		Total 14 years and over	Single	Married	Widowed	Divorced
MALE						
1958[1]..................	...	100.0	24.5	69.8	3.9	1.8
1955[1]..................	22.7	100.0	24.1	69.9	4.2	1.8
1950[1]..................	22.8	100.0	26.2	68.2	4.0	1.6
1940..................	24.3	100.0	34.8	59.7	4.2	1.2
1930[2]..................	24.3	100.0	35.8	58.4	4.5	1.1
1920[2]..................	24.6	100.0	36.9	57.6	4.6	0.6
1910[2]..................	25.1	100.0	40.4	54.2	4.4	0.5
1900[2]..................	25.9	100.0	42.0	52.8	4.5	0.3
1890[2]..................	26.1	100.0	43.6	52.1	3.8	0.2
FEMALE						
1958[1]..................	...	100.0	18.8	66.0	12.8	2.3
1955[1]..................	20.2	100.0	18.2	66.9	12.6	2.3
1950[1]..................	20.3	100.0	19.6	66.1	12.1	2.2
1940..................	21.5	100.0	27.6	59.5	11.3	1.6
1930..................	21.3	100.0	28.4	59.5	10.8	1.3
1920..................	21.2	100.0	29.4	58.9	10.8	0.8
1910..................	21.6	100.0	31.8	57.1	10.3	0.6
1900..................	21.9	100.0	33.3	55.2	10.9	0.5
1890..................	22.0	100.0	34.1	54.8	10.6	0.4

[1]Figures for 1950, 1955, and 1958 refer to the civilian population only.

[2]Percentages do not add exactly to 100 percent because statistics for "marital status not reported" have not been distributed.

Source: U.S. Census, Current Population Reports, Series P-20, No. 35, 62, and 87.

lating the current age at which this proportion of young people are married.) Column 1 of Table 10-1 shows that for males the median age at first marriage declined from 26.1 in 1890 to 22.8 in 1950. Among women a similar, though smaller, change took place.

Of special importance for the analysis which this chapter undertakes is the fact that about one-half of the total 60-year change in marital status, 1890-1950, occurred in the single decade between 1940 and 1950. During the years of World War II and immediately thereafter, the proportion of persons never married and the median age at first marriage declined by as much as they had during the entire preceding half-century. For men, 45 percent of the 60-year decline in median age at marriage occurred in the single decade 1940 to 1950; for women, 71 percent of the decline occurred in this decade. Thus, two revolutionary changes in marital status took place during the 1940 to 1950 decade: (a) the number of spinsters

and bachelors declined greatly; and (b) it became customary to get married younger. In addition, the long-term upward trend in the divorce rate accelerated somewhat. In 1950 the proportion of the population which was divorced (1.6 percent) was 8 times the proportion so reported at the census of 1890. As will be seen below, the increase in widowhood has been due entirely to the aging of the population.

Another aspect of marital status that is worthy of particular notice is the category "separated." As defined in the census of 1950 and in recent sample surveys, this category measures roughly the number of marriages that have been disrupted by marital discord but which have not been terminated permanently by divorce. Statistics for the separated population are reported in Table 10-5. As of 1957, about 1.4 percent of all adult males and 1.9 percent of all adult females were separated, and about equally large proportions were living apart from their spouses because of work away from home, military service, and for other reasons. The number of separated persons is about 80 percent as large as the number who are divorced. Hence, as a measure of broken marriages, the statistics for divorce are very inadequate. At any one time the number of marriages that are effectively broken (even if temporarily) is almost twice the number indicated by the number of divorced persons. Also, in discussing married persons it is well to remember that 3 to 4 percent of all married persons are not living with their spouses, because of marital discord, military service, work away from home, etc.

THE AGE PATTERN OF MARITAL STATUS

Each of the marital statuses has a characteristic age pattern. Figures 10-2, 10-3, and 10-4 illustrate these patterns. Until about age 15, almost all of the population is single. In the 10 years between 15 and 25 the proportion married rises very swiftly, and reaches a peak at about age 30 to 35. The loss of marriage partners through death begins to be evident at about age 30, and at each year of age thereafter a larger proportion of the population is widowed. The proportion divorced also increases in size during the middle-aged years. Finally, at the years 85 and over the majority of the population is widowed, a comparatively small part is single, and the bal-

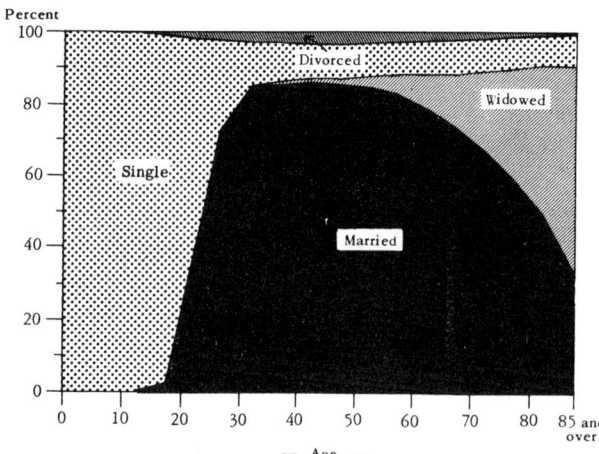

FIGURE 10-2. MARITAL STATUS BY AGE OF THE MALE POPULATION OF THE UNITED STATES: 1950

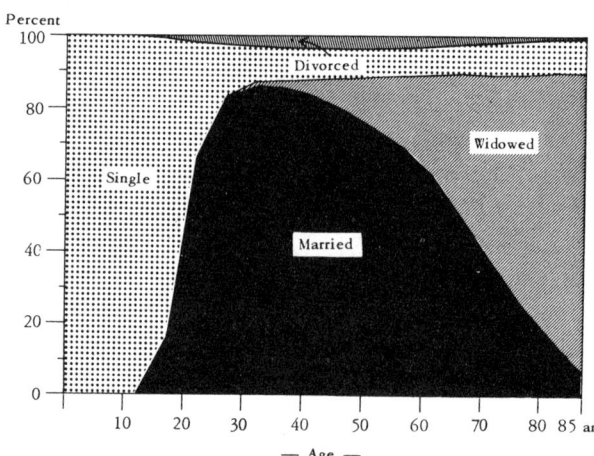

FIGURE 10-3. MARITAL STATUS BY AGE OF THE FEMALE POPULATION OF THE UNITED STATES:1950

ance is married. Tables 10-2 to 10-5 provide the statistical details of this pattern, and show how they can vary from one group to another among the population. These intergroup differences are analyzed later as "differentials in marital status."

Two factors are responsible for the 60-year trends noted above. First, the gradual aging of the population (described in Chapter 6) has caused a smaller percentage of the population to be in the ages of late adolescence and early adulthood, and a larger percentage to be in the older ages where a higher proportion of the population is either married, widowed, or divorced. The second factor is a very real increase in (a) the proportion of the population of each younger age group that is married and (b) the proportion of the population that ever marries.

Because marriage is an event that tends to occur at a particular phase of the life cycle, a precise comparison of the marital statuses of two or more populations, or of the sex, color, or urban-rural residence groupings of the population, requires that age differences be controlled. For this reason, most of the statistical tables in this chapter show the marital status of the various population groups subclassified by age, or standardized for age. Inasmuch as marital status changes very rapidly between the ages of 14 and 30, many of the tables report marital status by single years of age.

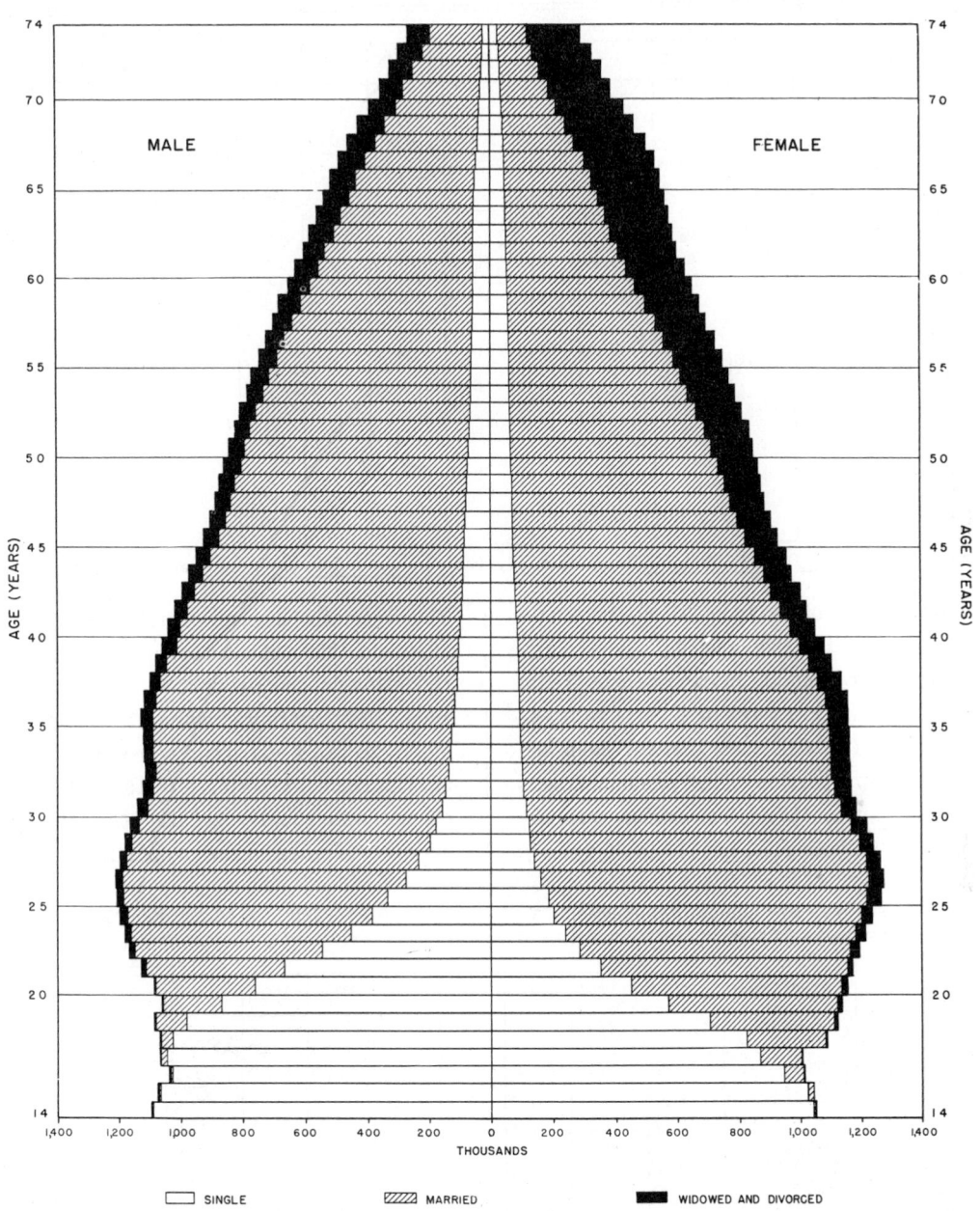

FIGURE 10-4. MARITAL STATUS OF PERSONS 14 TO 74 YEARS OLD, BY SINGLE
YEARS OF AGE AND SEX, FOR THE UNITED STATES:1950

Source: 1950 United States Census of Population, Special Reports, Marital Status.

Table 10-2.—PERCENT OF THE POPULATION CLASSIFIED AS SINGLE, BY AGE: 1890 TO 1950

Marital status and age	Male 1950	1940	1930	1920	1910	1900	1890	Female 1950	1940	1930	1920	1910	1900	1890
Percent single														
Total..........	26.4	34.8	35.8	36.9	40.4	42.0	43.6	20.0	27.6	28.4	29.4	31.8	33.3	34.1
14 years...........	99.1	99.9	99.9	99.7	99.9	99.9	100.0	99.3	99.7	99.6	99.4	99.6	99.4	99.8
15 to 19 years......	96.7	98.3	98.0	97.7	98.3	98.8	99.4	82.9	88.1	86.8	87.0	87.9	88.7	90.3
20 to 24 years......	59.1	72.2	70.8	70.7	74.9	77.6	80.7	32.3	47.2	46.0	45.6	48.3	51.6	51.8
25 to 29 years......	23.8	36.0	36.7	39.4	42.8	45.8	46.0	13.3	22.8	21.7	23.0	24.9	27.5	25.4
30 to 34 years......	13.2	20.7	21.2	24.1	26.0	27.6	26.5	9.3	14.7	13.2	14.9	16.1	16.6	15.2
35 to 39 years......	10.1	15.3	15.4	16.1	16.7	17.0	15.3	8.4	11.2	10.4	11.4	11.4	11.1	9.9
40 to 44 years......	9.0	12.6	13.1					8.3	9.5	9.5				
45 to 49 years......	8.7	11.2	11.9	12.0	11.1	10.3	9.1	7.9	8.6	9.0	9.6	8.5	7.8	7.1
50 to 54 years......	8.3	11.0	10.9					7.7	8.7	9.2				
55 to 59 years......	8.3	10.8	10.3	9.8	8.3	7.6	6.8	7.7	8.7	9.0	8.4	7.1	6.6	5.8
60 to 64 years......	8.6	10.5	9.9					8.2	9.3	8.9				
65 to 69 years......	8.7	10.3	9.3	7.3	6.2	5.7	5.6	8.4	9.4	8.4	7.1	6.3	6.0	5.6
70 to 74 years......	8.3	9.9	8.6					9.0	9.5	8.4				
75 to 79 years......	8.1	9.5	7.0					9.4	9.2	7.3				
80 to 84 years......	7.4	8.7						9.4	9.2					
85 years and over...	7.7	7.9						9.7	8.0					

Source: U.S. Census of Population: 1950, Volume II, Part 1, U.S. Summary, Chapter C, Table 102.

The marital status of the population, by single years of age from 14 to 30, and by 5-year age groups at ages older than 30, in each decade from 1890 to 1950, is shown in Tables 10-2 through 10-4. A study of Table 10-2 will show that for each age up to 45 a smaller proportion of the population was single in 1950 than in 1890. The change was especially large at the younger ages (15 to 30 years).

The dramatic change which took place between 1940 and 1950, noted above, is seen to be a great reduction in the proportion single at the younger ages. For example, whereas 72.2 percent of the males 20 to 24 years old were single in 1940, only 59.1 percent were single in 1950. For women, the change was equally great. The steady increase over the decades in the proportion married at each

Table 10-3.—PERCENT OF THE POPULATION CLASSIFIED AS MARRIED, BY AGE: 1890 TO 1950

Marital status and age	Male 1950	1940	1930	1920	1910	1900	1890	Female 1950	1940	1930	1920	1910	1900	1890
Percent married														
Total..........	67.5	59.7	58.4	57.6	54.2	52.8	52.1	65.8	59.5	59.5	58.9	57.1	55.2	54.8
14 years...........	0.6	0.1	0.1	0.3	0.1	0.1	...	0.7	0.3	0.4	0.5	0.4	0.5	0.2
15 to 19 years......	3.1	1.7	1.7	2.1	1.1	1.0	0.5	16.7	11.6	12.6	12.5	11.3	10.9	9.5
20 to 24 years......	39.9	27.4	28.1	28.3	24.0	21.6	18.9	65.6	51.3	51.6	52.3	49.7	46.5	46.7
25 to 29 years......	74.2	62.7	61.3	58.7	55.5	52.6	52.7	83.3	74.1	74.3	73.4	71.8	68.9	71.4
30 to 34 years......	84.3	77.2	76.0	73.2	71.4	69.8	71.3	86.2	80.4	81.5	80.1	79.0	78.0	79.8
35 to 39 years......	86.8	81.6	81.0	79.8	79.2	78.8	80.9	85.5	81.5	82.3	80.3	80.1	79.5	80.6
40 to 44 years......	87.1	83.2	82.1					83.1	80.6	80.6				
45 to 49 years......	86.2	83.6	82.1	81.0	81.5	82.2	84.3	79.8	78.3	77.6	74.0	74.8	73.9	73.9
50 to 54 years......	85.0	81.9	81.0					75.0	73.3	72.3				
55 to 59 years......	83.1	79.9	79.5	77.9	79.0	79.7	82.3	69.1	67.2	66.2	61.2	62.2	60.5	60.4
60 to 64 years......	79.3	76.7	76.2					60.1	58.0	56.9				
65 to 69 years......	74.0	71.9	71.5	64.7	65.6	67.1	70.5	48.9	46.5	46.6	33.9	35.0	34.2	35.4
70 to 74 years......	67.5	64.9	64.7					36.6	34.3	35.0				
75 to 79 years......	59.0	56.1	50.4					24.7	23.0	18.2				
80 to 84 years......	48.2	45.8						14.2	13.5					
85 years and over...	33.6	33.0						7.0	6.7					

Source: U.S. Census of Population: 1950, Volume II, Part 1, U.S. Summary, Chapter C, Table 102.

of these ages may be observed from Table 10-3. In 1940, for example, only 51.3 percent of the girls 20 to 24 were married, but by 1950 65.6 percent of this age group were married.

In 1890 young people were considerably less likely to be married than in 1940. From 1890 to 1920 there was a gradual increase in the tendency toward earlier marriage. This trend leveled off between 1920 and 1930 (especially among females), and was reversed during the years of economic depression, 1930 to 1940. The leveling off and eventual reversal of this trend, especially the 1920 to 1930 phase, is a phenomenon worthy of analysis and interpretation by sociologists and social psychologists. Why should a long-time trend toward younger marriage be halted during a time of great economic prosperity? It is reasonable to suppose that during the severe economic depression of the 1930's unemployment, low incomes, and the need for older children to contribute to the support of their parents and to help support their younger brothers and sisters prevented many young people from marrying, or at least caused them to postpone their marriages for a few years. But why the prosperity that followed World War I did not create a boom in marriage is not clear. The marriage boom in the 1940 to 1950 decade appears to have compensated not only for the reversal of the 1930 to 1940 period, but also for the leveling off of the 1920 to 1930's. The marital status composition in 1950 is about what it would have been if the average changes of 1890 to 1920 had persisted uninterrupted until 1950.

One of the questions asked of the demographer is, "What proportion of today's young adult population will get married at sometime in its life?" Only an approximate answer can be given to this question. A first approximation could be obtained by computing the percent ever married for the age group which was 85 years old in 1950, and assuming that the present younger generations will equal this mark. But the proportion obtained in this way may be too large. It is well known that married persons live longer than single persons. Therefore, the group which survived to be enumerated at age 85 in 1950 may contain an excess number of

married persons. A more accurate approximate measure, which is also useful for fertility analysis, is obtained if we use the proportion of persons at the close of the childbearing period (45 to 49 or 50 to 54 years) who have ever been married. The estimated proportions for the various time periods are as follows:

Proportion ever married at age 45 to 54

	Male	Female
1958.........	92.9	92.3
1955.........	91.5	93.2
1950.........	89.9	92.2
1940.........	88.9	91.3
1930.........	88.6	90.9
1920.........	88.0	90.4
1910.........	88.9	91.5
1900.........	89.7	92.2
1890.........	89.9	92.9

The proportion ever married seems to have been high in 1890, to have declined gradually to 1920, and then to have risen rather slowly to the present. This suggests that at some earlier date-- perhaps during the high fertility period prior to the Civil War, or even earlier--the proportion ever married at each age (especially for women) may have been much greater than it was by the end of the 19th century and the beginning of this century. The higher proportion of bachelors in the population during the intervening time may have been related to the mass immigration of single persons from abroad and to the rapid urbanward migration, and to an urban culture that placed great emphasis upon postponing marriage in order to achieve greater economic security for one's wife and children or to care for aged parents. Now, under present high levels of living, the population appears to be able to "have its cake and eat it too"--to enjoy economic security and comfort and yet to be married. Under present conditions, an estimated 92 percent of young women will marry at some time in their lives, and an estimated 93 percent of men. These figures indicate a situation which is not very different from that which existed in 1890.

If the proportions remaining single at each 5-year age group over 30 are compared for 1940 and 1950, it is clear that a greater proportion of persons of each age were married in 1950 than in

1940. This can only mean that spinsters and bachelors of all ages tended to marry during this decade. Undoubtedly, the economic depression in 1930 to 1940 had the effect of postponing or preventing marriage. The prosperity of the war years appears not only to have reversed any such tendency but also to have caused a much higher proportion of the older persons to marry than had done so at any time during this century. A part of this increase was inevitable. If the proportion ever marrying had been increasing for several years, it follows that of the people who were passing into each older age group a higher proportion would be married than of the people who were just passing out of that age group. But the changes between 1940 and 1950 were so great, especially at ages under 50, that a genuine epidemic of marriages seems to have swept through the unmarried middle age adult population, as well as through the younger population.

An incidental by-product of this marriage boom was that widowhood tended to decrease because of remarriage (Table 10-4). Widowed persons as well as unmarried persons apparently were caught up in the marriage boom, with the result that at each age a smaller proportion of persons were

Table 10-4.—PERCENT OF THE POPULATION CLASSIFIED AS WIDOWED OR DIVORCED, BY AGE: 1890 TO 1950

Marital status and age	Male							Female						
	1950	1940	1930	1920	1910	1900	1890	1950	1940	1930	1920	1910	1900	1890
Percent widowed														
Total	4.1	4.2	4.5	4.6	4.4	4.5	3.8	11.8	11.3	10.8	10.8	10.3	10.9	10.6
14 years	0.2	...	...	...	...	...	...	0.1	...	...	...	...	...	...
15 to 19 years	0.1	...	...	...	...	...	...	0.1	0.1	0.2	0.3	0.2	0.2	0.1
20 to 24 years	0.2	0.1	0.3	0.5	0.4	0.4	0.2	0.4	0.6	1.0	1.4	1.2	1.4	1.2
25 to 29 years	0.3	0.4	0.8	1.1	1.1	1.2	1.0	0.9	1.3	2.1	2.6	2.4	2.9	2.8
30 to 34 years	0.4	0.7	1.3	1.8	1.8	2.0	1.8	1.6	2.5	3.3	3.9	3.9	4.6	4.5
35 to 39 years	0.7	1.3	2.0	3.0	3.2	3.6	3.3	2.7	4.6	5.3	7.2	7.5	8.6	8.9
40 to 44 years	1.2	2.1	3.0					5.0	7.3	8.0				
45 to 49 years	2.1	3.2	4.3	5.8	6.4	6.8	6.0	8.6	10.7	11.6	15.3	15.7	17.6	18.4
50 to 54 years	3.7	5.1	6.3					13.9	15.9	16.9				
55 to 59 years	5.9	7.4	8.4	11.2	11.7	11.9	10.2	20.5	22.4	23.4	29.5	30.0	32.3	33.3
60 to 64 years	9.6	11.1	12.4					29.7	31.3	33.1				
65 to 69 years	15.0	16.2	17.8	26.9	27.1	26.4	23.3	41.1	43.1	44.1	58.4	58.1	59.3	58.6
70 to 74 years	22.2	23.8	25.4					53.3	55.5	55.9				
75 to 79 years	31.4	33.3	41.5					65.1	67.3	73.9				
80 to 84 years	43.3	44.7						75.9	77.1					
85 years and over	57.9	58.5						82.9	85.1					
Percent divorced														
Total	2.0	1.2	1.1	0.6	0.5	0.3	0.2	2.4	1.6	1.3	0.8	0.6	0.5	0.4
14 years	0.1	...	...	...	...	...	...	...	...	...	...	...	...	...
15 to 19 years	0.1	...	...	...	...	...	...	0.3	0.1	0.2	0.1	0.1	0.1	...
20 to 24 years	0.9	0.3	0.4	0.2	0.1	0.1	...	1.7	0.9	1.1	0.6	0.5	0.4	0.2
25 to 29 years	1.7	0.9	1.0	0.5	0.4	0.2	0.2	2.5	1.8	1.8	0.9	0.7	0.6	0.4
30 to 34 years	2.1	1.4	1.4	0.7	0.5	0.4	0.2	3.0	2.4	1.9	1.0	0.8	0.7	0.5
35 to 39 years	2.4	1.8	1.5	0.9	0.7	0.5	0.3	3.5	2.8	1.9	1.1	0.9	0.7	0.6
40 to 44 years	2.7	2.0	1.6					3.7	2.7	1.8				
45 to 49 years	2.9	2.0	1.7	1.0	0.8	0.6	0.4	3.6	2.4	1.7	1.0	0.8	0.6	0.5
50 to 54 years	3.0	2.0	1.6					3.3	2.0	1.5				
55 to 59 years	2.7	1.9	1.6	1.0	0.8	0.6	0.5	2.7	1.7	1.3	0.8	0.6	0.5	0.4
60 to 64 years	2.5	1.7	1.5					2.1	1.4	1.0				
65 to 69 years	2.3	1.6	1.3					1.5	1.0	0.8				
70 to 74 years	1.9	1.3	1.1					1.1	0.7	0.5				
75 to 79 years	1.5	1.1	0.8	0.7	0.7	0.5	0.4	0.7	0.4	0.3	0.4	0.4	0.3	0.3
80 to 84 years	1.1	0.8						0.5	0.3					
85 years and over	0.8	0.6						0.4	0.2					

Source: U.S. Census of Population: 1950, Volume II, Part 1, U.S. Summary, Chapter C, Table 102.

widowed in 1950 than in 1940. (The over-all increase in widowhood for ages 14 and over combined, reported in Table 10-4 to have taken place between 1890 and 1950, is misleading. As demonstrated below, it is entirely a result of the aging of the population.) A part of this decrease in widowhood may be attributed to the greater longevity of the population (and the resultant greater joint survival of married couples), but even when allowance is made for this factor it is evident that widowed persons of most ages (and especially the younger ages) are more inclined to remarry than they formerly were.[3] The phenomenon of remarriage will be discussed more fully in a later section of this chapter.

As the popularity of marriage zoomed between 1940 and 1950, the number of divorces also rose impressively. At all ages, the proportion of divorced persons was higher in 1950 than in 1940 (Table 10-4, bottom panel). Thus, the population seems not only to have become much more inclined to marry than it used to be, but it also seems much more inclined to dissolve marriages that are unsatisfactory to one or both of the partners. In 1950 the highest proportion divorced occurred at ages 50 to 54 among men (3.0 percent) and at ages 40 to 44 among women (3.7 percent). At ages older than this the proportion divorced was smaller. Apparently the older generations were less inclined to become divorced. Also, the remarriage of divorced and widowed persons returns a certain proportion of the older ages to the "married" category; and higher death rates among divorced persons causes them to become a smaller share of the total population at advanced years. The higher proportion of women than of men who are divorced at each age suggests that the rate of remarriage is higher among divorced men than among divorced women. (Data to be presented later in this chapter will show that this is true.)

Since the trends between 1890 and 1950 have been said to be a product of changing age compo-

sition as well as of changing marriage patterns, it is logical to ask the question, "What part of the total change has been due to changing age composition and what part has been due to changing marriage patterns?" One way of answering this question is to compute what proportion of the population would have been married, single, widowed, or divorced at each census if the age composition had remained constant through all censuses. This is done by "standardizing" the statistics for marital status (applying the proportions in each marital status at each age to the age composition of one year which is taken as a standard.) The following are age-standardized statistics, for which the age composition of the 1950 census was used as a standard.

Marital status of the population standardized for age				
Month and year	Single	Married	Widowed	Divorced
Male				
March, 1957...	24.5	70.3	3.5	1.8
April, 1955...	25.1	69.3	3.9	1.7
April, 1950...	26.2	68.0	4.2	1.7
April, 1940...	31.1	62.8	4.8	1.3
April, 1930...	30.9	62.1	5.6	1.2
January, 1920.	31.8	61.3	6.1	0.7
April, 1910...	32.5	60.4	6.2	0.5
June, 1900....	33.1	59.9	6.4	0.4
June, 1890....	32.8	61.2	5.6	0.3
Female				
March, 1957...	18.6	67.7	11.5	2.3
April, 1955...	18.6	67.4	11.8	2.3
April, 1950...	19.6	66.1	12.2	2.2
April, 1940...	24.3	61.0	12.9	1.7
April, 1930...	23.7	61.2	13.7	1.3
January, 1920.	24.1	60.4	14.6	0.8
April, 1910...	24.5	60.1	14.7	0.6
June 1900.....	25.0	58.7	15.7	0.5
June, 1890....	24.3	59.4	15.9	0.4

Source: *Statistical Abstract of the United States, 1958*, Table 43.

A comparison of the above tabulation with the corresponding figures of Table 10-1 shows that if changing marriage patterns alone had been operating, (age composition held constant) there would have been a much less spectacular decrease in the single population between 1890 and 1950 than is reported in Table 10-1. Also, there would have been a large decline in the proportion widowed, instead of the increase reported in Table 10-1. Thus, the gradual aging of the population (due pri-

---

[3] At ages below 40, probably the major share of the decrease in widowhood has been due to increased longevity, but at the older ages remarriage is primarily responsible.

marily to falling birth rates) has had almost as great a part in increasing the proportion married as have the changing marital patterns. This aging of the population tends to mask a substantial decline in widowhood that has taken place within each age group. During the period 1890 to 1950, changing age composition had <u>more</u> effect than changing marriage patterns upon the status of being married or widowed; but during the dramatic decade 1940 to 1950, the drastic change in marriage customs greatly overshadowed the influence of changing age composition.

CHANGES IN MARITAL STATUS SINCE 1950[*]

Since the 1950 census, the changes which took place in the 1940 to 1950 decade have continued, but apparently at a decelerating rate. Table 10-5 shows that in 1957 a higher proportion of the population in each of the three broad age groups that span the child-rearing period was married than had been in 1950. In 1957, 92.3 percent of the male population and 93.0 percent of the female population had been married at some time in its

life; this represented further substantial increases over 1950 in the proportions ever married.

These increases may be attributed partly to changing age composition. The fact that the small cohorts of children born during the depression years have been entering the adult population during the years since 1950 means that there would have been a decline in the number of single persons even if marriage rates had remained unchanged. However, the statistics for marital status in 1956, standardized for age (shown in the preceding section), show that since 1950 there have been further increases in the proportion married and ever married, and further declines in the proportions single and widowed.

There is evidence that the trend toward earlier marriage has about run its course. It is reasonable to suppose that there is a culturally-specified lower limit to early marriage, and that this limit is several years past puberty. The continued pressure for higher educational attainment, and the greater participation of women in the labor force are only two of several forces that would tend to keep the proportions married at each age

Table 10-5.—MARITAL STATUS, BY SEX, OF SELECTED AGE GROUPS OF THE CIVILIAN POPULATION: 1957, AND CHANGE IN MARITAL STATUS: 1950 TO 1957

Sex and marital status	Marital status: 1957				Change in marital status: 1950 to 1957			
	All ages	18 and 19 years	20 to 24 years	45 to 54 years	All ages	18 and 19 years	20 to 24 years	45 to 54 years
Male..................	100.0	100.0	100.0	100.0				
Single...................	23.9	92.0	51.8	7.7	-2.3	-0.4	-4.3	-2.9
Married..................	70.5	8.0	47.7	87.4	2.5	0.7	4.4	3.7
Spouse present..........	67.8	6.7	45.5	83.9	1.9	-0.4	3.8	2.8
Spouse absent...........	2.7	1.2	2.2	3.6	0.6	-1.1	0.6	0.6
Separated............	1.4	0.7	1.3	1.6	...	...	...	...
Other................	1.3	0.5	0.9	1.9	...	...	...	...
Widowed..................	3.8	...	...	2.1	-0.4	...	...	1.0
Divorced.................	1.8	...	0.5	2.8	0.1	...	...	0.2
Female...............	100.0	100.0	100.0	100.0				
Single...................	18.6	69.7	29.0	7.0	-1.0	-1.8	-2.6	-0.8
Married..................	66.6	29.9	69.1	79.0	0.5	1.7	2.9	1.7
Spouse present..........	62.9	26.8	63.1	74.7	-0.5	-2.7	...	0.6
Spouse absent...........	3.7	3.1	6.1	4.4	1.0	1.0	3.0	1.2
Separated............	1.9	1.0	2.4	2.3	...	...	...	...
In armed forces......	0.4	1.8	2.1	...	...	...	...	...
Other................	1.4	0.4	1.6	2.0	...	...	...	...
Widowed..................	12.6	0.1	0.2	10.5	-0.4	...	-0.2	1.7
Divorced.................	2.3	0.3	1.7	3.4	0.1	1.4	-0.1	-0.6

Source: <u>Current Population Reports</u>, Series P-20, No. 81, March, 1958, Table 1.

*See also "Marital Status in 1958" at the end of this chapter.

from rising very far above the present levels. Certainly, the average annual change between 1950 and 1957 is much smaller than it was between 1940 and 1950, when the effect of age is controlled. On the other hand, a serious economic recession could very easily cause the remarkable trends of the years since 1946 to be sharply reversed, and could cause widespread postponement of marriage with a consequent rise in the age at marriage.

DIFFERENTIALS IN MARITAL STATUS

The marital status composition of the population varies widely among the various social and economic groups. From Tables 10-6 to Table 10-11, inclusive, it is possible to infer what some of the basic differences in marital status among these groups were in 1950, and how they varied with age.

In some cases, differences in marital status between groups having particular social or economic traits are due simply to differences in age composition. In other cases, marital status differences of a particular kind may exist at the younger ages, while at the older ages there may either be no differential at all, or a differential of another kind. Hence, in examining marital status differences between groups, it is desirable to note the differences for each of several age groups, rather than simply to standardize for age or to report data for all ages combined.

The sex differential. Men tend to be single (never married) in greater proportions than women (Table 10-2). At each age, women tend to be married, widowed, or divorced in greater proportions than men. This generalization is valid for the rural-nonfarm and the rural-farm populations at all but the most advanced ages, for both

Table 10-6.—MARITAL STATUS BY SEX OF THE URBAN WHITE POPULATION OF THE UNITED STATES: 1950

Age in years	Male				Female			
	Percent single	Percent married	Percent widowed	Percent divorced	Percent single	Percent married	Percent widowed	Percent divorced
14 years...............	98.9	0.7	0.2	0.1	99.4	0.5	0.1	...
15 to 19 years..........	96.9	2.9	0.1	0.1	85.3	14.3	0.1	0.3
15 years..............	98.9	0.8	0.2	0.1	98.5	1.4	0.1	...
16 years..............	98.9	0.8	0.1	0.1	95.3	4.6	0.1	0.1
17 years..............	98.6	1.3	0.1	0.1	89.4	10.3	0.1	0.2
18 years..............	96.6	3.3	0.1	0.1	80.2	19.2	0.1	0.5
19 years..............	91.8	8.0	0.1	0.2	68.8	30.3	0.1	0.7
20 to 24 years..........	60.3	38.7	0.1	0.9	36.6	61.3	0.3	1.8
20 years..............	83.3	16.2	0.1	0.4	56.2	42.4	0.2	1.2
21 years..............	72.1	27.2	0.1	0.6	44.2	53.9	0.3	1.5
22 years..............	61.0	38.0	0.1	0.9	34.5	63.3	0.3	1.9
23 years..............	49.4	49.3	0.1	1.2	27.2	70.3	0.3	2.1
24 years..............	40.3	58.2	0.2	1.4	22.3	75.0	0.4	2.3
25 to 29 years..........	24.2	73.7	0.2	1.8	15.3	81.1	0.7	2.8
25 years..............	33.1	65.1	0.2	1.6	19.0	78.0	0.5	2.5
26 years..............	28.2	69.8	0.2	1.8	16.9	79.8	0.6	2.7
27 years..............	23.3	74.7	0.2	1.8	14.8	81.6	0.7	2.8
28 years..............	19.9	78.0	0.2	1.9	13.6	82.6	0.9	2.9
29 years..............	16.7	81.1	0.2	2.0	12.0	83.9	1.0	3.2
30 to 34 years..........	13.1	84.4	0.3	2.3	20.9	84.3	1.3	3.5
35 to 39 years..........	9.9	86.9	0.5	2.7	9.9	83.6	2.3	4.1
40 to 44 years..........	8.7	87.3	1.0	3.0	9.9	81.1	4.5	4.5
45 to 49 years..........	8.5	86.3	1.8	3.4	9.3	78.0	8.2	4.5
50 to 54 years..........	8.2	85.1	3.3	3.3	9.2	72.8	14.0	4.0
55 to 59 years..........	8.2	83.1	5.7	3.0	9.0	66.3	21.4	3.3
60 to 64 years..........	8.5	79.2	9.5	2.8	9.5	56.6	31.4	2.5
65 to 69 years..........	8.6	73.9	15.0	2.5	9.8	45.7	42.6	1.8
70 to 74 years..........	8.2	67.0	22.8	2.0	10.5	33.2	55.1	1.2
75 to 79 years,.........	7.8	57.9	32.6	1.6	10.9	22.1	66.2	0.8
80 to 84 years..........	7.2	47.1	44.6	1.2	10.8	12.6	76.1	0.5
85 years and over........	7.0	33.0	59.1	0.8	10.5	6.3	82.7	0.5

the white and the nonwhite populations. It is also valid for the urban white population up to about age 40. Since unmarried white women tend to be urban dwellers, the differential is reversed in cities among the middle-aged and older populations.

The basic explanation for the differential is simple: women tend to marry at younger ages than men. Hence, by the time they have attained any given age, a smaller proportion of women than of men have remained single. However, by the time age 40 is reached about the same proportion of men as of women have married, so the differential has become quite small by this age. The differential is largest, of course, at those ages when quite a few girls are marrying but a large proportion of boys are remaining single. These ages are 15 to 19 and 20 to 24. Among the white population at these youngest ages the sex differential is

greater among the rural than among the urban population, because rural boys (especially farm boys) are more inclined to postpone marriage than city boys. Among the nonwhite population there is a sex differential among all urban-rural groupings, but it is about equally large in all of them and shows no tendency to be unusually large among the farm population. Because of this fact, the sex differential in marital status at the young adult ages tends to be greater among whites than among nonwhites in rural areas. In urban areas the sex differential in marital status for the white and nonwhite population is about equal.

Because women live longer than men, a greater proportion of women than of men are widowed at any age. Part of this differential between the sexes may be due to a greater tendency for widowed men than for widowed women to remarry.

Tables 10-6 through 10-11 show that a higher

Table 10-7.—MARITAL STATUS BY SEX OF THE URBAN NONWHITE POPULATION OF THE UNITED STATES: 1950

Age in years	Male				Female			
	Percent single	Percent married	Percent widowed	Percent divorced	Percent single	Percent married	Percent widowed	Percent divorced
14 years,	99.4	0.4	0.1	0.1	98.9	1.0	0.1	...
15 to 19 years	95.6	4.3	0.1	0.1	79.0	20.4	0.2	0.3
15 years	99.2	0.6	0.1	...	97.3	2.6	0.1	0.1
16 years	99.1	0.8	0.1	...	91.7	8.1	0.1	0.1
17 years	97.8	2.1	0.1	...	82.0	17.4	0.2	0.3
18 years	94.2	5.6	0.1	0.1	69.9	29.2	0.4	0.5
19 years	86.9	12.9	0.1	0.1	57.5	41.4	0.4	0.7
20 to 24 years	53.5	44.9	0.5	1.1	31.4	65.1	1.1	2.3
20 years	75.3	23.8	0.3	0.5	45.7	52.4	0.5	1.4
21 years	62.8	36.0	0.5	0.6	37.4	60.1	0.9	1.6
22 years	53.6	44.6	0.5	1.3	30.5	66.0	1.2	2.3
23 years	44.6	53.6	0.6	1.1	24.8	71.0	1.4	2.8
24 years	37.0	60.9	0.6	1.5	21.2	73.9	1.6	3.3
25 to 29 years	24.8	72.6	0.6	2.0	14.5	79.2	2.3	4.0
25 years	32.7	65.2	0.5	1.6	18.7	76.0	1.8	3.6
26 years	27.7	69.8	0.6	1.9	16.5	77.8	1.8	3.9
27 years	23.7	73.5	0.6	2.1	13.3	80.6	2.1	4.0
28 years	21.2	76.0	0.7	2.2	12.4	80.7	2.8	4.1
29 years	18.2	78.7	0.8	2.3	11.0	81.3	2.9	4.7
30 to 34 years	14.0	82.2	1.1	2.8	9.2	81.7	4.3	4.8
35 to 39 years	10.3	84.5	1.9	3.3	7.2	79.9	7.6	5.3
40 to 44 years	8.9	84.6	3.2	3.4	5.9	75.3	13.6	5.1
45 to 49 years	8.4	83.3	5.1	3.3	5.0	69.1	21.2	4.6
50 to 54 years	7.0	81.3	8.3	3.3	4.2	61.2	30.7	3.8
55 to 59 years	6.4	78.6	11.7	3.3	4.4	53.1	39.5	3.0
60 to 64 years	6.4	73.6	17.3	2.8	4.3	43.2	50.2	2.3
65 to 69 years	5.9	67.1	24.7	2.2	4.1	32.0	62.1	1.8
70 to 74 years	5.5	59.9	32.7	1.9	4.2	22.0	72.9	0.9
75 to 79 years	5.2	54.1	39.4	1.3	5.4	15.1	78.7	0.8
80 to 84 years	5.4	44.5	49.2	0.9	4.1	9.7	85.7	0.6
85 years and over	11.9	30.7	56.4	0.9	12.4	4.8	82.4	0.4

proportion of women than of men are divorced at each age up to about age 60. This is a result of the combined effects of the earlier age at which women marry, the greater survival rates among women, and the greater tendency for divorced men than for divorced women to remarry. Beyond age 60 the proportion of men who are divorced is greater than the proportion of women. This is difficult to explain. Perhaps more elderly divorced women than men tend to report themselves as widowed.

Urban-rural differentials. Among the white population, marriage of girls at the very young ages tends to be a rural rather than an urban phenomenon. The 1950 census reported, for instance, that among girls aged 17, 12.5 percent of rural-farm and 16.9 percent of rural-nonfarm white girls were married. But among urban white girls of this age only 10.3 percent were married. Also,

a lower proportion of white urban than of white rural women ever marry. Among nonwhite women, the proportion married at the young ages and the proportion ever married do not differ a great deal between urban and rural residence.

Among males, the situation is very different. Farm boys tend to marry unusually late in life, while rural-nonfarm males tend to marry younger than either the farm boys or the city boys. This pattern is present for both white and nonwhite males, but it is much more pronounced among the former than among the latter.

At each age, the proportion of the population that is widowed or divorced is highest in urban areas and lowest in rural-farm areas. This difference is greater for women than for men, and for white men and women than for nonwhite.

The above differences lead to the following generalization: The social and economic position of an

Table 10-8.—MARITAL STATUS BY SEX OF THE RURAL-NONFARM WHITE POPULATION OF THE UNITED STATES: 1950

Age in years	Male				Female			
	Percent single	Percent married	Percent widowed	Percent divorced	Percent single	Percent married	Percent widowed	Percent divorced
14 years..................	99.0	0.7	0.2	0.1	99.3	0.7	...	...
15 to 19 years...........	96.2	3.5	0.1	0.1	78.1	21.5	0.1	0.3
15 years.................	99.2	0.6	0.1	0.1	97.4	2.5	...	...
16 years.................	99.0	0.8	0.1	0.1	91.9	7.9	...	0.1
17 years.................	98.3	1.5	0.1	0.1	82.8	16.9	0.1	0.2
18 years.................	95.5	4.3	0.1	0.1	66.7	32.7	0.1	0.5
19 years.................	89.5	10.3	0.1	0.2	49.0	50.1	0.2	0.7
20 to 24 years...........	54.3	44.5	0.1	1.1	21.6	76.7	0.4	1.3
20 years.................	79.7	19.7	0.1	0.5	35.8	63.0	0.3	1.0
21 years.................	66.1	33.0	0.1	0.8	26.4	72.1	0.3	1.2
22 years.................	52.5	46.2	0.1	1.2	20.0	78.2	0.4	1.4
23 years.................	39.8	58.7	0.1	1.4	15.5	82.9	0.4	1.3
24 years.................	31.7	66.5	0.2	1.6	12.1	85.8	0.5	1.6
25 to 29 years...........	18.9	79.0	0.2	1.8	8.1	89.4	0.8	1.7
25 years.................	25.8	72.3	0.2	1.7	10.1	87.7	0.5	1.7
26 years.................	21.8	76.3	0.2	1.7	8.8	88.8	0.7	1.7
27 years.................	18.2	79.6	0.2	1.9	8.0	89.5	0.8	1.7
28 years.................	15.6	82.2	0.3	1.9	6.9	90.5	0.9	1.7
29 years.................	13.2	84.7	0.2	1.8	6.5	90.6	1.0	1.9
30 to 34 years...........	10.9	86.9	0.3	1.8	5.8	91.0	1.3	1.9
35 to 39 years...........	9.0	88.4	0.5	2.1	5.8	89.7	2.2	2.2
40 to 44 years...........	8.7	87.9	1.0	2.4	6.2	87.4	3.9	2.4
45 to 49 years...........	8.8	86.6	1.9	2.8	6.5	83.7	7.2	2.6
50 to 54 years...........	9.0	84.6	3.4	3.0	6.5	79.2	11.8	2.5
55 to 59 years...........	9.4	81.8	5.8	3.0	6.6	73.3	18.1	2.1
60 to 64 years...........	10.1	77.9	9.3	2.7	7.0	65.0	26.3	1.7
65 to 69 years...........	10.4	72.8	14.4	2.4	7.2	54.2	37.3	1.3
70 to 74 years...........	9.8	66.9	21.1	2.1	7.5	42.6	48.9	1.0
75 to 79 years...........	9.6	59.3	29.5	1.6	7.8	29.2	62.2	0.7
80 to 84 years...........	9.0	49.2	40.6	1.3	8.2	17.3	74.0	0.5
85 years and over........	9.1	34.4	55.6	0.9	8.6	8.3	82.6	0.4

Table 10-9.—MARITAL STATUS BY SEX OF THE RURAL-NONFARM NONWHITE POPULATION OF THE UNITED STATES: 1950

Age in years	Male				Female			
	Percent single	Percent married	Percent widowed	Percent divorced	Percent single	Percent married	Percent widowed	Percent divorced
14 years..................	99.7	0.2	...	...	98.7	1.2	...	0.1
15 to 19 years...........	95.5	4.3	0.1	0.1	76.7	22.8	0.3	0.2
15 years................	99.5	0.4	0.1	...	96.0	3.8	0.1	0.1
16 years................	99.3	0.7	...	...	89.1	10.8	0.1	0.1
17 years................	97.6	2.2	0.1	0.1	79.5	20.1	0.3	0.1
18 years................	93.6	6.2	0.2	0.1	65.6	33.7	0.3	0.4
19 years................	88.1	11.6	0.2	0.2	52.5	46.4	0.5	0.6
20 to 24 years...........	57.9	40.8	0.6	0.7	29.2	68.2	1.2	1.3
20 years................	77.3	22.1	0.4	0.3	40.1	58.1	0.9	0.9
21 years................	65.0	33.8	0.6	0.7	34.2	63.7	0.9	1.3
22 years................	57.9	40.8	0.4	0.8	28.9	68.4	1.4	1.4
23 years................	47.2	51.3	0.6	0.8	22.5	74.6	1.4	1.5
24 years................	40.1	58.0	0.8	1.1	19.3	77.3	1.7	1.7
25 to 29 years...........	28.2	69.5	0.9	1.4	13.4	81.9	2.7	2.0
25 years................	34.6	63.6	0.7	1.0	16.3	79.2	2.4	2.1
26 years................	32.5	65.4	1.0	1.0	14.4	80.6	2.8	2.2
27 years................	26.4	71.2	0.8	1.5	12.9	82.6	2.5	2.0
28 years................	23.7	73.6	1.0	1.6	11.3	84.5	2.4	1.8
29 years................	22.3	75.1	0.9	1.6	11.4	83.1	3.4	2.1
30 to 34 years...........	17.3	79.5	1.2	2.0	8.8	84.7	4.3	2.2
35 to 39 years...........	12.8	83.0	2.2	2.1	7.7	82.2	7.5	2.6
40 to 44 years...........	11.3	83.1	3.3	2.2	6.4	79.0	12.2	2.4
45 to 49 years...........	10.3	82.2	5.1	2.3	6.0	73.1	18.5	2.4
50 to 54 years...........	9.3	79.7	8.6	2.4	4.9	67.6	25.3	2.2
55 to 59 years...........	8.2	77.9	11.7	2.2	4.8	59.7	33.6	1.9
60 to 64 years...........	8.3	73.5	16.3	1.9	4.2	51.6	42.9	1.3
65 to 69 years...........	6.5	69.7	22.1	1.7	3.6	40.6	54.9	0.9
70 to 74 years...........	5.6	63.7	29.2	1.5	3.5	30.2	65.0	1.2
75 to 79 years...........	5.6	59.1	34.4	0.9	4.7	23.3	71.4	0.6
80 to 84 years...........	5.3	50.8	42.8	1.0	3.7	16.0	79.8	0.5
85 years and over........	11.1	38.8	49.3	0.8	7.9	8.4	83.0	0.8

unmarried adult woman in rural-farm society is not a comfortable one. If she does not succeed in marrying at an early age, she migrates to the city. If she loses her husband through death or divorce, she either marries or migrates to the city. Among farm males, marriage tends to be postponed until the retirement of the parent who has been the head of the household and the operator of the farm. Since farming is usually a family enterprise, if the farmer loses his spouse through death or divorce he tends to remarry or to migrate to rural-nonfarm or urban areas. As a consequence, cities tend to have an excess of unmarried older women and of widowed or divorced men and women. Because farm men have somewhat greater longevity than city men, they tend to survive, and this helps to account for the comparative scarcity of widowed females in farm areas. Among the rural-nonfarm population of almost every age, the proportion that is married is unusually high and the proportion divorced is much smaller than in urban areas. This is due in part to the fact that this population has a large suburban element. Movement to the suburbs is usually a family movement, in which both husband and wife are young, are living together, and have children; the likelihood of divorce or widowhood in the immediate future is fairly remote.

The color differential. Nonwhite women tend to marry at considerably younger ages than white women. There is a similar color differential among males, but it is much smaller. The following table summarizes the proportions of girls at age 17 and boys at age 19 who were married, by color and residence in 1950:

Residence	Females-17 years		Males-19 years	
	White	Nonwhite	White	Nonwhite
Urban	10.3	17.4	8.0	12.9
Rural nonfarm	16.9	20.7	10.3	11.6
Rural farm	12.5	18.4	8.1	14.0

Table 10-10.—MARITAL STATUS BY SEX OF THE RURAL-FARM WHITE POPULATION OF THE UNITED STATES: 1950

Age in years	Male				Female			
	Percent single	Percent married	Percent widowed	Percent divorced	Percent single	Percent married	Percent widowed	Percent divorced
14 years.................	99.4	0.4	0.1	0.1	99.3	0.7	...	...
15 to 19 years...........	97.4	2.5	0.1	0.1	83.8	15.9	0.1	0.2
15 years................	99.4	0.4	0.1	0.1	97.9	2.1	...	...
16 years................	99.3	0.6	...	...	93.9	6.0	0.1	...
17 years................	98.5	1.4	...	...	87.3	12.5	0.1	0.2
18 years................	96.3	3.6	0.1	0.1	72.5	27.0	0.1	0.3
19 years................	91.7	8.1	...	0.2	54.2	45.2	0.2	0.5
20 to 24 years...........	64.4	34.7	0.1	0.7	25.7	72.9	0.4	1.0
20 years................	83.8	15.9	0.1	0.3	41.0	57.9	0.3	0.8
21 years................	74.1	25.2	0.1	0.5	30.3	68.3	0.3	1.1
22 years................	64.0	35.1	0.1	0.8	23.4	75.2	0.4	1.1
23 years................	52.2	46.8	0.1	0.9	18.6	79.9	0.4	1.1
24 years................	43.6	55.0	0.3	1.1	14.6	83.8	0.5	1.1
25 to 29 years...........	28.8	69.8	0.3	1.2	9.2	89.0	0.7	1.2
25 years................	37.7	60.9	0.2	1.1	11.8	86.4	0.6	1.2
26 years................	33.5	64.8	0.3	1.3	10.6	87.6	0.6	1.2
27 years................	28.2	70.4	0.2	1.1	8.8	89.3	0.7	1.2
28 years................	23.9	74.5	0.3	1.3	7.7	90.4	0.7	1.1
29 years................	20.4	78.3	0.3	1.1	7.2	91.0	0.7	1.1
30 to 34 years...........	16.9	81.4	0.4	1.2	6.0	92.1	0.9	1.0
35 to 39 years...........	12.5	85.7	0.6	1.3	5.1	92.7	1.3	0.9
40 to 44 years...........	10.7	86.9	1.0	1.4	4.9	92.0	2.2	0.9
45 to 49 years...........	9.9	87.1	1.6	1.5	4.9	90.3	3.9	0.9
50 to 54 years...........	9.1	86.7	2.8	1.5	4.5	88.1	6.5	0.8
55 to 59 years...........	8.3	86.0	4.2	1.5	4.6	84.2	10.4	0.8
60 to 64 years...........	8.6	82.9	7.1	1.5	5.1	77.4	16.7	0.8
65 to 69 years...........	9.1	77.9	11.7	1.4	5.8	66.8	26.8	0.6
70 to 74 years...........	8.4	71.9	18.6	1.2	6.4	51.7	41.2	0.6
75 to 79 years...........	8.0	62.4	28.6	1.0	6.5	34.4	58.7	0.4
80 to 84 years...........	6.8	49.9	42.5	0.8	5.7	18.9	75.2	0.2
85 years and over........	6.5	33.4	59.5	0.6	6.5	8.8	84.4	0.3

Also, a higher proportion of the nonwhite than of the white population marries at some time during its childbearing years. The proportions ever married at ages 55 to 59, by color and residence, were as follows in 1950:

Residence	Females		Males	
	White	Nonwhite	White	Nonwhite
Urban	91.0	95.6	91.8	93.6
Rural nonfarm	93.4	95.2	90.6	91.8
Rural farm	95.4	97.1	91.7	96.1

Marriages are much less stable among the non-white population than among the white population. Although higher death rates among the nonwhite population tend to increase widowhood, this instability is due much more largely to the greater impermanence of marriage among the nonwhite population. Most of this impermanence results from separation, rather than from divorce. Separation due to marital discord is more than 6 times as prevalent among the nonwhite than among the white population, as the following statistics show:

Proportion of population 14 years of age and over with broken marriages

Sex and color	Total	Married, spouse absent			Di-vorced	Widowed
		Total	Sepa-rated	Other		
Male						
White......	8.0	2.1	0.9	1.3	1.8	4.1
Nonwhite...	16.0	8.9	5.7	3.2	1.7	5.4
Female						
White......	18.2	3.6	1.5	2.0	2.2	12.4
Nonwhite...	31.0	13.6	9.4	4.2	2.5	14.9

Source: Current Population Reports, Series P-20, No. 62, April, 1955.

For each nine nonwhite married couples living together there is one nonwhite married couple that is separated because of marital discord, desertion, or for other similar reasons. The corresponding ratio for white couples is only 13 in 1000 couples.

Sociologists have often commented on this phenomenon, and have attributed it to the cultural patterns which developed during slavery and to the lower socio-economic position of the nonwhite population. For the first time, the 1960 census will provide data with which to measure changes, and changing differentials, in broken marriages among the nonwhite population.

CHANGES IN MARITAL STATUS: 1940 TO 1950

What segments of the population created the marriage boom that occurred during the 1940 to 1950 decade? Tables 10-12 through 10-17 provide some of the information necessary to the answering of this question; they show the percentage-point change in marital status by age, sex, color, and urban-rural residence. The following example will make clear the meaning of these figures. In

Table 10-6 it was reported that 42.4 percent of the white urban females aged 20 in 1950 were married. If one computes this same proportion for 1940, he will find it to be 28.2 percent. Subtraction of the proportion married in 1940 from the proportion married in 1950 shows that there has been an increase of 14.2 percentage points in the proportion of this group that is married. These differences, or changes in proportions for each marital status, are reported in Tables 10-12 through 10-17 for age, sex, color, and residence groups.

The marriage boom affected all but a very few age-sex-color-residence groups. This may be verified by noting the almost universal decline in the proportions single and the increase in the proportions married at each age in each table (see also Figure 10-5 for an over-all picture of the change in proportions married.)

The decreases in the proportion single were

Table 10-11.—MARITAL STATUS BY SEX OF THE RURAL-FARM NONWHITE POPULATION OF THE UNITED STATES: 1950

Age in years	Male				Female			
	Percent single	Percent married	Percent widowed	Percent divorced	Percent single	Percent married	Percent widowed	Percent divorced
14 years................	99.7	0.3	...	...	98.7	1.2	0.1	...
15 to 19 years..........	95.8	4.1	0.1	...	80.1	19.5	0.2	0.2
15 years..............	99.6	0.4	...	...	96.4	3.5	...	...
16 years..............	99.3	0.7	...	...	90.2	9.7	0.1	0.1
17 years..............	97.1	2.8	0.1	...	81.1	18.4	0.3	0.2
18 years..............	94.2	5.6	0.1	...	68.6	30.8	0.4	0.2
19 years..............	85.8	14.0	0.1	...	55.2	43.7	0.5	0.5
20 to 24 years..........	55.3	43.8	0.4	0.4	32.4	65.6	1.1	0.9
20 years..............	75.1	24.4	0.3	0.3	44.4	54.3	0.6	0.6
21 years..............	63.8	35.4	0.4	0.3	36.7	61.5	1.0	0.8
22 years..............	53.0	46.3	0.4	0.4	30.8	67.2	1.2	0.8
23 years..............	41.8	57.2	0.6	0.5	26.1	71.4	1.3	1.2
24 years..............	34.7	63.9	0.6	0.8	20.5	76.9	1.6	1.1
25 to 29 years..........	23.6	75.0	0.7	0.7	13.0	83.8	2.0	1.2
25 years..............	28.9	69.7	0.6	0.7	16.8	80.3	1.7	1.1
26 years..............	27.6	71.0	0.6	0.9	14.7	82.4	1.7	1.2
27 years..............	22.2	76.7	0.6	0.5	12.3	84.1	2.1	1.5
28 years..............	20.4	78.2	0.7	0.7	11.2	85.7	2.3	0.8
29 years..............	17.1	81.1	0.9	0.9	9.2	87.4	2.3	1.2
30 to 34 years..........	13.1	85.0	1.1	0.8	7.1	89.1	2.6	1.1
35 to 39 years..........	8.5	89.1	1.5	0.9	4.8	90.0	4.2	0.9
40 to 44 years..........	7.5	89.2	2.3	1.1	4.0	88.2	6.9	0.8
45 to 49 years..........	6.4	88.7	3.8	1.1	3.6	85.4	10.3	0.8
50 to 54 years..........	5.2	88.4	5.7	0.8	3.0	80.4	15.8	0.9
55 to 59 years..........	3.9	88.2	7.1	0.8	2.9	75.7	20.6	0.8
60 to 64 years..........	4.5	84.0	10.6	0.9	3.0	68.1	28.1	0.7
65 to 69 years..........	4.3	80.8	14.2	0.7	3.2	55.5	40.7	0.5
70 to 74 years..........	3.9	74.9	20.6	0.7	3.2	40.3	55.8	0.6
75 to 79 years..........	4.0	68.5	26.9	0.7	3.8	30.7	65.2	0.2
80 to 84 years..........	3.5	59.0	36.9	0.6	4.1	16.9	78.7	0.3
85 years and over........	5.7	41.6	51.9	0.8	4.6	9.0	86.3	0.1

Table 10-12.—PERCENTAGE POINT CHANGE IN MARITAL STATUS OF THE URBAN WHITE POPULATION, BY SEX: 1940 TO 1950

Age in years	Male				Female			
	Single	Married	Widowed	Divorced	Single	Married	Widowed	Divorced
14 years.....................	-1.0	0.6	0.2	0.1	-0.4	0.4	0.1	...
15 to 19 years.............	-1.8	1.7	0.1	0.1	-6.4	6.2	0.1	0.2
15 years..................	-1.0	0.7	0.2	0.1	-0.9	0.9	0.1	...
16 years..................	-0.9	0.6	0.1	0.1	-2.7	2.6	0.1	0.1
17 years..................	-0.9	0.8	0.1	0.1	-5.2	5.0	0.1	0.1
18 years..................	-1.9	1.9	0.1	0.1	-8.0	7.6	...	0.3
19 years..................	-4.3	4.2	0.1	0.2	-11.5	11.0	...	0.4
20 to 24 years.............	-15.2	14.6	...	0.6	-17.5	16.8	...	0.8
20 years..................	-8.5	8.1	0.1	0.3	-14.8	14.2	...	0.6
21 years..................	-12.6	12.1	...	0.4	-17.9	17.1	...	0.7
22 years..................	-15.9	15.3	...	0.6	-18.9	18.0	...	0.9
23 years..................	-17.6	16.9	...	0.8	-18.0	17.2	-0.1	0.8
24 years..................	-17.6	16.8	0.1	0.8	-16.4	15.7	-0.1	0.8
25 to 29 years.............	-14.1	13.3	-0.1	0.8	-11.8	11.2	-0.2	0.7
25 years..................	-17.0	16.2	...	0.9	-14.8	14.1	-0.1	0.8
26 years..................	-15.2	14.3	...	0.9	-12.8	12.1	-0.1	0.7
27 years..................	-14.0	13.2	...	0.8	-11.3	10.7	-0.1	0.7
28 years..................	-12.5	11.8	-0.1	0.8	-10.5	10.0	-0.1	0.6
29 years..................	-10.9	10.3	-0.1	0.8	-9.1	8.8	-0.2	0.6
30 to 34 years.............	-8.2	7.9	-0.2	0.7	-6.7	6.9	-0.6	0.4
35 to 39 years.............	-5.6	5.5	-0.5	0.6	-3.6	4.5	-1.5	0.6
40 to 44 years.............	-3.9	4.0	-0.8	0.7	-1.5	2.6	-2.1	1.1
45 to 49 years.............	-2.7	2.6	-1.1	1.2	-1.2	1.9	-2.3	1.5
50 to 54 years.............	-2.6	2.9	-1.5	1.1	-1.4	2.3	-2.3	1.4
55 to 59 years.............	-2.4	2.8	-1.4	0.9	-1.6	2.7	-2.3	1.1
60 to 64 years.............	-1.8	2.4	-1.6	0.9	-1.8	2.8	-1.9	0.9
65 to 69 years.............	-1.8	2.3	-1.4	0.8	-1.7	3.2	-2.2	0.6
70 to 74 years.............	-1.7	2.8	-1.6	0.6	-0.9	2.4	-2.0	0.4
75 to 79 years.............	-1.4	2.5	-1.7	0.5	...	1.7	-2.1	0.3
80 to 84 years.............	-1.2	2.3	-1.3	0.4	...	0.7	-1.0	0.2
85 years and over.........	-0.8	1.0	-0.5	0.2	1.1	0.4	-1.8	0.3

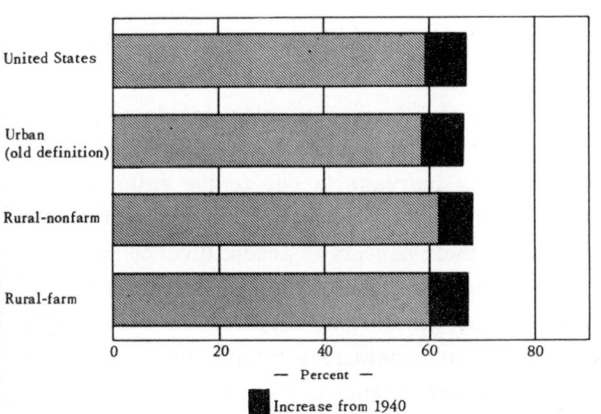

FIGURE 10-5. PERCENT MARRIED, POPULATION 14 YEARS
OF AGE AND OVER, BY URBAN AND RURAL RESIDENCE,
1940 AND 1950

greater at most ages for the populations of urban areas than of rural areas, and was greater in rural-farm than in rural-nonfarm areas. The changes in urban areas were especially impress-ive, for they were large and covered a much greater age range. The marriage boom affected the white population much more than it did the non-white. Thus, the marriage boom affected most the very groups which, during the 1930's, had been the most inclined to remain single or to postpone marriage. The change was greater for females than for males. However, caution must be used in interpreting these estimates of urban and rural changes. In 1950 large numbers of young men were in military service abroad, and their marital status is not considered here. In computing these tables, moreover, the definition of urban used for 1940 was perforce the old definition, whereas the definition used for 1950 was the new definition of the urban population. Had the new definition been used in 1940 also, a somewhat higher proportion of the population would have been reported as married at that time and, hence, the increases in proportion married would have been smaller for the urban population than Table 10-12 reports.

Table 10-13.—PERCENTAGE POINT CHANGE IN MARITAL STATUS OF THE URBAN NONWHITE POPULATION, BY SEX: 1940 TO 1950

Age in years	Male				Female			
	Single	Married	Widowed	Divorced	Single	Married	Widowed	Divorced
14 years..................	-0.5	0.3	0.1	0.1	-0.7	0.6	0.1	...
15 to 19 years...........	-1.4	1.4	0.1	0.1	-4.6	4.6	-0.1	...
15 years..................	-0.5	0.3	0.1	...	-1.0	1.0	...	0.1
16 years..................	-0.3	0.3	0.1	...	-2.7	2.7	...	...
17 years..................	-0.8	0.8	0.1	...	-4.8	4.5	...	0.1
18 years..................	-2.0	1.9	0.1	0.1	-5.8	5.7	-0.1	0.1
19 years..................	-4.1	4.0	...	...	-7.8	8.0	-0.3	0.1
20 to 24 years...........	-9.1	8.3	0.1	0.7	-9.7	9.5	-0.8	0.9
20 years..................	-6.8	6.3	0.1	0.4	-9.1	9.3	-0.6	0.4
21 years..................	-9.1	8.4	0.2	0.3	-9.3	9.3	-0.5	0.5
22 years..................	-8.8	7.7	0.2	0.9	-9.6	9.4	-0.6	0.8
23 years..................	-8.2	7.3	0.2	0.6	-9.4	9.2	-0.9	1.1
24 years..................	-8.3	7.4	...	0.9	-9.1	8.9	-1.1	1.3
25 to 29 years...........	-8.2	7.5	-0.4	1.1	-7.7	8.7	-2.3	1.4
25 years..................	-7.9	7.4	-0.3	0.8	-9.0	9.4	-1.7	1.4
26 years..................	-8.3	7.5	-0.3	1.1	-7.5	8.1	-1.9	1.3
27 years..................	-8.7	7.8	-0.3	1.2	-8.2	9.2	-2.3	1.3
28 years..................	-8.4	7.8	-0.4	1.2	-7.6	8.6	-2.5	1.4
29 years..................	-8.4	7.6	-0.4	1.2	-6.8	8.2	-3.3	1.8
30 to 34 years...........	-9.2	8.7	-0.7	1.4	-5.2	8.1	-4.5	1.6
35 to 39 years...........	-8.3	7.8	-1.1	1.6	-2.9	7.8	-6.9	2.0
40 to 44 years...........	-6.6	7.0	-1.7	1.5	-1.9	7.8	-8.0	2.0
45 to 49 years...........	-4.6	5.3	-1.9	1.3	-1.4	6.5	-7.1	1.9
50 to 54 years...........	-4.8	5.3	-2.0	1.4	-1.5	6.0	-6.3	1.7
55 to 59 years...........	-4.4	4.5	-1.7	1.6	-0.7	4.4	-5.0	1.2
60 to 64 years...........	-3.5	3.4	-1.1	1.3	-0.9	3.7	-3.8	1.0
65 to 69 years...........	-3.2	2.3	...	0.9	-0.6	3.6	-3.9	0.9
70 to 74 years...........	-3.2	2.9	-0.6	0.9	-0.3	3.0	-3.0	0.4
75 to 79 years...........	-3.6	4.3	-1.0	0.2	1.0	1.1	-2.6	0.4
80 to 84 years...........	-3.1	1.6	1.3	0.1	-0.2	1.2	-1.3	0.4
85 years and over........	4.4	-3.4	-1.4	0.3	8.8	-0.7	-8.4	0.2

The differences are so large, however, that the change in definition or in the military population could not account for all of them.

The decade 1940 to 1950 also witnessed a general decline in widowhood; the proportion of persons of each age who were widowed was smaller in 1950 than it had been in 1940, in spite of the war casualties. This decline could be a result of the increased longevity of males, but it must also be due in part to a greater tendency for widowed persons to remarry.[4] This decline was characteris-tic both of the white and nonwhite men and women living in both urban and rural residences.

For almost all age-sex-color-residence groups the proportion of divorced persons increased. Part of this increase is due to the aging of cohorts--the younger generations are more inclined than were their parents to accept divorce as a way out of domestic difficulties. As these more divorce-prone generations displace the older, less divorce-prone generations, the proportion divorced in each age group tends to rise, and the proportion of the total population that is divorced tends to increase.

The increases in the proportion divorced which are reported in these tables do not measure adequately the actual increase in the occurrence of divorce. Underreporting was a factor, and there is also good evidence (see below) of an increased tendency for divorced persons to remarry during the decade; in a way, this latter factor is analo-

---

[4] It is believed that little of this change can be due to the method of asking the marital status question or to assigning a marital status to those persons for whom the census enumerator did not obtain information. In both 1940 and 1950 the Census Bureau estimated the marital status on the basis of other information on the schedule. Because of slight changes in the assignment procedure, some persons who would have been classified as single under the 1940 procedure would have been classified as "married, spouse absent" or "widowed" in 1950.

gous to the finding for widowed persons.

The increases in the proportion of divorced persons of any age are much greater in urban than in rural areas. In both rural-farm and rural-nonfarm areas, the increase in the proportion divorced was very small.

In interpreting these changes, the role of migration must not be forgotten. There may be a very strong tendency for widowed and divorced persons (especially women) to migrate from rural to urban areas shortly after the loss of their spouses. Hence, one can infer nothing about changes in divorce rates and widowhood rates from these statistics concerning change in marital status.

ADDITIONAL DIFFERENTIALS IN MARITAL STATUS AND CHANGE IN MARITAL STATUS

The marital status of the population varies markedly according to several other characteristics--educational attainment, occupation, and income. Each of these differentials is discussed later in this chapter. Part III is devoted to these particular aspects of population composition.

REGIONAL DIFFERENCES IN MARITAL STATUS

A refined study of regional differences in marital status would require that age differences be controlled. Such control would involve an extended calculation to standardize the data simultaneously for age, color, and urban-rural residence. In the absence of the facilities needed for this calculation, it is possible only to discuss the actual differences observed and to infer indirectly the extent to which age composition and differences in marital patterns underlie these differences. The data needed for this task are contained

Table 10-14.—PERCENTAGE POINT CHANGE IN MARITAL STATUS OF THE RURAL-NONFARM WHITE POPULATION, BY SEX: 1940 TO 1950

Age in years	Male				Female			
	Single	Married	Widowed	Divorced	Single	Married	Widowed	Divorced
14 years..................	-0.9	0.6	0.2	0.1	-0.4	0.4	...	...
15 to 19 years...........	-1.9	1.6	0.1	0.1	-6.9	6.7	...	0.1
15 years..................	-0.7	0.5	0.1	0.1	-1.3	1.2	...	...
16 years..................	-0.7	0.5	0.1	0.1	-3.3	3.2	...	0.1
17 years..................	-1.0	0.8	0.1	0.1	-5.8	5.7	...	0.1
18 years..................	-2.2	2.1	0.1	0.1	-10.6	10.4	...	0.3
19 years..................	-4.3	4.2	0.1	0.1	-15.6	15.3	...	0.3
20 to 24 years...........	-12.9	12.2	...	0.7	-15.9	15.5	...	0.5
20 years..................	-7.2	6.8	...	0.4	-17.2	16.8	...	0.4
21 years..................	-11.0	10.4	...	0.6	-17.4	17.0	-0.1	0.5
22 years..................	-15.1	14.3	...	0.8	-16.4	15.9	...	0.6
23 years..................	-16.9	16.0	...	0.9	-14.2	14.1	-0.1	0.3
24 years..................	-16.0	15.0	...	1.0	-12.5	12.1	-0.1	0.5
25 to 29 years...........	-10.8	9.9	-0.1	0.9	-8.1	7.9	-0.2	0.4
25 years..................	-14.2	13.3	...	1.0	-10.8	10.4	-0.2	0.6
26 years..................	-12.3	11.5	-0.1	0.9	-9.3	9.0	-0.1	0.4
27 years..................	-10.3	9.3	-0.1	1.0	-7.6	7.4	-0.2	0.4
28 years..................	-9.2	8.3	...	1.0	-7.0	6.9	-0.2	0.3
29 years..................	-7.8	7.2	-0.2	0.8	-5.8	5.7	-0.3	0.4
30 to 34 years...........	-5.4	5.1	-0.3	0.5	-4.5	4.9	-0.6	0.2
35 to 39 years...........	-3.4	3.5	-0.6	0.5	-2.4	3.6	-1.5	0.2
40 to 44 years...........	-2.6	3.2	-0.9	0.4	-1.4	3.2	-2.2	0.3
45 to 49 years...........	-2.5	3.1	-1.2	0.6	-0.9	2.5	-2.3	0.6
50 to 54 years...........	-2.9	3.7	-1.5	0.8	-1.1	3.3	-2.8	0.7
55 to 59 years...........	-2.6	3.2	-1.5	0.9	-1.1	3.9	-3.2	0.5
60 to 64 years...........	-1.6	2.8	-1.9	0.7	-1.0	4.2	-3.6	0.4
65 to 69 years...........	-1.0	2.1	-1.7	0.5	-0.7	4.3	-3.9	0.3
70 to 74 years...........	-1.1	2.4	-2.0	0.6	-0.6	4.6	-4.3	0.3
75 to 79 years...........	-0.8	2.8	-2.5	0.4	-0.1	3.2	-3.4	0.2
80 to 84 years...........	-0.4	2.0	-2.0	0.5	0.2	1.7	-2.2	0.2
85 years and over........	0.4	-0.2	-0.4	0.2	0.9	0.8	-2.0	0.2

Table 10-15.—PERCENTAGE POINT CHANGE IN MARITAL STATUS OF THE RURAL-NONFARM NONWHITE POPULATION, BY SEX: 1940 TO 1950

Age in years	Male				Female			
	Single	Married	Widowed	Divorced	Single	Married	Widowed	Divorced
14 years..................	-0.2	0.1	...	...	-0.5	0.4	...	0.1
15 to 19 years............	-1.5	1.4	0.1	0.1	-2.2	2.4	-0.2	-0.1
15 years.................	-0.3	0.2	0.1	...	-0.7	0.6	...	...
16 years.................	-0.2	0.2	...	...	-2.1	2.3	-0.1	...
17 years.................	-1.1	0.9	0.1	0.1	-1.9	2.2	-0.1	-0.2
18 years.................	-2.4	2.3	0.2	...	-3.1	3.4	-0.3	...
19 years.................	-2.9	2.8	0.1	0.1	-4.6	5.0	-0.5	0.1
20 to 24 years............	-2.8	2.4	0.1	0.3	-5.0	5.8	-1.0	...
20 years.................	-3.7	3.5	0.2	0.1	-6.0	6.6	-0.6	...
21 years.................	-4.9	4.2	0.3	0.4	-4.6	5.4	-0.8	0.2
22 years.................	-1.7	1.4	-0.2	0.4	-3.9	4.7	-0.8	0.1
23 years.................	-2.8	2.5	-0.1	0.3	-5.5	6.5	-1.1	0.1
24 years.................	-3.1	2.7	...	0.4	-4.7	5.9	-1.3	0.1
25 to 29 years............	-3.1	2.7	-0.2	0.5	-4.1	5.5	-1.4	...
25 years.................	-3.5	3.3	-0.2	0.3	-6.0	6.9	-1.1	0.3
26 years.................	-2.5	2.2	...	0.2	-4.2	4.8	-0.8	0.2
27 years.................	-3.8	3.4	-0.3	0.5	-4.0	5.7	-1.6	-0.1
28 years.................	-3.7	3.3	-0.2	0.5	-4.3	6.3	-1.7	-0.3
29 years.................	-2.7	2.4	-0.5	0.7	-2.0	3.6	-1.8	0.1
30 to 34 years............	-4.4	4.4	-0.7	0.8	-3.0	6.1	-2.9	-0.2
35 to 39 years............	-4.7	5.1	-0.8	0.5	-0.7	5.1	-4.4	...
40 to 44 years............	-3.4	5.0	-2.0	0.3	-0.4	6.4	-5.9	-0.1
45 to 49 years............	-2.4	3.9	-1.9	0.3	0.4	5.3	-5.8	0.1
50 to 54 years............	-2.8	4.0	-1.7	0.5	-0.4	6.7	-6.7	0.4
55 to 59 years............	-2.6	4.2	-2.0	0.5	...	4.0	-4.4	0.4
60 to 64 years............	-1.8	2.9	-1.4	0.3	-0.5	4.5	-4.1	0.1
65 to 69 years............	-2.0	2.8	-1.2	0.4	-0.5	4.2	-3.6	-0.2
70 to 74 years............	-2.2	3.7	-1.8	0.4	-0.2	3.5	-4.0	0.5
75 to 79 years............	-2.8	4.9	-2.0	-0.1	0.7	3.0	-3.8	0.1
80 to 84 years............	-2.9	4.9	-2.5	0.4	-0.1	1.9	-2.0	0.1
85 years and over.........	3.7	0.9	-4.9	0.2	4.4	-0.1	-4.8	0.6

in the Appendix tables to this report. Tables 10-18 and 10-19 are abstracted from these appendix materials.

Percent single (never married). The top line of Table 10-18 shows that in 1950 there was comparatively little variation among the regions in regard to the proportions of their populations which were single. However, two geographic divisions have somewhat above-average proportions of single persons, and two have somewhat below-average proportions of single persons. The two divisions which contain proportionately more bachelors and spinsters are the New England and the Middle Atlantic states, and the two divisions which have proportionately fewer unmarried people are the Pacific and the West South Central divisions. In both cases, these deviations are the opposite of what one would expect on the basis of

age composition. Since the two northeastern divisions have an older population composition, one would expect them to have below-average proportions of single people (because of the shortage of persons in their early teens and the preponderance of persons above 35 years of age). In the West and Southwest one would presume that the recent migrations and the younger age composition would cause a great surplus of unmarried persons, but this assumption also proves to be false. It must be concluded, therefore, that these are regional differences in marital status, and that they are understated, rather than exaggerated, by differences in age composition. Apparently, bachelorhood and spinsterhood are more widely accepted ways of life in New England and the Middle Atlantic states (the areas of most intense urban settlement and earliest urban settlement) than in the rest of

Table 10-16.—PERCENTAGE POINT CHANGE IN MARITAL STATUS OF THE RURAL-FARM WHITE POPULATION,
BY SEX: 1940 TO 1950

Age in years	Male				Female			
	Single	Married	Widowed	Divorced	Single	Married	Widowed	Divorced
14 years..................	-0.5	0.3	0.1	0.1	-0.3	0.3	...	...
15 to 19 years............	-0.7	0.7	0.1	0.1	-2.6	2.5	...	0.1
15 years.................	-0.5	0.3	0.1	0.1	-0.5	0.5	...	...
16 years.................	-0.4	0.3	...	...	-1.1	1.1	0.1	...
17 years.................	-0.7	0.6	...	...	-1.6	1.6	...	0.1
18 years.................	-1.3	1.2	0.1	0.1	-6.1	5.9	...	0.1
19 years.................	-2.5	2.4	...	0.2	-13.3	13.1	...	0.2
20 to 24 years............	-9.7	9.2	-0.1	0.5	-15.2	14.9	-0.1	0.4
20 years.................	-5.0	4.9	...	0.2	-15.6	15.2	...	0.4
21 years.................	-7.2	6.8	...	0.3	-16.7	16.2	-0.1	0.6
22 years.................	-9.7	9.2	-0.1	0.6	-15.5	15.3	-0.1	0.5
23 years.................	-12.5	12.1	-0.1	0.6	-13.1	12.8	-0.2	0.4
24 years.................	-13.4	12.6	...	0.7	-11.6	11.5	-0.2	0.3
25 to 29 years............	-10.5	10.2	-0.2	0.6	-8.1	8.1	-0.3	0.4
25 years.................	-12.1	11.5	-0.1	0.6	-10.2	9.9	-0.2	0.4
26 years.................	-10.5	9.8	-0.1	0.7	-8.7	8.6	-0.3	0.4
27 years.................	-9.9	9.6	-0.3	0.5	-8.0	7.9	-0.3	0.4
28 years.................	-10.1	9.6	-0.2	0.6	-7.1	7.1	-0.4	0.2
29 years.................	-8.9	8.9	-0.3	0.4	-5.8	5.9	-0.4	0.3
30 to 34 years............	-6.8	6.8	-0.4	0.3	-4.6	5.2	-0.7	0.1
35 to 39 years............	-4.5	5.1	-0.7	0.2	-2.5	3.6	-1.2	...
40 to 44 years............	-2.6	3.3	-1.0	0.2	-1.2	2.7	-1.6	0.1
45 to 49 years............	-1.3	2.3	-1.3	0.4	-0.3	2.1	-1.9	0.1
50 to 54 years............	-2.0	3.5	-1.7	0.2	-0.7	3.1	-2.6	0.1
55 to 59 years............	-2.7	4.9	-2.3	0.2	-0.7	3.9	-3.3	0.1
60 to 64 years............	-2.1	4.5	-2.5	0.2	-0.6	4.6	-4.2	0.2
65 to 69 years............	-1.2	3.7	-2.5	0.2	-0.4	5.8	-5.5	0.1
70 to 74 years............	-1.5	4.5	-3.0	0.2	-0.3	5.4	-5.4	0.2
75 to 79 years............	-1.7	5.0	-3.4	0.1	±0.2	4.2	-4.1	0.1
80 to 84 years............	-2.2	4.1	-2.1	0.1	-1.2	1.8	-0.6	...
85 years and over........	-1.6	2.7	-1.1	...	...	0.9	-1.1	0.1

the nation. In the Far West and the Southwest--areas of new and rapid population growth--the unmarried status appears to be less tolerable than it is elsewhere in the nation. These interregional differences are largest among the urban populations of the respective regions, although the rural populations tend also to reflect them to a smaller degree. This regional pattern is extraordinarily consistent for both white and nonwhite males and females, and for each sex-color group in urban, rural-nonfarm, and rural-farm areas. It should be reemphasized, however, that these deviations from the national average are comparatively small--all regions appear to have roughly the same marriage patterns.

Percent change in the number of single persons: 1940-50. Table 10-19 shows the percent change between 1940 and 1950 in the number of single

persons of each sex-color, and urban and rural, group for each geographic division. This table shows that not only changing marital patterns, but also changing age composition and streams of interregional migration operated to produce the rates observed. An outstanding feature of this table is its demonstration that, in almost every region, above-average declines in the number of never-married persons were occurring in the rural-farm and the urban parts of the region, while there was an increase in the number of single persons in rural-nonfarm areas. Young persons (many of them unmarried) were leaving farms at a very rapid rate. This migration, coupled with the new pattern of earlier age at marriage, caused the single population of rural-farm areas to decline by 41 percent in this one decade. In the cities there were large declines in

Table 10-17.—PERCENTAGE POINT CHANGE IN MARITAL STATUS OF THE RURAL-FARM NONWHITE POPULATION, BY SEX, 1940 TO 1950

Age in years	Male				Female			
	Single	Married	Widowed	Divorced	Single	Married	Widowed	Divorced
14 years..................	-0.1	0.1	...	...	-0.4	0.3	0.1	...
15 to 19 years............	-0.8	0.7	0.1	...	1.1	-0.8	-0.2	-0.1
15 years.................	-0.2	0.2	...	...	-0.3	0.4	-0.1	...
16 years.................	-0.1	0.1	...	...	-0.6	0.7	-0.1	...
17 years.................	-1.3	1.3	0.1	...	0.2	-0.1	-0.1	...
18 years.................	-1.1	1.0	...	...	1.6	-1.1	-0.3	-0.2
19 years.................	-3.0	3.1	...	0.1	-0.9	1.4	-0.5	-0.1
20 to 24 years............	-2.6	2.6	-0.2	-0.1	-0.4	1.3	-0.9	...
20 years.................	-3.7	3.7	...	0.1	-0.2	1.0	-0.8	-0.1
21 years.................	-1.9	1.8	...	0.1	-0.9	1.4	-0.6	...
22 years.................	-2.2	2.4	-0.2	...	...	1.2	-1.0	-0.2
23 years.................	-3.3	3.5	-0.2	0.1	1.0	-0.2	-0.9	0.1
24 years.................	-3.0	3.2	-0.4	0.3	-0.7	1.9	-1.1	0.1
25 to 29 years............	-2.3	2.8	-0.6	0.1	-1.4	2.7	-1.3	...
25 years.................	-3.8	4.0	-0.5	0.2	-1.4	2.6	-1.2	-0.1
26 years.................	-0.9	1.4	-0.6	0.3	-1.5	2.7	-1.3	...
27 years.................	-2.3	3.2	-0.7	-0.2	-1.1	2.0	-1.2	0.3
28 years.................	-2.2	2.8	-0.7	...	-1.0	2.8	-1.4	-0.4
29 years.................	-1.9	2.2	-0.4	0.2	-1.1	2.8	-1.5	...
30 to 34 years............	-3.8	4.8	-0.9	...	-1.7	4.4	-2.6	-0.3
35 to 39 years............	-4.0	5.3	-1.3	-0.1	-1.0	4.8	-3.5	-0.3
40 to 44 years............	-1.9	4.0	-2.0	0.1	-0.5	5.7	-4.9	-0.3
45 to 49 years............	-0.7	2.3	-1.7	0.1	0.2	4.9	-4.8	-0.2
50 to 54 years............	-1.1	3.4	-2.1	-0.1	-0.4	6.0	-5.5	...
55 to 59 years............	-1.7	4.5	-2.7	-0.1	-0.1	5.8	-5.7	...
60 to 64 years............	-0.8	3.4	-2.7	...	-0.5	7.6	-7.2	...
65 to 69 years............	-0.2	3.1	-2.8	-0.1	-0.2	7.2	-7.0	-0.1
70 to 74 years............	-0.7	4.3	-3.5	...	-0.4	5.8	-5.7	0.2
75 to 79 years............	-0.8	4.8	-4.0	0.1	0.1	6.1	-6.2	-0.2
80 to 84 years............	-1.7	5.9	-4.3	0.1	0.3	3.2	-3.6	...
85 years and over........	0.7	-1.0	...	0.4	1.2	0.8	-1.8	-0.1

the single population, despite the fact that great numbers of unmarried migrants were pouring in from the rural areas. This decline could have occurred only if the urban population of each region were undergoing a drastic change in age at marriage. It is possible to determine approximately, from Table 10-19, which of the regions experienced the greatest change in marriage patterns as a result of the simultaneous influences of migration and changing age composition. These were the New England, the Middle Atlantic, and the East North Central divisions (the most urban). The least change occurred in the South Atlantic and East South Central divisions (the more rural). The great South-to-North migration would lead one to expect (if all regions had adopted the younger marriage pattern to an equal degree) that the rate of decline in the single population would be great-

est in the southern (sending) and smallest in the northern (receiving) regions. But the exact reverse of this situation exists--the greatest negative rates are found for the New England, Middle Atlantic, and East North Central (migrant receiving) states. Thus, the regions where the population previously had been most inclined to postpone or forego marriage were the very regions which made the greatest change toward earlier marriage. Thus, the trend toward younger marriages in the 1940 to 1950 decade involved a differential regional element that acted to reduce interregional differences in marital status.

The increase in number of single persons among the rural-nonfarm population can be attributed to general population growth and to migration.

Negro migration into the urban areas of the northeastern and western sections of the nation

Table 10-18.—PERCENT OF THE POPULATION 14 YEARS OF AGE AND OVER THAT IS SINGLE (NEVER MARRIED), BY SEX, COLOR, AND URBAN-RURAL RESIDENCE, FOR GEOGRAPHIC DIVISIONS: 1950

Sex, color, and residence	United States total	Geographic division								
		New England	Middle Atlantic	East North Central	West North Central	South Atlantic	East South Central	West South Central	Mountain	Pacific
All sex-color groups..	23.1	26.9	25.1	22.1	23.2	23.9	22.8	20.9	22.4	20.1
Urban..................	22.7	27.5	25.2	21.9	22.5	22.1	20.7	19.8	21.0	19.4
Rural nonfarm..........	22.3	23.9	24.0	20.8	21.7	23.5	21.7	20.7	23.0	21.9
Rural farm.............	26.1	27.5	27.0	24.8	26.0	29.1	26.1	24.0	26.1	23.4
White males..........	26.0	28.6	27.2	24.9	26.6	26.4	25.9	24.5	26.3	24.1
Urban..................	24.9	28.8	27.0	24.1	24.0	23.8	22.5	22.8	23.8	22.6
Rural nonfarm..........	26.2	27.0	27.0	24.3	25.5	27.2	25.2	25.2	28.0	28.2
Rural farm.............	30.6	32.4	31.7	29.8	32.1	32.1	30.2	28.2	31.6	28.3
Nonwhite males.......	28.7	33.2	30.0	25.1	26.0	31.1	27.5	26.0	34.5	30.9
Urban..................	26.0	31.9	28.9	24.0	23.8	27.2	24.0	23.0	29.3	27.4
Rural nonfarm..........	32.9	43.5	44.2	41.2	36.9	32.6	28.9	28.2	37.4	44.9
Rural farm.............	33.9	39.9	33.8	31.2	32.5	37.0	31.0	30.5	37.4	46.2
White females........	20.0	25.2	22.9	19.5	20.0	19.5	19.2	16.9	17.7	15.6
Urban..................	20.8	26.4	23.4	20.2	21.4	19.6	19.2	17.2	18.2	16.1
Rural nonfarm..........	17.4	20.8	20.3	16.8	17.7	17.5	17.2	15.2	16.3	13.4
Rural farm.............	19.7	21.8	21.6	19.0	18.7	22.5	21.0	17.9	18.4	15.8
Nonwhite females.....	20.8	23.8	23.3	16.9	18.2	23.4	20.0	18.3	23.2	17.4
Urban..................	19.1	23.3	23.1	16.6	16.9	20.9	17.7	16.1	18.3	16.7
Rural nonfarm..........	22.0	29.7	27.3	23.6	26.0	23.2	19.8	18.9	25.5	21.7
Rural farm.............	26.0	28.0	23.6	20.7	23.6	29.4	23.6	23.2	26.9	24.0

Source: Statistical appendix to this study; derived from census data.

Table 10-19.—PERCENT CHANGE IN THE SINGLE (NEVER MARRIED) POPULATION 14 YEARS OF AGE AND OVER, BY SEX, COLOR, AND URBAN-RURAL RESIDENCE, FOR GEOGRAPHIC DIVISIONS: 1940 TO 1950

Sex, color, and residence	United States total	Geographic division								
		New England	Middle Atlantic	East North Central	West North Central	South Atlantic	East South Central	West South Central	Mountain	Pacific
All sex-color groups..	-17.6	-18.6	-20.8	-19.6	-24.8	-11.5	-18.5	-18.8	-12.2	-1.1
Urban..................	-18.7	-21.0	-24.7	-20.9	-16.4	-13.3	-12.1	0.5	-6.4	-12.7
Rural nonfarm..........	12.6	3.3	5.9	10.2	-13.7	25.9	14.3	...	8.4	63.9
Rural farm.............	-41.1	-47.7	-42.4	-41.8	-41.5	-36.9	-36.3	-49.3	-41.3	-40.9
White males..........	-18.4	-19.4	-23.8	-21.9	-24.8	-8.7	-15.7	-15.6	-13.9	-2.7
Urban..................	-20.7	-22.1	-28.0	-23.5	-16.4	-14.9	-11.0	7.0	-6.1	-15.5
Rural nonfarm..........	14.7	4.7	4.3	9.8	-9.9	34.8	22.9	4.5	7.1	60.2
Rural farm.............	-40.4	-47.5	-42.7	-42.1	-39.2	-35.8	-34.1	-47.8	-42.1	-40.4
Nonwhite males.......	-8.7	11.1	15.5	21.4	-10.1	-13.5	-22.8	-23.6	10.2	13.4
Urban..................	4.1	22.4	14.0	21.9	-6.0	-5.0	-10.8	7.1	7.4	18.1
Rural nonfarm..........	22.4	31.0	44.7	54.5	-2.0	15.2	5.3	16.8	52.5	164.1
Rural farm.............	-41.0	-73.7	-58.9	-47.2	-46.6	-36.0	-38.5	-50.7	-31.3	-52.8
White females........	-18.8	-18.6	-21.1	-20.4	26.0	-13.4	-19.1	-20.5	-12.4	-1.5
Urban..................	-20.6	-21.0	-25.5	-23.0	-17.6	-15.9	-12.8	-1.9	-8.0	-13.9
Rural nonfarm..........	7.6	1.1	5.7	8.6	-19.3	20.0	9.1	-12.1	1.8	57.2
Rural farm.............	-43.0	-47.7	-41.3	-41.3	-45.5	-40.6	-38.3	-52.0	-42.3	-37.7
Nonwhite females.....	-8.4	4.6	18.2	23.2	-2.7	-13.8	-22.5	-23.7	21.4	37.7
Urban..................	1.8	8.3	18.9	25.0	0.6	-9.6	-15.6	-15.6	12.7	44.9
Rural nonfarm..........	16.6	7.2	20.0	42.7	7.2	14.6	2.1	10.1	102.1	192.9
Rural farm.............	-37.2	-66.1	-40.9	-41.4	-39.5	-33.5	-35.7	-46.0	-25.6	-56.2

Source: Statistical appendix to this study; derived from census data.

was so large that it caused an increase in the number of single nonwhites. But the rates of growth for single nonwhites in these areas are far below those that pertain to the population generally. It must be concluded that although the marriage boom had a strong effect on all groups in all regions, its impact was most revolutionary in the cosmopolitan centers. In the cities, where bachelor society had become most highly developed and institutionalized, the greatest changes were wrought.

PART II

MARRIAGE AND DIVORCE AS DEMOGRAPHIC EVENTS[5]

The preceding discussion has treated marriage and divorce as statuses which people occupy at the time of a census or other enumeration. In this section they are studied as events, or as changes in marital status. They have an incidence that can

---

[5] In the United States, statistics concerning marriage and divorce are grossly incomplete and inadequate. The National Office of Vital Statistics receives much less cooperation from municipal, county, and state governments in its attempt to obtain records of marriage and divorce than it does in its collection of birth and death statistics. No impelling motive is involved (such as the maintenance of public health) which might persuade local officials to comply. The records are kept by different branches of government (county and municipal clerks, and clerks of courts, for instance), and in many cases the levels of efficiency, competence, and devotion to public welfare are low because the officials are appointed on the basis of political rather than professional qualifications. Also, in some areas, workers in the judicial branches of government seem to resent having to report statistics through their local health departments, which, in turn, lack the legal power to force compliance.

As of 1955, a count of the marriages performed in every county was available for only 33 states. For 10 additional states, information was available concerning the number of marriage licenses issued (which usually tends to exceed the number of marriages by 1 to 3 percent or more). In 11 states there were no central files of marriage and divorce records; here data were collected by means of special surveys sponsored by state registrars of vital statistics. It is necessary to try to remedy gaps, inadequacies, and known errors in the data by use of a variety of estimates and adjustments. Under these conditions the data can be only approximate and suggestive, rather than precise. The total number of marriages

be measured and correlated with other demographic events and with socio-economic variables. Each year during the 1950 to 1960 decade, about 1,550,000 marriages and 380,000 divorces occurred in the United States. The National Office of Vital Statistics, whose duty it is to assemble information on marriage and divorce from each of the 48 states, publishes an annual summary which includes data concerning certain characteristics of the brides and grooms. A "crude marriage rate" and a "crude divorce rate"--the number of marriages or divorces per 1,000 total population as of midyear--are the official marriage and divorce rates published by the National Office of Vital Statistics. Table 10-20 reports estimates of the number of marriages and divorces, accompanied by crude rates, which have taken place from 1870 to 1958. Figure 10-6 illustrates the annual fluctuations that have occurred during that time. The general picture indicates a steady rise during the period, the attainment of an all-time peak in 1946, and a decline from 1946 to the present. Toward the close of the 1950 to 1960 decade, an annual crude marriage rate of 9.3 and a crude divorce rate of 2.3 per 1,000 total population were considered normal.

The chief value of the crude rates mentioned above has been said to lie in the fact that they reflect year-to-year changes, since age composition cannot change greatly within the short periods involved. A close examination of the data in Table 10-20 and Figure 10-6 shows that there is much year-to-year variation both in the numbers of marriages and divorces and in the rates at which they occur. In general, marriage rates rise dur-

---

and divorces, and the rates of marriage and divorce, which are published are actually only estimates. Experts at the National Office of Vital Statistics are forced to guess at the number of marriages that occurred among populations for which there are no data, and to adjust the reported data according to known deficiencies. The poor statistics on marriage and divorce in the United States contrast sharply with the excellent data available in several European nations. As poor as they are, the statistics which are available at present are of much higher quality than those of only a few years ago.

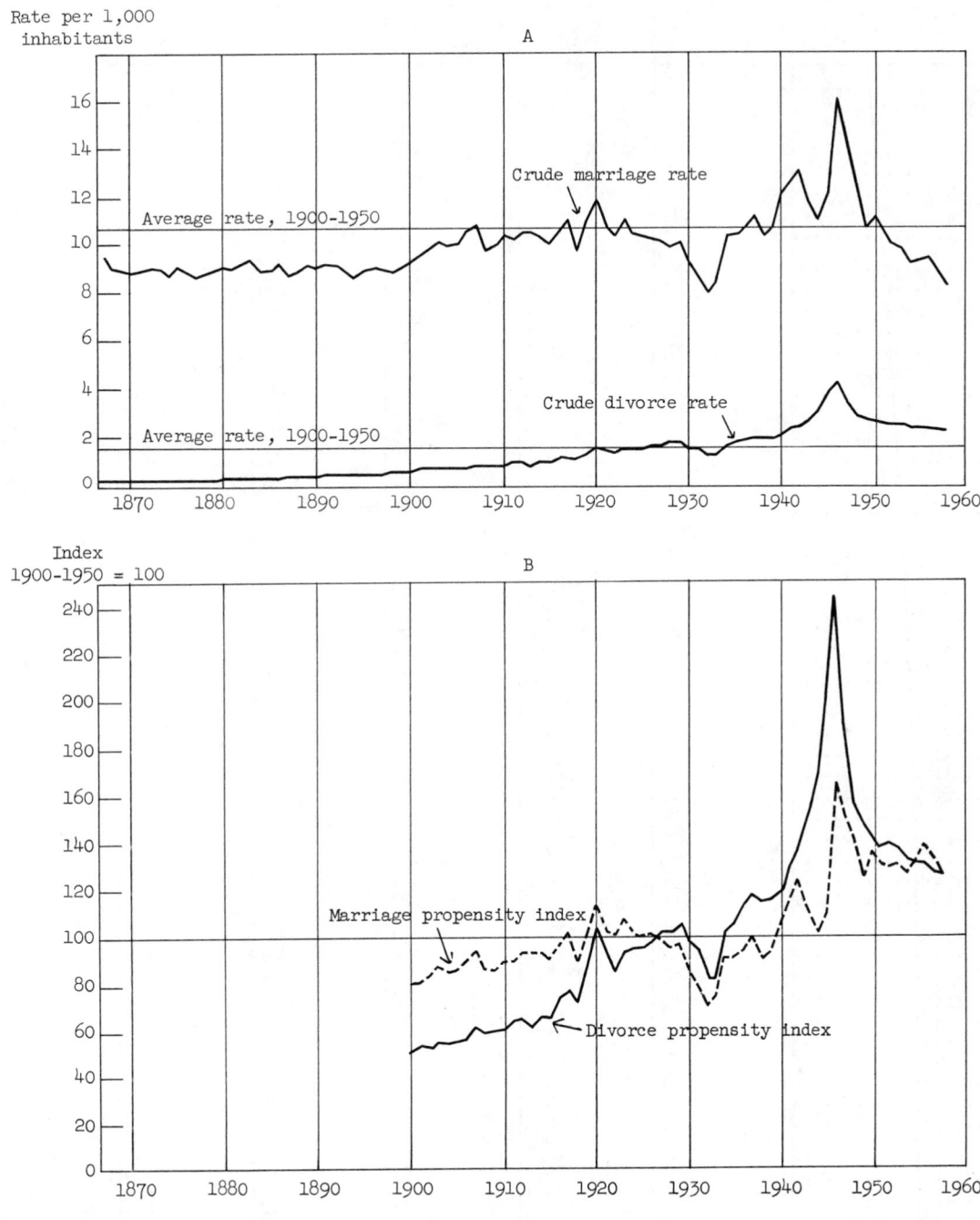

FIGURE 10-6. CRUDE MARRIAGE AND DIVORCE RATES, 1867-1957 AND MARRIAGE
AND DIVORCE PROPENSITY INDEXES, 1890-1957

Table 10-20.—NUMBER OF MARRIAGES AND DIVORCES, CRUDE MARRIAGE AND DIVORCE RATES, AND PROPENSITY INDEXES FOR MARRIAGE AND DIVORCE: 1870 TO 1958

Year	Marriages			Divorces		
	Number (000)	Crude rate per 1,000	Propensity index	Number (000)	Crude rate per 1,000	Propensity index
1958 (estimated).........	1,438	8.3	127	376	2.2	127
1957 (provisional).......	1,516	8.9	134	378	2.2	128
1956.....................	1,585	9.4	139	382	2.3	132
1955.....................	1,531	9.3	133	377	2.3	132
1954.....................	1,490	9.2	128	379	2.4	134
1953.....................	1,546	9.8	132	390	2.5	138
1952.....................	1,539	9.9	130	392	2.5	140
1951.....................	1,595	10.4	132	381	2.5	138
1950.....................	1,667	11.1	136	385	2.6	142
1949.....................	1,580	10.6	125	397	2.7	148
1948.....................	1,811	12.4	142	408	2.8	155
1947.....................	1,992	13.9	151	483	3.4	189
1946.....................	2,291	16.4	167	610	4.3	244
1945.....................	1,613	12.2	112	485	3.5	201
1944.....................	1,452	10.9	101	400	2.9	167
1943.....................	1,577	11.7	111	359	2.6	152
1942.....................	1,772	13.2	125	321	2.4	138
1941.....................	1,696	12.7	117	293	2.2	129
1940.....................	1,596	12.1	108	264	2.0	119
1939.....................	1,404	10.7	95	251	1.9	116
1938.....................	1,331	10.3	90	244	1.9	115
1937.....................	1,451	11.3	100	249	1.9	118
1936.....................	1,369	10.7	94	236	1.8	114
1935.....................	1,327	10.4	92	218	1.7	107
1934.....................	1,302	10.3	91	204	1.6	101
1933.....................	1,098	8.7	77	165	1.3	83
1932.....................	982	7.9	71	164	1.3	83
1931.....................	1,061	8.6	79	188	1.5	94
1930.....................	1,127	9.2	86	196	1.6	99
1929.....................	1,233	10.1	97	206	1.7	106
1928.....................	1,182	9.8	95	200	1.7	104
1927.....................	1,201	10.1	99	196	1.6	103
1926.....................	1,203	10.2	101	185	1.6	99
1925.....................	1,188	10.3	100	175	1.5	96
1924.....................	1,185	10.4	102	171	1.5	96
1923.....................	1,230	11.0	108	165	1.5	93
1922.....................	1,134	10.3	100	149	1.4	86
1921.....................	1,164	10.7	103	160	1.5	94
1920.....................	1,274	12.0	114	171	1.6	104
1919.....................	1,150	11.0	102	142	1.3	89
1918.....................	1,000	9.7	89	116	1.1	73
1917.....................	1,144	11.1	103	122	1.2	78
1916.....................	1,076	10.6	97	114	1.1	74
1915.....................	1,008	10.0	91	104	1.0	68
1914.....................	1,025	10.3	94	101	1.0	68
1913.....................	1,021	10.5	94	91	0.9	63
1912.....................	1,005	10.5	94	94	1.0	67
1911.....................	955	10.2	90	89	1.0	65
1910.....................	948	10.3	90	83	0.9	62
1909.....................	897	9.9	87	80	0.9	61
1908.....................	857	9.7	87	77	0.9	60
1907.....................	937	10.8	95	77	0.9	62
1906.....................	895	10.5	91	72	0.8	58
1905.....................	842	10.0	87	68	0.8	57
1904.....................	815	9.9	86	66	0.8	57
1903.....................	818	10.1	88	65	0.8	57
1902.....................	776	9.8	85	61	0.8	55
1901.....................	742	9.6	83	61	0.8	56

Table 10-20.—NUMBER OF MARRIAGES AND DIVORCES, CRUDE MARRIAGE AND DIVORCE RATES, AND PROPENSITY INDEXES
FOR MARRIAGE AND DIVORCE: 1870 TO 1958-Continued

Year	Marriages			Divorces		
	Number (000)	Crude rate per 1,000	Propensity index	Number (000)	Crude rate per 1,000	Propensity index
1900......................	709	9.3	81	56	0.7	53
1895......................	620	8.9	...	40	0.6	...
1890......................	570	9.0	...	33	0.5	...
1885......................	507	8.9	...	23	0.4	...
1880......................	453	9.0	...	20	0.4	...
1875......................	409	9.1	...	14	0.3	...
1870......................	352	8.8	...	11	0.3	...

Source: Vital Statistics of the United States: 1950, Vol. I, Tables 5.01 and 5.08; also annal reports in this series 1951 to 1956. Data for 1957 and 1958 based upon preliminary estimates from a sample.

ing times of increasing economic prosperity and fall during periods of economic decline. The lowest crude marriage rate on record is that of 1932, a year of great financial and economic panic. Wars also have affected the marriage rate markedly. Mobilization for defense has tended to cause a rise in marriages, followed by a drop when the men were shipped to combat centers and, hence, were no longer available for marriage. As the men returned and were demobilized, marriage rates rose sharply. This kind of cycle occurred during World War I (1916-1920), again during World War II (1939-1946) and, though fewer people were involved, at the time of the Korean conflict (1950).

Crude divorce rates have tended to rise over the years; their annual fluctuations, though showing a slight lag, have roughly paralleled those of the marriage rate. Since a certain proportion of each year's marriages terminates in divorce, there is a rise in the number of divorces following a rise in the number of marriages. The conditions that seem to encourage high marriage rates seem also to favor an increase in divorce; poor economic conditions appear to discourage divorce as well as marriage, while unusually prosperous times seem to cause an increase in both. The greatest fluctuations, however, are associated with wars and with postwar demobilization. Immediately after both World War I and World War II and, apparently, even after the Civil War the divorce rate increased sharply, perhaps reflecting the hastiness with which many marriages had been entered

into, and the results of prolonged separation. The peak rate of 4.3, reached in 1946, was almost 75 percent above the level of about 2.5 at which the rate has remained since 1950. The fact that the divorce rate has been about 70 percent higher since 1950 than it was during the 1920's seems to indicate that as marriage has become more popular, it has also become less durable.

The divorce rate seems to have begun to rise about 1875 (before that time it had been low, remaining on a plateau and fluctuating little). The upward trend became slowly but steadily more pronounced during the "gay nineties" and the first decade of the twentieth century. After reaching a post-World War peak in 1920, and then subsiding for a year, the divorce rate climbed at an even faster rate. It dipped sharply during the early depression years, but by 1935 it was as high as it had been before the depression. The rate continued to climb until it reached another postwar peak in 1946.

Marriage and divorce are influenced by factors other than economic conditions and wars, however. During the years 1923 to 1929, which witnessed such a great rise in the nation's prosperity, the marriage rate declined--perhaps because the attitudinal climate of the "roaring twenties" made marriage less appealing. It should also be noted that the marriage rate recovered, and resumed its long-term trend, several years before the economic depression of the 1930's ended. Apparently, couples will postpone marriage only for a limited number of months or years because of economic hardship, and then will marry despite unfavorable economic conditions. A similar pattern appears to be followed with respect to divorce.

General Marriage and Divorce Rates and Indexes. The crude marriage and divorce rates cited above are completely unreliable as data with which to chart long-run trends, and in recent years they have become very inadequate even as guides to the significance of short-run changes. Their major shortcoming is that the base on which the rates are calculated includes many millions of children and other people who are not eligible to marry or to divorce. Actually, the only persons who are "exposed" to the possibility of marriage are those who are single, widowed, or divorced; and, even in these categories, comparatively few persons marry after age 55. By the same token, only those who are married are "exposed" to the possibility of divorce, and comparatively few divorces occur after age 55. A valid general rate, therefore, could be one based upon the following principle.

General marriage rate =
$$\frac{\text{Number of marriages of females aged 18 to 54 that occurred during a period}}{\text{Number of single, widowed, or divorced females aged 18 to 54 years at the midpoint of that period}}$$

General divorce rate =
$$\frac{\text{Number of divorces of females aged 18 to 54 that occurred during a period}}{\text{Number of married females aged 18 to 54 years at the midpoint of that period}}$$

Since all but a small fraction of marriages, and almost all divorces, occur within these ages, the rates are fairly reliable (but not exact) measures of the probability that an unmarried woman aged 18 to 54 will marry, or that a married woman of this age will get divorced, in a given year. Since complete marriage and divorce data tabulated by age of bride or of wife are not available even now, it is not possible to compute precisely the number

of women occupying these statuses. A rough approximation of the general marriage rate may be calculated by placing all marriages and all divorces in the numerators of the formulas given above. This method results in a slight exaggeration of the rates, but since the exaggeration tends to be constant from year to year it does not reduce the usefulness of the rates with respect to the study of trends. Such a procedure has been followed in preparing the "propensity indexes." The use of data from the decennial censuses, and also from the annual estimates of the number of marriages, made it possible to estimate the denominators which were needed to establish the above rates (the number of married and not married persons) for each year from 1900 to 1958. By dividing these denominators into the total number of marriages and divorces that were estimated to have occurred, a set of quasi-general marriage and divorce rates was established. Finally, using the statistics computed from marriage and divorce rates for the half-century 1900 to 1950 as a base of 100, an index value of marriage propensity and of divorce propensity has been calculated, and is reported in Table 10-20 and Figure 10-6.[6] These indexes are sensitive measures of the relative variation, from year to year, in the probability of an unmarried person marrying and of a married person obtaining a divorce.

---

[6] The procedure for making these estimates was as follows. Starting at each decennial census with the number of not-married women (single, widowed, divorced) 18 to 54 years of age, the estimated number of women who reached the age of 18 during each year of the following decade was added, the number of marriages during each year was subtracted, the number of divorces during each year was added, and the estimated number of women who reached age 55 during each year while still not married was subtracted. By this process it was possible to estimate the number of women aged 18 to 54 who were eligible to marry on July 1 of each year--assuming, for the purposes of this calculation, that no deaths had occurred. If these calculations are begun at a given census (and if all the statistics were absolutely complete and accurate), then at the subsequent decennial census the actual census count of not-married women aged 18 to 54 will exceed our estimate by a number equal to the number of not-married women aged 18 to 54 who died during this 10-year period. By comparing the

The picture presented by these more refined measures is very different in several respects from that indicated by the crude rates, and reveals in the following ways the weaknesses of the latter rates:

(a) The crude marriage rate implies that there has been a decline in the propensity to marry since 1950, whereas the marriage propensity index indicates that this propensity has remained on a plateau, making a dip in each of the recession years 1954 and 1957-58.

(b) The crude marriage rate at the present time is about equal to what it was in 1900, namely 9.3 percent. According to the marriage propensity index, however, the probability that unmarried persons would marry within one year was 70

percent greater in 1956 than in 1900. The difference between the crude marriage rate and the marriage propensity index is due to the fact that the "supply" of eligible marriage partners is now much smaller, in comparison with the size of the population, than it was before the "marriage boom." Stated another way, including in the base of the crude marriage rate all of the babies added by the recent baby boom gives the rate a downward bias that does not necessarily reflect actual trends.

(c) The crude divorce rate is now roughly three times as high as it was in 1900, but the divorce propensity index is now only a little more than twice as high as it was in 1900. Thus, the rate at which marriages dissolve has not risen as much as the crude rate has implied.

(d) The known weaknesses of the divorce rate have caused disputes as to whether the incidence of divorce has increased, decreased, or remained the same since 1950. The divorce propensity index suggests that it remained about the same from 1953 to 1954, and that it has declined slowly since 1954.

The radical change which has taken place in the age composition of the population in recent years, combined with the great increases in the proportion who are married, have made the crude rates a most unsatisfactory measure, even for the charting of year-to-year changes.

The economic recession of 1957 to 1958 affected the probabilities of persons marrying and getting divorced, but not nearly as strongly as the crude rates would suggest. However, the unmistakably depressing effect of this fairly severe economic reversal may be regarded as rather clear evi-

---

Footnote 6 continued

number of not-married women aged 18 to 54 who are enumerated at the subsequent census with the number estimated by the above "bookkeeping" procedure, a total discrepancy (due to deaths and to errors in the data) for the decade was measured. This discrepancy was then distributed proportionately throughout the years of the decade. Subtracting the adjustment for each year from the number of not-married women estimated by the "bookkeeping" process makes it possible to obtain an estimate of the number of not-married women living on July 1 of each calendar year. This estimate is completely consistent with the count for each census. Consequently, it is an appropriate denominator for use in computing a "probability of marriage" index. Estimates for the years since 1950 were made by applying a correction factor, arrived at by extrapolating the trend exhibited by the correction factor in the preceding decades.

The number of married women living each year was obtained by subtracting the estimated number of not-married women, obtained by the process just described, from the total number of women aged 18 to 54 on July 1 of that year. This procedure provides the denominator for a probability of divorce measure.

The procedure contains a "built-in" correction for errors in census counting, for underregistration, and for other inconsistencies in the data. In spite of the fact that it is only a rough approximation (it would have been possible to use a much more refined process of aging forward not-married women of each age group), it is sufficiently precise to reveal a generally correct picture of the changes that have taken place and of the annual fluctuations in the probability that an unmarried woman will marry and that a married woman will get divorced; in each case the calculation was restricted to the age group 18 to 54 years of age.

Note: The National Office of Vital Statistics publishes marriage rates per 1,000 unmarried female population 15 years of age and over and divorce rates per 1,000 female population 15 years of age and over from 1920 to date. These rates are similar to the ones computed here, but still includes much "unexposed" population. A similar marriage rate, based only on women 15 to 44 years of age has been published for years since 1940. It includes some unexposed population at the younger ages and excludes much exposed population at the upper ages.

dence that the "new" marriage patterns which have prevailed since 1940 are based on a relatively high level of economic prosperity.

FIRST MARRIAGE AND REMARRIAGE

Only about 70 percent of the marriages that occur are first marriages for both bride and groom. In all other cases, one or both of the partners have been married previously. Table 10-21, based on a tabulation of marriage returns for 25 states in 1956, shows that among both males and females only about 76 to 77 percent of all marriages are

Table 10-21.—PREVIOUS MARITAL STATUS OF BRIDE, BY PREVIOUS MARITAL STATUS OF GROOM: TOTAL OF 25 REPORTING STATES, 1956

Previous marital status of groom	Total	Previous marital status of bride			
		Single	Widowed	Divorced	Not stated
Total.....	100.0	76.2	6.2	15.3	2.3
Single........	77.1	69.1	1.6	6.2	0.1
Widowed.......	5.5	1.3	2.7	1.5	0.1
Divorced.......	15.1	5.7	1.8	7.4	0.2
Not stated.....	2.3	0.1	0.1	0.2	2.0

Source: National Office of Vital Statistics, _Vital Statistics of the United States, 1956_.

first marriages. A summary of the previous marital status of marriage partners may be made as follows:

	Percent
First marriage for both bride and groom....	69
First marriage for bride, not for groom....	7
First marriage for groom, not for bride....	8
Remarriage for both bride and groom........	13
Previous marital status not reported.......	2
Total..........................	100

It is important to realize the fact that widows and divorcees have been much more prone to remarry since World War II than they were previously. Among those members of the population who remarry, the ratio of divorced persons to widows is almost 3 to 1. Since this ratio is much higher than that found among the general population, it must be concluded that divorced persons are much more inclined to remarry than widowed

persons. A major element in this differential, of course, is the fact that divorced persons are considerably younger than widowed persons. There appears to be a tendency for previously married persons to marry persons who also have been married before. In fact, there seems to be a tendency for widowed persons to marry widowed persons, and for divorced persons to marry divorced persons.

AGE AT MARRIAGE

Table 10-22 reports the marriage rates that prevailed in 1950 in each of several age groups, for brides and grooms separately. The rates for first marriages and for remarriages are given separately. In computing these age-specific marriage rates, at each age the unmarried population has been used as the denominator. Similarly, the rates of first marriage have been based on the single (never married) population, while the rates of remarriage have been based on the widowed and divorced population. In the United States it has been possible to make these computations only in census years, when data from the census can be combined with data concerning marriages performed. In 1950, however, data concerning only 15 states were available for this tabulation. The rates reported are probably not exactly the same as the national rates, but the age patterns are probably very similar to the national age patterns. For this reason the table is worth careful study.

According to the estimates of Table 10-22, the rates for first marriages begin low, climb quickly to reach a peak in the years 20 to 24, and then decline gradually with advancing age. The peak rate was reached much earlier in the case of females than in the case of males. Between the ages of 20 and 24, the probability that a single woman would marry within a year was greater than 1 in 4. But after they passed their twenties, single women had rates which were much lower than those of men, and which declined more swiftly. Between 40 and 44 years of age, the probability of a single woman marrying during a one-year period was only 1/10

Table 10-22.—MARRIAGE RATES PER 1,000 PERSONS EXPOSED BY AGE OF BRIDE AND GROOM AT FIRST MARRIAGE: 15 REPORTING STATES, 1950[1]

Age	All marriages		First marriage		Remarriages	
	Bride	Groom	Bride	Groom	Bride	Groom
15 years and over........	82.7	87.1	114.9	85.9	42.2	90.9
15 to 19 years...............	102.6	21.6	100.6	21.5	448.4	40.4
20 to 24 years...............	277.2	190.8	267.5	187.5	401.3	335.5
25 to 29 years...............	196.2	204.9	167.2	188.0	286.3	372.2
30 to 34 years...............	129.7	156.5	89.5	120.0	198.3	324.5
35 to 39 years...............	85.7	113.5	49.2	68.4	129.0	245.5
40 to 44 years...............	56.2	86.1	26.1	40.9	82.5	178.7
45 to 49 years...............	36.5	65.0	16.0	25.0	48.5	128.4
50 to 54 years...............	21.8	49.1	8.2	15.2	27.3	88.5
55 and over.................	5.0	18.8	2.4	5.0	5.5	25.2

[1]Rates for all marriages based on population aged 15 years and over; for first marriages or single (never married) population; for remarriages, or widowed and divorced population. Marriages refer to state of occurrence.

Source: National Office of Vital Statistics, Vital Statistics of the United States: 1950, Vol I, Table 5.05, page 69.

as great as at ages 20 to 24, and at ages beyond 55 the probabilities were less than 1/100 as great.

Before age 25 the rates for males were well below those for females, but at ages older than this they were above those for females. Beyond age 45, single men married at a rate nearly twice as high as that of single women.

Rates of remarriage are not very trustworthy before age 25, since the number of previously married persons is small and may be grossly misstated. Table 10-22 shows that the rate of remarriage is higher for females than for males at the younger ages, but that after age 25 it is much higher for males. As a group, previously married men remarry at a rate that is more than twice as high as that of previously married women. Despite the fact that a very high proportion of remarriages occur after age 30 (see below), the rate of remarriage is at its peak in the twenties, and declines with advancing age. At every age the rate of remarriage is higher, both for men and women, than the rate of first marriage. This implies that once they have entered the married state, both sexes try to remain there. If their marriage is broken they tend to remarry rather promptly.[7]

Remarriage as a Percent of All Marriages, by Age. Remarriage varies directly with the age of the couple. At ages below 20, almost all marriages are first marriages, but at older ages the extent of remarriage becomes progressively greater (see Table 10-23). At age 30, more than one-half of all brides are marrying for the second, or higher order, time. By the time age 45 is reached, more than 75 percent of all marriages are remarriages.

According to Table 10-23, remarriage appears to be a smaller percent of all marriage among the nonwhite population than among the white population. This is true at every age, and the differential is large.

Indirect evidence concerning the extent of remarriage is furnished by Table 10-24, the data in

---

[7] The reader must be warned that the rates of Table 10-22 are illustrative only, because they are for selected states and are based on place of occurrence rather than on place of residence, and hence cannot be accepted as precise estimates of the first marriage rates and remarriage rates. In Chapter 7 of his census monograph American Families, (John Wiley and Sons, 1957), Paul Glick reports first marriage rates and remarriage rates for widowed and divorced persons, by age, sex, color, and other characteristics. These rates were estimated from census data and from special survey materials, and have the same general shape as the curves presented in Figure 10-7, although the rates reported by Glick are lower.

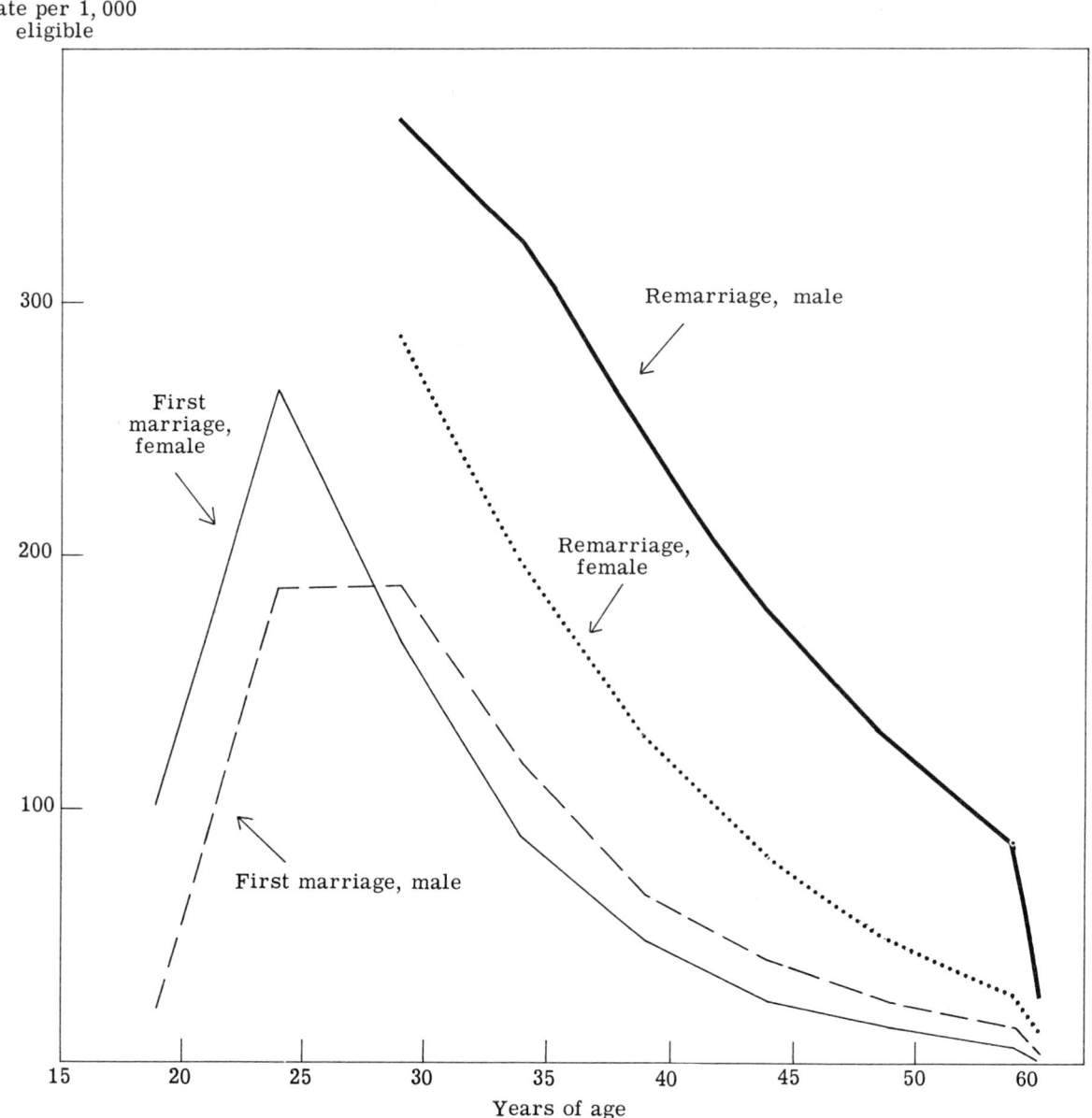

FIGURE 10-7. AGE PROFILE OF MARRIAGE RATES: FIRST MARRIAGE AND REMARRIAGE, BY SEX, AND AGE, 15 REPORTING STATES

which were taken from census materials. An estimated 14 percent of all married women 15 to 59 years of age who were living with their husbands are reported as having been previously married.

More urban women than rural women are reported to have been married before. Table 10-24 also seems to indicate that there has been more remarriage among the nonwhite population than among the white population, which is in direct contradiction to the implication of Table 10-23. There appears to have been a serious misreporting of previous marital status among the nonwhite population, either at the time of marriage registration or at the census. The nature of the error would indicate that most of it is connected with the registration data.

Age at Marriage and Previous Marital Status. The number of times brides and grooms have been married previously varies greatly with age, as shown by Table 10-25. At ages below 19 years, about 95 percent of all marriages consist of first marriages. During the years 20 to 29, first marriages are predominant, but an increased proportion of the total consists of remarriage of divorced

Table 10-23.—PERCENT OF ALL MARRIAGES THAT ARE REMARRIAGES, BY AGE, RACE, AND SEX: 23 REPORTING STATES, 1956

Age	Bride					Groom				
	Total	White	Nonwhite			Total	White	Nonwhite		
			Total	Negro	Other			Total	Negro	Other
Total..............	23.2	23.3	21.9	21.9	21.4	22.0	21.8	22.8	22.9	18.8
Under 15 years..........	0.2	0.3	....	...	...	...	...	...	...	...
15 years.................	0.5	0.6	0.1	0.1	...	...	...	...	...	...
16 years.................	0.5	0.6	0.1	0.1	...	0.1	...	0.8	0.8	...
17 years.................	1.1	1.2	0.5	0.5	...	0.2	0.2	...	...	...
18 years.................	1.9	2.0	0.7	0.7	2.9	0.3	0.3	0.1	0.1	...
19 years.................	3.5	3.7	1.3	1.3	1.1	0.6	0.6	0.5	0.5	2.4
20 years.................	5.2	5.5	3.2	3.2	6.2	1.2	1.3	1.0	1.0	4.1
21 years.................	7.7	8.1	4.9	4.8	12.4	2.2	2.4	2.3	2.4	3.4
22 years.................	12.1	12.8	7.2	.7.2	5.5	3.8	4.0	4.0	3.9	7.9
23 years.................	16.7	17.7	10.8	10.7	11.5	5.7	5.9	6.3	6.3	4.5
24 years.................	22.5	23.5	16.3	16.3	17.0	8.2	8.4			
25 years.................	28.4	29.6	21.1	20.9	28.0	10.9	11.2	8.5	8.5	9.8
26 years.................	34.2	35.9	25.1	25.0	27.8	14.4	14.8	11.9	12.0	2.3
27 years.................	40.4	42.2	30.9	30.8	37.9	18.2	18.7	14.9	15.9	17.1
28 years.................	45.4	47.7	33.9	33.9	37.5	23.9	24.5	19.9	20.0	16.7
29 years.................	49.9	52.4	38.3	38.4	33.3	28.2	29.1	22.4	22.6	12.2
30 years.................	53.7	56.4	41.2	41.3	39.1	32.7	33.6	27.5	27.5	30.0
31 years.................	57.4	59.4	47.7	47.2	77.8	38.2	39.4	31.4	31.3	36.0
32 years.................	60.8	62.8	51.2	51.2	53.8	41.5	42.9	34.0	33.8	44.4
33 years.................	63.9	66.0	53.7	53.9	33.3	45.0	46.6	37.3	37.1	46.2
34 years.................	65.5	67.4	56.8	56.9	46.2	48.1	49.8	39.5	39.9	23.8
35 years.................	68.6	70.9	57.1	57.1	58.3	52.5	54.2	44.0	44.0	50.0
36 years.................	69.5	72.3	56.2	55.8	83.3	55.8	51.9	46.1	46.6	8.3
37 years.................	72.2	74.7	61.5	61.5	58.3	58.5	59.9	53.0	52.0	57.1
38 years.................	73.2	75.6	62.6	62.8	53.8	60.0	62.0	50.7	50.4	75.0
39 years.................	75.9	78.4	63.1	62.8	100.0	64.4	65.8	56.5	56.4	60.0
40 years.................	75.3	77.0	67.4	67.4	66.7	65.4	67.0	57.3	57.3	55.6
41 years.................	78.4	79.8	70.5	70.4	80.0	68.0	70.3	56.9	56.7	100.0
42 years.................	78.9	80.3	71.2	71.2	75.0	68.3	69.7	62.4	62.6	40.0
43 years.................	80.6	82.0	73.5	73.3	100.0	70.9	72.3	64.0	63.9	80.0
44 years.................	80.8	82.1	73.9	73.8	100.0	73.2	74.4	67.5	67.6	60.0
45 to 49 years..........	82.3	83.7	75.1	75.1	72.7	76.2	77.3	71.6	71.6	68.4
50 to 54 years..........	86.5	87.4	80.9	81.0	66.7	81.4	82.7	75.1	75.1	78.6
55 to 59 years..........	89.0	89.4	86.5	86.4	100.0	84.6	85.5	80.2	80.1	88.9
60 to 64 years..........	90.2	90.5	88.2	88.0	100.0	89.0	89.9	83.8	83.8	85.7
65 to 69 years..........	92.7	93.4	86.7	86.6	100.0	91.4	92.5	85.8	85.8	75.0
70 to 74 years..........	93.7	94.2	89.0	88.9	100.0	94.0	94.8	89.1	89.4	60.0
75 years and over........	95.2	96.0	87.5	87.5	...	95.9	96.4	96.5	93.2	100.0
Not stated..............	48.6	56.6	23.2	23.2	...	47.4	53.1	26.0	25.2	60.0

Source: National Office of Vital Statistics, *Vital Statistics of the United States, 1956.*

Table 10-24.—PERCENT OF WOMEN 15 TO 59 YEARS OLD
MARRIED AND HUSBAND PRESENT WHO HAVE MARRIED
MORE THAN ONCE, BY COLOR AND AGE AT MARRIAGE;
MEDIAN AGE AT MARRIAGE

Age at last marriage	All races			Nonwhite		
	Total	Urban and rural non-farm	Rural farm	Total	Urban and rural non-farm	Rural farm
Total.....	13.8	14.2	11.7	24.0	24.7	20.9
14 to 19 yrs...	4.7	4.7	5.0	6.8	6.7	7.0
20 to 24 yrs...	8.3	8.4	8.0	16.0	15.7	17.6
25 to 29 yrs...	19.2	19.2	18.7	34.2	33.9	35.8
30 to 34 yrs...	35.7	36.4	30.3	47.4	48.6	41.6
35 to 59 yrs...	63.5	64.0	59.7	75.4	76.0	71.4
Median age at marriage......	21.8	21.9	20.8	21.7	22.0	20.4
Married once.	20.9	21.0	20.0	20.1	20.2	19.3
Married more than once...	27.8	28.0	26.4	29.1	29.5	27.2

Source: U.S. Bureau of the Census, U.S. Census of
Population: 1930, Vol. IV, Special Reports, Part 2,
Chapter E, Duration of Current Marital Status,
Table 1.

persons. By age 30 to 34 among women, and age
35 to 39 among men, the majority of marriages
are remarriages, and the great bulk of these are
remarriages of divorced persons. However, the
remarriage of widowed persons is a much more
frequent occurrence during the age span 30 to 44,
and by age 40 to 44 among women and age 50 to 54
among men it surpasses first marriages in importance. Among persons of both sexes who are
aged 60 or more, the remarriage of widowed persons accounts for a very great majority of the few
marriages that occur. At age 75 and over, 88
percent of all marriages among women and 82
percent of all marriages among men are remarriages of widowed persons.

At each age beyond age 45, a much higher proportion of the men who remarry have been divorced than is the case among women. On the
other hand, a much larger share of the women who
remarry after age 45 have been widowed.

Number of Times Married, by Age at Marriage.
One might want to know what proportions, among
the population that marries, are marrying for the
first, second, third, etc. time. Table 10-26 gives
approximate answers to this question with respect
to 16 reporting states, by means of statistics for
1956, by age. For one of the spouses involved,
roughly 18 percent of all marriages are second
marriages, 2.7 percent of all marriages are third
marriages, and 0.4 percent of all marriages are
fourth marriages. These proportions vary greatly
with age. Among women, first marriages predominate until age 31, at which age the number of
second marriages is larger than the number of
first marriages. Beyond age 37 for women, and
age 44 for men, more than 10 percent of all marriages are third marriages. Fourth marriages
become quite frequent beyond age 50; at age 60 to
64, 4.1 percent of brides and 3.2 percent of
grooms are marrying for the fourth or more time.

Age Distribution of Brides and Grooms. The
nature of the age patterns described above means
that the age distribution of brides and grooms at
the time of marriage varies with previous marital
status. The age distribution of marriage partners,
by previous marital status, is reported for 23
states in Table 10-27.

(a) First marriages are highly concentrated in the very young ages. Almost 75 percent
of brides who are marrying for the first time are
15 to 24 years of age, and among grooms about the
same proportion are 20 to 29 years of age. Comparatively few first marriages occur after age 40,
largely because at these ages all but a very small
fraction of the population has already married.

(b) Remarriages are distributed rather
widely among all ages above 20. In general, remarriages of divorced persons tend to be concentrated in the years between 20 and 44 for brides,
and 20 to 49 for grooms. On the other hand, widowed persons tend to remarry later--between the
ages of 30 to 64 for women and 40 to 74 for men.

Further insight into the relationships that exist
between previous marital status and age at marriage may be obtained from Table 10-28, in which
the median ages of bride and groom at time of
marriage are reported by previous marital status
and by number of present marriage. According to
this table the average bride who is marrying for

Table 10-25.—PREVIOUS MARITAL STATUS OF BRIDES AND GROOMS AT MARRIAGE, BY AGE: 19 REPORTING STATES, 1953

Age	Brides					Grooms				
	Total	Single	Widowed	Di-vorced	Not stated	Total	Single	Widowed	Di-vorced	Not stated
Total...............	100.0	73.4	6.8	16.7	3.1	100.0	74.5	6.0	16.4	3.1
Under 19 years...........	100.0	93.8	0.1	1.9	4.2	100.0	94.8	...	0.4	4.8
20 to 24 years...........	100.0	87.1	0.8	9.5	2.6	100.0	93.2	0.1	3.4	3.3
25 to 29 years...........	100.0	62.3	4.2	31.4	2.1	100.0	80.7	1.0	15.9	2.4
30 to 34 years...........	100.0	41.6	9.8	46.9	1.7	100.0	60.0	3.3	34.5	2.2
35 to 39 years...........	100 0	30.0	16.7	51.7	1.6	100.0	43.2	7.3	47.7	1.8
40 to 44 years...........	100.0	22.7	26.5	48.8	2.0	100.0	32.4	12.8	52.8	2.0
45 to 49 years...........	100.0	17.8	38.6	41.9	1.7	100.0	24.2	21.4	52.4	2.0
50 to 54 years...........	100.0	12.5	52.1	33.4	2.0	100.0	18.4	33.3	46.3	2.0
55 to 59 years...........	100.0	10.0	62.6	25.2	2.2	100.0	13.6	49.1	35.5	1.8
60 to 64 years...........	100.0	9.1	73.0	15.7	2.2	100.0	10.1	62.2	25.7	2.0
65 to 69 years...........	100.0	6.9	78.2	13.0	1.9	100.0	7.3	70.6	20.0	2.1
70 to 74 years...........	100.0	5.4	83.8	8.7	2.1	100.0	4.4	78.8	14.9	1.9
75 years and over........	100.0	5.9	87.8	4.4	1.9	100.0	3.3	82.2	12.4	2.1

Source: National Office of Vital Statistics, Vital Statistics of the United States, 1953, Vol I, Table 7, page 60-61.

the first time is 20.5 years of age and her husband is 2.8 years older (23.3 years). But the bride who has been divorced and is remarrying is 11 years older, and the groom is 12.3 years older, than the members of the first-marriage couple. A typical previously-widowed bride is 27 years older, and a previously-widowed groom is 33 years older, than the bride and groom in the first-marriage couple. Persons marrying for the third, fourth, etc., time are considerably older, on the average, than those who are being married for the second time.

SEX DIFFERENCES IN AGE AT MARRIAGE

To say that, on the average, the groom tends to be two years older than the bride, is to make a very crude generalization. The age difference between the marriage partners varies according to the age group concerned and also according to whether the marriage is a first marriage or a remarriage. Table 10-29 reports the median age of spouse for brides and grooms of various ages, in those cases involving a first marriage for both partners. This table indicates that when a very

young girl marries, she tends to marry a man who is four or five years older than she is. Older brides tend to marry men more nearly their own age; at about age 30 to 35 the median age of brides is only about 1 year lower than the median age of their husbands. Among grooms, exactly the reverse situation holds: when a very young man marries, his bride tends to be about the same age, and men who marry at older ages tend to select brides who are considerably younger than they. The older the groom, the greater the age differential becomes. For example, men who are marrying for the first time at 34 years of age, and who are marrying women who also are marrying for the first time, tend to select brides who are 6 years younger than they are.

Many of the differences in age distribution between marriage partners are hidden by Table 10-29, which deals only with medians. Much of the missing information is provided by Table 10-30, in which the age of the groom is reported according to how many years older or younger he is than his bride. The table is divided into two sections. Section A compares the ages of brides and grooms in marriages which are first marriages for both partners. Section B compares the

Table 10-26.—NUMBER OF PRESENT MARRIAGE OF BRIDE AND GROOM, BY AGE: 16 REPORTING STATES, 1956

| Age | Number of present marriage | | | | | | | | | |
| | Bride | | | | | Groom | | | | |
	Total	First	Second	Third	Fourth or more	Total	First	Second	Third	Fourth or more
Total...............	100.0	78.9	18.1	2.7	0.4	100.0	79.9	17.3	2.4	0.4
Under 15 years...........	100.0	99.7	0.3	...	...	100.0	100.0	...	...	...
15 years.................	100.0	99.4	0.5	...	...	100.0	100.0	...	...	...
16 years.................	100.0	99.5	0.5	...	...	100.0	100.0	...	...	...
17 years.................	100.0	99.0	1.0	...	...	100.0	99.8	0.2	...	...
18 years.................	100.0	98.4	1.6	...	...	100.0	99.7	0.3	...	...
19 years.................	100.0	97.0	2.9	0.1	...	100.0	99.4	0.6	...	...
20 years.................	100.0	95.6	4.3	0.1	...	100.0	99.0	1.0	...	...
21 years.................	100.0	93.4	6.4	0.2	...	100.0	97.9	2.0	...	...
22 years.................	100.0	89.3	10.1	0.6	...	100.0	96.7	3.2	0.1	...
23 years.................	100.0	85.3	13.9	0.7	...	100.0	94.9	4.9	0.1	...
24 years.................	100.0	79.7	19.2	1.1	0.1	100.0	92.7	7.1	0.2	...
25 years.................	100.0	74.3	23.6	1.9	0.2	100.0	90.2	9.5	0.3	...
26 years.................	100.0	68.7	28.9	2.2	0.2	100.0	87.0	12.4	0.5	...
27 years.................	100.0	63.6	33.1	3.1	0.3	100.0	83.3	16.0	0.8	...
28 years.................	100.0	57.6	38.1	3.9	0.5	100.0	78.2	20.2	1.5	0.1
29 years.................	100.0	52.9	42.0	4.4	0.7	100.0	73.6	24.8	1.5	0.2
30 years.................	100.0	48.4	45.6	5.4	0.6	100.0	69.8	27.6	2.4	0.2
31 years.................	100.0	45.2	46.9	6.8	1.0	100.0	64.3	31.7	3.7	0.3
32 years.................	100.0	42.6	49.7	6.8	0.9	100.0	60.8	35.3	3.5	0.4
33 years.................	100.0	39.0	52.2	7.9	0.9	100.0	58.4	37.2	4.0	0.5
34 years.................	100.0	37.0	53.2	8.8	1.0	100.0	54.5	39.7	5.1	0.8
35 years.................	100.0	34.1	55.3	9.4	1.2	100.0	50.0	44.1	5.3	0.5
36 years.................	100.0	31.7	57.2	9.9	1.2	100.0	46.0	47.0	6.2	0.8
37 years.................	100.0	29.0	59.2	10.1	1.7	100.0	43.5	48.9	6.6	1.0
38 years.................	100.0	27.7	59.2	11.4	1.7	100.0	42.7	48.8	7.7	0.7
39 years.................	100.0	24.8	61.8	11.4	1.9	100.0	38.6	52.6	7.6	1.1
40 years.................	100.0	25.2	60.7	12.3	1.8	100.0	36.7	54.0	8.2	1.1
41 years.................	100.0	22.8	61.9	13.3	2.0	100.0	34.2	55.2	8.9	1.7
42 years.................	100.0	22.1	62.9	13.5	1.6	100.0	33.1	56.1	9.3	1.5
43 years.................	100.0	19.8	64.8	13.2	2.2	100.0	31.5	57.3	9.6	1.6
44 years.................	100.0	18.8	64.6	14.3	2.3	100.0	27.4	60.1	11.0	1.5
45 to 49 years...........	100.0	17.4	65.6	14.6	2.3	100.0	24.5	62.0	11.8	1.7
50 to 54 years...........	100.0	12.9	67.7	16.2	3.2	100.0	18.4	65.2	13.8	2.6
55 to 59 years...........	100.0	10.4	68.8	18.0	2.8	100.0	14.1	68.8	14.4	2.7
60 to 64 years...........	100.0	7.7	69.7	18.5	4.1	100.0	9.7	70.1	17.1	3.2
65 to 69 years...........	100.0	6.2	69.5	20.1	4.2	100.0	7.1	71.3	18.4	3.3
70 to 74 years...........	100.0	5.1	67.7	22.7	4.4	100.0	4.5	73.1	18.1	4.3
75 years and over........	100.0	4.6	56.5	32.7	6.2	100.0	2.3	66.3	25.0	6.5
Not stated...............	100.0	47.6	45.7	6.1	0.6	100.0	45.3	46.0	8.8	...

Source: National Office of Vital Statistics, Vital Statistics of the United States, 1956.

ages of brides and grooms whose marriages involve a remarriage for one or both partners.

The highest degree of similarity between the ages of bride and groom at first marriage is found among brides who marry at age 21; among this group 18 percent of the couples are of the same age and in an additional 24 percent the age of the groom is within 1 year, plus or minus, of the bride's age. At ages younger than 20 the groom tends to be considerably older than the bride, while at ages older than 20 the correlation between the ages of bride and groom becomes progressively lower and rather large disparities become much more common. In the case of brides who

Table 10-27.—PERCENTAGE DISTRIBUTION OF MARRIAGES BY AGE OF BRIDE AND OF GROOM, BY PREVIOUS MARITAL STATUS: 23 REPORTING STATES, 1956
(Excludes cases for which age was not stated.)

Age	Total	Previous marital status			
		Single	Widowed	Divorced	Not stated
Bride					
Total.......	100.0	100.0	100.0	100.0	100.0
Under 15 yrs...	0.3	0.4	...	...	0.7
15 to 19 yrs...	35.5	44.4	0.5	4.1	48.0
20 to 24 yrs...	33.7	39.2	3.4	19.2	30.7
25 to 29 yrs...	10.6	8.9	6.2	20.9	7.5
30 to 34 yrs...	5.9	3.3	8.6	17.8	3.4
35 to 39 yrs...	4.3	1.7	11.0	14.4	2.5
40 to 44 yrs...	3.2	0.9	13.2	10.2	2.3
45 to 49 yrs...	2.4	0.6	14.6	6.7	1.7
50 to 54 yrs...	1.6	0.3	12.9	3.4	1.1
55 to 59 yrs...	1.1	0.2	11.0	1.8	0.7
60 to 64 yrs...	0.8	0.1	8.6	0.9	0.6
65 to 69 yrs...	0.5	...	6.2	0.4	0.4
70 to 74 yrs...	0.2	...	2.7	0.1	0.2
75 and over....	0.1	...	1.1	...	...
Groom					
Total.......	100.0	100.0	100.0	100.0	100.0
Under 15 yrs...	...	...	...	...	...
15 to 19 yrs...	10.5	13.2	...	0.3	15.7
20 to 24 yrs...	43.3	52.7	1.0	10.0	50.5
25 to 29 yrs...	19.8	21.3	2.6	19.3	16.3
30 to 34 yrs...	8.1	6.4	4.4	18.2	5.8
35 to 39 yrs...	5.0	2.8	6.3	15.6	3.0
40 to 44 yrs...	3.6	1.5	8.2	12.8	2.1
45 to 49 yrs...	2.8	0.9	10.9	9.7	2.0
50 to 54 yrs...	2.0	0.5	12.0	6.1	1.2
55 to 59 yrs...	1.6	0.3	13.9	3.8	1.0
60 to 64 yrs...	1.2	0.2	13.5	2.2	0.8
65 to 69 yrs...	1.1	0.1	13.9	1.4	0.8
70 to 74 yrs...	0.6	...	8.0	0.5	0.4
75 and over....	0.3	...	5.3	0.3	0.2

Source: National Office of Vital Statistics, Annual Report, 1956.

are 34 years of age, for example, 3 percent of the grooms are 10 to 14 years younger, and 9 percent are 10 or more years older, than the bride.

When one or both of the parties involved are marrying for a second or third time, the correlation between the ages of bride and groom is much lower than it is when the marriage is a first marriage for both. Among those who remarry, the ages deviate in either direction--the groom may be considerably younger than the bride, or he may be considerably older. Such small correlation as

Table 10-28.—MEDIAN AGE OF BRIDE AND OF GROOM AT MARRIAGE, BY PREVIOUS MARITAL STATUS AND BY NUMBER OF PRESENT MARRIAGE: 1956

(Median age under 45 years computed on data by single years of age; 45 years and over, on data by 5-year age groups.)

Previous marital status and number of present marriage	Bride	Groom
PREVIOUS MARITAL STATUS		
Total: 23 states[1]...........	21.5	24.5
Single....................	20.5	23.3
Widowed..................	47.4	56.7
Divorced.................	31.5	35.6
NUMBER OF PRESENT MARRIAGE		
Total: 16 states[2]..........	21.4	24.2
First.....................	20.4	23.1
Second....................	33.7	38.2
Third.....................	41.1	46.9
Fourth or more............	44.3	51.1

[1]Includes marriages for which previous marital status was not stated.

[2]Includes marriages for which number of present marriage was not stated.

Source: National Office of Vital Statistics, Annual Report, 1956.

Table 10-29.—SPECIFIED AGE OF BRIDE AND OF GROOM BY MEDIAN AGE OF SPOUSE, AT FIRST MARRIAGE OF BOTH: 25 REPORTING STATES, 1956

(Computed on data by single years of age.)

Specified age of bride	Median age of groom	Specified age of groom	Median age of bride
15 years.........	19.7	18 years.........	18.0
16 years.........	20.3	19 years.........	18.5
17 years.........	20.8	20 years.........	18.9
18 years.........	21.4	21 years.........	19.4
19 years.........	21.9	22 years.........	20.2
20 years.........	22.7	23 years.........	20.7
21 years.........	23.3	24 years.........	21.2
22 years.........	24.2	25 years.........	21.7
23 years.........	25.1	26 years.........	22.1
24 years.........	25.8	27 years.........	22.7
25 years.........	26.6	28 years.........	23.3
26 years.........	27.4	29 years.........	24.0
27 years.........	28.1	30 years.........	24.7
28 years.........	29.1	31 years.........	25.5
29 years.........	29.9	32 years.........	26.4
30 years.........	30.8	33 years.........	26.8
31 years.........	31.9	34 years.........	27.9

Source: National Office of Vital Statistics, Annual Report, 1956.

Table 10-30.—(A) AGE OF GROOM IN RELATION TO AGE OF BRIDE: FIRST MARRIAGES, PERCENT DISTRIBUTION (25 STATES REPORTING + 5 STATES ESTIMATED)

Age of bride	Groom younger than bride									Same	Groom older than bride								
	15 years -over	14 to 10 years	9 to 8 years	7 to 6 years	5 years	4 years	3 years	2 years	1 years		1 years	2 years	3 years	4 years	5 years	6 to 7 years	8 to 9 years	10 to 14 years	15 years -over
15 years	...	...	...	...	...	...	...	...	...	0.3	3.6	12.5	20.9	17.8	11.8	20.1	7.9	4.3	0.8
16 years	...	...	...	...	...	...	...	...	...	1.4	6.1	19.4	18.9	13.9	15.8	14.8	5.7	3.3	0.5
17 years	...	...	...	...	...	...	...	...	0.5	4.0	14.7	17.7	16.4	17.0	10.1	12.2	4.4	2.6	0.4
18 years	...	...	...	...	...	...	...	0.1	1.2	10.2	14.8	15.3	21.7	12.3	8.8	9.3	3.7	2.2	0.5
19 years	...	...	...	...	...	...	...	...	0.5	4.3	11.5	15.1	19.8	15.2	11.4	7.9	8.6	3.3	2.2
20 years	...	...	...	...	...	...	0.2	1.5	5.2	12.1	18.9	16.8	13.7	10.4	7.2	8.3	3.1	2.2	0.5
21 years	...	...	...	...	...	0.1	0.7	2.0	5.3	18.3	18.4	15.4	11.9	8.9	6.6	7.1	2.9	2.0	0.5
22 years	...	...	...	...	...	0.4	1.1	3.0	9.5	16.8	16.4	14.1	11.1	8.4	6.0	6.8	3.2	2.5	0.7
23 years	...	...	...	...	0.2	0.7	1.7	5.5	10.3	15.6	15.0	13.4	10.4	7.8	5.6	6.8	3.2	3.0	0.8
24 years	...	...	...	0.2	0.5	1.3	3.9	6.5	10.6	15.4	14.5	11.9	9.4	7.2	4.9	6.3	3.4	3.0	1.0
25 years	...	...	...	0.7	0.8	2.8	4.8	7.3	11.4	14.5	12.8	10.4	8.0	6.5	4.8	6.5	3.7	3.9	1.3
26 years	...	...	0.2	1.1	2.5	3.1	6.2	8.1	10.9	13.4	11.7	9.6	7.9	6.2	4.0	6.3	3.5	4.0	1.4
27 years	...	...	0.5	2.1	2.7	4.3	6.3	8.8	11.2	12.7	10.1	8.5	6.6	5.4	4.7	6.1	4.2	4.4	1.4
28 years	...	0.2	0.5	3.5	3.3	5.4	6.2	8.3	9.9	11.7	9.7	7.9	6.7	5.6	4.1	6.4	3.8	4.8	2.2
29 years	...	0.1	1.5	4.8	3.7	5.4	7.7	8.8	8.8	10.4	8.4	6.8	6.3	5.1	4.0	6.8	4.3	4.6	2.4
30 years	...	0.5	1.7	4.9	4.7	6.6	6.8	7.2	9.3	10.3	8.5	6.6	5.4	5.0	4.6	6.2	4.1	5.6	2.2
31 years	...	1.0	2.3	5.7	4.1	5.2	7.0	7.7	7.9	10.3	8.2	6.4	6.3	5.4	4.1	6.0	4.2	5.6	2.5
32 years	...	2.0	3.4	6.4	4.7	5.8	4.7	6.0	7.8	9.7	6.8	6.8	7.0	5.2	4.3	6.1	4.9	5.6	2.6
33 years	...	2.1	3.2	6.1	4.5	5.3	6.5	6.0	8.7	9.1	6.5	7.9	5.9	4.7	3.9	6.4	4.4	5.4	3.1
34 years	...	3.1	3.8	6.0	5.1	6.3	6.4	6.7	7.5	9.3	8.0	6.0	4.	4.0	3.2	6.8	4.3	5.5	3.2

(B) AGE OF GROOM IN RELATION TO AGE OF BRIDE: REMARRIAGES, PERCENT DISTRIBUTION (30 STATES, ALL MARRIAGES, MINUS 25 + 5 STATES, FIRST MARRIAGES)

Age of bride	Groom younger than bride									Same	Groom older than bride								
	15 years -over	14 to 10 years	9 to 8 years	7 to 6 years	5 years	4 years	3 years	2 years	1 years		1 years	2 years	3 years	4 years	5 years	6 to 7 years	8 to 9 years	10 to 14 years	15 years -over
15 to 19 years	...	...	...	...	...	...	...	0.1	0.1	3.4	2.6	8.4	30.2	10.4	9.3	12.5	8.4	9.5	5.1
20 to 21 years	...	...	...	...	...	0.1	0.4	0.9	0.3	4.1	8.0	5.4	7.1	8.2	7.9	15.2	13.2	17.6	11.5
22 to 24 years	...	...	...	0.1	0.4	0.6	2.0	3.7	6.6	6.2	6.5	6.5	7.0	7.4	6.9	12.0	9.4	14.1	10.8
25 years	...	...	...	0.5	0.7	2.7	4.0	5.9	5.9	6.5	7.8	6.6	6.6	6.0	5.9	10.0	7.6	13.3	9.8
26 years	...	...	0.2	0.6	1.8	3.3	4.7	5.6	6.8	7.8	6.9	7.2	6.1	5.8	5.6	9.1	6.6	12.0	9.7
27 years	...	...	0.2	2.2	2.6	3.6	5.3	5.3	5.9	7.5	6.8	6.7	6.2	5.6	5.1	8.9	7.0	12.0	9.1
28 years	...	0.1	0.5	3.3	2.6	3.7	4.8	5.8	6.2	7.5	6.8	6.3	5.7	6.0	4.7	8.4	6.9	11.4	9.4
29 years	...	0.2	1.4	3.1	3.0	4.0	4.6	4.9	6.7	7.0	6.5	6.3	6.0	5.6	4.9	8.0	6.8	11.3	9.6
30 years	...	0.3	1.9	4.2	3.2	4.1	4.4	5.4	6.0	7.7	6.2	5.9	5.5	4.9	4.7	8.0	6.6	11.3	9.8
31 years	...	1.1	1.9	4.7	3.3	4.0	4.3	5.2	5.7	6.8	6.6	6.1	5.1	5.2	4.5	8.1	6.8	11.5	9.2
32 years	...	1.4	2.7	4.6	3.0	4.6	4.4	5.3	5.7	6.9	5.4	5.7	5.4	4.7	4.5	7.7	6.8	11.2	9.8
33 years	...	1.8	2.5	4.1	3.2	3.9	5.3	4.9	6.0	5.8	5.8	6.2	5.3	5.1	4.4	8.3	6.8	11.3	9.1
34 years	0.1	2.7	3.3	5.5	3.4	3.8	4.0	4.6	5.2	6.7	6.5	5.5	5.3	4.6	4.3	7.8	6.3	11.6	8.9

Source: Derived by interpolation and estimation for 5 states for which data were not available in full age detail, from National Office of Vital Statistics, Vital Statistics of the United States, 1956.

does exist tends to reach its highest point at about age 26 or 27, and then becomes progressively lower as age of bride increases. Among brides 34 years of age, for example, when the marriage is a remarriage for one of the partners, only about 18 percent of the couples are of the same age or have an age difference of only plus or minus 1 year. On the other hand, 20 percent of the grooms are 10 or more years older than their brides. When there is a great discrepancy between the ages of bride and groom, among first marriages it is about equally distributed between grooms who are younger than their brides and grooms who are older than their brides; among remarriages, however, the groom tends to be considerably older than the bride.

MONTH AND SEASON OF MARRIAGE

If couples considered no one particular month of the year more appropriate than any other as a time to marry, roughly 1/12 (8.3 percent) of all marriages would occur during each month. Variations in the number of days in the month would affect these proportions slightly, and the monthly proportions would probably vary from year to year as a result of changes in the number of week ends in the respective months. Table 10-31 reports an index of seasonal variation, showing which months are preferred for marriage, and by how much. When they are ranked in descending order of preference, the months fall into the following order:

June

August

September

May

December

November

October

July

April

February

January

March

Table 10-31.—MONTH OF MARRIAGE

Month	Index of seasonal variation, July 1946 to June 1950	Percent distribution of marriage preformed in 1950 (29 reporting states
Total.........	100.0	100.0
January.............	80.7	5.8
February............	83.1	6.2
March...............	80.5	5.2
April...............	95.2	7.8
May.................	103.1	7.5
June................	135.2	11.5
July................	98.8	9.2
August..............	114.1	9.9
September...........	109.9	11.3
October.............	99.2	8.8
November............	99.4	8.1
December............	100.7	8.7

Source: National Office of Vital Statistics, Vital Statistics of the United States, 1950, Vol. I, Table 5.04, Vol. II, Table 4.

The month of June is so popular that it attracts 35 percent more marriages than its number of days would suggest, while March is so unpopular that it has 20 percent fewer marriages than are its proportionate share. This concentration of marriages in the summer and early autumn months tends to have a slight seasonal effect on the distribution of births by months.

A FEW FACTS ABOUT DIVORCE

Grounds for Divorce. Each of the 48 states has its own laws regulating divorce, and the states differ greatly as to the severity of their divorce laws and the grounds upon which they permit a pe-

tition for divorce to be filed. Table 10-32 reports the grounds on which divorces actually were granted in 24 states in 1953. Cruelty and desertion are the two leading grounds; adultery, nonsupport, and drunkenness are grounds that are used comparatively less often. It must be emphasized that these are merely the legal grounds on which the plea was made and on which the decree was granted, and not necessarily the actual reasons for the divorce.

Table 10-32.—DIVORCES, BY LEGAL GROUNDS FOR DECREE: 24 REPORTING STATES, 1953

Legal grounds for decree	Percent of divorces
Total......................	100.0
Adultery...........................	1.3
Bigamy.............................	0.4
Conviction of crime.................	0.5
Cruelty............................	47.0
Desertion..........................	18.4
Drunkenness........................	2.1
Fraud..............................	0.3
Insanity...........................	0.1
Nonsupport.........................	1.5
Under age..........................	0.1
Other and not stated...............	28.3

Source: Vital Statistics of the United States: Vol. I, Table 13, p. 74.

Duration of Marriage and Divorce. Ideally, it would be desirable if divorce rates were expressed in terms of length of marriage. But the only official data available are percentage distributions by duration of marriage, as shown in Table 10-33. Divorce appears to be much more prevalent among couples who have been married less than 7 years than among couples who have been married longer than this. One-fourth of all divorces are granted to couples who have been married less than three years. However, it must not be concluded that couples who have lived together for a long time are immune to divorce. In 1953, 5 percent of all divorces in 23 states were granted to couples who had been married for 25 years or more, and about 1/5 of all divorces were granted to couples who had been married for 15 years or longer.

Children Involved in Divorces. Children are involved in about 45 percent of all divorce cases

Table 10-33.—PERCENTAGE DISTRIBUTION OF DIVORCES
AND ANNULMENTS BY DURATION OF MARRIAGE:
REPORTING STATES, 1950 AND 1953

Duration of marriage	23 reporting states, 1953	16 reporting states, 1950
Total..............	100.0	100.0
Under 1 year...........	6.8	6.3
Median.................	6.1	5.8
1 year.................	10.0	10.1
2 years................	9.7	10.1
3 years................	8.0	9.8
4 years................	7.1	9.2
5 years................	6.9	5.8
6 years................	6.6	4.4
7 years................	6.0	4.2
8 years................	3.9	4.2
9 years................	3.0	3.5
10 years...............	2.9	3.0
11 years...............	3.0	2.5
12 years...............	2.6	2.3
13 years...............	2.2	2.1
14 years...............	1.9	1.9
15 to 19 years.........	7.5	7.1
20 to 24 years.........	4.5	5.1
25 to 29 years.........	3.1	3.0
30 to 34 years.........	1.5	1.7
35 to 39 years.........	0.7	0.7
40 years and over......	0.5	0.5
Not stated.............	1.5	2.1

Source: Vital Statistics of the United States:
1953, Vol. I, Table 16, page 76, Vital Statistics
of the United States: 1950, Vol. II, Table 9,
page 30.

(Table 10-34). In about 1/2 of the cases which involve children, (23 percent of all cases), two or more children are affected by the divorce. In one divorce in eleven, there are three or more chil-

Table 10-34.—PERCENTAGE DISTRIBUTION OF DIVORCES
AND ANNULMENTS BY NUMBER OF CHILDREN
REPORTED: REPORTING STATES, 1950 AND 1953

Reported number of children	22 reporting states, 1953	16 reporting states, 1950
Total.............	100.0	100.0
None..................	54.5	54.0
1 child...............	22.3	22.9
2 children...........	13.6	11.7
3 children...........	5.7	4.8
4 children...........	2.2	1.6
5 or more children......	1.6	1.3
Not stated..........	...	3.6

Source: Vital Statistics of the United States:
1953, Vol. I, Table U, page XXXIV, Vital Statistics
of the United States: 1950, Table 12, page 33.

dren in the family. If the data in Table 10-34, concerning 22 states which reported in 1953, reflect conditions throughout the nation, then each year about 350,000 children are members of families broken by divorce. This figure amounts to an average of one child per divorce.

PART III

MARITAL STATUS IN RELATION TO EDUCATION,
OCCUPATION, AND INCOME

Educational attainment, occupation, and income are each discussed in a separate chapter in this volume. These chapters, however, do not focus explicitly on the question, "How is marital status related to the amount of education the population has received, to the occupations in which the population is engaged, and to the income level of the population?" This chapter concludes, therefore, with a brief review of the proportions of the population, at each of the various educational, occupational, and income levels, who are single, married, widowed, or divorced.

Educational Attainment and Marriage. Younger adults who have had very little education (failed to graduate from high school) and those who have acquired an extraordinarily large amount (completed 4 or more years of college) seem more inclined to remain single than young adults who have graduated from elementary school or attended 1 to 3 years of high school. (See Table 10-35.) Among women, a large amount of education seems to decrease the prevalence of marriage more markedly than it does among men, since completion of college appears to be associated, for women, with an especially strong tendency to remain single. This differential between women who have graduated from college and those who have not is larger among women in the older age groups than it is among the younger women, which suggests that the differential is decreasing with the passage of time. Nevertheless, in 1957, among women 25 to 34 years of age, the proportion of college graduates who were single (never married) was 2 1/2 times as great as the corresponding proportion for the age group as a whole. A college degree seems to have a similar, though slighter, effect upon men.

Table 10-35.—PERCENT OF POPULATION SINGLE (NEVER MARRIED) BY AGE, SEX, AND EDUCATIONAL ATTAINMENT: 1957

Age	Total	Years of school completed					
		Elementary:		High school:		College:	
		Less than 8 years	8 years	1 to 3 years	4 years	1 to 3 years	4 years or more
MALE							
Total, 14 years old and over....	23.9	21.4	22.5	34.3	19.4	26.3	16.0
14 to 19 years old................	97.5	98.6	98.1	97.6	93.5	98.9	100.0
20 to 24 years old................	51.8	49.3	46.2	40.7	47.0	72.7	56.2
25 to 34 years old................	17.9	22.5	15.9	14.0	15.7	18.5	24.4
35 to 44 years old................	8.6	13.0	9.2	6.0	7.9	5.1	9.2
45 to 64 years old................	7.7	8.2	8.1	7.0	6.2	5.7	8.1
65 years old and over.............	7.3	6.5	7.3	6.6	5.0	1.9	5.7
FEMALE							
Total, 14 years old and over....	18.6	13.7	18.4	26.4	14.8	19.0	24.4
14 to 19 years old................	87.0	88.7	92.7	87.6	76.2	91.2	60.0
20 to 24 years old................	29.0	30.3	20.5	14.1	27.6	52.8	55.5
25 to 34 years old................	9.1	13.3	9.8	3.9	8.3	8.6	23.9
35 to 44 years old................	6.4	6.6	5.7	3.7	6.5	5.3	16.2
45 to 64 years old................	7.1	4.7	5.3	4.9	8.1	9.2	21.9
65 years old and over.............	8.0	4 3	6.8	8.3	11.7	16.0	29.9

Source: Current Population Reports, Series P-20, No. 81, March, 1958, Table 3.

In the long run, college education probably tends to delay marriage, rather than to cause permanent spinsterhood or bachelorhood.

Among the married population who are high school or college graduates, the proportion who become divorced is smaller than among the population as a whole. This is true among both males and females in age groups over 35 years of age, where the great bulk of broken marriages are found. Thus, there seems to be evidence in support of the generalization that marriages between more highly educated persons tend to be more

Table 10-36.—PERCENT WIDOWED AND DIVORCED OF MARRIED PERSONS, BY AGE, SEX, AND EDUCATIONAL ATTAINMENT: 1957

Age	Total	Years of school completed					
		Elementary:		High school:		College:	
		Less than 8 years	8 years	1 to 3 years	4 years	1 to 3 years	4 years or more
MALE							
Total, 14 years old and over....	8.0	15.0	9.9	4.8	3.8	5.1	3.4
25 to 34 years....................	2.3	1.9	3.2	2.4	1.7	3.1	1.9
35 to 44 years....................	3.3	4.0	3.9	3.2	3.0	4.1	1.5
45 to 64 years....................	7.1	9.8	7.3	6.0	5.2	5.0	1.9
65 years and over.................	35.4	41.7	31.4	21.4	21.3	25.6	23.1
FEMALE							
Total, 14 years old and over....	22.3	44.8	31.7	16.4	11.4	15.2	15.3
25 to 34 years....................	3.7	5.3	4.4	4.3	2.9	3.4	4.1
35 to 44 years....................	7.9	10.0	7.6	8.6	7.0	7.9	7.3
45 to 64 years....................	26.8	34.4	25.7	25.3	21.1	24.2	23.2
65 years and over.................	152.3	164.3	140.0	145.9	141.0	102.8	116.7

Source: Current Population Reports, Series P-20, No. 81, March, 1958, Table 3.

Table 10-37.—PERCENT OF POPULATION SINGLE (NEVER MARRIED) BY AGE, SEX, AND MAJOR OCCUPATION GROUP (EMPLOYED PERSONS ONLY): 1957

Major occupation group	Total, 14 years and over	14 to 19 years	20 to 24 years	25 to 34 years	35 to 44 years	45 to 64 years	65 years and over
MALE	16.6	95.3	45.0	16.2	7.2	6.4	5.2
Professional, technical, and kindred workers	16.5	98.2	46.0	21.6	8.2	8.1	5.6
Farmers and farm managers	11.3	100.0	30.9	15.8	13.9	8.0	5.9
Managers, officials, proprietors, exc. farm	5.7	66.7	37.6	10.8	3.1	3.5	3.0
Clerical and kindred workers	24.0	94.7	50.3	22.2	10.9	11.3	2.4
Sales workers	20.3	98.3	49.7	13.4	3.5	2.5	6.8
Craftsmen, foremen, and kindred workers	8.7	82.5	37.5	11.2	4.4	3.7	4.7
Operatives and kindred workers	17.5	91.5	42.6	14.9	6.4	7.0	5.8
Private household workers	42.9	100.0	...	....	60.0	20.0	...
Service workers, except private household	21.1	99.2	53.3	18.6	9.2	7.5	6.7
Farm laborers and foremen	55.0	98.6	63.1	33.3	23.1	22.3	7.8
Laborers, except farm and mine	26.9	95.2	46.8	20.9	13.2	9.2	4.9
FEMALE	25.0	88.9	48.8	21.4	12.5	12.9	17.4
Professional, technical, and kindred workers	35.8	87.5	67.1	36.9	23.2	26.7	36.6
Farmers and farm managers	5.0	100.0	....	...	10.5	...	8.3
Managers, officials, proprietors, exc. farm	10.8	37.5	33.3	15.3	7.7	8.1	22.0
Clerical and kindred workers	33.4	86.6	47.2	25.4	17.9	19.4	20.2
Sales workers	21.6	93.8	50.8	16.1	5.1	6.5	9.7
Craftsmen, foremen, and kindred workers	20.9	85.7	52.9	23.9	16.9	7.3	75.0
Operatives and kindred workers	16.7	76.6	35.7	14.0	12.9	9.8	18.5
Private household workers	27.0	97.5	50.4	17.7	8.8	10.0	17.3
Service workers, except private household	16.5	89.7	47.4	12.9	3.7	6.5	9.6
Farm laborers and foremen	13.6	91.3	45.2	9.6	5.1	4.4	...
Laborers, except farm and mine	21.4	57.1	50.0	10.3	16.2	16.7	...

Source: Current Population Reports, Series P-20, No. 81, March, 1958, Table 4.

stable marriages. Speculation could produce a variety of theories as to why the above generalization might be a valid one. At present, however, the available data are so scarce that it is not possible to evaluate precisely the forces underlying this very definite and interesting differential which exists between the various educational strata of the population with respect to broken marriages.

Occupation and Marital Status. Among male members of the labor force, those employed as clerical, private household service, or farm workers are much more inclined to remain unmarried than those in other occupations. Men engaged in sales work tend to marry at an older age than other males. On the other hand, managers, officials, proprietors, craftsmen, and operatives seem more inclined to marry at an earlier age, and less inclined to remain bachelors at older ages, than men in other occupations. Some of these differences may represent differences in

working conditions, some of them may be due to an occupational selection of unmarried persons for particular jobs (such as private household work), and some may be due to differences between occupations with respect to income paid for work.

Among women, the occupational groups differ much more than they do among men as to the proportion in each group who are single. Women who are professional and clerical workers are much more inclined to remain unmarried than women in other occupations, while women who are managers, sales workers, operatives, or service workers show an above-average propensity to marry. This may reflect three things: women with well-paying jobs in the professions or with responsible positions as clerks, may be less inclined to marry; married women from lower-income families may enter factories and stores to help supplement the family income; working conditions in certain oc-

Table 10-38.—PERCENT SINGLE BY TOTAL MONEY INCOME IN 1956, URBAN AND RURAL NONFARM, MALE: 1957

Income	Total, 14 years and over	Age						
		14 to 19 years	20 to 24 years	25 to 34 years	35 to 44 years	45 to 64 years	65 years and over
MALE								
Total, those with income........	17.2	95.2	46.8	15.8	7.0	6.6	6.2
$1 to $1,999.....................	41.6	97.4	70.1	38.2	23.4	16.1	7.7
$2,000 to $3,999.................	15.7	75.3	40.0	19.5	9.6	8.0	4.9
$4,000 to $5,999.................	7.4	70.0	23.1	11.7	6.0	4.1	2.5
$6,000 and over..................	3.3	...	25.3	7.3	1.7	2.5	2.0

Source: Current Population Reports, Series P-20, No. 81, March, 1958, Table 5.

cupations, such as school teaching, may play a part in causing women to withdraw from the labor market when they marry.

Income and Marital Status. There is a very consistent differential between the various income levels as regards propensity to marry: men with low incomes are less inclined to marry, while above-average proportions of males with high incomes are married. (See Table 10-37.) This differential, which exists in each male age group, is a very large one. For example, among men 35 to 44 years of age with incomes of $2,000 to $3,000, about 10 percent had never married as of 1957. Among men in the same age group who were earning $6,000 or more, 2 percent, or only 1/5 of that share were still bachelors in 1957. This suggests that a large proportion of the population gets married almost as soon as its income permits, and that marriage is postponed by a large proportion of the men whose incomes are lower.

MARITAL STATUS IN 1958

Demographers are trying hard to learn the part which economic prosperity is playing in keeping marriage rates high. Since mid-1957, the nation has been undergoing a sharp recession. A similar, but milder, recession took place in 1954. If there were a tendency for young persons to postpone marriage when unemployment became high, it should be reflected in an increased percentage who remain single at ages 14-17, 18-19, and perhaps even 20-24. By comparing the percentage of persons reported as never married at these early ages, reported each year by the Bureau of

the Census in its Current Population Survey, it should be possible to determine whether troubled economic times seem to cause a higher proportion of young people to remain single. Following are the data for each year, 1950 to 1958:

Sex and year	Percent single		
	14 to 17 years	18 and 19 years	20 to 24 years
Male			
1950............	99.7	92.4	55.8
1951............	99.7	92.9	51.7
1952............	99.0	89.9	48.3
1953............	99.6	91.5	48.7
1954............	99.5	92.4	54.2
1955............	99.8	90.6	48.8
1956............	99.7	91.8	49.2
1957............	99.6	92.0	51.8
1958............	99.6	91.6	52.1
Female.			
1950............	93.7	67.8	31 6
1951............	95.3	67.9	31.2
1952............	94.4	67.8	29.6
1953............	95.5	66.2	29.5
1954............	95.0	70.2	30.7
1955............	94.7	67.0	29.1
1956............	93.8	66.0	28.6
1957............	94.9	69.7	29.0
1958............	95.3	66.4	29.0

When allowance is made for sample fluctuations, one can conclude from these data that perhaps the trend toward younger marriage was suspended between 1953 and 1956, and that the recent recession has caused a slight reversal, or tendency toward postponement. If there had been a major change in marriage patterns, there would have been a very noticeable increase in the percentage of both males and females aged 18 and 19 years of age who were single. But the tendency, if it exists, is very slight, and does not represent a major development as yet.

Chapter 11

HOUSEHOLD AND FAMILY STATUS

With respect to most items of census information, the members of a population are enumerated as individuals and the demographic characteristics for which statistics are tabulated involve such personal traits as age, sex, or educational attainment. However, there are certain groups of persons about which it is important to obtain information. In such cases, the primary unit of tabulation is not the individual, but the group. The number of people in the group, its size, and others of its characteristics (including any changes in its numbers, size, or other characteristics) are the objects of investigation. If the person is considered at all in the analysis of a group, it is to ascertain his status in the group--the role he plays in the group organization. Unfortunately, because so much emphasis has been placed on the statistics which refer to individuals, many demographers have tended to think that the statistics which concern population groups are of only secondary importance. To so evaluate group statistics is a serious mistake, for many comparatively unexplored but very important aspects of population can be illuminated only by making the group the unit of analysis. Two of the most important groups about which the census collects information (and about which there is also widespread general interest) are households and families, i.e., residential groups--clusters of people who occupy a residence jointly. This chapter can serve only as a brief introduction to this very large field of demographic study.

HOUSEHOLDS AND DWELLING UNITS

Each member of a population has a dwelling place and a set of living arrangements. The arrangements under which the members of a population live are of considerable importance to those who are concerned with family relationships, housing problems, marketing, and city planning. In census terminology, each separate dwelling place is termed a "dwelling unit," and the group of persons that inhabits it constitutes a "household."

"A household includes all the persons who occupy a house, an apartment or other group of rooms, or a room that constitutes a dwelling unit. In general, a group of rooms occupied as separate living quarters is a dwelling unit if it has separate cooking equipment or a separate entrance; a single room occupied as separate living quarters is a dwelling unit if it has separate cooking equipment or if it constitutes the only living quarters in the structure. A household includes the related family members and also the unrelated persons, if any, such as lodgers, foster children, wards, or employees who share the dwelling unit. A person living alone in a dwelling unit, or a group of unrelated persons sharing a dwelling unit as partners, is also counted as a household." [1]

-----

[1] U. S. Bureau of the Census, U.S. Census of Population: 1950, Vol. II, Characteristics of the Population, Part 1, U.S. Summary, Chapter C, p. 43.

The household is important as a unit of study for several reasons. Sociologists and anthropologists have a direct interest in living arrangements, in the composition of households, and in the relationships between the members of the household. In the United States, the "normal" household is generally thought of as a man and his wife living together with their children. However, many households consist of one person, or of two unrelated persons--unmarried working girls, for example--occupying a dwelling unit. Moreover, some households include a married son or daughter and spouse, and their children. A widow living alone is an example of the one-person household, and some households consist of "normal" families that rent a spare room to a lodger, or employ a maid or housekeeper who lives in the house. Whereas anthropologists must usually rely on faulty and incomplete samples and on general observation for the facts about the system of living arrangements among the people they are studying, such facts concerning the people of the United States are available in full detail in the United States Census reports. It provides information about the household units themselves--their number, size, and composition--as well as data concerning the nature of the household in which the individual members of the population live.

Economists, market analysts, public utility companies, and persons concerned with the subject of housing are especially interested in household statistics, because the household, rather than the person, is often the principal unit with which they deal. Telephone service, gas, water, and electricity are distributed to household units. Many products, such as television sets, washing machines, and house furnishings, are manufactured to satisfy the needs of household units. In the designing of houses and apartments, information about the size, composition, and characteristics of households is very important to architects, contractors, and real estate firms. (For example, it is becoming apparent that a high proportion of the houses built in the past 15 years are too small to accomodate today's larger families comfortably, which means that greater emphasis must be placed on the building of larger units with more rooms.)

The living arrangements of elderly persons are of interest to those who study the problems of the aged. Social agencies which are concerned with crowded housing conditions, and the general quality of living arrangements, also strive to gather as much information as they can about the nation's households.

The Census Bureau recognizes two types of households: households and quasi households. The household is the group defined above--the occupants of a dwelling unit. A quasi household is a particular kind of residential unit whose specific purpose is to house large numbers of unrelated individuals. Hotels, large lodging or boarding houses, institutions, labor camps, and military barracks are examples of quasi households. A house with at least 5 lodgers was defined as a quasi household in the census of 1950 (in the 1940 census, a dwelling place was classified as a quasi household if it included 11 or more lodgers).

As of 1958 there were about 50.4 million households in the population, and an average of 3.35 persons per household. With respect to the composition of these households, the following differentials exist (Table 11-1):

(a) Nonfarm households are about 15 percent smaller in their average size than farm households.

(b) White households are about 15 percent smaller in their average size than nonwhite households.

During the 7 decades since 1890, there has been a rather steady decline in the average size of the household. Today's household contains only 65 percent as many persons as the average household of 1890, which had 5 members. This decline has been due (before 1945) to lower fertility rates, to a tendency toward "undoubling" in household occupancy, and to an increased longevity which creates a great many households occupied by elderly couples. Since 1920, the size of the household has declined much more rapidly among the white than among the nonwhite population.

Table 11-1.—TRENDS IN NUMBER OF HOUSEHOLDS AND IN COLOR AND RESIDENCE OF HOUSEHOLDS: 1890 TO 1958

Year	Number of households (000)	Percent of households:		Population per household				
		Nonwhite	Nonfarm	Total	Color		Residence	
					White	Nonwhite	Nonfarm	Farm
1958 (CPS).........	50,402	(a)	89.7	3.4	3.3	3.9	3.3	3.9
1956 (CPS).........	48,785	8.2	88.4	3.3	3.3	3.8	3.3	(a)
1950 (CPS).........	43,554	(a)	85.6	3.4	(a)	(a)	(a)	(a)
1950 (Census)......	42,826	8.8	86.6	3.5	3.5	4.2	3.4	4.0
1940 (Census)......	34,949	9.4	79.6	3.8	3.7	4.1	3.7	4.3
1930 (Census)......	29,905	9.8	77.9	4.1	4.1	4.3	4.0	4.6
1920 (Census)......	24,352	10.4	72.3	4.3	4.3	4.3	4.2	4.7
1910 (Census)......	20,256	(a)	69.8	4.5	(a)	(a)	(a)	(a)
1900 (Census)......	15,964	11.9	64.4	4.8	4.8	4.8	(a)	(a)
1890 (Census)......	12,690	11.3	62.4	5.0	4.9	5.5	(a)	(a)

(a) Not available.
Source: Current Population Reports, Series P-20, Nos, 67, 68, 72, 76, 81, and U.S. Census of Housing: 1950 Vol. I, General Characteristics, Part 1, U.S. Summary, Tables J, K, and 4.

Between 1950 and 1958, the number of households in the population increased at the rate of about 850,000, or almost 2 percent, per year. This growth represents the net balance between an increase of about 1 million households per year among the urban and rural-nonfarm population and a decrease of about 150,000 households per year among the rural-farm population. An annual increment of this size has some important implications. For example, it is a means of estimating the number of new dwelling units that must be provided annually to take care of population growth and changing living habits, aside from the new construction required to replace dilapidated, obsolete, or substandard housing. This increase is also an index of the expansion in the demand for refrigerators, television sets, telephones, and other household items.

HOUSEHOLD STATUS CATEGORIES

The general view of households is that they are internally organized, and that each person stands in some fixed status with respect to a central person who is designated as the head of the household. The Census Bureau recognizes the following range of statuses within households:

1. Head of household.--One person in each household is designated as the "head." The number of heads, therefore, is equal to the number of households. The head is usually the person regarded as the head by the members of the household. Married women are not classified as heads if their husbands are living with them at the time of the census.

2. Wife.--The category "Wife" in the relationship table includes only wives of heads of households.

3. Child.--This category includes sons and daughters, stepchildren and adopted children of the head regardless of their age or marital status. It excludes sons-in-law and daughters-in-law and, of course, any children of the head no longer living in the household.

4. Grandchild.--This category comprises all persons living in the household who are sons, daughters, stepchildren, or adopted children of a child of the head.

5. Parent.--This class comprises both parents and parents-in-law of the head if living in the household.

6. Other relative.--This group includes such relatives of the head as sons-in-law, sisters-in-law, nephews, brothers, aunts, grandchildren, cousins, and great-grandchildren, if these are members of the household.

7. Lodger.--All persons in households who are not related to the head, except resident employees and their families, are counted as lodgers. Among these persons are lodgers, roomers,

and boarders, and their relatives residing in the same household. Also included are partners, foster children, and wards.

8. <u>Resident employee</u>.--This category consists of all employees of the head of the household who usually reside in the household with their employer, and their relatives residing in the same household. The main types of such employees are cooks, maids, nurses, and hired farm hands.

Quasi households, unlike households, are not regarded as being internally organized. Instead, they are managed or directed. The only status within this class that is separately recognized in census statistics is the manager or director--the quasi household head. The definition of this status is:

9. <u>Head of quasi household</u>.--Heads of quasi households are usually managers or officers in institutions, hotels, lodginghouses, and similar establishments. If the landlady in a rooming house reported herself as the head but her husband was a member of the quasi household, he was designated as head for consistency with the treatment of married heads and wives of heads of households. The number of heads of quasi households also represents the number of quasi households.

FAMILIES AND FAMILY STATUS CATEGORIES

The household status definitions fail to identify family units, which are characterized by kinship ties--blood relationship, marriage, or adoption-- rather than by living arrangements. Because there is considerable interest in family statistics, as distinct from household statistics, the Census Bureau identified families and tabulated a considerable body of family statistics during the 1950 census. The following basic concepts pertain to the interpretation of these data:

<u>Family</u>. A family, as defined in the 1950 census, is a group of two or more persons related by blood, marriage, or adoption and living together; all such persons are regarded as members of one family. If the son of the head of the household and the son's wife are members of the household, they are treated as part of the head's family. A lodger

and his wife who are not related to the head of the household, or a resident employee and his wife living in, are considered as a separate family, however. Thus, a household may contain more than one family. A household head living alone or with nonrelatives only is not regarded as a family. Some households, therefore, do not contain a family.

A <u>primary family</u> comprises the head of a household and all (one or more) other persons in the household who are related to the head. The primary family may include one or more "subfamilies," as defined below. <u>Secondary families</u> are families whose head is not also the household head. Such families are generally the families of roomers or of resident employees who are living in ordinary homes or rooming houses.

A <u>subfamily</u> is a married couple with or without children, or one parent with one or more children under 18 years old, living in a household; a <u>subfamily</u> is related to, but does not include, the head of the household or his wife. A widowed or divorced daughter and her children, living in her father's home, or a young married couple living with the parents of one of the couple, would be examples of a subfamily. The number of subfamilies is not included in the count of families. Instead, the subfamily is considered part of the primary family.

A <u>married couple</u>, as defined for census purposes, is a husband and his wife who are enumerated as members of the same household or quasi household. A married couple is classified as "with own household" if the husband is the head of the household. The expression "husband-wife" before the term "household," "family," or "subfamily" indicates that the head of the household, family, or subfamily is a married man whose wife lives with him.

An <u>unrelated individual</u> is a person (other than an inmate of an institution) who is not living with any relative. There are two types of such persons: (a) primary individuals, and (b) secondary individuals, each of which is defined below.

<u>Primary individual</u>. A primary individual is a household head living alone, or with nonrelatives

only. Examples of primary individuals living with nonrelatives include a single woman who shares her apartment with a partner or a housekeeper, or a widow in whose house a lodger occupies a room.

Secondary individual. A secondary individual is a person (other than a primary individual or an inmate of an institution) who is not related to any other person in the household or quasi household. Secondary individuals include lodgers, resident employees, hotel guests, students living in college dormitories, members of the armed forces living in military barracks, resident staff members of institutions, and other persons living apart from relatives.

Inmate of institution. This category includes persons who are inmates in such places as homes for delinquent or dependent children, homes and schools for the mentally or physically handicapped, places providing specialized medical care, homes for the aged, prisons, and jails. Persons in this category exclude staff members and their families.[2]

Within each family each member has a designated status. The following family status categories are recognized by the Census:

    Head of family
    Wife of family head
    Child of family head
    Son-in-law or daughter-in-law of family head
    Grandchild of family head
    Parent of family head
    Other relative of family head

The definitions of these categories parallel those of the household status categories, except that relationship to family head, rather than to household head, is the basis of classification. The number of heads of families is equal to the number of families. The number of women who are wives of family heads is the same as the number of "husband-wife" families. The number of married wo-

men who live with their husbands but who are not wives of family heads is the same as the number of "husband-wife subfamilies;" these subfamilies consist of primary family members who are sharing the living quarters of a relative who is a household head.

The concepts and definitions listed above make it possible to discuss the population's living units in terms of types and trends, and to classify the entire population according to its household status and its family status.

LIVING ARRANGEMENTS OF THE POPULATION, AND TRENDS IN TYPES OF HOUSEHOLD AND FAMILY UNITS

Of the nearly 50 million households which the United States contained as of March, 1957, a vast majority (87 percent) were made up of primary families and only a minority (13 percent) consisted of primary individuals (Table 11-2). However, households comprised of primary individuals (unrelated persons, or persons living alone or with nonrelatives) have long been on the increase. In 1940 only about 10 percent of all households were occupied by primary individuals. This increase reflects several factors. Improved economic conditions permit many unmarried working persons to live in their own apartments rather than as lodgers in private households. Social Security and other pension plans permit widowed persons to live alone in their own households after their spouses have died, rather than move in to the home of one of their children.

Among the households that consist of families, about 90 percent have a male head and 10 percent have a female head. The husband-wife family (which may or may not contain children) accounts for 76 percent of all households and for 87 percent of all families.

Secondary families are very few in number (235,000 in 1957) and have been decreasing rapidly and, apparently, steadily since 1940. A high proportion of such families (32 percent) consist of a mother and her child, living as lodgers or servants in a private household or rooming house.

[2]The above definitions have been abstracted from U.S. Bureau of the Census, U.S. Census of Population: 1950, Marital Status, Vol. IV, Special Reports, Part 2, Chapter D.

Table 11-2.—TYPES OF HOUSEHOLD AND FAMILY UNITS: 1940, 1950, AND 1957, AND PERCENT CHANGE: 1940 TO 1950 AND 1950 TO 1957

Type of unit	Number of units (000)			Percent distribution			Percent change	
	March, 1957	March, 1950	April, 1940	March, 1957	March, 1950	April, 1940	1950 to 1957	1940 to 1950
HOUSEHOLDS								
Total.............	49,543	43,554	34,949	100.0	100.0	100.0	13.8	24.6
Primary families........	43,210	38,838	31,491	87.2	89.2	90.1	11.3	23.3
Husband-wife...........	37,711	34,075	26,571	76.1	78.2	76.0	10.7	28.2
Other male head........	1,208	1,169	1,510	2.4	2.7	4.3	3.3	-22.7
Female head...........	4,291	3,594	3,410	8.7	8.3	9.8	19.4	5.4
Primary individuals......	6,333	4,716	3,458	12.8	10.8	9.9	34.3	36.4
Male.................	1,984	1,668	1,599	4.0	3.8	4.6	18.9	4.3
Female...............	4,349	3,048	1,859	8.8	7.0	5.3	42.7	64.0
FAMILIES								
Total.............	43,445	39,303	32,166	100.0	100.0	100.0	10.5	22.2
Husband-wife...........	37,849	34,440	26,971	87.1	84.0	83.8	9.9	27.7
Other male head.........	1,230	1,184	1,579	2.8	4.9	4.9	3.9	-25.0
Female head............	4,366	3,679	3,616	10.1	11.2	11.3	18.7	1.7
SECONDARY FAMILIES								
Total.............	235	465	675	100.0	100.0	100.0	-49.5	-31.1
Husband-wife...........	138	365	400	58.7	78.5	59.3	-62.2	-8.8
Other male head.........	22	15	69	9.4	3.2	10.2	...	-78.3
Female head............	75	85	206	31.9	18.3	30.5	...	-58.7
SUBFAMILIES								
Total.............	1,802	2,402	2,062	100.0	100.0	100.0	-25.0	16.5
Husband-wife...........	1,091	1,651	1,546	60.5	68.7	75.0	-33.9	6.8
Other male head.........	95	113	52	5.3	4.7	2.5	...	117.3
Female head............	616	638	464	34.2	26.6	22.5	-3.4	37.5
MARRIED COUPLES								
Total.............	38,940	36,091	28,517	100.0	100.0	100.0	7.9	26.6
With own household.......	37,711	34,075	26,571	96.8	94.4	93.2	10.7	28.2
Without own household....	1,229	2,016	1,946	3.2	5.6	6.8	-39.0	3.6
Percent without own household...........	3.3	5.6	6.8	0.1	0.2	0.2	...	-17.6
UNRELATED INDIVIDUALS								
Total.............	9,780	9,136	9,277	100.0	100.0	100.0	7.0	-1.5
Male...................	4,002	4,209	4,942	40.9	46.1	53.3	-4.9	-14.8
Female.................	5,778	4,927	4,335	59.1	53.9	46.7	17.3	13.7
SECONDARY INDIVIDUALS								
Total.............	3,447	4,420	5,819	100.0	100.0	100.0	-22.0	-24.0
Male...................	2,018	2,541	3,343	58.5	57.5	57.4	-20.6	-24.0
Female.................	1,429	1,879	2,476	41.5	42.5	42.6	-23.9	-24.1

Source: <u>Current Population Reports</u>, Series P-20, No. 76, July, 1957.

The program of Aid to Dependent Children, the greater pension benefits for widows, and the increased level of prosperity have probably all cooperated to help the secondary family move out of the household of someone else and into a home of their own (in which case they become a primary family).

About 4.2 percent of all families contain a subfamily. In 1957 there were 1.8 million subfamilies. In a high proportion of cases (34 percent) the subfamily has a female head, usually a daughter who is living, with her child, in her father's household. When the head is a male, he is usually a son, or son-in-law, and his wife who live in the home of one of the parents. The existence of a large number of subfamilies is an indication of a housing shortage, of military mobilization, or low income. The number of subfamilies increased between 1940 and 1950 (reaching an all-time peak in the period 1945 to 1948, during the critical housing shortage immediately after demobilization). Since 1950 the number of subfamilies has declined sharply, during a period when the total number of families was growing rapidly, which indicates that the housing shortage has been greatly reduced. The sharpest decline has been in the husband-wife subfamily, which is a bona fide "doubled-up" family.

Another measure of the decline in the housing shortage is the change in the proportion of married couples who do not have their own households. In 1940, 6.8 percent of all married couples did not have their own households (were living either as subfamilies or as secondary families in the households of someone else). By 1957 this proportion had declined by more than one-half.

The number of secondary individuals (lodgers, etc.) declined sharply between 1940 and 1950, and again between 1950 and 1957. The operators of boarding and rooming houses have suffered from this decrease very severely during the past two decades, because the number of lodgers and other secondary individuals is now only about 60 percent as large as it was in 1940. The marriage boom, the end of the housing shortage, and a generally higher level of prosperity have combined to reduce the number of secondary individuals. The decline has been as sharp among male as among female individuals.

The total number of unrelated individuals living in households has tended to remain constant, or to grow slightly. This situation is the net result of two opposite trends: the tendency for the number of primary individuals to increase, and for the number of secondary individuals to decrease.

Considered together, the findings given by Table 11-2 indicate that, in general, the living arrange-

ments of the American population are much more comfortable and satisfying now than they were in 1950 and, very probably, more comfortable than they have ever been. Fewer persons are forced to live as lodgers or members of secondary families in other persons' homes, or as subfamilies in the homes of their relatives. More elderly people, even those who are widowed, seem able to retain separate living quarters. The "doubling up" which was necessitated by the housing shortage has been greatly reduced. If there is dissatisfaction with the type of living arrangements (without regard to the quality of the living quarters), it probably is concentrated among the 3.4 million secondary individuals, or the 0.2 million secondary families, who still live as lodgers or resident employees, and the 1.8 million subfamilies who live in the homes of relatives.

DIFFERENTIALS IN HOUSEHOLD AND FAMILY RESIDENCE OF THE POPULATION: 1950

Table 11-3 gives information about the number of households and families which existed in 1950, by urban and rural residence. At that time, 96.2 percent of the population was residing in households; the remaining 3.8 percent lived in quasi households. About 1.0 percent of the population lived in institutions. Almost 92 percent of the population were members of families.

In rural-farm areas, almost all of the population was living in families; it is primarily in the urban and rural-nonfarm areas that a significant proportion of the population lives in quasi households or as unrelated individuals in private households. The average household consisted of 3.38 members, while the average family contained 3.6 members. Rural-farm families and households were larger, on the average, than urban or rural-nonfarm families and households. Urban families and households were smaller than those in rural-nonfarm places.

In considering the household and family status of the population, it is imperative that the factor of age be controlled, for family status varies with the stages of the life cycle. Figures 11-1 and 11-2 illustrate the extent to which household status

Table 11-3.—RESIDENCE OF THE UNITED STATES POPULATION IN HOUSEHOLDS, QUASI HOUSEHOLDS, AND FAMILIES: 1950

Household and family	Total, U.S.	Urban	Rural nonfarm	Rural farm
Total.................................	100.0	100.0	100.0	100.0
Percent of population in households...........	96.2	95.8	95.0	99.7
Percent of population in quasi households.....	3.8	4.2	5.0	0.3
Pct. of population in institutions..........	1.0	0.8	2.5	....
Pct. of population in other quasi households	2.7	3.4	2.4	0.3
Number of households........................	42,857,335	28,509,435	8,580,048	5,767,852
Population per household.....................	3.38	3.24	3.45	3.98
Number of families..........................	38,310,980	25,373,215	7,517,570	5,420,195
Percent of population in families............	91.6	90.5	91.0	97.2
Population per family........................	3.60	3.44	3.78	4.13

Source: U.S. Census of Population: 1950, Vol. II, Characteristics of the Population, Part 1, U.S. Summary, Table 47.

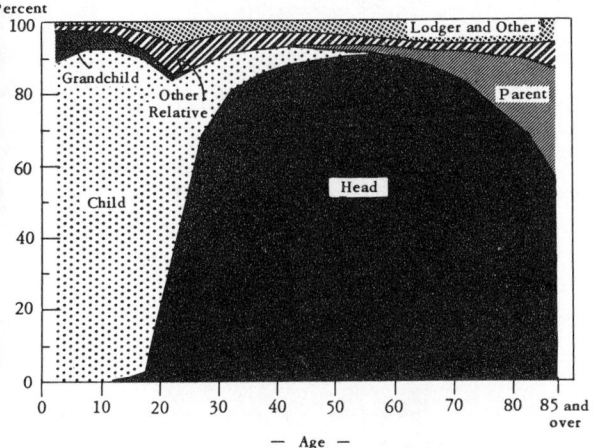

FIGURE 11-1. HOUSEHOLD STATUS BY AGE OF THE MALE POPULATION OF THE UNITED STATES, 1950

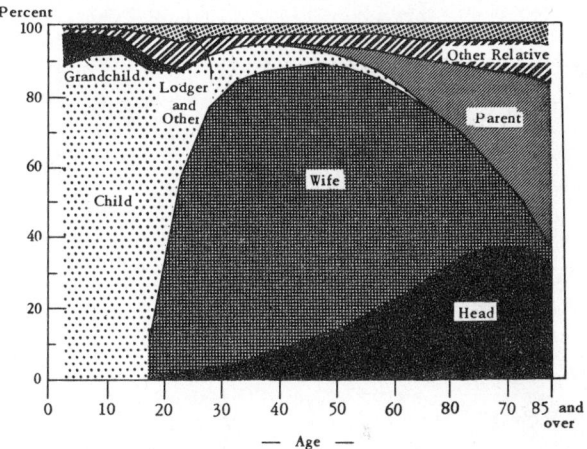

FIGURE 11-2. HOUSEHOLD STATUS BY AGE OF THE FEMALE POPULATION OF THE UNITED STATES, 1950

changes with age. In the following pages, each of the household statuses will be considered separately. The proportion of the population living in each status, by age, sex, color, and urban-rural residence, will be presented in a single table. A table of similar format will show the percentage-point change which took place between 1940 and 1950.

DIFFERENTIALS IN HOUSEHOLD STATUS: HEAD

According to Table 11-4, more than one-half of all males were household heads in 1950. Only about one woman in twelve was the head of a household. A smaller proportion of nonwhite males than of white males were household heads;

consequently, a higher proportion of nonwhite women than of white women were household heads.

By census definition, a person cannot be classed as the head of a household until he is 14 years old. Very few males assume this responsibility in their teens. At the age of 20, however, the men begin to marry, and by the time they are 30 years old more than 70 percent of the males have become household heads. The largest proportion of males are classed as household heads at about age 55 to 59, when more than 90 percent of the white males and more than 85 percent of the nonwhite males are household heads. Beyond age 60, the proportion classed as household heads declines. Widowed men tend to become parents of household heads

Table 11-4.—PERCENT OF PERSONS LIVING IN HOUSEHOLDS WHO ARE CLASSIFIED AS HEAD, BY FIVE-YEAR AGE GROUPS, COLOR, SEX, AND URBAN-RURAL RESIDENCE: 1950

Color and age	Male				Female			
	Total	Urban	Rural nonfarm	Rural farm	Total	Urban	Rural nonfarm	Rural farm
White...................	51.9	53.7	50.8	46.1	8.3	9.8	6.9	3.1
Under 5 years..........	...	...	...	...	...	...	...	...
5 to 9 years...........	...	...	....	...	...	...	...	...
10 to 14 years.........	0.1	0.1	0.1	0.1	...	...	...	...
15 to 19 years.........	2.1	2.1	2.7	1.3	0.5	0.7	0.3	0.1
20 to 24 years.........	37.0	36.7	46.2	26.1	2.2	2.8	1.2	0.2
25 to 29 years.........	70.4	69.6	78.0	61.8	3.1	3.9	2.0	0.5
30 to 34 years.........	82.2	81.6	86.9	77.2	4.5	5.5	3.1	0.9
35 to 39 years.........	86.7	86.2	89.7	84.3	6.4	7.8	4.9	1.5
40 to 44 years.........	88.9	88.6	90.9	87.8	9.1	10.9	6.9	2.6
45 to 49 years.........	90.3	89.9	91.8	90.2	12.1	14.3	9.8	4.2
50 to 54 years.........	90.9	90.5	92.1	91.5	15.6	18.0	13.2	6.0
55 to 59 years.........	91.1	90.5	92.1	92.2	19.2	21.8	17.2	8.4
60 to 64 years.........	89.5	88.7	90.9	90.7	23.7	26.6	22.0	11.2
65 to 69 years.........	86.8	85.9	88.7	87.4	29.4	32.0	29.1	15.3
70 to 74 years.........	83.0	81.7	86.4	82.9	34.7	36.9	35.8	19.8
75 years and over......	71.5	70.4	77.1	66.8	36.7	37.9	41.0	21.9
Nonwhite...............	40.8	43.0	40.1	35.9	11.6	14.2	11.3	4.2
Under 5 years..........	...	...	...	...	...	...	...	...
5 to 9 years...........	...	...	...	...	...	...	...	...
10 to 14 years.........	...	0.1	0 1	...	...	...	...	...
15 to 19 years.........	2.1	1.7	3.0	2.2	0.7	1.0	0.7	0.2
20 to 24 years.........	29.5	27.7	36.0	29.4	4.6	5.9	3.6	0.9
25 to 29 years.........	57.3	55.1	63.9	60.5	9.3	11.1	7.5	2.3
30 to 34 years.........	70.5	68.1	75.7	76.1	13.1	15.5	10.1	4.0
35 to 39 years.........	77.1	73.9	81.9	85.5	17.3	20.1	15.5	6.2
40 to 44 years.........	80.7	77.6	85.2	89.0	21.0	24.3	19.2	8.3
45 to 49 years.........	82.8	79.9	86.5	91.0	25.0	28.6	24.3	10.7
50 to 54 years.........	84.0	80.9	87.8	92.2	28.0	31.7	28.4	13.9
55 to 59 years.........	85.3	82.0	88.6	92.9	30.9	34.7	32.8	16.2
60 to 64 years.........	84.2	80.7	87.2	91.0	33.3	36.5	37.5	18.4
65 to 69 years.........	82.9	78.2	87.9	88.9	38.1	41.3	44.9	21.0
70 to 74 years.........	80.1	74.9	86.3	84.9	39.8	41.3	48.5	25.2
75 years and over......	71.4	66.0	80.6	72.5	36.8	37.4	48.3	21.7

Source: U.S. Census of Population: 1950, Vol. II, Characteristics of the Population, Part 1, U.S. Summary, Table 107; Sixteenth Census of the United States: 1940, Vol. IV, Characteristics by Age.

rather than to be heads themselves, to have the status of lodger, or to live in quasi households.

The change which took place between 1940 and 1950 in the proportion of persons classed as household heads is shown in Table 11-5. In the construction of this table, a table exactly like Table 11-4 was prepared from the 1940 census materials. Each proportion for 1940 was then subtracted from the corresponding percentage for 1950, and the difference was entered in the matching cell of Table 11-5. Although this procedure cannot yield precise results, because of changes in definitions and procedures between the two censuses, the pattern of differences that emerges is sufficiently consistent and plausible to warrant the assumption that it measures roughly the changes that actually took place.[3]

---

[3] The "total" rows in Table 11-5, which give information for all age groups combined, include the population under 14 years of age. The changing proportion of children in the total population affects the percentage point change. For this reason, the changes for all, or most, of the individual ages in a column sometimes have signs that differ from the sign connected with the change for "total." This is only one of the many instances in which the conclusions reached will be incorrect if detailed data, by age, are not studied. A similar discrepancy in change may be observed between the "total" column for a set of specific ages and the individual columns for urban, rural nonfarm, and rural farm, a discrepancy due to the differential growth of these areas.

Table 11-5.—PERCENTAGE POINT CHANGE, 1940 TO 1950, OF PERSONS LIVING IN HOUSEHOLDS WHO ARE CALSSIFIED AS HEAD, BY FIVE-YEAR AGE GROUPS, COLOR, SEX, AND URBAN-RURAL RESIDENCE

Color and age	Male				Female			
	Total	Urban	Rural nonfarm	Rural farm	Total	Urban	Rural nonfarm	Rural farm
White....................	4.8	4.9	2.5	4.1	0.4	0.2	-0.4	-0.5
Under 5 years..........	...	...	...	...	...	...	...	...
5 to 9 years...........	...	...	...	...	...	...	...	...
10 to 14 years.........	0.1	0.1	0.1	0.1	...	...	...	...
15 to 19 years.........	1.2	1.4	1.5	0.3	0.3	0.4	0.1	0.1
20 to 24 years.........	15.7	17.1	16.9	7.2	0.8	0.9	...	-0.1
25 to 29 years.........	13.9	15.1	11.4	9.9	0.3	0.3	-0.1	-0.1
30 to 34 years.........	8.2	9.0	5.8	7.1	-0.1	-0.3	-0.4	-0.4
35 to 39 years.........	5.3	6.0	3.4	4.8	-0.8	-1.0	-1.1	-1.0
40 to 44 years.........	3.3	4.0	1.8	2.1	-0.8	-1.0	-1.9	-1.3
45 to 49 years.........	2.1	2.8	1.3	0.9	-0.7	-0.8	-2.2	-1.6
50 to 54 years.........	2.3	2.9	1.7	1.6	-0.8	-1.1	-2.6	-2.2
55 to 59 years.........	2.5	2.9	2.0	2.4	-1.1	-1.5	-3.0	-2.6
60 to 64 years.........	2.1	2.5	1.8	1.7	-1.2	-1.4	-3.2	-3.3
65 to 69 years.........	2.0	2.8	1.6	0.9	-1.1	-1.5	-3.0	-3.5
70 to 74 years.........	2.3	3.2	2.1	0.8	-0.8	-0.8	-3.1	-3.6
75 years and over......	2.5	3.1	2.0	0.4	...	...	-2.6	-1.8
Nonwhite................	1.1	2.1	-1.7	-1.3	0.8	-0.6	0.1	-0.7
Under 5 years..........	...	...	...	...	...	...	...	...
5 to 9 years...........	...	...	...	...	...	...	...	...
10 to 14 years.........	...	0.1	0.1	...	...	...	...	...
15 to 19 years.........	...	0.4	0.7	-0.5	0.1	0.1	-0.1	...
20 to 24 years.........	0.8	5.3	3.5	-4.8	0.9	0.6	-0.5	-0.3
25 to 29 years.........	1.0	6.6	2.4	-5.8	0.7	-0.4	-0.1	-0.6
30 to 34 years.........	2.9	7.3	2.3	-2.0	-0.6	-2.1	-1.5	-1.4
35 to 39 years.........	3.2	6.0	2.8	1.1	-1.5	-3.3	-1.5	-2.3
40 to 44 years.........	2.8	5.1	2.4	1.0	-1.7	-3.3	-2.5	-3.6
45 to 49 years.........	1.0	3.6	0.8	...	-0.4	-2.2	-2.3	-3.3
50 to 54 years.........	0.5	3.2	1.3	0.6	0.1	-1.3	-2.4	-3.3
55 to 59 years.........	0.2	2.6	0.9	0.9	0.8	-0.6	-0.9	-3.0
60 to 64 years.........	-0.2	2.4	0.2	0.2	0.9	-0.4	-0.9	-3.7
65 to 69 years.........	-0.2	2.0	1.9	...	1.4	0.6	-0.1	-4.7
70 to 74 years.........	1.4	3.4	3.0	1.3	2.1	0.6	...	-1.5
75 years and over......	2.5	3.3	3.4	2.2	3.0	2.1	1.7	-2.5

Source: U.S. Census of Population: 1950, Vol. II, Characteristics of the Population, Part 1, U.S. Summary, Table 107; Sixteenth Census of the United States: 1940, Vol. IV, Characteristics by Age.

The changes at the younger ages reflect, among men, the marriage boom and the tendency toward earlier marriage. Among older groups these changes imply that greater proportions of older men were maintaining their own households in 1950 than in 1940. This latter situation could be a result of the greater economic security provided by Social Security, increased health and vigor at the older ages, and of greater longevity accompanied by the recently increased propensity for widowed persons (men as well as women) to remarry. A slightly higher proportion of males were classed as household heads in 1950 than in 1940, in every age group, and in both urban and rural areas. However, the greatest gains were made in the younger age groups, 20 to 25 and 25 to 29 years. The gains in almost all age groups were greater for urban residents than for rural-nonfarm, and greater for rural-nonfarm than for rural-farm.

At most ages younger than 35 years, nonwhite males made a smaller gain than white males in the proportion classed as household heads, but tended to make an equal or greater gain at the older ages, especially in urban and rural-nonfarm areas. Among the rural-farm nonwhite population there were losses at the younger ages, and sizable increases at the older ages. Among urban nonwhites, the gains were comparatively large at all ages, which could denote a rise in the level of living and the availability of more adequate living arrangements for the nonwhites who are flowing into urban places.

There were only minor changes in the proportions of women who were household heads. The proportion classed as head tended to be slightly greater in 1950 than in 1940 among white women 30 years of age or less. This increase may reflect earlier departure from home, an increase in divorce at young ages, and an increased amount of widowhood resulting from World War II. The proportion of women reported as head in 1950 was slightly less than it had been in 1940 among women older than age 30. This decline in headship among women of the middle and older ages seems to be related to the increased tendency for these groups to marry, and also to the increased longevity of their spouses. This change occurred among women of all ages, and among white and nonwhite women aged 30 to 64. The decline in the older years was greater for rural-farm than for other areas. Thus, one aspect of the decline in the farm population appears to have been a tendency toward fewer farm households headed by women. (The change in the farm definition, to exclude dwelling units rented for cash, may account for a part of this difference.)

DIFFERENTIALS IN HOUSEHOLD STATUS: WIFE

In 1950, 46.5 percent of the white and 32.3 percent of the nonwhite women over 14 years of age were classed as wives of household heads (see Table 11-6). In general, the age pattern, the color pattern, and the urban-rural pattern tend to follow those described in Chapter 10 in connection with percent of women married. It is evident that the proportion of women who are married must always be equal to, or greater than, the proportion who are wives of heads. At the younger ages, the difference between the two proportions is a measure of the number of families who are "doubled up," a situation in which a wife may be the spouse of a son of the head, or may herself be a daughter of

the head. At the older ages, the difference between the two percentages is a measure of the tendency for aged couples to live with a son or a daughter. A comparison of the statistics in Table 11-6 with the statistics in Chapter 10 concerning the percent of women of each age who are married will show that at the extremely young ages (15 to 19 years) a large share--as much as 50 percent or more--of the couples appeared to be living with parents, and that at the oldest ages (70 to 74) 10 percent or more appeared to be living with children. At the intermediate ages, all but a comparatively small fraction of the married women are wives of household heads. The tendency for young couples to live with parents, and for older persons to live with children, appears to be more characteristic of farm areas than of urban and rural-nonfarm areas. Among nonwhite couples, the tendency toward doubling up is much greater than it is among white couples, especially at the older ages.

The widespread tendency for the proportion of women classified as wives to increase between 1940 and 1950, especially among the white population of the younger ages, (shown in the right-hand columns of Table 11-6), was due to the increased propensity to marry, to increased longevity of males, and to an increase in the proportion of older people who maintain a separate residence rather than live with children or in homes for the aged.

DIFFERENTIALS IN HOUSEHOLD STATUS: CHILD

In 1950 about 94 percent of white children under 5 to 14 years of age lived in households of which either the father or the mother was the head (Table 11-7). Among nonwhite children, a much smaller proportion (about 80 percent) lived under these arrangements. With increasing age, a decreasing proportion of the population was classed as child of the head. As people enter the labor force, go away to school, or marry, they appear to change their household status from that of "child" to "head," "wife," "lodger," etc. Hence, beginning at about age 19 for boys, and at about

Table 11-6.—PERCENT OF FEMALES LIVING IN HOUSEHOLDS WHO ARE CLASSIFIED AS WIFE IN 1950, AND PERCENTAGE-POINT CHANGE, 1940 TO 1950, BY FIVE-YEAR AGE GROUPS, COLOR, SEX, AND URBAN-RURAL RESIDENCE

Color and age	Percent, 1950				Percentage-point change, 1940 to 1950			
	Total	Urban	Rural nonfarm	Rural farm	Total	Urban	Rural nonfarm	Rural farm
White..................	46.5	46.3	47.3	46.5	4.1	4.3	3.5	4.4
Under 5 years..........	...	...	...	...	...	...	...	...
5 to 9 years...........	...	...	...	...	...	...	...	...
10 to 14 years.........	...	...	0.1	...	...	...	0.1	...
15 to 19 years.........	11.8	10.6	16.5	9.9	4.5	5.2	5.6	1.4
20 to 24 years.........	57.3	53.5	69.1	58.7	15.8	17.1	15.8	12.9
25 to 29 years.........	76.0	73.1	83.8	79.8	10.0	11.6	8.2	8.6
30 to 34 years.........	81.0	78.2	87.2	86.2	6.4	7.5	5.4	5.7
35 to 39 years.........	81.6	78.8	86.6	88.6	4.2	5.1	3.9	3.6
40 to 44 years.........	80.0	77.0	84.7	88.8	2.5	3.1	3.5	2.3
45 to 49 years.........	77.3	74.2	81.4	87.8	1.6	2.3	3.1	1.9
50 to 54 years.........	72.7	69.2	76.9	85.5	1.9	2.8	3.9	2.8
55 to 59 years.........	66.9	63.0	71.0	81.3	2.5	3.6	4.7	3.5
60 to 64 years.........	57.6	53.1	62.7	73.8	2.6	3.5	5.1	4.0
65 to 69 years.........	46.5	42.2	51.7	62.1	3.0	3.8	5.0	4.9
70 to 74 years.........	34.1	30.2	40.2	46.3	2.6	3.0	5.0	4.1
75 years and over......	16.5	14.6	20.3	20.6	1.4	1.6	2.5	1.9
Nonwhite...............	32.3	32.3	32.3	32.3	0.7	2.5	-0.6	-1.3
Under 5 years..........	...	...	...	...	...	...	...	...
5 to 9 years...........	...	...	...	...	...	...	...	...
10 to 14 years.........	0.1	...	0.1	0.1	...	...	...	...
15 to 19 years.........	9.8	8.1	13.7	10.4	-0.8	1.2	0.7	-3.4
20 to 24 years.........	40.3	36.9	49.0	44.7	-0.2	5.1	2.7	-6.2
25 to 29 years.........	56.1	52.3	63.9	66.5	1.3	6.6	2.6	-4.1
30 to 34 years.........	62.6	58.1	70.1	77.4	3.3	7.4	4.7	0.8
35 to 39 years.........	63.7	58.8	69.0	81.2	3.1	6.7	3.8	2.3
40 to 44 years.........	61.9	56.5	66.8	80.7	2.8	6.0	4.3	3.5
45 to 49 years.........	58.5	53.0	61.7	78.8	0.9	4.6	2.9	2.9
50 to 54 years.........	53.7	47.7	57.0	73.7	0.7	4.2	3.8	3.8
55 to 59 years.........	48.9	42.3	52.0	69.4	0.2	3.5	2.9	3.6
60 to 64 years.........	41.5	34.5	44.8	62.6	0.4	3.0	3.6	6.4
65 to 69 years.........	31.5	24.9	34.7	49.0	1.1	3.1	3.6	5.5
70 to 74 years.........	22.1	16.7	25.7	34.7	1.2	2.5	2.9	4.9
75 years and over......	11.3	8.1	14.1	17.1	0.9	1.1	1.3	3.6

Source: U.S. Census of Population: 1950, Vol. II, Characteristics of the Population, Part 1, U.S. Summary, Table 107; Sixteenth Census of the United States: 1940, Vol. IV, Characteristics by Age.

age 17 to 18 in the case of girls, there is a swift drop in the proportion classed as child of the household head. By age 30, less than 10 percent of the population of 1950 retained this status. Persons who continue to be classified as child of the head after age 30 are unmarried children who work or keep house in their parental home, invalids and physically handicapped persons, and other adults who live with their parents and acknowledge the parent as head.

Beyond age 35, the proportion classed as "child" was higher among women than among men. Apparently the responsibility of living with elderly parents is more frequently assumed by unmarried women than by bachelors. The pattern was characteristic of both nonwhite and white women, in both rural and urban places. This difference cannot be attributed to marital status, for at each of these ages the proportion of women who have ever married exceeded the proportion of men. The tendency to remain at home with an aged parent appears to be more characteristic of white than of nonwhite children, for a higher proportion of whites than of nonwhites were classed as children at each adult age.

Nonwhite youths appear to begin leaving home at an earlier age than white youths. Among males, the tendency to retain the status of child in adult-

Table 11-7.—PERCENT OF PERSONS LIVING IN HOUSEHOLDS WHO ARE CLASSIFIED AS CHILD, BY FIVE-YEAR AGE GROUPS, COLOR, SEX, AND URBAN-RURAL RESIDENCE: 1950

Color and age	Male				Female			
	Total	Urban	Rural nonfarm	Rural farm	Total	Urban	Rural nonfarm	Rural farm
White..................	39.1	36.7	41.7	45.2	34.9	32.7	37.4	41.3
Under 5 years..........	91.5	91.3	92.8	90.4	91.4	91.1	92.6	90.4
5 to 9 years...........	93.8	93.7	94.4	93.5	93.6	93.3	94.2	93.5
10 to 14 years.........	93.8	93.8	94.0	93.8	94.1	93.8	94.4	94.6
15 to 19 years.........	89.2	89.0	88.9	90.0	77.6	78.0	73.3	81.3
20 to 24 years.........	48.5	47.6	41.8	61.6	29.2	31.5	20.9	30.3
25 to 29 years.........	19.0	18.7	14.5	28.9	13.9	15.3	9.3	13.4
30 to 34 years.........	10.3	10.0	7.8	15.9	9.4	10.5	6.3	8.5
35 to 39 years.........	6.8	6.5	5.6	9.6	7.1	7.8	5.2	6.0
40 to 44 years.........	4.7	4.4	4.3	6.5	5.4	5.9	4.4	4.7
45 to 49 years.........	3.0	2.8	3.0	3.8	3.7	3.9	3.5	3.3
50 to 54 years.........	1.7	1.5	1.9	1.9	2.4	2.5	2.6	2.1
55 to 59 years.........	0.8	0.8	1.0	0.9	1.4	1.4	1.6	1.2
60 to 64 years.........	0.4	0.3	0.5	0.4	0.8	0.7	0.8	0.7
65 to 69 years.........	0.2	0.2	0.2	0.2	0.4	0.3	0.5	0.4
70 to 74 years.........	...	...	...	...	...	...	...	...
75 years and over......	...	...	...	...	...	....	...	...
Nonwhite..............	38.9	33.9	42.4	48.8	35.6	30.8	39.2	46.8
Under 5 years..........	74.8	73.4	76.5	76.5	74.3	72.9	76.3	75.8
5 to 9 years...........	79.7	79.0	79.9	80.8	79.6	78.4	79.7	81.6
10 to 14 years.........	81.1	80.6	79.4	82.8	81.4	80.1	80.5	84.0
15 to 19 years.........	78.1	76.7	76.6	81.2	67.4	65.5	64.9	72.8
20 to 24 years.........	41.9	37.9	41.0	54.0	30.1	28.2	29.3	38.1
25 to 29 years.........	18.1	16.0	19.4	26.1	15.4	14.2	16.3	19.8
30 to 34 years.........	9.4	8.2	11.1	13.4	9.3	8.7	10.5	10.8
35 to 39 years.........	5.5	4.9	6.8	6.8	5.6	5.2	7.0	6.1
40 to 44 years.........	3.5	3.2	4.6	3.9	4.0	3.7	5.1	4.3
45 to 49 years.........	2.1	1.8	2.9	2.3	2.6	2.3	3.7	2.9
50 to 54 years.........	1.3	1.2	2.0	1.2	1.8	1.7	2.5	1.6
55 to 59 years.........	0.6	0.6	0.9	0.6	1.0	0.9	1.5	1.1
60 to 64 years.........	0.4	0.4	0.5	0.5	0.6	0.4	1.0	0.5
65 to 69 years.........	0.3	0.3	0.4	0.2	0.4	0.4	0.4	0.5
70 to 74 years.........	...	...	...	...	...	...	...	...
75 years and over......	....	...	...	...	...	...	...	...

Source: U.S. Census of Population: 1950, Vol. II, Characteristics of the Population, Part 1, U.S. Summary, Table 107; Sixteenth Census of the United States; 1940, Vol. IV, Characteristics by Age.

hood was much greater in rural-farm areas than in rural-nonfarm or urban areas. Among white females this tendency was considerably greater in urban than in rural areas. Unmarried farm girls appear to have left home at an earlier age, and in much greater proportions, than unmarried city girls.

Because of the marriage boom, the proportion of the population classed as "child" (especially in the young white population) decreased markedly between 1940 and 1950. Most of this change was due to an increase in the proportion of persons aged 15 to 25 who were married persons in their own households instead of unmarried children in a parental household (Table 11-8). The decrease was greater among women than among men, and, at most ages, tended to be greater in urban than in rural areas. Beyond age 25, there were only minute changes. Among the nonwhite population, in the age range 25 to 50, there was a small but consistent tendency for the proportion classed as "child" to increase.

In noting how rapidly the number of persons holding the status of "child" decreases after age 30, it should be kept in mind that when a person attains this age his parents are usually 55 years of age or over; therefore, even if the living arrangement is a satisfactory one, it is increasingly

Table 11-8.—PERCENTAGE-POINT CHANGE, 1940 TO 1950, OF PERSONS LIVING IN HOUSEHOLDS WHO ARE CLASSIFIED AS CHILD, BY FIVE-YEAR AGE GROUPS, COLOR, SEX, AND URBAN-RURAL RESIDENCE

Color and age	Male				Female			
	Total	Urban	Rural nonfarm	Rural farm	Total	Urban	Rural nonfarm	Rural farm
White..................	-3.0	-2.9	-1.2	-2.3	-3.3	-3.0	-1.7	-3.1
Under 5 years..........	0.6	0.7	0.3	0.3	0.6	0.7	0.3	0.4
5 to 9 years...........	0.6	0.7	0.3	0.5	0.5	0.6	0.3	0.5
10 to 14 years.........	...	...	-0.1	0.5	0.6	0.5	0.8	0.8
15 to 19 years.........	-1.3	-2.3	-1.6	1.1	-4.1	-5.1	-4.5	-0.7
20 to 24 years.........	-14.6	-16.8	-14.4	-3.9	-13.0	-14.3	-11.2	-10.9
25 to 29 years.........	-10.2	-11.2	-7.4	-5.9	-6.5	-7.6	-4.5	-5.9
30 to 34 years.........	-4.6	-4.8	-3.1	-3.8	-3.3	-3.7	-2.6	-3.5
35 to 39 years.........	-2.0	-2.1	-1.2	-2.1	-1.3	-1.5	-1.2	-1.6
40 to 44 years.........	-0.5	-0.6	-0.2	-0.1	-0.3	-0.3	-0.4	-0.2
45 to 49 years.........	0.1	...	0.2	0.4	-0.1	-0.1	-0.1	0.3
50 to 54 years.........	...	-0.1	...	0.1	-0.1	-0.1	...	0.1
55 to 59 years.........	-0.1	-0.1	-0.1	...	...	...	-0.1	0.1
60 to 64 years.........	...	-0.1	...	...	0.1	...	-0.1	0.1
65 to 69 years.........	0.2	0.2	0.2	0.2	0.4	0.3	0.5	0.4
70 to 74 years.........	...	...	...	...	...	...	...	...
75 years and over......	...	...	...	...	...	...	...	...
Nonwhite...............	-0.8	0.6	2.5	1.3	-1.1	0.7	1.9	0.9
Under 5 years..........	-2.7	-0.6	-1.9	-3.3	-2.9	-0.4	-2.1	-4.1
5 to 9 years...........	-1.2	-0.6	-0.8	-1.2	-1.1	-0.4	-0.9	-0.8
10 to 14 years.........	-1.0	-0.9	-1.9	-0.1	-0.5	0.1	-0.4	-0.1
15 to 19 years.........	0.5	...	...	2.3	0.5	...	1.3	3.1
20 to 24 years.........	-2.5	-4.4	-1.1	6.4	-0.1	-0.9	1.8	4.8
25 to 29 years.........	0.5	-0.4	2.1	6.3	1.1	0.6	2.5	3.7
30 to 34 years.........	0.1	-0.3	1.4	2.7	0.5	0.5	1.3	0.9
35 to 39 years.........	0.4	0.3	0.9	1.0	0.5	0.4	1.1	0.4
40 to 44 years.........	0.4	0.5	0.7	0.5	0.7	0.7	1.0	0.9
45 to 49 years.........	0.3	0.2	0.6	0.6	0.6	0.4	1.1	1.0
50 to 54 years.........	0.2	0.1	0.4	0.2	0.3	0.3	0.6	0.2
55 to 59 years.........	...	...	...	0.1	0.1	0.1	0.3	0.2
60 to 64 years.........	0.1	0.1	...	0.3	-0.1	-0.2	0.2	-0.2
65 to 69 years.........	0.3	0.3	0.4	0.2	0.4	0.4	0.4	0.5
70 to 74 years.........	...	...	...	...	...	...	...	...
75 years and over......	...	...	...	...	...	...	...	...

Source: U.S. Census of Population: 1950, Vol. II, Characteristics of the Population, Part 1, U.S. Summary, Table 107; Sixteenth Census of the United States: 1940, Vol. IV, Characteristics by Age.

likely to be broken by death. Upon the death of both parents, the "child" automatically becomes a household head unless the home is dissolved. Only one-half of one percent of the population 60 to 64 years of age is still classed as "child of the head;" at this age, all but a small fraction of the population has left its parental home, and all but a comparatively few parents are either deceased or are too aged and dependent to avoid being classified as "parent of the head" rather than "head."

DIFFERENTIALS IN HOUSEHOLD STATUS: GRANDCHILD

Under some circumstances, children live in the households of grandparents. They may be or-phans, the illegitimate children of a son or daughter, the children of a son or daughter whose marriage has been broken either through widowhood or divorce, or they may simply be married sons or daughters who are living, with their children, in the household of parents or parents-in-law. This situation is much more common among very young children (under 5 years) than among older children, for two reasons. First, young parents may live with their own parents while their children are still very young, but as they establish themselves financially and increase the size of their family they move into households of their own. A second reason is that the grandparents of a child who is 10 years old tend to be 60 years of age or older; hence they are subject not only to higher rates of mortality but to poorer health, which lessens their ability to maintain a household for their grandchildren. Beyond age 30, almost no fraction of the population lives in the household of its grandparents.

Among the nonwhite population in 1950, almost one child in five was living in the household of a grandparent (Table 11-9). At each age, the proportion of nonwhite children living in grandparents' households was about 3 times that of white children. Among nonwhite families there are more crowded living conditions, lower incomes, higher rates of illegitimacy, more desertion of families, and a higher proportion of marriages broken by death. All of these factors contribute to the kind of situation in which the grandparent, rather than the parent, is the household head.

Among the white population between 1940 and 1950, the proportion of children living in grandparents' homes increased, though negligibly (Table 11-10). At each individual age among the white population there was a decrease in the proportion of persons living in the household of a grandparent. This seeming inconsistency--a slight, over-all increase while each age group showed a decline--is a result of the baby boom: in

1950, a much larger percent of the population was in the 0 to 9 age group (where the status of grandchild has the most members) than had been in it in 1940. Among the nonwhite population, the proportion of children living with grandparents increased by about 20 percent; the greatest increases occurred in rural areas and among the youngest age groups. Greater mobility, increased migration, and an acute housing shortage among Negroes may have helped to account for this situation.

DIFFERENTIALS IN HOUSEHOLD STATUS: PARENT

Persons classed as "parent of the head" live in the households of their children or their children-in-law. As Table 11-11 shows, in 1950 less than 1 percent of any age group younger than age 40 for women and age 50 for men had this kind of living arrangement. Beyond these ages, the proportion climbed fairly rapidly; at ages of 75 and over, about 33 percent of women and 14 to 19 percent of men were living with their children. The fact that the proportion of persons in this status almost doubled with each additional five or six years after age 70 indicates that the status is associated with poor health and the consequent need for daily care and assistance.

Table 11-9.—PERCENT OF PERSONS LIVING IN HOUSEHOLD WHO ARE CLASSIFIED AS GRANDCHILD, BY FIVE-YEAR AGE GROUPS, COLOR, SEX, AND URBAN-RURAL RESIDENCE: 1950

Color and age	Male				Female			
	Total	Urban	Rural nonfarm	Rural farm	Total	Urban	Rural nonfarm	Rural farm
White...................	1.7	1.6	1.7	2.0	1.5	1.4	1.5	1.9
Under 5 years..........	6.8	6.9	5.7	8.0	6.8	6.9	5.8	7.9
5 to 9 years...........	4.5	4.6	4.0	4.8	4.6	4.7	4.0	4.8
10 to 14 years.........	3.2	3.2	3.1	3.3	3.2	3.3	3.0	3.0
15 to 19 years.........	2.3	2.3	2.4	2.1	2.0	2.0	1.9	1.8
20 to 24 years.........	1.0	0.9	1.0	1.1	0.6	0.6	0.5	0.6
25 to 29 years.........	0.2	0.2	0.2	0.3	0.2	0.2	0.2	0.2
Nonwhite...............	5.8	4.8	7.1	7.4	5.2	4.3	6.3	7.0
Under 5 years..........	18.0	17.4	18.2	19.0	18.0	17.4	17.8	19.4
5 to 9 years...........	13.9	13.2	14.4	14.7	13.5	12.9	14.6	13.9
10 to 14 years.........	10.7	9.5	12.5	11.4	10.1	9.2	12.0	10.3
15 to 19 years.........	7.2	6.3	9.0	7.5	5.8	5.1	7.3	6.0
20 to 24 years.........	2.7	2.3	3.8	3.1	1.9	1.7	2.4	2.0
25 to 29 years.........	0.8	0.7	1.4	0.9	0.7	0.6	1.0	0.7

Source: U.S. Census of Population: 1950, Vol. II, Characteristics of the Population, Part 1, U.S. Summary, Table 107; Sixteenth Census of the United States: 1940, Vol. IV, Characteristics by Age.

Table 11-10.—PERCENTAGE-POINT CHANGE; 1940 TO 1950, IN PERSONS LIVING IN HOUSEHOLDS WHO ARE CLASSIFIED AS GRANDCHILD, BY FIVE-YEAR AGE GROUPS, COLOR, SEX, AND URBAN-RURAL RESIDENCE

Color and age	Male				Female			
	Total	Urban	Rural nonfarm	Rural farm	Total	Urban	Rural nonfarm	Rural farm
White..................	0.1	0.1	0.1	...	...	...	...	-0.1
Under 5 years..........	-0.3	-0.4	-0.1	-0.1	-0.5	-0.5	-0.2	-0.3
5 to 9 years...........	-0.2	-0.3	-0.1	-0.2	-0.2	-0.2	-0.1	-0.2
10 to 14 years........	-0.2	-0.3	-0.2	-0.2	-0.2	-0.2	-0.3	-0.3
15 to 19 years........	...	...	...	...	...	-0.1	-0.2	...
20 to 24 years........	-0.1	-0.1	-0.1	0.1	-0.1	-0.1	-0.1	...
25 to 29 years........	-0.1	-0.1	-0.1	-0.1	...	...	...	...
30 to 34 years........	-0.1	-0.1	-0.1	-0.1	-0.1	-0.1	-0.1	-0.1
35 to 39 years........	...	...	...	...	...	...	...	...
Nonwhite..............	1.1	1.2	1.8	1.4	0.9	1.1	1.5	1.4
Under 5 years..........	2.4	1.7	2.7	3.3	2.5	1.8	2.5	3.9
5 to 9 years...........	1.6	2.2	1.4	1.7	1.7	2.0	2.0	1.5
10 to 14 years........	1.4	1.5	1.8	1.4	1.4	1.5	1.9	1.2
15 to 19 years........	1.3	1.2	1.8	1.3	1.1	0.8	1.5	1.2
20 to 24 years........	0.5	0.4	1.0	0.8	0.5	0.4	0.7	0.6
25 to 29 years........	0.2	0.2	0.5	0.2	0.2	0.2	0.4	0.2
30 to 34 years........	-0.3	-0.2	-0.4	-0.3	-0.2	-0.2	-0.3	-0.2
35 to 39 years........	-0.1	-0.1	-0.2	-0.1	-0.1	-0.1	-0.1	-0.1

Source: U.S. Census of Population: 1950, Vol. II, Characteristics of the Population, Part 1, U.S. Summary, Table 107; Sixteenth Census of the United States: 1940, Vol. IV, Characteristics by Age.

At each age, a higher proportion of women than of men are classed as parent of the head. It appears that as long as the male parent is alive he, or he and his spouse, tend to maintain a separate residence. When a male parent dies, his wife is more inclined to give up her own household and move in with a child. In other words, a mother seems more inclined than a father to abandon the parental household at the death of the spouse.

Elderly white male parents live with children in a higher proportion of cases than do elderly nonwhite male parents. Among females, the reverse is true--elderly white females are found living with children in slightly smaller proportions than elderly nonwhite females. A larger proportion of mothers live in the household of a child in rural-farm areas than in other areas. The proportion is also higher in urban areas than in rural-nonfarm areas. These facts seem to indicate that, when their spouses die, many elderly women migrate from the country to the city to live with their children.

Between 1940 and 1950, there was a slight over-all increase in the proportion of the total popula-

tion classed as parent of the head. Yet Table 11-12 reports that almost every age-color-sex-residence group had a smaller proportion of persons in this category in 1950 than in 1940. This seeming contradiction is due to the over-all aging, during the decade, of the population. In 1950, parents of every age were less dependent upon their children for a place to live than they had been in 1940. The extension of Social Security benefits, greater longevity, and better general economic conditions were probably the factors primarily responsible for their increased independence. The changes in this direction were greatest in the older age groups, among all males, and among nonwhite women.

DIFFERENTIALS IN HOUSEHOLD STATUS: OTHER RELATIVE

In some cultures, the normal household contains relatives other than the head, his wife, their children and (possibly) parents. In the United States, only a comparatively few persons live with brothers, sisters, uncles, aunts, cousins, or other

Table 11-11.—PERCENT OF PERSONS LIVING IN HOUSEHOLDS WHO ARE CLASSIFIED AS PARENT, BY FIVE-YEAR AGE GROUPS, COLOR, SEX, AND URBAN-RURAL RESIDENCE: 1950

Color and age	Male				Female			
	Total	Urban	Rural nonfarm	Rural farm	Total	Urban	Rural nonfarm	Rural farm
White...................	1.1	1.1	0.9	1.2	2.8	3.0	2.2	2.6
30 to 34 years.........	...	...	...	...	...	...	...	...
35 to 39 years.........	...	...	...	...	0.1	0.1	0.1	0.1
40 to 44 years.........	0.1	0.1	0.1	0.1	0.4	0.5	0.4	...
45 to 49 years.........	0.3	0.3	0.3	0.2	1.2	1.3	1.1	0.7
50 to 54 years.........	0.7	0.7	0.8	0.5	2.9	3.1	2 6	1.9
55 to 59 years.........	1.4	1.5	1.5	1.1	5.3	5.8	4.6	3.9
60 to 64 years.........	2.9	3.0	2.7	2.4	9.3	10.0	7.7	7.8
65 to 69 years.........	5.1	5.4	4.6	4.9	13.8	14.6	11.2	14.2
70 to 74 years.........	8.7	9.2	6.9	9.1	19.9	20.6	15.2	24.2
75 years and over......	18.7	19.2	14.6	23.3	33.3	33.2	27.1	44.9
Nonwhite...............	0.7	0.7	0.6	0.7	2.5	2.7	2.0	2.3
30 to 34 years.........	...	0.1	...	...	0.1	0.1	0.1	0.1
35 to 39 years.........	0.1	0.1	0.1	0.1	0.5	0.5	0.4	0.5
40 to 44 years.........	0.2	0.2	0.2	0.2	1.4	1.5	1.3	1.2
45 to 49 years.........	0.5	0.6	0.4	0.4	2.9	3.2	2.4	2.4
50 to 54 years.........	0.9	0.9	0.9	0.7	5.5	5.9	4.4	4.8
55 to 59 years.........	1.4	1.6	1.3	1.0	8.6	9.4	6.3	7.5
60 to 64 years.........	2.7	2.9	2.7	2.1	12.7	14.3	8.7	11.0
65 to 69 years.........	4.5	5.1	3.4	4.0	17.0	18.4	11.3	19.0
70 to 74 years.........	7.1	8.0	5.3	6.9	23.0	24.6	15.2	26.7
75 years and over......	14.1	15.4	9.5	15.9	32.8	33.3	23.5	42.2

Source: U.S. Census of Population: 1950, Vol. II, Characteristics of the Population, Part 1, U.S. Summary, Table 107; Sixteenth Census of the United States: 1940, Vol. IV, Characteristics by Age.

Table 11-12.—PERCENTAGE-POINT CHANGE, 1940 TO 1950, IN PERSONS LIVING IN HOUSEHOLDS WHO ARE CLASSIFIED AS PARENT, BY FIVE-YEAR AGE GROUPS, COLOR, SEX, AND URBAN-RURAL RESIDENCE

Color and age	Male				Female			
	Total	Urban	Rural nonfarm	Rural farm	Total	Urban	Rural nonfarm	Rural farm
White...................	0.1	0.1	...	0.2	0.3	0.3	0.1	0.3
35 to 39 years.........	...	...	...	...	...	...	...	...
40 to 44 years.........	...	...	...	...	...	...	...	-0.3
45 to 49 years.........	...	...	...	...	...	...	-0.1	-0.1
50 to 54 years.........	-0.1	-0.2	...	...	...	-0.1	-0.2	-0.1
55 to 59 years.........	-0.3	-0.3	-0.2	-0.1	-0.2	-0.2	-0.6	-0.3
60 to 64 years.........	-0.3	-0.6	-0.5	...	-0.3	-0.3	-0.9	-0.4
65 to 69 years.........	-0.8	-1.0	-0.8	-0.2	-1.2	-1.0	-1.5	-1.4
70 to 74 years.........	-1.2	-1.5	-1.3	-0.4	-1.6	-1.5	-1.7	-0.7
75 years and over......	-1.6	-1.6	-1.3	-0.3	-1.5	-1.2	-0.5	-0.5
Nonwhite...............	0.1	...	...	0.1	0.1	0.1	...	...
30 to 34 years.........	...	0.1	...	...	0.1	0.1	0.1	0.1
35 to 39 years.........	...	...	...	...	-0.1	-0.1	-0.3	-0.2
40 to 44 years.........	...	...	...	...	-0.4	-0.3	-0.4	-0.6
45 to 49 years.........	...	0.1	-0.1	0.1	-0.6	-0.6	-0.7	-0.8
50 to 54 years.........	...	-0.2	-0.1	0.1	-0.8	-1.0	-0.9	-1.0
55 to 59 years.........	-0.2	-0.3	-0.4	-0.2	-0.8	-1.3	-1.0	-0.8
60 to 64 years.........	...	-0.3	0.2	...	-1.2	-1.1	-1.8	-2.4
65 to 69 years.........	-0.1	-0.5	-0.5	...	-2.7	-2.7	-2.8	-2.0
70 to 74 years.........	-0.9	-1.3	-0.9	-0.8	-3.4	-2.7	-2.9	-3.4
75 years and over......	-1.8	-1.5	-1.8	-1.4	-4.9	-3.9	-4.0	-2.1

Source: U.S. Census of Population: 1950, Vol. II, Characteristics of the Population, Part 1, U.S. Summary, Table 107; Sixteenth Census of the United States: 1940, Vol. IV, Characteristics by Age.

more distant relatives. Among the white population, only 3.7 percent lived in this kind of a household in 1950; among the nonwhite population, the proportion was 7.1--almost twice as great (Table 11-13).[4]

Only 1 to 2 percent of white children 0 to 9 years of age lived with relatives other than their parents or grandparents, but about 5 percent of nonwhite children were living this way.

The status of "other relative" seems to be a common one among migrants. When a young person (20 to 29 years old) migrates, it appears that he often travels first to the home of a relative who lives in a city, and resides there until he finds work and gets "on his feet." The fact that there are higher proportions in the status of "other relative" among urban persons 20 to 24 and 25 to 29 than there are at other ages, and among other

Table 11-13.—PERCENT OF PERSONS LIVING IN HOUSEHOLDS WHO ARE CLASSIFIED AS OTHER RELATIVE, BY FIVE-YEAR AGE GROUPS, COLOR, SEX, AND URBAN-RURAL RESIDENCE: 1950

Color and age	Male				Female			
	Total	Urban	Rural nonfarm	Rural farm	Total	Urban	Rural nonfarm	Rural farm
White.................	3.7	3.9	3.1	3.5	3.7	4.0	3.0	3.7
Under 5 years..........	1.1	1.1	1.0	1.1	1.2	1.3	1.1	1.2
5 to 9 years...........	1.1	1.2	1.0	1.1	1.3	1.3	1.1	1.2
10 to 14 years.........	2.1	2.2	2.1	1.8	1.9	2.0	1.8	1.6
15 to 19 years........	4.0	4.2	4.1	3.3	5.4	5.4	5.5	5.5
20 to 24 years.........	7.6	7.9	7.3	6.8	6.6	6.6	5.4	8.7
25 to 29 years.........	6.5	7.0	5.0	6.3	4.3	4.4	3.3	5.3
30 to 34 years.........	5.1	5.5	3.7	5.0	3.3	3.5	2.3	3.6
35 to 39 years.........	4.2	4.6	3.2	4.3	3.0	3.3	2.2	3.0
40 to 44 years.........	3.8	4.0	3.0	3.8	3.1	3.4	2.2	2.9
45 to 49 years.........	3.5	3.7	3.0	3.7	3.4	3.6	2.5	3.1
50 to 54 years.........	3.4	3.5	2.9	3.7	3.9	4.2	2.8	3.5
55 to 59 years.........	3.2	3.2	2.8	3.5	4.3	4.6	3.3	4.0
60 to 64 years.........	3.3	3.3	3.1	3.6	5.2	5.5	4.1	5.0
65 to 69 years.........	3.6	3.5	3.4	4.1	6.0	6.3	4.7	6.3
70 to 74 years.........	4.0	4.0	3.5	4.5	7.2	7.5	5.9	7.7
75 years and over......	4.8	4.7	4.3	6.1	8.7	8.9	7.6	9.7
Nonwhite................	7.1	7.9	6.4	5.4	7.2	7.9	6.3	6.2
Under 5 years..........	5.1	5.9	4.2	3.9	5.4	6.2	4.8	4.1
5 to 9 years...........	4.8	5.3	4.7	4.0	5.3	6.2	4.7	4.1
10 to 14 years.........	6.3	7.1	6.6	5.1	6.6	7.7	6.2	5.0
15 to 19 years........	9.1	10.6	8.8	7.0	11.9	13.6	10.4	9.5
20 to 24 years.........	15.6	18.0	13.6	10.3	13.3	14.0	11.3	12.4
25 to 29 years.........	12.0	12.9	10.4	9.4	9.0	9.4	7.1	9.0
30 to 34 years.........	9.1	9.6	8.5	7.6	6.7	7.1	5.5	6.2
35 to 39 years.........	6.9	7.5	6.3	5.2	5.5	5.8	4.6	4.6
40 to 44 years.........	5.6	6.0	5.0	4.4	5.0	5.4	4.3	3.9
45 to 49 years.........	4.7	5.0	4.5	3.6	4.7	5.1	4.3	3.6
50 to 54 years.........	4.2	4.5	4.0	3.2	4.9	5.2	4.2	4.2
55 to 59 years.........	3.9	4.3	3.7	3.0	5.1	5.5	4.6	4.1
60 to 64 years.........	3.9	4.1	4.1	3.3	6.1	6.6	4.9	5.4
65 to 69 years.........	4.1	4.4	3.5	3.7	7.2	7.4	5.6	8.2
70 to 74 years.........	4.9	5.2	4.1	4.8	9.2	9.3	7.5	10.7
75 years and over......	7.0	7.5	5.1	7.8	13.0	13.1	10.5	15.7

Source: U.S. Census of Population: 1950, Vol. II, Characteristics of the Population, Part 1, U.S. Summary, Table 107; Sixteenth Census of the United States: 1940, Vol. IV, Characteristics by Age.

[4]Although grandchildren are often tabulated as "other relatives," they are treated separately in these tables. Hence, they are not included in the present discussion.

residence groups at these same ages, indicates that the above generalization is a valid one. The very large net migration of Negroes to cities between 1940 and 1950 makes the proportion in the status of "other relative" (14 to 18 percent) among urban nonwhites especially meaningful. Table 11-14 also gives evidence that the greater increases in this status between 1940 and 1950 occurred among the nonwhite population in the migration ages (20 to 35).

After they pass the migration ages, and until they reach age 60, from 3 to 5 percent of men and women live as "other relatives;" beyond age 60, the proportion rises. This rise reflects the tendency for families to take care of their more distant elderly relatives who have no children, or whose children cannot care for them.

A smaller proportion of the white population lived with "other relatives" in 1950 than in 1940, but among the nonwhite population the situation was reversed (Table 11-14). As noted above, the migration of nonwhites was probably a major factor in this difference.

DIFFERENTIALS IN HOUSEHOLD STATUS: LODGER

An unusually large proportion of lodgers are either young persons 20 to 29 years of age or older persons 60 years of age or over. (See Table 11-15.) Many migrants live as lodgers until they marry or move into households of their own. Many

Table 11-14.—PERCENTAGE-POINT CHANGE, 1940 TO 1950, IN PERSONS LIVING IN HOUSEHOLDS WHO ARE CLASSIFIED AS OTHER RELATIVE, BY FIVE-YEAR AGE GROUPS, COLOR, SEX, AND URBAN-RURAL RESIDENCE

Color and age	Male				Female			
	Total	Urban	Rural nonfarm	Rural farm	Total	Urban	Rural nonfarm	Rural farm
White.....................	-0.3	-0.5	-0.3	-0.2	-0.4	-0.4	-0.2	-0.2
Under 5 years..........	...	...	0.1	...	0.1	0.1	0.1	0.1
5 to 9 years..........	-0.1	...	-0.1	-0.1	...	-0.1	-0.1	...
10 to 14 years........	0.3	0.5	0.4	-0.1	-0.1	-0.1	-0.2	-0.3
15 to 19 years........	0.3	0.5	0.3	-0.2	0.4	0.5	0.4	0.2
20 to 24 years........	0.3	0.3	-0.2	0.6	-0.4	-0.3	-0.5	0.2
25 to 29 years........	-0.8	-1.0	-1.0	-0.3	-1.0	-1.1	-0.5	-1.1
30 to 34 years........	-0.9	-1.1	-0.7	-0.7	-0.8	-0.9	-0.4	-0.9
35 to 39 years........	-0.8	-0.9	-0.5	-0.5	-0.5	-0.6	-0.1	-0.4
40 to 44 years........	-0.4	-0.6	-0.2	-0.3	-0.2	-0.3	-0.1	-0.1
45 to 49 years........	-0.2	-0.2	0.1	...	...	-0.2	0.1	0.1
50 to 54 years........	-0.2	-0.2	-0.1	...	-0.1	-0.3	-0.2	...
55 to 59 years........	-0.4	-0.5	-0.3	-0.3	-0.3	-0.5	-0.2	-0.1
60 to 64 years........	-0.3	-0.4	-0.1	-0.2	-0.3	-0.6	-0.2	0.1
65 to 69 years........	-0.3	-0.4	-0.1	-0.1	-0.4	-0.6	-0.5	0.1
70 to 74 years........	0.1	0.1	...	0.2	0.3	0.2	0.2	0.6
75 years and over.....	0.3	0.3	0.3	0.7	0.5	0.5	0.6	0.6
Nonwhite...............	0.9	0.9	0.3	0.2	0.7	0.8	0.3	0.3
Under 5 years..........	0.9	1.0	-0.1	0.3	0.9	0.9	0.4	0.3
5 to 9 years..........	0.3	0.4	0.2	-0.1	0.3	0.5	-0.3	-0.2
10 to 14 years........	0.5	1.1	0.8	-0.6	0.1	0.4	-0.4	-0.6
15 to 19 years........	0.3	0.8	-0.2	-0.8	1.1	1.4	0.1	...
20 to 24 years........	3.4	3.0	1.7	1.1	2.2	1.8	1.7	2.3
25 to 29 years........	2.3	1.6	1.3	2.2	1.2	0.8	0.4	2.1
30 to 34 years........	2.0	1.4	2.0	2.2	0.8	0.8	0.5	1.0
35 to 39 years........	1.4	1.4	0.9	0.9	1.1	1.0	0.6	0.8
40 to 44 years........	1.2	1.2	0.8	0.8	1.0	1.1	0.9	0.5
45 to 49 years........	1.0	0.9	0.9	0.7	1.1	1.1	1.2	0.7
50 to 54 years........	0.7	0.6	0.6	0.4	0.9	0.7	0.7	0.8
55 to 59 years........	0.8	0.7	0.7	0.5	1.0	...	1.0	0.4
60 to 64 years........	0.8	0.6	0.9	0.6	1.1	1.3	0.7	0.5
65 to 69 years........	0.8	0.7	0.1	0.7	1.0	1.3	0.4	1.3
70 to 74 years........	1.0	0.9	0.7	0.9	1.4	2.0	1.6	1.0
75 years and ovdr.....	1.4	2.1	0.5	1.4	1.9	3.0	1.8	2.0

Source: U.S. Census of Population: 1950, Vol. II, Characteristics of the Population, Part 1, U.S. Summary, Table 107; Sixteenth Census of the United States: 1940, Vol. IV, Characteristics by Age.

Table 11-15.—PERCENT OF PERSONS LIVING IN HOUSEHOLDS WHO ARE CLASSIFIED AS LODGER, BY FIVE-YEAR AGE GROUPS, COLOR, SEX, AND URBAN-RURAL RESIDENCE: 1950

Color and age	Male				Female			
	Total	Urban	Rural nonfarm	Rural farm	Total	Urban	Rural nonfarm	Rural farm
White..................	2.4	3.0	1.7	1.2	1.8	2.3	1.2	0.6
Under 5 years..........	0.6	0.7	0.5	0.4	0.6	0.7	0.5	0.4
5 to 9 years...........	0.6	0.6	0.5	0.6	0.6	0.6	0.5	0.5
10 to 14 years.........	0.7	0.6	0.6	0.8	0.7	0.7	0.7	0.6
15 to 19 years.........	2.0	2.4	1.6	1.6	2.4	3.0	2.0	0.9
20 to 24 years.........	5.5	6.9	3.5	2.1	3.9	4.8	2.4	1.0
25 to 29 years.........	3.6	4.4	2.2	1.4	2.3	2.9	1.1	0.5
30 to 34 years.........	2.3	2.9	1.4	1.0	1.6	2.1	0.8	0.4
35 to 39 years.........	2.1	2.6	1.4	0.9	1.5	1.9	0.8	0.3
40 to 44 years.........	2.3	2.8	1.6	1.0	1.5	1.9	0.9	0.4
45 to 49 years.........	2.6	3.2	1.8	1.1	1.6	2.0	1.0	0.4
50 to 54 years.........	3.1	3.7	2.1	1.2	1.8	2.2	1.2	0.4
55 to 59 years.........	3.2	3.9	2.5	1.2	2.0	2.4	1.2	0.5
60 to 64 years.........	3.7	4.6	2.7	1.6	2.4	3.0	1.5	0.7
65 to 69 years.........	4.0	4.9	2.9	2.1	2.9	3.6	1.7	0.9
70 to 74 years.........	4.2	5.1	3.1	2.6	3.3	4.1	2.0	1.3
75 years and over......	4.8	5.6	3.9	3.4	4.3	4.9	3.4	2.4
Nonwhite...............	6.5	9.4	3.1	1.5	4.8	6.9	2.0	0.9
Under 5 years..........	2.1	3.3	1.0	0.5	2.3	3.5	1.0	0.5
5 to 9 years...........	1.6	2.4	1.0	0.5	1.6	2.4	0.9	0.4
10 to 14 years.........	1.7	2.6	1.2	0.7	1.7	2.7	1.1	0.5
15 to 19 years.........	3.3	4.6	2.5	1.8	4.0	6.1	2.4	1.0
20 to 24 years.........	10.0	13.9	5.3	2.7	8.7	12.0	3.6	1.5
25 to 29 years.........	11.5	15.1	4.5	2.4	8.5	11.1	3.0	1.3
30 to 34 years.........	10.6	13.7	4.3	2.2	7.1	9.3	2.5	1.1
35 to 39 years.........	10.0	13.2	4.5	1.8	6.3	8.3	2.4	1.0
40 to 44 years.........	9.6	12.7	4.5	1.9	5.5	7.2	2.1	1.0
45 to 49 years.........	9.5	12.3	5.1	2.2	4.9	6.4	2.2	1.0
50 to 54 years.........	9.2	12.1	4.8	2.0	4.7	6.2	2.1	1.1
55 to 59 years.........	8.2	11.1	4.9	1.9	4.3	5.8	1.8	1.2
60 to 64 years.........	8.2	11.4	5.0	2.3	4.6	6.2	2.2	1.4
65 to 69 years.........	7.8	11.5	4.5	2.6	4.9	6.8	2.3	1.8
70 to 74 years.........	7.6	11.5	3.9	2.9	5.2	7.2	2.5	2.1
75 years and over......	7.2	10.7	4.5	3.4	5.7	7.6	3.0	3.2

Source: U.S. Census of Population: 1950, Vol. II, Characteristics of the Population, Part 1, U.S. Summary, Table 107; Sixteenth Census of the United States: 1940, Vol. IV, Characteristics by Age.

older persons who have lost their families are inclined to rent rooms in private households; perhaps in this way they regain, under controlled conditions, some of the family life they have lost through the death of a spouse. More men than women, and more nonwhites than whites, are lodgers. Lodgers are extremely rare in rural-farm areas, and are most plentiful in cities. In 1950, lodgers comprised 9.4 percent of the nonwhite males living in cities.

Between 1940 and 1950 the proportion of the population classed as lodgers declined substantially, in all age-sex-color-residence groups (see Table 11-16). This change may have been due, in part, to a change in census definitions. In 1940, houses with 5 to 10 lodgers were classed as households, whereas in 1950 they were classed as quasi households. Other things being equal, this new definition would tend to decrease the "lodger" population and to increase the quasi household population. Improved economic conditions, earlier age at marriage, and the increased proportion of persons of all ages who were married were also partly responsible for this change.

Table 11-16.—PERCENTAGE-POINT CHANGE, 1940 TO 1950, IN PERSONS LIVING IN HOUSEHOLDS WHO ARE CLASSIFIED AS LODGER, BY FIVE-YEAR AGE GROUPS, COLOR, SEX, AND URBAN-RURAL RESIDENCE

Color and age	Male				Female			
	Total	Urban	Rural nonfarm	Rural farm	Total	Urban	Rural nonfarm	Rural farm
White.................	-1.2	-1.7	-1.1	-0.7	-0.6	-0.8	-0.7	-0.4
Under 5 years..........	-0.2	-0.3	-0.2	-0.3	-0.3	-0.3	-0.2	-0.3
5 to 9 years...........	-0.2	-0.3	-0.3	-0.2	-0.3	-0.4	-0.3	-0.2
10 to 14 years.........	-0.3	-0.3	-0.3	-0.5	-0.3	-0.3	-0.3	-0.3
15 to 19 years.........	...	0.4	-0.2	-0.5	0.3	0.5	-0.2	-0.3
20 to 24 years.........	-0.5	-0.3	-2.1	-1.0	-1.1	-1.0	-2.5	-1.2
25 to 29 years.........	-2.3	-2.9	-2.7	-1.3	-1.7	-1.9	-2.2	-0.9
30 to 34 years.........	-2.2	-2.8	-1.9	-1.0	-1.3	-1.7	-1.3	-0.5
35 to 39 years.........	-2.2	-3.0	-1.5	-0.9	-0.9	-1.2	-0.8	-0.3
40 to 44 years.........	-2.1	-2.8	-1.3	-0.7	-0.5	-0.8	-0.4	-0.1
45 to 49 years.........	-1.8	-2.5	-1.4	-0.6	-0.3	-0.5	-0.2	-0.1
50 to 54 years.........	-1.6	-2.3	-1.5	-0.8	-0.2	-0.5	-0.1	-0.2
55 to 59 years.........	-1.4	-2.0	-1.2	-0.9	-0.2	-0.5	-0.2	-0.1
60 to 64 years.........	-1.0	-1.5	-1.0	-0.7	-0.2	-0.5	-0.1	-0.1
65 to 69 years.........	-0.9	-1.6	-0.8	-0.7	-0.3	-0.7	-0.2	-0.2
70 to 74 years.........	-1.0	-1.7	-0.8	-0.6	-0.5	-0.8	-0.4	-0.2
75 years and over......	-1.2	-1.8	-0.9	-0.8	-0.5	-1.0	-0.2	-0.2
Nonwhite...............	-1.9	-4.6	-2.7	-1.2	-1.4	-3.5	-1.6	-0.5
Under 5 years..........	-0.6	-2.1	-0.8	-0.3	-0.5	-2.2	-0.9	-0.3
5 to 9 years...........	-0.7	-2.0	-0.7	-0.4	-0.9	-2.2	-0.9	-0.5
10 to 14 years.........	-1.0	-1.9	-1.0	-0.6	-1.1	-2.2	-1.2	-0.5
15 to 19 years.........	-1.5	-2.2	-2.1	-1.4	-1.1	-2.6	-2.0	-0.5
20 to 24 years.........	-1.3	-3.7	-4.5	-2.2	-1.6	-4.6	-3.1	-0.7
25 to 29 years.........	-3.1	-7.2	-5.4	-2.0	-2.7	-5.9	-2.9	-0.7
30 to 34 years.........	-3.9	-7.6	-4.5	-1.8	-2.6	-4.9	-2.1	-0.6
35 to 39 years.........	-4.1	-7.0	-3.7	-2.0	-1.7	-3.4	-1.2	-0.5
40 to 44 years.........	-3.8	-6.2	-3.2	-1.5	-1.4	-3.0	-1.2	-0.3
45 to 49 years.........	-1.9	-4.4	-1.7	-0.7	-0.8	-2.3	-0.4	-0.2
50 to 54 years.........	-1.0	-3.5	-1.9	-0.9	-0.7	-2.2	-0.6	-0.3
55 to 59 years.........	-0.6	-2.8	-1.0	-1.0	-0.6	-2.0	-0.6	...
60 to 64 years.........	-0.4	-2.7	-1.1	-0.8	-0.6	-2.1	-0.6	-0.3
65 to 69 years.........	-0.4	-2.5	-1.7	-0.6	-0.8	-2.2	-0.8	-0.3
70 to 74 years.........	-1.1	-2.9	-2.7	-1.1	-1.0	-2.2	-1.1	-0.8
75 years and over......	-1.8	-3.9	-2.0	-1.8	-0.7	-2.1	-0.8	-0.5

Source: U.S. Census of Population: 1950, Vol. II, Characteristics of the Population, Part 1, U.S. Summary, Table 107; Sixteenth Census of the United States: 1940, Vol. IV, Characteristics by Age.

DIFFERENTIALS IN HOUSEHOLD STATUS: RESIDENT EMPLOYEE

The status of resident employee (servant, cook, housekeeper, hired hand) was not common in 1950 (Table 11-17); less than 1 percent of the population held this status. It was found among women twice as frequently as among men, and among nonwhites about twice as frequently as among whites. In urban areas, only older males were found as resident employees in any meaningful numbers, whereas in rural-farm areas a few young men also held this status. In urban and rural-nonfarm areas, only elderly white women and middle-aged nonwhite women were resident employees to any significant extent.

Between 1940 and 1950, the percentage of the population classed as resident employee dropped by more than 50 percent. Table 11-18 reports large declines for most age-sex-color-residence groups. The depression of 1930 to 1940 forced a great many people to work as domestic servants; the manpower shortages and improved wage scales of the 1940's caused a great decrease in this kind of employment.

Table 11-17.—PERCENT OF PERSONS LIVING IN HOUSEHOLDS WHO ARE CLASSIFIED AS RESIDENT EMPLOYEE, BY FIVE-YEAR AGE GROUPS, COLOR, SEX, AND URBAN-RURAL RESIDENCE: 1950

Color and age	Male				Female			
	Total	Urban	Rural nonfarm	Rural farm	Total	Urban	Rural nonfarm	Rural farm
White..................	0.2	...	0.1	0.9	0.4	0.4	0.4	0.4
Under 5 years..........	...	...	...	0.1	...	...	...	0.1
5 to 9 years...........	...	...	...	0.1	...	...	0.1	0.1
10 to 14 years.........	0.1	...	0.1	0.1	0.1	...	0.1	0.1
15 to 19 years.........	0.4	...	0.1	1.7	0.4	0.4	0.5	0.4
20 to 24 years.........	0.4	...	0.2	2.4	0.3	0.3	0.4	0.5
25 to 29 years.........	0.2	...	0.1	1.2	0.2	0.2	0.2	0.4
30 to 34 years.........	0.1	...	0.1	0.9	0.2	0.2	0.3	0.3
35 to 39 years.........	0.2	...	0.1	0.9	0.3	0.3	0.4	0.3
40 to 44 years.........	0.2	...	0.1	0.9	0.4	0.4	0.4	0.4
45 to 49 years.........	0.2	0.1	0.2	1.0	0.6	0.6	0.7	0.5
50 to 54 years.........	0.2	0.1	0.2	1.1	0.7	0.7	0.8	0.6
55 to 59 years.........	0.3	0.1	0.2	1.1	0.9	0.9	0.9	0.7
60 to 64 years.........	0.3	0 1	0.2	1.3	1.1	1.2	1.2	0.9
65 to 69 years.........	0.3	0.1	0.2	1.2	1.1	1.1	1.1	0.9
70 to 74 years.........	0.2	0.1	0.2	0.8	0.8	0.8	0.9	0.7
75 years and over......	0.1	...	0.1	0.4	0.5	0.4	0.5	0.5
Nonwhite...............	0.3	0.2	0.3	0.3	0.7	0.9	0.7	0.3
Under 5 years..........	...	...	0.1	0.1	...	...	...	0.1
5 to 9 years...........	...	...	...	...	0.1	0.1	0.1	...
10 to 14 years.........	0.1	0.1	0.2	0.1	0.1	0.1	0.1	0.1
15 to 19 years.........	0.2	0.1	0.2	0.3	0.5	0 6	0.5	0.2
20 to 24 years.........	0.3	0.2	0.3	0.5	1.1	1.3	0.9	0.4
25 to 29 years.........	0.3	0.2	0.4	0.7	1.1	1.2	1.2	0.4
30 to 34 years.........	0.3	0.3	0.4	0.6	1.0	1.2	1.1	0.4
35 to 39 years.........	0.4	0.3	0.4	0.7	1.1	1.3	1.2	0.4
40 to 44 years.........	0.4	0.4	0.4	0.7	1.3	1.4	1.4	0.5
45 to 49 years.........	0.5	0.4	0.6	0.5	1.4	1.5	1.4	0.6
50 to 54 years.........	0.4	0.4	0.5	0.6	1.4	1.6	1.5	0.7
55 to 59 years.........	0.5	0.4	0.7	0.7	1.3	1.5	1.0	0.5
60 to 64 years.........	0.5	0.5	0.5	0.8	1.2	1.5	0.9	0.7
65 to 69 years.........	0.4	0.4	0.4	0.6	0.8	1.0	0.8	0.6
70 to 74 years.........	0.4	0.3	0.4	0.5	0.8	0.9	0.5	0.6
75 years and over......	0.4	0.4	0.2	0.4	0.4	0.4	0.5	0.3

Source: U.S. Census of Population: 1950, Vol. II, Characteristics of the Population, Part 1, U.S. Summary, Table 107; Sixteenth Census of the United States: 1940, Vol. IV, Characteristics by Age.

DIFFERENTIALS IN FAMILY STATUS OF THE POPULATION

Sociologists and social workers, among others, frequently find that the information which is available to them concerning household status is unsatisfactory because it fails to reveal the nature of the family groupings within the household. The definitions which the Census has devised (presented earlier in this chapter) enable it to gather data concerning the family status of individuals. The Census has combined these definitions with its concepts concerning household status in such a way that information about these two aspects of the nation's households can be examined simultaneously. Tables 11-19 through 11-23 summarize the information that was made available by the 1950 census concerning the United States population 14 years of age and over, by sex, color, and age. The tabulations are confined to the population 14 years of age and over because the population under this age tends to have the status of "child" or "grandchild" in a primary family, which was described above. Comparable data for 1940 are not available, nor are data with respect to urban-rural residence. In the following analysis of these

Table 11-18.—PERCENTAGE-POINT CHANGE, 1940 TO 1950, IN PERSONS LIVING IN HOUSEHOLDS WHO ARE CLASSIFIED AS RESIDENT EMPLOYEE BY FIVE-YEAR AGE GROUPS, COLOR, SEX, AND URBAN-RURAL RESIDENCE

Color and age	Male				Female			
	Total	Urban	Rural nonfarm	Rural farm	Total	Urban	Rural nonfarm	Rural farm
White.....................	-0.3	-0.1	...	-0.9	-0.7	-0.8	-0.6	-0.3
Under 5 years..........	...	...	...	0.1	...	...	...	0.1
5 to 9 years...........	...	...	...	0.1	...	...	0.1	...
10 to 14 years.........	0.1	...	0.1	...	0.1	...	0.1	0.1
15 to 19 years.........	-0.3	...	...	-0.8	-1.2	-1.4	-1.3	-0.7
20 to 24 years.........	-0.9	-0.1	-0.1	-2.9	-2.0	-2.2	-1.7	-1.0
25 to 29 years.........	-0.6	-0.1	-0.1	-2.5	-1.2	-1.3	-1.0	-0.5
30 to 34 years.........	-0.4	-0.1	-0.1	-1.5	-0.8	-0.9	-0.6	-0.5
35 to 39 years.........	-0.3	-0.1	-0.1	-1.1	-0.7	-0.8	-0.5	-0.4
40 to 44 years.........	-0.2	-0.1	-0.1	-0.9	-0.7	-0.7	-0.7	-0.4
45 to 49 years.........	-0.3	...	...	-0.8	-0.6	-0.7	-0.6	-0.4
50 to 54 years.........	-0.4	...	...	-1.0	-0.7	-0.8	-0.8	-0.4
55 to 59 years.........	-0.3	...	-0.1	-1.1	-0.7	-0.8	-0.8	-0.4
60 to 64 years.........	-0.3	...	-0.1	-0.8	-0.6	-0.6	-0.6	-0.3
65 to 69 years.........	-0.2	...	...	-0.3	-0.2	-0.3	-0.3	-0.2
70 to 74 years.........	-0.1	...	0.1	-0.1	-0.1	-0.1	-0.1	-0.1
75 years and over......	...	-0.1	...	...	0.1	...	...	0.1
Nonwhite.................	-0.4	-0.4	-0.4	-0.5	-0.8	-1.1	-1.5	-0.2
Under 5 years..........	...	...	0.1	0.1	...	...	...	0.1
5 to 9 years...........	...	...	...	...	0.1	0.1	0.1	...
10 to 14 years.........	0.1	0.1	0.2	...	0.1	0.1	...	0.1
15 to 19 years.........	-0.5	-0.1	-0.2	-0.9	-0.7	-0.9	-1.6	-0.3
20 to 24 years.........	-0.9	-0.5	-0.7	-1.3	-1.8	-2.4	-3.3	-0.5
25 to 29 years.........	-1.0	-0.8	-0.9	-0.9	-1.7	-2.0	-3.0	-0.5
30 to 34 years.........	-1.0	-0.8	-1.0	-1.0	-1.5	-1.6	-2.8	-0.6
35 to 39 years.........	-0.7	-0.6	-0.9	-0.8	-1.2	-1.3	-2.3	-0.5
40 to 44 years.........	-0.6	-0.4	-0.8	-0.7	-0.9	-1.1	-1.9	-0.5
45 to 49 years.........	-0.3	-0.3	-0.3	-0.6	-0.7	-1.0	-1.7	-0.3
50 to 54 years.........	-0.5	-0.3	-0.4	-0.5	-0.6	-0.8	-1.3	-0.2
55 to 59 years.........	-0.3	-0.2	-0.1	-0.3	-0.5	-0.6	-1.6	-0.4
60 to 64 years.........	-0.3	-0.1	-0.2	-0.3	-0.5	-0.6	-1.2	-0.3
65 to 69 years.........	-0.3	-0.1	-0.2	-0.4	-0.4	-0.3	-0.7	-0.3
70 to 74 years.........	-0.2	-0.2	-0.1	-0.3	-0.2	-0.1	-0.6	-0.3
75 years and over......	-0.1	...	-0.2	-0.3	-0.3	-0.3	-0.1	-0.3

Source: U.S. Census of Population: 1950, Vol. II, Characteristics of the Population, Part 1, U.S. Summary, Table 107; Sixteenth Census of the United States: 1940, Vol. IV, Characteristics by Age.

tables, only new conclusions, not derivable from household status information alone, will be discussed.

In 1950, about 86.9 percent of the white male population 14 years of age and over were members of primary families (Table 11-19). An additional 1.4 percent were members of secondary families. (One-half of this 1.4 percent lived as residents of households and one-half as residents of quasi households.) The remaining 12 percent of the population lived alone or with persons to whom they were not related. Four groups of people comprise most of this last class: the residents of hotels, dormitories, barracks, and other non-institutional quasi households (3.9 percent); "primary individuals" living alone or with persons unrelated to them (3.3 percent); lodgers, without their families, living in households (2.8 percent); and inmates of institutions (1.6 percent). These proportions indicate just how widely living with one's primary family is accepted in the United States as the normal residential status.

The proportions in each of the family and household statuses which are named above vary with age. Table 11-20 shows this age pattern. In general, persons in their late teens and their twenties were more inclined than any other age group to live outside a family. These are the ages most

Table 11-19.—DETAILED FAMILY STATUS OF MALES 14 YEARS OLD AND OVER, BY AGE, FOR THE UNITED STATES: 1950

(Based on 3 1/3 percent sample. Percent not shown where less than 0.1 or where base is less than 3,000.)

Detailed family status	14 years and over	14 to 17 years	18 and 19 years	20 to 24 years	25 to 29 years	30 to 34 years	35 to 44 years	45 to 54 years	55 to 64 years	65 to 74 years	75 and over
MALE, TOTAL.........	100.0	100.0	100.0	100.0	100.0	100.0	100.0	100.0	100.0	100.0	100.0
In households............	93.8	97.0	83.0	86.6	93.8	95.6	96.0	95.3	94.8	94.5	92.1
In primary families..........	86.9	95.5	78.9	79.9	87.8	90.9	90.6	88.1	85.0	80.6	75.2
Head.......................	62.4	0.4	3.5	30.2	63.2	75.9	81.2	81.9	79.3	70.7	53.5
Child......................	18.2	88.4	68.3	41.3	17.7	9.8	5.3	2.2	0.6	0.1	...
Son- or daughter-in-law.....	1.3	...	0.6	2.8	3.4	2.5	1.5	0.6	0.2	0.1	...
Grandchild.................	0.5	3.2	2.1	1.0	0.3	0.1	...	...	...	...	...
Parent.....................	1.3	...	...	...	...	...	0.1	0.5	2.0	6.2	17.2
Other relative.............	3.2	3.4	4.4	4.5	3.3	2.6	2.6	2.8	2.9	3.5	4.5
Primary individuals..........	3.3	0.2	0.5	1.2	1.6	1.6	2.3	3.7	5.9	9.5	12.2
In secondary families.........	0.7	0.4	0.5	1.1	1.1	0.8	0.7	0.6	0.5	0.4	0.4
Lodger.....................	0.6	0.4	0.5	1.1	1.1	0.8	0.6	0.5	0.4	0.4	0.4
Resident employee...........	...	0.1	...	...	...	...	0.1	0.1	...	...	...
Secondary individuals.........	3.0	0.9	3.1	4.4	3.2	2.3	2.4	3.0	3.4	3.9	4.3
Lodger.....................	2.8	0.8	2.6	4.1	3.1	2.2	2.2	2.7	3.2	3.7	4.2
Resident employee...........	0.2	0.2	0.5	0.3	0.1	0.1	0.1	0.2	0.2	0.2	0.1
In quasi households......	6.2	3.0	17.0	13.4	6.2	4.4	4.0	4.7	5.2	5.5	7.9
In secondary families.........	0.7	0.5	0.6	0.8	0.8	0.7	0.7	0.7	0.6	0.6	0.5
Secondary individuals.........	3.9	1.3	15.2	11.1	4.0	2.3	2.0	2.5	2.7	2.8	2.6
Inmates of institutions.......	1.6	1.2	1.2	1.4	1.4	1.3	1.3	1.5	1.9	2.2	4.8

Source: U.S. Census of Population: 1950, Special Reports, Marital Status, Table 1.

frequently associated with military service, attendance at college, and migration to unfamiliar communities. Accordingly, above-average proportions of these age groups lived in households or quasi households as secondary individuals; comparatively few of these persons lived alone, or as primary individuals living with nonrelatives.

The greatest proportion of the population lived in primary families at age 30 to 44, when all but about 9 to 10 percent had this status. At the older ages, the maturing of children and increasing mortality caused the dissolution of primary families and, thereby, a large increase in the number of primary individuals--parents who are alone in the home after the children have gone and the spouse has died. At age 65 to 74, 9.5 percent of males and 17.4 percent of females were primary individuals. (In more than half the cases, it is the male's death that brings about the dissolution of the family.) At the oldest ages there was also a small rise in the proportion residing in quasi households, since at these ages an increased proportion of the population resides in hospitals, homes for the aged, etc.

Comparing the proportions in Table 11-19 with those in Table 11-20 shows that males of each age were more inclined than females of the same ages to live outside families--that a higher proportion of males than of females lived as residents of quasi households and as lodgers. On the other hand, beyond the age of 30, women were more inclined than men to live as primary individuals, i.e., as household heads living alone or with nonrelatives.

A considerably smaller share of the nonwhite than of the white population lived in primary families. (Compare Tables 11-21 and 11-22 for nonwhites with Tables 11-19 and 11-20 for the total population.) A greater proportion of the nonwhite than of the white population of each age lived in quasi households (including institutions), and in households in which they were lodgers or resident

Table 11-20.—DETAILED FAMILY STATUS OF FEMALES 14 YEARS OLD AND OVER, BY AGE, FOR THE UNITED STATES: 1950

(Based on 3 1/3 percent sample. Percent not shown where less than 0.1 or where base is less than 3,000.)

Detailed family status	14 years and over	14 to 17 years	18 and 19 years	20 to 24 years	25 to 29 years	30 to 34 years	35 to 44 years	45 to 54 years	55 to 64 years	65 to 74 years	75 and over
FEMALE, TOTAL........	100.0	100.0	100.0	100.0	100.0	100.0	100.0	100.0	100.0	100.0	100.0
In households............	96.6	98.1	89.5	94.5	97.5	97.8	97.7	97.3	96.8	96.0	92.1
In primary families..........	88.4	96.6	84.6	88.7	92.8	93.6	92.5	88.9	83.4	74.7	68.2
Head......................	6.0	...	0.3	1.1	2.2	3.5	5.7	8.7	11.1	13.3	14.2
Wife......................	58.4	...	20.8	52.5	72.1	77.6	77.3	71.5	59.6	38.9	14.8
Child.....................	15.4	89.9	54.5	27.6	13.7	9.0	6.0	2.9	1.1	0.2	...
Son- or daughter-in-law.....	0.9	...	2.7	3.2	1.9	1.1	0.5	0.2	...	...	...
Grandchild.................	0.4	3.0	1.6	0.7	0.2	0.1	...	...	...	...	...
Parent.....................	3.6	...	...	...	...	...	0.3	2.1	7.1	15.9	30.9
Other relative.............	3.7	3.7	4.7	3.8	2.7	2.3	2.7	3.5	4.4	6.3	8.1
Primary individuals...........	5.2	0.1	0.6	1.2	1.5	1.8	2.9	5.8	10.1	17.4	19.4
In secondary families.........	0.7	0.4	1.1	1.4	1.1	0.8	0.6	0.5	0.4	0.4	0.3
Lodger.....................	0.6	0.4	1.0	1.3	1.0	0.7	0.6	0.4	0.4	0.3	0.3
Resident employee...........	0.1	...	0.1	0.1	0.1	0.1	0.1	0.1	0.1	...	...
Secondary individuals.........	2.3	1.0	3.2	3.1	2.1	1.6	1.7	2.1	2.8	3.6	4.0
Lodger.....................	1.9	0.8	2.7	2.8	1.9	1.4	1.4	1.5	1.9	2.8	3.7
Resident employee...........	0.5	0.2	0.5	0.3	0.2	0.2	0.4	0.6	0.9	0.8	0.4
In quasi households......	3.4	1.9	10.5	5.5	2.5	2.2	2.3	2.7	3.2	4.0	7.9
In secondary families.........	0.6	0.4	0.7	0.9	0.8	0.6	0.6	0.6	0.6	0.5	0.4
Secondary individuals.........	1.8	0.7	9.3	4.1	1.3	1.0	1.0	1.2	1.5	1.6	1.8
Inmates of institutions.......	1.0	0.8	0.5	0.4	0.5	0.6	0.7	0.9	1.2	1.9	5.8

Source: U.S. Census of Population: 1950, Special Reports, Marital Status, Table 1.

employees. Status within the primary family also varied with color. At most ages a higher proportion of the nonwhite than of the white population was living as "other relative," "son-or daughter-in-law," and "grandchild." Also, the secondary family was a much more common living arrangement among the nonwhite than among the white households.

Tables 11-19 through 11-22 are valuable reference tables. Glancing down any column enables one to ascertain the household status and the family status of a particular age-sex group. For example, one may find that elderly nonwhite women were, in about equal proportions (approximately 20 percent), heads of primary families, wives, or parents of family heads, and that most of the remaining elderly nonwhite women were primary individuals. Reading any row horizontally makes it possible to discover the stage in the life cycle at which the largest share of the population was characterized by a given family status.

FAMILY STATUS AND MARITAL STATUS

A person's family status may be expected to change, of course, with any change in his marital status, but a change in marital status may affect family status in a variety of ways. Tables 11-23 and 11-24 provide information which makes it possible to determine the ways in which these two statuses were interrelated in 1950.

Single persons tended to be a child in a primary family, to live in a quasi household, to be an "other relative" in a primary family, or to be a lodger in a household. This was true of both single men and single women, and of both white and nonwhite. However, single women were more inclined than single men to live with relatives.

A married couple living together constituted the center of a primary family in all but a small proportion of cases. The man was head and the woman was wife of the family head in all but about 7 percent of such couples. About 3.5 percent of the

Table 11-21.—DETAILED FAMILY STATUS OF NONWHITE MALES 14 YEARS OLD AND OVER, BY AGE,
FOR THE UNITED STATES: 1950

(Based on 3 1/3 percent sample. Percent not shown where less than 0.1 or where base is less than 3,000.)

Detailed family status	14 years and over	14 to 19 years	20 to 24 years	25 to 34 years	35 to 44 years	45 to 54 years	55 to 64 years	65 to 74 years
NONWHITE MALE, TOTAL.....	100.0	100.0	100.0	100.0	100.0	100.0	100.0	100.0
In households................	91.3	93.9	85.6	88.8	91.9	92.7	93.7	94.9
In primary families..............	78.1	90.6	74.9	75.4	77.9	76.5	76.5	73.5
Head...........................	50.2	1.3	23.6	53.2	67.9	70.2	70.2	61.2
Child..........................	18.4	74.1	35.4	12.4	4.2	1.5	0.5	0.1
Son- or daughter-in-law..........	1.5	0.3	3.6	3.0	1.3	0.5	0.2	0.1
Grandchild.....................	1.4	7.2	2.3	0.5	...	...	...	...
Parent.........................	0.9	...	...	...	1.0	0.6	2.0	7.5
Other relative.................	5.8	7.8	10.0	6.4	4.4	3.6	3.5	4.7
Primary individuals..............	4.9	0.3	1.8	3.1	4.6	7.0	9.0	13.6
In secondary families............	2.4	1.1	3.2	3.8	2.7	2.0	1.2	0.9
Lodger.........................	2.2	1.0	3.1	3.6	2.5	1.8	1.1	0.9
Resident employee..............	0.1	...	0.1	0.1	0.2	0.2	0.1	...
Secondary individuals............	6.0	1.9	5.8	6.5	6.7	7.3	7.0	6.9
Lodger.........................	5.7	1.8	5.6	6.3	6.5	6.9	6.7	6.5
Resident employee..............	0.2	0.1	0.2	0.1	0.2	0.3	0.3	0.4
In quasi households...........	8.7	6.1	14.4	11.2	8.1	7.3	6.3	5.1
In secondary families..............	2.0	1.3	2.5	2.9	2.3	1.7	1.3	1.0
Secondary individuals..............	3.8	2.9	8.1	4.3	3.2	3.1	2.0	2.2
Inmates of institutions...........	2.9	1.9	3.8	3.9	2.7	2.5	2.4	2.0

Source: U.S. Census of Population: 1950, Special Reports, Marital Status, Table 1.

couples were living with parents or parents-in-law. Only about 0.6 percent of the married couples living together were classed as parents of the family head. This is clear evidence that not many parents move in with children, unless the parents are widowed or divorced.

Tables 11-23 and 11-24 are especially informative concerning the family status of persons whose marriage has been disrupted. When a marriage has been broken by separation or divorce, both the husband and wife tend to return to their parental homes, or to live with another relative, in a substantial number of cases. In about 30 percent of such cases the woman assumes the headship of the family and preserves it as a unit. Widowed persons are somewhat more inclined than separated or divorced persons to live alone or with nonrelatives. Lodgers, in a high proportion of cases, are men who are separated or divorced.

CHARACTERISTICS OF HOUSEHOLDS AND FAMILIES BY TYPE: 1957

In August, 1958, the Bureau of the Census released one of its most comprehensive tabulations of the characteristics of households and families, based upon the Current Population Survey for March, 1957. These materials make it possible to note that there are several current differences in the composition of the various types of households and families. Tables 11-25 and 11-26 summarize information obtained from this report.

Urban-rural differences. Households and families with female heads are much more common in urban than in rural areas, and are least common in rural-farm areas. The following tabulation shows what proportion of households and families have female heads, by urban-rural residence.

Table 11-22.—DETAILED FAMILY STATUS OF NONWHITE FEMALES 14 YEARS OLD AND OVER, BY AGE, FOR THE UNITED STATES: 1950

(Based on 3 1/3 percent sample. Percent not shown where less than 0.1 or where base is less than 3,000.)

Detailed family status	14 years and over	14 to 19 years	20 to 24 years	25 to 34 years	35 to 44 years	45 to 54 years	55 to 64 years	65 to 74 years
NONWHITE FEMALE, TOTAL...	100.0	100.0	100.0	100.0	100.0	100.0	100.0	100.0
In households............	95.3	95.7	92.8	94.6	95.8	96.4	96.1	96.4
In primary families......	82.7	91.7	82.3	83.2	82.8	81.1	78.6	73.2
Head.....................	9.9	0.4	2.9	7.3	12.4	15.8	18.2	19.2
Wife.....................	43.9	7.8	37.3	56.2	60.0	54.4	44.1	22.4
Child....................	16.8	66.6	27.9	11.8	4.7	2.2	0.9	0.2
Son- or daughter-in-law..	1.2	1.8	3.7	1.5	0.5	0.2	0.1	...
Grandchild...............	1.2	6.1	1.8	0.5	...	...	...	...
Parent...................	3.4	...	...	...	0.8	4.0	10.2	22.3
Other relative...........	6.4	8.9	8.8	5.9	4.5	4.5	5.1	9.1
Primary individuals......	5.9	0.2	1.5	3.1	6.1	9.4	12.1	17.4
In secondary families....	2.4	1.8	4.3	3.8	2.4	1.3	0.8	0.7
Lodger...................	2.3	1.8	4.1	3.5	2.2	1.1	0.7	0.7
Resident employee........	0.1	...	0.1	0.2	0.2	0.2	0.1	...
Secondary individuals....	4.3	2.0	4.8	4.6	4.5	4.5	4.7	5.2
Lodger...................	3.4	1.7	3.8	3.9	3.5	3.4	3.5	4.6
Resident employee........	0.8	0.3	0.9	0.7	1.0	1.1	1.2	0.6
In quasi households......	4.7	4.3	7.2	5.4	4.2	3.6	3.9	3.6
In secondary families....	2.1	1.7	3.4	2.9	2.0	1.5	1.2	0.8
Secondary individuals....	1.7	1.9	3.1	1.7	1.3	1.2	1.3	1.2
Inmates of institutions..	0.9	0.7	0.7	0.8	0.9	1.0	1.4	1.6

Source: U.S. Census of Population: 1950, Special Reports, Marital Status, Table 1.

Type of living arrangement and residence	Percent with female head
Households:	
Urban........................	9.8
Rural nonfarm................	6.9
Rural farm...................	5.7
Families:	
Urban........................	11.7
Rural nonfarm................	7.8
Rural farm...................	6.1

Secondary families are primarily an urban and rural-nonfarm phenomenon; almost none are found in rural-farm areas (data not shown). Although subfamilies are distributed almost proportionately among the urban and rural areas, a much higher percentage of the subfamilies in rural-farm areas are of the husband-wife type (child and his spouse living with the parents) than in urban areas, where subfamilies with female heads are more common. Unrelated individuals (persons living in a household where they have no relatives) are also distributed proportionately among urban and rural areas. But in rural-farm areas a much higher proportion of these persons are secondary individuals (lodgers) than in urban areas, where they tend to live as primary individuals in separate dwelling units instead of with a primary family.

Color. A smaller proportion of nonwhite than of white households and families are of the conventional husband-wife type. In 1957, 20 percent of all nonwhite families had female heads; this is twice their proportionate share.

Size. As of 1957 the average household contained 3.34 persons and the average family contained 3.61 persons. The largest households and families are those of the conventional husband-wife type; those which have a female head, or a male head other than a husband living with his wife, are much smaller. Comparatively few households (11 percent) contain only 1 person. A substantial number of families now contain 5 or

Table 11-23.—DETAILED FAMILY STATUS OF PERSONS 14 YEARS OLD AND OVER, BY MARITAL STATUS AND SEX, FOR THE UNITED STATES: 1950

Detailed family status	Single		Married				Widowed		Divorced	
			Spouse present		Separated					
	Male	Female	Male	Female	Male	Female	Male	Female	Male	Female
Total..................	100.0	100.0	100.0	100.0	100.0	100.0	100.0	100.0	100.0	100.0
In households............	85.9	90.8	99.3	99.3	82.9	93.4	89.5	95.4	79.4	93.5
In primary families.........	74.3	78.3	98.5	98.6	40.7	67.3	54.3	63.9	41.0	62.2
Head.....................	3.4	3.3	93.4	...	9.9	31.8	26.0	31.0	10.5	29.4
Wife.....................	...	...	...	93.6	...	...	...	...	...	...
Child....................	62.0	63.0	1.5	2.2	17.2	19.9	1.9	2.3	18.4	19.6
Son- or daughter-in-law....	...	...	2.0	1.4	0.2	0.2	0.2	0.1	0.1	0.2
Grandchild................	1.7	1.6	...	0.1	0.3	0.5	...	...	0.2	0.3
Parent...................	...	...	0.6	0.6	2.5	5.7	20.0	24.6	2.1	4.5
Other relative...........	7.2	10.4	0.9	0.7	10.6	9.2	6.2	5.9	9.7	8.3
Primary individuals.........	4.5	5.8	...	...	21.5	14.5	25.1	25.7	21.0	21.1
In secondary families........	0.5	0.6	0.8	0.7	1.0	2.1	0.5	0.4	0.7	1.4
Lodger....................	0.5	0.5	0.7	0.7	1.0	1.8	0.5	0.4	0.7	1.1
Resident employee..........	...	0.1	...	0.1	...	0.3	...	0.1	...	0.3
Secondary individuals........	6.6	6.1	...	...	19.7	9.4	9.6	5.3	16.7	8.8
Lodger....................	6.0	5.0	...	...	19.0	7.6	9.2	4.0	15.9	6.9
Resident employee..........	0.6	1.1	...	...	0.6	1.8	0.4	1.2	0.7	1.9
In quasi households.......	14.1	9.2	0.7	0.7	17.1	6.6	10.5	4.6	20.6	6.5
In secondary families........	0.5	0.5	0.7	0.7	0.8	1.4	0.4	0.4	0.6	0.8
Secondary individuals........	10.3	6.6	...	...	11.8	3.4	5.8	2.0	14.2	4.1
Inmates of institutions......	3.3	2.1	...	...	4.5	1.8	4.2	2.2	5.8	1.6

Source: U.S. Census of Population: 1950, Special Reports, Marital Status, Table 1.

more members, as a consequence of the increased fertility to be discussed in the next chapter. However, the average size of household is still decreasing, because there is a steady counter-tendency toward an increase in the number of one-person and two-person households which are comprised of unrelated individuals and retired couples.

Children under 18 years of age. Almost one-half of the households (48 percent), and a surprisingly large share of the families (41 percent) contain no children under 18 years of age. Childless couples (many of whom have just married and are awaiting their first child) and couples whose families have grown up and moved away comprise a very large share of all families. Among the families which contained children, the average number of children per family in 1957 was 2.26.

Age of head. During the decade 1950 to 1960, household and family heads tended to be quite old. The median age of household heads was 47 years and that of family heads was 45 years in 1957. About 1/6 of all household heads were past retirement age (65 years or older). This high average age is a result of the low fertility which characterized the 1930's; the small cohorts of infants that were born during those years comprise the present younger generation of householders. Increased longevity has also had a great effect upon household composition. Instead of being widowed, a higher proportion of persons survive as couples to advanced ages. In 1957, one household in 9 was a man-wife household with a male head 65 years of age or older.

Marital status. In 1957, only slightly more than three-fourths of all household heads were heads of

Table 11-24.—DETAILED FAMILY STATUS OF NONWHITE PERSONS 14 YEARS OLD AND OVER, BY MARITAL STATUS AND SEX, FOR THE UNITED STATES: 1950

Detailed family status	Single		Married				Widowed		Divorced	
	Male	Female	Spouse present		Separated		Male	Female	Male	Female
			Male	Female	Male	Female				
Nonwhite total..........	100.0	100.0	100.0	100.0	100.0	100.0	100.0	100.0	100.0	100.0
In households.............	86.2	92.9	97.3	97.3	86.5	93.2	90.8	95.8	82.9	92.7
In primary families..........	71.9	80.6	93.9	94.0	37.5	63.7	45.3	66.1	36.8	59.1
Head.....................	2.3	3.5	86.0	...	9.6	30.0	23.7	36.2	11.2	29.9
Wife.....................	...	...	...	86.4	...	...	...	...	...	...
Child....................	54.8	59.3	2.3	2.9	15.1	18.5	2.7	3.0	12.0	15.6
Son- or daughter-in-law....	...	...	2.6	2.2	0.3	0.2	0.3	0.1	0.2	0.1
Grandchild................	4.5	4.4	0.1	0.2	0.5	1.0	0.1	0.1	0.5	0.6
Parent...................	...	...	0.6	0.5	0.9	2.9	9.9	18.4	1.2	2.9
Other relative............	10.4	13.3	2.3	1.8	11.1	11.1	8.6	8.2	11.8	10.0
Primary individuals..........	4.2	3.7	...	...	21.8	14.6	27.7	21.5	21.0	17.9
In Secondary families.......	1.1	1.5	3.4	3.3	1.4	2.6	0.9	0.8	1.0	2.1
Lodger...................	1.1	1.4	3.2	3.1	1.4	2.5	0.9	0.8	1.0	1.9
Resident employee..........	...	0.1	0.2	0.2	...	0.1	...	...	...	0.2
Secondary individuals........	9.0	7.0	...	...	25.8	12.3	16.9	7.4	24.1	13.7
Lodger...................	8.5	5.6	...	...	25.4	10.7	16.3	6.1	23.3	10.0
Resident employee..........	0.4	1.4	...	...	0.4	1.6	0.6	1.3	0.8	3.7
In quasi households.......	13.8	7.1	2.7	2.7	13.5	6.8	9.2	4.2	17.1	7.3
In secondary families........	1.2	1.4	2.7	2.7	1.1	2.2	1.0	1.0	1.1	1.8
Secondary individuals........	7.6	4.1	...	...	8.2	3.5	4.9	2.1	10.4	3.7
Inmates of institutions......	5.0	1.6	...	...	4.2	1.1	3.3	1.1	5.6	1.8

Source: U.S. Census of Population: 1950, Special Reports, Marital Status, Table 1.

husband-wife households. In about 13 percent of the households the head was widowed, and many household heads were either single (5 percent) or divorced (2.5 percent). Almost 60 percent of female household heads were widowed, and another 25 percent were either single or divorced. When a couple is separated, or when the male spouse is absent because of military service, because of the nature of his work, or for other reasons, the wife is the household head. Wives who were heads under these circumstances comprised 14 percent of all households and 21 percent of all families.

Education. In general, household heads tend to be somewhat better educated than primary individuals who live alone or with nonrelatives (Table 11-25), although this difference is small. In general, primary individuals are found at all educational levels.

Occupation. Primary individuals are highly concentrated in four occupational classes: professional, clerical, operative, and service. A large share of these persons are probably teachers, stenographers, and restaurant waitresses.

Income. Primary individuals are concentrated at the lower end of the income distribution. Perhaps inadequacy of income is one reason why such persons are not married. The higher the income level, the higher the proportion of persons who are married. That part of the population which has a high family income also has an extraordinarily high proportion of families of the husband-wife type. The high income of such families undoubtedly is due in part to working wives.

Residence. Primary individuals are highly concentrated in urban areas; they account for a comparatively small share of the rural-nonfarm and rural-farm populations.

ORPHANHOOD

Orphanhood is related to the topics discussed above, although the census does not make a sepa-

Table 11-25.—CHARACTERISTICS OF HOUSEHOLDS AND FAMILIES, BY TYPE: 1957

Subject	Households				Families			
	All house-holds	Husband-wife house-holds	Other house-holds, male head	House-holds, with fe-male head	All families	Husband-wife families	Other families, male head	Families with fe-male head
COLOR								
Total...................	100.0	100.0	100.0	100.0	100.0	100.0	100.0	100.0
White.....................	90.6	92.2	86.4	85.2	90.8	92.1	88.9	80.0
Nonwhite..................	9.4	7.8	13.6	14.8	9.2	7.9	11.1	20.0
SIZE								
Total...................	100.0	100.0	100.0	100.0	100.0	100.0	100.0	100.0
1 person...................	11.0	...	52.4	43.7	...	...	...	...
2 persons..................	28.8	29.4	26.5	27.2	32.8	30.3	55.0	47.7
3 persons..................	19.7	21.9	10.2	13.3	21.9	21.7	20.4	24.5
4 persons..................	18.4	22.0	5.3	7.1	20.7	21.9	12.6	12.4
5 persons..................	11.1	13.4	2.8	4.0	12.4	13.2	6.3	7.2
6 persons..................	5.7	7.0	1.2	2.2	6.4	6.8	2.4	3.8
7 persons or more...........	5.3	6.3	1.7	2.5	5.8	6.0	3.3	4.3
Average (mean) number........	3.34	3.75	1.92	2.21	3.61	3.69	2.94	3.12
RELATED CHILDREN UNDER 18								
Total...................	100.0	100.0	100.0	100.0	100.0	100.0	100.0	100.0
No related children under 18..	48.4	39.3	87.3	73.6	40.9	39.5	66.8	46.2
1 related child under 18......	17.3	19.7	6.1	11.1	19.9	19.6	15.8	23.3
2 related children under 18...	16.6	19.9	3.3	7.2	19.0	19.8	8.6	14.5
3 related children under 18...	9.5	11.4	1.9	3.7	10.8	11.4	5.1	7.4
4 or more children under 18...	8.2	9.7	1.4	4.3	9.4	9.7	3.7	8.7
Average (mean) per family.....	...	...	...	...	1.34	1.38	0.65	1.14
Average per family with children....................	...	...	...	...	2.26	2.28	1.97	2.12
AGE OF HEAD								
Total...................	100.0	100.0	100.0	100.0	100.0	100.0	100.0	100.0
Under 25 years...............	4.7	5.0	3.9	3.9	4.9	5.0	4.7	4.5
25 to 29 years...............	8.6	10.0	4.9	3.9	9.4	10.0	5.0	5.5
30 to 34 years...............	10.7	12.4	5.9	4.6	11.7	12.4	5.8	6.9
35 to 44 years...............	22.1	25.0	12.9	13.1	24.1	24.9	15.8	19.1
45 to 54 years...............	20.5	21.0	18.4	18.9	21.0	21.0	19.1	22.0
55 to 64 years...............	16.7	15.2	20.3	21.4	15.6	15.3	17.6	17.9
65 to 74 years...............	11.5	8.6	20.6	20.9	9.6	8.6	19.3	15.7
75 years and over............	5.2	2.8	13.2	13.2	3.6	2.8	12.7	8.5
Median age...................	46.9	44.0	57.0	57.6	44.9	44.0	54.8	51.4
MARITAL STATUS OF HEAD								
Total...................	100.0	100.0	100.0	100.0	100.0	100.0	100.0	100.0
Married, spouse present.......	76.1	100.0	...	...	87.1	100.0	...	...
Married, spouse absent........	3.6	...	16.5	14.3	2.5	...	15.4	20.9
Separated....................	2.0	...	9.4	7.8	1.3	...	5.6	11.5
Other.......................	1.6	...	7.1	6.5	1.2	...	9.8	9.4
Husband in armed forces...	0.2	...	...	1.2	0.2	...	...	1.7
Other.....................	1.4	...	7.1	5.3	1.0	...	9.8	7.7
Widowed......................	12.7	...	36.0	59.7	6.8	...	42.0	56.3
Divorced.....................	2.5	...	10.7	10.5	1.5	...	6.0	13.2
Single.......................	5.1	...	36.8	15.5	2.0	...	36.6	9.6

Source: Current Population Reports, _Marital Status, Economic Status, and Family Status, March 1957_, Series P-20, No. 81.

Table 11-26.—CHARACTERISTICS OF HOUSEHOLD HEADS: 1957

Subject	Households	Primary individuals	Families	
			All families	Husband-wife families
EDUCATION OF HEAD				
Total.....................................	100.0	100.0	100.0	100.0
Elementary: 0 to 7 years.....................	22.8	29.2	21.8	20.6
8 years.............................	18.4	19.8	18.1	18.0
High school: 1 to 3 years.....................	18.0	13.8	8.6	18.6
4 years..........................	23.1	18.3	23.8	24.4
College: 1 to 3 years.....................	7.6	8.1	7.5	7.8
4 years or more....................	8.9	8.6	8.9	9.5
School years not reported....................	1.3	0.2	1.1	1.1
Median school years completed...................	10.4	9.2	10.5	10.8
MAJOR OCCUPATION OF HEAD				
Total with employed civilian heads..........	100.0	100.0	100.0	100.0
Professional, technical, and kindred workers......	10.4	15.5	9.9	9.9
Farmers and farm managers......................	7.4	3.4	7.7	7.8
Managers, officials, and proprietors, exc. farm...	14.2	8.3	14.7	15.3
Clerical and kindred workers.....................	8.2	18.9	7.2	6.3
Sales workers.................................	5.4	4.3	5.5	5.6
Craftsmen, foremen, and kindred workers..........	19.2	6.5	20.3	21.5
Operatives and kindred workers...................	19.7	15.5	20.1	20.2
Service workers, including private household......	8.1	21.9	6.9	5.4
Farm laborers and foremen......................	1.4	1.7	1.4	1.4
Laborers, except farm and mine....................	6.1	4.1	6.3	6.6
FAMILY INCOME				
Total.....................................	100.0	100.0	100.0	100.0
Under $2,000..........................	21.3	61.1	15.5	12.9
$2,000 to $3,999...........................	22.8	23.4	22.7	21.9
$4,000 to $5,999...........................	26.4	11.4	28.5	29.8
$6,000 and over...............................	29.6	4.1	33.3	35.4
RESIDENCE				
Total.....................................	100.0	100.0	100.0	100.0
Urban..	64.9	76.1	63.3	62.1
Rural nonfarm.................................	24.6	18.7	25.4	26.3
Rural farm....................................	10.5	5.2	11.3	11.7

Source: Current Population Reports, Marital Status, Economic Status, and Family Status, March 1957, Series P-20, No. 81.

rate estimate of orphans. Lack of specific data on the subject makes it necessary to form estimates. In 1954, Louis O. Shudde and Lenore A. Epstein of the Social Security Administration estimated that there were 2.9 million children under age 18 who had lost one or both of their parents by death. This amounted to 5 percent of the nation's children, or 1 in 20. But the number of orphans has declined greatly in recent decades, and the percent of children who are orphans has declined sharply. These estimates showed the following trends:

Year	Total orphans, one or both parents dead		Complete orphans, both parents dead	
	Number (000)	Percent of child population	Number (000)	Percent of child population
1953 (July)	2,870	5.4	66	.12
1949 (Oct.)	2,930	6.1	81	.17
1940.......	3,840	9.5	290	.7
1930.......	5,050	11.7	450	1.1
1920.......	6,400	16.3	750	1.9

Source: Louis O. Shudde and Lenore A. Epstein, "Orphanhood,—A Diminishing Problem," Research and Statistics Note No. 33, Social Security Administration Division of Research and Statistics, December 27, 1954.

The change indicated above has been a direct result of the reduction of adult mortality during the ages at which adults are parents of young children. Orphanhood, once a major social problem, has been sharply reduced within the short span of only 3 decades, decades during which the size of the population was growing very rapidly. In commenting on these findings, the authors point out that further reductions in orphanhood may be expected in the future. One reason for this view is the fact that, at the present time, a disproportionately large share of orphans belong to the nonwhite population, in which additional large mortality reductions may be expected. At the present time, the nonwhite population has twice its proportionate share of orphans. These estimates do not involve any speculation concerning either the remarriage of widowed parents or adoptions. They are intended merely to measure the decline in the phenomenon of orphanhood itself.

These statistics indicate that one of the most noticeable by-products of increased longevity has been the virtual disappearance from the American scene of the orphanage as a quasi household. The number of complete orphans has declined to such an extent that a large proportion of them are in foster homes.

CONCLUSION

The above discussion has attempted to furnish a picture of the number and the types of residential groups in the population, and of the recent changes in each type. The status or role that a person occupies within his household and his family varies with age, sex, color, and urban-rural residence. These differentials, and the changes which have taken place in these differentials, have been described. Finally, it has been shown that households and families have differential characteristics, such as the education, income, and occupation of the head, the number of earners, the number of young children, etc., which are worthy of independent study.

Note. The reader who is interested in the topic of household and family statistics should read Paul C. Glick's excellent monograph, American Families, Census Monograph Series, John Wiley, 1957. Estimates of the future number of families and future household formation will be found in Chapter 26 of the present study.

Chapter 12

THE FERTILITY OF THE UNITED STATES POPULATION

INTRODUCTION

Human fertility is one of the three variables of population change. The other two are mortality and migration. In some ways fertility is now the most important of the three variables; under present conditions, variations in fertility largely determine what the nation's population will be in the future. Its effect is felt at all times and in all segments of the economy. For example, an acute shortage of school rooms in the period from 1952 to 1957 reflected the surge of births in prior years. Different segments of the population are growing at uneven rates because of differential fertility. The ancient problem of an unequal distribution of births and resources is still present in America, although much reduced in severity.

In recent decades, much information has been obtained on fertility, on social and psychological factors affecting fertility, and on physical processes which have long been little understood. There is still a vast field of unanswered questions, however, and much basic research on the subject remains to be done. The present chapter is not intended to be a summary of specialized knowledge in various fields relating to fertility. All it seeks to do is to outline some of the fundamental trends in American fertility, as they relate to the world setting and to other factors, to exhibit a few "trees" in a very large forest. The data used are largely limited to census data on ratios of young children, to census data on number

of children ever born to the women, and to national vital statistics on births.

A BRIEF SUMMARY OF FERTILITY CONDITIONS IN THE UNITED STATES SHORTLY AFTER THE MIDCENTURY

The United States had many births per year in the period from 1954 to 1957 as compared with the annual number in the previous 30 years. In these years, 1954 to 1957, there were 4.1 to 4.3 million births (corrected for underregistration), the largest annual numbers on record to that time. They compare with a decline from an estimated 3.0 million births in 1924 to 2.3 million in 1933, a plateau of 2.4 to 2.6 million births yearly between 1934 and 1940, a wartime surge to 3.1 million in 1943 followed by a decline to 2.9 million in 1945, and the postwar surge to 4.1 million in 1954. The average level of the crude birth rate (births per 1,000 population) was about 25 in most of the postwar years through 1957, about 21 during the war, and about 19 during the economic depression of the 1930's. The low birth rate during the 1930's occurred after a long-time decline from a rate of about 55 in 1810. Thus, the increase after 1940 interrupted at least temporarily a long-time downward trend.

---

[1]The views expressed herein are those of Mr. Grabill and are not necessarily those of the Bureau of the Census.

Judging from statements in newspapers and popular magazines, usually in connection with economic prospects, many people believed that the post-1940 surge in annual births reflected an immediate increase in the average size of families, reversing the long-time trend toward smaller families. Instead, much of the early increase reflected a change in the "timing" of births. First births per 1,000 women of each age occurred at a rate that was too high to persist indefinitely, because such a persistence would in time require the impossible lifetime production of more than one first birth per woman. The average size of completed families did not increase until some years after the surge in annual births began.

Demographers noted from vital statistics on order of birth (births classified by whether they were the mother's first, second, or subsequent child) that the bulk of the postwar increase in annual births was traceable to first, second, and third births and did not involve a return of the once-common large families of five children or more. (Figure 12-1.) There were differences of opinion among demographers as to whether the many additional first and second children meant that young women were merely having children earlier than usual, with no eventual increase in the size of completed families. It has since been established, by census and survey data on women classified by number of children ever born, that when some large groups of women complete the childbearing ages they will contain proportionately fewer childless (no children ever born) women and 1-child women, and more 2-child and 3-child women, than some predecessor groups. For example, among the ever-married women who were 30 to 34 years old in 1952 there was already a smaller percent childless (14.7) than among the women 40 to 44 years old (19.8). In this sense, families were becoming larger. In March 1957, the women 35 to 39 years old who had ever been married had an average of 2.61 children ever born as compared with an average of 2.40 for the ever-married women 45 to 49 years old. Thus, there no longer was any doubt that the average number of children ever born to women of completed fer-

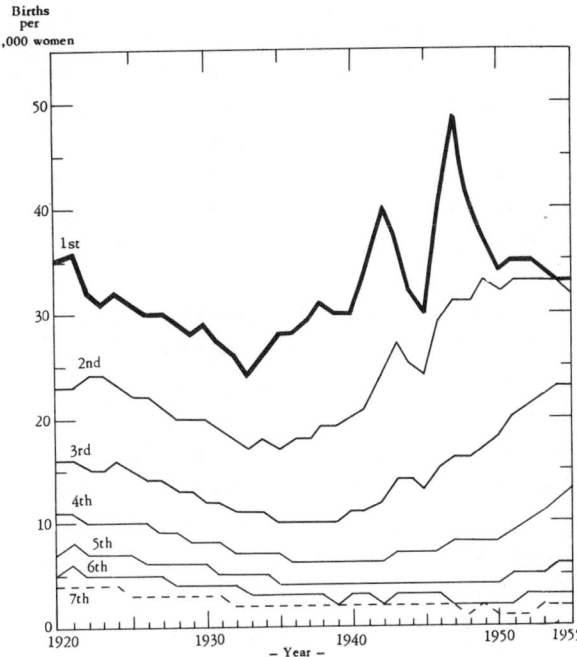

FIGURE 12 - 1. BIRTHS PER 1,000 NATIVE WHITE WOMEN 15 TO 44 YEARS OLD, BY BIRTH ORDER, FOR THE UNITED STATES, 1920 TO 1953

(Adjusted for underregistration, and for states not in Birth Registration Area prior to 1933.)

Source: National Office of Vital Statistics, "Births by Age of Mother, Color, and Live-Birth Order: United States, 1955, Vital Statistics-Special Reports, Vol. 46, No. 18, October 11, 1957, Table 9. The rates for 1920 to 1939 in this source were derived by P. K. Whelpton.

tility would increase when the younger groups of women reached the end of the childbearing age in their turn.

Early marriage and early childbearing were considered by some writers to be the main factors in the baby boom. Though important, they were only two of many factors and in that sense they were an over-simplified explanation. Census data show that ratios of young children to women of childbearing age increased considerably between 1940 and 1950 in groups which already had marriage patterns leading to early and virtually universal marriage, such as rural-farm nonwhites, and in groups which already had very high fertility, such as the white people in the Appalachian mountain area whose large 1935-1940 ratios implied a potential doubling of population each generation from natural increase. The high-fertility groups are cited here only as an indication of the complexity of the changes. Although the nation's rural-farm population participated in the increase in fertility, the relatively infertile urban population had a much larger increase. In fact, the fertility of most segments of the population responded in dramatic fashion to the improved economic conditions after 1940, particularly after World War II.

Census data indicate that between 1940 and 1950 the large increases in the average number of children ever born to women under 35 years old occurred chiefly as a result of increases in the proportion of women of each age who were married. (Table 12-1.) This is evident from the much larger percent increases in fertility rates which are present when the data are for women of all marital classes than when the data are limited to ever-married women. Between 1950 and 1957, large percent increases also occurred but this time they were of approximately the same size for the women of all marital classes and for the ever-married women, indicating that increased fertility of the ever-married women was the main cause rather than a reduction in the proportion of unmarried women.

With mortality similar to that prevailing in 1953, each woman who reaches age 45 years should have borne 3.4 children in order to support a long-run natural population increase at the recently prevailing level of about 1.7 percent per year. If the women who were 25 to 29 years old in 1957 were about 55 percent through their eventual lifetime childbearing, as were the women of this age in 1940, then they may end their childbearing careers with an average of 3.6 children. (If some were only having their children at an earlier age than has been customary, 3.6 is too high an estimate.) A corresponding estimate for women who were 25 to 29 years old in 1952 is 3.0 children. The women aged 30 to 34 years in 1952 were expected, on the basis of calculations made several years ago, to have borne an average of about 2.5 children by the time they reached menopause, but they attained this average sooner, by 1957, at age 35 to 39.

With about the same mortality rates as those prevailing in 1953, women should bear an average of 2.2 children as they pass through life to maintain the population at a zero rate of change, assuming that there is no net immigration or emigration. Most of the present cohorts of women

Table 12-1.—NUMBER OF CHILDREN EVER BORN PER 1,000 WOMEN 15 TO 49 YEARS OLD, BY AGE AND MARITAL STATUS OF WOMAN, FOR THE UNITED STATES: MARCH 1957, APRIL 1950, AND APRIL 1940

(Minus sign (-) denotes decrease)

Marital status and age of woman	1957	1950	Percent increase, 1950 to 1957	1940	Percent increase, 1940 to 1950
All marital classes					
15 to 44 years....................	1,696	1,395	21.6	1,238	12.7
15 to 19 years....................	108	105	2.9	68	54.4
20 to 24 years....................	971	738	31.6	522	41.4
25 to 29 years....................	1,900	1,436	32.3	1,132	26.9
30 to 34 years....................	2,249	1,871	20.2	1,678	11.5
35 to 39 years....................	2,457	2,061	19.2	2,145	-3.9
40 to 44 years....................	2,342	2,170	7.9	2,490	-12.9
45 to 49 years....................	2,237	2,292	-2.4	2,740	-16.4
Ever married					
15 to 44 years....................	2,218	1,859	19.3	1,904	-2.4
15 to 19 years....................	672	604	11.3	572	5.6
20 to 24 years....................	1,368	1,082	26.4	987	9.6
25 to 29 years....................	2,139	1,654	29.3	1,463	13.1
30 to 34 years....................	2,425	2,059	17.8	1,964	4.8
35 to 39 years....................	2,612	2,247	16.2	2,414	-6.9
40 to 44 years....................	2,514	2,364	6.3	2,754	-14.2
45 to 49 years....................	2,401	2,492	-3.7	2,998	-16.9

Source: Derived from Bureau of the Census, Current Population Reports, Series P-20, No. 84, August, 1958, "Fertility of the Population: March 1957."

have high rates, which suggest that they will produce much more than this minimum. Only the women who married in the early 1930's have a near-replacement averate number of children.

THE UNITED STATES SITUATION WITH RESPECT TO PAST TRENDS [2]

1. The colonial and early federal periods. For more than two centuries, from the time of the first permanent settlements in America to the early decades of the nineteenth century, the fertility of the American people ranked among the world's highest. Estimates made by both contemporary and modern authorities, utilizing a variety of techniques and data, place the annual birth rate in the colonial and early federal periods at 50 to 57 births per 1,000 inhabitants. The women of completed fertility are estimated, in various ways and by various persons, to have had an average of about eight children ever born.

The contemporary explanation for America's high fertility in those years is illustrated by the remarks of the Chevalier Felix de Beaujour, a former French consular official in the United States, who declared in 1814:

"Everything in the United States favours the progress of population; the emigrations from Europe, the disasters of the European colonies, but, above all, the abundance of the means of subsistence. Marriages are there easier than in Europe, births more multiplied, and deaths relatively less frequent. It is calculated that out of sixty individuals, two are married annually, that one is born out of every twenty, and that the proportion of deaths is only one in forty. This last report, founded on careful observations, seems incredible in a country so recently cleared and naturally not healthy; but it is nonetheless true, because it accords with the number of births, which there is greater

than in Europe. In the United States, more children are necessarily born than among us, because the inhabitants, in such an extent of country, finding the means of subsistence more abundant, marry at an earlier age. No human consideration there operates as a hindrance to reproduction, and the children swarm on the rich land in the same manner as do insects." Chevalier Felix de Beaujour, Sketch of the United States of North America, published in England, 1814.

In a much earlier year (1751), Benjamin Franklin wrote:

"Tables of the proportion of Marriages to Births, of Deaths to Births, of Marriages to the number of inhabitants, &c., form'd on observations made upon the Bills of Mortality, Christenings, &c., of populous cities, will not suit countries; nor will tables form'd on observations made in full settled old countries, as Europe, suit new countries, as America.

"2. For people increase in proportion to the number of marriages, and that is greater in proportion to the ease and convenience of supporting a family....

..."which charges are greater in the cities, as Luxury is more common; many live single during life, and continue servants to families, journeymen to Trades, &c., hence cities do not by natural generation supply themselves with inhabitants; the deaths are more than the births.

"4. In countries full settled, the case must be nearly the same; all Lands being occupied and improved to the heighth; those who cannot get land must labour for others that have it; when laborers are plenty, their wages will be low; by low wages a family is supported with difficulty; this difficulty deters many from marriage, who therefore long continue servants and single. Only as the Cities take supplies of people from the country, and thereby make a little more room in the country; Marriage is a little more encourag'd there, and the births exceed the deaths....

"7. Hence, marriages in America are more

[2] Portions of this section were written several years ago for joint use in this chapter and in Wilson H. Grabill, Clyde V. Kiser and P. K. Whelpton, The Fertility of American Women, John Wiley and Sons, Inc., New York, 1958.

general and more generally early, than in Europe. And if it is reckoned there, that there is but one marriage per annum among one hundred persons, perhaps we may here reckon two; and if in Europe they have but four Births to a marriage (many of their marriages being late) we may here reckon eight of which if one half grow up, and our marriages are made, reckoning one with another at twenty years of age our people must be at least doubled every twenty years." -- Benjamin Franklin, "Observations Concerning The Increase of Mankind, The Peopling of Countries, &c., " The Magazine of History, with Notes and Quotes, Extra Number, No. 63, 1755.

Beaujour's data probably were based in part on estimates made by Samuel Blodget, which are reproduced in Table 12-2 as an example of the work done in early times.[3]

Franklin's references to Europe also have a factual basis on data from an investigation of parish records in several countries by a clergyman

who was much interested in population data.[4] Franklin's remarks about urban and rural differences in marriages, etc., were evidently in regard to Europe; fragmentary data indicate that American cities of the time had something like 2 births for every death. Also, the colonial population did double every 23 years or so after 1660.

It is instructive that Franklin and some of his contemporaries spoke of a doubling of population every few decades, and gave relatively little attention to the role played by migration of population from abroad. The implication is that even in 1751 births were so much more numerous than immigrants that bountiful natural increase was regarded as the main source of future growth. A birth rate of about 55 and a population of about 1, 207, 000 in 1750 meant about 66, 000 births per year at that time, as compared with an annual net immigration amounting to perhaps 4, 000. Experimental computations indicate that the annual births could easily have been twice as numerous as any steady amount of annual net immigration within 10 years after the initial settlements were made. Even though immigration was not steady, it is likely that the proportion of the population that was native born increased rapidly. The relatively steady rate of decennial population increase after 1660 suggests that despite large fluctuations of immigration, steady natural increase was the major factor in population growth. Various colonial censuses show nearly equal numbers of males and females in the population, probably as a result of natural increase, whereas European data on emigration to the New World showed that among emigrants there was a large majority of males. In 1790, if not at a much earlier date, the proportion of the population that was American born was well over 90 percent as determined by experimental

[3]No effort has been made to remove printing errors and other errors that appear in Blodget's table. Blodget probably made his estimates somewhat as follows: He began with data from the first two censuses of the United States (1790 and 1800) and figured the average annual percent increase in population (3 percent) from these figures. This percentage was then applied in a chain computation to obtain annual population estimates and annual amounts of numerical increase. Blodget obtained custom house data and port records on "passengers arriving, " and allowed for the fact that many of such persons were representing Americans returning from business abroad, were aliens in transit to Canada, were here temporarily, etc. (Blodget placed net immigration at about half of total immigration.) Subtraction of the (net) immigration from the annual population increase gave the annual natural increase. Blodget published death ratios (population per death) for various scattered localities in the United States, based on bills of mortality, and from these he estimated the national death rate to be "near 2 1/2 percent." The births seem to be a residual estimate, obtained by adding deaths to the estimated annual natural increase, since the birth estimates are the only component of population growth shown to the last digit. Also, the birth rate appears, by recomputation, to be between 52 and 53 per 1,000 population instead of the "near 5 3/4 percent" stated in the column heading for births.

[4]Johann Peter Süssmilch, Die Göttliche Ordnung ... (Of God's Way), Berlin, 1741 and later editions. For an extended account in English, see Frederick S. Crum, "The Statistical Work of Süssmilch, " Quarterly Publications of the American Statistical Association, Vol. VII, New Series, No. 55, September 1901.

Table 12-2.—ABSTRACT OF SAMUEL BLODGET'S ESTIMATES OF ANNUAL POPULATION INCREASE, BIRTHS, DEATHS, AND NET IMMIGRATION, FOR THE UNITED STATES: 1790 TO 1805

Year	Free persons	Slaves, increase yearly near 2 percent	Free blacks and persons of color	Annual migrations, free men and slaves	Births in each year near 5 3/4 percent	Deaths in each year near 2 1/2 percent	Total population including Louisiana in the year 1804	Total increase each year, near 3 percent
1790............	3,232,303	697,697	59,511	3,500	...	...	3,930,000	...
1791............	3,333,761	714,139	63,500	4,000	215,900	101,000	4,047,900	117,900
1792............	3,438,237	731,000	67,500	5,000	220,937	103,500	4,169,337	121,337
1793............	3,446,417	748,000	71,600	3,600	227,680	107,100	4,294,417	125,180
1794............	3,657,189	766,000	75,700	3,500	235,382	110,200	4,423,249	128,632
1795............	3,771,946	784,000	79,800	3,900	242,197	113,400	4,555,946	132,697
1796............	3,890,124	802,500	84,900	4,500	249,117	117,000	4,692,624	136,678
1797............	4,012,902	820,500	89,900	3,500	257,516	120,300	4,833,402	140,776
1798............	4,940,404	837,000	95,000	3,800	266,202	124,000	4,978,404	145,002
1799............	4,273,756	854,000	100,600	4,000	273,334	128,000	5,127,756	149,352
1800............	4,404,798	876,790	105,843	3,800	282,132	132,100	5,281,588	153,823
1801............	4,544,300	898,300	110,800	4,000	290,712	136,200	5,440,100	158,512
1802............	4,682,313	921,000	115,900	4,500	299,113	140,400	5,603,313	163,213
1803............	4,727,412	944,000	121,900	3,900	308,749	144,550	5,771,412	168,099
1804............	5,000,100	999,900	126,000	9,500	810,500	149,000	6,000,000	228,588
1805............	5,156,000	1,024,900	131,000	...	321,000	153,000	6,180,000	180,000

Source: Samuel Blodget, Economica: A Statistical Manual for the United States of America, Washington, 1806, p. 58. No correction has been made for printing errors and other errors in the source table.

computations. Further evidence of the existence of a largely native-born population appears in the 1820 Census, which counted only 53, 687 "foreigners not naturalized" in the population of 9,638, 453.

Lest what has just been said seem an underestimation of the very important role played by immigration, we hasten to mention the Beards' estimate made from fragmentary European data, that between 1600 and 1770 about 750,000 persons journeyed from Europe to the New World. [5] Other estimates of immigration during these years exceed 2,000,000. Certain difficulties are involved in using such data. Many of the out-migrants from Europe died enroute. Others went to Canada, the Carribean, or South America instead of to the Colonies destined to form the United States. Many found conditions not to their liking and returned to Europe, while some died in America without progeny. Basically, the only migrants who represented a permanent contribution to the population were those who contributed children. There were enough immigrants of the family type to account for the fact that a much larger population growth took place in the American Colonies than in other colonies.

2. The nineteenth and twentieth centuries. In the absence of national birth statistics until the twentieth century, we are fortunate to have decennial census data since 1790 on the population classified by age and sex. Ratios of young children to women of childbearing age, computed from such data, are fully as useful for many purposes as birth rates, although they must be used with due regard to their limitations. These ratios vary over time, not only because of changes in birth rates, but also because of changes in infant mortality, changes in the proportion of women in the more fertile portions of the childbearing age range, and changes in the completeness with which young children have been enumerated in censuses. These ratios are also affected by such factors as migration of population between the time of the children's birth and the date of the census. However, these disturbing factors are not sufficiently important to hide the fertility trends for the nineteenth and twentieth centuries. For example,

[5] Charles A. and Mary R. Beard, The Beards' Basic History of the United States, Doubleday, Doran and Company, New York, 1944.

standardization for age of women would change the national ratios of children under 5 years old to white women 15 to 44 years old by only about 4 percent between 1800 and 1940. Ratios of young children to women are sometimes described as measures of effective fertility because they show what the situation was after most of the children have passed the first few months of life, a period during which death rates were especially high in the early days of the nation.

Table 12-3 presents a series of ratios of children under 5 years old per 1,000 women 20 to 44 years old for the period from 1800 to 1950, computed by P. K. Whelpton.[6] These ratios show clearly that fertility declined nationally after 1810, if it had not already begun to fall during earlier decades. In 1800 the ratios were so relatively low in the New England states as to suggest that fertility in that area had already been declining for some time. It is known from old bills of mortality that New England had an average level of contemporary mortality; hence, the ratios were not depressed from this source. The ratios of children to women in 1800 were intermediate in value for such long-settled areas as the Middle Atlantic states and the South Atlantic states. They were high indeed in the thinly populated newer areas of settlement--the East North Central states and the East South Central states in 1800, and the West North Central states in 1910. These frontier areas had

astonishingly high ratios, of about 1,900 children under 5 years old per 1,000 women 20 to 44 years old. The high ratios in these "new" areas were probably due in part to the recent heavy migration of young married women who had been brought in as brides from longer-settled areas. The frontier areas contained perhaps 125 men 20 to 29 years old per 100 women of this age; the developing rural economy depended for prosperity on family efforts, and widowed women with children were regarded as matrimonial prizes.

The general magnitude of the early ratios of young children to women can best be appreciated by comparison with modern data for the Hutterites, a small religious sect in the Midwest that has extraordinarily high fertility.[7] The Hutterites have long had an average of about 8.9 children ever born per married woman 45 years old and over. They also have a fairly low rate of infant mortality--only 5 percent of infants died in the first year of life between 1946 and 1950. Despite the high fertility and the low infant mortality, the Hutterite women in 1950 had "only" 1,438 children under 5 years old per 1,000 women 20 to 44 years old.

The West South Central Division in 1810 and the Mountain and Pacific Divisions in 1850 may appear to be exceptions to the general rule that highest fertility occurred in new areas of settlement. The Pacific Division may have been an exception. The other two divisions were not exactly new areas of settlement. About one-fourth of the 1810 enumerated population of the West South Central Division was in the then century-old city of New Orleans; the remainder was in the rest of Louisiana, and in a few settlements in Arkansas. New Orleans was then a comparatively unhealthful place with a high incidence of cholera, malaria, and other diseases. Infant mortality probably was high as a consequence; this alone would tend to depress the ratio of children to women. The Spanish-Americans of

---

[6] In interpreting the ratios shown in Table 3, those for 1800 to 1820 might be increased by about 4 percent to correspond to the age-standardized ratios shown for 1830 and later. The ratios for 1800 to 1820 are estimated from data on the number of children under 10 years old and on women 16 to 24 years old and 25 to 44 years old; the national increase in the ratios between 1800 and 1810 may be an artifact rather than a real phenomenon. The 1850 census shows consistently low ratios compared with those for 1840 and 1860; this difference may reflect the change in enumeration procedures in 1850 from a household basis to an individual basis. It was noted in 1850 that some enumerators began the age count with 1 year for infants, contrary to instructions to enter ages in fractions of a year when under 1 year old as of June 1. The 1890 census also has ratios which are relatively low. In 1890 only, the instructions were to report age as of the nearest birthday, with the result that a larger than usual proportion of children over 4 1/2 years old were reported as 5 years old.

[7] See Joseph W. Eaton and Albert J. Mayer, "The Social Biology of a Very High Fertility Among the Hutterites; The Demography of a Unique Population," Human Biology, Vol. 25, No. 3, pp. 206-264, September 1953.

Table 12-3.—CHILDREN UNDER 5 YEARS OF AGE PER 1,000 WOMEN 20 TO 44 YEARS OF AGE, BY RACE, FOR THE UNITED STATES, BY DIVISIONS: 1800 TO 1950

(In an attempt to improve the comparability of white and Negro ratios, all ratios have been adjusted for under-enumeration of children, and all except those for whites in 1800 to 1820 have been standardized indirectly to the age distribution of women in the United States in 1930. The number of enumerated white children under 5 have been increased by 5 percent, and of Negro children 13 percent, these being factors obtained from a study of data for 1925 to 1930. (Dots indicates that data are not available.)

Year	United States	New England	Middle Atlantic	East North Central	West North Central	South Atlantic	East South Central	West South Central	Mountain	Pacific	Negro, United States
1800......	1,342	1,164	1,334	1,918	...	1,402	1,875	...	...	...	...
1810......	1,358	1,111	1,365	1,777	1,915	1,382	1,794	1,446	...	...	...
1820......	1,295	980	1,244	1,683	1,768	1,330	1,708	1,483	...	...	...
1830......	1,145	826	1,044	1,473	1,685	1,189	1,530	1,369	...	...	...
1840......	1,085	770	951	1,280	1,446	1,162	1,424	1,310	...	...	...
1850......	892	636	776	1,037	1,122	957	1,115	1,061	875	896	1,087
1860......	905	639	784	1,016	1,118	940	1,056	1,103	1,054	1,035	1,072
1870......	814	564	702	892	1,012	833	922	953	982	916	997
1880......	780	520	648	781	930	879	952	1,066	892	808	1,090
1890......	685	456	563	668	797	802	873	994	770	600	930
1900......	666	497	567	620	731	802	855	942	742	532	845
1910......	631	505	554	576	650	780	836	861	680	478	736
1920......	604	543	562	570	605	720	760	706	686	447	608
1930......	506	467	447	482	520	618	680	586	582	357	554
1940......	419	365	337	407	452	480	556	492	546	358	513
1950......	587	552	507	586	642	601	666	644	699	576	706

Source: P.K. Whelpton, Forecasts of the Population of the United States, 1945-1975, page 16, Bureau of the Census, (U.S. Government Printing Office, Washington, D.C., 1947) and computations from 1950 Census of Population, Volume II, Characteristics of the Population, Parts 1-50, Table 13, each state.

New Mexico predominated in the Mountain Division in 1850, and the Mormons of Utah were an important minority group. If infant mortality was as high among the Spanish-Americans in the Mountain Division as it was in Mexico as late as 1930, it easily accounted for the relatively low ratios of young children to women in the Mountain Division in 1850; the Spanish-Americans and the Mormons were, and still are, groups of relatively high fertility.

California's population constituted the bulk of the population of the Pacific Division in 1850, as it does now. The Gold Rush of 1849 and the subsequent rapid growth of commerce may have resulted in a migration, partly selective, of materialistic and sophisticated people who did not want large families. The Boston and New York newspapers of the day contained many advertisements of "fast-sailing ships" bound for the gold fields, and some "bride" ships sailed from these areas, where the birth rate already was low. Whatever the cause, since 1850 California (and in lesser degree, the neighboring states of Washington and Oregon) has been characterized by relatively low ratios of young children to white women.

The Negro population of the United States, as shown in Table 12-3 for censuses since 1850, had an "effective" fertility which changed little before 1890. Perhaps it had not changed much for a hundred years or so. The Census of 1870 is an exception; the low fertility ratio in 1870, relative to 1860 and 1880, reflects both the enumeration problems and the low fertility which were caused by the unsettled living conditions in the South following the Civil War. (Ratios for white women in the three southern divisions were also relatively low in 1870.) The ratios for Negroes from 1850 to 1880 do not compare in magnitude with the much higher ones noted for whites from 1800 to 1830. This probably reflects much higher infant mortality among the Negroes rather than any lesser fertility. Glover's life tables indicate that as recently as 1910 about one-fourth of Negro infants died in the first year of life. (In contrast, the best available evidence is that around 1789 only about one-seventh of white infants died in the first year of life in Massachusetts and New Hampshire.) Data from the 1910 Census, on children ever born, indicate that the Negro women then 70 to 74 years old actually had been a very fertile group, with an average of about 7.5 children ever born among women in rural-farm areas, even though many of them had been slaves when they were young adults.

It should be clear from Table 12-3 that the bulk of the decline in current fertility occurred in the nineteenth century among white women and in the twentieth century among nonwhite women. There was some apparent leveling off of the fertility ratios for whites between 1880 and 1920 in the New England states and the Middle Atlantic states. This local leveling off possibly was due to the temporary masking effect of fairly high fertility among millions of recently-arrived foreign-born white women; sharp declines occurred between 1920 and 1930 following the restriction of immigration in 1921. The ratios in 1940 were adversely affected everywhere by the economic depression, and in some cases were considerably below the level needed for permanent population maintenance. Then came World War II and the postwar resurgence of fertility, which was of unprecedented magnitude. The resurgence is reflected in the higher ratios shown for 1950 than for 1940.

In terms of local data, birth registration in America has a long history. The Colony of Massachusetts Bay made birth registration a government responsibility in 1642. Churches in many places kept baptismal records. One who examines these records can scarcely avoid being impressed by the fairly large number of women whose names appear as mothers year after year. However, the early data are seriously incomplete and not very adaptable to statistical purposes.

The early civic data were kept for legal purposes, such as cases involving inheritance of property by the oldest living son. Massachusetts in 1842 began state-wide birth registration, primarily for the purpose of providing vital statistics. A few other states also established reporting systems in the nineteenth century. Essentially,

however, large-scale birth data of adequate reliability became available with the establishment of the Birth Registration Area in 1915, when ten states and the District of Columbia were admitted on the basis of a showing of virtually complete registration (90 percent or better). It was not until 1933 that nation-wide coverage was achieved. Many people have made estimates of national births for years before 1933. Some estimates have been made for years as far back as 1774. These are of uncertain reliability. They have been estimated from census data on young children, from birth rates for "representative" small areas applied to national population figures, and by other methods.

Official estimates of births for years since 1915 are reproduced in Table 12-4. The estimates shown for 1956 to 1957 are provisional.

In essence, the Birth Registration Area picked up the story after the crude birth rate had declined from a level of about 55 in 1810 to about 29.5 in 1915. The absolute numbers of births increased considerably between these two dates, however, because increases in population more than offset decreases in birth rates. Just before or after World War I the long series of increasing annual numbers of births reached a true turning point and began to decline in earnest. (Another turning point occurred about 1933.)

The annual birth rates for 1915 to 1957 were affected by a trend toward fewer children per marriage, two world wars, peace, a so-called "cold war," depressions, prosperity, and curtailment of immigration. It is possible that during this period the tendency for families to have few children, a trend which had been developing for more than 100 years, became fairly universal. (In 1952, according to the Current Population Survey, only 13.4 percent of ever-married women 45 to 49 years old had 5 or more children ever born.) Since 1930, annual fertility has fluctuated with the changes in economic and psychological conditions. During the depression of the 1930's, births and birth rates were low because people postponed marriage or childbearing. Between 1946 and 1957, on the other hand, the birth rates were high. In fact, each year

Table 12-4.—LIVE BIRTHS AND BIRTH RATES ADJUSTED FOR UNDERREGISTRATION, BY COLOR, FOR THE UNITED STATES:
1915 TO 1957

(Includes estimates for Statesmnot in the Birth-Registration Area prior to 1933. Figures rounded to nearest
1,000 without adjustment to total. Rates per 1,000 enumerated population as of April 1 for 1940 and 1950 and
per 1,000 estimated population as of July 1 for other years.)

Year	Number			Rate[1]		
	Total	White	Nonwhite	Total	White	Nonwhite
1957	4,310,000	...	...	25.3	...	...
1956	4,203,000	3,583,000	619,000	25.1	24.0	34.0
1955	4,104,000	3,488,000	617,000	24.8	23.7	34.6
1954	4,078,000	3,475,000	603,000	25.3	24.1	34.9
1953	3,965,000	3,389,000	575,000	25.0	24.0	34.1
1952	3,913,000	3,358,000	555,000	25.1	24.1	33.6
1951	3,823,000	3,277,000	546,000	24.9	23.9	33.8
1950	3,632,000	3,108,000	524,000	24.1	23.0	33.3
1949	3,649,000	3,136,000	513,000	24.5	23.6	33.0
1948	3,637,000	3,141,000	495,000	24.9	24.0	32.4
1947	3,817,000	3,347,000	469,000	26.6	26.1	31.2
1946	3,411,000	2,990,000	420,000	24.1	23.6	28.4
1945	2,858,000	2,471,000	388,000	20.4	19.7	26.5
1944	2,939,000	2,545,000	394,000	21.2	20.5	27.4
1943	3,104,000	2,704,000	400,000	22.7	22.1	28.3
1942	2,989,000	2,605,000	384,000	22.2	21.5	27.7
1941	2,703,000	2,330,000	374,000	20.3	19.5	27.3
1940	2,559,000	2,199,000	360,000	19.4	18.6	26.7
1939	2,466,000	2,117,000	349,000	18.8	18.0	26.1
1938	2,496,000	2,148,000	348,000	19.2	18.4	26.3
1937	2,413,000	2,071,000	342,000	18.7	17.9	26.0
1936	2,355,000	2,027,000	328,000	18.4	17.6	25.1
1935	2,377,000	2,042,000	334,000	18.7	17.9	25.8
1934	2,396,000	2,058,000	338,000	19.0	18.1	26.3
1933	2,307,000	1,982,000	325,000	18.4	17.6	25.5
1932	2,440,000	2,099,000	341,000	19.5	18.7	26.9
1931	2,506,000	2,170,000	335,000	20.2	19.5	26.6
1930	2,618,000	2,274,000	344,000	21.3	20.6	27.5
1929	2,582,000	2,244,000	339,000	21.2	20.5	27.3
1928	2,674,000	2,325,000	349,000	22.2	21.5	28.5
1927	2,802,000	2,425,000	377,000	23.5	22.7	31.1
1926	2,839,000	2,441,000	398,000	24.2	23.1	33.4
1925	2,909,000	2,506,000	403,000	25.1	24.1	34.2
1924	2,979,000	2,577,000	401,000	26.1	25.1	34.6
1923	2,910,000	2,531,000	380,000	26.0	25.2	33.2
1922	2,882,000	2,507,000	375,000	26.2	25.4	33.2
1921	3,055,000	2,657,000	398,000	28.1	27.3	35.8
1920	2,950,000	2,566,000	383,000	27.7	26.9	35.0
1919	2,740,000	2,387,000	353,000	26.1	25.3	32.4
1918	2,948,000	2,588,000	360,000	28.2	27.6	33.0
1917	2,944,000	2,587,000	357,000	28.5	27.9	32.9
1916	2,964,000	2,599,000	...	29.1	28.5	...
1915	2,965,000	2,594,000	...	29.5	28.9	...

[1]For 1917-19 and 1941-46, based on population including Armed Forces overseas. For other years, based on
population excluding Armed Forces overseas.

Source: National Office of Vital Statistics, Vital Statistics of the United States: 1950, Volume I, Table
6.02, page 78, for data from 1915 to 1950, (U.S. Government Printing Office, Washington, D. C., 1954.) The
estimates for 1915 to 1934 were prepared by P. K. Whelpton. The data for 1956 and 1957 are provisional
figures from the National Office of Vital Statistics. The data for 1951 to 1955 are from the National Office
of Vital Statistics, Vital Statistics Special Reports, Volume 44, Number 8, "Births by Age of Mother, Race,
and Live-Birth Order;" July 24, 1956, Table 6, and from population bases provided by the Bureau of the Census.

from 1954 to 1957 set new records for the absolute number of births. The trend between 1946 and 1957 reflected the return of millions of veterans of World War II and the favorable post-war economic and psychological conditions.

Thus far we have dealt with trends in current fertility, as shown by the ratios of young children to women and by the annual births and birth rates. These are cross-sectional measures which refer to conditions of a given year, and do not trace the fertility behavior of real cohorts of women from beginning to end of the 30-year child-bearing period. Cohort fertility can be studied from annual birth statistics by means of a chain computation based on data for women age 15 in a specified year, age 16 the following year, etc., and allowing for deaths and net migration among the women. An

approach of this sort was used by Whelpton in his classic monograph Cohort Fertility, and is being used in his continuing study. His results indicate the general trends in cohort fertility from year to year, and are excellent for studying the effect of the depression, war, and prosperity on the cumulative fertility of various cohorts of women in 1915.

The population census data on women by number of children ever born, data which have been published for 1910, 1940, 1950, 1952, 1954, and 1957, provide direct evidence of changes in the average size of biological families. Some pertinent rates for women of completed fertility are shown in Table 12-5.

It may be noted that within each census grouping shown by Table 12-5 the last line refers to the

Table 12-5.—CHILDREN EVER BORN PER 1,000 WOMEN OF COMPLETED FERTILITY, BY AGE COHORTS AND COLOR, FOR THE UNITED STATES: 1957, 1950, 1940, AND 1910

(Data based on Current Population Survey 1957, and samples, 1950, 1940, and 1910.)

Census or survey date and age of women	Period when women were 28 years old, (the approximate mean age of childbearing)	Children ever born per 1,000 women		
		Total	White	Nonwhite
1957				
45 to 49 years......................	1936 to 1940	2,237	...	...
50 to 51 years......................	1934 to 1935	2,234	...	...
52 to 56 years......................	1929 to 1933	2,358	...	...
1950				
45 to 49 years......................	1929 to 1933	2,292	2,251	2,633
50 to 54 years......................	1924 to 1928	2,497	2,451	2,981
55 to 59 years......................	1919 to 1923	2,728	2,689	3,214
1940[1]				
45 to 49 years......................	1919 to 1923	2,740	2,704	3,120
50 to 54 years......................	1914 to 1918	2,870	2,821	3,452
55 to 59 years......................	1909 to 1913	3,014	2,962	3,718
60 to 64 years......................	1904 to 1908	3,076	3,017	3,922
65 to 69 years......................	1899 to 1903	3,270	3,186	4,236
70 to 74 years......................	1894 to 1898	3,442	3,349	4,793
1910				
40 to 44[2] years...................	1894 to 1898	3,904	3,778	5,160
45 to 49 years......................	1889 to 1893	4,295	4,139	5,864
50 to 54 years......................	1884 to 1888	4,529	4,371	6,281
55 to 59 years......................	1879 to 1883	4,816	4,675	6,586
60 to 64 years......................	1874 to 1878	4,847	4,701	6,529
65 to 69 years......................	1869 to 1873	4,982	4,850	6,762
70 to 74 years......................	1864 to 1868	5,001	4,885	6,576

[1] All data for 1940 revised to include estimates of children ever born for women who had no report on this subject.

[2] Age 40 to 44 normally is associated with 90 percent completed fertility or more.

Source: U.S. Census of Population: 1950, Volume IV, Special Reports, Part 5c, Fertility, Tables 4 and 6; U.S. Census of Population: 1940, Special Reports, Differential Fertility, 1940 and 1910--Fertility for States and Large Cities, Tables 1 to 4.

same birth cohort of women as does the first line of the next census grouping, or to the survivors thereof. The rates from the early census usually are a little higher than are the rates for those women who survived to the next census. Perhaps the fertility of older women is often reported to the census taker by a daughter, another relative, or a nonrelative, who may not be aware of a child that died in infancy many years earlier. The rates for different censuses and surveys seem to compare well when an age as old as 70 years is not involved. The 1910-1940 comparison of women who were age 40 to 44 in 1910 and 70-74 in 1940 involved almost a 50 percent loss through death and shows a particularly large "loss" in average fertility per woman. In addition to differential mortality and underreporting of children ever born to old women, it is possible that the 1910 Census was at fault. It may have included a few stillbirths and adopted children or stepchildren because of the indefinite wording of the question which was used: "Mother of how many children: a. Number born? b. Number living?"

The census data show not only the total fertility but also the distributions of women by number of children ever born. From these data one can measure the decline in the proportion of women with many children and the rise in the proportion of those with few (see Table 12-6). It may be noted that a much larger proportion of nonwhite than of white women have remained childless and that the nonwhite women reported 0, 1, 2, children in that order of frequency in 1950, whereas white women reported 2, 1, 0, children. The data for whites are thought to indicate a general preference by married couples for 2 children, while the data for nonwhites may reflect some sterility due to poor health conditions among nonwhites before the advent of antibiotics.

Table 12-7 presents gross and net reproduction rates; intrinsic rates of birth, death and natural increase; and crude rates of birth, death and natural increase, for dates from 1905 to 1952.

The gross and net reproduction rates are more fully explained in the following section, "The United States in the World Situation." It may be noted here, however, that they measure the strength of current age-specific birth rates, in terms of the number of daughters expected in a second generation per woman in a first generation, with and without allowance for mortality of daughters before they reach their mother's age. It may be noted that in the economic-depression years of 1930-1935 and 1935-1940 the net reproduction rate was too low to insure the one surviving daughter per woman that was needed to replace women in the next generation. Even if mortality was not allowed for (gross reproduction rate), at this low rate there would just be one daughter per woman. After 1945, the reproduction rates implied a con-

Table 12-6.—PERCENT DISTRIBUTION OF WOMEN 45 TO 49 YEARS OLD, EVER MARRIED, BY NUMBER OF CHILDREN EVER BORN, BY COLOR OF WOMAN, FOR THE UNITED STATES: 1950, 1940, AND 1910
(Statistics based on samples)

Children ever born	Total			White			Nonwhite		
	1950	1940	1910	1950	1940	1910	1950	1940	1910
Total women ever married...	100.0	100.0	100.0	100.0	100.0	100.0	100.0	100.0	100.0
No children..................	20.4	16.7	9.5	19.5	16.1	9.6	28.1	23.4	8.7
1 child......................	19.8	16.2	10.3	20.1	16.4	10.4	17.9	14.2	9.5
2 children...................	21.7	19.1	12.1	22.6	19.6	12.5	13.7	13.4	8.3
3 children...................	13.8	14.7	11.3	14.2	15.1	11.7	10.3	10.9	7.6
4 children...................	8.7	10.3	10.7	8.8	10.5	11.0	7.3	8.8	7.9
5 and 6 children.............	8.4	12.2	17.3	8.3	12.1	17.6	9.4	13.0	13.8
7 to 9 children..............	5.0	7.7	17.6	4.6	7.4	17.4	8.3	10.2	18.8
10 or more children..........	2.2	3.1	11.2	1.9	2.8	9.8	4.9	6.3	25.4

Source: U.S. Census of Population: 1950, Volume IV, Special Reports, Part 5c, Fertility, Tables 2, 4, and 6; U.S. Census of Population: 1940, Special Reports, Differential Fertility, 1940 and 1910—Fertility for States and Large Cities, Table 2. Data for 1940 officially revised to include estimates of children for women who had no report on children ever born.

Table 12-7.—REPRODUCTION RATES, INTRINSIC RATES, AND CRUDE RATES, FOR THE UNITED STATES, BY COLOR: 1905 TO 1910, 1930 TO 1935, 1935 TO 1940, AND ANNUALLY, 1940 TO 1952

(Intrinsic rates and crude rates per 1,000 total population. Intrinsic rates for 1946 to 1952 computed by approximate methods. Reproduction rates and intrinsic rates for 5-year periods computed from census data on women by own children under 5 years old)

Year and color	Reproduction rate		Intrinsic rate			Crude rate		
	Gross	Net	Natural increase	Birth	Death	Natural increase	Birth	Death
Total								
1952...................	1.64	1.56	16.2	24.1	7.9	15.5	25.1	9.6
1951...................	1.59	1.52	15.3	23.5	8.2	15.2	24.9	9.7
1950...................	1.51	1.44	13.2	22.1	8.9	14.5	24.1	9.6
1949...................	1.52	1.44	13.2	22.2	9.0	14.8	24.5	9.7
1948...................	1.51	1.44	13.2	22.3	9.1	15.0	24.9	9.9
1947...................	1.59	1.51	14.8	23.6	8.8	16.5	26.6	10.1
1946...................	1.43	1.34	10.6	20.8	10.2	14.1	24.1	10.0
1945...................	1.22	1.14	4.9	17.4	12.5	9.8	20.4	10.6
1944...................	1.26	1.17	5.8	18.1	12.3	10.6	21.2	10.6
1943...................	1.33	1.23	7.8	19.5	11.7	11.8	22.7	10.9
1942...................	1.28	1.19	6.5	18.6	12.1	11.9	22.2	10.3
1941...................	1.17	1.08	2.7	16.6	13.9	9.8	20.3	10.5
1940...................	1.12	1.02	0.9	15.7	14.8	8.6	19.4	10.8
1935 to 1940..........	1.10	0.98	-0.7	15.5	16.2	7.8	18.8	11.0
1930 to 1935..........	1.11	0.98	([1])	([1])	([1])	8.6	19.6	11.0
1905 to 1910..........	1.79	1.34	10.1	26.9	16.8	14.7	29.9[2]	15.2[3]
White								
1952...................	1.58	1.51	15.1	23.1	8.0	14.7	24.1	9.4
1951...................	1.53	1.47	14.1	22.5	8.4	14.4	23.9	9.5
1950...................	1.45	1.39	12.0	21.0	9.0	13.5	23.0	9.5
1949...................	1.46	1.40	12.0	21.2	9.2	14.1	23.6	9.5
1948...................	1.47	1.40	12.5	21.7	9.2	14.3	24.0	9.7
1947...................	1.57	1.49	14.4	23.1	8.7	16.2	26.1	9.9
1946...................	1.41	1.33	10.2	20.3	10.1	13.8	23.6	9.8
1945...................	1.18	1.11	3.8	16.5	12.7	9.5	19.9	10.4
1944...................	1.22	1.14	4.8	17.3	12.5	10.1	20.5	10.4
1943...................	1.30	1.21	7.1	18.8	11.7	11.4	22.1	10.7
1942...................	1.25	1.17	5.9	18.0	12.1	10.4	21.5	10.1
1941...................	1.13	1.05	1.9	15.8	13.9	9.3	19.5	10.2
1940...................	1.08	1.00	0.0	14.9	14.9	8.2	18.6	10.4
1935 to 1940..........	1.06	0.96	-1.5	14.7	16.2	7.4	18.0	10.6
1930 to 1935..........	1.08	0.97	([1])	([1])	([1])	8.2	18.8	10.6
1905 to 1910..........	1.74	1.34	10.1	26.0	15.9	13.8	28.8[2]	15.0[3]
Nonwhite								
1952...................	2.06	1.89	23.3	31.2	7.9	22.6	33.6	11.0
1951...................	2.02	1.86	23.1	31.1	8.0	22.7	33.8	11.1
1950...................	1.94	1.78	21.3	29.8	8.5	22.1	33.3	11.2
1949...................	1.91	1.74	20.7	29.6	8.9	18.8	33.0	11.2
1948...................	1.85	1.68	19.4	28.7	9.3	21.0	32.4	11.4
1947...................	1.77	1.59	17.4	27.4	10.0	19.8	31.2	11.4
1946...................	1.60	1.44	13.3	24.8	11.5	17.3	28.4	11.1
1945...................	1.56	1.38	12.5	24.7	12.2	14.6	26.5	11.9
1944...................	1.58	1.38	12.7	25.2	12.5	15.0	27.4	12.4
1943...................	1.58	1.38	12.8	25.7	12.9	15.5	28.3	12.8
1942...................	1.51	1.32	10.8	24.2	13.4	15.0	27.7	12.7
1941...................	1.47	1.25	8.9	23.6	14.7	13.8	27.3	13.5
1940...................	1.41	1.20	7.3	22.7	15.4	12.9	26.7	13.8
1935 to 1940..........	1.41	1.14	4.4	22.1	17.7	11.6	26.0	14.4
1930 to 1935..........	1.34	1.07	([1])	([1])	([1])	11.6	26.5	14.9
1905 to 1910..........	2.24	1.33	10.1	34.6	24.5	14.7	38.1[2]	23.4[3]

[1]Not available.

[2]Estimated.

[3]Death Registration Area.

Source: Population Index, Vol. 21, No. 2, April 1955, pp. 152-153. U.S. Census of Population: 1940, Special Reports, Differential Fertility, 1940 and 1910—Standardized Fertility Rates and Reproduction Rates, Tables 7 and 9. Bureau of the Census, Statistical Abstract of the United States: 1955, Tables 58 and 69. P. K. Whelpton, "Births and Birth Rates in the Entire United States;" National Office of Vital Statistics, Vital Statistics—Special Reports, Vol. 33, No. 8, September 29, 1950, Table 1. National Office of Vital Statistics, Vital Statistics of the United States: 1950, Vol. I, Table 8.40.

siderable potential population increase per generation. It must be emphasized, however, that the raw materials used--the age-specific birth rates (and death rates)--are very changeable over time, and may contain "hidden" biases. Hence, the reproduction rates have limited value for analytical purposes when they are based on cross-sectional data for a short period of time.

If the age-specific birth (and death) rates of a particular date were to continue unchanged, which is not likely to happen, the population eventually would attain a fixed distribution by age; thereafter it would have a constant annual number of births, deaths, and thus a constant natural increase per 1,000 population. These potential constant rates are the "intrinsic" rates shown in the table. Sometimes they are interpreted as being the vital rates from which the vagaries of present age distributions have been removed. The intrinsic rates are on a per annum basis and in that respect they can be more fairly compared for different populations or for different times than can the reproduction rates, which are on a variable "per generation" basis. The potential age distributions differ for the different populations, however, so the intrinsic rates would still not be completely comparable. Thus, one population may have a certain intrinsic rate of natural increase due to low birth and death rates, and another population may have the same intrinsic rate of increase due to high birth and death rates.

THE UNITED STATES IN THE WORLD SITUATION

Reliable national data on fertility exist for only a small part of the world's population. Around 1947, data of good quality on registered births existed for the United States, Canada, Japan, northwest-central Europe, and Southern Europe. Data of fair quality were available for most countries of Eastern Europe and Latin America for this date. In most of Asia and Africa, however, such data were either lacking or were seriously deficient. Even in these areas, however, there were a number of small-scale local studies which gave at least a rough idea of general conditions. Using

such data, and with a wide margin for possible error, the United Nations has estimated the crude birth rate for 1947 in various regions of the world to be about as shown in Table 12-8.

Table 12-8.—ESTIMATED CRUDE BIRTH RATE FOR VARIOUS REGIONS OF THE WORLD: 1947

Region	Births per 1,000 population
Africa..................................	40-45
America	
United States and Canada..............	25
Latin America........................	40
Asia (excluding the Asiatic part of the U.S.S.R.)	
Near East.............................	40-45
South-Central Asia....................	40-45
Japan.................................	31
Remaining Far East....................	40-45
Europe (including the Asiatic part of the U.S.S.R.)	
North-West-Central Europe.............	19
Southern Europe.......................	23
Eastern Europe, including U.S.S.R.....	28
Oceania................................	28

Source: United Nations, Demographic Yearbook, 1949-50, p. 14.

It may be noted that most of the regions with relatively low birth rates are economically or technically advanced, while those with relatively high birth rates are generally regions with relatively undeveloped rural economies. This is an over-simplification of the relation. There is no perfect correlation among nations between the level of fertility and the degree of technical advancement, industrialization, urbanization, educational attainment of the population, or "civilization."

The western nations have relatively low birth rates as compared with other parts of the world. The year 1947 presents an atypical picture, since the birth rates in these nations had surged as a result of the return to civilian life of millions of World War II veterans. In the United States the crude birth rate of 26.6 (corrected) in 1947 compares with one of about 22 in 1942-45 and one of about 19 during most of the depression years of the 1930's. In north-west-central Europe as a whole, the swing was from a depression low of about 16 in the 1930's to a high of about 19 in 1946-47. Small though this swing was, it brought a welcome if temporary respite to several countries which earlier had anticipated an imminent decline in population. Other nations, such as Italy and Greece in southern Europe and Japan in Asia, also participated in the postwar surge.

The so-called "Demographic Revolution" is defined as a transition from high birth and death rates to low birth and death rates. The nations of north-west-central Europe are regarded as having neared the end of this process. The nations of southern and eastern Europe, after a later start, are fast approaching the same condition. In Asia, Africa, and Latin America the demographic revolution has just begun at most, and in many places it may not really have started. The stages which are popularly supposed to constitute the typical demographic revolution are (1) an initial decline in death rates, accompanied by a period of rapid population growth, and (2) a subsequent decline in birth rates, with a slowing down of population growth. The nations of western civilization apparently followed this pattern with the important exceptions of France and the United States where fertility declined as early as the beginning of the nineteenth century, prior to any large declines in mortality. In north-west-central Europe, France excepted, recorded crude birth rates fluctuated around a level of 30 to 35 (41 in Finland) from the earliest available date to the last quarter of the nineteenth century, and then declined. The data for Sweden go back to the eighteenth century, and for England and Wales to about 1840. (It is entirely possible that the data for these early years were incomplete. It is possible that at some time the unrecorded rates were at a level of 40 or more.) Southern and eastern Europe in general had later declines in birth rates, from a level of about 40 at the beginning of the twentieth century, with particularly rapid declines after World War I. In other parts of the world where birth rates are still above 40, it is quite possible that the general level of fertility has changed little for centuries. (Most areas have customs that tend to keep the birth rate from approaching its biologically possible upper limit.)

In recent years the death rate has declined in many parts of the world, as it has in India and parts of South America, where death rates formerly were very high. Some of the decline is traceable to simple and inexpensive measures such as the spraying of houses in malaria-ridden areas with DDT and the instruction of natives in sanitation practices; supplies and technical advisors have been provided by nations in which these techniques are well-established. Whether such efforts will lead to the sequence of events which are typical of the demographic revolution remains to be seen. In a genuine revolution of this type the declining death rates are symptomatic of changes in ways of living, of changes in fundamental attitudes and values in a population which is seeking to control its own destiny. Efforts are now being made in various nations of the world to educate the people, to introduce technical advances which in time may help the masses of people to secure more than a simple subsistence from agricultural life. There are indications that conditions in India may slowly improve. Parts of South America appear to be in the throes of a genuine industrial or social revolution.

Some demographers fear that it is dangerous to attempt to reduce death rates in less fortunate nations without first trying to reduce birth rates. They assert that the security of the remainder of the world is endangered by the resulting "explosive" growth of underdeveloped populations. The governments are forging ahead with mortality-reducing programs despite this philosophy. Explosive population growth is occurring in some parts of the world; this has happened in the past, however, and has been checked either by the age-old Malthusian factors of sporadic famine, disease, and warfare or by the adoption of family limitation practices.

It is sometimes said that modern industrial Japan is the only country not inhabited by whites which has a history of declining fertility.[8] This, of course, disregards those countries which have important minority racial groups, such as the United States with its large Negro minority and the U.S.S.R. which has a large Asian element in its population. The U.S.S.R. had a recorded birth rate of about 50 in its European area at the end of the nineteenth century. Its official birth rate had fallen to 38.3 for the whole country in 1938, and to an estimated rate of about 26 in 1953. The birth rate has declined in the U.S.S.R. despite strong policies and programs designed to encourage fertility, such as "Mother Heroine" medals for women with many children, pensions for the third and subsequent children, and government-run nurseries and kindergartens to enable the mother to work. The experience of the U.S.S.R. seems to indicate that the traditional kinship system of the Asians (with its premium on many sons) and other value systems that are favorable to high fertility can be weakened by the forces that tend to bring death rates and birth rates more nearly in balance with each other. The raising of women from the status of a mere household chattel and permitting them to participate in public activities is a fundamental aspect of this change. It seems likely that Communist China may eventually go through the same cycle. In fact, the Chinese government recently established clinics that instruct the people in methods of birth control. Although Africa presents special problems because many of its population live in small groups with very simple economies, there is no reason to expect that a drastic reduction in its present high death rates would not be followed by a corresponding downward adjustment of fertility.

Table 12-9 presents gross and net reproduction rates for a few of the nations of the world. The gross reproduction rate shows how many daughters would be born to a group of 1000 women who started life at the same time, if all members of this group survived to the end of the childbearing ages and if they were subject to the age-specific birth rates prevailing at a particular date. One may double the gross reproduction rate to obtain a rough approximation of the total number of children, including sons, the group would bear. The data vary in adequacy and should be used with considerable caution. The completeness of birth and death registration varies from country to country. Even the concept of "birth" may differ among countries; some countries require prompt regis-

Table 12-9.—GROSS AND NET REPRODUCTION RATES FOR SELECTED COUNTRIES

Country and year	Reproduction rates		Efficiency ratio (NRR/GRR)
	Gross	Net	
NORTH AMERICA			
United States, 1950.......	1.50	1.44	.96
Canada, 1948..............	1.67	...	...
1945..............	1.46	1.33	.91
Jamaica, 1947.............	1.89	1.48	.78
Trinidad and Tobago, 1946.	2.36	1.95	.83
SOUTH AMERICA			
Chile, 1943...............	2.02	1.18	.58
EUROPE			
Belgium, 1951.............	1.11	1.01	.91
Denmark, 1952.............	1.23	1.12	.91
Finland, 1948.............	1.67	1.40	.84
France, 1947.............	1.46	1.31	.90
Ireland, 1945-47..........	1.63	1.38	.85
Netherlands, 1949.........	1.56	1.43	.92
Norway, 1950.............	1.21	1.11	.92
Portugal, 1951............	1.49	1.09	.73
Spain, 1953..............	1.43	1.10	.77
Sweden, 1947.............	1.21	1.13	.93
Switzerland, 1946.........	1.29	1.16	.90
United Kingdom:			
England and Wales, 1946.	1.16	1.07	.92
Scotland, 1947.........	1.50	1.35	.90
ASIA			
India, 1941...............	2.76	1.30	.47
Palestine:			
Jews, 1945.............	1.72	1.61	.94
Moslems, 1940..........	3.81	2.17	.57
AFRICA			
Union of South Africa, white, 1940............	1.50	1.35	.90
OCEANIA			
Australia, 1950..........	1.49	1.36	.91
New Zealand, 1951........	1.65	1.54	.93

Source: Population Index, Vol. 20, No. 2, April 1954. The Index obtained much of its data from United Nations publications.

[8]United Nations, The Determinants and Consequences of Population Trends, Document No. ST/SOA/Ser. A/17. Population Studies No. 17. Sales No. 1953. XIII. 3 New York, 1953, p. 72, par. 14.

tration of every live birth, while others permit reports with a lag of some time and may ignore those infants who die soon after birth. The gross reproduction rate for Chile, 2.02, suggests a total of only 4 children whereas the true figure probably should be about 6 or 7. The gross reproduction rates for Portugal and Spain also seem to be too low. Table 12-9 shows that at current fertility patterns the United States is replacing itself at a comparatively rapid rate. Even though its gross yearly rate may be lower than that of many nations of Asia, Africa, and South America, its net reproduction rate is higher because of its low mortality rates. However, it is well to remember that in 1935-1940 the net reproduction rate of the United States was .98. In a population where family planning is an accepted custom, birth and reproduction rates can fluctuate within a wide range.

The net reproduction rate shows the number of daughters a group of women would have during their lifetime if they were subject to the birth and death rates that prevailed at each age in a particular year or period. For replacement from generation to generation, the rate should be one daughter per woman. The net rate differs from the gross reproduction rate only in the allowance for mortality; the "efficiency ratio" shown indicates the proportion of females who live to pertinent childbearing ages. India had a large loss from death. Because the birth rates and death rates at

each age in a particular year or period may be atypical, the reproduction rate for a particular date may not reflect long-run tendencies. In view of her long history of virtual balance of births and deaths, it is surprising that France had a net reproduction rate as high as 1.31 in 1947.

A few countries have data on women by number of children ever born. Because of differences in detail, comparisons are sometimes difficult to make. England and Wales, for example, show data in terms of children ever born to the present marriage, by duration of marriage, without regard for the age of the woman. In some countries where consensual marriages are common, the data are necessarily in terms of all women, without regard to marital status. In the United States census data on children ever born are obtained for ever-married women, and it is assumed that single women are childless. Comparisons with three other countries are given in Table 12-10. These data are for women 45 to 49 years of age at the time of the census, which means that they refer to women of recently completed fertility. The data for France show an inadequate level of fertility for replacement. The women should have about 2,060 children per 1,000 women to insure 1,000 daughters; a further allowance is needed for mortality. The data for Brazil correctly show a population of high fertility. The data for Mozambique are typical of small families in some African

Table 12-10.—PERCENT DISTRIBUTION OF WOMEN 45 TO 49 YEARS OLD BY NUMBER OF CHILDREN EVER BORN, FOR SELECTED COUNTRIES

(Data include single women)

Children ever born	United States, 1950	France, 1946	Brazil, 1940	Mozambique (Portugese East Africa), 1940
Total women...............	100.0	100.0	100.0	100.0
No children....................	26.8	23.0	14.9	15.4
1 child.......................	18.3	24.2	5.5	10.8
2 children....................	19.9	21.7	5.9	13.2
3 children....................	12.7	12.8	6.1	13.7
4 children....................	8.0	7.2	6.6	13.2
5 or more children............	14.4	11.0	61.0	33.8
Children ever born 1,000 women.	2,292	2,078	6,189	3,586

Source: U.S. Census of Populations: 1950, Volume IV, Special Reports, Part 5c, Fertility. United Nations, Demographic Yearbook: 1949-50, Institut National de la Statistique et des Etudes Economiques, Resultats Statistiques du Recensement General de la Population, Mars 1946, Volume IV, Familles, Presses Universitaires de France, Paris, 1953.

tribes, and probably reflect mostly the births which survive to a fair age and take little account of infants lost through normal death as well as through certain tribal practices; they may also reflect some impairment of fecundity by poor health conditions.

Thus, at the present time fertility in the United States is moderately high in comparison with most nations of Europe, but is well below that of most nations of Asia, Africa, or South and Central America. However, because of its very low death rates, the moderate fertility of the United States is making possible a very rapid population growth. At the present time, some high-birth-rate nations are experiencing a decline in mortality. There is hope that, within a few decades, they will undergo a fertility transition similar to that which took place in the western world and bring their fertility rates to an intermediate low level. Meanwhile, the fertility situation in the United States is such that the population could greatly restrict its births, if conditions should make this seem desirable. Although the present rate of growth in the United States is high, it is entirely possible that a severe depression could cause it to decline substantially.

BASIC DIFFERENCES WITHIN THE POPULATION

Urban and rural differences.--Urban populations probably have had a lower level of fertility than rural populations ever since the first fair-sized town came into being. Differences of this type can be inferred for ancient Rome and have been noted in recent times for places which still have ancient living customs, such as parts of India and China. They can be noted in some American Colonial censuses (Table 12-11).

Urban-rural differences in fertility have many causes, not all of which involve family limitation. Thus, the influx to cities of young unmarried persons (especially of women) in search of jobs tends to make city populations slightly less "married" than rural populations, and also tends to increase the average age at marriage of women in cities as compared with rural areas. Years ago (the difference is less today) health conditions were not so favorable for childbearing in congested urban areas as in rural areas. Rickets, undulant fever, certain fly-borne diseases, and dietary deficiencies impaired the ability of some urban women to produce live-born children. In general, however,

Table 12-11.--TOTAL NUMBER OF INHABITANTS AND NUMBER OF WHITE CHILDREN UNDER 16 YEARS OLD PER 1,000 WHITE WOMEN 16 YEARS OLD AND OVER, FOR NEW YORK COUNTY AND THE REMAINDER OF THE COLONY OR STATE OF NEW YORK, 1703 TO 1771

(New York City contained almost all of the population of New York County at each census)

Year	New York County		Remainder of the colony of New York	
	Population	Children per 1,000 women	Population	Children per 1,000 women
1771	21,863	1,279	146,154	1,886
1756	13,046	1,260	83,544	2,022
1749	13,294	1,441	60,054	2,025
1746	11,717	1,426	49,872[1]	2,179
1723	7,248	1,564	33,316	1,968
1712[2]	5,841	1,743	13,563[3]	2,057
1703	4,375	1,906	16,290	2,446

[1]Albany County excluded as "not possible to be enumerated on account of the enemy."

[2]"The returns of this census are deemed imperfect, the people being deterred by a simple superstition, and observation that sickness followed upon the last numbering of the people."

[3]Kings and Richmond counties excluded as their data lack age detail.

Source: Computed from a series of early New York Colony enumerations presented in Bureau of the Census, A Century of Population Growth. U.S. Government Printing Office, Washington, D. C., 1909.

conscious family limitation has probably been the major factor in urban and rural differentials, with urban people either wanting fewer children or being more efficient in limitation than rural people. The higher cost of raising a child in urban areas than in rural areas has been noted by many writers as a major reason for limitation. Within both urban and rural areas, however, the people who have most severely limited their families have more often been those who have a fair economic status than those who are poor. (See section on Income and Wealth.)

Some demographers believe that the small family system began in urban areas and spread to the surrounding rural areas. The reference here is not to the age-old urban and rural differentials in fertility but to the progressively greater family limitation that accompanied the later stages of the evolution of modern civilization. Actually, it is by no means certain that the rural population of the United States lagged behind the urban population, provided that one allows for a "normal" differential at the start. Ratios of young children to white women declined very early in the rural population, and in 1800 they were already low in New England as compared with other geographic divisions. (Table 12-12.) Between 1810 and 1840, on a national basis, both the urban and rural ratios of children under 5 years old per 1,000 women 20 to 44 years old declined by about 200 children per 1,000 women; between 1840 and 1910 the decline amounted to about 230 in the urban population and 350 in the rural population; and between 1910 and 1940 the decline amounted to about 160 in the urban population and 230 in the rural population. Thus, absolute differences in urban and rural fertility (in terms of data on young children) narrowed over the years. Table 12-12 makes it unmistakably clear that the urban-rural difference is one of very long standing. It also gives unmistakable evidence that birth rates in rural areas began to fall almost a century and one-half ago, and that the trend was parallel (at a higher level) to the falling of the urban rates.

A somewhat modified picture is obtained when one compares relative changes in fertility. In 1810, the urban ratio (900) was 68 percent as high as the rural ratio (1,329), and by 1940 the urban ratio (311) had "declined" to 56 percent of the rural ratio (551). Trends in percentages of this type do not necessarily indicate absolute widening or narrowing, because they fail to take into account changes in the size of the bases.

Data on women by number of children ever born may also be used for an examination of changing differences in urban and rural fertility. (Table 12-13.)

The decrease between 1910 and 1950 in rates of children ever born for women 45 to 49 years old was greater for the United States as a whole than for any component part, because of the change in the urban-rural composition of the population.

If women at successive ages in a single census are compared, the urban areas may sometimes appear to have had more of a decline in fertility than the rural areas. Such a comparison must allow for the migration of widows from rural-farm areas to other areas, the differential mortality of women with many children and women with few, and other factors. The writer thinks that there is less bias when one compares data for women in the same age group at several censuses than when one compares data for women in successive age groups in a single census.

Another theory is that a considerable part of the nation's decline in fertility came from "urbanization," or from an increase in the proportion of the population residing in urban areas, which made the normally low fertility of the urban population more significant. Between 1810 and 1940, for example, the proportion of the nation's white women 20 to 44 years old who were residing in urban areas increased from about 9 percent to 63 percent. It is obvious that the urban population has become the largest element in the nation. But what has been the effect of this urbanization on national fertility? According to Table 12-12, the urban and rural ratios of young children to women in 1940 were 311 and 551, respectively. If we multiply these ratios by the corresponding 1810 weights of 8 percent urban and 91 percent rural among women 20 to 44 years old and add the

Table 12-12.—NUMBER OF CHILDREN UNDER 5 YEARS OLD PER 1,000 WHITE WOMEN 20 TO 44 YEARS OLD, FOR THE UNITED STATES AND GEOGRAPHIC DIVISIONS, URBAN AND RURAL: 1800 TO 1840 AND 1910 TO 1950

(Data for 1800 to 1840 partly estimated from broad age groups. Urban-rural classification based on old (1940 Census) definition)

Area	1950	1940	1930	1920	1910	1840	1830	1820	1810	1800
United States..................	551	400	485	581	609	1,070	1,134	1,236	1,290	1,281
Urban...........................	479	311	388	471	469	701	708	831	900	845
Rural...........................	673	551	658	744	782	1,134	1,189	1,276	1,329	1,319
New England....................	516	347	441	518	482	752	812	930	1,052	1,098
Urban,..........................	486	321	417	500	468	592	614	764	845	827
Rural...........................	612	443	541	602	566	800	851	952	1,079	1,126
Middle Atlantic................	471	320	424	539	533	940	1,036	1,183	1,289	1,279
Urban...........................	432	286	386	501	495	711	722	842	924	852
Rural...........................	596	457	590	680	650	1,006	1,100	1,235	1,344	1,339
East North Central.............	552	388	458	548	555	1,270	1,467	1,608	1,702	1,840
Urban...........................	491	326	400	485	470	841	910	1,059	1,256	...
Rural...........................	679	533	605	668	672	1,291	1,484	1,616	1,706	1,840
West North Central.............	600	431	495	584	630	1,445	1,678	1,685	1,810	...
Urban...........................	514	324	365	416	426	705	1,181	...	...	...
Rural...........................	702	538	614	711	760	1,481	1,703	1,685	1,810	...
South Atlantic.................	572	464	593	694	760	1,140	1,174	1,280	1,325	1,345
Urban...........................	450	305	401	458	485	770	767	881	936	861
Rural...........................	677	596	744	851	894	1,185	1,209	1,310	1,347	1,365
East South Central.............	631	539	655	734	817	1,408	1,519	1,631	1,700	1,799
Urban...........................	494	333	414	441	469	859	863	1,089	1,348	...
Rural...........................	720	648	781	846	922	1,424	1,529	1,635	1,701	1,799
West South Central.............	607	474	584	686	845	1,297	1,359	1,418	1,383	...
Urban...........................	542	342	410	445	504	846	877	866	727	...
Rural...........................	703	591	723	823	977	1,495	1,463	1,522	1,557	...
Mountain........................	663	526	582	664	661	...	...	...	...	...
Urban...........................	584	404	428	470	466	...	...	...	...	...
Rural...........................	754	643	712	807	810	...	...	...	...	...
Pacific........................	539	339	360	425	460	...	...	...	...	...
Urban...........................	478	283	306	344	360	...	...	...	...	...
Rural...........................	652	466	507	603	640	...	...	...	...	...

Source: Wilson H. Grabill, "Progress Report on Fertility Monograph," in Current Research on Human Fertility, 1954, Milbank Memorial Fund, New York, 1955, page 84, and records for Mountain and Pacific divisions.

products, 529 is an approximation of what the 1940 national ratio could be "expected" to have been if the urban-rural distribution of women had not changed since 1810. Compare the expected figure of 529 with the actual national ratio of 400 in 1940. The difference between 529 and 400--129--measures the approximate effect of "urbanization." Compared with the national ratio of 400

in 1940 this difference is large, but it is small compared with the national change between 1810 and 1940 (1,290 - 400 = a decline of 890 in the ratios). Urbanization thus accounted for only slightly more than 14 percent of the total decline in ratios of young children to white women between 1810 and 1940.

Are urban areas consumers rather than produc-

Table 12-13.—NUMBER OF CHILDREN EVER BORN PER 1,000 WOMEN 45 TO 49 YEARS OLD, FOR THE UNITED STATES, URBAN AND RURAL: 1950, 1940, AND 1910

(Statistics based on samples)

Census year	United States	Old definition of urban		
		Urban	Rural nonfarm	Rural farm
1950	2,292	1,947	2,519	3,560
1940	2,740	2,295	2,986	3,962
1910	4,295	3,615	4,270	5,553
Decrease, 1910 to 1950	-2,003	-1,668	-1,751	-1,993

Source: U.S. Census of Population: 1950, Vol. IV, Part 5C, Fertility, Tables 4 and 6, and U.S. Census of Population: 1940, Special Reports, Differential Fertility, 1940 and 1910--Fertility for States and Large Cities, Table 4.

ers of people? Much has been written since the eighteenth century about "inadequate" urban fertility. Textbooks on population declare that cities must adapt themselves to family life if they are ever to cease being dependent on in-migration for the maintenance of their population. The general theme is that modern cities have such small families that only a favorable age distribution of population which is caused by migration keeps the larger cities from having more deaths than births. The conclusion that urban fertility is inadequate has generally been based on the use of replacement indexes and on conventional net reproduction rates, both of which reflect the conditions existing during a short period of time. For example, Thompson noted from the 1920 Census data that the number of children under 5 years old per 1,000 native white women 20 to 44 years old in large cities was substantially below permanent replacement needs.[9] He provided the following data in data in support of his argument:

Area	Index showing percent of excess (or deficit) of ratios of children of native white women over permanent replacement needs, 1920
United States	15
Cities of 100,000 and over	-30
25,000 to 100,000	-15
10,000 to 25,000	-10
2,500 to 10,000	...
Rural	55

The Bureau of the Census placed the net reproduction rate for the urban population as a whole at only 937 for the period 1905-10, at 747 for 1930-35, and at 726 for 1935-40. Subsequently, the net reproduction rate for the urban population rose to 1,186 in 1944-49.[10]

The net reproduction rates pertain to age-specific birth (and death) rates in a particular year, and may not reflect the lifetime fertility of actual cohorts of women. In terms of children ever born, urban women 45 to 49 years old (women of completed fertility) in 1950 had an average of 1.9 children, compared with 2.3 children for urban women of this age in 1940, and with 3.6 children in 1910, using the old urban definition (1940) throughout.[11] Even by the more comprehensive and realistic 1950 definition of urban, which includes residents of the thickly populated fringe areas around large cities and also unincorporated places of 2,500 or more, urban women 45 to 49 years old averaged only 2.0 children ever born.

Without a life table we know that an average of 1.9 or 2.0 children is inadequate for the replacement of population. An average of 2.06 children is needed merely to insure one female birth for each woman, since about 106 boys are born for every 100 girls. Replacement from generation to generation, however, further requires that enough daughters survive to become potential mothers. Replacement quotas can easily be approximated as follows: The women who were 45 to 49 years old

[9] Warren S. Thompson, Ratio of Children to Women: 1920, Census Monograph XI. U. S. Government Printing Office, Washington, D.C., 1931, p. 168.

[10] U. S. Census of Population: 1940, Special Reports, Differential Fertility, 1940 and 1910--Standardized Fertility Rates and Reproduction Rates, p. 20. Bureau of the Census, Current Population Reports, Series P-20, No. 27, "Marital Fertility: April, 1949." February 3, 1950, p. 1.

[11] The data reflect conditions existing at the time of the census rather than those existing at the time the children were born. Women 45 to 49 years old were the survivors of a slighty larger group of women who lived during the childbearing ages. Also, women migrated between urban and rural areas, and some rural towns were reclassified as urban when the population attained a size of 2,500 people.

in 1950 had been at the average age of childbearing, about 28 years, in 1929. (This 28 years is the mean age of childbearing, which is a year or so more than the median age of childbearing, 26 or 27 years.) This serves as a rough average date of birth for all of their children, who actually were born between 1915 and 1949. According to United States life tables for 1929-31, about 87 percent of female births should survive to age 28 years.[12] On this basis, a replacement quota for the lifetime experience of women who were 45 to 49 years old in 1950 is 2.06 divided by .87=2.4 children. The average which was actually reported, of 2.0 children ever born, was thus about 83 percent of replacement needs. The experience of a single cohort like the women 45 to 49 years old in 1950 does not, of course, prove that urban areas have become consumers of people. Not only urban residence, but also the effect on lifetime fertility of past conditions such as the economic depression of the 1930's was involved. Some additional replacement quotas are 2.1 children, based on 1949 life tables, and 2.7 children based on Glover's life tables for females in 1901-1909 in the original Death Registration states. A quota of 3.0 children might be a maximum need for whites as far back as 1810. Data for women in age groups older than 45 to 49 years in 1950 and for women of various ages in the 1940 and 1950 Censuses indicate that urban areas, nationally, long have had an adequate amount of lifetime fertility among women. Data for women under 45 years old in the 1950 Census indicate that there is a good chance for these women to attain an adequate level of lifetime fer-

tility by the time they reach age 45 years. This generalization does not apply to women in certain large cities, however. (See section on "Distributional Aspects.")

Color, race, and nativity.--Fertility data for white and nonwhite women have already been shown in several places in this chapter. Negroes comprised about 96 percent of the nonwhite women, nationally, in 1950 and 1940. It has already been noted that whereas the white women had sharply declining current fertility beginning at least as early as 1810, Negroes had little change in ratios of young children to women until after 1880 (see Table 12-3, page 295. Because of high infant mortality, however, ratios of children under 5 years old to nonwhite women 20 to 44 years old did not exceed a level of 1,100 nationally between the Censuses of 1850 and 1880. The nonwhite women actually were a very fertile group, as may be seen from the fact that the nonwhite women who were 50 to 54 years old in the 1910 Census were the first nonwhite group to complete the childbearing ages with fewer than 6,500 children ever born per 1,000 women (Table 12-5, page 298). It may be noted parenthetically, that the expectation of life at birth has increased for Negro females from 37.7 years in 1909-11 to 63.2 years in 1950; corresponding figures for white females are 53.6 years and 72.4 years.[13]

Despite a very large decline in current fertility after 1880, nonwhite women in 1950 had relatively more children ever born and more annual births than did white women, age for age:

Age of woman (years)	Children ever born per 1,000 women, United States: 1950		Births per 1,000 women, United States: 1950 (corrected for underregistration)	
	White	Nonwhite	White	Nonwhite
15 to 19...	92	195	70	164
20 to 24...	701	1,012	190	243
25 to 29...	1,409	1,654	165	174
30 to 34...	1,847	2,079	103	113
35 to 39...	2,030	2,310	51	64
40 to 44...	2,132	2,509	15	21
45 to 49...	2,251	2,663	1	3

[12]Computed from U. S. Bureau of the Census, United States Life Tables, 1930. United States Government Printing Office, Washington, D.C., 1936. Tables IB and ID. The children of the women 45 to 49 years old actually were subject not to the mortality conditions embodied in a life table for 1929-31, but to a different experience in each year and age of the children's existence. A generation life table was not available. Such a table might take into account mortality at age 0 in 1929-31, age 1 in 1930-32, age 2 in 1931-33, etc. Little error results from the use of the table for 1929-31, however, because the bulk of mortality occurred in infancy. In 1929-31, about 94 percent of female children reaching the age of 2 years would be expected to survive to age 28; using a 1949 life table, 96 percent would be expected to survive from age 2 to age 28.

[13]National Office of Vital Statistics, Vital Statistics of the United States: 1950, Vol. I., U. S. Government Printing Office, Washington, D.C., 1954, p. 152.

It is hard to evaluate the fertility of nonwhite women in urban areas in 1950, because some of them were recent in-migrants from rural areas. There may be a typical pattern according to which the nonwhite urban women tend to have more births at ages under 20 years than do white urban women, with the white women at least temporarily overtaking the nonwhite women in respect to the average number of children ever born by about age 30. In 1950, urban nonwhite women 30 to 34 years old, ever married, had 1,806 children ever born per 1,000 women, as compared with 1,821 for white women. At age 35 to 39 years, the corresponding rates were 1,879 for nonwhite women and 1,943 for white women. These particular groups of urban nonwhite women seem likely to reach the end of their childbearing with insufficient children for replacement of their generation. A large proportion of nonwhite women in urban areas reported that no children had been born to them. For example, in 1950 one-third of urban nonwhite women 40 to 44 years old, ever married, were childless. In 1950, 69.7 percent of nonwhite women 15 to 59 years old resided in urban areas as compared with 66.5 percent of white women. Back in 1910, about two-thirds of nonwhite women lived in rural areas. The urbanization of rural nonwhite women may have involved them in a

struggle toward a higher plane of living that could not be as easily reached if they had many children. There was a relatively low percent of childlessness among nonwhite urban women in 1910; this suggests that much of the subsequent childlessness may have been voluntary.

In 1950 the national population still contained 1.3 million foreign-born white women of childbearing age. About one-half of this group was 35 to 44 years old. The foreign-born white population, however, is not as important a factor as it was in the days of unrestricted immigration. The immigration quotas that went into effect in 1921 and 1924 have changed the character of the immigration and have severely limited the annual number of immigrants admitted. Since then, immigrants have come largely from nations where birth rates are low. Also, the immigration laws may tend to select low fertility migrants from each nation. On a standardized-for-age basis, the ever-married foreign-born white women 15 to 44 years old were less fertile than the nation's native white women in 1950. (See Table 12-14.) A very large proportion of the foreign-born white women (82 percent) lived in urban areas where birth rates were relatively low in 1950.

Table 12-14 also shows that the small Asian and Indian populations are relatively fertile.

Table 12-14.—RACE-NATIVITY OF WOMAN: STANDARDIZED DISTRIBUTION OF WOMEN 15 TO 44 YEARS OLD, EVER MARRIED, BY NUMBER OF CHILDREN EVER BORN, FOR THE UNITED STATES: 1950

(Standardized for age of woman on the basis of the distribution by age of women of all races in 1950. Statistics based on sample.)

Subject	Native white	Foreign-born white	Negro	Other races-urban (largely Asiatic)	Other races-rural (largely Indian)
Number of women ever married............	21,810,110	1,033,810	2,766,150	42,480	51,210
Percent (standardized)............	100.0	100.0	100.0	100.0	100.0
No children ever born..................	21.9	22.4	30.8	21.2	12.9
1 child..............................	27.1	29.9	22.1	25.5	17.5
2 children...........................	25.7	25.5	16.0	21.0	16.3
3 children...........................	12.7	12.0	10.0	16.4	13.1
4 children...........................	6.0	4.9	6.6	4.8	12.3
5 and 6 children.....................	4.3	3.3	7.6	8.4	14.7
7 to 9 children......................	1.7	1.3	4.9	2.0	10.5
10 or more children..................	0.5	0.6	1.9	0.6	2.6
Children ever born per 1,000 women ever married (standardized)................	1,829	1,707	2,119	2,047	3,304

Source: Derived from U.S. Census of Population: 1950, Vol. IV, Part 5C, Fertility, Table 12.

Social and economic differentials. Income and wealth.

"That the poor have more children than the rich is a well-established fact. It was noted by students of population as early as the eighteenth century and since about 1900 has been confirmed by many statistical studies. However, ...the methods employed have often been far from adequate. Since fertility data have rarely been available for groups differentiated by income or property, various indirect measures of "wealth" have been used..."--United Nations. [14]

It seems well to note some of the various types of evidence that exist concerning the important topic of fertility variations by income or wealth, because American economists seem to be increasingly skeptical about the theory that poor families actually have more children than do wealthy families. The situation seems to be changing, reflecting both the weakening of an ancient fertility pattern and an improvement in planes of living. Present income differentials may seem small because the sharp and often tragic distinctions between the "poor" and the "wealthy" do not now exist in their former proportions. An "indirect" method of measuring income differentials makes use of tax lists, rental levels of real estate, data on per capita income, and plane of living indices to classify particular areas as relatively "poor" or "wealthy." Birth rates or other measures of fertility such as ratios of young children to women are then computed for each type of area. Almost invariably, fertility has been found to be greater in the "poor" areas, with some exceptions such as a recent study of New York City. The following data illustrate the point that patterns of relatively high fertility in "poor" areas have a long history.

Some economists and housing analysts have failed to find a relation between the economic status of various areas in a large city and the average size of households. They usually have not controlled important variables such as age of women, type of household, and marital status. In cities it often happens that a certain area contains small dwelling units and therefore small households, regardless of economic conditions. Or a district may contain many rooming houses and efficiency apartments occupied largely by unattached adults. It is easier for renters to move about as their needs change than for the living quarters to be expanded. Note that Jaffe grouped together pertinent parts of cities. Also, he used data on young children (as approximations to annual births) rather than data on households. His area comparisons are suggestive but not conclusive; the wealthy areas may have contained some unmarried servants or a number of low-income families, and a few large estates that raised the average "wealth." Guesses, sometimes justified, are involved in an assumption that low birth rates in wealthy areas mean that wealthy families are small.

Data for particular social and economic groups have been studied for fertility differences. Notables in "Who's Who" have been found to have rather small families, on the average, as have college alumni. These people are selected for reasons other than income or wealth, and not all of them are wealthy. Hence, they may not typify wealthy persons in general. Achievement is sometimes a result of long struggle, with no time or inclination for marriage, or desire for children, until late in life. At the other extreme, families helped by charitable or relief agencies have been noted to contain relatively many children. Here also, there is some selection; families with many children have a more difficult time "making ends meet" on a given small income than those with few or no children. For this reason, low income families with few children may not qualify for assistance.

Direct data on income or wealth for the general population in relation to fertility are rare. Where such data exist, a J-shaped relation of fertility with economic status has often been noted. (See Figure 12-2.) That is, fertility tends to be successively less in population groups of successively higher economic status until a certain status is reached; then it either levels off, or increases as still higher economic status is reached. Some

---

[14]United Nations, The Determinants and Consequences of Population Trends, op. cit., p. 86.

Table 12-15.—STANDARDIZED REPRODUCTION RATES OF THE WHITE POPULATION, BY PLANE OF LIVING, FOR SELECTED GEOGRAPHICAL AREAS IN THE UNITED STATES: 1800 TO 1840

(The standardized reproduction rates are computed from census data on number of young children and on women by age. They correspond roughly to gross reproduction rates reduced by 2 1/2 years of infant mortality and put on an index basis, with the rate for "lowest" areas set at 100.)

Area, date, and plane of living	Standardized reproduction rate	Area, date, and plane of living	Standardized reproduction rate
Urban areas:		Rural areas:	
New York City, 1820		New York State, 1820	
Lowest	100	Lowest	100
Intermediate	82	Intermediate	95
Highest	80	Highest	86
New York City, 1840		North Carolina, 1800	
Lowest	100	Lowest	100
Intermediate low	83	Intermediate	88
Intermediate high	73	Highest	76
Highest	57	North Carolina, 1820	
Boston, 1830		Lowest	100
Lowest	100	Intermediate	85
Intermediate	85	Highest	79
Highest	58	Georgia, 1800	
Providence, 1830		Lowest	100
Lowest	100	Intermediate	86
Intermediate	95	Highest	86
Highest	72	Georgia, 1820	
Providence, 1830 (married women)		Lowest	100
Lowest	100	Intermediate	92
Highest	79	Highest	85
		South Carolina, 1800	
		Lowest	100
		Intermediate low	89
		Intermediate high	83
		Highest	66

Source: A. J. Jaffe, "Differential Fertility in the White Population in Early America," Journal of Heredity (An Organ of the American Genetic Association), Washington, D. D. Vol. XXXI, No. 9, September 1940, page 410.

demographers have used this fertility-income regression to speculate that when the small family system has diffused throughout the nation, fertility may become directly related to income or wealth. They regard the J-shaped pattern as evidence of the emergence of a direct pattern. Evidence in support of this theory was obtained in a local survey in the city of Indianapolis in 1941. This survey found a direct relation between fertility and the husband's average annual earnings since marriage, but only for couples who claimed that they had been successful in controlling the number and spacing of all their children.[15] Poor people who knew how to limit their families had fewer chil-

[15] Clyde V. Kiser and P. K. Whelpton, "Fertility Planning and Fertility Rates by Socio-Economic Status," Social and Psychological Factors Affecting Fertility. IX. Milbank Memorial Fund Quarterly, Vol. XXVII, No. 2, April 1949. Pages 388 and 395. The data are limited to wives who were Protestant, native white, married between 1920 and 1929, marriage unbroken at the time of the intensive interview in 1941, wife under 30 and husband under 40 at marriage, neither previously married, both resident in a large city most of the time since marriage, and both with at least a full grammar school education.

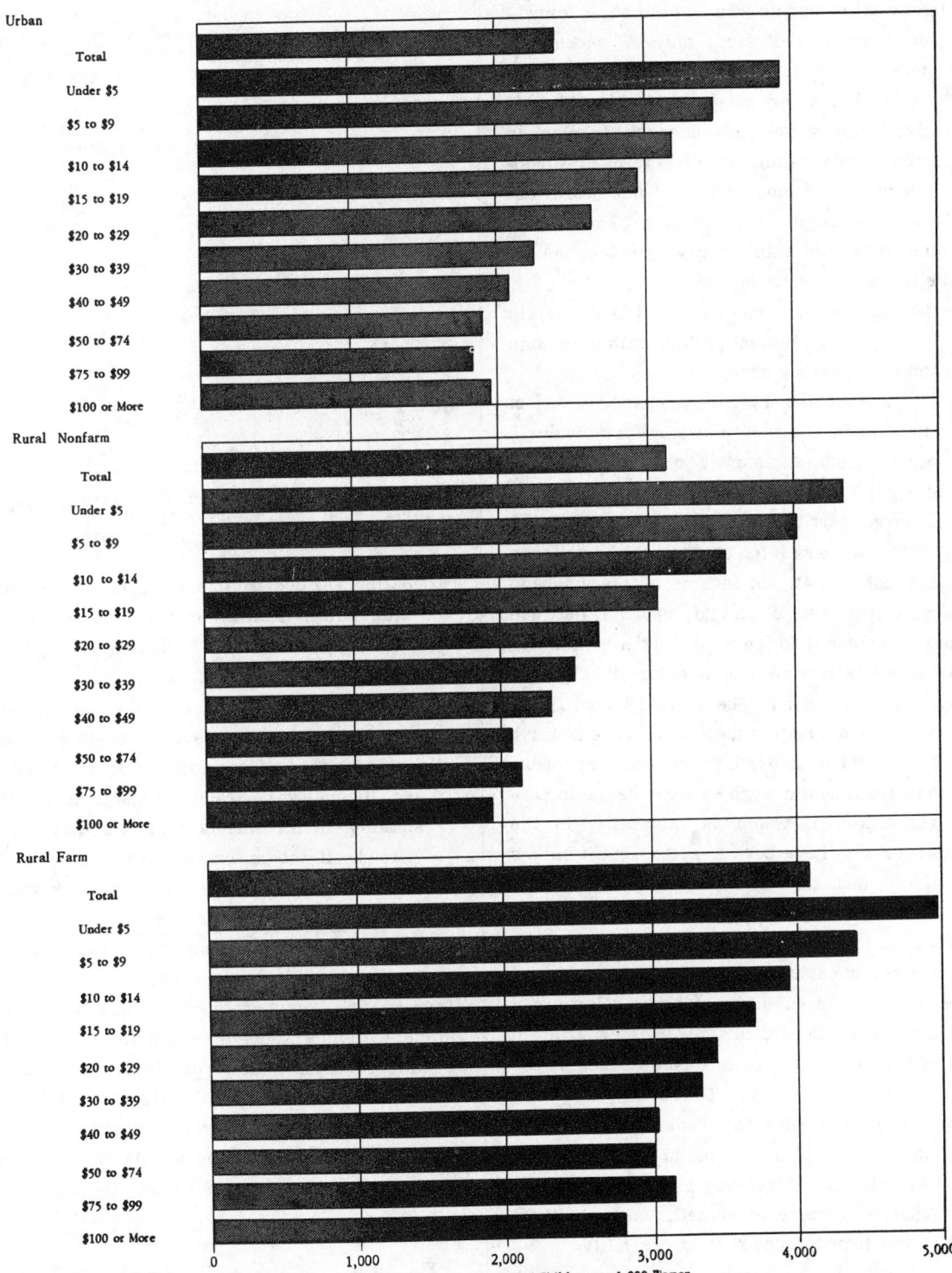

FIGURE 12 - 2. MONTHLY RENTAL VALUE OF HOME BY NUMBER OF CHILDREN EVER BORN PER
1, 000 NATIVE WHITE WOMEN EVER MARRIED, 45 TO 49 YEARS OLD,
FOR THE UNITED STATES, URBAN AND RURAL, 1940

(Data based on sample. Limited to women living in private households and related to household head.)

Source: U.S. Census of Population: 1940, Special Reports, Differential Fertility, 1940 and 1910--Women by Number of Children Ever Born, Table 60.

dren than wealthy people who had the same knowledge. However, in that study only 17 percent of the couples in the lowest income group (under $1,200) and 45 percent of those in the highest group ($3,000 or more) had successfully planned the number and spacing of all their children. Much larger proportions had tried but were not completely successful. (Perhaps control measures are sometimes only indifferently practiced until a child or two has been born).

The J-shaped pattern was observed in France in 1906. It may be an ancient pattern rather than an indication of impending change.

The Bureau of the Census prepared data on family income in relation to own children under 5 years old in a sample survey of the population made in April 1949. A strong inverse relation between current fertility and family income was found.[16] Three years later another sample survey that made use of data on income of the husband only found patterns of virtual equality between husband's income and current fertility and between husband's income and number of children ever born to their wives. (See Table 12-16.) There was a two-year overlap in the two surveys of birth dates of the children under 5 years old; there were also other reasons why such sudden change in patterns was expected. Sampling variability in the two surveys may have been a factor, but it seems more likely that the different types of income studied were the major cause of the difference between the results of the two surveys. Family income is sometimes high because of working wives and because of the earnings of other relatives of the family head. Should income be measured in terms of family income, or in terms of income for the head of the family only? The family income is closely associated with the rental value of the home and the plane of living, but high incomes are somewhat selective of working wives without children. That is, income is sometimes an indirect result rather than a "cause" of low fertility.

Table 12-16.—MONEY INCOME IN 1951 FOR MEN 20 TO 59 YEARS OLD, MARRIED AND WIFE PRESENT, BY NUMBER OF OWN CHILDREN UNDER 5 YEARS OLD, PER 1,000 MEN STANDARDIZED FOR AGE OF MAN, FOR THE UNITED STATES: APRIL, 1952

(Statistics based on sample. Standard is distribution of total men married and wife present.)

Money income	Percent distribution of men	Own children under 5 years old per 1,000 men
Total............	100.0	519
Under $1,000........	6.8	528
$1,000 to $1,999....	11.0	495
$2,000 to $2,999....	20.7	530
$3,000 to $3,999....	27.0	528
$4,000 to $4,999....	16.1	532
$5,000 to $5,999....	8.6	506
$6,000 to $6,999....	3.9	532
$7,000 and over.....	6.0	540

Source: Bureau of the Census, Current Population Reports, P-20, No. 46, "Fertility of the Population: April, 1952," December 31, 1953, Table 17.

Education.--Education is indirectly a major factor in fertility. It may or may not be associated with a struggle for a high plane of living, culturally, materially, or spiritually.

"...when nearly every individual is seeking supremely that perseverance 'extravagantly high standard of comfort,' with all the energy and ingenuity he can command, many things standing in the way of it must and will be sacrificed. If the marriage or parental relationship is thought in any way to conflict with this object, it must be sacrificed! "...[17]

The American people have been a relatively literate group since early times, slaves and some immigrants excepted. In part, this was because some religious sects stressed the desirability of reading the Bible. However, free public education early became a matter of civic rather than religious concern. According to the 1850 Census, 92 percent of the total white population 20 years old and over could read and write. By way of con-

---

[16]U. S. Bureau of the Census, Current Population Reports, Series P-20, No. 27, "Marital Fertility: April 1949," Feb. 3, 1950, p. 10.

---

[17]Dr. Nathan Allen, "Lessons on Population Suggested by Grecian and Roman History," in The Congregational Quarterly, October, 1871. (An article on the declining birth rate among natives of New England and an analogy to the fall of ancient Greece and Rome.)

trast, 38,031 men and 56,965 women out of a total of 118,825 couples marrying in England and Wales in 1842 affixed their marks instead of signatures to marriage records. In the French army of 1851, of 311,218 conscripts, only 59.5 percent could read and write. [18]

It may be presumed that many of the adults who lived during the past century saw the newspaper advertisements on contraceptives and abortifacients that appeared between 1810 and the passage of the Comstock Law in 1873. [19] Or they may have read the several pamphlets that offered a moral and health justification for family limitation, as well as methods for accomplishing it. At least one of these pamphlets received considerable notoriety from the political attacks on its congressman-author in the 1840's.

Since the American people were largely literate and yet had a much higher birth rate than the people of Europe until well into the nineteenth century, it appears that for a long time the factors sustaining the birth rate, such as abundant subsistence, outweighed the factors tending to depress the birth rate. The small or moderate-size family did not become "fashionable" all at once.

The 1910 Census obtained data on children ever born in relation to literacy of women, for example:

Table 12-17.—NUMBER OF CHILDREN EVER BORN PER 1,000 WOMEN 45 TO 49 YEARS OLD, BY LITERACY AND RACE-NATIVITY OF WOMAN, FOR THE UNITED STATES: 1910

(Statistics based on sample)

Literacy	Native white	Foreign-born white[1]	Negro
Literate...........	3,753	4,836	5,279
Illiterate.........	6,075	6,195	6,329
Percent illiterate..	4.6	14.2	53.7

[1]Foreign-born white women 45 to 54 years old.

Source: U.S. Census of Population: 1940, Special Reports, Differential Fertility, 1940 and 1910-- Women by Number of Children Ever Born, U.S. Government Printing Office, Washington, D.C., 1943, Tables 54, 55, and 56.

The above figures for 1910 represent a large change from conditions in colonial times when white women were estimated to have had an average of 8 children. It is likely that the fertility of

the illiterate as well as that of the literate declined over the years before 1910.

Table 12-18 illustrates the general inverse relation between the amount of formal schooling women have received and their subsequent lifetime fertility. The inverse pattern appears also in Puerto Rico, where birth rates have changed very little for many decades, and where most of the people are of the Roman Catholic faith.

Table 12-18.—NUMBER OF CHILDREN EVER BORN PER 1,000 WOMEN OF COMPLETED FERTILITY BY YEARS OF SCHOOL COMPLETED, FOR THE UNITED STATES AND PUERTO RICO: 1950

(Statistics for the United States based on sample)

Years of school completed	United States		Puerto Rico, women 45 years old and over
	White women 45 to 49 years old	White women ever married 45 to 49 years old	
Total.........	2,251	2,456	5,809
Elementary:			
0 to 7 years....	3,232	3,422	6,088
8 years.........	2,487	2,643	3,566
High school:			
1 to 3 years....	2,148	2,290	3,154
4 years.........	1,643	1,818	2,319
College:			
1 year or more..	1,336	1,602	1,801

Source: U.S. Census of Population: 1950, Vol. IV, Part 5C, Fertility, U.S. Government Printing Office, Washington, D.C., 1955. Table 20. Special report of 1950 Census, "Fertility by Social and Economic Status, for Puerto Rico: 1950," Series PC-14, No. 21, June 24, 1954, Tables 1 and 2.

In Puerto Rico as well as in the United States, the level of fertility of women who had some college education was well below replacement. To

---

[18] U. S. Census Office, Statistical View of the United States, Being a Compendium of the Seventh Census (1850), A.O.P. Nicholson, Public Printer, Washington, D.C., 1854, p. 149.

[19]The Comstock Law, an act prohibiting the use of the mails for obscene literature and the dissemination of information on contraception, was enacted on the last day of the second session of the 39th Congress, at the instigation of the noted Vice Crusader, Anthony Comstock, supported mainly by the Y.M. C.A. Comstock's concern was for the temptations faced by young men away from home.

some extent this pattern results from the fact that higher education is selective of women who expect to pursue a career, such as school teaching, and from delayed marriage. The data for women probably show a stronger inverse relation between fertility and education than would appear in similar data for men.

There was a time, in the United States, when many local communities would hire only single women as school teachers, and their social life had to be very circumspect. Hence, a large proportion of women college graduates did not marry during the economic depression of the 1930's. A teacher shortage during and after World War II caused these restrictions almost to disappear. Women college graduates married in large numbers, including many who had graduated years earlier. The college graduates had the largest ratios of own children under 5 years old to women 30 years old and over in 1950 (Figure 12-3).

Major occupation groups of men.--Data on major occupation groups indicate that there is no clear-cut relation between fertility and social and economic status (see Table 12-19). Fertility tends to be comparatively low in the so-called "white-collar" occupation groups and comparatively high

in the so-called "blue-collar" groups. It is relatively low in nonfarm occupation compared with farm occupations. But clerical and sales workers have one of the lowest levels of cumulative fertility (children ever born), although they do not rank at the top in prestige or average income. This has led sociologists to speculate that the greatest pressure to limit births was not felt by the uppermost social classes, but by those that are just below the top strata. It is from these groups that the coveted entrance into the upper classes is made. In terms of current fertility (own children under 5 years old in 1952), the prestige groups, "professionals, technicians, and kindred workers" and "managers, officials, and proprietors, except farm," have levels of fertility that are roughly the same as those of the blue collar group - "craftsmen, foremen, and kindred workers." All occupation groups participated in the surge in current fertility after World War II.

It should be kept in mind that occupation is not a fixed characteristic. Over a lifetime, a person may be attached to several different occupation groups. Workers shift from one group to another as a result of such factors as changing economic and technological conditions, sporadic job changes,

Table 12-19.—MAJOR OCCUPATION GROUP OF EMPLOYED CIVILIAN MEN, MARRIED AND WIFE PRESENT, BY NUMBER OF CHILDREN EVER BORN TO THE WIFE AND NUMBER OF OWN CHILDREN UNDER 5 YEARS OLD OF THE WIFE, FOR THE UNITED STATES: APRIL, 1952

(Statistics based on sample. Standards are distributions by age of total wives or husbands.)

Major occupation employed group of husband	Number of wives 15 to 44 years old (1,000's)	Children ever born per 1,000 wives 15 to 44 years old, standardized for age of woman	Own children under 5 of wife per 1,000 husbands 20 to 59 years old, standardized for age of man	
			1952	1947
Total...	21,618	1,985	529	467
Professional, technical and kindred workers.........	1,764	1,653	492	470
Farmer and farm managers.........................	1,830	2,704	687	555
Managers, officials, and proprietors, except farm...	2,710	1,759	492	417
Clerical and kindred workers......................	1,362	1,574	438	393
Sales workers....................................	1,164	1,535	479	400
Craftsmen, foremen, and kindred workers.............	4,832	1,932	480	459
Operatives and kindred workers....................	5,030	2,076	555	474
Service workers, including private household........	926	1,805	516	410
Farm laborers and foremen........................	384	3,153	747	639
Laborers, except farm and mine....................	1,616	2,380	597	507

Source: U.S. Bureau of the Census, Current Population Reports, Series P-20, No. 46, "Fertility of the Population: April, 1952," Dec. 31, 1953, Tables 3 and 16.

Years of School Completed

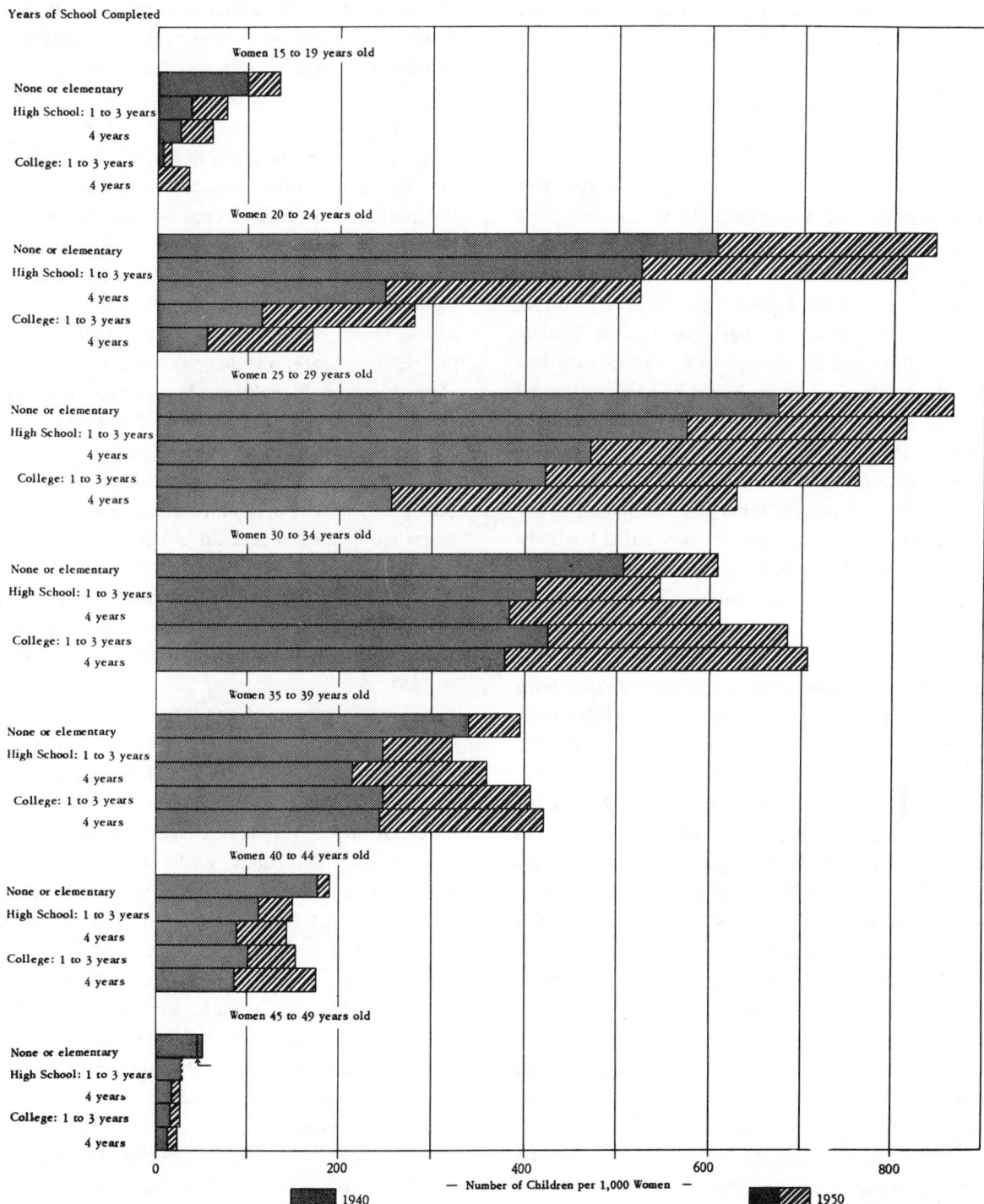

FIGURE 12 - 3. NUMBER OF OWN CHILDREN UNDER 5 YEARS OLD PER 1,000 WHITE WOMEN 15 TO 49 YEARS OLD
BY YEARS OF SCHOOL COMPLETED AND AGE OF WOMEN, FOR THE UNITED STATES, 1950 AND 1940

(Statistics based on samples Data for white women in 1950 and native white women in 1940.)

Source: U.S. Census of Population: 1950, Vol. IV, Special Reports, Part 5C, Fertility, Table 44, and U.S. Census of Population: 1940, Special Reports, Differential Fertility, 1940 and 1910--Women by Number of Children Under 5 Years Old, Table 25.

and long-term "upward" movements associated with increasing age, skill, and experience.

SOME DISTRIBUTIONAL ASPECTS

States

It has already been indicated that the fertility of the population has varied widely by geographical divisions since the early days of the United States (Table 12-3, page 295). The current fertility of women in the early 1800's was relatively low in New England, high in the long-settled Middle Atlantic and South Atlantic states, and extraordinarily high for a while in areas of new settlement because of selective migration of young married women. During the 150 years of fertility decline before 1935, fertility declined more in some parts of the country than in others. By virtue of a slower decline in fertility, the largely rural Southern and Mountain states became the areas with relatively fertile populations. Since 1910, four states have usually been in the lead with respect to children ever born per 1,000 white women: Utah with its largely Mormon population; New Mexico with its largely Roman-Catholic and one-third Spanish-American or Mexican population; North Dakota with its many fertile rural-farm people; and Arkansas with its Ozark mountaineers. (Figure 12-4). At the other extreme, the District of Columbia (wholly urban) and a few highly urban and industrial states usually have had the lowest rates of children ever born. The New England states have been overtaken by other states with respect to low fertility. In terms of rates of children ever born, Vermont was the thirteenth most fertile state in 1950, and Maine occupies a middle position. One of the southern states, Florida, had a fairly low rank in 1950, probably because of heavy inmigration of people from the North.

In 1950, among white women 45 to 49 years old, twenty-two states and the District of Columbia had rates of children ever born that were below a national replacement quota of 2,360 children ever born per 1,000 women, figured from 1929-31 United States life tables. In 1940, eight states and the District of Columbia had rates below the calculated

replacement quota, which was then about 2,450. Women who are now young may complete the childbearing ages with larger families than did the women who were 45 to 49 years old in 1950, in view of the increase in births after 1940.

Because of fluctuations in births, differences in the distribution of the population by age and marital status, and similar factors, states do not always rank in a consistent fashion with respect to different measures and dates for fertility. For example, in 1950 and 1951 the District of Columbia had a crude birth rate (corrected) that was above the nation's rate, in sharp contrast to its last-place position in respect to average number of children ever born per woman. The District has a relatively large proportion of women of childbearing age. (Some of the difficulties in allocating births to residence of mother may result from the fact that nearby Maryland suburbs have Washington, D.C. post office service.) Different measures of fertility vary widely in other states, too, however. Arkansas, which ranks at the top in Figure 12-3, ranked 15th in respect to the crude birth rate in 1951.

Counties

The Bureau of the Census published net reproduction rates for the white population in 1935-40, on a county basis, computed from data on children under 5 years old and women by 5-year age groups. The rates, while old, are useful as a general indication of broad county patterns of variation. In the period from 1935 to 1940 all but three states had some counties with net reproduction rates below replacement needs (Figure 12-5). The exceptions were Utah, New Mexico, and Arizona. North Dakota came close to being an exception, with only one county having a rate below replacement. Relatively moderate or low fertility existed in a broad band of counties, extending from the northeast westward through Nebraska and Kansas. The whole Pacific Coast area, Nevada, the Piedmont region of the South, and northern and central Texas also had relatively moderate or low fertility. All this was at a time (1935 to 1940) when the net reproduction rate of the nation's white population (978) was slightly below the replacement

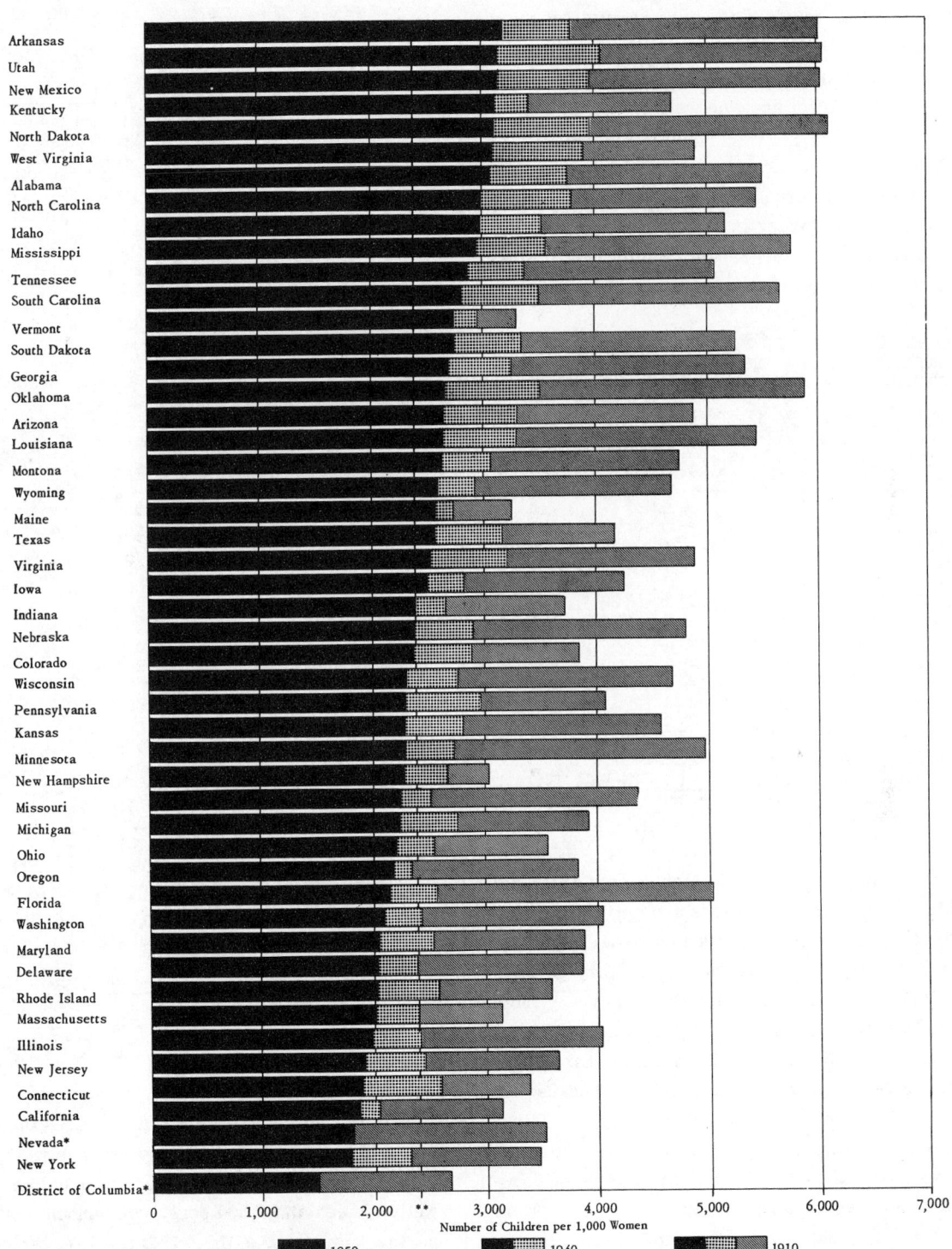

FIGURE 12 - 4. NUMBER OF CHILDREN EVER BORN PER 1,000 WHITE WOMEN 45 TO 49 YEARS
OLD, FOR STATES, 1950, 1940, AND 1910

(Data based on samples.)

*Rates for 1950 and 1940 approximately equal.

*Replacement quota for 1950, from life tables for 1929-1931. (2360)

Source: U.S. Census of Population: 1950, Vol. IV, Special Reports, Part 5C, Fertility, Table 32, and U.S. Census of Population: 1940,
Special Reports, Differential Fertility, 1940 and 1910--Fertility for States and Large Cities, Tables 31 and 32.

level, (1,000). The map represents a distorted picture in that much of the area consists of thinly populated counties, whereas the bulk of the population is concentrated in a few small areas (large cities) which do not show up well.

Size of Place of Residence and Individual Cities

Birth rates, ratios of young children to women, and rates of children ever born tend to be lowest in large cities, larger in places of moderate size, and largest in rural areas. Table 12-20 illustrates the pattern in terms of crude birth rates.

Table 12-20.—BIRTHS PER 1,000 INHABITANTS, URBAN AND RURAL, BY SIZE OF URBAN PLACE, BY COLOR, FOR THE UNITED STATES: 1950

(Rates adjusted for underregistration)

Area	All races	White	Non-white
Total................	24.1	23.0	33.3
Urban....................	22.9	22.0	30.6
Places of:			
250,000 or more........	21.6	20.3	29.6
100,000 to 250,000.....	23.4	22.4	31.2
50,000 to 100,000......	23.1	22.3	31.2
25,000 to 50,000.......	23.1	22.6	29.7
10,000 to 25,000.......	24.2	23.6	32.1
2,500 to 10,000........	24.6	23.9	33.2
Rural....................	25.8	24.5	37.1

Source: National Office of Vital Statistics, Vital Statistics of the United States: 1950, Vol. I, Table 6.24 (U.S. Government Printing Office, Washington, D.C., 1954.)

The variation by size of place is only a general tendency. Frequent exceptions are noticeable when individual cities are arranged in order by size. One city may have a large fertile foreign-born population, or may differ in some other way from other cities. For example, the adjacent cities of Minneapolis and St. Paul differ somewhat in respect to fertility of their populations because of different proportions of "white-collar" and "blue-collar" workers, among other reasons. Some of the wide variations that exist in the size of completed families in large cities may be seen from the following data from the 1940 Census (similar tabulations were not made in 1950). See Table 12-12.

Table 12-21.—NUMBER OF CHILDREN EVER BORN PER 1,000 WOMEN 45 TO 49 YEARS OLD, BY COLOR, FOR CITIES OF 250,000 OR MORE: 1950

(Data based on sample. Rate not shown where base is less than 3,000 women.)

City	Children ever born per 1,000 women 45 to 49 years old, 1940	
	White	Nonwhite
Atlanta, Ga..............	2,196	2,140
Baltimore, Md............	2,211	1,777
Birmingham, Ala..........	2,228	...
Boston, Mass.............	2,341	...
Buffalo, N.Y.............	2,499	...
Chicago, Ill.............	2,215	1,703
Cincinnati, Ohio.........	1,799	...
Cleveland, Ohio..........	2,570	1,961
Columbus, Ohio...........	1,955	...
Dallas, Texas............	1,961	...
Denver, Colo.............	1,863	...
Detroit, Mich............	2,458	1,949
Houston, Texas...........	2,202	...
Indianapolis, Ind........	1,845	...
Jersey City, N.J.........	2,532	...
Kansas City, Mo..........	1,687	...
Los Angeles, Calif.......	1,613	...
Louisville, Ky...........	1,909	...
Memphis, Tenn............	2,001	2,318
Milwaukee, Wis...........	2,284	...
Minneapolis, Minn........	1,989	...
Newark, N.J..............	2,614	...
New Orleans, La..........	2,247	2,548
New York, N.Y............	2,221	1,727
Oakland, Calif...........	1,806	...
Philadelphia, Pa.........	2,324	2,075
Pittsburgh, Pa...........	2,669	...
Portland, Oreg...........	1,608	...
Providence, R.I..........	2,375	...
Rochester, N.Y...........	2,131	...
St. Louis, Mo............	1,822	1,833
St. Paul, Minn...........	2,062	...
San Antonio, Texas.......	2,504	...
San Francisco, Calif.....	1,441	...
Seattle, Wash............	1,738	...
Toledo, Ohio.............	1,969	...
Washington, D.C..........	1,473	1,903

Source: U.S. Census of Population: 1940, Special Reports, Differential Fertility, 1940 and 1910-- Fertility for States and Large Cities, Table 41. (U.S. Government Printing Office, Washington, D.C., 1943.)

Note that in many of these large cities the average number of children ever born was well below replacement needs (about 2,450 children per 1,000 white women and 2,800 per 1,000 nonwhite women, on the basis of the United States life tables for 1919-21). The rates for some cities were also inadequate as compared with a quota of 2,060 children that assumes no mortality between birth and the childbearing ages (the 2,060 children would yield about 1,000 daughters to replace 1,000 women, and 1,060 sons).

SOME FACTORS AFFECTING FERTILITY

1. <u>Age and Fecundity</u>. Biologically, reproduction is possible among women from an average age of about 13 years to an average age of about 47 years, or between puberty and the menopause. Within this age range the fecundity (ability to conceive) varies widely. There is evidence from certain African tribes and Oriental groups that conception is not easily accomplished before the age of 16 years. Other data suggest that fecundity reaches a peak at about age 19. Thereafter it declines, slowly at first. By about age 35, it is declining rapidly. Fecundity may be affected by such things as a hormone inbalance. A woman's actual childbearing usually is far below her potentiality, because it depends on marital status, the number and spacing of children wanted, the efficiency of family limitation practices, and on her and her husband's health. The general pattern of relation between birth rates and age for all women is illustrated in Figure 12-5, which also shows the changes that occurred between 1940 and 1950. Note the substantial increase for young women and the declines for women in their forties. The increased rates for younger women are due in part to the higher proportion of girls marrying at younger ages (see below). Some demographers believe that these increased rates may be due to a change in the "timing" of births, reflecting a recent fashion which leads more women to have children about a year after marriage. (Census data on the children ever born by duration of marriage cast some doubt on this theory.) If one could forecast what the fertility rates of women who are now 20 to 29 years of age will be when they are 30 to 39 years of age, a much more secure interpretation could be placed upon the recent upsurge in fertility. According to our data for 1950, many of the women in their forties were completing quite large families; mothers of this age in 1950 were

having their sixth child, on the average. Figure 12-5 compares the birth rates of two specific years, but the rates for 1940 are roughly similar in magnitude to those for the depression years of the 1930's, and the rates for 1950 are roughly similar to those for years from 1946 to 1954.

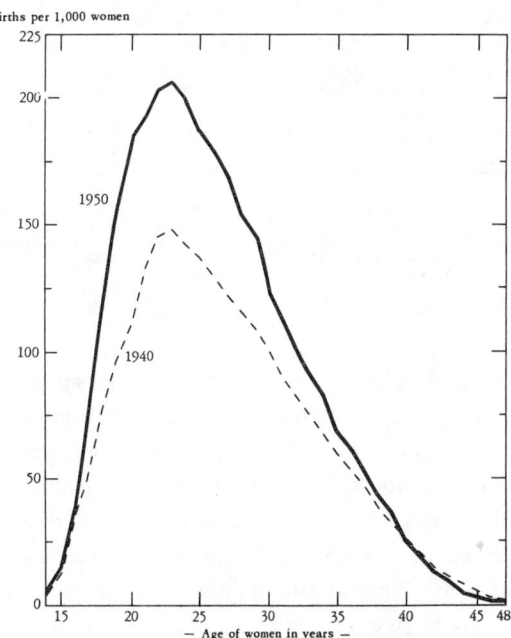

FIGURE 12 - 5. BIRTHS PER 1,000 WOMEN BY SINGLE YEARS OF AGE, FOR THE UNITED STATES, 1950 AND 1940
(Adjusted for underregistration)

Source: Information for births in 1950 obtained from National Office of Vital Statistics tabulations of births by single years of age of mother and from census data on women by single years of age. Information for births in 1940 obtained from the same sources as for 1950, tabulated by 5-year age groups. The rates for single years of age in 1940 were mathematically interpolated from the 5-year age groups.

2. <u>Marriage</u>. Age-specific birth rates changed between 1940 and 1950 in part because the percent of the population that was married increased for every age group, as indicated by the following data for women of all races in the United States. A small part of the increase in percent married at the older ages came from reductions in mortality of men, which resulted in relatively fewer widows. In 1950, 91.7 percent of the women 40 to 44 years old were reported as married, widowed, or divorced, compared with 90.5 percent in 1940. Increases in the percentage of women who were married were smaller than increases in total fer-

tility. This indicates that other factors helped to account for increases in fertility.

Age of woman	Percent married 1950 1940		Percent change in proportion married	Percent change in age-specific birth rates, 1940 to 1950
15 to 19 years	16.7	11.6	44.0	50.8
20 to 24 years	65.6	51.3	27.9	45.0
25 to 29 years	83.3	74.1	12.4	35.3
30 to 34 years	86.2	80.4	7.2	24.3
35 to 39 years	85.5	81.5	4.9	14.3
40 to 44 years	83.1	80.6	3.1	-3.2

Source: U.S. Bureau of the Census, 1950 Census of Population, Vol. II, Characteristics of the Population, Part 1, United States Summary, pp. 1-179. National Office of Vital Statistics, Vital Statistics Statistics of the United States: 1950, Vol. 1, P. 83.

According to census data on children ever born, the proportion of women who are childless declines rapidly with the duration of marriage, and the proportion of women who have at least a first child rises. It may be deduced from data on changes in percent childless that the bulk of first births are spread out over a three or four year period, beginning about a year after the marriage.

This deduction suggests a different interpretation than is usually made of correlation studies which have shown correlation coefficients of well over .90 between fluctuations in annual marriages and fluctuations in first births a year later. Perhaps economic conditions cause similar variations in first-birth rates among women married for one, two, and three years, and hence account for the high total correlation.

The length of time women have been married is highly correlated with variations in their fertility. Comparisons of data on children ever born for women in 1950 at successive years of marriage indicate that the birth rate is highest in the second year of marriage (this comprises women "married one year") and remains high through the fifth year. After the fifth year, the birth rate declines considerably (Table 12-22).

3. Family limitation. The low proportion of women with very large families in the United States indicates that the practice of some form of family limitation is virtually universal. The Indianapolis Study in 1941 found that among middle-aged Protestants in that city, about 90 percent of the married women had used contracep-

Table 12-22.—NUMBER OF CHILDREN EVER BORN PER 1,000 WHITE WOMEN 15 TO 44 YEARS OLD, MARRIED ONCE AND HUSBAND PRESENT, BY DURATION OF MARRIAGE, FOR THE UNITED STATES: 1950

(Data based on sample)

Years married	Children per 1,000 women married once, husband present	First differences of previous column (Approximation to annual births per 1,000 women)	Percent of women with no children ever born	First differences of previous column (Approximation to percentage of women who had their first child in given year of marriage)
Under 1 year.......	130	130	90.7	9.3
1 year.............	430	300	60.8	29.9
2 years............	679	249	41.4	19.4
3 years............	973	294	28.3	13.1
4 years............	1,209	236	22.5	5.8
5 years............	1,371	162	20.5	2.0
6 years............	1,565	194	17.3	3.2
7 years............	1,695	130	15.5	1.8
8 years............	1,770	75	15.2	0.3
9 years............	1,964	194	12.2	3.0
10 to 14 years.....	2,198	94[1]	13.1	-0.4[1]
15 to 19 years.....	2,534	67[1]	11.4	0.3[1]
20 or more years...	3,046	73[1]	9.4	0.3[1]

[1]First difference of previous column, divided by interval in years between mid-points of successive age groups.

Source: Derived from U.S. Census of Population: 1950, Vol. IV, Special Reports, Part 5C, Fertility Table 18. (U.S. Government Printing Office, Washington, D. C., 1955.)

ion at some stage in their marriage, and that most of the remainder were women who were relatively sterile. Stix and Notestein observed that 85 to 96 percent of (largely urban) patients at birth control clinics had practiced contraception before admission, but had come to the clinic because they wanted a safer or a more satisfactory method.[20] In rural areas somewhat smaller percentages may practice limitation, but many rural areas have fertility indexes that are not very much higher than nearby urban areas. "Folk" methods were more widely used in Indianapolis than methods recommended by clinics. Most methods used were relatively effective, in that 90 percent or more of possible conceptions were prevented, as compared with conception rates among control groups of women not practicing contraception.[21] Yet, more than one-half of the women had at least one conception while they were practicing contraception. If any of the promising new drugs designed to cause harmless temporary sterility come into common use, a few women will undoubtedly "forget" to take them on occasion.

Norman Himes has shown that several "modern" forms of contraception have long histories, dating back to medieval times or earlier.[22] He also noted that ineffective mystic charms were recommended in olden times, and that social and philosophical justifications for family limitation were, in the main, a nineteenth century development.

Himes thought that knowledge of contraception was limited largely to the elite in medieval times, and that its spread in the nations of western civilization was a nineteenth and twentieth century phenomenon. His "evidence" was the differential birth rate between the poor and the well-to-do in early times, and the nineteenth century declines in national fertility. One wonders whether Himes's statement that houses of prostitution were arsenals of linen sheaths, etc., does not indicate that more people than the elite knew of such devices. (Himes regarded these devices as insurance against venereal disease only.) Also, one wonders how it happened that in eighteenth century Prussia, Sussmilch could find no more than four christening records per marriage record in church files, and why Swedish data showed a relatively low birth rate of only 35 per 1,000 population and relatively low proportions of children in the population. (Perhaps infants who died soon after birth were not registered.) Similarly, one wonders why New England in 1800 had relatively low fertility as compared with other parts of the United States. All these situations existed well before the appearance of the pamphlets cited by Himes, which presented a moral and social justification for birth control as well as a rudimentary knowledge of how to practice it.

Number of Children Desired

The number of children desired by the average American couple is not constant. In normal times there may be some visualization before marriage of an ideal size family of three or four children, the first child not being desired until the couple is financially ready for it. Economic conditions and unplanned pregnancies may cause a change in the number and timing of children desired, and the number desired may change several times during the marriage. Long postponement of childbearing may lower the number of children wanted and early childbearing may raise the number wanted (or may raise the number born to more nearly match the number wanted). It is possible that for the next two or three years the expectations of the average American couple may come close to being realized.

The Gallup polls have shown several times that most people (81 to 85 percent) consider from two to four children to be an "ideal" number. The most common "ideal" number, noted by only 31 percent at each date, was two children in 1941 and three children in 1945. This trend toward a larger ideal

---

[20] Regine N. Stix and Frank W. Notestein, Controlled Fertility, the William and Wilkins Co., Baltimore, 1940.

[21] Charles F. Westoff, Lee F. Herrera, and P. K. Whelpton, "XX. The Use, Effectiveness, and Acceptability of Methods of Fertility Control," Social and Psychological Factors Affecting Fertility, Vol. Four, pp. 898, 905, 936. The Milbank Memorial Fund, New York, 1954.

[22] Norman E. Himes, Medical History of Contraception. The Williams and Wilkins Co., Baltimore, 1936.

size could have been due to sampling variability and, in any case, probably did not foreshadow the baby boom. Only 1 percent thought one child an ideal number, and 14 to 18 percent desired five children or more. Census data for 1950 indicate that of the women who marry at some time during their life, about two-thirds actually bear fewer than 3 children. (In Puerto Rico in 1950 a family of two or three children was also almost universally regarded as an ideal size according to the results of a private study, but the women had an average of five or six children.) The Indianapolis Study tested the psychological effect on fertility of such variables as the sex of the first child (if not a boy, does the couple try again?), feelings of eco-nomic insecurity, fear of childbirth, whether the parents themselves came from large or small families, etc. At best, each item was able to explain only a little of the variation in fertility, independent of other variables. In the aggregate, only 18 to 20 percent of the variations in fertility were "predictable" in a population group where fertility was relatively well controlled. It appears, then, that the motives for human behavior are extremely complex. Further studies which are planned by private organizations may some day give us a clearer picture of the human motives that determine family size, and of the forces that motivate people to change their expectations concerning family size.

Chapter 13

SCHOOL ENROLLMENT AND EDUCATIONAL ATTAINMENT*

Free public education, at the elementary level and later at the high school level, has been hailed as a major strength of the United States. Encouraging all young people to delay full-time participation in the labor force until they have devoted a certain amount of time to study has paved the way for rapid scientific and technological progress. It is intended that this educational system shall bring to light, and provide an opportunity for, exceptionally talented children who otherwise might be obscured because of their economic status, their ethnic background, or their social class. The public education system also raises the general level of ability in the population as a whole, and feeds into the labor force more workers who are prepared to comprehend and carry out tasks requiring skill, judgment, and knowledge. Occupational experts have stated, for example, that persons who have not completed the equivalent of the fifth grade of elementary school are "functionally illiterate;" that is, they are not equipped to participate in our technologically advanced society except as unskilled workmen. Education is also considered essential to the functioning of a democratic form of government, in the sense that only citizens who are able to read and who have some background in the fields of history, government, and certain other general subjects can vote intelligently. For these reasons it is important to maintain an inventory of the educational status of the population. The decennial census has been the vehicle used for gathering this information, and in recent years the data thus obtained has been supplemented by information from the Current Population Surveys. Educational statistics are now considered an integral part of the population census, and are one of the basic topics of population analysis. Two bodies of information concerning educational status are collected: (a) data about school enrollment, and (b) data about educational attainment. The first body of information relates to the present school attendance of children who are of school age, while the second refers to the amount of education completed by all members of the population, both children and adults. Both of these topics are discussed in this chapter, a separate section being devoted to each.

SCHOOL ENROLLMENT[1]

School enrollment rates (the percent of children of school age who are enrolled in school) have risen steadily since 1910, the year of the first census at which statistics on this subject were assembled. Some of the rapid changes of the past

---

* A tabulation which presents statistics concerning educational attainment, by sex and color, for total, urban, rural-nonfarm, and rural-farm areas of each geographic division, for both 1950 and 1940, is contained in the statistical appendix.

[1] The Census Bureau's current statistics concerning school enrollment (data gathered since the 1950 census) are based on the enumerator's inquiry as to whether the person being interviewed had been enrolled, at any time during the current term or school year, in any type of day or night school, public, parochial, or other private school, belonging to the "regular" school system. This system, as defined by the Census Bureau, includes kindergartens, elementary schools, high

half century have taken place in the years since the last census, and changes are continuing to take place. The record of these increases in school enrollment, covering nearly half a century, is summarized in the following table:

Year	Percent of population aged 7 to 19 years enrolled in school
1958.................	90.0
1950.................	83.0
1940.................	79.1
1930.................	78.3
1920.................	72.1
1910.................	67.4

[1] Continued

schools, colleges, universities, and professional schools. (Only since 1954 have children enrolled in kindergarten been included in the totals.)

The above definition differs slightly from the definition used in the 1950 census. At that census, taken in April, the enumerator asked, "Has he attended school at any time since February 1?" School attendance was limited to "regular" schools of the type enumerated above. Persons enrolled in vocational, trade, or business schools were excluded from the enrollment figures in the census, unless such schools were graded and considered a part of a regular school system; the Census Bureau's current statistics reports do not include persons attending these "special" schools in the enrollment figures, but they do show them separately. Persons who were receiving on-the-job training or were enrolled in correspondence courses were not counted by the census as enrolled in school, and in the Bureau's current statistics they are neither reported as enrolled nor included in the "special" category. Students who had enrolled in regular school but were not attending because of illness, and those who were receiving tutoring at home as a substitute for regular school attendance, were included in the enrollment statistics at the 1950 census.

The data from the 1950 census are approximately comparable with the results of the surveys which have been taken since 1950, and with earlier censuses. The censuses of 1910, 1920, and 1930 specified a somewhat longer time interval in their questions concerning school attendance (the period since September 1 of the year preceding the census), and had fewer restrictions as to the kind of school the person was attending. In 1940, the question specified the period from March 1 to the date of the census enumeration. It was discovered that this period was too short, since some rural schools had closed by March 1. Fortunately, school enrollment has increased so greatly that the trends and the differentials stand out in spite of these minor variations in the definitions.

When interpreting the statistics of school enrollment by urban and rural areas, one must keep in mind the fact that at the 1950 census college students were (and have been since 1950) allocated to the community where they were attending school, rather than to their parents' residence, as they had been in previous years.

The above series indicates that there was a great increase in school attendance between 1910 and 1930. During these 20 years the proportion of students aged 7 to 19 years who were enrolled in school increased from 67 to 78 percent (by 11 percentage points). In the eight years from 1950 to 1958 the proportion enrolled in school jumped from 83 to 90 percent, or by 7 percentage points. A part of this increase was due to the changing age composition of the school-age population (a larger proportion being concentrated in the age group 7 to 13, the group whose attendance rate has always been the highest). Nevertheless, it is true that a higher proportion of young people in each age group are now enrolled in school than at any previous time in the nation's history. In 1910 universal public education was still an abstract concept; in the years since, it has become, for all practical purposes, a reality.

Age and School Enrollment. There is a definite age pattern connected with school enrollment (see Figure 13-1 and Table 13-1). Nearly all children who are between the ages of 7 and 14 (second to eighth grades) are attending school. The law of almost every state compels school attendance at these ages, and in several states attendance is mandatory until age 16. The completion of grammar school is now considered the very minimum desirable amount of schooling in most communities. Attendance at these ages has not always been so nearly universal, however. In 1910, parents appear to have been much less insistent than they are today that their children between 6 and 9 years of age attend school, and at age 11 (now the age at which attendance is at its peak rate) only 91 percent were enrolled in school. In those days there was also much less emphasis upon completing grammar school. From age 14 to age 15, among both boys and girls, there was a sharp drop in school attendance. At these ages children were economically useful for farm work and could be of genuine assistance in lightening the housework connected with large families.

Since 1910 there has been a persistent upward trend in the proportion of children remaining in school after passing the age of compulsory attendance. For example, in 1910 only 34 percent of

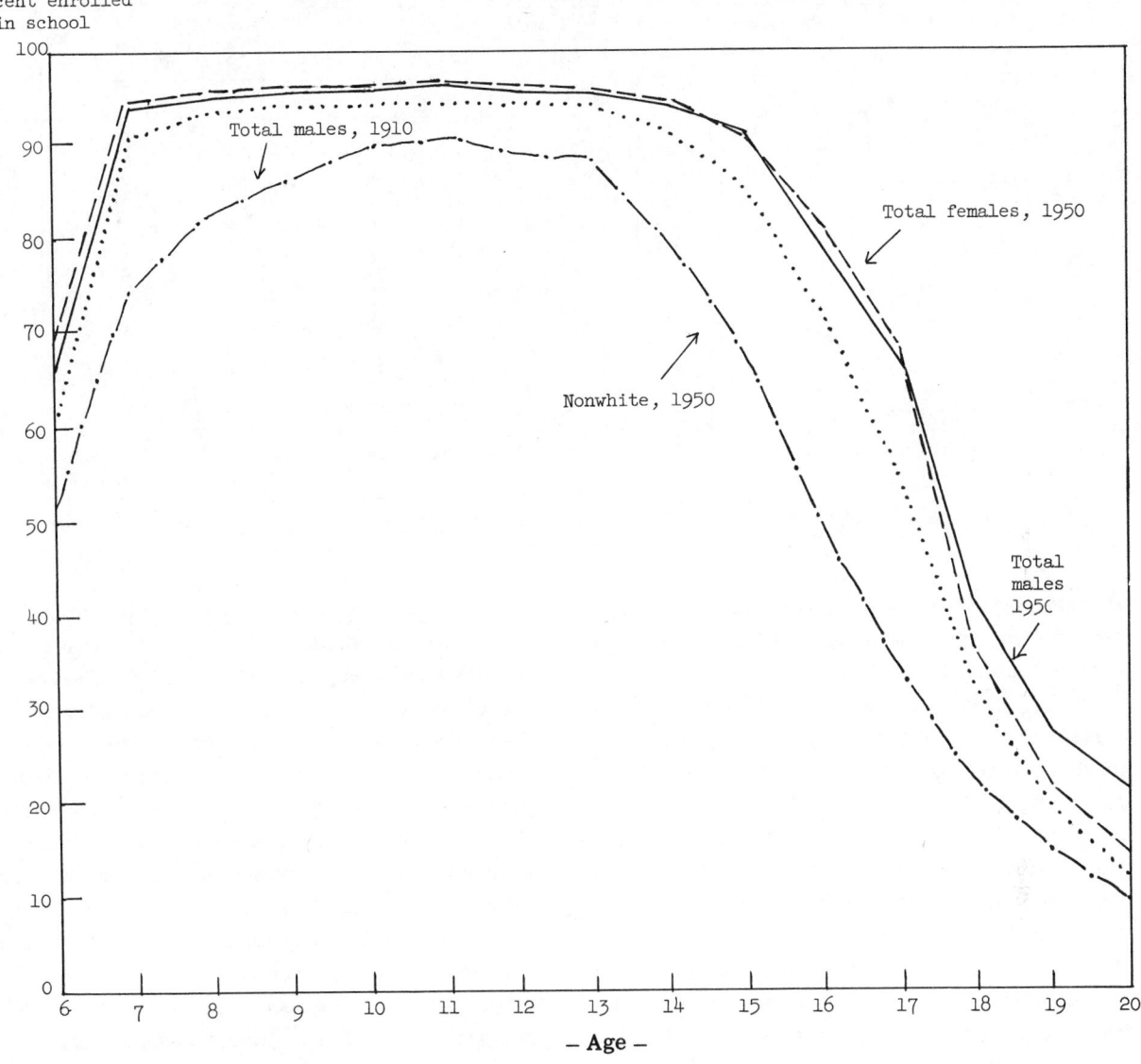

FIGURE 13-1.—PERCENT ATTENDING SCHOOL, FOR SELECTED POPULATION GROUPS,
BY AGE: 1910 AND 1950

boys 17 years of age were still in school, but by 1950 this proportion had doubled. Although it is still true that beyond age 13 the school attendance rate drops as age increases, the drop is not nearly so precipitous as it used to be. Moreover, the point in the life span at which the rate drops to zero is later now: in 1910 school attendance for most persons was over by the time they reached age 20, but at the present time a substantial proportion of persons in their late twenties or even in their thirties are still attending school, largely because of the greater emphasis which is now placed on postgraduate study. How the more recent changes in school enrollment fit into the long-range trend may be evaluated by studying Table 13-2. Since 1950 there have been dramatic increases in the enrollment of children 5 to 6 years of age (preschool and kindergarten, as well as first grade). Also, the increases in the enrollment of children of grammar school age have been

Table 13-1.—PERCENT ENROLLED IN SCHOOL BY SINGLE YEARS OF AGE AND SEX, FOR THE UNITED STATES: 1910 TO 1950

Age	Both sexes		Male					Female				
	1950	1940	1950	1940	1930	1920	1910	1950	1940	1930	1920	1910
Total, 5 to 20 years..	72.7	70.8	73.4	71.2	70.2	64.1	59.1	72.0	70.4	69.7	64.5	59.4
5 years................	10.5	18.0	10.2	17.5	19.5	18.3	16.7	10.8	18.4	20.5	19.3	17.4
6 years................	67.6	69.1	66.9	68.2	65.5	62.8	51.7	68.2	70.1	67.1	63.9	52.4
7 years................	94.4	92.4	94.2	92.2	89.0	83.1	74.7	94.5	92.7	89.7	83.5	75.2
8 years................	95.6	94.8	95.6	94.7	94.0	88.3	82.5	95.7	95.0	94.3	88.6	82.8
9 years................	96.1	95.6	96.0	95.5	95.4	90.3	86.1	96.2	95.7	95.7	90.5	86.3
10 years................	96.0	95.7	95.9	95.6	96.9	92.9	89.6	96.2	95.8	97.2	93.2	90.4
11 years................	96.3	95.9	96.1	95.8	97.4	93.8	90.9	96.4	96.0	97.6	94.1	91.5
12 years................	95.9	95.5	95.6	95.3	96.9	93.0	89.2	96.3	95.7	97.3	93.4	90.3
13 years................	95.9	94.8	95.7	94.6	96.4	92.4	88.3	96.0	95.1	96.7	92.7	89.3
14 years................	94.8	92.5	94.7	92.2	92.9	86.2	80.7	94.9	92.8	92.9	86.5	81.8
15 years................	91.4	87.6	91.5	87.3	84.8	71.9	67.5	91.2	88.0	84.5	73.9	69.0
16 years................	80.9	76.2	80.6	75.7	65.8	48.2	49.3	81.1	76.8	66.8	53.3	51.9
17 years................	68.2	60.9	67.9	60.5	47.1	32.1	34.0	68.4	61.3	48.8	37.2	36.6
18 years................	39.8	36.4	42.4	38.1	31.1	20.5	22.1	37.2	34.7	30.3	22.8	23.0
19 years................	24.7	20.9	27.8	23.2	20.8	14.0	14.8	21.8	18.7	18.8	13.6	14.1
20 years................	17.9	12.5	21.2	14.4	14.6	9.3	9.3	14.9	10.6	11.7	7.5	7.5

Source: U.S. Census of Population: 1950, Vol. II, Characteristics of the Population, Part 1, U.S. Summary, Table 110.

so substantial that there is now almost 100 percent enrollment at these ages. Finally, there has been a continuation of the trend toward an ever-increasing proportion of children completing high school, and also of the tendency of a larger share to go on to college. This trend toward participation in higher education by a greater proportion of the population was greatly accelerated by the G. I. Bill which was connected with World War II, by the Korean G. I. Bill, and by other programs designed to further the education of war veterans. The tendency seems to be persisting, and is apparently being strengthened and increased by the momentum which these programs created and by the high level of economic prosperity. Today our culture seems to have accepted it as normal for schooling to extend through grammar school and high school, and to agree that the children of all social strata should attend college if they have the necessary qualifications. Just how long children should stay in school (especially those with average or below-average scholarship abilities) is a topic about which there is little agreement. It is obvious, however, that the trend is toward encouraging youngsters to take more, rather than fewer, years of schooling.

Sex Differences in School Enrollment. Until about age 17, girls have a slightly higher rate of school enrollment than boys, but the difference is small (Figure 13-1). At ages 18 and above, boys have a substantially higher enrollment rate than girls. This change results largely from the fact that many girls beyond the age of 17 withdraw from school to marry, especially after they have graduated from grammar or high school. The proportion of female high school graduates who enter college is much smaller than the corresponding proportion of males.

In 1910 the difference between the sexes with respect to school enrollment was not very large, but since 1940 it has grown rapidly. Table 13-3, which provides data for single years of age up to age 29, demonstrates that the increase in enrollment at older ages has been due primarily to an increased enrollment of males. (Nevertheless, it should not be overlooked that young adult females have made very substantial increases in enrollment, despite the fact that males have made even greater increases.)

The change between 1950 and 1957 in the direction of greater school attendance affected the two sexes almost equally between ages 5 and 17, but

Table 13-2.—SCHOOL ENROLLMENT RATES BY AGE AND SEX: 1910 TO 1957

Sex and year	Total 5 to 20 years	7 to 19 years	5 and 6 years	7 to 13 years	14 to 17 years	18 and 19 years	20 years
BOTH SEXES							
1957........................	...	89.7	78.6	99.5	89.5	34.9	...
1950........................	72.7	83.0	39.3	95.7	83.5	32.3	17.9
1940........................	70.8	79.1	43.0	95.0	79.3	28.9	12.5
1930........................	69.9	78.3	43.2	95.3	73.1	25.4	13.1
1920........................	64.3	72.1	41.0	90.6	61.6	17.8	8.3
1910........................	59.2	67.4	34.6	86.1	58.9	18.7	8.4
MALE							
1957........................	...	91.7	78.3	99.5	91.1	43.3	...
1950........................	73.4	83.6	38.8	95.6	83.8	35.2	21.2
1940........................	71.2	79.4	42.3	94.8	78.9	30.8	14.4
1930........................	70.2	78.4	42.5	95.1	72.8	26.0	14.6
1920........................	64.1	71.7	40.4	90.4	60.2	17.3	9.3
1910........................	59.1	67.1	34.2	85.8	57.9	18.6	9.3
FEMALE							
1957........................	...	87.7	79.0	99.5	87.8	28.1	...
1950........................	72.0	82.4	39.8	95.8	84.0	29.5	14.9
1940........................	70.4	78.9	43.7	95.2	79.7	26.9	10.6
1930........................	69.7	78.2	43.9	95.5	73.4	24.7	11.7
1920........................	64.5	72.5	41.6	90.8	63.1	18.3	7.5
1910........................	59.4	67.8	34.9	86.4	59.8	18.8	7.5

Source: 1950 Census of Population: 1950, Vol. II, Characteristics of the Population, U.S. Summary, Table 110. Current Population Reports, Series P-20, No. 80, February, 1958.

beyond age 17 it was largely the male students who accounted for the extraordinarily great increases in school attendance rates. The following summary, comparing the 1950 attendance rates of boys and girls with the 1957 rates, for age groups beyond 18 years, shows not only that males have had the highest rates of attendance, but that the attendance rates of males have increased much more than those of females. Hence, the change since 1950 has been consistent with the long-range trend.

Age	Percent enrolled in school 1957	1950	Change, 1950-1957
Male:			
18 and 19.........	43.3	35.2	8.1
20 to 24..........	21.3	14.2	7.1
25 to 29..........	9.5	5.9	3.6
30 to 34..........	2.6	1.5	1.1
Female:			
18 and 19.........	28.1	24.3	3.8
20 to 24..........	8.2	4.6	3.6
25 to 29..........	1.9	0.4	1.5
30 to 34..........	1.1	0.4	0.7

Source: Current Population Reports, Series P-20, No. 80, February 1958.

Color Differences in School Enrollment. In 1950, at all ages, the attendance rate for the nonwhite population was lower than the attendance rate for the white population (see Figure 13-1 and Table 13-3). The differential was not large at ages below 14 years. At age 15 and above, however, the school attendance rate of the nonwhite population was consistently lower than that of the white population. The relative size of the differential increased with increasing age. At age 18, for example, the proportion of nonwhite children in school was only 75 percent as large as the proportion of white children in school. The school enrollment pattern of nonwhites in 1950 was about what the enrollment pattern of the nation as a whole had been in 1920. Generally speaking, it is fair to say that the educational facilities provided for Negroes and other nonwhite populations, and the degree of importance attached to the education and participation of these populations are lagging behind those provided for the white population by about three decades. Nevertheless, the 1940 to 1950 decade witnessed a revolutionary increase in the proportions of the nonwhite population enrolled

Table 13-3.—SCHOOL ENROLLMENT, BY SINGLE YEARS OF AGE, COLOR, AND SEX, FOR THE UNITED STATES, URBAN AND RURAL: 1950

Sex and age	Total		Urban		Rural nonfarm		Rural farm	
	White	Nonwhite	White	Nonwhite	White	Nonwhite	White	Nonwhite
BOTH SEXES								
Total, 5 to 29 years..	49.5	48.5	48.1	45.7	49.1	48.2	55.5	55.2
5 years.................	10.3	11.8	10.1	11.7	10.0	11.5	11.4	12.3
6 years.................	67.9	65.6	71.7	69.9	63.2	61.1	61.6	60.5
7 years.................	94.8	91.3	96.4	93.6	94.1	89.6	93.4	87.9
8 years.................	95.9	93.8	96.2	95.4	95.8	92.7	95.2	91.5
9 years.................	96.3	94.7	96.5	95.7	96.4	93.8	95.7	93.6
10 years................	96.3	94.5	96.5	95.8	96.3	93.4	95.6	93.2
11 years................	96.4	94.9	96.7	96.2	96.3	93.6	95.9	93.9
12 years................	96.2	94.5	96.4	95.5	96.0	93.5	95.5	93.6
13 years................	96.1	94.2	96.5	95.7	96.1	93.2	95.2	92.4
14 years................	95.2	91.9	96.1	94.6	95.0	90.6	93.0	88.5
15 years................	92.1	85.9	94.5	90.4	90.9	82.5	87.3	80.7
16 years................	82.1	72.6	86.1	78.4	79.0	68.1	74.8	65.5
17 years................	69.9	55.8	74.3	61.4	64.4	50.7	63.5	48.8
18 years................	40.8	32.3	44.8	35.2	34.4	28.0	34.6	93.6
19 years................	25.3	19.7	30.4	22.0	17.4	16.4	14.3	16.8
20 years................	18.6	12.5	23.4	14.3	11.0	10.8	7.1	9.3
21 years................	15.4	10.2	19.2	11.9	9.0	8.5	5.1	6.4
22 years................	12.9	8.3	15.9	9.7	7.7	6.5	4.7	4.8
23 years................	11.1	7.7	13.3	8.8	6.7	6.0	5.0	4.7
24 years................	9.6	7.1	11.4	8.1	5.9	5.7	4.7	4.0
25 years................	8.3	6.7	9.9	7.6	5.3	5.0	4.5	4.1
26 years................	7.3	6.4	8.5	7.1	4.7	5.6	4.3	3.7
27 years................	6.4	6.4	7.4	6.9	4.4	5.5	4.4	3.7
28 years................	5.8	5.6	6.7	6.1	3.9	4.5	4.2	4.2
29 years................	5.2	5.1	5 8	5.7	3.7	4.2	4.0	3.1
MALE								
Total, 5 to 29 years..	52.3	50.5	52.2	49.4	50.6	48.0	55.1	54.9
5 years.................	10.0	11.4	9.8	11.4	9.8	11.1	10.8	11.7
6 years.................	67.2	64.6	71.2	69.3	62.6	60.1	60.7	59.2
7 years.................	94.7	90.7	95.3	93.4	94.1	88.9	93.2	86.9
8 years.................	95.9	93.5	96.2	95.3	95.7	92.4	95.1	91.3
9 years.................	96.3	94.5	96.5	95.6	96.2	93.4	95.6	93.5
10 years................	96.1	94.2	96.4	95.7	96.1	92.6	95.5	92.7
11 years................	96.4	94.4	96.6	95.7	96.2	92.3	95.7	93.5
12 years................	95.8	94.2	96.1	95.6	95.6	93.0	95.2	92.8
13 years................	96.0	93.7	96.4	95.6	96.1	92.6	95.0	91.3
14 years................	95.1	91.2	96.3	94.9	95.2	90.0	92.4	86.2
15 years................	92.3	85.8	95.0	91.9	91.7	82.8	86.1	78.0
16 years................	81.8	72.2	87.2	80.7	79.3	67.5	71.3	61.8
17 years................	69.6	55.0	76.5	63.7	62.9	48.9	59.3	44.4
18 years................	43.7	32.4	50.4	38.2	35.8	26.9	33.2	26.2
19 years................	28.7	20.1	36.0	24.7	19.9	15.3	14.8	14.8
20 years................	22.2	13.7	29.0	16.9	13.3	10.8	7.7	8.7
21 years................	20.5	11.9	26.5	14.8	11.9	8.8	5.9	6.4
22 years................	20.1	11.3	25.5	14.2	16.6	8.1	6.3	5.5
23 years................	18.3	11.7	22.6	14.2	10.8	8.3	6.9	6.0
24 years................	16.0	11.3	19.4	13.3	9.7	8.7	6.9	5.9
25 years................	13.9	10.9	16.7	12.9	8.6	7.8	6.7	5.9
26 years................	11.9	10.4	14.1	11.9	7.4	8.8	6.5	5.7
27 years................	10.3	9.9	12.1	11.2	6.7	8.2	6.6	5.5
28 years................	9.2	8.9	10.6	9.9	6.0	7.2	6.6	5.9
29 years................	8 0	8.1	9.0	9.1	5.6	6.4	6.1	4.5

Table 13-3.—SCHOOL ENROLLMENT, BY SINGLE YEARS OF AGE, COLOR, AND SEX, FOR THE UNITED STATES, URBAN AND RURAL: 1950-Continued

Sex and age	Total		Urban		Rural nonfarm		Rural farm	
	White	Nonwhite	White	Nonwhite	White	Nonwhite	White	Nonwhite
FEMALE								
Total, 5 to 29 years..	46.7	46.6	44.1	42.5	47.6	48.4	56.0	43.5
5 years..................	10.6	12.2	10.2	11.9	10.2	11.9	12.1	13.0
6 years..................	68.5	66.5	72.2	70.5	63.8	62.2	62.5	61.8
7 years..................	94.9	91.8	95.5	93.9	94.2	90.3	93.6	88.9
8 years..................	95.9	94.0	96.1	95.6	95.9	93.0	95.3	92.0
9 years..................	96.4	94.9	96.4	95.8	96.6	94.2	95.8	93.8
10 years.................	96.4	94.9	96.5	95.9	96.6	94.2	95.7	93.7
11 years.................	96.5	95.6	96.7	96.7	96.4	94.9	96.2	94.3
12 years.................	96.5	94.8	96.8	95.4	96.4	94.1	95.9	94.3
13 years.................	96.2	94.7	96.5	95.8	96.1	93.8	95.4	93.4
14 years.................	95.2	92.7	96.0	94.3	94.9	91.2	93.6	90.9
15 years.................	92.0	86.1	93.9	89.0	90.1	82.3	88.6	83.4
16 years.................	82.4	73.0	85.0	76.4	78.7	68.7	79.0	69.4
17 years.................	70.1	56.6	72.2	59.4	66.0	52.4	68.5	53.7
18 years.................	37.9	32.3	39.8	32.6	32.9	29.2	36.4	33.7
19 years.................	22.1	19.3	25.7	20.0	14.4	17.5	13.5	18.8
20 years.................	15.3	11.6	18.7	12.4	8.5	10.8	6.5	9.9
21 years.................	10.5	8.7	12.7	9.4	5.9	8.1	4.2	6.4
22 years.................	6.0	5.7	7.1	6.3	3.6	4.7	2.8	4.2
23 years.................	4.1	4.3	4.7	4.6	2.7	3.6	2.7	3.5
24 years.................	3.5	3.4	4.0	3.9	2.3	2.4	2.3	2.3
25 years.................	3.1	3.1	3.5	3.4	2.1	2.2	2.2	2.5
26 years.................	3.0	2.8	3.4	3.1	2.2	2.2	2.0	2.0
27 years.................	2.8	3.0	3.1	3.2	2.1	2.7	2.1	2.0
28 years.................	2.6	2.7	2.9	2.9	1.9	1.6	2.0	2.6
29 years.................	2.5	2.6	2.8	2.8	1.8	1.8	2.0	2.0

Source: U.S. Census of Population: 1950, Characteristics of the Population, U.S. Summary, Table 111.

in school. In 1940 the differences between the school attendance rates of whites and nonwhites were immense, at all ages. By 1950 these differentials had been greatly diminished. The upward direction of these trends since 1950 has only been a continuation of the major innovation that was initiated during the 1940's.

Table 13-4 shows the extent to which the color differential seems to have been reduced since 1950. In 1957, at each age between 7 and 18 years, the proportion of the nonwhite population enrolled in school much more nearly corresponded to the proportion of the white population thus enrolled than it had in 1950 or in 1940. The following summary, which shows the school attendance rate of the nonwhite population as a percentage of the attendance rate of the white population, measures the extent of the differential that still exists.

Age	School attendance rate of non-white population as a percentage of the school attendance rate of white population		
	Both sexes	Male	Female
5 and 6 years.......	94	92	95
7 to 13 years.......	98	98	98
14 to 17 years......	94	92	96
18 and 19 years.....	106	88	130
20 to 24 years.....	60	45	92
25 to 29 years.....	81	61	206
30 to 34 years......	63	44	100

Source: Current Population Reports, Series P-20, No. 80, February 1958, Table 3.

As regards grammar school attendance, the differential between the white and the nonwhite populations seems almost to have disappeared. Even with respect to high school attendance, the differential is small--8 or 10 percent. Only in terms of kindergarten and college attendance does the non-

Table 13-4.—SCHOOL ENROLLMENT RATES OF THE WHITE AND NONWHITE POPULATIONS, BY AGE AND SEX: 1940, 1950, AND 1957

Sex and age	White			Nonwhite			Difference (white minus nonwhite)			Change 1950 to 1957		Change 1940 to 1950	
	1957	1950	1940	1957	1950	1940	1957	1950	1940	White	Non-white	White	Non-white
BOTH SEXES													
5 to 24 years......	75.2	60.9	58.3	71.9	58.4	53.4	3.3	2.5	4.9	14.3	13.5	2.6	5.0
7 to 19 years....	90.0	83.5	79.9	87.7	79.6	73.3	2.3	3.9	6.6	6.5	8.1	3.6	6.3
5 and 6 years..	79.3	39.4	44.0	74.3	38.7	36.6	5.0	0.7	7.4	39.9	35.6	-4.6	2.1
7 to 13 years..	99.7	95.9	95.5	98.2	93.9	91.2	1.5	2.0	4.3	3.8	4.3	0.4	2.7
14 to 17 years...	90.1	84.9	80.7	84.8	76.8	68.2	5.3	8.1	12.5	5.2	8.0	4.2	8.6
18 and 19 years..	34.6	33.0	29.8	36.7	26.3	21.1	-2.1	6.7	8.7	1.6	10.4	3.2	5.2
20 to 24 years.....	14.7	13.4	6.9	8.8	9.1	3.8	5.9	4.3	3.1	1.3	-0.3	6.5	5.3
MALE													
5 to 24 years......	79.3	63.1	59.2	73.6	59.7	53.4	5.7	3.4	5.8	16.2	13.9	3.9	6.3
7 to 19 years....	92.2	84.1	80.3	88.3	79.7	72.5	3.9	4.4	7.8	8.1	8.6	3.8	7.2
5 and 6 years..	79.1	38.9	43.4	73.1	38.0	35.3	6.0	0.9	8.1	40.2	35.1	4.5	2.7
7 to 13 years..	99.7	95.8	95.4	98.2	93.6	90.5	1.5	2.2	4.9	3.9	4.6	0.4	3.1
14 to 17 years...	91.9	84.8	80.5	84.7	76.3	65.9	7.2	8.5	14.6	7.1	8.4	4.3	10.4
18 and 19 years..	44.0	36.2	32.1	38.5	26.6	20.5	5.5	9.6	11.6	7.8	11.9	4.1	6.1
20 to 24 years.....	22.9	19.4	8.7	10.3	12.0	4.1	12.6	7.4	4.6	3.5	-1.7	10.7	7.9
FEMALE													
5 to 24 years......	71.1	58.7	57.4	70.4	57.2	53.3	0.7	1.5	4.1	12.4	13.2	1.3	3.9
7 to 19 years....	87.8	82.9	79.5	87.0	79.6	74.0	0.8	3.3	5.5	4.9	7.4	3.4	5.6
5 and 6 years..	79.5	39.8	44.6	75.6	39.4	37.9	3.9	0.4	6.7	39.7	36.2	-4.8	1.5
7 to 13 years..	99.7	96.1	95.6	98.2	94.3	91.8	1.5	1.8	3.8	3.6	3.9	0.5	2.5
14 to 17 years...	88.2	85.0	80.9	85.0	77.3	70.4	3.2	7.7	10.5	3.2	7.7	4.1	6.9
18 and 19 years..	27.0	29.9	27.6	35.1	26.0	21.6	-8.1	3.9	6.0	-2.9	9.1	2.3	4.4
20 to 24 years.....	8.3	7.8	5.2	7.6	6.7	3.5	0.7	1.1	1 7	0.5	0.9	2.6	3.2

Source: Current Population Reports, Series P-20, No. 80, February, 1958 and U.S. Census of Population: 1950, Characteristics of the Population, U.S. Summary, Table 110.

white population now seem to be at a definite disadvantage; and if the small sample on which the statistics in the above summary are based can be trusted, it is only the nonwhite male who is at a disadvantage in attending college, for a larger percentage of nonwhite girls than of white girls aged 20 and over were in school in 1957. However, there is a substantial white-nonwhite differential for males at these ages; only about one-half as many nonwhite males as white males aged 20 and over were enrolled in school in 1957. A careful study of Table 13-4 will show that the nonwhite population appears to have made almost no progress since 1950 in increasing the proportion of males 20 to 24 attending school, whereas the white population seems to have made considerable progress. The sample numbers are too small to permit an evaluation of this inference, however.

It is possibly true that, because of the current boom in college attendance, the nonwhite population is unable to keep pace with the rising enrollment rates of the white population.

The economic and social implications of the possible future disappearance of these color differentials are worthy of careful reflection. The idea that most Negroes, and most members of other nonwhite races, are semi-literate, incompetent, and inexperienced persons who are unable to comprehend or take part in the technology and the complex civilization being created by their dominant white brothers appears to be rapidly losing ground. When today's generation of nonwhite children reach adulthood, their level of education will enable them to participate in every phase of the economy under much less of a handicap than was borne by preceding generations.

Differences in Urban and Rural Residence. At every age, school attendance rates were higher in urban areas than in rural areas in 1950, and this difference still existed in 1957, although by then it was somewhat diminished. Within rural areas, the school attendance rate of the rural-nonfarm population is greater than that of the rural-farm. Table 13-3 provides data concerning school enrollment in 1950 in urban, rural-nonfarm, and rural-farm areas by age, sex, color, and single years of age. The kind of urban-rural differential described above appears at almost every age, for each sex and for both whites and nonwhites. At ages beyond 18, the very low school attendance rates of the rural populations (and especially of the rural-farm population) are due in large part to the fact that in many areas no educational facilities beyond the high school level are available locally, which makes it necessary for residents of such areas to migrate to urban places if they wish to attend college.

It is of interest to note that the sex and color differentials described above persist at almost every age group within the urban, the rural-nonfarm, and the rural-farm populations individually. However, between the ages of 6 and 18 the color differential is considerably smaller in urban areas than in rural areas. Thus, the recent urbanization of the nonwhite population may have been responsible, in large part, for the rapid rise of nonwhite school attendance rates and the resultant shrinking of the white-nonwhite differential.

The following summary shows that as of 1957 there were only comparatively small differences, at the grammar school level, between the school enrollment rates of urban and rural areas. Rural areas were only a few points behind urban areas in junior high school enrollment. However, rural boys still appear to be considerably less inclined than urban boys to complete high school. Country girls 18 to 19 years of age, on the other hand, appear to be somewhat less willing than their city cousins to drop out of senior high school (presumably to get married) before graduation.

Age	Percent enrolled in school by urban-rural residence		
	Urban	Rural nonfarm	Rural farm
5 years.............	73.8	47.9	31.0
6 years.............	98.2	96.7	96.0
7 to 9 years........	99.7	99.6	98.7
10 to 13 years......	99.7	99.6	98.9
14 and 15 years.....	98.2	96.0	95.5
16 and 17 years.....	82.5	78.1	77.6
18 and 19 years.....	35.9	33.6	32.6
Male...............	47.8	39.6	35.2
Female.............	27.9	27.6	29.6

Source: Current Population Reports, Series P-20, No. 80, 1958, Table 2.

Grade in Which Enrolled. Students usually enter elementary school when they are six years of age (or when they will be six within a few months). If they perform acceptably they progress, by one grade each year, until they graduate. Thus, the "normal" student can expect to graduate from elementary school at the age of 13 or 14 years, from high school at the age of 17 or 18 years, and from college at the age of 21 or 22 years.[2] Actually, many students deviate rather markedly from this theoretical progression. A few, whose abilities demand more challenge, are "accelerated" by being enrolled in grades whose members are older than their own age group. A larger number become retarded, either because they fail to master the material, or because of illness or other factors which prevent steady attendance. Table 13-5 reports the actual grade distribution of students enrolled in school in 1950. The diagonal line in this table indicates roughly the theoretical line of progress. Cells that fall to the right of this line represent acceleration, while cells that fall to the left represent retardation. On this basis, one might conclude that in 1950 the population had the following over-all record of progress in school:

---

[2] Students who are enumerated in April of a census year have been attending school for almost 8 months, and hence are rather evenly divided (in the first grade, for example) between age 6+G and 7+G, G being the grade in which they are enrolled.

Age	On schedule	Retarded	Accelerated	Not reported
6 years.........	89.2	...	4.5	6.2
7 years.........	92.6	...	3.9	3.5
8 years.........	86.8	6.6	3.9	2.7
9 years.........	82.6	11.2	3.8	2.4
10 years.......	77.8	15.7	4.2	2.2
11 years.......	75.6	18.0	4.1	2.2
12 years.......	71.9	21.6	4.4	2.1
13 years.......	69.5	23.6	4.7	2.1
14 years.......	67.1	25.0	5.9	2.1
15 years.......	65.6	26.4	5.9	2.1
16 years.......	67.0	24.6	6.2	2.2
17 years.......	72.3	22.0	3.2	2.6
18 years.......	70.4	23.4	5.6	0.6
19 years.......	55.1	36.8	7.7	0.4
20 years.......	54.1	37.1	8.5	0.4
21 years.......	45.7	50.8	3.1	0.5

The rough method of calculation used here indicates that, at most ages, only about 5 to 7 percent of the students are accelerated and that a much larger proportion are retarded. At ages 13 to 14 (the normal time for graduation from elementary school), about 1 pupil in 4 is retarded by one year or more. (Inspection of Table 13-5 shows that about one-half of these students are retarded by one year, one-fourth by two years, and one-fourth by three years or more.) At the normal time of graduation from high school a somewhat smaller proportion of students are retarded, presumably because many retarded pupils have withdrawn from school. Many college students are retarded because they have stayed out of school to work, or are working and attending college only on a part-time basis. Thus, at age 21, less than one-half of the students are "on schedule." The situation may have been somewhat unusual in 1950 because of the G. I. Bill, which paid an allowance to veterans of World War II who wished to return to school. Because of this program many veterans completed high school and entered college who otherwise would not have done so.

Another way of measuring progress through school, but an even less exact way, is to compute the median grade in which the persons of each age are enrolled.[3] This information is reported in Table 13-6 for each age group, by sex, color, and urban-rural residence. Although the data are crude, it enables one to summarize some of the differences between various population groups with re-

spect to school progress. The following findings may be derived from Table 13-6.

(a) More students were accelerated at each age in urban areas than in rural areas, and more rural-nonfarm students than rural-farm students were accelerated at each age. Retardation in school was disproportionately concentrated in rural, and especially in rural-farm, areas.

(b) White students were more accelerated at each age than nonwhite students. The color-achievement differential was greatest in rural areas and smallest in urban places, but it was large in all areas. It tended to vary markedly with with age. At the age when it is "normal" to graduate from elementary school, nonwhite students were more retarded by one full year than white students, on an average. At the normal age for graduation from high school, this differential had been extended to almost 1 1/2 years, and at the time of graduation from college it was almost 2 1/2 years. A variety of explanations may be advanced for the retardation of nonwhite, as compared with white, students: poorer health, lower motivation, poorer schools, need to work while attending school, less encouragement from parents, etc.

(c) At all ages below 22 years, male students were retarded in comparison with female students. This was true of both white and nonwhite students, and in urban, rural-nonfarm, and rural-farm areas. At some ages these differences were quite large, amounting to as much as 0.6 years. At ages beyond 16 years, this difference could have resulted from selective withdrawal from school, i.e., a tendency for the less scholarly girls to withdraw in order to marry. However, the fact that the differential also existed, in a smaller but nevertheless unmistakable degree, at ages 7 to 13 (when almost 100 percent of all young people

---

[3] In both Table 13-5 and Table 13-6, the retardation of persons who had withdrawn from school was disregarded. It is probable that a very high proportion of the students who dropped out were severely retarded, and that many of them did so for this reason.

Table 13-5.—YEAR OF SCHOOL IN WHICH ENROLLED, BY SINGLE YEARS OF AGE, COLOR, AND SEX, FOR THE UNITED STATES: 1950

Age	Persons enrolled in school	Year of school in which enrolled																	Not reported	Median school year in which enrolled
		Elementary school								High school				College						
		1	2	3	4	5	6	7	8	1	2	3	4	1	2	3	4	5 or more		
Percent....	100.0	10.5	9.8	9.0	8.4	7.9	7.7	7.2	7.0	6.0	5.6	4.7	5.5	2.0	1.8	1.4	1.5	0.7	3.1	6.4
5 to 24 years..	100.0	10.8	10.1	9.3	8.6	8.1	7.9	7.4	7.1	6.0	5.7	4.8	5.1	1.9	1.6	1.2	1.1	0.3	3.2	6.2
5 years......	100.0	25.9	1.8	1.1	...	...	...	...	...	...	...	...	...	...	...	...	...	...	71.1	1.6
6 years......	100.0	89.2	3.9	0.4	0.3	...	...	...	...	...	...	...	...	...	...	...	...	...	6.3	1.5
7 years......	100.0	37.2	55.4	3.4	0.4	0.2	...	...	...	...	...	...	...	...	...	...	...	...	3.5	2.2
8 years......	100.0	6.6	37.0	49.8	3.3	0.4	0.2	...	...	...	...	...	...	...	...	...	...	...	2.7	3.1
9 years......	100.0	2.1	9.1	36.9	45.7	3.2	0.4	0.2	...	...	...	...	...	...	...	...	...	...	2.4	4.0
10 years....	100.0	1.0	3.2	11.5	35.7	42.1	3.4	0.4	0.4	...	...	...	...	...	...	...	...	...	2.2	4.9
11 years....	100.0	0.5	1.3	4.2	12.0	34.2	41.4	3.2	0.7	0.2	...	...	...	...	...	...	...	...	2.2	5.9
12 years....	100.0	0.4	0.8	2.2	5.4	12.8	33.9	38.0	3.7	0.5	0.2	...	...	...	...	...	...	...	2.1	6.8
13 years....	100.0	0.4	0.5	1.2	2.6	5.7	13.2	32.2	37.3	3.9	0.6	0.2	...	...	...	...	...	...	2.1	7.8
14 years....	100.0	0.6	0.3	0.6	1.4	2.7	5.9	13.5	31.8	35.3	4.9	0.6	0.4	...	...	...	...	...	2.1	8.8
15 years....	100.0	0.5	0.6	0.4	0.8	1.4	2.9	6.2	13.6	29.5	36.1	4.9	0.9	0.1	...	...	...	...	2.1	9.8
16 years....	100.0	0.3	0.4	0.6	0.5	0.7	1.4	2.7	6.1	11.9	30.8	36.2	5.9	0.2	0.1	...	...	...	2.2	10.8
17 years....	100.0	0.3	0.3	0.4	0.4	0.4	0.7	1.2	2.7	4.5	11.1	30.4	41.9	2.8	0.3	0.1	...	...	2.6	12.0
18 years....	100.0	0.2	0.2	0.2	0.3	0.2	0.4	0.6	1.4	2.1	4.7	13.0	45.3	25.1	4.8	0.6	0.2	...	0.6	12.6
19 years....	100.0	0.2	0.3	0.3	0.3	0.2	0.4	0.5	1.2	1.3	2.7	5.4	24.1	24.3	30.9	6.2	1.2	0.3	0.4	13.5
20 years....	100.0	0.2	0.4	0.4	0.4	0.3	0.4	0.6	1.3	1.2	2.1	2.9	15.0	11.9	25.9	20.2	7.6	0.9	0.4	14.5
21 years....	100.0	0.2	0.3	0.4	0.5	0.4	0.6	0.7	1.8	1.6	2.3	2.6	12.5	10.0	16.9	20.9	24.0	3.1	0.5	14.9
22 years....	100.0	0.2	0.3	0.4	0.6	0.5	0.7	1.0	2.6	2.0	2.8	3.0	13.7	9.4	15.6	17.2	23.0	6.6	0.5	14.8
23 years....	100.0	0.2	0.3	0.4	0.7	0.6	0.9	1.4	3.2	2.3	3.3	3.3	13.0	7.0	11.3	16.4	24.7	9.1	0.6	15.0
24 years....	100.0	0.3	0.3	0.5	0.7	0.7	1.0	1.3	3.4	2.7	4.1	3.9	15.0	6.3	9.3	13.4	25.1	11.5	0.6	15.0
25 to 29 years.	100.0	0.4	0.5	0.7	1.0	1.1	1.5	2.1	5.1	3.0	4.4	4.2	19.4	6.4	8.5	9.2	13.2	13.6	0.8	14.0

Source: U.S. Census of Population, Characteristics of the Population, U.S. Summary, Table 112.

are in school) forces the conclusion that girls are retarded in school considerably less frequently than boys.

Enrollment in Public and Private Schools. The extent to which private schools perform the task of educating the population is a topic which is often discussed.[4] The following summary shows that in 1957, at the elementary school level, about 1 pupil in 6 was enrolled in a private school, and that at the high school level only 1 pupil in 10 was in a private school. At the college level 1 student in 3 was attending a private college or university. Thus, private schools participate most fully at the lower and upper educational levels, and least fully at the intermediate and high school levels. The 34.5 percent of students who were attending private colleges or professional schools as of 1957 can be divided into two categories, since 14.0 percent were attending denominational schools and 20.6 percent were enrolled in other kinds of private schools. The nonwhite population depends very heavily on public schools for its elementary and high school education, since only a comparatively small proportion of nonwhite students are enrolled in private schools. According to the above table, the enrollment of the nonwhite population in private elementary schools is only about one-third as large as would be expected if nonwhite students were enrolled in private schools in the same proportions as the white population. The number of nonwhite students attending private high schools is only 1/5 as large as would be expected under the terms of the above comparison.

Level of schooling	Total	Public schools	Private schools
Total population			
Elementary school....	100.0	84.4	15.6
High school.........	100.0	90.0	10.0
College.............	100.0	65.5	34.5
Nonwhite population			
Elementary school....	100.0	95.6	4.4
High school.........	100.0	97.7	2.3
College.............	100.0	64.1	35.9

Source: Current Population Survey, Series P-20, No. 80, February 1958.

Enrollment in Adult Education Classes. Along with the boom in school enrollment has come a

[4] A public school is defined by the census as any educational institution operated by publicly elected or appointed school officials and supported by public funds. The educational institutions which are non-public are defined as private schools.

Table 13-6.—MEDIAN SCHOOL YEAR IN WHICH ENROLLED, BY SINGLE YEARS OF AGE, COLOR AND SEX,
FOR THE UNITED STATES, URBAN AND RURAL: 1950

Sex and age	Total				White				Nonwhite			
	Total	Urban	Rural nonfarm	Rural farm	Total	Urban	Rural nonfarm	Rural farm	Total	Urban	Rural nonfarm	Rural farm
MALE												
5 to 24 years.......	6.2	6.7	5.7	5.6	6.4	6.8	5.8	5.9	5.0	5.7	4.6	4.2
5 years..........	1.6	1.5	1.6	1.8	1.6	1.5	1.6	1.6	1.5	1.5	1.6	1.6
6 years..........	1.5	1.5	1.5	1.5	1.5	1.5	1.5	1.5	1.5	1,5	1.5	1.5
7 years..........	2.2	2.3	2.0	2.0	2.2	2.3	2.1	2.1	2.0	2.2	1.8	1.7
8 years..........	3.0	3.2	2.9	2.8	3.1	2.9	2.9	2.9	2.7	3.0	2.5	2.4
9 years..........	3.9	4.1	3.8	3.7	4.0	4.1	3.8	3.8	3.5	3.8	3.3	3.0
10 years.........	4.8	5.0	4.7	4.6	4.9	5.0	4.7	4.7	4.2	4.6	4.0	3.6
11 years.........	5.8	6.0	5.6	5.5	5.9	6.0	5.7	5.6	5.1	5.5	4.8	4.3
12 years.........	6.7	6.9	6.5	6.4	6.8	6.9	6.6	6.5	5.8	6.4	5.5	4.9
13 years.........	7.6	7.8	7.5	7.4	7.7	7.9	7.5	7.5	6.6	7.2	6.2	5.6
14 years.........	8.6	8.8	8.4	8.3	8.7	8.9	8.5	8.5	7.5	8.2	7.2	6.4
15 years.........	9.6	9.8	9.4	9.2	9.7	9.9	9.5	9.4	8.4	9.1	8.0	7.2
16 years.........	10.6	10.8	10.5	10.3	10.7	10.8	10.5	10.5	9.4	10.1	8.9	8.0
17 years.........	11.7	11.8	11.6	11.4	11.8	11.9	11.6	11.6	10.4	11.0	10.0	8.9
18 years.........	12.5	12.7	12.3	1 .1	12.6	12.7	12.4	12.2	11.3	11.7	11.2	10.0
19 years.........	13.4	13.7	12.9	12.3	13.5	13.7	13.0	12.4	12.2	12.5	11.8	10.6
20 years.........	14.4	14.5	13.9	12.5	14.5	14.6	14.0	12.6	12.6	13.0	12.5	11.0
21 years.........	14.7	14.9	14.1	12.5	14.8	14.9	14.2	12.7	12.7	13.0	12.3	10.3
22 years.........	14.8	14.9	14.2	12.3	14.9	15.0	14.3	12.5	12.6	12.9	12.5	9.0
23 years.........	15.2	15.4	14.4	11.8	15.3	15.5	14.6	12.1	12.4	12.7	11.9	8.6
24 years.........	15.3	15.5	14.2	11.7	15.4	15.7	14.5	12.1	12.2	12.6	10.6	8.0
FEMALE												
5 to 24 years.......	6.2	6.5	5.8	5.9	6.3	6.6	5.9	6.1	5.4	6.0	5.0	4.7
5 years..........	1.6	1.5	1.6	1.6	1.6	1.5	1.6	1.6	1.6	1.6	1.6	1.5
6 years..........	1.5	1.5	1.5	1.5	1.5	1.5	1.5	1.5	1.5	1.6	1.5	1.5
7 years..........	2.2	2.3	2.1	2.1	2.2	2.3	2.1	2.1	2.1	2.3	1.9	1.8
8 years..........	3.2	3.2	3.0	3.0	3.2	3.3	3.1	3.1	2.9	3.1	2.7	2.5
9 years..........	4.1	4.2	4.0	3.9	4.1	4.2	4.0	4.0	3.7	4.0	3.5	3.3
10 years.........	5.0	5.2	4.9	4.8	5.1	5.2	4.9	4.9	4.5	4.9	4.2	3.9
11 years.........	6.0	6.1	5.8	5.8	6.1	6.2	5.9	5.9	5.4	5.8	5.2	4.7
12 years.........	6.9	7.1	6.8	6.7	7.0	7.1	6.8	6.8	6.3	6.7	6.0	5.5
13 years.........	7.9	8.1	7.8	7.6	8.0	8.1	7.8	7.8	7.2	7.6	6.9	6.3
14 years.........	8.9	9.1	8.7	8.6	9.0	9.1	8.8	8.8	8.1	8.6	7.8	7.3
15 years.........	10.0	10.1	9.8	9.6	10.0	10.1	9.9	9.8	9.1	9.6	8.7	8.1
16 years.........	11.0	11.1	10.8	10.7	11.0	11.1	10.9	10.9	10.1	10.6	9.6	9.0
17 years.........	12.0	12.1	11.9	11.7	12.1	12.2	12.0	11.9	11.1	11.6	10.7	10.0
18 years.........	12.6	12.8	12.5	12.2	12.7	12.9	12.5	12.3	12.0	12.4	11.7	10.8
19 years.........	13.7	13.9	13.1	12.4	13.8	14.0	13.2	12.6	12.6	13.0	12.4	11.2
20 years.........	14.7	14.8	14.2	12.5	14.8	14.9	14.3	12.7	13.2	14.0	12.9	11.7
21 years.........	15.4	15.5	14.7	12.4	15.5	15.6	14.9	12.6	14.0	14.3	14.2	11.2
22 years.........	15.0	15.3	13.4	12.4	15.1	15.4	13.3	12.5	13.3	13.8	14.1	11.9
23 years.........	13.7	14.3	12.5	11.9	13.9	14.5	12.5	12.1	12.7	12.8	12.6	10.2
24 years.........	13.0	13.6	12.4	11.7	13.1	13.8	12.4	12.0	12.4	12.6	11.6	...

Source: U.S. Census of Population: 1950, Characteristics of the Population, U.S. Summary, Table 112.

greatly heightened participation by adults in the education classes and group meetings designed especially for them. In its Current Population Survey of October, 1957, the Bureau of the Census obtained information concerning the extent to which the population was taking part in adult education, by means of a project carried on in cooperation with the Office of Education. It was found that 8.3 million persons 14 years of age or over (7.8 percent) were enrolled in adult education classes. The extent of enrollment was found to be inversely related to age:

Age	Percent enrolled in adult education
Total...................	7.8
14 to 19 years...........	13.6
20 to 29 years...........	10.3
30 to 44 years...........	9.9
45 to 59 years...........	7.0
60 to 74 years...........	2.8
75 years and over........	1.1

Source: Current Population Survey, Series P,20, No. 80, February, 1958, Table G.

Marital Status of Students. Before World War II, comparatively few students married while they were in school. The veterans, many of them married, who enrolled in the colleges in such great numbers after World War II seem to have established a new cultural pattern on the nation's campuses; the proportion of students who marry during their junior or senior year in college, or during their postgraduate training, is much greater now than it was before World War II. This change is also due in part to the greatly increased emphasis on,and the higher rates of enrollment in, postgraduate training. In 1957, as the following data show, 41 percent of the male and 18 percent of the female students were married. Almost all of these were college students. Thus, at the present time about one student in 3 who is 20 to 34 years of age is married.

Marital status	Percent of college students 20 to 34 years of age		
	Total	Male	Female
Total...............	100.0	100.0	100.0
Single.................	664.0	58.7	77.5
Married, spouse present	34.3	40.9	17.7
Other.................	1.6	0.4	4.8

Source: Current Population Survey, Series P-20, No. 80, February, 1958.

Regional Variations in School Enrollment. Different sections of the country appear to place varying degrees of emphasis on school enrollment (see Table 13-7). In 1950, rates of school enrollment were higher in the regions of the Northeast, the North Central, and the West than they were in the South. At ages 7 to 13, the ages of compulsory attendance, the interregional differences were comparatively small. At the high school and col-

lege ages, however, the regions showed considerable diversity with respect to enrollment. The West made an especially good showing in high school attendance--its rates of school enrollment at ages 14 to 19 were greater than those of any other region. The South had much lower enrollment rates at the high school ages than the other regions. At the ages of college attendance, the Northeast and the West had above-average rates of enrollment, while the South's enrollment rates again were very much below average. The South's position is due in part (but not entirely) to the fact that it has a large rural population and a large nonwhite population; both of these groups have been shown to have rates of attendance which are below-average in comparison with those of the general population.

However, it does not seem to be true, as many persons believe, that the white-nonwhite differential in rates of school enrollment is greater in the South than it is elsewhere in the nation. Following are the 1950 differences between the percent of white children and the percent of nonwhite children attending school, for the South and for the nation, by urban-rural residence for selected age selected age groups:

Age	Difference in percent enrolled in school (white minus nonwhite)					
	Urban		Rural nonfarm		Rural farm	
	U.S.	South	U.S.	South	U.S.	South
7 years..	2.8	1.4	4.5	1.4	5.5	2.8
10 years.	0.7	0.5	2.9	1.2	2.4	1.0
14 years.	1.5	1.5	4.4	2.3	4.5	2.5
16 years.	7.7	6.0	10.9	4.4	9.3	4.5
18 years.	9.6	9.0	6.4	2.5	...	2.5
20 years.	9.1	7.7	0.2	-0.1	...	...
25 years.	2.3	1.8	0.3	0.7	...	...

Source: Computed from U.S. Census of Population: 1950, Characteristics of the Population, U.S. Summary, Table 151.

These figures show that, when the measurement is made separately for urban and rural areas, the South actually had a smaller white-nonwhite differential in school enrollment in 1950 than the other regions. However lax the South may have been in past decades with respect to providing

Table 13-7.—PERCENT ENROLLED IN SCHOOL BY SINGLE YEARS OF AGE, BY COLOR AND SEX, FOR THE UNITED STATES, URBAN, AND RURAL: 1950

Age, color, and area	Regions - Both sexes					Regions - Male					Regions - Female				
	North-east	North Central	South Total	South Non-white	West	North-east	North Central	South Total	South Non-white	West	North-east	North Central	South Total	South Non-white	West
Total......	48.8	50.0	49.0	50.3	50.2	52.4	52.8	51.1	52.0	52.9	45.3	47.3	46.8	48.7	47.5
5 years.......	12.4	9.9	9.2	11.2	11.7	12.1	9.4	9.0	10.6	11.6	12.8	10.3	9.4	11.7	11.7
6 years.......	75.7	68.8	60.0	63.0	71.3	75.2	67.9	59.2	62.0	71.0	76.1	69.6	60.9	64.0	71.5
7 years.......	94.8	95.6	92.4	90.8	95.8	94.7	95.5	92.1	90.1	95.8	94.8	95.7	92.7	91.5	95.8
8 years.......	95.6	96.3	94.8	93.8	96.6	95.6	96.4	95.7	93.5	96.5	95.6	96.3	94.9	94.1	96.7
9 years.......	95.8	96.7	95.6	94.9	96.8	95.9	96.6	95.4	94.6	96.8	95.7	96.8	95.7	95.2	96.7
10 years.......	95.8	96.6	95.5	94.7	96.9	95.7	96.5	95.2	94.4	96.7	95.8	96.6	95.7	95.1	97.1
11 years.......	95.9	96.7	95.8	95.3	97.1	95.8	96.7	95.8	94.8	96.8	96.0	96.8	96.0	95.7	97.5
12 years.......	95.7	96.5	95.3	94.8	96.9	95.4	96.2	95.0	94.4	96.7	96.0	96.8	95.7	95.3	97.1
13 years.......	95.8	96.7	94.9	94.1	97.0	95.7	96.6	94.7	93.5	96.9	95.9	96.8	95.1	94.6	97.0
14 years.......	95.7	95.8	92.7	91.0	96.8	95.8	95.8	92.4	89.9	97.0	95.7	95.9	93.1	92.2	96.6
15 years.......	94.4	93.4	86.7	83.7	94.8	94.6	93.3	86.7	83.0	95.4	94.1	93.5	86.7	84.4	94.1
16 years.......	85.7	84.4	72.8	68.9	88.2	85.7	83.5	72.2	67.6	89.5	85.6	85.2	73.4	70.1	86.8
17 years.......	72.4	73.9	58.0	52.2	76.3	72.8	73.5	57.1	50.3	77.0	72.0	74.4	59.0	54.0	75.5
18 years.......	41.2	41.8	35.4	31.2	45.2	45.5	45.3	36.3	29.9	47.8	37.2	38.4	34.6	32.4	42.3
19 years.......	26.7	24.7	22.3	19.4	27.3	31.0	28.5	24.3	19.1	29.6	22.8	21.4	20.3	19.7	24.8
20 years.......	20.5	18.0	15.4	12.3	19.7	25.3	21.7	17.8	12.6	22.0	16.4	14.7	13.1	12.0	17.1
21 years.......	16.9	15.2	12.2	9.7	16.6	23.1	20.2	15.8	10.6	20.9	11.2	10.6	8.6	8.8	11.9
22 years.......	13.9	12.5	10.3	7.7	14.5	21.9	19.3	16.0	10.5	21.7	6.5	6.0	4.9	5.3	7.3
23 years.......	11.6	10.4	9.5	7.4	12.6	19.3	17.0	15.7	11.4	20.2	4.4	4.0	3.6	4.0	5.1
24 years.......	9.9	9.1	8.3	6.9	10.9	16.6	15.2	13.9	11.5	17.7	3.7	3.3	3.1	3.1	4.3
25 years.......	8.9	7.9	7.5	6.4	9.6	14.4	13.0	12.7	10.8	15.6	3.3	3.0	2.8	2.7	3.8
26 years.......	7.4	6.7	6.9	6.0	8.6	12.3	10.7	11.4	10.2	13.6	3.0	2.9	2.7	2.4	3.9
27 years.......	6.6	5.8	6.3	6.2	7.6	10.6	9.3	10.1	10.1	11.7	3.0	2.5	2.5	2.7	3.6
28 years.......	6.0	5.2	5.8	5.5	6.8	9.5	8.2	9.4	9.2	10.3	2.7	2.4	2.4	2.4	3.5
29 years.......	5.3	4.6	5.2	4.8	6.1	8.1	7.0	8.3	8.0	9.0	2.6	2.3	2.3	2.1	3.2
Nonwhite:															
Total......	43.7	45.4	...	50.3	44.4	47.1	48.1	...	52.0	46.1	40.7	42.9	...	48.7	42.6
5 years.......	14.7	11.6	...	11.2	15.7	14.3	11.7	...	10.6	15.6	15.0	11.4	...	11.7	15.7
6 years.......	74.2	72.9	...	63.0	66.0	74.0	71.9	...	62.0	65.7	74.3	74.0	...	64.0	66.3
7 years.......	93.1	94.3	...	90.8	86.2	92.7	94.2	...	90.1	86.2	93.5	94.3	...	91.5	86.3
8 years.......	94.6	95.4	...	93.8	88.0	94.4	95.6	...	93.5	87.4	94.7	95.3	...	94.1	88.7
9 years.......	94.5	96.1	...	94.9	89.9	95.0	95.9	...	94.6	89.9	94.0	96.3	...	95.2	89.9
10 years.......	94.5	95.3	...	94.7	89.5	94.2	94.7	...	94.4	89.0	94.9	96.0	...	95.1	90.1
11 years.......	94.8	95.7	...	95.3	90.3	94.0	94.9	...	94.8	88.2	95.6	96.4	...	95.7	92.7
12 years.......	93.4	95.7	...	94.8	90.1	93.4	95.7	...	94.4	90.9	93.4	95.8	...	95.3	89.3
13 years.......	94.9	96.3	...	94.1	89.5	94.3	96.1	...	93.5	88.4	95.4	96.5	...	94.6	90.7
14 years.......	94.6	95.4	...	91.0	91.3	94.8	95.6	...	89.9	92.6	94.5	95.2	...	92.2	90.0
15 years.......	92.3	92.2	...	83.7	89.8	93.0	93.4	...	83.0	92.3	91.6	91.0	...	84.4	87.5
16 years.......	82.6	81.7	...	68.9	82.6	84.1	82.9	...	67.6	86.5	81.0	80.5	...	70.1	79.0
17 years.......	62.8	63.1	...	52.2	73.6	62.5	65.9	...	50.3	77.0	63.0	60.4	...	54.0	70.1
18 years.......	31.1	34.8	...	31.2	44.5	33.9	38.4	...	29.9	48.6	28.6	31.8	...	32.4	40.2
19 years.......	17.0	20.4	...	19.4	26.1	18.9	22.7	...	19.1	27.7	15.5	18.6	...	19.7	24.5
20 years.......	11.5	12.2	...	12.3	17.8	13.9	15.0	...	12.6	20.6	9.7	9.9	...	12.0	14.9
21 years.......	10.5	10.2	...	9.7	14.8	13.4	13.1	...	10.6	17.9	8.1	7.6	...	8.8	11.5
22 years.......	8.9	8.6	...	7.7	11.9	12.2	11.5	...	10.5	16.1	6.4	6.0	...	5.3	7.5
23 years.......	7.6	7.8	...	7.4	10.3	11.8	11.6	...	11.4	14.3	4.2	4.5	...	4.0	6.5
24 years.......	6.9	7.0	...	6.9	9.1	10.4	11.2	...	11.5	12.4	4.1	3.3	...	3.1	5.9
25 years.......	6.9	6.6	...	6.4	8.7	11.1	10.2	...	10.8	12.8	3.4	3.4	...	2.7	4.5
26 years.......	7.2	6.3	...	6.0	7.9	11.8	9.9	...	10.2	10.8	3.3	3.1	...	2.4	5.0
27 years.......	6.0	6.0	...	6.2	7.7	9.4	9.4	...	10.1	10.8	3.2	2.9	...	2.7	4.5
28 years.......	6.0	5.5	...	5.5	5.7	9.3	8.2	...	9.2	7.5	3.1	3.0	...	2.4	3.7
29 years.......	5.8	4.8	...	4.8	6.4	8.7	7.4	...	8.0	8.3	3.3	2.4	...	2.1	4.4
Urban:															
Total......	48.2	48.2	46.0	46.7	49.7	52.3	52.2	50.2	50.8	53.6	44.2	44.2	42.1	43.6	45.8
5 years.......	12.9	8.1	8.2	9.9	12.2	12.5	8.1	8.0	9.4	12.0	13.4	8.1	8.4	10.3	12.4
6 years.......	77.3	71.1	62.9	64.9	75.5	76.9	70.3	62.4	64.1	75.3	77.8	71.9	63.5	65.6	75.8
7 years.......	94.7	95.9	94.3	93.2	96.7	94.6	95.7	94.2	92.8	96.6	94.7	96.0	94.4	93.6	96.7
8 years.......	95.3	96.5	95.9	95.5	97.2	95.3	96.7	96.0	95.4	97.0	95.4	96.4	95.9	95.7	97.4
9 years.......	95.6	96.8	96.3	95.7	97.3	95.7	96.8	96.3	95.4	97.3	95.5	96.8	96.4	96.0	97.3
10 years.......	95.5	96.8	96.6	96.2	97.3	95.4	96.8	96.5	96.3	97.1	95.5	96.7	96.6	96.0	97.4
11 years.......	95.6	96.9	96.8	96.6	97.7	95.6	96.8	96.8	96.3	97.5	95.7	97.0	96.8	96.8	97.9
12 years.......	95.5	96.7	96.4	95.9	97.3	95.3	96.4	96.1	96.0	97.1	95.8	97.0	96.6	95.8	97.5
13 years.......	95.5	97.0	96.2	95.6	97.5	95.3	96.9	96.3	95.7	97.2	95.7	97.0	96.1	95.4	97.7
14 years.......	95.5	96.6	95.0	93.9	97.4	95.5	96.7	95.4	94.2	97.5	95.5	96.4	94.6	93.6	97.3
15 years.......	94.7	95.1	90.8	88.1	96.0	95.1	95.5	92.1	89.9	96.6	94.4	94.7	89.4	86.6	95.5
16 years.......	86.9	86.7	78.5	74.0	90.6	87.5	87.5	80.7	76.0	92.5	86.2	86.0	76.5	72.2	88.8
17 years.......	73.7	75.9	64.4	57.4	80.4	75.1	78.1	67.4	59.4	83.2	72.3	73.8	61.7	55.7	77.8
18 years.......	42.3	44.8	41.3	34.3	50.0	47.8	51.1	45.5	35.9	55.6	37.5	39.5	37.6	33.0	44.6
19 years.......	28.5	30.0	28.7	22.9	32.9	33.9	36.4	33.1	24.9	37.7	23.9	25.1	25.0	21.3	28.5
20 years.......	22.2	22.6	21.3	15.2	24.7	28.1	28.5	26.0	17.1	29.2	17.3	18.0	17.4	13.9	20.5
21 years.......	18.4	19.1	16.7	12.2	20.7	25.7	26.2	23.0	14.7	27.5	12.0	12.9	11.1	10.3	14.3
22 years.......	15.2	15.5	13.9	9.8	17.6	24.2	24.6	22.8	14.7	27.1	7.0	7.1	6.2	6.1	8.8
23 years.......	12.6	12.7	12.3	9.2	15.0	21.1	21.3	21.4	15.4	24.8	4.8	4.6	4.2	4.4	5.8
24 years.......	10.7	11.1	10.4	8.7	12.9	18.1	18.7	18.2	15.0	21.4	4.0	3.9	3.5	3.7	5.0
25 years.......	9.3	9.4	9.4	8.0	11.2	15.7	15.8	16.3	14.3	18.8	3.5	3.4	3.3	3.1	4.3
26 years.......	8.1	8.0	8.4	7.0	9.9	13.4	13.0	14.3	12.5	16.0	3.2	3.3	3.1	2.6	4.3
27 years.......	7.2	6.8	7.3	7.4	8.6	11.7	11.0	12.3	12.6	13.6	3.1	2.9	2.8	3.0	3.9
28 years.......	6.5	6.1	6.7	6.3	7.7	10.4	9.7	11.1	11.0	11.8	3.0	2.7	2.6	2.4	3.9
29 years.......	5.7	5.2	6.0	5.7	6.9	8.8	8.0	9.6	9.9	10.3	2.7	2.6	2.6	2.3	3.4

Table 13-7.—PERCENT ENROLLED IN SCHOOL BY SINGLE YEARS OF AGE, BY COLOR AND SEX, FOR THE UNITED STATES, URBAN, AND RURAL: 1950-Continued

Age, color, and area	Regions - Both sexes					Regions - Male					Regions - Female				
	North-east	North Central	South		West	North-east	North Central	South		West	North-east	North Central	South		West
			Total	Non-white				Total	Non-white				Total	Non-white	
Rural nonfarm:															
Total......	50.2	50.6	47.6	49.0	48.8	53.4	52.5	48.8	49.4	48.7	48.0	48.8	46.4	48.6	48.8
5 years........	10.8	11.1	9.2	11.4	10.5	10.7	10.8	8.9	10.9	10.5	11.0	11.4	9.6	11.9	10.4
6 years........	71.2	65.1	57.7	62.9	64.5	70.6	64.6	56.8	61.9	64.2	71.7	65.7	58.6	64.0	64.7
7 years........	95.0	95.4	91.9	90.8	94.4	95.0	95.3	91.7	90.1	94.3	95.1	95.5	92.0	91.4	94.4
8 years........	96.4	96.2	94.7	93.8	95.5	96.5	96.0	94.4	93.3	95.7	96.2	96.3	95.0	94.2	95.4
9 years........	96.5	96.7	95.5	94.7	96.2	96.5	96.5	95.2	94.2	96.1	96.6	96.9	95.8	95.2	96.3
10 years........	96.7	96.5	95.4	94.4	96.4	96.4	96.2	95.0	93.8	96.2	97.0	96.8	95.7	95.0	96.6
11 years........	96.4	96.6	95.5	94.7	96.2	96.2	96.6	95.2	93.9	95.6	96.7	96.5	95.7	95.5	96.8
12 years........	96.2	96.1	95.2	94.6	96.1	95.6	95.6	94.9	94.0	95.8	96.8	96.7	95.5	95.3	96.3
13 years........	96.7	96.5	94.8	93.9	96.2	96.6	96.5	94.7	93.4	96.3	96.7	96.6	95.0	94.4	96.1
14 years........	96.5	95.8	92.5	90.7	96.0	96.7	95.6	92.6	89.8	96.5	96.4	95.9	92.5	91.7	95.5
15 years........	93.8	93.2	85.8	81.9	92.8	94.2	93.5	86.8	81.9	93.9	93.3	92.8	84.8	82.0	91.7
16 years........	83.4	83.7	70.5	67.0	83.6	82.7	83.0	71.1	66.3	85.3	84.1	84.4	69.9	67.7	81.8
17 years........	69.6	72.2	53.9	49.3	66.0	67.3	70.7	52.6	47.2	64.3	72.0	73.8	55.2	51.3	68.2
18 years........	38.3	38.0	30.0	28.0	32.6	40.1	40.7	30.8	26.9	31.8	36.3	35.2	29.1	29.1	33.7
19 years........	21.5	16.7	16.5	16.5	15.0	23.8	20.4	18.7	15.7	15.5	19.2	13.1	14.0	17.2	14.1
20 years........	14.9	10.1	10.4	10.5	9.3	17.2	13.1	12.5	10.3	10.1	12.8	7.3	8.1	10.6	7.9
21 years........	11.6	8.4	8.6	8.3	7.3	15.3	11.5	11.1	8.5	8.7	8.0	5.6	5.8	8.2	5.3
22 years........	9.2	6.8	7.4	6.4	7.0	14.2	10.2	11.2	8.2	10.3	4.3	3.6	3.6	4.6	3.3
23 years........	7.7	5.7	6.8	6.0	6.5	12.7	8.9	10.9	8.8	9.5	2.9	2.8	2.7	3.5	3.1
24 years........	6.4	5.2	6.2	5.8	5.7	10.7	8.5	9.9	9.3	9.0	2.4	2.0	2.6	2.4	2.3
25 years........	5.4	4.8	5.5	4.9	5.1	8.9	7.8	9.0	8.0	7.5	2.1	1.9	2.0	2.0	2.6
26 years........	4.7	4.0	5.3	5.9	4.9	7.7	6.0	8.4	9.4	7.2	2.0	2.1	2.2	2.3	2.5
27 years........	4.2	3.6	5.0	5.6	4.9	6.5	5.5	7.7	8.4	6.9	2.1	1.8	2.2	2.8	2.7
28 years........	3.7	3.0	4.5	4.8	4.2	5.7	4.6	7.1	7.9	6.0	1.9	1.5	1.9	1.8	2.3
29 years........	3.5	2.8	4.3	4.3	3.9	5.2	4.3	6.6	6.9	5.6	1.8	1.4	2.0	1.8	2.2
Rural farm:															
Total......	54.3	55.6	55.3	55.6	56.9	54.0	54.8	55.0	55.2	57.3	54.6	56.5	55.7	55.9	56.4
5 years........	11.3	13.6	10.6	12.3	11.2	11.2	11.8	10.4	11.7	11.4	11.4	15.6	10.9	12.9	11.0
6 years........	68.5	65.8	58.1	61.1	61.4	68.4	64.7	57.0	59.9	61.3	68.6	67.0	59.3	62.3	61.4
7 years........	95.3	95.2	90.3	88.4	93.9	94.9	95.2	89.6	87.3	94.3	95.7	95.2	91.0	89.4	93.5
8 years........	96.4	96.1	93.3	92.0	95.6	96.5	95.9	93.2	91.8	95.5	96.2	96.2	93.5	92.3	95.8
9 years........	96.4	96.4	94.6	94.2	95.7	96.5	96.3	94.4	94.0	95.5	96.3	96.5	94.7	94.3	96.0
10 years........	96.4	96.2	94.3	93.6	96.1	96.7	96.1	94.1	93.1	96.0	96.1	96.3	94.6	94.1	96.2
11 years........	97.2	96.4	94.8	94.3	96.3	96.7	96.4	94.5	94.0	96.0	97.8	96.5	95.2	94.7	96.7
12 years........	96.7	96.2	94.3	93.9	96.2	96.5	96.1	93.8	93.2	96.0	97.0	96.4	94.9	94.8	96.3
13 years........	96.5	96.2	93.5	92.8	96.1	96.5	96.0	93.0	91.8	96.5	96.5	96.5	94.0	93.8	95.7
14 years........	96.1	94.1	90.4	88.6	95.5	96.2	93.6	89.1	86.1	95.6	95.9	94.6	91.8	91.1	95.4
15 years........	92.0	89.4	83.0	80.5	92.4	91.4	88.0	81.1	77.5	93.0	92.6	91.0	85.0	83.6	91.7
16 years........	77.8	79.0	68.3	65.1	84.8	74.3	74.8	64.6	61.1	84.2	82.1	84.0	72.4	69.3	85.6
17 years........	65.3	70.3	53.6	48.4	75.2	61.4	65.2	49.4	43.6	74.5	70.0	76.5	58.5	53.7	76.0
18 years........	34.3	35.3	31.4	29.6	45.0	33.2	33.8	28.9	25.8	46.1	35.7	37.3	34.2	33.8	43.6
19 years........	14.3	11.6	15.7	16.8	19.8	15.1	11.8	15.5	14.7	21.6	13.3	11.3	15.9	18.9	17.5
20 years........	8.3	5.7	8.1	9.2	9.6	8.0	6.3	8.2	8.5	11.1	8.6	5.0	8.0	9.9	7.5
21 years........	6.6	4.6	5.4	6.2	6.5	7.4	5.1	6.0	6.1	7.9	5.7	3.8	4.8	6.3	4.7
22 years........	5.5	4.1	4.7	4.8	6.2	7.3	5.3	6.2	5.4	8.3	3.3	2.7	3.1	4.3	3.6
23 years........	4.9	4.1	5.3	4.8	5.9	7.3	5.6	7.2	6.0	8.3	2.1	2.4	3.2	3.6	3.0
24 years........	6.1	3.9	4.9	4.0	4.8	9.1	5.6	7.2	5.9	6.2	2.6	1.9	2.4	2.3	3.2
25 years........	4.7	3.9	4.6	4.1	4.8	6.8	5.6	7.1	6.0	7.0	2.4	2.2	2.2	2.5	2.4
26 years........	3.7	3.5	4.6	3.7	4.9	5.8	5.1	7.1	5.7	7.4	1.7	1.9	2.1	2.0	2.2
27 years........	4.0	3.6	4.7	3.7	5.0	5.5	5.5	7.1	5.6	7.4	2.4	1.7	2.2	1.8	2.4
28 years........	3.7	3.5	4.7	4.3	4.6	5.5	5.4	7.3	6.1	6.9	1.8	1.8	2.3	2.7	2.2
29 years........	3.7	3.5	4.3	3.2	3.6	4.9	5.2	6.7	4.6	5.2	2.5	1.8	2.0	1.9	2.0

Source: U.S. Census of Population: 1950, Characteristics of the Population, U.S. Summary, Table 151.

equal opportunities for its large nonwhite population to enroll in school, it is now less remiss in this respect than its northern and western neighbors. As residents of a less wealthy, more rural, and less education-minded region, both white and nonwhite children in the South have below-average attendance rates.

EDUCATIONAL ATTAINMENT OF THE ADULT POPULATION

One of the most widely useful population variables is the level of educational attainment of the adult population. Educational attainment has a high correlation with income, with occupation, with status or social position in the community, with certain buying habits, with many attitudes and opinions, and with a great variety of other elements in human life. It is essential, therefore, that sociologists, economists, and analysts in other related fields comprehend the recent changes that have taken place in the level of educational attainment, and the further changes that may be expected. The direction of this educational trend is connected with several other recent changes, and is one "cause" of these other changes. A question concerning educational attainment was included in a decennial census for the first time in 1940. It replaced a question on literacy, which had been abandoned because all but a very small fraction of the population was literate. In any case, persons who report completing not even one year of schooling may be considered as corresponding roughly to those who would be in an "illiterate" category. Thus, by shifting from a literacy question to a "years of schooling completed" question, the census provided a much richer body of information concerning the educational attainment of the population.

By the time they have attained the age of 25 years, almost all persons have completed the amount of education to which they aspire, which they can afford, or which they have been required to obtain, and hence they are no longer enrolled in school. For this reason, statistics concerning the educational attainment of the adult (out-of-school) population are often analyzed in terms of the population aged 25 years and over. One often-used measure involves data concerning the "median years of school completed." For example, the figure relating to median years of schooling completed by the population aged 25 years and over has risen steadily during the period for which data are available:

Year	Median years of school completed
1957...........	10.6
1950...........	9.3
1940...........	8.6

The above data indicate that in 1940, one-half of the population had less than 8.6 years of school-

ing. In 1957, this level had risen by two full years. Two of the comments which can be made about these statistics are worthy of emphasis. First, few other nations, if any, have achieved such a high average level of educational accomplishment. Second, the level of educational attainment has not yet reached a peak; it is still rising, and may be expected to continue to rise for several decades. Only a few years before 1940, the average citizen was a graduate of elementary school. By about 1965 the average citizen will be a high school graduate. By that time the proportion of citizens with less than a complete elementary school education will be very small. This situation has a variety of profound implications.

A much more adequate measure of educational attainment than "median years of school completed" is a percentage distribution which shows what proportion of the population has reached each level of schooling. The following summary pictures succinctly the status as of 1957 and the changes that have taken place since 1940.

Years of school completed	1957 (CPS)	1950 (census)	1940 (census)	Change, 1940-57
Total............	100.0	100.0	100.0	...
College:				
4 years or more...	7.5	6.0	4.6	2.9
1 to 3 years......	7.3	7.2	5.4	1.9
High school:				
4 years...........	26.0	20.2	14.1	11.9
1 to 3 years......	17.7	16.9	15.0	2.7
Elementary school:				
8 years...........	17.9	20.2	27.8	-9.9
5 to 7 years......	12.8	15.9	18.3	-5.5
1 to 4 years......	6.6	8.3	9.8	-3.2
No school years completed.........	2.4	2.5	3.7	-1.3
School years not reported..........	1.9	2.8	1.4	0.5

Source: Current Population Report, Series P-20, No. 77, 1957, and the 1950 and 1940 decennial censuses.

In March, 1957, among persons aged 25 and over, 1 person in every 13 was a college graduate and 1 person in 7 had completed one or more years of college. At the other extreme, only slightly more than 2 percent of the population had had no schooling at all (were illiterate) and only about 9 percent were "functionally illiterate" (had completed less than 5 years of elementary school). (The number of functional illiterates was slightly larger than the number of college graduates in 1957.) The great mass of the population had completed the eighth grade of elementary school or had attended high school. Fully one-fourth of the population had completed high school without going on to college.

Swift progress was made in raising the educational level of the population during the 17 years between 1940 and 1957. The proportion of the population classified as functional illiterates decreased by one-third, while the proportion of persons who had completed college increased by approximately 65 percent. The percentage of persons who had achieved only a grammar school education declined drastically during this period, and the percentage of persons who had attended or completed high school increased by 50 percent. Thus, the proportion of citizens with little education has been reduced until it is now only a very small fraction of its former size, while the percentage of citizens with an intermediate or advanced education has been greatly increased.

The educational attainment of a particular group of persons reflects the rates of school enrollment which its members had when they were young, modified somewhat by death and migration. As has been demonstrated in the preceding section of this chapter, although children drop out of school at all ages they do so according to a pattern of age-rates that has been changing over the years. If a high proportion of the members of a particular group remained in school until they were 18 to 25 years of age, the whole group's level of educational attainment would be higher than if the majority had dropped out when they were very young. Thus, the socio-economic differentials which are connected with educational attainment today are nothing more than a reflection of the socio-economic differentials which were connected with yesterday's school enrollment. According to this principle, today's differentials in school enrollment will become tomorrow's differentials in educational attainment. Persons migrate from one

community to another, members of certain socio-economic groups tend to die at younger ages than members of other groups, and some persons are able to move from one socio-economic group to another between the time they are in school and the time they are enumerated as adults by the census; the extent to which these factors operate determines the degree of correspondence between school enrollment and educational attainment, a correspondence which is never exact. The currently rising level of educational attainment noted above is, therefore, a consequence of the rising level of school enrollment over the past half century.

Age Pattern of School Attainment. In keeping with the lower rates of school enrollment which they had in their youth, the older age groups have lower levels of educational attainment than the younger age groups, as indicated by the following summary of the median years of school completed by persons of each age.

Age	Median years of school completed		
	1940	1950	1957
25 to 29 years..	10.3	12.1	12.3
30 to 34 years..	9.5	11.6	12.2
35 to 39 years..	8.8	10.7	12.0
40 to 44 years..	8.6	9.8	
45 to 49 years..	8.5	8.9	10.0
50 to 54 years..	8.4	8.7	
55 to 59 years..	8.3	8.5	8.7
60 to 64 years..	8.3	8.4	
65 to 69 years..	8.2	8.2	
70 to 74 years..	8.1	8.2	8.3
75 years-over...	8.0	8.1	

The least-educated persons are much more heavily concentrated in the older ages than might be imagined. For example, almost one-half of the persons who have had no schooling are in the age group 65 and over, and 35 percent of the functional illiterates (those with 1 to 4 years of schooling) are 65 or more years old. On the other hand, of the persons who have had a college education, the greatest proportion is concentrated in the younger age groups. The educational level of the population as a whole rises as the older, less-educated generations die out and are replaced by younger, more-educated generations. Thus, 40 years from now, when the population which is currently aged 35 years of age and over will be 75 years of age and over, no age group will have a median level of less than 12.0 years of schooling--provided the enrollment rates do not drop in the meantime.

Sex Differences in Educational Attainment. As would be expected in view of the sex differences in school enrollment, a larger proportion of males than of females have graduated from college or attended college, but a considerably larger percentage of females than of males have graduated from high school without attending college. Because they have a greater propensity to drop out of elementary school and to be retarded in school, a higher proportion of boys than of girls have only an elementary school education. This general pattern of sex differences was present in 1950 and 1940, as well as in 1957. Over the 17 years for which data are available, the sex differential has diminished considerably at the high school and elementary school levels, but at the college level it has increased greatly. This means that at the upper end of the educational attainment continuum the educational achievement level of males is rising faster than that of females. The recent changes in the sex differential may be summarized succinctly as follows:

Years of school completed	Sex differential (male-female)			
	1957 (CPS)	1950 (census)	1940 (census)	Change, 1940-57
Total.........	100.0	100.0	100.0	...
College:				
4 years or more.	3.7	2.1	1.7	2.0
1 to 3 years....	-0.2	-0.7	-1.2	1.0
High school:				
4 years or more.	-7.4	-5.0	-4.2	-3.2
1 to 3 years....	-0.8	-1.0	-1.4	0.6
Elementary school:				
8 years.........	1.0	0.9	1.3	-0.3
5 to 7 years....	0.9	1.0	0.9	...
1 to 4 years....	1.7	1.9	2.2	-0.5
No school years completed........	0.3	0.2	0.3	...
School years not reported........	0.6	0.7	0.4	0.2

Source: Current Population Reports, Series P-20, No, 77, 1957, and U.S. Census of Population: 1950, U.S. Summary, Detailed Characteristics, Table 115.

Table 13-9 reports the median years of school completed by the white and nonwhite population of each age, by urban and rural residence. In all the possible comparisons, the nonwhite population falls well below the white.

Color Differences in Educational Attainment. A very large differential in educational attainment exists between the white and the nonwhite populations. Among the most poorly educated persons, a disproportionately large share are nonwhite, and nonwhites comprise a disproportionately small share of the most highly educated people. For example, in 1957 only 2.8 percent of the nonwhite population aged 25 and over had completed 4 years of college, but for the total population the corresponding percentage was 2 1/2 times as great. At the other extreme in the area of educational attainment, in 1957 more than one-fourth of the nonwhite population was functionally illiterate--a proportion that was almost 3 times as great as that found among the general population. At the present time, the over-all color differential in educational attainment is not shriveling; rather, it is growing. A careful study of Table 13-8 shows that since 1940 the increase in the proportion of college graduates has been much more rapid among the total population than among the nonwhite population. Despite the fact that the educational level of the Negro population is rising, it is not rising nearly rapidly enough to reduce the white-nonwhite educational differential. However, this differential is a temporary phenomenon which the current pattern of school enrollment rates will probably reverse within a decade or so.

In part, the color differential can be traced back to the situation that existed after the Civil War. Despite major efforts to extend education to the newly-freed slaves and their children and grandchildren, it was a long time before nearly equal opportunities for enrollment in elementary school and high school were provided; in most states such opportunities have been available for only a few years, and it is not certain that they are available yet, in some states. Attendance at college is a privilege which only a comparatively small proportion of nonwhites have been able to enjoy. As a

Table 13-8.—YEARS OF SCHOOL COMPLETED BY PERSONS 25 YEARS OF AGE AND OVER, BY COLOR: 1940, 1950, AND 1957

| Years of school completed | Percent distribution | | | | | | Difference (total minus nonwhite) | | | |
| | Total | | | Nonwhite | | | 1957 | 1950 | 1940 | Change, 1940 to 1957 |
	1957	1950	1940	1957	1950	1940				
Total..............	100.0	100.0	100.0	100.0	100.0	100.0	...	...	...	...
College:										
4 years or more.......	7.5	6.0	4.6	2.8	2.2	1.3	4.7	3.8	3.3	1.4
1 to 3 years..........	7.3	7.2	5.4	3.1	2.9	1.9	4.2	4.3	3.5	0.7
High school:										
4 years..............	26.0	20.2	14.1	11.9	8.1	4.4	14.1	12.1	9.7	4.4
1 to 3 years..........	17.7	16.9	15.0	16.5	13.0	8.5	1.2	3.9	6.5	-5.3
Elementary school:										
8 years..............	17.9	20.2	27.8	12.2	11.5	11.7	5.7	8.7	16.1	-10.4
5 to 7 years..........	12.8	15.9	18.3	23.6	27.2	29.4	-10.8	-11.3	-11.1	0.3
1 to 4 years..........	6.6	8.3	9.8	20.1	24.9	30.7	-13.5	-16.6	-20.9	7.4
None.................	2.4	2.5	3.7	6.8	6.6	10.3	-4.4	-4.1	-6.6	2.2
Not reported..........	1.9	2.8	1.4	3.0	3.6	1.8	-1.1	-0.8	-0.4	-0.7

Source: U.S. Census of Population: 1950, Characteristics of the Population, U.S. Summary, Table 115; Current Population Reports, P-20, No-77, 1957.

result, among the older age groups of the nonwhite population the level of educational attainment is extremely low. As these older generations die out, and are replaced by younger nonwhites whose level of educational attainment is much closer to that of their white peers, the color differential may be expected to shrink. Many years would be required, however--perhaps a century or more-- for its complete disappearance, even if the differentials in school enrollment were suddenly to trend toward zero.

Tables 13-10 and 13-11 have been prepared in order to facilitate the more precise tracing of what is happening to the educational level of the white and the nonwhite populations. Table 13-10 was computed by subtracting the percentage of the population which had reached each educational level in 1950 from the corresponding percentage in 1957. The calculation was made for each age group. In the preparation of Table 13-11, this procedure was followed for the nonwhite population. A comparison of these two sets of differences makes it possible to discover whether the recent changes in educa-

tional attainment are tending to lessen or to increase the white-nonwhite differential at each age.

(a) Among the young nonwhite population, the average level of educational attainment has risen faster than among the young white population. For example, between 1950 and 1957 the median years of school completed by the nonwhite population aged 25 to 29 increased by 1.2 years, while among the general population of the same ages it increased by only 0.2 years. A similar gain was reported for ages 30 to 34. However, at ages 35 and above, the white population made larger gains than the nonwhite. This last differential reflects the fact that a great improvement in school facilities was extended to the white population but was denied to the nonwhite population until recently. The gradual dying out of that portion of the nonwhite population which will be 45 years of age or more in 1960 will help to lessen the white-nonwhite differential.

(b) The above finding is reflected in the much greater increases which have taken place among the nonwhite than among the white popula-

Table 13-9.—MEDIAN YEARS OF SCHOOL COMPLETED BY POPULATION 25 YEARS OLD AND OVER, BY SEX, AGE, COLOR, AND URBAN-RURAL RESIDENCE: 1950

Sex and age	Total				White				Nonwhite			
	Total	Urban	Rural nonfarm	Rural farm	Total	Urban	Rural nonfarm	Rural farm	Total	Urban	Rural nonfarm	Rural farm
MALE												
25 years and over.	9.0	10.0	8.7	8.6	9.3	10.3	8.8	8.4	6.4	7.5	5.1	4.3
25 to 29 years.....	12.0	12.2	10.8	8.9	12.4	12.3	11.1	9.5	7.4	9.2	7.1	5.6
30 to 34 years.....	11.4	12.1	10.4	8.7	11.9	12.2	10.7	8.9	7.8	8.6	6.4	5.1
35 to 39 years.....	10.3	11.1	9.3	8.5	10.7	11.7	9.8	8.7	7.1	8.0	5.7	4.7
40 to 44 years.....	9.4	10.3	8.8	8.3	9.9	10.7	9.0	8.5	6.5	7.4	5.2	4.7
45 to 49 years.....	8.9	9.1	8.6	8.2	8.9	9.6	8.9	8.3	6.0	6.7	4.7	4.2
50 to 54 years.....	8.6	8.8	8.5	8.1	8.7	8.9	8.6	8.3	5.6	6.4	4.5	4.0
55 to 59 years.....	8.4	8.6	8.3	8.0	8.5	8.7	8.4	8.2	5.1	6.0	4.2	3.9
60 to 64 years.....	8.3	8.4	8.2	7.8	8.3	8.5	8.2	8.0	4.7	5.6	3.9	3.8
65 to 69 years.....	8.1	8.3	8.3	7.3	8.2	8.3	8.1	7.8	4.0	4.8	3.3	3.3
70 to 74 years.....	8.0	8.2	7.8	7.1	8.1	8.3	8.0	7.6	3.9	4.5	3.1	3.3
75 years and over...	7.9	8.1	7.5	6.8	8.1	8.2	7.8	7.2	3.1	3.9	2.4	2.4
FEMALE												
25 years and over.	9.6	10.2	9.0	8.5	10.0	10.6	9.3	8.7	7.2	8.0	5.9	5.4
25 to 29 years.....	12.1	12.2	11.6	10.1	12.2	12.3	12.0	10.8	8.9	9.9	7.6	6.7
30 to 34 years.....	11.8	12.1	11.0	9.3	12.1	12.2	11.4	10.0	8.1	9.0	7.2	6.3
35 to 39 years.....	10.7	11.3	10.8	8.9	11.2	11.8	10.6	9.3	7.8	8.4	6.7	6.0
40 to 44 years.....	10.1	10.6	9.5	8.7	10.5	10.9	9.9	8.9	7.2	7.9	6.1	5.7
45 to 49 years.....	9.0	9.6	8.8	8.5	9.5	10.0	9.0	8.6	6.7	7.3	5.6	5.3
50 to 54 years.....	8.8	8.9	8.7	8.4	8.9	9.0	8.8	8.5	6.1	6.7	5.0	4.9
55 to 59 years.....	8.6	8.7	8.5	8.3	8.7	8.7	8.6	8.4	5.8	6.5	4.8	4.7
60 to 64 years.....	8.4	8.5	8.4	8.2	8.5	8.6	8.4	8.3	5.3	6.0	4.4	4.3
65 to 69 years.....	8.3	8.4	8.2	7.9	8.4	8.5	8.3	8.1	4.5	5.2	3.7	3.8
70 to 74 years.....	8.3	8.4	8.2	7.8	8.4	8.5	8.3	8.1	4.2	4.8	3.4	3.5
75 years and over...	8.2	8.4	8.1	7.3	8.3	8.4	8.2	7.8	3.4	4.1	2.3	2.5

tion in the proportion attending high school and graduating from high school, for ages 25 to 29 and 30 to 34. It is also reflected in the greater decline, among nonwhites of all ages, in the proportions which have reached only a very low level of educational attainment.

(c) However, the comparatively low rate of college entrance among Negroes has persisted, and is still characteristic of all age groups. For example, between 1950 and 1957 the percentage of nonwhite males aged 25 to 29 who had obtained college degrees increased by only 0.8 percentage points, whereas among the general population the increase was 4.0 percentage points, or 5 times as much. This is unmistakable evidence that the white-nonwhite differential in the area of higher education is currently increasing at a very rapid rate. The differential is increasing because there has been a much greater increase in college at-

tendance among the white than among the nonwhite population.

Urban-Rural Differences in Educational Attainment. At each age, the average level of educational attainment in urban areas is considerably above that of rural areas. The differences are especially large at the younger ages, 25 to 39 years of age (Table 13-9). Within the rural areas, the educational attainment of the rural-nonfarm population is higher than that of the rural-farm population, and here too the differences are large.

Table 13-9 is noteworthy for its demonstration that the age, sex, color and urban-rural differentials are all valid simultaneously, and independently of each other. Thus, the least-educated group in the population is the rural nonwhite population aged 75 years of age and over (whose median is only 2.3 years of school). The most-educated group is made up of white urban persons

Table 13-10.—PERCENTAGE-POINT CHANGE IN PERCENT DISTRIBUTION OF EDUCATIONAL ATTAINMENT FOR THE TOTAL POPULATION (25 YEARS OLD AND OVER): 1950 TO 1957

| Age | None | Elementary school | | | High school | | College | | School years not reported | Median school yrs. completed |
		1 to 4 years	5 to 7 years	8 years	1 to 3 years	4 years	1 to 3 years	4 years or more		
TOTAL										
25 years and over...	-0.1	-1.7	-3.1	-2.3	0.8	5.8	0.1	1.5	-0.9	1.3
25 to 29 years....	...	-1.8	-2.1	-1.9	-0.9	5.0	0.2	2.8	-1.2	0.2
30 to 34 years....	-0.1	-1.2	-3.4	-3.8	0.5	6.4	0.6	2.5	-1.4	0.5
35 to 44 years....	-0.1	-1.9	-5.1	-4.6	0.7	11.8	0.4	1.1	-1.3	1.7
45 to 54 years....	-0.6	-2.7	-14.1	-3.2	2.6	6.6	0.8	1.6	-1.0	1.2
55 to 64 years....	-1.0	-3.0	-2.4	-0.6	1.7	3.9	0.8	1.2	-0.5	0.3
65 years and over.	0.6	-0.6	-2.0	-0.8	1.0	1.1	0.2	0.7	0.2	0.1
MALES										
25 years and over...	-0.1	-1.8	-3.2	-2.3	0.9	4.5	0.4	2.3	-0.9	1.3
25 to 29 years....	-0.1	-2.0	-1.7	-1.6	-1.4	3.5	0.4	4.0	-1.3	0.2
30 to 34 years....	-0.1	-1.4	-2.7	-4.2	1.9	2.2	0.8	5.2	-1.7	0.6
35 to 44 years....	-0.3	-2.0	-5.2	-4.5	0.6	10.4	0.5	1.8	-1.5	1.8
45 to 54 years....	-0.4	-2.5	-4.4	-3.2	2.3	5.8	1.1	2.1	-0.8	0.9
55 to 64 years....	-0.8	-3.4	-2.4	-0.1	2.1	3.0	0.7	1.2	-0.5	0.1
65 years and over.	0.6	-0.2	-2.2	-0.6	1.0	0.3	-0.3	1.3	0.2	0.1
FEMALES										
25 years and over...	-0.2	-1.6	-3.1	-2.4	0.7	6.9	-0.1	0.7	-0.8	1.2
25 to 29 years....	...	-1.8	-2.5	-2.2	-0.5	6.5	-0.1	1.6	-1.1	0.2
30 to 34 years....	-0.2	-1.0	-3.9	-3.6	-0.8	10.3	0.4	-0.1	-1.2	0.4
35 to 44 years....	...	-1.9	-5.0	-4.9	0.6	13.1	-1.3	0.4	-1.2	1.4
45 to 54 years....	-0.9	-2.8	-3.8	-3.2	2.9	7.2	0.6	1.1	-1.2	1.4
55 to 64 years....	-1.1	-2.6	-2.4	-1.2	1.2	4.6	0.8	1.3	-0.5	0.3
65 years and over.	0.7	-0.9	-1.8	-1.1	0.9	1.6	...	0.2	0.3	0.1

Source: Current Population Reports, P-20, No-77, 1957.

Note: The differences shown here were computed by subtracting the percent distribution by columns in 1950 from the corresponding percent distribution in 1957.

aged 25 to 29 years of age (whose median is 12.3 years of schooling).

The urban-rural differential with respect to educational attainment is changing only very slowly. The rural-farm areas are gradually adopting the pattern of the urban areas, where almost all of the population completes grammar school.

| Years of school completed | Difference between total and rural farm population | | |
	1957	1950	Change, 1950-57
College:			
4 years or more...	5.1	4.0	1.1
1 to 3 years......	2.7	2.9	-0.2
High school:			
4 years..........	7.8	7.6	0.2
1 to 3 years......	2.7	2.9	-0.2

Continued

| Years of school completed | Difference between total and rural farm population | | |
	1957	1950	Change, 1950-57
Elementary school:			
8 years..........	-6.5	-5.8	-0.7
5 to 7 years......	-6.9	-6.8	-0.1
1 to 4 years......	-5.3	-5.4	0.1
No school years completed.........	-0.8	-0.6	-0.2
School years not reported..........	1.2	1.2	...

Source: Current Population Reports, Series P-20, No. 77, 1957, Tables 1, 2, and 4.

Regional Differences in Educational Attainment. The age, sex, color, and urban-rural differences noted above are present in each region. However, there is also a set of inter-regional differences.

Table 13-11.—PERCENTAGE-POINT CHANGE IN PERCENT DISTRIBUTION OF EDUCATIONAL ATTAINMENT FOR THE NONWHITE POPULATION (25 YEARS OLD AND OVER): 1950 TO 1957

| Age | None | Elementary school | | | High school | | College | | School years not reported | Median school yrs. completed |
		1 to 4 years	5 to 7 years	8 years	1 to 3 years	4 years	1 to 3 years	4 years or more		
TOTAL										
25 years and over...	0.2	-4.8	-3.6	0.7	3.5	3.8	0.4	0.6	-0.6	0.9
25 to 29 years....	-0.9	-6.3	-6.0	1.0	4.0	5.9	0.5	1.2	0.4	1.2
30 to 34 years....	-1.3	-6.1	-5.6	0.8	6.1	8.2	0.2	-0.5	-2.1	1.2
35 to 44 years....	-0.2	-5.8	-6.1	-0.1	5.4	5.6	0.5	1.5	-0.9	1.1
45 to 54 years....	-0.5	-6.8	-1.9	1.8	3.1	2.4	0.5	1.0	0.2	0.8
55 to 64 years....	3.6	-4.6	-0.3	1.0	2.3	0.4	-0.2	-0.8	-1.5	0.2
65 years and over.	0.2	0.6	-0.1	-0.2	-0.8	...	-0.6	0.4	0.4	-0 1
MALES										
25 years and over...	0.5	-5.5	-2.8	0.3	3.5	3.4	0.2	0.6	-0.2	0.9
25 to 29 years....	-1.1	-7.8	-3.5	0.6	4.7	4.2	0.4	0.8	1.9	1.0
30 to 34 years....	-1.6	-5.8	-3.5	0.1	5.8	8.7	0.1	-1.2	-2.4	1.1
35 to 44 years....	-0.1	-6.9	-4.6	0.3	5.5	3.6	0.6	2.7	-1.1	1.2
45 to 54 years....	-0.3	-7.8	-2.0	1.4	2.9	3.5	1.0	0.4	1.1	1.0
55 to 64 years....	4.2	-4.7	0.6	-0.6	3.0	0 2	-0.6	-1.0	-1.2	0.1
65 years and over.	2.3	0.7	-2.2	-1.0	-1.3	0.6	-0.8	0.6	1.1	-0.3
FEMALES										
25 years and over...	...	-4.0	-4.4	1.2	3.3	4.2	0.2	0.6	-1.0	0.9
25 to 29 years....	-0.5	-5.0	-8.0	1.5	3.3	7.4	0.6	1.8	-1.0	1.4
30 to 34 years....	-0.9	-6.3	-7.3	1.5	6.5	7.8	0.4	0.3	-1.8	1.2
35 to 44 years....	-0.1	-4.7	-7.5	-0.5	5.2	7.4	0.4	0.3	-0.7	1.1
45 to 54 years....	-0.5	-5.6	-1.8	2.2	3.3	1.3	0.2	1.6	-0.7	0.7
55 to 64 years....	3.1	-4.4	-1.2	2.4	1.8	0.5	0.3	-0.6	-1.8	0.3
65 years and over.	-1.6	0.6	1.8	0.6	-0.3	-0.5	-0.3	0.3	-0.3	0.2

Source: Current Population Reports, P-20, No-77.

Note: The differences shown here were computed by subtracting the percent distribution (by columns) in 1950 from the corresponding percent distribution in 1957.

At each age, the educational attainment of the population in the South is below that of the other regions, while in the West the level of educational attainment at each age is generally higher than it is in other regions. In the South, the white-nonwhite differential is unusually large. This differential in amount of education completed is due to past neglect with respect to educational opportunities for nonwhites; at the present time nonwhites suffer no more neglect, educationally, in the South than they do in other regions (see Part I of this chapter). These regional differences are due in part to differences in urban-rural composition, in part to differences in the quality and quantity of educational facilities provided, and in part to the fact that so many of the better educated persons migrate from regions of lower opportunity to regions of higher opportunity.

In interpreting these interregional differences, one must keep in mind the fact that they are a net resultant of conditions that have existed over the past 50 to 75 years. These differences should not be used to evaluate the current educational programs of the various regions. Such programs are best evaluated in terms of school enrollment data, or educational attainment data, for young adults 20 to 24 or 25 to 29 years of age.

CONCLUSION

This brief introduction to the subject of educational enrollment and educational attainment demonstrates that large and meaningful differences are present among the various population groups. In later chapters, the educational variable will be

Table 13-12.—MEDIAN YEARS OF SCHOOL COMPLETED BY THE POPULATION 25 YEARS OF AGE AND OVER, IN EACH REGION, BY AGE, SEX, AND COLOR: 1950

Age and sex	Northeast		North Central		South		West	
	Total	Nonwhite	Total	Nonwhite	Total	Nonwhite	Total	Nonwhite
Male...............	9.4	8.3	9.0	8.2	8.4	5.3	10.7	8.5
25 to 29 years..........	12.1	9.9	12.2	10.1	10.1	7.1	12.4	11.0
30 to 34 years..........	12.0	9.0	12.0	9.3	9.5	6.5	12.3	10.3
35 to 39 years..........	10.7	8.5	10.8	8.6	8.7	5.9	12.1	8.8
40 to 44 years..........	9.9	8.1	9.9	8.1	8.4	5.5	11.0	8.2
45 to 49 years..........	8.9	7.7	8.8	7.6	8.1	4.9	9.8	7.6
50 to 54 years..........	8.7	7.4	8.7	7.2	8.0	4.7	9.1	7.2
55 to 59 years..........	8.6	7.0	8.5	6.7	7.7	4.3	8.8	6.9
60 to 64 years..........	8.3	6.6	8.3	6.3	7.3	4.1	8.6	6.8
65 to 69 years..........	8.3	6.0	8.2	5.7	6.6	3.6	8.5	6.2
70 to 74 years..........	8.2	5.5	8.2	5.1	6.5	3.4	8.4	5.7
75 years and over.......	8.1	5.1	8.1	4.4	6.1	1.6	8.3	3.9
Female.............	9.7	8.5	9.9	8.6	8.7	6.3	11.7	8.9
25 to 29 years..........	12.2	10.3	12.2	10.6	10.8	8.0	12.4	11.7
30 to 34 years..........	12.0	9.4	12.1	9.8	10.1	7.5	12.3	10.5
35 to 39 years..........	10.6	8.7	11.3	8.9	9.4	7.0	12.2	9.4
40 to 44 years..........	10.0	8.3	10.6	8.5	8.9	6.4	12.0	8.6
45 to 49 years..........	9.0	8.0	9.3	8.1	8.5	5.9	10.9	8.2
50 to 54 years..........	8.8	7.5	8.8	7.7	8.3	5.4	10.3	8.0
55 to 59 years..........	8.5	7.2	8.6	7.3	8.1	5.1	9.3	7.6
60 to 64 years..........	8.4	6.8	8.5	6.8	8.0	4.7	8.9	6.8
65 to 69 years..........	8.4	6.3	8.4	6.1	7.3	4.1	8.8	6.2
70 to 74 years..........	8.4	5.8	8.4	5.5	7.4	3.8	8.7	5.5
75 years and over.......	8.3	5.4	8.3	5.0	7.0	1.8	8.6	4.1

Source: U. S. Census of Population: 1950, Characteristics of the Population, U. S. Summary, Table 154.

so employed as to show that it is a major differentiator with respect to income, occupation, fertility, marital status, and other population factors. Despite the fact that these data cannot reflect the quality of the education which is available, or indicate how well the various members of the population have mastered the materials presented to them, they are an excellent rough measure of the rising level of general competence among the population.

Note: The future educational attainment of the population is discussed in Chapter 26.

Chapter 14

INTERNATIONAL MIGRATION AND NATIONAL ORIGINS OF THE POPULATION

A BRIEF HISTORY OF UNITED STATES IMMIGRATION

As a nation whose population is composed of immigrants and the descendants of immigrants, the United States has a complex migration history. An understanding of this history is indispensable to anyone attempting to appreciate the present ethnic and racial background of the population. Moreover, ethnic origin is still an important factor in the lives of a great many people. The fact that all but a small fraction of United States citizens are now native born (93.3 percent in 1950), and that the proportion of foreign-born persons is declining (see Chapter 7), does not mean that complete cultural homogeneity has been achieved. The number of foreign-born persons is still quite large, and the number who are children and grandchildren of foreign-born persons is much larger still. To use a familiar metaphor, this nation has been the "melting pot" of many racial, national, and ethnic groups, each of which has its distinctive cultural traits. These groups have become adjusted to each other generation by generation, and a dominant American culture has gradually emerged. The fact that the population no longer contains large numbers of foreign-born persons does not mean that ethnicity has disappeared; the children and grandchildren of many foreign-born persons retain some of their unique cultural traits, and some are forced, by their ethnic backgrounds, to occupy lower statuses than they might otherwise achieve. One has only to watch the enthusiasm with which a St. Patrick's Day parade is put on by Irishmen who never saw Ireland, or to observe the customs of French Canadians who have never been to France, to appreciate how important cultural origins can be in explaining a population's behavior. The politician knows that he must say and do certain specific things if he is to get the "Italian vote," the "Polish vote," and the votes of many other such ethnic groups composed of the second- and third-generation offspring of immigrants. To reemphasize: the phenomenon of "cultural pluralism" is not entirely a thing of the past; immigrants from many different cultures are continuing to arrive in the United States each year, and the children of immigrants comprise a substantial percentage of the population. Although the flow of immigration is now controlled, it is still large in comparison with the number of immigrants admitted by most other nations of the world. In recent years there have been large migrations from Puerto Rico and Mexico, and a relaxation of immigration quotas in order to admit some of the many thousands of displaced persons and refugees left by World War II, and these new kinds of migrants have joined the streams coming from the more traditional sources.

In 1790, when the Republic was formed, the white population was preponderantly British in descent. There were comparatively few Germans, Irish, and Dutch, very small groups of French, Canadians, Belgians, Swiss, Mexicans, and Swedes--and almost no others. The following estimated distribution indicates the composition of the population in 1790.

Country of origin	Percent of white population
Total.........................	100.0
Great Britain and Northern Ireland	77.0
Germany.......................	7.4
Irish Free State..............	4.4
Netherlands...................	3.3
France........................	1.9
Canada........................	1.6
Belgium.......................	1.5
Switzerland...................	0.9
Mexico........................	0.7
Sweden........................	0.5
All other.....................	0.8

Source: 70th Congress, 2nd Session, Senate Document 259. Immigration Quotas on the Basis of National Origin, p.5 (as reported by W. S. Thompson and P. K. Whelpton in Population Trends in the United States, 1933, p. 91).

In addition to the white population, there was a substantial population consisting of involuntary immigrants and their children--19 percent of the total population in 1790 was Negro.

The "Old" Migration. Because official immigration records are not available for years prior to 1820, the volume of immigration between 1790 and 1820 is not known, nor is there any way of knowing which countries the migrants came from. However, it is believed that there were very few migrants, and that they came primarily from England and Ireland. The statistical record of immigration, by country of origin, is summarized in Table 14-1.[1] According to this table, not until the nineteenth century was well underway (about 1830) did the many and diverse national groups begin their massive exodus to the United States. In about 1830 the Germans and the Irish began to arrive in greatly increasing numbers, far outstripping the migrants from England. The Irish immigration reached a peak near the middle of the century; a total of 1,350,000 Irish are recorded as having arrived in the United States during the 8 years from 1847 to 1854. The German immigration reached its peak between 1880 and 1892 (although it had been very high since 1830); in these 12 years more than 1,770,000 Germans came to this country. Large numbers of both Irish and German immigrants continued to arrive for some time even after these peak years but in somewhat less than "flood" proportions.

The Chinese migration began in about 1855, and continued at a rather impressive rate for 30 years. Landing on the West Coast, these migrants provided much of the unskilled labor and the muscle power needed for the swift development of the West. Scandinavians joined the stream of immigrants heading for America's Midwest, and, immediately after the Civil War, great numbers of Swedes, Norwegians, and Danes flowed into Wisconsin, Minnesota, the Dakotas, Iowa, Nebraska, and the territory even farther west.

Between 1830 and 1885, the immigration came preponderantly from Northwestern Europe and from Germany. Since there was comparatively

---

[1] Official statistics concerning immigration are notoriously incomplete and inexact with respect to the era of mass immigration. This fact has already been noted in Chapter 7, but must be restated here with particular reference to country of origin. The statistics often classify persons according to country of debarkation rather than country of birth or of previous residence. The fact that early statistics were kept only for third-class, or steerage passengers may also have biased the statistics which show country of origin. Moreover, it is known that there has been a considerable amount of unregistered immigration among particular ethnic or national groups, as in the case of Chinese and Mexicans who entered the country in violation of the regulations.

Immigration from Canada has always been a rather large but vaguely defined stream. During the nation's early years no record whatsoever was kept of this movement; but ever since records of overland movement have been maintained, little cognizance has been taken of the fact that many so-called Canadian immigrants have been immigrants from other parts of the world who have used Canada as a stopover point for a few years on their way to the United States.

Many immigrants to the United States eventually returned home, and although there must have been rather large differences in this respect among the various ethnic and national groups, no data are available concerning return-emigrants according to country of origin. For all the above-mentioned reasons, although Table 14-1 provides a generally informative picture of the nations and cultures from which the United States drew her immigrants, it must be remembered that the picture is very rough and is only approximate. Extensive research could refine it, but as yet such research has not been completed except in the case of a few specific nationality groups.

Table 14-1.—NUMBER OF IMMIGRANTS TO THE UNITED STATES, BY CONTINENT, REGION, AND NATION OF ORIGIN: 1820 TO 1957

Year	All countries	Europe, total	Northwestern Europe				Central Europe		
			Great Britain	Ireland[2]	Scandinavia	Other northwestern	Germany	Poland	Other central
1955 to 1957...	886,282	437,082	58,789	19,056	16,539	50,876	134,358	963	29,915
1950 to 1954...	1,099,035	716,759	83,141	21,471	27,054	57,027	381,010	1,232	57,444
1945 to 1949...	653,019	375,466	107,921	21,029	19,212	49,587	91,322	5,395	18,756
1940 to 1944...	203,589	97,577	17,074	1,471	3,288	24,524	28,184[1]	2,182	5,332
1935 to 1939...	272,422	185,754	9,769	3,703	4,876	14,631	73,156[1]	9,060	19,372
1930 to 1934...	426,953	259,519	44,466	32,070	12,069	17,463	45,951	16,495	17,836
1925 to 1929...	1,520,910	789,407	117,654	125,281	84,051	44,625	237,531	39,435	32,452
1920 to 1924...	2,774,600	1,787,303	220,015	81,456	120,684	93,503	149,103	183,881	178,836
1915 to 1919...	1,172,679	532,391	63,348	29,035	58,511	35,814	13,032	(3)	25,074
1910 to 1914...	5,174,701	4,524,169	308,530	137,410	179,764	125,999	161,195	(3)	1,129,653
1905 to 1909...	4,947,239	4,538,980	340,041	178,059	226,042	114,415	173,794	(3)	1,217,983
1900 to 1904...	3,255,149	3,095,445	129,477	166,881	262,166	65,753	154,928	(3)	783,393
1895 to 1899...	1,373,649	1,310,941	92,500	171,788	122,614	30,095	121,178	10,372	233,823
1890 to 1894...	2,320,645	2,269,017	236,259	233,922	268,115	91,532	457,894	97,421	300,236
1885 to 1889...	2,210,974	2,138,362	410,704	308,854	294,496	88,037	524,966	23,900	176,239
1880 to 1884...	3,037,594	2,501,695	400,196	365,207	377,287	112,760	920,215	19,010	138,548
1875 to 1879...	855,636	645,947	152,882	108,046	71,993	47,541	172,919	3,478	30,443
1870 to 1874...	1,886,501	1,606,250	425,565	314,218	136,108	70,830	578,850	7,538	29,684
1865 to 1869...	1,374,018	1,222,768	338,625	212,195	86,170	48,935	519,615	1,434	2,868
1860 to 1864...	707,243	655,085	194,361	215,224	10,320	22,299	204,119	452	477
1855 to 1859...	897,027	812,339	205,828	220,426	9,678	42,160	321,821	721	...
1850 to 1854...	1,917,527	1,807,435	239,494	809,060	15,751	80,928	654,251	366	...
1845 to 1849...	1,027,306	989,259	154,983	474,441	8,926	63,616	284,897	22	...
1840 to 1844...	400,031	380,045	63,589	181,704	4,134	28,123	100,537	83	...
1835 to 1839...	307,939	281,709	49,985	116,621	1,432	26,057	85,469	275	...
1830 to 1834...	230,442	141,070	24,365	54,051	644	19,100	39,257	91	...
1825 to 1829...	89,813	72,265	17,131	39,965	162	9,281	38,41	3	...
1820 to 1824...	38,689	27,026	9,205	11,652	102	2,694	1,912	16	...

Source: Historical Statistics of the United States, 1789-1945, Table B-304 and Statistical Abstract of the United States, 1958, Table 108. For details of changing definitions see footnotes to sources.

[1]Austria included with Germany, 1938 to 1945.
[2]Includes Northern Ireland.
[3]From 1899 to 1919 Poland is included with Austria-Hungary, Germany, and Russia.

little restriction on immigration, the number of new arrivals varied with the changes that took place, both in the United States and in Europe, in economic and political conditions. As Figure 14-1 illustrates, the flow of immigrants was very erratic--in some years it was a veritable flood and in other years it was, comparatively, a trickle. When there was financial panic, depression, or war in the United States, migration from Europe slackened; when there was famine or political upheaval across the Atlantic and prosperity in the United States, migration tended to be large. New

land to settle was not the only opportunity the United States offered to immigrants; there were railroads to build, forests to convert into lumber, mines to work, and cities to build. The course of economic development paced the flow of immigration.

The "New" Immigration. Although many of these migrants from Northwestern Europe and Germany met with temporary hostility and, in scattered instances, with mistreatment, it was recognized that they were needed to help man the expanding economy, and they were generally accepted as poten-

Table 14-1.—NUMBER OF IMMIGRANTS TO THE UNITED STATES, BY CONTINENT, REGION, AND NATION OF ORIGIN: 1820 TO 1957—Continued

Year	Eastern Europe		Southern Europe		Asia, total	Asia			
	U.S.S.R. and Baltic states	Other eastern	Italy	Other southern		Turkey	China	Japan	Other Asia
1955 to 1957...	1,561	1,086	90,326	33,613	48,270	179	4,052	16,946	27,093
1950 to 1954...	2,536	827	54,331	30,686	31,742	74	2,660	10,610	18,398
1945 to 1949...	2,603	1,175	44,485	13,981	25,075	107	14,132	1,098	9,738
1940 to 1944...	2,076	1,070	6,024	6,352	4,839	105	1,940	459	2,335
1935 to 1939...	3,406	2,572	34,814	10,395	7,006	90	2,050	506	4,360
1930 to 1934...	5,869	4,642	50,239	12,419	10,960	349	3,824	2,177	4,610
1925 to 1929...	14,479	8,799	67,489	17,611	17,798	311	7,925	3,421	6,141
1920 to 1924...	73,923	78,205	460,644	147,053	92,572	23,769	22,723	38,636	7,444
1915 to 1919...	52,390	4,572	125,083	125,532	66,546	5,668	11,116	46,561	3,201
1910 to 1914...	1,054,608	107,323	1,104,833	214,854	132,041	83,900	9,800	30,564	7,777
1905 to 1909...	936,676	105,188	1,092,051	154,731	128,018	37,823	8,011	73,306	8,878
1900 to 1904...	564,625	48,641	838,424	81,157	109,962	28,320	11,873	66,406	3,363
1895 to 1899...	203,978	5,479	298,950	20,164	38,530	20,349	9,074	8,860	247
1890 to 1894...	246,123	4,928	304,811	27,776	19,208	3,614	6,194	5,138	4,262
1885 to 1889...	133,127	6,400	159,444	12,195	3,698	1,089	216	1,516	877
1880 to 1884...	49,571	822	108,216	9,863	66,073	9	65,581	67	416
1875 to 1879...	26,872	155	19,976	11,642	68,756	50	68,408	20	278
1870 to 1874...	8,305	164	26,320	8,668	65,053	13	64,731	173	136
1865 to 1869...	1,159	80	6,310	5,377	27,439	2	27,221	137	79
1860 to 1864...	511	47	3,543	3,732	26,842	...	26,807	1	34
1855 to 1859...	384	52	5,596	5,673	22,826	...	22,788	...	38
1850 to 1854...	39	42	3,047	4,457	13,160	...	13,145	...	15
1845 to 1849...	299	21	902	1,152	48	...	20	...	28
1840 to 1844...	221	24	574	1,056	28	...	12	...	16
1835 to 1839...	50	4	381	1,435	33	...	8	...	25
1830 to 1834...	230	4	1,844	1,484	14	...	...	...	14
1825 to 1829...	41	10	224	1,607	8	...	2	...	6
1820 to 1824...	45	9	206	1,185	7	...	1	...	6

tial good citizens. However, in about 1880, the ethnic and national composition of the migration streams began to change drastically; the flow of immigrants from Italy, Poland, Russia, the Baltic States, and Southern Europe began to assume substantial proportions, and by 1900 these new arrivals dwarfed migration from all other sources. In 1907, for example, the estimated 1,200,000 migrants who were received from Europe were divided by origin as follows:

"Old" sources	Number of persons
Northwestern Europe..............	190,000
Germany.........................	38,000

"New" sources	Number of persons
Poland and other Central Europe...	338,000
Italy............................	286,000
Russia and Baltic States.........	259,000
Other Eastern and Southern Europe.	89,000

Thus, only about one-fifth of the total flow of immigrants was coming from the sources which had provided the "old" immigration. Whereas a large proportion of the "old" migration were Protestants (except for Irish Catholics and some Catholic Germans), an overwhelming percentage of the new immigrants were Catholic, Jewish, or Greek Orthodox in their religious affiliation. Meanwhile, beginning in about 1900, the Japanese

Table 14-1.—NUMBER OF IMMIGRANTS TO THE UNITED STATES, BY CONTINENT, REGION, AND NATION OF ORIGIN: 1820 TO 1957—Continued

Year	America, total	America			Africa, total	Austral- asia, total	Australasia		All other countries
		Canada and New- foundland	Mexico	Other			Australia and New Zealand	Other	
1955 to 1957...	389,309	121,152	154,343	113,814	4,154	3,832	3,331	501	3,635
1950 to 1954...	326,108	152,275	69,804	104,029	4,862	6,542	3,082	3,460	13,022[4]
1945 to 1949...	230,545	107,857	37,873	84,815	5,228	12,841	12,334	507	3,864
1940 to 1944...	97,890	53,054	18,285	26,551	1,492	1,421	1,218	203	370
1935 to 1939...	77,488	53,131	10,765	13,592	770	950	865	85	454
1930 to 1934...	152,831	109,572	21,944	21,315	1,350	2,290	2,185	105	3
1925 to 1929...	708,219	422,433	243,171	42,615	2,445	3,041	2,881	160	...
1920 to 1924...	883,059	526,853	255,774	100,432	3,917	6,819	6,458	361	930
1915 to 1919...	564,113	379,399	96,976	87,738	2,882	6,515	5,939	576	232
1910 to 1914...	506,426	329,316	88,358	88,752	5,985	5,824	5,341	483	256
1905 to 1909...	233,797	117,600	28,358	87,839	5,224	7,959	7,637	302	33,261
1900 to 1904...	44,012	5,467	2,830	35,715	1,102	4,396	3,534	862	232
1895 to 1899...	22,291	2,487	625	19,179	193	1,477	990	487	217
1890 to 1894...	15,059	611	109	14,339	239	3,227	2,235	992	13,895
1885 to 1889...	60,360	38,405	323	21,632	526	7,680	3,196	4,484	348
1880 to 1884...	464,466	454,460	2,082	7,924	237	4,681	4,075	606	442
1875 to 1879...	135,638	125,617	2,707	7,314	189	4,916	4,640	276	190
1870 to 1874...	209,372	198,693	2,426	8,253	182	5,080	4,329	751	564
1865 to 1869...	108,257	101,020	1,173	6,064	182	...	...	...	15,372
1860 to 1864...	22,035	16,958	784	4,293	225	...	...	...	3,056
1855 to 1859...	36,416	28,690	1,988	5,738	73	...	...	...	25,373
1850 to 1854...	47,729	35,481	1,458	10,790	11	...	...	...	49,192
1845 to 1849...	32,684	24,240	1,324	7,120	18	...	...	...	5,297
1840 to 1844...	17,832	10,045	1,745	6,042	43	...	...	...	2,083
1835 to 1839...	18,483	8,688	3,021	6,774	42	...	...	...	7,672
1830 to 1834...	13,422	3,187	4,166	6,069	8	...	...	...	75,928
1825 to 1829...	7,646	1,378	3,680	2,588	12	...	...	...	9,882
1820 to 1824...	2,009	919	155	935	3	...	...	...	9,644

[4]Philippine Islands included with "All other countries" through 1954; beginning in 1955 included in "Other Asia."

began to arrive in greatly increased numbers, and in 1908 Mexicans began to cross the border in unprecedently large mass immigrations. Once the first arrivals had established themselves, all of these "new" sources began to account for large quantities of each year's immigrants. Native-born Americans and immigrants from Northwestern Europe began to be apprehensive, feeling that this different and unprecedently large flood of new-comers was somehow a threat to the cultural and economic progress of the nation. They attempted to set up restrictions and regulations concerning which nationalities, and how many of each, could enter, and this led to the imposition of the migra-tion "quotas." (Figure 14-2 illustrates the change in the sources of immigrants between 1820 and 1957.)

Immigration by Quota. After the turn of the century, public sentiment in favor of restricting the numbers, and regulating the source, of immigration became extremely intense and widespread. The empty lands of the Midwest had all been homesteaded, and the colonization of the West and the Southwest was well underway. The great rail-roads had been built, and the end of the forests was already in sight. The "new migration" flowed into the large cities, where ethnic islands were established. New York City, Chicago, and other

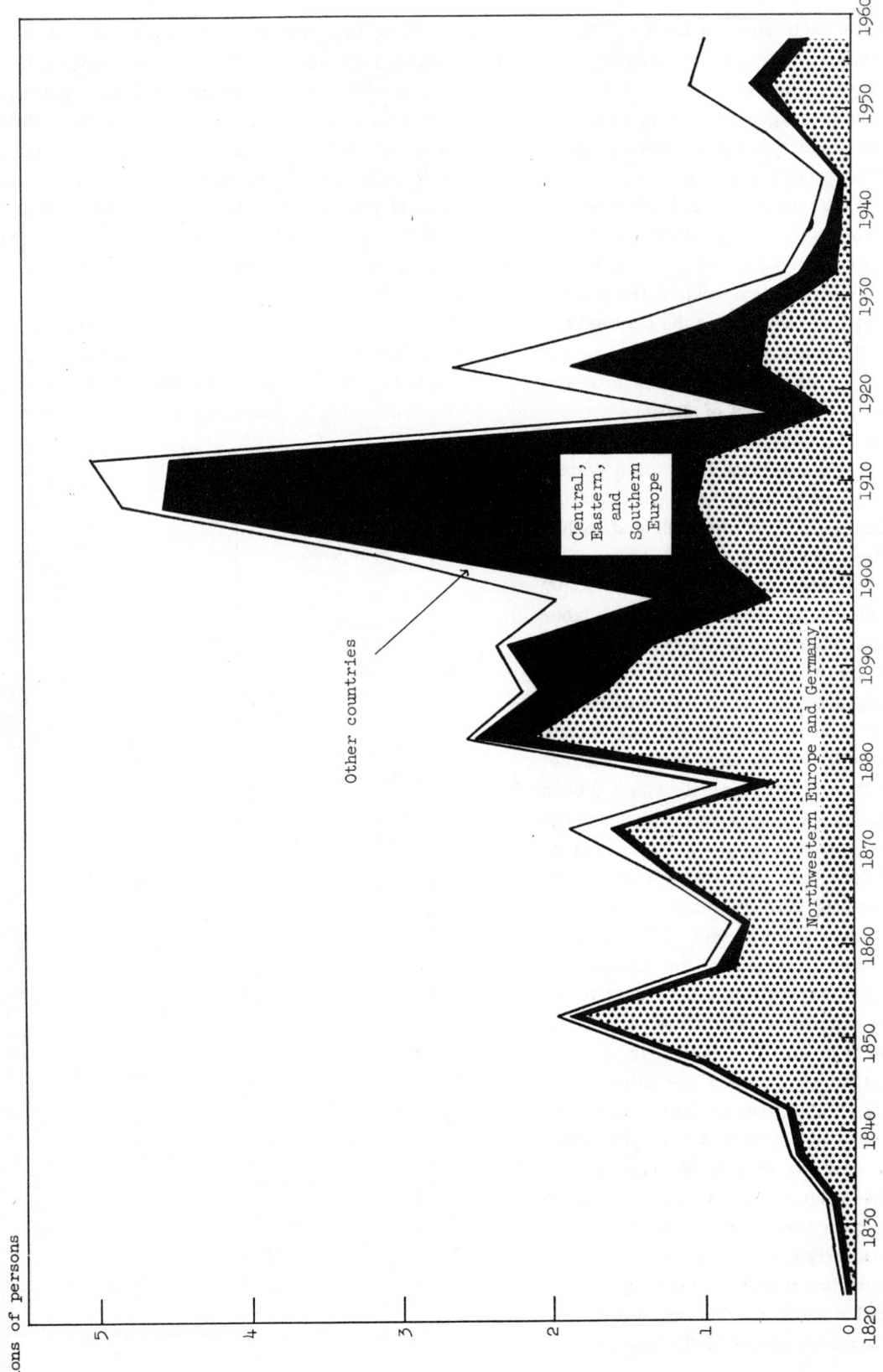

FIGURE 14-1. NUMBER OF IMMIGRANTS (5-YEAR TOTALS) TO THE UNITED STATES, BY REGION OF ORIGIN: 1820 TO 1957

large metropolises each came to have its "Little Italy, " "Little Poland, " etc., which were separate neighborhoods and communities. In these enclaves, the native languages and the customs connected with dress, food, and ritual were kept alive. Schools, newspapers, and churches were established to serve the needs of particular ethnic groups. The community at large developed antipathies toward these groups, and students of society predicted that this separatism would make assimilation very slow and difficult for the members of such colonies. Prejudice against the Chinese had already led to their exclusion by law and treaty, beginning in 1882. The inflow of Japanese workmen was "voluntarily" curtailed by Japan in 1907, in response to pressure from the United States. Sentiment in favor of limiting immigration from Southern and Eastern Europe mounted, and such a limitation was imposed by the Immigration Act of 1921. Support for this action came from many different segments of the population--from labor unions and labor groups, from farmers and businessmen, and from "race haters"--and arguments in its favor ranged all the way from economics to eugenics. The annual "quota" of immigrants which the act established for each country was set at 3 percent of the number of people who had been born in that country and who were residents in the United States as reported by the 1910 Census of Population. (Before this time, the restrictions on immigration were largely qualitative, and were intended to exclude certain classes of defective or undesirable persons, irrespective of national origins.) Since the quotas of 1921 still gave to the "new" migration sources a large share of the total 150,000 persons to be admitted each year, the law was revised in 1924; it followed the same principle as the Act of 1921, but based the quotas on the national origins of the foreign-born population as of 1890. (In 1890 the stream of "new" immigrants had not been flowing long enough to build up a large foreign-born population of Southern and Eastern European origin.) The Act of 1924 also called for a study that would determine more exactly the national origins of the population, and specified that, beginning July 1, 1929, the number

comprising the quota of any country should have the same ratio to 150,000 as the number of persons in the United States of that national origin had to the total population of the United States. This act also established minimum quotas of 100 persons for all quota areas, and continued the exclusion of Orientals. The quotas which were established in 1929, and which were in effect for nearly a quarter of a century (until 1952), are reported in Table 14-2.

There has been much criticism of the quota system and of the philosophy on which the quotas are based. Many argue that cultural homogeneity is not necessarily a good thing (and that perhaps it

Table 14-2.—ANNUAL IMMIGRATION QUOTAS BY COUNTRY: 1929 AND 1952

Country	Quota effective 1929	1952 Immigration and Nationality Act
All countries........	153,714	154,657
Europe..................	150,591	149,667
Austria..............	1,413	1,405
Belgium..............	1,304	1,297
Bulgaria.............	100	100
Czechoslovakia........	2,874	2,859
Denmark..............	1,181	1,175
Finland..............	569	566
France...............	3,086	3,069
Germany..............	25,957	25,814
Great Britain........	65,721	65,361
Greece...............	307	308
Hungary..............	869	865
Iceland..............	100	100
Ireland..............	17,853	17,756
Italy................	5,802	5,645
Netherlands..........	3,153	3,136
Norway...............	2,377	2,364
Poland...............	6,524	6,488
Portugal.............	440	438
Rumania..............	295	289
Spain................	252	250
Sweden...............	3,314	3,295
Switzerland..........	1,707	1,698
Turkey...............	226	225
U.S.S.R..............	2,784	2,697
Yugoslavia...........	845	933
Other Europe.........	1,538	1,534
Asia..................	1,323	2,990
Africa................	1,200	1,400
Australia.............	200	600
All others...........	400	...

Source: Statistical Abstract of the United States: 1958, Table 103.

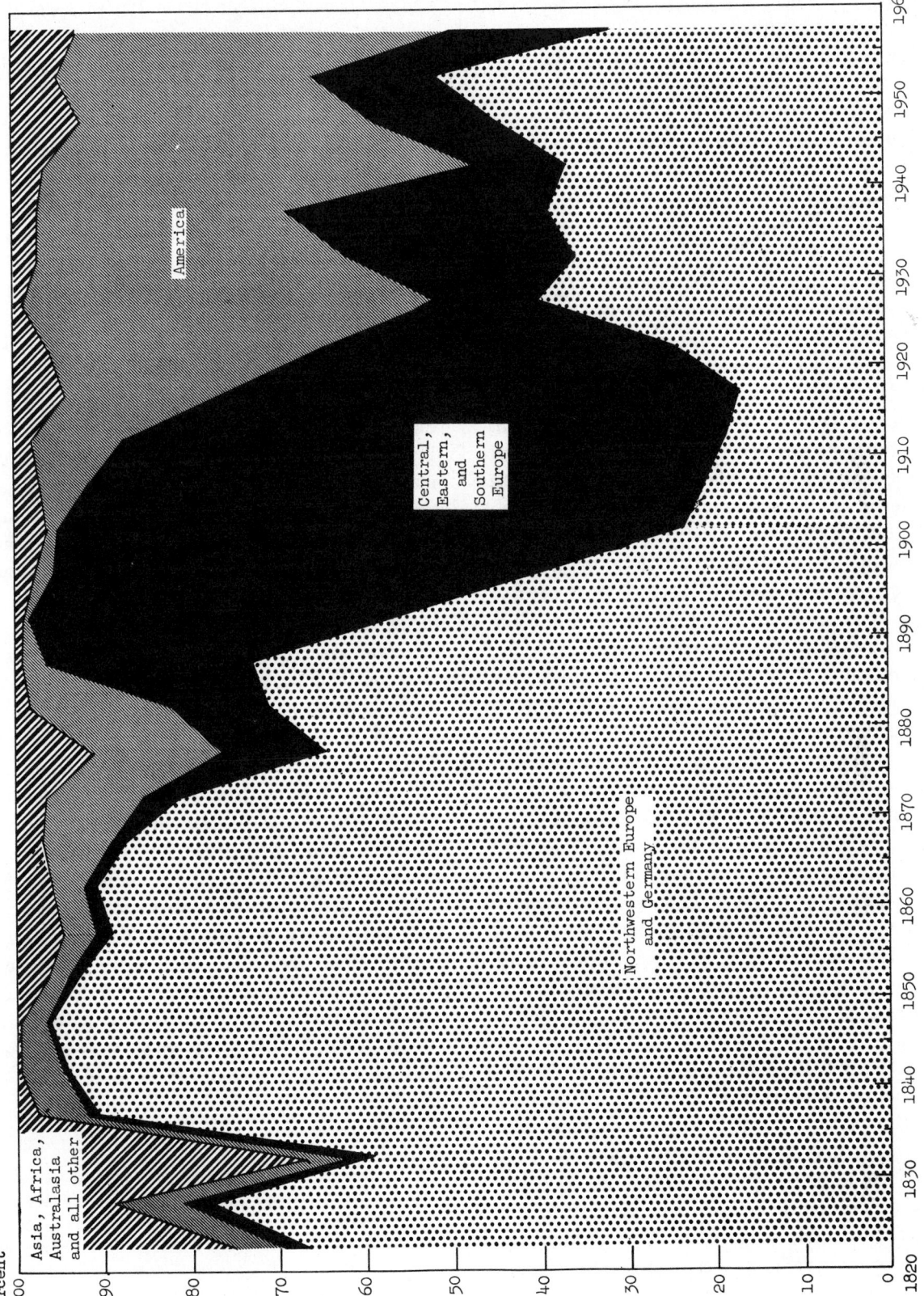

Percent

FIGURE 14-2.   PERCENT COMPOSITION OF IMMIGRATION, BY REGION OF ORIGIN: 1820 TO 1957

is perilous to a democracy in times like the present), and that the United States should continuously absorb persons from all of the world's cultures in order to avoid losing insight into the problems faced by other peoples.

Whatever opinions one may have concerning the course of events which it set in motion, the quota system did have the intended effect of curtailing sharply the flow of immigration from Southern, Eastern, and Central Europe (except Germany). However, it did not revive migration from the "old" sources. The quotas set for the nations of Northern and Western Europe were larger than the numbers applying for admission, and these nations failed regularly to fill their allotted quotas; in almost every year between 1925 and the present the total quota allotted to these nations has been undersubscribed by a rather large margin. During the years of the economic depression, 1930 to 1939, the margin was very wide. For example, the volume of migration from Great Britain has been so small that only between 5 and 40 percent of the large quota of 65,000 has been used in any year since 1925. Thus, a part of the great decline in immigration during the years 1925 to 1945 was not a direct result of the quota system. Part of this decline was caused by economic recession, war, and the disinclination of Northwestern Europeans to leave the country of their birth and seek citizenship in America. This reluctance has been due, in no small part, to the greatly improved level of living achieved by many of these countries. Life today in Sweden, England, or Denmark may be less luxurious in certain ways than it is in the United States, but the economic opportunities for the citizen with education or skill may be just as great, or greater, there than in the United States.

In addition to the quota immigration, a substantial number of persons enter each year as nonquota immigrants. This category consists of immigrants born in Canada, Mexico, Cuba, Haiti, the Dominican Republic, the Canal Zone, and the countries of Central and South America, and their spouses and children under age 21 if accompanying, or following to join, such immigrants; spouses and children of citizens of the United States; ministers of religious denominations and their spouses and children if accompanying, or following to join, such ministers; and certain refugees admitted by special legislation.

Immigration after World War II: Displaced Persons and Refugees. World War II caused many millions of people to be "transferred" from one nation to another. For example, millions of Germans were removed from Eastern Europe and Poland to what is now Western Germany, and, in the process, many thousands of them were left homeless or stateless. The nations of the world, as an act of humanity and under stimulus from the United Nations, cooperated to provide asylum for these refugees. In the United States, the Displaced Persons Act of 1948 authorized the entry of displaced persons and other refugees without regard to the current availability of places for them on the quotas of their countries of origin, but made their entry chargeable against future annual quotas. [2] Between 1948 and 1955, 406,000 persons entered the United States under this program. The program was renewed in 1953 and the original act was replaced by a new Displaced Persons Act which authorized the issuance of 214,000 special nonquota visas to refugees and expellees from the Soviet Union and other Communist-dominated countries. Between 1954 and 1957 a total of 187,700 persons were granted asylum under this program. Thus, since 1948, the number of immigrants coming to this country from certain nations has been considerably in excess of the quotas allotted to the nations they came from, and most of these nations are those which have been historically considered sources of the "new" migration rather than of the "old" migration. A very large percentage of these displaced persons and refugees were born in Poland, Germany, the U.S.S.R.,

---

[2] Because many of the nations from which these refugees came had very small quotas, the program quickly created the absurd situation in which some countries had used up the quotas which were to have lasted well into the twenty-first century.

Yugoslavia, Latvia, Lithuania, Hungary, Estonia, Czechoslovakia, Rumania, Greece, and Austria. Table 14-1 reports that almost 2 million immigrants were admitted between 1950 and 1957. In only 6 of the 40 years of mass immigration (between 1830 and 1870) did the number of immigrants exceed the 327,867 admitted by the United States in 1957. Nevertheless, many people believe that the United States has been far too slow and cautious in admitting refugees and displaced persons--that the number admitted should have been much greater, and that the two special acts should have set up requirements for eligibility which were much fewer in number and which involved less "red tape."

Meanwhile, the quota system has remained in effect to regulate the immigration of persons other than refugees. In 1952, the quotas were revised slightly to give a token quota to nations of the Orient and Africa (see Table 14-2). As of 1957, about 20,000 of the visas made available by the Displaced Persons Act of 1953 had not been used, and in 1957 an extension was granted permitting refugees to use them in the next few years. Presumably, after the termination of this special program, immigration will again be regulated by the quota system as revised in 1953, unless new legislation is passed.

Recent Immigration. In the year 1956 to 1957, immigrants came to the United States from the nations listed below. The immigrants are classified by country of birth, and the nations are ranked in descending order according to volume of migration.

Country	1956	1957
Mexico	65,047	49,154
Germany	38,390	45,230
Canada	29,533	33,203
Italy	39,789	19,061
West Indies	19,022	18,056
England	15,605	19,533
Poland	8,453	11,225
Yugoslavia	8,723	9,842
South America	6,846	9,002
Ireland	6,483	9,124
Greece	10,531	4,952
Japan	5,586	6,354
Hungary	2,261	8,705
Scotland	4,245	5,946

Many persons may not realize that, since 1950, a greatly increasing number of Spanish-speaking immigrants have come to the United States. In fact, immigration from Italy, Poland, etc., can now be called the "old" migration; the "new" migration is that of Mexicans, Puerto Ricans, and South Americans. As was true in many past years, in recent years several nations of Western Europe have not used the immigration quotas allotted to them. For example, in the year 1957 the following nations of Northwestern Europe failed to use more than 60 percent of their quotas:

Great Britain
Ireland
Sweden

In the case of those Northwestern European countries whose quotas are more fully utilized, many of the quota migrants were once refugees or displaced persons from Eastern or Central Europe, but have resided in one or another of these Northwestern European countries long enough to qualify as quota migrants. Among the nations which have filled, or nearly filled, their quotas in recent years are the following:

Germany	Denmark
France	Switzerland
The Netherlands	Finland
Belgium	Austria
Norway	Asia
	Africa

In the year 1957, only 30 percent of all immigrants to the United States were quota immigrants. Most of the remainder came as refugees, brides of servicemen, relatives of American citizens, or as nonquota immigrants from Western Hemisphere countries.

CHARACTERISTICS OF IMMIGRANTS

Prior to the imposition of quotas, immigrants to the United States were predominantly male; most of them were young, and a large proportion of them came from the lower socio-economic strata of their native countries. The following examples of sex and age information illustrate the predominance of young males among immigrants:

Year	Percent Male	Percent over 45
Before quotas:		
1820.........	70	14[1]
1849.........	60	10[1]
1875.........	62	13[1]
1900.........	68	5
1907.........	72	4
1914.........	66	6
After quotas:		
1925.........	56	10
1950.........	48	19
1957.........	48	12

[1]Percent age 40 and over.

Source: Historical Statistics of the United States, 1789 to 1945, Table B 331, and Statistical Abstract of the United States, 1958, Table 111.

Unfortunately, the evidence concerning the socio-economic origins of the earlier immigrants is only informal, but it does strongly indicate that a very large share of them had rural peasant and urban proletarian backgrounds.

The quota system and the nonquota immigration regulations (the latter specify what persons shall have priority in entering the country) have combined to alter the composition of the immigrating cohorts. During the years 1946 to 1950, when the volume of refugees and brides of servicemen (who are allowed to enter the country as nonquota immigrants) was at its height, only 40 percent of the immigrants were male. Since the establishment of the quotas, a higher percentage of immigrants have been professional or other white-collar workers. If immigration regulations are supposed to see to it that the nation is supplied with comparatively unskilled manpower that cannot be recruited at home, the quota system has failed, because it has not delivered this kind of worker to our shores. The following statistics summarize some of the pertinent characteristics of immigrants in recent periods.

Characteristics	1936-1940	1946-1950	1957
Sex: percent male............	45.2	40.2	47.5
Age: percent under 16 years...	15.3	15.9	24.5
percent 45 yrs. and over.	18.6	17.5	12.0
Literacy: percent illiterate.	1.7	0.9	0.2

Characteristics	1936-1940	1946-1950	1957
(Continued)			
Occupational composition:[1]			
Professional, technical.....	19.1	16.2	16.1
Farmers and farm managers...	3.6	9.1	2.3
Proprietors, managers, and officials.................	19.7	7.1	4.0
Clerical, sales.............	11.6	17.5	16.9
Craftsmen, foremen..........	17.9	15.0	17.6
Operatives.................		15.7	12.7
Private household workers...	14.2	7.5	7.5
Service wrks. exc. domestic.	5.3	4.9	5.7
Farm laborers and foremen...	1.4	1.6	3.0
Laborers, exc. farm and mine	7.1	5.3	14.3

[1]Occupation reported for only 47 percent in 1957, 46 percent in 1946-1950, and 44 percent in 1936-1940. Many female immigrants, of course, had no occupation to report.

Source: Statistical Abstract of the United States, 1958, Table 111.

EMIGRATION

It would certainly be incorrect to leave the impression that all immigrants to the United States have remained here and become citizens. Large numbers found the country not to their liking, and returned home. Many came with the sole intention of working for a few years in order to save some money, or to send money home which would support their families over a financial crisis; many of these immigrants returned when they had accomplished such objectives. As a result, each major stream of immigration from a nation has had its back-flow. The size of this back-flow has depended on a variety of factors; the most important factor at any given time, of course, has been the total number of foreign-born persons of a particular nationality who have recently immigrated and are present in the country. Probably the largest emigration in the nation's history occurred right after the turn of the century. For example, during the 8 years from 1908 to 1915, a total of 2.3 million aliens departed from the United States, most of whom were undoubtedly dissatisfied or homesick Italians, Poles, Germans, etc.

Unfortunately, statistics concerning emigration have been kept only for recent years, and even hese give much less information than is needed. The following statistics are a summary of immigration and emigration from 1908 to 1915, and for he years since 1936. During the economic depression, 1936 to 1940, the back-flow was quite arge, but since 1955 it has been comparatively small. Since 1935, the back-flow has averaged roughly 20,000 to 25,000 persons per year (except during World War II). As of 1957, there was one emigrant for every 14 immigrants.

Year	Emigrants (000)	Immigrants (000)	Ratio emigrants to immigrants
1908 to 1915....	2,268	7,036	.32
1936 to 1940....	136	308	.44
1941 to 1945....	43	171	.25
1946 to 1950....	114	864	.13
1951 to 1955....	134	1,088	.12
1955..........	31	238	.13
1956..........	23	322	.07
1957..........	24	327	.07

Source: Statistical Abstract of the United States, 1958, Table 111.

Emigrants tend to be older than immigrants, and higher in the socio-economic scale. Also, a higher proportion of them are men. These characteristics of emigrants are illustrated by the following summary, which should be compared with the summary of characteristics of immigrants reported above.

Characteristics	1957
Sex: percent male.........................	54.8
Age: percent under 16 years................	11.5
percent 45 years and over............	22.8
Occupational composition:[1]	
Professional and technical............	37.7
Farmers and farm managers.............	1.5
Proprietors, managers, and officials....	18.0
Clerical, sales.......................	10.5
Craftsmen, foremen....................	5.5
Operatives...........................	4.6
Service workers, except domestic........	6.8
Private household workers.............	4.9
Farm laborers and foremen.............	2.4
Laborers, except farm and mine.........	8.1

[1]Occupations were reported for only 41 percent of the emigrants.
Source: Statistical Abstract of the United States, 1958, Table 111.

These data seem to indicate that the typical emigrant from the United States is a middle-aged or elderly male white-collar worker, who has met with some financial and occupational success and is returning to his country of origin to spend his last days among the relatives and friends he left when he immigrated to America.

COUNTRY OF BIRTH OF THE FOREIGN-BORN POPULATION

Comparative Size of the Nationality Groups. The immigration described above injected into the population of the United States large numbers of foreign-born persons who came from many different nations. Some of these national groups were quite large, and became very influential cultural and political factors in the communities in which they settled, while other nationalities were represented by comparatively small groups. Table 14-3 reports the number of foreign-born persons enumerated in 1950, by country of birth, and shows the percentage distribution of the foreign-born population at each decade from 1870 to 1950.[3] (Prior to 1910, the data refer to all foreign-born persons; the data concerning 1910, and subsequent censuses, refer only to the foreign-born white population.)

In 1870, foreign-born persons of Irish and German origin together comprised 64 percent of all foreign-born residents, but by 1950 they accounted for only 15 percent, or less than 1/4 of their former share. Likewise, persons of English origin made up only about 1/2 as large a proportion of the foreign-born population in 1950 as they had in 1870. The foreign-born population who had come from Eastern Europe jumped from 0.5 percent of all foreign-born persons in 1880 to 13 percent in 1920. Likewise, the proportion of foreign-born from Southern Europe leaped from 0.9

[3] Lack of comparability from census to census, due to changing national boundaries, makes it impossible to discuss meaningfully only the larger differences.

Table 14-3.—COUNTRY OF BIRTH OF THE FOREIGN-BORN POPULATION OF THE UNITED STATES: 1870 TO 1950

Country of birth	Total number in 1950 (000)	Percentage distribution								
		Foreign-born white					Total foreign born			
		1950	1940	1930	1920	1910	1900	1890	1880	1870
All countries.......	10,161	100.0	100.0	100.0	100.0	100.0	100.0	100.0	100.0	100.0
Northeastern Europe......	2,319	23.0	24.7	26.7	28.1	31.8	40.6	47.2	52.1	55.8
England and Wales.....	585	5.8	5.8	6.2	6.4	7.2	9.0	10.9	11.2	11.3
Scotland..............	244	2.4	2.4	2.5	1.9	2.0	2.3	2.6	2.5	2.5
Northern Ireland......	15	0.2	0.9	1.3						
Ireland (Eire)........	505	5.0	5.0	5.3	7.6	10.1	15.6	20.2	27.8	33.3
Norway................	202	2.0	2.3	2.5	2.7	3.0	3.3	3.5	2.7	2.1
Sweden................	325	3.2	3.9	4.3	4.6	5.0	5.6	5.2	2.9	1.7
Denmark[1]............	108	1.1	1.2	1.3	1.4	1.4	1.5	1.4	1.0	0.5
Netherlands[2]........	102	1.0	1.0	1.0	1.0	0.9	0.9	0.9	0.9	0.8
Belgium...............	53	0.5	0.5	0.5	0.5	0.4	0.3	0.2	0.2	0.2
Switzerland...........	72	0.7	0.8	0.8	0.9	0.9	1.1	1.1	1.3	1.3
France................	108	1.1	0.9	1.0	1.1	0.9	1.0	1.2	1.6	2.1
Central Europe..........	2,944	28.9	30.4	30.3	31.5	34.3	35.1	35.0	32.2	32.1
Germany...............	984	9.7	10.8	11.5	12.3	17.3[3]	25.8	30.1	29.4	30.4
Poland................	861	8.5	8.7	9.1	8.3	7.0[3]	3.7	1.6	0.7	0.3
Czechoslovakia........	278	2.7	2.8	3.5	2.6	...	...	...	...	...
Austria...............	409	4.0	4.2	2.7	4.2	6.3[3]	4.2	2.6	1.9	1.3
Hungary...............	268	2.6	2.5	2.0	2.9	3.7	1.4	0.7	0.2	0.1
Yugoslavia............	144	1.4	1.4	1.5	1.2	...	...	...	...	...
Eastern Europe..........	1,224	12.0	12.6	11.6	13.0	10.4	4.8	2.0	0.5	0.1
U.S.S.R.[4]...........	895	8.8	9.1	8.2	10.2	8.9[3]	4.1	2.0	0.5	0.1
Lithuania.............	148	1.5	1.5	1.4	1.0					
Finland...............	96	0.9	1.0	1.0	1.1	1.0	0.6			
Rumania...............	85	0.8	1.0	1.0	0.7	0.5	0.1			
Southern Europe.........	1,696	16.6	16.5	14.9	13.9	11.5	5.2	2.3	0.9	0.5
Greece................	169	1.7	1.4	1.2	1.3	0.8	0.1	...	...	...
Italy.................	1,427	14.0	14.2	12.8	11.7	10.1	4.7	2.0	0.7	0.3
Spain.................	46	0.4	0.4	0.4	0.4	0.2	0.1	0.1	0.1	0.1
Portugal..............	54	0.5	0.5	0.5	0.5	0.4	0.3	0.2	0.1	0.1
Other Europe([1]) ([4])......	86	0.9	0.5	0.5	0.3	0.2[5]	0.1	0.2	0.2	0.1
Asia[6]....................	180	1.8	1.4	1.1	0.8	0.7	1.3	1.2	1.6	1.2
Canada—French...........	238[7]	2.3[7]	2.4	2.7	2.2	2.9	3.8[7]	3.3[7]	10.7[7]	8.9[7]
Canada—Other[7]..........	756	7.4	6.9	6.7	6.0	6.1	7.6	7.3		
Mexico...................	451	4.4	3.3	4.6	3.5	1.6	1.0	0.8	1.0	0.8
Other American..........	120	1.2	0.6	0.5	0.3	0.2	0.3	0.3	0.3	0.3
Remainder of world and not reported...........	147	1.5	0.5	0.5	0.5	0.3	0.3	0.3	0.3	0.3

[1]Iceland included with Denmark prior to 1930; included with Other Europe 1930 to 1950
[2]Listed as Holland prior to 1910.
[3]Persons reported in 1910 as of Polish mother tongue born in Austria, Germany, and U.S.S.R. have been deducted from their respective countries and combined as Poland.
[4]Latvia and Estonia included with U.S.S.R. from 1860 to 1920 and with Other Europe from 1930 to 1950.
[5]Includes 4,635 persons born in Serbia and 5,363 persons born in Montenegro, which became parts of Yugoslavia in 1918.
[6]Includes Turkey in Europe.
[7]Includes Newfoundland.

Source: U.S. Census of Population: 1950, Vol. II, General Characteristics, U.S. Summary, Table 49.

percent in 1880 to 13.9 percent in 1920. The arrival of foreign-born persons from Italy, Poland, and Russia was the leading source of this change. Other countries from the "new migration" sources contributed smaller, but greatly increased, percentages of the foreign-born population during this period. Throughout the entire 80 years from 1870 to 1950, representatives of almost all the European nations have been present in substantial numbers, and have contributed to the economic and cultural development of the nation. Table 14-3 illustrates how extremely heterogeneous the composition of the foreign-born population has been with respect to its country of birth, especially since 1890.

As of 1950, the largest foreign-born groups in the United States (ranked in descending order of size) were as follows:

Country of birth	Percent of all foreign-born white
Italy	14.0
Canada	9.7
Germany	9.7
U.S.S.R.	8.8
Poland	8.5
England and Wales	5.8
Ireland	5.2
Mexico	4.4
Austria	4.0
Sweden	3.2
Czechoslovakia	2.7
Hungary	2.6
Scotland	2.4
Norway	2.0

Thus, in 1950, one or two nationalities did not thoroughly dominate the foreign-born population, as the Irish and the Germans did in 1870.

Urban-rural Residence of the Nationality Groups. There is a great deal of diversity among the foreign-born population with respect to the urban-rural distribution of the various nationality groups. The distribution of a particular national group often depended partly on what state of economic development the nation had reached when the stream of migration from that country was at its peak. Much of the diversity also appears to be due to the fact that there is a stronger preference for city living among immigrants from some sources. Among the foreign-born population in 1950, the country-of-birth groups which were most urban were (ranked in descending order):

Country of birth	Percent urban, 1950
U.S.S.R.	92
Ireland	92
Italy	91
Greece	90
Poland	88
Scotland	86

The least urbanized nationalities were the Mexicans, the Scandinavians, and the immigrants from Holland, Belgium, and Switzerland. All of these groups were either 69 or 70 percent urban. However, there was no such thing as a predominantly rural country-of-birth group among the foreign-born population. All of the groups had a much higher proportion of urbanism than was found in the general population.

Regional Distribution. The regional distribution of the foreign-born population as a whole has already been described in Chapter 7. Table 14-4 shows the country of birth of the foreign-born population of each geographic division, in 1950. The regional distribution has changed greatly over the years, of course. As each nationality group arrived, it tended to establish "colonies," either in certain cities or in particular sections of states, and friends and relatives coming from abroad settled in these colonies because it made their adjustment easier. The concentration of Scandinavians in Minnesota and Wisconsin is a familiar example of this kind of settlement. The "new immigration" (especially from Russia, Poland, and Italy) settled in metropolitan centers in the Middle Atlantic States of New York, New Jersey, and Pennsylvania. Many of them also went to Chicago, but otherwise they did not settle very extensively in the Midwest. However, large numbers of them flowed on across the country and settled in the Mountain and Pacific states.

Mexicans dominate the foreign-born population of the West South Central Division (60 percent of all foreign born) and comprise a substantial percentage of the foreign born in both the Mountain and the Pacific divisions. Canadians are an im-

Table 14-4.—COUNTRY OF BIRTH OF FOREIGN-BORN WHITE POPULATION BY GEOGRAPHIC DIVISIONS: 1950

Country of birth	U.S., total	Geographic division								
		New England	Middle Atlantic	East North Central	West North Central	South Atlantic	East South Central	West South Central	Mountain	Pacific
All countries.........	100.0	100.0	100.0	100.0	100.0	100.0	100.0	100.0	100.0	100.0
Northwestern Europe........	22.8	23.8	19.5	21.9	38.5	22.7	23.2	9.4	30.9	28.8
England, Scotland, and Wales................	8.2	9.3	7.2	8.0	5.1	12.3	12.7	4.2	10.9	10.7
Northern Ireland........	0.2	0.2	0.2	0.1	0.1	0.1	0.1	...	0.1	0.2
Ireland (Eire)..........	5.0	8.9	6.7	2.9	2.1	3.1	2.8	1.1	2.4	2.7
Norway, Sweden, and Denmark..............	6.3	3.9	2.9	6.7	26.8	3.4	2.7	1.8	12.3	10.2
Netherlands, Belgium, and Switzerland.......	2.2	0.7	1.5	3.5	3.7	2.0	2.5	1.1	3.8	3.3
France...............	1.1	0.8	1.1	0.8	0.7	1.8	2.3	1.1	1.3	1.6
Central Europe............	28.9	13.0	34.0	41.4	30.9	25.7	25.6	13.1	17.3	15.0
Germany................	9.7	3.0	10.4	12.2	17.3	10.4	15.6	6.9	7.8	7.3
Poland.................	8.5	7.1	10.5	12.6	3.7	6.9	4.5	1.9	1.9	2.2
Czechoslovakia, Austria, Hungary, and Yugoslavia	10.8	3.0	13.1	16.6	9.9	8.4	5.6	4.3	7.7	5.5
Eastern Europe............	12.0	10.0	15.2	10.8	12.7	14.0	8.2	2.9	9.0	8.8
U.S.S.R...............	8.8	6.3	12.4	6.0	8.8	10.9	6.6	2.4	7.2	6.4
Lithuania, Finland, and Rumania..............	3.2	3.7	2.8	4.8	3.9	3.1	1.7	0.5	1.8	2.4
Southern Europe...........	16.7	20.1	23.0	11.2	5.2	15.5	13.7	5.5	10.2	12.7
Italy..................	14.0	16.0	20.9	9.0	4.0	10.1	9.5	4.3	6.7	9.2
Greece, Spain, and Portugal..............	2.7	4.2	2.1	2.2	1.2	5.3	4.1	1.3	3.6	3.5
Other Europe[1]............	0.9	0.8	0.7	1.0	1.2	1.4	3.0	0.5	0.6	0.8
Asia[2]...................	1.8	2.1	1.5	1.4	0.9	3.5	4.5	1.6	1.3	2.7
Canada[3]..................	9.8	27.7	3.8	9.7	6.8	8.2	6.9	2.9	9.7	14.1
Mexico..................	4.4	...	0.2	1.1	1.8	0.4	1.1	59.6	18.5	13.1
Other American...........	1.2	0.5	1.4	0.4	0.4	5.1	2.8	1.9	0.7	1.7
Remainder of world........	1.4	1.9	0.7	1.0	1.5	3.5	11.0	2.5	1.7	2.5

[1]Includes Iceland, Lativia, and Estonia.
[2]Includes Turkey in Europe.
[3]Includes Newfoundland.

Source: U.S. Census of Population: 1950, Vol. II, General Characteristics, U.S. Summary, Table 49.

portant segment of the foreign-born population in all states along the Canadian border, and are especially numerous in New England and in the Pacific and Mountain states.

The Future of the Foreign-born Ethnic Groups. As Table 14-5 indicates, almost all of the country-of-birth groups in the foreign-born population declined in size between 1940 and 1950, but some of them declined by a larger percentage than others. The groups showing the largest declines were those whose members had arrived in greatest number before 1900, and those whose flow had been most sharply curtailed by the system of quotas. These nations were:

Country of birth	Percent change in foreign born, 1940 to 1950
Sweden, Norway, Denmark..........	-25
Germany...........................	-20
Lithuania, Finland, Rumania.......	-18
U.S.S.R...........................	-14
Poland............................	-13
Italy.............................	-12
Czechoslovakia, Austria, Hungary..	-12

Table 14-5.—COUNTRY OF BIRTH OF FOREIGN-BORN POPULATION, PERCENT DISTRIBUTION, 1950, AND PERCENT CHANGE, 1940 TO 1950, BY URBAN-RURAL RESIDENCE

Country of birth	Percent distribution: 1950				Percent change: 1940 to 1950			
	Total	Urban	Rural nonfarm	Rural farm	Total	Urban	Rural nonfarm	Rural farm
All countries............	100.0	83.5	11.0	5.4	-11.0	-7.1	-18.3	-39.5
Northwestern Europe..........	100.0	80.7	13.2	6.1	-17.7	-12.4	-23.0	-50.1
England and Wales..........	100.0	82.1	14.2	3.7	-11.5	-7.4	-23.3	-40.4
Scotland.................	100.0	86.4	11.0	2.5				
Northern Ireland..........	100.0	89.4	8.0	2.5	-85.5	-84.8	-89.2	-91.2
Ireland (Eire).............	100.0	91.9	6.6	1.6	-11.7	-9.7	-24.2	-45.7
Norway, Sweden, and Denmark	100.0	71.4	17.4	11.2	-24.9	-16.5	-21.8	-55.8
Netherlands, Belgium, and Switzerland..............	100.0	70.4	16.3	13.3	-10.6	-0.7	-10.9	-41.3
France...................	100.0	82.4	12.9	4.8	4.9	11.2	-9.4	-32.9
Central Europe..............	100.0	83.1	10.9	6.1	-15.7	-10.8	-25.3	-42.8
Germany..................	100.0	78.9	13.3	7.8	-20.5	-15.6	-22.6	-48.4
Poland...................	100.0	88.5	7.0	4.4	-13.3	-10.8	-25.3	-34.0
Czechoslovakia, Austria, Hungary, and Yugoslavia...	100.0	82.6	11.6	5.8	-12.2	-6.3	-27.8	-39.6
Eastern Europe..............	100.0	88.9	6.9	4.3	-15.1	-12.9	-12.4	-45.2
U.S.S.R...................	100.0	91.7	5.2	3.1	-14.0	-12.6	-12.6	-43.3
Lithuania, Finland and Rumania.................	100.0	81.1	11.4	7.5	-17.7	-14.1	-12.1	-47.2
Southern Europe.............	100.0	91.0	6.8	2.2	-10.6	-7.3	-32.7	-38.8
Italy....................	100.0	91.2	6.8	2.0	-12.1	-9.0	-34.3	-38.7
Greece, Spain, and Portugal	100.0	89.8	6.9	3.3	-1.6	3.1	-23.7	-39.0
Other Europe[1]................	100.0	77.0	13.7	9.3	42.7	32.6	95.3	87.2
Asia[2].......................	100.0	90.3	6.8	2.9	16.7	16.5	21.5	9.5
Canada—French[3]...............	100.0	80.5	14.9	4.7	-6.7	-2.9	-10.0	-37.0
Canada—Other..................	100.0	79.3	15.5	5.3				
Mexico.......................	100.0	68.7	18.3	12.9	19.4	30.1	3.5	-2.2
Other American...............	100.0	90.9	7.1	2.0	79.7	83.5	51.3	39.9
Remainder of world and not reported...................	100.0	69.7	18.5	11.7	150.4	146.0	238.4	92.0

[1]Includes Iceland, Latvia, and Estonia.
[2]Includes Turkey in Europe.
[3]Includes Newfoundland.

Source: U.S. Census of Population: 1950, Vol. II, General Characteristics, U.S. Summary, Table 49.

However, not all foreign-born population groups declined. The following four nationality groups increased in number between 1940 and 1950:

Country of birth	Percent change in foreign born, 1940 to 1950
America (except Canada and Mexico).	80
Mexico..........................	19
Asia............................	17
France..........................	5

In the future, large declines may be expected in the foreign-born population from the countries of Southern and Eastern Europe and from Poland. The composition of the foreign-born population will tend, in general, to approach more closely the proportions of the official quotas, although the special programs for refugees and nonquota immigrants will prevent the correspondence from being exact. We may also look forward to greatly increased immigration from the countries of the Americas, now that the first colonies of persons from these areas have become firmly established.

THE SECOND GENERATION: PARENTAGE

The term "parentage" is used by the Census to indicate the ethnic background of the children of immigrants. If both of a person's parents were born abroad, he is classed as "native born of foreign parentage." If a person had one foreign-born parent and one native-born parent, he is said to be "native born of mixed parentage." The terms "foreign parentage" and "mixed parentage" are used to identify these two groups which, together, constitute the "foreign white stock" in the population. This section discusses the populations of foreign parentage and of mixed parentage with respect to country of origin. Persons of foreign parentage are assigned the country of origin of the father, and persons of mixed parentage are classified according to the country of origin of the foreign-born parent.

Children of immigrants tend to be bi-cultural, since they are exposed to the folkways and traditions of their parents' ethnic group and, at the same time, to the American culture in which they live. Sociologically, one of the most amazing facts in the migration history of the United States has been the alacrity with which the children of immigrants have adopted English as their language and have sought to become Americans with respect to customs as well as to legal citizenship. Nevertheless, as was suggested earlier, their complete assimilation often requires more than two generations. Despite their efforts, many persons of foreign or mixed parentage have characteristics which differ from the characteristics of those native-born persons whose parents were both native born. Thus, it is desirable to compare the adjustment of the second generation with that of the first generation, and to compare the characteristics of second-generation Americans with those of native-born Americans. Fortunately, the "parentage" statistics reported by the census, which provide a count of the number of persons of foreign or mixed parentage and some indication of their characteristics, make possible a limited comparison of this type.

It would be a mistake to think that the number of native-born persons whose parents are Polish or German, for instance, is strictly proportional to the total number of Polish or German immigrants. A variety of factors must be considered in the process of explaining parentage statistics. At the time of their arrival, immigrants from various countries differ with respect to age, sex, and marital status. Moreover, fertility rates are higher among some immigrant groups than among others. Immigrants who arrived many years ago, and who are now deceased, have left behind children who are also now deceased and whose grandchildren are therefore native born of native parents. Immigrants who have arrived more recently, of course, tend to have larger numbers of children of foreign or mixed parentage.

As of 1950, exactly 3/4 of the white population was "native stock"--native born and of native parentage; the other 25 percent of the white population was "foreign white stock"--either born abroad or having one foreign-born parent. Table 14-6 reports the nativity and parentage of the population as recorded since 1890. In 1950 a higher proportion of the population was native born than at any preceding census, which reflected the long-run effects of the decrease in the number of immigrants after 1925. The proportion of native-born persons with foreign parents was also smaller in 1950 than it had been previously (17.5 percent of the population). Approximately 2/3 of the members of this group (11 percent of the total population) reported that both their parents had been born abroad, while the remaining 1/3 (6.5 percent of the total population) reported only one foreign-born parent. Table 14-6 illustrates the change that has taken place and is continuing to take place. These data, which show that one person in four is either foreign born or has at least one foreign-born parent, are the basis for the assertion in the opening paragraph of this chapter that "cultural pluralism is not entirely a thing of the past."

The number of persons of foreign parentage declined during the 1930 to 1940 decade and also

Table 14-6.—NATIVITY AND PARENTAGE OF THE WHITE POPULATION: 1890 TO 1950
(Data for 1950 based on 20 percent sample.)

Year	Total white	Native white						Foreign born white
		Total native white	Native parentage	Foreign or mixed parentage				
				Total	Both parents foreign	Mixed parentage		
TOTAL-NUMBER(000)								
1950	134,478	124,383	100,805	23,578	14,816	8,763		10,095
1940	118,702	107,282	84,125	23,158	15,184	7,974		11,419
1930	110,287	96,303	70,401	25,902	17,408	8,495		13,983
1920	94,821	81,108	58,422	22,686	15,695	6,992		13,713
1910	81,732	68,386	49,489	18,898	12,916	5,982		13,346
1900	66,809	56,595	40,949	15,646	10,632	5,014		10,214
1890	55,101	45,979	34,476	11,504	8,085	3,419		9,122
PERCENT OF INCREASE								
1940 to 1950	13.3	15.9	19.8	1.8	-2.5	9.9		-11.6
1930 to 1940	7.6	11.4	19.5	-10.6	-12.8	-6.1		-18.3
1920 to 1930	16.3	18.7	20.5	14.2	10.9	21.5		2.0
1910 to 1920	16.0	18.6	18.1	20.0	21.5	16.9		2.7
1900 to 1910	22.3	20.8	20.9	20.8	21.5	19.3		30.7
1890 to 1900	21.2	23.1	18.8	36.0	31.5	46.7		12.0
PERCENT OF TOTAL WHITE POPULATION								
1950	100.0	92.5	75.0	17.5	11.0	6.5		7.5
1940	100.0	90.4	70.9	19.5	12.8	6.7		9.6
1930	100.0	87.3	63.8	23.5	15.8	7.7		12.7
1920	100.0	85.8	61.6	23.9	16.6	7.4		14.5
1910	100.0	83.7	60.6	23.1	15.8	7.3		16.3
1900	100.0	84.7	61.3	23.4	15.9	7.5		15.3
1890	100.0	83.4	62.6	20.9	14.7	6.2		16.6

Source: U.S. Census of Population: 1950, Special Reports, Nativity and Parentage.

during the 1940 to 1950 decade, while the number of persons of mixed parentage increased slightly. This increase was probably made up largely of the children of those members of the armed forces who had married foreign-born spouses while on military duty abroad. The population reached its most heterogeneous point, with respect to both nationality groups and ethnic groups, between 1910 and 1920. During this period about 16 percent of the total population was foreign born, about 23 percent was of either foreign or mixed parentage, and only 61 percent was native born of native parents. Perhaps as many as 1/2 or 2/3 of the persons comprising this 61 percent had a grandparent who was foreign born. Thus, those members of the population whose ancestors for the last three generations have been native born are a comparatively small minority among the population.

As the mass immigration phase recedes further and further into the past, a swift decline may be expected in the number of persons of foreign or mixed parentage (children of immigrants). Unfortunately, no statistics have been kept for grandchildren of immigrants which show their national averages with respect to income, education, and other such characteristics. One cannot help wondering whether they have really blended indistinguishably into the general population, or whether some social and economic differences may not have persisted even into the third and fourth generations. The next section reviews evidence concerning the assimilation of the second generation, which suggests that at least some significant differences may still exist in the third generation, even though data with which to measure these differences are not available.

Table 14-7 reports the country of origin of the foreign white stock and also of the children of immigrants. The country-of-origin composition of the second generation is similar to that of the

Table 14-7.—THE FOREIGN WHITE STOCK, BY COUNTRY OF ORIGIN: 1950

Country of origin	Total foreign white stock (000)	Native white of foreign or mixed parentage (000)	Percent distribution Total foreign white stock	Native white of foreign or mixed parentage
Total, all countries....................	33,751	23,589	100.0	100.0
England and Wales...............................	2,028	1,443	6.0	6.1
Scotland.......................................	708	463	2.1	2.0
Ireland (Northern Ireland and Eire)...............	2,442	1,921	7.2	8.1
Norway...	855	652	2.5	2.8
Sweden...	1,190	865	3.5	3.7
Denmark..	427	319	1.3	1.4
Netherlands....................................	375	273	1.1	1.2
Switzerland....................................	287	216	0.9	0.9
France...	362	254	1.1	1.1
Germany..	4,727	3,743	14.0	15.9
Poland...	2,786	1,925	8.3	8.2
Czechoslovakia.................................	984	706	2.9	3.0
Austria..	1,225	816	3.6	3.5
Hungary..	705	437	2.1	1.8
Yugoslavia.....................................	384	240	1.1	1.0
Russia...	2,542	1,647	7.5	7.0
Lithuania......................................	398	250	1.2	1.1
Finland..	268	172	0.8	0.7
Rumania..	215	130	0.6	0.5
Greece...	364	195	1.1	0.8
Italy..	4,571	3,143	13.5	13.3
Canada-French..................................	758	519	2.2	2.2
Canada-other...................................	2,224	1,468	6.6	6.2
Mexico...	1,343	892	4.0	3.8
Other America..................................	222	101	0.7	0.4
All other and not reported.....................	1,364	798	4.0	3.4

Source: U.S. Census of Population: 1950, Special Reports, Nativity and Parentage, Table 13.

foreign-born population, although there are some differences. Among persons of foreign or mixed parentage in 1950, the ten largest ethnic groups were:

Population (000)	Country of origin	Percent of all second generation population, 1950
3,743	Germany...............	15.9
3,143	Italy.................	13.3
1,987	Canada (total)........	8.4
1,921	Ireland..............	8.1
1,647	Russia...............	7.0
1,443	England and Wales.....	6.1
892	Mexico...............	3.8
865	Sweden...............	3.7
816	Austria..............	3.5
652	Norway...............	2.8

ASSIMILATION OF IMMIGRANTS

To what extent has each of the various nationality and ethnic groups been assimilated into the general population? Which groups are most completely assimilated and which are least assimilated? How do the second generations of these groups (persons of foreign or mixed parentage) vary in the extent of their assimilation according to country of origin? Data which make it possible to give approximate answers to these questions are contained in Table 14-8. This table shows selected population characteristics for the foreign born (first generation) and for the children of the foreign born (second generation) of several different nationality and racial groups. In order to remove from the analysis as many disturbing factors as possible, the comparison is restricted to persons who were 25 to 44 years of age, and were living in urban places, in 1950. However, since this restriction permits the comparison to include one of the nation's largest groups of persons with foreign or mixed parentage, such an analysis

Table 14-8.—COMPARISON OF THE NATIVE AND FOREIGN STOCK BY COUNTRY OF ORIGIN AND ETHNIC GROUPS: 1950

(Selected characteristics of the native white population of native parentage aged 25-44 years of age and living in urban areas, and of the foreign born and native born population of foreign or mixed parentage aged 25-44 years of age and living in urban areas; for selected countries of origin and ethnic groups.)

Characteristic	U.S. total-white			U.S. urban-white, 25-44 years			England and Wales		Ireland		Norway	
	Native of native parentage	Native of foreign parentage	Foreign born	Native of native parentage	Native of foreign parentage	Foreign born	Foreign or mixed parentage	Foreign born	Foreign or mixed parentage	Foreign born	Foreign or mixed parentage	Foreign born
MARITAL STATUS												
Male.....................	100.0	100.0	100.0	100.0	100.0	100.0	100.0	100.0	100.0	100.0	100.0	100.0
Single...................	27.8	27.1	12.9	12.4	18.5	15.8	13.0	12.0	25.4	28.9	15.0	20.8
Married..................	66.8	67.7	75.2	84.4	79.2	81.5	84.1	85.1	72.2	69.4	81.6	76.5
Widowed or divorced.......	5.4	5.2	11.9	3.2	2.3	2.6	2.8	2.9	2.4	1.7	3.4	2.7
Female...................	100.0	100.0	100.0	100.0	100.0	100.0	100.0	100.0	100.0	100.0	100.0	100.0
Single...................	21.0	21.7	8.0	10.3	14.7	10.8	12.0	9.2	23.1	20.9	11.8	12.7
Married..................	66.6	65.5	65.4	83.3	80.6	83.3	81.9	85.8	72.5	74.0	82.1	82.3
Widowed or divorced.......	12.4	12.7	26.6	6.4	4.6	5.9	6.0	5.0	4.4	5.1	6.0	4.9
YEARS OF SCHOOL COMPLETED												
Male.....................	100.0	100.0	100.0	100.0	100.0	100.0	100.0	100.0	100.0	100.0	100.0	100.0
No school years completed..	1.1	0.8	8.8	0.4	0.4	2.2	0.2	0.4	0.2	0.5	0.2	0.6
Elementary: 1 to 4 years...	5.7	4.3	15.5	2.3	2.0	6.2	1.1	1.4	1.3	3.2	1.1	2.0
5 to 7 years...	19.1	13.4	18.4	7.9	8.3	13.2	4.9	5.6	4.9	16.2	4.2	12.1
8 years.......	21.5	22.6	23.7	12.3	16.3	19.7	10.7	14.5	13.4	31.5	16.2	29.0
High school: 1 to 3 years..	19.7	21.6	9.1	21.1	24.1	16.4	22.4	19.3	22.4	14.6	19.9	14.8
4 years..	15.1	21.1	11.5	28.7	28.0	21.1	32.6	30.6	34.0	20.5	32.3	22.0
College: 1 to 3 years......	8.3	7.9	3.8	11.9	9.5	7.9	13.2	11.8	10.8	5.0	13.2	8.5
4 years or more..	6.4	7.2	5.0	12.1	10.5	10.3	14.2	13.6	12.0	5.2	12.3	8.2
School years not reported..	3.2	1.1	4.2	3.4	0.9	2.9	0.7	2.7	0.9	3.3	0.6	2.7
Median school years completed.	10.1	10.2	8.2	12.2	11.8	10.3	12.3	12.2	12.2	8.9	12.3	10.0
Female...................	100.0	100.0	100.0	100.0	100.0	100.0	100.0	100.0	100.0	100.0	100.0	100.0
No school years completed..	0.9	0.7	10.4	0.5	0.5	2.6	0.2	0.4	0.2	0.7	0.2	0.4
Elementary: 1 to 4 years...	4.1	3.9	14.6	1.8	1.9	6.8	1.1	1.0	1.1	3.1	0.7	1.2
5 to 7 years...	12.5	12.7	18.4	6.9	8.6	14.0	4.1	5.9	4.0	17.6	2.7	11.6
8 years.......	17.4	22.1	24.1	10.8	16.8	20.3	9.2	17.2	11.3	32.0	11.4	27.5
High school: 1 to 3 years..	22.6	21.3	9.9	20.9	23.3	16.9	21.9	19.0	20.5	15.2	19.0	16.6
4 years.......	26.1	27.1	13.6	36.8	35.2	25.6	42.0	39.7	44.6	20.6	43.9	29.7
College: 1 to 3 years......	8.8	7.0	3.3	11.5	7.4	6.5	11.8	8.7	9.7	3.5	14.2	6.5
4 years or more...	5.1	4.2	2.4	8.4	5.3	4.9	8.7	5.7	7.8	3.0	7.2	4.3
School years not reported..	2.4	1.0	3.3	2.4	0.9	2.4	0.9	2.4	0.7	4.2	0.7	2.2
Median school years completed.	10.8	10.4	8.2	12.2	11.8	9.9	12.3	12.1	12.3	8.8	12.4	10.5
EMPLOYMENT STATUS												
Male.....................	100.0	100.0	100.0	100.0	100.0	100.0	100.0	100.0	100.0	100.0	100.0	100.0
In labor force.............	78.6	83.0	75.3	93.2	95.1	94.6	95.3	95.1	94.3	95.0	95.2	93.3
Not in labor force.........	21.4	17.0	24.7	6.8	4.9	5.4	4.7	4.9	5.7	5.0	4.8	6.7
Female...................	100.0	100.0	100.0	100.0	100.0	100.0	100.0	100.0	100.0	100.0	100.0	100.0
In labor force.............	27.8	31.7	22.1	36.0	36.2	35.1	35.4	31.5	40.5	39.1	35.9	30.6
Not in labor force.........	72.2	68.3	77.9	64.0	63.8	64.9	64.6	68.5	59.5	60.9	64.1	69.4
UNEMPLOYMENT												
Male-percent of civilian labor labor force unemployed......	4.3	5.3	5.7	3.7	4.7	6.0	3.4	3.7	5.4	0.4	4.3	5.1
Female-percent of civilian labor labor force unemployed......	3.9	4.5	4.7	3.3	4.0	4.6	3.7	4.3	3.0	2.4	2.9	3.5
MAJOR OCCUPATION GROUP												
Male.....................	100.0	100.0	100.0	100.0	100.0	100.0	100.0	100.0	100.0	100.0	100.0	100.0
Profess.,tech.,kindred wrks...	7.8	8.6	6.1	12.4	10.7	10.8	14.9	16.6	11.4	5.6	13.1	8.0
Farmers and farm managers.....	11.8	7.0	4.5	0.3	0.2	0.2	0.2	0.1	...	0.1	0.3	0.2
Mgrs.,offs.,propr's,exc. farm.	10.7	12.8	15.1	12.8	13.8	15.8	14.0	16.0	10.5	8.2	14.4	12.7
Clerical and kindred workers..	13.8	15.5	8.8	18.2	17.0	12.8	19.7	18.5	23.2	14.1	17.3	8.3
Craftsmen,foremen,kindred wrks	19.1	20.4	22.8	23.5	22.1	23.2	23.0	23.0	19.2	22.0	26.3	36.3
Operatives and kindred wrks...	19.7	20.9	20.1	22.2	24.3	21.4	19.4	16.7	19.2	21.3	18.2	16.6
Private household workers.....	0.1	0.1	0.3	...	...	0.2	...	0.3	...	0.3	...	0.7
Service workers.............	4.4	5.5	9.5	4.4	5.1	7.6	4.3	5.2	10.4	15.3	3.9	5.0
Farm laborers,unpaid family... / Farm laborers exc. unpaid wrks	6.0	2.3	3.1	0.4	0.3	1.0	0.2	0.2	0.1	0.3	0.3	0.2
Laborers, exc. farm and mine..	6.4	6.2	9.0	4.8	5.9	6.7	3.6	2.8	5.3	12.1	5.7	11.3
Occupation not reported.......	1.2	0.7	0.8	0.8	0.5	0.7	0.5	0.5	0.6	0.7	0.6	0.7
Female...................	100.0	100.0	100.0	100.0	100.0	100.0	100.0	100.0	100.0	100.0	100.0	100.0
Profess.,tech.,kindred wrks...	14.5	11.3	8.6	15.5	10.8	10.7	17.0	13.2	17.8	12.6	16.3	10.4
Farmers and farm managers.....	0.7	0.4	0.7	0.1	...	0.1	...	...	...	0.1	0.1	...
Mgrs.,off.,propr's,exc. farm.	4.6	4.5	6.4	4.5	4.5	5.2	5.0	5.2	3.4	2.8	4.6	3.3
Clerical and kindred workers..	41.1	42.7	20.7	44.8	42.4	30.0	50.1	49.0	56.5	20.7	49.1	30.2
Craftsmen,foremen,kindred wrks	1.5	1.9	2.3	1.7	2.2	2.3	1.7	2.0	1.7	1.3	1.6	2.5
Operatives and kindred workers	17.4	23.0	31.4	18.6	28.3	31.4	14.6	17.0	11.8	13.4	11.9	14.2
Private household workers.....	3.6	3.2	10.4	1.8	1.5	6.1	1.3	3.1	1.1	21.6	2.9	21.5
Service workers.............	11.5	9.4	15.3	11.0	8.4	12.2	8.4	8.9	6.6	25.5	12.1	16.5
Farm laborers,unpaid family...	2.0	1.3	1.0	0.1	...	...	...	...	...	...	...	0.2
Farm labor., exc. unpaid,fore.	0.5	0.3	0.5	...	0.1	0.2	...	0.1	...	0.1	0.1	...
Laborers, exc.farm and mine..	0.7	0.7	0.9	0.6	0.7	0.8	0.5	0.4	0.3	0.6	0.4	0.2
Occupation not reported.......	2.0	1.3	1.7	1.4	1.0	1.2	1.2	0.9	0.8	1.2	1.0	1.0
INCOME IN 1949												
Persons with income...........	100.0	100.0	100.0	100.0	100.0	100.0	100.0	100.0	100.0	100.0	100.0	100.0
Less than $500.............	17.4	12.4	13.4	9.0	7.2	8.1	7.9	8.9	6.3	7.6	8.4	6.6
$500 to $999...............	12.8	10.6	13.3	7.4	6.3	7.9	5.9	7.6	5.9	8.9	6.2	6.5
$1,000 to $1,499...........	10.8	9.4	9.8	8.5	7.2	8.5	6.4	7.7	6.1	10.8	6.7	7.5
$1,500 to $1,999...........	10.3	9.8	9.4	9.9	8.8	9.4	7.5	8.7	8.2	11.8	7.8	7.9
$2,000 to $2,499...........	11.5	12.3	11.7	13.2	13.2	12.7	11.1	11.5	13.3	13.3	11.2	10.2
$2,500 to $2,999...........	9.1	10.7	10.0	12.3	13.4	11.3	12.1	10.3	14.0	11.7	11.5	10.3
$3,000 to $3,999...........	14.6	17.8	16.5	21.6	23.9	21.0	24.6	21.3	26.5	21.2	24.9	24.9
$4,000 to $4,999...........	6.2	7.6	7.0	9.2	9.9	9.8	12.0	10.7	10.5	8.9	12.0	13.7
$5,000 to $5,999...........	3.0	3.9	3.7	4.1	4.7	5.1	5.7	5.5	4.8	3.3	5.4	6.4
$6,000 and over............	4.4	5.5	5.4	4.8	5.4	6.3	6.9	7.9	4.4	2.4	5.9	6.0
Median income..............	$1,938	$2,314	$2,181	$2,581	$2,771	$2,654	$2,967	$2,775	$2,861	$2,409	$2,925	$3,040

Source: U.S. Census of Population: 1950, Special Reports, Nativity and Parentage, Tables 10 and 23. Data for occupational composition of the native white of native parentage were obtained by summing occupational data for various sizes of urban places in the Special Report Characteristics by Size of Place, subtracting nonwhite from total to get white and then subtracting the occupational data for the foreign stock.

Table 14-8.—COMPARISON OF THE NATIVE AND FOREIGN STOCK BY COUNTRY OF ORIGIN AND ETHNIC GROUPS: 1950—Continued

(Selected characteristics of the native white population of native parentage aged 25-44 years of age and living in urban areas, and of the foreign born and native born population of foreign or mixed parentage aged 25-44 years of age and living in urban areas; for selected countries of origin and ethnic groups.)

Characteristics	Sweden		Germany		Poland		Czechoslovakia		Austria		U.S.S.R.		Italy	
	Foreign or mixed parentage	Foreign born	Foreign or mixed parentage	Foreign born	Foreign or mixed parentage	Foreign born	Foreign or mixed parentage	Foreign born	Foreign or mixed parentage	Foreign born	Foreign or mixed parentage	Foreign born	Foreign or mixed parentage	Foreign born
MARITAL STATUS														
Male..................	100.0	100.0	100.0	100.0	100.0	100.0	100.0	100.0	100.0	100.0	100.0	100.0	100.0	100.0
Single................	14.5	15.5	13.3	14.8	21.7	17.5	19.7	15.5	21.9	16.1	16.3	11.7	18.6	12.9
Married...............	82.6	80.7	84.0	83.2	76.4	80.3	78.4	82.1	75.9	81.3	82.0	86.0	79.6	85.3
Widowed or divorced...	3.0	3.8	2.7	2.0	1.9	2.2	1.9	2.4	2.3	2.6	1.7	2.3	1.7	1.8
Female................	100.0	100.0	100.0	100.0	100.0	100.0	100.0	100.0	100.0	100.0	100.0	100.0	100.0	100.0
Single................	13.7	11.6	12.4	9.8	13.9	8.5	14.2	8.3	15.0	9.6	13.0	10.1	16.3	8.5
Married...............	81.0	82.2	81.9	85.3	82.2	85.6	81.5	86.3	80.6	84.3	83.0	83.8	80.2	87.0
Widowed or divorced...	5.4	6.2	5.7	4.9	3.9	5.9	4.3	5.3	4.4	6.1	4.0	6.2	3.5	4.5
YEARS OF SCHOOL COMPLETED														
Male..................	100.0	100.0	100.0	100.0	100.0	100.0	100.0	100.0	100.0	100.0	100.0	100.0	100.0	100.0
No school years completed..	0.1	0.2	0.2	0.7	0.3	3.3	0.3	1.7	0.2	1.3	0.3	2.1	0.5	2.0
Elementary: 1 to 4 years...	0.9	1.1	1.3	1.6	1.8	6.2	1.5	4.2	1.3	2.7	1.0	4.1	2.2	10.4
5 to 7 years...	3.3	9.7	7.2	5.5	10.8	16.4	8.8	14.0	7.2	9.5	3.0	9.5	11.6	22.0
8 years........	12.0	30.3	19.1	24.7	21.1	21.3	19.5	23.8	15.3	19.2	8.0	18.9	20.6	24.3
High school: 1 to 3 years..	21.1	17.2	23.7	14.1	27.1	15.2	27.1	17.5	22.9	15.2	16.7	17.1	28.7	16.6
4 years......	35.5	24.1	28.1	28.9	23.8	18.0	28.2	20.7	28.8	20.6	31.1	20.7	24.9	13.9
College: 1 to 3 years......	13.1	7.1	9.6	10.0	7.1	6.8	7.0	5.5	10.3	9.6	15.3	9.5	5.4	3.5
4 years or more..	13.3	7.0	10.0	11.9	7.2	9.8	6.1	9.8	13.0	19.1	23.5	14.9	5.3	4.5
School years not reported..	0.8	3.3	0.8	2.5	0.7	3.0	1.6	2.7	0.8	2.7	1.1	3.2	0.8	2.3
Median school years completed.	12.3	10.2	11.8	12.1	10.7	9.3	11.1	9.8	12.1	12.0	12.7	11.4	10.5	8.6
Female................	100.0	100.0	100.0	100.0	100.0	100.0	100.0	100.0	100.0	100.0	100.0	100.0	100.0	100.0
No school years completed..	0.2	0.6	0.2	0.8	0.3	3.8	0.3	1.9	0.3	2.1	0.3	3.3	0.5	3.4
Elementary: 1 to 4 years...	0.8	0.7	1.2	1.4	1.8	8.4	1.5	5.5	1.3	3.9	1.0	5.8	2.2	15.2
5 to 7 years...	2.0	8.3	6.4	6.1	12.4	18.6	10.3	18.0	7.4	11.0	3.0	11.4	13.2	26.1
8 years........	9.1	28.5	18.5	27.4	24.4	22.8	21.4	28.8	16.4	22.8	8.8	20.4	23.3	24.2
High school: 1 to 3 years..	18.9	19.0	23.8	16.9	26.4	14.9	27.5	15.8	23.2	15.5	17.2	18.2	27.3	13.8
4 years......	47.3	29.6	35.1	32.0	26.7	20.7	31.0	20.5	37.2	25.3	47.6	26.7	27.6	11.9
College: 1 to 3 years......	12.8	6.4	8.4	7.5	4.4	4.7	4.6	4.4	7.7	8.8	11.1	6.6	2.9	1.8
4 years or more..	8.2	4.2	5.7	5.8	2.9	3.6	2.9	3.3	5.7	8.5	10.0	5.1	2.2	1.7
School years not reported..	0.8	2.7	0.8	2.1	0.6	2.5	0.6	1.7	0.8	2.1	1.0	2.5	0.8	1.8
Median school years completed.	12.4	10.7	11.9	11.4	10.2	8.8	10.8	8.8	12.0	10.8	12.4	10.3	10.1	8.2
EMPLOYMENT STATUS														
Male..................	100.0	100.0	100.0	100.0	100.0	100.0	100.0	100.0	100.0	100.0	100.0	100.0	100.0	100.0
In labor force............	95.7	96.0	96.1	96.2	95.1	95.0	95.8	95.4	95.1	95.3	95.7	96.0	95.0	95.6
Not in labor force........	4.5	3.8	3.9	3.8	4.9	5.0	4.2	4.6	4.9	4.7	4.3	4.0	5.0	4.4
Female................	100.0	100.0	100.0	100.0	100.0	100.0	100.0	100.0	100.0	100.0	100.0	100.0	100.0	100.0
In labor force............	36.6	36.9	36.0	35.7	38.2	33.0	37.1	36.4	34.9	37.5	29.1	31.0	36.4	35.2
Not in labor force........	63.4	63.1	64.0	64.3	61.8	67.0	62.9	63.6	65.1	62.5	70.9	69.0	63.6	64.8
UNEMPLOYMENT														
Male-percent of civilian labor force unemployed.......	3.1	9.6	3.1	3.0	5.2	6.1	3.8	4.5	4.8	3.9	3.3	4.2	5.7	4.6
Female-percent of civilian labor force unemployed.......	2.7	3.4	3.0	3.7	3.9	6.0	3.4	5.4	4.2	5.0	4.6	6.0	4.4	4.3
MAJOR OCCUPATION GROUP														
Male..................	100.0	100.0	100.0	100.0	100.0	100.0	100.0	100.0	100.0	100.0	100.0	100.0	100.0	100.0
Profess.,tech.,kindred wrks..	14.8	9.5	11.4	11.3	7.8	8.5	7.8	9.3	12.5	16.3	12.9	18.5	6.7	5.3
Farmers and farm managers.....	0.5	0.1	0.3	0.3	0.1	0.2	0.1	0.1	0.1	0.1	0.2	0.1	0.2	0.2
Mgrs.,off.,propr's, exc. farm..	14.6	12.3	13.7	17.8	9.8	20.7	7.9	11.6	14.5	20.8	33.3	28.2	12.0	12.8
Clerical and kindred workers..	18.7	8.3	16.4	13.2	13.8	13.5	13.4	10.8	17.7	14.5	18.2	24.4	14.8	9.3
Craftsmen, foremen,kindred wrk	26.2	39.9	27.1	31.0	23.9	19.7	27.8	26.6	21.1	20.5	13.8	11.2	22.6	25.5
Operatives and kindred workers	16.9	17.1	21.8	17.0	32.7	26.4	30.8	28.5	24.1	18.0	15.7	12.6	28.4	26.6
Private household workers.....	0.1	0.4	...	0.1	...	0.1	0.1	0.1	0.1	0.1	...	...	...	0.1
Service workers.............	3.5	5.7	4.1	6.5	4.4	4.8	4.3	5.3	4.2	5.8	3.2	2.5	6.6	9.5
Farm laborers, unpaid family..														
Farm laborers exc.unpaid wrks.	0.2	0.3	0.3	0.2	0.1	0.3	0.1	0.2	0.1	0.2	0.1	0.1	0.2	0.2
Laborers, exc. farm and mine..	4.0	5.4	4.4	2.3	6.8	4.9	7.1	6.8	5.0	3.1	1.8	1.9	7.9	9.8
Occupation not reported..	0.5	1.0	0.5	0.6	0.5	0.8	0.5	0.7	0.5	0.6	0.7	0.5	0.6	0.6
Female................	100.0	100.0	100.0	100.0	100.0	100.0	100.0	100.0	100.0	100.0	100.0	100.0	100.0	100.0
Profess.,tech.,kindred workers	16.7	11.0	12.3	11.8	7.0	6.6	8.0	6.8	10.3	12.8	9.7	14.3	5.8	4.0
Farmers and farm managers.....	...	...	0.1	0.1	...	...	...	...	...	0.1	...	0.1	...	...
Mgrs.,off.,propr's, exc. farm.	4.1	5.5	5.1	6.3	3.6	6.3	3.4	4.4	5.1	6.7	10.0	8.2	3.4	4.1
Clerical and kindred workers..	54.3	30.3	47.8	31.7	31.7	26.9	38.5	22.0	45.2	31.7	41.9	56.7	34.0	15.7
Craftsmen,foremen,kindred wrks	1.6	2.5	2.2	2.3	2.7	1.9	2.6	2.7	2.2	3.6	2.2	1.6	2.9	3.3
Operatives and kindred workers	10.8	17.5	19.1	24.2	42.4	42.0	32.5	40.7	25.7	29.7	26.6	11.6	44.3	63.7
Private household workers.....	2.1	16.5	2.3	6.8	1.3	3.3	2.3	6.7	1.5	3.2	1.7	0.8	0.6	0.5
Service workers.............	8.8	15.0	9.5	14.5	9.0	10.7	10.7	14.3	8.3	10.7	6.1	5.4	7.1	6.6
Farm laborers, unpaid family..	...	0.1	...	0.2	...	...	...	0.1	...	...	...	...	...	...
Farm laborers exc.unpaid wrks.	0.1	...	0.1	0.1	...	0.1	0.1	0.1	...	0.1	0.1	0.1	...	0.1
Laborers, exc. farm and mine..	0.4	0.1	0.6	0.5	1.2	0.8	0.9	1.0	0.7	0.4	0.3	0.3	0.9	1.1
Occupation not reported......	0.9	1.4	1.1	1.4	0.9	1.4	1.0	1.4	0.8	1.0	1.1	1.0	1.0	1.0
INCOME IN 1949														
Persons with income.........	100.0	100.0	100.0	100.0	100.0	100.0	100.0	100.0	100.0	100.0	100.0	100.0	100.0	100.0
Less than $500..........	7.9	6.7	7.6	7.2	6.8	9.1	6.9	8.6	7.0	6.7	6.9	6.2	6.5	5.7
$500 to $999..............	5.6	5.7	5.5	6.5	6.2	8.3	5.7	7.4	5.9	5.9	5.8	4.9	6.7	6.3
$1,000 to $1,499..........	5.7	6.5	6.0	6.9	7.1	7.8	6.7	7.8	7.0	7.1	6.2	5.5	8.3	8.1
$1,500 to $1,999..........	6.7	6.8	7.4	8.1	9.0	8.2	8.5	9.7	8.3	7.8	7.4	6.6	10.7	10.2
$2,000 to $2,499..........	11.1	10.3	11.1	10.9	13.9	11.7	13.4	13.2	12.9	11.8	10.5	11.1	15.7	15.6
$2,500 to $2,999..........	11.7	10.6	12.1	10.4	14.7	10.9	15.3	12.6	13.5	10.4	9.9	11.3	15.0	14.4
$3,000 to $3,999..........	25.0	25.2	25.5	22.2	26.1	20.9	26.5	22.0	23.8	21.8	20.7	20.8	23.3	23.9
$4,000 to $4,999..........	13.1	15.0	12.3	12.8	9.2	9.6	10.1	9.8	10.2	11.3	11.0	11.3	7.9	8.7
$5,000 to $5,999..........	6.2	6.8	5.8	6.8	3.6	6.0	3.8	4.0	5.0	7.0	8.8	8.8	3.2	3.5
$6,000 and over..........	6.9	6.4	6.7	8.2	3.5	7.7	3.1	4.9	6.3	10.2	12.8	13.5	2.8	3.6
Median income..........	$3,047	$3,136	$3,005	$3,002	$2,740	$2,728	$2,788	$2,630	$2,826	$3,013	$3,160	$3,213	$2,573	$2,643

Table 14-8.—COMPARISON OF THE NATIVE AND FOREIGN STOCK BY COUNTRY OF ORIGIN AND ETHNIC GROUPS: 1950—Continued.

(Selected characteristics of the native white population of native parentage aged 25-44 years of age and living in urban areas, and of the foreign born and native born population of foreign or mixed parentage aged 25-44 years of age and living in urban areas; for selected countries of origin and ethnic groups.)

Characteristic	Canada-French Foreign or mixed parentage	Canada-French Foreign born	Canada-other Foreign or mixed parentage	Canada-other Foreign born	Mexico Foreign or mixed parentage	Mexico Foreign born	Puerto Rico Foreign or mixed parentage	Puerto Rico Foreign born	Negro	Japanese	Chinese	Filipino	Indian
MARITAL STATUS													
Male....................	100.0	100.0	100.0	100.0	100.0	100.0	100.0	100.0	100.0	100.0	100.0	100.0	100.0
Single..................	16.9	13.8	15.4	12.3	18.4	14.9	22.9	18.0	14.2	34.6	28.8	38.4	22.2
Married.................	80.3	83.2	81.1	84.6	78.1	81.0	73.1	79.3	81.3	64.0	69.3	55.5	71.1
Widowed or divorced......	2.8	2.9	3.4	3.1	3.5	4.0	4.0	2.7	4.5	1.4	1.9	6.1	6.7
Female.................	100.0	100.0	100.0	100.0	100.0	100.0	100.0	100.0	100.0	100.0	100.0	100.0	100.0
Single..................	16.5	13.5	12.9	11.1	12.5	10.1	15.7	11.1	9.4	21.5	11.8	8.8	10.2
Married.................	78.6	80.8	80.8	82.9	79.8	79.8	78.1	79.5	79.2	75.7	84.5	86.5	79.5
Widowed or divorced......	4.9	5.7	6.3	6.0	7.7	10.0	6.2	9.4	11.4	2 7	3.7	4.7	10.3
YEARS OF SCHOOL COMPLETED													
Male....................	100.0	100.0	100.0	100.0	100.0	100.0	100.0	100.0	100.0	100.0	100.0	100.0	100.0
No school years completed..	0.4	0.7	0.3	0.2	6.2	11.7	2.2	3.7	2.2	0.7	9.2	3.0	3.4
Elementary: 1 to 4 years...	2.2	4.9	1.1	1.5	20.2	26.7	6.9	17.7	15.9	1.3	10.3	11.4	8.1
5 to 7 years...	21.2	24.7	5.4	5.5	23.6	23.4	15.1	25.4	26.3	2.5	13.3	19.2	14.6
8 years........	21.9	23.9	11.2	12.9	12.4	10.0	16.7	20.9	13.5	5.2	9.7	12.4	16.3
High school: 1 to 3 years..	23.6	19.5	22.0	23.0	19.0	10.4	22.0	13.5	19.0	10.6	11.7	19.3	20.3
4 years..	19.9	14.6	31.0	29.7	12.3	8.8	18.0	8.5	12.0	45.0	15.0	17.5	19.5
College: 1 to 3 years......	5.8	5.3	13.6	12.2	3.6	3.4	7.5	2.8	4.3	16.9	9.2	7.2	8.0
4 years or more..	4.3	4.9	14.7	12.9	1.7	2.3	5.7	2.4	2.6	15.0	14.6	4.2	4.7
School years not reported..	0.7	1.5	0.8	2.1	1.1	3.2	6.0	5.1	4.2	2.8	7.0	5.8	5.0
Median school years completed.	9.5	8.8	12.3	12.2	7.9	6.3	9.8	8.0	8.3	12.6	10.0	9.2	9.7
Female.................	100.0	100.0	100.0	100.0	100.0	100.0	100.0	100.0	100.0	100.0	100.0	100.0	100.0
No school years completed..	0.3	0.5	0.2	0.3	8.4	13.1	2.5	5.2	1.4	1 1	11.9	2.3	2.6
Elementary: 1 to 4 years...	1.9	4.5	1.2	1.3	21.5	27.6	8.2	19.7	11.3	1.4	9.0	9.3	5.8
5 to 7 years...	21.0	24.3	5.2	5.0	24.2	24.8	13.8	26.4	25.8	2.5	10.8	14.9	17.5
8 years........	23.0	23.0	9.4	11.5	11.5	9.5	16.9	20.3	14.1	5.7	8.5	13.2	16.3
High school: 1 to 3 years..	22.2	18.9	20.3	24.4	17.7	9.6	20.7	11.9	22.1	9.5	9.4	18.6	23.8
4 years..	23.0	18.4	40.3	37.0	12.8	9.4	22.8	8.5	14.7	55.8	26.2	20.8	20.2
College; 1 to 3 years......	5.1	5.1	13.2	11.9	1.9	2.2	5.6	2.5	4.4	13.0	8.6	9.0	6.3
4 years or more..	2.8	3.2	9.5	6.8	1.0	1.6	4.6	2.0	3.2	8.6	12.1	10.1	4.6
School years not reported..	0.7	2.0	0.6	1.6	1.1	2.0	4.9	3.6	3.0	2.2	3.3	1.9	2.8
Median school years completed.	9.5	8.9	12.3	12.2	7.4	6.0	9.9	7.7	8.7	12.5	11.6	10.5	9.8
EMPLOYMENT STATUS													
Male....................	100.0	100.0	100.0	100.0	100.0	100.0	100.0	100.0	100.0	100.0	100.0	100.0	100.0
In labor force............	95.4	95.8	94.3	95.0	90.6	92.8	84.2	85.9	88.8	87.9	83.4	89.0	75.0
Not in labor force........	4.6	4.2	5.7	5.0	9.4	7.2	15.8	14.1	11.2	12.1	16.6	11.0	25.0
Female.................	100.0	100.0	100.0	100.0	100.0	100.0	100.0	100.0	100.0	100.0	100.0	100.0	100.0
In labor force............	43.0	41.1	36.0	36.2	28.3	29.3	36.8	44.5	52.7	50.6	32.8	28.7	32.0
Not in labor force........	57.0	58.9	64.0	63.8	71.7	70.7	63.2	55.5	47.3	49.4	67.2	71.3	68.0
UNEMPLOYMENT													
Male-percent of civilian labor force unemployed.......	6.5	5.9	4.7	4.0	10.7	8.5	10.2	14.7	9.2	3.8	7.2	10.9	13.5
Female-percent of civilian labor force unemployed.......	5.0	5.6	3.8	3.6	9.9	8.1	9.7	9.1	7.9	2.9	4.4	11.4	7.7
MAJOR OCCUPATION GROUP													
Male....................	100.0	100.0	100.0	100.0	100.0	100.0	100.0	100.0	100.0	100.0	100.0	100.0	100.0
Profess.,tech.,kindred wrks...	5.4	6.0	15.1	14.9	2.8	3.9	7.4	4.2	2.9	12.0	9.8	2.8	7.0
Farmers and farm managers....	0.2	0.2	0.3	0.1	0.4	0.5	1.5	0.1	0.2	5.4	0.4	1.2	3.0
Mgrs.,off.,propr's, exc. farm.	8.9	9.4	13.1	15.5	3.9	6.1	6.1	5.2	2.4	12.0	23.0	2.5	4.7
Clerical and kindred workers..	12.2	9.4	17.9	17.5	8.9	6.8	15.0	8.1	6.8	15.0	11.7	4.3	7.1
Craftsmen, foremen,kindred wrk	24.6	27.7	22.7	24.6	19.7	17.6	17.5	11.8	10.8	13.1	4.4	7.2	20.6
Operatives and kindred workers	36.0	35.5	20.7	18.4	28.3	24.4	28.9	32.3	29.0	13.9	15.6	14.0	24.9
Private household workers.....	...	0.2	...	...	0.1	0.2	...	0.1	1.1	1.3	1.0	2.4	0.5
Service workers............	5.6	5.4	4.8	4.1	6.6	7.2	13.3	26.9	16.8	6.5	31.2	46.6	8.1
Farm laborers, unpaid family..⎫ Farm laborers, exc.unpaid wrks⎭	0.4	0.3	0.3	0.2	5.9	11.1	0.4	1.9	1.0	4.0	0.4	7.4	3.4
Laborers, exc. farm and mine..	6.0	5.6	4.4	4.0	22.7	21.6	7.8	7.8	27.7	15.9	1.3	3.6	19.3
Occupation not reported......	0.6	0.3	0.6	0.6	0.7	0.7	2.1	1.4	1.4	0.7	1.0	7.9	1.4
Female..................	100.0	100.0	100.0	100.0	100.0	100.0	100.0	100.0	100.0	100.0	100.0	100.0	100.0
Profess.,tech.,kindred wrks...	8.5	12.3	18.5	18.5	4.3	5.4	9.4	3.4	6.0	10.4	14.1	13.8	10.2
Farmers and farm managers....	0.1	...	...	0.1	...	0.1	1.7	...	...	0.8	0.1	0.1	0.1
Mgrs.,off.,propr's, exc. farm.	2.3	3.1	4.8	4.9	3.5	5.1	3.1	1.2	1.4	5.0	9.0	5.2	2.6
Clerical and kindred workers..	23.9	19.5	44.4	44.0	23.4	16.7	28.7	8.3	6.7	34.4	35.7	24.1	17.7
Craftsmen,foremen,kindred wrks	2.2	1.9	1.5	1.7	2.0	2.5	2.2	1.6	0.8	1.1	0 6	0.7	1.6
Operatives and kindred workers	51.8	45.8	17.9	13.5	37.9	39.8	35.0	75.4	18.9	23.6	21.0	25 0	26.2
Private household workers.....	1.4	3.6	1.8	3.4	8.4	11.4	3.6	1.7	40.3	11.1	5.2	9.0	15.2
Service workers............	7.7	11.5	9.5	12.5	15.1	13.3	13.9	6.5	22.1	8.4	12.2	18.1	22.3
Farm laborers, unpaid family..	...	...	...	...	...	...	...	0.1	...	1.1	...	0.4	...
Farm laborers, exc.unpaid wrks	...	...	...	0.1	2.0	2.1	...	0.1	0.6	2.4	0.1	1.1	0.6
Laborers, exc. farm and mine..	1.0	1.7	0.6	0.4	1.8	2.1	...	0.8	1.7	0.8	0.4	1.2	1.6
Occupation not reported......	1.0	0.6	0.9	1.0	1.5	1.5	2.2	0.9	1.3	1.0	1.8	1.3	1.9
INCOME IN 1949													
Persons with income..........	100.0	100.0	100.0	100.0	100.0	100.0	100.0	100.0	100.0	100.0	100.0	100.0	100.0
Less than $500....	8.4	8.4	9.0	8.6	12.5	12.1	7.9	7.8	18.3	8.1	8.9	6.6	17.2
$500 to $999.............	7.7	7.9	6.8	6.8	14.6	14.8	11.2	12.6	19.2	8.7	10.9	8.7	16.1
$1,000 to $1,499...........	9.7	9.6	7.3	7.4	15.1	14.5	11.4	17.9	17.3	10.5	12.7	14.7	14.2
$1,500 to $1,999...........	12.5	11.9	8.9	8.3	13.8	13.1	14.0	21.6	15.1	11.7	15.4	15.2	13.3
$2,000 to $2,499...........	17.3	16.3	11.8	11.5	14.9	14.6	18.3	19.3	13.5	16.4	16.9	18.4	12.7
$2,500 to $2,999...........	14.6	13.4	11.9	10.9	10.8	10.1	13.5	9.5	8.1	13.5	10.3	12.8	9.8
$3,000 to $3,999...........	19.1	20.0	22.4	22.0	13.4	14.1	16.5	8.1	6.8	19.1	13.6	16.5	10.2
$4,000 to $4,999...........	6.2	6.8	10.5	11.5	3.2	3.7	3.5	1.7	1.1	5.9	5.6	4.8	3.6
$5,000 to $5,999...........	2.4	3.0	5.1	5.9	0.8	1.3	1.9	0.7	0.3	2.9	2.6	1.2	1.4
$6,000 and over............	2.1	2.6	6.3	7.2	0.9	1.6	1.8	0.8	0.3	3.1	3.1	1.0	1.5
Median income..............	$2,338	$2,374	$2,759	$2,841	$1,784	$1,824	$2,149	$1,768	$1,362	$2,334	$2,060	$2,129	$1,596

should be a reliable indication of the extent to which assimilation has taken place among the second generation.

In the analysis of this table, "assimilation" has been measured in terms of the extent to which each of the ethnic groups, of mixed parentage and of foreign parentage, has achieved a socio-economic status equal or superior to that of the native white population of native parentage. (Throughout this section this latter group is called "native stock," while the first- or second-generation ethnic groups are referred to as "foreign stock.") Thus, if a particular ethnic group whose members were of foreign parentage has as much education, as high an average level of income, and as high a socio-economic level of occupational composition as native-born persons with native parents (native stock), then this particular ethnic group can be said to have reached a very advanced stage of assimilation.[4] If a specific group with foreign or mixed parentage has, on the average, a level of education, income, and occupation that is lower than that of the native stock, the assimilation achieved by the foreign-parentage group may be considered incomplete. Thus, the extent to which each of the first- and second-generation members of each of the various nationality groups differs from the native stock, and from each member of the other ethnic groups, is a general (even if partial) measure of the kind of adjustment a group has made and of the extent of its assimilation.

Careful study of Table 14-8 will show that the first generation of most nationality groups has characteristics that differ markedly from those of the second generation--and that both the first and the second generations tend to differ in composition from the native stock. Particular foreign-stock groups have a higher socio-economic status than the native stock, and the first generation of some national groups has as high a socio-economic status as the second generation, partly because the direct and indirect selectivity of the quota system favors educated and white-collar persons. Also, the refugees who were admitted under the special programs contained a large segment of well educated white-collar workers. The kinds and amounts of variation that exist between the various ethnic groups, and between the first and second generations of each ethnic group, can be appreciated more clearly by means of the following short interpretative comments concerning each ethnic group which have been extracted from the statistics of Table 14-8.

England and Wales. This group seems to encounter almost no problems with respect to adjustment or assimilation. In fact, immigrants born in England and Wales tend to surpass the native stock in socio-economic status. They are more highly educated, more of them are concentrated in the professional and other white-collar occupations, and they have higher incomes than native Americans of native parents.

Ireland. Both Irish immigrants and their children are unique in that an extraordinarily high percentage of them have never married or have married late in life. The proportion single in this group is more than twice as high as it is among native white persons of native parentage. Although Irish immigrants tend to have little education, their children achieve as much education as the native stock does. There is a very strong emphasis on graduating from high school, though the proportion attending college is somewhat lower than it is among the native stock. The Irish immigrant is predominantly a blue-collar worker. His children tend to be highly concentrated in the clerical and service occupations, and a substantial proportion of them are professional managerial workers, craftsmen, or operatives. Although a comparatively high percentage of immigrant Irish women are employed as private household

[4] A group may be said to have achieved complete assimilation if it shows no compositional disadvantages, and if there is a comparative absence of residential segregation within its community of residence. Any interpretation of the comparisons made here must involve a clear understanding of the fact that we are not comparing the adjustment of parents with the adjustment of their children, but are comparing persons of the same generation (age). The difference is one of place of birth and place of birth of parents.

workers, their daughters appear to avoid this occupation. The income of Irish immigrants and their children is below that of the native stock, and shows a high concentration in the middle-income range.

Norway and Sweden. Immigrants from Scandinavia seem to place very great emphasis on the education of their children. Among native-born persons with Swedish and Norwegian parents, as among the native-born children of English immigrants, a higher proportion had received a college education than among the native-born children of native parents. This achievement is even more impressive when one realizes that the Scandinavian immigrant himself is not nearly as well educated as the German or English immigrant. A relatively high percentage of Scandinavian immigrants are craftsmen, but their children go into all of the white-collar occupations as well as into the craft occupations. The income level of both the foreign-born and the second-generation Scandinavians is higher than that of the native stock.

Germany. Americans of German ancestry (both first and second generation) have a slightly higher socio-economic status than is found among the native white stock. Although they lag slightly behind some other groups with respect to getting an advanced education and entering the professional occupations, they seem to be more highly concentrated in the managerial and craft occupations and to have above-average incomes. German women, both foreign born and native born, avoid private household work. Among the Germans, as among the English, the socio-economic status of the foreign-born generation is as high as that of the second generation.

Poland. Immigrants from Poland are among the less-educated ethnic groups, and the second generation has attained a considerably lower educational level than has the native white stock. Among second-generation Poles, the proportion failing to complete grammar school is much larger than it is among the general population, and the proportion entering college is also much smaller. Nevertheless, the second generation does show a marked shift toward the American pattern. Polish immigrants are employed primarily as operatives, managers, and craftsmen. In 1950, the second generation of urban Poles 25 to 44 years of age had a lower socio-economic status than first-generation Poles of the same age. A very large percentage of Polish immigrant women who are employed work as factory or clerical workers.

Czechoslovakia. Persons of Czechoslovakian background show a pattern of adjustment very similar to that of Polish immigrants, except that second-generation Czech women reach a slightly higher educational and occupational level than second-generation Polish women.

Austria. Persons born in Austria and residing in the United States tend to have above-average educational attainments (in 1950, 19 percent were college graduates). Likewise, a considerably larger share of professionals are found among Austrian immigrants than among the native white stock. The second-generation Austrian, however, tends to be much closer to the educational and occupational average attained by the native stock. A large percentage of the foreign-born Austrians who were 25 to 44 years of age in 1950 had entered this country as refugees, a fact which helps to account for this pattern.

U.S.S.R. The foreign-born population of Russian origin surpasses all other ethnic groups, both first and second generation, and also surpasses the native stock, in socio-economic status. In 1950, 71 percent of the first-generation Russians were white-collar workers (compared with 43 percent for the native white stock). Their income and their level of educational attainment are also well above average, and are higher than those of any other group. The second generation is especially outstanding. This differential may be explained in part by the fact that the Russian group contains large refugee and Jewish components, and that a large proportion of such immigrants place great value on obtaining an education and a white-collar position.

Italy. Italian immigrants, like the Irish, Poles, and Czechs, were poorly educated when they arrived, and most of them hold jobs as operatives, craftsmen, or laborers. The second generation is considerably better educated than the first, and its occupational composition represents a marked rise in the socio-economic scale. Like those of Irish origin, a very large proportion of Italian immigrants remain single or delay marriage for a longer time than the members of most other immigrant groups.

Canada. Most demographers think that the division between French-Canadian and English-Canadian immigration is too poorly maintained in the census enumeration to warrant separate tabulation. Table 14-8, however, suggests that the division is a most important one, and that the two groups are very unlike as to characteristics and have made very different adjustments to living in the United States. Compared with English Canadians, the French Canadians (both first and second generation) have much less education, are more heavily concentrated in the blue-collar and service occupations, and have lower incomes. The English Canadians (both first and second generation) are one of the best-educated groups in the nation's population, and their socio-economic status and income level are also among the highest in the population. With respect to these characteristics they far surpass the level, as a group, attained by the native stock.

Mexico. As a group, immigrants from Mexico have a very low educational attainment. Although the educational attainment of the second generation is somewhat higher than that of the first generation, it is still far below that of the native stock or of any other immigrant group. Mexicans are employed largely as unskilled laborers, and there is not a great deal of difference between the first and the second generations in this respect. The Mexican is the most poorly educated member of the nation's population, with an educational level lower than that of the Puerto Rican. His is the only ethnic group for which a comparison of the characteristics of the first and second generations fails to show a substantial intergenerational rise in socio-economic status. Hence, at the present time, the assimilation of the Mexican population seems to be proceeding very slowly.

Puerto Rico. Although Puerto Rico is not a foreign nation, its migrants are treated here as a separate ethnic group. Since 1940, migrants from Puerto Rico have become very numerous in the population: between 1940 and 1950 their numbers increased by 157,000, which was an increase of 223 percent during the period. Since 1950 the flow has continued at what appears to be an even more accelerated rate, and because of their extremely high fertility rates the Puerto Rican second generation is growing very rapidly. It seems reasonable, therefore, to expect that the 1960 census will find between 0.7 to 1.2 million persons of Puerto Rican ancestry, which will represent another tremendous increase. The presence of this increasingly large Spanish-speaking group, together with the greatly increased immigration of Mexicans, is creating a new ethnic element in the population-- an element which may eventually become large enough to modify quite significantly the nation's racial attitudes and inter-ethnic relations.

Contrary to what may be popular opinion, Puerto Ricans are about as well educated when they arrive as the immigrants from Italy or Poland were, and are far above the Mexicans in socio-economic status. In other words, a strong selectivity seems to operate, in that the more talented and skilled Puerto Ricans migrate to the United States. They are employed as operatives, service workers, and laborers. As yet, the number of adult second-generation Puerto Ricans is small, but the characteristics reported for this group in Table 14-8 suggest a rapid assimilation. The educational attainment, income, and occupational level of second-generation Puerto Ricans is clearly superior to that of the Negro population as a whole. In fact, although the evidence is skimpy, it suggests that Puerto Ricans may become assimilated as fast as the Italians, the Polish, and the Czechs have, and much faster than the Negroes and Mexicans.

Japanese. Among the Japanese population, the level of schooling is superior to that of the native stock. The occupational composition of this group is unique: there is an above-average concentration of professional persons, and also an above-average concentration of unskilled laborers. The average income is below that of the native stock. An extraordinarily high percentage of persons of Japanese ancestry, both male and female, are single. There is much evidence that although this group has struggled hard toward assimilation-- foregoing marriage, and making many sacrifices in order to get an education--they have been only moderately successful in entering well-paying white-collar occupations.

Chinese. With respect to educational attainment, occupation, and income, persons of Chinese background are below the Japanese group and also below the native stock. There is great diversity within the Chinese group, however: although a large percentage have very little education, a significant percentage have college degrees. In comparison with the Japanese, a higher proportion of the Chinese are proprietors. As is true among the Japanese, although Chinese parents seem very anxious to enable their children to attain an education, the absorption of the children into the general economic system appears to be limited by ethnic prejudice.

Philippine Islands. Filipino immigrants and their children are somewhat less educated than the Chinese, but are well above the Negro and Mexican populations in this respect. The men are highly concentrated in the service occupations.

American Indians. Although Indians and Negroes are not foreign-origin nationality groups, data concerning them are included in Table 14-8 in order that their socio-economic status may be compared with that of the other immigrant and ethnic groups. The educational attainment of American Indians who are 25 to 44 years of age and living in urban areas is roughly similar to that of immigrants from Ireland, Poland, and Italy, and the occupations they hold are of approximately the same type. The sample on which these statistics are based is small, however. The enumeration of Indians in urban areas is thought to be grossly incomplete, and possibly biased. However, these data suggest that at least a substantial segment of the urban Indian population has made significant steps toward assimilation.

Negro. Despite the fact that almost all Negroes are native born of native parents, and have an American ancestry dating back through many more generations than that of most of the white population, the indexes of assimilation and adjustment for Negroes shows that they are below the second generation of every nationality group. The second generations of urban Mexicans, Puerto Ricans, Chinese, Japanese, and American Indians are clearly above them with respect to income, education, and occupational level. Thus, unless one subscribes to the theory that Negroes are genetically inferior, it must be presumed that the culture of slavery, and the repressive actions and attitudes to which Negroes have been subjected since slavery, have caused their assimilation to proceed far more slowly than that of any ethnic group. As has been shown in preceding chapters, and as will be shown in chapters that follow, the progress of the Negro toward improving his socio-economic status has been especially rapid since 1950.

CONCLUSION

This chapter has presented data tracing the arrival in the United States of immigrants who have come from many nations and who represent a multitude of diverse cultures. It has been demonstrated that differences associated with ethnic origins still exist in the population, and that millions of persons are still in the process of being assimilated. The data concerning all ethnic foreign-stock groups except Mexicans show evidence of substantial improvement in socio-economic status between the first and second generations. Some of these groups have managed to attain a socio-economic level higher than that of the native-born population of native parentage; others are still striving toward equal socio-economic status. The following lists show the major ethnic groups, ranked in estimated order with respect to the extent of their socio-economic assimilation:

A. Socio-economic level equal to or greater than that of the native white population of native parentage (ranked according to socio-economic status)

Second generation (foreign or mixed parentage)	First generation (foreign born)
Russia (Jewish)	Russia (Jewish)
Sweden	Austria
England and Wales	England and Wales
Norway	Canada-English
Canada-English	Germany
Germany	
Austria	
Ireland	

B. Socio-economic level below that of the native white population of native parentage (ranked according to socio-economic status)

Second generation (foreign or mixed parentage)	First generation (foreign born)
Japan	Sweden
Czechoslovakia	Norway
Poland	Poland
Italy	Czechoslovakia
China	Canada-French
Canada-French	Italy
Puerto Rico	Ireland
American Indian	Puerto Rico
Filipino	Mexican
Mexican	
Negro	

It must be kept in mind that the above ranking is only approximate, and that it is based on data concerning only those persons who were aged 25 to 44 years and residing in urban areas in 1950. It is to be hoped that similar and even more detailed data will be made available from the 1960 census, especially for the rapidly growing Puerto Rican and Mexican populations, for the populations of Polish, Italian, and Czechoslovakian ancestry, and for the other ethnic groups whose socio-economic level is still below that of the native stock.

Almost without exception among the various foreign-stock groups, a larger proportion of males were unmarried than among males of native stock, and bachelorhood was even more pronounced among the second generation than among the first. Bachelorhood was extraordinarily common among the second generations of Irish, Austrian, Polish, Czech, and Italian groups. A similar situation exists among second-generation women of almost every nationality. However, in all but a very few nationality groups, a higher proportion of foreign-born women are married than of women of native stock. This postponement or rejection of marriage by members of the second generation may reflect their ambition to achieve a higher socio-economic status than that attained by the first generation.

The process by which the second generation achieves assimilation often seems to involve the clerical occupations as a way of obtaining a foothold in the white-collar occupations, and also seems to be accomplished by a rise from laborer to operative and from operator to craftsmen. Although immigrant women of many ethnic groups are employed as domestic servants and in other menial work, the second-generation women of these groups tend to avoid such occupations.[5]

---

[5] For more details of occupational assimilation of ethnic immigrant groups, see E. P. Hutchinson, Immigrants and Their Children, John Wiley, 1956.

Chapter 15

INTERNAL MIGRATION AND RESIDENTIAL MOBILITY [*]

HOW INTERNALLY MOBILE IS THE POPULATION OF THE UNITED STATES?

Few, if any, populations in the world are so mobile, on a routine basis, as the residents of the United States. During the course of a single year, between 19 and 22 percent of the nation's inhabitants move from one house or apartment to another, and about 5 to 7 percent of them move from one county to another in the process of changing their residence. Not more than 2 or 3 percent of the adult population has spent its entire life in one house or apartment, and perhaps not more than 10 to 15 percent live their entire lives within the same county. The present chapter undertakes to show that this residential flux is not simply a whimsical or aimless wandering, but that it has a definite pattern and is intimately related to the structuring of the population and to social change and adjustment. Because of the fundamental role it plays in population change and redistribution, residential mobility is a topic worthy of widespread study.

Migration is a tradition in the United States. Beginning on the Atlantic seaboard, the colonists settled the land by a process of westward migration that lasted for more than three centuries. Throughout our entire national history, as a part of the growing-up process, young men and women have asked themselves seriously whether or not they could better their fortunes by moving to some other place and by "striking out on their own" among strangers--often with no personal resources except ambition and courage. The legend of great statesmen, scholars, and businessmen beginning their careers by coming to a big city almost penniless has been reenacted by American youngsters many millions of times, all over the country. The fact that such a large share of the population are children of immigrants may also be connected with this propensity to be "on the move."

Population students divide all residential mobility into two parts: (a) <u>local moving</u>, or the changing of residence from one part of a community to another, and (b) <u>migration</u>, or the changing of residence from one community to another. For the sake of greater ease in collecting statistics concerning mobility, it has become customary to define as a migrant any person who changes his residence from one county to another, and as a local mover any person who changes residence within the same county. Both of these types of residential mobility are significant and worthy of attention. Migration usually involves the complete severance of a person's economic and social ties with the community he leaves, and requires that he adjust to a new job, a new set of community institutions, and a new group of people. Also, migration can change the size or the composition of

---

[*] In preparing this chapter, the author has drawn freely from two monographs, <u>Streams of Migration Between Subregions</u>, by Donald J. Bogue, Henry S. Shryock, and Siegfried Hoermann, and <u>Differential Migration in the Corn and Cotton Belts</u>, by Donald J. Bogue and Margaret J. Hagood, both published by the Scripps Foundation, Miami University, Oxford, Ohio. Special acknowledgments are due the co-authors of these studies for extensive use of materials they helped to prepare and analyze.

a particular population rather quickly. Such changes can result from a mass exodus of people, a mass invasion of people, or a large-scale selective interchange of people with other areas. For these reasons and for other reasons elaborated below, migration tends to receive more popular, as well as more scientific, attention than local moving. Nevertheless, local moving can change the internal distribution of population within a community, and can cause particular neighborhoods to undergo rather dramatic changes within a comparatively short time. For this reason, local moving is coming to the fore as a subject considered worthy of more intensive research.

Table 15-1 reports the mobility status of the civilian population from 1935 to 1958, as measured by censuses and special surveys. By comparing the place of residence at the time of enumeration with the place of residence at some specified earlier date, it is possible to determine what percentage of the population are migrants (living in a different county), what percentage are local mov-

ers (living in a different house in the same county), and what share are nonmobile (living in the same house). This table shows that the percentages cited in the second sentence of this chapter have been valid with respect to each year's migration experience between 1947 and 1958. Because the migration interval (the span of time over which movement is measured) varied in length before 1947, the data concerning the period 1935 to 1947 are only roughly comparable with the data for the period 1947 to 1958; during the latter period, annual surveys covered movement which had occurred within the past year. Therefore, it cannot be determined whether the annual rates prevailing from 1947 to 1958 are about the same as the average rate has been for the past 20 or 30 years, or whether they are inflated as a result of postwar adjustment and economic prosperity. Certainly these annual rates from 1947 to 1958 are higher than the estimated average annual rates for the 1935 to 1940 period and the 1940 to 1947 period, which were obtained by dividing the rate for each period by the number of years the period covers

Table 15-1.—MOBILITY STATUS OF THE CIVILIAN POPULATION FROM 1935 TO 1958

(Civilian population includes members of the Armed Forces living off post and with their families on post)

| Migration interval | Length of migration interval (years) | Percent of the population alive at beginning of interval | | | | Percent migrants are of all mobile population |
| | | Nonmobile | Total[1] | Mobile | | |
				Local movers	Migrants[1]	
April, 1935 to April, 1940[2]	5	62.0[a]	38.0[a]	24.6[a]	13.4	35[a]
April, 1940 to April, 1947	7	42.5	57.5	36.2	21.3	37
April, 1947 to April, 1948	1	79.8	20.2	13.6	6.7	33
April, 1948 to April, 1949	1	80.8	19.1	13.0	6.1	32
March, 1949 to March, 1950	1	80.9	19.0	13.1	5.9	31
April, 1950 to April, 1951	1	78.8	21.2	13.9	7.3	34
April, 1951 to April, 1952	1	79.7	20.2	13.2	7.0	35
April, 1952 to April, 1953	1	79.4	20.6	13.5	7.1	34
April, 1953 to April, 1954	1	80.7	19.2	12.2	7.0	36
April, 1954 to April, 1955	1	79.6	20.5	13.3	7.2	35
March, 1955 to March, 1956	1	79.0	21.0	13.7	7.3	36
April, 1956 to April, 1957	1	80.1	19.4	13.1	6.2	32
March, 1957 to March, 1958	1	79.7	49.8	13.1	6.7	30

(a) Estimated from ratio of migrants to total population for later years. Migration for 1935-40 included an estimated 1,500,000 persons who moved between a city of 100,000 or more and the balance of the county combining the city. If an adjustment were made to remove these "quasi-county" migrants, it would lower all rates for 1935-40 by about 9 or 10 percent.

[1]Includes persons abroad at the beginning of the migration interval who entered the continental United States during the interval.

[2]Includes military population.

Source: U.S. Bureau of the Census, Current Population Reports, Series P-20, Nos. 14, 61, 73, 82, and 86.

(these earlier enumerations were for a longer interval of time, and the fact that they show lower average annual rates is undoubtedly due, at least in part, to circular migration and to problems of response).

The mobility rates for each year are large enough to indicate that, over a period of a very few years, a large proportion of the population changed residence one or more times. This conclusion is confirmed by the data for 1935 to 1940 and for 1940 to 1947. More than one-half of the population changed residence between 1940 and 1947, and during this period more than one-fifth of the population were migrants (changing county as well as residence). This was not a typical period, since it included wartime movements; but the rates which prevailed from April, 1947, to March, 1958, would have made possible a turnover of the total population at twice the extent indicated in Table 15-1. A very high proportion of the population does change its place of residence in the course of a lifetime, as was demonstrated by a recent census report that "nine out of every ten persons 1 year old and over in the United States in April, 1952, had moved at least once in their lifetime." This same report found that less than 2 percent of the population 25 years of age and over had always lived in the same house.[1]

The year-to-year fluctuations in the rate of total mobility, the rate of local moving, and the rate of migration, as shown by the eleven-year series of annual rates, have been surprisingly small, even though the largest of these fluctuations are statistically significant. The low rates for the year 1953 to 1954 appear to reflect a decrease in business activity. Local moving (which is sensitive to the volume of residential construction) tends to have greater year-to-year fluctuations than migration has.

To summarize: The frequently-made statement that the population of the United States is a fluid one appears to be justified by the facts. However,

it is local moving more than long-distance migration which gives it this character. Although the present rates of residential mobility are not high enough to indicate that every person is moving or migrating every year, they are so high that the annual volume of movement and migration involves many millions of persons. Over a period of only a few years, mobility involves a majority of the population; over a period of a lifetime, it involves almost everybody.

WHICH SEGMENTS OF THE POPULATION ARE MOST MOBILE?

Census surveys taken in recent years have provided data about the total residential mobility of the population, classified according to several characteristics.[2]

Sex Differences. During almost every interval between 1940 and 1958, men appear to have been more mobile with respect to residence than women, but the difference in rates between the sexes is very small (Table 15-2). This difference has consisted largely of a tendency for males to be slightly more migratory than females. There is very little evidence that either sex, at the local level, has been a great deal more mobile than the other. During the period 1935 to 1958 the migration rates for males have been about 3 percent higher than for females, whereas over the period 1940 to 1958 the rates of local movement for the sexes were almost identical. The year-to-year fluctuations in mobility rates tended to affect each sex in the same way and by about the same amount.

Color Differences. Total residential mobility for the nonwhite population has been somewhat higher than for the white population, during ten of the eleven mobility periods between 1940 and 1958 for which mobility data were collected by color.

---

[1] Current Population Reports, Series P-20, No. 47, September, 1953.

[2] Several of the characteristics discussed in this section are the subjects of later chapters. They will be discussed here only insofar as they are associated with mobility, and the mobility aspects of these topics are omitted in the later chapters.

Table 15-2.—PERCENT OF THE CIVILIAN POPULATION CLASSIFIED AS RESIDENTIALLY MOBILE BY COLOR, SEX, AND TYPE OF MOBILITY: 1940 TO 1958

(Civilian population includes members of the Armed Forces living off post and with their families on post)

Type of mobility and mobility interval	Percent of population alive at the beginning of the interval								
	Sex			Color					
				White			Nonwhite		
	Both sexes	Male	Female	Both sexes	Male	Female	Both sexes	Male	Female
ALL RESIDENTIAL MOBILITY									
April, 1940 to April, 1947(a)	57.0	57.3	56.7	56.8	...	...	58.7	...	...
April, 1947 to April, 1948(a)	19.9	20.1	19.7	...	...	...	...	...	...
April, 1948 to April, 1949	18.8	18.9	18.6	18.9	18.9	18.8	18.3	19.1	17.6
March, 1949 to March, 1950	18.7	19.0	18.5	18.6	18.8	18.4	19.9	20.3	19.5
April, 1950 to April, 1951	21.0	21.3	20.7	20.9	21.2	20.6	21.7	22.3	21.2
April, 1951 to April, 1952	19.8	20.0	19.7	19.8	19.8	19.7	20.5	21.3	19.8
April, 1952 to April, 1953	20.1	20.1	20.1	19.1	19.2	18.9	27.9	27.4	28.3
April, 1953 to April, 1954	18.6	18.8	18.5	18.3	18.6	18.2	20.8	21.1	20.6
April, 1954 to April, 1955	19.9	20.1	19.6	19.5	19.8	19.3	22.4	22.8	22.0
March, 1955 to March, 1956	20.5	20.6	20.4	20.0	20.1	19.9	24.8	25.0	24.6
April, 1956 to April, 1957	19.4	19.6	19.1	19.0	19.2	18.9	22.2	23.1	21.4
March, 1957 to March, 1958	19.8	20.3	19.4	19.2	19.7	18.7	25.1	25.2	24.9
LOCAL MOVERS									
April, 1940 to April, 1947(a)	36.2	36.6	35.9	36.1	...	...	36.9	...	...
April, 1947 to April, 1948(a)	13.6	13.6	13.5	...	...	...	...	...	...
April, 1948 to April, 1949	13.0	12.9	13.1	13.0	12.8	13.1	13.6	13.9	13.3
March, 1949 to March, 1950	13.1	13.1	13.1	12.9	12.9	12.9	15.2	15.4	15.1
April, 1950 to April, 1951	13.2	14.1	13.8	13.7	13.9	13.5	16.1	16.3	16.0
April, 1951 to April, 1952	13.2	13.2	13.2	13.0	12.9	13.0	15.5	16.2	14.8
April, 1952 to April, 1953	13.5	13.5	13.6	12.4	12.4	12.4	21.7	21.2	22.2
April, 1953 to April, 1954	12.2	12.3	12.1	11.8	11.9	11.7	16.0	16.3	15.8
April, 1954 to April, 1955	13.3	13.4	13.2	12.7	12.9	12.6	18.0	18.2	17.8
March, 1955 to March, 1956	13.7	13.6	13.9	13.0	12.9	13.1	19.9	19.9	19.9
April, 1956 to April, 1957	13.1	13.3	13.0	12.5	12.7	12.4	17.8	18.3	17.4
March, 1957 to March, 1958	13.1	13.3	13.0	12.3	12.5	12.1	19.8	19.3	20.2
MIGRANTS[1]									
April, 1935 to April, 1940[2]	13.1	13.3	12.9	13.5	...	...	9.5	...	...
April, 1940 to April, 1947(a)	20.8	20.7	20.8	20.7	...	...	21.8	...	...
April, 1947 to April, 1948(a)	6.4	6.5	6.2	...	...	...	...	...	...
April, 1948 to April, 1949	5.8	6.0	5.5	5.9	6.1	5.7	4.7	5.2	4.3
March, 1949 to March, 1950	5.6	5.9	5.4	5.7	5.9	5.5	4.7	4.9	4.4
April, 1950 to April, 1951	7.1	7.2	6.9	7.2	7.3	7.1	5.6	6.0	5.2
April, 1951 to April, 1952	6.6	6.8	6.5	6.8	7.0	6.6	5.1	5.1	5.0
April, 1952 to April, 1953	6.6	6.7	6.5	6.7	6.8	6.6	6.2	6.2	6.1
April, 1953 to April, 1954	6.4	6.5	6.3	6.6	6.7	6.5	4.8	4.8	4.8
April, 1954 to April, 1955	6.6	6.7	6.4	6.8	7.0	6.7	4.4	4.6	4.2
March, 1955 to March, 1956	6.8	7.0	6.5	7.0	7.2	6.8	4.9	5.1	4.7
April, 1956 to April, 1957	6.2	6.3	6.2	6.5	6.5	6.4	4.4	4.8	4.0
March, 1957 to March, 1958	6.7	7.0	6.4	6.9	7.2	6.6	5.3	5.9	4.7

(a) Data by color not available.

[1]Excludes persons abroad at the beginning of the migration interval who entered the continental United States during the interval.

[2]Includes military population.

Source: U.S. Bureau of the Census, Current Population Reports, Series P-20, Nos. 14, 36, 49, 61, and 73.

This difference is an average of two different patterns, however. The nonwhite population, on the average, was about 3 or 4 percentage points more mobile locally (within the same county) than the white population. On the other hand, the white population averaged about 2 percentage points higher with respect to migration than the nonwhite population between 1935 and 1958. This latter difference has not been found by all surveys, however. During the years from 1940 to 1947 the nonwhite population is reported to have been slightly more migratory than the white, a tendency which was especially marked with respect to interstate, as contrasted with intrastate, migration. World War II seems to have provided an unusually strong stimulus to out-migration on the part of Negroes from the South. To summarize: Under most circumstances, the nonwhite population tends to be less migratory than the white, but to be somewhat more mobile locally than the white population.

Urban-rural Differences. All but one of the surveys taken to date show that the rural-nonfarm population has been residentially more mobile than either the urban or the rural-farm population. (It must be kept in mind that the urban-rural classification of Table 15-3 applies to residence at the end of the migration interval, and that the rates in the table are rates of in-migration, not of out-migration, to urban and rural areas.) This differential seems to reflect the growth of suburbs and the building up of more dense settlements in the vicinity of metropolises, rather than a flow of population to open country, villages, or hamlets. As new subdivisions are created in suburban areas, they attract a flow of families from the central city. Such subdivisions tend to be classed as rural-nonfarm rather than urban.

Rates of movement to rural-farm residences and to urban residences were about equal during the 1940's, in terms of both local mobility and migration. This does not necessarily imply that rural-farm and urban populations were making the same net gains or losses in population, however. It merely indicates that the people residing in rural-farm homes were tending to change residence about as frequently as those living in urban areas. A high proportion of this rural-farm mobility consists of short-distance moves from one farm to another. Since 1949, the rural-farm population has tended to be less mobile than it was in the 1940's, and less mobile (both with respect to local moving and migration) than the urban population. As the farm population has continued to shrink, the rural-farm areas have declined in the rate at which they attract migrants.

Table 15-3.—PERCENT OF THE CIVILIAN POPULATION CLASSIFIED AS RESIDENTIALLY MOBILE, BY URBAN-RURAL RESIDENCE AT DESTINATION AND TYPE OF MOBILITY: 1940 TO 1958

Type of mobility and mobility interval	Percent of population alive at beginning of the interval			
	Total	Type of residence at destination		
		Urban	Rural non-farm	Rural farm
ALL RESIDENTIAL MOBILITY				
April, 1940 to April, 1947.	57.0	56.4	62.9	52.1
April, 1947 to April, 1948.	19.9	18.3	24.0	20.1
April, 1948 to April, 1949.	18.8	17.8	22.2	18.2
March, 1949 to March, 1950.	18.7	18.5	21.4	16.2
April, 1950 to April, 1951.	21.0	21.3	23.7	16.0
April, 1951 to April, 1952.	19.8	20.5	19.7	17.0
April, 1952 to April, 1953.	20.1	20.7	22.9	13.3
April, 1953 to April, 1954.	18.6	18.6	20.9	14.9
April, 1954 to April, 1955.	19.9	20.2	22.1	14.5
March, 1955 to March, 1956.	20.5	20.5	23.8	14.3
April, 1956 to April, 1957.	19.4	19.4	21.7	13.9
March, 1957 to March, 1958.	19.8	19.7	22.8	14.4
LOCAL MOVERS				
April, 1940 to April, 1947.	36.2	36.7	37.4	33.3
April, 1947 to April, 1948.	13.6	12.7	16.1	13.1
April, 1948 to April, 1949.	13.0	12.7	15.3	11.5
March, 1949 to March, 1950.	13.1	13.3	13.8	11.6
April, 1950 to April, 1951.	13.9	14.7	14.8	9.4
April, 1951 to April, 1952.	13.2	14.2	12.0	10.5
April, 1952 to April, 1953.	13.5	14.4	14.2	8.4
April, 1953 to April, 1954.	12.2	12.5	12.7	10.2
April, 1954 to April, 1955.	13.3	13.9	14.0	9.5
March, 1955 to March, 1956.	13.7	14.2	14.7	9.7
April, 1956 to April, 1957.	13.1	13.7	13.7	9.1
March, 1957 to March, 1958.	13.1	13.8	13.7	8.6
MIGRANTS[1]				
April, 1935 to April, 1940[2]	13.1	11.9	18.5	11.3
April, 1940 to April, 1947.	20.8	19.7	25.5	18.8
April, 1947 to April, 1948.	6.4	5.6	7.9	7.0
April, 1948 to April, 1949.	5.8	5.1	6.9	6.7
March, 1949 to March, 1950.	5.6	5.2	7.6	4.6
April, 1950 to April, 1951.	7.1	6.5	8.9	6.6
April, 1951 to April, 1952.	6.6	6.3	7.8	6.5
April, 1952 to April, 1953.	6.6	6.3	8.7	5.0
April, 1953 to April, 1954.	6.4	6.1	8.3	4.7
April, 1954 to April, 1955.	6.6	6.3	8.2	5.0
March, 1955 to March, 1956.	6.8	6.3	9.1	4.6
April, 1956 to April, 1957.	6.2	5.8	8.0	4.8
March, 1957 to March, 1958.	6.7	5.9	9.1	5.8

[1]Excludes persons abroad at the beginning of the migration interval who entered the continental United States during the interval.

[2]Includes military population.

Source: U.S. Bureau of the Census, Current Population Reports, Series P-20, Nos. 14, 22, 28, 36, 47, 49, 57, 61, 73, 82, 86, and tabulations of the Bureau of the Census.

Age Differences. Persons in their late teens, their twenties, and their early thirties are more mobile than the general population. Persons who are 14 to 17 years old, and those who are 35 years old and over, tend to be less mobile than average. The validity of these statements has been documented frequently. It is not generally recognized, however, that local mobility also has a higher rate among persons at the young adult ages, and that it varies with age according to much the same pattern as migration. Table 15-4 and Figure 15-1

Table 15-4.—PERCENT OF THE CIVILIAN POPULATION CLASSIFIED AS RESIDENTIALLY MOBILE, BY AGE AND TYPE OF MOBILITY: 1940 TO 1958

(Civilian population includes members of the Armed Forces living off post and with their families on post)

Type of mobility and mobility interval	Percent of population alive at the beginning of the interval									
	Total all ages	Age (years)								
		Under 14	14 to 17	18 and 19	20 to 24	25 to 29	30 to 34	35 to 44	45 to 64	65 and over
ALL RESIDENTIAL MOBILITY										
April, 1940 to April, 1947...	57.0	63.2[1]	53.2	56.3	67.3	74.2		59.8	42.5	38.0
April, 1947 to April, 1948...	19.9	20.6	16.0	27.1	34.9	27.4		17.6	12.0	11.5
April, 1948 to April, 1949...	18.8	20.1	14.7	26.6	35.0	26.0		16.4	10.9	9.6
March, 1949 to March, 1950...	18.7	20.5	16.6	23.3	34.0	25.9		16.5	10.8	9.4
April, 1950 to April, 1951...	21.0	23.0	17.6	29.8	37.7	33.6	25.5	18.3	12.4	9.7
April, 1951 to April, 1952...	19.8	22.0	16.9	28.5	37.8	31.6	24.2	17.1	11.3	8.9
April, 1952 to April, 1953...	20.1	22.7	17.0	28.2	40.5	33.4	23.9	18.2	10.5	8.8
April, 1953 to April, 1954...	18.6	20.4	14.9	25.5	38.1	30.5	22.7	15.5	11.3	9.6
April, 1954 to April, 1955...	19.9	21.8	16.4	28.9	41.8	31.3	23.6	16.3	12.3	9.8
March, 1955 to March, 1956...	21.0	22.8	18.1	29.8	47.6	33.8	25.5	17.7	12.3	10.0
April, 1956 to April, 1957...	19.4	21.7	16.4	26.9	41.2	32.0	23.2	16.5	10.8	9.2
March, 1957 to March, 1958...	19.8	21.9	15.6	28.7	42.6	34.6	23.2	16.6	11.5	9.7
LOCAL MOVERS										
April, 1940 to April, 1947...	36.2	41.5[1]	35.5	35.0	39.6	44.6		37.5	28.8	26.1
April, 1947 to April, 1948...	13.6	14.1	10.7	18.0	22.3	18.8		11.9	8.7	7.8
April, 1948 to April, 1949...	13.0	13.9	10.3	17.2	24.4	17.6		11.6	7.8	6.7
March, 1949 to March, 1950...	13.1	14.6	11.5	15.4	22.9	17.4		12.0	7.8	7.2
April, 1950 to April, 1951...	13.9	15.0	12.6	18.2	24.1	21.0	16.4	12.9	8.6	7.3
April, 1951 to April, 1952...	13.2	14.4	11.5	17.2	24.0	19.9	15.6	11.9	8.3	6.9
April, 1952 to April, 1953...	13.5	15.1	12.3	17.0	23.5	22.3	16.1	13.1	7.3	6.6
April, 1953 to April, 1954...	12.2	13.7	10.2	15.0	22.3	19.5	14.9	10.4	8.0	6.3
April, 1954 to April, 1955...	13.3	14.9	11.2	17.9	26.1	20.2	15.7	11.0	8.7	6.8
March, 1955 to March, 1956...	13.7	15.4	12.2	18.7	26.5	21.9	16.0	11.5	8.6	7.2
April, 1956 to April, 1957...	13.1	14.9	11.6	16.0	26.2	20.9	15.4	11.5	7.8	6.4
March, 1957 to March, 1958...	13.1	14.6	10.6	17.6	26.8	21.7	15.7	11.0	8.0	7.0
MIGRANTS (a)										
April, 1935 to April, 1940 (b)	13.1	12.5[2]	10.5	13.6	18.4	19.0		13.6	9.1	6.9
April, 1940 to April, 1947...	20.8	21.7[1]	17.7	21.3	27.7	29.6		22.3	13.7	11.9
April, 1947 to April, 1948...	6.4	6.5	5.3	9.1	12.6	8.6		5.7	3.3	3.7
April, 1948 to April, 1949...	5.8	6.2	4.4	9.4	10.6	8.4		4.8	3.1	2.9
March, 1949 to March, 1950...	5.6	5.9	5.1	7.9	11.1	8.5		4.5	3.0	2.2
April, 1950 to April, 1951...	7.1	8.0	5.0	11.6	13.6	12.5	9.0	5.4	3.8	2.4
April, 1951 to April, 1952...	6.6	7.6	5.4	11.3	13.8	11.7	8.6	5.2	3.1	2.0
April, 1952 to April, 1953...	6.6	7.6	4.7	11.2	17.0	11.1	7.8	5.2	3.2	2.2
April, 1953 to April, 1954...	6.4	6.7	4.7	10.5	15.8	11.0	7.8	5.1	3.3	3.3
April, 1954 to April, 1955...	6.6	6.9	5.3	11.0	15.7	11.1	7.9	5.3	3.6	3.0
March, 1955 to March, 1956...	7.3	7.4	5.9	11.1	21.1	11.9	9.5	6.2	3.7	2.8
April, 1956 to April, 1957...	6.2	6.8	4.8	10.9	15.0	11.0	7.8	5.0	3.1	2.8
March, 1957 to March, 1958...	6.7	7.3	5.0	11.1	15.8	12.9	7.5	5.6	3.5	2.7

[1] 7 to 13 years.

[2] 5 to 13 years.

(a) Excludes persons abroad at the beginning of the migration interval who entered the continental United States during the interval.

(b) Includes military population.

Source: U.S. Bureau of the Census, Current Population Reports, Series P-20, Nos. 14, 22, 28, 36, 39, 47, 49, 61, 73, 82, and 86.

show that several of the recent mobility tabulations of the census reveal this same pattern. Thus, all residential mobility is primarily a phenomenon of late adolescence and early maturity. The high degree of mobility prevailing among the young adult population is a fundamental aspect of population dynamics. Each year, 35 to 40 percent of that part of the population which is aged 20 to 24 changes residence, and about 14 to 16 percent of this change is migratory. By way of contrast, 7 percent or less of the population aged 65 years and over changes residence within a year, and only about 3 percent or less become migrants. The higher-than-average mobility of children under 14 years of age is evidently due to the movement, both local and migratory, of their parents. The age pattern of mobility is understandable in view of the fact that 18 years is the median age for graduating from high school and, thus, for either going to college or seeking work, that the median age of marriage falls in the interval 20 to 24, and that the gradual transitions from smaller-to-larger living quarters and from the status of renter to home-owner are made by a great many families while the adult members are between the ages of 25 and 35. Most marriages involve a change of residence for two people, and the arrival of a second or third child may require a family comprising four or five persons to change residence. Note that migration is a much larger proportion of all mobility between the ages of 18 and 29 than at other ages.

The two types of mobility do not have identical age patterns, however. The child population and the older adult population tend to exhibit rates of local mobility that are nearer the average for all ages than are the migration rates of these two age groups.

Educational Differences. Information concerning the educational attainment of each mobility group is presented for only two periods, 1935 to 1940 and 1940 to 1947 (Table 15-5). There is a considerable variation between age groups with respect to the level of educational attainment. Because older people had fewer opportunities in their youth to obtain a secondary education than did the generations following them, the population at the older ages has a lower average attainment than the young adult population. Inasmuch as mobility status varies sharply with age, some control over the age factor should be a part of any examination of mobility differences between educational groups. Such a control may consist of presenting the data separately for each age group. Table 15-5 shows data for the age groups 25 to 34 years of age only. The relationships which are shown to exist through study of the data concerning this group are roughly representative of the relationships which characterize mobility and education for most of the other age groups.[3]

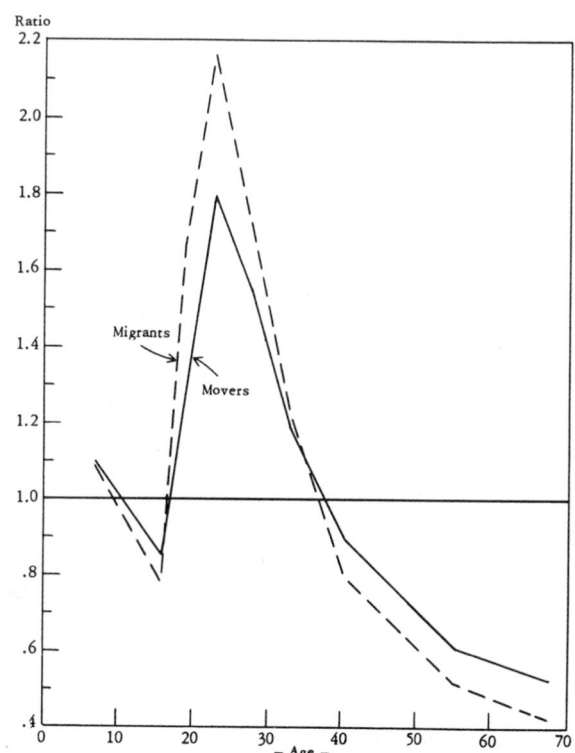

FIGURE 15-1. RATIO OF MIGRATION AND LOCAL MOVER RATES FOR EACH AGE GROUP TO THE AVERAGE RATE FOR ALL AGES, UNITED STATES: 1947 TO 1955

[3] More detailed information is presented below, in Table 15-18, for the year 1949-50.

Table 15-5.—PERCENT OF THE CIVILIAN POPULATION 25 TO 34 YEARS OF AGE CLASSED AS RESIDENTIALLY MOBILE, BY YEARS OF SCHOOL COMPLETED AND TYPE OF MOBILITY: 1940 TO 1947 AND 1935 TO 1940

Type of mobility and mobility interval	Total, 25 to 34 years of age	Years of school completed				
		Grade school		High school		College 1 year or more
		Not rptd. and less than 7 yrs	7 and 8 years	1 to 3 years	4 years	
April, 1940 to April, 1947						
Total mobility..................	74.2	83.2	72.1	73.1	74.9	77.7
Local movers....................	44.6	46.0	50.3	46.2	45.2	32.1
Migrants........................	29.6	27.2	21.8	26.9	29.7	45.6
April, 1935 to April, 1940						
Migrants........................	19.0	13.8	14.4	17.8	21.3	33.0

Source: U.S. Bureau of the Census, Current Population Reports, Series P-20, No. 14, Table 9, and Sixteenth Census, Social Characteristics of Migrants, Table 7.

Although the most mobile segment of the population appears to be the portion with above-average educational attainment, no one educational segment is a great deal more mobile than the others on the basis of total mobility. However, the pattern for local moving differs in detail from the pattern associated with migration. The rates for local moving are highest at the center and the lower end of the educational-attainment scale, and lowest at the upper end. The reverse is true for migration; by far the highest rates of migration are those for groups with some college training, and the lowest rates are for those with no more than grade school education. Migration exhibited a similar pattern between 1935 and 1940. Thus, it seems that rates of local moving are much higher among those segments of the population with average or below average educational attainment, whereas rates of migration are higher among those with above-average educational attainment.

Differences in Labor Force Status and Employment Status. Even though the labor force participation pattern is quite different for men and for women, the mobility patterns of both sexes in the various employment statuses are quite similar. Among both men and women, one of the most mobile segments of the population since 1940 has been that part which is unemployed. (See Table 15-6.) One of the least mobile segments has been that part which is not in the labor force. Both of these differences undoubtedly reflect, at least in part, the unique age composition of that portion of the population which is seeking work, and of that portion which is not in the labor force. The unemployed population, at any given moment, consists in part of young people seeking their first job or transferring from a part-time to a full-time job. Persons who are not in the labor force are largely students, persons who are in ill health, housewives, and persons who have retired. Note that in Table 15-6 unemployed women are shown to be consistently more spatially mobile than unemployed men (the period 1935 to 1954 is an exception to this pattern). This difference could be a reflection of the fact that a higher proportion of the female than of the male labor force is concentrated in the younger ages, where mobility rates are highest. In general, employed persons have not tended to be exceptionally mobile, either locally or as migrants. Since employment status and labor force status are determined as of the end of the mobility interval, and no indication is given as as to what these statuses were at the beginning of the interval, no decisive statement can be made either about the effect of mobility on employment status or the effect of employment status on migration. Scattered evidence does indicate that an above-average proportion of unemployed persons are in-migrants, in comparison with the general population, even after the factor of age is controlled. This may be due in part to the fact that some migrants had arrived so recently that they had not yet found a job when they were enumerated. During the period 1947 to 1958, unemployed

Table 15-6.—PERCENT OF THE CIVILIAN POPULATION CLASSIFIED AS RESIDENTIALLY MOBILE, BY SEX AND LABOR FORCE STATUS: 1940 TO 1958

(Civilian population includes members of the Armed Forces living off post and with their families on post)

Type of mobility and mobility interval	Male					Female.				
	14 yrs. old and over	Labor force			Not in labor force	14 Yrs. old and over	Labor force			Not in labor force
		Total	Em-ployed	Unem-ployed			Total	Em-ployed	Unem-ployed	
ALL RESIDENTIAL MOBILITY										
April, 1940 to April, 1947....	56.5	58.2	57.9	59.9	48.6	55.7	56.7	56.4	65.8	55.3
April, 1947 to April, 1948....	20.0	20.7	19.8	29.0	16.9	19.3	20.4	20.0	31.2	18.8
April, 1948 to April, 1949....	18.8	19.4	18.7	24.1	16.3	18.1	18.4	17.6	33.1	18.0
March, 1949 to March, 1950....	18.5	18.9	17.9	25.0	16.8	17.9	18.7	18.1	27.8	17.6
April, 1950 to April, 1951....	20.3	21.0	20.9	25.7	16.9	19.9	21.4	21.0	32.2	19.2
April, 1951 to April, 1952....	19.2	20.3	20.2	23.3	14.4	18.9	19.7	19.5	28.4	18.5
April, 1952 to April, 1953....	19.4	20.7	20.4	31.2	13.8	19.0	20.2	19.9	34.3	18.5
April, 1953 to April, 1954....	18.2	19.4	18.3	27.6	13.0	17.9	19.1	18.4	30.1	17.3
April, 1954 to April, 1955....	19.4	20.2	19.3	23.7	16.4	18.9	19.3	18.7	33.7	18.6
March, 1955 to March, 1956....	20.0	21.1	19.9	33.2	15.3	19.6	20.2	19.6	34.4	19.2
April, 1956 to April, 1957....	19.0	19.9	19.0	29.7	15.4	...	...	...	...	...
March, 1957 to March, 1958....	19.7	20.6	18.8	31.7	16.1	...	...	...	...	...
LOCAL MOVERS										
April, 1940 to April, 1947....	35.8	37.2	37.4	34.9	29.6	35.1	35.3	35.2	37.0	35.0
April, 1947 to April, 1948....	13.5	14.3	14.0	16.9	10.0	13.2	14.8	14.6	19.5	12.5
April, 1948 to April, 1949....	12.8	13.6	13.3	15.3	9.1	12.8	13.7	13.3	21.3	12.4
March, 1949 to March, 1950....	12.6	13.4	12.9	17.4	9.3	12.7	13.9	13.6	17.6	12.2
April, 1950 to April, 1951....	13.6	14.3	14.3	15.9	10.7	13.4	15.1	14.8	21.0	12.6
April, 1951 to April, 1952....	12.7	13.8	13.7	14.5	8.0	12.8	14.2	14.2	14.5	12.2
April, 1952 to April, 1953....	12.9	13.9	13.8	18.7	8.3	12.9	14.7	14.6	20.1	12.1
April, 1953 to April, 1954....	11.9	12.8	12.5	14.9	7.8	11.6	13.4	13.0	20.1	10.7
April, 1954 to April, 1955....	12.8	13.7	13.4	13.5	9.2	12.6	14.0	13.6	22.0	11.9
March, 1955 to March, 1956....	13.0	13.8	13.3	19.4	9.9	13.2	14.3	14.0	21.4	12.7
April, 1956 to April, 1957....	12.7	13.5	13.1	19.3	9.7	...	...	...	...	...
March, 1957 to March, 1958....	12.7	13.5	12.7	20.0	9.7	...	...	...	...	...
MIGRANTS										
April, 1935 to April, 1940[1]...	13.3	13.7	14.0	11.9	11.7	12.9	13.8	14.3	10.8	12.6
April, 1940 to April, 1947....	20.7	21.0	20.5	25.0	19.0	20.6	21.4	21.2	28.8	20.3
April, 1947 to April, 1948....	6.5	6.4	5.8	12.1	6.9	6.1	5.6	5.4	11.7	6.3
April, 1948 to April, 1949....	6.0	5.8	5.4	8.8	7.2	5.3	4.7	4.3	11.8	5.6
March, 1949 to March, 1950....	5.9	5.5	5.0	7.6	7.5	5.2	4.8	4.5	10.2	5.4
April, 1950 to April, 1951....	6.6	6.7	6.6	9.8	6.2	6.5	6.3	6.1	11.2	6.6
April, 1951 to April, 1952....	6.5	6.6	6.5	8.8	6.4	6.0	5.5	5.2	13.8	6.3
April, 1952 to April, 1953....	6.5	6.7	6.6	12.5	5.5	6.1	5.5	5.3	14.2	6.4
April, 1953 to April, 1954....	6.3	6.6	5.7	12.5	5.2	6.3	5.7	5.4	10.0	6.6
April, 1954 to April, 1955....	6.6	6.5	5.9	10.2	7.2	6.3	5.3	5.0	11.7	6.7
March, 1955 to March, 1956....	7.0	7.4	6.6	13.8	5.4	6.3	5.9	5.6	13.0	6.5
April, 1956 to April, 1957....	6.2	6.4	5.9	10.4	5.7	...	...	...	...	...
March, 1957 to March, 1958....	7.0	7.1	6.1	11.7	6.4	...	...	...	...	...

[1]Rates are based upon populations that include "Migration Status Not Reported."

Source: U.S. Bureau of the Census, Current Population Reports, Series P-20, Nos. 14, 36, 39, 47, 49, 57, 61, 82, and 86; Series P-50, Nos. 10 and 20; and Sixteenth Census, Economic Characteristics of Migrants, 1935-40, Table 1.

persons of both sexes had higher rates of migration, as well as higher rates of local moving, than employed persons. This was a reversal of the situation prevailing in the 1935 to 1940 period, when the unemployed were comparatively less migratory. Those persons who are not in the labor force have also shown a surprisingly high degree of migration in recent years, in comparison with earlier years. The differences between the two periods may be accounted for in part by differences in the length of the time intervals, but it is also reasonable to assume that the unfavorable economic conditions between 1935 and 1940 may have discouraged jobless persons from migrating.

<u>Occupational Differences.</u> Men and women are so unlike in their occupational composition, and so unlike with respect to their mobility in the several occupational groups, that the mobility of each occupational group is analyzed separately for each sex. Statistics concerning the mobility of employed workers in each occupational group are available for six intervals, covering the years 1940 to 1951 and 1955 to 1956. Table 15-7 presents the rates for male workers and Table 15-8 presents those for female workers.

(a) <u>Males</u>: One of the most mobile segments of the employed male population is that portion whose members are in professional or semiprofessional

Table 15-7.—PERCENT OF THE CIVILIAN MALE POPULATION CLASSIFIED AS RESIDENTIALLY MOBILE, BY MAJOR OCCUPATION GROUP AND TYPE OF MOBILITY: 1940 TO 1956

(Civilian population includes members of the Armed Forces living off post and with their families on post)

Type of mobility and mobility interval	Major occupation group of the employed male									
	Total employed males	Professional, technical, and kindred workers	Farmers and farm managers	Managers, officials and proprietors, except farm	Clerical, sales, and kindred workers	Craftsmen, foremen, and kindred workers	Operatives and kindred workers	Service workers	Farm laborers, and foremen	Laborers, except farm and mine
ALL RESIDENTIAL MOBILITY										
Apr. 1940 to Apr. 1947..	57.9	64.1	46.3	56.8	58.4	59.3	61.8	57.7	55.7	59.9
Apr. 1947 to Apr. 1948..	19.8	21.6	14.9	17.3	19.0	19.9	21.5	17.6	26.8	23.5
Apr. 1948 to Apr. 1949..	18.7	22.0	11.7	14.4	20.6	16.8	21.8	17.5	25.8	23.1
Mar. 1949 to Mar. 1950..	17.9	22.7	10.9	14.9	18.4	17.0	20.4	19.0	21.8	21.2
Apr. 1950 to Apr. 1951..	21.0	22.5	11.8	17.7	21.0	21.7	23.8	18.6	26.3	24.7
Apr. 1951 to Apr. 1952[2].	...	...	...	...	...	...	...	...	...	...
Apr. 1952 to Apr. 1953[2].	...	...	...	...	...	...	...	...	...	...
Apr. 1953 to Apr. 1954[2].	...	...	...	...	...	...	...	...	...	...
Apr. 1954 to Apr. 1955[2].	...	...	...	...	...	...	...	...	...	...
Mar. 1955 to Mar. 1956[3].	16.6	16.9	8.0	15.1	14.8	15.3	19.7	17.2	26.9	17.5
LOCAL MOVERS										
Apr. 1940 to Apr. 1947..	37.4	31.7	31.1	35.1	38.9	38.6	41.8	38.8	34.2	38.6
Apr. 1947 to Apr. 1948..	14.0	11.6	10.6	12.6	14.2	14.6	15.6	12.2	15.4	17.0
Apr. 1948 to Apr. 1949..	13.3	12.1	7.8	10.4	14.6	12.6	16.7	12.8	16.1	16.5
Mar. 1949 to Mar. 1950..	12.9	13.6	7.5	10.0	13.0	12.8	16.0	13.4	14.3	16.0
Apr. 1950 to Apr. 1951..	14.3	12.6	7.1	13.3	14.4	14.5	16.7	14.2	12.4	18.5
Apr. 1951 to Apr. 1952[2].	...	...	...	...	...	...	...	...	...	...
Apr. 1952 to Apr. 1953[2].	...	...	...	...	...	...	...	...	...	...
Apr. 1953 to Apr. 1954[2].	...	...	...	...	...	...	...	...	...	...
Apr. 1954 to Apr. 1955[2].	...	...	...	...	...	...	...	...	...	...
Mar. 1955 to Mar. 1956[3].	11.2	10.4	5.6	9.5	10.7	10.2	14.1	13.3	13.4	12.2
MIGRANTS										
Apr. 1935 to Apr. 1940[1].	14.0	25.4	8.2	15.4	15.8	13.4	12.6	17.9	16.0	12.0
Apr. 1940 to Apr. 1947..	20.5	32.4	15.2	21.7	19.5	20.7	20.0	18.9	21.5	21.3
Apr. 1947 to Apr. 1948..	5.8	10.0	4.3	4.7	4.8	5.3	5.9	5.4	11.4	6.5
Apr. 1948 to Apr. 1949..	5.4	9.9	3.9	4.0	6.0	4.2	5.1	4.7	9.7	6.6
Mar. 1949 to Mar. 1950..	5.0	9.1	3.4	4.9	5.4	4.2	4.4	5.6	7.5	5.2
Apr. 1950 to Apr. 1951..	6.7	9.9	4.6	4.3	6.5	7.2	7.1	4.5	13.9	6.2
Apr. 1951 to Apr. 1952[2].	...	...	...	...	...	...	...	...	...	...
Apr. 1952 to Apr. 1953[2].	...	...	...	...	...	...	...	...	...	...
Apr. 1953 to Apr. 1954[2].	...	...	...	...	...	...	...	...	...	...
Apr. 1954 to Apr. 1955[2].	...	...	...	...	...	...	...	...	...	...
Mar. 1955 to Mar. 1956[3].	5.4	6.5	2.4	5.5	4.2	5.2	5.5	4.0	13.4	5.2

[1]Rates are based upon populations that include "Migration Status Not Reported."

[2]Information not tabulated.

[3]Information based upon males 20 to 64 years of age employed in March, 1956, who worked in 1955, by occupation group of longest job held in 1955. Data for clerical workers does not include sales workers.

Source: U.S. Bureau of the Census, Current Population Reports, Series P-20, Nos. 14, 36, 39, and 73; Series P-50, Nos. 10 and 20, and Sixteenth Census, Economic Characteristics of Migrants, 1935-40, Table 5.

occupations. Since 1940, laborers (both farm and nonfarm) and operatives have also shown above-average mobility. The above-average mobility of operatives and of nonfarm laborers is due to a higher rate of local movement. Farm laborers are one of the most migratory of all occupational groups. The least mobile occupational group (with respect to both local mobility and migration) is comprised of farmers and farm managers. Pro-

prietors, managers, and officials also tend to have below-average mobility, as an occupational group.

As was found to be true of educational-attainment groups, occupational groups also vary with respect to kind of mobility. Operatives, service workers, and laborers consistently have had higher rates of moving than the general population. Professional, proprietary, and managerial occupations, on the other hand, have had lower-than-

Table 15-8.—PERCENT OF THE CIVILIAN FEMALE POPULATION CLASSIFIED AS RESIDENTIALLY MOBILE, BY MAJOR OCCUPATION GROUP AND TYPE OF MOBILITY: 1940 TO 1955

(Civilian population includes members of the Armed Forces living off post and with their families on post)

Type of mobility and mobility interval	Major occupation group of the employed female										
	Total employed females	Professional, technical, kindred workers	Farmers and farm managers	Managers, officials, proprietors, exc. farm	Clerical, sales, and kindred workers	Craftsmen, foremen, and kindred workers	Operatives and kindred workers	Private household workers	Service workers	Farm laborers and foremen	Laborers, except farm and mine
ALL RESIDENTIAL MOBILITY											
Apr.1940 to Apr.1947..	56.4	57.0	36.3	54.9	55.6	52.2	56.7	59.1	62.5	47.6	56.4
Apr.1947 to Apr.1948..	20.0	21.7	14.2	17.0	19.9	9.2	19.0	...	23.4	15.5	...
Apr.1948 to Apr.1949..	17.6	21.8	6.3	13.3	16.9	12.1	14.8	...	23.6	8.8	...
Mar.1949 to Mar.1950..	18.1	18.3	5.5	14.2	19.1	10.3	17.4	...	19.7	11.4	...
Apr.1950 to Apr.1951..	21.4	25.0	18.3	17.3	21.5	20.0	19.4	21.0	27.0	13.0	...
Apr.1951 to Apr.1952[2].	...	...	...	...	...	...	...	...	...	...	...
Apr.1952 to Apr.1953[2].	...	...	...	...	...	...	...	...	...	...	...
Apr.1953 to Apr.1954[2].	...	...	...	...	...	...	...	...	...	...	...
Apr.1954 to Apr.1955[2].	...	...	...	...	...	...	...	...	...	...	...
LOCAL MOVERS											
Apr.1940 to Apr.1947..	35.2	24.8	25.7	35.0	34.8	37.1	38.6	39.1	38.6	30.6	29.5
Apr.1947 to Apr.1948..	14.6	11.2	10.6	11.9	15.0	5.4	15.6	...	16.6	11.4	...
Apr.1948 to Apr.1949..	13.3	13.6	4.2	9.5	12.8	9.7	12.6	...	17.8	6.2	16.5
Mar.1949 to Mar.1950..	13.6	12.2	4.4	11.0	14.9	8.1	14.0	...	14.0	8.0	...
Apr.1950 to Apr.1951..	15.1	15.3	6.7	11.4	15.0	13.6	15.8	15.7	17.8	8.8	...
Apr.1951 to Apr.1952[2].	...	...	...	...	...	...	...	...	...	...	...
Apr.1952 to Apr.1953[2].	...	...	...	...	...	...	...	...	...	...	...
Apr.1953 to Apr.1954[2].	...	...	...	...	...	...	...	...	...	...	...
Apr.1954 to Apr.1955[2].	...	...	...	...	...	...	...	...	...	...	...
MIGRANTS											
Apr.1935 to Apr.1940[1].	14.3	23.9	5.7	12.9	11.8	8.9	7.8	17.9	18.1	9.9	11.0
Apr.1940 to Apr.1947..	21.2	32.2	10.6	19.9	20.8	15.1	18.1	20.0	23.9	17.0	26.9
Apr.1947 to Apr.1948..	5.4	10.5	3.6	5.1	4.9	3.8	3.4	...	6.8	4.1	...
Apr.1948 to Apr.1949..	4.3	8.2	2.1	3.8	4.1	2.4	2.2	...	5.8	2.6	...
Mar 1949 to Mar.1950..	4.5	6.1	1.1	3.2	4.2	2.2	3.4	...	5.7	3.4	...
Apr.1950 to Apr.1951..	6.3	9.7	11.5	5.9	6.5	6.4	3.6	5.3	9.2	4.2	...
Apr.1951 to Apr.1952[2].	...	...	...	...	...	...	...	...	...	...	...
Apr.1952 to Apr.1953[2].	...	...	...	...	...	...	...	...	...	...	...
Apr.1953 to Apr.1954[2].	...	...	...	...	...	...	...	...	...	...	...
Apr.1954 to Apr.1955[2].	...	...	...	...	...	...	...	...	...	...	...

[1]Rates are based upon populations that include "Migration Status Not Reported."

[2]Information not tabulated.

Source: U.S. Bureau of the Census, Current Population Reports, Series P-20, Nos. 14, 36, 39; Series P-50, Nos. 10 and 20, and Sixteenth Census, Economic Characteristics of Migrants, 1935-40, Table 5.

average rates of moving. Clerical workers, and craftsmen and foremen, have shown about average local mobility. In summary, the high total mobility of the professional group results from a high rate of migration. The high mobility of the laborer group derives from moderately high rates of both moving and migration. Farm operators and farm managers have low rates with respect to both types of mobility. Clerical workers and craftsmen have about average rates for both types of mobility. Operatives have lower-than-average rates of migration, but higher-than-average rates of local movement.

These inter-occupational differences are probably, in part, a reflection of the differences in the average age of members of the particular occupational groups involved. The pattern of differences probably varies also with changing economic conditions. For example, laborers were much less migratory during the period 1935 to 1940, in comparison with the other occupation groups, than they were in the period 1940 to 1950.

(b) Females: Among women workers, there has been a higher proportion of mobility in the service and the professional occupations than in the other occupations. Female service workers have been both more migratory and more locally mobile than has the employed female population generally. Professional female workers, like professional male workers, have been much more migratory but considerably less locally mobile than the employed population as a whole. Women craft and operative workers tend to have about average local mobility, but low rates of migration. Apparently, the women who are employed in these latter types of work are recruited locally, or else do not move a great distance to take these kinds of jobs. Female workers in clerical occupations tend to have average mobility, both locally and as migrants.

Income Differences. As yet, only scanty data are available concerning the incomes received by mobile and nonmobile persons. The evidence presented in Table 15-9, based on a single survey, leads to the hypothesis that among adult workers 25 years of age and over, the median income of mobile workers is smaller than the income of non-

mobile workers. This seemed to be the case among both the male and the female workers. Migrants had a smaller median income than movers, and movers, in turn, had a smaller median income than the nonmobile population. Thus, these data suggest that an inverse relationship may exist between degree of mobility and average size of income. Much of this difference could be accounted

Table 15-9.—MEDIAN INCOME OF THE CIVILIAN LABOR FORCE, BY MOBILITY STATUS, AGE, AND SEX FOR THE UNITED STATES: MARCH, 1949 TO MARCH, 1950

Sex and type of mobility	Median income, by age			
	All ages[1]	14 to 24 years	25 to 44 years	45 to 64 years
Male, total....	$2,536	$1,334	$2,864	$2,685
Nonmobile....	2,578	1,240	2,900	2,732
Local mover..	2,456	1,809	2,762	2,393
Migrant......	2,071	1,343	2,621	1,813
Female, total..	$1,467	$1,191	$1,650	$1,483
Nonmobile....	1,505	1,239	1,676	1,511
Local mover..	1,417	1,240	1,646	1,231
Migrant......	947	831	1,176	([2])

[1]Includes civilian labor force of all ages, including those 65 years of age and over.
[2]No data reported.

Source: U.S. Bureau of the Census, Current Population Reports, Series P-20, No. 36, Table 9.

for by the younger average age of migrants (incomes are lower among younger workers), but since this relationship persists within each of two broad age groups, 20 to 44 years and 45 to 64 years, the difference is probably not due solely to the different age compositions of the various income groups. However, this need not force one to conclude that moving or migration has the effect of reducing income. It should be kept in mind that the migration-interval and the earnings-interval both refer to the same span of time--the year preceding enumeration. The mobile person may lose his job and then move, or he may move because of low earnings. Both the loss of income and the movement may be indirect consequences of unemployment. In addition, if moving requires a person to be off work, it can act to reduce his income. On the other hand, these data do not give any evidence that movement acts to increase earnings, at least within the year of the move. Whether movement eventually tends to increase earnings cannot be determined by means of these data.[4]

Differences in Marital Status. Data concerning differences in mobility according to marital status categories, with a necessary control on age, have been published in two Current Population Surveys. Evidence for two age classes, summarized in Table 15-10, indicates that unmarried persons tended to be less residentially mobile than married, widowed, or divorced persons. Divorced persons were found to be more mobile than widowed persons, and widowed persons more mobile than married persons. The direction of cause and effect cannot be determined here in all cases. The act of marrying involves mobility for at least one member of each couple. On the other hand, it is possible that purchasing a home, moving to a larger house or apartment, or moving to the suburbs may cause married persons to be more locally mobile, age-for-age, than single persons. On the other hand, it is also possible that persons who have migrated as unmarried persons tend to marry at an earlier age than nonmigrants.[5] Summary: There is great variation within the population in degree of mobility--both local movement and migration. There are variations associated with sex, color, age, educational attainment, employment status, occupation, income, and marital status. These differences tend to be patterned, and to persist year after year. Differential local mobility is not always identical with differential migration mobility, either in pattern or intensity. In many instances, local movement seems to be a poor man's substitute for migration. Persons toward the lower end of the socio-economic scale seem to move locally under certain circumstances which would cause persons higher in the socio-economic scale to migrate.

Table 15-10.—PERCENT OF THE CIVILIAN POPULATION CLASSIFIED AS RESIDENTIALLY MOBILE, BY TYPE OF MOBILITY AND MARITAL STATUS, FOR TWO AGE GROUPS: 1948

Age period and type of mobility	Marital status				
	Total	Single	Married	Widowed	Divorced
1947 to 1948					
25-34 years old					
Total mobility.	27.4	14.9	30.0	21.8	32.1
Movers.......	18.8	8.7	20.9	12.3	21.0
Migrants.....	8.6	6.2	9.1	9.5	11.1
35-44 years old					
Total mobility.	17.6	15.3	17.3	22.8	31.3
Movers.......	11.9	8.9	11.9	15.5	21.0
Migrants.....	5.7	6.4	5.4	7.3	10.3

Source: U.S. Bureau of the Census, Current Population Reports, Series P-20, No. 22.

THE EFFECT OF INTERNAL MIGRATION UPON THE REGIONAL DISTRIBUTION OF POPULATION

Internal migration both brings people to a community from other places (in-migration) and takes them away from a community to live in other places (out-migration).[6] Its effect, therefore, is made most clear by an examination of net migration, which is in-migration minus out-migration. If migration were a completely random process, one would expect every place to receive as many in-migrants as the out-migrants it loses, and would expect the net effect to be zero. That this certainly has not happened in the United States is shown by Table 15-11, which reports the estimated net gain or loss of population through migration, for each of the economic regions described in Chapter 5, for the 1940 to 1950 decade. The map of Figure 15-2 graphs the net migration rate in

---

[4] More data concerning this topic will be presented in Table 15-18, below.

[5] The Current Population Survey Report, Series P-20, No. 82, also contains data for the year 1956-57; these data indicate patterns very similar to those discussed here for the year 1948. The 1948 data are given because they report more detail both for age and for marital status.

[6] The terms "in-migration" and "out-migration" are used in the analysis of internal migration to avoid confusion with international "immigration" and "emigration."

Table 15-11.—ESTIMATED NUMBER OF NET MIGRANTS AND NET MIGRATION RATE FOR EACH ECONOMIC REGION: 1940 TO 1950

Economic region	Region number	Net migration per 100 population			Number of net migrants (000)		
		Total	Metropolitan areas	Non-metropolitan areas	Total	Metropolitan areas	Non-metropolitan areas
U.S. Total...............................	....	0.4	9.2	-9.3	589	6,397	-5,808
Atlantic Metropolitan Belt Region.................	I	4.3	4.2	5.9	1,169	1,054	115
Eastern Great Lakes and Northeastern Upland Region.	II	-1.7	-1.1	-2.2	-146	-41	-105
Lower Great Lakes Region..........................	III	2.2	3.1	-1.1	411	455	-44
Upper Great Lakes Region.........................	IV	-5.1	2.1	-8.0	-239	28	-266
North Center (Corn Belt) Region....................	V	-2.7	7.8	-7.2	-383	328	-711
Central Plains Region.............................	VI	-7.1	22.0	-12.5	-342	163	-505
Central and Eastern Upland Region.................	VII	-9.3	5.8	-16.8	-1,231	258	-1,490
Southeast Coastal Plain Region....................	VIII	-11.4	8.7	-17.2	-1,570	266	-1,836
Atlantic Flatwoods and Gulf Coast Region..........	IX	14.7	26.9	1.4	852	814	38
South Center and Southwest Plains Region..........	X	-15.1	25.1	-22.8	-1,219	325	-1,544
Rocky Mountain and Intermountain Region...........	XI	-0.8	18.9	-3.9	-23	78	-101
Pacific Northwest Region..........................	XII	24.1	27.2	21.2	675	367	308
Pacific Southwest Region..........................	XIII	37.8	39.4	29.5	2,633	2,300	334

Source: Donald J. Bogue, Components of Population Change, 1940-50: Estimates of Net Migration and Natural Increase for Each Standard Metropolitan Area and State Economic Area. (Oxford, Ohio, Scripps Foundation, Miami University) 1957, Table II-A.

each of the state economic areas.[7] For example, the Pacific Southwest Region had a net gain of 2,633,000 persons, whereas the Southeast Coastal Plains Region (the "Old South") lost 1,570,000 persons. This represented a gain through migration alone of 37.8 percent on the part of the first region, and a loss of 11.4 percent through migration alone to the second region. It is clear that these population changes are of major consequence, especially in view of the fact that they took place within the short span of ten years. However, they are only extreme instances of an over-all pattern of migration which is causing a major interregional redistribution of the population. Each of the economic regions had a unique

[7] These materials are drawn from a monograph, Components of Population Change, 1940-50: Estimates of Net Migration and Natural Increase for each Standard Metropolitan Area and State Economic Area, by Donald J. Bogue. (Oxford, Ohio: The Scripps Foundation, Miami University), 1957. This source reports the estimated net migration, 1940 to 1950, for each state economic area, economic subregion, and economic region. It also provides similar data for the central city and suburban ring of each individual standard metropolitan area, by age, sex, and color.

migration situation, a situation intimately related to the social and economic changes occurring within the region and within each of the other regions.

Three major interregional flows of internal migration have been operating in the United States, not only during the 1940 to 1950 decade, but for several decades; the behavior of these flows between 1940 and 1950 may be inferred from Figures 15-1 and 15-2 and Table 15-11:

(a) The Westward Movement. There has been a high-volume flow of persons into the Pacific Southwest and Pacific Northwest Regions. These migrants have been drawn heavily from the Corn Belt and Central Plains Regions, but substantial numbers also have come from the southern regions and from all of the regions of the northeastern portion of the nation. Until 1940 this flow consisted primarily of white persons, but after 1940 many Negroes joined the stream.

(b) The Northward Movement from the Southern Province. The great industrial and commercial expansion that has taken place in the Atlantic Metropolitan Belt Region and the Lower Great Lakes Region has attracted many millions of persons from the three economic regions of the South, who have settled in northern industrial centers in or-

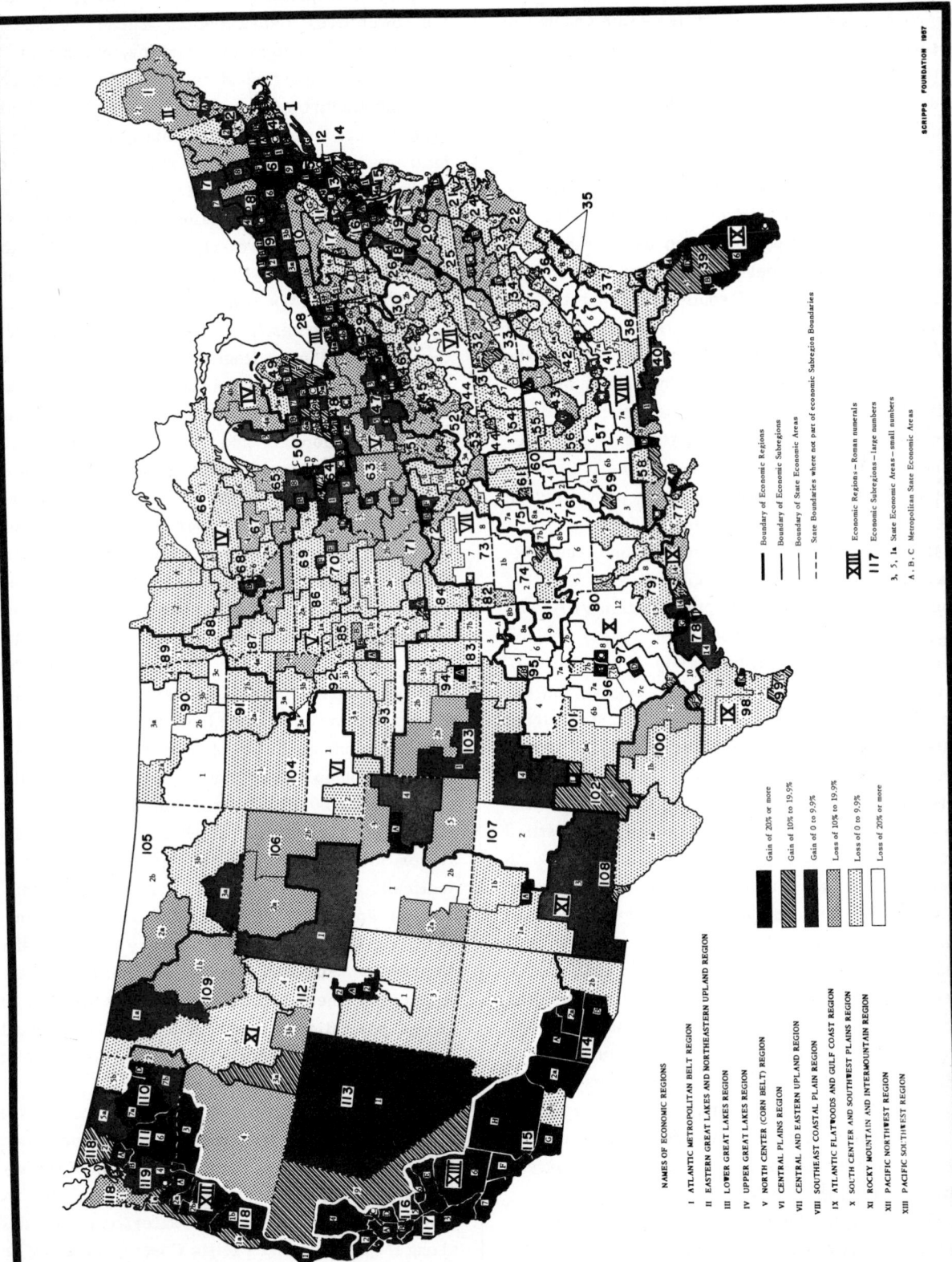

FIGURE 15-2. RATE OF NET MIGRATION FOR STATE ECONOMIC AREAS OF THE UNITED STATES: 1940 TO 1950

der to raise their level of living. Both white and Negro migrants have flowed along this channel in great numbers.

(c) The Southward Movement to the Gulf Coast and the Southern Atlantic Seaboard. The entire Gulf Coast--from the mouth of the Rio Grande in Texas, past Corpus Christi and Houston, across the coastal portions of lower Louisiana, Mississippi, and Alabama, and on to the southern tip of Florida--has undergone a much more rapid and intensive economic development than the remainder of the southern and southeastern parts of the United States that lies further from the coast. A similar development has taken place along the Atlantic Seaboard in Florida. The development of this southern coastal region has attracted migrants from all regions lying to the north. Between 1940 and 1950 it enjoyed a positive rate of net migration second only to those prevailing in the regions of the Pacific Coast.

Between 1940 and 1950 three regions, the Central and Eastern Upland Region (Region VII), the Southeast Coastal Plain Region (Region VIII), and the South Center and Southwest Plains Region (Region X), lost population heavily through net out-migration. These are all of the regions of the Southern Province, except the Gulf Coast. During this decade, the entire Southern Province underwent great agricultural and industrial changes. One facet of this change was that more than 4 million persons left these three regions and settled in other economic regions. In Region X, the South Center and Southwest Plains Region, one person in 7 who had lived in this broad territory in 1940 had migrated elsewhere by 1950 and had not been replaced by an in-migrant. This region contains the greater part of Mississippi and the cotton-farming sections of Texas, Oklahoma, Arkansas, and Tennessee. Mechanization of agriculture in the Mississippi Delta and other farming areas, a rapid increase in livestock farming, and the attractiveness of the industrial wages prevailing in metropolitan centers seem to have almost "emptied" some parts of this region of its population.

Two regions experienced small rates of net gain from migration. They were Region I, the

Atlantic Metropolitan Belt Region, and Region III, the Lower Great Lakes Region. These are the two most populous regions in the nation, and contain a very large proportion of the nation's commerce and manufacturing. Even though their rates of migration were comparatively small, the number of migrants they gained at the expense of the rest of the nation was quite large--1.56 million. Many of the migrants they gained came from the South.

The remaining five regions--Region II, the Eastern Great Lakes-Northeastern Upland Region, Region IV, the Upper Great Lakes Region, Region V, the North Center (Corn Belt) Region, Region VI, the Central Plains Region, and Region XI, the Rocky Mountain-Intermountain Region--suffered moderately small population losses through migration. Regions II and IV are relatively rural dairying regions, with quite a bit of deforested woodland and few large metropolitan centers; these two regions have experienced a long-time migration deficit. Regions V and VI, which are agricultural regions with a high level of living, have lost population because of progressive farm mechanization and the concomitant increase in average size of farms and in farm consolidation. The net migration loss in Region VI (the Great Plains) was much greater than in Region V. In the latter region, an influx of new manufacturing industries tended to hold that segment of the population which was departing from the farms. In Region VI, agricultural adjustment to the wide fluctuations in annual rainfall (an adjustment dramatically accelerated by the droughts of the mid-1930's) appears to have continued. The Rocky Mountain Region, perhaps contrary to the general impression, suffered a small net migration loss. Apparently, the pull exerted by the Pacific regions on the population of this region was strong enough to more than counterbalance the in-migration coming from regions to the east.

The regional migration picture can be viewed (from a broad perspective) in yet another way: The population flowed from the interior of the nation toward the old as well as the newly established commercial and industrial waterfronts located along the Atlantic and Pacific Coasts, and along the

Gulf Coast and the Lower Great Lakes. Meanwhile, population flowed from the non-industrial, mountainous, and deforested areas which offered few job opportunities to new entrants into the labor force, and out of those agricultural regions where adjustments to farm mechanization and to the realities of climate and weather had made it economically unprofitable for the agricultural labor force to be increased in size.

Migration to Metropolitan Areas and from Nonmetropolitan Areas. Within each of the regions, there has been a long-term flow of migrants from nonmetropolitan to metropolitan areas. For example, between 1940 and 1950, the principal standard metropolitan areas (those having a total population of 100,000 or more in 1950) gained 6.4 million persons through migration (Table 15-11, column 6). The remainder (the nonmetropolitan part) of the nation--which comprises the vast majority of the nation's land area but contains only about one-half of its population--lost 5.8 million persons through net out-migration. This "metropolitanization" of the population was an almost universal process; the metropolitan portions of every region except one (Region II) experienced net gains from migration, while the nonmetropolitan portions of every region except the rapidly growing Gulf Coast and Pacific Coast Regions and the Atlantic Metropolitan Belt Region experienced net out-migration. This tendency for the population to cluster around a few large centers has been a long-run trend, and has been noted and described before.[8]

This metropolitanization has been almost entirely the result of migration. In fact, if migration were not in the picture, the nonmetropolitan areas would have grown faster than the metropolitan areas, for rural areas traditionally have had higher rates of fertility than urban areas.

Interregional differences in metropolitan and nonmetropolitan growth are largely a product of migration, although in some instances (such as the Rocky Mountain Region) a high level of fertility has compensated for a part of the migration losses and has caused the region to grow at about average rates. In those areas where high rates of in-migration coincide with moderately high birth rates (as in some of the metropolitan areas), the result is a virtual population "explosion." But regional differences and metropolitan-nonmetropolitan differences do not account for all the variations in internal migration. A careful study of Figure 15-2 will show that within each region some metropolitan areas gained migrants at a faster rate than others, and that some nonmetropolitan areas suffered much larger net migration losses than others. To find an explanation for these local (but nevertheless sizable) variations in the migration process, it would be necessary to study the variations existing among these subareas with respect to environmental conditions, and to examine the changes in economic balance occurring among them. Although these variations have been measured, as yet they have not been adequately explained.

Interregional Migration Between 1935 and 1940. The picture presented above for the period 1940 to 1950 is not unique. In fact, the net interregional redistribution of population through net migration is very similar in most respects to the migration pattern that may be inferred from the census data concerning migration between 1935 and 1940. Figures 15-4, 15-5, and 15-6 show the rates of in-, out-, and net migration for this earlier period, by population subregions.[9]

In order to indicate which population subregions are similar to each other and which are relatively

---

[8] See for example, Donald J. Bogue, Population Growth in Standard Metropolitan Areas: 1900-1950, With an Explanatory Analysis of Urbanized Areas, Housing and Home Finance Agency, 1953.

[9] Population subregions were units of homogeneous area, analagous to state economic areas, as delimited for the 1950 census. The population subregions were used in the census of 1940 to identify the origin and destination of migrants. These maps have been reproduced from the monograph, Streams of Migration Between Subregions, op. cit.

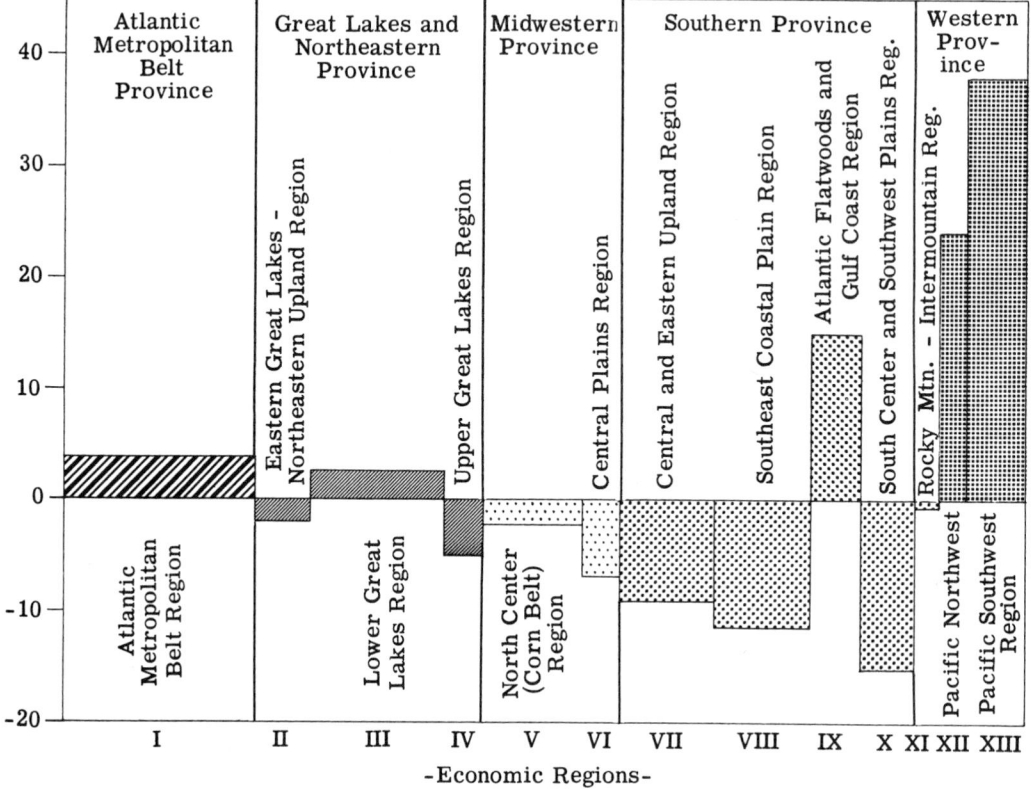

FIGURE 15-3. RATE OF NET MIGRATION FOR EACH ECONOMIC REGION, 1940 TO 1950

Note: The width of the bars is proportional to the population size in mid-decade.

unlike each other, the boundaries of the 13 major economic regions have been superimposed on these maps. An examination of the maps shows that much of the variation among these subregions was systematic; areas having similar physical characteristics and lying in the same economic region tended to have a similar migration experience.

The western half of the United States, and especially the Pacific regions, tended to have rates of in-migration that were much higher than the national average of 12 per 100 (Map 15-4). Florida, and most of the Gulf Coast across the southern portions of Alabama, Mississippi, and Texas, were also areas of heavy in-migration. In general, the Upper South, the Midwest, and the Northeast had below-average rates of in-migration.

Throughout the nation, the rates of in-migration tended to be higher for metropolitan than for non-metropolitan areas.

Out-migration rates (Map 15-5) were very high in certain subregions which formed a belt extending downward from Canada into the Panhandle and the central areas of Texas. Rates of out-migration were above average in most of the Central Plains Region, and in much of the territory to the west of it. Moderately high out-migration rates also characterized many parts of the South and the Upper Great Lakes area. Along the Eastern Seaboard, around the lower Great Lakes, throughout the Appalachian and Piedmont areas, and along the

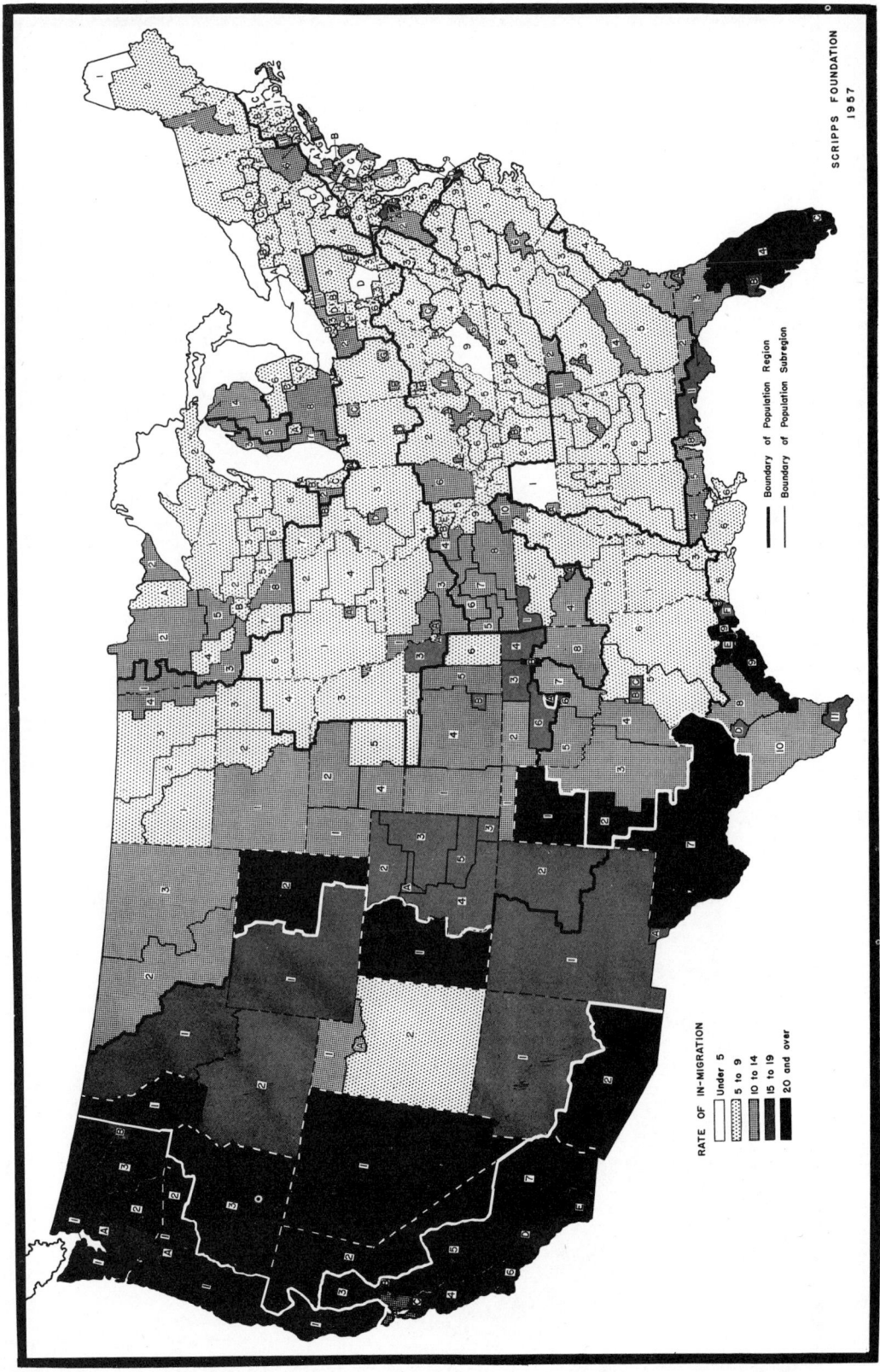

FIGURE 15-4. RATE OF IN-MIGRATION FOR EACH POPULATION SUBREGION OF THE UNITED STATES: 1935 TO 1940

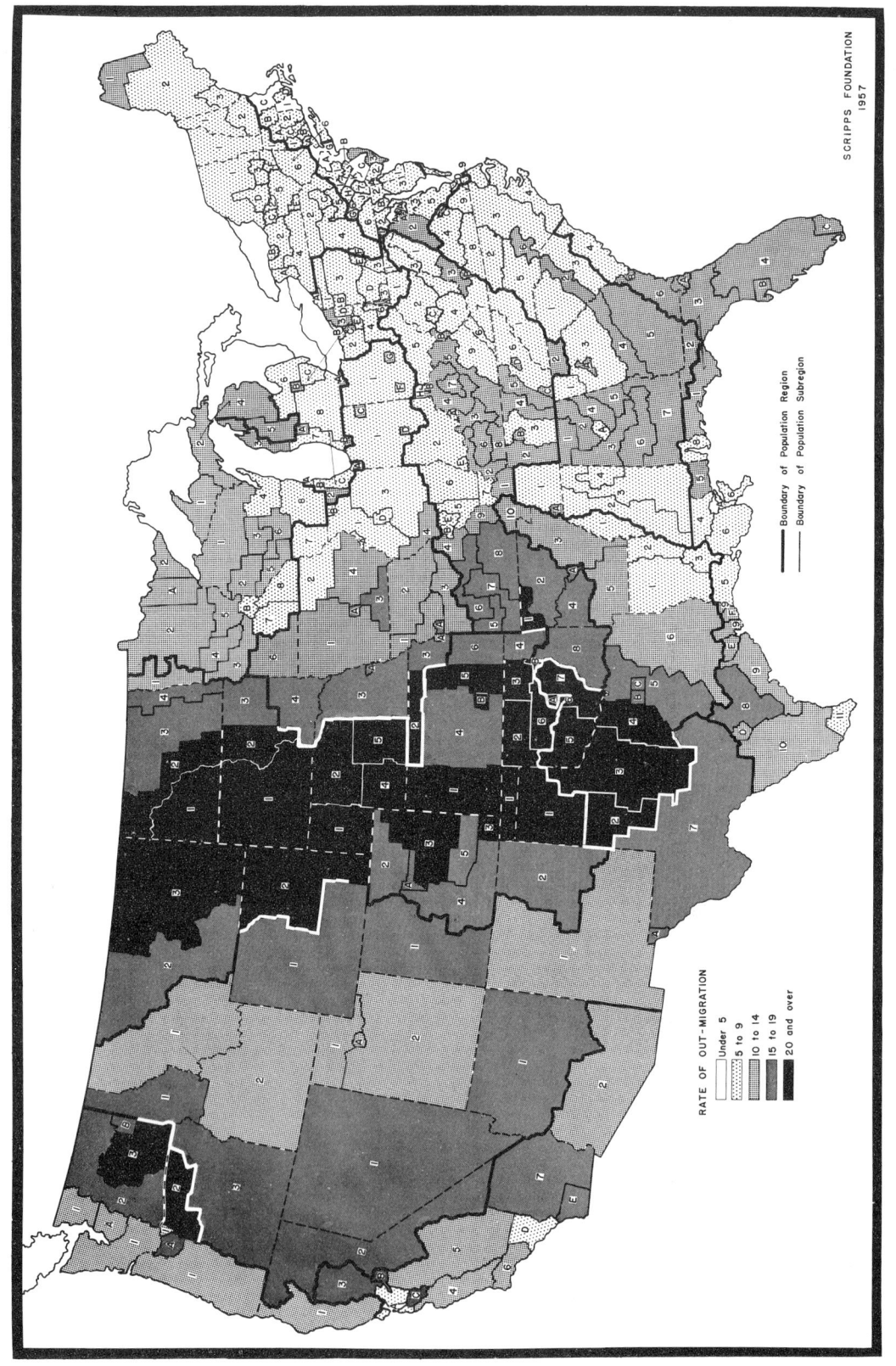

FIGURE 15-5. RATE OF OUT-MIGRATION FOR EACH POPULATION SUBREGION OF THE UNITED STATES: 1935 TO 1940

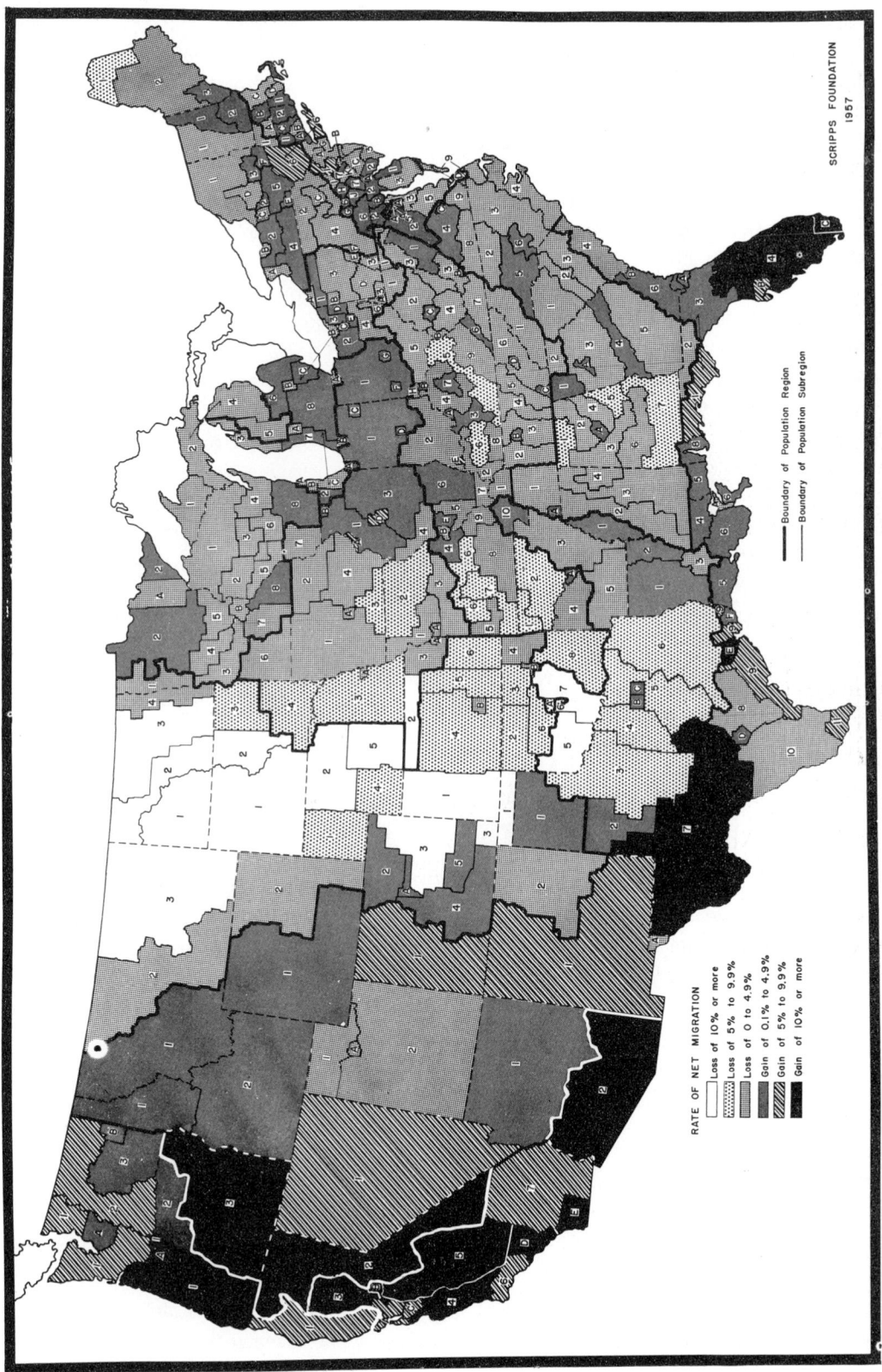

FIGURE 15-6.   RATE OF NET MIGRATION FOR EACH POPULATION SUBREGION OF THE UNITED STATES: 1935 TO 1940

lower Mississippi River, out-migration rates were below average.

The net balance of in- and out-migration is shown in Map 15-6. Extraordinarily rapid population growth resulting from migration was characteristic of two major areas--the West Coast and the lower Gulf Coast of Florida. Almost all subregions of the Pacific Southwest, the Pacific Northwest, and the Gulf Coast regions had high rates of net in-migration. Smaller gains from net migration were found along the lower Great Lakes, within the Atlantic Metropolitan Belt, and in the lower Mississippi River and northern Florida areas. Most metropolitan areas, irrespective of regional location, experienced a net migration gain.

At the other extreme, severe net losses due to migration were suffered by a majority of the subregions in the Central Plains Region. Losses of 5 to 10 percent were characteristic of subregions in the Upper Great Lakes Region, throughout the hilly and mountainous portions of the eastern part of the nation, and in much of the South.

Economic Areas vs. States as Units of Area for Measuring Migration. The inter-area variations illustrated by the four maps indicate that some areas were receiving migrants at a much more rapid rate than others, that some areas were losing population through out-migration at a much more rapid rate than others, and that these differences led to large inter-area differences in population growth. A most important fact to note is that these variations do not follow state lines (either in the 1935 to 1940 period or the 1940 to 1950 period). A careful study of the maps, state by state, will show that there was considerable internal diversity within most states with respect to rates of in-, out-, and net migration. A review of four of the most striking examples will illustrate this diversity.

(1) In the Gulf Coast States, the population subregions bordering on the Gulf Coast had an above-average rate of in-migration and received a substantial net population gain through migration. The population subregions lying away from the Gulf, but within these same states, had much lower rates of in-migration and showed a tendency to have a net out-migration. A state-by-state tabulation for the Gulf States would have struck a net balance between the coastal areas and the inland areas, and would have presented a much less informative picture. Thus, a subdivision of the states into homogeneous subregions permits the data to show more specifically where migration gains and losses were concentrated.

(2) The large out-migration from the Central Plains Region is shown to have been much more severe in some parts of the states that were affected than in others. Figure 15-5, for example, shows that the rate of out-migration is greater for the western than for the eastern portion of the tier of states running from North Dakota south to Oklahoma. A state-wide average presents an unduly bright picture for the western segment of each state and an unduly pessimistic picture for the eastern part.

(3) In the states which are partly Great Plains and partly Rocky Mountain (Montana, Wyoming, Colorado, and New Mexico), the net migration rates tend to be negative for the eastern (plains) and positive for the western (mountainous) area.

(4) The metropolitan areas in many states showed a positive balance with respect to migration, while the nonmetropolitan areas in the same state showed a net loss due to migration.

Thus, the subdivision of states into metropolitan and nonmetropolitan areas, the further subdivision of the nonmetropolitan part into more homogeneous population subregions, and the use of this system of areas for tabulating migration information, are refinements that greatly increase the precision and detail of the information available concerning migrants. State-by-state tabulations cannot provide this important information.

INTERREGIONAL MIGRATION: 1950 TO 1958

Estimates of the net migration between April 1, 1950 and July 1, 1958 are given in Table 15-12 for each geographic division. Separate estimates are

Table 15-12.—ROUGH ESTIMATES OF NET MIGRATION FOR GEOGRAPHIC DIVISIONS, BY COLOR:
APRIL 1, 1950 TO JULY 1, 1958.

Geographic division	Estimated net migration (000)			Migrants per 1,000 residents in 1950		
	Total	White	Nonwhite	Total	White	Nonwhite
New England...............................	-348	-388	40	-3.7	-4.2	26.1
Middle Atlantic............................	-142	-390	248	-0.5	-1.4	12.9
East North Central........................	1,242	809	433	4.1	2.8	23.3
West North Central........................	-390	-444	54	-2.8	-3.3	11.1
South Atlantic............................	669	1,023	-354	3.1	6.4	-6.9
East South Central........................	-1,356	-912	-444	-11.8	-10.4	-16.4
West South Central........................	-330	-182	-148	-2.3	-1.5	-5.9
Mountain..................................	596	562	34	11.7	11.6	14.8
Pacific...................................	2,485	2,278	207	17.2	16.6	27.3

presented for the white and the nonwhite population.[10] Some very large streams of migration have flowed since the 1950 census. Five geographic divisions have lost population, and four have gained population, through migration. The losers are the New England, Middle Atlantic, West North Central, East South Central, and West South Central states. The gainers are the Pacific, Mountain, South Atlantic, and East North Central states. As usual, the Pacific Division hogged far more than its share. It is estimated to have gained

[10] These estimates were prepared by the author. The method used was as follows: An estimate was made of the white and nonwhite population of each geographic division, using the "vital statistics" method of estimating. The estimates by color were then forced to equal both the Census Bureau's estimates for total state populations and the Census Bureau's estimates of the white and the nonwhite population in the nation. By accumulating births and deaths from April, 1950 to the date of the estimate, the population change attributable to natural increase was estimated. Net migration was estimated by subtracting natural increase from the total population change. An adjustment was made which allocated net immigration by color. Since the year 1956 was the latest year for which vital statistics were available, the calculations were made for July 1, 1956. The net migration estimates were then extended to 1958 by inflating the 1950 to 1956 estimates, on the assumption that the amount of migration in 1957 and 1958 would be the same as the average annual amount which had occurred from 1950 to 1956. This procedure is admittedly very rough, but it is believed to be accurate enough to reveal the broad outlines of the recent migratory movements.

2.5 million persons through migration (creating a 17.2 percent increase in population in 8 1/4 years due to migration alone). Most of these migrants flowed to California. More than half a million persons migrated into the Mountain States (primarily Arizona, Nevada, and New Mexico). A surprising result of these estimates is their indication of a net in-migration of 1.2 million persons to the East North Central states. This is a departure from past migration patterns, with respect to color as well as numbers. For several decades this division has received many thousands of Negro migrants, but not since 1920 had it gained white migrants. A majority of the white migrants who have recently come to the East North Central states are from the South. The East South Central states, in particular, have had a very heavy northward movement of white as well as nonwhite migrants.

It may appear surprising at first that the South Atlantic Division gained white population through net migration. However, the large migration flow attracted to this division is concentrated very heavily in Florida and in the Baltimore-Washington metropolitan areas.

Rates of net interregional migration are much higher for the nonwhite than for the white population. Almost 1 million nonwhite persons left the South during this 8-year period, and they migrated to all of the other geographic divisions. The major recipients of this migration were the Middle Atlantic, the East North Central, and the Pacific

Divisions. The nonwhite migrants were attracted to the large industrial and commercial centers located in the northeast and around the Great Lakes, and to the metropolitan areas on the Pacific Coast. The out-migration rate of Negroes has been heaviest for the East South Central States--Mississippi, Alabama, Tennessee, and Kentucky (and probably also Arkansas, in the West South Central Division). Contrary to what may be popular opinion, this out-migration has not been heavy enough to cause the Negro population of these areas to decline appreciably in size.[11] But it is large enough to drain off almost all the natural increase. Thus, the South is exporting most of its nonwhite population growth to other divisions, but is maintaining the seedbed.

HISTORY OF INTERREGIONAL MIGRATION IN THE UNITED STATES

Good data with which to trace the migration streams that flowed from 1790 until the Civil War are not available. But both the direction and the nature of these streams are well-known--they were made up of frontiersmen pushing out from the original colonies and the places of older settlement to exploit the nation's unclaimed forests, minerals, and wild game; these streams also included farmers and ranchers rushing to stake out claims for land. By 1870 most of the land had been claimed and was in the process of being developed, and this date marks the time when reasonably adequate statistics for net migration, which are now available, began to be collected.[12] After 1890 to 1910, migration was guided primarily by a phase of technological and industrial development and interregional commercial integration, in which rapid urbanization through migration was an outstanding characteristic. In the Dakotas, Nebraska, and Kansas, the last of the migration-to-settle-the-land movement took place between 1870 and 1890. Oklahoma and the Mountain and Pacific states had almost completed their land-claiming phase by 1910. The maps of Figures 15-7 and 15-8 show the centers where there was pressure resulting in out-migration, and the location of the socioeconomic vacuums that attracted both white and nonwhite migrants, at various dates. Estimates of the net migration of the white and nonwhite populations for each decade, 1870 to 1950 (and also for the period 1950 to 1958), are presented for each geographic division in Table 15-13. It is easy to see, from these maps and from the table, that the westward movement, the northward movement, and the movement to Florida and the Gulf Coast have all been underway continuously since 1870.[13] The northward movement of Negroes from the South was already widespread in the decade after the Civil War, and has continued uninterruptedly right up to the present time. Even the westward movement of Negroes was underway by 1900, and it has also continued during each decade since that time. The unique feature of northward and westward Negro migration, both during the 1940 to 1950 decade and the 1950 to 1960 decade, has been its huge volume; the number of Negroes leaving the South now is about three times what it was between 1910

---

[11] This is a generalization about the South as a whole. The 1960 census probably will show an absolute decrease in the nonwhite populations of Mississippi and Arkansas, where poor economic conditions and a hostile race situation have combined to cause an unusually large exodus.

[12] Dorothy S. Thomas, Simon Kuznets, Everett S. Lee, and associates have prepared a most valuable historical series of data concerning net migration. The materials of this section rely heavily upon data summarized from the report, Population Redistribution and Economic Growth, United States: 1870-1950, by Everett S. Lee, Ann Ratner Miller, Carol P. Brainerd, and Richard A. Easterlin, American Philosophical Society, 1957. The techniques used by these authors were developed and refined by C. Horace Hamilton and Edward P. Hutchinson.

[13] The estimates of Lee, et al., op. cit., show that Florida and the District of Columbia (and, more recently, both Virginia and Maryland) have both been major destinations of migrants at each decade since 1870, despite negative net migration for the South Atlantic Division as a whole.

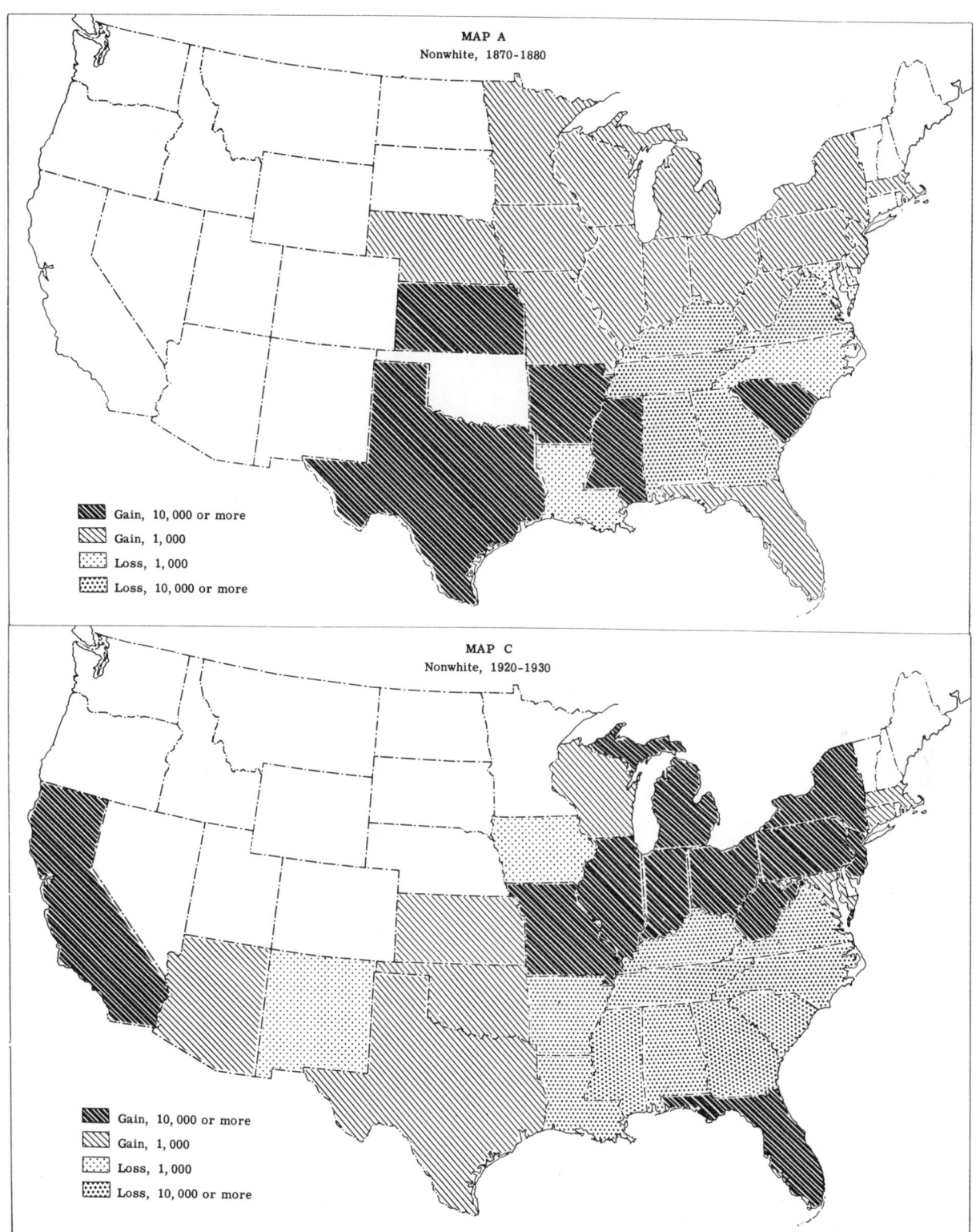

FIGURE 15-7. CLASSIFICATION OF STATES ACCORDING TO WHETHER THEY WERE GAINING OR LOSING NONWHITE POPULATION THROUGH NET MIGRATION, FOR SELECTED DECADES: 1870 TO 1950

Source: Compiled from data in Everett S. Lee and others, Population Redistribution and Economic Growth, American Philosophical Society, 1957, Table 1.14.

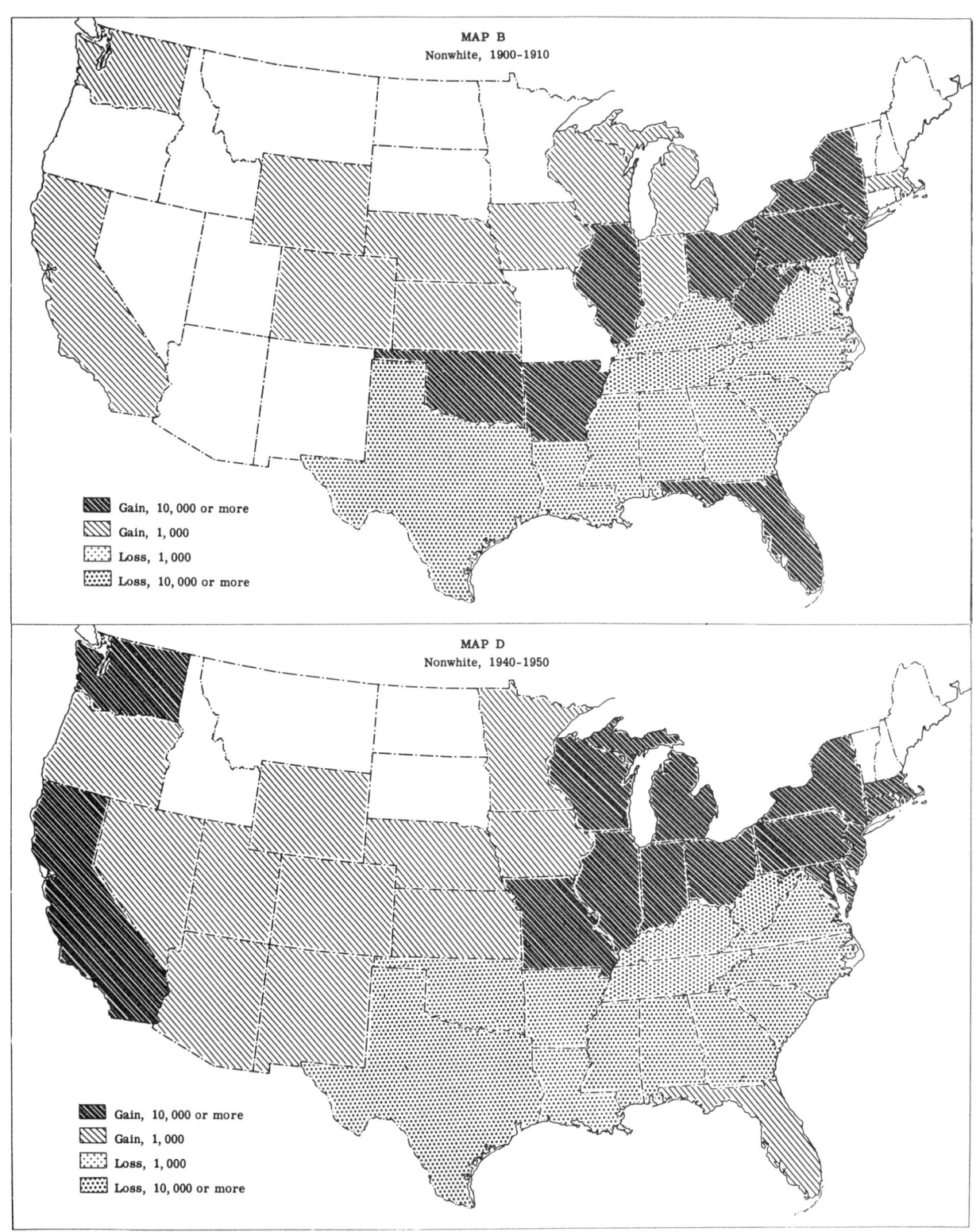

FIGURE 15-7. CLASSIFICATION OF STATES ACCORDING TO WHETHER THEY WERE GAINING OR
LOSING NONWHITE POPULATION THROUGH NET MIGRATION, FOR SELECTED
DECADES: 1870 TO 1950-Continued

Source: Compiled from data in Everett S. Lee and others, Population Redistribution and Economic
Growth, American Philosophical Society, 1957, Table 1.14.

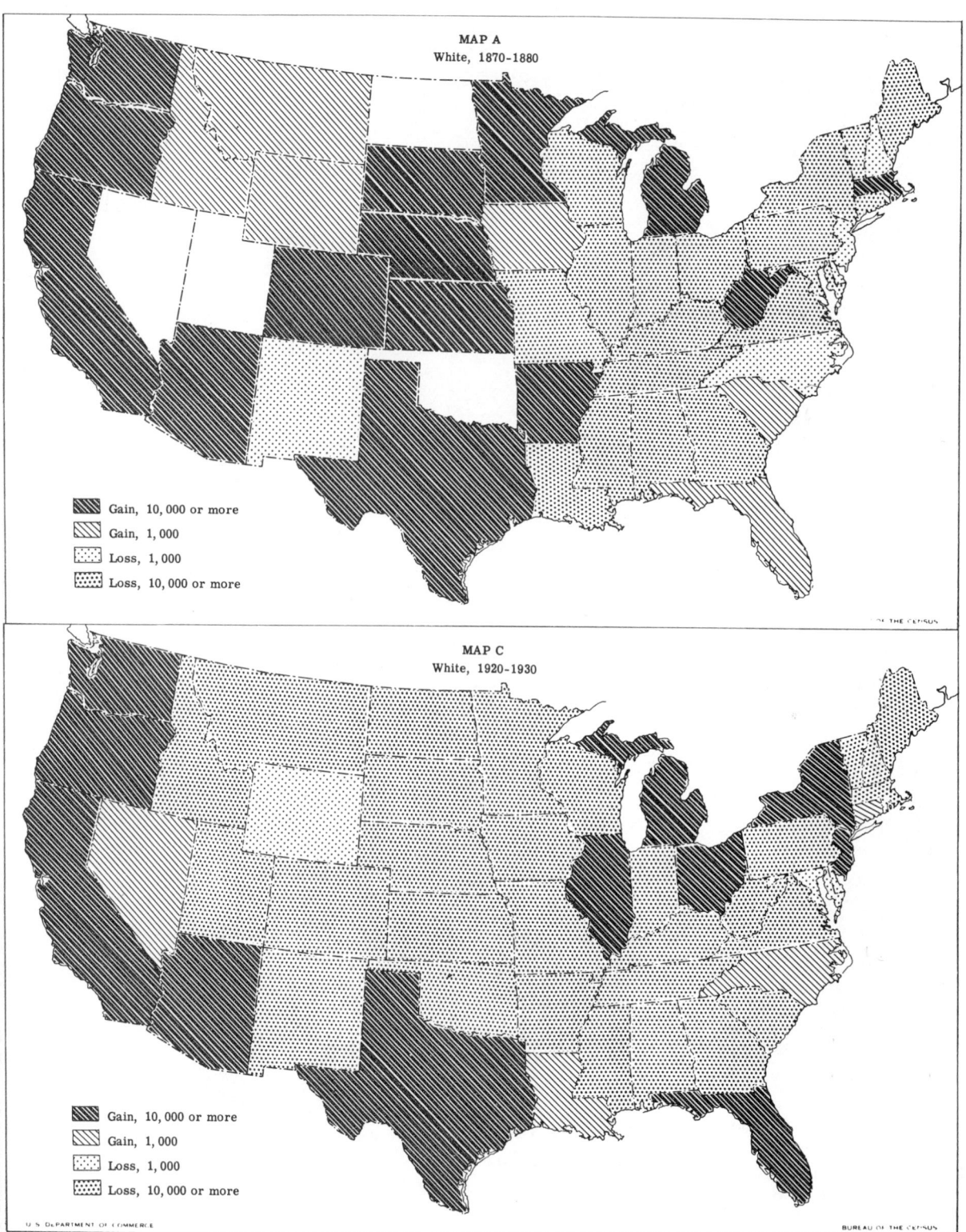

FIGURE 15-8. CLASSIFICATION OF STATES ACCORDING TO WHETHER THEY WERE GAINING OR LOSING WHITE POPULATION THROUGH NET MIGRATION, FOR SELECTED DECADES: 1870 TO 1950

Source: Compiled from data in Everett S. Lee and others, Population Redistribution and Economic Growth, American Philosophical Society, 1957, Table 1.11.

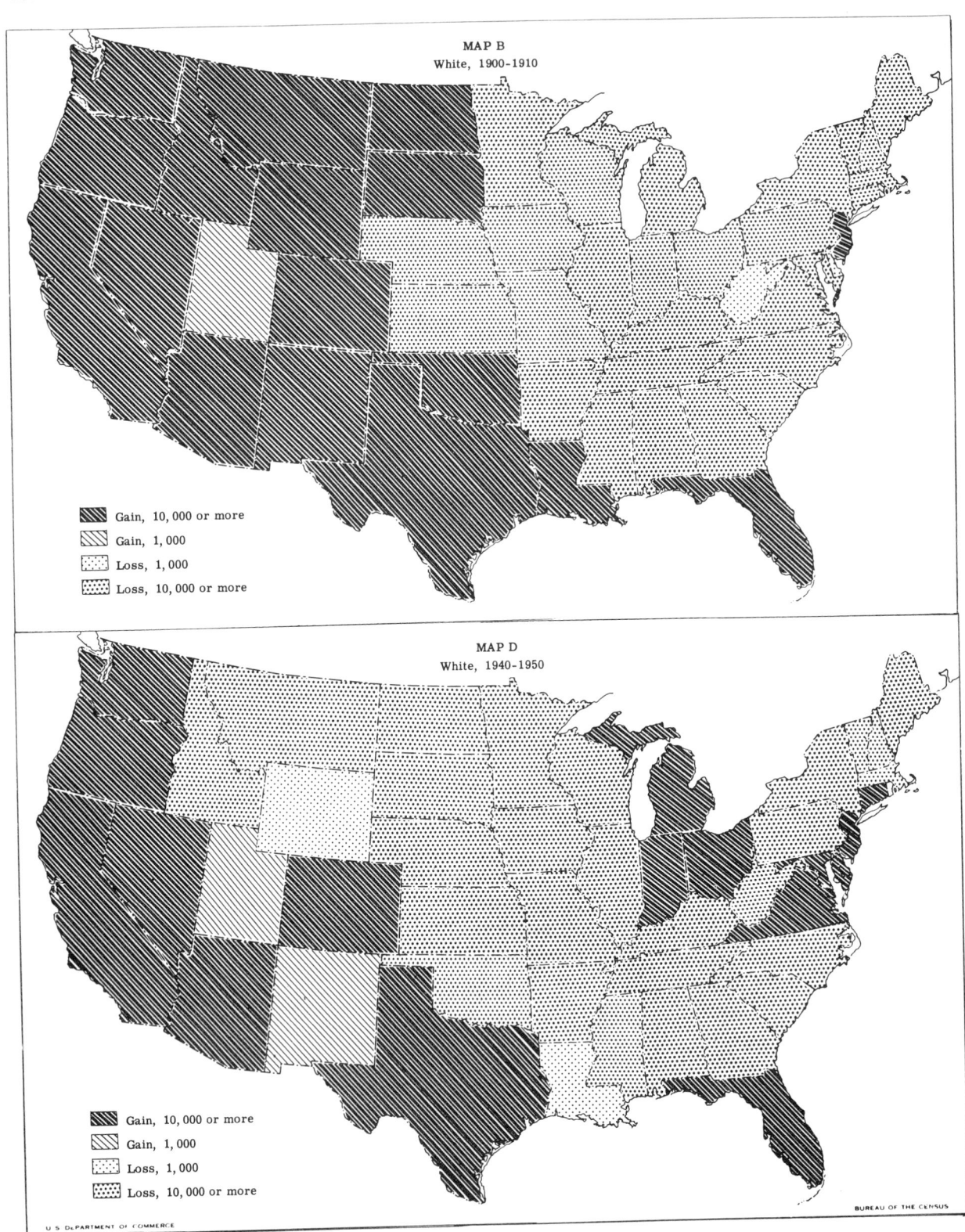

FIGURE 15-8. CLASSIFICATION OF STATES ACCORDING TO WHETHER THEY WERE GAINING OR
LOSING WHITE POPULATION THROUGH NET MIGRATION, FOR SELECTED DECADES:
1870 TO 1950 - Continued

Source: Compiled from data in Everett S. Lee and others, Population Redistribution and Economic
Growth, American Philosophical Society, 1957, Table 1.11.

Table 15-13.—ESTIMATED INTERCENSAL NET MIGRATION FOR GEOGRAPHIC DIVISIONS, BY COLOR: 1870 to 1958

	Total	Interval								
	1870 to 1950	1950 to 1958	1940 to 1950	1930 to 1940	1920 to 1930	1910 to 1920	1900 to 1910	1890 to 1900	1880 to 1890	1870 to 1880
NATIVE WHITE:										
New England...............	-534	-388	-105	-23	-190	-53	-84	21	-33	-67
Middle Atlantic...........	-1825	-390	-714	-139	-59	-205	-182	-37	-207	-282
East North Central........	-1190	809	-218	-102	283	303	-487	-46	-483	-440
West North Central.......	-2622	-444	-932	-568	-708	-444	-475	-374	403	471
South Atlantic............	326	1023	465	282	-158	51	-101	-86	-106	-21
East South Central........	-2497	-912	-571	-241	-391	-374	-342	-213	-211	-155
West South Central........	462	-182	-397	-335	10	--63	437	431	104	275
Mountain..................	897	562	70	37	-153	156	364	120	187	116
Pacific...................	6950	2278	2402	1090	1274	629	869	184	509	102
NONWHITE:										
New England...............	82	40	25	5	7	12	8	14	7	4
Middle Atlantic...........	1301	248	387	166	342	170	87	91	39	19
East North Central........	1249	433	494	108	324	201	46	39	16	21
West North Central.......	197	54	35	20	41	44	10	24	8	5
South Atlantic............	-1684	-354	-424	-175	-509	-162	-110	-182	-73	-49
East South Central........	-1305	-444	-485	-122	-181	-248	-110	-43	-60	-56
West South Central........	-280	-148	-336	-50	-61	-46	50	57	-61	45
Mountain..................	40	34	20	6	-1	10	5	...	...	...
Pacific...................	396	207	284	43	37	18	14	...	...	...

[1]The Data for 1870 to 1950 refer to migrants 10 years of age and over, and exclude immigrants. The data for 1950 to 1948 are for all ages and include immigrants.

Source: Data for 1870 to 1950 summarized from data reported in Population Redistribution and Economic Growth, by Everett S. Lee, Ann Ratner Miller, Carol P. Brainerd and Richard A. Easterlin, (The American Philosophical Society, 1957) Tables 1.11 and 1.14. Data for 1950 to 1958 from Table 15.12.

and 1940.[14] Thus, almost the only unique aspect of current interregional migration during the 1950 to 1960 decade is the renewed flow, mentioned in the preceding section, of white migrants into Ohio, Michigan, Illinois, Indiana, and Wisconsin. This inflow has consisted of white workers who have come from the South in numbers so great as to more than compensate for the number of residents who have been leaving for the West.[15]

It must be reemphasized strongly that since 1940, most interregional migration has been metropolis-oriented. Few members of the migration streams flowing westward have remained long in agricultural occupations. Instead, they have swelled the populations of Los Angeles and the other metropolitan areas in the Pacific and Mountain Divisions. The northward movement of Negroes and southern whites has been to metropolitan centers, and not to the outlying parts of states.

[14] Note from Table 15-13 that the northward movement of Negroes, especially from the South Atlantic states, was also very large during the 1920 to 1930 decade. The economic depression of the 1930's slackened the flow to about one-third of what it had been between 1920 and 1930. The current large volume of the northward flow may be regarded as a development that began during and after World War I, was temporarily slowed by economic hard times, but has been greatly accelerated in recent years by unusually high prosperity and rapid economic expansion. The low birth rates which prevailed in northern industrial centers during the 1930's helped to create a demand in the 1950's for outside labor, because there were not enough local young people in the oncoming generations to satisfy the demands of the labor market.

[15] If they are correct in smaller details, the estimates of Table 15-12 also suggest that the New England states have recently been losing white population at a much faster rate than in previous decades, and that the industrialization of the South Atlantic states, together with the continued development of Florida and the growth of Washington, D.C. and Baltimore, have recently been attracting much larger numbers of white in-migrants than they used to.

For example, between 1950 and 1958 the Chicago Standard Metropolitan Area received an estimated increase of 175,000 nonwhite persons through net migration. This number amounts to 40 percent of the total net number of nonwhite migrants estimated to have entered the East North Central Division during these years.[16] Observation and indirect data both make it evident that the remaining 60 percent went to Detroit, Cleveland, Toledo, Indianapolis, and the other industrial metropolitan centers in the division. Moreover, these same metropolises have claimed the equivalent of the total net migration of white population that has flowed into the East North Central Divisions.[17] These statistics show that the state is peculiarly inappropriate as a unit of area through which to analyze current migration events.

The data presented here make it clear not only that migration has a definite interregional pattern, but also that this pattern is quite stable, changing only slowly and in response to changes in the industrial, commercial, and technological development and balance of the various regions.

THE EFFECT OF MIGRATION UPON POPULATION DISTRIBUTION AND COMPOSITION IN METROPOLITAN AREAS

Certain procedures make it possible to estimate the net migration of population with respect to the central cities and suburban rings of standard metropolitan areas. Table 15-14 presents such data for the decade 1940 to 1950, and Table 15-15 divides this net migration into its racial components of white and nonwhite. Central cities, as a whole, lost population through net migration during the 1940 to 1950 decade, but their suburbs made impressively large migration gains. The total loss of central cities, as estimated from Table 15-14, was 671,000, an amount equal to 1.6 percent of their total 1940 population. Therefore, the central city growth of 13.5 percent between 1940 and 1950, reported by the Census, was due entirely to the reproductive change (excess of births over deaths) which took place among the metropolitan population, and to annexation.[18] In fact, these central cities grew in spite of migration conditions, not because of them. The central cities of only four economic regions--the Atlantic Flatwoods and Gulf Coast Region (Region IX), the Rocky Mountain and Intermountain Region (Region XI), the Pacific Northwest Region (Region XII), and the Pacific Southwest Region (Region XIII)--the four regions with the highest over-all rates of growth--were able to attract more migrants than they lost. Even so, only the central cities of the two Pacific Coast regions made gains that were impressive. (The recent growth of central cities may be purely temporary. The increase consists entirely of infants and children under ten years of age, who may move to the suburbs themselves when they attain adulthood.)

The suburban portions of standard metropolitan areas gained population through net migration in every economic region, which would seem to indicate that suburbanization through migration has been an almost universal phenomenon. A total of 7,068,000 persons are estimated to have moved into the suburban rings in the 1940 to 1950 decade. This means that for each three persons living in

---

[16] These estimates are based on research by Dr. Beverly Duncan, reported in Population Growth in the Chicago Standard Metropolitan Area, 1950-57, A Report to the Department of City Planning, City of Chicago, The Chicago Community Inventory, February, 1958.

[17] This may be inferred from the small rates of current growth of nonmetropolitan areas, and from the negative net migration of nonmetropolitan state economic areas from 1940 to 1950.

[18] Suburban rings lost more than 1.4 million persons to central cities during this decade through annexation. For several decades prior to 1940, annexation had come to an almost complete halt. During the 1940 to 1950 decade, however, it was revived and is now a major component that must be considered in analyzing metropolitan and urban growth. If accurate computations of the components of growth are to be made in future decades, it will be necessary to prepare estimates of the population of annexed territories.

Table 15-14.—ESTIMATED NUMBER OF NET MIGRANTS AND NET MIGRATION RATE FOR CENTRAL CITY AND SUBURBAN RING PORTION OF METROPOLITAN AREAS IN EACH OF THE ECONOMIC REGIONS; 1940 to 1950

Economic Region	Region Number	Net migration per 100 population			Number of net migrants (000)		
		S.M.A. Total	Central Cities	Suburban Rings	S.M.A. Total	Central Cities	Suburban Rings
U.S. Total..........................	....	9.2	-1.6	26.7	6,397	-671	7,068
Atlantic Metropolitan Belt Region...........	I	4.2	-2.8	15.3	1,054	-438	1,492
Eastern Great Lakes and Northeastern Upland Region.......................................	II	-1.1	-6.4	5.7	-41	-137	97
Lower Great Lakes Region.....................	III	3.1	-4.3	14.8	455	-392	847
Upper Great Lakes Region.....................	IV	2.1	-6.7	28.0	28	-67	94
North Center (Corn Belt) Region.............	V	7.8	-2.0	30.3	328	-58	386
Central Plains Region.......................	VI	22.0	5.4	80.3	163	31	132
Central and Eastern Upland Region...........	VII	5.8	-5.6	19.6	258	-136	395
Southeast Coastal Plain Region..............	VIII	8.7	-4.5	29.5	266	-84	350
Atlantic Flatwoods and Gulf Coast Region....	IX	26.9	1.7	91.4	814	38	776
South Center and Southeast Plains Region....	X	25.1	-0.3	145.9	325	-3	328
Rocky Mountain and Intermountain Region	XI	18.9	2.8	54.6	78	8	70
Pacific Northwest Region....................	XII	27.2	9.3	63.8	367	84	284
Pacific Southwest Region....................	XIII	39.4	15.5	66.6	2,300	484	1,816

Source: Donald J. Bogue, Components of Population Change, 1940 to 1950: Estimates of Net Migration and Natural Increase for Each Standard Metropolitan Area and State Economic Area. (Oxford, Ohio, Scripps Foundation, Miami University) 1957, 2967, Table II-A.

the suburbs in 1940, an additional one moved in during the next ten years.

It was shown above that during the 1940 to 1950 decade, the population was being "metropolitanized"--that metropolitan areas were attracting large numbers of migrants, while nonmetropolitan areas were suffering a rather severe loss from migration. It is now clear that, in most regions, all of this growth accrued to the suburbs, and that in most regions the central cities themselves added a net increment to suburban growth through net out-migration to the suburbs. Figure 15-9 illustrates the situation.

It has often been said that the suburbs were "draining the central cities" of their population. Since the central cities lost 671,000 and the suburbs gained 7,068,000, it is obvious that less than 10 percent of the suburban gain came from the central cities--the heavy net drain was on the nonmetropolitan areas. Nevertheless, as will be shown later, central cities appear to have been "exporting" their long-term residents to the suburbs and, at the same time, attracting migrants from nonmetropolitan areas; thus, the figure 671,000 represents only the net loss in what appears to have been a very large population turnover.

Change in Color Composition as a Result of Net Migration. In order to demonstrate the remarkable changes migration can make in population composition in a short time, Tables 15-15 and 15-16 summarize the net migration to standard metropolitan areas, between 1940 and 1950, by age and color. From these tables it may be concluded that:

(a) The net loss of central cities, described above, is the net result of a very severe net out-migration of white population (probably from 2.0 to 2.2 million persons) and a large in-migration to the central city of nonwhite population (estimated at 1.3 million persons). The process by which the central city lost one net migrant to the suburbs was actually the end result of a larger process whereby for each two nonwhite persons moving into the central city about three white persons moved out. However, although this pattern held for a majority of the regions, it was not true of all regions (see below).

(b) The net migration gain of suburban rings was predominantly a gain of white population. Of

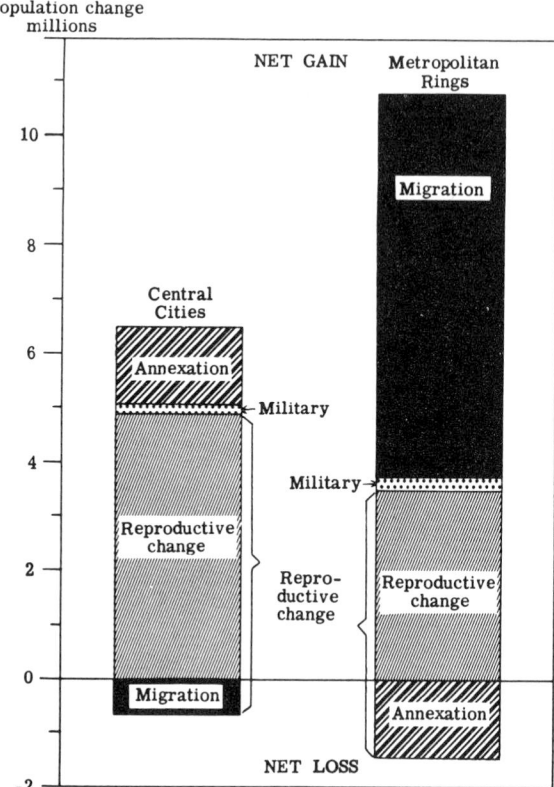

FIGURE 15-9. COMPONENTS OF POPULATION CHANGE
IN CENTRAL CITIES AND METROPOLITAN
RINGS: 1940 TO 1950

tended to be heavily concentrated in ages 20 to 24 and 25 to 29. (Since this was their age group in 1950, the median age of migrants at the time of migration was much younger than the figures indicate. If an equal amount of the migration occurred during each year of the decade, then the median age of the migrants was about 21 years at the time of migration.)

(d) The age composition of the Negro net migrants differed a great deal from that of the white. Although the peak age of migrants was 25 to 29 for both groups, a higher proportion of nonwhite than of white migrants were in the ages 30 to 59 and 10 to 14. Thus, a higher proportion of nonwhite than of white migrants to metropolitan areas appear to have been adults with children.

(e) Central cities gained nonwhite migrants of all ages, but lost white population of all ages except for the 15 to 29 age group. There was strong

an estimated net influx of 7.2 million migrants, only 347,000 (4.8 percent) were nonwhite and the balance (95.2 percent) were white.

Proportionately, the nonwhite migrants may appear to have been a very small part of all migrants to suburbs, but the settling of 1/3 of a million nonwhites in metropolitan suburbs during one decade may indicate the start of a new trend in population distribution. A surprisingly large share (21.6 percent) of all net nonwhite migration to metropolitan areas accrued to the suburban rings. The population of a vast majority of the suburban rings was preponderantly white in 1940. It is entirely possible that during the 1950 to 1960 decade, and later, this tendency will be accelerated and extended to more standard metropolitan areas.

(c) The net in-migrants to metropolitan areas had the typical age distribution of migrants. They

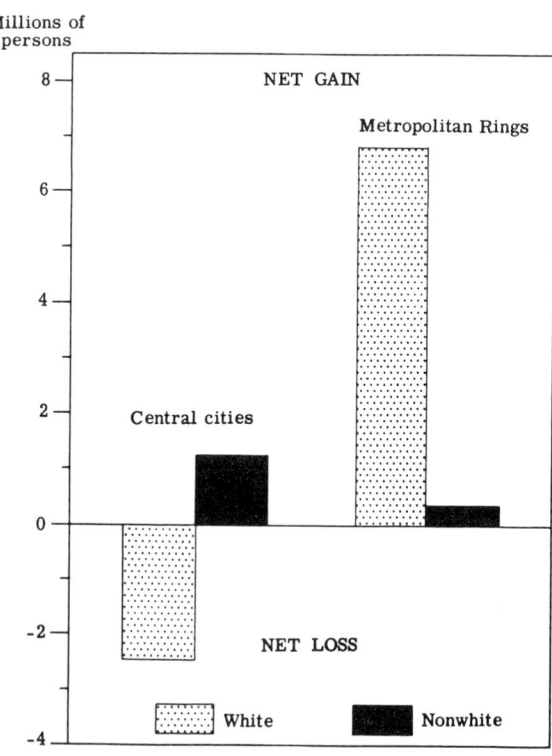

FIGURE 15-10. NUMBER OF NET MIGRANTS, CENTRAL
CITIES AND METROPOLITAN RINGS, BY
COLOR: 1940 TO 1950

evidence that the families who moved from central cities to the suburbs were white families with children under 10 years of age. The central city seemed able to continue to attract a large part of the incoming young white migrants (1/2 to 2/3 of all the white arrivals to the S.M.A. who were in these age groups), but appeared to be having heavy losses among members of the age group 30 to 74 and their children.

(f) The assumption that the net loss of the central city flowed directly to the suburbs makes it possible to subdivide the white net migrants to the suburbs into two groups: those coming from the central city, and those coming from nonmetropolitan areas. The following summary shows this estimate:

Age	Net migrants to suburbs		Percent distribution	
	No. from central city (000)	No. from nonmetropolitan areas (000)	From central cities	From nonmetropolitan areas
Total...	3,301	3,563	100.0	100.0
0-9........	1,342	211	40.7	5.9
10-14......	190	285	5.8	8.0
15-19......	...	362	...	10.2
20-24......	...	426	...	12.0
25-29......	...	756	...	21.2
30-34......	261	601	7.9	16.9
35-39......	321	358	9.7	10.0
40-44......	258	243	7.8	6.8
45-49......	194	158	5.9	4.4
50-54......	157	111	4.8	3.1
55-59......	155	47	4.7	1.3
60-64......	126	29	3.8	0.8
65-69......	97	13	2.9	0.4
70-74......	98	-29	3.0	-0.8
75-over....	102	-8	3.1	-0.2

Although the above figures are only crude approximations, they indicate that suburban rings are the destination of large numbers of the migrants who come directly from nonmetropolitan areas. Of the 6.9 million white migrants gained by suburbs, an estimated 3.3 million came from the central city and 3.6 million (more than one-half) came directly from nonmetropolitan areas. The white migrants coming directly to the suburbs from nonmetropolitan areas were of all ages under 60, but tended to be less concentrated in the age group 20 to 29 than were all white migrants to

the S.M.A. Because of the numbers of whole families among them, the former group appeared to be more of a general cross-section of the population. Thus, the old theory that the metropolitan area grows largely by outward radial expansion from the center is no longer valid. At least one-half of the growth in 1940 to 1950 came from direct accretion at the edges, without benefit of mediation through the central city.

In this connection, it should not be inferred that all of the 3.3 million estimated net white migrants to the suburbs from central cities had migrated to the central city at an earlier period; a large proportion had been born and reared in the central city.

The extraordinarily high proportion of children among the migrants who move to the metropolitan ring from the central city (40.7 percent) seems to testify dramatically to the fact that many parents do not want to rear their children under conditions prevailing in many neighborhoods at the heart of the metropolis. However, the white population had no monopoly on this concern. Table 15-15 shows that the proportion of children and adolescents among the nonwhite in-migrants to the suburbs was higher than among the white.

The above summary presents the picture for metropolitan areas as a whole. Table 15-16 gives estimates of migrants to the S.M.A.'s, the central cities, and the suburban metropolitan rings of each economic region, by color. The following observations may be derived from these materials:

(a) The tendency for central cities to lose large amounts of white population appears to be strongest in the older and more industrialized S.M.A.'s of the Northeast (especially Regions I and III), but it exists in almost all S.M.A.'s outside of the rapidly-growing West.

(b) The exodus of Negroes from the Southern Coastal Plain (Region VIII) was so great that it drew from the metropolitan as well as from the nonmetropolitan parts of this region. In all other S.M.A.'s there was at least some gain of nonwhite population.

(c) The tendency for S.M.A.'s to attract large numbers of nonwhite migrants was strongest in the industrialized S.M.A.'s of Regions I and III, and

Table 15-15.—SUMMARY OF NET MIGRATION: STANDARD METROPOLITAN AREAS, CENTRAL CITIES AND METROPOLITAN SUBURBAN RINGS, FOR THE UNITED STATES, BY AGE AND COLOR: 1940-50

Age	Standard metropolitan area,total			Central cities			Rings		
	Total	White	Nonwhite	Total	White	Nonwhite	Total	White	Nonwhite
ALL AGES	6,029,154	4,423,523	1,605,631	-1,184,926	-2,443,741	1,258,815	7,214,080	6,867,264	346,816
0-9.......	366,863	211,249	155,614	-1,268,835	-1,341,748	72,913	1,635,698	1,552,997	82,701
10-14.....	416,074	284,900	131,174	-94,154	-190,349	96,195	510,228	475,249	34,979
15-19.....	525,432	394,876	130,556	132,086	33,083	99,003	393,346	361,793	31,553
20-24.....	1,152,651	904,642	248,009	689,855	478,691	211,164	462,796	425,951	36,845
25-29.....	1,415,629	1,101,203	314,426	624,829	345,281	279,548	790,800	755,922	34,878
30-34.....	832,514	601,029	231,485	-58,658	-260,895	202,237	891,172	861,924	29,248
35-39.....	515,483	358,238	157,245	-191,258	-321,346	130,088	706,741	679,584	27,157
40-44.....	333,015	243,176	89,839	-190,602	-258,352	67,750	523,617	501,528	22,089
45-49.....	213,625	158,143	55,482	-155,596	-193,635	38,039	369,221	351,778	17,443
50-54.....	143,912	111,434	32,478	-135,906	-156,773	20,867	279,818	268,207	11,611
55-39.....	69,102	47,048	22,054	-141,214	-155,353	14,139	210,316	202,401	7,915
60-64.....	51,262	29,674	21,588	-109,452	-125,827	16,375	160,714	155,501	5,213
65-69.....	13,962	14,208	-246	-97,761	-96,738	-1,023	111,723	110,946	777
70-74.....	-25,163	-28,853	3,690	-95,345	-98,164	2,819	70,182	69,311	871
75-84.....	-9,377	-19,054	9,677	-88,379	-95,263	6,884	79,002	76,209	2,793
85-over...	14,170	11,610	2,560	-4,536	-6,353	1,817	18,706	17,963	743
				Ratio of each age group to total					
ALL AGES	100.0	100.0	100.0	-100.0	-100.0	100.0	100.0	100.0	100.0
0-0.......	6.1	4.8	9.7	-107.1	-54.9	5.8	22 7	22.6	23.8
10-14.....	6.9	6.4	8.2	-7.9	-7.8	7.6	7.1	6.9	10.1
15-19.....	8.7	8.9	8.1	11.1	1.4	7.9	5.5	5.3	9.1
20-24.....	19.1	20.5	15.4	58.2	19.6	16.8	6.4	6.2	10.6
25-29.....	23.5	24.9	19.6	52.7	14.1	22.2	11.0	11.0	10.1
30-34.....	13.8	13.6	14.4	-5.0	-10.7	16.1	12.4	12.6	8.4
35-39.....	8.5	8.1	9.8	-16.1	-13.1	10.3	9.8	9.9	7.8
40-44.....	5.5	5.5	5.6	-16.1	-10.6	5.4	7.3	7.3	6.4
45-49.....	3.5	3.6	3.5	-13.1	-7.9	3.0	5.1	5.1	5.0
50-54.....	2.4	2.5	2.0	-11.5	-6.4	1.7	3.9	3.9	3.3
55-59.....	1.1	1.1	1.4	-11.9	-6.4	1.1	2.9	2.9	2.3
60-64.....	0.9	0.7	1.3	-9.2	-5.1	1.3	2.2	2.3	1.5
65-69.....	0.2	0.3	...	-8.3	-4.0	-0.1	1.5	1.6	0.2
70-74.....	-0.4	-0.7	0.2	-8.0	-4.0	0.2	1.0	1.0	0.3
75-84.....	-0.2	-0.4	0.6	-7.5	-3.9	0.5	1.1	1.1	0.8
85-over...	0.2	0.3	0.2	-0.4	-0.3	0.1	0.3	0.3	0.2

in the Pacific Southwest Region (XIII). Moderately large gains of nonwhite population were experienced in the semi-industrial Regions V and VII, and along the Gulf Coast (Region IX). The S.M.A.'s in Regions IV, VI, X, and XI had comparatively little attraction for nonwhite migrants. For the most part, these S.M.A.'s are small and are located in rural and agricultural areas.

(d) The rapid suburbanization of the white population is evident in all regions. In no region did the suburban rings of the S.M.A.'s fail to gain white population, even in regions where the central cities suffered severe losses.

(e) The nonwhite population also showed a surprising tendency toward suburbanization. The righthand column of Table 15-16 shows what proportion of all nonwhite net migration to the S.M.A.'s went to the suburban rings. In four S.M.A.'s it was well above 25 percent. In two regions of the South, Regions IX and X, the number of nonwhite migrants going to the suburbs was several times the number going to the central city. Only in the S.M.A.'s of the urban Northeast (Regions I, III, and IV) and of the Pacific Northwest (Region XII)--places where racial tolerance is above average--were Negroes failing to join the white population in the suburbanization movement to the extent of 25 percent or more. However, even in these areas the amount of suburbanization of nonwhite migrants was greater than might have been expected.

Table 15-16.—SUMMARY OF NET MIGRATION: STANDARD METROPOLITAN AREAS, CENTRAL CITIES, AND METROPOLITAN SUBURBAN RINGS, FOR EACH ECONOMIC REGION, BY COLOR: 1940 TO 1950 (Thousands of net migrants)

Region name and province	Region number	Standard metropolitan area			Central cities			Rings			Percent of total non-white net migration going to ring
		Total	White	Non-white	Total	White	Non-white	Total	White	Non-white	
ATLANTIC METROPOLITAN BELT PROVINCE											
Atlantic Metropolitan Belt Region (Identical with the province).........	I	886.6	330.4	556.3	-677.7	-1,158.1	480.4	1,564.3	1,488.4	75.9	14
GREAT LAKES AND NORTHEASTERN PROVINCE											
Eastern Great Lakes and Northeastern Upland Region......................	II	-98.5	-128.7	30.3	-173.4	-199.8	26.5	74.9	71.1	3.8	13
Lower Great Lakes Region...............	III	306.6	-185.7	492.4	-487.8	-910.6	422.8	794.4	724.9	69.5	14
Upper Great Lakes Region...............	IV	30.0	25.1	4.9	-66.7	-71.1	4.3	97.6	96.2	0.5	10
MIDWEST PROVINCE											
North Center (Corn Belt) Region........	V	298.9	233.4	65.5	-83.3	-134.7	51.4	382.2	368.1	14.1	22
Central Plains Region..................	VI	170.5	157.0	13.5	36.2	26.0	10.2	134.3	131.0	3.3	9
SOUTHERN PROVINCE											
Central and Eastern Upland Region.......	VII	189.7	122.5	67.3	-184.4	-233.7	49.3	374.1	356.1	18.0	27
Southeast Coastal Plain Region..........	VIII	276.0	307.2	-31.2	-105.1	-94.2	-10.8	381.1	401.4	-20.4	..
Atlantic Flatwoods and Gulf Coast Region	IX	819.8	736.5	83.3	9.3	-2.4	11.7	810.6	739.0	71.6	86
South Center and Southwest Plains Region	X	345.2	337.5	7.7	-12.5	-13.9	1.4	357.6	351.3	6.3	82
WESTERN PROVINCE											
Rocky Mountain and Intermountain Region.	XI	89.4	85.3	4.0	7.7	4.5	3.2	81.6	80.8	0.8	20
Pacific Northwest Region...............	XII	386.8	364.7	22.1	79.8	59.6	20.2	307.0	305.1	1.8	8
Pacific Southwest Region...............	XIII	2,728.0	2,038.3	289.6	472.7	284.6	188.2	1,855.2	1,753.8	101.5	35

MIGRATION STREAMS IN RELATION TO URBANIZATION AND METROPOLITANIZATION

It has been evident throughout the preceding discussion that migration which terminates in urban communities, and especially in metropolitan urban communities, is one of the most pronounced characteristics of internal migration at the present time. In their study of migration streams for the 1935 to 1940 period, Bogue, Shryock and Hoermann developed some special estimates that permitted them to arrive at a series of generalizations concerning this phenomenon.[19] The data upon which their findings were based are too voluminous, and the procedure they used requires too elaborate an explanation, to be repeated in full detail here. However, the following summary of their conclusions concerning migration between urban and rural areas from 1935 to 1940 is probably a valid characterization of all internal migration in the United States from 1920 to the present time.

---

[19] Bogue, Shryock, and Hoermann, Migration Streams, op. cit.

(a) The largest single type of migration among rural and urban areas was not the flow of migrants from rural to urban areas, as might be supposed. It was the flow of migrants between cities. Table 15-18 provides data which estimate the size of each of the nine urban-rural streams. The volume of urban-to-urban migration amounted to about one-third (32.5 percent) of all migration, and was more than twice as large as the migration between any other combination of urban and rural places of origin and destination. The migrants originating in urban areas amounted to 50.9 percent of all migrants.

Since the population of the United States was more than 50 percent urban during this period, it is not surprising to find that intercity migration constituted such a large part of all migration. On the other hand, this finding may be significant in view of the fact that migration has traditionally been thought of in terms of a rural-to-urban redistribution of the population and the concomitant social changes. The adjusted figures show that there was an intercity flow of more than 5 million persons during the five-year period 1935 to 1940. This movement appears to have had no profound

Table 15-17.—STREAMS OF INTERNAL MIGRATION AMONG URBAN AND RURAL AREAS: 1935 TO 1940

Urban-rural origins and destinations	Number of migrants	Percent distribution	Migration rate (adjusted)	Stream velocity
	Adjusted for reporting bias	Adjusted		
Total internal migration.....................	15,734,798	100.0	13.0	13.0
In-migration to urban.....................	8,230,003	52.3	11.9	11.9
In-migration to rural nonfarm.............	4,467,409	28.4	18.2	18.2
In-migration to rural farm...............	3,037,386	19.3	11.2	11.2
Out-migration from urban....................	8,016,641	50.9	11.5	11.5
To urban.................................	5,110,451	32.5	7.4	12.9
To rural nonfarm.........................	2,195,105	14.0	3.2	15.8
To rural farm............................	711,085	4.5	1.0	4.4
Out-migration from rural nonfarm............	3,933,048	25.0	16.0	16.0
To urban.................................	2,053,492	13.1	8.4	14.7
To rural nonfarm.........................	1,439,517	9.1	5.9	29.2
To rural farm............................	440,039	2.8	1.8	8.0
Out-migration from rural farm...............	3,785,109	24.1	13.9	13.9
To urban.................................	1,066,060	6.8	3.9	6.8
To rural nonfarm.........................	832,787	5.3	3.1	15.3
To rural farm............................	1,886,262	12.0	6.9	30.7
Net migration				
Urban....................................	213,362	1.4[1]	0.4	0.4
Rural nonfarm............................	534,361	3.4[1]	2.2	2.2
Rural farm...............................	-747,723	-4.8[1]	-2.7	2.7

[1]Percent of total internal migration that accrued to this type of population as a migration gain or loss.

Source: Donald J. Bogue, Henry Shryock, Jr., and Siegfried A. Hoermann, Subregional Migration in the United States, 1935-40, Vol. I, Streams of Migration, 1957.

effect on the urban population as a whole—no effect of the kind that would almost certainly have resulted from a rural-farm to urban migration of the same size—although this large flow undoubtedly had very pronounced effects on the particular cities that lost or gained large numbers of migrants. Since few of the migration studies made before 1940 even hint at the existence of so large a group of intercity migrants, few hypotheses or theories have as yet been developed to explain it.

(b) The volume of migration from rural to urban areas in the 5-year period was comparatively small. The "corrected" number of rural-to-urban migrants is only 3,119,552, or 19.9 percent, of all migrants for the period (the sum of "to urban" in the "out-migration from rural nonfarm" and the "out-migration from rural farm" sections of Table 15-18). About two-thirds of these rural-to-urban migrants came from rural-nonfarm areas. Other

types of migration, such as urban to rural nonfarm, rural nonfarm to rural nonfarm, and rural farm to rural farm, surpass in volume one or both of the rural-to-urban-types. These statistics illustrate how great was the decline in rural-to-urban migration during the depression decade 1930 to 1940. Rates as low as those of the 1930 to 1940 period could not possibly have prevailed in the preceding decades of rapid urban growth.

(c) One of the most common forms of migration was the "circulation" of migrants among communities of the same type. The large volume of movement from one urban place to another has already been noted. In addition, 49.8 percent of the migrants who reported that they had come from rural-farm areas were residing in rural-farm areas in 1940. Similarly, 36.6 percent of the migrants who reported having come from rural-nonfarm residences were residing in rural-nonfarm residences in 1940. If no tendency toward migrating to a particular type of community (preference for a particular type of destination) were present, one would expect to find the urban-rural composition of migrants' destinations to be the same as the urban-rural composition of the general population. This similarity would be expected because the proportion of migrants exposed to the likelihood of settling in a particular type of community would be the same as the proportion which that type of community was of the total population. The proportion of migrants having the same type of community of origin and of destination, in excess of the proportion which that type of community constitutes in the general population, measures the extent of the tendency toward circulation. That this tendency was present in the urban, rural-nonfarm, and rural-farm populations is shown by the following summary:

Percentage of U.S. population 5 yrs. old and over

    Type of residence
      Urban........................ 57.3
      Rural nonfarm................ 20.2
      Rural farm................... 22.5

Percent of out-migrants from each type of residence having same type of community of destination

    Type of residence
      Urban........................ 63.7
      Rural nonfarm................ 36.6
      Rural farm................... 49.8

Excess of migrants having same type of community of origin and destination

    Type of residence
      Urban........................ 6.4
      Rural nonfarm................ 16.4
      Rural farm................... 27.4

Hence, rural areas showed this tendency more markedly than urban areas, and among rural-farm populations the tendency was stronger than among rural-nonfarm populations. It should be kept in mind that the "circulation" of migrants among communities of the same urban or rural type could involve changes with respect to region of location, size of place, economic functions of place, type of neighborhood, and many other characteristics. To conclude without investigation that this type of migration accomplished nothing, for either the mi-

grants or the communities involved, would be unwise.

(d) Biases in the data prevent an exact estimation of the part which migration played in augmenting the population of cities during this period. However, it is valid to assert that migration probably contributed less to city growth (except in the suburbs) during the period 1935 to 1940 than did the natural increase which occurred within the cities themselves. The data show a small gain for the urban population, a gain of 2.2 percent for the rural-nonfarm population, and a loss of 2.7 percent for the rural-farm population. Between 1930 and 1940 the nation's urban population actually increased by 7.9 percent. On the assumption that one-half of this growth, or 3.9 percent, occurred between 1935 and 1940 (a conservative assumption in the present case, since cities are thought to have been less attractive to migrants during the first half than during the second half of the decade), one could estimate that net migration to cities accounted for no more than one-fourth of the total urban growth during the period. Of the total of the 3.9 percent by which cities grew, a net increase of only 0.4 percent is attributed to migration by Table 15-17. It appears also that net migration made a 2.2 percent contribution to the rather large growth of the rural-nonfarm population. Moreover, the estimates indicate that the streams of urban-rural migration which flowed during the 5-year period caused a net loss of about 750,000 persons to the rural-farm population.

(e) The next to last column of Table 15-17 shows rates of migration between the urban and rural types of community. The first 4 rates in this column are in-migration rates (which include circulatory migration), and the next 12 are out-migration rates (which also include circulatory migration). The urban population appeared to be definitely less mobile than the rural population, as is indicated by its lower out-migration rate. Once they had arrived in a city, people may have tended to leave only if they moved to another city or to a rural-nonfarm (probably suburban) residence. More than one-half of the above rate of in-migration to rural-nonfarm areas was accounted for by migrants from cities, and more than one-half of the rather high out-migration rate for the rural-farm population is shown to have been a result of movement from one farm to another.

(f) The data make it possible to measure the 5-year rates of flow of the urban-rural streams. The rate at which a stream of migrants flows (its velocity) from a particular place of origin to a particular place of destination during the 5-year interval may be indicated by the following equation:

$$V= \frac{M}{P_o} \frac{P_d}{P_t} \ 100, \text{ or } V= \frac{M}{P_d} \frac{P_o}{P_t} \ 100, \text{ where}$$

V= the rate of flow (velocity) of the migration stream

M= the number of migrants in the stream

P_o= the population in the area of origin

P_d= the population in the area of destination

P_t= the total population of all potential areas of destination, including the area of origin (destination of nonmigrants)

(This is an abstract measure that takes the viewpoint neither of the place of origin nor of the place of destination; the same result may be obtained by using either the in-migration or the out-migration rate.)[20]

The last column of Table 15-17 reports the velocities for the nine urban-rural streams. Note that the conventional in-, out-, and net migrations (without sign) are also velocities.[21] Two streams had outstandingly high velocities--the rural-farm to rural-farm stream and the rural-nonfarm to rural-nonfarm stream. Three streams had unusually low velocities; they were the urban to rural-farm, the rural-farm to urban, and the rural-nonfarm to rural-farm streams.

These estimates provide evidence that the present urban-rural distribution of the population may make it very easy to expect too much from internal migration as a source of urban growth. A rapid depopulation of rural areas would be required if a high rate of growth in the urban areas

were to be maintained on the basis of migration alone, even for one decade. On the other hand, demographers may have tended in the past to overlook the part which the city plays in contributing to its own growth. The fact that cities have continued to have higher fertility than mortality rates has given them a positive "natural increase." City populations grew moderately between 1930 and 1940 as a result of their own fertility, even though their birth rates were low. During this decade, natural increase probably contributed at least three times as much to urban growth as did the process of internal migration.

With the increasing urbanization of the population and the gradual narrowing of the fertility differential between urban and rural populations, the growth of the urban population will depend more

---

[20]

Proof: $\dfrac{M}{P_o} \div \dfrac{P_d}{P_t} = \dfrac{M}{P_d} \div \dfrac{P_t}{P_o}$, hence $\dfrac{MP_t}{P_o P_d} = \dfrac{MP_t}{P_d P_o}$

These equations, by adjusting the rate of a particular stream, can take into account the size of the population at either the place of destination or the place of origin. For purposes of comparison, the migration rate of the total population becomes the standard. The way this formula is used can be clarified by two examples: (a) Compute the velocity of the stream of migration from urban areas to urban areas. Table 15-17 shows the basic rate to be 7.4 per 100. In 1940, the urban population 5 years of age or older amounted to 57.3 percent of all the population in this age group. Hence, 7.4 is divided by 57.3, resulting in a velocity of 12.9 per 100. This velocity rate is almost equal to the average rate of 13.0 for all areas. Thus, the rate of flow of migrants from city to city almost exactly equalled the average rate for all streams. Therefore, the large volume of city-to-city migration noted above is not the result of high-velocity streams flowing between places with small populations, but of average-velocity streams flowing between places with large populations. (b) Compute the velocity of the stream of migration from rural-farm to rural-nonfarm areas. Table 15-17 shows the out-migration rate to be 3.1. The rural-nonfarm population 5 years of age or older was 20.2 percent of the total population in this age group. Accordingly, 3.1 is divided by 20.2, giving a velocity of 15.3.

[21] Velocity is given no sign because its value does not depend on the direction of the flow between two areas, and because it is reported without reference either to origin or to destination.

on the level of urban fertility and the reclassification of rural territory as urban, and less on rural-urban migration. Anything causing an interruption in the flow of migrants from rural to urban areas--a depression, for example--might alter drastically the growth patterns of rural areas and create hardships for rural youth, but such an interruption would have a much smaller effect on urban growth patterns. Moreover, the lowered growth rates in urban places during such times of economic depression as the 1935 to 1940 decade resulted in greater part from lowered birth rates in the cities themselves than from decreases in the rates of out-migration from rural areas to cities.

Viewing the urban-rural origins and destinations of migrants in the 1935 to 1940 period from the perspective of probable future developments makes it clear that the study of internal migration involves a much broader expanse than its traditional treatment indicates. Much migration behavior is comparatively unexplained and has had relatively little study. A theory of migration should be developed which accounts for the large volume of out-movement originating in urban areas, and for the large volume of circulation occurring among communities of the same type.

(g) The total net effect of the flow of the nine urban-rural streams of migration during the 1935 to 1940 period was to move an estimated 748, 000 persons from rural-farm areas to nonfarm areas. More than two-thirds of this net change was gained by rural-nonfarm areas; cities received less than one-third. (Note that in the process of adjusting for reporting bias, the net migration balance of cities changes from a loss of 3/4 million persons to an estimated gain of almost 1/4 million persons.) There is general evidence that this net gain of the rural-nonfarm population was due to suburban movement, and did not betoken a resurgence of growth in villages and hamlets located in the open country outside the environs of large cities.

Most of the findings described under these seven points have apparently remained valid between 1940 and 1958. The only modification imposed on these findings by the events that have occurred since 1940 are (a) a resumption of the movement from rural-farm to nonfarm places; this movement has become much stronger (although it is still only a secondary source of urban growth) than it was during the 1935 to 1940 decade, and (b) the greatly stepped-up tempo of suburbanization, which actually underscores the findings concerning the 1935 to 1940 period. Instead of depending for population growth on migrants from farms, the large metropolises are now pulling people from villages and small cities throughout the nation.

HOW MIGRATION SELECTIVITY VARIES WITH AGE

The first section of this chapter showed that migration was selective of persons with certain specific traits, i.e., persons having a particular marital status, level of educational attainment, occupational status, or income level. These differences between migrants and nonmigrants may be due in part to differences between the two groups with respect to age composition, and may not be a direct result of migration. On the other hand, differences in age composition may hide large differences directly connected with migration selectivity.[22] If a migration differential persists at every age, or over a large segment of the age range in a particular category, it may be taken as strong evidence that the differential is a basic one--the result of a condition fundamentally related to the migration situation. Therefore, a full understanding of differential migration requires an examination of migration rates that are computed for each of the major population characteristics, by age. Table 15-18 presents such statistics; they are derived from the 1950 census of migration, which refers to the year April 1, 1949 to April 1,

---

[22] Selective migration is strongly affected also by the composition of the population at the place of origin, the composition of the population at the place of destination, and by the economic conditions that exist at the place of origin and destination. These and other aspects of selective migration are simultaneously studied in relation to age, sex, and color and each of the major population characteristics in the monograph Differential Migration in the Corn and Cotton Belts, by Donald J. Bogue and Margaret J. Hagood, op. cit.

Table 15-18.—PERCENTAGE OF POPULATION CLASSED AS MIGRANT, BY AGE AND SELECTED POPULATION CHARACTERISTICS: 1949 TO 1950

Characteristics	Total 14 years and over	Age						
		14 to 19 years	20 to 24 years	25 to 29 years	30 to 34 years	35 to 44 years	45 to 64 years	65 years and over
Total.............................	5.7	6.9	11.3	9.4	6.7	4.7	3.0	2.6
COLOR AND SEX								
White: Male...........................	6.2	7.2	12.1	10.7	7.8	5.4	3.3	2.5
Female.........................	5.5	7.2	11.4	8.9	6.3	4.3	2.9	2.8
Nonwhite: Male.........................	4.4	4.8	8.3	6.6	5.0	3.7	2.4	1.8
Female.........................	3.7	5.0	6.9	5.1	3.6	2.7	2.0	1.9
MARITAL STATUS								
Male...........................	6.0	6.9	11.7	10.3	7.5	5.2	3.2	2.6
Single...........................	7.2	6.7	10.4	9.0	6.4	5.0	3.7	2.6
Married, wife present....................	5.2	13.4	13.0	10.2	7.1	4.7	2.7	1.8
Other...........................	8.0	10.8	18.7	17.0	14.4	11.1	6.5	3.6
Female...........................	5.3	6.9	10.9	8.5	6.0	4.2	2.8	2.7
Single...........................	5.2	5.4	7.5	6.0	4.8	3.7	2.7	2.4
Married, husband present................	5.4	16.2	12.3	8.7	5.9	4.0	2.4	1.7
Other...........................	5.0	13.7	14.6	11.2	8.2	5.6	4.2	3.3
RELATIONSHIP TO HOUSEHOLD HEAD								
Head..............................	4.5	15.6	13.3	10.0	6.9	4.5	2.4	1.4
Male..............................	4.8	14.6	13.2	10.1	7.0	4.6	2.5	1.5
Female.............................	2.6	19.5	14.1	8.2	5.6	3.5	1.9	1.2
Wife..............................	5.1	17.0	12.2	8.5	5.8	3.8	2.2	1.4
Other relative.....................	5.0	3.7	6.3	6.8	5.6	4.9	5.9	5.3
Unrelated member of household......	13.0	23.2	22.4	17.0	13.1	10.6	8.0	5.4
Member of quasi household..........	16.6	36.0	21.3	19.0	15.6	12.2	7.9	4.7
EDUCATION BY COLOR[1]								
White.............................	4.9	...	...	9.8	7.0	4.8	3.1	2.6
Elementary: Less than 5 years..........	3.5	...	...	8.6	7.2	5.2	2.8	2.2
Elementary: 5-8 years..................	3.7	...	...	8.2	6.0	4.1	2.8	2.4
High school...........................	5.2	...	...	8.4	6.3	4.6	3.3	3.0
College...............................	8.1	...	...	16.2	10.9	6.8	4.2	3.6
School years not reported.............	3.8	...	...	7.1	5.5	4.0	2.8	2.9
Nonwhite.............................	3.3	...	...	5.8	4.3	3.1	2.2	1.9
Elementary: Less than 5 years..........	3.0	...	...	6.0	4.7	3.6	2.4	1.8
Elementary: 5-8 years..................	3.0	...	...	5.3	3.9	2.9	2.0	1.7
High school...........................	3.7	...	...	5.5	3.9	2.9	2.2	2.5
College...............................	5.6	...	...	9.6	7.0	4.2	2.8	2.6
School years not reported.............	2.9	...	...	4.6	3.6	2.8	2.3	2.2
EMPLOYMENT STATUS								
Male..............................	6.0	6.9	11.7	10.3	7.5	5.2	3.2	2.4
Employed..........................	5.2	6.2	10.0	9.1	6.5	4.7	2.8	1.5
Unemployed........................	9.2	8.0	12.5	13.0	11.2	9.2	6.4	3.6
Armed forces......................	29.7	42.6	29.8	26.8	22.3	22.8	13.6	2.1
Not in labor force................	6.1	5.3	12.4	13.9	13.4	8.4	5.4	3.0
Female............................	5.3	6.9	10.9	8.5	6.0	4.2	2.8	2.7
Employed[2].......................	5.0	7.8	9.2	7.1	5.0	3.5	2.6	2.1
Unemployed........................	9.6	9.0	13.2	12.4	10.3	8.3	6.8	5.4
Not in labor force................	5.3	6.6	12.0	9.1	6.4	4.4	2.9	2.7

[1]Data on "Education by Color": relates to persons 25 years and over.

[2]Includes members of the armed forces.

Table 15-18.—PERCENTAGE OF POPULATION CLASSED AS MIGRANT, BY AGE AND SELECTED POPULATION CHARACTERISTICS: 1949 TO 1950 (Continued)

Characteristics	Total 14 years and over	Age						
		14 to 19 years	20 to 24 years	25 to 29 years	30 to 34 years	35 to 44 years	45 to 64 years	65 years and over
MAJOR OCCUPATION GROUP								
Male, employed....................	5.2	6.4	9.9	9.0	6.4	4.6	2.7	1.4
Professional, technical and kindred workers............................	9.3	12.4	20.1	18.7	11.3	6.8	3.8	2.4
Farmers and farm managers.............	3.1	4.7	7.2	5.8	4.3	3.2	2.2	1.1
Managers, off. and prop'r, exc. farm...	4.6	8.0	12.4	9.9	7.1	5.0	2.7	1.2
Clerical and kindred workers..........	4.5	5.7	8.4	7.5	5.0	3.3	1.9	1.2
Sales workers.........................	6.5	4.0	11.1	11.6	8.4	5.9	3.4	1.6
Craftsmen, foremen, and kindred workers	4.8	8.0	9.5	7.9	6.1	4.6	2.6	1.4
Operatives and kindred workers.........	4.6	6.7	8.7	6.9	5.0	3.6	1.9	0.9
Service workers........................	4.5	8.6	11.1	7.8	5.5	4.0	2.6	1.2
Farm laborers and foremen.............	8.1	5.8	9.8	10.9	10.2	9.8	7.8	4.1
Laborers, except farm and mine.........	5.3	7.4	9.3	8.0	6.0	4.6	2.7	1.3
Occupation not reported...............	5.5	5.3	10.0	8.7	7.1	4.6	3.4	2.0
PERSONAL INCOME OF MALES								
Total.....................	6.0	6.9	11.7	10.3	7.5	5.2	3.2	2.4
Under $500[3]...........................	5.8	5.6	10.6	9.7		7.0	4.8	2.8
$500-$999...............................	8.6	14.6	15.2	12.2		7.8	5.2	2.5
$1,000-$1,499...........................	9.0	13.2	15.7	12.4		7.0	4.4	2.5
$1,500-$1,999...........................	7.4	8.8	12.2	11.1		6.1	3.6	2.1
$2,000-$2,499...........................	5.7	7.6	9.2	8.7		4.8	2.6	1.8
$2,500-$2,999...........................	4.7	7.1	8.1	7.1		4.0	2.1	1.6
$3,000-$3,999...........................	4.5	8.0	8.6	7.1		3.8	2.1	1.7
$4,000-$5,999...........................	5.0	7.6	11.8	8.7		5.0	2.6	2.0
$6,000 and over.........................	4.8	8.5	12.6	9.8		5.8	3.0	1.9
Income not reported....................	6.2	7.1	11.5	8.6		5.5	3.7	3.0

[3]Includes persons without income as well as those with a loss or with $1 to $499.

1950. The following additional comments about selective migration are based on these materials:

Color and Sex. Males were slightly more migratory than females between the ages of 20 and 64. At ages older or younger than this, females were as migratory as males, or more so. Although the white population was more migratory than the nonwhite at every age, the greatest disparity in rate between the two groups was found at ages 20 to 24 years. At these ages young white persons were more or less freely wandering, in search of their fortunes, but many nonwhite youths were being forced to accept whatever opportunities were available in their local communities. However, when they had attained the age of about 30, nonwhite persons tended to become only slightly less migratory than white persons of the same age.

Marital Status. Single (never married) persons were considerably less mobile than those who had married, at all ages under 45 years. At ages 45 and above, however, single persons were more mobile than those who were married and living with their spouses. Widowed, separated, and divorced persons were more mobile at all ages than either the single or the married group--probably, in large part, because the marriage dissolution itself induced migration.

Household Status. At all ages, nonfamily members of private households and residents of quasi households were much more migratory than persons who were members of private families. Male household heads were more migratory than female household heads, at all ages over 25 years.

Educational Attainment. The fact that more persons with a high school or a college education tended to migrate was found to be not solely a function of age, but a trait persisting within each age group. The greater the amount of education attained, the greater seemed to be the propensity to migrate. The only exception to this general pattern was the rather high migration rate for persons with less than 5 years of elementary education; this may have been due to the movement out of the South of low-income white families and Negroes. When the factor of age is controlled, the educational attainment differential becomes much greater for males than for females. In fact, among women, education seemed strongly related to migration only between the ages of 25 and 34.

Employment Status. Unemployed persons at all ages had a higher rate of migration than employed persons or persons not in the labor force. This differential existed among both males and females.

Major Occupation Group. Professional workers, farm laborers, and sales workers were the most mobile of the occupation groups; almost every age group, individually, showed above-average rates of migration for these occupations. The least mobile occupation groups were farm operators and managers, nonfarm laborers, clerical workers, and service workers older than 25 years.

Income of Individuals. At each age, the least migratory segments of the population were those with large (above-average) incomes and those with almost no income. This would seem to indicate that a person might be "too poor to migrate" as well as "so rich that he has no need to migrate." On the other hand, the same situation that is responsible for an adult person's poverty might prevent him from migrating, even if he wanted to. There was also some evidence that members of the very wealthiest groups may be somewhat more migratory than persons in the upper-middle income brackets.

Age. Last, but not least, is the age differential itself. In Table 15-18, each category of each characteristic shows a distinctive age pattern. In most cases this pattern indicates that there are low migration rates during adolescence, middle age, and the retirement years, and higher rates for persons 20 to 34 years of age. Thus, the age differential is perhaps the most fundamental of all the aspects of migration selectivity.

FACTORS UNDERLYING INTERNAL MIGRATION

Why do people migrate? Under what conditions do persons and families decide to change their residence and go elsewhere? Answers to these questions have been hinted at throughout the preceding section. This final section is devoted to an attempt to make a more systematic and integrated (and somewhat more theoretical) statement.

Economic Opportunity. Undoubtedly the strongest and most universal factor behind migration is economic opportunity--or, comparative economic opportunity. People must be able to obtain a livelihood when they arrive in a new community, so employment, occupation, and salary are considerations which play an important part in their decision to move. Much migration is based on the individual's expectation, or hope, that a change in his community of residence will improve his economic status--if not immediately, at least eventually. This phenomenon may be observed on all sides. Any kind of economic expansion, if it increases employment, attracts migrants. This expansion may be industrial, commercial, or not-for-profit. (Even the rumor of potential economic opportunities can stimulate migration.) Economic contraction, or "hard times," tends to depress migration. In both the westward movement and the South-to-North movement, economic opportunity has been one of the major driving forces.[23] During any given period, migrants tend to avoid (or at least not to remain in) communities where economic conditions are bad, and tend to be attracted to communities where economic opportunities are more plentiful. For example, the rate of net migration to metropolitan areas during the period 1935 to 1940 (using population subregions as the

---

[23] The role of economic opportunity in internal migration was well documented by Carter Goodrich and associates in Migration and Economic Opportunity, University of Pennsylvania Press, 1936.

unit of analysis) was found to have the following correlations with the rate of unemployment:[24]

```
Total, with respect to all subregions........ -.55
With respect to other metropolitan areas..... -.47
With respect to nonmetropolitan areas........ -.50
```

Thus, net migration to metropolitan areas was positive, and highest where the rate of unemployment was lowest, both with respect to movement between metropolitan areas and with respect to migration from nonmetropolitan to metropolitan areas. This variable was found to persist as a significant factor even when more than a dozen other variables were simultaneously held constant.

Basic Social and Economic Changes. When one segment of the economy suffers a marked disequilibrium with respect to the other segments, migration may bring about at least a partial readjustment. For example, shrinkage in the farm labor force has been causing extensive off-farm migration, as was demonstrated when the net migration statistics for nonmetropolitan state economic areas were correlated with the percent of employed labor force in agriculture in 1950. The correlation was -.52.[25] Thus, if a high proportion of the labor force in a state economic area derived its livelihood from farming, the rate of net migration tended to be negative, or very low, and in places where the percentage of nonfarm workers was high, the rate of net migration tended to be positive and large.

Level of Living. Comfortable living conditions appear to attract migrants, irrespective of the existence of specific employment opportunities (although adequate living conditions and concrete job opportunities are usually found together). For example, the rate of net out-migration from nonmetropolitan areas tended to be highest (most negative) in areas where the farm operator level-of-living index was lowest. It tended to be less negative, and in some cases actually positive, in areas where the level of living of farm operators was higher. The correlation between net migration and farm operator level of living was .58.[26] Moreover, there was a high and consistently positive correlation between the level of income and the rate of net migration (.65 for all state economic areas).[27] Net migration flowed toward centers of high income, and away from centers of low income. The directions taken by this flow cannot be considered a result of regional differences, because the calculation was also made for each economic region separately, and was found to hold within each.

Routine Functioning of the Economy. The very large intercity migration reported in a preceding section indicates that the smooth and routine functioning of our urbanized and metropolitanized economy requires a certain amount of movement on the part of the nation's population. The fact that urban-to-urban migrants are better educated than the average migrant, and are more often holders of specialized jobs, leads to the conclusion that one of the major factors underlying internal migration among cities and metropolitan areas is our economy's continuing need to distribute and redistribute the specialists, experts, and managers (both the actual and the potential) in such a way that their abilities can be used most profitably. Only by a process of migration can the most talented persons be extracted from the population, congregated for training in universities and other educational centers, and then dispersed to the places where their specialized services are needed. This is true not only of doctors, lawyers, engineers, teachers, accountants, and other business specialists, but also of such specialized persons as sales managers, plant foremen, and supervisors in firms having numerous branch plants.

Change in Personal Status. The study of differential migration made by Bogue and Hagood un-

[24] Bogue, Shryock, and Hoermann, op. cit., p. 68.

[25] Bogue, Components of Population Change, op. cit., pages 24-29.

[26] Ibid.

[27] Ibid.

covered many situations in which migration was strongly selective of persons for noneconomic reasons (at least, the reasons were only indirectly economic).[28] Failing health and old age appear to bring many migrants to institutions that are located in the city. Inability to work brings adults into the city from farms. A death in a family can send young children to an orphanage, and can force an older adult to live with one of his or her children. A criminal often migrates to escape punishment, and the fear of imprisonment makes migrants of many offenders. Many girls migrate at the time of marriage, and after marriage the amount of migrating they do often depends more on their husbands' situations than on their wishes. Divorce causes migration, and necessitates it in some states. The existence of these "noneconomic" factors does not disprove the theory that much migration is motivated by desire to take advantage of economic opportunities, and that in many areas the lack of sufficient opportunities at home stimulates out-migration. It does show,

however, that economic opportunity is only one of several factors in migration, and that for some members of the population it may be of secondary importance.

CONCLUSION

The materials presented here have demonstrated that internal migration is one of the fundamental mechanisms by means of which population changes take place, and also that such migration is fundamental to the maintenance of a particular population balance. If internal migration were suddenly to cease, population would begin to pile up in areas of high fertility (which, all too often, are areas of low economic opportunity). If migration were suddenly to become random, unpatterned and unselective, many fundamental social changes would stop taking place, many persons would immediately experience acute hardships, and many social institutions would cease to function efficiently. Because it is such a central aspect of so many different social and economic phenomena, the intensive study of internal migration is one of the most important responsibilities of demography.

[28] Op. cit., Part II.

Chapter 16

THE LABOR FORCE AND ITS COMPOSITION

INTRODUCTION TO THE STUDY OF THE LABOR FORCE

The labor force of a nation is that part of the population which is engaged in the production of economic goods and services at a particular time. It is the totality of persons who at a given moment are performing (or seeking an opportunity to perform) work for which a wage, salary, or other money income usually is received. Those who are unemployed but seeking work are included. Also included are unpaid family workers who perform gainful work but who receive no money pay. Self-employed persons such as doctors, lawyers, and entrepreneurs are a part of the labor force as well as those who are employed at wage or salary jobs. In short, the breadwinners of a population are its labor force. Members of the armed forces are included as a part of the labor force, although they are often excluded when a discussion is limited to the civilian labor force. Not included in the labor force are: dependent children, housewives who have no job other than keeping house, students who are not working, adults who are retired or unable to work because of ill health or for other reasons, and inmates of institutions--jails, hospitals, sanitoria, etc.

A great many persons and agencies are interested in the labor force. The size and distribution of the labor force, and the characteristics of its members, can provide much information about the economic and social well-being of a nation or a community at a given moment, and can reveal how the population has organized itself to earn its livelihood. Equally important and interesting are changes in the size, distribution, or composition of the labor force, because such changes reflect shifts in the level of economic well-being and disclose new patterns of economic and social organization. It is not surprising, therefore, to find that for this group of population statistics the demand is steady and the customers numerous. Their concern involves more than an interest in knowing the total number of jobs, the number of people who are with and without jobs, and the changes in these totals. They want to know: the age at which youths begin to work and at which elderly people retire; the participation in the labor force of women (unmarried, married but childless, and married with children); the number of hours worked per week, and the number of weeks worked per year, by various subgroups of workers and these subjects are only a sample of the topics that labor force experts explore. Fortunately, a splendid body of statistics concerning the present status of the labor force, and its recent trends and changes, has been assembled for the United States. Statisticians, labor economists, and others interested in the field of labor statistics have cooperated to develop definitions and procedures for obtaining detailed and continuous information. Their work has been encouraged and financed by an interested public.

419

The economic depression of the 1930's demonstrated that previous concepts and modes of measurement were seriously deficient when it came to measuring unemployment. During the years of World War II there was a chronic shortage of manpower; efforts were made to sharpen the concepts so that pools of surplus manpower could be more easily found, and so that industry could attract those marginal workers who had removed themselves from the labor force. Since the end of World War II this country has been continuously concerned with the maintenance of a high level of prosperity. Congress has authorized the use of funds for the maintenance of a constant statistical vigil, so that if "soft spots" begin to develop immediate steps can be taken to correct the situation. Each of these crises and programs has emphasized a different aspect of employment, and each has required the collection of new bodies of information. To meet the growing need for comprehensive information, the censuses of 1940 and 1950 each had several questions on labor force topics. The demand for labor force information has been continuous, and the Bureau of the Census has been empowered to conduct a special sample survey of the labor force once each month. The sample upon which these surveys are based is relatively large, and can provide much information about labor force characteristics. The results of these surveys are released jointly by the U. S. Department of Commerce and the Department of Labor. More detailed information about each month's findings is published by the Census Bureau in a series entitled Current Population Reports, Labor Force, Series P-50 and P-57. Once each year there is a special report in the P-50 series entitled Annual Report on the Labor Force. These more detailed reports furnish data about occupation, income, and other economic characteristics of workers (as well as much general population information not necessarily related to the labor force-- some of which has been summarized in other parts of this book). Much valuable information is contributed by other organizations, such as the Bureau of Labor Statistics of the Department of Labor.

This chapter and the three chapters that follow undertake to summarize what has been learned about the United States labor force. The present chapter will concentrate upon the following topics:

Labor force participation
Unemployment
Weeks worked per year
Hours worked per week
Multiple and part-time jobholding
Seasonal variatons in employment
Labor mobility
Length of working life

Later chapters will deal with occupation, industry, and unemployment, respectively.

LABOR FORCE PARTICIPATION

As presently defined, the civilian labor force of the United States includes all civilian persons 14 years of age or over who are not inmates of institutions, and are either employed or unemployed (according to the definitions stated below) during the calendar week preceding the census or survey. The total labor force includes the civilian labor force plus members of the Armed Forces stationed either in the United States or abroad. Persons in the labor force are called collectively "labor force participants," and the proportion of the total noninstitutional population 14 years of age or over that is participating in the labor force is called the "labor force participation rate."[1] Employed persons comprise all civilians 14 years old and over who, during the week preceding enumeration, (a) did any work at all as paid employees or in their own business or profession, or on their own farm, or who worked 15 hours or more as unpaid workers on a farm or in a business operated by a member of the family, or (b) "all those who were not working or looking for work, but who had jobs or businesses from which they were temporarily absent because of vacation, illness, bad

---

[1] A close approximation, the proportion of population 14 years of age and over that is participating (including the small institutional population), frequently is used when statistics for the noninstitutional population are not available.

weather, or labor-management dispute, or because they were taking time off for other reasons.

Unemployed persons include those who did not work at all during the survey week and who were looking for work.[2]

Armed Forces are persons on active duty with the United States Army, Air Force, Navy, Marine Corps, or Coast Guard.

The civilian labor force consists of the sum of the employed and unemployed components of the labor force, and the civilian labor force participation rate is the number of employed and unemployed persons combined and divided by the total civilian (noninstitutional) population 14 years of age and over. These rates can be computed for particular parts of the population, such as age groups, sex groups, color groups, etc.

TRENDS IN THE WORK FORCE SINCE 1820, AND PROJECTIONS TO 1975

Labor force concepts were first introduced during the 1930's; before that time a more general inquiry concerning "usual occupation" had been used for more than a century to obtain information about the nation's work force. Although the "gainful workers" who were reported as a result of this

questioning were not necessarily working or actively seeking work at the time of the census, the total numbers of workers who were reported according to the old and the new definitions correspond rather well, as the estimates reported in Table 16-1 (and illustrated in Figure 16-1) show.[3] Together, the statistics which were reported concerning "gainful workers" prior to the 1930's and the statistics which have since been based on "labor force" provide a good over-all picture of the trends in the United States working force. In addition, the Bureau of the Census has calculated estimates of what the labor force will be in 1960, 1965, 1970, and 1975 if the average annual rates of change in labor force participation rates which have been observed between 1950 and 1955 continue unchanged. These estimates are also reported.

The most conspicuous trend has been the very large increase in the size of the work force. For every member of the labor force a century ago, there are 9 working persons today. Simple growth of the population is by far the major cause of this growth. However, a somewhat larger proportion of the population is in the labor force today than was the case a century or so ago, and the labor force participation rate is higher. By 1970 about 58 percent of the total noninstitutional population aged 14 and over will be labor force participants, whereas it is estimated that a century earlier the labor force participation rate was about 52 per-

---

[2] Those who had made efforts to find jobs within the preceding 60-day period--by such means as registering at a public or private employment agency, writing letters of application, canvassing for work, etc.--and who, during the survey week, were awaiting the results of these efforts, are also regarded as looking for work. Also included as unemployed are those who did not work at all during the survey week and--
   a. were waiting to be called back to a job from which they had been laid off, or
   b. were waiting to report to a new wage or salary job scheduled to start within the following 30 days (and were not in school during the survey week); or
   c. would have been looking for work except that they were temporarily ill or believed no employment was available in their line of work or in their community.
For a more detailed discussion of basic definition of labor force concepts, the reader is referred to "Concepts and Methods Used in the Current Employment and Unemployment Statistics," prepared by the Bureau of the Census, Current Population Reports, Series P-23, No. 5, May, 1958.

---

[3] For a full discussion of the differences between the "gainful worker" and the "labor force" approach to the measurement of the working force, see A. J. Joffee and Charles D. Stewart, Manpower Resources and Utilization; Appendix D, "Comparison of the Labor Force and Gainfully Occupied Procedures," John Wiley and Sons, 1951. In general, the gainful worker approach has no specific time referent and tends to include retired or disabled persons and to undercount the number of new workers (persons seeking their first job), the unemployed, and the occasional workers. The labor force approach refers to a specific period of time, and therefore permits the calculation of rates and facilitates the measurement of short-run changes in employment levels. It tends to count the labor force precisely at one instant in time, but excludes seasonal or other part-time workers if they are not working or actively seeking work at the time of the census or survey.

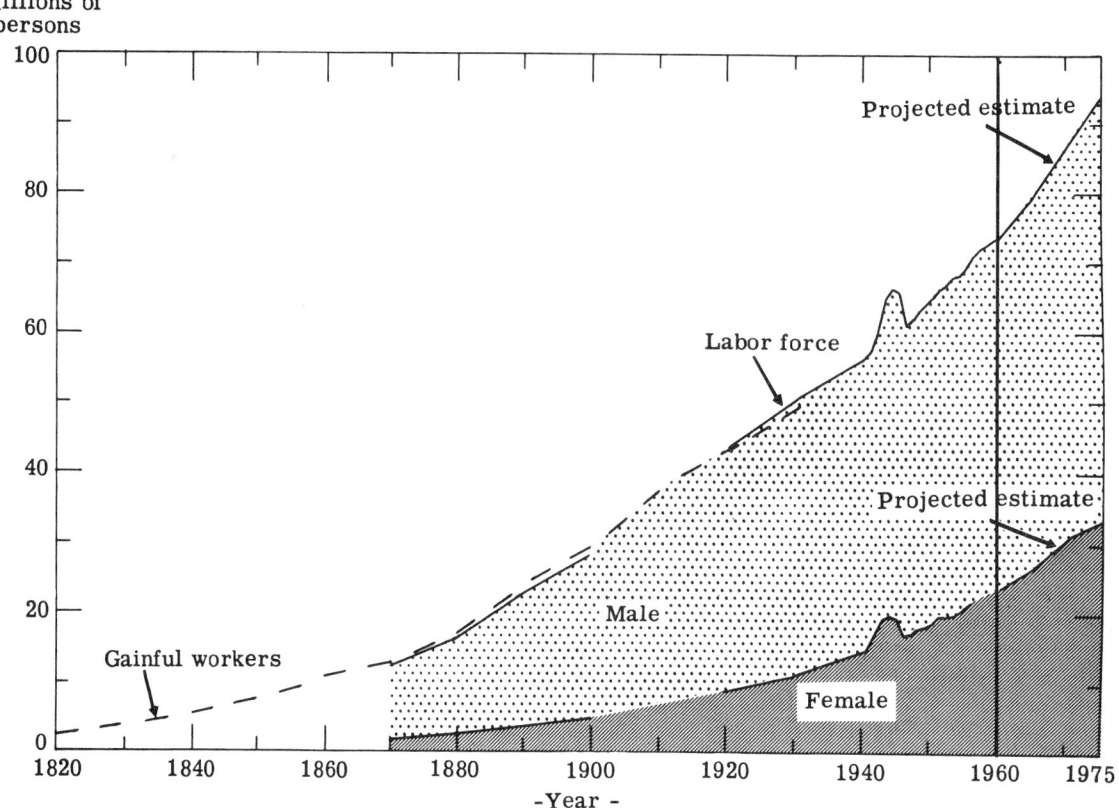

Figure 16 - 1. WORK FORCE OF THE UNITED STATES: 1820 TO 1957, AND PROJECTED WORK FORCE: 1960 TO 1975

Source: Gertrude Bancroft, "Projections of the Labor Force in the United States, 1955 to 1975, " U. S. Bureau of the Census, P-50, No. 69, 1956.

cent. A most impressive aspect of Table 16-1 and Figure 16-1 is the fact that the number of workers is scheduled to increase by almost 20 million in the 15 years between 1960 and 1975. During these years the much larger cohorts of children born since the "baby boom" of 1946 will be entering the labor force and swelling its ranks.

A good over-all measure of economic self-sufficiency among a population is the percentage of the total population that is in the work force. Thus, if 33 percent of the population is in the labor force, this means that each worker has an average of about 2 dependents. For many decades there has been a steady decline in dependency as measured in this way; today each worker has only about 1.4 dependents, whereas in 1870 he had about 2.0 dependents. This decline has resulted from two major changes: due to lower birth rates the ratio of children to adults is now smaller, and women now have a much higher rate of participation in the labor force than they had formerly. By 1960 the labor force participation rate for women will be more than twice as high as it was in 1870, and many experts believe that by 1975 it will rise even to 40 percent. Whereas women comprised only 15 percent of the total labor force of 1870, by 1975 one worker in 3 will be female if recent trends continue. Meanwhile, the participation rate for men has declined markedly over the past century (from 86 in 1870 to about 81 in 1960), and is expected to decline further. Earlier retirement and the delaying of entrance into the labor force in order to obtain more education are the two principal causes of the lower labor force participation among men.

Table 16-1.—THE WORK FORCE IN THE UNITED STATES; 1820 TO 1975

Year	Gainful workers (000) (1)	Total labor force (000) Total (2)	(000) Male (3)	(000) Female (4)	Percent of total population (5)	Percent of workers female (6)	Participation rate Total (7)	Male (8)	Female (9)
1820	2,881	...	...	...	29.9	...	...	...	...
1830	3,932	...	...	...	30.6	...	...	...	...
1840	5,420	...	...	...	31.8	...	...	...	...
1850	7,697	...	...	...	33.2	...	...	...	...
1860	10,533	...	...	...	33.5	...	...	...	...
1870	12,925	12,557	10,699	1,858	31.5	14.8	51.5	86.2	15.5
1880	17,392	16,896	14,328	2,568	33.7	15.2	52.5	87.3	16.3
1890	23,318	22,653	18,757	3,896	36.0	17.2	54.2	87.3	19.2
1900	29,073	28,282	23,168	5,114	37.2	18.1	55.0	87.7	20.4
1910	37,371	...	...	...	...	...	...	...	...
1920	42,434	42,660	33,957	8,703	38.7	20.4	55.8	85.9	24.1
1930	48,830	50,080	39,062	11,018	39.5	22.0	54.6	83.4	25.1
1940	...	56,030	41,870	14,160	42.5	25.3	55.9	83.9	28.2
1941	...	57,380	42,740	14,640	43.1	25.5	56.6	84.8	28.7
1942	...	60,230	44,110	16,120	45.0	26.8	58.8	86.6	31.3
1943	...	64,410	45,600	18,810	48.0	29.2	62.2	88.7	36.1
1944	...	65,890	46,520	19,370	49.6	29.4	63.1	89.8	36.8
1945	...	65,140	45,870	19,270	49.2	29.6	61.8	88.0	36.2
1946	...	60,820	43,980	16,840	43.4	27.7	57.2	83.7	31.3
1947	...	61,608	44,694	16,915	42.9	27.5	57.3	84.4	31.0
1948	...	62,748	45,150	17,599	43.0	28.0	57.8	84.6	31.9
1949	...	63,571	45,524	18,048	42.8	28.4	58.0	84.5	32.4
1950	...	64,599	45,919	18,680	42.7	28.9	58.3	84.4	33.1
1951	...	65,832	46,524	19,309	42.9	29.3	58.8	84.8	33.8
1952	...	66,426	46,868	19,559	42.6	29.4	58.7	84.6	33.9
1953	...	67,362	47,692	19,668	42.5	29.2	58.5	84.4	33.6
1954	...	67,818	47,847	19,970	42.1	29.4	58.4	83.9	33.7
1955	...	68,896	48,054	20,842	41.9	30.3	58.7	83.6	34.8
1956	...	70,387	48,579	21,808	42.1	31.0	59.3	83.7	35.9
1957	...	70,746	48,649	22,097	41.5	31.2	58.7	82.7	35.9
1960	...	73,372	49,751	23,621	41.3	32.2	58.1	80.7	36.5
1965	...	79,442	52,536	26,906	41.7	33.9	57.9	78.7	38.2
1970	...	86,604	56,213	30,391	42.3	35.1	58.3	77.9	39.8
1975	...	93,705	60,104	33,601	42.3	35.9	59.0	77.9	41.1

Source: (a) Historical Statistics of the United States, 1789-1945, Table D-10;
(b) Continuation to 1952 of Historical Statistics of the United States, Table 1;
(c) Alba M. Edwards, Comparative Occupation Statistics for the United States, 1870 to 1940, p. 13, 91.
(d) John D. Durand, The Labor Force in the United States, 1890-1960;
(e) Current Population Reports, Labor Force, P-50, No. 42 and 69;
(f) Statistical Abstract of the United States, 1957, Tables 239, 240, 1, 2, and 3;
(g) Data for 1870, 1880, and 1890, estimated by the author by use of ratios and trends;
(h) Statistical Abstract of the United States, 1958, Tables 254 and 2.

DIFFERENTIALS IN LABOR FORCE PARTICIPATION

The above statistics reveal only in a very general way the size and composition of the labor force. Some subgroups of the population have considerably higher participation rates than other groups. These differentials are of considerable importance in understanding the composition of the labor force and the changes which are taking place in this composition.

Sex differences in labor force participation. Table 16-1 reports that in 1950, 84 percent of males and 33 percent of females aged 14 years of age and over were in the labor force (the 1950 census showed a participation rate of 78 percent for males and 29 percent for females).[4] This large sex difference in labor force participation is a result of two conditions: (a) by cultural definition women tend to be accepted as economic dependents and are not generally required to earn their own livelihood, and (b) childbearing and housekeeping remove from the labor force many women who otherwise would participate. However, this differential has lessened steadily since 1870. At that time only about 15.5 percent of the women 14 years of age and over were in the labor force (one in six). Today the rate is more than twice that (one in three), and is still rising. The increasing participation rates for women and the decreasing participation rates for men act together to diminish the sex differential in labor force participation, although it is now very large and probably will remain so.

Age differences in labor force participation. Labor force participation varies a great deal with age. Table 16-2 shows that during the years of adolescence (14 to 19 years) only about 50 percent of the males and 30 percent of the females to be in the labor force (as of 1955-60). The age composition of the labor force, and a more detailed picture of the age pattern, is shown in Tables 16-3 to 16-7. Tables 16-5 and 16-6, compiled from the 1950 census, show participation rates and age composition for the populations of urban and rural

---

[4] The statistics reported in Table 16-1 are derived from the monthly sample surveys conducted by the Bureau of the Census. It is thought that the more carefully selected, better trained, and more experienced sample survey enumerators do a more thorough job of counting part-time and marginal workers than do the decennial census enumerators; therefore, despite the fact that these data are drawn from only a small fraction of the population, the data from the Current Population Reports (sample data) are generally conceded to be more nearly correct than the 1950 or 1940 census reports. They tend to yield higher rates of participation than the official decennial census tabulations, reported in Table 16-2 and later tables. In general, the sample data are useful to indicate the level and the over-all rates of labor force participation, by age and sex. The census data are useful as the only source from which to obtain detailed information concerning differentials in participation, especially for small areas.

areas, by sex and color. The data in Table 16-6, which reports participation rates for single years during the ages of labor force entry, shows that for both men and women the participation rate rises rapidly as age 20 is attained; this rise reflects departure from school, and the shift from dependency to self-support. For each sex, the labor force participation rates have a distinctive age-curve. Figure 16-2 illustrates the curves with data from the 1950 census. For males the curve climbs quickly toward 100 percent and remains on a high plateau through ages 25 to 44, after which it falls slowly as disabilities gradually remove men from work, although it continues to be high right up to age 60. This pattern reflects the adherence to the cultural dictum that if an adult male is not sick or disabled he should work. Women have a lower participation rate, at all ages, than men. The rate for females climbs to its highest point at about 20 years and then begins to descend. Women tend to work in greatest numbers between the time they leave school and the time they marry or have their first child; at both of these latter times many women withdraw from the labor force. The rate for females tends to rise again between ages 35 to 54, and then declines again at the older ages. This second rise is due to a tendency for women to re-enter the labor force after their children are in school or have left home.

Trends in age differentials and age composition in the labor force. When the United States was an agrarian society, and was in the early phase of the industrial revolution, it was customary for children to begin work at a young age. It was not at all uncommon to find children 8 or 10 years of age gainfully employed. There has been a long-term decline in the participation of children in the work force; in most states legislation specifies the minimum age and otherwise regulates the employment of children (usually those under 16 years of age). Census employment statistics before 1940 reported data for all persons 10 years of age or older. In 1890 about 18 percent of the children 10 to 15 years of age were gainfully employed (26 percent of boys and 10 percent of girls). When the

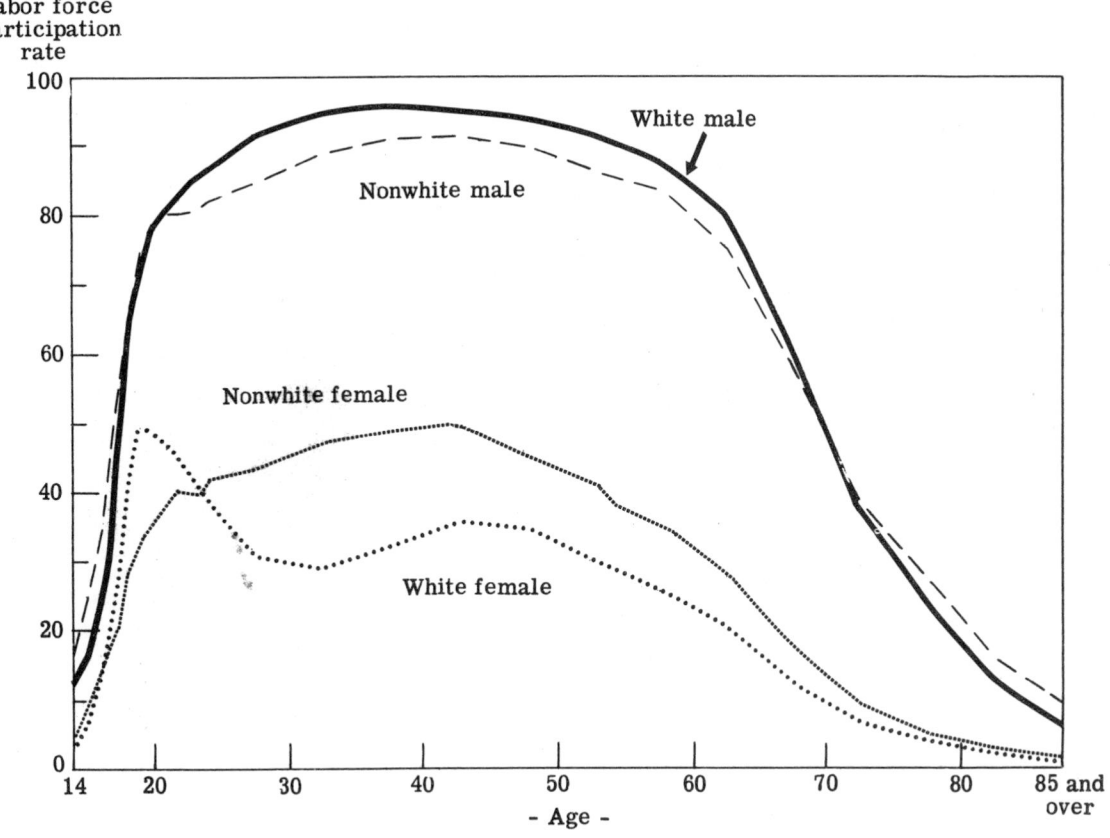

Labor force
participation
rate

FIGURE 16 - 2. LABOR FORCE PARTICIPATION RATE FOR THE POPULATION 14 YEARS OF AGE
AND OVER, BY AGE, SEX, AND COLOR, 1950

labor force definitions of 1940 were established, age 14 (instead of age 10) was chosen as the youngest age for which it was worthwhile to collect employment data. In 1940, only 13 percent of boys 14 years of age were in the labor force (4.1 percent of girls 14 years of age). (The year 1940 may have provided an artificially low set of statistics, because in years of economic depression children tend to be driven out of the labor force.) During the wartime emergency, however, the youth of the nation proved to be a most valuable source of manpower. A great many teen-agers worked a shift in a factory or held some other job, while attending school. As Table 16-2 indicates, 70 percent of the boys 14 to 19 years of age and 42 percent of the girls were in the labor force. This

represented a jump in rate of participation within 4 years of 59 percentage points for boys and 83 percent for girls. Since 1945 the young teen-agers have been withdrawing from the labor force; their withdrawal has been very gradual however, so their present participation rates are still well above those of 1940--and many demographers expect them to remain at that level until 1965 or longer. It is difficult to know whether this greater participation by youth is one of the causes, or simply one of the effects, of the recent decline in the age at marriage which is described in Chapter 10.

Until very recently the conditions of life were hard, and few workers managed to save enough to retire in their old age; traditionally, therefore, a

Table 16-2.—LABOR FORCE PARTICIPATION RATES, BY AGE AND SEX: 1900 TO 1955, AND PROJECTIONS FOR 1960 AND 1975

Age	1900	1920	1940	1944	1950	1955	1960	1975
Both sexes..........	55.0	55.8	55.9	63.1	58.3	58.7	58.1	59.0
MALE......................	87.7	85.9	83.9	89.8	84.4	83.6	80.7	77.9
14 to 19 years..............	63.6	52.6	44.2	70.0	53.2	49.5	46.0	40.3
20 to 24 years..............	91.7	91.0	96.1	98.5	89.0	90.8	88.2	84.5
25 to 34 years..............	96.3	97.2	98.1	99.0	96.2	97.7	96.8	97.5
35 to 44 years..............			98.5	99.0	97.6	98.4	97.3	98.3
45 to 54 years..............	93.3	93.8	95.5	97.1	95.8	96.4	95.7	97.1
55 to 64 years..............			87.2	92.1	87.0	88.3	87.4	90.0
65 years and over..........	68.3	60.1	45.0	52.2	45.8	40.6	33.4	21.8
FEMALE......................	20.4	24.1	28.2	36.8	33.1	34.8	36.5	41.1
14 to 19 years..............	26.8	28.4	23.3	42.0	31.5	29.9	28.7	27.1
20 to 24 years..............	32.1	38.1	49.5	55.0	46.1	46.0	46.5	46.4
25 to 34 years..............	18.1	22.4	35.2	39.0	34.0	34.9	35.8	39.1
35 to 44 years..............			28.8	40.5	39.1	41.6	44.0	50.9
45 to 54 years..............	14.1	17.1	24.3	35.8	38.0	43.8	49.2	62.8
55 to 64 years..............			18.7	25.4	27.0	32.5	37.5	50.1
65 years and over..........	9.1	8.0	7.4	9.8	9.7	10.6	11.1	13.4

Source: Data for 1940-55 from Current Population Reports, Series P-50, Nos.61 and 72; data for 1960 and 1975 from Ibid., No. 69; data for 1920 from U.S. Census, 1940, Vol. III, The Labor Force, Part 1, United States Summary, Table 8, p. 26; Data for 1900 from U.S. Census, 1940, Comparative Occupational Statistics for the U.S., 1870-1940.

high percentage of older workers remained in the labor force until death or physical disability overtook them. For example, in 1890 about 68 percent of males 65 years of age and over were still in the working force. The establishment of Social Security and other pension plans has permitted, or required, increasing proportions of older men to retire. By 1940 the percentage of men 65 and over who were still in the labor force had dropped to about 45 percent, and by 1960 it will have declined to less than 40 percent. If recent trends continue, by 1975 only about 20 to 25 percent of the males in these retirement ages will be labor force participants. Instead of being a luxury enjoyed by only a few, retirement is now a normal and significantly large segment of the life cycle of most men, and will become even more important in the future (see section on length of working life, below).

The increase in the number of women in the labor force extends even into the retirement ages. Consequently, the labor force participation rate for women 65 years of age or older is roughly 50 percent higher than it was in 1940, and may continue to rise even more. It should be noted that the labor force participation of teen-age girls is no higher now than it was in 1900. The major increases have come in the ages 25 to 64.

The age composition of the labor force has changed a great deal because of these changes in the age pattern of participation rates (see Table 16-3). It has also been affected by the rise in the average age of the population. Among males, the proportion of the labor force which is comprised of teen-age youngsters has declined to about 7 1/2 percent. Because the 1960-75 period will see a great influx of younger people into the labor force, this percentage will remain fairly stable, despite declining participation rates for teen-agers. At the other end of the age range, progressively rising rates of retirement are causing a smaller and smaller proportion of the labor force to be comprised of men 65 years of age. However, there is a slight rise in the proportion between the ages of 55 and 64. In summary, the ages 20 to 64 are coming to be generally recognized as the span of working life, and persons who are younger than this or older than this tend to be excluded.

The age composition of the female segment of the labor force is quite different from that of the male segment, and is changing rapidly. Whereas

Table 16-3.—AGE COMPOSITION OF THE LABOR FORCE, BY SEX: 1940 TO 1975

Age	Male				Female			
	Census		Estimated		Census		Estimated	
	1940	1950	1960	1975	1940	1950	1960	1975
All ages.............	100.0	100.0	100.0	100.0	100.0	100.0	100.0	100.0
14 and 15 years...............	0.5	0.8	} 7.6	7.7	0.4	0.7	} 9.7	8.9
16 and 17 years...............	1.8	1.8			2.4	2.2		
18 and 19 years...............	4.1	3.3			7.9	5.8		
20 to 24 years...............	12.5	10.6	10.1	13.7	20.7	15.3	11.0	13.1
25 to 34 years...............	25.1	24.5	21.9	25.3	27.7	23.4	17.3	17.9
35 to 44 years...............	21.7	22.8	22.9	18.1	19.2	22.9	22.8	16.9
45 to 54 years...............	18.3	18.1	19.6	18.2	13.0	17.3	22.2	22.5
55 to 64 years...............	11.4	12.7	13.2	13.8	6.6	9.4	12.9	15.9
65 years and over............	4.6	5.5	4.8	3.2	2.1	3.1	4.1	4.8

Source: Current Population Reports, Labor Force, Series P-50, No. 69, 1956, Table 2, and Statistical Abstract of the United States, 1957, Table 238.

in the past females have been highly concentrated in the young adult years, they are now rapidly taking on an age pattern more nearly resembling that of males. By 1975 the female working force will have only a moderately younger age composition than the male working force.

Color differences in labor force participation. There are marked differences between the labor force participation of the white and the nonwhite populations. (See Tables 16-4 to 16-6.) Nonwhite males enter the labor force at an earlier age than white males. At ages 14 to 17, this differential is of substantial size, and reflects the early withdrawal of nonwhite boys from school to get jobs. By age 20, however, white males are participating at the same rates as nonwhite males, and thereafter the rates for white males are higher than for nonwhite up to age 70. Beyond age 70 the non-

Table 16-4.—LABOR FORCE PARTICIPATION RATES FOR CIVILIAN MALES, BY AGE AND COLOR FOR THE UNITED STATES, URBAN AND RURAL: 1950

Age	All males	A. White males				B. Nonwhite males				Percent total males in civilian labor force by age			
		Total	Urban	Rural non-farm	Rural farm	Total	Urban	Rural non-farm	Rural farm	Total	Urban	Rural non-farm	Rural farm
Total, 14 years and over.......	78.9	79.2	79.8	74.7	82.9	76.5	76.9	67.6	83.4	100.0	100.0	100.0	100.0
14 to 19 years....	39.3	38.8	35.5	38.8	47.6	43.3	33.7	42.1	59.8	5.5	4.3	5.7	10.1
20 to 24 years....	81.9	82.1	78.8	85.8	92.6	80.3	78.5	75.5	91.3	10.1	9.8	10.9	10.1
25 to 29 years....	90.3	91.0	90.5	90.4	95.4	84.5	84.9	75.3	93.7	12.2	12.8	13.0	9.3
30 to 34 years....	93.9	94.5	94.7	92.6	96.6	88.2	88.7	79.3	95.5	12.1	12.5	12.9	9.6
35 to 39 years....	94.6	95.1	95.4	92.9	97.0	90.4	90.7	82.6	96.7	12.0	12.3	12.6	10.6
40 to 44 years....	94.3	94.7	95.1	91.8	96.8	90.7	90.8	83.8	96.3	11.1	11.3	11.1	10.1
45 to 49 years....	93.2	93.5	94.0	89.8	96.2	89.7	89.9	82.1	95.9	9.8	10.1	9.3	9.3
50 to 54 years....	90.6	91.0	91.8	85.4	94.2	86.9	86.7	78.6	94.7	8.7	9.0	7.8	8.5
55 to 59 years....	86.7	87.0	87.9	79.4	91.8	82.9	82.2	73.2	92.7	7.3	7.5	6.4	7.7
60 to 64 years....	79.4	79.7	80.5	70.1	87.3	76.0	73.9	66.8	89.1	5.6	5.6	5.0	6.3
65 to 69 years....	59.8	60.0	59.2	48.8	76.4	58.1	52.1	47.6	79.6	3.4	3.2	3.1	4.6
70 to 74 years....	38.7	38.6	36.0	29.8	61.0	40.2	32.4	30.0	64.9	1.5	1.3	1.4	2.4
75 to 79 years....	24.2	23.9	21.3	17.3	44.5	27.6	20.1	20.1	50.3	0.6	0.4	0.6	1.1
80 to 84 years....	13.2	12.9	11.0	9.0	26.9	16.7	11.7	11.3	32.8	0.2	0.1	0.2	0.3
85 years and over.	6.9	6.6	5.8	4.6	13.0	9.8	7.6	7.0	16.9	...	...	...	0.1

Source: U.S. Census of Population: 1950, Vol. II, Detailed Characteristics of the Population, Part 1, U.S. Summary, Chapter C, Table 118.

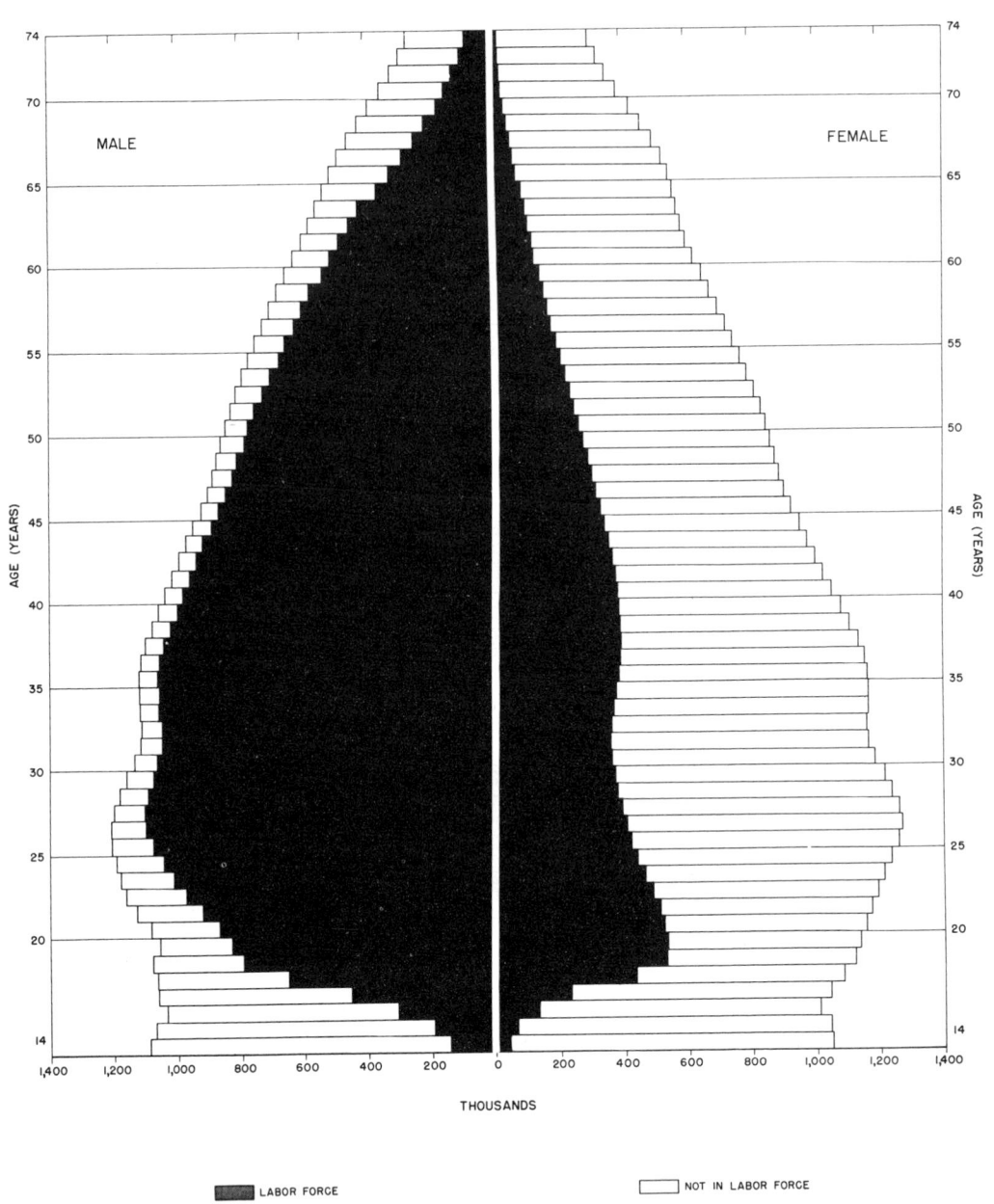

Figure 16 - 3. LABOR FORCE STATUS OF PERSONS 14 TO 74 YEARS OLD, BY SINGLE YEARS OF AGE AND SEX, FOR THE UNITED STATES: 1950

Source: Reproduced from U.S. Census of Population: 1950, Vol. IV,   Special Reports, Part 1, Chapter A , Employment and Personal Characteristics, 1953.

whites have higher participation rates than whites; this probably reflects the poorer economic status of the nonwhites and their need to continue working during ages at which white males are retired. For all ages combined, the percentage of nonwhite adult males in the labor force is 2.4 percent smaller than the corresponding percentage of white males. There is no easy explanation for the lower participation rates of nonwhite males than of white males during the major working years 20 to 65. This differential remains even when place of residence (urban-rural) and other intervening factors that might account for it are controlled. An uncharitable explanation is that a higher proportion of nonwhite than of white adult males are shiftless and inclined to let someone support them. A more charitable explanation is that unemployment rates are higher among nonwhite than among white males, and that a certain percentage of the unemployed are reported as "not in the labor force" instead of as "seeking work." These differentials in the participation of white and nonwhite persons give the labor force a unique color composition that varies with age and with urban and rural residence. Table 16-7, reporting the percent of the civilian labor force of each age that was nonwhite in the 1950 census, reveals this pattern. Among younger male workers, nonwhites comprise a higher proportion than they do at older ages. Among female workers, nonwhites comprise an above-average proportion of the workers in the childbearing ages and (in rural areas) at the youngest ages.

Among women, the white-nonwhite differences are almost the reverse of those just described for men. Although a larger proportion of nonwhite girls are participants at ages 14, 15 and 16 than are white girls, at ages 17 to 23 a larger proportion of white girls are in the labor force. This may be because white girls have more job opportunities at these ages, and because nonwhite girls marry earlier than white girls. After age 19 the labor force participation rate for white women declines, but that of nonwhite women continues to rise and reaches a peak of 48 to 49 percent at ages 35 to 44 years. At all ages beyond age 24, the labor force participation rate of nonwhite women is much higher than that of white women. The economic position of the nonwhite family appears to be such that in a high proportion of cases the wife and mother must continue to work in order to attain the desired level of living. As the economic well-being of the nonwhite population increases, and since the occupations in which nonwhite female workers are concentrated (domestic service) are now under social security, the color differential among women workers may lessen. At the present time, however, the differential is large; at all ages beyond 24 years, at least 30 percent more of the nonwhite than of the white women are in the labor force.

Urban-rural differences in labor force participation: Males. In rural-farm households, a higher proportion of men are participants in the labor force than is the average for the nation (see Table 16-4). Farm boys begin to work at an earlier age than other boys. A great majority of farm men continue to work after they reach age 65, and during the major years of labor participation (25 to 64) the participation rates for farm men are considerably higher than for urban and rural-nonfarm men. Figure 16-4 provides visual comparison between the participation rates of rural-farm, rural-nonfarm, and urban workers throughout the life cycle. Several factors probably account for the life-long high participation rate for farm men. One of the most important factors might be that farm workers, and particularly farm operators, have an opportunity to stay in the labor force, if they so desire, even though they may not work very intensively. A nonfarm worker usually must choose between full-time work and complete retirement, whereas an elderly farm operator can be severely incapacitated and still report himself as working, so long as he participates in management or chores. On the other hand, farm laborers who become physically incapacitated may find that they cannot earn a living on the farm and must migrate to some other type of residence in search of work they can do.

This urban-rural differential is even more pronounced among nonwhite men than among white

Table 16-5.—LABOR FORCE PARTICIPATION RATES FOR FEMALES, BY AGE AND COLOR, FOR THE UNITED STATES, URBAN AND RURAL: 1950

Age	All fe-males	A. White females				B. Nonwhite females				Percent total females in civilian labor force by age			
		Total	Urban	Rural non-farm	Rural farm	Total	Urban	Rural non-farm	Rural farm	Total	Urban	Rural non-farm	Rural farm
ToTotal, 14 years and over.......	29.0	28.1	32.2	22.2	15.1	37.0	42.8	29.4	22.0	100.0	100.0	100.0	100.0
14 to 19 years....	22.6	23.3	28.1	18.0	13.2	18.2	19.1	16.6	17.3	8.7	8.0	9.7	14.0
20 to 24 years....	43.2	43.6	50.2	31.1	24.3	39.6	45.2	30.8	25.8	15.3	15.7	14.4	13.3
25 to 29 years....	32.6	31.3	36.0	22.6	17.0	42.9	48.3	33.5	24.6	12.3	12.7	11.7	10.2
30 to 34 years....	30.9	29.1	32.9	23.2	16.7	46.3	52.5	36.7	24.2	11.0	11.0	11.2	10.3
35 to 39 years....	33.9	32.1	36.1	27.4	17.8	48.6	54.9	40.5	25.9	11.7	11.6	12.2	11.6
40 to 44 years....	36.2	34.9	39.3	29.9	18.4	48.1	54.5	40.1	26.5	11.2	11.2	11.4	11.0
45 to 49 years....	34.8	33.6	37.9	29.2	17.2	45.3	50.9	39.1	26.2	9.6	9.6	9.5	9.4
50 to 54 years....	30.8	29.8	33.8	25.5	14.8	40.9	45.7	36.1	25.6	7.7	7.8	7.4	7.5
55 to 59 years....	25.9	25.2	28.7	21.0	12.5	34.9	38.8	31.4	23.7	5.6	5.7	5.5	5.6
60 to 64 years....	20.5	20.0	22.9	16.1	10.0	27.6	30.5	25.4	19.2	3.7	3.8	3.8	3.6
65 to 69 years....	12.8	12.5	14.2	9.6	7.3	16.4	17.6	14.9	14.0	2.0	2.0	2.1	2.2
70 to 74 years....	6.6	6.5	7.3	4.9	5.1	8.4	8.7	7.7	8.3	0.7	0.7	0.8	0.9
75 to 79 years....	3.5	3.4	3.8	2.6	3.1	5.1	5.3	4.4	5.4	0.2	0.2	0.3	0.4
80 to 84 years....	1.7	1.6	1.7	1.4	1.8	2.4	2.8	1.8	2.3	0.1	0.1	0.1	0.1
85 years and over.	1.2	1.2	1.2	0.8	1.2	2.1	2.4	2.0	1.4	...	...	...	...

Source: U.S. Census of Population: 1950, Vol. II, Detailed Characteristics of the Population, Part 1, U.S. Summary, Chapter C, Table 118.

men. Nonwhite rural-farm men are much younger than white men when they enter the labor force, and a much greater proportion of nonwhite than of white farm men continue to work beyond the retirement years. Between the ages of 20 and 50 the labor force participation rates for white and nonwhite farm residents are almost equal, and between the ages of 50 and 65 the male nonwhite farm population has a higher participation rate than its white counterpart. This means that the color differential, described above, applies to the urban and rural-nonfarm populations, but not to the rural-farm population.

Urban males enter the labor force later than rural-nonfarm boys, probably largely because they remain in school longer. Beyond age 25, however, the labor force participation rate of urban men (both white and nonwhite) is higher than that of their rural-nonfarm counterparts. Thus, a disproportionately large share of adult males of all ages who are not in the labor force are living in rural-nonfarm areas.

Nonwhite men have lower participation rates than white men, as noted above; the nonwhite par-

ticipation rate is especially low for the rural-nonfarm population, particularly at ages 20 to 44 years. Small country villages or suburban settlements appear to be the homes of nonwhite men who cannot, who need not, or who will not work.

Among white men living in rural-nonfarm areas, labor force participation declines more rapidly after age 60 than among urban white men. This group shows evidence of much earlier retirement than does the population at large. This situation may be due to a process of selection: many farmers and businessmen who want to retire resettle in villages and suburbs. Older nonwhite males in rural-nonfarm areas do not exhibit this pattern: their labor force participation remains as high as that of the urban nonwhite males.

Urban-rural differences in labor force participation: Females. The farm offers comparatively few employment opportunities to women, and for this reason women living in rural-farm households have labor force participation rates that are below those of urban and rural-nonfarm women. This is true for both white and nonwhite women at almost all ages (see Table 16-6). At all ages a higher

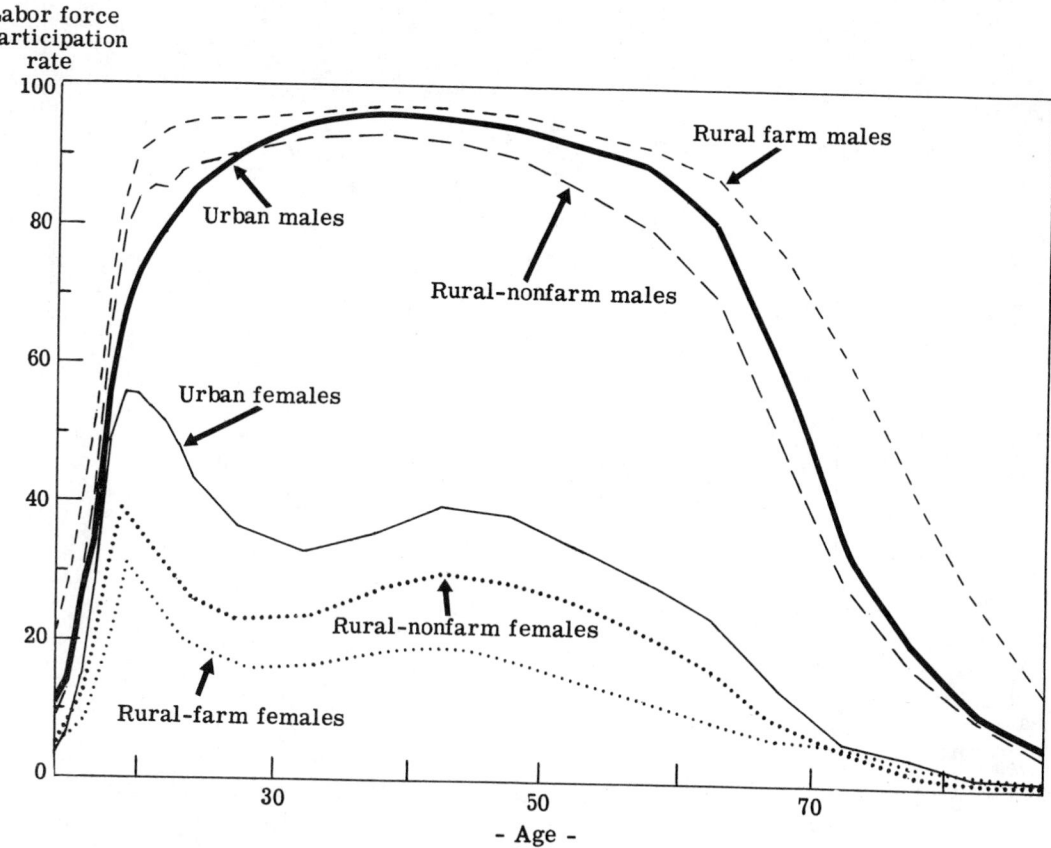

FIGURE 16 - 4. LABOR FORCE PARTICIPATION RATE FOR THE WHITE POPULATION 14 YEARS
OF AGE AND OVER BY AGE AND SEX FOR URBAN, RURAL - NONFARM AND
RURAL FARM, 1950

proportion of nonwhite farm women than of white farm women are in the labor force.

It is in the city that women find employment; the labor force participation rates for white urban women are about twice those for rural-farm women, and about 50 percent greater than those for rural-nonfarm women. In addition, city women enter the labor force at a younger average age than do rural women. At the most advanced ages (at which all but a few women are retired) the urban-rural differences are smaller.

Nativity and labor force participation. Table 16-8, which reports the labor force participation for native white and foreign-born white populations by urban and rural residence, shows that the differences between the two groups are small when age and urban-rural residence are taken into account. On an over-all basis, the foreign-born male population has a lower participation rate than the native white population (75.3 percent in comparison with 79.7 percent). But this difference is due largely to the fact that the foreign-born population is older and more urban in its composition. In general, the teen-age foreign-born boy is more inclined to enter the labor force than the teen-age native white boy, but in the years 18 to 24 he participates less than the native white boy (perhaps because he is more often in school). At ages 35 to 64 the participation rates of foreign-born males tend to be higher than those of native white males. Beyond age 65 the labor force participation rate of foreign-born men is lower than

Table 16-6.—CIVILIAN LABOR FORCE PARTICIPATION RATES OF PERSONS 14 TO 25 YEARS OLD, BY SINGLE YEARS OF AGE, COLOR, AND SEX, FOR THE UNITED STATES, URBAN AND RURAL: 1950

Age and sex	Total	A. White				B. Nonwhite				Color differential: (A-B÷A)			
		Total	Urban	Rural non-farm	Rural farm	Total	Urban	Rural non-farm	Rural farm	Total	Urban	Rural non-farm	Rural farm
MALES													
14 years.......	13.2	12.7	10.8	8.9	21.1	16.8	7.3	12.6	33.8	-32.3	32.4	-41.6	-60.2
15 years.......	17.9	17.0	14.2	12.9	28.8	23.8	12.6	20.1	43.6	-40.0	11.3	-55.8	-51.4
16 years.......	29.3	28.3	24.1	25.1	41.6	36.2	23.4	33.0	57.6	-27.9	2.9	-31.5	-38.5
17 years.......	42.5	41.4	36.6	42.4	52.8	50.1	38.7	48.9	69.4	-21.0	-5.7	-15.3	-31.4
18 years.......	60.8	60.4	55.5	64.0	70.4	64.2	56.0	63.2	78.6	-6.3	-0.9	1.2	-11.6
19 years.......	72.9	72.8	67.6	78.0	84.4	73.9	67.7	74.0	86.3	-1.5	-0.1	5.1	-2.2
20 years.......	78.4	78.4	73.4	84.0	90.3	78.3	74.7	76.1	89.1	0.1	-1.8	9.4	1.3
21 years.......	80.2	80.2	76.0	85.2	91.8	80.4	77.7	77.2	91.3	-0.2	-2.2	9.4	0.6
22 years.......	81.3	81.4	77.9	85.1	92.9	80.4	78.5	75.5	92.2	1.2	-0.8	11.3	0.8
23 years.......	83.6	83.9	81.2	87.0	93.9	80.6	79.4	74.6	92.0	3.9	2.2	14.3	2.0
24 years.......	85.7	86.2	84.4	87.8	94.5	81.5	81.2	73.7	92.8	5.5	3.8	16.1	1.8
FEMALES													
14 years.......	4.1	3.8	3.6	3.8	4.4	5.9	3.0	5.5	11.1	-55.3	16.7	-44.7	-152.3
15 years.......	6.2	5.9	5.8	6.1	5.8	8.5	5.6	8.9	13.4	-44.1	3.4	-45.9	-131.0
16 years.......	12.9	12.9	14.8	11.7	8.9	13.2	11.1	13.9	16.7	-2.3	25.0	-18.8	-87.6
17 years.......	22.5	22.9	27.4	18.8	13.4	20.0	20.3	19.2	19.9	12.7	25.9	-2.1	-48.5
18 years.......	40.1	41.8	48.4	32.7	25.1	28.3	32.1	25.0	22.2	32.3	33.7	23.6	11.6
19 years.......	47.4	49.2	55.6	37.9	31.5	33.6	38.5	28.2	23.9	31.7	30.8	25.6	24.1
20 years.......	47.0	48.5	55.0	36.3	29.8	36.2	41.7	29.2	25.4	25.4	24.2	19.6	14.8
21 years.......	45.7	46.5	53.0	33.8	27.2	39.0	44.5	30.0	26.6	16.1	16.0	11.2	2.2
22 years.......	44.1	44.6	51.5	31.5	23.6	40.5	45.9	31.8	27.2	9.2	10.9	-1.0	-15.2
23 years.......	41.1	41.2	47.8	28.3	21.3	40.3	45.8	30.7	25.9	2.2	4.2	-8.5	-21.6
24 years.......	38.3	37.8	43.9	26.3	19.1	41.7	47.5	32.4	24.0	-10.3	-8.2	-23.2	-25.6

Source: U.S. Census of Population: 1950, Vol. II, _Detailed Characteristics of the Population_, Part 1, U.S. Summary, Chapter C, Table 119.

that of native white men - perhaps because the former have poorer health, or perhaps because they are better cared for by their children.

Foreign-born women, especially older foreign-born women, do not participate in the labor force to the same extent as native-born white women. This is especially true in rural-nonfarm areas. (In rural-farm areas foreign-born women have higher participation rates than native-born women, which may reflect the Old World custom among farm mothers and daughters of working in the fields as unpaid family workers.) There are at

Table 16-7.—PERCENT OF THE CIVILIAN LABOR FORCE NONWHITE, BY AGE AND URBAN-RURAL RESIDENCE: 1950

Age	U.S. total		Urban		Rural nonfarm		Rural farm	
	Male	Female	Male	Female	Male	Female	Male	Female
Total..............	9.5	12.8	9.3	12.7	7.5	10.6	12.4	18.3
14 to 15 years..........	15.7	17.9	9.0	11.0	14.2	14.3	23.2	33.8
16 and 17 years..........	14.8	11.9	11.4	9.1	12.9	11.4	20.8	26.0
18 and 19 years..........	12.4	8.5	10.5	7.5	11.2	8.5	17.5	16.5
20 to 24 years..........	10.7	10.9	10.2	10.5	9.1	9.5	14.7	19.1
25 to 34 years..........	9.5	15.1	9.8	15.6	6.8	11.5	11.8	18.0
35 to 44 years..........	9.7	14.6	10.1	15.1	7.2	10.9	11.6	16.8
45 to 54 years..........	9.2	12.4	9.4	12.4	7.2	10.6	10.9	17.2
55 to 64 years..........	7.2	9.3	6.7	8.7	6.3	9.3	9.6	16.2
65 years and over........	8.0	10.0	6.4	8.6	7.5	11.8	12.2	19.3

Source: U.S. Census of Population: 1950, Vol. II, _Detailed Characteristics of the Population_, Part 1, U.S. Summary, Chapter C, Table 118.

Table 16-8.—LABOR FORCE PARTICIPATION RATES FOR THE NATIVE WHITE AND FOREIGN-BORN WHITE POPULATION, BY AGE AND SEX, FOR THE UNITED STATES, URBAN AND RURAL: 1950

(Based on 3 1/3 percent sample)

Age	A. Native white				B. Foreign-born white				Differential: (A-B÷A)			
	Total	Urban	Rural non-farm	Rural farm	Total	Urban	Rural non-farm	Rural farm	Total	Urban	Rural non-farm	Rural farm
MALES												
Total 14 years and over.............	79.7	80.2	75.5	83.0	75.3	76.8	60.9	81.6	5.5	4.2	19.3	1.7
14 to 17 years......	24.7	21.3	22.1	35.6	35.5	30.9	42.2	59.5	-43.7	-45.1	-91.0	-67.1
18 to 19 years......	67.0	62.0	71.4	77.3	60.4	54.3	68.3	...	9.9	12.4	4.3	...
20 to 24 years......	82.1	78.9	85.8	92.6	78.2	75.8	78.6	96.0	4.8	3.9	8.4	-3.7
25 to 29 years......	91.1	90.6	90.7	95.6	89.2	89.4	85.2	94.4	2.1	1.3	6.1	1.3
30 to 34 years......	94.6	94.8	92.6	96.8	94.1	94.5	90.3	96.6	0.5	0.3	2.5	0.2
35 to 44 years......	95.0	95.3	92.6	96.9	95.6	96.0	91.4	97.3	-0.6	-0.7	1.3	-0.4
45 to 54 years......	92.1	92.6	87.9	95.1	93.6	94.3	85.3	96.0	-1.6	-1.8	3.0	-0.9
55 to 64 years......	83.6	84.4	75.8	89.7	83.8	85.2	69.7	89.6	-0.2	-0.9	8.0	0.1
65 to 74 years......	52.1	50.1	41.6	70.7	48.7	49.0	35.4	71.1	6.5	2.2	14.9	-0.6
75 years and over...	19.8	17.5	13.8	35.9	14.2	12.9	10.0	34.3	28.3	26.3	27.5	4.5
FEMALES												
Total 14 years and over.............	28.7	33.5	22.6	15.2	22.0	23.2	15.3	14.5	23.4	30.8	32.3	4.6
14 to 17 years......	11.4	13.2	9.9	7.8	14.8	14.8	13.2	...	-29.8	-12.1	-33.3	...
18 to 19 years......	45.4	52.0	35.0	27.6	47.1	51.0	...	...	-3.7	1.9	...	...
20 to 24 years......	43.5	50.0	31.0	24.4	40.7	45.1	20.4	17.9	6.4	9.8	34.2	26.6
25 to 29 years......	31.3	36.1	22.8	17.3	32.4	35.2	16.8	18.5	-3.5	2.5	26.3	-6.9
30 to 34 years......	29.1	33.0	23.3	16.9	31.5	33.6	21.2	17.4	-8.2	-1.8	9.0	-3.0
35 to 44 years......	33.4	37.9	28.8	17.9	34.1	35.5	26.5	20.8	-2.1	6.3	8.0	-16.2
45 to 54 years......	32.1	36.9	27.8	15.9	30.2	31.3	23.6	20.7	5.9	15.2	15.1	-30.2
55 to 64 years......	23.7	28.0	19.3	11.4	19.6	20.5	14.6	13.2	17.3	26.8	24.4	-15.8
65 to 74 years......	10.5	12.3	8.0	6.1	8.6	8.8	6.8	10.1	18.1	28.5	15.0	-65.6
75 years and over...	2.6	2.9	1.9	2.4	2.2	2.2	2.0	2.4	15.4	24.1	-5.3	...

Source: U.S. Census of Popultion: 1950, Vol. IV, Special Reports, Part 1, Chapter A, Employment and Personal Characteristics, Table 5.

least two equally plausible explanations for the fact that a smaller proportion of foreign-born than of native-born white women of any age are in the labor force. (a) The belief that "a woman's place is in the home" may be more prevalent among foreign-born than among native-born white families, and thus the wife and daughters may be discouraged from seeking work. (b) Many of the jobs available to women require rather full acculturation and/or special training - school teaching, secretarial work, and beautician work are examples. Women born abroad are at a definite disadvantage in competing for such jobs. Many of them must be content to work in factories, as domestic servants, or at other service occupations--and even so they must compete with native white and Negro women for the jobs that are available. Possibly each of the sets of reasons accounts for a part of the differential.

Marital status and labor force participation. Almost all white males 25 to 50 years of age who are married and living with their spouses are in the labor force (95 to 97 percent). For single men of these ages, the degree of labor force participation is much smaller (80 to 85 percent). And for men who are separated, widowed, or divorced it is even lower (75 to 80 percent). Among nonwhite men there is a similar, but even more marked, set of differences between those who are living with their wives and those who are single or whose marriages are broken. These differences are found in urban, rural-nonfarm, and rural-farm areas alike. (In the rural areas the single and the separated-widowed-or-divorced group tends to have about equally low rates of participation. Also, the marital status differential is smaller for the rural-farm population than for the urban or rural-nonfarm populations.) Without attempting to consider the riddle of cause and effect--whether "having a wife keeps a man working" or whether "having a job makes a man's thoughts turn toward marriage"--it is readily apparent that a high proportion of the adult males who are not in the labor force are either single, separated, widowed, or divorced.

Exactly the reverse situation exists for females. Labor force participation rates are much lower among married women living with their husbands than among unmarried women, or among women whose marriages have been disrupted by separation, widowhood, or divorce. Separated, widowed, or divorced white women have lower participation rates than single women, possibly because some of them have dependent children or are receiving income from the ex-husband or his estate. These differences are quite large; a very high percentage of the women who do not have husbands in their households must be their own breadwinners. For example, in 1950 only 21 percent of the white wives 30 to 34 years of age and living with their spouses were in the labor force, but 78 percent of the single (never married) and 62 percent of the separated, widowed, or divorced women were in the labor force. Among nonwhite women the same set of differences exist, but are smaller than for white women. Women at all ages living in urban, rural-nonfarm, and rural-farm areas follow this same pattern. As yet the phenomenon of the working wife is comparatively rare in rural-farm areas (13 percent of white and 18 percent of nonwhite women living with spouse); it is much more frequent in urban and rural nonfarm areas.

It should be noted that the color differences in labor force participation, noted above, remain generally valid for males in each of the three marital statuses, in urban and rural nonfarm. For example, married nonwhite males 25 to 50

years of age have lower labor force participation rates than their white counterparts.

Table 16-9 supports the finding that it is the nonwhite married women living with their husbands who are primarily responsible for the higher labor force participation rates of nonwhite than of white women. Single nonwhite women have lower rates of labor force participation than single white women, and nonwhite separated, widowed, or divorced women have about the same rates as white women of the same marital status and urban-rural residence. This tendency for a higher proportion of all married nonwhite women to be in the labor force appears to be due to a desire on the part of married nonwhite women to increase the family income and raise its standard of living. It is difficult to explain exactly why fewer of the unmarried nonwhite than of the unmarried white girls are in the labor force.

Between 1940 and 1950 there were marked increases in the labor force participation rates of married women. Table 16-10 shows that white married women living with their husbands had labor force participation rates in 1950 that were 66 percent higher than they had been in 1940. These increases were especially large for women aged 35 to 64 years. For example, the rate for white married women aged 45 to 54 years, spouse present, was 120 percent higher in 1950 than in 1940. In addition, very young girls and older women (under 20 and older than 54 years) were much more frequent participants in 1950 than in 1940, irrespective of their marital status. Only single, widowed, separated, or divorced women aged 20 to 54 did not have large increases in labor force participation rates during this decade. Whereas earlier events emancipated women so that they could choose between a husband and a career, events during the 1940-50 decade enabled them to aspire to both a home and a job.

Male workers tended to have lower labor force participation rates in 1950 than in 1940, for most combinations of age and marital status. The greatest declines were for men not married or not living with their wives. During the postwar period there was a higher proportion of the men of each

Table 16-9.—LABOR FORCE PARTICIPATION RATES FOR MALES BY MARITAL STATUS, AGE, AND COLOR FOR THE UNITED STATES, URBAN AND RURAL: 1950

Age	All	Single				Married, spouse present				Separated, widowed, or divorced			
		Total	Urban	Rural non-farm	Rural farm	Total	Urban	Rural non-farm	Rural farm	Total	Urban	Rural non-farm	Rural farm
WHITE MALES													
Total 14 years and over.......	79.2	59.2	58.8	53.7	67.0	90.0	90.3	87.3	92.4	58.7	61.0	48.6	65.4
14 to 19 years....	38.8	37.4	34.1	37.2	46.7	89.4	88.7	90.7	89.3	71.5	70.6	73.2	71.8
20 to 24 years....	82.1	75.4	70.8	80.0	90.6	93.0	91.9	94.3	96.7	80.1	80.3	76.6	89.3
25 to 29 years....	91.0	82.0	81.3	77.1	91.5	95.0	94.5	95.3	97.4	77.1	78.0	70.6	89.4
30 to 34 years....	94.5	84.6	86.1	73.0	91.0	97.0	96.9	96.7	98.0	79.9	81.8	70.3	91.6
35 to 39 years....	95.1	83.6	85.4	69.7	91.7	97.5	97.6	97.0	98.0	80.3	82.0	70.3	92.2
40 to 44 years....	94.7	82.0	84.3	66.1	90.9	97.3	97.4	96.4	97.8	80.0	81.8	69.1	91.0
45 to 49 years....	93.5	80.0	82.4	61.9	91.1	96.3	96.6	95.0	97.0	79.6	81.4	68.0	90.8
50 years and over.	70.5	57.6	59.6	39.0	75.8	78.0	78.8	69.3	84.9	46.1	48.1	35.1	55.3
NONWHITE MALES													
Total 14 years and over.......	76.5	57.8	55.7	51.5	68.4	89.1	88.9	84.9	93.3	67.0	70.2	49.8	76.2
14 to 19 years....	43.3	41.8	31.9	40.6	58.7	88.3	85.4	89.6	92.1	68.8	64.9	65.4	81.8
20 to 24 years....	80.3	74.3	71.5	69.6	88.4	91.6	90.1	91.7	96.0	71.8	73.5	58.5	88.0
25 to 29 years....	84.5	73.5	75.0	59.3	86.5	91.9	91.1	90.8	96.7	72.2	75.9	52.5	89.4
30 to 34 years....	88.2	74.9	78.1	56.6	85.4	93.9	93.1	93.4	97.6	75.7	79.8	52.9	92.4
35 to 39 years....	90.4	76.5	79.4	58.1	88.6	95.1	94.5	94.3	97.9	78.9	82.5	56.6	92.7
40 to 44 years....	90.7	76.0	78.4	59.3	87.2	95.1	94.6	94.5	97.5	80.2	83.2	60.0	92.4
45 to 49 years....	89.7	74.5	77.7	54.3	86.2	94.4	93.8	92.6	97.4	79.4	81.8	60.9	90.2
50 years and over.	69.7	56.7	59.1	40.0	70.4	77.8	77.2	66.9	86.4	53.7	55.2	40.9	64.5

Source: U.S. Census of Population: 1950, Vol. II, Detailed Characteristics of the Population, Part 1, U.S. Summary, Chapter C, Table 121.

age, without wives, who were in school, retired, or unable to work than there had been in 1940. The change in this respect was especially pronounced for unmarried nonwhite men of all ages. There was a similar change for unmarried nonwhite women.[5]

The only major exception to this pattern of decreased labor force participation among males was in the case of boys 14 to 17 years of age. This group had a considerably higher rate of participation in 1950 than in 1940, possibly as a result of precedents established during World War II.

[5]These comparisons between the 1940 and 1950 census statistics must be accepted with caution and reservations. Differences in census procedures and definitions make the data only very roughly comparable. Also, in 1950 large numbers of young men were veterans attending school.

The tendency toward a greater and greater participation of married women has continued since the 1950 census. The following data for the year 1956, taken from the Census Bureau's Current Population Survey, are pertinent:

Marital status of women	Labor force participation rate	
	March 1956	Change, 1950-56
Total........	34.2	2.8
Single............	46.4	-4.1
Married..........	30.2	5.4
Spouse present...	29.0	5.2
Spouse absent....	49.1	1.7
Widowed and divorced.........	36.9	0.9

In releasing these statistics, the Bureau of the Census made the following comment:

"In March, 1956, some 10.5 million married couples out of the total of 38.3 million were working couples. This compares with 9.8 million a year earlier and only 6.5 million working couples in 1957. The proportion of all couples with both husband and wife in the labor force has risen from 19.5 percent in 1947 to 27.4 percent in 1956.

While the labor market behavior of wives is influenced in part by the employment status of their husbands, the pattern differs by age. For example, the greater tendency of wives to be in the labor market when the head is unemployed or on part-time shows up mainly among younger couples. Also among the younger couples, the wife is still more likely to work if the husband is not in the labor force at all, whereas the reverse is true in the older group. The practice has grown for young wives to help support the family while their husbands are completing their education. Older husbands not in the labor force, on the other hand, are mostly retired and their wives would also be past normal working age.

In general, the higher a husband's income, the less likely his wife is to be a member of the labor force. Thus, among all wives, the proportion working in March 1956 ranged from a high of about 31 percent for those whose husbands had money incomes of less than $5,000 the previous year to about 12 percent for those with money incomes of $10,000 or more. The relationship between income of husbands and participation of wives is far more pronounced among families with young children. For example, among wives 20 to 24 years of age with children under 6, the proportion in the labor force ranged from about one-fourth if the husband's income was very low (under $1,000) to only 3 percent if his income was $10,000 or more.

This relationship between the income of the husband and the labor force participation of the wife is much less pronounced than it was only a few years ago. This is because recent increases in participation among wives have been much sharper higher up on the income scale. Between 1951 and 1956, for example, the labor force rate for women whose husbands received between $7,000 and $10,000 just about tripled—from 7 percent to 21 percent. Among women whose husbands were in the $2,000-$3,000 bracket, on the other hand, the increase in the rate was only from 28 percent to 34 percent."[6]

Presence and age of children and labor force participation. Having a preschool child in the household is a major barrier to a wife's participation in the labor force (Tables 16-12 and 16-13). Married women who have no children, or those who have only teen-age children, have much higher rates of participation than married women with young children or children of grammar-school age. Nevertheless, the recent rise in labor force participation rates of married women living with husbands has taken place among women with young children, as well as among wives with only older children or no children.

The presence of children of grammar-school age is less of a deterrent to participation than the presence of very young children. Having both very young children and teen-age children is more favorable toward the wife's working than having only young children—possibly because a larger family means a greater need for income, or because the older children provide free baby-sitting services for a part of the day.

Having children in the household is much more of a deterrent to working for white wives than for nonwhite wives, and for urban wives than for rural wives (who have lower participation rates anyway).[7]

The recent upsurge in the participation of married women appears to have taken place largely

---

[6]Current Population Reports, Labor Force, "Marital and Family Status of Workers: 1956", Series P-50, No. 73, April, 1957.

[7]Much of the work done by farm wives would classify them as unpaid family workers; and because of the nature of the work, the presence of young children may not be much of a deterrent.

Table 16-10.—LABOR FORCE PARTICIPATION RATES FOR FEMALES BY MARITAL STATUS, AGE, AND COLOR, FOR THE UNITED STATES, URBAN AND RURAL: 1950

Age	All	Single				Married, spouse present				Separated, widowed, or divorced			
		Total	Urban	Rural non-farm	Rural farm	Total	Urban	Rural non-farm	Rural farm	Total	Urban	Rural non-farm	Rural farm
WHITE FEMALES													
Total 14 years and over.......	28.1	47.6	55.2	33.7	23.2	20.7	23.1	18.7	12.5	33.1	36.9	24.3	18.0
14 to 19 years....	23.3	23.5	28.1	18.6	13.6	19.8	26.1	14.0	9.3	38.2	45.5	29.5	21.8
20 to 24 years....	43.6	75.6	78.8	68.5	56.3	26.2	31.2	19.4	12.1	55.9	62.2	43.4	32.8
25 to 29 years....	31.3	81.1	86.3	64.6	52.2	21.1	23.8	17.4	12.3	59.6	65.2	44.4	37.9
30 to 34 years....	29.1	78.4	84.4	59.9	46.0	20.9	22.7	19.3	13.9	62.4	67.5	46.3	40.8
35 to 39 years....	32.1	76.6	83.1	57.6	42.7	24.2	26.2	23.5	15.5	65.3	70.4	49.2	42.5
40 to 44 years....	34.9	75.8	82.5	55.9	40.9	26.4	28.9	25.7	16.1	65.5	70.3	50.2	41.5
45 to 49 years....	33.6	72.6	79.8	52.8	36.4	24.5	26.8	24.3	14.8	60.4	64.9	47.5	36.1
50 years and over.	18.7	44.8	50.2	30.0	21.2	12.8	14.1	12.1	8.8	21.2	23.7	15.6	11.8
NONWHITE FEMALES													
Total 14 years and over.......	37.0	36.0	42.3	28.4	24.1	31.8	37.4	26.4	17.9	47.2	51.4	35.9	33.6
14 to 19 years....	18.2	17.7	18.0	16.6	17.7	16.2	18.9	12.9	13.3	34.4	37.6	33.3	25.2
20 to 24 years....	39.6	57.0	63.5	47.1	40.4	26.0	30.6	19.4	15.8	50.4	54.4	42.9	34.2
25 to 29 years....	42.9	66.5	72.7	53.9	44.0	32.6	37.7	25.0	18.0	58.6	61.6	50.2	42.7
30 to 34 years....	46.3	67.2	74.0	51.7	41.3	37.5	43.4	30.7	19.4	64.2	67.2	52.3	48.4
35 to 39 years....	48.6	66.2	73.3	47.8	43.1	39.3	45.5	34.9	20.7	67.7	70.6	55.1	56.5
40 to 44 years....	48.1	64.9	71.7	48.2	43.8	38.1	44.2	33.9	20.9	66.1	69.0	53.3	55.7
45 to 49 years....	45.3	58.5	66.7	38.8	36.3	34.7	39.8	32.8	20.3	61.6	64.2	50.9	52.9
50 years and over.	26.7	37.1	42.6	26.2	24.1	22.3	26.2	20.7	14.9	29.3	32.1	22.7	23.1

Source: U.S. Census of Population: 1950, Vol. II, Detailed Characteristics of the Population, Part 1, U.S. Summary, Chapter C, Table 121.

Table 16-11.—PERCENT CHANGE IN LABOR FORCE PARTICIPATION RATES, BY AGE, COLOR, SEX, AND MARITAL STATUS FOR THE UNITED STATES: 1940 TO 1950

Age	Male						Female					
	Single		Married, spouse present		Separated, widowed, or divorced		Single		Married, spouse present		Separated, widowed, or divorced	
	White	Non-white	White	Non-white	White	Non-white	White	Non-white	White	Non-white	White	Non-white
Total......	-5.4	-10.8	-1.2	-3.5	-6.8	-7.3	3.5	-13.8	65.6	16.5	9.9	-11.5
14 to 17 years.	42.9	-2.8	10.3	...	116.5	...	59.2	-17.4	178.0	8.9	49.4	-27.1
18 to 19 years.	1.7	-6.6	0.6	-1.9	16.1	3.8	12.8	-15.4	157.5	-7.0	20.5	-15.1
20 to 24 years.	-11.6	-12.0	-4.1	-5.9	-4.8	-9.8	2.3	-12.9	60.5	1.2	3.5	-21.4
25 to 29 years.	-10.3	-14.2	-3.0	-5.5	-9.0	-11.2	2.0	-10.4	23.4	3.2	-2.8	-16.9
30 to 34 years.	-5.7	-11.8	-0.9	-3.4	-7.3	-6.9	1.0	-7.4	28.8	19.2	-4.0	-11.6
35 to 44 years.	-3.8	-8.7	0.3	-1.0	-4.8	-4.9	3.9	-7.5	83.3	26.9	9.9	-4.3
45 to 54 years.	-1.5	-7.9	0.2	-0.6	-4.9	-3.7	12.6	-8.5	119.8	29.0	26.3	-1.9
55 to 64 years.	-2.0	-13.3	-2.8	-3.7	-10.6	-9.4	22.0	-6.0	96.9	15.5	40.5	-5.8
65 to 74 years.	7.3	-12.2	9.2	-8.0	13.9	-7.7	29.7	-11.5	74.1	0.9	43.8	-16.8
75 years-over..	-3.2	-22.1	2.5	-3.4	1.7	-7.9	1.5	-37.0	36.4	-27.7	16.7	-22.2

Source: U.S. Census of Population: 1950, Vol. IV, Special Reports, Part 1, Chapter A, Employment and Personal Characteristics, Table 11.

Table 16-12.—LABOR FORCE PARTICIPATION RATES OF MARRIED WOMEN, HUSBAND PRESENT, BY AGE AND PRESENCE OF CHILDREN IN THE HOUSEHOLD: 1948 TO 1956

Age and presence of children	Year			
	April, 1948	March, 1950	March, 1956	Change, 1948 to 1956
All married women......................	22.0	23.8	29.0	7.0
Under 35 years........................	22.9	25.0	27.5	4.6
35 to 44 years........................	27.3	28.5	34.3	13.0
45 to 64 years........................	19.4	21.8	31.5	22.1
65 years and over.....................	6.1	6.4	7.8	1.7
No children under 6 years..............	27.6	29.6	35.7	11.1
Children under 6 years.................	10.7	11.9	15.9	5.2

Source: Current Population Reports, Series P-50, No. 73 (1957).

among women 35 years of age and over who have time to spare because all of their children are in school. The older these children are, the greater appears to be the inclination of the mother to get a job.

The fact that 1 mother in 6 who has preschool children, and 1 mother in 3 who has an adolescent child, is in the labor force has implications which touch upon family life, child rearing, juvenile delinquency, and other subjects. The exact reasons why more women are working are not known, nor are the desirable and undesirable effects that their working has upon the home. These are sociological topics upon which more research is needed.

Household status and labor force participation. Labor force participation rates differ according to the household status of the individual, as well as according to marital status (Table 16-14). For example, single persons who are also the head of a private household, or who are living in a private household as a lodger or other nonrelative of the head, tend to have higher rates than unmarried relatives of the head (sons or daughters, etc.). Conversely, being a relative of the head is generally conducive to below-average labor force participation, because a certain proportion of such relatives are economically dependent upon the head of the household, even though they may be widowed, divorced, or estranged from a spouse. This is especially true for female relatives, who frequently return to their parents' home after a marital disruption.

Persons who are married but whose spouses are absent tend to have higher labor force participation rates, whether they are relatives of the head or not, than single persons or persons who are widowed or divorced. Similarly, single persons tend to have higher participation rates than widowed or divorced persons of the same household status.

Table 16-13.—LABOR FORCE PARTICIPATION RATES OF MARRIED WOMEN, HUSBAND PRESENT, BY PRESENCE OF CHILDREN IN HOUSEHOLD, COLOR, AND URBAN-RURAL RESIDENCE: 1956

Color and urban-rural residence	None 6 to 17	With own children under 6		With no own children under 6		
		Some 6 to 11 only	Some 12 to 17 only	Some 6 to 11 only	Some 12 to 17 only	No children under 17
All married women with husband present..	15.6	15.0	22.0	32.4	40.5	35.3
White..............................	14.2	14.0	20.2	31.3	39.3	34.3
Nonwhite...........................	31.3	25.4	...	...	58.0	46.5
Urban..............................	15.5	15.7	26.1	32.6	43.8	38.2
Rural nonfarm......................	15.8	12.6	...	29.6	38.4	31.0
Rural farm.........................	15.8	17.0	...	40.4	30.1	27.5

Source: Current Population Reports, Series P-50, No. 73 (1957).

Table 16-14.—LABOR FORCE PARTICIPATION RATES OF THE POPULATION CLASSIFIED ACCORDING TO HOUSEHOLD STATUS, BY SEX, COLOR, AND MARITAL STATUS

Marital status and household status	Male		Female	
	White	Nonwhite	White	Nonwhite
SINGLE				
Head of household...................	78.8	81.3	69.8	64.8
Relative of head....................	56.8	55.0	42.4	30.1
Not relative of head................	75.9	78.0	77.3	67.3
Resident of quasi-household.........	51.2	45.4	45.6	34.2
MARRIED, SPOUSE PRESENT				
Wife of head.......................	...	...	20.1	30.9
Head of household..................	90 5	89.9	...	...
Relative of head (other than spouse)......	82.6	83.1	28.1	33.1
Not relative of head...............	84.0	88.4	39.7	46.9
Resident of quasi-household........	81.0	87.4	39.9	38.4
MARRIED, SPOUSE ABSENT				
Head of household..................	76.1	82.8	47.8	61.4
Relative of head...................	73.2	79.5	40.4	48.9
Not relative of head...............	81.9	85.6	65.9	71.1
Resident of quasi-household........	48.7	42.0	20.3	37.3
WIDOWED OR DIVORCED				
Head of household..................	58.9	64.7	34.8	46.1
Relative of head...................	48.2	49.9	21.8	27.6
Not relative of head...............	68.8	69.9	54.0	58.4
Resident of quasi-household........	45.8	44.9	31.8	36.3

Source: U.S. Census of Population: 1950, Volume IV. Special Reports, Part I. Chapter A, Employment and Personal Characteristics, Table 6.

This set of differences is characteristic both of white and nonwhite persons of both sexes. It is also true for almost all age groups of each sex and color (data by age are not shown).

It may be of interest to note that for women the highest rates of labor force participation are found among single women who are heads of households (many of whom live alone), and among single, married (spouse absent), widowed, or divorced women who are living in private households but who are not related to the head. The lowest rates are found, of course, among wives who are living with their husbands.

School enrollment and labor force participation. Students who are attending school are workers only about one-third as frequently as youths who are not attending school. Very few young students (14 to 15 years of age), especially young girl students, are in the labor force. However, the participation rates for youngsters of these ages who are not enrolled in school are considerably higher. With each additional year of age, the nonparticipation of students diminishes; a majority of male students 25 years of age or older are in the labor force, many of them probably on a part-time basis.

In the high school as well as the college attendance ages (14 to 25 years) a higher proportion of nonwhite than of white male students are working. The opposite situation exists among girls; a higher proportion of white than of nonwhite girls who are enrolled in school are also working.

A high proportion of girls who have passed their 20th birthday leave school to get married; for women aged 21 and over, therefore, being in school is associated with above-average labor force participation.

Table 16-15 brings out another very interesting point: a considerable number of adolescent boys who are not enrolled in school are not in the labor force either. For example, at ages 14 to 16, a very large proportion of the boys who are not in school are neither working nor looking for work. Even at ages 17 and 18, about 20 percent of the boys who are not in school are also not in the labor force. This indicates that a large group of boys and young men in their late teens and early twenties are "floating" or "loafing," a situation

Table 16-15.—LABOR FORCE PARTICIPATION RATES OF PERSONS ENROLLED AND NOT ENROLLED IN SCHOOL, BY AGE, SEX, AND COLOR FOR THE UNITED STATES: 1950

Age	Male				Female			
	White		Nonwhite		White		Nonwhite	
	En-rolled	Not en-rolled	En-rolled	Not en-rolled	En-rolled	Not en-rolled	En-rolled	Not en-rolled
Total 14 years and over..	27.5	91.3	27.3	84.5	14.5	38.6	11.6	39.8
14 years...............	11.9	26.1	13.8	48.8	3.7	7.2	4.8	14.5
15 years...............	15.0	44.0	18.1	61.6	5.4	13.4	6.7	21.0
16 years...............	20.3	64.6	22.7	71.2	9.8	27.7	8.2	28.2
17 years...............	25.5	77.7	26.5	79.5	15.9	38.4	11.3	31.4
18 years...............	28.8	85.3	28.9	81.7	21.9	53.9	11.9	35.5
19 years...............	31.5	90.0	34.7	84.1	27.6	55.1	18.5	38.2
20 years...............	33.5	90.9	36.5	85.1	31.6	51.4	23.4	38.1
21 years...............	34.5	91.6	42.9	86.0	33.5	47.6	28.0	39.7
22 years...............	38.4	92.3	45.8	84.9	45.4	43.9	36.7	40.9
23 years...............	42.4	93.0	43.9	85.3	49.6	40.7	36.5	40.5
24 years...............	48.1	93.4	49.0	85.6	52.6	37.4	41.1	41.2
25 years...............	52.9	94.0	49.5	86.0	48.6	34.4	36.7	40.7
26 years...............	57.5	94.2	59.2	87.2	45.3	32.0	43.9	41.8
27 years...............	65.8	94.5	61.3	87.1	43.2	30.3	50.0	42.9
28 years...............	70.1	94.7	60.8	87.9	42.3	29.3	49.3	43.4
29 years...............	73.8	95.0	61.4	87.6	41.9	28.8	49.5	43.2

Source: U.S. Census of Population: 1950, Volume IV, Special Reports, Part I, Chapter A, Employment and Personal characteristics, Table 12.

which may have important implications for studies of crime and delinquency. [8]

There have been some extensive changes since 1940 in the labor force participation rates of students and nonstudents. The following tabulation of participation rates for persons 14 to 19 years of age for 1940 and selected dates since 1940 shows what has happened:

School enrollment and sex	Oct. 1956	1950	April 1944	April 1940
Enrolled in school				
Both sexes..........	24.9	25.3	34.0	6.6
Male...............	29.7	30.8	49.5	8.8
Female.............	19.8	19.2	19.9	4.2
Not enrolled in school				
Both sexes..........	69.1	73.5	79.4	66.1
Male...............	87.1	92.9	95.4	87.9
Female.............	56.7	57.9	69.4	45.0

At the time of the 1940 census students had low participation rates; only 6.6 percent of all students 14 to 19 years old were in the labor force. Mobilization for war altered this situation drastically, as shown by the data for the column headed "April, 1944." During World War II it became very common for boys and girls attending high school or college to have a part-time or even a full-time job (working an evening shift). This custom has continued since the war, with only a moderate reduction in the participation rates. In 1956 the participation rate of boys 14 to 19 years of age stood at 29.7; this is 19.8 points below the rate which prevailed at the time of peak manpower mobilization in 1944, but it is 20.9 points above the rate which this age group had in 1940. For girls the 1956 rate was 19.8, which is only 1.1 points below the 1944 peak.

It would be incorrect to assume that the increased labor force participation of students has been due simply to the employment of students of college age (18 years and older). The statistical facts reveal that increasing proportions of high school students as well as college students have been participating.

---

[8] A portion of these "floaters" may be looking for work, but their families (who are the ones who report to the census enumerators concerning the boys' activities) may not know of it or may not remember to report it.

Year	Participation rate	
	High school ages (14 to 17 years)	College ages (18 to 24 years)
1956............	23.4	40.0
1950............	24.0	33.7
1948............	19.2	24.3
1947............	16.9	(not available)

Source: Current Population Reports, Series P-50, No. 71, Table A

At the start of the fall term in October, 1956, the Census Bureau's Current Population Survey found that an estimated 3.4 million students were enrolled in school and were also gainfully employed--at least part time. Of these, about 1.9 million were of high school age (14 to 17 years) and 1.5 million were older students (18 to 34 years). This is a very large increase over the rates that prevailed in 1948.

In interpreting these statistics, it is important to remember that this change has taken place during a period in which the rate of school enrollment also has been rising. Thus, the greater participation of students has not been achieved at the expense of education. As one of the important sources of reserve manpower, students may be drawn into the labor force during periods of manpower shortage; during recessions and business slumps they may also be among the first to be discharged from regular jobs. In some measure, no doubt, the higher participation rates of college age students can be attributed to the growing tendency for students to marry while they are still in school, and therefore to need greater incomes.

In sharp contrast to the students, the youths of high school age who are not attending school have had a declining labor force participation rate. The following summary shows this trend:

Year	Participation rate of persons not in school	
	14 to 17 years	18 to 24 years
1956............	62.5	68.8
1950............	68.7	71.2
1948............	72.5	69.6

It is not known exactly why this decline has taken place, or what kinds of activities are engaging the

estimated 400,000-450,000 youngsters 14 to 17 years of age who are neither in school nor working.

Because of the changes just described, a larger proportion of the labor force is now comprised of students 14 to 19 years of age than in 1940. The following tabulation illustrates the change that has taken place:

Year	Percent of labor force comprised of students 14 to 19 years of age		
	Both sexes	Male	Female
April, 1940......	1.1	1.0	1.3
April, 1944......	4.1	4.0	4.3
October, 1948....	2.5	2.3	3.1
October, 1950....	3.2	2.8	4.1
October, 1954....	2.9	2.6	3.6
October, 1956....	3.6	3.3	4.3

Educational attainment and labor force participation. For adult workers who have completed their education, the highest labor force participation rates are found among those who have completed high school or attended college. The lowest labor force participation rates are found among those with only an elementary school education. Table 16-16 provides data for the year 1957 that show this to be true for every age group, and for both males and females. Among women workers, the level of educational attainment is an especially potent factor influencing the level of participation. For example, among women 45 to 64 years of age, only 31 percent of those with less than 5 years of elementary school education were in the labor force in 1957. Among women of this age who had had 4 years or more of college the rate was 62 percent, or almost twice as great. With each increment in educational attainment, a higher proportion of the women in every age group are found in the labor force.

Several factors may account for this set of differentials. Among men, a higher proportion of those with less educational attainment may have become disabled in industrial accidents or may be suffering from poor health or inability to participate. Among women, those with less educational attainment may be operating under these same disadvantages, and many of them may have left

Table 16-16.—LABOR FORCE PARTICIPATION RATES ACCORDING TO EDUCATIONAL ATTAINMENT, BY SEX AND AGE: 1957

Years of school completed and sex	18 years and over total	Participation rates by educational attainment						
		Elementary school			High school		College	
		Less than 5 years	5 to 7 years	8 years	1 to 3 years	4 years	1 to 3 years	4 years or more
BOTH SEXES Total, 18 years and over.	60.0	45.4	55.1	57.5	61.1	62.2	62.1	77.3
18 to 24 years.........	60.3	57.3	63.4	60.8	54.0	66.1	50.8	72.4
25 to 34 years.........	64.4	62.6	67.1	67.5	65.0	58.3	65.6	80.1
35 to 44 years.........	69.2	68.1	68.4	70.0	68.4	66.5	69.2	80.7
45 to 64 years.........	66.2	58.7	61.6	65.4	65.7	67.7	70.6	81.6
65 years and over......	23.4	18.5	22.4	23.5	23.9	26.2	28.4	42.9
MALE Total, 18 years and over.	86.0	65.2	81.7	83.8	90.7	93.6	83.2	92.3
18 to 24 years.........	79.1	81.0	91.7	92.0	80.1	86.4	55.4	68.0
25 to 34 years.........	97.0	88.8	97.1	98.7	98.4	98.5	92.5	95.5
35 to 44 years.........	97.8	90.7	96.2	97.5	98.2	98.7	99.1	99.4
45 to 64 years.........	92.7	82.5	91.4	92.8	94.7	96.4	94.9	96.8
65 years and over......	37.4	29.0	36.5	37.6	42.1	45.0	48.8	55.9
FEMALE Total, 18 years and over.	36.6	22.0	28.7	31.5	35.6	41.3	42.0	55.3
18 to 24 years.........	45.5	...	33.7	33.8	33.5	53.7	45.1	76.1
25 to 34 years.........	34.8	24.3	31.9	34.8	34.0	33.0	37.8	50.8
35 to 44 years.........	42.6	39.3	40.7	40.7	41.4	42.7	40.1	54.4
45 to 64 years.........	41.1	30.9	32.4	37.2	40.5	46.7	51.1	62.1
65 years and over......	11.5	6.9	9.7	11.7	11.6	16.4	16.2	22.6

Source: U.S. Bureau of the Census, Current Population Reports, Series P-50, No. 78. Table 3, November, 1957.

school early to get married. Also, the less educated women may have more children to keep them at home and may have a more difficult time re-entering the labor force after their children are old enough to be in school. It has been shown in Chapter 10 that a smaller proportion of women with above-average education ever marry, and this fact would indirectly encourage a higher participation rate among women with more education. Undoubtedly, the current trend toward a re-entry of married women into the labor force is highly selective, favoring those who have special skills and a high school or college education. Thus, the fact that an unprecedentedly large proportion of the women who are just now entering the period in which some of their children are mature (women 35 to 54 years of age) are also educated women with previous work experience may account for their high rates of re-entry.

This set of differentials, coupled with the rapidly rising general level of educational attainment, discussed in Chapter 14, is causing the labor force of the United States to have a progressively higher level of educational attainment. Table 16-17 shows this trend from 1940-57. The following short summary of that table shows that the proportion of semi-illiterate workers (those with less than 5 years of elementary school) is declining very rapidly, while there is a very large increase in the proportion of workers with high school or college degrees.

Year	Proportion of workers with educational attainment of:					
	Less than 5 yrs. of elementary school		4 yrs. high school or 1 to 3 yrs. college		4 yrs. or more of college	
	Male	Female	Male	Female	Male	Female
1957.........	6.3	3.9	35.7	46.6	9.6	8.4
1940.........	9.6	6.3	23.4	38.0	6.2	7.2
Change, 1940 to 1957.	-3.3	-2.4	12.3	8.6	3.4	1.2

In future years, as older workers with below-average educational attainment continue to retire from the labor force and are replaced by younger persons who have completed above-average

Table 16-17.—EDUCATIONAL ATTAINMENT OF PERSONS 18 TO 64 YEARS OLD IN THE CIVILIAN LABOR FORCE: 1940, 1948, 1952, AND 1957

Year	Median school years completed	Percent distribution by educational attainment						
			Elementary school		High school		College	
		Total	Less than 5 years	5 to 8 years	1 to 3 years	4 years	1 to 3 years	4 years or more
BOTH SEXES:								
1940 (April).......	9.3	100.0	8.7	39.4	18.1	20.3	7.0	6.4
1948 (October).....	10.6	100.0	7.3	32.4	19.7	26.5	7.4	6.7
1952 (October).....	11.2	100.0	6.8	29.5	19.0	27.9	8.6	8.2
1957 (October).....	11.8	100.0	5.6	26.2	19.8	30.5	8.8	9.2
MALE:								
1940 (April).......	8.8	100.0	9.6	42.7	18.1	17.2	6.2	6.2
1948 (October).....	10.2	100.0	7.9	34.0	20.7	23.6	7.1	6.7
1952 (October).....	10.7	100.0	7.6	31.6	19.4	24.7	8.4	8.4
1957 (October).....	11.3	100.0	6.3	28.2	20.1	27.2	8.5	9.6
FEMALE:								
1940 (April).......	10.2	100.0	6.3	30.4	18.1	28.7	9.3	7.2
1948 (October).....	11.7	100.0	5.7	28.6	17.3	33.4	8.2	6.8
1952 (October).....	12.0	100.0	5.2	25.1	18.2	34.7	9.1	7.8
1957 (October).....	12.1	100.0	3.9	21.9	19.1	37.3	9.3	8.4

Source: U.S. Census Bureau, Current Population Reports, Series P-50, No. 78, March, 1957, Table A.

amounts of education, the educational level of the labor force will continue to rise. It is a most impressive fact that by 1960 the average member of the labor force in the United States will be a high school graduate, and that at least 1 in 10 will be a college graduate. As recently as about 1930 the average worker was a graduate of elementary school, and only 5 percent had completed college.

Table 16-17 makes it clear that women with above-average education have been the principal female participants for many years; even in 1940 the average educational attainment of women workers was much higher than that of men workers. This tendency for the average woman worker to have more education than the average man worker is due in part to the fact that the older (and hence the less educated) women have withdrawn in favor of marriage and childbearing. Also, the present stage of economic development in the United States may make it much harder for an older person with less education to get a job if that person is a woman.

Size of place and labor force participation. Size of place as such does not seem to influence the rate of labor force participation of males, since above-average rates are found for the open-country farm population and for the population in places of 100,000 or more (Table 16-18). However, larger places seem to provide women workers with a somewhat greater opportunity to enter the labor force than smaller places. Women in rural villages have higher rates of participation than farm women, and each size of urban place category has a higher rate of participation than the rural villages and the other urban places smaller than itself. This is true as regards both white and nonwhite women.

Table 16-18 also shows that the very low participation rate of nonwhite males in rural-nonfarm areas, noted above, is attributable to the open country segment rather than to the village segment of the rural-nonfarm population.

TRENDS IN AGRICULTURAL AND NONAGRICULTURAL EMPLOYMENT

Under normally prosperous conditions, all but a small fraction of the labor force (3 to 5 percent) is employed. The employed workers are distributed throughout various occupations and industries. The next two chapters (Chapters 17 and 18) will analyze the occupational and industrial composition of the employed labor force, while Chapter 19 will discuss unemployment. The remainder of

Table 16-18.—LABOR FORCE PARTICIPATION RATES OF POPULATION CLASSIFIED BY SIZE OF PLACE, SEX, AND COLOR: 1950

Type and size of place	Male		Female	
	White	Nonwhite	White	Nonwhite
Total.............................	79.2	76.6	28.1	37.1
URBAN AREAS...........................	79.8	77.0	32.2	42.8
In urbanized areas................................	80.7	77.8	32.7	42.5
Places of 100,000 or more......................	80.3	77.9	34.4	42.5
Places of 50,000 or more.......................	80.0	77.5	33.7	44.9
Places of 25,000 or more.......................	81.7	80.1	30.6	42.9
Places of 2,500 to 25,000.....................	81.8	78.5	28.0	41.7
Other urban....................................	81.9	75.0	27.0	38.5
Not in urbanized areas............................	77.5	74.3	30.9	43.8
Places of 25,000 or more......................	77.8	75.4	32.9	44.9
Places of less than 25,000....................	77.4	73.9	30.2	43.4
Rural nonfarm.....................................	74.7	67.6	22.2	29.4
Places of 1,000 to 2,500......................	75.7	72.3	25.2	36.4
Other rural nonfarm............................	74.2	66.3	20.5	26.8
Rural farm..	82.9	83.3	15.1	22.1
Places of 1,000 to 2,500......................	79.3	81.2	19.5	31.7
Other rural farm..............................	83.0	83.3	15.1	22.0

Source: U.S. Census of Population: 1950, Volume IV, Special Reports, Part 1, Chapter A. Employment and Personal Characteristics, Table 4.

this chapter is devoted to a general description of employment trends, and especially certain selected aspects of employment such as hours worked per week, weeks worked per year, multiple jobholding, labor mobility, and the "length of working life."

In April, 1950, the total civilian employed labor force stood at almost exactly 60 million employed civilian workers. At that time 95 percent of the labor force was employed and 5 percent was unemployed. Since 1950 the employed labor force has grown rather steadily, so that by 1956 there were 65 million employed civilian workers, and 3.8 percent of the labor force was unemployed.

The number of persons who are employed at any one time is a function of two things: the number of persons who are offering their services on the labor market (the total number of persons in the labor force), and the demand for labor services. If the demand is great, almost all members of the labor force will be employed, and the proportion remaining unemployed will be small. But if economic conditions are poor, unemployment will be high and fewer persons may be employed--even though a great many more people may have entered the labor force. The following statistics are informative in this respect:

Year	Total labor force	Employed, civilian	Unemployed	Percent unemployed
1929......	49,440	47,630	1,550	3.2
1930......	50,080	45,480	4,340	8.7
1933......	51,840	38,760	12,830	24.9
1940......	56,030	47,520	8,120	14.6
1944......	65,890	53,960	670	1.2
1950......	64,599	59,957	3,142	5.0
1952......	66,426	61,293	1,673	2.7
1954......	67,818	61,238	3,230	5.0
1956......	70,387	64,979	2,551	3.8
1957......	70,746	65,011	2,936	4.3
1958......	71,284	63,966	4,681	6.8
1959 (Feb)	70,062	62,722	4,749	6.1

Source: Statistical Abstract of the United States, 1957, Table 239, Current Population Reports, monthly releases.

Thus, our total labor force jumped by 20 million persons between 1930 and 1956, and all but 1 million of this increase was absorbed either into the ranks of the civilian employed or into military service. The rate of unemployment was essentially the same in 1956 as in 1929.

The above set of data are noteworthy for their portrayal of what happened to employment during the years of the economic depression, 1930-40. Throughout this period of economic hardship the total labor force (the number of people wanting to work) increased, but the economy was unable to absorb it. In fact, in 1933 the number of civilian employed persons was smaller by about 9,000,000 than it had been only 4 years earlier in 1929, and the total number of unemployed persons stood at about 12,830,000. At this time, one worker in 4 was unemployed (either actively seeking work or on public emergency work).

During the war years employment zoomed upward, and the backlog of unemployed workers who had suffered such hardships during the 1930's was almost completely absorbed. In the year 1944 (when the nation was at peak wartime mobilization) an unprecedentedly high total of 54 million persons were employed, with an extraordinarily low unemployment rate of only 1.2 percent. Due to continued population growth and the entry of women into the labor force, the number of employed persons has continued to grow.

Each recession or downturn in business is immediately reflected in a rise in the proportion of the labor force that is unemployed, as conditions during the year 1954 demonstrated. The year 1958 developed an even more threatening backlog of unabsorbed workers. Periodic fluctuations in unemployment such as these will be reviewed in more detail in Chapter 19, and the question "What kinds of people are unemployed?"--in terms of age, sex, color, marital status, educational attainment, occupation, industry, and other traits--will be answered there.

As would be expected in view of the materials presented in earlier chapters, there has been a steady decline in the proportion of the employed labor force that is engaged in agricultural industries. Instead, there has been a steady rise in the proportion of workers engaged in nonagricultural commerce and industry, as the following series shows:

Year	Percent of employed workers in nonagricultural activities
1958	90.9
1957	90.4
1956	89.9
1954	89.4
1950	87.5

con. Year	Percent of employed workers in nonagricultural activities
1945	83.8
1940	80.2
1935	78.5
1930	77.2
1925	76.2
1920	74.4
1915	71.6
1910	69.6
1905	67.9
1900	67.1

Source: Computed from Historical Statistics of the United States, Series D 62-76 (adapted from National Industrial Conference Board) and from Statistical Abstract of the United States, 1957, Table 239, and Statistical Abstract of the United States, 1958.

Figure 16-5, based upon the Census Bureau's Monthly Report of the Labor Force, illustrates for the period 1946-57 (a) the generally upward trend in the size of the employed labor force and (b) the cyclical pattern of unemployment, both of which have just been described. In addition, it portrays another aspect of employment that has not yet been discussed, namely, the fact that there is a strong annual cycle or seasonal fluctuation in employment and unemployment. The agricultural industries employ many temporary workers during the planting, tilling, and harvest seasons, and dismiss them for the winter months. During the time of peak agricultural operations in June and July, about 3 million more persons are employed in agricultural industries than at the period of lowest agricultural employment in December-January. Similarly, the construction and transportation industries, and many manufacturing industries, have a distinctly seasonal pattern, in which operations are greatly expanded during one or more seasons (usually the spring and summer months). In addition, nonagricultural employment usually receives a boost from the shopping and commercial activities associated with the Thanksgiving, Christmas, and New Year's holidays. It should be noted, in this connection, that the size of the total labor force, as well as total employment and unemployment, fluctuates with the seasons. This means that during the months when there is less work, several millions of persons (primarily women, students, unmarried persons, and older persons)

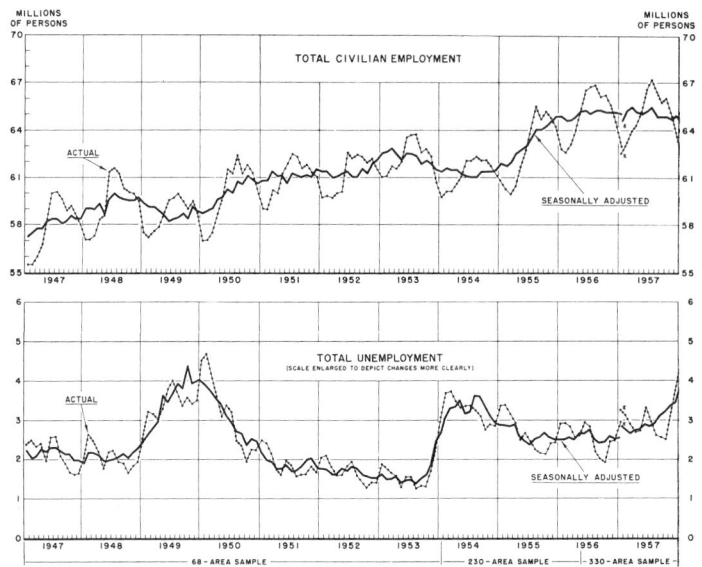

FIGURE 16-5. TRENDS IN EMPLOYMENT AND UNEMPLOYMENT, ACTUAL AND SEASONALLY
ADJUSTED: JANUARY 1947 TO DATE

Source: Current Population Reports, Labor Force, Series P-50, No. 85, 1958.

withdraw from the labor force rather than remain in the status of unemployed.

Year	Number of workers (000)			Ratio of agricultural to total
	Total	Agricultural	Nonagricultural	
1957.......	66,005	6,837	59,168	10.4
1956.......	64,979	6,585	58,394	10.1
1954.......	61,238	6,504	54,734	10.6
1950.......	59,957	7,507	52,450	12.5
1945.......	52,820	8,580	44,240	16.2
1940.......	53,466	10,580	42,886	19.8
1935.......	51,769	11,130	40,639	21.5
1930.......	49,006	11,172	37,834	22.8
1925.......	45,009	10,725	34,284	23.8
1920.......	41,897	10,718	31,179	25.6
1915.......	40,083	11,371	28,712	28.4
1910.......	38,133	11,610	26,523	30.4
1905.......	33,653	10,795	22,858	32.1
1900.......	29,025	9,552	19,473	32.9

Figure 16-4 also shows that the armed forces are, and have been, a most important source of employment. About 8 to 10 percent of all employment consists of military service. A very large proportion of civilians, of course, are employed in supplying the needs of the military forces. If "peace were to break out" suddenly, the economy would be forced to undergo an immediate and very sizable readjustment.

THE STATUS OF NONWORKERS

What do the people do who are not in the labor force? Why are they not working? These questions are answered, at least in part, by the data in Table 16-19, which shows the status of nonworkers by age, sex, color, and urban-rural residence. Four categories of status outside the labor force were recognized in 1950: keeping house, unable to work (because of age or chronic illness), inmates of institutions, and other and not reported (this last category includes students, the retired, and those too old to work). The Bureau of the Census has warned that the statistics for some of these categories have a low degree of reliability. For this reason only the largest differences are accepted here as being valid.

If a man is not in the labor force, it is because he is either (a) unable to work, (b) is a student, (c) is retired, or (d) is in an institution. If a woman is not in the labor force it can be for one of the above reasons, or because she is keeping house.

At ages below 25, almost all boys and almost all unmarried girls who are not in the labor force are absent from it because of being students. At these

Table 16-19.—STATUS OF NONWORKERS BY SEX, AGE, COLOR, AND URBAN-RURAL RESIDENCE: 1950

URBAN, WHITE

Age	Male, 14 years old and over						Female, 14 years old and over					
	Not in labor force, total	Keeping house	Unable to work	Inmates of institutions	Other	Not reported	Not in labor force, total	Keeping house	Unable to work	Inmates of institutions	Other	Not reported
Total.........	100.0	2.2	21.7	5.1	65.1	5.9	100.0	80.1	4.3	1.2	12.9	1.6
14 to 19 years....	100.0	0.5	0.7	1.2	93.2	4.3	100.0	13.7	0.6	0.8	81.4	3.5
20 to 24 years....	100.0	1.1	3.1	3.3	86.9	5.5	100.0	82.2	0.8	0.5	14.4	2.1
25 to 29 years....	100.0	2.7	8.0	7.4	71.9	9.9	100.0	94.3	0.7	0.4	3.2	1.5
30 to 34 years....	100.0	3.6	14.9	13.5	48.9	19.2	100.0	95.0	0.6	0.6	2.3	1.5
35 to 39 years....	100.0	5.0	19.8	17.0	36.7	21.4	100.0	95.1	0.8	0.7	2.2	1.3
40 to 44 years....	100.0	4.8	24.2	17.0	35.1	18.9	100.0	94.5	1.0	0.8	2.4	1.4
45 to 49 years....	100.0	5.2	27.8	14.7	34.9	17.4	100.0	93.9	1.3	0.9	2.6	1.4
50 to 54 years....	100.0	4.7	34.8	12.7	37.4	10.4	100.0	92.9	1.9	1.0	3.0	1.2
55 to 59 years....	100.0	4.4	39.1	9.9	39.2	7.4	100.0	91.2	2.8	0.9	3.8	1.2
60 to 64 years....	100.0	3.8	41.3	7.1	43.0	4.8	100.0	86.9	5.5	1.2	5.1	1.3
65 to 69 years....	100.0	3.1	41.0	3.9	49.1	2.8	100.0	80.4	9.7	1.4	7.3	1.1
70 to 74 years....	100.0	2.8	43.2	3.3	48.4	2.3	100.0	70.3	16.9	2.6	9.1	1.2
75 years and over.	100.0	2.4	51.3	5.6	39.2	1.6	100.0	49.5	31.4	6.3	11.5	1.3

URBAN, NONWHITE

Age	Male, 14 years old and over						Female, 14 years old and over					
	Not in labor force, total	Keeping house	Unable to work	Inmates of institutions	Other	Not reported	Not in labor force, total	Keeping house	Unable to work	Inmates of institutions	Other	Not reported
Total.........	100.0	3.1	23.2	8.1	59.7	5.9	100.0	68.3	9.1	1.2	19.5	2.0
14 to 19 years....	100.0	1.0	1.1	2.0	92.1	3.9	100.0	20.1	1.1	0.9	74.8	3.0
20 to 24 years....	100.0	4.2	5.9	11.7	70.3	8.0	100.0	76.4	2.2	0.7	18.5	2.2
25 to 29 years....	100.0	4.0	9.3	16.2	63.6	6.8	100.0	86.5	2.2	0.8	8.4	2.1
30 to 34 years....	100.0	5.0	13.0	21.0	49.3	11.7	100.0	86.7	3.0	1.1	7.6	1.7
35 to 39 years....	100.0	4.2	17.0	19.8	46.7	12.3	100.0	86.5	3.7	1.0	6.8	2.0
40 to 44 years....	100.0	3.9	25.0	16.3	43.9	10.9	100.0	85.0	5.2	1.5	6.5	1.8
45 to 49 years....	100.0	7.7	32.6	16.0	34.2	9.5	100.0	83.1	7.7	1.2	6.1	1.9
50 to 54 years....	100.0	3.6	42.9	11.8	34.3	7.4	100.0	80.4	10.3	1.5	6.3	1.4
55 to 59 years....	100.0	4.6	46.5	9.8	33.5	5.7	100.0	76.4	13.3	1.8	7.4	1.1
60 to 64 years....	100.0	4.1	53.0	5.0	32.4	5.5	100.0	68.9	20.5	1.7	7.0	1.9
65 to 69 years....	100.0	3.7	57.3	3.1	33.3	2.6	100.0	56.2	33.3	1.0	8.2	1.3
70 to 74 years....	100.0	2.2	62.1	1.9	30.8	3.1	100.0	47.1	41.3	1.5	8.9	1.3
75 years and over.	100.0	3.2	67.8	3.0	24.6	1.3	100.0	31.2	54.9	2.6	10.0	1.3

RURAL NONFARM, WHITE

Age	Male, 14 years old and over						Female, 14 years old and over					
	Not in labor force, total	Keeping house	Unable to work	Inmates of institutions	Other	Not reported	Not in labor force, total	Keeping house	Unable to work	Inmates of institutions	Other	Not reported
Total.........	100.0	2.1	26.4	15.1	52.9	3.5	100.0	79.4	4.3	3.0	11.9	1.4
14 to 19 years....	100.0	0.6	1.1	4.4	89.8	4.0	100.0	22.4	0.7	1.9	71.6	3.4
20 to 24 years....	100.0	2.1	6.5	21.1	65.0	5.3	100.0	90.0	0.8	1.3	6.4	1.5
25 to 29 years....	100.0	3.2	12.4	31.1	46.6	6.7	100.0	94.5	0.7	1.5	2.1	1.2
30 to 34 years....	100.0	3.3	17.3	40.0	30.9	8.6	100.0	95.1	0.6	1.8	1.5	1.0
35 to 39 years....	100.0	3.7	20.9	41.6	25.5	8.3	100.0	94.2	0.9	2.3	1.6	1.0
40 to 44 years....	100.0	3.6	24.5	40.7	26.2	5.0	100.0	93.1	1.0	3.3	1.5	1.1
45 to 49 years....	100.0	3.1	26.4	37.8	27.3	5.4	100.0	92.2	1.4	3.3	1.9	1.1
50 to 54 years....	100.0	3.5	30.8	33.3	28.6	3.9	100.0	90.8	2.2	3.8	2.0	1.2
55 to 59 years....	100.0	3.3	36.0	25.2	32.6	2.8	100.0	89.3	3.1	4.0	2.7	0.9
60 to 64 years....	100.0	2.5	39.0	20.1	35.8	2.5	100.0	86.2	5.4	4.1	3.4	1.0
65 to 69 years....	100.0	2.7	44.8	10.3	40.7	1.5	100.0	80.7	9.9	4.0	4.3	1.1
70 to 74 years....	100.0	2.4	51.5	7.4	37.2	1.5	100.0	71.8	16.8	4.8	5.6	1.0
75 years and over.	100.0	2.1	59.9	9.8	26.9	1.4	100.0	48.6	34.5	8.5	7.3	1.2

RURAL NONFARM, NONWHITE

Age	Male, 14 years old and over						Female, 14 years old and over					
	Not in labor force, total	Keeping house	Unable to work	Inmates of institutions	Other	Not reported	Not in labor force, total	Keeping house	Unable to work	Inmates of institutions	Other	Not reported
Total.........	100.0	2.3	24.4	29.9	40.3	3.1	100.0	68.1	9.1	4.3	16.7	1.7
14 to 19 years....	100.0	0.9	1.2	11.3	83.3	3.5	100.0	27.0	1.0	2.2	66.3	3.4
20 to 24 years....	100.0	4.8	5.3	46.5	37.3	6.2	100.0	81.7	1.1	3.4	11.8	2.0
25 to 29 years....	100.0	2.8	6.8	56.4	29.7	4.2	100.0	87.2	1.8	4.5	4.9	1.5
30 to 34 years....	100.0	1.7	9.0	63.4	24.0	1.9	100.0	88.1	1.8	5.3	3.6	1.2
35 to 39 years....	100.0	3.0	14.6	59.9	19.4	3.2	100.0	86.3	3.3	5.3	3.9	1.2
40 to 44 years....	100.0	2.9	17.6	59.6	16.8	3.1	100.0	86.1	3.1	6.5	3.4	0.9
45 to 49 years....	100.0	2.2	21.9	53.5	20.0	2.4	100.0	85.1	5.0	5.1	3.3	1.5
50 to 54 years....	100.0	2.8	31.6	43.3	19.3	3.0	100.0	82.2	6.9	6.1	4.1	0.7
55 to 59 years....	100.0	2.5	44.1	33.5	17.9	2.0	100.0	79.6	10.2	5.2	3.3	1.6
60 to 64 years....	100.0	3.1	50.5	25.3	17.6	3.6	100.0	70.5	17.9	6.2	4.4	1.0
65 to 69 years....	100.0	2.8	60.0	10.4	25.2	1.7	100.0	60.6	30.7	2.8	4.6	1.3
70 to 74 years....	100.0	2.3	71.2	6.4	18.8	1.3	100.0	46.6	43.7	3.5	5.5	0.6
75 years and over.	100.0	2.0	77.3	5.9	14.0	0.9	100.0	29.7	59.3	5.4	3.6	1.9

Table 16-19.—STATUS OF NONWORKERS BY SEX, AGE, COLOR, AND URBAN-RURAL RESIDENCE: 1950—Continued

RURAL FARM, WHITE

Age	Male, 14 years old and over						Female, 14 years old and over					
	Not in labor force, total	Keeping house	Unable to work	Inmates of institutions	Other	Not reported	Not in labor force, total	Keeping house	Unable to work	Inmates of institutions	Other	Not reported
Total.........	100.0	2.5	30.5	...	63.2	3.8	100.0	81.2	4.0	...	13.0	1.8
14 to 19 years....	100.0	0.6	1.2	...	94.5	3.8	100.0	22.8	0.8	...	73.2	3.2
20 to 24 years....	100.0	4.0	15.8	...	73.7	6.5	100.0	91.2	0.8	...	0.3	7.7
25 to 29 years....	100.0	7.7	29.5	...	53.5	9.3	100.0	95.8	0.9	...	2.4	0.9
30 to 34 years....	100.0	8.2	36.5	...	44.2	11.1	100.0	96.7	0.8	...	1.7	0.8
35 to 39 years....	100.0	10.5	41.2	...	38.2	10.1	100.0	96.9	0.8	...	1.6	0.7
40 to 44 years....	100.0	10.8	43.3	...	38.4	7.6	100.0	97.2	0.8	...	1.2	0.8
45 to 49 years....	100.0	11.2	48.8	...	33.1	6.9	100.0	96.6	1.2	...	1.4	0.8
50 to 54 years....	100.0	6.9	56.9	...	32.0	4.2	100.0	96.2	1.6	...	1.4	0.8
55 to 59 years....	100.0	5.2	58.2	...	32.9	3.7	100.0	95.1	2.5	...	1.5	0.9
60 to 64 years....	100.0	4.8	58.5	...	33.5	3.2	100.0	92.0	4.8	...	2.3	0.9
65 to 69 years....	100.0	3.6	64.7	...	29.7	2.0	100.0	85.6	10.0	...	3.2	1.2
70 to 74 years....	100.0	2.6	69.0	...	26.4	2.0	100.0	73.5	20.9	...	4.2	1.4
75 years and over.	100.0	1.9	77.6	...	19.3	1.3	100.0	46.0	45.8	...	6.4	1.7

RURAL FARM, NONWHITE

Age	Male, 14 years old and over						Female, 14 years old and over					
	Not in labor force, total	Keeping house	Unable to work	Inmates of institutions	Other	Not reported	Not in labor force, total	Keeping house	Unable to work	Inmates of institutions	Other	Not reported
Total.........	100.0	3.4	27.9	...	64.8	3.8	100.0	72.7	6.2	...	19.7	1.4
14 to 19 years....	100.0	0.9	1.8	...	94.2	3.1	100.0	29.9	0.8	...	67.2	2.1
20 to 24 years....	100.0	9.2	13.1	...	68.3	9.5	100.0	83.9	1.2	...	13.4	1.4
25 to 29 years....	100.0	10.1	21.2	...	62.0	6.7	100.0	92.1	1.3	...	5.4	1.1
30 to 34 years....	100.0	14.5	33.6	...	42.7	9.1	100.0	93.9	1.7	...	3.6	0.9
35 to 39 years....	100.0	13.5	37.5	...	37.5	11.5	100.0	94.6	1.9	...	2.4	1.1
40 to 44 years....	100.0	12.9	39.8	...	40.9	6.5	100.0	93.5	2.2	...	2.9	1.5
45 to 49 years....	100.0	21.9	47.9	...	22.9	7.3	100.0	92.9	2.8	...	3.6	0.7
50 to 54 years....	100.0	8.4	60.7	...	22.4	8.4	100.0	91.2	4.8	...	2.4	1.5
55 to 59 years....	100.0	4.8	67.5	...	19.0	8.7	100.0	90.9	5.0	...	3.0	1.0
60 to 64 years....	100.0	6.5	65.3	...	25.9	2.4	100.0	83.2	11.8	...	3.9	1.1
65 to 69 years....	100.0	3.1	75.8	...	19.6	1.5	100.0	69.1	24.5	...	5.1	1.3
70 to 74 years....	100.0	3.5	77.2	...	16.8	2.6	100.0	53.3	39.7	...	5.6	1.4
75 years and over.	100.0	2.0	86.8	...	10.0	1.2	100.0	26.7	65.7	...	5.8	1.8

ages there is comparatively little disability. At ages 30 and over, being disabled, being in an institution, and being in the category of "retired and other" are important reasons why men are not in the labor force. Being an inmate of an institution becomes increasingly important as a reason at ages beyond 30 years. A substantial portion of the men in the younger age groups who are in institutions are prisoners, and this fact accounts for most of the difference which exists between the sexes with respect to the status of being in an institution. Among nonwhite males, being unable to work and being an inmate are more frequent explanations for nonparticipation than they are among the white population, while being a student, being retired, or being too old to work are less frequent explanations among the nonwhite males. Nonwhite women report "keeping house" as a reason for not being in the labor force much less often than white women, but report "being unable to work" much more frequently.

In rural areas, being unable to work is reported much more frequently by nonwhite males than by white males. Inasmuch as many prisons, sanitaria, and other institutions are located in rural areas and are nonfarm by definition, a very high proportion of the total institutional population is rural nonfarm. It is for this reason that 15 percent of the white and 30 percent of the nonwhite rural-nonfarm men who are not in the labor force are reported in Table 16-17 as being institutionalized.

Being retired, or being too old to work ("Other" for advanced years) are much more urban than rural phenomena. Also, they are much more common among the white than among the nonwhite populations.

HOURS WORKED PER WEEK: PART-TIME WORKERS

Historically, there has been a long-term decline in the average length of the workweek. During the last decade of the 19th century (and presumably long before that time) a very high proportion of workers put in a 60-hour week--six 10-hour days. Throughout the current century the length of the workweek has declined rather steadily; at the present time the 40-hour week is the average, and in many places the 35-hour week is coming to be regarded as the norm. The following series (comprised of three different series that are not strictly comparable) outlines roughly the change that has taken place in hours worked per week.

Year	Total	Nonagricultural industries	Agricultural industries
1890	58.4	...	...
1900	57.3	...	...
1910	54.6	...	...
1920	50.4	...	...
1930	...	42.1	...
1934	...	34.6	...
1940	...	38.1	...
May 1948	43.4	41.9	52.5
May 1950	42.5	41.3	50.1
May 1954	41.6	40.6	49.3
May 1955	41.9	40.9	49.5
May 1956	41.5	40.9	46.3
May 1957	41.1	40.5	46.3
May 1958	41.0	40.0	49.6

Source: Historical Statistics of the United States: 1789-1945, Series D 121-133 (from Paul H. Douglas); D 117-120 (from Department of Labor); and Current Population Reports.

In 1958, the average American worker was working about 17 hours per week less than the average worker of 1890. This decline has taken place both in agricultural and in nonagricultural industries, but the nonfarm worker still works about 8 hours per week less than his country cousin on the farm. As recently as 1948 the average farm workweek was 52 hours, and even now the farmer puts in more than the equivalent of six 8-hour days during his peak season. In 1934, during the economic depression, the number of hours in the nonagricultural workweek fell to as few as 35. This happened because employers followed a policy of "spreading the work" by giving more employees a limited amount of work, or of working a plant only a few days each week. During the recent war boom with its manpower shortages it became customary for many workers to work overtime, and

hence the length of the average workweek in nonagricultural industries has remained slightly above 40 hours, until the 1958 recession.

Many persons who are employed do not have full-time jobs. Instead, they may work only a few hours per day or a few days each week. The Bureau of the Census, which collects data concerning hours worked as a part of its monthly survey of the labor force, defines full-time work as a total of 35 hours or more per week. Workers who work less than 35 hours per week are classed as part-time workers. The 40-hour week has come to be regarded as standard, and Census statistics as to the number of workers who work 41 hours or more per week are regarded as being a measure of the amount of "overtime" work.

The following summary of part-time, full-time, and overtime workers presents the picture of hours worked, by sex and color, as of 1956. (These statistics, and others from the Current Population Survey which are reported here, are averages of the results of the 12 monthly surveys for the year 1956.)

Sex	Part time (1 to 34 hours)	Full time (35 to 40 hours)	"Overtime" 41 hours or more	Average
Male........	12.3	48.1	39.7	43.0
White......	11.6	47.6	40.8	43.3
Nonwhite...	18.6	53.9	27.5	39.7
Female......	26.5	51.7	22.0	36.7
White......	24.9	53.0	22.1	37.1
Nonwhite...	37.4	41.8	20.8	33.8
White (both sexes).....	15.9	49.3	34.8	41.3
Nonwhite....	26.1	49.0	24.9	37.3

Source: U.S. Bureau of the Census. Annual Report on the Labor Force, P-50, No. 72, Tables 18 and 20.

A much higher proportion of women than of men are part-time workers. More nonwhite males than white males, and more nonwhite females than white females, are part-time workers. Note also that more men workers than women workers put in overtime, and that nonwhite workers (especially males) have much less overtime than white workers of the same sex. For these reasons (much part-time work and less overtime), the average workweek of women workers is about 10 hours shorter than that of men, and the average workweek of nonwhite workers is about 4 hours shorter than that of white workers. In assembling this information, the Census also asks the reason for working part time. Two categories of reasons are recognized: Economic reasons--slack work, inability to find full-time work, material shortages, repairs to plant or equipment, beginning or termination of job during the week. Other reasons--labor disputes, bad weather, own illness, vacation, demands of home housework, attendance at school, no desire for full-time work, full-time worker only during peak season, legal or religious holiday, and other such reasons. Furthermore, the census classifies the workers who were found to be working part time during the week of the census monthly survey according to whether they are regularly part-time workers or usually full-time workers. The results for 1957 are as follows:

| Sex and color | | Worked 1 to 34 hours during survey week | | | |
| | | | Usually work full time | | Usually work part time | |
	Total	For economic reasons	For other reasons	For economic reasons	For other reasons
		Percent of workers			
Total......	18.6	2.2	4.6	1.8	10.1
White (both sexes)	16.5	1.9	4.2	1.3	9.1
Nonwhite (both sexes)	25.5	3.7	4.9	6.0	10.9
Male.......	12.5	2.1	4.3	1.3	4.8
White........	12.0	1.9	4.2	1.1	4.8
Nonwhite.....	18.1	4.1	5.7	4.0	4.3
Female.....	27.0	2.2	4.1	2.6	18.1
White........	25.8	2.1	4.1	1.8	17.8
Nonwhite.....	36.4	3.2	3.9	8.9	20.4

Source: U.S. Bureau of the Census, Annual Report on the Labor Force, 1958, Series P-50, No. 72, Tables 18 and 20.

A much higher proportion of women than of men work part time--not primarily for economic reasons, but because of the demands of housework, no desire for full-time work, etc. That a greater proportion of nonwhite than of white workers are employed only part time may be attributed both to economic and to other reasons, but the differences between white and nonwhite workers are due more largely to economic reasons--the fact that fewer nonwhite workers are apparently able to find full-time work, shortened workweeks, etc. If irregular attendance at work were inferred from the proportion of workers who usually worked full time but were working only part time during the survey week for noneconomic reasons, it would have to be concluded that women are somewhat less regular in attendance than men, and that nonwhite workers are less regular than white.[9]

Table 16-20 presents a classification of part-time and full-time workers by age. The part-time workers, among both males and females, are the very young and the very old. Almost three-fourths of the boys and girls 14 to 17 years of age are part-time workers; they are usually part-time workers for noneconomic reasons (school attendance). More than one-fourth of retirement-age male workers (65 years of age or over), and more than 40 percent of older female workers of the same age, are part-time employees--and again the reasons are largely noneconomic. Two impressive facts about these older workers are (a) a great many of them are holding down full-time jobs, and (b) their attendance at work appears to be fully as regular as that of the younger people.

The preceding discussion, based upon sample data from the monthly labor force surveys, cannot provide information about differences in hours worked for groups having various combinations of sex, color, age, and urban and rural-residence. A special tabulation from the 1950 census makes available such information which is presented here as Table 16-21. In 1950 the tendency to work long workweeks was a characteristic of all the age-sex-color groups in the farm population, in comparison with the urban and the rural-nonfarm pop-

---

[9]Another reason for intermittent attendance at work among women and nonwhites is that both of these groups have more of a tendency to be in occupations which involve irregular work schedules--day laborers, domestic service, etc.

Table 16-20.—PERCENT DISTRIBUTION OF WORKERS IN NONAGRICULTURAL INDUSTRIES ACCORDING TO FULL-TIME
AND PART-TIME STATUS, BY AGE AND SEX: 1956
(Annual average of 12 monthly surveys)

Sex and age	Total at work	Worked 1 to 34 hours during survey week					Worked 35 hours or more during survey week			Average hours
		Total	Usually work full time		Usually work part time		Total	35 to 40 hours	41 hours or more	
			For economic reasons	For other reasons	For economic reasons	For other reasons				
Male, total........	100.0	12.3	1.9	4.4	1.2	4.8	87.8	48.1	39.7	43.0
14 to 17 years....	100.0	74.5	1.3	2.2	7.3	63.7	25.5	14.7	10.8	21.5
18 to 24 years....	100.0	17.3	2.5	4.0	1.6	9.2	82.7	49.4	33.3	40.4
25 to 34 years....	100.0	7.9	1.7	4.4	0.6	1.2	92.0	49.3	42.7	44.3
35 to 44 years....	100.0	7.7	1.8	4.5	0.6	0.8	92.4	49.1	43.3	44.8
45 to 54 years....	100.0	8.6	1.8	4.6	1.0	1.2	91.4	49.3	42.1	44.5
55 to 64 years....	100.0	11.3	2.1	4.8	1.4	3.0	88.8	51.2	37.6	43.1
65 years and over.	100.0	26.6	1.4	4.1	2.6	18.5	73.5	41.8	31.7	38.3
Female, total.......	100.0	26.5	2.1	4.5	2.6	17.3	73.7	51.7	22.0	36.7
14 to 17 years....	100.0	71.1	1.4	2.0	5.5	62.2	28.8	19.5	9.3	21.0
18 to 24 years....	100.0	19.3	1.9	5.0	2.1	10.3	80.8	63.0	17.8	37.3
25 to 34 years....	100.0	22.6	2.2	5.1	2.2	13.1	77.6	57.6	20.0	37.3
35 to 44 years....	100.0	25.2	2.3	4.5	2.4	16.0	74.8	52.3	22.5	37.3
45 to 54 years....	100.0	25.2	2.2	4.4	2.5	16.1	74.7	49.7	25.0	37.9
55 to 64 years....	100.0	26.0	1.9	4.0	3.0	17.1	74.1	46.6	27.5	38.1
65 years and over.	100.0	41.7	1.1	3.2	2.9	34.5	58.3	28.5	29.8	33.9

Source: U.S. Bureau of the Census, Annual Report on the Labor Force, 1956, Series P-50, No. 72, 1957,
Table 18.

ulation.[10] The rural-nonfarm employed population, in its turn, had a longer workweek than the urban. This pattern in which the length of the workweek decreased as contact with agriculture decreased was true for both white and nonwhite males and females. In rural areas, and especially in rural-farm areas, a much higher proportion of teen-age children were full-time labor force participants than in urban areas. Of the farm boys 14 to 17 years of age, one in six worked 60 hours during the week preceding the 1950 census enumeration. This could reflect the fact that the census was taken in a month of peak agricultural activity.

Nonwhite teen-agers, especially boys, worked longer workweeks than white teen-agers. This difference reflects the fact that nonwhite children

leave school, and become full-time workers, at an earlier age.

Among the central working ages (35 to 44 years), the patterns described above with respect to the total nonagricultural working force in 1956 also prevailed in 1950. All but a few men worked full time, and there was a larger proportion of part-time workers among the nonwhite than among the white male workers. A much higher proportion of the women workers of this age were part-time workers, and a larger share of nonwhite than of white women were part-time workers.

Among workers 65 to 74 years of age, rural workers (and especially those in the rural-farm category) worked the longest workweek. At this advanced age the sex difference was much smaller--the proportion of part-time workers among men was not a great deal smaller than among women. At these oldest ages, the white workers continued to have a longer workweek than the nonwhite.

In the future, as more and more women enter the labor force, the number and proportion of

---

[10]Despite the fact that a much higher percentage of farm workers work longer hours compared with nonfarm workers, the total number of workers spending long hours at their occupation is greater in nonfarm areas, simply because there are so many more nonfarm workers.

Table 16-21.—HOURS WORKED DURING CENSUS WEEK: EMPLOYED PERSONS BY SEX, COLOR, AND SELECTED AGES, FOR THE UNITED STATES: 1950

Hours worked	Total				Urban				Rural nonfarm				Rural farm			
	Male		Female		Male		Female		Male		Female		Male		Female	
	White	Non-white	White	Non-white	White	Non-white	White	Non-white	White	Non-white	White	Non-white	White	Non-white	White	Non-white
All ages.........	100.0	100.0	100.0	100.0	100.0	100.0	100.0	100.0	100.0	100.0	100.0	100.0	100.0	100.0	100.0	100.0
1 to 14 hours......	1.9	2.4	4.2	6.4	1.8	2.2	3.8	5.7	2.4	3.5	6.0	10.7	2.0	2.2	4.6	6.2
15 to 29 hours.....	4.4	6.5	8.8	15.9	3.4	5.3	7.5	14.2	5.5	9.2	9.8	18.3	7.1	8.2	21.0	25.7
30 to 34 hours.....	3.1	4.8	5.3	9.2	2.4	3.6	4.7	8.2	4.1	6.9	6.7	11.2	5.0	6.8	8.4	14.8
35 to 39 hours.....	2.8	2.6	7.5	5.7	2.3	2.5	8.0	5.8	2.3	2.5	5.8	6.1	2.3	2.8	5.2	4.5
40 hours...........	40.4	40.8	45.7	32.1	47.3	49.5	49.0	35.4	36.9	38.7	36.5	22.1	17.2	18.5	28.3	19.9
41 to 48 hours.....	19.0	17.5	16.7	16.5	21.0	20.9	16.9	18.2	19.6	15.0	17.4	13.0	10.2	9.9	12.3	8.1
49 to 59 hours.....	10.4	11.1	4.2	5.8	9.2	7.0	3.8	5.2	11.4	10.7	5.8	7.5	13.8	22.7	6.1	8.6
60 hours or more....	15.6	11.7	4.5	4.9	9.4	6.2	3.3	4.1	15.1	10.8	8.3	7.1	40.0	27.2	9.5	8.5
Hours not reported..	2.4	2.6	3.1	3.4	2.4	2.9	2.9	3.2	2.6	2.7	3.6	4.0	2.3	1.8	4.6	3.7
Ages 14 to 17....	100.0	100.0	100.0	100.0	100.0	100.0	100.0	100.0	100.0	100.0	100.0	100.0	100.0	100.0	100.0	100.0
1 to 14 hours......	23.0	8.6	29.9	15.3	36.0	22.0	32.3	22.2	27.9	11.5	32.9	20.1	4.5	1.4	14.9	6.2
15 to 29 hours.....	27.1	19.8	22.7	27.7	23.6	21.0	19.5	22.4	23.0	19.7	22.2	22.6	33.5	19.3	38.4	35.3
30 to 34 hours.....	6.7	8.9	4.6	10.5	4.2	5.6	4.0	7.9	6.0	9.4	4.3	10.2	10.2	10.3	7.7	13.3
35 to 39 hours.....	2.7	2.7	4.0	4.0	2.2	2.2	4.5	4.4	2.0	2.2	2.5	6.4	3.5	3.1	3.6	2.6
40 hours...........	13.6	17.7	18.8	17.4	13.8	16.2	21.6	17.5	15.2	20.7	14.9	14.6	12.6	17.5	11.2	18.6
41 to 48 hours.....	6.4	10.7	8.2	8.4	6.2	15.9	8.4	11.5	7.7	10.7	9.0	7.0	5.9	8.3	6.2	5.9
49 to 59 hours.....	5.1	14.7	2.6	5.9	1.9	5.1	2.0	4.8	4.8	12.6	3.3	4.8	9.3	19.9	4.5	7.5
60 hours or more....	8.2	13.4	1.8	5.2	1.8	5.0	0.9	3.9	5.7	9.0	2.7	6.4	17.4	18.7	4.5	6.0
Hours not reported..	7.1	3.4	7.3	5.5	10.3	7.0	6.7	5.3	7.6	4.1	8.2	8.0	3.0	1.5	9.0	4.5
Ages 35 to 44....	100.0	100.0	100.0	100.0	100.0	100.0	100.0	100.0	100.0	100.0	100.0	100.0	100.0	100.0	100.0	100.0
1 to 14 hours......	0.8	1.5	3.3	5.4	0.6	1.3	3.0	4.8	1.2	2.0	4.8	9.3	1.2	2.1	3.8	5.4
15 to 29 hours.....	2.6	4.5	9.3	15.4	2.0	3.9	8.0	14.2	3.9	6.9	10.5	18.5	3.8	4.8	20.8	23.2
30 to 34 hours.....	2.5	4.2	6.0	9.3	1.9	3.4	5.5	8.3	3.6	5.8	7.5	12.0	3.8	6.0	9.0	15.5
35 to 39 hours.....	2.6	2.6	7.7	6.2	2.9	2.5	8.2	6.2	2.3	2.6	5.9	6.6	1.8	2.9	5.9	5.3
40 hours...........	40.7	44.4	44.9	32.7	46.7	52.1	48.2	35.6	37.3	41.8	36.0	21.2	17.9	17.1	29.1	19.9
41 to 48 hours.....	19.9	18.9	16.6	17.2	22.0	21.7	16.9	18.4	20.3	16.1	17.1	14.6	10.1	10.5	11.5	8.8
49 to 59 hours.....	11.3	10.0	4.3	5.8	10.3	6.4	3.8	5.2	12.6	10.6	5.8	7.5	14.3	23.2	6.2	9.7
60 hours or more....	17.5	11.6	5.1	5.0	11.5	6.2	3.7	4.2	16.7	11.8	9.4	7.0	45.0	31.7	9.7	9.7
Hours not reported..	2.0	2.3	2.8	3.0	2.0	2.5	2.7	3.0	2.1	2.4	3.0	3.2	2.0	1.7	4.0	2.5
Ages 55 to 64....	100.0	100.0	100.0	100.0	100.0	100.0	100.0	100.0	100.0	100.0	100.0	100.0	100.0	100.0	100.0	100.0
1 to 14 hours......	1.7	2.7	4.7	10.0	1.1	2.1	4.2	9.1	2.8	4.4	6.9	16.2	2.6	3.0	5.7	7.2
15 to 29 hours.....	4.6	7.2	10.8	20.5	3.5	6.2	9.4	19.6	6.4	10.8	10.5	22.3	7.0	7.4	26.8	24.1
30 to 34 hours.....	3.7	5.2	6.3	9.8	2.9	3.9	5.8	8.9	4.9	8.6	7.5	11.3	5.6	6.3	9.2	13.8
35 to 39 hours.....	3.2	2.2	7.1	6.0	3.5	2.3	7.5	5.3	2.5	2.0	6.4	5.3	2.6	2.2	4.8	2.7
40 hours...........	40.7	38.0	36.6	24.2	48.7	47.6	40.2	26.2	36.0	36.5	25.9	17.4	15.6	16.3	17.0	19.8
41 to 48 hours.....	17.9	16.5	16.9	13.6	20.1	19.9	17.4	15.6	18.7	13.6	17.4	8.5	9.5	10.1	9.5	6.8
49 to 59 hours.....	9.6	11.0	6.0	6.4	8.4	7.5	5.6	6.1	10.0	10.1	7.6	5.7	13.8	20.1	7.1	9.3
60 hours or more....	16.0	14.4	8.2	6.6	9.3	7.5	6.6	5.2	15.6	11.1	13.8	8.9	40.9	32.5	15.0	12.6
Hours not reported..	2.7	2.8	3.5	3.9	2.6	3.1	3.3	3.8	3.2	2.8	4.1	4.4	2.4	2.2	4.9	3.9
Ages 65 to 74....	100.0	100.0	100.0	100.0	100.0	100.0	100.0	100.0	100.0	100.0	100.0	100.0	100.0	100.0	100.0	100.0
1 to 14 hours......	3.8	5.7	7.6	15.7	2.6	6.0	6.9	15.1	5.7	8.1	10.7	22.9	5.3	4.5	8.2	8.2
15 to 29 hours.....	8.5	11.5	12.6	23.5	6.0	9.7	11.0	22.4	10.8	16.8	14.2	26.0	12.8	11.5	26.2	25.7
30 to 34 hours.....	5.6	7.6	6.3	11.1	4.1	5.0	6.0	9.9	6.2	10.5	6.2	10.8	8.7	9.7	9.4	17.5
35 to 39 hours.....	3.6	3.3	5.6	5.4	3.7	3.3	5.9	5.8	3.0	2.7	4.4	4.6	3.9	3.5	5.0	4.4
40 hours...........	33.0	27.6	28.9	19.0	42.7	37.2	32.5	21.0	26.5	23.4	19.5	14.0	14.4	17.8	11.7	16.9
41 to 48 hours.....	17.4	14.3	16.3	10.2	20.8	19.9	17.5	11.8	17.8	10.6	14.7	7.0	9.0	9.0	7.7	7.1
49 to 59 hours.....	9.2	12.2	6.3	5.3	8.0	6.3	5.9	4.5	9.3	11.8	7.6	5.4	11.9	19.5	8.0	8.7
60 hours or more....	15.5	14.3	10.5	6.3	8.6	8.7	8.7	6.6	16.5	12.6	16.1	4.7	31.4	21.7	16.5	7.1
Hours not reported..	3.4	3.4	5.9	3.5	3.5	3.8	5.6	3.0	4.1	3.5	6.6	4.7	2.6	2.8	7.4	4.4

part-time workers will probably increase. Many employers, especially those in retail trade, are coming to appreciate the fact that they can tap a large reserve of high-quality and experienced workers simply by permitting mothers to work 4 to 6 hours per day instead of 7 or 8. Such an arrangement may become institutionalized in future years.

In regard to the interpreting of figures concerning hours worked per week, and the trends indicated by such figures, three warnings are in order. First, one cannot determine precisely from such statistics what constitutes an average full-time workweek, because of the large number of part-time workers and the possibility that workers may be working overtime temporarily. Second, when interpreting the gradual shortening of the workweek one should realize that the time involved is the time spent on the job, and not the total time spent away from home. Many persons now spend 10 to 20 hours per week commuting from their residence to work and, consequently, have no more free hours in the week to relax, to play with their children, to pursue a hobby, or to practice a sport than the workman of 1890. Third, in times of economic crisis and depression, the statistics for length of the working week tend to reflect the unavailability of full-time work rather than the change in work habits and working arrangements.

WEEKS WORKED PER YEAR: YEAR-ROUND, PART-YEAR, AND INTERMITTENT WORKERS

The number of persons who are at work during any particular week of a year is much smaller than the total number of persons in the population who work at some time during the same year. This is because many workers are employed for less than a full year. Throughout a year new workers continuously enter the labor force, and older workers retire; by definition, such people work less than a full year. In addition, some workers are only seasonally employed and others are sporadically employed--many irregularly employed people are "extras" who are called to meet peak loads or to substitute for regular workers who are ill or on vacation. Many students find summer jobs which they leave when school opens in the fall. As a result of all these situations combined, the Bureau of the Census, when conducting its annual special survey once each year to measure the "work experience" of the civilian population during the preceding year, finds that a very large number of the people have had at least some employment. For example, during 1957 the average of the Census Bureau's monthly estimates of the number of civilian persons employed was 65.0 million persons; but an estimated 77.7 million different persons reported in February, 1958, that they had worked during one week or more during the year 1957. Almost 2/3 of the popula-

tion 14 years old and over (86 percent of males and 47 percent of females) had been gainfully employed at some time during 1957. This is not an unusual example; the annual survey of work experience, conducted since 1950, has shown that part-year work is very common, and that during any one year there is a large turnover in the personnel comprising the labor force. Hence, some most worthwhile insights concerning the labor force can be obtained by classifying the population according to the number of weeks worked during a year. The Bureau of the Census defines anyone who worked during 50-52 weeks as a "year-round" worker, and anyone who worked during 1-49 weeks as a "part-year" worker. The workers may also be classified according to whether they worked primarily at full-time jobs (35 hours or more per week during a majority of the weeks worked), or primarily at part-time jobs (less than 35 hours per week during a majority of the weeks worked). These classifications make it possible to arrive at tabulations of the number of year-round and part-time workers, and the number of weeks worked by full-time and part-time workers. Table 16-22 is a summary of such data for 1956. By grouping the various items of this table it is possible to recognize a category of "nonworkers" (persons who did not work at all during the year) and the following 5 categories of workers:

Type of worker	Percent of persons who worked in 1957
FULL-TIME WORKERS (35 hours or more per week)......................	81.0
Year-round full-time workers—worked primarily at full-time jobs for 50 or more weeks during the year.............	55.1
Part-year full-time workers—worked primarily at full-time jobs for less than 50 weeks but more than 26 weeks........	15.5
Intermittent workers—worked primarily at full-time jobs, but for 26 weeks or less...................................	10.4
PART-TIME WORKERS (less than 35 hours per week)..................	19.0
Year-round part-time workers............	6.4
Part-year part-time workers............	12.6

Table 16-22.—PERSONS WITH WORK EXPERIENCE DURING 1957, BY WEEKS WORKED AND FULL- OR PART-TIME EMPLOYMENT, FOR THE UNITED STATES

(Thousands of persons 14 years of age and over)

Work experience in 1957	1957					
	Both sexes		Male		Female	
	Number	Percent	Number	Percent	Number	Percent
Total civilian population.....	118,788	100.0	56,639	100.0	62,149	100.0
Worked in 1957.........................	77,664	65.4	48,709	86.0	28,955	46.6
Did not work in 1957...................	41,124	34.6	7,930	14.0	33,194	53.4
Total who worked..................	77,664	100.0	48,709	100.0	28,955	100.0
Full time:						
50 to 52 weeks......................	42,818	55.1	32,089	65.9	10,729	37.0
27 to 49 weeks......................	11,981	15.5	7,350	15.1	4,631	16.0
Part time or intermittent..............	22,865	29.4	9,270	19.0	13,595	47.0
1 to 26 weeks at full-time jobs......	8,075	10.4	3,447	7.1	4,628	16.0
At part-time jobs....................	14,790	19.0	5,823	12.0	8,967	31.0
50 to 52 weeks....................	4,989	6.4	2,135	4.4	2,854	9.9
27 to 49 weeks....................	2,872	3.7	1,115	2.3	1,757	6.1
14 to 26 weeks....................	2,693	3.5	1,030	2.1	1,663	5.7
1 to 13 weeks....................	4,236	5.5	1,543	3.2	2,693	9.3

Source: Current Population Reports, Series P-50, No. 86, September, 1958.

Only slightly more than one half (55.1 percent in 1957) of all workers who are employed during any year may be called year-round full-time workers. Yet all but a small fraction of jobs are full-time (full workweek) jobs--only 19.0 percent of the workers were employed primarily at part-time jobs, and only 6.4 percent (1 worker in 16) had the equivalent of permanent part-time work. Thus, most part-year work consists of full-time jobs which are held for periods of time shorter than a year.

Intermittent and irregular workers are primarily very young workers, very old workers, and women. Table 16-23, which provides information about weeks worked during the year 1956 for three selected age groups, shows that it is primarily the young (students and new workers) among whom there are above-average concentrations of workers who work less than 26 weeks, either at full-time or part-time jobs. Also, as workers approach retirement a larger proportion of them become part-year workers. It should be noted that a very high proportion of males 35 to 44 years are year-round, full-time workers (80 percent), and that only 4 to 5 percent are intermittent workers or part-time workers. Another especially in-

teresting facet of Table 16-23 are the statistics for year-round part-time work among women. Between 11 and 15 percent of the women workers of all ages fall in this category. As pointed out above, future years may see a growing tendency to employ mothers and housewives on a permanent but part-time basis. The Census Bureau reports that there has been an "uptrend in part-time work among those who prefer or are available only for that type of employment... Other studies indicate that this increase has been primarily among housewives and students who want only part-time work." [11]

Differentials in hours worked may be found between urban and rural areas and between white and nonwhite workers. In urban areas a higher proportion of the workers are employed year-round at full-time jobs than in rural areas. This is true both for males and females (Table 16-24).

A smaller proportion of the nonwhite population with work experience has year-round full-time employment than of the white population. This pattern prevails for both men and women, and in

[11] Current Population Reports, Series P-50, No. 77, Nov. 1957.

Table 16-23.—PERCENT DISTRIBUTION OF WORK EXPERIENCE IN 1956 BY NUMBER OF WEEKS WORKED AND EXTENT OF EMPLOYMENT, BY AGE AND SEX

Work experience in 1956	Male			Female		
	14 to 17 years	35 to 44 years	60 to 64 years	14 to 17 years	35 to 44 years	60 to 64 years
Total civilian population.........	100.0	100.0	100.0	100.0	100.0	100.0
Worked in 1956.....................	51.4	98.5	87.3	34.8	52.6	38.0
Did not work in 1956...............	48.6	1.5	12.7	65.2	47.4	62.0
Total who worked in 1956......	100.0	100.0	100.0	100.0	100.0	100.0
Worked at full-time jobs..............	26.7	97.7	90.2	30.7	72.1	65.8
13 weeks or less.....................	14.7	0.7	1.7	17.3	6.5	5.9
14 to 26 weeks.......................	4.8	1.8	3.8	7.5	7.5	4.3
27 to 39 weeks.......................	1.9	4.2	4.8	2.7	7.6	7.0
40 to 47 weeks.......................	1.2	7.0	7.3	0.9	5.8	5.7
48 and 49 weeks......................	0.2	4.4	3.4	0.1	2.8	3.1
50 to 52 weeks.......................	3.8	79.6	69.3	2.2	41.9	39.8
Worked at part-time jobs..............	73.3	2.3	9.8	69.3	27.9	34.2
13 weeks or less.....................	25.8	0.2	1.7	33.9	6.6	6.3
14 to 26 weeks.......................	13.9	0.5	1.9	15.6	4.4	5.8
27 to 39 weeks.......................	6.0	0.2	1.4	4.9	3.0	3.2
40 to 47 weeks.......................	3.5	0.3	0.6	1.7	2.0	2.8
48 and 49 weeks......................	1.1	0.1	0.3	1.4	0.8	1.4
50 to 52 weeks.......................	23.0	1.0	3.8	11.8	11.1	14.7

Source: Current Population Reports, Series P-50, No. 77, November, 1957, Table 1.

urban, rural-nonfarm, and rural-farm areas. The following summary from Table 16-24 reports the following differentials:

Sex and residence	Percent of workers who are employed year-round full-time		
	White	Nonwhite	Difference
Total, male.....	68.8	55.4	13.4
Urban............	70.2	57.5	12.7
Rural nonfarm.....	66.8	48.7	18.1
Rural farm........	66.1	53.8	12.3
Female, total...	38.6	29.1	9.5
Urban............	43.7	36.3	7.4
Rural nonfarm.....	33.8	23.2	10.6
Rural farm........	18.7	9.8	8.9

At the time of the 1950 census, information was collected concerning the number of weeks worked during 1949 by persons who were members of the labor force at the time of the census. This puts the consideration of weeks worked on a slightly different basis, because it excludes persons who were not in the labor force at the exact time of the 1950 census but who had worked at some time during the preceding year. Nevertheless, it pro-

vides a useful basis for estimating the work experience of a cross-section of the labor force and and for measuring simultaneously the differentials of sex, color, age, and urban-rural residence. The statistics needed for this comparison are reported in Table 16-25. This table shows that the sex, age, and color differentials described above were all present to a marked degree in 1950 for adult ages 20 to 74 years, and that the urban-rural differential held for females but not for males. Moreover, at these ages the differentials held simultaneously in almost all cases. For example, the color differential is valid for all but a very few combinations of age, sex, and residence within the individual age groups from 20 to 74 years; the sex differential is valid for all combinations of age, color, and residence; and the age differential is valid for all combinations of sex, color, and residence. Thus, part-year workers, and especially intermittent workers, are comprised predominantly of women workers, young workers, nonwhite workers, and rural workers. From Table 16-25 it is also worth noting that in the younger ages (14 to 17 years) part-time work consists pre-

Table 16-24.—PERCENT DISTRIBUTION OF WORK EXPERIENCE IN 1956 BY NUMBER OF WEEKS WORKED AND EXTENT OF EMPLOYMENT, BY SEX, COLOR, AND URBAN-RURAL RESIDENCE

Sex, color, and urban-rural residence	Percent of population that worked in 1956	Percent distribution of those with work experience				
		Total	Worked at full-time jobs			Worked at part-time jobs
			50 weeks or more	27 to 49 weeks	1 to 26 weeks	
MALE						
Total...............................	86.0	100.0	67.5	15.1	6.5	10.9
White................................	86.1	100.0	68.8	14.5	6.4	10.3
Nonwhite.............................	85.2	100.0	55.4	20.6	8.0	16.0
Urban................................	85.2	100.0	68.9	15.6	6.6	8.8
White................................	85.3	100.0	70.2	14.8	6.6	8.4
Nonwhite.............................	84.3	100.0	57.5	22.2	7.1	13.2
Rural nonfarm.......................	86.0	100.0	65.5	15.9	6.9	11.6
White................................	86.3	100.0	66.8	15.6	6.6	11.0
Nonwhite.............................	82.5	100.0	48.7	20.7	10.8	19.7
Rural farm..........................	89.8	100.0	64.5	11.3	5.7	18.5
White................................	89.5	100.0	66.1	10.8	5.3	17.8
Nonwhite.............................	91.8	100.0	53.8	14.9	8.5	22.8
FEMALE						
Total...............................	45.7	100.0	37.3	16.3	16.9	29.4
White................................	44.2	100.0	38.6	16.4	16.8	28.2
Nonwhite.............................	58.7	100.0	29.1	16.2	17.6	37.1
Urban................................	46.4	100.0	42.7	17.2	16.0	24.1
White................................	45.3	100.0	43.7	17.3	16.2	22.9
Nonwhite.............................	56.1	100.0	36.3	16.6	14.8	32.3
Rural nonfarm.......................	40.5	100.0	32.7	16.3	19.5	31.5
White................................	39.1	100.0	33.8	16.6	19.7	29.8
Nonwhite.............................	56.6	100.0	23.2	13.8	17.7	45.3
Rural farm..........................	51.4	100.0	17.0	12.1	17.5	53.3
White................................	48.1	100.0	18.7	11.0	15.3	55.1
Nonwhite.............................	72.5	100.0	9.8	17.1	27.2	45.9

Source: Current Population Reports, Series P-50, No. 77, November 1957, Table 4.

dominantly of participation for less than 26 weeks, while among the oldest workers (65 and over) part-time work is heavily concentrated in the 27 to 49 week categories. Workers give several reasons for part-time work, and the reasons they give vary with sex, color, age, and urban-rural residence (Table 16-26). Among males, unemployment or layoff is the primary reason (40 percent), and illness or disability and going to school are the second and third most important reasons. Among women, taking care of the home accounts for more than one-half of all part-time work. The other reasons given by women are much the same as those given by the men workers, and are ranked in the same way. Only 15 percent of the men and 9 percent of the women worked part time because they had voluntarily taken unpaid absences. These

low proportions prevailed among all sex, color, and residence groups. The miscellaneous category of "other reasons" contains primarily those who have entered the labor force or have retired during the year, or who are working part time in the civilian labor force because of military service.

Among nonwhite workers, part-time work is attributed much more to unemployment or layoffs and to illness or disability than among the white population. A considerably smaller proportion of the nonwhite than of the white workers reported school attendance as the reason for being employed part-time.

Unemployment or layoff is a much more important reason for part-time work among males (while illness or disability is a somewhat less im-

Table 16-25.—WEEKS WORKED IN 1949 BY PERSONS IN THE LABOR FORCE IN 1950, BY COLOR, SEX, AND URBAN-RURAL RESIDENCE, FOR SELECTED AGE GROUPS

Weeks worked in 1949	United States, total				Urban				Rural farm			
	Male		Female		Male		Female		Male		Female	
	White	Non-white	White	Non-white	White	Non-white	White	Non-white	White	Non-white	White	Non-white
All ages, total.........	100.0	100.0	100.0	100.0	100.0	100.0	100.0	100.0	100.0	100.0	100.0	100.0
1 to 13 weeks.........	3.3	4.4	7.5	8.9	3.0	4.0	6.9	8.0	3.8	4.6	9.9	13.0
14 to 26 weeks........	6.8	9.9	10.9	15.3	6.2	9.8	10.4	13.6	6.4	8.5	12.8	25.3
27 to 39 weeks........	7.3	10.3	10.8	12.8	6.8	9.9	9.8	11.8	6.2	10.2	14.7	19.2
40 to 49 weeks........	13.0	17.2	13.2	14.0	13.1	16.1	13.3	14.2	10.7	20.0	11.0	14.8
50 to 52 weeks........	69.6	58.2	57.6	48.9	70.9	60.1	59.6	52.5	72.9	56.7	51.7	27.7
Ages 14 to 17 years.....	100.0	100.0	100.0	100.0	100.0	100.0	100.0	100.0	100.0	100.0	100.0	100.0
1 to 13 weeks.........	26.3	18.4	34.6	27.9	28.2	27.3	33.9	33.8	19.2	12.9	34.9	18.9
14 to 26 weeks........	21.0	22.5	24.9	27.6	21.6	21.1	25.3	20.3	19.0	23.1	23.8	35.9
27 to 39 weeks........	9.1	14.0	9.5	13.4	9.0	9.7	9.7	11.2	8.8	16.8	9.1	17.7
40 to 49 weeks........	7.9	13.5	7.5	9.7	7.9	8.1	7.8	8.2	7.9	15.7	5.9	11.3
50 to 52 weeks........	35.7	31.6	23.4	21.4	33.3	33.7	23.2	26.5	45.1	31.6	26.3	16.2
Ages 20 to 24 years.....	100.0	100.0	100.0	100.0	100.0	100.0	100.0	100.0	100.0	100.0	100.0	100.0
1 to 13 weeks.........	5.8	5.7	7.0	12.2	6.4	6.3	6.6	11.2	4.6	4.9	8.7	16.8
14 to 26 weeks........	11.0	11.9	11.0	18.6	11.4	13.3	10.5	17.4	8.6	8.7	12.2	24.3
27 to 26 weeks........	9.9	11.3	9.5	13.8	9.9	11.7	8.6	12.8	8.6	10.6	13.8	20.8
40 to 49 weeks........	14.4	17.7	12.4	12.4	14.3	16.0	12.2	12.2	13.8	22.5	12.5	15.5
50 to 52 weeks........	58.9	53.3	60.0	42.9	58.0	52.8	62.0	46.4	64.4	53.4	52.8	22.6
Ages 35 to 44 years.....	100.0	100.0	100.0	100.0	100.0	100.0	100.0	100.0	100.0	100.0	100.0	100.0
1 to 13 weeks.........	1.5	2.9	6.4	7.0	1.3	2.8	5.9	6.3	2.1	3.6	7.6	10.6
14 to 26 weeks........	4.5	8.1	9.6	13.6	3.9	8.2	9.2	12.3	4.4	5.6	11.6	22.6
27 to 39 weeks........	6.3	9.6	11.5	12.4	5.6	9.4	10.2	11.6	5.5	8.2	17.9	19.7
40 to 49 weeks........	12.9	17.7	13.9	14.7	12.7	16.8	14.0	14.9	10.8	19.8	12.0	16.0
50 to 52 weeks........	74.7	61.7	58.5	52.2	76.5	62.8	60.8	55.0	77.1	62.8	50.9	31.1
Ages 55 to 64 years.....	100.0	100.0	100.0	100.0	100.0	100.0	100.0	100.0	100.0	100.0	100.0	100.0
1 to 13 weeks.........	2.8	3.7	5.3	6.9	2.3	3.5	4.7	5.8	3.1	3.5	7.2	8.4
14 to 26 weeks........	6.6	9.0	8.7	14.1	6.0	9.1	8.5	11.8	5.6	5.8	9.4	21.5
27 to 26 weeks........	7.2	10.0	11.0	12.3	6.9	9.4	10.1	11.1	5.4	9.2	12.1	18.5
40 to 49 weeks........	13.2	16.8	14.3	14.2	13.7	15.5	14.7	14.8	9.7	19.7	8.9	13.7
50 to 52 weeks........	70.2	60.5	60.8	52.5	71.1	62.5	61.9	56.4	76.2	61.8	62.4	38.0
Ages 65 to 74 years.....	100.0	100.0	100.0	100.0	100.0	100.0	100.0	100.0	100.0	100.0	100.0	100.0
1 to 13 weeks.........	4.3	5.6	5.6	10.5	3.5	5.9	5.0	8.4	4.5	4.0	6.5	13.7
14 to 26 weeks........	8.0	11.8	9.2	15.5	7.2	11.6	9.0	13.4	6.7	9.5	7.3	22.0
27 to 39 weeks........	7.4	9.4	9.5	10.1	7.4	7.4	9.0	9.0	5.4	11.0	10.6	17.6
40 to 49 weeks........	11.9	15.8	13.1	13.4	12.7	12.8	14.0	12.9	8.8	20.2	6.5	14.8
50 to 52 weeks........	68.3	57.3	62.6	50.5	69.2	62.3	63.1	56.2	74.5	55.4	69.2	31.9
Ages 75 years and over..	100.0	100.0	100.0	100.0	100.0	100.0	100.0	...	100.0	100.0	...	...
1 to 13 weeks.........	5.7	7.9	6.2	17.3	4.5	6.8	6.0	...	5.0	7.1	...	...
14 to 26 weeks........	8.8	13.0	7.9	11.8	7.9	12.9	7.7	...	8.0	13.3	...	...
27 to 26 weeks........	6.2	9.8	8.1	9.1	6.0	9.4	7.4	...	6.1	10.0	...	...
40 to 49 weeks........	10.1	14.4	10.4	12.7	11.2	10.1	11.0	...	8.2	18.4	...	...
50 to 52 weeks........	69.1	54.8	67.4	49.1	70.5	60.8	67.9	...	72.6	51.1	...	...

Source: U.S. Census of Population: 1950, Volume IV, Special Reports, Part 1, Chapter A, Employment and Personal Characteristics, 1953, Table 14.

portant reason) in urban and rural-nonfarm areas than in rural-farm areas. Farm women much more often give household responsibilities as their reason for working part time than do urban or rural-nonfarm women. Young workers work part time primarily because of school attendance and

Table 16-26.—REASONS FOR PART-YEAR WORK BY WORKERS WHO WERE EMPLOYED LESS THAN 50 WEEKS IN 1956, BY SEX, COLOR, AND URBAN-RURAL RESIDENCE

Sex, color, and residence	Total	Percent who did not work a full year because of--					
		Unemployment or layoffs	Illness or disability	Unpaid absence from work	Taking care of home	Going to school	Other reasons
MALE							
Total..............	100.0	39.9	21.7	15.3	...	22.8	17.3
White...................	100.0	38.1	21.7	15.4	...	23.8	17.9
Nonwhite...............	100.0	51.0	21.8	14.8	...	16.2	13.7
Urban..............	100.0	41.3	21.8	15.5	...	21.8	16.4
White...................	100.0	38.6	21.9	15.6	...	23.3	17.2
Nonwhite...............	100.0	57.8	21.5	14.7	...	12.3	11.6
Rural nonfarm.......	100.0	41.0	20.3	15.5	...	23.0	18.4
White...................	100.0	40.0	19.9	16.0	...	23.5	18.8
Nonwhite...............	100.0	50.7	23.5	11.2	...	18.8	15.1
Rural farm.........	100.0	30.6	24.3	14.1	...	27.2	19.6
White...................	100.0	31.8	24.9	12.9	...	27.0	19.5
Nonwhite...............	100.0	25.0	21.0	19.7	...	28.3	20.0
FEMALE							
Total..............	100.0	16.8	12.8	8.6	56.7	16.3	5.3
White...................	100.0	16.3	11.9	9.1	56.4	16.9	5.6
Nonwhite...............	100.0	19.8	18.4	6.2	58.2	12.3	4.0
Urban..............	100.0	19.0	14.4	9.9	51.8	15.6	5.8
White...................	100.0	17.8	13.0	10.1	51.9	16.8	6.1
Nonwhite...............	100.0	26.7	23.8	8.3	51.0	7.9	4.0
Rural nonfarm.......	100.0	15.2	11.0	7.3	63.6	14.8	4.6
White...................	100.0	14.9	10.6	7.8	63.6	15.4	4.5
Nonwhite...............	100.0	18.0	13.7	3.6	63.7	10.1	5.2
Rural farm.........	100.0	9.5	8.5	5.2	67.5	21.4	4.3
White...................	100.0	10.9	8.1	5.9	66.5	20.6	4.6
Nonwhite...............	100.0	5.7	9.9	3.3	70.4	23.4	3.3

Source: Current Population Reports, Series P-50, No. 77, November, 1957, Table 9.

unemployment or layoff, while older workers (65 and over) give illness as the primary reason for part-time work, followed by unemployment or layoff (data by age not shown). Voluntary unpaid absence from work, though not given as a reason by a very sizable number in any age group, occurs most frequently among workers 25 to 44 and 45 to 64 years of age.

In general, part-time work among men appears to be largely involuntary, a consequence of employment conditions, while among women it seems to result from a combination of employment conditions and the need to care for a home. There is comparatively little evidence that any particular age, sex, color, or residence group works part time because it prefers part-time work, except for persons who are attending school or working under some other special circumstances.

MULTIPLE JOBHOLDING

About one in every twenty workers holds two or more jobs simultaneously. In its monthly survey for July, 1957, the Bureau of the Census estimated that 3 1/2 million persons (5 percent of the total employed workers) were employed at two or more jobs during the week of the survey. For most categories of workers, this can be accepted as the most adequate measure available of working at two or more jobs at once. [12]

[12]There are some rather large methodological problems in collecting statistics for multiple jobs. Probably there is a very large seasonal variation, and perhaps other cyclical variations also. The data presented here represent a summer month during a year of full employment.

"The group designated as multiple jobholders includes wage and salary workers with more than one employer during the week, as well as persons with both a wage and salary job and either self-employment or unpaid work in a family enterprise. Persons who worked for more than one private family (as a maid, laundress, babysitter, odd job worker, etc.) but held no other job during the survey week were counted as having only one job and excluded from the count of multiple jobholders. Most of the group were persons who had a full-time job during regular working hours and also did some part-time work in the evenings or on weekends. A number, however, were persons who either shifted jobs during the week or who made up a full week's work through a combination of part-time jobs. Finally, the total includes some--mainly school teachers--who had taken temporary summer jobs while on vacation from their regular ones."[13]

The Census Bureau calculates a "rate of multiple jobholding" by dividing the number of workers holding two or more jobs at the same time by the total number of employed persons. This measure makes it possible to learn what kinds of workers are most inclined to be "eager beavers" or "moonlighters" in the labor force.

Workers whose primary work is agricultural had a much higher rate of multiple jobholding than nonagricultural workers.

Industry and class of worker of primary job	Rate of multiple jobholding
Total............................	5.3
Agricultural.....................	11.0
Wage and salary workers..............	12.1
Self-employed workers (farm operators)	10.7
Unpaid family workers................	10.0
Nonagricultural industries..............	4.6
Wage and salary workers..............	4.7
Self-employed workers................	3.7
Unpaid family workers................	3.9

Source: Current Population Reports, Series P-50, No. 80, February, 1958.

Farm operators are only a little less inclined than farm wage workers to be multiple jobholders. The Census Bureau comments, "With the flexibility in hours possible in agriculture, large numbers of farmers were able to earn money in a wage or salary job while operating their farms, probably with the aid of family members. Around 900,000 persons, or about a quarter of all multiple jobholders, were self-employed farmers on either their primary or secondary jobs."[14] By comparison, workers whose primary jobs were in the nonagricultural industries were only about one-half as likely to hold two jobs.

The rate of multiple jobholding varies with sex, age, and color, and marital status.

Characteristic of worker	Rate of multiple jobholding	
	Male	Female
Total....................	6.6	2.5
COLOR		
White........................	6.6	2.3
Nonwhite.....................	7.1	4.1
MARITAL STATUS		
Single.......................	5.9	3.1
Married, spouse present.......	7.0	2.1
Separated, widowed, divorced..	3.5	3.0
AGE		
14 to 17 years...............	9.1	5.5
18 and 19 years..............	6.0	3.6
20 to 24 years...............	5.6	1.8
25 to 34 years...............	7.1	2.2
35 to 44 years...............	7.5	2.4
45 to 54 years...............	6.5	2.4
55 years and over............	4.8	2.4

Source: Op. Cit., Table 2.

Among males the rate is about 2 1/2 times as high as among females. Nonwhite workers are much more inclined than white workers to hold two jobs at the same time. (This is especially true for nonwhite women workers.) Married men living with their wives have a much higher rate of multiple jobholding than single, separated, widowed, or divorced men, but married women have lower rates than single, separated, widowed, or divorced

[13]Current Population Reports, Series P-50, No. 80, Feb. 1958.

[14]Op. cit.

women. Multiple jobholding is at its peak in adolescence, is lower during the 20's, and then becomes high again between ages 35 and 44. Thereafter, among males, it declines with increasing
age, but among women it remains on a plateau
during the ages after 35. The high rate of multiple
jobholding reported for teenagers probably does
not represent multiple jobholding as much as it
reflects a tendency on the part of youngsters to
shift from one temporary job to another during the
summer vacation.

From the statistics available, it is not clear just
how much of multiple jobholding is genuine "moonlighting" (doing extra work at night in addition to a
regular daytime job), how much is the combining
of two or more part-time jobs in order to fill out
a full workweek, and how much is due to normal
labor turnover--workers ending one job and starting another. Nor are statistics available as yet
concerning the number of hours per week worked
by the multiple-jobholders.

Despite the high rates of multiple jobholding
among agricultural workers, by far the greater
share (45 percent) of all multiple jobholders are
industrial workers, both in the primary and secondary jobs. (Agricultural workers comprise
about 25 percent of all multiple jobholders.) Although they have a lower rate of multiple jobholding, the number of nonagricultural workers is so
much greater than the number of agricultural
workers that the typical multiple jobholder is a
nonagricultural worker. Another very large group
of multiple jobholders (about 17 percent) combine
nonagricultural wage and salary work with some
form of nonfarm self-employment.

THE LENGTH OF WORKING LIFE

Once a male workman enters the labor force, he
tends to remain there continuously until the time
of his permanent retirement or his withdrawal because of incurable illness or disability. The
number of years that the average workman spends
in the labor force once he has entered it is called
his "length of working life." During the 19th century and before, the average life expectancy was

short, and most men worked until they died. However, during the past half-century an unprecedentedly large proportion of people have been surviving infancy to pass into the working years, and
have also been surviving the working years to pass
into the ages at which it is customary to be retired. The causes of this change, of course, are
the great improvements that have taken place in
medicine, public health protection, and the level of
living. During this same period, the practice has
developed of requiring workmen to retire when
they attain the age of 65 or thereabouts, if they do
not do so voluntarily. Retirement benefits such as
insurance and Social Security have assured more
and more workers of a minimum income in their
old age. These two developments are having an
impact in two very important ways upon American
breadwinners and ex-breadwinners.

First, the economy has benefited because each
person born, and each person reared to adulthood,
has been able to contribute more years of productive work. The infectious diseases used to carry
away many thousands of children before they could
enter the labor force and repay society for the
costs of bearing, feeding, clothing, and educating
them. Moreover, even after a workman had survived long enough to enter the labor force, his life
was often snuffed out after only a very short span
of work. The conquest of the diseases which were
responsible for this excessive mortality during the
years of early adulthood meant that a much higher
proportion of those who entered the labor force
survived to retire at age 65. Society has benefited
greatly from these advances, because the "wastage" involved in rearing and training persons who
do not in turn contribute to the nation's economy
has been greatly reduced. Also, the working years
which are gained when a workingman's life is
saved and he is returned to his job are, in large
part, experienced working years, in which skills
and "know how" which have been accumulated over
a period of apprenticeship and working can continue to produce and to be available for the training of younger workers. This development is not
without its problems, however. Many industries
like to employ only younger men, and would prefer

to have no workmen older than 45 or 50 years of age. The greatly increased number and proportion of older workmen mean that employment must be found for those unskilled and semi-skilled men who have passed their 40th birthday and who have lost their jobs. Many companies do not like to hire older persons because of the effect of such workers on the program of retirement pensions, and also because they prefer younger men with more strength and better education.

The second major result of the increased life span and the practice of withdrawing from the labor force at a fixed age is that retirement has become a status which most workmen normally expect to achieve.

"...many older workers now withdraw from the labor force before they die. Fifty years ago death and disability accounted for practically all labor force separations. Only a small proportion of the population survived to the age which is now considered conventional for retirement. Moreover, in an agrarian economy, where self-employment predominated, those who reached an older age were often in a position to continue to to do some work. Today, most important among the reasons for men 55 and over leaving the labor force are: age restrictions in hiring practices, compulsory retirement ages in private pension plans, widespread availability of social security for older persons, and inability to go on working (which tends to rise with age)."[15]

A more precise measurement of these two changes--the increasing length of working life and the increasing length of retirement--can be made by constructing a "table of working life," which is an elaboration and modification of the standard life tables. Whereas the standard life table summarizes the effect that current mortality rates at each age would have upon a hypothetical population of 100,000 newborn infants exposed throughout their lives to these rates, the tables of working life summarize the joint effect that current rates

at each age of mortality, of entering the labor force, and of withdrawal from the labor force would have upon a hypothetical population of 100,000 newborn infants exposed throughout their lives to these rates. In other words, the tables of working life follow a cohort of 100,000 persons through successive ages, showing at each age the number that would be alive and also in the labor force. By counting up the total number of person-years of labor force participation yet to be experienced by the group as a whole, as it reaches each age, and dividing by the total number of persons alive at that age, it is possible to compute an "average length of working life." Such a calculation can be made not only for the infant at birth, but at any age. Such tables were reported by Seymour Wolfbein for the labor force of 1940, and have since become a standard procedure for analyzing work experience in terms of the life-span of the worker.[16] For the purposes of the present analysis the most important columns of this table are the three right-hand columns. These tables show, for example, that the total life expectancy of a 20 year old workman in 1940 and in 1950 was as follows:

Year	Total life expectancy	Work life expectancy	Retirement expectancy
1940	46.8	41.3	5.5
1950	48.9	43.2	5.7

In 1950, such a man could expect to live to about age 69, and to spend 43 years working and almost 6 years in retirement before his death.

Garfinkle reports computations of working life expectancy for the year 1900, and estimates, or projects, concerning working life expectancies to the year 2000.[17] The table in which these compu-

---

[15] Stuart Garfinkle, "Changes in Working Life of Men, 1900 to 2000," Monthly Labor Review, March, 1955, p. 299.

[16] Length of Working Life for Men, Bulletin No. 1001, U. S. Bureau of Labor Statistics, August, 1950.

[17] Ibid. His estimates for the year 2000 assume a continuation of labor force participation rates as they prevailed in the spring of 1954, except for a drop of 10 percentage points among men 65 and over; they assume continuation of mortality trends which have prevailed from 1920 to 1950.

Table 16-27.—TABLE OF WORKING LIFE, MALES; 1940 AND 1950

Age	Number living of 100,000 born alive			Accessions to the labor force per 1,000 in population	Separations from the labor force (per 1,000 in labor force)			Average number of remaining years of--		
	In population	In labor force			Due to all causes	Due to death	Due to retirement	Life	Labor force participation	Retirement
		Number	Percent of population							
	(Within age interval)			(Between successive age intervals)				(At beginning of age interval)		
1940										
10 to 14 years	461,865	6,196	(1)	...	8.2	8.2	...	...	...	...
15 to 19 years	458,100	205,229	44.8	431.0	12.0	12.0	...	51.3	45.8	5.5
20 to 24 years	452,589	405,067	89.5	441.6	14.9	14.9	...	46.8	41.3	5.5
25 to 29 years	445,845	429,795	96.4	68.0	17.6	17.6	...	42.4	36.8	5.6
30 to 34 years	438,014	425,750	97.2	7.9	28.0	21.9	6.1	38.0	32.3	5.7
35 to 39 years	428,373	413,808	96.6	...	37.8	29.7	8.1	33.7	28.0	5.7
40 to 44 years	415,611	398,155	95.8	...	53.3	42.1	11.2	29.6	23.8	5.8
45 to 49 years	398,028	376,933	94.7	...	80.2	60.8	19.4	25.5	19.8	5.7
50 to 54 years	373,582	346,684	92.8	...	117.8	85.9	31.9	21.8	16.0	5.8
55 to 59 years	340,970	305,850	89.7	...	211.6	115.7	95.9	18.3	12.4	5.9
60 to 64 years	299,545	241,134	80.5	...	376.7	148.9	227.8	15.1	9.2	5.9
65 to 69 years	248,456	150,316	60.5	...	495.5	191.8	303.7	12.2	6.8	5.4
70 to 74 years	189,583	75,833	40.0	...	576.4	262.4	314.0	9.6	5.6	4.0
75 years-over	232,278	44,830	19.3	...	...	...	...	...	...	...
1950										
10 to 14 years	477,806	21,000	(1)	...	5.3	5.3	...	...	...	...
15 to 19 years	475,282	251,899	53.0	483.5	8.5	8.5	...	53.6	47.9	5.7
20 to 24 years	471,255	418,003	88.7	354.0	9.8	9.8	...	48.9	43.2	5.7
25 to 29 years	466,652	448,453	96.1	73.3	10.7	10.7	...	44.4	38.6	5.8
30 to 34 years	461,671	446,436	96.7	6.0	15.1	14.1	1.0	39.8	34.0	5.8
35 to 39 years	455,169	439,693	96.6	...	23.3	21.3	2.0	35.2	29.3	5.9
40 to 44 years	445,488	429,450	96.4	...	42.6	33.4	9.2	30.8	24.9	5.9
45 to 49 years	430,539	411,165	95.5	...	70.9	51.5	19.4	26.6	20.6	6.0
50 to 54 years	408,140	382,019	93.6	...	116.5	77.4	38.9	22.6	16.6	6.0
55 to 59 years	375,956	337,608	89.8	...	195.5	109.7	85.8	19.0	13.0	6.0
60 to 64 years	332,858	271,612	81.6	...	337.2	142.3	194.9	15.7	9.7	6.0
65 to 69 years	279,537	180,022	64.4	...	485.9	180.1	305.8	12.7	7.2	5.5
70 to 74 years	217,261	92,553	42.6	...	558.6	247.5	311.1	10.1	5.9	4.2
75 years-over	287,742	61,289	21.3	...	...	...	...	...	...	...

(1) Only persons 14 years old and over are enumerated in the labor force.

Source: Monthly Labor Review. March, 1955, Table 2, p.300.

tations are reported (Table 16-28) shows that in 1900 a labor force participant who was 20 years of age could expect to live another 32 years, of which only 3 would be spent in retirement. Thus, during the past half-century the length of working life has increased by about 4 years (increased by 10 percent), and the length of retirement has increased by almost 3 years (doubled). Looking ahead to the next half-century, Garfinkle anticipates that the working life expectancy of 20-year olds will increase to 45 years, and that an additional 3 years will be added to retirement ex-

pectancy. Thus, in the year 2000 the average length of retirement will be about 3 times what it was in 1900. Great caution must be used in forecasting a continued lengthening of the working life. The emphasis on college education may ultimately cause the average age of entrance into the labor force to become considerably older than at present. Also, future years may see a considerable increase in the number of workers who retire before age 65. If the latter possibility were to materialize, the average number of years spent in retirement could rise even more.

Table 16-28.—AVERAGE LIFE AND WORK-LIFE EXPECTANCY FOR MEN: 1900 TO 2000

| Year | At birth | | | At age 20 | | |
| | Average number of remaining years of-- | | | Average number of remaining years of-- | | |
	Life	Working life	Outside labor force	Life	Working life	Retirement
1900..............................	48.2	32.1	16.1	42.2	39.4	2.8
1940..............................	61.2	38.3	22.9	46.8	41.3	5.5
1950..............................	65.5	41.9	23.6	48.9	43.2	5.7
1955..............................	66.5	42.0	24.5	49.5	43.0	6.5
2000..............................	73.2	45.1	28.1	53.8	45.1	8.7
Change:						
1900-1950..........................	17.3	9.8	7.5	6.7	3.8	2.9
1950-2000..........................	7.7	3.2	4.5	4.9	1.9	3.0

Source: Stuart Garfinkle, "Changes in Working Life of Men, 1900-2000," Monthly Labor Review, March, 1955, Table 1, p. 299.

Because both the length of working life and the length of retirement are increasing, the proportion of the total life span that is "unproductive" (years lived from birth to entrance into the labor force plus years lived in retirement after withdrawal from the labor force) has not changed a great deal. Both in 1900 and in 1950 about 35 percent of the total life span of the male was spent outside the working force. In 1950, however, a much larger proportion of the non-working years consisted of old-age retirement financed from savings and pensions, and a much smaller proportion consisted of childhood dependency financed from the current income of another worker.

It is not possible to construct for women a table concerning length of working life like the one reported for men in Table 16-27. It cannot be assumed that women remain in the labor force continuously once they have entered, nor that they stay out of the labor force forever when they withdraw. Both of these assumptions, which are generally valid for men, must be made before a table can be constructed concerning length of working life remaining to working persons. The fact that a great many women withdraw from the labor force when they marry or when they have their first child, and then re-enter it when their children are partially grown, makes these assumptions invalid for female workers. A substitute measure, called "work years remaining," has been devised by Garfinkle, and is reported in Table 16-29. It is a measure of the average years of working life re-

maining at each age to all women (not just to those in the labor force). This measure is an average of the work experience of all women--those who remain in the labor force, those who leave and re-enter it one or several times, and those who never work. Hence, the measure can in no way be used to estimate the number of years of work remaining to women currently employed. Nevertheless, this measure is invaluable as a device for showing the contribution that women workers make to the economy. Under the conditions which prevailed in 1950, the average girl aged 15 may be expected to spend almost 16 years (more than one-third of her life span from 15 to 65) in the labor force before she dies. This is 3 years more than could have been expected in 1940, and the biggest gain has been made among married women. The following statistics, reported by Wolfbein, indicate that this working-life expectancy is more than 2 1/2 times as long as that which prevailed for women in 1900, and also that the working-life expectancy of women has increased by 20 percent in the 5 years from 1950 to 1955.

Year	Life expectancy	Remaining work years expectancy	Years outside labor force
1900	50.7	6.3	44.4
1940	65.9	12.1	53.8
1950	71.0	15.2	55.8
1955	72.9	18.2	54.7

Source: Seymour Wolfbein, "The Length of Working Life," paper read at Fourth International Gerontological Conference, Merano, Italy, July, 1957.

Table 16-29.—AVERAGE REMAINING LIFETIME FOR ALL WOMEN AND AVERAGE NUMBER OF YEARS OF WORK REMAINING, AT SPECIFIED AGES, BY MARITAL STATUS: 1950 AND 1940

| Age | 1950 | | | | | Change, 1940-1950 | | | | |
| | Average remaining lifetime, all women | Average number of years of work remaining | | | | Average remaining lifetime, all women | Average number of years of work remaining | | | |
		All women	Single women	Married, husband present	Widowed, separated, divorced		All women	Single women	Married, husband present	Widowed, separated, divorced
15..............	58.5	15.8	16.0	13.2	25.6	3.5	2.9	3.0	4.4	2.5
20.............	53.7	14.5	15.1	12.2	24.1	3.3	2.6	1.1	3.7	2.1
25.............	49.0	12.4	18.3	10.9	21.7	3.1	2.7	3.1	3.4	2.3
30.............	44.3	10.9	21.6	9.7	18.9	2.9	2.8	5.7	3.2	2.5
35.............	39.6	9.4	20.6	8.4	15.9	2.6	2.8	5.3	3.0	2.6
40.............	35.1	7.8	17.6	7.0	12.8	2.4	2.5	4.1	2.6	2.5
45.............	30.6	6.1	14.1	5.4	9.7	2.1	1.9	2.9	1.9	2.2
50.............	26.4	4.5	10.8	4.0	7.0	2.0	1.4	2.2	1.4	1.8
55.............	22.3	3.2	7.8	2.8	4.6	1.8	1.0	1.5	0.9	1.3
60.............	18.5	2.0	5.1	1.8	2.6	1.6	0.6	1.1	0.6	0.8

Source: Stuart H. Garfinkle, "Tables of Working Life for Women, 1950," Monthly Labor Review, October, 1956, Table 12.

LABOR MOBILITY

The composition of the labor force, far from being static, is in a continuous process of turnover. Labor force dynamics is a very large subject, and can be summarized here only very briefly. There are several distinct types of labor mobility. The following classification identifies the principal ones:

A. Accession to the labor force[18]--becoming a labor force participant. When possible, it is desirable to distinguish between first entry and re-entry.

B. Separation from the labor force[19]--ceasing to be a labor force participant.

C. Inter-establishment mobility (or "job mobility")--a change of employer.

1. Employer mobility--a change of employer involving movement only within the same industry.

2. Industry mobility--a change of employer involving movement from one industry to another.

D. Intra-establishment mobility--a change of job without a change of employer, due to promotion, transfer, or demotion within the same establishment.

E. Occupational mobility--a change in occupation. This may involve either inter-establishment mobility or intra-establishment mobility.

A. Accession to the labor force. Direct statistics concerning the number of persons who join the labor force each year are not available, but accession rates can be estimated from the changes which take place in labor force participation with age, and are one by-product of the table of working life. Most accession, especially for men, occurs before age 30. Table 16-27 reports the accession rates of men for 1940 and 1950. In general, about 48 percent of men enter the labor force between the ages of 15 and 19, an additional 35 percent between 20 and 24, and almost all of the remainder between 25 and 29 years of age. If a man has not entered the labor force by the time he is 35, the probabilities are very high that he never will be a labor force participant. Garfinkle reports 1950 accession rates for women (subdivided into 3 cate-

---

[18]Some experts would not call these movements "labor mobility,' but would restrict the discussion of mobility to change of status within the labor force. Certainly "labor mobility rates" usually exclude accession and separation.

[19]Ibid.

gories, according to factors that are related to entrance) as follows:

Estimated annual accessions to the female labor force by selected demographic factors: 1950 (per 1,000 in the stationary female population)

Age	Total accessions per thousands	Accessions related to:		
		Age	Children reaching school age	Loss of husband
14 to 19 years.	86.3	85.1	0.5	0.7
20 to 24 years.	23.1	16.9	4.8	1.4
25 to 29 years.	10.1	3.5	6.0	0.6
30 to 34 years.	9.3	0.4	7.7	1.2
35 to 39 years.	9.4	0.2	7.3	1.9
40 to 44 years.	7.5	...	4.9	2.6
45 to 49 years.	4.7	...	1.8	2.9
50 to 54 years.	3.0	...	...	3.0
55 to 59 years.	3.0	...	...	3.0

Source: Julius Garfinkle, "Tables of Working Life for Women," Bulletin No. 1204, U.S. Department of Labor, 1956, Table 8.

Almost three-fourths of the women who ever enter the labor force do so before they reach the age of 20; after that age the rate of entry is much lower. Unlike males, however, they trickle in at all ages, up to age 60. When women enter between the ages of 30 and 45, it is usually because their children have reached school age; most of these women are re-entering the labor force. Entrance after age 45 is related primarily to widowhood.

B. Separations from the labor force. For men, the rates of separation from the labor force in 1950 are presented in Table 16-27, which reports separately the rates of separation which are due to death and those which are due to retirement. Note that for each age up to age 60 to 64 the rate for separation due to death is greater than the rate due to retirement; thereafter, retirement is the larger source of attrition. Both rates are comparatively small prior to age 45; after age 55 they both increase rapidly.

Estimated rates of separation from the female labor force have been prepared by Garfinkle. His estimates recognize four reasons for separation: marriage, childbirth, death, and other (illness, improved earning capacity of husband, and permanent retirement).

Estimated annual separation from the female labor force by selected demographic factors, 1950 (per 1,000 in the stationary female labor force)

Age	Total separation	Separation related to:			
		Marriage	Childbirth	Death	Retirement and other
14 to 19 years..	58.3	13.1	36.4	0.8	8.0
20 to 24 years..	107.6	28.6	71.4	1.0	6.4
25 to 29 years..	62.3	12.1	43.6	1.2	5.4
30 to 34 years..	18.1	...	12.7	1.7	3.7
35 to 39 years..	9.2	...	...	2.4	6.9
40 to 44 years..	25.5	...	...	3.5	21.9
45 to 49 years..	37.9	...	...	5.3	32.6
50 to 54 years..	49.6	...	...	7.7	42.0
55 to 59 years..	63.3	...	...	11.4	51.9

Source: Julius Garfinkle, "Tables of Working Life for Women," Bulletin No. 1204, U.S. Department of Labor, 1956, Table 9.

At all ages below 30, the rate of separation for women is high, illustrating in another way that a large number of women enter the labor force for only a brief interval immediately after they leave school, or before, and then withdraw. There is a very high rate of separation for women at ages 20 to 24, which is associated with marriage and childbirth. Among women workers, the lowest rates of separation are found at ages 35 to 39. After age 45 the rates of separation increase rapidly, the increase being due primarily to the "other" factors rather than to death. Among women, the death rates are so low at most ages below 60 that death is a comparatively minor reason of separation from the labor force. Because so many of them are secondary earners, relatively few women have to remain in the labor force until age 65 in order to qualify for a pension. For this reason they tend to "retire" at a younger age than men, as is demonstrated by the comparatively high rates of separation for "other" reasons between ages 40 to 59 years.

C. Inter-establishment mobility (job mobility). The Bureau of the Census collected information concerning workers who changed jobs during the year 1955. Of 75.3 million persons who worked at some time during 1955, 8 1/2 million workers (11 percent) shifted jobs at least once during the year.[20] The kinds of shifts that were made, and the proportion of all shifts that were of each type are indicated by the following summary:

Pattern of job shift	Percent distribution		
	Total job shifts	Job shifts by men	Job shifts by women
Total.............	100.0	100.0	100.0
Same occupation and industry...............	27.5	26.7	29.6
Same occupation, different industry.......	19.6	19.1	20.8
Same industry, different occupation.....	8.1	7.4	10.0
Different occupation and industry.........	44.8	46.7	39.7

The above statistics are not precise, because they include 3 1/2 million workers who were holding two or more jobs simultaneously. Nevertheless, they are adequate to demonstrate that almost one-half of all labor mobility involves a complete shift of employment as regards both occupation and industry. This phenomenon, which has been observed in several other studies of labor mobility, is especially prevalent among young workers. Such workers often "shop around" to find work that is satisfying, and many leave the part-time work which they did while attending school in order to find full-time permanent jobs. In only about a quarter of all job shifts do workers change from one firm to another within the same industry and continue to work at the same occupation. Workers seem to be more industry-mobile than occupation-mobile; only about 8 percent of the mobile workers remained in the same industry after they changed occupation, although more than double this proportion remained in the same occupation after they changed industry. In commenting on its survey the Census Bureau reported:

"The survey results clearly show that job mobility varies considerably among different groups in the population.... Men tend to change jobs more often than women. Overall, about 18 percent of the men but only 11 percent of the women had more than one job in 1955.... Job mobility is much greater for younger workers than for those who are advanced in years. Over one-fourth of the workers between 18 and 24 years old had more than one job in 1955 as compared with about one-seventh of those between 35 and 54 years of age.... About one-fifth of the farmers as compared with only one-tenth of the nonfarm self-employed had more than one job during the year. The larger proportion for farmers reflects their tendency to take nonfarm jobs part of the year in addition to operating their farms.

"The main reason persons gave for shifting jobs was to improve their status, either by getting a more interesting or higher paying job or to escape certain unpleasant circumstances on their previous job. About two-fifths of all job shifts were attributable to this factor. Economic causes, such as layoffs due to lack of work, business failure, etc., accounted for one-fifth to one-quarter of the job shifts and an additional one-fifth gave termination of a temporary job as the reason for leaving."[21]

Additional information on inter-establishment mobility, and the nature of this mobility, is provided by the statistics of monthly labor turnover in manufacturing industries, published by the Bureau of Labor Statistics. The following summary of the annual average monthly turnover, by reason for turnover, shows that each month about 3.5 workers in manufacturing industries change employers (either to another manufacturing industry or to a nonmanufacturing industry). Of course, much of this mobility is caused by the repeated moves of a core of highly mobile workers.

Year	Accession	Separation:				
		Total	Quit	Discharge	Layoff	Misc. (incl. military)
1956..	3.4	3.5	1.6	0.3	1.5	0.2
1950..	4.4	3.5	1.9	0.3	1.1	0.2
1945..	6.3	8.3	5.1	0.6	2.3	0.3

---

[20] U. S. Bureau of the Census, Current Population Reports, "Job Mobility of Workers in 1955," Series P-50, No. 70, Feb. 1957.

[21] Ibid.

These accessions and separations are based upon changes in the payrolls of a sample of manufacturing firms who report changes in personnel. Voluntary quits comprise almost one-half of all separations, and are the largest single source of labor mobility. Involuntary layoffs are almost as numerous as quits, however. Less than 10 percent of all labor turnover is caused by firing of workers.

The most detailed information about labor mobility yet to become available was furnished by a special survey of six cities--Chicago, Los Angeles, New Haven, Philadelphia, St. Paul, and San Francisco--sponsored by the Social Science Research Council.[22] Work histories covering a ten-year period were collected by the Bureau of the Census according to specifications designed by an inter-university research committee. The findings confirm, at every point, the 1955 study of one-year mobility summarized above.[23] In addition, this study found that only 33 percent of the men and 35 percent of the women in the six cities had had only one job (no mobility) during the ten years 1940-49. About 35 percent of the workers had had 3 jobs or more.[24]

D. Intra-establishment mobility. Employers and labor unions are placing more and more emphasis upon encouraging workers to remain with the same employer and to make their job advances within one particular firm. Seniority rights, equity in the company, pension schemes, longer vacations, automatic pay raises for tenure, and other policies all tend to encourage the worker to re-

main with a particular firm. As yet, however, only scanty data are available concerning the amount, types, and rates of intra-establishment mobility. This area of labor mobility is in great need of further extensive research.

E. Occupational mobility. This topic will be discussed in the next chapter, which deals with occupations.

SEASONAL VARIATIONS IN THE LABOR FORCE, EMPLOYMENT, AND UNEMPLOYMENT

The Bureau of the Census has recently developed improved methods for measuring seasonal variations in labor force data. The Census Bureau's own clear and concise interpretation of these season variations is quoted in full:

"Employment and unemployment--like most other measures of economic activity--are subject to appreciable seasonal variations, that is, fluctuations that recur fairly regularly at certain times of the year.

"....The seasonal variations for the two largest aggregates for which factors are provided--civilian labor force and total employment--are quite similar, as might be expected since these categories are almost co-extensive in periods of high employment. Both are at a low point in the first quarter of the year, rising slowly with the usual spring expansion in agriculture, construction, and other outdoor work (table A). A sharp upturn occurs in May and again in June, with the large-scale entry of students into the summer labor market, with both series finally reaching a peak in July. The downturn thereafter results from the reversal of these earlier developments, first the withdrawal of students from the labor force at the start of the school term in September and later the curtailment in outdoor activities. The range from seasonal low to high of around 5 to 6 percent in these two series represents the equivalent of 3 1/2 to 4 million workers.

"As already indicated, fluctuations in agricultural employment are one of the principal factors in the seasonal pattern for the labor force as a whole. From a low point in the winter period

[22] Gladys L. Palmer, Labor Mobility in Six Cities, Social Science Research Council, 1954.

[23] For example, the job changes that occurred over a 10-year period had the following pattern of percent distribution:

Total..................... 100
Same occupation and industry 18
Same occupation, different industry........ 17
Same industry, different occupation........ 5
Different occupation or industry........... 55
Source: Ibid., p. 78.

[24] Ibid., p. 49.

Table 16-30.—SEASONAL ADJUSTMENT FACTORS FOR THE LABOR FORCE AND ITS MAJOR COMPONENTS
TO BE USED FOR 1957 AND 1958

(Applicable to figures based on new definitions)

Month	Civilian labor force	Employment			Unemployment	
		Total	Agri-culture	Nonagri-cultural industries	Total	Rate[1]
January...............................	97.6	96.8	80.7	98.7	114.3	116.9
February..............................	97.6	96.9	81.6	98.8	113.2	115.7
March.................................	98.2	97.7	85.8	99.1	108.3	110.2
April.................................	98.7	98.7	93.5	99.3	99.0	100.3
May...................................	100.1	100.2	106.1	99.5	98.5	98.6
June..................................	102.6	102.0	118.7	100.1	116.0	113.4
July..................................	103.0	102.9	117.2	100.9	105.5	102.6
August................................	101.8	102.4	110.8	101.4	89.6	88.1
September.............................	100.5	101.3	111.6	100.3	83.1	82.5
October...............................	100.8	101.8	112.7	100.6	78.5	77.8
November..............................	100.1	100.3	97.0	100.7	95.5	95.0
December..............................	99.3	99.3	84.4	100.9	98.6	99.0

[1]Unemployment as percent of civilian labor force.

Source: Current Population Reports, Series P-50, No. 82, 1958.

(December through February), the farm work force rises more or less steadily to a peak in June. There is a wide range of about 40 percentage points between the factors for these months. The retreat from the early summer peak is irregular. There is a temporary lull in agricultural employment in midsummer, between the period when cultivation of major crops has been completed and the start of fall harvesting. A secondary peak occurs during the peak harvest period in September and October--before the cold-weather cutback sets in.

"Fluctuations in nonagricultural employment are relatively small compared with those in agriculture. The range from the low point--which also occurs in the first quarter--to the peak in August is only about 2 1/2 percentage points. After the withdrawal of students in September, a secondary peak is reached in the final months of the year with the expansion in retail trade and related activities for the Christmas holidays.

"The seasonal pattern in unemployment is the most irregular of all. Joblessness is high in the first quarter, when economic activity in general and outdoor work in particular are in their slack period. A gradual improvement occurs up through May, but unemployment is boosted again in June as a result of jobseeking among students and re-

cent graduates. The level gradually subsides again until the annual low point is reached in October, after which the wintertime rise gets under way. The pattern is, of course, similar for the unemployment rate. However, the rate reaches a somewhat higher peak in the first quarter, since the high point in unemployment coincides with the seasonal low in the labor force."

CONCLUSION

The labor force is such a large and multi-sided topic that it has been possible to present here only the most basic and fundamental facts concerning long-range trends and current conditions. Moreover, since the labor force situation tends to change rapidly, new developments which have not been mentioned here will continue to emerge. The reader is encouraged to study reports for the last 12-month period in the Census Bureau's Labor Force P-50 and P-57 series, and to examine the annual summary of the labor force and other labor data to be found in the Monthly Labor Review and the Statistical Abstract of the United States. By so doing, he can up-date the materials presented in this chapter and can also gain knowledge of many details that could not be included here for lack of space.

Chapter 17

OCCUPATIONAL COMPOSITION AND OCCUPATIONAL TRENDS

Labor force concepts separate the economically active members of the population from the inactive members, and determine whether or not the economically active are employed. These concepts do not, however, designate the kinds of jobs members of the labor force perform or the types of firms for which they work. The gathering of this information requires two additional bodies of statistics, data concerning occupation and industry. The present chapter discusses the occupational composition of the population. The chapter which follows deals with industrial composition.

Census enumerators are instructed to record the exact kind of work performed by employed persons, or (if the person is unemployed) the kind of work performed on the last job. Specially trained census clerks, supervised by occupational statisticians, classify and code these responses in terms of meaningful occupational groups. The system of occupational classification now in use is a product of many years of experimentation, research, and critical review of the results yielded by preceding classifications. Foremost among the statisticians responsible for the present relatively high quality and great usefulness of the occupational statistics was Dr. Alba M. Edwards. He compiled long lists of occupational names with the corresponding job descriptions, in order to designate meaningful common elements on the basis of which occupational classifications could be established. During this painstaking labor Dr. Edwards did not lose sight of the immense sociological significance of the population's occupational characteristics. His own comment on this point is so

well expressed that it is better quoted than paraphrased.

"The most nearly dominant single influence in a man's life is probably his occupation. More than anything else, perhaps, a man's occupation determines his course and his contribution in life. And when life's span is ended, quite likely there is no other single set of facts that will tell so well the kind of man he was and the part he played in life as will a detailed and chronological statement of the occupation, or occupations, he pursued. Indeed, there is no other single characteristic that tells so much about a man and his status--social, intellectual, and economic--as does his occupation. A man's occupation not only tells, for each workday, what he does during one-half of his waking hours, but it indicates, with some degree of accuracy, his manner of life during the other half--the kind of associates he will have, the kind of clothes he will wear, the kind of house he will live in, and even, to some extent, the kind of food he will eat. And, usually, it indicates, in some degree, the cultural level of his family.

---

*The author is indebted to Mr. David L. Kaplan of the Bureau of the Census for advise and assistance in assembling the materials for this chapter and in handling problems of intercensal comparability in the data.

**A tabulation presenting statistics for occupational composition, by sex, for urban, rural-nonfarm, and rural-farm areas of each geographic division for both 1950 and 1940 is contained in the statistical appendix.

"In similar manner there probably is no single set of closely related facts that tell so much about a nation as do detailed statistics of the occupations of its workers. The occupations of a people influence directly their lives, their customs, their institutions--indeed, their very numbers. In fact, the social and the economic status of a people is largely determined by the social and economic status of its gainful workers. And, were the figures available, the social and industrial history of a people might be traced more accurately through detailed statistics of the occupations of its gainful workers than through records of its wars, its territorial conquests, and its political struggles.

"With present-day interest in social problems and in their statistical measurement, it has become quite evident that statistics which show the actual life conditions of 40 percent of the population for one-third of each workday, and which give at least a rough index of their life conditions for the balance of the time--as well as giving a rough index of the life conditions of those dependent upon them--are far too important to be neglected. "[1]

In answer to the question, "What kind of work does he do?" census enumerators receive a great multitude of different responses concerning occupation. It has been estimated that, at the present time, there may be as many as 25,000 different occupations in a modern industrialized nation. It would be both impossible and undesirable to tabulate statistics for each item in such a long list. Since many occupations are very similar to each other, the solution to this multiplicity is to develop a classification scheme which groups similar occupations into one category. In the United States, occupational data are gathered by several different federal agencies, as well as by private organizations; consequently, classification must be standardized if comparability is to be achieved. In fact,

the need for comparability of occupational classifications is international in scope, and has led to the setting up of major programs aimed at achieving an international classification scheme. Within the Federal Government a Joint Committee on Occupational Classification (sponsored by the Bureau of the Budget and the American Statistical Association) has functioned to bring about a standard system for classifying occupations. The occupational categories employed by the Bureau of the Census were developed in consultation with this committee and other government and private agencies. In general, this system is able to present statistics on three different levels of detail:

a. Detailed occupational classification--469 highly specific categories of occupations, or of subgroupings of occupations, according to industry.

b. Intermediate occupational classification-- Combinations of the categories of the detailed occupational classification, in which similar occupations are grouped and in which detailed occupations that contain only a few workers are merged with larger categories which they resemble. In the 1950 census there were 158 categories for male workers and 67 categories for female workers.

c. Major occupational classification--11 broad categories of occupation, consisting of groupings of the intermediate (and, hence, of the detailed) occupational categories.

A listing of the major occupational categories will be found in Table 17-1. Table 17-A-1 (end of the chapter) is a slightly condensed listing of the detailed occupational classification, while Table 17-A-3 uses the intermediate occupational classification.

Since new inventions and scientific discoveries are constantly being made, since technological progress continues to offer improved ways of accomplishing the nation's tasks, and since economic, social, and political organization changes, these classifications must be revised at each decennial census. Moreover, the number and proportion of workers falling in each of the occupa-

---

[1] Alba M. Edwards, "Preface" to Comparative Occupation Statistics for the United States, 1870 to 1940, U.S. Census of Population: 1940, p. xi.

tions which do continue to be recognized will change with changing conditions. The new occupations must be added, and old occupations must be reevaluated to assure that they are still in the proper groupings. Hence, strict comparability cannot, and should not, be maintained from census to census. However, by estimating the effect of changes in classification, and by using groupings of occupational categories, general trends in occupational composition can be charted.

In attempting to portray the occupational composition of the working force and the changes in that composition, the present chapter presents data for all three levels of occupational classification--the major, the intermediate, and the detailed. All too often information is presented only for the major occupational categories, which gives only a general (and often superficial) overview of the changes that are taking place. Inasmuch as the statistical tables for the intermediate and the detailed occupational classifications are very lengthy and run for several pages, they are placed in a special statistical appendix at the end of this chapter, and are identified as Tables 17-A-1 to 17-A-6, inclusive.[2]

PRESENT OCCUPATIONAL STRUCTURE

One of the United States' most unique characteristics is the occupational composition of its population. It is almost the only nation to have achieved a tremendously high level of living while remaining comparatively self-sufficient in terms of producing its own food and most of its basic raw materials; its occupational structure reveals, in one form, the "secret" of this achievement. Economists from all over the world have compared the occupational composition of their own nations with that of the United States in order to point out some of the things which a nation must accomplish if it is to attain "economic development." It is well, therefore, to learn what proportions of the nation's people are in each of the major kinds of jobs.[3]

During the month of July, 1957, civilian employment in the United States reached a peacetime high of 67,221,000 persons, and unemployment was at a low level. During the months since then, until the time of the present writing (1959), the nation has been undergoing an economic recession involving severe unemployment among certain occupational groups (see the chapter on unemployment). Hence, the occupational composition as of July, 1957 (rather than for a later date for which statistics are available) is taken as the "normal" occupational structure of the United States economy at the present time.

---

[2]The reader is urged to read and study these tables, comparing the various indices for the detailed occupations with each other and with the averages for all workers. By so doing, he can learn to appreciate the great amount of diversity and variation that exists within each of the various major occupational categories of the working force. In the analysis that follows, only the extreme cases of variation will be discussed. Tracing a particular occupation through all of these tables will reveal a great deal of information about it.

[3]Several approaches can be taken toward reporting occupational composition. (1) The occupations of employed persons can be reported. This approach reveals the occupational composition of the economy (jobs actually being filled) at a particular time. (2) The occupations of the "experienced labor force" (employed persons plus unemployed persons who have held a job previously) can be reported. This reveals the occupational composition of the labor force, exclusive of new workers. (3) The occupational composition of the population with work experience at some time in the recent past or the present. This approach includes not only employed and unemployed persons, but also persons who once worked but who are no longer in the labor force. Under conditions of high employment the first two approaches yield almost identical results, and both are used here almost interchangeably (because data concerning particular topics are sometimes available for one, and sometimes for the other). In examining occupational composition it is best to restrict the analysis to the civilian population, because military occupations do not fit easily into the classification system and because fluctuations in military manpower should not be confused with changes in civilian occupational composition.

Major occupation	Thousands of employed persons	Percent distribution
Total	67, 221	100. 0
Profess'l, techn'l, kindred wrks .	6, 129	9. 1
Farmers and farm managers.....	3, 524	5. 2
Mgrs., offs., prop'rs, exc. farm...	6, 913	10. 3
Clerical and kindred workers	9, 302	13. 8
Sales workers	4, 159	6. 2
Craftsmen, foremen, kindred wrks.	8, 799	13. 1
Operatives and kindred workers ..	12, 632	18. 8
Private household workers.......	2, 021	3. 0
Service wrks., exc. priv. hshld....	5, 715	8. 5
Farm laborers and foremen......	3, 963	5. 9
Laborers, except farm and mine .	4, 064	6. 0

Source: Bureau of the Census, Current Population Reports; The Monthly Report on the Labor Force: July, 1957.

Even a hasty glance at these statistics will show some of the outstanding features of this well-to-do industrial nation. One might describe the system succinctly by stating that a comparatively small group of managers, officials, and proprietors (10 percent) organize and administer the work of a somewhat more numerous body of skilled and specially trained foremen, craftsmen, inspectors, and other "key employees" (13 percent) who, in turn, supervise the work of a much larger body of semi-skilled and less trained operatives (19 percent). Distribution to the consumer is accomplished by a comparatively small sales personnel (6 percent) working under the supervision of some of the proprietors and managers. But the tasks of production, management, distribution. and administration are so great that a large cadre of clerical workers (14 percent) is required to keep books, type letters, cash checks, operate telephone switchboards, ship and receive goods, calculate payrolls, etc. Meanwhile, food is produced by a small number of farmers and farm managers (5 percent) assisted by farm laborers (6 percent). In this system, the "common laborer" (6 percent)

who has little to offer except unskilled muscle power plays only a minor role.

However, a description of the production and distribution of material goods does not tell the full story of the nation's material well-being. The entire system must be "serviced" by two major groups of persons who are useful in less tangible ways. The first of these is composed of the professional and technical personnel (physicians, lawyers, actors, engineers, architects, teachers, clergymen) who plan, teach, advise, consult, do research, entertain, and heal (9 percent). The second group comprises nonprofessional "service workers," including policemen, firemen, waiters and waitresses, attendants of all kinds, barbers and beauticians, etc., who provide needed personal and similar services (12 percent). A few members of this latter group are workers in private households who serve as maids, housecleaners, baby sitters, etc. (3 percent).

This brief description cannot give the reader adequate information concerning the full detail of the occupational structure. If he wishes to learn exactly what occupations are contained in each of the 11 major occupational groups listed above, the reader is urged to read through the full list of detailed occupations provided in Table 17-A-4.

Within each of the major occupational groups, some occupational categories are much more important than others in terms of the numbers of working persons who hold certain types of jobs. Table 17-A-1 at the end of this chapter contains statistics which show what proportion of all workers are in each detailed occupation class, and also what proportion of all workers within each major occupation group are in each of the detailed occupations categories of which the group is comprised. One of the most impressive aspects of this table is the fact that no one of the detailed occupations is impressively large, either numerically or proportionately. A few catch-all categories, such as "farmers" (the census fails to distinguish among the many kinds of farmers and farm operations) and "operatives, unclassified manufacturing industries," contain as much as 5 percent of the workers; but aside from these, most of the really specifically detailed occupations contain less than one-half of one percent of all workers. The following detailed occupational categories contained one-half of one percent or more of the total employed labor force in 1950, and hence are the largest occupational groups:

Major occupation	Percent of all employed workers
PROFES'L, TECHN'L, KINDRED WKRS.	
Accountants and auditors	0.67
Engineers, technical.	0.93
Nurses, professional	0.71
Teachers-exc. college and music . . .	1.91
FARMERS AND FARM MANAGERS	
Farmers (owners and tenants)	7.60
MGRS., OFFS., PROP'RS, EXC. FARM	
Prop'rs of food and dairy pr. stores	0.71
Prop'rs of eating, drinking places. .	0.51
CLERICAL AND KINDRED WORKERS	
Bookkeepers	1.28
Shipping and receiving clerks	0.51
Stenographers, typists, secretaries .	2.83
Telephone operators	0.64
SALES WORKERS	
Insurance agents and brokers	0.54
Sales wkrs. (n. e. c.)-manufacturing.	0.57
Sales wkrs. (n. e. c.)-wholesale trade	0.72
Sales wkrs. (n. e. c.)-retail trade . . .	4.35
CRAFTSMEN, FOREMEN, KINDRED WRKS.	
Carpenters	1.62
Electricians	0.55
Foremen, manufacturing.	0.91
Machinists.	0.91
Mechanics, automobile.	1.16
Painters, construction, maintenance	0.69
OPERATIVES AND KINDRED WORKERS	
Laundry and dry cleaning.	0.76
Coal mine operatives and laborers .	0.64
Truck and tractor drivers	2.36
Operatives, unclassified, mfg.	9.61
Opers., unclass., wholesale-ret. tr. .	0.51
PRIVATE HOUSEHOLD WORKERS	
Private household wkrs. except housekeepers and laundresses	2.13
SERVICE WKRS. EXC. PRIV. HOUSEHOLD	
Barbers, beauticians, manicurists .	0.68
Cooks, except private household . . .	0.77
Janitors and sextons	0.81
Waiters and waitresses	1.18
FARM LABORERS AND FOREMEN	
Farm laborers, wage workers	2.60
Farm laborers, unpaid family wrks.	1.62
LABORERS, EXCEPT FARM AND MINE	
Laborers, unclassified, manufact. . .	1.94
Laborers, unclassified, const	1.16
Labor's, unclass., wholesale, ret. tr.	0.56

The above categories constitute only about one-tenth of the detailed occupational categories, but account for more than one-half (57 percent) of the jobs.

Many of the occupations in the list of detailed occupations have very few members, although these members may be so famous or so essential that they are a very important group. In the entire United States, less than 15,000 members (roughly 3/10 of one percent) were reported for each of the following specific detailed occupations at the 1950 census:

Professional, technical, and kindred workers
    Actors and actresses
    Airplane pilots and navigators
    Athletes
    Chiropractors
    Engineers, metallurgical
    Engineers, mining
    Farm and home management advisors
    Optometrists
    Osteopaths
    Veterinarians

Managers, officials, and proprietors, except farm
    Floormen and floor managers, store
    Inspectors, state public administration
    Managers (salaried) of repair services other than auto

Clerical and kindred workers
  Attendants and assistants, library
  Baggagemen, transportation
  Telegraph messengers
Sales workers
  Auctioneers
  Demonstrators
  Stock and bond salesmen
Craftsmen, foremen, and kindred workers
  Electrotypers and stereotypers
  Engravers, except photoengravers
  Forgemen and hammermen
  Furriers
  Glaziers
  Inspectors--construction
  Millers, grain, flour, feed
  Piano and organ tuners and repairmen
  Stone cutters and stone carvers
Operatives and kindred workers
  Blasters and powdermen
  Boatmen, canalmen, and lock keepers
  Chainmen, rodmen, and axmen, surveying
  Conductors, bus and street railway
  Heaters, metal
  Milliners
Service workers
  Bootblacks
  Marshalls and constables
  Midwives
  Watchmen (crossing) and bridge tenders
Laborers, in such manufacturing industries as:
  Fabricated nonferrous metal products
  Office and store machinery and equipment
  Aircraft and parts
  Photographic equipment and watches
  Confectionery and related products
  Knitting mills
  Dyeing and finishing of textiles
  Chemicals--production of synthetic fibers
  Chemicals--production of drugs and medicine
  Chemicals--production of paints, varnishes
  Leather--footwear, except rubber
  Leather--products, except footwear
Some of these "small" occupational groups have few members because the services rendered by one person, or by only a few persons, can serve the needs of millions. A half-dozen movie stars supported by the necessary "extras," or a TV camera crew and a few entertainers, can provide recreation for millions. In other cases, the entire national economy needs only a very few units of certain highly specialized occupations; examples are metallurgical engineers, piano tuners, and lock keepers on canals. Finally, some of these occupations involve trades which are dying, or jobs for which there is very little demand. For example, the highly skilled and precise business of making watches or cameras provides few opportunities for unskilled laborers, even though the census recognizes such an occupation.

Just because a particular occupation has only a few members in it, one should not conclude either that it is unimportant or that it is unknown and unappreciated by the public. The highly specialized job, performed as an integrated part of a vast network of other interdependent and highly specialized jobs, is the very essence of modern industrial society. Many occupational experts consider that the detailed occupational classification of the Census Bureau is a terribly coarse and inexact scheme which fails to reveal the full extent of occupational differentiation that actually exists, but to most users of census data it appears to provide a much greater mass of information than most minds are able or willing to absorb.

CHANGES IN OCCUPATIONAL COMPOSITION:
1950-1957 AND 1820-1950

Changes between 1950 and 1957. (See Tables 17-1 and 17-2.) Between 1950 and 1957, while the total number of jobs was rising quite rapidly (8 percent), certain of the major occupation classes made extraordinarily large increases, and hence became a larger proportion of all occupations than they previously had been. These fast-growing categories of occupation are:

Professional, technical, and kindred
  workers (grew 43 percent)
Clerical and kindred workers (grew
  19 percent)

Table 17-1.—OCCUPATIONAL COMPOSITION OF THE EXPERIENCED LABOR FORCE; 1900 TO 1957

Major occupation group	Current population survey[1]		Decennial Census					
	1957	1950	1950	1940	1930	1920	1910	1900
Total.................................	100.0	100.0	100.0	100.0	100.0	100.0	100.0	100.0
Professional, technical, and kindred workers.	9.7	7.3	8.6	7.5	6.8	5.4	4.7	4.3
Farmers and farm managers.....................	4.9	7.0	7.4	10.4	12.4	15.3	16.5	19.9
Managers, officials, and propr's, exc. farm..	10.0	10.4	8.7	7.3	7.4	6.6	6.6	5.8
Clerical and kindred workers.................	13.9	12.6	12.3	9.6	8.9	8.0	5.3	3.0
Sales workers................................	6.3	6.3	7.0	6.7	6.3	4.9	4.7	4.5
Craftsmen, foremen, and kindred workers......	13.3	13.0	14.2	12.0	12.8	13.0	11.6	10.5
Operatives and kindred workers...............	19.8	20.8	20.4	18.4	15.8	15.6	14.6	12.8
Private household workers....................	3.2	3.2	2.6	4.8	4.1	3.3	5.0	5.4
Service workers, exc. private household......	8.6	8.0	7.9	7.0	5.7	4.5	4.6	3.6
Farm laborers and foremen....................	4.2	5.1	4.4	7.0	8.8	11.7	14.4	17.7
Laborers, exc. farm and mine.................	6.0	6.4	6.6	9.4	11.0	11.6	12.0	12.5

[1]Data are based on estimates for four quarterly months: January, April, July, and October.

Source: Current Population Reports, Series P-50, No. 85, June 1958, Table F and, U. S. Bureau of the Census. Occupational Trends in the United States, 1900 to 1950, by David L. Kaplan and M. Claire Casey. Bureau of the Census Working Paper No. 5, 1958.

Service workers, except household
(grew 16 percent)

Meanwhile, the following occupations have actually lost members or have grown very slowly, and are now a smaller proportion of the total than formerly.

Farmers and farm managers (declined 25 percent)

Farm laborers and foremen (declined 11 percent)

Laborers, except farm and mine (grew 1 percent)

The following occupations (those remaining) grew at about average rates, and in 1957 were about as large a part of the total as in 1950.

Managers, officials, and proprietors, except farm (grew 4 percent)

Sales workers (grew 8 percent)

Craftsmen, foremen, and kindred workers (grew 10 percent)

Operatives and kindred workers (grew 3 percent)

Private household workers (grew 8 percent)

During the period of full employment that pre-

Table 17-2.—INTERCENSAL PERCENT CHANGE IN EACH OF THE MAJOR OCCUPATION GROUPS: 1900 TO 1957

Major occupation group	Percent change during the interval							
	1950 to 1957	1930 to 1950	1900 to 1930	1940 to 1950	1930 to 1940	1920 to 1930	1910 to 1920	1900 to 1910
Total..............................	8	21.2	67.7	14.0	6.3	15.4	13.2	28.5
Professional, technical, and kindred workers.	43	53.5	168.2	31.0	17.2	45.0	29.9	42.4
Farmers and farm managers.....................	-25	-27.5	4.7	-18.4	-11.1	-6.4	4.5	7.0
Managers, officials, and propr's, exc. farm..	4	42.7	113.0	36.7	4.3	28.9	13.8	45.1
Clerical and kindred workers.................	19	66.8	394.4	45.2	14.9	28.1	70.3	126.6
Sales workers................................	8	35.1	134.1	19.8	12.8	48.6	17.3	34.3
Craftsmen, foremen, and kindred workers......	10	33.7	104.0	34.6	-0.7	13.9	27.0	41.0
Operatives and kindred workers...............	3	56.4	106.8	26.4	23.8	16.8	21.1	46.3
Private household workers....................	8	-23.0	26.5	-36.2	20.7	41.6	-23.8	17.2
Service workers, except private household....	16	67.3	165.0	26.9	31.8	45.9	11.1	63.4
Farm laborers and foremen....................	-11	-39.9	16.3	-29.0	-15.3	-13.3	-7.9	4.8
Laborers, exc. farm and mine.................	1	27.2	47.4	-20.3	-8.6	8.7	9.6	23.7

Source: Current Population Reports, Series P-50, No. 85, June 1958, Table F and, U. S. Bureau of the Census, Occupational Trends in the United States, 1900 to 1950, by David L. Kaplan and M. Claire Casey. Bureau of the Census Working Paper No. 5, 1958.

vailed between 1950 and 1957 there was a tendency to substitute machines for common unskilled labor, both in agriculture and nonagricultural industries. This led to a decline of 11 percent in the number of farm laborers, and to a decline of 25 percent in the number of farmers. A change which removes 1/4 of the workers from one big occupation, such as farming, and redistributes them among others--all within a span of only 7 years--is most revolutionary indeed! Expanding opportunities in cities have permitted many thousands of operators of poor and submarginal farms (including Negro sharecroppers) to quit the land forever. Also, technological advance has tended to diminish the farm labor force. Mechanization has increased the "optimum size" of farms and, hence, has made it desirable for farms to be larger and fewer. Many farms have been consolidated since 1950, the displaced farmers being forced into other occupations. Mechanization also resulted in only a very small growth in the laborer occupations at a time when all employment was increasing much more rapidly. Since 1950, laborers have enjoyed an excellent opportunity to climb into a high occupational category if they were qualified, and have had little incentive to remain laborers.

The very large increase of 43 percent for professional and technical workers, within a period of only 7 years, is truly impressive. This rate of gain is about twice that which took place during the period 1930 to 1950, and hence represents a very greatly stepped-up demand for professional and technical services. Instead of being a small, thin "upper crust" of society as they were before World War II, professional and technical persons now comprise a broad thick strata, and are so numerous as to be much less awe-inspiring than they formerly were.

The moderate gains made by the central core of the economic system--the workers in business and production and marketing (proprietors, sales workers, craftsmen, and operatives)--represent the growth of the total economy. The growth of employment in the service occupations betokens the continued rise in level of living and the increased use of personal services by the populace.

Changes between 1900 and 1950. There has been little novelty in the occupational changes that have taken place since 1950. "Professional," "clerical," and "service" workers (excluding household workers) have increased steadily since 1900. Similarly, unskilled laborers, farm laborers, and farmers have been among the slowest growing occupations in each decade, and in some cases have actually declined. Today, the proportions of professional, technical, or kindred workers and service workers are more than twice the size they were in 1900, and the proportion of clerical workers is more than three times what it was in 1900. On the other hand, farmers and farm laborers today are less than 1/4 the proportion they were at the turn of the century, and unskilled laborers comprise less than one-half as large a share. Thus, most of the changes since 1950 are simply extensions of trends that are more than half a century old. Nevertheless, the sharp downturn since 1950 in the number of farmers, and the sharp upturn in the numbers of professional workers, represent a major acceleration of past trends.

A few of the occupational groups that did not show extensive change between 1950 and 1957 had experienced moderate rates of growth during the earlier decades. These were:

Managers and officials--slow, steady growth
Sales workers--slow, steady growth
Craftsmen--slow, steady growth
Operatives--slow, steady growth until 1940, rapid growth between 1940 and 1950

These changes are associated with the long-time trends of population growth, industrialization, and urbanization of the economy which have already been described in earlier chapters.

Employment as private household workers, which also showed little change since 1950, tends to fluctuate with economic conditions. It tends to bulk large during periods of economic depression, and to decrease when there are acute labor shortages--i.e., when more pleasant and more profitable jobs are available. The growth of 8 percent in this group between 1950 and 1957 probably is related to the greatly increased participation of women in the labor force, discussed in the pre-

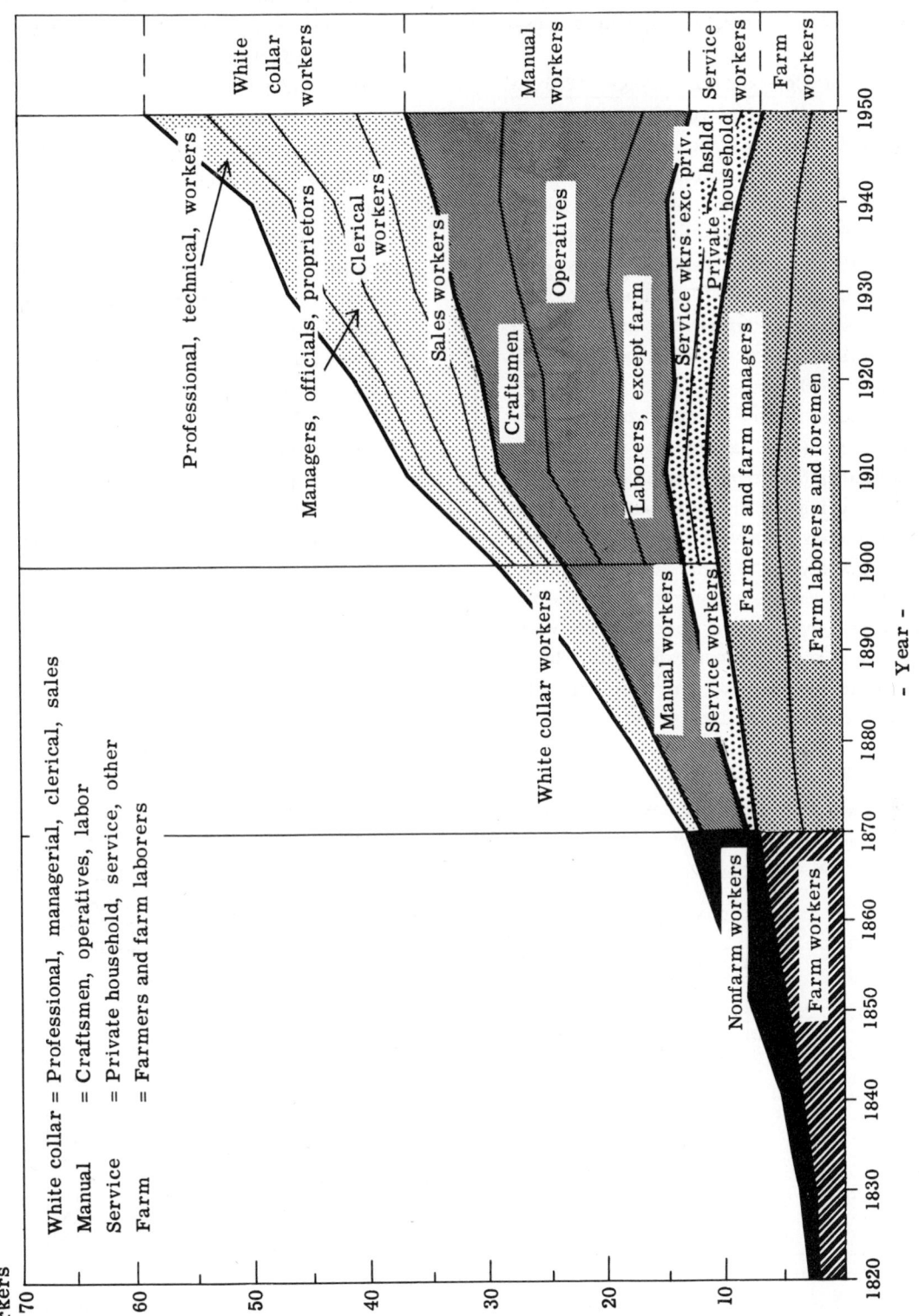

FIGURE 17-1. OCCUPATIONAL COMPOSITION OF THE EXPERIENCED LABOR FORCE, 1820 TO 1950.

ceding chapter. Working women tend to hire housekeepers and baby sitters to help with domestic duties.

An Overview of Occupational Change, 1820 to 1950. The use of estimating procedures makes it possible, without doing great violence to the facts, to obtain data for four broad categories of occupation from 1870 to the present, and for two major divisions of occupation (agricultural and nonagricultural) from 1820 to 1870. Table 17-3 presents this information, and Figure 17-1 illustrates the dramatic expansion and differential growth of the nation's occupational structure during the 130 years preceding 1950.

a. During each decade since 1820, the nonfarm occupations have grown much more rapidly than the farm occupations. In other words, during our much-discussed frontier period, when thousands of migrants were rushing westward to homestead the land, so many people were turning to nonfarm occupations that these occupations were growing at an even more rapid rate. In no decade of the last 130 years did the nonfarm occupations fail to grow at least 25

percent faster than the agricultural occupations, and in most decades they grew twice as fast or even faster. It is this very large and persistent differential that has caused the percentage of farm workers to decline from 72 percent of all workers in 1820 to 1/8 of this share, or only 9 percent, in 1957. The steady decrease in the number of farm workers since 1910 was preceded by two decades of very slow growth, while the number of nonfarm workers was continuing to grow very rapidly.

b. Among the nonfarm workers the white collar workers grew most rapidly, at least after 1870. In every decade between 1870 and 1930 the white collar occupations grew more rapidly than either manual workers or service workers.

c. The manual worker has grown, both in numbers and at a moderately rapid rate, during each decade since 1870. Large numbers of farm workers who were not needed to till the farms, and many millions of immigrants who flowed in from other countries, found work as "blue collar" em-

Table 17-3.—PERCENT DISTRIBUTION AMONG FOUR BROAD GROUPINGS OF OCCUPATION FOR THE EXPERIENCED LABOR FORCE, AND INTERCENSAL RATES OF CHANGE: 1820 TO 1950

| Year | Percent of workers classed as: | | | | | Percent change during preceding decade | | | | |
| | Farm workers | Nonfarm workers | | | | Farm workers | Nonfarm workers | | | |
		Total	White-collar workers	Manual workers	Service workers		Total	White-collar workers	Manual workers	Service workers
1950	11.8	88.2	36.6	41.1	10.5	-22.7	21.8	34.3	17.8	1.8
1940	17.4	82.6	31.1	39.8	11.7	-12.9	11.4	12.3	6.9	27.2
1930	21.2	78.8	29.4	39.6	9.8	-9.4	24.5	36.0	13.5	44.1
1920	27.0	72.9	24.9	40.2	7.8	-1.2	19.6	32.2	19.2	-7.0
1910	30.9	69.2	21.4	38.2	9.6	5.9	42.0	55.7	36.8	35.6
1900	37.5	62.4	17.6	35.8	9.0	10.6	34.7	46.1	34.4	17.5
1890	42.2	57.8	15.0	33.2	9.6	15.9	51.5	62.8	48.2	46.6
1880	48.9	51.2	12.4	30.0	8.8	25.4	44.6	59.3	47.2	21.6
1870	52.4	47.5	10.4	27.4	9.7	9.1	42.3	(a)	(a)	(a)
1860	59.0	41.0	(a)	(a)	(a)	26.7	54.3	(a)	(a)	(a)
1850	63.6	36.4	(a)	(a)	(a)	31.7	64.7	(a)	(a)	(a)
1840	68.6	31.4	(a)	(a)	(a)	34.3	46.6	(a)	(a)	(a)
1830	70.5	29.5	(a)	(a)	(a)	33.8	43.2	(a)	(a)	(a)
1820	71.9	28.1	(a)	(a)	(a)	(a)	(a)	(a)	(a)	(a)

(a) Data not available.

Source: Bureau of the Census, Historical Statistics of the United States 1789-1945, Tables D-47-61 and D-90-106, Alba M. Edwards, Comparative Occupation Statistics for the United States, 1980 to 1940, Tables xxxi, 9; U. S. Bureau of the Census, Occupational Trends in the United States, 1900 to 1950, by David L. Kaplan and M. Claire Casey. Bureau of the Census Working Paper No. 5, 1958.

ployees in factories, mines, on railroads, and at construction jobs. This group of workers is still the largest single category, although by 1960 the number of white collar workers may equal or slightly surpass the number of manual workers.

d. Service workers have grown irregularly and only moderately rapidly, and in 1950 comprised only about the same proportion of all workers as they had in 1870. Many service occupations outside private households did not begin to grow rapidly until after 1920.

In short, the occupational changes we see about us today have their roots in a fundamental reorganization of the mode of gaining a livelihood, a reorganization that has been underway persistently for much more than a century.

RAPIDLY-EXPANDING VERSUS SLOWLY-GROWING OR DECLINING SPECIFIC OCCUPATIONS: 1940 TO 1950

The process of continuous technological, economic, and social change is creating new occupations and is making others obsolete or unnecessary. Observing which of the detailed occupations enjoyed the most rapid rates of growth between two censuses makes it possible to appreciate better some of the changes that have taken place. Below are two lists of occupations. List 1 enumerates occupations that grew very rapidly between 1940 and 1950 (by 50 percent or more). List 2 enumerates occupations that declined or grew very slowly (less than 5 percent).

List 1.—RAPIDLY EXPANDING OCCUPATIONS: 1940 TO 1950 (Those increasing by 50 percent or more)

Detailed occupation	Percent change 1940 to 1950
PROFESS'L, TECHN'L, AND KINDRED WORKERS	
Accountants and auditors	70.8
Airplane pilots and navigators	217.8
Athletes	61.1
College pres., prof'rs, and inst. (n.e.c.)	66.2
Draftsmen	67.8
Editors and reporters	51.3
Engineers, technical	90.8
Chemical	157.7
Electrical	73.6
Industrial	244.1
Metallurgical, metallurgists, and mining	99.8
Not elsewhere classified	116.4
Entertainers	60.0
Librarians	53.7
Photographers	59.4
Radio operators	160.5
Sports instructors and officials	110.8
Surveyors	89.8
Technicians, medical and dental and testing	125.6
Technicians (n.e.c.)	173.0
Profess'l, techn'l, and kindred wrks. (n.e.c.)	113.8
MGRS., OFFS., AND PROPRIETORS, EXC. FARM	
Buyers and department heads, store	102.7
Floormen and floor managers, store	57.3
Inspector, public administration	
Local public administration	76.0

List 2.—SLOWLY-GROWING OR DECLINING OCCUPATIONS: 1950 TO 1950 (Those declining or increasing by less than 5 percent)

Detailed occupation	Percent change 1940 to 1950
PROFESS'L, TECHN'L, AND KINDRED WORKERS	
Funeral directors and embalmers	3.8
Lawyers and judges	1.6
Osteopaths	-14.3
Religious workers	2.6
FARMERS AND FARM MANAGERS	
Farmers (owners and tenants)	-16.4
Farm managers	-5.6
MGRS., OFFICIALS, AND PROPR'S, EXC. FARM	
Buyers and shippers, farm products	-29.6
Inspectors, public administration	
State public administration	-11.4
Managers and superintendents, building	-4.6
Postmasters	0.2
Mgrs., offs., and propr's, (n.e.c.)-salaried	
Retail trade	
Gasoline service stations	2.3
CLERICAL AND KINDRED WORKERS	
Collectors, bill and account	-43.9
Express messengers and railway mail clerks	-14.7
Messengers and office boys	-0.8
Telegraph messengers	-48.4
Telegraph operators	-11.0
SALES WORKERS	
Advertising agents and salesmen	-14.1

List 1.—Continued

Purchasing agents and buyers (n. e. c.)	99. 7

Managers, offs., and prop., (n. e. c.)-salaried

Construction	81. 4
Manufacturing	55. 0
Transportation	68. 9
Wholesale trade	54. 4
Retail trade	
Furniture, home furnishings, and equip. stores..	72. 8
Motor vehicles and accessories retailing	81. 4
Insurance and real estate	79. 9
Business services	92. 4
Miscellaneous repair services	139. 5
PPersonal services	68. 7
All other industries (incl. not reported)	55. 8

CLERICAL AND KINDRED WORKERS

Agents (n. e. c.)	79. 1
Office machine operators	137. 8
Stenographers, typists and secretaries	50. 2
Telephone operators	79. 0
Clerical and kindred workers (n. e. c.)	71. 6

SALES WORKERS

Auctioneers	61. 1
Demonstrators	65. 8
Newsboys	74. 9

CRAFTSMEN, FOREMEN, AND KINDRED WRKS.

Brickmasons, stonemasons, and tile setters	85. 9
Carpenters	67. 5
Cement and concrete finishers	96. 8
Decorators and window dressers	59. 0
Electricians	64. 5
Excavating, grading, and road machinery operators	105. 5
Foremen (n. e. c.)	62. 3
Manufacturing	74. 6
Metal ind., mach'y, incl. elect. and trans. equip	96. 2
Other nondurable goods (incl. not spec. mfg.)	65. 8
Telecommunic'n, util. and sanitary services	56. 0
Other industries (incl. not reported)	72. 9
Glaziers	54. 7
Heat treaters, annealers and temperers	74. 1
Linemen and servicemen, t'graph, t'phone, power	97. 9
Mechanics and repairmen	105. 1
Airplane	174. 2
Automobile	74. 2
Not elsewhere classified	139. 5
Opticians, and lens grinders and polishers	72. 7
Piano and organ tuners and repairmen	60. 0
Plasterers	61. 0
Plumbers and pipe fitters	64. 0
Roofers and slaters	87. 0
Tinsmiths, coppersmen, and sheet metal wkrs	58. 6
Toolmakers, and die makers and setters	62. 1
Upholsterers	60. 8

List 2.—Continued

Hucksters and peddlers	-54. 9
Stock and bond salesmen	-34. 3

CRAFTSMEN, FOREMEN, AND KINDRED WRKS.

Bakers	-1. 9
Forgemen and hammermen	-29. 1
Furriers	-13. 4
Inspectors (n. e. c.)	
Transport. exc. r. r., commun., other pub. util..	-4. 4
Millers, grain, flour, feed, etc.	-34. 9
Molders, metal	-17. 2
Paperhangers	-17. 6
Shoemakers and repairers, except factory	-7. 0
Stone cutters and stone carvers	-4. 4
Tailors and tailoresses	-22. 9

OPERATIVES AND KINDRED WORKERS

Apprentices	
Machinists and toolmakers	-17. 7
Chainmen, rodmen and axmen, surveying	-8. 2
Conductors, bus and street railway	-33. 3
Deliverymen and routemen	-8. 7
Dressmakers and seamstresses, except factory	3. 5
Dyers	0. 5
Milliners	-6. 2
Mine operatives and laborers (n. e. c.)	-11. 4
Motormen, street, subway, and elevated railway	-27. 8
Power station operators	0. 2

Operatives and kindred workers (n. e. c.)

Manufacturing	
Durable goods	
Metal industries	
Fabricated metal ind. (incl. not spec. metal)	
Not specified metal industries	-64. 1
Transportation equipment	
Ship and boat building and repairing	-26. 0
Nondurable goods	
Tobacco manufactures	-14. 6
Textile mill products	
Knitting mills	-15. 9
Miscellaneous textile mill products	-5. 6
Chemicals and allied products	
Synthetic fibers	-11. 6
Leather and leather products	
Leather: tanned, curried and finished	-1. 3
Not specified manufacturing industries	-33. 7

PRIVATE HOUSEHOLD WORKERS

Housekeepers, private hshld, living in and living out	-61. 8
Laundresses, private hshld, living in and living out.	-62. 5
Private hshld. wrks. (n. e. c.) living in and living out	-22. 0

SERVICE WORKERS, EXCEPT PRIVATE HSHLD.

Barbers, beauticians and manicurists	-8. 0
Boarding and lodging house keepers	-59. 9
Bootblacks	-2. 8

List 1.—Continued

OPERATIVES AND KINDRED WORKERS

Apprentices

Carpenters	80.4
Electricians	188.4
Plumbers and pipe fitters	157.4
Printing trades	62.5
Asbestos and insulation workers	192.8
Blasters and powdermen	142.5
Boatmen, canalmen and lock keepers	51.5
Furnacemen, smeltermen and pourers	92.0
Laundry and dry cleaning operatives	52.0
Oilers and greasers, except auto	64.0
Photographic process workers	97.0
Sawyers	113.8
Welders and flame cutters	115.6
Operatives and kindred workers (n.e.c.)	54.6
Manufacturing	50.1
Durable goods	85.4
Sawmills, pl'g mills, misc. wood products	111.0
Saw and planing mills and millwork	154.4
Furniture and fixtures	74.3
Stone, clay, and glass products	61.8
Glass and glass products	52.2
Cement, and concrete, gypsum, plaster prod.	139.4
Structural clay products	53.3
Misc. nonmetallic mineral and stone prod	69.8
Metal industries	58.3
Primary metal industries	
Other primary iron and steel industries	62.0
Primary nonferrous industries	112.0
Machinery, except electrical	124.3
Agricultural machinery and tractors	160.1
Office and store machines and devices	69.7
Miscellaneous machinery	128.8
Electrical machinery, equipment and supplies	153.4
Transportation equipment	80.4
Motor vehicles and motor vehicle equipment	81.7
Aircraft and parts	149.3
Railroad and misc. transportation equipment	66.9
Profess'l and photographic equip., watches	
Profess'l and photographic equip., supplies	101.0
Watches, clocks, clockwork-operated devices	} 58.4
Miscellaneous manufacturing industries	
Nondurable goods	
Food and kindred products	62.4
Meat products	52.6
Dairy products	77.5
Canning, preserving fruits, veg., sea foods	92.8
Grain-mill products	107.3
Bakery products	58.4
Beverage industries	63.7
Misc. food prep. kindred pr., not spec. food	87.2

List 2.—Continued

Marshals and constables	-25.6
Private policemen and detectives	3.9
Porters	4.1

FARM LABORERS AND FOREMEN

Farm foremen	1.6
Farm laborers, wage workers	-23.8
Farm laborers, unpaid family workers	-21.9

LABORERS, EXCEPT FARM AND MINE

Longshoremen and stevedores	3.2
Teamsters	-10.9
Laborers (n.e.c.)	
Manufacturing	-17.5
Durable goods	-18.1
Saw and planing mills, and misc. wood prod.	-29.7
Saw and planing mills and millwork	-29.8
Miscellaneous wood products	-28.9
Furniture and fixtures	-34.1
Stone, clay and glass products	-13.8
Glass and glass products	-20.5
Cement, and concrete, gypsum, plaster prod.	-0.9
Structural clay products	-16.5
Pottery and related products	1.4
Misc. nonmetallic mineral, stone products	-28.1
Metal industries	-13.6
Primary metal industries	
Blast furnaces, steel works, rolling mills	-15.5
Other primary iron and steel industries	-5.4
Primary nonferrous industries	-19.3
Fabricated metal ind. (incl. not spec. metal)	
Not specified metal industries	-82.6
Machinery, except electrical	4.6
Office and store machines and devices	-11.4
Miscellaneous machinery	-1.8
Transportation equipment	-23.2
Motor vehicles and motor vehicle equip.	-18.6
Aircraft and parts	-2.5
Ship and boat building and repairing	-38.7
Railroad and misc. transportation equip.	-27.8
Profess'l, and photographic equip., supplies	-15.9
Watches, clocks, clockwork-oper. devices.	-27.4
Nondurable goods	-13.8
Food and kindred products	-5.1
Meat products	-13.5
Dairy products	-6.8
Can. and preserving fruits, veg., sea foods.	-12.1
Grain-mill products	-0.5
Confectionary and related products	-41.6
Misc. food prep., kindred prod., not spec. food industries	-7.4
Tobacco manufactures	-37.0
Textile mill products	-24.8
Knitting mills	-42.3

List 1.—Continued

    Paper and allied products 52.9
      Paperboard containers and boxes 63.2
      Misc. paper and pulp products 125.3
    Chemicals and allied products............... 72.8
      Drugs and medicines...................... 112.3
      Paints, varnishes and related products 57.6
    Petroleum and coal products 58.0
      Petroleum refining 60.7
    Rubber products 57.1
Nonmanufacturing industries (incl. not reported).. 100.2
    Construction............................... 133.3
    Transportation, except railroad 62.8
    Telecommun., and util. and sanitary services .. 120.8
    Wholesale and retail trade 127.1
    Business and repair services................. 52.0
    Personal services.......................... 181.3
    Public administration 412.7
    All other industries (incl. not reported) 55.4

SERVICE WRKS., EXC. PRIVATE HOUSEHOLD

Attendants, hospital and other institution 119.6
Attendants, profess'l, and personal serv. (n.e.c.) .. 64.3
Bartenders.................................... 70.2
Charwomen and cleaners 89.1
Cooks except private household.................. 57.2
Practical nurses.............................. 51.0
Service wrks., exc. private household (n.e.c.) 61.4

LABORERS, EXCEPT FARM AND MINE

Laborers
  Manufacturing
    Nondurable
      Paper and allied products
        Miscellaneous paper and pulp products....... 65.9
  Nonmanufacturing industries (incl. not reported)
    Construction 50.6
    Business and repair services................. 120.8
    Public administration...................... 127.6

List 2.—Continued

    Dyeing and finishing textiles, exc. knit. goods -30.3
    Carpets, rugs and other floor coverings... -10.5
    Yarn, thread and fabric mills .... -23.0
    Miscellaneous textile mill products .... -40.3
  Apparel and other fabricated textile products -5.5
    Apparel and accessories................. -4.4
    Miscellaneous fabricated textile products.. -8.8
  Paper and allied products.................. -15.9
    Pulp, paper, and paperboard mills........ -30.6
  Chemicals and allied products.............. -17.6
    Synthetic fibers .... -39.4
    Drugs and medicines .... -16.4
    Paints, varnishes and related products.... -11.6
  Petroleum and coal products .... -8.7
    Petroleum refining...................... -6.7
    Miscellaneous petroleum and coal prod.... -16.3
  Rubber products .... -3.5
  Leather and leather products............... -38.5
    Leather: tanned, curried, and finished .... -31.1
    Footwear, except rubber................. -46.9
    Leather products, except footwear........ -34.2

A comparison of the above two lists permits the following observations to be made:

During the 1940 to 1950 period there was a great boom in all things pertaining to:

    Aeronautics
    Automation in industry
    Automobiles
    Education and advanced professional training
    Electronics
    Engineering--technical ability to apply
      scientific principles
    Home construction and furnishing

Increased levels of living

Mechanization of agriculture

Medical and health care, including dental care and care of eyes

Personal services for individuals and families

Planning and regulation--greater control, analysis, and regulation of the operation of individual businesses

Recreation, hobbies, increased use of leisure time

Scientific research

Synthetic materials and chemical products

Travel, transportation by motor truck and motor bus

Urbanization, growth of cities

The 1940 to 1950 decade witnessed a decline in almost all forms of employment in agriculture, and in many "menial" occupations in which rates of pay are very low and conditions of work are not desirable--such as messengers, office boys, boot blacks, maids, laundresses. Shortages of workers in plants producing materials for defense and war enabled workers to desert these jobs and get better ones, if they had the necessary qualifications. Many women who had been supporting themselves in these less desirable kinds of jobs married and became housewives. The marriage boom caused a decline in boarding and lodging house keepers. Mechanization and automation in industry and commerce led to a large decline in the use of the muscle power of laborers. The long list of occupations in which there are fewer persons employed in 1950 than there were in 1940 (List 2) is most impressive testimony to the great technological advances that were made during this decade.

But the laborer occupations were not the only ones victimized by a decline due to advances in technology. Different methods of marketing farm products, of collecting overdue bills, of sending messages from one city to another, of advertising,

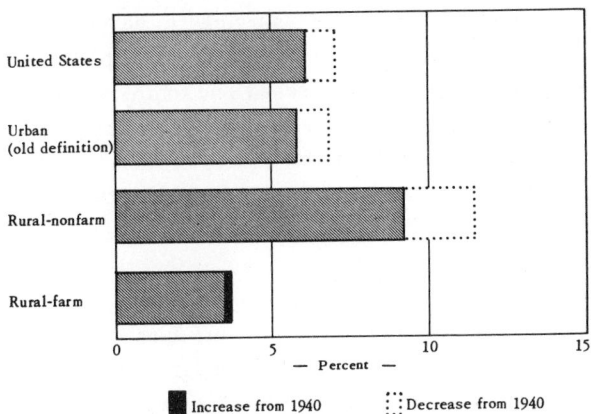

FIGURE 17-3. PERCENT OF EMPLOYED WORKERS IN LABORER (EXCEPT FARM AND MINE) OCCUPATIONS, BY URBAN AND RURAL RESIDENCE, 1940 AND 1950

of selling food, and of investing savings caused large declines in particular detailed occupation categories among managers, clerical workers, and sales workers. Changed methods of production, and the substitution of machines for men, permitted operatives to do work that had previously been done only by skilled craftsmen. Long-established occupations such as bakers, millers, paperhangers, tailors, stonecutters, furriers, and shoemakers had fewer members at the end of the decade than at the beginning. (As will be shown later, many of these occupations were skills which foreign born craftsmen had brought with them from Europe.) The independent milliner or dressmaker tended to disappear in favor of the factory which produced ready-to-wear clothes. The substitution of motor busses for street cars led to a great decline in the number of conductors and motormen. Automation in textile manufacturing, in metal fabrication, in controlling chemical processes, and in fabricating shoes and other leather products made many craftsmen and operatives unnecessary. Mechanization of mines and automation of control in electric power stations has made it possible to produce more power with fewer workers.

Meanwhile, a great increase took place in the number of workers who are engaged neither in "primary" extraction (farming, forestry, mining) nor in "secondary" fabrication (manufacture or commerce), but are employed in "tertiary" occu-

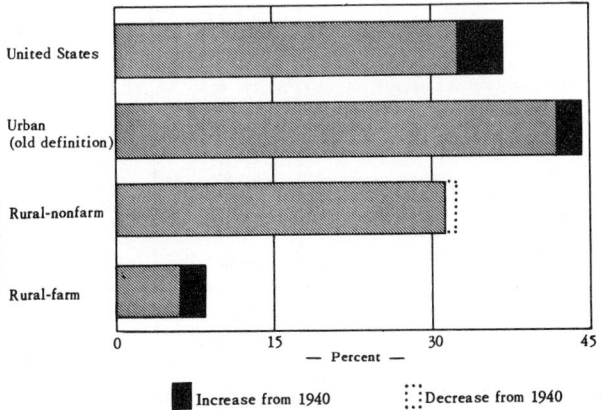

FIGURE 17-2. PERCENT OF EMPLOYED WORKERS IN WHITE COLLAR OCCUPATIONS, BY URBAN AND RURAL RESIDENCE, 1940 AND 1950

pations--jobs that furnish services to persons or to primary and secondary businesses. Stepped-up scientific research, increased and improved education at all levels, better medical care, improved methods of controlling the quality of factory output and of regulating the flow of goods and the size of inventories, and a tremendously improved level of living--all these advances mean that there are millions of cars, TV sets, toasters, etc., to be repaired, and that there is an increase in dining out, in the use of hospitals and other medical facilities, and a greater demand for dry cleaning, laundry, haircuts, and beauty treatments.

Comparable data concerning detailed occupations will not be available until the 1960 Census. It may safely be assumed (given the generally similar nature of the change in the major occupation groups) that the specific occupations which have grown rapidly since 1950, and those that have grown only very slowly or declined, are of the same types as those enumerated in Lists 1 and 2, respectively.

LONG-RUN TRENDS IN SPECIFIC OCCUPATIONS: 1900 TO 1950

In 1958 the Bureau of the Census released a unique tabulation, prepared by David E. Kaplan and Claire Casey, which estimates the volume of employment in the detailed occupation groups (in some cases combinations have been made in order to achieve comparability) for each decade of the half-century from 1900 to 1950.[4] These tables permit the measurement of long-term changes in occupational composition, in terms of detailed occupations. Below are two lists (Lists 3 and 4), of rapidly-expanding occupations and of slowly-growing or declining occupations. These lists correspond to Lists 1 and 2, above, except that they span a period of 50 years instead of a decade. Also, rates of growth are computed separately for

---

[4] U. S. Bureau of the Census. Occupational Trends in the United States, 1900 to 1950, by David L. Kaplan and M. Clair Casey. Bureau of the Census Working Paper No. 5, 1958.

the first 30 years of the period and the last 20, in order to determine when rapid growth or decline began.

During the 50 years after 1900, the number of experienced persons in the labor force increased by almost exactly 100 percent. Any occupation that grew at 3 times this rate was considered to have grown with extraordinary rapidity, while one that grew by 50 percent or less was defined as slowly-growing.

List 3.--OCCUPATIONS THAT GREW BY 300 PERCENT OR MORE: 1900 TO 1950

Occupation	Increase, 1900 to 1950		Percent increase	
	Percent	No. of persons (000)	1930 to 1950	1900 to 1930
PROFESS'L, TECHN'L, KINDRED WRKS.				
Accountants and auditors	1,603.7	368	103.8	736.0
Authors.................................	467.8	14	33.0	326.8
Chemists	796.0	68	71.1	423.5
College pres., prof'rs, instr's(n.e.c.)	1,652.9	120	105.9	751.3
Designers and draftsmen	834.3	150	71.1	445.9
Engineers, civil	536.0	108	45.7	336.4
Engineers: civil, chemical, metallurgical and metallurgists, and mining...........	1,698.8	53	302.3	347.1
Engineers: electrical, industrial, aeronautical, mechanical, (n.e.c.)...........	2,404.4	345	210.2	707.5
Librarians.............................	1,850.3	54	92.0	915.9
Nurses, professional and student profess'l .	4,059.0	479	66.9	2,392.3
Surveyors..............................	350.2	21	84.7	143.7
Technicians, medical, dental, testing(n.e.c.)	185,952.0	186	818.9	20,148.0
Dietitians, nutritionists, foresters and conservationists, natural scientists(n.e.c.) personnel and labor relations workers, social scientists, professional, technical, and kindred workers	2,408.0	290	312.4	508.1
MGRS., OFFS., PROPR'S, EXC. FARM				
Credit men	1,593.8	32	50.6	1,024.5
Floormen and floor managers, store.......	465.4	9	83.0	209.0
Inspectors(n.e.c.), fed. pub. admin. and postal service, offs., admin. (n.e.c.), fed. public admin. and postal service..........	331.4	60	96.6	119.4
Inspectors (n.e.c.), state publ. admin., offs., admin. (n.e.c.), state publ. administration .	704.8	29	123.7	259.7
Purchasing agents, buyers (n.e.c.)........	805.9	58	127.0	299.1
Construction	408.6	238	48.7	242.1
Telecommun., utilities, sanitary services..	1,140.6	63	75.8	605.6
Wholesale trade	336.9	264	126.1	93.3
Insurance and real estate	729.9	103	77.4	367.8
Business serv., all other ind. (incl. not rep.)	792.2	286	129.6	288.5
CLERICAL AND KINDRED WORKERS				
Attendants and assistants, library	928.5	12	597.6	47.4
Bookkeepers, cashiers	328.3	762	34.6	218.3
Mail carriers	501.9	142	40.6	328.2
Stenographers, typists, secretaries	1,139.3	1,527	51.4	718.7
Telephone operators	1,855.6	356	50.5	1,199.1
Off. mach. operators, shipping, receiving clerks, bank tellers, dispatchers starters, vehicle, clerical, kindred wrks. (n.e.c,) ..	1,447.0	3,396	111.3	632.2
SALES WORKERS				
Demonstrators	348.3	11	91.6	134.0
Newsboys...............................	1,368.3	94	159.6	465.7
Real estate agents and brokers	331.4	111	-3.7	347.9
CRAFTSMEN, FOREMEN, KINDRED WRKS.				
Decorators and window dressers	1,410.6	43	128.8	560.2
Electricians............................	554.1	281	31.2	398.5
Foremen(n.e.c.)	435.1	705	57.2	240.4
Metal ind., mach. incl. electrical, transp. equip,, other durable goods, textiles, text. prods., apparel, other nondurable goods (ind. not specified manufacturing)	480.8	434	79.0	224.5

List 3.—Continued

Transport., exc. r. r., telecommunications, utilities and sanitary services	533.3	52	38.6	356.9
Other industries (incl. not reported)	579.9	140	85.7	266.1
Insp., scalers graders, log and lumber	1,115.8	17	149.5	387.3
Inspectors (n. e. c.)	351.0	77	26.8	255.7
Construction	787.7	7	17.5	655.3
Transportation exc. railroad, commun. and other public utilites	1,211.1	12	-8.8	1,377.1
Linemen, servicemen, t'graph, t'phone, power	1,138.5	202	106.2	500.5
Job setters, metal; machinists; mechanics: and repairmen: airplane, auto., office machine, radio-telvision, r. r. and car shop, (n. e. c.); toolmakers, die makers, setters..	733.8	2,231	82.8	356.2
Millwrights	661.4	53	46.4	420.3
Rollers and roll hands, metal	398.1	25	2.6	385.6
Roofers and slaters	462.1	41	112.4	164.7
Structural metal workers	1,429.4	54	73.7	780.4
OPERATIVES AND KINDRED WORKERS				
Apprentice carpenters	617.1	10	167.9	167.7
Apprentice plumbers, pipe fitters	348.1	10	112.9	110.5
Apprentices, printing trade	352.7	12	45.0	212.1
Blasters and powdermen	1,419.1	11	74.4	771.0
Dyers	391.6	21	46.8	235.0
Filers, grinders and polishers, metal	840.5	143	103.2	362.9
Furnacemen, smelters, and pourers	337.8	45	190.7	50.6
Laundry and dry cleaning operations	405.7	370	74.3	190.1
Meat cutters, exc. slaughter, packing houses	438.1	146	49.9	259.0
Photographic process workers	1,512.8	28	277.7	327.0
Sawyers	450.4	82	176.7	98.9
Operatives and kindred wrks. (n. e. c.)	311.0	9,439	82.8	124.8
Furniture and fixtures	599.8	113	82.5	283.5
Cement, concrete, gypsum, plaster products	525.8	25	163.6	137.4
Motor vehicles, motor veh. equip; ship and boat bldg., repairing; blast furnaces, steel works, rolling mills; other primary iron and steel industries; fabricated steel prod. office and store mach. and devices; misc. machinery; not specified metal inds.; agri, mach. and tractors; aircraft and parts; r. r. and misc. transport. equip.; primary nonferrous industries	1,009.7	1,226	124.4	376.2
Fabricated nonferrous metal products	825.1	88	191.9	216.9
Electrical mach., equip. and supplies	1,912.0	338	203.5	563.0
Meat prod., can., preserving fruits, veg., and sea foods	2,059.7	217	189.0	647.2
Dairy products	368.0	48	139.9	95.1
Grain-mill products	674.4	29	386.3	59.3
Bakery products	1,391.4	64	144.8	509.2
Beverage industries	334.8	44	698.3	-45.5
Misc. food preparations and kindred prods., not specified food industries	2,024.1	49	72.5	1,131.4
Pulp, paper, paperboard mills; misc. paper and pulp products	700.8	146	106.7	287.4
Printing, publishing, allied industries	400.4	64	56.4	219.9
Paints, varnishes, related products	550.9	16	122.2	192.9
Drugs, medicines; misc. chemicals, allied	1,499.7	139	180.9	469.5
Petroleum refining	5,774.5	47	76.6	3,226.7
Misc. petroleum and coal products	325.5	5	327.9	-0.6
Rubber products	731.8	111	56.5	431.4
Nonmanufacturing	423.9	631	75.2	199.0
Construction	981.1	65	374.8	127.7
Railroad, railway express service; transportation, exc. railroad; telecomm. utilites, sanitary services; wholesale and retail trade; business and repair serv...	301.8	413	112.3	89.2
Personal services, all other industries (including not reported)	1,857.4	99	-36.6	2,987.0
SERVICE WORKERS EXC. PRIVATE HSHLD				
Attendants and ushers: recreation, amuse..	1,480.9	87	223.1	389.3
Charwomen and cleaners	332.9	98	145.9	76.0
Cooks, except private household	309.8	362	63.9	150.1
Elevator operators	663.3	84	43.2	432.8
Firemen, fire prevention	672.6	98	53.8	402.3
Janitors and sextons	752.3	426	55.7	447.3
Porters	326.9	137	18.8	259.4
Counter, fountain wrks., waiters, waitresses	680.8	729	101.4	287.7
Service wrks., exc. private hshld. (n. e. c.)	502.5	468	116.1	178.8
LABORERS, EXCEPT FARM AND MINE				
Gardeners, exc. farm and grounds keepers.	564.0	135	-5.2	600.4
Meat products, can., preserving fruits, veg. and sea foods	416.7	52	-7.0	455.6

List 3.—Continued

Misc. food preparations and kindred prod., not specified food industries	718.5	21	-10.5	814.6
Misc. fabricated textile products	356.3	2	117.5	109.8
Paperboard containers and boxes	677.0	9	278.4	105.3
Drugs and medicines, misc. chemical and allied products	306.2	46	-24.4	437.1
Petroleum refining	379.6	20	-37.8	671.6
Construction	3,756.1	768	11.0	3,375.2
Wholesale and retail trade	403.7	276	36.4	269.3
Business and repair services	1,399.4	14	-1.0	1,415.3

It may surprise the reader to discover just how many of the "revolutionary" changes in occupational composition that are associated with the "modern" (automobile-aviation-electronic-atomic) era originated and began to develop during the days of the horse and buggy and the gas light, when ways of living and methods of economic organization were both "old fashioned." The rates of change which are shown to have prevailed between 1900 and 1930 for many of the professional and other white-collar occupations are proportionately much higher, in many instances, than the rates shown for these occupations during the more recent period (even though the numerical increase may have been larger in the years since 1930).

However, the occupational growth between 1900 and 1930 is not identical in all its aspects with the growth described above for the most recent years. In the earlier decades much more emphasis was placed on developments in commerce (retail and wholesale trade), in rail transportation, and in basic production processes (processes that required large numbers of foremen, mechanics, electricians, and inspectors). The decades since 1930 have produced the great class of operatives who man the labor-saving machines and thereby replace unskilled workmen. The boom in the tertiary (professional and clerical) occupations did not _follow_ the growth of secondary (commercial and producer) occupations, as frequently is asserted; it has been underway continuously since 1900, and has paralleled the expansion of commerce and manufacturing.

The following list of slowly-growing or declining occupations testifies to the great technological change that has taken place.

List 4.—OCCUPATIONS THAT DECLINED OR GREW BY LESS THAN 50 PERCENT: 1900 TO 1950

Occupation	Change, 1900 to 1950		Percent change	
	Percent	No. of persons (000)	1930 to 1950	1900 to 1930
FARMERS AND FARM MANAGERS				
Farmers (owners and tenants)	-24.6	-1,413	-27.6	4.2
MGRS., OFFS., PROPR'S, EXC. FARM				
Conductors, railroad	32.2	14	-22.6	70.8
Off., pilots, pursers, engineers, ship	-1.1	...	-12.1	12.5
CLERICAL AND KINDRED WORKERS				
Baggagemen, transportation	-56.8	-11	-10.5	-51.7
Messengers, office boys, t'graph messeng..	3.8	3	-28.7	45.6
Telegraph operators	-36.4	-20	-47.6	21.5
SALES WORKERS				
Hucksters and peddlers	-68.9	-53	-57.9	-26.1
CRAFTSMEN, FOREMEN, KINDRED WRKS.				
Boilermakers	29.2	9	-19.4	60.3
Bookbinders	26.5	7	70.5	-25.8
Brickmasons, stonemasons, tile setters	21.2	32	5.7	14.6
Blacksmiths, forgemen, hammermen	-72.8	-160	-56.0	-38.1
Railroads and railway express service	45.1	17	-33.8	119.1
Locomotive: engineers and firemen	22.8	24	-23.1	59.7
Millers, grain, flour, feed, etc.	-60.8	-15	-37.7	-37.1
Molders, metal	-32.6	-32	-38.1	8.8
Paperhangers	6.7	1	-17.9	30.0
Shoemakers, repairmen, exc. factory	-40.8	-41	-21.3	-24.7
Stone cutters and stone carvers	-75.2	-28	-59.5	38.9
Tailors and tailoresses	-34.4	-46	-48.0	26.2
Craftsmen and kindred wrks. (n.e.c.)	26.6	16	76.3	-28.2
OPERATIVES AND KINDRED WORKERS				
Apprentices: machinists and toolmakers; auto mechanics; bricklayers, masons; mech., exc. auto; building trades(n.e.c.); metal working trades(n.e.c.); other spec. trades; trade not specified	28.5	16	17.7	9.2
Boatmen, canalmen, and lock keepers	-34.1	-4	53.1	-57.0
Brakemen, r.r.; switchmen, railroad	35.0	38	-16.1	61.0
Conductors, bus and street railway	-51.7	-12	-68.4	52.7
Dressmakers, seamstresses, exc. factory..	-64.5	-267	26.1	-52.0
Milliners	-82.3	-62	47.0	-66.7
Mine operatives and laborers (n.e.c.)				
Mining and quarrymen except fuel	-6.1	-41	-30.5	35.0
Motormen, mine, factory, logging camp, etc.	-27.4	-10	-53.1	54.9
Sailors and deck hands	37.4	15	-15.6	62.7
Weavers, textiles	32.0	50	-53.1	45.1
Tobacco manufacturers	-39.0	-45	-32.1	-10.3
Misc. textile mill products	2.7	1	-10.6	15.0
Leather: tanned, curried, and finished	23.5	6	9.0	13.3
Not spec. manufacturing industries	-35.4	-24	-68.9	107.5
PRIVATE HOUSEHOLD WORKERS				
Laundresses, private hshld. -living out	-73.0	-204	-78.1	23.1
Housekeepers: private hshld. -living in, living out; private hshld. wrks.(n.e.c.)-living in, living out	12.6	164	-11.6	27.3
SERVICE WRKS. EXC. PRIVATE HSHLD				
Boarding and lodging housekeepers	-58.2	-42	-79.4	102.5
FARM LABORERS AND FOREMEN				
Farm laborers: wage wrks., unpaid family workers	-50.1	-2,564	-40.1	16.8
LABORERS, EXCEPT FARM AND MINE				
Fishermen and oystermen	8.2	6	1.8	6.3
Teamsters	-93.9	-351	-81.1	-67.8
Laborers (n.e.c.)	9.2	278	-29.7	55.4
Saw and planing mills, millwork, misc. wood products	21.9	31	-41.8	109.5
Glass and glass products	6.0	1	-44.2	89.9
Structural clay products	-31.1	-13	-52.0	43.4
Pottery and related products	19.2	1	-38.8	94.8
Misc. nonmetallic mineral, stone products..	31.0	2	16.6	12.3
Profess'nl equipment and supplies; photographic equip., supplies; watches, clocks, clockwork-operated devices; misc. manufacturing industries	-26.5	-8	-70.2	146.4
Confectionery and related products	36.3	1	-23.9	79.1
Tobacco manufacturers	-26.6	-4	-51.8	52.3
Knitting mills	-16.2	-1	-67.6	158.6
Dyeing, finishing textiles, exc. knit goods ..	-64.4	-6	-57.4	-16.4
Yarn, thread and fabric mills	12.8	6	-47.0	112.9
Miscellaneous textile mill products	-25.2	-1	-25.8	0.8
Misc. petroleum and coal products	-45.2	-5	28.0	-57.2
Leather: tanned, curried, and finished	-52.5	-8	-55.3	6.3
Footwear, except rubber	7.7	...	-67.9	235.6
Leather products, except footwear	-33.2	-1	-38.7	9.1
Not spec. manufacturing industries	-85.8	-68	-90.1	43.1
Nonmanufacturing ind. (incl. not reported) ..	-9.0	-205	-23.4	18.9
Railroads and railway express service	3.2	9	-40.3	72.9
Personal services; all other industries (including not reported)	-84.8	-1,548	67.9	-52.6

The substitution of automobile for rail transportation, and of electronic for telegraphic communication, has caused a sharp decline in the number of jobs related to railroading and telegraphy. Many time-honored crafts, such as shoemaker, flour miller, stonecutter, blacksmith, and dressmaker, have suffered large decreases. Many of the slowly-growing occupations grew moderately fast until 1930, and declined thereafter. This pattern was especially noticeable among the laborer occupations; many of them were expanding until after World War I, when the phase of rapid automation and mechanization began.

The long-term process of urbanization, described in Chapter 3, is intimately related to the long-run trends in occupational change. The agricultural occupations have declined, and the cities have grown because they were able to manufacture and distribute vast quantities of goods produced by craft methods which used much human labor. During the last 20 years urbanization has continued, accompanied by stepped-up mechanization and automation, and a need for ever-increasing numbers of white collar workers, especially professionals and clerks.

SEX DIFFERENCES IN OCCUPATIONAL COMPOSITION

The greatly increased participation of women in the labor force was discussed in Chapter 16. It is now possible to discover what occupations women enter as they flock into the labor market. Table 17-4 reports separately the occupational composition of the male and female employed workers, and shows what proportion of workers in each occupational group are women. The data refer to

Table 17-4.—MAJOR OCCUPATION GROUP OF EMPLOYED PERSONS, BY SEX: JULY, 1957

Major occupation group	Percent distribution		Proportion female
	Male	Female	
Total employed...	100.0	100.0	32.0
Professional, technical, and kindred workers.................	8.7	10.1	35.3
Farmers and farm managers................................	7.3	0.9	5.5
Managers, officials, and proprietors, except farm...........	12.9	4.7	14.5
Clerical and kindred workers................................	6.6	29.2	67.5
Sales workers...	5.6	7.5	38.9
Craftsmen, foremen, and kindred workers.....................	18.7	1.2	2.9
Operatives and kindred workers.............................	20.0	16.2	27.5
Private household workers..................................	0.1	9.2	97.5
Service workers, except private household..................	6.2	13.4	50.4
Farm laborers and foremen.................................	5.2	7.4	39.9
Laborers, except farm and mine............................	8.7	0.4	2.0

Source: Current Population Reports, "The Monthly Report on the Labor Force: July 1957," Series P-57, No. 181, Table 15, August 1957.

July, 1957, a date which (as noted above) is considered representative of "normal" recent occupational development.

Although women workers are present in significant numbers in each of the major occupational groups, they are particularly concentrated (in comparison with males) in three major occupational groups:

Clerical and kindred workers (68 percent female)

Private household workers (98 percent female)

Service workers, except private household (50 percent female)

Also, women tend to be mildly concentrated (in comparison with their proportion in all occupations combined) in three additional groups:

Professional, technical, and kindred workers (35 percent female)

Sales workers (39 percent female)

Farm laborers (40 percent female)

Women workers are comparatively rare in four classes of occupations:

Managers, officials, and proprietors (15 percent female)

Farmers and farm managers (6 percent female)

Craftsmen, foremen, and kindred workers (3 percent female)

Laborers, except farm (2 percent female)

The occupations falling in the "operative" category tend to be neither unusually favorable to nor unusually exclusive of women. Jobs as operatives (most of which are in factories) are now the second largest source of employment for women.

Sex Composition and the Detailed Occupations. Table 17-A-1 (Appendix to this chapter) reports what proportion of workers in each of the detailed occupational groups are women. It is readily evident that within each of the major occupational groups there is a great deal of variation in the extent to which women are accepted as (or want to be) workers. Following are two lists of occupations; the first, List 5, enumerates occupations in which almost no women are found, and the second, List 6, enumerates occupations in which women outnumber men.

List 5.—DETAILED OCCUPATION HELD PREPONDERANTLY BY MEN: 1950

Detailed occupation	Percent female 1950
PROFESS'L, TECHN'L, AND KINDRED WORKERS	
Airplane pilots and navigators...................	1.3
Architects	3.8

List 6.—DETAILED OCCUPATION IN WHICH WOMEN OUTNUMBER MEN: 1950

Detailed occupation	Percent female 1950
PROFESS'L, TECHN'L, AND KINDRED WORKERS	
Dancers and dancing teachers	71.1
Dietitions and nutritionists......................	94.0

List 5.—Continued

Clergymen	4.0
Dentists	2.7
Engineers, technical	1.2
Aeronautical	1.9
Chemical	1.9
Civil	1.6
Electrical	1.2
Industrical	1.1
Mechanical	0.5
Metallurgical and metallurgists	2.1
Mining	1.0
Not elsewhere classified	1.3
Foresters and conservationists	3.2
Lawyers and judges	3.5
Surveyors	3.7

FARMERS AND FARM MANAGERS

Farmers (owners and tenants)	2.7

MANAGERS, OFFICIALS, AND PROPR'S, EXC. FARM

Buyers and shippers, farm products	2.1
Conductors, railroad	0.6
Inspectors, public administration	4.1
Federal public admin. and postal service	3.1
State public administration	3.8
Officers, pilots, pursers, and engineers, ship	3.0
Managers, offs., propr's(n.e.c.)-salaried	
Construction	2.3
Transportation	3.6
Retail trade	
Motor vehicles and accessories retailing	3.4
Gasoline service stations	1.8
Hardware, farm impl., bldg. material retail	3.6
Automobile repair services and garages	1.7
Managers, offs., propr's(n.e.c.)-self-employed	
Construction	1.3
Transportation	4.7
Telecommun., and util. and sanitary services	4.5
Wholesale trade	4.1
Retail trade	
Motor vehicles and accessories retailing	2.6
Gasoline service stations	3.7
Hardware, farm impl., and bldg. material retail	4.9
Banking and other finance	4.7
Automobile repair services and garages	1.8
Miscellaneous repair services	4.4

CLERICAL AND KINDRED WORKERS

Baggagemen, transportation	1.9
Express messengers and railway mail clerks	1.5
Mail carriers	2.1

SALES WORKERS

Newsboys	4.0
Salesmen and sales clerks (n.e.c.)	
Wholesale trade	3.7

List 6.—Continued

Librarians	88.6
Musicians and music teachers	50.7
Nurses, professional	97.6
Nurses, student professional	97.9
Religious workers	69.6
Social and welfare workers, except group	69.2
Teachers (n.e.c.)	74.5
Technicians, medical and dental	56.7

CLERICAL AND KINDRED WORKERS	62.3
Attendants and assistants, library	74.4
Attendants, physician's and dentist's office	95.0
Bookkeepers	77.1
Cashiers	81.1
Office machine operators	82.3
Stenographers, typists, and secretaries	94.4
Telephone operators	95.5

SALES WORKERS

Demonstrators	81.9

CRAFTSMEN, FOREMEN, AND KINDRED WRKS.

Bookbinders	56.1

OPERATIVES AND KINDRED WORKERS

Dressmakers and seamstresses, except factory	97.2
Fruit, nut, and veg. graders and packers, exc. factory	60.2
Laundry and dry cleaning operatives	67.1
Milliners	89.4
Spinners, textile	75.0
Operatives and kindred workers (n.e.c.)	
Manufacturing	
Durable goods	
Electrical machinery, equip., and supplies	53.8
Profess'l and photographic equip., watches	
Watches, clocks, clockwork-oper. devices	59.2
Miscellaneous manufacturing industries	52.1
Nondurable goods	52.8
Food and kindred products	
Can. and preserving fruits, veg., sea foods.	62.6
Bakery products	52.9
Confectionery and related products	65.4
Not specified food industries	57.9
Tobacco manufactures	70.1
Textile mill products	53.3
Knitting mills	72.1
Apparel and other fabricated textile prod.	80.1
Apparel and accessories	81.1
Miscellaneous fabricated textile products	71.8
Chemicals and allied products	
Drugs and medicines	60.1
Leather and leather products	
Footwear, except rubber	52.8
Leather products, except footwear	55.3
Nonmanufacturing industries (incl. not reported)	
Personal services	56.2

List 5.—Continued

CRAFTSMEN, FOREMEN, AND KINDRED WRKS. .	3.0
Blacksmiths	0.5
Boilermakers	0.9
Brickmasons, stonemasons, and tile setters	0.6
Cabinetmakers	1.5
Carpenters	0.5
Cement and concrete finishers	0.6
Cranemen, derrickmen, and hoistmen	0.8
Electricians	0.7
Electrotypers and stereotypers	3.7
Excavating, grading, and road machinery operators	0.5
Foremen (n.e.c.)	
Construction	0.5
Manufacturing	
Metal industries	2.1
Transportation equipment	1.7
Railroads and railway express service	0.5
Transportation, except railroad	1.2
Telecommun., and util. and sanitary services	2.4
Forgemen and hammermen	2.0
Glaziers	3.2
Heat treaters, annealers, and temperers	1.4
Inspectors, scalers, and graders, log and lumber	4.3
Inspectors (n.e.c.)	
Construction	1.0
Railroads and railway express service	0.4
Transport., exc. r.r., commun., other public util.	3.9
Job setters, metal	1.2
Linemen and servicemen, t'graph, t'phone, power	2.3
Locomotive engineers	0.6
Locomotive firemen	0.4
Loom fixers	1.1
Machinists	1.6
Mechanics and repairmen	1.2
Airplane	1.6
Automobile	0.6
Office machine	1.5
Radio and television	2.7
Railroad and car shop	0.5
Not elsewhere classified	1.6
Millers, grain, flour, feed, etc.	0.7
Millwrights	0.4
Molders, metal	1.1
Motion picture projectionists	1.8
Painters, construction and maintenance	2.1
Pattern and model makers, except paper	3.4
Photoengravers and lithographers	3.7
Piano and organ tuners and repairmen	3.4
Plasterers	0.8
Plumbers and pipe fitters	0.7
Pressmen and plate printers, printing	4.3
Rollers and roll hands, metal	2.2
Roofers and slaters	0.5

List 6.—Continued

PRIVATE HOUSEHOLD WORKERS

Housekeepers private household	96.2
Living in	98.9
Living out	94.6
Laundresses	96.9
Living in	99.2
Living out	96.9
Private household workers (n.e.c.)	94.5
Living in	92.6
Living out	94.8

SERVICE WORKERS, EXCEPT PRIVATE HOUSEHOLD

Attendants, hospital and other institution	59.3
Att., professional and personal service (n.e.c.)	66.4
Boarding and lodging housekeepers	73.0
Charwomen and cleaners	60.4
Cooks, except private household	55.8
Counter and fountain workers	51.3
Housekeepers and stewards, except private hshld	78.3
Midwives	82.9
Practical nurses	95.9
Waiters and waitresses	82.1
Service workers, exc. private household (n.e.c.)	61.5

List 5.—Continued

Shoemakers and repairers, except factory.........	3.8
Stationary engineers	0.7
Stone cutters and stone carvers	2.6
Structural metal workers	0.5
Tinsmiths, coppersmiths, and sheet metal workers	0.9
Toolmakers, and die makers and setters	0.7
Craftsmen and kindred workers (n.e.c.)	1.6

OPERATIVES AND KINDRED WORKERS

Apprentices	2.7
Auto mechanics.............................	4.0
Bricklayers and masons	0.4
Carpenters.................................	0.8
Electricians...............................	0.9
Machinists and toolmakers..................	1.0
Plumbers and pipe fitters..................	4.5
Building trades (n.e.c.)	0.8
Metalworking trades (n.e.c.)...............	1.1
Printing trades	2.6
Other specified trades	3.7
Trade not specified	4.9
Asbestos and insulation workers..............	2.7
Attendants, auto service and parking..........	2.8
Blasters and powdermen......................	0.8
Boatmen, canalmen, and lock keepers	2.5
Brakemen, railroad..........................	0.4
Bus drivers	3.2
Chainmen, rodmen and axmen, surveying	2.3
Conductors, bus and street railway............	1.8
Deliverymen and routemen....................	1.8
Dyers	4.3
Filers, grinders, and polishers, metal	4.5
Furnacemen, smeltermen, and pourers..........	2.2
Heaters, metal..............................	4.5
Meat cutters, except slaughter and packing houses .	2.0
Mine operatives and laborers (n.e.c.)	0.8
Coal mining...............................	0.4
Crude petroleum and natural gas extraction......	0.4
Mining and quarrying auto	2.7
Motormen, mine, factory, logging camp, etc......	0.9
Motormen, street, subway, and elevated railway...	1.3
Oilers and greasers, except auto	1.6
Power station operators	3.9
Sailors and deck hands	1.9
Sawyers	2.0
Stationary firemen..........................	0.9
Switchmen, railroad	0.8
Taxicab drivers and chauffeurs.................	1.7
Truck and tractor drivers	0.6
Welders and flame-cutters.....................	3.6
Operatives and kindred workers (n.e.c.)	
Manufacturing	
Durable goods	
Saw and planning mills, misc. wood products	
Sawmills, planning mills, and mill work...	3.5

List 5.—Continued

Stone, clay and glass products	
Cement, and concrete, gypsum, plaster prod.	3.1
Metal industries	
Primary metal industries	
Blast furnaces, steel works, rolling mills	4.6
Transportation equipment	
Ship and boat building and repairing.......	4.2
Nondurable goods	
Petroleum and coal products	2.7
Petroleum refining.....................	2.5
Miscellaneous petroleum and coal prod....	3.9
Nonmanufacturing industries (incl. not reported)	
Construction	2.2
Railroads and railway express service	1.3

SERVICE WORKERS, EXC. PRIVATE HOUSEHOLD

Bootblacks....................................	3.4
Firemen, fire protection	0.4
Guards, watchmen, and doorkeepers..............	2.2
Marshals and constables.......................	2.8
Policemen and detectives.......................	1.8
Government..................................	1.4
Porters......................................	2.2
Sheriffs and bailiffs	4.1
Watchmen (crossing) and bridge tenders...........	4.0

FARM LABORERS AND FOREMEN

Farm foremen	2.7

LABORERS, EXCEPT FARM AND MINE 3.7

Fishermen and oystermen	1.4
Garage laborers, and car washers and greasers ...	3.4
Gardeners, except farm and groundskeepers.......	2.3
Longshoremen and stevedores...................	1.1
Lumbermen, raftsmen, and wood choppers	0.9
Teamsters....................................	1.5
Laborers (n.e.c.)	4.1
Manufacturing	
Durable goods	4.3
Saw and planning mills, and misc. wood prod.	2.5
Sawmills, planning mills, and mill work ..	1.7
Stone, clay, and glass products.............	3.9
Cement, and concrete, gypsum, plaster prod.	0.8
Structural clay products	2.5
Misc. nonmetallic mineral and stone prod..	2.9
Metal industries	3.0
Primary metal industries.................	1.4
Blast furnaces, steel works, rolling mills	1.1
Other primary iron and steel industries .	1.6
Primary nonferrous industries	2.3
Machinery, except electrical...............	3.7
Agricultural mach. and tractors...........	3.0
Miscellaneous machinery	3.7
Transportation equipment..................	4.0
Motor vehicles and motor vehicle equip ...	4.8
Ship and boat building and repairing.......	1.2

List 5.—Continued
- Railroad and misc. transportation equip... 2.9

Nondurable goods
  Food and kindred products
  - Dairy products 4.8
  - Grain-mill products.................... 1.5
  - Beverage industries.................... 3.0
  - Misc. food preparations and kindred prod.. 4.6
  Textile mill products
  - Dyeing and finishing textiles, exc. knit goods 3.9
  Paper and allied products
  - Pulp, paper, and paperboard mills 2.9
- Chemicals and allied products.............. 4.2
  - Misc. chemicals and allied products 3.5
- Petroleum and coal products 1.1
  - Petroleum refining..................... 1.0
  - Misc. petroleum and coal products 1.5
- Nonmanufacturing industries (incl. not reported). 2.8
- Construction 0.8
- Railroads and railway express service 2.5
- Transportation, except railroad.............. 2.0
- Telecomm., and utilities and sanitary services 1.2
- Business and repair services 4.4
- Public administration 2.5

List 5 gives occupations in which less than 5 percent of the persons employed in 1950 were women. Noting the characteristics of the occupations on this list makes it possible to generalize that women have been excluded from occupations of the following types:

a. Hazardous occupations
b. Occupations requiring heavy physical exertion
c. Occupations involving great public or financial trust or responsibility, or important decision-making
d. Occupations requiring expert or extensive technical knowledge
e. Occupations requiring a broad and deep educational background
f. Occupations involving extremely uncomfortable working conditions--extreme heat, cold, humidity, and large amounts of fumes, odors, noise, dirt, etc.
g. Occupations requiring fairly continuous mobility, such as traveling sales workers, itinerant inspectors, train conductors
h. Occupations requiring the worker to supervise or "boss" large numbers of other employees
i. Occupations based on a traditional craft, requiring apprenticeship or special "trade school" preparation

A similar study of List 6 leads to the generalization that women have entered the following types of occupations in extraordinarily large numbers:

a. Occupations that resemble the traditional role of housekeeper and mother (cleaning, sewing, cooking, canning)
b. Occupations that are not hazardous or uncomfortable, and that do not require lifting, carrying or other strenuous exertion.
c. Occupations that are sedentary, and involve much patience and waiting (receptionists, sales workers, telephone operators)
d. Occupations that require manual dexterity, skilled and rapid use of the hands, or highly trained reflex action of the hands

(electronics and electrical assembly, operation of office machines, etc.)

e. Occupations that have a distinctive welfare, cultural, or not-for-profit orientation (social workers, nurses, librarians, religious workers)

f. Occupations that require contact with very young children (elementary school teachers)

g. Occupations in which the use of feminine "sex appeal" is essential or profitable (receptionists, attendants, actresses, sales workers, waitresses, stewardesses)

These generalizations refer to a changing situation, however, rather than to a static one. Women have made tremendous strides toward entering some occupations from which they have previously been excluded. The decade 1940 to 1950 witnessed an extreme wartime shortage of manpower and, hence, an increased use of womanpower. This emergency caused many occupational barriers to be relaxed. Despite this fact, however, some occupations remained almost completely unavailable to women. One way to learn which occupations were favorable to increased participation by women and which were not is to compare the percent increase in employment for men and women during the decade 1940 to 1950. List 7 and List 8, which follow, enumerate the occupations which were unusually favorable to increased participation by women and those which did not change their sex composition by admitting more women.

List 7.–DETAILED OCCUPATIONS MOST FAVORABLE TO THE INCREASED PARTICIPATION OF WOMEN: 1940 TO 1950

Detailed occupation	Percent change 1940 to 1950	
	Male	Female
PROFESS'L, TECHN'L, KINDRED WORKERS		
Accountants and auditors	58.8	204.7
Architects	22.3	95.6
Athletes	55.5	267.2
Chemists	28.3	350.5
Clergymen	20.5	115.3
Dentists	5.7	95.3
Draftsmen	59.4	491.9
Engineers, technical	88.9	787.0
Chemical	153.5	1,512.8
Civil	41.7	911.5
Electrical	72.0	654.3
Metallurgical and metallurgists	98.0	373.0
Not elsewhere classified	114.8	898.4
Entertainers (n. e. c.)	42.0	133.3
Funeral directors and embalmers	2.5	25.0
Lawyers and judges	0.4	49.4
Musicians and music teachers	9.8	30.9
Pharmacists	8.4	125.8
Physicians and surgeons	13.8	54.0
Radio operators	140.1	1,427.8
Surveyors	84.0	836.6
Veterinarians	17.9	953.2
MGRS., OFFS., PROPR'S, EXC. FARM		
Credit men	3.2	104.7
Floormen and floor managers, store	24.5	126.9

List 8.–DETAILED OCCUPATIONS LEAST FAVORABLE TO THE INCREASED PARTICIPATION OF WOMEN: 1940 TO 1950

Detailed occupation	Percent change 1940 to 1950	
	Male	Female
PROFESS'L, TECHN'L, KINDRED WRKS.	42.3	30.4
Actors and actress	38.5	6.6
Chiropractors	26.3	-1.6
College pres., professors, inst. (n. e. c.)	73.8	45.4
Dancers and dancing teachers	113.7	26.6
Designers	37.5	32.7
Librarians	73.1	51.5
Nurses, professional	49.0	34.4
Religious workers	35.4	-7.2
Teachers (n. e. c.)	15.5	8.8
MGRS., OFFS., PROPR'S, EXC. FARM		
Conductors, railroad	19.9	...
Officials, lodge, society, union, etc.	14.5	-28.7
CLERICAL AND KINDRED WORKERS		
Attendants and assistants, library	61.6	29.3
Attendants, physician's and dentist's off.	46.2	25.4
Baggagemen, transportation	30.3	...
Office machine operators	203.6	127.2
CRAFTSMEN, FOREMEN, KINDRED WRKS.		
Inspectors (n. e. c.)		
Construction	11.4	-26.3
Structural metal workers	49.6	46.7
OPERATIVES AND KINDRED WORKERS		
Apprentices	41.1	39.4
Other specified trades	35.7	-20.2

List 7.—Continued

Inspectors, public administration.........	33.0	109.2
Federal public admin. and postal service	35.2	137.7
Local public administration............	70.7	284.3
Off., pilots, pursers, engineers, ship......	20.8	1,063.9
Officials, admin. (n.e.c.), public adm.		
State public administration	9.7	63.1
Postmasters	-0.9	1.8
Mgrs., off'ls, propr's (n.e.c.)-salaried		
Construction.......................	79.7	321.1
Retail trade	18.1	55.1
Food, dairy pr. stores, milk retailing...	6.3	36.1
Gen. merchandise, five-ten cent stores .	5.6	76.7
Apparel and accessories stores........	18.7	76.0
Gasoline service stations	1.7	25.3
Other retail trade....................	7.5	58.3
Banking and other finance	9.9	111.8
Miscellaneous repair services..........	132.9	498.1
All other industries (incl. not reported)..	41.2	157.3

CLERICAL AND KINDRED WORKERS

Bookkeepers	-1.5	71.9
Mail carriers	35.6	127.0
Shipping and receiving clerks	32.5	129.4
Ticket, station, and express agents.......	19.5	255.4
Clerical and kindred workers (n.e.c.)	37.5	132.4

SALES WORKERS ....

	14.2	65.8
Auctioneers...........................	54.0	2,171.5
Insurance agents and brokers	22.8	98.1
Newsboys..............................	71.2	265.8
Real estate agents and brokers...........	19.3	97.7
Salesmen and sales clerks (n.e.c.)	-14.1	64.5

CRAFTSMEN, FOREMEN, KINDRED WRKS.

Boilermakers	30.1	335.6
Cabinetmakers	43.8	194.7
Carpenters............................	67.1	244.7
Compositors and typesetters.............	7.2	49.2
Electricians...........................	63.9	218.5
Electrotypers and stereotypers...........	43.4	457.7
Engravers, except photoengravers........	15.8	96.0
Excavating, grading, road mach. operators	104.8	395.3
Foremen (n.e.c.)		
Construction	28.5	107.0
Railroads and railway express service...	10.3	144.6
Transportation, except railroad........	36.6	135.0
Glaziers..............................	52.1	220.8
Heat treaters, annealers, temperers	72.8	240.0
Inspectors, scalers, graders, log, lumber...	16.6	103.9
Inspectors (n.e.c.)		
Railroad and railway express service....	29.6	112.0
Linemen, servicemen, t'graph, t'phone, pow.	95.1	396.0
Loom fixers...........................	34.2	257.9
Machinists............................	11.0	83.1

List 8.—Continued

Dressmakers, seamstresses, exc. factory.	63.9	2.4
Switchmen, railroad	32.9	...
Operatives and kindred workers (n.e.c.)		
Manufacturing-durable goods		
Saw and planing mills, misc. wood prod.	112.1	100.0
Metal industries		
Primary metal industries		
Blast furnaces, steel wrks, roll. mills	39.2	21.8
Manufacturing-nondurable goods		
Food and kindred products		
Dairy products	77.8	75.8
Can. preserving, fruits, veg., seafoods	98.5	89.5
Grain-mill products.................	107.4	106.9
Confectionery and related products ...	19.0	10.2
Beverage industries.................	66.8	50.2
Textile mill products		
Dyeing, finishing text., exc., knit goods.	16.2	3.6
Carpets, rugs, other floor coverings ..	30.6	20.7
Apparel, other fabricated text. products		
Misc. fabricated textile products	53.8	37.6
Paper and allied products	55.3	48.0
Pulp, paper, and paperboard mills ...	31.7	-0.6
Paperboard containers and boxes	82.9	44.5
Misc. paper and pulp products	142.4	110.0
Printing, publishing, allied industries..	54.3	38.6
Chemicals and allied products	81.2	49.2
Drugs and medicines	121.0	86.2
Petroleum and coal products		
Misc. petroleum and coal products ...	41.9	18.5

SERVICE WRKS., EXC. PRIVATE HSHLD.

Firemen, fire protection	35.6	...

LABORERS, EXCEPT FARM AND MINE

Laborers (n.e.c.)

Manufacturing-durable goods		
Stone, clay and glass products		
Pottery and related products	1.9	-2.5
Manufacturing-nondurable goods		
Food and kindred products		
Bakery products....................	31.5	31.4
Beverage industries.................	21.0	-19.2
Paper and allied products		
Paperboard containers and boxes	10.1	-11.9
Misc. paper and pulp products	73.8	25.8
Printing, publishing, allied industries..	31.4	22.2
Nonmanufacturing industries		
Personal services....................	34.7	19.6

List 7.—Continued

Mechanics and repairmen	103.5	405.7
Airplane	171.0	880.3
Automobile	73.7	243.3
Not elsewhere classified	137.2	446.4
Millwrights	45.8	170.8
Motion picture projectionists............	16.0	88.3
Painters, construction and maintenance ...	21.7	265.9
Pattern and model makers, except paper ..	25.1	389.4
Photoengravers and lithographers	33.6	145.3
Piano and organ tuners and repairmen	56.0	491.1
Plasterers	60.4	196.4
Plumbers and pipe fitters	63.4	272.1
Pressmen and plate printers, printing	45.1	318.5
Rollers and roll hands, metal............	4.4	510.2
Stationary engineers	17.3	177.4
Tinsmiths, coppersmiths, sheet metal wrks	57.8	250.3
Upholsterers	54.6	181.5

OPERATIVES AND KINDRED WORKERS

Apprentices

Trade not specified...................	31.3	145.2
Attendants, auto service and parking	6.3	71.6
Blasters and powdermen	141.2	600.0
Boatsmen, canalmen, lock keepers	49.7	185.9
Dyers	-1.1	62.0
Furnacemen, smeltermen and pourers	89.3	401.6
Heaters, metal........................	13.1	205.9
Meat cutters, exc. slaughter, packing house	19.0	252.7
Motormen, mine, factory, logging camp etc.	32.0	448.7
Oilers and greasers, except auto	62.3	379.0
Painters, exc. construction, maintenance..	25.1	81.5
Power station operators	-0.8	33.7
Sailors and deck hands	13.8	450.4
Stationary firemen.....................	9.3	188.5
Taxicab drivers and chauffeurs...........	35.9	175.8
Welders and flame-cutters...............	111.4	358.6

Operatives and kindred workers (n.e.c.)

  Manufacturing-durable goods

    Stone, clay and glass products

Structural clay products	39.5	167.6

    Transportation equipment

Aircraft and parts	128.1	612.0

  Manufacturing-nondurable goods

Textile mill products	0.6	15.7
Yarn, thread, and fabric mills	7.9	33.6
Leather and leather products	-5.0	22.2
Footwear, except rubber	-7.3	21.4

  Nonmanufacturing industries(incl. not rep.)

Construction.........................	130.6	391.8
Railroads, railway express service	38.6	179.4
Transportation, except railroad	51.5	215.7
Telecomm., utilities, sanitary services .	112.3	409.1
Business and repair services..........	42.1	175.0

List 7.—Continued

SERVICE WRKS., EXC., PRIVATE HSHLD.

Attendants, hospital, other institution......	53.0	213.0
Attendants, recreation and amusement....	28.6	93.0
Bartenders............................	62.8	333.3
Cooks, except private household	20.1	108.4
Elevator operators	-3.1	112.3
Policemen and detectives	27.3	122.6
Government..........................	30.9	168.8
Private.............................	1.7	63.7
Porters		
Sheriffs and bailiffs	15.6	97.1
Ushers, recreation and amusement	4.1	94.7
Waiters and waitresses.................	-6.6	63.5
Watchmen (crossing), bridge tenders......	20.4	248.9

FARM LABORERS AND FOREMEN

Farm foremen.........................	0.3	89.8

LABORERS, EXCEPT FARM AND MINE

Fishermen and oystermen	20.7	143.5
Garage laborers, car washers, greasers..	17.6	444.9
Gardeners, exc. farm, groundskeepers ...	7.6	133.1
Longshoremen and stevedores...........	2.6	120.5
Lumbermen, raftsmen, wood choppers....	34.3	308.3
Laborers (n.e.c.)		
Manufacturing		
Durable goods		
Machinery, except electrical.........	3.9	26.0
Agricultural machinery, tractors ...	31.9	265.1
Nonmanufacturing ind. (incl. not rep'td) ..	33.7	122.2
Railroads and railway express service .	14.1	351.2
Transportation, except railroad	32.3	167.5
Telecomm., utilites, sanitary services ..	38.9	225.8
Public administration.................	124.0	487.3

Comparing these lists might lead to the conclusion that during the 1940 to 1950 decade women invaded many new occupational fields, and made important advances toward entering almost all of the better-paying, more prestigeful, and more responsible positions from which they had been excluded because of sex-prejudice or custom. Large differentials still exist, however, and probably will continue to exist, because it is more difficult for a woman to combine family rearing and the role of wife and mother with some types of jobs than with others. Also, the temperament which our society associates with femininity may be somewhat incompatible with the behavior the same society expects of the holders of some types of occupations. The only fields in which women did not make substantial gains are:

    a. Those in which occupational prejudice has almost disappeared already

    b. Occupations that previously had been dominated by women, and are now being invaded by men—nurses, office machine operators, stenographers

    c. Hazardous, strenuous, or disagreeable occupations which most workers, whether they are men or women, do not value highly.

In short, during this decade women made progress on all the occupational fronts that presented them with a challenge.

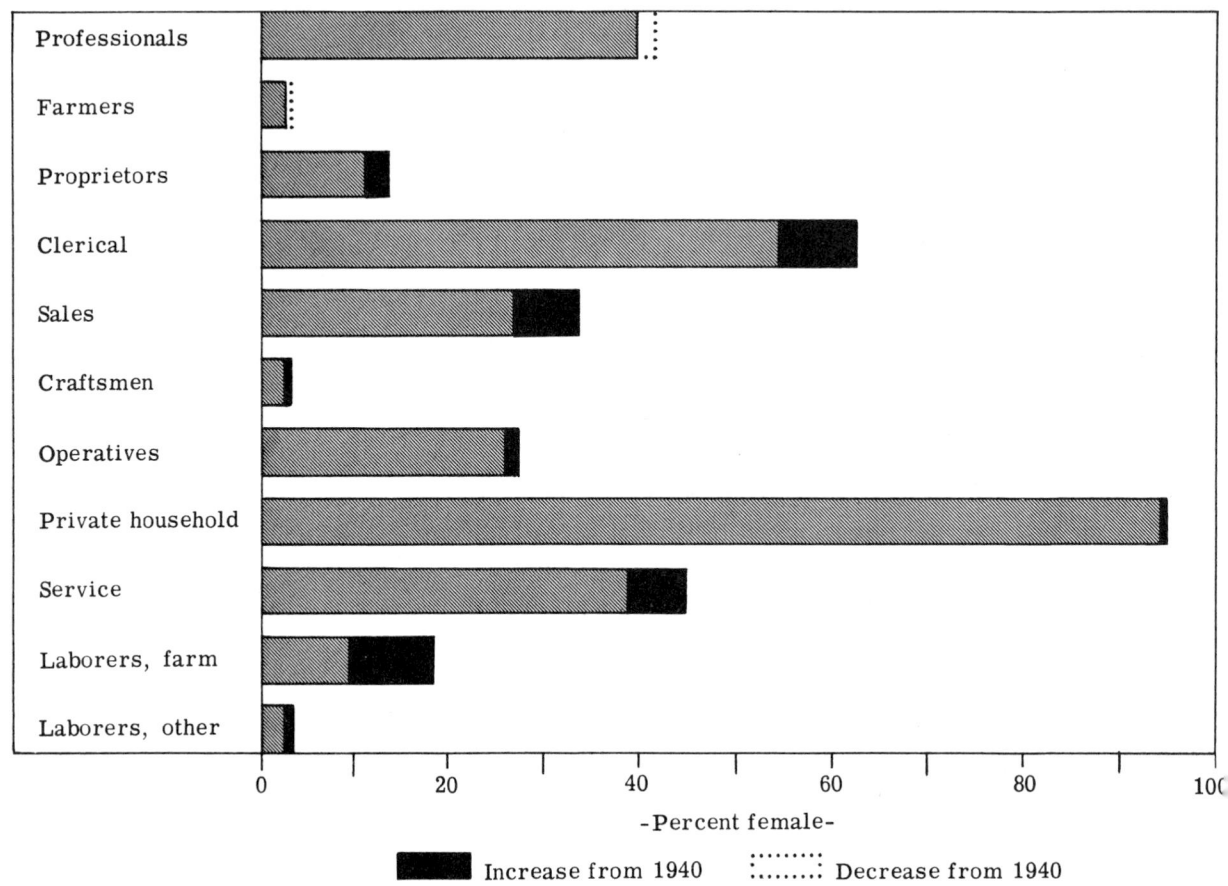

FIGURE 17 - 4. PERCENT OF FEMALE WORKERS IN EACH MAJOR OCCUPATION GROUP,
1940 AND 1950

The changes which have taken place in the sex composition of major occupational groups since 1950, noted above, suggest that this generalization about detailed occupations may be made for the period since 1950; these changes also suggest that the process has probably been accelerated somewhat with respect to some of the top-prestige occupations. When the statistics for detailed occupations become available from the 1960 census, perhaps they will show that women have enjoyed a decade of unprecedented progress toward entering all of those fields which they want to enter but from which, heretofore, they have been generally excluded.

OCCUPATIONS OF WOMEN IN THE LABOR FORCE:
YEARS BEFORE 1940

Women were entering the labor force long before 1940, and the above discussion fails to reveal the kinds of work they were doing prior to the time when they began to expand the scope of their activity. Table 17-A-6 reports what proportion of the workers in each detailed occupation were women at the censuses of 1900, 1930, and 1950, with change in percent female from 1900 to 1950. The "occupations of early entrance" may be identified as those in which the percentage of women workers was as much as 20 percent or more in 1900.

Under this definition, the following occupations were among the first to welcome women workers:

Major occupation	Females as a percent of all workers
PROFES'L, TECHN'L, KINDRED WKRS.	
Nurses, professional and student	93.6
Teachers (n.e.c.)	74.6
Librarians	72.5
Musicians and music teachers	56.8
Authors	45.0
Artists and art teachers	44.3
Dieticians and nutritionists, prof. and tech. wkrs. (n.e.c.)	24.0
Dancers and dancing teachers	21.6
MGRS., PROP'RS, AND KINDRED WKRS.	
Postmasters	33.4
Floormen and floor managers, store	30.1
CLERICAL AND KINDRED WORKERS	
Telephone operators	80.0
Attendants and assistants, library	79.8
Stenographers, typists, secretaries	64.2
Bookkeepers, cashiers	31.4
SALES WORKERS	
Demonstrators	66.1
Sales clerks (n.e.c.)	20.2
CRAFTSMEN, FOREMEN, KINDRED WKRS.	
Bookbinders	51.9
OPERATIVES AND KINDRED WORKERS	
Milliners	100.0
Dressmakers, seamstresses, etc., fac'y	99.9
Spinners, textile	65.0
Laundry and dry cleaning operatives	61.4
Weavers, textile	47.9
Photographic process workers	27.3
OPERATIVES (n.e.c.)	
Paperboard containers and boxes	84.1
Knitting mills	77.6
Misc. fabricated textile products	71.3
Apparel and accessories	69.7
Carpets, rugs, and other floor covering	61.8
Yarn, thread, and fabric mills	58.2
Bakery products	47.6
Misc. textile mill products	43.9
Electrical machinery, equipment, supplies	43.3
Rubber products	42.3
Pulp, paper, paper products	40.0
Watches, clocks, photographic equipment	36.8
Footwear, except rubber	36.1
Tobacco manufactures	35.0
Printing, publishing	31.7
Confectionery and related products	30.4
Drugs and medicines	30.2
Miscellaneous food preparation	29.0
Cann'g., preserv. fruits, veg., meat prod.	28.8
Pottery and related products	25.5
SERVICE WORKERS	
Laundresses	99.3
Housekeepers, priv. hshld. wkrs.	96.1
Midwives	89.5
Charwomen and cleaners	84.1
Boarding and lodging house keepers	83.4
Housekeepers, stewards, exc. priv. hshld.	77.8
Serv. wkrs., exc. priv. hshld. (n.e.c.)	48.7
Waiters and waitresses, counter and fountain workers	40.0
Cooks, except private household	39.7
LABORERS	
Paperboard containers and boxes	60.3
Apparel and accessories	59.9
Knitting mills	48.4
Footwear, except rubber	25.4
Miscellaneous fabricated textile products	24.4
Printing, publishing, and allied industries	20.6
Tobacco manufactures	20.6

Again, a study of the historical record leads to the discovery that women were at work in many places and at a variety of jobs long before they had the right to vote. Nevertheless, it is evident that the occupations through which they could enter the labor force were restricted in scope: a large number of jobs were simply "women's work" that had been transferred from the home to the factory or service establishment. The making of clothes, the preparation of food, and "housekeeping" in public buildings comprised a very large share of their work. Their earliest gains in the white-collar field seem to have been made in the artistic, educational, and nursing professions, in the retail

Table 17-5.—FEMALES AS A PERCENT OF ALL WORKERS IN THE EXPERIENCED LABOR FORCE, BY MAJOR OCCUPATION GROUP: 1900 TO 1950

Major occupation group	Percent female					
	1950	1940	1930	1920	1910	1900
All workers....................................	27.9	24.3	22.1	20.5	20.0	18.3
Professional, technical, and kindred workers........	39.5	41.5	44.8	44.1	41.3	35.2
Farmers and farm managers............................	2.7	2.9	4.4	4.3	4.5	5.4
Managers, officials, and proprietors, except farm...	13.6	11.0	8.1	6.8	6.1	4.4
Clerical and kindred workers.........................	62.3	54.2	51.8	47.7	34.6	24.2
Sales workers..	34.3	26.8	24.1	26.3	21.6	17.4
Craftsmen, foremen, and kindred workers.............	3.0	2.2	1.7	1.9	2.5	2.5
Operatives and kindred workers......................	27.3	25.8	24.3	26.5	31.3	34.0
Private household workers...........................	94.8	94.4	95.6	96.4	96.4	96.7
Service workers, except private household...........	44.7	38.9	37.7	37.0	36.8	34.3
Farm laborers and foremen...........................	18.7	9.7	15.0	18.0	16.7	13.6
Laborers, except farm and mine......................	3.7	2.7	3.0	4.1	2.4	3.8

Source: David Kaplan and Claire Casey, "Occupational Trends in the United States: 1900-1910," Bureau of the Census Working Paper No. 5, 1958.

store, and under the protective wing of the Federal Government as postal employees.

Table 17-5 charts the entrance of women workers into each of the major occupation groups, by decades. Their biggest gains since 1900 have been in the areas of clerical, sales, and managerial work, where they now comprise a proportion of the total that is two or three times as large as their share was in 1900. They have made moderate gains in service and professional work, fields which were already strongholds of feminine employment a half century ago.

Sometimes it is forgotten that women workers have been used very widely as factory operatives for a very long time. In 1900 the proportion of women operatives was higher than it is today. But American women have not been employed as common laborers (except agricultural) to any great extent, at least during the half century for which data are available.

Table 17-A-6 compares the proportion of women in each occupation in 1900 with the corresponding proportions in 1930 and 1950, thus permitting the reader to note the occupations that welcomed the woman worker in this century, especially between 1900 and 1940.

AGE AND OCCUPATION

Some occupations have a high proportion of very young people, while others are filled with middle-aged or older persons. As a result, each occupation tends to have a distinctive age composition. Table 17-6 demonstrates this fact in its reporting of the age composition of each of the major occupational groups for 1950, separately for males and females. These occupational groups have an age structure that may be characterized as follows:

a. Professional, technical, and kindred workers--deficit of very young and (among males) very old workers, with concentration between ages 25 to 44.

b. Farmers and farm managers--deficit of young and adult workers, with a very large concentration at older ages, especially at ages 60 and over.

c. Managers and officials--concentration at all ages above 35 years, with deficit at all ages younger than 35. These are positions into which workers are promoted after several years of experience in lower echelon occupations.

d. Clerical and kindred workers--concentrated in young age groups, 18 to 34. Deficit in extremely young, middle-aged, and older groups.

e. Sales workers--concentration in all young age groups. For men, a deficit at all ages above 35 years; this is an important occupation for middle-aged and older women.

f. Craftsmen--concentration in adult and older ages, large deficit of very young workers.

g. Operatives and kindred workers--no special concentration at any age; a general concentration at all younger ages, with deficits at ages above 45 years. This is a result of the manufacturers' well-known preference for young workers and discrimination against the older worker.

h. Private household workers--a young girl's and older woman's occupation, with a definite shortage in the adult years 18 to 45. A similar pattern prevails for the few male private household workers.

i. Service workers, except private household-- concentration of very young and middle-aged or older persons--45 years and older.

j. Farm laborers--this is the major occupation of youngsters, and among men there is very heavy concentration at ages under 25 years. Among women there is a large concentration at the very young ages, with a small concentration at ages above 55.

k. Laborers, except farm--an occupation for young men, in which strength and stamina count. However, a surprising proportion of middle-aged and older men are found in this group. They are poorly educated or untrained men who grew up during the era before advanced education became widespread, and men who have lost their jobs as craftsmen or operatives and have been demoted to unskilled tasks.

One need only review hastily Table 17-A-2, appended to this chapter, to appreciate the fact that age composition varies much more among the detailed occupations than among the major occupation groups. Following are Lists 9 and 10, which enumerate the occupations that are held primarily by young adults (persons aged 25 to 34 years) and by middle-aged and older adults (persons aged 35 to 64 years) respectively.

List 9.--YOUNG ADULT OCCUPATIONS: OCCUPATIONS FOR WHICH THE PROPORTION OF EMPLOYED PERSONS 25 TO 34 YEARS OF AGE IS 20 PERCENT GREATER THAN THE AVERAGE FOR ALL OCCUPATIONS: 1950

Intermediate occupation classification	Percent aged 25 to 34 years
PROFESS'L, TECHN'L, AND KINDRED WORKERS.	31.0
Accountants and auditors	31.5
Artists and art teachers	33.3
Authors, editors and reporters	29.7
Chemists	40.7
College pres., prof'rs, and instr's (n.e.c.)	34.7
Designers and draftsmen	40.3
Engineers, aeronautical	55.7
Engineers, electrical	35.5
Engineers, mechanical	35.2
Other technical engineers	37.2
Musicians and music teachers	31.1
Natural scientists (n.e.c.)	41.2
Social scientists	33.0
Surveyors	31.3
Teachers (n.e.c.)	32.3
Technicians, medical and dental	38.7
Other profess'l, techn'l, and kindred workers	33.7
CLERICAL AND KINDRED WORKERS	
Bookkeepers	31.1

List 10.--OLDER WORKERS OCCUPATIONS: OCCUPATIONS FOR WHICH THE PROPORTION OF EMPLOYED PERSONS 55 TO 64 YEARS OF AGE IS 25 PERCENT GREATER THAN THE AVERAGE FOR ALL OCCUPATIONS: 1950

Intermediate occupation classification	Percent aged 55 to 64 years
MALE	
PROFESS'L, TECHN'L, AND KINDRED WORKERS	
Architects	17.2
Clergymen	16,4
Dentists	17.1
Pharmacists	16.7
FARMERS AND FARM MANAGERS	18.4
MGRS., OFFS., AND PROPR'S, EXCEPT FARM...	16.7
Officials and inspectors, state and local	23.0
Other specified managers and officials	19.0
Mgrs., offs., and propr's (n.e.c.)-salaried	
Finance, insurance, and real estate	17.0
Other industries (incl. not reported)	16.2
Mgrs., offs., and propr's (n.e.c.)-self-employed	17.7
Construction	17.7
Manufacturing	18.8
Wholesale trade	18.5
Eating and drinking places	17.4
Retail trade, exc. eating and drinking	17.2
Other industries (incl. not reported)	18.2

List 9.—Continued

SALES WORKERS

Insurance agents and brokers 29.8

Salesmen and sales clerks (n.e.c.)

    Manufacturing............................... 30.9

    Wholesale trade 30.5

CRAFTSMEN, FOREMEN, AND KINDRED WORKERS

Linemen and servicemen, t'graph, t'phone, power... 40.6

Locomotive firemen........................... 36.0

Mechanics and repairmen, airplane.............. 49.8

Mechanics and repairmen, auto 35.3

Mechanics and repairmen, radio and television..... 42.4

Structural metal workers....................... 30.1

Tinsmiths, coppersmiths, sheet metal workers..... 33.2

Toolmakers and die makers and setters 30.4

OPERATIVES AND KINDRED WORKERS

Apprentices.................................. 32.9

Bus drivers.................................. 31.9

Filers, grinders, and polishers, metal 29.5

Truck drivers and deliverymen.................. 33.1

Welders and flame-cutters..................... 34.4

Operatives and kindred workers (n.e.c.)

    Manufacturing

        Durable goods

            Fabricated metal (incl. not specified)....... 30.1

            Machinery except electrical............... 29.8

            Machinery, electrical.................... 33.0

            Motor vehicles and motor vehicle equipment. 30.9

            Transportation equip. exc. motor vehicle ... 34.0

        Nondurable goods

            Paper and allied products................. 29.7

            Chemicals and allied products.............. 32.4

SERVICE WORKERS EXC. PRIVATE HOUSEHOLD

Firemen, fire protection 32.5

LABORERS EXCEPT FARM AND MINE

Laborers (n.e.c.)

    Manufacturing

        Nondurable

            Chemicals and allied products 29.9

FEMALE

PROFESS'L, TECHN'L, AND KINDRED WORKERS

Actresses, dancers, and entertainers (n.e.c.)..... 33.4

Chemists and natural scientists (n.e.c.)........... 40.1

Designers and draftsmen 30.7

Nurses, professional.......................... 29.8

Physicians and surgeons........................ 28.1

Social scientists 29.9

Technicians, medical and dental................. 32.8

CLERICAL AND KINDRED WORKERS

Stenographers, typists, and secretaries........... 29.0

List 10.—Continued

SALES WORKERS

Real estate agents and brokers.................. 24.0

CRAFTSMEN, FOREMEN, AND KINDRED WORKERS

Blacksmiths, forgemen, and hammermen 24.9

Boilermakers 20.1

Cabinetmakers and patternmakers............... 17.4

Carpenters 18.0

Foremen (n.e.c.)

    Nonmanufacturing (incl. not reported).......... 17.4

Locomotive engineers........................... 40.4

Millwrights................................... 16.4

Painters (const.), paperhangers, and glaziers..... 16.5

Shoemakers and repairers, except factory......... 22.0

Stationary engineers 19.3

Tailors and furriers 30.1

OPERATIVES AND KINDRED WORKERS

Stationary firemen............................. 21.7

Operatives and kindred workers (n.e.c.)

    Manufacturing

        Nondurable goods

            Apparel and other fabricated textile products 18.0

PRIVATE HOUSEHOLD WORKERS 17.5

SERVICE WORKERS, EXC. PRIVATE HSHLD..... 18.0

Barbers, beauticians, and manicurists 21.3

Charwomen, janitors, and porters................ 23.1

Elevator operators............................. 24.3

Guards and watchmen 30.3

FEMALE

PROFESS'L, TECHN'L, AND KINDRED WORKERS

College pres., prof'rs, and instr's (n.e.c.)....... 13.7

Dietitians and nutritionists....................... 13.1

Lawyers and judges............................ 12.6

Librarians.................................... 13.9

Musicians and music teachers.................... 15.1

Physicians and surgeons........................ 12.2

Social, welfare, and recreation workers 12.3

Therapists and healers (n.e.c.).................. 14.1

FARMERS AND FARM MANAGERS............... 23.1

MGRS., OFFS., AND PROPR'S, EXCEPT FARM.. 15.8

Specified managers and officials................. 16.7

Mgrs., offs., and propr's (n.e.c.)-salaried....... 12.9

    Other industries (incl. not reported)........... 14.1

Mgrs., offs., and propr's (n.e.c.)-self-employed. 17.4

    Eating and drinking places 12.4

    Wholesale and retail trade, exc. eat. and drink... 18.4

    Other industries (incl. not reported)........... 19.7

SALES WORKERS

Insurance and real estate agents and brokers....... 16.8

.ist 9.—Continued

OPERATIVES AND KINDRED WORKERS

Operatives and kindred workers (n.e.c.)	28.1
Manufacturing	28.3
Durable goods	32.9
Metal industries	33.2
Machinery including electrical	35.5
Other durable goods	31.0
Nondurable goods	
Other nondurable goods	28.3
Not specified manufacturing industries	29.7

SERVICE WRKS. EXC. PRIVATE HOUSEHOLD

Barbers, beauticians and manicurists	34.5
Waitresses, bartenders, and counter workers	30.2

List 10.—Continued

OPERATIVES AND KINDRED WORKERS

Dressmakers and seamstr., except factory	27.4

PRIVATE HOUSEHOLD WORKERS. 14.3

Private household workers-living in	20.9
Private household workers-living out	13.1

SERVICE WRKS. EXCEPT PRIVATE HOUSEHOLD. 12.6

Charwomen, janitors, and porters	25.0
Cooks, except private household	18.3
Housekeepers and stewards, exc. private hshld	29.2
Practical nurses and midwives	24.3
Other service workers, exc. private household	15.1

A comparison of these two lists will show that younger workers are concentrated in:

a. New and rapidly expanding occupations. Much occupational change is due to the fact that the younger generations enter new fields that are just opening up, and avoid fields that are declining in importance. Foremost in these new fields at the present time are the professional occupations.

b. "Junior" occupations which, in some firms, are prerequisites to better occupations. (Before a man can become a sales manager he must have been a salesman; before he can be a foreman he must have been a worker on the line; before he can be a craftsman he must have been an apprentice, etc.)

c. Part-time and temporary jobs. Jobs that can be held during a summer vacation, or on Saturdays, evenings, and holidays while the worker is attending school.

d. Jobs requiring unusual speed, physical exertion, stamina, or those involving intense heat, pressure, or other uncomfortable and hazardous conditions.

Table 17-6.—AGE COMPOSITION OF EMPLOYED PERSONS, BY OCCUPATION AND SEX, UNITED STATES: 1950

Major occupation group	Total employed	Age (years)											Median age
		14 and 15	16 and 17	18 and 19	20 to 24	25 to 29	30 to 34	35 to 44	45 to 54	55 to 59	60 to 64	65 and over	
MALE, total	100.0	0.7	1.5	2.7	9.7	12.2	12.2	23.5	18.8	7.4	5.6	5.6	39.7
Professional, technical, and kindred workers	100.0	0.1	0.1	0.7	7.2	15.7	15.2	26.8	18.4	6.3	4.5	4.9	39.0
Farmers and farm managers	100.0	0.2	0.4	0.9	5.2	8.6	10.0	22.7	21.0	9.9	8.5	12.5	45.1
Managers, officials, and propr's, exc. farm	100.0	...	0.1	0.3	3.1	7.6	11.2	28.4	26.0	9.9	6.8	6.5	44.7
Clerical and kindred workers	100.0	0.2	1.1	3.9	14.2	14.9	12.7	21.1	16.5	6.6	4.7	4.0	36.4
Sales workers	100.0	2.5	2.5	3.1	10.4	13.9	13.0	21.9	16.8	6.3	4.6	5.0	37.1
Craftsmen, foremen, and kindred workers	100.0	0.1	0.3	1.2	7.7	12.5	13.3	25.9	20.9	8.0	5.9	4.4	40.8
Operatives and kindred workers	100.0	0.2	1.2	3.5	13.5	14.9	14.0	24.3	16.0	5.7	4.0	2.7	36.1
Private household workers	100.0	2.4	2.6	2.6	6.1	6.7	7.5	20.2	22.7	9.2	8.3	11.7	45.9
Service workers except private household	100.0	0.9	2.4	2.8	7.6	9.1	9.2	20.1	20.4	9.6	8.4	9.6	44.0
Farm laborers and foremen	100.0	7.6	11.3	11.3	17.4	10.3	7.4	13.0	9.8	3.9	3.6	5.4	26.6
Laborers, except farm and mine	100.0	0.6	2.4	4.8	13.6	12.6	11.0	20.8	16.7	6.8	5.5	5.0	37.4
FEMALE, total	100.0	0.6	1.9	5.6	15.2	12.4	11.1	23.3	17.5	5.7	3.8	3.0	36.4
Professional, technical, and kindred workers	100.0	0.1	0.3	3.0	15.4	12.8	10.2	25.1	19.9	6.3	4.0	3.0	36.4
Farmers and farm managers	100.0	0.5	0.6	0.9	3.0	4.2	6.2	20.3	25.5	12.6	10.5	15.6	50.6
Managers, officials, and propr's, exc. farm	100.0	...	0.2	0.7	4.3	6.7	9.7	29.3	27.7	9.6	6.2	5.7	44.7
Clerical and kindred workers	100.0	0.1	1.2	9.1	24.7	15.8	10.7	19.5	13.0	3.2	1.8	1.0	29.7
Sales workers	100.0	0.7	5.0	7.3	12.0	9.3	10.2	24.0	19.0	6.1	3.8	2.7	37.3
Craftsmen, foremen, and kindred workers	100.0	0.1	0.7	2.7	10.0	11.4	12.0	27.9	21.1	6.8	4.3	3.1	39.7
Operatives and kindred workers	100.0	0.1	1.3	4.3	13.0	13.3	13.4	26.3	17.3	5.4	3.4	2.2	36.7
Private household workers	100.0	2.5	3.5	3.7	8.1	8.7	9.6	22.4	20.1	7.8	6.5	6.9	41.1
Service workers except private household	100.0	0.5	2.7	4.8	11.1	10.7	11.5	23.4	18.5	7.3	5.3	4.1	38.7
Farm laborers and foremen	100.0	4.8	5.9	5.2	10.4	10.2	11.0	22.5	17.1	6.0	3.7	3.2	36.1
Laborers, except farm and mine	100.0	0.6	2.2	5.1	13.6	12.7	12.6	24.6	16.8	5.5	3.6	2.7	36.3

Source: 1950 Census of Population, Vol. II, <u>Characteristics of Population</u>, Part 1, United States Summary, Table 127.

e. Low-paying occupations which are wanted only by new and inexperienced workers, and which mature workers with families to support cannot afford to accept.

In contrast, older workers are concentrated in:

a. Occupations that are dying out or declining--blacksmiths, tailors, farmers.
b. Occupations into which one is promoted or to which one is appointed after many years of service or experience.
c. Occupations that require prolonged training and experience (and perhaps also investment capital).
d. Jobs which, through custom, have tended to become "old folks'" occupations--guards, elevator operators in certain types of structures, charwomen, practical nurses, etc.
e. Low-paying occupations that can supplement a small pension, or that will support one or two persons, but not a family.

There is little that is necessarily permanent about the age structure of most of the occupations. In fact, the age composition is very likely to change from decade to decade. When an occupation first emerges it is populated with a cohort of young recruits. As time passes these incumbents grow older, and the occupation ceases to attract new personnel because its importance declines. Finally, as it becomes an obsolete or unattractive occupation, it is occupied only by older workers. The current wave of young adult technical and professional workers illustrates this pattern. Nevertheless, some age differentials between occupations do remain more or less indefinitely, because of the educational and physical prerequisites, and the experience which is required for entrance. For example, there will always be comparatively few 20-year-old lawyers, physicians, and other similar professional and technical people. Likewise, there will always be few 50-year-old dancers and athletes. Because women must "take time out to have a family," the age composition of the women workers will tend to be different from that of the men in a given occupation.

RACE AND OCCUPATIONAL COMPOSITION

Race Differences in Occupational Composition, 1958. A great deal has been said and written about racial discrimination in employment, and about the tendency to exclude persons from a given occupation because of racial or ethnic origin. Some occupations have been held so exclusively by particular racial groups (such as Negro waiters and porters on Pullman railroad cars or Chinese hand laundrymen) that these occupations are regarded almost as racial property. In general, the nonwhite races have occupied the occupations which are lowest in the socio-economic scale, while the white population has tended to be more concentrated toward the upper end of this scale. That this is true at the present time may be observed from Table 17-7, which gives the occupational composition of the white and the nonwhite populations, by sex, for April, 1958.[5]

In comparison with the white population, the nonwhite workers are extraordinarily concentrated in the nonfarm laborer, private household worker, farm laborer, service worker, and operative categories. There are disproportionately few nonwhite workers in the four upper occupational groups--professional, proprietor and manager, clerical, and craftsmen and foremen. This differential is extremely large. Before the occupational distribution of the nonwhite population could match that of the white population, it would be necessary to raise 27 percent of the nonwhite workers from a lower to a higher occupational category. The reasons for this differential are many and complex; racial prejudice is only one aspect of the

[5]Sample statistics for occupation by color first became available from the Census Bureau, Current Population Survey in 1958, and hence it was impossible to use July, 1957, as the point for comparison, as in the preceding section. Because the business recession of 1957 to 1958 is known to have affected nonwhite workers much more severely than white, the comparisons made here tend to understate the number and proportion of nonwhite workers in operative and craft occupations, where unemployment is being felt most seriously.

situation, though it is probably a major one. Under present conditions, differences between white and nonwhite workers with respect to educational attainment, health, and motivation are also involved. (These differences are not necessarily biological, but are connected with the prevailing cultural arrangements.) Because a very high proportion of the nonwhite workers lack the necessary training, aptitude, and interest, they probably could not "hold down" a job in one of these upper groups if it were given them, although their sons and daughters will probably be able to do so. On the other hand, sociologists and anthropologists have taught us that this lack of aptitude, training, and interest are themselves indirect products of prejudice--that nonwhite children have not been given adequate schooling, and that the interests and hopes of young people with colored skins have

been directed into channels which are consistent with the limitations of present reality, rather than with the national philosophy of unlimited opportunity and reward in proportion to talent and drive. Outright discrimination has been exhibited throughout the nation's history by employers, both in the North and the South: if two equally qualified persons of the same age, one white and one nonwhite with equally satisfactory character references, were to apply for a job, a disproportionately large number of employers would give the job to the white applicant. This kind of direct discrimination has diminished greatly within the past two or three decades, but it still exists in all regions and in all sectors of the economy.

Changes in Color Differential For Occupations, 1950 to 1958. Since the census of 1950 the occupational composition of the nonwhite population has

Table 17-7.—OCCUPATIONAL COMPOSITION OF WHITE AND NONWHITE EMPLOYED PERSONS, APRIL, 1958 AND PERCENT CHANGE IN OCCUPATIONAL COMPOSITION: 1950 TO 1958

Major occupation group	White			Nonwhite			Difference between white and nonwhite
	Both sexes	Male	Female	Both sexes	Male	Female	
PERCENT DISTRIBUTION, 1958							
Total............................	100.0	100.0	100.0	100.0	100.0	100.0	...
Professional, technical, and kindred workers.	11.9	11.2	13.5	4.3	3.3	5.8	-7.6
Farmers and farm managers....................	5.1	7.2	0.6	4.1	6.3	0.8	-1.0
Managers, officials, and propr's, exc. farm..	11.5	14.3	5.6	2.5	2.9	1.9	-9.0
Clerical and kindred workers.................	15.3	6.8	33.4	6.0	4.7	8.0	-9.3
Sales workers................................	7.1	6.7	8.0	1.4	1.5	1.4	-5.7
Craftsmen, foremen, and kindred workers......	14.3	20.5	1.1	5.5	8.7	0.7	-8.8
Operatives and kindred workers...............	17.2	18.4	14.6	20.2	24.6	13.3	3.0
Private household workers....................	2.3	0.1	7.1	16.3	0.6	40.2	14.0
Service workers, except private household....	7.7	5.3	12.7	18.0	15.5	21.9	10.3
Farm laborers and foremen....................	3.0	3.0	3.1	7.2	8.6	5.2	4.2
Laborers, except farm and mine..............	4.6	6.5	0.5	14.5	23.4	0.9	9.9
PERCENT CHANGE, 1950 TO 1958							
Total............................	7.3	2.1	20.4	6.5	0.2	17.7	-0.8
Professional, technical, and kindred workers.	57.9	70.9	39.3	49.4	68.0	36.4	-8.5
Farmers and farm managers....................	-28.2	-27.7	-39.8	-55.5	-53.1	-72.2	-27.3
Managers, officials, and propr's, exc. farm..	4.5	3.2	12.3	10.4	4.7	26.3	5.9
Clerical and kindred workers.................	16.6	-12.3	36.0	68.6	31.4	125.8	52.0
Sales workers................................	5.6	10.6	-2.3	24.3	39.0	6.1	18.7
Craftsmen, foremen, and kindred workers......	12.0	11.9	15.7	23.2	20.7	100.0	11.2
Operatives and kindred workers...............	-10.0	-10.3	-9.0	12.3	13.8	8.4	22.3
Private household workers....................	65.3	-47.2	76.4	-7.9	-71.2	-3.1	-73.2
Service workers, except private household....	13.6	-1.2	31.0	19.7	9.2	33.5	6.1
Farm laborers and foremen....................	-6.9	-17.6	27.2	-21.0	-8.6	-41.0	-14.1
Laborers, except farm and mine..............	11.6	10.1	75.0	12.1	11.4	43.8	0.5

Source: Estimated from data in Bureau of the Census, Current Population Reports, "Monthly Report on the Labor Force, April, 1950" and "Monthly Report on the Labor Force, April, 1958," Series P-57, Nos. 94 and 190.

undergone a revolutionary change. Table 17-7, which reports the percent change in the number of workers in each occupation, by color and sex, 1950 to 1958, provides the data which verify this statement. The number of nonwhite male farmers (largely sharecroppers in the South) was estimated to have declined by 55 percent, and the number of farm laborers by 21 percent, within the short period of 8 years. The Negro woman, even more than the Negro man, was emancipated from low-income farm jobs during this period. This wholesale desertion of agriculture--the abandonment of farms in the South and the migration to cities in the North, West, and also in the South--has altered profoundly the occupational picture of the nonwhite population. The rate of growth of Negro workers in the urban occupations has been impressively large. The number of nonwhite workers now employed in the following occupations is substantially greater than the number thus employed in 1950:

> Professional and technical workers (49 percent increase)
>
> Clerical and kindred workers (69 percent increase)
>
> Sales workers (24 percent increase)
>
> Craftsmen (20 percent increase)
>
> Operatives (12 percent increase)
>
> Service workers (20 percent increase)
>
> Laborers, except farm (12 percent increase)

As their numbers in the city have increased, Negroes have been admitted to the professional and technical occupations, to business offices, and to factories as skilled, semi-skilled and unskilled workers to an extent that is amazing, considering the situation of only a few years ago. If exclusion were still being as widely practiced as it was then, the rate of increase since 1950 in nonwhite employment for occupations at the top of the list would have been nearly zero. Instead, these rates nearly equal, and in some cases surpass, those achieved by the white population. Despite the fact that the occupational differential between white and nonwhite workers is still very large, during the short period of 8 years since 1950 some very substantial changes have been made, which have greatly increased the flow of nonwhite workers in

all urban occupations and have reduced the occupational differential between the races. Since 1950 several labor unions have adopted or have carried out the intent of previously adopted resolutions concerning nondiscrimination. The Federal Government has exerted strong pressure against discrimination in employment by means of its military contracts. The Negro stenographer, switchboard operator, business machine operator, and receptionist have become commonplace in many cities. Jobs as laboratory technicians in hospitals and in industrial plants, as bus drivers, and as policemen are now freely available to nonwhite persons, at least in larger cities. As the income and the purchasing power of the nonwhite groups rise, retailers find it uneconomical to continue discriminatory hiring practices, and the Negro saleswoman and salesman have already made their appearance. Negro workers are helping to fill the rapidly growing occupations of beautician, social worker, practical nurse, etc.

Yet the occupational progress of the nonwhite population should not be exaggerated. As this population has flowed off the farm and into the city, it has not been able to command the best jobs. Many of these people have managed only to swell the ranks of the unskilled laborer group in the city, or to obtain work as janitors, porters, etc. Even if there were no racial prejudice in hiring, these kinds of jobs are the only ones which many of these newcomers to the city are equipped to do. Having worked only at chopping cotton, and having had only an elementary school education, they cannot compete for the better jobs and must, therefore, accept the poorer ones. Their children, however, like the children of the immigrants from Europe, are attending better schools, and remaining in school longer, and are acquiring a better education than their parents had and, hence, will be in a much stronger position to compete for middle-class and upper-income jobs only a few short years from now.

Perhaps the most impressive aspect of Table 17-7 is the occupational progress which has been made by the nonwhite woman. Instead of staying exclusively in the occupations of housemaid, laundress, or field worker on a farm, she has invaded the business world as a secretary or other clerical worker, as a professional worker, or as a service worker. She is very often a manager or proprietor (in fact, a disproportionately large share of female managers and proprietors are nonwhite). Negro men have also made great progress toward increasing their numbers as professional workers and as workers in business and industry. At one time, the number of male nonwhite businessmen, salesmen, craftsmen and clerical workers was almost negligible; this is no longer true.

Changes in Occupational Composition, 1940 to 1950. It would be a serious mistake to think that the trend toward reducing the differential between white and nonwhite workers has been in operation only since 1950, however. Most of the changes described above were taking place throughout the 1940 to 1950 decade. Between the end of the Civil War and 1930, slow progress was made toward permitting nonwhite workers to enter white-collar and skilled occupations. This process was accelerated during the 1930's, but not until the labor shortages and the mass northward migrations began to be felt, about 1940, did the transition start to acquire its present speed. The changes that took place between 1940 and 1950 may be noted from Table 17-8, and are also illustrated in Figure 17-5. Large declines took place in the farmer and farm laborer occupations, and large gains were achieved in the professional, managerial, and clerical groups. Rapid urbanization caused a growth in the laborer and service occupations.

This comparison of growth rates for white and nonwhite workers can be deceiving, however, because it can exaggerate the amount of change in

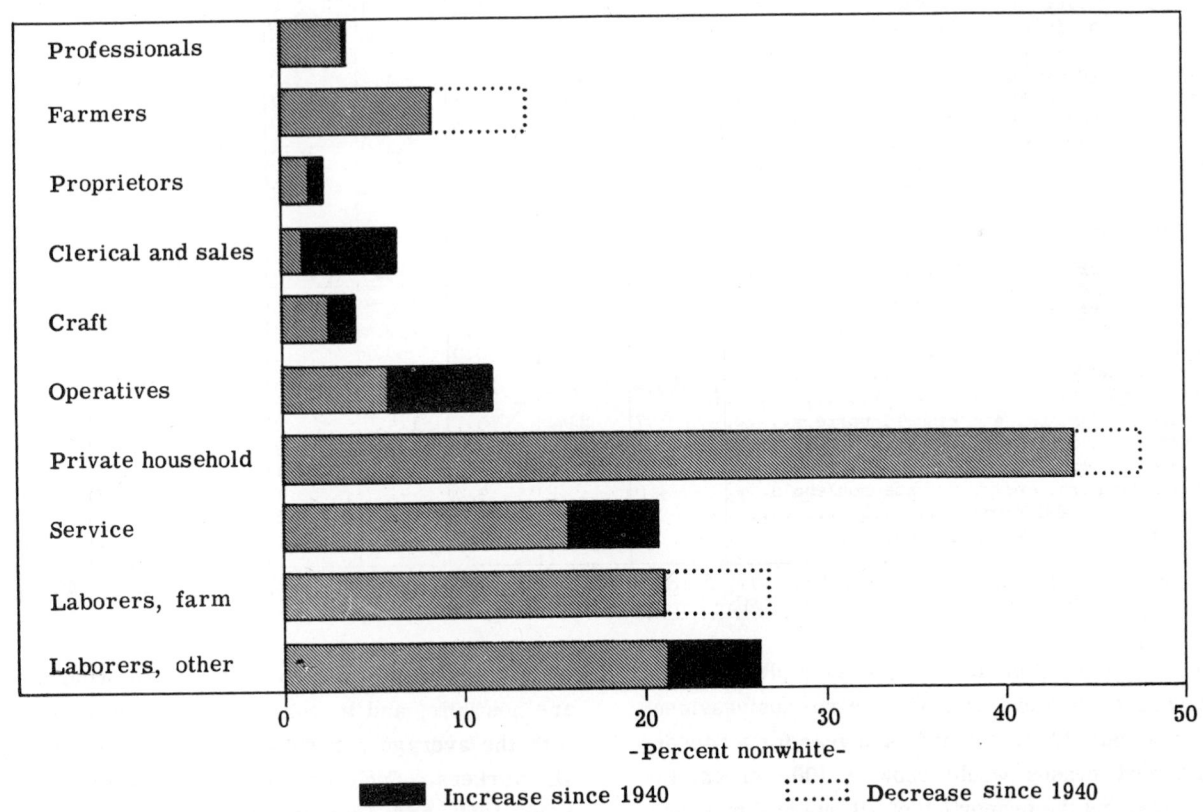

FIGURE 17-5. PERCENT OF NONWHITE PERSONS IN EACH MAJOR OCCUPATION GROUP, 1940 AND 1958

Table 17-8.—PERCENT OCCUPATIONAL DISTRIBUTION OF EMPLOYED LABOR FORCE, 1950 AND 1940, AND PERCENT CHANGE OF EMPLOYMENT IN EACH MAJOR OCCUPATION, 1940 TO 1950, BY SEX AND COLOR

Major occupation group	Total	White			Nonwhite			Difference between white and nonwhite
		Both sexes	Male	Female	Both sexes	Male	Female	
PERCENT DISTRIBUTION, 1950								
Total...............................	100.0	100.0	100.0	100.0	100.0	100.0	100.0	...
Professional, technical, and kindred workers.	8.8	9.4	7.9	13.5	3.5	2.3	5.8	-5.9
Farmers and farm managers....................	7.8	7.6	10.2	0.6	9.5	13.5	1.7	1.9
Managers, officials, and propr's, exc. farm..	9.0	9.8	11.7	4.8	2.0	2.3	1.4	-7.8
Clerical and kindred workers.................	12.4	13.4	6.8	31.1	3.6	3.1	4.4	-9.8
Sales workers...............................	7.1	7.7	7.0	9.6	1.3	1.2	1.5	-6.4
Craftsmen, foremen, and kindred workers......	14.0	15.0	19.9	1.6	5.3	7.7	0.6	-9.7
Operatives and kindred workers...............	20.1	20.2	20.2	20.2	18.9	20.9	15.1	-1.3
Private household workers....................	2.5	1.2	0.1	4.1	14.8	1.1	41.3	13.6
Service workers except private household.....	7.7	6.9	5.2	11.5	15.4	13.5	19.0	8.5
Farm laborers and foremen....................	4.3	3.7	4.3	2.2	9.8	10.9	7.8	6.1
Laborers, except farm and mine..............	6.2	5.1	6.7	0.7	15.9	23.4	1.5	10.8
PERCENT DISTRIBUTION, 1940								
Total...............................	100.0	100.0	100.0	100.0	100.0	100.0	100.0	...
Professional, technical, and kindred workers.	7.5	8.0	5.9	14.9	2.7	1.9	4.3	-5.3
Farmers and farm managers....................	11.5	11.1	14.1	1.1	15.1	21.2	3.1	4.0
Managers, officials, and propr's, exc. farm..	8.4	9.2	10.7	4.4	1.4	1.7	0.8	-7.8
Clerical and kindred workers................. }	16.8	18.5	14.0	33.2	2.0	2.2	1.6	-16.5
Sales workers............................... }								
Craftsmen, foremen, and kindred workers......	11.3	12.3	15.7	1.1	3.0	4.4	0.2	-9.3
Operatives and kindred workers...............	18.4	19.4	19.0	20.6	10.5	12.5	6.7	-8.9
Private household workers....................	4.7	2.7	0.2	11.1	21.9	3.0	59.1	19.2
Service workers except private household.....	7.7	7.3	5.9	11.6	11.8	12.5	10.5	4.5
Farm laborers and foremen....................	6.9	5.7	7.0	1.2	17.7	20.1	13.1	12.0
Laborers, except farm and mine..............	6.8	6.0	7.6	0.9	14.0	20.7	0.8	8.0
PERCENT CHANGE, 1940 TO 1950								
Total...............................	23.9	24.5	18.6	43.5	18.8	17.8	20.7	-5.7
Professional, technical, and kindred workers.	46.8	46.5	58.8	30.5	54.1	45.9	61.0	7.6
Farmers and farm managers....................	-16.3	-14.9	-14.8	-19.4	-25.3	-24.8	-32.0	-10.4
Managers, officials, and propr's, exc. farm..	33.8	33.2	30.0	58.1	72.6	62.3	115.6	39.4
Clerical and kindred workers................. }	43.9	42.1	17.4	75.9	191.0	132.7	351.3	148.9
Sales workers............................... }								
Craftsmen, foremen, and kindred workers......	53.7	52.1	50.7	114.9	113.2	108.4	364.1	61.1
Operatives and kindred workers...............	35.1	30.1	26.6	40.8	113.9	97.9	173.2	83.8
Private household workers....................	-33.3	-46.3	-32.4	-46.9	-19.4	-57.5	-15.6	26.9
Service workers, except private household....	24.0	18.2	4.0	41.7	54.4	27.1	118.7	36.2
Farm laborers and foremen....................	-22.3	-18.0	-27.7	162.1	-34.3	-36.3	-28.4	-16.3
Laborers, except farm and mine..............	11.5	5.2	4.8	15.1	35.1	33.4	118.6	29.9

Source: 1950 Census of Population, Vol. II, Characteristics of the Population, Part 1, U.S. Summary, Table 128
1940 Census of Population, Vol. III, The Labor Force, Part 1, U.S. Summary, Table 62.

the occupational structure. For example, if at one census there were only 100 Negro businessmen, and if only 10 were added each year for a decade, the next census would show a 100 percent increase, but the proportion of all businessmen who are Negro would remain almost unchanged. One way of assessing the extent to which nonwhites are being admitted to the various occupations is to find out what percent of the workers in each occupation are nonwhite, and to compare these proportions with the average percent who are nonwhite among all workers. Such information is reported for 1940, 1950, and 1958 in Table 17-9. These data show that sizable shifts have taken place in the 18 years since 1940. In no one of the upper occupational groups is the percentage of nonwhites now

Table 17-9.—PERCENT NONWHITE EMPLOYED PERSONS BY OCCUPATION AND SEX: 1940, 1950, AND 1958

Major occupation group	Both sexes			Male			Female		
	April 1958	1950	1940	April 1958	1950	1940	April 1958	1950	1940
Total.............................	10.1	9.9	10.4	9.1	9.1	9.1	12.2	12.2	14.2
Professional, technical, and kindred workers.	3.9	3.9	3.7	2.8	2.8	3.0	5.6	5.6	4.6
Farmers and farm managers...................	8.3	12.2	13.6	8.0	11.7	13.1	15.5	28.0	31.6
Managers, officials, and propr's, exc. farm..	2.4	2.2	1.7	2.0	1.9	1.5	4.5	3.9	2.9
Clerical and kindred workers................	4.2	2.8 } 1.2		6.4	4.3 } 1.5		3.2	1.9 } 0.8	
Sales workers...............................	2.2	1.8		2.2	1.7		2.4	2.1	
Craftsmen, foremen, and kindred workers......	4.2	3.8	2.7	4.1	3.7	2.7	8.3	5.1	2.4
Operatives and kindred workers..............	11.6	9.4	5.9	11.7	9.3	6.2	11.2	9.4	5.1
Private household workers...................	43.8	58.1	48.1	37.7	53.2	64.4	44.0	58.4	46.9
Service workers except private household.....	20.9	19.8	15.9	22.5	20.7	17.6	19.3	18.7	13.0
Farm laborers and foremen...................	21.1	22.5	26.6	22.2	20.2	22.3	18.9	32.6	63.9
Laborers, except farm and mine..............	26.2	25.7	21.2	26.4	25.8	21.5	20.2	22.8	13.4

Source: Basic data from tables 17-7 and 17-8.

negligible, and there have been substantial gains in the proportion who are nonwhite in almost all categories. (The professional and clerical occupations have been growing very rapidly because of technological and economic expansion; therefore, it might have been expected that the growth rates of the nonwhite groups, although high, would be lower than those of the whites. In general, this has not proved to be the case. In the clerical occupations especially, the nonwhite population has made extraordinarily large gains.) During this period the Negro was admitted to the factory and to the office. He entered these places at the lower levels--as an operative and as a clerical worker. Already significant advances have been made toward admitting him to the craft and the managerial positions. So rapid has been this progress that, if it were to continue unabated for another two decades, the differential in occupational composition between the nonwhite and the white populations would be so greatly reduced that the directly discriminatory aspects of the occupational situation would have almost disappeared. Because of the rising educational level of the nonwhite population, and because the initial phase of "invasion" has already been accomplished, it seems entirely plausible that further changes of the kind described here will continue to occur at a very rapid pace.

Nonwhite workers have been admitted to some of the detailed occupations much more readily than to others. Certain of the detailed occupations which are lower in the occupational scale have been relegated to the colored races. In order to help assess the present occupational situation of the younger generation of nonwhite workers, the percent nonwhite has been computed for each of the detailed occupations for workers 25 to 34 years of age only. This information is reported at the end of the chapter in Table 17-A-4. By consulting these data the reader can determine which of the specific occupations are most favorable toward the entrance of young nonwhite workers of each sex and which are least favorable.[6]

---

[6]These statistics must be used with extreme caution. They were tabulated by the Bureau of the Census from a very small sample (3 1/3 percent). Tabulating these data according to the detailed occupation classification, and cross-classifying them by age, color, and sex simultaneously, subdivided the data so much that the entries for individual age-sex-color-occupation groups (such as number of nonwhite male dentists 25 to 34 years of age) are subject to extremely large errors of sampling variability. It is fervently to be hoped that the U. S. Census soon abandons its policy of using extremely small samples and performs its special "analytical" tabulations, which are so essential to the proper study and interpretation of the basic and important changes that are taking place in the nation. Both in 1940 and in 1950, the samples used for these tabulations were grossly inadequate to support a rigorous analysis.

Table 17-10.—PERCENTAGE OF FOREIGN-BORN WORKERS IN EACH MAJOR OCCUPATION GROUP, BY SEX: 1950

Major occupation group	Foreign-born white		Difference from average percent foreign born	
	Male	Female	Male	Female
Total...	9.2	6.7	...	...
Professional, technical, and kindred workers...........	7.4	4.6	-1.8	-2.1
Farmers and farm managers.......................	4.0	5.8	-5.2	-0.9
Managers, officials, and proprietors, except farm......	12.9	9.7	3.7	3.0
Clerical and kindred workers...........................	5.5	3.2	-3.7	-6.5
Sales workers...	7.1	6.1	-2.1	-0.6
Craftsmen, foremen, and kindred workers................	10.9	9.7	1.7	3.0
Operatives and kindred workers........................	9.2	11.1	...	4.4
Private household workers..............................	15.9	8.2	6.7	1.5
Service workers, except private household..............	15.9	8.3	6.7	1.6
Farm laborers and foremen.............................	6.7	4.0	-2.5	-2.7
Laborers, except farm and mine........................	10.0	8.2	0.8	1.5

Source: United States Census of Population: 1950, Special Reports, _Occupational Characteristics_, Table 2.

NATIVITY AND OCCUPATIONAL COMPOSITION

Immigrants to the United States have tended to better themselves by climbing the occupational ladder. Of the many thousands who started as farm laborers in the Midwest, a high proportion are now farm operators. Of those who began as factory hands, a high proportion are now craftsmen or proprietors. A moderately large share of the foreign-born population is concentrated toward the middle and bottom of the occupational ladder, as compared with the general population; nevertheless, it is evident that immigrants now have better jobs than they did when they began working in the United States. Table 17-10 reports what proportion of the workers in each occupational group is foreign-born, by sex. Male immigrants (most of whom had resided in this country for 5 years or more before the 1950 census) were concentrated in the following occupations:

> Mgrs., officials, and propr's. (13 percent)
> Craftsmen, foremen, kindred wkrs. (11 pct.)
> Service workers, exc. priv. hshld. (16 pct.)

Women immigrants were concentrated in the following occupations:

> Managers, officials, propr's. (10 percent)
> Craftsmen, foremen, kindred wkrs. (10 pct.)
> Operatives (11 percent)
> Private household workers (8 percent)
> Service wkrs., exc. priv. hshld. (8 percent)
> Laborers, except farm (8 percent)

Because they lacked the educational background, the number of foreign-born persons rising to professional occupations has been disproportionately small. Under these circumstances, the major avenue to success lay in becoming the proprietor of a store or factory, or in developing a craft skill. The following list (List 11) of detailed occupations indicates the nature of this specialization. This list shows that the proportion of workers in these occupations who are foreign born is twice or more the average proportion of foreign born among all workers.

List 11.—OCCUPATIONS IN WHICH THE PROPORTION OF FOREIGN BORN WORKERS IS TWICE THE AVERAGE POPULATION OF FOREIGN BORN AMONG ALL WORKERS, FOR ONE SEX OR THE OTHER: 1950

Detailed occupation	Percent of employed persons foreign born	
	Male	Female
PROFESS'L, TECHN'L, KINDRED WRKS.		
Actors and actresses....................	18.9	13.6
Physicians and surgeons................	11.4	18.3
Designers.............................	18.3	23.0
Religious workers	17.0	13.9
Therapists and healers (n.e.c.)..........	14.7	16.4
MGRS., OFFS., PROPR'S, EXC. FARM		
Managers, superintendents, building......	30.5	19.8
Managers, propr's (n.e.c.)-manufacturing	20.1	15.8
Managers, propr's (n.e.c.)-wholesale tr..	22.1	18.6

List 11.—Continued

Managers, propr's (n.e.c.)-retail trade...	18.8	13.6
Food, dairy products stores, milk ret'l..	24.0	16.1
General merchandise, five, ten cent store	21.0	14.3
Apparel and accessories stores.........	33.5	19.1
Eating and drinking places.............	24.9	11.8
Personal services	23.7	11.8

SALES WORKERS

Hucksters and peddlers	24.4	3.4

CRAFTSMEN, FOREMEN, KINDRED WRKS.

Bakers	27.7	13.6
Cabinetmakers.......................	20.2	3.6
Furriers.............................	43.7	25.0
Jewelers, watchmakers, gold-silversmiths.	18.6	11.5
Shoemakers and repairers, exc. factory ..	39.3	13.9
Tailors and tailoresses.................	65.7	31.3
Toolmakers, die makers and setters	19.3	11.4

OPERATIVES AND KINDRED WORKERS

Conductors, bus and street railway.......	23.5	16.7
Dressmakers, seamstresses, exc. factory	33.8	16.7
Dyers	20.4	8.1
Milliners	44.9	32.0
Sailors and deck hands	18.7	12.1
Operatives and kindred workers (n.e.c.)		
Manufacturing		
Confectionery and related products	22.1	10.5
Apparel, other fab'd textile products ...	40.6	19.4
Leather and leather products..........	20.2	9.7

PRIVATE HOUSEHOLD WORKERS

Housekeepers, private hshld.-living in	16.7	18.7
Laundresses, private hshld.-living in	...	15.4
Private hshld wrks. (n.e.c.)-living in.....	36.3	27.2

SERVICE WRKS., EXC. PRIVATE HSHLD.

Barbers, beauticians, and manicurists....	22.7	6.0
Boarding and lodging house keepers.......	29.9	13.7
Charwomen and cleaners	20.4	25.2
Cooks, except private household	27.2	7.9
Elevator operators	27.4	4.8
Housekeepers, stewards, exc. priv. hshld.	17.6	14.0
Janitors and sextons	16.1	18.6
Waiters and waitresses.................	26.1	4.8

LABORERS, EXCEPT FARM AND MINE

Gardeners, exc. farm and groundkeepers..	20.2	18.7
Longshoremen and stevedores	19.9	7.7
Laborers (n.e.c.)		
Manufacturing		
Can., preserv. fruits, veg., sea foods ..	15.7	14.7
Textile mill pr.-carpets, rugs, other floor coverings....................	21.9	15.4

OCCUPATION AND EDUCATIONAL ATTAINMENT

In each of the occupations the workers tend to be concentrated at a particular level of education, and this level varies widely from occupation to occupation. In many occupations, a certain minimum amount of schooling is necessary if the worker is to comprehend and master the job, to pass the examination for a practicing license, or to obtain a certification of proficiency. This applies not only to such obvious examples as physicians, lawyers, teachers in schools and universities, and engineers, but also to many jobs at the clerical, craft, and operative levels. The ability to read a blueprint, to make computations involving common fractions and decimals, and to spell and punctuate correctly are required in offices and machine shops. Once employers were known to discriminate against job applicants who did not have at least a grammar school diploma. Now many doors are closed to those who lack a high school diploma, and a college degree is becoming a common requirement for an increasing variety of jobs.

Table 17-11 reports the educational attainment of workers in each of the major occupations. One half of the professional workers have 4 years or more of college. A disproportionately large number of managers, proprietors, and officials also have 4 years or more of college education. At the other extreme, the least educated persons are highly concentrated in six major occupational groups:

Farmers and farm managers
Operatives and kindred workers
Private household workers
Service workers, exc. private household
Farm laborers
Laborers, except farm

A grammar school education, or less, is adequate preparation for a majority of the detailed classes of jobs in these categories, and the persons who fill these jobs tend to be those who cannot compete for better paying jobs because they lack the educational requirements and other qualifications. Farmers and farm managers have a low educa-

Table 17-11.—EDUCATIONAL COMPOSITION OF EACH OF THE MAJOR OCCUPATION GROUPS, BY SEX AND COLOR, 1950, FOR 25 YEARS OF AGE AND OVER

Major occupation group	Median years of school completed	Total	College 4 or more years	College 1 to 3 years	High school 4 years	High school 1 to 3 years	Elementary school 8 years	Elementary school 5 to 7 years	Elementary school Less than 5 years	Education not reported
MALE AND FEMALE, total..............	10.1	100.0	8.1	7.8	21.3	17.7	19.7	14.8	8.9	1.8
Professional, technical, and kindred workers.	16.+	100.0	51.7	19.6	15.5	5.3	3.1	1.5	0.9	2.3
Farmers and farm managers.................	7.3	100.0	1.5	3.3	11.3	12.5	28.4	23.5	18.2	1.3
Managers, officials, and propr's, exc. farm..	11.3	100.0	11.4	13.9	27.7	17.4	15.3	8.2	4.3	1.9
Clerical and kindred workers...............	11.4	100.0	6.7	14.5	44.0	17.5	10.5	3.8	1.5	1.6
Sales workers.............................	11.2	100.0	8.2	13.7	32.5	20.0	14.3	6.6	2.9	1.9
Craftsmen, foremen, and kindred workers......	8.3	100.0	1.8	4.7	22.1	22.8	25.0	15.8	6.2	1.6
Operatives and kindred workers.............	7.7	100.0	0.8	2.6	16.5	22.4	25.4	20.7	10.1	1.6
Private household workers..................	6.9	100.0	0.9	1.9	9.5	14.9	20.9	29.1	20.5	2.3
Service workers except private household.....	7.8	100.0	1.5	4.3	18.2	20.6	24.0	18.7	10.5	2.2
Farm laborers and foremen..................	6.6	100.0	0.8	2.2	8.9	10.9	22.6	24.1	27.9	2.6
Laborers, except farm and mine..............	7.0	100.0	0.7	1.7	9.6	14.8	22.8	25.3	22.9	2.2
MALE, total.........................	9.5	100.0	7.8	7.1	19.4	17.6	20.7	15.6	9.8	1.9
Professional, technical, and kindred workers.	16.+	100.0	54.6	15.7	15.3	5.7	3.6	1.8	1.0	2.2
Farmers and farm managers.................	8.3	100.0	1.4	3.2	11.4	12.5	28.6	23.4	18.1	1.3
Managers, officials, and propr's, exc. farm..	12.2	100.0	12.0	14.1	27.0	17.2	15.4	8.2	4.3	1.9
Clerical and kindred workers...............	12.2	100.0	7.8	13.8	34.8	19.2	14.2	6.4	2.2	1.5
Sales workers.............................	12.3	100.0	10.8	16.3	31.6	17.7	12.6	6.1	3.0	1.8
Craftsmen, foremen, and kindred workers......	9.3	100.0	1.8	4.7	22.0	22.8	25.0	15.9	6.3	1.6
Operatives and kindred workers.............	8.7	100.0	0.9	2.8	16.6	22.1	24.8	20.4	10.8	1.5
Private household workers..................	8.1	100.0	2.1	2.8	12.1	12.9	20.1	24.9	21.6	3.4
Service workers except private household.....	8.7	100.0	1.6	4.2	16.6	18.2	24.0	20.1	13.0	2.3
Farm laborers and foremen..................	7.4	100.0	0.8	1.8	8.0	10.2	21.8	24.0	30.6	2.8
Laborers, except farm and mine..............	8.0	100.0	0.6	1.6	9.4	14.6	22.7	25.5	23.3	2.2
FEMALE, total.........................	11.3	100.0	8.7	9.8	26.3	17.8	16.7	12.4	6.3	2.1
Professional, technical, and kindred workers.	15.8	100.0	46.9	26.1	15.9	4.6	2.4	1.0	0.8	2.4
Farmers and farm managers.................	8.1	100.0	3.2	5.1	10.4	11.6	21.2	24.1	22.0	2.4
Managers, officials, and propr's, exc. farm..	12.1	100.0	7.3	12.6	31.8	18.9	15.1	8.3	4.0	2.0
Clerical and kindred workers...............	12.4	100.0	5.9	15.1	50.9	16.1	7.6	1.9	0.9	1.6
Sales workers.............................	11.6	100.0	2.9	8.3	34.3	24.7	17.9	7.5	2.6	1.9
Craftsmen, foremen, and kindred workers......	9.9	100.0	2.9	5.2	24.3	23.8	23.8	13.1	4.2	2.7
Operatives and kindred workers.............	8.7	100.0	0.6	1.9	16.1	23.3	26.9	21.3	8.2	1.6
Private household workers..................	7.9	100.0	0.8	1.9	9.3	15.0	21.0	29.3	20.4	2.3
Service workers except private household.....	9.1	100.0	1.4	4.3	20.3	23.6	24.0	17.0	7.2	2.1
Farm laborers and foremen..................	7.9	100.0	0.9	3.6	11.6	12.9	25.2	24.0	19.8	2.0
Laborers, except farm and mine..............	8.6	100.0	1.3	2.4	15.0	20.2	24.5	20.8	13.4	2.5
MALE—NONWHITE, total....................	6.6	100.0	2.3	2.7	7.6	11.9	11.3	27.2	34.4	2.7
Professional, technical, and kindred workers.	15.9	100.0	47.3	12.7	11.7	8.0	5.0	6.7	4.4	4.2
Farmers and farm managers.................	4.1	100.0	0.3	0.5	1.5	3.7	5.8	27.0	59.4	1.7
Managers, officials, and propr's, exc. farm..	8.4	100.0	6.5	6.7	12.8	14.7	12.2	22.7	21.5	3.0
Clerical and kindred workers...............	12.0	100.0	7.0	14.8	28.4	18.2	10.2	12.5	6.9	1.9
Sales workers.............................	9.4	100.0	6.1	9.2	17.9	18.1	10.1	18.7	17.5	2.5
Craftsmen, foremen, and kindred workers......	7.8	100.0	1.4	3.9	11.5	16.0	14.3	27.2	23.4	2.4
Operatives and kindred workers.............	7.1	100.0	0.6	2.1	8.3	15.4	13.5	29.8	28.2	2.3
Private household workers..................	7.0	100.0	0.8	2.2	8.7	12.4	14.7	28.5	29.3	3.4
Service workers except private household.....	8.0	100.0	1.2	3.6	11.2	16.8	15.5	27.3	21.6	2.7
Farm laborers and foremen..................	4.1	100.0	0.2	0.4	2.4	4.4	6.5	24.5	58.6	3.0
Laborers, except farm and mine..............	6.0	100.0	0.3	1.0	4.7	10.7	11.2	30.9	38.4	2.8
FEMALE—NONWHITE, total.................	7.9	100.0	4.2	4.2	10.8	15.6	12.9	28.3	21.6	2.5
Professional, technical, and kindred workers.	16.+	100.0	54.2	23.7	9.2	4.2	1.8	2.4	1.7	2.7
Farmers and farm managers.................	4.8	100.0	0.1	0.4	1.6	4.6	5.7	34.6	51.6	1.4
Managers, officials, and propr's, exc. farm..	8.6	100.0	3.5	7.9	14.1	17.2	13.9	26.4	14.5	2.5
Clerical and kindred workers...............	12.6	100.0	12.0	21.8	40.5	12.8	5.2	3.5	2.1	2.3
Sales workers.............................	10.3	100.0	2.3	8.0	26.0	21.7	11.7	19.4	8.2	2.9
Craftsmen, foremen, and kindred workers......	8.9	100.0	1.8	5.0	21.3	18.9	16.0	23.7	9.2	4.1
Operatives and kindred workers.............	8.4	100.0	1.0	2.9	14.3	21.0	15.6	27.7	15.3	2.2
Private household workers..................	7.0	100.0	0.5	1.2	6.7	14.4	14.2	34.0	26.7	2.3
Service workers except private household.....	8.4	100.0	1.0	3.8	13.9	21.6	15.3	26.9	15.1	2.5
Farm laborers and foremen..................	5.2	100.0	0.2	0.6	2.3	6.7	7.2	35.3	46.0	1.7
Laborers, except farm and mine..............	7.6	100.0	0.6	2.3	11.4	15.5	14.3	28.4	24.2	3.2

Source: U.S. Census of Population, 1950, Special Report, _Education_, Table 11.

tional level, but to some extent it is low for a different reason than applies to the other three groups--farmers are a much older group of workers, and hence they matured at a time when educational attainment was generally low. The younger generation of farmers has attained a much higher level of education than their fathers did.

Clerical and sales workers have an intermediate level of education. An eighth grade education is almost the minimum requirement acceptable for entrance into these occupations, and a high school diploma is strongly desired by many employers. Those who begin college but do not complete all 4 years also tend to get jobs in these middle income white collar occupations.

Craft workers tend also to be graduates of high school, although many have had no more than 8 years of school, and some have had only 5 to 7 years of elementary school training.

Sex and Color Differences in Education and Occupation. Table 17-11 reports the educational composition of white and nonwhite male and female workers in each occupation. The differences described above apply equally to both sexes, and are approximately correct for the nonwhite as well as for the white population. In general, however, the nonwhite workers in each occupation classification have a lower level of educational attainment than the general population. For example, the nonwhite professional worker tends to have fewer years of education than the white professional worker. This fact should not be accepted as evidence that there is no racial discrimination in employment. These data might lead one to conclude that, given its level of education attainment, the nonwhite population is working at occupations that are higher in the socio-economic scale than is the population generally, and therefore, that what is often called racial discrimination is simply inadequate educational preparation. This conclusion is partially correct; in order to measure the amount of difference, however, one should compare the occupational accomplishments of persons with equal amounts of education, not the educational attainments of persons with the same occupation. In other words, one should ask the questions, "What

kinds of jobs do people obtain who have had 4 years of high school (or any other specified amount of schooling)?" and "How do white and nonwhite workers differ in the kinds of jobs they obtain when they have completed equal amounts of schooling?" The information in Table 17-12 answers this question, and Figure 17-6 illustrates the very close relationship between the amount of schooling completed and the type of job obtained.

Women who have had a high school education, or more, tend to obtain jobs as professional workers and as clerical workers in considerably greater proportions than men with the same educational background. Disproportionately few women with these above-average levels of education tend to enter managerial and proprietary or sales occupations. At the lowest levels of educational attainment (less than a grammar school education), women tend to be highly concentrated in jobs as operatives, household workers, and service workers. About one-half of employed women, and about one-fifth of employed nonwhite women, who have an 8th grade education work as operatives, primarily in factories. The least-educated men tend to be moderately concentrated in these same occupations (compared to all men), but they tend also to be laborers, farm laborers, and farmers.

There seems to be little evidence of over-all discrimination against the nonwhite worker with respect to entrance into the professional and clerical categories of occupations, but there does seem to be some discrimination with respect to his entrance into the managerial and sales occupations. Table 17-12 demonstrates the existence of this situation, if one compares the percentage of nonwhite workers who have had a high school education, or more, and who are employed as managers or as sales workers, with the percentage of white workers of the same sex and education who are so employed. It will be observed that the proportion of nonwhite college graduates who achieve professional occupations is roughly the same as the proportion of white persons having the same sex and educational attainment, but that the proportion of nonwhite college graduates achieving managerial or sales occupations is much smaller. Among

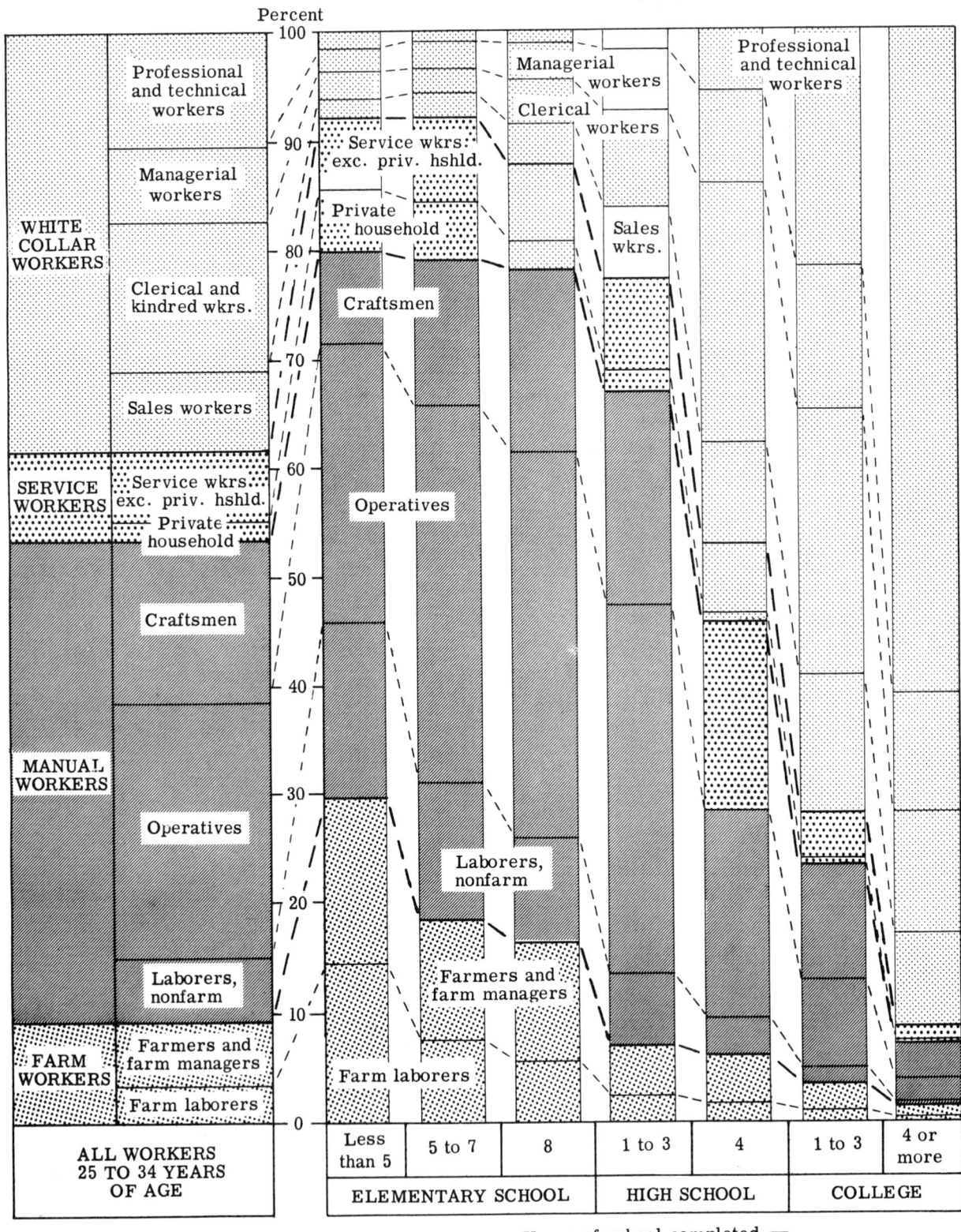

FIGURE 17-6. OCCUPATIONAL COMPOSITION OF WORKERS 15 TO 34 YEARS OF AGE
WHO HAVE ATTAINED SPECIFIED LEVELS OF EDUCATION: 1950

nonwhite workers who have only a high school diploma or a partial college education, a much smaller proportion than of the white population succeed in climbing into the professional category;

they appear to enter the clerical occupations as a substitute for a profession.

At the lower educational levels, nonwhite persons are much more heavily concentrated in the

Table 17-12.—OCCUPATIONAL COMPOSITION OF PERSONS 25 TO 34 YEARS OF AGE, BY EDUCATIONAL ATTAINMENT, SEX, AND COLOR: 1950

Major occupation group	Total	College		High school		Elementary school		
		4 years or more	1 to 3 years	4 years	1 to 3 years	8 years	5 to 7 years	Less than 5 years
TOTAL...........................	100.0	100.0	100.0	100.0	100.0	100.0	100.0	100.0
Professional, technical, and kindred workers.	10.2	61.0	21.9	5.7	1.9	1.0	0.9	1.5
Farmers and farm managers....................	6.0	1.0	2.5	4.5	4.6	11.0	11.0	15.2
Managers, officials, and propr's, exc. farm..	6.9	10.7	13.1	8.4	5.5	3.4	2.4	2.0
Clerical and kindred workers.................	13.9	11.1	24.4	24.0	8.8	4.0	2.2	2.5
Sales workers................................	7.1	8.4	12.7	9.2	6.4	3.6	2.2	1.8
Craftsmen, foremen, and kindred workers......	14.9	3.3	10.5	17.2	19.6	16.8	13.3	8.4
Operatives and kindred workers...............	23.5	2.1	8.0	19.0	33.8	35.3	34.6	25.5
Private household workers....................	1.8	0.1	0.4	0.8	2.0	2.6	5.4	5.7
Service workers except private household.....	6.4	1.4	4.1	6.2	8.5	7.2	7.8	6.5
Farm laborers and foremen....................	3.3	0.3	0.9	1.6	2.3	5.5	7.6	14.8
Laborers, except farm and mine..............	5.9	0.5	1.6	3.3	6.6	9.6	12.8	16.0
WHITE MALES......................	100.0	100.0	100.0	100.0	100.0	100.0	100.0	100.0
Professional, technical, and kindred workers.	10.1	58.0	18.4	5.5	1.9	0.9	1.0	1.8
Farmers and farm managers....................	7.8	1.3	3.6	6.7	6.2	14.6	14.1	16.0
Managers, officials, and propr's, exc. farm..	9.0	13.7	17.5	11.0	6.8	4.0	3.0	3.0
Clerical and kindred workers.................	7.7	7.4	14.0	11.3	5.9	3.0	2.1	2.2
Sales workers................................	7.7	10.8	16.3	9.6	5.6	2.9	2.2	2.4
Craftsmen, foremen, and kindred workers......	21.0	4.4	14.7	25.1	26.7	21.9	19.7	13.0
Operatives and kindred workers...............	23.8	2.3	9.5	20.8	33.0	33.1	35.1	28.1
Private household workers....................	...	...	...	...	...	...	0.1	0.1
Service workers except private household.....	3.6	1.1	3.2	4.1	4.3	3.5	3.5	3.8
Farm laborers and foremen....................	3.1	0.3	1.0	1.7	2.3	5.4	7.1	15.4
Laborers, except farm and mine..............	6.2	0.6	1.8	4.1	7.2	10.6	12.0	14.2
WHITE FEMALES....................	100.0	100.0	100.0	100.0	100.0	100.0	100.0	100.0
Professional, technical, and kindred workers.	13.4	69.2	31.1	6.4	2.2	1.3	1.5	5.5
Farmers and farm managers....................	0.3	0.1	0.2	0.2	0.2	0.6	0.8	0.9
Managers, officials, and propr's, exc. farm..	3.3	3.0	4.0	3.7	3.2	2.2	2.3	2.8
Clerical and kindred workers.................	35.3	21.9	49.9	53.1	20.1	8.7	4.2	13.0
Sales workers................................	8.2	2.5	5.5	9.4	11.1	7.9	5.7	5.6
Craftsmen, foremen, and kindred workers......	1.7	0.5	0.8	1.6	2.6	2.5	1.9	1.8
Operatives and kindred workers...............	22.9	1.0	3.0	14.3	38.8	48.9	55.7	40.5
Private household workers....................	1.8	0.1	0.5	1.0	2.1	4.4	5.4	9.1
Service workers except private household.....	10.1	1.4	4.0	8.7	16.5	15.8	14.7	12.2
Farm laborers and foremen....................	2.1	0.2	0.8	1.3	2.1	6.0	5.9	7.3
Laborers, except farm and mine..............	0.8	0.1	0.1	0.5	1.2	1.6	1.7	1.4
NONWHITE MALES....................	100.0	100.0	100.0	100.0	100.0	100.0	100.0	100.0
Professional, technical, and kindred workers.	2.6	57.4	9.0	3.1	1.1	0.5	0.3	0.2
Farmers and farm managers....................	10.9	1.5	1.9	2.8	4.2	7.0	13.8	22.1
Managers, officials, and propr's, exc. farm..	1.7	5.6	4.5	3.3	2.1	1.4	1.1	0.7
Clerical and kindred workers.................	4.7	13.8	22.5	13.0	5.1	2.8	1.5	0.7
Sales workers................................	1.1	3.3	4.8	2.2	1.3	1.0	0.5	0.3
Craftsmen, foremen, and kindred workers......	8.7	2.8	11.6	12.7	10.5	9.8	7.7	5.8
Operatives and kindred workers...............	25.8	5.2	19.3	26.4	32.8	29.2	26.2	21.0
Private household workers....................	0.8	0.4	0.6	0.9	0.8	1.1	0.7	0.6
Service workers except private household.....	12.1	8.0	15.3	17.9	16.5	14.5	10.4	6.2
Farm laborers and foremen....................	7.3	0.4	0.9	2.3	2.8	5.2	8.6	15.3
Laborers, except farm and mine..............	24.1	1.6	9.7	15.4	22.9	27.5	29.1	27.1

Table 17-12.—OCCUPATIONAL COMPOSITION OF PERSONS 25 TO 34 YEARS OF AGE, BY EDUCATIONAL ATTAINMENT, SEX, AND COLOR: 1950—Continued

Major occupation group	Total	College		High school		Elementary school		
		4 years or more	1 to 3 years	4 years	1 to 3 years	8 years	5 to 7 years	Less than 5 years
NONWHITE FEMALES..................	100.0	100.0	100.0	100.0	100.0	100.0	100.0	100.0
Professional, technical, and kindred workers.	7.0	74.1	28.8	3.9	1.4	0.8	0.4	0.9
Farmers and farm managers..................	0.8	...	...	0.2	0.3	0.4	1.3	2.5
Managers, officials, and propr's, exc. farm..	1.1	0.9	1.8	1.4	1.0	1.0	0.9	0.8
Clerical and kindred workers...............	6.3	14.2	26.4	17.0	2.9	1.7	0.6	0.7
Sales workers.............................	1.6	0.5	1.6	3.7	2.0	1.3	0.7	0.6
Craftsmen, foremen, and kindred workers......	0.8	0.2	0.7	1.3	0.9	1.0	0.7	0.3
Operatives and kindred workers..............	18.5	3.2	11.4	21.4	22.6	22.3	18.2	14.4
Private household workers..................	35.5	3.4	9.7	23.6	37.5	43.7	46.3	45.3
Service workers except private household.....	20.7	3.2	18.2	24.5	26.9	22.8	18.9	15.1
Farm laborers and foremen..................	6.1	0.2	0.6	1.4	3.0	3.5	10.2	17.6
Laborers, except farm and mine.............	1.5	0.1	0.7	1.6	1.5	1.6	1.8	1.9

Source: U.S. Census of Population, 1950, Vol. IV, Special Reports, Part 5, Chapter B, Education, 1953, Table 11.

laborer, farm laborer, service, and private household occupations than are white workers of the same educational levels. Correspondingly, a much smaller percentage of less-educated nonwhite workers than of less-educated white workers are in the craft and operative jobs. This suggests that the uneducated nonwhites tend to hold the poorest jobs in the economy, and that the uneducated whites tend to hold the next-to-poorest jobs.

The above observations concerning the occupational level which nonwhite workers are able to achieve with a particular educational attainment must be tempered by a consideration of the facts about the quality of education. Many nonwhite persons received their education in schools that were definitely substandard and in which the quality of instruction was poor. Employers may be much less impressed by the average high school record of a nonwhite applicant than of a white applicant. Even a transcript of grades is not revealing, because an "A" average from an all-Negro high school in the rural South may denote less knowledge than a "C" average from a mixed Negro-white high school in the North. Hence, it would be incorrect to insist that all of the differences in occupational attainment shown in Table 17-12 are due directly to racial discrimination in occupational situations. Instead, these differences may be due to the kind of discrimination that provides Negroes with a poorer quality of education.

OCCUPATION AND INCOME

In Chapter 19, which discusses the distribution of income among the population, an analysis is made of the distribution of income among the various occupational groups. The reader may be especially interested in the discussion of the incomes received by workers in each of the detailed occupation groups. Chapter 19 contains lists of "poverty" occupations--occupations that offer an income too small to support a family; "meager livelihood" occupations--occupations that permit only a meager living for a family, a living which is barely above the poverty level; and the "wealthy" occupations--those that provide an income sufficient to permit luxurious or affluent living. The information upon which much of this discussion is based is published in Table 17-A-3 at the end of the present chapter.

CLASS OF WORKER AND OCCUPATION

The Bureau of the Census recognizes 4 classes of workers:

Private wage or salary workers (71 percent of all workers)

Government workers (10 percent of all workers)

Self-employed workers (17 percent of all workers)

Table 17-13.—CLASS-OF-WORKER COMPOSITION OF EACH MAJOR OCCUPATION GROUP: 1950

Major occupation group	Total	Private wage and salary workers	Government workers	Self-employed workers	Unpaid family workers
Total......................................	100.0	70.9	9.9	17.2	2.0
Professional, technical, and kindred workers......	100.0	52.1	34.5	13.3	0.1
Farmers and farm managers......................	100.0	0.8	...	99.2	...
Managers, officials, and proprietors, except farm.	100.0	42.3	6.4	51.0	0.3
Clerical and kindred workers....................	100.0	78.4	20.0	1.1	0.5
Sales workers..................................	100.0	86.8	0.4	11.0	1.8
Craftsmen, foremen, and kindred workers..........	100.0	84.0	6.3	9.6	0.1
Operatives and kindred workers..................	100.0	93.2	3.3	3.3	0.2
Private household workers......................	100.0	97.6	...	2.2	0.3
Service workers except private household.........	100.0	72.2	19.7	7.4	0.7
Farm laborers and foremen......................	100.0	61.1	0.6	0.4	38.0
Laborers, except farm and mine.................	100.0	86.3	10.0	3.3	0.3

Source: U.S. Census of Population: 1950, Vol. II, Characteristics of the Population, U.S. Summary, Table 128.

Unpaid family workers (2 percent of all workers)

The workers in each of the various occupations tend to be concentrated in one or another of these four classes. (See Table 17-13). Almost all farmers are self-employed, and almost all operatives, private household workers, and service workers are wage or salary workers. About one-half of all managers and proprietors are self-employed; the remainder are paid either by private industry (42 percent) or by government (6 percent). Clerical workers are either private wage or salary workers (about 78 percent) or government workers (20 percent). Professional workers and craftsmen are the only groups of which sizable proportions are distributed among three of the classifications. County and state governments, and the Federal Government, hire many professionals, and many professionals are self-employed. Craftsmen tend either to work for wages or to be self-employed; only 6 percent work for the government. Almost all unpaid family workers are farm laborers.

Included in the "self-employed" class are not only physicians, lawyers, and proprietors of large business concerns, but also the managers of many very small and not too profitable enterprises. In fact, self-employment may represent underemployment or unemployment. Persons who are unable to obtain work which satisfies them often "go into business for themselves," and earn a very meager living as their own employers. Many farmers living on small submarginal farms are self-employed, but are not necessarily solvent.

SEASONAL AND PART-YEAR OCCUPATIONS

Some occupations have such definitely seasonal or irregular schedules that the persons who are employed in them must either be idle for a part of each year or seek work in another occupation. As Table 17-14 shows, the occupations which are lowest in the occupational scale tend to have the most irregular working schedules.[7] Only about one-half of the laborers (both farm and nonfarm) are able to obtain a full year's work. Among operatives in factories and other establishments, only 60 percent of the men and 47 percent of the women had a full year's work in 1949. People employed in private households have a particularly difficult time obtaining a full year's work. On the other hand, in the professional, proprietary and managerial, and

[7]Part-year work according to occupation must be measured indirectly, by cross-classifying present occupation (at time of enumeration) against weeks worked during the previous year. This method assumes that the previous year's work was in the same occupational classification as the present occupation, an assumption which is valid often enough to permit this approach to be used as a rough measure of part-time occupations.

Table 17-14.—PERCENT OF WORKERS WHO WORKED LESS THAN A FULL YEAR (50 TO 52 WEEKS) IN 1949, BY MAJOR OCCUPATION GROUP AND SEX

Major occupation group	Percent of workers who worked 50 to 52 weeks in 1949		Deviation from average percent for all workers	
	Male	Female	Male	Female
Total...	31.7	43.4	...	...
Professional, technical, and kindred workers..........	23.1	56.9	-8.6	13.5
Farmers and farm managers.............................	20.0	38.1	-11.7	-5.3
Managers, officials, and proprietors, except farm.....	14.1	22.5	-17.6	-20.9
Clerical and kindred workers..........................	21.9	27.5	-9.8	-15.9
Sales workers...	23.8	43.2	-7.9	-0.2
Craftsmen, foremen, and kindred workers...............	34.1	36.1	2.4	-7.3
Operatives and kindred workers........................	39.5	52.9	7.8	9.5
Private household workers.............................	40.3	51.0	8.6	7.6
Service workers, except private household.............	30.6	49.0	-1.1	5.6
Farm laborers and foremen.............................	47.5	54.8	5.8	11.4
Laborers, except farm and mine........................	50.2	52.1	18.5	8.7

Source: U. S. Census of Population: 1950, Special Reports, Occupational Characteristics, Table 16.

clerical occupations—i. e., in all of the white-collar occupations—the proportion of part-time workers is well below average. (Professional women are an exception, since many of them are school teachers and work only 8 or 10 months each year.)

But each of the major occupational groups includes certain detailed occupations that are especially likely to have seasonal and part-year working schedules. List 12 enumerates these occupations.

List 12.—OCCUPATIONS PROVIDING ONLY PART-YEAR EMPLOYMENT: 1950 (OCCUPATIONS WHERE LESS THAN 50 PERCENT OF MEN OR 35 PERCENT OF WOMEN WORKED 50 TO 52 WEEKS IN 1949)

Detailed occupation	Percent worked 50 to 52 weeks in 1949	
	Male	Female
PROFESS'L, TECHN'L, KINDRED WRKS.		
Actors and actresses.....................	32.1	18.4
Athletes	32.7	...
Dancers and dancing teachers............	41.6	23.0
Entertainers (n. e. c.)	46.6	34.2
Musicians and music teachers............	45.9	33.7
Sports instructors and officials	52.9	31.4
Teachers (n. e. c.).......................	49.7	23.5
SALES WORKERS		
Demonstrators	...	27.9

	Male	Female
CRAFTSMEN, FOREMEN, KINDRED WRKS.		
Brickmasons, stonemasons, tile setters....	37.2	...
Carpenters.............................	40.3	...
Cement finishers	35.5	...
Painters...............................	38.2	50.0
Paperhangers	23.7	...
Plasterers.............................	36.3	...
Rollers and roll hands, metal............	34.9	...
Roofers and slaters	36.7	...
Structural metal workers	48.6	...
OPERATIVES AND KINDRED WORKERS		
Apprentices		
Bricklayers	36.7	...
Carpenters	42.3	...
Building trades (n. e. c.)..............	34.4	...
Plasters and powdermen.................	31.3	...
Fruit, nut, vegetable graders and packers except factory	35.5	13.0
Furnacemen, smeltermen, and pourers...	47.8	...
Heaters, metal.......................	44.0	...
Mine operatives (n. e. c.)		
Coal mining	12.0	...
Mining and quarring, except fuel........	49.3	...
Motormen, mine, factory, logging camp ..	18.3	...
Sailors and deck hands	35.6	...
Sawyers	49.4	...
Operatives and kindred workers(n. e. c.)		
Manufacturing		
Blast furnaces, steel works, rolling mills	33.8	...
Motor vehicles and motor veh. equip...	46.9	41.9
Can. preserving fruits, veg., sea foods ..	42.7	17.5
Apparel, other fab'd textile products ...	44.9	38.7
Leather products, except footwear.....	49.6	36.0
Nonmanufacturing-construction	48.5	...

List 12.—Continued

SERVICE WORKERS, EXC. PRIVATE HSHLD.

Attendants, recreation and amusement....	34. 1	45. 8
Ushers	40. 1	27. 6

FARM LABORERS AND FOREMEN

Farm laborers, wage workers	50. 6	22. 9

LABORERS, EXCEPT FARM AND MINE

Fishermen and oystermen	35. 8	...
Longshoremen and stevedores	39. 5	...
Lumbermen..........................	32. 8	...
Teamsters...........................	48. 5	...
Laborers (n. e. c.)		
Manufacturing		
Sawmills, planing mills, mill work.....	45. 8	...
Blast furnaces, steel works, rolling mills	29. 7	...
Motor vehicles and motor vehicle equip.	46. 3	...
Can. preserving fruits, veg., sea foods..	35. 3	21. 0
Nonmanufacturing		
Construction........................	38. 7	40. 4
Business and repair services..........	44. 7	...
Personal services...................	37. 0	51. 1

For example, the professional occupations as a whole tend to provide full-time year-round work, but the occupations which deal with the arts and with entertainment--drama, athletics, dancing, music--tend to provide less than full-time employment. Among the craftsmen, operatives, and laborers, all of the occupations connected with construction--brickmasons, carpenters, painters, plasterers, construction laborers, etc.--have a seasonal and, hence, part-year pattern of employment. Jobs related to packing, canning, or preserving fruits and vegetables are extremely seasonal. Lumbering, mining, sawmill work, fishing, and recreation are all seasonal industries, and a very large proportion of the occupations associated with them are part-year jobs. Even occupations in many of the leading manufacturing industries, such as motor vehicles, provide only part-year work because of retooling and style changes, which require annual periods of layoff.

OCCUPATION AND MARITAL STATUS

Although there is no necessary correlation between marital status and occupation, some types of jobs almost demand that the person holding them be unmarried. In some occupations the rate of pay is so low that it would not enable a married person to support a family. Some of these low-paying jobs are held by very young workers who are attending school. Other occupations require prolonged isolation, or separation from family (seagoing workers or workers in forests). Still other occupations require the worker to live in the employer's household. Listed below are some specific occupations which employ an unusually large proportion of unmarried workers:

Occupation	Percent married, 1950
Ushers, recreation and amusement.....	7. 4
Newsboys...........................	8. 0
Farm laborers, unpaid family workers..	9. 9
Telegraph messengers	14. 7
Attendants, recreation and amusement ment places........................	21. 9
Bootblacks..........................	26. 1
Messengers and office boys	31. 4
Attendants and assistants, library......	31. 5
Nurses, student professional..........	34..4
Counter and fountain workers	38. 9
Dancers and dancing teachers	39. 2
Sailors and deck hands	41. 1
Athletes............................	42. 7
Laborers, manufacture of apparel and other fabricated textile products	42. 7
Apprentices—bricklayers, carpenters, other specified trades................	45. 7
Laundresses, living in	46. 0
Farm laborers, wage workers	46. 3
Attendants, physicians' and dentists' offices	46. 8
Librarians	47. 4
Waiters and waitresses..............	47. 7
Laborers, manufacture of machinery....	48. 0
Practical nurses.....................	49. 1
Private household workers, living out...	49. 5
Religious workers...................	50. 5
Surveying chainmen, rodmen, and axmen	51. 5
Dressmakers and seamstresses, except factory............................	52. 3
Laborers, retail and wholesale trade ...	53. 3
Garage laborers and car washers and greasers	55. 0

OCCUPATION AND MIGRATION

People who work at some types of jobs are required by their employers to travel from place to place in the course of their work, or to change their residence frequently. Other kinds of jobs tend to be of short duration, so that the worker must often move from one job to another. Consequently, some occupations contain a great many more migratory workers than are found in others. In 1950, holders of the following detailed occupations were reported as having an unusually large rate of migration.

Occupation	Percent living in a different county in 1949
Members of armed forces	40.2
Athletes	23.8
Mining engineers	22.8
Nurses, student, professional	21.1
Airplane pilots and navigators	20.1
Crude petroleum and natural gas extraction operatives and laborers	19.3
Private household workers, living in	19.1
Natural scientists (n.e.c.)	17.8
Clergymen	17.7
Housekeepers, living in	15.9
Sports instructors and officials	15.5
Radio operators	15.2
Farm and home management advisors	15.1
Religious workers	15.0
Entertainers (n.e.c.)	14.8
Aeronautical engineers	13.8
College presidents, professors, and instructors (n.e.c.)	13.5
Dancers and dancing teachers	13.4
Authors	13.2
Chemical engineers	13.2
Retail trade–general merchandise and five and ten cent stores	13.0
Recreation and group workers	12.6
Civil engineers	12.1
Surveyors	12.0
Actors and actresses	11.9
Sailors and deckhands	11.7
Technicians (n.e.c.)	11.7
Foresters and conservation workers	11.4
Attendants and assistants, library	11.4
Farm laborers, wage	11.4
Apprentices, carpenter	11.2
Editors and reporters	11.0
Engineers, technical	10.9
Physicians and surgeons	10.7
Housekeepers	10.6
Inspectors (n.e.c.)–Construction	10.5
Waiters and waitresses	10.4
Technicians, medical and dental	10.4
Electrical engineers	10.4
Nurses, professional	10.2
Optometrists	10.2
Social scientists	10.2
Excavating, grading, and road machinery operators	10.0
Managers, officials and proprietors (n.e.c.)–salaried–construction	9.9
Officials and administrators (n.e.c.), public administration–federal public administration and postal service	9.9
Dietitians and nutritionists	9.8
Chainmen, rodmen, and axmen, surveying	9.8
Engineers (n.e.c.)	9.7
Musicians and music teachers	9.7
Apprentices, trades not specified	9.7

OCCUPATIONAL COMPOSITION IN URBAN AND RURAL AREAS

Each of the urban, rural-nonfarm, and rural-farm populations has a distinctive occupational structure; information demonstrating this is provided by Table 17-15. In the city, of course, the occupations of farmer and farm laborer are almost nonexistent. Urban areas contain proportionately more professional, managerial, clerical, sales, and service workers than rural areas. Among rural-nonfarm workers, in comparison with urban workers, there are proportionately more laborers (both farm and nonfarm) and operatives, and proportionately fewer white-collar-workers of all types.

Table 17-15.—OCCUPATIONAL COMPOSITION OF THE URBAN AND RURAL EMPLOYED LABOR FORCE, 1950, AND ESTIMATED PERCENT CHANGE: 1940 TO 1950

Major occupation group	Percent distribution, 1950			Estimated percent change		
	Urban	Rural nonfarm	Rural farm	Urban	Rural nonfarm	Rural farm
Total..................................	100.0	100.0	100.0	27.6	49.6	-19.8
Professional, technical, and kindred workers.	9.3	6.1	1.2	44.9	35.5	0.5
Farmers and farm managers....................	0.4	3.0	56.3	...	...	-19.6
Managers, officials, and propr's, exc. farm..	13.0	10.7	2.0	35.9	33.0	-0.9
Clerical and kindred workers................	8.4	4.3	1.0	21.7	45.4	28.1
Sales workers...............................	8.2	5.1	1.1	6.1	40.0	5.3
Craftsmen, foremen, and kindred workers......	21.2	21.6	5.5	42.7	74.6	31.3
Operatives and kindred workers..............	21.8	25.0	7.8	28.5	52.4	33.5
Private household workers....................	0.2	0.2	0.1	...	...	...
Service workers except private household.....	7.6	4.3	0.8	13.6	38.7	5.4
Farm laborers and foremen....................	0.6	6.5	19.1	...	56.0	-44.9
Laborers, except farm and mine..............	8.2	11.8	4.0	8.2	28.2	-15.3
Occupation not reported.....................	1.0	1.4	1.1	...	...	...

Source: Statistical appendix to this monograph.

Contrary to what might be anticipated, the rural-farm labor force is not composed exclusively of farmers and farm laborers. In fact, 25 percent of the employed rural-farm population had nonagricultural occupations in 1950. Craftsmen, operatives, and nonfarm laborers comprised more than two-thirds of these people who were living on farms but were not obtaining their living from agriculture. This phenomenon is due to at least four sets of circumstances. (a) A person may own or rent a place which he calls a "farm," but which is not in production, or he may rent his farmland to a neighbor for agricultural use. (b) One or more members of a bona fide farm household may be employed elsewhere than on the farm. Thus, a farmer father may have sons and daughters (and even a wife) who are living at home and working in a nearby town. (c) There are many part-time farmers and part-time farm laborers in rural areas, especially just outside the fringes of large cities and in mining areas. These "farmers" till their land in the spring and summer, and work at other jobs the rest of the year. Many of them work a full work week in an industrial plant, a mine, or a business and do their farming on weekends or in the evening. Poultry, vegetable, and specialty crop farms can be adapted particularly well to this kind of operation. (d) Many farm laborers live on farms as tenants. They work full time as farm hands during peak seasons of planting and harvesting, but may seek nonagricultural work during the winter and early spring months. Since the census is taken in early April, when the need for farm labor is not at its peak, many nonfarm occupations will be reported by this group.

Some analysts, disturbed by the fact that the farm population is not exclusively agricultural, have blamed past census definitions and procedures for this situation. The definition of the farm population will probably be changed for the 1960 census, in an effort to attain a closer correspondence between definition and actuality. Changing the census definition will not eliminate the situation entirely, however, and may not even improve it very much. The Census Bureau classifies entire households as being either farm or nonfarm, but defines occupations in terms of the activities of the individual members of each household during a particular week, selecting the job at which most hours were worked. Hence, a change in criteria on the basis of which a farm is defined will affect the household, but not the individuals in the household. Thus, a revised definition will decrease the confusion resulting from some of the circumstances described above--it will modify (a) and, to a lesser extent, (c), but will have almost no effect on situations (b) and (d). It is inevitable, therefore, that a sizable element of the farm population will continue to have nonagricultural occupations in the week preceding the census, regardless of the definitions used.

A study of the tables in the Appendix to this volume, and of the following summary, will show that the tendency for farm populations to contain some nonagricultural population is especially strong along the Atlantic Seaboard:

Geographic division	Percent of employed persons among the rural farm population having nonagricultural occupations: 1950
Total.............	32. 7
New England	44. 9
Middle Atlantic........	44. 7
East North Central.....	35. 0
West North Central	20. 9
South Atlantic	40. 3
East South Central	32. 9
West South Central.....	28. 5
Mountain..............	25. 1
Pacific	35. 8

OCCUPATIONAL COMPOSITION OF GEOGRAPHIC
DIVISIONS, AND CHANGE: 1940 TO 1950

To this point, the discussion of occupations has focused solely upon the national population as a whole and has disregarded the internal variations among regions and geographic divisions. The existence and magnitude of these variations may be verified by studying, in the statistical appendix at the end of this volume, the occupational information for 1950 and 1940 which is given for each geographic division by sex and urban and rural residence.

The greatest single factor in inter-divisional diversity is the degree to which an area is urbanized (or agricultural). The urbanized divisions-- the Northeast and the West--have a much smaller proportion of farmers and farm laborers than the rest of the nation has, and the highly agricultural West North Central and East South Central divisions have quite small proportions of white collar workers, manual workers in nonagricultural in-

dustries, and service workers. This means that other interregional differences in occupational composition should be examined by comparing the urban, rural-nonfarm, and rural-farm populations of the various divisions. The information needed for this comparison is in the Appendix cited above.

In general, the urban and the rural-nonfarm populations of all geographic divisions have similar occupational compositions, in terms of the major occupational categories. The divisions which contain a large amount of manufacturing tend to have a larger proportion of craftsmen and operatives than the divisions which contain less manufacturing. In the geographic divisions where there is much farming and ranching, the urban and rural-nonfarm populations tend to contain above-average proportions of sales and proprietary workers. The geographic divisions containing major metropolitan centers which have nationwide dominance (New York, Chicago, Los Angeles, etc.), tend to have a larger proportion of professional and service workers. Finally, in the South, where there is a large pool of underemployed nonwhite persons, the proportion of women who are employed in private households is unusually large.

Another factor involved in the variation between regions is the extent to which farming is done by farm operators working alone or with family help, or by hired farm labor. In the highly mechanized West North Central Division, the ratio of farm operators to farm laborers is 3 to 1. In the Northeast there is much truck gardening and dairying, which require help, and the ratio is about 2 to 1. In the Pacific and Southwest areas, where many special crops and winter crops are grown, farm labor is used much more extensively, and the ratio approaches 1 to 1.

Thus, the interregional and interdivisional differences in occupation can be explained almost entirely in terms of five factors:

a. The balance between agricultural and nonagricultural activities

b. The balance between manufacturing and commerce within cities

c. The balance between smaller cities and major metropolitan centers

d. The availability of a low income group, which has no alternative source of employment, for use as domestic servants

e. The extent of mechanization in agriculture, and the type of farming

To be sure, these factors offer only a crude explanation of interdivisional differences in occupational composition. Each of the cities within a geographic division has its own unique "economic base"--particular industries upon which it depends for a livelihood and which reflect its unique resources and history. Examining the occupational composition of each community in terms of the detailed occupational classification, rather than in terms of the major occupational categories cited here, will show that the inter-area variation is vastly greater than this discussion indicates, and that the factors which must be recognized in accounting for this variation are much more numerous and varied than the five leading ones that have been cited.

The economic and social effects of the population changes that have been occurring within each of the geographic divisions can be appreciated more readily after a study of the percent change which has taken place in each occupation in each geographic division, and in the urban, rural-nonfarm, and rural-farm parts of each geographic division.

a. In the South, rapid urbanization has resulted in very large decreases in the agricultural population (both farmers and farm laborers), and equally impressive increases in the number of clerical, craft, and operative workers. This urbanization has also helped to bring about a decline in the number of workers in private households. Managers, clerical workers, and sales workers have increased at below-average rates in those areas of the nation that contain older and more established urban centers. The Pacific Division, because of its extremely rapid growth, has gained in all nonagricultural occupations (except private household workers).

b. The increase that has occurred in the rural-nonfarm population is most accurately interpreted as suburban growth. The occupational groups that have been increasing at the most rapid rates in the suburbs recently have not been the upper class or high income groups, as was the case in the past, but the groups belonging to the great and growing middle-class--clerical and kindred workers, sales workers, craftsmen and foremen, and service workers.

c. The data concerning changes in the rural-farm population show, of course, a large decline in the agricultural population. They also provide new information by showing that the decline was roughly twice as great for farm laborers as for farm operators. But these statistics are also informative as to which of the occupations belonging to the nonagricultural groups have been entered by members of the farm population. Large rates of increase between 1940 and 1950 are shown for clerical, craft, and operative workers in the farm populations of all divisions except New England. Thus, the large and growing nonagricultural element in the farm population (as in the rural-nonfarm population) consists of middle-class workers.

The automobile, and the great improvement in the national level of living, have permitted the average city dweller--the lower echelon white collar worker and the factory worker--to join the rush to the suburbs and to small farms on the outer fringes of the suburbs.

CONCLUSION

It has been possible in this chapter to present only the major facts connected with the very broad subject of occupational composition and the trends in occupational composition. Even the statistical tables which have been presented contain much information that could not be discussed. The two principal objects have been (a) to encourage the use of detailed occupational classifications in analyzing occupations, and (b) to demonstrate that occupational analysis involves a very large and important demographic element which neither demographers nor labor force experts should neglect.

Table 17-A-1. DETAILED OCCUPATION OF THE EXPERIENCED CIVILIAN LABOR FORCE AND OF EMPLOYED PERSONS, BY SEX, FOR THE UNITED STATES: 1950

Detailed occupation	Total employed (000)	Percent female	Percent of total employed — Total	Male	Female	Percent of maj. occ. group of employed — Total	Male	Female	Percent of experienced labor force unemployed, 1950 — Total	Male	Female	Percent change, 1940-1950 — Total	Male	Female
TOTAL.................	56,225.3	28.0	100.0	100.0	100.0	...	...	...	4.7	4.8	4.4	25.3	20.0	41.1
PROFESSIONAL, TECHNICAL AND KINDRED WKRS.	4,909.2	39.5	8.73	7.33	12.34	100.0	100.0	100.0	1.6	1.8	1.3	37.4	42.3	30.4
Accountants and auditors	376.5	14.8	0.67	0.79	0.35	7.67	10.80	2.87	1.9	1.9	1.5	70.8	58.8	204.7
Actors and actresses	14.9	34.1	0.03	0.02	0.03	0.30	0.33	0.26	19.3	18.0	21.7	25.7	38.5	6.6
Airplane pilots and navigators	13.7	1.3	0.02	0.03	...	0.28	0.46	0.01	3.3	3.3	6.6	217.8	217.0	262.7
Architects	24.8	3.8	0.04	0.06	0.01	0.51	0.80	0.05	1.0	0.9	2.2	24.0	22.3	95.6
Artists and art teachers	77.5	38.2	0.14	0.12	0.19	1.58	1.61	1.52	3.8	3.8	3.9	47.6	38.9	64.2
Athletes	11.6	6.1	0.02	0.03	...	0.24	0.37	0.04	6.6	6.6	7.4	61.1	55.5	267.2
Authors	15.7	38.7	0.03	0.02	0.04	0.32	0.32	0.31	3.3	3.6	2.8	34.8	22.7	60.0
Chemists	74.4	10.0	0.13	0.17	0.05	1.52	2.26	0.38	1.7	1.7	2.3	38.2	28.3	350.5
Chiropractors	12.9	14.3	0.02	0.03	0.03	0.26	0.37	0.09	1.4	1.0	3.8	21.4	26.3	-1.6
Clergymen	167.5	4.0	0.30	0.40	0.04	3.41	5.41	0.35	0.6	0.6	1.0	22.7	20.5	115.3
College presidents, professors, and instr. (n.e.c.)	124.7	23.2	0.22	0.24	0.18	2.54	3.22	1.49	0.7	0.6	0.9	66.2	73.8	45.4
Dancers and dancing teachers	16.1	71.1	0.03	0.01	0.07	0.33	0.16	0.59	6.6	7.4	6.3	43.6	113.7	26.6
Dentists	74.9	2.7	0.13	0.18	0.01	1.53	2.45	0.11	0.2	0.2	1.5	7.0	5.7	95.3
Designers	38.7	26.5	0.07	0.07	0.06	0.79	0.96	0.53	3.5	2.9	4.9	36.2	37.5	32.7
Dietitians, nutritionists	22.4	94.0	0.04	...	0.13	0.46	0.05	1.09	1.9	3.2	1.8	(1)	(1)	(1)
Draftsmen	121.7	6.9	0.22	0.28	0.05	2.48	3.81	0.43	2.5	2.4	2.9	67.8	59.4	491.9
Editors and reporters	89.3	32.0	0.16	0.15	0.18	1.82	2.04	1.47	2.4	2.3	2.4	51.3	37.1	93.9
Engineers, technical	525.3	1.2	0.93	1.28	0.04	10.70	17.47	0.33	1.7	1.7	2.7	90.8	88.9	787.0
Aeronautical	17.6	1.9	0.03	0.04	...	0.36	0.58	0.02	1.6	1.6	1.5	(2)	(2)	(2)
Chemical	32.5	1.9	0.06	0.08	0.01	0.66	1.07	0.03	1.7	1.6	4.4	157.7	153.5	1,512.8
Civil	123.3	1.6	0.22	0.30	...	2.51	4.09	0.10	1.8	1.8	1.8	43.6	41.7	911.5
Electrical	106.5	1.2	0.19	0.26	0.01	2.17	3.54	0.06	1.5	1.5	2.6	73.6	72.0	654.3
Industrial	40.2	1.1	0.07	0.10	...	0.82	1.34	0.02	1.9	1.9	2.4	242.4	242.4	508.1
Mechanical	110.2	0.5	0.20	0.27	...	2.24	3.69	0.03	2.2	2.2	3.5	(2)	(2)	(2)
Metallurgical, and metallurgists	11.3	2.1	0.02	0.03	...	0.23	0.37	0.01	1.3	1.3	3.6	} 99.8	} 98.0	} 373.0
Mining	10.8	1.0	0.02	0.03	...	0.22	0.36	0.01	2.1	1.9	14.2			
Not elsewhere classified	72.8	1.3	0.13	0.18	0.01	1.48	2.42	0.05	1.1	1.1	1.6	116.4	114.8	898.4
Entertainers (n.e.c.)	14.9	28.7	0.03	0.03	0.03	0.30	0.36	0.22	8.4	8.6	8.1	60.0	42.0	133.3
Farm and home management advisors	12.2	49.3	0.02	0.02	0.04	0.25	0.21	0.31	0.6	0.3	0.9	9.9	6.2	13.9
Foresters and conservationists	26.1	6.7	0.05	0.06	0.01	0.53	0.85	0.04	3.4	3.4	3.4	(1)	(1)	(1)
Funeral directors and embalmers	39.4	3.5	0.07	0.09	0.02	0.80	1.24	0.14	1.3	1.3	1.3	3.8	2.5	25.0
Lawyers and judges	180.5	3.5	0.32	0.43	0.04	3.68	5.86	0.32	0.4	0.4	1.2	1.6	0.4	49.4
Librarians	55.3	88.6	0.10	0.02	0.31	1.13	0.21	2.53	0.8	1.4	0.7	53.7	73.1	51.5
Musicians and music teachers	152.5	50.7	0.27	0.19	0.50	3.11	2.55	4.01	4.9	7.4	2.2	19.6	9.8	30.9
Natural scientists (n.e.c.)	40.1	14.6	0.07	0.08	0.04	0.82	1.15	0.30	1.6	1.5	2.0	(1)	(1)	(1)
Nurses, professional	398.5	97.6	0.71	0.02	2.47	8.12	0.32	20.06	1.3	2.5	1.3	} 34.7	} 49.0	} 34.4
Nurses, student professional	76.1	97.9	0.14	...	0.47	1.55	0.05	3.85	0.7	2.2	0.7			

Table 17-A-1. DETAILED OCCUPATION OF THE EXPERIENCED CIVILIAN LABOR FORCE AND OF EMPLOYED PERSONS, BY SEX, FOR THE UNITED STATES: 1950--Con.

Detailed occupation	Total employed (000)	Percent female	Percent of total employed			Percent of maj. occ. group of employed		Percent of experienced labor force unemployed, 1950			Percent change, 1940-1950		
			Total	Male	Female	Male	Female	Total	Male	Female	Total	Male	Female
PROFESSIONAL, TECH. AND KINDRED WKRS.--Con.													
Optometrists	14.6	5.7	0.03	0.03	0.01	0.46	0.04	0.8	0.8	0.9	42.6	40.9	76.4
Osteopaths	5.1	15.2	0.01	0.01	...	0.15	0.04	0.3	0.3	0.9	-14.3	-11.0	-28.9
Personnel and labor relations workers	52.1	28.8	0.09	0.09	0.10	1.25	0.77	1.5	1.4	1.6	(1)	(1)	(1)
Pharmacists	88.1	8.2	0.16	0.20	0.05	2.72	0.37	1.0	1.0	1.3	13.3	8.4	125.8
Photographers	52.5	17.3	0.09	0.11	0.06	1.46	0.47	4.1	4.1	4.1	59.4	53.4	96.6
Physicians and surgeons	191.9	6.1	0.34	0.44	0.07	6.07	0.60	0.2	0.2	0.6	15.6	13.8	54.0
Radio operators	15.9	9.3	0.03	0.04	0.01	0.49	0.08	3.1	3.3	1.7	160.5	140.1	1,427.8
Recreation and group workers	16.0	41.7	0.03	0.02	0.04	0.31	0.35	4.5	3.9	5.2	(3)	(3)	(3)
Religious workers	41.4	69.6	0.07	0.03	0.18	0.42	1.49	0.6	1.0	0.5	2.6	35.4	-7.2
Social and welfare workers, except group	75.5	69.2	0.13	0.06	0.33	0.78	2.69	1.3	1.5	1.2	31.6	29.5	32.7
Social scientists	35.2	32.3	0.06	0.06	0.07	0.80	0.59	1.9	1.8	2.3	(1)	(1)	(1)
Sports instructors and officials	45.0	24.7	0.08	0.08	0.07	1.14	0.57	1.8	2.0	1.2	110.8	93.6	188.3
Surveyors	25.3	3.7	0.05	0.06	0.01	0.82	0.05	3.5	3.4	5.0	89.8	84.0	836.6
Teachers (n.e.c.)	1,120.6	74.5	1.99	0.71	5.31	9.62	43.06	0.6	0.8	0.6	10.3	15.1	8.8
Technicians, medical and dental	76.3	56.7	0.14	0.08	0.28	1.11	2.23	2.2	2.9	1.6	125.6	110.9	152.5
Technicians, testing	75.5	22.2	0.13	0.14	0.11	1.98	0.87	1.9	1.8	2.2			
Technicians (n.e.c.)	26.9	15.8	0.05	0.06	0.03	0.76	0.22	2.1	2.2	1.6	173.0	153.0	370.9
Therapists and healers (n.e.c.)	24.4	49.4	0.04	0.03	0.08	0.42	0.62	1.8	1.8	1.7	43.2	29.4	60.8
Veterinarians	13.4	6.2	0.02	0.03	0.01	0.42	0.04	0.8	0.7	2.7	24.8	17.9	953.2
Professional, technical, and kindred wkrs.(n.e.c.)	114.3	19.0	0.20	0.23	0.14	3.12	1.12	2.4	2.4	2.2	113.8	108.3	131.0
FARMERS AND FARM MANAGERS	4,306.3	2.7	7.66	10.34	0.74	100.00	100.00	0.3	0.3	0.9	-16.3	-16.1	-23.4
Farmers (owners and tenants)	4,271.4	2.7	7.60	10.26	0.73	99.22	98.12	0.3	0.3	0.9	-16.4	-16.1	-24.4
Farm managers	34.8	6.3	0.06	0.08	0.01	0.78	1.88	0.8	0.7	1.4	-5.6	-9.5	170.0
MANAGERS, OFFICIALS, & PROP.,EXC. FARM	5,017.5	13.5	8.92	10.72	4.31	100.00	100.00	1.2	1.2	1.2	38.4	34.6	69.6
Buyers and department heads, store	142.2	25.4	0.25	0.26	0.23	2.44	5.34	1.7	1.2	3.1	102.7	101.8	105.5
Buyers and shippers, farm products	28.2	2.1	0.05	0.07	...	0.64	0.09	2.2	1.7	21.6	-29.6	-30.2	15.9
Conductors, railroad	55.7	0.6	0.10	0.14	...	1.28	0.05	0.6	0.6	2.8	20.6	19.9	
Credit men	32.9	21.7	0.06	0.06	0.05	0.59	1.06	1.3	1.2	1.5	15.6	3.9	104.7
Floormen and floor managers, store	10.8	46.2	0.02	0.01	0.03	0.10	0.74	2.2	2.8	1.5	57.3	24.5	126.9
Inspectors, public administration	55.9	4.1	0.10	0.13	0.01	1.24	0.33	1.6	1.4	5.1	35.0	33.0	109.2
Federal public administration and postal service	26.8	3.1	0.05	0.06	0.01	0.60	0.12	1.8	1.5	8.2	37.1	35.2	137.7
State public administration	9.5	3.8	0.02	0.02	...	0.21	0.05	1.1	1.5	1.1	-11.4	-11.0	-21.0
Local public administration	19.6	5.5	0.03	0.05	0.01	0.43	0.16	1.6	1.4	3.8	76.0	70.7	284.3

Table 17-A-1. DETAILED OCCUPATION OF THE EXPERIENCED CIVILIAN LABOR FORCE AND OF EMPLOYED PERSONS, BY SEX, FOR THE UNITED STATES: 1950-Con.

Detailed occupation	Total employed (000)	Per-cent female	Percent of total employed			Percent of maj. off. group of employed		Percent of experienced labor force unemployed, 1950			Percent change, 1940-1950		
			Total	Male	Female	Male	Female	Total	Male	Female	Total	Male	Female
MANAGERS, OFFICIALS, & PROP., EXC. FARM—Con.													
Managers and superintendents, building........	65.7	34.1	0.12	0.11	0.14	1.00	3.31	1.4	1.4	1.3	-4.6	7.3	-21.4
Officers, pilots, pursers, and engineers, ship.....	38.1	3.0	0.07	0.09	0.01	0.85	0.17	7.9	8.1	2.6	24.1	20.8	1,063.9
Officials & administrators (n.e.c.), public adm....	153.9	17.1	0.27	0.31	0.17	2.94	3.89	0.9	0.9	0.9	32.6	27.3	66.4
Federal public administration and postal service.	49.5	10.7	0.09	0.11	0.03	1.02	0.79	1.0	1.0	1.1	34.2	30.8	70.1
State public administration......	23.1	12.1	0.04	0.05	0.02	0.47	0.41	0.7	0.8	0.4	14.3	9.7	63.1
Local public administration......	81.2	22.4	0.14	0.16	0.12	1.45	2.69	1.5	0.9	0.9	38.0	31.6	65.9
Officials, lodge, society, union, etc.....	26.6	10.8	0.05	0.06	0.02	0.55	0.43	1.5	1.5	2.2	7.4	14.5	-28.7
Postmasters......	38.7	43.1	0.07	0.05	0.11	0.51	2.46	0.3	0.4	0.3	0.2	-0.9	1.8
Purchasing agents and buyers (n.e.c.)......	63.0	9.1	0.11	0.14	0.04	1.32	0.84	1.7	1.7	2.4	99.7	97.9	120.5
Managers, officials, & prop. (n.e.c.)-salaried (4).	1,787.6	12.0	3.18	3.88	1.36	36.25	31.58	1.3	1.3	2.9	39.7	35.4	79.3
Construction......	85.6	2.3	0.15	0.21	0.01	1.93	0.29	2.9	3.0	1.8	81.4	79.7	321.2
Manufacturing......	412.5	6.4	0.73	0.95	0.17	8.90	3.89	1.0	0.9	1.5	55.0	51.7	128.5
Transportation......	95.8	3.6	0.17	0.23	0.02	2.13	0.51	0.9	0.9	1.2	68.9	66.1	181.0
Telecommunications, & utilities & sanitary serv..	61.4	9.7	0.11	0.14	0.04	1.28	0.88	0.3	0.3	0.6	27.4	24.6	62.9
Wholesale trade......	157.1	5.7	0.28	0.37	0.06	3.41	1.33	1.0	1.0	1.5	54.4	51.7	133.8
Retail trade......	513.8	15.3	0.91	1.07	0.50	10.03	11.60	1.4	1.4	1.7	23.0	18.1	55.1
Food and dairy products stores, & milk ret'lng.	101.7	12.1	0.18	0.22	0.08	2.06	1.82	1.3	1.3	1.5	10.3	6.3	36.1
General merchandise and five & ten cent stores.	59.4	22.3	0.11	0.11	0.08	1.06	1.96	1.2	1.2	1.4	15.8	5.6	76.7
Apparel and accessories stores......	42.0	32.2	0.07	0.07	0.09	0.66	2.00	1.2	1.0	1.8	32.1	18.7	76.0
Furniture, home furnishings, and equip. stores.	27.6	9.2	0.05	0.06	0.02	0.58	0.37	0.9	0.8	1.7	72.8	70.1	107.1
Motor vehicles and accessories retailing......	56.4	3.4	0.10	0.13	0.01	1.26	0.28	1.0	1.0	0.9	81.4	79.5	176.8
Gasoline service stations......	35.4	1.8	0.06	0.09	...	0.80	0.09	1.8	1.8	1.6	2.3	1.7	25.3
Eating and drinking places......	68.7	28.2	0.12	0.12	0.12	1.14	2.87	3.2	3.5	2.4	37.7	32.5	54.0
Hardware, farm implement, & bldg.mat'l. retail.	43.7	3.6	0.08	0.10	0.01	0.97	0.23	0.6	0.5	0.6	37.9	36.2	88.9
Other retail trade......	78.9	16.9	0.14	0.16	0.08	1.51	1.97	1.2	1.2	1.6	13.8	7.5	58.3
Banking and other finance......	118.7	10.4	0.21	0.26	0.08	2.45	1.83	0.5	0.4	0.6	15.2	9.9	111.8
Insurance and real estate......	70.1	16.5	0.12	0.14	0.07	1.35	1.71	0.4	0.4	0.7	79.9	67.8	200.5
Business services......	27.7	18.3	0.05	0.06	0.03	0.52	0.75	1.8	1.7	2.1	92.4	85.8	136.6
Automobile repair services and garages......	23.7	1.7	0.04	0.06	...	0.54	0.06	1.3	1.3	1.7	31.4	30.9	65.1
Miscellaneous repair services......	4.3	5.2	0.01	0.01	...	0.09	0.03	1.0	0.9	2.2	139.5	132.9	498.1
Personal services......	65.0	33.4	0.12	0.11	0.14	1.00	3.21	2.5	2.5	2.6	68.7	59.4	96.5
All other industries (incl. not reported)......	151.6	24.5	0.27	0.28	0.24	2.64	5.50	2.5	2.4	3.0	55.8	41.2	157.3
Managers, officials, & propr's (n.e.c.)-self-emp.	2,518.4	13.4	4.48	5.39	2.14	50.27	49.71	0.9	1.0	0.5	(4)	(4)	(4)
Construction......	199.5	1.3	0.35	0.49	0.02	4.53	0.39	1.8	1.8	0.9	...	...	...
Manufacturing......	237.5	6.1	0.42	0.55	0.09	5.14	2.14	0.7	0.7	0.5	...	...	...
Transportation......	51.3	4.7	0.09	0.12	0.02	1.13	0.35	1.2	1.3	0.6	...	...	...

Refers only to last three columns.

Table 17-A-1. DETAILED OCCUPATION OF THE EXPERIENCED CIVILIAN LABOR FORCE AND OF EMPLOYED PERSONS, BY SEX, FOR THE UNITED STATES: 1950-Con.

Detailed occupation	Total employed (000)	Per-cent female	Percent of total employed			Percent of maj. occ. group of employed		Percent of experienced labor force unemployed, 1950			Percent change, 1940-1950		
			Total	Male	Female	Male	Female	Total	Male	Female	Total	Male	Female
MANAGERS, OFFICIALS, & PROP., EXC. FARM-Con.													
Telecommunications, & utilities & sanitary serv..	5.7	4.5	0.01	0.01	...	0.13	0.04	1.0	1.1	...	...	...	...
Wholesale trade..	177.9	4.1	0.32	0.42	0.05	3.93	1.09	0.8	0.8	0.6	...	...	...
Retail trade..	1,414.5	17.1	2.52	2.90	1.54	27.02	35.71	0.8	0.9	0.5	...	...	...
Food and dairy products stores, & milk ret'ling.	398.0	17.9	0.71	0.81	0.45	7.53	10.50	0.8	0.9	0.3	...	...	...
General merchandise and five & ten cent stores.	65.2	21.5	0.12	0.13	0.09	1.18	2.07	0.5	0.6	0.3	...	...	...
Apparel and accessories stores..	84.7	30.6	0.15	0.15	0.16	1.35	3.82	0.6	0.8	0.3	...	...	...
Furniture, home furnishings, & equipment stores	68.3	8.3	0.12	0.15	0.04	1.44	0.84	0.4	0.4	0.4	...	...	...
Motor vehicles and accessories retailing..	59.8	2.6	0.11	0.14	0.01	1.34	0.23	0.5	0.5	0.3	...	...	...
Gasoline service stations..	146.5	3.7	0.26	0.35	0.03	3.25	0.80	0.9	0.9	0.4	...	...	...
Eating and drinking places..	288.6	26.3	0.51	0.53	0.48	4.90	11.20	1.4	1.6	0.7	...	...	...
Hardware, farm implement, & bldg.mat'l. retail.	84.9	4.9	0.15	0.20	0.03	1.86	0.62	0.3	0.3	0.2	...	...	...
Other retail trade..	218.6	17.4	0.39	0.45	0.24	4.16	5.62	0.7	0.8	0.4	...	...	...
Banking and other finance..	21.9	4.7	0.04	0.05	0.01	0.48	0.15	0.4	0.4	0.1	...	...	...
Insurance and real estate..	44.9	13.2	0.08	0.10	0.04	0.90	0.88	0.3	0.3	0.3	...	...	...
Business services..	33.8	14.1	0.06	0.07	0.03	0.67	0.70	0.8	0.8	0.9	...	...	...
Automobile repair services and garages..	60.1	1.8	0.11	0.15	0.01	1.36	0.16	0.6	0.8	0.5	...	...	...
Miscellaneous repair services..	29.6	4.4	0.05	0.07	0.01	0.65	0.19	0.7	0.6	0.5	...	...	...
Personal services..	144.3	27.2	0.26	0.26	0.25	2.42	5.81	0.8	0.9	0.5	...	...	...
All other industries (incl. not reported)..	97.4	14.6	0.17	0.21	0.09	1.92	2.10	1.3	1.4	0.5	...	...	...
CLERICAL AND KINDRED WORKERS..	6,894.4	62.3	12.26	6.42	27.31	100.00	100.00	2.5	2.8	2.3	57.3	28.8	81.5
Agents (n.e.c.)..	121.3	15.5	0.22	0.26	0.12	4.03	0.45	1.4	1.4	1.7	79.1	68.8	168.0
Attendants and assistants, library..	12.2	74.4	0.02	0.01	0.06	0.12	0.21	3.4	2.8	3.6	36.3	61.6	29.3
Attendants, physician's and dentist's office..	40.8	95.0	0.07	0.01	0.25	0.08	0.90	2.6	3.1	2.5	26.3	46.2	25.4
Baggagemen, transportation..	7.9	1.9	0.01	0.02	...	0.30	...	2.3	2.3	1.9	32.8	30.3	...
Bank tellers..	64.0	44.8	0.11	0.09	0.18	1.36	0.67	0.8	0.9	0.7	(5)	(5)	(5)
Bookkeepers..	721.0	77.1	1.28	0.41	3.54	6.33	12.96	2.1	2.7	1.9 }	47.8 }	-1.5	71.9
Cashiers..	226.4	81.1	0.40	0.11	1.17	1.65	4.28	3.4	3.1	3.4			
Collectors, bill and account..	23.4	14.8	0.04	0.05	0.02	0.77	0.08	2.4	2.5	2.3	-43.9	-48.1	4.0
Dispatchers and starters, vehicle..	30.8	11.5	0.05	0.07	0.02	1.05	0.08	2.4	2.1	4.4	(5)	(5)	(5)
Express messengers and railway mail clerks..	18.7	1.5	0.03	0.05	...	0.71	0.01	1.0	1.0	2.8	-14.7	-15.6	138.5
Mail carriers..	165.4	2.1	0.29	0.40	0.02	6.21	0.08	1.6	1.6	4.2	36.8	35.6	127.0
Messengers and office boys..	55.4	18.2	0.10	0.11	0.06	1.74	0.24	5.8	6.2	3.9	-0.8	-15.1	300.1
Office machine operators..	142.1	82.3	0.25	0.06	0.74	0.97	2.72	2.7	2.5	2.7	137.8	203.6	127.2
Shipping and receiving clerks..	284.5	7.0	0.51	0.65	0.13	10.17	0.46	4.3	4.3	3.8	36.6	32.5	129.4
Stenographers, typists, and secretaries..	1,589.5	94.4	2.83	0.22	9.55	3.40	34.98	2.0	2.6	2.0	50.2	26.6	51.9
Telegraph messengers..	7.2	10.5	0.01	0.02	...	0.25	0.02	10.7	11.1	6.7	-48.4	-53.1	261.1
Telegraph operators..	34.3	21.7	0.06	0.07	0.05	1.03	0.18	1.7	1.5	2.2	-11.0	-11.4	-9.6

Table 17-A-1. DETAILED OCCUPATION OF THE EXPERIENCED CIVILIAN LABOR FORCE AND OF EMPLOYED PERSONS, BY SEX, FOR THE UNITED STATES: 1950-Con.

Detailed occupation	Total employed (000)	Per-cent female	Percent of total employed			Percent of maj. occ. group of employed		Percent of experienced labor force unemployed, 1950			Percent change, 1940-1950		
			Total	Male	Female	Male	Female	Total	Male	Female	Total	Male	Female
CLERICAL AND KINDRED WORKERS—Con.													
Telephone operators	357.9	95.5	0.64	0.04	2.17	0.62	7.96	2.1	2.1	2.2	79.0	51.0	80.6
Ticket, station, and express agents	59.3	12.9	0.11	0.13	0.05	1.98	0.18	1.0	0.9	1.7	30.7	19.5	255.4
Clerical and kindred workers (n.e.c.)	2,929.7	49.1	5.21	3.68	9.16	57.25	33.55	2.7	2.9	2.6	71.6	37.5	132.4
SALES WORKERS	3,926.5	33.9	6.98	6.41	8.46	100.00	100.00	2.9	2.6	3.5	27.7	14.2	65.8
Advertising agents and salesmen	32.4	14.1	0.06	0.07	0.03	1.07	0.34	4.0	3.5	7.0	-14.1	-20.8	75.7
Auctioneers	5.3	8.6	0.01	0.01	...	0.19	0.03	3.2	2.6	8.8	61.1	54.0	217.5
Demonstrators	13.4	81.9	0.04	0.01	0.07	0.09	0.82	4.6	5.1	4.4	65.8	55.0	68.4
Hucksters and peddlers	22.0	11.0	0.04	0.05	0.02	0.73	0.23	5.4	5.2	6.2	-54.9	-59.3	31.7
Insurance agents and brokers	304.0	8.5	0.54	0.69	0.16	10.71	1.95	1.1	1.1	1.4	26.9	22.8	98.1
Newsboys	96.2	4.0	0.17	0.23	0.02	3.55	0.29	3.1	3.1	2.3	74.9	71.2	265.8
Real estate agents and brokers	140.6	14.4	0.25	0.30	0.13	4.63	1.52	1.4	1.4	1.5	26.5	19.3	97.7
Stock and bond salesmen	11.0	9.9	0.02	0.02	0.01	0.38	0.08	2.5	2.2	5.5	-34.3	-39.4	185.8
Salesmen and sales clerks (n.e.c.)	3,301.8	38.1	5.87	5.04	8.01	78.64	94.72	3.1	2.8	3.6	29.2	-14.1	64.5
Manufacturing	320.7	7.0	0.57	0.74	0.14	11.49	1.69	1.9	1.8	3.0	...	...	...
Wholesale trade	406.8	3.7	0.72	0.97	0.10	15.09	1.13	1.9	1.8	2.7	...	...	...
Retail trade	2,445.4	48.8	4.35	3.09	7.59	48.26	89.67	3.4	3.2	3.5	...	...	...
Other industries (incl. not reported)	128.8	23.1	0.23	0.24	0.19	3.82	2.23	4.8	4.1	7.0	...	...	...
CRAFTSMEN, FOREMEN AND KINDRED WORKERS	7,772.6	3.0	13.82	18.61	1.50	100.00	100.00	4.7	4.7	4.0	50.9	49.6	108.2
Bakers	119.8	11.7	0.21	0.26	0.09	1.40	5.95	4.0	4.0	4.2	-1.9	-6.1	48.0
Blacksmiths	43.5	0.5	0.08	0.11	...	0.57	0.08	3.6	3.6	4.3	(6)	(6)	(6)
Boilermakers	35.5	0.9	0.06	0.09	...	0.47	0.14	8.7	8.7	11.9	30.9	30.1	335.6
Bookbinders	31.2	56.1	0.06	0.08	0.11	0.18	7.42	3.8	3.9	3.6	(7)	(7)	(7)
Brickmasons, stonemasons, and tile setters	165.3	0.6	0.29	0.41	0.01	2.18	0.39	6.0	6.0	8.7	85.9	85.5	202.0
Cabinetmakers	73.3	1.5	0.13	0.18	0.01	0.96	0.45	4.1	4.1	5.1	44.8	43.8	194.7
Carpenters	912.5	0.6	1.62	2.24	0.03	12.04	2.04	7.4	7.4	7.0	67.5	67.1	244.7
Cement and concrete finishers	29.5	0.6	0.05	0.07	...	0.39	0.08	9.7	9.7	12.7	96.8	96.1	285.4
Compositors and typesetters	175.4	6.3	0.31	0.41	0.07	2.18	4.70	1.8	1.8	1.9	9.1	7.2	49.2
Cranemen, derrickmen, and hoistmen	103.0	0.8	0.18	0.25	...	1.36	0.33	3.6	3.6	6.2	(8)	(8)	(8)
Decorators and window dressers	43.3	30.0	0.08	0.07	0.08	0.40	5.52	3.7	3.9	3.3	59.0	43.7	111.4
Electricians	309.2	0.7	0.55	0.76	0.01	4.07	0.94	4.6	4.6	6.4	44.5	63.9	218.5
Electrotypers and stereotypers	11.8	3.7	0.02	0.03	...	0.15	0.18	1.6	1.4	6.9	47.4	43.4	457.7
Engravers, except photoengravers	9.7	12.7	0.02	0.02	0.01	0.11	0.52	3.1	2.9	4.2	22.1	15.8	96.0
Excavating, grading, and road machinery operators	105.4	0.5	0.19	0.26	...	1.39	0.21	5.1	5.1	4.8	105.5	104.8	395.3
Foremen (n.e.c.)	843.1	8.1	1.50	1.91	0.43	10.28	28.85	1.2	1.1	2.0	62.3	60.2	89.9
Construction	58.6	0.5	0.10	0.14	...	0.77	0.11	3.1	3.1	3.3	28.7	28.5	107.0
Manufacturing	510.6	9.9	0.91	1.14	0.32	6.11	21.37	1.2	1.0	2.2	74.6	73.5	85.4

Table 17-A-1. DETAILED OCCUPATION OF THE EXPERIENCED CIVILIAN LABOR FORCE AND OF EMPLOYED PERSONS, BY SEX, FOR THE UNITED STATES: 1950—Con.

Detailed occupation	Total employed (000)	Per-cent female	Percent of total employed			Percent of maj. occ. group of employed		Percent of experienced labor force unemployed, 1950			Percent change, 1940–1950		
			Total	Male	Female	Male	Female	Total	Male	Female	Total	Male	Female
CRAFTSMEN, FOREMEN AND KINDRED WKRS.—Con.													
Metal industries................	83.3	2.1	0.15	0.20	0.01	1.08	0.73	0.8	0.8	1.5	} 96.2	93.8	196.0
Machinery, including electrical.....	80.2	5.9	0.14	0.19	0.03	1.00	2.00	0.8	0.7	1.3			
Transportation equipment.........	50.0	1.7	0.09	0.12	0.01	0.65	0.36	1.2	1.1	3.2	54.7	52.1	220.8
Other durable goods.............	75.5	7.4	0.13	0.17	0.04	0.93	2.38	1.3	1.3	2.0	(9)	(9)	(9)
Textiles, textile products, and apparel...	69.0	30.5	0.12	0.12	0.13	0.64	8.93	1.9	1.8	2.1	49.7	42.6	68.6
Other nondurable goods (incl. not specified mfg)	152.7	10.7	0.27	0.34	0.10	1.81	6.96	1.2	1.0	2.7	65.8	64.4	80.3
Railroads and railway express service.	53.9	0.5	0.10	0.13	...	0.71	0.10	0.4	0.4	1.7	10.6	10.3	144.6
Transportation, except railroad......	19.8	1.2	0.04	0.05	...	0.26	0.10	1.0	1.0	1.7	37.2	36.6	135.0
Telecommunications,& utilities & sanitary service.	40.2	2.4	0.07	0.10	0.01	0.52	0.42	0.4	0.4	0.4	56.0	55.2	92.4
Other industries (incl. not reported)....	159.9	9.9	0.28	0.36	0.10	1.91	6.74	1.2	1.1	1.6	72.9	70.1	105.5
Forgemen and hammermen............	13.1	2.0	0.02	0.03	...	0.17	0.11	3.7	3.7	4.1	-29.1	-29.5	117.0
Furriers.........................	11.0	14.4	0.02	0.02	0.01	0.13	0.67	14.6	15.0	11.6	-13.4	-13.8	-10.6
Glaziers.........................	10.3	3.2	0.02	0.02	...	0.13	0.14	3.6	3.6	3.9	54.7	52.1	220.8
Heat treaters, annealers, and temperers...	17.8	1.4	0.03	0.04	...	0.23	0.08	3.0	2.9	5.6	74.1	72.8	240.0
Inspectors, scalers, and graders, log and lumber...	17.2	4.3	0.03	0.04	...	0.22	0.31	3.7	3.5	6.1	18.8	16.6	103.9
Inspectors (n.e.c.)..............	95.8	7.0	0.17	0.22	0.04	1.18	2.86	1.6	1.4	4.1	24.8	22.9	57.6
Construction....................	8.0	1.0	0.01	0.02	...	0.11	0.04	2.9	2.9	5.6	10.8	11.4	-26.3
Railroads and railway express service..	36.8	0.4	0.07	0.09	...	0.49	0.07	0.6	0.6	1.9	29.8	29.6	112.0
Transport.exc.r.r., communica'n, & other pub.util...	12.5	3.9	0.02	0.03	...	0.16	0.21	1.1	1.0	2.8	-4.4	-3.0	-29.9
Other industries (incl. not reported).....	38.5	15.6	0.07	0.08	0.04	0.43	2.55	2.3	2.0	4.2	37.0	31.5	77.2
Jewelers, watchmakers, goldsmiths, and silversmiths..	45.7	5.4	0.08	0.11	0.02	0.57	1.04	4.4	4.2	8.7	42.5	40.5	90.0
Job setters, metal...............	24.4	1.2	0.04	0.06	...	0.32	0.13	2.3	2.2	4.2	(10)	(10)	(10)
Linemen & servicemen, telegraph, telephone & power....	212.7	2.3	0.38	0.51	0.03	2.76	2.10	1.5	1.5	1.4	97.9	95.1	396.0
Locomotive engineers.............	72.8	0.6	0.13	0.18	...	0.96	0.18	0.6	0.6	2.9	14.7	14.0	...
Locomotive firemen..............	54.1	0.4	0.10	0.13	...	0.72	0.08	3.4	3.4	4.9	23.5	23.0	...
Loom fixers.....................	30.3	1.1	0.05	0.07	...	0.40	0.14	2.2	2.1	5.3	35.2	34.2	257.9
Machinists......................	513.2	1.6	0.91	1.25	0.05	6.70	3.45	3.8	3.8	5.1	11.7	11.0	83.1
Mechanics and repairmen...........	1,706.5	1.2	3.04	4.16	0.13	22.36	8.90	3.5	3.4	4.2	105.1	103.5	405.7
Airplane.......................	70.7	1.6	0.13	0.17	0.01	0.92	0.49	4.1	4.0	10.7	174.2	171.0	880.3
Automobile.....................	650.6	0.6	1.16	1.60	0.03	8.58	1.73	4.0	4.0	5.0	74.2	73.7	243.3
Office machine.................	15.9	1.5	0.03	0.04	...	0.21	0.10	2.4	2.4	2.5	(11)	(11)	(11)
Radio and television............	74.8	2.7	0.13	0.18	0.01	0.97	0.86	4.4	4.4	3.8	(11)	(11)	(11)
Railroad and car shop...........	47.5	0.5	0.08	0.12	...	0.63	0.09	1.8	1.8	6.0	14.6	14.1	...
Not elsewhere classified.........	847.0	1.6	1.51	2.06	0.08	11.06	5.62	3.0	3.0	3.4	139.5	137.2	446.4

Table 17-A-1. DETAILED OCCUPATION OF THE EXPERIENCED CIVILIAN LABOR FORCE AND OF EMPLOYED PERSONS, BY SEX, FOR THE UNITED STATES: 1950-Con.

Detailed occupation	Total employed (000)	Per-cent female	Percent of total employed			Percent of maj. occ. group of employed		Percent of experienced labor force unemployed, 1950			Percent change, 1940-1950		
			Total	Male	Female	Male	Female	Total	Male	Female	Total	Male	Female
CRAFTSMEN, FOREMEN, AND KINDRED WKRS.--Con.													
Millers, grain, flour, feed, etc.	9.6	0.7	0.02	0.02	...	0.13	0.03	1.8	1.8	...	-34.9	-35.0	-17.3
Millwrights	57.9	0.4	0.10	0.14	...	0.77	0.10	3.7	3.7	5.1	46.1	45.8	170.8
Molders, metal	60.5	1.1	0.11	0.15	...	0.79	0.28	4.8	4.7	6.3	-17.2	-17.7	93.3
Motion picture projectionists	26.1	1.8	0.05	0.06	...	0.34	0.20	1.7	1.7	1.8	16.8	16.0	88.3
Opticians, and lens grinders and polishers	19.2	13.1	0.03	0.04	0.02	0.22	1.07	3.3	3.0	5.1	72.7	64.7	154.1
Painters, construction and maintenance	390.1	2.1	0.69	0.94	0.05	5.07	3.44	9.5	9.6	6.1	21.7	21.7	265.9
Paperhangers	20.9	14.0	0.04	0.04	0.02	0.24	1.25	7.1	7.7	3.2	-17.6	-24.6	91.3
Pattern and model makers, except paper	35.9	3.4	0.06	0.09	0.01	0.46	0.51	3.9	4.0	3.5	28.3	25.1	389.4
Photoengravers and lithographers	28.5	3.7	0.05	0.07	0.01	0.36	0.45	1.7	1.6	3.3	35.9	33.6	145.3
Piano and organ tuners and repairmen	7.7	3.4	0.01	0.02	...	0.10	0.11	3.1	3.1	2.6	60.0	56.0	491.1
Plasterers	60.3	0.8	0.11	0.15	...	0.80	0.21	6.3	6.3	7.2	61.0	60.4	196.4
Plumbers and pipe fitters	277.9	0.7	0.49	0.68	0.01	3.66	0.84	6.1	6.1	6.8	64.0	63.4	272.1
Pressmen and plate printers, printing	49.1	4.3	0.09	0.12	0.01	0.62	0.90	2.2	2.2	2.8	49.3	45.1	318.5
Rollers and roll hands, metal	30.4	2.2	0.05	0.07	...	0.39	0.28	2.1	2.1	3.9	6.3	4.4	510.2
Roofers and slaters	44.4	0.5	0.08	0.11	...	0.59	0.10	8.6	8.6	9.5	87.0	86.7	169.3
Shoemakers and repairers, except factory	57.1	3.8	0.10	0.14	0.01	0.73	0.91	3.0	2.7	11.0	-7.0	-9.6	266.7
Stationary engineers	213.9	0.7	0.38	0.52	0.01	2.82	0.61	1.9	1.9	3.1	17.7	17.3	177.4
Stone cutters and stone carvers	8.7	2.6	0.02	0.02	...	0.11	0.10	4.1	4.0	5.4	-4.4	-6.5	451.2
Structural metal workers	49.2	0.5	0.09	0.12	...	0.65	0.11	10.7	10.7	16.0	49.5	49.6	46.7
Tailors and tailoresses	82.5	19.5	0.15	0.16	0.10	0.88	6.81	4.0	4.2	3.2	-22.9	-27.8	7.0
Tinsmiths, coppersmiths, and sheet metal workers	122.8	0.9	0.22	0.30	0.01	1.61	0.49	5.3	5.2	7.8	58.6	57.8	250.3
Toolmakers, and die makers and setters	152.6	0.7	0.27	0.37	0.01	2.01	0.45	2.8	2.8	4.7	62.1	61.7	183.2
Upholsterers	61.2	8.5	0.11	0.14	0.03	0.74	2.22	4.1	4.1	1.6	60.8	54.6	181.5
Craftsmen and kindred workers (n.e.c.)	69.5	1.6	0.12	0.17	0.01	0.91	0.48	6.1	6.0	12.5	(7)	(7)	(7)
Members of the armed forces	...	...	...	...	...	...	...	...	...	...	...	...	...
OPERATIVES AND KINDRED WORKERS	11,146.2	27.1	19.82	20.06	19.21	100.00	100.00	4.9	4.8	5.0	38.7	35.4	48.7
Apprentices	115.2	2.7	0.20	0.28	0.02	1.38	0.10	3.9	3.8	5.7	41.1	41.1	39.4
Auto mechanics	3.7	4.0	0.01	0.01	...	0.04	...	4.8	4.8	5.8	(12)	(12)	(12)
Bricklayers and masons	6.1	0.4	0.01	0.02	...	0.08	...	5.1	5.0	8.3	(12)	(12)	(12)
Carpenters	10.0	0.8	0.02	0.02	...	0.12	...	7.3	7.3	7.9	80.4	80.3	90.7
Electricians	8.9	0.9	0.02	0.02	...	0.11	0.01	3.7	3.6	9.3	188.4	188.1	225.0
Machinists and toolmakers	15.3	1.0	0.03	0.04	...	0.19	0.02	2.7	2.6	9.1	-17.7	-18.3	117.8
Mechanics, except auto	6.3	7.3	0.01	0.01	...	0.07	0.02	3.9	3.4	10.2	(12)	(12)	(12)
Plumbers and pipe fitters	11.9	4.5	0.02	0.03	...	0.14	0.02	3.7	3.7	2.9	157.4	152.0	371.7
Building trades (n.e.c.)	4.0	0.8	0.01	0.01	...	0.05	...	6.0	6.0	11.8	(12)	(12)	(12)
Metalworking trades (n.e.c.)	6.6	1.1	0.01	0.01	...	0.08	...	3.3	3.3	5.3	(12)	(12)	(12)
Printing trades	15.2	2.6	0.03	0.04	...	0.18	0.01	2.3	2.2	4.4	62.5	62.1	78.6
Other specified trades	12.6	3.7	0.02	0.03	...	0.15	0.02	4.0	3.9	4.8	32.8	35.7	-20.2
Trade not specified	14.6	4.9	0.03	0.03	0	0.17	0.02	3.3	3.2	4.4	34.3	31.3	145.2

Table 17-A-1. DETAILED OCCUPATION OF THE EXPERIENCED CIVILIAN LABOR FORCE AND OF EMPLOYED PERSONS, BY SEX, FOR THE UNITED STATES: 1950—Con.

Detailed occupation	Total employed (000)	Per-cent female	Percent of total employed			Percent of maj. occ. group of employed		Percent of experienced labor force unemployed, 1950			Percent change, 1940-1950		
			Total	Male	Female	Male	Female	Total	Male	Female	Total	Male	Female
OPERATIVES AND KINDRED WORKERS.—Con.													
Asbestos and insulation workers	15.2	2.7	0.03	0.04	...	0.18	0.01	7.5	7.5	7.5	192.8	189.2	440.0
Attendants, auto service and parking	236.0	2.8	0.42	0.57	0.04	2.82	0.22	4.6	4.7	2.4	7.4	6.3	71.6
Blasters and powdermen	10.9	0.8	0.02	0.03	...	0.13	...	5.0	5.0	6.2	142.5	141.2	600.0
Boatmen, canalmen, and lock keepers	8.1	2.5	0.01	0.02	...	0.10	0.01	4.1	4.2	0.5	51.5	49.7	185.9
Brakemen, railroad	78.4	0.4	0.14	0.19	...	0.96	0.01	2.6	2.6	5.0	12.4	12.0	...
Bus drivers	155.0	3.2	0.28	0.37	0.03	1.85	0.16	1.4	1.4	5.0	(13)	(13)	(13)
Chainmen, rodmen, and axmen, surveying	7.0	2.3	0.01	0.02	...	0.08	0.01	6.0	6.1	3.6	-8.2	-10.1	757.9
Conductors, bus and street railway	11.3	1.8	0.02	0.03	...	0.14	0.01	1.4	1.3	3.7	-33.3	-33.9	35.1
Deliverymen and routemen	238.6	1.8	0.42	0.58	0.03	2.88	0.14	3.6	3.6	4.2	-8.7	-9.5	70.9
Dressmakers and seamstresses, except factory	138.1	97.2	0.25	0.01	0.85	0.05	4.45	3.2	4.8	3.2	3.5	63.9	2.4
Dyers	24.2	4.3	0.04	0.06	0.01	0.29	0.03	4.6	4.6	4.6	0.5	-1.1	62.0
Filers, grinders, and polishers, metal	147.7	4.5	0.26	0.35	0.04	1.74	0.22	5.1	5.1	6.1	42.8	41.3	84.3
Fruit, nut, & vegetable graders & packers, ex.fac.	28.7	60.2	0.05	0.03	0.11	0.14	0.57	16.4	13.6	18.1	37.4	27.8	44.5
Furnacemen, smeltermen, and pourers	55.4	2.2	0.10	0.13	0.01	0.67	0.04	3.7	3.8	3.3	92.0	89.3	401.6
Heaters, metal	9.3	4.5	0.02	0.02	...	0.11	0.01	4.2	4.2	4.3	17.0	13.7	205.9
Laundry and dry cleaning operatives	428.3	67.1	0.76	0.35	1.83	1.73	9.52	4.5	5.0	4.3	52.0	50.5	52.7
Meat cutters, except slaughter and packing house	170.6	2.0	0.30	0.41	0.02	2.06	0.11	3.2	3.2	2.9	20.6	19.0	252.7
Milliners	12.3	89.4	0.02	...	0.07	0.02	0.37	4.0	3.9	4.1	-6.2	100.8	-11.8
Mine operatives and laborers (n.e.c.)	573.4	0.8	1.02	1.40	0.03	7.00	0.16	5.2	5.2	5.0	-11.4	-11.9	163.7
Coal mining	362.1	0.4	0.64	0.89	0.01	4.44	0.04	5.3	5.3	7.4	}	}	}
Crude petroleum and natural gas extraction	102.6	0.4	0.18	0.25	...	1.26	0.01	5.5	5.3	6.6	}	}	}
Mining and quarrying, except fuel	108.7	2.7	0.19	0.26	0.02	1.30	0.10	5.5	5.6	3.7	}	}	}
Motormen, mine, factory, logging camp, etc.	23.9	0.9	0.04	0.06	...	0.29	0.01	1.9	1.9	6.1	32.9	32.0	448.7
Motormen, street, subway, and elevated railway	26.5	1.3	0.05	0.06	...	0.32	0.01	1.0	0.9	5.4	-27.8	-28.4	86.2
Oilers and greasers, except auto	58.8	1.6	0.10	0.14	0.01	0.71	0.03	4.4	4.4	4.6	64.0	62.3	379.0
Painters, except construction and maintenance	116.7	11.4	0.21	0.26	0.08	1.27	0.44	5.0	5.0	5.1	29.8	25.1	81.5
Photographic process workers	28.0	44.5	0.05	0.04	0.08	0.19	0.41	4.3	4.6	4.7	97.0	63.2	150.7
Power station operators	21.5	3.9	0.04	0.05	0.01	0.25	0.03	0.7	0.6	1.2	0.2	-0.8	33.7
Sailors and deck hands	40.3	1.9	0.07	0.10	...	0.49	0.02	21.2	21.3	11.8	15.6	13.8	450.4
Sawyers	93.7	2.0	0.17	0.23	0.01	1.13	0.06	4.0	4.0	5.3	113.8	111.7	300.6
Spinners, textile	80.8	75.0	0.14	0.05	0.39	0.25	2.01	4.8	6.8	4.2	(7)	(7)	(7)
Stationary firemen	121.8	0.9	0.22	0.30	0.01	1.49	0.04	3.9	3.9	4.7	9.9	9.3	188.5
Switchmen, railroad	61.3	0.8	0.11	0.15	...	0.75	0.02	1.3	1.3	2.1	33.9	32.9	...
Taxicab drivers and chauffeurs	202.1	1.7	0.36	0.49	0.02	2.44	0.11	4.9	4.9	5.3	36.5	35.9	175.8
Truck and tractor drivers	1,329.2	0.6	2.36	3.25	0.05	16.26	0.27	4.8	4.8	5.9	(13)	(13)	(13)
Weavers, textile	97.9	39.4	0.17	0.15	0.25	0.73	1.28	4.6	5.0	3.9	(7)	(7)	(7)
Welders and flame-cutters	260.3	3.6	0.46	0.62	0.06	3.09	0.31	5.5	5.5	5.5	115.6	111.4	358.6

Table 17-A-1. DETAILED OCCUPATION OF THE EXPERIENCED CIVILIAN LABOR FORCE AND OF EMPLOYED PERSONS, BY SEX, FOR THE UNITED STATES: 1950—Con.

Detailed occupation	Total employed (000)	Per-cent female	Percent of total employed			Percent of maj. occ. group of employed		Percent of experienced labor force unemployed, 1950			Percent change, 1940-1950		
			Total	Male	Female	Male	Female	Total	Male	Female	Total	Male	Female
OPERATIVES AND KINDRED WORKERS—Con.													
Operatives and kindred workers (n.e.c.)......	6,119.6	38.9	10.88	9.24	15.13	46.03	78.78	5.0	4.9	5.2	54.6	54.5	54.7
Manufacturing......	5,405.5	41.0	9.61	7.88	14.09	39.26	73.37	4.9	4.8	5.1	50.1	49.9	50.3
Durable goods......	2,407.5	26.3	4.28	4.38	4.04	21.82	21.01	4.7	4.7	4.8	85.4	75.4	120.8
Sawmills, planing mills, & misc.wood prod...	184.8	8.5	0.33	0.42	0.10	2.08	0.52	4.2	4.1	5.3	111.0	112.1	100.0
Sawmills, planing mills, and mill work...	142.6	3.5	0.25	0.34	0.03	1.69	0.16	3.8	3.8	5.1	151.4	151.4	280.3
Miscellaneous wood products......	42.2	25.2	0.08	0.08	0.07	0.39	0.35	5.4	5.5	5.4	33.9	26.1	63.7
Furniture and fixtures......	123.8	21.2	0.22	0.24	0.17	1.20	0.87	4.1	4.0	4.4	74.3	62.5	138.2
Stone, clay, and glass products......	182.2	25.7	0.32	0.33	0.30	1.67	1.55	3.2	3.2	3.2	61.8	55.3	84.1
Glass and glass products......	72.3	30.1	0.13	0.12	0.14	0.62	0.72	3.1	2.9	3.6	52.2	43.6	78.8
Cement, & concrete, gypsum & plaster prod.	28.4	3.1	0.05	0.07	0.01	0.34	0.03	4.0	3.5	3.7	139.4	136.8	263.3
Structural clay products......	21.2	18.8	0.04	0.04	0.03	0.21	0.13	4.0	4.1	3.6	53.3	39.5	167.6
Pottery and related products......	33.3	42.5	0.06	0.05	0.09	0.24	0.47	2.9	3.2	2.6	41.8	32.8	56.3
Misc. nonmetallic mineral & stone prod...	27.0	22.3	0.05	0.05	0.04	0.26	0.20	3.2	3.2	3.0	69.8	56.0	145.5
Metal industries......	523.2	17.6	0.93	1.06	0.58	5.31	3.04	4.1	4.1	4.3	58.3	53.7	84.2
Primary metal industries......	258.1	7.2	0.46	0.59	0.12	2.95	0.61	3.6	3.6	4.4	(a)	(a)	(a)
Blast furnaces, steel works, & roll.mills	126.6	4.6	0.23	0.30	0.04	1.49	0.19	2.9	2.8	4.2	38.2	39.2	21.8
Other primary iron and steel industries.	69.7	5.9	0.12	0.16	0.03	0.81	0.11	5.2	5.2	5.0	62.0	56.8	84.8
Primary nonferrous industries......	61.9	13.9	0.11	0.13	0.05	0.66	0.28	3.4	3.2	4.3	112.0	104.1	143.9
Fabricated metal ind.(incl.not spec.metal)	265.1	27.7	0.47	0.47	0.47	2.36	2.43	4.6	4.7	4.2	(a)	(a)	(a)
Fabricated steel products......	231.5	26.0	0.41	0.42	0.38	2.11	1.99	4.5	4.6	4.2	(16)	(16)	(16)
Fabricated nonferrous metal products...	30.1	40.6	0.05	0.04	0.08	0.22	0.41	5.3	6.0	4.3	(17)	(17)	(17)
Not specified metal industries......	3.5	24.3	0.01	0.01	0.01	0.03	0.03	5.1	5.0	5.4	-64.1	-67.0	-50.2
Machinery, except electrical......	343.4	17.9	0.61	0.70	0.39	3.47	2.03	3.7	3.6	4.1	124.3	115.9	173.2
Agricultural machinery and tractors......	50.0	6.6	0.09	0.12	0.02	0.58	0.11	1.9	1.8	2.7	160.1	153.0	335.4
Office and store machinery and devices...	37.1	33.6	0.07	0.06	0.08	0.30	0.41	4.1	3.6	5.1	69.7	60.9	90.2
Miscellaneous machinery......	256.3	17.8	0.46	0.52	0.29	2.59	1.51	4.0	4.0	4.0	128.8	117.5	201.1
Electrical machinery, equipment, and supp...	334.6	53.8	0.60	0.38	1.15	1.90	5.96	3.6	4.0	3.3	153.4	122.3	188.1
Transportation equipment......	427.3	15.5	0.76	0.89	0.42	4.44	2.19	6.7	6.7	7.0	80.4	72.6	138.9
Motor vehicles and motor vehicle equip...	336.6	16.7	0.60	0.69	0.36	3.45	1.87	6.4	6.4	6.4	81.7	75.7	118.8
Aircraft and parts......	62.2	12.5	0.11	0.13	0.05	0.67	0.26	5.1	4.2	11.1	149.3	128.1	612.0
Ship and boat building and repairing......	12.8	4.2	0.02	0.03	...	0.15	0.02	13.4	13.4	13.5	-26.0	-27.9	94.6
Railroad and misc.transportation equip...	15.7	9.1	0.03	0.04	0.01	0.18	0.05	13.1	13.6	7.8	66.9	61.0	162.8
Professional & photographic equip.& watches.	74.5	47.2	0.13	0.10	0.22	0.48	1.16	5.0	4.8	5.2	...	...	...
Professional equipment and supplies......	40.1	45.2	0.07	0.05	0.12	0.27	0.60	3.8	3.9	3.6	101.0	99.7	102.7
Photographic equipment and supplies......	15.7	37.8	0.03	0.02	0.04	0.12	0.20	4.7	3.4	6.8			
Watches, clocks, & clockwork-operated dev.	18.7	59.2	0.03	0.02	0.07	0.09	0.37	7.7	8.8	6.8	58.4	41.1	78.0
Miscellaneous manufacturing industries......	213.6	52.1	0.38	0.25	0.71	1.26	3.69	6.8	6.7	6.9	(18)	(18)	(18)

Table 17-A-1. DETAILED OCCUPATION OF THE EXPERIENCED CIVILIAN LABOR FORCE AND OF EMPLOYED PERSONS, BY SEX, FOR THE UNITED STATES: 1950-Con.

Detailed occupation	Total employed (000)	Percent female	Percent of total employed			Percent of maj. occ. group of employed		Percent of experienced labor force unemployed, 1950			Percent change, 1940-1950		
			Total	Male	Female	Male	Female	Total	Male	Female	Total	Male	Female
OPERATIVES AND KINDRED WKRS.—Con.													
Operatives and kindred workers (n.e.c.)—Con.													
Manufacturing—Con.													
Nondurable goods..........	2,960.6	52.8	5.27	3.45	9.95	17.20	51.77	5.1	5.0	5.2	31.7	28.5	34.7
Food and kindred products..........	489.8	38.0	0.87	0.75	1.19	3.73	6.17	7.7	6.0	10.5	62.4	59.8	66.8
Meat products......	123.7	28.7	0.22	0.22	0.23	1.08	1.18	4.1	3.8	4.6	52.6	40.9	91.9
Dairy products......	58.5	16.0	0.10	0.12	0.06	0.60	0.31	3.1	2.7	2.7	77.5	77.8	75.8
Canning & preserving fruits, veg. & seafood	68.8	62.6	0.12	0.06	0.27	0.32	1.43	21.8	19.3	23.2	92.8	98.5	89.5
Grain-mill products..........	31.5	15.1	0.06	0.07	0.03	0.33	0.16	3.6	3.2	5.8	107.3	107.4	106.9
Bakery products..........	63.2	52.9	0.11	0.07	0.21	0.37	1.11	4.8	5.3	4.4	58.4	55.0	62.6
Confectionery and related products...	44.9	65.4	0.08	0.04	0.19	0.19	0.97	8.5	8.8	8.4	13.1	19.0	10.2
Beverage industries......	52.9	17.1	0.09	0.11	0.06	0.54	0.30	5.2	5.2	5.9	63.7	66.8	50.2
Misc. food preparations and kindred prod...	35.0	43.5	0.06	0.05	0.10	0.24	0.50	6.5	7.3	5.5	87.2	63.6	123.4
Not specified food industries......	11.3	57.9	0.02	0.01	0.04	0.06	0.22	6.5	5.5	7.2			
Tobacco manufactures........	61.7	70.1	0.11	0.05	0.27	0.23	1.43	8.8	9.2	8.6	-14.6	-9.8	-16.5
Textile mill products......	665.1	53.3	1.18	0.77	2.26	3.82	11.75	4.3	4.5	4.2	8.1	0.6	15.7
Knitting mills......	145.5	72.1	0.26	0.10	0.67	0.50	3.48	3.7	3.7	3.1	-15.9	-28.7	-9.6
Dyeing & finishing textiles, exc. knit goods	24.2	22.3	0.04	0.05	0.03	0.23	0.18	4.0	4.2	3.4	13.1	16.2	3.6
Carpets, rugs, and other floor coverings...	24.5	43.3	0.04	0.03	0.07	0.17	0.35	2.7	2.4	3.0	26.1	30.6	20.7
Yarn, thread, and fabric mills......	441.4	49.9	0.79	0.55	1.40	2.73	7.29	4.7	4.7	4.8	19.3	7.9	33.6
Miscellaneous textile mill products...	29.5	46.8	0.05	0.04	0.09	0.19	0.46	5.1	4.6	4.6	-5.6	-19.2	16.8
Apparel and other fabricated textile prod...	811.8	80.7	1.44	0.39	4.17	1.93	21.71	5.1	8.2	4.3	39.0	19.6	44.7
Apparel and accessories......	758.2	81.4	1.35	0.35	3.93	1.74	20.43	5.1	8.5	4.2	38.8	16.8	45.1
Miscellaneous fabricated textile products...	53.6	71.8	0.10	0.04	0.24	0.19	1.27	5.3	5.8	5.1	41.8	53.8	37.6
Paper and allied products......	218.4	32.4	0.39	0.36	0.45	1.82	2.35	3.2	2.7	4.0	52.9	55.3	48.0
Pulp, paper, and paperboard mills......	101.7	15.5	0.18	0.21	0.10	1.06	0.52	2.1	2.1	4.9	25.4	31.7	-0.6
Paperboard containers and boxes......	59.1	45.4	0.11	0.08	0.17	0.40	0.89	4.5	4.2	3.6	63.2	82.9	44.5
Miscellaneous paper and pulp products...	57.6	49.1	0.10	0.07	0.18	0.36	0.94	3.3	3.0	3.6	125.3	142.1	110.0
Printing, publishing, and allied industries...	74.9	44.2	0.13	0.10	0.21	0.51	1.10	4.3	3.9	4.8	47.0	54.3	38.6
Chemicals and allied products......	183.3	22.6	0.33	0.35	0.26	1.75	1.37	3.5	3.0	5.1	72.8	81.2	49.2
Synthetic fibers......	25.6	32.4	0.05	0.04	0.05	0.21	0.27	3.2	2.5	4.5	-11.6	-9.7	-15.3
Drugs and medicines......	11.3	60.1	0.03	0.01	0.05	0.07	0.29	2.9	2.4	3.1	112.3	121.0	86.2
Paints, varnishes, and related products...	17.4	15.1	0.03	0.04	0.02	0.18	0.09	3.4	3.3	3.8	57.6	56.3	65.1
Miscellaneous chemicals and allied prod...	125.9	17.4	0.22	0.26	0.14	1.29	0.72	3.7	3.1	6.3	(19)	(19)	(19)
Petroleum and coal products......	52.6	2.7	0.09	0.13	0.01	0.63	0.05	2.1	2.0	5.2	58.0	56.9	109.2
Petroleum refining......	46.2	2.5	0.08	0.11	0.01	0.55	0.04	1.9	1.8	5.2	60.7	59.3	150.2
Miscellaneous petroleum and coal products...	6.4	3.9	0.01	0.02	...	0.08	0.01	3.3	3.3	4.2	40.8	41.9	18.5
Rubber products......	119.1	30.4	0.21	0.20	0.23	1.02	1.20	3.6	3.5	4.0	57.1	54.5	63.5
Leather and leather products......	283.9	49.4	0.50	0.35	0.89	1.77	1.64	5.2	5.9	4.5	6.8	-5.0	22.2
Leather: tanned, curried, and finished...	29.4	15.8	0.05	0.06	0.03	0.30	0.15	4.6	4.6	5.0	-1.3	-5.4	28.4
Footwear, except rubber......	209.7	52.8	0.37	0.24	0.70	1.22	3.67	4.7	5.6	3.9	5.8	-7.3	21.4

TABLE 17-A-1. DETAILED OCCUPATION OF THE EXPERIENCED CIVILIAN LABOR FORCE AND OF EMPLOYED PERSONS, BY SEX, FOR THE UNITED STATES: 1950-Con.

Detailed occupation	Total employed (000)	Percent female	Percent of total employed			Percent of maj. occ. group of employed		Percent of experienced labor force unemployed, 1950			Percent change, 1940-1950		
			Total	Male	Female	Male	Female	Total	Male	Female	Total	Male	Female
OPERATIVES AND KINDRED WORKERS-Con.													
Operatives and kindred workers (n.e.c.)-Con.													
Leather products, except footwear........	44.8	55.3	0.08	0.05	0.16	0.25	0.82	7.8	8.8	6.9	17.5	9.2	25.1
Not specified manufacturing industries........	37.5	47.3	0.07	0.05	0.11	0.24	0.59	9.7	9.2	10.2	-33.7	-35.3	-31.7
Nonmanufacturing industries (incl.not reported)	714.1	22.9	1.27	1.36	1.04	6.78	5.41	5.8	5.6	6.5	100.2	87.8	157.7
Construction........	64.0	2.2	0.11	0.15	0.01	0.77	0.05	7.5	7.6	5.8	133.3	130.6	391.8
Railroads and railway express service........	90.9	1.3	0.16	0.22	0.01	1.10	0.04	3.3	3.3	4.5	39.5	38.6	179.4
Transportation, except railroad........	34.3	13.4	0.06	0.07	0.03	0.37	0.15	5.2	4.8	7.8	62.8	51.5	215.7
Telecommunications,& utilities & san.services	49.8	6.6	0.09	0.11	0.02	0.57	0.11	2.8	2.7	4.0	120.8	112.3	409.1
Wholesale and retail trade........	284.5	37.9	0.51	0.44	0.69	2.17	3.57	5.8	5.5	6.2	127.1	114.1	152.1
Business and repair services........	49.6	13.4	0.09	0.11	0.04	0.53	0.22	5.3	5.4	4.4	52.0	42.1	175.0
Personal services........	19.9	56.2	0.04	0.02	0.07	0.11	0.37	5.6	7.3	4.3	181.3	177.3	184.5
Public administration........	50.3	12.3	0.09	0.11	0.04	0.54	0.21	4.2	3.9	6.5	412.7	405.0	474.7
All other industries (incl. not reported)....	70.8	29.6	0.13	0.12	0.13	0.61	0.69	10.8	11.2	9.8	55.4	41.5	102.4
PRIVATE HOUSEHOLD WORKERS........	1,407.5	94.8	2.50	0.18	8.49	100.00	100.00	5.4	5.8	5.4	-32.6	-37.2	-32.3
Housekeepers, private household........	139.7	96.2	0.25	0.01	0.86	7.19	10.08	3.9	10.6	3.7			
Living in........	52.8	98.9	0.09	...	0.33	0.78	3.91	...	...	...			
Living out........	87.0	94.6	0.15	0.01	0.52	6.41	6.17	6.2	11.7	5.9	-61.8	82.0	-62.9
Laundresses, private household........	71.2	96.9	0.13	0.01	0.44	3.01	5.17	3.1	4.6	3.1			
Living in........	0.6	99.2	...	...	...	0.01	0.05	...	...	...			
Living out........	70.5	96.9	0.13	0.01	0.43	3.00	5.12	3.2	4.6	3.1	-62.5	-35.4	-63.0
Private household workers (n.e.c.)........	1,196.6	94.5	2.13	0.16	7.20	89.80	84.75	5.7	5.4	5.7			
Living in........	162.1	92.6	0.29	0.03	0.96	16.34	11.26	...	...	...			
Living out........	1,034.4	94.8	1.84	0.13	6.24	73.46	73.50	6.5	6.5	6.5	-22.0	-40.4	-20.5
SERVICE WORKERS, EXCEPT PRIVATE HSHLD....	4,287.7	44.6	7.63	5.86	12.18	100.00	100.00	5.0	5.2	4.7	34.5	20.9	56.3
Attendants, hospital and other institution....	204.4	59.3	0.36	0.21	0.77	3.50	6.33	3.0	3.4	2.8	119.6	53.0	213.0
Attendants, professional & personal serv.(n.e.c.)	47.6	66.4	0.08	0.04	0.20	0.67	1.65	5.0	4.3	5.3	64.3	50.7	72.2
Attendants, recreation and amusement.....	58.8	8.1	0.10	0.13	0.03	2.28	0.25	8.4	8.6	5.6	32.1	28.6	93.0
Barbers, beauticians, and manicurists.....	382.5	49.6	0.68	0.48	1.21	8.11	9.92	1.6	1.4	3.4	-8.0	-8.0	-8.1
Bartenders........	193.5	6.9	0.34	0.44	0.09	7.59	0.70	6.9	7.2	3.1	70.2	62.8	333.3
Boarding and lodging house keepers........	28.8	73.0	0.05	0.02	0.13	0.33	1.10	1.2	1.6	1.0	-59.9	-25.7	-65.7
Bootblacks........	13.8	3.4	0.02	0.03	...	0.56	0.02	6.4	6.4	6.4	-2.8	-4.1	59.2
Charwomen and cleaners........	119.3	60.4	0.21	0.12	0.46	1.99	3.77	4.0	5.5	3.1	89.1	63.6	110.5
Cooks, except private household........	434.8	55.8	0.77	0.47	1.54	8.10	12.66	6.1	9.1	3.6	57.2	20.1	108.4
Counter and fountain workers........	86.5	51.3	0.15	0.10	0.28	1.77	2.32	6.9	8.2	5.6	(14)	(14)	(14)

Table 17-A-1. DETAILED OCCUPATION OF THE EXPERIENCED CIVILIAN LABOR FORCE AND OF EMPLOYED PERSONS, BY SEX, FOR THE UNITED STATES: 1950-Con.

Detailed occupation	Total employed (000)	Percent female	Percent of total employed			Percent of maj. occ. group of employed		Percent of experienced labor force unemployed, 1950			Percent change, 1940-1950		
			Total	Male	Female	Male	Female	Total	Male	Female	Total	Male	Female
SERVICE WORKERS, EXCEPT PRIVATE HSHLD.-Con.													
Elevator operators	89.1	30.2	0.16	0.15	0.17	2.62	1.41	5.4	5.5	5.2	16.0	-3.1	112.3
Firemen, fire protection	109.9	0.4	0.20	0.27	...	4.61	0.02	0.8	0.8	2.2	36.2	35.6	...
Guards, watchmen, and doorkeepers	237.2	2.2	0.42	0.57	0.03	9.77	0.27	4.7	4.8	2.6	25.6	21.9	63.0
Housekeepers and stewards, except private hshld.	105.8	78.3	0.19	0.06	0.53	0.97	4.33	2.9	5.2	2.2	36.3	26.9	39.2
Janitors and sextons	454.5	11.7	0.81	0.99	0.34	16.91	2.78	3.7	3.8	2.8	31.2	29.8	42.5
Marshals and constables	6.5	2.8	0.01	0.02	...	0.27	0.01	1.3	1.3	0.5	-25.6	-26.7	65.5
Midwives	1.7	82.9	...	...	0.01	0.01	0.07	6.5	2.4	7.3	(15)	(15)	(15)
Policemen and detectives	192.2	1.8	0.34	0.47	0.02	7.95	0.18	1.1	1.1	2.6	28.3	27.3	122.6
Government	172.3	1.4	0.31	0.42	0.02	7.16	0.12	0.8	0.8	1.4	31.8	30.9	168.8
Private	19.8	5.7	0.04	0.05	0.01	0.79	0.06	3.9	3.9	5.1	3.9	1.7	63.7
Porters	161.9	2.2	0.29	0.39	0.02	6.67	0.19	6.8	6.8	6.8	4.1	3.1	88.0
Practical nurses	135.9	95.9	0.24	0.01	0.83	0.24	6.81	5.8	5.9	5.8	51.0	50.5	51.0
Sheriffs and bailiffs	18.5	4.1	0.03	0.04	...	0.75	0.04	1.3	1.3	1.0	17.6	15.6	97.1
Ushers, recreation and amusement	23.3	33.7	0.04	0.04	0.05	0.65	0.41	7.6	7.9	7.1	23.4	4.1	94.7
Waiters and waitresses	664.8	82.1	1.18	0.29	3.47	5.02	28.50	6.8	7.0	6.7	40.8	-6.6	63.5
Watchmen (crossing) and bridge tenders	11.5	4.0	0.02	0.03	...	0.47	0.02	1.8	1.8	2.6	23.6	20.4	248.9
Service workers, except private household (n.e.c.)	505.0	61.5	0.90	0.48	1.98	8.19	16.23	6.8	9.5	5.0	61.4	40.1	78.4
FARM LABORERS AND FOREMEN	2,399.8	18.7	4.27	4.81	2.86	100.00	100.00	4.6	4.7	3.8	-22.7	-30.0	40.1
Farm foremen	16.7	2.7	0.03	0.04	...	0.84	0.10	2.3	1.7	21.3	1.6	0.3	89.8
Farm laborers, wage workers	1,465.6	8.9	2.60	3.29	0.83	66.36	29.00	6.7	6.3	10.6	-23.8	-26.9	33.9
Farm laborers, unpaid family workers	910.4	34.9	1.62	1.46	2.02	30.39	70.68	0.9	1.1	0.7	-21.9	-37.1	42.2
Farm service laborers, self-employed	9.1	10.8	0.02	0.02	0.01	0.42	0.22	5.5	3.5	19.2	(7)	(7)	(7)
LABORERS, EXCEPT FARM AND MINE	3,417.2	3.7	6.08	8.12	0.81	100.00	100.00	8.9	8.9	8.7	10.1	9.6	24.7
Fishermen and oystermen	67.5	1.4	0.12	0.16	0.01	2.02	0.76	6.7	6.8	5.6	21.5	20.7	143.5
Garage laborers, and car washers and greasers	65.1	3.4	0.12	0.16	0.01	1.91	1.75	7.2	7.2	7.0	20.8	17.6	444.9
Gardeners, except farm, and groundskeepers	145.5	2.3	0.26	0.35	0.02	4.32	2.59	6.1	6.1	8.9	8.9	7.6	133.1
Longshoremen and stevedores	62.7	1.1	0.11	0.15	...	1.88	0.52	10.2	10.2	11.0	3.2	2.6	120.5
Lumbermen, raftsmen, and wood choppers	172.1	0.9	0.31	0.42	0.01	5.18	1.24	8.9	9.0	6.5	35.1	34.3	308.3
Teamsters	21.2	1.5	0.04	0.05	...	0.63	0.25	4.9	4.9	7.4	-10.9	-11.8	161.7
Laborers (n.e.c.)	2,883.2	4.1	5.13	6.83	0.75	84.04	92.88	9.1	9.1	8.8	8.9	8.5	19.4
Manufacturing	1,091.4	6.2	1.94	2.53	0.43	31.12	53.12	7.0	6.8	8.7	-17.5	-17.8	-11.3
Durable goods	686.2	4.3	1.22	1.62	0.19	19.96	23.33	6.6	6.6	6.3	-18.1	-19.2	17.1
Sawmills, planing mills, & misc. wood products	156.2	2.5	0.28	0.38	0.02	4.63	3.08	5.6	5.6	6.2	-29.7	-30.6	41.8
Sawmills, planing mills, and mill work	139.9	1.7	0.25	0.34	0.01	4.18	1.82	5.4	5.4	6.4	-29.8	-30.5	66.6
Miscellaneous wood products	16.3	9.8	0.03	0.04	0.01	0.45	1.25	7.3	7.4	5.8	-28.9	-31.8	16.5
Furniture and fixtures	19.7	7.1	0.04	0.05	0.01	0.56	1.11	5.7	5.7	4.9	-34.1	-36.4	22.9

Table 17-A-1. DETAILED OCCUPATION OF THE EXPERIENCED CIVILIAN LABOR FORCE AND OF EMPLOYED PERSONS, BY SEX, FOR THE UNITED STATES: 1950-Con.

Detailed occupation	Total employed (000)	Per-cent female	Percent of total employed			Percent of maj. occ. group of employed		Percent of experienced labor force unemployed, 1950			Percent change, 1940-1950		
			Total	Male	Female	Male	Female	Total	Male	Female	Total	Male	Female
LABORERS, EXCEPT FARM AND MINE.-Con.													
Stone, clay, and glass products	77.7	3.9	0.14	0.18	0.02	2.27	2.40	5.3	5.3	5.0	-13.8	-14.4	3.4
Glass and glass products	14.3	8.8	0.03	0.03	0.01	0.40	0.99	6.3	6.4	5.9	-20.5	-22.0	-0.2
Cement, & concrete, gypsum,& plaster prod.	21.8	0.8	0.04	0.05	...	0.66	0.14	5.1	5.1	2.7	-0.9	-1.1	52.5
Structural clay products	26.6	2.5	0.05	0.06	...	0.79	0.52	4.7	4.6	5.2	-16.5	-17.3	34.7
Pottery and related products	6.3	11.2	0.01	0.01	...	0.17	0.56	5.8	6.2	2.6	1.4	1.9	-2.5
Misc.nonmetallic mineral & stone prod.	8.7	2.9	0.02	0.02	...	0.26	0.20	5.6	5.6	7.4	-28.1	-28.0	-30.7
Metal industries	263.6	3.0	0.47	0.63	0.05	7.77	6.31	6.4	6.4	5.8	-13.6	-14.7	47.5
Primary metal industries	207.1	1.4	0.37	0.50	0.02	6.21	2.23	6.3	6.3	7.8	(a)	(a)	(a)
Blast furnaces, steel works,& roll.mills	132.5	1.1	0.24	0.32	0.01	3.98	1.17	5.8	5.8	8.2	-15.5	-16.0	72.0
Other primary iron and steel industries	48.6	1.6	0.09	0.12	...	1.45	0.60	7.9	7.9	8.0	-5.4	-7.5	57.7
Primary nonferrous industries	26.0	2.3	0.05	0.06	...	0.77	0.47	5.8	5.8	6.5	-19.3	-20.0	7.2
Fabricated metal ind.(incl.not spec.metal)	56.5	9.2	0.10	0.13	0.03	1.56	4.08	6.8	7.0	4.7	(16)	(16)	(16)
Fabricated steel products	51.0	9.1	0.09	0.11	0.03	1.41	3.66	6.7	6.9	4.8	(17)	(17)	(17)
Fabricated nonferrous metal products	4.6	10.4	0.01	0.01	...	0.13	0.38	7.7	8.1	4.6	...	...	-61.6
Not specified metal industries	0.9	6.5	...	0.01	...	0.02	0.04	6.0	6.0	5.1	-82.6	-83.3	26.0
Machinery, except electrical.	53.4	3.7	0.09	0.13	0.01	1.56	1.56	5.3	5.4	3.7	4.6	3.9	265.1
Agricultural machinery and tractors	12.8	3.0	0.02	0.03	...	0.38	0.30	3.3	3.3	2.5	34.5	31.9	-50.9
Office and store machines and devices	1.6	8.4	...	...	...	0.05	0.11	6.5	6.6	4.9	-11.4	-4.4	22.7
Miscellaneous machinery	39.0	3.7	0.07	0.09	0.01	1.14	1.15	5.9	6.0	3.9	-1.8	-2.6	22.7
Electrical mach., equipment, and supplies	29.5	16.6	0.05	0.06	0.03	0.75	3.86	6.7	6.7	6.6	12.7	11.2	21.3
Transportation equipment	66.1	4.0	0.12	0.16	0.02	1.93	2.09	11.5	11.5	10.3	-23.2	-23.9	-2.3
Motor vehicles and motor vehicle equip.	45.8	4.8	0.08	0.11	0.01	1.33	1.72	8.0	8.0	7.9	-18.6	-19.0	-10.7
Aircraft and parts	3.6	5.4	0.01	0.01	...	0.10	0.15	7.6	7.6	6.8	-2.5	-5.7	146.2
Ship and boat building and repairing	12.0	1.2	0.02	0.03	...	0.36	0.11	21.0	20.7	37.1	-38.7	-39.1	36.9
Railroad & misc.transportation equipment.	4.8	2.9	0.01	0.01	...	0.14	0.11	19.1	19.3	12.7	-27.8	-28.9	50.0
Professional & photographic equip.& watches.	4.4	17.2	0.01	0.01	...	0.11	0.59	4.7	4.8	4.6	(a)	(a)	(a)
Professional equipment and supplies.	2.5	17.7	...	0.01	...	0.06	0.35	3.9	4.1	3.3	-15.9	-16.3	-13.7
Photographic equipment and supplies.	1.0	11.9	...	0.01	...	0.03	0.10	4.8	3.8	11.3			
Watches,clocks,& clockwork-operated dev.	0.8	22.6	...	...	...	0.02	0.15	7.0	8.2	2.6	-27.4	-28.5	-22.0
Miscellaneous manufacturing industries.	15.6	18.9	0.03	0.03	0.02	0.38	2.33	7.7	7.7	8.1	(18)	(18)	(13)
Nondurable goods	396.1	9.3	0.70	0.89	0.23	10.92	28.99	7.4	7.1	10.3	-13.8	-12.7	-22.9
Food and kindred products	141.5	7.7	0.25	0.32	0.07	3.97	8.53	9.2	9.0	11.6	-5.1	-3.6	-20.6
Meat products	34.2	9.1	0.06	0.08	0.02	0.94	2.46	5.6	5.8	4.5	-13.5	-12.8	-20.0
Dairy products	14.2	4.8	0.03	0.03	...	0.41	0.54	4.1	4.1	4.3	-6.8	-6.8	-8.1
Canning & preserv.fruits,veget.,& sea food	19.3	16.0	0.03	0.04	0.02	0.49	2.42	22.6	22.3	24.1	-12.1	-8.6	-26.7
Grain-mill products	18.2	1.5	0.03	0.04	...	0.55	0.21	5.9	5.8	9.2	-0.5	0.2	-32.0
Bakery products	8.7	13.2	0.02	0.02	...	0.23	0.91	6.0	6.3	3.8	31.5	31.5	31.4
Confectionery and related products	3.7	16.2	0.01	0.01	...	0.09	0.47	9.8	9.9	9.2	-41.6	-32.1	-66.2

Table 17-A-1. DETAILED OCCUPATION OF THE EXPERIENCED CIVILIAN LABOR FORCE AND OF EMPLOYED PERSONS, BY SEX, FOR THE UNITED STATES: 1950-Con.

Detailed occupation	Total employed (000)	Per-cent female	Percent of total employed			Percent of major occ. group of employed		Percent of experienced labor force unemployed, 1950			Percent change, 1940-1950		
			Total	Male	Female	Male	Female	Total	Male	Female	Total	Male	Female
LABORERS, EXCEPT FARM AND MINE-Con.													
Nondurable goods- Con.													
Food and kindred products-Con.													
Beverage industries	22.7	3.0	0.04	0.05	...	0.67	0.54	7.3	7.3	7.2	19.2	21.0	-19.2
Misc.food prep. and kindred products	17.7	4.6	0.03	0.04	0.01	0.51	0.64	9.5	9.6	6.2}	-7.4	-9.3	33.7
Not specified food industries	2.9	15.8	0.01	0.01	...	0.07	0.36	8.9	9.4	6.0}			
Tobacco manufactures	7.1	23.7	0.01	0.01	0.01	0.16	1.33	22.7	15.6	39.1	-37.0	-38.0	-33.8
Textile mill products	60.2	13.9	0.11	0.13	0.05	1.57	6.59	5.9	6.1	4.4	-21.8	-23.6	-31.7
Knitting mills	2.8	30.2	...	...	0.01	0.06	0.67	5.5	6.5	3.2	-42.3	-40.2	-46.7
Dyeing & finishing text.,exc.knit goods	3.0	3.9	0.01	0.01	...	0.09	0.09	5.0	5.0	5.6	-30.3	-29.5	-45.1
Carpets, rugs, & other floor coverings	5.7	7.9	0.01	0.01	...	0.16	0.36	3.2	3.2	3.4	-10.5	-7.9	-32.8
Yarn, thread, and fabric mills	45.2	14.3	0.08	0.10	0.04	1.18	5.09	6.4	6.5	4.6	-23.0	-21.8	-29.5
Miscellaneous textile mill products	3.5	13.6	0.01	0.01	...	0.09	0.37	6.4	6.7	4.4	-40.3	-42.7	-19.4
Apparel & other fab. textile products	10.4	37.3	0.02	0.02	0.02	0.20	3.05	7.8	9.1	5.5	-5.5	-0.4	-12.9
Apparel and accessories	7.9	42.0	0.01	0.02	0.02	0.11	2.60	7.9	9.6	5.3	-4.4	2.8	-12.7
Misc. fabricated textile products	2.5	22.3	...	0.01	0.02	0.06	0.44	7.6	7.9	6.7	-8.8	-7.3	-13.7
Paper and allied products	44.1	7.1	0.08	0.10	0.02	1.24	2.45	4.8	4.8	4.8	-15.9	-15.5	-21.3
Pulp, paper, and paperboard mills	27.2	2.9	0.05	0.07	0.01	0.80	0.62	4.2	4.3	3.2	-30.6	-29.7	-52.2
Paperboard containers and boxes	8.9	14.9	0.02	0.02	0.01	0.23	1.05	6.1	6.2	5.5	6.1	10.1	-11.9
Miscellaneous paper and pulp products	7.9	12.4	0.01	0.02	0.01	0.21	0.77	5.3	5.3	5.2	65.9	73.8	25.8
Printing, publishing, & allied indust.	11.1	10.6	0.02	0.02	0.01	0.30	0.93	5.1	5.2	4.5	30.4	31.4	22.2
Chemicals and allied products	63.2	4.2	0.11	0.15	0.02	1.84	2.09	6.0	5.7	12.2	-17.6	-17.2	-25.6
Synthetic fibers	3.1	6.8	0.01	...	...	0.09	0.16	5.6	5.8	4.1	-39.4	-38.8	-46.3
Drugs and medicines	1.9	16.6	...	...	...	0.05	0.25	3.7	3.6	4.3	-16.4	-15.9	-27.0
Paints, varnishes, and related products	4.6	5.5	0.01	0.01	...	0.13	0.19	5.7	5.6	7.5	-11.6	-13.6	46.4
Misc.chemicals and allied products	53.7	3.5	0.10	0.13	0.01	1.58	1.49	6.1	5.8	14.7	(19)	(19)	(19)
Petroleum and coal products	29.0	1.1	0.05	0.07	...	0.87	0.24	5.5	5.5	8.6	-8.7	-9.3	99.4
Petroleum refining	23.4	1.0	0.04	0.06	...	0.70	0.18	5.4	5.3	9.7	-6.7	-7.2	88.2
Misc. petroleum and coal products	5.6	1.5	0.01	0.01	...	0.17	0.07	6.2	6.2	5.7	-16.3	-17.1	137.1
Rubber products	16.0	13.2	0.03	0.03	0.01	0.42	1.66	5.7	5.6	6.2	-3.5	-2.5	-9.8
Leather and leather products	13.7	19.7	0.02	0.03	0.02	0.33	2.13	8.5	7.8	11.5	-38.5	-40.1	-31.0
Leather: tanned, curried,& finished	6.6	9.3	0.01	0.01	...	0.18	0.48	9.2	8.0	25.9	-31.1	-35.1	74.1
Footwear, except rubber	5.3	30.6	0.01	0.01	0.01	0.11	1.27	7.7	8.8	5.2	-46.9	-47.9	-44.7
Leather products, except footwear	1.8	26.0	...	...	...	0.04	0.38	8.5	8.1	9.5	-34.2	-36.5	-26.6
Not specified manufacturing industries	9.1	11.3	0.02	0.02	0.01	0.24	0.80	15.5	15.3	16.6	-64.4	-64.2	-66.3
Nonmanufacturing industries (incl.not rep'td)	1,791.7	2.8	3.19	4.30	0.32	52.92	39.76	10.4	10.4	9.0	35.2	33.7	122.2
Construction	654.4	0.8	1.16	1.60	0.03	19.74	3.97	13.1	13.1	13.8	50.6	50.1	149.0
Railroads and railway express service	262.9	2.5	0.47	0.63	0.04	7.79	5.11	7.4	7.4	5.5	16.3	14.1	351.2
Transportation, except railroad	104.3	2.0	0.19	0.25	0.01	3.11	1.67	8.9	8.9	9.3	33.7	32.3	167.5
Telecommunications,& util.& sanitary serv.	125.7	1.2	0.22	0.31	0.01	3.77	1.20	4.8	4.7	9.0	39.9	38.9	225.8

Table 17-A-1. DETAILED OCCUPATION OF THE EXPERIENCED CIVILIAN LABOR FORCE AND OF EMPLOYED PERSONS, BY SEX, FOR THE UNITED STATES: 1950-Con.

Detailed occupation	Total employed (000)	Per-cent female	Percent of total employed			Percent of major occ. group of employed		Percent of experienced labor force unemployed, 1950			Percent change, 1940-1950		
			Total	Male	Female	Male	Female	Total	Male	Female	Total	Male	Female
LABORERS, EXCEPT FARM AND MINE.-Con.													
Nonmanufacturing industries-Con.													
Wholesale and retail trade...............	312.3	5.4	0.56	0.73	0.11	8.98	13.35	6.7	6.7	6.0	46.6	43.9	120.4
Business and repair services.............	13.5	4.4	0.02	0.03	...	0.39	0.46	7.4	7.6	3.6	120.8	118.2	196.5
Personal services.......................	71.7	8.6	0.13	0.16	0.04	1.99	4.87	9.9	10.3	5.6	33.2	34.7	19.6
Public administration...................	98.2	2.5	0.17	0.24	0.02	2.91	1.97	6.1	5.9	12.6	127.6	124.0	487.3
All other industries (incl. not rep'td.)	148.8	6.1	0.26	0.35	0.06	4.25	7.15	18.6	18.9	14.8	-17.7	-20.7	101.2
OCCUPATION NOT REPORTED.................	740.5	38.1	1.32	1.13	1.80	100.00	100.00	45.8	49.4	38.7	77.4	87.4	65.2

(a) Information not available.
1. Combined with "Professional, technical, and kindred workers (n.e.c.).".
2. Combined with "Engineers, technical--Not elsewhere classified."
3. Combined with "Social and welfare workers, except group."
4. Appears in two parts--salaried and self-employed--in the 1950 occupational classification; comparable separation not shown in the 1940 system.
5. Combined with "Clerical and kindred workers (n.e.c.)."
6. Combined with "Forgemen and hammermen."
7. Data not available for adequate 1940 estimate; for purposes of major group comparability, however, a rough allowance for this occupation has been included in the major group total.
8. Combined with "Excavating, grading, and road machinery operations."
9. "Other durable goods" combined with "Other nondurable goods (incl. not specified mfg.)"
10. Combined with "Machinists."
11. Combined with "Mechanics and repairmen - Not elsewhere classified."
12. Combined with "Apprentices-Other specified trades."
13. Combined with "Taxicab drivers and chauffeurs" and "Truck and tractor drivers."
14. Combined with "Waiters and waitresses."
15. Combined with "Practical nurses."
16. Combined with "Other primary iron and steel industries."
17. Combined with "Primary nonferrous industries."
18. Combined with "Watches, clocks and clockwork-operated devices."
19. Combined with "Drugs and medicines."
Source: U. S. Census of Population: 1950, U. S. Summary, Detailed Characteristics. Tables 124 and 125.

Table 17-A-2. PERCENT AGE DISTRIBUTION OF EMPLOYED POPULATION, AND PERCENT NEGRO, BY OCCUPATION AND SEX, FOR THE UNITED STATES: 1950

Detailed occupation	Percent Negro	Percent age distribution								Total (Coef. of dis-placement)
		Total	14-19 years	20-24 years	25-34 years	35-44 years	45-54 years	55-64 years	65 years and over	
MALE, 14 YEARS OLD AND OVER.........	8.6	100.0	4.9	9.7	24.5	23.5	18.8	13.0	5.6	
PROFESSIONAL, TECHNICAL, AND KINDRED WKRS.	2.5	100.0	0.9	7.2	31.0	26.8	18.4	10.8	4.9	9.8
Accountants and auditors.........	0.3	100.0	0.3	6.8	31.5	26.5	19.8	11.6	3.5	11.0
Architects......................	0.6	100.0	0.3	4.0	22.3	27.0	21.3	17.2	7.9	12.5
Artists and art teachers........	1.2	100.0	1.3	9.4	33.3	26.1	15.8	9.6	4.5	11.4
Authors, editors, and reporters.	0.8	100.0	1.0	7.6	29.7	27.8	18.4	10.3	5.2	9.5
Chemists........................	1.0	100.0	0.7	9.0	40.7	27.8	13.4	6.5	1.9	20.5
Clergymen.......................	11.3	100.0	0.2	3.2	21.1	27.1	21.5	16.4	10.5	14.6
College pres.,prof'rs,instr's (n.e.c.)	2.6	100.0	0.2	5.6	34.7	27.1	17.9	10.6	3.9	13.8
Dentists........................	2.1	100.0	...	0.9	20.9	23.8	27.2	17.1	10.1	17.3
Designers and draftsmen.........	0.4	100.0	1.8	15.4	40.3	20.7	12.4	7.1	2.3	21.5
Engineers, aeronautical.........	0.2	100.0	0.1	6.2	55.7	27.4	7.8	2.6	0.4	34.9
Engineers, civil................	0.4	100.0	0.3	6.0	25.0	27.2	22.6	14.1	4.6	9.3
Engineers, electrical...........	0.3	100.0	0.2	7.2	35.5	27.2	20.0	8.4	1.5	15.9
Engineers, mechanical...........	0.3	100.0	0.1	5.3	35.2	25.2	19.4	11.6	3.2	13.0
Other technical engineers.......	0.2	100.0	0.1	4.9	37.2	23.9	17.5	9.1	2.3	18.1
Lawyers and judges..............	0.8	100.0	...	0.9	19.7	30.8	23.5	14.4	10.7	18.5
Musicians and music teachers....	7.4	100.0	4.0	12.6	31.1	25.8	11.5	8.0	4.0	11.8
Natural scientists (n.e.c.).....	1.4	100.0	0.5	8.0	41.2	28.0	13.5	6.7	2.1	21.2
Pharmacists.....................	1.4	100.0	0.2	3.0	17.7	28.0	26.0	16.7	8.4	18.2
Physicians and surgeons.........	2.1	100.0	...	1.7	25.4	29.0	19.9	12.9	11.1	13.0
Social scientists...............	1.3	100.0	0.4	6.1	33.0	30.5	17.9	9.3	2.8	15.5
Social, welfare, & recreation workers	6.3	100.0	1.6	8.7	28.9	28.1	17.1	10.9	4.7	9.0
Surveyors.......................	0.6	100.0	4.1	21.3	31.3	20.3	12.2	6.8	4.0	18.4
Teachers (n.e.c.)...............	6.6	100.0	0.4	7.5	32.3	29.2	19.0	9.4	2.3	13.7
Technicians, medical and dental.	3.8	100.0	2.5	16.1	38.7	22.8	12.8	5.5	1.6	20.6
Other professional, technical and kindred wkrs.	2.7	100.0	2.5	11.4	33.7	25.0	14.6	8.8	4.0	12.4
FARMERS AND FARM MANAGERS.......	11.1	100.0	1.5	5.2	18.7	22.7	21.0	18.4	12.5	14.5
MGRS.,OFFS., & PROP'RS, EXCEPT FARM.....	1.6	100.0	0.4	3.1	18.9	26.4	26.0	16.7	6.5	16.7
Offs. & inspectors, State and local.....	0.9	100.0	0.2	2.3	13.7	21.4	25.2	23.0	14.2	25.0
Other specified managers and officials..	1.6	100.0	0.5	3.4	19.8	26.1	24.9	19.0	6.3	15.4
Mgrs.,offs.,props. (n.e.c.)-salaried....	1.0	100.0	0.6	4.3	21.8	29.8	25.0	14.1	4.4	13.6
Manufacturing..........	0.3	100.0	0.3	2.7	19.5	31.6	26.7	15.1	4.1	18.1
Wholesale and retail trade.........	1.1	100.0	0.9	6.1	26.6	30.3	21.5	11.0	3.6	11.6
Finance, insurance, and real estate.....	0.9	100.0	0.2	2.4	16.9	28.0	28.7	17.0	6.8	19.6
Other industries (incl. not reported)...	1.7	100.0	0.7	2.9	19.4	28.2	26.7	16.2	4.9	15.8
Mgrs.,offs., props.(n.e.c.)-self-employed	1.9	100.0	0.2	3.3	16.8	28.4	27.0	17.7	7.6	19.8
Construction...........	1.7	100.0	0.2	2.1	18.2	28.5	26.6	17.7	6.7	18.6
Manufacturing..........	0.5	100.0	0.2	1.7	15.7	27.9	27.4	18.8	8.3	21.5
Wholesale trade........	1.5	100.0	0.2	1.9	15.5	27.9	28.1	18.5	7.9	21.5

Table 17-A-2. PERCENT AGE DISTRIBUTION OF EMPLOYED POPULATION, AND PERCENT NEGRO, BY OCCUPATION AND SEX, FOR THE UNITED STATES: 1950-Con.

Detailed occupation	Percent Negro	Percent age distribution								Total (Coef. of displacement)
		Total	14-19 years	20-24 years	25-34 years	35-44 years	45-54 years	55-64 years	65 years and over	
MGRS.,OFFS.,& PROP'RS, EXCEPT FARM-Con.										
Eating and drinking places	4.0	100.0	0.2	2.3	17.2	29.7	28.8	17.4	4.4	20.6
Retail trade, exc. eat'g & drinking	1.6	100.0	0.3	2.5	17.3	28.6	26.1	17.2	8.0	19.0
Other industries (incl. not reported)	2.8	100.0	0.2	2.2	16.0	27.4	27.9	18.2	8.1	20.7
CLERICAL AND KINDRED WORKERS	4.1	100.0	5.3	14.2	27.6	21.1	16.5	11.3	4.0	8.0
Bookkeepers	0.5	100.0	3.7	17.6	31.1	19.1	13.6	9.6	5.3	14.5
Mail carriers	7.5	100.0	0.7	7.9	28.9	23.2	20.8	15.3	3.2	8.7
Other clerical and kindred workers	4.1	100.0	5.7	14.4	27.2	21.1	16.4	11.2	4.0	8.2
SALES WORKERS	1.5	100.0	8.1	10.4	26.9	21.9	16.8	10.9	5.0	6.3
Insurance agents and brokers	2.0	100.0	0.5	6.9	29.8	23.8	20.2	12.7	6.1	7.5
Real estate agents and brokers	1.7	100.0	0.4	2.7	13.6	18.5	25.0	24.0	15.8	27.4
Other specified sales workers	3.7	100.0	51.9	4.4	11.5	10.7	9.9	7.8	3.8	47.0
Salesmen and sales clerks (n.e.c.)	1.2	100.0	6.3	11.8	28.4	22.8	16.3	10.1	4.3	7.4
Manufacturing	0.4	100.0	1.2	7.2	30.9	26.5	19.0	11.3	3.9	9.6
Wholesale trade	0.4	100.0	0.9	7.2	30.5	27.4	19.0	11.0	4.0	10.1
Retail trade	1.7	100.0	9.4	14.5	27.2	20.3	14.6	9.5	4.5	12.0
Other industries (incl. not reported)	1.0	100.0	3.2	9.3	28.1	23.8	19.0	11.7	4.9	4.1
CRAFTSMEN, FOREMEN, KINDRED WKRS.	3.6	100.0	1.5	7.7	25.8	25.8	20.9	13.9	4.4	6.6
Bakers	5.7	100.0	3.9	11.7	23.3	24.5	18.6	13.9	4.1	3.9
Blacksmiths,forgemen, hammermen	4.6	100.0	0.9	4.5	15.8	19.2	20.6	24.9	14.1	22.2
Boilermakers	2.2	100.0	0.5	4.5	21.6	24.6	25.1	20.1	3.6	14.5
Cabinetmakers and patternmakers	2.2	100.0	2.0	7.8	25.0	20.5	18.2	17.4	9.1	8.4
Carpenters	3.8	100.0	1.6	6.6	22.1	22.9	21.3	18.0	7.5	9.4
Compositors and typesetters	1.4	100.0	2.9	10.8	23.4	25.9	19.5	13.0	4.5	4.2
Cranemen, hoist'n, const. mach. oper.	4.5	100.0	1.0	7.6	28.4	31.4	20.7	9.4	1.5	13.7
Electricians	1.1	100.0	0.9	8.2	29.2	27.4	22.0	10.4	1.9	11.8
Foremen (n.e.c.)	1.1	100.0	0.3	2.3	18.3	33.0	27.5	15.3	3.3	20.5
Manufacturing, durable goods	0.8	100.0	0.4	1.9	19.3	35.4	26.6	13.8	2.8	20.5
Mfg., nondurable (incl. not. spec.)	1.0	100.0	0.4	2.9	19.6	35.3	25.4	13.6	2.8	19.0
Nonmanufacturing (incl. not reported)	1.5	100.0	0.2	2.3	16.5	30.3	29.4	17.4	3.9	21.8
Linemen & servicemen, t'graph, etc	0.9	100.0	2.1	19.3	40.6	18.1	13.8	5.6	0.5	25.7
Locomotive engineers	0.5	100.0	...	0.6	7.1	11.6	29.8	40.4	10.5	43.3
Locomotive firemen	4.1	100.0	0.4	7.0	36.0	28.5	17.9	8.7	1.5	16.5
Machinists and job setters	1.5	100.0	0.9	6.0	27.5	25.6	21.5	14.6	3.9	16.5
Masons, tile setters, stone cutters	10.4	100.0	2.2	10.7	25.4	21.4	19.7	14.8	5.8	4.8

Table 17-A-2. PERCENT AGE DISTRIBUTION OF EMPLOYED POPULATION, AND PERCENT NEGRO, BY OCCUPATION AND SEX, FOR THE UNITED STATES: 1950-Con.

Detailed occupation	Percent Negro	Percent age distribution								Total (coef. of dis- placement)
		Total	14-19 years	20-24 years	25-34 years	35-44 years	45-54 years	55-64 years	65 years and over	
CRAFTSMEN, FOREMEN, KINDRED WKRS.--Con.										
Mechanics and repairmen, airplane	1.5	100.0	0.7	8.4	49.8	26.0	10.8	3.8	0.5	27.8
Mechanics and repairmen, auto	5.9	100.0	2.3	11.9	35.3	28.0	16.1	5.5	0.9	17.5
Mechanics and repairmen, radio and television	3.3	100.0	3.6	20.0	42.4	22.6	8.6	2.3	0.5	28.2
Other mech. and repair., & loom fixers	3.4	100.0	1.6	8.3	26.4	26.3	20.1	13.2	4.1	6.2
Millwrights	1.7	100.0	0.4	3.6	21.5	30.2	23.8	16.4	4.1	15.1
Molders, metal	18.2	100.0	1.0	7.0	28.3	25.9	18.2	15.9	3.7	9.1
Painters (const.), paperhangers, glazers	5.4	100.0	2.0	6.6	19.7	25.2	23.4	16.5	6.6	10.8
Plasterers and cement finishers	19.3	100.0	2.1	9.2	24.1	23.9	22.5	14.0	4.2	5.1
Plumbers and pipe fitters	3.0	100.0	0.9	6.4	25.4	27.6	22.0	14.0	3.7	9.2
Print craft., exc. compos. & typeset	1.2	100.0	2.3	10.5	25.7	26.7	19.2	12.0	3.6	5.6
Shoemakers & repairers, exc. factory	9.3	100.0	2.6	6.0	15.7	19.8	21.5	22.0	12.4	18.5
Stationary engineers	1.9	100.0	0.4	4.1	19.1	24.9	25.8	19.3	6.4	15.5
Structural metal workers	2.4	100.0	1.1	6.9	30.1	28.4	20.6	10.8	2.1	12.3
Tailors and furriers	6.2	100.0	0.8	3.8	12.9	14.8	21.1	30.1	16.5	30.3
Tinsmiths, coprsm., sheet metal workers	1.1	100.0	1.8	9.4	33.2	24.7	16.6	11.0	3.3	9.9
Toolmakers, & die makers & setters	0.3	100.0	0.5	4.1	30.4	25.8	20.7	14.7	3.8	11.8
Other craftsmen and kindred workers	3.9	100.0	2.6	9.8	26.2	24.3	19.3	13.3	4.5	3.4
OPERATIVES AND KINDRED WORKERS	9.1	100.0	4.9	13.5	28.9	24.3	16.0	9.7	2.7	9.0
Apprentices	1.8	100.0	19.5	39.9	32.9	5.1	1.5	0.8	0.3	53.2
Attendants, auto service & parking	8.9	100.0	17.7	24.3	28.7	15.2	7.9	4.2	2.0	31.6
Brakemen and switchmen, railroad	2.6	100.0	0.5	6.9	28.7	24.7	20.1	15.9	3.2	9.6
Bus drivers	3.9	100.0	1.3	5.8	31.9	31.1	19.0	9.2	1.7	15.2
Filers, grinders, & polishers, metal	5.9	100.0	1.9	9.4	29.5	25.2	17.2	12.5	4.3	6.7
Furnacemen, smeltermen, & heaters	19.4	100.0	1.2	8.1	27.4	28.0	19.7	13.1	2.5	8.4
Laundry and dry cleaning operatives	31.7	100.0	6.9	14.4	27.3	23.2	15.5	9.4	3.3	9.5
Meat cutters, except slaughter & pack	3.7	100.0	3.1	11.7	26.5	25.6	16.8	11.9	4.4	6.1
Mine operatives and laborers (n.e.c.)	6.5	100.0	2.7	12.1	28.0	26.2	18.2	11.1	1.7	8.6
Motormen, street, subway, & elev. rwy	4.3	100.0	4.0	12.4	26.0	24.1	18.2	12.0	3.3	4.8
Painters, exc. const. & maintenance	7.1	100.0	3.9	12.9	28.5	23.4	16.7	11.0	3.6	7.2
Power station operators	0.7	100.0	0.5	5.3	22.1	29.0	26.4	14.7	2.0	14.8
Sailors and deck hands	10.8	100.0	3.9	19.8	28.5	22.2	16.4	7.4	1.8	14.1
Sawyers	22.1	100.0	6.1	12.8	23.7	24.0	17.7	11.6	4.1	4.8
Spinners and weavers, textile	0.7	100.0	3.6	12.3	26.4	23.2	17.5	13.3	3.7	4.8
Stationary firemen	13.8	100.0	0.8	5.3	18.1	21.8	24.0	21.7	8.3	16.6
Taxicab drivers and chauffeurs	14.6	100.0	1.3	10.1	28.1	27.7	21.6	9.3	1.9	11.0
Truck drivers and deliverymen	11.2	100.0	5.4	14.7	33.1	26.7	13.9	5.1	1.1	17.3
Welders and flame-cutters	3.7	100.0	1.5	9.4	34.4	33.1	15.4	5.4	0.8	19.5
Other spec. operat. & kindred workers	6.7	100.0	4.0	12.4	26.0	24.1	18.2	12.0	3.3	4.8

Table 17-A-2. PERCENT AGE DISTRIBUTION OF EMPLOYED POPULATION, AND PERCENT NEGRO, BY OCCUPATION AND SEX, FOR THE UNITED STATES: 1950-Con.

Detailed occupation	Percent Negro	Percent age distribution								Total (coef. of displacement)
		Total	14-19 years	20-24 years	25-34 years	35-44 years	45-54 years	55-64 years	65 years and over	
OPERATIVES AND KINDRED WKRS.-Con.										
Operatives and kindred workers (n.e.c.)	8.6	100.0	5.0	13.6	27.7	23.0	16.2	11.1	3.4	7.2
Manufacturing	7.9	100.0	4.7	13.8	28.2	23.3	16.0	10.8	3.2	7.8
Durable goods	8.2	100.0	4.1	13.8	29.3	23.3	15.8	10.6	3.1	8.9
Saw & pln'g mills, misc.wood products	22.8	100.0	8.2	16.1	24.7	21.4	15.7	10.6	3.8	9.9
Furniture and fixtures	6.9	100.0	7.5	16.2	26.4	20.3	11.6	10.6	4.4	11.0
Stone,clay, & glass products	7.5	100.0	4.0	13.8	28.2	23.6	16.1	10.8	3.5	7.9
Primary metal industries	13.0	100.0	2.0	10.3	28.4	26.5	17.9	12.3	2.6	7.5
Fab'd metal (incl.not specified)	5.5	100.0	4.2	14.1	30.1	22.8	15.2	10.4	3.2	10.0
Machinery, except electrical	2.6	100.0	2.9	12.4	29.8	23.9	16.6	10.4	3.3	8.4
Electrical mach'y, equip, supplies	2.7	100.0	4.3	15.2	33.0	23.5	14.2	8.2	1.6	11.0
Motor vehicles & motor vehicle equip	9.6	100.0	3.3	15.4	33.0	22.5	15.4	10.0	2.5	12.1
Transp. equipment, exc. motor vehicle	5.0	100.0	1.8	10.1	34.0	26.6	15.8	9.7	2.0	13.0
Other durable goods	4.0	100.0	5.8	14.8	29.1	20.6	14.4	11.0	4.3	10.6
Nondurable goods	7.6	100.0	5.4	13.7	26.8	23.3	16.2	11.2	3.4	6.8
Food and kindred products	12.6	100.0	6.8	15.1	26.5	22.4	16.0	10.2	3.0	9.3
Yarn, thread, & fabric mills	3.6	100.0	5.4	14.4	26.8	24.3	16.1	9.9	3.1	8.3
Knit'g & other textile mill products	3.7	100.0	5.6	14.7	27.1	25.6	14.2	9.6	3.2	10.4
Apparel & other fab'd textile products	5.2	100.0	5.8	11.7	21.3	19.5	17.5	18.0	6.2	8.5
Paper and allied products	6.4	100.0	4.5	16.2	29.7	23.2	14.8	9.0	2.6	11.7
Chemicals and allied products	12.5	100.0	2.7	12.7	32.4	27.1	15.4	8.0	1.7	14.5
Leather and leather products	2.7	100.0	7.5	12.8	21.5	20.8	16.9	15.0	5.5	7.7
Other nondurable goods	8.9	100.0	4.4	11.6	28.5	24.7	17.8	10.6	2.4	7.1
Not specified manufacturing industries	10.4	100.0	5.2	15.0	28.8	23.1	17.8	9.4	3.3	9.9
Nonmanufacturing (including not reported)	12.7	100.0	6.7	12.4	24.4	21.6	17.7	12.7	4.5	4.5
Transportation, comm., other public util.	10.7	100.0	2.4	10.1	22.9	23.0	21.8	16.0	3.8	6.4
Wholesale and retail trade	13.2	100.0	11.1	14.3	23.8	19.9	14.8	11.2	4.9	10.8
Other ind. (including not reported)	13.8	100.0	6.3	12.7	26.3	22.0	16.8	11.3	4.6	6.2
PRIVATE HOUSEHOLD WORKERS	49.3	100.0	7.5	6.1	14.2	20.2	22.8	17.5	11.7	17.2
SERVICE WORKERS, EXC. PRIVATE HOUSEHOLD	19.6	100.0	6.1	7.6	18.3	20.1	20.3	18.0	9.6	11.7
Barbers, beauticians, & manicurists	8.5	100.0	0.6	4.6	15.3	22.5	26.1	21.3	9.6	19.6
Charwomen, janitors, and porters	40.6	100.0	4.9	6.2	13.3	16.7	20.4	23.1	15.4	21.5
Cooks, except private household	22.9	100.0	3.2	8.1	20.9	26.0	23.6	14.7	3.5	9.0
Elevator operators	19.1	100.0	2.7	6.1	12.6	16.7	21.5	24.3	16.1	24.5
Firemen, fire protection	1.3	100.0	0.2	5.7	32.5	30.3	20.3	9.5	1.5	16.3
Guards and watchmen	4.2	100.0	0.5	2.4	9.8	14.7	20.3	30.3	19.9	35.2
Policemen, sheriffs, and marshals	1.9	100.0	0.1	4.7	28.7	26.9	22.9	12.3	4.4	11.7
Waiters, bartenders, & counter workers	12.4	100.0	7.3	10.6	23.8	24.3	18.6	11.7	3.7	4.1
Other service workers, exc. private hshld	21.1	100.0	19.4	13.5	17.9	15.4	14.9	12.6	6.3	19.0

Table 17-A-2. PERCENT AGE DISTRIBUTION OF EMPLOYED POPULATION, AND PERCENT NEGRO, BY OCCUPATION AND SEX, FOR THE UNITED STATES: 1950-Con.

Detailed occupation	Percent Negro	Total	\multicolumn{7}{c}{Percent age distribution}	Total (Coef. of displacement)
			14-19 years	20-24 years	25-34 years	35-44 years	45-54 years	55-64 years	65 years and over	
FARM LABORERS AND FOREMEN	18.5	100.0	29.2	17.4	17.7	13.0	9.8	7.5	5.4	32.0
Farm laborers, unpaid family workers	19.4	100.0	57.3	18.7	10.0	4.3	2.7	2.8	4.2	61.4
Farm laborers, except unpaid, & foremen	18.1	100.0	17.0	16.9	20.9	16.8	12.8	9.6	6.0	19.7
LABORERS, EXCEPT FARM AND MINE	25.2	100.0	7.9	13.6	23.6	20.8	16.7	12.4	5.0	6.9
Fishermen and oystermen	8.2	100.0	5.4	9.9	22.0	24.8	19.8	12.5	5.6	3.0
Longshoremen and stevedores	34.2	100.0	1.0	5.2	21.5	29.5	25.3	14.4	3.1	13.9
Lumbermen, raftsmen, wood choppers	25.4	100.0	10.1	15.1	24.1	22.1	16.1	9.5	3.0	10.6
Other specified laborers	25.4	100.0	9.3	11.3	18.4	17.6	16.5	15.3	11.6	14.3
Laborers (n.e.c.)	25.4	100.0	7.8	14.0	24.2	20.6	16.5	12.2	4.7	7.2
Manufacturing	24.7	100.0	6.4	15.5	26.2	20.8	15.5	11.9	3.7	9.0
Durable goods	25.4	100.0	6.1	15.3	25.7	20.7	15.6	12.5	3.9	8.0
Furn., saw & plg mills, wood products	36.0	100.0	10.0	16.9	23.7	20.8	15.6	9.7	3.3	12.3
Stone, clay, and glass products	18.4	100.0	6.4	16.8	27.3	20.3	14.7	10.6	3.9	11.4
Primary metal industries	27.2	100.0	3.1	13.4	26.8	22.0	16.6	14.4	3.7	7.4
Fabricated metal (incl. not specified)	15.8	100.0	6.6	15.9	25.6	19.6	14.5	13.1	4.7	9.1
Machinery, incl. electrical	11.6	100.0	5.8	15.6	25.1	19.0	14.0	13.2	4.9	8.4
Transportation equipment	26.8	100.0	4.0	14.1	27.4	20.8	16.4	13.2	4.1	7.5
Other durable goods	11.0	100.0	10.2	17.1	23.7	16.6	13.7	13.6	5.1	13.3
Nondurable goods	23.7	100.0	7.0	15.8	27.0	21.0	15.0	10.8	3.4	10.7
Food and kindred products	20.6	100.0	8.1	16.1	25.8	20.5	15.4	10.8	3.3	10.9
Textile mill products & apparel	20.3	100.0	9.2	16.0	24.4	19.7	14.3	11.6	4.8	10.6
Chemicals and allied products	34.5	100.0	4.2	15.1	29.9	22.7	15.3	10.2	2.6	10.8
Other nondurable goods	23.1	100.0	5.9	15.6	28.5	21.2	11.8	10.8	3.2	10.9
Not specified manufacturing industries	22.3	100.0	6.6	16.5	26.1	21.0	15.1	11.2	3.5	10.1
Nonmanufacturing (incl. not reported)	25.7	100.0	8.7	13.1	22.8	20.5	17.2	12.5	5.2	7.2
Construction	25.3	100.0	7.1	14.1	24.9	22.0	16.9	11.1	3.9	7.0
Railroads & railway express service	27.9	100.0	3.0	11.1	21.9	23.6	21.8	15.1	3.5	6.6
Transportation, except railroad	20.4	100.0	7.6	14.9	26.2	21.9	16.3	10.1	3.0	9.6
Telecommun., utilities, sanitary serv	24.0	100.0	4.0	12.6	23.9	20.2	17.8	15.0	6.5	5.8
Wholesale and retail trade	20.5	100.0	19.7	15.4	21.4	17.1	13.3	9.2	3.9	20.5
Other ind. (including not reported)	32.1	100.0	8.4	10.1	19.1	18.0	17.6	16.0	10.8	12.1
OCCUPATION NOT REPORTED	11.1	100.0	10.8	12.0	22.1	18.7	15.7	12.2	8.5	11.1
FEMALE, 14 YEARS OLD AND OVER	11.9	100.0	8.1	15.2	23.4	23.3	17.5	9.5	3.0	5.3
PROFESS'L, TECH'L, KINDRED WORKERS	5.4	100.0	3.3	15.4	22.9	25.2	19.9	10.3	3.0	5.3
Accountants and auditors	0.7	100.0	3.4	14.9	25.9	25.8	20.1	8.1	1.8	7.6
Actresses, dancers, entert. (n.e.c.)	3.5	100.0	8.6	24.2	33.4	18.6	9.3	4.3	1.6	19.5
Artists and art teachers	1.3	100.0	2.7	18.6	27.1	22.0	16.5	9.2	3.9	8.0
Authors, editors, and reporters	0.6	100.0	2.2	14.9	27.9	23.2	17.3	9.6	4.9	6.5
Chemists and natural scientists (n.e.c.)	2.3	100.0	1.1	26.5	40.1	16.9	10.3	4.0	1.1	28.0
College pres, prof'rs, instr's (n.e.c.)	5.2	100.0	0.5	9.6	23.7	25.1	23.6	13.7	3.8	13.2

Table 17-A-2. PERCENT AGE DISTRIBUTION OF EMPLOYED POPULATION, AND PERCENT NEGRO, BY OCCUPATION AND SEX, FOR THE UNITED STATES: 1950-Con.

Detailed occupation	Percent Negro	Percent age distribution								Total (Coef. of displacement)
		Total	14-19 years	20-24 years	25-34 years	35-44 years	45-54 years	55-64 years	65 years and over	
PROF'L, TECH'L, KINDRED WORKERS—Con.										
Designers and draftsmen	1.7	100.0	3.1	19.3	30.7	22.3	16.0	6.8	1.8	11.4
Dietitians and nutritionists	8.2	100.0	1.8	14.0	25.5	21.2	21.0	13.1	3.4	9.6
Lawyers and judges	1.3	100.0	0.3	4.3	22.9	29.4	25.4	12.6	5.1	19.2
Librarians	3.0	100.0	5.6	12.0	17.9	23.4	20.5	13.9	6.7	11.2
Musicians and music teachers	3.8	100.0	3.6	10.6	19.3	22.7	21.4	15.1	7.3	13.8
Nurses, professional	3.2	100.0	0.6	18.1	29.8	24.0	16.1	8.8	2.6	10.0
Nurses, student professional	3.1	100.0	46.2	43.7	5.1	2.4	1.5	0.8	0.3	66.6
Physicians and surgeons	2.2	100.0	0.5	5.9	28.1	25.7	20.8	12.2	6.8	16.9
Social scientists	2.7	100.0	1.8	16.1	29.9	25.5	17.6	7.4	1.7	9.7
Social welfare, & recreation workers	7.6	100.0	0.9	13.0	22.9	26.2	21.5	12.3	3.2	9.9
Teachers (n.e.c.)	8.1	100.0	0.9	11.5	19.4	29.5	24.5	11.7	2.5	15.4
Technicians, medical and dental	3.0	100.0	5.2	31.1	32.8	17.9	9.0	3.3	0.7	25.3
Therapists and healers (n.e.c.)	4.0	100.0	1.0	10.9	23.8	23.2	21.0	14.1	6.0	11.5
Other professional, technical, and kindred wkrs	3.5	100.0	3.2	15.5	26.0	22.3	17.4	10.3	5.3	6.0
FARMERS AND FARM MANAGERS	26.6	100.0	2.0	3.0	10.4	20.3	25.6	23.1	15.6	34.3
MGRS., OFFS., & PROPR'S, EXC. FARM	3.6	100.0	0.9	4.3	16.4	29.2	27.7	15.8	5.7	25.1
Specified managers and officials	2.0	100.0	1.4	6.7	16.8	26.0	25.8	16.7	6.6	21.8
Mgrs.,offs.,props. (n.e.c.)-salaried	2.6	100.0	1.5	6.5	19.7	29.8	25.9	12.9	3.7	19.0
Wholesale and retail trade	3.3	100.0	1.4	6.2	20.8	32.5	25.1	11.1	2.9	18.4
Other industries (incl. not reported)	2.2	100.0	1.6	6.8	18.9	28.0	26.4	14.1	4.2	19.4
Mgrs.,offs.,props.(n.e.c.)-self-employed	4.9	100.0	0.3	1.9	14.1	30.2	29.5	17.4	6.6	30.4
Eating and drinking places	9.0	100.0	0.4	2.3	17.6	35.6	29.1	12.4	2.6	26.8
Wholesale & retail trade,exc.eat.& drinking	3.9	100.0	0.3	1.8	13.5	29.1	29.5	18.4	7.4	31.1
Other industries (incl. not reported)	3.2	100.0	0.3	1.7	12.5	27.3	30.0	19.7	8.5	32.2
CLERICAL AND KINDRED WORKERS	1.7	100.0	10.4	24.7	26.4	19.5	13.0	5.0	1.0	14.8
Bookkeepers	0.5	100.0	7.8	20.9	26.4	22.9	15.1	5.6	1.3	8.7
Cashiers	2.1	100.0	12.1	19.0	25.0	22.9	14.2	5.7	1.1	9.4
Stenographers, typists, secretaries	1.4	100.0	10.7	28.0	29.0	17.5	10.5	3.6	0.7	21.0
Telephone operators	0.7	100.0	11.5	27.1	21.2	19.7	11.9	5.0	0.6	15.3
Other clerical and kindred workers	2.5	100.0	10.6	23.1	25.4	19.6	11.0	6.0	1.3	12.4
SALES WORKERS	1.9	100.0	13.0	12.0	19.5	23.9	19.0	9.9	2.7	7.4
Insur. & real estate agents & brokers	6.4	100.0	2.2	7.8	15.4	23.9	26.6	16.8	7.3	21.3
Other specified sales workers	3.9	100.0	14.4	10.7	23.7	22.3	17.2	9.1	2.6	6.6
Salesmen & sales clerks (n.e.c.), retail	1.7	100.0	13.5	12.2	19.5	24.1	18.7	9.6	2.4	7.5
Salesmen & sales clerks (n.e.c.), exc. retail	2.7	100.0	10.8	11.8	21.3	23.2	19.1	10.5	3.3	5.6

Table 17-A-2. PERCENT AGE DISTRIBUTION OF EMPLOYED POPULATION, AND PERCENT NEGRO, BY OCCUPATION AND SEX

Detailed occupation	Percent Negro	Total	Percent age distribution							Total (coef. of displacement)
			14-19 years	20-24 years	25-34 years	35-44 years	45-54 years	55-64 years	65 years and over	
CRAFTSMEN, FOREMEN, KINDRED WKRS.	4.9	100.0	3.4	10.0	23.3	28.0	21.1	11.1	3.1	10.0
Foremen (n.e.c.)	2.5	100.0	1.4	5.7	22.7	35.0	23.6	9.6	2.0	17.9
Other craftsmen and kindred workers	5.9	100.0	4.2	11.7	23.6	25.1	20.2	11.7	3.5	7.4
OPERATIVES AND KINDRED WORKERS	9.1	100.0	5.7	13.0	26.7	26.3	17.3	8.8	2.2	6.3
Dressmakers & seamstresses, exc. factory	7.6	100.0	1.0	3.0	9.7	18.7	25.0	27.4	15.2	37.6
Laundry and dry cleaning operatives	34.4	100.0	5.8	11.6	24.0	26.7	19.0	10.3	2.6	6.3
Spinners and weavers, textile	0.4	100.0	2.9	10.3	26.9	31.7	19.4	7.6	1.2	13.8
Other spec. operat. & kindred workers	7.3	100.0	6.3	13.6	27.0	25.9	16.7	8.2	2.3	6.2
Operatives and kindred wkrs. (n.e.c.)	6.5	100.0	6.0	13.8	28.1	26.4	16.6	7.6	1.5	7.8
Manufacturing	6.1	100.0	5.9	13.9	28.3	26.5	16.5	7.6	1.4	8.1
Durable goods	5.1	100.0	5.1	11.7	32.9	26.6	14.3	5.5	0.9	12.8
Metal industries	5.2	100.0	4.1	13.7	33.2	27.7	14.8	5.6	0.9	14.2
Machinery, incl. electrical	3.2	100.0	5.2	15.8	35.5	25.9	12.8	4.3	0.5	15.3
Other durable goods	6.7	100.0	5.3	14.1	31.0	26.8	15.2	6.4	1.2	11.1
Nondurable goods	6.4	100.0	6.3	13.6	26.4	26.4	17.4	8.3	1.6	6.1
Food and kindred products	10.0	100.0	6.6	13.3	27.3	26.3	16.6	7.6	1.3	6.9
Knitting mills	1.8	100.0	8.5	16.3	27.7	26.6	13.9	5.8	1.2	9.1
Textile mill products, exc. knit	1.7	100.0	4.5	12.2	27.5	28.7	17.7	8.0	1.4	9.7
Apparel and other fab'd text. pr.	8.1	100.0	6.4	12.9	25.2	25.8	18.5	9.3	1.9	5.3
Leather and leather products	3.3	100.0	7.8	14.3	24.5	26.5	17.3	8.7	1.9	3.3
Other nondurable goods	8.2	100.0	5.6	14.8	28.3	25.5	16.2	7.2	1.4	8.1
Not specified manufacturing industries	15.1	100.0	5.8	15.5	29.7	25.8	15.4	6.6	1.2	9.1
Nonmanufacturing (incl. not reported)	12.1	100.0	7.3	12.6	24.0	25.5	18.3	9.8	2.5	3.9
PRIVATE HOUSEHOLD WORKERS	58.0	100.0	9.8	8.1	18.3	22.5	20.1	14.3	6.9	13.0
Private household workers—living in	21.3	100.0	6.9	9.5	13.1	16.6	20.4	20.9	13.6	24.9
Private household workers—living out	64.6	100.0	10.3	8.1	19.2	23.5	20.1	13.1	5.7	11.3
SERVICE WORKERS, EXC. PRIVATE HSHLD.	18.4	100.0	8.0	11.1	22.3	23.4	18.5	12.6	4.1	5.3
Attendants, hospital and other institutions	15.9	100.0	11.4	13.8	19.5	21.6	19.0	11.7	3.0	7.0
Barbers, beauticians, & manicurists	14.0	100.0	3.1	12.4	34.5	29.8	14.4	4.8	1.0	17.6
Charwomen, janitors and porters	27.5	100.0	2.5	3.3	12.0	22.1	27.3	25.0	7.8	30.1
Cooks, except private household	24.9	100.0	1.7	4.3	15.7	28.0	27.7	18.3	4.3	25.0
Housekeepers and stewards, exc. private hshld.	7.5	100.0	1.1	4.6	9.9	16.4	26.8	29.2	12.0	38.0
Practical nurses and midwives	12.3	100.0	2.6	6.5	12.3	18.7	24.3	24.3	11.3	29.9
Waitresses, bartenders, counter workers	7.0	100.0	14.8	17.5	30.2	22.9	10.2	3.7	0.7	15.8
Other service workers, exc. private household	35.2	100.0	8.0	9.8	18.6	22.4	20.5	15.1	5.6	11.2

Table 17-A-2. PERCENT AGE DISTRIBUTION OF EMPLOYED POPULATION, AND PERCENT NEGRO, BY OCCUPATION AND SEX, FOR THE UNITED STATES: 1950-Con.

Detailed occupation	Percent Negro	Percent age distribution								Total (Coef. of dis- placement)
		Total	14-19 years	20-24 years	25-34 years	35-44 years	45-54 years	55-64 years	65 years and over	
FARM LABORERS AND FOREMEN............	31.1	100.0	15.9	10.4	21.2	22.5	17.1	9.7	3.2	8.2
Farm laborers, unpaid family workers...........	22.9	100.0	15.5	9.1	21.0	23.0	17.9	10.3	3.2	8.8
Farm laborers, exc. unpaid, and foremen........	50.8	100.0	16.9	13.5	21.8	20.8	15.3	8.4	3.3	9.1
LABORERS, EXCEPT FARM AND MINE............	22.4	100.0	7.9	13.6	25.3	24.6	16.8	9.1	2.7	3.2
OCCUPATION NOT REPORTED..................	10.9	100.0	11.9	11.4	21.2	21.0	16.8	10.9	6.8	9.0

Source: U. S. Census of Population, 1950. U. S. Summary, Part I, Vol.II. Detailed Characteristics of the Population. Tables 127 and 128.

Occupation and sex	Total	Income distribution							Median income
		Destitute (Less-$1,000)	Meager ($1,000-$1,999)	Adequate ($2,000-$2,999)	Comfortable ($3,000-$4,999)	Abundant ($5,000-$6,999)	Affluent ($7,000-$9,999)	Wealthy ($10,000)	
Male, experienced civilian labor force	100.0	15.3	18.0	24.6	31.0	6.6	2.2	2.3	2,668
PROFESSIONAL, TECHNICAL, AND KINDRED WORKERS	100.0	5.8	9.3	14.6	37.3	17.4	7.5	8.0	3,958
Accountants and auditors	100.0	3.0	5.5	13.6	48.1	19.0	6.2	4.5	4,002
Architects	100.0	3.4	5.8	8.0	23.3	26.6	14.9	18.1	5,580
Artists and art teachers	100.0	9.9	12.9	15.6	33.8	15.8	6.8	5.2	3,543
Authors, editors, and reporters	100.0	6.5	8.2	11.4	31.0	21.5	11.2	10.3	4,469
Chemists	100.0	3.7	5.8	12.5	44.9	21.3	7.7	4.1	4,373
Clergymen	100.0	14.0	23.5	27.9	27.5	5.1	1.4	0.7	2,412
College presidents, professors, and instr's (n.e.c.)	100.0	4.3	9.2	11.1	36.8	23.3	10.1	5.1	4,348
Dentists	100.0	2.6	3.9	6.6	19.2	23.0	20.1	24.6	6,232
Designers and draftsmen	100.0	3.9	7.4	19.2	51.8	13.5	2.8	1.4	3,600
Engineers, aeronautical	100.0	1.8	4.2	6.5	40.7	32.2	11.0	3.5	4,851
Engineers, civil	100.0	2.5	5.4	10.0	42.0	26.4	8.8	4.8	4,518
Engineers, electrical	100.0	2.5	4.6	8.2	40.8	28.9	10.7	4.3	4,690
Engineers, mechanical	100.0	2.8	5.0	8.4	41.1	27.5	9.7	5.5	4,633
Other technical engineers	100.0	2.3	3.8	6.9	40.3	28.4	11.2	7.1	4,834
Lawyers and judges	100.0	3.5	5.4	7.0	20.1	20.5	15.4	28.1	6,257
Musicians and music teachers	100.0	17.3	19.0	18.9	28.4	9.3	3.9	3.1	3,189
Natural scientists (n.e.c.)	100.0	5.3	9.2	13.7	37.2	19.8	9.0	5.7	4,138
Pharmacists	100.0	3.6	6.6	13.0	40.0	21.5	8.3	7.1	4,246
Physicians and surgeons	100.0	5.5	6.6	6.8	13.1	12.7	14.3	41.0	8,115
Social scientists	100.0	3.4	6.3	10.3	36.0	23.2	13.1	7.7	4,617
Social, welfare, and recreation workers	100.0	9.1	12.7	22.7	40.2	10.3	3.2	1.8	3,186
Surveyors	100.0	10.7	17.1	27.5	36.8	5.5	1.6	0.8	2,805
Teachers (n.e.c.)	100.0	5.3	11.6	19.6	47.3	12.7	2.6	0.9	3,456
Technicians, medical and dental	100.0	7.8	15.3	29.4	36.6	7.3	2.3	1.2	2,915
Other professional, technical, and kindred workers	100.0	8.8	12.9	19.2	37.0	12.5	5.2	4.4	3,358
FARMERS AND FARM MANAGERS	100.0	35.9	27.0	16.1	12.9	4.1	2.0	1.9	1,455
MANAGERS, OFFICIALS, & PROP., EXCEPT FARM	100.0	6.0	9.6	15.9	33.3	16.5	7.7	11.0	3,944
Officials and inspectors, State and local adm'n	100.0	5.0	10.0	22.5	44.3	11.7	4.1	2.3	3,382
Other specified managers and officials	100.0	4.1	7.3	13.1	43.0	20.0	7.1	5.6	4,111
Managers, officials, & propr's (n.e.c.)-salaried	100.0	3.2	5.8	13.1	36.4	20.0	9.5	11.9	4,406
Manufacturing	100.0	1.8	2.9	7.5	31.8	23.4	13.5	19.7	5,460
Wholesale and retail trade	100.0	3.9	7.7	18.0	39.8	15.7	6.7	8.2	3,828
Finance, insurance, and real estate	100.0	1.5	2.7	8.1	33.7	24.0	12.7	17.4	5,278
Other industries (incl. not reported)	100.0	4.2	7.2	8.1	37.3	21.3	8.4	8.2	4,393
Managers, officials & propr's (n.e.c.)-self-employed	100.0	8.6	13.0	18.3	28.0	13.3	6.6	12.1	3,975
Construction	100.0	6.8	10.6	16.4	30.1	14.8	7.7	13.6	3,863
Manufacturing	100.0	6.9	8.9	12.4	22.9	16.0	9.1	23.7	4,827
Wholesale trade	100.0	8.4	9.0	13.2	24.5	16.0	8.7	20.2	4,382
Eating and drinking places	100.0	11.0	16.0	21.2	29.3	12.1	5.0	5.4	3,077
Retail trade, exc. eating and drinking places	100.0	8.9	14.3	20.3	29.6	12.5	5.8	8.6	3,287
Other industries (incl. not reported)	100.0	8.8	13.7	18.1	26.8	12.5	6.7	13.3	3,462

Table 17-A-3. INCOME DISTRIBUTION OF THE EXPERIENCED CIVILIAN LABOR FORCE, BY OCCUPATION AND SEX, FOR THE UNITED STATES: 1950-Con.

Occupation and sex	Total	Income distribution							Median income
		Destitute (Less-$1,000)	Meager ($1,000-$1,999)	Adequate ($2,000-$2,999)	Comfortable ($3,000-$4,999)	Abundant ($5,000-$6,999)	Affluent ($7,000-$9,999)	Wealthy ($10,000)	
Male-Con.									
CLERICAL AND KINDRED WORKERS....	100.0	7.7	12.5	29.4	43.7	4.9	1.1	0.7	3,010
Bookkeepers....	100.0	7.2	15.2	33.2	38.6	4.3	0.9	0.6	2,847
Mail carriers....	100.0	3.9	5.9	20.7	66.2	2.5	0.5	0.2	3,465
Other clerical and kindred workers....	100.0	8.0	12.8	29.8	42.5	5.1	1.2	0.7	2,982
SALES WORKERS....	100.0	13.3	14.0	22.0	32.6	10.7	4.0	3.4	3,028
Insurance agents and brokers....	100.0	4.5	9.0	17.1	42.4	16.3	5.5	5.1	3,764
Real estate agents and brokers....	100.0	8.8	13.0	16.0	28.7	15.9	8.0	9.7	3,665
Other specified sales workers....	100.0	57.6	10.1	9.4	12.4	5.2	2.5	2.8	869
Salesmen and sales clerks (n.e.c)....	100.0	11.5	15.0	24.0	32.9	10.0	3.6	2.9	2,980
Manufacturing....	100.0	5.2	7.6	15.8	39.9	17.4	7.3	6.8	3,890
Wholesale trade....	100.0	4.6	8.3	19.2	42.2	15.4	5.8	4.6	3,695
Retail trade....	100.0	15.3	19.0	27.5	28.1	6.5	2.1	1.5	2,537
Other industries (incl. not reported)....	100.0	9.9	13.9	22.4	36.0	11.1	3.8	3.0	3,145
CRAFTSMEN, FOREMEN, AND KINDRED WORKERS....	100.0	7.1	13.1	25.3	45.1	7.8	1.1	0.4	3,125
Bakers....	100.0	6.7	14.5	31.5	42.0	3.9	0.8	0.6	2,917
Blacksmiths, forgemen, and hammermen....	100.0	14.3	17.4	26.3	37.7	3.5	0.6	0.2	2,701
Boilermakers....	100.0	3.2	7.8	22.4	59.1	6.7	0.6	0.2	3,385
Cabinetmakers and patternmakers....	100.0	8.8	16.6	27.9	40.8	4.8	0.6	0.4	2,881
Carpenters....	100.0	14.3	22.6	27.1	32.1	3.2	0.5	0.2	2,456
Compositors and typesetters....	100.0	4.1	8.2	19.0	46.5	19.2	2.1	0.8	3,742
Cranemen, hoistmen, & const. machinery operators....	100.0	3.9	11.5	29.9	46.5	7.1	1.0	0.2	3,115
Electricians....	100.0	4.5	8.6	20.6	53.5	11.2	1.2	0.4	3,449
Foremen (n.e.c.)....	100.0	1.4	3.7	15.0	56.5	19.7	2.9	0.8	3,949
Manufacturing, durable goods....	100.0	1.2	2.7	11.2	56.9	23.8	3.5	0.8	4,202
Mfg., nondurable goods (incl. not spec. mfg.)....	100.0	1.3	3.4	15.4	57.1	19.1	2.9	0.8	3,945
Nonmanufacturing industries (incl. not reported)....	100.0	1.7	4.8	18.1	55.9	16.6	2.2	0.7	3,740
Linemen & servicemen, t'graph, t'phone, & power....	100.0	2.9	6.7	26.2	55.6	7.9	0.5	0.1	3,363
Locomotive engineers....	100.0	1.0	1.6	6.0	54.6	33.9	2.5	0.4	4,590
Locomotive firemen....	100.0	2.7	7.0	16.9	61.1	11.6	0.5	0.1	3,688
Machinists and job setters....	100.0	3.4	7.8	26.3	58.1	3.9	0.4	0.1	3,242
Masons, tile setters, and stone cutters....	100.0	10.4	18.0	24.0	37.2	8.8	1.1	0.5	2,895
Mechanics and repairmen, airplane....	100.0	2.5	5.8	19.8	66.1	5.0	0.7	0.1	3,437
Mechanics and repairmen, automobile....	100.0	8.5	18.3	33.5	36.3	2.6	0.4	0.2	2,689
Mechanics and repairmen, radio and television....	100.0	13.9	19.9	29.3	32.8	3.3	0.5	0.3	2,059
Other mechanics and repairmen, and loom fixers....	100.0	5.5	12.2	32.1	45.1	4.3	0.6	0.2	3,005
Millwrights....	100.0	2.3	5.4	21.9	63.3	6.4	0.5	0.2	3,413
Molders, metal....	100.0	5.6	13.9	37.4	40.8	1.9	0.1	0.1	2,826
Painters (construction), paperhangers, & glaziers....	100.0	16.7	24.5	27.7	27.9	2.4	0.5	0.4	2,295
Plasterers and cement finishers....	100.0	11.4	18.8	23.2	35.5	9.2	1.2	0.7	2,842

Table 17-A-3. INCOME DISTRIBUTION OF THE EXPERIENCED CIVILIAN LABOR FORCE, BY OCCUPATION IN 1949

Occupation and sex	Total	Income distribution							Median income
		Destitute (Less-$1,000)	Meager ($1,000-$1,999)	Adequate ($2,000-$2,999)	Comfortable ($3,000-$4,999)	Abundant ($5,000-$6,999)	Affluent ($7,000-$9,999)	Wealthy ($10,000)	
Male-Con.									
CRAFTSMEN, FOREMEN, KINDRED WKRS.—Con.									
Plumbers and pipe fitters	100.0	5.9	11.2	21.8	47.9	11.3	1.3	0.7	3,344
Printing craftsmen, exc. compositors & typesetters	100.0	3.2	5.4	14.0	43.6	25.4	7.0	1.4	4,211
Shoemakers and repairers, except factory	100.0	18.0	29.4	28.9	19.9	2.6	0.8	0.4	2,079
Stationary engineers	100.0	2.4	6.3	19.3	56.5	11.5	2.6	1.4	3,604
Structural metal workers	100.0	4.3	9.5	20.5	53.0	11.6	1.0	0.2	3,428
Tailors and furriers	100.0	8.2	17.3	29.1	36.4	6.5	1.7	0.8	2,841
Tinsmiths, coppersmiths, and sheet metal workers	100.0	5.1	10.1	26.3	52.1	5.6	0.6	0.3	3,203
Toolmakers, and die makers and setters	100.0	2.1	4.2	14.8	65.3	11.9	1.2	0.4	3,741
Other craftsmen and kindred workers	100.0	9.0	14.8	25.4	42.9	6.2	1.1	0.6	3,022
OPERATIVES AND KINDRED WORKERS	100.0	10.5	19.4	32.9	33.9	2.7	0.4	0.2	2,607
Apprentices	100.0	16.2	23.4	35.0	23.8	1.2	0.2	0.1	2,286
Attendants, auto service and parking	100.0	23.6	30.0	30.9	14.1	1.1	0.2	0.2	1,791
Brakemen and switchmen, railroad	100.0	2.6	6.3	18.7	65.0	7.0	0.3	0.1	3,592
Bus drivers	100.0	8.2	12.2	23.7	53.4	2.1	0.2	0.1	3,116
Filers, grinders, and polishers, metal	100.0	6.5	12.4	30.2	47.9	2.7	0.3	0.1	3,019
Furnacemen, smeltermen, and heaters	100.0	4.4	11.7	34.5	44.5	4.0	0.6	0.2	2,985
Laundry and dry cleaning operatives	100.0	15.1	31.0	32.9	18.0	2.0	0.5	0.4	2,099
Meat cutters, except slaughter and packing house	100.0	6.9	11.8	30.9	41.7	4.4	0.9	0.5	2,920
Mine operatives and laborers (n.e.c.)	100.0	10.9	21.3	39.0	25.3	2.8	0.4	0.3	2,415
Motormen, street, subway, and elevated railway	100.0	0.9	2.5	16.8	77.1	2.4	0.2	0.1	3,278
Painters, except construction and maintenance	100.0	8.4	17.8	33.8	37.6	2.0	0.3	0.1	2,715
Power station operators	100.0	1.2	3.5	17.2	69.7	7.6	0.6	0.2	3,655
Sailors and deck hands	100.0	13.3	23.1	31.9	27.4	3.5	0.6	0.2	2,376
Sawyers	100.0	27.1	34.3	22.4	14.8	1.1	0.2	0.1	1,624
Spinners and weavers, textile	100.0	7.8	22.0	45.5	23.1	1.1	0.2	0.2	2,409
Stationary firemen	100.0	6.1	17.1	33.7	40.8	1.9	0.2	0.1	2,804
Taxicab drivers and chauffeurs	100.0	12.4	28.7	36.8	20.5	1.2	0.2	0.2	2,212
Truck drivers and deliverymen	100.0	12.8	21.3	29.8	31.6	3.5	0.6	0.4	2,499
Welders and flame-cutters	100.0	4.8	10.8	27.6	51.6	4.5	0.6	0.2	3,746
Other specified operatives and kindred workers	100.0	8.9	17.7	35.8	33.7	3.2	0.5	0.3	2,655
Operatives and kindred workers (n.e.c.)	100.0	9.5	18.5	34.5	34.7	2.2	0.3	0.2	2,695
Manufacturing	100.0	8.8	18.1	34.8	35.5	2.2	0.3	0.2	2,671
Durable goods	100.0	8.8	16.6	34.3	38.0	2.0	0.2	0.1	2,742
Sawmills, planing mills, & misc. wood prod.	100.0	25.9	33.1	23.2	16.3	1.0	0.1	0.2	1,701
Furniture and fixtures	100.0	13.9	30.8	35.7	18.6	0.8	0.1	0.1	2,128
Stone, clay, and glass products	100.0	7.6	18.2	36.9	34.1	2.7	0.3	0.2	2,652
Primary metal industries	100.0	5.2	12.7	40.5	39.5	1.9	0.2	0.1	2,815
Fabric'd metal ind. (incl. not spec. metal)	100.0	8.0	16.3	39.2	34.2	1.9	0.3	0.2	2,681
Machinery, except electrical	100.0	5.9	12.8	34.9	44.0	1.9	0.2	0.1	2,908

Table 17-A-3. INCOME DISTRIBUTION OF THE EXPERIENCED CIVILIAN LABOR FORCE, BY OCCUPATION AND SEX, FOR THE UNITED STATES: 1950-Con.

Occupation and sex	Total	Income distribution							Median income
		Destitute (Less-$1,000)	Meager ($1,000-$1,999)	Adequate ($2,000-$2,999)	Comfortable ($3,000-$4,999)	Abundant ($5,000-$6,999)	Affluent ($7,000-$9,999)	Wealthy ($10,000-)	
Male-Con.									
OPERATIVES AND KINDRED WORKERS-Con.									
Electrical machinery, equipment, & supplies.	100.0	7.3	12.9	32.8	44.3	2.3	0.2	0.1	2,919
Motor vehicles and motor vehicle equipment.	100.0	5.0	10.5	30.7	51.2	2.2	0.2	0.1	3,063
Transportation equipment, exc. motor vehicle	100.0	5.0	11.1	32.8	48.2	2.6	0.3	0.1	3,023
Other durable goods	100.0	10.7	19.8	35.1	31.5	2.3	0.3	0.2	2,549
Nondurable goods	100.0	8.9	20.1	35.5	32.4	2.6	0.3	0.2	2,575
Food and kindred products	100.0	11.1	19.5	34.5	32.5	1.7	0.4	0.3	2,564
Yarn, thread, and fabric mills	100.0	9.3	31.8	45.0	13.1	0.6	0.1	0.1	2,158
Knitting, and other textile mill products	100.0	8.1	19.8	36.8	29.7	4.8	0.5	0.2	2,575
Apparel and other fabricated textile prod.	100.0	9.9	21.2	30.1	30.9	6.5	1.0	0.4	2,593
Paper and allied products	100.0	6.3	13.3	39.0	38.9	2.1	0.2	0.2	2,797
Chemicals and allied products	100.0	6.5	12.9	31.8	46.5	1.9	0.2	0.1	2,965
Leather and leather products	100.0	10.3	27.2	39.3	21.7	1.1	0.2	0.1	2,284
Other nondurable goods	100.0	6.8	11.9	27.4	49.1	4.3	0.4	0.2	3,104
Not specified manufacturing industries	100.0	11.5	20.8	36.0	29.8	1.5	0.2	0.2	2,481
Nonmanufacturing industries (incl. not rptd)	100.0	13.4	20.4	32.9	30.3	2.2	0.5	0.3	2,481
Transport., commun., & other public utilities	100.0	6.0	14.1	35.2	42.8	1.6	0.2	0.1	2,863
Wholesale and retail trade	100.0	17.4	23.5	32.0	24.2	2.1	0.4	0.3	2,262
Other industries (incl. not reported)	100.0	16.0	23.0	31.9	25.2	2.9	0.7	0.4	2,324
PRIVATE HOUSEHOLD WORKERS	100.0	43.6	34.7	15.4	5.2	0.5	0.2	0.3	1,176
SERVICE WORKERS, EXCEPT PRIVATE HOUSEHOLD	100.0	17.0	26.1	31.7	22.8	1.8	0.4	0.2	2,195
Barbers, beauticians, and manicurists	100.0	10.0	25.9	34.2	25.4	3.4	0.8	0.4	2,370
Charwomen, janitors, and porters	100.0	18.9	34.9	34.6	10.8	0.6	0.1	0.1	1,904
Cooks, except private household	100.0	14.9	26.6	31.5	23.7	2.6	0.5	0.2	2,241
Elevator operators	100.0	9.9	27.3	48.6	13.6	0.4	0.1	...	2,232
Firemen, fire protection	100.0	1.3	3.7	26.5	63.9	4.1	0.5	0.1	3,298
Guards and watchmen	100.0	8.3	20.8	38.6	30.6	1.5	0.2	0.1	2,536
Policemen, sheriffs, and marshals	100.0	2.9	7.4	27.2	57.5	3.9	0.8	0.2	3,228
Waiters, bartenders, and counter workers	100.0	19.2	25.5	31.8	20.4	2.1	0.6	0.4	2,154
Other service workers, except private household	100.0	34.6	32.2	23.0	8.5	1.0	0.3	0.3	2,463
FARM LABORERS AND FOREMEN	100.0	58.0	27.6	9.9	3.6	0.5	0.2	0.2	863
Farm laborers, unpaid family workers	100.0	79.2	14.0	4.1	1.9	0.4	0.2	0.1	633
Farm laborers, except unpaid, and farm foremen	100.0	53.3	30.7	11.2	3.9	0.6	0.2	0.2	940
LABORERS, EXCEPT FARM AND MINE	100.0	22.7	28.4	31.9	15.7	0.9	0.2	0.1	1,961
Fishermen and oystermen	100.0	31.6	29.2	17.7	15.1	4.0	1.5	0.8	1,575

TABLE 1/-A-/. INCOME DISTRIBUTION OF THE ...

Occupation and sex	Total	Income distribution							Median income
		Destitute (Less $1,000)	Meager ($1,000-$1,999)	Adequate ($2,000-$2,999)	Comfortable ($3,000-$4,999)	Abundant ($5,000-$6,999)	Affluent ($7,000-$9,999)	Wealthy ($10,000)	
Male-Con.									
LABORERS, EXCEPT FARM AND MINE-Con.									
Longshoremen and stevedores..............	100.0	10.9	22.5	30.4	32.5	3.2	0.3	0.1	2,501
Lumbermen, raftsmen, and wood choppers....	100.0	42.1	32.2	13.4	10.0	1.6	0.4	0.3	1,200
Other specified laborers.................	100.0	29.7	31.6	25.7	11.8	0.9	0.2	0.1	1,638
Laborers (n.e.c.)........................	100.0	21.0	28.1	33.9	16.0	0.8	0.2	0.1	2,023
Manufacturing.........................	100.0	14.8	26.1	38.5	19.7	0.7	0.1	0.1	2,217
Durable goods.......................	100.0	15.5	26.0	38.9	18.7	0.7	0.1	0.1	2,204
Furniture, saw & plan'g mills, misc.wood pr.	100.0	31.7	38.9	19.6	9.0	0.6	0.2	0.1	1,427
Stone, clay, and glass products.........	100.0	12.2	27.1	41.5	18.3	0.8	0.1	...	2,230
Primary metal industries...............	100.0	7.7	20.0	50.3	21.2	0.6	0.1	...	2,420
Fabric'd metal ind. (incl. not spec. metal).	100.0	12.3	24.5	43.6	18.7	0.6	0.1	0.1	2,276
Machinery, including electrical.........	100.0	10.9	20.5	44.1	23.5	0.9	0.1	0.1	2,406
Transportation equipment...............	100.0	9.6	17.8	40.8	30.5	1.2	0.1	0.2	2,592
Other durable goods....................	100.0	14.5	27.0	39.2	18.4	0.5	0.1	0.1	1,917
Nondurable goods......................	100.0	13.6	26.1	37.7	21.7	0.7	0.1	0.1	2,245
Food and kindred products..............	100.0	15.9	24.9	36.6	21.9	0.6	0.1	0.1	2,239
Textile mill products and apparel......	100.0	13.9	38.9	37.7	9.0	0.4	0.1	0.1	1,945
Chemicals and allied products..........	100.0	14.2	26.3	37.0	21.8	0.6	0.1	0.1	2,236
Other nondurable goods.................	100.0	10.5	20.5	39.5	28.3	0.9	0.1	0.1	2,452
Not specified manufacturing industries...	100.0	18.7	29.6	36.3	14.3	0.8	0.2	0.1	2,038
Nonmanufacturing industries (incl. not reported)...	100.0	24.6	29.2	31.2	13.9	0.8	0.2	0.1	1,874
Construction..........................	100.0	24.6	32.4	27.7	13.8	1.1	0.2	0.2	1,787
Railroads and railway express service..	100.0	11.4	24.9	48.2	14.9	0.4	0.1	...	2,252
Transportation, except railroad........	100.0	18.9	25.2	32.4	22.1	1.0	0.3	0.3	2,177
Telecommunications, & utilities & sanitary serv.	100.0	14.7	27.7	37.8	18.8	0.8	0.2	0.1	2,184
Wholesale and retail trade.............	100.0	28.3	28.8	27.6	14.3	0.8	0.2	0.1	1,764
Other industries (incl. not reported)..	100.0	37.7	28.3	25.2	8.2	0.4	0.1	0.1	1,424
OCCUPATION NOT REPORTED.............	100.0	35.0	26.0	19.6	14.4	2.9	1.1	1.1	1,572
FEMALE, EXPERIENCED CIVILIAN LABOR FORCE.	100.0	31.9	32.6	25.0	8.9	1.0	0.3	0.3	1,575
PROFESSIONAL, TECHNICAL, AND KINDRED WKRS...	100.0	19.5	21.3	31.7	23.7	2.8	0.6	0.4	2,262
Accountants and auditors.................	100.0	7.1	17.5	38.7	32.2	3.3	0.9	0.3	2,632
Actresses, dancers, and entertainers (n.e.c.).	100.0	36.0	24.3	18.6	13.8	3.7	1.6	2.1	1,532
Artists and art teachers.................	100.0	24.9	22.2	23.1	23.6	4.4	1.1	0.7	2,271
Authors, editors, and reporters..........	100.0	23.6	18.3	22.0	24.0	7.2	2.4	2.5	2,329
Chemists and natural scientists (n.e.c.)...	100.0	10.3	16.6	27.7	39.4	4.6	0.9	0.5	2,838
College presidents,prof'rs, & instructors (n.e.c.).	100.0	11.0	14.6	21.4	41.5	8.8	1.9	0.9	3,106
Designers and draftsmen..................	100.0	13.3	18.8	32.1	26.2	5.3	2.0	2.3	2,504
Dietitians and nutritionists.............	100.0	20.5	31.0	28.4	17.5	2.1	0.3	0.1	1,951
Lawyers and judges.......................	100.0	10.0	10.5	15.7	31.5	18.2	7.6	6.6	3,616

Table 17-A-3. INCOME DISTRIBUTION OF THE EXPERIENCED CIVILIAN LABOR FORCE, BY OCCUPATION AND SEX, FOR THE UNITED STATES: 1950-Con.

Occupation and sex	Total	Income distribution							Median income
		Destitute (Less-$1,000)	Meager ($1,000-$1,999)	Adequate ($2,000-$2,999)	Comfortable ($3,000-$4,999)	Abundant ($5,000-$6,999)	Affluent ($7,000-$9,999)	Wealthy ($10,000)	
Female-Con.									
PROF., TECHNICAL, AND KINDRED WKRS.-Con.									
Librarians	100.0	22.4	21.5	26.6	26.3	2.5	0.5	0.2	2,220
Musicians and music teachers	100.0	45.8	22.7	16.4	12.4	1.8	0.5	0.5	1,555
Nurses, professional	100.0	19.0	25.2	38.3	16.4	0.9	0.2	0.1	2,127
Nurses, student professional	100.0	81.1	13.1	4.2	1.3	0.1	0.1	...	617
Physicians and surgeons	100.0	17.9	13.7	12.7	18.5	13.6	9.7	13.9	3,475
Social scientists	100.0	9.6	14.6	32.5	33.8	6.7	2.0	0.8	2,870
Social welfare, and recreation workers	100.0	12.9	17.3	36.9	29.0	2.9	0.7	0.4	2,497
Teachers (n.e.c.)	100.0	15.8	20.4	32.9	27.6	2.8	0.4	0.2	2,394
Technicians, medical and dental	100.0	16.4	27.8	39.6	14.9	0.8	0.4	0.2	2,122
Therapists and healers (n.e.c.)	100.0	20.1	25.3	27.2	24.4	2.1	0.3	0.5	2,152
Other professional, technical, and kindred wkrs.	100.0	21.2	20.7	27.2	24.6	4.3	1.1	0.8	2,270
FARMERS AND FARM MANAGERS	100.0	65.9	17.7	7.1	5.0	1.9	1.0	1.4	759
MANAGERS, OFFICIALS, AND PROP.,EXC. FARM.	100.0	22.2	24.4	23.6	19.7	5.3	2.1	2.6	2,122
Specified managers and officials	100.0	17.0	24.0	28.7	22.7	4.9	1.6	1.1	2,283
Managers, officials, and prop.(n.e.c.)-salaried	100.0	15.5	23.8	28.7	23.9	4.8	1.7	1.8	2,332
Wholesale and retail trade	100.0	17.1	26.3	29.1	20.3	4.1	1.6	1.5	2,192
Other industries (incl. not reported)	100.0	14.1	22.3	28.4	26.3	5.2	1.8	2.0	2,435
Managers, officials,& prop.(n.e.c.)-self-employed	100.0	30.0	25.2	17.3	15.0	5.8	2.7	4.0	1,764
Eating and drinking places	100.0	34.7	26.9	16.6	13.1	4.3	2.0	2.4	1,482
Wholesale & retail trade,exc. eating & drinking	100.0	30.4	26.0	17.5	14.6	5.4	2.4	3.6	1,721
Other industries (incl. not reported)	100.0	25.5	22.3	17.4	17.3	7.6	3.8	6.1	2,106
CLERICAL AND KINDRED WORKERS	100.0	15.9	32.1	39.4	11.6	0.7	0.2	0.2	2,042
Bookkeepers	100.0	14.8	34.2	37.8	11.7	0.9	0.3	0.2	2,020
Cashiers	100.0	28.0	40.2	25.4	5.8	0.4	0.1	0.1	1,585
Stenographers, typists, and secretaries	100.0	13.5	29.4	42.5	13.4	0.8	0.2	0.2	2,138
Telephone operators	100.0	13.9	30.8	43.9	10.8	0.6	0.1	0.1	2,093
Other clerical and kindred workers	100.0	17.4	33.2	37.7	10.9	0.6	0.2	0.1	1,986
SALES WORKERS	100.0	39.6	39.3	15.3	4.4	0.8	0.3	0.2	1,244
Insurance and real estate agents and brokers	100.0	21.4	25.0	26.4	18.4	5.2	2.0	1.6	2,112
Other specified sales workers	100.0	52.1	23.0	15.3	7.6	1.2	0.6	0.3	960
Salesmen and sales clerks (n.e.c.), retail trade	100.0	40.2	40.6	14.7	3.6	0.5	0.2	0.2	1,222
Salesmen and sales clerks (n.e.c.),exc.retail tr.	100.0	38.3	31.3	18.6	8.5	2.0	0.8	0.5	1,368

Table 17-A-3. INCOME DISTRIBUTION OF THE EXPERIENCED CIVILIAN LABOR FORCE, BY OCCUPATION AND SEX, FOR THE UNITED STATES: 1950—Con.

Occupation and sex	Total	Income distribution							Median income
		Destitute (Less-$1,000)	Meager ($1,000-$1,999)	Adequate ($2,000-$2,999)	Comfortable ($3,000-$4,999)	Abundant ($5,000-$6,999)	Affluent ($7,000-$9,999)	Wealthy ($10,000-)	
Female—Con.									
CRAFTSMEN, FOREMEN, AND KINDRED WKRS......	100.0	17.5	32.5	33.4	14.4	1.6	0.3	0.3	1,999
Foremen (n.e.c.)........	100.0	7.2	29.5	41.6	19.5	1.7	0.3	0.2	2,268
Other craftsmen and kindred workers......	100.0	22.0	33.8	29.9	12.3	1.5	0.3	0.3	1,847
OPERATIVES AND KINDRED WORKERS......	100.0	26.8	44.0	24.9	3.9	0.2	0.1	0.1	1,541
Dressmakers and seamstresses, except factory.....	100.0	45.2	36.2	15.1	3.0	0.3	0.1	0.1	1,126
Laundry and dry cleaning operatives......	100.0	39.7	47.6	11.1	1.3	0.2	0.1	0.1	1,183
Spinners and weavers, textile......	100.0	18.1	44.2	33.7	3.7	0.2	0.1	0.1	1,770
Other specified operatives and kindred workers.....	100.0	32.9	33.3	24.4	8.4	0.6	0.2	0.1	1,511
Operatives and kindred workers (n.e.c.).....	100.0	24.4	44.5	26.6	4.1	0.2	0.1	0.1	1,596
Manufacturing........	100.0	23.7	44.8	27.0	4.1	0.2	0.1	0.1	1,608
Durable goods.......	100.0	20.6	36.1	36.4	6.5	0.2	0.1	0.1	1,837
Metal industries......	100.0	17.7	36.8	39.8	5.3	0.2	0.1	0.1	1,901
Machinery, including electrical.....	100.0	20.0	32.5	40.5	6.6	0.3	0.1	...	1,933
Other durable goods.....	100.0	22.0	38.7	32.1	6.9	0.2	0.1	0.1	1,751
Nondurable goods........	100.0	24.9	48.3	23.4	3.2	0.2	0.1	0.1	1,533
Food and kindred products.....	100.0	35.9	37.7	23.2	2.8	0.2	0.1	0.1	1,378
Knitting mills.......	100.0	25.9	51.6	19.4	2.8	0.2	0.1	0.1	1,460
Textile mill products, except knitting......	100.0	20.0	48.5	28.6	2.6	0.1	0.1	0.1	1,677
Apparel & other fabricated textile products.	100.0	25.5	51.2	19.4	3.5	0.2	0.1	0.1	1,449
Leather and leather products......	100.0	23.6	54.7	19.3	2.1	0.1	...	0.1	1,487
Other nondurable goods......	100.0	19.4	43.2	33.2	4.0	0.2	0.1	0.1	1,756
Not specified manufacturing industries.....	100.0	28.1	45.1	23.0	3.4	0.2	0.2	0.1	1,505
Nonmanufacturing industries (incl. not reptd)...	100.0	33.4	40.8	21.1	4.2	0.2	0.1	0.1	1,401
PRIVATE HOUSEHOLD WORKERS......	100.0	76.8	19.9	2.6	0.5	0.1	0.1	0.1	652
Private household workers—living in......	100.0	56.1	37.2	5.6	0.7	0.2	0.1	0.2	892
Private household workers—living out......	100.0	80.6	16.7	2.1	0.4	0.1	0.1	...	621
SERVICE WORKERS, EXCEPT PRIVATE HOUSEHOLD.	100.0	47.6	36.8	12.1	2.9	0.4	0.1	0.1	1,054
Attendants, hospital and other institution......	100.0	34.3	42.3	19.8	3.3	0.1	0.1	0.1	1,320
Barbers, beauticians, and manicurists......	100.0	34.6	35.7	20.1	7.8	1.3	0.3	0.2	1,417
Charwomen, janitors, and porters......	100.0	40.7	41.7	15.4	1.9	0.2	0.1	0.1	1,197
Cooks, except private household......	100.0	50.5	35.3	11.0	2.6	0.3	0.1	0.1	991
Housekeepers and stewards, exc. private household.	100.0	28.9	43.1	21.9	5.4	0.5	0.2	0.1	1,466
Practical nurses and midwives......	100.0	47.7	36.1	12.7	2.9	0.3	0.1	0.2	1,056
Waitresses, bartenders, and counter workers...	100.0	55.5	34.5	7.9	1.6	0.2	0.1	0.1	902
Other service workers, except private household...	100.0	50.4	37.1	9.4	2.4	0.4	0.2	0.1	993

Table 17-A-3. INCOME DISTRIBUTION OF THE EXPERIENCED CIVILIAN LABOR FORCE, BY OCCUPATION AND SEX, FOR THE UNITED STATES: 1950—Con.

Occupation and sex	Total	Income distribution							Median income
		Destitute (Less-$1,000)	Meager ($1,000-$1,999)	Adequate ($2,000-$2,999)	Comfortable ($3,000-$4,999)	Abundant ($5,000-$6,999)	Affluent ($7,000-$9,999)	Wealthy ($10,000-)	
Female—Con.									
FARM LABORERS AND FOREMEN...........	100.0	87.0	9.2	2.2	1.1	0.2	0.1	0.1	576
Farm laborers, unpaid family workers.........	100.0	86.7	8.5	2.6	1.6	0.3	0.1	0.2	578
Farm laborers, except unpaid, and farm foremen....	100.0	87.2	9.7	2.0	0.8	0.1	0.1	0.1	574
LABORERS, EXCEPT FARM AND MINE...........	100.0	34.6	37.0	23.6	4.2	0.3	0.1	0.1	1,425
OCCUPATION NOT REPORTED...........	100.0	58.7	24.1	11.6	4.1	0.8	0.4	0.3	853

Source: **U. S. Census of Population: 1950, U. S. Summary,** Vol.II, Detailed Characteristics, Table 129.

Table 17-A-4. DETAILED OCCUPATION BY SELECTED CHARACTERISTICS OF THE EXPERIENCED LABOR FORCE: 1950

Detailed occupation	Percent of migrant workers in 1949	Years of school completed		Median years of school completed		Percent married spouse present		Percent full-time workers at work, 1949 50-52 weeks		Percent foreign born	
		Less than 8	4 yrs. college or more	Male	Female	Male	Female	Male	Female	Male	Female
TOTAL	5.7	22.6	7.0	9.7	11.8	74.0	46.6	68.3	56.6	9.2	6.7
PROFESSIONAL, TECHNICAL AND KINDRED WKRS	9.6	2.4	49.3	16.+	15.4	79.0	40.7	76.9	43.1	7.4	4.6
Accountants and auditors	6.2	1.6	31.9	14.4	12.7	80.3	40.7	86.3	80.9	5.8	2.7
Actors and actresses	11.9	6.0	25.0	12.8	13.2	59.6	40.4	32.1	18.4	18.9	13.6
Airplane pilots and navigators	20.0	1.5	16.2	13.4	...	82.4	60.0	81.6	...	2.2	...
Architects	7.5	1.6	63.1	16.+	...	82.1	40.0	82.1	...	10.8	13.3
Artists and art teachers	8.2	2.8	31.0	13.0	14.4	71.4	40.7	70.4	49.7	13.5	6.0
Athletes	23.8	5.4	11.0	12.5	...	42.7	15.0	32.7	...	3.8	15.0
Authors	13.2	1.7	47.6	15.7	16.+	64.6	45.6	68.3	58.5	15.2	5.2
Chemists	8.2	2.1	63.5	16.+	16.+	79.3	37.0	83.5	73.4	8.3	7.7
Chiropractors	7.7	1.7	60.5	16.+	...	83.6	39.3	75.0	...	7.9	4.9
Clergymen	17.7	6.5	60.2	16.+	12.8	74.3	45.1	89.0	74.0	11.8	4.5
College presidents, professors, & instrs.(n.e.c.)	13.5	0.3	89.1	16.+	16.+	77.4	29.4	58.6	39.2	9.1	6.8
Dancers and dancing teachers	13.4	3.5	10.3	12.5	12.5	39.2	38.4	41.6	23.0	3.9	6.0
Dentists	3.1	1.1	88.8	16.+	...	87.2	47.9	76.2	...	7.2	13.7
Designers	5.2	6.7	17.4	12.7	12.5	78.6	47.1	77.9	59.0	18.3	23.0
Dietitians and nutritionists	9.8	5.1	41.0	...	14.5	57.7	37.3	...	64.5	11.5	6.8
Draftsmen	6.2	1.8	14.2	12.9	12.8	75.0	37.1	81.4	76.9	7.3	2.1
Editors and reporters	11.0	1.4	45.5	15.6	15.4	75.5	38.4	81.5	70.7	6.9	4.8
Engineers, technical	10.9	2.5	53.4	16.+	14.5	85.0	54.0	84.1	71.0	6.7	6.3
Aeronautical	13.8	0.7	57.3	16.+	...	85.9	38.5	83.2	...	6.7	7.7
Chemical	13.2	0.9	81.3	16.+	...	82.8	52.4	85.2	...	5.0	14.3
Civil	12.1	3.0	52.5	16.+	...	84.6	48.3	82.8	...	5.6	8.6
Electrical	10.4	2.0	54.2	16.+	...	83.1	46.3	85.5	...	6.7	...
Industrial	9.4	1.6	43.9	15.3	16.+	87.3	70.6	84.4	...	5.9	11.8
Mechanical	9.6	3.6	49.9	16.+	...	84.8	61.5	82.1	...	9.2	7.7
Metallurgical, and metallurgists	6.4	1.4	57.7	16.+	14.6	87.9	44.4	82.1	...	5.8	...
Mining	22.8	4.2	65.9	16.+	...	88.2	50.0	80.8	...	5.9	...
Not elsewhere classified	9.7	2.5	48.7	15.9	...	87.5	69.7	87.4	...	6.3	3.0
Entertainers (n.e.c.)	14.8	14.5	6.1	10.8	12.2	61.5	53.4	46.6	34.2	10.7	9.7
Farm and home management advisors	15.1	2.2	81.6	16.+	16.+	85.5	29.7	85.7	73.0	1.6	1.2
Foresters and conservationists	11.4	14.1	34.5	12.7	...	79.7	77.8	72.1	...	1.9	2.8
Funeral directors and embalmers	6.0	6.0	14.8	13.0	...	83.0	57.3	85.9	...	2.0	4.9
Lawyers and judges	4.3	1.3	87.1	16.+	16.+	84.5	41.6	87.6	81.7	5.3	5.6
Librarians	7.5	1.3	48.5	15.8	15.9	47.4	30.0	62.4	62.9	4.7	4.1
Musicians and music teachers	9.7	3.9	33.4	12.8	14.6	62.4	38.6	45.9	33.7	11.8	4.3
Natural scientists (n.e.c.)	17.8	2.6	70.0	16.+	16.+	80.1	38.7	81.3	76.5	6.3	5.4
Nurses, professional	10.2	2.0	19.4	12.8	13.4	58.6	43.0	70.3	55.3	9.3	7.2
Nurses, student professional	21.1	1.2	4.6	...	12.9	34.4	3.6	...	46.4	11.5	1.5

Table 17-A-4. DETAILED OCCUPATION BY SELECTED CHARACTERISTICS OF THE EXPERIENCED LABOR FORCE: 1950-Con.

Detailed occupation	Percent of migrant workers in 1949	Years of school completed		Median years of school completed		Percent married spouse present		Percent full-time workers at work, 1949 50-52 weeks		Percent foreign born	
		Less than 8	4 yrs. college or more	Male	Female	Male	Female	Male	Female	Male	Female
PROFESSIONAL, TECHNICAL, & KINDRED WKRS.-Con.											
Optometrists	10.2	1.6	64.9	16.+	...	83.8	44.8	80.5	...	8.1	3.4
Osteopaths	1.8	1.8	88.8	16.+	...	90.5	39.1	78.2	...	2.7	17.4
Personnel and labor relations workers	5.5	1.6	36.4	14.7	13.4	87.8	37.3	91.1	82.4	3.8	4.4
Pharmacists	5.9	1.6	52.6	16.+	12.4	84.5	48.8	86.8	71.2	9.6	6.1
Photographers	8.4	5.4	8.6	12.4	12.4	71.5	48.6	76.4	65.0	10.5	8.8
Physicians and surgeons	10.7	0.7	92.4	16.+	16.+	85.0	40.3	83.6	72.9	11.4	18.3
Radio operators	15.2	2.9	8.2	12.6	...	78.2	46.4	84.2	...	4.5	...
Recreation and group workers	12.6	1.6	46.1	15.6	15.7	68.1	31.8	71.1	53.8	4.2	3.5
Religious workers	15.0	6.1	29.2	14.0	12.9	50.5	22.4	80.4	74.4	17.0	13.9
Social and welfare workers, except group	9.2	2.9	56.3	16.+	16.+	75.2	40.6	78.1	74.6	7.4	5.0
Social scientists	10.2	1.5	53.9	16.+	15.5	81.4	43.9	84.8	71.8	7.8	7.4
Sports instructors and officials	15.5	3.8	67.4	16.+	16.+	75.3	29.9	52.9	31.4	4.4	1.6
Surveyors	12.0	6.2	10.5	12.5	...	65.6	59.1	69.3	...	2.4	...
Teachers (n.e.c.)	8.6	1.3	65.5	16.+	16.+	78.8	44.2	49.7	23.5	4.0	2.4
Technicians, medical and dental	10.4	2.7	23.4	12.5	11.2	71.0	34.6	81.0	69.2	10.1	4.7
Technicians, testing	5.5	4.2	11.5	12.5	12.5	73.3	47.4	77.9	71.2	5.2	3.3
Technicians (n.e.c.)	11.7	2.1	18.5	12.7	13.7	76.4	36.2	78.4	75.9	5.2	5.4
Therapists and healers (n.e.c.)	9.6	4.9	43.9	15.4	14.9	81.8	32.0	72.2	58.8	14.7	16.4
Veterinarians	7.8	3.4	67.5	16.+	...	86.1	43.8	78.7	...	5.2	12.5
Professional, technical, and kindred wkrs. (n.e.c.)	12.2	4.2	38.1	14.0	15.9	72.3	36.0	73.6	62.8	7.7	6.6
FARMERS AND FARM MANAGERS	3.3	41.0	1.4	8.1	8.3	84.5	33.8	80.0	61.9	4.0	5.8
Farmers (owners and tenants)	3.2	41.1	1.4	8.1	8.3	84.5	33.8	80.0	61.7	4.0	5.9
Farm managers	7.0	19.6	10.1	10.7	...	86.8	31.6	86.1	...	7.3	3.8
MANAGERS, OFFICIALS, AND PROPRIETORS, EXC. FARM	4.9	12.1	11.2	12.1	12.2	87.7	57.3	85.9	77.5	12.9	9.7
Buyers and department heads, store	6.5	4.4	14.2	12.6	12.5	88.2	44.7	89.6	82.7	8.2	5.8
Buyers and shippers, farm products	5.6	22.2	2.8	9.4	...	86.8	70.6	74.5	...	6.5	...
Conductors, railroad	2.0	18.5	1.0	9.4	...	88.3	50.0	72.1	...	3.7	...
Credit men	6.7	2.4	18.9	13.0	12.6	88.7	49.1	87.2	86.4	5.3	2.7
Floormen and floor managers, store	5.3	6.7	5.8	12.3	11.2	88.1	51.5	82.6	75.7	7.7	4.3
Inspectors, public administration	6.5	7.3	13.9	12.4	...	86.1	44.0	88.5	...	4.5	10.7
Federal public administration and postal service	9.5	6.2	16.0	12.5	...	86.8	43.3	88.5	...	3.3	3.3
State public administration	4.3	4.0	15.1	12.5	...	86.4	42.9	85.1	...	3.2	14.3
Local public administration	3.5	10.3	10.4	12.3	...	84.9	44.7	85.3	...	6.8	14.9
Managers and superintendents, building	4.2	24.8	6.3	9.0	9.8	82.0	53.7	86.9	84.4	30.5	19.8
Officers, pilots, pursers, and engineers, ship	6.8	17.5	4.4	10.6	...	70.1	48.8	60.7	...	17.5	12.2
Officials and administrators (n.e.c.), public admin'n.	5.6	5.8	21.6	12.7	12.7	87.1	47.6	87.6	77.4	5.7	3.1
Federal public administration and postal service	9.9	3.5	29.3	13.4	12.9	87.2	42.4	91.5	88.5	8.1	4.7

Table 17-A-4. DETAILED OCCUPATION BY SELECTED CHARACTERISTICS OF THE EXPERIENCED LABOR FORCE: 1950 -Con.

Detailed occupation	Percent of migrant workers in 1949	Years of school completed		Median years of school completed		Percent married spouse present		Percent full-time workers at work, 1949 50-52 weeks		Percent foreign born	
		Less than 8	4 yrs. college or more	Male	Female	Male	Female	Male	Female	Male	Female
MANAGERS, OFFS., PROPR'S., EXC. FARM-Con.											
State public administration	5.5	3.2	27.0	13.0	•••	90.5	45.1	90.4	•••	2.1	1.4
Local public administration	3.0	7.9	15.6	12.3	12.7	85.9	49.3	83.8	73.7	5.3	2.9
Officials, lodge, society, union, etc.	6.4	9.9	11.7	11.8	•••	83.6	52.4	84.6	•••	11.1	4.8
Postmasters	0.8	6.6	7.6	12.2	12.2	86.7	63.7	90.8	82.1	3.1	1.4
Purchasing agents and buyers (n.e.c.)	4.9	4.4	11.9	12.7	12.4	88.1	40.1	89.7	84.1	6.5	5.8
Managers, offs.,& propr's.(n.e.c.)-salaried	6.6	6.7	15.6	12.5	12.4	87.5	48.3	88.6	75.7	7.8	6.1
Construction	9.9	11.0	11.4	12.1	•••	85.7	53.8	74.6	•••	7.4	4.6
Manufacturing	5.7	5.0	21.7	12.7	12.5	90.6	44.0	90.9	81.2	8.2	8.4
Transportation	5.6	6.6	10.0	12.2	12.5	90.0	43.9	92.5	85.3	5.3	5.8
Telecommunications, & utilities & san.serv.	4.8	5.2	18.7	12.6	12.4	92.3	42.3	93.4	88.5	3.6	3.2
Wholesale trade	7.1	5.9	14.9	12.5	12.5	89.4	50.9	90.8	82.1	8.9	6.1
Retail trade	7.2	8.5	8.5	12.3	12.1	85.8	54.9	88.1	73.4	8.7	7.0
Food and dairy prod. stores,& milk retail	5.6	12.7	4.0	11.9	11.0	86.2	62.7	88.5	74.7	10.8	10.4
Gen. mdse. and five and ten cent stores	13.0	4.0	14.8	12.7	12.3	84.9	49.1	89.1	80.2	6.1	5.8
Apparel and accessories stores	7.4	4.9	9.3	12.5	12.3	86.6	55.3	90.6	74.7	15.1	6.6
Furniture, home furnishings,& equip.stores	7.9	4.2	12.1	12.5	•••	89.3	58.2	90.6	•••	7.6	2.9
Motor vehicles and accessories retailing	6.7	4.3	8.8	12.4	•••	92.4	53.8	91.0	•••	3.5	3.8
Gasoline service stations	7.6	11.5	3.1	11.3	•••	83.4	50.0	83.5	•••	2.1	9.1
Eating and drinking places	6.7	15.6	4.8	11.3	10.6	75.0	58.5	79.3	61.4	19.0	8.2
Hardware, farm implement, & bldg.mat.retail	5.1	4.8	11.2	12.4	•••	92.3	52.1	92.7	•••	4.5	4.2
Other retail trade	6.7	7.4	11.7	12.4	12.3	84.6	49.1	88.7	76.2	8.1	5.3
Banking and other finance	4.1	1.4	23.0	13.0	12.6	88.6	40.9	92.6	88.0	5.3	2.4
Insurance and real estate	6.1	4.0	22.3	12.9	12.5	90.1	36.7	92.2	88.9	6.9	3.3
Business services	7.7	3.0	29.0	13.9	12.9	83.2	43.5	88.4	78.9	5.9	6.2
Automobile repair services and garages	5.8	9.3	3.1	11.8	•••	90.5	41.8	88.4	•••	3.8	•••
Miscellaneous repair services	6.6	10.5	2.6	12.1	•••	90.9	77.8	87.3	•••	7.7	•••
Personal services	6.6	11.6	8.1	12.2	11.8	80.2	51.5	83.2	71.1	13.8	6.1
All other industries (incl. not reported)	7.7	7.9	22.7	12.6	12.7	78.9	43.2	82.4	64.6	7.0	5.5
Managers,offs.,& propr's.(n.e.c.)-self-emp'd.	3.6	16.7	7.6	11.5	11.1	88.4	66.1	84.4	77.4	17.8	13.1
Construction	3.8	14.8	8.4	11.1	•••	91.1	60.9	66.8	•••	13.9	11.5
Manufacturing	2.9	13.0	13.3	12.2	12.3	90.0	59.3	85.0	75.1	20.1	15.8
Transportation	3.1	17.7	4.8	10.3	•••	88.1	59.5	79.9	•••	9.2	7.6
Telecommunications, & util. & sanitary serv.	7.0	23.1	9.1	10.9	•••	89.6	62.5	88.0	•••	7.4	•••
Wholesale trade	3.2	15.1	11.4	12.1	12.4	87.8	61.6	85.5	81.1	22.1	18.6
Retail trade	3.5	18.3	5.2	11.2	10.5	88.1	68.4	87.8	77.9	18.8	13.6
Food and dairy prod.stores,& milk retail	2.8	26.2	2.6	9.3	9.0	88.8	74.1	89.4	82.6	24.0	16.1
Gen. mdse. and five and ten cent stores	3.6	17.1	6.7	11.4	11.5	88.8	61.7	91.2	84.1	21.0	14.3
Apparel and accessories stores	2.6	11.2	8.5	12.2	12.1	89.0	57.7	89.6	76.4	33.5	19.1

Table 17-A-4. DETAILED OCCUPATION BY SELECTED CHARACTERISTICS OF THE EXPERIENCED LABOR FORCE: 1950—Con.

Detailed occupation	Percent of migrant workers in 1949	Years of school completed		Median years of school completed		Percent married spouse present		Percent full-time workers at work, 1949 50-52 weeks		Percent foreign born	
		Less than 8	4 yrs. college or more	Male	Female	Male	Female	Male	Female	Male	Female
MANAGERS,OFF.,PROPR'S.,EXC.FARM—Con.											
Furniture, home furnishings, & equip.stores.	3.2	9.1	9.1	12.3	12.2	90.0	69.9	90.0	80.4	14.8	12.9
Motor vehicles and accessories retailing...	3.0	8.6	9.8	12.2	...	93.2	76.1	90.7	...	6.9	6.5
Gasoline service stations..............	4.4	15.8	2.5	10.7	10.5	88.2	76.2	86.2	83.0	4.5	4.1
Eating and drinking places............	5.3	20.4	2.5	11.4	9.9	84.9	70.1	83.4	72.1	24.9	11.8
Hardware, farm imp., & bldg.mat'l. retail.	2.9	9.3	10.2	12.5	11.8	92.3	66.4	90.0	83.7	9.9	8.0
Other retail trade...................	2.7	15.2	9.2	11.9	12.1	85.9	61.1	87.0	76.3	17.2	10.8
Banking and other finance............	2.9	6.4	27.0	13.3	...	87.0	50.0	87.7	...	11.0	...
Insurance and real estate............	2.1	7.4	19.0	12.7	12.5	87.9	45.2	87.7	88.3	14.0	10.5
Business services...................	3.3	7.2	23.9	12.7	12.8	88.9	50.6	84.8	81.3	12.9	9.4
Automobile repair services and garages...	2.8	14.5	2.7	10.1	...	89.4	81.6	85.8	...	9.0	5.3
Miscellaneous repair services........	2.8	14.8	4.1	10.6	...	85.8	64.6	82.3	...	14.4	10.4
Personal services...................	5.8	18.5	6.4	10.6	11.2	86.5	67.2	84.7	75.4	23.7	11.8
All other industries (incl. not reported).	5.0	16.3	11.6	11.8	12.2	85.5	51.4	74.5	69.8	10.8	9.3
CLERICAL AND KINDRED WORKERS........	5.1	4.3	5.6	12.2	12.5	68.8	41.4	78.1	72.5	5.5	3.2
Agents (n.e.c.)......................	8.0	4.2	21.2	12.8	12.7	84.3	46.9	85.4	74.8	4.6	4.6
Attendants and assistants, library...	11.4	3.5	24.0	...	13.7	31.5	25.7	...	50.4	6.5	4.6
Attendants, physician's and dentist's office.	5.6	2.9	5.5	...	12.5	46.8	42.8	...	63.4	3.8	2.8
Baggagemen, transportation...........	3.9	23.8	2.1	9.0	...	75.3	30.0	79.4	...	8.9	10.0
Bank tellers........................	4.0	1.6	6.6	12.6	12.5	71.6	41.5	88.7	87.0	3.1	3.2
Bookkeepers.........................	5.0	1.8	5.9	12.7	12.5	67.1	46.2	78.3	75.7	5.5	3.7
Cashiers............................	5.7	5.4	2.5	12.2	12.1	66.1	47.6	74.2	63.6	8.4	4.3
Collectors, bill and account........	7.5	11.0	5.7	12.2	12.2	76.4	50.0	73.5	68.2	6.8	6.2
Dispatchers and starters, vehicle...	3.7	10.7	2.3	11.1	10.6	82.4	49.3	82.0	63.2	4.7	4.3
Express messengers and railway mail clerks.	3.6	5.8	3.7	12.3	...	82.9	40.0	85.1	...	2.4	...
Mail carriers.......................	1.7	6.9	3.2	12.2	11.9	82.2	67.0	86.6	...	2.5	3.6
Messengers and office boys..........	4.2	11.3	1.3	10.8	12.2	31.4	24.2	57.3	55.2	6.3	2.2
Office machine operators............	5.2	2.2	2.3	12.4	12.4	59.0	42.4	77.2	73.2	3.9	3.4
Shipping and receiving clerks.......	3.7	14.4	1.2	10.6	11.1	68.0	51.6	74.3	64.3	8.6	5.8
Stenographers, typists, and secretaries...	6.1	1.3	6.7	12.7	12.6	62.9	37.8	82.5	73.8	5.0	3.1
Telegraph messengers................	4.7	18.0	2.2	9.9	...	14.7	46.2	57.5	...	4.0	7.7
Telegraph operators.................	9.9	7.6	2.0	11.7	12.3	77.3	43.6	79.1	77.4	4.2	1.2
Telephone operators.................	4.7	4.1	1.0	12.1	12.2	67.0	44.0	80.6	74.3	6.2	2.2
Ticket, station, and express agents.	6.6	5.6	6.4	12.2	12.5	84.2	39.9	88.3	76.4	3.8	2.7
Clerical and kindred workers (n.e.c.)...	4.7	5.2	6.0	12.3	12.4	67.4	41.8	77.2	70.9	5.4	3.3
SALES WORKERS.................	6.2	8.9	7.1	12.2	11.7	72.8	53.1	76.2	56.8	7.1	6.1
Advertising agents and salesmen.	8.8	4.0	20.0	12.9	12.7	75.9	38.2	76.8	60.8	5.3	6.7

Detailed occupation	Percent of migrant workers in 1949	Years of school completed Less than 8	Years of school completed 4 yrs. college or more	Median years of school completed Male	Median years of school completed Female	Percent married spouse present Male	Percent married spouse present Female	Percent full-time workers at work, 1949 50-52 weeks Male	Percent full-time workers at work, 1949 50-52 weeks Female	Percent foreign born Male	Percent foreign born Female
SALES WORKERS-Con.											
Demonstrators	5.9	6.6	3.8	...	12.1	67.0	65.5	...	27.9	9.4	4.9
Hucksters and peddlers	3.3	41.7	0.6	8.1	...	59.0	45.7	52.4	47.4	24.4	3.4
Insurance agents and brokers	7.1	4.5	18.6	12.7	12.6	86.1	43.2	83.2	75.1	6.0	4.2
Newsboys	2.6	25.2	0.6	8.8	9.5	8.0	34.8	60.1	58.7	2.3	5.8
Real estate agents and brokers	3.7	7.5	14.1	12.5	12.6	84.6	56.0	77.8	63.9	10.3	7.5
Stock and bond salesmen	5.4	4.6	23.8	13.0	...	81.9	47.4	82.8	...	9.0	5.3
Salesmen and sales clerks (n.e.c.)	6.3	8.7	5.8	12.2	11.6	73.6	53.3	76.1	56.6	7.1	6.1
Manufacturing	8.2	5.3	14.9	12.6	12.1	82.0	52.7	81.9	57.9	6.7	7.8
Wholesale trade	7.3	5.9	11.3	12.5	12.1	84.4	51.1	82.7	61.4	7.6	10.2
Retail trade	5.8	9.6	3.6	12.1	11.6	68.2	53.5	72.7	56.7	7.2	6.0
Other industries (incl. not reported)	8.4	7.5	9.0	12.3	11.8	75.2	46.4	74.7	49.3	5.6	5.1
CRAFTSMEN, FOREMEN AND KINDRED WORKERS	5.3	21.3	1.7	9.5	10.4	81.8	53.1	65.9	63.9	10.9	9.7
Bakers	4.8	25.9	0.9	8.8	9.2	73.8	57.8	75.2	60.0	27.7	13.6
Blacksmiths	3.9	40.6	0.6	8.3	...	79.1	52.5	61.9	...	17.8	37.5
Boilermakers	6.2	27.9	0.5	8.8	...	83.1	50.0	57.4	...	13.9	50.0
Bookbinders	4.2	16.7	1.8	10.0	9.4	72.4	46.8	82.3	65.0	16.2	6.3
Brickmasons, stonemasons, and tile setters	6.0	31.5	0.9	8.8	...	77.9	70.4	37.2	...	17.7	22.2
Cabinetmakers	5.3	23.3	1.4	9.0	...	78.6	64.3	63.7	...	20.2	3.6
Carpenters	6.6	29.1	0.9	8.7	11.3	81.4	60.1	60.1	50.8	10.5	10.5
Cement and concrete finishers	7.3	42.2	0.1	8.3	...	79.0	66.7	35.5	...	14.2	33.3
Compositors and typesetters	4.8	8.5	2.5	11.7	12.0	76.4	45.8	82.6	67.9	8.6	3.4
Cranemen, derrickmen, and hoistmen	3.9	30.2	0.4	8.7	...	83.2	54.2	53.2	...	10.9	4.2
Decorators and window dressers	6.9	8.8	7.0	12.1	12.4	67.9	50.0	73.1	60.1	10.9	5.3
Electricians	5.2	12.0	1.8	11.1	...	84.0	55.1	69.1	...	5.9	7.2
Electrotypers and stereotypers	6.1	15.2	0.8	10.4	...	79.9	43.8	83.4	...	7.5	6.2
Engravers, except photoengravers	6.7	13.0	2.7	11.3	...	72.7	39.6	76.4	...	11.3	6.2
Excavating, grading, and road machinery oper'or	10.0	25.7	0.4	8.9	...	84.3	54.6	54.9	...	3.1	9.1
Foremen (n.e.c.)	3.6	17.1	3.2	10.1	10.2	91.0	52.6	85.8	75.3	9.7	9.0
Construction	9.4	21.7	1.9	9.1	...	88.4	66.7	70.0	...	7.9	11.1
Manufacturing	2.6	15.5	3.5	10.4	9.9	91.2	54.1	87.5	74.5	10.5	9.3
Metal industries	1.7	16.8	3.2	9.9	...	90.8	49.1	83.0	...	11.0	5.3
Machinery, including electrical	2.7	9.9	3.8	11.2	10.9	91.7	61.3	89.2	78.6	10.3	6.5
Transportation equipment	1.9	9.5	4.0	11.2	...	93.5	52.0	89.4	...	10.9	16.0
Other durable goods	2.7	19.0	2.2	9.6	10.4	90.0	46.8	84.5	73.2	9.3	6.3
Textiles, textile products, and apparel	3.1	24.7	2.4	9.1	9.4	90.7	54.0	86.7	69.9	14.4	12.8
Other nondurable goods (incl. not spec. mfg.)	2.8	13.8	4.4	10.6	10.2	91.1	55.5	90.6	78.2	9.3	6.8
Railroads and railway express serivce	4.6	25.6	1.4	8.8	...	92.0	40.0	88.3	...	12.0	...
Transportation, except railroad	4.4	18.4	2.7	9.9	...	92.8	77.8	87.1	...	9.9	22.2
Telecommunications, & utilities & san.serv.	4.1	15.2	3.5	10.6	...	92.7	32.4	92.1	...	7.0	5.9
Other industries (incl. not reported)	4.2	17.8	3.3	10.0	11.1	90.3	48.7	83.5	77.4	8.0	8.4

Table 17-A-4. DETAILED OCCUPATION BY SELECTED CHARACTERISTICS OF THE EXPERIENCED LABOR FORCE: 1950-Con.

Detailed occupation	Percent of migrant workers in 1949	Years of school completed — Less than 8	Years of school completed — 4 yrs. college or more	Median years of school completed — Male	Median — Female	Percent married spouse present — Male	Female	Percent full-time workers at work, 1949 50-52 weeks — Male	Female	Percent foreign born — Male	Female
CRAFTSMEN, FOREMEN & KINDRED WKRS.—Con.											
Forgemen and hammermen	2.5	30.9	0.8	8.6	...	83.8	57.1	60.5	...	16.2	28.6
Furriers	4.5	19.1	2.0	9.4	...	82.9	32.8	55.1	...	43.7	25.0
Glaziers	7.1	20.8	0.3	9.7	...	75.4	44.4	70.4	...	9.8	9.8
Heat treaters, annealers, and temperers	2.0	23.9	0.5	8.9	...	84.3	85.7	65.4	...	12.5	14.3
Inspectors, scalers, & graders, log and lumber	5.6	28.4	1.7	9.1	...	79.2	46.2	59.5	57.8	5.0	2.6
Inspectors (n.e.c.)	4.2	18.9	3.9	10.0	10.2	83.6	54.5	73.9	...	9.2	7.4
Construction	10.5	8.5	7.3	12.3	...	78.3	50.0	79.0	...	6.1	...
Railroads and railway express service	3.1	25.1	1.5	8.9	...	84.9	40.0	80.1	...	10.3	20.0
Transport,exc.r.r. communi'cn,& other pub.util	3.7	13.6	5.3	10.8	...	87.6	61.5	89.6	...	7.7	7.7
Other industries (incl. not reported)	4.2	16.7	5.1	10.9	10.1	82.1	54.5	61.0	57.8	9.3	7.2
Jewelers, watchmk'rs,goldsmiths and silversmiths	6.9	11.6	2.5	11.6	...	77.8	56.3	75.9	...	18.6	11.5
Job setters, metal	1.9	18.8	0.6	9.3	...	86.6	70.0	72.8	...	15.2	15.2
Linemen & servicemen, telegr., teleph., & power	7.0	8.9	1.5	12.1	12.0	79.5	52.9	87.3	82.7	3.0	4.7
Locomotive engineers	2.3	22.7	1.4	8.8	...	88.2	50.0	70.7	...	5.5	...
Locomotive firemen	4.5	14.9	0.9	10.5	...	82.9	53.3	58.7	...	3.2	6.7
Loom fixers	4.1	51.7	0.1	7.7	...	89.6	73.3	71.4	...	10.3	13.3
Machinists	3.3	16.6	1.1	10.0	10.0	83.2	52.8	72.9	60.2	12.8	6.7
Mechanics and repairmen	5.8	19.5	1.2	9.8	10.9	80.8	55.3	74.0	62.3	7.3	10.0
Airplane	7.6	6.7	2.7	12.2	...	80.9	60.6	84.1	...	3.5	12.1
Automobile	6.6	21.0	0.5	9.4	11.2	81.2	55.6	74.7	72.1	4.8	6.2
Office machine	7.8	8.4	2.7	12.1	...	72.5	46.7	78.7	...	6.3	13.3
Radio and television	7.8	6.8	3.6	12.2	...	65.8	54.7	67.5	...	4.6	1.6
Railroad and car shop	3.6	31.5	0.6	8.7	...	82.0	100.0	69.7	...	15.8	66.7
Not elsewhere classified	4.9	20.2	1.4	9.5	10.2	81.9	54.9	73.4	60.2	9.4	11.7
Millers, grain, flour, feed, etc.	3.2	27.4	2.3	8.7	...	83.2	...	78.7	...	5.5	...
Millwrights	2.7	23.4	0.7	8.9	...	88.8	70.0	61.2	...	13.6	...
Molders, metal	2.9	38.5	0.2	8.4	...	81.8	50.0	58.2	...	16.4	9.1
Motion picture projectionists	4.9	15.1	1.4	10.4	...	71.8	40.0	79.5	...	7.1	6.7
Opticians, and lens grinders and polishers	5.6	9.8	4.6	11.6	11.7	78.2	44.4	82.8	...	9.5	4.9
Painters, construction and maintenance	5.8	27.9	1.3	8.8	...	76.7	58.6	38.2	50.0	13.2	8.2
Paperhangers	3.5	34.7	0.5	8.4	...	76.3	82.4	23.7	...	11.6	2.2
Pattern and model makers, except paper	3.4	14.1	1.5	10.5	...	84.3	43.9	62.9	...	14.2	2.4
Photoengravers and lithographers	4.1	9.9	2.2	11.8	...	80.6	34.9	84.6	...	12.1	2.3
Piano and organ tuners and repairmen	6.1	12.2	5.0	11.5	...	75.8	34.9	60.8	...	9.2	...
Plasterers	6.0	32.4	0.6	8.7	...	77.8	47.4	36.3	...	15.1	6.2
Plumbers and pipe fitters	5.3	22.0	1.0	9.3	...	83.9	37.5	63.6	...	7.5	8.2
Pressmen and plate printers, printing	4.4	12.6	1.2	10.4	...	77.7	69.4	80.9	...	8.1	6.1
Rollers and roll hands, metal	2.4	30.4	0.5	8.8	...	80.1	66.7	34.9	...	13.3	12.5

TABLE I/-A-4. DETAILED OCCUPATION BY SELECTED CHARACTERISTICS OF THE EXPERIENCED LABOR FORCE, 1950--Con.

Detailed occupation	Percent of migrant workers in 1949	Years of school completed: Less than 8	Years of school completed: 4 yrs. college or more	Median years of school completed: Male	Median years of school completed: Female	Percent married spouse present: Male	Percent married spouse present: Female	Percent full-time workers at work, 1949 50-52 weeks: Male	Percent full-time workers at work, 1949 50-52 weeks: Female	Percent foreign born: Male	Percent foreign born: Female
CRAFTSMEN, FOREMEN & KINDRED WKRS.-Con.											
Shoemakers and repairers, except factory	5.0	40.6	0.7	8.3	...	77.2	70.8	78.7	...	39.3	13.9
Stationary engineers	4.8	19.8	9.9	10.0	...	86.9	50.8	83.8	...	10.3	1.6
Stone cutters and stone carvers	2.9	31.0	1.6	8.7	...	75.8	37.5	65.0	...	2.3	...
Structural metal workers	9.1	22.9	0.9	9.4	...	79.8	50.0	48.6	...	12.1	...
Tailors and tailoresses	2.9	38.2	1.6	8.4	8.7	78.0	51.0	68.4	54.7	65.7	31.3
Tinsmiths, coppersmiths, and sheet metal wkrs.	4.9	17.1	0.8	10.1	...	81.3	50.0	65.8	...	10.1	9.3
Toolmakers, and die makers and setters	3.0	11.4	1.6	10.9	...	85.6	68.6	73.8	...	19.3	11.4
Upholsterers	5.4	21.1	1.2	9.4	9.6	76.4	64.7	62.8	47.8	16.4	3.8
Craftsmen and kindred workers (n.e.c.)	5.7	22.4	1.2	9.3	...	78.3	60.4	60.6	...	12.8	7.5
Members of the armed forces	40.2	14.5	3.2	10.5	...	26.4	15.8	59.1	...	2.3	5.3
OPERATIVES AND KINDRED WORKERS	4.7	28.3	0.7	8.9	8.9	74.1	55.0	60.5	47.1	9.2	11.1
Apprentices	6.9	6.0	1.8	12.2	11.9	49.2	39.8	58.3	52.3	2.6	6.0
Auto mechanics	8.6	9.4	1.6	11.0	...	52.5	83.3	54.6	...	1.6	...
Bricklayers and masons	6.6	10.5	0.4	11.8	...	43.6	...	36.7	...	3.1	...
Carpenters	11.2	6.0	0.3	12.0	...	45.5	50.0	42.3	...	2.9	25.0
Electricians	6.4	4.6	1.2	12.2	...	56.9	33.3	62.8	...	1.2	33.3
Machinists and toolmakers	3.6	2.8	0.4	12.3	...	46.2	33.3	59.7	...	0.8	...
Mechanics, except auto	6.8	9.2	6.4	12.1	...	61.7	65.2	65.1	...	3.5	8.7
Plumbers and pipe fitters	6.0	5.2	2.0	12.1	...	65.5	56.5	70.3	...	3.2	4.3
Building trades (n.e.c.)	9.2	9.2	0.8	11.4	...	42.3	...	34.4	...	3.1	...
Metalworking trades (n.e.c.)	4.7	4.3	0.8	12.1	...	52.2	25.0	58.1	...	2.4	25.0
Printing trades	3.6	4.9	0.9	12.2	...	47.0	21.7	73.5	...	2.7	...
Other specified trades	9.6	7.1	5.6	12.1	...	45.7	16.7	57.9	...	3.7	...
Trade not specified	9.7	6.6	...	12.3	...	37.8	30.0	54.3	...	3.0	5.0
Asbestos and insulation workers	5.8	22.2	0.9	9.4	...	79.3	47.1	53.9	...	6.7	11.8
Attendants, auto service and parking	8.4	17.9	0.9	10.3	10.6	57.2	75.7	61.2	68.6	2.3	3.8
Blasters and powdermen	7.9	41.3	...	8.3	...	80.7	33.3	31.3	...	12.4	...
Boatmen, canalmen, and lock keepers	4.0	26.7	1.1	8.7	...	78.6	57.1	77.0	...	6.8	...
Brakemen, railroad	3.9	19.1	0.5	9.9	...	82.7	35.7	58.4	...	3.1	...
Bus drivers	3.8	17.7	0.9	9.7	10.4	86.8	70.7	74.6	22.2	4.8	2.0
Chainmen, rodmen, and axmen, surveying	9.8	17.9	2.1	11.3	...	51.5	...	50.7	...	3.5	...
Conductors, bus and street railway	2.1	14.7	0.8	8.9	...	81.2	58.3	87.2	...	23.5	16.7
Deliverymen and routemen	4.6	18.4	1.4	10.4	10.3	68.1	48.3	72.0	62.4	5.7	9.1
Dressmakers and seamstresses, except factory	4.1	21.5	1.7	8.9	9.1	52.3	41.5	63.7	50.4	33.8	16.7
Dyers	3.8	36.4	1.1	8.5	...	76.1	56.8	65.9	...	20.4	8.1
Filers, grinders, and polishers, metal	3.8	25.2	0.8	9.0	9.7	79.6	55.1	58.0	49.8	14.3	7.4
Fruit, nut, & veg. graders & packers, exc.fac.	6.7	36.8	0.5	8.3	8.8	67.1	62.6	35.5	13.0	17.9	9.2
Furnacemen, smeltermen, and pourers	3.3	35.6	0.3	8.6	...	78.7	54.5	47.8	...	13.3	9.1
Heaters, metal	1.0	28.5	0.7	8.8	...	82.4	69.2	44.0	...	13.8	15.4

Table 17-A-4. DETAILED OCCUPATION BY SELECTED CHARACTERISTICS OF THE EXPERIENCED LABOR FORCE: 1950-Con.

Detailed occupation	Percent of migrant workers in 1949	Years of school completed		Median years of school completed		Percent married spouse present		Percent full-time workers at work, 1949 50-52 weeks		Percent foreign born	
		Less than 8	4 yrs. college or more	Male	Female	Male	Female	Male	Female	Male	Female
OPERATIVES AND KINDRED WORKERS—Con.											
Laundry and dry cleaning operatives	4.9	33.1	0.8	9.0	8.6	65.8	50.1	69.0	58.8	11.6	6.9
Meat cutters, exc.slaughter and packing house	5.5	17.2	0.8	10.0	10.0	79.8	57.1	78.2	69.4	15.1	15.1
Milliners	3.0	18.3	1.9	...	9.2	75.5	42.4	...	39.6	44.9	32.0
Mine operatives and laborers (n.e.c.)	7.2	43.6	0.7	8.2	10.2	78.1	51.5	27.8	49.3	7.6	6.1
Coal mining	3.6	51.2	0.2	7.7	...	78.7	44.7	12.0	...	9.0	6.4
Crude petroleum and natural gas extraction	19.3	23.8	1.9	9.6	...	80.2	77.8	60.8	...	1.0	...
Mining and quarrying, except fuel	7.8	37.0	1.1	8.5	...	74.0	50.0	49.3	...	9.0	7.1
Motormen, mine, factory, logging camp, etc.	4.2	48.3	0.2	8.0	...	89.0	66.7	18.3	...	6.2	...
Motormen, street, subway, and elevated railway	1.9	18.7	0.9	9.2	...	86.7	63.6	87.3	...	15.4	9.1
Oilers and greasers, except auto	6.2	34.1	0.9	8.7	...	74.1	51.9	59.1	...	9.8	11.1
Painters, except construction and maintenance	4.7	27.3	0.6	8.8	9.8	76.2	54.3	63.4	46.9	12.3	5.5
Photographic process workers	5.2	7.1	2.4	12.1	12.1	60.4	46.3	74.5	67.3	7.6	4.7
Power station operators	3.8	11.2	2.5	11.5	...	91.1	51.5	90.8	...	5.9	17.1
Sailors and deck hands	11.7	28.4	1.0	9.0	...	41.1	58.8	35.6	...	18.7	12.1
Sawyers	7.5	53.0	0.4	7.4	6.5	73.3	58.8	49.4	...	4.2	4.7
Spinners, textile	3.4	58.0	0.5	7.9	6.5	76.8	68.7	59.3	48.9	11.7	7.0
Stationary firemen	3.6	38.6	0.6	8.4	...	80.4	58.0	73.3	...	13.5	10.0
Switchmen, railroad	3.6	18.5	0.6	9.9	...	84.2	58.3	70.4	...	4.2	...
Taxicab drivers and chauffeurs	4.5	25.0	0.8	9.9	10.5	74.4	54.9	64.7	...	8.1	3.5
Truck and tractor drivers	5.9	28.8	0.4	8.8	9.4	76.7	59.7	65.6	56.2	3.6	3.1
Weavers, textile	3.9	44.5	0.5	8.2	8.2	78.2	62.9	61.6	52.8	17.6	11.4
Welders and flame cutters	6.0	20.1	0.6	9.4	10.1	82.9	62.0	60.1	46.7	7.1	3.0
Operatives and kindred workers (n.e.c.)	4.0	27.8	0.8	8.9	9.0	72.9	55.9	61.3	45.4	11.8	11.5
Manufacturing	3.8	27.8	0.7	8.9	8.9	73.3	56.1	60.7	45.1	12.2	11.5
Durable goods	4.2	24.1	0.8	9.0	9.7	73.1	56.4	57.3	48.0	10.3	7.7
Sawmills,planing mills,& misc.wood products	6.8	46.5	0.3	8.1	8.8	68.7	62.1	52.2	41.7	4.7	3.8
Sawmills, planing mills, and mill work	7.2	49.1	0.3	7.9	8.8	68.9	63.4	51.6	38.7	3.8	6.0
Miscellaneous wood products	5.6	37.7	0.4	8.4	8.9	67.8	61.4	51.1	43.3	8.9	2.7
Furniture and fixtures	5.3	34.3	0.7	8.5	8.9	69.2	55.8	58.4	46.5	8.9	5.9
Stone, clay, and glass products	4.1	28.6	0.7	8.7	9.5	75.7	55.2	64.3	49.0	8.1	4.7
Glass and glass products	3.7	24.9	0.5	8.9	9.4	74.8	52.5	63.4	48.8	7.1	3.0
Cement,& conc.,gypsum, & plaster products	4.5	40.5	1.0	8.3	...	75.0	69.6	66.1	...	6.7	4.3
Structural clay products	4.8	32.2	0.7	8.5	10.5	74.8	63.1	60.5	47.7	7.3	5.4
Pottery and related products	4.3	23.2	0.7	8.9	9.4	75.6	54.4	64.2	46.3	7.3	5.2
Misc.nonmetallic mineral & stone products	4.2	29.0	0.8	8.7	9.4	79.7	61.1	67.4	56.3	13.7	10.0
Metal industries	3.5	27.4	0.6	8.8	9.2	75.6	56.8	52.7	49.9	13.0	8.9
Primary metal industries	3.0	31.3	0.6	8.7	9.4	77.5	55.4	46.2	44.2	13.5	8.6
Blast furnaces,steel wks., & roll.mills	2.8	30.8	0.5	8.8	9.4	77.6	47.8	33.8	36.7	14.0	9.1
Other primary iron & steel industries	2.9	35.2	0.8	8.5	9.3	76.4	53.8	58.5	41.5	12.2	8.1
Primary nonferrous industries	3.6	27.8	0.7	8.8	9.4	78.6	61.1	58.1	50.2	14.3	8.5

Table 17-A-4. DETAILED OCCUPATION BY SELECTED CHARACTERISTICS OF THE EXPERIENCED LABOR FORCE: 1950-Con.

Detailed occupation	Percent of migrant workers in 1949	Years of school completed — Less than 8	Years of school completed — 4 yrs. college or more	Median years of school completed — Male	Median years of school completed — Female	Percent married spouse present — Male	Percent married spouse present — Female	Percent full-time workers at work, 1949 50-52 weeks — Male	Percent full-time workers at work, 1949 50-52 weeks — Female	Percent foreign born — Male	Percent foreign born — Female
OPERATIVES AND KINDRED WORKERS-Con.											
Metal industries-Con.											
Fabricated metal ind.(incl.not spec.met.)	3.9	23.7	0.7	9.0	9.2	73.2	57.1	60.6	51.3	12.3	9.0
Fabricated steel products	3.9	24.1	0.7	8.9	9.2	73.4	58.4	60.6	52.4	12.5	9.0
Fabricated nonferrous metal products	3.9	21.3	0.3	9.2	9.3	71.9	50.5	60.6	46.9	10.7	8.3
Not specified metal industries	8.0	19.7	...	...	...	71.0	56.8	...	...	9.7	13.6
Machinery, except electrical	3.5	18.4	0.9	9.6	9.8	76.1	56.1	64.0	51.2	9.8	6.7
Agricultural machinery and tractors	4.8	18.4	0.7	9.3	9.0	77.4	57.5	63.0	64.0	5.8	6.3
Office and store machines and devices	2.4	13.2	1.2	10.2	10.0	75.1	53.8	74.4	56.6	12.6	8.4
Miscellaneous machinery	3.4	19.2	0.8	9.5	9.9	75.9	56.6	65.1	48.7	10.3	6.2
Electrical machinery, equipment, & supplies	3.9	13.4	1.0	10.4	10.2	69.6	57.4	66.7	48.3	8.6	6.1
Transportation equipment	4.7	20.1	1.0	9.6	9.9	73.8	61.5	51.2	43.7	10.5	8.1
Motor vehicles and motor vehicle equip.	4.8	21.0	0.9	9.4	9.8	72.9	62.5	46.9	41.9	10.9	8.5
Aircraft and parts	5.2	10.3	1.7	11.6	10.5	77.6	55.6	70.3	55.5	6.6	6.0
Ship and boat building and repairing	3.7	33.1	1.5	8.7	...	75.9	54.5	56.7	...	11.6	9.1
Railroad & misc.transportation equip.	3.0	25.6	0.3	8.9	...	76.1	60.7	58.9	...	15.4	8.3
Professional & photog.equip.,& watches	2.9	14.8	1.4	10.3	10.1	71.6	50.8	71.2	57.1	12.9	8.3
Profess. equipment and supplies	3.1	16.9	1.7	9.7	10.0	70.5	51.7	71.8	58.2	13.7	7.8
Photographic equipment and supplies	2.0	12.1	0.9	10.9	10.4	75.4	47.4	72.8	55.6	12.3	10.7
Watches, clocks, & clockwork-op.devices	3.2	12.9	1.1	10.8	10.0	69.3	51.2	67.2	56.0	11.6	7.8
Miscellaneous manufacturing industries	4.0	23.3	0.7	9.0	9.2	66.1	53.1	59.7	44.6	15.0	11.5
Nondurable goods	3.4	31.0	0.6	8.7	8.8	73.5	56.0	65.0	44.0	14.6	13.1
Food and kindred products	4.4	29.2	0.7	8.8	8.8	70.4	56.2	68.0	42.4	11.5	9.7
Meat products	4.3	31.5	0.5	8.7	8.7	75.1	60.4	73.8	54.8	12.8	9.1
Dairy products	15.6	18.9	1.2	9.4	9.0	74.6	51.8	77.1	50.2	7.1	5.0
Canning & preserv.fruits,veget.& seafood	5.1	38.3	0.6	8.5	8.5	62.4	60.9	42.7	17.5	13.0	12.9
Grain-mill products	4.0	30.7	0.5	8.6	9.5	75.7	59.4	74.7	47.7	5.4	7.1
Bakery products	5.2	24.7	0.2	9.0	9.3	54.9	50.9	67.0	59.4	11.2	8.7
Confectionery and related products	2.9	25.3	0.7	8.7	9.0	66.4	52.2	60.4	45.1	22.1	10.5
Beverage industries	3.1	26.4	0.8	8.8	8.9	70.1	53.8	64.4	48.1	10.9	3.9
Misc.food preparations & kindred prod.	3.8	33.7	0.7	8.5	8.7	71.9	55.0	65.2	46.7	14.2	8.1
Not specified food industries	6.1	20.6	2.6	9.4	9.1	63.3	51.9	65.9	51.4	10.9	7.8
Tobacco manufacture	1.7	45.8	0.4	7.2	8.3	71.5	56.7	67.8	49.3	11.7	8.0
Textile mill products	3.2	41.4	0.4	8.1	8.6	75.3	61.6	63.3	47.0	10.4	8.1
Knitting mills	3.4	28.5	0.3	8.9	8.9	74.2	58.8	58.4	44.9	9.2	6.2
Dyeing & finishing text.,exc. knit goods	2.5	33.1	0.1	8.7	8.7	71.4	59.6	62.8	55.2	17.1	8.5
Carpets, rugs, & other floor coverings	3.2	33.5	0.7	8.8	8.6	66.9	60.6	70.5	48.5	15.7	13.9
Yarn, thread, and fabric mills	3.2	46.9	0.4	7.4	8.4	76.7	63.4	64.3	47.8	9.1	8.5
Miscellaneous textile mill products	3.0	35.2	0.7	8.6	8.6	70.2	55.6	56.9	45.9	21.2	12.9
Apparel & other fabric. textile products	3.3	29.7	0.6	8.6	8.8	71.0	54.1	44.9	38.7	40.6	19.4
Apparel and accessories	3.3	29.5	0.6	8.6	8.8	71.9	54.2	43.5	38.4	43.1	19.7

Table 17-A-4. DETAILED OCCUPATION BY SELECTED CHARACTERISTICS OF THE EXPERIENCED LABOR FORCE: 1950-Con.

Detailed occupation	Percent of migrant workers in 1949	Years of school completed		Median years of school completed		Percent married spouse present		Percent full-time workers at work, 1949 50-52 weeks		Percent foreign born	
		Less than 8	4 yrs. college or more	Male	Female	Male	Female	Male	Female	Male	Female
OPERATIVES AND KINDRED WORKERS-Con.											
Nondurable goods-Con.											
Miscellaneous fab. textile products....	3.2	31.6	0.5	8.8	8.7	61.7	53.1	59.3	42.8	17.4	13.6
Paper and allied products....	3.7	25.6	0.6	8.9	9.2	74.2	50.5	72.9	55.4	8.8	6.4
Pulp, paper, and paperboard mills....	3.6	28.1	0.6	8.9	9.5	79.4	55.6	73.9	59.9	8.2	6.3
Paperboard containers and boxes....	4.1	24.7	0.6	9.0	9.0	63.3	48.1	70.2	53.6	9.8	5.7
Misc. paper and pulp products....	3.6	22.1	0.5	9.1	9.4	71.1	50.2	72.6	54.9	9.4	7.3
Printing, publishing, and allied indus....	3.6	17.3	1.6	10.0	9.9	61.7	45.9	70.2	61.5	9.6	7.2
Chemicals and allied products....	3.8	27.1	0.9	8.9	9.6	78.8	51.3	74.7	60.2	7.9	7.7
Synthetic fibers....	3.2	27.8	0.5	8.9	9.9	84.7	55.1	72.8	60.5	0.7	1.0
Drugs and medicines....	2.8	11.8	1.2	9.2	10.4	68.1	48.2	77.5	63.5	7.8	5.2
Paints, varnishes, and related products....	4.8	24.6	0.6	9.0	...	73.1	58.2	73.1	...	12.2	11.0
Misc.chemicals and allied products....	3.9	28.7	1.0	8.9	9.1	79.2	50.3	75.1	58.0	8.5	10.8
Petroleum and coal products....	3.3	19.3	1.6	10.4	...	86.0	63.6	85.9	...	5.7	4.5
Petroleum refining....	3.4	17.2	1.7	10.7	...	87.2	63.9	89.1	...	5.0	2.8
Misc.petroleum and coal products....	2.7	33.6	0.9	8.7	...	77.4	62.5	82.2	...	11.3	12.5
Rubber products....	3.0	22.2	0.9	9.1	9.7	79.4	56.9	68.0	53.7	10.3	8.2
Leather and leather products....	2.9	26.2	0.4	8.7	8.9	69.6	56.9	55.9	43.9	20.2	9.7
Leather: tanned, curried, and finished....	2.7	37.6	...	8.4	8.6	74.8	57.0	67.4	43.5	26.2	17.1
Footwear, except rubber....	2.7	24.3	0.4	8.7	8.8	69.1	59.2	54.5	45.7	17.4	8.4
Leather products, except footwear....	3.9	27.7	0.7	8.8	8.8	66.2	46.8	49.6	36.0	26.6	13.8
Not specified manufacturing industries....	4.6	21.6	0.7	8.9	9.3	64.8	52.4	58.1	47.1	9.3	12.5
Nonmanufacturing industries (incl.not rept'd).	5.3	27.8	1.2	8.9	9.2	71.1	52.7	64.7	49.6	9.5	10.5
Construction....	8.6	29.4	1.1	8.8	...	74.0	58.5	48.5	...	7.3	13.2
Railroads and railway express service....	3.3	35.8	0.7	8.5	...	79.7	47.1	63.2	...	10.5	15.7
Transportation, except railroad....	5.8	25.1	1.3	9.0	10.0	76.7	59.8	72.3	36.1	9.5	7.9
Telecomm., & utilities & sanitary services....	4.3	27.3	1.6	9.0	12.0	79.7	48.7	80.4	69.5	8.6	5.1
Wholesale and retail trade....	5.1	26.9	0.8	9.0	9.0	65.0	52.1	64.0	46.3	11.2	11.6
Business and repair services....	5.8	22.0	1.6	9.5	9.9	67.9	60.1	65.3	57.6	6.8	10.5
Personal services....	4.3	28.6	0.7	8.7	8.9	57.7	52.5	65.5	57.0	13.7	10.5
Public administration....	5.0	24.5	1.1	9.1	10.9	80.6	50.8	81.2	76.3	5.3	9.3
All other industries (incl. not reported)....	6.1	27.9	2.9	8.9	9.7	60.6	53.4	56.0	50.4	9.9	8.5
PRIVATE HOUSEHOLD WORKERS....	6.5	45.5	0.8	8.2	8.2	48.7	33.2	59.7	49.0	15.9	8.2
Housekeepers, private household....	10.6	36.0	1.3	8.9	8.5	42.3	20.2	48.5	57.1	6.5	13.5
Living in....	15.9	28.6	1.7	...	8.7	...	3.2	...	66.8	16.7	18.7
Living out....	7.4	40.3	1.0	...	8.4	49.5	30.5	...	50.7	4.8	10.3
Laundresses, private household....	2.2	67.0	0.3	...	5.8	46.1	41.9	...	55.6	9.2	2.8
Living in....	7.7	38.5	15.4	...	...	...	...	...	...	...	15.4
Living out....	2.2	67.2	0.2	...	5.8	46.1	42.1	...	55.6	9.2	2.7
Private household workers (n.e.c.)....	6.2	45.3	0.8	8.2	8.2	49.2	34.2	60.3	47.6	16.6	7.9

Table 17-A-4. DETAILED OCCUPATION BY SELECTED CHARACTERISTICS OF THE EXPERIENCED LABOR FORCE: 1950-Con.

Detailed occupation	Percent of migrant workers in 1949	Years of school completed		Median years of school completed		Percent married spouse present		Percent full-time workers at work, 1949 50-52 weeks		Percent foreign born	
		Less than 8	4 yrs. college or more	Male	Female	Male	Female	Male	Female	Male	Female
PRIVATE HOUSEHOLD WORKERS (n.e.c.)-Con.											
Private household workers (n.e.c.)-Con.											
Living in.................	19.1	30.9	1.7	8.7	8.7	46.0	6.5	74.9	64.5	36.3	27.2
Living out................	4.4	47.5	0.6	8.0	8.1	49.9	38.2	56.8	45.0	12.0	5.1
SERVICE WORKERS, EXC. PRIVATE HOUSEHOLD...	6.0	26.9	1.4	8.8	9.6	64.4	46.4	69.4	51.0	15.9	8.3
Attendants, hospital and other institutions.....	8.2	17.5	2.1	9.3	10.6	58.5	42.6	73.0	60.7	7.7	6.5
Attendants, prof. and personal service (n.e.c.).	7.2	17.4	6.4	11.1	11.6	54.6	43.0	60.7	51.2	6.2	6.2
Attendants, recreation and amusement............	7.4	24.0	1.5	9.3	10.5	21.9	37.9	34.1	45.8	3.9	8.0
Barbers, beauticians, and manicurists...........	4.2	17.4	1.3	8.8	12.0	81.2	55.7	77.7	60.3	22.7	6.0
Bartenders......................................	4.7	21.2	1.2	9.5	9.3	67.9	65.1	67.9	65.2	14.1	10.0
Boarding and lodging house keepers..............	4.2	25.2	3.9	8.9	9.3	72.0	37.1	75.6	80.2	29.9	13.7
Bootblacks......................................	5.8	51.2	...	7.5	...	26.1	40.0	53.9	...	11.9	6.7
Charwomen and cleaners..........................	3.1	48.0	0.5	7.9	8.1	59.2	47.3	57.9	64.7	20.4	25.2
Cooks, except private household.................	6.6	32.3	0.8	8.7	8.6	59.9	54.7	61.3	46.2	27.2	7.9
Counter and fountain workers....................	7.9	15.7	1.0	10.2	10.4	38.9	41.2	54.2	42.7	17.9	6.5
Elevator operators..............................	3.0	29.0	1.1	8.5	10.5	62.4	39.1	74.6	64.3	27.4	4.8
Firemen, fire protection........................	1.7	11.9	1.4	11.2	...	87.1	70.0	92.5	...	3.9	5.0
Guards, watchmen, and doorkeepers...............	3.6	34.5	1.1	8.5	9.7	76.4	40.0	75.6	44.5	14.5	9.1
Housekeepers and stewards, exc.private household	6.4	16.9	5.4	10.7	10.2	65.6	31.5	69.0	65.6	17.6	14.0
Janitors and sextons............................	3.1	44.2	0.9	8.2	8.3	69.0	52.9	71.0	65.1	16.1	18.6
Marshals and constables.........................	2.4	20.0	1.5	9.4	...	84.4	46.2	85.3	...	2.1	...
Midwives..	...	59.3	1.9	...	...	60.0	49.0	...	...	...	8.2
Policemen and detectives........................	3.6	10.2	4.1	11.7	12.4	86.7	49.2	88.5	67.5	4.4	4.6
Government....................................	3.4	9.5	4.1	11.9	...	87.3	53.4	89.6	...	4.2	...
Private.......................................	5.0	16.2	3.6	10.0	...	82.1	40.5	78.2	...	6.3	14.3
Porters...	3.9	46.7	1.0	8.1	8.6	60.4	46.0	70.4	64.8	12.3	7.1
Practical nurses................................	8.4	15.0	2.6	8.9	10.7	49.1	32.5	60.9	42.6	9.2	9.0
Sheriffs and bailiffs...........................	1.9	15.5	4.5	10.7	...	85.5	56.5	86.1	...	4.3	...
Ushers, recreation and amusement................	4.6	8.7	0.2	10.4	10.6	7.4	11.1	40.1	27.6	1.4	2.0
Waiters and waitresses..........................	10.4	16.7	0.8	9.6	10.3	47.7	48.5	53.6	41.7	26.1	4.8
Watchmen (crossing) and bridge tenders..........	1.9	33.7	0.7	8.6	...	78.1	46.7	78.1	...	11.8	6.7
Service workers, exc. private household (n.e.c.)	7.3	36.0	1.1	8.6	8.5	36.2	43.5	50.7	53.3	18.6	10.0
FARM LABORERS AND FOREMEN............	8.6	47.6	0.6	8.0	8.2	35.9	65.5	52.5	45.2	6.7	4.0
Farm foremen....................................	6.0	34.1	3.4	8.8	...	85.9	47.6	79.5	...	9.9	14.3
Farm laborers, wage workers.....................	11.4	51.7	0.6	7.7	6.5	46.3	47.2	50.6	22.9	9.0	4.7
Farm laborers, unpaid family workers............	4.1	41.4	0.4	8.3	8.4	9.9	73.8	56.6	56.8	1.3	3.7
Farm service laborers, self-employed............	6.1	22.3	2.0	8.8	...	76.9	47.8	54.7	...	4.0	4.3

Table 17-A-4. DETAILED OCCUPATION BY SELECTED CHARACTERISTICS OF THE EXPERIENCED LABOR FORCE: 1950-Con.

Detailed occupation	Percent of migrant workers in 1949	Years of school completed — Less than 8	Years of school completed — 4 yrs. college or more	Median years of school completed — Male	Median years of school completed — Female	Percent married spouse present — Male	Percent married spouse present — Female	Percent full-time workers at work, 1949 50-52 weeks — Male	Percent full-time workers at work, 1949 50-52 weeks — Female	Percent foreign born — Male	Percent foreign born — Female
LABORERS, EXCEPT FARM AND MINE	6.0	43.7	0.6	8.2	8.8	62.9	52.1	49.8	47.9	10.0	8.2
Fishermen and oystermen	5.1	49.7	0.4	7.7	...	67.8	58.6	35.8	...	13.0	3.4
Garage laborers, & car washers and greasers	7.7	36.3	0.5	...	...	55.0	47.3	57.5	...	3.8	1.4
Gardeners, except farm, and groundkeepers	4.6	41.4	1.6	8.3	8.5	61.7	43.9	51.3	43.2	20.2	18.7
Longshoremen and stevedores	2.5	47.8	0.5	8.0	...	69.8	50.0	39.5	...	19.9	7.7
Lumbermen, raftsmen, and wood choppers	8.9	56.2	0.4	7.0	...	62.1	51.7	32.8	...	4.2	10.3
Teamsters	6.7	47.4	0.5	8.0	...	73.6	78.6	48.5	...	2.1	7.1
Laborers (n.e.c.)	5.9	43.0	0.6	8.3	8.8	62.8	52.3	51.2	48.6	9.7	8.0
Manufacturing	5.0	42.0	0.5	8.3	8.8	65.4	55.0	53.2	45.2	11.2	8.0
Durable goods	5.2	42.8	0.5	8.3	9.0	65.1	54.6	47.9	43.2	11.7	7.1
Sawmills, planing mills, & misc. wood prod.	7.9	56.7	0.3	6.9	8.7	63.3	60.6	46.3	41.4	3.7	3.8
Sawmills, planing mills, & mill work	8.2	56.9	0.4	6.9	...	63.0	58.8	45.8	...	3.2	1.2
Miscellaneous wood products	5.4	54.4	...	7.0	...	61.0	63.8	51.2	...	7.8	8.5
Furniture and fixtures	7.6	41.0	0.4	8.3	...	61.3	58.8	57.6	...	7.1	2.0
Stone, clay, and glass products	5.1	41.3	0.4	8.3	8.9	67.7	52.6	59.6	...	9.3	2.6
Glass and glass products	5.4	35.4	0.2	8.5	...	64.9	37.8	60.7	...	8.6	...
Cement, & conc., gypsum, & plaster prod.	5.4	42.9	0.5	8.2	...	69.7	71.4	62.3	...	9.7	28.6
Structural clay products	5.0	44.9	0.4	8.2	...	67.7	65.0	56.1	...	8.0	...
Pottery and related products	4.9	31.4	...	8.6	...	61.7	59.3	59.4	...	13.3	...
Misc. nonmetallic mineral & stone prod.	4.8	44.4	0.3	8.2	...	71.2	60.0	61.5	...	11.2	6.7
Metal industries	3.8	41.7	0.5	8.3	8.8	66.8	51.3	41.0	42.2	15.8	8.7
Primary metal industries	3.7	42.9	0.4	8.3	8.8	67.4	48.3	38.0	38.1	16.5	8.6
Blast furn., steel wks., & roll.mills.	3.4	41.4	0.5	8.4	...	66.1	50.9	29.7	...	17.7	3.5
Other prim.iron and steel industries	3.9	49.2	0.3	7.9	...	69.8	44.1	55.3	...	13.3	17.6
Primary nonferrous industries	5.2	39.1	0.5	8.4	...	69.8	48.0	53.5	...	15.8	8.0
Fab.metal ind.(incl.not spec.metal)	4.2	36.9	0.5	8.5	8.9	61.4	53.1	53.1	44.7	12.9	8.8
Fab. steel products	4.4	37.1	0.5	8.4	8.9	61.8	52.8	53.2	42.9	13.4	9.4
Fab. nonferrous metal products	3.2	32.9	...	8.8	...	58.6	61.5	55.3	...	8.3	...
Not specified metal industries	...	42.9	3.6	...	...	70.4	...	...	...	11.1	...
Machinery, except electrical	5.2	32.1	1.2	8.6	...	65.1	67.9	53.9	...	14.5	12.5
Agricultural machinery and tractors	6.6	24.9	2.4	8.8	...	64.4	81.8	55.0	...	7.1	9.1
Office and store machinery and devises	2.0	15.7	...	...	...	48.0	65.9	53.6	46.7	16.0	...
Miscellaneous machinery	4.9	35.0	0.8	8.6	...	65.9	54.2	62.5	...	16.8	13.6
Elec. machinery, equip., and supplies	3.2	25.2	1.0	8.9	...	62.2	...	...	...	15.1	7.7
Transportation equipment	4.7	36.3	0.6	8.5	...	64.3	57.8	51.0	...	13.3	7.8
Motor veh., and motor veh. equipment	5.6	33.9	0.5	8.6	...	64.2	61.4	46.3	...	13.5	7.1
Aircraft and parts	5.9	23.7	2.2	9.4	...	65.6	85.7	68.1	...	10.9	14.3
Ship & boat building and repairing	1.8	47.6	0.4	8.1	...	64.5	30.0	61.8	...	12.0	10.0
Railroad and misc.transpor. equipment	2.8	36.9	...	8.4	...	65.0	...	51.3	...	17.3	...
Prof. & photographic equip. & watches	5.5	29.0	0.7	8.7	...	72.9	81.5	64.4	...	16.9	11.1
Professional equipment and supplies	7.4	25.0	1.5	...	9.7	66.1	83.3	...	...	14.3	16.7

Table 17-A-4. DETAILED OCCUPATION BY SELECTED CHARACTERISTICS OF THE EXPERIENCED LABOR FORCE: 1950—Con.

Detailed occupation	Percent of migrant workers in 1949	Years of school completed		Median years of school completed		Percent married spouse present		Percent full-time workers at work, 1949 50-52 weeks		Percent foreign born	
		Less than 8	4 yrs. college or more	Male	Female	Male	Female	Male	Female	Male	Female
LABORERS, EXCEPT FARM AND MINE—Con.											
Photographic equipment and supplies......	1.9	34.0	...	...	...	83.0	83.3	...	...	21.3	16.7
Watches, clocks, & clockwork-oper.devices...	8.3	29.2	...	...	...	66.7	77.8	...	...	13.3	...
Miscellaneous manufacturing industries......	4.3	32.9	0.7	8.6	8.6	51.8	38.9	55.8	...	15.2	8.9
Nondurable goods..........	4.5	40.8	0.5	8.4	8.7	66.1	55.5	62.9	46.8	10.2	8.6
Food and kindred products..........	5.2	37.6	0.6	8.4	8.7	64.9	59.2	59.6	41.0	10.1	10.8
Meat products..........	5.6	35.8	0.7	8.5	8.8	67.2	60.9	66.2	...	10.0	7.0
Dairy products..........	6.3	28.0	0.8	8.7	...	67.4	65.4	65.6	...	6.0	11.5
Canning & preserv.fruits, veg.,& seafoods...	4.8	44.4	0.6	8.2	8.3	59.9	57.3	35.3	21.0	15.7	14.7
Grain-mill products..........	6.4	41.2	0.2	8.3	...	72.4	88.9	66.9	...	4.2	3.1
Bakery products..........	7.6	33.1	1.1	8.7	...	52.4	46.9	66.1	...	8.5	...
Confectionery and related products......	6.1	33.8	0.7	8.7	...	64.0	52.2	65.8	...	12.0	26.1
Beverage industries..........	2.7	34.2	0.8	8.6	...	60.4	66.7	60.4	...	9.9	9.5
Misc.food preparations & kindred products...	4.4	45.9	0.3	8.1	...	67.0	58.3	58.1	...	12.7	11.1
Not specified food industries......	4.1	24.6	1.6	8.9	...	64.4	61.9	...	...	14.9	4.8
Tobacco manufactures..........	1.8	59.9	...	6.8	...	62.9	54.3	62.3	...	6.9	2.2
Textile mill products..........	3.4	52.9	0.2	7.3	8.3	66.2	58.8	61.6	53.5	11.8	9.4
Knitting mills..........	6.7	43.3	...	...	...	57.4	54.5	...	...	14.7	...
Dyeing & finishing textiles, exc.knit goods...	2.0	45.5	1.0	...	...	57.0	83.5	...	...	17.2	15.4
Carpets, rugs, and other floor coverings...	1.9	35.9	0.5	8.6	...	68.4	53.8	69.0	...	21.9	9.7
Yarn, thread, and fabric mills......	3.6	56.2	0.1	6.8	8.2	66.9	58.8	60.8	51.9	9.4	20.0
Miscellaneous textile mill products......	2.1	50.5	1.1	8.3	8.8	67.1	60.0	55.3	45.5	18.8	9.4
Apparel and other fabricated textile products...	2.9	36.7	0.7	8.5	9.0	46.5	56.2	55.3	45.8	14.2	9.9
Apparel and accessories......	1.9	33.4	0.3	...	...	42.7	57.0	...	...	15.2	5.6
Miscellaneous fabricated textile products...	6.4	47.9	2.1	...	...	55.3	50.0	...	...	11.8	4.4
Paper and allied products......	4.6	39.4	0.3	8.4	...	68.0	54.4	65.3	...	9.4	4.8
Pulp, paper, and paperboard mills......	3.5	43.2	0.3	8.3	...	73.5	61.9	66.8	...	8.9	...
Paperboard containers and boxes......	7.0	32.1	0.6	8.7	...	50.6	51.2	62.6	...	8.6	...
Miscellaneous paper and pulp products......	5.2	35.0	...	8.5	...	66.5	53.8	62.4	...	11.9	11.5
Printing, publishing, and allied industries...	5.6	24.0	1.2	9.5	...	52.4	55.3	68.5	...	10.5	7.9
Chemicals and allied products......	5.0	44.1	0.6	8.2	...	68.4	43.0	65.0	...	9.1	8.0
Synthetic fibers......	5.1	44.1	1.7	8.2	...	82.1	50.0	...	...	3.6	...
Drugs and medicines......	4.7	18.8	...	...	...	62.7	46.2	...	...	9.8	28.6
Paints, varnishes, and related products......	2.3	35.3	0.8	8.8	...	56.3	...	57.3	...	17.5	8.1
Miscellaneous chemicals and allied products...	5.2	45.6	0.5	8.1	...	68.6	45.9	61.4	...	8.9	...
Petroleum and coal products......	3.8	37.2	0.6	8.7	...	77.0	46.7	76.5	...	7.7	...
Petroleum refining......	3.7	35.1	0.7	8.9	...	78.8	50.0	81.7	...	7.7	...
Miscellaneous petroleum and coal products...	4.0	46.9	...	8.1	...	68.8	40.0	51.6	...	7.6	...
Rubber products......	3.9	31.5	0.4	8.7	...	68.2	50.9	61.8	...	14.0	7.3
Leather and leather products......	3.5	32.2	0.2	8.5	...	57.1	46.1	56.2	...	13.1	7.9

Table 17-A-4. DETAILED OCCUPATION BY SELECTED CHARACTERISTICS OF THE EXPERIENCED LABOR FORCE: 1950-Con.

Detailed occupation	Percent of migrant workers in 1949	Years of school completed		Median years of school completed		Percent married spouse present		Percent full-time workers at work, 1949 50-52 weeks		Percent foreign born	
		Less than 8	4 yrs. college or more	Male	Female	Male	Female	Male	Female	Male	Female
LABORERS, EXC.FARM AND MINE—Con.											
Leather: tanned, curried, and finished..	2.1	39.7	...	8.4	...	67.2	66.7	56.6	...	16.1	22.2
Footwear, except rubber.........	4.0	25.7	...	8.7	...	46.8	42.9	52.5	...	7.1	6.1
Leather products, except footwear......	6.2	28.1	1.6	...	...	45.7	44.4	...	...	17.4	5.6
Not specified manufacturing industries......	8.5	34.4	0.6	8.5	...	55.8	47.8	45.6	...	11.9	10.9
Nonmanufact'ng industries (incl. not rep.)....	6.5	43.5	0.6	8.2	8.8	61.4	48.6	50.1	53.5	8.9	8.1
Construction........	7.7	44.4	0.6	8.2	8.5	63.0	55.9	38.7	40.4	8.7	6.9
Railroads and railway express service.....	6.0	48.1	0.3	8.0	8.3	67.8	36.4	60.7	63.5	11.9	10.2
Transportation, except railroad......	6.4	36.1	0.4	8.5	...	60.7	71.2	56.3	0	9.3	8.2
Telecommunications, & util. & san.services.	5.1	48.1	0.5	8.0	...	70.1	42.9	69.6	...	11.3	4.8
Wholesale and retail trade.....	5.6	34.3	0.7	8.7	9.8	53.3	52.5	56.5	54.9	6.7	6.7
Business and repair services.....	8.7	34.3	0.8	8.7	...	54.1	61.9	44.7	...	7.0	4.8
Personal services.....	5.1	59.4	0.4	6.4	8.4	48.1	36.8	37.0	51.1	6.1	5.5
Public administration.....	3.9	38.5	0.8	8.5	...	70.7	38.2	70.5	...	7.8	7.4
All other industries (incl. not reported)..	7.4	47.4	1.0	8.0	8.7	53.0	50.9	43.6	48.9	9.0	12.7
OCCUPATION NOT REPORTED.....	8.2	26.1	3.9	9.0	10.1	51.4	47.5	39.2	33.6	7.5	5.8

Table 17-A-5. DETAILED OCCUPATION BY SELECTED CHARACTERISTICS OF THE EMPLOYED PERSONS

Detailed occupation	Total employed	Percent urban	Class of worker				Percent part time at work 1-34 hrs.		Percent Negro 25-34 yrs.	
			Private wage and salary	Government	Self-employed	Unpaid	Male	Female	Male	Female
EMPLOYED TOTAL................	55,754,760	68.4	71.2	9.8	16.9	2.1	9.9	19.9	9.1	14.5
PROFESSIONAL, TECHNICAL, & KINDRED WKRS.....	4,857,810	80.6	52.0	34.9	13.0	1.6	8.2	22.6	2.5	8.1
Accountants and auditors........	376,770	91.3	75.4	15.2	9.4	...	2.6	5.4	0.5	1.2
Actors and actresses............	13,530	91.6	82.0	7.5	10.0	0.4	39.3	45.4	1.4	2.0
Airplane pilots and navigators..	13,650	81.5	85.1	7.3	7.7	...	39.9	12.5	0.4	...
Architects......................	23,550	86.3	47.9	11.1	41.0	...	2.2	6.9	3.0	...
Artists and art teachers........	78,600	89.3	60.6	15.0	24.0	0.3	10.7	25.8	1.3	2.7
Athletes........................	10,770	84.1	85.2	1.7	12.5	0.6	35.6	61.5	9.2	20.0
Authors.........................	15,360	81.2	33.6	3.7	62.3	0.4	19.7	40.2	...	...
Chemists........................	75,360	86.6	85.0	12.9	2.1	...	3.2	6.3	2.0	4.0
Chiropractors...................	12,420	85.0	12.3	...	87.4	0.3	10.8	31.0	1.1	50.0
Clergymen.......................	164,580	67.2	93.9	1.3	4.8	...	10.7	29.5	4.2	1.9
College presidents, prof., and instrs. (n.e.c.).	122,910	84.7	44.3	55.0	0.7	...	21.3	28.7	3.2	9.2
Dancers and dancing teachers....	15,120	92.5	72.6	3.0	23.4	1.0	33.6	52.2	14.8	3.8
Dentists........................	66,670	84.6	10.1	3.1	86.8	0.2	9.0	17.4	2.8	...
Designers.......................	38,760	89.9	84.5	2.4	12.8	...	2.7	14.9	1.7	6.7
Dietitians and nutritionists....	21,960	83.5	61.1	37.8	1.0	0.1	4.2	8.7	28.6	13.2
Draftsmen.......................	116,160	89.7	83.8	14.5	1.6	0.1	3.4	4.0	1.3	2.1
Editors and reporters...........	89,070	87.1	86.4	5.7	7.7	0.2	4.9	19.3	0.6	0.7
Engineers, technical............	517,770	85.6	76.9	18.8	4.3	...	1.9	11.2	0.6	3.9
Aeronautical....................	17,670	87.9	84.6	15.1	0.3	...	1.2	...	0.2	...
Chemical........................	30,840	85.3	90.8	6.0	3.2	...	1.6	15.8	0.2	...
Civil...........................	121,200	84.7	49.7	44.4	5.8	...	2.3	21.1	1.2	20.0
Electrical......................	105,240	86.3	83.6	14.1	2.2	0.1	1.9	5.0	1.0	...
Industrial......................	40,170	86.5	90.8	6.6	2.6	...	1.1	6.7	...	...
Mechanical......................	107,220	86.0	85.6	10.2	4.2	...	1.5	9.1	0.4	...
Metallurgical, ad metallurgists.	12,600	84.5	93.6	4.5	1.9	...	1.2	...	...	...
Mining..........................	11,100	74.6	87.6	5.7	6.8	...	3.9	...	...	...
Not elsewhere classified........	71,730	86.3	80.1	12.8	7.2	...	2.7	10.7	0.5	...
Entertainers (n.e.c.)...........	15,420	79.2	74.3	1.9	22.4	1.4	29.0	38.3	12.6	13.3
Farm and home management advisors.	10,740	63.7	21.5	76.8	1.7	...	2.1	5.5	1.5	11.5
Foresters and conservationists..	26,040	38.5	16.0	81.2	2.8	...	4.3	11.8	0.8	...
Funeral directors and embalmers.	37,860	78.0	50.9	0.5	48.3	0.3	5.2	17.1	7.4	20.0
Lawyers and judges..............	171,480	89.2	25.6	14.1	60.3	...	3.9	9.3	0.7	1.8
Librarians......................	56,790	84.1	32.5	67.1	0.1	0.3	33.7	27.0	4.3	6.2
Musicians and music teachers....	154,380	83.8	51.9	18.2	29.8	0.1	46.1	61.5	7.3	6.1
Natural scientists (n.e.c.).....	37,860	82.0	48.5	45.2	6.2	0.1	4.5	9.3	1.9	5.6
Nurses, professional............	403,470	84.0	73.4	22.0	4.4	0.4	5.9	10.4	6.5	4.3
Nurses, student professional....	76,770	94.1	79.6	20.4	...	...	14.0	7.9	4.8	4.2

Table 17-A-5. DETAILED OCCUPATION BY SELECTED CHARACTERISTICS OF THE EMPLOYED PERSONS.-Con.

Detailed occupation	Total employed	Percent urban	Class of worker				Percent part time at work 1-34 hrs.		Percent Negro 23-34 yrs.	
			Private wage and salary	Government	Self-employed	Unpaid	Male	Female	Male	Female
PROFESSIONAL, TECHNICAL, & KIND.WKRS.-Con.										
Optometrists	14,880	90.5	28.4	0.6	71.0	...	5.2	24.1	1.4	...
Osteopaths	5,100	82.4	14.7	2.4	82.9	...	7.7	31.8	...	...
Personnel and labor relations workers	52,410	91.0	63.6	34.6	1.4	0.2	1.3	2.9	0.9	1.5
Pharmacists	84,480	86.1	53.2	2.7	43.9	0.2	4.0	12.3	2.8	4.8
Photographers	50,250	88.0	52.7	5.9	40.8	0.7	8.5	19.5	2.3	2.7
Physicians and surgeons	178,950	85.4	21.8	14.0	64.2	...	3.7	11.9	2.5	8.6
Radio operators	16,080	85.3	42.0	57.1	0.9	...	4.0	7.7	0.8	...
Recreation and group workers	16,410	90.9	57.0	40.0	2.2	0.7	16.3	24.3	7.4	6.3
Religious workers	40,950	78.4	85.3	1.5	10.0	3.2	11.7	22.2	6.6	2.2
Social and welfare workers, except group	76,890	86.1	34.8	64.3	0.5	0.4	4.7	8.1	8.3	13.6
Social scientists	33,780	89.3	54.0	41.5	4.4	0.1	4.2	10.1	1.2	6.0
Sports instructors and officials	44,370	75.4	31.4	64.8	3.8	...	16.1	24.8	3.2	4.8
Surveyors	24,120	70.5	44.3	49.5	6.1	0.1	6.8	15.8	1.2	...
Teachers (n.e.c.)	1,122,570	65.9	16.3	82.5	1.0	0.1	17.0	29.9	8.0	13.6
Technicians, medical and dental	78,390	91.0	73.0	19.1	7.7	0.2	7.5	7.5	4.7	6.5
Technicians, testing	75,420	78.8	90.2	8.5	1.2	0.1	5.5	8.5	1.6	3.2
Technicians (n.e.c.)	26,610	84.4	60.3	36.9	2.8	...	7.3	11.3	1.5	7.1
Therapists and healers (n.e.c.)	23,400	88.7	41.0	21.4	37.4	0.1	12.3	23.9	6.4	3.3
Veterinarians	11,370	59.1	17.7	15.6	66.5	0.3	6.8	20.0	1.0	...
Professional, tech.,& kindred wkrs. (n.e.c.)	115,830	86.7	62.8	31.4	5.6	0.1	11.6	16.6	1.2	2.5
FARMERS AND FARM MANAGERS	4,284,360	2.8	0.8	0.1	99.1	...	12.7	37.2	12.2	33.4
Farmers (owners and tenants)	4,248,300	2.7	...	...	100.0	...	12.7	37.2	12.3	33.6
Farm managers	36,060	23.5	94.3	5.1	...	0.6	6.5	33.9	4.2	...
MANAGERS, OFF., & PROP'S., except farm	4,893,750	78.6	42.6	6.6	50.5	0.4	3.4	9.4	1.9	5.2
Buyers and department heads, store	141,510	90.7	93.1	0.3	6.3	0.3	2.0	3.1	0.5	1.7
Buyers and shippers, farm products	26,310	47.2	28.7	0.6	70.6	0.1	10.1	30.8	0.8	33.3
Conductors, railroad	54,720	84.6	98.6	1.4	...	...	5.2	...	1.0	...
Credit men	33,900	94.5	98.1	0.8	1.1	...	1.6	3.2	0.4	...
Floormen and floor managers, store	10,560	91.8	99.1	...	0.9	...	4.8	6.3	4.2	...
Inspectors, public administration	56,670	81.9	...	100.0	...	...	2.6	18.3	1.2	8.3
Federal public administration & postal serv.	26,940	81.1	...	100.0	...	...	1.3	4.3	1.1	...
State public administration	9,660	73.9	...	100.0	...	...	4.2	16.7	...	...
Local public administration	20,070	86.8	...	100.0	...	...	3.6	26.2	1.9	12.5
Managers and superintendents, building	65,970	95.1	69.7	2.5	27.4	0.5	6.4	17.2	14.7	8.9
Officers, pilots, pursers, and engrs., ship	38,010	82.5	84.9	6.8	8.3	...	4.4	13.2	1.8	...
Officials & admin'rs.,(n.e.c.), pub. admin'trn.	152,070	73.4	...	100.0	...	...	4.1	9.9	3.4	1.5
Federal pub. admin. and postal service	48,450	83.7	...	100.0	...	...	1.9	3.6	3.8	2.4
State public administration	22,230	70.3	...	100.0	...	...	3.4	1.5	0.8	...
Local public administration	81,390	68.1	...	100.0	...	...	5.8	12.7	4.2	1.2

Table 17-A-5. DETAILED OCCUPATION BY SELECTED CHARACTERISTICS OF THE EMPLOYED PERSONS -Con.

Detailed occupation	Total employed	Percent urban	Class of worker				Percent part time at work 1-34 hrs.		Percent Negro 25-34 yrs.	
			Private wage and salary	Government	Self-employed	Unpaid	Male	Female	Male	Female
MGRS., OFF., & PROPRIETORS, EXC. FARM-Con.										
Officials, lodge, society, union, etc.	28,290	87.5	100.0	...	...	...	5.1	14.0	5.1	14.3
Postmasters	38,490	26.3	...	100.0	...	...	1.4	11.0	3.4	3.6
Purchasing agents and buyers (n.e.c.)	64,110	87.5	88.4	8.5	3.0	...	1.6	5.2	2.0	2.1
Managers, off., & prop. (n.e.c.)-salaried	1,747,290	82.7	96.3	3.7	...	...	2.3	8.4	1.3	3.3
Construction	84,570	76.1	87.0	13.0	...	...	4.4	6.5	3.5	6.7
Manufacturing	406,620	85.0	99.7	0.4	...	...	1.9	5.7	0.4	1.6
Transportation	93,660	88.7	96.0	4.0	...	...	1.2	4.5	0.6	3.0
Telecomm., & utilities & sanitary services	58,410	78.6	86.7	13.3	...	...	1.1	1.1	0.5	...
Wholesale trade	152,070	83.8	99.7	0.3	...	...	2.0	8.4	0.6	3.4
Retail trade	501,030	81.2	98.8	1.1	...	...	1.5	6.4	1.5	3.8
Food and dairy products stores, & milk ret.	98,400	79.5	99.3	0.7	...	...	1.4	6.1	2.0	10.8
Gen. mdse. and five and ten cent stores	58,080	82.6	98.8	1.2	...	...	1.6	2.7	0.4	1.0
Apparel and accessories stores	41,310	93.2	99.6	0.4	...	...	1.4	1.3	...	...
Furniture, home furn., & equipment stores	27,300	86.2	99.9	0.1	...	...	1.4	10.1	0.6	...
Motor vehicles and accessories retailing	54,930	82.6	99.7	0.3	...	...	0.4	5.2	2.0	6.0
Gasoline service stations	33,660	69.2	99.2	0.9	...	...	1.7	9.5	5.4	...
Eating and drinking places	68,670	83.7	98.6	1.4	...	...	2.1	11.7	0.3	...
Hardware, farm imp., & bldg. material retail	42,990	69.5	99.7	0.3	...	...	1.2	6.7	1.6	...
Other retail trade	75,690	82.7	96.7	3.3	...	...	2.4	7.2	...	4.4
Banking and other finance	111,360	79.8	96.0	4.0	...	...	3.6	8.3	...	...
Insurance and real estate	70,620	91.6	97.1	2.9	...	...	2.1	6.7	3.3	...
Business services	27,090	91.7	99.0	0.1	...	...	2.8	10.8	2.8	...
Automobile repair services and garages	23,700	75.8	98.5	1.5	...	...	0.6	6.7	2.4	...
Miscellaneous repair services	4,530	89.4	98.0	2.0	...	...	3.6	...	4.6	9.5
Personal services	61,440	86.4	99.2	0.8	...	...	2.8	8.2	2.3	3.9
All other industries (incl. not reported)	152,190	77.6	82.5	17.5	...	...	5.5	16.6	...	...
Managers, off., & prop., (n.e.c.)-self-employed	2,435,850	75.2	...	...	99.3	0.7	4.2	10.3	2.4	7.8
Construction	191,910	80.4	...	...	100.0	...	8.1	22.2	1.8	5.9
Manufacturing	231,660	79.0	...	...	99.8	0.2	4.8	14.6	1.1	2.0
Transportation	51,090	80.8	...	...	99.7	0.3	7.8	7.6	4.9	...
Telecomm., & utilities & sanitary services	4,260	62.0	...	...	98.6	1.4	7.6	28.6	7.7	...
Wholesale trade	175,020	84.7	...	...	99.7	0.3	5.8	17.3	1.9	10.3
Retail trade	1,356,780	72.3	...	...	99.2	0.8	2.5	9.0	2.2	8.5
Food and dairy products stores, & milk ret.	379,560	71.3	...	...	99.0	1.0	2.1	7.6	2.9	8.1
Gen. mdse. and five and ten cent stores	63,840	55.9	...	...	98.6	1.4	2.4	11.8	0.9	3.2
Apparel and accessories stores	82,200	91.3	...	...	99.7	0.3	1.9	9.4	1.6	2.0
Furniture, home furn., & equipment stores	66,240	85.0	...	...	99.6	0.4	2.0	12.7	...	...
Motor vehicles and accessories retailing	58,620	77.6	...	...	99.9	0.1	1.5	9.8	...	...

Table 17-A-5. DETAILED OCCUPATION BY SELECTED CHARACTERISTICS OF THE EMPLOYED PERSONS -Con.

Detailed occupation	Total employed	Percent urban	Class of worker: Private wage and salary	Government	Self-employed	Unpaid	Percent part time at work 1-34 hrs. Male	Female	Percent Negro 25-34 yrs. Male	Female
MGR.,OFF.,& PROPRIETORS,EXC.FARM-Con.										
Managers,off., & prop. (n.e.c.)-self-emp-Con..										
Gasoline service stations	143,280	59.7	...	...	99.6	0.4	1.3	9.0	1.1	8.6
Eating and drinking places	273,930	72.4	...	...	98.4	1.6	2.4	7.1	4.5	12.3
Hardware, farm imp.,& bldg.material retail	79,020	66.6	...	...	99.8	0.2	3.1	15.7	...	...
Other retail trade	210,090	77.1	...	...	99.4	0.6	4.3	12.7	2.1	7.7
Banking and other finance	20,910	84.5	...	...	99.3	0.7	8.8	12.7	...	...
Insurance and real estate	45,030	91.1	...	...	99.1	0.9	8.9	11.5	0.9	7.7
Business services	33,420	92.8	...	...	99.6	0.4	5.9	13.9	3.6	7.4
Automobile repair services and garages	59,640	67.5	...	...	99.8	0.2	2.7	21.6	1.3	...
Miscellaneous repair services	29,100	84.3	...	...	99.8	0.2	8.5	9.5	2.2	...
Personal services	139,560	73.1	...	...	98.2	1.8	4.1	11.7	9.8	7.9
All other industries (incl. not reported)	97,470	65.8	...	...	99.2	0.8	8.6	14.5	3.5	3.6
CLERICAL AND KINDRED WORKERS	6,864,600	86.3	78.4	20.0	1.1	0.5	5.6	9.1	5.7	2.9
Agents (n.e.c.)	120,960	84.5	66.8	29.0	4.0	0.2	3.5	18.2	0.9	5.8
Attendants and assistants, library	11,610	84.8	37.8	60.8	1.6	...	60.7	45.6	4.0	3.8
Attendants, physician's and dentist's office	42,090	86.2	90.7	4.0	2.1	3.3	15.5	14.6	4.8	3.0
Baggagemen, transportation	8,310	89.5	96.4	2.5	0.7	0.4	3.8	...	34.3	25.0
Bank tellers	61,710	84.8	96.5	3.4	...	...	3.1	6.6	0.3	...
Bookkeepers	715,860	81.1	89.2	5.6	3.1	2.1	4.7	11.4	2.6	1.0
Cashiers	230,310	88.2	91.9	4.6	1.9	1.6	10.0	18.6	4.1	4.1
Collectors, bill and account	23,820	88.4	88.9	3.3	7.3	0.5	9.2	30.6	4.1	14.8
Dispatchers and starters, vehicle	31,530	89.9	86.2	12.2	1.0	0.7	2.8	10.9	0.9	4.8
Express messengers and railway mail clerks	17,850	84.7	21.0	79.0	...	...	3.6	10.0	7.5	...
Mail carriers	164,070	73.4	...	100.0	...	...	7.6	39.8	10.8	4.8
Messengers and office boys	55,200	90.5	83.7	15.2	0.8	0.3	22.3	16.2	35.0	3.7
Office machine operators	142,530	93.0	84.1	15.6	0.3	...	5.2	3.7	4.7	4.1
Shipping and receiving clerks	287,400	86.2	98.7	1.0	0.2	0.1	3.6	8.5	8.1	7.2
Stenographers, typists, and secretaries	1,579,770	89.4	79.1	19.8	0.8	0.3	6.1	6.8	5.3	2.6
Telegraph messengers	7,800	92.7	100.0	...	...	...	27.8	33.3	21.4	...
Telegraph operators	34,380	70.2	97.7	2.4	...	...	3.4	6.3	0.6	...
Telephone operators	356,760	83.4	95.7	4.1	0.2	0.1	8.3	8.2	6.5	1.3
Ticket, station, and express agents	61,800	74.3	95.6	3.2	1.1	0.1	1.6	4.8	0.8	...
Clerical and kindred workers (n.e.c.)	2,910,840	86.9	73.7	25.0	0.8	0.4	5.3	9.6	5.5	4.2
SALES WORKERS	3,893,400	81.6	86.7	0.4	10.8	0.2	10.4	24.4	1.4	3.2
Advertising agents and salesmen	34,290	89.5	87.9	1.3	10.5	0.3	6.0	13.3	0.7	...
Auctioneers	5,250	66.3	48.6	1.1	49.7	0.6	25.0	27.3	...	...
Demonstrators	13,440	85.7	92.6	1.3	5.6	0.5	8.4	53.1	4.8	6.1

Table 17-A-5. DETAILED OCCUPATION BY SELECTED CHARACTERISTICS OF THE EMPLOYED PERSONS -Con.

Detailed occupation	Total employed	Percent urban	Class of worker				Percent part time at work 1-34 hrs.		Percent Negro 25-34 yrs.	
			Private wage and salary	Government	Self-employed	Unpaid	Male	Female	Male	Female
SALES WORKERS-Con.										
Hucksters and peddlers	22,170	80.6	48.2	...	50.9	0.9	29.6	43.4	20.3	9.1
Insurance agents and brokers	301,680	85.8	84.5	14.4	0.9	0.1	4.9	19.4	1.6	12.4
Newsboys	104,610	83.7	91.5	...	8.5	...	80.0	54.3	8.2	3.7
Real estate agents and brokers	139,080	85.3	52.3	0.5	46.7	0.5	7.7	23.4	2.5	4.8
Stock and bond salesmen	10,830	89.5	87.8	2.2	9.4	0.6	5.6	11.8	1.8	...
Salesmen and sales clerks (n.e.c.)	3,262,050	80.9	88.5	0.4	8.7	2.4	7.8	24.2	1.3	3.0
Manufacturing	315,210	88.9	95.1	0.1	4.6	0.3	4.2	30.5	0.5	1.8
Wholesale trade	398,820	88.7	91.7	...	8.0	0.2	3.5	20.6	0.5	3.7
Retail trade	2,421,660	78.4	87.1	0.3	9.5	3.1	10.1	23.9	1.8	3.0
Other industries (incl. not reported)	126,360	83.1	87.4	3.6	7.6	1.5	7.2	31.6	1.0	4.1
CRAFTSMEN, FOREMEN, & KINDRED WKRS.	7,700,760	74.4	84.0	6.4	9.5	0.1	7.9	11.6	3.9	7.5
Bakers	115,410	88.8	87.5	1.8	10.3	0.3	4.9	16.9	8.6	23.7
Blacksmiths	41,010	51.6	65.2	4.5	30.1	0.2	12.9	12.5	2.2	...
Boilermakers	35,070	84.4	93.9	5.0	1.1	...	5.9	...	2.0	...
Bookbinders	32,190	91.2	93.8	4.2	2.0	...	5.2	11.9	3.3	6.5
Brickmasons, stonemasons, and tile setters	164,430	71.9	83.7	1.6	14.5	0.1	23.9	32.0	13.3	25.0
Cabinetmakers	72,060	74.9	79.6	2.3	18.0	0.2	8.4	3.8	3.3	12.5
Carpenters	902,430	58.2	78.7	3.3	17.8	0.2	16.8	16.2	3.3	5.0
Cement and concrete finishers	28,380	80.0	90.2	3.7	6.0	0.1	20.0	16.7	24.3	100.0
Compositors and typesetters	172,590	86.8	90.5	2.3	7.0	0.2	4.5	11.1	2.3	3.5
Cranemen, derrickmen, and hoistmen	102,960	73.1	95.7	3.7	0.6	...	5.7	...	7.4	...
Decorators and window dressers	42,360	88.0	83.9	3.7	11.3	0.3	7.7	17.9	3.9	8.5
Electricians	304,260	74.2	80.2	10.4	9.4	...	7.7	6.2	3.2	...
Electrotypers and stereotypers	11,070	83.5	98.4	1.6	...	...	6.2	14.3	1.2	...
Engravers, except photoengravers	9,600	88.4	89.7	2.8	7.5	...	4.8	4.5	2.9	6.7
Excavating, grading, and road mach. operators	105,090	44.7	70.1	25.7	4.1	0.1	8.3	...	3.5	...
Foremen (n.e.c.)	840,660	76.1	93.6	6.4	...	...	2.1	5.0	1.1	3.8
Construction	58,470	63.3	71.9	28.1	...	...	4.1	...	0.8	...
Manufacturing	506,610	79.8	99.4	0.6	...	...	1.8	4.8	0.7	4.7
Metal industries	82,350	83.2	99.2	0.8	...	...	1.7	2.0	1.3	...
Machinery, including electrical	80,190	85.0	99.9	0.1	...	...	1.5	1.8	0.6	...
Transportation equipment	48,330	85.8	96.8	3.2	...	...	0.9	4.2	1.0	...
Other durable goods	75,270	68.9	99.8	0.1	...	...	2.5	6.1	0.8	6.0
Textiles, textile products and apparel	69,360	74.2	99.7	0.2	...	...	3.5	5.3	0.3	5.2
Other nondurable goods (incl. not spec. mfg.)	151,110	81.4	99.5	0.5	...	...	1.4	5.1	0.5	3.1
Railroads and railway express service	55,020	63.9	98.7	1.3	...	...	2.3	...	0.8	...
Transportation, except railroad	20,250	83.1	88.9	10.8	...	0.3	1.3	...	2.1	...
Telecomm., & utilities & sanitary services	42,300	80.0	82.6	17.4	...	...	...	...	1.3	...
Other industries (incl. not reported)	158,010	71.0	84.8	15.0	...	0.2	3.0	6.1	2.5	4.2

Table 17-A-5. DETAILED OCCUPATION BY SELECTED CHARACTERISTICS OF THE EMPLOYED PERSONS -Con.

Detailed occupation	Total employed	Percent urban	Class of worker				Percent part time at work 1-34 hrs.		Percent Negro 25-34 yrs.	
			Private wage and salary	Government	Self-employed	Unpaid	Male	Female	Male	Female
CRAFTSMEN, FOREMEN, & KINDRED WKRS.-Con.										
Forgemen and hammermen	13,650	78.0	96.7	1.3	2.0	...	6.9	16.7	4.4	...
Furriers	11,370	91.8	91.8	0.8	7.1	0.3	12.4	10.9	2.7	...
Glaziers	10,620	81.1	86.2	2.3	10.5	1.1	8.1	14.3	3.7	...
Heat treaters, annealers, and temperers	18,720	84.3	99.4	0.3	0.3	...	6.8	7.1	4.6	...
Inspectors, scalers, and graders, log and lumber	17,370	48.4	97.6	1.2	1.2	...	8.2	11.4	8.3	46.2
Inspectors (n.e.c.)	93,360	78.4	85.2	14.8	...	...	2.6	7.6	2.9	1.5
Construction	7,110	70.0	25.7	74.3	...	...	1.3	25.0	...	...
Railroads and railway express service	36,300	77.8	99.2	0.7	...	...	1.3	8.3	2.4	...
Transport.exc. r.r.,communic'n, & other pub.ut	11,190	84.2	60.9	39.1	...	...	1.1	8.3	5.1	...
Other industries (incl. not reported)	38,760	78.8	89.9	10.1	...	...	4.7	7.4	3.2	1.7
Jewelers	45,120	83.6	67.6	0.9	31.3	0.2	9.6	14.9	1.6	17.4
Job setters, metal	21,420	85.5	99.3	0.7	...	0.4	3.1	20.0	0.9	...
Linemen & servicemen, teleg, telephone, & power	210,240	77.4	94.3	5.3	...	...	1.5	4.9	1.1	2.3
Locomotive engineers	71,220	83.2	99.2	0.6	...	...	6.8	28.6	0.3	...
Locomotive firemen	53,760	87.8	99.4	0.3	...	...	7.3	28.6	0.4	...
Loom fixers	29,100	72.9	99.0	0.3	0.7	...	7.1	6.8	1.8	5.3
Machinists	503,520	81.4	92.6	5.8	1.5	...	3.7	...	...	...
Mechanics and repairmen	1,690,980	73.0	81.5	10.0	8.3	0.1	4.8	12.7	4.5	8.4
Airplane	70,560	83.8	62.2	36.9	0.8	...	3.0	8.0	1.6	18.2
Automobile	642,840	65.0	81.8	4.4	13.6	0.1	4.6	7.0	5.8	4.7
Office machine	17,040	88.7	87.7	7.4	4.9	...	3.3	...	1.0	...
Radio and television	75,860	82.6	70.1	10.8	18.9	0.2	7.2	13.1	3.0	14.3
Railroad and car shop	48,030	78.7	94.4	5.5	0.1	...	2.4	6.9	6.9	...
Not elsewhere classified	838,650	76.7	83.1	12.3	4.5	0.1	5.1	15.1	3.8	8.1
Millers, grain, flour, feed, etc	9,150	43.6	84.3	0.3	15.4	...	5.6	10.0	8.8	50.0
Millwrights	55,280	71.8	98.4	1.0	0.6	...	4.1	14.3	1.8	25.0
Molders, metal	57,810	78.3	98.6	0.7	0.7	0.1	13.6	35.7	21.6	11.5
Motion picture projectionists	26,910	79.7	95.8	2.1	2.0	0.1	21.2	11.1	6.9	8.8
Opticians, and lens grinders and polishers	19,230	89.5	88.3	0.8	10.9	...	3.8	24.9	1.5	...
Painters, construction and maintenance	389,610	75.8	63.6	5.8	30.4	0.2	18.6	64.7	6.6	12.5
Paperhangers	20,490	68.7	38.2	...	61.1	0.7	37.0	...	13.2	...
Pattern and model makers, except paper	33,810	79.1	91.4	2.9	5.6	0.1	2.9	5.1	1.4	...
Photoengravers and lithographers	30,420	92.5	92.6	2.2	5.2	...	2.2	...	1.1	66.7
Piano and organ tuners and repairmen	8,190	83.2	50.5	2.2	47.3	...	27.2	11.8	...	50.0
Plasterers	60,630	78.5	78.5	1.2	20.2	...	22.0	7.7	17.2	5.6
Plumbers and pipe fitters	273,930	75.2	78.2	6.5	15.2	0.1	8.4	19.5	3.3	...
Pressmen and plate printers, printing	50,190	89.5	95.1	3.6	1.3	...	4.3	9.2	1.5	...
Rollers and roll hands, metal	32,070	81.5	99.4	0.3	0.2	0.1	6.6	21.7	11.7	...
Roofers and slaters	43,380	82.3	81.3	0.9	17.8	...	30.9	40.0	4.9	...
Shoemakers and repairers, except factory	54,480	81.3	39.9	0.9	58.3	0.8	8.1	12.5	20.9	33.3

Table 17-A-5. DETAILED OCCUPATION BY SELECTED CHARACTERISTICS OF THE EMPLOYED PERSONS.—Con.

Detailed occupation	Total employed	Percent urban	Class of worker				Percent part time at work 1-34 hrs.		Percent Negro 25-34 yrs.	
			Private wage and salary	Government	Self-employed	Unpaid	Male	Female	Male	Female
CRAFTSMEN, FOREMEN & KINDRED WKRS.—Con.										
Stationary engineers	214,320	70.5	85.2	13.7	1.0	...	2.0	3.5	1.8	5.0
Stone cutters and stone carvers	9,120	70.7	88.8	1.0	10.2	...	10.5	...	5.3	...
Structural metal workers	48,420	78.9	89.2	9.2	1.7	...	12.1	...	1.0	...
Tailors and tailoresses	80,400	94.0	71.6	1.5	26.5	0.3	7.7	17.5	16.4	19.4
Tinsmiths, coppersmiths, and sheet metal wkrs	118,710	82.3	85.0	8.6	6.4	...	6.1	4.4	1.0	...
Toolmakers, and die makers and setters	153,870	85.0	96.6	1.7	1.7	...	3.1	6.5	0.4	...
Upholsterers	60,330	82.1	79.6	1.5	18.3	0.5	9.0	14.2	3.7	11.3
Craftsmen and kindred workers (n.e.c.)	72,990	83.4	85.3	9.0	5.6	0.1	9.5	29.3	4.7	8.3
Members of the armed forces	...	...	...	...	...	...	...	...	...	...
OPERATIVES AND KINDRED WORKERS	11,065,800	72.8	93.1	3.3	3.3	0.2	9.7	16.9	9.7	12.1
Apprentices	115,470	83.2	95.0	4.6	...	0.4	9.6	14.7	2.5	12.5
Auto mechanics	3,750	72.8	94.4	3.2	...	2.4	14.4	20.0	3.1	...
Bricklayers and masons	6,540	83.5	100.0	3.3	...	...	26.5	...	6.2	...
Carpenters	10,050	77.9	96.7	3.3	...	...	14.5	...	1.1	...
Electricians	9,540	79.9	91.8	8.2	...	...	7.3	...	0.9	...
Machinists and toolmakers	14,640	82.8	95.1	4.9	...	0.4	4.4	...	0.6	...
Mechanics, except auto	7,350	80.0	87.8	11.8	...	0.4	5.5	19.0	5.2	...
Plumbers and pipe fitters	11,640	85.6	96.4	3.4	...	0.2	6.9	10.0	1.3	...
Building trades (n.e.c.)	3,720	86.3	96.0	3.2	...	0.8	23.5	...	13.3	...
Metalworking trades (n.e.c.)	7,290	87.7	90.9	8.6	...	0.4	6.9	...	1.3	...
Printing trades	14,820	86.8	98.8	1.0	...	0.2	6.2	14.3	0.6	...
Other specified trades	12,120	83.9	93.8	5.2	...	1.0	11.7	13.3	6.3	...
Trade not specified	14,010	84.8	95.1	4.1	...	0.9	7.4	31.2	1.6	...
Asbestos and insulation workers	15,330	76.5	94.3	2.5	3.1	...	9.7	7.7	2.7	...
Attendants, auto service and parking	236,340	67.5	93.6	0.6	3.4	2.3	13.4	20.8	10.2	4.3
Blasters and powdermen	10,530	39.9	96.3	1.9	1.7	...	21.4	42.9	7.6	...
Boatmen, canalmen, and lock keepers	7,950	61.1	55.1	36.6	8.3	...	3.6	9.1	6.2	...
Brakemen, railroad	77,250	79.7	99.1	0.9	...	...	7.7	55.8	2.2	23.1
Bus drivers	153,030	69.6	64.4	34.0	1.5	1.0	12.7	66.7	4.5	7.0
Chainmen, rodmen, and axmen, surveying	6,390	60.1	61.5	37.1	0.5	...	13.9	1.5	1.5	...
Conductors, bus and street railway	11,040	98.1	30.4	69.6	...	1.0	3.7	9.1	22.1	16.7
Deliverymen and routemen	238,500	82.4	94.6	0.3	5.0	0.2	12.7	30.9	7.5	8.9
Dressmakers and seamstresses, except factory	139,420	84.3	66.0	2.5	31.0	0.5	19.7	27.0	18.7	18.7
Dyers	23,100	72.2	99.1	...	1.0	...	15.3	20.6	7.4	9.1
Filers, grinders, and polishers, metal	142,620	79.6	96.7	0.5	2.7	0.1	7.1	5.3	8.4	4.9
Fruit, nut, & veg. graders & packers, exc.factory	27,600	62.8	98.3	0.8	0.8	0.2	23.7	43.7	8.4	5.7
Furnacemen, smeltermen, and pourers	55,410	79.6	99.2	0.4	0.4	...	6.9	10.0	20.8	15.4
Heaters, metal	7,800	82.3	99.2	0.4	0.4	...	4.6	8.3	8.1	50.0
Laundry and dry cleaning operatives	425,190	84.5	90.5	3.2	5.5	0.8	8.3	15.0	39.0	47.4
Meat cutters, except slaughter and packing house	167,700	81.2	87.8	0.8	11.2	0.3	6.2	15.6	5.3	...

Table 17-A-5. DETAILED OCCUPATION BY SELECTED CHARACTERISTICS OF THE EMPLOYED PERSONS -Con.

Detailed occupation	Total employed	Percent urban	Class of worker				Percent part time at work 1-34 hrs.		Percent Negro 25-34 yrs.	
			Private wage and salary	Government	Self-employed	Unpaid	Male	Female	Male	Female
OPERATIVES AND KINDRED WORKERS-Con.										
Milliners	13,410	95.3	89.0	0.2	10.3	0.5	9.3	16.9	12.5	13.9
Mine operatives and laborers (n.e.c.)	563,160	32.2	97.4	0.3	2.3	...	25.6	18.2	6.1	6.4
Coal mining	355,710	26.3	98.1	...	1.7	...	36.2	31.0	7.1	9.1
Crude petroleum and nat. gas extraction	100,830	46.4	97.9	0.1	2.0	...	5.4	5.9	0.7	...
Mining and quarrying, except fuel	106,620	38.2	94.3	1.0	4.6	...	9.0	14.7	9.0	6.3
Motormen, mine, factory, logging camp, etc.	25,290	33.7	98.6	1.3	0.1	...	27.3	42.9	5.6	...
Motormen, street, subway, and elevated railway	27,210	95.0	55.6	44.3	0.1	...	2.5	...	7.0	20.0
Oilers and greasers, except auto	61,680	64.2	95.0	4.7	0.3	...	6.0	3.8	6.2	7.7
Painters, except construction and maintenance	115,770	77.8	95.9	1.5	2.5	0.1	5.8	12.1	7.9	8.1
Photographic process workers	29,550	90.4	84.1	8.2	6.1	1.7	6.7	17.3	4.8	8.4
Power station operators	21,420	67.6	85.1	14.7	0.1	...	1.1	10.5	1.4	33.3
Sailors and deck hands	39,210	85.8	89.1	9.3	1.3	0.2	7.0	22.2	15.0	10.0
Sawyers	93,060	32.1	93.3	0.4	6.0	0.3	17.1	18.2	25.1	8.0
Spinners, textile	81,390	59.3	99.3	0.5	0.3	...	12.6	27.2	2.8	0.6
Stationary firemen	121,800	70.5	84.3	15.7	...	...	3.7	8.5	12.7	14.3
Switchmen, railroad	59,160	84.6	97.6	2.3	...	...	3.9	9.1	1.6	...
Taxicab drivers and chauffeurs	202,650	89.1	84.3	5.6	10.0	0.1	5.3	23.3	14.4	18.4
Truck and tractor drivers	1,315,410	65.1	82.4	7.3	10.2	0.1	11.2	21.4	11.2	11.8
Weavers, textile	97,470	62.7	96.3	0.2	3.3	0.2	11.3	15.2	0.4	7.0
Welders and flame-cutters	257,430	73.8	92.0	3.2	4.7	...	5.4	7.4	4.8	7.0
Operatives and kindred workers (n.e.c.)	6,080,310	76.5	97.1	1.8	1.0	0.1	8.3	16.1	9.8	8.7
Manufacturing	5,366,070	76.6	98.9	0.3	0.6	0.1	8.1	15.9	9.0	8.2
Durable goods	2,385,630	77.6	98.8	0.4	0.8	0.1	6.8	9.4	9.2	6.8
Sawmills, plan'ng mills,& misc.wood prod.	184,710	38.2	96.2	...	3.3	0.4	13.8	15.6	24.5	24.5
Sawmills, planing mills, & mill work	142,680	32.1	96.3	...	3.2	0.5	14.5	13.8	25.1	25.5
Miscellaneous wood products	42,030	58.9	96.1	...	3.7	0.2	10.4	16.4	21.3	24.1
Furniture and fixtures	122,550	68.0	98.5	0.1	1.3	0.1	7.0	9.9	8.0	14.2
Stone, clay, and glass products	176,790	68.1	98.2	0.1	1.6	0.1	7.4	14.8	9.2	4.1
Glass and glass products	70,800	74.9	99.2	...	0.8	...	5.7	10.7	3.4	6.1
Cement, & conc.,gypsum,& plaster products	28,980	55.8	95.7	0.4	3.9	...	6.8	9.5	17.2	...
Structural clay products	20,160	56.3	97.6	0.1	1.9	0.3	7.9	9.2	20.9	2.4
Pottery and related products	30,720	69.3	98.6	...	1.2	0.1	14.0	26.6	1.9	...
Misc.nonmetallic mineral & stone prod.	26,130	69.3	98.6	0.1	1.1	0.1	6.1	6.3	7.7	5.4
Metal industries	520,470	82.5	98.9	0.6	0.4	...	6.7	7.9	10.5	7.1
Primary metal industries	255,840	80.7	99.9	...	0.1	...	7.3	9.4	14.1	6.1
Blast furn.,steel works,& roll.mills	122,580	83.7	99.9	...	...	...	6.6	6.9	12.7	6.6
Other primary iron and steel indust.	70,050	79.9	99.9	...	0.1	...	10.7	14.1	21.5	12.0
Primary nonferrous industries	63,210	75.7	99.7	0.1	0.2	...	4.7	8.5	8.1	2.3
Fabricated metal ind.(incl.not spec.met)	264,630	84.2	98.0	1.3	0.7	...	6.0	7.6	6.2	7.4
Fabricated steel products	230,970	84.3	97.9	1.4	0.6	...	6.0	7.3	6.3	6.4
Fab.nonferrous metal products	30,000	84.3	99.0	0.1	0.8	0.1	4.7	8.6	6.0	13.9

Table 17-A-5. DETAILED OCCUPATION BY SELECTED CHARACTERISTICS OF THE EMPLOYED PERSONS.-Con.

Detailed occupation	Total employed	Percent urban	Class of worker				Percent part time at work 1-34 hrs.		Percent Negro 25-34 yrs.	
			Private wage and salary	Government	Self-employed	Unpaid	Male	Female	Male	Female
OPERATIVES AND KINDRED WKRS.-Con.										
Not specified metal industries	3,660	81.1	98.4	...	1.6	...	11.4	10.5	...	3.8
Machinery, except electrical	344,940	80.2	99.6	...	0.3	...	5.1	5.8	3.4	3.8
Agricultural machinery and tractors	52,350	74.4	99.8	...	0.1	0.1	4.5	4.2	3.4	5.1
Office and store machines and devices	37,170	83.9	99.9	...	...	0.1	5.3	7.0	1.6	1.5
Miscellaneous machinery	255,420	80.9	99.6	...	0.4	...	5.2	5.7	3.2	4.2
Electrical machinery, equipment, & supplies	329,580	83.7	99.9	...	0.1	...	4.8	6.8	4.6	4.4
Transportation equipment	421,950	83.4	98.8	1.2	0.1	...	5.6	9.5	9.9	5.6
Motor vehic. and motor vehic. equipment	334,260	82.7	99.9	...	0.1	...	6.1	10.5	11.3	6.0
Aircraft and parts	60,480	87.4	99.8	1.2	...	...	2.7	3.4	2.1	1.1
Ship and boat building and repairing	11,520	84.4	63.5	35.7	0.8	...	7.1	...	20.4	20.0
Railroad & misc. transportation equipment	15,690	81.6	100.0	...	...	...	6.8	10.2	10.0	13.3
Professional & photog. equip. and watches	71,190	86.6	99.3	0.1	0.5	...	4.8	8.5	2.7	3.8
Professional equipment and supplies	37,350	87.5	99.2	...	0.7	0.1	4.5	5.9	3.7	5.2
Photographic equip. and supplies	15,840	86.2	99.8	0.2	...	...	3.8	5.1	1.7	3.6
Watches, clocks, &clockwork-operated dev.	18,000	85.0	99.2	0.2	0.7	...	6.8	14.3	1.4	1.6
Miscellaneous manufacturing industries	213,450	84.9	98.0	0.1	1.7	0.2	6.7	13.9	7.2	11.5
Nondurable goods	2,943,210	75.8	99.1	0.3	0.5	0.1	9.8	18.6	8.7	8.7
Food and kindred products	478,410	77.6	98.5	0.1	1.1	0.2	7.6	21.9	11.1	14.0
Meat products	122,550	81.6	98.7	0.2	1.1	0.5	6.6	15.4	21.9	17.7
Dairy products	56,010	61.2	96.9	0.1	2.5	0.5	3.6	17.7	4.2	3.8
Canning & pres. fruits, veget.,& sea foods	67,140	63.8	99.0	...	0.7	0.2	17.1	38.7	11.7	26.3
Grain-mill products	30,840	62.7	97.5	0.2	1.9	0.4	6.1	25.3	15.6	8.6
Bakery products	60,060	89.2	98.9	0.1	0.5	0.5	9.7	15.7	13.5	8.2
Confectionery and related products	43,860	91.5	98.7	...	1.2	0.1	9.3	20.0	10.9	9.4
Beverage industries	52,380	83.5	98.8	0.2	0.8	0.1	7.8	21.8	5.9	5.4
Misc. food preparations & kindred products	35,010	80.4	99.2	...	0.6	0.2	8.1	18.8	17.7	14.5
Not specified food industries	10,560	85.2	98.3	...	1.1	0.6	5.1	12.2	19.2	2.8
Tobacco manufactures	61,170	81.9	99.6	...	0.3	...	19.2	28.0	31.0	19.3
Textile mill products	661,320	63.8	99.7	...	0.2	...	13.6	22.1	4.9	2.6
Knitting mills	146,580	64.2	99.8	...	0.2	...	16.1	26.5	0.8	2.8
Dyeing & finishing textiles, exc. knit goods	24,240	74.1	99.5	...	0.5	...	15.6	17.4	2.4	2.2
Carpets, rugs, & other floor coverings	24,000	75.9	97.8	...	2.0	0.2	5.5	12.3	6.2	10.6
Yarn, thread, and fabric mills	438,210	60.6	99.8	...	0.1	...	13.2	20.8	5.5	1.7
Miscellaneous textile mill products	28,290	80.6	99.6	...	0.4	...	17.3	19.4	12.4	11.7
Apparel and other fabricated textile products	817,200	81.9	99.2	0.3	0.4	...	11.9	17.4	7.3	11.1
Apparel and accessories	765,830	81.7	99.4	0.3	0.3	0.1	12.1	17.5	6.9	11.0
Miscellaneous fab. textile products	53,370	85.2	97.8	0.1	2.1	...	10.1	15.9	10.8	13.6
Paper and allied products	218,910	74.1	99.8	...	0.2	...	4.5	10.0	7.0	6.5
Pulp, paper, and paperboard mills	101,010	62.5	99.9	...	0.1	...	4.2	7.2	6.7	4.4
Paperboard containers and boxes	59,100	85.8	99.7	...	0.3	...	5.1	14.2	10.3	6.8
Miscellaneous paper & pulp products	58,800	82.4	99.7	0.1	0.3	...	4.5	7.4	4.4	7.3
Printing, publishing, & allied industries	75,340	90.3	93.9	4.9	0.9	0.4	10.0	10.9	8.8	16.9

Table 17-A-5. DETAILED OCCUPATION BY SELECTED CHARACTERISTICS OF THE EMPLOYED PERSONS.-Con.

Detailed occupation	Total employed	Percent urban	Class of worker				Percent part time at work 1-34 hrs.		Percent Negro 25-34 yrs.	
			Private wage and salary	Government	Self-employed	Unpaid	Male	Female	Male	Female
OPERATIVES AND KINDRED WKRS.-Con.										
Chemicals and allied products........	182,340	74.8	98.2	1.5	0.3	...	3.3	7.0	12.3	7.2
Synthetic fibers.....................	25,290	50.2	100.0	...	...	...	3.5	6.2	1.1	1.0
Drugs and medicines..................	14,190	89.0	99.4	...	0.4	...	1.9	5.3	15.1	3.6
Paints, varnishes, & related products..	17,970	89.6	99.7	0.2	0.2	...	2.4	8.0	11.3	18.8
Miscellaneous chem. and allied products..	124,890	76.1	97.5	2.2	0.3	...	3.5	7.8	14.1	10.0
Petroleum and coal products..........	51,990	79.6	99.7	...	0.2	...	2.6	7.5	3.9	...
Petroleum refining...................	45,780	78.8	99.7	...	0.2	0.1	2.4	9.1	2.8	...
Miscellaneous petroleum and coal prod...	6,210	85.0	99.5	...	0.5	0.1	4.7	...	14.3	...
Rubber products......................	118,440	80.2	99.7	0.1	0.2	...	12.0	12.6	7.8	4.7
Leather and leather products.........	277,890	77.1	99.4	...	0.5	...	16.0	19.6	4.0	3.9
Leather: tanned, curried, & finished..	27,480	81.6	98.9	...	1.1	...	9.3	8.6	9.8	17.9
Footwear, except rubber..............	205,620	74.1	99.7	...	0.3	...	18.9	21.1	1.2	1.7
Leather products, except footwear....	44,790	88.5	98.4	0.1	1.4	0.1	10.1	15.0	11.0	11.2
Not specified manufacturing industries..	37,230	73.2	99.5	0.2	0.3	...	5.4	11.6	15.3	22.8
Nonmanufacturing industries (incl. not reported)	714,240	76.5	83.0	12.6	3.8	0.6	9.1	19.4	11.9	17.8
Construction.........................	63,000	64.0	75.8	11.2	12.3	0.5	14.1	13.5	11.0	...
Railroads and railway express service..	92,010	74.3	99.3	0.7	...	...	2.6	2.0	10.8	28.6
Transportation, except railroad......	33,990	74.8	85.3	12.6	1.5	0.5	7.2	20.8	11.4	31.4
Telecomm., & utilities & sanitary services..	50,850	76.8	69.2	30.0	0.6	0.1	2.4	7.0	9.5	16.1
Wholesale and retail trade...........	284,490	82.5	96.6	0.2	2.8	0.4	11.5	19.6	16.5	16.6
Business and repair services.........	46,540	79.2	84.0	0.7	13.4	1.9	11.4	18.4	14.3	8.9
Personal services....................	19,260	80.2	87.8	0.9	9.0	2.2	14.3	21.8	29.6	32.5
Public administration................	50,490	71.1	...	100.0	...	...	3.7	6.3	24.7	21.0
All other industries (incl. not reported)..	71,610	67.5	79.4	15.9	3.5	1.2	16.1	25.1	15.9	17.4
PRIVATE HOUSEHOLD WORKERS........	1,431,930	75.2	97.5	...	2.2	0.3	26.7	42.8	68.9	77.0
Housekeepers, private household......	144,810	66.7	98.4	...	0.9	0.7	25.5	19.8	18.8	53.0
Living in............................	56,220	75.2	99.1	...	0.3	0.6	5.6	3.9	100.0	20.3
Living out...........................	88,590	62.6	98.1	...	1.2	0.7	29.3	30.1	13.3	65.2
Laundresses, private household.......	73,350	65.2	73.2	...	26.7	0.1	34.8	73.7	23.1	71.5
Living in............................	390	76.9	100.0	...	...	...	34.8	30.8	...	...
Living out...........................	72,960	65.1	73.1	...	26.9	0.1	34.8	73.9	23.1	71.5
Private household workers (n.e.c.)...	1,213,770	76.9	98.8	...	1.0	0.3	26.5	43.7	73.6	78.9
Living in............................	166,440	78.9	99.4	...	0.3	0.3	6.4	5.9	69.2	41.0
Living out...........................	1,047,330	76.5	...	...	...	...	31.6	49.7	74.8	83.4
SERVICE WORKERS, EXCEPT PRIVATE HOUSEHOLD...	4,271,190	81.7	98.7	...	1.0	0.3	10.4	22.2	24.9	25.7
Attendants, hospital and other institution..	199,440	73.3	44.2	55.1	0.3	0.3	3.5	8.1	29.5	30.0
Attendants, prof. and personal service (n.e.c.)..	46,710	86.9	81.5	13.9	3.9	0.7	23.5	30.7	19.3	47.6
Attendants, recreation and amusement..	60,990	81.6	95.4	2.0	2.2	0.5	50.2	50.6	21.4	7.9
Barbers, beauticians, and manicurists..	386,400	80.6	51.3	0.7	47.8	0.2	6.5	23.1	15.3	12.1

Table 17-A-5. DETAILED OCCUPATION BY SELECTED CHARACTERISTICS OF THE EMPLOYED PERSONS -Con.

Detailed occupation	Total employed	Percent urban	Class of worker				Percent part time at work 1-34 hrs.		Percent Negro 25-34 yrs.	
			Private wage and salary	Government	Self-employed	Unpaid	Male	Female	Male	Female
SERVICE WORKERS, EXCEPT PRIVATE HSHLD.-Con.										
Bartenders	188,820	79.1	81.5	0.6	16.3	1.6	6.5	19.0	5.0	8.9
Boarding and lodging house keepers	31,050	81.8	19.8	2.3	77.3	0.6	6.2	12.0	...	10.5
Bootblacks	14,370	88.3	83.5	0.2	16.3	...	32.7	14.3	91.5	100.0
Charwomen and cleaners	119,220	86.4	82.8	12.7	4.2	0.3	22.4	45.0	27.1	54.3
Cooks, except private household	437,280	73.4	79.3	14.6	4.8	1.3	4.5	20.0	31.2	45.7
Counter and fountain workers	85,860	89.2	90.7	6.0	2.5	0.8	25.7	30.7	8.1	16.1
Elevator operators	88,170	95.6	91.3	8.7	...	...	3.9	8.6	27.7	54.3
Firemen, fire protection	106,620	94.7	2.2	97.7	0.1	...	1.1	...	2.0	20.0
Guards, watchmen, and doorkeepers	234,690	78.5	76.1	23.7	0.1	...	4.7	22.0	6.3	18.2
Housekeepers and stewards, exc. private hshld	107,790	84.7	77.6	20.9	1.0	0.5	7.6	15.7	7.4	20.0
Janitors and sextons	454,170	80.8	67.8	31.6	0.5	0.1	13.1	36.2	50.4	43.9
Marshals and constables	6,120	48.5	...	100.0	...	...	4.8	...	...	...
Midwives	1,500	56.0	48.0	10.0	42.0	...	25.0	42.9	...	6.1
Policemen and detectives	188,050	90.1	9.5	89.7	0.8	...	2.4	20.5	2.9	3.7
Government	169,350	90.1	...	100.0	...	...	2.1	25.0	2.8	...
Private	19,320	89.6	92.2	...	7.6	0.2	5.2	10.5	4.7	16.7
Porters	161,400	96.2	94.1	5.4	0.3	0.1	6.3	13.4	85.1	66.7
Practical nurses	134,010	76.8	81.6	10.5	7.3	0.6	10.0	12.9	12.0	24.3
Sheriffs and bailiffs	17,040	67.4	...	100.0	...	...	4.7	9.1	2.2	...
Ushers, recreation and amusement	23,550	87.0	99.1	0.5	0.1	0.2	67.6	73.6	17.6	17.6
Waiters and waitresses	657,750	80.7	92.2	3.2	2.6	2.1	20.4	23.8	38.3	8.7
Watchmen (crossing) and bridge tenders	12,240	79.7	65.7	36.0	0.4	...	3.1	30.8	4.9	33.3
Service workers, exc. private household (n.e.c.)	507,630	83.0	85.2	11.1	2.1	1.7	16.5	21.5	37.4	61.4
FARM LABORERS AND FOREMEN	2,416,500	8.1	60.4	0.5	0.4	38.6	23.0	57.8	18.9	32.2
Farm foremen	17,040	21.8	96.5	3.4	...	...	4.3	43.8	3.6	66.7
Farm laborers, wage workers	1,455,690	12.2	99.2	0.8	...	...	18.8	46.8	19.4	56.8
Farm laborers, unpaid family workers	933,930	1.1	...	...	...	100.0	32.3	61.7	17.3	22.3
Farm service laborers, self-employed	9,840	45.4	...	...	100.0	...	24.6	22.5	5.5	20.0
LABORERS, EXCEPT FARM AND MINE	3,372,450	65.2	86.2	10.0	3.3	0.4	15.6	18.7	28.0	26.1
Fishermen and oystermen	68,880	39.5	49.3	1.2	48.6	0.8	22.6	45.8	9.9	14.3
Garage laborers, and car washers and greasers	64,800	76.5	94.1	3.0	1.9	1.1	14.2	33.9	54.9	70.6
Gardeners, except farm, and groundskeepers	139,530	71.9	67.6	19.6	11.7	1.1	24.6	36.0	24.1	...
Longshoremen and stevedores	59,730	94.6	95.6	4.1	0.3	...	42.4	32.0	40.3	33.3
Lumbermen, raftsmen, and wood choppers	171,180	13.6	87.1	0.5	11.7	0.7	26.0	17.0	27.4	7.7
Teamsters	21,780	37.2	78.5	3.6	17.8	0.1	24.0	14.3	23.0	...
Laborers (n.e.c.)	2,846,550	67.9	87.6	8.2	1.3	3.2	13.8	17.7	27.8	26.2
Manufacturing	1,081,080	69.1	98.8	0.9	0.2	...	8.9	13.9	27.3	17.6

Table 17-A-5. DETAILED OCCUPATION BY SELECTED CHARACTERISTICS OF THE EMPLOYED PERSONS -Con.

Detailed occupation	Total employed	Percent urban	Class of worker				Percent part time at work 1-34 hrs.		Percent Negro 25-34 yrs.	
			Private wage and salary	Government	Self-employed	Unpaid	Male	Female	Male	Female
LABORERS, EXCEPT FARM AND MINE.-Con.										
Laborers (n.e.c.)-Con.										
Durable goods	630,610	67.2	98.6	0.1	0.3	0.9	9.2	10.2	27.7	16.2
Sawmills, planing mills,& misc.wood prod.	153,780	32.2	98.7	0.1	0.9	0.2	16.1	16.7	38.8	25.0
Sawmills, planing mills, & mill work.	138,390	29.8	98.5	0.2	1.2	0.1	16.4	16.2	38.0	15.8
Miscellaneous wood products	15,390	54.2	100.0	...	...	...	13.5	17.4	47.6	44.4
Furniture and fixtures	20,310	65.6	99.9	...	0.1	...	6.6	23.4	27.6	31.2
Stone, clay, and glass products	78,000	57.4	99.5	0.2	0.2	...	8.8	10.6	17.0	20.0
Glass and glass products	15,060	68.1	100.0	...	...	...	7.2	9.8	3.4	15.4
Cement, & conc.,gypsum, & plaster prod.	22,440	58.8	98.8	0.7	0.4	...	8.2	14.3	18.1	33.3
Structural clay products	25,860	49.0	99.7	...	0.3	...	8.2	10.5	21.1	42.9
Pottery and related products	6,270	59.8	100.0	...	...	...	15.6	8.7	8.0	...
Misc.nonmetallic mineral & stone prod.	8,370	58.8	100.0	...	...	...	10.4	14.3	30.8	20.0
Metal industries	264,210	82.7	99.4	0.5	...	...	7.2	9.7	28.3	15.6
Primary metal industries	208,260	83.2	99.9	...	...	...	7.1	9.9	30.5	32.4
Blast furn.,steel wks.,& rolling mills	135,180	86.2	100.0	...	...	...	6.7	7.8	28.8	38.5
Other primary iron and steel ind.	46,800	81.0	99.9	...	...	...	9.8	16.7	43.6	41.7
Primary nonferrous industries	26,280	71.9	99.8	0.2	...	...	4.5	5.0	18.1	11.1
Fab. metal ind. (incl.not spec. metal).	55,950	80.8	97.4	2.3	0.3	...	7.3	9.7	19.8	5.4
Fabricated steel products	50,640	80.3	97.4	2.4	0.2	...	7.2	9.8	19.7	3.7
Fabricated nonferrous metal products	4,470	80.0	99.3	...	0.6	...	7.5	...	16.0	...
Not specified metal industries	840	78.6	100.0	...	...	...	11.5	100.0	30.8	100.0
Machinery, except electrical	51,210	77.2	99.8	0.1	0.1	...	5.6	12.0	15.8	5.9
Agricultural machinery and tractors	12,300	74.1	99.8	...	...	...	4.6	10.0	16.1	...
Office and store machines and devices	1,350	84.4	100.0	...	...	0.3	4.5	100.0	...	...
Miscellaneous machinery	37,560	78.0	99.8	0.2	...	...	5.9	10.3	16.5	7.1
Electrical machinery, equipment, & supp.	27,240	79.0	99.9	...	...	0.1	5.1	5.8	7.3	7.4
Transportation equipment	67,050	83.7	91.8	8.1	...	...	6.5	4.5	31.8	25.0
Motor vehicles & motor vehicle equip.	46,500	83.8	99.9	0.1	...	...	5.8	5.9	29.8	23.8
Aircraft and parts	3,750	74.4	98.4	1.6	...	...	5.2	...	16.7	...
Ship and boat bldg. and repairing	12,450	85.5	57.1	42.6	...	...	8.6	...	44.6	50.0
RR. and misc. transportation equipment	4,350	84.8	99.3	0.6	0.2	...	9.0	...	28.0	...
Prof. & photographic equip., & watches.	4,140	75.4	98.6	0.7	...	0.7	7.4	7.4	12.0	14.3
Prof. equipment and supplies	1,920	78.1	100.0	...	...	...	7.7	8.3	11.1	16.7
Photographic equip. and supplies	1,560	73.1	96.2	...	...	1.9	7.7	...	15.4	...
Watches,clocks,& clockwork-op.devices.	660	72.7	100.0	...	...	...	2.3	11.1	...	...
Miscellaneous manufacturing industries.	14,670	75.3	99.2	0.6	...	0.2	8.4	6.2	13.0	12.0
Nondurable goods	392,310	72.4	99.2	0.5	0.2	...	8.5	17.3	26.6	18.6
Food and kindred products	141,600	72.4	99.5	...	0.4	...	9.7	23.4	24.1	18.0
Meat products	36,000	81.9	99.7	...	0.3	...	7.1	15.5	30.6	26.3
Dairy products	14,640	57.2	98.8	...	1.3	...	7.5	32.0	7.7	...
Canning & preserv.fruits,veg.,& seafoods	19,020	58.0	99.8	...						

Table 17-A-5. DETAILED OCCUPATION BY SELECTED CHARACTERISTICS OF THE EMPLOYED PERSONS-Con.

Detailed occupation	Total employed	Percent urban	Class of worker				Percent part time at work 1-34 hrs.		Percent Negro 25-34 yrs.	
			Private wage and salary	Government	Self-employed	Unpaid	Male	Female	Male	Female
LABORERS, EXCEPT FARM AND MINE.-Con.										
Laborers (n.e.c.)-Con.										
Grain-mill products.............	18,720	62.0	99.6	0.3	0.1	...	8.6	37.5	20.7	...
Bakery products.................	7,920	84.0	98.9	0.4	...	0.8	13.8	28.1	36.2	...
Confectionery and related products......	4,110	78.1	99.3	...	0.8	...	1.8	15.8	23.3	12.5
Beverage industries.............	21,390	81.1	99.9	...	0.1	...	11.4	22.2	16.4	20.0
Misc.food preparations & kindred products.....	16,560	73.2	98.7	0.2	0.9	0.2	7.6	16.7	34.3	10.0
Not specified food industries......	3,240	78.7	99.9	...	0.9	...	11.5	22.2	14.3	...
Tobacco manufactures.............	7,350	86.5	100.0	...	...	...	13.3	29.2	77.8	80.0
Textile mill products...........	59,220	65.3	99.9	...	...	...	10.2	15.9	28.4	9.3
Knitting mills..................	2,550	68.2	100.0	...	...	...	7.9	15.0	13.3	11.1
Dyeing and finishing text.,exc.knit goods	2,820	84.0	100.0	...	...	...	16.1	...	14.8	...
Carpets,rugs, and other floor coverings..	5,970	76.9	99.5	0.5	...	...	2.2	15.4	13.6	...
Yarn, thread, and fabric mills........	45,150	62.1	100.0	...	...	...	11.4	16.3	32.6	5.2
Misc. textile mill products.........	2,730	70.3	100.0	...	...	...	3.8	20.0	34.8	5.2
Apparel & other fabricated textile products	11,430	78.0	98.2	1.8	...	...	11.0	13.2	28.9	60.0
Apparel and accessories...........	8,820	76.9	97.6	2.4	...	...	14.6	14.1	29.6	34.8
Misc.fabricated textile products......	2,610	81.6	100.0	...	...	...	2.9	6.3	27.8	31.0
Paper and allied products...........	44,040	65.6	99.8	0.1	0.1	...	5.0	4.7	28.3	75.0
Pulp, paper, and paperboard mills.....	27,120	58.5	99.7	...	0.2	...	5.2	...	28.7	9.4
Paperboard containers and boxes......	8,640	77.4	100.0	...	...	...	3.3	7.7	23.3	...
Misc.paper and pulp products........	8,280	76.4	100.0	...	...	...	6.0	4.0	31.2	15.8
Printing, publishing, and allied industries	11,580	94.0	93.8	6.2	...	...	15.2	15.2	22.1	25.0
Chemicals and allied products.......	62,190	73.5	98.2	1.5	0.1	0.1	6.6	12.1	31.6	13.2
Synthetic fibers.................	3,390	40.7	100.0	...	...	...	5.7	15.4	11.4	...
Drugs and medicines.............	1,890	79.4	100.0	...	...	...	8.0	...	12.9	...
Paints, varnishes, and related products..	3,540	83.1	100.0	...	...	...	6.2	12.9	35.4	17.2
Miscellaneous chemicals and allied prod..	53,370	74.7	97.9	1.8	0.1	0.2	6.7	8.3	22.0	33.3
Petroleum and coal products........	28,350	78.9	99.6	0.4	...	...	3.3	...	18.7	33.3
Petroleum refining..............	23,250	78.2	99.6	0.4	...	...	2.7	...	38.5	33.3
Misc. petroleum and coal products.....	5,100	82.4	99.4	0.6	...	...	6.1	20.0	15.4	6.7
Rubber products................	14,820	79.4	99.8	0.2	...	...	9.2	10.2	18.3	10.0
Leather and leather products.......	11,730	69.3	100.0	...	...	...	10.3	24.2	17.0	...
Leather: tanned, curried, and finished..	5,220	66.1	100.0	...	...	...	6.2	42.9	4.3	...
Footwear, except rubber..........	4,860	65.4	100.0	...	...	...	17.7	26.7	50.0	14.3
Leather products, except footwear.....	1,650	90.9	100.0	...	...	...	5.4	7.1	50.0	...
Not specified manufacturing industries.....	8,160	68.0	100.0	...	...	...	5.4	2.4	33.9	25.0
Nonmanufacturing industries (incl.not reported)	1,765,470	67.2	80.8	16.7	2.0	0.5	16.7	22.9	28.1	43.3
Construction...................	645,090	63.4	80.8	16.8	2.0	0.3	18.3	21.8	27.6	48.7
Railroads and railway express service......	265,680	62.3	98.8	1.2	...	...	4.8	5.0	28.8	61.0
Transportation, except railroad.......	103,200	79.8	92.0	5.0	2.0	0.9	14.6	15.3	21.9	12.5

Table 17-A-5. DETAILED OCCUPATION BY SELECTED CHARACTERISTICS OF THE EMPLOYED PERSONS -Con.

Detailed occupation	Total employed	Percent urban	Class of worker				Percent part time at work 1-34 hrs.		Percent Negro 25-34 yrs.	
			Private wage and salary	Government	Self-employed	Unpaid	Male	Female	Male	Female
LABORERS, EXCEPT FARM AND MINE—Con.										
Nonmanufacturing—Con.										
Telecommunications,& util.& sanitary serv..	123,720	75.8	58.3	49.5	2.1	0.1	7.0	13.5	23.4	60.0
Wholesale and retail trade..	305,160	74.9	97.0	0.3	1.4	1.3	19.8	28.5	26.2	38.0
Business and repair services..	13,320	71.4	89.4	0.2	9.7	0.8	21.1	21.1	22.9	11.1
Personal services..	71,910	67.3	94.7	0.4	4.0	0.9	50.7	21.3	54.1	63.8
Public administration..	95,070	75.1	...	100.0	...	...	6.8	5.2	37.9	7.1
All other industries (incl. not reported)..	142,320	54.5	78.9	14.4	6.1	0.6	26.6	36.4	29.7	31.6
OCCUPATION NOT REPORTED..	702,210	60.1	93.6	5.0	1.0	0.3	12.5	15.2	14.0	13.0

Table 17-A-6. OCCUPATIONAL CHANGE, 1900 TO 1950, BY DETAILED OCCUPATIONS

Detailed occupation	Percent female 1950	Percent female 1930	Percent female 1900	Change (000) 1900–1950	Percent change 1900–1950	Percent change 1900–1930	Percent change 1930–1950
TOTAL	27.9	22.1	18.3	29,969	103.2	67.7	21.2
PROFESSIONAL, TECHNICAL, AND KINDRED WORKERS	39.5	44.8	35.2	3,846	311.6	168.2	53.5
Accountants and auditors	14.8	8.9	6.1	368	1,603.7	736.0	103.8
Actors and actresses							
Athletes							
Dancers and dancing teachers	32.4	35.5	21.6	83	264.1	144.2	49.1
Entertainers (n.e.c.)							
Sports instructors and officials							
Airplane pilots and navigators	1.4	1.1	(b)	14	(b)	(b)	137.5
Architects	3.9	1.9	0.9	15	139.7	116.0	11.0
Artists and art teachers	38.4	37.8	44.3	6	231.8	130.2	44.1
Authors	38.7	43.8	45.0	14	467.8	326.8	35.0
Chemists	10.2	4.2	2.9	68	796.0	423.5	71.1
Clergymen	31.7	24.1	4.1	195	171.5	93.4	40.4
Religious workers							
Recreation and group wkrs., social and welfare wkrs. ex. group	23.4	32.5	6.4	120	1,652.9	751.3	105.9
College presidents, professors, and instructors (n.e.c.)	2.8	1.8	2.7	46	156.0	139.5	6.9
Dentists	11.9	9.4	5.2	150	834.3	445.9	71.1
Designers	32.2	24.3	7.8	61	193.1	90.1	54.2
Draftsmen	1.6	0.3	0.2	108	536.0	336.4	45.7
Editors and reporters	1.9	...	0.1	53	1,698.8	347.1	302.3
Engineers, civil	1.0	0.1	0.2	345	2,404.4	707.5	210.2
Engineers, chemical							
Engineers, metallurgical, and metallurgists							
Engineers, mining							
Engineers, electrical							
Engineers, industrial							
Engineers: aeronautical, mechanical, (n.e.c.)							
Farm and home management advisors	49.6	24.6	2.0	13	(b)	(b)	181.1
Funeral directors and embalmers	6.8	5.7	0.4	24	150.3	110.8	18.7
Lawyers and judges	3.5	2.1		76	70.6	49.2	14.3
Librarians	88.6	91.4	72.5	54	1,850.3	915.9	92.0
Musicians and music teachers	49.2	48.2	56.8	74	80.0	79.1	0.5
Nurses, professional	97.6	98.1	93.6	479	4,059.0	2,392.3	66.9
Nurses, student professional	5.8	3.7	(b)	15	(b)	(b)	78.1
Optometrists	8.3	3.1	1.4	44	95.6	81.6	7.8
Pharmacists	17.4	15.3	12.2	31	123.5	31.3	70.2
Photographers							
Physicians and surgeons	11.5	9.2	4.7	107	81.5	43.2	26.7
Osteopaths							
Chiropractors							
Therapists and healers (n.e.c.)							
Radio operators	9.2	0.9	(b)	17	(b)	(b)	238.2
Surveyors	3.8	...	0.2	21	350.2	143.7	84.7
Teachers (n.e.c.)	74.6	81.8	74.6	713	163.7	139.6	10.0

Table 17-A-6.　OCCUPATIONAL CHANGE, 1900 TO 1950, BY DETAILED OCCUPATIONS -Con.

Detailed occupation	Percent female			Change (000)	Percent change		
	1950	1930	1900	1900–1950	1900–1950	1900–1930	1930–1950
PROFESSIONAL, TECHNICAL AND KINDRED WKRS.—Con.							
Technicians, medical and dental; Technicians, testing; Technicians (n.e.c.)	36.0	48.5	...	186	185,952.0	20,148.0	818.9
Veterinarians	6.4	0.1	0.2	6	67.6	45.3	15.3
Dietitians and nutritionists; foresters and conservationists; natural scientists (n.e.c.); personnel and labor relations workers; social scientists; professional, technical, and kindred workers (n.e.c.)	26.3	25.9	24.0	290	2,408.0	508.1	312.4
FARMERS AND FARM MANAGERS	2.7	4.4	5.4	-1,388	-24.1	4.7	-27.5
Farmers (owners and tenants)	2.7	4.4	5.4	-1,413	-24.6	4.2	-27.6
Farm managers	6.4	1.9	11.7	25	239.5	285.0	-11.8
MANAGERS, OFFICIALS, AND PROPR'S., EXC. FARM	13.6	8.1	4.4	3,459	203.8	113.0	42.7
Buyers and department heads, store	26.0	25.1	(a)	(a)	(a)	(a)	320.0
Buyers and shippers, farm products	2.8	0.2	0.1	17	137.0	237.7	-29.8
Conductors, railroad	0.7	...	...	14	32.2	70.8	-22.6
Credit men	21.9	8.4	...	32	1,593.8	1,024.5	50.6
Floormen and floor managers, store	46.0	34.3	30.1	9	465.4	209.0	83.0
Inspectors (n.e.c.), public administration; officials (n.e.c.), public administration	13.7	8.9	5.9	158	273.8	116.1	73.0
Inspectors (n.e.c.), Federal public administration and postal service; Officials and administrators (n.e.c.), Federal public administration and postal service	8.2	2.1	0.8	60	331.4	119.4	96.6
Inspectors (n.e.c.), State public administration; Officials and administrators (n.e.c.), State pub. adm.	9.7	7.1	6.6	29	704.8	259.7	123.7
Inspectors (n.e.c.), local public administration; Officials and administrators (n.e.c.), local public ad.	19.2	13.2	1.6	68	193.4	97.4	48.6
Managers and superintendents, building	34.2	29.9	(a)	(a)	(a)	(a)	-4.9
Officers, pilots, pursers, and engineers, ship	2.8	...	...	...	-1.1	12.5	-12.1
Officials, lodge, society, union, etc.	11.0	20.7	(a)	(a)	(a)	(a)	89.5
Postmasters	43.2	39.5	33.4	21	109.7	83.0	14.5
Purchasing agents and buyers (n.e.c.)	9.2	7.1	2.8	58	805.9	299.1	127.0
Managers, officials, and proprietors (n.e.c.)	12.8	7.3	4.4	2,908	192.5	106.0	42.0
Construction	1.6	0.3	0.2	238	408.6	242.1	48.7
Manufacturing	6.3	3.1	1.8	490	281.2	156.3	48.7
Transportation	4.0	0.8	0.5	85	129.4	49.3	53.7
Telecommunications, and utilities and sanitary services	9.4	8.1	5.5	63	1,140.6	605.6	75.8
Wholesale trade	4.9	1.7	1.3	264	336.9	93.3	126.1
Eating and drinking places	26.6	24.2	6.0	260	236.4	50.3	123.8

Table 17-A-6. OCCUPATIONAL CHANGE, 1900 TO 1950, BY DETAILED OCCUPATIONS—Con.

Detailed occupation	Percent female			Change (000)	Percent change		
	1950	1930	1900	1900–1950	1900–1950	1900–1930	1930–1950
MANAGERS, OFFICIALS, AND PROPRIETORS, EXC. FARM—Con.							
Food and dairy products stores, and milk retailing; General merchandise and five and ten cent stores; Apparel and accessories stores; Motor vehicles and accessories retailing; Gasoline service stations; Furniture, home furnishings, and equipment stores; Hardware, farm implements, and building material retailing	14.4	8.4	5.2	787	96.0	73.9	12.7
Other retail trade	9.6	5.0	0.7	67	87.8	128.0	-17.7
Banking and other finance	15.4	6.2	2.5	103	729.9	367.8	77.4
Insurance and real estate	1.8	0.6	(b)	86	(b)	(b)	-7.9
Automobile repair services and garages	4.6	7.0	(a)	...	(a)	(a)	302.9
Miscellaneous repair services	29.3	20.8	13.3	144	199.8	45.4	106.3
Personal services; Business services	19.9	8.5	4.9	286	792.2	288.5	129.6
All other industries (including not reported)	62.3	51.8	24.2	6,355	724.6	394.4	66.8
CLERICAL AND KINDRED WORKERS							
Agents (n.e.c.)	15.5	6.6	6.0	93	156.7	143.8	5.3
Collectors, bill and account	74.5	73.1	79.8	12	928.5	47.4	597.6
Attendants and assistants, library; Attendants, physician's and dentist's office	95.0	94.7	(b)	43	(b)	(b)	54.8
Baggagemen, transportation	1.9	..	0.1	-11	-56.8	-51.7	-10.5
Bookkeepers and cashiers	78.1	63.1	31.4	762	328.3	218.3	34.6
Express messengers and railway mail clerks	1.5	..	(b)	19	(b)	(b)	25.2
Mail carriers	2.2	0.9	0.9	142	501.9	328.2	40.6
Stenographers, typists, and secretaries	94.4	93.8	64.2	1,527	1,139.3	718.7	51.4
Messengers and office boys	16.9	5.1	6.7	3	3.8	45.6	-28.7
Telegraph messengers; Telegraph operators	22.0	23.8	12.9	-20	-36.4	21.5	-47.6
Telephone operators	95.5	94.5	80.0	356	1,855.6	1,199.1	50.5
Ticket, station, and express agents	15.1	4.9	2.4	34	125.9	43.0	57.9
Office machine operators; Shipping and receiving clerks; Bank tellers; disp., starters, veh.; clerical, kindred wkrs. (n.e.c.)	46.7	26.3	4.7	3,396	1,447.0	632.2	111.3
SALES WORKERS	34.3	24.1	17.4	2,826	216.3	134.1	35.1
Advertising agents and salesmen	14.8	7.1	2.4	22	180.7	227.9	-14.4
Auctioneers	9.3	0.1	0.1	3	98.2	52.5	30.0
Demonstrators	81.9	76.2	66.1	11	348.3	134.0	91.6
Hucksters and peddlers	14.3	3.2	3.8	-53	-68.9	-26.1	-57.9
Insurance agents and brokers	8.6	5.0	1.4	234	298.2	227.9	21.5
Newsboys	4.0	1.1	1.0	94	1,368.3	465.7	159.6
Real estate agents and brokers	14.5	6.2	2.5	111	331.4	347.9	-3.7
Stock and bond salesmen	10.4	1.0	...	7	186.8	459.6	-48.8
Salesmen & clks. (n.e.c.); mfg.; wholesale tr.; ret. tr.; other ind. (including not reported)	38.6	28.3	20.2	2,396	220.1	127.9	40.4

Table 17-A-6. OCCUPATIONAL CHANGE, 1900 TO 1950, BY DETAILED OCCUPATIONS-Con.

Detailed occupation	Percent female			Change (000)	Percent change		
	1950	1930	1900	1900–1950	1900–1950	1900–1930	1930–1950
CRAFTSMEN, FOREMEN, AND KINDRED WORKERS	3.0	1.7	2.5	5,289	172.8	104.0	33.7
Bakers	11.8	6.3	2.5	57	81.8	100.4	-9.3
Boilermakers	0.9	...	...	9	29.2	60.3	-19.4
Bookbinders	56.2	54.4	51.9	7	26.5	-25.8	70.5
Brickmasons, stonemasons, and tile setters	0.6	...	0.1	32	21.2	14.6	5.7
Cabinetmakers	1.5	...	0.2	43	119.4	76.6	24.2
Carpenters	0.5	...	0.1	421	70.6	54.0	10.8
Cement and concrete finishers	0.7	...	(b)	34	(b)	(b)	119.6
Electrotypers and stereotypers	4.0	0.2	0.9	9	282.5	146.7	55.1
Engravers, except photographers							
Photoengravers and lithographers	6.0	4.6	7.4	137	100.9	79.3	12.1
Compositors and type setters							
Pressmen and plate printers, printing	30.0	31.0	9.7	43	1,410.6	560.2	128.8
Decorators and window dressers	0.7	...	0.8	281	554.1	398.5	31.2
Electricians							
Cranemen, derrickmen, and hoistmen; excavating, grading, and road machinery operators	0.7	...	0.1	311	232.6	119.6	51.5
Stationary engineers							
Blacksmiths; forgemen and hammermen	0.8	...	0.1	-160	-72.8	-38.1	-56.0
Foremen (n.e.c.)	8.2	6.5	8.4	705	435.1	240.4	57.2
Construction; manufacturing	0.5	0.1	(b)	62	(b)	(b)	44.2
Metal industries; machinery, including electrical; transportation equipment							
Textiles, textile products, and apparel	10.1	9.5	13.4	434	480.8	224.5	79.0
Other durable goods; other nondurable goods (including not specified manufacturing)							
Railroads and railway express service	0.5	0.1	...	17	45.1	119.1	-33.8
Transportation, except railroad	2.0	0.5	1.1	52	533.3	356.9	38.6
Telecommunications, and utilities and sanitary services	10.1	8.3	5.6	140	579.9	266.1	85.7
Other industries (including not reported)	13.9	13.0	11.8	7	99.4	69.1	17.9
Furriers							
Painters, construction and maintenance	2.0	...	0.1	237	107.5	102.0	2.7
Glaziers	1.5	...	(b)	19	(b)	(b)	211.5
Heat treaters, annealers, and temperers	4.5	3.1	...	17	1,115.8	387.3	149.5
Inspectors, scalers, and graders, log and lumber	7.3	4.6	...	77	351.0	255.7	26.8
Inspectors (n.e.c.)	1.1	...	...	7	787.7	655.3	17.5
Construction	0.4	...	...	17	87.4	96.5	-4.6
Railroads and railway express service							
Transportation except railroad, communication, and other public utilities	4.0	8.9	(b)	12	1,211.1	1,337.1	-8.8
Other industries (including not reported)	16.1	13.3	(b)	40	(b)	(b)	129.7
Jewelers, watchmakers, goldsmiths, and silversmiths	5.8	3.2	8.5	25	108.7	64.8	26.6
Linemen and servicemen, telegraph, telephone, and power	2.3	...	...	202	1,138.5	500.5	106.2
Locomotive engineers	0.5	...	...	24	22.8	59.7	-23.1
Locomotive firemen							
Loom fixers	1.2	0.2	...	22	232.7	102.9	64.0

Table 17-A-6. OCCUPATIONAL CHANGE, 1900 TO 1950, BY DETAILED OCCUPATIONS.-Con.

Detailed occupation	Percent female			Change (000)	Percent change		
	1950	1930	1900	1900–1950	1900–1950	1900–1930	1930–1950
CRAFTSMEN, FOREMEN, AND KINDRED WORKERS—Con.							
Job setters, metal; machinists							
Mechanics and repairmen, airplane							
Mechanics and repairmen, automobile	1.3	...	0.2	2,231	733.8	356.2	82.8
Mechanics and repairmen, railroad and car shop							
Mechanics and repairmen, office machine; mechanics and repairmen, radio and television; mechanics and repairmen (n.e.c.)							
Toolmakers, and die makers and setters	0.7	0.3	0.1	-15	-60.8	-37.1	-37.7
Millers, grain, flour, feed, etc.	0.4	...	...	53	661.4	420.3	46.4
Millwrights	1.1	...	0.6	-32	-32.6	8.8	-38.1
Molders, metal	1.9	...	(b)	27	(b)	(b)	35.0
Motion picture projectionists	13.5	10.5	8.7	14	218.7	97.0	61.8
Opticians and lens grinders and polishers	13.4	5.1	1.1	1	6.7	30.0	-17.9
Paperhangers	3.4	0.1	1.4	23	152.2	97.4	28.3
Pattern and model makers, except paper	3.3	0.4	1.0	4	96.1	58.9	23.4
Piano and organ tuners and repairmen	0.8	...	0.1	31	87.3	98.3	-5.5
Plasterers	0.7	...	0.1	212	230.0	157.9	27.9
Plumbers and pipe fitters	2.2	...	...	25	398.1	385.6	2.6
Rollers and roll hands, metal	0.5	...	...	41	462.1	116.7	112.4
Roofers and slaters	4.2	0.3	2.0	-41	-40.8	-24.7	-21.3
Shoemakers and repairmen, except factory	2.7	...	...	-28	-75.2	38.9	-59.5
Stone cutters and stone carvers	0.6	...	...	54	1,429.4	780.4	73.7
Structural metal workers	19.4	12.9	19.8	-46	-34.4	26.2	-48.0
Tailors and tailoresses	1.0	4.4	4.9	84	170.3	69.6	59.4
Tinsmiths, coppersmiths, and sheet metal workers	8.7	0.1	0.1	39	153.2	62.7	55.6
Upholsterers	1.8	...	...	16	26.6	-28.2	76.3
Craftsmen and kindred workers (n.e.c.)	1.7	...	...	38	...	...	...
Members of the armed forces	...	...	...	...	...	...	...
OPERATIVES AND KINDRED WORKERS	27.3	24.3	34.0	8,310	223.4	106.8	56.4
Apprentice carpenters	0.8	0.1	0.3	10	617.1	167.7	167.9
Apprentice electricians	1.0	0.2	(b)	9	(b)	(b)	103.7
Apprentice plumbers and pipe fitters	4.5	...	...	10	348.1	110.5	112.9
Apprentices, printing trades	2.7	3.2	2.5	12	352.7	212.1	45.0
Apprentice machinists and tool makers; apprentice auto mechanics; apprentice brick layers and masons; apprentice mechanics, except auto; apprentices, building trade (n.e.c.); apprentices, metal working trades (n.e.c.); apprentices, other specified trades	3.1	7.5	11.6	16	28.5	9.2	17.7
Apprentices, trade not specified							
Asbestos and insulation workers	2.7	...	(b)	17	(b)	(b)	564.6
Attendants, auto service and parking	2.8	1.4	(b)	253	(b)	(b)	76.5
Blasters and powdermen	0.9	...	...	11	1,419.1	771.0	74.4
Boatmen, canalmen, and lock keepers	2.4	0.7	0.6	-4	-34.1	-57.0	53.1

Table 17-A-6. OCCUPATIONAL CHANGE, 1900 TO 1950, BY DETAILED OCCUPATIONS -Con.

Detailed occupation	Percent female			Change (000) 1900–1950	Percent change		
	1950	1930	1900		1900–1950	1900–1930	1930–1950
OPERATIVES AND KINDRED WORKERS-Con.							
Brakemen, railroad	0.6	0.1	...	38	35.0	61.0	-16.1
Switchmen, railroad	2.3	...	(b)	8	(b)	(b)	111.2
Chainmen, rodmen, and axmen, surveying	1.9	...	0.1	-12	-51.7	52.7	-68.4
Conductors, bus and street railway	1.8	0.1	0.3	86	51.6	12.3	34.9
Deliverymen and routemen	...	...	...	...	...	...	...
Dressmakers and seamstresses, except factory	97.2	99.8	99.9	-267	-64.5	-52.0	-26.1
Dyers	4.3	1.7	2.8	21	391.6	235.0	46.8
Filers, grinders, and polishers, metal	4.6	3.0	3.8	143	840.5	362.9	103.2
Fruit, nut, and vegetable graders and packers, except factory	62.0	61.9	(b)	37	(b)	(b)	266.3
Furnacemen, smeltermen, and pourers	2.2	...	...	45	337.8	50.6	190.7
Heaters, metal	4.6	...	...	5	98.1	198.8	-33.7
Laundry and dry cleaning operatives	67.1	68.4	61.4	370	405.7	190.1	74.3
Meat cutters, except slaughter and packing house	2.0	0.2	0.1	146	438.1	259.0	49.9
Milliners	89.5	100.0	100.0	-62	-82.3	-66.7	-47.0
Mine operatives and laborers (n.e.c.); coal mining; crude petroleum and natural gas extraction; mining and quarrying, except fuel	0.8	...	0.2	-41	-6.1	35.0	-30.5
Motormen, mine, factory, logging camp, etc.	1.0	...	(b)	25	(b)	(b)	48.1
Motormen, street, subway, and elevated railway	1.4	...	(b)	-10	-27.4	54.9	-53.1
Oilers and greasers, except auto	1.6	0.1	(b)	63	127.9	50.3	101.5
Painters, except construction and maintenance	11.6	5.6	2.7	71	1,512.8	327.0	51.7
Photographic process workers	44.9	41.8	27.3	28	(b)	(b)	277.7
Power station operators	3.9	...	(b)	22	37.4	62.7	-23.1
Sailors and deck hands	1.7	...	0.2	15	450.4	98.9	-15.6
Sawyers	2.1	0.2	...	82	56.1	44.6	176.7
Spinners, textile	74.5	59.2	65.0	31	78.6	75.4	7.9
Stationary firemen	0.9	...	...	57	(b)	(b)	1.8
Bus drivers; taxicab drivers and chauffeurs; truck and tractor drivers	1.0	0.2	(b)	1,808	(b)	(b)	85.9
Weavers, textile	39.2	42.8	47.9	50	32.0	45.1	-53.1
Welders and flame-cutters	3.6	...	(b)	283	(b)	(b)	670.3
Operatives and kindred workers (n.e.c.)	39.1	35.6	37.5	9,439	311.0	124.8	82.8
Sawmills, planing mills, and mill work	8.6	10.6	6.5	122	163.3	21.2	117.2
Miscellaneous wood products	21.4	12.6	10.2	113	599.8	283.5	82.5
Furniture and fixtures	30.4	17.9	8.2	51	205.4	63.6	86.7
Glass and glass products	3.2	2.9	2.1	25	525.8	137.4	163.6
Cement and concrete, gypsum, and plaster products	18.8	10.5	3.7	25	223.4	84.5	75.3
Structural clay products	...	...	...	16	251.1	132.4	51.1
Pottery and related products	42.6	28.9	25.5	25	220.1	10.5	257.6
Miscellaneous nonmetallic mineral and stone products	22.4	0.1	1.1	20	...	...	...

Table 17-A-6. OCCUPATIONAL CHANGE, 1900 TO 1950, BY DETAILED OCCUPATIONS -Con.

Detailed occupation	Percent female			Change (000)	Percent change		
	1950	1930	1900	1900–1950	1900–1950	1900–1930	1930–1950
OPERATIVES AND KINDRED WORKERS-Con.							
Motor vehicles and motor vehicle equipment							
Ship and boat building and repairing							
Blast furnaces, steel workers, and rolling mills							
Other primary iron and steel industries; fabricated steel prod.							
Office and store machines and devices							
Miscellaneous machinery	16.1	11.9	5.6	1,226	1,009.7	376.2	124.4
Not specified metal industries							
Agricultural machinery and tractors							
Aircraft and parts							
Railroad and miscellaneous transportation equipment	22.9	23.7	7.4	88	825.1	216.9	191.9
Primary nonferrous industries; fabricated nonferrous metal prod.	53.7	38.6	43.3	338	1,912.0	563.0	203.5
Electrical machinery, equipment, and supplies							
Professional equipment and supplies; photographic equipment and supplies	51.1	36.9	36.8	215	210.3	67.6	85.1
Watches, clocks, and clockwork-operated devices; miscellaneous manufacturing industries							
Meat products	43.8	33.9	28.8	217	2,059.7	647.2	189.0
Canning and preserving fruits, vegetables, and sea foods							
Dairy products	16.6	17.0	3.9	48	368.0	95.1	139.9
Grain-mill products	15.6	8.0	2.7	29	674.4	59.3	386.3
Bakery products	52.8	54.8	47.6	64	1,391.4	509.2	144.8
Confectionery and related products	65.5	60.9	30.4	24	88.1	63.8	14.8
Beverage industries	17.3	10.8	6.2	44	334.8	-45.5	698.3
Miscellaneous food preparations and kindred products; not specified food industries	46.9	46.7	29.0	49	2,024.1	1,131.4	72.5
Tobacco manufactures	70.1	65.5	35.0	-45	-39.0	-10.3	-32.1
Knitting mills	72.1	68.5	77.6	114	278.4	215.9	19.8
Dyeing and finishing textiles, except knit goods	22.3	28.9	18.5	13	100.7	52.5	31.6
Carpets, rugs, and other floor covering	43.7	52.4	61.8	15	146.5	62.1	52.1
Yarn, thread, and fabric mills	50.1	53.4	58.2	274	135.7	60.3	47.0
Miscellaneous textile mill products	46.9	36.1	43.9	1	2.7	15.0	-10.6
Apparel and accessories	80.6	70.6	69.7	599	266.4	87.9	95.0
Miscellaneous fabricated textile products	71.7	59.9	71.3	38	181.8	-29.8	301.2
Pulp, paper, and paperboard mills	28.1	30.4	40.0	146	700.8	287.4	106.7
Miscellaneous paper and pulp products							
Paperboard containers and boxes	45.8	59.6	84.1	44	229.3	-26.1	345.5
Printing, publishing, and allied industries	44.7	38.5	31.7	64	400.4	219.9	56.4
Synthetic fibers	33.1	51.8	(b)	27	(b)	(b)	29.1
Paints, varnishes, and related products	15.3	12.4	15.5	16	550.9	192.9	122.2
Drugs and medicines; miscellaneous chemicals and allied products	22.4	31.8	30.2	139	1,449.7	469.5	180.9
Petroleum refining	2.7	1.8	3.1	47	5,774.5	3,226.7	76.6
Miscellaneous petroleum and coal products	4.0	0.9	1.0	5	325.5	-0.6	327.9
Rubber products	30.8	26.3	42.3	111	731.8	431.4	56.5
Leather: tanned, curried, and finished	16.0	12.4	5.8	6	23.5	13.3	9.0
Footwear, except rubber	52.5	38.8	36.1	128	131.0	114.4	7.8

Table 17-A-6. OCCUPATIONAL CHANGE, 1900 TO 1950, BY DETAILED OCCUPATIONS -Con.

Detailed occupation	Percent female			Change (000)	Percent change		
	1950	1930	1900	1900–1950	1900–1950	1900–1930	1930–1950
OPERATIVES AND KINDRED WORKERS-Con.							
Leather products, except footwear.....	54.9	25.3	6.3	19	61.2	-16.6	93.3
Not specified manufacturing industries....	47.9	46.1	43.4	-24	-35.4	107.5	-68.9
Nonmanufacturing....	23.2	14.2	17.5	631	423.9	199.0	75.2
Construction....	2.1	0.2	0.2	65	981.1	127.7	374.8
Railroads and railway express service....; Transportation, except railroad....; Telecommunications, and utilities and sanitary services....; Wholesale and retail trade....	24.8	12.5	18.9	413	301.8	89.2	112.3
Business and repair services....; Public administration....; Personal services....	12.8	10.1	(b)	54	(b)	(b)	789.3
All other industries (including not reported)....	34.8	18.4	3.3	99	1,857.4	2,987.0	-36.6
PRIVATE HOUSEHOLD WORKERS.......	94.8	95.6	96.7	-41	-2.6	26.5	-23.0
Laundresses, priv.hshld.--living in; laundresses,priv.hshld.-- living out....	96.9	99.7	99.3	-204	-73.0	23.1	-78.1
Housekeepers, priv.hshld.--living in; housekeepers, priv.hshld.-- living out.--	94.7	94.7	96.1	164	12.6	27.3	-11.6
Priv.hshld.workers (n.e.c.)--living in; priv.hshld.workers (n.e.c.)-- living out....							
SERVICE WORKERS, EXCEPT PRIVATE HOUSEHOLD....	44.7	37.7	34.3	3,594	343.4	165.0	67.3
Attendants, hospital and other institution....	74.3	81.7	89.5	258	236.3	81.0	85.8
Midwives; practical nurses....; Attendants, professional and personal services (n.e.c.)....	66.8	63.3	(b)	52	(b)	(b)	1,101.4
Attendants, recreation and amusement....; Ushers, recreation and amusement....	15.1	11.4	1.6	87	1,480.9	389.3	223.1
Barbers, beauticians, and manicurists....	50.0	30.2	5.5	264	198.4	179.0	7.0
Bartenders....	6.7	(b)	0.5	125	141.2	100.0	(b)
Boarding and lodging house keepers....	73.0	88.2	83.4	-42	-58.2	102.5	-79.4
Bootblacks....	3.4	0.2	1.0	7	85.0	128.2	-19.0
Charwomen and cleaners....	59.9	66.8	84.1	98	332.9	76.0	145.9
Cooks, except private household....	54.1	39.0	39.7	362	309.8	150.1	63.9
Elevator operators....	30.3	18.3	0.2	84	663.3	432.8	43.2
Firemen, fire prevention....; Guards, watchmen, and doorkeepers....	0.4	...	...	98	672.6	402.3	53.8
Policemen and detectives, government....; Policemen and detectives, private....; Marshals and constables....	2.0	0.9	0.7	343	297.2	161.5	51.9
Housekeepers and stewards, except private household....	77.8	69.5	77.8	78	232.4	80.1	84.6
Janitors and sextons....	11.7	11.6	14.2	426	752.3	447.3	55.7
Porters....	2.3	0.2	...	137	326.9	259.4	18.8
Sheriffs and bailiffs....	4.1	1.8					

Table 17-A-6. OCCUPATIONAL CHANGE, 1900 TO 1950, BY DETAILED OCCUPATIONS—Con.

Detailed occupation	Percent female			Change (000)	Percent change		
	1950	1930	1900	1900–1950	1900–1950	1900–1930	1930–1950
SERVICE WORKERS, EXCEPT PRIVATE HOUSEHOLD.—Con.							
Counter and fountain workers; waiters and waitresses	78.5	57.9	40.0	729	630.8	287.7	101.4
Watchmen (crossing) and bridge tenders	4.0	1.5	0.3	7	166.8	180.9	-5.0
Service workers, except private household (n.e.c.)	60.3	59.9	48.7	468	502.5	178.8	116.1
FARM LABORERS AND FOREMEN	18.7	15.0	13.6	-2,547	-49.7	-16.3	-39.9
Farm foremen	3.5	0.8	5.4	11	165.3	323.3	-37.3
Farm laborers, wage workers	18.8	15.1	13.6	-2,564	50.1	16.8	-40.1
Farm laborers, unpaid family workers	13.3	...	4.7	6	136.0	19.2	97.9
Farm service laborers, self-employed	3.7	3.0	3.8	265	7.3	47.4	27.2
LABORERS, EXCEPT FARM AND MINE							
Fishermen and oystermen	1.4	0.3	0.7	6	8.2	6.3	1.8
Garage laborers, and car washers and greasers	3.4	0.2	(b)	72	(b)	(b)	-5.7
Gardeners, except farm, and groundskeepers	2.4	1.2	2.1	135	564.0	600.4	-5.2
Longshoremen and stevedores	1.1	...	0.1	43	147.9	152.7	-1.9
Lumbermen, raftsmen, and wood choppers	0.9	0.1	0.2	79	67.6	25.8	33.2
Teamsters	1.5	...	1.1	-351	-93.9	-67.8	-81.1
Laborers (n.e.c.)	4.1	3.3	4.5	278	9.2	55.4	-29.7
Manufacturing	6.4	5.8	5.4	486	67.1	171.0	-38.3
Sawmills, planing mills, and mill work	2.5	2.0	0.6	31	21.9	109.5	-41.8
Miscellaneous wood products							
Furniture and fixtures	7.1	3.7	2.0	14	190.4	437.9	-46.0
Glass and glass products	8.8	6.2	3.3	1	6.0	89.9	-44.2
Cement and concrete, gypsum, and plaster products	0.8	0.4	0.9	11	86.7	206.4	-39.1
Structural clay products	2.5	1.3	0.5	-13	-31.1	43.4	-52.0
Pottery and related products	10.8	8.1	5.9	1	19.2	94.8	-38.8
Miscellaneous nonmetallic mineral and stone products	3.0	0.1	0.6	2	31.0	12.3	16.6
Motor vehicles and motor vehicle equipment							
Ship and boat building and repairing							
Blast furnaces, steel works, and rolling mills							
Other primary iron and steel industries; fabricated steel prod							
Office and store machines and devices	3.3	1.9	1.2	247	170.0	335.8	-38.0
Miscellaneous machinery							
Not specified metal industries							
Agricultural machinery and tractors							
Aircraft and parts							
Railroad and miscellaneous transportation equipment							
Primary nonferrous industries; fabricated nonferrous metal products	3.5	2.4	0.7	18	122.1	159.3	-11.4
Electrical machinery, equipment, and supplies	16.7	9.6	11.4	24	290.3	341.1	-11.5
Professional equipment and supplies; photographic equipment and supplies							
Watches, clocks, and clockwork-operated devices; misc. manufacturing industries	18.8	7.8	9.3	-8	-26.5	146.4	-70.2

Table 17-A-6. OCCUPATIONAL CHANGE, 1900 TO 1950, BY DETAILED OCCUPATIONS -Con.

Detailed occupation	Percent female			Change (000)	Percent change		
	1950	1930	1900	1900-1950	1900-1950	1900-1930	1930-1950
LABORERS, EXCEPT FARM AND MINE—Con.							
Meat products	12.2	14.2	9.9	52	416.7	455.6	-7.0
Canning and preserving fruits, vegetables, and sea foods	4.8	5.2	2.3	10	176.6	218.1	-13.0
Dairy products	1.6	1.0	0.4	10	96.9	58.5	24.3
Grain-mill products	12.9	12.7	8.2	6	185.5	269.6	-22.7
Bakery products	16.1	26.5	17.7	1	36.3	79.1	-23.9
Confectionery and related products	3.0	2.6	2.0	13	102.5	31.6	196.1
Beverage industries / Miscellaneous food preparations and kindred products; not specified food industries	5.9	15.0	6.4	21	718.5	814.6	-10.5
Tobacco manufactures	31.8	31.5	20.6	-4	-26.6	52.3	-51.8
Knitting mills	29.5	37.5	48.4	-1	-16.2	158.6	67.6
Dyeing and finishing textiles, except knit goods	4.0	4.1	3.0	-6	-64.4	-16.4	-57.4
Carpets, rugs, and other floor coverings	8.0	12.3	8.6	4	248.3	177.5	25.5
Yarn, thread, and fabric mills	14.1	15.8	18.7	6	12.8	112.9	-47.0
Miscellaneous textile mill products	13.3	11.1	19.7	-1	-25.2	0.8	-25.8
Apparel and accessories	40.8	46.4	59.9	3	61.8	158.7	-37.5
Miscellaneous fabricated textile products	22.2	14.3	24.4	2	356.3	109.8	117.5
Pulp, paper, and paperboard mills	5.1	5.7	6.5	23	165.4	294.7	-32.8
Miscellaneous paper and pulp products	14.9	23.2	60.3	9	677.0	105.3	273.4
Paperboard containers and boxes	10.6	12.8	20.6	8	185.4	156.4	11.3
Printing, publishing, and allied industries	6.7	10.3	(b)	3	(b)	(b)	-32.9
Synthetic fibers	5.6	2.5	3.8	3	128.3	187.2	-20.5
Paints, varnishes, and related products	4.4	3.3	3.0	46	306.2	437.1	-24.4
Drugs and medicines; miscellaneous chemical and allied products	1.0	0.4	0.3	20	379.6	671.6	-37.8
Petroleum refining	1.5	0.2	0.1	-5	-45.2	-57.2	28.0
Miscellaneous petroleum and coal products	13.4	10.8	13.9	12	196.5	395.3	-40.1
Rubber products	12.1	3.1	1.5	-8	-52.5	6.3	-55.3
Leather: tanned, curried, and finished	29.7	25.8	25.4	•••	7.7	235.6	-67.9
Footwear, except rubber	26.5	10.1	5.0	-1	-33.2	9.1	-38.7
Leather products, except footwear	11.6	10.6	7.0	-68	-85.8	43.1	-90.1
Not specified manufacturing industries	2.8	1.5	4.2	-205	-9.0	18.9	-23.4
Nonmanufacturing industries (including not reported)	0.8	•••	0.5	768	3,756.1	3,375.2	11.0
Construction	2.4	0.7	0.4	9	3.2	72.9	-40.3
Railroads and railway express service / Transportation, except railroad	1.7	0.4	0.1	168	196.0	190.3	2.0
Telecommunications, and utilities and sanitary services	5.4	3.7	0.8	276	403.7	269.3	36.4
Wholesale and retail trade	4.2	0.2	•••	14	1,399.4	1,415.3	1.0
Business and repair services / Public administration / Personal services	2.8	0.8	(b)	107	(b)	(b)	-19.7
All other industries (including not reported)	6.6	3.1	5.2	1,548	-84.8	-52.6	67.9

(a) No answer.
(b) Estimated to be zero in 1900 or 1930 or both.

Source: U. S. Bureau of the Census, Occupational Trends in the United States, 1900 to 1950, by David L. Kaplan and M. Claire Casey, Bureau of the Census Working Paper No. 5, 1958.

Chapter 18

INDUSTRIAL COMPOSITION*

Jobs may be classified not only according to the kind of work involved (occupation), but also according to the business (industry) of the employer. Thus, three men may work as carpenters, but each may be in a different industry. One may be employed in a furniture factory (manufacturing industry); one may work for a contractor who builds houses (construction industry); and one may work for a wholesale firm which makes crates for shipping bulky items (trade industries). For many purposes, it is as desirable to know the kinds of business or industry in which people are employed as it is to know what kinds of work they do. Until the 1940 census, a clear distinction was not made between these two aspects of employment, and "occupational statistics" were actually a combination of occupation and industry. This distinction was made explicit in the 1940 and 1950 censuses, and two separate and distinct series of data were recognized: occupational statistics (kind of work) and industry statistics (kind of business in which employed). Separate data for industry of employment have been made available by these two censuses. For many years the Bureau of Labor Statistics in the U. S. Department of Labor has emphasized industry statistics, and has published data concerning the amount of employment and other information about each nonagricultural industry. Interagency committees within the Federal Government, working in cooperation with private experts, have developed a Standard Industrial Classification (SIC) for use in publishing official statistics, which has promoted the comparability of the data published by various agencies. The categories used to tabulate the industrial statistics which are released by the Bureau of the Census and the Bureau of Labor Statistics are consistent with the Standard Industrial Classification, although they tend to be combinations of the very detailed SIC classifications.

The industrial classification of employed persons is made on the basis of the job at which a person was employed during the week to which the labor force enumeration applies. (Persons holding two or more jobs are classified according to the job at which they worked the greatest number of hours.) Unemployed persons are classified on the basis of the last job they held. Unemployed persons who have never worked are given the special category "new worker," and no industrial information can be tabulated concerning them.

As is the case of occupational classification, industrial classification is made at three levels:

   Detailed industrial classification--148 categories

   Intermediate industrial classification-- 77 categories

   Major industrial classification--12 categories

A listing of the major industrial groups is given below. Table 18-A-1 (end of the chapter) makes use of the intermediate industrial classification (the Bureau of the Census did not make extensive use of the detailed classification). Examples of

---

*A tabulation presenting statistics for industrial composition, by sex, for urban, rural-nonfarm, and rural-farm areas of each geographic divisions for both 1950 and 1940 is contained in the statistical appendix.

the intermediate industrial classification will be used throughout the discussion of this chapter. The 12 major categories, with the percent of the employed population which each category contained in 1950 and the percent change in employment in each between 1940 and 1950, are as follows:

Major industry	Percent of employed persons	Percent change, 1940 to 1950
Total.....................	100.0	25.3
Agriculture, forestry, fisheries..	12.5	-17.5
Mining......................	1.7	1.7
Construction	6.1	65.8
Manufacturing.................	25.9	37.9
Durable goods...............	13.8	51.6
Nondurable goods............	11.9	27.1
Not spec. manufacturing ind....	0.2	-33.4
Transport., commun., and other public utilities	7.8	40.6
Wholesale and retail trade.......	18.8	39.8
Finance, insurance, real estate..	3.4	30.1
Business and repair services	2.5	58.4
Personal services..............	6.2	-12.2
Entertainment, recreation serv...	1.0	32.1
Professional and related services.	8.3	42.1
Public administration	4.4	77.0
Industry not reported.........	1.5	15.4

This classification, with the intermediate and detailed classifications that form a part of the system, is an extremely valuable addition to the body of official Federal statistics. Perhaps many demographers and human ecologists do not adequately appreciate it. The nation's work is not performed by individuals working independently of and in isolation from each other, but by persons working in groups as members of establishments, firms, and institutions. Much has been written about the division of labor in modern society, and how minutely divided tasks are integrated and organized under one roof, or several roofs, to accomplish useful functions. The occupational statistics give us information about the division of work; the industrial statistics give us information about the integration of occupations and the types of units into which work is organized. What a

community does to earn its living, what kinds of economic institutions form its "economic base," and what it requires in the way of imports and exports with respect to other areas, can best be determined on the basis of industrial classification. Also, basic changes in the economy, or fluctuations in economic activity, tend to have an industrial rather than an occupational pattern. During times of economic depression, it is the firm--the industry (such as construction or coal mining industry)--that is depressed; the individual worker loses his job because of the financial difficulties of his firm, not because of the particular work he performs in that firm. Not infrequently, one industry will be laying off persons who perform a certain kind of work and another industry will be hiring them. If a community undergoes a radical change in its mode of earning a living, it is usually because major units of industry have been added or subtracted--because particular firms decide either to locate there or to go out of business.

This brief discussion should be sufficient to show that industrial statistics are as important as occupational statistics, and that both are essential if the social scientist is to understand how a nation or a community is organized to earn its living and how changes take place in that organization.

In portraying the industrial composition of the working force and the recent changes in that composition, the present chapter presents data concerning all three levels of industrial classification--the major, the intermediate, and the detailed. All too often information is presented only for the major industrial categories, with the result that the full content of industrial composition is not grasped. Since the statistical tables for the detailed industrial classifications are very lengthy and run to several pages, they are placed in a special statistical appendix at the end of this chapter, and are identified as Tables 18-A-1 to 18-A-4, inclusive.

PRESENT INDUSTRIAL STRUCTURE

The data presented above show that, as of 1950, the largest single industry group is the one engaged in manufacturing; about one-fourth of the working population is engaged in the fabricating of goods. This work ranges all the way from canning or preserving foods to operating blast furnaces and steel rolling mills. Not all of these people are production workers in shops or on the assembly line, however. Some of them are proprietors and managers of manufacturing firms and their staffs of accountants, stenographers, clerks, and other white-collar workers. Also included are a large number of people who do not actually fabricate goods: packers, shipping and stockroom workers, the truck drivers who haul the product away (if they are employed by the firm), and the janitors who clean up after the production and administrative forces. Manufacturing activities are subdivided into two major categories, the production of durable goods and of nondurable goods. The durable goods industries are those that manufacture lumber, furniture, cement, products made of stone, clay, and glass, steel, machinery, motor vehicles, and other similar commodities that have a considerable lifetime of use. Nondurable goods industries produce food, textiles, apparel, paper, chemicals, leather products, and similar items that are consumed rather quickly. In the American economy these two major branches of production are of about equal size, although the number of workers in the durable goods industries is somewhat larger than the number in the nondurable goods industries.

Only a little smaller than the manufacturing force is the group of workers who were engaged in trade (wholesale and retail) in 1950--19 percent. In this category fall not only food stores, department stores and drug, apparel, shoe, furniture, liquor, jewelry, and other stores common to most large shopping centers, but also filling stations, restaurants, taverns, and wholesaling establishments of all types. Thus, the task of assembling, displaying, and offering for sale at convenient points the commodities which are produced on farms and in factories requires almost as many workers as the task of fabrication.

Agriculture is the third largest industry; in 1950 it occupied 12 percent of the working force. The position of agriculture in modern industrial organization is sometimes described by the statement that each farm worker is feeding many nonfarm workers (8 in 1950). This does not tell the whole story, however, because it is the nonfarm workers who produce the machinery, the fertilizer, and the equipment which make this feat possible, and who carry out the scientific research and engineering that enable a smaller and smaller proportion of persons to be engaged in agricultural production. In fact, the process of feeding the population involves not less than 1/4 of the population more or less directly. In addition to the agricultural workers noted above, there are:

2.5 percent employed in the manufacture of food products

3.1 percent employed in food retailing

6.7 percent employed in the wholesaling of food items and farm raw materials

0.8 percent employed in the manufacture of farm machinery

Ranked after the "big three" of the industrial structure--manufacture, trade, and agriculture--is a series of major industries each of which employs 4 to 8 percent of all workers. Construction (6 percent) includes the activities connected with the building of highways and bridges as well as the construction of business buildings and homes. About 8 percent of all workers are in the transportation industries, which include taxi and bus drivers, persons employed in warehousing and storage, and the employees of petroleum pipe line companies as well as of trucking firms, railways, airlines, and steamship lines. Professional services--medical, educational, legal, religious, welfare, engineering, architectural, etc.--employ 8 percent of all workers. Public administration (4 percent) includes the employees of the Federal, state, and local governments, and of the postal service. Personal services (6 percent) include workers in private households, hotels and lodging places, and laundering and dry cleaning establishments, as well as dressmakers, workers in shoe repair shops, barber and beauty shops, etc.

The remaining classes of industry, though of fundamental importance to the economy, offer employment to only a comparatively small fraction of workers. Only 2 percent of the working force is needed in the mining which extracts the ores and fuels needed by the economy. The 3 percent of workers who are employed in finance do the banking, insurance, and real estate work of the nation, while entertainment is provided by 1 percent of the working force.

This brief description of the major industrial groups is only an introduction to the industrial structure. In order to learn which of the more detailed industries have been classed under each of these major headings, and how large each one is, the reader is referred to Table 18-A-1 at the end of this chapter. This table reports the total number of persons employed in each industry in 1950, and shows what proportion of all the total employed persons worked in each industry at that time.

CHANGES IN INDUSTRIAL COMPOSITION: 1950-1957 AND 1940-1950

As indicated in Chapter 17, since 1820 the agricultural industries have grown more slowly than

(a change of -17.5 percent), but it appears to have been even more severe between 1950 and 1957 (a decline from 7.2 to 5.1 million workers, for an implied loss of 29 percent in 8 years). Since 1950, the farm population has declined at an average rate of almost 3 percent per year, a faster rate of decline than took place in any previous decade.

The Bureau of the Census does not report statistics concerning the individual classes of nonagricultural industry in its monthly Current Population Survey. The data provided by the Bureau of Labor Statistics, however, makes it possible to measure the above changes.

According to BLS reports, employment in the nonagricultural industries increased by 17 percent between 1950 and 1957 (see Table 18-1).[1] Few of the industrial groups grew at this rate. Those that grew considerably faster were:

Finance, insurance, real estate (29 percent)

Service industries (25 percent)

Government--state and local (32 percent)

The industrial classes that have grown most slowly since 1950 are:

Mining (a loss of 9 percent)

Manufacturing, nondurable goods (1 percent)

Table 18-1.—PRESENT INDUSTRIAL COMPOSITION (1957): AND RECENT CHANGES IN INDUSTRIAL COMPOSITION OF THE NONAGRICULTURAL WORKING FORCE: 1950 TO 1957

Industry group	Number of employees		Percent change 1950 to 1957	Percent distribution	
	1957 (000)	1950 (000)		1957	1950
Total...................................	52,162	44,738	16.6	100.0	100.0
Mining.................................	809	889	-9.0	1.6	2.0
Contract construction..................	2,808	2,333	20.4	5.4	5.2
Manufacturing.........................	16,782	14,967	12.1	32.2	33.5
Durable goods......................	9,821	8,085	21.5	18.8	18.1
Nondurable goods...................	6,961	6,882	1.1	13.3	15.4
Transportation, communication, and public utilities....	4,151	3,977	4.4	8.0	8.9
Wholesale and retail trade............	11,302	9,645	17.2	21.7	21.6
Wholesale trade....................	3,065	2,571	19.2	5.9	5.7
Retail trade.......................	8,237	7,074	16.4	15.8	15.8
Finance, insurance, real estate........	2,348	1,824	28.7	4.5	4.1
Service and miscellaneous.............	6,336	5,077	24.8	12.1	11.3
Government............................	7,626	6,026	26.6	14.6	13.5
Federal............................	2,217	1,928	15.0	4.2	4.3
State and local....................	5,409	4,098	32.0	10.4	9.2

the nonagricultural industries. Since 1910 there has been an actual decline in the number of persons employed in agricultural industries. This decline was very sharp between 1940 and 1950

[1] These statistics are based upon the averages of the 12 monthly reports for the years 1950 and 1957. The 1950 figures have been revised to make them comparable with the new bench mark which was established in 1956.

Transportation, communications, public utilities (4 percent)

Only the following few industries grew at approximately the national average rate for all industries:

Contract construction (20 percent)
Manufacturing, durable goods (22 percent)
Trade, wholesale and retail (17 percent)
Government, federal (15 percent)

The over-all effect of this differential growth has been that mining, nondurable goods manufacture, and transportation have each become smaller sources of employment than they used to be, and that finance, services, and state and local government have each gained a larger share of workers than they previously employed.

To many persons it is a source of concern that the government now employs one of every seven nonagricultural workers, and that the government labor force is growing at a considerably faster rate than the nongovernmental labor force. Many people who are worried about these statistics, however, fail to realize that state and local governments together employ more than twice as many workers as the Federal Government, and that the highest rates of growth in employment are among state and local governments. Between 1950 and 1957, employment in the Federal Government grew by 15 percent, while in the state and local government field it grew by 32 percent, or more than twice as much. Moreover, if they knew the specific occupations to which the added government workers have been assigned (see below), perhaps most citizens would approve the expansion.

Rates of change between 1940 and 1950, for each of the major nonagricultural industry groups, have been presented above; a review of these rates will make it evident that the changes since 1950 are largely an extension, with some modifications, of changes which were already underway in the 1940 to 1950 decade. Between 1940 and 1950 the fastest-growing industries were public administration (government), construction, business services, and professional services.[2] Manufacturing, trade, finance, and entertainment grew at a rate which was about the same as the national average for all nonagricultural industries. This picture is essentially the same as the one that has been described for 1950 to 1957. However, transportation grew much more rapidly in the 1940 to 1950 decade than it has grown since 1950. Between 1940 and 1950 truck transportation was burgeoning, and air transportation was growing from an infant to a giant industry.

Table 18-A-1, at the end of this chapter, contains statistics concerning the rate of change in each intermediate industrial class, 1940-50. From the data in this table two lists of industries have been compiled, one of fast-growing industries (those that grew twice as fast as the national average) and one of slow-growing industries (those that grew less than half as fast as the national average).

List 18-1.—FAST GROWING INDUSTRIES (Growing twice the average national rate): 1940 to 1950

Detailed industry	Percent change 1940 to 1950
MANUFACTURES	
Cement and concrete, gypsum, and plaster products	60.1
Primary nonferrous metal industries	54.1
Machinery, except electrical	79.0
Electrical machinery	112.9
Motor vehicles	52.1
Aircraft	140.0
Canning and preserving fruits, vegetables, and sea foods	60.7

List 18-2.—SLOW GROWING OR DECLINING INDUSTRIES (Growing less than one-half as rapidly as the national average): 1940 to 1950

Detailed industry	Percent change 1940 to 1950
AGRICULTURE, FORESTRY, FISHERIES	
Agriculture	-18.1
Forestry	-3.2

[2] In this decade, employment in the Federal Government grew much more rapidly than employment in state and local governments.

List 1.-Continued

Paperboard boxes.................. 62.2
Drugs and medicines 65.2

TRANSPORTATION

Warehousing 76.7
Taxicabs........................ 95.2
Air transportation 323.9
Telephone (wire and radio)......... 90.1

WHOLESALE AND RETAIL TRADE

Wholesale trade, total............. 64.4
Retail tr., five and ten cent stores ... 113.9
Retail tr., furniture, hshld. furnishing 51.5
Household appliances and radios..... 101.2
Motor vehicles and accessories 58.4
Eating and drinking places 51.4
Hardware and farm implements 62.8
Lumber and building materials, ret.. 55.8
Liquor stores 85.8
Retail florists................... 54.8
Jewelry stores 74.1

BUSINESS AND REPAIR SERVICES

Advertising 52.2
Accounting, auditing, bookkeeping... 101.6

PERSONAL SERVICES

Laundering, cleaning, and dyeing.... 53.2

ENTERTAINMENT

Radio broadcasting and T.V......... 152.2

PROFESSIONAL SERVICES

Medical services and hospitals 59.3
Educational services, private....... 56.9
Welfare and religious services 80.0

PUBLIC ADMINISTRATION

Federal......................... 230.3

Some of these industries were affected by the introduction of new products or new lines of production (T.V., aircraft, air conditioners, etc.) and others by the development of improved modes of accomplishing certain desired results. For example, the electric refrigerator, the deep freeze, and the oil furnace together dealt a severe blow to the ice and coal companies that were an established part of every city's industrial complement.

List 2.-Continued

MINING

Metal mining..................... -22.3
Coal mining...................... -3.5

MANUFACTURING

Miscellaneous wood industries 9.0
Ship and boat building and repairing.. 2.6
Tobacco manufactures .... -13.8
Textiles--knitting mills .... -10.7
Textiles--yarn, thread, fabric mills . 9.9
Pulp, paper, and paperboard mills .. 12.0
Chemicals--synthetic fibers 4.5
Leather and leather pr. (incl. footwear) 8.2

RETAIL TRADE

Dairy products stores, milk retail... -13.9
Gasoline service stations.......... 11.9
Fuel and ice retailing .... -11.7

PERSONAL SERVICES

Private households................. -29.9
Hotels and lodging places 1.1
Dressmaking, shoe repair, misc.
  personal services .... -4.8

URBAN AND RURAL INDUSTRIAL COMPOSITION

It must be remembered that the census statistics for population refer to the place where the worker lives and not to the location of the place where he works. Hence, the urban-rural distribution of employed persons in each industry provides only a very approximate idea of the urban-rural distribution of the places that employ these workers. This is especially true with respect to suburban populations, for vast numbers of metropolitanites live in communities which differ greatly from the places where their work is located. Table 18-2 provides information about industrial composition by urban and rural residence of the workers. From this information one may infer that the industrial compositions of the urban and the rural-nonfarm populations are generally similar, except for about 9 percent of the rural-nonfarm population which is engaged in agriculture and about 5 percent which is engaged in mining. If one excludes these two industries he will find that the rural-nonfarm and urban populations have similar industrial structures. In comparison with the urban population, the rural-nonfarm population has a small deficit of persons employed in finance and entertainment services and a small excess of workers in professional services and construction. These differences are a consequence of the fact that the major financial institutions and public entertainment establishments are highly concentrated at the center of the city, and that a disproportionately large share of new construction is taking place in the suburbs.

As Chapter 17 revealed, not all workers living on farms are farm workers. In 1950, only 71 percent of the rural-farm population was employed in agricultural industry; a significant proportion of farm residents--in view of their proportion in the general working population--were in each of the other industrial classifications. A disproportionately large share of the rural-farm population who are not farmers are manufacturing workers or miners who operate farms either part-time or at a subsistence level. A disproportionately small share are in finance, trade, entertainment, personal services, and public administration.

The estimated change in employment in each industry, 1940 to 1950, according to urban and rural areas shows that the rural-nonfarm population has increased very rapidly in all categories except personal services and mining. (This change may indicate suburbanization of residence rather than suburbanization of industries.) The rural-farm population also made large gains in all the nonextractive industries except personal services and professional services. In the case of the rural-nonfarm population these changes are due, at least in part, to the increased number of suburban homes and the rapid growth of outlying shopping centers. Employment changes among the rural-farm population are due almost entirely to the fact that "living on a farm in the country" has become a residential arrangement for vast quantities of nonagricultural workers and their families. This

Table 18-2.—INDUSTRIAL COMPOSITION AND PERCENT CHANGE IN EMPLOYMENT OF MAJOR INDUSTRIES, BY URBAN AND RURAL RESIDENCE: 1940 TO 1950

Major industry group	Percent distribution, 1950				Percent change, 1940 to 1950			
	Total	Urban	Rural nonfarm	Rural farm	Total	Urban	Rural nonfarm	Rural farm
Total..........................	100.0	100.0	100.0	100.0	25.3	30.9	52.9	-16.9
Agriculture, forestry, and fisheries.......	12.5	1.1	9.1	71.0	-17.5	-13.9	72.7	-25.1
Mining..................................	1.7	0.9	4.9	1.3	1.7	-4.6	19.5	-6.1
Construction............................	6.1	6.0	8.9	3.1	65.8	38.2	89.6	28.7
Manufacturing..........................	25.9	29.4	25.6	9.4	37.9	15.2	57.1	30.0
Durable goods......................	13.8	15.5	14.0	5.4	51.6			
Nondurable goods..................	11.9	13.7	11.4	3.9	27.1			
Not specified.....................	0.2	0.2	0.2	0.1	-33.4			
Transport., commun., and other public util.	7.8	9.0	7.4	2.1	40.6	26.7	54.5	24.9
Wholesale and retail trade..............	18.8	21.9	18.0	4.3	39.8	22.1	57.3	23.6
Finance, insurance, and real estate.......	3.4	4.4	1.9	0.5	30.1	24.5	42.5	38.7
Business and repair services.............	2.5	2.7	3.1	0.8	58.4	45.9	74.8	27.7
Personal services.....................	6.2	7.2	5.9	1.7	-12.2	-24.2	6.3	-50.8
Entertainment and recreation services......	1.0	1.2	0.8	0.1	32.1	19.9	39.0	4.1
Professional and related services..........	8.3	9.5	8.4	2.7	42.1	27.5	47.8	-12.0
Public administration.....................	4.4	5.2	4.0	1.2	77.0	50.4	81.4	50.0
Industry not reported.....................	1.5	1.3	1.9	1.8	15.4	28.2	43.2	79.2

way of life seems to have been adopted at a very rapid rate during the 1940 to 1950 decade. People of all socio-economic levels took part in the movement. One of the largest groups of participants was made up of manufacturing workers (see Figure 18-1). Although no data are available for the years since 1950, it is very likely (in view of the vast amount of other evidence about suburbanization) that this movement has continued and perhaps has even accelerated.

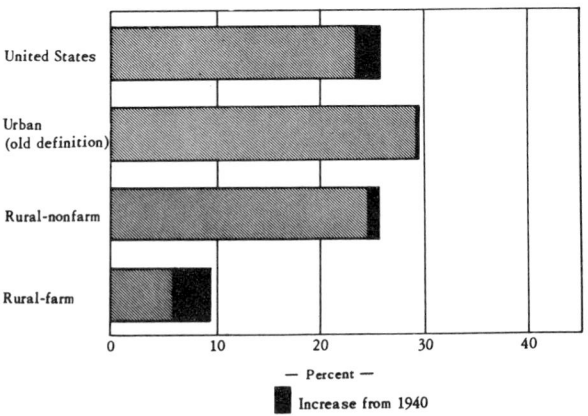

FIGURE 18-1.   PERCENT OF EMPLOYED WORKERS IN
MANUFACTURING INDUSTRIES, BY URBAN AND
RURAL RESIDENCE, 1940 AND 1950

SEX COMPOSITION OF INDUSTRIES

Certain industries, such as agriculture, mining, construction, transportation, public utilities, and sanitary services have a very small proportion of female employees (see Table 18-3). The hazards, discomforts, and hard labor involved in these industries are the primary reasons for this differential. Durable goods manufacturing, wholesale trade, and business and repair services also employ a disproportionately small number of women; in these cases tradition, as well as the nature of the work, may be responsible for the differential. Above-average concentrations of woman workers are found in nondurable goods manufacture (especially of foods and textiles), finance (bank tellers, bookkeepers), personal services (domestic servants and maids in hotels), and professional services (nurses and school teachers). A compari-

son of the percent change, 1940 to 1950, for male and female workers in each industry group shows that the employment of woman workers increased at a much faster rate than the employment of male workers in every industry which is mentioned above as having a comparative deficit of women. In fact, woman workers increased at a faster rate than men in every industry group except two: private household and education are two of the industries where woman workers already greatly outnumbered men. Thus, the 1940 to 1950 decade witnessed a sizable decline in the ratio of men to women in most industries. However, this decline is not evidence that women were taking on the tasks formerly performed by men; it may only mean that male-dominated industries hired women receptionists, typists, and similar workers at a faster rate than other industries. For an analysis of sex differentials in work assignment and of changes in these differentials, the reader is referred to Chapter 17, which discusses sex differentials in occupation.

RACE COMPOSITION OF INDUSTRIES

As column 4 in Table 18-3 shows, Negroes are excluded from none of the major industry groups. The proportion of Negroes in agriculture has declined, and is now not a great deal higher than that of white workers. In the nonagricultural industries the race differential is much smaller than the sex differential. Also, the race differential is considerably smaller by industry than by occupation, which implies that the preferential employment of white workers is more closely connected with occupation than with industry. Perhaps every industry has certain occupations for which it will hire Negroes, and other occupations from which it will exclude them. For example, a large department store which does not hesitate to employ Negro stockroom boys, elevator operators, dishwashers, and janitors may refuse to hire Negro sales personnel or office workers. It is this willingness to hire Negroes for at least some jobs that causes race differentials to be smaller between industries than between occupations.

Table 18-3.—SELECTED CHARACTERISTICS OF EMPLOYEES IN MAJOR INDUSTRY GROUPS: 1950

Industry group	Percent female, 1950	Percent change, 1940 to 1950		Percent Negro, 1950 (male)	Percent self-employed (male)	Number of weeks worked, 1949 (male)	
		Male	Female			1 to 26 weeks	50 to 52 weeks
Total...........................	28.0	20.0	41.1	8.6	21.2	10.5	68.2
Agriculture, forestry, and fisheries.........	8.4	-20.0	20.7	13.5	66.2	11.7	70.2
Mining.................................	2.5	0.4	111.9	4.7	3.8	20.4	39.1
Construction..........................	2.9	63.9	170.5	8.7	19.2	17.3	46.1
Manufacturing.........................	25.0	32.6	56.6	7.5	3.4	8.4	67.5
Durable goods.......................	16.0	42.9	122.1	8.1	3.1	8.7	63.4
Nondurable goods....................	35.3	22.1	37.7	6.6	3.7	7.9	73.7
Transport., commun., and other public util...	15.6	33.3	100.2	8.5	5.3	7.5	73.0
Transportation.....................	6.6	30.3	150.3	9.4	6.7	8.4	69.4
Telecommunications.................	60.6	55.9	90.6	2.3	0.6	3.5	87.5
Utilities and sanitary services...........	12.2	38.5	66.6	7.1	1.0	5.2	82.4
Wholesale and retail trade..................	33.7	26.8	75.1	6.1	25.6	9.3	75.6
Wholesale trade.....................	19.2	56.4	109.2	5.4	15.4	7.0	78.5
Retail trade........................	37.0	20.1	71.7	6.3	28.6	10.0	74.7
Finance, insurance, and real estate..........	40.7	11.7	71.1	5.2	15.8	6.3	82.5
Business and repair services.................	12.9	51.4	132.4	5.9	30.1	9.4	73.1
Personal services..........................	66.7	2.0	-17.9	20.6	27.7	13.3	68.7
Private households..................	87.4	-23.2	-30.7	44.8	4.8	26.8	50.0
Hotels and lodging places.............	48.6	-0.1	2.4	17.7	17.8	15.0	64.3
Other personal services.............	48.6	14.1	22.3	14.5	38.5	8.7	76.0
Entertainment and recreation services........	25.5	22.8	67.4	8.4	13.3	20.5	57.7
Professional and related services............	58.2	37.3	45.6	7.5	20.2	8.4	71.1
Medical and health.....................	63.8	39.1	73.5	8.7	37.5	6.7	78.1
Educational............................	63.8	41.9	28.1	7.5	1.9	10.5	57.9
Other.................................	36.5	30.5	51.1	6.3	25.8	7.5	80.7
Public administration......................	26.2	67.3	111.3	7.4	...	5.1	84.3

Source: U.S. Census of Population: 1950, Characteristics of the Population, U.S. Summary, Tables 130, 131, 132, 133, and 135.

Nevertheless, there are some significant differentials between industries, many of which have an indirect occupational basis. Disproportionately few Negroes are employed in mining, wholesale trade, finance, and business services--and disproportionately many work in personal services. Negroes are somewhat more numerous in the manufacture of durable goods than in the production of nondurable goods, which may be due to the fact that they are often employed to work around hot metal in steel mills and foundries, and to do other jobs in the durable goods industries which involve unusual discomfort. Also, much of the nondurable goods manufacturing (especially textiles) is located in the South, where hiring practices are more severely preferential.

No statistics are available with which to evaluate recent changes in the differentials between industries. The evidence presented in Chapter 17,

however, concerning the decline since 1950 in race differentials among occupational groups, makes it seem almost inevitable that the race differentials among industry groups have also shown a very large decline since 1950.

AGE COMPOSITION AND INDUSTRY

Certain industries welcome extremely young workers while other industries (especially those that are stable or are declining in size) have above-average concentrations of older workers (Table 18-4). The following industries tend to employ a disproportionately large share of young workers (teenagers):

Agriculture (unpaid family workers, temporary farm laborers)

Manufacturing, nondurable goods (printing, bakeries, textiles)

Table 18-4.—AGE COMPOSITION OF MAJOR INDUSTRY GROUPS: 1950

Industry group	All ages	Percent distribution by age, males				
		14 to 19 years	20 to 24 years	25 to 44 years	45 to 64 years	65 years and over
Total..........................	100.0	4.9	9.7	47.9	31.8	5.6
Agriculture, forestry, and fisheries..........	100.0	10.2	9 2	38.2	32.2	10.1
Mining..	100.0	2.1	10.3	54.3	31.0	2.2
Construction....................................	100.0	2.9	9.3	49.1	33.6	5.1
Manufacturing...................................	100.0	4.0	10.7	51.7	29.8	3.7
Durable goods...............................	100.0	3.0	10.6	52.8	29.9	3.7
Nondurable goods............................	100.0	5.5	10.9	50.0	29.7	3.8
Transportation, commun. and public utilities...	100.0	1.9	9.4	49.7	35.5	3.5
Transportation..............................	100.0	1.8	8.6	49.6	36.3	3.7
Telecommunications..........................	100.0	3.9	14.6	52.8	27.7	1.0
Utilities and sanitary services............	100.0	1.9	10.4	49.2	34.9	3.5
Wholesale and retail trade.....................	100.0	6.1	10.5	48.9	29.7	4.7
Wholesale trade.............................	100.0	2.9	9.8	52.7	30.4	4.2
Retail trade................................	100.0	7.1	10.8	47.8	29.5	4.9
Finance, insurance, and real estate...........	100.0	1.9	7.0	42.1	39.7	9.4
Business and repair service....................	100.0	3.4	10.8	56.0	26.2	3.7
Personal services..............................	100.0	4.9	8.3	40.2	37.4	9.3
Private households..........................	100.0	8.3	5.4	29.3	40.9	16.1
Hotels and lodging places...................	100.0	4.4	8.6	35.6	41.1	10.3
Other.......................................	100.0	4.1	9.0	45.2	34.9	6.8
Entertainment and recreation services.........	100.0	14.2	11.0	42.5	27.5	4.9
Professional and related services.............	100.0	2.1	6.9	48.5	34.2	8.4
Medical and health.........................	100.0	1.7	6.3	47.9	35.2	8.9
Educational.................................	100.0	2.7	9.0	51.1	31.3	5.9
Other.......................................	100.0	1.6	4.9	45.7	36.8	11.1
Public administration.........................	100.0	0.8	7.0	53.5	34.1	4.7

Retail trade (gasoline stations, grocery stores, drug stores, ten-cent stores)

Private household service (baby sitters)

Entertainment and recreation (ushers, attendants)

Older workers (65 years of age or older) tend to make up an unusually large share of all workers in the following industries:

Agriculture (farm operators)

Finance, insurance, and real estate

Private household service

Personal service, except household

Professional service

Young adult and adult workers (25-44 years of age) are employed in unusually large numbers in the following industries:

Manufacturing, durable goods

Mining

Transportation

Telecommunications

Utilities and sanitary services

Wholesale trade

Business repair services

Educational services

Public administration

These differences are expressed here only in terms of major industrial groupings. Appendix A-18-2 at the end of this chapter reports the age composition of each intermediate industry, by sex. A study of that table will show the existence of a much greater variation than is indicated by Table 18-4.

INCOME AND INDUSTRY

A later chapter, which discusses the distribution of income among various segments of the population, analyzes the distribution of income among the various industry groups. This analysis includes both the major and the intermediate classifications of industries. The information upon which much of this discussion is based is published in Table 18-A-3 at the end of the present chapter.

CLASS OF WORKER AND INDUSTRY

Opportunities for self-employment are highest in the following industries:

	Percent of males self employed
Agriculture	66. 2
Retail trade	28. 6
Business and repair services	30. 1
Personal serv., other than domestic, hotel	38. 5
Medical and health services	37. 5

A very high proportion of the people in all other industries are wage or salary workers, except those in public administration and educational services, many of whom work for local, state, or Federal government (see Table 18-3).

PART-YEAR WORK AND INDUSTRY OF EMPLOYMENT

Some industries are notorious for offering only part-year employment, because the work involved depends on seasonal or cyclical factors, or on an irregular demand. List 18-3 enumerates the industries that appear to offer the smallest degree of full-year employment, and List 18-4 enumerates the industries that appear to offer the greatest amount of year-round employment.

List 18-3.—DETAILED INDUSTRY CLASSES THAT OFFER THE LEAST FULL-YEAR EMPLOYMENT: 1950

Industry	Percent of workers working:	
	Less than 27 weeks	Less than 50 weeks
Total, all industries	10. 5	31. 8
Fisheries	21. 1	53. 2
Mining, coal	30. 6	82. 0
Nonmetallic mining and quarrying, except coal	8. 5	42. 9
Construction	17. 3	53. 9
Mfg.--Logging	23. 5	68. 0
Mfg.--Sawmills	14. 1	47. 8
Mfg.--Primary iron, steel	7. 2	52. 8
Mfg.--Motor vehicles	7. 3	42. 8
Mfg.--Apparel	11. 9	41. 9
Water transportation	17. 3	51. 8
Retail tr.: eating places	14. 0	34. 3
Personal serv.: priv. hshld.	26. 8	50. 0
Personal services: hotels	15. 0	35. 7
Entertainment	20. 5	42. 3
Professional services	8. 4	28. 9

List 18-4.—DETAILED INDUSTRY CLASSES THAT OFFER THE GREATEST DEGREE OF FULL-YEAR EMPLOYMENT: 1950

Industry	Percent of workers working 50 to 52 weeks
Mfg.--Electrical machinery	75. 8
Mfg.--Aircraft and parts	77. 6
Mfg.--Meat	77. 1
Mfg.--Bakery	78. 0
Mfg.--Paper	75. 9
Mfg.--Chemicals	79. 2
Mfg.--Petroleum	85. 1
Street railways	80. 4
Air transportation	84. 1
Telecommunications	87. 5
Electric and gas utilities	84. 0
Water supply	78. 6
Wholesale and retail trade	75. 6
Finance, insurance, real estate	82. 5
Business services	76. 0
Laundry	75. 5
Professional services: medical	78. 1
Professional services: welfare	80. 4
Professional services: legal	81. 1
Public administration	84. 3

OCCUPATIONAL COMPOSITION OF INDUSTRIES

Inasmuch as each industry is an organization of occupations, integrated so as to perform a particular kind of function, industries can be expected to vary greatly in occupational composition. Some require large quantities of unskilled laborers, while others need white collar workers almost exclusively. The occupational composition of each of the major industry groups is reported in Table 18-5. In general, industries tend to fall into two broad types: those employing unusually large proportions of manual workers and those employing unusually large proportions of white-collar workers.

The manual worker industries are:

Mining

Construction

Manufacturing

Transportation

Business and repair services

Private household service

The white-collar industries are:

Wholesale trade

Retail trade

Finance, insurance, and real estate

Entertainment services

Professional services

Public administration

Of course, white-collar workers are found in the first group in significant proportions, and manual workers are found in all industries listed in the second group. The division is made on the basis of the average distribution of manual and white-collar workers among all industries.

Table 18-A-5, at the end of this chapter, provides statistics concerning the occupational composition of each detailed industry group. This table shows that the following industries use particularly large proportions of (unskilled) laborers.

Agriculture

Forestry

Construction

Manufacturing--logging

Manufacturing--sawmills, planing mills, etc.

Manufacturing--stone and clay products

Manufacturing--primary iron and steel ind.

Railroads and railway express service

Water transportation

Water supply, sanitary services

Personal services, private household

Operatives make up an unusually large proportion of the workers in the following industries:

Mining, all types

Manufacturing--most durable goods industries

Manufacturing--most nondurable goods industries

Transportation--rail, street, truck, water

Retail trade--gasoline service stations

Laundering, cleaning, and dyeing services

Craftsmen are exceptionally numerous in the following industries:

Mining--petroleum, mining, and quarrying, except fuel

Construction

Manufacturing--most durable goods

Manufacturing--printing and publishing

Manufacturing--bakery products

Railroads and railway express

Air transportation

Telecommunications

Electric and gas utilities

Auto repair service

Miscellaneous repair services

Sales workers, as would be expected, are found primarily in:

Wholesale trade

Retail trade, exc. gasoline service stations and eating and drinking places

Finance, insurance, real estate, exc. banking

Printing and publishing

Clerical workers are employed in all industries, but are especially concentrated in:

Transportation--rail, air

Telecommunication

Electric and gas utilities

Wholesale trade

Retail trade--general stores

Finance--banking

Personal services--hotels

Public administration--postal service and Federal Government

Managers, proprietors and officials are essential to all industries, but are especially important in:

Agriculture

Water transportation

Wholesale trade

Retail trade (except drugstores)

Finance, insurance, and banking

Business and repair services

Personal services--hotels

Personal services--laundries and cleaning establishments

Entertainment

State and local government

Professional and technical workers are an unusually large proportion of the employees in these categories:

Professional services--medical, educational, welfare, legal

Forestry

Mining--crude petroleum and gas

Manufacturing--electrical machinery, equip., and supplies

Manufacturing--aircraft and parts

Manufacturing--chemicals and allied products

Manufacturing--petroleum and coal products

Air transportation

Telecommunications

Drug stores

Business services

Personal service--except domestic, hotel, laundry

Entertainment

Public administration, except postal

INDUSTRY COMPOSITION AND CHANGE IN GEOGRAPHIC DIVISIONS

No single characteristic more effectively expresses the principal ways in which regions and sections of the country differ from each other than does industrial composition. Table 18-6 gives the industry statistics for each geographic division. Three of the divisions stand out as being highly specialized in manufacturing (33-39 percent of the employed labor force) and as offering comparatively little employment in agriculture. They are:

New England Division

Middle Atlantic Division

East North Central Division

In three of the divisions there is a high speciali-

Table 18-5.—BROAD OCCUPATIONAL COMPOSITION OF MAJOR INDUSTRY GROUPS: 1950

Industry group	Percent of males employed as:			Percent of females employed as:		
	White collar workers	Manual workers	Service workers	White collar workers	Manual workers	Service workers
Total...........................	41.2	51.6	6.0	53.1	24.4	20.7
Agriculture, forestry, and fisheries..........	66.4	33.5	0.1	22.3	76.9	0.7
Mining...........................	10.8	88.3	0.7	82.3	14.4	3.0
Construction......................	14.0	85.3	0.5	75.1	22.9	1.8
Manufacturing.....................	21.9	75.4	2.2	28.2	70.4	1.0
Durable goods....................	18.9	78.8	1.9	38.5	59.8	1.3
Nondurable goods.................	26.4	70.7	2.6	22.7	76.1	0.8
Transportation, commun., and other public util.	24.1	72.2	3.4	90.2	6.4	3.1
Transportation...................	22.6	73.2	3.8	77.6	15.1	7.1
Telecommunication................	34.3	63.2	2.1	96.6	1.9	1.4
Utilities and sanitary services....	26.2	71.3	1.9	90.0	7.4	2.3
Wholesale and retail trade..................	61.8	28.9	9.0	69.2	7.8	22.7
Wholesale trade..................	62.5	36.0	1.2	75.2	23.4	1.1
Retail trade.....................	61.6	26.9	11.3	68.5	5.9	25.3
Finance, insurance, and real estate..........	82.0	7.7	10.1	91.5	0.9	7.4
Business and repair services..................	30.3	66.7	2.7	85.4	11.2	3.0
Personal services.............................	24.1	38.7	37.0	8.7	15.2	76.0
Private households......................	2.1	61.1	36.5	0.9	0.7	98.2
Hotels and lodging places..............	34.6	13.3	51.9	27.6	3.0	69.3
Other.................................	26.5	42.1	31.2	17.9	52.1	29.7
Entertainment and recreation services..........	53.5	20.7	25.6	74.0	4.1	21.6
Professional and related services.............	71.3	10.6	17.9	80.3	1.8	17.6
Medical and Health........................	62.9	12.6	24.3	70.0	2.8	27.1
Educational..............................	69.4	12.5	17.9	88.3	1.0	10.6
Other....................................	81.8	6.5	11.6	81.7	2.4	15.7
Public administration........................	55.0	23.1	20.8	92.9	2.5	4.1

Table 18-6.—INDUSTRIAL CHARACTERISTICS OF THE EMPLOYED LABOR FORCE, BY GEOGRAPHIC DIVISIONS: 1950

Major industry group	United States total	Northeast		North Central		South			West	
		New England	Middle Atlantic	East North Central	West North Central	South Atlantic	East South Central	West South Central	Mountain	Pacific
Total employed....................	100.0	100.0	100.0	100.0	100.0	100.0	100.0	100.0	100.0	100.0
Agriculture, forestry, and fisheries.........	12.5	4.0	3.3	8.9	24.8	16.7	27.4	19.6	18.1	8.6
Mining..................................	1.7	0.1	1.7	0.9	0.9	2.4	3.0	3.2	4.0	0.7
Construction............................	6.1	5.6	5.5	5.0	5.8	6.6	5.9	7.9	8.2	7.7
Manufacturing..........................	25.9	38.5	33.0	35.2	15.4	21.7	18.4	13.3	9.5	20.2
Durable goods.......................	13.8	18.2	16.0	24.5	6.9	7.7	8.6	5.8	4.8	12.0
Nondurable goods....................	11.9	20.1	16.8	10.3	8.3	13.9	9.6	7.4	4.6	8.1
Transport., commun., and other public util...	7.8	6.4	8.6	7.8	8.3	6.7	6.2	7.8	9.6	8.4
Wholesale and retail trade..................	18.8	18.1	19.3	18.3	19.4	16.9	15.4	20.1	20.1	21.9
Finance, insurance, and real estate..........	3.4	3.9	4.7	3.0	3.0	2.6	2.0	2.9	2.9	4.3
Business and repair services................	2.5	2.4	2.7	2.4	2.7	2.0	1.9	2.5	3.0	3.2
Personal services......................	6.2	5.3	5.9	4.8	4.8	8.4	7.4	7.9	6.1	6.4
Entertainment and recreation services.......	1.0	0.8	1.0	0.9	0.9	0.8	0.7	0.9	1.3	1.7
Professional and related services...........	8.3	9.4	8.7	7.8	8.6	7.5	6.9	8.0	9.7	9.6
Public administration.....................	4.4	4.3	4.2	3.5	3.7	6.1	3.2	4.2	5.9	6.0
Industry not reported.....................	1.5	1.2	1.4	1.4	1.9	1.5	1.7	1.6	1.7	1.3

Source: U.S. Census of Population: 1950, Characteristics of the Population, U.S. Summary, Chapter B, Table 80.

zation in agriculture, a secondary emphasis on wholesale and retail trade, and comparatively little manufacturing. These three divisions are:

West North Central Division
East South Central Division
West South Central Division

The remaining three divisions cannot be described as a unit, since each is unique. The South Atlantic Division (the "Old South") does a moderate degree of manufacturing and has only a slightly greater-than-average proportion of its workers in agriculture. In comparison with the nation as a whole it is deficient in trade, finance, transportation, and business services, and has an excess of workers in personal services and public administration. The Mountain and Pacific Divisions lack manufacturing, but because they have been growing rapidly they have a large construction industry. A high proportion of the population is also employed in professional services, trade, and business services.

The more one studies Table 18-6, the more one realizes that each geographic division has an industrial composition that is not exactly duplicated by any other division, and that in none of the divisions do the proportions employed in specific categories resemble even closely the national averages. The "industrial structure" of the nation, therefore, is merely an abstraction--an average of the many different regional industrial struc-

tures. The regional structures, in turn, are also abstractions--averages of the industrial structures of many separate communities.

Some profound changes in the industrial structures of the various regional and geographic divisions of the nation took place between 1940 and 1950. The changes, noted earlier, which took place in the nation were not distributed uniformly over the country, but tended to be localized.

(a) Although the decline in agricultural employment was felt by all of the geographic divisions except one (there was a slight increase in the Pacific Division), its effects were particularly severe in the South, where the West South Central states (Oklahoma, Arkansas, Texas, and Louisiana) suffered unusually sharp declines. During this decade the entire South was changing from a predominantly agricultural region to a more industrial and commercial one.

(b) Manufacturing employment increased most markedly in the Midwest, West, and Southwest-- the very areas in which it had previously been a small proportion of the total. Thus, the 1940 to 1950 decade witnessed a slight but significant change in the direction of a more even distribution of manufacturing industries.

(c) The South experienced a rapid growth in all the industries that reflect urbanization and "economic development" -- transportation, finance, business and repair services, and professional

Table 18-7.—PERCENT CHANGE IN NUMBER OF EMPLOYED PERSONS IN EACH MAJOR INDUSTRY GROUP, BY GEOGRAPHIC DIVISIONS: 1940 TO 1950

Major industry group	United States total	Northeast		North Central		South			West	
		New England	Middle Atlantic	East North Central	West North Central	South Atlantic	East South Central	West South Central	Mountain	Pacific
Total..........................	25.3	18.5	21.6	28.6	18.9	24.7	12.9	21.5	39.6	53.8
Agriculture, forestry, and fisheries........	-17.5	-11.8	-14.4	-14.9	-8.7	-19.4	-25.0	-31.0	-4.7	4.8
Mining...................................	1.7	4.1	-13.3	-4.7	3.2	18.5	7.6	37.0	-12.9	-34.0
Construction..............................	65.8	41.4	38.3	54.5	69.6	73.9	70.3	106.6	115.0	93.7
Manufacturing.............................	37.9	19.1	30.3	43.1	48.4	30.0	42.6	59.1	57.3	70.8
Transport., commun., and other public util...	40.6	29.3	29.7	37.3	37.1	46.6	44.1	58.0	57.5	58.5
Wholesale and retail trade...................	39.8	25.6	28.3	33.9	31.2	57.7	54.3	49.8	59.3	56.9
Finance, insurance, and real estate..........	30.1	26.8	14.6	25.9	24.3	50.0	47.4	50.3	71.3	50.8
Business and repair services................	58.4	49.6	46.2	57.0	50.0	77.0	71.8	62.0	78.7	83.7
Personal services..........................	-12.2	-25.1	-19.8	-14.2	-23.1	-7.8	-11.6	-7.4	15.5	9.9
Entertainment and recreation services.......	32.1	23.1	19.5	32.8	27.5	48.0	62.8	46.1	74.1	24.4
Professional and related services...........	42.1	28.9	27.5	40.2	28.8	55.5	53.6	53.3	60.5	74.0
Public administration.......................	77.0	51.3	53.1	62.7	46.7	96.7	77.2	108.9	104.3	145.4

services. In the Northeast region and the East North Central Division these industries were already very concentrated and therefore grew more slowly.

(d) The West grew rapidly with respect to almost all industries, because of the great population explosion and economic expansions that were occurring there.

The changes that took place in industrial composition during this decade reflected a lessening of regional specialization in agriculture, a wider distribution of manufacturing and other nonagricultural industries throughout the geographic divisions, and the population increase which had taken place.

CONCLUSION

This chapter has attempted to encourage demographers to pay more attention to the field of industry statistics, and to encourage economists who are experts in the field of industry analysis to pay more attention to the demographic aspects of industrial composition. There are unmistakable differences among the categories of industry; they vary in size, in composition (sex, race, age, urban-rural income, and degree of self employment), and with respect to distribution (regional and urban-rural). Moreover, all of these aspects tend to change over time, and there are large inter-industry differentials in the rates at which they change. A full appreciation of these differentials, and of the changes which they undergo, requires that the subject be approached in terms of a more detailed classification than is provided by the 12-category major industry classification.

Table 18-A-1.—DETAILED INDUSTRY OF THE EMPLOYED LABOR FORCE, FOR THE UNITED STATES: 1950

Detailed industry	Total employed (000)	Percent female	Percent of total employed			Percent change, 1940 to 1950		
			Total	Male	Female	Total	Male	Female
Total 14 years old and over...........	56,225.3	28.0	100.00	100.00	100.00	25.3	20.0	41.1
AGRICULTURE, FORESTRY, AND FISHERIES...	6,996.2	8.4	12.44	15.81	3.75	-17.7	-20.0	20.7
Agriculture...........................	6,875.8	8.5	12.23	15.53	3.72	-18.1	-20.4	20.1
Forestry..............................	43.5	7.2	0.08	0.10	0.02	-3.2	-7.3	121.5
Fisheries.............................	76.8	3.1	0.14	0.18	0.01	27.8	25.4	208.4
MINING................................	929.5	2.5	1.65	2.24	0.15	1.7	0.4	111.9
Metal mining..........................	92.7	2.2	0.16	0.22	0.01	-22.3	-23.2	62.6
Coal mining...........................	509.7	1.1	0.91	1.24	0.04	-3.5	-4.0	71.7
Crude petroleum and natural gas extraction...	233.0	5.3	0.41	0.54	0.08	26.5	23.2	143.6
Nonmetallic mining and quarrying, except fuel...	94.1	3.3	0.17	0.22	0.02	15.2	13.2	135.7
CONSTRUCTION..........................	3,440.7	2.9	6.12	8.25	0.63	65.8	63.9	170.5
MANUFACTURING.........................	14,570.8	25.0	25.91	26.98	23.17	37.9	32.6	56.6
Durable goods.........................	7,754.0	16.0	13.79	16.08	7.88	51.6	42.9	122.1
Lumber and wood products, except furniture...	860.5	4.6	1.53	2.03	0.25	28.1	26.1	90.1
Logging...............................	171.9	1.3	0.31	0.42	0.01	21.5	21.0	74.1
Sawmills, planing mills, and mill work...	586.4	3.4	1.04	1.40	0.13	34.4	32.4	136.3
Miscellaneous wood products...........	102.3	16.6	0.18	0.21	0.11	9.0	2.8	56.0
Furniture and fixtures................	330.2	15.6	0.59	0.69	0.33	42.7	34.9	107.6
Stone, clay, and glass products.......	461.9	17.4	0.82	0.94	0.51	36.0	28.8	84.9
Glass and glass products..............	141.8	23.8	0.25	0.27	0.21	36.8	28.1	75.2
Cement, and concrete, gypsum, and plaster products...	105.0	5.1	0.19	0.25	0.03	60.1	57.8	118.4
Structural clay products..............	77.9	11.0	0.14	0.17	0.05	15.1	8.5	129.4
Pottery and related products..........	55.5	35.1	0.10	0.09	0.12	44.2	33.9	68.1
Misc. nonmetallic mineral and stone products...	81.7	16.1	0.15	0.17	0.08	26.9	18.2	106.1
Metal industries......................	2,005.2	11.2	3.57	4.40	1.42	34.1	29.1	93.4
Primary metal industries..............	1,166.7	6.5	2.07	2.69	0.48	...	...	...
Blast furnaces, steel works, and rolling mills...	662.7	5.4	1.18	1.55	0.23	21.3	18.7	94.7
Other primary iron and steel industries...	288.0	5.9	0.51	0.67	0.11	44.0	38.2	93.3
Primary nonferrous industries.........	215.9	10.7	0.38	0.48	0.15	54.1	46.7	124.2
Fabricated metal industries (incl. not spec. metal)..	838.6	17.6	1.49	1.71	0.94	...	...	...
Fabricated steel products.............	721.9	17.2	1.28	1.48	0.79	(1)	(1)	(1)
Fabricated nonferrous metal products..	104.2	20.6	0.19	0.20	0.14	(1)	(1)	(1)
Not specified metal industries........	12.5	14.6	0.02	0.03	0.01	-68.7	-70.1	-57.1
Machinery, except electrical..........	1,296.4	13.4	2.31	2.77	1.10	79.0	70.3	167.5
Agricultural machinery and tractors...	175.9	10.0	0.31	0.39	0.11	101.4	91.6	276.0
Office and store machines and devices...	105.6	23.8	0.19	0.20	0.16	66.4	60.1	90.1
Miscellaneous machinery...............	1,014.9	12.9	1.81	2.18	0.83	77.0	68.0	178.6
Electrical machinery, equipment, and supplies...	788.2	34.9	1.40	1.27	1.75	112.9	90.1	174.3

Table 18-A-1.—DETAILED INDUSTRY OF EMPLOYED LABOR FORCE, FOR THE UNITED STATES: 1950-Con.

Detailed industry	Total employed (000)	Percent female	Percent of total employed			Percent change, 1940 to 1950		
			Total	Male	Female	Total	Male	Female
MANUFACTURING—Continued								
Transportation equipment..........	1,347.1	11.7	2.40	2.94	1.01	53.7	45.5	166.4
Motor vehicles and motor vehicle equipment....	869.0	12.6	1.55	1.87	0.70	52.1	45.5	121.9
Aircraft and parts..........	257.1	12.7	0.46	0.55	0.21	140.0	119.0	608.6
Ship and boat building and repairing..........	157.4	5.9	0.28	0.37	0.06	-12.6	-1.4	200.4
Railroad and misc. Transportation equipment..........	63.6	10.5	0.11	0.14	0.04	43.3	35.3	189.0
All other durable goods..........	664.5	35.7	1.18	1.05	0.42	63.1	53.3	84.2
Professional equipment and supplies..........	120.1	30.9	0.21	0.20	0.24	78.3	68.8	105.1
Photographic equipment and supplies..........	46.9	28.4	0.08	0.08	0.08			
Watches, clocks, and clockwork-operated devices..........	34.7	45.0	0.06	0.05	0.10	58.5	48.2	79.3
Miscellaneous manufacturing industries..........	462.8	36.9	0.82	0.72	1.09			
Nondurable goods..........	6,698.9	35.3	11.91	10.69	15.06	27.2	22.1	37.7
Food and kindred products..........	1,401.2	22.7	2.49	2.67	2.03	28.3	21.2	60.8
Meat products..........	273.9	20.4	0.49	0.54	0.36	30.3	22.1	76.4
Dairy products..........	161.7	16.3	0.29	0.33	0.17	39.7	36.2	61.1
Canning and preserving fruits, veg., and sea foods....	146.4	39.8	0.26	0.22	0.37	60.7	50.8	78.6
Grain-mill products..........	116.5	12.7	0.21	0.25	0.09	29.5	24.7	75.8
Bakery products..........	273.2	22.9	0.49	0.52	0.40	13.0	3.9	60.2
Confectionery and related products..........	77.8	49.9	0.14	0.10	0.25	9.7	7.6	11.8
Beverage industries..........	200.2	11.8	0.36	0.44	0.15	25.3	20.7	47.0
Miscellaneous food preparations and kindred products....	113.8	21.9	0.20	0.22	0.16	37.9	25.0	100.8
Not specified food industries..........	37.5	34.0	0.07	0.06	0.08			
Tobacco manufactures..........	94.1	52.9	0.17	0.11	0.32	-13.8	-11.9	-15.4
Textile mill products..........	1,241.4	42.6	2.21	1.76	3.36	6.2	3.1	10.7
Knitting mills..........	193.7	62.2	0.34	0.18	0.77	-10.7	-17.2	-6.1
Dyeing and finishing textiles, except knit goods....	53.7	17.5	0.10	0.11	0.06	14.7	13.9	18.6
Carpets, rugs, and other floor coverings....	65.2	31.1	0.12	0.11	0.13	24.8	25.6	23.1
Yarn, thread, and fabric mills....	872.6	41.0	1.55	1.27	2.28	9.9	5.6	16.6
Miscellaneous textile mill products....	56.2	36.2	0.10	0.09	0.13	-4.4	-12.2	13.5
Apparel and other fabricated textile products....	1,065.2	70.8	1.89	0.77	4.80	35.6	15.8	45.9
Apparel and accessories..........	980.3	72.1	1.74	0.68	4.50	34.7	12.1	46.1
Miscellaneous fabricated textile products....	84.9	55.9	0.15	0.09	0.30	47.1	51.6	43.7
Paper and allied products..........	466.4	23.5	0.83	0.88	0.70	41.4	38.3	52.7
Pulp, paper, and paperboard mills....	227.8	12.4	0.41	0.49	0.18	12.0	13.0	5.2
Paperboard containers and boxes....	112.5	32.7	0.20	0.19	0.23	62.2	68.9	50.0
Miscellaneous paper and pulp products....	126.1	35.2	0.22	0.20	0.28	121.3	122.8	118.6
Printing, publishing, and allied industries....	859.0	24.9	1.53	1.59	1.36	35.0	28.0	61.7
Chemicals and allied products....	659.1	19.5	1.17	1.31	0.82	54.7	51.0	71.9
Synthetic fibers..........	52.7	23.7	0.09	0.10	0.08	4.5	6.3	-0.8
Paints, varnishes, and related products....	58.4	17.9	0.10	0.12	0.07	32.5	25.8	75.8
Drugs and medicines..........	55.4	39.3	0.10	0.08	0.14			
Miscellaneous chemicals and allied products....	492.6	17.1	0.88	1.01	0.54	65.2	60.6	87.7

Table 18-A-1.—DETAILED INDUSTRY OF EMPLOYED LABOR FORCE, FOR THE UNITED STATES: 1950-Con.

Detailed industry	Total employed (000)	Percent female	Percent of total employed			Percent change, 1940 to 1950		
			Total	Male	Female	Total	Male	Female
MANUFACTURING—Continued								
Petroleum and coal products	287.2	11.2	0.51	0.63	0.21	41.3	35.2	120.0
Petroleum refining	259.0	11.7	0.46	0.56	0.19	45.5	38.8	129.0
Miscellaneous petroleum and coal products	28.1	7.0	0.05	0.06	0.01	11.8	10.3	37.0
Rubber products	237.5	25.3	0.42	0.44	0.38	49.8	45.7	63.6
Leather and leather products	387.8	44.2	0.69	0.53	1.09	8.2	-2.2	24.8
Leater: tanned, curried, and finished	49.7	15.3	0.09	0.10	0.05	-4.8	-9.7	35.3
Footwear, except rubber	271.8	49.1	0.48	0.34	0.85	8.7	-3.0	24.3
Leather products, except footwear	66.3	45.6	0.12	0.09	0.19	17.7	12.3	24.7
Not specified manufacturing industries	117.8	30.3	0.21	0.20	0.23	-35.8	-39.5	-25.4
TRANSPORT., COMMUNICATION, AND OTHER PUBLIC UTIL.	4,368.9	15.6	7.77	9.10	4.34	40.6	33.3	100.2
Transportation	2,940.5	6.6	5.23	6.78	1.24	34.5	30.3	150.3
Railroads and railway express service	1,387.0	5.2	2.47	3.24	0.46	22.2	19.5	104.0
Street railways and bus lines	324.0	8.0	0.58	0 74	0.17	45.5	39.0	212.7
Trucking service	599.7	5.5	1.07	1.40	0.21	36.7	34.0	110.8
Warehousing and storage	97.5	15.0	0.17	0.20	0.09	76.7	66.6	169.5
Taxicab service	163.9	5.7	0.29	0.38	0.06	95.2	88.3	397.2
Water transportation	209.8	5.3	0.37	0.49	0.07	15.6	12.9	103.3
Air transportation	98.2	19.6	0.17	0.19	0.12	323.9	278.3	738.7
Petroleum and gasoline pipe lines	19.7	5.9	0.04	0.05	0.01	12.6	8.0	240.3
Services incidental to transportation	40.6	18.3	0.07	0.08	0.05	44.9	31.3	169.6
Telecommunications	646.4	60.6	1.15	0.63	2.49	75.2	55.9	90.6
Telephone (wire and radio)	599.4	62.6	1.07	0.55	2.39	90.1	78.8	97.5
Telegraph (wire and radio)	47.0	35.1	0.08	0.08	0.10	-12.2	-19.7	6.3
Utilities and sanitary services	782.0	12.2	1.39	1.69	0.61	41.4	38.5	66.6
Electric light and power, and electric-gas utilities	456.1	14.1	0.81	0.97	0.41	44.3	41.7	61.9
Other and not specified utilites	34.7	18.9	0.06	0.07	0.04	}	}	
Gas and steam supply systems	113.1	13.7	0.20	0.24	0.10	31.0	26.5	69.2
Water supply	72.6	9.0	0.13	0.16	0.04	40.7	38.3	108.8
Sanitary services	105.5	2.5	0.19	0.25	0.02	}	}	
WHOLESALE AND RETAIL TRADE	10,550.0	33.7	18.76	17.28	22.60	39.8	26.8	75.1
Wholesale trade	1,980.2	19.2	3.52	3.95	2.42	64.4	56.4	109.2
Motor vehicles and equipment	56.1	15.9	0.10	0.11	0.06			
Drugs, chemicals, and allied products	86.4	27.4	0.15	0.15	0.15			
Dry goods and apparel	119.2	33.2	0.21	0.20	0.25			
Food and related products	582.3	19.5	1.04	1.16	0.72			
Electrical goods, hardware, and plumbing equipment	162.4	20.5	0.29	0.32	0.21	64.4	56.4	109.2
Machinery, equipment, and supplies	139.8	17.0	0.25	0.29	0.15			
Petroleum products	161.8	13.2	0.29	0.35	0.14			
Farm products-raw materials	103.2	11.9	0.18	0.22	0.08			
Miscellaneous wholesale trade	504.6	17.0	0.90	1.03	0.54			
Not specified wholesale trade	64.6	28.4	0.11	0.11	0.12			

Table 18-A-1.—DETAILED INDUSTRY OF EMPLOYED LABOR FORCE, FOR THE UNITED STATES: 1950—Con.

Detailed Industry	Total employed (000)	Percent female	Percent of total employed			Percent change, 1940 to 1950		
			Total	Male	Female	Total	Male	Female
WHOLESALE AND RETAIL TRADE—Continued								
Retail trade	8,569.8	37.0	15.24	13.33	20.18	35.1	20.1	71.7
Food stores, except dairy products	1,583.4	29.2	2.82	2.77	2.94	18.9	5.3	73.4
Dairy products stores and milk retailing	136.0	14.1	0.24	0.29	0.12	-13.9	-17.4	16.3
General merchandise stores	955.2	65.2	1.70	0.82	3.97	33.0	12.7	47.2
Five and ten cent stores	183.6	78.9	0.33	0.10	0.92	113.9	64.3	132.6
Apparel and accessories stores, except shoe stores	529.7	59.3	0.94	0.53	2.00	26.2	1.6	51.4
Shoe stores	89.1	26.6	0.16	0.16	0.15	26.6	12.7	92.3
Furniture and housefurnishings stores	266.2	23.0	0.47	0.51	0.39	51.5	43.4	86.9
Household appliance and radio stores	214.2	18.3	0.38	0.43	0.25	101.5	92.8	150.0
Motor vehicles and accessories retailing	526.4	11.5	0.94	1.15	0.39	58.4	54.2	100.9
Gasoline service stations	456.7	4.8	0.81	1.07	0.14	11.9	10.2	59.9
Drug stores	296.6	42.9	0.53	0.42	0.81	32.0	-0.9	136.3
Eating and drinking places	1,686.1	51.2	3.00	2.03	5.49	51.4	29.3	80.7
Hardware and farm implement stores	230.4	15.9	0.41	0.48	0.23	62.8	55.2	120.0
Lumber and building material retailing	343.4	11.6	0.61	0.75	0.25	55.8	53.0	80.3
Liquor stores	77.4	16.0	0.14	0.16	0.08	85.8	75.0	174.8
Retail florists	60.6	42.2	0.11	0.09	0.16	54.8	28.1	116.5
Jewelry stores	106.7	33.2	0.19	0.18	0.23	74.1	50.1	156.5
Fuel and ice retailing	158.9	10.5	0.28	0.35	0.11	-11.7	-14.8	27.7
Miscellaneous retail stores	463.6	31.0	0.82	0.79	0.91	46.3	33.5	85.9
Not specified retail trade	205.7	48.8	0.37	0.26	0.64	5.1	-12.9	33.9
FINANCE, INSURANCE, AND REAL ESTATE	1,915.1	40.7	3.41	2.80	4.97	30.1	11.7	71.1
Banking and credit agencies	529.4	49.0	0.94	0.67	1.65	} 30.2	} 1.1	} 96.2
Security, commodity brokerage, and investment companies	89.5	29.3	0.16	0.16	0.17			
Insurance	760.1	44.0	1.35	1.05	1.31	43.4	24.6	77.8
Real estate (incl. real estate-insurance-law offices)	536.2	30.0	0.95	0.93	1.02	14.7	8.9	31.1
BUSINESS AND REPAIR SERVICES	1,412.8	12.9	2.51	3.04	1.16	58.6	51.4	132.4
Advertising	113.4	33.1	0.20	0.19	0.24	52.2	36.8	96.8
Accounting, auditing, and bookkeeping services	102.4	24.5	0.18	0.19	0.16	} 101.6	} 85.4	} 153.9
Miscellaneous business services	243.0	32.0	0.43	0.41	0.49			
Automobile repair services and garages	667.1	3.7	1.19	1.59	0.16	39.1	37.8	83.9
Miscellaneous repair services	287.0	6.3	0.51	0.66	0.11	73.4	68.4	210.2
PERSONAL SERVICES	3,487.7	66.8	6.20	2.86	14.82	-12.3	2.0	-17.9
Private households	1,631.7	87.4	2.90	0.51	9.08	-29.9	-23.2	-30.7
Hotels and lodging places	523.9	48.6	0.93	0.66	1.62	1.1	-0.1	2.4
Laundering, cleaning, and dyeing services	678.5	53.3	1.21	0.78	2.30	53.2	40.3	66.7
Dressmaking shops	48.4	95.1	0.09	0.01	0.29	} -4.8	} -1.7	} -8.5
Shoe repair shops	68.7	6.2	0.12	0.16	0.03			
Miscellaneous personal services	536.6	43.9	0.95	0.74	1.50			

Table 18-A-1.—DETAILED INDUSTRY OF EMPLOYED LABOR FORCE, FOR THE UNITED STATES: 1950-Con.

Detailed industry	Total employed (000)	Percent female	Percent of total employed			Percent change, 1940 to 1950		
			Total	Male	Female	Total	Male	Female
ENTERTAINMENT AND RECREATION SERVICES.........	552.7	25.5	0.98	1.02	0.90	31.8	22.8	67.4
Radio broadcasting and television.........	62.0	25.0	0.11	0.12	0.10	152.2	139.1	202.7
Theaters and motion pictures.........	209.4	34.8	0.37	0.34	0.46	25.0	11.2	62.9
Bowling alleys, and billard and pool parlors.........	68.1	6.6	0.12	0.16	0.03 }	23.7	18.4	53.2
Miscellaneous entertainment and recreation services.....	213.2	22.7	0.38	0.41	0.31			
PROFESSIONAL AND RELATED SERVICES.........	4,671.2	58.2	8.31	4.82	17.29	42.0	37.3	45.6
Medical and other health services, except hospitals.....	644.2	52.0	1.15	0.76	2.13 }	59.3	39.1	73.5
Hospitals.........	984.9	71.6	1.75	0.69	4.49			
Educational services, government.........	1,539.0	64.8	2.74	1.34	6.35	26.0	34.4	21.9
Educational services, private.........	531.2	61.0	0.94	0.51	2.06	56.9	65.9	51.7
Welfare and religious services.........	400.4	39.6	0.71	0.60	1.01 }	50.0	40.6	66.7
Nonprofit membership organizations.........	184.7	40.5	0.33	0.27	0.48			
Legal services.........	233.5	36.4	0.42	0.37	0.54			
Engineering and architectural services.........	84.7	14.8	0.15	0.18	0.08 }	21.9	19.2	28.1
Miscellaneous professional and related services.........	68.5	35.2	0.12	0.11	0.15			
PUBLIC ADMINISTRATION.........	2,488.8	26.2	4.43	4.53	4.15	77.0	67.3	111.3
Postal service.........	454.3	11.6	0.81	0.99	0.33	48.4	47.3	57.8
Federal public administration.........	1,009.3	33.7	1.80	1.65	2.16	230.3	226.0	238.9
State public administration.........	264.3	37.9	0.47	0.41	0.64 }	29.0	23.5	48.3
Local public administration.........	760.9	21.0	1.35	1.48	1.01			
INDUSTRY NOT REPORTED.........	840.9	39.1	1.50	1.26	2.09	15.5	13.6	18.6

[1]Fabricated steel products combined with fabricated nonferrous metal products.

Source: U.S. Census of Population: 1950, U.S. Summary, Detailed Characteristics, Tables 130 and 131.

Table 18-A-2.—PERCENT AGE DISTRIBUTION AND RACE COMPOSITION OF THE EMPLOYED PERSONS AND WEEKS WORKED BY THE EXPERIENCED CIVILIAN LABOR FORCE BY INDUSTRY AND SEX FOR THE UNITED STATES: 1950

Industry and sex	Total	Age percent distribution							Percent of employed		Percent who worked in 1949:	
		14 to 19	20 to 24	25 to 34	35 to 44	45 to 54	55 to 64	65 and over	Negro	Self-employed	1 to 26 weeks	50 to 52 weeks
MALE, EMPLOYED	100.0	4.9	9.7	24.4	23.5	18.8	13.0	5.6	8.6	21.2	10.5	68.2
AGRICULTURE, FORESTRY, AND FISHERIES	100.0	10.2	9.2	18.5	19.7	17.4	14.8	10.1	13.5	66.2	11.7	70.2
Agriculture	100.0	10.2	9.2	18.5	19.6	17.4	14.9	10.2	13.5	66.8	11.5	70.7
Forestry and fisheries	100.0	6.2	10.1	22.0	24.8	19.3	12.3	5.3	14.1	33.8	21.1	46.8
MINING	100.0	2.1	10.3	27.0	27.3	19.5	11.5	2.2	4.7	3.8	20.4	39.1
Coal mining	100.0	2.2	9.9	26.8	27.7	19.7	12.0	1.7	6.0	2.6	30.6	18.0
Crude petroleum and natural gas extraction	100.0	1.9	11.2	28.6	27.1	19.9	9.6	1.8	0.7	5.9	7.0	72.3
Mining and quarrying, except fuel	100.0	2.2	10.1	25.8	26.8	18.6	12.7	3.8	6.1	4.8	8.5	57.1
CONSTRUCTION	100.0	2.9	9.3	24.5	24.6	20.1	13.5	5.1	8.7	19.2	17.3	46.1
MANUFACTURING	100.0	4.0	10.7	27.0	24.7	17.9	11.9	3.7	7.5	3.4	8.4	67.5
Durable goods	100.0	3.0	10.6	27.9	24.9	17.9	12.0	3.7	8.1	3.1	8.7	63.4
Logging	100.0	8.2	14.0	25.1	23.5	16.3	9.7	3.2	20.0	14.9	23.5	32.0
Sawmills, planing mills, and mill work	100.0	7.0	13.9	24.0	23.2	17.2	10.8	3.9	24.9	6.7	14.1	52.2
Miscellaneous wood products	100.0	5.0	11.3	22.1	22.3	18.7	14.1	6.6	16.3	6.3	11.2	62.5
Furniture and fixtures	100.0	5.4	13.3	26.1	21.9	16.3	11.8	5.2	6.0	5.4	10.8	64.3
Glass and glass products	100.0	3.6	12.6	26.7	24.7	16.8	11.5	4.1	3.2	1.9	9.0	70.2
Stone and clay products	100.0	3.3	11.6	26.9	24.1	17.9	11.9	4.2	9.7	4.0	7.8	68.6
Primary iron and steel industries	100.0	1.6	9.1	26.8	26.0	19.1	14.0	3.4	13.1	0.5	7.2	47.2
Primary nonferrous industries	100.0	1.8	8.7	27.5	27.2	18.6	12.7	3.4	7.3	1.1	8.3	66.8
Fabric'd metal ind.(incl. not spec. metal)	100.0	2.8	10.6	28.4	24.8	17.4	12.0	3.9	4.4	3.3	8.2	68.8
Machinery, except electrical	100.0	2.0	9.2	28.4	25.1	18.5	12.6	4.1	2.3	2.7	7.0	72.7
Electrical machinery, equip. and supplies	100.0	2.6	11.3	31.6	25.3	18.1	9.9	2.3	2.3	1.3	7.1	75.8
Motor vehicles and motor vehicle equip.	100.0	2.3	11.5	28.5	24.6	18.3	11.6	3.0	8.3	0.5	7.3	57.2
Aircraft and parts	100.0	1.1	8.2	38.1	29.5	14.4	7.1	1.6	1.6	0.3	5.4	77.6
Ship and boat building and repairing	100.0	0.9	4.9	25.5	27.0	23.8	14.7	3.1	8.8	2.7	10.6	67.6
Railroad and misc. transportation equip.	100.0	1.2	6.5	25.3	25.2	20.5	16.5	4.8	5.1	0.8	8.0	66.8
All other durable goods	100.0	3.9	10.9	28.1	23.4	16.9	12.0	4.8	2.9	7.3	8.6	72.2
Nondurable goods	100.0	5.5	10.9	25.5	24.5	17.8	11.9	3.8	6.6	3.7	7.9	73.7
Meat products	100.0	3.2	12.2	26.7	25.3	18.3	11.5	2.8	15.1	2.5	6.1	77.1
Bakery products	100.0	5.8	12.7	26.8	25.8	16.5	9.7	2.8	6.4	5.5	7.3	78.0
Other food industries	100.0	4.2	11.3	26.0	24.9	18.2	11.6	3.8	7.2	4.8	8.6	73.3
Tobacco manufactures	100.0	2.2	9.3	21.9	24.2	21.2	15.0	6.1	25.3	2.7	9.2	73.0
Knitting mills	100.0	5.5	12.8	25.4	28.1	15.9	8.9	3.4	2.3	3.7	8.3	66.5
Yarn, thread, and fabric mills	100.0	4.3	11.7	25.1	25.1	17.7	11.9	4.0	4.9	1.0	9.4	67.9
Other textile mill products	100.0	3.3	11.2	25.1	23.2	17.7	14.1	5.4	5.2	2.3	8.0	70.9
Apparel and other fabric'd textile pr.	100.0	4.9	10.5	21.3	20.7	18.9	17.4	6.3	5.8	10.0	11.9	58.1
Paper and allied products	100.0	3.5	12.7	27.6	24.7	17.0	11.0	3.6	7.6	1.3	6.5	75.9

Table 18-A-2.—PERCENT AGE DISTRIBUTION AND RACE COMPOSITION OF THE EMPLOYED PERSONS AND WEEKS WORKED BY THE EXPERIENCED CIVILIAN LABOR FORCE BY INDUSTRY AND SEX FOR THE UNITED STATES: 1950—Con.

Industry and sex	Total	Age percent distribution							Percent of employed		Percent who worked in 1949:	
		14 to 19	20 to 24	25 to 34	35 to 44	45 to 54	55 to 64	65 and over	Negro	Self-employed	1 to 26 weeks	50 to 52 weeks
MANUFACTURING—Continued												
Nondurable goods—Con.												
Printing, publishing, and allied ind.....	100.0	16.2	10.2	21.1	21.0	16.1	10.9	4.5	3.0	6.7	8.5	78.8
Chemicals and allied products.....	100.0	2.0	9.7	30.3	27.9	17.5	10.1	2.5	9.8	2.2	6.0	79.2
Petroleum and coal products.....	100.0	0.9	7.7	29.1	28.3	21.3	11.4	1.4	5.4	0.9	3.7	85.1
Rubber products.....	100.0	1.8	9.0	28.8	26.3	19.6	12.1	2.5	6.5	0.7	5.5	73.2
Footwear, except rubber.....	100.0	7.8	12.4	20.3	21.2	17.9	14.9	5.5	1.5	1.9	9.9	60.6
Leather and leather pr. exc. footwear.....	100.0	4.0	9.6	22.4	22.7	18.3	16.1	6.8	6.3	5.2	10.1	66.5
Not specified manufacturing industries.....	100.0	3.2	10.3	25.9	24.0	18.6	12.8	5.1	8.6	5.1	9.8	69.7
TRANSPORT., COMMUN., OTHER PUBLIC UTIL.	100.0	1.9	9.4	25.6	24.1	21.3	14.2	3.5	8.5	5.3	7.5	73.0
Railroads and railway express service.....	100.0	1.3	7.1	19.4	21.1	25.0	21.0	5.0	10.5	0.1	6.9	71.0
Street railways and bus lines.....	100.0	1.1	5.8	27.6	28.5	21.2	12.8	2.9	6.4	1.8	3.5	80.4
Trucking service and warehousing.....	100.0	3.0	11.8	31.8	28.2	15.9	7.1	2.3	7.5	22.2	10.4	67.1
Water transportation.....	100.0	1.8	9.7	22.8	26.0	22.7	13.3	3.7	14.8	1.7	17.3	48.2
Air transportation.....	100.0	1.7	11.4	49.0	24.6	8.7	3.6	0.9	4.5	2.8	5.2	84.1
All other transportation.....	100.0	1.6	10.1	28.9	27.8	20.4	8.9	2.3	9.1	13.9	10.4	65.8
Telecommunications.....	100.0	3.9	14.6	33.2	19.6	18.7	9.0	1.0	2.3	0.6	3.5	87.5
Electric and gas utilities.....	100.0	1.8	11.7	27.2	24.8	21.2	11.6	1.6	3.7	0.3	4.3	84.0
Water supply, sanitary services, other util.	100.0	2.2	7.3	20.0	22.4	22.6	17.6	8.0	15.6	3.6	7.3	78.6
WHOLESALE AND RETAIL TRADE.....	100.0	6.1	10.5	24.9	24.0	18.3	11.4	4.7	6.1	25.6	9.3	75.6
Wholesale trade.....	100.0	2.9	9.8	27.0	25.7	19.1	11.3	4.2	5.4	15.4	7.0	78.5
Food, dairy product stores, milk retailing.	100.0	11.6	11.0	22.0	22.3	16.5	11.5	5.1	4.4	34.0	10.2	76.8
General merchandise and five-ten cent stores	100.0	7.6	12.8	24.2	21.5	16.5	11.6	5.8	5.7	16.5	9.3	77.6
Apparel and accessories stores.....	100.0	5.4	9.7	19.6	21.1	20.0	16.0	8.2	5.0	30.4	9.2	76.8
Furniture, home furnishings, equip. stores..	100.0	3.4	11.8	30.0	25.0	17.0	9.0	3.7	4.2	23.7	8.6	75.7
Motor vehicles and accessories retailing....	100.0	2.7	11.0	31.9	26.2	18.5	7.9	1.8	5.0	17.1	6.4	79.1
Gasoline service stations.....	100.0	10.2	16.5	28.5	22.8	13.4	6.2	2.4	6.9	35.4	11.5	71.9
Drug stores.....	100.0	15.7	17.8	17.8	21.7	18.3	6.2	5.8	8.0	28.8	12.0	75.8
Eating and drinking places.....	100.0	5.2	8.1	20.9	25.1	21.9	14.3	4.4	11.2	31.5	14.0	65.7
Hardware, farm implem't, bldg, mater'l ret.	100.0	3.7	10.5	26.3	24.2	18.2	11.8	5.3	5.2	20.9	7.3	76.9
All other retail trade.....	100.0	5.1	9.3	23.7	23.4	19.0	13.0	6.6	6.4	32.9	9.4	76.0
FINANCE, INSURANCE, AND REAL ESTATE.....	100.0	1.9	7.0	20.2	21.9	22.5	17.2	9.4	5.2	15.8	6.3	82.5
Banking and other finance.....	100.0	3.1	9.9	20.5	22.5	22.3	14.8	6.9	2.3	7.2	5.1	86.1
Insurance and real estate.....	100.0	1.4	5.7	20.0	21.6	22.6	18.1	10.5	6.4	19.3	6.9	81.1
BUSINESS AND REPAIR SERVICES.....	100.0	3.4	10.8	30.2	25.8	17.4	8.8	3.7	5.9	30.1	9.4	73.1
Business services.....	100.0	2.5	9.0	28.7	24.4	19.0	11.6	4.8	2.7	30.4	9.5	76.0
Automobile repair services and garages.....	100.0	4.0	12.2	32.4	26.9	16.6	6.2	1.6	8.4	23.6	8.6	73.4
Miscellaneous repair services.....	100.0	2.9	9.5	26.7	24.4	17.2	11.6	7.7	3.6	45.2	11.2	69.1

Table 18-A-2.—PERCENT AGE DISTRIBUTION AND RACE COMPOSITION OF THE EMPLOYED PERSONS AND WEEKS WORKED BY THE EXPERIENCED CIVILIAN LABOR FORCE BY INDUSTRY AND SEX FOR THE UNITED STATES: 1950—Con.

Industry and sex	Total	Age percent distribution							Percent of employed		Percent who worked in 1949:	
		14 to 19	20 to 24	25 to 34	35 to 44	45 to 54	55 to 64	65 and over	Negro	Self-employed	1 to 26 weeks	50 to 52 weeks
PERSONAL SERVICES..........	100.0	4.9	8.3	18.7	21.5	20.9	16.5	9.3	20.6	27.7	13.3	68.7
Private households..........	100.0	8.3	5.4	12.0	17.3	21.4	19.5	16.1	44.8	4.8	26.8	50.0
Hotels and lodging places..........	100.0	4.4	8.6	15.6	20.0	22.4	18.7	10.3	17.7	17.8	15.0	64.3
Laundering, cleaning, and dyeing services...	100.0	5.1	11.5	25.9	24.8	17.7	10.8	4.2	18.0	24.5	8.8	75.5
All other personal services..........	100.0	3.2	6.8	18.4	22.0	22.2	18.3	9.1	11.6	50.5	8.6	76.4
ENTERTAINMENT AND RECREATION SERVICES..	100.0	14.2	11.0	21.3	21.2	16.7	10.8	4.9	8.4	13.3	20.5	57.7
PROFESSIONAL AND RELATED SERVICES......	100.0	2.1	6.9	24.4	24.1	19.8	14.4	8.4	7.5	20.2	8.4	71.1
Medical and other health services..........	100.0	1.7	6.3	24.2	23.7	20.4	14.8	8.9	8.7	37.5	6.7	78.1
Educational services, government......	100.0	2.3	8.5	27.6	24.4	18.7	13.0	5.4	7.7	...	10.1	56.4
Educational services, private..........	100.0	3.7	10.0	26.8	22.0	17.4	12.9	7.2	6.8	6.9	11.7	62.1
Welfare, religious, membership organiz'ns...	100.0	1.9	5.0	18.4	23.2	21.0	17.8	12.6	10.2	3.1	7.8	80.4
Legal, engineering, and misc. profess'l serv	100.0	1.1	4.8	24.2	26.9	20.7	13.3	9.0	1.2	55.9	7.2	81.1
PUBLIC ADMINISTRATION..........	100.0	0.8	7.0	28.5	25.0	20.1	14.0	4.7	7.4	...	5.1	84.3
Postal service..........	100.0	0.6	7.3	28.2	24.3	20.9	15.4	3.2	10.6	...	4.2	86.1
Federal public administration..........	100.0	0.7	8.2	34.5	26.3	17.5	10.9	2.0	9.3	...	5.4	83.8
State and local public administration.......	100.0	0.9	5.7	23.4	24.1	22.0	16.0	7.9	4.2	...	5.4	83.8
INDUSTRY NOT REPORTED..........	100.0	10.3	10.9	20.7	19.0	16.4	13.5	9.2	10.8	2.7	35.4	35.8
FEMALE, EMPLOYED..........	100.0	8.1	15.2	23.4	23.3	17.5	9.5	3.0	11.9	6.1	19.2	56.5
AGRICULTURE, FORESTRY, AND FISHERIES...	100.0	12.8	9.0	19.2	22.2	18.8	12.4	5.6	29.2	19.8	31.8	48.1
Agriculture..........	100.0	12.9	9.0	19.1	22.1	18.9	12.4	5.6	29.4	19.9	31.8	48.1
Forestry and fisheries..........	100.0	6.4	12.6	24.6	27.1	17.8	9.1	2.4	11.9	11.0	30.3	49.8
MINING..........	100.0	5.8	22.1	31.4	20.9	13.2	5.2	1.3	2.0	3.0	10.9	73.4
Coal mining..........	100.0	6.0	20.4	30.2	20.1	14.0	7.7	1.5	3.9	2.6	16.5	59.4
Crude petroleum and natural gas extraction..	100.0	5.0	23.8	33.9	21.3	11.6	3.5	0.9	0.7	2.5	8.4	79.7
Mining and quarrying, except fuel..........	100.0	7.7	19.9	26.6	20.8	16.3	6.5	2.2	3.3	4.6	11.1	72.2
CONSTRUCTION..........	100.0	5.8	16.2	26.6	24.1	16.9	7.9	2.4	4.6	11.0	16.7	64.9
MANUFACTURING..........	100.0	6.5	16.6	28.3	24.8	15.6	6.8	1.4	4.8	1.0	17.8	54.6
Durable goods..........	100.0	6.1	18.8	32.0	23.7	13.4	5.1	0.9	3.8	0.9	16.3	59.5
Logging..........	100.0	10.0	15.0	25.0	21.9	17.7	8.6	1.8	14.2	9.4	28.8	36.4
Sawmills, planing mills, and mill work....	100.0	7.3	17.4	28.0	25.5	14.9	5.5	1.3	11.0	3.0	17.3	58.0

Table 18-A-2.—PERCENT AGE DISTRIBUTION AND RACE COMPOSITION OF THE EMPLOYED PERSONS AND WEEKS WORKED BY THE EXPERIENCED CIVILIAN LABOR FORCE BY INDUSTRY AND SEX FOR THE UNITED STATES: 1950—Con.

Industry and sex	Total	Age percent distribution							Percent of employed		Percent who worked in 1949:	
		14 to 19	20 to 24	25 to 34	35 to 44	45 to 54	55 to 64	65 and over	Negro	Self-employed	1 to 26 weeks	50 to 52 weeks
MANUFACTURING—Continued												
Durable goods—Con.												
Miscellaneous wood products	100.0	5.9	15.8	28.1	27.3	15.3	6.3	1.4	17.4	2.0	21.0	49.6
Furniture and fixtures	100.0	7.2	17.7	28.3	24.9	14.6	6.2	1.2	6.6	1.8	19.0	55.8
Glass and glass products	100.0	6.3	20.9	33.6	23.1	11.0	4.4	0.8	3.1	0.5	16.4	57.5
Stone and clay products	100.0	5.9	17.8	28.6	24.3	14.8	7.0	1.6	2.2	2.7	16.2	59.2
Primary iron and steel industries	100.0	6.0	22.4	31.7	21.2	12.7	5.1	0.9	4.6	0.3	9.9	62.9
Primary nonferrous industries	100.0	5.1	18.6	32.5	23.7	13.8	5.4	0.9	2.3	0.5	15.4	63.6
Fabric'd metal ind.(incl. not spec.metal)	100.0	5.9	18.2	31.5	24.3	13.8	5.3	0.9	3.6	0.8	15.5	60.8
Machinery, except electrical	100.0	5.8	20.1	31.3	22.9	13.7	5.2	1.0	2.8	0.6	13.4	66.8
Electrical machinery, equip. and supplies	100.0	6.5	20.1	35.0	22.9	11.4	3.7	0.5	2.8	0.6	19.4	57.5
Motor vehicles and motor vehicle equip.	100.0	4.3	16.6	34.7	25.9	13.5	4.4	0.6	3.9	0.2	13.2	55.4
Aircraft and parts	100.0	2.7	15.4	39.5	25.6	12.9	3.6	0.4	1.3	0.1	11.1	69.7
Ship and boat building and repairing	100.0	3.8	15.6	32.1	23.3	18.0	6.2	1.0	4.0	1.2	7.0	80.6
Railroad and misc. transportation equip.	100.0	5.1	19.5	30.0	23.5	14.7	6.3	1.0	3.1	1.4	12.6	68.3
All other durable goods	100.0	7.2	17.8	29.2	23.4	14.5	6.4	1.4	5.4	1.8	18.7	56.0
Nondurable goods	100.0	6.7	15.5	26.4	25.4	16.7	7.7	1.6	5.2	1.0	18.6	52.0
Meat products	100.0	6.2	16.3	30.2	26.7	14.6	5.4	0.7	11.2	0.6	16.4	60.6
Bakery products	100.0	9.2	17.0	26.2	24.6	14.9	6.7	1.3	5.7	3.8	15.9	63.6
Other food industries	100.0	7.1	16.1	25.8	24.8	16.9	7.8	1.5	7.0	1.6	28.8	47.7
Tobacco manufactures	100.0	4.9	12.3	25.0	29.2	18.7	8.5	1.5	20.3	0.2	19.5	51.5
Knitting mills	100.0	8.6	16.7	27.5	26.2	14.0	5.8	1.2	1.9	0.4	19.1	48.3
Yarn, thread, and fabric mills	100.0	4.2	14.0	27.9	29.1	17.5	7.3	1.1	1.4	0.3	18.2	51.0
Other textile mill products	100.0	5.4	14.0	24.5	25.1	18.1	10.0	2.9	4.3	5.5	16.8	55.7
Apparel and other fabric'd textile pr	100.0	6.7	13.5	25.1	25.6	18.2	9.0	1.8	7.6	0.7	20.4	41.6
Paper and allied products	100.0	7.3	18.9	28.3	23.6	14.4	6.2	1.3	3.8	0.3	14.5	62.9
Printing, publishing, and allied ind.	100.0	9.0	18.9	23.3	21.6	16.5	8.3	2.5	3.3	2.7	13.9	69.3
Chemicals and allied products	100.0	6.2	21.6	31.0	22.3	12.8	5.1	1.0	3.0	0.9	12.3	71.1
Petroleum and coal products	100.0	4.9	25.3	34.1	20.2	11.8	3.3	0.4	0.9	0.4	6.6	83.8
Rubber products	100.0	4.6	16.6	31.7	25.7	15.1	5.6	0.8	3.4	0.1	13.7	62.1
Footwear, except rubber	100.0	8.5	16.0	24.1	24.9	16.7	8.1	1.6	1.4	0.2	16.8	47.9
Leather and leather pr. exc. footwear	100.0	7.6	14.6	26.3	23.9	16.8	8.7	2.1	8.9	1.1	21.0	46.2
Not specified manufacturing industries	100.0	6.7	18.0	28.8	23.7	15.1	6.4	1.3	10.1	1.3	18.2	57.8
TRANSPORT., COMMUN., OTHER PUBLIC UTIL.	100.0	9.9	26.8	24.0	18.9	14.2	5.4	0.8	2.5	1.0	9.7	76.1
Railroads and railway express service	100.0	2.1	13.3	24.7	21.2	24.9	11.9	2.1	7.9	0.1	7.7	76.3
Street railways and bus lines	100.0	5.2	15.2	26.1	26.0	17.9	7.8	1.8	6.8	2.0	10.7	67.8
Trucking service and warehousing	100.0	9.4	20.4	27.4	21.8	14.0	5.5	1.4	3.5	6.3	17.3	66.2
Water transportation	100.0	5.6	20.6	27.4	22.4	16.2	6.2	1.5	5.4	2.0	11.6	72.8
Air transportation	100.0	3.7	31.7	44.0	13.2	5.5	1.6	0.3	2.2	0.9	8.2	77.2
All other transportation	100.0	6.4	16.7	28.6	23.7	16.6	6.5	1.4	7.9	9.7	17.5	64.0
Telecommunications	100.0	12.4	31.1	21.9	17.7	12.4	4.1	0.4	1.0	0.1	9.0	77.6
Electric and gas utilities	100.0	10.2	28.1	25.0	18.3	12.9	4.9	0.6	1.4	0.2	9.0	79.3
Water supply, sanitary services, other util.	100.0	7.5	21.4	22.4	20.4	17.3	8.8	2.1	3.1	1.4	9.0	78.2

Table 18-A-2.—PERCENT AGE DISTRIBUTION AND RACE COMPOSITION OF THE EMPLOYED PERSONS AND WEEKS WORKED BY THE INDUSTRIAL LABOR FORCE BY INDUSTRY AND SEX FOR THE UNITED STATES: 1950-Con.

Industry and sex	Total	Age percent distribution							Percent of employed		Percent who worked in 1949:	
		14 to 19	20 to 24	25 to 34	35 to 44	45 to 54	55 to 64	65 and over	Negro	Self-employed	1 to 26 weeks	50 to 52 weeks
WHOLESALE AND RETAIL TRADE	100.0	10.3	14.2	22.7	24.2	17.4	8.8	2.3	5.4	11.2	21.2	58.8
Wholesale trade	100.0	8.0	20.0	26.6	22.7	15.2	6.2	1.4	3.4	3.4	16.9	64.9
Food, dairy product stores, milk retailing	100.0	9.9	11.1	21.4	26.7	18.9	9.3	2.6	4.0	24.5	18.0	65.7
General merchandise and five-ten cent stores	100.0	14.3	15.3	21.4	21.9	17.2	9.3	2.4	2.7	2.9	21.6	60.5
Apparel and accessories stores	100.0	6.9	10.4	19.6	24.4	22.6	13.7	4.3	4.0	12.0	20.4	58.1
Furniture, home furnishings, equip. stores	100.0	7.1	15.4	17.8	25.4	17.5	8.1	2.1	3.2	11.9	18.2	63.9
Motor vehicles and accessories retailing	100.0	8.8	22.0	24.4	23.2	12.6	3.7	0.7	0.9	5.6	13.7	70.9
Gasoline service stations	100.0	5.9	11.4	29.1	28.7	18.6	8.3	2.3	3.1	33.4	15.5	69.8
Drug stores	100.0	21.1	17.3	24.7	21.0	12.5	4.9	1.1	4.2	5.9	24.1	56.0
Eating and drinking places	100.0	9.1	12.9	22.2	25.9	16.3	7.7	1.6	12.3	12.7	26.8	47.1
Hardware, farm implem't, bldg, mater'l ret.	100.0	7.9	16.6	26.5	24.4	18.1	8.2	2.3	1.0	11.4	13.4	71.8
All other retail trade	100.0	8.9	13.6	22.4	23.7	18.9	10.3	3.3	2.9	17.2	20.8	61.8
FINANCE, INSURANCE, AND REAL ESTATE	100.0	13.2	25.4	20.9	16.8	13.8	7.4	2.4	3.1	3.9	11.8	75.3
Banking and other finance	100.0	14.0	29.9	23.4	15.6	11.6	4.4	1.0	1.0	0.6	10.4	77.8
Insurance and real estate	100.0	12.7	22.8	19.5	17.5	15.1	9.1	3.3	4.4	5.8	12.6	73.9
BUSINESS AND REPAIR SERVICES	100.0	7.5	19.0	26.5	23.1	15.5	6.6	1.9	2.4	12.9	17.2	65.2
Business services	100.0	7.7	20.3	26.9	21.9	15.0	6.4	1.8	1.7	11.3	17.6	64.8
Automobile repair services and garages	100.0	8.2	17.0	25.6	25.9	16.1	5.7	1.5	5.1	13.5	14.6	69.4
Miscellaneous repair services	100.0	5.0	11.0	24.2	28.2	18.9	9.5	3.2	3.4	25.3	17.3	63.0
PERSONAL SERVICES	100.0	7.5	8.9	20.0	23.6	20.0	13.8	6.3	42.3	10.2	25.0	52.3
Private households	100.0	9.3	7.9	17.7	22.1	20.4	15.2	7.4	55.2	2.8	29.0	47.8
Hotels and lodging places	100.0	3.3	7.5	17.3	23.3	23.8	17.6	7.2	22.5	16.0	19.7	59.0
Laundering, cleaning, and dyeing services	100.0	6.4	12.2	24.2	27.0	18.6	9.4	2.2	28.4	6.5	17.9	60.1
All other personal services	100.0	3.4	10.8	28.6	27.0	16.4	9.3	4.6	13.3	46.4	19.5	57.8
ENTERTAINMENT AND RECREATION SERVICES	100.0	17.2	16.8	24.1	19.4	13.5	6.9	2.0	6.2	8.3	26.9	51.5
PROFESSIONAL AND RELATED SERVICES	100.0	5.4	15.5	21.0	23.4	19.7	11.5	3.6	7.7	3.3	15.4	47.0
Medical and other health services	100.0	8.1	18.9	23.3	20.5	16.3	9.9	3.2	8.1	3.3	18.3	61.5
Educational services, government	100.0	2.6	12.6	18.8	27.7	23.9	12.1	2.4	9.1	...	13.3	26.3
Educational services, private	100.0	4.7	13.9	19.6	22.2	20.0	13.6	6.0	5.6	11.8	14.6	42.6
Welfare, religious, membership organiz'ns.	100.0	4.9	12.2	19.8	20.4	19.7	15.3	7.6	6.0	1.7	14.4	69.3
Legal, engineering, and misc.profess'l serv.	100.0	7.9	20.1	26.3	21.3	15.0	6.9	2.5	1.5	11.5	14.2	70.0
PUBLIC ADMINISTRATION	100.0	3.2	13.9	27.5	24.1	19.5	9.6	2.0	6.6	...	11.4	75.9
Postal service	100.0	1.1	5.4	17.0	25.5	28.8	18.1	4.2	5.4	...	11.3	77.0
Federal public administration	100.0	2.4	14.4	33.2	25.0	17.4	6.8	0.8	8.2	...	11.2	76.9
State and local public administration	100.0	4.7	15.1	22.1	22.8	20.5	11.6	3.2	4.8	...	11.9	74.5
INDUSTRY NOT REPORTED	100.0	11.5	13.0	21.8	20.7	16.2	10.5	6.4	10.0	0.8	39.7	37.5

Source: U.S. Census of Population: 1950, U.S. Summary, Vol. II, Detailed Characteristics, Tables 132, 133, and 135.

Table 18-A-3A.--INCOME DISTRIBUTION OF THE EXPERIENCED MALE CIVILIAN LABOR FORCE BY INDUSTRY, FOR THE UNITED STATES: 1950

Industry	Total	Destitute (less-$1,000)	Meager ($1,000-$1,999)	Adequate ($2,000-$2,999)	Comfortable ($3,000-$4,999)	Abundant ($5,000-$6,999)	Affluent ($7,000-$9,999)	Wealthy ($10,000 and over)	Median income (dollars)
TOTAL EMPLOYED	100.0	15.2	18.0	24.6	31.0	6.6	2.2	2.3	2,668
AGRICULTURE, FORESTRY, AND FISHERIES	100.0	41.8	27.2	14.5	10.5	3.2	1.4	1.4	1,260
Agriculture	100.0	42.0	27.2	14.5	10.3	3.2	1.4	1.4	1,254
Forestry and fisheries	100.0	31.2	28.3	17.2	16.8	4.2	1.5	0.8	1,605
MINING	100.0	8.7	17.2	34.0	31.7	5.7	1.7	1.2	2,691
Coal mining	100.0	10.2	21.0	42.4	21.3	3.5	0.9	0.5	2,401
Crude petroleum and natural gas extraction	100.0	5.1	8.6	15.8	51.6	11.8	3.9	3.1	3,675
Mining and quarrying, except fuel	100.0	8.1	17.2	32.0	36.4	4.1	1.1	1.0	2,772
CONSTRUCTION	100.0	14.2	21.9	25.0	29.2	6.5	1.7	1.4	2,510
MANUFACTURING	100.0	8.3	14.4	28.4	38.6	6.6	2.0	1.8	3,108
Durable goods	100.0	8.2	14.0	28.5	40.2	5.9	1.7	1.5	2,978
Logging	100.0	34.9	29.5	16.0	15.0	2.9	0.9	0.9	1,438
Sawmills, planing mills, and mill work	100.0	27.0	32.2	19.6	17.1	2.4	0.8	0.9	1,671
Miscellaneous wood products	100.0	14.9	30.6	29.8	19.5	2.9	1.0	1.3	2,132
Furniture and fixtures	100.0	11.3	24.6	32.0	25.9	3.5	1.0	1.6	2,397
Glass and glass products	100.0	6.3	13.5	31.0	40.4	6.1	1.6	1.2	2,974
Stone and clay products	100.0	7.4	17.5	34.6	33.1	4.3	1.4	1.6	2,724
Primary iron and steel industries	100.0	4.2	11.0	36.6	41.2	4.7	1.3	0.9	2,953
Primary nonferrous industries	100.0	5.0	11.5	33.5	41.9	5.2	1.6	1.3	2,999
Fabric'd metal ind. (incl. not specified metal)	100.0	6.0	12.2	31.1	40.5	6.3	1.9	2.0	3,017
Machinery, except electrical	100.0	4.5	9.8	28.4	46.4	7.0	2.1	1.9	3,178
Electrical machinery, equipment and supplies	100.0	5.0	9.3	25.8	47.1	8.3	2.7	1.9	3,245
Motor vehicles and motor vehicle equipment	100.0	4.1	8.4	24.8	53.0	7.1	1.8	0.9	3,251
Aircraft and parts	100.0	3.2	6.6	23.2	54.6	9.0	2.4	1.0	3,383
Ship and boat building and repairing	100.0	6.9	11.9	26.4	47.9	5.0	1.2	0.6	3,111
Railroad and misc. transportation equipment	100.0	3.8	9.8	28.5	49.0	6.1	1.7	1.1	3,176
All other durable goods	100.0	7.5	14.2	28.4	37.1	7.6	2.4	2.9	2,997
Nondurable goods	100.0	8.6	14.8	28.1	36.2	7.8	2.3	2.3	2,949
Meat products	100.0	6.3	13.2	33.6	39.2	5.1	1.4	1.2	2,918
Bakery products	100.0	7.6	13.2	28.3	39.7	8.1	1.9	1.2	3,028
Other food industries	100.0	9.1	16.3	28.4	37.1	5.5	1.7	1.9	2,866
Tobacco manufactures	100.0	12.3	28.4	33.2	19.9	3.5	1.2	1.4	2,236
Knitting mills	100.0	8.0	20.4	26.8	31.5	8.5	2.1	2.7	2,773
Yarn, thread, and fabric mills	100.0	7.9	26.1	40.8	20.4	2.7	0.9	1.3	2,331
Other textile mill products	100.0	6.2	14.8	37.9	32.5	5.0	1.6	2.1	2,763
Apparel and other fabric'd textile products	100.0	9.1	18.2	26.5	29.2	9.3	3.0	4.7	2,846
Paper and allied products	100.0	6.2	12.0	32.6	39.7	5.8	1.7	1.9	2,978

Table 18-A-3A.—INCOME DISTRIBUTION OF THE EXPERIENCED MALE CIVILIAN LABOR FORCE BY INDUSTRY, FOR THE UNITED STATES: 1950-Con.

Industry	Total	Destitute (less-$1,000)	Meager ($1,000-$1,999)	Adequate ($2,000-$2,999)	Comfortable ($3,000-$4,999)	Abundant ($5,000-$6,999)	Affluent ($7,000-$9,999)	Wealthy ($10,000 and over)	Median income (dollars)
MANUFACTURING-Continued									
Nondurable goods-Con.									
Printing, publishing, and allied industries	100.0	16.7	9.0	16.7	34.3	15.4	4.6	3.3	3,354
Chemicals and allied products	100.0	5.7	11.0	24.8	44.3	8.6	2.9	2.7	3,231
Petroleum and coal products	100.0	2.5	4.6	14.0	59.4	13.1	3.9	2.6	3,909
Rubber products	100.0	3.9	8.8	29.0	49.0	6.3	1.8	1.2	3,192
Footwear, except rubber	100.0	9.9	26.5	36.8	21.8	2.7	0.9	1.4	2,324
Leather and leather products, exc. footwear	100.0	7.9	18.8	35.3	29.7	4.4	1.4	2.5	2,649
Not specified manufacturing industries	100.0	8.7	16.1	29.6	33.3	6.5	2.3	3.4	2,845
TRANSPORT., COMMUN., AND OTHER PUBLIC UTIL.	100.0	6.7	12.8	26.5	44.6	6.7	1.7	0.9	3,108
Railroads and railway express service	100.0	4.5	10.3	27.1	49.6	7.0	1.3	0.3	3,204
Street railways and bus lines	100.0	5.0	8.8	25.5	58.3	3.2	0.7	0.5	3,236
Trucking service and warehousing	100.0	11.6	18.2	26.5	35.8	5.1	1.4	1.5	2,759
Water transportation	100.0	9.3	17.5	26.4	33.9	8.4	2.9	1.6	2,869
Air transportation	100.0	4.4	8.1	20.8	47.5	10.8	4.2	4.1	3,534
All other transportation	100.0	12.3	26.7	32.2	23.6	3.3	0.9	1.0	2,297
Telecommunications	100.0	4.4	6.8	21.2	47.4	14.5	4.5	1.3	3,597
Electric and gas utilities	100.0	3.9	8.5	24.7	51.5	8.2	2.1	1.0	3,322
Water supply, sanitary services, other utilities	100.0	8.9	19.5	35.7	31.2	3.2	1.0	0.5	2,604
WHOLESALE AND RETAIL TRADE	100.0	12.7	17.9	25.4	29.7	8.0	2.9	3.5	2,752
Wholesale trade	100.0	8.0	13.8	24.3	34.6	10.4	3.8	5.2	3,143
Food, dairy product stores, milk retailing	100.0	17.1	18.4	24.9	30.1	6.1	1.8	1.5	2,554
General merchandise and five and ten cent stores	100.0	12.3	18.4	26.6	27.9	8.0	3.0	3.9	2,708
Apparel and accessories stores	100.0	11.5	14.5	22.4	30.6	11.4	4.1	5.6	3,065
Furniture, home furnishings, equipment stores	100.0	9.8	16.5	26.6	31.4	9.0	3.2	3.5	2,887
Motor vehicles and accessories retailing	100.0	7.1	13.5	25.5	35.3	9.5	3.5	3.5	3,135
Gasoline service stations	100.0	17.0	24.9	28.9	23.0	4.0	1.3	0.9	2,250
Drug stores	100.0	19.7	15.0	16.1	26.8	13.0	4.9	4.4	2,947
Eating and drinking places	100.0	18.5	24.8	26.4	21.9	4.9	1.7	1.7	2,225
Hardware, farm implem't, bldg, mater'l retailing	100.0	8.9	17.6	28.7	30.2	7.7	3.0	3.9	2,807
All other retail trade	100.0	13.6	18.8	25.3	27.7	8.1	3.0	3.4	2,669
FINANCE, INSURANCE, AND REAL ESTATE	100.0	7.2	13.4	20.9	32.8	13.2	5.3	7.2	3,371
Banking and other finance	100.0	5.2	10.2	20.5	35.4	12.1	7.0	9.5	3,572
Insurance and real estate	100.0	8.0	14.7	21.0	31.8	13.3	5.0	6.3	3,284
BUSINESS AND REPAIR SERVICES	100.0	11.9	19.2	27.8	30.0	6.1	2.2	2.7	2,662
Business services	100.0	8.9	12.7	19.3	32.6	13.4	5.5	7.7	3,379
Automobile repair services and garages	100.0	11.4	21.2	32.4	29.6	3.4	1.0	1.0	2,504
Miscellaneous repair services	100.0	16.6	22.0	27.1	28.1	4.2	1.1	0.8	2,397

Table 18-A-3A.—INCOME DISTRIBUTION OF THE EXPERIENCED MALE CIVILIAN LABOR FORCE BY INDUSTRY, FOR THE UNITED STATES: 1950—Con.

Industry	Total	Destitute (less-$1,000)	Meager ($1,000-$1,999)	Adequate ($2,000-$2,999)	Comfortable ($3,000-$4,999)	Abundant ($5,000-$6,999)	Affluent ($7,000-$9,999)	Wealthy ($10,000 and over)	Median income (dollars)
PERSONAL SERVICES	100.0	21.5	26.8	25.7	19.4	3.9	1.3	1.3	2,055
Private households	100.0	48.3	30.2	15.5	5.1	0.5	0.2	0.3	1,052
Hotels and lodging places	100.0	20.9	31.0	24.7	16.3	3.8	1.4	1.9	1,942
Laundering, cleaning, and dyeing services	100.0	12.2	23.1	29.4	26.9	5.4	1.6	1.5	2,455
All other personal services	100.0	15.0	25.0	29.3	23.3	4.5	1.5	1.4	2,301
ENTERTAINMENT AND RECREATION SERVICES	100.0	23.5	19.6	18.2	22.3	9.1	3.4	4.0	2,338
PROFESSIONAL AND RELATED SERVICES	100.0	10.5	17.8	21.6	26.8	10.7	4.6	8.0	3,009
Medical and other health services	100.0	9.0	18.4	22.5	18.7	10.4	5.7	15.4	3,006
Educational services, government	100.0	9.3	16.7	23.1	36.8	10.2	3.0	0.9	3,071
Educational services, private	100.0	13.9	19.5	21.2	28.6	10.1	3.9	2.9	2,760
Welfare, religious, membership organizations	100.0	15.6	23.8	25.2	25.1	6.6	2.4	1.4	2,372
Legal, engineering, and misc. profess'l services	100.0	6.5	9.0	11.4	24.8	19.2	9.3	19.8	4,816
PUBLIC ADMINISTRATION	100.0	5.0	10.1	26.6	48.4	6.9	2.2	0.8	3,221
Postal service	100.0	3.8	5.8	21.2	65.3	3.1	0.6	0.2	3,489
Federal public administration	100.0	5.3	10.4	26.0	42.5	10.9	3.9	1.1	3,252
State and local public administration	100.0	5.3	12.2	29.9	44.9	5.3	1.6	0.9	3,063
INDUSTRY NOT REPORTED	100.0	37.0	25.8	18.4	13.9	2.8	1.0	1.2	1,456

Source: U.S. Census of Population: 1950, U.S. Summary, Vol. II, Detailed Characteristics, Table 136.

Table 18-A-3B.—INCOME DISTRIBUTION OF THE EXPERIENCED FEMALE CIVILIAN LABOR FORCE BY INDUSTRY, FOR THE UNITED STATES: 1950

Industry	Total	Destitute (less-$1,000)	Meager ($1,000-$1,999)	Adequate ($2,000-$2,999)	Comfortable ($3,000-$4,999)	Abundant ($5,000-$6,999)	Affluent ($7,000-$9,999)	Wealthy ($10,000 and over)	Median income (dollars)
TOTAL EMPLOYED	100.0	31.9	32.6	25.0	8.9	1.0	0.3	0.3	1,575
AGRICULTURE, FORESTRY, AND FISHERIES	100.0	77.6	13.2	4.8	2.8	0.8	0.4	0.6	430
Agriculture	100.0	78.2	13.0	4.4	2.6	0.8	0.4	0.6	426
Forestry and fisheries	100.0	43.3	22.7	22.5	9.4	1.4	0.4	0.3	1,289
MINING	100.0	11.8	21.8	40.3	22.6	1.8	0.6	1.1	2,357
Coal mining	100.0	16.4	29.6	38.4	12.6	1.8	0.7	0.5	2,083
Crude petroleum and natural gas extraction	100.0	8.6	15.9	43.0	28.7	1.7	0.7	1.4	2,562
Mining and quarrying, except fuel	100.0	15.1	28.3	35.6	17.4	2.4	0.4	0.9	2,149
CONSTRUCTION	100.0	20.9	27.7	32.5	15.2	2.3	0.7	0.8	2,037
MANUFACTURING	100.0	20.1	39.4	32.3	7.2	0.5	0.2	0.2	1,784
Durable goods	100.0	16.7	32.0	40.8	9.6	0.5	0.2	0.2	2,026
Logging	100.0	39.0	29.0	18.1	11.9	0.7	0.5	0.7	1,377
Sawmills, planing mills, and mill work	100.0	26.0	33.4	28.8	9.8	1.2	0.4	0.5	1,740
Miscellaneous wood products	100.0	33.8	45.2	16.3	4.0	0.3	0.1	0.2	1,324
Furniture and fixtures	100.0	22.9	40.1	29.2	6.9	0.5	0.2	0.2	1,718
Glass and glass products	100.0	17.4	40.5	35.5	6.0	0.3	0.1	0.1	1,845
Stone and clay products	100.0	17.8	40.1	33.9	7.1	0.6	0.2	0.3	1,841
Primary iron and steel industries	100.0	9.5	26.8	49.7	12.8	0.8	0.2	0.2	2,215
Primary nonferrous industries	100.0	13.7	28.4	44.9	11.8	0.7	0.3	0.3	2,142
Fabric'd metal ind. (incl. not specified metal)	100.0	15.3	33.9	41.7	8.0	0.6	0.2	0.3	2,013
Machinery, except electrical	100.0	12.0	29.4	46.3	11.2	0.7	0.2	0.2	2,146
Electrical machinery, equipment and supplies	100.0	18.3	30.1	43.2	7.9	0.3	0.1	0.1	2,027
Motor vehicles and motor vehicle equipment	100.0	10.2	19.3	51.2	18.5	0.5	0.2	0.1	2,404
Aircraft and parts	100.0	9.0	17.0	55.1	17.9	0.6	0.2	0.2	2,447
Ship and boat building and repairing	100.0	7.6	17.5	50.3	22.6	1.3	0.3	0.3	2,530
Railroad and misc. transportation equipment	100.0	12.7	25.4	46.8	13.3	1.1	0.2	0.4	2,196
All other durable goods	100.0	21.6	39.8	31.3	6.4	0.4	0.2	0.2	1,754
Nondurable goods	100.0	21.9	43.3	27.9	6.0	0.5	0.2	0.2	1,676
Meat products	100.0	20.3	30.6	41.0	7.6	0.3	0.1	0.1	1,976
Bakery products	100.0	23.4	39.2	31.4	5.0	0.6	0.2	0.2	1,722
Other food industries	100.0	33.3	35.6	25.0	5.2	0.5	0.2	0.2	1,494
Tobacco manufactures	100.0	26.6	49.9	21.6	1.7	0.1	0.1	0.2	1,522
Knitting mills	100.0	24.7	50.4	20.9	3.5	0.3	0.1	0.1	1,504
Yarn, thread, and fabric mills	100.0	18.0	46.5	31.7	3.4	0.1	0.1	0.1	1,742
Other textile mill products	100.0	21.2	37.7	34.5	5.9	0.3	0.2	0.2	1,800
Apparel and other fabric'd textile products	100.0	24.4	49.4	21.0	4.5	0.3	0.4	0.2	1,496
Paper and allied products	100.0	16.1	41.0	36.3	5.8	0.5	0.2	0.2	1,863

Table 18-A-3B.—INCOME DISTRIBUTION OF THE EXPERIENCED FEMALE CIVILIAN LABOR FORCE BY INDUSTRY, FOR THE UNITED STATES: 1950—Con.

Industry	Total	Destitute (less $1,000)	Meager ($1,000-$1,999)	Adequate ($2,000-$2,999)	Comfortable ($3,000-$4,999)	Abundant ($5,000-$6,999)	Affluent ($7,000-$9,999)	Wealthy ($10,000 and over)	Median income (dollars)
MANUFACTURING—Continued									
Nondurable goods—Con.									
Printing, publishing, and allied industries	100.0	18.6	33.0	32.8	12.8	1.8	0.5	0.5	1,960
Chemicals and allied products	100.0	13.2	27.4	44.2	13.6	0.9	0.3	0.3	2,172
Petroleum and coal products	100.0	6.1	15.2	43.9	32.0	2.0	0.5	0.4	2,636
Rubber products	100.0	13.0	33.0	46.2	7.2	0.3	0.1	0.1	2,062
Footwear, except rubber	100.0	21.6	55.0	20.6	2.4	0.1	0.1	0.1	1,538
Leather and leather products, exc. footwear	100.0	24.7	47.5	22.6	4.4	0.4	0.1	0.2	1,548
Not specified manufacturing industries	100.0	21.8	38.7	29.9	8.1	0.9	0.3	0.3	1,755
TRANSPORT., COMMUN., AND OTHER PUBLIC UTIL.	100.0	12.1	25.8	44.6	16.4	0.6	0.2	0.1	2,222
Railroads and railway express service	100.0	6.6	13.7	43.0	35.7	0.8	0.2	0.1	2,720
Street railways and bus lines	100.0	19.6	27.3	38.0	14.0	0.7	0.2	0.2	2,069
Trucking service and warehousing	100.0	22.4	32.8	32.4	10.2	1.2	0.4	0.6	1,867
Water transportation	100.0	11.4	24.5	45.5	16.7	1.4	0.3	0.2	2,268
Air transportation	100.0	8.0	18.1	54.2	18.6	0.7	0.2	0.1	2,417
All other transportation	100.0	24.4	31.4	29.9	12.0	1.4	0.5	0.4	1,818
Telecommunications	100.0	11.5	26.8	46.9	14.0	0.6	0.1	0.1	2,194
Electric and gas utilities	100.0	10.6	27.3	44.8	16.3	0.7	0.2	0.1	2,218
Water supply, sanitary services, other utilities	100.0	12.5	30.1	42.8	13.4	0.8	0.2	0.2	2,134
WHOLESALE AND RETAIL TRADE	100.0	35.6	37.2	19.4	6.0	1.0	0.4	0.4	1,378
Wholesale trade	100.0	20.8	32.0	34.1	10.8	1.4	0.4	0.5	1,927
Food, dairy product stores, milk retailing	100.0	38.7	35.2	18.3	6.0	1.0	0.4	0.4	1,299
General merchandise and five and ten cent stores	100.0	31.6	43.1	19.4	4.7	0.7	0.3	0.2	1,431
Apparel and accessories stores	100.0	29.3	39.4	21.0	7.5	1.6	0.6	0.6	1,530
Furniture, home furnishings, equipment stores	100.0	26.8	37.4	25.0	8.0	1.6	0.6	0.6	1,659
Motor vehicles and accessories retailing	100.0	17.0	33.1	35.2	11.6	1.7	0.6	0.8	2,000
Gasoline service stations	100.0	39.8	31.4	17.6	8.4	1.5	0.6	0.8	1,323
Drug stores	100.0	41.7	39.4	13.4	4.2	0.8	0.3	0.2	1,191
Eating and drinking places	100.0	50.9	34.4	10.2	3.3	0.6	0.3	0.3	983
Hardware, farm implem't, bldg, mater'l retailing	100.0	21.5	37.9	28.2	9.2	1.7	0.7	0.7	1,786
All other retail trade	100.0	33.6	36.1	20.6	7.1	1.5	0.5	0.6	1,469
FINANCE, INSURANCE, AND REAL ESTATE	100.0	17.2	37.8	34.2	9.0	1.0	0.4	0.4	1,901
Banking and other finance	100.0	13.3	36.8	39.5	9.3	0.7	0.2	0.2	1,998
Insurance and real estate	100.0	19.5	38.4	31.2	8.9	1.2	0.5	0.5	1,841
BUSINESS AND REPAIR SERVICES	100.0	22.3	30.8	30.3	12.7	2.4	0.8	0.7	1,912
Business services	100.0	21.0	29.5	31.5	13.9	2.5	0.9	0.7	1,985
Automobile repair services and garages	100.0	25.4	37.2	26.2	8.3	1.7	0.6	0.5	1,689
Miscellaneous repair services	100.0	30.2	34.3	24.8	8.1	1.2	0.6	0.7	1,612

Table 18-A-3B.—INCOME DISTRIBUTION OF THE EXPERIENCED FEMALE CIVILIAN LABOR FORCE BY INDUSTRY, FOR THE UNITED STATES: 1950-Con.

Industry	Total	Destitute (less-$1,000)	Meager ($1,000-$1,999)	Adequate ($2,000-$2,999)	Comfortable ($3,000-$4,999)	Abundant ($5,000-$6,999)	Affluent ($7,000-$9,999)	Wealthy ($10,000 and over)	Median income (dollars)
PERSONAL SERVICES...............	100.0	61.8	28.1	7.4	2.1	0.4	0.2	0.1	786
Private households..............	100.0	75.5	20.4	3.1	0.7	0.1	0.1	0.1	586
Hotels and lodging places.......	100.0	42.1	39.2	12.5	4.4	1.0	0.4	0.4	1,174
Laundering, cleaning, and dyeing services......	100.0	36.9	47.1	13.0	2.4	0.3	0.2	0.1	1,246
All other personal services.....	100.0	42.3	32.6	16.9	6.4	1.1	0.4	0.3	1,220
ENTERTAINMENT AND RECREATION SERVICES......	100.0	42.0	26.9	18.0	9.6	1.9	0.7	0.9	1,279
PROFESSIONAL AND RELATED SERVICES..............	100.0	25.3	27.9	28.1	16.3	1.7	0.4	0.3	1,892
Medical and other health services......	100.0	26.8	34.0	28.0	9.7	0.9	0.3	0.3	1,686
Educational services, government........	100.0	18.6	22.1	30.8	25.4	2.6	0.5	0.1	2,278
Educational services, private......	100.0	42.2	25.3	19.1	11.2	1.4	0.5	0.3	1,306
Welfare, religious, membership organizations.....	100.0	32.6	31.4	24.0	10.1	1.3	0.4	0.2	1,564
Legal, engineering, and misc. profess'l services..	100.0	17.7	28.0	34.5	16.0	2.2	0.8	0.9	2,103
PUBLIC ADMINISTRATION...........	100.0	13.1	19.6	42.8	22.6	1.4	0.4	0.1	2,425
Postal service..................	100.0	18.4	23.8	28.8	27.9	0.8	0.2	0.1	2,269
Federal public administration...	100.0	11.5	12.5	46.4	27.0	1.8	0.5	0.1	2,649
State and local public administration....	100.0	14.0	27.6	41.2	15.6	1.1	0.3	0.2	2,167
INDUSTRY NOT REPORTED...........	100.0	54.1	25.3	14.3	4.8	0.9	0.3	0.4	897

Source: U.S. Census of Population: 1950, U.S. Summary, Vol. II, Detailed Characteristics, Table 136.

Table 18-A-4.—MAJOR OCCUPATION DISTRIBUTION OF EMPLOYED PERSONS, BY INDUSTRY AND SEX FOR THE UNITED STATES: 1950

Industry and sex	Total, 14 years old and over	Profess'l techn'l and kindred workers	Managers, offs., and proprietors, incl.farm	Clerical and kindred workers	Sales workers	Crafts-men,fore-men, and kindred workers	Oper-atives and kindred workers	Service workers, including private hshld.	Laborers, except mine	Occu-pation not re-ported
MALE, EMPLOYED	100.0	7.3	21.1	6.4	6.4	18.6	20.1	6.0	12.9	1.1
AGRICULTURE, FORESTRY, AND FISHERIES	100.0	0.7	65.5	0.1	0.1	0.3	0.8	0.1	32.4	0.1
Agriculture	100.0	0.5	66.6	0.1	0.1	0.3	0.7	0.1	31.6	0.1
Forestry and fisheries	100.0	13.7	3.6	1.1	0.3	3.1	3.9	1.0	73.1	0.2
MINING	100.0	3.6	4.1	2.9	0.2	17.7	70.5	0.7	0.1	0.2
Coal mining	100.0	0.9	2.1	1.9	0.1	14.0	80.4	0.4	0.1	0.2
Crude petroleum, natural gas extraction	100.0	9.8	8.2	5.2	0.4	22.7	52.8	0.5	0.1	0.3
Mining and quarrying, except fuel	100.0	3.5	4.6	2.8	0.4	22.0	64.4	1.7	0.3	0.3
CONSTRUCTION	100.0	3.8	8.6	1.3	0.3	58.0	7.7	0.5	19.6	0.2
MANUFACTURING	100.0	5.7	6.0	6.6	3.6	24.8	39.5	2.2	11.1	0.4
Durable goods	100.0	5.7	4.9	6.5	1.8	27.5	38.4	1.9	12.9	0.4
Logging	100.0	1.0	3.7	0.7	0.2	5.3	10.7	0.7	77.7	0.1
Sawmills, planing mills, and mill work	100.0	0.7	6.2	2.5	0.7	10.9	45.0	1.3	32.3	0.5
Miscellaneous wood products	100.0	1.2	7.3	3.5	1.2	17.5	49.2	1.8	17.8	0.4
Furniture and fixtures	100.0	1.6	6.3	4.4	2.6	27.9	48.5	1.6	6.7	0.5
Glass and glass products	100.0	4.3	4.1	6.2	1.7	18.3	50.7	2.2	12.2	0.4
Stone and clay products	100.0	4.1	6.5	4.2	2.0	17.5	41.1	1.5	22.7	0.4
Primary iron and steel industries	100.0	3.9	2.2	6.3	0.6	31.7	32.7	2.0	20.0	0.5
Primary nonferrous industries	100.0	5.5	3.8	6.4	1.2	26.7	40.2	2.5	13.4	0.5
Fabric'd metal ind.(incl.not spec.mt)	100.0	5.3	6.3	7.0	2.6	28.9	40.1	1.9	7.5	0.3
Machinery, except electrical	100.0	7.5	5.6	7.6	2.8	35.4	34.3	1.8	4.6	0.3
Electrical mach., equip. and supplies	100.0	13.3	4.9	9.5	2.3	26.8	35.9	2.4	4.8	0.4
Motor vehicles and motor veh. equip.	100.0	4.4	2.6	7.5	1.1	25.3	50.1	2.4	6.0	0.5
Aircraft and parts	100.0	16.6	2.1	8.3	0.4	39.0	29.9	1.8	1.5	0.5
Ship and boat building and repairing	100.0	5.2	2.8	5.8	0.2	55.1	19.4	2.6	8.5	0.4
Railroad and misc. transport. equip.	100.0	6.9	3.5	8.7	0.9	32.3	36.5	2.6	8.2	0.5
All other durable goods	100.0	6.8	10.1	7.1	4.9	25.6	39.2	1.9	3.9	0.4
Nondurable goods	100.0	5.6	7.7	6.8	6.3	20.9	41.4	2.6	8.4	0.4
Meat products	100.0	2.3	7.2	7.7	6.2	9.6	49.2	2.9	14.3	0.4
Bakery products	100.0	1.0	7.4	5.3	6.5	36.7	36.1	3.2	3.7	0.2
Other food industries	100.0	3.6	10.9	6.3	6.3	15.5	40.0	2.6	14.3	0.4
Tobacco manufactures	100.0	1.7	6.9	7.0	4.9	16.8	45.3	4.6	12.2	0.6
Knitting mills	100.0	1.2	7.3	5.7	2.8	16.6	60.2	3.2	2.7	0.3
Yarn, thread, and fabric mills	100.0	1.8	3.2	3.8	1.2	17.8	60.9	3.3	7.6	0.3
Other textile mill products	100.0	3.0	4.8	6.1	2.2	14.8	57.2	2.4	9.0	0.6
Apparel and other fabric'd text. pr.	100.0	1.8	14.2	8.2	5.6	12.6	52.8	2.3	2.1	0.2
Paper and allied products	100.0	4.0	5.2	6.6	3.0	18.2	48.1	2.3	12.0	0.4

Table 18-A-4.—MAJOR OCCUPATION DISTRIBUTION OF EMPLOYED PERSONS, BY INDUSTRY AND SEX FOR THE UNITED STATES: 1950-Con.

Industry and sex	Total, 14 years old and over	Profess'l, techn'l and kindred workers	Managers, offs., and proprietors, incl.farm	Clerical and kindred workers	Sales workers	Craftsmen, foremen, and kindred workers	Operatives and kindred workers	Service workers, including private hshld.	Laborers, except mine	Occupation not reported
MANUFACTURING—Continued										
Nondurable goods—Con.										
Printing, publishing, and allied ind..	100.0	8.9	9.7	8.5	18.1	40.4	11.1	1.5	1.6	0.3
Chemicals and allied products.........	100.0	12.9	7.3	7.3	5.1	18.6	33.4	3.3	11.6	0.6
Petroleum and coal products...........	100.0	14.5	6.0	9.1	2.5	23.8	30.0	2.3	11.4	0.4
Rubber products.......................	100.0	6.4	4.5	7.7	2.8	17.2	50.0	2.9	7.9	0.6
Footwear, except rubber...............	100.0	1.2	4.5	4.8	2.5	9.2	72.7	2.0	2.7	0.5
Leather and leather pr. exc. footwear.	100.0	2.0	7.7	5.1	2.7	10.3	60.6	1.7	9.5	0.4
Not specified manufacturing industries..	100.0	6.4	8.3	8.6	6.3	22.0	31.2	6.8	9.4	1.0
TRANSPORT., COMMUN., OTHER PUBLIC UTIL.	100.0	3.8	8.0	11.8	0.5	25.0	32.3	3.4	14.9	0.4
Railroads and railway express service...	100.0	1.5	7.3	16.4	0.1	29.4	20.4	5.0	19.7	0.3
Street railways and bus lines..	100.0	1.5	4.2	7.6	0.1	16.3	64.1	2.9	3.1	0.2
Trucking service and warehousing......	100.0	0.8	9.6	7.1	0.7	5.8	62.2	1.0	12.6	0.1
Water transportation..................	100.0	2.2	18.1	7.6	0.3	6.4	25.3	7.7	30.8	1.6
Air transportation....................	100.0	22.8	10.0	17.5	0.9	32.7	5.2	6.3	3.9	0.7
All other transportation..............	100.0	2.1	7.2	6.6	0.6	6.6	70.1	2.2	4.4	0.2
Telecommunications....................	100.0	10.0	9.8	13.8	0.7	58.0	3.2	2.1	2.0	0.4
Electric and gas utilities............	100.0	9.8	5.4	12.8	1.4	42.9	15.9	2.0	9.4	0.5
Water supply,sanitary serv.,other util..	100.0	5.0	6.9	6.2	0.4	19.4	21.1	1.6	38.7	0.8
WHOLESALE AND RETAIL TRADE........	100.0	2.5	29.8	5.5	24.0	8.6	15.7	9.0	4.6	0.2
Wholesale trade.......................	100.0	2.7	24.4	10.7	24.7	7.2	20.8	1.2	8.0	0.3
Food, dairy pr. stores, milk retailing..	100.0	0.4	34.7	3.5	28.6	4.4	23.4	1.2	3.7	0.2
General merchandise,five-ten cent stores	100.0	1.8	33.5	11.2	27.5	9.6	5.5	6.7	3.9	0.2
Apparel and accessories stores.......	100.0	0.7	33.9	3.2	39.1	15.1	4.1	2.7	1.0	0.1
Furniture, home furn., equip. stores..	100.0	1.0	25.0	4.3	36.0	20.6	8.5	1.2	3.1	0.2
Motor veh. and accessories retailing..	100.0	1.1	26.8	4.6	37.2	20.6	4.4	1.6	3.4	0.2
Gasoline service stations.............	100.0	0.2	40.6	0.7	1.2	4.6	48.7	0.6	3.2	0.1
Drug stores...........................	100.0	45.4	11.0	2.9	22.6	1.1	5.7	9.6	1.6	0.2
Eating and drinking places............	100.0	1.2	32.1	1.2	1.2	0.9	5.7	61.7	0.7	0.2
Hardware,farm impl,bldg,mater'l ret..	100.0	1.3	26.1	6.3	27.0	15.4	12.9	1.0	9.7	0.3
All other retail trade................	100.0	2.2	32.4	4.5	29.5	10.4	13.5	2.5	4.7	0.3
FINANCE, INSURANCE, AND REAL ESTATE..	100.0	4.6	24.0	17.6	35.8	3.8	0.9	10.1	3.0	0.2
Banking and other finance.............	100.0	6.6	39.6	39.9	4.0	1.9	0.8	6.5	0.3	0.4
Insurance and real estate.............	100.0	3.7	17.5	8.3	49.0	4.6	1.0	11.6	4.0	0.2
BUSINESS AND REPAIR SERVICES........	100.0	9.7	13.7	3.7	3.2	53.1	10.0	2.7	3.6	0.2
Business services.....................	100.0	35.6	16.7	10.4	7.8	12.3	7.3	8.5	1.2	0.3
Automobile repair serv. and garages...	100.0	0.5	12.9	1.5	2.0	67.6	8.9	0.9	5.6	0.1
Miscellaneous repair services.........	100.0	1.1	12.2	1.1	0.6	66.7	15.8	0.3	1.9	0.3

Table 18-A-4.—MAJOR OCCUPATION DISTRIBUTION OF EMPLOYED PERSONS, BY INDUSTRY AND SEX FOR THE UNITED STATES: 1950-Con.

Industry and sex	Total, 14 years old and over	Profess'l techn'l and kindred workers	Managers, offs., and proprietors, incl. farm	Clerical and kindred workers	Sales workers	Crafts-men, fore-men, and kindred workers	Oper-atives and kindred workers	Service workers, including private hshld.	Laborers, except mine	Occu-pation not re-ported
PERSONAL SERVICES..........	100.0	6.8	13.0	3.1	1.2	8.8	20.3	37.0	9.6	0.2
Private households.......	100.0	0.8	0.9	0.3	0.1	3.4	9.8	36.5	47.9	0.2
Hotels and lodging places......	100.0	2.2	22.3	9.8	0.3	7.8	3.0	51.9	2.5	0.2
Laundering, cleaning, dyeing services....	100.0	0.5	22.8	2.0	3.0	7.3	60.7	1.8	1.6	0.2
All other personal services.......	100.0	18.9	4.4	0.7	0.9	13.9	3.9	56.6	0.5	0.1
ENTERTAINMENT AND RECREATION SERVICES	100.0	26.2	20.7	4.7	1.9	11.4	3.6	25.6	5.7	0.3
PROFESSIONAL AND RELATED SERVICES....	100.0	63.0	4.1	3.9	0.3	5.5	3.1	17.9	2.0	0.2
Medical and other health services......	100.0	56.2	3.1	3.4	0.2	6.7	3.9	24.3	2.0	0.3
Educational services, government.......	100.0	64.3	1.8	3.0	0.1	6.6	3.3	18.6	2.0	0.2
Educational services, private........	100.0	60.7	4.3	3.7	1.0	7.6	3.2	15.9	3.4	0.2
Welfare, religious, membership organiz..	100.0	54.4	10.6	6.5	0.6	3.2	2.5	19.7	2.4	0.2
Legal, engineering, misc. profes'l serv.	100.0	88.6	2.5	3.2	0.4	2.2	1.7	0.9	0.4	0.1
PUBLIC ADMINISTRATION........	100.0	12.2	10.2	32.4	0.2	11.0	5.8	20.8	6.3	1.1
Postal service............	100.0	0.3	6.9	83.9	0.1	1.4	1.0	2.8	3.4	0.2
Federal public administration.........	100.0	20.0	9.7	26.2	0.2	20.2	8.8	6.0	6.5	2.3
State and local public administration....	100.0	11.7	12.2	10.7	0.3	8.0	5.7	43.1	7.8	0.5
INDUSTRY NOT REPORTED.........	100.0	3.3	4.3	2.7	2.2	4.7	4.6	2.1	10.4	65.7
FEMALE EMPLOYED............	100.0	12.3	5.0	27.3	8.5	1.5	19.2	20.7	3.7	1.8
AGRICULTURE, FORESTRY, AND FISHERIES.	100.0	0.4	19.5	2.2	0.2	0.1	1.0	0.7	75.8	0.1
Agriculture..............	100.0	0.3	19.7	1.8	0.2	0.1	0.9	0.7	76.2	0.1
Forestry and fisheries........	100.0	8.8	3.7	36.7	0.9	0.6	15.7	4.4	28.7	0.3
MINING...............	100.0	5.4	3.3	73.1	0.5	2.1	12.2	3.0	0.1	0.3
Coal mining..............	100.0	2.3	2.6	59.5	1.2	3.3	26.7	4.1	0.1	0.2
Crude petroleum, natural gas extraction.	100.0	7.2	3.3	82.0	0.1	1.2	4.1	1.8	0.1	0.2
Mining and quarrying, except fuel......	100.0	4.3	4.0	66.5	0.9	2.9	16.2	4.5	0.1	0.6
CONSTRUCTION............	100.0	3.1	6.0	65.3	0.7	14.7	2.8	1.8	5.4	0.2
MANUFACTURING...........	100.0	2.3	1.3	23.8	0.8	3.6	64.9	1.0	1.9	0.4
Durable goods............	100.0	2.3	1.3	34.4	0.5	3.5	53.8	1.3	2.5	0.5
Logging...............	100.0	1.1	3.0	28.1	0.5	2.5	4.1	15.9	44.7	...
Sawmills, planing mills, and mill work	100.0	1.1	2.9	47.3	0.4	4.0	28.7	2.4	12.9	0.4
Miscellaneous wood products......	100.0	0.5	1.5	18.5	0.3	2.9	65.8	0.7	9.4	0.5
Furniture and fixtures........	100.0	0.9	2.0	29.6	0.6	6.3	56.4	0.8	2.8	0.6

Industry and sex	Total, 14 years old and over	Profess'l, techn'l and kindred workers	Managers, offs., and proprietors, incl. farm	Clerical and kindred workers	Sales workers	Crafts-men, fore-men, and kindred workers	Oper-atives and kindred workers	Service workers, including private hshld.	Laborers, except mine	Occu-pation not re-ported
MANUFACTURING—Continued										
Durable goods—Con.										
Glass and glass products	100.0	4.1	0.7	22.4	0.3	1.6	65.3	1.3	3.8	0.6
Stone and clay products	100.0	4.3	2.2	29.4	0.5	2.2	55.8	1.1	3.9	0.5
Primary iron and steel industries	100.0	4.1	1.2	60.5	0.3	4.4	21.3	3.6	4.4	0.3
Primary nonferrous industries	100.0	3.3	1.2	48.1	0.3	2.5	39.9	1.7	2.6	0.4
Fabric'd metal ind.(incl.not spec.mt.)	100.0	1.7	1.3	35.7	0.4	2.8	53.1	1.1	3.6	0.4
Machinery, except electrical	100.0	2.5	1.5	51.8	0.4	3.2	37.6	1.5	1.2	0.5
Electrical mach.,equip. and supplies	100.0	1.8	0.6	23.5	0.3	3.2	67.3	0.9	1.8	0.4
Motor vehicles and motor veh. equip.	100.0	1.8	0.6	36.1	0.2	2.6	54.4	1.9	2.0	0.5
Aircraft and parts	100.0	6.3	0.7	57.9	0.1	5.6	26.6	1.7	0.6	0.4
Ship and boat building and repairing	100.0	4.4	2.3	74.8	0.4	5.6	7.6	3.1	1.5	0.5
Railroad and misc. transport. equip.	100.0	2.8	1.7	56.1	0.2	2.6	24.9	9.0	2.1	0.5
All other durable goods	100.0	1.9	1.9	23.8	1.0	4.6	64.1	0.6	1.6	0.6
Nondurable goods	100.0	2.3	1.2	18.2	1.0	3.6	70.9	0.8	1.6	0.3
Meat products	100.0	1.1	0.8	25.0	0.5	1.0	64.0	1.4	5.6	0.5
Bakery products	100.0	0.5	2.9	18.1	6.3	12.0	55.4	2.4	1.8	0.4
Other food industries	100.0	2.3	2.1	27.5	0.9	2.3	59.5	1.6	3.3	0.4
Tobacco manufactures	100.0	0.4	0.3	7.0	0.1	1.3	85.6	1.4	3.4	0.3
Knitting mills	100.0	0.3	0.6	7.1	0.4	2.2	88.0	0.4	0.7	0.3
Yarn, thread, and fabric mills	100.0	0.7	0.3	7.5	0.1	1.1	87.2	0.9	1.8	0.4
Other textile mill products	100.0	1.3	0.9	19.4	0.4	2.2	72.5	0.8	2.2	0.4
Apparel and other fabric'd text. pr.	100.0	0.7	0.8	6.0	0.4	2.9	88.1	0.3	0.5	0.4
Paper and allied products	100.0	1.8	0.9	25.1	0.4	2.5	64.9	0.7	2.9	0.3
Printing, publishing, and allied ind.	100.0	11.2	3.7	49.3	3.8	14.4	16.0	0.7	0.6	0.3
Chemicals and allied products	100.0	7.8	2.3	47.2	2.6	2.4	33.0	2.0	2.2	0.4
Petroleum and coal products	100.0	6.7	1.5	81.8	0.5	1.2	4.9	2.2	1.0	0.2
Rubber products	100.0	2.1	0.6	27.7	0.2	3.0	60.9	1.3	3.5	0.6
Footwear, except rubber	100.0	0.7	0.4	10.9	0.2	2.2	83.8	1.2	1.2	0.6
Leather and leather pr. exc. footwear.	100.0	0.7	1.3	13.5	0.4	2.8	78.0	0.4	2.9	0.5
Not specified manufacturing industries	100.0	3.8	2.0	32.5	1.5	2.8	51.0	2.6	2.8	1.1
TRANSPORT., COMMUN., OTHER PUBLIC UTL	100.0	2.2	1.9	85.7	0.4	1.6	3.2	3.1	1.6	0.2
Railroads and railway express service	100.0	1.8	1.5	75.5	0.3	2.1	3.1	6.5	9.0	0.3
Street railways and bus lines	100.0	1.8	2.7	62.9	0.6	1.4	19.2	9.0	2.3	0.2
Trucking service and warehousing	100.0	1.0	5.4	73.8	0.6	0.8	13.0	2.5	2.7	0.2
Water transportation	100.0	3.5	4.0	69.7	0.9	1.2	6.3	9.8	4.1	0.5
Air transportation	100.0	6.3	2.6	65.0	1.1	1.9	1.6	20.7	0.6	0.3
All other transportation	100.0	4.0	6.7	68.0	1.2	0.8	14.6	2.4	1.9	0.4
Telecommunications	100.0	1.6	1.3	93.5	0.2	1.4	0.4	1.4	0.1	0.2
Electric and gas utilities	100.0	4.5	1.4	83.5	1.0	2.8	3.5	2.4	0.7	0.3
Water supply,sanitary serv., other util.	100.0	3.8	3.1	80.1	0.8	2.1	3.0	1.9	4.9	0.4

Table 18-A-4.—MAJOR OCCUPATION DISTRIBUTION OF EMPLOYED PERSONS, BY INDUSTRY AND SEX FOR THE UNITED STATES: 1950-Con.

Industry and sex	Total, 14 years old and over	Profess'l techn'l and kindred workers	Managers, offs., and proprietors, incl.farm	Clerical and kindred workers	Sales workers	Crafts-men,foremen, and kindred workers	Operatives and kindred workers	Service workers, including private hshld.	Laborers, except mine	Occupation not reported
WHOLESALE AND RETAIL TRADE	100.0	1.1	10.8	22.9	34.4	1.3	6.0	22.7	0.5	0.2
Wholesale trade	100.0	1.9	5.3	63.8	4.2	1.3	20.8	1.1	1.3	0.3
Food, dairy pr. stores, milk retailing	100.0	0.2	17.6	17.0	56.5	0.9	4.2	2.9	0.5	0.2
General merchandise,five-ten cent stores	100.0	1.4	7.0	21.3	59.9	1.5	4.4	4.0	0.4	0.2
Apparel and accessories stores	100.0	0.7	14.2	13.1	50.8	2.8	16.1	1.8	0.4	0.2
Furniture, home furn., equip. stores	100.0	1.9	9.5	43.7	30.9	3.4	6.8	3.1	0.4	0.2
Motor veh. and accessories retailing	100.0	2.0	6.2	81.0	7.5	0.9	1.1	0.8	0.4	0.2
Gasoline service stations	100.0	0.3	27.5	35.7	5.3	0.6	27.9	1.4	0.9	0.2
Drug stores	100.0	4.3	3.8	11.7	55.8	0.2	0.6	23.3	0.2	0.2
Eating and drinking places	100.0	0.6	11.2	3.8	1.1	0.3	0.3	82.3	0.3	0.2
Hardware, farm impl.,bldg, mater'l ret	100.0	0.9	8.1	61.1	25.9	1.0	1.2	1.0	0.7	0.1
All other retail trade	100.0	1.2	15.6	25.9	49.2	2.2	2.6	2.4	0.7	0.3
FINANCE, INSURANCE, AND REAL ESTATE	100.0	1.5	6.9	77.2	5.9	0.3	0.4	7.4	0.2	0.2
Banking and other finance	100.0	1.5	4.9	89.6	0.3	0.2	0.5	2.8	0.1	0.2
Insurance and real estate	100.0	1.5	8.0	70.0	9.1	0.4	0.4	10.1	0.3	0.2
BUSINESS AND REPAIR SERVICES	100.0	11.2	7.3	65.0	1.9	4.8	5.7	3.0	0.7	0.3
Business services	100.0	13.9	7.3	67.6	1.8	2.2	3.3	3.4	0.2	0.2
Automobile repair serv. and garages	100.0	3.2	6.3	70.1	1.1	8.4	4.9	2.6	3.2	0.2
Miscellaneous repair services	100.0	1.3	8.6	38.5	3.7	20.1	25.9	0.6	1.0	0.5
PERSONAL SERVICES	100.0	1.2	2.7	4.3	0.5	0.4	14.4	76.0	0.4	0.1
Private households	100.0	0.6	0.1	0.2	...	...	0.4	98.2	0.3	0.1
Hotels and lodging places	100.0	1.4	12.8	13.0	0.4	0.4	2.2	69.3	0.4	0.2
Laundering, cleaning, dyeing services	100.0	0.2	5.7	13.6	1.8	1.7	74.9	0.8	1.0	0.3
All other personal services	100.0	5.0	2.8	4.8	0.9	0.7	19.1	66.3	0.2	0.1
ENTERTAINMENT AND RECREATION SERVICES	100.0	23.4	7.5	38.4	4.7	1.0	2.5	21.6	0.6	0.3
PROFESSIONAL AND RELATED SERVICES	100.0	59.8	1.5	18.9	0.1	0.2	1.4	17.6	0.2	0.2
Medical and other health services	100.0	50.0	1.3	18.6	0.1	0.2	2.4	27.1	0.2	0.2
Educational services, government	100.0	79.0	1.0	9.2	0.1	0.1	0.4	9.9	0.1	0.1
Educational services, private	100.0	68.8	2.0	14.3	0.2	0.3	1.1	12.7	0.4	0.2
Welfare, religious, membership organiz.	100.0	31.0	4.0	38.3	0.4	0.3	2.6	22.7	0.4	0.2
Legal, engineering, misc.profess'l serv.	100.0	18.4	1.3	77.0	0.1	0.2	0.5	2.2	0.1	0.2
PUBLIC ADMINISTRATION	100.0	10.3	6.4	76.0	0.2	0.5	1.5	4.1	0.5	0.5
Postal service	100.0	0.5	31.4	62.8	0.1	0.2	0.7	3.4	0.4	0.4
Federal public administration	100.0	6.9	1.9	84.9	0.3	0.7	2.0	2.4	0.4	0.5
State and local public administration	100.0	16.8	7.2	67.1	0.2	0.3	0.9	6.5	0.5	0.4
INDUSTRY NOT REPORTED	100.0	2.2	1.4	14.5	1.1	0.5	2.1	2.7	1.0	74.6

Chapter 19

UNEMPLOYMENT AND CHARACTERISTICS OF THE UNEMPLOYED

Not all members of the labor force have jobs; some are unemployed. A very sensitive indicator of the economy's well-being is the percent of the labor force that is employed and the percent that is unemployed (the latter of which is commonly called the rate of unemployment).[1] When added together, these two percentages equal 100 percent, so it is necessary only to report either the rate of employment or the percent employed, but not both. Some unemployment is inevitable, and at any given instant in time a considerable number of workers will be seeking work--even under conditions of so-called "full employment." This minimal amount of unemployment has several causes. Each year a new cohort of workers joins the labor force for the first time, most of them as unemployed persons seeking work. Many migrate from one community to another in search of better jobs, and many workers who have been fired because of inefficiency or non-cooperation, move from job to job. Workers who have lost their jobs because of bankruptcy or retrenchment of operation in the firm that employed them, or who have quit to look for a better job in the same community, also add to routine unemployment. Many persons--housewives, students, and elderly people, for example--work only intermittently, and such workers reenter the labor force periodically or seasonally to seek a job. There is a continuous process of turnover and change in business, as unsuccessful industries and firms die or shrink in size, new ones are born, and established firms expand their operations. The flow of workers from one establishment to another, in adjustment to these changing conditions, makes some unemployment inevitable. However, this so-called "frictional unemployment" is not very great, involving perhaps 2 to 4 percent of all workers. As soon as the unemployment rate (the percent of the labor force that is unemployed) rises much above this minimum, it becomes a subject of immediate and serious concern, since such a rise may betoken the onset of a severe business depression or a panic. One of the major reasons why the Bureau of Labor Statistics and the Bureau of the Census conduct the Current Population Survey once each month is that they want to keep a vigilant watch on the level of unemployment. Not only must this survey show the total amount of unemployment; it must also indicate

---

[1] It will be recalled that in Chapter 16, which concerned employment status, unemployed persons included those who did not work at all during the week preceding the visit of the census enumerator, and who were looking for work. Also included among the unemployed are those who did not work at all during this particular week but were waiting to be called back to a job from which they had been laid off; those who were waiting to report to a new wage or salary job scheduled to start within the following 30 days (and were not in school during the week preceding enumeration); and those who would have been looking for work except for temporary illness or the belief that no job was available in their line of work. This definition, which has been in effect throughout 1957 and the years since, differs slightly from the definition that had been used previously. Under the earlier definition most of the persons who had been laid off for definite periods of less than 30 days, and all of those persons waiting to report to a wage or salary job scheduled to start within 30 days, were classified as employed rather than as unemployed. This change in definition increases the rate of unemployment by about 0.3 percentage points (0.2 or 0.3 points for males, and 0.4 or 0.5 points for females).

what kinds of people, and which occupations and industries, are most affected by changes in the over-all unemployment level. Although the data on unemployment that are collected at the time of the decennial census refer to only one week out of a total span of ten years, they are valuable in that they reveal the comparative unemployment rates of small areas and the detailed characteristics of unemployed persons. However, when these data are used they must be presumed to be representative of inter-area differentials and inter-group differences in other years and at other seasons of the year.[2]

TRENDS IN UNEMPLOYMENT

Since World War II, the rate of unemployment has fluctuated between 2.4 and 5.2 percent of the employed labor force. This rate has reflected the economy's vaccilation between a high level of prosperity (nearly full employment) and mild recession. Between 1947 and 1959 there were three "recessions" and three periods of nearly full employment. The years 1949 to 1950, 1954, and 1957 to 1958 were years of above-average unemployment and economic set-back, while the years 1947 to 1948, 1951 to 1953, and 1956 were years of extraordinarily low unemployment and great prosperity. Figure 19-1 charts the monthly fluctuations in employment and unemployment, both as actually measured and as adjusted for seasonal variations.

On March 15, 1959, 6 percent of the nation's labor force was unemployed. This represented a substantial improvement, compared to the situation that had existed a year earlier when the nation seemed to be heading into its most serious postwar economic slump. On April 1, 1959, labor experts were predicting that the recession was ending, and that another phase of low unemployment lay ahead. However, the rate of unemployment as of that moment was still higher than it had been most of the time in recent years.

No one knows exactly to what height the rate of unemployment rose during the depths of the economic depression of the 1930's, or how many millions of workers were without jobs. Labor force concepts had not yet been developed in those years, and no procedure had been established for taking a representative sample of the population. The Census Bureau's Monthly Report of the Labor Force for March, 1940, showed that 15.9 percent of male and 13.9 percent of female civilian work-

---

[2] The collection of high-quality statistics concerning unemployment is a very difficult task, for a variety of reasons.

(a) The phenomenon being measured involves a comparatively small part of the labor force--2 to 6 percent in most years. The sampling error of such a small proportion tends to be quite large even though the size of the sample (the number of persons interviewed) is very large.

(b) The entire set of labor force concepts is rather complex, and interviewers who are incompetent or poorly trained tend to do an extraordinarily bad job of obtaining data about unemployment. Proof of this statement is the fact that, when the survey and the census have been taken simultaneously, the rates of unemployment indicated by the sample surveys made by the Bureau of the Census have been much higher than the rates of unemployment indicated by the decennial census. In 1950, for example, the decennial census showed rates of unemployment that were 20 percent lower than those shown by the Current Population Survey. The difference has been attributed to the fact that the Current Population Survey enumerators were more competent, more thoroughly trained, and had had longer experience with census operations.

(c) The results obtained depend in no small degree on the exact definition of unemployment that is used, the way the questions are worded, the sequence in which they are asked, and the instructions given for handling special cases. Should the substitute schoolteacher who is a housewife between emergency calls be termed unemployed? What about the lumberjack or construction worker who has a job, and is expecting to be called as soon as a current spell of bad weather ends? What about the housewife who wants to work and has left her name at several employment agencies, but is not out actively seeking work and is content to keep house unless she is offered a job that pleases her?

(d) The nature of the enumeration process itself often leads to error. One respondent, usually a housewife, is asked to report the economic activities which all the members of a household engaged in during the preceding week. She may not know all the facts concerning these activities.

For an excellent discussion of these problems, see Gertrude Bancroft, "Current Unemployment Statistics of the Census Bureau and Some Alternatives" in The Measurement and Behavior of Unemployment, a report of a conference sponsored by the National Bureau of Economic Research (Published by Princeton University Press, 1957).

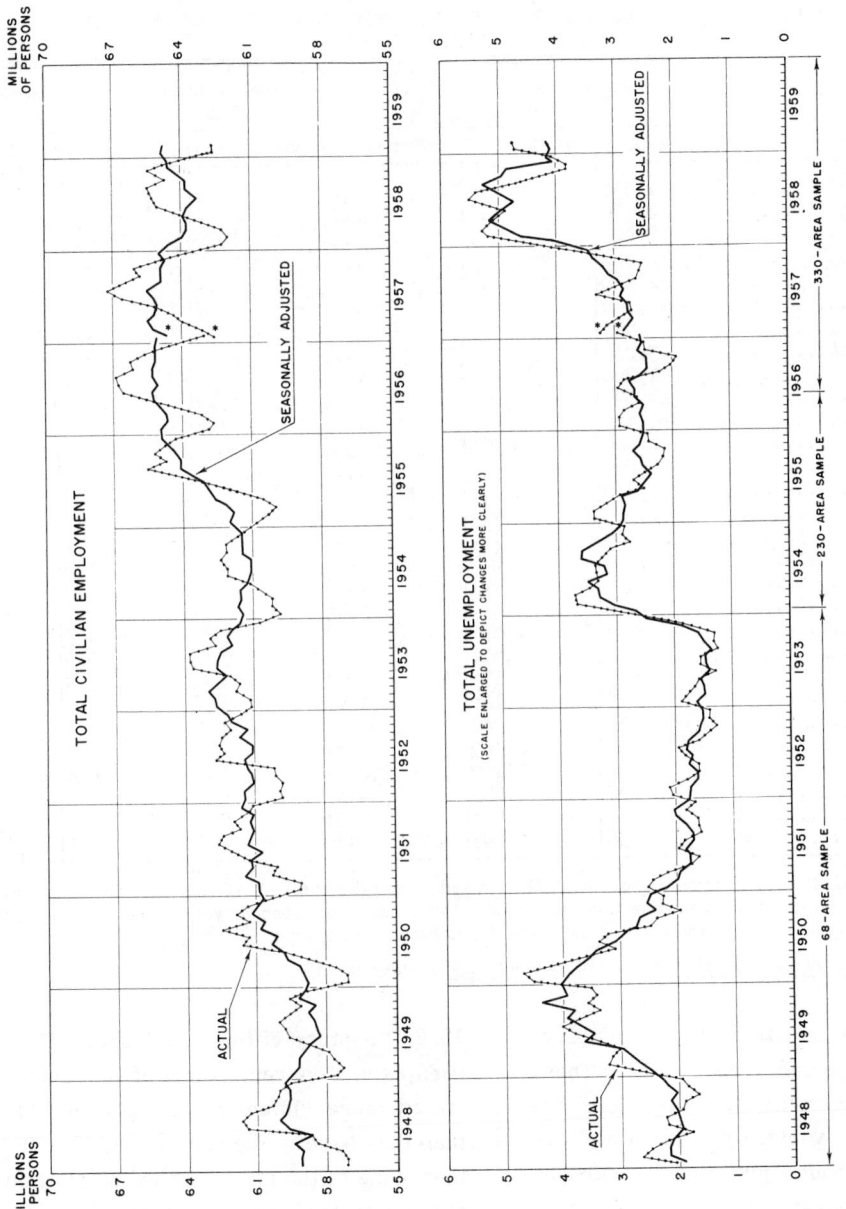

FIGURE 19-1. TRENDS IN EMPLOYMENT AND UNEMPLOYMENT, ACTUAL AND SEASONALLY ADJUSTED: JANUARY 1948 TO DATE

Source: Current Population Reports, Labor Force, Series P-57, No. 200, March, 1959.

ers were unemployed. Labor force experts claim, on the basis of carefully-made estimates using available data, that 24.9 percent of all labor force members were unemployed in 1933. Table 19-1 presents estimates of the annual average number

Various labor force experts have attempted to extend estimates of unemployment backward, to years before the 1930's. Among the most successful of these efforts are the estimates made by Stanley Lebergott, which are graphed as Figure

Table 19-1.—ANNUAL AVERAGE OF NUMBER OF UNEMPLOYED PERSONS AND RATE OF UNEMPLOYMENT, BY SEX: 1929 TO 1957

Year	Number of unemployed persons (000)			Rate of unemployment: Percent of labor force unemployed		
	Both sexes	Male	Female	Both sexes	Male	Female
1929	1,550	...	...	3.2	...	...
1930	4,340	...	...	8.7	...	...
1931	8,020	...	...	15.9	...	...
1932	12,060	...	...	23.6	...	...
1933	12,832	...	...	24.9	...	...
1934	11,340	...	...	21.7	...	...
1935	10,610	...	...	20.1	...	...
1936	9,030	...	...	16.9	...	...
1937	7,700	...	...	14.3	...	...
1938	10,390	...	...	19.0	...	...
1939	9,480	...	...	17.2	...	...
1940	8,120	5,930	2,190	14.6	14.3	15.5
1941	5,560	...	...	9.9	...	...
1942	2,660	...	...	4.7	...	...
1943	1,070	...	...	1.9	...	...
1944	670	...	...	1.2	...	...
1945	1,040	620	420	1.9	1.8	2.2
1946	2,270	...	...	3.9	...	...
1947	2,142	...	...	3.6	...	...
1948	2,064	1,430	633	3.4	3.3	3.6
1949	3,395	2,415	981	5.5	5.5	5.4
1950	3,142	2,155	987	5.0	4.9	5.3
1951	1,879	1,123	756	3.0	2.6	3.9
1952	1,673	1,062	611	2.7	2.4	3.1
1953	1,602	1,069	533	2.5	2.4	2.7
1954	3,230	2,160	1,070	5.0	4.8	5.4
1955	2,654	1,752	903	4.0	3.9	4.3
1956	2,551	1,608	943	3.8	3.5	4.3
1957[1]	2,936	1,893	1,043	4.3	4.1	4.7

[1]A change in definitions and procedures in 1957 caused a slight degree of noncomparability with previous years. It is estimated that the changes cause the number of unemployed to be 243,000 higher than under the old definitions, which increases the rate of unemployment from 4.0 to 4.

Source: Statistical Abstract of the United States: 1957, Table 239.

of unemployed persons and the rate of unemployment, by sex, for the period 1929 to 1957. These estimates indicate that when the economic depression was at its worst, approximately one worker in four was without a job. Under conditions of full employment, the rate of unemployment is only one-fifth or one-sixth as large as it was in 1933. When the unemployment rate rises above 4 percent, or when as many as 3 million persons are unemployed, both the economists and the general public begin to get alarmed.

19-2.[3] A study of this graph shows that, if the estimates are correct, rates of unemployment fluctuated more violently in the pre-depression years than they have in the post-World War II years, and that some of the economic low points that occurred earlier in the century actually were quite severe

[3] Stanley Lebergott, "Annual Estimates of Unemployment in the United States," in The Measurement and Behavior of Unemployment, op. cit., pp. 213 to 239.

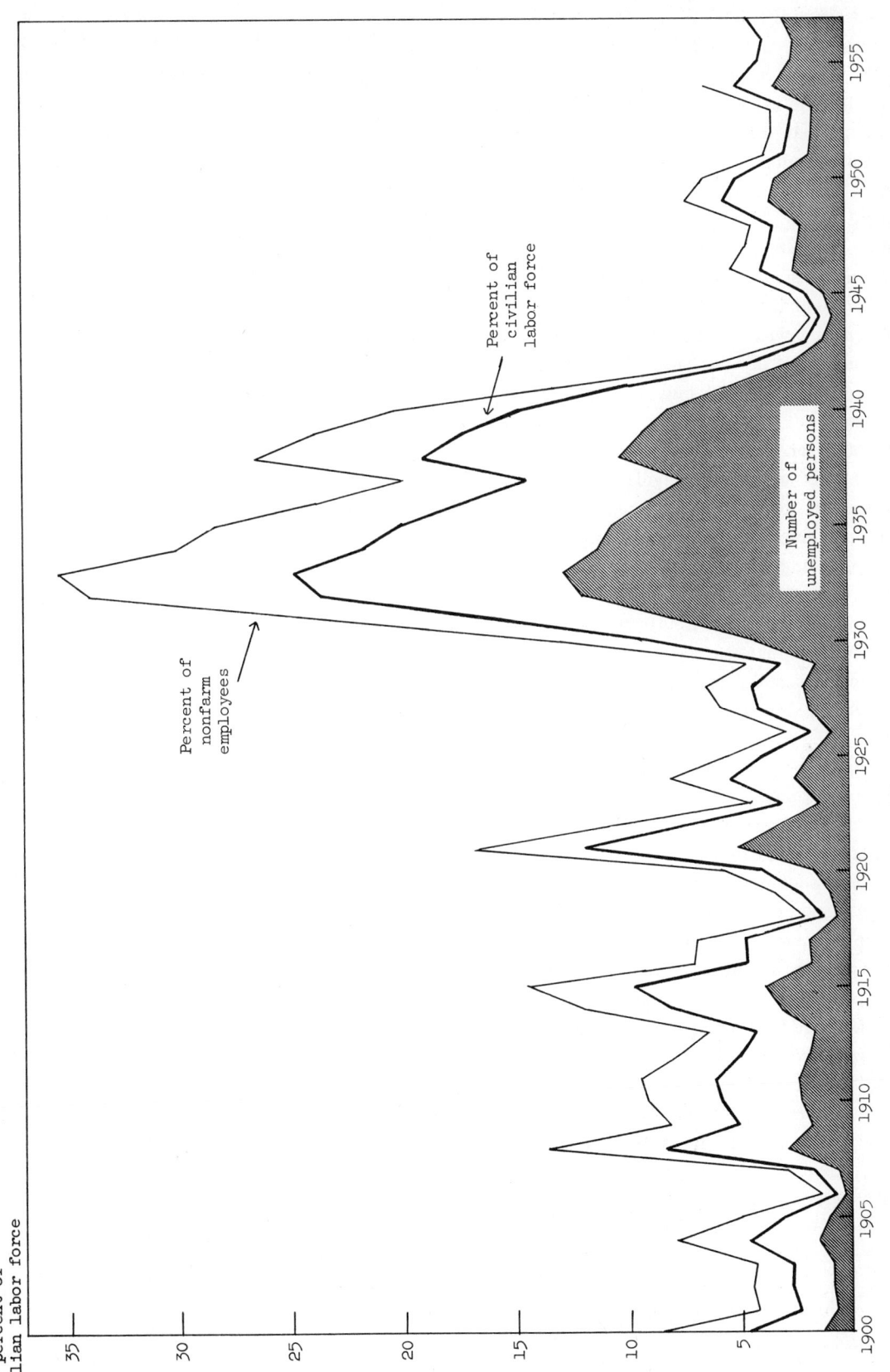

Million of persons
or percent of
civilian labor force

FIGURE 19-2. ANNUAL AVERAGE NUMBER OF UNEMPLOYED PERSONS, AND UNEMPLOYMENT RATES; 1900 TO 1957

Source: Data for 1900-1928 from Stanley Lebergott, "Annual Estimates of Unemployment in the United States, 1900-1950," in Measurement and Behavior of Unemployment, 1957. Data for 1929-57 from Statistical Abstract of the United States.

and caused extensive unemployment. For example, the "hard times" of 1908 to 1911, 1914 to 1915, and 1921 to 1922 appear to have been considerably more severe than the recent "recessions." Moreover, it appears that the average level of unemployment among nonfarm workers, even during "good times," was considerably higher than it has been in recent years. Thus, the decade 1947 to 1957 is unique, and stands out as the longest period of low unemployment during this century. The long-run evidence that is available seems to indicate that the nation will be lucky if things stay as they are and unlucky if things change, since a very great change can probably be only in one direction--for the worse.

Seasonal Variations in Unemployment Trends. Unemployment has a rather regular seasonal cycle. The number of jobless persons, and the rate of unemployment, tends to rise above the yearly average during the months of January, February, and March. These are the "slow" months with respect to employment. Retail trade is at a low ebb; winter weather hampers construction; agricultural activity, and many types of manufacturing, are suspended or greatly curtailed because of bad weather. The arrival of spring reverses the situation, and unemployment drops sharply during April and May. Unemployment tends to rise again during June, when the schools close and pour out a new generation of graduates seeking jobs and a flood of students seeking part-time summer employment. By August or September the new workers have been absorbed into the labor force; unemployment sinks to its lowest level of the year during the last quarter, when students are in school and when retail trade and other industries are at their peak in preparation for the holidays. This seasonal pattern makes it necessary to adjust the measured rate of unemployment before comparing it with that of preceding months.[4] Businessmen, labor union officials, and government leaders anxiously watch the month-by-month changes in the seasonally-adjusted rate of unemployment.

DIFFERENTIALS IN UNEMPLOYMENT

Unemployment is much more prevalent among some segments of the population than among others. Certain categories of workers are relatively secure in their jobs, whereas others lead a very precarious existence. Some types of workers are involved in frictional unemployment much more often than other types. In order to understand the problem of unemployment more fully, it is necessary to answer the question, "Who are the unemployed?" This will be done by examining the differences in rates of unemployment among various subgroupings of the population. Subgroups with above-average rates of unemployment are said to have a positive differential in unemployment, while those with below-average rates are said to have a negative differential. Differentials will be presented for age, sex, color, nativity, urban-rural residence, industry, and occupation. Differentials in unemployment can vary widely, both from region to region and from one stage of the business cycle to another. The differentials discussed here refer to the nationwide situation that has characterized the postwar years. As yet, insufficient data exist to make possible an ade-

---

[4] The following seasonal adjustment factors were used to adjust the unemployment statistics for 1957 and 1958:

Month	Number of unemployed	Rate
January	114.3	116.9
February	113.2	115.7
March	108.3	110.2
April	99.0	100.3
May	98.5	98.6
June	116.0	113.4
July	105.5	102.6
August	89.6	88.1
September	83.1	82.5
October	78.5	77.8
November	95.5	95.0
December	98.6	99.0

Source: U. S. Bureau of the Census Annual Report of the Labor Force, 1957, Series P-50, No. 85, page 16.

quate discussion of the long-range trends and the fluctuations in the differentials.

Age Differences in Rates of Unemployment. The highest rates of unemployment are found among young people. At ages 14 to 25 years, they are leaving school and entering the labor force to seek their first full-time jobs. Many persons of these ages are searching for part-time work they can do while they attend school, or for temporary vacation work. At these ages workers are highly mobile, and they seem to move from job to job with comparatively little stimulation, seeking work that pleases them or is better suited to their needs. Under these conditions, it is not surprising that among young workers 14 to 19 years old the rates of unemployment are usually between 2 and 3 times as great as the rate for the labor force as a whole.[5]

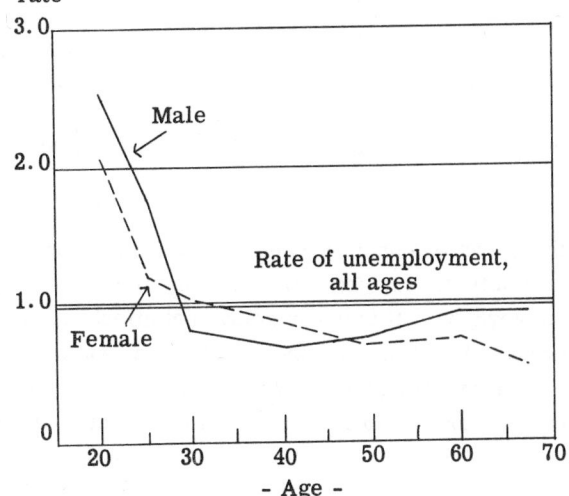

FIGURE 19-3. AGE PATTERN OF UNEMPLOYMENT RATES, BY SEX: AVERAGE FOR THE YEARS 1948 TO 1957, INCLUSIVE

By the time they reach age 25 most workers have passed through this phase of high mobility, and unemployment has more serious implications. Unemployment rates at this age are much lower-- they have been only 2 to 5 percent in the postwar years. For male workers these rates refer to the prevalence of joblessness among principal bread-winners, for whom unemployment tends to mean either involuntary loss of job or dissatisfaction with a particular job. Most male workers aged 25 or over are already married or are planning to marry shortly, and are intent on obtaining--and retaining--satisfactory employment. Between the ages of 35 and 44, among male workers, the rate of unemployment tends to be at its low point. Beyond age 45 the unemployment rate for males rises somewhat, probably reflecting the decreased employability of older men. Beyond age 70 unemployment rates are quite low; if an elderly worker does not have a job, he tends to report himself as not being in the labor force rather than as unemployed.

Because men greatly outnumber women in the labor force, the set of age differentials just described for men characterizes the labor force generally. To what extent, and in what ways, the age pattern for women workers differs from this general pattern will be discussed later in this section.

Evidence validating the picture of age differentials that has just been described is presented in Tables 19-2 and 19-3. Table 19-2 shows the rates of unemployment for each age group of workers for each year, 1948 to 1958, by sex. Data for the prewar year 1940 are also included, to make possible an examination of the age pattern under conditions of higher unemployment. A comparison, for each year, of the differences in rates between age groups reveals that the same general pattern characterizes each year.

One might be inclined to ask the questions, "Does the age differential change with changes in the level of unemployment?" "When unemployment rises, which age groups are most affected?" "When unemployment is at a low ebb, does the age

---

[5] In November, 1958, for example, at a time when the average rate of unemployment among males was 5.6 percent, the rate for boys 18 and 19 years of age was 16.0 percent. Among girls 16 and 17 years of age it was 15.4 percent.

Table 19-2.—UNEMPLOYMENT RATES, BY AGE AND SEX, FOR THE UNITED STATES, SELECTED DATES: 1940 TO 1958

Sex and year	All ages	Age						
		14 to 19 years	20 to 24 years	25 to 34 years	35 to 44 years	45 to 54 years	55 to 69 years	65 years and over
MALE								
1958[1].............								
1957.............	4.1	11.3	7.8	3.3	2.8	3.3	3.5	3.4
1956.............	3.5	9.6	6.3	2.9	2.3	2.7	3.2	3.3
1955.............	3.9	9.9	7.0	3.0	2.8	3.0	4.1	3.7
1954.............	4.9	11.2	9.8	4.4	3.7	3.9	4.9	4.2
1953.............	2.4	6.8	4.3	1.9	1.7	1.9	2.4	2.0
1952.............	2.4	7.6	4.0	1.8	1.7	1.8	2.1	2.7
1951.............	2.6	7.0	3.5	2.0	1.7	2.1	2.5	3.3
1950.............	4.9	11.0	7.7	4.2	3.3	3.9	4.7	4.6
1949.............	5.5	11.9	9.9	4.7	3.8	3.9	4.9	4.9
1948.............	3.3	8.3	6.3	2.5	2.1	2.3	2.8	3.0
1940.............	14.3	32.8	18.1	10.9	11.3	12.4	14.9	10.0
FEMALE								
1958[1].............								
1957.............	4.7	10.1	6.0	5.3	3.8	3.2	3.0	3.4
1956.............	4.3	9.9	5.6	4.3	3.4	3.2	3.2	2.1
1955.............	4.3	9.0	5.4	4.7	3.6	3.1	3.3	1.8
1954.............	5.4	10.0	6.6	5.8	4.6	4.0	3.9	2.9
1953.............	2.7	6.0	3.7	2.9	2.0	1.8	2.0	1.3
1952.............	3.1	7.0	3.9	3.1	2.5	2.0	2.1	1.9
1951.............	3.9	7.4	3.8	4.1	3.3	3.1	3.5	2.5
1950.............	5.3	10.4	6.3	5.3	4.0	4.2	3.9	3.4
1949.............	5.4	11.2	6.7	5.3	4.2	3.5	3.8	3.4
1948.............	3.6	7.3	4.2	3.7	2.5	2.5	2.7	1.9
1940.............	15.3	27.8	19.9	13.3	9.8	14.6	10.9	2.1

[1]Provisional

Source: U.S. Bureau of the Census, Annual Report on the Labor Force, Series P-50, Nos. 85, 72, 67, 59, 45, 40, 31, 19, 13, and Monthly Report on the Labor Force, Nos. 187 through 198.

pattern tend to become less distinct or does it become more pronounced?" Table 19-3 presents data which provide a tentative answer to these questions. For this table, the rates of Table 19-2 were grouped into four categories and converted to an index:[6]

Postwar years: High unemployment--1949, 1950, 1954, 1957

Postwar years: Medium level of unemployment--1948, 1955, 1956

Postwar years: Low level of unemployment--1951, 1952, 1953

Prewar years: 1940

According to Table 19-3, the age differential in unemployment does appear to change as the level of unemployment changes. When unemployment is at a low ebb, the age pattern becomes more definite; everybody has a job except the very youngest and the very oldest people. The workers in

these two age groups seem to have the greatest difficulty finding jobs even during times of full employment. Rising unemployment affects all age groups, but it causes the greatest percentage increase of unemployed among workers in the central age groups 25 to 54 years of age. Thus, when

---

[6] Years of high unemployment (high in relation to the postwar average) were defined as years in which the average annual unemployment rate was more than 4.0 percent. Years of low unemployment were defined as those years in which the average annual rate was less than 3.0 percent; and years of medium unemployment were defined as years in which the rate was between 3.0 and 4.0 percent. An index of age differential was computed by summing the rates for the years in each of these three groups by age groups, and dividing the sum for each age group by the sum for all ages. The pattern of differential unemployment among age groups, as shown by this index for the years 1948 to 1957, is charted in Figure 19-4.

Table 19-3.—INDEX OF DIFFERENTIAL AGE COMPOSITION OF THE UNEMPLOYED, BY PHASE OF THE BUSINESS CYCLE
AND SEX: 1940 TO 1957

(Index = unemployment rate for specific ages divided by unemployment rate for all ages.)

Sex and level of unemployment, and years	All ages	Age						
		14 to 19 years	20 to 24 years	25 to 34 years	35 to 44 years	45 to 54 years	55 to 64 years	65 years and over
MALE								
Postwar, 1948 to 1957..........	1.00	2.52	1.78	0.81	0.69	0.77	0.94	0.94
High-1949, 1950, 1954, 1957...	1.00	2.34	1.81	0.86	0.70	0.77	0.93	0.88
Medium-1948, 1955, 1956.......	1.00	2.60	1.83	0.79	0.67	0.75	0.94	0.93
Low-1951, 1952, 1953..........	1.00	2.89	1.59	0.77	0.69	0.78	0.95	1.08
Prewar-1940...................	1.00	2.29	1.27	0.76	0.79	0.87	1.04	0.70
FEMALE								
Postwar, 1948 to 1957..........	1.00	2.07	1.22	1.04	0.79	0.72	0.74	0.58
High-1949, 1950, 1954, 1957...	1.00	2.00	1.23	1.04	0.80	0.72	0.70	0.63
Medium-1948, 1955, 1956.......	1.00	2.15	1.25	1.04	0.78	0.72	0.75	0.48
Low-1951, 1952, 1953..........	1.00	2.10	1.18	1.04	0.80	0.71	0.78	0.59
Prewar-1940...................	1.00	1.79	1.28	0.86	0.63	0.94	0.70	0.14
DIFFERENCE-MALE MINUS FEMALE								
Postwar, 1948 to 1957..........	...	0.45	0.56	-0.23	-0.10	0.05	0.20	0.36
High-1949, 1950, 1954, 1957...	...	0.34	0.58	-0.18	-0.10	0.05	0.23	0.25
Medium-1948, 1955, 1956.......	...	0.45	0.58	-0.25	-0.11	0.03	0.19	0.45
Low-1951, 1952, 1953..........	...	0.79	0.41	-0.27	-0.11	0.07	0.17	0.49
Prewar-1940	...	0.50	-0.01	-0.10	0.16	-0.07	0.34	0.56

Source: U.S. Bureau of the Census, Annual Report on the Labor Force, Series P-50, Nos. 85, 72, 67, 59, 45, 40, 31, 19, 13, and Monthly Report on the Labor Force, Nos. 187 through 198.

the over-all rate of unemployment rises, all age groups are affected; however, the proportional increases in joblessness are greatest among adult workers, and the major breadwinners become much less secure. Nevertheless, during times of recession the largest absolute (rate-point) change in unemployment rates is found among the younger workers.

As noted above, the age differentials are not identical for the two sexes. Many women are only marginal or secondary participants in the labor force, because they are married and are supported by their husbands; thus, when they lose their jobs they tend to behave differently than men. Male workers have a considerably larger differential ages 14 to 19 and ages 20 to 24 than female workers of these ages; also, the tendency among males for the unemployment rate to rise after age 45 does not exist among the female workers. When middle-aged and elderly females lose their jobs, they apparently tend to withdraw from the labor force (or to report themselves as not seeking work) rather than to look for other jobs. This re-

action on the part of older female workers is especially pronounced during periods of high unemployment. In fact, during periods of high unemployment the tendency to report oneself as not in the labor force rather than as unemployed seems to characterize elderly workers of both sexes.

It would be incorrect to infer that all of the age differential in unemployment reflects a differential loss of jobs due to layoff, shutdown, or firing. Most of the differential at the younger ages is due to the fact that new workers are continuously entering the labor force and that high rates of labor mobility characterize these younger ages. A part of the differential at the older ages may be due to the re-entry of workers after periods of retirement or illness.

Color Differences in Rates of Unemployment. Nonwhite participants in the labor force have much higher rates of unemployment than white workers (see Figure 19-4). All available evidence indicates that this phenomenon is so universal as to be almost a "social law" underlying the operation of

Percent of
labor force
unemployed

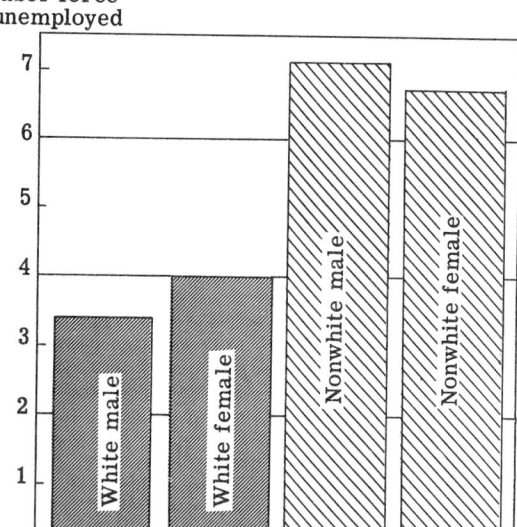

FIGURE 19.4. TEN-YEAR AVERAGE RATES OF
UNEMPLOYMENT (PERCENT OF LABOR FORCE
UNEMPLOYED) BY SEX AND COLOR: 1948-1957

American society. It applies to each age group individually, and to both males and females. Furthermore, the 1950 census materials show that
this phenomenon existed in urban, rural-nonfarm,
and rural-farm areas, and that it was present in
each age and sex group. It has persisted throughout the span of time for which unemployment statistics have been collected. All this evidence
seems to indicate that, on a gross basis at least
(not considering differences in other characteristics) the slogan, "Negroes are the last to be hired
and the first to be fired," has a solid basis in fact.
Whether this particular differential is due to race
prejudice alone, or whether some of it is due, indirectly, to other factors associated with race--
educational attainment, work experience, level of
skill, health, etc.--is a matter that has not yet
been explored adequately.[7]

Documentation of the above generalizations is
contained in Tables 19-4, 19-5, 19-6, and 19-7.[8]

Table 19-4, which reports unemployment rates
by color and sex, shows that in every one of the
postwar years the unemployment rates for nonwhite workers have been much higher than the
corresponding rates for white workers. The following text table summarizes the extent of these
differences:

Level of unemployment	Sex and color differences in employment rate during periods of high, medium, and low unemployment: 1947 to 1957		
	Both sexes	Male	Female
Difference: Nonwhite minus white			
Total..............	3.2	3.5	2.6
High unemployment.......	4.0	4.6	2.9
Medium unemployment.....	3.3	3.4	3.0
Low unemployment........	2.0	2.2	1.6
Ratio: Nonwhite ÷ white			
Total..............	1.90	2.01	1.66
High unemployment.......	1.87	2.02	1.60
Medium unemployment.....	1.98	2.04	1.84
Low unemployment........	1.80	1.96	1.51

Note: The years 1947 to 1957 were each classified
into one of the three categories, "high," "medium,"
and "low." 1949, 50, 54, and 57 were years of high
unemployment, 1947, 48, 55, and 56 were years of
medium unemployment, while the years 1951, 52, and
53 were years of low unemployment.

Thus, throughout the 11-year period from 1947 to
1957, inclusive, the rate of unemployment for nonwhite workers has been 90 percent higher than the

---

[7] For a good discussion of the factors that might be able to
account for the color differential in unemployment, see "Foci
of Discrimination in the Employment of Nonwhite," by Ralph
Turner, American Journal of Sociology, November, 1952.

[8] Tables 15-5 through 15-9 are based on the 1950 census;
this census, as was discussed above, seriously understated the
level of unemployment. These census data are used here only
to make possible a discussion of differentials in unemployment,
and on the assumption that the undercount in the 1950 census
was, roughly, proportionally equal among all segments of the
population. Tables 19-2 and 19-4 furnish the best estimates
available of the true size of the unemployment rates according
to age, color, and sex categories; in order to examine these
variables simultaneously, however, it is necessary to use the
census tabulations.

Table 19-4.—UNEMPLOYMENT RATES, BY COLOR AND SEX: ANNUAL AVERAGES, 1947 TO 1957

Year	White			Nonwhite		
	Both sexes	Male	Fe-male	Both sexes	Male	Fe-male
1957....	4.0	3.8	4.5	8.7	9.2	8.0
1956....	3.4	3.2	3.9	8.2	7.9	8.7
1955....	3.6	3.4	3.9	7.9	8.2	7.5
1954....	4.5	4.4	4.9	8.9	9.2	8.2
1953....	2.3	2.2	2.6	4.1	4.4	3.7
1952....	2.4	2.2	2.9	4.6	4.5	4.8
1951....	2.8	2.4	3.7	4.8	4.4	5.4
1950....	4.6	4.5	4.9	8.5	8.9	7.8
1949....	5.2	5.2	5.2	8.2	8.8	7.2
1948....	3.2	3.1	3.4	5.2	5.1	5.2
1947....	3.3	3.5	3.0	5.4	5.7	4.7

Source: Current Population Reports, Labor Force, Series P-50, No. 66, 72, and 85.

rate for white workers. On the average, this has meant that 3 percent more nonwhite than white workers were without jobs. During periods of recession, the unemployment rates for nonwhite workers increased by a larger amount than the rates for white workers, although the percentage increase was about the same for the two groups. During periods of full employment, the color differential diminished somewhat. Thus, the nonwhite population feels the effect of a recession with considerably greater force than does the white population.

The color differential in employment is more severe for nonwhite male workers than for nonwhite women workers, and in times of recession there is a great deal more unemployment among nonwhite men than among nonwhite women. Throughout the 11 years covered by the above summary, unemployment rates among nonwhite males were almost exactly twice as high as unemployment rates among white males in the labor force.

An examination of Tables 19-5, 19-6, and 19-7 for 1950 indicates that this discrimination in employment appears to be greatest at the youngest ages (25 to 40 years for men and 20 to 40 for women), and suggests that the nonwhite worker finds it much harder to obtain a satisfactory job when he first enters the labor force than does the white worker.

Sex Differentials in Rates of Unemployment. During most of the postwar years, the unemployment rate for female workers has been about 10 to 15 percent higher than the unemployment rate for males. In 1940, it was 8 percent higher. Only during the postwar demobilization period, 1946 to

Table 19-5.—UNEMPLOYMENT RATES FOR MALES IN THE CIVILIAN LABOR FORCE, BY AGE AND COLOR FOR THE UNITED STATES, URBAN AND RURAL: 1950

Age	All males	A. White males				B. Nonwhite males			
		Total	Urban	Rural nonfarm	Rural farm	Total	Urban	Rural nonfarm	Rural farm
Total, 14 years and over................	5.0	4.7	5.3	5.2	1.5	7.8	10.2	6.8	1.2
14 to 19 years...........	10.9	10.8	13.7	13.8	3.3	11.5	22.7	10.8	1.6
20 to 24 years...........	8.0	7.6	8.5	7.9	3.2	11.4	15.6	8.8	2.1
25 to 29 years...........	5.0	4.6	5.0	4.7	1.9	9.0	11.1	6.7	1.6
30 to 34 years...........	3.8	3.4	3.8	3.6	1.3	7.5	9.3	5.6	1.0
35 to 39 years...........	3.6	3.3	3.6	3.6	1.1	6.5	8.1	5.1	0.9
40 to 44 years...........	3.7	3.4	3.8	3.8	1.1	6.1	7.7	5.3	0.9
45 to 49 years...........	4.0	3.7	4.2	4.2	1.1	6.5	8.1	5.9	1.0
50 to 54 years...........	4.2	4.0	4.5	4.5	1.1	6.3	7.9	6.3	0.9
55 to 59 years...........	4.6	4.4	5.0	5.1	1.0	6.8	8.7	7.4	1.0
60 to 64 years...........	5.2	5.1	6.0	6.0	1.0	6.4	8.8	6.8	0.7
65 to 69 years...........	5.5	5.4	6.9	6.1	0.7	6.6	10.2	7.8	0.9
70 to 74 years...........	4.3	4.3	5.9	4.7	0.4	4.7	8.3	6.2	0.4
75 to 79 years...........	3.4	3.4	5.0	3.8	0.3	3.6	7.8	3.5	0.3
80 to 84 years...........	2.4	2.3	3.5	2.5	0.3	3.5	5.4	6.2	1.2
85 years and over........	2.5	2.3	4.3	0.2	0.3	4.4	8.4	...	0.7

Source: U.S. Census of Population: 1950, Vol. II, Detailed Characteristics of the Population, Part 1, U.S. Summary, Chapter C, Table 118.

1947, and during the recession year of 1949, were a greater percentage of male than of female labor force participants unemployed.

The following summary, in which the ratio of female to male rates of unemployment is shown for each of several age groups and for phases of high, medium, and low unemployment, demonstrates that sex differentials in rates of unemployment tend to vary both with age and with the level of unemployment.

Age	Ratio of rate for female to male workers: 10-year average			
	Total	Level of unemployment		
		High	Medium	Low
All ages........	1.14	1.07	1.14	1.31
14 to 19 years.....	0.93	0.92	0.94	0.95
20 to 24 years.....	0.78	0.73	0.78	0.97
25 to 34 years.....	1.45	1.31	1.51	1.77
35 to 44 years.....	1.31	1.22	1.32	1.53
45 to 54 years.....	1.06	0.99	1.10	1.19
55 to 64 years.....	0.89	0.81	0.91	1.09
65 years and over..	0.70	0.77	0.58	0.71
White, total.......	1.16	1.09	1.15	1.35
Nonwhite, total....	0.94	0.86	1.01	1.05

Note: Years of high unemployment: 1949, 50, 54, and 57; Years of medium unemployment: 1948, 55, and 56. Years of low unemployment: 1951, 52, and 53.

At ages 14 to 24 years, and at 55 years and over, women have had lower rates of unemployment than men. Only between the ages of 25 and 54 years (and especially between the ages of 25 and 44 years) have unemployment rates been higher for women than for men. Between 24 and 34 years this differential reaches its peak, and at these ages women have had rates almost 50 percent higher than those of men. Moreover, the intensity of this differential varies with the national level of unemployment. During periods of prosperity (low unemployment) the sex differential has been greatest, and during periods of recession (high unemployment) it has been smallest. Thus, when jobs are plentiful a disproportionately large share of women aged 25 to 54 are among the residual of unemployed; when the level of unemployment rises, however, and men of all ages are thrown into the unemployed category, the sex differential diminishes at ages 25 to 54.

The sex differential with respect to unemployment is restricted almost entirely to the white population; among the nonwhite population, men have rates of unemployment that are as high as, or even higher than, those of women, except during

Table 19-6.—UNEMPLOYMENT RATES FOR FEMALES IN THE CIVILIAN LABOR FORCE, BY AGE AND COLOR FOR THE UNITED STATES, URBAN AND RURAL: 1950

Age	All fe-males	A. White females				B. Nonwhite females			
		Total	Urban	Rural nonfarm	Rural farm	Total	Urban	Rural nonfarm	Rural farm
Total, 14 years and over.................	4.7	4.2	4.2	4.3	3.2	8.0	8.8	7.2	3.3
14 to 19 years..........	9.7	9.0	8.7	10.7	8.3	16.4	22.5	13.7	4.6
20 to 24 years..........	5.3	4.5	4.4	5.1	4.7	11.8	13.3	9.5	4.2
25 to 29 years..........	4.7	4.0	4.0	4.2	3.1	9.1	9.9	7.6	3.7
30 to 34 years..........	4.2	3.6	3.7	3.4	2.2	7.4	8.0	6.2	3.3
35 to 39 years..........	3.9	3.4	3.5	3.2	2.2	6.6	7.1	5.9	2.6
40 to 44 years..........	3.5	3.1	3.2	3.1	1.9	5.8	6.3	5.2	2.4
45 to 49 years..........	3.6	3.3	3.4	3.1	1.9	5.8	6.2	5.8	2.7
50 to 54 years..........	3.7	3.5	3.7	3.4	1.6	5.3	5.7	5.6	2.1
55 to 59 years..........	3.9	3.7	3.9	3.5	1.7	5.3	5.6	5.8	2.9
60 to 64 years..........	4.0	4.0	4.3	3.4	1.5	4.7	5.1	5.2	1.6
65 to 69 years..........	3.9	3.7	4.1	3.2	0.8	5.2	5.6	6.2	2.4
70 to 74 years..........	3.2	3.2	3.7	2.3	0.7	3.8	4.8	2.6	1.4
75 to 79 years..........	3.2	3.1	3.7	2.1	0.6	3.8	4.5	4.4	0.7
80 to 84 years..........	2.1	2.2	2.6	2.0	...	1.1	1.8	...	...
85 years and over.......	2.1	2.3	2.8	1.9	...	0.9	...	...	...

Source: U.S. Census of Population: 1950, Vol. II, Detailed Characteristics of the Population, Part 1, U.S. Summary, Chapter C, Table 118.

periods of nearly full employment. This sex differential may reflect, in part, a greater tendency for white women not to report themselves as a part of the labor force unless they have a job. Tables 19-5, 19-6, and 19-7 suggest that this may be the case. More white women are financially able to make working or not working a matter of choice--for many of them, a job has partially the nature of a pastime. To a higher proportion of nonwhite women, however, working is a matter of economic necessity, and when they are without work they report themselves as unemployed members of the labor force rather than as housewives. Among the nonwhite civilian labor force in 1950, women had a higher rate of unemployment than men at the ages of 14 to 35 years, but a lower rate of unemployment at ages older than this. Thus, the high rates of unemployment found among nonwhite males may be due not so much to the difficulties they encounter in entering the labor force as to the difficulties they experience because they are among the first to be laid off during economic recession.

Table 19-7 shows unemployment rates by single years of age, by sex, color, and urban-rural residence; it is worthy of intensive study, particularly with reference to unemployment in relation to first entry into the labor force. Apparently, girls 14 and 15 years old actively seek work more aggressively than boys of these ages. This is especially true of nonwhite youths, and of young people living in urban areas. By ages 17 and 18 the situation is reversed; boys enter the labor force in larger numbers than girls, and have higher rates of unemployment.

Urban-rural Differences in Rates of Unemployment. Tables 19-5, 19-6, and 19-7 all report that in 1950 the rural-farm male population had much lower unemployment rates than did the urban and the rural-farm male populations. Other studies

Table 19-7.—UNEMPLOYMENT RATES FOR PERSONS 14 TO 25 YEARS OLD, IN THE CIVILIAN LABOR FORCE, BY SINGLE YEARS OF AGE, COLOR, AND SEX, FOR THE UNITED STATES, URBAN AND RURAL: 1950

Age and sex	Total	A. White				B. Nonwhite			
		Total white	Urban	Rural nonfarm	Rural farm	Total nonwhite	Urban	Rural nonfarm	Rural farm
MALES									
14 years.............	4.4	4.5	6.3	6.8	1.3	4.0	12.9	5.1	0.8
15 years.............	6.7	6.8	9.5	10.7	1.6	6.2	17.0	7.7	0.8
16 years.............	11.7	12.0	16.7	16.6	3.0	9.7	22.7	11.1	1.2
17 years.............	13.1	13.1	17.0	16.9	3.7	13.0	26.0	10.9	2.0
18 years.............	12.2	11.9	14.6	14.8	3.9	14.2	25.3	12.5	2.0
19 years.............	10.5	10.2	12.1	11.7	3.9	12.9	20.7	11.3	1.9
20 years.............	9.8	9.5	11.1	10.3	3.8	12.6	18.8	9.3	2.7
21 years.............	9.0	8.7	9.9	9.1	3.7	12.1	17.4	8.8	1.9
22 years.............	8.1	7.7	8.8	7.8	3.2	11.7	15.8	9.4	2.4
23 years.............	7.1	6.7	7.4	6.9	2.8	10.9	14.5	8.5	1.9
24 years.............	6.4	6.0	6.7	6.2	2.5	10.1	12.9	8.1	1.6
FEMALES									
14 years.............	7.9	7.7	9.2	9.2	3.0	8.7	22.5	11.4	1.6
15 years.............	11.7	11.5	13.0	12.6	6.1	12.3	23.4	12.5	4.2
16 years.............	15.4	15.2	16.3	15.4	9.9	16.5	27.7	13.8	4.5
17 years.............	13.0	12.2	12.1	13.8	10.3	19.1	27.0	15.5	5.0
18 years.............	9.5	8.7	8.2	10.3	9.6	18.2	23.2	14.8	5.1
19 years.............	7.0	6.2	5.9	7.5	7.1	15.7	18.4	12.3	6.4
20 years.............	6.1	5.4	5.1	6.4	5.8	13.5	15.7	10.8	5.1
21 years.............	5.5	4.7	4.5	5.4	4.6	13.2	15.2	10.3	3.7
22 years.............	5.2	4.4	4.3	4.9	4.5	11.5	12.9	9.7	4.0
23 years.............	4.8	4.0	4.0	4.2	4.2	10.9	12.1	8.3	4.0
24 years.............	4.9	4.1	4.1	4.3	3.6	10.4	11.4	8.5	4.1

Source: U.S. Census of Population: 1950, Vol. II, Detailed Characteristics of the Population, Part 1, U.S. Summary, Chapter C, Table 119.

have found the presence of this differential to be practically universal. The data in these tables show that it exists at all ages, for both white and nonwhite men. It is also present, to a more limited extent, among white and nonwhite women. This difference, it is known, does not imply that there are greater employment opportunities in rural-farm areas than in nonfarm areas. Rather, it reflects the greater prevalence of self-employment in rural areas. A farm operator can always find something to do, even if he is earning only a bare subsistence from his farm. Thus, he would be likely to report himself as a member of the labor force and as employed, even if he were seriously underemployed (or mal-employed) from the viewpoint of his optimum economic well-being. This tendency among farm operators is a basic characteristic of employment statistics, and must be kept continuously in mind. If two regions differ with respect to the proportion of their labor force that is unemployed, the difference may be due

solely to the fact that one of the regions has a much larger agricultural population than the other.

Among white workers in 1950, unemployment was about equally prevalent in urban areas and in rural-nonfarm areas, and at almost all ages. However, among nonwhite workers, there was much more unemployment in the urban than in the rural-nonfarm areas. For nonwhite men this difference was present at all ages, whereas for women it was confined largely to ages 14 to 45 years. Large numbers of Negroes were migrating to the cities around 1950, and the high rate of nonwhite unemployment in urban areas may have been a reflection of the fact that a great number of new arrivals were seeking work there, rather than an indication that employment conditions were poorer in cities.

Nativity Differences in Rates of Unemployment. In 1950, unemployment was considerably higher among foreign-born than among native-born white persons, at all ages over 25 years. (Few foreign-

Table 19-8.—UNEMPLOYMENT RATES FOR THE NATIVE WHITE AND FOREIGN-BORN WHITE POPULATION, BY AGE, AND SEX, FOR THE UNITED STATES, URBAN AND RURAL: 1950 (Based on 3 1/3 percent sample)

Age and sex	A. Native white				B. Foreign-born white				Nativity differential, A—B ÷ A			
	Total	Urban	Rural nonfarm	Rural farm	Total	Urban	Rural nonfarm	Rural farm	Total	Urban	Rural nonfarm	Rural farm
MALES												
Total, 14 years and over........	4.5	5.1	5.2	1.5	5.7	6.0	5.9	1.6	-26.7	-17.6	-13.5	-6.7
14 to 17 years......	10.6	14.4	14.9	2 6	6.0	6.0	...	...	43.4	58.3	...	...
18 and 19 years.....	10.9	13.0	13.4	4.0	8.3	8.6	...	...	23.8	33.8	...	...
20 to 24 years......	7.6	8.5	7.7	3.3	7.6	8.7	6.8	1.9	...	-2.4	11.7	42.4
25 to 29 years......	4.5	4.9	4.5	1.8	5.7	5.8	5.2	5.0	-26.7	-18.4	-15.6	-177.8
30 to 34 years......	3.3	3.6	3.6	1.3	4.9	5.1	5.0	1.4	-48.5	-41.7	-38.9	-7.7
35 to 44 years......	3.3	3.7	3.7	1.0	4.3	4.5	4.1	1.2	-30.3	-21.6	-10.8	-20.0
45 to 54 years......	3.7	4.2	4.4	1.0	4.8	5.0	4.4	1.8	-29.7	-19.0	....	-80.0
55 to 64 years......	4.1	4.9	5.2	0.8	6.4	6.6	7.4	1.7	-56.1	-34.7	-42.3	-112.5
65 to 74 years......	4.1	5.6	5.2	0.6	7.6	8.4	7.9	1.0	-85.4	-50.0	-51.9	-66.7
75 years and over...	2.8	4.4	2.9	0.3	5.3	6.8	3.8	1.3	-89.3	-54.5	-31.0	-333.3
FEMALES												
Total, 14 years and over........	4.1	4.1	4.3	3.3	4.8	4.9	4.5	1.9	-17.1	-19.5	-4.6	42.4
14 to 17 years......	12.7	13.3	13.7	8.2	13.7	15.9	...	...	-7.9	-19.5	...	...
18 and 19 years.....	7.1	6.7	8.5	8.1	6.0	5.7	...	...	15.5	14.9	...	....
20 to 24 years......	4.5	4.4	5.1	5.0	5.7	5.4	9.8	...	-26.7	-22.7	-92.2	...
25 to 29 years......	3.9	3.9	4.0	2.6	4.7	4.7	4.5	...	-20.5	-20.5	-12.5	...
30 to 34 years......	3.7	3.9	3.4	2.2	5.8	5.7	7.4	...	-56.8	-46.2	-117.6	...
35 to 44 years......	3.2	3.2	3.3	2.0	4.6	4.7	4.5	1.6	-43.8	-46.9	-36.4	20.0
45 to 54 years......	3.2	3.3	3.2	1.9	4.6	4.7	3.9	3.2	-43.8	-42.4	-21.9	-68.4
55 to 64 years......	3.6	3.8	3.4	1.9	4.9	5.2	3.9	0.8	-36.1	-36.8	-14.7	57.9
65 to 74 years......	3.2	3.6	2.6	0.8	4.4	4.7	3.9	...	-37.5	-30.6	-50.0	...
75 years and over...	2.4	2.6	2.9	0.7	4.8	5.9	...	...	-100.0	-126.9	...	...

Source: U.S. Census of Population: 1950, Vol. IV, Special Reports, Part 1, Chapter A, Employment and Personal Characteristics, Table 5.

born persons are less than 25 years of age.) Table 19-8 shows that in 1950 this situation existed in urban, rural-nonfarm, and rural-farm areas, and applied to both sexes. For most age groups, the unemployment rates among the foreign born were higher by 30 percent or more than the rates for the native-born population. This differential was greater among women than among men, for most age groups above 20 years of age. For all ages combined, the differential was greater in urban than in rural areas, although for some age groups the differential was larger for rural than for urban populations.

The above findings must be interpreted with great caution. Chapter 14 (International Migration) showed that some migrant groups have levels of education, occupation, and income that are considerably above the averages for the nation, while others are well below the national averages. It must be presupposed that the high unemployment among the foreign born is most heavily concentrated among those groups which have below-average socio-economic status. Thus, one would expect persons of Mexican, Italian, and Polish ancestry (and immigrants from the other nations of eastern and southern Europe) to have very high rates of unemployment, and immigrants from England, Scandinavia, Germany, and other northwestern European countries to have average or below-average rates of unemployment.

Industry and Class-of-worker Differentials in Rate of Unemployment. Asking unemployed persons a few questions about their last job and their last employer makes it possible to establish differentials by industry, by class-of-worker, and by occupation. The following table summarizes the unemployment differentials, as manifested in 1957, by industry group and class of worker:

Industry group and class of worker	Rate of unemployment	Ratio to average rate
Experienced civilian labor force	3.9	1.00
Agriculture......................	2.1	0.54
Wage and salary workers..........	6.7	1.72
Self-employed workers............	0.2	0.05
Unpaid family workers............	0.2	0.05

Con.

Industry group and class of worker	Rate of unemployment	Ratio to average rate
Experienced civilian labor force continued.		
Nonagricultural industries........	4.1	1.05
Wage and salary workers..........	4.5	1.15
Forestry, fisheries, mining....	6.3	1.62
Construction..................	9.8	2.51
Manufacturing.................	5.0	1.28
Durable goods...............	4.9	1.26
Nondurable goods............	5.3	1.36
Transportation, communication, and public utilities..........	3.1	0.79
Wholesale and retail trade.....	4.5	1.15
Service industries............	3.2	0.82
Public administration..........	2.0	0.51
Self-employed and unpaid family workers........................	1.0	0.26

Source: Annual Report on the Labor Force, 1957, Series P-50, No. 85, 1958.

Most of the unemployment is found among wage and salary workers; self-employed workers have very low rates of unemployment, both in the agricultural and the nonagricultural industries. Among wage and salary workers, those who had been employed in the construction industries had by far the greatest rate of unemployment. Other industries with above-average rates of unemployment were mining, forestry, fisheries, manufacturing, and wholesale and retail trade. The differentials that have been pointed out here are present almost every year, because they represent differences among the industries in rates of labor turnover and in other operating conditions. However, there are substantial year-to-year fluctuations in the comparative sizes of the industry differentials in relation to the average rate. An analysis of these fluctuations is beyond the scope of this book, because it would involve a study of why and how business cycles occur.

Occupation Differentials in Rates of Unemployment. Persons in some occupations are comparatively immune to unemployment, whereas persons in other occupations seem to be "sitting ducks" each time an economic downturn comes along. Following are the unemployment differentials for each of a selected list of occupations, for the year

1957; they are fairly typical of most postwar years:

UNEMPLOYMENT RATES BY OCCUPATION GROUP: ANNUAL AVERAGE, 1957

Occupation group	Annual av- erage[1]	Ratio to total annual average
Experienced civilian labor force.	3.9	1.00
Profess'l, techn'l, kindred wrks...	1.2	0.31
Medical and other health workers..	1.4	0.36
Teachers, except college..........	0.7	0.18
Other profess'l, techn'l, kindred.	1.3	0.33
Farmers and farm managers.........	0.3	0.08
Mgrs, offs., and propr's, exc. farm	1.0	0.26
Salaried workers..................	0.9	0.23
Self-employed wrks. in ret. trade.	0.9	0.23
Self-emp. wrks. exc. ret. trade...	1.0	0.26
Clerical and kindred workers.......	2.8	0.72
Stenographers,typists,secretaries.	2.3	0.59
Other clerical and kindred wrks...	3.0	0.77
Sales workers.....................	2.6	0.67
Retail trade......................	3.3	0.85
Other sales workers...............	1.4	0.36
Craftsmen, foremen, kindred wrks...	3.8	0.97
Carpenters........................	8.0	2.05
Const. craftsmen, exc. carpenters.	6.4	1.64
Mechanics and repairmen...........	2.8	0.72
Metal craftsmen, exc. mechanics...	3.2	0.82
Other craftsmen...................	2.3	0.59
Foremen, not elsewhere classified.	1.7	0.44
Operatives and kindred workers.....	6.3	1.62
Drivers and deliverymen...........	4.2	1.08
Other operatives and kindred wrks.	6.8	1.74
Durable goods manufacturing......	6.6	1.69
Nondurable goods manufacturing...	7.3	1.87
Other industries.................	6.4	1.64
Private household workers..........	3.7	0.95
Service workers, exc. prov. hshld..	5.1	1.31
Protective service workers........	1.9	0.49
Waiters, cooks, and bartenders....	6.7	1.72
Other service workers............	5.0	1.28
Farm laborers and foremen..........	3.7	0.95
Paid workers......................	6.5	1.67
Unpaid family workers.............	0.1	0.03
Laborers, except farm and mine.....	9.4	2.41
Construction......................	12.6	3.23
Manufacturing.....................	8.3	2.12
Other industries.................	6.5	1.67

[1]Based on January, April, July, and October.

The occupations which appear to be most vulnerable to unemployment, ranked in descending order of vulnerability, are as follows:[9]

---

[9] For data concerning unemployment rates for specific detailed occupations, the reader is referred to the special appendix of statistics for detailed occupations, at the end of Chapter 17.

	Ratio to average rate
Laborers, construction industries......	3.23
Laborers, manufacturing industries.....	2.12
Carpenters.............................	2.05
Operatives, nondurable goods manufac- tures.................................	1.87
Waiters, cooks, and bartenders........	1.72
Operatives, durable goods manufactures.	1.69
Laborers, other industries except manufactures and construction........	1.67
Farm laborers, paid workers...........	1.67
Construction craftsmen, exc. carpenters	1.64
Service workers, exc. protective , waiters, cooks, and bartenders........	1.28
Operatives, except manufacturing.......	1.64
Drivers and deliverymen...............	1.08

Following are the occupations having the least unemployment in 1957, listed in ascending order of vulnerability to unemployment:

	Ratio to average rate
Unpaid family workers, farm...........	0.03
Farmers and farm managers.............	0.08
Teachers, except college..............	0.18
Managers and officials--salaried wrks..	0.23
Propr's, self employed in ret. trade...	0.23
Mgrs, offs., and propr's, self employed except retail trade..................	0.26
Professional, technical, exc. medical and teachers elsewhere classified.....	0.33
Mediaal and other health workers.......	0.36
Sales workers, except retail trade.....	0.36
Foremen................................	0.44
Protective service workers............	0.49
Stenographers, typists, secretaries....	0.59

DESCRIPTION OF UNEMPLOYMENT

Duration of Unemployment. Some unemployed workers have been without work for a much longer span of time than others. Table 19-9 provides two measures of duration of unemployment, according to certain characteristics of the workers. This table shows that during 1957 the average duration of unemployment was more than 10 weeks, and that workers with the following characteristics had been unemployed longest:

Older workers; men over 45 years of age

Nonwhite workers

Workers in manufacturing industries

Workers in mining, fisheries, forestry

Once they lose their jobs, workers with the above characteristics or occupational backgrounds had more difficulty finding employment than other

Table 19-9.—RATE OF LONG-TERM UNEMPLOYMENT AND AVERAGE DURATION OF UNEMPLOYMENT, BY SELECTED CHARACTERISTICS: ANNUAL AVERAGE, 1957

Age, color, sex, and industry	Rate of long-term unem-ployment[1]	Average duration (weeks)[2]	Age, color, sex, and industry	Rate of long-term unem-ployment[1]	Average duration (weeks)[2]
Total, 14 years and over.......	19.1	10.3	INDUSTRY		
			Wage and salary workers in nonagricultural industries, total........................	19.7	10.5
AGE AND SEX					
Male, 14 years and over...........	20.4	11.1	Construction.....................	17.6	9.4
14 to 17 years..................	12.0	7.5	Manufacturing....................	23.0	11.7
18 to 24 years..................	14.5	8.3	Durable goods................	23.6	11.9
25 to 44 years..................	18.8	10.1	Nondurable goods.............	22.0	11.4
45 to 64 years..................	27.6	14.8	Transportation, communication,		
65 years and over..............	38.6	18.6	and other public utilities.......	18.2	10.4
Female, 14 years and over........	16.7	9.0	Wholesale and retail trade........	16.5	9.6
			Service industries...............	16.1	9.2
COLOR			Other industries[3]................	28.6	15.6
White...........................	18.5	10.1			
Nonwhite........................	21.2	11.0			

[1]Percent of unemployed in each category who were out of work 15 weeks or longer.
[2]Arithmetic mean based on distributions by single weeks of unemployment.
[3]Includes forestry and fisheries, mining, and public administration.

Source: Annual Report on the Labor Force, 1957, Series P-50, No. 85, 1958.

workers. Periods of generally high unemployment bring an increase both in the average duration of unemployment and in the percentage of workers who have been unemployed for a long time.

Volume of Unemployment. The number of different workers who are unemployed at various times during the course of a given year is much greater than the number who are unemployed at any one time during that year. For example, the total number of different persons who had been unemployed at some time during the year 1957 was 11.6 million, which was 4 times as large as the average monthly number of unemployed (2.9 million). This illustrates the rapid turnover that takes place among unemployed workers. About one-half of the persons who became unemployed during 1957 remained jobless for less than 5 weeks during any one period of unemployment. As these persons found work, their places in the ranks of the jobless were filled by new members of the unemployed population. Once a person has been employed, he tends to become a "repeater"; almost 40 percent of the persons who became jobless at some time during 1957 were unemployed two or more times during that year.

Unemployment and Part-year Work. In the chapter concerning the labor force, it was reported that a substantial proportion of persons work for only part of a year. Unemployment is the leading reason for part-year work. For example, 45 percent of the men and 20 percent of the women who had worked less than 50 weeks during 1957 gave layoff or some other form of unemployment as their reason for not having worked full time.

Age and Marital Status Composition of the Unemployed. The above discussion of differentials, or differences in rates of unemployment, fails to show adequately the population composition of the body of unemployed workers. Tables 19-10 and 19-11 attempt to remedy this by showing the age and marital status composition of the unemployed, in comparison with the employed. Although the rates of unemployment are highest among the very young, single, etc., the great majority (65 percent) of unemployed males are adult workers in the prime working ages—20 to 64 years of age, most of whom have family responsibilities. Similarly, 68 percent of unemployed females, despite their rate differences, fall within this age span. More than 60 percent of unemployed men are

Table 19-10.—AGE COMPOSITION OF THE UNEMPLOYED AND EMPLOYED BY SEX: ANNUAL AVERAGE FOR 1957

Age	Both sexes		Male		Female	
	Unemployed	Employed	Unemployed	Employed	Unemployed	Employed
Total......................	100.0	100.0	100.0	100.0	100.0	100.0
14 and 15 years....................	2.6	1.4	2.7	1.4	2.4	1.4
16 and 17 years....................	7.9	2.5	7.4	2.3	8.6	3.0
18 and 19 years....................	9.1	3.3	8.4	2.6	10.2	4.9
20 to 24 years....................	14.6	8.7	14.9	7.6	14.1	10.9
25 to 34 years....................	19.5	21.9	18.4	23.2	21.5	19.2
35 to 44 years....................	17.0	23.6	16.1	23.7	18.7	23.4
45 to 54 years....................	15.2	20.5	16.0	20.1	14.0	21.3
55 to 59 years....................	5.8	7.6	6.4	7.7	4.5	7.2
60 to 64 years....................	4.5	5.6	5.2	5.9	3.2	5.0
65 to 69 years....................	2.4	2.8	2.7	3.0	2.0	2.3
70 years and over.................	1.4	2.1	1.7	2.5	0.8	1.4

Source: Current Population Reports, Series P-50, No. 85, 1958.

married and living with their wife (and most of them have children). Thus, the above analysis, which showed above-average unemployment rates for the groups with least family responsibilities, should not be allowed to leave an incorrect impression; the tragedy of unemployment befalls families with dependents much more often than it does unattached individuals with only themselves to support. This happens, despite the pattern of differences in rates because there are so many more workers with families than there are unattached individuals in the labor force. Beyond a doubt, the phenomenon of the working wife is, at least in part, an unemployment insurance device which helps to assure at least some protection to the family if the husband loses his job. In many other cases it is a response to the husband's unemployment.

Table 19-11.—MARITAL STATUS OF EMPLOYED AND UNEMPLOYED, BY SEX: MARCH, 1958

Marital status	Unemployed	Employed
Male, total.................	100.0	100.0
Single..........................	30.0	16.7
Married.........................	64.7	79.7
Wife present...................	60.6	77.3
Wife absent....................	4.1	2.4
Widowed and divorced...........	5.3	3.6
Female, total.................	100.0	100.0
Single..........................	19.7	24.7
Married.........................	68.3	58.6
Husband present...............	57.2	53.5
Husband absent in armed forces	1.3	0.4
Husband absent, other reasons.	9.8	4.7
Widowed and divorced...........	12.0	16.7

Source: Current Population Reports, Series P-50, No. 87, 1959.

SUMMARY

The economic well-being of the population is intimately related to its ability to support itself through some form of employment. The members of some subgroups in the population find it very difficult to get jobs, or to get steady and secure jobs, and this situation creates problems that affect many other aspects of the lives of persons in such groups. Despite the recent high levels of propserity, there is still a great deal of job insecurity among the population. In 1957, not less than 15 percent of the persons who worked at some time during the year experienced one or more episodes of unemployment. Hence, statistics showing that only 3 or 4 percent of the population is unemployed at any one time fail to measure the actual amount of livelihood that is lost, and the hardship that is created, through unemployment.

Unemployment hits most heavily certain categories of the labor force. Young wage and salary workers; elderly, nonwhite, or foreign-born workers; young female workers; and unskilled and semi-skilled blue collar workers employed in construction, manufacturing, or trade, are subject to a much higher risk of unemployment than are the self-employed, skilled, or white collar workers.

In this chapter it has not been possible to analyze in detail the problem of the partially unemployed labor force. Some experts believe that, at any one time, the number of partially unemployed workers (those who work less than full time but who desire full-time work, or who would like to work more hours than they are able to find employment for) is considerably greater than the volume of wholly unemployed workers, and that the purchasing power and the self-support lost as a result of underemployment is equal, as far as the nation's economy is concerned, to the burden of unemployment. Among this underemployed group are many farm operators, and many middle-aged and elderly men and women, housewives, and students living in nonfarm areas.

Chapter 20

INCOME AND POPULATION COMPOSITION

INCOME AS A MEASURE OF ECONOMIC WELL-BEING

Money income is a sensitive measure of economic well-being in today's technologically advanced nations. In such societies it is roughly synonymous with "livelihood, " because very few families or individuals are able to maintain economic self-sufficiency and because barter exchange has almost disappeared. Except for a certain amount of household consumption of the produce from farms and vegetable gardens, there is comparatively little production-for-own-use (self-sufficiency). Only a few arrangements involving barter or "payment in kind" persist within these modern societies, and almost all obligations are now discharged by means of money payments. The few exceptions (such as farmers who are given the use of a dwelling as part of the rent bargain, or restaurant workers who get meals as a part of their pay) only emphasize the comparative infrequency of moneyless exchange. This situation means that statistics concerning money income are an excellent measure of the level-of-living potential among the population, the only major exception being found in the rural-farm population-- and even there a study of income distribution can provide much insight.

Average Level of Economic Well-Being: Per Capita Income. After having suffered a severe set-back during the economic crisis of 1930 to 1933, the general income level of the United States population has risen to unprecedented heights. In the years 1956 and 1957, the nation's population enjoyed a higher level of living than at any time in its history.[1] No other nation in the world matches it with respect to average level of material comforts. (Despite this fact, there are probably some nations where the proportion of people living in poverty is smaller than it is in the United States. The Scandinavian countries, for example, have low poverty levels, even though much smaller proportions of the populations live in luxury in these countries than in the United States.)

A valuable statistical series, permitting one to trace changes in the level of economic well-being in the United States population, are the annual per capita estimates of disposable personal income that are prepared by the Department of Commerce in collaboration with other government agencies and with private research organizations. These estimates are arrived at by the following process: from the nation's total personal income that is available for spending are subtracted the personal payments for taxes and other obligations, and the resulting figure is divided by the number of inhabitants in the nation. It is a measure of the number of dollars which each inhabitant, on the average, can spend to satisfy his material needs and wants. The changing level of economic well-being may be traced in the following estimates of

---

[1] Since income statistics refer to one complete year, the latest year for which data are available is one year earlier than the current year. Thus, 1957 is the latest year for which final estimates are available until December, 1959, when the data for 1958 will be released.

per capita disposable income for selected years, 1929 to 1957:

Year	Per capita disposable personal income:	
	At current 1957 dollars	At constant (1947) dollars
1929..................	682	927
1933..................	364	679
1940..................	576	981
1945..................	1,075	1,283
1950..................	1,359	1,280
1954..................	1,567	1,331
1955..................	1,635	1,384
1956..................	1,708	1,422
1957 (preliminary)....	1,756	1,416

Source: Statistical Abstract of the United States, 1958, Table 383.

These figures illustrate the extent to which prosperity increased after World War II: they show that in 1957, after all taxes had been paid, each man, woman, and child in the nation had $1,756 to spend for self-maintenance, education, recreation, and other goods and services. This is more than twice the amount the average person had during the depression year of 1933; it is 60 percent more than the average amount available in 1929, a year which held the all-time record for prosperity before the economic depression of 1930 to 1939. A comparison of this data with that of earlier years reflects a real change in purchasing power, for the adjustment of the data has taken into account changing price levels. One could truthfully say that, in the light of present-day standards, all but a small fraction of today's grandparents were once almost paupers. The statistics presented suggest that actual purchasing power declined in 1957 (in 1958 it may decline even more)--the result, it is assumed, of a business recession accompanied by inflation.

INCOME DISTRIBUTION

The economic well-being of the population cannot be measured exclusively in terms of the average income available per citizen, however. The distribution of the income must also be discovered, by means of such questions as, "To what extent do a very few persons receive very large incomes and a great many persons receive very small incomes?" "What percentage of persons receive less than the per capita share as measured above, and how much less do how many persons receive?" Revolutionary changes have taken place recently in income distribution, as well as in the nation's general level of economic well-being.

Beginning in the mid-1940's, the Bureau of the Census began to collect statistics concerning the income received from all sources by families and individuals, and it is these data which provide detailed information about income distribution.[2] During the calendar year 1957, 7 out of every 10 persons who were 14 years of age and over (70.7 percent) received at least some money income. It

---

[2] Despite their great utility, and the current intensive use being made of them by analysts in many different fields, income statistics are of very recent origin. The census of 1940, which introduced so many other innovations, was the first decennial census which undertook to collect information concerning income. Even in 1940, however, the census obtained information concerning only wage or salary income, and an indication as to whether as much as $50.00 or more had been earned from self-employment and other sources. The first reliable "complete" income statistics (combined income from all sources) for the individuals and families of the nation were collected on a sample basis during the 1940's. Each year since then these data have been collected, and they have been expanded with respect to both scope and detail until they now yield a variety of quite precise and very useful facts. The 1950 census also undertook to obtain the complete incomes of families as well as of individuals. It succeeded moderately well, although the sample data and the census data are not strictly comparable. The data used in this chapter have been taken primarily from the Current Population Survey, although the 1950 census data are used for a more detailed examination of some of the income differences.

It is known that the incomes enumerated for persons and families are smaller than the incomes actually received, and that they may be underreported by as much as 20 percent. Little is known about the origin or nature of this error, or about its effect on the validity of the data if such data is to be used as a basis for inferences concerning differences between groups of the population or changes over periods of time. These data can be defended only in the sense that the uniform and "logical" sequences they present are sufficiently consistent with general observation and theoretical expectations that their "face value" validity seems very high.

may surprise the reader to learn that so large a percentage of the population receives income. The percentage of persons who are fully dependent on others for a livelihood is much smaller than it used to be, primarily because such a large proportion of housewives are now employed, such a large percentage of young persons attending school are working part time, and such a large percentage of persons 65 years of age and over (both male and female) regularly receive pensions or other similar kinds of payments. The percentage of the population that is dependent decreased substantially between 1945 and 1957, the span of time concerning which data are available.

The median income for individuals in 1957 was $2,452, or $204 per month, and for families it was $4,971, or about $415 per month; however, the dispersion from these midpoints is very wide. The distribution of income among individuals and among families who did receive income is shown in Table 20-1.[3] There is a characteristic "income curve" describing the distribution of income among individuals, and it indicates that a large proportion of the population receive very modest incomes and a small proportion of the population receive very large incomes. Figure 20-1 illustrates this curve very roughly (it would emphasize the concentration which exists at the low income level if it were plotted in units of 100 dollars instead of 500 dollars). For centuries, economists have speculated as to why the income curve for individuals has its characteristic skewed shape, with such a large proportion of income recipients concentrated toward the lower end of the income scale. It is now rather generally agreed that a variety of factors interact to produce this distribution. Among these factors are:

a. Differences in ability, intelligence, initiative, skill, health, and other characteristics that influence income-earning ability. That great individual differences in productive ability exist among the population can be observed on every hand. There is no general agreement concerning the extent to which these differences arise from inherited limitations or capabilities and the extent to which they reflect the particular environment

and experience of each individual. Whatever the origin of these differences, lack of productive capacity does curtail severely the earning power of some individuals, and extraordinary skill or talent does enable a few individuals to obtain larger than average incomes. It has often been pointed out, however, that differences in ability could not possibly be the only factor responsible for income differences, since differential abilities are known to be distributed among the population according to a "normal curve," rather than according to the kind of very skewed curve that is shown in Figure 20-1.

---

[3] Note concerning units for which incomes are reported: persons, families, and unrelated individuals: Since income is paid to persons, the most basic income statistics that can be collected are those referring to the total money income received by individuals over one-year periods. Such data are called "personal" or "individual" income statistics. However, for a very large percentage of the population the family, rather than the person, is the unit of consumption and livelihood. Since one-half of all today's families have two or more earners, one can gain a much more accurate picture of the livelihood situation by assembling income data in terms of family units. Hence, income statistics tabulated for families are an important type of income information. (Often these family statistics are cross-classified according to the socio-economic characteristics of the family head.) But many individuals do not live in families; they live alone in single-person households, as lodgers or tenants in private homes, hotels, and rooming houses, or as employees who live in the private household of the employer. If a tabulation of family incomes is prepared, an income tabulation must also be made for this residue of "unrelated individuals" or nonfamily persons.

Thus, there are two major kinds of income tabulations:
    Incomes of persons (income recipients)
    Incomes of families and of unrelated individuals
        (nonfamily persons)
Sometimes families and unrelated individuals have been treated as equivalent units, and their incomes reported in a single distribution (1950 census). However, it is extremely difficult to interpret such data, because one never knows to what extent the differences in income that are observed to exist between two or more population groups are due to real differences in income level, and to what extent they result simply from a difference between the groups in the proportionate mixture of families and unrelated individuals. In recent years the Census Bureau has adopted the practice of reporting separate tabulations for families and for unrelated individuals.

Table 20-1.—PERCENT DISTRIBUTION OF MONEY INCOME AMONG FAMILIES AND INDIVIDUALS: 1950 AND 1957

Total money income[1]	Income of families			Income of individuals		
	1957	1950	Change, 1950 to 1957	1957	1950	Change, 1950 to 1957
Total....................	100.0	100.0	...	100.0	100.0	...
Under $500.........................	3.0	4.0	11.0	16.2	16.0	0.2
$500 to $999.......................	3.4	5.0	-1.6	12.3	11.3	1.0
$1,000 to $1,499...................	4.0	5.2	-1.2	8.2	9.3	-1.1
$1,500 to $1,999...................	4.5	5.8	-1.3	6.7	7.2	-0.5
$2,000 to $2,499...................	5.2	6.3	-1.1	7.3	8.8	-1.5
$2,500 to $2,999...................	4.4	7.5	-3.1	5.6	9.3	-3.7
$3,000 to $3,499...................	5.7	7.5	-1.8	6.9	7.5	-0.6
$3,500 to $3,999...................	6.1	9.4	-3.3	5.9	7.8	-2.0
$4,000 to $4,499...................	7.3	8.1	-0.8	6.4	6.3	0.1
$4,500 to $4,999...................	6.8	7.2	-0.4	4.9	4.4	0.5
$5,000 to $5,999...................	14.5	10.6	3.9	8.3	4.8	3.5
$6,000 to $6,999...................	10.3	7.7	2.6	9.0	6.5	2.5
$7,000 to $9,999...................	16.3	9.9	6.4			
$10,000 to $14,999................	6.5					
$15,000 to $24,999................	1.4	5.8	2.6	2.4	0.7	1.7
$25,000 and over..................	0.5					

[1]The data for 1950 have been adjusted for change in price level; the income classes are expressed in 1957 dollars.

Source: Current Population Reports, Series P-60, Nos. 9, 28, and 30.

b. **Differences in the "market value" of various occupations.** Higher rates of pay are awarded to persons who perform certain essential activities that require highly specialized training and for which applicants are scarce. Lower rates of pay are the general rule in less specialized occupations that require less skill and experience, and for which manpower can easily be recruited.

c. **Custom, tradition, and the "power structure" of the society.** The nation's economy may be regarded as a giant factory turning out a measurable quantity of those goods and services that are required for the satisfaction of the needs and desires of the population. The manner in which the product of this "factory" is divided, and the proportionate share awarded to each group of workers, is determined largely by custom and tradition, and by comparative "bargaining power." For example, specific laws governing the transmission of property from generation to generation through the custom of inheritance help to determine the extent to which individuals who have very modest ability but wealthy parents are able to enjoy large incomes, and the extent to which other individuals who have a great deal of inate ability but who inherit only poverty are prevented from acquiring the technical training necessary to develop their talents. Corporations and labor unions that are highly organized, and that hold a very strong position within the economy, are able to capture a larger share of the wealth produced than can individual workers or small businesses, because the latter have less power to demand higher pay for their services. If it were necessary to select one element as the single factor underlying the recent and current changes in the pattern of income distribution, the interplay of the forces involved in this "power structure" would have to be considered as one of the leading contenders.

d. **Labor turnover and part-time, part-year employment.** Since some workers are continuously entering and leaving the labor force, they receive incomes for only a part of the particular calendar year concerning which statistics are collected. Many others work only a few hours per week, and receive small incomes for this reason. Women workers and young workers who are attending school account for much of the large concentration at the low income level. Periods of unemployment also reduce the earnings of some

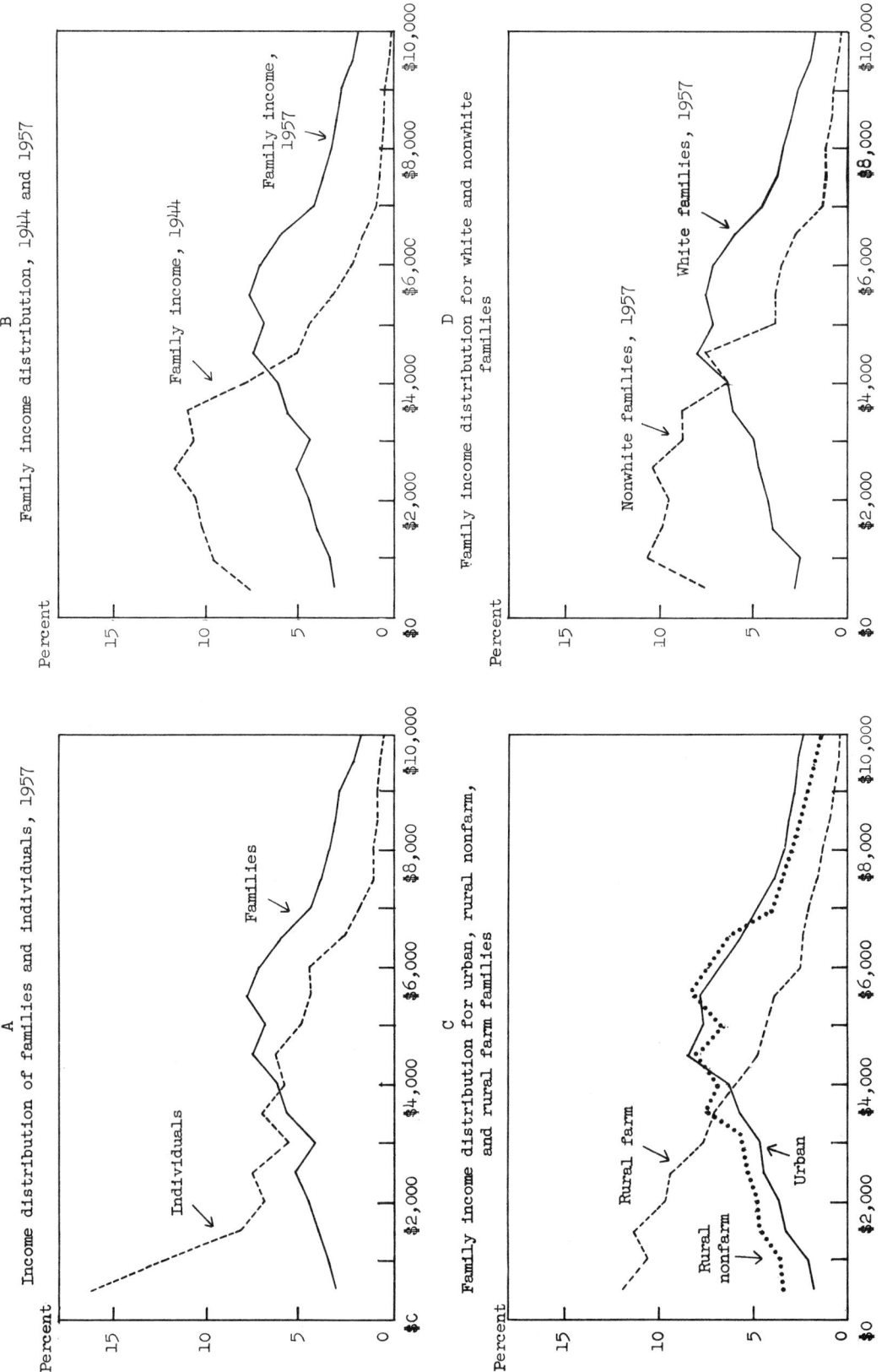

FIGURE 20-1. INCOME DISTRIBUTION OF SELECTED POPULATIONS, 1944 AND 1957

workers. Although these factors alone cannot account for the shape of the income curve, they certainly increase the number of persons earning small incomes.

Studying income distribution in terms of families rather than in terms of individuals produces a somewhat different picture. Figure 20-1 shows that family income distribution is not concentrated at the lowest income levels, but takes the shape of a long distribution with a small hump in the middle. This difference between individual and family income distributions makes it evident that a large percentage of the individuals who receive exceptionally small incomes are members of families, and are partially dependent upon others for their livelihood. Hence, if one wishes to gain a realistic picture of the livelihood level of the population, the income distributions for families and for unrelated individuals will yield more information than will the income distributions for all persons as individuals. It is for this reason that great emphasis is placed on family income in the present chapter.

RECENT CHANGES IN INCOME DISTRIBUTION

Since 1940 there has been an almost miraculous shift in the distribution of the income received by the nation's population. Before 1940, the concentration of population at the lowest levels of the income scale was much more pronounced than at present. (This generalization is based on a comparison of the curves illustrating wage or salary income in 1940 and in 1950; the data on which these curves are based are not shown here.) Using data prepared by the Bureau of Labor Statistics, in conjunction with a special tabulation of census materials, Miller estimates that in 1946 about 26 percent of "city worker" families had incomes below the median figure at which it was considered possible to maintain a minimum desirable level of living.[4] Since the level of living of

"city worker" families is higher than that of the rural population, it can only be concluded that at least this 26 percent of the nation's families were living in a state of poverty or semi-poverty in 1946; and it seems reasonable to conclude that, before this date, the proportion living at this level must have been even larger. The political slogan which, in the 1930's, called "one-third of a nation ill-fed, ill-clothed, and ill-housed" was apparently not inconsistent with the facts.

Since 1940 the concentration of population at the extreme bottom of the income scale has been decreasing, a change which has not only diminished substantially the proportion of the population living under conditions of destitution, but has also created and continued to augment a large "middle income" class. It is difficult to demonstrate statistically this process and the changes resulting from it, because statistics concerning income from all sources were not available until 1944, and by that time a substantial improvement in the population's living level had already taken place. The steady decrease in the purchasing power of the dollar, due to inflation, also makes the comparison of data for different years rather hazardous. Panel B of Figure 20-1 illustrates the nature of the change that has taken place in income level, although the actual change is exaggerated in this figure because the data are not corrected for the above-mentioned decrease in purchasing power. In Table 20-1, the income distribution statistics for 1950 have been adjusted to make them comparable with those of 1957, the 1957 dollar being used as the unit of measure. According to this table, the proportion of the population in the lower income brackets was reduced substantially between 1950 and 1957, with respect both to families and to individuals. Family income has made especially large gains. However, poverty and need have not yet been eradicated. In 1946, 25 percent of the nation's families had incomes amounting to less than the figure that was considered the minimum required for the maintenance of health, comfort, and decent living; if the same standards are used, it can be said that in 1957 about 15 to 20 percent of the nation's families (one in five or six) were still in this predicament.

---

[4]Miller, Herman P. Income of the American People, John Wiley and Sons, 1955, p. 95.

A somewhat more adequate proof that the shape of the income distribution curve has changed, and is still changing, is provided by Table 20-2, in which the median and quartile incomes, corrected for changing price levels, are reported for selected years, 1944 to 1956. These data indicate the changes between 1944 and 1956-1957 in the purchasing power of (a) the one-fourth of persons and families with smallest incomes, (b) the one-fourth of persons and families with largest incomes, and (c) the families at the median level. This table shows that the income level of the families in the lowest quartile rose at a considerably faster rate than the income level of those in the median or upper quartiles, which suggests a decrease in the concentration of families at the lower end of the income scale. Also, the fact that the upper quartile grew at a faster rate than the median suggests an increase in the concentration of persons in the middle-income group. The combined effect of these changes has been to reduce the proportion of "proletarian" families, and thereby to transfer the families no longer classifiable as "proletarian" into the "bourgeois," or middle-class, category. One of the most significant changes, both socially and economically, during the period 1940 to 1960 has been the rapid development of a very large, and definitely recognizable, American middle class; this class now outnumbers the low-income class, and its members are sufficiently educated and alert to vote for the kind of governmental policies that tend further to expand the middle-income class.

The following short summary indicates the estimated change which took place during the period 1935-36 to 1954 with respect to the income received by each of the quintiles of consumer units (not families), ranked in order of size (value of dollar held constant). It shows even more clearly the very rapid improvement in the economic level of the lowest 40 percent of the population, the rapid improvement in the middle-income groups, and the much-slower-than-average growth of the very wealthiest families and other consumer units:

Table 20-2.—MEDIAN AND QUARTILE INCOME OF PERSONS, FAMILIES, AND UNRELATED INDIVIDUALS, ADJUSTED FOR CHANGING PRICE LEVELS: SELECTED YEARS 1944 to 1957

(Purchasing power of the dollar in 1947 to 1949 = $1,000.)

Median and quartile and type of income	Change, 1944 to 1956	Year								Percent change, 1944 to 1956
		1957	1956	1955	1954	1952	1950	1947	1944	
LOWER QUARTILE INCOME										
Persons - male............	126	1,343	1,415	1,296	1,262	1,404	1,235	1,229	1,289	9.8
Persons - female..........	-153	387	392	388	409	392	379	435	545	-28.1
Families.................	683	2,533	2,530	2,334	2,155	1,783	1,960	1,957	1,847	37.1
Unrelated individuals.......	52	...	577	537	492	537	433	424	525	9.9
MEDIAN INCOME										
Persons - male............	385	3,065	3,106	2,928	2,786	2,736	2,501	2,335	2,721	14.1
Persons - female..........	-222	998	987	974	1,011	1,011	927	1,065	1,209	-18.4
Families.................	753	4,136	4,122	3,860	3,629	3,426	3,229	3,176	3,369	22.4
Unrelated individuals.......	-55	...	1,247	1,144	1,067	1,173	965	1,029	1,302	-4.2
UPPER QUARTILE INCOME										
Persons - male............	514	4,509	4,537	4,282	4,055	3,797	3,615	3,418	4,023	12.8
Persons - female..........	60	2,126	2,135	2,082	2,016	2,017	1,931	1,895	2,075	2.9
Families.................	1,302	5,799	6,303	5,797	5,296	4,978	4,709	4,643	5,001	26.0
Unrelated individuals.......	297	...	2,704	2,501	2,395	2,388	2,218	2,115	2,407	12.3

Source: Computed from: Current Population Reports, P-60, Nos. 27, 28, and 30, 1958. Correction for change in price level made by multiplying values for each year by the "Purchasing Power of the Dollar - Consumer Prices" index reported in Statistical Abstract of the United States, 1958, Table 418.

All consumer units ranked by size of income	Percent change in average income (1950 dollars)		
	1935-36 to 1954	1935-36 to 1944	1941 to 1954
Total.............	64	25	32
Lowest fifth........	95	23	59
Second fifth........	105	28	59
Third fifth.........	94	36	43
Fourth fifth........	75	33	32
Highest fifth.......	42	18	20
Top 5 percent.......	27	13	12

Source: Statistical Abstract of the United State States, 1958, Table 379.

The recent trends in income distribution can be summarized by a statement of the two major changes that have been, and still are, taking place: (a) the general level of income is rising, and (b) the income distribution curve for families is gradually becoming less skewed toward the lower incomes, and is following the same pattern for individual workers who are employed full time. The apparent increase between 1950 and 1957 in the proportion of workers with very low incomes is due to the increase in the proportion of part-time workers.

DIFFERENTIALS IN INCOME DISTRIBUTION

Sex Differences in Income Distribution. A much smaller proportion of women than of men receive incomes; this difference, of course, is due primarily to the lower rates of labor force participation among women. For example, the percentage of the total population 14 years of age or over who received some income during the calendar year of 1957 was as follows:

	Both sexes	Males	Females
Total....................	70.7	91.5	52.4
Urban and rural nonfarm....	71.5	92.0	53.9
Rural farm..............	65.0	88.1	40.8

Of those persons receiving income, women received much smaller incomes than men. Table 20-3 shows the income distribution in 1956 with respect to both men and women, by urban and rural residence; it demonstrates that most of the male income recipients are rather evenly distributed over a range that includes incomes from $500 to $6,000, with a smaller proportion having incomes larger than $6,000, whereas the women recipients are highly concentrated at the lower end of the scale. Less than one-half of the women recipients received as much as $1,200 per year, and only 7 percent received more than $4,000. This sex differential is present in urban, rural-nonfarm, and rural-farm areas. It is produced by a variety of conditions, among which are the lower rates of pay which women commonly receive (often for the kind of work performed by men at higher rates), more part-time work, more part-year employment, and the large numbers of widows who receive small pensions.

Limiting the comparison to year-round, full-time workers gives an approximate picture of the over-all sex differential in wage rates and income payments, some of the other factors being held constant:

	Both sexes	Male	Female	Percent female is of male
Total..........	$4,041	4,462	2,828	63
Urban..........	$4,239	4,807	2,935	61
Rural nonfarm..	$4,168	4,489	2,637	59
Rural farm.....	$2,052	2,041	2,092	102

As this comparison shows, the average woman worker who is employed full time earns slightly less than 2/3 as much money as the average male worker. This is due in part to differences in the composition of the labor force among various occupations and industries (women are often assigned to less responsible posts where rates of pay are smaller, and many of them work in industries in which pay levels are lower).

Income Distribution and Urban and Rural Residence. The largest money incomes are found in urban areas, and the smallest in rural-farm areas. Inasmuch as a large share of the rural-farm population receives a certain amount of economic goods and services, in the form of housing and food, for which it does not pay money, the statistics concerning money income tend to understate the total rural-farm income. Even when a generous allowance is made for the value of housing and food, however, it is still obvious that the income of farm families is very low in compar-

Table 20-3.—INCOME DISTRIBUTION OF INDIVIDUALS BY SEX AND URBAN-RURAL RESIDENCE: 1956

Income	Total, both sexes	Male				Female			
		Total	Urban	Rural nonfarm	Rural farm	Total	Urban	Rural nonfarm	Rural farm
Total...............	100.0	100.0	100.0	100.0	100.0	100.0	100.0	100.0	100.0
Less than $500...........	16.3	9.1	6.0	9.2	24.1	27.6	21.7	35.1	53.5
$500 to $999.............	12.5	8.1	6.6	8.2	15.4	19.3	19.3	20.1	17.7
$1,000 to $1,499........	8.0	6.2	5.4	5.6	11.4	10.6	11.2	10.0	8.1
$1,500 to $1,999........	6.8	5.5	4.7	5.5	9.7	8.7	9.4	7.8	5.8
$2,000 to $2,499........	7.4	6.4	5.9	6.7	8.1	9.0	10.0	7.6	5.2
$2,500 to $2,999........	6.1	5.7	5.6	5.6	7.0	6.7	7.4	5.4	4.6
$3,000 to $3,499........	7.0	7.4	7.7	7.8	5.2	6.5	7.7	4.5	2.0
$3,500 to $3,999........	6.3	7.4	7.9	7.6	4.6	4.5	5.2	3.4	1.1
$4,000 to $4,499........	6.8	9.2	10.5	9.3	3.1	3.0	3.5	2.2	1.4
$4,500 to $4,999........	4.6	6.7	7.7	6.2	3.0	1.3	1.6	1.1	0.3
$5,000 to $5,999........	7.8	11.9	13.3	12.8	3.2	1.5	1.8	1.4	0.1
$6,000 to $6,999........	4.0	6.2	7.2	5.9	2.0	0.5	0.6	0.6	0.1
$7,000 to $9,999........	4.1	6.5	7.4	6.3	2.0	0.4	0.5	0.5	...
$10,000 and over........	2.3	3.6	3.1	3.3	1.3	0.2	0.2	0.5	...
Median income...........	$2,432	$3,608	$4,010	$3,592	$1,461	$1,146	$1,402	$871	$468

Source: Current Population Reports, Series P-60, No. 27, 1958, Table 16.

ison with that of urban and rural-nonfarm families. For example, the median income of families in 1956, by color and by urban and rural residence, was as follows:

	All families
Total...............	$4,783
Urban...............	5,221
Rural nonfarm.......	4,619
Rural farm..........	2,371

The average rural-farm family receives only one-half as much money as the average United States family. It is doubtful whether the value of the food and rent that is produced or furnished on the farm accounts for more than a small fraction of this differential. Therefore, one seems forced to conclude that a disproportionately large number of the nation's "pockets of poverty" are found in rural-farm areas. Panel C of Figure 20-1 illustrates the differences in income distribution between urban, rural-nonfarm, and rural-farm populations.

Income and Age. Young and inexperienced workers are paid at lower rates and, consequently, their annual earnings are low. At these ages there is much irregularity of employment, and a high proportion of younger workers are employed only part time. Periods of unemployment are more frequent and of longer duration, because young

workers are more inclined than older workers to leave jobs they dislike in order to seek more enjoyable or more remunerative work, and also because they are the first to be laid off during slack seasons. With increasing age, the average level of earnings rises until it reaches a peak between the ages of 35 and 45 years, after which it declines. The decline in income after age 40 is due to the increasing prevalence of illness and disability, to reductions in pay because of loss of speed, stamina, and strength, and to the use of younger workers in new kinds of work which usually offer higher pay. Thus, the age distribution of the nation's income has the shape of an inverted "U." Figure 20-2 illustrates how median income varies with age. Each age group, of course, has its own income distribution; Figure 20-2 merely illustrates where the mid-points of these distributions lie.

Income and Economic Welfare. All too often, in reading a discussion of income distribution, the reader notes what proportion of families fall in each income interval without stopping to consider what significance these income figures have in terms of the level of comfort and decency at which they permit families to live. Income statistics should be able to tell us how large a part of the

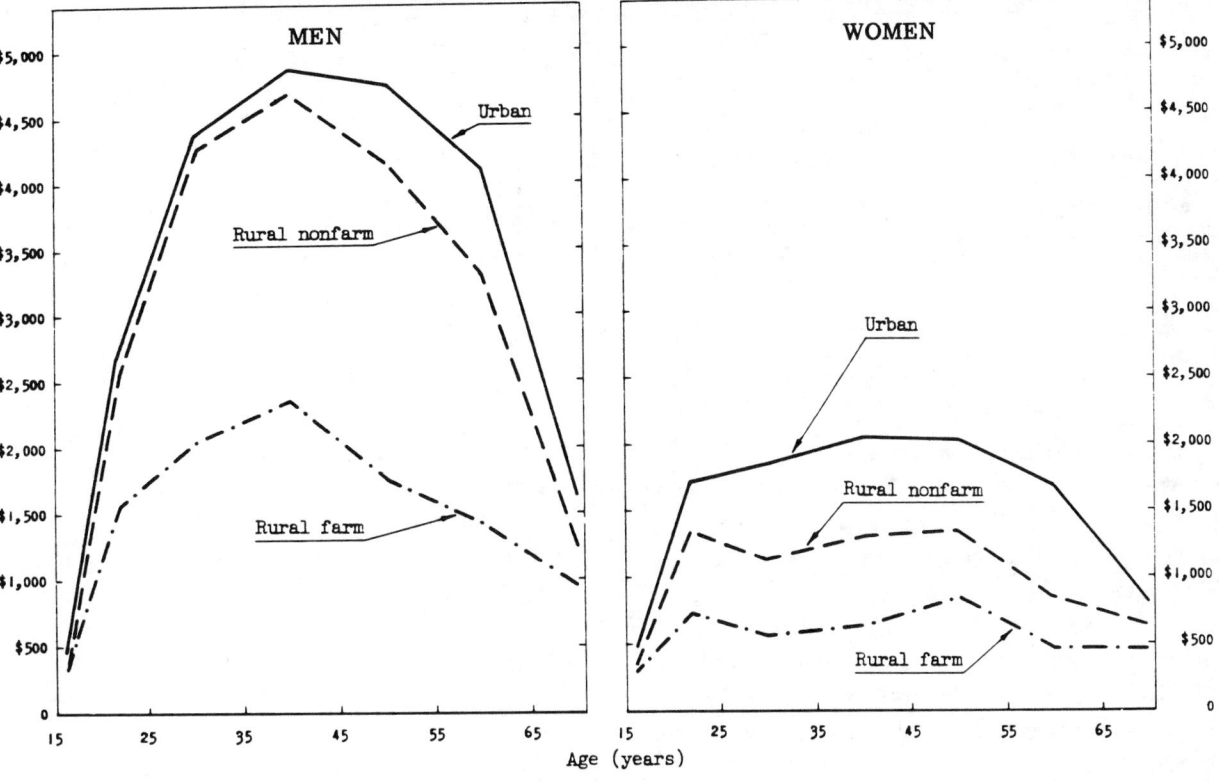

FIGURE 20-2. MEDIAN INCOME OF MEN AND WOMEN, BY AGE AND RESIDENCE: 1956

Source: Current Population Reports, Series P-60, No. 27, 1958.

population is not receiving enough income to support itself at a level considered adequate for the maintenance of health and welfare. As an attempt to approximate the socio-economic significance of income, in Table 20-4 the incomes of families have been divided into 6 major "livelihood status" categories; the families are classified by age of head and by livelihood status. The income intervals assigned to each of the six livelihood status classes were selected on a "common sense" basis, guided somewhat by data from certain level-of-living studies made by the Department of Labor.[5]

[5] Although many income experts would undoubtedly object strongly to such a subjective procedure, this approach does succeed in adding meaning to income statistics, and the results probably are quite valid, in terms of the livelihood interpretation placed upon income by the populace at large.

According to Table 20-4, about one family in 16 is living in a state of destitution--that is, two or more members of the family are receiving incomes which, combined, total less than $1,000 per year. In addition, about one family in 7 receives only a meager livelihood. Thus, about 1/5 of the nation's families have less than the minimum desirable livelihood. Almost one-half of the families whose head is elderly (65 years of age or over) have an inadequate livelihood, in terms of the standards established in Table 20-4. Although these elderly ages are the ages at which families are small, they also are the ages at which expenses for health care are large. A high proportion of these families of elderly persons must subsist on small pensions and on the income from property or savings. Since their income in terms of dollars is rather inflexibly fixed, they have

Table 20-4.—LIVELIHOOD STATUS OF FAMILIES BY AGE OF HEAD: 1956

Livelihood status of families	Range of money income	Age of head (years)						
		All ages	14 to 24	25 to 34	35 to 44	45 to 54	55 to 64	65-over
All families.............	....	100.0	100.0	100.0	100.0	100.0	100.0	100.0
Destitute..................	Less than $1,000..	6.5	6.4	4.4	4.1	5.7	7.7	15..
Meager livelihood...........	$1,000 to $2,499..	14.0	17.7	9.2	8.2	11.7	15.4	34.2
Minimum adequate livelihood.	$2,500 to $3,999..	17.6	30.0	18.7	15.5	14.1	18.6	18.6
Comfortable livelihood......	$4,000 to $5,999..	28.6	30.0	36.1	32.5	26.1	24.8	15.6
Abundant..................	$6,000 to $9,999..	25.4	14.8	27.5	30.3	29.9	23.4	11.6
Affluent and rich...........	$10,000 or more...	7.9	1.0	4.0	9.1	12.5	10.2	4.9
Median income..............	....	$4,783	$3,789	$4,930	$5,360	$5,411	$4,568	$2,550

Source: Current Population Reports, Series P-60, No. 27, 1958.

been the groups most severely penalized by the "creeping inflation" of recent years.

The proportion earning only a meager livelihood also tends to be above-average among those families in which the head is very young, a situation that reflects the fact that the chief earner has not yet reached peak earning power. It should be noted, however, that the proportion of destitute families is not much greater among the families with young heads than among families where the head is more mature.

About one-third of the families receive an "abundant" income or are sufficiently "affluent" to permit it to enjoy some luxuries and to have few if any financial worries.[6] These families are concentrated between the ages of 25 and 64; families where the heads are very young or of retirement age are conspicuously scarce in the "abundance" stratum.

Thus, not only has poverty not yet been eradicated from the population, but its burdens fall most heavily upon young families at the ages where childbearing is at its peak and upon older families where the head can no longer obtain employment. But poverty is not completely absent from any age group; even at the peak earning ages

---

[6] Many readers undoubtedly would not define an income of $6,000 for a family of 4 persons as an "abundant" living, but in an effort to avoid presenting an unduly pessimistic picture of life at the lower end of the income scale, for the price levels of 1956 this seemed to be the most appropriate cutting point between "comfort" and "abundance".

of 35 to 44 years, in 1956 one family in 8 appeared to be either destitute or received only a meager livelihood.

Color and Income. In 1956 the average nonwhite family received only slightly more than one-half as much income as the average white family, and achieved even this low income because both the nonwhite husband and wife (or other family members) were employed in a high proportion of cases. The following figures describe the differential which existed between median incomes of white and nonwhite families in 1956.

	White	Nonwhite	Ratio nonwhite to white
Total............	$4,993	$2,628	.53
Urban............	5,413	3,250	.60
Rural nonfarm....	4,871	2,268	.47
Rural farm.......	2,648	1,104	.42

The differential is considerably smaller in urban than in rural areas, although it is extraordinarily large in both places. In order to explain the existence of such a tremendous difference between the incomes of two groups of citizens, it would be necessary to discuss not only economic discrimination, but also the average differences between the races with respect to education, skill, aptitude, and performance on the job. Although these factors are not necessarily biologically determined, and are probably subject to rather swift change from one generation to the next, all of them appear to be partly responsible for the existence of this differential.

The significance of the color differential is more clearly illustrated by Table 20-5, in which the proportion of families falling in each of the

Table 20-5.—LIVELIHOOD STATUS OF FAMILIES, BY COLOR AND REGION: 1956

Livelihood status of families[1]	United States			Region						
	Total	White	Nonwhite	North-east	North Central	South			West
						Total	White	Nonwhite	
All families........	100.0	100.0	100.0	100.0	100.0	100.0	100.0	100.0	100.0
Destitute..............	6.5	5.4	18.2	3.0	4.8	12.1	9.2	25.8	4.6
Meager.................	14.0	12.5	29.6	10.2	12.0	20.7	17.2	36.5	11.2
Minimum adequate........	17.6	17.0	23.5	16.3	16.7	20.4	20.1	21.5	15.5
Comfortable.............	28.6	29.6	18.9	31.9	29.3	24.7	27.4	12.2	29.2
Abundant................	25.4	27.0	8.8	29.1	28.1	17.7	20.7	3.9	29.5
Affluent or rich........	7.9	8.6	1.0	9.6	9.1	4.4	5.4	0.2	10.0
Median income...........	$4,783	$4,993	$2,628	$5,296	$5,111	$3,742	$4,219	$1,975	$5,222

[1]For income intervals to which each status refers, see Table 20-4.
Source: Current Population Reports, Series P-60, No. 27, 1958, Table 12.

livelihood status categories is reported. Panel D of Figure 20-1 also illustrates the large difference in income distribution between the white and nonwhite populations. Whereas only 5.4 percent of the white families fall in the "destitute" group, 18.2 percent of the nonwhite families are so classified. (In the South, 26 percent of the nonwhite families are in this class.) Moreover, the proportion of families classed as earning only a meager livelihood is more than twice as great among the nonwhite as among the white population. At the upper end of the scale, 65 percent of the white population enjoys a comfortable, an abundant, or an affluent livelihood, while only 29 percent of the nonwhite population is so fortunate.

These statistics for families are matched by data concerning individual income. Table 20-6, which gives data from the 1950 census in regard to median income for the white and nonwhite population by age, sex, and urban-rural residence, shows just how universal and how large is this differential between the white and nonwhite populations. The median individual incomes of elderly nonwhite persons are almost unbelievably low and, even at the ages of peak earning power, nonwhite persons receive incomes that are only about one-half (or less) as large as those received by white earners of the same age, sex, and residence.

Is this large differential in income between the white and nonwhite races diminishing? The available evidence suggests that, as far as wage or salary income is concerned, the differential has remained almost constant since 1951, and has diminished slightly since 1939. If, during the recent period of rising income, the incomes of white and nonwhite families had increased by the same amounts, the effect would have been to diminish the differential substantially. However, this kind of increase did not take place. Between 1939 and 1956 the median income from wages or salaries increased by $3,350 among white families, but it increased by only $1,940 among nonwhite families:

Year	Median income of primary families and individuals		
	White	Nonwhite	Ratio of nonwhite to white
1956..........	$4,685	$2,429	.52
1951..........	3,673	1,943	.53
1939..........	1,325	489	.37

Taking into account the fact that the proportion of total income derived from sources other than wages or salaries has increased since 1939, and that this increase has been concentrated largely among the white population, might lead one to conclude that the income differential has remained almost constant over the past twenty years. However, one very impressive fact should not be overlooked--that during the recent period of prosperity the income of the nonwhite population increased by about the same percentage as that of the white population. This increase has brought a remarkable improvement in the well-being of the nonwhite population, the long-run effects of which

Table 20-6.—MEDIAN INCOME IN 1949 OF PERSONS, BY AGE, COLOR, AND SEX, FOR THE UNITED STATES, FARM AND NONFARM: 1950

Age and residence	Both sexes			Males			Females		
	Total	White	Nonwhite	Total	White	Nonwhite	Total	White	Nonwhite
United States..........	1,917	2,053	961	2,434	2,572	1,341	1,029	1,137	584
14 to 19 years........	429	440	354	435	442	389	419	437	313
20 to 24 years........	1,503	1,585	873	1,669	1,750	1,130	1,276	1,386	551
25 to 34 years........	2,288	2,419	1,238	2,737	2,878	1,627	1,309	1,448	750
35 to 44 years........	2,489	2,681	1,259	3,073	3,208	1,697	1,358	1,504	742
45 to 54 years........	2,398	2,565	1,146	2,979	3,123	1,601	1,316	1,456	641
55 to 64 years........	2,062	21,70	914	2,551	2,670	1,260	1,006	1,092	497
65 years and over......	847	883	473	1,128	1,212	593	602	630	390
Urban and rural nonfarm..	2,043	2,157	1,121	2,613	2,741	1,571	1,104	1,200	672
14 to 19 years........	452	460	386	462	464	435	441	454	335
20 to 24 years........	1,569	1,638	976	1,772	1,842	1,280	1,323	1,422	514
25 to 34 years........	2,370	2,495	1,354	2,850	2,962	1,790	1,366	1,497	817
35 to 44 years........	2,619	2,803	1,400	3,207	3,332	1,882	1,426	1,568	810
45 to 54 years........	2,531	2,704	1,314	3,140	3,269	1,821	1,391	1,525	712
55 to 64 years........	2,210	2,307	1,065	2,766	2,871	1,529	1,077	1,154	572
65 years and over......	877	907	530	1,246	1,314	692	631	654	415
Rural farm.............	1,099	1,273	443	1,339	1,489	577	458	533	311
14 to 19 years........	344	357	298	356	365	319	320	338	268
20 to 24 years........	987	1,137	441	1,090	1,212	582	657	889	308
25 to 34 years........	1,486	1,681	565	1,719	1,880	788	525	742	324
35 to 44 years........	1,567	1,784	563	1,850	2,034	758	547	732	329
45 to 54 years........	1,425	1,625	501	1,697	1,884	680	542	693	327
55 to 64 years........	1,166	1,289	470	1,354	1,463	585	481	549	321
65 years and over......	644	717	367	789	860	406	399	421	308

upon the nonwhite population--in terms of escape from slum housing, improved health, increased school attendance, and great emphasis on education--may well be far greater than the effects of the additional comfort and luxury which have been achieved, during the same period of prosperity, among the white population.

Regional Differences in Income Distribution. The Northeastern Region had the highest average level of income in the nation in 1956. According to Table 20-5, the proportion of "destitute" families in this region in 1956 was only about one-half the proportion in the nation, and a higher percentage of the population was living in comfort, abundance, or affluence here than in any other region. However, its position was very nearly equalled by the West and the North Center regions. The South, by contrast, had a much lower average income level; 1/6 of its families were "destitute" and an additional 1/5 were earning only a meager liveli-

hood. This situation is accounted for, in part, by the fact that the South has a large concentration of both nonwhite and rural populations. However, the statistics in Table 20-7 indicate the existence of a regional effect that is independent of race or rural-urban residence. This table compares the median incomes of the white families in the South's urban, rural-nonfarm, and rural-farm areas with the median incomes of all the families in the urban, rural-nonfarm, and rural-farm areas of the other regions, and shows that in terms of each of these residence categories the median incomes of the South's white families were much smaller.

The lower section of Table 20-7, which provides data concerning individuals, shows that there is a male-female and a white-nonwhite differential--and a substantial one--in every region. The smallest sex differential and the largest color differential appear to exist in the South, as the fol-

Table 20-7.—MEDIAN INCOME OF FAMILIES BY URBAN-RURAL RESIDENCE AND OF INDIVIDUALS BY SEX, FOR REGIONS: 1956

Color, sex, and urban-rural residence	United States	Regions						
		North-east	North Central	South			West
				Total	White	Nonwhite	
FAMILIES							
All families............................	4,783	5,296	5,111	3,742	4,219	1,975	5,222
Urban families.......................	5,221	5,373	5,570	4,328	4,740	2,473	5,500
Rural nonfarm families................	4,619	5,341	4,931	4,027	4,449	2,143	4,824
Rural farm families...................	2,371	3,369	2,911	1,725	2,074	1,075	3,979
INDIVIDUALS							
(Year round full-time workers)							
Males, total...........................	4,462	4,646	4,691	3,710	...	...	5,209
White..................................	4,677	4,742	4,761	4,067	...	...	5,289
Nonwhite...............................	2,763	3,398	3,698	2,048	...	...	([1])
Females, total.........................	2,828	2,851	2,969	2,493	...	...	3,299
White..................................	2,942	2,914	3,006	2,735	...	...	3,337
Nonwhite...............................	1,631	([1])	([1])	980	...	...	([1])

([1]) Median not reported because of small sample for this category.
Source: Current Population Reports, Series P-60, No. 27, 1958, Tables 12 and 25.

lowing ratios demonstrate:

Region	Ratios of median incomes:	
	Female to male	Nonwhite to white (males)
U.S. total.........	.63	.59
Northeast...........	.61	.73
North Central.......	.63	.78
South..............	.67	.50
West...............	.63	.76[1]

[1]Based upon all recipients rather than on year-round full-time workers.

Size of Urban Place and Income Distribution. Among urban areas, there is a persistent tendency for incomes to be bigger in larger communities than in smaller communities. For example, Table 20-8, which reports the median incomes of families and individuals (year-round full-time workers), shows that in urbanized areas of 1 million or more persons the median income of families was larger by $1,239 (24 percent) than it was in the urban places with less than 25,000 inhabitants. Income differential does not vary continuously with size; among cities whose populations range from 25,000 to 999,999, size appears to have only a negligible effect on income level. It is possible that one of the major reasons for the lower median incomes in medium-size and small cities is the

Table 20-8.—MEDIAN INCOME OF FAMILIES AND INDIVIDUALS, LIVING IN URBAN PLACES, CLASSIFIED ACCORDING TO SIZE OF PLACE: 1956

Urban places, by size of place	Median income			Ratio to total			Ratio, female to male
	Families	Individuals		Families	Individuals		
		Male	Female		Male	Female	
United States urban total..............	$5,953	$4,807	$2,935	1.00	1.00	1.00	.61
Urbanized areas, 1,000,000 and over..........	$6,480	$5,057	$3,134	1.09	1.05	1.07	.62
Urbanized areas, 250,000 to 999,999..........	$5,836	$4,647	$2,969	.98	.97	1.01	.64
Urbanized areas, under 250,000...............	$6,012	$4,852	$2,866	1.01	1.01	.98	.59
Other urban areas, 25,000 and over...........	$5,819	$4,775	$2,757	.98	.99	.94	.58
Other urban areas, under 25,000..............	$5,241	$4,384	$2,531	.88	.91	.86	.58

Note: The above statistics are based upon families where the head was a full-time year round worker and upon individuals who were year round full-time workers.
Source: Current Population Reports, Series P-60, No. 27, 1958, Tables 1 and 16.

comparative scarcity of manufacturing and whole-sale activities in such places. As yet, no fully adequate, tested theory has been advanced to explain why incomes should be above average in the largest places. Some theories have explained the differential as a form of bonus which repays the workers in the largest metropolises for the extra time and money they spend in commuting to their work. It is very possible that if some of the additional costs connected with working in the largest places were taken into account, the income differentials according to size of urban place would be almost negligible among places above 25,000, and that the differentials between the latter places and the communities whose populations are below 25,000 would be seen to result from a lack of industrial base in places with less than 25,000 inhabitants.

The size-of-city differential appears to be somewhat larger and more regular for females than for males. Also, the largest places (those with a quarter-million or more inhabitants) seem to be somewhat less discriminatory with respect to pay received by the female labor force, the sex differential in income being somewhat lower in these places than in the smaller cities.

Educational Attainment and Income. Rich rewards are paid by the American economy to those who attain an advanced education. For example, in 1956 the median income of males who completed 4 years or more of college was $6,980, which was 2.2 times the median income of those who had completed less than 8 grades and 43 percent greater than the median income of those who had graduated from high school. A senior in high school, debating whether it would be worth his while to go to college, could note from Table 20-9 that the median income of college graduates is $2,093 per year greater than that of high school graduates. Thus, he could reasonably expect to receive a lifelong bonus of about $500 per year for each year he spent in college, or of almost $2.00 per college year for each working day of his life. The rewards that can be expected for completing grammar school and high school can also be calculated in terms of money.

At the other extreme, persons who do not graduate from elementary school receive very low incomes. Each increase in educational attainment is accompanied by a substantial increase in average income level, for both males and females and in urban, rural-nonfarm, and rural-farm areas. Although many highly educated people receive small incomes, and many people with little education receive high incomes, they only provide exceptions to what is a very marked and a very consistent relationship.

Perhaps the economic significance of education can be demonstrated more clearly by reporting the livelihood status of families according to the educational attainment of the head, as is done in Table 20-10. This table indicates that 15 percent of the families whose head has completed less than 8 years of schooling are "destitute," and that an additional 27 percent of the families in this educational category have only a meager livelihood. As the educational level rises, the picture brightens; among families whose head has had 5 years or more of college, only about 3 percent fall in either one of these two lowest income categories. More than two-thirds of the families whose head is in this most-highly-educated category live in abundance or affluence, but only about 16 percent of families whose head is classified as least-educated reach these economic levels (only 3 percent reach the "affluent" level). Among families of which the head is a high school graduate, a very large proportion are concentrated in the "comfortable" and "abundant" groups, and comparatively few are in either the extremely poor or the most wealthy groups. In general, it seems that graduation from high school tends to assure a comfortable living, and that graduation from college tends to assure an abundant living. Most persons who do not complete elementary school face careers in which their income will never allow them to live above the level of poverty or near-poverty.

Occupation and Income Distribution. Occupations differ markedly as to the level of income which they provide (see Table 20-11). The professional and managerial categories provide a very high percentage of their occupants with a

Table 20-9.—MEDIAN TOTAL MONEY INCOME IN 1956 OF PERSONS 14 YEARS OF AGE AND OVER, BY YEARS OF SCHOOL COMPLETED AND SEX FOR THE UNITED STATES, URBAN, AND RURAL

Educational attainment	Males				Females			
	Total [2]	Urban	Rural nonfarm	Rural farm	Total [2]	Urban	Rural nonfarm	Rural farm
Total...................	4,462	4,010	3,592	1,461	2,828	1,402	871	468
Elementary school, all grades.	3,579	3,121	2,453	1,198	2,152	941	694	603
Less than 8 years..........	3,120	2,654	1,996	944	1,811	830	631	571
8 years....................	4,035	3,631	3,240	1,734	2,408	1,178	809	667
High school, all grades.......	4,720	4,263	4,076	2,025	2,895	1,673	1,040	774
1 to 3 years..............	4,514	3,858	3,568	1,653	2,583	1,111	817	646
4 years...................	4,887	4,563	4,475	2,441	3,021	2,093	1,495	972
College, total...............	6,060	5,301	5,333	2,742	3,610	2,298	2,365	1,567
1 to 3 years..............	5,457	4,526	4,706	2,240	3,440	1,775	1,901	[1]
4 years or more...........	6,980	6,176	5,906	[1]	3,809	3,090	3,121	[1]

[1] Not reported due to insufficient number of cases in sample.
[2] The totals for males and females are based upon year round full-time workers, while the data for urban and rural areas, by sex, are based upon all income recipients.

Source: Current Population Reports, Series P-60, No. 27, 1958, Table 20.

comfortable, abundant, or affluent livelihood, while a very high percentage of the nation's destitution and meager livelihood is found among families whose heads are farm laborers or workers in private households. The families of nonfarm unskilled workers and service workers also tend to have a meager livelihood, or a minimum adequate livelihood, in a high proportion of cases. The clerical, sales, craft, and operative occupations tend to provide a comfortable or abundant livelihood, assuring a comparative lack of economic hardship but also little luxury.

Among the professional occupations, self-employment offers the greatest opportunity for achieving an unusually high level of wealth (52 percent of self-employed persons are in the "affluent" category), but it also entails a greater risk of low income (8 percent of self-employed persons are in the two lowest income categories). Very few salaried professionals, on the other hand, have extremely low incomes, but in comparison with self-employed professionals, few of them are extremely wealthy--most of them are highly concentrated in the "abundant" rather than in the "af-

Table 20-10.—LIVELIHOOD STATUS OF FAMILIES, CLASSIFIED BY EDUCATIONAL ATTAINMENT OF THE HEAD

Educational attainment of family head	Total	Livelihood status					
		Destitute	Meager	Minimum adequate	Comfortable	Abundant	Affluent or rich
All families.................	100.0	6.5	14.0	17.6	28.6	25.4	7.9
Elementary school, all grades......	100.0	11.3	22.9	21.5	23.6	16.8	4.0
Less than 8 years..............	100.0	14.6	27.1	21.6	20.4	13.2	2.9
8 years.....................	100.0	6.9	17.6	21.5	27.3	21.2	5.4
High school, all grades...........	100.0	4.0	8.9	16.7	34.6	29.2	6.6
1 to 3 years..................	100.0	4.7	11.1	19.3	34.7	24.9	5.2
4 years......................	100.0	3.3	7.1	14.7	34.3	32.6	7.8
College, total...................	100.0	1.5	4.9	9.4	25.2	37.3	21.4
1 to 3 years..................	100.0	2.0	7.0	11.5	30.3	34.9	14.3
4 years......................	100.0	1.4	3.4	8.0	21.6	41.3	24.3
5 years or more...............	100.0	0.6	2.6	7.5	19.7	36.0	33.7

Source: Current Population Reports, Series P-60, No. 27, 1958, Table 8.

Table 20-11.—LIVELIHOOD STATUS OF FAMILIES, CLASSIFIED BY OCCUPATION OF FAMILY HEAD: 1956

Occupation of family head	Total	Livelihood status					
		Desti-tute	Meager	Minimum adequate	Comfort-able	Abundant	Affluent or rich
Total employed civilians................	100.0	4.2	9.9	16.9	31.3	28.6	9.0
Professional, technical, and kindred workers.	100.0	1.0	2.3	7.8	25.2	42.1	21.6
Self employed...........................	100.0	2.8	5.2	6.8	11.6	21.9	51.9
Salaried................................	100.0	0.7	2.0	8.0	27.0	44.5	17.8
Farmers and farm managers..................	100.0	25.0	32.0	20.7	12.2	7.2	3.0
Managers, officials, and prop'rs, exc. farm..	100.0	3.3	6.2	11.2	23.6	33.4	22.2
Self employed...........................	100.0	5.8	10.1	14.7	23.4	26.5	19.5
Salaried................................	100.0	0.9	2.4	7.7	23.7	40.1	25.1
Clerical and kindred workers................	100.0	1.3	4.3	16.5	39.5	32.7	5.7
Sales workers..............................	100.0	1.4	4.5	15.1	29.5	36.6	12.7
Craftsmen, foremen, and kindred workers......	100.0	0.9	4.9	12.7	38.0	36.6	6.9
Operatives and kindred workers..............	100.0	1.3	8.3	22.0	37.9	26.1	4.4
Private household workers....................	100.0	32.4	35.8	16.1	13.5	2.1	...
Service workers, except private household....	100.0	3.5	14.4	24.1	36.6	18.2	3.2
Farm laborers and foremen...................	100.0	22.8	35.5	22.9	13.7	4.9	0.3
Laborers, except farm and mine..............	100.0	5.0	19.3	28.0	29.8	15.8	2.0
Heads unemployed in March 1957.............	100.0	8.8	24.8	29.4	20.2	15.4	1.3
In Armed Forces or not in labor force in March 1957................................	100.0	18.6	34.2	19.2	15.2	9.7	3.2

Source: Current Population Reports, Series P-60, No. 27, 1958, Table 9.

fluent" class. Among managers and officials, self-employment is neither as secure nor as rewarding, on the average, as a salaried position: a larger share of self-employed managers and officials are in the very lowest income brackets, and a smaller share are in the highest income brackets, than is the case among salaried managers and officials.

Despite their lower average level of educational attainment, family heads who are in the operative or craftsmen categories tend to earn at about the same average level as heads who are sales workers or clerical workers. Thus, although education has a very strong influence on the level of income received, occupation also has a significantly large, and perhaps more direct, independent effect.

Table 20-11 provides information only for broad occupational groupings. A great deal of interest has been expressed in the incomes received by persons who are employed in each of the more specifically detailed occupation classes. Statistics which make possible this kind of detailed study are provided in the appendix to Chapter 17, "Occupational Composition," where the estimated

livelihood status, as of 1950, is reported for each detailed occupation.[7]

From the income information of the 1950 census it is possible to compile a list of "destitution occupations," or occupations within which a high proportion of persons receive far less money than is necessary to support a family. The following is such a list; in these occupations, the percentage of workers receiving less than $1,000 in 1949 was 50 percent higher than the average for all occupations.

----

[7] The "livelihood status" categories used in the appendix to Chapter 17 have different income limits from those of this chapter. This arises from an effort to approximate the price level of 1950 (the categories of the present chapter refer to 1956-57) and also to indicate roughly the livelihood implications supporting a family, using income data collected for individuals. The categories and intervals used in this chapter are regarded as being more adequate than those used in Chapter 17, and for this reason in Chapter 17 the actual income intervals are reported together with the rough livelihood categories.

List 20-A. DESTITUTION OCCUPATIONS: Occupations for which the proportion of persons in the experienced civilian labor force with income of less than $1,000 is more than 50 percent above the average for all occupations

Occupation	Percent
MALE, EXPERIENCED CIVILIAN LABOR FORCE	
Farmers and farm managers	35.9
Sales workers:	
Other specified sales workers	57.6
Operatives and kindred workers:	
Attendants, auto service and parking	23.6
Sawyers	27.1
Operatives and kindred wkrs. (n.e.c.)	
Sawmills, planing mills, and misc. wood products	25.9
Private household workers	43.6
Service wkrs., except priv. hshld:	
Other service wkrs., exc. priv. hshld	34.6
Farm laborers and foremen:	58.0
Farm laborers, unpaid family wkrs.	79.2
Farm laborers, except unpaid, and farm foremen	53.3
Laborers, except farm and mine:	
Fishermen and oystermen	31.6
Lumbermen, raftsmen and wood choppers	42.1
Other specified laborers	29.7
Laborers (n.e.c.):	
Furniture, saw and plan'g mills, misc. wood products	31.7
Nonmanufacturing	24.6
Construction	24.6
Wholesale and retail trade	28.3
Other industries (incl. not rept'd)	37.7
FEMALE, EXPERIENCED CIVILIAN LABOR FORCE	
Professional, technical, and kindred workers:	
Nurses, student professional	81.1
Farmers and farm managers	65.9
Sales workers:	
Others (n.e.c.)	52.1
Private household worker:	
Private hshld wkrs-living in	56.1
Private hshld wkrs-living out	80.6
Service wkrs., except priv. household:	
Waitresses, bartenders, and counter workers	55.5
Other service wkrs., exc. priv. hshld	50.4
Farm laborers and foremen:	
Farm laborers, unpaid family wkrs	86.7
Farm laborers, exc. unpaid and farm foremen	87.2

The workers in many of the "destitution occupations" are part-time workers who are not supporting a family, persons who work at the particular occupation during only part of a year or on a part-time basis, or workers who receive other compensation (such as student nurses and unpaid family workers). A second group, the "meager livelihood" occupations, are perhaps more typical of the work in which the heads of poverty-ridden families are most often employed, when they are working. In these occupations the percentage of workers receiving incomes of "$1,000 to $1,999" was 50 percent higher than the average for all workers in the experienced labor force.

List 20-B. OCCUPATIONS AFFORDING A MEAGER LIVELIHOOD: Occupations for which the proportion of persons in the experienced civilian force with income of $1,000-$1,999 is 50 percent or more than the average for all occupations

Occupation	Percent
MALE EXPERIENCED CIVILIAN LABOR FORCE	
Farmers and farm managers	27.0
Craftsmen, foremen and kindred wkrs:	
Shoemakers and repairers, except factory	29.4
Operatives and kindred workers:	
Attendants, auto service and parking	30.0

List 20-B. Continued

Operatives and kindred workers: Continued

Laundry and dry cleaning operatives	31.0
Sawyers	34.3
Taxicab drivers and chauffeurs......	28.7

Operatives and kindred workers (n. e. c):

Sawmills, plan'g mills, and misc. wood products..................	33.1
Furniture and fixtures.............	30.8
Yarn, thread and fabric mills........	31.8
Leather and leather products.......	27.2

Private household workers...........	34.7

Service wkrs., except private hshld:

Charwomen, janitors and porters....	34.9
Elevator operators.................	27.3
Other service wkrs., exc. priv. hshld .	32.2

Farm laborers and foremen:

Farm laborers, exc. unpaid and farm foremen...................	30.7

Laborers, except farm and mine:	28.4
Fishermen and oystermen..........	29.2
Lumbermen, raftsmen, and wood choppers.......................	32.2
Other specified laborers...........	31.6
Laborers (n. e. c.).................	28.1

Furniture, saw and plan'g mills, misc. wood products.........	38.9
Stone, clay, and glass products	27.1
Other durable goods...........	27.0
Textile mill prod. and apparel.	38.9
Not specified mfg. industries	29.6

Nonmanufacturing industries (incl. not reported):

Construction.................	32.4
Telecommunications, and utilities and sanitary services.........	27.7
Wholesale and retail trade......	28.8
Other industries (incl. not rept'd)	28.3

FEMALE, EXPERIENCED CIVILIAN LABOR FORCE

Operatives and kindred workers:

Knitting mills.................	57.6
Apparel and other fabricated textile products..............	51.2
Leather and leather products....	54.7

Finally, List 20-C enumerates the high-income occupations, in which the percentage of persons earning more than $10,000 is 50 percent greater than the average for all workers:

List 20-C. HIGH INCOME OCCUPATIONS: Occupations for which the proportion of persons in the experienced civilian force with income of $10,000 and over is 50 percent or more than the average for all occupations

Occupation	Percent
MALE, EXPERIENCED CIVILIAN LABOR FORCE	
Professional, technical and kindred workers	8.0
Accountants and auditors.............	4.5
Architects.........................	18.1
Artists and art teachers.............	5.2
Authors, editors, and reporters	10.3
Chemists..........................	4.1
College presidents, prof'rs and inst'rs. (n. e. c.)...........................	5.1
Dentists...........................	24.6
Engineers, aeronautical	3.5
Engineers, civil...................	4.8
Engineers, electrical...............	4.3
Engineers, mechanical	5.5
Other technical engineers............	7.1
Lawyers and judges	28.1
Natural scientists (n. e. c)............	5.7
Pharmacists	7.1
Physicians and surgeons	41.0
Social scientists...................	7.7
Other professional, technical and kindred workers	4.4
Managers, off'ls, and props., exc. farm:	11.0
Other specified mgrs. and officials ...	5.6
Mgr., off'ls, and props (n. e. c.) - salaried:	
Manufacturing....................	19.7
Wholesale and retail trade..........	8.2
Finance, insurance and real estate ..	17.4
Other industries (incl. not rep'td)....	8.2
Mgrs., off's, and props. (n. e. c.) - self-employed:	
Construction	13.6

List 20-C. Continued

Mgrs., off's, and props. (n.e.c.)-
 self-employed: Continued
  Manufacturing...................... 23.7
  Wholesale trade................... 20.2
  Eating and drinking places......... 5.4
  Retail trade, exc. eating and drink-
    ing places 8.6
  Other industries (incl. not rep'td).... 13.3

Sales workers:
  Insurance agents and brokers......... 5.1
  Real estate agents and brokers........ 9.7
  Salesmen and sales clerks (n.e.c.):
    Manufacturing..................... 6.8
    Wholesale trade................... 4.6

FEMALE, EXPERIENCED CIVILIAN
LABOR FORCE

Prof., tech., and kindred workers: 0.4
  Actresses 2.1
  Artists and art teachers............ 0.7
  Authors, editors, and reporters 2.5
  Chemists and natural scientists(n.e.c.) 0.5
  College pres., prof'rs., and instr's
    (n.e.c.)......................... 0.9
  Designers and draftsmen............. 2.3
  Lawyers............................ 6.6
  Musicians and music teachers 0.5
  Physicians and surgeons 13.9
  Special scientists 0.8
  Social, welfare, and recreation wkrs.. 0.4
  Therapists and healers (n.e.c.)....... 0.5
  Other prof., tech., and kindred wkrs .. 0.8
Farmers and farm managers.......... 1.4
Managers, offls., and props., exc.farm 2.6
  Specified managers and officials...... 1.1
  Managers, offls. and props., (n.e.c.)-
    salaried......................... 1.8
  Wholesale and retail trade......... 1.5
  Other industries (incl. not rep'td)... 2.0
  Mgrs., offls., and props.(n.e.c.)-
    self-employed.................... 4.0
  Eating and drinking places......... 2.4
  Wholesale and retail trade, exc.
    eating and drinking places....... 3.6
  Other industries (incl. not rep'td).. 6.1

Clerical and kindred workers:
  Bookkeepers..................... 2.2

Sales workers:
  Insurance and real estate agents and
    brokers......................... 1.6
  Salesmen and sales clerks (n.e.c.)
    exc. retail trade................. 0.5

Physicians far outstrip all other occupations with respect to high income. In 1950, 41 percent of physicians reported an income of more than $10,000. Lawyers and judges were a poor second, only 28 percent being in this income group. The ten highest-income occupations of 1950, in descending order, were:

	Percent earning $10,000 or more 1949
Physicians and surgeons.............	41.0
Lawyers and judges.................	28.1
Dentists..........................	24.6
Managers, officials, proprietors-- manufacturing-- self-employed......	23.7
Managers, officials, proprietors-- wholesale trade-- self-employed....	20.2
Managers, officials, proprietors-- manufacturing-- salaried..........	19.7
Architects........................	18.1
Managers, officials, proprietors-- finance, insurance and real estate salaried..........................	17.4
Managers, officials, proprietors-- construction-- self-employed.......	13.6
Authors, editors, and reporters.....	10.3

Industry and Income Distribution. Family heads employed in the mining, manufacturing, wholesale trade, finance, professional, and public administration industries receive high incomes in a much higher percentage of cases than do family heads employed in other industries. An above-average proportion of family heads employed in agriculture and personal services receive only a meager livelihood, or less. The smallest amount of economic hardship is found among employees of the manufacturing, transportation, professional service, finance, and public administration industries; 8 percent, or less, of the families whose heads were employed in these industries had incomes placing them at the "destitution" or "meager" level. The very large family incomes are con-

Table 20-12.—LIVELIHOOD STATUS OF FAMILIES, CLASSIFIED BY INDUSTRY OF FAMILY HEAD: 1956

Industry of family head	Total	Livelihood status					
		Destitute	Meager	Minimum adequate	Comfortable	Abundant	Affluent or rich
Total employed civilians...............	100.0	4.2	9.9	16.9	31.3	28.6	9.0
Agriculture, forestry, and fisheries.........	100.0	24.1	32.3	21.0	12.7	7.3	2.6
Mining....................................	100.0	1.4	9.2	14.0	35.2	28.7	11.5
Construction..............................	100.0	2.4	11.3	18.1	30.4	28.9	8.9
Manufacturing.............................	100.0	0.9	5.0	14.4	35.5	34.6	9.7
Transportation, commun., and other pub. util.	100.0	1.4	4.1	15.5	37.9	33.7	7.4
Wholesale trade...........................	100.0	1.2	8.3	17.7	32.1	29.9	10.8
Retail trade..............................	100.0	3.4	9.7	21.3	29.9	27.7	7.8
Finance, insurance, and real estate.........	100.0	2.0	5.7	12.7	26.2	35.1	18.4
Business and repair services................	100.0	2.8	10.9	20.1	31.3	24.1	10.8
Personal services.........................	100.0	12.1	23.2	20.0	27.2	12.8	4.8
Entertainment and recreation services[1].......							
Professional and related services...........	100.0	1.6	7.1	16.5	31.2	28.0	15.7
Public administration......................	100.0	0.9	3.7	14.0	38.4	34.6	8.3

[1]Percent not shown where there were fewer than 100 cases in the sample reporting on income.

Source: Current Population Reports, Series P-60, No. 27, 1958, Table 10.

centrated among the families whose heads work in finance, professional service, and mining.

These inter-industry differences in income are due in part to differences in occupational composition. They are also due, of course, to differences in the wage and salary levels of various industries. The object here is not to explain the reasons for these differences (the factors underlying them are many and complex), but only to call attention to the fact that they do exist and, thereby, to help explain why some communities have higher income levels than others.

Unemployment and Income. Workers who were unemployed at the time of the 1957 income survey tended to fall at the lower end of the income scale. Nevertheless, one-third of the families with unemployed heads had received incomes capable of providing a comfortable level of living, or better, and less than 10 percent of families with unemployed heads were "destitute." These data suggest that, although many of those who were unemployed in 1957 may have been marginal workers, a majority had had well-paying jobs during the preceding year, and that their lack of work in 1957 did not indicate membership in a more or less permanent body of unemployable persons.

Part-Year and Part-Time Work in Relation to Income. A great many workers who receive low incomes are part-year or part-time workers. The following data show the median incomes, in 1956, of males who worked at full-time jobs (35 hours or more per week) according to the number of weeks worked in 1956.

Weeks worked	Median income	
	Full-time workers	Part-time workers
50-52 weeks...................	$4,462	$1,112
40-49 weeks...................	3,892	1,259
27-39 weeks...................	2,654	887
14 to 26 weeks...............	1,696	557
13 weeks or less.............	704	369

The data for females present a similarly consistent picture of decreasing income with decreasing amounts of full-time work and decreasing number of weeks worked.

Nevertheless, low incomes are not uncommon even among full-time, full-year workers, as the following summary shows:

Income group	Percent of workers	
	Male	Female
Total.....................	100.0	100.0
Less than $1,000...............	5.2	8.7
$1,000 to $1,999...............	5.8	15.8
$2,000 to $2,999...............	10.6	30.5
$3,000 to $3,999...............	17.4	27.1
$4,000 and over...............	61.1	17.8

In spite of being employed at full-time, full-year work, about 1 male worker in 9 and 1 female worker in 4 earned less than $2,000 in 1956. This suggests that the "meager livelihood" occupations listed above (and other occupations that are not listed) are perpetuators of chronic economic hardship.

Veteran Status and Income. Veterans of World War II have considerably higher incomes, on the average, than nonveterans of the same age and type of residence:

Age	Median income (1956)	
	Veterans	Nonveterans
TOTAL[1]		
25 to 34 years.................	$4,944	$4,150
35 to 44 years.................	5,122	3,443
URBAN		
25 to 34 years.................	4,838	3,911
35 to 44 years.................	4,985	4,614
RURAL FARM		
25 to 34 years.................	2,440	1,899
35 to 44 years.................	2,150	1,753

[1] The statistics for "Total" concern year-round, full-time workers; the statistics for residence subgroups concern all income recipients.

Source: Current Population Reports, Series P-60, No.27, 1958, Table 18.

The reasons for this differential can only be guessed. Perhaps it is due in part to the advantages available to the veterans of World War II (additional education and training, assistance in getting started in business, on-the-job training, loans for purchasing homes, etc.). Or it may be due to poorer health and a greater prevalence of physical handicaps among nonveterans than among veterans. Whatever the reasons for the difference, it is abundantly clear that veterans as a group are advantaged rather than disadvantaged, economically.

Number of Earners and Family Income. In 1956 almost one-half of all families had two or more earners:

Number of earners:	Percent of families	Median income, 1956
Total.............	100.0	$4,783
No earners...........	6.0	1,394
1 earner.............	48.5	4,328
2 earners............	35.4	5,576
3 or more earners......	10.0	6,946

Source: Current Population Reports, Series P-60, No.27, 1958, Table 7.

Thus, in 1956 a second worker in a family added about $1,250 per year to the family income, on an average. Undoubtedly the recent increase in the number of multi-worker families has been one of the major factors behind the rapid rise in family purchasing power. "Between 1948 and 1956 the proportion of families with more than one earner increased from 41 percent to 46 percent among nonfarm families and from 37 percent to 42 percent among farm families" (U. S. Census, Series P-60, No.27). Chapter 16 of the present monograph, which concerns the Labor Force, shows that nonwhite families are especially inclined to have two or more earners. Probably as much of the economic well-being gained by the nonwhite population has been acquired through multiple-earners in families as through increased rates of pay.

Moreover, multiple-earner families do not exist only at the low-income and medium-income levels; in fact, among families with high incomes there tends to be an above-average percentage of multiple-earner families:

Family income	Percent of families with more than one earner
Total....................	45
$1,000 to $1,999...............	26
$4,000 to $4,999...............	40
$6,000 to $6,999...............	59
$10,000 to $14,999.............	69
$15,000 and over..............	50

Source: Ibid., Table B.

Size of Family and Income. Unfortunately for their own welfare, large families with 6 or more members receive less income than medium-size families. In 1956, the median income received by families of various sizes whose head was a full-time, year-round worker was as follows:

Size of family	Median income	Income per member
2 persons.....................	$5,235	$2,618
3 persons.....................	5,559	1,853
4 persons.....................	5,666	1,417
5 persons.....................	5,750	1,150
6 persons.....................	5,587	931
7 persons or more.............	4,991	Less than 713

Source: Current Population Reports, Series P-60, No.27, 1958, Table 5.

These data make it readily apparent that a very large percentage of the families with 5 or more members have a meager livelihood. This aspect of income statistics has not yet been adequately explored. Although it is true that certain economies can be effected in large families, and that some members of large families are almost always in the very young age groups where per capita expenses are low, it is still very doubtful whether the livelihood status of 4-member families is as high as that of 3-member or 2-member families. These data illustrate, from another angle, the oft-noted fact that families of low socioeconomic status tend to be among the most fertile segments of the population.

Source of Income. In addition to finding out the total amount of income received by a family, the Bureau of the Census obtains approximate information concerning the sources of this income. Statistics for families, classified by source of income, are reported in Table 20-13. Only about one-half (48 percent) of the families rely solely on wages or salary for their income, and an additional 5.3 percent rely on self-employment only. All other families (47 percent) receive their income from two or more sources.

The most common sources of supplementary income are pensions, interest, dividends, and other income from annuities, estates, or trusts; net income from boarders or lodgers, and from rental properties; unemployment or sickness benefits, public assistance, and alimony. About one-third of all families which receive wage or salary income also receive income from one of the other above-mentioned sources. Some wage and salary workers (about 10 percent) also receive income from self-employment.

An even larger fraction (almost 3/5) of the families receiving income from nonfarm self-employment also receive income from wages or salaries, or from sources other than employment.

Even the self-employed rural-farm family derives much of its income from nonagricultural sources. A total of 7.0 percent of all families reported some income from farm self-employment. But almost one-half of the families in this 7.0 percent also reported receiving income from wages, and an additional one-fifth received income from sources other than wages.

Unfortunately, it is not yet possible to collect accurate statistics concerning the amounts of each type of income received, and for this

Table 20-13.—DISTRIBUTION OF FAMILIES ACCORDING TO SOURCE OF INCOME IN 1956, FOR THE UNITED STATES, URBAN AND RURAL

Source of income	All families	Families, by residence		
		Urban	Rural nonfarm	Rural farm
Total..................................	100.0	100.0	100.0	100.0
Earnings only, total...........................	60.7	59.1	64.4	63.5
Wages or salary only...........................	47.6	51.5	52.8	15.0
Self employment only...........................	5.3	3.2	4.0	19.8
Nonfarm self employment.......................	2.9	3.0	3.5	0.9
Farm self employment..........................	2.3	0.1	0.4	17.6
Wages or salary and self employment.............	7.7	4.4	6.6	28.0
With nonfarm self employment.................	4.0	4.1	5.2	1.2
With farm self employment....................	3.4	0.3	1.2	25.0
Earnings and income other than earning............	33.3	34.7	30.2	33.0
Wages or salary and other income...............	25.7	29.6	24.4	7.8
Self employment and other income...............	3.4	2.3	2.6	11.1
Nonfarm self employment......................	2.0	2.2	2.2	0.5
Farm self employment.........................	1.3	0.1	0.3	9.7
Wages or salary, self employment and other income..................................	4.2	2.8	3.2	14.1
Other income; no earnings......................	5.2	5.5	5.4	3.6

Source: Current Population Reports, Series P-60, No. 27, 1958, Table 11.

reason one cannot infer <u>how much</u> income of each type is received by families. The fact that such a high percentage of families derive their income from more than one source is due to a variety of factors, including an increase in the number of working wives, more inclusive pension plans, the changed pattern of income distribution (which permits more families to hold investments or own property), and the shortening of working hours (which permits multiple job holding.

CONCLUSION

Additional materials concerning income are contained in other chapters which provide income statistics for the topics with which they are especially concerned. (The interested reader may locate these topics in the Index.) It is hoped that this brief exposition of income, supplemented by the materials presented in other chapters, makes it abundantly clear that income differences are one of the leading factors that help to explain differences in human behavior.

Chapter 21

THE POPULATION IN INSTITUTIONS

THE INSTITUTIONAL POPULATION DEFINED

At any given moment, about 1 percent of the population (which would amount to roughly 1.75 million persons, as of 1958) is in the custody of institutions. These inmates have certain disabilities which are considered, by the community at large, to constitute hazards to their own welfare or to the welfare of other members of the community. Because the expense connected with the care of such persons, and the task of rehabilitating and returning them to society as self-sustaining individuals, are responsibilities borne by the larger community, there is considerable general interest regarding the size and composition of this group. As a part of the process of taking the national decennial census, each institutional establishment is located and its residents are enumerated. Compiling separately the census reports concerning institutions makes it possible to obtain information about the persons who reside in them. All institutions, of course, are quasi households (see Chapter 10). Four major criteria are used in determining whether or not the residents of a particular quasi household are to be classified as inmates of institutions. They are (a) length of stay, (b) usual place of residence, (c) labor force status, and (d) type of public responsibility. The official census definition is as follows: The institutional population "constitutes the inmate population of certain places which provide care for persons suffering from various types

of disabilities in which the length of stay is relatively long; in which by virtue of the length of stay and disability persons under care are classified as usual residents and excluded from the labor force; and in which some general public interest attaches to the type of disability involved. Specifically, it includes persons under care in:

    Correctional institutions (penitentiaries and jails)
    Hospitals for mental diseases
    Tuberculosis hospitals
    Homes for the aged and dependent
    Nursing, rest, and convalescent homes
    Schools for the mentally and physically handicapped
    Homes for neglected and dependent children
    Training schools for juvenile delinquents
    Detention homes
    Homes for unwed mothers[1]

Members of the resident staff and their families are excluded from this population. Also excluded are persons living in convents and monasteries, and in all institution-like facilities operated by the armed forces.

As of April 1, 1950, there were 1,567,000 inmates of institutions. These were distributed, by type, as follows:

---

[1] U. S. Census of Population: 1950, Special Reports. Institutional Population, "Introduction." Prepared by Henry D. Sheldon.

Type of institution	Number of inmates	Percent distri- bution
Total.....................	1,566,846	100.0
Correctional...................	264,557	16.9
Prisons and reformatories.....	178,065	11.4
Jails and workhouses..........	86,492	5.5
Mental hospitals................	613,628	39.2
Tuberculosis hospitals..........	76,291	4.9
Other special hospitals........	20,084	1.3
Homes for aged and dependent....	296,783	18.9
Homes and schools for mentally handicapped...................	134,189	8.6
Homes and schools for physically handicapped...................	20,999	1.3
Homes for neglected and de- pendent children..............	96,300	6.1
Public training schools for Juvenile delinquents...........	29,042	1.9
Other institutions for juveniles	14,973	1.0

Source: U.S. Census of Population: 1950, Special Reports; Institutional Population, "Introduction."

This summary shows that almost one-half of the nation's institutional population is under such care because of mental illness or mental defect (the combined populations of mental hospitals and of homes and schools for mentally handicapped persons). Inmates of homes for the aged and of correctional institutions are each roughly one-half as numerous as the inmates of mental hospitals. Thus, mental disability, crime and delinquency, and old age are the three major reasons why these members of the population are in institutions.

Trends in institutional population can be traced only very approximately. A report on the institutional population was prepared as a part of the 1940 census, but because that census differed from the 1950 census both in its classification of institutions and in its procedures, comparisons cannot easily be made. A gross comparison between the total numbers of inmates 14 years and over at the two censuses yields the following statistics:

Year	Total	Male	Female
Number of inmates:			
1950..............	1,444,238	879,219	565,091
1940..............	1,176,993	767,474	409,519
Percent of total population 14 yrs. old and over:			
1950..............	1.3	1.6	1.0
1940..............	1.2	1.5	0.8
Percent change, 1940 to 1950.......	22.7	14.6	38.0

The institutional population appears to have grown at a rate roughly 50 percent higher than the average growth rate for the total population, which was 14.2 percent. A part of this apparent growth, however, may be due to more complete coverage and to changes in those definitions that decide which quasi households are to be treated as institutions.

COMPOSITION OF THE INSTITUTIONAL POPULATION

Selected compositional characteristics of the institutional population, by type of institution, are reported in Table 21-1.

Sex. Unlike the general population, the institutional population is disproportionately masculine. The outstanding instance of this situation is supplied by correctional institutions, in which 96 percent of all inmates are males. Other institutions with a strong preponderance of males are training schools for juvenile delinquents (65 percent), and tuberculosis hospitals (62 percent). In all other kinds of institutions the numbers of male and female inmates were almost equal, although there was still a slight majority of males (homes for the aged had almost an exact 50-50 sex composition).

Color. A disproportionately large share of the nonwhite population is in correctional institutions and public training schools for juvenile delinquents. The differential is very large: In 1950, the number of nonwhite inmates in correctional institutions was 3.5 times the proportion one would expect if whites and nonwhites had the same percentages of their total populations in institutions. A similar comparison shows that the number of nonwhite inmates of training schools for juvenile delinquents was more than 2 times the number to be expected. However, the nonwhite population is underrepresented in homes for the aged, schools for the mentally handicapped, and homes for neglected and dependent children.

Age. Taken as a whole, the institutional population has a very peculiar age distribution. Almost equal proportions fall in each age group from 15 to 64 years, with a large excess at ages 65 and over and a deficit at ages 0 to 9. However,

Table 21-1.—NUMBER AND CHARACTERISTICS OF INMATES OF INSTITUTIONS, BY TYPE OF INSTITUTION: 1950

Number and percentage composition	U.S. total population	Total institutional population	Correctional institutions	Mental hospitals	Tuberculosis hospitals	Homes for the aged and dependent	Schools for the mentally handicapped	Schools for the physically handicapped	Homes for neglected and dependent children	Public training schools for juvenile delinquents, etc.
NUMBER (000)										
Total.....................	150,697	1,567	178	614	76	297	134	21	96	37
Male, white......................	67,129	950	111	288	39	141	65	10	51	18
Female, white....................	67,813	617	4	253	23	144	62	9	40	11
Male, nonwhite...................	7,704	158	60	41	8	7	4	1	3	6
Female, nonwhite.................	8,051	57	3	32	6	4	3	1	2	2
Percent male.....................	49.7	60.6	96.1	53.6	62.2	50.0	51.2	53.4	55.9	64.8
Percent nonwhite.................	10.5	13.9	35.3	11.8	18.4	3.8	5.1	10.6	5.6	22.4
AGE										
Total.....................	100.0	100.0	100.0	100.0	100.0	100.0	100.0	100.0	100.0	100.0
Under 5 years....................	10.7	1.1				0.2	1.6	4.7	10.1	0.6
5 to 9 years.....................	8.8	3.0	0.2	0.6	4.2	0.3	6.1	25.4	30.0	1.4
10 to 14 years...................	7.4	5.0				0.3	11.6	30.9	42.3	27.1
15 to 19 years...................	7.0	6.3	6.8	1.2	4.6	0.4	15.2	24.5	16.3	64.8
20 to 24 years...................	7.6	6.7	21.4	3.1	10.7	0.5	13.3	4.3	0.4	3.9
25 to 29 years...................	8.1	7.2	20.2	5.5	12.9		11.3			
30 to 34 years...................	7.6	6.7	14.5	7.2	10.8	1.3	9.3			
35 to 39 years...................	7.5	6.8	11.6	8.8	10.0		7.8			
40 to 44 years...................	6.8	6.6	8.7	9.4	9.2	2.4	6.4			
45 to 49 years...................	6.0	6.5	6.6	10.0	8.3		5.2	10.1	0.9	2.2
50 to 54 years...................	5.5	6.7	4.1	10.7	7.8	6.4	4.0			
55 to 59 years...................	4.8	6.7	2.5	10.8	7.2		2.9			
60 to 64 years...................	4.0	6.3	1.6	9.7	5.6	14.8	2.2			
65 years and over................	8.1	24.6	1.7	23.0	8.6	73.3	3.1			
RACE AND NATIVITY										
All classes.................	100.0	100.0	100.0	100.0	100.0	100.0	100.0	100.0	100.0	100.0
Native white.....................	82.8	71.8	61.7	72.8	72.4	73.2	92.7	85.7	93.6[1]	
Foreign-born white...............	6.7	15.3	3.4	15.5	10.1	22.8	1.6	3.1	1.0	
Negro............................	10.0	12.3	33.9	11.2	15.4	3.7	5.3	10 0	3.7	
Other races......................	0.5	0.6	1.0	0.4	2.1	0.3	0.3	1.1	1.7	
YEARS OF SCHOOL COMPLETED										
Total, 25 years old and over...	100.0	100.0	100.0	100.0	100.0	100.0	100.0	100.0	100.0	100.0
Elementary: Under 5 years........	10.8	15.8	18.2	13.0	9.7	14.2				
5 to 7 years..........	15.9	13.1	20.4	11.1	14.0	14.0				
8 years...............	20.2	15.2	15.8	15.6	11.8	18.2				
High school: 1 to 3 years.........	16.9	7.8	17.1	6.3	11.7	6.0				
4 years.............	20.2	6.7	6.7	6.9	9.8	6.9	N.A.	N.A.	N.A.	N.A.
College: 1 to 3 years..........	7.2	2.2	2.6	1.8	4.2	2.6				
4 years..............	6.0	1.7	0.7	1.7	2.8	2.3				
School years not reported.........	2.8	37.4	18.4	43.7	36.1	35.7				
Median school years completed......	9.3	8.2	8.1	8.3	8.7	8.2				
MARITAL STATUS										
Total, 14 years old and over..	100.0	100.0	100.0	100.0	100.0	100.0	100.0	100.0	100.0	100.0
Single...........................	23.1	48.9	47.1	47.6	33.2	31.4				
Married..........................	66.6	28.3	39.2	35.0	47.9	13.9	N.A.	N.A.	N.A.	N.A.
Widowed..........................	8.1	17.1	3.8	11.9	10.0	50.1				
Divorced.........................	2.2	5.8	10.0	5.6	8.8	4.6				
MOBILITY STATUS										
Total.....................	100.0	100.0	100.0	100.0	100.0	100.0	100.0	100.0	100.0	100.0
Same house as in 1949............	82.3	76.2	63.9	86.7	58.3	76.9	91.5	73.9	79.2[1]	
Different house, same county......	11.4	9 5	3.4	4.0	20.2	15.2	0.8	5.5	10.4	
Different county, same state......	...	11.3	24.3	8.3	18.2	5.4	7.0	15.7	8.3	
Different state or abroad.........	6.3	3.1	8.3	0.9	3.3	2.4	0.7	4.9	2.2	
METROPOLITAN AREA RESIDENCE										
Total.....................	100.0	100.0	100.0	100.0	100.0	100.0	100.0	100.0	100.0	100.0
In standard metropolitan areas	56.8	55.3	39.5	53.3	62.1	63.7	34.3	66.6	71.1	52.1
Urban...........................	42.8	34.2	16.5	28.6	32.4	48.2	16.1	58.9	54.9	15.8
Rural...........................	12.0	21.2	23.0	24.7	29.7	15.5	18.1	7.8	16.2	37.3
Outside standard metropolitan areas	43.2	44.7	60.5	46.7	37.9	36.3	65.7	33.4	28.9	47.9
Urban...........................	14.2	15.5	16.6	16.4	5.5	14.6	19.9	21.7	12.5	6.5
Rural...........................	29.0	29.2	43.9	30.3	32.4	21.7	45.8	11.7	16.4	40.4
Total.....................	100.0	100.0	100.0	100.0	100.0	100.0	100.0	100.0	100.0	100.0
Percent urban, total..............	64.0	49.6	33.1	45.0	37.8	62.9	36.0	80.5	67.3	22.3
Percent rural, total..............	36.0	50.4	66.9	55.0	62.2	37.1	64.0	19.5	32.7	77.7

[1] Combined in census tables.

N.A. Not tabulated.

Source: U.S. Census of Population, 1950, Special Reports, Institutional Population, Tables 3,4,5,6,7,8,9,10,11,19, 20,21,22,23, and 24.

this equality of age distribution is due to the averaging-out effect of combining the various types of institutional population, each of which has a more or less unique age composition. For example, the population in correctional institutions is very heavily concentrated in ages 20 to 44 years of age, with a comparative deficit for older years. By contrast, patients in mental hospitals and homes for the aged are heavily concentrated at ages above 40. It is the age composition of these last two groups that is largely responsible for the fact that, of the total institutional population, 1 inmate in 4 (24.6 percent) was aged 65 and over in 1950. Patients in tuberculosis hospitals have an excess at every age above 20, with a deficit at the younger ages. Homes and schools for the handicapped, and for neglected and delinquent children, have comparatively small populations above the age of 20 years. The inmates of institutions caring for juvenile delinquents are very heavily concentrated in the age group 10 to 19 (92 percent). Each of the other groups of institutionalized juvenile populations has a larger proportion in the 0 to 5 age range and, hence, a less heavy concentration in the teen-age years.

Educational Attainment. In comparison with the population at large, adult inmates of institutions are poorly educated. (Data are reported only for the population 25 years of age and over.) Despite the fact that for a very large proportion of the institutional population the number of years of schooling attained are not reported, there is enough data to show that among the inmates of institutions the percentage who have had only 7 years or less of grammar school education is larger than it is among the population at large. At the other end of the scale, the percentage of inmates with a high school or college education is much smaller than it is among the general population. Unless one is willing to concede that all of the persons for whom no information was reported concerning educational attainment were high school and college graduates, one can only conclude that rates of institutionalization are highest among the least-educated population, and that they decline at each higher level of educational attainment. The significance of this differential is difficult to evaluate. It may mean that persons who are able to attain only limited amounts of education are more likely to have, or to acquire, disabilities that cause them to be institutionalized; it may mean that less-educated persons have smaller incomes and cannot afford to take preventive action which might help them to avoid institutionalization; or it may mean that less-educated persons live more often in environments that produce a need for institutionalization than do members of the more-educated group.

Marital Status. Adult inmates of institutions are much more inclined to be single than the general adult population. Inmates of correctional institutions and mental hospitals are especially inclined to remain unmarried; in 1950, 47 to 49 percent of these persons were single. In the case of correctional institutions, this situation may have been due partially to the younger age composition of the inmates. Among inmates of homes for the aged, 86 percent were either single, widowed, or divorced. The fact that they were not married was undoubtedly one of the reasons why many of these persons were in such institutions.

Migration and Mobility. Becoming an inmate of an institution requires a change of residence (and, very often, a change in the county of residence), so it is not surprising that a large share of the institutional population is reported as having changed residence or having migrated during the past year. The mobility statistics in Table 21-1 give a rough measure of institutional turnover. Tuberculosis hospitals and correctional institutions show the greatest turnover; mental hospitals and schools for the mentally handicapped show the least turnover.

Residence. The institutional population as a whole is rather evenly divided between urban and rural-nonfarm residence. (By census definition, no institutional population is defined as rural farm, even though some of the institutional establishments may operate a large agricultural enterprise.) Homes for the aged, schools for the physically handicapped, and homes for neglected and dependent children tend to be located in urban areas, whereas correctional institutions, mental hospitals, tuberculosis hospitals, and schools for the mentally handicapped tend to be located in rural (often suburban) areas.

RECENT TRENDS IN THE NUMBER OF PRISONERS IN STATE AND FEDERAL PRISONS

As of January 1, 1957, there were 188,730 prisoners in state and federal prisons, which amounted to 114 prisoners for each 100,000 of the civilian population. By far the majority (89 percent) were in state jails, prisons and institutions, and only 11 percent in federal institutions. In the years since 1950 the number of persons sentenced to prison has increased at a rate roughly equal to the nation's population growth. During World War II the number of prisoners declined from 179,047 in 1939 to a low of 131,884 in 1944, a decrease of 23 percent in 5 years. Thus, one of the by-products of the war was a temporary relief from the growing burden of prison population. After demobilization the number climbed rapidly and steadily; in the 12 years from 1944 to 1956 the prison population increased by 42 percent. The following statistics summarize the changing size of the prison population since 1939:

Year	Number of prisoners (000)
1939	179
1940	173
1942	150
1944	132
1946	139
1948	155
1950	165
1952	167
1954	182
1956	189

Source: Statistical Abstract of the United States: 1958, Table 190.

RECENT TRENDS IN THE NUMBER OF PATIENTS IN HOSPITALS FOR MENTAL DISEASES AND IN INSTITUTIONS FOR MENTAL DEFECTIVES AND EPILEPTICS

Although the fact may not be widely known, the number of persons in mental hospitals and mental institutions is roughly 3.5 times as large as the number of prisoners in state and federal prisons. In 1955 there were 632,000 inmates of mental institutions, in comparison with 182,000 prisoners. The number of persons in mental institutions has grown steadily and swiftly since 1931, the year from which the available statistics date. The following is a summary of the trend:

Year	Number of patients (000)
1931	355
1935	421
1940	483
1945	520
1948	555
1950	578
1952	596
1954	623
1955	632

Source: Statistical Abstract of the United States: 1958, Table 90.

During the 24 years from 1931 to 1955, the number of patients in mental hospitals and institutions increased by more than a quarter-million, or by 78 percent. This growth rate was about three times the rate at which the total population grew. If this rate of growth continues, by 1975 there will be more than a million persons in hospitals for mental disease and in institutions for mental defectives and epileptics. The rapid growth of this segment of the population indicates that the growing prevalence of mental illness is one of the nation's major current social problems.

CONCLUSION

The composition of the institutional population differs greatly from that of the general population: A higher percentage of the institutional population than of the general population is male, nonwhite, poorly educated, and single or divorced. The inmates of institutions are unable to live a "normal" social or economic life. They cannot marry, have families, or support themselves by being in the labor force. Children in institutions have no opportunity to benefit from family living. Since institutional establishments tend to be large, the presence of such a unit in a census tract, city, county, or other small area can affect markedly the over-all composition of the community's population, and its rates of mortality, fertility, and migration.

The fact that the institutional population is growing more rapidly than the general population reflects the increasing seriousness of three of the nation's major social problems: poor health in old age, mental ill-health at all adult ages, and crime and delinquency among teenagers and young men.

Chapter 22

ILLNESS: ITS INCIDENCE AND PREVALENCE

A general knowledge of how much illness there is among the nation's population, and of the differences between various socio-economic sub-groupings of the population in rates of morbidity for various types of illness, should be a part of the information which the well-trained sociologist, demographer, economist, or other analyst of human events brings to bear on the problems he studies. The level of health that prevails and the types of sickness that occur among the population are highly correlated with almost every type of human behavior one cares to examine. In some cases, illness is a causal factor in behavior, while in others it is a result of certain socio-economic conditions; in some cases, illness is both cause and effect. Hence, the widespread and growing scientific attention currently being given to the subject of illness is based on more than the fact that people have a general desire to maintain health and avoid illness. Additional reasons for such study are: (a) Illness is regarded by many of those concerned with public welfare as one of the major social problems of the day. The safety and the efficient functioning of the community, and the security of the individual against avoidable discomfort and hardship, are both objectives in the minds of those who want to lessen the frequency and severity of illness; (b) Since illness is a precondition of mortality, a familiarity with health trends and with the prospects for reduction of the major types of disabling illness is one means of understanding and predicting the future course of the death rate; (c) Poor health on the part of one spouse, or of both spouses, is an important consideration in the refined analysis of fertility differences, because illness lessens the desire and the capacity for bearing children; and (d) Sickness is a relevant factor in a wide variety of sociological, psychological, and economic researches. It may be just as potent as education, religion, or occupation in explaining why a person has a high income, holds a particular attitude on a given issue, or buys or fails to buy a particular commodity.[1] Hence, the view that health and morbidity statistics are a special branch of analysis with which social scientists need not be familiar is a narrow one. The leading exponent of demographic studies of illness has been Mortimer Spiegelman, of Metropolitan Life.

Statistics concerning the frequency of onset of illness (incidence) and the proportion of the population that is ill at any one time (prevalence) are far less complete and detailed than statistics concerning mortality. There has been no established program for registering cases of illness in order to furnish reliable and complete morbidity statistics on a routine basis. (Certain diseases have been classified as "notifiable" diseases, for each

---

[1] For an excellent statement of health as a research variable, see Jacob J. Feldman, "Barriers to the use of Health Survey Data in Demographic Analysis," Milbank Memorial Fund Quarterly, July, 1958. He concludes that "...it is unfortunate that social scientists working in the field of health should devote all their energies in trying to explain medical phenomena in terms of social processes. It might well benefit both social science and medicine if more frequently the orientation were reversed and attention were paid to the physiological factors bearing on the social environment." This statement certainly is worthy of serious consideration by students of population.

new case of which the physician should notify public health officials. However, the list of notifiable diseases is comparatively short and does not include the major killers--cancer, heart diseases, and other chronic ailments.) Data concerning illness can be obtained only by conducting special surveys or by making special clinical examinations of samples of the population. Both of these procedures are costly, and both involve methodological problems.[2] However, a major development is now taking place, and will eventually alter

substantially the present situation in which only partial and incomplete data are available. In June, 1957, the U. S. Public Health Service began to collect statistics concerning illness from a representative cross-section of the population. This National Health Survey, directed by Forrest E. Linder, interviews a part of its sample each week, and thus is continuously collecting information about illness, disability, hospitalization, medical care, and dental care from a probability sample of the population. This program has been in operation for such a short time that, as yet, only a few preliminary results are available. In the following pages are summarized the results that have been released to date from this survey. These findings are supplemented with isolated bits of information from other surveys taken in particular local communities.

---

[2] Surveys which make use of interviewers without formal medical training, and which ask questions of only one person in each household concerning the health of all household members, have several limitations. Among them are the following: (a) Some diseases are almost asymptomatic, especially in their early stages, and the respondent may have disorders of which he is unaware and which only a thorough physical examination and clinical screening would reveal. (b) The respondent may have experienced some symptoms of illness, but may not yet have seen a doctor. He can only describe his feelings and subjective observations to the interviewer. At some stage these symptoms must be translated into a diagnosis, usually by a coder working without benefit of medical help. (c) The patient may know the correct diagnosis for his disorder, but may evade, falsify, or mislead the interviewer because of shame, modesty, or reluctance to admit he is ill. This is particularly true for particular types of disorders such as tuberculosis or syphilis, or disorders that affect particular sites. (d) The respondent may be ignorant of the correct diagnosis even though he has seen a doctor, because the physician may not have given him the information or he may not have understood it correctly. (e) One member of a household usually is not fully informed about all the disorders that have affected all the other members of the household. Since the other persons usually are away at work or at school when the interviewer calls, it is impossible to obtain the information which they may have been given by a physician but which they have not reported to the respondent. (f) Episodes of illness are rapidly forgotten, especially if they have left no sensible after-effect. Differential forgetting leads to severe underreporting of particular types of illness, if the survey tries to cover the events of more than a few days or weeks. (g) People find it very difficult to make a systematic and complete inventory of all their ailments. Some people become accustomed to having physical disabilities and often overlook them. It requires a rather lengthy and detailed probing operation by a skilled interviewer to elicit the desired information. (h) People differ markedly in recognizing and reporting their symptoms. Their reactions may vary all the way from a Spartan-like refusal to recognize pain or discomfort to the pathological illness sensations of the hypochondriac. (i) Many disorders, such as those of mental illness, have symptoms that the average respondent would not define as indications of illness. (j) The above difficulties can be handled correctly, if at all, only by unusually intelligent, conscientious, and sensitive interviewers who have undergone intensive training. It is very difficult to assemble a sufficient number of such persons to conduct a reliable illness survey on a large scale.

Even statistics based on clinical examinations, where data are collected by physicians and nurses, have serious deficiencies. Individual physicians differ in their diagnoses of a given set of symptoms, especially when the condition is rather vaguely defined. The task of standardizing the examination, and the diagnostic and reporting procedures, is very great. In addition, getting a representative cross-section of the population to cooperate fully in submitting to a clinical examination has proved to be almost impossible thus far. If such examination is voluntary, usually only a comparatively small fraction of the original sample (and probably a biased part) will appear at the clinic for examination. If the examination is nonvoluntary, as are the selective service or military physical examinations, the sample usually is not representative of any general segment of the population.

Thus, the collection of reliable and complete statistics concerning illness is a complex task, and is bound to encounter many technical and methodological problems. Experimentation toward the perfection of methods for avoiding or controlling many of the biases and shortcomings connected with present survey and clinical procedures is still underway. The next decade should see this branch of investigation make giant forward strides because of the work of the National Health Survey and other research groups.

DISABILITY DUE TO ILLNESS

During the year July, 1957 to June, 1958, the average civilian experienced 20 days of restricted activity due to illness or injury.[3] The aggregate for the year among the total population was 3.4 billion illness days. If this illness were spread evenly over the year, it would mean that on any average day 5.5 percent of the population was in a state of restricted activity due to some physical problem. The prevalence of disabling illness is highly concentrated in the autumn and winter months (see Figure 22-1). Also, it is highly concentrated in the upper age groups (see Figure 22-2). These results are based on data reported in Health Statistics From the U. S. National Health Survey, Selected Survey Topics, (Series B-5, U. S. Public Health Service, November, 1958). Almost 40 percent of these restricted-activity days were also bed-disability days, or days in which the per-

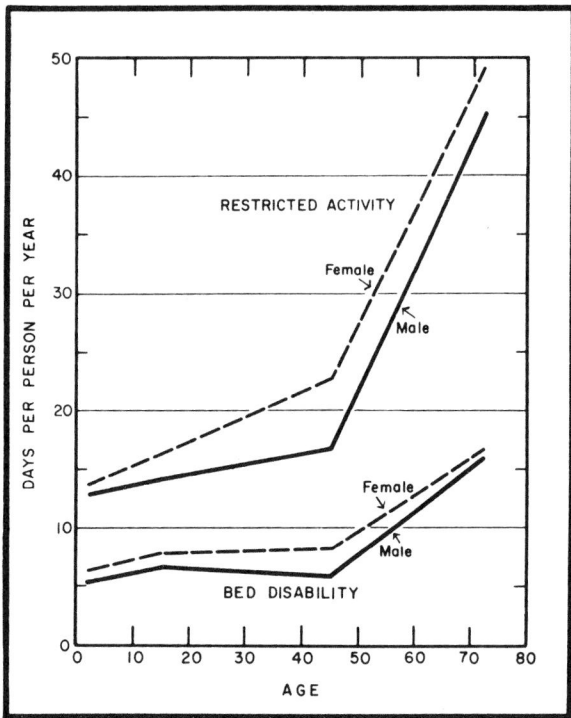

FIGURE 22-2. NUMBER OF DAYS OF RESTRICTED ACTIVITY AND BED DISABILITY PER PERSON PER YEAR BY SEX AND AGE

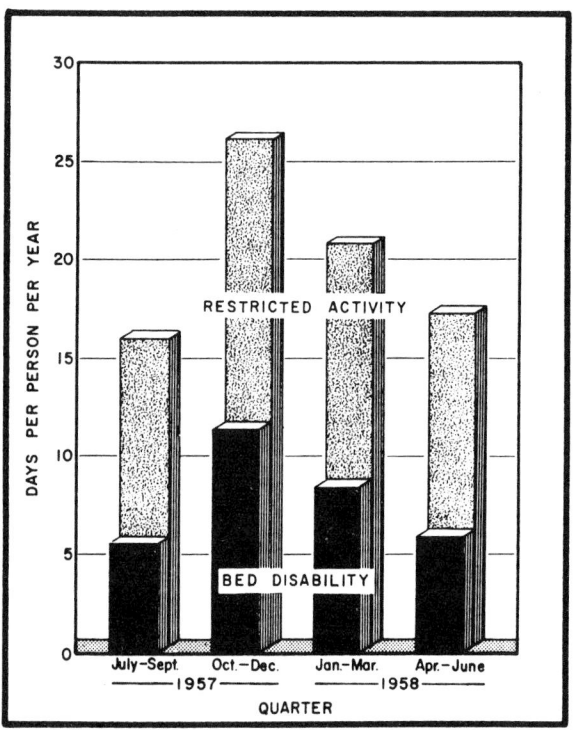

FIGURE 22-1. NUMBER OF DAYS OF RESTRICTED ACTIVITY AND BED DISABILITY PER PERSON PER YEAR BY QUARTER

son spent all or most of the day in bed because of an illness or an injury. The average person had 7.8 bed-disability days in the year, which amounted to an aggregate of 1.3 billion days of bed disability among the civilian noninstitutional population. Bed disability has a seasonal prevalence similar to that of restricted activity. Its age pattern is somewhat different, however; from age 15 to age 45, bed disability does not increase with age, and after age 45 it increases rather rapidly with advancing age.

The National Health Survey obtained data for two additional types of disability days: work-loss days and school-loss days. The first of these measures

---

[3] All days in which a person's customary daily activities were restricted for the whole of the day because of an illness or an injury were counted as restricted-activity days.

the number of days of work lost by adults who usually are employed, and who would have been at work if they had not been ill. The second refers to the number of days of school lost, due to illness, by students aged 6 to 16. The average usually-employed person lost 10.1 days of work because of disabling illness in the survey year 1957-58, and the average student lost 8.4 days of school.[4] Table 22-1 summarizes the statistics concerning seasonal variations in disability, as measured by the four types of disability.

is possible that males do not consider their health needs as carefully as women, and do not reduce their activity during mild attacks of illness.

Age	Restricted-activity days		Bed-disability days	
	Male	Female	Male	Female
All ages......	17.7	22.2	6.9	8.7
Under 5 years......	12.8	13.7	5.2	6.4
5 to 24 years......	14.1	16.4	6.6	7.8
25 to 64 years.....	16.8	22.9	5.8	8.2
65 years and over..	45.2	49.1	16.0	16.6

Source: National Health Survey, Report B-5, 1958.

Table 22-1.—AVERAGE NUMBER OF DAYS OF DISABILITY PER PERSON PER YEAR, BY QUARTER, AGE OF PERSONS, AND RESIDENCE, UNITED STATES: JULY, 1957-JUNE, 1958

Quarter, age, and residence	Restricted activity days	Bed disability days	Work loss days[1]	School loss days[2]
QUARTER				
Annual average....................	20.0	7.8	10.1	8.4
July-September, 1957.........................	15.9	5.5	8.5	1.1
October-December, 1957......................	26.1	11.4	13.6	17.5
January-March, 1958.........................	20.9	8.5	11.1	8.8
April-June, 1958............................	17.3	5.8	7.0	6.2
AGE				
Under 5 years...............................	13.2	5.8	...	...
5 to 24 years...............................	15.3	7.2	11.6[1]	...
25 to 64 years..............................	19.9	7.1	9.2	...
65 years and older..........................	47.3	16.3	21.4	...
RESIDENCE				
Urban.......................................	19.7	7.9	9.8	9.0
Rural nonfarm...............................	20.0	7.5	9.9	7.8
Rural farm..................................	21.5	7.6	12.2	7.3

[1]Computed for persons 17 years of age and over. These data refer to disability among persons who reported "working" as their major activity day the 12 month period preceding the week of the interview.
[2]Computed for children 6 to 16 years of age.

Source: U.S. National Health Survey, Report, Series B-5, Nov. 1958.

As shown by Figure 22-2, and by the following summary, men have 20 to 25 percent fewer restricted-activity days, and also fewer bed-disability days per year than women. It cannot be concluded on the basis of these data alone that men are more healthy than women, or that they suffer from fewer and less severe episodes of illness; it

Data from the National Health Survey also indicate that the rural-farm population tends to have more restricted-activity days and more work-loss days per year, because of illness, than the urban or the rural-nonfarm population. However, the size of these urban-rural differentials is not great.

Color and Disability Due to Illness. The non-white population has a rate of disability resulting from illness that is roughly 50 to 60 percent greater than that of the white population. This differential is shown by the following indexes of relative prevalence of disabling illness among the civilian noninstitutional population aged 14 to 64

---

[4] These data may be moderately higher than the average for a typical current year because of a mild epidemic of Asian influenza that reached peak intensity in October-December of 1957-58. For this reason, the data for the fourth quarter of 1957 may exaggerate the extent of seasonal fluctuations in illness.

years of age, by sex, derived from a special sample survey of the noninstitutional population of the United States in February, 1949:

Sex	Total	White	Nonwhite
Both sexes.............	100	95	153
Male................	105	102	133
Female..............	95	88	171

Note: Prevalence in the entire civilian noninstitutional population aged 14 to 64 is taken as 100. Each relative prevalence is adjusted for differences in age composition among the various groups.

Source: Theodore D. Woolsey, "Estimates of Disabling Illness Prevalence in the United States," Public Health Reports, Vol. 65, No. 6, Feb. 10, 1950. The data were collected by the U.S. Bureau of the Census in conjunction with its February, 1949, Current Population Survey, in collaboration with the U.S. Public Health Service.

According to these indexes, nonwhite females experience almost twice as much disabling illness as white females, and more than 25 percent more days of disabling illness than nonwhite males.[5] (At time of writing, comparable data had not yet been published from the National Health Survey.)

The 1949 sample survey of disabling illness also showed that unemployed persons and unmarried women have much higher rates of disabling illness than other groups in the population:

	Relative prevalence of disabling illness:
Employed, total................	55
Employed in agriculture......	71
Employed in nonagricultural industries..................	53
Unemployed....................	127
Married females..............	86
Unmarried females............	117

Source: Computed from Health in California, State of California, Department of Public Health, 1957, page 41.

---

[5] Note that in this survey white males are reported as having more disability from illness than white females. This inconsistency with the results of the National Health Survey may be due to differences in the wording of the questions, to seasonal factors, or to both. The 1949 survey asked about "inability to do one's regular work or other duties because of illness or disability," and referred to a single day. The National Health Survey determines disability over a two-week period, after probing intensively for all the kinds of illness which may have occurred during the previous two weeks.

These data seem to indicate that unemployed persons are even more disadvantaged than has been realized: persons who do not have jobs appear also to have much more severe health problems than the employed population. The population employed in agricultural industry had more than 20 percent more days of disabling illness than workers employed in nonagricultural industries. Thus, both the National Health Survey and the survey of 1949 seem to suggest that farming may not be as healthful an occupation as has been popularly supposed.

Income and Disability Due to Illness. The extent of disabling illness varies inversely with income: the smaller the income, the greater the number of days of disabling illness per year. The existence of this relationship has been demonstrated in numerous surveys. For example, a recent survey of health in California showed the following differentials between income groups as to number of days of disabling illness, expressed as a percentage of the average number of days for all persons:

	Index of disabling illness
Total.....................	100
Family income less than $2,000...	190
Family income $2,000 to $4,000...	90
Family income $5,000 or more.....	85

Source: Computed from Health in California, State of California, Department of Public Health, 1957, page 41.

Although the facts make it clear that there is a relationship between illness and income, the reasons for the differential among income groups are not fully understood. Most experts believe that a substantial proportion of it is due to the environment in which low-income persons live--poorer housing, greater overcrowding, lack of adequate preventative medical care, inadequate diet, less healthful working conditions, and other environmental factors not conducive to good health. However, experts also acknowledge that poor health is an important cause of low income. If a family's principal earner suffers prolonged or frequent disability due to illness, the family suffers loss of income. If this earner becomes totally incapacitated, the family may be forced to depend on public welfare for a meager subsistence, even though the family income may have been large only a few years before. Whatever the direction of causation, the California survey found that the lowest income group was least prepared to bear the burdens of illness. The proportion of such families who had at least some health insurance was less than one-half as great as it was among the persons in the next higher income group, and less than one-third as great as it was among persons in the group earning $5,000 or more. Moreover, the illnesses in the lowest income group were probably more severe than the illnesses in the other groups, since more hospitalization was reported for the lowest group.[6]

ILLNESS DUE TO ACUTE CONDITIONS

The National Health Survey has followed the established practice of classifying all morbid conditions according to two classes--acute and chronic. An acute condition is an illness or an injury which has lasted less than three months at the time of the interview, and which is not on the list of organic disorders or disabilities that are usually considered chronic because of their long duration (see below).[7] The acute conditions may be subdivided, according to general type, into five categories. Following is the number of millions of cases of acute conditions that occurred in the 1957-58 survey year of the National Health Survey, by type of condition:

Condition	Millions of cases	Rate per 100 persons
Total.....................	437.9	260.1
Infectious and parasitic.......	38.6	22.9
Respiratory....................	284.5	169.0
Digestive......................	24.0	14.3
Injuries.......................	47.6	28.3
All other acute conditions.....	43.1	25.6

6 State of California, Department of Public Health, Health in California, California State Printing Office, 1957, pp. 40-41.

Thus, the average person had 2.6 different attacks due to acute conditions during the year. Respiratory conditions (common colds, influenza, pneumonia, acute bronchitis) accounted for well over one-half of all the acute conditions that had their onset during the year. (The common cold is by far the leading acute source of disabling illness.) Data for each of the major classes of acute conditions, by age and sex, are reported in Table 22-2. Figure 22-3 shows that there is a marked seasonal variation in the incidence of respiratory conditions, but that the other acute conditions fluctuate comparatively little and tend to have a

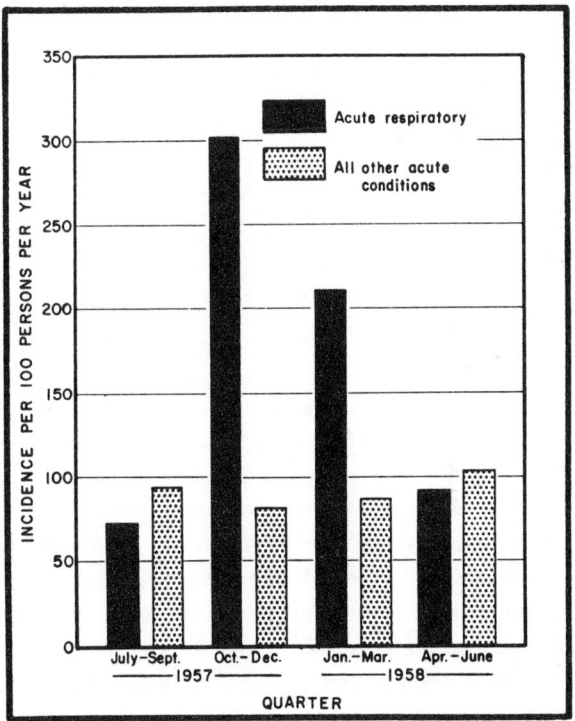

FIGURE 22-3. INCIDENCE OF ACUTE CONDITIONS PER 100 PERSONS PER YEAR BY QUARTER

[7] Minor acute conditions for which a doctor was not consulted, and which caused no days of restricted activity, were arbitrarily excluded from the National Health Survey statistics because they were not sufficiently severe to be reliably reported throughout the population.

Table 22-2.—INDIDENCE OF ACUTE CONDITIONS AND DISABILITY DAYS PER 100 PERSONS PER YEAR BY
CONDITION GROUP, SEX, AND AGE: JULY, 1957-JUNE, 1958

Age, sex, and days of disability	Total acute conditions	Condition group				
		Infectious and parasitic	Respiratory	Digestive	Injuries	All other acute conditions
Both sexes						
All ages............................	260.1	22.9	169.0	14.3	28.3	25.6
Under 5 years........................	403.9	53.5	266.2	23.7	28.7	31.6
5 to 24 years........................	320.6	34.3	203.5	17.5	33.6	31.7
25 to 64 years.......................	202.0	11.5	133.7	9.9	25.4	21.5
65 years and over....................	162.6	2.6	105.4	13.5	23.6	17.3
Male						
All ages............................	247.5	21.8	158.0	13.2	33.9	20.5
Under 5 years........................	405.9	56.2	259.7	20.3	35.7	34.0
5 to 24 years........................	312.1	30.9	191.4	17.7	44.4	27.4
25 to 64 years.......................	178.2	10.3	116.4	8.4	29.5	13.6
65 years and over....................	155.1	1.3	114.1	12.5	14.4	12.7
Female						
All ages............................	272.0	24.0	179.4	15.3	22.9	30.4
Under 5 years........................	401.8	50.7	273.0	27.3	21.5	29.1
5 to 24 years........................	328.9	37.5	215.1	17.2	23.1	35.8
25 to 64 years.......................	224.2	12.7	149.7	11.4	21.5	28.8
65 years and over....................	168.9	3.7	98.1	14.4	31.4	21.1
Disability days per 100 persons[1]						
Restricted activity days..............	...	113.0	696.2	47.0	146.6	139.2
Bed disability days...................	...	53.3	352.3	19.7	42.9	50.4
Work loss days........................	...	33.0	367.1	22.9	113.4	62.2
School loss days......................	...	124.4	565.2	23.9	37.3	37.4

[1]See footnotes to Table 22-1.

Source: U.S. National Health Survey, Report Series B-5, Nov. 1958.

lower incidence in winter than in summer. This is because certain of the infectious diseases tend to reach a seasonal peak in the summer months.

The incidence of acute conditions decreases with increasing age (Table 22-2 and Figure 22-4). The rate for persons aged 65 and over is less than 1/2 that for children under 5 years of age.

Acute respiratory conditions cost the nation 1,172 billion days of restricted activity, 593 million days of bed disability, 219 million days of lost work, and 196 million days of school attendance in the year 1957-58. These figures amount to an average of 1 week of restricted activity, and 3.5 days in bed, for each member of the total population. For each working adult, the cost was 3.7 days of lost work. Inasmuch as acute respiratory disorders are considered preventable conditions, this large volume of illness may be regarded as potentially unnecessary. It may constitute an extensive erosion, year after year, of the health of the population, and, as such, it eventually may contribute to more serious organic disorders.

Perhaps the most important single finding of Table 22-2 is the low rate of incidence of the infectious and parasitic diseases. Not only have these diseases lost their ability to kill the population, but also they no longer infect the population as frequently as they used to. However, they should not be considered "dead." If precautionary measures were relaxed even briefly, any one of them could emerge again as a major source of illness. Also, certain diseases (such as tuberculosis) still have a large new-case rate among particular population groups, even though modern medical practice prevents them from being a major cause of death.

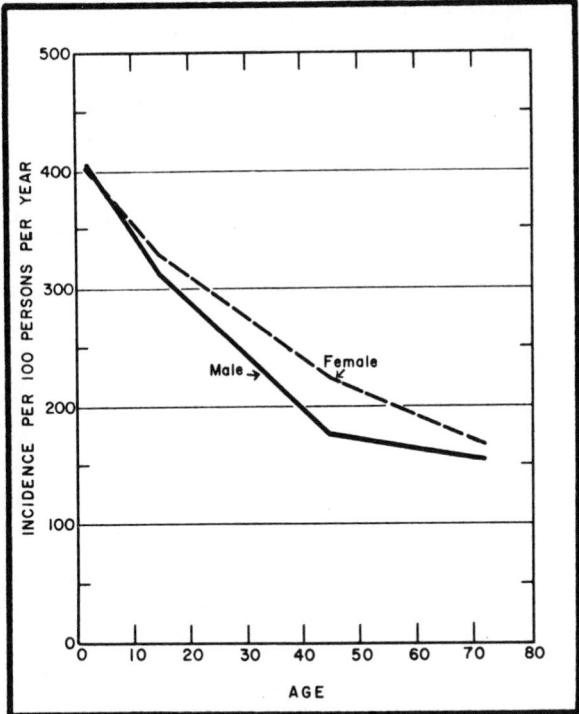

FIGURE 22-4. INCIDENCE OF ACUTE CONDITIONS
PER 100 PERSONS PER YEAR BY SEX AND AGE

Injuries. Injuries are a special class of acute condition, in that they are externally caused and that their control depends more upon non-medical than upon medical action. Table 22-2 reports that from July, 1957, to June, 1958, the rate of injury among the population was 28 injuries per 100 persons, causing 1.5 days of restricted activity and 0.4 bed-days per person. Injuries cost working persons an average of 1.1 day of employment each. In a special report concerning the last half of 1957, the National Health Survey estimated that motor vehicle accidents accounted for 9.8 percent of the total injuries received. Home accidents caused 40.3 percent of all injuries; 16.7 percent of injuries were work-connected, and 33.1 percent occurred in other types of accidents or in non-accidental situations.[8] As Table 22-2 reports, the

injury rate is almost 50 percent higher for males than for females. Among males it is highest during youth, and decreases with increasing age. Females have a reverse age pattern: their injury rate remains low until about age 65, and then increases substantially.

ILLNESS DUE TO CHRONIC CONDITIONS

Chronic conditions are long-term illnesses and illnesses of an organic or functional nature. Among the most common of these disorders are the following:

Asthma or hay fever
Tuberculosis
Chronic bronchitis
Repeated attacks of sinus trouble
Rheumatic fever
Hardening of the arteries
High blood pressure
Heart trouble
Stroke
Trouble with varicose veins
Hemorrhoids or piles
Chronic gallbladder or liver trouble
Stomach ulcer
Any other chronic stomach trouble
Kidney stones or chronic kidney trouble
Arthritis or rheumatism
Prostate trouble
Diabetes
Thyroid trouble or goiter
Any allergy
Epilepsy
Mental or nervous trouble
Tumor or cancer, cyst or growth
Chronic skin trouble
Hernia or rupture

The following impairments are also considered chronic disorders:

Deafness or serious trouble with hearing
Serious trouble with seeing, even with glasses
Conditions present since birth, such as cleft palate or club foot
Stammering or other trouble with speech
Missing fingers, hand, or arm
Missing toes, foot, or leg

[8] Health statistics from the National Health Survey, Report B-3, "Preliminary Report on Number of Persons Injured, July-December, 1957," U. S. Public Health Service, 1958.

Cerebral palsy

Paralysis of any kind

Repeated trouble with back or spine

Any permanent stiffness or deformity of the
foot, leg, fingers, arm, or back

As of January 1, 1959, no data concerning the prevalence of chronic disorders had been published by the Public Health Survey. However, Table 22-3 reports, from this survey, preliminary data concerning the number of days of disability associated with each of five different chronic conditions, per 100 persons per year. Although the data in this table are not additive (a person may suffer restricted activity as a result of having two or more disorders simultaneously), the chronic disorders appear to account for a slightly greater number of restricted-activity days, for two more bed-disability days, and for slightly more work-loss days than do the acute disorders. Disorders of the circulatory system (heart disease, hypertension, etc.) are the largest single source of disability among the chronic disorders; arthritis and rheumatism are in second place. Table 22-3 is notably deficient in its lack of data about illness from cancer.

5 reports estimated rates of the incidence of cancer, by age and sex, for 10 urban areas in the United States. From this figure it is evident that the rate of cancer illness is moderately low at the younger ages, that it takes a sharp upward turn between the ages of 35 and 50, and then climbs steadily and steeply with increasing age. The National Cancer Institute estimates that an average male born in 1950 has a 1 in 5 chance of eventually developing cancer, and a 1 in 8 chance of eventually dying from it. The corresponding probabilities for women are 1 in 4 and 1 in 7. The Institute also reports studies from Iowa, Connecticut, and New York, which show that cancer illness has a much higher incidence rate in urban than in rural areas. This differential holds not only for cancer of the respiratory system (as associated with air pollution), but for almost all other major cancer sites. The exact cause of this urban-rural differential is not known, as yet. In their survey of 10 urban areas, Dorn and Cutler also discovered evidence of regional differences.[10] For example, cancer of the digestive system had higher rates in the North than in the South, whereas cancer of the skin had much higher rates in the South and the

Table 22-3.—NUMBER OF DAYS OF DISABILITY ASSOCIATED WITH CHRONIC CONDITIONS PER 100 PERSONS PER YEAR BY CONDITION GROUP: UNITED STATES, JULY, 1957-JUNE, 1958

Chronic condition group	Restricted-activity days	Bed-disability days	Work-loss days	School-loss days
Circulatory..	287.6	98.9	116.2	6.0
Digestive...	129.2	47.6	91.3	1.7
Arthritis and rheumatism.........................	151.5	39.9	52.0	...
Impairments and other effects of injuries.........	95.5	22.2	65.8	3.8
Other impairments................................	135.8	45.0	54.0	5.7
All other chronic conditions.....................	582.5	200.1	272.9	74.1

Source: U.S. National Health Survey, Report Series B-5, Nov. 1958.
Note: See footnotes to Table 22-1.

A recent publication prepared by the Biometry Branch of the National Cancer Institute, U. S. Public Health Service, provides some additional facts about illness from this disease.[9] Figure 22-

West than in the North. Chances of surviving cancer illness are closely related to the site affected, and to whether or not diagnosis is made early while the cancer is still localized. Persons affected with cancer of the esophagus, stomach, or lung have poor survival prospects, whereas per-

---

[9] For documentation of this summary, the reader is referred to "The Extent of Cancer Illness in the United States," by the Biometry Branch of the National Cancer Institute, Public Health Census Publication, No. 547, 1958.

---

[10] See source of data for Table 22-5.

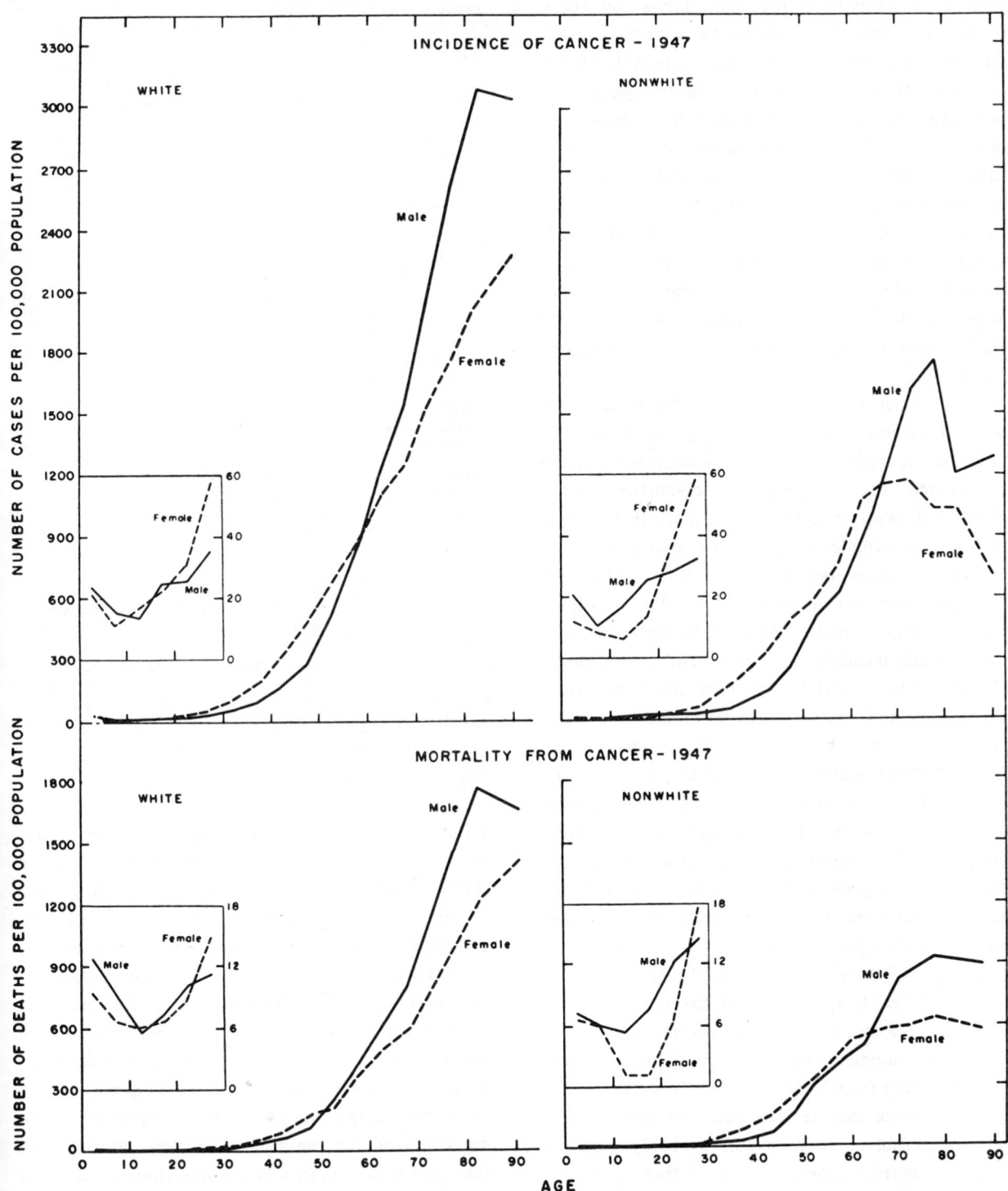

FIGURE 22-5. CANCER INCIDENCE AND MORTALITY RATES, BY AGE, SEX, AND RACE, 1947

sons with cancer of the skin, large intestine, breast, or body of the uterus have much brighter survival prospects. When cancer is detected while it is still localized, the survival prospects are only moderately poorer than the prospects of normal life expectancy. Persons who survive cancer illness at one site seem to have only a slightly greater than average propensity to develop a second cancer at another site. Hence, a nationwide program leading to early detection could add materially to the number of years of survival of persons who develop cancer illness, and thus could lead to further moderate increases in life expectancy.

An illustration of the probable differential impact of chronic illness on the population is provided by Table 22-4, which presents indexes of the prevalence and the extent of disability due to chronic illness, as measured by a clinical examination of a sample of the population of Baltimore, Maryland. These data show that chronic illness is most prevalent among persons 65 and over, that it affects women somewhat more often than men, that the nonwhite population has more chronic ailments but suffers less disability from them than the white population, and that chronic ailments are most prevalent among the lowest income groups.

The Baltimore study found that 65 percent of the sample of persons examined had a chronic ailment of some kind, although it was often mild and non-disabling. The sample group had an average of 1.6 conditions per person. This is a much higher rate of prevalence than the rates that have been found by survey-interview methods.

Chronic ailments are the major focus of the attention of health specialists at the present time. Since the leading causes of death are chronic in nature, the future course of the death rate depends on the extent to which the incidence and severity of these diseases can be lessened. Progress in the field of chronic disorders will probably take the form of retarding the progress of these diseases after their initial onset, and of limiting the extent of the disability they cause, rather than complete elimination of the disorders and their effects. The chronic diseases are especially important for ad-

Table 22-4.—DIFFERENTIAL IMPACT OF CHRONIC DISEASE UPON THE POPULATION: RELATIVE PREVALENCE OF CHRONIC DISEASE AMONG A CROSS-SECTION OF BALTIMORE POPULATION GIVEN CLINICAL SCREENING EXAMINATIONS

Age, sex, color, and income	Differential prevalence of chronic illness[1]	Differential limitation of daily living[2]
Total...............	100	100
Age		
Under 15 years.........	26	28
15 to 34 years.........	77	26
35 to 64 years.........	140	95
65 years and over......	258	695
Sex		
Male..................	92	49
Female................	107	144
Color		
White.................	99	116
Nonwhite..............	103	58
Annual family income		
Under $2,000..........	115	191
$2,000 to $3,999......	102	65
$4,000 to $5,999......	97	58
$6,000 and over.......	91	165

[1]Differential is the ratio of the rate per 1,000 persons in the specific group divided by the average rate per 1,000 persons for all groups combined, multiplied by 100.
[2]Differential is the percentage of the specific groups whose activities and daily living are limited by a chronic disease, divided by the corresponding percentage for all groups combined.

Source: Commission on Chronic Illness, Chronic Illness in a Large City, Harvard University Press, 1957.

ditional reasons. Because of their long-term nature and their tendency to permanently handicap their victims, they often have a devastating economic effect on a family. Diseases of this type can wipe out a lifetime's savings, as well as remove the source of the family's economic support. The patient who is afflicted with a chronic disorder often experiences mental depression, and develops psychological problems resulting from prolonged illness, from loss of earning power, and from the regimen of reduced activity which is often required for the rest of his life. Children in the family of a victim of chronic illness may lose their opportunity to attend college; wives may ruin their own health while working and caring for a family whose male breadwinner is incapacitated, and older children may be called on to spend a large percentage of their income and savings for the prolonged care, either at home or in an institution, of an elderly parent affected by a chronic disease. Since these diseases usually cannot be traced to any particular cause, and are often quite unrelated to the degree of preventative medical care a person has had throughout his life, and because they affect many "innocent bystanders" such as children and other relatives, they are coming more and more to be looked upon as "acts of God" from the results of which the victims and their dependents should be protected by a nation-wide program of insurance or prepaid medical care. After he recovers from a chronic illness, a person often needs to be retrained for a different kind of work, and he then encounters the problem of trying to find suitable employment in an economy which regularly exercises economic discrimination against the older worker and the handicapped worker. This situation is leading to enlarged programs for rehabilitating the victims of these diseases in order that they may be able to support themselves at least partially, instead of becoming objects of public charity.

CONCLUSION

It is regrettable that data are not yet available from the National Health Survey concerning the incidence and prevalence of each of the specific acute and chronic disorders, by age, sex, color, socio-economic characteristics, and place of residence. Sufficient evidence has been assembled and presented, however, to show that there is much variation among the various population groups with respect to the extent and severity of illness. Unfortunately, the method of collecting the data and the sampling procedures used in other studies affect the results so greatly that it is not possible to state reliably, as yet, exactly how large these differentials are. Exact measurements, especially for chronic disorders, probably can never be obtained by means of survey interviews conducted by nonmedical interviewers. The methods used in such surveys usually result in the reporting of only the most serious or the most advanced chronic ailments. The available data suggest that much illness is avoidable; therefore, a large amount of "excess morbidity" and unnecessary suffering could be avoided if every ill person could afford the medical service his condition calls for, and the treatment which science has developed for his particular disorder. The data also suggests that a person's state of health is an important factor in determining his behavior in many aspects of his life. It is to be hoped that greater attention will be paid in the near future to longitudinal studies of morbidity, in which the illness history of an entire life can be investigated. Also, surveys of sickness need to give much more attention to terminal illness, and to the illness events immediately preceding it. By concentrating on illnesses among the noninstitutional population, survey methods are furnishing comparatively little information concerning death-producing morbidity and the circumstances surrounding it. Other researchers, however, are making intensive studies in this latter area, and eventually their methods may produce data that will be more helpful in the further reduction of mortality than the household-survey approach seems to be.

Chapter 23

RELIGIOUS AFFILIATION

Most sociologists consider religious affiliation a factor of paramount importance in explaining many aspects of human behavior. Like the factors of educational attainment, occupation, and income, it is an axis around which much of a person's life is oriented. Even for the purposes of formal demography, a knowledge of the religious affiliations of the population is important, since it helps to explain the level and trend of fertility, the willingness of some persons to migrate to particular localities, etc. Many nations of the world collect statistics concerning religious affiliation, and report them in full detail as a part of the regular official census.[1] The United States, unfortunately, is not one of those nations.[2]

In March of 1957, the U. S. Bureau of the Census included the question, "What is your religion?" on its monthly Current Population Survey. The Census wanted to determine the attitude of the public toward answering such a question, and also to experiment with the wording in case the question should become an item on the 1960 census. Only a negligible number refused to answer, and much

[*] The author acknowledges with pleasure the assistance of Jacob J. Feldman, Senior Study Director, National Opinion Research Center, in the preparation of materials for this chapter. As described below, a majority of the data presented here was obtained through special retabulations, made according to the writer's specifications, of data collected on surveys which Mr. Feldman designed. Mr. Feldman wrote tabulation instructions, and kindly reviewed the manuscript of this chapter.

[1] "Among the countries with 500,000 or more inhabitants for which censuses have been published in recent years...about half have included at least one question on religion. By continental divisions, these totaled seven in North America, three in South America, twelve in Europe (including all the German governments as one), sixteen in Africa, and two in Oceania." Dorothy Good, "Questions on Religion in the United States Census," Population Index, January, 1959.

[2] Despite strong appeals from a wide array of analysts and administrators (including leaders of religious groups), a question on religious affiliation has never been included in the regular decennial census enumerations. For example, the American Sociological Society, the Census Users Advisory Committee (representing more than 75 professional organizations), and the Population Association of America supported the asking of a question on religious affiliation in the 1960 census. The Bureau of the Census has received strong representation directly and indirectly, through purse-string-holding congressmen, not to include questions on religion in its enumerations. It has been held by some that to ask a census question on religious affiliation would violate those constitutional rights of the citizen which assure freedom of religious belief. A small minority has feared that, at some future date, census records showing religious affiliation could be used as a weapon against persons belonging to particular religious groups. This is a fallacious argument. The religious affiliation of almost every citizen, or of his family, is already recorded or indicated in a number of different places. The titles of the ministers, priests, and rabbis who perform wedding ceremonies, the names of cemeteries and funeral directors on death certificates, the membership registers of churches, census records showing the birthplace of parents, the records of grammar schools, high schools, and colleges--even military and veterans' records--contain information that could be used to determine religious affiliation. Finally, if a dictator were abroad in the land, he probably would not rely on out-of-date census records, but would call for a new and compulsory registration involving severe penalties for noncompliance or falsification. This is what happened in Germany before World War II.

valuable information was obtained concerning the general religious affiliation of the population. Sample surveys made by private research organizations routinely ask questions concerning religion; their experience has been that it is one of the easiest questions to enumerate, and causes no more anxiety or resentment than questions on such matters as age or marital status. A question on religious affiliation will not appear in the 1960 census, but its absence is due to policy considerations, not technical problems.

This brief chapter is an attempt to document the proposition that much scientific knowledge would be gained by including a question on religious affiliation once each year in the sample surveys, and also in the decennial census.[3] This chapter is based on the fraction of the results of the Census survey of March, 1957 that was released, and on a tabulation of the data concerning religious affiliation that were collected by the National Opinion Research Center of the University of Chicago in two of its recent nationwide surveys.[4]

CENSUS MATERIALS ON RELIGION:
NUMBER AND DISTRIBUTION

Table 23-1 and Figure 23-1 show the religious composition of the population. Summarized in its

_____

[3] This could be done at no additional cost, by substituting the question on religious affiliation for the question on veterans' status, which yielded such unreliable information at the 1950 census that detailed tabulations were not published.

[4] In February, 1958, the Bureau of the Census published a report, "Religion Reported by the Civilian Population of the United States: March, 1957," Current Population Reports, Series P-20, No. 79. These data furnish much of the material for this chapter. The release stated: "This is the first report containing nationwide statistics on religion of the population, based on data collected from individuals by the Bureau of the Census... Other reports presenting results of this survey are being prepared." When the supplementary reports of the Census Bureau are released, they will replace the NORC tabulations presented in this chapter, which were assembled only because the additional reports mentioned in the first census report had not yet been made available.

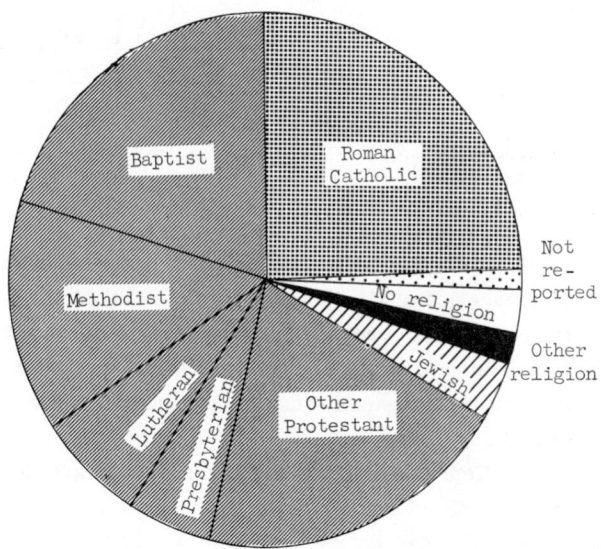

FIGURE 23-1. RELIGION REPORTED BY PERSONS 14 YEARS OLD AND OVER: CIVILIAN POPULATION, MARCH, 1957

Source: Current Population Reports, Series P-20, No. 79, Table 1, Feb. 1958.

broadest terms, the religious affiliation of persons 14 years old and over is as follows:

Religion	Total	White	Nonwhite
Total.............	100.0	100.0	100.0
Protestant..........	66.2	63.9	87.5
Roman Catholic.......	25.7	27.9	6.5
Jewish..............	3.2	3.6	...
Other religion.......	1.3	1.2	1.5
No religion..........	2.7	2.5	3.5
No information.......	0.9	0.9	1.0'

Thus, two of every three persons 14 years of age or older identifies himself with one of the Protestant denominations, while about one in four reports himself as a Roman Catholic. The Jewish group is much smaller; only about one person in 31 in the population is Jewish. Almost all of the population (96.4 percent) claimed some religious affiliation; only 2.7 percent reported themselves as having no religion.

Within the Protestant class, the Bureau of the Census identified four major denominations:

	Percent of population 14 and over		
	Total	White	Nonwhite
Baptist.........	19.7	15.2	60.7
Lutheran........	7.1	7.8	0.2
Methodist.......	14.0	13.7	17.3
Presbyterian....	5.6	6.2	0.9
Other Protestant	19.8	21.1	8.5

This shows that about one-third of the population (and one-half of all Protestants) is either Methodist or Baptist, one-eighth is either Lutheran or Presbyterian, while about one-fifth belongs to the many dozens of smaller denominations or hundreds of sects.

The Census Bureau's inquiry carefully avoided mention of membership, so that the statistics of Table 23-1 can be used only as a rough guide to membership. Membership statistics, as compiled from records of the individual religious organizations by the National Council of the Churches of Christ in the United States of America, are summarized in Table 23-2. From this table certain items of additional information, noted below, can be obtained. Within each of the major Protestant groups (Baptist, Methodist, etc.) there are numerous subgroupings. Seven religious groups, in addition to the "big four" named above, claim 1 million or more members. They are:

Christ Unity Science Church ("Christian Science")

Churches of Christ

Congregational Christian Churches ("Christian Church")

Disciples of Christ

Greek Archdiocese of North and South America ("Greek Orthodox")

Latter Day Saints ("Mormon")

Protestant Episcopal Church ("Episcopal")

The largest remaining denominations (those containing less than 1 million but as many as 100,000 members) are as follows:

Seventh-Day Adventist

Assemblies of God

Church of the Brethren

Churches of God

Church of God in Christ

Church of the Nazarene

Evangelical and Reformed Church

Evangelical United Brethren Church

International Church of the Foursquare Gospel

Jehovah's Witnesses

Pentecostal bodies

Reformed bodies

Salvation Army

Table 23-1.—RELIGION REPORTED FOR PERSONS 14 YEARS OLD AND OVER, BY COLOR AND SEX, FOR THE UNITED STATES: CIVILIAN POPULATION, MARCH 1957

(In this report, the "civilian population" includes about 809,000 members of the Armed Forces living off post or with their families on post, but excludes all other members of the Armed Forces. Four largest Protestant groups shown separately. Percent not shown where less than 0.1.)

Religion	Total (000)	White (000)		Nonwhite (000)		Percent distribution					
		Male	Female	Male	Female	Total	White		Nonwhite		Percent non-white
							Male	Female	Male	Female	
Total, 14 years and over........	119,333	51,791	55,570	5,679	6,293	100.0	100.0	100.0	100.0	100.0	100.0
Protestant.........	78,952	32,320	36,155	4,851	5,626	66.2	62.4	65.1	85.4	89.4	13.3
Baptist..........	23,525	7,822	8,450	3,354	3,899	19.7	15.1	15.2	59.1	62.0	30.8
Lutheran.........	8,417	4,084	4,301	17	15	7.1	7.9	7.7	0.3	0.2	0.4
Methodist........	16,676	6,788	7,821	968	1,099	14.0	13.1	14.1	17.0	17.5	12.4
Presbyterian......	6,656	3,000	3,549	57	50	5.6	5.8	6.4	1.0	0.8	1.6
Other Protestant..	23,678	10,626	12,034	455	563	19.8	20.5	21.7	8.0	8.9	4.3
Roman Catholic......	30,669	14,396	15,499	361	413	25.7	27.8	27.9	6.4	6.6	2.5
Jewish.............	3,868	1,860	1,999	1	8	3.2	3.6	3.6	...	0.1	0.2
Other religion......	1,545	688	676	88	93	1.3	1.3	1.2	1.5	1.5	11.7
No religion.........	3,195	2,051	730	306	108	2.7	4.0	1.3	5.4	1.7	13.0
Religion not rept...	1,104	476	511	72	45	0.9	0.9	0.9	1.3	0.7	11.5

Table 23-2.—RELIGIOUS BODIES--NUMBER OF CHURCHES AND MEMBERSHIP: 1956

Religious body	Number of churches reported	Church membership
Total..	308,647	103,224,954
Bodies with membership of 50,000 or over.................................	289,446	101,627,542
Adventist Bodies: Seventh-day Adventists....................	2,880	283,140
Apostolic Overcoming Holy Church of God....................	300	75,000
Assemblies of God......................................	7,916	470,361
Baptist Bodies:		
American Baptist Convention........................	6,372	1,528,210
Southern Baptist Convention........................	30,797	8,700,481
National Baptist Convention, U.S.A., Ind............	25,603	4,557,416
National Baptist Convention of America..............	11,398	2,668,799
American Baptist Association........................	3,000	600,000
Baptist General Conference of America...............	441	59,304
Conservative Baptist Association of America..........	1,000	250,000
Free Will Baptists..................................	2,054	163,619
General Association of Regular Baptist Churches......	759	129,100
General Baptists....................................	722	55,300
National Baptist Evangelical Life and Soul Saving Assembly of U.S.A.......................................	264	57,674
National Primitive Baptist Convention of the U.S.A.............	1,019	80,000
North American Baptist Association..................	1,778	261,202
Primitive Baptists..................................	1,000	72,000
United Baptists....................................	568	63,641
United Free Will Baptist Church....................	836	100,000
Brethren (German Baptist): Church of the Brethren..............	1,052	197,290
Buddhist Churches of America...........................	48	[2]63,000
Christ Unity Science Church............................	4,481	1,581,286
Christian and Missionary Alliance......................	954	[2]57,109
Churches of God:		
Church of God (Cleveland, Tenn.)...................	2,939	147,929
Church of God (Anderson, Ind.).....................	2,195	127,395
The Church of God.................................	1,818	70,941
Church of God in Christ................................	3,500	360,428
Church of the Nazarene.................................	4,169	277,618
Churches of Christ.....................................	16,250	1,700,000
Congregational Christian Churches......................	5,549	1,379,394
Disciples of Christ, International Convention..........	7,982	1,922,484
Eastern Churches:		
American Carpatho-Russian Orthodox Greek Catholic Church.........	70	100,000
Armenian Apostolic Church of America...............	61	102,900
Greek Archdiocese of North and South America.......	378	1,150,000
Romanian Orthodox Episcopate of America............	51	50,000
The Russian Orthodox Church Outside Russia.........	81	[3]55,000
The Russian Orthodox Greek Catholic Church of America.............	359	760,000
Serbian Eastern Orthodox Church....................	53	100,000
Syrian Antiochian Orthodox Church..................	80	110,000
Ukrainian Orthodox Church of U.S.A.................	91	83,000
Evangelical and Reformed Church........................	2,736	784,270
Evangelical Mission Covenant Church of America........	493	55,311
Evangelical United Brethren Church.....................	4,354	742,537
Federated Churches....................................	508	88,411
Friends: Five Years Meeting of Friends................	486	73,095
Independent Fundamental Churches of America............	400	[4]65,000
International Church of the Foursquare Gospel.........	692	110,568
Jehovah's witnesses....................................	3,597	189,517
Jewish Congregations..................................	4,079	5,500,000
Latter-day Saints:		
Church of Jesus Christ of Latter-Day Saints........	2,869	1,289,581
Reorganized Church of Jesus Christ of Latter-day Saints...........	850	142,480

Table 23-2.—RELIGIOUS BODIES--NUMBER OF CHURCHES AND MEMBERSHIP: 1956—Continued.

Religious body	Number of churches reported	Church membership
Bodies with membership of 50,000 or over—Continued		
Lutheran:		
Lutheran Synodical Conference of N.A.:		
Lutheran Church, Missouri Synod	4,898	2,076,550
Evangelical Lutheran Joint Synod of Wisconsin and other States	858	339,106
American Lutheran Church	1,938	871,446
Augustana Evangelical Lutheran Church	1,177	549,604
Evangelical Lutheran Church	2,468	1,021,058
Lutheran Free Church	360	78,155
United Evangelical Lutheran Church	169	[1]54,098
United Lutheran Church in America	4,050	2,174,500
Mennonite Bodies: Mennonite Church	468	70,513
Methodist Bodies:		
African Methodist Episcopal Church	5,878	1,166,301
African Methodist Episcopal Zion Church	3,083	761,000
Christian Methodist Episcopal Church	2,469	392,167
Free Methodist Church of North America	1,225	54,014
The Methodist Church	39,845	9,422,893
Moravian Bodies: Moravian Church in America (Unitas Fratrum)	159	56,449
Old Catholic Churches: North American Old Roman Catholic Church	62	84,142
Pentecostal Assemblies:		
Pentecostal Assemblies of the World, Inc	395	60,000
Pentecostal Church of God of America, Inc	900	103,500
United Pentecostal Church, Inc	1,500	125,000
Polish National Catholic Church of America	157	250,000
Presbyterian Bodies:		
Cumberland Presbyterian Church	997	85,651
Presbyterian Church in the U.S	3,875	829,570
Presbyterian Church in the U.S.A	8,329	2,717,320
United Presbyterian Church of N.A	833	251,344
Protestant Episcopal Church	6,708	2,852,965
Reformed Bodies:		
Christian Reformed Church	495	211,454
Reformed Church in America	845	208,999
Roman Catholic Church	21,121	34,563,851
Salvation Army	1,282	247,964
Spiritualists: International General Assembly of Spiritualists	209	164,072
Unitarian Churches	373	101,549
Universalist Church of America	388	70,516
Bodies with membership of less then 50,000	19,201	1,597,412

[1]1955 data.
[2]1954 data.
[3]1951 data.
[4]1946 data.

Source: National Council of the Churches of Christ in the United States of America: Yearbook of American Churches, September 1957, as reported in Statistical Abstract of the United States, 1958.

Spiritualist

Unitarian

These listings demonstrate that the one-fifth reported above as "Other Protestant" is divided into many small parts. As Table 23-2 indicates, many of the small "splinter" denominations and sects consist of only a few hundred or, in some cases, a few dozen people. The Negro "storefront" church, a common sight in large cities, is the most extreme example of the minute subdivision under Protestantism.

Distribution of Religious Groups. The religious composition of the population of the four census regions is reported in Table 23-3; the composition

Table 23-3.—REGION OF RESIDENCE OF PERSONS 14 YEARS OLD AND OVER, BY RELIGION REPORTED: CIVILIAN POPULATION, MARCH 1957

Religion	United States (000)	Northeast (000)	North Central (000)	South (000)	West (000)
Total, 14 years old and over............	119,333	31,264	34,825	36,551	16,693
Protestant................................	78,952	13,225	24,025	30,249	11,453
White..................................	68,475	11,675	21,978	24,037	10,785
Nonwhite...............................	10,477	1,550	2,047	6,212	668
Roman Catholic............................	30,669	14,106	8,587	4,254	3,722
Jewish....................................	3,868	2,671	460	299	438
Other religion...........................	1,545	647	410	269	219
No religion..............................	3,195	358	1,024	1,108	705
Religion not reported....................	1,104	257	319	372	156
PERCENT BY RELIGION					
Total, 14 years old and over............	100.0	100.0	100.0	100.0	100.0
Protestant................................	66.2	42.3	69.0	82.8	68.6
White..................................	57.4	37.3	63.1	65.8	64.6
Nonwhite...............................	8.8	5.0	5.9	17.0	4.0
Roman Catholic............................	25.7	45.1	24.7	11.6	22.3
Jewish....................................	3.2	8.5	1.3	0.8	2.6
Other religion...........................	1.3	2.1	1.2	0.7	1.3
No religion..............................	2.7	1.1	2.9	3.0	4.2
Religion not reported....................	0.9	0.8	0.9	1.0	0.9
PERCENT BY RESIDENCE					
Total, 14 years old and over............	100.0	26.2	29.2	30.6	14.0
Protestant................................	100.0	16.8	30.4	38.3	14.5
White..................................	100.0	17.1	32.1	35.1	15.8
Nonwhite...............................	100.0	14.8	19.5	59.3	6.4
Roman Catholic............................	100.0	46.0	28.0	13.9	12.1
Jewish....................................	100.0	69.1	11.9	7.7	11.3
Other religion...........................	100.0	41.9	26.5	17.4	14.2
No religion..............................	100.0	11.2	32.1	34.7	22.1
Religion not reported....................	100.0	23.3	28.9	33.7	14.1

by urban and rural areas is shown in Table 23-4. From the information in these tables, it may be concluded that:

(a) The South is strongly Protestant in its religious affiliation. Only 12 percent of the South's population is Roman Catholic, and less than 1 percent is Jewish.

(b) Roman Catholics are heavily concentrated in the Northeastern states. In the population of the North Central states and the West, they constitute just about the same proportion as they do of the nation's total population. Roman Catholics are predominantly urban; they are concentrated in and about large cities, and are comparatively scarce in rural areas.

(c) Persons of Jewish religion are highly concentrated in Northeastern states and in large cities. There are almost no Jewish farmers, and very few Jewish residents of rural-nonfarm areas.

(d) The "Other Religion" category has a distribution pattern roughly similar to that of the Roman Catholics. Persons whose religious belief is other than Protestant, Catholic, or Jewish are somewhat concentrated in the Northeast and in large urban centers. Because of its large Oriental population, the West also has a slight concentration of persons in the "Other Religion" category.

POPULATION CHARACTERISTICS OF RELIGIOUS GROUPS: CENSUS MATERIALS

Sex Composition (Table 23-1). A slightly higher percentage of men than of women claim no religion. Among men and women who do identify

Table 23-4.—URBAN-RURAL RESIDENCE OF PERSONS 14 YEARS OLD AND OVER, BY RELIGION REPORTED, FOR THE UNITED STATES: CIVILIAN POPULATION, MARCH 1957

| Religion | United States | Urban | | | Rural nonfarm | Rural farm |
		Total	Urbanized areas of 25,000 or more	Other urban		
PERCENT BY RESIDENCE						
Total, 14 years old and over..........	100.0	63.9	36.6	27.3	24.4	11.7
Protestant................................	100.0	56.6	27.2	29.5	28.7	14.7
White..................................	100.0	55.2	24.5	30.7	30.1	14.7
Nonwhite...............................	100.0	66.1	44.6	21.6	19.3	14.5
Roman Catholic...........................	100.0	78.8	53.9	24.9	15.8	5.4
Jewish...................................	100.0	96.1	87.4	8.7	3.6	0.2
Other religion...........................	100.0	77.4	52.9	24.5	14.9	7.7
No religion..............................	100.0	54.2	29.5	24.7	31.3	14.5
Religion not reported....................	100.0	68.2	49.5	18.7	23.4	8.4

themselves with a religious group, there is almost no difference between the sexes with respect to religious affiliation, although a slightly higher percentage of women than of men are members of Protestant denominations. This sex imbalance is greatest in the Methodist and the "Other Protestant" churches.

Color Composition (Table 23-1). The nonwhite population is almost exclusively Protestant (87.5 percent). Only about one nonwhite person in 16 is a Roman Catholic. More than 60 percent of the nonwhite population belongs to one denomination, the Baptist, and an additional 17 percent belongs to the Methodist denomination. (Approximately 31 percent of all Baptists are nonwhite.) Hence, more than 3/4 of all nonwhites belong to these two denominations. A very small percentage of the membership of the Lutheran, Presbyterian, Roman Catholic, and Jewish groups is nonwhite. The remaining nonwhite population tends to belong to one of the many minor sects or small denominations. Nonwhite males and females both are more inclined than is the white population to report that they have no religion.

Age Composition. Inasmuch as almost all of the population reported one religion or another, any differences between religious groups with respect to age composition must be due entirely to the operation of basic demographic processes--fertility, mortality, immigration--within the groups. (As noted below, there is comparatively little evidence that persons change their religious affiliation after they reach maturity.) Assuming that mortality has only a minor differentiating effect, being roughly the same in all groups (with the possible exception of nonwhite Protestants), fertility and immigration seem the logical factors by means of which to explain age differences. An examination of Table 23-5 shows that the Roman Catholic and the nonwhite Protestant groups contain disproportionately large numbers of persons aged 14 to 34, in comparison with the general population. This situation is due to the higher fertility of these groups. In the case of Roman Catholics, it may also be due partially to immigration, for there has been a large immigration of Puerto Rican and Mexican families to the United States in recent years. (On the other hand, the presence in the population of many elderly Italian and Polish immigrants who arrived in the United States shortly after the turn of the century helps to account for the fact that there is a larger percentage of Catholics than of nonwhite Protestants in the age group 65 and over.)

Religion of Married Partners. Husbands and wives tend to belong to the same religious groups. Considering only three major religious divisions, the Protestant, the Roman Catholic, and the Jewish, the census survey showed the following percentages:

Table 23-5.—AGE OF PERSONS 14 YEARS OLD AND OVER, BY RELIGION REPORTED, FOR THE UNITED STATES: CIVILIAN POPULATION, MARCH 1957

Religion	Total 14 years and over (000)	14 to 19 years (000)	20 to 24 years (000)	25 to 34 years (000)	35 to 44 years (000)	45 to 64 years (000)	65 years and over (000)	Median age (years)
Total......................	119,333	13,960	9,743	23,437	23,113	34,399	14,681	40.4
Protestant..................	78,952	9,334	6,332	15,188	14,919	22,907	10,272	40.8
White....................	68,475	7,850	5,288	12,916	12,899	20,181	9,341	41.3
Nonwhite.................	10,477	1,484	1,044	2,272	2,020	2,726	931	37.2
Roman Catholic..............	30,669	3,707	2,675	6,555	6,407	8,266	3,059	38.7
Jewish......................	3,868	350	233	660	729	1,393	503	44.5
Other religion and not reported.....	2,649	280	209	424	482	847	407	43.5
No religion.................	3,195	289	294	610	576	986	440	42.0
PERCENT BY AGE								
Total......................	100.0	11.7	8.2	19.6	19.4	28.8	12.3	...
Protestant..................	100.0	11.8	8.0	19.2	18.9	29.0	13.0	...
White....................	100.0	11.5	7.7	18.9	18.8	29.5	13.6	...
Nonwhite.................	100.0	14.2	10.0	21.7	19.3	26.0	8.9	...
Roman Catholic..............	100.0	12.1	8.7	21.4	20.9	27.0	10.0	...
Jewish......................	100.0	9.0	6.0	17.1	18.8	36.0	13.0	...
Other religion and not reported.....	100.0	10.6	7.9	16.0	18.2	32.0	15.4	...
No religion.................	100.0	9.0	9.2	19.1	18.0	30.9	13.8	...

Religion	Percentage of married couples
Husband and wife in the same major religious group..........	93.6
Husband and wife in different major religious groups.........	6.4

Protestant Intermarriage. Where at least one spouse is Protestant, the census reports the following distribution for the religion of the other spouse:

	Percent
Total...............................	100.0
Protestant (both spouses Protestant)..	91.4
Roman Catholic.......................	8.4
Jewish...............................	0.2

Thus, approximately 1 married Protestant in 12 currently has a religion different from that of his spouse.

Catholic Intermarriage. In families where one spouse is Roman Catholic, the religion of the other spouse is as follows:

	Percent
Total............................	100.0
Roman Catholic (both spouses Catholic)	78.5
Protestant...........................	21.2
Jewish...............................	0.4

Thus, a higher percentage of Catholics than of Protestants have married across religious lines.

Jewish Intermarriage. In families where one spouse is Jewish, the religion of the other spouse is as follows:

	Percent
Total...............................	100.0
Jewish (both spouses Jewish).........	92.8
Protestant...........................	4.2
Roman Catholic.......................	3.0

The Jewish group seems to be more endogamous than either of the other two groups. Thus, on an absolute basis, Roman Catholics are considerably more exogamous than Protestant or Jewish persons. This characteristic seems to be due largely to the fact that a majority of their potential mates are non-Catholic. On a relative basis, taking into account the difference in the number of potential mates of their own religions, and of religious affiliations, Catholics and Protestants tend to marry outside their group to about the same general extent, while out-marriage is much less frequent among Jewish persons.

FERTILITY OF RELIGIOUS GROUPS: CENSUS MATERIALS

Demographers have long been interested in the differences between religious groups with respect to fertility, because of the different attitudes toward family size and family planning that are expressed or implied by the ideologies of the various groups. Table 23-6 reports measures of the fertility of each of the leading religious groups, in terms of the number of children ever born per 1,000 women of each group who are married and living with the husbands. Data are reported separately for women still in the childbearing ages (15 to 44), standardized for age, and for women past the ages of fertility (45 years old and over).

Comparison of these measures with the corresponding measures for earlier periods of American history, and with those of other nations that have high fertility (Chapter 12) makes it very obvious that no one of the religious groups is subject to uncontrolled fertility. The practices of family planning and family limitation have evidently become widely diffused throughout the population. Although the fertility of every religious group is above the replacement level, no group is characterized by rates of children ever born that imply an average of 5 or 6 children per married woman, an average which is typical of high fertility groups. Thus, fertility control is a widely-accomplished fact throughout all major American religious groups.

Baptists are the most fertile group; their standardized measures of fertility are 9 to 11 percent above the national average. A part of this differential is due to the fact that about one-third of the Baptists are Negroes; the fertility of Negroes is 40 percent higher than that of whites, so it boosts the average. In addition, a large share of the white Baptists either now live in rural areas of the South, or were born and reared in those areas, where fertility rates for the white population are above the national average.

Among older women, Roman Catholics are more fertile than any other religious group except Baptists, although this differential is much smaller (only 9 percent) than many people have believed. Moreover, younger Catholic women appear to have adopted the family-planning practices of the general population to such an extent that their age-standardized fertility measure in 1957 was only 1 percent above that of the nation. This is due in part, but not entirely, to the fact that the national level of fertility has climbed somewhat and is thus closer to the moderately higher Roman Catholic level.

The lowest rates of fertility shown are for Jewish and Presbyterian women. These groups are 20 to 25 percent below the general population in fer-

Table 23-6.—NUMBER OF CHILDREN EVER BORN PER 1,000 WOMEN, MARRIED AND HUSBAND PRESENT,
BY RELIGION: 1957

Religion	Women 15 to 44 years old		Women 45 years old and over	Ratio to nation	
	Per 1,000 women	Per 1,000 women, standardized for age[1]	Per 1,000 women	Standardized, women 15-44	Women 45 years old and over
Total.........................	2,218	2,188	2,798	1.00	1.00
Protestant.........................	2,220	2,206	2,753	1.01	.98
Baptist...........................	2,359	2,381	3,275	1.09	1.11
Lutheran..........................	2,013	1,967	2,382	.90	.85
Methodist.........................	2,155	2,115	2,638	.97	.94
Presbyterian......................	2,001	1,922	2,188	.88	.78
Other Protestant..................	2,237	2,234	2,702	1.02	.97
Roman Catholic....................	2,282	2,210	3,056	1.01	1.09
Jewish............................	1,749	(2)	2,218	.79	.79
Other, none, and not reported.......	2,069	2,075	2,674	.95	.96

[1]Standard is the distribution by age of all women of corresponding marital status in the United States in 1950.
[2]Standardized rate not computed where there are fewer than 150,000 women in several component 5-year age groups.
[3]Rate not shown where base is less than 150,000.
Source: Department of Commerce, Bureau of the Census; Current Population Reports, Series P-20.

tility, and are scarcely reproducing themselves. Lutherans also have moderately low rates of fertility--about 10 percent below the national average. Methodists have average fertility.

A substantial share of the differences in fertility among the religious groups is due to differences in urban-rural residence. For example, the fact that Lutherans tend to be more urban than Methodists in distribution may account for most, if not all, of the differences between them. The differential between Roman Catholics and Protestants probably would be larger if these two groups were compared separately by urban and rural residence, because a much higher percentage of Protestants than of Catholics live in rural areas and are farmers. Also, compositional factors as well as distributional factors may underlie some of the fertility differences between religious groups. Intergroup differences with respect to age at marriage, occupation, and education must be controlled simultaneously in a fertility analysis before it can be claimed that such an analysis has measured the independent effect of religious affiliation upon fertility. For example, the very low fertility level of Jewish and Presbyterian women may be due to a combination of other factors associated with low fertility--their residence in large metropolises, and the fact that their husbands are well-educated, hold white-collar jobs, and have high incomes (see section following).

In reviewing the census materials on fertility recently, Paul C. Glick, Census expert on family and fertility statistics, concluded, "...the differences between the major religious groups with respect to fertility patterns reflect differences in the age, color, geographic, and socio-economic distributions of these groups--perhaps as much as, or more than, they reflect differences in religious doctrines with regard to family behavior....Differences between rates for those under and over childbearing age suggest a trend toward convergence of the fertility levels among women in the major religious groups."[5] There is also unmistakable evidence that differences in religious doctrines do stimulate fertility differences, independently of these other traits. One of the unfinished

and important tasks of demography is to measure and analyze the independent effect of religious affiliation upon fertility. It is to be hoped that the necessary data will be made available soon--if not by the Bureau of the Census, then by private research organizations.

N.O.R.C. MATERIALS ON RELIGION: NUMBER AND DISTRIBUTION

The special tabulation of materials from the National Opinion Research Center used the results of two nationwide sample surveys--study 335, conducted in the summer of 1953, and study 367, conducted in the summer of 1955. Jacob J. Feldman, Senior Study Director, was the principal designer, the supervisor of coding, and the analyst for both these surveys. In each case there was a sample of approximately 2,500 households. In both surveys a question was asked concerning the religious preference of the respondent (and, presumably, of the entire household), who was also questioned as to the standard population characteristics of the household head.[6] Hence, by retabulating the data from these surveys it was possible to obtain information concerning the spatial distribution and the population characteristics of household heads, according to their religious preference.[7]

---

[5] "Intermarriage and Fertility Patterns among Persons in the Major Religious Groups," unpublished paper presented at the annual meeting of the American Sociological Society held in Seattle, Washington, August, 1958.

[6] These questions were answered in a straightforward and matter-of-fact way in each survey. It is the experience of NORC that such questions are among the easier items on its interviews attempt to obtain information.

[7] These tabulations were made separately for each survey, and the desired analytical tables were prepared independently from each survey's results. These duplicate tables were then compared, item by item. In most cases the twin tables were simply averaged to obtain the most accurate possible unbiased estimate; for a few cells in most of the tables, however, the results of one survey were arbitrarily accepted in preference

The NORC statistics given for Protestants and Roman Catholics, as total groups, have only small sampling variances. However, the statistics for individual Protestant denominations are subject to a larger sampling error. And the data for the three small groups-- "Jewish," "No Religion," and "Other Religion"--are subject to very large sampling errors, since the data for each of these groups are based on less than 75 households in each survey. However, as modern sampling theory asserts, and as has been demonstrated empirically hundreds of times, probability samples of this size are capable of yielding much valuable information about particular homogeneous groups, so the results concerning these three smallest groups should not be disregarded entirely.

The close correspondence between the results of the NORC surveys and the Census Bureau's survey of March, 1957, may be observed from the following comparison of religious composition as reported by each survey:

Religion	NORC surveys	Census Bureau survey	Difference (NORC minus Census)
Total...............	100.0	100.0	...
Protestant............	71.5	66.2	5.3
Baptist.............	22.0	19.7	2.3
Methodist..........	17.4	14.0	3.4
Presbyterian........	6.7	5.6	1.1
Lutheran............	7.6	7.1	1.1
Episcopal...........	2.8	(n.a.)	-2.1
Other Protestant....	14.9	19.8	
Roman Catholic........	21.1	25.7	-4.6
Jewish...............	3.0	3.2	-0.2
Other................	1.4	1.3	0.1
No religion..........	2.8	2.7	0.1
Religion not reported.	...	0.9	-0.9

[7]Continued
to those of the other survey--if one survey had a substantial number of cases with which to make the particular calculation and the other survey, as a result of sampling fluctuations, had almost none. Although this procedure yields results that are internally consistent in almost every way, and which agree remarkably well with the much larger sample taken by the Bureau of the Census in its March, 1957 survey, it must be kept in mind that the possibility of large sampling errors exists, especially for some of the more detailed cross-tabulations. These NORC data are submitted as tentative evidence, until statistics based upon larger samples of the population are available.

Considering that the NORC data refer to household heads (most of whom are male, and heavily concentrated at ages above 35 years), whereas the Census data refer to all persons aged 14 and over, much of the overcount of Protestants and undercount of Catholics in the NORC sample, in comparison with the Census data, may be attributed to differences in the age composition of the two samples. Also, the training of NORC interviewers, who are taught to probe until their questions are answered fully, may have meant that a considerable number of persons who belong to small offshoots of the Baptist and Methodist denominations (see Table 23-2) were correctly allocated to those denominations rather than grouped with "Other Protestant." Also, minor differences in coding instructions could create small differences in the final distribution.

Region of Residence of Household Heads (Table 23-7). A comparison of Table 23-7 (NORC) and Table 23-3 (Census), with respect to regional distribution of household heads by religious affiliation, shows very similar proportions for the major religious groups in the two surveys. However, Table 23-7 provides additional valuable information by showing the regional distribution of the individual Protestant denominations. Nearly two-thirds of all Baptists are concentrated in the South, and one-half of those living outside the South are found in the North Central states (to which southerners have been migrating). Baptists are a minority religious group outside these two regions, but within these two regions they are quite numerous. Methodists and Presbyterians tend to be more widely distributed among all regions; however, a slightly above-average share of Methodists live in the South, and the Presbyterians have a similar concentration in the Northeast and North Central regions. The membership of the Episcopal religion is quite concentrated in the Northeast and the West, although there is a substantial share in every region. Lutherans, by contrast, are almost nonexistent in the South; they are heavily concentrated in the North Central states, which have large populations of German descent.

Table 23-7.—REGION OF RESIDENCE OF HOUSEHOLD HEADS, BY RELIGIOUS AFFILIATION

Religion	All	Region			
		North-east	North-central	South	West
TOTAL..	100.0	25.4	28.8	31.2	14.6
Protestant total.................................	100.0	17.6	29.2	40.0	13.2
Baptist...	100.0	8.3	15.6	69.4	6.7
Methodist.......................................	100.0	20.1	32.6	35.2	12.2
Presbyterian....................................	100.0	30.1	32.0	21.6	16.4
Episcopal.......................................	100.0	37.2	15.6	26.4	21.0
Lutheran..	100.0	24.0	54.4	6.6	15.0
Other Protestant................................	100.0	15.0	33.5	29.6	21.8
Roman Catholic...................................	100.0	46.0	29.8	7.7	16.6
Jewish...	100.0	61.2	11.4	9.4	18.0
Other..	100.0	34.2	34.4	6.0	25.4
No religion......................................	100.0	20.8	30.6	22.6	26.0

Source: Special tabulations of survey data from National Opinion Research Center, Jacob J. Feldman, Senior Study Director.

To summarize: All religious groups for which data are available, except three, tend to be rather widely distributed among the regions, and to show only a moderate degree of concentration. Four generalizations that may be made concerning the distribution of religious groups are:

Baptists are concentrated in the South, and are very scarce in the Northeast and the West.
Lutherans are concentrated in the Midwest, and are very scarce in the South.
Jews are concentrated in the Northeast, and are very scarce in the South.
Roman Catholics are concentrated in the Northeast, and are very scarce in the South.

Religious Affiliation and Metropolitan and Non-metropolitan Residence. In Table 23-8 the household heads of each religious affiliation are classified according to residence inside or outside a standard metropolitan area (S.M.A.). Those living inside standard metropolitan areas are further dichotomized, according to whether the S.M.A. in which they live had more or less than 1 million in-

habitants at the 1950 census. Nonmetropolitan areas are also dichotomized, according to whether the largest city in the county contained more or fewer than 10,000 inhabitants in 1950. Approximately one-fourth of the NORC sample of households falls into each of these four categories. Three religious groups stand out as having exceptionally high concentrations of their membership in metropolitan areas: Jewish, Episcopal, and Roman Catholic. Whereas roughly one-half of the total sample of households falls in the S.M.A.'s, 98 percent of Jewish, 78 percent of Episcopal, and 74 percent of Roman Catholic household heads lived in an S.M.A. Moreover, all three of these groups were much more heavily concentrated in the very largest S.M.A.'s than they were in the smaller ones; 23 percent of the household heads in the total sample lived in S.M.A.'s having a population of one million or more, but 84 percent of Jewish, 53 percent of Episcopal, and 45 percent of Roman Catholic household heads live in these largest places. Also, persons reporting "other religion" and "no religion" are highly concentrated in places with one million or more inhabitants.

Table 23-8.—TYPE OF COUNTY OF RESIDENCE OF HOUSEHOLD HEAD BY RELIGIOUS AFFILIATION

Religion	Total	Metropolitan areas		Non metropolitan areas	
		Large-1 million or more inhabitants	Small-less than 1 million inhabitants	Largest town in county 10,000 or more	Largest town in county less than 10,000
Total.........................	100.0	30.4	28.2	19.2	22.2
Protestant total....................	100.0	22.8	28.8	21.6	26.8
Baptist...........................	100.0	15.6	31.7	22.8	30.0
Methodist.........................	100.0	21.6	29.0	19.0	30.4
Presbyterian......................	100.0	29.9	32.8	16.0	21.2
Episcopal.........................	100.0	52.7	25.0	8.8	13.6
Lutheran..........................	100.0	30.1	21.8	29.6	18.5
Other Protestant..................	100.0	22.4	26.0	22.4	29.0
Roman Catholic.....................	100.0	45.3	28.4	14.7	11.6
Jewish............................	100.0	84.0	14.8	1.2	...
Other.............................	100.0	55.8	28.1	8.4	7.7
No religion.......................	100.0	38.2	26.4	19.4	16.0

Source: Special tabulations from National Opinion Research Center, Jacob J. Feldman, Senior Study Director.

Baptists, as one would suspect from their regional distribution, have a substantial concentration in the nonmetropolitan areas and the small S.M.A.'s. Methodists have a similar tendency to be concentrated in these areas. Presbyterians tend to be slightly metropolitanized, but a substantial share of their membership also lives in nonmetropolitan areas.

Religious Affiliation and Degree of Industrialization of Community of Residence. Table 23-9 classifies household heads by religion, and also according to the degree of industrialization of the county in which they reside. (Industrialization is measured in terms of the percentage of employed persons who were working in mining or manufacturing industries at the time of the 1950 census.) The outstanding fact brought out by this table is that Roman Catholics comprise a disproportionately large share of the population in the most heavily industrialized areas, whereas the other highly urbanized and metropolitanized populations--the Jewish and the Episcopal--tend to be distributed in the counties that are moderately, but not extremely, industrialized. Methodists and Presbyterians tend to be concentrated toward each of the two extremes; disproportionately large shares of these groups are found both in the more-industrialized and in the less-industrialized counties.

RELIGIOUS PREFERENCE AND EDUCATIONAL
ATTAINMENT (N.O.R.C. MATERIALS)

Two religious groups stand out above all others as well-educated: those with Jewish and those with Episcopal religious preference. A third group, the Presbyterian, had attained an educational level considerably above the average. More than one-fifth of the members of each of these groups were college graduates (Table 23-10), and only a comparatively small percent had less than 8 years of schooling. More than 60 percent of the household heads in each of these groups were high school graduates, whereas among the general population only 40 percent had this much schooling.

Among the white population, Protestant household heads showed a slightly higher level of education than Roman Catholic: Proportionately fewer Protestants had less than a grammar school education, and proportionately more Protestants had a college education, than was the case among Catholics (Table 23-10). This difference may be due in part to the fact that among the Roman Catholics there were many elderly and less-educated immigrants.

Baptists reported a much lower level of educational attainment than any other denomination or religious group. Almost one-fifth of the white Baptists had less than 7 years of schooling, where-

Table 23-9.—DEGREE OF INDUSTRIALIZATION OF COUNTY OF RESIDENCE, BY RELIGIOUS AFFILIATION

Religion	All county resi- dence	Percentage of employed labor force in county of residence who are employed in mining or manufacturing industries							
		44.3 percent or more	37.2 to 42.8 percent	31.9 to 37.1 percent	27.3 to 31.9 percent	23.5 to 27.0 percent	18.0 to 23.3 percent	11.1 to 17.8 percent	Less than 11.1 percent
Total.............	100.0	13.0	12.4	12.5	11.7	12.3	12.8	11.7	13.7
Protestant..............	100.0	12.2	11.9	10.8	12.0	11.0	14.0	12.4	15.5
Baptist.............	100.0	6.8	11.7	15.4	12.1	10.4	17.7	14.4	11.5
Methodist............	100.0	12.0	10.2	10.4	16.8	8.7	11.5	10.2	20.2
Presbyterian.........	100.0	13.3	14.5	6.6	8.4	12.7	17.5	15.1	12.0
Episcopal...........	100.0	12.2	12.2	12.2	9.5	20.3	14.9	12.2	6.8
Lutheran.............	100.0	18.8	11.6	8.2	13.5	11.6	3.9	14.0	18.4
Other Protestant......	100.0	15.3	13.1	8.7	8.7	11.6	15.2	11.0	16.5
Roman Catholic.........	100.0	15.9	14.9	15.5	10.0	14.9	8.3	11.4	9.2
Jewish.................	100.0	10.1	6.1	31.3	20.2	22.2	8.1	...	2.0
Other.................	100.0	20.8	14.6	4.2	6.2	14.6	22.9	8.3	8.3
No religion............	100.0	8.8	11.2	12.5	7.5	13.8	15.0	11.2	20.0

Source: Special tabulations of survey materials from National Opinion Research Center, Jacob J. Feldman, Senior Study Director.

as only about one-eighth of the Protestant population as a whole had this small an amount of education. Although 42 percent of Protestants had graduated from high school or attended college, only 31 percent of Baptists had attained this level.

Lutherans and Presbyterians were noteworthy for having a great concentration of their household heads near the average level of education; this group contained comparatively few very poorly-educated persons, as well as a somewhat below-average percentage of college-trained persons.

The various religious groups could be ranked as follows with respect to their average level of educational attainment:

Table 23-10.—EDUCATIONAL COMPOSITION OF HOUSEHOLD HEADS, BY RELIGIOUS AFFILIATION 1955 TO 1956

Religious preference	Total	Education: Highest grade of school completed						
		Elementary School			High School		College	
		0-4 years	5-6 years	7-8 years	1-3 years	4 years	1-3 years	4 or more
Total..............	100.0	8.9	7.8	24.0	20.2	21.1	9.6	8.4
Protestant Total......	100.0	8.8	7.8	24.2	20.6	20.8	9.8	8.2
Baptist.............	100.0	16.9	11.6	26.0	20.4	14.8	6.1	4.2
Methodist...........	100.0	5.3	6.2	20.9	21.5	26.0	11.6	8.6
Presbyterian........	100.0	3.2	3.2	17.6	23.6	24.6	14.9	13.0
Episcopal...........	100.0	2.0	4.2	16.4	10.3	23.2	21.2	22.6
Lutheran............	100.0	5.4	5.2	29.3	22.4	22.4	8.5	7.0
Other Protestant....	100.0	6.7	8.7	27.0	18.5	20.5	9.2	9.4
Roman Catholic........	100.0	8.0	7.4	25.8	20.6	22.4	8.9	6.8
Jewish...............	100.0	8.3	4.2	13.4	13.2	27.8	10.9	22.3
Other................	100.0	23.4	13.6	11.0	11.0	22.4	5.7	12.8
No religion..........	100.0	10.7	8.7	23.4	20.4	16.9	8.8	11.0

Source: Special tabulations of survey materials from National Opinion Research Center, Jacob J. Feldman, Senior Study Director.

Episcopal
Jewish
Presbyterian
Methodist
Other Protestant
Lutheran
No Religion
Roman Catholic
Baptist

Undoubtedly, the "Other Protestant" category hides some denominations which, if tabulated separately, using samples large enough to be reliable, would rank near the top with the Episcopal and Jewish groups. Unitarians, for example, might well out-rank both. Such groups as Christian Scientist and Congregationalist might rank near, or even above, the Presbyterian and Methodist groups.

Table 23-11, which shows separately the educational attainment of white and nonwhite persons in each religious group, shows that the average level of educational attainment is much lower among nonwhite household heads where the head is a Baptist than where he is a member of some other

denomination. This suggests that as Negroes obtain more education and move out of the rural South, they or their children tend to change their religious preference.

RELIGIOUS PREFERENCE AND OCCUPATIONAL COMPOSITION (N. O. R. C. MATERIALS)

Quite a large amount of diversity exists among the various religious groups with respect to occupational composition of household heads (see Table 23-12). Three religions stand out distinctively as having large percentages of their groups in "white-collar" employment: the Episcopal, the Jewish, and the Presbyterian. Of these three, the Episcopal group contains the largest percentage of professional and technical persons, while the Jewish group has substantial proportions in managerial and proprietary jobs. At the other extreme are three religions with above-average proportions of "blue-collar" workers: Baptists, Methodists, and Lutherans. All three of these last-named groups contain substantial numbers of farmers, craftsmen, operatives, and unskilled workers.

Table 23-11.—EDUCATIONAL ATTAINMENT OF HOUSEHOLD HEAD, BY COLOR AND RELIGIOUS AFFILIATION

| Religious preference | Total | Education: Highest grade of school completed | | | | | | |
| | | Elementary school | | | High school | | College | |
		0-4 years	5-6 years	7-8 years	1-3 years	4 years	1-3 years	4 or more years
WHITE, TOTAL	100.0	6.8	6.6	24.2	20.5	22.4	10.3	9.1
Protestant total	100.0	6.0	6.1	24.6	21.0	22.4	10.8	9.1
Baptist	100.0	10.4	8.4	28.3	22.1	17.7	7.6	5.4
Methodist	100.0	4.3	5.2	21.0	21.8	26.5	12.2	9.0
Presbyterian	100.0	3.2	3.2	17.4	23.6	24.7	15.1	12.8
Episcopal	100.0	2.1	2.9	17.1	8.8	22.5	23.1	23.5
Lutheran	100.0	5.4	5.1	29.2	21.8	22.5	8.5	7.5
Other Protestant	100.0	6.1	7.1	26.9	19.0	21.4	9.8	9.8
Roman Catholic	100.0	7.5	7.6	25.8	20.8	22.5	9.0	6.8
Jewish	100.0	8.3	4.2	13.4	13.2	28.2	10.8	21.8
Other	100.0	25.2	13.4	12.4	9.8	21.2	3.7	14.2
No religion	100.0	11.0	9.5	23.6	19.1	16.3	9.5	11.0
NONWHITE:	100.0	27.1	18.0	21.4	17.5	10.7	3.4	2.1
Baptist	100.0	32.0	18.4	21.6	16.4	7.8	2.8	1.2
Other	100.0	18.6	17.6	20.6	18.9	16.4	4.3	3.6

Source: Special tabulations of survey data from National Opinion Research Center, Jacob J. Feldman, Senior Study Director.

Table 23-12.—OCCUPATIONAL COMPOSITION OF HOUSEHOLD HEADS, BY RELIGIOUS AFFILIATION

Religious affiliation	Total	Occupation - percent distribution									
		Prop. prof. tech.	Farm oper. or mgrs.	Mgrs. off. prop.	Clerical workers	Sales wkrs.	Crafts- men	Oper- atives	Serv- ice wkrs.	Farm labor- ers	Labor- ers, non- farm
TOTAL............	100.0	10.0	10.8	12.6	6.4	4.8	19.4	20.3	7.6	2.0	6.1
Protestant total....	100.0	9.5	12.9	11.8	6.3	4.5	19.2	19.7	7.4	1.6	7.0
Baptist...........	100.0	6.0	13.3	7.6	4.1	3.0	18.2	25.3	10.0	2.4	10.0
Methodist.........	100.0	10.2	15.7	13.2	7.5	4.8	19.2	16.6	5.6	1.4	5.5
Presbyterian......	100.0	15.3	8.0	16.1	8.2	10.6	16.7	15.8	4.8	1.2	3.6
Episcopal.........	199.9	19.6	1.5	20.4	11.0	5.4	16.7	9.6	10.7	...	5.3
Lutheran..........	100.0	8.0	15.6	15.4	5.4	4.4	24.0	15.1	6.2	0.6	5.2
Other Protestant..	100.0	10.4	11.6	10.2	7.0	3.4	19.9	21.6	6.8	2.4	6.8
Roman Catholic......	100.0	9.6	5.4	11.4	7.6	4.6	21.6	23.8	8.6	3.0	4.6
Jewish.............	100.0	17.6	1.3	36.0	9.6	15.0	7.2	12.0	...	...	1.3
Other..............	100.0	17.7	4.6	15.2	2.2	3.0	18.0	16.9	14.4	1.2	6.8
No religion........	100.0	11.7	13.0	13.0	0.8	4.2	20.2	19.6	10.8	3.7	3.0

Source: Special tabulations of survey data from National Opinion Research Center, Jacob J. Feldman, Senior Study Director.

Except for a comparative scarcity of farmers, and a compensating small excess of factory workers and service workers, Roman Catholics and Protestants tend to have quite similar occupational compositions. In the past, there has been a tendency to think of Catholics as being considerably lower in socio-economic status than Protestants. A close examination of Table 23-12 will show that in the Catholic group the proportion of household heads who are professional, proprietary, and clerical workers is about as large as it is among Protestants. The major difference is that such Protestant religions as Baptist, Methodist, and Lutheran contain a large proportion of farmers; Catholics have an excess of urban working-class persons, which compensates for the scarcity of Catholic farmers.

To what extent are the occupational differences noted above due to religious affiliation, and to what extent are they due simply to the fact, noted in the preceding section, that some religious groups have had more education than others? For example, are Baptist household heads concentrated in the blue-collar occupational group because they are Baptists, or because a preference for the Baptist religion is more common among socio-economic groups whose members have not had an opportunity to complete as many years of schooling as

the rest of the population? A completely valid answer to this question would require much more detailed data than are available at the present time; it would require a simultaneous cross-tabulation of religious affiliation by single years of schooling, by occupation (using a fairly detailed breakdown), by color, by sex, and by age. The sample of data available at the present time is much too small to permit a full control even of education as a general factor in explaining the broad occupational groups.[8] Table 23-13 shows the median years of schooling completed by the members of each religious group who are in each of the broad occupational categories. These data permit only a few tentative statements. It seems that educational attainment is a much more powerful factor in determining occupation than is religious preference. Support for this conclusion is provided in Table 23-12, which shows that household heads employed in a particular occupation have generally reached the same educational level, irrespective of their religious preference. Some variations, however, are too large to be explained

---

[8] This is especially true for the Jewish, the "Other Religion" and the "No Religion" groups, where the number of cases in the sample is extremely small.

Table 23-13.—MEDIAN YEARS OF SCHOOL COMPLETED BY HOUSEHOLD HEADS, BY OCCUPATION AND RELIGIOUS AFFILIATION: 1955

Religious affiliation	Total	Median years of school completed by occupation									
		Prop. prof. tech.	Farm oper. or mgrs.	Mgrs. off. prop.	Cleri-cal wkrs.	Sales wkrs.	Crafts-men	Oper-atives	Serv-ice wkrs.	Farm labor-ers	Labor-ers, non-farm
TOTAL..........	9.5	16+	7.4	11.2	11.5	11.4	9.0	7.9	7.4	6.2	6.7
Protestant total...	9.5	16+	7.6	11.2	11.5	11.6	9.0	8.0	7.3	6.9	6.7
Baptist..........	7.8	15.0	6.4	10.5	11.0	11.0	8.2	7.2	7.0	5.1	6.0
Methodist........	10.7	16+	8.1	11.4	11.7	11.6	9.6	9.4	7.8	8.0	7.0
Presbyterian.....	11.0	16+	9.5	11.4	11.9	12.0	9.8	8.8	7.5	7.5	8.2
Episcopal........	11.8	16+	13.5	12.5	12.2	13.5	11.6	8.8	9.5	...	7.2
Lutheran.........	9.6	16+	7.4	10.8	10.6	11.4	8.7	9.2	7.0	7.0	7.5
Other Protestant.	9.3	16+	8.2	10.0	11.8	11.6	9.0	7.6	7.1	6.6	7.0
Roman Catholic.....	9.4	14.6	7.0	10.7	11.3	11.0	9.2	8.0	8.2	5.4	6.5
Jewish............	11.4	16+	...	11.4	11.6	9.2	8.2	8.6	...	...	9.2
Other............	8.8	12.8	5.0	8.5	...	...	7.2	5.5	2.0	5.0	...
No religion........	9.2	16+	7.2	11.0	12.0	12.5	8.8	8.0	7.4	6.7	5.3

Note: Each median is based upon comparatively few cases. The over-all pattern of differences between entire rows or entire columns may be considered as general evidence. Individual cells should not be accepted as precise estimates.

Source: Special tabulations of survey data from National Opinion Research Center, Jacob J. Feldman, Senior Study Director.

on the basis of sampling error, and are not easily accounted for except by attributing them to variations within the occupational groups. These variations probably arise from the fact that the Census fails to count postgraduate college training separately. For example, a person with an A. B. degree and a person with an M. D. or Ph. D. degree are both simply classed as having had "4 years or more of college." The fact that professional persons, except Baptists and Roman Catholics, have an average educational attainment of four years of college does not necessarily mean that these two religious groups have a "special pipeline" that allows their members to reach the nation's upper socio-economic levels without bothering to complete the amount of schooling that is generally considered a prerequisite. Instead, it probably means that a high proportion of Jewish, Episcopal, and Presbyterian professionals are physicians, college professors, or lawyers, while an unusually high percentage of Baptist and Catholic professionals may be artists, entertainers, photographers, or employed in other occupations which are classified by the Census as "professional" but which require much less schooling. Similarly,

household heads who are Roman Catholic, Baptist, or Lutheran appear to have reached a status enabling them to be classified as proprietors, managers, or officials with the aid of less formal education than was obtained by the members of other religious groups who are classified as proprietors, managers or officials. It is quite possible that Episcopal, Jewish, and Presbyterian household heads, again because of higher educational achievement, hold very responsible positions in banks, manufacturing concerns, or as self-employed proprietors in wholesale and retail establishments, and that a higher proportion of Baptist, Catholic, and Lutheran workers with less education may be employed as railroad conductors, postmasters, or managers, or may be owners of small neighborhood grocery stores, restaurants, or filling stations--jobs which the Census also classifies as managerial or proprietary.[9]

---

[9] Also, the use of median education, which does not show the full education distribution for each combination of occupation and religion, is a very crude approach to this problem, but is made necessary by lack of a larger sample.

From the materials in Table 23-13, one might expect to obtain the answer to a different kind of question: "Are the members of any religious group discriminated against, in their efforts to find employment, simply because of their particular religious preference?" One might conclude that they are if, in any religious group, the household heads have jobs that are low in the socio-economic scale and levels of educational attainment that are extraordinarily high. An examination of Table 23-13 shows that three groups seem to fit this pattern: the Presbyterian, the Methodist, and the Episcopal.[10] If the data are accepted as valid, one would be forced to conclude that the Episcopal group is more severely discriminated against than any other. Common-sense reflection suggests that such is not the case; if there is discrimination of the type defined above, it should show up among the Baptists, a group having a very large Negro population. Probably nothing more is involved than the fact that Episcopalians, Presbyterians, and Methodists place a stronger emphasis on educational achievement than many other religious groups do, and, hence, that their members tend to attain above-average educational levels irrespective of the occupational levels at which they may eventually work.

To summarize: The meager data available gives little evidence either that any religious group is extraordinarily favored, or that there is severe discrimination (independent of any other factors) against any religious group because of its beliefs--with respect to broad categories of occupational attainment. Although the religious groups differ substantially with respect to occupational composition, in general the members of each religion seem to be located just about as high on the occupational ladder as the level of their educational attainment would lead one to expect.

---

[10] However, it will be shown in the next section that there are proportionately few Episcopalians and Presbyterians with low socio-economic status.

RELIGIOUS PREFERENCE AND INCOME
(N.O.R.C. MATERIALS)

There is a high concentration of poverty among the Baptist population, while being in the upper income brackets is closely related to a preference for the Episcopal or Jewish religion (see Table 23-14). Methodists, Presbyterians, and Roman Catholics tend to be concentrated in the upper middle income brackets, while Lutherans and other Protestants seem to be in the lower-middle grades. Persons who claim no religion tend to be distributed more or less evenly throughout all income levels. This means that, in comparison with the general population, disproportionately large numbers of people who have no religious preference are located at the extremely high and the extremely low income levels. If one were to rank and classify the leading religions according to "high income," "median income," and "low income" these groups would be listed as follows:

Religion

High income
Jewish
Episcopal
Presbyterian

Median income
Catholic
Lutheran
No religion
Methodist

Low income
Baptist
Small Protestant sects

How much of this income difference between religious groups is due to the differences in occupational composition that are described above? Here again, an answer to this question requires a multiple-variable cross-tabulation, which the sample of NORC data was too small to support. Since the measure of income employed here is family income, such items as the number of earners in the family, the occupational and educational level of the secondary earners, etc., could also affect the comparisons. Even such aspects of family structure and composition as age of head and family reaction to poverty (some groups sup-

Table 23-14.—INCOME DISTRIBUTION OF HOUSEHOLD HEADS BY RELIGIOUS AFFILIATION

Religious affiliation	Total	Income							
		Less than $1,000	$1,000 to $1,999	$2,000 to $2,999	$3,000 to $3,999	$4,000 to $4,999	$5,000 to $7,499	$7,500 to $9,999	$10,000 and over
TOTAL.........................	100.0	7.3	10.0	13.8	17.4	17.7	21.3	7.0	5.6
Protestant total...............	100.0	8.2	11.0	14.6	17.6	17.4	19.8	6.4	5.2
Baptist.......................	100.0	12.6	15.2	19.0	17.8	15.2	13.8	4.0	2.1
Methodist.....................	100.0	7.0	9.6	11.3	18.2	16.6	24.0	7.5	5.9
Presbyterian..................	100.0	2.4	8.5	9.2	18.0	20.8	23.5	9.0	8.7
Episcopal.....................	100.0	6.4	8.4	10.9	11.2	15.8	23.6	9.7	14.1
Lutheran......................	100.0	3.6	8.1	13.2	19.4	19.2	23.0	8.2	5.2
Other Protestant..............	100.0	8.4	9.6	15.7	16.2	20.2	18.6	6.2	5.2
Roman Catholic.................	100.0	5.0	7.2	11.7	18.4	19.6	25.0	8.4	4.6
Jewish.........................	100.0	1.3	7.3	6.2	11.6	11.8	31.5	11.4	18.9
Other..........................	100.0	2.2	16.4	17.4	16.2	15.1	22.1	7.2	3.4
No religion....................	100.0	10.2	7.2	13.0	12.2	19.7	18.4	7.6	11.6

Source: Special tabulations from National Opinion Research Center, Jacob J. Feldman, Senior Study Director.

port elderly low-income parents in their own households, while other groups may allow them to live apart) may affect these data to a marked degree. As a very rough substitute for completely adequate evidence, Table 23-15 reports the median family income for each occupational group, subdivided according to religious preference. Except in the case of the Baptists, most of the income differentials between religions, mentioned above, tend to disappear and become simply income differentials between occupations.

When comparisons are made for all categories in the occupational scale, household heads whose religious preference is Roman Catholic tend to receive higher incomes than those who are Protestant. For example, the family incomes of

Table 23-15.—MEDIAN INCOMES OF HEADS OF HOUSEHOLDS BY OCCUPATION AND RELIGIOUS AFFILIATION

Religious affiliation	Total	Median income by occupation									
		Prof. and Tech.	Farm oper. or mgrs.	Mgrs. off. or Prop.	Cleri-cal wkrs.	Sales wkrs.	Crafts-men	Oper-atives	Serv-ice wkrs.	Farm labor-ers	Labor-ers, non-farm
TOTAL..........	4,094	5,876	2,838	5,936	4,032	4,882	4,462	3,762	2,610	1,779	2,852
Protestant total...	3,933	5,457	2,703	5,570	3,960	4,893	4,418	3,656	2,399	1,726	2,659
Baptist..........	3,174	4,529	1,639	4,116	4,111	4,250	4,056	3,310	1,868	1,798	2,311
Methodist........	4,235	5,586	3,134	5,992	3,901	4,929	4,756	4,018	2,155	2,000	3,326
Presbyterian.....	4,586	5,794	4,479	6,405	4,958	5,178	3,916	4,106	3,750	2,000	2,666
Episcopal........	5,000	6,156	...	7,208	5,500	4,750	5,250	3,146	3,375	...	2,000
Lutheran.........	4,278	5,858	2,854	5,802	4,333	6,372	4,662	3,800	2,375	...	2,834
Other Protestant.	4,008	5,458	2,708	5,188	3,778	3,916	4,574	3,613	2,842	2,250	2,598
Roman Catholic.....	4,340	6,334	4,250	6,281	4,118	5,688	4,636	3,964	3,562	1,792	3,450
Jewish...........	5,954	7,333	...	6,924	4,775	4,300	5,000	3,792	...	...	...
Other............	3,875	...	4,000	5,334	...	...	4,000	3,625	2,542	...	...
No religion.......	4,320	10,000+	3,250	6,010	...	4,125	4,250	3,854	2,125	2,000	...

Note: Each median is based upon comparatively few cases. The over-all pattern of differences between entire rows or entire columns may be considered as general evidence. Individual cells should not be accepted as precise estimates.

Source: Special tabulations of survey data from National Opinion Research Center, Jacob J. Feldman, Senior Study Director.

Catholic craft workers tend to be higher than the family incomes of Protestant craft workers, and so on for most occupational groups. Since Catholics have a lower educational level than Protestants, one might expect that some factor specifically associated with religion as such would explain this situation. However, the facts that most farmers have small cash incomes, and that most farmers are Protestants, probably constitute one of the major reasons for this differential. Also, because they have more children, there may be more earners in Catholic families (working children as well as working mothers) than in Protestant families.

Jewish and Episcopal household heads who are employed as professional, proprietary, or managerial workers tend to have higher median incomes than the members of other religious groups employed in these same broad occupational categories. This is probably due to the kind of internal variation between occupations within each of the broad occupational categories that was described and illustrated in connection with educational attainment. Thus, occupation is a much more potent factor than religious preference in determining the income level of household heads.

How completely do inter-faith differences with respect to educational attainment explain the differences in income between religious groups? Table 23-16, which reports the median income of each educational group, for each religion, provides very rough data with which to examine this question. This table shows that the differences in income between religious groups are greatly reduced when the factor of education is introduced. A general, over-all difference does seem to remain, however. Roman Catholic household heads tend to have higher incomes, for a given amount of schooling completed, than Protestant household heads. Similarly, Jewish household heads tend to receive larger incomes than Catholic household heads for a given amount of schooling completed. The difference between the Roman Catholic and the Protestant groups are of about the same magnitude as those between the Catholic and the Jewish. Within the protestant group, the Episcopalians, Presbyterians, and Methodists who had had college educations received higher incomes than the Baptists. All of these differences may be due to differences in age of head, number and type of secondary earners, family structure, and occupation-- as well as to cultural factors associated with religious affiliation. Clarification of this point must await the availability of data.

Table 23-16.—MEDIAN INCOME OF HEADS OF HOUSEHOLDS, BY EDUCATIONAL ATTAINMENT AND RELIGIOUS AFFILIATION

Religious affiliation	Total	Elementary school			High school		College	
		0-4 years	5-6 years	7-8 years	1-3 years	4 years	1-3 years	4 or more years
TOTAL....................	4,012	1,932	2,560	3,320	4,050	4,644	5,134	6,500
Protestant total...............	3,850	1,710	2,360	3,096	3,946	4,588	4,935	5,900
Baptist.....................	3,032	1,629	2,312	2,839	3,670	4,034	4,128	4,614
Methodist...................	4,077	2,688	2,208	3,088	4,019	4,670	5,260	6,245
Presbyterian...............	4,494	2,250	3,125	3,500	4,282	4,682	5,625	6,000
Episcopal..................	4,750	...	...	3,250	3,375	5,475	4,584	7,062
Lutheran...................	4,230	1,688	3,300	3,526	4,103	4,759	5,458	6,584
Other Protestant............	3,916	1,734	2,274	3,242	4,036	4,628	4,538	5,416
Roman Catholic..............	4,354	2,710	3,219	3,992	4,368	4,612	5,644	6,789
Jewish.....................	5,956	2,916	...	4,334	5,500	5,472	6,050	8,500
Other.......................	3,822	2,292	2,500	3,500	4,875	3,875	4,000	6,667
No religion.................	4,184	2,666	2,125	3,300	3,708	6,000	4,875	8,638

Note: Each median is based upon comparatively few cases. The over-all pattern of differences between entire rows or entire columns may be considered as general evidence. Individual cells should not be accepted as precise estimates.

Source: Special tabulations of survey data from National Opinion Research Center, Jacob J. Feldman, Senior Study Director.

It should not be concluded hastily that any of the socio-economic differences shown here are due directly to religious membership as such. The kind of occupational use to which a given amount of educational attainment is put has a great deal to do with the amount of income received. People with college degrees who choose law, medicine, or business administration as a career (as a high proportion of Jewish and Episcopal members do), and who have spent 5 to 8 years in college, will almost certainly receive much larger incomes than other college graduates who have spent 4 years in college and have chosen to teach elementary school or to hold other kinds of low-paying jobs as professionals or officials. Moreover, persons who live in large metropolitan areas (as a high proportion of Jews and Episcopalians do) receive higher incomes for a given occupation than workers living in other places. To summarize: education is a much more potent factor than religious preference in determining the income level of households, and even observed differences between religious groups, when amount of education is controlled, may be due to "intervening variables" other than religious affiliation.

SUMMARY AND CONCLUSION

The various religious groups differ greatly from each other in their distribution among regions, metropolitan and nonmetropolitan areas, and with respect to the size of places in which they live. They also differ as to age of the family head, ethnic composition, propensity to intermarry, and educational, occupational, and income levels. However, these differences are not due solely to religious affiliation as such. For example, it has been demonstrated in this chapter that occupational differences and educational differences each "explain" a large part of the income difference between religious groups. (Data were not available with which to measure how much of the total income differences between religious groups would be explained by both occupation and education considered simultaneously, but these factors probably

would explain by far the larger part of these differences, if detailed occupation and education categories were used in the analysis.) There is comparatively little evidence that any particular group is receiving favored social or economic treatment simply on the basis of its religious affiliation. Neither is there much evidence to support a conclusion that any major religious group is being persecuted or disadvantaged in an economic sense solely because of its beliefs. Nevertheless, there is evidence that some economic and other differences between religious groups would still be found to persist, independent of other variables.

It would be very wrong to assert that because religious affiliation does not always have a strong effect, independent of all other variables, it is not an important variable for demographic and sociological analysis. This chapter has made it abundantly clear that unique "clusters of traits" are associated with each of the various religious groups. The hypothesis that these clusters are part of a tradition or culture which is transmitted from one generation to another is plausible, and is worthy of test and study. For example, in order to explain the results of this chapter it is almost mandatory to develop the hypothesis that members of the Episcopal, Jewish, and Presbyterian religions place a very high value on obtaining as much education as possible, that they strive to gain employment in the professional, managerial, or proprietary occupations, and that they attempt to save from current income so they can invest and increase their future income. This complex of traits or ambitions may lead to later marriage, fewer children, metropolitan residence, greater willingness to migrate, the accumulation of above-average amounts of wealth, and many other demographic and social phenomena reflecting values that our society deems praiseworthy. On the other hand, if we are familiar with the population composition of particular denominations, it helps us to understand the position these groups take with respect to particular social and economic issues. For this reason, and because religion sometimes is an important explanatory factor even when it is considered independently of other variables (as in the case of fertility analysis), much scientific and public good could be accomplished if religion were added as an item on the decennial census.

The analysis presented in this chapter concerning the interrelationships between religious affiliation and other population variables has had to be based on incomplete and inadequate data. These materials have enabled the analysis to demonstrate only that some highly meaningful relationships exist; as data with which to measure the magnitude of these relationships, however, they have permitted only approximate conclusions. There was not enough data to permit exploration of the reasons behind the existence of these relationships, and how they varied with changes in other circumstances. Further research must await more adequate information. It is to be hoped that the Bureau of the Census will give a high priority to this item in 1970, as penance for the policy forced on it in 1960.

Chapter 24

HOUSING AND POPULATION

Since there is a very close relationship between population trends and housing trends, persons who are interested in one of these subjects are, almost of necessity, interested in the other. The demographer needs to be informed concerning the residential situation and the living arrangements of the population, and the housing specialist must rely upon demography for an understanding of many of the forces that underlie changes in the quantity and the distribution of housing. The processes of family formation and dissolution, and other social and economic processes that affect the number and the composition of households, are topics for population study, as Chapters 10 and 11 have illustrated. They are also a part of the foundation upon which all housing analysis is built. The present chapter, by discussing housing trends in the light of population trends, is aimed at meeting some of the joint needs of demographers and housing experts.[1] During the years 1956 and 1957 the U. S. Bureau of the Census conducted a National Housing Inventory, which provided housing information on a sample basis for the nation as a whole, for regions, for standard metropolitan areas, and for nonmetropolitan areas. (The survey statistics refer to the housing situation as of December 31, 1956.) These recently-published materials provide the basis for much of the following discussion of the current situation.

THE DECLINING SIZE OF HOUSEHOLD[2]

As of March, 1958, the population of the United States was living in about 50.4 million dwelling units.[3] This represented an over-all average of 3.35 persons per dwelling unit. For almost seven decades, the number of dwelling units has increased faster than the population, with the result that the average number of persons per household has declined. Data to support this finding are given in Table 24-1, which shows, for example, that between 1950 and 1957 the number of dwelling units increased by 16.5 percent, whereas the population increased by 12.1 percent. In this one period, the supply of living quarters increased 36 percent faster than the number of people. A similar change took place between 1940 and 1950; during that decade the number of dwelling units in-

---

[1] If he has not already done so, the reader of this chapter should read Chapter 10, "Marriage and Marital Status" and Chapter 11, "Households and Families."

[2] In the United States, the first census of housing was taken in 1940. A second census of housing was taken in 1950. Materials for earlier decades, and for 1958, are inferred indirectly from household information obtained in population censuses.

[3] The term "dwelling unit" used in the housing census was the equivalent of the concept "household" used in assembling population data. In general, a dwelling unit is a group of rooms or a single room occupied or intended for occupancy as separate living quarters by a household, a family, or other group of persons living together, or by a person living alone. Ordinarily, a dwelling unit is a house, an apartment, or a flat. A dwelling unit may be located in a business structure devoted primarily to business or other nonresidential use. When used as residences, trailers, boats, tents, and railroad cars are defined as dwelling units.

Table 24-1.—OCCUPIED DWELLING UNITS AND POPULATION, BY COLOR OF OCCUPANTS: 1890 TO 1958

Color of occupants and year	Housing-occupied dwelling units		Total population		Population per occupied dwelling unit	Ratio of housing growth to population growth
	Number (000)	Percent increase over preceding period	Number (000)	Percent increase over preceding period		
TOTAL						
1958 (March).............	50,402	...	...	...	3.35	...
1957 (January 1).........	49,874	16.5	168,950	12.1	3.39	1.36
1950.....................	42,826	22.9	150,697	14.5	3.53	1.58
1940.....................	34,855	16.6	131,669	7.2	3.77	2.31
1930.....................	29,905	22.8	122,775	16.1	4.11	1.42
1920.....................	24,352	20.2	105,711	14.9°	4.34	1.36
1910.....................	20,256	26.9	91,972	21.0	4.54	1.28
1900.....................	15,964	25.8	75,995	20.7	4.76	1.25
1890.....................	12,690	...	62,948	...	4.93	...
WHITE						
1958 (March).............	45,635	...	...	...	3.29	...
1957 (January 1)........	45,541	16.6	150,480	11.5	3.30	1.44
1950.....................	39,044	23.7	134,942	14.1	3.46	1.68
1940.....................	31,561	17.0	118,215	7.2	3.75	2.36
1930.....................	26,983	23.6	110,287	16.3	4.09	1.45
1920.....................	21,826	([1])	94,821	16.0	4.34	([1])
1910.....................	([1])	([1])	81,732	22.3	([1])	([1])
1900.....................	14,064	25.0	66,809	21.2	4.75	1.18
1890.....................	11,255	...	55,101	...	4.90	...
NONWHITE						
1958 (March).............	4,767	...	...	...	3.90	...
1957 (January 1)........	4,333	14.5	18,470	17.2	4.26	0.84
1950.....................	3,783	14.9	15,755	17.1	4.16	0.87
1940.....................	3,293	12.7	13,454	7.7	4.09	1.65
1930.....................	2,922	15.7	12,488	14.7	4.27	1.07
1920.....................	2,526	([1])	10,890	6.3	4.31	([1])
1910.....................	(1)	([1])	10,240	11.5	([1])	(1)
1900.....................	1,900	32.4	9,185	17.1	4.83	1.89
1890.....................	1,435	...	7,846	...	5.47	...

[1]Not available.

Note: Data for 1958 refers primarily to civilian population living in private occupied households, whereas the data for earlier years refers to total population divided by total number of occupied dwelling units.

Source: 1950 Census of Housing, Vol. I, Part 1, Table J, p. xxix; National Housing Inventory, U.S. Summary; Current Population Reports, Series P-20, No. 88, 1958.

creased at a rate 50 percent faster than the rate of population growth. Over the years, this trend has been impressively steady. In 1890, there were 5 persons per household; by 1958, the average household contained only 2/3 as many persons as it had in 1890.

This decline in average size of household has taken place in spite of the recent upswing in fertility and its resulting increase in the number of families having 2, 3, or 4 children. The factors that have caused this decline in household size are described in more detail in Chapter 11, but among them are:

(a) Greater longevity, meaning that more elderly people are surviving to live in their own households after their children have grown and departed.

(b) Greater economic security for elderly people, enabling them to live apart, either alone or with their spouse, rather than with a child or other relative.

(c) A decline in the number and proportion of households with extraordinarily large families--6 or more children.

(d) A decline in the number of subfamilies and secondary families. Young married couples tend to live with their parents less frequently now, and fewer domestic servants "live in" in the households of their employers.

(e) A decline in the proportion of unmarried persons who live as lodgers in private homes or rooming houses, and a resulting increase in the tendency for unmarried persons to live in their own apartments, either alone or with someone else.

(f) Younger age at marriage, which means that children are departing earlier from the parental household and establishing their own families, rather than remaining at home. This situation results in a larger number of husband-wife households without children among the population aged 45 and over.

(g) Aging of the population. An increased share of the population is now concentrated in the age groups where childless households are most common--age 45 and over.

There is a limit, however, to which the population desires to extend, or is capable of extending, several of the above changes, and apparently this limit is rapidly being approached. Meanwhile, the nation's fertility continues to be high, and the number of 3-child and 4-child families is increasing. As a result, this long-term trend toward smaller households seems destined to 'be suspended or reversed in the near future. Details concerning this situation are given in Chapter 26.

HOUSING IN METROPOLITAN AND NONMETROPOLITAN AREAS IN COMPARISON WITH POPULATION

The National Housing Inventory of 1956-1957 was tabulated to provide information for each of the following types of areas, as well as for regions:

	Occupied dwelling units	Estimated population Dec.31,'56	Average persons per unit
U. S. Total........	100.0	100.0	3.39
Standard metropolitan areas..............	59.7	59.1	3.36
Central cities......	31.1	31.2	3.41
Metropolitan rings..	28.6	27.9	3.31
Nonmetropolitan areas.	40.3	40.9	3.44

The above summary, together with the statistics of Table 24-2, furnish the basis for the following observations:

(a) Housing and population are distributed in almost identical proportions between metropolitan and nonmetropolitan areas, and between central cities and metropolitan rings.

(b) This distribution implies, in turn, that the average number of persons per dwelling unit is roughly the same in both areas. The average nonmetropolitan household is slightly larger than the metropolitan household, and the central city

Table 24-2.—DWELLING UNITS INSIDE AND OUTSIDE STANDARD METROPOLITAN AREAS: 1940 TO 1956

Dwelling units	U.S. total	Standard metropolitan areas			Nonmetropolitan areas
		Total	Central cities	Metropolitan rings	
Dwelling units, 1956 (000),.....................	55,342	31,615	16,286	15,329	23,727
Net change, 1950 to 1956 (000)...................	9,355	5,985	1,163	4,822	3,370
Net change, 1940 to 1950 (000)...................	8,658	5,648	2,417	3,231	3,010
Percent change, 1950 to 1956....................	20.3	23.4	7.7	45.9	16.6
Percent change, 1940 to 1950....................	23.2	28.3	19.0	44.4	17.3
Percent distribution of change, 1950 to 1956......	100.0	64.0	12.4	51.5	36.0
Percent distribution of change, 1940 to 1950......	100.0	65.2	27.9	37.3	34.8
Percent distribution of dwelling units, 1956......	100.0	57.1	29.4	27.7	42.9
Percent distribution of dwelling units, 1940......	100.0	53.5	34.0	19.5	46.5
Population, percent distribution, 1956...........	100.0	59.1	31.2	27.9	40.9
Population, percent change, 1900 to 1956.........	11.6	17.5	5.6	34.7	4.0
Ratio of housing growth to population growth......	1.75	3.37	1.38	1.32	4.15

Source: National Housing Inventory, Vol. III, and 1950 Census of Housing, Vol. I, Part 1, Table G.

household is slightly larger than the suburban household.

(c) The pattern of housing growth is very similar to the pattern of population growth, showing a huge increase in suburban areas and a moderate growth in nonmetropolitan areas and central cities. Because the nonmetropolitan population has grown comparatively little (an estimated 4 percent during the period 1950 to 1956) while nonmetropolitan housing has grown at almost the national rate, the ratio of housing growth to population growth is much higher in nonmetropolitan than in metropolitan areas. This high nonmetropolitan housing ratio is probably due to the fact that nonmetropolitan areas have grown rapidly in rings just outside metropolitan areas, and to the out-migration that has taken place from the less-promising nonmetropolitan areas.

REGIONAL DISTRIBUTION OF HOUSING IN COMPARISON WITH POPULATION

Estimates of the quantity of dwelling units and of the comparative distribution of housing and population for the four geographic regions, as of

December 31, 1956, are shown in Table 24-3 and in the following summary:

	Occupied dwelling units	Estimated population Dec.31,'56	Average persons per unit
U.S. Total....	100.0	100.0	3.39
Northeast........	25.7	25.1	3.31
North Center.....	28.6	29.8	3.53
South............	30.1	30.6	3.45
West.............	15.6	14.5	3.13

As was the case with respect to metropolitan and nonmetropolitan areas, housing is also distributed among regions in quantities that are almost exactly proportionate to the size of the various regional populations. In the highly urbanized Northeast and West, the average size of household is slightly below the national average, while in the South and the North Center the average size of household is slightly above the national average.

Housing growth has closely paralleled the regional pattern of population growth, described in Chapter 4. However, in the 1950 to 1957 period, housing grew more rapidly than population in the Northeast and in the South. These are the two regions with the lowest rates of population growth. Thus, at the present time, housing growth ap-

Table 24-3.—DISTRIBUTION OF DWELLING UNITS BY CENSUS REGION: 1956, 1950, AND 1940

Dwelling units	U.S. total	Regions			
		Northeast	North Central	South	West
Total dwelling units, 1956 (000).............	55,342	14,201	15,843	16,638	8,660
In metropolitan areas............................	31,615	10,749	8,686	6,728	5,451
In nonmetropolitan areas........................	23,727	3,451	7,157	9,910	3,209
Net change in dwelling units (000)					
1950 to 1956.....................	9,355	2,150	2,097	2,984	2,128
1940 to 1950.....................	8,658	1,737	2,149	2,778	1,994
Percent change in dwelling units					
1950 to 1956.....................	20.3	15.1	13.2	17.9	24.6
1940 to 1950.....................	23.2	16.8	18.5	25.5	43.9
Percent distribution of dwelling units					
1956..	100.0	25.7	28.6	30.1	15.6
1950..	100.0	26.2	29.9	29.6	14.2
1940..	100.0	27.6	31.1	29.1	12.1
Population, percent distribution, 1956............	100.0	25.1	29.8	30.6	14.5
Population, percent change, 1950 to 1956.........	11.6	6.5	12.2	9.7	24.7
Ratio of housing growth to population growth......	1.75	2.32	1.08	1.85	1.00

pears to be spread among the regions a little more evenly than population growth. This difference is probably due to out-migration from New England and the South to metropolitan centers-- both nearby and distant ones. This migration, of course, frees housing at the places of origin and creates a demand for additional housing at the places of destination.

THE KINDS OF HOUSING IN WHICH THE POPULATION LIVES

Age of Structure. The postwar housing boom has caused a remarkable change to take place in the average age of housing. No less than 30 percent of all the living units in existence on December 31, 1956 had been erected since 1945, and one in four was less than 10 years old. This is in sharp contrast to the situation as it was in 1940, or even in 1950, as Table 24-3 and the following summary show:

Approximate age of structure	Percent distribution, selected dates			
	Dec. 31 1956	Apr. 1 1950	Apr. 1 1940	Percent change 1940- 1956
Total..........	100.0	100.0	100.0	59.7
10 years or less..	23.6	20.7	15.9	160.1
10 to 19 years....	13.4	13.3	24.6	-13.9
20 to 29 years....	11.2	20.1	18.6	-4.4
30 to 39 years....	14.9	14.3	17.6	33.6
40 to 49 years....	11.6	13.6	10.3	79.2
50 years or more..	22.6	17.9	13.0	176.2

Source: Estimated by the author, using data from National Housing Inventory and Census of Housing for 1950 and 1940.

Building activity fluctuated greatly during the decades preceding 1956, as shown by the following tabulation of the periods in which the housing in existence on December 31, 1956 had been built:

Year in which built	Dwelling units Dec. 31, 1956	Percent
Total................	55,342	100.0
1950 to 1956............	10,946	19.9
1945 to 1949............	5,774	10.5
1940 to 1944............	3,523	6.4
1930 to 1939............	4,990	9.1
1920 to 1929............	8,894	16.1

Year in which built	Dwelling units Dec. 31, 1956	Percent
Continued 1910 to 1919............	6,485	11.7
1900 to 1909............	6,153	11.1
Before 1900.............	8,107	14.6
No information.........	407	0.8

Source: National Housing Inventory and Census of Housing for 1950 and 1940. Data for 1929 and for earlier years are rough extrapolations of data from the 1950 and 1940 censuses.

From 1945, when wartime restrictions on building materials were relaxed, to December 31, 1956, a net total of 16.7 million living units were added to the housing supply. This addition represented an increase more than twice as large as that of any previous decade except the 1920 to 1929 decade, which also saw a great postwar housing boom. Following the 1920 spurt, housing experienced a decade of stagnation during the 1930's. Most of the housing built before 1930 is now 30 years old or more, and most of the housing built after 1930 is 15 years old or less. As a result of the decline in home construction during the 1930's, the nation is now in an odd situation: the amount of very young housing and the amount of older housing are increasing simultaneously, and at very large rates. Old housing and young housing each increased by more than 150 percent during the 17 years between 1940 and 1957. This increase in old housing took place despite a very ambitious nation-wide program of urban renewal and slum clearance. Unfortunately, a high percentage of the oldest structures that are still standing were neither well-designed nor well-built, nor was their architecture of the quality that has encouraged owners of some old structures to restore them and keep them up-to-date and in good repair. As a consequence, the housing situation seems to be getting worse (more obsolete housing) and getting better (more new housing) at the same time! Housing experts are forced to take an ambivalent view of the years since World War II. They can look with pride upon the vast amount of new construction, but they must also look with dismay at the rapid accumulation of over-age, obsolete, and substandard buildings dating from the nineteenth century and the early part of the twentieth century.

Type of Structure. The single-family house, detached from all other structures, is by far the nation's most popular living arrangement (see Table 24-3). More than two-thirds of American families live in such houses, and the new housing being built is overwhelmingly of this type, except for the new construction connected with public housing and slum clearance programs. This emphasis on detached dwellings makes housing in the United States very unlike that of many other nations, where multiple-unit dwellings are overwhelmingly in the majority. Moreover, the estimates of percent change in each type of housing since the 1950 census, shown in Table 24-4, indicate that all net growth has been in this type of housing. Construction of apartments is barely keeping abreast of the razing and abandonment of duplexes and other old multiple-unit structures. (However, units located in large apartment buildings are increasing at a rate that is impressively high.)

Even within the central cities of standard metropolitan areas, the single-family house provides shelter for more families than any other type of structure. Nevertheless, it comprises a much smaller percentage (38.5 percent) of all housing here than it does in the suburbs or in nonmetropolitan areas. Within the central city the duplex, the small apartment, and the large apartment each comprise roughly one-fifth of all living units. In

Table 24-4.—SELECTED CHARACTERISTICS OF DWELLING UNITS, BY LOCATION WITHIN OR OUTSIDE STANDARD METROPOLITAN AREAS, DECEMBER 31, 1956 AND APRIL, 1950

Characteristic	U.S. total	Standard metropolitan areas			Nonmetropolitan areas	April, 1950
		Total	Central cities	Suburban rings		
TYPE OF STRUCTURE						
Total.........................	100.0	100.0	100.0	100.0	100.0	100.0
1 dwelling unit, detached..........	68.1	56.6	38.5	75.9	83.5	63.3
1 dwelling unit, attached..........	2.1	3.1	4.5	1.6	0.7	17.6
2 dwelling units....................	12.3	15.0	18.6	11.1	8.7	
3 and 4 dwelling units.............	6.8	9.0	13.1	4.7	3.7	7.3
5 to 9 dwelling units..............	4.4	6.0	8.9	3.0	2.1	4.6
10 to 19 dwelling units............	2.0	3.2	5.2	1.1	0.5	2.4
20 or more dwelling units..........	3.9	6.5	11.2	1.5	0.3	4.0
Trailers...........................	0.5	0.5	0.1	1.0	0.4	0.7
YEAR BUILT						
Total.........................	100.0	100.0	100.0	100.0	100.0	100.0
1955 to 1956.......................	6.0	6.5	2.7	10.6	5.3	...
1950 to 1954.......................	14.0	15.0	8.3	22.2	12.5	...
1945 to 1950.......................	10.5	9.9	7.2	12.7	11.4	13.4
1940 to 1944.......................	6.4	6.5	5.1	7.9	6.4	7.3
1930 to 1939.......................	9.1	8.5	7.9	9.2	9.9	13.3
1929 or earlier....................	54.0	53.6	68.8	37.4	54.6	65.9
NUMBER OF ROOMS.................	100.0	100.0	100.0	100.0	100.0	100.0
1 and 2 rooms......................	7.8	7.5	10.1	4.7	8.2	10.4
3 rooms............................	12.9	13.2	16.7	9.5	12.4	14.9
4 rooms............................	22.0	21.6	21.6	21.5	22.8	21.9
5 rooms............................	24.8	26.3	24.2	28.5	22.9	21.2
6 rooms............................	19.0	19.8	17.7	22.0	17.9	16.8
7 or more rooms....................	13.5	11.7	9.7	13.8	15.8	14.8
NUMBER OF BEDROOMS..............	100.0	100.0	100.0	100.0	100.0	...
No bedroom.........................	3.2	3.3	4.1	2.3	3.2	...
1 bedroom..........................	19.5	20.7	26.7	14.2	17.8	...
2 bedrooms.........................	39.2	38.9	39.2	38.7	39.6	...
3 bedrooms.........................	28.4	29.6	23.9	35.6	26.9	...
4 bedrooms or more.................	9.7	7.5	6.1	9.1	12.5	...

Source: National Housing Inventory.

Table 24-5.—DWELLING UNITS, BY TYPE OF STRUCTURE: 1956, 1950, AND 1940

Type of structure	Number of dwelling units (000)			Percent change		Percent distribu-tion, 1940
	Dec. 31, 1956	April 1, 1950	April 1, 1940	1950 to 1956	1940 to 1950	
Total........................	55,342	48,983	37,325	13.0	31.2	100.0
1 dwelling unit, detached..........	37,715	29,116	23,731	29.4	22.7	63.6
1 dwelling unit, attached..........	1,145	1,210	1,413	-5.4	-14.4	3.8
2 dwelling units..................	6,798	6,891	5,356	-1.3	28.7	14.3
3 and 4 dwelling units.............	3,739	3,374	2,729	10.8	23.6	7.3
5 to 9 dwelling units.............	2,410	2,138	1,492	12.7	43.3	4.0
10 to 19 dwelling units............	1,126	1,085	854	3.8	27.0	2.3
20 or more dwelling units..........	2,141	1,855	1,582	15.4	17.3	4.2
Trailers.........................	265	315	167	-12.1	88.6	0.4

Source: 1956 National Housing Inventory, 1950 Census of Housing, Vol. I, Table 17, 1940 Census of Housing, Vol. II, Table 4 (partly estimated).

suburban areas, more than three-fourths of all housing is of the single-family type, and less than 3 percent of the living units are in large apartment buildings. Outside the S.M.A.'s, almost all housing is of the single-family type; apartments are almost nonexistent, and there are comparatively few (8.7 percent) two-unit structures.

Much has been written about the problem of residential deconcentration and decongestion in American cities. The fact is that American cities are already among the most spread-out and the least-densely settled cities in the world. Almost no other nation has such a large percentage of families living in houses each of which has its own yard. One of the reasons behind the high cost of today's municipal services is this low-density pattern of living. Much of our traffic congestion is due to our residential decongestion.

Size of Living Unit. The big, old-fashioned house with 7 or more rooms fell into disfavor after World War I, when fertility declined and families became smaller. The later age at marriage, the larger number of childless couples, and the small-size families that characterized the late 1920's and the 1930's made the small "efficiency" or "kitchenette" apartment and the 4-room house or apartment popular. The baby boom has reversed this trend, and builders are now emphasizing the 5- and 6-room house. Between 1940 and 1950, the 4-room unit increased in number much faster than either the 3-room or the 5-room; building during this decade seemed oriented to-

ward the one-child family. Since 1950, there has been a great increase in the number of 5-room and 6-room units; 4-room units are being built much less frequently now than they were during the last decade. Even the 7-room units have experienced a reversed rate of growth. These changes may be noted from the following summary:

Number of rooms	1956	1950	1950	Estimated percent change 1950-56[1]	Percent change 1940-50
Total...	100.0	100.0	100.0	...	...
1 room.....	7.8	2.9	3.5	-8.0	-0.8
2 rooms....		7.5	8.7		-5.3
3 rooms....	12.9	14.9	14.5	6.3	25.1
4 rooms....	22.0	21.9	18.7	24.0	42.4
5 rooms....	24.8	21.2	19.8	43.8	30.4
6 rooms....	19.0	16.8	17.2	38.3	19.6
7 rooms or more......	13.5	14.8	17.5	11.6	2.9

[1]Not adjusted for differences in "not reported."

A smaller percentage of the population is single, and a higher percentage of married couples have one, two, three, etc., children, than was the case in 1940. Under these circumstances the dwelling unit with only 1 to 3 rooms is completely inadequate, so the new construction is emphasizing larger units. In fact, one of the greatest needs at the present time is economical housing for families with three and four children. As would be expected, small dwelling units with only 1 to 3 rooms are highly concentrated inside the central city. These smaller units are occupied by single individuals, unrelated persons sharing an apartment, or elderly couples. The slow increase in the number of such households has kept the construction of 3-room units moderately active (and will continue to do so in the near future). However, no one seems to like 1-room or 2-room apartments now; these kinds of units declined in number between 1940 and 1950, and between 1950 and 1957. Both the very new and the older structures that have 5 to 7 rooms are concentrated in the suburbs. Nonmetropolitan areas have a disproportionately large share of the very large, and also of the smaller (3 to 4 rooms) dwelling units (tenant farmers' houses are often small, as are the homes of laborers in small towns).

Number of Bedrooms. As houses become more and more modern in design, and as the size of the family increases again, the size and adequacy of a house may come to be rated in terms of the number of bedrooms. A trend in this direction is indicated by the fact that the National Housing Authority introduced a question on number of bedrooms for the first time in its December 31, 1956, survey. The results, reported in Table 24-4, show that the 2-bedroom unit is by far the most common (39 percent), and that at the present time only about one-fifth of living units have only one bedroom. Three-bedroom places now comprise 28 percent of the total, and are definitely on the increase. Almost no 1-bedroom units seem to be under construction; this situation is evidenced, indirectly, by data showing that in suburban rings 1-bedroom units are comparatively scarce, while the frequency of 3-bedroom units is much greater than average.

How many bedrooms do today's families actually need? The answer to this question can be computed on a theoretical basis, using data on household composition furnished by the Census Bureau's Current Population Survey. Assume that two children in a family may share a bedroom if they are of the same sex, and that they should have separate bedrooms if they are of opposite sexes. Assume, further, that the head and his wife sleep in a separate bedroom, that each additional adult (other relative or nonrelative) should have a separate bedroom, and that two unrelated persons shar-

ing a living unit will share a single bedroom; these assumptions make it possible to compute how many 1-, 2-, 3-, and 4-bedroom units are needed. However, these assumptions do not take into account accomodations for guests; therefore, compute a second theoretical distribution, by assuming further that one-half of the households have a separate guest bedroom and that the other one-half use a "hide-a-bed" or "roll-away" bed for guests. These two theoretical distributions may be compared with the actual distribution, as follows:

Number of bedrooms	Actual number of dwelling units	Theoretical distribution	
		No provision for guests	One-half of units have a guest room
Total.....	100.0	100.0	100.0
1 redroom....	22.6	36.3	18.1
2 redrooms...	39.2	35.5	35.9
3 bedrooms...	28.4	22.0	28.8
4 bedrooms...	9.7	6.2	17.2

These calculations are made, of course, without respect to the ability of the families to pay rental or to purchase such units, or to the location of such units. If every family were put in the house ideally suited for it, and if no provision were made for guests, the present supply of housing would provide sufficient bedrooms. If one-half of the households were to have a guest room, the supply would still be adequate except for a moderate shortage of 4-bedroom units.

OWNER-RENTER STATUS

More than 60 percent of all occupied dwelling units are occupied by owners; renters are now in the minority, comprising only 40 percent of all householders. Following is a summary of the percent of all occupied dwelling units that were owner-occupied on December 31, 1956:

Percent of occupied units owner-occupied	Total	White	Nonwhite
Total: 1950..............	60.4	60.7	36.1
Inside S.M.A.'s.............	58.0	60.2	35.5
Center of cities..........	45.4	47.6	31.1
Metropolitan rings........	71.7	72.5	52.2
Nonmetropolitan areas.......	63.9	66.4	37.0

This is a very different situation from that prevailing in 1940, when these proportions were almost reversed, and when almost 60 percent of occupied dwelling units were rented. Between 1940 and 1957, the various governmental home financing programs of the Housing and Home Finance Agency, the loans for veterans' housing, etc., caused a steady and dramatic increase in the amount of home ownership. The rising level of living and the higher real income of the average workingman are also partially responsible for this development. Following is a summary of the rates of change in owner-occupied and tenant-occupied units:

Dwelling units by type of occupancy and color of occupants, 1957; and by percent change 1950 to 1956 and 1940 to 1950

Types of occupancy and color of occupants	Number of dwelling units (000) Dec. 31, 1956	Percent change	
		1950 to 1956	1940 to 1950
All dwelling units..	55,342	20.3	23.2
Occupied dwelling units	49,874	16.5	22.9
Owner-occupied.......	30,121	27.8	55.0
White..............	28,557	28.4	54.3
Nonwhite...........	1,564	18.6	69.5
Renter-occupied......	19,753	2.5	-2.0
White..............	16,984	1.1	-2.0
Nonwhite...........	2.770	12.4	-2.1
Vacant dwelling units..	5,468	73.2	27.8

The number of tenant-occupied units was almost as large in 1940 as in 1956. The growth which has occurred in owner-occupied housing since 1940 is almost equal to the amount by which all housing has grown since 1940.

There is a much higher rate of ownership in suburban areas than inside the central city, where a majority of people still rent (see Table 24-6). The percentage of home ownership in nonmetropolitan areas is higher than it is inside the central city, but is lower than the percentage of home ownership in metropolitan suburban rings.

As yet, only slightly more than one-third of the houses occupied by nonwhite households are owned by the occupants. Since 1940, the rate of home ownership has increased moderately rapidly among the nonwhite population (the relative gains were greater between 1940 and 1950 than between 1950 and 1957). As of December, 1956, home ownership among nonwhite residents of suburban metropolitan rings was much higher than among nonwhite residents of other areas; at that time, 31.1 percent of the nonwhite population of central cities were home owners. The development of more home ownership among nonwhites has been aided by a slow change in the treatment which nonwhite persons receive at the hands of the private mortgage banking business, as well as by a rapid rise in the economic well-being of these groups, described in other chapters of this book.

QUALITY OF HOUSING

Short of a costly appraisal by a specially trained expert, housing is very difficult to rate according to its livability or quality. Two rough substitute measures have been used in housing censuses, and together they provide a crude assessment of the amount of undesirable living quarters. These measures are "condition of structure" statistics ("dilapidated" or "not dilapidated") and statistics concerning the adequacy of plumbing, bath, and toilet facilities.[4] When used together, these two sets of data may be used to classify units as either "standard" or "substandard." A dwelling unit is

---

[4] "A dwelling unit was reported as dilapidated when it had serious deficiencies, was rundown or neglected, or was of inadequate original construction, so that it did not provide adequate shelter or protection against the elements or endangered the safety of the occupants. A dwelling unit was reported as dilapidated if, because of either deterioration or inadequate original construction, it was below the generally accepted minimum standard for housing and should be torn down or extensively repaired or rebuilt."

"Dwelling units 'with all facilities' consist of those which have: both a flush toilet and a bathtub or shower inside the structure for the exclusive use of the occupants, and hot running water. Units 'lacking facilities' consist of those which lack one or more of the plumbing facilities or which lack exclusive use of these facilities. For example, included as 'lacking facilities' would be a downstairs apartment with hot running water but whose occupants share the bathroom with the occupants of the upstairs apartment." Bureau of the Census, 1956 National Housing Inventory, Vol.1, Part 1, pp. 5-6.

Table 24-6.—DWELLING UNITS CLASSIFIED BY OCCUPANCY STATUS: 1940, 1950, AND 1956

| Occupancy status | National Housing Inventory, 1956 | | | | | Census, April, 1950 | Census, April, 1940 |
| | United States total | Standard metropolitan areas | | | Nonmetro-politan areas | | |
		Total	Central cities	Metro-politan rings			
TYPE OF OCCUPANCY							
All dwelling units..............	100.0	100.0	100.0	100.0	100.0	100.0	100.0
Occupied dwelling units............	90.1	94.2	95.2	93.1	84.7	93.1	93.4
Owner occupied..................	54.4	54.6	43.2	66.8	54.1	51.2	40.7
White.......................	51.6	51.7	39.2	64.9	51.5	48.4	38.6
Nonwhite....................	2.8	3.0	4.0	1.9	2.6	2.9	2.1
Renter occupied.................	35.7	39.5	52.0	26.3	30.7	41.9	52.7
White.......................	30.7	34.2	43.1	24.6	26.1	36.5	45.9
Nonwhite....................	5.0	5.4	8.9	1.7	4.5	5.4	6.7
Vacant dwelling units.............	9.9	5.8	4.8	6.9	15.3	6.9	6.6

Source: National Housing Inventory and 1940 and 1950 Censuses of Housing.

said to be substandard if it is either located in a dilapidated structure or if it lacks some or all plumbing facilities, or both. Table 24-7 shows that on December 31, 1956, one dwelling unit in four (23.7 percent) throughout the nation was substandard, according to the above classification. One dwelling unit in 14 (7.6 percent) was located in a dilapidated structure; an additional 16.1 percent of units, although not located in dilapidated structures, lacked plumbing facilities.[5]

---

[5] As stated above, these two items are only rough indexes of quality. Many dwelling units are located in dilapidated structures, or share a bath with the occupants of an adjoining dwelling unit, and yet are beautifully furnished and completely comfortable. However, these items correlate highly with physical deterioration, poor maintenance, overcrowding, and other aspects of poor housing. When used to rate housing in the aggregate--in terms of a city block, a census tract, or an entire city, state, or nation--they give results that are reliable within usefully narrow limits. Thus, although the assertion that 1/4 of the nation lives in poor-quality housing is not based upon careful inspection and rating of each structure, it nevertheless has a solid basis in observation of the prevalence of indexes of poor quality housing. When it is realized that roughly 1/4 of the nation's dwelling units are located in structures that are 50 years old or older, and that there are, in addition, many thousands of tarpaper shacks and other buildings of inadequate original construction, the assumptions upon which the index of substandard housing rests seem quite plausible.

As discouragingly high as these proportions of substandard housing may seem, they represent a marked improvement over the situation that existed in 1950. At that time, more than one-third of the nation's housing was substandard; the years between 1950 and 1957 witnessed a decline of 29 percent in the quantity of substandard housing, and an increase of 45 percent in the quantity of standard housing. Moreover, the greatest declines that have taken place in substandard housing have been among the units of lowest quality: places with no running water, or with only cold water, and located in dilapidated structures without adequate plumbing facilities.[6]

The largest quantity of substandard housing is found in nonmetropolitan areas, and especially in rural areas. This poorer quality is due both to a greater degree of dilapidation and to lack of plumbing, bath, and toilet facilities. More than two-thirds of all substandard housing, and only

---

[6] Because it is very difficult to get census enumerators to rate structures uniformly with respect to dilapidation or non-dilapidation, the consistency of the data is affected by the type and the amount of training and instruction the enumerators have received. A part (though certainly not all) of the increase in standard housing between 1950 and 1957 may have been due to the changes that occurred in rating procedures during that period.

Table 24-7.—CONDITION OF STRUCTURE AND PLUMBING OF DWELLING UNITS, BY LOCATION: 1950 AND 1956

Condition of structure and plumbing	National Housing Inventory					Percent distri- bution, 1950	Percent change, 1950 to 1956
	United States total	Standard metropolitan areas			Nonmetro- politan areas		
		Total	Central cities	Metro- politan rings			
Total......................	100.0	100.0	100.0	100.0	100.0	100.0	20.0
STANDARD: Not dilapidated, with private bath, hot and cold water..	76.3	87.0	86.1	87.9	61.7	63.1	45.0
SUBSTANDARD, total................	23.7	13.0	13.9	12.1	38.3	36.9	-28.9
Not dilapidated, with toilet and bath, cold water only..........	1.9	1.6	1.7	1.5	2.2	3.2	-30.0
Not dilapidated, lacking toilet and bath......................	8.9	6.3	7.2	5.3	12.4	12.3	-13.6
Not dilapidated, no running water.........................	5.3	0.9	0.2	1.6	11.4	11.5	-45.0
Dilapidated, with private toilet and bath, hot and cold water....	1.7	1.9	2.6	1.1	1.4	1.4	43.4
Dilapidated, lacking hot water or toilet and bath.............	5.9	2.4	2.3	2.5	10.8	8.3	-15.0
Total......................	100.0	57.9	29.9	28.0	42.1	...	...
STANDARD: Not dilapidated, with private bath, hot and cold water..	100.0	66.0	33.8	32.2	34.0	...	...
SUBSTANDARD, total................	100.0	31.8	17.0	14.8	68.2	...	...
Not dilapidated, with toilet and bath, cold water only..........	100.0	50.6	27.7	22.9	49.4	...	...
Not dilapidated, lacking toilet and bath......................	100.0	41.1	24.3	16.8	58.9	...	...
Not dilapidated, no running water.........................	100.0	9.5	0.9	8.6	90.5	...	...
Dilapidated, with private toilet and bath, hot and cold water....	100.0	63.8	45.4	18.4	36.2	...	...
Dilapidated, lacking hot water or toilet and bath.............	100.0	23.1	11.5	11.6	76.9	...	...
Not reported, units excluded for which no information was requested	100.0	36.1	15.4	20.7	63.9	...	...

Source: National Housing Inventory, U.S. Summary.

one-third of all standard housing, is located in nonmetropolitan areas. In nonmetropolitan areas the housing is much older than it is in metropolitan areas, a situation largely responsible for this differential. Also relevant is the fact that, until recently, there have been no building codes or health ordinances governing the construction of living units in rural areas; in most rural areas, there are still no minimum standards. Thus, the contention that we have large quantities of "rural slums" appears to be justified by the data. They are less obviously offensive and create less agitation because they are more widely dispersed and, hence, less easily visible, and because there

is a "double standard" of what constitutes adequate housing in urban and in rural areas.

The central cities contain a disproportionately large share of the older housing found within metropolitan areas; despite this fact, the central cities have only a slightly greater percentage of substandard dwelling units than have the suburban rings. There are two reasons for this situation: (a) Major drives are now underway in the nation's central cities to raze inadequate housing and to renew and upgrade older structures; accompanied by the competitive pressures of an expanding housing supply in the suburbs, these drives have caused many hundreds of the poorest dwelling units to be destroyed or removed from the market. (b) Metropolitan rings are not exclusively occupied by newly-built suburban developments containing modern homes. Many parts of these rings are very old industrial centers, containing much over-age housing and, in many cases, substantial quantities of temporary housing that was poorly built to begin with. Many suburban homes lack adequate plumbing facilities. In 1957, of the 32 percent of all substandard housing located in S.M.A.'s, the central cities contained 17 percent and the suburbs contained 15 percent. Inside the central city, 5 percent of all housing was dilapidated; in the suburbs, 4 percent was dilapidated.

VACANCIES AND VACANCY RATES

In 1957, one dwelling unit in 10 was vacant. This was a 50 percent increase in the vacancy rate, compared to either 1940 or 1950, when only about 5-6 percent of the nation's dwelling units were vacant. One side effect of the current housing boom has been the creation of more competition in the housing business. Many housing experts are hoping that this competition will continue and even increase, thus helping to drive substandard units off the market and to lower the prices the Federal Government and the cities must pay when they buy such units for razing.

However, the highest vacancy rates were found in nonmetropolitan areas, and were a result of out-migration to metropolitan areas rather than of unusually active building in the nonmetropolitan areas. Inside central cities, where the demand for rental housing is always highest, the vacancy rate in December, 1956 was still only 4.8 percent, and in suburban rings it was 6.8 percent.

The vacancy rate at any given time is a product of many factors. If new construction exceeds the amount needed to provide housing for the new families being added each year, to replace the housing being razed, and to furnish housing for the increased number of single and nonfamily persons occupying dwelling units, then an increment is made to vacancies. However, a high vacancy rate is not generally regarded as undesirable, because it appears that the only economical way in which much of the nation's substandard housing can be removed is to let it lose its monetary value through competitive processes and prolonged vacancy. Unfortunately, there is only a very low correlation between vacancy rates and quality of housing. Since Negroes and other nonwhite persons are not permitted to rent many of the vacant units, they must continue to compete for substandard housing; this situation means that the vacancy rates in the slums remain only a very little lower than the rates prevailing in non-slum neighborhoods. Thus, differential treatment of the races in the housing market is keeping the rising vacancy rate from having its full impact with respect to hastening the removal of the most inadequate units, a fact that points up one of the major weaknesses of the "filtering down" theory of housing. (This is a theory asserting that when housing is provided for upper socio-economic groups, a "filtering down" process sees to it that used housing is occupied, and thus benefits all groups.)

CHARACTERISTICS OF SUBSTANDARD DWELLING UNITS

Tables 26-8 and 26-9 undertake to answer the question, "What kinds of dwelling units are substandard?" In general, a disproportionately large share of substandard units are:

(a) Single-family units, or multiple-unit buildings housing five to nine households.
(b) Small units having less than 5 rooms, and especially those having only 1 or 2 rooms.
(c) Units with 1 bedroom or no bedroom.

That these are the outstanding characteristics may be noted most directly in Table 24-8, which shows the "rate of substandardness" for housing of each type. The rates are highest for structures with 1 family unit, or with five to nine family units; for units with only 1 or 2 rooms; and for units with 1 bedroom or less. Inadequate plumbing and small rooms are especially common among the older multiple-unit structures that contain five to nine dwelling units. Single-family houses are more

Table 24-8.—PERCENT OF UNITS DILAPIDATED AND SUBSTANDARD, BY CHARACTERISTICS OF HOUSING

Housing characteristics	Percent of units substandard					Percent of units dilapidated				
	U.S. total	Standard metropolitan areas			Non-metro-politan areas	U.S. total	Standard metropolitan areas			Non-metro-politan areas
		Total	Central cities	Metro-politan rings			Total	Central cities	Metro-politan rings	
NUMBER OF DWELLING UNITS IN STRUCTURE:................	23.7	13.0	13.9	12.1	38.3	7.6	4.2	4.8	3.6	12.2
1 dwelling unit..........	25.1	9.7	6.7	11.4	40.2	8.3	3.2	2.7	3.5	13.3
2 dwelling units.........	18.7	14.2	13.8	15.1	29.1	5.1	4.6	4.5	4.8	6.4
3 and 4 dwelling units....	21.2	20.4	21.6	16.9	23.8	6.0	6.1	6.5	5.1	5.6
5 to 9 dwelling units.....	29.5	29.3	33.6	15.9	30.1	8.1	7.9	9.7	2.2	8.9
10 or more dwelling units.	15.5	14.8	16.1	6.1	25.9	6.1	5.8	6.7	...	4.8
NUMBER OF BEDROOMS IN UNIT:										
0 to 1 bedroom...........	38.3	26.8	25.7	28.8	56.6	13.3	7.9	7.6	8.5	21.7
2 bedrooms...............	22.5	11.1	10.7	11.6	38.2	7.5	4.0	4.3	3.7	12.3
3 or more bedrooms........	16.2	6.3	6.1	6.5	28.9	4.4	2.1	2.7	1.7	7.3
NUMBER OF ROOMS IN UNIT:										
1 or 2 rooms.............	57.9	47.9	47.4	49.2	70.7	19.9	12.7	11.6	15.4	29.1
3 rooms..................	35.0	22.4	20.9	25.1	53.4	13.4	8.3	8.4	8.0	20.8
4 rooms..................	26.5	12.9	11.5	14.4	44.3	9.3	4.2	4.1	4.3	16.0
5 rooms..................	16.2	7.2	7.8	6.8	30.0	4.7	2.4	3.1	1.8	8.2
6 or more rooms..........	14.9	5.8	4.7	6.6	26.6	3.5	2.1	2.3	1.9	5.4

Source: National Housing Inventory.

frequently substandard because of dilapidation than because of inadequate facilities, especially in central cities.

Table 24-9 shows what percentage of substandard dwelling units have each characteristic. Thus, roughly 75 percent of all substandard units were in single-family structures; about 35 percent of substandard units had 1 bedroom or no bedroom; 19 percent had only 1 or 2 rooms; and an additional 20 percent had only 3 rooms. A much smaller percentage of standard dwelling units had each of these characteristics.

The frequency with which these characteristics occurs varies according to whether the unit is substandard because of dilapidation or because of lack of plumbing facilities, and according to whether it is located in a central city, in a metropolitan suburban ring, or in a nonmetropolitan area. Within central cities the highest rates of substandard housing are found for multiple-unit structures, while in nonmetropolitan areas it is the single-family houses that have the highest rates of inade-

quacy. In all areas, however, the rates are much higher for units with only 1 or 2 rooms and with 1 bedroom. Almost everywhere, the lowest rates for substandard housing are found among apartment building with 10 or more dwelling units and among units with 6 or more rooms.

CHARACTERISTICS OF OCCUPANTS OF SUBSTANDARD HOUSING

Persons and families who live in substandard housing tend to have one or more of the following characteristics:

(a) Poverty--An extremely disproportionately large share earn incomes of less than $2,000.

(b) Elderly--A very high percentage are 65 years of age or older.

(c) Nonwhite--A disproportionately large percentage of substandard houses are occupied by Negroes and other nonwhite population.

Table 24-9.—SELECTED CHARACTERISTICS OF STANDARD AND SUBSTANDARD DWELLING UNITS, BY LOCATION INSIDE OR OUTSIDE STANDARD METROPOLITAN AREAS: DECEMBER 31, 1956

Number of dwelling units, number of rooms, and number of bedrooms	United States total			Standard metropolitan areas									Nonmetropolitan areas		
				S.M.A. total			Central city			Metropolitan ring					
	Stand-ard	Substandard		Stand-ard	Substandard		Stand-ard	Substandard		Stand-ard	Substandard		Stand-ard	Substandard	
		Lacking facili-ties	Dilapi-dated		Lacking facili-ties	Dilapi-dated		Lacking facili-ties	Dilapi-dated		Lacking facili-ties	Dilapi-dated		Lacking facili-ties	Dilapi-dated
NUMBER OF DWELLING UNITS															
Total...............	100.0	100.0	100.0	100.0	100.0	100.0	100.0	100.0	100.0	100.0	100.0	100.0	100.0	100.0	100.0
1 dwelling unit..........	69.0	73.5	77.0	62.6	44.3	45.9	46.7	19.0	24.5	79.2	73.3	76.8	81.5	87.0	91.7
2 dwelling units.........	13.2	10.5	8.4	14.7	16.3	16.3	18.6	18.8	17.5	10.6	13.4	14.7	10.2	7.8	4.6
3 and 4 dwelling units....	7.1	6.5	5.4	8.3	14.6	13.2	11.9	21.7	17.6	4.4	6.5	6.7	4.7	2.7	1.8
5 to 9 dwelling units.....	4.1	5.9	4.7	4.9	14.8	11.3	6.9	23.4	17.8	2.9	4.9	1.9	2.5	1.8	1.6
10 or more dwelling units.	6.7	3.7	4.5	9.5	10.0	13.3	15.9	17.0	22.6	2.8	1.9	...	1.1	0.7	0.3
NUMBER OF BEDROOMS															
Total...............	100.0	100.0	100.0	100.0	100.0	100.0	100.0	100.0	100.0	100.0	100.0	100.0	100.0	100.0	100.0
0 to 1 bedroom..........	17.8	34.5	38.5	19.7	49.9	43.8	26.1	60.2	47.8	12.9	38.1	38.1	14.3	27.3	36.0
2 bedrooms..............	38.9	35.9	37.7	39.1	30.9	36.2	39.9	26.9	34.4	38.1	35.4	38.8	38.5	38.2	38.5
3 bedrooms..............	41.1	27.5	21.5	39.3	17.5	18.3	32.2	11.0	16.6	46.8	24.9	20.8	44.6	32.1	23.1
Not reported.............	2.2	2.1	2.2	2.0	1.7	1.7	1.8	1.8	1.3	2.2	1.6	2.3	2.7	2.3	2.4
NUMBER OF ROOMS															
Total...............	100.0	100.0	100.0	100.0	100.0	100.0	100.0	100.0	100.0	100.0	100.0	100.0	100.0	100.0	100.0
1 to 2 rooms.............	4.2	18.2	20.1	4.5	29.8	22.5	6.2	39.9	24.4	2.6	18.2	19.7	3.8	12.8	18.9
3 rooms.................	10.8	17.1	22.4	11.6	20.8	25.6	15.2	22.7	28.8	7.9	18.6	20.8	9.3	15.4	20.9
4 rooms.................	21.1	23.5	26.8	21.5	21.2	21.3	22.1	17.4	18.3	20.9	25.6	25.7	20.4	24.6	29.4
5 rooms.................	27.4	17.9	15.3	28.0	14.4	14.9	25.9	12.5	15.4	30.1	16.7	14.2	26.3	19.5	15.4
6 or more rooms.........	36.2	23.0	15.1	34.1	13.2	15.4	30.4	7.3	12.9	37.9	19.8	18.9	40.2	27.6	15.0
Not reported.............	0.3	0.4	0.3	0.3	0.6	0.3	0.2	0.1	0.1	0.5	1.2	0.7	0.1	0.3	0.3

Source: National Housing Inventory.

(d) Renters--A disproportionately much higher percentage of substandard houses are renter-occupied than owner-occupied.

(e) Broken homes--A disproportionately high percentage of substandard houses are occupied by households whose head is a woman, or by households that are not of the usual husband-wife variety.

(f) Rural residence--A disproportionately high share of substandard houses are located in rural areas, especially in rural-farm areas.

(g) Residence in the South--A much higher percentage of houses are substandard in the South than in any other part of the nation.

Statistical data in support of these generalizations are contained in Tables 24-10, 24-11, 24-12, and 24-13. Each of these differentials shows strong signs of being at least partially independent of each of the others, so the groups occupying the very poorest housing are the groups possessing two, three, or even more of these traits simultaneously. Although data are not available, one suspects that the housing situation of the average elderly, poor, nonwhite, renter-occupied household where the head is a woman, living in the rural South, must be very bad indeed. Conversely, the highest percentages of standard housing would be expected in areas where all of these characteristics were comparatively scarce.

Perhaps few average citizens realize just how far below the housing of the white population the housing of the average nonwhite family falls. In 1950, almost three-fourths of nonwhite households were living in substandard dwellings (see Table 24-12). One-third of all nonwhite dwelling units were in structures rated as dilapidated, and an additional four-fifths lacked plumbing facilities. In urban areas housing conditions for nonwhite families, while still not good, were much better than in rural areas. In rural areas almost no nonwhite family was able to command a standard house; 94 percent of all rural-nonfarm, and 98

Table 24-10.—QUALITY OF HOUSING BY OWNER-RENTER AND HOUSEHOLD STATUS AND AGE OF HEAD: DECEMBER 31, 1956

Area, household status, and age of head	Owner occupied					Renter occupied				
	Total owner occupied	Standard units	Substandard			Total renter occupied	Standard units	Substandard		
			Total	Lacking facilities	Dilapidated			Total	Lacking facilities	Not dilapidated
United States, total.......	100.0	83.6	16.4	12.7	3.7	100.0	71.5	28.5	18.3	10.2
Male head, wife present, no nonrelatives................	100.0	85.6	14.4	11.4	3.0	100.0	74.9	25.1	16.3	8.8
Less than 65 years of age..	100.0	87.0	13.0	10.3	2.7	100.0	75.5	24.5	15.8	8.6
65 years old and over......	100.0	76.6	23.4	18.5	4.9	100.0	68.5	31.5	20.9	10.7
Other head..................	100.0	75.5	24.5	18.2	6.3	100.0	63.4	36.6	23.0	13.6
Less than 65 years of age..	100.0	77.2	22.8	16.8	6.0	100.0	65.9	34.1	21.1	13.1
65 years of age and over...	100.0	73.2	26.8	20.2	6.7	100.0	56.8	43.2	28.2	14.9
Standard metropolitan areas,total..............	100.0	92.8	7.2	5.3	1.9	100.0	81.1	19.0	12.5	6.5
Male head, wife present, no nonrelatives................	100.0	94.0	6.0	4.5	1.5	100.0	85.0	15.0	9.9	5.1
Less than 65 years of age..	100.0	94.5	5.5	4.1	1.4	100.0	85.4	14.6	9.7	4.9
65 years old and over......	100.0	90.2	9.8	7.5	2.3	100.0	81.0	19.0	12.6	6.4
Other head..................	100.0	87.2	12.7	8.9	3.8	100.0	72.8	27.2	17.7	9.4
Less than 65 years of age..	100.0	88.1	11.9	8.3	3.5	100.0	74.3	25.7	16.6	9.1
65 years of age and over...	100.0	85.8	14.2	9.9	4.3	100.0	68.2	31.5	21.3	10.5
Central cities in S.M.A.'s, total..................	100.0	94.7	5.3	3.9	1.4	100.0	80.6	19.4	12.5	6.9
Male head, wife present, no nonrelatives................	100.0	95.6	4.4	3.3	1.1	100.0	85.3	14.7	9.4	5.3
Less than 65 years of age..	100.0	96.1	3.9	2.8	1.2	100.0	85.5	14.5	9.3	5.2
65 years old and over......	100.0	93.1	6.9	6.0	0.8	100.0	83.4	16.6	10.3	6.2
Other head..................	100.0	91.5	8.5	6.0	2.5	100.0	72.2	27.8	18.0	9.8
Less than 65 years of age..	100.0	92.4	7.6	4.7	2.9	100.0	73.2	26.8	17.2	9.6
65 years of age and over...	100.0	90.2	8.8	8.0	1.9	100.0	68.3	31.7	21.2	10.5
Metropolitan rings, total..	100.0	91.5	8.5	6.2	2.2	100.0	82.0	18.0	12.4	5.6
Male head, wife present, no nonrelatives................	100.0	93.0	7.0	5.2	1.7	100.0	84.4	15.6	10.9	4.7
Less than 65 years of age..	100.0	93.7	6.3	4.9	1.5	100.0	85.1	14.9	10.4	4.5
65 years old and over......	100.0	87.3	12.7	8.9	3.8	100.0	74.9	25.1	18.3	6.7
Other head..................	100.0	82.5	17.5	12.2	5.3	100.0	74.9	25.1	16.7	8.4
Less than 65 years of age..	100.0	83.4	16.6	12.3	4.3	100.0	77.7	22.3	14.8	7.5
65 years of age and over...	100.0	81.1	18.9	12.0	6.9	100.0	68.0	32.0	21.5	10.5
Nonmetropolitan areas, total..................	100.0	71.0	29.0	22.9	6.1	100.0	54.4	45.4	28.7	16.9
Male head, wife present, no nonrelatives................	100.0	73.4	26.6	21.3	5.3	100.0	58.5	41.5	26.6	14.9
Less than 65 years of age..	100.0	75.6	24.4	19.6	4.8	100.0	59.6	40.4	25.8	14.6
65 years old and over......	100.0	61.7	38.3	30.6	7.8	100.0	46.4	53.6	35.3	18.2
Other head..................	100.0	62.0	38.0	29.0	9.1	100.0	42.8	57.2	34.6	22.6
Less than 65 years of age..	100.0	62.5	37.5	28.2	9.3	100.0	44.3	55.7	32.5	23.3
65 years of age and over...	100.0	61.4	38.6	29.7	8.9	100.0	40.1	59.9	38.5	21.4

Source: National Housing Inventory.

percent of all rural-farm, nonwhite housing was substandard in 1950.[7] About one-half of this was due to dilapidation. In 1950, dilapidation rates were about 5 times as high among houses occupied by nonwhites as among houses occupied by whites.

[7] At the time of writing, the National Housing Inventory data concerning the quality of housing had not yet been fully tabulated, so changes since 1950 cannot be measured. However, it is believed that through migration, urban renewal, and "invasion" of new neighborhoods, a substantial improvement has been made.

Table 24-11.—QUALITY OF HOUSING BY INCOME OF OCCUPANTS: 1956

Condition and occupancy	Income in 1956							
	Total	Less than $2,000	$2,000 to $3,999	$4,000 to $5,999	$6,000 to $7,999	$8,000 to $9,999	$10,000 or more	Income not reported
CONDITION AND OCCUPANCY								
United States, total...............	100.0	100.0	100.0	100.0	100.0	100.0	100.0	100.0
Owner occupied units, total.............	60.7	52.0	51.0	63.1	69.6	74.6	80.6	59.5
Standard...........................	50.3	28.7	28.5	56.9	66.3	72.0	78.9	52.4
Substandard, total....................	10.4	23.3	12.7	6.2	3.3	2.5	1.8	7.1
Not dilapidated, lacking facilities.	8.1	17.8	10.2	4.8	2.8	1.8	1.3	5.3
Dilapidated.........................	2.3	5.5	2.5	1.4	0.5	0.7	0.5	1.8
Renter occupied.......................	39.3	48.0	49.0	36.8	30.4	25.4	19.4	40.5
Standard...........................	27.7	20.5	33.6	31.1	27.3	24.1	18.4	31.4
Substandard, total....................	11.6	27.4	15.4	5.7	3.1	1.3	1.0	9.2
Not dilapidated, lacking facilities.	7.4	15.9	10.5	4.2	2.1	0.9	0.6	6.0
Dilapidated.........................	4.2	11.5	4.9	1.5	1.0	0.4	0.4	3.2

Source: National Housing Inventory.

The housing differential between whites and non-whites is reduced greatly when the nonwhite person owns his own home, although even in these cases the differential remains large. In 1950, the following comparison between white and nonwhite renter-occupied houses, in percent of dwelling units dilapidated, is worthy of attention:

Urban-rural residence	Percent of rented units in dilapidated structures	
	White households	Nonwhite households
Total.........................	9.2	38.1
Urban...........................	6.2	32.1
Rural-nonfarm....................	16.5	51.3
Rural-farm......................	20.2	50.6

Comparatively few of the owners of these rental units, either in the North or in the South, are themselves nonwhite.

There is also a large regional differential in quality of housing (see Table 24-13). In the three geographic divisions of the South, and in the West North Central states, the quality of housing in 1950 was much below the national average, while in the New England, Middle Atlantic, and Pacific states it was much above-average. The smallest amount of substandard housing was found in the Pacific states, where the proportions of dilapidated

houses, and houses lacking facilities, were less than half the national average. The worst housing conditions in 1950 existed in the East South Central states, where more than two-thirds of all dwelling units were substandard, and almost one-fourth were dilapidated.

In each geographic division, the renter-occupied units were much more likely to be substandard than were the owner-occupied units. As a consequence, much more than one-half of the rental housing in the South and in the West North Central states was substandard.

SIZE OF HOUSEHOLD

Over the years, there has been a steady change in the number of persons occupying dwelling units. This change may be summarized as follows:

Number of persons per household	1956	1950	1940
Total.....................	100.0	100.0	100.0
1 person....................	11.4	9.3	7.7
2 persons...................	28.3	28.1	24.8
3 persons...................	20.4	22.8	22.4
4 persons...................	18.5	18.4	18.1
5 persons...................	11.0	10.4	11.5
6 or more person.............	10.3	11.1	15.6
6 persons...................	...	5.3	6.8
7 persons...................	...	2.7	3.8
8 persons...................	...	1.4	2.2
9 persons...................	...	0.8	1.3
10 or more persons............	...	0.9	1.5
Median number...............	...	3.1	3.3

Table 24-12.—QUALITY OF HOUSING (PERCENT SUBSTAND-
ARD) BY URBAN-RURAL RESIDENCE, OWNER-RENTER
STATUS AND COLOR: 1950

Housing quality, owner-renter status and color	Percent substandard			
	U.S. total	Urban	Rural non-farm	Rural farm
ALL OCCUPIED UNITS				
Total...............	35.4	21.9	53.6	75.7
Lacking facilities.....	26.4	15.5	40.9	58.6
Dilapidated...........	9.0	6.4	12.7	17.1
White, total........	31.8	18.2	50.4	72.8
Lacking facilities.....	25.1	13.9	40.0	59.4
Dilapidated...........	6.7	4.3	10.4	13.4
Nonwhite, total.....	73.2	61.2	94.4	98.1
Lacking facilities.....	39.8	33.7	51.1	52.1
Dilapidated...........	33.4	27.5	43.3	46.0
OWNER-OCCUPIED UNITS				
White, total........	28.7	12.4	44.5	68.6
Lacking facilities.....	23.8	9.7	37.5	58.1
Dilapidated...........	4.9	2.7	7.0	10.5
Nonwhite, total.....	68.4	52.2	92.5	96.3
Lacking facilities.....	43.9	34.3	58.5	59.5
Dilapidated...........	24.5	17.9	34.0	36.8
RENTER-OCCUPIED UNITS				
White, total........	36.0	24.7	61.0	82.6
Lacking facilities.....	26.8	18.5	44.5	62.4
Dilapidated...........	9.2	6.2	16.5	20.2
Nonwhite, total.....	75.8	65.6	95.9	99.0
Lacking facilities.....	37.7	33.5	44.6	48.4
Dilapidated...........	38.1	32.1	51.3	50.6

Source: U.S. Census of Housing: 1950, Vol. I,
Part 1, Table 7.

Since 1940 there has been a steady increase in the number of 1-person and 2-person households, and an equally steady decrease in the proportion of households with 6 persons or more. This has resulted from the combination of trends enumerated earlier in this chapter, in the discussion concerning changes in average size of household. It is entirely probable that the percentage of 6-person households will reverse its long-term downward trend and increase in the near future, as a result of higher fertility.

Table 24-14 shows that a considerably higher-than-average proportion of 1-person households are renter-occupied, and that households having 4 or 5 members are inclined to be owner-occupied households. One-person households are much more common in central cities and in nonmetropolitan areas than in suburban metropolitan rings, where a very high percentage of dwellings are occupied by husband-wife families. Conversely, there is a comparative shortage of 5-person and 6-person households inside central cities; apparently there is a tendency for many families of this size to move to the suburbs. In comparison with metropolitan areas, nonmetropolitan areas tend to have concentrations both of 1-person households and of households with 5 or more persons. The first of these concentrations is probably due to the residence of widows in small towns and villages, and the second to higher fertility in nonmetropolitan areas.

Table 24-13.—QUALITY OF HOUSING BY GEOGRAPHIC DIVISION OF RESIDENCE AND OWNER-RENTER STATUS: 1950

Geographic Division	All units			Owner-occupied			Renter-occupied		
	Total substandard	Lacking facilities	Dilapidated	Total substandard	Lacking facilities	Dilapidated	Total substandard	Lacking facilities	Dilapidated
U. S. total........	36.9	27.1	9.8	30.9	24.9	6.0	41.1	28.2	12.9
New England..........	26.1	21.3	4.8	18.4	15.2	3.2	29.4	23.4	6.0
Middle Atlantic.......	20.5	15.5	5.0	15.4	12.6	2.8	22.8	16.0	6.8
East North Central....	33.9	27.6	6.3	28.4	24.3	4.1	38.4	29.8	8.6
West North Central....	49.1	41.3	7.8	42.0	36.9	5.1	56.2	46.3	9.9
South Atlantic........	51.2	35.3	15.9	44.2	34.9	9.3	58.1	36.6	21.5
East South Central....	67.3	44.3	23.0	60.0	46.2	13.8	74.0	43.5	30.5
West South Central....	52.4	34.4	18.0	44.8	33.5	11.3	58.9	35.9	23.0
Mountain..............	37.7	27.1	10.6	31.6	24.2	7.4	40.3	28.3	12.0
Pacific..............	16.4	10.5	5.9	11.0	7.4	3.6	20.4	12.6	7.8

Source: U. S. Census of Housing, 1950, Vol. 1, Part 1, Table 18.

Table 24-14.—NUMBER OF PERSONS IN DWELLING UNITS, BY OWNER-RENTER STATUS AND BY LOCATION IN METROPOLITAN AND NONMETROPOLITAN AREAS: 1956

Owner-renter status and location	Total	Number of persons in dwelling units					
		1 person	2 persons	3 persons	4 persons	5 persons	6 or more persons
DISTRIBUTION BY NUMBER OF PERSONS							
All occupied units, total..........	100.0	11.4	28.3	20.4	18.5	11.0	10.3
In standard metropolitan areas..........	100.0	10.9	28.9	21.2	19.2	10.9	8.9
Central cities......................	100.0	13.9	31.5	20.8	16.6	9.3	7.9
Metropolitan rings..................	100.0	7.6	26.1	21.6	22.1	12.7	10.0
In nonmetropolitan areas..............	100.0	12.2	27.4	19.4	17.4	11.2	12.4
Owner-occupied units..............	100.0	8.2	28.6	20.5	20.3	12.1	10.3
In standard metropolitan areas..........	100.0	6.6	27.9	21.4	22.1	12.6	9.5
Central cities......................	100.0	8.3	31.4	21.1	19.6	11.0	8.7
Metropolitan rings..................	100.0	5.4	25.5	21.6	23.7	13.7	10.1
In nonmetropolitan areas..............	100.0	10.4	29.5	19.3	17.9	11.5	11.4
Renter-occupied units..............	100.0	16.3	27.8	20.4	15.8	9.4	10.3
In standard metropolitan areas..........	100.0	16.8	30.3	20.9	15.4	8.6	8.1
Central cities......................	100.0	18.6	31.6	20.5	14.1	7.8	7.3
Metropolitan rings..................	100.0	13.0	27.6	21.5	18.1	10.2	9.7
In nonmetropolitan areas..............	100.0	15.4	23.5	19.6	16.6	10.7	14.2
DISTRIBUTION BY LOCATION							
All dwelling units, total..........	100.0	100.0	100.0	100.0	100.0	100.0	100.0
In standard metropolitan areas..........	59.7	57.0	61.0	61.8	62.1	59.0	51.6
Central cities......................	52.1	66.7	56.8	51.2	44.9	44.2	46.3
Metropolitan rings..................	47.9	33.3	43.2	48.8	55.1	55.8	53.7
In nonmetropolitan areas..............	40.3	43.0	39.0	38.2	27.9	41.0	48.4
Owner-occupied units..............	100.0	100.0	100.0	100.0	100.0	100.0	100.0
In standard metropolitan areas..........	57.4	46.0	56.0	59.8	62.4	59.5	52.9
Central cities......................	40.8	51.1	45.9	40.2	36.3	35.7	37.0
Metropolitan rings..................	59.2	48.9	54.1	59.8	63.7	64.3	63.0
In nonmetropolitan areas..............	42.6	54.0	44.0	40.2	37.6	40.5	47.1
Renter-occupied units..............	100.0	100.0	100.0	100.0	100.0	100.0	100.0
In standard metropolitan areas..........	63.3	65.4	69.0	64.7	61.5	58.1	49.5
Central cities......................	67.7	75.1	70.6	66.7	62.0	61.6	61.4
Metropolitan rings..................	32.3	24.9	29.4	33.3	38.0	38.4	38.6
In nonmetropolitan areas..............	36.7	34.6	31.0	35.3	38.5	41.9	50.5

Source: National Housing Inventory.

OVERCROWDING

By taking into account simultaneously the number of rooms and the number of persons in a household, it is possible to estimate the extent of overcrowding. The most conventional measure is the "number of persons per room," obtained for each household individually by dividing the number of occupants by the number of rooms. A ratio of 1.0 persons per room is regarded as the maximum desirable under present standards, while 1.51 or more persons per room is regarded as evidence of definite overcrowding. In 1950 and 1940, the Census reported the following measures of overcrowding:

Persons per room	Total 1950	Tenant occupied	Owner occupied	Total 1940
Total				
1.0+persons per room..	15.7	21.4	11.0	20.3
1.51+persons per room.	6.2	9.2	3.7	9.0
Urban				
1.0+persons per room..	13.3	18.1	8.5	15.9
1.51+persons per room.	4.7	7.0	2.3	5.8
Rural nonfarm				
1.0+persons per room..	19.4	28.1	14.4	22.6
1.51+persons per room.	8.6	13.5	5.7	11.1
Rural farm				
1.0+persons per room..	22.3	34.5	15.9	30.4
1.51+persons per room.	10.2	18.0	6.1	16.1

Thus, almost 1 household in 6 was overcrowded to some extent, and 1 in 16 was definitely overcrowded. Overcrowding was much less common in urban than in rural areas. Almost twice as large a proportion of residences are overcrowded in rural-farm areas as in urban areas. Also, there is roughly twice as much overcrowding in tenant households as in owner households. As a result, the most crowded households are those of rural-farm tenants, and the least crowded are the owner-occupied urban households.

The current wave of building is helping to reduce overcrowding, and many of the nation's slum clearance and urban renewal programs are aimed at alleviating this difficulty. Between 1940 and 1950 there was a substantial reduction (25 to 50 percent) in overcrowding, as may be observed from the right-hand column of the above summary. This reduction took place in all types of areas, and in tenant-occupied as well as owner-occupied units (data not shown).

Overcrowding is a much more serious problem among the nonwhite than among the white population. In 1940, the following set of white-nonwhite differentials with respect to crowding existed in urban and rural areas:

Area	Persons per room					
	Total		White		Nonwhite	
	1.01+	1.51+	1.01+	1.51+	1.01+	1.51+
Total.......	20.3	9.0	18.2	7.5	40.0	23.2
Urban.........	15.9	5.8	14.4	4.8	31.2	16.0
Rural nonfarm..	22.6	11.1	21.1	9.9	41.6	25.6
Rural farm.....	30.4	16.1	26.5	13.0	53.9	34.7

These differentials have continued to prevail, although they are all now at a much lower level. Table 24-15 examines regional differentials, by color, for renter-occupied units. The regional pattern of crowding is what one would expect—high in the South and high for non-whites in all regions. (Data with which to examine this differential in 1957 are not available.)

Table 24-15 reports the percentage of tenant-occupied dwelling units that were at least partially overcrowded (with 1.01+ persons per room) and the percent that were definitely overcrowded (with 1.51+ persons per room), by color, by urban-rural residence, and by region, in 1940. Throughout the entire United States, 22 percent of all white and 42 percent of all nonwhite households indicated at least some crowding; 9 percent of the white households and 25 percent of the nonwhite

Table 24-15.—PERCENTAGE OF TENANT-OCCUPIED DWELLING UNITS OVERCROWDED, BY COLOR, URBAN-RURAL, RESIDENCE, AND REGION: 1940

Urban-rural residence and color	United States total		Northeast and North Central		South		West	
	1.01+ persons per room	1.51+ persons per room	1.01+ persons per room	1.51+ persons per room	1.01+ persons per room	1.51+ persons per room	1.01+ persons per room	1.51+ persons per room
All renter-occupied units..................	24.9	11.4	17.7	6.0	39.9	22.0	20.3	9.9
White..........................	22.3	9.4	17.1	5.6	36.6	18.9	19.9	9.6
Nonwhite.......................	42.4	25.0	28.1	12.9	47.7	29.4	31.9	18.0
Urban, renter-occupied units................	19.7	7.6	17.1	5.4	30.5	15.3	15.0	6.2
White..........................	17.9	6.3	16.3	4.9	26.8	12.3	14.7	6.0
Nonwhite.......................	34.1	18.0	27.2	12.0	40.0	23.0	25.1	12.4
Rural-nonfarm, renter-occupied units.........	29.6	15.0	19.4	7.8	40.7	22.3	28.9	16.0
White..........................	27.7	13.4	19.1	7.6	39.3	20.5	28.6	15.7
Nonwhite.......................	45.4	28.4	35.9	20.6	46.4	29.2	44.1	29.7
Rural-farm, renter-occupied units...........	40.4	22.8	20.0	8.3	51.7	30.7	37.1	21.7
White..........................	35.6	18.7	19.7	8.0	49.0	27.4	36.3	21.0
Nonwhite.......................	55.9	36.0	44.3	30.2	56.1	36.1	54.1	35.2

Source: 1940 Census of Housing, Vol. II, Part 1, Table 10.

households appeared to be definitely overcrowded. Overcrowding, among both white and nonwhite households, was much higher in rural than in urban areas, and much higher in rural-farm than in rural-nonfarm areas. In all categories, crowding was greatest in the South and least in the Northeast. As a result, the least overcrowding was found among urban white households in the Northeast (4.9 percent definitely overcrowded), and the most severe overcrowding was found among rural-farm nonwhite households in the South, where 36 percent of the households were definitely overcrowded.

The over-all picture of housing that has been presented here for the nonwhite resident of the South--almost universally substandard housing, and widespread overcrowding--makes plausible the hypothesis that one major incentive for out-migration from the South is the hope of obtaining more livable housing conditions. These same statistics show that only a comparatively small share of these migrants can realize this ambition in the North; in the North, also, substandard housing and overcrowding are "normal living conditions" for nonwhite citizens.

Overcrowding in 1957. The extent of overcrowding in 1957 can be inferred from Table 24-16, in which households are cross-classified by number of rooms and number of persons. All households above the diagonal line contain more than 1.0 persons per room. This table shows that there is almost no overcrowding in households with 3 persons or less. Overcrowding is much more prevalent among 6-person households than among any other group; more than two-thirds of such households are overcrowded at least to some extent. More than 45 percent of 5-person households, and 18 percent of 4-person households, are at least partially overcrowded.

INCOME IN RELATION TO HOUSING

On December 31, 1956, the median rent paid by the general renting public was $60 per month (see Table 24-17). However, the amount varied greatly according to the income level. Persons making less than $2,000 per year paid only two-thirds as much as this median rent, while those with an income of $10,000 or more per year paid two-thirds more than the median amount. These data indicate the truth of the widely-known generalization that the higher a person's income is the more money he spends for housing, and the more adequate his housing is. There is widespread interest

Table 24-16.—NUMBER OF ROOMS IN DWELLING UNIT BY NUMBER OF PERSONS IN DWELLING UNIT

Occupancy and number of rooms	United States total	Number of persons in dwelling unit					
		1	2	3	4	5	6 or more persons
TOTAL, OWNER-OCCUPIED	100.0	100.0	100.0	100.0	100.0	100.0	100.0
1 or 2 rooms	1.8	9.7	1.6	1.2	0.9	0.3	0.8
3 rooms	4.2	9.7	6.2	3.4	1.8	2.2	3.1
4 rooms	18.5	21.6	22.3	19.6	17.2	15.0	10.2
5 rooms	30.2	24.8	31.6	32.8	32.3	29.2	22.2
6 rooms	25.7	18.3	22.5	25.7	28.6	30.1	29.3
7 or more rooms	19.4	15.3	15.6	17.0	19.0	23.1	34.0
Not reported	0.2	0.5	0.3	0.2	0.1	0.2	0.4
TOTAL, RENTER-OCCUPIED	100.0	100.0	100.0	100.0	100.0	100.0	100.0
1 or 2 rooms	13.0	43.4	13.1	6.8	2.5	1.9	3.6
3 rooms	23.9	30.6	33.7	23.7	15.2	11.8	11.6
4 rooms	27.1	14.3	27.2	31.9	32.4	29.3	27.8
5 rooms	19.1	6.7	15.4	21.3	26.3	28.4	24.9
6 rooms	16.6	4.8	10.4	16.0	23.2	28.4	31.9
Not reported	0.2	0.2	0.2	0.3	0.3	0.1	0.2

Source: National Housing Inventory.

Table 24-17.—GROSS MONTHLY RENT BY INCOME IN 1956

Gross monthly rent	Total	Income in 1956 (dollars)						Income not reported
		Less than $2,000	$2,000 to $3,999	$4,000 to $5,999	$6,000 to $7,999	$8,000 to $9,999	$10,000 or over	
Total...................	100.0	100.0	100.0	100.0	100.0	100.0	100.0	100.0
Less than $30......................	10.2	32.0	7.9	3.2	0.9	0.6	0.7	8.0
$30 to $39.........................	9.8	18.3	12.4	5.0	5.1	2.6	0.8	2.8
$40 to $49.........................	14.1	19.1	18.6	10.9	8.2	4.0	3.5	13.2
$50 to $59.........................	15.8	12.2	19.1	17.7	14.3	11.1	6.2	15.6
$60 to $79.........................	20.9	12.5	29.3	35.2	30.8	26.8	16.3	29.0
$80 to $99.........................	13.9	3.6	8.7	20.0	23.1	26.6	23.2	16.0
$100 or more......................	9.3	2.3	4.0	8.1	17.7	28.2	49.3	15.5
Median rent......................	60.0	39.9	55.8	63.8	74.0	83.7	99.4	...

Source: National Housing Inventory.

in the relationship between income and housing, and in the amounts of additional housing that are purchased as additional income is received. Table 24-17 summarizes the income-rent relationship for December 31, 1956. Table 24-18 demonstrates that although it is no longer necessary to be rich to own one's own home, owners do have a considerably larger income than renters. In 1956 the median income of owners was $4,800, and the median income of renters was only about 3/4 of that amount.

Housing statisticians are fond of using the "rent-income ratio," which is determined by dividing the annual gross rent by the annual family income, and multiplying the result by 100 to form a percent. Table 24-18 presents the distribution of these rent-income ratios for central cities, metropolitan rings, and nonmetropolitan areas. It is easy to see that rent takes a bigger "bite" out of the consumer's dollar in metropolitan areas than in nonmetropolitan areas, and that rent is a relatively greater source of expense in central cities than in suburban metropolitan rings. The fact that the rent-income ratio has risen considerably since 1950 could mean either that people have become willing to spend a larger percentage of their income for housing, or that rents have risen faster than other expenses.

The lower panel of Table 24-19 shows that poor people must spend a larger percentage of their to-

Table 24-18.—MEDIAN INCOME OF OWNERS AND RENTERS AND RENT-INCOME RATIOS, BY PLACE OF RESIDENCE: 1956

Income and gross rent as percent of income	National Housing Inventory					April 1, 1950
	United States total	Standard metropolitan areas			Nonmetropolitan areas	
		Total	Central cities	Metropolitan rings		
Median income in 1956:						
Total................................	$4,300	$5,000	$4,600	$5,300	$3,400	$2,900
Owner occupied..........................	4,800	5,500	5,300	5,700	3,700	3,100
Renter occupied.........................	3,600	4,100	4,000	4,300	2,800	2,700
Gross rent as percent of income..........	100.0	100.0	100.0	100.0	100.0	100.0
Less than 10 percent..................	7.5	6.2	6.6	5.2	10.4	14.4
10 to 14 percent.....................	19.5	19.7	19.9	19.4	19.0	23.4
15 to 19 percent.....................	23.0	22.9	21.7	25.8	23.3	20.9
20 to 24 percent.....................	16.9	17.9	17.6	18.7	14.6	21.2
25 to 29 percent.....................	10.2	10.2	10.0	10.7	10.2	
30 to 39 percent.....................	9.3	9.7	9.7	9.7	9.4	20.2
40 percent or more...................	13.3	13.4	14.7	10.6	13.1	

Source: National Housing Inventory.

Table 24-19.—GROSS RENT AS PERCENT OF INCOME, BY SELECTED CHARACTERISTICS OF OCCUPANTS, DECEMBER 31, 1956

Characteristics	Total	Gross rent as percentage of income					
		Less than 10 percent	10 to 14 percent	15 to 19 percent	20 to 29 percent	30 percent or more	Not available
Total...........................	100.0	5.4	14.2	16.8	19.7	16.6	27.3
NUMBER OF PERSONS							
1 person........................	100.0	4.0	7.2	7.6	14.5	31.1	35.6
2 persons.......................	100.0	5.4	16.5	15.6	17.1	16.8	28.6
3 persons.......................	100.0	5.8	15.5	19.1	20.9	12.4	26.4
4 persons.......................	100.0	5.5	16.5	20.9	24.2	10.3	22.7
5 persons.......................	100.0	5.6	13.6	19.9	26.0	11.2	23.9
6 or more persons...............	100.0	7.1	13.7	22.7	21.2	14.9	20.4
SEX AND AGE OF HOUSEHOLD HEAD							
Male head, wife present, no nonrelatives......	100.0	6.2	16.8	20.3	21.1	10.4	25.2
Under 35 years..................	100.0	5.6	17.2	24.4	26.2	9.1	17.5
35 to 64 years..................	100.0	7.3	18.2	18.5	17.5	8.1	30.3
65 years and over..............	100.0	2.0	7.0	10.6	17.8	29.9	32.8
Other head......................	100.0	3.9	8.5	9.3	16.6	30.0	31.7
Under 65 years of age..........	100.0	4.7	9.8	11.2	18.3	26.2	29.8
65 years and over..............	100.0	1.6	5.0	4.1	12.1	40.4	36.8
YEAR MOVED INTO UNIT							
1955-56.........................	100.0	4.4	13.2	19.1	24.0	18.5	20.8
1950-54.........................	100.0	6.0	15.2	16.6	19.8	15.5	26.9
1945-49.........................	100.0	8.8	17.4	14.9	13.8	14.3	30.8
1944 or earlier.................	100.0	6.9	15.6	13.0	11.9	17.6	34.9
INCOME IN 1956							
Less than $2,000................	100.0	1.1	2.8	4.9	12.3	55.6	23.4
$2,000 to $3,999................	100.0	2.8	10.4	20.8	37.2	19.3	9.4
$4,000 to $5,999................	100.0	6.9	23.6	31.3	27.3	3.0	7.8
$6,000 to $7,999................	100.0	18.5	38.3	25.7	10.6	0.2	6.7
$8,000 to $9,999................	100.0	27.6	43.3	15.4	6.7	0.5	6.5
$10,000 or more.................	100.0	...	...	...	...	...	100.0

Source: National Housing Inventory.

tal income for rent than well-to-do people; hence, low rent-income ratios are generally found among high-income families, while high rent-income ratios are usually found among low-income families. This same table tells us that households with high rent-income ratios tend to be single-person households (such as old-age pensioners), or families with 6 or more persons; they also tend to be recent movers, to be elderly, and to be headed by a woman or by a person other than a husband with wife present. These are the characteristics of low-income groups.

COMPONENTS OF CHANGE IN THE HOUSING INVENTORY

One unique aspect of the Census Bureau's 1956-57 National Housing Inventory was its analy-sis of housing change in terms of components, which was accomplished by comparing each dwelling unit in the Inventory sample with the 1950 Census returns. This comparison, supplemented by inquiries made of the 1956 occupants, or of informed neighbors, permitted each dwelling unit which had been in existence in 1950 to be classified in the 1956 Inventory under one of the following five categories:

Same unit as in 1950

Unit changed by conversion

Unit changed by merger

Unit lost through demolition

Unit lost through other means

Similarly, all the units in the Inventory sample could be classified according to the following categories:

Same unit
Unit changed by conversion
Unit changed by merger
Unit added through new construction
Unit added through other sources

An entire set of publications, ten reports of Volume 1, of the National Housing Inventory is devoted to statistics concerning the components of change between April 1, 1950 and December 31, 1956.

Space does not permit an analysis of these data. However, the following notes, some quoted or some paraphrased from the "Summary of Findings" of the National Housing Inventory may serve as a guide to those interested only in the general over-all result. Tables 24-20 to 24-23, reproduced from the census report, document these notes and provide additional information.

. . . .

Of the 55,342,000 dwelling units reported for the United States in 1956, approximately 41,453,000, or 74.9 percent, consist of "same" units, that is, those which existed in 1950 and which were reported as essentially unchanged in 1956. [100 percent minus this figure is a measure of the proportion of units that did not exist in 1950 or were changed in some way through conversion, merger, or other sources.]

One-tenth of the Nation's 1950 dwelling units were reported as demolished, converted, merged, or otherwise changed.

Conversion is the process of changing existing dwelling units into a larger number of dwelling units. The net number of units added to the housing inventory through conversion was 708,000.

Merger is the process of changing existing units into a smaller number of dwelling units. The net number of units lost through mergers was 672,000. Thus, gains through conversions were largely offset by losses through mergers.

New construction was by far the most important single factor of change in the housing inventory. Dwelling units added through new construction totaled 10,920,000, or 19.7 percent of the 1956 inventory. This represents an annual aver-

age of 1,618,000 new dwelling units over the 6 3/4 year period.

About 943,000 dwelling units, or 1.7 percent of the 1956 inventory, were added through "other sources," such as nonresidential space, rooming houses, or transient accomodations.

Approximately 1,131,000 units or 2.5 percent of the Nation's 1950 housing inventory were lost through demolition, and 1,413,000 units or 3.1 percent were lost through "other sources"--abandonment, disaster, or other means, such as changing dwelling units into nonresidential space, rooming houses, or transient accomodations.

Characteristics of Units Created or Removed

Virtually all of the increment of dwelling units created by conversion became additions to the renter-occupied sector.

With respect to the quality of dwelling units involved in conversion, the number of units reported as "not dilapidated, with all plumbing facilities" doubled (from 494,000 to 911,000) while the number of units either dilapidated or lacking some plumbing facilities tripled (from 146,000 to 434,000).

Mergers tended to remove units exclusively from the renter supply, while leaving the number of owner-occupied units unchanged. Mergers tended to improve the over-all quality of housing by reducing the number of dwelling units (from 772,000 to 185,000) which were dilapidated or lacked some plumbing facilities. This reduction was greater inside than outside standard metropolitan areas.

About 85 percent of the 1,131,000 units demolished in the period 1950 to 1956 had been renter-occupied or vacant in 1950. Of the demolished units, approximately three-quarters had been dilapidated or lacked some plumbing facilities in 1950. The total number of units demolished inside central cities was far greater than the number demolished in standard metropolitan areas outside central cities.

Although only 9 percent of the Nation's occupied housing was occupied by nonwhites in 1950, about 27 percent (256,000) of the units demolished between 1950 and 1956 had been occupied by non-whites.

Of the renter-occupied units demolished, approximately four-fifths had rented for less than $40 per month.

Of the units lost through "other means," approximately 73 percent were reported as dilapidated or lacking plumbing facilities in 1950. Of the renter-occupied units lost through "other means," approximately four-fifths had rented for less than $40 per month.

For nonwhites, the major source of additional housing between 1950 and 1956 came from units formerly occupied by white households--approximately 745,000 units came from this source. Inside standard metropolitan areas, 31 percent of the housing occupied by nonwhites in 1956 had been occupied by white households in 1950, compared with only 14 percent outside standard metropolitan areas. This type of shift varied widely by regions; for the South the figure was 12 percent; for the West it was 53 percent; for the North Central, 41 percent; and for the Northeast, 33 percent.

At the same time, about 140,000 units in the United States occupied by nonwhites in 1950 were occupied by white households in 1956.

With respect to condition and plumbing facilities, the over-all quality of "same" units in 1956 showed improvement over 1950. Nevertheless,

some downgrading as well as upgrading took place. About 3,412,000 units were upgraded from "lacking facilities or dilapidated" to "not dilapidated, with all facilities" between 1950 and 1956. During the same period, about 1,285,000 units were downgraded from "not dilapidated, with all facilities" to "lacking plumbing facilities or dilapidated." With respect both to numbers and to relative rate, the upgrading that took place outside standard metropolitan areas exceeded that occurring inside standard metropolitan areas. Of the units that were downgraded within standard metropolitan areas, a greater number were located within the central cities than outside of them. The North Central region showed the greatest relative improvement, with four times as many units upgraded as downgraded; the South was next, and the West and the Northeast were last. Generally, improvement was greater among units that were owner occupied in 1950 than it was among those that were renter occupied.

. . . .

ECONOMIC, SOCIOLOGICAL, AND PSYCHOLOGICAL
FORCES UNDERLYING HOUSING CHANGES

It would be a mistake to contend that demographic forces are the only causes of the rapid changes currently taking place in the housing of

Table 24-20.—SOURCE OF THE 1956 HOUSING INVENTORY

Area	Total dwelling units, 1956 (000)	Same units 1950 and 1956 (000)	Units changed by--		Units added through--		Percent distribution					
			Conversion (000)	Merger (000)	New construction (000)	Other sources (000)	Total dwelling units, 1956	Same units, 1950 and 1956	Units changed by--		Units added through--	
									Conversion	Merger	New construction	Other sources
United States.............	55,342	41,453	1,376	649	10,920	943	100.0	74.9	2.5	1.2	19.7	1.7
Inside standard metrop. areas.....	31,615	23,149	880	371	6,763	451	100.0	73.2	2.8	1.2	21.4	1.4
In central cities..............	16,286	13,410	573	266	1,783	255	100.0	82.3	3.5	1.6	10.9	1.6
Not in central cities..........	15,329	9,740	307	106	4,980	196	100.0	63.5	2.0	0.7	32.5	1.3
Outside standard metrop. areas....	23,727	18,304	496	277	4,157	492	100.0	77.1	2.1	1.2	17.5	2.1
Northeast..................	14,201	11,116	412	170	2,364	139	100.0	78.3	2.9	1.2	16.6	1.0
Inside standard metrop. areas.....	10,749	8,495	304	124	1,743	84	100.0	79.0	2.8	1.2	16.2	0.8
Outside standard metrop. areas....	3,451	2,622	109	46	620	55	100.0	76.0	3.2	1.3	18.0	1.6
North Central..............	15,843	12,513	452	216	2,425	238	100.0	79.0	2.9	1.4	15.3	1.5
Inside standard metrop. areas.....	8,686	6,566	274	112	1,629	105	100.0	75.6	3.2	1.3	18.8	1.2
Outside standard metrop. areas....	7,157	5,946	178	104	796	132	100.0	83.1	2.5	1.5	11.1	1.8
South..................	16,638	11,969	378	204	3,770	317	100.0	71.9	2.3	1.2	22.7	1.9
Inside standard metrop. areas.....	6,728	4,452	217	105	1,847	107	100.0	66.2	3.2	1.6	27.5	1.6
Outside standard metrop. areas....	9,910	7,518	161	98	1,923	209	100.0	75.9	1.6	1.0	19.4	2.1
West..................	8,660	5,855	133	60	2,362	250	100.0	67.6	1.5	0.7	27.3	2.9
Inside standard metrop. areas.....	5,451	3,637	85	31	1,544	155	100.0	66.7	1.6	0.6	28.3	2.8
Outside standard metrop. areas....	3,209	2,218	49	29	817	95	100.0	69.1	1.5	0.9	25.5	3.0

Source: 1956 National Housing Inventory, Vol.1, Part 1, Table A.

Table 24-21.—DISPOSITION OF THE 1950 HOUSING INVENTORY

Area	Total dwelling units, 1950 (000)	Same units, 1950 and 1956 (000)	Units changed by--		Units lost through--		Percent distribution					
			Conversion (000)	Merger (000)	Demolition (000)	Other means (000)	Total dwelling units, 1956	Same units, 1950 and 1956	Units changed by--		Units lost through--	
									Conversion	Merger	Demolition	Other means
United States	45,986	41,453	668	1,321	1,131	1,413	100.0	90.1	1.5	2.9	2.5	3.1
Inside standard metrop. areas	25,630	23,149	422	765	643	651	100.0	90.3	1.6	3.0	2.5	2.5
In central cities	15,123	13,410	271	544	512	387	100.0	88.7	1.8	3.6	3.4	2.6
Not in central cities	10,507	9,740	151	221	131	264	100.0	92.7	1.4	2.1	1.2	2.5
Outside standard metrop. areas	20,356	18,304	246	556	488	762	100.0	89.9	1.2	2.7	2.4	3.7
Northeast	12,051	11,116	199	349	207	179	100.0	92.2	1.7	2.9	1.7	1.5
Inside standard metrop. areas	9,220	8,495	143	260	197	126	100.0	92.1	1.6	2.8	2.1	1.4
Outside standard metrop. areas	2,851	2,622	56	89	10	54	100.0	92.6	2.0	3.1	0.4	1.9
North Central	13,746	12,513	215	422	255	342	100.0	91.0	1.6	3.1	1.9	2.5
Inside standard metrop. areas	7,262	6,566	130	219	170	177	100.0	90.4	1.8	3.0	2.3	2.4
Outside standard metrop. areas	6,484	5,946	85	202	85	165	100.0	91.7	1.3	3.1	1.3	2.5
South	13,658	11,969	184	431	516	558	100.0	87.6	1.3	3.2	3.8	4.1
Inside standard metrop. areas	5,151	4,452	102	223	222	152	100.0	86.4	2.0	4.3	4.3	3.0
Outside standard metrop. areas	8,508	7,518	82	208	294	407	100.0	88.4	1.0	2.4	3.5	4.8
West	6,532	5,855	71	120	153	333	100.0	89.6	1.1	1.8	2.3	5.1
Inside standard metrop. areas	3,998	3,637	48	63	54	196	100.0	91.0	1.2	1.6	1.4	4.9
Outside standard metrop. areas	2,534	2,218	23	57	99	130	100.0	87.5	0.9	2.3	3.9	5.4

Source: 1956 National Housing Inventory, Vol. 1, Part 1, Table B.

the population. Nor can these changes be considered simply a reaction to the physical aspects of dwelling units. Many sociological, economic, and psychological forces influence the quantity, type, and location of housing demanded, and determine who lives where in the supply of existing houses. Large numbers of residents may move out of one community in response to factors having little relevance to the quality of the housing or to the changing size and composition of the families involved. Conversely, other neighborhoods persist as integral units in spite of strong external economic pressures and other factors. It is possible to understand and interpret these events only by explicitly introducing into the study of housing an analysis of economic, sociological, and psychological factors which help to determine the changes that occur. The dramatic flow of people into suburban areas, the persistence of ethnic neighborhoods, and the abandonment of neighborhoods containing standard housing in the face of Negro invasion are only extreme examples of the influence of these non-demographic forces.

In 1956 the author participated in a pilot study that undertook to measure some of the non-material forces involved in such changes. A few results of that research are indicated briefly here, in order to illustrate the basic assertion made above. The Hyde Park-Kenwood area of Chicago, in which the University of Chicago is located, was scheduled to undergo urban renewal and redevelopment. The National Opinion Research Center made a sample survey of the residents of the community in order to gain a factual basis on which the redevelopment could be planned.[8] At the urging of the study directors, the sponsors of the study allowed the following questions to be asked:

1. Generally speaking, do you like or dislike living in this area?
2. Would you say that, in general, you like living in this neighborhood better than, worse than, or about the same as you might like living in other areas in Chicago and the suburbs--leaving out those areas you couldn't possibly afford?
3. What things do you like about living in this particular house (apartment)?
4. And what do you dislike about living in this house?

---

[8] See report entitled the Hyde Park-Kenwood Urban Renewal Survey, National Opinion Research Center, University of Chicago, 1956. Senior study directors for the project were Eli S. Marks and Donald J. Bogue. The field work was under the supervision of Selma F. Monsky.

Table 24-22.—NET CHANGES IN THE HOUSING INVENTORY, 1950 TO 1956

Area	Inventory of dwelling units (000)		Net increase (000)		Units added through-- (000)				Units lost through-- (000)			
	Dec.31, 1956	April 1, 1950	Total	Percent	Total added	New construction	Conversion	Other sources	Total lost	Demolition	Merger	Other means
United States.....	55,342	45,986	9,355	20.3	12,571	10,920	708	943	3,216	1,131	672	1,413
Inside standard metropolitan areas........	31,615	25,630	5,985	23.4	7,672	6,763	458	451	1,688	643	394	651
In central cities....	16,286	15,123	1,163	7.7	2,340	1,783	302	255	1,177	512	278	387
Not in central cities	15,329	10,507	4,822	45.9	5,332	4,980	156	196	510	131	115	264
Outside standard metropolitan areas........	23,727	20,356	3,370	16.6	4,899	4,157	250	492	1,529	488	279	762
Northeast..........	14,201	12,051	2,151	17.9	2,716	2,364	213	139	565	207	179	179
Inside standard metropolitan areas........	10,749	9,220	1,529	16.6	1,988	1,743	161	84	459	197	136	126
Outside standard metropolitan areas........	3,451	2,831	621	21.9	728	620	53	55	107	10	43	54
North Central......	15,843	13,746	2,097	15.3	2,900	2,425	237	238	803	255	206	342
Inside standard metropolitan areas........	8,686	7,262	1,424	19.6	1,878	1,629	144	105	454	170	107	177
Outside standard metropolitan areas........	7,157	6,484	673	10.4	1,021	796	93	132	348	85	98	165
South.............	16,638	13,658	2,980	21.8	4,281	3,770	194	317	1,301	516	227	558
Inside standard metropolitan areas........	6,728	5,151	1,578	30.6	2,069	1,847	115	107	492	222	118	152
Outside standard metropolitan areas........	9,910	8,508	1,401	16.5	2,211	1,923	79	209	810	294	110	407
West..............	8,660	6,532	2,128	32.6	2,674	2,362	62	250	546	153	60	333
Inside standard metropolitan areas........	5,451	3,998	1,454	36.4	1,736	1,544	37	155	282	54	32	196
Outside standard metropolitan areas........	3,209	2,534	675	26.6	938	817	26	95	263	99	28	136

Source: 1956 National Housing Inventory, Vol. I, Part 1, Table C.

5. What things do you like about living in this particular neighborhood?

6. And what things do you dislike about living in this neighborhood?

The results of this survey showed that persons' choices of neighborhoods in which to live, and the decisions of residents whether to remain in their present neighborhood or move to another, are affected by such considerations as the following:

(a) Quality of schools, elementary and high

(b) Playgrounds and recreational facilities

(c) Intellectual and educational level of adults

(d) Friendliness and sociability of residents

(e) Common interests--professional associations

(f) Community spirit

(g) Racial biases

(h) Delinquency and crime

(i) Police and fire protection

(j) Street lighting

(k) Garbage collection

(l) Parking problems

(m) Dirt and air pollution

(n) Volume of traffic and traffic safety

(o) Transportation facilities

(p) Shopping facilities

(q) Distance to work

A comparison of the responses to questions 3 and 4 with the responses to questions 5 and 6 suggested that some of the strongest forces influencing the movement of families are quite independent of the quality or adequacy of the housing involved. Many of the motives for change in residence are noneconomic, and, if acted upon, actually result in a reduction of the family's real income.

Table 24-23.—SUMMARY CHARACTERISTICS OF SELECTED COMPONENTS OF CHANGE, 1956 AND 1950

("..." indicates too few sample cases for reliable median)

Area and subject	1956		1950		1956		1950		1956		1950	
	New construction	Same	Demolition and other loss	Same	New construction	Same	Demolition and other loss	Same	New construction	Same	Demolition and other loss	Same
	Total				Inside standard metropolitan areas				Outside standard metropolitan areas			
UNITED STATES												
Total number of units (000)....	10,920	41,453	2,544	41,453	6,763	23,149	1,294	23,149	4,157	18,304	1,250	18,304
Owner occupied(percent of occupied).	76.3	58.2	27.6	58.9	77.6	54.2	23.5	54.5	74.1	64.0	32.7	64.9
Not dilap.,with all facil.(percent of total reporting)..	90.8	74.7	27.1	68.6	96.1	86.4	40.0	82.7	81.8	58.7	14.2	49.3
Median number of rooms............	4.8	4.9	3.3	4.9	4.9	4.9	3.3	4.8	4.5	5.0	3.3	4.9
Median value of owner-occupied units (nonfarm)...	$14,100	$10,700	(1)	$7,900	$14,700	$12,200	...	$9,000	$12,300	$7,800	...	$5,800
Median contract rent (nonfarm)....	$70	$50	$27	$38	$78	$53	$30	$40	$55	$37	$22	$29
	Inside standard metropolitan areas--Total				Inside standard metropolitan areas--In central cities				Inside standard metropolitan areas--Not in central cities			
UNITED STATES												
Total number of units (000)....	6,763	23,149	1,294	23,149	1,783	13,410	899	13,410	4,980	9,740	395	9,740
Owner occupied(percent of occupied).	77.6	54.2	23.5	54.5	61.2	45.0	14.5	45.4	83.6	67.7	45.5	67.8
Not dilap.,with all facil.(percent of total reporting)..	96.1	86.4	40.0	82.7	98.7	86.8	39.8	84.5	95.2	85.8	40.6	80.1
Median number of rooms............	4.9	4.9	3.3	4.8	4.6	4.7	3.3	4.7	5.0	5.1	3.4	5.0
Median value of owner-occupied units (nonfarm)...	$14,700	$12,200	...	$9,000	$14,300	$11,300	...	$8,700	$14,800	$13,000	...	$9,500
Median contract rent (nonfarm)....	$78	$53	$30	$40	$78	$54	$30	$40	$78	$51	...	$39

[1] Less than $4,000.

Source: 1956 National Housing Inventory, Vol. I, Part 1, Table O.

As the quality of housing improves, and as the poverty-stricken segment of the population shrinks, such factors of choice and taste as are listed above will undoubtedly become even more potent in shaping the direction of housing trends.

CONCLUSION

This brief picture of the housing situation has been intended to serve demographers who have only a limited knowledge of the residential aspect of the population's activities. In order to confine the discussion to one short chapter, it has been necessary to be incomplete and to treat topics in a somewhat oversimplified way. A second objective has been to indicate to housing specialists the many points at which a correct interpretation of housing trends rests directly upon demographic analysis. Not only must the origin of the current housing boom be traced to the revolutionary shifts that have occurred in the demographic picture since 1940, but the prospect for the future is also destined to be dictated in part by these same demographic events. Chapter 26 will show how future rates of family formation, the changing pattern of fertility, and other demographic developments will affect the number, size and distribution of the dwelling units needed to house the population. As the last section of the present chapter indicates, these population factors will interact with economic, sociological, and psychological factors to determine housing trends in the future.

Chapter 25

THE POPULATION OF ALASKA AND HAWAII

The admission of Alaska as the 49th state, and the general expectation that Hawaii will soon enter as the 50th, has greatly increased the need and the desire of the residents of the 48 states to know more about their fellow-citizens who live in these outlying areas. This chapter undertakes to supply at least some of this information. Since the presentation is confined primarily to the demographic aspects of Alaska and Hawaii, with only a very brief resumé of their physical characteristics and economic base as these factors affect population, the reader is encouraged to suplement the materials in this chapter by reading a good discussion of the geography, economy, and history of each area. The materials are organized in the following way: First, each area is introduced separately, in order to detail its unique characteristics; then the vital processes and the population composition of the two territories are discussed jointly, in order that the two areas may be compared with each other and with the 48 states.

ALASKA

Alaska was acquired in 1867 by purchase from Russia. It was organized as a territory in 1912, and was admitted to statehood in 1958. Alaska has a land area of 571,065 square miles, which is 18.9 percent (more than one-sixth) as large as the territory of the 48 states. Two areas the size of the state of Texas could be accommodated within its borders, with enough space left over to squeeze in an area the size of Louisiana. As yet, Alaska is not heavily populated; on July 1, 1958, the population was estimated to be 214,000.[1] This is a smaller population than that of Nevada, the least populous of the 48 states, but it is considerably larger than the population many states had at the time they acquired statehood. Moreover, the population has grown very rapidly since 1940, as the following summary shows:

Date	Population (000)	Percent increase since preceding date
1958 (July)...........	214.0	66.3
1950 (April).........	128.6	77.4
1939 (October).......	72.5	22.3
1929 (October).......	59.3	7.7
1920 (January).......	55.0	-14.5
1910.................	64.4	1.2
1900.................	63.6	98.4
1890.................	32.1	-4.1
1880.................	33.4	...

After the gold rushes of the 1890 to 1900 decade there was a decade of relative population stability, followed by a decade of sharp decline. Between 1920 and 1930, a part of the loss was regained, but not until World War II and the postwar world situation made Alaska of strategic military importance did it begin to develop rapidly. Its largest recorded numerical growth has taken place since 1950--an average gain of more than 10,000 persons per year, and an annual growth rate of more than 8 percent. Much of this population ex-

---

[1] Estimate based on data in Current Population Reports, Series P-25, No. 189, Nov. 1958.

pansion has resulted from the needs of national defense activities. The building of military installations brought many thousands of construction workers, and, later, a labor force to man the installations. The U. S. Government is the state's largest single industry, and the dominant employer. These government activities are causing the area's resources to be developed more rapidly and accelerating the diversification of the economy.

Urban-rural Distribution. At the 1950 census, six places were defined as urban, and together they contained 26.6 percent of the total population. Among the 48 states, only in North Dakota and Mississippi is the population composition as rural as this. All the other states are much more urbanized. It is essential to realize the extent to which Alaska differs, in this respect, from most of the other states. The six Alaskan cities recognized in the 1950 census are:

City	Population 1950	Percent increase in population, 1940 to 1950
Anchorage............	11,254	222.0
Juneau..............	5,956	4.0
Fairbanks............	5,771	67.0
Ketchikan............	5,305	13.0
Eastchester..........	3,096	...
Mountain View........	2,880	...

Unlike the situation in the 48 states, between 1940 and 1950 the rural parts of Alaska, as well as the urban places, grew very rapidly:

Year	Urban places	Rural places
1939 to 1950..........	97.2	71.1
1929 to 1939..........	121.6	7.2
1920 to 1929..........	156.3	-1.0
1910 to 1920..........	-50.2	-10.7
1900 to 1910..........	-60.7	21.3
1890 to 1900..........	...	49.7

However, during the two preceding decades (1920 to 1940) there had been a major trend toward urbanization, with the cities growing extremely fast and the rural areas stagnating.

Regional Distribution of Population. All of Alaska is not a frozen expanse of useless land, as many people imagine. It has a variety of resources that augurs well for the development of a balanced economy. Many persons who are familiar with Alaska think of it in terms of three regions, each with a different type of economy and population.

a. The Pacific Seaboard. This region comprises a long narrow strip of land and water about 30 miles wide, curving up the coast and including the Alaska Peninsula and the Aleutian Islands. It measures about 3,000 miles from tip to tip. Throughout this territory the rainfall is heavy and the climate is extraordinarily mild, considering the northerly latitude. Warm ocean currents flowing along the coast make the winters considerably less severe than winters in northern Minnesota and North Dakota. The salmon industry, lumbering, and some farming are the principal economic activities. Unfortunately, the coastline is very rugged and mountainous, so that the region has only a comparatively small amount of agricultural land with which to take advantage of the longer growing season and the ample rainfall.

b. Bering Sea and Arctic Coastline. Like the Pacific Seaboard, this region is a narrow strip of land bordering on water. It follows the Bering Sea coastline north from the Alaska Peninsula, up and around along the northern coastline bordering on the Arctic Ocean. The land here is an expanse of low hills; there is comparatively little rainfall. Winters are more severe than in the first region, although the weather is moderated considerably by the region's proximity to large bodies of water. Mining, fishing, and hunting are the leading activities.

c. Interior Alaska. Since this section of Alaska is isolated from the moderating effects of the ocean currents, it experiences extremes of cold in winter and of heat in summer. Winters in interior Alaska are severe, and temperatures of 40 degrees below zero are not uncommon. Summer temperatures often reach 90 degrees Fahrenheit. Much of the land is swamp or tundra, and only a few inches below the topsoil there is permanent frost. If a particular plat of land is farmed, or if sharp seasonal changes take place there, these perma-frost conditions change, causing the land to settle or to form hummocks. This unpredictability of contour is an annoyance to

ALASKA—SECTION 1

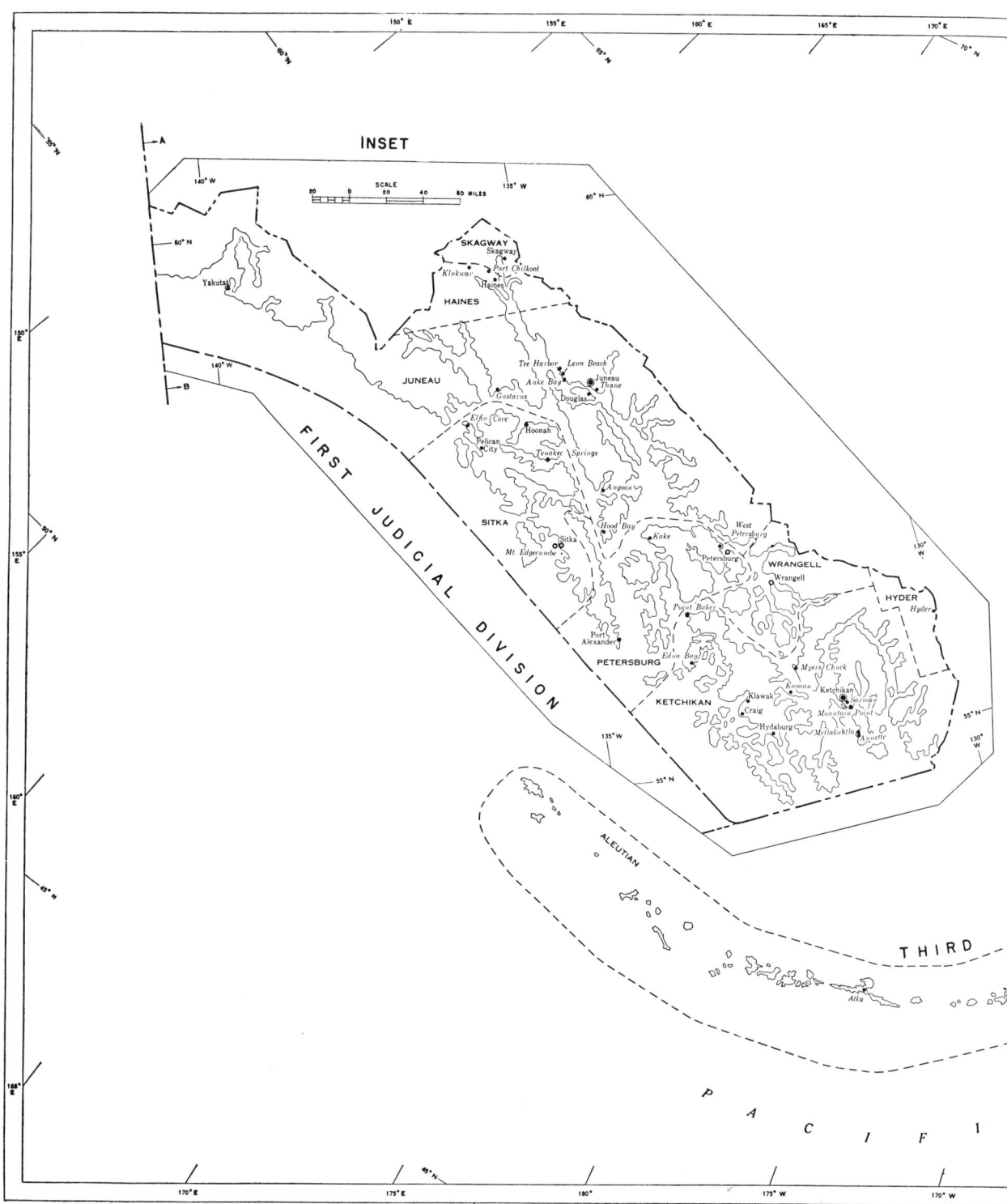

FIGURE 25-1. ALASKA

ALASKA—SECTION 2

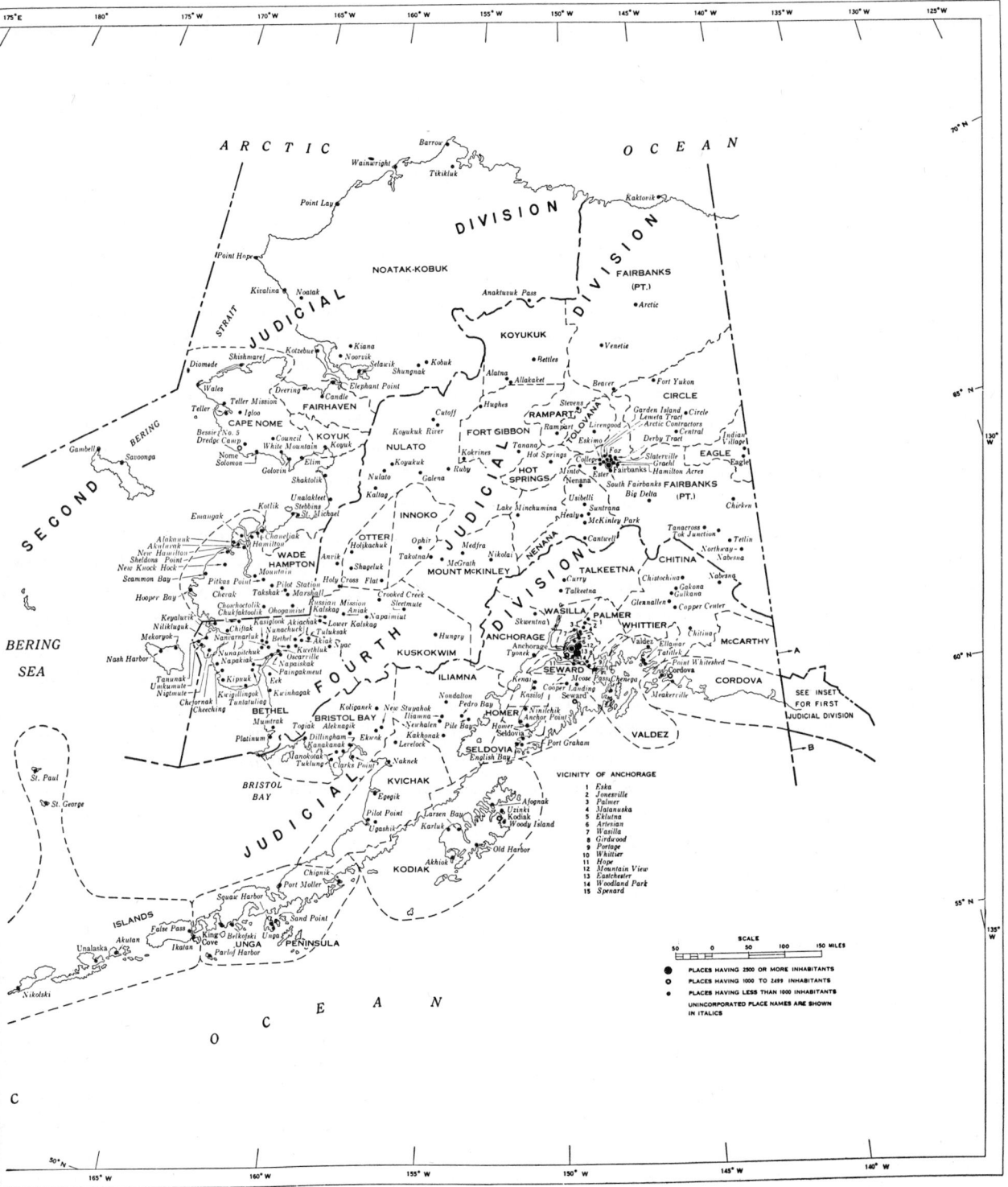

FIGURE 25-1. ALASKA-Continued

builders and farmers. Oddly, it is not the milder coastal region that furnishes Alaska with opportunities for agricultural development, but this interior area. Although its growing season is comparatively short, its location near the Arctic Circle gives the summer days more hours of sunlight, so the crops mature more quickly. Mantauska Valley, near Anchorage, and Tannana Valley, near Fairbanks, are the leading farming areas. Dairying constitutes about one-half of the farming activity; potatoes and garden vegetables are grown, and there is even some raising of beef cattle and hogs.

How is the population of Alaska distributed among these three regions? This question may be answered, approximately, by means of statistics concerning the judicial divisions (analogous to counties) and the districts (analogous to townships). Alaska is divided into four judicial divisions, each of which is subdivided into several districts. A delimitation approximating these three regions was devised by grouping these units. Table 25-1 presents population data for each regional grouping, to show the present regional distribution and the growth trends. This table shows that the Pacific Seaboard region (including the Alaska Peninsula and the Aleutian Islands) contains more than two-thirds of the population, and has grown more rapidly in recent years than the other regions. This region contains five of Alaska's six cities: Anchorage, Juneau, Ketchikan,

Eastchester, and Mountain View. The region stretching along the Bering Sea and the Arctic Ocean is the least populous, and is completely rural. In recent years it has experienced very little population growth, although it was once the scene of feverish mining activities. Interior Alaska has one city--Fairbanks--and has grown very rapidly since 1940.

Industrial Base. The largest single source of employment in Alaska is the Federal Government. In 1950, 31 percent of the employed labor force was employed by a local or territorial government, or the Federal Government; all but a small part of this 31 percent were employed by military establishments, either as members of the armed forces or as civilian employees. Aside from national defense, with its concomitant vast construction industry, Alaskans rely for their livelihood mainly on fishing, mining, hunting, trapping, and forestry (see Table 25-2). Salmon fishing is the largest single private industry, and the canning of salmon is a highly mechanized industry. The volume of the catch has declined in recent years, and this decrease is considered due to overfishing. Mining, especially gold mining, has been a major economic force and has attracted many people to Alaska. Although mining now employs only a small part of the labor force, it is still a major source of income. Experts believe that Alaska has deposits of copper, tungsten, silver, oil, and even coal which have not as yet been ade-

Table 25-1.—POPULATION AND POPULATION GROWTH OF ALASKA, BY REGIONS: 1929 TO 1950

Region	Population percent distribution 1950	Number of inhabitants			Population percent change	
		1950	1939	1929	1939 to 1950	1929 to 1939
Alaska, total..................................	100.0	128,643	72,524	59,278	77.4	22.3
Pacific Coastal Region...........................	68.2	87,721	44,553	35,613	96.9	25.1
First judicial division........................	21.9	28,203	25,241	19,304	11.7	30.8
Third judicial division........................	46.3	59,518	19,312	16,309	208.2	18.4
Bering Sea and Arctic Coast Region...............	12.6	16,167	15,109	13,480	7.0	12.1
Second judicial division......................	9.5	12,272	11,877	10,127	3.3	17.3
Bethel district of fourth judicial district......	3.0	3,895	3,232	3,353	20.5	-3.6
Interior Alaska.................................	19.2	24,755	12,862	10,185	92.5	26.3
Fourth judical district, exc. Bethel district....	19.2	24,755	12,862	10,185	92.5	26.3

Source: U.S. Census of Population: 1950, Vol. II, Parts 51-54, Territories and Possessions, Alaska, Tables 3 and 4.

Table 25-2.—INDUSTRY GROUP OF EMPLOYED PERSONS IN ALASKA, BY SEX, COLOR, AND URBAN-RURAL RESIDENCE: 1950

Industry group	Employed labor force					Urban		Rural	
	Total	Male	Female	White	Non-white	White	Non-white	White	Non-white
Employed, total....................	100.0	100.0	100.0	100.0	100.0	100.0	100.0	100.0	100.0
Agriculture, forestry, and fisheries......	13.3	17.2	2.4	7.3	37.3	3.9	10.9	9.6	39.7
Agriculture, except hunting and trapping.....	1.2	1.5	0.5	1.3	0.8	0.3	0.3	2.0	0.8
Hunting and trapping.........................	4.5	5.7	1.0	0.4	20.8	...	...	0.7	22.7
Forestry..................................	0.2	0.3	0.1	0.3	...	0.3	0.1	0.2	...
Fisheries.................................	7.4	9.7	0.8	5.3	15.7	3.3	10.5	6.7	16.2
Mining....................................	3.2	4.1	0.6	3.3	2.4	1.3	...	4.7	2.6
Construction..............................	13.3	17.1	2.7	15.4	4.9	13.1	8.1	16.9	4.6
Manufacturing.............................	9.3	9.0	10.2	6.2	22.8	4.9	16.0	7.0	22.5
Transportation, communication, public utilities...............................	12.8	15.2	5.9	14.5	6.9	16.4	13.3	13.0	5.3
Wholesale and retail trade...............	12.8	10.2	20.1	14.6	5.8	19.4	14.9	11.2	4.9
Wholesale trade..........................	1.1	1.3	0.7	1.3	0.2	1.8	0.3	1.0	0.2
Retail trade.............................	11.7	8.9	19.5	13.3	5.6	17.6	14.6	10.2	4.7
Food and dairy products..................	1.9	1.8	2.2	2.2	1.0	2.9	1.7	1.6	0.9
Eating and drinking places...............	4.0	2.5	8.1	4.5	1.9	5.8	10.8	3.6	1.1
Other retail trade.......................	5.8	4.6	9.1	6.6	2.7	8.9	2.1	5.0	2.7
Finance, insurance, real estate..........	1.3	0.9	2.4	1.5	0.2	2.4	1.9	0.9	0.1
Business and repair services.............	1.7	1.9	1.0	2.0	0.3	2.4	0.9	1.8	0.2
Personal services........................	4.1	1.8	10.5	4.9	5.0	5.4	14.9	2.8	4.1
Private households.......................	1.1	0.1	3.8	0.6	3.1	0.7	5.4	0.5	2.9
Hotels and lodging places................	1.1	0.7	2.3	1.2	0.8	1.6	5.1	0.9	0.4
Other personal services..................	1.9	1.0	4.4	2.1	1.1	3.1	4.4	1.4	0.8
Entertainment and recreation services.....	0.8	0.7	1.2	0.9	0.5	1.3	3.0	0.7	0.2
Professional and related services........	7.2	3.9	16.6	7.8	4.6	8.9	7.2	7.8	4.4
Public administration....................	17.0	15.8	20.3	19.8	5.7	19.5	6.5	19.9	5.6
Industry not reported....................	3.4	2.3	6.2	2.8	5.5	1.9	2.3	3.5	5.7

Source: U. S. Census of Population: 1950, Vol. II, Parts 51-54, Territories and Possessions, Alaska, Tables 19 and 20.

quately developed. Hunting and trapping are major part-time seasonal activities, especially among the Eskimos, Indians, and other native peoples, for whom hunting, trapping, and fishing are a major source of subsistence livelihood. The chief commercial item gained from these activities is the annual harvest of 60,000 to 70,000 young bull seals which are hunted around the Pribilof Islands; they are selected and killed under the supervision of the U. S. Fish and Wildlife Service.

Forestry is important economically in a few areas along the lower coast, although in general the timber logs are not large. As mentioned above, agriculture is still important as a source of livelihood in only a few somewhat scattered areas.

Ethnic Composition. Alaska is populated by white American immigrants, and by three native groups who occupied the territory long before the arrival of the whites. Indians have lived for many decades along the lower section of the Pacific

Coast and, in the interior, around Fairbanks. They are related ethnically to the Indians of the Pacific Northwest and the Vancouver area. Eskimos have lived along the coasts of the Bering Sea and the Arctic Ocean for a long time. The Alaska Peninsula and the Aleutian Islands are inhabited by the Aleuts, a group related to the Eskimos. Contact with white men has had some near-disastrous consequences for both the Eskimos and the Aleuts; infectious diseases, excessive use of alcohol, brutal treatment, and exploitation have decimated and impoverished them. Programs designed to raise the economic and social level at which these peoples live are now underway. The various censuses have enumerated the native ethnic groups as follows:

Year	Total	Eskimo	Indian	Aleut
1950..........	33,863	15,882	14,089	3,892
Urban.......	1,933	234	1,647	52
Rural.......	31,930	15,648	12,442	3,840
1939..........	32,458	15,576	11,283	5,599
1929..........	29,983	n(1)	(1)	(1)
1920..........	26,558	13,698	9,918	2,942

[1]Not available.
Source: 1950 Census of Population, Vol. II, Territories and Possessions, Alaska, Table 6.

In 1950 the Eskimos were the most numerous of the aboriginal populations, and the Aleuts were the smallest group. Both the Eskimos and the Aleuts appear to be experiencing comparatively little population growth, while the Indians seem to be increasing more rapidly. At the 1960 census, the Indians will probably outnumber the Eskimos.

Both the Eskimos and the Aleuts live almost entirely in rural areas. Although they have adopted many of the ways of the white populations, they still rely heavily on hunting, fishing, and trapping for a large portion of their livelihood.

The Indians of Alaska are more urbanized than the other two aboriginal groups. A great many of them are employed in salmon fishing or in the fish-canning industry. Others hunt and trap. The Indians who are city dwellers are employed primarily as restaurant workers, domestic servants in private households, and at other "blue-collar" jobs.

Note: Further details concerning birth and death rates, and a more detailed discussion of

Alaska's population characteristics, are presented later in this chapter. See the sections following the brief introduction to Hawaii.

HAWAII

Hawaii, a group of islands lying in the mid-Pacific a little more than 2,000 miles west of San Francisco, became a territory of the United States in 1900. The native government had requested, in 1898, that Hawaii become a part of the United States. The group includes seven inhabited islands, two uninhabited islands having 1 square mile or more of territory, and many smaller uninhabited islands whose land area is only a fraction of a square mile. The combined population of the inhabited islands was estimated to be 637,000 on July 1, 1958. This is almost three times the population of Alaska. However, the combined land area--6,407 square miles--is very small in comparison with that of most states. When Hawaii is admitted to the Union, only three states will have smaller land areas--Rhode Island, Delaware, and Connecticut.

Hawaii now has a larger population than five of the existing states, and if it had only a few thousand more persons it would be as large as four of the other states. When admitted to the Union it will have a larger population than most of the states had when they were admitted, the only exceptions being a very few of the more populous among the 13 original states. Following are population census counts for selected dates during the past century:

Date	Number of inhabitants	Percent increase since preceding date
1958 (estimated....	637,000	27.5
1950...............	499,794	18.1
1940...............	423,330	14.9
1930...............	368,336	43.9
1920...............	255,912	33.4
1910...............	191,909	24.6
1900...............	154,001	...
1890...............	89,990	...
1860...............	69,800	...
1850...............	84,165	...

Note: Censuses prior to 1900 were taken under the direction of the Hawaiian Government.

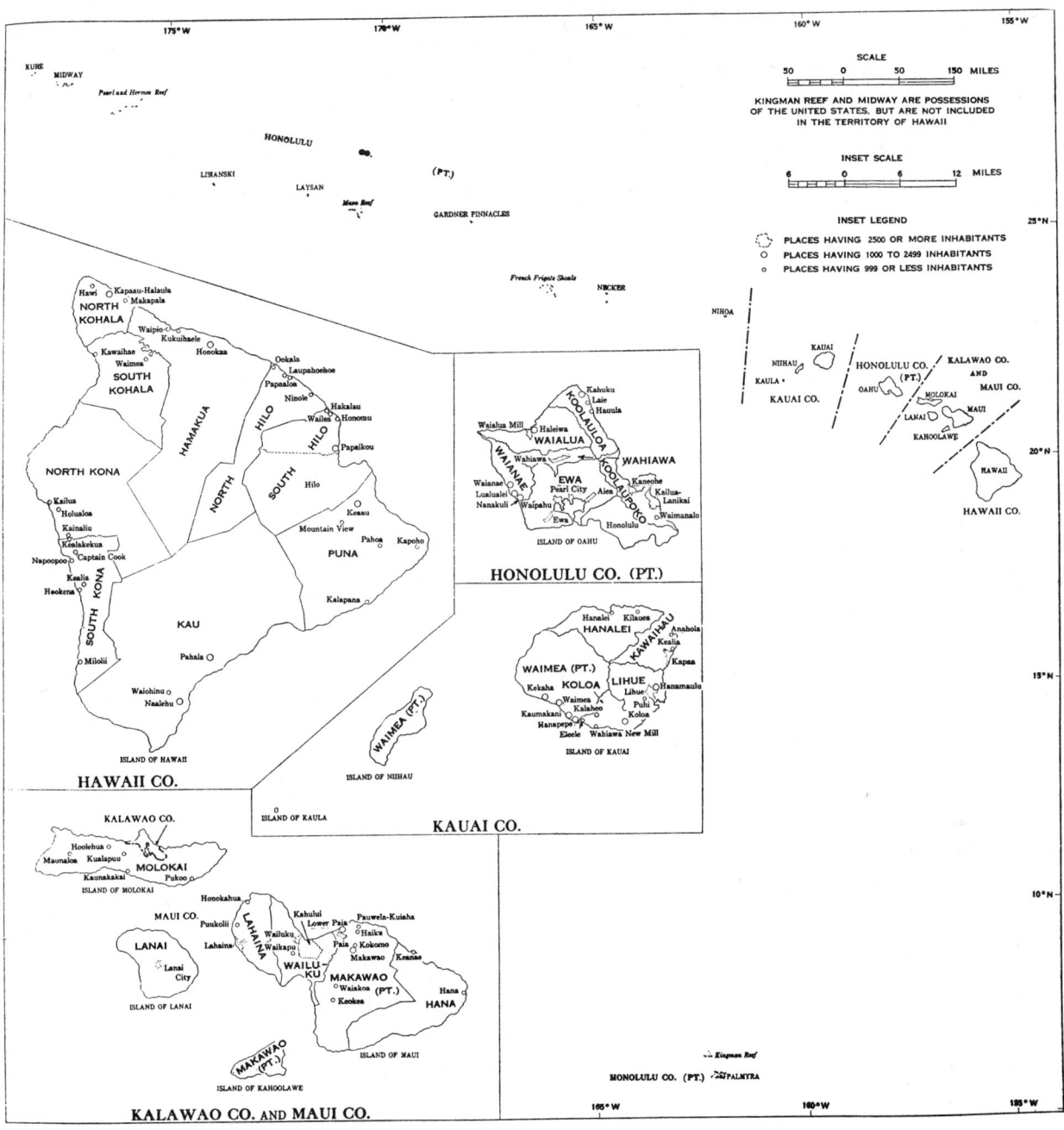

FIGURE 25-2. HAWAII

It is estimated that between the time of the 1950 census and July 1, 1958, the population increased by 137,000, or 27.5 percent. This figure represents a larger average annual numerical increase than had occurred at any time in the statistical history of the islands.

Approximately 10 percent of Hawaii's population is military, and 90 percent is civilian. (A substantial proportion of the civilian population is employed by the military establishments.) Between the time of the 1950 census and July 1, 1958, the civilian population increased by an estimated

21.2 percent--somewhat more slowly than the military population.

The land area, the 1950 population, and the population growth which took place from 1940 to 1950, are distributed among the principal islands as follows:

Island	Population, 1950	Land area, 1950 (square miles)	Population per square mile
Total...............	499.8	6,407	78.0
Oahu....................	353.0	589	599.4
Hawaii.................	68.4	4,021	17.0
Maui...................	40.1	728	55.1
Kauai..................	29.7	551	53.9
Molokai................	5.3	259	20.4
Lanai..................	3.1	141	22.2
Niihau.................	0.2	72	3.1
Kahoolawe..............	...	45	...
Palmyra................	...	1	...

Island	Percent distribution Population	Percent distribution Land Area	Population percent change 1940-50
Total............	100.0	100.0	...
Oahu.................	70.6	9.1	37.0
Hawaii...............	13.7	62.8	-6.7
Maui.................	8.0	11.4	-14.5
Kauai................	5.9	8.6	-16.7
Molokai..............	1.1	4.0	-1.1
Lanai................	0.6	2.2	-15.7
Niihau...............	...	1.1	22.0
Kahoolawe............	...	0.7	...
Palmyra..............	...	...	...

Urban and Rural Composition. Hawaii is predominantly urban. In 1950 there were 17 urban places, which together contained 69.0 percent of the population. One of these (Honolulu) is a metropolis, and six of the others are cities of substantial size. The remainder are small places with less than 5,000 inhabitants. The seven largest places are as follows:

City	Island	Population, 1950
Honolulu...................	Oahu	248,034
Hilo......................	Hawaii	27,198
Wahiawa...................	Oahu	8,369
Kailua-Lanikai............	Oahu	7,740
Wailuku..................	Maui	7,424
Waipahu..................	Oahu	7,169
Kahului..................	Maui	6,306

In recent decades the islands have become urbanized very rapidly, and the rural sections have lost population through large-scale rural-to-urban migrations:

Decade	Percent change, urban	Percent change, rural
1940-50........	30.5	-2.6
1930-40........	33.5	-6.6

A part of the change that occurred between 1940 and 1950 was stimulated by the transfer of population among the islands during World War II. The islands differ greatly from each other in the extent to which they are urban:

Island	Percent urban, 1950
Oahu.............	81.3
Hawaii...........	39.8
Maui.............	52.2
Kauai............	23.7
Molokai..........	...
Lanai............	87.6
Niihau...........	...

Molokai and Niihau are entirely rural, while Oahu and Lanai are almost entirely urban or suburban.

Factors Influencing Population Distribution. The Hawaiian Islands are of volcanic origin. In general, the interior of each island is mountainous or hilly and is rather densely forested. Less than 10 percent of the total land area is under cultivation; this land lies in strips located near the coast. The climate is subtropical, with very heavy rainfall on the upper slopes of the windward (north and northeastern) side of each island, and moderate to light rainfall on the leeward (south and southwest) side of each. Under this combination of circumstances it is not surprising that a high proportion of the islands' inhabitants are distributed along the shore, and that the interior is more sparsely settled.

Economic Base. National defense, sugar production, pineapple growing and canning, and tourism are the leading industries of the islands. Pearl Harbor Naval Base, one of the largest in the world, is a major link in the nation's chain of Pacific defenses. It necessitates the presence of a large military population, and is also, together with the other military establishments on the islands, a major source of employment for civilians. The climate favors the growing of sugar cane and pineapple, both of which are produced in huge quantities on large corporate farms where scientific and intensive cultivation are combined with the employment of large numbers of farm-contract laborers. At the present time, the wages and benefits given these workers compare favorably with those received by agricultural workers in other parts of the world. A very large percentage of the workers in the sugar cane and pineapple industries are Filipinos. Coffee is also an important secondary crop. In 1950, 19 percent of the total employed labor force was engaged in agriculture. One worker in 10 was employed on a sugar cane farm; the processing of sugar cane and the canning of pineapple accounts for 5.8 percent of the islands' employment.

Hawaii's beautiful landscape, delightful climate, and the unique and colorful culture of its native population have made it a favorite vacation spot for tourists and a popular stop-over for world travelers. It even has been recommended as a very favorable spot in which to spend one's retirement years. The many activities connected with the serving of travelers and vacationers has grown into a large and prosperous industry, and is now a leading source of employment and income.

Racial and Ethnic Composition. At the time of its discovery in 1778, Hawaii had a very homogeneous population. Its people were of Polynesian descent; they had lived in isolation for many generations, and had developed a distinctive culture and had become physically homogeneous. Today the situation is exactly reversed; Hawaii's population is a mixture of many different races, and there has been so much intermarriage that ethnic classification can be only a rough indication of cultural and racial background. There have been three major migrations to Hawaii, and in each case the principal attraction was the opportunity to work on the large sugar plantations.

(a) The Chinese came between 1850 and 1883. This was a spontaneous migration (not encouraged by Hawaii), and was stopped by legislative action.

(b) The Japanese came between 1885 and 1900. They were encouraged at first, but were eventually restricted by legislation.

(c) In recent decades, the Filipinos have been encouraged to come and fill the need for agricultural manpower which was created when the inflow of Chinese and Japanese was stopped.

In addition, there have been smaller migrations of Portuguese, Puerto Ricans, Koreans, Negroes, and other ethnic groups. The "Caucasian" population (the term used in the census to designate the "white" population) is a polyglot array of nationalities and cultures.

It has been estimated that there were perhaps as many as 300,000 native Hawaiians inhabiting the islands at the time of their discovery. Contact with the white race brought disease and disorganization, and the Hawaiian population shrank to a small part of its former size. Today, the number of native (Polynesian) "Hawaiians" is increasing, but a very high percentage of persons so classified are only part Hawaiian; the number of full-blooded Hawaiians is small and is still diminishing. Hawaiians have intermarried freely, both with the Caucasians and with the Asiatic groups.

Table 25-3 presents a picture of the racial composition of the population as obtained by the 1950 Census. Persons were asked to classify the members of their household by race and, in addition, were asked the question, "Is this person of mixed race?" Persons of mixed race were classified according to the race of the nonwhite parent. If

Table 25-3.—ETHNIC COMPOSITION OF HAWAII'S POPULATION: 1950

Ethnic group	Population 1950	Percent distribution	Percent change 1940-50	Percent mixed race	Percent urban 1950
Total....	499,769	100.0	18.1	18.9	69.0
Hawaiian....	86,090	17.2	33.9	85.8	66.3
Caucasian...	114,793	23.0	10.6	...	66.2
Chinese.....	32,376	6.5	12.5	8.9	91.7
Filipino....	61,062	12.2	16.2	12.6	53.6
Japanese....	184,598	36.9	16.9	2.2	73.2
Korean......	7,030	1.4	2.6	} 27.3	} 69.0
Negro.......	2,651	0.5	...		
Puerto Rican	9,551	1.9	15.1		
All other...	1,618	0.3	...		

Source: U. S. Census of Population: 1950, Vol. II, Parts 51-54, Territories and Possessions, Hawaii, Tables A, 8, 9.

both parents were nonwhite, the race of the male parent was used to categorize the person. In 1950, more than 85 percent of the Hawaiians reported themselves as having mixed parentage. Thus, there are now only about 12,000 to 15,000 full-blooded Hawaiians in the islands, whereas there were originally a quarter-million or more.

The native Hawaiians (full-blooded and part-Hawaiian) now comprise only about one-sixth of Hawaii's population. They are outnumbered both by the Japanese and by the Caucasians. The Japanese are the most numerous group, and comprise more than one-third of the total population. The Chinese are a much smaller group (6 percent of the total), while Filipinos are about one-third as numerous as Japanese.

The Chinese and Japanese populations have largely deserted the sugar farms, and most of them are now found in the cities. The Filipinos are less urbanized comparatively than the other populations.

Because of the mixed racial situation, rates of growth based on the classifications of two successive censuses are not very reliable. Column 3 of Table 25-3 presents such rates, but they should be accepted with reservations. The very high rates of growth reported for native Hawaiians may be to a certain extent fictitious, since many persons of mixed nonwhite racial background may have claimed Hawaiian ancestry rather than iden-

tifying themselves as members of some one of the other nonwhite races. The Japanese and Filipino populations appear to have been growing at moderate rates, while the Chinese and the Caucasians seem to have grown somewhat more slowly.

BIRTH AND DEATH RATES

Births. Both Alaska and Hawaii contain two or more populations with extremely high fertility rates. In Alaska the nonwhites (Indians, Eskimos, and Aleuts) have a gross reproduction rate of 3.2, which is extraordinarily high. (It means that 1,000 women would produce 3,200 daughters in their time, if all of the 1,000 women lived through the childbearing period. This represents a growth factor of 220 percent per generation, not considering deaths before age 49.) Native Hawaiians have a gross reproduction rate of 2.8, which is also very high. In 1950 the 48 states had a gross reproduction rate of 1.5, which is generally regarded as a moderately high level of fertility. Table 25-4 reports the age-specific birth rates for each ethnic group in Alaska and Hawaii. This table shows that among nonwhites in Alaska and among Hawaiians in Hawaii, much childbearing takes place during the teen years. The fertility rate rises to a much higher peak among these ethnic groups than it does in the 48 states; it then declines slowly throughout the remaining

Table 25-4.—BIRTH RATES BY AGE, COLOR, AND ETHNIC GROUP AND GROSS REPRODUCTIVE RATE FOR ALASKA, HAWAII, AND THE 48 STATES: 1950

(Corrected for underregistration)

Age	Alaska			Hawaii					48 states		
	Total	White	Non-white	Total	Hawaiian and part Hawaiian	Caucasian	Japanese	All other	Total	White	Non-white
All ages........	160.2	132.9	225.7	125.3	204.8	103.5	95.8	151.3	106.2	102.3	137.3
10-14..............	0.3	...	0.5	0.8	0.7	0.4	0.4	1.6	1.0	0.4	5.1
15-19..............	118.5	133.2	112.0	57.9	125.8	60.2	11.6	78.6	81.6	70.0	163.5
20-24..............	290.4	259.4	346.1	200.7	392.2	192.3	116.2	244.6	196.6	190.4	242.6
25-29..............	225.6	190.4	330.1	198.6	329.8	159.3	174.0	229.2	166.1	165.1	173.8
30-34..............	141.6	112.9	246.6	125.7	160.1	98.0	121.4	155.2	103.7	102.6	112.6
35-39..............	90.5	60.6	197.0	64.3	92.4	47.4	59.4	80.2	52.9	51.4	64.3
40-44..............	26.5	14.7	77.2	17.2	30.6	10.1	14.2	22.5	15.1	14.5	21.2
45 and over........	6.1	2.9	18.7	1.0	2.0	...	0.8	2.0	1.2	1.0	2.6
Gross reproduction rate.............	2.2	1.9	3.2	1.6	2.8	1.4	1.2	1.9	1.5	1.4	1.9

childbearing years, instead of dropping sharply after age 35 as it does among the lower-birth-rate populations.

In Alaska, the white population also has comparatively high birth rates. In 1950 the gross reproduction rate was 1.9, or 35 percent higher than the gross reproduction rate for whites in the 48 states. In Hawaii, the Caucasian and the Japanese populations have fertility levels equal to, or lower than, those of the 48 states. But the "other races" group (primarily Filipino) have very high fertility. Thus, in Alaska the over-all picture is one of generally high fertility among both whites and natives. In Hawaii the white and the Japanese populations (the two largest) have lower fertility rates; the Chinese and the Filipinos are the only sizable groups having high fertility.

Deaths. After it is adjusted for differences in age composition, the death rate is more than 40 percent higher in Alaska than in the 48 states, while in Hawaii it is 6 percent lower than in the 48 states. In both places, however, death rates vary greatly among the ethnic groups. In Alaska the age-adjusted death rate for nonwhites is more than twice as high as the corresponding rate in the 48 states. Among the white population of Alaska death rates are also higher than they are among the white population of the 48 states, but by a factor of only 25 percent instead of the 100 percent by

which the nonwhite Alaskan death rate exceeds that of the 48 states. The nonwhite populations of Alaska live under conditions that are distinctly unhealthful; death rates that reach this high a level routinely, year after year, have not characterized the United States population in this century.

In Hawaii the over-all death rate is below that of the 48 states. However, the native Hawaiians have unusually high death rates (the age-adjusted rate is 60 percent higher than the rate of Hawaii as a whole, and 50 percent higher than that of the 48 states). Hawaiians of Japanese ancestry, in contrast, have unusually low death rates. Unfortunately, the National Office of Vital Statistics relegates the death statistics for the Chinese and Filipino populations to the "other races" category. The available evidence makes it seem probable that the Chinese have very low death rates, similar to those of the Japanese, while the Filipinos have high death rates--although the Filipino rates are probably somewhat lower than those of the Hawaiians.

Table 25-5 reports age-specific death rates for each ethnic group. An unusual feature of the death rates for native Hawaiians is that they are not unusually high during the early years of life (0 to 20 years), but that beyond age 35 they are very much higher than the rates for the general population. This could mean (a) that a substantial reduction in

Table 25-5.—DEATH RATES BY AGE, COLOR, AND ETHNIC GROUP FOR ALASKA, HAWAII, AND THE 48 STATES: 1950

Age	Alaska			Hawaii					48 states		
	Total	White	Non-white	Total	Hawaiian and part Hawaiian	Cauca-sian	Japan-ese	All other	Total	White	Non-white
All ages........	9.7	7.1	17.0	5.8	6.7	5.5	5.3	6.4	9.6	9.5	11.2
Under 1 year......	55.8	27.2	100.4	26.7	33.2	35.7	15.9	27.8	33.0	29.9	53.7
1-4 years.........	6.8	1.2	15.6	1.6	2.0	1.3	1.6	1.3	1.4	1.2	2.5
5-14 years........	2.2	0.4	4.0	0.5	0.4	0.3	0.5	0.7	0.6	0.6	0.9
15-24 years......	3.9	2.0	9.3	1.1	1.5	1.3	0.7	1.2	1.3	1.1	2.5
25-34 years......	4.5	2.5	15.1	1.3	2.5	0.9	1.2	1.3	1.8	1.5	4.4
35-44 years......	6.1	3.9	15.3	3.1	5.7	2.4	2.0	3.6	3.6	3.1	8.1
45-54 years......	11.9	9.8	19.8	8.0	16.2	6.7	5.8	7.9	8.5	7.7	17.1
55-64 years......	21.9	20.3	25.3	20.5	35.7	19.4	17.0	20.5	19.1	18.0	33.7
65-74 years......	52.4	56.0	45.3	40.1	65.2	39.3	35.4	42.4	40.7	40.2	46.0
75-84 years...... }	113.0	123.3	94.3	83.3	128.8	87.6	71.7	90.8	93.3	94.2	80.4
85 years and over. }				164.3	233.3	178.4	144.4	150.2	202.0	206.8	144.7
Age-standardized death rate......	11.9	9.8	17.7	7.9	13.0	7.7	6.4	8.2	8.4		

Source: Vital Statistics of the United States: 1950, Vol. I, Tables 8.40; 9.16; 10.15.

mortality has taken place among the younger generation, but has affected the older generations less, or (b) that middle-aged Hawaiians are unusually subject to death from degenerative diseases. It is entirely possible that both of these explanations are valid. That the second explanation is at least one of the factors involved is evidenced by the following death rates for each of the ten leading causes of death:

Cause	Rate Alaska	Hawaii
Diseases of heart...................	112.1	174.1
Malignant neoplasms................	37.1	86.6
Vascular lesions...................	30.1	48.8
Accidents..........................	134.0	34.6
Diseases of early infancy..........	69.9	40.2
Influenza and pneumonia............	37.4	18.7
General arteriosclerosis...........	2.4	5.7
Diabetes Mellitus..................	3.4	14.9
Congenital malformations...........	10.7	12.3
Cirrhosis of liver.................	5.8	7.9

This summary suggests rather clearly that in Hawaii (and, presumably, especially among native Hawaiians) heart disease, cancer, vascular lesions, diabetes, and cirrhosis of the liver (all degenerative diseases) take a much heavier toll than they do in Alaska. In Alaska, on the other hand, rates of death from accidents, diseases of early infancy, and influenza and pneumonia are much higher than in Hawaii. Table 25-5 reveals that from birth to about age 45, the age-specific death rates among Alaska's Eskimos, Indians, and Aleuts are from 4 to 10 times as high as the corresponding rates in the 48 states.

COMPOSITION OF POPULATION OF ALASKA AND HAWAII IN COMPARISON WITH THE 48 STATES

Sex Composition. Unlike the 48 states, both Alaska and Hawaii have a much larger male than female population. In each place the economy is conducive to the employment of large numbers of unmarried males; in the process of migration, single men have been attracted to the plantations of Hawaii and to the mines, forests, and fisheries of Alaska. In 1950 there were 162 men for each 100 women in Alaska, and in Hawaii the sex ratio was 121 men per 100 women. As Table 25-6 shows, these sex-composition imbalances are confined almost entirely to the immigrant populations--a large excess of males is found only among the white population of Alaska, and among the non-Hawaiian population of Hawaii. The sex ratios among the native stocks are more "normal," as is shown by the following data for 1950:

	Sex ratio
Hawaiian........	98.8
Eskimo..........	106.7
Indian..........	105.6
Aleut..........	118.4

Table 25-6.--SEX RATIOS BY AGE, RACE, AND COLOR FOR ALASKA AND HAWAII, IN COMPARISON WITH THE 48 STATES: 1950

Place, race, and color	All ages	Sex ratio by age								
		Under 5 years	5-9 years	10-19 years	20-29 years	30-39 years	40-49 years	50-64 years	65-74 years	75 yrs. and over
ALASKA, total...............	161.6	104.8	102.5	164.1	217.0	156.9	160.8	195.4	231.1	253.2
White....................	86.3	105.6	99.0	232.3	252.9	168.5	167.3	221.2	324.3	485.8
Nonwhite.................	107.6	103.4	106.8	110.3	123.6	113.8	137.1	127.6	115.0	90.0
HAWAII, total..............	121.2	105.3	105.8	108.6	115.9	132.0	160.4	131.3	150.2	163.6
Hawaiian.................	98.8	102.3	108.2	98.0	95.5	96.2	91.2	93.7	92.5	87.2
Caucasian................	132.4	108.7	103.8	157.9	171.2	136.1	118.0	110.3	91.9	75.5
Chinese..................	111.2	105.8	106.8	99.2	90.8	107.5	119.7	133.5	188.1	369.1
Filipino.................	248.7	104.2	107.2	107.1	161.2	599.3	831.5	754.0	534.8	339.3
Japanese.................	102.1	104.9	104.4	100.6	89.0	101.0	113.8	96.1	155.3	175.0
FORTY-EIGHT STATES, total...	98.6	103.9	103.5	101.9	95.3	95.9	99.2	100.2	92.9	82.6
White....................	99.0	104.4	104.1	102.5	96.3	96.7	99.4	99.9	92.7	81.9
Nonwhite.................	95.7	100.5	99.5	98.0	87.9	89.0	97.0	104.5	95.9	93.0

Source: Population Census of the United States: 1950, Vol. II, Territories and Possessions, Alaska, Table 29, Hawaii, Table 32.

(The moderately high sex ratio among the Aleut population is difficult to explain, except as the result of a problem connected with census enumeration. The sex ratio for this group was somewhat less extreme in the census of 1939--112.8.)

In Hawaii the sex ratio is extremely imbalanced among the Filipino population (249), and reflects the arrival in recent decades of large numbers of men without families who migrated to Hawaii to work on the sugar and pineapple plantations, as described earlier. At particular adult ages, the sex ratio among Filipinos is extremely distorted (831 at age 40 to 49). The Chinese and Japanese immigrations to Hawaii are now several decades in the past, so at the younger ages the number of men and women is roughly equal, because the population is native born. Only at the most advanced ages were the sex ratios for Japanese and Chinese strongly imbalanced in favor of males. By 1960, when most of the remnants of the old cohorts of family-less migrants from the Orient will have died out, this imbalance will disappear from Hawaii except among the Caucasian and Filipino populations.

Large male-predominant sex imbalances are found among the white population of Alaska (186) and the Caucasian population of Hawaii (132). They are due, in large part, to the fact that these particular populations comprise the most recent group of immigrants; these imbalances are also a result of the presence of the large numbers of military personnel stationed in both Alaska and Hawaii.

Age Composition. Due to a combination of high birth rates and recent immigration, Alaska and Hawaii both have populations whose age composition is much younger than that of the 48 states (see Table 25-7). The white immigrants to Alaska, and the Caucasian and Filipino immigrants to Hawaii, have not lived there long enough to accumulate a large number of elderly people. The high fertility of the native populations in both places also increases the percentage of young persons. In comparison with the 48 states, Alaska has a very large concentration of persons 20 to 39 years of age, and a corresponding deficit of persons 50 years old or older. In comparison with the 48 states, Hawaii has a very heavy excess of children and of young adults less than 30 years of age, and a deficit at ages older than this. Since the Chinese and Japanese populations arrived in Hawaii before the heavy influx of Filipinos and Caucasians, both of the two first-named groups have a higher percentage of older persons than the other ethnic groups. Thus, due to its combination of demographic circumstances, Hawaii and Alaska each

Table 25-7.—AGE COMPOSITION OF THE POPULATION OF ALASKA AND HAWAII, BY RACE AND COLOR, IN COMPARISON WITH THE 48 STATES: 1950

Place, race, and color	Median age	Total	Age							
			Under 10 years	10-19 years	20-29 years	30-39 years	40-49 years	50-64 years	65-74 years	75 yrs. and over
ALASKA, total..............	25.8	100.0	20.4	14.5	24.2	17.9	11.0	8.3	2.7	1.0
White....................	28.1	100.0	16.4	11.1	27.1	20.4	12.3	9.0	2.7	1.0
Nonwhite.................	18.4	100.0	30.4	23.2	17.1	11.4	7.7	6.3	2.7	1.2
HAWAII, total..............	25.0	100.0	23.2	16.9	20.0	15.1	10.8	8.0	2.9	1.2
Hawaiian.................	16.6	100.0	34.3	22.8	15.2	11.8	7.6	6.2	1.5	0.5
Caucasian................	27.9	100.0	18.6	12.1	24.3	20.1	11.8	9.4	2.6	1.0
Chinese..................	27.0	100.0	21.8	15.5	18.9	16.6	11.5	9.8	3.1	2.8
Filipino.................	27.0	100.0	20.1	15.6	13.4	16.1	21.4	11.9	1.2	0.2
Japanese.................	25.0	100.0	22.0	17.6	21.4	15.7	8.5	9.3	4.0	1.6
FORTY-EIGHT STATES, total..	30.2	100.0	19.5	14.4	15.7	15.1	12.8	14.3	5.6	2.6
White....................	30.8	100.0	19.1	14.1	15.6	15.2	12.9	14.8	5.8	2.7
Nonwhite.................	26.1	100.0	22.8	17.2	16.7	14.9	12.1	10.7	4.1	1.6

Source: Population Census of the United States: 1950, Vol. II, Territories and Possessions, Alaska, Table 29, Hawaii, Table 32.

has an age composition in which the median age is 5 years, or more, lower than that of the white population of the 48 states. Two of the ethnic groups have amazingly young age structures. The nonwhite population of Alaska had a median age of 18.4 in 1950, and the Hawaiian population of Hawaii had a median age of 16.6 years at that time. Since there has been little migration in the recent history of these two groups, such extraordinarily young age compositions are the results of very high fertility and of recently, or currently, high mortality.

Marital Status. Males in both Alaska and Hawaii tend to marry at a considerably older age, or more often tend never to marry at all, than males in the 48 states. That this postponement of marriage, indicated by Table 25-8, is not due to differences in age composition is made clear by Table 25-9. However, there is considerable variation among the ethnic groups with respect to marital status. Alaska has a very large concentration of never-married white males, especially at ages 20 to 29 and at age 45 and over. Nonwhite males in Alaska tend to postpone marriage, but many bachelors seem to marry after age 40 (or else the single men die off, leaving only the married ones). In Hawaii males also tend to postpone marriage, but only among the native Hawaiian and Filipino men

do substantial proportions tend to remain bachelors throughout their lives. The Filipino men are much more inclined to remain unmarried than the men of any of the other ethnic groups, either in Alaska or Hawaii. Caucasians and Japanese men tend, eventually, to marry in as large proportions as do the males in the 48 states. Thus, both Alaska and Hawaii are well-stocked with eligible bachelors. Their status is partly a matter of necessity, considering the imbalanced sex ratio, and it is undoubtedly also partly a result of the kind of work they do. Hunters, trappers, fishermen, and plantation laborers may find a family a very heavy economic burden.

Unmarried females, in contrast, are comparatively scarce--especially in Alaska. In 1950, only 12 percent of the white Alaskan female population 14 years of age and over had never married, and a sizable percentage of these "spinsters" were girls between the ages of 14 and 18 years. Although the nonwhite women in Alaska tend to marry at a later age than the white women, almost 100 percent marry eventually, and their age at marriage is earlier than that of the nonwhite female population in the 48 states.

Hawaiian, Filipino, and Caucasian women tend to marry at an earlier age than the women in the 48 states, and almost all of them eventually marry.

Table 25-8.—MARITAL STATUS OF POPULATION 14 YEARS OF AGE AND OVER, BY RACE AND COLOR, ALASKA AND HAWAII IN COMPARISON WITH THE 48 STATES: 1950

Place, race, and color	Male					Female				
	Total	Single	Married	Wid-owed	Di-vorced	Total	Single	Married	Wid-owed	Di-vorced
ALASKA, total..................	100.0	43.4	48.4	3.2	4.9	100.0	16.8	73.6	6.3	3.3
White.......................	100.0	42.9	49.1	2.3	5.6	100.0	12.0	79.5	4.5	4.1
Nonwhite....................	100.0	45.8	45.4	7.1	1.7	100.0	28.2	59.5	10.8	1.5
HAWAII, total.................	100.0	41.4	52.3	3.7	2.6	100.0	28.3	61.6	7.6	2.5
Hawaiian....................	100.0	43.9	48.5	4.5	3.1	100.0	28.9	60.4	7.2	3.5
Caucasian...................	100.0	35.6	58.8	1.8	3.8	100.0	18.6	69.4	8.0	4.0
Chinese.....................	100.0	38.4	55.8	4.1	1.7	100.0	28.7	59.4	9.8	2.1
Filipino....................	100.0	49.8	41.7	5.2	3.3	100.0	30.9	65.5	2.0	1.6
Japanese....................	100.0	40.9	54.2	3.9	1.0	100.0	33.2	57.3	8.2	1.3
FORTY-EIGHT STATES, total.....	100.0	26.4	67.5	4.1	2.0	100.0	20.0	65.8	11.8	2.4
White.......................	100.0	26.1	67.9	4.0	2.0	100.0	19.9	66.2	11.5	2.4
Nonwhite....................	100.0	28.5	64.4	5.2	1.9	100.0	20.7	62.0	14.6	2.7

Source: Population Census of the United States: 1950, Vol. II, Territories and Possessions, Alaska, Table 33 and Hawaii, Table 36.

Table 25-9.—PERCENTAGE MALES EVER MARRIED, BY AGE AND ETHNIC GROUP: 1950

Place and ethnic group	All ages	Age								
		15-19 years	20-24 years	25-29 years	30-34 years	35-39 years	40-44 years	45-54 years	55-64 years	65 yrs. and over
MALES										
ALASKA, total................	57.3	2.7	20.5	67.2	81.2	85.2	86.9	83.6	77.9	68.1
White.....................	57.5	3.1	19.9	67.2	82.0	85.5	87.2	82.4	74.7	61.3
Nonwhite..................	56.3	1.6	24.0	61.3	76.4	83.9	85.6	89.3	92.8	92.7
HAWAII, total................	59.7	1.3	21.6	59.7	78.9	76.6	75.4	82.3	88.2	84.5
Hawaiian..................	58.5	1.7	33.7	66.2	74.8	84.8	83.4	89.1	91.6	92.3
Caucasian.................	65.0	2.4	23.1	75.6	87.0	89.0	90.1	90.2	91.2	89.6
Chinese...................	62.9	0.8	20.3	57.5	78.4	81.4	85.9	89.1	93.9	66.1
Filipino..................	50.9	1.6	28.3	51.3	64.5	47.8	49.1	62.3	69.1	67.5
Japanese..................	60.4	0.4	12.5	47.3	76.0	89.2	92.9	96.1	95.7	90.7
FORTY-EIGHT STATES, total.....	73.6	3.3	41.0	76.2	86.8	89.1	91.0	91.5	91.6	...
White.....................	73.9	3.2	40.5	76.4	86.9	89.9	91.0	91.4	91.3	...
Nonwhite..................	71.5	4.4	45.3	74.8	85.6	89.6	91.0	92.3	93.8	...
FEMALES										
ALASKA, total................	84.9	22.3	79.1	91.8	94.1	94.7	95.1	95.4	96.3	96.3
White.....................	89.1	30.2	84.9	92.7	94.2	94.3	94.7	94.5	95.0	94.8
Nonwhite..................	74.7	16.7	68.3	88.8	93.8	96.2	96.6	98.0	99.3	97.9
HAWAII, total................	73.6	8.0	51.7	81.4	90.6	92.4	93.5	95.4	96.1	95.1
Hawaiian..................	74.1	11.6	69.0	89.5	94.5	95.9	95.4	96.1	96.3	93.3
Caucasian.................	82.5	17.1	74.3	88.0	90.6	89.6	89.8	89.5	89.1	89.8
Chinese...................	72.9	4.7	43.3	78.0	90.1	92.4	92.5	95.8	97.8	98.5
Filipino..................	72.3	14.8	73.3	93.5	97.6	98.0	98.5	98.8	99.7	97.2
Japanese..................	68.4	1.9	32.6	73.6	88.4	92.3	95.0	98.7	99.5	98.7
FORTY-EIGHT STATES, total.....	80.0	17.1	67.7	86.7	90.7	91.6	91.7	92.2	92.1	...
White.....................	80.1	16.5	67.6	86.9	90.7	91.5	91.4	91.8	91.8	...
Nonwhite..................	79.3	21.1	68.8	85.9	91.1	93.1	94.3	95.5	95.8	...

Source: Population Census of the United States: 1950, Vol. II, Territories and Possessions, Alaska, Table 33 and Hawaii, Table 36.

Chinese and Japanese women, on the other hand, tend to marry at a later age, although almost all of them marry eventually, too.

Widowhood is the lot of a disproportionately larger share of Alaskan nonwhite women than of women among the 48 states, considering the young age composition of the nonwhite Alaskan population. Divorce seems to be much more common among the white population of Alaska, and among the Caucasian, Hawaiian, and Filipino populations of Hawaii (again, considering their younger age composition) than it is in the 48 states.

School Enrollment. Both in Alaska and Hawaii, children are given excellent educational opportunities, and a high percentage of the children of elementary and high school age are enrolled in school. In fact, as Table 25-10 reveals, Hawaii outstrips the 48 states with respect to the proportions of children aged 7 to 15 who are enrolled in school. White children in Alaska are enrolled at rates higher than those of the white children in the 48 states at every age up to age 16, after which white Alaskans tend to show lower enrollment rates. Nonwhite children in Alaska are enrolled at somewhat lower rates than are those of the white Alaskan population, or even than the young people in the nonwhite population of the 48 states. But Alaska's school enrollment rates are impressively high in view of the primitive economy by which many of these students' families support themselves, and the very low educational attainment of their parents (see below).

The Chinese and Japanese populations of Hawaii appear to be especially eager to educate their

Table 25-10.—PERCENT OF CHILDREN ENROLLED IN SCHOOL, BY AGE, RACE, AND COLOR, ALASKA AND HAWAII, IN COMPARISON WITH THE 48 STATES: 1950

Place and ethnic group	Percent enrolled in school, selected ages										
	6 years	8 years	10 years	12 years	14 years	15 years	16 years	17 years	18 years	19 years	20 years
ALASKA, total.................	47.2	89.9	90.7	91.6	89.6	87.1	76.5	57.1	20.1	7.0	4.1
White......................	57.4	97.2	96.9	97.4	97.4	94.9	87.6	67.3	14.2	4.3	2.7
Nonwhite...................	34.6	81.8	84.9	86.8	83.6	81.5	68.8	48.5	32.7	17.5	11.3
HAWAII, total.................	68.0	97.8	97.7	98.1	97.6	96.4	90.5	81.4	52.6	22.6	12.2
Hawaiian...................	64.5	98.0	97.4	97.7	96.5	96.5	84.0	72.2	48.1	20.3	8.8
Caucasian..................	65.0	98.4	97.1	97.4	95.8	94.0	88.0	70.2	28.9	8.4	4.4
Chinese....................	66.9	95.5	98.2	97.0	98.9	99.1	96.5	91.7	71.1	45.4	32.9
Filipino...................	68.2	96.9	98.7	99.1	97.9	94.4	90.7	71.8	50.0	17.9	10.7
Japanese...................	72.8	98.5	97.8	98.6	98.3	96.8	95.3	93.0	66.8	34.8	19.8
FORTY-EIGHT STATES. total.....	67.6	95.6	96.0	95.9	94.8	91.4	80.9	68.2	39.8	24.7	17.9
White......................	67.9	95.9	96.3	96.2	95.2	92.1	82.1	69.9	40.8	25.3	18.6
Nonwhite...................	65.6	93.8	94.5	94.5	91.9	85.9	72.6	55.8	32.3	19.7	12.5

Source: Population Census of the United States: 1950, Vol. II, Territories and Possessions, Alaska, Table 36 and Hawaii, Table 40.

children. Not only do they send their children to elementary school and high schools at much higher rates than do the white populations of either Hawaii or the 48 states, but they also send an extraordinarily large percentage on to college. Among the Hawaiian and Filipino populations enrollment rates are high for the elementary school years, but are moderately below average for the years of high school and are very low at the college ages. Here again, the record of these groups is impressive, in view of their low socio-economic status and the parents' lack of education.

Thus, Hawaii has a better over-all school attendance record among its young people than Alaska. In both places, however, completing grammar school is the "normal" level of education, and substantial percentages of native as well as white populations are going on to secondary school and to college. As the educational program now under way in each of these areas continues, it will raise the education level rapidly.

Educational Attainment of Youth. As a direct consequence of the fact that children in Hawaii are more inclined to remain in school beyond the eighth grade than are children in the 48 states, by the time Hawaiian youths have attained the age of 18 or 20 years they have completed as many grades of schooling as their peers on the mainland, if not more. In Alaska, the children have accumu-

lated about one or one and one-half fewer grades of schooling than children in the 48 states by the time they reach the age of 16 or 18. This difference may be due to the lower attendance rates of the nonwhite children in Alaska, or to the fact that progress through the grades may be slower there. (Data with which to test this hypothesis were not tabulated for Alaska, although they were tabulated for Hawaii. See Table 25-11.)

The 1950 census reflected a rather sharp difference between the educational attainment of Japanese, Chinese, and Hawaiian young people and that of Filipino youth. By the time they had reached age 20, the three former groups had an average equivalent to a high school education (12 years or more), but the Filipinos had the equivalent of only two years of high school. However, the younger generations of all Hawaii's nonwhite populations, including the Filipino, were considerably superior in their educational attainment to the nonwhite population of the 48 states. In fact, at age 18 the average Filipino youth, who is low man on Hawaii's educational totem pole, had completed two more grades of schooling than the average American Negro of the same age.

Educational Attainment of Adults. The adult populations of both Alaska and Hawaii have educational backgrounds that are very modest in comparison with the accomplishments of their chil-

Table 25-11.—MEDIAN YEARS OF SCHOOL COMPLETED FOR MALES 8 TO 24 YEARS OF AGE, SELECTED AGES, BY COLOR AND RACE, ALASKA AND HAWAII IN COMPARISON WITH THE 48 STATES: 1950

Place and ethnic group	Median school years completed, selected ages								
	8 years	10 years	12 years	14 years	16 years	18 years	20 years	22 years	24 years
ALASKA..............................	1.6	3.2	5.0	6.3	8.1	10.1	12.1	11.0	11.3
White..............................	(1)	(1)	(1)	(1)	(1)	(1)	(1)	(1)	(1)
Nonwhite...........................	(1)	(1)	(1)	(1)	(1)	(1)	(1)	(1)	(1)
HAWAII..............................	2.2	4.0	5.0	7.7	9.6	11.3	12.1	11.7	11.0
Hawaiian...........................	2.1	3.9	5.7	7.5	9.3	10.9	12.0	9.0	9.9
Caucasian..........................	2.1	3.9	5.8	7.7	9.2	10.6	11.6	11.0	11.0
Chinese............................	2.3	3.9	6.2	7.9	11.8	10.6	12.5	12.4	12.3
Filipino...........................	1.9	3.8	5.6	7.3	9.4	10.6	10.0	9.2	9.0
Japanese...........................	2.3	4.2	6.1	8.0	9.9	11.7	12.4	12.3	12.1
FORTY-EIGHT STATES...................	2.1	3.9	5.8	7.7	9.5	11.2	12.1	11.9	11.8
White..............................	2.2	4.0	5.9	7.8	9.6	11.4	12.2	12.1	12.1
Nonwhite...........................	1.8	3.3	4.9	6.5	8.0	8.7	8.7	8.6	8.6

[1]Not available.

Source: U. S. Census of Population: 1950, Vol. II, Territories and Possessions, Alaska, Table 38 and Hawaii, Table 42.

dren. This is especially true of the nonwhite ethnic groups in Alaska and Hawaii. (A comparison of Table 25-12 for adults with Table 25-11 for youths will show the magnitude of these intergenerational differences.) More than one-half of the Hawaiian adult population 25 years of age or older was functionally illiterate in 1950. Thirty percent had not attended school long enough to complete first grade, and an additional 25 percent had completed only one of the first four grades. A similar, but even more unfavorable, situation was found among the Filipino population, of which 34 percent had not completed first grade and an additional 33 percent had completed only one of the first four grades.

Except for these two outstanding examples of illiteracy, or semi-literacy, the adults of the ethnic groups were relatively well-educated in compari-

Table 25-12.—YEARS OF SCHOOL COMPLETED BY PERSONS 25 YEARS OLD AND OVER, BY RACE AND COLOR, FOR ALASKA AND HAWAII IN COMPARISON WITH THE 48 STATES: 1950

Place and ethnic group	Median school years completed	Total	Educational attainment									
			No education	Elementary				High school		College		Not reported
				1-4 years	5-6 years	7 years	8 years	1-3 years	4 years	1-3 years	4 or more years	
ALASKA.............	11.3	100.0	6.4	6.5	4.8	3.9	14.8	16.0	25.6	12.3	7.3	2.4
White............	12.2	100.0	0.7	1.9	2.7	3.4	16.1	18.3	30.7	15.0	9.0	2.2
Nonwhite.........	4.0	100.0	29.7	25.0	13.3	5.5	9.7	6.9	4.8	1.5	0.5	3.0
HAWAII.............	8.7	100.0	10.6	13.3	11.0	5.1	12.9	14.6	19.9	5.2	6.1	1.3
Hawaiian.........	8.8	100.0	2.1	12.1	13.9	8.0	16.9	21.2	18.7	3.2	2.4	1.4
Caucasian........	12.2	100.0	1.8	6.3	7.1	4.4	10.2	14.4	26.6	12.7	14.8	1.6
Chinese..........	9.9	100.0	14.1	10.6	8.6	2.5	8.5	12.6	28.9	4.6	8.8	0.8
Filipino.........	2.9	100.0	33.8	32.7	10.8	5.4	4.7	6.2	3.7	0.6	0.3	1.9
Japanese.........	8.6	100.0	9.4	11.5	13.2	4.8	17.7	16.1	20.8	2.4	3.0	1.0
FORTY-EIGHT STATES.	9.3	100.0	2.5	8.3	9.1	6.8	20.2	17.0	20.2	7.2	6.0	2.7
White............	9.7	100.0	2.1	6.6	8.2	6.6	21.2	17.4	21.4	7.6	6.4	2.6
Nonwhite.........	6.9	100.0	6.5	24.9	18.0	9.3	11.5	13.0	8.1	2.9	2.2	3.7

Source: U. S. Census of Population: 1950, Vol. II, Territories and Possessions, Alaska, Table 10 and Hawaii, Table 43.

son with the adult population of the 48 states. A substantial proportion of the older Chinese and Japanese residents in Hawaii have had no schooling, or very little schooling, but this deficiency is compensated for by the unusually high educational attainment of the younger generations. By 1960 most of these two groups of this poorly-educated generation of Oriental citizens will have died out, and the Japanese and Chinese adult populations of Hawaii will be two of the best-educated groups in any state.

In both Alaska and Hawaii the white population has an outstandingly high level of educational attainment--considerably above the average for the 48 states. This is due in large part to the selective assignment of the military personnel sent to these places, and to the presence of the many civilian technicians and specialists employed in the local industries and military installations. In Hawaii, 1 Caucasian adult in 7 was a college graduate, and in Alaska, 1 in 11. (In the 48 states only 1 in 17 was a college graduate.)

This discussion should make it abundantly clear that the native populations of Alaska and Hawaii (especially of Alaska) are being transformed in many ways by the education which is now available to them. The oncoming generations of Eskimo, Aleut, Indian, Filipino, and Hawaiian children may be expected to be very different in outlook, interests, and ambitions from their illiterate or semiliterate elders, who did not have such educational opportunities.

Labor Force Status. Of the adult populations in both Alaska and Hawaii in 1950, a higher percentage were in the labor force than was the case among the adult population of the 48 states (see Table 25-13). This difference was due largely to the preponderance of males in Alaska's and Hawaii's populations, and to the younger age composition of these populations which meant the presence of few retired persons. When these compositional differences are taken into account, the labor force participation rates of males in these places turn out to be approximately the same as those in the 48 states. In Alaska, however, white women had extraordinarily high labor force participation rates, despite the fact that most of them were married. In Hawaii, Chinese and Japanese women have high labor force participation rates, while Filipino women have low labor force participation rates.

Unemployment rates were almost twice as high in Alaska and Hawaii in 1950 as they were in the 48 states. This deprivation fell most heavily on

Table 25-13.—LABOR FORCE STATUS OF THE POPULATION 14 YEARS OF AGE AND OVER, BY SEX, RACE, AND COLOR, FOR ALASKA AND HAWAII IN COMPARISON WITH THE 48 STATES: 1950

Place and ethnic group	Percent in labor force		Percent of civilian labor force unemployed		Percent of labor force military	
	Male	Female	Male	Female	Male	Female
ALASKA, total	87.7	36.8	10.2	8.4	36.8	0.5
White	91.5	41.6	8.6	6.3	41.7	0.6
Nonwhite	71.1	25.3	16.2	16.6	9.4	0.1
HAWAII, total	79.4	33.1	10.1	7.9	14.4	0.6
Hawaiian	70.7	27.6	18.0	14.3	3.0	0.1
Caucasian	88.5	29.2	6.5	6.7	41.8	2.4
Chinese	72.1	37.6	7.9	7.0	1.6	0.1
Filipino	85.9	19.7	15.8	21.4	2.0	0.2
Japanese	74.3	39.4	5.8	5.4	1.0	...
FORTY-EIGHT STATES, total	78.7	28.9	4.9	4.6	2.2	0.2
White	79.0	28.1	4.6	4.1	2.3	0.2
Nonwhite	76.1	36.7	7.8	7.9	1.6	0.1

Source: U. S. Census of Population: 1950, Vol. II, Territories and Possessions, Alaska, Table 41 and Hawaii, Table 47.

the nonwhite populations. For example, among the nonwhite population of Alaska the unemployment rate was 4 times the unemployment rate of the white population in the 48 states, and the rate of the Filipino workers in Hawaii was almost 5 times the rate found among the white workers in the 48 states. Hawaiians were also hit hard by unemployment, but their unemployment rate was only 3 1/2 times that of white workers on the mainland.

Both in Alaska and Hawaii, more than 40 percent of the men belonging to the labor force were in military service in 1950. These proportions have probably not declined since then.

Occupation--males. In Alaska, the largest occupational groups are unskilled laborers, semi-skilled operatives, and craftsmen (Table 25-14). However, there is a larger proportion of professional and technical workers, and of managers and officials, than in the 48 states. The members of these latter groups are specialists of all kinds, experts who are needed in the military as well as the economic development programs. Alaska is almost devoid of agricultural workers, and has comparatively few clerical and sales workers.

In both Alaska and Hawaii, occupation varies sharply according to ethnic background. In Alaska, white men hold the white-collar jobs and do the skilled work, while the jobs calling for semi-skilled operatives and unskilled laborers are held by nonwhite persons. As has been noted, a large percentage of this latter group have only very limited education, and lack certain kinds of background experience that would fit them for other types of work.

Hawaii's occupational structure resembles that of the 48 states much more closely than does Alaska's. The major difference between Hawaii and the mainland in occupational composition is the almost complete absence in Hawaii of farm managers, and the existence of a very large body of farm laborers. As is the case in Alaska, Hawaii's white population is heavily concentrated in the jobs giving higher prestige and salary, while the nonwhite populations are concentrated in the lower status jobs. However, this generalization does not apply as widely to the Chinese and Japanese groups; they are distributed among all occupational groups, and show a concentration in the white-collar as well as the blue-collar jobs.

Occupation--females. Both in Hawaii and Alaska, women workers are employed most often in teaching school, doing clerical work, as oper-

Table 25-14.—OCCUPATIONAL COMPOSITION OF EMPLOYED MALE LABOR FORCE, BY RACE AND COLOR, OF ALASKA AND HAWAII IN COMPARISON WITH THE 48 STATES: 1950

Place and ethnic group	Total	Prof. and tech.	Farmers and farm mgrs.	Mgrs. off., and prop.	Clerical wkrs.	Sales wkrs.	Craft. and foremen	Operatives	Service wkrs.	Farm laborers	Labor other	Occ. not reported
ALASKA..............	100.0	10.4	0.9	11.3	4.1	2.3	22.7	19.8	6.1	0.4	19.8	2.1
White..........	100.0	12.7	1.1	13.4	4.9	2.7	26.8	14.5	6.5	0.4	15.2	1.9
Nonwhite.........	100.0	1.7	0.2	3.0	1.1	1.0	6.7	40.3	4.5	0.8	37.7	3.0
HAWAII..............	100.0	7.3	3.1	9.5	7.3	5.1	20.9	16.0	7.7	12.5	10.0	0.5
Hawaiian..........	100.0	5.7	7.9		7.2	2.7	22.9	20.1	10.0	22.6		0.8
Caucasian.........	100.0	16.9	18.5		7.7	6.4	21.3	12.7	6.7	8.9		0.9
Chinese...........	100.0	10.7	20.0		17.3	8.8	18.4	11.3	7.8	5.3		0.4
Filipino..........	100.0	1.2	3.0		2.0	1.3	7.5	19.9	11.2	53.6		0.4
Japanese..........	100.0	5.4	15.1		8.5	6.5	27.7	14.9	5.3	16.3		0.4
FORTY-EIGHT STATES..	100.0	7.3	10.3	10.7	6.4	6.4	18.6	20.0	6.1	4.9	8.2	1.1
White.............	100.0	7.8	10.0	11.6	6.8	6.9	19.7	20.0	5.2	4.2	6.6	1.1
Nonwhite.........	100.0	2.3	13.3	2.3	3.1	1.2	7.6	20.6	14.4	10.7	23.1	1.5

Source: U. S. Census of Population: 1950, Vol. II, Territories and Possessions, Alaska, Table 17 and Hawaii, Tables 20 and 55.

Table 25-15.—OCCUPATIONAL COMPOSITION OF EMPLOYED FEMALE LABOR FORCE, BY RACE AND COLOR, FOR ALASKA AND HAWAII IN COMPARISON WITH THE 48 STATES: 1950

Place and ethnic group	Total	Occupation - Females										
		Prof. and tech.	Farmers and farm mgrs.	Mgrs. off., and prop.	Clerical wkrs.	Sales wkrs.	Craft. and foremen	Operatives	Service wkrs.	Farm laborers	Labor other	Occ. not reported
ALASKA............	100.0	15.2	0.3	7.6	30.0	6.7	0.8	13.0	18.9	0.1	1.3	6.0
White...........	100.0	17.8	0.3	8.5	36.0	7.7	0.9	5.9	17.3	0.1	0.7	4.7
Nonwhite........	100.0	3.5	0.1	3.5	3.5	2.4	0.5	44.2	26.6	...	3.9	11.7
HAWAII............	100.0	16.3	1.3	5.3	25.6	10.0	1.5	12.4	22.2	3.7	0.9	0.9
Hawaiian........	100.0	16.4	4.6		26.2	5.3	2.1	14.5	27.0		2.6	1.3
Caucasian.......	100.0	36.0	6.6		29.3	7.0	1.1	4.3	13.8		0.8	1.0
Chinese.........	100.0	20.7	7.9		36.5	10.9	1.3	8.5	12.2		1.2	0.8
Filipino........	100.0	6.5	6.2		15.6	8.9	1.8	17.0	36.4		5.9	1.6
Japanese........	100.0	8.6	6.8		23.0	12.4	1.5	15.3	24.7		7.1	0.6
FORTY-EIGHT STATES.	100.0	12.3	0.7	4.3	27.3	8.5	1.5	19.2	20.7	2.9	0.8	1.8
White...........	100.0	13.3	0.6	4.7	30.5	9.4	1.6	19.8	15.3	2.2	0.7	1.8
Nonwhite........	100.0	5.7	1.7	1.4	4.3	1.4	0.6	14.8	59.2	7.6	1.5	1.7

Source: U. S. Census of Population: 1950, Vol. II, Territories and Possessions, Alaska, Table 17 and Hawaii, Tables 20 and 55.

atives in the canning of fish (Alaska) or pineapple (Hawaii), and in the service occupations. In Alaska, nonwhite women qualify only for the operative and service worker categories; almost all of the female white-collar workers are white. In Hawaii, the Hawaiian, Chinese, Japanese, and Filipino women have much more opportunity to hold white-collar jobs than the nonwhite women in the 48 states.

Income of Males. Caucasian men in Hawaii, and white men in Alaska, have higher average incomes than white men in the 48 states. In both places a smaller percentage of the people have extremely small incomes, and the percentage of persons with incomes of $5,000 or more is larger than it is in the 48 states. However, the nonwhite people of Alaska have extremely small cash incomes. More than 60 percent of them received less than $1,000

Table 25-16.—INDIVIDUAL INCOME OF MALES, BY RACE AND COLOR, FOR ALASKA AND HAWAII IN COMPARISON WITH THE 48 STATES: 1950

Place and ethnic group	Median income	Total	Percent income distribution - males with income								
			Less than $1,000	$1,000 to $1,499	$1,500 to $1,999	$2,000 to $2,499	$2,500 to $2,999	$3,000 to $3,999	$4,000 to $4,999	$5,000 to $6,999	$7,000 and over
ALASKA											
White............	2,625	100.0	15.9	25.7			13.5	14.0	11.3	13.7	5.9
Nonwhite.........	784	100.0	60.8	19.7			8.9	5.3	2.4	2.2	0.7
HAWAII............	2,340	100.0	16.7	11.4	10.9	16.2	10.9	17.7	6.9	5.3	4.0
Hawaiian.........	2,369	100.0	22.6	8.8	8.5	13.6	12.0	21.5	7.1	3.7	2.2
Caucasian........	2,856	100.0	9.8	16.8	8.0	9.5	8.3	18.3	10.1	11.0	8.2
Chinese..........	2,964	100.0	17.6	6.1	6.8	9.7	10.5	22.9	11.9	7.6	6.8
Filipino.........	1,995	100.0	18.1	11.6	20.5	29.6	10.6	7.6	1.2	0.5	0.2
Japanese.........	2,427	100.0	18.6	7.8	9.5	16.5	13.1	21.0	6.9	3.7	2.9
FORTY-EIGHT STATES..	2,434	100.0	20.9	9.6	9.2	11.7	10.7	19.2	8.4	5.9	4.0
White............	2,572	100.0	19.2	9.0	8.7	11.5	11.0	20.5	9.2	6.5	4.5
Nonwhite.........	1,344	100.0	38.9	16.2	14.2	13.3	8.0	7.2	1.2	0.5	0.3

Source: U. S. Census of Population: 1950, Vol. II, Territories and Possessions, Alaska, Table 22 and Hawaii, Table 63.

in 1949, a situation reflecting the subsistence economy by which a large number of these peoples live. The only cash income received by many of them consists of payments received for furs trapped in winter, or of wages earned in the salmon-canning factories during the canning season. Since living costs are quite high in Alaska, even the white citizen's higher average income is counterbalanced by the higher prices he must pay for commodities. Hence, it may be concluded that white Alaskans and Hawaiians enjoy a level of living approximately the same as that of white persons in the 48 states, while the nonwhite population of Alaska lives in what can only be considered according to current standards, dire poverty and economic distress.

In Hawaii, the Filipino population is at the bottom of the income scale, while the highest average income is received by the Chinese group. Between these extremes fall the other ethnic groups. The Hawaiians have below-average incomes, but are better off than the Filipinos. All the nonwhite populations in Hawaii have more favorable income distributions than has the nonwhite population in the 48 states.

SUMMARY

Alaska and Hawaii both have young, highly fertile, and rapidly growing populations. Except for the Indian and other nonwhite populations of Alaska, and the Filipino and Hawaiian populations of Hawaii, the inhabitants of both places show every demographic trait that is considered characteristic of modern, progressive, well-educated, technologically sophisticated populations. The nonwhite populations of Alaska definitely displace the Negro population of the 48 states as the nation's most underprivileged group. In Hawaii, the Filipino population occupies a social and economic position considerably below those of the other groups. But even these "less-developed" populations show many evidences of rapid progress and change, patterned after the model of the now-dominant groups. In Hawaii, all ethnic groups show signs of at least equalling the Negro population of the 48 states in degree of advancement; in many respects these ethnic groups have progressed quite a bit farther than the Negro population, especially in terms of education. The Chinese population, the oldest of Hawaii's immigrant groups, has made an outstanding economic advancement, while the Japanese population, the next earliest arrival, is only slightly less advanced.

In both Alaska and Hawaii the oncoming generations--the youngsters who are now in school--may be expected to create remarkable changes. Since they are receiving education and more adequate medical care, and are being helped to take part more fully in the broader social and economic life of the nation, it seems likely that they will strive to live at a level very different from that of their ancestors. As the older generations die out and are replaced by these newer generations, rapid improvement may be expected to take place with respect to health and to other aspects of life that are considered indexes of socio-economic well-being. Meanwhile, the white populations of Alaska and Hawaii, in all of their demographic characteristics, differ little from the white populations of the 48 states.

Chapter 26

FUTURE POPULATION: IMPLICATIONS OF THE POTENTIAL PAROXYSM OF GROWTH *

THE POTENTIAL PAROXYSM OF GROWTH

The people of the United States are standing on the threshhold of what looks as though it may be an era of almost runaway population growth. The generation of parents who, during the 1920's and 1930's, controlled fertility to a point below the replacement level has now completed its reproductive cycle. It has been replaced by younger generations whose members have been bearing many more babies each year and have also been enjoying lower death rates than prevailed when their parents were going through the reproductive cycle. As a consequence, the growth rate of the population has risen to about 1.7 percent per year from the low of about 0.6 percent per year that it reached during 1932. The oldest of the larger annual cohorts of babies that have been born since 1941 has aged; the baby boom is now a greatly enlarged body of children and adolescents 0 to 18

years of age, the majority of whom are less than 15 years of age. Beginning in the period 1962 to 1965, these infants of yesterday will be attaining adulthood, marrying in large numbers, and having babies of their own. If this second generation of the baby boom maintains a fertility that is only the same as that of its parents, or even slightly lower, the numerical growth in population will dwarf any previous growth the nation has known. This process will resemble the action of a two-stage rocket, with the momentum provided by the baby boom becoming simply the starting point for a second spurt of growth.

This kind of development is implicit in the combination of demographic events that exists now. To illustrate the point, Table 26-1 reports and Figure 26-1 illustrates what the population size would be at various dates in the future if the fertility and immigration rates prevailing in the 1955 to 1957 period were to continue for only a few decades, under conditions favorable to a slow decrease in mortality. As of 1960 the United States will have been in existence 170 years, and will have gained about 175 million persons. If it continues to grow at the present rates, only about 50 additional years would be required to gain another 175 million persons. After that, the third set of 175 million persons would be produced in only 25 years, and a fourth set would require only about 12 years, etc. This spiraling numerical growth results, of course, from the continuous increase in the base population to which the vital rates apply; even a moderate rate of increase applied to a huge base gives a sizable amount of growth. Feature writers in our Sunday newspapers and magazines often talk about

---

* Many of the ideas expressed in this chapter were derived from a symposium "The Population Situation in the United States in 1975," in Applications of Demography, Donald J. Bogue (editor), Scripps Foundation, 1957. The contributors to this symposium were: Conrad Taeuber (Future Size and Age and Sex Composition); Daniel O. Price (Future Color and Nativity Composition); Jacob S. Siegel (Future Distribution by States and Regions); Ray P. Cuzzort, (Future Size and Distribution of Standard Metropolitan Areas); David L. Kaplan (Future Labor Force); Louis J. Ducoff (Future Farm Population); Leo F. Schnore (Journey to Work in the Future); Carl M. Frisen (Future School and College Enrollment); Emanual Landau (Future Marriage and Housing Boom); S. T. Hitchcock (Future Highway Traffic and Traffic Fatalities); Bruce Waxman (Future Aged Population).

Table 26-1.—PROJECTION OF THE U. S. POPULATION FOR 1960 TO THE YEAR 2100, ON THE ASSUMPTION THAT FERTILITY CONTINUES AT THE AVERAGE LEVEL OF 1955-57, THAT THE LEVEL OF MORTALITY DECLINES MODERATELY, AND THAT NET IMMIGRATION AVERAGES 300,000 PER YEAR

Year of projection	Total	White	Nonwhite	Percent nonwhite
1950	151,132	135,343	15,789	10.4
1960	180,126	159,800	20,300	11.3
1970	213,810	188,337	25,473	11.9
1980	259,981	226,931	33,050	12.7
1990	312,338	269,998	42,340	13.6
2000	375,238	321,031	54,207	14.4
2025	593,627	493,397	100,230	16.9
2050	939,117	754,675	184,441	19.6
2075	1,485,684	1,148,105	337,579	22.7
2100	2,350,352	1,736,185	614,167	26.1

the "population explosions" in Japan, India, China, and many other "underdeveloped" countries of the world. Actually, under current trends, the United States is exhibiting one of the world's greatest numerical increases. It is potentially able to make one of the biggest bangs when the "population bombs" go off.

It may seem a little absurd to worry about overpopulation when our nation is plagued with vast surpluses of food and our population is living at a level of comfort unknown anywhere else in the world. Our common sense tells us that a people with enough acumen to attain its present advantaged position would certainly do something about the threat of a "standing room only" population long before it became critical. However, as has just been illustrated, the full impact of a reproductive increase is not felt until a quarter-century or so later. As a nation, we would be well-advised to inform ourselves fully about the long-run consequences of our current growth, in order that these anticipated future developments may be considered in making today's plans for tomorrow. The goal of this chapter is to provide as comprehensive and detailed a spelling out of probable future population developments, together with as brief a statement of their possible meaning as can be made without resorting to the crystal ball. The author has no population policy of his own that he wants to preach; he is interested neither in scaring the reader with the bogey of Malthusianism nor in helping to perpetuate the myth, popular among businessmen today, that population growth is

necessary to a sustained economic prosperity. The analysis will be organized around two basic questions, "What will the population situation be, in terms of details that have been discussed in earlier chapters of this book, if present trends continue?" and "Since the present trend appears to be an impossible and implausible long-range course for population growth, what can reasonably be expected to happen?"

However, even if the over-all population growth were to be sharply curtailed now, a number of phenomenal demographic changes would, nevertheless, take place. These changes would be caused by the infants and children who are already in existence as a result of the baby boom. With each new year, that segment of the population born during the baby boom period puts an additional strain on a different sector of the economy and, therefore, affects a different aspect of community life. Until now the members of this baby-boom generation have created problems related only to childhood and adolescence, but in the next few decades they will create problems associated with late adolescence and adulthood. In still later decades they will create problems related to middle age and old age. These changes of the next few years are certain to take place, for the people who will create them are already born.

In addition to spelling out the long-run implications of present growth trends, this chapter attempts to describe in rather full detail what will happen in the next 20 years from 1960 to 1980 as a result of this great body of children who will grow

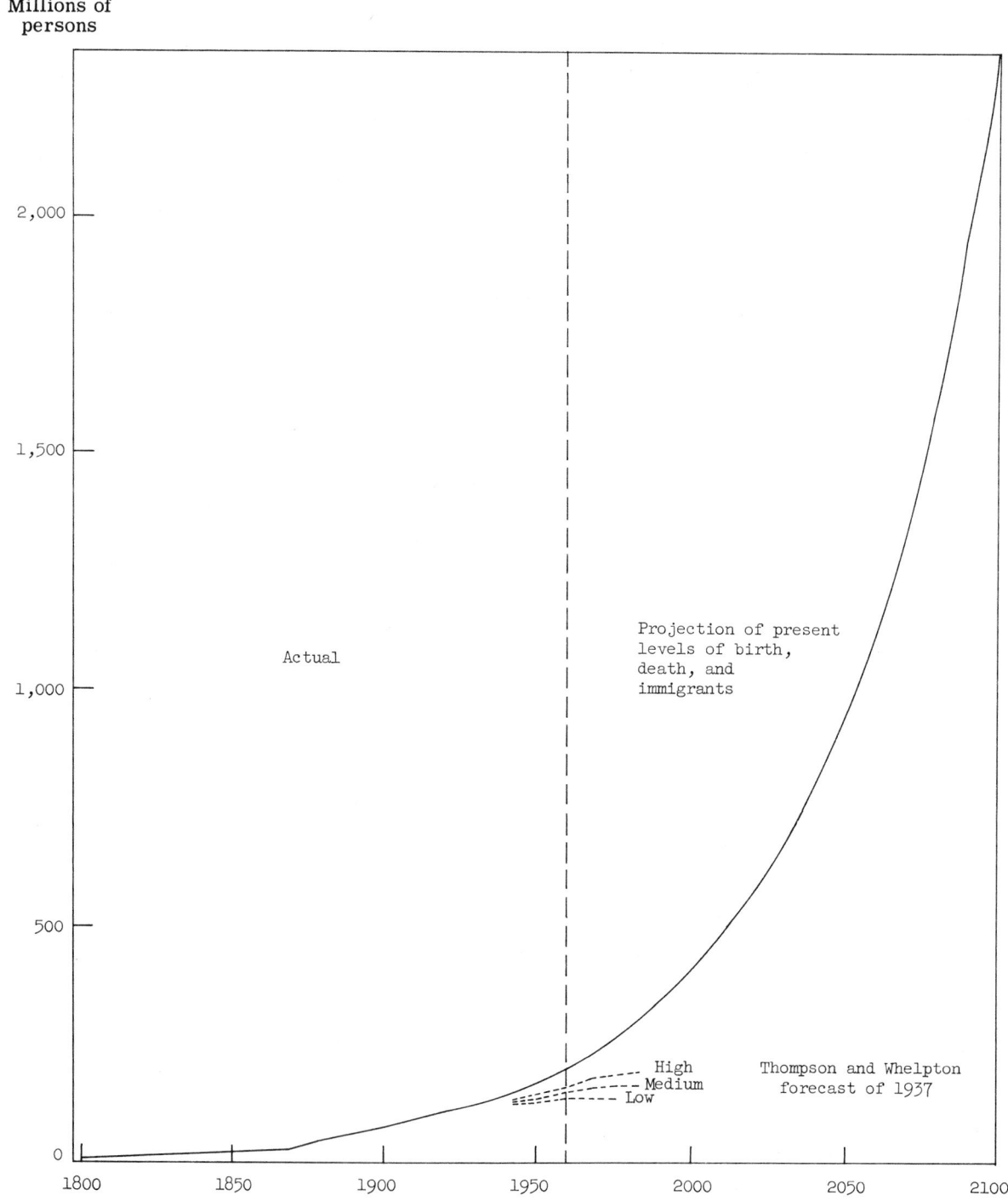

FIGURE 26-1. POPULATION OF THE UNITED STATES, 1790-1960, AND PROJECTION OF 1955-1957
GROWTH COMPONENTS TO FUTURE YEARS

up and enter adulthood, thus replacing a much smaller older generation.

ESTIMATES OF FUTURE POPULATION

One responsibility which the general public has delegated to the demographer is that of peering into the future and attempting to predict what population changes lie ahead, and of interpreting these changes in such a way that their significance can be appreciated by interested persons who are not demographers. So widespread has become the interest in, and the need for, work of this type that the U. S. Bureau of the Census has accepted as one of its specialized activities the analysis of probable and possible future developments. However, instead of calling its reports on future population "estimates," "predictions," or "forecasts," the Bureau of the Census uses the term "illustrative projections." This term is supposed to warn the potential user (who usually is impatient and pays little heed to footnotes explaining all of the pitfalls) that the components of population growth are much too dynamic, and too responsive to unpredictable changes in the economic, political, and sociological aspects of the nation's situation, ever to be predicted with a high degree of assurance.[1] The present chapter draws upon several recent reports of the Census Bureau, the object being to integrate and interpret them. From among the projections were selected those that seemed most plausible and, hence, that could be used as rough estimates of what actually will happen; these selected projections were then analyzed, to learn what kinds and amounts of change they implied. In this way, an attempt was made to build up a picture of probable future population change.

---

[1] It is difficult to overemphasize the frailties of population forecasts. The reader who wishes to develop his critical faculties with respect to forecasts should read Harold F. Dorn's "Pitfalls in Population Forecasts and Projections," *Journal of the American Statistical Association*, September, 1950; and John Hajnal's "The Prospects for Population Forecasts," *Journal of the American Statistical Association*, March, 1955.

Any discussion concerning the future population of the nation should be prefaced by a statement of two basic principles:

(a) Whether or not the population grows rapidly will be determined largely by the future course of birth rates. Death rates at the ages between birth and the end of the reproductive years have now become extremely low--so low that even if they were reduced to zero, they would add only moderately to the nation's population growth. Immigration from abroad is restricted to a small constant annual amount that will account directly for only a very minute fraction of the years beyond 1960, if present trends continue. (Indirectly, the fertility of immigrants can have a somewhat greater long-range impact on growth, especially if immigrants are drawn from high fertility nations.) But the most important factor in the determining of future population trends is fertility, and this is a most difficult item to predict.

(b) More than 90 percent of the nation knows how to limit the size of its families, and almost 100 percent of the population would take family-limiting action if the necessity to do so arose. Such limitation could take the form of an almost universal practice of birth control that would restrict family size to the number of children desired. Other possibilities are the delay of marriage, or the acceptance of lifelong spinsterhood and bachelorhood, by a larger percentage of the population. The well-known responsiveness of marriage rates and birth rates to changing economic conditions makes highly plausible the blunt assertion that the American people would not knowingly and stupidly reproduce themselves (like fruit flies) into a state of semi-starvation, or even endanger their present level of living. Almost at the first signs of such a development they would probably take decisive steps to reduce fertility. Hence, although it is difficult to imagine a rise in population growth exceeding that illustrated in Figure 26-1, one can easily visualize a situation involving a sharp and sudden curtailment of growth on very short notice. In fact, population growth could be reduced to zero within a period as short as 5 years under conditions of acute economic hardship. All that would be required would be for the population to return to its former age at marriage, for the share of couples remaining childless to return to the former percentage, and for most other couples to decide that they should not have a third or higher order child. THERE-FORE, THE PROJECTION OF FIGURE 26-1 IS IN NO WAY A PREDICTION, BUT ONLY AN EX-TRAPOLATION OF PRESENT TRENDS.[2] Although the American population is aboard a swiftly-moving demographic escalator, it is culturally, psychologically, and technologically prepared and able to step off at any point if it "gets tired of the ride." This is the major difference between the implications of the "population bomb" in the United States and in most other rapidly-growing countries; we can de-fuse the bomb almost at will, although undoubtedly the members of our population would differ widely as to the speed with which they would reduce their fertility and the extent of the reduction.

THE CENSUS BUREAU'S POPULATION PROJECTIONS TO 1980

Although the Bureau of the Census does not at present make long-range projections of the population, it does make a series of illustrative projections covering a period of 20 to 25 years, and revises them at intervals of two to four years. As will be demonstrated shortly, these data are capable of generating a gold-mine of information. The most recent estimates available in 1959 are a newly prepared set, released late in 1958, covering the period 1960 to 1980.[3] To develop the projections, a "components" method was used.[4] In

---

[2] Figure 26-1 illustrates just how radically the perspective on future population growth has changed since the low fertility days of the 1930's. In 1937, forecasts of the future population to the year 1980 were prepared by W. S. Thompson and P. K. Whelpton; they anticipated a drastic slowing down and, finally, a suspension of population growth. (Published in National Resources Committee, Population Statistics: National Data, October, 1937.) The "high," "medium," and "low" estimates of these forecasts are plotted in Figure 26-1 as offshoots of the curve of actual and extrapolated growth. The Thompson-Whelpton "medium" forecast called for a population of around 160 million persons by 1980, with population growth almost zero at that date. The nation actually achieved this population in 1953, just 16 years after the publication of the forecasts; it has since grown at a rate more than twice as fast as the rate in effect when the forecasts were made, and there are few signs of a major reduction. No demographic expert, unless he had prophetic powers, could have predicted the postwar fertility behavior of the population in 1937. At the time Thompson and Whelpton made their forecast, there had been more than a century of monotonously regular fertility decline. Birth rates had fallen sharply in the late 1920's, for four or five years be-fore the economic crash, so that the low level of birth rates during the 1930's was not attributable solely to economic hardship. In the cities the birth rates were lowest, and ur-banization was a universal trend. Hence, it was easy to fore-see continued urbanization and continued fertility decline. A demographer who made any other inference from the empiri-cal evidence would have been suspected of prejudice by his colleagues.

Some modern population observers have become so accus-tomed to sustained population growth that they cannot visualize any other situation; they should take a lesson from the previ-ous reversal. A shift to the former pattern, or to an even sharper curtailment of fertility, could come at any time--and very abruptly. It could come either independently or as a con-sequence of an economic depression.

---

[3] U. S. Bureau of the Census, "Illustrative Projections of the Population of the United States, by Age and Sex: 1960 to 1980," prepared by Meyer Zitter and Jacob J. Siegel, Current Population Reports, Series P-25, No. 187, November, 1958.

[4] "This method involves the preparation of separate pro-jections of each of the components of population change (i. e., births, deaths, and net immigration) on the basis of certain assumptions and the combination of the projections of change with estimates of the current population. More specifically, a 'cohort survival' procedure was used to carry forward the population, age by age, by 5-year time periods to future dates. This procedure yields population projections for the desired projection dates, by 5-year age groups and sex." Op. cit., p. 6. This method of estimating future population was developed by P. K. Whelpton and W. S. Thompson, who collaboratively em-ployed it to produce two widely used series of forecasts for the nation. See W. S. Thompson and P. K. Whelpton, (1) Estimates of Future Population by States, 1934; and (2) Popu-lation Statistics--1. National Data, 1937 (both reports pub-lished by National Resources Committee). Mr. Whelpton col-laborated with Hope Tisdale Eldridge and Jacob S. Siegel of the Bureau of the Census in the preparation of the first Census-sponsored projections, Forecasts of the Population of the United States, 1945-75, 1947. An alternative method of mak-ing population projections, the "cohort method" would make use of assumptions concerning the future fertility and mor-tality of cohorts, and follow each age group longitudinally throughout life. Experimental work with this method has been done by P. K. Whelpton, Scripps Foundation, and Joseph Schachter, National Office of Vital Statistics.

making its latest projections, the Bureau of the Census prepared not one set of estimates, but four sets, each set reflecting a different level and a different trend with respect to future fertility. A single set of assumptions about mortality and net immigration was used in all four sets of estimates.[5] (The research upon which this single set of assumptions was made was prepared by T. N. E. Greville. See Illustrative United States Population Projections, Actuarial Study No. 46, U. S. Department of Health, Education, and Welfare, 1957.)

For purposes of most practical application, the present author believes that only two of the four sets of projections are needed. They are the projections identified by the census as Series II and Series IV.[6]

Set II is here adopted as a reasonably good "high" (upper limit of population size) estimate of what might materialize, while Series IV is adopted as a reasonably good "medium" (most probable) estimate of what may happen in the next 20 years if economic conditions remain about as they are in 1959 and there is no war, major epidemic, or other population-affecting calamity.[7] The author

believes it is impossible (at the present time) to specify a plausible or possible "low" set of estimates, for reasons stated above--if economic or social conditions were to persuade the population of the wisdom of such a course, reproductive growth could be suspended within a very few years. Such a development could begin at any time.[8]

The Census Bureau's Series II (here taken to be a "high" estimate) and Series IV projections, (adopted as a medium estimate) with their underlying assumptions, are reported in Table 26-2. These estimates call for the following growth in total size, between 1960 and 1980:

Year	Total population		Total growth		Percent increase	
	High (II)	Medium (IV)	High (II)	Medium (IV)	High (II)	Medium (IV)
1950.......	151.7	151.7	19.0	19.0	14.5	14.5
1960.......	180.1	179.4	28.4	27.7	18.8	18.5
1970.......	213.8	202.5	33.7	23.1	18.7	12.7
1980.......	260.0	230.8	46.2	28.3	21.6	14.0

This summary shows that under the "high" assumptions--great economic prosperity and a continued propensity toward high fertility--the 1960 to 1970 decade would see almost 34 million persons added to the population, with a growth rate almost identical to that of the present decade. Under "medium" assumptions, the addition to the population would be 23 million, which implies a

---

[5] "Since the possible range of variation in the number of deaths and migrants for this group is small compared to the possible range of future fertility, it was considered unnecessary to make alternative allowances for these components." Op. cit., p. 2.

[6] Series I specifies a level of fertility that has not characterized the population of the United States since about 1900, and hence is unrealistically high as a forecast of what may actually happen. It has been the unfortunate fate of almost all official and widely known forecasts to be too low. The Census Bureau seems to have generated Set I with tongue in cheek, and with a determination that, for once at least, population growth would not top possible expectations. Since the object of this chapter is to specify the developments that could reasonably be expected to occur, this projection (at the risk of making the error that seems to be "the demographer's disease"--underestimating the power of the American female to reproduce herself) is not considered seriously.

[7] Admittedly, there is not enough evidence to allow one to say what will happen in future years. These choices are merely "best guesses," made (after reviewing the entire history and the current demographic situation in the preceding chapters) in an effort to help the layman choose more discriminately among the alternatives that are offered, almost without guidance, by the census.

[8] In fact, a movement in the direction of lowering fertility appears to have begun in 1958, as a result of the rising levels of unemployment. Both nuptiality rates and fertility rates declined moderately, but nevertheless persistently, during 1958.

Table 26-2.—ESTIMATES AND PROJECTIONS OF THE TOTAL POPULATION OF THE UNITED STATES INCLUDING ARMED FORCES OVERSEAS, BY AGE: 1950 TO 1980

Age	Age composition					
	1950	1960	1970		1980	
			High (Class II)	Medium (Class IV)	High (Class II)	Medium (Class IV)
United States total..............	151,683	179,420	213,810	202,541	259,981	230,834
Under 5 years...........................	16,320	19,285	24,190	17,136	31,991	22,242
5 to 9 years...........................	13,299	19,159	22,089	18,576	28,940	20,749
10 to 14 years...........................	11,144	17,217	20,893	20,191	25,080	18,066
15 to 19 years...........................	10,680	13,406	19,262	19,262	22,186	18,690
20 to 24 years...........................	11,620	11,311	17,343	17,343	21,001	20,304
25 to 29 years...........................	12,314	10,946	13,640	13,640	19,441	19,441
30 to 34 years...........................	11,612	11,878	11,582	11,582	17,554	17,554
35 to 39 years...........................	11,298	12,434	11,118	11,118	13,792	13,792
40 to 44 years...........................	10,271	11,549	11,872	11,872	11,608	11,608
45 to 49 years...........................	9,115	11,050	12,214	12,214	10,982	10,982
50 to 54 years...........................	8,298	9,796	11,092	11,092	11,464	11,464
55 to 59 years...........................	7,300	8,372	10,271	10,271	11,443	11,443
60 to 64 years...........................	6,124	7,238	8,695	8,695	9,973	9,973
65 to 69 years...........................	4,953	5,877	6,900	6,900	8,646	8,646
70 to 74 years...........................	3,444	4,383	5,376	5,376	6,654	6,654
75 to 79 years...........................	2,144	3,035	3,764	3,764	4,593	4,593
80 to 84 years...........................	1,158	1,597	2,158	2,158	2,784	2,784
85 years and over.......................	588	887	1,351	1,351	1,849	1,849

Source: U. S. Bureau of the Census, Illustrative Projections of the Population of the United States, by Age and Sex: 1960 to 1980, prepared by Meyer Zitter and Jacob Siegel, Series P-25, No. 187, Nov. 10, 1958.

growth rate of about 13 percent--roughly comparable with that of the 9940 to 9950 decade.[9]

---

[9] The Census Bureau's "high" series postulates a growth of about 1.76 percent per year from 1957 on. According to the latest estimates of the population, available in March of 1959, the rate of growth was about 1.65 for the year 1958. This rate represented a 6 percent decline from the actual growth during the years 1955 to 1957, the growth upon which the "high" series of estimates is based. Thus, in 1958 the population was growing at a rate slower than that projected by the Series II estimates. It now seems probable that the population will not attain the schedule of growth specified by the Census Bureau's projection Series II, and that the growth rates indicated by its Series I (based on fertility rates that are 10 percent higher than those on which Series II is based) are therefore completely unattainable. As of March, 1959, the actual annual rate of growth appeared to lie almost midway between the assumptions of Series II and Series IV, and at that date there was a strong prospect for further declines in the average annual rate of growth. On the assumption that at least some of these prospects for lower fertility would actually materialize, the Series IV estimates were chosen as the best single crude prediction of what actually will happen. They call for an increase of almost 80 million persons in the 20 years from 1960 to 1980, and for a total population of 231 million persons in 1980.

These projections make no allowance for an economic recession. The Bureau of the Census explicitly states on page 1 of its report, "It is further assumed that there will be no major economic depression; in fact, the projections are designed to be consistent with high employment and high economic activity." However, users of population projections must always remember that recessions can happen, and that either a severe economic depression or a major military mobilization would sharply curtail population growth.[10] If an economic "crash" similar to that of 1929 were to happen in 1959 or shortly thereafter, population growth during the 1960 to 1970 decade could easily sink to 5 percent, which would give a growth of

---

[10] From experimental work recently performed by Dudley Kirk, and others, it is evident that during the late 1950's, fertility rates have been at least somewhat responsive to changing economic conditions. However, the exact degree of correspondence is not as yet measured precisely, and no one cares to speculate upon how much depression it would take to cause long-run replacement rates to equal unity.

about 9 million instead of the 23 to 33 million mentioned above. Hence, the lowest of the official Census projections should be regarded as a medium estimate of what might actually happen.

FUTURE COLOR COMPOSITION

The nonwhite population is now growing at a rate about 60 percent higher than that of the white population. If this differential continues undiminished into the future, and if both groups continue to grow at their 1955 to 1957 rates, there will be a slow but steady increase in the proportion of the population that is nonwhite. However, no drastic changes in the color composition can be expected in the immediate future. This is because the nonwhite population is so much smaller than the white population that even a growth differential of 60 percent can cause only a comparatively small change in the color composition of the total population. The present differential would have to continue until about the year 2050 in order for the nonwhite population to equal the same percentage of the population (19 percent) as it did in 1790, assuming the present rates of growth continue.

Our political, economic, and social life will undoubtedly be modified at least slightly by the fact that in 1980 one citizen in eight (rather than one in nine, as in 1960) will be nonwhite; some subtle changes in these areas seem already to have occurred, as a result of the change in these proportions from one in ten in 1940. However, this kind of change is only a slow and almost imperceptible shift in the balance of political and economic influence, and is not in any sense a drastic or major change in the racial situation.

If future birth rates were to be reduced sharply because of economic or other conditions, it is quite possible that the decline in fertility would be proportionately greater among the white than among the nonwhite population. If this were to happen, the percent of nonwhite population would increase a little bit faster than Table 26-1 indicates. However, during the depression years of the 1930's, fertility declined among the nonwhite population as well as among the white, so one can expect the nation to follow a similar pattern in the event of a future economic collapse. On the other hand, the nonwhite population is now undergoing rapid urbanization, and is becoming increasingly concentrated in metropolitan areas. It seems reasonable to expect such a situation to lead to a shrinking of the fertility differential and, consequently, to a slower rise in the percentage of nonwhite population than is indicated in Table 26-1. On balance, one might expect the change in the percentage of population that is nonwhite to follow approximately the course outlined in Table 26-1.

Meanwhile, the absolute size of the nonwhite population will grow very rapidly, as will that of the white. If present trends continue, one may expect that by 1980 there will be a total of 33 million nonwhite citizens, instead of the 20.3 million of 1960 or the 15.8 million of 1950. The increase in the nonwhite population in the 30 years from 1950 to 1980 will equal the total growth within the national boundaries of the nonwhite population in all of the centuries prior to 1950. Moreover, it is very likely that a large part, if not all, of this increase will be concentrated in a few of the largest metropolitan areas, and that it may have a profound effect on the social, political, and economic life of particular communities. Meanwhile, as the educational and other differentials between the nonwhite and white populations shrink, the social, economic, and political significance of color differences may be greatly reduced and changed in future years.

FUTURE SEX COMPOSITION

Women will continue to outnumber men in future years, and the surplus of women will become even larger than it is at present--both in absolute terms and in percentage terms. The following schedule of sex ratios illustrate the changes in sex composition that may be expected under conditions of high fertility and medium mortality:

Year	Sex ratio		Surplus of female (000)	
	High fertility (II)	Low fertility (IV)	High fertility (II)	Low fertility (IV)
1950.....	99.2	99.2	623	623
1960.....	97.9	97.9	1,902	1,918
1970.....	97.3	96.9	2,894	3,139
1980.....	97.6	96.8	3,135	3,766

As described in Chapter 7, the principal cause of the tendency for women to outnumber men is the greater longevity of women. If present fertility trends continue, the sex ratio will decline only 0.3 points between 1960 and 1980. It would be sustained by the predominance of males among the large crops of infants born under these high fertility conditions. However, if fertility declines to the point indicated in the medium mortality projections, by 1980 the sex ratio could decline by as much as 1.1 additional points, to 96.8. In this latter case, there would be.fewer male infants to offset the mortality differential among adults with respect to sex.

By 1980, there will almost certainly be at least 3.1 million more women than men in the population, and the differential will probably be even greater. Most of this surplus will be concentrated at ages above 55 years of age (see Table 26-3). The more the birth rate declines, the larger becomes the size of the female surplus, so the above prediction is comparatively "safe."

FUTURE AGE COMPOSITION

The population will almost certainly have a _younger_ average age composition in the immediate future than it has had in the past, unless the actual future course of fertility is considerably lower than it has been at any time since 1946. The future age composition implied by the "high" and "medium" projections described above is furnished for 10-year intervals, from 1960 to 1980, in Table 26-2. Tables 26-4, 26-5, and 26-6 are designed to show some of the changes and developments that will take place if these projections materialize. Both the "high" and the "medium" series schedule a decline in the median age of the

Table 26-3.—SEX RATIOS BY AGE, PROJECTED TO 1980 UNDER ASSUMPTIONS OF HIGH AND MEDIUM FERTILITY

Age	Sex ratio					
	1950	1960	1970		1980	
			High (Class II)	Medium (Class IV)	High (Class II)	Medium (Class IV)
United States total......	99.2	97.9	97.3	96.9	97.6	96.8
Under 5 years.................	103.9	103.8	104.1	103.9	104.3	104.1
5 to 9 years..................	103.6	104.3	104.4	104.4	104.5	104.5
10 to 14 years................	103.6	104.4	104.2	104.2	104.3	104.3
15 to 19 years................	101.8	103.1	103.8	103.8	103.9	103.9
20 to 24 years................	98.5	101.7	102.8	102.8	102.8	102.7
25 to 29 years................	96.4	99.1	100.4	100.4	101.6	101.6
30 to 34 years................	96.4	97.4	99.7	99.7	101.1	101.1
35 to 39 years................	96.7	95.8	98.3	98.3	99.6	99.6
40 to 44 years................	98.9	95.7	96.8	96.8	99.1	99.1
45 to 49 years................	99.6	95.2	94.6	94.6	97.1	97.1
50 to 54 years................	99.5	95.7	92.9	92.9	94.2	94.2
55 to 59 years................	100.1	94.1	90.3	90.3	90.0	90.0
60 to 64 years................	100.3	90.9	87.7	87.7	85.8	85.8
65 to 69 years................	94.5	87.8	82.4	82.4	79.9	79.9
70 to 74 years................	91.1	84.9	76.5	76.5	74.6	74.6
75 to 79 years................	87.2	77.4	71.4	71.4	67.8	67.8
80 to 84 years................	80.9	73.2	67.7	67.7	61.5	61.5
85 years and over............	69.7	68.6	61.0	61.0	56.6	56.6

Source: U. S. Bureau of the Census, _Illustrative Projections of the Population of the United States, by Age and Sex: 1960 to 1980_, prepared by Meyer Zitter and Jacob Siegel, Series P-25, No. 187, Nov. 10, 1958.

population (see Table 26-6). Under the "high" assumptions, the median age is expected to be about 26.1 years in 1970 and 25.2 years in 1980; this would represent a decline of 4.0 years from 1960 and 5.0 years from 1950. Under the "medium" assumptions, the median age will decline by about one year between 1960 and 1970 and then begin to rise again slowly.

Since those members of the population who will be 0 to 19 years of age in 1980 must all be born in the period 1960 to 1980, the assumptions that are made concerning fertility are of utmost importance in determining the size of these younger age groups. If the high fertility assumptions turn out to be accurate, there will be an even greater concentration in the age groups under 20 years than there is at present. But if the medium fertility assumptions correctly indicate the course population trends will take, there will be a gradual decrease in the proportion of the total population in the younger ages. Under these latter circumstances, the percentage of children under 5 years of age would be about the same in 1980 as it was in 1945 (see Table 26-4).

By 1960, the wave of infants born during and since World War II will have begun to enter the age group 15 to 19 in large numbers; they will be marrying, and starting the second round of population growth described in the introduction to this chapter. By 1970, this group will be age 25 to 29 years old and, together with younger oncoming groups, will be making a very large reproductive contribution. The war and postwar group will be preceded by the unusually small cohorts of persons born during the 1930's. By 1980, this older and smaller group, born in the depression, will have almost completed its childbearing. After 1980 there will be a succession of large cohorts of young couples entering the reproduction stage of their lives. At this point, about 1980 to 1990, really fantastic amounts of population growth will begin to occur unless fertility is reduced. Thus, not until shortly after 1980 will the full reproductive effect of the second round of the baby boom be felt. This is indicated by the data in the right-hand column of Table 26-5, where the fluctuations in growth rates for persons of various ages may be observed.

Table 26-4.—AGE COMPOSITION OF THE POPULATION PROJECTED TO 1980

| Age | Percent distribution | | | | | | |
	1940	1950	1960	1970 High (Class II)	1970 Medium (Class IV)	1980 High (Class II)	1980 Medium (Class IV)
United States total	100.0	100.0	100.0	100.0	100.0	100.0	100.0
Under 5 years	8.0	10.7	10.7	11.3	8.5	12.3	9.6
5 to 9 years	8.1	8.8	10.7	10.3	9.2	11.1	9.0
10 to 14 years	8.9	7.4	9.6	9.8	10.0	9.6	7.8
15 to 19 years	9.4	7.0	7.5	9.0	9.5	8.5	8.1
20 to 24 years	8.8	7.6	6.3	8.1	8.6	8.1	8.8
25 to 29 years	8.4	8.1	6.1	6.4	6.7	7.5	8.4
30 to 34 years	7.8	7.6	6.6	5.4	5.7	6.8	7.6
35 to 39 years	7.2	7.5	6.9	5.2	5.5	5.3	6.0
40 to 44 years	6.7	6.8	6.4	5.6	5.9	4.5	5.0
45 to 49 years	6.3	6.0	6.2	5.7	6.0	4.2	4.8
50 to 54 years	5.5	5.5	5.5	5.2	5.5	4.4	5.0
55 to 59 years	4.4	4.8	4.7	4.8	5.1	4.4	5.0
60 to 64 years	3.6	4.0	4.0	4.1	4.3	3.8	4.3
65 to 69 years	2.9	3.3	3.3	3.2	3.4	3.3	3.7
70 to 74 years	2.0	2.3	2.4	2.5	2.7	2.6	2.9
75 to 79 years	2.0	1.4	1.7	1.8	1.9	1.8	2.0
80 to 84 years		0.7	0.9	1.0	1.1	1.1	1.2
85 years and over		0.4	0.5	0.6	0.7	0.7	0.8

Source: U. S. Bureau of the Census, Illustrative Projections of the Population of the United States, by Age and Sex: 1960 to 1980, prepared by Meyer Zitter and Jacob Siegel, Series P-25, No. 187, Nov. 10, 1958.

Table 26-5.—ESTIMATED AND PROJECTED PERCENT INTERDECADE CHANGES IN POPULATION, BY AGE: 1950 TO 1980

Age	1950 to 1960	Percent change during decade			
		1960 to 1970		1970 to 1980	
		High (Class II)	Medium (Class IV)	High (Class II)	Medium (Class IV)
U. S. total........................	18.3	18.7	12.9	21.6	14.0
Under 5 years..........................	18.2	21.0	-11.1	32.2	29.8
5 to 9 years...........................	44.1	15.3	-3.0	31.0	11.7
10 to 14 years.........................	54.5	21.4	17.3	20.0	-10.5
15 to 19 years.........................	25.5	43.7	43.7	15.2	-3.0
20 to 24 years.........................	-2.7	53.3	53.3	21.1	17.1
25 to 29 years.........................	-11.1	24.6	24.6	42.5	42.5
30 to 34 years.........................	2.3	-2.5	-2.5	51.6	51.6
35 to 39 years.........................	10.1	-10.6	-10.6	24.1	24.1
40 to 44 years.........................	12.4	2.8	2.8	-2.2	-2.2
45 to 49 years.........................	21.2	10.5	10.5	-10.1	-10.1
50 to 54 years.........................	18.1	13.2	13.2	3.4	3.4
55 to 59 years.........................	14.7	22.7	22.7	11.4	11.4
60 to 64 years.........................	18.2	20.1	20.1	14.7	14.7
65 to 69 years.........................	18.7	17.4	17.4	25.3	25.3
70 to 74 years.........................	27.3	22.7	22.7	23.8	23.8
75 to 79 years.........................	41.6	24.0	24.0	22.0	22.0
80 to 84 years.........................	37.9	35.1	35.1	29.0	29.0
85 years and over......................	50.9	52.3	52.3	36.9	36.9

Source: Current Population Reports, Population Estimates, Series P-25, No. 187, Table 1.

The proportion of persons 65 years of age and over is expected to increase steadily to 1980, because of the continued effect of past fertility declines and the anticipated reductions in mortality rates at the upper ages. By 1980 the aged will probably account for between 9.5 and 10.5 percent of the total population. If birth rates remain high, the proportion of persons in this category will not increase a great deal; if they fall, however, the proportion of aged will rise.

The two series of estimates imply some interesting changes in future dependency ratios. (Dependency ratios are found by expressing the population 0 to 19 years of age and 65 years of age and over, respectively, as percentages of the population 20 to 64 years of age. For a full discussion, see Chapter 6, on age composition.) Table 26-6 shows that if the fertility assumptions are accurate, the dependency ratio will rise steadily, and will reach a point well above 100 by 1980. This means that there would be more dependents than supporters in the population, and suggests a level of dependency that is very high. However, it must be noted that the dependency ratio has jumped from 73 to 90 in the 10 years between 1950 and

1960, and that the projected additional dependency is less than the increase that has occurred in the past 10 years. All but a small fraction of this increase is the result of the growing number and proportion of children.

Under the medium assumptions concerning fertility, the expected schedule of dependency takes on a character quite different from that indicated when high fertility assumptions are used. If events were to follow the medium course outlined by projection IV, the dependency load would rise to a peak of about 95 in 1965 and would then slowly decline. By 1980 it would have fallen to about the general level prevailing in 1955. Following is a summary of what may be expected if the medium estimates become valid:

Year	Dependency ratio		
	Total	Youth	Old age
1940..............	70.4	58.6	11.8
1950..............	72.5	58.5	14.0
1955..............	81.3	65.8	15.5
1960..............	89.7	73.0	16.7
1965..............	94.8	77.0	17.8
1970..............	87.8	69.7	18.1
1975..............	84.2	65.5	18.7
1980..............	82.4	63.0	19.4

Table 26-6.—SUMMARY MEASURES OF ESTIMATED AND PROJECTED AGE COMPOSITION: 1950 TO 1980

Item	1940	1950	1960	1970		1980	
				High (Class II)	Medium (Class IV)	High (Class II)	Medium (Class IV)
Median age......................	29.0	30.2	29.2	26.1	28.2	25.2	29.0
Dependency ratio, total...........	70.4	72.5	89.7	98.3	87.8	104.3	82.4
Youth...........................	56.8	58.5	73.0	80.2	69.7	85.0	63.0
Old age.........................	11.8	14.0	16.7	18.1	18.1	19.3	19.4
Percent distribution..............	100.0	100.0	100.0	100.0	100.0	100.0	100.0
0-4 years......................	8.0	10.8	10.7	11.3	8.5	12.3	9.6
5-19 years.....................	26.4	23.2	27.7	29.1	28.7	29.3	24.9
20-44 years....................	38.9	37.7	32.4	30.7	32.4	32.1	35.8
45-64 years....................	19.8	20.3	20.3	19.8	20.9	16.9	19.0
65 years and over..............	6.9	8.1	8.8	9.1	9.7	9.4	10.6

Source: U. S. Bureau of the Census, Illustrative Projections of the Population of the United States, by Age and Sex: 1960 to 1980, prepared by Meyer Zitter and Jacob Siegel, Series P-25, No. 187, Nov. 10, 1958.

The growth in the number and percentage of the population aged 65 and over will contribute a small amount of additional dependency to the total borne by the population, but the aging of the population is a comparatively small source of additional dependency, and will remain so in the immediate future. However, if some future date should bring a sharp drop in birth rates, the population would again enter a phase of rapid aging.

FUTURE OF THE FOREIGN-BORN POPULATION

It is not difficult to forecast, in general, the magnitude of the foreign-born population. Because of immigration restrictions there is every likelihood that it will remain small and will constitute a continuously diminishing percentage of the population. However, it will not shrink almost to zero and disappear, as a mere mechanical extrapolation of the recent trends would suggest. Piecing together various bits of evidence makes it seem plausible that in the immediate future the number of foreign-born inhabitants will remain almost stationary--in the neighborhood of 9 to 11 million inhabitants. This statement is based on the assumption that future net immigration will be between 200,000 and 300,000 per year. Rough estimates indicate that, under an assumption of 300,000 persons per year from 1958 to 1980, the size of the foreign-born population at selected future dates would be roughly as follows:

Year	Foreign-born population	Percent foreign born is of total
1950..................	10,200	6.7
1960..................	10,400	5.8
1970..................	10,500	5.2
1980..................	10,750	4.7

If net immigration averages over 200,000 per year, the size of the foreign-born population will be about 9 million instead of 11 million persons.

In 1960, the age composition of the foreign-born population shows an unusual concentration at the older ages, because of the aging of large cohorts remaining from the pre-quota era. By 1980 almost all of this older group will have died out, and the age structure will show a more even distribution among the adult ages, as may be noted from the following summary:

Percent distribution of foreign-born Population by age: 1950-1980

Age	1950	1960	1970	1980
Total.......	100	100	100	100
Under 20.......	3	7	8	8
20-34..........	9	13	17	19
35-44..........	13	13	16	18
45-54..........	23	16	16	18
55-64..........	26	21	15	15
65 and over....	26	30	27	21

Note: Assume a net immigration of 300,000 per year, distributed by age according to Bureau of Census assumptions reported in P-25, No. 187.

Source: Current Population Report, P-25, No. 187, Table J. Immigrants.

An unknown quantity that is nevertheless a major factor in estimating the future foreign-born population is the future size of the nonquota immigration from Canada and Latin America. The very recent tendency for larger numbers of persons to immigrate to the United States from Latin America may cause the size of the foreign-born population to rise somewhat above the amounts scheduled, provided new legislation does not place more severe restrictions upon immigrants from the nations in the Western Hemisphere.

THE FUTURE NUMBER OF HOUSEHOLDS

Between 1962 and 1968 an accelerating volume of first marriages will usher in an entirely new era with respect both to the number of new households and new families formed each year and the total number of households and families in existence. This finding is based upon a report, "Illustrative Projections of the Number of Households and Families: 1960 to 1980," prepared by David M. Heer and Paul C. Glick of the Bureau of the Census.[11] Dr. Heer and Dr. Glick have selected certain ones of the official projections and, by making reasonable assumptions concerning future trends in proportions of persons marrying at each age and in the living arrangements of persons not married, have transformed them into projections concerning the number of households and families that will be in existence in each of certain selected dates. The report cited furnishes four series of projections, identified as A, B, C, and D. A careful study of these data leads to the conclusion that Series B can be adopted as a reasonably good estimate of what may be expected to be a "high" set of estimates concerning household and family formation, and that Series C may be adopted as a reasonably good "medium" (most-likely-to-happen) estimate of what actually will

develop.[12] Following the argument laid down earlier, no useful "low" estimate of future developments is thought to be possible. A recession could cause widespread postponement of marriage and a doubling up of families in households, and could drive large numbers of unmarried persons from households into their parents' homes or into lodging houses--and on comparatively short notice.

Table 26-7 summarizes the estimates of the future number of households to be expected under the high (Series B) and medium (Series C) estimates. This table also summarizes the actual trend since 1930, for comparison. Beginning in about 1962, the rate at which new households are added each year will begin to rise rapidly; by the year 1968 it will have definitely exceeded the rate of any previous year except the historic 1945 to 1946 period of demobilitzation. The cause of this rise, of course, is the arrival at marriage age of the first of the infants born in the period 1941 to 1944, at the start of the baby boom. Each year thereafter a new and larger wave of the postwar birth cohorts, now grown to adulthood, will arrive at the nubile age. Since the median age of

---

[11] U. S. Bureau of the Census, Current Population Reports, Series P-20, No. 90, December 28, 1958.

---

[12] The Series A projections were based on the assumption that all trends in family formation would continue unabated to 1965, after which time one-half or more of the average age annual change would continue to 1980. This projection was regarded as a poor estimate of what might actually materialize, because there is evidence that the kind of very far-reaching changes that have taken place in the field of living arrangements have begun to stabilize; the median age at first marriage has almost stopped falling, and the movement of unmarried persons out of lodging houses and of widows and elderly couples into their own houses has largely been accomplished. However, because the Series D projections make no provision for any further change of this type, they were rejected as plausible average future developments. By this process of elimination, Series B and C were designated as the "high" and "medium" estimates. Series C allows for the uninterrupted continuation, until 1980, of about one-third or one-fourth of the average annual change that occurred from 1950 to 1956-58 in the process of household formation. This is a realistic assumption, and it is very plausible that such a continuation could occur.

Table 26-7.—TRENDS IN THE NUMBER OF HOUSEHOLDS, 1930 TO 1960, AND PROJECTED TRENDS TO 1980

Year	Number of households		Net annual increase since preceding date		Percent change over preceding date	
	High (Series B)	Medium (Series C)	High	Medium	High	Medium
DECADES:						
1930.............................	29,905		542			
1940.............................	34,949		504		16.9	
1950.............................	43,554		861		24.6	
1955.............................	47,788		833		9.7	
1960.............................	51,877	51,614	767	701	19.1	18.5
1970.............................	61,094	59,689	922	808	17.8	15.6
1980.............................	73,085	70,544	1,199	1,086	19.6	18.2
1975.............................	67,003	64,906	1,182	1,043	9.7	8.7
1980.............................	73,085	70,544	1,216	1,128	9.1	8.7
ANNUAL, 1960-70:						
1960.............................	51,877	51,614	767	701	8.6	8.0
1961.............................	52,424	52,096	547	482	1.1	0.9
1962.............................	53,253	52,826	829	730	1.6	1.4
1963.............................	54,227	53,683	974	857	1.8	1.6
1964.............................	55,224	54,561	997	878	1.8	1.6
1965.............................	56,076	55,311	852	750	1.5	1.4
1966.............................	56,966	56,087	890	776	1.6	1.4
1967.............................	57,960	56,954	994	867	1.7	1.5
1968.............................	59,127	57,973	1,167	1,019	2.0	1.8
1969.............................	60,079	58,803	952	830	1.6	1.4
1970.............................	61,094	59,689	1,015	886	1.7	1.5

Source: David M. Heer and Paul C. Glick, "Illustrative Projections of the Number of Households and Families," Current Population Reports, Series P-20, No. 90, December, 1958.

women at first marriage at the present time is about 20.2 years, the onset of this new marriage boom may be expected about 18 years after the onset of the baby boom, and may be expected to reach a sustained new plateau of intensity about 22 years after 1946. Thus, the year 1968 will mark the end of the transition to the new era, and thereafter the volume of new family formation will be very large in comparison with that of the past. An examination of the first four columns of Table 26-2 in comparison with 26-7 will indicate that this is the pattern that may reasonably be expected.[13]

Columns 3 and 4 of Table 26-5 may be taken as crude estimates of the net annual demand for increments in housing, needed as a result of new household information.[14] Throughout the 1970 to 1975 period, the annual demand for new dwellings will be 1,043,000 per year, according to the medium assumptions. During the 1975 to 1980 period the demand will be boosted to 1,128,000 units per year. These figures indicate only what will be required in the way of additional units, and do not

take into account the dwellings that will be needed

[13] It must be kept in mind that the timing of these events, as well as the amounts involved, depends on an assumption that there will be only very moderate changes in previous trends. A reversal of these trends could cause a sharp drop in family formation. However, as the depression years of the 1930 decade demonstrated, the major effect of such a reversal would be to postpone marriage, rather than to cancel it. Hence, most of the new households scheduled in Table 26-7 will be formed irrespective of economic conditions, although the date at which they arrive at this new plateau could be pushed back from 1 to 3 years by a severe economic recession.

[14] As the Census Bureau takes care to point out in each of its estimates of this type, however, "...the increase in the number of households which may take place between now and 1980 may not be identical with the volume of new housing construction during this period. The number of housing units constructed is likely to differ from the net increase in occupied dwelling units because of change in the number of vacant housing units, demolition of existing units, and change, through conversions, in the number of dwelling units in existing structures." Ibid., p. 2.

to replace obsolete and substandard housing, or to raise the average level of quality in housing. Between 1975 and 1980, a great transformation may be expected. Our rapid growth has caused us comparatively little concern so far, because these additional members of the population are still dependent, and are "hidden" in the households of their parents; we have been forced to recognize them only by voting bonds for elementary and high school expansion and by starting to plan for college expansion (see below). However, when this accumulation of young people begins to go househunting, the result can be either a prolonged spree of residential construction or an agonizing shortage of housing such as now exists in many other parts of the world. In fact, if birth rates have not already been brought nearer to death rates, the developments of the late 1960's and 1970's may make every citizen acutely aware of the fact that they must be, eventually.

AGE OF HOUSEHOLD HEAD

Because of the nation's changing age composition, a major share of the households added to the population during the period 1958 to 1965 will have heads 55 years of age or over, as the following summary shows:

Age of head	Increase in households 1948 to 1965		Percent increase 1958 to 1965	
	High estimate Series B	Medium estimate Series C	High estimate Series B	Medium estimate Series C
Total..........	5,674	4,909	11.3	9.7
Under 25 years.....	1,242	1,062	51.9	44.4
25 to 44 years.....	1,554	1,156	5.0	3.7
55 years and over..	2,878	2,691	17.2	16.0

The increase in the number of households with heads aged 25 to 44 will comprise only 23 to 28 percent of the total increase; more than one-half of total household growth will be accounted for by households with heads 55 years of age and over. Heer and Glick comment, "These facts have significant implications for the type of housing in demand during the early years of the next decade because of the fact that neither young nor older heads of households have large families, on the average."

However, the very high rate of increase for young household heads should be noted in the above summary; after 1970, the number of younger household heads will increase very rapidly. A large share of the housing that will be needed in 1965 and after will be housing for families in the later stages of the reproductive cycle, designed to accomodate families of the size that will then be considered desirable. The construction of 3- and 4-bedroom dwelling units may be much more appropriate after 1965 than the building of 2-bedroom units.

THE FUTURE NUMBER OF FAMILIES AND OF INDIVIDUALS LIVING OUTSIDE FAMILIES

Table 26-8 shows projections, prepared by Heer and Glick as a part of the report just described, of the number of primary families, primary individuals, families, and secondary individuals that may be expected to exist from 1960 to 1980, reported at 5-year intervals.[15] The B and C series of estimates, for reasons already stated, have been adopted as indicating what is most likely to happen; the C estimates seem somewhat more realistic than the B, which are thought to be a little on the "high" side. According to this table, the number of husband-wife families (which may or may not have children) may be expected to reach the following numbers:

Year	Millions of families
1960..	39
1965..	42
1970..	45
1975..	49
1980..	53

[15] The reader who is not familiar with these terms should refer to the beginning sections of Chapter 11, where they are all defined.

In a 20-year period, the number of married couples living together under conditions where the husband is head of a household is expected to increase by about 14 million, or about 35 percent. Between 1950 and 1958, the annual net increase in the number of married couples averaged only 386,000, but by 1980 will be about 900,000 or 1,000,000. The small number of couples added in recent years has been due to the low fertility of the 1930's. The greatly increased number of married couples expected after 1968 is due, of course, to the high fertility prevailing since 1946.

Table 26-8 also anticipates a large increase in the number of primary families with a female as head, and in the number of female individuals living with nonrelatives in households. These developments are by-products of the changing sex ratio, described above. As elderly women outlive and outnumber men in increasing numbers and proportions, they will become household heads and primary individuals more frequently.

FUTURE AVERAGE SIZE OF HOUSEHOLD AND FAMILY

Since the average size of households and fam-

ilies depends very directly upon the assumptions made concerning family formation among persons already born, they are doubly tenuous. However, the data available suggest that the long-term trend toward smaller sizes of households will be reversed between 1955 and 1965, so that households will contain slightly more members than previously. This development will be due entirely to fertility and to the presence of more children in the household, for almost all other family-formation trends are operating in the opposite direction. The expected average sizes of households in 1965 and 1975 are as follows:

Year	Average number of persons in household		Average number of persons in family	
	High estimate Series B	Medium estimate Series C	High estimate Series B	Medium estimate Series C
1940................	3.67	3.67	3.76	3.76
1950................	3.37	3.37	3.54	3.54
1958................	3.35	3.35	3.65	3.65
1965................	3.40	3.41	3.75	3.73
1975................	3.43	3.44	3.81	3.75

Table 26-8.—NUMBER OF HOUSEHOLD AND FAMILY UNITS, FOR THE UNITED STATES: MARCH 1958, AND PROJECTIONS, JULY 1960 TO 1980

(In thousands)

Date and series	Households						Families	Secondary individuals
	Total	Primary families			Primary individuals			
		Husband-wife	Other male head	Female head	Male	Female		
March 1958..................	50,402	37,967	1,246	4,232	2,274	4,683	43,714	3,490
July 1960:								
Series B..................	51,877	39,008	1,277	4,509	2,172	4,911	45,021	3,439
Series C..................	51,614	38,898	1,283	4,489	2,141	4,803	44,911	3,527
July 1965:								
Series B..................	56,076	41,793	1,278	4,874	2,319	5,812	48,133	3,314
Series C..................	55,311	41,477	1,275	4,831	2,235	5,493	47,820	3,573
July 1970:								
Series B..................	61,094	45,422	1,314	5,235	2,491	6,632	52,149	3,453
Series C..................	59,689	44,801	1,317	5,174	2,340	6,057	51,559	3,874
July 1975:								
Series B..................	67,003	49,748	1,392	5,642	2,742	7,479	56,963	3,512
Series C..................	64,906	48,853	1,400	5,543	2,509	6,601	56,092	4,227
July 1980:								
Series B..................	73,085	54,460	1,512	6,043	2,981	8,089	62,212	4,002
Series C..................	70,544	53,182	1,536	5,938	2,749	7,139	60,980	4,606

Source: David M. Heer and Paul C. Glick, "Illustrative Projections of the Number of Households and Families," Current Population Reports, Series P-20, No.90.

A substantial increase in average size of household would have occurred more than a decade ago, had it not been for the very strong countermovements described in Chapters 14 and 24. It is now expected that these countermovements will cease to exert as much influence as previously, so accumulating fertility can only be expected to result in larger families and larger households.

The average size of family (but not of household) has already increased between 1950 and 1958, and the most important factor in this change is fertility. Further increases are expected. Almost all of the expected increase in size of family reported in the above schedule is caused by the increased number of persons under 18 years of age.

FUTURE SCHOOL ENROLLMENTS

Due to the enlarged birth cohorts, enrollments in elementary schools have been climbing rapidly and steadily since the late 1940's. High school enrollments have been expanding since the mid-1950's. Starting in the 1960's, college and professional school enrollments will begin a strong upward thrust because of population growth (see Figure 26-2). The upward trends in high school and college enrollment have been strengthened by

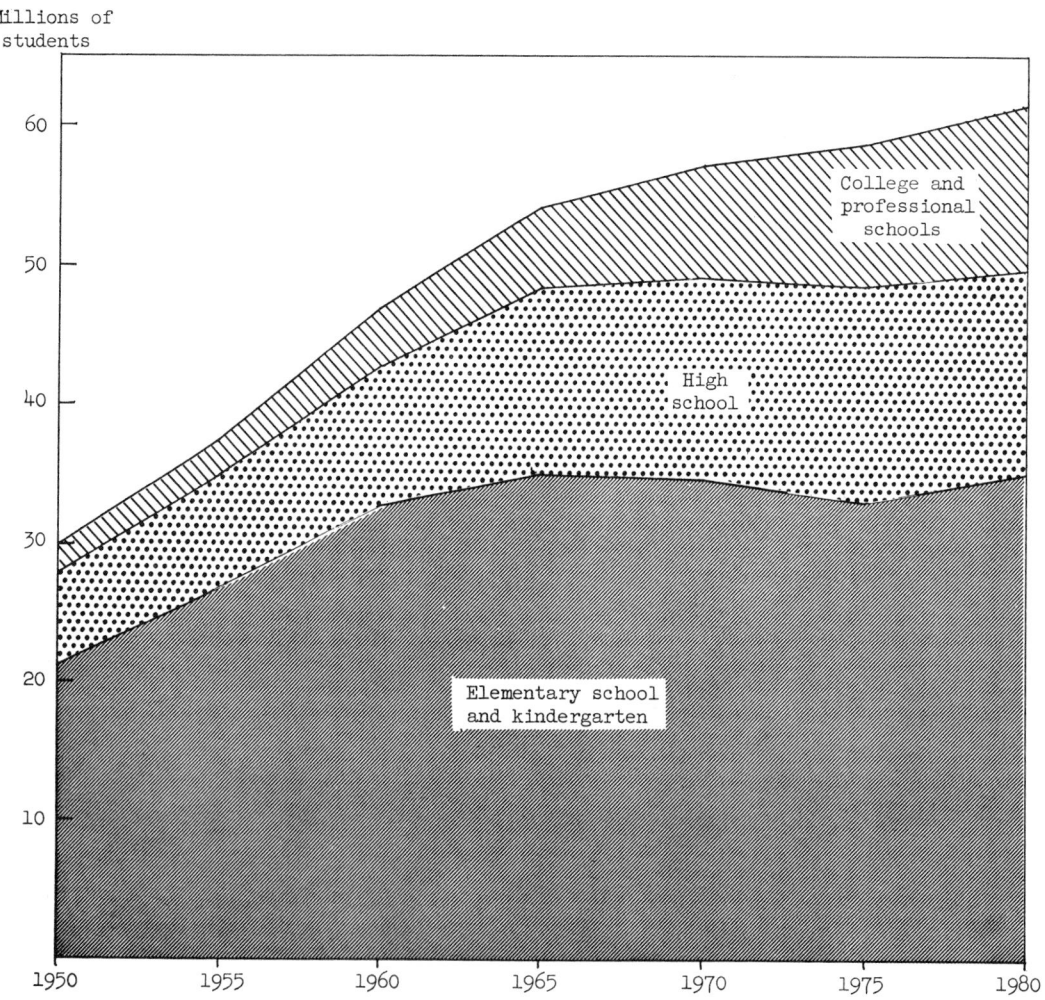

FIGURE 26-2. ESTIMATED SCHOOL ENROLLMENT, BY TYPE OF SCHOOL: 1950 TO 1980

a steady rise in the percentage of students above 16 years of age that remain in school. A higher percentage of students now graduate from high school, and a higher percentage now enroll in college, than ever before, and these proportions are still increasing. Combining these two factors-- larger oncoming generations and rising enrollment rates--makes it obvious how desirable is the attempt to foresee the nature and magnitude of the nation's future need for educational facilities. Tables 26-9 and 26-10 report estimates of enrollments in future years. They have been prepared, by the author, on the assumption that the Census Bureau's Series IV projections will materialize and that the trends prevailing between 1953 and 1958 in school enrollment, by age, will continue until 1980.[16] Table 26-10 was developed from Table 16-9 by assuming that the percentage of persons of each age attending each type of school would be identical with the respective proportions for 1958.

Future Enrollment in Elementary Schools. If the Census Bureau's projection IV turns out to be approximately correct, enrollments in elementary schools will level off in the early 1960's, and will be no larger in 1980 than in 1965. However, if birth rates remain high, a continued expansion may be expected.

Future Enrollment in High Schools. High schools are just now beginning to get the larger generations of students born in the early 1940's. Their enrollments will increase by more than 3 million students between 1960 and 1965, and will rise by another 2.2 million before leveling off in about 1975. If fertility rates do not decline, there will be no leveling off in 1975, but a continued steady and rapid rise.

Future Enrollments in Colleges and Professional Schools. It is estimated that college and professional school enrollments will grow by 2 1/2 times between 1960 and 1980, from 4 million to 11.5 million students. The greatest percentage increases to date are now occurring in the late 1950's, and will continue in the early 1960's as a result of rapidly rising enrollment rates and the arrival at the freshman and sophomore level of the very first of the larger birth cohorts of 1940, 1941, and 1942. Undergraduate schools will experience a rapid expansion in enrollment, which will become most acute (in terms of annual amounts of increase) in about 1965 to 1966. Professional and graduate schools will begin to feel

Table 26-9.—ESTIMATED FALL SCHOOL ENROLLMENT BY AGE: 1950 TO 1980

Age	Estimated Fall school enrollment (000)						
	1950	1955	Est. 1960	Est. 1965	Est. 1970	Est. 1975	Est. 1980
Total, 5 to 34 years........	30,276	37,426	46,843	54,065	57,476	58,495	61,516
5 to 29 years..................	30,176	37,235	46,558	53,733	57,059	57,931	60,673
5 to 13 years................	20,716	26,548	32,002	34,102	33,400	31,614	34,022
5 and 6 years.............	4,061	5,520	6,331	6,993	6,569	6,464	7,556
7 to 13 years.............	16,655	21,028	25,671	27,109	26,831	25,150	26,466
14 to 17 years.............	6,953	7,970	10,140	13,286	14,986	15,168	14,103
18 and 19 years.............	1,190	1,232	1,998	3,028	3,780	4,579	4,574
20 to 24 years.............	959	1,010	1,674	2,228	3,243	4,021	4,650
25 to 29 years.............	358	475	744	1,089	1,650	2,549	3,324
30 to 34 years.............	100	192	285	332	417	564	843

[16] Specifically, it was assumed that the percentage decline occurring between 1953 and 1958 in the proportion of persons of each age group who were not enrolled in school would be repeated in each 5-year period from 1960 to 1980.

the impact of the baby boom about 1963 to 1966, with peak expansion taking place about 1969 to 1971. As in the case of high school and elementary school enrollments, if fertility rates decline, then expansion in college enrollment may be expected to diminish about 18 to 20 years after the lowering of the birth rates.

Table 26-10.—ESTIMATED FALL SCHOOL ENROLLMENT (ASSUMING MEDIUM FUTURE FERTILITY), BY TYPE OF SCHOOL: 1950 TO 1980

Date	Estimated enrollment				Percent change since preceding date			
	Total	Elementary school and kindergarten	High school	College and prof. schools	Total	Elementary school and kindergarten	High school	College and prof. schools
1950.....................	30,276	21,389	6,656	2,231	...	...	...	...
1955.....................	37,426	27,086	7,961	2,379	23.6	26.6	19.6	6.6
1960.....................	46,843	32,603	10,171	4,069	25.2	20.4	27.8	71.0
1965.....................	54,065	35,063	13,282	5,720	15.4	7.5	30.6	40.6
1970.....................	57,476	34,594	15,077	7,805	6.3	-1.3	13.5	36.5
1975.....................	58,495	32,902	15,556	10,037	1.8	-4.9	3.2	28.6
1980.....................	61,516	35,162	14,811	11,543	5.2	6.9	-4.8	15.0

Source: Current Population Reports: P-20, No.40, Table 7; P-20, No.89, Table 5.

THE FUTURE EDUCATIONAL LEVEL OF THE POPULATION

Although it already has one of the most educated populations on the earth, between 1960 and 1980 the United States will continue to make steady and substantial gains in the level of educational attainment. The process by which this will be accomplished has already been described in Chapter 13; as the older age groups which have received less education are replaced by younger generations who have acquired more education, the over-all average for adults will rise. This process will continue as long as we keep improving our educational system and making it possible for the members of each new generation to obtain more education than was available to their parents. By making reasonable assumptions about probable future trends in the amount of schooling that will be attained by persons who are already born, or will be born in the next few years, and by aging the entire population forward to various dates into the future, Charles B. Nam has recently completed the first official projection of the Bureau of the Census concerning future educational attainment.[17] Table 26-11 summarizes the projections.

In making these projections, two sets of projections were used, a series A and a Series B. Series A assumed a continuation of recent increases in school enrollment, especially at ages 20 to 29, whereas Series B assumed a smaller increase. In this chapter, only the series A projections are used, because it is thought that the nation is only now facing up to the problem of providing a college education for those of its citizens who want and can benefit from schooling beyond high school, and is only beginning to accept public responsibility for providing this education in the interests of national welfare and progress. Actual events may cause the Series A assumptions (here reported as a single "medium" set of likely-to-happen events) to be somewhat on the low side.

These projections show that large changes in educational level are in store. The percentage of the total population aged 25 years or more that has graduated from college is expected to rise from 7.6 percent in 1960 to 11.0 percent in 1980. At the lower extreme, the percentage of functional illiterates (persons with less than 5 years of schooling) will decline from 8.1 percent in 1960 to 3.9 percent in 1980. In 1980, 60 percent of the total population either will have graduated from high school or will have attended at least 1 year of college. By 1980, only about 1 person in 9 will lack a complete elementary school education.

One needs only to exercise a little imagination to visualize some of the implications of such a

[17] U. S. Bureau of the Census, "Projections of Educational Attainment in the United States: 1960 to 1980," Current Population Reports, Series P-20, No. 91, January, 1959. Prepared by Charles B. Nam.

Table 26-11.—PROJECTED YEARS OF SCHOOL COMPLETED BY PERSONS 25 YEARS OLD AND OVER, BY SEX: 1950 TO 1980

School years completed and sex	Year				
	1950	1960	1970 (Series A)	1980 (Series A)	Change 1960 to 1980
MEDIAN SCHOOL YEARS COMPLETED					
Both sexes..................................	9.3	10.8	12.0	12.3	1.5
Male.......................................	9.0	10.5	11.9	12.3	1.8
Female.....................................	9.6	11.0	12.1	12.2	1.2
EDUCATIONAL DISTRIBUTION					
Both sexes, total..........................	100.0	100.0	100.0	100.0	...
College: 4 years or more...................	6.2	7.6	9.2	11.0	3.4
1 to 3 years......................	7.3	8.2	9.3	10.6	2.4
High school: 4 years or more...............	20.7	26.4	32.2	38.1	11.7
1 to 3 years.................	17.4	18.9	19.9	20.0	1.1
Elementary school: 8 years.................	20.8	17.5	13.2	9.2	-8.3
5 to 7 years............	16.4	13.3	10.4	7.2	-6.1
1 to 4 years............	8.6	6.3	4.5	3.1	-3.2
No school years completed..................	2.6	1.8	1.2	0.8	-1.0
MALES, total..................................	100.0	100.0	100.0	100.0	...
College: 4 years or more...................	7.3	9.5	11.8	14.5	5.0
1 to 3 years......................	7.0	8.3	9.8	11.6	3.3
High school: 4 years or more...............	18.1	23.0	28.0	32.9	9.9
1 to 3 years.................	16.9	18.6	19.6	19.8	1.2
Elementary school: 8 years.................	21.4	18.3	13.7	9.4	-8.9
5 to 7 years............	17.0	13.5	10.6	7.4	-6.1
1 to 4 years............	9.6	7.0	5.1	3.5	-3.5
No school years completed..................	2.7	1.8	1.3	0.9	-0.9
FEMALES, total...............................	100.0	100.0	100.0	100.0	...
College: 4 years or more...................	5.1	5.8	6.7	7.7	1.9
1 to 3 years......................	7.7	8.2	8.9	9.6	1.4
High school: 4 years or more...............	23.1	29.6	36.0	42.8	13.2
1 to 3 years.................	17.8	19.2	20.2	20.3	1.1
Elementary school: 8 years.................	20.3	16.7	12.8	8.9	-7.8
5 to 7 years............	15.8	13.1	10.1	7.1	-6.0
1 to 4 years............	7.6	5.6	4.0	2.7	-2.9
No school years completed..................	2.5	1.7	1.2	0.8	-0.9

Source: "Projections of Educational Attainment in the United States: 1960 to 1980," by Charles B. Nam, Current Population Reports, Series P-20, No. 91, Jan. 12, 1959, Table 2.

continued rapid rise in educational level. It means that our labor force will be better equipped to participate in an economy that places a premium on knowledge and technical abilities. It indicates, at least on a logical basis, a greatly increased future interest in and support of cultural activities--art, music, literature, drama. It may be expected to cause a greatly increased proportion of people to have hobbies and to join community groups based on various common recreational interests. This increase in educational level may even mean that we will be better-informed and more critical vot-

ers, and that politicians will be forced to use more logic and less mob psychology in their efforts to get elected. It probably means that we will have to mechanize, or otherwise eliminate, the nastiest and most disagreeable of the unskilled jobs, because there may not be enough persons willing to do them (unless our immigration policy is changed).

No less important than the over-all rise in educational attainment will be the sharp reduction in socio-economic differentials with respect to educational attainment. The next 20 years may be expected to bring about the virtual disappearance of the stereotype of the illiterate Negro, the factory worker who has a vocabulary that barely enables him to read a newspaper, and of "hillbillies" from the rural South whose parents did not think it important that they finish even the 8 grades of schooling available in the one-room schoolhouse with its limited curriculum. Another social result of this educational change may be a reduction in the great and widespread lack of understanding between generations. Even now this situation is rapidly improving. Table 26-12 shows how, over the next 20 years, the proportion of elderly people with only an elementary school education or less will decline until it amounts to less than one-half of the present population. By 1980, the educational attainment of persons 65 years of age or older will be slightly higher than that of the United States population as a whole in 1950. In 1980, the adolescent youngsters who look upon their parents as ignorant and backward individuals incapable of understanding the world about them will have less objective evidence on which to base such a view.

However, the educational level will continue to rise long beyond 1980. A comparison of the youngest and the oldest age groups for 1980, in Table 26-12, yields convincing evidence that the process will very probably continue well into the 21st century.

THE FUTURE LABOR FORCE

The projected future size of the labor force has already been discussed in Chapter 16, so a detailed analysis is not necessary here. It need only to be pointed out that the same enlarged cohorts of young people who will be marrying, going to college, and having children will also be seeking jobs, and that as a consequence the labor force is inevitably destined to undergo a great expansion. Throughout the entire 1960 to 1970 decade, each June will see a larger mass of young people graduate from school and seek steady employment than the year before. The following summary, from Gertrude Bancroft's "Projections of the Labor Force in the United States: 1955 to 1975," illustrates what may be expected to take place:[18]

Year	Estimated total labor force (000)	Average net annual increase (000) during preceding 5 years
1955	69,899	860
1960	73,372	1,095
1965	79,442	1,214
1970	86,604	1,432
1975	93,705	1,420
1980[1]	100,228	1,305

[1]Estimated by applying Bancroft's projected participation rates to Census age-sex projections.

Each year from 1950 to 1955, a net average of 860,000 new workers entered the labor force. Between 1955 and 1960, this annual average will have jumped to 1,095,000 workers per year.[19] This great increase has been due in large part to the fact that the earliest of the larger birth cohorts of the period 1941 to 1946 had already begun to seek jobs, although not as yet in large numbers. The really big increase is yet to come--from 1962 onward. The average annual addition to the labor force will be greater by about 440,000 workers between 1965 and 1970 than it has been between 1955 and 1960. Even assuming a substantial reduction in fertility, the labor force promises to number more than 100,000,000 by 1980. If it is assumed that fertility will decline in the 20 years from 1960 to 1980, the number of workers will increase by about 27 million. If fertility does not decline, but remains at 1956-57 levels, it can be assumed that the labor force in 1980 will number about 113,000,000--a gain of 40 million workers in two decades. Irrespective of whether the in-

[18] U. S. Bureau of the Census, Current Population Reports, Series P-50, No. 69, October, 1956. Prepared by Gertrude Bancroft.

[19] These estimates presuppose that labor force participation rates and trends, among both male and female workers, will continue as in the recent past.

Table 26-12.—PROJECTED YEARS OF SCHOOL COMPLETED BY YOUNG PERSONS (25-29 YEARS) AND OLDER PERSONS (65 AND OVER) TO 1980

Years of school completed	1960		1980		Change 1960-80	
	25 to 29 years	65 years and over	25 to 29 years	65 years and over	25 to 29 years	65 years and over
Median school years completed..	12.3	8.4	12.5	9.5	+0.2	1.1
Total..................	100.0	100.0	100.0	100.0	...	...
College: 4 years or more..........	10.9	4.2	14.6	6.6	+3.7	+2.4
1 to 3 years.............	10.7	5.0	12.7	7.8	+2.0	+2.8
High school: 4 years or more.......	39.9	11.5	46.9	20.1	+7.0	+8.6
1 to 3 years..........	20.9	12.0	18.6	18.8	-1.3	+6.8
Elementary school: 8 years........	8.0	26.9	2.9	21.2	-5.1	-4.7
5 to 7 years....	6.7	21.3	2.4	16.4	-4.3	-4.9
1 to 4 years....	2.1	13.9	1.4	7.4	-0.7	-6.5
No school years completed..........	0.8	5.2	0.5	1.7	-0.3	-3.5

Source: "Projections of Educational Attainment in the United States: 1960 to 1980," by Charles B. Nam, Current Population Reports, Series P-20, No. 91, Jan. 12, 1959, Table 2.

crease is 27 million or 40 million, never in the history of the nation will so many new workers have been placed on the labor market each year for such a prolonged period of time. What will be the effect of this change? Will it cause a large body of unemployed workers to accumulate? Will some well-planned program be necessary to help channel these vastly increased numbers of workers into jobs, or can the labor market handle the task without help? These are questions for which satisfactory answers have not yet been developed.

THE FUTURE POPULATION OF GEOGRAPHIC DIVISIONS AND STATES

Many persons are interested in knowing the probable future population of particular regions or states. Although the arithmetic required to construct a projection concerning the future population of a state or region is no more laborious than that needed for a projection for a nation, the result is even less trustworthy. The principal reason for the difference is that the internal migration component is even harder to predict than the fertility component. Nevertheless, although short-run projections made for states by means of the components method (making assumptions about the future trends of birth, death, and migration rates in each state) have a large range of error,

they are sufficiently reliable to be useful. The reason for this is that the factors causing a particular area to gain or lose population through migration at a particular time tend to persist for several decades, and the demographer is generally justified in assuming that recent trends in each state will continue for at least another ten or fifteen years. This permits him to glance a short distance ahead.

Meyer Zitter of the U. S. Bureau of the Census has prepared such projections, which are reported in a publication, "Illustrative Projections of the Population, by States: 1960, 1965 and 1970."[20] The principal results of these projections are summarized in Tables 26-13 and 26-14. Since these data are based on an earlier set of basic population projections for the nation as a whole, projections which have since been revised, the sum of the estimates for the individual states does not exactly equal the total reported above as the latest census projections. However, the series of state projections that correspond most closely to the "medium" estimate for the entire nation have been adopted as a "medium" estimate of the population

[20] U. S. Bureau of the Census, Current Population Reports, Series P-25, No. 160, August, 1957.

Table 26-13.—PROJECTED POPULATION OF GEOGRAPHIC DIVISIONS TO 1970 AND ESTIMATED PERCENT CHANGE 1950 TO 1960 AND 1960 TO 1970

Geographic division	Population (000)				Percent change		Ratio to U.S. rate	
	1950	1960	1965	1970	1950-60	1960-70	1950-60	1960-70
United States..........	150,697	178,479	189,363	203,687	18.4	14.1	...	...
New England..................	9,314	10,057	10,649	11,264	8.0	12.0	0.43	0.85
Middle Atlantic..............	30,164	34,604	36,218	38,481	14.7	11.2	0.80	0.79
East North Central..........	30,399	37,118	39,504	42,883	22.1	15.5	1.20	1.10
West North Central..........	14,061	15,665	15,951	16,604	11.4	6.0	0.62	0.43
South Atlantic..............	21,182	25,619	27,243	29,386	20.9	14.7	1.14	1.04
East South Central..........	11,477	11,881	12,119	12,382	3.5	4.2	0.19	0.30
West South Central..........	14,538	16,760	17,436	18,471	15.3	10.2	0.83	0.72
Mountain....................	5,075	6,789	7,366	8,192	33.8	20.7	1.84	1.47
Pacific.....................	14,487	19,986	22,877	26,024	38.0	30.2	2.07	2.14

Source: U. S. Bureau of the Census, <u>Current Population Reports</u>, "Illustrative Projections of the Population, by States, 1960, 1965, and 1970," prepared by Meyer Zitter, P-25, No.160, August, 1957.

of the individual states.[21] Population projections for states and regions have so large a margin of error that their usefulness would not be materially improved by adjusting them to the revised United States totals. According to these projections, in the 20 years between 1950 and 1970 the following states are expected to grow at a rate 50 percent or more in excess of the national average rate:

State	Expected percent increase, 1950-1970
Nevada..........................	147
Arizona.........................	122
Florida.........................	98
California......................	89
Delaware........................	73
Maryland........................	64
New Mexico......................	63
Utah............................	62
Oregon..........................	60
Michigan........................	58
Colorado........................	56

The following states are expected to grow at less than one-half the national rate during this time:

State	Expected increase, 1950-1970
Arkansas................................	-20
Oklahoma................................	-9
Mississippi.............................	-7
West Virginia...........................	3
Vermont.................................	4
Kentucky................................	6
North Dakota............................	6
Alabama.................................	8
Maine...................................	9
Iowa....................................	9
South Dakota............................	14
Nebraska................................	14
Rhode Island............................	16

There is absolutely no assurance that some of the factors causing the states in the first list to grow rapidly, or that some of the factors retarding growth in the second group of states, may not suddenly be sufficiently altered as to change completely the course of growth. For example, the St. Lawrence Seaway may quite possibly change very drastically the rather drab growth prospects suggested by Table 26-13 for Illinois, New York, Pennsylvania, Wisconsin, and Minnesota. On the other hand, the long-term rush to Florida and California may slow down because of insufficient employment opportunities or severe setbacks during recessions, and may cause growth in these states to slacken in comparison with the growth of other areas.

In general, however, the forces that are currently guiding the regional redistribution of population appear to be strong and promise to continue operating for quite a while. These forces favor a continued very rapid growth of the Mountain and Pacific states, and an extraordinarily slow growth in the East South Central, West South Central, West North Central, and New England states. The two remaining divisions—the East North Central and the South Atlantic—are scheduled to grow at rates slightly above the national average.

---

[21] The estimates used here are Zitter's Series 2, which assume that net migration will continue at the 1940 to 1955 level, that fertility will continue at about the 1950 to 1953 level, and that mortality will decline moderately.

Table 26-14.—PROJECTED POPULATION IN 1970, AND IMPLIED PERCENT CHANGE, 1950 TO 1970, BY STATES

State	Number of inhabitants (000)			Percent change 1950-70	Ratio of rate to U.S.rate
	1950	1970	Change 1950-70		
United States, total......................	...	...	...	...	...
New England					
Maine.......................................	914	994	80	8.8	0.25
New Hampshire...............................	533	642	109	20.4	0.58
Vermont.....................................	378	394	16	4.2	0.12
Massachusetts...............................	4,691	5,514	823	17.5	0.50
Rhode Island................................	792	918	126	15.9	0.45
Connecticut.................................	2,007	2,802	795	39.6	1.13
Middle Atlantic					
New York....................................	14,830	19,354	4,524	30.5	0.87
New Jersey..................................	4,835	6,772	1,937	40.1	1.14
Pennsylvania................................	10,498	12,355	1,857	17.7	0.50
East North Central					
Ohio..	7,947	11,681	3,734	47.0	1.34
Indiana.....................................	3,934	5,561	1,627	41.4	1.18
Illinois....................................	8,712	11,142	2,430	27.9	0.76
Michigan....................................	6,372	10,043	3,671	57.6	1.64
Wisconsin...................................	3,435	4,456	1,021	29.7	0.84
West North Central					
Minnesota...................................	2,982	3,709	727	24.4	0.69
Iowa..	2,621	2,863	242	9.2	0.26
Missouri....................................	3,955	4,737	782	19.8	0.56
North Dakota................................	620	660	40	6.5	0.18
South Dakota................................	653	743	90	13.8	0.39
Nebraska....................................	1,326	1,511	185	14.0	0.40
Kansas......................................	1,905	2,380	475	24.9	0.71
South Atlantic					
Delaware....................................	318	550	232	73.0	2.07
Maryland....................................	2,343	3,844	1,501	64.1	1.82
District of Columbia........................	802	1,049	247	30.8	0.88
Virginia....................................	3,319	4,462	1,143	34.4	0.98
West Virginia...............................	2,006	2,070	64	3.2	0.09
North Carolina..............................	4,062	5,070	1,008	24.8	0.70
South Carolina..............................	2,117	2,690	573	27.1	0.77
Georgia.....................................	3,445	4,156	711	20.6	0.59
Florida.....................................	2,771	5,496	2,725	98.3	2.79
East South Central					
Kentucky....................................	2,945	3,107	162	5.5	0.16
Tennessee...................................	3,292	3,921	629	19.1	0.54
Alabama.....................................	3,062	3,318	256	8.4	0.24
Mississippi.................................	2,179	2,036	-143	-6.6	...
West South Central					
Arkansas....................................	1,910	1,522	-388	-20.3	...
Louisiana...................................	2,684	3,586	902	33.6	0.95
Oklahoma....................................	2,233	2,031	-202	-9.0	...
Texas.......................................	7,711	11,331	3,620	46.9	1.33
Mountain					
Montana.....................................	591	730	139	23.5	0.67
Idaho.......................................	589	727	138	23.4	0.66
Wyoming.....................................	291	382	91	31.3	0.89
Colorado....................................	1,325	2,064	739	55.8	1.59
New Mexico..................................	681	1,112	431	63.3	1.80
Arizona.....................................	750	1,669	919	122.5	3.48
Utah..	689	1,114	425	61.7	1.75
Nevada......................................	160	395	235	146.9	4.17

Table 26-14.—PROJECTED POPULATION IN 1970, AND IMPLIED PERCENT CHANGE, 1950 TO 1970, BY STATES-Con.

State	Number of inhabitants (000)			Percent change 1950-70	Ratio of rate to U.S.rate
	1950	(000) 1970	Change 1950-70		
Pacific					
Washington....................................	2,379	3,594	1,215	51.1	1.45
Oregon..	1,521	2,433	912	60.0	1.70
California....................................	10,586	19,997	9,411	88.9	2.53

Source: U. S. Bureau of the Census, Current Population Reports, "Illustrative Projections of the Population by States, 1960, 1965, and 1970," prepared by Meyer Zitter, P-25, No. 160, August, 1957.

THE FUTURE OF URBAN AND RURAL POPULATION

There are almost no signs that the current trend toward urbanization will slacken in the next two decades. The 1960 census will show that roughly 67 to 69 percent of the population is urban--a jump of 3 to 5 percentage points above the 64.0 percent that was urban in 1950. Assuming that 90 percent of the projected increase in the 1960 to 1970 and the 1970 to 1980 decades accrues to urban places, the urban populations would be as follows:

Year	Urban population (millions)	Percent urban
1950.........................	98	64
1960.........................	121	68
1970.........................	142	70
1980.........................	168	73

If the urbanization movement turns out to be somewhat less rapid, the proportion urban in 1980 may be as low as 70 percent; if it is even more rapid than estimated, the urban population may account for as much as 75 percent of the total, or even more. It is very likely that by 1980 there will be at least 165 cities with a population of 100,000 or more, instead of only 106 as in 1950.

THE FUTURE POPULATION OF METROPOLITAN AREAS

In a recent article entitled "The Size and Distribution of Standard Metropolitan Areas in 1975," Ray P. Cuzzort estimated that in 1975 a possible 66 percent of the population will reside in principal standard metropolitan areas (S.M.A.'s with a total population of 100,000 or more inhabitants), and that such places may number as many as 200.[22] This estimate implies a population of 133 to 138 million persons living in standard metropolitan areas in 1975. Cuzzort made further projections on the basis of recent growth trends of central cities and suburbs, and concluded that by 1975 the population of metropolitan suburban rings would comprise more than one-half (56 percent) of the total S.M.A. population, if recent differentials in growth continue. This will cause central cities to decline markedly in relative importance, not only within the total national economy, but also even within their own metropolitan areas. As manufacturing, retail trade, and services move out into the suburban areas, the central city will become less and less of a single, central, integrating focal point; instead, the number of focal points within each metropolitan area will multiply.

These projections also indicate that there seems to be no limitation on the size to which metropolitan areas may be expected to grow. By 1980, the New York-Northeastern Standard Metropolitan Area may have almost 20 million inhabitants, and the nation may have 30 metropolitan areas with as many as 1 million inhabitants (instead of only 14, as in 1950). Chicago will probably be "small" compared with Los Angeles by 1980, and many other rapidly growing places situated along the Gulf Coast and in the West will have surpassed in size

---

[22] Chapter 12 in Applications of Demography, The Population Situation in the U. S. in 1975, op. cit.

quite a few metropolitan areas that now are much larger than they.[23]

The urbanization of the population will bring many more metropolitan areas to the South, the Midwest, and the West, and the metropolitan population will thus be much more evenly distributed among the regions and less concentrated in the Northeast than it has been. Cuzzort estimated that in 1975 the metropolitan population of the South will be double what it was in 1950.

Hence, it is probable that by 1980 the population will be even more metropolitanized than it is now, that it will be concentrated in larger agglomerations which are more widely distributed regionally, and that the metropolitan units will be more decentralized than they are at present.

THE FUTURE OF THE RURAL FARM POPULATION

Few experts on farm population can foresee any trend except a continued decline in the size of the farm population, in spite of the rapid growth of the total population. In a recent article, "The Farm Population and Agricultural Labor Force in 1975, " Louis Ducoff of the Agriculture Marketing Service reported as follows: "From 1910 to 1956, the farm population declined from 32 million to a little over 22 million. . . . Unofficial projections which we made on the assumption of a continuation of the average annual percentage rate of decline experienced during the 40 year period 1916-56 (Projection I), and alternatively the average annual percentage rate observed during the period 1933-56 (Projection II). The two projections would imply a farm population in 1975 of 16. 3 million to 18. 6 million. "[24]

The above estimates were made on the assumption that the same definition of the rural-farm population used in the 1950 census and earlier censuses would continue to be used in the future. As reported in Chapter 3, a new definition of farm population will be employed in the 1960 census, and probably later censuses; this change in definition will remove a net total of about 4 million persons from the rural farm population. Ducoff's estimates may be adjusted very roughly, to the new definition by subtracting 4.0 millions from each one. With this adjustment, the estimated future farm population would be:

Year	Projection I upper limit	Projection II lower limit
1960......................	18.0	16.5
1970......................	15.0	13.3
1980......................	13.2	11.2

It must be emphasized that these projections are based upon extrapolation, and may be upset by unforeseen developments in agricultural economics. It may be that the decline of the farm population will slow down as it approaches a lower limit of land occupancy that is economically and sociologically desirable. A severe and prolonged economic depression could make it impossible for farm youth to migrate to urban areas, thereby causing a slackening in the decline of the farm population. On the other hand, additional labor-saving devices for farming, and new ways of producing large quantities of food cheaply (including synthetic processes), may be developed and may become so widely adopted in the next few decades that the farm population will decline at a rate even faster than that prevailing during the past 40 years. For other, less drastic, reasons one can expect a continued decline. There are still large pockets of underemployed farm folk in the South (especially Negroes), and in the Middle West. The process of farm mechanization does not yet seem to be completed, and in some areas the actual average size of farm is still much smaller than the optimal economic size of farm. To many observers, it seems that the farm policy of the Federal Govern-

---

[23] The prospects for new urban and metropolitan developments are especially high for the South. See Rupert Vance and Nicholas Demerath, The Urban South, University of North Carolina Press, 1956.

[24] Louis J. Ducoff, "The Farm Population and the Agricultural Labor Force in 1975, " in Applications of Demography, op. cit., p. 71.

ment and of other administrators encourages large factory-type farming operations, which squeeze out the many small operators who now comprise a very large share of the farm population. For these and other reasons, Ducoff's estimates that the long-term trend will continue for at least another 20 years appears to be realistic.

SOME OBSERVATIONS ABOUT POPULATION AS A FACTOR IN PROSPERITY

What will it mean to have 230,000,000 to 280,000,000 persons by 1980, with the prospect of very large numerical increases each year after that for an indefinite period? The market analyst who sees each new infant only as a new customer who someday will buy a house, a car, a color TV set, etc., is ecstatically optimistic over the prospect, and predicts unparalleled prosperity based on population trends. The economist who is studying such basic resources as supplies of petroleum and other non-replaceable gifts of nature, who is considering the nation's food-growing facilities-- or who is weighing the future need for ordinary living-space--may become gloomy at the prospect.

A look at other times and other places fails to confirm the easy credo that a pure increase in numbers brings prosperity. There is no high correlation between level of material comfort and reproductivity, even among the technologically well-developed nations where private enterprise is the preferred mode of life. One need look no farther than the Netherlands or Italy to learn that runaway population growth is regarded as an enemy of high per-capita real income, and of profit on business investments. Why should it be different in the United States in the long run?

Contrary to what may be popular opinion, future population growth is not expected to create a sudden "economic boom"; rather, it will be just a steady upward thrust in numbers. This kind of increase will not cause a crisis in housing and consumers' goods similar to that which followed World War II; rather, it will call for much smaller relative increases in productive effort each year. Only comparatively moderate annual ex-

pansions in plants and facilities would be required to handle it.

There is nothing inevitable about the timing of the effects to be felt from population growth. Marriage can be postponed. Childbearing can be postponed or foregone. If a recession begins to develop, the population factor can actually aggravate the situation, rather than correct it. Postponement of marriage may depress the market for rental housing for several years. By postponing or foregoing children, couples may completely remove the pressure for housing with more rooms. Such a contraction could leave many segments of the economy with surplus capacity--schools with empty rooms, factories with overextended long-range expansion programs, and planned residential subdivisions that would not be needed for many years. And there is plenty of latitude for postponement of marriage and childbearing. Although at present it is the custom for girls to marry between ages 18 and 20, they could easily return to the old custom of marrying between 21 and 23 years of age. If this were to happen, it would be economically equivalent to having no marriages and no family formation for three or four years. If a serious depression begins to develop, this change in age at marriage may occur. Thus, in just a few short months, population change could become a major element in the economic situation, and the circular downward spiraling of the population could deepen a recession into a depression.

Economists often forget that there is no chicken-or-the-egg riddle about the relationship between population growth and economic well-being. The jobs must come first, before the economy can feel the wonderful secondary effects of increased purchases, expanding markets, etc. A major problem, by 1965 and thereafter, is going to be the providing of employment for the tremendous crops of young people pouring out of high schools and colleges seeking work. The events of the summer of 1958 showed that this can be a very serious problem.

There is a tendency for investors to overcapitalize the "demographic goodwill" generated by the baby boom. As millions of businessmen make their independent calculations, each may overestimate the value that will accrue to his enterprise and underestimate the number of competitors he will have, the total expansion that others will make, and the number of pieces into which the pie must be cut. If all the individual anticipations and planned expansions were added up, it would probably show that too much profit is already being expected to result from the baby boom. This same type of miscalculation was being made in the 1920's, and population growth was a key part of the philosophy that prosperity would be eternal. It is entirely possible that this miscalculation is now being repeated, and perhaps on an even larger scale (even if it is more subtly expressed and more carefully hidden).

Therefore, upon closer examination, the close correlation that has previously been supposed to exist between population growth and economic prosperity turns out to be more a matter of coincidence than of cause and effect. Economists and businessmen who have been relying heavily on population growth to solve the economic problems of the 1960's and 1970's may be destined to be greatly disappointed.

SOME OBSERVATIONS ABOUT POPULATION AS A FACTOR IN SOCIAL PROBLEMS

Population growth causes an increase not only in material needs and business activity but also in the social problems of the nation. For example, the nation can look forward to a 50 percent increase in the number of juvenile delinquents in the 12 years from 1958 to 1970, simply on the basis of the increased number of children who will be living at the ages when delinquency occurs. Actually, the great urbanization movement that has brought many thousands of Negro youngsters into a strange and disorganizing environment may result in an even greater increase. Between 1960 and 1980 the number of murders, robberies, and other serious crimes committed each year (and, presumably, the number of prisoners arrested and sentenced to prison each year) will double--again because of population growth. These changes will take place even if delinquency rates and crime rates remain unchanged.

Similarly, the rapid growth of our elderly population will require an expansion of our hospitals and mental hospitals to provide for the admission, during each year of the 1960 to 1970 decade, of at least 25 percent more elderly persons than these institutions care for at present; and in the 1970 to 1980 decade, this capacity will have to be increased by another 20 to 25 percent.

When the marriage and homebuilding boom begins, serious problems will develop concerning traffic, automobile accidents, and commuting times and distances. The need to provide shelter for the newly-formed families will make it harder to tear down slums and raise the quality of housing. These are only some of the tensions that will arise in many sectors of community life as a result of future population growth.

Meanwhile, as the various chapters of this report have made plain, some serious problems still remain to be solved. Poverty still afflicts a substantial number and proportion of individuals. Much mortality, especially among breadwinners and the mothers of growing children, is unnecessary. At all times there are one or more million of families suffering because their principal earner is unemployed. Substantial segments of the population live in housing that is either inadequate or downright unhealthy. Many young persons are unable to realize ambitions which they are exceptionally qualified to fulfill, solely because they are unable to afford the necessary training or because they are members of a nonwhite race. Many elderly people are spending their last days in joyless loneliness, with inadequate income and inadequate care, because inflation has all but nullified their retirement pensions. Thousands of marriages are dissolved each year because of stresses and strains resulting from inadequate upbringing or unfavorable environmental situations. Under conditions of slow population growth it might be much easier to "do something about" each of these problems than it would be under conditions of rapid growth, because rapid growth would require continuous expenditures merely to expand existing facilities and would allow little opportunity for improvements. Thus, the potential paroxysm of growth must be an element in the consideration of almost every problem facing the nation.

FUTURE POPULATION OF THE UNITED STATES IN COMPARISON WITH THE WORLD

How big will the United States population be in comparison with the population of the world and of the major nations of the world in future years? Only a few years ago the answer to this question could not even have been guessed, but excellent materials for making an evaluation are now available. Very recently the United Nations completed the monumental task of making population estimates and projections for the world, continents, and world regions from 1950 to 2000, and for major individual nations from 1955 to 1975.[25] These estimates, summarized in Tables 26-15 and 26-16 make explicit a situation which the world's citizens are only now beginning to comprehend; world population is growing by amounts that are becom-

ing so huge that it is almost impossible to believe that trends can continue along their present course for more than just a few more decades. Even when assumptions are made that the high fertility nations of the world will make moderate reductions in their birth rates, at a pace that seems consistent with their cultural patterns, level of literacy, and degree of economic development, the projected growth is astounding. The United Nations' calculations (in comparison with the medium estimates for the United States) specify the following.

Year	U.N. projection World population (millions)	Census projection U.S. population (millions)	Percent U.S. is of world population
1950..............	1,497	151.1	6.1
1975..............	3,828	235.2	5.6
2000..............	6,267	375.2	4.7

In commenting on its estimates, the United Nations report states, "Never in the history of mankind have numbers of the human species multiplied as rapidly as in the present century, nor can it easily be conceived that the people of the earth will continue at a similar pace in the century which follows.... Even if it is conceded that population growth, after its peak near the end of our century, might diminish gradually and cease within another century, world population would not stop growing until it had reached between 10,000 and 25,000 million. One cannot say that such further growth is utterly impossible, but the vast changes in human organization required to sustain it can hardly be conceived at the present time."

Stated succinctly, the projected growth of world population is so large that the professional demographers can scarcely bring themselves to believe their own best estimates of what is likely to take place. Yet, because the high fertility populations have not yet become acculturated to the idea of family planning, they cannot foresee any alternative to such growth other than a rise in death rates, caused by famine, war, malnutrition, and other poverty engendered diseases. This is the general context within which the future growth of

---

[25] United Nations, Department of Economic and Social Affairs, The Future Growth of World Population, Population Studies, No. 28, 1958. Chapter 2 of this report, only 6 pages long, is "must" reading for anyone interested in the future population situation. The making of population projections for major regions of the world, and of evaluating prospects for future population growth, is currently a major program of demography. Although it lies outside the scope of this book, it is a most fascinating and important topic. The interested reader should consult United Nations, Determinants and Consequences of Population Growth, 1951. Another excellent source is Philip M. Hauser (ed.), Population and World Politics, with articles by John Durand (World Population Trends); Frank Notestein (Regional Population Trends); W. S. Woytinsky (World Resources and Population); Simon Kuznets (Economic Trends and Population); Dorothy S. Thomas (International Migration); J. J. Spengler (Population as a Factor in Economic Growth); Kingsley Davis (Population and Power); Frank Lorimer (Population Policy in the Communist World); Irene Taeuber (Population and Politics in Underdeveloped Areas); and Quincy Wright (Population and Foreign Policy). Published by Free Press, Glencoe, Ill. A third excellent item is Ansley J. Coale and E. M. Hoover's Population Growth and Economic Development in Low-income Countries. A Case Study in India's Prospects, Princeton University Press, 1958.

Table 26-15.—ESTIMATED POPULATION AND POPULATION PROJECTED BY THE MEDIUM ASSUMPTION, OF CONTINENTS AND THE WORLD, 1900, 1925, 1950, 1975 and 2000

Estimate and year	World total	World continents					
		Africa	North America[1]	Latin America[1]	Asia[2]	Europe and U.S.S.R.[2]	Oceania
Estimated population (millions)							
1900.........................	1,550	120	81	63	857	423	6
1925.........................	1,907	147	126	99	1,020	505	10
1950.........................	2,497	199	168	163	1,380	574	13
1975.........................	3,828	303	240	303	2,210	751	21
2000.........................	6,267	517	312	592	3,870	947	29
ESTIMATED PERCENT INCREASE							
1900-1925.....................	23	22	56	57	19	19	57
1925-1950.....................	31	35	33	65	35	14	36
1950-1975.....................	53	52	43	86	60	31	59
1975-2000.....................	64	71	30	95	75	26	40
1900-1950.....................	61	66	107	159	61	36	117
1950-2000.....................	151	160	86	263	180	65	113
ESTIMATED PERCENTAGE OF WORLD POPULATION CONTAINED IN EACH CONTINENT							
1900.........................	100.0	7.7	5.2	4.1	55.3	27.3	0.4
1925.........................	100.0	7.7	6.6	5.2	53.5	26.5	0.5
1950.........................	100.0	8.0	6.7	6.5	55.2	23.0	0.5
1975.........................	100.0	7.9	6.3	7.9	57.7	19.6	0.5
2000.........................	100.0	8.2	5.0	9.4	61.8	15.1	0.5
ESTIMATED INCREASE							
1900-1950.....................	947	79	87	100	523	151	7
1950-2000.....................	3,770	318	144	429	2,490	373	16
PERCENT OF INCREASE IN EACH CONTINENT							
1900-1950.....................	100	8	9	11	55	16	1
1950-2000.....................	100	8	4	11	66	10	1

[1] Mexico is included with Latin America.
[2] Asiatic part of U.S.S.R. included with Europe.
Source: United Nations, Department of Economic and Social Affairs, The Future Growth of World Population, Tables 5, 6, 7.

the United States population may be expected to take place.

As the above summary shows, if the United States follows the course of medium fertility described earlier in this chapter, it will grow considerably more slowly than the world, and hence the United States population probably will become an even smaller percentage of the world population than it is now. (If the 1955 to 1957 rate were to be maintained indefinitely, as specified by the high (series II) estimates, the rate of growth of the United States population would be almost identical with the projected growth of world population, so that in the year 2000 the United States population would still be about 6.0 percent of the total, as at present.)

The anticipated great increase in world population is destined to take place in all parts of the world. But as Table 26-15 indicates, growth will be especially rapid in Latin America, Africa, and Asia.

How this growth probably will be distributed among the individual major nations, and which nations will be growing faster and which growing slower than the United States (according to the United Nations estimates) may be learned from Table 26-16, which provides data for the 37 largest nations whose past growth trends were summarized in the first chapter of this volume (Table 1-2). By 1975, the United States would still be the fourth largest nation. Meanwhile, China and India, the two largest nations, each will have grown by

Table 26-16.—POPULATION PROJECTION TO 1975, USING MEDIUM ASSUMPTIONS, OF 37 LARGEST NATIONS, AND COMPARISON OF THE IMPLIED GROWTH WITH THAT OF THE UNITED STATES

Nation	Projected population (millions) 1960	Projected population (millions) 1975	Percent change 1960-1975	Difference in rate from U.S. rate	Projected increase (millions)
China	654,000	894,000	37	+16	240,000
India	417,000	563,000	35	+14	146,000
U.S.S.R.	215,000	275,000	28	+7	60,000
United States	179,000	217,000	21	...	38,000
Japan	95,100	116,000	22	+1	20,900
Indonesia	89,300	122,000	37	+16	32,700
Pakistan	92,200	128,000	39	+18	35,800
Germany	73,000	80,500	10	-11	7,500
Brazil	67,100	102,000	52	+31	34,900
United Kingdom	51,600	55,500	8	-13	3,900
Italy	49,500	56,100	13	-8	6,600
France	44,500	49,100	10	-11	4,600
Nigeria	34,000	42,300	24	+3	8,300
Korea	31,500	43,000	37	+16	11,500
Mexico	34,200	53,300	56	+35	19,100
Spain	30,000	34,400	15	-6	4,400
Poland	29,400	34,400	17	-4	5,000
Viet Nam	29,100	40,400	39	+18	11,300
Turkey	27,500	40,000	45	+24	12,500
Egypt	26,000	38,300	47	+26	12,300
Philippines	24,400	34,100	40	+19	9,700
Thailand	22,900	32,100	40	+19	9,200
Burma	20,700	27,400	32	+11	6,700
Argentina	21,300	27,200	28	+7	5,900
Federated West Africa	20,200	24,700	22	+1	4,500
Iran	24,300	34,300	41	+20	10,000
Yugoslavia	19,000	22,600	19	-2	3,600
Romania	18,500	21,700	17	-4	3,200
Canada	17,600	22,300	27	+6	4,700
Union of South Africa	15,200	21,900	44	+23	6,700
Czechoslovakia	13,700	15,500	13	-8	1,800
Afghanistan	12,800	16,900	32	+11	4,100
Colombia	14,300	21,600	51	+30	7,300
Belgian Congo	13,900	17,600	27	+6	3,700
Ethiopia	12,200	14,400	18	-3	2,200
Netherlands	11,300	12,800	13	-8	1,500
Sudan	10,500	12,200	16	-5	1,700

Source: United Nations, Department of Economic and Social Affairs, The Future Growth of World Population, Tables 5, 6, 7.

amounts that are unprecedented. Between 1960 and 1975, China is scheduled to grow by an amount equal to the expected total size of the United States population in 1975, while India is expected to grow by an amount equal to the actual size of the United States population in 1947. Whether these nations can absorb such fantastic amounts of population growth in the 15-year period from 1960 to 1975 without experiencing a sharp compensating rise in the death rate is a debatable question which only time will be able to answer. The U.S.S.R. is scheduled to grow at a rate moderately higher than the United States, and with its slightly larger population, it will make an increase roughly 60 per-

cent greater than that of the United States. In this nation also, it is debatable whether such a large population can be absorbed without lowering the already low level of material comfort and well-being. Following is a list of nations, scheduled to grow at rates faster than the United States, ranked in order of expected rate of growth during the 1960 to 1975 period:

	Estimated percent change 1960-1975
Mexico	56
Brazil	52
Colombia	51
Egypt	47
Turkey	45

(Continued on next page)

	Estimated percent change 1960-1975
Union of South Africa.........	44
Iran.........................	41
Philippines..................	40
Thailand.....................	40
Pakistan.....................	39
Viet Nam.....................	39
Indonesia....................	37
China........................	37
Korea........................	37
India........................	35
Burma........................	32
Afghanistan..................	32
Argentian....................	28
U.S.S.R......................	28
Belgian Congo................	27
Canada.......................	27
Nigeria......................	24
French West Africa...........	22
Japan........................	22
UNITED STATES................	21

Of the nations in this list (including the United States), only Canada might be said to have the potential for absorbing the expected growth without substantially burdening its economy. Experts foresee a very desperate and troubled situation in most of the nations toward the top of this list.

The aspect of Table 26-16 that really worries many population experts is that it measures only 15 years of growth, and that the expected growth in the ensuing 15 years (after 1975) is scheduled, by United Nations projections, to be substantially larger than reported in Table 26-16. Even if all of the world's peoples were to be converted to the small family system at a pace that is optimistic, in view of the time required in the past to make this transition among similar populations, by the year 2000 world growth rates would only have reached their peak and only then would start to decline.

This unprecedented growth is developing because death rates are being lowered in many countries through advances in medical care and public health, while fertility rates remain high. As the situation develops, the various national governments are coming to realize the uncomfortable choice with which they are presented- either to

reduce fertility or to see death rates return to their former level after wiping out much (if not all) of the progress made thus far toward raising the level of living.

CONCLUSION

These somewhat pessimistic comments about the economic and social problems that may be expected because of the current rapid population growth have been submitted, in a somewhat exaggerated way, in order to counteract partially the uncritically optimistic attitude many people seem to have toward rapid population growth. However, as explained above, there is probably little need to worry about the spectre of overpopulation in the United States. When the economic and social consequences of the demographic events of the present and the recent past begin to make themselves universally felt, the American citizenry may be expected to react. If these consequences seem to presage a lowered level of material comfort and the loss of a preferred way of living, it is very likely that reproductive behavior will be modified to avoid these undesired effects. The next few years will also begin to make clear the nature of some of the repercussions that will follow from the explosive growth of the economically less developed parts of the world. As our domestic population problems unfold, may we not discover that they differ only in degree, rather than kind, from those faced by the unfortunate nations where growth is rapid and the prospects of accomplishing a quick adjustment are small.

It is hoped that the review of past trends and future possibilities presented in this volume may be partly responsible, at least in a small way, for a wider interest in and a clearer perception of what is happening- and for an increased awareness of the implications which population changes have for so many different aspects of our international, national, and community life.

TABLE 1

PERCENT DISTRIBUTION: RACE, NATIVITY, MARITAL STATUS, HOUSEHOLD DATA, RESIDENCE IN 1949, FAMILY INCOME, AND COUNTRY OF BIRTH FOR THE TOTAL POPULATION OF THE UNITED STATES, BY GEOGRAPHIC DIVISIONS: 1950

Subject	United States	New England	Middle Atlantic	East North Central	West North Central	South Atlantic	East South Central	West South Central	Mountain	Pacific
TOTAL, 1950......................................	100.0	100.0	100.0	100.0	100.0	100.0	100.0	100.0	100.0	100.0
Male..	49.7	48.9	49.0	49.8	50.0	49.6	49.5	49.9	51.1	50.3
Female..	50.3	51.1	51.0	50.2	50.0	50.4	50.5	50.1	48.9	49.7
White...	89.5	98.4	93.6	93.9	96.5	75.7	76.4	82.8	95.5	94.8
Nonwhite......................................	10.5	1.6	6.4	6.1	3.5	24.3	23.6	17.2	4.5	5.2
RACE AND NATIVITY...............................	100.0	100.0	100.0	100.0	100.0	100.0	100.0	100.0	100.0	100.0
Native white.................................	82.8	84.5	80.7	86.8	92.5	74.0	76.0	80.5	90.8	86.1
Foreign-born white............................	6.7	13.8	13.0	7.1	4.0	1.7	0.5	2.3	4.7	8.7
Negro...	10.0	1.5	6.2	5.9	3.0	24.1	23.5	16.7	1.3	3.5
Other races, total...........................	0.5	0.1	0.2	0.2	0.4	0.2	0.1	0.5	3.2	1.7
MARITAL STATUS, ALL SEX-COLOR GROUPS	100.0	100.0	100.0	100.0	100.0	100.0	100.0	100.0	100.0	100.0
Single.......................................	23.1	26.9	25.1	22.1	23.2	23.9	22.8	20.9	22.4	20.1
Married......................................	66.7	62.7	65.1	67.6	66.8	66.5	67.4	68.8	68.0	68.0
Widowed and divorced.........................	10.2	10.4	10.0	10.4	10.0	9.6	9.9	10.3	9.6	11.9
MARITAL STATUS, WHITE MALE..................	100.0	100.0	100.0	100.0	100.0	100.0	100.0	100.0	100.0	100.0
Single.......................................	26.0	28.6	27.2	24.9	26.6	26.4	25.9	24.5	26.3	24.1
Married......................................	68.0	65.0	67.0	68.5	67.4	68.7	69.1	70.0	67.3	68.5
Widowed and divorced.........................	6.0	6.4	5.8	6.6	6.1	4.9	5.0	5.5	6.4	7.4
MARITAL STATUS, WHITE FEMALE................	100.0	100.0	100.0	100.0	100.0	100.0	100.0	100.0	100.0	100.0
Single.......................................	20.0	25.2	22.9	19.5	20.0	19.5	19.2	16.9	17.7	15.6
Married......................................	66.2	60.8	63.6	66.9	66.5	67.1	67.6	69.3	69.4	67.9
Widowed and divorced.........................	13.8	14.0	13.5	13.6	13.5	13.4	13.1	13.8	12.9	16.4
MARITAL STATUS, NONWHITE MALE..............	100.0	100.0	100.0	100.0	100.0	100.0	100.0	100.0	100.0	100.0
Single.......................................	28.7	33.2	30.0	25.1	26.0	31.1	27.5	26.0	34.5	30.9
Married......................................	64.1	58.6	63.6	66.1	63.3	62.9	65.7	65.8	57.6	61.4
Widowed and divorced.........................	7.2	8.2	6.5	8.8	10.7	6.0	6.7	8.2	7.9	7.7
MARITAL STATUS, NONWHITE FEMALE...........	100.0	100.0	100.0	100.0	100.0	100.0	100.0	100.0	100.0	100.0
Single.......................................	20.8	23.8	23.3	16.9	18.2	23.4	20.0	18.3	23.2	17.4
Married......................................	62.0	58.4	60.7	64.6	61.1	60.5	62.3	62.7	63.3	66.5
Widowed and divorced.........................	17.2	17.7	16.0	18.5	20.7	16.1	17.7	19.0	13.4	16.1
HOUSEHOLD DATA										
Married couples, with own household.......	93.4	92.8	91.7	93.5	95.3	92.0	93.2	94.6	95.6	95.3
Married couples, without own household....	6.6	7.2	8.3	6.5	4.7	8.0	6.8	5.4	4.4	4.7
Families.....................................	0.9	0.9	0.9	0.9	0.9	0.9	0.9	0.9	0.9	0.9
Unrelated individuals.......................	9.8	10.1	9.4	9.4	10.3	9.6	7.0	8.9	11.3	14.0
Number of households........................	1.1	1.1	1.1	1.1	1.1	1.1	1.1	1.1	1.2	1.2
Population in households....................	96.2	95.3	96.1	96.4	96.6	96.0	97.5	97.0	96.1	95.0
Institutional population....................	1.0	1.4	1.2	1.1	1.0	0.9	0.7	0.7	0.8	1.1
RESIDENCE IN 1949										
Population 1 year old and over, 1950......	100.0	100.0	100.0	100.0	100.0	100.0	100.0	100.0	100.0	100.0
Same house as in 1950.......................	81.0	87.0	87.4	83.3	81.6	78.2	78.1	75.1	73.9	72.9
Different house, same county................	11.2	7.7	6.8	10.6	10.2	12.7	14.3	14.5	13.6	16.1
Different county or abroad..................	6.2	3.8	3.8	4.7	6.6	7.3	6.1	9.1	11.1	9.0
Residence not reported.....................	1.6	1.5	1.9	1.4	1.6	1.8	1.4	1.4	1.4	2.0
INCOME IN 1949 OF FAMILIES										
Number reporting............................	100.0	100.0	100.0	100.0	100.0	100.0	100.0	100.0	100.0	100.0
Less than $500............................	8.3	6.2	6.6	5.9	7.9	11.8	17.3	10.3	7.0	5.6
$500-$999.................................	6.4	3.7	3.3	4.2	6.8	9.4	13.9	11.4	5.9	4.2
$1,000-$1,499.............................	7.1	5.2	4.6	5.1	8.1	9.8	12.4	10.9	7.1	5.3
$1,500-$1,999.............................	7.5	6.6	5.7	5.7	8.4	9.9	10.9	9.9	7.8	6.1
$2,000-$2,499.............................	9.7	10.5	9.4	8.6	11.0	11.1	10.5	10.4	10.1	8.0
$2,500-$2,999.............................	9.4	11.5	10.4	9.7	9.9	9.0	7.6	8.1	9.8	8.4
$3,000-$3,499.............................	11.0	12.8	12.5	12.6	11.1	8.8	7.0	8.5	11.8	11.5
$3,500-$3,999.............................	8.4	9.2	9.1	9.8	8.2	6.4	4.9	6.6	9.1	10.4
$4,000-$4,499.............................	7.1	7.8	8.1	8.4	6.9	5.3	3.8	5.5	7.3	8.7
$4,500-$4,999.............................	5.0	5.6	5.5	6.0	4.7	3.8	2.6	3.9	5.2	6.4
$5,000-$5,999.............................	7.8	8.4	9.3	9.4	6.8	5.7	3.7	5.5	7.4	9.7
$6,000-$6,999.............................	4.3	4.4	5.1	5.3	3.6	3.2	2.0	3.1	4.0	5.7
$7,000-$9,999.............................	4.9	4.9	6.3	5.9	4.0	3.6	2.0	3.3	4.3	6.3
$10,000 and over..........................	3.1	3.2	4.1	3.5	2.8	2.4	1.5	2.6	3.1	3.6
Income not reported..........................	4.9	5.8	5.4	4.9	4.5	5.2	4.0	4.4	4.5	4.4
COUNTRY OF BIRTH OF FOREIGN-BORN.............	100.0	100.0	100.0	100.0	100.0	100.0	100.0	100.0	100.0	100.0
Northwestern Europe	22.8	23.8	19.5	21.9	38.5	22.7	23.2	9.4	30.9	28.8
England, Scotland, and Wales.............	8.2	9.3	7.2	8.0	5.1	12.3	12.7	4.2	10.9	10.7
Irish Free State (Eire)..................	5.0	8.9	6.7	2.9	2.1	3.1	2.8	1.1	2.4	2.7
Northern Ireland.........................	0.2	0.2	0.2	0.1	0.1	0.1	0.1	0.0	0.1	0.2
Norway, Sweden, Denmark..................	6.3	3.9	2.9	6.7	26.8	3.4	2.7	1.8	12.3	10.2
France	1.1	0.8	1.1	0.8	0.7	1.8	2.3	1.1	1.3	1.6
Other....................................	2.2	0.7	1.5	3.5	3.7	2.0	2.5	1.1	3.8	3.3
Central Europe..............................	26.9	13.0	34.0	41.4	30.9	25.7	25.6	13.1	17.3	15.0
Germany..................................	9.7	3.0	10.4	12.2	17.3	10.4	15.6	6.9	7.8	7.3
Poland...................................	8.5	7.1	10.5	12.6	3.7	6.9	4.5	1.9	1.9	2.2
Austria, Hungary, Czechoslovakia, and	10.8	3.0	13.1	16.6	9.9	8.4	5.6	4.3	7.7	5.5
Eastern Europe Yugoslavia	12.0	10.0	15.2	10.8	12.7	14.0	8.2	2.9	9.0	8.8
Russia (U.S.S.R.)........................	8.8	6.3	12.4	6.0	8.8	10.9	6.6	2.4	7.2	6.4
Other....................................	3.2	3.7	2.8	4.8	3.9	3.1	1.7	0.5	1.8	2.4
Southern Europe	16.7	20.1	23.0	11.2	5.2	15.5	13.7	5.5	10.2	12.7
Italy....................................	14.0	16.0	20.9	9.0	4.0	10.1	9.5	4.3	6.7	9.2
Greece, Spain, Portugal..................	2.7	4.2	2.1	2.2	1.2	5.3	4.1	1.3	3.6	3.5
Other Europe	0.9	0.8	0.7	1.0	1.2	1.4	3.0	0.5	0.6	0.8
Asia	1.8	2.1	1.5	1.4	2.9	3.5	4.5	1.6	1.3	2.7
Canada	9.8	27.7	3.8	9.7	6.8	8.2	6.9	2.9	9.7	14.1
Mexico	4.4	0.0	0.2	1.1	1.8	0.4	1.1	59.6	18.5	13.1
Other America	1.2	0.5	1.4	0.4	0.4	5.1	2.8	1.9	0.7	1.7
Remainder of World.........................	1.4	1.9	0.7	1.0	1.5	3.5	11.0	2.5	1.7	2.5

TABLE 2

PERCENT DISTRIBUTION: RACE, NATIVITY, MARITAL STATUS, HOUSEHOLD DATA, RESIDENCE IN 1949, FAMILY INCOME, AND COUNTRY OF BIRTH FOR THE URBAN POPULATION OF THE UNITED STATES, BY GEOGRAPHIC DIVISIONS: 1950

Subject	United States	New England	Middle Atlantic	East North Central	West North Central	South Atlantic	East South Central	West South Central	Mountain	Pacific
TOTAL, 1950	100.0	100.0	100.0	100.0	100.0	100.0	100.0	100.0	100.0	100.0
Male	48.6	48.3	48.5	49.0	48.2	48.0	47.5	48.7	49.5	49.2
Female	51.4	51.7	51.5	51.0	51.8	52.0	52.5	51.3	50.5	50.8
White	89.9	98.1	92.6	91.7	94.7	76.4	74.2	83.8	97.4	94.2
Nonwhite	10.1	1.9	7.4	8.3	5.3	23.6	25.8	16.2	2.6	5.8
RACE AND NATIVITY	100.0	100.0	100.0	100.0	100.0	100.0	100.0	100.0	100.0	100.0
Native white	81.1	82.8	78.0	83.1	90.2	73.5	73.4	81.0	92.2	84.8
Foreign-born white	8.8	15.3	14.6	8.6	4.5	2.9	0.8	2.8	5.1	9.3
Negro	9.7	1.8	7.3	8.1	5.1	23.5	25.7	16.0	1.8	4.3
Other races, total	0.3	0.1	0.2	0.2	0.2	0.1	0.0	0.2	0.8	1.6
MARITAL STATUS, ALL SEX-COLOR GROUPS	100.0	100.0	100.0	100.0	100.0	100.0	100.0	100.0	100.0	100.0
Single	22.7	27.5	25.2	21.9	22.5	22.1	20.7	19.8	21.0	19.4
Married	66.1	61.9	64.7	67.0	65.8	66.7	67.2	68.5	67.9	67.6
Widowed and divorced	11.5	10.6	10.1	11.1	11.6	11.2	12.1	11.7	11.1	13.0
MARITAL STATUS, WHITE MALE	100.0	100.0	100.0	100.0	100.0	100.0	100.0	100.0	100.0	100.0
Single	24.9	28.8	27.0	24.1	24.0	23.8	22.5	22.8	23.8	22.6
Married	68.9	64.9	67.3	69.2	69.5	71.0	72.1	71.5	69.5	69.7
Widowed and divorced	6.2	6.3	5.7	6.7	6.6	5.3	5.4	5.7	6.7	7.6
MARITAL STATUS, WHITE FEMALE	100.0	100.0	100.0	100.0	100.0	100.0	100.0	100.0	100.0	100.0
Single	20.8	26.4	23.4	20.2	21.4	19.6	19.2	17.2	18.2	16.1
Married	64.0	59.3	62.6	65.1	62.9	64.9	64.7	67.1	66.7	65.8
Widowed and divorced	15.2	14.3	14.0	14.7	15.7	15.5	16.1	15.8	15.1	18.1
MARITAL STATUS, NONWHITE MALE	100.0	100.0	100.0	100.0	100.0	100.0	100.0	100.0	100.0	100.0
Single	26.0	31.9	28.9	24.0	23.8	27.2	24.0	23.0	29.3	27.4
Married	66.2	59.9	64.6	67.3	65.3	66.0	68.1	68.0	61.3	64.8
Widowed and divorced	7.8	8.2	6.4	8.7	10.9	6.8	7.9	9.0	9.4	7.8
MARITAL STATUS, NONWHITE FEMALE	100.0	100.0	100.0	100.0	100.0	100.0	100.0	100.0	100.0	100.0
Single	19.1	23.3	23.1	16.6	16.9	20.9	17.7	16.1	18.3	16.7
Married	61.9	58.7	60.7	64.8	61.1	60.4	61.0	62.1	63.4	66.6
Widowed and divorced	18.9	18.0	16.1	18.6	21.9	18.6	21.4	21.8	18.3	16.8
HOUSEHOLD DATA										
Married couples, with own household	92.8	92.7	91.4	92.7	94.5	91.4	92.3	94.0	5.5	95.1
Married couples, without own household	7.2	7.3	8.6	7.3	5.5	8.6	7.7	6.0	4.5	4.9
Families	0.9	0.9	0.9	0.9	0.9	0.9	0.9	0.9	0.9	0.9
Unrelated individuals	11.3	10.3	9.9	10.6	12.9	12.6	10.4	11.1	12.7	14.6
Number of households	1.1	1.1	1.1	1.1	1.1	1.1	1.1	1.1	1.1	1.1
Population in households	95.8	95.3	96.3	96.1	95.1	94.8	96.3	96.2	95.5	95.3
Institutional population	0.8	1.1	0.8	0.7	1.0	0.9	0.7	0.7	0.8	0.8
RESIDENCE IN 1949										
Population 1 year old and over, 1950	100.0	100.0	100.0	100.0	100.0	100.0	100.0	100.0	100.0	100.0
Same house as in 1950	81.0	87.4	87.9	82.7	79.3	76.8	76.3	72.6	72.0	73.2
Different house, same county	11.4	7.7	6.7	11.4	11.9	13.0	15.2	16.1	15.1	16.8
Different county or abroad	5.8	3.3	3.6	4.4	7.1	8.1	6.9	9.7	11.5	8.0
Residence not reported	1.7	1.5	1.9	1.4	1.8	2.2	1.5	1.5	1.4	2.0
INCOME IN 1949 OF FAMILIES										
Number reporting	100.0	100.0	100.0	100.0	100.0	100.0	100.0	100.0	100.0	100.0
Less than $500	6.0	5.7	6.2	5.0	5.8	7.1	8.5	6.9	5.5	5.1
$500-$999	4.0	3.1	2.8	3.0	4.1	5.6	7.5	7.2	4.4	3.6
$1,000-$1,499	5.1	4.5	4.1	3.7	5.2	7.2	9.1	8.3	5.5	4.7
$1,500-$1,999	6.1	5.9	5.2	4.3	6.1	8.7	10.3	8.9	6.5	5.4
$2,000-$2,499	8.9	10.0	8.7	7.4	9.5	10.5	11.6	10.7	9.0	7.3
$2,500-$2,999	9.6	11.5	10.1	9.2	10.3	9.6	9.7	9.0	9.7	8.0
$3,000-$3,499	12.0	13.1	12.6	13.0	12.7	10.2	9.8	9.9	12.5	11.4
$3,500-$3,999	9.5	9.6	9.3	10.4	10.1	7.8	7.5	8.0	10.1	10.7
$4,000-$4,499	8.3	8.3	8.5	9.2	8.4	6.7	6.0	6.8	8.3	9.1
$4,500-$4,999	5.9	5.9	5.8	6.7	6.1	5.1	4.3	5.0	6.2	6.9
$5,000-$5,999	9.4	9.0	10.0	10.8	8.8	7.9	6.2	7.3	8.8	10.6
$6,000-$6,999	5.3	4.7	5.6	6.2	4.6	4.6	3.4	4.1	4.9	6.3
$7,000-$9,999	6.1	5.3	6.9	7.0	4.8	5.4	3.6	4.4	5.0	7.0
$10,000 and over	3.9	3.3	4.4	4.1	3.5	3.6	2.5	3.5	3.4	3.8
Income not reported	5.1	5.7	5.5	5.0	5.2	5.7	4.4	4.6	4.5	4.3
COUNTRY OF BIRTH OF FOREIGN-BORN	100.0	100.0	100.0	100.0	100.0	100.0	100.0	100.0	100.0	100.0
Northwestern Europe	22.0	23.9	19.2	21.1	35.1	21.9	23.9	10.7	32.0	28.5
England, Scotland, and Wales	8.1	9.0	6.9	8.0	5.8	11.7	13.1	4.9	12.2	11.4
Irish Free State (Eire)	5.5	9.7	6.9	3.1	2.7	3.3	3.4	1.4	2.9	3.0
Northern Ireland	0.2	0.2	0.2	0.1	0.1	0.1	0.1	0.0	0.1	0.2
Norway, Sweden, Denmark	5.3	3.7	2.7	6.2	23.2	3.2	2.6	1.9	11.5	9.6
France	1.0	0.7	1.1	0.7	0.8	1.8	2.2	1.4	1.2	1.7
Other	1.9	0.6	1.4	3.0	2.4	1.8	2.4	1.1	4.0	2.7
Central Europe	28.6	12.5	33.1	41.1	30.4	24.4	25.0	11.2	17.9	15.7
Germany	9.1	2.7	10.1	11.4	14.7	9.8	14.9	6.1	8.2	7.4
Poland	9.0	7.0	10.6	13.3	4.8	7.1	5.0	1.9	2.2	2.5
Austria, Hungary, Czechoslovakia, and Yugoslavia	10.7	2.8	12.5	16.4	10.9	7.5	5.1	3.2	7.5	5.8
Eastern Europe	12.8	10.4	15.9	11.1	12.9	15.7	10.1	3.3	8.9	9.4
Russia (U.S.S.R.)	9.7	7.1	13.2	6.6	9.1	12.5	8.2	2.7	7.1	7.1
Other	3.1	3.4	2.8	4.5	3.7	3.2	1.9	0.6	1.7	2.3
Southern Europe	18.2	21.9	23.8	12.2	7.6	16.6	16.1	6.7	10.8	12.8
Italy	15.3	17.4	21.6	9.8	5.7	10.6	10.6	5.0	6.9	9.3
Greece, Spain, Portugal	2.8	4.4	2.2	2.5	1.9	6.0	5.4	1.7	3.9	3.4
Other Europe	0.8	0.8	0.7	1.0	1.1	1.1	1.6	0.4	0.6	0.7
Asia	1.9	2.3	1.6	1.6	1.3	3.7	5.4	2.0	1.6	2.8
Canada	9.3	26.0	3.4	9.5	7.2	8.0	7.3	3.4	9.6	14.2
Mexico	3.6	0.0	0.2	1.2	2.4	0.4	0.8	57.3	16.2	12.0
Other America	1.3	0.5	1.4	0.4	0.6	5.7	3.0	2.6	0.8	1.9
Remainder of World	1.2	1.8	0.7	0.9	1.4	2.6	6.8	2.3	1.6	2.0

TABLE 3

PERCENT DISTRIBUTION: RACE, NATIVITY, MARITAL STATUS, HOUSEHOLD DATA, RESIDENCE IN 1949, FAMILY INCOME, AND COUNTRY OF BIRTH FOR THE RURAL-NONFARM POPULATION OF THE UNITED STATES, BY GEOGRAPHIC DIVISIONS: 1950

Subject	United States	New England	Middle Atlantic	East North Central	West North Central	South Atlantic	East South Central	West South Central	Mountain	Pacific
TOTAL, 1950	100.0	100.0	100.0	100.0	100.0	100.0	100.0	100.0	100.0	100.0
Male	50.9	50.2	50.6	50.8	50.0	50.8	50.0	50.6	52.4	53.7
Female	49.1	49.8	49.4	49.2	50.0	49.2	50.0	49.4	47.6	46.3
White	91.3	99.2	97.7	98.4	98.1	79.4	83.4	84.1	93.4	97.0
Nonwhite	8.7	0.8	2.3	1.6	1.9	20.6	16.6	15.9	6.6	3.0
RACE AND NATIVITY	100.0	100.0	100.0	100.0	100.0	100.0	100.0	100.0	100.0	100.0
Native white	87.7	90.3	91.4	94.6	93.8	78.5	83.1	82.3	89.1	90.9
Foreign-born white	3.6	8.9	6.3	3.7	4.2	0.9	0.4	1.8	4.3	6.1
Negro	8.0	0.6	2.1	1.3	0.9	20.5	16.5	15.2	0.8	1.3
Other races, total	0.7	0.1	0.2	0.3	1.1	0.2	0.1	0.7	5.8	1.6
MARITAL STATUS, ALL SEX-COLOR GROUPS	100.0	100.0	100.0	100.0	100.0	100.0	100.0	100.0	100.0	100.0
Single	22.3	23.9	24.0	20.8	21.7	23.5	21.7	20.7	23.0	21.9
Married	68.1	66.1	66.9	69.3	66.8	67.9	68.6	69.0	68.2	69.0
Widowed and divorced	9.6	10.0	9.1	9.9	11.4	8.6	9.7	10.3	8.8	9.1
MARITAL STATUS, WHITE MALE	100.0	100.0	100.0	100.0	100.0	100.0	100.0	100.0	100.0	100.0
Single	26.2	27.0	27.0	24.3	25.5	27.2	25.2	25.2	28.0	28.2
Married	67.7	66.4	66.8	68.8	67.3	68.3	69.9	69.1	65.4	64.7
Widowed and divorced	6.1	6.6	6.2	6.9	7.3	4.5	4.9	5.7	6.6	7.1
MARITAL STATUS, WHITE FEMALE	100.0	100.0	100.0	100.0	100.0	100.0	100.0	100.0	100.0	100.0
Single	17.4	20.8	20.3	16.8	17.7	17.5	17.2	15.2	16.3	13.4
Married	69.9	66.0	67.6	70.3	66.9	71.0	69.9	71.4	72.5	75.2
Widowed and divorced	12.7	13.3	12.1	12.9	15.5	11.6	12.8	13.4	11.2	11.4
MARITAL STATUS, NONWHITE MALE	100.0	100.0	100.0	100.0	100.0	100.0	100.0	100.0	100.0	100.0
Single	32.9	43.5	44.2	41.2	36.9	32.6	28.9	28.2	37.4	44.9
Married	59.7	47.5	48.9	48.8	52.3	61.2	63.4	63.1	55.7	47.4
Widowed and divorced	7.4	8.9	6.9	10.0	10.7	6.2	7.7	8.8	6.9	7.7
MARITAL STATUS, NONWHITE FEMALE	100.0	100.0	100.0	100.0	100.0	100.0	100.0	100.0	100.0	100.0
Single	22.0	29.7	27.3	23.6	26.0	23.2	19.8	18.9	25.5	21.7
Married	60.7	54.8	59.1	58.6	56.8	60.6	60.4	61.5	63.2	65.1
Widowed and divorced	17.3	15.5	13.6	17.8	17.2	16.1	19.7	19.6	11.2	13.2
HOUSEHOLD DATA										
Married couples, with own household	95.0	93.9	93.7	96.0	96.4	93.8	94.6	95.4	96.1	96.5
Married couples, without own household	5.0	6.1	6.3	4.0	3.6	6.2	5.4	4.6	3.9	3.5
Families	0.9	0.9	0.9	0.9	0.9	0.9	0.9	0.9	0.9	0.9
Unrelated individuals	9.0	9.7	7.6	7.8	10.8	8.7	7.2	8.5	11.2	13.6
Number of households	1.1	1.2	1.1	1.2	1.2	1.1	1.1	1.1	1.2	1.2
Population in households	95.0	94.6	93.9	95.3	96.1	95.3	96.1	96.4	95.3	91.9
Institutional population	2.5	2.7	4.2	3.3	2.2	1.7	1.9	1.6	1.3	3.0
RESIDENCE IN 1949										
Population 1 year old and over, 1950	100.0	100.0	100.0	100.0	100.0	100.0	100.0	100.0	100.0	100.0
Same house as in 1950	78.0	84.7	84.3	81.5	79.4	76.8	75.0	74.3	72.5	67.7
Different house, same county	12.1	8.3	8.2	10.4	10.8	13.3	15.8	13.8	13.5	16.2
Different county or abroad	8.1	5.5	5.1	6.6	8.1	8.2	7.5	10.4	12.6	13.8
Residence not reported	1.8	1.5	2.4	1.5	1.7	1.7	1.7	1.5	1.5	2.3
INCOME IN 1949 OF FAMILIES										
Number reporting	100.0	100.0	100.0	100.0	100.0	100.0	100.0	100.0	100.0	100.0
Less than $500	9.6	7.2	7.3	7.5	9.7	11.7	16.3	11.4	8.0	6.2
$500-$999	8.6	5.0	4.7	6.1	9.3	10.3	14.0	14.6	7.4	5.5
$1,000-$1,499	9.2	6.6	6.1	7.0	9.6	11.1	13.5	13.0	8.2	7.1
$1,500-$1,999	9.5	8.4	7.7	7.6	9.8	11.4	12.4	11.0	8.8	7.8
$2,000-$2,499	11.8	12.2	12.2	11.1	12.6	13.0	12.2	10.9	11.4	9.7
$2,500-$2,999	10.5	12.0	12.6	11.5	10.8	10.3	8.2	7.9	10.5	9.8
$3,000-$3,499	10.8	12.2	12.8	13.1	10.8	9.1	7.0	8.1	12.2	12.5
$3,500-$3,999	7.7	8.4	8.7	9.4	7.3	6.0	4.5	6.5	9.1	10.5
$4,000-$4,499	5.9	6.7	6.9	7.1	5.6	4.6	3.3	4.9	6.5	7.9
$4,500-$4,999	3.9	4.7	4.7	4.7	3.5	3.0	2.1	3.0	4.5	5.4
$5,000-$5,999	5.3	6.7	6.8	6.5	4.6	4.2	2.8	3.6	5.8	7.5
$6,000-$6,999	2.7	3.2	3.4	3.2	2.3	2.1	1.4	1.9	3.0	3.9
$7,000-$9,999	2.7	3.6	3.7	3.1	2.5	2.0	1.3	1.8	2.8	3.9
$10,000 and over	1.7	3.0	2.3	1.8	1.7	1.2	1.0	1.2	1.9	2.1
Income not reported	4.5	6.4	4.7	4.7	3.7	4.6	3.6	3.9	4.2	4.4
COUNTRY OF BIRTH OF FOREIGN-BORN	100.0	100.0	100.0	100.0	100.0	100.0	100.0	100.0	100.0	100.0
Northwestern Europe	27.3	25.3	23.9	26.9	41.7	27.5	24.5	7.9	28.8	30.9
England, Scotland, and Wales	9.8	12.1	10.8	9.6	4.7	16.2	13.8	3.7	10.0	9.7
Irish Free State (Eire)	3.0	5.1	4.8	1.6	1.4	2.5	1.8	0.6	1.9	2.0
Northern Ireland	0.1	0.2	0.1	0.1	0.1	0.1	0.1	0.0	0.1	0.1
Norway, Sweden, Denmark	9.9	5.6	4.2	9.2	29.9	4.3	3.1	1.6	12.5	13.4
France	1.2	1.2	1.4	1.1	0.7	1.9	2.9	0.9	1.4	1.4
Other	3.3	1.0	2.5	5.3	4.9	2.5	2.7	1.1	3.0	4.3
Central Europe	28.6	14.5	41.2	40.2	31.0	29.4	25.9	14.3	16.2	12.6
Germany	11.7	4.4	12.8	16.4	20.4	12.4	16.3	7.6	6.5	6.9
Poland	5.5	6.8	9.1	7.3	1.8	5.6	3.3	1.7	1.4	1.1
Austria, Hungary, Czechoslavakia, and Yugoslavia	11.4	3.3	19.3	16.5	8.9	11.4	6.3	5.0	8.3	4.6
Eastern Europe	7.5	6.6	7.3	8.2	12.9	6.4	4.8	2.1	7.4	5.9
Russia (U.S.S.R.)	4.1	2.3	4.8	2.7	9.2	3.8	3.4	1.8	5.1	3.2
Other	3.3	4.3	2.5	5.6	3.6	2.7	1.3	0.3	2.2	2.7
Southern Europe	10.3	11.4	16.6	7.4	2.3	12.3	8.3	3.4	9.7	10.4
Italy	8.7	8.8	15.5	6.5	2.0	9.3	6.5	2.9	6.8	7.3
Greece, Spain, Portugal	1.7	2.6	1.1	0.9	0.4	3.0	1.8	0.6	2.9	3.2
Other Europe	1.1	0.7	1.1	1.1	1.2	1.9	4.1	0.7	0.8	0.8
Asia	1.1	1.1	0.9	0.7	0.6	2.7	3.5	1.1	1.0	1.8
Canada	13.6	37.2	7.0	12.1	7.0	9.9	7.5	2.5	10.5	15.8
Mexico	7.4	0.1	0.1	1.0	1.3	0.6	1.1	63.8	23.2	17.5
Other America	0.8	0.6	0.7	0.4	0.3	2.7	3.2	0.9	0.6	1.0
Remainder of World	2.4	2.5	1.2	2.0	1.6	6.5	17.1	3.3	1.9	3.3

TABLE 4

PERCENT DISTRIBUTION: RACE, NATIVITY, MARITAL STATUS, HOUSEHOLD DATA, RESIDENCE IN 1949, FAMILY INCOME, AND COUNTRY OF BIRTH FOR THE RURAL-FARM POPULATION OF THE UNITED STATES, BY GEOGRAPHIC DIVISIONS: 1950

Subject	United States	New England	Middle Atlantic	East North Central	West North Central	South Atlantic	East South Central	West South Central	Mountain	Pacific
TOTAL, 1950	100.0	100.0	100.0	100.0	100.0	100.0	100.0	100.0	100.0	100.0
Male	52.4	53.3	52.8	52.9	53.6	51.3	51.2	52.2	54.0	54.0
Female	47.6	46.7	47.2	47.1	46.4	48.7	48.8	47.8	46.0	46.0
White	85.5	99.7	99.0	99.5	99.0	69.4	73.7	79.1	92.9	95.5
Nonwhite	14.5	0.3	1.0	0.5	1.0	30.6	26.3	20.9	7.1	4.5
RACE AND NATIVITY	100.0	100.0	100.0	100.0	100.0	100.0	100.0	100.0	100.0	100.0
Native white	83.1	89.5	93.1	96.2	96.1	69.1	73.6	77.4	89.0	86.9
Foreign-born white	2.4	10.2	5.9	3.2	2.9	0.4	0.2	1.7	3.9	8.6
Negro	13.7	0.3	0.9	0.4	0.6	30.0	26.2	20.1	0.4	0.6
Other races, total	0.8	0.1	0.1	0.1	0.4	0.6	0.1	0.8	6.7	3.9
MARITAL STATUS, ALL SEX-COLOR GROUPS	100.0	100.0	100.0	100.0	100.0	100.0	100.0	100.0	100.0	100.0
Single	26.1	27.5	27.0	24.8	26.0	29.1	26.1	24.0	26.1	23.4
Married	67.2	63.7	65.6	68.5	68.7	63.9	66.7	69.2	68.0	69.6
Widowed and divorced	6.7	8.8	7.4	6.7	5.3	7.0	7.2	6.8	5.9	7.0
MARITAL STATUS, WHITE MALE	100.0	100.0	100.0	100.0	100.0	100.0	100.0	100.0	100.0	100.0
Single	30.6	32.4	31.7	29.8	32.1	32.1	30.2	28.2	31.6	28.3
Married	64.5	60.7	62.4	64.7	63.7	63.5	65.2	67.2	63.2	65.8
Widowed and divorced	4.9	6.9	5.8	5.5	4.2	4.4	4.5	4.6	5.3	5.9
MARITAL STATUS, WHITE FEMALE	100.0	100.0	100.0	100.0	100.0	100.0	100.0	100.0	100.0	100.0
Single	19.7	21.8	21.6	19.0	18.7	22.5	21.0	17.9	18.4	15.3
Married	71.9	67.3	69.3	72.9	74.8	67.8	69.6	73.9	75.3	75.8
Widowed and divorced	8.4	11.0	9.1	8.1	6.5	9.7	9.3	8.2	6.4	8.4
MARITAL STATUS, NONWHITE MALE	100.0	100.0	100.0	100.0	100.0	100.0	100.0	100.0	100.0	100.0
Single	33.9	39.9	33.8	31.2	32.5	37.0	31.0	30.5	37.4	46.2
Married	61.1	52.4	59.4	59.5	59.3	58.7	64.1	63.5	55.3	47.7
Widowed and divorced	5.1	7.7	6.7	9.3	8.2	4.3	4.9	6.1	7.4	6.1
MARITAL STATUS, NONWHITE FEMALE	100.0	100.0	100.0	100.0	100.0	100.0	100.0	100.0	100.0	100.0
Single	26.0	28.0	23.6	20.7	23.6	29.4	23.6	23.2	26.9	24.0
Married	63.3	59.3	66.8	66.4	66.7	60.6	65.1	65.4	63.4	66.8
Widowed and divorced	10.7	12.7	9.5	12.9	9.7	9.9	11.3	11.4	9.7	9.1
HOUSEHOLD DATA										
Married couples, with own household	93.9	90.4	91.0	94.4	96.1	91.3	93.3	95.2	94.9	95.1
Married couples, without own household	6.1	9.6	9.0	5.6	3.9	8.7	6.7	4.8	5.1	4.9
Families	1.0	1.0	1.0	1.0	0.9	1.0	1.0	1.0	1.0	1.0
Unrelated individuals	4.0	7.6	5.9	4.2	4.1	3.0	2.5	3.4	6.4	8.1
Number of households	1.1	1.1	1.1	1.1	1.1	1.0	1.0	1.1	1.1	1.1
Population in households	99.7	98.9	99.4	99.8	99.9	99.8	99.9	99.7	99.5	98.5
Institutional population	-	-	-	-	-	-	-	-	-	-
RESIDENCE IN 1949										
Population 1 year old and over, 1950	100.0	100.0	100.0	100.0	100.0	100.0	100.0	100.0	100.0	100.0
Same house as in 1950	85.1	90.3	89.7	89.2	88.1	83.4	82.4	81.9	82.5	81.4
Different house, same county	9.1	5.2	5.6	5.9	6.3	11.1	12.1	10.9	8.9	9.8
Different county or abroad	4.8	3.6	3.5	4.1	4.6	4.2	4.3	6.2	7.5	7.6
Residence not reported	1.1	0.9	1.2	0.9	1.0	1.2	1.1	1.1	1.1	1.2
INCOME IN 1949 OF FAMILIES										
Number reporting	100.0	100.0	100.0	100.0	100.0	100.0	100.0	100.0	100.0	100.0
Less than $500	17.2	11.6	11.4	9.2	10.7	24.5	29.4	18.4	10.3	9.6
$500-$999	14.4	8.6	7.9	8.8	10.3	18.3	21.9	19.6	8.5	6.9
$1,000-$1,499	13.4	11.1	10.2	11.2	12.7	14.9	15.8	16.0	10.9	8.8
$1,500-$1,999	11.1	11.5	10.8	11.1	11.8	10.9	10.5	11.5	11.2	9.2
$2,000-$2,499	10.6	12.7	12.2	12.2	12.5	9.7	7.8	9.3	11.9	11.6
$2,500-$2,999	7.2	9.7	9.8	9.7	8.4	5.8	4.4	5.6	8.6	9.3
$3,000-$3,499	6.7	8.3	9.2	9.4	8.3	4.9	3.4	3.0	8.7	9.8
$3,500-$3,999	4.2	5.4	5.9	6.4	5.0	2.8	1.9	3.0	5.6	7.4
$4,000-$4,499	3.6	4.6	4.8	5.3	4.7	2.2	1.4	2.6	4.8	6.0
$4,500-$4,999	2.2	3.2	3.2	3.4	2.8	1.3	0.8	1.5	3.0	3.7
$5,000-$5,999	3.3	4.5	4.9	5.1	4.5	1.9	1.2	2.3	5.0	5.8
$6,000-$6,999	1.9	2.5	2.9	2.9	2.7	0.9	0.6	1.4	2.8	3.2
$7,000-$9,999	2.4	3.4	3.8	3.4	3.4	1.0	0.6	1.8	4.3	4.4
$10,000 and over	1.8	2.9	3.0	1.8	2.2	0.8	0.5	1.8	4.2	4.3
Income not reported	4.5	6.0	5.3	4.8	3.9	4.8	3.6	4.3	5.2	5.5
COUNTRY OF BIRTH OF FOREIGN-BORN	100.0	100.0	100.0	100.0	100.0	100.0	100.0	100.0	100.0	100.0
Northwestern Europe	25.8	15.4	18.3	24.5	45.1	22.3	17.5	5.4	30.1	27.9
England, Scotland, and Wales	5.0	6.1	6.7	4.9	3.2	11.1	8.6	1.9	7.1	5.1
Irish Free State (Eire)	1.4	2.6	2.7	1.0	1.0	1.9	1.2	0.3	1.3	1.4
Northern Ireland	0.1	0.1	0.1	0.0	0.1	0.1	0.1	0.0	0.0	0.1
Norway, Sweden, Denmark	12.9	4.7	3.7	10.7	34.0	3.7	2.9	1.7	15.4	11.1
France	0.9	0.8	0.9	0.7	0.5	2.0	1.6	0.5	1.7	1.6
Other	5.4	1.1	4.2	7.2	6.4	3.5	3.1	1.1	4.5	8.6
Central Europe	32.3	21.0	49.7	49.2	32.2	36.9	28.7	19.7	16.7	12.3
Germany	13.9	4.2	15.4	17.8	21.8	15.6	17.6	9.1	8.2	7.0
Poland	6.8	11.8	14.5	12.1	2.3	8.0	3.7	2.0	1.4	1.1
Austria,Hungary,Czechoslovakia,and Yugoslavia	11.5	5.0	19.8	19.3	8.1	13.4	7.5	8.5	7.1	4.3
Eastern Europe	9.5	13.0	9.3	10.7	12.2	9.1	3.7	2.0	12.8	7.0
Russia (U.S.S.R.)	5.1	3.6	6.0	3.4	7.3	6.6	2.6	1.8	11.3	4.0
Other	4.4	9.4	3.3	7.3	4.9	2.5	1.1	0.3	1.6	3.0
Southern Europe	6.7	8.1	10.5	3.0	1.0	6.8	9.2	3.0	8.5	15.6
Italy	5.1	5.2	9.7	2.6	0.8	5.2	8.3	2.8	5.3	10.3
Greece, Spain, Portugal	1.6	3.0	0.8	0.4	0.2	1.6	0.9	0.2	3.2	5.3
Other Europe	1.4	1.1	1.7	1.4	1.5	4.6	8.4	0.8	0.8	0.8
Asia	0.9	1.2	0.6	0.4	0.3	1.4	1.2	0.3	0.7	3.0
Canada	9.2	37.6	8.2	8.2	5.4	5.7	3.6	1.2	8.3	9.4
Mexico	10.6	0.1	0.1	0.6	0.6	0.3	3.2	64.7	20.0	16.6
Other America	0.4	0.3	0.5	0.2	0.2	1.7	1.3	0.4	0.5	0.7
Remainder of World	3.1	2.2	1.2	1.8	1.5	11.2	23.2	2.4	1.6	6.8

APPENDIX

TABLE 5

PERCENT CHANGE: RACE, NATIVITY, MARITAL STATUS, COUNTRY OF BIRTH AND PARENTAGE OF THE TOTAL POPULATION OF THE UNITED STATES, BY GEOGRAPHIC DIVISIONS: 1940-50

Characteristic	United States	New England	Middle Atlantic	East North Central	West North Central	South Atlantic	East South Central	West South Central	Mountain	Pacific
TOTAL	14.5	10.4	9.5	14.2	4.0	18.8	6.5	11.3	22.3	48.8
Male	13.3	9.6	7.9	12.7	3.0	18.3	5.8	10.5	20.6	46.3
Female	15.6	11.2	11.1	15.7	5.1	19.4	7.2	12.0	24.1	51.5
White	14.1	10.0	7.6	11.8	3.5	22.5	9.7	13.9	21.8	46.5
Nonwhite	17.1	41.8	47.9	69.1	19.7	8.7	-2.8	0.2	34.1	109.0
RACE AND NATIVITY										
Native white	16.8	15.3	12.0	15.0	5.5	22.4	9.7	13.8	24.0	51.9
Foreign-born white	-11.0	-14.2	-13.6	-16.4	27.7	27.3	18.6	15.2	-9.1	8.5
Negro	16.9	40.8	47.8	68.7	20.9	8.4	-2.9	0.3	82.4	275.6
Other races, total	21.1	56.1	51.5	83.3	12.2	57.9	108.0	-2.2	21.0	11.0
Indian	2.8	42.8	33.3	12.6	5.8	-70.1	45.2	-13.4	16.4	14.2
Japanese	11.7	115.3	119.2	1860.3	262.6	215.2	662.8	136.5	66.0	-12.5
Chinese 7	51.8	44.7	47.8	76.2	69.5	132.3	86.8	104.1	31.4	45.1
All other	118.4	143.0	56.7	76.8	96.8	2054.7	1945.7	455.2	133.9	38.3
MARITAL STATUS, ALL SEX-COLOR GROUPS	11.1	7.0	6.7	9.9	0.9	17.0	5.1	9.3	18.2	39.4
Single	-17.6	-18.6	-20.8	-19.6	-24.8	-11.5	-18.5	-18.8	-12.2	-1.1
Married	24.3	21.1	20.2	22.4	12.8	30.8	15.2	20.6	32.0	57.3
Widowed and divorced	23.5	21.2	24.1	23.8	11.6	26.7	12.8	18.0	26.2	45.0
MARITAL STATUS, WHITE MALE	9.1	5.3	2.7	5.6	-0.9	20.0	7.9	11.0	15.1	34.4
Single	-18.4	-19.4	-23.8	-21.9	-24.8	-8.7	-15.7	-15.6	-13.9	-2.7
Married	23.8	20.2	17.8	19.6	12.3	35.2	19.7	24.1	31.5	54.2
Widowed and divorced	22.0	18.4	20.8	19.5	7.4	34.3	18.1	18.0	23.9	41.9
MARITAL STATUS, WHITE FEMALE	12.6	7.9	7.0	9.7	2.0	22.1	10.4	13.5	20.4	40.1
Single	-18.8	-18.6	-21.1	-20.4	26.0	-13.4	-19.1	-20.5	-12.4	-1.5
Married	24.6	21.1	19.1	20.3	12.7	35.7	20.7	24.3	31.8	54.5
Widowed and divorced	25.1	21.8	22.9	22.3	12.3	35.0	21.8	24.2	27.0	42.5
MARITAL STATUS, NONWHITE MALE	12.7	38.5	42.7	61.6	12.6	4.3	-8.3	-5.3	29.8	77.4
Single	-8.7	11.1	15.5	21.4	-10.1	-13.5	-22.8	-23.6	10.2	13.4
Married	24.2	55.6	58.0	83.0	20.9	15.0	-1.3	2.8	43.5	138.6
Widowed and divorced	27.8	75.3	67.5	72.7	42.7	14.8	-0.4	7.4	41.4	128.3
MARITAL STATUS, NONWHITE FEMALE	15.1	37.3	45.8	63.3	16.9	6.1	-5.7	-2.3	34.7	124.8
Single	-8.4	4.6	18.2	23.2	-2.7	-13.8	-22.5	-23.7	21.4	37.7
Married	25.4	56.6	59.5	81.6	22.3	16.3	0.9	4.5	42.0	169.8
Widowed and divorced	16.3	39.8	47.7	54.8	22.8	6.9	-4.3	3.4	27.5	123.4
WHITE POPULATION BY NATIVITY AND PARENTAGE, 1940 (Percent Distribution)										
MALE	100.0	100.0	100.0	100.0	100.0	100.0	100.0	100.0	100.0	100.0
Native	89.9	82.2	82.2	89.3	93.5	97.6	99.4	97.1	92.9	86.6
Native parentage	70.6	48.0	53.1	67.6	73.2	93.1	97.7	89.9	75.1	64.9
Foreign or mixed parentage	19.4	34.2	29.1	21.6	20.3	4.5	1.6	7.2	17.7	21.9
Foreign parentage	12.8	23.1	21.2	14.2	11.9	2.7	0.9	4.1	9.8	12.8
Mixed parentage	6.6	11.1	8.0	7.4	8.4	1.8	0.8	4.1	9.8	12.8
Father foreign	4.4	6.1	5.3	5.0	5.9	1.2	0.6	3.2	8.0	9.1
Mother foreign	2.3	4.9	2.7	2.4	2.5	0.6	0.2	2.2	5.1	5.9
Foreign born	10.1	17.8	17.8	10.7	6.5	2.4	0.6	2.9	7.1	13.2
FEMALE	100.0	100.0	100.0	100.0	100.0	100.0	100.0	100.0	100.0	100.0
Native	90.8	82.0	83.4	90.7	94.6	98.0	97.4	99.5	94.1	88.6
Native parentage	71.2	48.2	54.0	68.5	74.4	93.6	90.2	97.8	76.1	65.7
Foreign or mixed parentage	19.7	33.8	29.4	22.2	20.2	4.4	7.2	1.7	17.9	22.9
Foreign parentage	12.8	22.8	21.2	14.4	11.6	2.6	4.0	0.8	9.6	13.3
Mixed parentage	6.8	11.0	8.2	7.8	8.6	1.8	3.2	0.8	8.4	9.7
Father foreign	4.5	6.2	5.5	5.2	6.0	1.2	2.2	0.6	5.5	6.3
Mother foreign	2.3	4.8	2.7	2.5	2.6	0.6	1.0	0.2	2.9	3.4
Foreign born	9.2	18.0	16.6	9.3	5.4	2.0	2.6	0.5	5.9	11.4
COUNTRY OF BIRTH OF FOREIGN-BORN	-11.0	-14.2	-13.6	-16.4	-27.7	27.3	18.6	15.2	-9.1	8.5
Northwestern Europe	-17.7	-21.7	-17.6	-20.8	-32.9	28.6	8.3	4.3	-20.5	-5.8
England, Scotland, and Wales	-11.5	-18.7	-16.5	-14.1	-21.7	34.8	29.0	30.9	-18.9	0.9
Irish Free State (Eire)	-11.7	-20.8	-9.4	-10.5	-24.1	12.0	-11.4	1.8	-17.3	2.7
Northern Ireland	-85.5	-82.3	-87.9	-84.7	-88.4	-77.5	-78.0	-82.8	-86.0	78.9
Norway, Sweden, Denmark	-24.9	-21.2	-18.4	-29.1	-35.9	25.1	-14.3	-20.4	-25.8	-12.4
France	4.9	7.9	-3.0	-3.7	-12.5	67.7	20.7	3.3	8.1	3.8
Other	-10.6	-0.6	-7.2	-18.4	-24.9	40.8	-9.9	-4.3	-4.5	0.9
Central Europe	-15.7	-11.2	-14.6	-20.6	-30.8	14.9	0.1	-12.2	-9.5	9.8
Germany	-20.5	-7.8	-14.9	-29.3	-36.4	15.5	0.7	-13.9	-13.8	-5.6
Poland	-13.3	-13.8	-13.6	-18.4	-17.9	9.7	8.0	15.2	17.2	45.2
Austria, Hungary, Czechoslavakia, and Yugoslavia	-12.2	-8.3	-14.1	-14.5	-23.5	18.9	-7.0	-18.1	-10.0	24.2
Eastern Europe	-15.1	-14.9	-18.1	-17.6	-27.2	12.0	-13.6	-11.4	13.3	13.1
Russia (U.S.S.R.)	-14.0	-17.0	-17.4	-15.9	-25.4	10.7	-14.6	-14.3	-9.7	21.1
Other	-17.7	-11.0	-21.1	-19.7	-30.9	16.9	-9.8	4.5	-25.0	-3.8
Southern Europe	-10.6	-10.7	-12.7	-10.4	-17.1	5.6	-11.3	-13.2	-12.4	-0.6
Italy	-12.1	-11.0	-14.0	-12.4	-18.9	0.8	-15.8	-16.3	-16.7	1.3
Greece, Spain, Portugal	-1.6	-9.3	3.0	-0.9	-10.6	15.9	0.9	-0.8	-3.0	-5.1
Other Europe	42.7	28.3	36.5	28.7	53.8	136.8	286.7	124.3	39.9	53.4
Asia	16.7	-4.9	4.9	3.6	28.0	57.6	21.0	22.4	76.0	76.7
Canada	-6.7	-14.7	-7.0	-10.3	-20.1	50.8	31.6	31.5	3.0	13.9
Mexico	19.4	138.9	13.2	32.7	-8.9	106.6	42.8	22.8	-0.2	21.8
Other America	79.7	51.4	50.6	94.5	151.2	106.6	118.9	162.5	154.0	132.3
Remainder of World	150.4	32.2	209.3	403.3	492.8	708.6	1954.2	892.8	202.4	50.1

TABLE 6

PERCENT CHANGE: RACE, NATIVITY, MARITAL STATUS, COUNTRY OF BIRTH AND PARENTAGE OF THE URBAN POPULATION OF THE UNITED STATES, BY GEOGRAPHIC DIVISIONS: 1940-50

Characteristic	United States	New England	Middle Atlantic	East North Central	West North Central	South Atlantic	East South Central	West South Central	Mountain	Pacific
TOTAL	19.5	7.8	7.1	14.6	17.1	30.0	28.9	48.0	39.8	43.3
Male	18.6	7.1	5.5	13.5	17.0	29.9	29.0	49.1	39.4	41.5
Female	20.4	8.5	8.6	15.6	17.2	30.1	28.8	47.0	40.2	45.0
White	17.2	7.2	4.5	11.1	16.3	30.9	31.2	51.1	38.9	39.7
Nonwhite	43.5	48.0	50.3	72.1	32.6	27.4	22.9	33.5	84.7	134.0
RACE AND NATIVITY										
Native white	22.6	13.2	10.4	15.7	19.1	31.7	31.8	52.5	42.5	46.7
Foreign-born white	-7.1	-14.0	-11.1	-13.8	-16.9	36.6	12.0	26.1	11.7	22.3
Negro	43.2	47.5	50.2	70.7	30.3	27.2	22.9	33.0	61.7	273.4
Other races, total	61.5	58.0	55.9	189.2	171.8	138.3	166.1	87.8	198.0	33.5
Indian	108.7	36.5	86.4	75.2	196.2	163.6	176.0	76.8	280.5	60.8
Japanese	44.6	143.0	78.2	2024.3	507.3	227.1	928.6	119.6	239.6	9.6
Chinese	55.8	44.9	46.5	72.8	68.5	111.7	114.9	102.1	53.2	53.1
All other	71.7	62.2	56.3	61.3	77.6	147.6	284.7	164.1	154.4	63.6
MARITAL STATUS, ALL SEX-COLOR GROUPS	15.4	5.0	4.6	10.7	12.9	26.1	23.9	41.0	33.7	34.9
Single	-18.7	-21.0	-24.7	-20.9	-16.4	-13.3	-12.1	0.5	-6.4	-12.7
Married	31.2	19.3	19.1	23.8	25.9	45.2	40.1	59.2	52.4	56.7
Widowed and divorced	29.5	22.9	24.3	27.8	23.2	32.7	27.1	40.3	36.2	37.0
MARITAL STATUS, WHITE MALE	11.9	3.2	0.3	6.1	11.8	26.2	26.4	44.7	32.0	29.5
Single	-20.7	-22.1	-28.0	-23.5	-16.4	-14.9	-11.0	7.0	-6.1	-15.5
Married	28.5	18.4	16.1	19.9	25.0	46.7	43.4	62.1	51.0	52.0
Widowed and divorced	29.7	20.4	23.1	26.6	22.9	42.4	36.8	48.7	38.9	38.8
MARITAL STATUS, WHITE FEMALE	14.8	5.5	4.2	8.9	12.6	28.6	28.0	44.3	33.8	33.7
Single	-20.6	-21.0	-25.5	-23.0	-17.6	-15.9	-12.8	-1.9	-8.0	-13.9
Married	29.6	19.1	17.4	20.7	25.8	47.9	45.2	63.7	51.7	52.9
Widowed and divorced	28.1	22.6	22.0	24.3	21.8	38.0	34.6	44.1	33.4	32.4
MARITAL STATUS, NONWHITE MALE	37.6	44.4	44.8	64.9	24.7	22.9	15.9	26.3	72.7	98.8
Single	4.1	22.4	14.0	21.9	-6.0	-5.0	-10.8	-7.1	7.4	18.1
Married	54.3	50.7	61.9	86.2	35.1	37.5	27.7	40.6	117.1	162.3
Widowed and divorced	58.8	136.7	69.3	79.1	65.7	39.3	27.8	44.9	167.6	146.8
MARITAL STATUS, NONWHITE FEMALE	36.8	43.3	47.8	65.7	26.8	20.9	15.0	23.4	74.5	145.3
Single	1.8	8.3	18.9	25.0	-0.6	-9.6	-15.6	-15.6	12.7	44.9
Married	54.9	58.0	62.9	84.9	35.4	38.0	29.4	41.0	105.7	203.1
Widowed and divorced	31.5	61.4	47.0	54.5	31.5	17.2	12.1	20.4	70.0	117.9
WHITE POPULATION BY NATIVITY AND PARENTAGE, 1940 (Percent Distribution)										
MALE	100.0	100.0	100.0	100.0	100.0	100.0	100.0	100.0	100.0	100.0
Native	85.9	80.2	79.3	86.2	92.4	95.3	98.3	95.7	92.2	85.7
Native parentage	60.9	42.5	46.5	60.6	72.7	86.9	94.3	86.1	73.3	62.4
Foreign or mixed parentage	25.0	37.7	32.8	25.6	19.8	8.4	4.1	9.6	18.8	23.3
Foreign parentage	17.1	26.2	24.1	17.4	11.8	5.3	2.3	5.4	10.4	13.7
Mixed parentage	7.9	11.5	8.6	8.2	8.0	3.1	1.8	4.2	8.5	9.5
Father foreign	5.2	6.5	5.8	5.5	5.5	2.1	1.4	2.8	5.4	6.1
Mother foreign	2.7	5.0	2.9	2.7	2.5	1.0	0.5	1.3	3.1	3.4
Foreign born	14.1	19.8	20.7	13.8	7.6	4.7	1.7	4.3	7.8	14.3
FEMALE	100.0	100.0	100.0	100.0	100.0	100.0	100.0	100.0	100.0	100.0
Native	87.3	80.1	80.9	88.2	93.7	96.2	98.8	96.1	93.1	87.4
Native parentage	62.1	43.1	48.0	61.9	72.9	87.9	94.8	86.4	73.5	63.1
Foreign or mixed parentage	25.2	37.0	32.9	26.2	20.9	8.2	4.0	9.6	19.6	24.4
Foreign parentage	17.1	25.6	24.1	17.6	12.3	5.1	2.1	5.4	10.6	14.3
Mixed parentage	8.1	11.4	8.8	8.6	8.6	3.1	1.9	4.3	9.0	10.1
Father foreign	5.4	6.4	5.9	5.8	6.0	2.1	1.5	2.9	5.8	6.5
Mother foreign	2.8	5.0	2.9	2.7	2.6	1.0	0.5	1.3	3.2	3.6
Foreign born	12.7	19.8	19.1	11.8	6.2	3.8	1.2	3.9	6.8	12.6
COUNTRY OF BIRTH OF FOREIGN-BORN	-7.1	-14.0	-11.1	-13.8	-16.9	36.6	12.0	26.1	11.7	22.3
Northwestern Europe	-12.4	-22.0	-14.6	-17.2	22.2	41.8	12.5	18.4	-5.3	6.3
England, Scotland, and Wales	-7.4	-19.9	-12.5	-11.7	-14.8	51.6	29.5	42.0	-6.0	10.9
Irish Free State (Eire)	-9.7	-20.6	-7.3	-8.6	-19.0	16.8	-7.9	6.8	-9.0	11.0
Northern Ireland	-84.8	-81.0	-87.3	-84.5	-87.7	-76.2	-81.9	-83.1	-83.5	-76.2
Norway, Sweden, Denmark	-16.5	-20.6	-15.8	-25.1	-25.0	40.4	2.3	-2.9	-9.5	0.9
France	11.2	4.9	7.5	3.1	3.9	84.6	17.7	15.6	34.6	13.9
Other	-0.7	-3.2	-2.5	-12.5	-6.9	59.0	1.2	19.1	22.1	25.0
Central Europe	-10.8	-8.8	-11.0	-18.2	-19.7	28.0	-4.1	11.6	14.1	24.7
Germany	-15.6	-6.9	-14.6	-26.2	-25.3	19.6	-8.3	6.3	6.1	6.6
Poland	-10.8	-12.5	-10.0	-17.2	-15.5	15.3	-2.5	17.0	34.9	57.8
Austria, Hungary, Czechoslovakia and Yugoslavia	-6.3	-0.7	-8.7	-12.5	-13.0	59.1	8.6	19.9	18.4	42.8
Eastern Europe	-12.9	-14.9	-17.6	-16.0	-18.1	13.6	-15.9	-5.1	14.6	27.1
Russia (U.S.S.R.)	-12.6	-16.7	-17.2	-15.6	-16.0	11.4	-16.9	-7.3	21.4	32.9
Other	-14.1	-10.9	-19.3	-16.6	-22.8	23.3	-11.0	5.4	-6.9	12.0
Southern Europe	-7.3	-9.2	-10.3	-8.9	-14.2	17.3	-5.1	-3.1	6.9	16.3
Italy	-9.0	-9.1	-11.5	-10.8	-15.5	11.7	-8.3	-4.4	3.0	15.5
Greece, Spain, Portugal	3.1	-9.7	4.0	-0.6	-10.0	28.9	1.9	0.8	14.5	18.7
Other Europe	32.6	19.8	28.1	18.7	64.6	100.7	95.7	71.2	70.3	62.5
Asia	16.5	-7.6	5.1	3.0	26.3	61.4	15.1	31.7	99.5	96.8
Canada	-2.9	-15.4	-3.4	-5.5	-12.1	68.0	43.1	42.0	19.2	26.2
Mexico	30.1	117.7	15.3	36.8	3.5	120.7	46.6	52.0	31.8	32.7
Other America	83.5	46.2	52.9	93.9	157.3	118.6	121.1	179.3	206.1	151.4
Remainder of World	146.0	20.2	200.2	374.7	489.5	585.3	1147.2	817.0	238.8	88.7

TABLE 7

PERCENT CHANGE: RACE, NATIVITY, MARITAL STATUS, COUNTRY OF BIRTH AND PARENTAGE OF THE RURAL-NONFARM POPULATION OF THE UNITED STATES, BY GEOGRAPHIC DIVISIONS: 1940-50

Characteristic	United States	New England	Middle Atlantic	East North Central	W. North Central	South Atlantic	East South Central	West South Central	Mountain	Pacific
				Geographic division						
TOTAL	43.2	35.5	32.0	45.8	16.3	55.2	42.8	28.2	35.9	99.5
Male	42.6	35.1	30.4	44.5	16.3	55.3	43.0	29.2	34.7	95.0
Female	43.7	36.0	33.6	47.2	16.3	55.0	42.5	27.2	37.3	104.8
White	43.4	35.7	31.9	45.5	16.4	59.6	46.6	26.9	32.8	97.3
Nonwhite	40.4	22.4	35.2	60.8	9.9	38.7	25.8	35.5	111.0	201.8
RACE AND NATIVITY										
Native white	45.3	39.9	34.9	47.6	17.9	60.0	46.5	26.6	34.6	101.2
Foreign-born white	-18.3	-3.7	-31.6	-15.6	-17.3	-2.1	37.8	24.3	-18.0	-20.2
Negro	38.0	15.3	31.6	58.3	-11.4	38.1	25.3	35.1	69.0	285.2
Other races, total	55.6	57.0	71.7	22.6	26.7	197.3	187.3	31.4	96.5	29.3
Indian	-6.4	46.6	8.7	-0.5	-4.8	-74.9	37.5	-25.6	10.2	5.5
Japanese	-28.4	39.6	433.4	672.7	57.9	191.2	534.5	152.6	7.8	-40.6
Chinese	12.6	39.0	107.2	179.1	78.4	404.2	65.7	113.7	-27.1	-21.6
All other	189.9	147.6	63.6	314.2	180.3	11,936.7	7925.0	1224.7	120.1	11.1
MARITAL STATUS, ALL SEX-COLOR GROUPS	37.7	30.3	28.4	38.5	12.5	51.0	38.9	23.8	30.7	85.8
Single	12.6	3.3	5.9	10.2	-13.7	25.9	14.3	0.0	8.4	63.9
Married	48.5	43.9	38.7	50.2	23.5	62.2	48.5	32.6	30.5	95.7
Widowed and divorced ..	43.9	34.6	38.9	43.7	21.9	56.9	45.8	30.7	34.9	82.6
MARITAL STATUS, WHITE MALE	37.1	29.4	25.6	36.2	-12.4	56.5	43.9	24.4	26.4	78.4
Single	14.7	4.7	4.3	9.8	-9.9	34.8	22.9	4.5	7.1	60.2
Married	48.1	42.9	36.8	48.8	23.0	66.7	52.4	33.0	34.4	88.1
Widowed and divorced ..	47.3	36.3	39.7	45.0	23.9	73.0	62.1	36.9	36.8	81.6
MARITAL STATUS, WHITE FEMALE	39.5	31.5	31.0	40.5	12.9	56.7	44.2	22.4	30.6	89.9
Single	7.6	1.1	5.7	8.6	-19.3	20.0	9.1	-12.1	1.8	57.2
Married	50.8	45.5	40.8	51.5	24.6	69.8	55.8	32.6	40.1	100.3
Widowed and divorced ..	44.4	34.1	39.4	42.9	21.6	63.2	52.3	29.5	31.9	82.4
MARITAL STATUS, NONWHITE MALE	32.2	26.3	39.7	54.0	2.2	26.8	16.8	26.7	83.7	167.5
Single	22.4	31.0	44.7	54.5	-2.0	15.2	5.3	16.8	52.5	164.1
Married	37.6	16.8	34.7	52.2	3.9	37.1	22.0	30.8	118.3	171.6
Widowed and divorced ..	37.9	71.4	47.5	61.6	9.8	33.7	25.4	33.9	64.9	163.6
MARITAL STATUS, NONWHITE FEMALE	31.6	11.0	30.6	51.8	5.3	31.5	17.9	25.0	105.3	218.2
Single	16.6	7.2	20.0	42.7	7.2	14.6	2.1	10.1	102.1	192.9
Married	38.6	9.1	35.7	54.1	5.7	40.0	23.7	31.1	114.6	230.9
Widowed and divorced ..	30.6	28.5	34.1	58.1	1.2	30.3	19.7	23.7	70.9	211.1
WHITE POPULATION BY NATIVITY AND PARENTAGE, 1940 (Percent distribution)										
MALE	100.0	100.0	100.0	100.0	100.0	100.0	100.0	100.0	100.0	100.0
Native	94.0	88.1	90.5	94.1	93.9	98.3	99.5	97.9	93.2	89.9
Native parentage	80.6	62.9	70.8	79.6	75.6	94.7	98.2	92.3	76.5	71.6
Foreign or mixed parentage ...	13.4	25.1	19.7	14.5	18.4	3.5	1.3	5.6	16.7	18.3
Foreign parentage	8.0	14.7	13.2	8.5	10.7	2.0	0.6	3.0	9.2	10.3
Mixed parentage	5.4	10.4	6.5	6.0	7.7	1.6	0.7	2.7	7.5	8.1
Father foreign	3.5	5.4	4.3	4.0	5.4	1.1	0.5	1.9	4.7	5.2
Mother foreign	1.9	5.0	2.2	2.0	2.3	0.5	0.2	0.8	2.8	2.9
Foreign born	6.0	11.9	9.5	5.9	6.1	1.7	0.5	2.1	6.8	10.1
FEMALE	100.0	100.0	100.0	100.0	100.0	100.0	100.0	100.0	100.0	100.0
Native	95.0	88.2	91.5	95.3	95.0	98.8	99.7	98.3	94.7	91.9
Native parentage	81.8	63.9	72.1	80.6	76.4	95.7	98.4	93.2	78.0	72.9
Foreign or mixed parentage ...	13.2	24.3	19.4	14.7	18.6	3.1	1.3	5.1	16.8	19.0
Foreign parentage	7.7	14.0	12.6	8.4	10.5	1.6	0.6	2.7	8.7	10.2
Mixed parentage	5.5	10.3	6.8	6.3	8.1	1.4	0.7	2.4	8.0	8.8
Father foreign	3.7	5.7	4.4	4.2	5.6	1.0	0.5	1.7	5.3	5.8
Mother foreign	1.9	4.6	2.3	2.1	2.4	0.4	0.2	0.7	2.8	3.0
Foreign born	5.0	11.8	8.5	4.7	5.0	1.2	0.3	1.7	5.3	8.1
COUNTRY OF BIRTH OF FOREIGN-BORN	-18.3	-8.7	-31.6	-15.6	-17.3	-2.1	37.8	24.3	-18.0	-20.2
Northwestern Europe	-23.0	-15.1	-33.2	-20.7	-19.0	2.7	10.7	-5.7	-23.2	-27.4
England, Scotland, and Wales	-23.3	-8.9	-35.2	-20.3	-21.6	3.7	29.3	19.9	-29.3	-30.5
Irish Free State (Eire) ...	-24.2	-19.5	-27.8	-22.4	-25.6	-3.5	-15.4	-12.5	-23.9	-29.4
Northern Ireland	-89.2	-87.3	-92.2	-85.5	-87.2	-80.0	-76.3	-75.8	-85.7	-89.9
Norway, Sweden, Denmark ..	-21.8	-15.7	-28.1	-22.1	-19.5	1.7	-22.2	-28.1	-22.1	-25.5
France	-9.4	28.6	-16.9	-14.8	-19.4	31.9	45.8	-20.9	-2.9	-23.5
Other	-10.9	25.1	-17.4	-15.1	-3.8	13.8	-6.7	-6.2	2.0	-16.3
Central Europe	-25.3	-14.0	-34.5	-18.3	-24.7	-15.1	14.6	8.1	-21.0	-25.2
Germany	-22.6	-3.6	-25.7	-25.0	-28.0	9.9	32.2	6.5	-17.3	-29.3
Poland	-25.3	-12.3	-38.2	-15.2	-1.2	-19.5	31.6	52.0	3.2	-3.9
Austria, Hungary, Czechoslavakia, and Yugoslavia	-27.8	-27.3	-37.6	-11.8	-20.0	-30.4	-19.1	0.4	-26.4	-21.7
Eastern Europe	-12.4	1.6	-25.9	-7.1	-0.4	-14.5	-15.9	-1.9	-6.2	-20.6
Russia (U.S.S.R.)	-12.6	-12.3	-20.0	-5.4	-2.8	-17.7	-18.8	-3.6	6.1	-25.6
Other	-12.1	11.3	-35.1	-7.9	6.2	-9.5	-7.3	7.8	-26.1	-13.5
Southern Europe	-32.7	-22.3	-38.0	-23.3	-29.4	-35.7	-22.2	-27.0	-29.1	-35.6
Italy	-34.3	-28.4	-39.2	-25.2	-32.1	-31.7	-25.8	-29.8	-30.4	-32.9
Greece, Spain, Portugal ..	-23.7	8.4	-16.3	-6.9	-11.9	-41.3	-5.5	-8.7	-25.9	-41.1
Other Europe	95.3	104.3	88.3	109.7	71.8	155.8	559.1	352.4	31.4	47.1
Asia	21.5	45.7	0.7	19.3	49.3	36.9	57.1	-12.1	30.8	22.9
Canada	-10.0	-5.1	-17.3	-16.2	-18.6	20.4	25.2	7.0	0.2	-13.9
Mexico	3.5	210.0	-8.1	18.4	-30.5	23.8	81.5	34.1	-22.0	-3.9
Other America	51.3	90.2	13.3	117.8	164.2	37.4	120.3	72.1	126.4	44.2
Remainder of World	238.4	147.8	278.0	563.9	587.8	861.4	2991.4	1450.8	232.8	38.4

•

TABLE 8

PERCENT CHANGE: RACE, NATIVITY, MARITAL STATUS, COUNTRY OF BIRTH AND PARENTAGE OF THE RURAL-FARM POPULATION OF THE UNITED STATES, BY GEOGRAPHIC DIVISIONS: 1940-50

Characteristic	United States	New England	Middle Atlantic	East North Central	West North Central	South Atlantic	East South Central	West South Central	Mountain	Pacific
TOTAL	-23.6	-28.7	-20.3	-19.0	-20.2	-23.2	-23.1	-36.1	-21.7	-11.1
Male	-24.1	-29.4	-22.2	-20.5	-20.6	-23.2	-23.2	-36.2	-22.5	-13.7
Female	-23.1	-28.0	-18.2	-17.3	-19.8	-23.1	-23.1	-36.1	-20.6	-7.9
White	-22.5	-28.5	-20.3	-19.0	-20.0	-22.2	-21.6	-34.8	-21.0	-9.8
Nonwhite	-29.8	-62.4	-26.0	-22.2	-34.0	-25.3	-27.1	-40.6	-29.7	-32.5
RACE AND NATIVITY										
Native white	-21.8	-27.4	-19.2	-17.8	-18.3	-22.3	-21.7	-35.2	-19.6	-6.7
Foreign-born white	-39.5	-32.8	-34.7	-43.5	-53.4	5.3	31.6	-19.9	-43.0	-33.9
Negro	-29.8	-24.7	-24.7	-21.0	-33.6	-25.8	-27.2	-40.7	53.8	45.1
Other races, total	-30.2	12.1	-36.1	-28.7	-34.7	21.8	50.6	-39.7	-32.3	-39.3
MARITAL STATUS, ALL SEX-COLOR GROUPS	-25.5	-32.2	-24.1	-22.6	-23.2	-24.2	-24.0	-36.6	-24.1	-16.3
Single	-41.1	-47.7	-42.4	-41.8	-41.5	-36.9	-36.3	-49.3	-41.3	-40.9
Married	-16.6	-21.9	-12.4	-11.6	-12.2	-16.5	-17.6	-30.3	-13.9	-1.8
Widowed and divorced	-28.4	-36.1	-26.1	-26.0	-30.3	-24.3	-25.8	-38.7	-28.6	-21.5
MARITAL STATUS, WHITE MALE	-25.0	-32.8	-26.1	-24.4	-23.6	-22.3	-21.3	-34.6	-25.2	-17.9
Single	-40.4	-47.5	-42.7	-42.1	-39.2	-35.8	-34.1	-47.8	-42.1	-40.4
Married	-14.3	-20.7	-12.8	-11.5	-11.7	-13.3	-13.8	-26.7	-12.4	-1.1
Widowed and divorced	-26.8	-37.3	-28.9	-28.2	-29.2	-17.7	-18.0	-35.6	-25.5	-22.5
MARITAL STATUS, WHITE FEMALE	-23.1	-31.1	-21.5	-20.3	-22.4	-21.9	-21.0	-34.4	-22.0	-11.5
Single	-43.0	-47.7	-41.3	-41.3	-45.5	-40.6	-38.3	-52.0	-42.3	-37.7
Married	-14.7	-22.7	-11.9	-11.6	-12.2	-13.5	-13.9	-27.8	-13.6	-1.3
Widowed and divorced	-25.3	-35.1	-23.7	-24.2	-30.7	-18.0	-19.7	-35.4	-30.5	-21.7
MARITAL STATUS, NONWHITE MALE	-34.6	-65.2	-39.3	-31.2	-38.8	-29.6	-32.4	-45.1	-27.8	-37.4
Single	-41.0	-73.7	-58.9	-47.2	-46.6	-36.0	-38.5	-50.7	-31.3	-52.8
Married	-30.1	-56.2	-16.7	-18.0	-32.9	-24.5	-28.6	-41.7	-26.1	-13.3
Widowed and divorced	-37.8	-57.8	-37.4	-31.7	-41.9	-33.8	-37.0	-46.7	-20.5	-48
MARITAL STATUS, NONWHITE FEMALE	-32.9	-60.4	-21.0	-20.2	-36.8	-28.6	-30.9	-42.9	-28.1	-32.2
Single	-37.2	-66.1	-40.9	-41.4	-39.5	-33.5	-35.7	-46.0	-25.6	-56.2
Married	-29.3	-58.9	-8.7	-11.6	-34.7	-24.0	-26.9	-41.0	-26.5	-18.5
Widowed and divorced	-40.7	-50.7	-27.7	-12.5	-43.3	-38.2	-40.2	-46.9	-41.8	-11.4
WHITE POPULATION BY NATIVITY AND PARENTAGE, 1940 (Percent Distribution)										
MALE	100.0	100.0	100.0	100.0	100.0	100.0	100.0	100.0	100.0	100.0
Native	96.1	88.4	92.3	95.0	94.6	99.6	99.8	98.1	93.5	86.6
Native parentage	85.0	68.1	78.5	79.7	72.5	98.7	99.4	92.3	76.3	64.8
Foreign or mixed parentage	11.0	20.3	13.8	15.3	22.0	0.8	0.5	5.8	17.2	21.8
Foreign parentage	6.5	11.9	9.3	9.1	12.8	0.4	0.2	3.4	9.5	13.2
Mixed parentage	4.5	8.5	4.5	6.2	9.3	0.4	0.2	2.5	7.7	8.7
Father foreign	3.1	4.6	2.9	4.2	6.6	0.3	0.2	1.7	5.1	5.9
Mother foreign	1.4	3.8	1.6	2.0	2.6	0.1	0.1	0.7	2.6	2.7
Foreign born	3.9	11.6	7.7	5.0	5.4	0.4	0.2	1.9	6.5	13.4
FEMALE	100.0	100.0	100.0	100.0	100.0	100.0	100.0	100.0	100.0	100.0
Native	96.8	88.4	92.9	95.7	95.7	99.7	99.9	98.5	95.0	89.6
Native parentage	86.8	67.8	79.9	81.7	75.3	98.9	99.5	92.8	78.8	67.9
Foreign or mixed parentage	10.0	20.6	13.0	14.1	20.4	0.7	0.4	5.6	16.2	21.7
Foreign parentage	5.7	11.8	8.2	8.0	11.5	0.3	0.2	3.1	8.6	12.8
Mixed parentage	4.3	8.8	4.7	6.0	8.9	0.4	0.2	2.5	7.5	8.9
Father foreign	3.0	4.7	3.1	4.2	6.4	0.3	0.2	1.7	5.1	6.1
Mother foreign	1.3	4.1	1.7	1.9	2.5	0.1	0.1	0.7	2.4	2.8
Foreign born	3.2	11.6	7.1	4.3	4.3	0.3	0.1	1.5	5.0	10.4
COUNTRY OF BIRTH OF FOREIGN-BORN	-39.5	-32.8	-34.7	-43.5	-53.4	5.3	31.6	-19.9	-43.0	-33.9
Northwestern Europe	-50.1	-41.4	-45.5	-49.8	-56.0	-18.8	-17.7	-42.6	-52.2	-45.4
England, Scotland, and Wales ..	-40.4	-35.6	-43.2	-40.3	-46.1	-16.2	24.1	-20.2	-50.1	-43.6
Irish Free State (Eire)........	-45.7	-42.0	-52.4	-43.0	-50.0	-27.8	-39.7	-36.6	-49.7	-36.6
Northern Ireland	-91.2	-92.4	-92.9	-89.1	-91.0	-86.0	-23.1	-87.3	-95.1	-89.3
Norway, Sweden, Denmark	-55.8	-45.2	-43.6	-55.8	-57.9	-28.8	-46.6	-55.0	-51.8	-54.0
France	-32.9	-16.0	-33.7	-42.7	-49.2	6.3	-6.7	-38.3	-24.6	-30.8
Other	-41.3	-28.2	-34.4	-44.9	-47.5	-5.6	-39.7	-46.6	-49.9	-32.4
Central Europe	-42.8	-33.1	-34.4	-43.4	-57.7	-8.9	2.7	-46.8	-46.3	-41.3
Germany	-48.4	-31.3	-28.1	-52.8	-55.8	-7.7	11.9	-49.3	-50.3	-46.1
Poland	-34.0	-31.7	-38.0	-35.7	-38.8	19.5	127.3	-9.9	-27.9	-28.0
Austria, Hungary, Czechoslavakia, and Yugoslavia	-39.6	-37.5	-36.1	-36.5	-50.9	-21.2	-29.7	-49.0	-43.9	-34.0
Eastern Europe	-45.2	-35.3	-30.4	-43.3	-57.1	58.6	52.4	-43.1	-51.8	-43.7
Russia (U.S.S.R.)	-43.3	-36.2	-25.9	-32.7	-58.1	101.3	97.8	-46.3	-50.3	-34.9
Other	-47.2	-34.9	-37.3	-47.2	-55.5	1.2	-2.7	-7.1	-60.1	-52.4
Southern Europe	-38.8	-33.0	-37.8	-30.3	-37.1	-28.4	-37.3	-50.3	-40.9	-41.4
Italy..........................	-38.7	-32.6	-39.4	-32.8	-39.2	-29.3	-39.2	-51.4	-47.7	-37.4
Greece, Spain, Portugal	-39.0	-33.6	-5.9	-9.9	-25.2	-25.3	-10.6	-24.6	-24.3	-47.8
Other Europe	87.2	100.4	163.3	90.5	23.2	559.7	1173.3	196.1	-0.4	0.6
Asia	9.5	24.5	-2.9	-2.4	11.0	39.8	54.9	-16.7	43.6	8.6
Canada	-37.0	-32.4	-29.4	-47.6	-43.2	-26.5	-22.5	-36.4	-35.9	-32.7
Mexico	-2.2	222.2	3.8	-15.5	-46.1	15.6	-24.1	-1.7	-20.0	11.4
Other America	39.9	26.4	20.6	56.1	97.5	29.9	91.5	100.0	22.3	24.5
Remainder of World	92.0	36.6	250.2	399.8	408.7	1281.9	5362.1	731.2	82.9	-6.0

TABLE 9.
POPULATION: RACE, NATIVITY, MARITAL STATUS, HOUSEHOLD DATA, RESIDENCE IN 1949, FAMILY INCOME, AND COUNTRY OF BIRTH OF THE TOTAL POPULATION OF THE UNITED STATES, BY GEOGRAPHIC DIVISIONS

Subject	Geographic division									
	United States	New England	Middle Atlantic	East North Central	West North Central	South Atlantic	East South Central	West South Central	Mountain	Pacific
TOTAL, 1950	150,697,361	9,314,453	30,163,533	30,399,368	14,061,394	21,182,335	11,477,181	14,537,572	5,074,998	14,486,527
Male	74,833,239	4,553,770	14,793,099	15,145,262	7,033,415	10,496,597	5,677,525	7,249,397	2,591,918	7,292,256
Female	75,864,122	4,760,683	15,370,434	15,254,106	7,027,979	10,685,738	5,799,656	7,288,175	2,483,080	7,194,271
White	134,942,028	9,161,156	28,237,528	28,543,307	13,576,077	16,041,709	8,770,570	12,037,250	4,845,634	13,728,797
Nonwhite	15,755,333	153,297	1,926,005	1,856,061	485,317	5,140,626	2,706,611	2,500,322	229,364	757,730
RACE AND NATIVITY										
Native white	124,780,860	7,875,105	24,329,729	26,394,273	13,013,365	15,671,174	8,717,310	11,703,526	4,607,527	12,468,851
Foreign-born white	10,161,168	1,286,051	3,907,799	2,149,034	562,712	370,535	53,260	333,724	238,107	1,259,946
Negro	15,042,286	142,941	1,875,241	1,803,698	424,178	5,094,744	2,698,635	2,432,028	66,429	504,392
Other races, total	713,047	10,356	50,764	52,363	61,139	45,882	7,976	68,294	162,935	253,338
MARITAL STATUS, ALL SEX-COLOR GROUPS	112,354,034	7,165,099	23,434,108	22,935,684	10,518,325	15,193,185	8,046,853	10,432,053	3,601,436	11,027,291
Single	25,972,345	1,925,602	5,878,993	5,062,142	2,440,964	3,630,237	1,831,093	2,179,489	805,709	2,218,116
Married	74,903,453	4,495,866	15,245,986	15,497,068	7,023,606	10,099,108	5,422,353	7,173,135	2,449,220	7,497,111
Widowed and divorced	11,478,236	743,631	2,309,129	2,376,474	1,053,755	1,463,840	793,407	1,079,429	346,507	1,312,064
MARITAL STATUS, WHITE MALE	49,979,010	3,397,388	10,670,690	10,656,093	5,050,619	5,794,568	3,081,056	4,345,426	1,761,392	5,221,778
Single	12,987,269	972,553	2,906,178	2,652,123	1,341,374	1,531,890	797,566	1,064,954	462,695	1,257,936
Married	33,980,608	2,208,307	7,149,324	7,304,553	3,402,442	3,980,472	2,130,574	3,042,384	1,185,565	3,576,987
Widowed and divorced	3,011,133	216,528	615,188	699,417	306,803	282,206	152,916	238,088	113,132	386,855
MARITAL STATUS, WHITE FEMALE	51,354,115	3,653,471	11,300,378	10,890,868	5,111,720	5,934,412	3,158,509	4,376,292	1,691,196	5,237,269
Single	10,272,018	920,401	2,585,674	2,119,179	1,021,119	1,160,107	607,333	739,054	299,567	819,584
Married	33,977,480	2,220,727	7,188,875	7,285,339	3,399,906	3,981,645	2,136,463	3,032,583	1,173,920	3,558,022
Widowed and divorced	7,104,617	512,343	1,525,829	1,486,350	690,695	792,660	414,713	604,655	217,709	859,663
MARITAL STATUS, NONWHITE MALE	5,332,607	57,842	690,131	684,465	173,712	1,664,055	856,334	818,318	78,879	308,871
Single	1,530,810	19,201	206,932	172,035	45,216	516,737	235,543	212,502	27,201	95,443
Married	3,419,009	33,880	438,684	452,163	109,977	1,047,460	563,006	538,692	45,416	189,731
Widowed and divorced	382,788	4,761	44,515	60,267	18,519	99,858	57,785	67,124	6,262	23,697
MARITAL STATUS, NONWHITE FEMALE	5,688,302	56,398	772,909	704,258	182,274	1,800,150	950,954	892,017	69,969	259,373
Single	1,182,248	13,447	180,209	118,805	33,255	421,503	190,651	162,979	16,246	45,153
Married	3,526,356	32,952	469,103	455,013	111,281	1,089,531	592,310	559,476	44,319	172,371
Widowed and divorced	979,698	9,999	123,597	130,440	·37,738	289,116	167,993	169,562	9,404	41,849
HOUSEHOLD DATA	35,006,330	2,090,655	7,060,950	7,296,380	3,340,355	4,629,760	2,528,080	3,383,040	1,157,985	3,519,125
Married couples, with own household	32,704,380	1,940,730	6,478,195	6,822,125	3,184,940	4,261,110	2,356,560	3,199,710	1,106,660	3,354,350
Married couples, without own household	2,301,950	149,925	582,755	474,255	155,415	368,650	171,520	183,330	51,325	164,775
Families	38,310,980	2,330,245	7,765,545	7,897,520	3,649,590	5,086,625	2,764,405	3,695,400	1,257,665	3,863,985
Unrelated individuals	11,051,050	721,565	2,202,270	2,156,675	1,080,385	1,454,720	561,025	929,070	406,335	1,539,005
Number of households	42,857,335	2,616,797	8,622,808	8,829,542	4,153,167	5,540,342	2,991,927	4,103,354	1,446,725	4,552,673
Population in households	145,030,888	8,880,812	28,987,149	29,306,167	13,581,307	20,344,644	11,193,665	14,102,683	4,877,377	13,757,084
Institutional population	1,566,718	125,822	375,811	331,061	142,261	199,042	85,241	104,632	42,447	160,401
RESIDENCE IN 1949										
Population 1 year old and over, 1950	147,162,995	9,099,790	29,535,750	29,639,335	13,734,175	20,678,275	11,209,130	14,184,320	4,933,040	14,149,180
Same house as in 1950	119,190,100	7,915,990	25,827,460	24,688,530	11,213,300	16,180,620	8,758,975	10,647,605	3,646,410	10,311,210
Different house, same county	16,476,275	701,710	2,019,935	3,138,505	1,394,260	2,616,485	1,601,010	2,049,890	670,910	2,283,570
Different county or abroad	9,074,960	346,370	1,117,215	1,406,100	910,990	1,502,665	687,475	1,286,465	548,145	1,269,535
Residence not reported	2,421,660	135,720	571,140	406,200	215,625	378,505	161,670	200,360	67,575	284,865
INCOME IN 1949 OF FAMILIES										
Number reporting	36,439,955	2,194,100	7,345,935	7,507,450	3,484,665	4,823,600	2,654,775	3,533,674	1,200,735	3,695,020
Less than $500	3,018,085	136,885	481,935	444,225	273,860	566,985	459,295	364,110	83,520	207,270
$500-$999	2,326,710	81,290	242,115	316,255	237,370	453,055	368,430	404,080	70,415	153,700
$1,000-$1,499	2,587,100	113,045	337,880	384,425	281,240	473,150	329,835	385,035	85,070	197,420
$1,500-$1,999	2,721,655	145,150	422,265	428,495	291,035	477,145	289,435	349,540	94,115	224,475
$2,000-$2,499	3,541,355	229,880	687,325	644,630	381,910	533,975	278,370	368,985	121,550	294,730
$2,500-$2,999	3,440,215	253,065	764,935	726,990	346,090	435,815	200,555	284,705	117,085	310,975
$3,000-$3,499	4,008,335	279,760	917,090	944,840	388,275	426,585	185,915	299,435	142,225	424,210
$3,500-$3,999	3,051,775	201,915	665,730	733,385	285,675	306,385	129,670	234,695	109,720	384,600
$4,000-$4,499	2,596,085	171,825	596,795	628,595	238,820	253,250	101,525	195,540	87,500	322,235
$4,500-$4,999	1,825,815	122,115	404,380	448,830	163,025	181,365	69,400	136,085	62,780	237,835
$5,000-$5,999	2,827,995	184,385	686,600	706,220	236,435	274,595	97,735	193,045	88,890	360,090
$6,000-$6,999	1,570,950	95,705	377,735	398,755	125,425	153,060	51,940	108,785	48,610	210,935
$7,000-$9,999	1,780,450	107,860	461,865	442,415	139,075	173,660	53,910	116,000	51,935	233,730
$10,000 and over	1,143,430	71,220	299,285	259,390	96,430	114,575	38,760	93,635	37,320	132,815
Income not reported	1,871,025	136,145	419,610	390,070	164,925	263,025	109,630	161,725	56,930	168,965
COUNTRY OF BIRTH OF FOREIGN-BORN	10,161,168	1,286,051	3,907,799	2,149,034	562,712	370,535	53,260	333,724	238,107	1,259,946
Northwestern Europe	2,318,772	305,844	762,175	470,323	216,694	84,288	12,343	31,308	73,536	362,261
England, Scotland and Wales	828,815	119,044	282,325	171,488	28,569	45,748	6,764	14,067	26,013	134,797
Irish Free State (Eire)	504,961	114,304	260,538	61,339	11,835	11,496	1,495	3,653	5,814	34,487
Northern Ireland	15,398	3,068	7,131	2,079	353	483	56	101	216	1,911
Norway, Sweden, Denmark	635,135	50,634	111,409	144,492	150,736	12,515	1,461	6,107	29,218	128,563
France	107,924	9,902	42,140	16,157	4,101	6,683	1,220	3,765	3,213	20,743
Other	226,539	8,892	58,632	74,768	21,100	7,363	1,347	3,615	9,062	41,760
Central Europe	2,944,546	167,709	1,329,488	890,497	173,666	95,292	13,652	43,646	41,196	189,400
Germany	984,331	38,187	406,016	262,695	97,472	38,699	8,283	22,911	18,419	91,649
Poland	861,184	91,363	411,416	271,120	20,573	25,599	2,382	6,250	4,471	28,010
Austria, Hungary, Czechoslavakia, Yugoslavia	1,099,031	38,159	512,056	356,682	55,621	30,994	2,987	14,485	18,306	69,741
Eastern Europe	1,223,067	128,811	593,046	231,499	71,714	51,929	4,383	9,695	21,508	110,482
Russia (U.S.S.R.)	894,844	81,638	484,996	129,203	49,625	40,442	3,499	7,948	17,128	80,365
Other	328,223	47,173	108,050	102,296	22,089	11,487	884	1,747	4,380	30,117
Southern Europe	1,696,130	259,028	899,118	241,517	29,100	57,308	7,280	18,462	24,309	160,008
Italy	1,427,145	205,388	817,214	194,257	22,233	37,545	5,078	14,212	15,856	115,362
Greece, Spain, Portugal	268,985	53,640	81,904	47,260	6,867	19,763	2,202	4,250	8,453	44,646
Other Europe	86,375	10,209	28,218	21,547	6,836	5,055	1,601	1,797	1,533	9,579
Asia	180,024	27,062	59,031	31,059	5,333	12,840	2,391	5,318	3,100	33,890
Canada	994,562	356,701	148,196	207,598	38,336	30,254	3,659	9,707	22,991	177,120
Mexico	450,562	626	6,110	23,811	10,326	1,565	611	198,932	44,108	164,473
Other America	120,297	6,067	53,153	8,971	2,479	18,856	1,506	6,460	1,783	21,022
Remainder of the world	146,833	23,994	29,264	22,212	8,228	13,148	5,834	8,399	4,043	31,711

TABLE 10.

POPULATION: RACE, NATIVITY, MARITAL STATUS, HOUSEHOLD DATA, RESIDENCE IN 1949, FAMILY INCOME, AND COUNTRY OF BIRTH OF THE URBAN POPULATION OF THE UNITED STATES, BY GEOGRAPHIC DIVISIONS

Subject	United States	New England	Middle Atlantic	East North Central	West North Central	South Atlantic	East South Central	West South Central	Mountain	Pacific
TOTAL, 1950	96,467,686	7,101,511	24,271,689	21,185,713	7,305,219	10,391,163	4,484,771	8,079,828	2,785,888	10,861,904
Male	46,891,782	3,430,186	11,780,081	10,385,705	3,520,930	4,988,722	2,132,258	3,931,912	1,379,146	5,342,842
Female	49,575,904	3,671,325	12,491,608	10,800,008	3,784,289	5,402,441	2,352,513	4,147,916	1,406,742	5,519,062
White	86,756,435	6,963,451	22,463,620	19,437,512	6,916,749	7,936,269	3,329,435	6,768,316	2,712,506	10,228,597
Nonwhite	9,711,251	138,060	1,808,069	1,748,201	388,470	2,454,894	1,155,356	1,311,512	73,382	633,307
RACE AND NATIVITY										
Native white	78,267,570	5,879,254	18,921,462	17,615,133	6,588,763	7,638,526	3,293,458	6,545,204	2,569,493	9,216,277
Foreign-born white	8,488,865	1,084,197	3,542,158	1,822,379	327,986	297,743	35,957	223,112	143,013	1,012,320
Negro	9,392,608	130,566	1,767,233	1,714,094	375,194	2,445,469	1,153,642	1,291,752	50,881	463,777
Other races, total	318,643	7,494	40,836	34,107	13,276	9,425	1,714	19,760	22,501	169,530
MARITAL STATUS, ALL SEX-COLOR GROUPS	74,249,865	5,531,937	19,093,698	16,303,460	5,636,742	7,899,115	3,354,696	5,981,959	2,045,826	8,402,432
Single	16,863,942	1,523,964	4,807,101	3,577,459	1,268,816	1,746,359	694,020	1,184,202	429,769	1,632,252
Married	49,105,685	3,423,622	12,356,579	10,923,150	3,711,507	5,267,795	2,254,335	4,098,044	1,389,905	5,680,748
Widowed and divorced	8,280,238	584,351	1,930,018	1,802,851	656,419	884,961	406,341	699,713	226,152	1,089,432
MARITAL STATUS, WHITE MALE	32,240,205	2,578,974	8,505,537	7,273,224	2,534,372	2,906,703	1,186,515	2,432,403	975,768	3,846,709
Single	8,013,863	743,230	2,295,910	1,752,936	607,171	690,700	267,073	554,544	232,271	870,028
Married	22,213,015	1,673,726	5,726,000	5,034,322	1,760,498	2,062,986	855,393	1,739,045	678,343	2,682,702
Widowed and divorced	2,013,327	162,018	483,627	485,966	166,703	153,017	64,049	138,814	65,154	293,979
MARITAL STATUS, WHITE FEMALE	34,818,431	2,849,875	9,213,464	7,721,970	2,809,134	3,199,537	1,331,243	2,598,052	1,016,053	4,079,103
Single	7,241,456	752,256	2,156,065	1,560,276	602,332	628,618	255,032	446,373	184,498	656,006
Married	22,292,849	1,688,755	5,770,711	5,025,315	1,765,895	2,075,242	861,575	1,742,184	677,923	2,685,249
Widowed and divorced	5,284,126	408,864	1,286,688	1,136,379	440,907	495,677	214,636	409,495	153,632	737,848
MARITAL STATUS, NONWHITE MALE	3,387,189	51,447	639,206	636,212	140,015	824,894	378,675	439,487	28,272	248,981
Single	880,586	16,437	184,991	152,864	33,348	224,585	90,940	100,899	8,284	68,238
Married	2,243,388	30,814	413,202	427,859	91,436	544,548	257,959	298,955	17,323	161,292
Widowed and divorced	263,215	4,196	41,013	55,489	15,231	55,761	29,776	39,633	2,665	19,451
MARITAL STATUS, NONWHITE FEMALE	3,804,040	51,641	735,491	672,054	153,221	967,981	458,263	512,017	25,733	227,639
Single	728,037	12,041	170,135	111,383	25,965	202,456	80,975	82,386	4,716	37,980
Married	2,356,433	30,327	446,666	435,654	93,678	585,019	279,408	317,860	16,316	151,505
Widowed and divorced	719,570	9,273	118,690	125,017	33,578	180,506	97,880	111,771	4,701	38,154
HOUSEHOLD DATA	22,888,935	1,598,900	5,741,420	5,139,745	1,756,430	2,379,030	1,033,955	1,916,060	656,880	2,666,515
Married couples, with own household	21,251,250	1,482,195	5,250,215	4,766,610	1,660,410	2,173,500	954,185	1,801,585	627,295	2,535,255
Married couples, without own household	1,637,685	116,705	491,205	373,135	96,020	205,530	79,770	114,475	29,585	131,260
Families	25,373,215	1,801,395	6,366,320	5,611,905	1,944,640	2,675,230	1,164,155	2,124,975	722,785	2,961,810
Unrelated individuals	8,411,855	569,675	1,887,965	1,735,160	729,170	996,175	348,140	661,680	259,585	1,224,305
Number of households	28,509,435	2,012,071	7,049,051	6,254,465	2,221,222	2,950,484	1,283,131	2,383,524	837,019	3,518,468
Population in households	92,414,222	6,770,415	23,379,577	20,359,302	6,946,709	9,854,485	4,319,394	7,769,618	2,660,155	10,354,567
Institutional population	773,036	77,775	187,719	149,594	75,966	91,297	30,085	53,578	23,667	83,355
RESIDENCE IN 1949										
Population 1 year old and over, 1950	94,262,470	6,948,075	23,792,805	20,663,800	7,132,065	10,148,730	4,374,680	7,877,000	2,710,880	10,614,435
Same house as in 1950	76,313,925	6,071,685	20,911,835	17,095,040	5,653,040	7,795,225	3,338,735	5,721,830	1,952,125	7,774,410
Different house, same county	10,774,750	534,730	1,584,780	2,367,925	846,315	1,314,735	666,170	1,271,910	409,910	1,778,275
Different county or abroad	5,535,795	236,195	847,165	903,280	503,120	820,070	302,785	765,070	310,870	847,240
Residence not reported	1,638,000	105,465	449,025	297,555	129,590	218,700	66,990	118,190	37,975	214,510
INCOME IN 1949 OF FAMILIES										
Number reporting	24,078,530	1,698,885	6,014,870	5,330,605	1,844,430	2,524,050	1,112,415	2,027,605	690,300	2,835,370
Less than $500	1,437,495	97,420	372,145	265,890	106,225	178,160	94,225	140,080	38,300	145,050
$500–$999	962,760	53,225	170,110	159,120	75,590	141,535	83,385	146,455	30,665	102,675
$1,000–$1,499	1,233,435	76,155	243,660	195,345	96,090	182,815	101,745	167,525	38,180	131,920
$1,500–$1,999	1,467,095	100,720	310,060	231,790	112,270	219,620	114,735	179,715	44,600	153,585
$2,000–$2,499	2,143,600	169,100	525,000	393,130	176,125	266,160	128,585	216,620	62,320	206,560
$2,500–$2,999	2,310,845	195,545	605,925	491,840	190,710	241,335	107,695	182,515	67,145	228,135
$3,000–$3,499	2,880,840	222,805	757,350	691,340	233,675	256,900	108,830	200,100	86,420	323,420
$3,500–$3,999	2,279,050	162,960	558,400	554,710	186,945	197,965	83,105	162,590	69,920	302,455
$4,000–$4,499	1,988,070	140,655	511,290	489,040	155,680	169,485	66,920	138,570	57,475	259,055
$4,500–$4,999	1,431,965	100,100	346,320	357,725	111,735	127,645	48,350	102,185	42,510	195,395
$5,000–$5,999	2,271,110	153,195	601,775	576,440	161,975	199,625	69,070	148,040	60,910	300,080
$6,000–$6,999	1,280,370	80,270	333,880	332,070	84,015	115,640	37,905	83,785	33,775	179,030
$7,000–$9,999	1,462,360	90,115	412,330	372,115	89,340	136,565	39,730	88,475	34,655	199,035
$10,000 and over	929,435	56,620	266,625	220,050	64,055	90,600	28,135	70,950	23,425	108,975
Income not reported	1,294,685	102,510	351,450	281,300	100,210	151,180	51,740	97,370	32,485	126,440
COUNTRY OF BIRTH OF FOREIGN-BORN	8,488,865	1,084,197	3,542,158	1,822,379	327,986	297,743	35,957	223,112	143,013	1,012,320
Northwestern Europe	1,870,749	258,805	679,498	385,395	115,186	65,149	8,579	23,878	45,717	288,542
England, Scotland and Wales	691,031	97,100	246,122	145,768	19,101	34,841	4,724	10,913	17,485	114,977
Irish Free State (Eire)	464,043	104,973	244,834	56,879	8,996	9,784	1,224	3,148	4,203	30,002
Northern Ireland	13,769	2,672	6,614	1,896	219	381	37	76	155	1,719
Norway, Sweden, Denmark	453,503	39,659	96,322	112,654	76,202	9,483	936	4,317	16,382	97,548
France	88,893	7,635	37,547	13,041	2,711	5,273	799	3,013	1,782	17,092
Other	159,510	6,766	48,059	55,157	7,957	5,387	859	2,411	5,710	27,204
Central Europe	2,446,396	135,824	1,171,953	748,302	99,652	72,622	8,981	24,945	25,627	158,490
Germany	776,525	29,472	357,053	207,422	48,193	29,146	5,373	13,672	11,696	74,498
Poland	762,289	75,542	373,813	241,557	15,794	21,119	1,786	4,208	3,145	25,325
Austria, Hungary, Czechoslavakia, Yugoslavia	907,582	30,810	441,087	299,323	35,665	22,357	1,822	7,065	10,786	58,667
Eastern Europe	1,086,780	112,914	564,698	201,629	42,197	46,799	3,631	7,400	12,677	94,835
Russia (U.S.S.R)	820,512	76,442	466,489	119,598	29,997	37,213	2,960	5,991	10,189	71,633
Other	266,268	36,472	98,209	82,031	12,200	9,586	671	1,409	2,488	23,202
Southern Europe	1,543,306	237,370	843,386	222,561	25,036	49,298	5,781	14,926	15,466	129,482
Italy	1,301,875	189,138	765,203	177,760	18,847	31,499	3,826	11,101	9,877	94,624
Greece, Spain, Portugal	241,431	48,232	78,183	44,801	6,189	17,799	1,955	3,825	5,589	34,858
Other Europe	66,502	8,563	23,661	17,456	3,659	3,234	593	967	787	7,582
Asia	162,570	24,847	56,107	29,149	4,230	11,076	1,949	4,535	2,252	28,425
Canada	791,208	281,391	121,746	172,922	23,678	23,728	2,630	7,615	13,727	143,771
Mexico	309,630	442	5,637	21,135	7,987	1,185	277	127,910	23,158	121,899
Other America	109,335	4,992	50,692	7,832	1,804	17,045	1,079	5,709	1,264	18,918
Remainder of the world	102,389	19,049	24,780	15,998	4,557	7,607	2,457	5,227	2,338	20,376

APPENDIX

TABLE 11.

POPULATION: RACE, NATIVITY, MARITAL STATUS, HOUSEHOLD DATA, RESIDENCE IN 1949, FAMILY INCOME, AND COUNTRY OF BIRTH OF THE RURAL-NON FARM POPULATION OF THE UNITED STATES, BY GEOGRAPHIC DIVISIONS

Subject	United States	Geographic division								
		New England	Middle Atlantic	East North Central	West North Central	South Atlantic	East South Central	West South Central	Mountain	Pacific
TOTAL, 1950	31,181,325	1,809,842	4,503,683	5,510,241	3,027,024	6,158,176	2,944,336	3,243,129	1,430,508	2,554,386
Male	15,862,847	908,930	2,280,153	2,799,286	1,513,253	3,129,161	1,471,392	1,640,312	748,984	1,371,376
Female	15,318,478	900,912	2,223,530	2,710,955	1,513,771	3,029,015	1,472,944	1,602,817	681,524	1,183,010
White	28,470,339	1,795,930	4,399,268	5,421,641	2,968,597	4,888,104	2,456,061	2,726,715	1,335,660	2,478,363
Nonwhite	2,710,986	13,912	104,415	88,600	58,427	1,270,072	488,275	516,414	94,848	76,023
RACE AND NATIVITY										
Native white	27,350,570	1,635,026	4,115,588	5,215,274	2,840,285	4,832,288	2,445,572	2,669,725	1,274,118	2,322,694
Foreign-born white	1,119,769	160,904	283,680	206,367	128,312	55,816	10,489	56,990	61,542	155,669
Negro	2,491,377	11,319	96,045	73,545	26,498	1,260,121	485,215	492,817	11,912	33,905
Other races, total	219,609	2,593	8,370	15,055	31,929	9,951	3,060	23,597	82,936	42,118
MARITAL STATUS, ALL SEX-COLOR GROUPS	22,219,813	1,335,782	3,331,114	3,972,744	2,254,982	4,232,841	2,009,335	2,261,113	975,694	1,846,208
Single	4,961,668	319,833	799,046	825,825	489,678	994,219	435,730	468,859	224,557	403,921
Married	15,122,182	882,825	2,227,389	2,751,708	1,507,372	2,874,360	1,378,463	1,560,384	665,208	1,274,473
Widowed and divorced	2,135,963	133,124	304,679	395,211	257,932	364,262	195,142	231,870	85,929	167,814
MARITAL STATUS, WHITE MALE	10,362,168	659,242	1,633,048	1,969,811	1,098,539	1,735,825	836,296	972,500	485,698	971,209
Single	2,713,209	177,725	441,384	478,141	279,715	471,337	210,596	245,051	135,771	273,489
Married	7,012,619	437,999	1,091,139	1,355,313	738,974	1,186,161	584,861	671,752	317,726	628,694
Widowed and divorced	636,340	43,518	100,525	136,357	79,850	78,327	40,839	55,697	32,201	69,026
MARITAL STATUS, WHITE FEMALE	10,043,719	666,355	1,619,246	1,935,838	1,117,844	1,665,226	842,184	945,189	432,778	819,059
Single	1,748,530	138,275	328,446	324,613	197,660	290,846	145,008	143,279	70,555	109,848
Married	7,017,381	439,670	1,094,298	1,361,110	747,400	1,181,659	588,970	673,907	313,607	615,808
Widowed and divorced	1,277,808	88,410	196,502	250,115	172,784	192,721	108,206	127,051	48,616	93,403
MARITAL STATUS, NONWHITE MALE	922,567	5,838	45,546	41,061	20,750	414,704	159,980	167,828	30,506	36,354
Single	303,579	2,542	20,121	16,927	7,668	135,069	46,258	47,267	11,407	16,330
Married	551,117	2,774	22,285	20,024	10,862	253,764	101,352	105,848	16,984	17,224
Widowed and divorced	67,871	522	3,140	4,110	2,230	25,871	12,370	14,713	2,115	2,800
MARITAL STATUS, NONWHITE FEMALE	891,359	4,347	33,274	26,034	17,849	417,086	170,875	175,596	26,712	19,586
Single	196,350	1,291	9,095	6,144	4,645	96,967	33,868	33,262	6,824	4,254
Married	541,065	2,382	19,667	15,261	10,136	252,776	103,280	107,925	16,891	12,747
Widowed and Divorced	153,944	674	4,512	4,629	3,068	67,343	33,727	34,409	2,997	2,585
HOUSEHOLD DATA	6,945,150	400,535	1,004,845	1,273,325	696,340	1,312,020	633,225	723,060	310,645	591,155
Married couples, with own household	6,598,950	376,050	941,540	1,221,925	671,505	1,230,300	599,035	689,665	298,530	570,400
Married couples, without own household	346,200	24,485	63,305	51,400	24,835	81,720	34,190	33,395	12,115	20,755
Families	7,517,570	433,080	1,072,710	1,363,090	768,540	1,428,045	696,610	790,630	336,535	628,330
Unrelated individuals	2,001,210	129,270	254,310	310,390	242,410	366,805	145,165	191,990	109,555	251,295
Number of households	8,580,048	500,021	1,219,212	1,576,555	933,007	1,565,261	766,013	900,209	390,969	728,821
Population in households	29,634,663	1,711,583	4,228,002	5,249,854	2,909,352	5,867,081	2,830,664	3,127,384	1,362,770	2,347,973
Institutional population	793,682	48,047	188,092	181,467	66,295	107,745	55,156	51,054	18,780	77,046
RESIDENCE IN 1949										
Population 1 year old and over, 1950	30,333,410	1,758,380	4,372,210	5,351,490	2,950,850	5,991,105	2,872,325	3,163,600	1,386,915	2,486,535
Same house as in 1950	23,674,640	1,488,980	3,686,090	4,360,755	2,342,820	4,601,635	2,154,215	2,351,540	1,005,040	1,683,565
Different house, same county	3,656,350	146,420	358,155	558,000	317,875	796,255	454,095	436,715	186,605	402,150
Different county or abroad	2,462,555	96,140	221,925	355,035	238,855	489,995	214,790	328,010	174,685	343,120
Residence not reported	539,865	26,840	106,040	77,700	51,300	103,120	49,225	47,335	20,585	57,720
INCOME IN 1949 OF FAMILIES										
Number reporting	7,183,025	405,160	1,022,000	1,298,865	740,105	1,362,970	671,360	759,440	322,385	600,740
Less than $500	691,130	29,030	74,610	97,885	71,530	158,920	109,125	86,725	25,885	37,420
$500-$999	619,070	20,355	47,695	79,775	68,850	140,260	94,285	110,985	23,725	33,140
$1,000-$1,499	660,425	26,875	62,595	90,580	71,130	151,165	90,695	98,370	26,385	42,630
$1,500-$1,999	682,260	34,085	78,695	99,305	72,575	155,105	83,370	83,630	28,410	47,085
$2,000-$2,499	848,625	49,365	124,585	144,150	93,250	177,325	82,115	82,895	36,815	58,125
$2,500-$2,999	755,175	48,745	128,635	149,975	79,605	140,440	54,950	60,290	33,720	58,855
$3,000-$3,499	778,670	49,460	131,200	170,665	79,675	123,975	47,285	61,765	39,355	75,290
$3,500-$3,999	553,245	34,090	89,055	122,390	53,745	81,895	30,395	49,355	29,265	63,055
$4,000-$4,499	422,715	27,045	70,650	92,610	41,095	63,085	22,320	37,220	20,960	47,750
$4,500-$5,999	279,265	19,170	48,275	60,980	25,860	41,095	13,980	22,610	14,555	32,740
$5,000-$5,999	383,420	27,140	69,810	85,005	34,050	57,420	18,530	27,705	18,655	45,105
$6,000-$6,999	191,680	13,145	34,940	41,280	16,965	28,525	9,090	14,705	9,515	23,515
$7,000-$9,999	194,655	14,655	37,895	40,775	18,840	27,340	8,815	13,910	9,165	23,240
$10,000 and over	122,690	11,980	23,360	23,490	12,935	16,460	6,425	9,275	5,975	12,790
Income not reported	334,545	27,920	50,710	64,225	28,435	65,075	25,250	31,190	14,150	27,590
COUNTRY OF BIRTH OF FOREIGN-BORN	1,119,769	160,904	283,680	206,367	128,312	55,816	10,489	56,990	61,542	155,669
Northwestern Europe	305,707	40,720	67,710	55,476	53,531	15,358	2,570	4,521	17,725	48,096
England, Scotland and Wales	109,971	19,454	30,740	19,843	6,024	9,020	1,452	2,118	6,144	15,176
Irish Free State (Eire)	33,088	8,249	13,518	3,248	1,808	1,397	192	358	1,166	3,152
Northern Ireland	1,238	356	408	123	72	83	9	16	48	123
Norway, Sweden, Denmark	110,573	9,013	12,031	18,999	38,396	2,397	330	901	7,675	20,801
France	13,881	1,931	3,845	2,288	900	1,075	309	504	847	2,182
Other	36,956	1,687	7,168	10,975	6,331	1,386	278	624	1,845	6,662
Central Europe	319,697	23,300	116,775	82,994	39,798	16,407	2,714	8,160	9,969	19,580
Germany	131,008	7,009	36,353	33,839	26,121	6,913	1,712	4,347	3,986	10,728
Poland	61,052	11,008	25,718	15,043	2,294	3,130	346	965	848	1,700
Austria, Hungary, Czechoslavakia, Yugoslavia	127,637	5,283	54,704	34,112	11,383	6,364	656	2,848	5,135	7,152
Eastern Europe	83,811	10,574	20,732	17,013	16,498	3,593	499	1,198	4,524	9,180
Russia (U.S.S.R.)	46,376	3,724	13,630	5,525	11,839	2,110	359	1,005	3,164	5,020
Other	37,435	6,850	7,102	11,488	4,659	1,483	140	193	1,360	4,160
Southern Europe	115,640	18,321	47,166	15,297	2,985	6,862	875	1,950	5,991	16,193
Italy	97,008	14,127	44,065	13,359	2,503	5,164	687	1,626	4,190	11,287
Greece, Spain, Portugal	18,632	4,194	3,101	1,938	482	1,698	188	324	1,801	4,906
Other Europe	11,863	1,199	3,130	2,361	1,553	1,036	435	380	473	1,296
Asia	12,273	1,743	2,447	1,471	760	1,525	363	603	611	2,750
Canada	152,413	59,929	19,733	24,868	8,951	5,553	785	1,443	6,478	24,673
Mexico	82,612	155	419	1,979	1,716	328	118	36,332	14,253	27,312
Other America	8,538	936	2,075	858	436	1,520	337	511	360	1,505
Remainder of the world	27,215	4,027	3,493	4,050	2,084	3,634	1,793	1,892	1,158	5,084

TABLE 12.

POPULATION: RACE, NATIVITY, MARITAL STATUS, HOUSEHOLD DATA, RESIDENCE IN 1949, FAMILY INCOME, AND COUNTRY OF BIRTH OF THE RURAL-FARM POPULATION OF THE UNITED STATES, BY GEOGRAPHIC DIVISIONS

Subject	United States	New England	Middle Atlantic	East North Central	West North Central	South Atlantic	East South Central	West South Central	Mountain	Pacific
					Geographic division					
TOTAL, 1950	23,048,350	403,100	1,388,161	3,703,414	3,729,151	4,632,996	4,048,074	3,214,615	858,602	1,070,237
Male	12,078,610	214,654	732,865	1,960,271	1,999,232	2,378,714	2,073,875	1,677,173	463,788	578,038
Female	10,969,740	188,446	655,296	1,743,143	1,729,919	2,254,282	1,974,199	1,537,442	394,814	492,199
White	19,715,254	401,775	1,374,640	3,684,154	3,690,731	3,217,336	2,985,094	2,542,219	797,468	1,021,837
Nonwhite	3,333,096	1,325	13,521	19,260	38,420	1,415,660	1,062,980	672,396	61,134	48,400
RACE AND NATIVITY										
Native white	19,162,720	360,825	1,292,679	3,563,866	3,584,317	3,200,360	2,978,280	2,488,597	763,916	929,880
Foreign-born white	552,534	40,950	81,961	120,288	106,414	16,976	6,814	53,622	33,552	91,957
Negro	3,158,301	1,056	11,963	16,059	22,486	1,389,154	1,059,778	647,459	3,636	6,710
Other races, total	174,795	269	1,558	3,201	15,934	26,506	3,202	24,937	57,498	41,690
MARITAL STATUS, ALL SEX-COLOR GROUPS	15,884,356	297,380	1,009,296	2,659,480	2,626,601	3,061,229	2,682,822	2,188,981	579,916	778,651
Single	4,146,735	81,805	272,846	658,858	682,470	889,659	701,343	526,428	151,383	181,943
Married	10,675,586	189,419	662,018	1,822,210	1,804,727	1,956,953	1,789,555	1,514,707	394,107	541,890
Widowed and divorced	1,062,035	26,156	74,432	178,412	139,404	214,617	191,924	147,846	34,426	54,818
MARITAL STATUS, WHITE MALE	7,376,637	159,172	532,105	1,413,058	1,417,708	1,152,040	1,058,245	940,523	299,926	403,860
Single	2,260,197	51,598	168,884	421,046	454,488	369,853	319,897	265,359	94,653	114,419
Married	4,754,974	96,582	332,185	914,918	902,970	731,325	690,320	631,587	189,496	265,591
Widowed and divorced	361,466	10,992	31,036	77,094	60,250	50,862	48,028	43,577	15,777	23,850
MARITAL STATUS, WHITE FEMALE	6,491,965	137,241	467,668	1,233,060	1,184,742	1,069,649	985,082	833,051	242,365	339,107
Single	1,282,052	29,870	101,163	234,290	221,127	210,643	207,293	149,402	44,514	53,730
Married	4,667,250	92,302	323,866	898,914	886,611	724,744	685,918	615,540	182,390	256,965
Widowed and divorced	542,683	15,069	42,639	99,856	77,004	104,262	91,871	68,109	15,461	28,412
MARITAL STATUS, NONWHITE MALE	1,022,851	557	5,379	7,192	12,947	424,457	317,679	211,003	20,101	23,536
Single	346,645	222	1,820	2,244	4,210	157,083	98,345	64,336	7,510	10,875
Married	624,504	292	3,197	4,280	7,679	249,148	203,695	133,889	11,109	11,215
Widowed and divorced	51,702	43	362	668	1,058	18,226	15,639	12,778	1,482	1,446
MARITAL STATUS, NONWHITE FEMALE	992,903	410	4,144	6,170	11,204	415,083	321,816	204,404	175,524	12,148
Single	257,861	115	979	1,278	2,645	122,080	75,808	47,331	4,706	2,919
Married	628,858	243	2,770	4,098	7,467	251,736	209,622	133,691	11,112	8,119
Widowed and divorced	106,184	52	395	794	1,092	41,267	36,386	23,382	1,706	1,110
HOUSEHOLD DATA	5,172,245	91,220	314,685	883,310	887,585	938,710	860,900	743,920	190,460	261,455
Married couples, with own household	4,854,180	82,485	286,440	833,590	853,025	857,310	803,340	708,460	180,835	248,695
Married couples, without own household	318,065	8,735	28,245	49,720	34,560	81,400	57,560	35,460	9,625	12,760
Families	5,420,195	95,770	326,515	922,525	936,410	983,350	903,640	779,795	198,345	273,845
Unrelated individuals	637,985	22,620	59,995	111,125	108,785	91,740	67,720	75,400	37,195	63,405
Number of households	5,767,852	104,705	354,545	998,542	998,938	1,021,597	942,783	819,621	218,737	305,384
Population in households	22,982,003	398,814	1,379,570	3,697,011	3,725,246	4,623,078	4,043,607	3,205,681	854,452	1,054,544
Institutional population	-	-	-	-	-	-	-	-	-	-
RESIDENCE IN 1949										
Population 1 year old and over, 1950	22,567,115	393,335	1,370,735	3,624,045	3,651,260	4,538,440	3,962,125	3,143,720	835,245	1,048,210
Same house as in 1950	19,201,535	355,325	1,229,535	3,232,735	3,217,440	3,783,760	3,266,025	2,574,235	689,245	853,235
Different house, same county	2,045,175	20,560	77,000	212,580	230,070	505,395	480,745	341,265	74,395	103,165
Different county or abroad	1,076,610	14,035	48,125	147,785	169,015	192,600	169,900	193,385	62,590	79,175
Residence not reported	243,795	3,415	16,075	30,945	34,735	56,685	45,455	34,835	9,015	12,635
INCOME IN 1949 OF FAMILIES										
Number reporting	5,178,400	90,055	309,065	877,980	900,130	936,580	871,000	746,630	188,050	258,910
Less than $500	889,460	10,435	35,180	80,450	96,105	229,905	255,945	137,305	19,335	24,800
$500-$999	744,880	7,710	24,310	77,360	92,930	171,260	190,760	146,640	16,025	17,885
$1,000-$1,499	693,240	10,015	31,625	98,500	114,420	139,170	137,395	119,140	20,505	22,870
$1,500-$1,999	572,300	10,345	33,510	97,400	106,190	102,420	91,330	86,195	21,105	23,805
$2,000-$2,499	549,130	11,415	37,740	107,350	112,535	90,490	67,670	69,470	22,415	30,045
$2,500-$2,999	374,195	8,775	30,375	86,175	75,775	54,080	37,910	41,900	16,220	23,985
$3,000-$3,499	348,825	7,495	28,540	82,835	74,925	45,710	29,800	37,570	16,450	25,500
$3,500-$3,999	219,480	4,865	18,275	56,285	44,985	26,525	16,170	22,750	10,535	19,090
$4,000-$4,499	185,200	4,125	14,855	46,945	42,045	20,680	12,305	19,750	9,065	15,430
$4,500-$4,999	114,585	2,845	9,785	30,125	25,430	12,625	7,070	11,290	5,715	9,700
$5,000-$5,999	173,465	4,050	15,015	44,775	40,410	17,550	10,135	17,300	9,325	14,905
$6,000-$6,999	98,900	2,290	8,915	25,405	24,445	8,895	4,945	10,295	5,320	8,390
$7,000-$9,999	123,435	3,070	11,640	29,525	30,895	9,755	5,365	13,615	8,115	11,455
$10,000 and over	91,305	2,620	9,300	15,850	19,440	7,515	4,200	13,410	7,920	11,000
Income not reported	241,795	5,715	17,450	44,545	36,280	46,770	32,640	33,165	10,295	14,935
COUNTRY OF BIRTH OF FOREIGN-BORN	552,534	40,950	81,961	120,288	106,414	16,976	6,814	53,622	33,552	91,957
Northwestern Europe	142,316	6,319	14,967	29,452	47,977	3,781	1,194	2,909	10,094	25,623
England, Scotland and Wales	27,813	2,490	5,463	5,877	3,444	1,887	588	1,036	2,384	4,644
Irish Free State (Eire)	7,830	1,082	2,186	1,212	1,031	315	79	147	445	1,333
Northern Ireland	391	40	109	60	62	19	10	9	13	69
Norway, Sweden, Denmark	71,059	1,932	3,056	12,839	36,138	635	195	889	5,161	10,214
France	5,150	336	748	828	490	335	112	248	584	1,469
Other	30,073	439	3,405	8,636	6,812	590	210	580	1,507	7,894
Central Europe	178,453	8,585	40,760	59,201	34,216	6,263	1,957	10,541	5,600	11,330
Germany	76,798	1,706	12,610	21,434	23,158	2,640	1,198	4,892	2,737	6,423
Poland	37,843	4,813	11,885	14,520	2,485	1,350	250	1,077	478	985
Austria, Hungary, Czechoslavakia, Yugoslavia	63,812	2,066	16,265	23,247	8,573	2,273	509	4,572	2,385	3,922
Eastern Europe	52,476	5,323	7,616	12,857	13,019	1,537	253	1,097	4,307	6,467
Russia (U.S.S.R.)	27,956	1,472	4,877	4,080	7,789	1,119	180	952	3,775	3,712
Other	24,520	3,851	2,739	8,777	5,230	418	73	145	532	2,755
Southern Europe	37,184	3,337	8,566	3,659	1,079	1,148	624	1,586	2,852	14,333
Italy	28,262	2,123	7,946	3,138	883	882	565	1,485	1,789	9,451
Greece, Spain, Portugal	8,922	1,214	620	521	196	266	59	101	1,063	4,882
Other Europe	8,010	447	1,427	1,730	1,624	785	573	450	273	701
Asia	5,181	472	477	439	343	239	79	180	237	2,715
Canada	50,941	15,381	6,717	9,808	5,707	973	244	649	2,786	8,676
Mexico	58,320	29	54	697	623	52	216	34,690	6,697	15,262
Other America	2,424	139	386	281	239	291	90	240	159	599
Remainder of the world	17,229	918	991	2,164	1,587	1,907	1,584	1,280	547	6,251

TABLE 13.

POPULATION: RACE, NATIVITY, MARITAL STATUS, COUNTRY OF BIRTH, AND PARENTAGE OF THE WHITE POPULATION, FOR THE TOTAL POPULATION OF THE UNITED STATES, BY GEOGRAPHIC DIVISIONS, 1940

Subject	United States	Geographic division								
		New England	Middle Atlantic	East North Central	West North Central	South Atlantic	East South Central	West South Central	Mountain	Pacific
TOTAL, 1940	131,669,275	8,437,290	27,539,487	26,626,342	13,516,990	17,823,151	10,778,225	13,064,525	4,150,003	9,733,262
Male..............................	66,061,592	4,154,760	13,710,692	13,438,325	6,829,335	8,870,589	5,366,024	6,558,293	2,149,398	4,984,176
Female............................	65,607,683	4,282,530	13,828,795	13,188,017	6,687,655	8,952,562	5,412,201	6,506,232	2,000,605	4,749,086
White.............................	118,214,870	8,329,146	26,237,622	25,528,451	13,111,519	13,095,227	7,993,755	10,569,596	3,978,913	9,370,641
Nonwhite..........................	13,454,405	108,144	1,301,865	1,097,891	405,471	4,727,924	2,784,470	2,494,929	171,090	362,621
RACE AND NATIVITY										
Native white	106,795,732	6,830,905	21,715,022	22,957,377	12,333,656	12,804,158	7,948,859	10,279,885	3,716,924	8,208,946
Foreign-born white	11,419,138	1,498,241	4,522,600	2,571,074	777,863	291,069	44,896	289,711	261,989	1,161,695
Negro	12,865,518	101,509	1,268,366	1,069,326	350,992	4,698,863	2,780,635	2,425,121	36,411	134,295
Other races, total................	588,887	6,635	33,499	28,565	54,479	29,061	3,835	69,808	134,679	228,326
MARITAL STATUS, ALL SEX-COLOR GROUPS..	101,102,924	6,693,807	21,963,558	20,877,417	10,420,305	12,981,252	7,658,677	9,547,782	3,046,790	7,913,336
Single	31,529,245	2,366,444	7,423,548	6,298,934	3,247,620	4,102,355	2,247,357	2,683,886	917,303	2,241,798
Married	60,282,822	3,713,910	12,679,087	12,659,325	6,228,385	7,723,962	4,707,710	5,948,883	1,854,961	4,766,599
Widowed and divorced	9,290,857	613,453	1,860,923	1,919,158	944,300	1,154,935	703,610	915,013	274,526	904,939
MARITAL STATUS, WHITE MALE	45,823,031	3,225,818	10,393,258	10,090,501	5,098,715	4,830,414	2,854,723	3,914,924	1,529,876	3,884,802
Single	15,915,844	1,205,938	3,813,865	3,397,495	1,783,547	1,677,048	945,821	1,262,488	537,160	1,292,482
Married	27,438,595	1,837,049	6,069,966	6,107,849	3,029,392	2,943,230	1,779,469	2,450,621	901,400	2,319,619
Widowed and divorced.............	2,468,592	182,831	509,427	585,157	285,776	210,136	129,433	201,815	91,316	272,701
MARITAL STATUS, WHITE FEMALE.......	45,605,134	3,385,147	10,556,563	9,932,021	5,011,443	4,859,703	2,861,883	3,855,114	1,404,209	3,739,051
Single...........................	12,645,291	1,130,347	3,278,015	2,663,321	1,379,569	1,339,289	750,675	929,635	342,085	832,355
Married	27,279,080	1,834,044	6,037,322	6,053,842	3,017,052	2,933,102	1,770,649	2,438,783	890,717	2,303,569
Widowed and divorced	5,680,763	420,756	1,241,226	1,214,858	614,822	587,312	340,559	486,696	171,407	603,127
MARITAL STATUS, NONWHITE MALE	4,730,717	41,770	483,479	423,676	154,234	1,594,723	933,488	864,516	60,750	174,081
Single...........................	1,677,535	17,276	179,175	141,689	50,315	597,147	305,000	278,080	24,681	84,172
Married	2,753,739	21,778	277,729	247,096	90,942	910,567	570,496	523,964	31,639	79,528
Widowed and divorced.............	299,443	2,716	26,575	34,891	12,977	87,009	57,992	62,472	4,430	10,381
MARITAL STATUS, NONWHITE FEMALE	4,944,042	41,072	530,258	431,219	155,913	1,696,412	1,008,583	913,228	51,955	115,402
Single	1,290,575	12,883	152,493	96,429	34,189	488,871	245,861	213,683	13,377	32,789
Married	2,811,408	21,039	294,070	250,538	90,999	937,063	587,096	535,515	31,205	63,883
Widowed and divorced	842,059	7,150	83,695	84,252	30,725	270,478	175,626	164,030	7,373	18,730
WHITE POPULATION BY NATIVITY AND PARENT AGE, 1940 (Percent Distribution)										
Male	59,695,815	4,112,232	13,142,936	12,938,824	6,664,181	6,583,188	4,010,462	5,356,120	2,072,401	4,815,471
Native	53,684,800	3,379,200	10,805,420	11,550,240	6,234,060	6,423,940	3,984,620	5,202,460	1,924,260	4,180,600
Native parentage..................	42,126,520	1,972,200	6,978,700	8,752,220	4,879,440	6,128,220	3,918,620	4,815,220	1,556,920	3,124,980
Foreign or mixed parentage........	11,558,280	1,407,000	3,826,720	2,798,020	1,354,620	295,720	66,000	387,240	367,340	1,055,620
Foreign parentage.................	7,613,220	950,860	2,781,020	1,834,960	793,540	179,260	34,780	217,920	202,340	618,540
Mixed parentage...................	3,945,060	456,140	1,045,700	963,060	561,080	116,460	31,220	169,320	165,000	437,080
Father foreign	2,600,980	252,880	695,980	650,460	393,200	79,880	23,600	117,780	105,020	282,180
Mother foreign	1,344,080	203,260	349,720	312,600	167,880	36,580	7,620	51,540	59,980	154,900
Foreign born	6,011,015	733,032	2,337,516	1,388,584	430,121	159,248	25,842	153,660	148,141	634,871
Female	59,005,743	4,258,589	13,198,264	12,694,110	6,490,642	6,552,821	4,003,074	5,251,071	1,920,068	4,637,104
Native	53,597,620	3,493,380	11,013,180	11,511,620	6,142,900	6,421,000	3,984,600	5,115,020	1,806,220	4,110,280
Native parentage..................	41,998,320	2,051,880	7,128,540	8,693,340	4,830,300	6,131,100	3,916,460	4,737,600	1,461,580	3,047,520
Foreign or mixed parentage........	11,599,300	1,441,500	3,884,640	2,818,280	1,312,600	289,900	67,560	377,420	344,640	1,062,760
Foreign parentage.................	7,570,520	971,000	2,798,300	1,832,480	755,000	172,640	33,660	208,920	183,960	614,560
Mixed parentage	4,028,780	470,500	1,086,340	985,800	557,600	117,260	33,900	168,500	160,680	448,200
Father foreign	2,666,160	264,180	723,520	666,440	391,480	81,200	25,620	117,320	105,060	291,340
Mother foreign	1,362,620	206,320	362,820	319,360	166,120	36,060	8,280	51,180	55,620	156,860
Foreign born	5,408,123	765,209	2,185,084	1,182,490	347,742	131,821	19,054	136,051	113,848	526,824
COUNTRY OF BIRTH OF FOREIGN-BORN	11,419,138	1,498,241	4,522,600	2,571,074	777,863	291,069	44,896	289,711	261,989	1,161,695
Northwestern Europe...............	2,816,681	390,430	925,045	594,201	323,058	65,562	11,396	30,021	92,492	384,476
England, Scotland, and Wales......	936,656	146,491	338,297	199,741	36,501	33,929	5,244	10,750	32,068	133,635
Irish Free State (Eire)..........	572,031	144,236	287,484	68,561	15,595	10,263	1,687	3,589	7,033	33,583
Northern Ireland..................	106,416	17,357	58,799	13,627	3,039	2,149	255	587	1,540	9,063
Norway, Sweden, Denmark	845,333	64,221	136,599	203,815	235,121	10,014	1,704	7,672	39,387	146,810
France	102,930	9,176	40,690	16,784	4,689	3,986	1,011	3,646	2,971	19,977
Other	253,315	8,949	63,176	91,673	28,113	5,231	1,495	3,777	9,493	41,408
Central Europe....................	3,482,449	188,940	1,556,947	1,121,325	250,923	82,919	13,643	49,711	45,515	172,526
Germany...........................	1,237,772	41,404	484,647	371,771	153,176	33,511	8,225	26,599	21,359	97,080
Poland............................	993,479	105,942	476,181	332,229	25,064	23,330	2,205	5,427	3,816	19,285
Austria, Hungary, Czechoslavakia, and Yugoslavia.....	1,251,198	41,594	596,119	417,325	72,683	26,078	3,213	17,685	20,340	56,161
Eastern Europe....................	1,439,805	151,350	724,167	280,975	98,454	46,356	5,075	10,946	24,816	97,656
Russia (U.S.S.R.).................	1,040,884	98,346	587,238	153,591	66,501	36,529	4,095	9,274	18,973	66,337
Other.............................	398,921	53,014	136,929	127,384	31,953	9,827	980	1,672	5,843	31,319
Southern Europe	1,896,886	289,998	1,029,922	269,436	35,113	54,293	8,212	21,267	27,749	160,896
Italy.............................	1,623,580	230,880	950,419	221,723	27,430	37,234	6,029	16,984	19,034	113,847
Greece, Spain, Portugal...........	273,306	59,118	79,503	47,713	7,683	17,059	2,183	4,283	8,715	47,049
Other Europe	60,511	7,957	20,675	16,744	4,445	2,135	414	801	1,096	6,244
Asia	154,321	28,470	56,288	29,988	4,168	8,146	1,976	4,346	1,761	19,178
Canada............................	1,065,480	418,657	159,399	231,432	147,986	20,058	2,780	7,380	22,321	155,467
Mexico	377,433	262	5,397	17,947	11,341	847	428	161,932	44,200	135,079
Other America	66,942	4,016	35,298	4,613	987	9,127	688	2,461	702	9,050
Remainder of World................	58,630	18,151	9,462	4,413	1,388	1,626	284	846	1,337	21,123

TABLE 14

POPULATION: RACE, NATIVITY, MARITAL STATUS, COUNTRY OF BIRTH, AND PARENTAGE OF THE WHITE POPULATION, FOR THE URBAN POPULATION OF THE UNITED STATES BY GEOGRAPHIC DIVISIONS, 1940

Subject	United States	New England	Middle Atlantic	East North Central	West North Central	South Atlantic	East South Central	West South Central	Mountain	Pacific
TOTAL, 1940	74,423,702	6,420,542	21,147,543	17,444,359	5,993,124	6,921,726	3,165,356	5,203,401	1,771,742	6,355,909
Male	36,363,706	3,123,605	10,401,473	8,610,589	2,886,820	3,312,404	1,499,898	2,504,345	876,780	3,147,792
Female	38,059,996	3,296,937	10,746,070	8,833,770	3,106,304	3,609,322	1,665,458	2,699,056	894,962	3,208,117
White	67,972,823	6,328,168	19,974,775	16,453,265	5,706,113	5,113,499	2,271,610	4,274,136	1,738,288	6,112,969
Nonwhite	6,450,879	92,374	1,172,768	991,094	287,011	1,808,227	893,746	929,265	33,454	242,940
RACE AND NATIVITY										
Native white	58,838,505	5,067,060	15,992,563	14,339,412	5,311,493	4,895,591	2,239,501	4,097,216	1,610,245	5,285,424
Foreign-born white	9,134,318	1,261,108	3,982,212	2,113,853	394,620	217,908	32,109	176,920	128,043	827,545
Negro	6,253,588	87,631	1,146,580	979,300	282,126	1,804,272	893,102	918,744	25,904	115,929
Other races, total	197,291	4,743	26,188	11,794	4,885	3,955	644	10,521	7,550	127,011
MARITAL STATUS, ALL SEX-COLOR GROUPS	59,690,675	5,133,875	17,091,172	13,964,768	4,814,560	5,479,781	2,476,470	4,059,374	1,372,054	5,298,621
Single	18,684,845	1,864,110	5,832,875	4,204,270	1,445,796	1,666,644	697,746	1,107,854	394,454	1,471,096
Married	35,025,758	2,804,939	9,789,540	8,413,222	2,853,512	3,226,150	1,485,796	2,474,426	828,393	3,149,780
Widowed and divorced	5,980,072	464,826	1,468,757	1,347,276	515,252	586,987	292,928	477,094	149,207	677,745
MARITAL STATUS, WHITE MALE	26,566,325	2,435,040	7,913,674	6,471,703	2,179,166	1,959,909	843,800	1,601,690	661,291	2,500,052
Single	9,027,045	921,864	2,900,372	2,116,308	689,096	644,494	258,740	485,415	212,051	798,685
Married	16,093,351	1,381,592	4,642,198	3,989,774	1,359,206	1,222,417	542,637	1,027,239	407,073	1,521,215
Widowed and divorced	1,445,929	131,564	371,104	365,621	130,864	92,998	42,423	89,036	42,167	180,152
MARITAL STATUS, WHITE FEMALE	28,106,206	2,628,007	8,260,578	6,718,854	2,406,587	2,134,335	939,760	1,732,931	684,028	2,601,126
Single	8,184,513	918,036	2,636,196	1,879,709	696,577	596,625	252,838	430,555	172,968	601,009
Married	16,070,469	1,384,141	4,629,300	3,966,966	1,359,778	1,226,572	542,182	1,028,760	407,293	1,525,477
Widowed and divorced	3,851,224	325,830	995,082	872,179	350,232	311,138	144,740	273,616	103,767	474,640
MARITAL STATUS, NONWHITE MALE	2,352,471	35,340	431,017	377,120	110,158	630,632	311,504	329,352	14,029	113,319
Single	797,013	13,296	157,459	121,567	34,591	218,275	95,786	100,863	6,084	49,092
Married	1,396,143	20,280	249,822	225,207	66,505	374,487	193,420	202,416	7,046	56,960
Widowed and divorced	159,315	1,764	23,736	30,346	9,062	37,870	22,298	26,073	899	7,267
MARITAL STATUS, NONWHITE FEMALE	2,665,673	35,488	485,903	397,091	118,649	754,905	381,406	395,401	12,706	84,124
Single	676,274	10,894	138,848	86,686	25,532	207,250	90,382	91,021	3,351	22,310
Married	1,465,795	18,926	268,220	231,275	68,023	402,674	207,557	216,011	6,981	46,128
Widowed and divorced	523,604	5,668	78,835	79,130	25,094	144,981	83,467	88,369	2,374	15,686
WHITE POPULATION BY NATIVITY AND PARENTAGE, 1940 (Percent Distribution)										
Male	33,431,308	3,087,138	9,883,188	8,138,998	2,772,289	2,481,304	1,088,376	2,077,653	863,964	3,038,398
Native	28,713,880	2,475,440	7,839,760	7,012,540	2,562,680	2,365,460	1,070,400	1,987,900	796,260	2,603,440
Native parentage	20,357,780	1,312,500	4,600,480	4,929,280	2,014,240	2,156,680	1,025,880	1,789,160	633,480	1,896,080
Foreign or mixed parentage	8,356,100	1,162,940	3,239,280	2,083,260	548,440	208,780	44,520	198,740	162,780	707,360
Foreign parentage	5,709,560	807,860	2,386,660	1,412,940	326,100	131,980	24,540	112,480	89,440	417,560
Mixed parentage	2,646,540	355,080	852,620	670,320	222,340	76,800	19,980	86,260	73,340	289,800
Father foreign	1,731,200	199,840	569,020	451,540	152,720	51,920	15,000	59,180	46,280	185,700
Mother foreign	915,340	155,240	283,600	218,780	69,620	24,880	4,980	27,080	27,060	104,100
Foreign born	4,717,428	611,698	2,043,428	1,126,458	209,609	115,844	17,976	89,753	67,704	434,958
Female	34,828,770	3,271,610	10,177,064	8,344,935	2,960,431	2,652,164	1,187,993	2,208,707	880,959	3,124,907
Native	30,411,880	2,622,200	8,238,280	7,377,540	2,775,420	2,550,100	1,173,860	2,121,540	820,620	2,732,320
Native parentage	21,624,460	1,411,680	4,888,720	5,181,980	2,157,040	2,332,540	1,125,760	1,908,780	647,560	1,970,400
Foreign or mixed parentage	8,787,420	1,210,520	3,349,560	2,195,560	618,380	217,560	48,100	212,760	173,060	761,920
Foreign parentage	5,949,080	837,880	2,451,460	1,476,340	363,300	135,560	25,320	118,660	93,600	446,960
Mixed parentage	2,838,340	372,640	898,100	719,220	255,080	82,000	22,780	94,100	79,460	314,960
Father foreign	1,864,420	210,580	600,160	485,040	177,060	56,100	17,280	64,940	51,100	202,160
Mother foreign	973,920	162,060	297,940	234,180	78,020	25,900	5,500	29,160	28,360	112,800
Foreign born	4,416,890	649,410	1,938,784	967,395	185,011	102,064	14,133	87,167	60,339	392,587
COUNTRY OF BIRTH OF FOREIGN-BORN	9,134,318	1,261,108	3,982,212	2,113,853	394,620	217,908	32,109	176,920	128,043	827,545
Northwestern Europe	2,134,768	331,677	796,131	465,542	148,051	45,955	7,623	20,160	48,265	271,364
England, Scotland, and Wales	746,533	121,276	281,238	165,009	22,431	22,977	3,647	7,685	18,608	103,662
Irish Free State (Eire)	513,926	132,130	264,156	62,248	11,101	8,380	1,329	2,948	4,617	27,017
Northern Ireland	90,504	14,037	52,044	12,230	1,784	1,598	204	450	937	7,220
Norway, Sweden, Denmark	543,249	49,969	114,452	150,340	101,575	6,756	915	4,445	18,103	96,694
France	79,940	7,275	34,937	12,653	2,609	2,856	679	2,607	1,324	15,000
Other	160,616	6,990	49,304	63,062	8,551	3,388	849	2,025	4,676	21,771
Central Europe	2,742,929	149,011	1,316,646	915,140	124,174	56,720	9,369	22,353	22,469	127,047
Germany	919,580	31,649	418,174	281,224	64,507	24,361	5,859	12,864	11,027	69,915
Poland	854,450	86,344	415,401	291,903	18,683	18,311	1,832	3,596	2,331	16,049
Austria, Hungary, Czechoslavakia, and Yugoslavia	968,899	31,018	483,071	342,013	40,984	14,048	1,678	5,893	9,111	41,083
Eastern Europe	1,248,451	132,734	685,236	239,994	51,516	41,183	4,316	7,797	11,066	74,609
Russia (U.S.S.R.)	938,516	91,790	563,613	141,694	35,709	33,408	3,562	6,460	8,395	53,885
Other	309,935	40,944	121,623	98,300	15,807	7,775	754	1,337	2,671	20,724
Southern Europe	1,664,165	261,424	940,030	244,247	29,167	42,012	6,092	15,406	14,470	111,317
Italy	1,429,898	208,003	864,890	199,194	22,293	28,203	4,174	11,612	9,589	81,940
Greece, Spain, Portugal	234,267	53,421	75,140	45,053	6,874	13,809	1,918	3,794	4,881	29,377
Other Europe	50,158	7,147	18,471	14,710	2,223	1,611	303	565	462	4,666
Asia	139,486	26,895	53,367	28,305	3,350	6,861	1,694	3,444	1,129	14,441
Canada	815,193	332,749	126,041	183,055	26,948	14,122	1,838	5,011	11,512	113,917
Mexico	237,985	203	4,889	15,451	7,717	537	189	99,570	17,567	91,862
Other America	59,567	3,414	33,146	4,039	701	7,797	488	2,044	413	7,525
Remainder of World	41,616	15,854	8,255	3,370	773	1,110	197	570	690	10,797

APPENDIX

TABLE 15.

POPULATION: RACE, NATIVITY, MARITAL STATUS, COUNTRY OF BIRTH, AND PARENTAGE OF THE WHITE POPULATION, FOR THE RURAL-NONFARM POPULATION OF THE UNITED STATES, BY GEOGRAPHIC DIVISIONS, 1940

Subject	United States	Geographic division								
		New England	Middle Atlantic	East North Central	West North Central	South Atlantic	East South Central	West South Central	Mountain	Pacific
TOTAL, 1940	27,029,385	1,484,686	4,638,745	4,598,539	2,848,621	4,863,219	2,344,478	2,823,807	1,277,059	2,150,231
Male	13,757,516	745,198	2,361,686	2,357,504	1,424,179	2,455,318	1,166,008	1,422,747	671,296	1,153,580
Female	13,271,869	739,488	2,277,059	2,241,035	1,424,442	2,407,901	1,178,470	1,401,060	605,763	996,651
White	24,778,585	1,472,099	4,528,317	4,516,861	2,788,420	3,839,809	1,911,527	2,390,889	1,226,707	2,103,956
Nonwhite	2,250,800	12,587	110,428	81,678	60,201	1,023,410	432,951	432,918	50,352	46,275
RACE AND NATIVITY										
Native white........................	23,407,379	1,295,947	4,113,482	4,272,384	2,633,338	3,782,771	1,903,918	2,345,026	1,151,660	1,908,853
Foreign-born white	1,371,206	176,152	414,835	244,477	155,082	57,038	7,609	45,863	75,047	195,103
Negro	2,109,630	10,935	105,554	69,398	35,006	1,020,063	431,886	414,960	8,139	13,689
Other races, total	141,170	1,652	4,874	12,280	25,195	3,347	1,065	17,958	42,213	32,586
MARITAL STATUS, ALL SEX-COLOR GROUPS	20,055,748	1,148,341	3,533,375	3,469,351	2,184,611	3,460,161	1,651,768	2,036,510	906,753	1,664,878
Single	5,792,327	358,243	1,113,042	958,331	635,876	1,023,355	449,010	537,407	263,248	453,815
Married	12,437,421	679,736	2,129,541	2,180,797	1,319,628	2,152,566	1,050,851	1,302,375	566,672	1,055,255
Widowed and divorced	1,826,000	110,362	290,792	330,223	229,107	284,240	151,907	196,728	76,833	155,808
MARITAL STATUS, WHITE MALE	9,405,804	568,343	1,754,868	1,745,278	1,064,525	1,386,864	664,134	873,439	465,319	883,034
Single	3,089,288	194,613	614,853	552,999	345,630	455,366	200,664	268,180	159,455	297,528
Married	5,788,069	338,316	1,046,216	1,080,238	649,296	876,221	435,121	560,276	277,808	524,577
Widowed and divorced	528,447	35,414	93,799	112,041	69,599	55,277	28,349	44,983	28,056	60,929
MARITAL STATUS, WHITE FEMALE	9,041,295	570,358	1,696,140	1,661,863	1,077,627	1,354,026	673,964	852,611	407,928	746,778
Single	2,208,119	160,099	467,717	383,749	276,398	337,192	161,335	187,615	91,276	142,738
Married	5,731,460	336,239	1,039,292	1,067,695	647,507	868,013	431,303	557,334	271,386	512,691
Widowed and divorced	1,101,716	74,020	189,131	210,419	153,722	148,821	81,326	107,662	45,266	91,349
MARITAL STATUS, NONWHITE MALE	811,513	5,013	43,401	35,942	22,927	360,274	152,046	150,872	18,778	22,260
Single	292,070	2,098	18,306	14,760	8,869	133,137	49,357	46,641	8,687	10,215
Married	462,601	2,592	22,309	17,809	11,785	205,571	91,820	91,808	8,619	10,288
Widowed and divorced	56,842	323	2,786	3,373	2,273	21,566	10,869	12,423	1,472	1,757
MARITAL STATUS, NONWHITE FEMALE	797,136	4,627	38,966	26,268	19,552	358,997	161,624	159,588	14,728	12,806
Single	202,850	1,433	12,166	6,823	4,979	97,660	37,654	34,971	3,830	3,334
Married	455,291	2,589	21,724	15,055	11,040	202,761	92,609	92,957	8,859	7,699
Widowed and divorced	138,995	605	5,076	4,390	3,513	58,576	31,363	31,660	2,039	1,773
WHITE POPULATION BY NATIVITY AND PARENT. AGE 1940 (Percent Distribution)										
Male	12,751,354	743,732	2,346,837	2,348,288	1,397,527	1,955,758	951,553	1,218,125	650,458	1,139,076
Native	11,991,260	655,020	2,123,040	2,209,060	1,312,840	1,921,540	946,820	1,192,480	606,040	1,024,420
Native parentage	10,278,740	468,160	1,661,660	1,868,920	1,056,260	1,852,340	934,340	1,123,800	497,720	815,540
Foreign or mixed parentage.........	1,712,520	186,860	461,380	340,140	256,580	69,200	12,480	68,680	108,320	208,880
Foreign parentage	1,024,800	109,600	309,480	199,400	149,140	38,500	6,140	36,100	59,620	116,820
Mixed parentage	687,720	77,260	151,900	140,740	107,440	30,700	6,340	32,580	48,700	92,060
Father foreign	449,200	40,060	100,560	94,860	75,140	21,560	4,800	23,160	30,340	58,720
Mother foreign	238,520	37,200	51,340	45,880	32,300	9,140	1,540	9,420	18,360	33,340
Foreign born......................	760,094	88,712	223,797	139,228	84,687	34,218	4,733	25,645	44,418	114,656
Female	12,215,452	742,540	2,241,618	2,218,549	1,395,135	1,900,680	963,216	1,178,118	581,149	994,447
Native	11,604,340	655,100	2,050,580	2,113,300	1,324,740	1,877,860	960,340	1,157,900	550,520	914,000
Native parentage	9,988,520	474,500	1,616,560	1,787,480	1,065,580	1,819,860	948,220	1,097,880	453,080	725,360
Foreign or mixed parentage	1,615,820	180,600	434,020	325,820	259,160	58,000	12,120	60,020	97,440	188,640
Foreign parentage	939,980	104,220	282,540	186,660	146,780	30,580	5,520	31,620	50,760	101,300
Mixed parentage	675,840	76,380	151,480	139,160	112,380	27,420	6,600	28,400	46,680	87,340
Father foreign	446,780	42,180	99,480	93,500	78,700	19,640	4,860	20,120	30,580	57,720
Mother foreign	229,060	34,200	52,000	45,660	33,680	7,780	1,740	8,280	16,100	29,620
Foreign born......................	611,112	87,440	191,038	105,249	70,395	22,820	2,876	20,218	30,629	80,447
COUNTRY OF BIRTH OF FOREIGN-BORN	1,371,206	176,152	414,835	244,477	155,082	57,038	7,609	45,863	75,047	195,103
Northwestern Europe	396,805	47,963	101,427	69,940	66,091	14,952	2,322	4,796	23,091	66,223
England, Scotland, and Wales	143,462	21,348	47,433	24,894	7,685	8,701	1,123	1,766	8,686	21,826
Irish Free State (Eire)	43,672	10,242	18,733	4,188	2,430	1,447	227	409	1,532	4,464
Northern Ireland	11,490	2,797	5,229	846	563	415	38	66	335	1,201
Norway, Sweden, Denmark	141,374	10,727	16,727	24,397	47,718	2,356	424	1,253	9,857	27,915
France	15,319	1,501	4,625	2,687	1,116	815	212	637	872	2,854
Other	41,488	1,348	8,680	12,928	6,579	1,218	298	665	1,809	7,963
Central Europe	427,714	27,092	178,153	101,577	52,843	19,323	2,369	7,551	12,622	26,184
Germany...........................	169,300	7,271	48,936	45,141	36,284	6,290	1,295	4,080	4,821	15,182
Poland	81,712	12,550	41,615	17,749	2,322	3,889	263	635	822	1,867
Austria, Hungary, Czechoslavakia, and Yugoslavia	176,702	7,271	87,602	38,687	14,237	9,144	811	2,836	6,979	9,135
Eastern Europe	95,666	10,403	27,981	18,313	16,570	4,204	593	1,221	4,823	11,558
Russia (U.S.S.R.)	53,086	4,248	17,040	5,839	12,181	2,565	442	1,042	2,983	6,746
Other	42,580	6,155	10,941	12,474	4,389	1,639	151	179	1,840	4,812
Southern Europe	171,953	23,594	76,122	19,940	4,231	10,678	1,125	2,672	8,452	25,139
Italy	147,546	19,725	72,418	17,858	3,684	7,784	926	2,317	6,022	16,812
Greece, Spain, Portugal...........	24,407	3,869	3,704	2,082	547	2,894	199	355	2,430	8,327
Other Europe	6,075	587	1,662	1,126	904	405	66	84	360	881
Asia	10,103	1,196	2,430	1,233	509	1,114	231	686	467	2,237
Canada	169,372	63,150	23,848	29,673	10,997	4,613	627	1,349	6,463	28,652
Mexico	79,834	50	456	1,671	2,469	265	65	27,085	18,262	29,511
Other America	5,642	492	1,832	394	165	1,106	153	297	159	1,044
Remainder of World	8,042	1,625	924	610	303	378	58	122	348	3,674

TABLE 16.

POPULATION: RACE, NATIVITY, MARITAL STATUS, COUNTRY OF BIRTH, AND PARENTAGE OF THE WHITE POPULATION, FOR THE RURAL-FARM POPULATION OF THE UNITED STATES, BY GEOGRAPHIC DIVISIONS, 1940

Subject	United States	Geographic division								
		New England	Middle Atlantic	East North Central	West North Central	South Atlantic	East South Central	West South Central	Mountain	Pacific
TOTAL, 1940....................	30,216,188	532,062	1,753,199	4,583,444	4,675,245	6,038,206	5,268,391	5,037,317	1,101,202	1,227,122
Male...................	15,940,370	285,957	947,533	2,470,232	2,518,336	3,102,867	2,700,118	2,631,201	601,322	682,804
Female.................	14,275,818	246,105	805,666	2,113,212	2,156,909	2,935,339	2,568,273	2,406,116	499,880	544,318
White.................	25,463,462	528,879	1,734,530	4,558,325	4,616,986	4,141,919	3,810,618	3,904,571	1,013,918	1,153,716
Nonwhite..............	4,752,726	3,183	18,669	25,119	58,259	1,896,287	1,457,773	1,132,746	87,284	73,406
RACE AND NATIVITY										
Native white..........	24,549,848	467,898	1,608,977	4,345,581	4,388,825	4,125,796	3,805,440	3,837,643	955,019	1,014,669
Foreign-born white....	913,614	60,981	125,553	212,744	228,161	16,123	5,178	66,928	58,899	139,047
Negro.................	4,502,300	2,943	16,232	20,628	33,860	1,874,528	1,455,647	1,091,417	2,368	4,677
Other races, total....	250,426	240	2,437	4,491	24,399	21,759	2,126	41,329	84,916	68,729
MARITAL STATUS, ALL SEX-COLOR GROUPS...	21,356,501	411,591	1,339,011	3,443,298	3,421,134	4,041,310	3,530,439	3,451,898	767,983	949,837
Single................	7,052,073	144,091	477,631	1,136,333	1,165,948	1,412,356	1,100,601	1,038,625	259,601	316,887
Married...............	12,819,643	229,235	760,006	2,065,306	2,055,245	2,345,246	2,171,063	2,172,082	459,896	561,564
Widowed and divorced..	1,484,785	38,265	101,374	241,659	199,941	283,708	258,775	241,191	48,486	71,386
MARITAL STATUS, WHITE MALE	9,850,902	222,435	724,716	1,873,520	1,855,024	1,483,641	1,346,789	1,439,795	403,266	501,716
Single................	3,799,511	90,603	297,480	729,215	747,794	577,188	486,417	508,893	164,581	197,340
Married...............	5,557,175	115,442	383,250	1,036,631	1,022,096	844,592	801,711	863,106	217,404	272,943
Widowed and divorced..	494,216	16,390	43,986	107,674	85,134	61,861	58,661	67,796	21,281	31,433
MARITAL STATUS, WHITE FEMALE	8,457,633	186,782	599,845	1,551,304	1,527,229	1,371,342	1,248,159	1,269,572	312,253	391,147
Single................	2,252,659	52,458	173,862	400,551	405,901	405,472	336,502	311,465	77,677	88,771
Married...............	5,477,151	112,640	369,749	1,018,682	1,010,260	838,517	797,164	852,689	212,192	265,249
Widowed and divorced..	727,823	21,684	56,234	132,071	111,059	127,353	114,493	105,418	22,384	37,127
MARITAL STATUS, NONWHITE MALE.........	1,566,733	1,417	9,061	10,614	21,149	603,817	469,938	384,292	27,943	38,502
Single................	588,452	720	4,570	4,335	7,882	245,735	159,857	130,576	10,983	23,794
Married...............	894,995	605	3,900	5,286	11,446	330,509	285,256	229,740	15,089	13,164
Widowed and divorced..	83,286	92	591	993	1,821	27,573	24,825	23,976	1,871	1,544
MARITAL STATUS, NONWHITE FEMALE	1,481,233	957	5,389	7,860	17,732	582,510	465,553	358,239	24,521	18,472
Single................	411,451	310	1,719	2,232	4,371	183,961	117,825	87,691	6,360	6,982
Married...............	890,322	548	3,107	4,707	11,434	331,628	286,932	226,547	15,211	10,208
Widowed and divorced..	179,460	92	563	921	1,927	66,921	60,796	44,001	2,950	1,282
WHITE POPULATION BY NATIVITY AND PARENTAGE, 1940 (Percent Distribution)										
Male.................	13,513,153	281,362	912,911	2,451,538	2,494,365	2,146,126	1,970,533	2,060,342	557,979	637,997
Native...............	12,979,660	248,740	842,620	2,328,640	2,358,540	2,136,940	1,967,400	2,022,080	521,960	552,740
Native parentage.....	11,490,000	191,540	716,560	1,954,020	1,808,940	2,119,200	1,958,400	1,902,260	425,720	413,360
Foreign or mixed parentage	1,489,660	57,200	126,060	374,620	549,600	17,740	9,000	119,820	96,240	139,380
Foreign parentage....	878,860	33,400	84,880	222,620	318,300	8,780	4,100	69,340	53,280	84,160
Mixed parentage......	610,800	23,800	41,180	152,000	231,300	8,960	4,900	50,480	42,960	55,220
Father foreign......	420,580	12,980	26,400	104,060	165,340	6,400	3,800	35,440	28,400	37,760
Mother foreign......	190,220	10,820	14,780	47,940	65,960	2,560	1,100	15,040	14,560	17,460
Foreign born........	533,493	32,622	70,291	122,898	135,825	9,186	3,133	38,262	36,019	85,257
Female...............	11,961,521	244,439	779,582	2,110,626	2,135,076	1,999,977	1,851,865	1,864,246	457,960	517,750
Native...............	11,581,400	216,080	724,320	2,020,780	2,042,740	1,993,040	1,849,820	1,835,580	435,080	463,960
Native parentage.....	10,385,340	165,700	623,260	1,723,880	1,607,680	1,978,700	1,842,480	1,730,940	360,940	351,760
Foreign or mixed parentage	1,196,060	50,380	101,060	296,900	435,060	14,340	7,340	104,640	74,140	112,200
Foreign parentage....	681,460	28,900	64,300	169,480	244,920	6,500	2,820	58,640	39,600	66,300
Mixed parentage......	514,600	21,480	36,760	127,420	190,140	7,840	4,520	46,000	34,540	45,900
Father foreign......	354,960	11,420	23,880	87,900	135,720	5,460	3,480	32,260	23,380	31,460
Mother foreign......	159,640	10,060	12,880	39,520	54,420	2,380	1,040	13,740	11,160	14,440
Foreign born	380,121	28,359	55,262	89,846	92,336	6,937	2,045	28,666	22,880	53,790
COUNTRY OF BIRTH OF FOREIGN-BORN	913,614	60,981	125,553	212,744	228,161	16,123	5,178	66,928	58,899	139,047
Northwestern Europe	285,108	10,790	27,487	58,719	108,916	4,655	1,451	5,065	21,136	46,889
England, Scotland, and Wales	46,661	3,867	9,626	9,838	6,385	2,251	474	1,299	4,774	8,147
Irish Free State (Eire)	14,433	1,864	4,595	2,125	2,064	436	131	232	884	2,102
Northern Ireland	4,422	523	1,526	551	692	136	13	71	268	642
Norway, Sweden, Denmark	160,710	3,525	5,420	29,078	85,828	892	365	1,974	11,427	22,201
France	7,671	400	1,128	1,444	964	315	120	402	775	2,123
Other................................	51,211	611	5,192	15,683	12,983	625	348	1,087	3,008	11,674
Central Europe	311,806	12,837	62,148	104,608	73,906	6,876	1,905	19,807	10,424	19,295
Germany	148,892	2,484	17,537	45,406	52,385	2,860	1,071	9,655	5,511	11,983
Poland	57,317	7,048	19,165	22,577	4,059	1,130	110	1,196	663	1,369
Austria, Hungary, Czechoslavakia, and Yugoslavia	105,597	3,305	25,446	36,625	17,462	2,886	724	8,956	4,250	5,943
Eastern Europe	95,688	8,223	10,950	22,668	30,368	969	166	1,928	8,927	11,489
Russia (U.S.S.R.)	49,282	2,308	6,585	6,058	18,611	556	91	1,772	7,595	5,706
Other	46,406	5,915	4,365	16,610	11,757	413	75	156	1,332	5,783
Southern Europe	60,768	4,980	13,770	5,249	1,715	1,603	995	3,189	4,827	24,440
Italy	46,136	3,152	13,111	4,671	1,453	1,247	929	3,055	3,423	15,095
Greece, Spain, Portugal	14,632	1,828	659	578	262	356	66	134	1,404	9,345
Other Europe.........................	4,278	223	542	908	1,318	119	45	152	274	697
Asia	4,732	379	491	450	309	171	51	216	165	2,500
Canada	80,915	22,758	9,510	18,704	10,041	1,323	315	1,020	4,346	12,898
Mexico	59,614	9	52	825	1,155	45	174	35,277	8,371	13,706
Other America	1,733	110	320	180	121	224	47	120	130	481
Remainder of World	8,972	672	283	433	312	138	29	154	299	6,652

TABLE 17
PERCENT DISTRIBUTION: AGE BY COLOR AND SEX FOR THE TOTAL POPULATION OF THE UNITED STATES, BY GEOGRAPHIC DIVISIONS: 1950

Age by color and sex	United States	New England	Middle Atlantic	East North Central	West North Central	South Atlantic	East South Central	West South Central	Mountain	Pacific
TOTAL, ALL GROUPS										
All ages	100.0	100.0	100.0	100.0	100.0	100.0	100.0	100.0	100.0	100.0
Under 5 years	10.7	9.8	9.4	10.5	10.6	11.7	12.1	11.7	12.2	10.5
5-9 years	8.8	8.0	7.7	8.4	8.6	9.8	10.3	9.8	10.0	8.2
10-14 years	7.4	6.5	6.4	7.0	7.4	8.4	9.3	8.4	8.4	6.4
15-19 years	7.0	6.7	6.4	6.5	7.1	8.0	8.5	7.9	7.6	6.1
20-24 years	7.6	7.5	7.4	7.5	7.3	8.3	7.9	7.9	7.7	7.3
25-29 years	8.1	8.0	8.2	8.2	7.5	8.5	7.6	8.0	8.0	8.5
30-34 years	7.6	7.7	8.0	7.8	7.0	7.7	6.9	7.2	7.5	8.2
35-39 years	7.5	7.3	7.9	7.4	6.9	7.4	6.9	7.3	7.2	8.0
40-44 years	6.8	6.7	7.3	6.8	6.5	6.4	6.2	6.6	6.3	7.1
45-49 years	6.0	6.1	6.6	6.2	6.0	5.5	5.4	5.8	5.4	6.3
50-54 years	5.5	5.9	6.3	5.7	5.7	4.7	4.6	4.9	4.7	5.6
55-59 years	4.8	5.4	5.4	5.2	5.2	3.9	3.9	4.1	4.2	4.9
60-64 years	4.0	4.6	4.5	4.3	4.5	3.1	3.2	3.3	3.6	4.3
65-69 years	3.3	3.7	3.5	3.4	3.8	2.8	3.0	3.0	2.9	3.5
70-74 years	2.3	2.7	2.4	2.4	2.7	1.8	2.0	2.0	2.0	2.4
75 years or older	2.6	3.3	2.6	2.7	3.3	2.0	2.2	2.2	2.2	2.6
WHITE MALE										
All ages	100.0	100.0	100.0	100.0	100.0	100.0	100.0	100.0	100.0	100.0
Under 5 years	10.8	10.3	9.8	10.7	10.8	11.5	11.9	11.6	12.1	10.6
5-9 years	8.8	8.4	8.0	8.6	8.8	9.5	10.2	9.7	9.9	8.3
10-14 years	7.4	6.7	6.6	7.2	7.6	8.1	9.2	8.2	8.3	6.4
15-19 years	7.0	6.8	6.4	6.5	7.1	7.8	8.4	7.9	7.4	6.3
20-24 years	7.5	7.5	7.2	7.2	7.1	8.4	7.8	7.8	7.5	7.3
25-29 years	8.0	7.9	7.9	7.9	7.4	8.5	7.8	8.0	7.8	8.2
30-34 years	7.6	7.7	7.8	7.5	6.9	7.9	7.1	7.3	7.4	8.1
35-39 years	7.4	7.3	7.7	7.3	6.8	7.5	7.0	7.3	7.2	7.9
40-44 years	6.8	6.7	7.3	6.8	6.5	6.6	6.3	6.7	6.5	7.1
45-49 years	6.1	6.1	6.6	6.2	5.9	5.5	5.4	5.9	5.5	6.4
50-54 years	5.6	5.9	6.4	5.8	5.7	4.8	4.6	5.0	4.9	5.7
55-59 years	5.0	5.4	5.6	5.4	5.3	4.1	4.0	4.2	4.4	5.0
60-64 years	4.2	4.6	4.7	4.6	4.6	3.3	3.3	3.4	3.9	4.4
65-69 years	3.3	3.6	3.5	3.5	3.7	2.7	2.9	2.8	3.0	3.5
70-74 years	2.3	2.5	2.3	2.4	2.7	1.9	2.0	1.9	2.0	2.3
75 years or older	2.4	2.8	2.3	2.6	3.2	1.9	2.1	2.1	2.1	2.4
WHITE FEMALE										
All ages	100.0	100.0	100.0	100.0	100.0	100.0	100.0	100.0	100.0	100.0
Under 5 years	10.2	9.4	9.0	10.2	10.3	10.9	11.4	11.2	12.1	10.3
5-9 years	8.4	7.7	7.4	8.2	8.4	9.1	9.8	9.4	9.9	8.1
10-14 years	7.0	6.2	6.1	6.8	7.3	7.8	8.8	8.0	8.3	6.3
15-19 years	6.8	6.5	6.3	6.6	7.1	7.5	8.3	7.7	7.6	5.9
20-24 years	7.6	7.4	7.5	7.6	7.4	8.2	8.1	8.0	7.8	7.1
25-29 years	8.2	7.9	8.3	8.2	7.5	8.7	8.0	8.2	8.2	8.6
30-34 years	7.8	7.7	8.1	7.8	7.1	8.0	7.2	7.4	7.7	8.2
35-39 years	7.5	7.4	7.9	7.4	6.9	7.5	7.1	7.4	7.3	8.0
40-44 years	6.8	6.8	7.3	6.7	6.5	6.6	6.3	6.7	6.3	7.0
45-49 years	6.0	6.2	6.5	6.1	6.0	5.6	5.4	5.8	5.3	6.1
50-54 years	5.6	6.1	6.3	5.7	5.7	4.9	4.7	4.9	4.1	5.7
55-59 years	4.9	5.5	5.4	5.2	5.2	4.2	4.0	4.2	4.2	5.0
60-64 years	4.2	4.6	4.5	4.4	4.5	3.5	3.4	3.5	3.5	4.4
65-69 years	3.5	4.0	3.7	3.6	3.8	3.0	3.0	3.0	2.9	3.7
70-74 years	2.5	3.0	2.6	2.5	2.8	2.1	2.1	2.1	2.0	2.6
75 years or older	2.9	3.8	3.0	3.1	3.6	2.3	2.4	2.4	2.3	3.1
NONWHITE MALE										
All ages	100.0	100.0	100.0	100.0	100.0	100.0	100.0	100.0	100.0	100.0
Under 5 years	12.9	10.9	10.9	11.2	11.2	13.7	14.2	13.5	14.2	11.2
5-9 years	10.4	8.1	8.2	8.4	9.1	11.5	11.7	11.1	11.5	7.4
10-14 years	9.3	7.9	7.4	7.3	8.6	10.3	10.6	9.9	10.4	6.2
15-19 years	8.1	7.0	6.7	6.3	7.1	8.9	9.2	8.6	9.2	6.0
20-24 years	7.8	9.4	8.1	8.3	7.3	8.0	7.2	7.3	8.9	8.4
25-29 years	8.1	10.5	9.9	9.9	7.8	7.8	6.5	6.8	7.9	10.6
30-34 years	7.1	8.5	8.6	8.6	6.8	6.8	5.7	5.9	6.4	9.3
35-39 years	7.3	7.4	8.6	8.5	7.2	7.0	6.3	6.4	6.0	9.3
40-44 years	6.4	6.1	7.8	7.4	6.7	5.9	5.7	6.0	5.1	8.3
45-49 years	5.8	5.7	7.0	6.9	6.4	5.1	5.2	5.7	4.7	7.0
50-54 years	4.8	5.4	5.9	5.8	5.7	4.2	4.5	4.7	3.9	5.0
55-59 years	3.6	4.2	3.9	4.2	4.8	3.1	3.6	3.9	3.2	3.3
60-64 years	2.7	3.2	2.7	2.8	3.7	2.4	2.7	3.0	2.7	2.8
65-69 years	2.6	2.6	2.0	2.2	3.4	2.4	3.1	3.3	2.5	2.3
70-74 years	1.5	1.7	1.1	1.2	2.0	1.4	1.8	1.8	1.6	1.4
75 years or older	1.6	1.6	1.0	1.1	2.1	1.4	2.0	2.0	1.9	1.2
NONWHITE FEMALES										
All ages	100.0	100.0	100.0	100.0	100.0	100.0	100.0	100.0	100.0	100.0
Under 5 years	12.3	11.0	9.9	10.9	10.8	12.9	13.2	12.7	15.0	12.6
5-9 years	10.0	8.2	7.7	8.3	8.8	11.0	10.9	10.5	12.6	8.5
10-14 years	8.8	7.4	6.8	7.1	8.0	9.7	9.9	9.2	10.7	6.7
15-19 years	8.2	7.0	6.8	6.8	7.6	8.9	9.0	8.6	9.7	6.6
20-24 years	8.7	9.2	9.5	9.3	8.2	8.7	8.1	8.1	9.0	9.5
25-29 years	8.6	10.2	10.7	10.5	8.3	8.2	7.1	7.4	7.9	11.7
30-34 years	7.7	8.6	9.6	9.2	7.5	7.2	6.3	6.7	6.8	10.2
35-39 years	7.8	7.9	9.4	8.8	7.7	7.4	7.0	7.2	6.2	9.0
40-44 years	6.4	6.3	7.7	7.2	6.9	5.9	6.0	6.3	4.9	6.5
45-49 years	5.7	5.7	6.6	6.3	6.3	5.2	5.4	5.7	4.3	5.3
50-54 years	4.5	4.8	5.1	4.9	5.3	4.2	4.5	4.5	3.5	4.1
55-59 years	3.2	3.8	3.4	3.5	4.1	2.9	3.2	3.5	2.6	3.1
60-64 years	2.5	3.2	2.5	2.5	3.2	2.3	2.5	2.7	2.1	2.3
65-69 years	2.7	2.9	2.1	2.2	3.3	2.6	3.2	3.4	1.9	1.9
70-74 years	1.4	1.8	1.2	1.2	1.9	1.4	1.7	1.6	1.2	1.0
75 years and older	1.6	2.0	1.2	1.3	2.1	1.5	2.0	1.9	1.7	1.1

TABLE 18

PERCENT DISTRIBUTION: AGE BY COLOR AND SEX FOR THE URBAN POPULATION OF THE UNITED STATES, BY GEOGRAPHIC DIVISIONS: 1950

Age by color and sex	United States	Geographic Division								
		New England	Middle Atlantic	East North Central	West North Central	South Atlantic	East South Central	West South Central	Mountain	Pacific
TOTAL, ALL GROUPS										
All ages	100.0	100.0	100.0	100.0	100.0	100.0	100.0	100.0	100.0	100.0
Under 5 years	10.1	9.5	9.1	10.2	10.2	10.6	11.1	11.6	11.7	10.3
5-9 years	7.8	7.6	2.3	7.8	7.6	8.1	8.4	8.8	8.9	7.7
10-14 years	6.3	6.2	6.0	6.3	6.2	6.5	7.0	6.9	7.3	5.8
15-19 years	6.4	6.6	6.2	6.2	6.6	6.8	7.2	7.2	7.0	5.6
20-24 years	8.0	7.7	7.6	7.9	8.3	8.8	9.0	8.9	8.2	7.3
25-29 years	8.7	8.1	8.4	8.7	8.4	9.5	9.1	9.2	8.6	8.9
30-34 years	8.1	7.8	8.2	8.1	7.4	8.6	7.9	7.9	7.9	8.5
35-39 years	7.8	7.4	8.1	7.7	7.1	8.2	7.8	7.7	7.4	8.2
40-44 years	7.1	6.8	7.5	7.1	6.7	7.2	7.0	6.9	6.6	7.3
45-49 years	6.4	6.3	6.8	6.4	6.2	6.1	6.0	6.0	5.6	6.4
50-54 years	5.8	6.1	6.5	5.9	5.8	5.3	5.1	5.0	5.0	5.8
55-59 years	5.0	5.6	5.5	5.3	5.3	4.2	4.1	4.0	4.4	5.0
60-64 years	4.2	4.7	4.5	4.4	4.5	3.4	3.3	3.2	3.8	4.4
65-69 years	3.4	3.8	3.5	3.4	3.7	2.9	3.0	2.8	3.1	3.6
70-74 years	2.3	2.7	2.3	2.2	2.6	1.9	1.9	1.8	2.2	2.5
75 years or older	2.5	3.2	2.4	2.5	3.2	2.0	2.1	2.0	2.4	2.8
WHITE MALE										
All ages	100.0	100.0	100.0	100.0	100.0	100.0	100.0	100.0	100.0	100.0
Under 5 years	10.5	10.0	9.5	10.5	10.8	10.9	11.4	11.9	12.0	10.6
5-9 years	8.1	8.1	7.6	8.0	8.0	8.2	8.6	9.0	9.2	7.9
10-14 years	6.4	6.4	6.2	6.4	6.4	6.3	6.9	7.0	7.4	5.9
15-19 years	6.2	6.6	6.1	6.0	6.3	6.4	6.8	7.1	6.6	5.7
20-24 years	7.8	7.7	7.3	7.6	8.1	8.7	8.8	8.8	7.9	7.2
25-29 years	8.6	8.2	8.1	8.5	8.6	9.6	9.5	9.4	8.6	8.6
30-34 years	8.0	7.8	7.9	7.9	7.5	8.8	8.3	8.1	7.9	8.4
35-39 years	7.7	7.4	7.9	7.6	7.1	8.1	7.7	7.6	7.3	8.1
40-44 years	7.1	6.8	7.5	7.0	6.7	7.2	7.0	7.0	6.7	7.3
45-49 years	6.4	6.2	6.9	6.5	6.1	6.1	5.9	5.9	5.6	6.6
50-54 years	5.9	6.0	6.6	6.1	5.4	5.4	5.1	5.0	5.0	5.9
55-59 years	5.2	5.6	5.8	5.6	5.3	4.4	4.2	4.0	4.4	5.1
60-64 years	4.3	4.7	4.8	4.6	4.6	3.5	3.4	3.2	3.8	4.4
65-69 years	3.3	3.6	3.5	3.4	3.6	2.7	2.7	2.5	3.1	3.5
70-74 years	2.2	2.4	2.2	2.2	2.5	1.8	1.8	1.7	2.1	2.3
75 years or older	2.2	2.6	2.1	2.2	2.9	1.8	1.8	1.8	2.3	2.4
WHITE FEMALE										
All ages	100.0	100.0	100.0	100.0	100.0	100.0	100.0	100.0	100.0	100.0
Under 5 years	9.5	8.9	8.6	9.7	9.7	9.8	10.3	11.0	11.4	9.8
5-9 years	7.4	7.2	7.0	7.5	7.2	7.4	7.8	8.4	8.7	7.4
10-14 years	6.0	5.9	5.7	6.1	5.9	5.9	6.4	6.6	7.2	5.6
15-19 years	6.4	6.5	6.1	6.3	7.0	6.6	7.3	7.3	7.2	5.6
20-24 years	8.1	7.6	7.7	8.0	8.5	8.8	9.5	9.2	8.4	7.3
25-29 years	8.7	8.0	8.4	8.6	8.2	9.5	9.3	9.3	8.6	8.8
30-34 years	8.1	7.8	8.2	8.1	7.4	8.6	8.0	7.9	7.9	8.3
35-39 years	7.8	7.5	8.1	7.7	7.1	8.1	7.6	7.7	7.4	8.1
40-44 years	7.1	6.9	7.5	7.0	6.7	7.2	7.0	6.9	6.5	7.2
45-49 years	6.3	6.3	6.8	6.3	6.2	6.1	5.9	5.9	5.5	6.3
50-54 years	5.9	6.3	6.5	5.9	5.9	5.4	5.1	4.9	5.0	5.8
55-59 years	5.2	5.6	5.6	5.3	5.3	4.6	4.3	4.1	4.3	5.2
60-64 years	4.3	4.7	4.6	4.4	4.6	3.8	3.6	3.4	3.8	4.6
65-69 years	3.6	4.0	3.7	3.6	3.9	3.3	3.1	2.9	3.2	3.9
70-74 years	2.5	3.0	2.6	2.5	2.8	2.3	2.2	2.0	2.2	2.8
75 years or older	3.0	3.7	2.9	3.0	3.7	2.6	2.6	2.4	2.7	3.3
NONWHITE MALE										
All ages	100.0	100.0	100.0	100.0	100.0	100.0	100.0	100.0	100.0	100.0
Under 5 years	11.9	11.2	11.0	11.4	10.8	12.4	12.9	12.8	11.4	11.6
5-9 years	8.9	8.2	8.2	8.4	8.4	9.5	9.8	9.6	8.2	7.5
10-14 years	7.6	7.7	7.3	7.2	7.7	8.1	8.3	8.0	7.3	6.1
15-19 years	6.8	6.8	6.4	6.1	6.5	7.3	7.6	7.3	7.0	5.6
20-24 years	7.9	9.0	7.8	8.1	7.2	8.1	7.7	7.8	9.0	8.0
25-29 years	9.2	10.6	9.9	9.9	8.2	9.0	7.8	8.2	9.4	11.0
30-34 years	8.2	8.5	8.7	8.8	7.2	8.1	6.9	7.1	8.3	9.8
35-39 years	8.3	7.5	8.8	8.7	7.7	8.4	7.6	7.5	7.7	9.6
40-44 years	7.4	6.2	8.0	7.5	7.3	7.2	6.9	6.9	6.6	8.3
45-49 years	6.6	5.8	7.1	7.0	6.8	6.1	6.2	6.4	5.8	6.9
50-54 years	5.4	5.4	6.0	5.8	6.1	5.0	5.3	5.2	4.9	5.0
55-59 years	3.9	4.1	3.9	4.1	5.0	3.5	3.9	4.1	4.0	3.3
60-64 years	2.8	3.2	2.7	2.8	3.8	2.5	2.9	2.9	3.4	2.7
65-69 years	2.4	2.6	2.0	2.1	3.4	2.3	2.9	3.0	3.0	2.2
70-74 years	1.3	1.7	1.1	1.1	2.0	1.3	1.6	1.6	2.0	1.3
75 years or older	1.3	1.5	0.9	1.0	2.0	1.2	1.7	1.7	1.8	1.1
NONWHITE FEMALES										
All ages	100.0	100.0	100.0	100.0	100.0	100.0	100.0	100.0	100.0	100.0
Under 5 years	10.9	11.0	9.8	10.9	10.1	11.0	11.2	11.4	12.4	12.2
5-9 years	8.3	8.1	7.6	8.2	7.9	8.6	8.7	8.8	8.9	8.1
10-14 years	7.2	7.2	6.7	7.0	7.1	7.5	7.6	7.4	7.5	6.2
15-19 years	7.2	6.9	6.7	6.7	7.0	7.7	7.8	7.6	7.6	6.3
20-24 years	9.2	9.4	9.5	9.4	8.5	9.3	8.9	9.0	9.3	9.7
25-29 years	9.9	10.4	10.9	10.7	8.8	9.5	8.4	8.7	9.6	12.2
30-34 years	8.8	8.8	9.7	9.4	8.0	8.6	7.6	7.8	8.7	10.5
35-39 years	8.8	7.9	9.5	8.9	8.2	8.8	8.4	8.2	8.0	9.5
40-44 years	7.2	6.3	7.7	7.2	7.3	7.1	7.1	7.1	6.3	6.8
45-49 years	6.3	5.7	6.6	6.3	6.7	6.2	6.3	6.4	5.4	5.4
50-54 years	4.9	4.8	5.1	4.9	5.6	4.7	5.1	4.8	4.7	4.1
55-59 years	3.4	3.8	3.3	3.4	4.3	3.2	3.5	3.5	3.6	3.0
60-64 years	2.5	3.1	2.5	2.4	3.3	2.4	2.7	2.7	2.6	2.2
65-69 years	2.6	2.8	2.0	2.2	3.4	2.6	3.2	3.3	2.4	1.9
70-74 years	1.4	1.8	1.1	1.2	1.8	1.4	1.7	1.6	1.4	1.0
75 years and older	1.5	1.9	1.2	1.2	2.0	1.5	1.9	1.8	1.7	1.0

TABLE 19

PERCENT DISTRIBUTION: AGE BY COLOR AND SEX FOR THE RURAL-NONFARM POPULATION OF THE UNITED STATES, BY GEOGRAPHIC DIVISIONS: 1950

Age by color and sex	United States	New England	Middle Atlantic	East North Central	West North Central	South Atlantic	East South Central	West South Central	Mountain	Pacific
TOTAL, ALL GROUPS										
All ages	100.0	100.0	100.0	100.0	100.0	100.0	100.0	100.0	100.0	100.0
Under 5 years	12.1	11.2	10.9	11.8	10.7	13.2	13.4	12.4	13.3	11.9
5-9 years	10.0	9.2	9.1	9.6	8.7	10.8	10.9	10.6	11.0	9.6
10-14 years	8.2	7.2	7.5	7.9	7.5	8.9	9.1	9.0	9.2	7.6
15-19 years	7.5	6.7	6.9	6.7	6.8	8.3	8.3	8.1	8.0	7.4
20-24 years	7.6	6.9	7.1	7.0	6.4	8.8	8.3	7.4	7.5	7.8
25-29 years	7.9	7.7	7.9	7.8	6.8	8.7	8.2	7.4	7.8	8.2
30-34 years	7.4	7.7	7.7	7.4	6.5	7.7	7.1	6.8	7.4	7.9
35-39 years	7.0	7.3	7.3	7.0	6.3	7.0	6.7	6.8	7.0	7.6
40-44 years	6.1	6.5	6.6	6.1	5.9	5.8	5.7	6.1	5.9	6.4
45-49 years	5.2	5.6	5.7	5.3	5.4	4.7	4.7	5.4	4.9	5.4
50-54 years	4.6	5.2	5.2	4.8	5.3	4.0	4.0	4.4	4.2	4.8
55-59 years	4.1	4.8	4.7	4.4	5.2	3.3	3.3	3.9	3.8	4.2
60-64 years	3.6	4.1	4.1	4.0	5.0	2.7	2.8	3.3	3.3	3.7
65-69 years	3.3	3.5	3.5	3.6	4.7	2.5	2.9	3.3	2.7	3.1
70-74 years	2.4	2.8	2.6	2.8	3.8	1.7	2.0	2.3	1.8	2.1
75 years and older	2.9	3.6	3.2	3.6	5.0	1.8	2.3	2.7	2.1	2.3
WHITE MALE										
All ages	100.0	100.0	100.0	100.0	100.0	100.0	100.0	100.0	100.0	100.0
Under 5 years	12.0	11.4	11.1	12.0	10.9	12.9	13.6	12.1	12.8	11.4
5-9 years	9.9	9.4	9.2	9.8	8.8	10.5	11.1	10.5	10.5	9.3
10-14 years	8.1	7.4	7.7	8.0	7.6	8.6	9.2	8.9	8.9	7.4
15-19 years	7.5	6.8	6.9	6.8	6.7	8.4	8.2	8.2	7.9	8.1
20-24 years	7.4	7.0	6.8	6.6	6.1	9.0	8.2	7.5	7.5	8.2
25-29 years	7.8	7.5	7.6	7.5	6.8	8.8	8.3	7.4	7.4	7.8
30-34 years	7.4	7.6	7.6	7.3	6.5	8.0	7.4	6.9	7.3	7.6
35-39 years	7.1	7.3	7.4	7.0	6.4	7.2	6.9	7.0	7.0	7.4
40-44 years	6.3	6.6	6.7	6.3	6.0	6.0	5.9	6.4	6.2	6.5
45-49 years	5.3	5.7	5.8	5.4	5.4	4.8	4.7	5.5	5.2	5.6
50-54 years	4.7	5.2	5.3	4.9	5.3	4.0	3.9	4.5	4.4	4.8
55-59 years	4.2	4.7	4.8	4.5	5.2	3.3	3.3	3.9	4.0	4.3
60-64 years	3.7	4.0	4.2	4.0	4.9	2.7	2.7	3.3	3.6	3.9
65-69 years	3.2	3.4	3.5	3.6	4.6	2.3	2.5	2.9	2.9	3.2
70-74 years	2.4	2.6	2.5	2.8	3.8	1.6	1.9	2.3	2.0	2.2
75 years and older	2.9	3.2	3.0	3.5	5.0	1.7	2.2	2.7	2.2	2.3
WHITE FEMALE										
All ages	100.0	100.0	100.0	100.0	100.0	100.0	100.0	100.0	100.0	100.0
Under 5 years	11.9	11.0	10.8	11.7	10.4	12.9	13.1	12.0	13.4	12.5
5-9 years	9.8	8.9	8.9	9.5	8.5	10.5	10.8	10.4	11.1	10.1
10-14 years	8.0	7.0	7.3	7.8	7.3	8.6	9.0	8.8	9.2	7.9
15-19 years	7.1	6.6	6.7	6.6	6.7	7.8	8.2	7.7	7.6	6.6
20-24 years	7.5	6.8	7.3	7.2	6.6	8.5	8.5	7.3	7.4	7.1
25-29 years	8.2	7.9	8.2	8.1	6.9	9.1	8.5	7.7	8.2	8.6
30-34 years	7.6	7.8	7.9	7.6	6.5	8.0	7.3	7.1	7.8	8.2
35-39 years	7.0	7.3	7.3	6.9	6.3	7.1	6.7	7.0	7.2	7.7
40-44 years	6.1	6.5	6.5	5.9	5.8	5.9	5.6	6.2	5.9	6.4
45-49 years	5.2	5.6	5.2	5.2	5.4	4.8	4.7	5.4	4.8	5.3
50-54 years	4.6	5.3	5.1	4.7	5.3	4.0	3.9	4.5	4.1	4.7
55-59 years	4.2	4.8	4.7	4.4	5.3	3.4	3.4	4.0	3.7	4.2
60-64 years	3.8	4.2	4.1	4.0	5.1	2.9	3.0	3.5	3.2	3.6
65-69 years	3.4	3.7	3.5	3.6	4.9	2.6	2.9	3.3	2.6	2.9
70-74 years	2.5	2.9	2.6	2.8	3.9	1.8	2.1	2.4	1.8	2.0
75 years and older	3.1	3.9	3.4	3.7	5.0	2.0	2.3	2.7	2.0	2.3
NONWHITE MALE										
All ages	100.0	100.0	100.0	100.0	100.0	100.0	100.0	100.0	100.0	100.0
Under 5 years	13.6	9.0	8.4	7.8	12.5	14.5	14.2	14.0	15.9	9.5
5-9 years	11.2	7.9	7.3	7.0	11.0	11.9	11.1	11.7	13.0	7.1
10-14 years	9.9	9.7	8.6	8.0	11.3	10.1	9.5	10.3	11.9	6.6
15-19 years	8.9	8.6	11.0	8.8	9.5	8.8	8.5	8.9	10.3	8.8
20-24 years	8.9	12.4	11.4	12.5	8.1	8.6	8.3	7.9	9.3	13.0
25-29 years	7.8	9.7	9.4	10.3	6.9	8.1	7.4	6.5	7.2	9.8
30-34 years	6.4	6.7	7.4	7.4	5.8	6.8	6.0	5.5	5.7	7.6
35-39 years	6.4	5.9	6.7	6.6	5.6	6.6	6.3	5.8	5.3	7.7
40-44 years	5.4	5.3	5.9	5.9	4.7	5.4	5.5	5.2	4.3	7.3
45-49 years	4.8	4.9	5.7	5.7	4.6	4.5	4.8	5.0	4.1	6.2
50-54 years	4.0	5.0	5.4	5.3	4.2	3.8	4.1	4.1	3.1	4.5
55-59 years	3.2	4.2	4.1	4.2	3.9	2.8	3.3	3.6	2.6	3.3
60-64 years	2.6	3.3	3.0	3.3	3.3	2.3	2.6	2.8	2.1	2.7
65-69 years	2.9	2.8	2.4	3.0	3.3	2.5	3.3	3.7	1.9	2.4
70-74 years	1.8	2.1	1.6	1.9	2.3	1.6	2.2	2.3	1.2	1.6
75 years and older	2.2	2.3	1.7	2.3	3.1	1.8	2.9	2.8	1.9	1.8
NONWHITE FEMALES										
All ages	100.0	100.0	100.0	100.0	100.0	100.0	100.0	100.0	100.0	100.0
Under 5 years	13.9	11.0	10.6	11.2	13.8	14.3	13.5	13.7	16.5	14.8
5-9 years	11.5	9.8	9.3	9.8	12.2	11.9	10.6	11.3	14.5	11.0
10-14 years	9.9	9.9	8.7	9.4	11.5	10.1	9.1	9.8	12.3	9.4
15-19 years	8.9	8.1	8.4	8.3	9.8	9.0	8.8	8.9	10.7	8.4
20-24 years	8.4	7.8	8.7	7.5	7.1	8.7	8.4	7.6	9.0	8.8
25-29 years	7.4	8.3	8.2	7.4	6.2	7.9	7.1	7.1	7.1	8.8
30-34 years	6.4	7.0	7.5	6.7	5.7	6.6	6.1	5.9	5.8	8.0
35-39 years	6.4	7.3	7.4	6.6	5.6	6.5	6.4	6.2	5.5	6.6
40-44 years	5.4	5.9	6.5	6.4	4.6	5.2	5.6	5.5	4.1	5.4
45-49 years	4.8	4.9	6.4	5.5	4.6	4.5	4.9	5.0	3.6	4.3
50-54 years	4.1	4.7	5.4	5.3	3.9	3.8	4.4	4.2	2.6	3.8
55-59 years	3.1	3.5	3.9	4.1	3.5	2.8	3.3	3.5	1.9	3.0
60-64 years	2.6	3.8	2.9	3.6	2.9	2.4	2.8	2.9	1.7	2.3
65-69 years	3.3	3.3	2.6	3.3	3.3	2.9	4.0	4.2	1.6	2.2
70-74 years	1.9	2.3	1.7	2.2	2.2	1.6	2.3	2.1	1.1	1.4
75 years and older	2.2	2.3	1.9	2.8	2.9	1.8	2.7	2.5	1.8	1.9

TABLE 20
PERCENT DISTRIBUTION: AGE BY COLOR AND SEX FOR THE RURAL-FARM POPULATION OF THE UNITED STATES, BY GEOGRAPHIC DIVISIONS: 1950

Age by color and sex	United States	New England	Middle Atlantic	East North Central	West North Central	South Atlantic	East South Central	West South Central	Mountain	Pacific
TOTAL, ALL GROUPS										
All ages	100.0	100.0	100.0	100.0	100.0	100.0	100.0	100.0	100.0	100.0
Under 5 years	11.4	9.7	10.2	10.3	11.2	12.1	12.2	11.5	12.3	10.0
5-9 years	11.1	9.4	9.8	10.1	10.5	12.1	12.0	11.5	11.6	9.9
10-14 years	10.7	8.9	9.2	9.6	9.7	12.1	11.9	11.2	10.7	9.2
15-19 years	9.2	8.3	8.4	8.2	8.3	10.3	10.1	9.5	9.1	7.8
20-24 years	6.1	6.0	6.5	5.7	6.0	6.6	6.3	5.8	6.4	5.6
25-29 years	5.9	5.9	6.4	6.4	5.9	6.2	5.8	5.6	6.4	5.9
30-34 years	6.0	6.1	6.3	6.3	6.5	5.7	5.6	5.7	6.5	6.5
35-39 years	6.5	6.3	6.4	6.6	6.9	6.2	6.2	6.8	6.8	7.3
40-44 years	6.1	6.2	6.1	6.2	6.5	5.6	5.8	6.4	6.2	7.0
45-49 years	5.6	5.8	5.8	5.9	6.0	5.0	5.2	5.9	5.4	6.6
50-54 years	5.2	5.8	5.7	5.8	5.7	4.5	4.6	5.1	4.8	6.3
55-59 years	4.7	5.6	5.3	5.5	5.1	3.9	4.0	4.6	4.5	5.7
60-64 years	3.9	4.9	4.6	4.7	4.1	3.2	3.3	3.7	3.7	4.8
65-69 years	3.2	4.1	3.8	3.7	3.1	2.9	3.1	3.1	2.6	3.4
70-74 years	2.1	3.1	2.6	2.5	2.0	1.9	2.0	1.9	1.5	2.1
75 years and older	2.3	3.7	3.0	2.8	2.2	2.0	2.2	2.1	1.5	2.1
WHITE MALE										
All ages	100.0	100.0	100.0	100.0	100.0	100.0	100.0	100.0	100.0	100.0
Under 5 years	10.5	9.4	9.9	10.1	10.7	10.6	11.0	10.4	11.4	9.5
5-9 years	10.4	9.2	9.5	9.9	10.1	11.1	11.2	10.7	10.8	9.6
10-14 years	10.2	8.9	9.1	9.5	9.4	11.4	11.5	10.7	10.2	9.0
15-19 years	9.2	8.6	8.7	8.5	8.6	10.2	10.3	9.5	9.1	8.0
20-24 years	6.2	6.3	6.7	6.0	6.3	6.5	6.3	5.9	6.4	5.7
25-29 years	5.7	5.8	6.1	5.6	6.0	5.7	5.6	5.4	6.0	5.5
30-34 years	5.9	5.8	6.1	5.9	6.2	5.7	5.6	5.6	6.2	6.0
35-39 years	6.5	6.1	6.3	6.4	6.7	6.3	6.3	6.6	6.8	6.9
40-44 years	6.2	6.1	6.0	6.1	6.5	6.0	6.0	6.6	6.3	6.8
45-49 years	5.8	5.9	5.8	5.9	6.1	5.3	5.3	6.0	5.7	6.6
50-54 years	5.4	5.8	5.6	5.8	5.8	4.9	4.8	5.4	5.1	6.4
55-59 years	5.1	5.7	5.5	5.6	5.3	4.4	4.4	5.0	4.9	6.1
60-64 years	4.4	5.1	4.8	5.0	4.4	3.8	3.8	4.3	4.3	5.3
65-69 years	3.6	4.3	4.0	4.0	3.4	3.3	3.3	3.4	3.1	3.9
70-74 years	2.4	3.3	2.8	2.7	2.2	2.3	2.3	2.2	1.8	2.3
75 years and older	2.5	3.7	3.1	2.9	2.3	2.3	2.3	2.2	1.6	2.2
WHITE FEMALE										
All ages	100.0	100.0	100.0	100.0	100.0	100.0	100.0	100.0	100.0	100.0
Under 5 years	11.1	10.1	10.5	10.7	11.8	10.8	11.3	11.0	12.8	10.4
5-9 years	10.9	9.7	10.1	10.4	10.9	11.2	11.3	11.2	12.0	10.3
10-14 years	10.5	9.0	9.3	9.7	10.1	11.3	11.4	10.9	11.0	9.5
15-19 years	8.5	7.9	8.0	7.8	7.9	9.3	9.5	8.8	8.8	7.6
20-24 years	5.7	5.7	6.1	5.5	5.7	5.9	6.0	5.4	6.1	5.2
25-29 years	6.2	6.0	6.6	6.2	6.5	6.0	6.1	5.9	6.7	6.2
30-34 years	6.6	6.5	6.6	6.7	6.9	6.3	6.2	6.4	7.0	7.0
35-39 years	6.9	6.5	6.6	6.8	7.1	6.8	6.7	7.2	7.1	7.7
40-44 years	6.4	6.3	6.2	6.6	6.6	6.2	6.2	6.8	6.3	7.1
45-49 years	5.8	5.8	5.7	6.0	6.0	5.6	5.5	6.2	5.4	6.5
50-54 years	5.4	5.9	5.7	5.9	5.6	5.0	4.9	5.3	4.7	6.2
55-59 years	4.8	5.6	5.3	5.4	4.9	4.4	4.2	4.7	4.2	5.4
60-64 years	3.9	4.7	4.4	4.5	3.8	3.6	3.5	3.7	3.2	4.2
65-69 years	3.0	3.9	3.5	3.4	2.7	3.1	3.0	2.8	2.1	2.9
70-74 years	2.0	2.8	2.4	2.2	1.7	2.1	2.0	1.8	1.2	1.8
75 years and older	2.3	3.8	3.0	2.6	2.0	2.3	2.2	2.0	1.3	2.0
NONWHITE MALE										
All ages	100.0	100.0	100.0	100.0	100.0	100.0	100.0	100.0	100.0	100.0
Under 5 years	14.9	6.9	10.5	9.7	13.7	15.1	15.4	14.4	14.8	9.6
5-9 years	13.8	7.2	9.3	10.3	12.6	14.3	13.9	13.3	13.0	7.1
10-14 years	13.4	13.3	10.0	12.2	12.3	13.9	13.5	12.9	11.8	6.4
15-19 years	11.1	8.2	8.4	8.5	9.7	11.6	11.0	10.9	9.9	6.3
20-24 years	6.7	9.1	8.8	6.1	7.1	7.2	6.3	6.0	8.3	6.3
25-29 years	5.1	7.9	8.0	4.5	5.3	5.6	4.7	4.4	6.9	7.0
30-34 years	4.5	4.7	6.8	4.0	4.9	4.8	4.2	4.2	5.3	6.1
35-39 years	5.2	4.7	6.9	5.3	4.9	5.2	5.0	5.0	5.1	8.6
40-44 years	4.8	5.4	6.2	5.7	4.9	4.4	4.7	5.1	4.3	10.4
45-49 years	4.4	4.9	5.8	6.3	4.9	3.8	4.4	5.1	4.4	9.5
50-54 years	3.8	6.5	5.0	6.2	4.7	3.4	3.9	4.3	3.8	6.7
55-59 years	3.3	7.1	4.3	6.0	4.1	2.9	3.4	3.9	3.0	4.1
60-64 years	2.7	4.6	3.8	5.3	3.5	2.3	2.6	3.1	2.9	4.3
65-69 years	3.0	4.3	2.9	4.4	3.2	2.5	3.2	3.5	2.7	3.8
70-74 years	1.7	2.0	1.7	2.7	1.9	1.5	1.8	1.9	1.7	2.2
75 years and older	1.8	3.2	1.6	2.9	2.2	1.4	2.0	2.0	2.1	1.6
NONWHITE FEMALES										
All ages	100.0	100.0	100.0	100.0	100.0	100.0	100.0	100.0	100.0	100.0
Under 5 years	15.2	10.8	12.2	10.9	14.9	15.4	15.3	14.8	15.9	14.8
5-9 years	14.0	8.5	10.5	11.2	13.0	14.5	13.8	13.5	14.2	11.2
10-14 years	13.0	10.4	10.4	11.5	12.6	13.5	12.9	12.6	12.1	9.4
15-19 years	10.7	9.9	9.1	8.5	10.6	11.1	10.4	10.3	10.7	8.9
20-24 years	7.2	6.7	8.2	4.8	7.0	7.6	7.0	6.6	8.5	8.3
25-29 years	5.8	6.2	8.1	4.5	5.7	6.1	5.5	5.2	6.9	9.2
30-34 years	5.2	6.9	7.4	5.8	5.4	5.2	5.0	5.0	5.7	7.7
35-39 years	5.7	5.7	7.2	6.5	5.6	5.6	5.8	5.8	5.3	5.3
40-44 years	4.8	7.1	6.4	6.5	5.1	4.4	5.0	5.4	4.2	4.2
45-49 years	4.4	6.9	5.2	6.7	4.8	4.0	4.5	5.0	4.0	4.5
50-54 years	3.8	6.7	4.7	5.9	4.0	3.5	3.9	4.1	3.4	5.0
55-59 years	2.9	4.1	3.4	5.4	3.2	2.6	2.9	3.3	2.7	4.5
60-64 years	2.2	3.4	2.5	4.0	2.6	2.0	2.1	2.4	2.0	2.8
65-69 years	2.5	2.8	2.0	3.2	2.3	2.1	2.7	2.9	1.8	1.8
70-74 years	1.3	2.3	1.2	2.3	1.4	1.1	1.4	1.4	1.1	1.1
75 years and older	1.5	1.8	1.5	2.5	1.6	1.3	1.7	1.7	1.5	1.3

TABLE 21
PERCENT CHANGE: AGE BY COLOR AND SEX FOR THE TOTAL POPULATION OF THE UNITED STATES, BY GEOGRAPHIC DIVISIONS: 1940-50

Age by color and sex	United States	Geographic Division								
		New England	Middle Atlantic	East North Central	West North Central	South Atlantic	East South Central	West South Central	Mountain	Pacific
TOTAL, ALL GROUPS										
All ages	14.5	10.4	9.5	14.2	4.0	18.8	6.5	11.3	22.3	48.8
Under 5 years	53.3	60.0	56.8	58.7	38.0	46.9	26.8	39.4	53.4	134.3
5-9 years	23.5	21.8	19.9	29.4	11.9	20.9	6.8	13.9	31.3	89.3
10-14 years	-5.3	-14.2	-15.9	-4.2	-11.2	-1.3	-7.0	-7.6	8.9	33.7
15-19 years	-13.9	-18.7	-22.1	-16.3	-19.9	-8.9	-12.8	-13.1	-3.2	12.8
20-24 years	-0.9	-4.6	-7.4	-1.0	-9.2	2.9	-7.0	-0.8	6.0	29.4
25-29 years	10.3	9.2	5.0	12.5	-0.5	14.8	-2.4	3.1	17.4	45.5
30-34 years	12.4	14.1	7.4	13.8	-1.0	20.1	-0.8	0.9	23.2	49.2
35-39 years	17.8	14.9	11.8	15.2	3.7	28.6	11.2	11.2	32.3	52.7
40-44 years	16.1	7.2	8.2	10.8	3.0	29.6	19.2	20.7	29.3	44.1
45-49 years	9.9	-0.3	4.4	4.1	-2.7	23.8	13.2	17.9	13.6	33.6
50-54 years	14.0	9.2	13.1	9.5	2.2	24.7	11.9	19.3	11.3	30.1
55-59 years	23.8	21.0	24.6	23.5	12.7	29.5	16.0	25.1	22.3	36.6
60-64 years	28.2	19.6	29.0	30.1	18.9	28.7	17.4	27.6	33.5	46.3
65-69 years	31.4	19.0	32.1	30.7	20.6	33.9	24.0	32.2	41.2	56.2
70-74 years	32.8	21.9	30.4	26.7	19.8	46.0	35.3	44.6	37.8	52.5
75 years and older	45.8	41.9	44.7	38.2	31.3	59.6	49.6	62.0	50.2	60.6
WHITE MALE										
All ages	12.9	9.2	6.0	10.3	2.5	21.8	8.9	13.1	20.0	44.3
Under 5 years	54.1	59.9	54.0	55.3	37.6	52.1	27.7	42.0	54.2	128.7
5-9 years	24.7	22.2	18.7	27.2	11.7	25.3	9.4	16.8	32.4	87.8
10-14 years	-6.0	-14.3	-17.2	-6.0	-11.6	-1.0	-6.1	-6.7	8.6	32.9
15-19 years	-15.0	-19.9	-25.2	-19.4	-21.7	-6.2	-11.5	-11.2	-4.5	15.2
20-24 years	-2.2	-5.4	-12.4	-6.1	-10.5	9.6	-3.6	3.1	4.1	26.6
25-29 years	9.4	8.0	0.9	7.6	-0.2	20.1	4.6	8.6	14.3	36.7
30-34 years	11.1	13.8	3.3	9.1	-1.9	23.7	4.8	5.0	19.0	42.3
35-39 years	16.5	14.5	7.7	11.2	3.5	32.9	17.9	15.3	29.7	45.5
40-44 years	14.5	6.7	4.8	7.5	2.2	32.9	24.3	23.7	28.6	39.5
45-49 years	6.2	-2.6	-0.4	-0.8	-5.4	22.9	14.0	17.8	10.7	29.8
50-54 years	8.8	4.7	6.4	3.2	-1.4	23.8	10.6	17.2	5.4	23.8
55-59 years	20.1	18.4	20.3	19.1	9.4	29.3	15.7	22.2	15.9	30.1
60-64 years	26.7	20.5	28.5	28.2	16.0	28.3	16.4	23.4	29.5	43.8
65-69 years	28.0	17.5	29.9	27.8	15.6	30.9	18.2	24.3	37.2	53.8
70-74 years	27.9	17.1	27.5	22.5	14.2	43.4	33.0	37.9	31.3	44.8
75 years and older	39.8	38.4	40.7	32.1	24.8	59.5	50.3	54.1	38.6	48.3
WHITE FEMALE										
All ages	15.4	10.8	9.2	13.3	4.6	23.2	10.5	14.7	23.7	48.8
Under 5 years	53.3	58.8	53.5	54.5	37.0	50.7	27.1	40.7	53.1	129.1
5-9 years	23.9	21.0	18.1	27.0	11.1	24.3	8.6	16.0	30.1	86.7
10-14 years	-6.7	-15.0	-18.4	-6.7	-12.3	-1.1	-6.4	-7.7	7.1	32.1
15-19 years	-14.7	-18.0	-22.9	-17.1	-19.5	-8.7	-12.3	-13.3	-4.7	8.8
20-24 years	-1.0	-5.5	-8.3	-2.9	-9.6	6.7	-1.8	2.1	5.3	25.9
25-29 years	11.2	8.3	3.1	10.0	-1.8	22.5	5.8	7.8	19.2	45.8
30-34 years	13.9	13.0	7.6	13.1	-0.7	24.3	6.2	5.3	26.8	49.6
35-39 years	17.2	14.7	13.6	15.5	3.6	33.3	17.4	17.1	35.0	54.7
40-44 years	17.1	7.6	9.0	10.9	3.4	34.6	24.9	26.1	30.2	44.0
45-49 years	10.8	1.5	4.9	4.4	-0.7	27.0	18.1	22.7	15.7	32.5
50-54 years	17.1	13.4	15.8	11.4	5.0	30.2	16.2	23.9	17.2	34.1
55-59 years	26.9	23.5	26.7	24.9	15.8	33.8	19.9	30.0	29.5	42.6
60-64 years	29.3	18.6	27.3	29.1	21.4	33.3	23.7	32.4	39.0	47.7
65-69 years	34.1	20.0	31.7	31.2	24.9	43.2	30.5	40.7	46.2	56.2
70-74 years	37.1	25.3	30.8	28.7	25.3	58.0	46.6	59.5	46.2	57.0
75 years and older	50.4	44.2	46.2	41.7	37.6	67.4	57.0	72.7	63.5	69.6
NONWHITE MALE										
All ages	16.5	43.1	47.1	68.7	18.5	8.4	-3.5	-0.7	33.2	91.7
Under 5 years	51.8	104.6	112.8	149.1	60.6	37.1	26.1	31.9	51.1	272.6
5-9 years	18.6	39.4	46.8	79.8	29.8	12.2	1.4	4.6	34.1	136.5
10-14 years	3.3	23.8	24.2	45.0	16.8	-1.3	-8.9	-8.5	32.3	60.0
15-19 years	-5.8	6.9	20.5	31.4	1.6	-12.2	-14.1	-15.6	26.6	24.4
20-24 years	4.3	68.2	60.0	91.2	19.0	-11.3	-19.7	-15.2	38.2	91.3
25-29 years	11.4	101.6	68.5	99.2	20.1	-3.0	-23.5	-18.2	35.2	106.9
30-34 years	9.5	74.6	38.5	70.3	7.0	6.0	-22.0	-20.5	30.6	77.6
35-39 years	14.3	38.5	22.9	47.0	6.5	17.1	-7.8	-11.5	28.0	87.1
40-44 years	17.2	7.0	22.2	34.2	3.4	17.4	2.8	-0.9	23.4	102.4
45-49 years	21.7	11.8	41.4	49.0	2.7	18.5	1.7	1.9	26.5	120.1
50-54 years	23.7	25.6	64.5	67.6	13.8	14.0	1.5	8.4	18.8	54.3
55-59 years	26.1	23.1	57.5	72.6	19.5	18.8	7.0	17.6	20.0	28.1
60-64 years	26.0	21.8	58.5	78.9	28.4	14.6	4.8	23.0	20.4	42.1
65-69 years	26.6	34.0	69.8	71.0	35.8	13.0	11.6	22.4	43.5	89.8
70-74 years	31.7	74.4	76.9	68.6	26.3	23.1	15.4	21.5	36.6	133.8
75 years and older	55.2	79.2	87.8	86.6	36.5	47.2	41.3	58.2	55.9	115.0
NONWHITE FEMALE										
All ages	17.7	40.4	48.7	69.4	20.9	9.1	-2.2	1.1	35.0	133.0
Under 5 years	49.9	101.4	110.4	146.8	60.4	35.3	23.8	31.1	46.8	277.5
5-9 years	17.9	37.9	47.3	79.3	25.6	11.6	0.7	4.4	30.6	136.4
10-14 years	1.3	9.9	19.0	40.6	11.9	-2.8	-9.2	-10.2	26.5	58.0
15-19 years	-6.3	0.5	20.4	33.7	5.4	-13.2	-15.8	-16.8	27.3	33.5
20-24 years	4.5	51.2	48.1	83.0	19.6	-9.6	-18.2	-14.1	33.2	121.1
25-29 years	9.7	79.0	50.4	85.3	15.6	-2.3	-23.3	-18.5	37.0	217.7
30-34 years	14.4	64.3	41.1	64.7	10.4	10.3	-16.7	-15.7	41.1	226.9
35-39 years	16.5	41.0	35.1	47.2	8.6	14.9	-5.1	-6.8	37.9	161.2
40-44 years	20.8	20.2	39.6	46.7	11.6	16.6	4.1	6.2	30.4	103.5
45-49 years	27.9	23.0	58.6	62.4	17.1	21.4	8.0	14.1	34.8	88.2
50-54 years	32.2	25.4	67.0	77.4	26.0	20.9	13.4	20.1	43.2	98.3
55-59 years	33.0	26.0	59.5	75.1	25.3	23.8	13.0	24.0	45.1	113.2
60-64 years	35.6	32.3	72.0	84.3	34.9	25.3	10.6	30.3	31.1	119.0
65-69 years	45.4	39.8	81.5	70.4	46.3	34.8	35.7	42.7	31.4	123.6
70-74 years	41.3	76.5	76.4	82.8	31.2	32.5	27.2	33.9	23.7	139.7
75 years and older	49.0	60.2	89.0	91.1	32.6	39.2	31.5	50.9	44.9	142.2

TABLE 22

PERCENT CHANGE: AGE BY COLOR AND SEX FOR THE URBAN POPULATION OF THE UNITED STATES, BY GEOGRAPHIC DIVISIONS: 1940-50

Age by color and sex	United States	Geographic Division								
		New England	Middle Atlantic	East North Central	West North Central	South Atlantic	East South Central	West South Central	Mountain	Pacific
TOTAL, ALL GROUPS										
All ages	19.5	7.8	7.1	14.6	17.1	30.0	28.9	48.0	39.8	43.3
Under 5 years	75.8	57.3	55.0	64.1	70.6	85.8	89.5	122.0	94.1	133.9
5-9 years	33.7	17.5	16.1	28.7	29.6	40.8	40.3	67.5	56.3	84.3
10-14 years	-5.5	-18.9	-19.9	-8.8	-3.8	2.2	4.9	20.8	21.3	24.8
15-19 years	-12.3	-22.0	-24.4	-17.7	-8.9	-3.0	2.5	14.0	8.0	5.6
20-24 years	5.9	-6.8	-9.1	1.0	10.5	14.9	21.3	39.6	26.0	24.2
25-29 years	14.5	6.4	0.8	11.5	13.2	20.4	18.5	39.5	35.6	38.8
30-34 years	13.5	10.5	2.3	10.7	5.9	21.8	12.6	28.3	36.1	39.6
35-39 years	17.5	10.7	7.3	11.6	9.2	29.9	21.9	35.8	42.8	42.9
40-44 years	15.9	3.3	4.4	8.7	10.4	33.1	31.2	46.7	40.1	37.5
45-49 years	12.1	-2.5	2.7	4.2	6.0	32.8	29.2	47.2	26.3	30.9
50-54 years	19.5	8.7	13.5	12.5	13.3	38.3	32.7	51.8	28.2	29.3
55-59 years	32.2	22.1	26.3	31.0	27.6	45.0	37.2	60.0	39.1	36.0
60-64 years	37.9	21.6	31.3	40.1	37.0	44.2	39.8	62.6	49.8	45.9
65-69 years	42.3	20.9	35.6	41.9	38.3	53.0	48.2	68.1	58.2	56.1
70-74 years	41.5	23.9	33.9	36.3	34.1	61.9	57.3	79.8	55.4	53.4
75 years and older	56.7	44.9	48.8	48.5	47.9	81.0	80.8	101.7	70.4	62.8
WHITE MALE										
All ages	16.2	6.5	3.0	10.0	16.2	30.2	30.8	51.8	38.5	38.1
Under 5 years	71.3	56.6	50.8	58.2	68.4	85.6	86.3	123.8	92.3	124.6
5-9 years	31.7	17.4	14.0	24.8	28.5	43.0	41.6	71.2	57.0	80.6
10-14 years	-8.2	-19.2	-22.2	-12.2	-5.2	-0.6	2.8	22.6	20.6	22.2
15-19 years	-16.4	-23.9	-28.4	-22.4	-14.0	-5.2	0.9	14.4	4.5	4.3
20-24 years	3.9	-7.8	-13.7	-2.5	14.1	21.0	28.8	47.5	27.8	20.0
25-29 years	13.5	6.0	-3.0	7.7	18.7	25.8	31.8	51.9	37.4	30.9
30-34 years	11.4	10.6	-2.5	6.1	7.6	24.0	20.9	38.2	34.5	32.9
35-39 years	14.1	10.3	2.0	6.4	10.1	30.5	27.5	42.3	41.2	34.9
40-44 years	12.0	2.2	-0.1	3.7	9.4	31.2	33.0	50.8	40.4	31.9
45-49 years	6.2	-5.5	-3.2	-2.8	1.9	27.0	26.5	47.0	23.5	26.9
50-54 years	12.2	3.5	6.0	4.4	8.2	32.8	26.5	48.9	23.6	23.7
55-59 years	27.5	19.7	22.0	26.0	23.6	43.0	33.9	56.5	33.8	30.4
60-64 years	37.4	24.2	32.0	40.0	35.8	43.0	35.8	57.6	47.4	45.0
65-69 years	40.3	20.6	35.0	41.4	35.2	48.9	42.6	60.5	57.6	55.5
70-74 years	37.2	19.2	32.5	33.3	29.8	56.9	53.8	72.3	50.1	46.6
75 years and older	50.0	42.6	45.9	42.1	39.5	76.7	78.8	92.5	56.6	51.2
WHITE FEMALE										
All ages	18.2	8.0	6.0	12.1	16.4	31.6	31.6	50.5	39.4	41.1
Under 5 years	71.2	55.9	50.6	57.9	69.7	84.7	86.3	121.3	92.7	126.4
5-9 years	31.4	16.6	13.4	25.1	28.7	42.3	41.3	69.9	53.8	80.0
10-14 years	-8.6	-19.7	-23.0	-12.3	-5.5	-0.8	3.2	20.9	20.4	21.7
15-19 years	-12.9	-21.0	-25.5	-19.1	-6.3	-2.2	4.8	17.0	9.5	2.9
20-24 years	2.4	-7.7	-11.5	-4.8	5.4	15.6	24.9	40.5	21.9	19.8
25-29 years	10.8	4.3	-3.1	5.0	6.6	23.9	24.5	41.6	31.6	34.6
30-34 years	11.8	8.6	1.6	7.5	3.2	22.6	16.4	30.2	35.3	36.3
35-39 years	17.9	10.1	8.7	11.0	7.8	33.4	27.6	41.8	42.7	41.8
40-44 years	16.1	3.9	5.0	8.8	10.7	36.8	37.7	52.1	38.7	36.0
45-49 years	12.2	-0.4	3.2	4.6	8.6	32.9	32.9	51.6	28.2	28.3
50-54 years	21.5	13.1	16.1	14.4	16.6	39.7	33.2	53.6	31.6	31.1
55-59 years	33.6	24.2	27.8	31.7	31.1	44.8	37.3	61.3	44.0	39.3
60-64 years	35.5	19.1	28.1	36.6	37.4	43.0	39.9	62.5	51.9	44.3
65-69 years	40.8	20.6	33.3	39.4	39.3	56.0	49.5	70.9	58.4	53.8
70-74 years	42.5	26.7	32.5	36.0	36.9	68.2	64.1	88.9	59.5	56.1
75 years and older	58.9	46.1	48.8	50.8	54.6	84.9	83.5	107.7	83.0	69.4
NONWHITE MALE										
All ages	44.5	49.4	49.6	72.1	32.2	29.0	24.2	35.7	83.9	115.8
Under 5 years	120.2	120.8	120.1	157.4	99.2	88.4	100.0	120.5	191.0	335.1
5-9 years	54.2	47.2	49.6	82.4	49.6	37.8	38.1	54.7	107.5	169.5
10-14 years	23.7	24.5	25.7	45.1	28.3	11.0	10.5	19.1	77.6	83.7
15-19 years	12.4	7.6	20.3	32.3	9.2	0.8	5.6	6.4	57.1	35.1
20-24 years	38.6	70.8	60.4	93.4	38.2	9.4	10.7	25.7	108.4	104.7
25-29 years	42.9	109.9	70.7	102.9	36.7	12.2	0.9	17.1	99.5	138.0
30-34 years	31.6	87.1	39.6	73.5	17.8	17.2	-2.5	5.4	85.1	108.4
35-39 years	29.3	47.2	24.2	48.8	14.1	25.5	8.5	10.3	80.9	118.9
40-44 years	30.2	10.9	24.5	36.4	13.0	28.3	18.0	22.0	68.3	118.2
45-49 years	41.5	17.0	44.7	52.9	11.7	39.4	21.1	30.9	43.4	129.8
50-54 years	53.9	32.6	69.2	72.9	26.8	43.9	35.1	51.0	44.2	70.6
55-59 years	57.4	30.6	61.3	78.0	30.6	52.2	45.2	68.5	49.7	45.0
60-64 years	62.0	27.9	62.2	88.1	41.2	48.8	49.5	81.5	57.7	65.1
65-69 years	63.4	44.3	77.6	80.0	57.1	46.6	45.0	71.6	82.5	106.3
70-74 years	68.2	78.8	84.2	78.8	49.0	56.0	46.0	70.0	94.0	146.8
75 years and older	96.5	81.2	97.9	102.3	58.8	89.0	89.1	118.7	75.7	136.3
NONWHITE FEMALE										
All ages	42.7	46.5	51.0	72.0	33.1	26.1	21.9	31.7	85.5	157.3
Under 5 years	117.5	111.9	116.8	155.5	102.5	86.0	95.5	117.9	199.3	342.9
5-9 years	52.8	42.8	50.3	82.0	46.5	35.4	37.5	53.1	107.0	169.2
10-14 years	19.5	13.2	21.0	41.3	22.7	7.6	8.2	14.7	62.5	83.6
15-19 years	12.0	5.4	22.9	36.8	16.2	-2.7	1.8	5.5	56.9	55.4
20-24 years	31.4	62.8	50.1	86.7	35.8	3.9	5.2	16.7	83.0	145.7
25-29 years	31.9	92.2	52.4	87.5	28.1	6.7	-7.3	3.9	94.5	228.6
30-34 years	31.5	76.4	42.4	65.9	16.8	18.4	-2.0	1.7	102.2	230.2
35-39 years	30.9	44.5	36.7	47.5	14.4	23.8	10.3	11.2	74.8	175.2
40-44 years	37.5	23.7	41.2	47.4	18.3	32.5	23.7	29.8	60.1	123.6
45-49 years	50.3	26.4	60.3	64.8	24.3	43.7	34.2	44.3	55.9	111.8
50-54 years	59.3	27.5	69.7	81.4	35.4	46.2	45.8	57.9	78.6	111.4
55-59 years	58.6	30.5	62.5	79.8	34.2	47.6	43.8	62.8	68.2	117.8
60-64 years	66.5	35.4	75.5	90.2	48.6	51.3	44.1	78.1	60.2	134.5
65-69 years	71.3	41.1	83.2	75.4	64.4	59.5	59.8	83.2	46.9	138.9
70-74 years	68.3	75.6	78.0	87.7	44.8	55.8	53.4	73.4	76.9	153.5
75 years and older	83.7	63.8	94.4	99.5	48.0	71.2	69.9	97.4	111.4	182.5

APPENDIX

TABLE 23

PERCENT CHANGE: AGE BY COLOR AND SEX FOR THE RURAL-NONFARM POPULATION OF THE UNITED STATES, BY GEOGRAPHIC DIVISIONS: 1940-50

Age by color and sex	United States	New England	Middle Atlantic	East North Central	West North Central	South Atlantic	East South Central	West South Central	Mountain	Pacific
TOTAL, ALL GROUPS										
All ages	43.2	35.5	32.0	45.8	16.3	55.2	42.8	28.2	35.9	99.5
Under 5 years	87.9	89.3	79.5	95.8	53.9	95.0	73.1	61.1	64.0	191.7
5-9 years	56.8	52.2	43.9	67.5	25.2	61.9	48.4	37.6	47.6	145.5
10-14 years	24.3	12.6	4.5	31.7	1.7	31.9	27.5	14.6	27.3	86.1
15-19 years	13.0	6.1	-4.9	13.2	-11.4	22.5	19.7	9.9	13.2	65.1
20-24 years	25.8	20.0	11.4	30.2	-3.0	37.2	27.2	12.6	15.2	79.0
25-29 years	38.5	33.6	33.7	47.0	9.0	51.3	29.6	9.0	24.0	94.8
30-34 years	40.4	39.5	37.9	45.6	8.4	54.4	28.1	6.8	33.1	102.3
35-39 years	47.9	43.9	41.4	49.5	14.3	62.9	43.1	20.4	45.8	108.1
40-44 years	47.6	35.7	37.8	47.6	14.6	65.3	55.0	33.5	44.9	92.9
45-49 years	36.3	22.3	25.6	35.3	7.9	55.3	47.0	32.8	27.4	71.8
50-54 years	36.5	28.3	28.3	34.0	13.0	56.0	45.2	35.0	22.9	63.4
55-59 years	44.9	38.1	37.9	41.8	25.3	62.3	51.3	42.7	35.2	72.5
60-64 years	48.8	33.9	42.2	43.7	31.7	62.6	55.6	46.2	50.2	86.7
65-69 years	51.9	33.8	42.0	41.8	33.9	68.9	65.4	56.2	58.7	98.4
70-74 years	54.5	37.0	41.1	40.3	34.5	85.5	85.4	73.0	52.5	92.3
75 years and older	67.4	58.3	56.6	53.2	43.6	103.7	103.8	92.5	65.1	97.3
WHITE MALE										
All ages	42.8	35.2	30.2	44.1	16.5	59.8	46.8	27.9	31.7	92.7
Under 5 years	88.7	90.8	80.7	96.4	55.8	98.8	73.1	56.6	61.2	188.5
5-9 years	58.0	53.7	44.8	67.8	25.6	65.7	51.5	35.8	44.4	144.3
10-14 years	24.4	13.2	5.9	32.4	2.2	32.3	29.2	12.4	24.2	85.2
15-19 years	15.8	7.7	-6.0	13.4	-10.5	30.1	25.7	16.9	13.6	74.2
20-24 years	27.3	22.9	5.7	25.1	-2.2	48.1	34.7	19.0	15.2	79.9
25-29 years	38.0	31.2	28.4	42.1	12.2	57.9	38.5	11.9	18.2	81.3
30-34 years	39.4	38.4	35.0	40.8	8.4	60.0	33.9	6.9	26.0	90.3
35-39 years	47.2	42.8	39.9	46.4	15.0	68.4	49.5	20.5	39.3	95.2
40-44 years	46.6	35.9	36.7	45.4	14.2	70.5	60.7	31.4	39.9	83.8
45-49 years	33.6	21.1	23.8	33.5	5.4	55.0	48.8	29.7	21.7	64.4
50-54 years	32.6	25.2	24.3	31.6	11.1	56.6	46.0	31.6	14.3	52.3
55-59 years	41.8	35.6	35.0	40.4	23.6	64.1	53.5	38.9	27.8	60.2
60-64 years	46.5	31.8	41.0	43.5	29.8	63.6	54.3	41.1	43.8	77.2
65-69 years	48.1	31.2	39.2	41.2	31.1	66.9	59.1	45.3	52.0	93.1
70-74 years	50.9	34.1	38.2	39.7	32.4	84.8	83.5	67.1	47.8	85.8
75 years and older	64.5	56.0	54.6	53.5	42.8	107.9	113.1	87.9	56.4	84.9
WHITE FEMALE										
All ages	44.1	36.2	33.7	47.0	16.4	59.3	46.4	25.8	34.1	102.5
Under 5 years	86.9	88.5	79.1	94.8	53.5	96.2	71.5	55.8	58.2	187.7
5-9 years	56.2	51.2	43.7	66.7	24.9	63.2	49.6	34.1	41.5	142.3
10-14 years	22.1	11.6	2.5	30.0	0.1	31.5	28.1	9.6	20.2	83.7
15-19 years	8.0	4.4	-5.3	12.3	-13.3	18.0	15.8	-2.6	2.9	51.3
20-24 years	24.4	16.6	15.0	33.0	-4.0	38.7	29.7	4.2	7.8	69.6
25-29 years	42.7	35.8	38.2	50.4	6.5	61.9	37.6	8.9	25.9	102.5
30-34 years	44.5	41.0	40.8	50.0	8.7	61.2	36.4	8.6	37.5	110.6
35-39 years	52.1	45.5	44.4	52.9	14.1	71.7	52.7	23.6	50.2	119.2
40-44 years	51.4	36.1	40.3	50.7	16.2	75.2	64.4	39.5	48.2	99.4
45-49 years	39.2	23.9	27.3	37.7	11.1	63.6	55.5	37.0	29.5	76.4
50-54 years	40.4	31.7	32.0	36.3	15.6	64.7	52.0	37.2	30.4	75.0
55-59 years	48.1	41.3	40.9	43.1	27.4	68.7	55.4	42.9	42.3	86.7
60-64 years	50.9	36.1	43.3	43.6	33.9	67.7	63.4	46.2	57.0	97.4
65-69 years	54.2	36.3	44.5	42.2	37.3	77.9	72.2	58.2	63.6	103.0
70-74 years	57.0	39.2	43.4	40.6	37.5	97.5	97.8	82.5	55.8	97.4
75 years and older	67.9	60.1	58.1	52.6	45.0	106.7	107.4	93.7	71.1	110.7
NONWHITE MALE										
All ages	41.0	28.4	39.0	61.7	9.1	38.2	25.9	36.8	105.1	185.6
Under 5 years	90.5	82.3	62.0	112.3	29.0	87.8	77.2	88.7	156.8	349.7
5-9 years	55.3	15.8	28.6	80.6	24.1	53.7	39.3	53.5	151.8	240.6
10-14 years	37.7	45.7	19.9	65.0	25.0	33.8	23.8	37.4	150.6	153.8
15-19 years	28.8	25.0	43.9	43.9	13.1	18.9	19.7	32.4	136.1	153.4
20-24 years	33.3	92.8	81.4	107.9	9.3	18.3	13.1	30.2	95.8	285.1
25-29 years	23.3	72.1	73.5	95.8	1.2	19.3	-2.6	5.3	66.7	208.1
30-34 years	20.2	19.2	42.8	60.9	-6.2	24.6	-5.9	-1.0	67.3	158.2
35-39 years	27.5	3.8	17.5	41.8	1.8	35.1	8.3	8.4	65.3	153.7
40-44 years	29.7	-3.2	7.1	22.0	-19.1	33.8	21.5	19.8	59.1	176.0
45-49 years	31.9	-1.1	18.8	22.1	-15.0	35.6	21.9	22.7	79.5	187.9
50-54 years	32.4	6.6	41.3	37.6	-9.0	32.8	21.0	31.1	58.7	100.7
55-59 years	42.5	4.6	41.7	53.8	9.0	39.2	33.9	52.1	57.3	89.7
60-64 years	46.2	7.7	43.7	46.1	20.3	41.9	35.5	61.7	57.7	104.6
65-69 years	50.4	3.9	34.5	42.7	13.0	42.2	45.4	69.3	106.8	138.7
70-74 years	57.1	77.9	52.6	40.0	6.5	55.8	53.7	61.3	81.9	178.9
75 years and older	94.6	81.1	66.2	70.5	25.8	99.0	88.8	113.2	137.4	113.8
NONWHITE FEMALE										
All ages	39.7	15.8	31.0	59.7	10.8	39.2	25.7	34.4	117.7	226.5
Under 5 years	87.2	61.9	64.8	103.2	29.9	83.4	76.3	86.5	139.7	346.8
5-9 years	52.9	23.7	28.3	80.0	19.2	52.1	36.6	50.2	138.1	235.5
10-14 years	32.0	8.8	5.1	51.9	18.6	29.7	20.3	31.4	139.3	145.5
15-19 years	18.8	-16.3	4.6	20.4	7.4	14.9	12.7	19.7	127.6	119.1
20-24 years	17.2	-3.0	31.6	63.0	-5.6	14.3	2.1	9.9	99.8	226.0
25-29 years	16.2	16.8	29.0	78.6	-6.9	19.6	-8.2	-2.4	84.8	338.2
30-34 years	24.9	0.2	29.5	65.2	5.3	32.1	-1.4	3.3	96.3	363.6
35-39 years	30.8	28.1	18.8	53.7	3.0	36.4	13.1	14.6	105.7	282.9
40-44 years	36.5	4.4	24.1	48.4	2.4	38.9	24.9	28.9	105.4	196.8
45-49 years	43.2	6.7	49.3	44.4	7.6	45.0	29.9	39.4	118.8	160.5
50-54 years	46.8	28.8	51.4	51.4	8.9	44.5	38.7	47.6	110.1	180.3
55-59 years	50.2	4.8	41.8	44.2	13.2	49.9	39.9	56.1	98.1	189.5
60-64 years	56.0	32.2	50.8	59.6	11.8	55.4	43.9	65.2	94.4	168.0
65-69 years	75.4	46.5	75.6	47.5	15.3	70.7	81.3	85.1	103.4	154.0
70-74 years	71.0	92.8	72.7	63.5	10.8	71.5	75.3	68.1	94.5	177.0
75 years and older	79.8	55.0	65.8	63.1	24.7	81.5	74.3	92.4	96.7	141.3

TABLE 24

PERCENT CHANGE: AGE BY COLOR AND SEX FOR THE RURAL-FARM POPULATION OF THE UNITED STATES, BY GEOGRAPHIC DIVISIONS: 1940-50

Age by color and sex	United States	New England	Middle Atlantic	East North Central	West North Central	South Atlantic	East South Central	West South Central	Mountain	Pacific
TOTAL, ALL GROUPS										
All ages	-23.6	-28.7	-20.3	-19.0	-20.2	-23.2	-23.1	-36.1	-21.7	-11.1
Under 5 years	-12.9	-1.1	8.5	1.1	-2.2	-17.6	-17.7	-32.2	-9.9	20.1
5-9 years	-18.7	-16.4	-6.2	-5.7	-11.3	-21.3	-22.4	-35.2	-15.6	10.4
10-14 years	-26.9	-32.9	-26.8	-22.1	-24.6	-25.6	-24.6	-39.3	-24.6	-12.5
15-19 years	-37.0	-41.5	-37.5	-36.5	-36.1	-35.0	-32.3	-46.7	-34.6	-32.8
20-24 years	-43.7	-45.3	-36.6	-41.1	-40.5	-43.0	-42.9	-55.6	-40.3	-35.7
25-29 years	-34.5	-32.0	-19.8	-25.6	-28.4	-34.5	-38.6	-51.6	-29.1	-22.2
30-34 years	-23.9	-22.7	-10.3	-11.8	-18.6	-22.6	-29.8	-43.5	-17.9	-7.8
35-39 years	-13.8	-19.0	-8.3	-07.3	-11.8	-10.1	-15.6	-30.4	-7.1	2.5
40-44 years	-14.6	-24.0	-18.1	-17.1	-15.2	-10.3	-8.7	-23.0	-10.9	-5.1
45-49 years	-21.3	-34.5	-27.7	-24.6	-21.2	-16.8	-14.5	-26.6	-24.1	-13.5
50-54 years	-21.5	-33.0	-27.4	-22.7	-19.4	-18.1	-16.8	-26.2	-28.7	-16.2
55-59 years	-16.4	-30.0	-22.1	-16.7	-14.5	-14.3	-12.5	-20.6	-18.9	-11.4
60-64 years	-15.0	-32.3	-21.4	-13.4	-13.7	-14.4	-12.2	-18.9	-12.3	-8.6
65-69 years	-14.2	-32.6	-20.5	-13.9	-15.3	-12.1	-8.0	-18.9	-11.4	-7.5
70-74 years	-12.3	-31.1	-22.0	-16.8	-17.3	-1.7	-0.2	-12.6	-18.9	-16.7
75 years and older	-6.3	-22.6	-13.6	-10.3	-11.9	3.4	6.7	-4.6	-17.2	-15.4
WHITE MALE										
All ages	-23.0	-29.1	-22.0	-20.4	-20.4	-22.2	-21.6	-34.8	-22.0	-12.2
Under 5 years	-11.3	0.7	8.9	1.8	-1.2	-19.3	-19.6	-32.7	-7.0	21.2
5-9 years	-16.7	-15.2	-6.7	-5.0	-10.2	-21.6	-22.1	-34.5	-12.6	13.2
10-14 years	-26.3	-32.5	-26.8	-21.6	-24.1	-26.3	-24.3	-39.0	-22.6	-9.5
15-19 years	-35.8	-41.1	-37.6	-36.2	-34.0	-33.8	-30.7	-45.6	-33.4	-29.5
20-24 years	-43.9	-46.9	-40.4	-44.3	-41.0	-42.0	-41.9	-54.0	-43.9	-37.4
25-29 years	-36.0	-36.4	-26.6	-32.0	-32.2	-35.4	-37.2	-50.8	-34.5	-28.7
30-34 years	-24.8	-25.7	-14.0	-17.0	-21.8	-24.1	-27.6	-43.1	-22.2	-12.7
35-39 years	-11.6	-19.3	-9.0	-8.2	-12.2	-6.8	-9.5	-26.4	-6.2	0.7
40-44 years	-11.8	-21.6	-16.8	-15.6	-14.1	-5.1	-2.7	-18.3	-8.2	-4.3
45-49 years	-20.4	-31.8	-26.6	-24.0	-20.5	-14.2	-12.2	-24.6	-23.6	-14.7
50-54 years	-22.0	-32.7	-29.1	-24.1	-19.6	-16.2	-16.2	-51.6	-31.1	-19.5
55-59 years	-16.8	-30.4	-24.4	-18.2	-14.2	-13.2	-10.5	-20.0	-21.9	-13.7
60-64 years	-14.5	-32.4	-23.0	-14.8	-13.3	-12.7	-9.1	-17.4	-11.1	-7.3
65-69 years	-15.1	-33.3	-22.4	-15.6	-16.2	-10.8	-9.3	-18.7	-10.4	-7.7
70-74 years	-13.8	-31.4	-23.7	-18.3	-18.8	1.0	2.2	-11.4	-20.4	-21.1
75 years and older	-7.6	-23.4	-15.6	-12.0	-13.0	9.3	11.0	-5.5	-20.1	-21.3
WHITE FEMALE										
All ages	-21.8	-27.8	-18.2	-17.3	-19.6	-22.2	-21.7	-34.9	-19.8	-6.8
Under 5 years	-12.5	-2.2	7.9	0.5	-2.6	-20.1	-20.3	-33.8	-8.1	19.4
5-9 years	-17.9	-17.1	-5.7	-6.3	-11.9	-22.4	-23.3	-35.5	-14.4	11.8
10-14 years	-27.2	-32.8	-26.8	-22.8	-25.0	-26.9	-25.5	-40.3	-24.9	-9.9
15-19 years	-38.7	-41.5	-37.3	-36.8	-38.5	-37.5	-34.4	-49.3	-36.2	-31.4
20-24 years	-42.1	-42.6	-31.3	-36.5	-39.7	-44.1	-42.4	-55.8	-37.6	-31.0
25-29 years	-28.0	-26.2	-10.6	-17.3	-23.3	-31.4	-32.5	-47.1	-22.9	-12.0
30-34 years	-17.6	-19.0	-5.2	-5.5	-14.3	-19.7	-23.1	-37.5	-10.7	3.9
35-39 years	-10.9	-18.0	-6.7	-6.2	-10.6	-9.7	-11.6	-25.9	-4.3	12.2
40-44 years	-14.4	-26.0	-19.1	-18.6	-15.9	-8.9	-6.3	-20.6	-10.8	-4.0
45-49 years	-21.0	-36.9	-28.9	-25.4	-21.7	-14.8	-11.3	-24.2	-24.7	-13.0
50-54 years	-18.9	-32.9	-25.2	-21.1	-18.9	-13.2	-12.7	-22.4	-26.1	-11.2
55-59 years	-13.9	-29.2	-19.0	-14.9	-14.5	-10.6	-9.1	-16.8	-14.5	-5.6
60-64 years	-12.9	-31.9	-19.3	-11.6	-14.0	-9.9	-7.1	-16.4	-12.2	-7.8
65-69 years	-11.6	-31.5	18.0	-11.5	-13.6	-5.5	-4.8	-15.8	-12.2	-8.4
70-74 years	-8.7	-30.7	-19.8	-14.8	-14.5	6.9	5.6	-6.2	-14.0	-13.1
75 years and older	-3.7	-21.6	-11.0	-7.9	-9.8	7.9	9.8	0.2	-13.7	-8.6
NONWHITE MALE										
All ages	-30.3	-63.6	-32.2	-25.6	-33.8	-25.5	-27.4	-41.3	-29.1	-34.2
Under 5 years	-16.6	-65.0	14.3	-10.2	-19.1	-13.7	-11.6	-29.0	-28.2	17.4
5-9 years	-24.3	-68.9	-6.9	-7.7	-25.2	-20.0	-21.1	-35.9	-33.1	-23.4
10-14 years	-27.1	-53.6	-24.6	-8.8	-27.2	-23.1	-23.8	-37.6	-32.3	-49.3
15-19 years	-35.4	-71.6	-45.5	-34.6	-35.9	-33.2	-30.9	-43.1	-35.1	-61.8
20-24 years	-48.8	-65.1	-41.9	-41.4	-43.5	-45.2	-46.7	-59.8	-28.5	-52.6
25-29 years	-48.8	-41.6	-46.3	-49.1	-47.3	-39.4	-50.6	-63.4	-24.5	-51.4
30-34 years	-42.9	-57.5	-44.4	-51.1	-44.7	-27.1	-45.8	-59.2	-31.1	-59.8
35-39 years	-29.3	-73.7	-39.8	-35.2	-42.1	-12.2	-29.9	-47.8	-31.4	-42.1
40-44 years	-22.6	-71.8	-42.6	-33.4	-38.7	-13.6	-19.3	-37.9	-32.2	-1.1
45-49 years	-25.5	-75.2	-30.5	-21.7	-39.0	-21.7	-22.4	-37.4	-22.9	30.7
50-54 years	-31.4	-65.6	-40.5	-17.6	-37.8	-30.2	-28.3	-37.6	-26.0	-25.4
55-59 years	-26.5	-63.3	-28.8	-16.1	-32.2	-23.2	-23.4	-31.6	-26.0	-48.4
60-64 years	-27.2	-62.2	-15.4	-16.3	-28.0	-26.5	-26.9	-27.9	-24.5	-38.3
65-69 years	-21.9	-62.9	-16.2	-18.2	-30.1	-25.8	-15.5	-26.0	-12.4	8.9
70-74 years	-17.3	-50.0	-22.5	-16.0	-38.1	-16.9	-12.4	-25.8	-19.3	51.7
75 years and older	-4.5	10.0	-31.1	-33.2	-28.7	-7.5	1.8	-6.6	-4.1	37.8
NONWHITE FEMALE										
All ages	-29.3	-60.6	-16.4	-18.0	-34.3	-25.1	-26.7	-39.9	-30.3	-29.3
Under 5 years	-17.7	-52.5	11.5	-9.4	-25.5	-14.6	-13.6	-29.1	-29.5	15.5
5-9 years	-24.9	-61.7	-12.7	-13.2	-32.3	-20.3	-22.0	-36.1	-34.9	-24.8
10-14 years	-28.1	-70.2	-16.1	-16.9	-31.1	-24.1	-23.9	-38.9	-35.1	-53.0
15-19 years	-37.1	-69.1	-30.0	-35.2	-37.7	-34.6	-32.8	-46.0	-32.2	-62.2
20-24 years	-44.8	-74.2	-20.8	-46.4	-43.6	-40.6	-43.1	-55.9	-30.6	-42.4
25-29 years	-42.9	-65.0	-11.5	-42.1	-46.5	-33.9	-45.4	-57.2	-27.9	20.0
30-34 years	-34.8	-51.9	-17.3	-21.2	-38.4	-21.9	-38.5	-51.0	-29.2	41.8
35-39 years	-28.1	-62.0	-17.5	-9.2	-36.4	-17.3	-28.2	-43.2	-28.8	30.5
40-44 years	-27.1	-54.7	-15.3	-8.9	-35.4	-24.1	-22.6	-35.2	-32.5	-54.7
45-49 years	-26.6	-45.8	-25.6	-3.3	-32.8	-24.8	-22.7	-32.9	-25.3	-50.8
50-54 years	-24.7	-53.2	-26.3	-7.4	-29.2	-24.5	-20.9	-30.8	-17.6	-16.8
55-59 years	-21.0	-51.1	-25.8	1.4	-28.7	-20.3	-19.5	-27.3	-5.5	26.3
60-64 years	-24.2	-65.3	-21.6	-10.5	-26.8	-21.9	-25.1	-27.9	-25.1	0.4
65-69 years	-13.5	-48.4	-8.6	-16.7	-30.1	-16.8	-2.6	-20.6	-22.9	-3.3
70-74 years	-18.2	9.1	-11.0	5.1	-28.7	-18.8	-12.7	-23.9	-40.6	13.3
75 years and older	-15.4	-55.0	-17.8	-6.6	-40.6	-18.1	-11.2	-15.4	-23.1	-8.3

TABLE 25

POPULATION: AGE BY COLOR AND SEX FOR THE TOTAL POPULATION OF THE UNITED STATES, BY GEOGRAPHIC DIVISIONS: 1950

Age by color and sex	United States	New England	Middle Atlantic	East North Central	West North Central	South Atlantic	East South Central	West South Central	Mountain	Pacific
TOTAL, ALL GROUPS										
All ages............	150,697,361	9,314,453	30,163,533	30,399,368	14,061,394	21,182,335	11,477,181	14,537,572	5,074,998	14,486,527
Under 5 years........	16,163,571	916,346	2,850,072	3,187,518	1,489,292	2,478,893	1,389,281	1,704,476	621,340	1,526,353
5-9 years........	13,199,685	746,441	2,324,909	2,551,212	1,211,857	2,070,091	1,184,284	1,422,115	505,804	1,182,972
10-14 years........	11,119,268	604,122	1,927,478	2,131,888	1,045,215	1,784,122	1,064,540	1,214,323	426,874	920,706
15-19 years........	10,616,598	620,680	1,922,554	1,986,674	1,000,110	1,688,853	978,520	1,149,846	385,185	884,176
20-24 years........	11,481,828	694,829	2,243,213	2,271,202	1,021,699	1,755,346	902,822	1,147,406	391,452	1,053,859
25-29 years........	12,242,260	741,444	2,486,192	2,490,536	1,049,916	1,794,472	877,099	1,158,035	406,893	1,237,703
30-34 years........	11,517,007	718,004	2,417,377	2,357,857	983,224	1,631,502	790,479	1,043,545	382,398	1,192,621
35-39 years........	11,246,386	683,944	2,383,284	2,261,566	967,832	1,572,562	796,908	1,054,774	364,572	1,160,944
40-44 years........	10,203,973	628,079	2,210,862	2,060,046	911,666	1,363,632	715,668	964,362	321,020	1,028,638
45-49 years........	9,070,465	569,654	1,990,537	1,872,225	838,639	1,157,345	616,910	846,902	272,268	905,985
50-54 years........	8,272,188	553,621	1,887,127	1,738,010	795,620	1,000,527	530,148	711,413	239,903	815,519
55-59 years........	7,235,120	504,874	1,628,154	1,573,546	733,557	821,010	444,467	600,524	214,150	714,838
60-64 years........	6,059,475	425,878	1,352,503	1,321,219	635,162	666,978	364,016	486,665	184,272	622,782
65-69 years........	5,002,936	348,760	1,057,548	1,048,326	528,427	589,256	343,304	429,835	148,095	509,385
70-74 years........	3,411,949	252,807	710,256	719,093	380,836	391,143	226,941	284,540	99,537	346,796
75 years and older...	3,854,652	305,000	771,467	828,450	468,342	416,603	251,494	318,811	111,235	383,250
WHITE MALE										
All ages............	67,129,192	4,475,977	13,871,634	14,227,210	6,794,416	7,993,766	4,370,610	6,036,001	2,472,330	6,887,248
Under 5 years........	7,244,211	460,193	1,355,145	1,524,308	734,268	916,634	519,334	702,581	299,647	732,101
5-9 years........	5,915,150	375,422	1,108,563	1,222,377	596,565	761,567	447,612	587,070	244,058	571,896
10-14 years........	4,944,535	301,994	914,449	1,019,506	513,266	646,637	401,542	497,732	205,733	443,676
15-19 years........	4,685,825	303,270	885,919	926,849	479,844	627,364	369,274	475,064	183,670	434,571
20-24 years........	5,002,782	335,280	992,351	1,024,396	483,581	668,231	339,508	473,035	186,267	500,133
25-29 years........	5,349,707	354,381	1,099,130	1,124,710	504,972	680,725	340,196	485,680	193,949	565,964
30-34 years........	5,080,610	343,139	1,077,158	1,072,298	468,979	629,508	309,495	439,852	183,838	556,343
35-39 years........	4,955,941	326,324	1,067,715	1,037,586	463,012	595,857	305,153	438,863	176,912	544,519
40-44 years........	4,573,529	299,541	1,012,639	961,058	438,952	526,037	277,220	407,223	159,982	490,877
45-49 years........	4,080,174	271,867	920,784	879,678	402,049	442,574	234,549	353,196	136,127	439,350
50-54 years........	3,756,125	262,178	881,283	825,357	384,473	386,501	201,963	300,536	120,099	393,735
55-59 years........	3,350,888	242,016	777,281	762,112	358,312	326,728	175,201	254,571	108,839	345,828
60-64 years........	2,829,399	203,671	650,488	647,599	312,152	265,059	144,826	207,829	95,194	302,581
65-69 years........	2,223,014	159,266	487,149	496,480	253,845	217,328	124,945	168,347	74,852	240,802
70-74 years........	1,513,308	111,510	319,099	336,228	182,845	149,584	87,366	117,200	50,026	159,450
75 years and older...	1,624,014	125,925	322,481	366,668	217,301	153,432	92,426	127,222	53,137	165,422
WHITE FEMALE										
All ages............	67,812,836	4,685,179	14,365,894	14,316,097	6,781,661	8,047,943	4,399,960	6,001,249	2,373,304	6,841,549
Under 5 years........	6,940,293	439,315	1,295,359	1,458,268	701,485	878,181	500,502	674,532	288,279	704,372
5-9 years........	5,681,442	358,512	1,064,131	1,174,634	571,909	731,552	430,432	565,044	234,164	551,064
10-14 years........	4,749,994	290,350	876,082	978,771	491,820	623,994	385,579	478,079	196,966	428,353
15-19 years........	4,644,695	306,653	906,106	938,309	484,548	603,316	363,776	459,972	179,922	402,093
20-24 years........	5,176,405	345,289	1,081,151	1,083,816	500,376	658,008	355,583	481,655	184,651	485,876
25-29 years........	5,575,097	371,199	1,187,991	1,176,887	505,853	703,087	352,955	494,826	194,898	587,401
30-34 years........	5,275,721	361,876	1,163,904	1,119,693	479,349	640,503	318,446	445,760	183,450	562,740
35-39 years........	5,102,532	345,953	1,141,828	1,063,333	468,695	605,272	311,288	445,795	173,615	546,753
40-44 years........	4,616,761	319,094	1,049,241	963,780	439,653	532,762	279,222	402,487	149,659	480,863
45-49 years........	4,089,180	289,074	938,800	869,910	405,746	451,117	238,823	350,280	125,781	419,649
50-54 years........	3,779,314	283,595	900,170	813,519	384,319	397,895	206,250	295,252	111,373	386,941
55-59 years........	3,344,844	256,728	781,150	740,657	353,721	338,279	176,979	253,976	98,645	344,709
60-64 years........	2,823,207	217,341	651,849	624,265	306,318	281,443	148,943	208,769	83,514	300,765
65-69 years........	2,362,572	185,280	531,092	510,615	258,406	244,316	133,734	178,389	68,158	252,582
70-74 years........	1,668,267	138,548	368,977	360,594	188,653	170,295	92,515	124,141	46,311	178,233
75 years and older...	1,982,512	176,372	428,063	439,046	240,810	187,923	104,933	142,292	53,918	209,155
NONWHITE MALE										
All ages............	7,704,047	77,793	921,465	918,052	238,999	2,502,831	1,306,915	1,213,396	119,588	405,008
Under 5 years.......	991,953	8,513	100,182	102,581	26,851	342,652	185,083	163,688	16,927	45,476
5-9 years..........	799,425	6,317	75,354	76,769	21,803	287,556	153,082	134,695	13,724	30,125
10-14 years........	715,864	6,161	68,623	66,663	20,477	257,446	139,126	119,793	12,447	25,128
15-19 years........	625,517	5,449	62,122	57,915	17,046	223,790	119,613	104,704	10,949	24,329
20-24 years........	603,511	7,300	74,681	76,212	17,497	199,782	94,645	88,494	10,695	34,205
25-29 years........	622,371	8,135	91,209	90,599	18,679	194,468	84,776	82,172	9,390	42,943
30-34 years........	544,113	6,468	79,576	79,192	16,362	171,146	73,900	72,067	7,697	37,705
35-39 years........	561,603	5,718	79,585	78,174	17,090	176,210	81,945	77,851	7,200	37,830
40-44 years........	496,740	4,718	71,978	67,901	16,111	148,158	74,835	73,183	6,054	33,802
45-49 years........	446,192	4,444	64,812	63,416	15,210	126,550	68,242	69,487	5,647	28,384
50-54 years........	372,523	4,188	54,478	52,873	13,741	106,128	58,755	57,360	4,614	20,386
55-59 years........	279,158	3,256	35,872	38,213	11,395	78,549	46,991	47,570	3,782	13,530
60-64 years........	208,439	2,485	25,059	26,152	8,868	59,833	35,427	35,860	3,283	11,472
65-69 years........	201,547	2,059	18,565	20,254	8,023	60,016	40,368	39,950	2,971	9,341
70-74 years........	115,521	1,353	10,457	10,727	4,762	35,107	23,593	22,022	1,899	5,601
75 years and older...	119,570	1,229	8,912	10,411	5,084	35,840	26,534	24,500	2,309	4,751
NONWHITE FEMALE										
All ages............	8,051,286	75,504	1,004,540	938,009	246,318	2,637,795	1,399,696	1,286,926	109,776	352,722
Under 5 years......	987,114	8,325	99,386	102,361	26,688	341,426	184,362	163,675	16,487	44,404
5-9 years.........	803,688	6,190	76,861	77,432	21,580	289,416	153,158	135,306	13,858	29,887
10-14 years.........	708,875	5,617	68,324	66,948	19,652	256,045	138,293	118,719	11,728	23,549
15-19 years........	660,561	5,308	68,407	63,601	18,672	234,783	125,857	110,106	10,644	23,183
20-24 years........	699,130	6,960	95,030	86,778	20,245	229,325	113,086	104,222	9,839	33,645
25-29 years........	695,085	7,699	107,862	98,340	20,412	216,192	99,172	95,357	8,656	41,395
30-34 years........	616,563	6,521	96,779	86,674	18,534	190,245	88,638	85,866	7,413	35,833
35-39 years........	626,310	5,949	94,156	82,473	19,035	195,223	98,522	92,265	6,845	31,842
40-44 years........	516,943	4,726	77,004	67,307	16,950	156,675	84,391	81,469	5,325	23,096
45-49 years........	454,919	4,269	66,141	59,221	15,634	137,104	75,296	73,959	4,713	18,602
50-54 years........	364,226	3,660	51,196	46,261	13,087	110,003	63,480	58,265	3,817	14,457
55-59 years........	260,230	2,874	33,851	32,564	10,129	77,454	45,296	44,407	2,884	10,771
60-64 years........	198,430	2,381	25,107	23,203	7,824	60,643	34,820	34,207	2,281	7,964
65-69 years........	215,803	2,155	20,742	20,977	8,153	67,596	44,257	43,149	2,114	6,660
70-74 years........	114,853	1,396	11,723	11,544	4,576	36,157	23,467	21,177	1,301	3,512
75 years and older...	128,556	1,474	12,011	12,325	5,147	39,408*	27,601	24,797	1,871	3,922

TABLE 26

POPULATION: AGE BY COLOR AND SEX FOR THE URBAN POPULATION OF THE UNITED STATES, BY GEOGRAPHIC DIVISIONS: 1950

Age by color and sex	United States	New England	Middle Atlantic	East North Central	West North Central	South Atlantic	East South Central	West South Central	Mountain	Pacific
TOTAL, ALL GROUPS										
All ages..........	96,467,686	7,101,511	24,271,689	21,185,713	7,305,219	10,391,163	4,484,771	8,079,828	2,785,888	10,861,904
Under 5 years........	9,772,719	674,785	2,218,717	2,152,836	745,821	1,104,720	499,240	934,916	325,777	1,115,907
5-9 years........	7,534,474	542,555	1,781,146	1,645,342	555,787	841,822	377,915	708,916	249,224	831,767
10-14 years........	6,072,441	437,664	1,460,507	1,339,625	454,506	674,715	312,899	561,308	203,147	628,070
15-19 years........	6,176,680	465,805	1,496,271	1,312,438	485,648	702,446	324,873	582,767	193,624	611,808
20-24 years........	7,713,937	545,557	1,833,386	1,673,523	604,613	911,703	402,395	719,458	228,511	794,791
25-29 years........	8,411,772	578,391	2,042,722	1,839,198	610,918	985,373	407,088	742,242	240,751	965,089
30-34 years........	7,822,116	553,937	1,980,729	1,715,710	542,745	892,022	354,889	640,395	220,500	921,189
35-39 years........	7,563,892	527,011	1,963,893	1,633,937	520,838	852,304	348,132	621,845	206,155	889,777
40-44 years........	6,891,449	484,977	1,828,573	1,493,922	492,001	746,236	312,854	560,501	183,101	789,284
45-49 years........	6,152,192	444,098	1,653,290	1,361,274	451,024	636,657	269,310	484,908	155,126	696,505
50-54 years........	5,636,546	435,256	1,572,841	1,257,643	425,100	548,463	229,034	402,771	138,485	626,953
55-59 years........	4,865,541	395,833	1,341,949	1,124,114	385,924	439,495	184,154	325,822	122,035	546,215
60-64 years........	4,028,648	331,477	1,103,430	923,837	331,025	350,545	147,624	259,216	104,912	476,582
65-69 years........	3,236,682	268,541	849,101	712,198	271,532	299,107	132,442	223,092	86,541	394,128
70-74 years........	2,173,537	190,529	558,469	472,340	191,321	196,873	86,388	146,322	59,953	271,342
75 years and older....	2,416,060	225,095	586,665	527,776	236,416	208,682	95,534	165,349	68,046	302,497
WHITE MALE										
All ages..........	42,249,894	3,360,946	10,924,891	9,530,141	3,333,142	3,835,515	1,595,780	3,313,670	1,341,190	5,014,619
Under 5 years........	4,419,776	337,158	1,037,843	998,613	359,492	418,202	182,507	395,586	160,899	529,476
5-9 years........	3,401,637	270,653	834,407	761,482	265,685	314,087	137,432	298,046	123,511	396,334
10-14 years........	2,705,101	216,585	678,224	614,043	214,846	243,063	110,521	231,700	99,555	296,564
15-19 years........	2,640,374	223,215	669,246	574,566	210,409	247,086	109,005	233,722	88,962	284,163
20-24 years........	3,277,636	258,970	792,321	725,449	268,493	335,053	141,165	290,109	106,437	359,639
25-29 years........	3,631,492	274,406	886,760	807,913	285,047	366,867	151,600	269,719	106,025	422,054
30-34 years........	3,396,275	261,792	863,927	755,753	248,990	336,087	131,928	253,211	98,476	407,919
35-39 years........	3,254,985	247,566	858,776	719,955	235,524	310,393	123,165	253,211	89,277	367,740
40-44 years........	3,014,533	227,203	820,007	669,218	222,692	275,811	111,606	230,979	89,277	367,740
45-49 years........	2,706,579	207,834	749,645	616,053	202,044	234,608	94,935	196,868	75,494	329,118
50-54 years........	2,509,587	202,648	722,428	578,152	192,341	205,453	80,680	165,864	67,017	295,004
55-59 years........	2,210,951	187,254	631,646	529,712	176,421	169,945	67,114	133,517	59,645	255,687
60-64 years........	1,836,192	156,626	522,826	439,561	151,675	133,927	53,512	105,363	51,019	221,683
65-69 years........	1,385,927	119,595	381,053	320,194	119,379	103,963	42,306	81,913	41,073	176,451
70-74 years........	912,179	80,779	242,282	206,297	82,887	70,094	28,783	55,623	28,054	117,380
75 years and older....	946,670	88,662	233,510	213,180	97,217	70,876	29,521	60,637	30,357	122,710
WHITE FEMALE										
All ages..........	44,506,541	3,602,505	11,538,729	9,907,371	3,583,607	4,100,754	1,733,635	3,454,646	1,371,316	5,213,978
Under 5 years........	4,247,785	322,281	992,590	959,421	345,936	401,004	178,135	381,319	156,186	510,913
5-9 years........	3,298,209	260,714	804,376	738,945	258,376	305,407	134,499	290,291	119,432	386,169
10-14 years........	2,650,284	210,825	655,748	601,849	210,994	240,812	110,742	228,802	99,292	290,259
15-19 years........	2,854,441	233,123	707,954	625,600	249,061	271,020	126,475	251,657	99,292	290,259
20-24 years........	3,599,050	273,877	883,174	795,416	305,536	362,664	165,042	318,626	115,360	379,355
25-29 years........	3,851,493	289,513	967,264	851,284	292,725	391,369	161,454	320,514	118,384	458,986
30-34 years........	3,600,705	280,181	949,190	801,330	261,197	350,677	139,132	273,020	108,220	434,758
35-39 years........	3,474,916	268,753	939,625	760,332	254,458	330,125	132,573	265,868	101,925	421,257
40-44 years........	3,169,603	249,184	866,881	696,052	240,698	295,478	120,808	237,693	89,084	373,525
45-49 years........	2,820,596	228,311	779,757	628,830	222,690	251,104	102,065	204,113	75,487	328,239
50-54 years........	2,626,276	225,526	751,001	586,204	209,991	223,332	88,102	170,894	67,968	303,258
55-59 years........	2,303,292	203,068	645,271	528,413	191,561	187,816	74,137	142,730	59,596	270,700
60-64 years........	1,935,661	170,530	533,958	438,850	165,685	156,222	62,184	117,334	51,678	239,220
65-69 years........	1,607,540	145,200	431,684	354,243	138,976	134,284	54,604	100,149	43,481	204,919
70-74 years........	1,131,223	107,334	295,951	246,004	101,059	94,615	38,654	70,089	30,646	146,871
75 years and older....	1,335,467	134,085	334,305	294,598	131,464	104,825	45,029	81,547	36,407	173,207
NONWHITE MALE										
All ages..........	4,641,888	69,240	855,190	855,564	187,788	1,153,207	536,478	618,242	37,956	328,223
Under 5 years........	553,406	7,757	94,460	97,492	20,197	142,707	69,208	79,119	4,311	38,155
5-9 years........	413,671	5,648	70,379	72,060	15,863	109,466	52,437	59,577	3,111	24,650
10-14 years........	354,555	5,303	62,832	61,233	14,476	93,470	44,730	49,635	2,764	20,112
15-19 years........	315,529	4,713	55,028	52,471	12,136	84,476	40,849	44,888	2,668	18,300
20-24 years........	368,566	6,263	67,317	69,048	13,543	93,492	41,148	48,071	3,434	26,250
25-29 years........	428,181	7,318	85,071	84,759	15,478	103,384	41,889	50,447	3,573	36,262
30-34 years........	379,231	5,910	74,721	74,900	13,592	93,764	37,027	43,847	3,160	32,310
35-39 years........	387,193	5,224	75,154	74,157	14,372	97,009	40,588	46,101	2,924	31,664
40-44 years........	341,938	4,262	68,045	64,246	13,666	82,536	36,790	42,610	2,518	27,265
45-49 years........	306,203	4,022	61,019	59,788	12,793	70,685	33,392	39,651	2,219	22,634
50-54 years........	252,836	3,750	50,949	49,475	11,493	58,120	28,512	32,433	1,848	16,256
55-59 years........	179,194	2,873	33,135	35,400	9,351	39,923	21,098	25,116	1,533	10,765
60-64 years........	128,478	2,189	23,000	23,898	7,124	28,630	15,393	18,036	1,301	8,907
65-69 years........	112,075	1,811	16,910	18,256	6,354	26,538	15,639	18,349	1,147	7,071
70-74 years........	61,382	1,171	9,376	9,481	3,668	14,461	8,555	9,737	762	4,171
75 years and older....	59,450	1,026	7,794	8,900	3,682	14,066	9,223	10,625	683	3,451
NONWHITE FEMALE										
All ages..........	5,069,363	68,820	952,879	892,637	200,682	1,301,687	618,878	693,270	35,426	305,084
Under 5 years........	551,752	7,589	93,824	97,310	20,196	142,807	69,390	78,892	4,363	37,363
5-9 years........	420,957	5,540	71,984	72,855	15,863	112,382	53,547	61,002	3,170	24,614
10-14 years........	362,501	4,951	63,703	62,500	14,190	97,370	46,906	51,171	2,658	19,052
15-19 years........	365,336	4,754	64,043	59,801	14,042	99,864	48,544	52,500	2,702	19,086
20-24 years........	468,685	6,447	90,574	83,610	17,041	120,494	55,040	62,652	3,280	29,547
25-29 years........	500,606	7,154	103,627	95,242	17,668	123,753	52,145	60,468	3,405	37,144
30-34 years........	445,905	6,054	92,891	83,727	15,966	111,494	46,802	53,809	3,095	32,067
35-39 years........	446,798	5,468	90,338	79,493	16,484	114,777	51,806	56,665	2,830	28,937
40-44 years........	365,375	4,328	73,640	64,406	14,745	92,411	43,650	49,219	2,222	20,754
45-49 years........	318,814	3,931	62,889	56,603	13,497	80,260	38,918	44,276	1,926	16,514
50-54 years........	247,847	3,332	48,463	43,812	11,275	61,558	31,740	33,580	1,652	12,435
55-59 years........	172,104	2,638	31,887	30,589	8,591	41,811	21,805	24,459	1,261	9,063
60-64 years........	128,317	2,132	23,646	21,528	6,541	31,766	16,535	18,483	914	6,772
65-69 years........	131,140	1,935	19,154	19,505	6,823	34,322	19,893	22,681	840	5,687
70-74 years........	68,753	1,245	10,860	10,558	3,707	17,703	10,396	10,873	491	2,920
75 years and older....	74,473	1,322	11,056	11,098	4,053	18,915	11,761	12,540	599	3,129

TABLE 27

POPULATION: AGE BY COLOR AND SEX FOR THE RURAL-NONFARM POPULATION OF THE UNITED STATES, BY GEOGRAPHIC DIVISIONS: 1950

Age by color and sex	United States	New England	Middle Atlantic	East North Central	West North Central	South Atlantic	East South Central	West South Central	Mountain	Pacific
TOTAL, ALL GROUPS										
All ages	31,181,325	1,809,842	4,503,683	5,510,241	3,027,024	6,158,176	2,944,336	3,243,129	1,430,508	2,544,386
Under 5 years	3,771,182	202,518	490,114	651,668	324,188	813,829	394,802	400,547	189,960	303,556
5-9 years	3,103,972	165,956	407,957	530,471	263,942	665,544	322,306	344,823	157,397	245,576
10-14 years	2,571,869	130,419	339,600	436,745	228,204	549,042	268,758	292,588	131,991	194,522
15-19 years	2,327,944	121,468	309,666	370,862	205,685	510,222	244,140	262,892	113,743	189,266
20-24 years	2,355,576	124,989	320,057	385,246	192,906	538,902	245,023	241,398	107,738	199,317
25-29 years	2,475,106	139,271	355,322	432,311	206,936	538,711	242,248	239,743	111,556	209,008
30-34 years	2,308,178	139,410	348,955	409,559	197,016	475,324	210,107	220,016	105,837	201,954
35-39 years	2,182,523	131,492	330,228	383,348	190,950	433,706	198,443	221,569	99,880	192,907
40-44 years	1,905,278	118,097	297,723	336,951	177,345	358,239	168,213	199,083	85,057	164,570
45-49 years	1,626,733	102,083	257,390	292,036	162,902	290,582	138,822	173,754	70,471	138,693
50-54 years	1,440,295	94,876	235,599	264,036	158,921	244,492	116,592	144,308	60,034	121,437
55-59 years	1,287,763	86,362	211,950	245,052	157,598	200,947	98,353	126,259	53,710	107,532
60-64 years	1,132,164	74,544	185,024	222,248	151,004	166,292	83,069	107,099	47,582	95,302
65-69 years	1,023,404	63,623	156,115	198,598	142,302	153,968	85,287	106,037	38,908	78,566
70-74 years	755,243	49,920	115,298	154,336	115,656	104,561	59,677	75,820	26,462	53,513
75 years and older	914,095	64,814	142,685	196,774	151,469	113,815	68,496	87,193	30,182	58,667
WHITE MALE										
All ages	14,489,275	901,136	2,221,370	2,747,083	1,482,395	2,494,901	1,232,474	1,385,822	699,378	1,324,716
Under 5 years	1,778,261	103,029	245,637	329,636	162,132	322,280	167,197	168,142	89,397	150,811
5-9 years	1,451,441	85,092	204,953	267,895	130,933	263,152	136,955	145,818	73,703	122,940
10-14 years	1,180,432	66,457	170,569	220,696	112,790	213,769	113,291	123,053	62,020	97,787
15-19 years	1,088,335	61,632	153,422	185,969	99,871	210,040	101,251	114,153	55,357	106,640
20-24 years	1,076,458	62,761	151,295	182,124	90,375	224,255	100,450	104,016	52,138	109,044
25-29 years	1,123,361	67,562	167,937	206,743	101,030	219,298	102,793	102,529	52,549	102,920
30-34 years	1,072,696	68,896	169,265	200,712	96,684	198,674	91,192	95,159	50,835	101,279
35-39 years	1,026,869	65,640	163,475	192,587	94,488	180,601	85,465	96,905	49,093	98,615
40-44 years	909,625	59,268	149,061	172,424	88,380	150,713	72,538	88,154	43,313	85,754
45-49 years	773,561	51,509	129,330	149,203	79,853	119,493	58,024	76,058	36,236	73,855
50-54 years	682,362	47,133	117,929	133,697	77,891	99,914	47,968	62,929	30,991	63,910
55-59 years	610,097	42,647	106,033	122,959	76,387	82,841	40,489	54,023	28,027	56,691
60-64 years	536,073	36,104	92,787	111,132	72,772	67,601	33,360	45,241	25,480	51,596
65-69 years	466,490	30,440	76,812	98,488	67,677	57,693	31,384	40,822	20,355	42,819
70-74 years	352,925	23,709	56,220	76,802	56,347	41,017	23,443	31,821	14,217	29,349
75 years and older	420,289	29,257	66,625	96,016	74,785	43,560	26,674	36,999	15,667	30,706
WHITE FEMALE										
All ages	13,961,064	894,794	2,177,898	2,674,558	1,486,202	2,393,203	1,223,567	1,340,893	636,282	1,153,647
Under 5 years	1,659,818	98,110	234,715	313,841	154,382	308,696	159,972	160,914	85,203	143,965
5-9 years	1,365,975	79,648	194,482	255,352	126,259	251,431	132,311	139,725	70,683	116,084
10-14 years	1,123,856	62,598	159,995	208,461	108,743	206,875	110,149	117,647	58,505	90,883
15-19 years	997,596	58,664	145,964	177,281	100,164	187,539	100,711	102,795	48,446	76,032
20-24 years	1,045,158	60,785	156,094	193,847	98,076	204,307	103,884	97,609	46,909	81,647
25-29 years	1,144,757	70,442	178,105	217,503	102,069	218,290	104,117	103,124	52,180	98,927
30-34 years	1,061,522	69,564	171,944	202,536	96,970	191,606	89,162	95,470	49,513	94,757
35-39 years	982,548	64,945	159,456	184,887	93,216	170,098	81,909	93,582	45,677	88,778
40-44 years	849,300	58,056	142,190	159,135	86,244	140,247	68,631	83,235	37,715	73,847
45-49 years	723,361	49,890	121,762	137,836	80,346	113,725	57,094	71,949	30,595	60,664
50-54 years	648,298	47,064	112,069	125,664	78,651	96,350	47,920	59,962	26,301	54,317
55-59 years	592,419	43,173	101,740	118,401	79,046	82,282	41,772	54,002	23,563	48,440
60-64 years	526,325	37,949	89,152	108,095	76,394	69,140	36,587	47,003	20,260	41,745
65-69 years	473,184	32,764	76,702	97,377	72,708	62,198	35,930	44,691	16,847	33,967
70-74 years	352,271	25,906	57,329	75,779	57,999	43,130	25,290	32,688	11,136	23,014
75 years and older	434,176	35,236	74,199	98,543	74,935	47,289	28,148	36,497	12,749	26,580
NONWHITE MALE										
All ages	1,373,572	7,794	58,783	52,203	30,858	634,260	238,918	254,490	49,606	46,660
Under 5 years	187,350	704	4,934	4,095	3,865	91,801	33,960	35,669	7,879	4,443
5-9 years	153,252	614	4,279	3,649	3,381	75,316	26,514	29,708	6,459	3,332
10-14 years	135,628	757	5,045	4,173	3,490	64,345	22,707	26,126	5,907	3,078
15-19 years	122,464	674	6,464	4,574	2,935	55,599	20,332	22,648	5,118	4,120
20-24 years	121,987	968	6,707	6,541	2,511	54,855	19,772	19,979	4,603	6,051
25-29 years	107,457	757	5,535	5,374	2,126	51,210	17,660	16,614	3,594	4,587
30-34 years	88,345	522	4,346	3,882	1,778	42,927	14,436	14,054	2,843	3,557
35-39 years	87,431	458	3,912	3,468	1,715	41,923	15,014	14,723	2,639	3,579
40-44 years	74,436	415	3,472	3,071	1,444	34,050	13,099	13,337	2,153	3,395
45-49 years	65,680	385	3,360	2,982	1,427	28,500	11,505	12,608	2,013	2,900
50-54 years	55,288	339	3,151	2,756	1,292	23,976	9,701	10,358	1,557	2,108
55-59 years	44,116	329	2,416	2,200	1,209	18,047	7,969	9,149	1,275	1,522
60-64 years	35,113	261	1,772	1,705	1,030	14,549	6,253	7,212	1,055	1,276
65-69 years	39,451	215	1,435	1,548	1,008	15,729	7,885	9,529	962	1,140
70-74 years	25,130	167	956	971	702	9,996	5,240	5,740	605	753
75 years and older	30,444	179	999	1,214	945	11,437	6,871	7,036	944	819
NONWHITE FEMALE										
All ages	1,337,414	6,118	45,632	36,397	27,569	635,812	249,357	261,924	45,242	29,363
Under 5 years	185,753	675	4,828	4,076	3,809	91,052	33,673	35,822	7,481	4,337
5-9 years	153,304	602	4,243	3,575	3,369	75,645	26,526	29,572	6,552	3,220
10-14 years	131,953	607	3,991	3,415	3,181	64,053	22,611	25,762	5,559	2,774
15-19 years	119,549	498	3,816	3,038	2,715	57,044	21,846	23,296	4,822	2,474
20-24 years	111,973	475	3,961	2,734	1,944	55,485	20,917	19,794	4,088	2,575
25-29 years	99,531	510	3,745	2,691	1,711	49,913	17,678	17,476	3,233	2,574
30-34 years	85,615	428	3,400	2,429	1,584	42,117	15,317	15,333	2,646	2,361
35-39 years	85,675	449	3,385	2,406	1,531	41,084	16,055	16,359	2,471	1,935
40-44 years	71,917	358	2,980	2,321	1,277	33,229	13,945	14,357	1,876	1,574
45-49 years	63,631	299	2,938	2,015	1,276	28,864	12,199	13,139	1,627	1,274
50-54 years	54,347	290	2,450	1,919	1,087	24,252	11,003	11,059	1,185	1,102
55-59 years	41,131	213	1,761	1,492	956	17,777	8,123	9,085	845	879
60-64 years	34,653	230	1,313	1,316	808	15,002	6,869	7,643	787	685
65-69 years	44,279	204	1,166	1,185	909	18,348	10,088	10,995	744	640
70-74 years	24,917	138	793	784	608	10,418	5,704	5,571	504	397
75 years and older	29,186	142	862	1,001	804	11,529	6,803	6,661	822	562

TABLE 28
POPULATION: AGE BY COLOR AND SEX FOR THE RURAL-FARM POPULATION OF THE UNITED STATES, BY GEOGRAPHIC DIVISIONS: 1950

Age by color and sex	United States	New England	Middle Atlantic	East North Central	West North Central	South Atlantic	East South Central	West South Central	Mountain	Pacific
TOTAL, ALL GROUPS										
All ages..............	23,048,350	403,100	1,388,161	3,703,414	3,729,151	4,632,996	4,048,074	3,214,615	858,602	1,070,237
Under 5 years..........	2,619,670	39,043	141,241	383,014	419,283	560,344	495,239	369,013	105,603	106,890
5-9 years.............	2,561,239	37,930	135,806	375,399	392,128	562,725	484,063	368,376	99,183	105,629
10-14 years...........	2,474,958	36,039	127,371	355,518	362,505	560,365	482,883	360,427	91,736	98,114
15-19 years...........	2,112,974	33,407	116,617	303,374	308,777	476,185	409,507	304,187	77,818	83,102
20-24 years...........	1,412,315	24,283	89,770	212,433	224,180	304,741	255,404	186,550	55,203	59,751
25-29 years...........	1,355,382	23,752	88,148	219,027	232,062	270,388	227,763	176,050	54,586	63,606
30-34 years...........	1,386,713	24,657	87,693	232,588	243,463	264,156	225,483	183,134	56,061	69,478
35-39 years...........	1,499,971	25,441	89,163	244,281	256,044	286,552	250,333	211,360	58,537	78,260
40-44 years...........	1,407,246	25,005	84,566	229,173	242,320	259,157	234,601	204,778	52,862	74,784
45-49 years...........	1,291,540	23,473	79,857	218,915	224,713	230,106	208,778	188,240	46,671	70,787
50-54 years...........	1,195,347	23,489	78,687	216,331	211,599	207,572	184,822	164,334	41,384	67,129
55-59 years...........	1,081,816	22,679	74,255	204,380	190,035	180,568	161,960	148,443	38,405	61,091
60-64 years...........	898,663	19,857	64,049	175,134	153,133	150,141	133,323	120,350	31,778	50,898
65-69 years...........	742,850	16,596	52,332	137,530	114,593	136,181	125,575	100,706	22,646	36,691
70-74 years...........	483,169	12,358	36,489	92,417	73,859	89,709	80,876	62,398	13,122	21,941
75 years and older....	524,497	15,091	42,117	103,900	80,457	94,106	87,464	66,269	13,007	22,086
WHITE MALE										
All ages	10,390,023	213,895	725,373	1,949,986	1,978,879	1,663,350	1,512,356	1,336,509	431,762	547,913
Under 5 years..........	1,086,174	20,006	71,665	196,059	212,644	176,152	169,630	138,853	49,351	51,814
5-9 years.............	1,082,052	19,677	69,203	193,000	199,947	184,328	173,225	143,206	46,844	52,622
10-14 years...........	1,059,002	18,952	65,656	184,767	185,630	189,805	177,730	142,979	44,158	49,325
15-19 years...........	957,116	18,423	63,251	166,314	169,564	170,238	159,018	127,189	39,351	43,768
20-24 years...........	648,688	13,549	48,735	116,823	124,713	108,923	97,893	78,910	27,692	31,450
25-29 years...........	594,854	12,413	44,433	110,054	118,895	94,560	85,803	72,338	26,011	30,347
30-34 years...........	611,639	12,451	43,966	115,833	123,305	94,747	86,375	74,974	26,978	33,010
35-39 years...........	674,087	13,118	45,464	125,044	133,000	104,863	96,523	88,747	29,343	37,985
40-44 years...........	649,371	13,070	43,551	119,416	127,880	99,513	93,076	88,090	27,392	37,383
45-49 years...........	600,034	12,524	41,829	114,422	120,152	88,473	81,590	80,270	24,397	36,377
50-54 years...........	564,176	12,397	40,926	113,508	114,241	81,134	73,315	71,743	22,091	34,821
55-59 years...........	529,840	12,115	39,592	109,441	105,504	73,942	67,598	67,031	21,167	33,450
60-64 years...........	457,134	10,941	34,875	96,906	87,705	63,531	57,954	57,225	18,695	29,302
65-69 years...........	370,597	9,231	29,284	77,798	66,789	55,672	51,255	45,612	13,424	21,532
70-74 years...........	248,204	7,022	20,597	53,129	43,611	38,473	35,140	29,756	7,755	12,721
75 years and older....	257,055	8,006	22,346	57,472	45,299	38,996	36,231	29,586	7,113	12,006
WHITE FEMALE										
All ages..............	9,325,231	187,880	649,267	1,734,168	1,711,852	1,553,986	1,442,738	1,205,710	365,706	473,924
Under 5 years..........	1,032,690	18,924	68,054	184,986	201,167	168,481	162,395	132,299	46,890	49,494
5-9 years.............	1,017,258	18,150	65,273	180,337	187,274	174,714	163,622	135,028	44,049	48,811
10-14 years...........	975,854	16,927	60,339	168,461	172,083	176,307	164,688	131,630	40,291	45,128
15-19 years...........	792,658	14,866	52,188	135,428	135,323	144,757	136,590	105,520	32,184	35,802
20-24 years...........	532,197	10,627	39,883	94,553	96,764	91,037	86,657	65,420	22,382	24,874
25-29 years...........	578,847	11,244	42,622	108,100	111,059	93,428	87,384	71,188	24,334	29,488
30-34 years...........	613,494	12,131	42,770	115,827	118,182	98,220	90,152	77,270	25,717	33,225
35-39 years...........	645,068	12,255	42,747	118,114	121,021	105,049	96,806	86,345	26,013	36,718
40-44 years...........	597,858	11,854	40,170	108,593	112,511	97,037	89,783	81,559	22,860	33,491
45-49 years...........	544,723	10,873	37,261	103,244	102,710	86,288	79,644	74,218	19,699	30,746
50-54 years...........	504,740	11,005	37,100	101,651	95,677	78,213	70,228	64,396	17,104	29,366
55-59 years...........	449,133	10,487	34,139	93,843	83,114	68,181	61,070	57,244	15,486	25,569
60-64 years...........	361,221	8,862	28,739	77,320	64,239	56,081	50,172	44,432	11,576	19,800
65-69 years...........	281,848	7,316	22,706	58,995	46,722	47,834	43,200	33,549	7,830	13,696
70-74 years...........	184,773	5,308	15,697	38,811	29,595	32,550	28,571	21,364	4,529	8,348
75 years and older....	212,869	7,051	19,559	45,905	34,411	35,809	31,756	24,248	4,762	9,368
NONWHITE MALE										
All ages..............	1,688,587	759	7,492	10,285	20,353	715,364	531,519	340,664	32,026	30,125
Under 5 years..........	251,197	52	788	994	2,789	108,144	81,915	48,900	4,737	2,878
5-9 years.............	232,502	55	696	1,060	2,559	102,294	74,131	45,410	4,154	2,143
10-14 years...........	225,681	101	746	1,257	2,511	99,631	71,689	44,032	3,776	1,938
15-19 years...........	187,524	62	630	870	1,975	83,315	58,432	37,168	3,163	1,909
20-24 years...........	112,958	69	657	623	1,443	51,435	33,725	20,444	2,658	1,904
25-29 years...........	86,733	60	603	466	1,075	39,874	25,227	15,111	2,223	2,094
30-34 years...........	76,537	36	509	410	992	34,455	22,437	14,166	1,694	1,838
35-39 years...........	86,979	36	519	549	1,003	37,278	26,343	17,027	1,637	2,587
40-44 years...........	80,366	41	461	584	1,001	31,572	24,946	17,236	1,383	3,142
45-49 years...........	74,309	37	433	646	990	27,365	23,345	17,228	1,415	2,850
50-54 years...........	64,399	49	378	642	956	24,032	20,542	14,569	1,209	2,022
55-59 years...........	55,648	54	321	613	835	20,579	17,924	13,305	974	1,243
60-64 years...........	44,848	35	287	549	714	16,654	13,781	10,612	927	1,289
65-69 years...........	50,021	33	220	450	661	17,749	16,844	12,072	862	1,130
70-74 years...........	29,009	15	125	275	392	10,650	9,798	6,545	532	677
75 years and older....	29,676	24	119	297	457	10,337	10,440	6,839	682	481
NONWHITE FEMALE										
All ages..............	1,644,509	566	6,029	8,975	18,067	700,296	531,461	331,732	29,108	18,275
Under 5 years..........	249,609	61	734	975	2,683	107,567	81,299	48,961	4,625	2,704
5-9 years.............	229,427	48	634	1,002	2,348	101,389	73,085	44,732	4,136	2,053
10-14 years...........	214,421	59	630	1,033	2,281	94,622	68,776	41,786	3,511	1,723
15-19 years...........	175,676	56	548	762	1,915	77,875	55,467	34,310	3,120	1,623
20-24 years...........	118,472	38	495	434	1,260	53,346	37,129	21,776	2,471	1,523
25-29 years...........	94,948	35	490	407	1,033	42,526	29,349	17,413	1,672	1,677
30-34 years...........	85,043	39	448	518	964	36,754	26,519	16,724	1,544	1,405
35-39 years...........	93,837	32	433	574	1,020	39,362	30,661	19,241	1,544	970
40-44 years...........	79,651	40	384	580	928	31,035	26,796	17,893	1,227	768
45-49 years...........	72,474	39	314	603	861	27,980	24,179	16,524	1,160	814
50-54 years...........	62,032	38	283	530	725	24,193	20,737	13,626	980	920
55-59 years...........	46,995	23	203	483	582	17,866	15,368	10,863	778	829
60-64 years...........	35,460	19	148	359	475	13,875	11,416	8,081	580	507
65-69 years...........	40,384	16	122	287	421	14,926	14,276	9,473	530	333
70-74 years...........	21,183	13	70	202	261	8,036	7,367	4,733	306	195
75 years and older....	24,897	10	93	226	290	8,964	9,037	5,596	450	231

APPENDIX

Age by color and sex	United States	New England	Middle Atlantic	East North Central	West North Central	South Atlantic	East South Central	West South Central	Mountain	Pacific
TOTAL, ALL GROUPS										
All ages	131,669,275	8,437,290	27,539,487	26,626,342	13,516,990	17,823,151	10,778,225	13,064,525	4,150,003	9,733,262
Under 5 years......	10,541,524	572,727	1,818,113	2,007,977	1,079,157	1,687,908	1,095,923	1,223,135	405,063	651,521
5-9 years	10,684,622	612,668	1,938,637	1,971,537	1,082,941	1,712,113	1,108,522	1,248,056	385,085	625,063
10-14 years	11,745,935	704,271	2,290,894	2,226,283	1,176,561	1,808,333	1,144,296	1,314,813	391,940	688,544
15-19 years	12,333,523	763,039	2,466,538	2,374,005	1,249,151	1,854,773	1,121,789	1,322,456	398,088	783,684
20-24 years	11,587,835	728,410	2,423,451	2,294,492	1,125,470	1,705,459	970,590	1,156,264	369,400	814,299
25-29 years	11,096,638	679,222	2,366,965	2,213,877	1,054,722	1,562,546	898,721	1,123,416	346,560	850,609
30-34 years	10,242,388	629,358	2,250,024	2,071,260	992,669	1,358,397	796,566	1,034,363	310,386	799,365
35-39 years	9,545,377	595,024	2,130,943	1,962,698	933,261	1,222,774	716,560	948,386	275,656	760,075
40-44 years	8,787,843	585,655	2,043,238	1,859,597	885,504	1,052,132	600,604	798,885	248,361	713,867
45-49 years	8,255,225	571,438	1,907,415	1,798,861	861,515	935,154	544,867	718,366	239,610	677,999
50-54 years	7,256,846	506,907	1,669,231	1,587,410	778,537	802,099	473,985	596,151	215,511	627,015
55-59 years	5,843,865	417,148	1,306,594	1,273,829	650,628	634,214	383,028	480,007	175,161	523,256
60-64 years	4,728,340	356,074	1,048,799	1,015,752	534,146	518,258	310,085	381,535	138,021	425,670
65-69 years	3,806,657	293,081	800,664	801,889	437,995	440,012	276,903	325,126	104,863	326,124
70-74 years	2,569,532	207,353	544,770	567,456	317,964	267,891	167,691	196,718	72,218	227,471
75 years and older....	2,643,125	214,915	533,211	599,419	356,769	261,088	168,095	196,848	74,080	238,700
WHITE MALE										
All ages	59,448,548	4,100,379	13,084,380	12,894,141	6,627,608	6,560,997	4,012,358	5,336,134	2,059,637	4,772,914
Under 5 years......	4,701,470	287,711	879,909	981,694	533,651	602,747	406,614	494,692	194,380	320,072
5-9 years	4,744,537	307,314	934,192	960,745	533,974	607,902	409,054	502,509	184,293	304,574
10-14 years	5,259,007	352,514	1,104,310	1,084,085	580,686	653,164	427,448	533,659	189,383	333,758
15-19 years	5,515,920	378,520	1,183,667	1,149,861	612,653	668,997	417,493	535,258	192,265	377,206
20-24 years	5,113,642	354,274	1,133,416	1,090,696	540,418	609,735	352,269	458,698	178,940	395,196
25-29 years	4,892,013	328,158	1,089,311	1,045,678	506,153	566,890	325,192	447,016	169,732	413,883
30-34 years	4,573,316	301,440	1,042,618	982,481	478,015	509,067	295,345	418,708	154,542	391,100
35-39 years	4,254,368	284,957	991,135	932,783	447,158	448,321	258,772	380,560	136,421	374,311
40-44 years	3,995,190	280,774	966,418	894,120	429,512	395,849	223,035	329,111	124,447	351,924
45-49 years	3,842,613	279,066	924,671	886,708	424,921	360,202	205,779	299,780	122,977	338,509
50-54 years	3,451,717	250,464	828,428	799,691	389,914	312,287	182,680	256,416	113,902	317,935
55-59 years	2,790,046	204,368	645,858	639,964	327,561	252,739	151,478	208,353	93,878	265,847
60-64 years	2,232,453	169,040	506,132	504,997	269,078	206,528	124,384	168,440	73,487	210,367
65-69 years	1,736,937	135,565	374,898	388,526	219,672	166,071	105,673	135,423	54,553	156,556
70-74 years	1,183,283	95,236	250,197	274,577	160,104	104,306	65,679	84,963	38,102	110,119
75 years and older....	1,162,036	90,978	229,220	277,585	174,138	96,192	61,483	82,548	38,335	111,557
WHITE FEMALE										
All ages	58,766,322	4,228,767	13,153,242	12,634,310	6,483,911	6,534,230	3,981,397	5,233,462	1,919,276	4,597,727
Under 5 years......	4,528,035	276,722	843,898	943,621	512,156	582,752	393,682	479,474	188,250	307,480
5-9 years	4,584,414	296,331	900,916	924,892	514,978	588,628	396,452	487,162	179,946	295,109
10-14 years	5,093,688	341,673	1,073,889	1,048,609	560,772	630,848	411,822	518,025	183,879	324,171
15-19 years	5,448,127	374,138	1,174,516	1,132,506	602,011	661,009	414,813	530,772	188,814	369,548
20-24 years	5,226,507	365,193	1,179,178	1,116,500	553,444	616,740	362,278	471,865	175,332	386,007
25-29 years	5,012,257	342,729	1,151,787	1,069,668	515,362	573,761	333,464	458,981	163,565	402,940
30-34 years	4,633,162	320,245	1,081,414	989,656	482,574	515,297	299,994	423,205	144,699	376,078
35-39 years	4,262,292	301,718	1,005,333	920,762	452,535	454,044	265,116	380,780	128,648	353,356
40-44 years	3,940,893	296,537	962,763	868,983	425,230	395,686	223,644	319,231	114,923	333,896
45-49 years	3,690,143	284,925	895,211	833,127	408,433	355,196	202,291	285,577	108,672	316,711
50-54 years	3,228,590	250,190	777,025	730,098	366,162	305,714	177,458	238,312	95,058	288,573
55-59 years	2,636,799	207,853	616,744	593,128	305,453	252,750	147,546	195,385	76,145	241,795
60-64 years	2,184,240	183,194	512,258	483,548	252,365	211,114	120,418	157,684	60,068	203,591
65-69 years	1,762,109	154,438	403,400	389,204	206,841	170,667	102,455	126,807	46,630	161,667
70-74 years	1,217,262	110,550	282,018	280,201	150,602	107,781	63,120	77,825	31,674	113,491
75 years and older....	1,317,804	122,331	292,892	309,807	175,023	112,243	66,844	82,377	32,973	123,314
NONWHITE MALE										
All ages..........	6,613,044	54,381	626,312	544,184	201,727	2,309,592	1,353,666	1,222,159	89,761	211,262
Under 5 years......	653,238	4,160	47,071	41,186	16,715	249,972	146,746	124,082	11,200	12,206
5-9 years	674,286	4,533	51,345	42,707	16,801	256,178	150,969	128,785	10,231	12,737
10-14 years	693,322	4,975	55,266	45,960	17,534	260,847	152,707	130,918	9,407	15,708
15-19 years	664,233	5,099	51,559	44,070	16,778	254,432	140,041	124,046	8,646	19,562
20-24 years	578,750	4,340	46,685	39,864	14,705	225,269	117,858	104,412	7,740	17,877
25-29 years	558,649	4,035	54,144	45,472	15,556	200,512	110,786	100,445	6,944	20,755
30-34 years	496,996	3,705	57,452	46,504	15,288	161,518	94,779	90,631	5,893	21,226
35-39 years	491,291	4,129	64,776	53,175	16,041	150,446	88,872	88,009	5,625	20,218
40-44 years	423,945	4,411	58,891	50,613	15,578	126,176	72,825	73,848	4,906	16,697
45-49 years	366,656	3,975	45,827	42,557	14,812	106,808	67,098	68,220	4,465	12,894
50-54 years	301,033	3,335	33,120	31,539	12,078	93,091	57,870	52,899	3,885	13,216
55-59 years	221,318	2,646	22,773	22,135	9,532	66,141	43,932	40,446	3,151	10,562
60-64 years	165,363	2,040	15,812	14,616	6,905	52,225	33,799	29,164	2,726	8,076
65-69 years	159,151	1,536	10,935	11,845	5,908	53,127	36,157	32,650	2,071	4,922
70-74 years	87,684	776	5,911	6,362	3,771	28,509	20,450	18,119	1,390	2,396
75 years and older....	77,029	686	4,745	5,579	3,725	24,341	18,777	15,485	1,481	2,210
NONWHITE FEMALE										
All ages..........	6,841,361	53,763	675,553	553,707	203,744	2,418,332	1,430,804	1,272,770	81,329	151,359
Under 5 years......	658,681	4,134	47,235	41,476	16,635	252,437	148,881	124,887	11,233	11,763
5-9 years	681,385	4,490	52,184	43,193	17,188	259,405	152,067	129,600	10,615	12,643
10-14 years	699,918	5,109	57,429	47,629	17,569	263,474	152,319	132,211	9,271	14,907
15-19 years	705,243	5,282	56,796	47,568	17,709	270,335	149,442	132,380	8,363	17,368
20-24 years	668,936	4,603	64,172	47,432	16,933	253,715	138,185	121,289	7,388	15,219
25-29 years	633,719	4,300	71,723	53,059	17,651	221,383	129,279	116,974	6,319	13,031
30-34 years	538,914	3,968	68,540	52,619	16,792	172,515	106,448	101,819	5,252	10,961
35-39 years	537,426	4,220	69,699	56,028	17,527	169,963	103,800	99,037	4,962	12,190
40-44 years	427,815	3,933	55,166	45,881	15,184	134,421	81,100	76,695	4,085	11,350
45-49 years	355,813	3,472	41,706	36,469	13,349	112,948	69,699	64,789	3,496	9,885
50-54 years	275,506	2,918	30,658	26,082	10,383	91,007	55,977	48,524	2,666	7,291
55-59 years	195,702	2,281	21,219	18,602	8,082	62,584	40,072	35,823	1,987	5,052
60-64 years	146,284	1,800	14,597	12,591	5,798	48,391	31,484	26,247	1,740	3,636
65-69 years	148,460	1,542	11,431	12,344	5,574	50,147	32,613	30,246	1,609	2,979
70-74 years	81,303	791	6,644	6,316	3,487	27,295	18,442	15,811	1,052	1,465
75 years and older....	86,256	920	6,354	6,448	3,883	28,312	20,991	16,438	1,291	1,619

TABLE 30
POPULATION: AGE BY COLOR AND SEX FOR THE URBAN POPULATION OF THE UNITED STATES, BY GEOGRAPHIC DIVISION: 1940

Age by Color and Sex	United States	New England	Middle Atlantic	East North Central	West North Central	South Atlantic	East South Central	West South Central	Mountain	Pacific
TOTAL, ALL GROUPS										
All ages	74,423,702	6,420,542	21,147,543	17,444,359	5,993,124	6,921,726	3,165,356	5,203,401	1,771,742	6,355,909
Under 5 years	5,007,137	419,047	1,309,165	1,212,119	414,399	494,114	236,156	396,872	145,997	379,268
5-9 years	5,083,240	450,388	1,407,559	1,182,273	406,886	500,155	240,191	398,924	137,815	359,049
10-14 years	5,854,770	526,700	1,687,831	1,366,568	451,322	563,708	267,539	439,547	145,876	405,679
15-19 years	6,493,936	581,537	1,852,184	1,499,984	515,047	633,453	289,421	479,642	160,023	482,645
20-24 years	6,755,377	569,021	1,897,020	1,567,797	529,138	696,768	305,439	488,464	163,214	538,516
25-29 years	6,725,909	531,424	1,884,682	1,547,744	515,138	697,501	311,659	505,955	156,907	574,899
30-34 years	6,286,218	488,152	1,791,469	1,452,565	487,879	621,875	283,742	475,503	142,148	542,885
35-39 years	5,906,293	463,264	1,702,923	1,378,497	455,352	564,971	257,826	437,598	127,020	518,842
40-44 years	5,490,678	456,691	1,634,491	1,299,511	426,837	487,790	216,117	366,323	116,257	486,661
45-49 years	5,107,261	443,812	1,510,408	1,243,288	409,952	423,053	190,596	317,407	110,485	458,260
50-54 years	4,419,140	389,808	1,306,728	1,069,918	363,280	353,643	159,160	256,453	97,929	422,221
55-59 years	3,462,821	315,995	1,003,588	824,306	293,869	271,491	123,979	197,499	80,148	351,946
60-64 years	2,758,293	266,024	795,979	635,648	235,814	219,504	98,401	154,866	64,381	287,676
65-69 years	2,152,883	216,883	594,367	485,223	191,977	177,498	83,914	128,904	50,503	223,614
70-74 years	1,455,824	150,175	395,962	335,099	139,686	110,798	51,546	79,398	35,823	157,337
75 years and older	1,463,922	151,621	373,187	343,819	156,548	105,404	49,670	80,046	37,216	166,411
WHITE MALE										
All ages	33,304,701	3,077,623	9,844,008	8,126,144	2,747,675	2,474,317	1,089,793	2,074,404	859,420	3,011,317
Under 5 years	2,308,303	210,147	625,684	579,892	201,910	179,153	86,118	166,764	72,874	185,761
5-9 years	2,314,899	224,892	667,580	561,076	195,607	175,956	84,650	161,245	68,000	172,893
10-14 years	2,666,858	261,794	802,433	646,665	215,929	200,976	94,385	178,789	71,978	193,909
15-19 years	2,890,343	284,826	869,752	691,703	235,360	221,750	98,636	187,538	75,513	225,265
20-24 years	2,916,452	271,897	862,565	702,420	227,552	240,220	100,140	185,104	75,114	251,440
25-29 years	2,917,917	253,237	847,837	701,191	229,053	242,573	103,152	194,503	74,616	271,755
30-34 years	2,758,874	230,666	813,852	663,857	219,436	221,724	96,418	185,617	69,022	258,282
35-39 years	2,592,711	218,685	776,915	632,921	203,403	196,695	85,142	169,667	61,046	248,237
40-44 years	2,462,992	216,432	760,588	605,627	193,985	176,355	74,207	146,528	56,256	233,014
45-49 years	2,353,512	214,329	722,060	598,376	190,013	157,780	66,981	128,773	54,636	220,564
50-54 years	2,083,026	190,756	640,116	526,939	171,369	134,360	57,591	107,485	48,944	205,466
55-59 years	1,623,679	152,581	487,605	401,715	138,306	104,435	45,728	82,680	40,490	170,139
60-64 years	1,257,630	123,174	374,771	301,567	108,724	83,272	36,247	64,910	31,700	133,265
65-69 years	932,256	96,965	267,609	218,383	86,269	62,540	27,572	49,565	23,968	99,385
70-74 years	627,969	66,381	173,317	149,158	62,467	40,263	17,445	31,486	17,271	70,181
75 years and older	597,280	60,861	151,324	144,654	68,292	36,265	15,381	30,750	17,992	71,761
WHITE FEMALE										
All ages	34,668,122	3,250,545	10,130,767	8,327,121	2,958,438	2,639,182	1,181,817	2,199,732	878,868	3,101,652
Under 5 years	2,222,094	201,863	599,623	558,691	192,847	173,022	84,055	162,757	70,753	178,483
5-9 years	2,255,850	217,808	647,842	544,474	190,403	172,905	83,242	161,477	67,426	170,273
10-14 years	2,629,977	256,301	785,907	636,265	213,118	199,952	94,302	179,741	71,382	193,009
15-19 years	3,028,611	287,893	887,457	727,183	257,031	238,033	108,887	206,107	81,698	234,322
20-24 years	3,246,296	289,558	934,736	786,726	279,667	268,481	120,099	217,158	85,170	264,701
25-29 years	3,158,974	271,069	921,527	756,066	261,470	259,546	115,343	215,507	79,218	279,228
30-34 years	2,927,168	250,976	861,472	697,107	243,686	236,032	105,527	200,169	70,315	261,884
35-39 years	2,699,471	237,371	802,070	643,973	225,430	207,598	92,219	179,604	63,187	248,019
40-44 years	2,520,514	233,029	769,370	604,812	208,694	184,559	78,354	150,336	57,512	233,848
45-49 years	2,341,743	223,034	708,772	572,820	198,000	164,278	69,555	130,298	53,437	221,549
50-54 years	2,028,243	193,697	609,398	491,176	174,805	141,034	60,458	108,039	47,077	202,559
55-59 years	1,625,352	159,218	476,819	386,488	142,241	115,425	49,732	86,095	38,125	171,209
60-64 years	1,350,276	139,591	394,328	310,585	117,790	98,138	41,200	70,393	31,457	146,794
65-69 years	1,081,242	117,286	307,128	246,043	97,658	77,541	33,997	57,202	25,478	118,909
70-74 years	753,545	82,442	211,760	175,270	72,281	50,977	21,939	36,347	17,975	84,554
75 years and older	798,766	89,409	212,558	189,442	83,317	51,661	22,908	38,502	18,658	92,311
NONWHITE MALE										
All ages	3,059,005	45,982	557,465	484,445	139,145	838,087	410,105	429,941	17,360	136,475
Under 5 years	237,304	3,497	41,770	36,641	9,897	70,532	32,606	33,516	1,189	7,656
5-9 years	252,809	3,812	45,679	38,079	10,344	74,212	35,587	35,970	1,182	7,944
10-14 years	271,070	4,229	48,373	40,863	11,007	78,457	38,073	39,151	1,234	9,683
15-19 years	265,431	4,344	44,369	38,496	10,833	78,219	36,606	39,081	1,387	12,096
20-24 years	252,258	3,646	40,875	34,821	9,594	79,580	35,299	35,554	1,393	11,496
25-29 years	285,869	3,457	48,745	40,792	11,063	86,267	39,563	40,716	1,552	13,714
30-34 years	275,196	3,118	52,371	42,188	11,320	75,214	36,159	39,417	1,486	13,923
35-39 years	286,478	3,507	59,247	48,769	12,339	72,852	35,606	39,701	1,395	13,062
40-44 years	251,738	3,785	53,551	46,174	11,913	60,718	29,726	33,201	1,289	11,381
45-49 years	207,760	3,393	41,270	38,392	11,257	47,986	26,225	28,913	1,326	8,998
50-54 years	158,040	2,794	29,407	28,065	8,922	38,293	20,168	20,509	1,101	8,781
55-59 years	109,271	2,212	20,015	19,395	7,026	24,781	13,903	14,268	889	6,782
60-64 years	76,170	1,710	13,780	12,405	4,967	18,191	9,889	9,546	731	4,951
65-69 years	65,727	1,263	9,272	9,909	3,980	17,033	10,352	10,235	550	3,133
70-74 years	34,962	655	4,949	5,170	2,418	8,754	5,638	5,503	335	1,540
75 years and older	28,922	560	3,792	4,286	2,265	6,998	4,705	4,660	321	1,335
NONWHITE FEMALE										
All ages	3,391,874	46,392	615,303	506,649	147,866	970,140	483,641	499,324	16,094	106,465
Under 5 years	239,436	3,540	42,088	36,895	9,745	71,407	33,377	33,835	1,181	7,368
5-9 years	259,682	3,876	46,458	38,644	10,532	77,082	36,712	37,232	1,207	7,939
10-14 years	286,865	4,376	51,118	42,775	11,268	84,323	40,779	41,866	1,282	9,078
15-19 years	309,551	4,474	50,606	42,602	11,823	95,451	45,292	46,916	1,425	10,962
20-24 years	340,371	3,920	58,844	43,830	12,325	108,487	49,901	50,648	1,537	10,879
25-29 years	363,149	3,661	66,573	49,695	13,552	109,115	53,601	55,229	1,521	10,202
30-34 years	324,980	3,392	63,774	49,413	13,437	88,905	45,638	50,300	1,325	8,796
35-39 years	327,633	3,701	64,691	52,834	14,180	87,826	44,859	48,626	1,392	9,524
40-44 years	255,434	3,445	50,982	42,898	12,245	66,158	33,830	36,258	1,200	8,418
45-49 years	204,246	3,056	38,306	33,700	10,682	53,009	27,835	29,423	1,086	7,149
50-54 years	149,831	2,561	27,807	23,738	8,184	39,956	20,943	20,420	807	5,415
55-59 years	104,519	1,984	19,149	16,708	6,296	26,850	14,616	14,456	644	3,816
60-64 years	74,217	1,549	13,100	11,091	4,333	19,903	11,065	10,017	493	2,666
65-69 years	73,658	1,369	10,358	10,888	4,070	20,384	11,993	11,902	242	2,187
70-74 years	39,348	697	5,936	5,501	2,520	10,804	6,524	6,062	245	1,062
75 years and older	38,954	791	5,513	5,437	2,674	10,480	6,676	6,134	245	1,004

APPENDIX

TABLE 31

POPULATION: AGE BY COLOR AND SEX FOR THE RURAL-NONFARM POPULATION OF THE UNITED STATES, BY GEOGRAPHIC DIVISIONS: 1940

Age by color and sex	United States	New England	Middle Atlantic	East North Central	West North Central	South Atlantic	East South Central	West South Central	Mountain	Pacific
TOTAL, ALL GROUPS										
All ages	27,029,385	1,484,686	4,638,745	4,598,539	2,848,621	4,863,219	2,344,478	2,823,807	1,277,059	2,150,231
Under 5 years	2,522,831	116,287	378,111	416,376	235,889	512,968	257,906	281,960	141,412	181,922
5-9 years	2,446,807	119,173	385,384	390,520	233,621	495,732	244,561	279,960	129,298	168,558
10-14 years	2,503,567	126,672	428,379	402,392	244,517	490,910	236,016	281,531	123,955	169,195
15-19 years	2,483,112	127,728	426,947	395,697	250,981	487,939	227,392	271,786	118,662	175,980
20-24 years	2,319,310	118,107	383,896	365,160	219,684	473,337	217,460	247,593	113,152	180,921
25-29 years	2,299,920	115,257	371,692	371,290	215,407	451,940	216,089	253,403	112,279	192,563
30-34 years	2,132,330	111,353	360,189	354,566	205,778	394,652	191,669	234,488	99,685	179,950
35-39 years	1,896,310	102,330	330,169	319,958	187,623	338,542	162,092	206,977	85,311	163,308
40-44 years	1,647,317	96,009	304,890	283,192	172,854	275,095	127,388	166,397	72,503	146,989
45-49 years	1,502,701	93,979	285,621	264,382	166,183	235,135	109,996	144,175	67,301	135,929
50-54 years	1,313,341	84,138	253,360	237,118	152,546	194,621	92,521	116,853	59,221	122,963
55-59 years	1,084,568	70,826	206,860	203,574	134,411	151,754	73,773	95,364	47,328	100,678
60-64 years	910,613	62,626	170,714	177,422	120,741	123,016	59,758	78,253	37,184	80,899
65-69 years	786,338	53,105	139,952	156,475	110,683	107,312	56,430	71,910	28,630	61,841
70-74 years	561,577	40,289	101,656	120,944	88,912	65,690	35,034	45,870	20,100	43,082
75 years and older	618,743	44,807	110,925	139,473	108,791	64,576	36,393	47,287	21,038	45,453
WHITE MALE										
All ages	12,627,240	738,653	2,304,124	2,311,776	1,392,365	1,944,551	954,619	1,211,227	644,227	1,125,698
Under 5 years	1,167,369	58,728	188,121	208,962	116,538	205,037	109,296	121,534	68,237	90,916
5-9 years	1,128,790	60,413	192,044	196,039	115,587	196,384	101,870	119,637	62,480	84,336
10-14 years	1,155,007	64,122	211,784	201,400	120,221	194,212	98,037	120,517	60,121	84,593
15-19 years	1,133,185	64,119	212,046	197,083	120,366	189,669	89,446	113,924	57,433	89,099
20-24 years	1,039,890	58,589	188,567	177,957	101,497	181,309	83,573	101,737	54,184	92,477
25-29 years	1,044,029	56,803	180,578	182,265	101,781	177,783	85,466	105,224	55,238	98,891
30-34 years	1,000,403	55,103	177,295	178,826	100,914	162,320	79,543	101,259	50,731	94,412
35-39 years	898,004	51,067	163,909	163,307	92,121	138,956	66,870	90,145	43,951	87,578
40-44 years	794,761	48,666	153,169	146,732	86,569	114,421	53,132	74,640	38,226	79,203
45-49 years	733,488	47,456	145,195	137,307	83,640	99,131	45,826	64,416	36,243	74,274
50-54 years	644,130	42,357	130,174	122,915	76,357	80,946	38,183	52,160	32,723	68,315
55-59 years	528,259	35,457	105,380	104,108	66,228	62,967	30,167	41,821	26,101	56,030
60-64 years	439,286	30,713	85,690	89,473	59,106	50,334	24,361	34,220	20,625	44,764
65-69 years	367,371	25,629	69,262	77,722	53,703	40,997	21,574	29,685	15,520	33,279
70-74 years	267,036	19,226	49,684	60,202	43,907	25,897	13,827	19,858	11,030	23,405
75 years and older	286,232	20,205	51,226	67,478	53,730	24,185	13,448	20,450	11,384	24,126
WHITE FEMALE										
All ages	12,151,345	733,446	2,224,193	2,205,085	1,396,055	1,895,258	956,908	1,179,662	582,480	978,258
Under 5 years	1,125,202	56,564	180,912	200,495	112,690	198,731	105,758	116,808	66,312	86,932
5-9 years	1,088,079	57,696	183,452	187,635	111,812	190,378	99,654	116,084	60,969	80,399
10-14 years	1,121,301	61,433	205,158	193,689	118,231	189,461	96,403	117,829	58,695	80,402
15-19 years	1,125,444	62,384	203,194	190,608	124,941	191,105	97,577	116,325	56,541	82,439
20-24 years	1,060,027	58,430	185,978	180,472	113,254	184,966	91,637	106,681	54,075	84,534
25-29 years	1,048,736	57,441	182,270	182,631	109,005	177,853	88,573	108,731	52,618	89,614
30-34 years	961,045	55,253	174,532	169,736	100,933	156,799	77,243	99,352	45,457	81,740
35-39 years	837,683	50,311	157,140	150,556	91,691	129,964	63,345	84,617	38,134	71,925
40-44 years	721,368	48,428	143,477	130,568	82,755	104,462	49,461	66,046	31,651	64,520
45-49 years	657,650	45,734	133,542	121,615	79,228	89,502	42,834	57,287	28,916	58,992
50-54 years	577,028	41,093	117,668	109,754	73,395	74,406	36,488	47,282	24,696	52,246
55-59 years	488,852	34,813	97,405	96,062	65,944	60,974	30,613	40,428	19,780	42,833
60-64 years	418,688	31,463	82,044	85,311	59,872	50,636	25,164	34,128	15,334	34,736
65-69 years	361,643	27,131	68,365	76,306	55,099	42,384	23,046	29,726	12,166	27,420
70-74 years	260,929	20,885	50,553	59,263	43,684	26,289	14,116	18,691	8,387	19,061
75 years and older	297,700	24,387	58,203	70,384	53,521	27,348	14,996	19,647	8,749	20,465
NONWHITE MALE										
All ages	1,130,276	6,545	57,562	45,728	31,814	510,767	211,389	211,520	27,069	27,882
Under 5 years	114,524	523	4,600	3,426	3,370	54,105	21,407	21,645	3,395	2,053
5-9 years	113,962	570	4,903	3,466	3,035	53,970	21,386	21,901	2,822	1,909
10-14 years	112,407	552	5,890	3,707	3,076	52,802	20,488	21,200	2,581	2,111
15-19 years	108,322	579	6,013	4,229	2,863	51,480	18,817	19,587	2,370	2,384
20-24 years	105,577	525	4,661	3,957	2,558	51,771	19,295	17,926	2,618	2,266
25-29 years	103,024	477	4,259	3,749	2,452	48,424	20,160	18,415	2,436	2,652
30-34 years	87,571	500	4,150	3,464	2,173	38,977	17,232	16,493	1,941	2,641
35-39 years	81,578	504	4,650	3,545	1,969	35,120	15,657	15,699	1,836	2,598
40-44 years	68,242	502	4,523	3,552	2,030	28,899	12,177	12,896	1,569	2,094
45-49 years	58,899	445	3,918	3,327	1,931	23,810	10,760	11,750	1,295	1,663
50-54 years	48,974	410	3,063	2,684	1,619	20,318	9,056	9,017	1,141	1,666
55-59 years	35,916	306	2,292	1,996	1,271	14,518	6,625	6,711	933	1,264
60-64 years	27,432	248	1,682	1,547	947	11,343	5,055	4,893	759	958
65-69 years	29,277	203	1,392	1,375	981	12,139	5,849	6,089	533	716
70-74 years	17,595	95	793	860	720	6,929	3,616	3,795	393	394
75 years and older	16,976	106	773	844	819	6,162	3,809	3,503	447	513
NONWHITE FEMALE										
All ages	1,120,524	6,042	52,866	35,950	28,387	512,643	221,562	221,398	23,283	18,393
Under 5 years	115,736	472	4,478	3,493	3,291	55,095	21,445	21,973	3,468	2,021
5-9 years	115,976	494	4,985	3,380	3,187	55,000	21,651	22,338	3,027	1,914
10-14 years	114,852	565	5,547	3,596	2,989	54,435	21,088	21,985	2,558	2,089
15-19 years	116,191	646	5,394	3,777	2,811	55,685	21,552	21,950	2,318	2,058
20-24 years	113,816	563	4,690	2,774	2,375	55,291	22,955	21,249	2,275	1,644
25-29 years	104,131	536	4,585	2,645	2,169	47,880	21,890	21,033	1,987	1,406
30-34 years	83,311	497	4,212	2,540	1,758	36,556	17,651	17,384	1,556	1,157
35-39 years	79,045	448	4,470	2,550	1,742	34,502	16,220	16,516	1,390	1,207
40-44 years	62,946	413	3,721	2,340	1,500	27,310	12,618	12,815	1,057	1,172
45-49 years	52,664	344	2,966	2,133	1,384	22,692	10,576	10,722	847	1,000
50-54 years	43,209	276	2,455	1,765	1,175	18,951	8,794	8,394	661	736
55-59 years	31,541	250	1,783	1,408	968	13,295	6,368	6,404	514	551
60-64 years	25,207	202	1,298	1,091	816	10,703	5,178	5,012	466	441
65-69 years	28,047	142	933	1,072	900	11,792	5,961	6,410	411	426
70-74 years	16,017	83	626	619	601	6,575	3,475	3,526	290	222
75 years and older	17,835	109	723	767	721	6,881	4,140	3,687	458	349

TABLE 32

POPULATION: AGE BY COLOR AND SEX FOR THE RURAL-FARM POPULATION OF THE UNITED STATES, BY GEOGRAPHIC DIVISION: 1940

Age by color and sex	United States	New England	Middle Atlantic	East North Central	West North Central	South Atlantic	East South Central	West South Central	Mountain	Pacific
TOTAL, ALL GROUPS										
All ages.............	30,216,188	532,062	1,753,199	4,583,444	4,675,245	6,038,206	5,268,391	5,037,317	1,101,202	1,227,122
Under 5 years.........	3,011,556	37,393	130,837	379,482	428,869	680,826	601,861	544,303	117,654	90,331
5-9 years.............	3,154,575	43,107	145,694	398,744	442,434	716,226	623,770	569,172	117,972	97,456
10-14 years...........	3,387,598	50,899	174,684	457,323	480,722	753,715	640,741	593,735	122,109	113,670
15-19 years...........	3,356,475	53,774	187,407	478,324	483,123	733,381	604,976	571,028	119,403	125,059
20-24 years...........	2,513,148	41,282	142,535	361,535	376,648	535,354	447,691	420,207	93,054	94,862
25-29 years...........	2,070,809	32,541	110,591	294,843	324,177	413,105	370,973	364,058	77,374	83,147
30-34 years...........	1,823,840	29,853	98,366	264,129	299,012	341,870	321,155	324,372	68,553	76,530
35-39 years...........	1,742,774	29,430	97,851	264,243	290,286	319,261	296,642	303,811	63,325	77,925
40-44 years...........	1,649,848	30,955	103,857	276,894	285,813	289,247	257,099	266,165	59,601	80,217
45-49 years...........	1,645,263	33,647	111,386	291,191	285,380	276,966	244,275	256,784	61,824	83,810
50-54 years...........	1,524,365	32,961	109,143	280,374	262,711	253,835	222,304	222,845	58,361	81,831
55-59 years...........	1,296,476	30,327	96,146	245,949	222,348	210,969	185,276	187,144	47,685	70,632
60-64 years...........	1,059,434	27,424	82,106	202,682	177,591	175,738	151,926	148,416	36,456	57,095
65-69 years...........	867,436	23,093	66,345	160,191	135,335	155,202	136,559	124,312	25,730	40,669
70-74 years...........	552,131	16,889	47,152	111,413	89,366	91,403	81,111	71,450	16,295	27,052
75 years and older....	560,460	18,487	49,099	116,127	91,430	91,108	82,032	69,515	15,826	26,836
WHITE MALE										
All ages.............	13,516,607	284,103	936,248	2,456,221	2,487,568	2,142,129	1,967,946	2,050,503	555,990	635,899
Under 5 years.........	1,225,798	18,836	66,104	192,840	215,203	218,557	211,200	206,394	53,269	43,395
5-9 years.............	1,300,848	22,009	74,568	203,630	222,780	235,562	222,514	218,627	53,813	47,345
10-14 years...........	1,437,142	26,598	90,093	236,020	244,536	257,976	235,026	234,353	57,284	55,256
15-19 years...........	1,492,392	29,575	101,869	261,075	256,927	257,578	229,411	233,796	59,319	62,842
20-24 years...........	1,157,300	23,788	82,284	210,319	211,369	188,206	168,556	171,857	49,642	51,279
25-29 years...........	930,067	18,118	60,896	162,222	175,319	146,534	136,574	147,289	39,878	43,237
30-34 years...........	814,039	15,671	51,471	139,798	157,665	125,023	119,384	131,832	34,789	38,406
35-39 years...........	763,653	15,205	50,311	136,505	151,534	112,670	106,760	120,748	31,424	38,496
40-44 years...........	737,437	15,676	52,661	141,761	148,958	105,070	95,696	107,943	29,965	39,707
45-49 years...........	755,613	17,281	57,416	151,025	151,268	103,291	92,972	106,591	32,098	43,671
50-54 years...........	724,561	17,351	58,138	149,837	142,188	96,981	86,906	96,771	32,235	44,154
55-59 years...........	638,108	16,330	52,873	134,141	123,027	85,337	75,583	83,852	27,287	39,678
60-64 years...........	535,537	15,153	45,671	113,957	101,248	72,922	63,776	69,310	21,162	32,338
65-69 years...........	437,310	12,971	38,027	92,421	79,700	62,534	56,527	56,173	15,065	23,892
70-74 years...........	288,278	9,629	27,196	65,217	53,730	38,146	34,407	33,619	9,801	16,533
75 years and older....	278,524	9,912	26,670	65,453	52,116	35,742	32,654	31,348	8,959	15,670
WHITE FEMALE										
All ages.............	11,946,855	244,776	798,282	2,102,104	2,129,418	1,999,790	1,842,672	1,854,068	457,928	517,817
Under 5 years.........	1,180,739	18,295	63,363	184,435	206,619	210,999	203,869	199,909	51,185	42,065
5-9 years.............	1,240,485	20,827	69,622	192,783	212,763	225,345	213,556	209,601	51,551	44,437
10-14 years...........	1,342,410	23,939	82,824	218,655	229,423	241,435	221,117	220,455	53,802	50,760
15-19 years...........	1,294,102	23,861	83,565	214,715	220,039	231,871	208,349	208,340	50,575	52,787
20-24 years...........	920,184	17,205	58,464	149,302	160,493	163,293	150,542	148,026	36,087	34,098
25-29 years...........	804,547	14,219	47,990	130,971	144,887	136,362	129,548	134,743	31,729	32,454
30-34 years...........	744,916	14,016	45,410	122,813	137,955	122,166	117,224	123,684	28,927	32,451
35-39 years...........	725,138	14,036	46,123	126,233	135,414	116,482	109,552	116,559	27,327	33,412
40-44 years...........	699,011	15,080	49,916	133,603	133,781	106,665	95,829	102,849	25,760	35,528
45-49 years...........	690,750	16,157	52,897	138,692	131,205	101,446	89,902	97,992	26,319	36,170
50-54 years...........	623,319	15,400	49,959	129,168	117,962	90,274	80,512	82,991	23,285	33,768
55-59 years...........	522,595	13,822	42,520	110,578	97,268	76,351	67,201	68,862	18,240	27,753
60-64 years...........	415,276	12,140	35,886	87,652	74,703	62,340	54,054	53,163	13,277	22,061
65-69 years...........	319,224	10,021	27,907	66,855	54,084	50,742	45,412	39,879	8,986	15,338
70-74 years...........	202,788	7,223	19,705	45,668	34,637	30,515	27,065	22,787	5,312	9,876
75 years and older....	221,338	8,535	22,131	49,981	38,185	33,234	28,940	24,228	5,566	10,538
NONWHITE MALE										
All ages.............	2,423,763	1,854	11,285	14,011	30,768	960,738	732,172	580,698	45,332	46,905
Under 5 years.........	301,510	140	701	1,119	3,448	125,335	92,733	68,921	6,616	2,497
5-9 years.............	307,515	151	763	1,162	3,422	127,996	93,996	70,914	6,227	2,884
10-14 years...........	309,845	194	1,003	1,390	3,451	129,588	94,146	70,567	5,592	3,914
15-19 years...........	290,480	176	1,177	1,345	3,082	124,733	84,618	65,378	4,889	5,082
20-24 years...........	220,915	169	1,149	1,086	2,553	93,918	63,264	50,932	3,729	4,115
25-29 years...........	169,756	101	1,140	931	2,041	65,821	51,063	41,514	2,956	4,389
30-34 years...........	134,229	87	931	852	1,795	47,327	41,388	34,721	2,166	4,662
35-39 years...........	123,235	118	879	861	1,733	42,474	37,609	32,609	2,394	4,558
40-44 years...........	103,965	124	817	887	1,635	36,559	30,922	27,751	2,048	3,222
45-49 years...........	99,997	137	639	838	1,624	35,012	30,113	27,557	1,844	2,233
50-54 years...........	94,019	131	650	790	1,537	34,640	28,646	23,373	1,613	2,769
55-59 years...........	76,131	128	466	744	1,235	26,842	23,404	19,467	1,329	2,516
60-64 years...........	61,761	82	350	664	991	22,691	18,855	14,725	1,236	2,167
65-69 years...........	64,147	70	271	561	947	23,955	19,956	16,326	988	1,073
70-74 years...........	35,127	26	169	332	633	12,826	11,196	8,821	662	462
75 years and older....	31,131	20	180	449	641	11,181	10,263	7,322	713	362
NONWHITE FEMALE										
All ages.............	2,328,963	1,329	7,384	11,108	27,491	935,549	725,601	552,048	41,952	26,501
Under 5 years.........	303,509	122	669	1,088	3,599	125,935	94,059	69,079	6,584	2,374
5-9 years.............	305,727	120	741	1,169	3,469	127,323	93,704	70,030	6,381	2,790
10-14 years...........	298,201	168	764	1,258	3,312	124,716	90,452	68,360	5,431	3,740
15-19 years...........	279,501	162	796	1,189	3,075	119,199	82,598	63,514	4,620	4,348
20-24 years...........	214,749	120	638	828	2,233	89,937	65,329	49,392	3,576	2,696
25-29 years...........	166,439	103	565	719	1,930	64,388	53,788	40,712	2,811	1,423
30-34 years...........	130,623	79	554	666	1,597	47,054	43,159	34,135	2,371	1,008
35-39 years...........	130,748	71	538	644	1,605	47,635	42,721	33,895	2,180	1,459
40-44 years...........	109,435	75	463	643	1,439	40,953	34,652	27,622	1,828	1,760
45-49 years...........	98,903	72	434	636	1,283	37,247	31,288	24,644	1,563	1,736
50-54 years...........	82,466	79	396	579	1,024	32,100	26,240	19,710	1,198	1,140
55-59 years...........	59,642	47	287	486	818	22,439	19,088	14,963	829	685
60-64 years...........	46,860	49	199	409	649	17,785	15,241	11,218	781	529
65-69 years...........	46,755	31	140	354	604	17,971	14,664	11,934	691	366
70-74 years...........	25,938	11	82	196	366	9,916	8,443	6,223	520	181
75 years and older....	29,467	20	118	244	488	10,951	10,175	6,617	588	266

TABLE 33

PERCENT DISTRIBUTION: EDUCATIONAL ATTAINMENT OF THE TOTAL POPULATION 25 YEARS OLD AND OVER, AND PERCENT OF THE TOTAL POPULATION 5-29 YEARS OLD ENROLLED IN SCHOOL, BY GEOGRAPHIC DIVISIONS: 1950

Educational Attainment and School Enrollment	Geographic Division									
	United States	New England	Middle Atlantic	East North Central	West North Central	South Atlantic	East South Central	West South Central	Mountain	Pacific
EDUCATIONAL ATTAINMENT, ALL GROUPS										
Total 25 years old and over	100.0	100.0	100.0	100.0	100.0	100.0	100.0	100.0	100.0	100.0
No school completed	2.5	2.7	3.0	1.5	1.0	3.2	3.4	4.6	2.4	1.5
Elementary school	44.5	37.5	43.5	44.0	47.5	50.9	57.7	47.0	36.8	32.3
1-4 years	8.3	5.2	6.4	5.8	5.2	14.6	16.9	13.3	6.1	4.7
5-6 years	9.1	7.4	8.3	7.5	6.8	14.0	14.8	12.1	6.2	5.5
7 years	6.8	5.8	6.4	5.9	6.3	10.2	8.5	8.4	5.2	4.6
8 years	20.3	19.1	22.5	24.8	29.3	12.1	17.5	13.3	19.2	17.5
High school	37.2	43.6	38.2	39.6	35.5	30.8	27.6	33.2	40.1	44.5
1-3 years	17.0	18.7	16.9	17.6	14.4	16.7	14.5	18.3	17.1	17.9
4 years	20.2	25.0	21.3	22.0	21.1	14.1	13.1	15.0	23.0	26.5
College	13.2	13.6	12.1	12.5	13.4	12.6	9.2	12.8	18.0	18.8
1-3 years	7.2	6.9	5.5	6.9	8.2	6.6	5.4	7.4	10.8	11.0
4 years or more	6.0	6.7	6.6	5.6	5.2	5.9	3.9	5.5	7.2	7.8
Not reported	2.7	2.6	3.2	2.4	2.6	2.6	2.1	2.4	2.7	2.9
EDUCATIONAL ATTAINMENT - MALE										
Total 25 years old and over	100.0	100.0	100.0	100.0	100.0	100.0	100.0	100.0	100.0	100.0
No school years completed	2.6	2.6	2.8	1.5	1.1	3.7	4.0	4.8	2.4	1.7
Elementary school	46.4	39.2	44.0	45.8	51.2	53.1	59.5	49.1	40.4	35.0
1-4 years	9.2	5.6	6.7	6.5	6.0	16.5	19.3	14.9	7.0	5.4
5-6 years	9.4	7.7	8.4	7.9	7.5	14.3	14.9	12.4	6.8	6.1
7 years	7.0	6.1	6.4	6.2	6.9	10.1	8.3	8.5	5.7	5.0
8 years	20.7	19.9	22.5	25.2	30.9	12.1	17.0	13.4	20.9	18.5
High school	34.0	40.9	35.6	36.4	31.9	27.6	24.9	30.0	36.4	40.6
1-3 years	16.4	19.1	16.7	17.1	13.8	15.6	13.6	17.0	16.5	17.4
4 years	17.6	21.8	18.8	19.3	18.1	12.0	11.3	13.0	19.8	23.2
College	13.9	14.5	14.0	13.4	12.8	12.7	9.0	13.2	17.7	19.4
1-3 years	6.8	6.3	5.7	6.7	6.9	6.1	4.8	7.1	9.8	10.5
4 years or more	7.1	8.1	8.3	6.7	6.0	6.6	4.3	6.0	8.0	8.8
Not reported	3.1	2.8	3.6	2.8	2.9	3.0	2.5	2.9	3.1	3.4
EDUCATIONAL ATTAINMENT - FEMALE										
Total 25 years old and over	100.0	100.0	100.0	100.0	100.0	100.0	100.0	100.0	100.0	100.0
No school years completed	2.4	2.8	3.2	1.4	0.9	2.7	2.8	4.3	2.5	1.4
Elementary school	42.7	36.0	43.1	42.3	43.8	48.9	56.0	45.0	33.1	29.6
1-4 years	7.4	4.9	6.1	5.2	4.4	12.7	14.6	11.7	5.3	4.0
5-6 years	8.8	7.1	8.1	7.1	6.1	13.8	14.8	11.8	5.7	5.0
7 years	6.7	5.6	6.3	5.6	5.6	10.3	8.8	8.3	4.7	4.3
8 years	19.8	18.3	22.5	24.4	27.7	12.1	17.9	13.1	17.5	16.5
High school	40.1	46.1	40.6	42.6	38.9	33.8	30.2	36.4	44.0	48.3
1-3 years	17.5	18.3	17.1	18.1	14.9	17.7	15.4	19.5	17.6	18.5
4 years	22.6	27.8	23.6	24.5	24.0	16.1	14.8	16.8	26.4	29.9
College	12.5	12.8	10.3	11.6	14.0	12.4	9.4	12.5	18.3	18.2
1-3 years	7.5	7.4	5.3	7.1	9.4	7.2	5.9	7.6	11.9	11.4
4 years or more	5.0	5.4	5.1	4.5	4.5	5.2	3.5	4.9	6.3	6.8
Not reported	2.3	2.3	2.8	2.0	2.4	2.2	1.6	1.9	2.2	2.4
EDUCATIONAL ATTAINMENT - WHITE										
Total 25 years old and over	100.0	100.0	100.0	100.0	100.0	100.0	100.0	100.0	100.0	100.0
No school years completed	2.1	2.7	3.0	1.4	0.9	1.9	2.1	3.6	1.8	1.4
Elementary school	42.5	37.3	42.9	43.4	47.1	45.6	53.3	43.0	36.5	31.7
1-4 years	6.6	5.2	6.0	5.3	4.8	9.7	12.1	10.1	5.8	4.3
5-6 years	8.2	7.3	7.8	7.1	6.5	12.2	13.1	10.8	6.0	5.2
7 years	6.6	5.8	6.2	5.7	6.2	10.2	8.5	8.1	5.1	4.5
8 years	21.2	19.1	22.9	25.3	29.7	13.4	19.5	14.0	19.5	17.7
High school	38.8	43.8	38.7	40.1	35.8	35.3	31.8	36.6	40.7	44.9
1-3 years	17.4	18.7	16.9	17.5	14.3	18.6	16.1	19.6	17.2	17.9
4 years	21.4	25.1	21.8	22.6	21.4	16.7	15.7	16.9	23.5	27.0
College	14.0	13.7	12.5	12.9	13.7	14.8	10.9	14.5	18.5	19.3
1-3 years	7.6	6.9	5.6	7.1	8.3	7.8	6.4	8.3	11.1	11.2
4 years or more	6.4	6.7	6.9	5.8	5.3	7.0	4.6	6.1	7.4	8.1
Not reported	2.6	2.5	3.0	2.3	2.6	2.4	1.9	2.3	2.5	2.8
EDUCATIONAL ATTAINMENT - NONWHITE										
Total 25 years old and over	100.0	100.0	100.0	100.0	100.0	100.0	100.0	100.0	100.0	100.0
No school years completed	6.5	4.1	3.0	2.6	3.5	7.7	8.2	9.7	19.5	4.5
Elementary school	63.6	48.2	53.9	54.4	57.4	70.2	73.4	67.7	44.7	44.6
1-4 years	24.9	10.4	13.6	14.4	15.8	32.0	33.7	29.6	13.7	11.3
5-6 years	18.0	12.5	15.3	14.6	14.8	20.4	20.9	19.1	12.2	11.8
7 years	9.3	8.6	9.2	9.1	9.0	10.1	8.6	9.6	6.7	7.3
8 years	11.5	16.6	15.8	16.4	17.8	7.7	10.2	9.4	12.2	14.1
High school	21.1	36.2	31.1	32.2	27.6	14.5	12.8	15.9	24.6	36.8
1-3 years	13.0	19.3	17.7	19.3	16.0	9.8	8.9	11.2	12.6	18.0
4 years	8.1	17.0	13.4	12.9	11.6	4.7	3.9	4.6	12.0	18.8
College	5.1	7.2	5.5	6.7	6.4	4.6	3.1	4.2	5.2	9.8
1-3 years	2.9	4.2	3.1	4.3	4.0	2.3	1.8	2.3	3.3	6.4
4 years or more	2.2	3.0	2.4	2.4	2.5	2.3	1.3	1.9	2.0	3.4
Not reported	3.7	4.3	6.4	4.1	5.1	3.0	2.5	2.6	6.0	4.4
PERCENT OF POPULATION ENROLLED IN SCHOOLS	49.4	49.7	48.5	49.5	50.9	48.1	50.3	49.2	51.6	49.6
5-6 years	39.3	43.1	44.6	39.6	39.7	35.6	36.3	32.8	35.0	44.2
7-13 years	95.5	95.8	95.5	96.6	96.1	95.4	93.7	95.0	95.4	97.2
14-15 years	92.9	94.9	94.9	95.7	92.1	90.5	87.5	89.9	93.1	96.6
16-17 years	74.4	76.9	79.4	80.1	76.9	64.1	63.5	68.7	77.1	84.1
18-19 years	32.2	38.2	32.6	32.9	33.9	27.6	30.0	30.1	35.7	36.3
20-24 years	12.9	16.3	13.9	12.8	13.1	10.8	11.1	11.5	14.4	14.9
25-29 years	6.5	6.6	6.8	6.0	6.1	6.0	6.5	6.8	7.5	7.8

TABLE 34

PERCENT DISTRIBUTION: EDUCATIONAL ATTAINMENT OF THE URBAN POPULATION 25 YEARS OLD AND OVER, AND PERCENT OF THE URBAN POPULATION 5-29 YEARS OLD ENROLLED IN SCHOOL, BY GEOGRAPHIC DIVISIONS: 1950

Educational Attainment and School Enrollment	Geographic Division									
	United States	New England	Middle Atlantic	East North Central	West North Central	South Atlantic	East South Central	West South Central	Mountain	Pacific
EDUCATIONAL ATTAINMENT, ALL GROUPS										
Total 25 years old and over	100.0	100.0	100.0	100.0	100.0	100.0	100.0	100.0	100.0	100.0
No school completed	2.3	2.9	3.3	1.6	1.0	2.3	2.4	3.7	1.5	1.4
Elementary school	39.5	37.4	42.3	40.8	39.9	41.6	45.8	39.2	32.3	29.7
1-4 years	6.8	5.5	6.6	5.9	4.7	10.3	11.6	10.5	5.1	4.3
5-6 years	8.0	7.7	8.2	7.4	6.2	11.3	11.7	10.1	5.5	5.1
7 years	6.0	6.0	6.1	5.5	5.3	7.9	7.1	7.1	4.5	4.2
8 years	18.7	18.1	21.3	22.1	23.7	12.1	15.4	11.6	17.2	16.0
High school	40.2	43.9	39.0	41.3	39.3	36.3	35.7	37.5	42.1	45.7
1-3 years	17.6	18.6	17.1	18.4	15.7	17.6	17.2	18.7	16.9	17.9
4 years	22.6	25.2	21.9	22.9	23.6	18.8	18.5	18.8	25.2	27.9
College	15.2	13.3	12.5	13.9	16.8	16.9	14.0	17.1	21.4	20.3
1-3 years	8.0	6.6	5.5	7.4	9.6	8.7	7.8	9.6	12.5	11.7
4 years or more	7.2	6.6	6.9	6.5	7.3	8.3	6.2	7.4	9.0	8.6
Not reported	2.7	2.6	3.0	2.4	3.0	2.9	2.2	2.6	2.6	2.8
EDUCATIONAL ATTAINMENT - MALE										
Total 25 years old and over	100.0	100.0	100.0	100.0	100.0	100.0	100.0	100.0	100.0	100.0
No school years completed	2.3	2.7	3.0	1.6	1.0	2.4	2.7	3.6	1.6	1.5
Elementary school	40.5	38.4	42.2	41.7	41.7	42.9	47.0	40.5	34.6	31.6
1-4 years	7.3	5.8	6.8	6.4	5.2	11.2	12.9	11.4	5.7	4.8
5-6 years	8.2	7.9	8.3	7.6	6.6	11.4	11.8	10.2	4.8	5.6
7 years	6.0	6.1	6.1	5.6	5.6	7.9	7.0	7.2	4.8	4.5
8 years	18.9	18.6	21.1	22.1	24.4	12.3	15.3	11.8	18.2	16.7
High school	37.3	41.4	36.5	38.3	36.0	33.2	32.8	34.3	38.5	42.0
1-3 years	17.3	19.1	17.0	18.0	15.4	17.0	16.5	17.7	16.5	17.4
4 years	19.9	22.3	19.5	20.3	20.6	16.2	16.3	16.6	22.0	24.5
College	16.9	14.6	14.9	15.7	17.8	18.1	14.7	18.4	22.3	21.6
1-3 years	8.0	6.4	6.0	7.7	9.1	8.3	7.5	9.7	12.0	11.6
4 years or more	8.8	8.3	8.9	8.0	8.7	9.8	7.2	8.6	10.3	10.0
Not reported	3.1	2.8	3.4	2.8	3.4	3.3	2.7	3.2	3.0	3.3
EDUCATIONAL ATTAINMENT - FEMALE										
Total 25 years old and over	100.0	100.0	100.0	100.0	100.0	100.0	100.0	100.0	100.0	100.0
No school years completed	2.3	3.1	3.5	1.6	0.9	2.1	2.1	3.7	1.5	1.3
Elementary school	38.7	36.4	42.4	40.0	38.2	40.5	44.7	38.0	30.1	27.9
1-4 years	6.4	5.3	6.4	5.4	4.2	9.5	10.4	9.7	4.6	3.8
5-6 years	7.9	7.6	8.2	7.1	5.8	11.1	11.6	10.0	5.2	4.7
7 years	5.9	5.9	6.2	5.4	5.1	7.9	7.2	7.0	4.2	3.9
8 years	18.6	17.7	21.6	22.0	23.1	11.9	15.5	11.4	16.1	15.4
High school	42.9	46.0	41.2	44.1	42.2	39.1	38.2	40.4	45.6	49.3
1-3 years	17.9	18.2	17.2	18.7	16.0	18.1	17.8	19.6	17.3	18.3
4 years	25.0	27.8	24.1	25.4	26.3	21.0	20.4	20.9	28.3	31.0
College	13.7	12.1	10.3	12.3	16.0	15.9	13.3	15.9	20.5	19.1
1-3 years	7.9	6.9	5.1	7.2	10.0	9.0	8.1	9.5	12.9	11.8
4 years or more	5.8	5.2	5.1	5.1	6.0	6.9	5.2	6.3	7.6	7.3
Not reported	2.3	2.4	2.7	2.0	2.7	2.5	1.7	2.0	2.2	2.4
EDUCATIONAL ATTAINMENT - WHITE										
Total 25 years old and over	100.0	100.0	100.0	100.0	100.0	100.0	100.0	100.0	100.0	100.0
No school years completed	2.1	2.9	3.3	1.5	0.8	1.3	1.1	3.0	1.5	1.2
Elementary school	37.5	37.2	41.4	39.7	39.0	35.0	38.4	34.5	31.9	28.9
1-4 years	5.5	5.4	6.1	5.2	4.1	6.0	6.5	7.8	4.9	4.0
5-6 years	7.1	7.7	7.7	6.8	5.7	8.9	9.0	8.5	5.3	4.8
7 years	5.6	5.9	5.9	5.2	5.1	7.3	6.4	6.5	4.4	4.0
8 years	19.3	18.1	21.7	22.6	24.0	12.8	16.5	11.8	17.2	16.2
High school	41.6	44.0	39.5	42.0	39.9	41.1	41.4	40.7	42.4	46.2
1-3 years	17.8	18.6	17.0	18.2	15.7	19.0	18.8	19.5	16.9	17.8
4 years	23.8	25.4	22.5	23.8	24.2	22.1	22.5	21.1	25.4	28.4
College	16.1	13.4	13.0	14.5	17.4	19.9	17.1	19.2	21.7	20.9
1-3 years	8.4	6.7	5.7	7.7	9.9	10.2	9.5	10.8	12.6	12.0
4 years or more	7.7	6.7	7.3	6.8	7.5	9.7	7.5	8.4	9.1	8.9
Not reported	2.6	2.6	2.9	2.3	2.9	2.7	2.1	2.6	2.6	2.8
EDUCATIONAL ATTAINMENT - NONWHITE										
Total 25 years old and over	100.0	100.0	100.0	100.0	100.0	100.0	100.0	100.0	100.0	100.0
No school years completed	4.6	3.8	3.0	2.4	2.9	5.7	6.2	7.2	5.2	3.8
Elementary school	58.9	47.9	54.6	54.2	55.6	64.8	68.2	63.9	47.4	43.3
1-4 years	19.4	10.4	13.6	14.3	14.6	25.7	26.9	24.6	12.7	10.5
5-6 years	16.9	12.5	15.5	14.6	14.4	19.8	20.0	18.5	12.6	11.6
7 years	9.4	8.5	9.4	9.1	9.0	10.0	9.3	10.1	7.7	7.5
8 years	13.1	16.4	16.0	16.2	17.6	9.4	12.0	10.6	14.3	13.6
High school	26.4	37.0	32.2	32.8	29.3	19.5	18.5	20.6	33.2	38.2
1-3 years	15.9	19.6	18.2	19.6	16.7	12.6	12.4	14.1	16.2	18.9
4 years	10.6	17.4	13.9	13.2	12.5	6.9	6.2	6.5	17.0	19.3
College	6.4	7.3	5.7	6.8	7.0	6.5	4.6	5.6	9.7	10.7
1-3 years	3.7	4.2	3.2	4.4	4.3	3.3	2.6	3.1	6.1	6.9
4 years or more	2.7	3.1	2.5	2.5	2.7	3.2	2.0	2.5	3.6	3.8
Not reported	3.6	4.1	4.6	3.8	5.2	3.4	2.5	2.7	4.5	4.1
PERCENT OF POPULATION ENROLLED IN SCHOOLS	47.8	49.2	47.8	48.0	48.6	45.5	47.3	45.9	51.1	49.3
5-6 years	41.1	44.1	45.6	40.7	38.7	37.1	37.6	32.5	36.0	46.3
7-13 years	96.1	95.8	95.2	96.7	96.3	96.2	96.2	95.6	96.8	97.4
14-15 years	94.8	95.3	94.8	96.2	94.1	93.5	93.2	91.3	94.8	97.1
16-17 years	78.8	77.7	80.7	82.0	78.7	71.6	71.6	70.2	79.9	87.2
18-19 years	36.5	39.7	34.0	35.8	40.7	34.9	36.0	34.1	42.8	40.6
20-24 years	15.8	17.5	15.1	15.1	18.5	14.7	15.4	14.5	19.8	17.5
25-29 years	7.6	7.1	7.4	6.8	8.0	7.3	8.0	7.7	9.5	8.7

TABLE 35

PERCENT DISTRIBUTION: EDUCATIONAL ATTAINMENT OF THE RURAL-NONFARM POPULATION 25 YEARS OLD AND OVER, AND PERCENT OF THE RURAL-NONFARM POPULATION 5-29 YEARS OLD ENROLLED IN SCHOOL, BY GEOGRAPHIC DIVISIONS: 1950

Educational Attainment and School Enrollment	United States	New England	Middle Atlantic	East North Central	West North Central	South Atlantic	East South Central	West South Central	Mountain	Pacific
EDUCATIONAL ATTAINMENT, ALL GROUPS										
Total 25 years old and over	100.0	100.0	100.0	100.0	100.0	100.0	100.0	100.0	100.0	100.0
No school completed	2.7	2.0	1.8	1.3	1.2	3.9	3.9	6.0	3.6	1.8
Elementary school	49.3	36.6	47.0	47.6	50.9	56.4	59.2	52.4	40.8	39.3
1-4 years	9.7	4.0	5.7	5.6	6.2	16.8	17.6	15.5	7.5	5.6
5-6 years	10.1	6.0	8.3	7.6	7.5	15.5	15.0	13.4	7.2	6.6
7 years	7.8	5.3	7.1	6.6	6.6	11.6	8.7	9.2	5.9	5.9
8 years	21.6	21.2	25.9	28.0	30.6	12.5	18.0	14.3	20.2	21.2
High school	33.9	43.5	35.6	37.7	32.6	27.7	25.8	30.1	37.9	41.2
1-3 years	16.7	18.9	16.4	16.9	13.6	16.9	14.0	18.8	17.5	18.6
4 years	17.2	24.7	19.2	20.8	19.0	10.8	11.8	11.3	20.5	22.6
College	10.9	15.3	10.8	10.2	12.3	9.3	8.4	9.1	14.7	14.2
1-3 years	6.3	8.0	5.3	6.1	7.7	5.2	5.0	5.3	9.0	8.6
4 years or more	4.7	7.3	5.5	4.1	4.5	4.2	3.4	3.7	5.7	5.5
Not reported	3.2	2.6	4.8	3.3	3.1	2.6	2.7	2.4	2.9	3.6
EDUCATIONAL ATTAINMENT - MALE										
Total 25 years old and over	100.0	100.0	100.0	100.0	100.0	100.0	100.0	100.0	100.0	100.0
No school years completed	3.0	2.1	1.9	1.5	1.3	4.4	4.5	6.5	3.5	2.0
Elementary school	51.7	39.8	49.2	50.0	54.2	58.4	60.4	54.2	44.6	43.0
1-4 years	10.9	4.6	6.4	6.5	7.2	18.7	19.5	17.2	8.5	6.6
5-6 years	10.6	6.6	8.9	8.2	8.3	15.7	14.8	13.5	7.9	7.4
7 years	8.0	5.9	7.5	6.8	7.1	11.5	8.4	9.2	6.4	6.3
8 years	22.1	22.7	26.5	28.5	31.6	12.5	17.6	14.3	21.9	22.7
High school	31.0	40.0	32.6	34.5	29.6	25.1	23.6	27.5	34.4	37.6
1-3 years	16.0	19.2	16.1	16.3	13.0	15.7	13.3	17.4	16.9	17.9
4 years	15.0	20.8	16.5	18.2	16.6	9.4	10.3	10.1	17.5	19.7
College	10.6	15.1	10.7	10.1	11.3	8.9	8.1	8.9	14.0	13.4
1-3 years	5.4	6.7	4.6	5.2	5.9	4.5	4.3	5.0	7.7	7.6
4 years or more	5.2	8.4	6.2	4.8	5.3	4.4	3.8	3.9	6.3	5.8
Not reported	3.8	3.1	5.5	3.9	3.6	3.1	3.4	2.9	3.5	4.0
EDUCATIONAL ATTAINMENT - FEMALE										
Total 25 years old and over	100.0	100.0	100.0	100.0	100.0	100.0	100.0	100.0	100.0	100.0
No school years completed	2.4	1.9	1.7	1.0	1.1	3.3	3.3	5.6	3.8	1.5
Elementary school	46.9	33.5	44.8	45.1	47.7	54.5	58.1	50.7	36.6	35.0
1-4 years	8.5	3.6	5.0	4.7	5.2	14.8	15.7	13.8	6.4	4.4
5-6 years	9.7	5.4	7.7	6.9	6.7	15.4	15.1	13.3	6.4	5.7
7 years	7.6	4.8	6.8	6.0	6.1	11.7	8.9	9.3	5.3	5.3
8 years	21.0	19.8	25.4	27.6	29.6	12.5	18.3	14.2	18.4	19.5
High school	36.8	46.9	38.6	40.8	35.4	30.4	28.0	32.6	41.8	45.4
1-3 years	17.4	18.6	16.8	17.5	14.1	18.1	14.7	20.2	18.1	19.5
4 years	19.4	28.3	21.9	23.4	21.3	12.3	13.2	12.4	23.7	25.9
College	11.3	15.5	10.8	10.4	13.2	9.7	8.6	9.2	15.5	15.0
1-3 years	7.1	9.2	6.0	6.9	9.4	5.8	5.6	5.7	10.5	9.8
4 years or more	4.1	6.3	4.8	3.4	3.7	3.9	3.0	3.6	5.0	5.2
Not reported	2.6	2.2	4.1	2.6	2.7	2.1	2.0	1.9	2.3	3.1
EDUCATIONAL ATTAINMENT - WHITE										
Total 25 years old and over	100.0	100.0	100.0	100.0	100.0	100.0	100.0	100.0	100.0	100.0
No school years completed	2.0	1.9	1.8	1.2	1.1	2.4	2.6	4.7	2.4	1.6
Elementary school	47.7	36.4	47.1	47.4	50.7	52.4	56.6	49.5	40.7	38.9
1-4 years	7.9	4.0	5.5	5.4	6.0	12.1	14.1	12.3	7.2	5.3
5-6 years	9.4	6.0	8.2	7.5	7.4	14.4	14.0	12.4	6.9	6.4
7 years	7.7	5.3	7.1	6.3	6.6	11.9	8.9	9.3	5.8	5.8
8 years	22.7	21.2	26.3	28.2	30.8	13.9	19.6	15.4	20.7	21.3
High school	35.7	43.7	36.2	37.9	32.7	31.9	29.0	33.4	38.8	41.6
1-3 years	17.4	18.9	16.6	17.0	13.6	19.1	15.4	20.6	17.8	18.8
4 years	18.3	24.8	19.6	21.0	19.2	12.8	13.6	12.8	21.1	22.8
College	11.6	15.4	11.0	10.3	12.4	10.9	9.4	10.1	15.3	14.4
1-3 years	6.6	8.0	5.4	6.1	7.8	6.1	5.6	6.0	9.4	8.8
4 years or more	4.9	7.4	5.6	4.2	4.6	4.8	3.8	4.1	5.9	5.6
Not reported	3.0	2.6	3.9	3.1	3.1	2.4	2.4	2.3	2.7	3.5
EDUCATIONAL ATTAINMENT - NONWHITE										
Total 25 years old and over	100.0	100.0	100.0	100.0	100.0	100.0	100.0	100.0	100.0	100.0
No school years completed	10.6	7.0	3.4	5.6	6.7	10.1	10.4	13.8	27.9	6.9
Elementary school	68.4	50.6	43.2	56.6	62.1	73.5	72.6	69.4	43.2	53.0
1-4 years	31.9	10.1	12.8	16.6	19.0	36.4	35.2	33.9	13.4	15.2
5-6 years	18.8	12.6	11.8	13.8	15.1	20.4	20.1	18.9	12.6	13.4
7 years	9.0	9.1	6.5	8.2	8.9	10.2	7.8	8.8	6.5	7.1
8 years	8.8	18.8	12.1	18.0	19.1	6.5	9.5	7.8	10.8	17.3
High school	12.2	29.0	16.2	21.9	21.2	10.3	9.9	10.9	19.9	28.3
1-3 years	8.5	16.0	9.7	13.8	13.5	7.7	7.1	8.4	11.3	14.7
4 years	3.7	13.0	6.5	8.2	7.7	2.6	2.7	2.5	8.7	13.6
College	3.0	6.7	3.0	4.2	3.9	2.8	2.9	3.0	2.6	4.9
1-3 years	1.7	3.8	1.7	2.9	2.6	1.4	1.7	1.5	1.6	3.4
4 years or more	1.4	2.9	1.3	1.3	1.3	1.4	1.2	1.4	1.1	1.4
Not reported	5.7	6.7	34.2	11.7	6.1	3.3	4.2	2.9	6.3	6.9
PERCENT OF POPULATION ENROLLED IN SCHOOLS	49.0	50.6	50.0	50.2	51.4	46.4	48.1	49.7	50.2	47.7
5-6 years	36.9	40.9	41.9	37.6	40.2	34.0	35.2	31.9	34.4	39.5
7-13 years	95.5	95.8	96.3	96.4	95.9	95.1	93.6	94.7	94.3	96.8
14-15 years	92.1	93.8	95.3	95.1	93.1	90.0	86.8	89.2	91.6	95.3
16-17 years	70.2	75.6	76.4	77.2	78.8	60.3	60.4	67.0	73.1	74.5
18-19 years	25.6	34.4	28.2	26.7	29.4	21.3	26.8	24.1	26.0	22.2
20-24 years	8.0	12.8	8.8	7.3	6.9	7.5	9.3	7.2	7.2	7.2
25-29 years	4.4	4.5	4.2	3.8	3.4	4.3	5.8	5.4	4.5	4.6

TABLE 36

PERCENT DISTRIBUTION: EDUCATIONAL ATTAINMENT OF THE RURAL-FARM POPULATION 25 YEARS OLD AND OVER, AND PERCENT OF THE RURAL-FARM POPULATION 5-29 YEARS OLD ENROLLED IN SCHOOL, BY GEOGRAPHIC DIVISIONS: 1950

Educational Attainment and School Enrollment	United States	New England	Middle Atlantic	East North Central	West North Central	South Atlantic	East South Central	West South Central	Mountain	Pacific
EDUCATIONAL ATTAINMENT, ALL GROUPS										
Total 25 years old and over	100.0	100.0	100.0	100.0	100.0	100.0	100.0	100.0	100.0	100.0
No school completed	3.1	2.4	1.8	1.0	0.8	4.8	4.4	5.6	3.7	2.3
Elementary school	62.5	44.8	57.0	58.9	61.2	69.5	72.4	63.1	46.8	45.6
1-4 years	13.7	4.9	5.8	5.8	5.4	23.4	23.4	18.7	7.6	6.7
5-6 years	13.0	6.8	9.2	8.2	7.5	19.6	18.8	16.4	7.3	7.3
7 years	9.8	5.6	8.2	7.6	8.0	14.7	10.3	11.1	6.6	6.5
8 years	26.0	27.5	33.9	37.3	40.3	11.9	19.8	16.9	25.2	25.1
High school	26.6	39.7	31.2	31.8	29.7	19.2	18.3	24.7	36.3	37.7
1-3 years	14.0	18.8	15.2	13.9	12.1	13.7	11.4	16.6	17.0	17.0
4 years	12.6	20.9	16.0	17.9	17.6	5.5	6.9	8.1	19.3	20.8
College	6.3	11.3	8.5	6.9	7.0	4.8	3.6	4.9	10.9	12.1
1-3 years	4.3	6.6	4.8	4.8	5.5	3.0	2.4	3.2	7.8	7.9
4 years or more	2.0	4.6	3.7	2.0	1.5	1.8	1.1	1.7	3.1	4.3
Not reported	1.5	1.8	1.5	1.3	1.3	1.6	1.4	1.7	2.3	2.2
EDUCATIONAL ATTAINMENT – MALE										
Total 25 years old and over	100.0	100.0	100.0	100.0	100.0	100.0	100.0	100.0	100.0	100.0
No school years completed	3.6	2.6	1.8	1.1	0.9	6.0	5.3	6.3	3.6	2.8
Elementary school	66.3	50.0	61.5	63.6	67.3	72.2	74.0	66.0	52.8	50.8
1-4 years	15.8	5.8	6.6	7.1	6.5	27.2	26.9	21.4	8.9	8.3
5-6 years	13.5	7.8	10.3	9.3	8.7	19.7	18.7	16.8	8.2	8.4
7 years	10.1	6.5	9.2	8.6	9.4	13.9	9.8	11.0	7.7	7.2
8 years	26.9	29.9	35.4	38.6	42.7	11.4	18.7	16.7	28.0	26.9
High school	23.5	36.2	27.8	28.5	25.8	16.2	16.2	21.7	32.3	33.4
1-3 years	12.8	18.8	14.5	13.0	11.3	11.7	10.3	14.9	16.0	15.7
4 years	10.7	17.3	13.3	15.4	14.5	4.5	5.9	6.9	16.3	17.7
College	4.9	9.3	7.1	5.3	4.5	3.8	2.8	4.1	8.6	10.3
1-3 years	3.1	4.8	3.6	3.4	3.2	2.2	1.8	2.6	5.8	6.4
4 years or more	1.8	4.5	3.5	1.9	1.3	1.5	1.0	1.4	2.8	3.9
Not reported	1.8	1.9	1.8	1.5	1.4	1.9	1.6	1.9	2.6	2.7
EDUCATIONAL ATTAINMENT – FEMALE										
Total 25 years old and over	100.0	100.0	100.0	100.0	100.0	100.0	100.0	100.0	100.0	100.0
No school years completed	2.6	2.3	1.7	0.9	0.7	3.7	3.4	4.9	3.9	1.7
Elementary school	58.4	38.9	52.1	53.8	54.1	66.8	70.6	60.0	39.4	39.3
1-4 years	11.4	3.8	4.8	4.5	4.2	19.4	19.7	15.7	6.0	4.8
5-6 years	12.4	5.6	8.0	7.0	6.1	19.5	19.0	16.0	6.2	5.9
7 years	9.5	4.6	7.2	6.5	6.3	15.4	10.9	11.2	5.4	5.6
8 years	25.1	24.9	32.2	35.8	37.5	12.4	21.0	17.1	21.8	23.0
High school	29.9	43.7	34.9	35.6	34.2	22.3	20.5	28.0	41.1	42.9
1-3 years	15.3	18.8	16.0	14.9	13.1	15.7	12.5	18.5	18.1	18.4
4 years	14.7	25.0	18.9	20.6	21.1	6.6	8.0	9.5	23.0	24.5
College	7.8	13.5	9.9	8.6	9.8	5.8	4.3	5.8	13.6	14.4
1-3 years	5.6	8.7	6.0	6.4	8.0	3.7	3.1	3.9	10.2	9.6
4 years or more	2.2	4.8	3.9	2.2	1.8	2.1	1.2	1.9	3.4	4.8
Not reported	1.3	1.6	1.4	1.2	1.2	1.3	1.2	1.4	2.0	1.7
EDUCATIONAL ATTAINMENT – WHITE										
Total 25 years old and over	100.0	100.0	100.0	100.0	100.0	100.0	100.0	100.0	100.0	100.0
No school years completed	2.1	2.4	1.7	1.0	0.8	3.1	2.8	4.2	2.1	2.0
Elementary school	60.5	44.7	56.9	58.9	61.1	66.1	69.7	60.4	47.0	45.3
1-4 years	10.3	4.9	5.6	5.8	5.3	16.9	17.8	14.5	7.1	6.2
5-6 years	11.9	6.7	9.1	8.2	7.4	18.7	17.7	15.5	7.1	7.0
7 years	9.9	5.6	8.2	7.6	8.0	16.2	11.0	11.6	6.7	6.5
8 years	28.4	27.5	34.0	37.3	40.5	14.2	23.3	18.9	26.1	25.5
High school	29.0	39.8	31.3	31.9	29.8	23.4	21.8	28.2	37.5	38.1
1-3 years	15.0	18.8	15.2	13.9	12.2	16.5	13.3	18.7	17.5	17.3
4 years	13.9	21.0	16.1	18.0	17.7	7.0	8.6	9.5	20.0	20.8
College	6.9	11.3	8.5	6.9	7.0	5.8	4.3	5.6	11.4	12.5
1-3 years	4.7	6.6	4.8	4.8	5.5	3.7	2.9	3.7	8.2	8.1
4 years or more	2.2	4.7	3.7	2.0	1.5	2.2	1.4	1.9	3.2	4.4
Not reported	1.5	1.8	1.6	1.3	1.3	1.6	1.4	1.6	2.0	2.1
EDUCATIONAL ATTAINMENT – NONWHITE										
Total 25 years old and over	100.0	100.0	100.0	100.0	100.0	100.0	100.0	100.0	100.0	100.0
No school years completed	10.7	7.0	6.5	3.6	6.6	10.0	9.8	12.4	30.9	9.7
Elementary school	78.1	54.7	67.9	67.0	74.9	80.0	81.5	75.7	42.4	50.7
1-4 years	40.4	12.5	23.0	17.9	27.9	42.9	42.9	38.4	15.6	16.7
5-6 years	21.5	14.1	18.0	16.0	19.7	22.2	22.6	20.7	10.9	12.3
7 years	9.0	10.2	9.4	9.4	8.8	10.1	8.0	8.9	5.3	5.6
8 years	7.2	18.0	17.5	23.8	18.3	4.8	8.0	7.8	10.6	16.1
High school	7.8	28.1	18.3	22.6	14.6	6.5	6.1	8.4	17.1	29.6
1-3 years	5.7	16.4	12.4	13.1	9.2	5.3	4.8	6.6	8.6	10.4
4 years	2.0	11.7	5.9	9.5	5.4	1.2	1.3	1.8	8.6	19.2
College	1.5	6.3	3.6	4.4	1.8	1.6	1.0	1.6	1.6	4.6
1-3 years	0.9	3.1	2.0	2.7	1.3	0.9	0.7	0.9	1.1	3.3
4 years or more	0.6	3.1	1.6	1.7	0.5	0.7	0.3	0.7	0.5	1.2
Not reported	1.9	3.9	3.6	2.4	2.1	1.8	1.6	1.8	8.0	5.5
PERCENT OF POPULATION ENROLLED IN SCHOOLS										
5-6 years	55.4	55.1	54.0	56.3	54.8	55.0	54.8	56.7	55.4	58.1
7-13 years	36.6	40.0	40.1	37.6	40.8	34.4	36.0	34.1	33.7	38.3
14-15 years	94.7	96.7	96.3	96.4	95.8	94.7	91.9	94.1	94.0	97.2
16-17 years	89.1	93.4	94.1	94.3	89.0	87.3	84.3	88.4	91.3	95.7
18-19 years	67.2	70.8	71.7	76.0	73.4	58.4	59.6	67.4	76.4	82.8
20-24 years	25.1	28.4	23.8	25.4	23.1	21.9	26.1	25.9	29.7	37.3
25-29 years	5.5	6.8	6.1	4.9	4.1	5.2	6.3	5.9	5.8	7.4
	4.2	4.2	3.9	3.8	3.4	4.2	4.8	5.0	4.5	4.5

TABLE 37

PERCENT CHANGE: EDUCATIONAL ATTAINMENT OF THE TOTAL POPULATION 25 YEARS OLD AND OVER AND SCHOOL ENROLLMENT OF THE TOTAL POPULATION 5-29 YEARS OLD, BY GEOGRAPHIC DIVISIONS: 1940-50

Educational Attainment and School Enrollment	Geographic Division									
	United States	New England	Middle Atlantic	East North Central	West North Central	South Atlantic	East South Central	West South Central	Mountain	Pacific
EDUCATIONAL ATTAINMENT, ALL GROUPS										
Total 25 years old and over	17.1	12.2	13.1	14.9	5.6	25.4	11.3	15.8	23.8	43.9
No school completed	-22.0	-22.0	-30.5	-23.1	-23.2	-20.3	-28.2	-10.2	-16.4	2.0
Elementary school	-6.6	-14.4	-13.2	-11.0	-14.3	8.0	-1.6	-0.2	-5.1	6.8
1-4 years	-0.5	-4.9	-0.6	-3.3	-10.4	2.0	-3.6	-1.4	3.0	27.1
4-6 years	-6.3	-3.8	-7.0	-13.6	-20.4	3.1	-6.9	-8.6	-4.7	15.9
7 years	16.4	19.1	21.1	20.6	8.7	8.1	21.9	-2.6	33.1	66.6
8 years	-14.5	-25.8	-23.9	-16.9	-17.2	23.1	-4.0	12.3	-14.0	-8.2
High school	49.7	38.4	57.7	49.3	31.9	58.2	48.1	34.4	49.5	65.8
1-3 years	32.9	21.6	34.3	29.6	11.3	56.4	36.9	26.1	27.9	47.5
4 years	67.5	54.4	82.8	69.9	51.1	60.5	62.8	46.1	71.0	80.9
College	54.3	56.8	52.0	51.8	32.9	59.3	39.8	49.1	59.6	84.0
1-3 years	53.7	60.7	53.8	51.6	31.7	54.4	36.8	43.1	57.2	89.2
4 years or more	55.1	52.9	50.6	52.0	34.8	65.1	44.1	58.1	63.3	77.3
Not reported	123.6	55.9	79.5	166.2	163.7	111.5	70.8	172.3	168.0	304.6
EDUCATIONAL ATTAINMENT - MALE										
Total 25 years old and over	13.9	9.4	9.7	11.5	2.8	22.7	8.9	13.1	19.4	39.1
No school years completed	-24.5	-27.6	-35.9	-26.5	-26.8	-19.9	-27.6	-12.0	-19.9	-1.9
Elementary school	-8.8	-16.5	-16.2	-13.2	-15.9	6.4	-3.1	-2.3	-7.9	3.5
1-4 years	-3.2	-10.4	-6.6	-6.7	-13.5	1.7	-4.1	-3.7	-1.0	20.0
5-6 years	-8.4	-7.2	-10.8	-15.5	-21.2	2.9	-7.4	-10.0	-8.7	10.1
7 years	14.7	18.4	18.8	20.0	8.1	5.6	21.2	-4.7	29.9	58.9
8 years	-16.9	-27.3	-26.4	-19.5	-19.0	19.4	-7.3	9.8	-16.3	-10.4
High school	47.6	38.3	55.5	46.2	32.5	55.8	45.6	30.5	46.6	63.6
1-3 years	31.4	21.4	33.5	28.0	11.5	52.8	36.1	22.5	27.0	41.8
4 years	66.9	57.5	82.3	67.4	54.9	59.9	58.9	42.6	68.3	79.4
College	54.2	52.9	49.2	51.5	32.9	61.1	42.7	53.7	63.2	81.9
1-3 years	59.2	67.5	59.2	57.1	34.1	61.2	41.7	50.6	64.4	90.0
4 years or more	49.8	43.2	43.0	46.3	31.6	61.1	43.9	57.7	61.8	73.1
Not reported	123.0	57.1	83.3	154.5	152.0	109.2	81.2	174.7	156.2	268.0
EDUCATIONAL ATTAINMENT - FEMALE										
Total 25 years old and over	20.3	14.9	16.4	18.5	8.5	28.1	13.7	18.4	28.7	49.0
No school years completed	-19.2	-16.8	-25.3	-19.4	-18.9	-20.8	-29.1	-8.0	-12.4	7.2
Elementary school	-4.2	-12.0	-10.2	-8.5	12.4	9.6	-0.1	2.2	-1.3	11.1
1-4 years	3.0	1.3	6.2	1.1	-6.0	2.3	-3.0	1.6	9.1	39.8
5-6 years	-4.1	- 0.2	-3.1	-11.4	-19.5	3.3	-6.5	-7.0	0.8	23.9
7 years	18.2	19.7	23.4	21.3	9.4	10.5	22.6	-0.4	37.6	76.5
8 years	-12.0	-24.4	-21.5	-14.2	-15.1	26.9	-0.9	14.9	-11.1	-5.6
High school	51.4	38.5	59.4	51.9	31.5	60.2	50.1	37.7	52.1	67.5
1-3 years	34.2	21.7	35.2	31.2	11.1	59.5	37.6	29.4	28.8	48.3
4 years	68.0	52.3	83.2	71.9	48.3	60.9	65.8	48.5	73.1	82.1
College	54.4	60.9	55.8	52.1	32.9	57.5	37.2	44.6	56.0	86.3
1-3 years	49.2	55.8	48.8	46.9	30.1	49.4	33.3	36.9	51.5	88.4
4 years or more	62.9	68.4	63.8	61.0	39.1	70.2	44.4	58.5	65.4	83.0
Not reported	124.3	54.6	75.1	183.5	179.2	114.5	57.5	168.8	187.2	368.8
EDUCATIONAL ATTAINMENT - WHITE										
Total 25 years old and over	16.8	11.9	11.3	12.8	5.3	29.1	15.9	19.0	23.5	41.6
No school years completed	-21.5	-21.9	-31.4	-24.3	-21.6	-14.2	-24.3	-2.6	-15.0	0.5
Elementary school	-8.3	-14.7	-15.0	-13.3	-14.8	8.3	0.6	1.3	-6.1	4.0
1-4 years	0.3	-5.5	-3.0	-7.8	-11.1	8.4	4.1	4.2	1.8	23.9
5-6 years	-8.1	-4.3	-9.4	-17.0	-21.3	2.2	-4.5	-7.3	-6.0	11.1
7 years	14.1	18.4	18.8	16.6	8.1	3.2	21.8	-4.4	31.5	61.2
8 years	-15.8	-26.0	-24.8	-17.9	-17.5	19.3	-5.3	10.8	-14.5	-9.5
High school	47.7	37.8	55.0	46.6	31.4	55.6	46.9	33.7	48.6	63.1
1-3 years	30.1	20.8	31.2	26.2	10.3	53.1	34.4	24.6	26.9	44.1
4 years	65.9	53.8	80.4	67.7	50.5	58.4	62.6	45.9	70.0	78.8
College	53.2	56.4	50.9	50.1	32.7	57.4	38.1	49.1	59.1	82.1
1-3 years	52.5	60.2	52.4	49.5	31.5	53.5	35.5	43.5	56.8	86.7
4 years or more	53.9	52.7	49.6	50.7	34.5	62.2	41.8	57.7	62.8	76.0
Not reported	120.3	54.3	67.2	152.7	152.6	130.2	82.8	193.6	160.1	300.2
EDUCATIONAL ATTAINMENT - NONWHITE										
Total 25 years old and over	20.6	41.3	48.7	63.6	16.0	13.8	-2.3	1.3	30.4	108.5
No school years completed	-23.5	-26.3	-13.5	-11.2	-33.4	-25.0	-31.4	-22.0	-19.5	11.8
Elementary school	6.8	10.7	17.3	33.4	-0.9	7.1	-6.8	-4.9	22.4	70.3
1-4 years	-2.4	16.2	19.1	35.3	-3.0	-4.2	-12.0	-10.1	18.7	64.1
5-6 years	2.6	22.0	16.7	26.3	-7.4	5.1	-11.9	-12.1	16.2	81.9
7 years	35.2	58.7	51.6	83.4	22.4	30.5	22.5	6.2	78.6	172.2
8 years	18.6	-11.8	2.8	19.7	-2.4	53.7	5.3	25.2	12.8	39.7
High school	97.2	114.6	132.3	134.0	57.8	85.9	59.1	43.9	103.8	169.3
1-3 years	84.2	102.1	106.6	114.3	42.1	83.3	55.9	41.7	77.0	168.3
4 years	122.8	130.8	177.8	170.2	86.0	91.8	66.8	49.6	142.2	170.3
College	93.5	118.4	108.1	133.3	50.9	83.9	64.8	47.8	115.6	206.2
1-3 years	88.1	149.3	104.9	140.3	50.6	66.4	54.6	36.1	102.8	234.1
4 years or more	101.3	104.8	112.6	121.9	51.6	106.1	81.5	65.3	141.1	165.0
Not reported	148.5	161.1	273.8	412.9	302.3	71.4	44.8	102.1	303.2	367.1
POPULATION ENROLLED IN SCHOOLS	8.3	0.4	-2.7	6.8	-2.6	14.7	15.8	6.2	17.6	46.6
5-6 years	19.7	0.3	6.7	7.1	-11.7	47.8	57.6	35.1	31.2	69.9
7-13 years	6.9	-2.4	-4.2	8.2	-2.6	9.2	11.3	2.7	17.2	54.9
14-15 years	-8.8	-19.9	-22.2	-10.8	-14.0	0.0	2.8	-7.9	3.6	17.7
16-17 years	-7.6	-15.4	-18.4	-11.3	-11.9	4.1	3.4	-5.4	-1.3	10.5
18-19 years	-3.4	8.1	-11.7	-6.6	-11.7	10.3	4.9	-5.0	-3.6	0.9
20-24 years	94.6	125.9	93.8	93.6	64.4	124.9	100.5	86.7	76.1	88.2
25-29 years	-	-	-	-	-	-	-	-	-	-

TABLE 38

PERCENT CHANGE: EDUCATIONAL ATTAINMENT OF THE URBAN POPULATION 25 YEARS OLD AND OVER AND SCHOOL ENROLLMENT OF THE URBAN POPULATION 5-29 YEARS OLD, BY GEOGRAPHIC DIVISIONS: 1940-50

Educational Attainment and School Enrollment	United States	New England	Middle Atlantic	East North Central	West North Central	South Atlantic	East South Central	West South Central	Mountain	Pacific
EDUCATIONAL ATTAINMENT, ALL GROUPS										
Total 25 years old and over	20.7	10.7	11.1	15.9	16.1	32.8	27.8	45.7	38.7	39.5
No school completed	-24.8	-24.9	-36.3	-28.4	-19.0	-17.3	-19.6	26.4	0.1	-4.6
Elementary school	-8.3	-15.8	-17.0	-12.1	-7.9	5.6	6.8	25.5	4.5	-0.9
1-4 years	6.1	-6.9	-2.1	-0.4	4.0	4.2	10.2	34.5	26.3	30.6
5-6 years	-3.5	-5.4	-7.0	-12.6	-12.0	1.9	1.5	16.9	8.5	13.5
7 years	26.0	15.6	18.2	26.3	25.2	17.5	42.7	26.1	65.1	83.2
8 years	-21.1	-27.9	-29.6	-20.6	-14.0	3.2	-3.3	25.7	-10.6	-21.0
High school	51.5	37.3	57.1	46.2	35.2	61.6	56.0	57.7	57.9	57.5
1-3 years	35.1	20.7	33.5	28.2	17.3	59.6	47.4	57.0	38.6	41.2
4 years	67.2	52.9	81.7	64.6	50.4	63.5	64.9	58.5	73.8	69.7
College	59.0	54.3	51.8	53.0	41.8	65.8	52.6	67.8	69.6	85.5
1-3 years	62.4	61.4	57.4	56.0	43.0	62.7	52.1	64.6	71.5	67.4
4 years or more	55.3	47.8	47.7	49.6	40.1	69.2	53.3	72.2	67.0	67.4
Not reported	161.8	52.2	85.6	259.9	247.4	179.6	200.4	295.3	228.7	382.5
EDUCATIONAL ATTAINMENT - MALE										
Total 25 years old and over	18.1	8.5	8.0	12.9	14.7	30.3	26.3	44.9	36.5	36.0
No school completed	-28.3	-30.6	-41.7	-32.0	-22.3	-16.9	-17.6	26.7	-5.8	-9.2
Elementary school	-10.7	-18.0	-20.1	-14.6	-9.6	3.1	5.3	24.2	2.0	-4.2
1-4 years	2.7	-12.2	-8.3	-3.7	0.2	3.2	11.4	34.3	20.8	22.4
5-6 years	-6.2	-8.7	-11.1	-14.6	-13.3	0.5	0.5	15.7	4.3	6.7
7 years	24.6	14.5	15.6	26.3	25.6	14.0	44.1	24.2	65.1	75.6
8 years	-23.5	-29.2	-32.1	-23.6	-15.9	-0.8	-7.5	22.9	-12.6	-23.2
High school	49.8	37.7	54.9	43.0	36.1	59.7	54.3	54.4	57.9	56.5
1-3 years	34.0	20.8	32.4	26.3	18.4	57.7	47.9	53.8	40.0	41.5
4 years	66.5	56.4	81.3	61.6	53.1	62.0	61.3	55.0	74.3	68.8
College	57.9	51.1	48.4	51.9	42.9	66.4	56.1	72.8	72.7	74.9
1-3 years	67.8	67.9	61.8	61.1	48.9	68.4	58.2	73.1	80.1	87.0
4 years or more	49.8	40.3	40.6	44.1	37.1	64.7	54.0	72.5	64.8	62.4
Not reported	167.6	51.0	92.1	268.8	236.4	174.2	206.9	317.1	227.7	348.1
EDUCATIONAL ATTAINMENT - FEMALE										
Total 25 years old and over	23.2	12.7	14.0	18.7	17.5	35.0	29.0	46.4	40.7	42.9
No school years completed	-21.4	-19.9	-31.3	-24.9	-15.4	-17.9	-22.0	26.2	6.4	0.4
Elementary school	-5.8	-13.7	-13.9	-9.6	-6.1	7.8	8.1	26.8	7.3	2.7
1-4 years	9.9	-1.3	4.6	3.3	8.4	5.0	8.8	34.6	33.3	41.4
5-6 years	-0.8	-2.1	-3.0	-10.7	-10.6	3.0	2.4	17.9	13.2	21.6
7 years	27.3	16.7	20.7	26.2	24.7	20.7	41.4	27.7	64.9	91.7
8 years	-18.7	-26.7	-27.2	-17.7	-12.1	6.9	0.5	28.4	-8.5	-18.7
High school	52.9	37.0	58.8	48.9	34.5	62.9	57.3	60.4	57.9	58.3
1-3 years	36.1	20.5	34.4	29.9	16.4	61.1	47.0	59.6	37.3	40.8
4 years	67.7	50.5	82.1	66.8	48.5	64.5	67.4	61.2	73.4	70.4
College	60.1	57.8	56.5	54.0	40.7	65.0	49.3	62.7	66.4	80.0
1-3 years	57.8	56.4	52.9	51.3	38.6	58.2	47.5	57.3	64.5	84.0
4 years or more	63.5	59.7	60.3	58.1	44.2	74.6	52.3	71.7	69.6	73.9
Not reported	155.0	53.5	78.6	249.0	261.0	185.8	191.5	267.1	229.7	435.9
EDUCATIONAL ATTAINMENT - WHITE										
Total 25 years old and over	18.8	10.2	8.8	12.8	15.6	33.9	31.1	49.4	38.0	36.1
No school years completed	-27.8	-25.0	-37.6	-30.4	-18.0	-14.8	-18.3	37.8	-2.2	-9.3
Elementary school	-11.7	-16.3	-19.5	-15.7	-8.9	3.2	7.1	28.4	3.4	-5.4
1-4 years	3.4	-7.7	-5.1	-6.7	3.6	15.2	22.7	45.1	21.7	23.6
5-6 years	-6.7	-6.0	-9.9	-17.5	-13.3	1.4	6.1	22.5	6.5	5.9
7 years	22.5	15.0	15.0	20.0	24.8	10.6	45.0	26.0	62.7	74.5
8 years	-23.1	-28.2	-31.0	-22.4	-14.6	-4.1	-7.2	24.6	-10.8	-23.0
High school	48.5	36.6	53.7	42.4	34.2	54.9	51.9	57.0	57.0	54.0
1-3 years	31.0	19.7	29.5	23.4	15.9	51.9	41.7	55.7	37.7	36.6
4 years	64.7	52.2	78.5	61.3	49.3	57.5	61.5	58.3	72.9	67.1
College	57.3	53.8	50.3	50.7	41.4	60.6	49.4	68.1	69.2	75.0
1-3 years	60.8	60.7	55.6	53.2	42.7	58.3	49.4	65.0	71.2	82.5
4 years or more	53.7	47.4	46.3	47.9	39.8	63.1	49.5	72.3	66.6	65.8
Not reported	152.0	50.3	76.4	238.7	239.0	181.8	195.3	327.5	225.9	371.6
EDUCATIONAL ATTAINMENT - NONWHITE										
Total 25 years old and over	41.7	47.2	48.6	66.6	26.2	29.4	19.0	28.5	72.0	131.1
No school years completed	-7.0	-20.2	-13.5	-10.1	-22.2	-10.1	-15.1	6.6	25.0	31.0
Elementary school	19.8	14.4	18.2	35.3	6.7	14.4	8.8	17.7	39.0	91.8
1-4 years	16.6	23.7	21.6	39.0	8.0	5.7	7.6	19.6	49.1	99.5
5-6 years	13.3	25.7	18.1	28.1	0.0	8.5	-0.3	4.8	46.9	109.1
7 years	51.2	36.2	54.1	91.6	30.8	37.9	39.9	26.0	135.1	220.3
8 years	15.8	-4.6	1.9	18.8	1.7	35.1	8.8	32.8	1.9	42.6
High school	111.3	120.8	134.8	136.1	64.0	97.7	73.7	65.1	121.2	173.2
1-3 years	97.9	108.0	108.5	116.6	47.5	94.7	70.3	67.0	89.8	180.1
4 years	135.2	137.4	181.0	172.5	92.8	103.4	81.1	61.3	161.1	166.8
College	102.8	130.8	107.5	133.9	55.8	93.5	66.1	62.2	126.4	203.9
1-3 years	102.1	158.1	104.3	141.1	57.0	80.8	59.5	56.0	116.5	235.9
4 years or more	103.8	101.3	111.8	122.3	54.1	108.2	75.6	70.6	144.9	158.4
Not reported	258.0	169.9	224.1	541.3	366.0	175.4	213.6	186.5	296.6	557.1
POPULATION ENROLLED IN SCHOOLS	11.2	-3.4	-5.3	4.8	9.7	27.5	32.2	43.5	36.9	42.6
5-6 years	14.4	-6.8	1.8	-0.4	-18.9	65.3	80.2	78.8	37.4	59.5
7-13 years	9.6	-7.4	-7.5	6.0	9.5	19.0	21.8	38.6	36.5	54.1
14-15 years	-14.3	-25.0	-27.2	-17.7	-13.0	-3.1	2.8	12.8	10.2	4.6
16-17 years	-13.4	-20.1	-23.4	-19.3	-12.3	3.0	8.6	11.5	-0.2	-4.3
18-19 years	3.7	8.9	-12.6	-4.8	12.1	27.8	35.9	34.6	15.7	-10.8
20-24 years	123.7	132.9	101.6	110.8	124.6	163.9	195.6	172.2	135.2	96.1

TABLE 39

PERCENT CHANGE: EDUCATIONAL ATTAINMENT OF THE RURAL-NONFARM POPULATION 25 YEARS OLD AND OVER AND SCHOOL ENROLLMENT OF THE RURAL-NONFARM POPULATION 5-29 YEARS OLD, BY GEOGRAPHIC DIVISIONS: 1940-50

Educational Attainment and School Enrollment	Geographic Division									
	United States	New England	Middle Atlantic	East North Central	West North Central	South Atlantic	East South Central	West South Central	Mountain	Pacific
EDUCATIONAL ATTAINMENT, ALL GROUPS										
Total 25 years old and over	43.2	33.8	35.5	42.3	17.6	59.6	45.2	28.1	35.7	89.1
No school completed	20.2	4.0	-4.3	14.1	-0.1	27.8	16.2	24.3	23.0	64.1
Elementary school	28.0	4.1	15.5	19.7	4.6	51.6	38.8	26.3	15.9	68.1
1-4 years	37.2	16.6	16.2	20.6	10.4	50.9	43.3	30.1	21.4	81.3
5-6 years	26.4	13.7	10.6	12.7	-1.9	45.7	33.3	17.1	17.1	72.3
7 years	48.7	43.7	46.6	47.9	32.3	50.9	62.4	18.3	50.5	108.3
8 years	19.6	-6.1	11.1	16.7	0.7	61.5	30.4	38.2	7.2	57.6
High school	66.7	59.2	69.2	77.9	36.0	82.8	67.1	31.2	56.0	105.5
1-3 years	54.6	41.7	49.5	54.6	16.5	91.0	60.7	32.0	39.3	92.0
4 years	80.9	76.1	92.4	104.2	54.9	71.6	75.6	29.8	74.7	119.4
College	54.8	81.3	59.3	62.1	23.8	56.1	37.5	18.1	52.6	108.2
1-3 years	54.9	79.6	57.4	61.9	25.6	57.6	39.5	16.2	50.9	112.4
4 years or more	54.7	83.2	61.3	62.5	20.8	54.3	34.7	21.0	55.4	102.1
Not reported	139.2	90.1	109.6	140.0	169.9	144.2	128.6	139.4	152.0	271.4
EDUCATIONAL ATTAINMENT - MALE										
Total 25 years old and over	39.0	29.1	30.9	37.9	14.4	55.6	41.5	25.1	30.0	79.7
No school years completed	18.1	-0.2	-9.5	11.8	-3.2	26.9	15.5	25.3	15.0	60.1
Elementary school	24.8	1.6	12.5	17.3	2.6	48.1	34.5	22.8	12.3	60.7
1-4 years	33.9	8.7	12.1	18.0	9.1	49.0	39.0	27.7	18.2	71.8
5-6 years	23.6	9.8	8.9	10.9	-2.3	43.2	29.7	14.6	13.8	64.6
7 years	46.0	44.8	45.1	47.8	31.1	46.4	59.9	13.9	46.5	99.2
8 years	15.9	-8.2	7.7	13.7	-2.1	55.1	24.9	32.4	3.4	50.5
High School	63.0	56.9	66.1	74.1	33.8	79.1	63.0	26.7	49.7	97.8
1-3 years	51.3	40.0	48.4	52.7	14.3	84.1	58.2	26.3	36.3	85.2
4 years	78.2	77.0	89.6	100.5	55.1	71.4	69.6	27.3	66.0	112.0
College	50.8	72.6	51.2	59.0	19.0	53.0	37.6	18.3	52.1	97.1
1-3 years	55.7	85.7	56.1	64.2	21.2	62.8	43.9	20.5	52.6	102.1
4 years or more	46.0	63.6	47.8	53.7	16.7	44.3	31.1	15.6	51.4	91.1
Not reported	132.3	107.0	109.4	116.1	162.2	139.2	144.3	124.2	135.6	232.9
EDUCATIONAL ATTAINMENT - FEMALE										
Total 25 years old and over	47.6	38.4	40.2	47.0	20.8	63.8	49.1	31.2	42.6	100.6
No school years completed	22.5	8.4	1.8	17.4	3.8	28.8	17.0	23.0	32.6	68.4
Elementary school	31.6	6.6	18.6	22.4	6.8	55.4	43.3	30.1	20.8	77.5
1-4 years	41.5	27.2	21.4	24.4	12.2	53.2	48.6	33.1	26.0	95.1
5-6 years	29.4	18.0	12.4	14.7	-1.3	48.3	36.9	19.6	21.5	82.3
7 years	51.5	42.3	48.1	47.8	33.6	55.6	64.8	22.9	55.9	120.2
8 years	23.6	-4.0	14.5	19.9	3.6	68.5	36.1	44.4	12.4	66.4
High school	70.0	61.1	72.1	81.3	37.8	86.2	70.8	35.1	62.6	114.6
1-3 years	57.7	43.2	50.7	56.4	18.6	97.5	63.0	37.2	42.8	100.3
4 years	83.1	75.9	95.0	107.2	54.8	72.1	80.5	31.7	83.0	128.1
College	58.8	89.8	68.0	65.3	28.0	59.2	37.6	17.9	53.5	121.2
1-3 years	54.5	76.1	58.7	60.2	28.5	54.3	36.7	12.6	50.3	123.8
4 years or more	66.8	114.3	82.1	76.8	26.9	67.1	39.2	27.4	61.0	116.4
Not reported	149.2	71.8	109.0	188.1	180.1	151.6	107.3	163.3	183.9	344.4
EDUCATIONAL ATTAINMENT - WHITE										
Total 25 years old and over	43.8	33.8	34.9	42.2	17.9	65.4	51.2	28.2	34.2	87.1
No school years completed	19.3	4.3	-4.5	15.4	3.9	37.8	24.5	26.5	3.0	62.5
Elementary school	27.6	4.0	15.5	19.6	4.8	55.7	45.2	27.0	14.7	65.9
1-4 years	38.2	17.1	16.6	21.2	11.4	60.5	57.2	34.2	19.9	78.7
5-6 years	26.1	13.6	10.6	12.8	-1.4	49.4	41.0	18.3	15.0	69.5
7 years	48.8	44.3	47.0	48.0	32.8	51.7	68.9	17.0	47.8	106.2
8 years	19.6	-6.2	11.0	16.4	0.7	62.6	32.7	36.4	6.8	55.8
High school	67.0	59.0	69.0	77.6	36.0	85.8	69.2	30.3	55.2	103.4
1-3 years	54.4	41.1	49.2	54.2	16.4	94.1	62.3	30.9	38.1	89.8
4 years	81.5	76.0	92.2	103.9	54.9	75.0	77.7	29.2	74.1	117.4
College	55.1	81.1	58.5	61.7	23.8	59.1	38.0	16.7	52.6	106.6
1-3 years	55.4	79.5	57.0	61.3	25.6	61.6	39.4	15.3	51.0	110.7
4 years or more	54.6	82.9	61.0	62.2	20.7	56.0	33.3	18.8	55.1	100.8
Not reported	135.2	89.1	82.7	138.2	168.0	175.3	152.6	145.0	141.7	269.6
EDUCATIONAL ATTAINMENT - NONWHITE										
Total 25 years old and over	36.6	21.8	63.7	50.1	2.3	36.3	20.3	27.4	77.2	183.5
No school years completed	15.3	-9.6	1.7	17.6	-25.4	6.1	2.2	21.8	96.5	120.7
Elementary school	29.9	-0.7	16.2	31.0	-6.6	35.1	16.3	24.1	48.9	163.3
1-4 years	27.7	-8.7	14.4	26.2	-4.2	27.5	17.4	24.1	40.2	156.9
5-6 years	23.7	9.3	12.3	21.8	-14.3	30.5	9.2	13.7	48.0	166.3
7 years	46.1	8.2	35.4	50.0	11.7	54.4	32.4	25.9	137.0	197.9
8 years	38.5	-5.6	14.1	37.1	-9.1	82.7	17.3	57.9	32.8	156.0
High school	72.6	72.9	83.9	99.0	28.6	83.5	54.2	40.9	105.4	247.7
1-3 years	70.2	66.0	69.3	85.8	22.3	87.1	53.6	42.9	99.9	236.0
4 years	78.3	82.2	113.0	127.9	41.9	73.7	55.8	34.6	113.2	262.0
College	69.7	124.6	100.7	106.5	17.4	64.0	86.0	43.4	66.7	228.9
1-3 years	56.7	103.0	98.5	120.7	14.0	44.0	68.7	29.2	50.1	246.8
4 years or more	89.5	161.9	103.7	82.1	25.1	91.1	118.5	63.3	101.1	196.4
Not reported	164.9	150.8	594.2	191.6	255.2	72.7	76.1	117.4	310.2	336.8
POPULATION ENROLLED IN SCHOOLS	35.6	27.9	15.6	40.2	5.5	48.2	51.4	25.8	29.3	93.1
5-6 years	56.1	37.4	29.3	47.7	9.6	92.0	113.9	66.2	49.4	109.7
7-13 years	37.0	27.9	17.0	44.4	10.0	44.5	47.4	25.2	31.6	102.1
14-15 years	22.5	8.5	2.6	26.1	-0.8	34.5	34.9	15.6	21.2	77.4
16-17 years	21.1	11.6	4.9	25.0	-2.8	35.2	31.4	17.3	21.2	68.6
18-19 years	10.3	23.1	-0.7	11.8	-23.5	32.6	30.8	-6.4	-3.2	47.4
20-24 years	80.4	136.2	65.4	78.3	-3.5	157.4	144.2	47.4	32.8	86.9

TABLE 40

PERCENT CHANGE: EDUCATIONAL ATTAINMENT OF THE RURAL-FARM POPULATION 25 YEARS OLD AND OVER AND SCHOOL ENROLLMENT OF THE RURAL-FARM POPULATION 5-29 YEARS OLD, BY GEOGRAPHIC DIVISIONS: 1940-50

Educational Attainment and School Enrollment	United States	New England	Middle Atlantic	East North Central	West North Central	South Atlantic	East South Central	West South Central	Mountain	Pacific
EDUCATIONAL ATTAINMENT, ALL GROUPS										
Total 25 years old and over	-20.0	-30.0	-20.4	-17.8	-18.1	-17.2	-18.1	-30.4	-19.5	-11.2
No school completed	-46.9	-51.6	-43.8	-42.9	-47.0	-45.9	-46.4	-50.1	-49.7	-36.1
Elementary school	-28.4	-14.3	-34.1	-31.8	-30.4	-19.2	-21.6	-34.6	-35.6	-31.1
1-4 years	-30.1	-39.8	-32.2	-36.6	-37.7	-25.0	-25.0	-38.7	-34.5	-27.0
5-6 years	-33.1	-37.2	-39.6	-40.4	-40.7	-23.2	-26.2	-41.0	-40.0	-32.4
7 years	-20.0	-9.5	-2.3	-15.5	-17.6	-23.8	-5.5	-36.6	-15.1	-7.7
8 years	-27.9	-50.5	-37.8	-31.5	-29.2	16.9	-21.1	-18.4	-38.6	-35.9
High school	9.5	-12.3	20.8	23.5	18.3	1.3	13.2	-15.7	10.7	19.4
1-3 years	-5.7	-24.0	-0.3	0.2	-7.4	5.6	4.1	-23.5	-10.5	-0.3
4 years	33.2	1.5	51.3	50.8	46.4	-8.0	32.4	6.3	39.7	42.6
College	6.6	4.6	16.6	12.5	8.7	-0.8	-4.7	-6.9	10.0	21.4
1-3 years	0.7	-2.5	2.2	6.2	6.4	-8.1	-8.7	-15.6	7.0	21.4
4 years or more	21.5	16.6	42.5	30.7	17.6	14.1	5.1	16.5	18.7	30.4
Not reported	-5.2	-7.9	-44.4	-17.4	17.3	-14.6	-22.3	29.2	73.2	68.4
EDUCATIONAL ATTAINMENT - MALE										
Total 25 years old and over	-21.7	-31.5	-23.7	-20.8	-19.9	-18.0	-19.1	-31.0	-22.1	-15.5
No school years completed	-45.7	-55.1	-48.2	-46.8	-48.7	-43.0	-44.6	-48.8	-49.2	-36.5
Elementary school	-28.6	-44.1	-35.2	-32.2	-29.8	-18.8	-21.6	-34.3	-35.6	-31.9
1-4 years	-29.4	-39.4	-34.5	-36.9	-37.5	-22.8	-22.7	-38.1	-34.7	-28.0
5-6 years	-32.6	-36.9	-40.5	-40.0	-38.5	-21.5	-25.1	-40.2	-41.1	-33.4
7 years	-19.4	-7.1	-1.5	-13.7	-14.3	-25.1	-5.9	-36.3	-14.3	-9.5
8 years	-29.1	-50.6	-39.1	-32.4	-29.3	13.8	-23.1	-18.1	-38.3	-36.7
High school	8.2	-10.2	19.2	21.6	21.1	-2.5	11.4	-17.5	8.6	15.8
1-3 years	-7.2	-21.7	-0.7	-1.0	-6.1	-0.2	3.1	-24.8	-11.2	-2.5
4 years	34.9	6.6	52.5	50.6	56.7	-8.2	29.8	4.3	38.8	39.1
College	3.7	1.8	17.2	8.4	0.9	-1.7	-8.7	-7.8	10.7	21.3
1-3 years	-2.3	0.7	5.2	2.3	-3.2	-8.4	-13.4	-15.6	7.2	19.1
4 years or more	15.9	3.0	32.9	21.1	13.1	10.3	1.0	11.6	18.8	25.2
Not reported	-3.9	-12.8	-43.9	-22.1	13.8	-10.3	-17.1	32.9	66.3	58.9
EDUCATIONAL ATTAINMENT - FEMALE										
Total 25 years old and over	-18.0	-28.4	-16.5	-14.4	-16.0	-16.3	-17.1	-29.6	-16.0	-5.6
No school years completed	-48.6	-46.4	-37.8	-36.9	-44.4	-50.1	-49.1	-51.9	-50.0	-35.6
Elementary school	-28.2	-44.9	-32.6	-31.2	-31.2	-19.7	-21.6	-34.9	-35.7	-29.9
1-4 years	-31.2	-40.6	-28.4	-36.2	-38.0	-27.8	-25.6	-39.4	-34.0	-24.9
5-6 years	-33.6	-37.8	-38.3	-41.0	-41.0	-24.9	-27.3	-41.8	-38.1	-30.7
7 years	-20.7	-13.0	-3.5	-17.9	-22.7	-22.5	-5.0	-36.8	-16.4	-4.9
8 years	-26.3	-50.3	-36.1	-30.3	-29.0	20.0	-19.2	-18.7	-38.9	-34.7
High school	10.6	-14.3	22.2	25.3	15.9	4.3	14.8	-14.1	13.0	23.1
1-3 years	-4.3	-26.5	0.1	1.4	-8.8	10.5	4.9	-22.3	-9.6	2.1
4 years	31.8	-2.3	50.3	51.0	39.1	-7.9	34.5	8.2	40.6	45.7
College	8.6	6.8	16.1	15.4	13.3	-0.1	-1.8	-6.1	9.7	27.2
1-3 years	2.7	-4.5	0.4	8.5	11.6	-7.9	-5.5	-15.5	7.0	23.4
4 years or more	27.0	35.1	53.2	41.6	21.6	17.0	8.9	21.0	18.6	35.7
Not reported	-6.9	-0.6	-45.1	-9.7	22.7	-20.2	-28.8	24.0	85.9	89.5
EDUCATIONAL ATTAINMENT - WHITE										
Total 25 years old and over	-18.5	-29.8	-20.3	-17.8	-17.9	-14.9	-14.5	-27.6	-19.0	-10.3
No school years completed	-43.2	-49.5	-43.9	-42.3	-45.0	-39.9	-42.7	-47.0	-42.8	-32.6
Elementary school	-28.4	-44.2	-34.1	-31.8	-30.3	-18.6	-19.6	-32.8	-36.3	-30.5
1-4 years	-28.2	-39.3	-32.2	-36.7	-37.5	-20.4	-17.9	-35.3	-36.3	-31.4
5-6 years	-33.8	-37.0	-39.6	-40.4	-40.6	-24.8	-24.7	-40.1	-40.6	-6.4
7 years	-20.8	-9.1	-2.2	-15.4	-17.5	-27.3	-6.0	-37.0	-15.7	-6.4
8 years	-28.5	-50.4	-37.8	-31.5	-29.2	11.5	-22.1	-18.7	-39.0	-35.6
High school	9.6	-12.3	20.8	23.6	18.4	-0.3	13.2	-15.3	9.9	19.4
1-3 years	-6.1	-24.0	-0.4	0.2	-7.4	3.8	2.9	-23.4	-11.0	0.2
4 years	33.6	1.5	51.4	50.9	46.4	-8.8	33.8	7.3	38.4	42.1
College	6.4	4.6	16.5	12.4	8.7	-2.8	-6.1	-5.9	9.7	24.2
1-3 years	0.8	-2.5	2.2	6.1	6.5	-9.0	-9.9	-14.2	6.7	20.9
4 years or more	20.8	16.6	42.4	30.6	17.7	9.6	3.3	16.5	18.2	30.7
Not reported	-0.2	-7.7	-42.8	-17.1	18.0	-1.7	-13.8	42.5	51.7	71.5
EDUCATIONAL ATTAINMENT - NONWHITE										
Total 25 years old and over	-29.9	-64.9	-31.0	-24.2	-37.2	-23.5	-28.7	-40.8	-26.8	-26.7
No school years completed	-51.8	-94.0	-39.3	-64.3	-64.8	-50.5	-49.8	-54.3	-55.6	-47.7
Elementary school	-28.4	-63.9	-33.0	-30.0	-38.3	-20.8	-27.1	-40.4	-19.2	-41.0
1-4 years	-33.7	-71.7	-29.6	-32.6	-42.1	-29.7	-31.3	-43.6	-15.9	-40.6
5-6 years	-29.9	-58.6	-40.1	-34.6	-42.9	-19.9	-30.0	-43.5	-33.2	-42.0
7 years	-11.9	-49.7	-12.9	-22.3	-25.9	-1.2	-2.9	-33.7	-1.8	-30.6
8 years	-1.3	-66.7	-37.1	-27.3	-31.0	107.5	-10.1	-13.6	-13.3	-43.6
High school	6.5	-18.5	23.0	19.6	1.7	21.7	14.3	-21.1	48.8	20.5
1-3 years	3.6	-24.5	25.9	8.6	-8.7	25.8	16.3	-23.4	13.2	-15.0
4 years	15.7	-8.5	17.3	38.8	26.2	6.9	7.4	-11.3	117.0	56.1
College	12.8	-12.5	30.0	37.7	-18.0	29.4	22.1	-19.1	67.8	40.5
1-3 years	-2.4	-23.4	13.8	21.7	-17.6	5.2	14.4	-33.5	58.3	57.3
4 years or more	49.0	1.9	58.9	72.8	-19.2	79.9	45.8	17.7	92.7	8.9
Not reported	-26.8	-35.8	-74.8	-36.6	18.8	-36.5	-39.9	-6.7	304.7	46.8
POPULATION ENROLLED IN SCHOOLS	-20.2	-28.3	-20.4	-17.4	-20.5	-19.7	-8.4	-34.7	-22.1	-11.4
5-6 years	-3.3	-15.7	0.7	-7.1	-14.9	-0.9	21.4	-17.3	-4.1	24.9
7-13 years	-20.2	-26.9	-18.9	-16.5	-20.1	-21.2	-9.1	-35.5	-20.3	-4.1
14-15 years	-23.3	-34.6	-30.1	-21.8	-22.6	-21.1	-11.0	-36.4	-24.2	-20.0
16-17 years	-21.2	-31.5	-24.5	-18.1	-17.2	-19.3	-12.5	-33.4	-25.5	-21.0
18-19 years	-41.0	-45.4	-40.6	-39.3	-45.2	-37.0	-29.0	-52.2	-46.6	-44.1
20-24 years	-33.7	-32.6	-10.7	-33.1	-46.7	-18.7	-19.6	-47.0	-53.3	-45.4

APPENDIX

TABLE 41

POPULATION: EDUCATIONAL ATTAINMENT OF THE TOTAL POPULATION 25 YEARS OLD AND OVER AND SCHOOL ENROLLMENT OF THE TOTAL POPULATION 5-29 YEARS OLD, BY GEOGRAPHIC DIVISIONS: 1950

Educational Attainment and School Enrollment	United States	New England	Middle Atlantic	East North Central	West North Central	South Atlantic	East South Central	West South Central	Mountain	Pacific
EDUCATIONAL ATTAINMENT, ALL GROUPS										
Total 25 years old and over	87,570,575	5,674,890	18,773,800	18,102,385	8,243,460	11,358,735	5,942,010	7,871,345	2,723,585	8,880,355
No school completed	2,184,355	154,415	561,480	263,295	80,685	362,065	201,625	360,345	66,695	133,750
Elementary school	38,973,875	2,128,895	8,174,370	7,971,520	3,914,315	5,785,690	3,427,595	3,698,975	1,002,405	2,870,110
1-4 years	7,270,465	296,970	1,205,270	1,056,890	427,830	1,654,610	1,002,690	1,043,405	167,085	415,715
5-6 years	7,975,945	418,770	1,554,425	1,359,480	558,080	1,592,140	880,180	952,685	170,035	490,150
7 years	5,985,955	331,430	1,194,825	1,061,520	516,195	1,159,600	507,155	659,280	141,470	411,480
8 years	17,741,510	1,081,725	4,219,850	4,490,630	2,412,210	1,379,340	1,037,570	1,043,605	523,815	1,552,765
High school	32,536,590	2,476,550	7,172,225	7,168,070	2,925,090	3,493,665	1,642,760	2,617,175	1,092,250	3,948,805
1-3 years	14,857,660	1,060,535	3,174,395	3,187,255	1,184,450	1,891,970	864,405	1,438,230	464,920	1,591,500
4 years	17,678,930	1,416,015	3,997,830	3,980,815	1,740,640	1,601,695	778,355	1,178,945	627,330	2,357,305
College	11,516,080	770,000	2,266,720	2,261,020	1,106,050	1,426,990	547,760	1,009,335	489,980	1,668,225
1-3 years	6,261,635	390,320	1,026,090	1,250,340	673,545	753,975	318,945	580,135	294,785	973,500
4 years or more	5,284,445	379,680	1,240,630	1,010,680	432,505	673,015	228,815	429,200	195,195	694,725
Not reported	2,329,675	145,030	599,005	438,480	217,320	290,325	122,270	185,515	72,265	259,465
EDUCATIONAL ATTAINMENT - MALE										
Total 25 years old and over	42,684,720	2,682,780	9,020,850	8,868,800	4,055,395	5,499,965	2,881,495	3,869,535	1,388,410	4,417,490
No school years completed	1,110,370	69,360	252,030	132,045	43,160	203,570	115,845	187,610	33,800	72,950
Elementary school	19,805,590	1,051,445	3,972,890	4,062,660	2,078,310	2,917,965	1,713,835	1,900,025	560,770	1,547,690
1-4 years	3,948,085	149,110	606,415	575,990	241,480	908,975	556,125	574,645	96,905	238,440
5-6 years	4,030,235	205,615	761,510	704,325	303,615	784,500	428,450	478,550	94,530	269,140
7 years	2,992,105	162,460	578,900	545,555	281,750	556,090	238,770	327,345	79,365	221,670
8 years	8,835,165	534,260	2,026,065	2,236,790	1,251,465	668,200	490,490	519,485	289,970	818,440
High school	14,526,960	1,097,435	3,209,990	3,232,760	1,294,410	1,515,400	718,240	1,162,380	504,810	1,791,575
1-3 years	7,005,480	512,310	1,510,890	1,517,030	560,485	856,595	392,665	658,320	229,360	767,825
4 years	7,521,480	585,125	1,699,100	1,715,690	733,925	658,805	325,575	504,060	275,450	1,023,750
College	5,930,250	388,480	1,259,535	1,191,860	520,815	698,785	260,655	508,965	246,225	854,935
1-3 years	2,903,135	170,295	511,495	596,055	278,175	333,270	137,640	275,640	135,735	464,830
4 years or more	3,027,120	218,185	748,040	595,805	242,640	365,515	123,015	233,325	110,490	390,105
Not reported	1,311,545	76,060	326,405	249,515	118,700	164,245	72,920	110,555	42,805	150,340
EDUCATIONAL ATTAINMENT - FEMALE										
Total 25 years old and over	44,885,855	2,992,110	9,752,950	9,233,585	4,188,065	5,858,770	3,060,515	4,001,810	1,335,185	4,462,865
No school years completed	1,073,985	85,055	309,450	131,250	37,525	158,495	85,780	172,735	32,895	60,800
Elementary school	19,168,285	1,077,450	4,201,480	3,908,860	1,836,005	2,867,725	1,713,760	1,798,950	441,635	1,322,420
1-4 years	3,322,380	147,860	598,855	480,900	186,350	745,635	446,565	468,760	70,180	177,275
5-6 years	3,945,710	213,155	792,915	655,155	254,465	807,640	451,730	474,135	75,505	221,010
7 years	2,993,850	168,970	615,925	518,965	234,445	603,310	268,385	331,935	62,105	189,810
8 years	8,906,345	547,465	2,193,785	2,253,840	1,160,745	711,140	547,080	524,120	233,845	734,325
High school	18,009,630	1,379,115	3,962,235	3,935,350	1,630,680	1,978,265	924,520	1,454,795	587,440	2,157,230
1-3 years	7,852,180	548,225	1,663,505	1,670,225	623,965	1,035,375	471,740	779,910	235,560	823,675
4 years	10,157,450	830,890	2,298,730	2,265,125	1,006,715	942,890	452,780	673,085	351,880	1,333,555
College	5,615,825	381,520	1,007,186	1,069,160	585,235	728,205	287,105	500,370	243,755	813,290
1-3 years	3,358,500	220,025	514,595	654,285	395,370	420,705	181,305	304,495	159,050	508,670
4 years or more	2,257,325	161,495	492,590	414,875	189,865	307,500	105,800	195,875	84,705	304,620
Not reported	1,018,130	68,970	272,600	188,965	98,620	126,080	49,350	74,960	29,460	109,125
EDUCATIONAL ATTAINMENT - WHITE										
Total 25 years old and over	79,396,835	5,588,120	17,625,730	17,028,010	7,968,615	8,875,720	4,637,125	6,613,265	2,623,210	8,437,040
No school years completed	1,649,080	150,830	526,525	235,515	70,965	170,540	95,175	238,375	47,165	113,990
Elementary school	33,775,910	2,087,110	7,555,190	7,387,040	3,756,575	4,043,220	2,469,870	2,846,970	957,520	2,672,415
1-4 years	5,237,345	287,915	1,049,050	902,190	384,360	861,070	563,280	670,570	153,355	365,555
5-6 years	6,506,500	407,935	1,378,765	1,202,730	517,385	1,084,545	607,310	712,390	157,820	437,620
7 years	5,227,740	323,980	1,088,880	967,225	491,510	908,900	394,880	538,680	134,765	378,920
8 years	16,804,325	1,067,280	4,038,495	4,314,895	2,363,320	1,188,705	904,400	925,330	511,580	1,490,320
High school	30,811,150	2,445,130	6,815,460	6,822,000	2,849,275	3,133,200	1,475,185	2,417,505	1,067,530	3,785,865
1-3 years	13,792,530	1,043,825	2,971,690	2,979,870	1,140,585	1,647,730	748,105	1,296,770	452,260	1,511,695
4 years	17,018,620	1,401,305	3,843,770	3,842,130	1,708,690	1,485,470	727,080	1,120,735	615,270	2,274,170
College	11,131,875	763,740	2,203,480	2,189,010	1,088,400	1,313,380	507,255	957,005	484,725	1,624,880
1-3 years	6,023,675	386,700	990,135	1,204,405	662,670	696,415	295,235	551,285	291,500	945,330
4 years or more	5,108,200	377,040	1,213,345	984,605	425,730	616,965	212,020	405,720	193,225	679,550
Not reported	2,028,820	141,310	525,075	394,445	203,400	215,380	89,640	153,410	66,270	239,890
EDUCATIONAL ATTAINMENT - NONWHITE										
Total 25 years old and over	8,173,740	86,770	1,148,070	1,074,375	274,845	2,483,015	1,304,885	1,258,080	100,385	443,315
No school years completed	535,275	3,585	34,955	27,780	9,720	191,525	106,450	121,970	19,530	19,760
Elementary school	5,197,965	41,785	619,180	584,480	157,740	1,742,470	957,725	852,005	44,885	197,695
1-4 years	2,033,120	9,055	156,220	154,700	43,470	793,540	439,410	372,835	13,730	50,160
5-6 years	1,469,445	10,835	175,660	156,750	40,695	507,595	272,870	240,295	12,215	52,530
7 years	758,215	7,450	105,945	97,295	24,685	250,700	112,275	120,600	6,705	32,560
8 years	937,185	14,445	181,355	175,735	48,890	190,635	133,170	118,275	12,235	62,445
High school	1,725,440	31,420	356,765	346,070	75,815	360,465	167,575	199,670	24,720	162,940
1-3 years	1,065,130	16,710	202,705	207,385	43,865	244,240	116,300	141,460	12,660	79,805
4 years	660,310	14,710	154,060	138,685	31,950	116,225	51,275	58,210	12,060	83,135
College	414,205	6,260	63,240	72,010	17,650	113,610	40,505	52,330	5,255	43,345
1-3 years	237,960	3,620	35,955	45,935	10,875	57,560	23,710	28,850	3,285	28,170
4 years or more	176,245	2,640	27,285	26,075	6,775	56,050	16,795	23,480	1,970	15,175
Not reported	300,855	3,720	73,930	44,035	13,920	74,945	32,630	32,105	5,995	19,575
POPULATION ENROLLED IN SCHOOLS	28,984,985	1,697,215	5,288,750	5,663,715	2,721,120	4,373,485	2,524,315	3,001,960	1,093,315	2,621,110
5-6 years	2,160,160	134,590	428,170	414,150	199,560	308,895	177,555	198,135	75,015	224,090
7-13 years	16,077,270	891,330	2,814,230	3,140,905	1,506,655	2,535,490	1,464,860	1,720,805	610,800	1,392,190
14-15 years	3,963,575	226,040	708,565	776,160	374,935	614,710	358,585	422,670	149,290	332,620
16-17 years	3,104,265	183,675	601,605	625,625	306,930	427,235	249,335	310,510	116,170	283,180
18-19 years	1,400,700	99,985	258,855	267,795	135,695	190,710	116,480	139,320	55,620	136,260
20-24 years	1,480,745	113,165	308,945	289,580	133,720	189,985	100,490	131,940	55,905	157,015
25-29 years	798,270	48,430	168,380	149,500	63,625	106,455	57,010	78,600	30,515	95,755

TABLE 42

POPULATION: EDUCATIONAL ATTAINMENT OF THE URBAN POPULATION 25 YEARS OLD AND OVER AND SCHOOL ENROLLMENT OF THE URBAN POPULATION 5-29 YEARS OLD, BY GEOGRAPHIC DIVISIONS: 1950

Educational Attainment and School Enrollment	Geographic division									
	United States	New England	Middle Atlantic	East North Central	West North Central	South Atlantic	East South Central	West South Central	Mountain	Pacific
EDUCATIONAL ATTAINMENT-ALL GROUPS										
Total 25 years old and over.....	58,851,820	4,400,325	15,406,030	12,952,545	4,430,770	6,128,405	2,553,115	4,551,065	1,576,060	6,853,505
No school completed............	1,359,185	128,305	500,705	203,145	42,490	138,145	60,930	166,240	24,420	94,805
Elementary school..............	23,262,585	1,644,265	6,515,535	5,288,575	1,766,570	2,550,005	1,168,695	1,784,340	508,755	2,035,845
1-4 years..................	4,010,225	243,590	1,013,960	763,490	206,995	633,785	295,585	476,435	80,715	295,670
5-6 years..................	4,727,770	340,525	1,269,010	956,540	273,110	691,395	181,485	321,955	70,820	288,850
7 years....................	3,505,530	263,015	946,315	710,965	236,235	485,890	198,805	526,915	270,430	1,098,780
8 years....................	11,019,060	797,135	3,286,250	2,857,580	1,050,230	738,935	392,805	1,706,075	663,985	3,134,745
High school...................	23,668,840	1,930,170	6,006,435	5,347,245	1,741,455	2,227,255	911,475	1,706,075	266,730	1,223,930
1-3 years..................	10,382,795	820,305	2,631,120	2,377,650	696,015	1,077,650	439,560	849,835	397,255	1,910,815
4 years....................	13,286,045	1,109,865	3,375,315	2,969,595	1,045,440	1,149,605	471,915	856,240	337,550	1,393,635
College.......................	8,955,920	583,935	1,921,170	1,803,620	745,730	1,037,435	356,490	437,460	196,310	803,295
1-3 years..................	4,697,635	291,740	851,085	962,740	424,450	531,375	199,180	338,895	141,240	590,340
4 years or more............	4,258,285	292,195	1,070,085	840,880	321,280	506,060	157,310	118,055	41,350	194,475
Not reported..................	1,605,290	113,650	462,185	309,960	134,525	175,565	55,525	118,055	41,350	194,475
EDUCATIONAL ATTAINMENT - MALE										
Total 25 years old and over.....	28,084,275	2,056,995	7,336,715	6,252,035	2,097,775	2,871,625	1,189,920	2,177,040	775,770	3,326,400
No school years completed......	637,015	55,765	220,475	97,090	21,515	70,230	32,480	79,075	12,095	48,270
Elementary school..............	11,361,065	790,190	3,094,935	2,607,915	874,935	1,231,005	559,255	882,180	268,160	1,052,570
1-4 years..................	2,053,255	119,090	497,940	399,145	108,100	322,960	153,935	247,175	43,950	160,960
5-6 years..................	2,306,020	162,750	606,125	477,930	137,500	328,435	140,325	222,435	45,315	185,205
7 years....................	1,690,525	121,865	446,135	348,350	117,235	227,690	83,175	155,970	37,360	149,745
8 years....................	5,311,265	383,485	1,544,655	1,382,490	512,100	351,920	181,820	256,600	141,535	556,660
High school...................	10,467,680	851,955	2,680,390	2,394,405	755,980	953,925	390,680	746,030	298,820	1,395,495
1-3 years..................	4,865,510	392,865	1,246,785	1,125,125	323,545	487,605	196,335	385,555	127,930	579,765
4 years....................	5,602,170	459,090	1,433,605	1,269,280	432,435	466,320	194,345	360,475	170,890	815,730
College.......................	4,734,575	300,935	1,093,055	979,310	373,290	520,850	175,075	399,685	173,110	719,265
1-3 years..................	2,257,205	130,735	438,205	478,580	191,130	239,080	89,105	211,390	92,995	385,985
4 years or more............	2,477,370	170,200	654,850	500,730	182,160	281,770	85,970	188,295	80,115	333,280
Not reported..................	883,940	58,150	247,940	173,315	72,055	95,615	32,430	70,050	23,585	110,800
EDUCATIONAL ATTAINMENT - FEMALE										
Total 25 years old and over.....	30,767,545	2,343,330	8,069,315	6,700,510	2,332,995	3,256,780	1,363,195	2,374,025	800,290	3,527,105
No school years completed......	722,170	72,540	280,230	106,055	20,975	67,915	28,450	87,145	12,325	46,535
Elementary school..............	11,901,520	854,075	3,420,680	2,680,660	891,635	1,319,000	609,440	902,160	240,595	983,275
1-4 years..................	1,956,970	124,500	516,020	364,345	98,895	310,825	141,650	229,260	36,765	134,710
5-6 years..................	2,421,750	177,775	662,885	478,610	135,610	362,960	158,495	236,600	41,475	167,340
7 years....................	1,815,005	138,150	500,180	362,615	119,000	258,200	98,310	165,985	33,460	139,105
8 years....................	5,707,795	413,650	1,741,595	1,475,090	538,130	387,015	210,985	270,315	128,895	542,120
High school...................	13,201,160	1,078,215	3,326,045	2,952,840	985,475	1,273,330	520,795	960,045	365,165	1,739,250
1-3 years..................	5,517,285	427,440	1,384,335	1,252,525	372,470	590,045	243,225	464,280	138,800	644,165
4 years....................	7,683,875	650,775	1,941,710	1,700,315	613,005	683,285	277,570	495,765	226,365	1,095,085
College.......................	4,221,345	283,000	828,115	824,310	372,440	516,585	181,415	376,670	161,440	674,370
1-3 years..................	2,440,430	161,005	412,880	484,160	233,320	292,295	110,075	226,070	103,315	417,310
4 years or more............	1,780,915	121,995	415,235	340,150	139,120	224,290	71,340	150,600	61,125	257,060
Not reported..................	721,350	55,500	214,245	136,645	62,470	79,950	23,095	48,005	17,765	83,675
EDUCATIONAL ATTAINMENT - WHITE										
Total 25 years old and over.....	53,328,225	4,321,795	14,337,530	11,936,175	4,199,915	4,771,075	1,919,320	3,829,525	1,535,430	6,477,460
No school years completed......	1,107,230	125,295	468,670	178,405	35,690	60,270	21,690	114,450	22,295	80,465
Elementary school..............	20,007,405	1,606,675	5,932,410	4,737,980	1,638,290	1,670,070	736,375	1,322,955	489,495	1,873,155
1-4 years..................	2,936,850	235,385	868,635	618,540	173,380	285,320	125,280	298,620	75,550	256,140
5-6 years..................	3,792,155	330,735	1,103,170	808,020	239,840	422,795	171,840	325,340	81,665	308,750
7 years....................	2,985,335	256,385	845,730	618,545	215,465	349,985	122,235	248,730	67,680	260,640
8 years....................	10,293,065	784,230	3,114,875	2,692,875	1,009,605	611,970	317,020	450,265	264,600	1,047,625
High school...................	22,207,225	1,901,135	5,662,740	5,013,965	1,673,860	1,962,165	793,950	1,557,705	650,495	2,991,210
1-3 years..................	9,506,135	804,915	2,436,325	2,178,185	657,380	906,805	361,190	748,390	260,140	1,152,805
4 years....................	12,701,090	1,096,220	3,226,415	2,835,780	1,016,480	1,055,360	432,760	809,315	390,355	1,838,405
College.......................	8,601,515	578,225	1,860,360	1,734,060	729,455	948,910	327,350	736,050	333,620	1,353,485
1-3 years..................	4,493,810	288,430	816,510	918,455	414,520	486,770	182,675	415,190	193,850	777,410
4 years or more............	4,107,705	289,795	1,043,850	815,605	314,935	462,140	144,675	320,860	139,770	576,075
Not reported..................	1,404,850	110,465	413,350	271,765	122,620	129,660	39,955	98,365	39,525	179,145
EDUCATIONAL ATTAINMENT-NONWHITE										
Total 25 years old and over.....	5,523,595	78,530	1,068,500	1,016,370	230,855	1,357,330	633,795	721,540	40,630	376,045
No school years completed......	251,955	3,010	32,035	24,740	6,800	77,875	39,240	51,790	2,125	14,340
Elementary school..............	3,255,180	37,590	583,125	550,595	128,280	879,935	432,320	461,385	19,260	162,690
1-4 years..................	1,073,375	8,205	145,325	144,950	33,615	348,465	170,305	177,815	5,165	39,530
5-6 years..................	935,615	9,790	165,840	148,520	33,270	268,600	126,980	133,695	5,125	43,795
7 years....................	520,195	6,690	100,585	92,420	20,770	135,905	59,250	73,225	3,410	28,210
8 years....................	725,995	12,905	171,375	164,705	40,625	126,965	75,785	76,650	5,830	51,155
High school...................	1,461,615	29,035	343,695	333,280	67,595	265,090	117,525	148,370	13,490	143,535
1-3 years..................	876,660	15,390	194,795	199,465	38,635	170,845	78,370	101,445	6,590	71,125
4 years....................	584,955	13,645	148,900	133,815	28,960	94,245	39,155	46,925	6,900	72,410
College.......................	354,405	5,710	60,810	69,560	16,275	88,525	29,140	40,305	3,930	40,150
1-3 years..................	203,825	3,310	34,575	44,285	9,930	44,605	16,505	22,270	2,460	25,885
4 years or more............	150,580	2,400	26,235	25,275	6,345	43,920	12,635	18,035	1,470	14,265
Not reported..................	200,440	3,185	48,835	38,195	11,905	45,905	15,570	19,690	1,825	15,330
POPULATION ENROLLED IN SCHOOLS...	17,178,935	1,265,420	4,119,540	3,752,385	1,319,600	1,873,865	864,880	1,525,200	570,255	1,887,790
5-6 years..................	1,297,670	99,755	335,145	274,255	90,035	135,000	59,845	99,180	38,065	166,790
7-13 years.................	9,002,225	646,185	2,136,540	1,999,465	674,260	995,930	460,225	829,690	297,710	962,220
14-15 years................	2,211,225	165,735	537,650	491,325	165,350	241,150	112,025	197,020	72,605	228,365
16-17 years................	1,839,365	137,605	469,945	408,450	140,985	186,525	86,550	149,400	58,075	201,830
18-19 years................	980,435	79,550	244,690	202,555	89,245	109,585	52,525	89,225	35,845	107,235
20-24 years................	1,215,615	95,440	275,380	251,495	111,045	133,755	61,515	103,715	44,945	138,325
25-29 years................	632,400	41,170	150,190	124,840	48,680	71,920	32,195	56,970	23,010	83,425

TABLE 43

POPULATION: EDUCATIONAL ATTAINMENT OF THE RURAL—NONFARM POPULATION 25 YEARS OLD AND OVER AND SCHOOL ENROLLMENT OF THE RURAL—NONFARM POPULATION 5–29 YEARS OLD, BY GEOGRAPHIC DIVISIONS: 1950

Educational Attainment and School Enrollment	Geographic division									
	United States	New England	Middle Atlantic	East North Central	West North Central	South Atlantic	East South Central	West South Central	Mountain	Pacific
EDUCATIONAL ATTAINMENT, ALL GROUPS										
Total 25 years old and over.....	16,896,415	1,046,355	2,600,035	3,093,845	1,795,700	3,064,355	1,467,960	1,692,485	721,945	1,413,735
No school completed	457,700	20,550	47,195	38,970	21,535	118,955	57,130	102,260	26,320	24,785
Elementary school..............	8,323,210	382,445	1,221,250	1,471,440	913,110	1,729,360	868,930	887,170	294,585	554,920
1–4 years	1,641,050	42,225	147,130	173,445	110,960	513,965	257,930	262,565	53,970	78,860
5–6 years	1,714,220	62,830	215,165	233,750	134,295	476,295	219,915	226,815	52,055	93,100
7 years...................	1,321,570	55,590	185,370	197,095	118,485	355,850	127,490	156,365	42,365	82,960
8 years	3,646,370	221,800	673,585	867,150	549,370	383,250	263,595	241,425	146,195	300,000
High school...............	5,728,265	455,680	926,525	1,166,005	584,650	850,245	379,405	509,255	273,785	582,715
1–3 years.............	2,823,175	197,330	426,610	523,185	243,690	518,175	206,160	318,435	125,995	263,595
4 years...............	2,905,090	258,350	499,915	642,820	340,960	332,070	173,245	190,820	147,790	319,120
College	1,845,300	160,355	280,490	316,085	220,020	285,855	122,800	153,360	106,225	200,110
1–3 years	1,057,705	83,475	138,345	188,340	138,970	158,385	72,870	89,980	65,310	122,030
4 years or more...........	787,595	76,880	142,145	127,745	81,050	127,470	49,930	63,380	40,915	78,080
Not reported.............	541,940	27,325	124,575	101,345	56,385	79,940	39,695	40,440	21,030	51,205
EDUCATIONAL ATTAINMENT – MALE										
Total 25 years old and over.....	8,426,460	505,560	1,284,615	1,541,525	874,475	1,527,935	717,975	838,410	379,280	756,685
No school years completed	252,115	10,480	24,295	22,825	11,705	67,780	32,115	54,480	13,220	15,215
Elementary school	4,353,095	201,120	632,350	770,815	474,085	892,395	433,485	454,330	169,320	325,215
1–4 years	920,925	23,015	81,930	100,750	62,835	286,230	139,885	144,420	32,165	49,695
5–6 years	891,070	33,505	114,410	126,150	72,220	239,505	106,505	113,020	29,970	55,785
7 years...................	677,600	29,765	96,075	104,505	62,285	175,350	60,615	77,040	24,100	47,865
8 years	1,863,500	114,835	339,915	439,410	276,745	191,310	126,480	119,850	83,085	171,870
High school...............	2,610,320	202,000	418,670	532,300	258,850	383,240	169,560	230,780	130,510	284,410
1–3 years.............	1,350,085	96,815	206,270	251,955	114,115	239,835	95,665	145,910	64,430	135,475
4 years	1,260,235	105,185	212,400	280,345	144,735	143,405	73,895	84,870	66,465	148,935
College	892,120	76,375	138,045	155,220	98,725	136,425	58,240	74,680	53,120	101,290
1–3 years	454,230	33,820	58,820	80,860	51,985	69,485	31,040	41,670	29,165	57,385
4 years or more	437,890	42,555	79,225	74,360	46,740	66,940	27,200	33,010	23,955	43,905
Not reported...........	318,810	15,585	71,275	60,365	31,110	48,095	24,575	24,140	13,110	30,555
EDUCATIONAL ATTAINMENT – FEMALE										
Total 25 years old and over.....	8,469,955	540,795	1,315,420	1,552,320	921,225	1,536,420	749,985	854,075	342,665	657,050
No school years completed	205,585	10,070	22,900	16,145	9,830	51,175	25,015	47,780	13,100	9,570
Elementary school..............	3,970,115	181,325	588,920	700,625	439,025	836,965	435,445	432,840	125,265	229,705
1–4 years.................	720,125	19,210	65,200	72,695	48,025	227,735	118,045	118,145	21,805	29,165
5–6 years.................	823,150	29,325	100,755	107,600	62,075	236,790	113,410	113,795	22,085	37,315
7 years...................	643,970	25,825	89,295	92,590	56,200	180,500	66,875	79,325	18,265	35,095
8 years	1,782,870	106,965	333,670	427,740	272,625	191,940	137,115	121,575	63,110	128,130
High school...............	3,117,945	253,680	507,855	633,705	325,800	467,005	209,845	278,475	143,275	298,305
1–3 years.............	1,473,090	100,515	220,340	271,230	129,575	278,340	110,495	172,525	61,950	128,120
4 years...............	1,644,855	153,165	287,515	362,475	196,225	188,665	99,350	105,950	81,325	170,185
College	953,180	83,980	142,445	160,865	121,295	149,430	64,560	78,680	53,105	98,820
1–3 years	603,475	49,655	79,525	107,480	86,985	88,900	41,830	48,310	36,145	64,645
4 years or more	349,705	34,325	62,920	53,385	34,310	60,530	22,730	30,370	16,960	34,175
Not reported...........	223,130	11,740	53,300	40,980	25,275	31,845	15,120	16,300	7,920	20,650
EDUCATIONAL ATTAINMENT – WHITE										
Total 25 years old and over.....	15,591,155	1,038,755	2,527,370	3,045,900	1,768,420	2,479,290	1,226,960	1,443,510	686,690	1,374,260
No school years completed	318,730	20,020	44,725	36,295	19,715	59,580	32,030	67,835	16,475	22,055
Elementary school..............	7,430,165	378,600	1,189,885	1,444,940	896,160	1,299,565	694,010	714,315	279,340	533,995
1–4 years	1,224,870	41,455	137,820	165,495	105,775	300,965	173,180	178,075	49,235	72,870
5–6 years	1,469,435	61,875	206,590	227,125	130,170	357,200	171,410	179,640	47,630	87,795
7 years...................	1,204,210	54,895	180,660	193,165	116,045	295,915	108,780	134,505	40,090	80,155
8 years	3,531,650	220,375	664,815	858,510	544,170	345,485	240,640	222,095	142,385	293,175
High school...............	5,568,770	453,475	914,720	1,155,485	578,875	790,120	355,645	482,145	266,755	571,550
1–3 years.............	2,711,825	196,115	419,555	516,580	240,005	473,280	188,935	297,530	122,020	257,805
4 years	2,856,945	257,360	495,165	638,905	338,870	316,840	166,710	184,615	144,735	313,745
College	1,805,885	159,845	278,310	314,080	218,950	269,505	115,770	145,945	105,295	198,185
1–3 years	1,036,010	83,185	137,105	186,960	138,250	150,225	68,730	86,125	64,755	120,675
4 years or more	769,875	76,660	141,205	127,120	80,700	119,280	47,040	59,820	40,540	77,510
Not reported...........	467,605	26,815	99,730	95,745	54,720	60,520	29,505	33,270	18,825	48,475
EDUCATIONAL ATTAINMENT – NONWHITE										
Total 25 years old and over	1,305,260	7,600	72,665	47,945	27,280	585,065	241,000	248,975	35,255	39,475
No school years completed	138,970	530	2,470	2,675	1,820	59,375	25,100	34,425	9,845	2,730
Elementary school..............	893,045	3,845	31,365	27,145	16,950	429,795	174,920	172,855	15,245	20,925
1–4 years	416,180	770	9,310	7,950	5,185	213,000	84,750	84,490	4,735	5,990
5–6 years	244,785	955	8,575	6,625	4,125	119,095	48,505	47,175	4,425	5,305
7 years...................	117,360	695	4,710	3,930	2,440	59,935	18,710	21,860	2,275	5,305
8 years	114,720	1,425	8,770	8,640	5,200	37,765	22,955	19,330	3,810	6,825
High school...............	159,495	2,205	11,805	10,520	5,775	60,125	23,760	27,110	7,030	11,165
1–3 years.............	111,350	1,215	7,055	6,605	3,685	44,895	17,225	20,905	3,975	5,790
4 years...............	48,145	990	4,750	3,915	2,090	15,230	6,535	6,205	3,055	5,375
College	39,415	510	2,180	2,005	1,070	16,350	7,030	7,415	930	1,925
1–3 years.............	21,695	290	1,240	1,380	720	8,160	4,140	3,855	555	1,355
4 years or more	17,720	220	940	625	350	8,190	2,890	3,560	375	570
Not reported...........	74,335	510	24,845	5,600	1,665	19,420	10,190	7,170	2,205	2,730
POPULATION ENROLLED IN SCHOOLS...	6,296,570	345,970	865,260	1,083,805	566,830	1,300,950	637,940	686,950	313,785	495,080
5–6 years	480,065	28,550	70,625	82,450	43,800	95,465	47,795	46,945	22,985	41,410
7–13 years	3,744,725	195,220	498,840	649,335	329,220	794,845	381,750	414,440	188,565	292,510
14–15 years	887,380	46,720	122,865	153,050	83,450	182,530	87,220	99,250	44,475	67,820
16–17 years	649,040	35,970	96,185	116,330	67,830	118,670	57,910	71,775	33,235	51,135
18–19 years	238,415	17,145	33,875	38,505	22,210	45,630	26,500	24,415	11,665	18,470
20–24 years	188,195	16,050	28,090	27,865	13,380	40,525	22,845	17,365	7,815	14,260
25–29 years	108,750	6,275	14,780	16,270	6,940	23,285	13,920	12,760	5,045	9,475

TABLE 44

POPULATION: EDUCATIONAL ATTAINMENT OF THE RURAL-FARM POPULATION 25 YEARS OLD AND OVER AND SCHOOL ENROLLMENT OF THE RURAL-FARM POPULATION 5-29 YEARS OLD, BY GEOGRAPHIC DIVISIONS: 1950

Educational Attainment and School Enrollment	United States	New England	Middle Atlantic	East North Central	West North Central	South Atlantic	East South Central	West South Central	Mountain	Pacific
EDUCATIONAL ATTAINMENT, ALL GROUPS										
Total 25 years old and over	11,822,340	228,210	767,735	2,055,995	2,016,990	2,165,975	1,920,935	1,627,795	425,590	613,115
No school completed	367,470	5,560	13,580	21,180	16,660	104,965	83,565	91,845	15,955	14,160
Elementary school	7,388,080	102,185	437,585	1,211,505	1,234,635	1,506,325	1,389,970	1,027,465	199,065	279,345
1-4 years	1,619,190	11,155	44,180	119,955	109,875	506,860	449,175	304,405	32,400	41,185
5-6 years	1,533,955	15,415	70,250	169,190	150,675	424,450	361,445	266,835	31,190	44,505
7 years	1,158,855	12,825	63,140	156,460	161,475	317,860	198,180	180,960	28,285	39,670
8 years	3,076,080	62,790	260,015	765,900	812,610	257,155	381,170	275,265	107,190	153,985
High school	3,139,485	90,700	239,265	654,820	598,985	416,165	351,880	401,845	154,480	231,345
1-3 years	1,651,690	42,900	116,665	286,420	244,745	296,145	218,685	269,960	72,195	103,975
4 years	1,487,795	47,800	122,600	368,400	354,240	120,020	133,195	131,885	82,285	127,370
College	744,860	25,710	65,060	141,315	140,300	103,700	68,470	79,620	46,205	74,480
1-3 years	506,295	15,105	36,660	99,260	110,125	64,215	46,895	52,695	33,165	48,175
4 years or more	238,565	10,605	28,400	42,055	30,175	39,485	21,575	26,925	13,040	26,305
Not reported	182,445	4,055	12,245	27,175	26,410	34,820	27,050	27,020	9,885	13,785
EDUCATIONAL ATTAINMENT - MALE										
Total 25 years old and over	6,173,985	120,225	399,520	1,075,240	1,083,145	1,100,405	973,600	854,085	233,360	334,405
No school completed	221,240	3,115	7,260	12,130	9,940	65,560	51,250	54,035	8,485	9,465
Elementary school	4,091,430	60,135	245,705	683,930	729,040	794,565	721,095	563,515	123,290	169,905
1-4 years	973,905	7,005	26,545	76,095	70,545	299,785	262,305	183,050	20,790	27,785
5-6 years	833,145	9,360	40,975	100,245	93,895	216,560	181,620	143,095	19,245	28,150
7 years	623,980	7,830	36,690	92,700	102,230	153,250	94,980	94,335	17,905	24,060
8 years	1,660,400	35,940	141,495	414,890	462,620	124,970	182,190	143,035	65,350	89,910
High school	1,448,960	43,480	110,930	306,015	279,580	178,235	158,000	185,570	25,480	111,670
1-3 years	789,885	22,630	57,835	139,950	122,825	129,155	100,665	126,855	37,385	52,585
4 years	659,075	20,850	53,095	166,065	156,755	49,080	57,335	58,715	38,095	59,085
College	303,560	11,170	28,435	57,330	48,800	41,510	27,340	34,600	19,995	34,380
1-3 years	191,700	5,740	14,470	36,615	35,060	24,705	17,495	22,580	13,575	21,460
4 years or more	111,860	5,430	13,965	20,715	13,740	16,805	9,845	12,020	6,420	12,920
Not reported	108,795	2,325	7,190	15,835	15,535	20,535	15,915	16,365	6,110	8,985
EDUCATIONAL ATTAINMENT - FEMALE										
Total 25 years old and over	5,648,355	107,985	368,215	980,755	933,845	1,065,570	947,335	773,710	192,230	278,710
No school years completed	146,230	2,445	6,320	9,050	6,720	39,405	32,315	37,810	7,470	4,695
Elementary school	3,296,650	42,050	191,880	527,575	505,345	711,760	668,875	463,950	75,775	109,440
1-4 years	645,285	4,150	17,635	43,860	39,330	207,075	186,870	121,355	11,610	13,400
5-6 years	700,810	6,055	29,275	68,945	56,780	207,890	179,825	123,740	11,945	16,355
7 years	534,875	4,995	26,450	63,760	59,245	164,610	103,200	86,625	10,380	15,610
8 years	1,415,680	26,850	118,520	351,010	349,990	132,185	198,980	132,230	41,840	64,075
High school	1,690,525	47,220	128,335	348,805	319,405	237,930	193,880	216,275	79,000	119,675
1-3 years	861,805	20,270	58,830	146,470	121,920	166,990	118,020	143,105	34,810	51,390
4 years	828,720	26,950	69,505	202,335	197,485	70,940	75,860	73,170	44,190	68,285
College	441,300	14,540	36,625	83,985	91,500	62,190	41,130	45,020	26,210	40,100
1-3 years	314,595	9,365	22,190	62,645	75,065	39,510	29,400	30,115	19,590	26,715
4 years or more	126,705	5,175	14,435	21,340	16,435	22,680	11,730	14,905	6,620	13,385
Not reported	73,650	1,730	5,055	11,340	10,875	14,285	11,135	10,655	3,775	4,800
EDUCATIONAL ATTAINMENT - WHITE										
Total 25 years old and over	10,477,455	227,570	760,830	2,045,935	2,000,280	1,625,355	1,490,845	1,340,230	401,090	585,320
No school years completed	223,120	5,515	13,130	20,815	15,560	50,690	41,475	56,090	8,395	11,470
Elementary school	6,338,340	101,835	432,895	1,204,765	1,222,125	1,073,585	1,039,485	809,700	188,685	265,265
1-4 years	1,075,625	11,075	42,595	118,155	105,205	274,785	264,820	193,875	28,570	36,545
5-6 years	1,244,910	15,325	69,005	167,585	147,375	304,550	264,060	207,410	28,525	41,075
7 years	1,038,195	12,760	62,490	155,515	160,050	263,000	163,865	155,445	26,995	38,125
8 years	2,979,610	62,675	258,805	763,510	809,545	231,250	346,740	252,970	104,595	149,520
High school	3,035,155	90,520	238,000	652,550	596,540	380,915	325,590	377,655	150,280	223,105
1-3 years	1,574,570	42,795	115,810	285,105	243,200	267,645	197,980	250,850	70,100	101,085
4 years	1,460,585	47,725	122,190	367,445	353,340	113,270	127,610	126,805	80,180	122,020
College	724,475	25,670	64,810	140,870	139,995	94,965	64,135	75,000	45,810	73,210
1-3 years	493,855	15,085	36,520	98,990	109,900	59,420	43,830	49,970	32,895	47,245
4 years or more	230,620	10,585	28,290	41,880	30,095	35,545	20,305	25,040	12,915	25,965
Not reported	156,365	4,030	11,995	26,935	26,060	25,200	20,180	21,775	7,920	12,270
EDUCATIONAL ATTAINMENT - NONWHITE										
Total 25 years old and over	1,344,885	640	6,905	10,060	16,710	540,620	430,090	287,565	24,500	27,795
No school years completed	144,350	45	450	365	1,100	54,275	42,110	35,755	7,560	2,690
Elementary school	1,049,740	350	4,690	6,740	12,510	432,740	350,485	217,765	10,380	14,080
1-4 years	543,565	80	1,585	1,800	4,670	232,075	184,355	110,530	3,830	4,640
5-6 years	289,045	90	1,245	1,605	3,300	119,900	97,385	59,425	2,665	3,430
7 years	120,660	65	650	945	1,475	54,860	34,315	25,515	1,290	1,545
8 years	96,470	115	1,210	2,390	3,065	25,905	34,430	22,295	2,595	4,465
High school	104,330	180	1,265	2,270	2,445	35,250	26,290	24,190	4,200	8,240
1-3 years	77,120	105	855	1,315	1,545	28,500	20,705	19,110	2,095	2,890
4 years	27,210	75	410	955	900	6,750	5,585	5,080	2,105	5,350
College	20,385	40	250	445	305	8,735	4,335	4,610	395	1,270
1-3 years	12,440	20	140	270	225	4,795	3,065	2,725	270	930
4 years or more	7,945	20	110	175	80	3,940	1,270	1,885	125	340
Not reported	26,080	25	250	240	350	9,620	6,870	5,245	1,965	1,515
POPULATION ENROLLED IN SCHOOLS	5,509,480	85,825	303,950	827,525	834,690	1,198,670	1,021,495	789,810	209,275	238,240
5-6 years	382,425	6,245	22,400	57,445	65,725	78,430	69,915	52,010	13,965	16,290
7-13 years	3,330,320	49,925	178,850	492,105	503,175	744,720	622,885	476,675	124,525	137,460
14-15 years	864,970	13,585	48,050	131,785	126,135	191,030	159,340	126,400	32,210	36,435
16-17 years	615,860	10,100	35,475	100,845	98,115	122,040	104,875	89,335	24,860	30,215
18-19 years	181,850	3,310	10,290	26,735	24,240	35,495	37,455	25,660	8,110	10,555
20-24 years	76,935	1,675	5,475	10,220	9,295	15,705	16,130	10,860	3,145	4,430
25-29 years	57,120	985	3,410	8,390	8,005	11,250	10,895	8,870	2,460	2,855

TABLE 45

POPULATION: EDUCATIONAL ATTAINMENT OF THE TOTAL POPULATION 25 YEARS OLD AND OVER AND SCHOOL ENROLLMENT OF THE TOTAL POPULATION 5-29 YEARS OLD, BY GEOGRAPHIC DIVISIONS: 1940

Educational Attainment and School Enrollment	Geographic division									
	United States	New England	Middle Atlantic	East North Central	West North Central	South Atlantic	East South Central	West South Central	Mountain	Pacific
EDUCATIONAL ATTAINMENT, ALL GROUPS										
Total 25 years old and over	74,775,836	5,056,175	16,601,854	15,752,048	7,803,710	9,054,565	5,337,105	6,799,801	2,200,427	6,170,151
No school completed	2,799,923	197,983	807,450	342,362	105,079	454,196	280,958	401,067	79,752	131,076
Elementary school	41,717,753	2,484,526	9,420,389	8,953,918	4,567,192	5,359,105	3,483,330	3,706,234	1,056,261	2,686,798
1-4 years	7,304,689	312,411	1,213,026	1,093,039	477,371	1,622,449	1,040,512	1,058,107	162,258	325,516
5-6 years	8,515,111	435,297	1,672,243	1,573,455	701,506	1,543,965	945,491	1,041,927	178,424	422,803
7 years	5,141,035	278,343	986,666	882,498	474,919	1,072,426	415,988	676,925	106,253	247,017
8 years	20,756,918	1,458,475	5,548,454	5,404,926	2,913,396	1,120,265	1,081,339	929,275	609,326	1,691,462
High school	21,733,675	1,789,471	4,549,367	4,801,418	2,216,861	2,207,953	1,109,301	1,947,320	730,387	2,381,597
1-3 years	11,181,995	872,262	2,362,827	2,458,705	1,064,526	1,209,787	631,336	1,140,426	363,486	1,078,640
4 years	10,551,680	917,209	2,186,540	2,342,713	1,152,335	998,166	477,965	806,894	366,901	1,302,957
College	7,482,515	491,170	1,490,914	1,489,646	832,156	896,034	391,946	677,045	307,060	906,544
1-3 years	4,075,184	242,898	667,152	824,654	511,245	488,392	233,165	405,493	187,542	514,643
4 years or more	3,407,331	248,272	823,762	664,992	320,911	407,642	158,781	271,552	119,518	391,901
Not reported	1,041,970	93,025	333,734	164,704	82,422	137,277	71,570	68,135	26,967	64,136
EDUCATIONAL ATTAINMENT - MALE										
Total 25 years old and over	37,463,087	2,451,320	8,223,272	7,957,457	3,945,420	4,481,346	2,644,845	3,421,234	1,162,913	3,175,280
No school years completed	1,471,290	95,749	393,202	179,541	58,933	254,091	159,923	213,299	42,180	74,372
Elementary school	21,718,390	1,259,629	4,743,577	4,682,699	2,470,996	2,742,331	1,768,595	1,945,655	608,895	1,496,013
1-4 years	4,079,100	166,389	649,323	617,192	279,198	893,602	579,972	596,775	97,908	198,741
5-6 years	4,399,910	221,609	853,955	833,889	385,448	762,369	462,493	532,206	103,496	244,445
7 years	2,607,902	137,196	487,396	454,700	260,634	526,672	197,022	343,705	61,105	139,472
8 years	10,631,478	734,435	2,752,903	2,776,918	1,545,716	559,688	529,108	472,969	346,386	913,355
High school	9,840,047	793,495	2,064,046	2,210,467	976,588	972,778	493,412	890,995	344,279	1,093,987
1-3 years	5,332,803	421,900	1,132,053	1,185,399	502,873	560,691	288,537	537,491	180,659	523,200
4 years	4,507,244	371,595	931,993	1,025,068	473,715	412,087	204,875	353,504	163,620	570,787
College	3,845,209	254,038	844,414	786,701	391,801	433,644	182,673	331,036	150,851	470,051
1-3 years	1,823,981	101,694	321,381	379,372	207,409	206,713	97,159	183,063	82,559	244,631
4 years or more	2,021,228	152,344	523,033	407,329	184,392	226,931	85,514	147,973	68,292	225,420
Not reported	588,151	48,409	178,033	98,049	47,102	78,502	40,242	40,249	16,708	40,857
EDUCATIONAL ATTAINMENT - FEMALE										
Total 25 years old and over	37,312,749	2,604,855	8,378,582	7,794,591	3,858,290	4,573,219	2,692,260	3,378,567	1,037,514	2,994,871
No school years completed	1,328,633	102,234	414,248	162,821	46,146	200,105	121,035	187,768	37,572	56,704
Elementary school	19,999,363	1,224,897	4,676,812	4,271,219	2,096,196	2,616,774	1,714,735	1,760,579	447,366	1,190,785
1-4 years	3,225,589	146,022	563,703	475,847	198,173	728,847	460,540	461,332	64,350	126,775
5-6 years	4,115,201	213,688	818,288	739,566	316,058	781,596	482,998	509,721	74,928	178,358
7 years	2,533,133	141,147	499,270	427,798	214,285	545,754	218,966	333,220	45,148	107,545
8 years	10,125,440	724,040	2,795,551	2,628,008	1,367,680	560,577	552,231	456,306	262,940	778,107
High school	11,893,628	995,976	2,485,321	2,590,951	1,240,273	1,235,175	615,889	1,056,325	386,108	1,287,610
1-3 years	5,849,192	450,362	1,230,774	1,273,306	561,653	649,096	342,799	602,935	182,827	555,440
4 years	6,044,436	545,614	1,254,547	1,317,645	678,620	586,079	273,090	453,390	203,281	732,170
College	3,637,306	237,132	646,500	702,945	440,355	462,390	209,273	346,009	156,209	436,493
1-3 years	2,251,203	141,204	345,771	445,282	303,836	281,679	136,006	222,430	104,983	270,012
4 years or more	1,386,103	95,928	300,729	257,663	136,519	180,711	73,267	123,579	51,226	166,481
Not reported	453,819	44,616	155,701	66,655	35,320	58,775	31,328	27,886	10,259	23,279
EDUCATIONAL ATTAINMENT - WHITE										
Total 25 years old and over	67,999,523	4,994,756	15,829,731	15,095,242	7,566,806	6,872,705	4,001,850	5,557,482	2,123,431	5,957,520
No school years completed	2,099,995	193,120	767,030	311,095	90,493	198,858	125,729	244,778	55,492	113,401
Elementary school	36,851,247	2,446,777	8,892,405	8,515,709	4,408,077	3,731,979	2,455,763	2,810,267	1,019,580	2,570,690
1-4 years	5,222,119	304,621	1,081,815	978,720	432,545	794,327	540,964	643,490	150,692	294,945
5-6 years	7,082,235	426,413	1,521,731	1,449,371	657,496	1,061,079	635,663	768,646	167,912	393,924
7 years	4,580,131	273,649	916,772	829,453	454,744	880,331	324,299	563,327	102,499	235,057
8 years	19,966,762	1,442,094	5,372,087	5,258,165	2,863,292	996,242	954,837	834,804	598,477	1,646,764
High school	20,858,925	1,774,830	4,395,810	4,653,543	2,168,811	2,014,074	1,003,961	1,808,542	718,256	2,321,098
1-3 years	10,603,592	863,994	2,264,733	2,362,153	1,033,657	1,076,515	556,744	1,040,568	356,334	1,048,894
4 years	10,255,333	910,836	2,131,077	2,291,390	1,135,154	937,559	447,217	767,974	361,922	1,272,204
College	7,268,466	488,429	1,460,531	1,458,777	820,463	834,249	367,361	641,647	304,623	892,386
1-3 years	3,948,681	241,446	649,604	805,538	504,022	453,808	217,833	384,297	185,922	506,211
4 years or more	3,319,785	246,983	810,927	653,239	316,441	380,441	149,528	257,350	118,701	386,175
Not reported	920,890	91,600	313,955	156,118	78,962	93,545	49,037	52,248	25,480	59,945
EDUCATIONAL ATTAINMENT-NONWHITE										
Total 25 years old and over	6,776,313	61,419	772,123	656,806	236,904	2,181,860	1,335,255	1,242,319	76,996	212,631
No school years completed	699,928	4,863	40,420	31,267	14,586	255,338	155,230	156,289	24,260	17,675
Elementary school	4,866,506	37,749	527,984	438,209	159,115	1,627,126	1,027,567	895,967	36,681	116,108
1-4 years	2,082,570	7,790	131,211	114,319	44,826	828,122	499,548	414,617	11,566	30,571
5-6 years	1,432,876	8,884	150,512	124,084	44,010	482,886	309,828	273,281	10,512	28,879
7 years	560,904	4,694	69,894	53,045	20,175	192,095	91,689	113,598	3,754	11,960
8 years	790,156	16,381	176,367	146,761	50,104	124,023	126,502	94,471	10,849	44,698
High school	874,750	14,641	153,557	147,875	48,050	193,879	105,340	138,778	12,131	60,499
1-3 years	578,403	8,268	98,094	96,552	30,869	133,272	74,592	99,858	7,152	29,746
4 years	296,347	6,373	55,463	51,323	17,181	60,607	30,748	38,920	4,979	30,753
College	214,049	2,741	30,383	30,869	11,693	61,785	24,585	35,398	2,437	14,158
1-3 years	126,503	1,452	17,548	19,116	7,223	34,584	15,332	21,196	1,620	8,432
4 years or more	87,546	1,289	12,835	11,753	4,470	27,201	9,253	14,202	817	5,726
Not reported	121,080	1,425	19,779	8,586	3,460	43,732	22,533	15,887	1,487	4,191
POPULATION ENROLLED IN SCHOOLS	26,759,099	1,689,746	5,437,451	5,301,499	2,792,794	3,813,689	2,179,471	2,826,552	929,753	1,788,144
5-6 years	1,805,211	134,240	401,117	386,529	225,910	209,006	112,673	146,691	57,157	131,898
7-13 years	15,034,695	913,611	2,936,471	2,903,121	1,547,316	2,322,402	1,315,851	1,675,677	521,350	898,896
14-15 years	4,347,665	282,189	910,323	870,177	436,216	614,511	348,783	458,688	144,139	282,639
16-17 years	3,361,206	217,108	736,879	705,382	348,277	410,454	241,061	328,152	117,692	256,201
18-19 years	1,449,485	92,502	293,230	286,746	153,730	172,855	110,990	146,671	57,671	135,090
20-24 years	760,837	50,096	159,431	149,544	81,345	84,461	50,113	70,673	31,744	83,420

TABLE 46

POPULATION: EDUCATIONAL ATTAINMENT OF THE URBAN POPULATION 25 YEARS OLD AND OVER AND SCHOOL ENROLLMENT OF THE URBAN POPULATION 5-29 YEARS OLD, BY GEOGRAPHIC DIVISIONS: 1940

Educational Attainment and School Enrollment	United States	New England	Middle Atlantic	East North Central	West North Central	South Atlantic	East South Central	West South Central	Mountain	Pacific
EDUCATIONAL ATTAINMENT, ALL GROUPS										
Total 25 years old and over	45,229,242	3,873,849	12,993,784	10,615,618	3,676,332	4,033,528	1,826,610	2,999,952	1,018,817	4,190,752
No school completed	1,606,239	164,552	702,791	261,559	49,750	135,687	65,956	125,513	21,030	79,401
Elementary school	23,001,057	1,888,244	7,195,844	5,625,284	1,830,577	2,045,190	983,840	1,356,447	422,093	1,653,538
1-4 years	3,471,964	253,869	961,890	722,452	190,915	514,014	241,882	339,022	56,709	191,211
5-6 years	4,464,991	349,107	1,262,911	1,023,199	295,556	571,423	263,180	243,606	69,704	256,305
7 years	2,589,169	221,867	752,643	537,082	182,305	355,579	117,349	243,802	39,108	139,434
8 years	12,474,933	1,063,401	4,218,400	3,342,551	1,161,801	604,174	361,429	400,017	256,572	1,066,588
High school	14,710,627	1,376,270	3,650,084	3,510,154	1,247,568	1,232,752	542,495	1,041,956	381,843	1,727,505
1-3 years	7,186,008	663,911	1,866,339	1,769,992	572,004	603,108	275,693	521,467	172,558	740,936
4 years	7,524,619	712,359	1,783,745	1,740,162	675,564	629,644	266,802	520,489	209,285	986,569
College	5,319,428	371,511	1,205,738	1,133,927	510,200	561,120	216,546	446,618	181,854	691,914
1-3 years	2,733,837	177,565	516,235	593,773	287,919	292,352	121,386	256,475	104,675	383,457
4 years or more	2,585,591	193,946	689,503	540,154	222,281	268,768	95,160	190,143	77,179	308,457
Not reported	591,891	73,272	239,327	84,694	38,237	58,779	17,773	29,418	17,997	38,394
EDUCATIONAL ATTAINMENT - MALE										
Total 25 years old and over	21,987,979	1,850,521	6,352,393	5,239,933	1,758,787	1,913,349	857,798	1,438,633	506,916	2,069,649
No school years completed	783,713	77,362	334,996	130,581	26,132	68,241	34,249	59,422	10,927	41,803
Elementary school	11,490,023	932,921	3,541,828	2,841,554	921,236	1,001,548	475,186	675,681	226,329	873,740
1-4 years	1,829,048	131,528	501,706	388,770	103,104	262,512	124,373	175,641	32,017	109,447
5-6 years	2,231,191	173,076	628,854	520,599	150,649	273,016	124,324	182,229	37,515	140,929
7 years	1,259,589	106,459	362,444	262,493	90,017	170,176	53,155	119,417	20,574	74,774
8 years	6,170,145	521,778	2,048,824	1,669,692	577,466	295,844	173,334	198,394	136,223	548,590
High school	6,568,705	606,788	1,650,436	1,603,141	537,197	531,296	234,307	463,984	171,315	770,241
1-3 years	3,388,212	318,204	891,068	847,609	263,038	274,727	122,451	240,613	81,769	348,733
4 years	3,180,493	288,584	759,368	755,532	274,159	256,569	111,856	223,371	89,546	421,508
College	2,826,677	195,615	700,933	618,461	253,093	279,746	103,899	223,006	91,493	360,431
1-3 years	1,272,433	76,625	258,869	285,739	124,546	127,058	52,230	117,765	47,313	182,288
4 years or more	1,554,244	118,990	442,064	332,722	128,547	152,688	51,669	105,241	44,180	178,143
Not reported	318,861	37,835	124,200	46,196	21,129	32,518	10,157	16,540	6,852	23,434
EDUCATIONAL ATTAINMENT - FEMALE										
Total 25 years old and over	23,241,263	2,023,328	6,641,391	5,375,685	1,917,545	2,120,179	968,812	1,561,319	511,901	2,121,103
No school years completed	822,526	87,190	367,795	130,978	23,618	67,446	31,707	66,091	10,103	37,598
Elementary school	11,511,034	955,323	3,654,016	2,783,730	909,341	1,043,642	508,654	680,766	195,764	779,798
1-4 years	1,642,866	122,341	460,184	333,682	87,811	251,502	117,509	163,381	24,692	81,764
5-6 years	2,233,800	176,031	634,057	502,600	144,907	298,407	138,856	191,377	32,189	115,376
7 years	1,329,580	115,328	390,199	274,589	92,288	185,403	64,194	124,385	18,534	64,660
8 years	6,304,788	541,623	2,169,576	1,672,859	584,335	308,330	188,095	201,623	120,349	517,998
High school	8,141,922	769,482	1,999,648	1,907,013	710,371	701,456	308,188	577,972	210,528	957,264
1-3 years	3,797,796	345,707	975,271	922,383	308,966	328,381	153,242	280,854	90,789	392,203
4 years	4,344,126	423,775	1,024,377	984,630	401,405	373,075	154,946	297,118	119,739	565,061
College	2,492,751	175,896	504,805	515,466	257,107	281,374	112,647	223,612	90,361	331,483
1-3 years	1,461,404	100,940	257,366	308,034	163,373	165,294	69,156	138,710	57,362	201,169
4 years or more	1,031,347	74,956	247,439	207,432	93,734	116,080	43,491	84,902	32,999	130,314
Not reported	273,030	35,437	115,127	38,498	17,108	26,261	7,616	12,878	5,145	14,960
EDUCATIONAL ATTAINMENT - WHITE										
Total 25 years old and over	41,493,140	3,821,189	12,291,196	10,018,170	3,496,689	3,043,051	1,317,096	2,464,456	998,380	4,042,913
No school years completed	1,352,041	160,870	667,212	235,067	41,264	55,776	22,515	79,600	19,630	70,107
Elementary school	20,416,026	1,855,927	6,716,809	5,228,647	1,712,893	1,323,989	605,239	984,126	410,478	1,577,918
1-4 years	2,596,882	247,336	845,695	620,720	160,436	206,567	91,225	197,662	53,773	173,468
5-6 years	3,681,174	341,433	1,126,583	910,313	263,021	340,012	142,392	253,203	66,753	237,464
7 years	2,258,516	217,023	688,802	489,703	166,702	262,191	76,567	188,395	37,909	131,224
8 years	11,879,454	1,050,135	4,055,729	3,207,911	1,122,734	515,219	295,055	344,866	252,043	1,035,762
High school	14,038,446	1,363,235	3,505,837	3,371,056	1,206,930	1,103,633	476,892	955,356	376,404	1,679,103
1-3 years	6,756,228	656,579	1,774,437	1,679,375	546,209	518,651	231,087	462,882	169,516	717,492
4 years	7,282,218	706,656	1,731,400	1,691,681	660,721	584,982	245,805	492,474	206,888	961,611
College	5,149,791	369,057	1,176,916	1,104,630	499,907	517,093	199,558	422,684	180,302	679,644
1-3 years	2,635,955	176,292	499,600	575,669	281,684	268,673	111,379	242,743	103,664	376,251
4 years or more	2,513,836	192,765	677,316	528,961	218,223	248,420	88,179	179,941	76,638	303,393
Not reported	536,836	72,100	224,422	78,770	35,695	42,560	12,892	22,690	11,566	36,141
EDUCATIONAL ATTAINMENT - NONWHITE										
Total 25 years old and over	3,736,102	52,660	702,588	597,448	179,643	990,477	509,514	535,496	20,437	147,839
No school years completed	254,198	3,682	35,579	26,492	8,486	79,911	43,441	45,913	1,400	9,294
Elementary school	2,585,031	32,317	479,035	396,637	117,684	721,201	378,601	372,321	11,615	75,620
1-4 years	875,082	6,533	116,195	101,732	30,479	307,447	150,657	141,360	2,936	17,743
5-6 years	783,817	7,674	136,328	112,886	32,535	231,411	120,788	120,403	2,951	18,841
7 years	330,653	4,844	63,841	47,379	15,603	93,388	40,782	55,407	1,199	8,210
8 years	595,479	13,266	162,671	134,640	39,067	88,955	66,374	55,151	4,529	30,826
High school	672,181	13,035	144,247	139,098	40,638	129,119	65,603	86,600	5,439	48,402
1-3 years	429,780	7,332	91,902	90,617	25,795	84,457	44,606	58,585	3,042	23,444
4 years	242,401	5,703	52,345	48,481	14,843	44,662	20,997	28,015	2,397	24,958
College	169,637	2,454	28,822	29,297	10,293	44,027	16,988	23,934	1,552	12,270
1-3 years	97,882	1,273	16,635	18,104	6,235	23,679	10,007	13,732	1,011	7,206
4 years or more	71,755	1,181	12,187	11,193	4,058	20,348	6,981	10,202	541	5,064
Not reported	55,055	1,172	14,905	5,924	2,542	16,219	4,881	6,728	431	2,253
POPULATION ENROLLED IN SCHOOLS	14,218,641	1,278,113	4,063,295	3,359,599	1,155,455	1,285,989	599,520	1,006,829	370,257	1,099,584
5-6 years	1,046,649	104,373	308,909	257,561	105,179	73,586	31,123	53,082	24,632	88,204
7-13 years	7,550,576	680,437	2,153,016	1,770,660	591,517	726,113	343,647	566,083	193,877	525,226
14-15 years	2,319,566	214,253	676,158	550,261	180,688	209,453	97,466	163,056	57,048	170,793
16-17 years	1,912,468	167,099	564,246	466,186	152,893	153,956	71,995	124,993	49,678	161,722
18-19 years	865,320	71,424	228,141	198,455	76,566	75,077	35,488	62,566	26,993	90,610
20-24 years	524,062	40,527	132,825	116,086	48,612	47,804	20,101	37,049	18,029	63,029

TABLE 47

POPULATION: EDUCATIONAL ATTAINMENT OF THE RURAL-NONFARM POPULATION 25 YEARS OLD AND OVER AND SCHOOL ENROLLMENT OF THE RURAL-NONFARM POPULATION 5-29 YEARS OLD, BY GEOGRAPHIC DIVISIONS: 1940

Educational Attainment and School Enrollment	Geographic Division									
	United States	New England	Middle Atlantic	East North Central	West North Central	South Atlantic	East South Central	West South Central	Mountain	Pacific
EDUCATIONAL ATTAINMENT, ALL GROUPS										
Total 25 years old and over	14,753,758	876,719	2,636,028	2,628,394	1,663,929	2,402,333	1,161,143	1,460,977	650,580	1,273,655
No school completed	500,352	22,966	80,220	43,551	23,885	124,160	58,671	91,312	26,765	28,822
Elementary school	8,380,066	427,039	1,554,414	1,547,604	962,674	1,446,340	724,264	778,491	322,995	616,245
1-4 years	1,511,983	41,357	185,427	180,684	110,159	432,123	207,190	222,837	55,814	76,392
5-6 years	1,755,199	63,352	291,858	265,426	151,881	419,051	192,100	216,382	56,357	98,792
7 years	1,101,454	43,011	168,965	159,899	96,681	299,219	88,799	147,518	33,665	63,697
8 years	4,011,430	279,319	908,164	941,595	603,953	295,947	236,175	191,754	177,159	377,364
High school	4,152,344	315,018	700,184	760,370	462,873	563,847	255,817	428,459	208,502	457,274
1-3 years	2,243,088	155,192	378,763	402,387	228,099	325,919	145,305	266,060	109,946	231,417
4 years	1,909,256	159,826	321,421	357,983	234,774	237,928	110,512	162,399	98,556	225,857
College	1,463,486	96,134	229,074	229,826	192,831	230,321	103,470	144,910	83,067	153,853
1-3 years	838,186	50,550	114,834	137,208	119,862	126,098	60,387	86,609	51,755	90,883
4 years or more	625,300	45,584	114,240	92,618	72,969	104,223	43,083	58,301	31,312	62,970
Not reported	257,510	15,562	72,136	47,043	21,666	37,665	18,921	17,805	9,251	17,461
EDUCATIONAL ATTAINMENT - MALE										
Total 25 years old and over	7,578,483	436,478	1,343,057	1,357,278	835,068	1,224,579	582,393	743,139	355,055	701,436
No school years completed	279,083	12,111	44,027	26,091	13,439	70,558	33,012	48,205	14,401	17,239
Elementary school	4,486,993	227,702	819,027	829,173	510,368	760,890	372,600	411,269	190,086	365,878
1-4 years	868,236	24,137	106,737	107,492	63,228	242,143	115,766	125,150	33,874	49,709
5-6 years	930,315	34,728	155,505	145,634	82,102	213,170	95,514	110,471	33,084	60,107
7 years	573,366	22,632	87,468	84,586	51,314	151,622	42,780	75,846	19,538	37,580
8 years	2,115,076	146,205	469,317	491,461	313,724	153,955	118,540	99,802	103,590	218,482
High School	1,930,917	140,690	320,045	355,280	208,608	258,424	117,128	201,813	103,173	225,756
1-3 years	1,092,942	76,420	182,366	196,178	109,078	156,426	68,316	128,039	56,615	119,504
4 years	837,975	64,270	137,679	159,102	99,530	101,998	48,812	73,774	46,558	106,252
College	725,569	47,931	119,084	115,258	90,334	111,633	48,784	70,462	41,222	80,861
1-3 years	355,146	19,621	48,672	57,784	46,637	52,643	24,692	38,515	22,532	44,050
4 years or more	370,423	28,310	70,412	57,474	43,697	58,990	24,092	31,947	18,690	36,811
Not reported	155,921	8,044	40,874	31,476	12,319	23,074	10,869	11,390	6,173	11,702
EDUCATIONAL ATTAINMENT - FEMALE										
Total 25 years old and over	7,175,275	440,241	1,292,971	1,271,116	828,861	1,177,754	578,750	717,838	295,525	572,219
No school years completed	221,269	10,855	36,193	17,460	10,446	53,602	25,659	43,107	12,364	11,583
Elementary school	3,893,073	199,337	735,387	718,431	452,306	685,450	351,664	367,222	132,909	250,367
1-4 years	643,747	17,220	78,690	73,192	46,931	189,980	91,424	97,687	21,940	26,683
5-6 years	824,884	28,624	136,353	119,792	69,779	205,881	96,586	105,911	23,273	38,685
7 years	528,088	20,379	81,497	75,313	45,367	147,597	46,019	71,672	14,127	26,117
8 years	1,896,354	133,114	438,847	450,134	290,229	141,992	117,635	91,952	73,569	158,882
High School	2,150,427	174,328	380,139	405,090	254,265	305,423	138,689	226,646	105,329	231,518
1-3 years	1,150,146	78,772	196,397	206,209	119,021	169,493	76,989	138,021	53,331	111,913
4 years	1,071,281	95,556	183,742	198,881	135,244	135,930	61,700	88,625	51,998	119,605
College	737,917	48,203	109,990	114,568	102,497	118,688	54,686	74,448	41,845	72,992
1-3 years	483,040	30,929	66,162	79,424	73,225	73,455	35,695	48,094	29,223	46,833
4 years or more	254,877	17,274	43,828	35,144	29,272	45,233	18,991	26,354	12,622	26,159
Not reported	101,589	7,518	31,262	15,567	9,347	14,591	8,052	6,415	3,078	5,759
EDUCATIONAL ATTAINMENT - WHITE										
Total 25 years old and over	13,634,321	869,621	2,576,761	2,582,521	1,633,283	1,918,557	938,276	1,239,813	627,660	1,247,829
No school years completed	354,590	22,266	76,143	39,835	20,914	58,661	30,780	59,126	21,078	25,787
Elementary school	7,567,595	422,494	1,512,660	1,515,828	941,521	1,087,186	556,283	620,319	310,843	600,461
1-4 years	1,125,490	40,352	172,721	170,817	103,876	242,170	126,611	145,537	51,760	71,646
5-6 years	1,519,101	62,343	279,817	256,728	146,187	315,556	142,110	168,694	52,807	94,879
7 years	1,008,378	42,268	163,969	156,133	94,202	256,111	73,237	127,879	32,600	62,019
8 years	3,914,626	277,531	896,153	932,150	597,256	273,369	214,325	178,249	173,676	371,917
High school	4,047,810	313,624	691,918	753,511	457,866	528,078	239,084	406,959	204,640	452,130
1-3 years	2,168,968	154,389	373,260	397,676	224,717	299,772	133,122	249,741	107,694	228,597
4 years	1,878,842	159,235	318,658	355,835	233,149	228,306	105,962	157,218	96,946	223,533
College	1,437,165	95,891	228,708	228,580	191,803	219,316	98,424	139,143	82,418	152,882
1-3 years	822,319	50,396	114,046	136,420	119,147	119,755	57,742	83,240	51,317	90,256
4 years or more	614,846	45,495	113,662	92,160	72,656	99,561	41,682	55,903	31,101	62,626
Not reported	227,161	15,346	68,332	44,767	21,179	25,316	12,705	14,266	8,681	16,569
EDUCATIONAL ATTAINMENT - NONWHITE										
Total 25 years old and over	1,119,437	7,098	59,267	45,873	30,646	483,776	222,867	221,164	22,920	25,826
No school years completed	145,762	700	4,077	3,716	2,971	65,499	27,891	32,186	5,687	3,035
Elementary school	812,471	4,545	41,754	31,776	21,153	359,154	167,981	158,172	12,152	15,784
1-4 years	386,493	1,005	12,706	9,867	6,283	189,953	80,579	77,300	4,054	4,746
5-6 years	236,098	1,009	12,041	8,698	5,694	103,515	49,990	47,688	3,550	3,913
7 years	93,076	743	4,996	3,766	2,479	43,108	15,562	19,679	1,065	1,678
8 years	96,804	1,788	12,011	9,445	6,697	22,558	21,850	13,505	3,483	5,447
High school	104,534	1,394	8,266	6,859	5,007	35,769	16,733	21,500	3,862	5,144
1-3 years	74,120	803	5,503	4,711	3,382	26,147	12,183	16,319	2,252	2,820
4 years	30,414	591	2,763	2,148	1,625	9,622	4,550	5,181	1,610	2,324
College	26,321	243	1,366	1,246	1,028	11,005	5,046	5,767	649	971
1-3 years	15,867	154	788	788	715	6,343	2,645	3,369	438	627
4 years or more	10,454	89	578	458	313	4,662	2,401	2,398	211	344
Not reported	30,349	216	3,804	2,276	487	12,349	6,216	3,539	570	892
POPULATION ENROLLED IN SCHOOLS	5,628,200	298,146	990,188	938,765	587,178	1,032,412	465,233	610,618	289,876	415,784
5-6 years	362,547	22,787	69,878	67,046	43,534	56,229	23,948	30,694	17,917	30,514
7-13 years	3,305,001	168,299	561,785	542,556	326,058	650,043	286,791	370,379	170,687	228,403
14-15 years	898,559	48,344	165,034	150,876	92,476	168,508	72,345	96,994	44,410	65,572
16-17 years	666,374	36,067	125,391	115,953	76,916	104,990	49,447	69,027	34,528	54,055
18-19 years	275,212	15,423	47,654	44,195	32,893	41,333	22,752	30,394	15,404	25,164
20-24 years	120,507	7,226	20,446	18,139	15,301	17,309	9,950	13,130	6,930	12,076

TABLE 48

POPULATION: EDUCATIONAL ATTAINMENT OF THE RURAL-FARM POPULATION 25 YEARS OLD AND OVER AND SCHOOL ENROLLMENT OF THE RURAL-FARM POPULATION 5-29 YEARS OLD, BY GEOGRAPHIC DIVISIONS: 1940

Educational Attainment and School Enrollment	Geographic division								
	United States	New England	Middle Atlantic	East North Central	West North Central	South Atlantic	East South Central	West South Central	Mountain	Pacific
EDUCATIONAL ATTAINMENT, ALL GROUPS										
Total 25 years old and over.....	14,792,836	305,607	972,042	2,508,036	2,463,449	2,618,704	2,349,352	2,338,872	531,030	705,744
No school completed.............	693,332	10,465	24,439	37,252	31,444	194,349	156,331	184,242	31,957	22,853
Elementary school...............	10,336,650	169,243	670,131	1,781,030	1,773,941	1,867,575	1,775,226	1,571,296	311,173	417,015
1-4 years..................	2,320,742	17,185	65,709	189,903	176,297	676,312	591,440	496,248	49,735	57,913
5-6 years..................	2,294,921	22,838	117,474	284,830	254,069	553,491	490,211	451,939	52,363	67,706
7 years....................	1,450,412	13,465	65,058	185,517	195,933	417,628	209,840	285,605	33,480	43,886
8 years....................	4,270,555	115,755	421,890	1,120,780	1,147,642	220,144	483,735	337,504	175,595	247,510
High School....................	2,870,704	98,183	199,099	530,894	506,420	411,354	310,989	476,905	140,042	196,818
1-3 years..................	1,752,899	53,159	117,725	286,326	264,423	280,760	210,338	352,899	80,982	106,287
4 years....................	1,117,805	45,024	81,374	244,568	241,997	130,594	100,651	124,006	59,060	90,531
College........................	699,601	23,525	56,102	125,893	129,125	104,593	71,930	85,517	42,139	60,777
1-3 years..................	503,161	14,783	36,083	93,673	103,464	69,942	51,392	62,409	31,112	40,303
4 years or more............	196,440	8,742	20,019	32,220	25,661	34,651	20,538	23,108	11,027	20,474
Not reported	192,569	4,191	22,271	32,967	22,519	40,833	34,876	20,912	5,719	8,281
EDUCATIONAL ATTAINMENT - MALE										
Total 25 years old and over.....	7,896,625	164,321	527,822	1,360,246	1,351,565	1,343,418	1,204,654	1,239,462	300,942	404,195
No school years completed......	408,494	6,276	14,179	22,869	19,362	115,292	92,662	105,672	16,852	15,330
Elementary school..............	5,741,374	99,006	382,722	1,011,972	1,039,392	979,893	920,809	858,705	192,480	256,395
1-4 years..................	1,381,766	10,724	40,880	120,930	112,866	388,947	339,833	295,984	32,017	39,585
5-6 years..................	1,238,404	13,805	69,596	167,656	152,697	276,183	272,655	239,506	32,897	43,409
7 years....................	774,947	8,025	37,484	107,641	119,303	204,874	101,087	148,442	20,993	27,118
8 years....................	2,346,257	66,452	234,762	615,765	654,526	109,889	237,234	174,773	106,573	146,283
High School...................	1,340,425	46,017	93,565	252,046	230,783	183,058	141,977	225,198	69,791	97,990
1-3 years..................	851,649	27,276	58,619	141,612	130,757	129,538	97,770	168,839	42,275	54,963
4 years....................	488,776	18,741	34,946	110,434	100,026	53,520	44,207	56,359	27,516	43,027
College........................	292,963	10,492	24,397	52,982	48,374	42,265	29,990	37,568	18,136	28,759
1-3 years..................	196,402	5,448	13,840	35,849	36,226	27,012	20,237	26,783	12,714	18,293
4 years or more............	96,561	5,044	10,557	17,133	12,148	15,253	9,753	10,785	5,422	10,466
Not reported..................	113,369	2,530	12,959	20,377	13,654	22,910	19,216	12,319	3,683	5,721
EDUCATIONAL ATTAINMENT - FEMALE										
Total 25 years old and over.....	6,896,211	141,286	444,220	1,147,790	1,111,884	1,275,286	1,144,698	1,099,410	230,088	301,549
No school years completed.......	284,838	4,189	10,260	14,383	12,082	79,057	63,669	78,570	15,105	7,523
Elementary school..............	4,595,256	70,237	287,409	769,058	734,549	887,682	854,417	712,591	118,693	160,620
1-4 years..................	938,976	6,461	24,829	68,973	63,431	287,365	251,607	200,264	17,718	18,328
5-6 years..................	1,056,517	9,033	47,878	117,174	101,372	277,308	217,556	212,433	19,466	24,297
7 years....................	675,465	5,440	27,574	77,896	76,630	212,754	108,753	137,163	12,487	16,768
8 years....................	1,924,298	49,303	187,128	505,015	493,116	110,255	246,501	162,731	69,022	101,227
High School...................	1,530,279	52,166	105,534	278,848	275,637	228,296	169,012	251,707	70,251	98,828
1-3 years..................	901,250	25,883	59,106	144,714	133,666	151,222	112,568	184,060	38,707	51,324
4 years....................	629,029	26,283	46,428	134,134	141,971	77,074	56,444	67,647	31,544	47,504
College........................	406,638	13,033	31,705	72,911	80,751	62,328	41,940	47,949	24,003	32,018
1-3 years..................	306,759	9,335	22,243	57,824	67,238	42,930	31,155	35,626	18,398	22,010
4 years or more............	99,879	3,698	9,462	15,087	13,513	19,398	10,785	12,323	5,605	10,008
Not reported..................	79,200	1,661	9,312	12,590	8,865	17,923	15,660	8,593	2,036	2,560
EDUCATIONAL ATTAINMENT - WHITE										
Total 25 years old and over.....	12,872,062	303,946	961,774	2,494,551	2,436,834	1,911,097	1,746,478	1,853,213	497,391	666,778
No school years completed.......	393,364	9,984	23,675	36,193	28,315	84,421	72,433	106,052	14,784	17,507
Elementary school..............	8,867,626	168,356	662,936	1,771,234	1,753,663	1,320,804	1,294,241	1,205,822	298,259	392,311
1-4 years..................	1,499,747	16,933	63,399	187,183	168,233	345,590	323,128	300,291	45,159	49,831
5-6 years..................	1,881,960	22,637	115,331	282,330	248,288	405,531	351,161	346,749	48,352	61,581
7 years....................	1,313,237	13,344	64,296	184,282	195,942	362,029	174,495	247,093	32,161	41,595
8 years....................	4,172,682	115,442	419,910	1,117,439	1,143,200	207,654	445,457	311,689	172,587	239,304
High School...................	2,772,669	97,971	198,055	528,976	504,015	382,363	287,985	446,227	137,212	189,865
1-3 years..................	1,678,396	53,026	117,036	285,102	262,731	258,092	192,535	327,945	79,124	102,805
4 years....................	1,094,273	44,945	81,019	243,874	241,284	124,271	95,450	118,282	58,088	87,060
College........................	681,510	23,481	55,907	125,567	128,753	97,840	68,379	79,820	41,903	59,860
1-3 years..................	490,407	14,758	35,958	93,449	103,191	65,380	48,712	58,314	30,941	39,704
4 years or more............	191,103	8,723	19,949	32,118	25,562	32,460	19,667	21,506	10,962	20,156
Not reported..................	156,893	4,154	21,201	32,581	22,088	25,669	23,440	15,292	5,233	7,235
EDUCATIONAL ATTAINMENT - NONWHITE										
Total 25 years old and over.....	1,920,774	1,661	10,268	13,485	26,615	707,607	602,874	485,659	33,639	38,966
No school years completed.......	299,968	481	764	1,059	3,129	109,928	83,898	78,190	17,173	5,346
Elementary school..............	1,469,004	887	7,195	9,796	20,278	546,771	480,985	365,474	12,914	24,704
1-4 years..................	820,995	252	2,310	2,720	8,064	330,722	268,312	195,957	4,576	8,082
5-6 years..................	412,961	201	2,143	2,500	5,781	149,960	139,050	105,190	4,011	6,125
7 years....................	137,175	121	762	1,235	1,991	55,599	35,345	38,512	1,319	2,291
8 years....................	97,873	313	1,980	3,341	4,442	12,490	38,278	25,815	3,008	8,206
High school...................	98,035	212	1,044	1,918	2,405	28,991	23,004	30,678	2,830	6,953
1-3 years..................	74,503	133	689	1,224	1,692	22,668	17,803	24,954	1,858	3,482
4 years....................	23,532	79	355	694	713	6,323	5,201	5,724	972	3,471
College........................	18,091	44	195	326	372	6,753	3,551	5,697	236	917
1-3 years..................	12,754	25	125	224	273	4,562	2,680	4,095	171	599
4 years or more............	5,337	19	70	102	99	2,191	871	1,602	65	318
Not reported..................	35,676	37	1,070	386	431	15,164	11,436	5,620	486	1,046
POPULATION ENROLLED IN SCHOOLS....	6,912,258	113,487	383,968	1,003,135	1,050,161	1,495,288	1,114,718	1,209,105	269,620	272,776
5-6 years..................	396,015	7,080	22,330	61,912	77,197	79,191	57,602	62,915	14,608	13,180
7-13 years.................	4,179,118	64,875	221,670	589,905	629,741	946,646	685,443	739,215	156,786	145,267
14-15 years................	1,129,540	19,592	69,131	168,650	163,052	242,550	178,972	198,638	42,681	46,274
16-17 years................	782,364	13,942	47,242	123,243	118,468	151,508	119,919	134,132	33,486	40,424
18-19 years................	308,953	5,655	17,435	44,096	44,271	56,445	52,750	53,711	15,274	19,316
20-24 years................	116,268	2,343	6,160	15,329	17,432	19,348	20,062	20,494	6,785	8,315

APPENDIX

TABLE 49

PERCENT DISTRIBUTION: EMPLOYMENT STATUS OF THE TOTAL POPULATION 14 YEARS OLD AND OVER AND MAJOR OCCUPATION GROUP AND MAJOR INDUSTRY GROUP OF THE TOTAL POPULATION OF THE UNITED STATES, BY GEOGRAPHIC DIVISIONS: 1950

Employment status, occupation and industry	Geographic Division									
	United States	New England	Middle Atlantic	East North Central	West North Central	South Atlantic	East South Central	West South Central	Mountain	Pacific
EMPLOYMENT STATUS, ALL GROUPS										
14 years old and over	100.0	100.0	100.0	100.0	100.0	100.0	100.0	100.0	100.0	100.0
Total labor force	53.5	54.4	53.9	54.3	52.6	54.4	50.4	51.2	52.5	54.3
Civilian labor force	52.6	53.7	53.6	54.0	52.4	52.4	49.6	50.0	51.2	52.2
Employed	50.1	50.4	50.5	51.8	50.9	50.4	47.7	48.0	48.5	48.2
Unemployed	2.5	3.3	3.0	2.2	1.5	2.0	1.9	2.1	2.7	4.0
Not in the labor force	46.5	45.6	46.1	45.7	47.4	45.6	49.6	48.8	47.5	45.7
EMPLOYMENT STATUS, WHITE MALES										
14 years old and over	100.0	100.0	100.0	100.0	100.0	100.0	100.0	100.0	100.0	100.0
Total labor force	79.0	77.5	78.8	80.4	79.4	79.3	77.7	78.6	78.4	78.4
Civilian labor force	77.2	76.1	78.1	79.9	78.9	74.7	75.9	76.0	76.0	74.3
Employed	73.7	71.1	73.7	76.9	76.7	72.2	73.4	73.1	71.9	69.0
Unemployed	3.5	5.0	4.5	3.0	2.2	2.4	2.5	2.8	4.0	5.3
Not in the labor force	21.0	22.5	21.2	19.6	20.6	20.7	· 22.3	21.4	21.6	21.6
EMPLOYMENT STATUS, WHITE FEMALES										
14 years old and over	100.0	100.0	100.0	100.0	100.0	100.0	100.0	100.0	100.0	100.0
Total labor force	28.1	32.8	29.9	28.5	26.3	28.1	21.9	23.7	25.7	29.6
Civilian labor force	28.0	32.8	29.9	28.5	26.3	28.0	21.8	23.6	25.7	29.6
Employed	26.9	31.2	28.6	27.5	25.7	27.0	21.1	22.9	24.4	27.4
Unemployed	1.1	1.6	1.3	1.0	0.6	1.0	0.8	0.7	1.2	2.2
Not in the labor force	71.9	67.2	70.1	71.5	73.7	71.9	78.1	76.3	74.3	70.4
EMPLOYMENT STATUS, NONWHITE MALES										
14 years old and over	100.0	100.0	100.0	100.0	100.0	100.0	100.0	100.0	100.0	100.0
Total labor force	76.1	74.1	73.9	76.3	70.0	78.4	76.9	73.6	71.7	77.0
Civilian labor force	74.9	70.4	73.1	75.7	69.3	77.2	76.4	72.5	67.9	72.4
Employed	69.0	61.5	64.2	67.1	62.6	73.4	72.5	67.7	61.3	62.1
Unemployed	5.8	8.9	8.9	8.6	6.8	3.8	3.9	4.8	6.6	10.3
Not in the labor force	23.9	·25.9	26.1	23.7	30.0	21.6	23.1	26.4	28.3	23.0
EMPLOYMENT STATUS, NONWHITE FEMALES										
14 years old and over	100.0	100.0	100.0	100.0	100.0	100.0	100.0	100.0	100.0	100.0
Total labor force	36.7	41.3	43.2	35.3	34.5	38.7	32.6	32.6	27.7	40.2
Civilian labor force	36.7	41.3	43.2	35.2	34.5	38.6	32.6	32.6	27.6	40.1
Employed	33.8	37.8	39.4	31.1	31.5	36.0	30.7	30.5	25.6	34.5
Unemployed	2.9	3.5	3.8	4.1	3.0	2.6	1.9	2.1	2.0	5.6
Not in the labor force	63.3	58.7	56.8	64.7	65.5	61.3	67.4	67.4	72.3	59.8
MAJOR OCCUPATION GROUP - MALE	100.0	100.0	100.0	100.0	100.0	100.0	100.0	100.0	100.0	100.0
Professional and technical workers	7.3	8.2	8.9	7.3	6.0	6.1	4.7	6.5	7.7	9.2
Farmers and farm managers	10.3	2.6	2.5	8.1	22.9	12.6	24.0	15.5	13.3	4.9
Managers, officials, and proprietors........	10.7	11.4	12.3	9.9	10.2	9.5	7.7	10.7	11.4	13.1
Clerical and kindred workers	6.4	7.0	8.4	6.9	5.6	5.4	4.0	5.1	5.3	6.3
Sales workers	6.4	7.1	7.0	6.1	6.1	5.9	4.9	6.1	5.9	7.9
Craftsmen and foremen	18.6	21.6	20.3	20.6	15.3	16.8	13.8	16.5	17.5	20.7
Operatives	20.0	24.9	22.4	23.9	13.8	20.2	18.0	16.0	15.5	16.5
Private household workers	0.2	0.2	0.2	0.1	0.1	0.3	0.2	0.2	0.1	0.2
Service workers, exc. household	5.9	6.7	7.5	5.7	4.5	5.2	4.0	5.0	5.7	6.6
Farm laborers, unpaid family workers	1.5	0.2	0.3	0.9	3.1	2.6	4.3	1.9	1.7	0.3
Farm laborers, paid, incl. foremen	3.4	1.8	1.3	2.0	4.4	4.6	4.7	5.8	6.6	4.5
Laborers, except farm and mine	8.2	7.4	8.0	7.3	6.8	9.6	8.3	9.5	8.2	8.9
Occupation not reported	1.1	0.9	1.0	1.1	1.3	1.3	1.3	1.2	1.2	0.9
MAJOR OCCUPATION - FEMALE	100.0	100.0	100.0	100.0	100.0	100.0	100.0	100.0	100.0	100.0
Professional and technical workers	12.3	12.5	11.9	11.7	13.9	11.3	11.6	12.6	15.6	14.2
Farmers and farm managers	0.7	0.2	0.2	0.5	1.0	0.9	2.5	1.3	1.1	0.7
Managers, officials, and proprietors	4.3	3.3	3.8	3.9	4.5	3.8	4.0	5.5	6.4	6.3
Clerical and kindred workers	27.3	27.4	30.1	29.7	26.9	21.9	18.9	24.6	27.6	31.6
Sales workers	8.5	7.2	7.5	9.3	9.5	7.5	8.0	9.6	9.8	9.3
Craftsmen and foremen	1.5	1.8	1.8	1.8	1.4	1.1	1.1	1.1	1.1	1.4
Operatives	19.2	30.7	25.4	19.6	12.7	20.2	17.3	9.8	7.8	12.1
Private household workers	8.5	5.2	6.8	5.8	6.1	14.2	15.2	13.4	6.7	6.5
Service workers, exc. household	12.2	9.1	9.8	12.9	14.5	11.1	12.2	15.1	17.5	14.0
Farm laborers, unpaid family workers	2.0	0.2	0.4	1.7	5.4	3.2	4.3	2.8	2.6	0.9
Farm laborers, paid, incl. foremen	0.8	0.2	0.2	0.3	0.6	2.3	1.7	1.5	0.8	0.9
Laborers, except farm and mine..............	0.8	0.8	0.7	1.0	0.8	0.8	0.8	0.7	0.6	0.7
Occupation not reported	1.8	1.3	1.4	1.8	2.7	1.8	2.4	2.0	2.3	1.4
MAJOR INDUSTRY GROUP - BOTH SEXES	100.0	100.0	100.0	100.0	100.0	100.0	100.0	100.0	100.0	100.0
Agriculture	12.5	4.0	3.3	8.9	24.8	16.7	27.4	19.6	18.1	8.6
Mining	1.7	0.1	1.7	0.9	0.9	2.4	3.0	3.2	4.0	0.7
Construction	6.1	5.6	5.5	5.0	5.8	6.6	5.9	7.9	8.2	7.7
Manufacturing, total.......................	25.9	38.5	33.0	35.2	15.4	21.7	18.4	13.3	9.5	20.2
Durable	13.8	18.2	16.0	24.5	6.9	7.7	8.6	5.8	4.8	12.0
Nondurable	11.9	20.1	16.8	10.3	8.3	13.9	9.6	7.4	4.6	8.1
Not specified	0.2	0.3	0.3	0.3	0.2	0.1	0.1	0.1	0.1	0.1
Transportation	7.8	6.4	8.6	7.8	8.3	6.7	6.2	7.8	9.6	8.4
Trade	18.8	18.1	19.3	18.3	19.4	16.9	15.4	20.1	20.1	21.9
Finance	3.4	3.9	4.7	2.4	3.0	2.6	2.0	2.9	2.9	4.3
Business services.........................	2.5	2.4	2.7	3.0	2.7	2.0	1.9	2.5	3.0	3.2
Personal services	6.2	5.3	5.9	4.8	4.8	8.4	7.4	7.9	6.1	6.4
Entertainment services	1.0	0.8	1.0	0.9	0.9	0.8	0.7	0.9	1.3	1.7
Professional services	8.3	9.4	8.7	7.8	8.6	7.5	6.9	8.0	9.7	9.6
Public administration	4.4	4.3	4.2	3.5	3.7	6.1	3.2	4.2	5.9	6.0
Industry not reported	1.5	1.2	1.4	1.4	1.9	1.5	1.7	1.6	1.7	1.3

TABLE 50

PERCENT DISTRIBUTION: EMPLOYMENT STATUS OF THE URBAN POPULATION 14 YEARS OLD AND OVER AND MAJOR OCCUPATION GROUP AND MAJOR INDUSTRY GROUP OF THE URBAN POPULATION OF THE UNITED STATES, BY GEOGRAPHIC DIVISIONS: 1950

Employment status, occupation and industry	United States	New England	Middle Atlantic	East North Central	West North Central	South Atlantic	East South Central	West South Central	Mountain	Pacific
EMPLOYMENT STATUS, ALL GROUPS										
14 years old and over	100.0	100.0	100.0	100.0	100.0	100.0	100.0	100.0	100.0	100.0
Total labor force	55.3	55.3	54.9	56.1	54.4	57.3	55.0	54.3	53.2	54.9
Civilian labor force	54.6	54.8	54.7	56.0	54.2	55.4	54.3	53.0	52.3	53.4
Employed	51.7	51.4	51.5	53.4	52.3	52.8	51.5	50.6	49.4	49.2
Unemployed	2.9	3.4	3.2	2.5	1.9	2.6	2.8	2.4	2.9	4.2
Not in the labor force	44.7	44.7	45.1	43.9	45.6	42.7	45.0	45.7	46.8	45.1
EMPLOYMENT STATUS, WHITE MALES										
14 years old and over	100.0	100.0	100.0	100.0	100.0	100.0	100.0	100.0	100.0	100.0
Total labor force	79.6	77.8	79.5	81.5	78.2	80.0	79.2	79.7	77.2	78.5
Civilian labor force	78.1	76.8	79.0	81.2	77.8	75.4	77.3	76.8	75.5	75.3
Employed	74.1	71.5	74.4	77.9	75.1	72.5	74.0	73.5	71.2	69.8
Unemployed	4.0	4.3	4.7	3.3	2.7	2.9	3.3	3.2	4.3	5.6
Not in the labor force	20.4	22.2	20.5	18.5	21.8	20.0	20.7	20.3	22.8	21.5
EMPLOYMENT STATUS, WHITE FEMALES										
14 years old and over	100.0	100.0	100.0	100.0	100.0	100.0	100.0	100.0	100.0	100.0
Total labor force	32.2	34.8	31.6	32.2	32.9	34.4	32.0	29.6	29.9	32.0
Civilian labor force	32.2	34.8	31.6	32.1	32.9	34.3	32.0	29.5	29.9	32.0
Employed	30.9	33.1	30.2	31.0	32.1	33.1	30.9	28.6	28.5	29.7
Unemployed	1.3	1.6	1.4	1.1	0.8	1.2	1.1	0.9	1.4	2.3
Not in the labor force	67.8	65.2	68.4	67.8	67.1	65.6	68.0	70.4	70.1	68.0
EMPLOYMENT STATUS, NONWHITE MALES										
14 years old and over	100.0	100.0	100.0	100.0	100.0	100.0	100.0	100.0	100.0	100.0
Total labor force	76.4	75.4	75.2	78.5	72.4	77.7	75.7	74.5	73.1	77.4
Civilian labor force	75.6	72.6	74.8	78.3	72.1	76.7	75.3	73.3	69.0	74.5
Employed	67.9	63.5	65.6	69.4	65.4	71.0	68.6	67.0	61.7	63.2
Unemployed	7.7	9.1	9.2	8.9	6.7	5.7	6.8	6.3	7.3	11.3
Not in the labor force	23.6	24.6	24.8	21.5	27.6	22.3	24.3	25.5	26.9	22.6
EMPLOYMENT STATUS, NONWHITE FEMALES										
14 years old and over	100.0	100.0	100.0	100.0	100.0	100.0	100.0	100.0	100.0	100.0
Total labor force	42.5	42.1	44.0	36.1	38.1	47.2	42.1	41.9	40.6	42.4
Civilian labor force	42.5	42.0	43.9	36.0	38.0	47.1	42.1	41.9	40.5	42.3
Employed	38.8	38.5	40.1	31.8	34.9	43.6	39.1	39.1	37.1	36.3
Unemployed	3.7	3.6	3.8	4.2	3.2	3.6	3.0	2.8	3.3	6.0
Not in the labor force	57.5	57.9	56.0	63.9	61.9	52.8	57.9	58.1	59.4	57.6
MAJOR OCCUPATION GROUP - MALE	100.0	100.0	100.0	100.0	100.0	100.0	100.0	100.0	100.0	100.0
Professional and technical workers	9.3	8.6	9.6	8.7	9.0	9.3	8.0	9.3	10.4	10.7
Farmers and farm managers	0.4	0.3	0.2	0.2	0.7	0.4	0.7	0.9	1.4	0.7
Managers, officials, and proprietors	13.0	11.9	13.3	11.3	13.8	13.3	12.6	14.6	15.0	14.7
Clerical and kindred workers	8.4	7.8	9.5	8.4	9.0	8.3	7.2	7.5	7.5	7.5
Sales workers	8.2	7.8	7.8	7.3	9.5	8.5	8.5	8.8	8.6	9.3
Craftsmen and foremen	21.2	22.0	20.4	22.5	21.0	20.0	20.3	20.2	21.4	22.0
Operatives	21.8	25.9	22.0	25.7	19.5	20.0	22.4	18.5	17.2	17.1
Private household workers	0.2	0.2	0.2	0.1	0.1	0.4	0.4	0.2	0.1	0.2
Service workers, exc. household	7.6	7.6	8.4	6.9	7.0	8.1	7.6	7.4	7.6	7.6
Farm laborers, unpaid family workers	0.0	0.0	0.0	0.0	0.0	0.0	0.0	0.0	0.1	0.0
Farm laborers, paid, incl. foremen	0.6	0.5	0.2	0.3	0.7	0.9	0.7	1.3	1.5	1.4
Laborers, except farm and mine	8.2	6.6	7.5	7.5	8.4	9.7	10.5	10.3	8.3	8.0
Occupation not reported	1.0	0.9	1.0	1.0	1.2	1.2	1.1	1.1	1.0	0.8
MAJOR OCCUPATION - FEMALE	100.0	100.0	100.0	100.0	100.0	100.0	100.0	100.0	100.0	100.0
Professional and technical workers	12.4	12.3	11.8	11.6	13.3	12.1	11.5	12.6	15.7	14.3
Farmers and farm managers	0.1	0.0	0.0	0.1	0.1	0.1	0.1	0.1	0.2	0.2
Managers, officials, and proprietors	4.2	3.1	3.8	3.9	4.3	3.9	4.0	5.4	6.1	6.1
Clerical and kindred workers	30.6	28.7	31.7	32.1	32.1	27.0	23.9	28.5	32.0	33.6
Sales workers	8.6	7.5	7.5	9.4	9.9	7.9	8.3	9.8	10.2	9.4
Craftsmen and foremen	1.6	1.9	1.8	1.9	1.6	1.2	1.3	1.2	1.2	1.5
Operatives	19.5	31.2	25.1	20.0	14.7	17.8	17.2	10.4	8.2	12.5
Private household workers	8.3	4.4	6.7	5.7	6.2	14.9	17.0	14.0	6.5	6.5
Service workers, exc. household	12.3	8.9	9.6	12.8	15.1	12.6	14.2	15.7	17.3	13.6
Farm laborers, unpaid family workers	0.0	0.0	0.0	0.0	0.0	0.0	0.0	0.0	0.1	0.1
Farm laborers, paid, incl. foremen	0.2	0.1	0.1	0.1	0.1	0.5	0.2	0.3	0.3	0.3
Laborers, except farm and mine	0.8	0.8	0.7	1.0	0.9	0.7	0.8	0.6	0.6	0.6
Occupation not reported	1.4	1.1	1.3	1.4	1.6	1.3	1.5	1.3	1.6	1.2
MAJOR INDUSTRY GROUP - BOTH SEXES	100.0	100.0	100.0	100.0	100.0	100.0	100.0	100.0	100.0	100.0
Agriculture	1.1	1.0	0.5	0.6	1.4	1.4	1.4	2.2	2.7	2.4
Mining	0.9	0.1	0.9	0.5	0.7	0.6	1.3	2.9	2.9	0.5
Construction	6.0	6.0	5.1	4.7	6.3	6.9	6.8	8.7	8.9	7.6
Manufacturing, total	29.4	39.7	33.8	39.1	22.8	22.0	23.9	15.5	11.4	20.8
Durable	15.5	18.6	15.9	27.2	10.2	7.2	10.1	5.8	5.3	11.6
Nondurable	13.7	20.9	17.6	11.6	12.2	14.7	13.6	9.5	6.0	9.1
Not specified	0.2	0.3	0.3	0.3	0.3	0.1	0.2	0.1	0.1	0.1
Transportation	9.0	6.7	9.0	8.6	11.1	8.8	9.3	9.9	11.5	9.0
Trade	21.9	19.4	20.6	20.2	25.2	21.9	23.0	25.7	25.3	24.1
Finance	4.4	4.2	5.2	3.6	4.5	3.9	3.5	4.1	4.1	5.1
Business services	2.7	2.3	2.7	2.5	3.1	2.3	2.4	3.0	3.5	3.5
Personal services	7.2	5.3	6.2	5.5	6.5	11.1	11.7	10.4	7.6	7.0
Entertainment services	1.2	0.8	1.1	1.0	1.2	1.2	1.1	1.3	1.7	2.0
Professional services	9.5	9.5	8.9	8.5	10.9	9.7	9.7	9.8	11.9	10.5
Public administration	5.2	4.6	4.5	3.9	4.8	8.8	4.5	5.3	7.2	6.5
Industry not reported	1.3	1.1	1.4	1.2	1.6	1.3	1.4	1.3	1.4	1.1

APPENDIX

TABLE 51

PERCENT DISTRIBUTION: EMPLOYMENT STATUS OF THE RURAL-NONFARM POPULATION 14 YEARS OLD AND OVER AND MAJOR OCCUPATION GROUP AND MAJOR INDUSTRY GROUP OF THE RURAL-NONFARM POPULATION OF THE UNITED STATES, BY GEOGRAPHIC DIVISIONS: 1950

Employment status, occupation and industry	United States	New England	Middle Atlantic	East North Central	West North Central	South Atlantic	East South Central	West South Central	Mountain	Pacific
EMPLOYMENT STATUS, ALL GROUPS										
14 years old and over	100.0	100.0	100.0	100.0	100.0	100.0	100.0	100.0	100.0	100.0
Total labor force	48.8	50.8	48.5	48.0	46.9	51.4	46.0	46.2	50.5	51.5
Civilian labor force	46.7	49.3	47.6	47.2	46.2	47.9	44.2	44.1	47.6	46.1
Employed	44.4	46.3	44.9	45.2	44.5	45.9	42.0	41.9	44.4	42.2
Unemployed	2.4	2.9	2.6	2.0	1.8	2.0	2.1	2.2	3.2	3.9
Not in the labor force	51.2	49.2	51.5	52.0	53.1	48.6	54.0	53.8	49.5	48.5
EMPLOYMENT STATUS, WHITE MALES										
14 years old and over	100.0	100.0	100.0	100.0	100.0	100.0	100.0	100.0	100.0	100.0
Total labor force	74.7	75.2	73.9	74.1	72.2	77.4	72.9	74.2	76.7	76.3
Civilian labor force	70.7	72.3	72.2	72.6	70.9	69.7	68.9	69.8	71.3	66.8
Employed	67.1	67.7	68.1	69.4	68.1	67.0	65.6	66.4	66.3	61.4
Unemployed	3.6	4.5	4.1	3.2	2.9	2.7	3.3	3.4	4.9	5.4
Not in the labor force	25.3	24.8	26.1	25.9	27.8	22.6	27.1	25.8	23.3	23.7
EMPLOYMENT STATUS, WHITE FEMALES										
14 years old and over	100.0	100.0	100.0	100.0	100.0	100.0	100.0	100.0	100.0	100.0
Total labor force	22.2	26.6	23.2	21.9	22.4	23.8	18.6	18.1	21.9	22.0
Civilian labor force	22.1	26.6	23.1	21.9	22.4	23.6	18.5	18.1	21.8	21.9
Employed	21.2	25.2	22.2	21.1	21.8	22.7	17.8	17.5	20.6	20.0
Unemployed	0.9	1.3	1.0	0.8	0.6	0.9	0.7	0.6	1.1	1.9
Not in the labor force	77.8	73.4	76.8	78.1	77.6	76.2	81.4	81.9	78.1	78.0
EMPLOYMENT STATUS, NONWHITE MALES										
14 years old and over	100.0	100.0	100.0	100.0	100.0	100.0	100.0	100.0	100.0	100.0
Total labor force	67.4	62.2	54.4	42.8	51.8	72.9	66.7	65.4	67.7	69.3
Civilian labor force	63.5	50.9	47.4	36.1	47.9	70.1	64.8	62.7	61.8	50.1
Employed	59.2	43.8	42.1	30.8	39.4	66.8	60.9	57.5	54.4	42.8
Unemployed	4.4	7.0	5.3	5.2	8.5	3.3	3.9	5.2	7.4	7.2
Not in the labor force	32.6	37.8	45.6	57.2	48.2	27.1	33.3	34.6	32.3	30.7
EMPLOYMENT STATUS, NONWHITE FEMALES										
14 years old and over	100.0	100.0	100.0	100.0	100.0	100.0	100.0	100.0	100.0	100.0
Total labor force	29.0	33.2	27.7	19.0	18.2	32.4	30.0	24.5	20.1	22.3
Civilian labor force	28.9	33.1	27.3	18.9	18.1	32.3	30.0	24.5	20.0	21.1
Employed	26.8	30.5	24.1	16.9	15.9	30.2	28.3	22.6	18.7	17.7
Unemployed	2.1	2.7	3.2	2.1	2.2	2.2	1.7	1.8	1.4	3.4
Not in the labor force	71.0	66.8	72.3	81.0	81.8	67.6	70.0	75.5	79.9	77.7
MAJOR OCCUPATION GROUP - MALE	100.0	100.0	100.0	100.0	100.0	100.0	100.0	100.0	100.0	100.0
Professional and technical workers	6.1	8.0	6.9	6.1	6.9	4.6	5.2	5.5	7.0	6.5
Farmers and farm managers	3.0	1.4	1.5	2.4	5.3	2.7	4.5	4.2	5.3	2.5
Managers, officials, and proprietors	10.7	11.7	9.8	10.7	15.6	8.8	9.4	10.5	11.4	11.2
Clerical and kindred workers	4.3	4.8	4.8	5.0	4.9	3.8	3.7	3.7	4.0	3.6
Sales workers	5.1	6.0	4.8	5.2	6.3	5.0	4.2	4.6	4.2	4.8
Craftsmen and foremen	21.6	23.4	23.8	23.8	20.8	20.1	18.6	20.3	20.0	21.7
Operatives	25.0	24.3	27.9	27.5	16.8	29.1	27.8	21.2	20.9	19.1
Private household workers	0.2	0.4	0.3	0.1	0.1	0.3	0.2	0.2	0.1	0.2
Service workers, exc. household	4.3	4.4	4.7	4.6	4.6	3.7	3.5	3.9	5.4	5.0
Farm laborers, unpaid family workers	0.5	0.1	0.2	0.3	0.7	0.5	0.9	0.6	0.9	0.2
Farm laborers, paid, incl. foremen	6.0	3.7	3.1	3.5	5.6	7.0	7.2	9.8	7.7	9.6
Laborers, except farm and mine	11.8	10.6	11.2	9.6	10.7	12.9	12.2	14.0	11.8	14.4
Occupation not reported	1.4	1.1	1.1	1.3	1.6	1.5	1.7	1.6	1.4	1.2
MAJOR OCCUPATION - FEMALE	100.0	100.0	100.0	100.0	100.0	100.0	100.0	100.0	100.0	100.0
Professional and technical workers	13.3	13.8	13.1	12.5	17.3	10.4	13.2	14.4	16.9	14.4
Farmers and farm managers	0.5	0.3	0.2	0.4	0.5	0.4	0.7	0.7	0.9	0.7
Managers, officials, and proprietors	5.7	4.5	4.4	5.4	7.2	4.5	5.6	7.4	8.9	8.6
Clerical and kindred workers	18.6	21.7	20.2	21.6	19.8	14.4	14.3	16.3	20.1	22.1
Sales workers	9.4	6.3	7.8	10.6	12.3	7.9	9.8	11.4	10.4	10.0
Craftsmen and foremen	1.3	1.6	1.6	1.7	1.2	1.0	1.0	0.9	0.8	1.1
Operatives	20.5	29.1	28.2	20.0	9.9	28.1	19.5	9.5	7.2	10.6
Private household workers	10.3	8.4	7.7	6.8	7.4	14.8	16.2	14.3	7.4	6.4
Service workers, exc. household	14.4	10.7	12.6	16.1	19.0	10.1	12.4	17.4	21.4	19.1
Farm laborers, unpaid family workers	0.5	0.1	0.2	0.4	0.8	0.6	0.7	0.8	1.1	0.5
Farm laborers, paid, incl. foremen	2.0	0.5	0.6	0.5	0.5	4.4	2.8	3.2	1.1	3.0
Laborers, except farm and mine	1.1	1.1	1.3	1.3	1.0	1.1	0.9	1.0	0.7	1.2
Occupation not reported	2.5	2.0	2.1	2.7	3.1	2.2	2.9	2.7	3.0	2.2
MAJOR INDUSTRY GROUP - BOTH SEXES	100.0	100.0	100.0	100.0	100.0	100.0	100.0	100.0	100.0	100.0
Agriculture	9.1	5.7	4.5	5.7	10.1	10.8	11.6	14.3	12.5	12.3
Mining	4.9	0.4	6.9	2.9	2.1	6.5	8.1	6.4	8.8	1.7
Construction	8.9	8.1	8.4	7.9	10.0	8.5	8.4	10.3	10.5	10.2
Manufacturing, total	25.6	37.6	33.0	32.8	11.5	28.1	22.3	15.3	9.7	22.3
Durable	14.0	18.1	18.3	22.6	5.2	10.3	11.9	8.3	5.9	16.5
Nondurable	11.4	19.2	14.5	9.5	6.2	17.7	10.3	6.8	3.7	5.7
Not specified	0.2	0.2	0.2	0.4	0.2	0.1	0.1	0.1	0.1	0.1
Transportation	7.4	5.9	7.5	7.8	9.5	5.9	6.8	7.6	10.2	7.9
Trade	18.0	14.7	15.0	19.1	25.5	15.7	17.0	19.4	19.2	18.5
Finance	1.9	2.9	2.2	1.9	2.4	1.5	1.4	1.5	1.6	2.1
Business services	3.1	3.1	2.9	3.2	4.5	2.4	2.8	2.9	3.3	3.1
Personal services	5.9	5.8	5.0	4.4	5.3	7.2	7.2	6.9	5.9	5.4
Entertainment services	0.8	0.7	0.7	0.8	1.0	0.7	0.6	0.8	1.1	1.0
Professional services	8.4	9.7	8.9	8.2	10.8	6.7	8.0	8.4	9.3	8.4
Public administration	4.0	3.7	3.4	3.3	4.6	4.1	3.6	4.0	5.9	5.3
Industry not reported	1.9	1.6	1.6	1.9	2.6	1.8	2.2	2.2	2.1	1.7

TABLE 52

PERCENT DISTRIBUTION: EMPLOYMENT STATUS OF THE RURAL-FARM POPULATION 14 YEARS OLD AND OVER AND MAJOR OCCUPATION GROUP AND MAJOR INDUSTRY GROUP OF THE RURAL-FARM POPULATION OF THE UNITED STATES, BY GEOGRAPHIC DIVISIONS: 1950

Employment status, occupation and industry	United States	New England	Middle Atlantic	East North Central	West North Central	South Atlantic	East South Central	West South Central	Mountain	Pacific
EMPLOYMENT STATUS, ALL GROUPS										
14 years old and over	100.0	100.0	100.0	100.0	100.0	100.0	100.0	100.0	100.0	100.0
Total labor force	51.1	52.9	52.7	52.3	53.8	51.1	47.9	47.9	53.5	54.3
Civilian labor force	51.1	52.8	52.7	52.2	53.8	51.0	47.8	47.9	53.4	54.2
Employed	50.2	50.7	51.1	51.4	53.3	50.3	47.2	47.0	52.1	52.1
Unemployed	0.9	2.1	1.6	0.9	0.5	0.8	0.7	0.9	1.3	2.1
Not in the labor force	48.9	47.1	47.3	47.7	46.2	48.9	52.1	52.1	46.5	45.7
EMPLOYMENT STATUS, WHITE MALES										
14 years old and over	100.0	100.0	100.0	100.0	100.0	100.0	100.0	100.0	100.0	100.0
Total labor force	82.7	80.7	82.0	83.8	87.0	80.5	79.9	80.3	85.1	82.9
Civilian labor force	82.6	80.5	81.9	83.7	86.9	80.4	79.8	80.2	85.0	82.7
Employed	81.3	77.5	79.6	82.5	86.3	79.3	78.8	78.9	83.3	80.0
Unemployed	1.3	3.0	2.3	1.2	0.6	1.0	1.0	1.3	1.7	2.7
Not in the labor force	17.3	19.3	18.0	16.2	13.0	19.5	20.1	19.7	14.9	17.1
EMPLOYMENT STATUS, WHITE FEMALES										
14 years old and over	100.0	100.0	100.0	100.0	100.0	100.0	100.0	100.0	100.0	100.0
Total labor force	14.9	20.7	19.2	16.3	14.3	16.1	11.0	11.4	15.0	19.0
Civilian labor force	14.8	20.7	19.2	16.3	14.3	16.0	11.0	11.4	14.9	19.0
Employed	14.4	19.6	18.5	15.8	14.0	15.6	10.6	11.1	14.3	17.9
Unemployed	0.5	1.0	0.7	0.5	0.3	0.5	0.4	0.3	0.7	1.1
Not in the labor force	85.1	79.3	80.8	83.7	85.7	83.9	89.0	88.6	85.0	81.0
EMPLOYMENT STATUS, NONWHITE MALES										
14 years old and over	100.0	100.0	100.0	100.0	100.0	100.0	100.0	100.0	100.0	100.0
Total labor force	82.8	72.5	82.6	71.3	73.4	85.0	83.5	78.5	75.7	85.0
Civilian labor force	82.7	72.2	82.4	71.2	73.3	85.0	83.5	78.4	75.7	84.9
Employed	81.7	66.4	77.2	66.5	68.8	84.3	83.0	77.2	71.2	80.6
Unemployed	1.0	5.7	5.2	4.7	4.5	0.7	0.5	1.2	4.5	4.3
Not in the labor force	17.2	27.5	17.4	28.7	26.6	15.0	16.5	21.5	24.3	15.0
EMPLOYMENT STATUS, NONWHITE FEMALES										
14 years old and over	100.0	100.0	100.0	100.0	100.0	100.0	100.0	100.0	100.0	100.0
Total labor force	21.5	32.4	32.6	16.0	12.6	24.9	20.4	16.4	20.2	28.9
Civilian labor force	21.5	32.4	32.6	15.9	12.5	24.9	20.4	16.4	20.2	28.9
Employed	20.8	29.5	29.9	14.9	10.9	24.1	20.0	15.6	19.3	27.1
Unemployed	0.7	2.9	2.6	1.1	1.6	0.8	0.5	0.8	0.9	1.8
Not in the labor force	78.5	67.6	67.4	84.0	87.4	75.1	79.6	83.6	79.8	71.1
MAJOR OCCUPATION GROUP - MALE	100.0	100.0	100.0	100.0	100.0	100.0	100.0	100.0	100.0	100.0
Professional and technical workers	1.2	2.3	2.1	1.3	0.6	1.2	1.1	1.1	1.2	1.8
Farmers and farm managers	56.3	40.3	42.0	55.6	69.5	49.7	59.7	58.6	56.0	43.7
Managers, officials, and proprietors	2.0	3.7	3.0	2.0	1.0	2.2	1.8	1.9	1.8	3.2
Clerical and kindred workers	1.0	1.8	1.7	1.4	0.6	1.1	0.9	0.9	0.8	1.3
Sales workers	1.1	1.8	1.5	1.1	0.6	1.4	1.0	1.1	0.8	1.6
Craftsmen and foremen	5.5	9.1	9.7	7.2	2.7	6.0	4.3	4.8	3.9	7.7
Operatives	7.8	12.1	13.4	10.3	2.9	10.6	7.7	5.8	4.2	7.7
Private household workers	0.1	0.2	0.2	0.1	0.0	0.1	0.1	0.1	0.1	0.1
Service workers, exc. household	0.8	1.4	1.3	0.9	0.3	0.9	0.6	0.6	0.8	1.3
Farm laborers, unpaid family workers	8.1	3.5	4.5	6.0	9.3	10.4	10.6	7.1	7.0	3.2
Farm laborers, paid, incl. foremen	11.0	14.8	13.3	9.4	9.6	10.0	7.4	12.9	18.9	21.1
Laborers, except farm and mine	4.0	7.9	6.4	3.6	1.8	5.4	3.8	4.0	3.2	6.2
Occupation not reported	1.1	1.1	1.1	1.1	1.1	1.2	1.2	1.3	1.2	1.0
MAJOR OCCUPATION - FEMALE	100.0	100.0	100.0	100.0	100.0	100.0	100.0	100.0	100.0	100.0
Professional and technical workers	10.0	12.4	10.8	10.1	11.9	8.1	10.0	9.6	11.8	10.9
Farmers and farm managers	8.5	7.1	5.9	6.7	7.3	6.7	12.1	11.0	8.6	11.1
Managers, officials, and proprietors	2.0	2.8	1.9	1.6	1.2	2.0	2.4	2.7	2.8	3.0
Clerical and kindred workers	10.2	17.5	14.8	14.8	7.8	7.3	6.9	8.3	11.8	15.7
Sales workers	4.6	4.2	4.5	4.9	3.2	4.5	4.8	5.4	4.8	5.4
Craftsmen and foremen	0.7	1.3	1.3	1.0	0.4	0.6	0.6	0.5	0.6	0.7
Operatives	13.3	23.1	23.4	13.5	5.0	18.5	15.1	5.8	6.2	7.7
Private household workers	7.1	10.8	7.9	5.5	3.8	9.3	7.8	7.3	6.7	6.5
Service workers, exc. household	5.9	7.0	6.9	6.8	4.5	4.5	4.9	7.0	9.7	9.1
Farm laborers, unpaid family workers	26.6	6.4	14.3	26.5	43.3	25.6	23.6	27.6	26.5	18.0
Farm laborers, paid, incl. foremen	5.5	3.5	3.8	2.7	3.0	8.2	5.8	8.6	4.4	7.3
Laborers, except farm and mine	0.7	1.1	1.3	0.9	0.4	0.7	0.5	0.6	0.4	0.8
Occupation not reported	5.1	2.9	3.2	5.0	8.3	4.1	4.5	6.2	5.6	3.6
MAJOR INDUSTRY GROUP - BOTH SEXES	100.0	100.0	100.0	100.0	100.0	100.0	100.0	100.0	100.0	100.0
Agriculture	71.0	52.4	54.3	66.3	84.5	65.6	73.6	75.6	77.4	64.6
Mining	1.3	0.3	2.6	1.1	0.4	1.9	1.9	1.2	0.9	0.4
Construction	3.1	4.4	4.5	2.9	1.8	3.6	2.8	3.4	2.8	4.1
Manufacturing, total	9.4	19.8	18.1	13.4	2.7	12.7	8.2	5.1	3.0	10.0
Durable	5.4	10.4	10.5	9.5	1.2	5.7	4.5	3.2	1.7	7.2
Nondurable	3.9	9.3	7.4	3.7	1.4	7.0	3.7	1.9	1.3	2.7
Not specified	0.1	0.2	0.1	0.3	0.1	0.1	0.1	0.0	0.0	0.1
Transportation	2.1	3.0	3.4	2.5	1.4	2.0	1.7	1.8	2.4	2.9
Trade	4.3	6.0	5.7	4.9	2.6	4.7	3.8	4.4	4.0	6.4
Finance	0.5	1.1	0.8	0.6	0.3	0.4	0.3	0.4	0.5	0.9
Business services	0.8	1.4	1.3	0.9	0.5	0.7	0.6	0.7	0.7	1.2
Personal services	1.7	3.4	2.4	1.4	0.8	2.5	1.6	1.6	1.7	2.1
Entertainment services	0.1	0.2	0.2	0.2	0.1	0.1	0.1	0.1	0.2	0.3
Professional services	2.7	4.3	3.7	2.8	2.1	2.6	2.4	2.4	2.9	3.5
Public administration	1.2	2.0	1.4	1.1	0.7	1.3	1.1	1.2	1.6	1.9
Industry not reported	1.8	1.6	1.6	1.8	2.1	1.8	1.7	2.1	1.9	1.6

TABLE 53

PERCENT CHANGE: EMPLOYMENT STATUS OF THE TOTAL POPULATION 14 YEARS OLD AND OVER AND MAJOR OCCUPATION GROUP AND MAJOR INDUSTRY GROUP OF THE EMPLOYED TOTAL POPULATION OF THE UNITED STATES, BY GEOGRAPHIC DIVISIONS: 1940-50

Employment Status, Occupation and Industry	Geographic Division									
	United States	New England	Middle Atlantic	East North Central	West North Central	South Atlantic	East South Central	West South Central	Mountain	Pacific
EMPLOYMENT STATUS, ALL GROUPS										
14 years old and over	11.1	7.0	6.7	9.9	0.9	17.0	5.1	9.3	18.2	39.4
Total labor force	13.8	7.8	7.0	15.1	5.9	18.6	4.1	10.8	24.1	45.4
Civilian labor force	12.5	6.8	6.6	14.8	5.7	15.6	2.8	9.0	21.8	42.0
Employed	25.3	18.5	21.6	28.6	18.9	24.7	12.9	21.5	39.6	53.8
Unemployed	-62.8	-57.7	-64.9	-66.8	-77.8	-59.0	-68.4	-68.0	-63.0	-26.7
Not in the labor force	8.3	6.2	6.4	4.2	-4.1	15.3	6.1	7.6	12.3	32.8
EMPLOYMENT STATUS, WHITE MALES										
14 years old and over	9.1	5.3	2.7	5.6	-0.9	20.0	7.9	11.0	15.1	34.4
Total labor force	9.2	4.5	2.2	7.1	-0.1	19.7	5.3	9.9	16.1	36.1
Civilian labor force	7.5	3.2	1.8	6.8	-0.4	14.9	3.3	7.4	13.3	31.8
Employed	20.1	15.2	16.0	19.6	11.9	24.1	14.6	19.4	30.8	42.2
Unemployed	-66.2	-58.3	-66.1	-71.5	-79.7	-64.0	-73.4	-69.8	-66.7	-37.8
Not in the labor force	8.6	8.1	4.3	-0.3	-4.1	21.0	18.2	15.0	11.9	28.6
EMPLOYMENT STATUS, WHITE FEMALES										
14 years old and over	12.6	7.9	7.0	9.7	2.0	22.1	10.4	13.5	20.4	40.1
Total labor force	31.0	14.3	13.8	32.3	28.3	43.7	37.9	44.6	59.2	65.9
Civilian labor force	30.8	14.2	13.7	32.2	28.2	43.0	37.7	44.2	58.8	65.5
Employed	44.3	24.6	27.6	43.9	41.7	55.8	56.7	65.6	77.2	75.9
Unemployed	-59.2	-57.3	-67.0	-59.7	-74.0	-57.1	-67.7	-71.2	-48.7	-5.4
Not in the labor force	6.8	5.1	4.4	2.6	-4.9	15.3	4.5	6.4	11.1	31.4
EMPLOYMENT STATUS, NONWHITE MALES										
14 years old and over	12.7	38.5	42.7	61.6	12.6	4.3	- 8.3	- 5.3	29.8	77.4
Total labor force	7.4	34.0	35.3	61.1	4.5	1.0	-13.8	-12.8	21.0	77.1
Civilian labor force	5.9	28.4	32.4	60.0	4.1	-0.3	-14.4	-14.1	17.3	67.6
Employed	19.2	57.6	78.9	122.9	41.4	8.0	-8.5	-4.9	36.7	75.0
Unemployed	-54.4	-43.8	-52.3	-49.9	-69.7	-59.8	-61.1	-63.7	-49.3	33.2
Not in the labor force	33.8	52.9	68.9	62.9	37.8	18.6	16.9	24.2	59.2	78.5
EMPLOYMENT STATUS, NONWHITE FEMALES										
14 years old and over	15.1	37.3	45.8	63.3	16.9	6.1	- 5.7	- 2.3	34.7	124.8
Total labor force	13.3	40.6	40.7	77.1	24.0	2.7	-13.0	- 5.7	27.4	154.5
Civilian labor force	13.2	40.5	40.6	77.0	24.0	2.5	-13.1	- 5.7	27.0	153.6
Employed	22.0	60.4	67.2	131.7	53.3	6.6	- 9.8	1.2	31.6	160.7
Unemployed	-38.4	-40.2	-47.3	-36.6	-58.9	-33.2	-44.9	-52.3	-12.2	117.5
Not in the labor force	16.1	35.1	49.8	56.7	13.5	8.4	-1.7	-0.6	37.7	108.4
MAJOR OCCUPATION GROUP - MALE	20.1	15.7	18.2	22.7	12.5	20.1	8.7	15.0	31.0	45.5
Professional and technical workers	43.1	36.7	34.8	39.4	29.2	54.4	46.5	53.4	55.5	65.1
Farmers and farm managers	-16.0	-16.9	-16.3	-13.7	- 7.8	-14.5	-19.7	-30.2	-10.3	-1.2
Managers, officials, and proprietors	34.3	26.7	32.7	27.4	16.3	48.2	36.1	35.7	43.6	57.9
Clerical and kindred workers	29.3	20.0	17.8	29.3	27.2	38.1	38.3	43.5	49.5	48.2
Sales workers	14.9	4.9	2.1	11.0	8.4	31.5	28.6	22.8	29.7	34.5
Craftsmen and foremen	50.0	27.7	34.4	41.8	52.1	65.5	65.1	81.8	77.3	77.2
Operatives	34.6	14.6	20.0	41.3	37.0	38.2	45.6	61.8	89.9	50.7
Private household workers	-35.7	-12.7	-26.1	- 8.4	-11.8	-45.9	-49.7	-65.8	29.9	-10.7
Service workers, except household	20.9	14.5	11.3	22.4	13.0	28.0	23.5	25.8	46.3	37.3
Farm laborers, unpaid family workers	-37.0	-37.0	-40.8	-40.7	-29.8	-30.8	-37.4	-55.3	-10.4	-17.1
Farm laborers, paid, incl. foremen	-26.0	-21.1	-23.7	-30.4	-28.1	-32.2	-32.1	-31.4	-5.7	-0.8
Laborers, except farm and mine	9.5	-3.9	-2.4	3.9	27.6	2.9	6.9	27.8	54.1	32.3
Occupation not reported	83.6	26.1	38.3	78.8	117.4	116.5	133.7	146.8	113.5	86.7
MAJOR OCCUPATION - FEMALE	41.1	25.1	30.3	47.7	42.1	37.5	27.9	45.8	74.7	79.3
Professional and technical workers	30.1	20.9	20.1	29.7	11.9	42.5	35.3	34.7	40.9	60.4
Farmers and farm managers	-23.3	-0.3	0.8	1.4	-17.2	-36.6	-35.2	-35.8	- 4.9	18.8
Managers, officials and proprietors	74.3	69.1	67.6	70.2	49.8	99.3	90.5	84.7	76.6	76.6
Clerical and kindred workers	82.1	54.5	59.0	76.5	74.4	104.7	109.0	127.2	128.1	125.8
Sales workers	63.9	44.1	36.4	57.3	62.9	96.0	93.7	87.7	99.0	84.8
Craftsmen and foremen	93.2	55.5	64.7	99.7	121.5	99.5	108.7	179.8	172.0	145.1
Operatives	49.5	26.6	39.2	64.5	59.4	43.2	57.0	91.8	66.5	95.1
Private household workers	-32.2	-48.2	-38.4	-38.5	-47.7	-24.2	-27.5	-27.5	-16.3	-7.1
Service workers, except household	56.1	27.5	29.6	52.7	50.8	77.2	88.4	81.6	91.0	72.8
Farm laborers, unpaid family workers	42.2	218.3	295.0	381.6	728.5	-1.9	-46.3	-12.7	433.6	134.3
Farm laborers, paid, incl. foremen	34.5	209.7	169.9	217.8	261.3	1.6	4.3	12.9	282.2	207.6
Laborers, except farm and mine	20.4	7.7	7.7	7.2	52.5	10.8	19.3	60.1	137.5	99.7
Occupation not reported	63.5	7.0	20.5	70.9	118.0	70.3	113.7	96.3	110.3	70.6
MAJOR INDUSTRY GROUP - BOTH SEXES	25.3	18.5	21.6	28.6	18.9	24.7	12.9	21.5	39.6	53.8
Agriculture	-17.5	-11.8	-14.4	-14.9	- 8.7	-19.4	-25.0	-31.0	- 4.7	4.8
Mining	1.7	4.1	-13.3	- 4.7	3.2	18.5	7.6	37.0	-12.9	-34.0
Construction	65.8	41.4	38.3	54.5	69.6	73.9	70.3	106.6	115.0	93.7
Manufacturing, total	37.9	19.1	30.3	43.1	48.4	30.1	42.6	59.1	57.3	70.8
Transportation	40.6	29.3	29.7	37.3	37.1	46.6	44.1	58.0	57.5	58.5
Trade	39.8	25.6	28.3	33.9	31.2	57.7	54.3	49.8	59.3	56.9
Finance	30.1	26.8	14.6	25.9	24.3	50.0	47.4	50.3	71.3	50.8
Business services	58.4	49.6	46.2	51.0	50.0	77.0	71.8	62.0	78.7	83.7
Personal services	-12.2	-25.1	-19.8	-14.2	-23.1	- 7.8	-11.6	- 7.4	15.5	9.9
Entertainment services	32.1	23.1	19.5	32.8	27.5	48.0	62.8	46.1	74.1	24.4
Professional services	42.1	28.9	27.5	40.2	28.8	55.5	53.6	53.3	60.5	74.0
Public administration	77.0	51.3	53.1	62.7	46.7	96.7	77.2	108.9	104.3	145.4
Industry not reported	15.4	-22.5	-19.8	23.5	50.8	29.7	56.0	49.1	41.4	32.9

TABLE 54

PERCENT CHANGE: EMPLOYMENT STATUS OF THE URBAN POPULATION 14 YEARS OLD AND OVER AND MAJOR OCCUPATION GROUP AND MAJOR INDUSTRY GROUP OF THE EMPLOYED URBAN POPULATION OF THE UNITED STATES, BY GEOGRAPHIC DIVISIONS: 1940-50

Employment Status, Occupation and Industry	Geographic Division									
	United States	New England	Middle Atlantic	East North Central	West North Central	South Atlantic	East South Central	West South Central	Mountain	Pacific
EMPLOYMENT STATUS, ALL GROUPS										
14 years old and over	15.4	5.0	4.6	10.7	12.9	26.1	23.9	41.0	33.7	34.9
Total labor force	26.0	8.3	11.1	21.3	21.0	42.6	33.4	47.3	56.8	63.9
Civilian labor force	15.9	4.8	3.8	15.2	16.7	21.0	20.4	38.1	39.3	37.8
Employed	30.9	17.2	19.6	29.8	33.8	32.1	35.2	56.2	61.3	50.0
Unemployed	-65.9	-60.6	-70.2	-68.9	-77.1	-63.2	-65.5	-62.9	-66.3	-35.4
Not in the labor force	13.5	4.3	5.4	5.4	-8.6	28.2	26.4	41.1	25.8	28.9
EMPLOYMENT STATUS, WHITE MALES										
14 years old and over	11.9	3.2	0.3	6.1	11.8	26.2	26.4	44.7	32.0	29.5
Total labor force	11.9	2.3	-0.5	7.4	12.2	20.6	25.4	44.7	33.7	30.7
Civilian labor force	10.5	1.3	-0.8	7.3	12.1	20.3	22.8	40.6	31.0	27.7
Employed	25.0	13.9	14.2	21.0	29.5	29.4	36.6	56.9	54.0	40.5
Unemployed	-69.2	-60.6	-71.2	-74.2	-79.0	-65.8	-69.3	-61.7	-70.7	-47.6
Not in the labor force	11.6	6.7	3.6	0.5	10.5	24.8	30.4	44.3	26.3	25.0
EMPLOYMENT STATUS, WHITE FEMALES										
14 years old and over	14.8	5.5	4.2	8.9	12.6	28.6	28.0	44.3	33.8	33.7
Total labor force	24.9	10.9	7.9	24.6	27.0	37.4	40.5	57.1	59.9	51.5
Civilian labor force	24.7	10.8	7.8	24.6	27.0	36.8	40.3	56.6	59.5	51.2
Employed	38.0	21.9	22.2	35.9	40.0	48.4	56.2	77.2	76.8	61.7
Unemployed	-65.8	-62.3	-74.3	-65.3	-75.7	-68.0	-70.8	-69.8	-53.9	-23.0
Not in the labor force	10.5	2.9	2.6	2.7	6.7	24.4	22.7	39.5	24.9	26.5
EMPLOYMENT STATUS, NONWHITE MALES										
14 years old and over	37.6	44.4	44.8	64.9	24.7	22.9	15.9	26.3	72.7	98.8
Total labor force	31.3	41.4	36.8	63.7	15.4	17.1	7.6	18.1	69.2	98.1
Civilian labor force	30.1	37.1	36.3	63.4	15.7	15.8	7.1	16.2	62.5	91.2
Employed	60.9	69.2	83.1	127.0	57.5	34.1	26.7	42.8	105.1	105.1
Unemployed	-54.6	-41.4	-53.5	-50.8	-69.0	-60.6	-60.7	-64.2	-53.5	36.7
Not in the labor force	62.5	54.5	75.8	69.4	57.9	48.1	51.4	58.1	83.0	101.4
EMPLOYMENT STATUS, NONWHITE FEMALES										
14 years old and over	36.8	43.3	47.8	65.7	26.8	20.9	15.0	23.4	74.5	145.3
Total labor force	25.1	50.4	41.4	78.0	28.1	6.2	1.4	3.0	76.8	159.0
Civilian labor force	25.0	50.2	41.3	77.9	28.1	6.1	1.4	3.0	76.3	158.6
Employed	39.7	74.7	69.9	133.3	59.0	12.7	8.9	12.9	98.5	170.6
Unemployed	-42.5	-41.2	-51.0	-38.0	-60.4	-39.3	-47.8	-56.1	-30.2	102.9
Not in the labor force	46.9	38.6	53.2	59.5	26.1	37.7	27.2	43.5	73.0	136.0
MAJOR OCCUPATION GROUP - MALE	27.6	14.6	17.1	25.4	30.6	30.7	34.3	54.7	54.9	43.2
Professional and technical workers	44.9	35.4	33.6	39.6	42.7	59.3	60.9	73.1	63.6	53.5
Farmers and farm managers	50.9	-34.2	55.4	46.5	78.1	50.2	60.6	69.8	59.8	67.7
Managers, officials, and proprietors	35.9	25.6	32.5	27.2	24.9	48.9	44.2	49.4	50.7	48.6
Clerical and kindred workers	21.7	18.1	13.1	21.6	24.6	23.1	29.5	41.0	43.1	32.5
Sales workers	6.1	0.0	-3.9	3.1	4.6	15.6	18.5	20.7	20.6	15.9
Craftsmen and foremen	42.7	22.7	28.4	33.2	47.8	56.1	57.3	97.2	85.1	72.5
Operatives	28.5	10.2	17.0	34.0	37.4	25.2	45.0	64.9	45.1	45.0
Private household workers	-39.9	-13.3	-26.6	-11.1	-16.5	-58.7	-56.2	-70.7	7.2	-30.5
Service workers, exc. household	13.6	12.6	5.3	15.5	12.0	14.0	14.5	25.7	44.1	20.5
Farm laborers, unpaid family workers	30.0	-62.8	-3.7	67.1	119.6	93.7	95.3	58.6	134.9	-4.3
Farm laborers, paid, incl. foremen	16.1	-25.6	22.1	18.7	32.3	10.2	2.2	22.1	47.9	3.3
Laborers, except farm and mine	8.2	-3.1	-4.5	0.1	25.5	0.4	2.5	48.9	72.4	29.6
Occupation not reported	70.8	17.9	33.7	79.4	129.2	119.5	106.8	132.7	92.1	77.4
MAJOR OCCUPATION - FEMALE	38.1	22.8	25.7	40.9	40.9	34.2	36.6	58.4	77.4	66.2
Professional and technical workers	32.8	18.8	17.7	36.3	29.9	47.4	45.6	57.3	52.0	48.8
Farmers and farm managers	149.6	11.0	182.4	200.7	148.8	172.3	103.6	120.3	215.0	176.3
Managers, officials, and proprietors	76.9	74.1	67.6	71.8	58.0	101.6	110.2	101.4	85.8	62.8
Clerical and kindred workers	73.7	51.4	52.9	68.1	72.2	88.7	100.7	128.4	122.1	110.1
Sales workers	50.0	36.1	27.1	45.1	54.8	70.5	73.2	84.4	85.6	64.7
Craftsmen and foremen	81.9	48.6	56.3	89.2	116.8	80.4	88.2	178.3	181.4	134.2
Operatives	39.0	21.1	31.7	50.8	51.3	29.1	35.0	81.0	99.4	84.8
Private household workers	-34.7	-49.9	-40.5	-39.1	-42.4	-35.1	-31.2	-25.4	-18.8	-20.2
Service workers, exc. household	45.8	23.1	22.5	42.5	45.8	59.5	75.5	76.9	84.0	54.8
Farm laborers, unpaid family workers	19.6	-3.6	82.9	34.3	35.9	-3.5	7.0	9.5	296.9	-20.0
Farm laborers, paid, incl. foremen	156.2	252.2	321.4	245.5	376.5	74.8	133.1	157.5	373.7	205.7
Laborers, except farm and mine	15.6	6.9	4.1	-0.2	38.8	14.0	19.6	69.9	156.3	95.4
Occupation not reported	43.3	-2.3	14.1	59.4	77.9	60.4	88.8	79.2	71.2	54.4
MAJOR INDUSTRY GROUP - BOTH SEXES	30.9	17.2	19.6	29.8	33.8	32.1	35.2	56.2	61.3	50.0
Agriculture	32.5	-13.9	40.9	26.0	50.6	24.3	28.1	47.1	60.0	24.6
Mining	13.1	-4.6	-12.0	-8.9	12.0	79.2	34.6	69.5	13.4	-21.6
Construction	63.3	38.2	35.4	50.0	66.4	66.2	64.7	119.7	141.8	96.2
Manufacturing, total	31.4	15.2	24.9	34.8	45.3	21.3	33.8	74.4	66.3	68.8
Transportation	35.5	26.7	26.2	32.5	38.1	34.2	36.6	61.3	51.0	46.1
Trade	33.7	22.1	23.4	27.5	31.4	44.6	48.5	54.8	55.6	42.7
Finance	22.8	24.5	9.8	19.0	21.5	36.2	40.9	49.3	59.2	31.5
Business services	55.1	45.9	42.9	46.0	53.7	65.8	67.4	73.8	84.2	75.4
Personal services	-15.5	-24.1	-22.5	-16.3	-19.5	-19.1	-16.1	-6.2	12.4	-6.2
Entertainment services	28.1	19.9	15.5	27.7	34.4	42.6	64.3	54.2	86.9	5.7
Professional services	44.8	27.5	25.6	41.6	45.4	59.3	69.0	74.8	76.0	65.8
Public administration	74.8	50.4	49.3	59.2	50.7	91.1	76.8	122.2	109.8	134.1
Industry not reported	-4.6	-28.2	-29.1	14.7	26.0	7.7	21.7	28.4	8.9	8.7

TABLE 55

PERCENT CHANGE: EMPLOYMENT STATUS OF THE RURAL-NONFARM POPULATION 14 YEARS OLD AND OVER AND MAJOR OCCUPATION GROUP AND MAJOR INDUSTRY GROUP OF THE EMPLOYED RURAL-NONFARM POPULATION OF THE UNITED STATES, BY GEOGRAPHIC DIVISIONS: 1940-50

Employment Status, Occupation and Industry	United States	New England	Middle Atlantic	East North Central	West North Central	South Atlantic	East South Central	West South Central	Mountain	Pacific
EMPLOYMENT STATUS, ALL GROUPS										
14 years old and over	37.7	30.3	28.4	38.5	12.5	51.0	38.9	23.8	30.7	85.8
Total labor force	38.9	31.1	29.0	43.8	15.9	50.4	33.3	20.1	33.8	91.0
Civilian labor force	35.5	28.4	27.6	42.5	15.0	45.0	29.6	17.3	29.2	81.6
Employed	52.9	40.1	42.3	63.9	37.9	57.6	49.8	37.0	52.1	95.0
Unemployed	-42.7	-39.4	-37.8	-49.3	-71.4	-35.6	-54.7	-60.9	-46.0	23.1
Not in the labor force	36.6	29.5	27.8	34.0	9.7	51.7	44.2	27.3	27.7	80.7
EMPLOYMENT STATUS, WHITE MALES										
14 years old and over	37.1	29.4	25.6	36.2	12.4	56.5	43.9	24.4	26.4	78.3
Total labor force	36.5	28.6	24.6	37.6	12.9	55.2	37.9	21.3	25.9	80.0
Civilian labor force	32.6	25.2	23.2	36.2	11.8	47.9	32.7	18.1	20.6	69.5
Employed	51.0	38.1	38.2	36.4	36.4	61.5	56.2	38.1	43.3	83.7
Unemployed	-44.9	-42.8	-40.3	-51.9	-72.5	-36.3	-55.6	-61.6	-50.0	10.6
Not in the labor force	38.7	31.7	28.3	32.4	11.0	60.8	63.5	34.6	28.1	73.1
EMPLOYMENT STATUS, WHITE FEMALES										
14 years old and over	39.5	31.5	31.0	40.5	12.9	56.7	44.2	22.4	30.6	89.9
Total labor force	54.6	38.5	42.1	70.3	29.2	65.0	51.5	31.3	60.6	110.9
Civilian labor force	54.1	38.4	41.9	69.9	29.0	63.7	51.2	31.0	59.9	110.1
Employed	68.4	45.9	53.6	84.9	43.6	77.4	75.8	54.7	79.3	118.3
Unemployed	-34.0	-25.9	-31.6	-34.9	-67.6	-28.6	-54.0	-67.8	-34.0	60.3
Not in the labor force	35.8	29.2	28.0	34.2	9.0	54.3	42.6	20.6	24.4	85.1
EMPLOYMENT STATUS, NONWHITE MALES										
14 years old and over	32.2	26.3	39.7	54.0	2.2	28.8	16.8	26.7	83.7	167.5
Total labor force	22.7	10.9	21.5	33.5	-12.9	24.2	5.4	11.3	66.9	174.7
Civilian labor force	16.8	-7.1	10.2	18.6	-18.2	19.9	2.6	7.2	56.5	127.9
Employed	34.0	8.9	40.6	70.1	25.9	32.3	15.4	26.4	92.6	147.3
Unemployed	-48.9	-48.8	-42.3	-36.5	-63.2	-52.1	-57.5	-53.1	-25.8	72.8
Not in the labor force	58.3	65.2	74.8	76.4	27.0	43.4	51.0	75.2	135.3	153.3
EMPLOYMENT STATUS, NONWHITE FEMALES										
14 years old and over	31.6	11.0	30.6	51.8	5.3	31.5	17.9	25.0	105.3	218.2
Total labor force	16.5	-11.6	17.0	43.2	-11.0	19.2	4.0	0.5	91.3	221.9
Civilian labor force	16.1	-11.7	16.0	42.6	-11.2	18.9	3.8	0.4	90.7	213.9
Employed	21.1	-10.1	19.4	82.6	3.4	22.0	7.8	7.0	103.8	219.4
Unemployed	-21.4	-26.4	-2.2	-21.7	-51.4	-10.8	-33.6	-39.7	7.9	190.7
Not in the labor force	39.3	28.7	37.3	54.1	9.9	38.5	25.3	36.3	109.2	217.2
MAJOR OCCUPATION GROUP - MALE	49.6	37.9	38.3	58.3	36.3	55.5	48.4	36.4	45.0	85.1
Professional and technical workers	35.5	48.3	35.0	39.6	6.3	38.4	32.9	13.4	37.3	78.9
Farmers and farm managers	106.8	129.5	102.3	116.7	138.2	106.8	93.9	57.6	69.7	173.0
Managers, officials, and proprietors	33.0	40.4	29.8	32.8	6.7	47.6	31.6	9.3	30.2	77.8
Clerical and kindred workers	45.4	31.5	28.3	63.3	31.7	53.4	47.0	37.5	47.9	69.6
Sales workers	40.0	34.9	25.4	48.7	17.4	56.8	44.6	21.4	33.4	71.0
Craftsmen and foremen	74.6	57.7	63.5	80.2	66.2	89.0	83.5	62.2	69.5	95.2
Operatives	52.4	38.6	37.6	71.7	39.5	57.6	50.8	56.8	23.3	77.5
Private household workers	-17.2	5.2	-7.7	13.2	9.3	-24.6	-40.0	-58.2	48.0	44.1
Service workers, exc. household	38.7	25.7	35.6	51.9	16.6	43.9	32.3	16.9	43.2	74.2
Farm laborers, unpaid family workers	220.4	290.4	192.9	273.6	361.0	231.3	206.1	102.2	165.9	327.7
Farm laborers, paid, incl. foremen	56.0	26.8	35.4	46.4	62.2	53.5	43.0	48.2	60.5	119.8
Laborers, except farm and mine	28.2	6.0	18.4	28.8	40.8	25.3	20.7	15.8	53.8	76.3
Occupation not reported	109.0	57.9	63.4	99.5	89.4	126.5	152.5	164.5	143.6	135.2
MAJOR OCCUPATION GROUP - FEMALE	62.5	45.1	42.3	84.9	42.9	62.1	53.3	41.3	80.4	120.0
Professional and technical workers	37.3	42.6	36.9	41.9	8.3	44.9	38.2	8.7	34.2	95.2
Farmers and farm managers	193.7	254.9	215.1	300.9	265.1	120.6	131.9	122.1	412.3	290.9
Managers, officials, and proprietors	73.1	68.4	68.7	69.7	38.2	102.6	76.0	51.8	70.2	122.3
Clerical and kindred workers	105.3	75.6	79.9	127.8	74.6	127.6	111.3	105.5	127.3	153.8
Sales workers	116.8	105.5	89.4	129.9	87.7	152.4	126.4	94.6	121.8	145.8
Craftsmen and foremen	131.9	102.7	108.7	164.4	126.2	135.9	143.1	151.8	128.9	147.6
Operatives	81.5	60.6	77.0	151.5	88.6	61.8	81.8	116.9	110.4	210.7
Private household workers	-10.4	-30.4	-18.6	-15.4	-31.6	1.0	-16.3	-26.9	5.0	47.3
Service workers, exc. household	94.4	59.8	70.5	110.4	67.8	113.5	110.7	89.7	106.2	134.8
Farm laborers, unpaid family workers	416.4	814.7	458.9	1060.9	1675.3	279.0	190.9	253.8	1535.8	382.5
Farm laborers, paid, incl. foremen	174.0	246.3	168.1	349.8	469.8	147.1	145.5	136.9	442.4	368.0
Laborers, except farm and mine	48.8	21.9	38.1	62.6	127.3	24.8	32.4	42.6	122.4	145.9
Occupation not reported	93.6	50.0	51.4	108.5	98.6	86.9	151.5	103.4	153.2	125.7
MAJOR INDUSTRY GROUP - BOTH SEXES	52.9	40.1	42.3	63.9	37.9	57.7	49.8	37.0	52.1	95.0
Agriculture	72.7	53.8	58.6	75.3	96.6	65.7	66.2	49.0	69.5	133.5
Mining	19.5	28.8	15.6	22.7	12.1	38.8	15.5	24.6	-6.1	19.2
Construction	89.6	69.4	63.8	88.0	90.5	106.6	94.4	97.6	104.4	114.8
Manufacturing, total	57.1	41.4	54.4	82.2	51.4	48.4	52.2	34.3	60.2	92.5
Transportation	54.5	46.8	41.7	58.7	34.9	65.9	56.2	45.5	63.0	91.9
Trade	57.3	48.9	46.7	61.9	31.5	80.6	63.1	34.4	58.8	91.1
Finance	42.5	40.8	20.7	56.3	24.1	57.3	41.6	30.2	79.3	86.8
Business services	74.8	74.4	63.6	76.4	49.1	107.8	92.2	46.2	71.4	106.4
Personal services	6.3	-15.2	-2.9	8.9	-11.9	14.7	-1.9	-9.2	26.6	60.2
Entertainment services	39.0	45.5	27.9	57.5	14.3	48.0	50.1	20.4	43.0	64.1
Professional services	47.8	44.8	41.8	50.8	20.3	58.8	54.4	28.9	45.7	96.6
Public administration	81.4	65.7	67.0	78.6	39.4	89.7	81.8	73.4	94.1	167.7
Industry not reported	43.2	-2.1	18.7	43.9	41.5	44.1	60.1	46.3	67.9	102.6

TABLE 56

PERCENT CHANGE: EMPLOYMENT STATUS OF THE RURAL-FARM POPULATION 14 YEARS OLD AND OVER AND MAJOR OCCUPATION GROUP AND MAJOR INDUSTRY GROUP OF THE EMPLOYED RURAL-FARM POPULATION OF THE UNITED STATES, BY GEOGRAPHIC DIVISIONS: 1940-50

Employment Status, Occupation and Industry	Geographic Division									
	United States	New England	Middle Atlantic	East North Central	West North Central	South Atlantic	East South Central	West South Central	Mountain	Pacific
EMPLOYMENT STATUS, ALL GROUPS										
14 years old and over	-25.5	-32.2	-24.1	-22.6	-23.2	-24.2	-24.0	-36.6	-24.1	-16.3
Total labor force.....................	-22.4	-29.5	-19.6	-16.9	-16.9	-22.0	-25.1	-36.0	-19.1	-10.8
Civilian labor force..................	-22.5	-29.4	-19.9	-17.0	-17.0	-21.9	-25.2	-36.0	-19.2	-10.8
Employed............................	-16.9	-24.0	-13.4	-10.8	-11.7	-16.8	-20.0	-31.0	-11.4	-3.9
Unemployed..........................	-83.6	-75.8	-76.3	-83.5	-89.2	-84.6	-86.0	-86.8	-81.4	-67.5
Not in the labor force................	-28.5	-35.1	-28.6	-27.9	-29.5	-26.2	-22.9	-37.1	-29.1	-22.0
EMPLOYMENT STATUS, WHITE MALES										
14 years old and over	-25.0	-32.8	-26.1	-24.4	-23.6	-22.3	-21.3	-34.6	-25.2	-17.9
Total labor force.....................	-23.5	-30.9	-23.2	-21.4	-20.3	-22.1	-22.5	-35.0	-21.5	-14.4
Civilian labor force..................	-23.5	-30.9	-23.4	-21.5	-20.5	-22.0	-22.5	-35.0	-21.7	-14.4
Employed............................	-17.7	-25.4	-17.3	-15.8	-15.8	-15.9	-16.0	-29.5	-14.4	-7.3
Unemployed..........................	-86.1	-77.8	-78.4	-85.9	-91.0	-88.2	-89.2	-88.5	-84.6	-73.0
Not in the labor force................	-31.7	-39.8	-36.9	-36.6	-39.9	-22.9	-16.1	-32.8	-41.1	-31.3
EMPLOYMENT STATUS, WHITE FEMALES										
14 years old and over	-23.1	-31.1	-21.5	-20.3	-22.4	-21.9	-21.0	-34.4	-22.0	-11.5
Total labor force	11.5	-20.0	3.4	26.4	26.0	3.6	1.9	-5.1	23.4	34.3
Civilian labor force..................	11.4	-20.1	3.3	26.3	25.9	3.4	1.8	-5.3	23.2	34.1
Employed............................	25.2	-15.1	12.3	37.4	40.3	17.0	20.2	12.3	42.1	45.8
Unemployed..........................	-74.1	-63.1	-65.8	-66.1	-80.7	-78.5	-80.1	-84.4	-68.3	-39.7
Not in the labor force................	-27.1	-33.6	-25.8	-25.6	-27.1	-25.4	-23.1	-36.9	-26.7	-18.0
EMPLOYMENT STATUS, NONWHITE MALES										
14 years old and over	-34.6	-65.2	-39.3	-31.2	-38.8	-29.6	-32.4	-45.1	-27.8	-37.4
Total labor force.....................	-34.8	-69.3	-19.3	-27.4	-41.1	-28.4	-33.3	-47.4	-30.8	-35.1
Civilian labor force..................	-34.7	-69.1	-20.0	-26.7	-40.8	-28.1	-33.3	-47.3	-29.1	-34.7
Employed............................	-32.6	-60.2	-10.3	-2.1	-28.3	-26.0	-32.1	-45.5	-21.2	-33.4
Unemployed..........................	-81.6	-93.8	-69.0	-83.4	-83.8	-84.9	-82.0	-83.2	-72.3	-51.7
Not in the labor force................	-33.5	-47.8	-71.7	-39.2	-31.5	-35.7	-27.6	-34.6	-16.2	-47.7
EMPLOYMENT STATUS, NONWHITE FEMALES										
14 years old and over	-32.9	-60.4	-21.0	-20.2	-36.8	-28.6	-30.9	-42.9	-28.1	-32.2
Total labor force	-37.4	-60.4	-0.4	-16.7	-18.7	-28.5	-45.0	-45.5	-48.2	-15.9
Civilian labor force..................	-37.5	-60.4	-0.5	-16.8	-18.8	-28.6	-45.0	-45.6	-48.3	-16.0
Employed............................	-36.5	-52.4	3.1	5.4	-0.1	-27.3	-44.6	-44.2	-48.6	-17.9
Unemployed..........................	-56.7	-86.8	-28.7	-77.8	-64.0	-53.6	-58.5	-62.8	-39.8	29.3
Not in the labor force................	-31.5	-60.3	-28.1	-20.8	-38.8	-28.7	-26.0	-42.4	-19.7	-37.2
MAJOR OCCUPATION GROUP - MALE	-19.8	-25.6	-17.3	-15.8	-15.9	-19.0	-20.6	-33.1	-14.9	-9.3
Professional and technical workers........	0.5	-6.4	11.8	0.2	-18.6	4.9	1.6	-10.7	1.3	31.7
Farmers and farm managers........	-19.6	-25.3	-21.6	-16.6	-11.1	-17.7	-22.0	-33.6	-16.6	-10.3
Managers, officials, and proprietors.....	-0.9	-24.3	10.7	3.0	-16.7	5.3	-1.4	-8.5	-2.2	12.5
Clerical and kindred workers............	28.1	-10.3	19.6	38.6	12.3	36.2	34.2	30.6	14.7	25.4
Sales workers........................	5.3	-22.1	8.2	2.5	-3.9	11.8	16.7	-2.7	-0.9	12.6
Craftsmen and foremen	31.5	-13.2	27.5	31.3	32.4	29.5	44.1	40.0	25.2	36.6
Operatives..........................	33.5	-3.9	13.7	35.8	15.3	45.7	54.8	45.9	-1.4	15.1
Private household workers	-53.5	-50.0	-50.2	-34.6	-36.1	-61.3	-66.8	-68.9	24.6	-28.1
Service workers, exc. household.........	5.4	-17.8	6.4	18.9	-8.9	-6.5	14.9	-5.6	3.0	3.3
Farm laborers, unpaid family workers......	-40.3	-45.0	-45.4	-44.2	-32.9	-33.8	-40.1	-57.8	-19.7	-24.1
Farm laborers, paid, incl. foremen......	-44.9	-41.9	-39.1	-44.5	-42.3	-53.4	-47.8	-51.3	-24.7	-27.4
Laborers, except farm and mine.........	-15.3	-28.4	-21.5	-18.6	2.2	-24.6	-5.6	-6.3	4.9	-11.5
Occupation not reported.............	97.7	30.1	27.6	55.3	131.1	101.8	149.4	156.3	114.8	51.6
MAJOR OCCUPATION GROUP - FEMALE	6.4	-15.4	12.2	37.2	39.9	-4.8	-16.9	-10.9	22.7	40.1
Professional and technical workers........	-16.7	-26.4	-17.5	-12.7	-36.8	-8.6	-1.0	-23.3	-13.3	20.1
Farmers and farm managers........	-33.0	-20.7	-18.2	-11.7	-26.5	-43.2	-39.1	-42.9	-27.8	-5.8
Managers, officials, and proprietors.....	43.9	-5.8	31.8	49.4	32.1	50.6	51.4	52.3	26.3	53.3
Clerical and kindred workers............	83.8	26.1	78.6	81.5	69.2	101.1	114.8	96.1	77.6	85.0
Sales workers........................	79.9	47.5	58.7	59.4	56.9	99.3	123.8	73.7	83.2	92.1
Craftsmen and foremen...................	120.2	57.5	88.7	103.6	163.9	100.5	175.3	257.4	132.6	140.2
Operatives..........................	64.3	20.4	45.9	88.9	84.3	62.0	102.3	140.9	-53.5	64.7
Private household workers	-61.9	-72.4	-65.8	-69.7	-81.0	-50.0	-51.1	-60.0	-55.2	-50.3
Service workers, exc. household	41.7	-25.1	2.5	33.2	29.5	54.0	91.5	79.6	48.6	48.7
Farm laborers, unpaid family workers......	38.5	248.9	305.1	382.1	731.9	-4.7	-47.9	-15.7	403.2	151.3
Farm laborers, paid, incl. foremen........	88.7	166.0	148.9	180.3	213.7	-40.7	-24.0	-25.0	202.0	144.8
Laborers, except farm and mine.........	-13.7	-29.2	-20.9	-29.0	25.2	-23.8	-13.5	61.9	41.9	
Occupation not reported.............	104.6	-0.7	17.9	79.4	218.3	73.8	119.4	124.5	159.7	75.2
MAJOR INDUSTRY GROUP - BOTH SEXES	-16.9	-24.0	-13.4	-10.8	-11.7	-16.8	-20.1	-31.0	-11.4	-3.9
Agriculture..........................	-25.1	-28.9	-24.6	-20.3	-13.7	-27.4	-29.5	-39.1	-15.5	-13.3
Mining..............................	-6.1	-29.5	-21.2	-18.3	-27.7	17.5	9.9	-4.1	-32.6	-55.2
Construction........................	28.7	-17.5	8.3	18.3	30.0	28.6	43.4	57.1	24.0	39.9
Manufacturing, total................	30.0	-2.9	26.6	42.3	49.0	22.2	47.7	31.1	-20.8	19.9
Transportation......................	24.9	-3.0	19.3	24.1	16.6	25.1	31.3	32.9	45.7	29.2
Trade..............................	23.6	-9.8	26.4	24.3	13.7	28.9	35.5	15.6	26.9	27.5
Finance............................	38.7	-3.2	21.4	37.9	38.8	55.5	55.3	41.8	59.4	38.5
Business services...................	27.7	0.7	26.5	31.5	28.3	28.1	35.0	12.9	31.6	46.3
Personal services...................	-50.8	-65.9	-56.3	-57.5	-72.2	-41.0	-39.5	-46.5	-38.5	-35.5
Entertainment services..............	4.1	-23.9	7.6	4.5	-12.8	6.0	30.3	-5.3	32.4	11.2
Professional services...............	-12.0	-22.4	-14.4	-10.5	-32.7	-3.5	-1.0	-15.2	-10.5	17.8
Public administration...............	50.0	-7.0	26.2	44.6	25.0	61.6	51.9	75.0	49.4	106.3
Industry not reported...............	79.2	-11.6	11.5	44.9	144.8	69.4	114.2	119.2	105.3	49.9

TABLE 57

POPULATION: EMPLOYMENT STATUS OF THE TOTAL POPULATION 14 YEARS OLD AND OVER AND MAJOR OCCUPATION GROUP AND MAJOR INDUSTRY GROUP OF THE EMPLOYED POPULATION OF THE UNITED STATES, BY GEOGRAPHIC DIVISIONS: 1950

Employment Status, Occupation and Industry	Geographic Division									
	United States	New England	Middle Atlantic	East North Central	West North Central	South Atlantic	East South Central	West South Central	Mountain	Pacific
EMPLOYMENT STATUS, ALL GROUPS										
14 years old and over	112,354,034	7,165,099	23,434,108	22,935,684	10,518,325	15,193,185	8,046,853	10,432,053	3,601,436	11,027,291
Total labor force	60,053,968	3,895,744	12,630,330	12,447,095	5,537,129	8,262,725	4,054,987	5,345,357	1,892,457	5,988,144
Civilian labor force	59,071,655	3,845,879	12,550,668	12,388,727	5,511,147	7,965,489	3,992,372	5,217,654	1,844,537	5,755,182
Employed	56,239,449	3,611,310	11,838,062	11,872,955	5,352,949	7,656,503	3,838,789	5,003,358	1,746,673	5,318,850
Unemployed	2,832,206	234,569	712,606	515,772	158,198	308,986	153,583	214,296	97,864	436,332
Not in the labor force	52,300,066	3,269,355	10,803,778	10,488,589	4,981,196	6,930,460	3,991,866	5,086,696	1,708,979	5,039,147
EMPLOYMENT STATUS, WHITE MALES										
14 years old and over	49,979,010	3,397,388	10,670,690	10,656,093	5,050,619	5,794,568	3,081,056	4,345,426	1,761,392	5,221,778
Total labor force	39,496,968	2,631,681	8,407,358	8,567,796	4,008,181	4,594,868	2,395,264	3,415,968	1,281,480	4,094,372
Civilian labor force	38,606,958	2,585,120	8,337,295	8,516,132	3,984,329	4,327,026	2,338,520	3,300,611	1,337,850	3,880,045
Employed	36,837,888	2,414,601	7,859,185	8,195,760	3,875,244	4,185,178	2,261,083	3,176,800	1,267,087	3,602,950
Unemployed	1,769,070	170,519	478,110	320,372	109,085	141,848	77,437	123,841	70,763	277,095
Not in the labor force	10,482,042	765,707	2,263,332	2,088,297	1,042,438	1,199,700	685,792	929,458	379,912	1,127,406
EMPLOYMENT STATUS, WHITE FEMALES										
14 years old and over	51,354,115	3,653,471	11,300,378	10,890,868	5,111,720	5,934,412	3,158,509	4,376,292	1,691,196	5,237,269
Total labor force	14,411,755	1,197,902	3,378,954	3,108,939	1,344,388	1,668,159	690,957	1,035,888	435,082	1,551,486
Civilian labor force	14,386,559	1,196,737	3,375,653	3,106,225	1,343,447	1,659,817	689,961	1,033,269	433,842	1,547,608
Employed	13,799,298	1,139,783	3,231,532	2,998,787	1,311,552	1,603,206	665,325	1,001,064	413,339	1,437,710
Unemployed	587,261	56,954	144,121	107,438	31,895	56,611	24,636	32,205	20,503	112,898
Not in the labor force	36,942,360	2,455,569	7,921,424	7,781,929	3,767,332	4,266,253	2,467,552	3,340,404	1,256,114	3,685,783
EMPLOYMENT STATUS, NONWHITE MALES										
14 years old and over	5,332,607	57,842	690,131	684,465	173,712	1,664,055	856,334	818,318	78,879	308,871
Total labor force	4,056,418	42,844	510,157	522,064	121,601	1,303,928	658,695	602,621	56,543	237,965
Civilian labor force	3,991,809	40,733	504,197	518,302	120,440	1,283,971	654,039	593,008	53,545	223,574
Employed	3,681,574	35,602	442,823	459,234	108,666	1,220,618	620,638	553,830	48,331	191,832
Unemployed	310,235	5,131	61,374	59,068	11,774	63,353	33,401	39,178	5,214	31,742
Not in the labor force	1,276,189	14,998	179,974	162,401	52,111	360,127	197,639	215,697	22,336	70,906
EMPLOYMENT STATUS, NONWHITE FEMALES										
14 years old and over	5,688,302	56,398	772,909	704,258	182,274	1,800,150	950,954	892,017	69,969	259,373
Total labor force	2,088,827	23,317	333,861	248,296	62,959	695,770	310,071	290,880	19,352	104,321
Civilian labor force	2,086,329	23,289	333,523	248,068	62,931	694,675	309,852	290,736	19,300	103,955
Employed	1,920,689	21,324	304,522	219,174	57,487	647,501	291,743	271,664	17,916	89,358
Unemployed	165,640	1,965	29,001	28,894	5,444	47,174	18,109	19,072	1,384	14,597
Not in the labor force	3,599,475	33,081	439,048	455,962	119,315	1,104,380	640,883	601,137	50,617	155,052
MAJOR OCCUPATION GROUP - MALE	40,519,462	2,450,203	8,302,008	8,654,994	3,983,910	5,405,796	2,881,721	3,730,630	1,315,418	3,794,782
Professional and technical workers	2,970,665	199,738	737,000	633,002	239,498	330,730	136,686	243,593	100,827	349,591
Farmers and farm managers	4,192,100	62,502	206,606	696,990	911,573	681,826	691,643	579,451	175,376	186,133
Managers, officials, and proprietors	4,340,679	280,226	1,018,259	858,650	404,435	511,022	223,208	399,119	149,670	496,090
Clerical and kindred workers	2,602,652	171,089	699,906	599,851	223,194	292,690	115,969	191,730	69,324	238,899
Sales workers	2,596,930	174,615	583,242	530,952	244,577	318,279	141,300	226,223	77,527	300,215
Craftsmen and foremen	7,546,894	529,134	1,687,203	1,786,991	609,904	905,780	397,926	614,940	230,621	784,395
Operatives	8,120,313	609,575	1,856,343	2,065,489	550,318	1,092,344	518,896	595,544	204,215	627,589
Private household workers	73,244	4,962	16,144	10,787	4,158	14,518	6,759	6,752	1,456	7,708
Service workers, exc. household	2,372,457	165,132	624,082	494,983	179,334	281,467	115,249	187,667	74,766	249,797
Farm laborers, unpaid family workers	592,905	5,348	21,696	75,770	121,760	140,790	123,184	69,233	22,084	13,040
Farm laborers, paid, incl. foremen	1,358,160	42,344	106,910	174,416	174,483	251,256	135,154	215,777	86,628	170,280
Laborers, except farm and mine	3,303,206	182,024	660,418	634,799	270,550	517,035	239,400	355,030	107,621	336,329
Occupation not reported	449,257	22,602	84,199	92,314	50,146	68,059	36,347	45,571	15,303	34,716
MAJOR OCCUPATION - FEMALE	15,719,987	1,161,107	3,536,054	3,217,961	1,369,039	2,250,707	957,068	1,272,728	431,255	1,524,068
Professional and technical workers	1,939,543	145,497	420,732	375,132	189,635	253,568	110,630	160,380	67,395	216,574
Farmers and farm managers	116,435	2,802	7,146	16,025	44,246	20,888	24,125	16,137	4,639	10,427
Managers, officials, and proprietors	677,357	38,339	134,377	126,578	61,237	85,005	38,657	69,806	27,753	95,605
Clerical and kindred workers	4,292,671	317,883	1,063,445	956,340	368,631	492,337	180,705	312,904	119,223	481,203
Sales workers	1,329,886	83,967	264,568	299,675	129,900	168,357	76,752	122,428	42,159	142,080
Craftsmen and foremen	236,096	21,454	62,702	58,380	19,401	23,784	10,635	13,913	4,711	21,116
Operatives	3,019,901	356,433	896,731	629,806	173,250	454,284	165,842	124,970	33,751	184,834
Private household workers	1,334,573	60,007	240,729	187,022	83,543	319,389	145,439	170,121	29,063	91,260
Service workers, exc. household	1,914,071	105,398	347,229	414,850	198,377	249,840	116,804	192,137	75,480	213,956
Farm laborers, unpaid family workers	317,453	2,031	13,667	53,939	74,456	71,404	41,424	36,095	11,244	13,193
Farm laborers, paid, incl. foremen	131,747	2,450	7,412	9,433	7,563	51,856	16,288	19,561	3,535	13,649
Laborers, except farm and mine	127,375	9,839	26,460	32,274	11,622	18,440	7,248	8,610	2,494	10,388
Occupation not reported	282,879	15,007	50,856	58,507	37,178	41,555	22,519	25,666	9,808	21,783
MAJOR INDUSTRY GROUP - BOTH SEXES	56,239,449	3,611,310	11,838,062	11,872,955	5,352,949	7,656,503	3,838,789	5,003,358	1,746,673	5,318,850
Agriculture	7,005,406	142,938	392,731	1,058,279	1,326,032	1,280,946	1,053,432	979,285	315,385	456,378
Mining	929,152	4,823	205,770	108,137	47,872	180,929	115,168	160,506	70,100	35,847
Construction	3,439,924	202,350	648,124	595,033	312,184	507,824	225,227	394,846	143,786	410,550
Manufacturing, total	14,575,703	1,391,846	3,910,047	4,177,752	824,911	1,661,847	705,352	664,637	166,592	1,072,719
Durable	7,756,928	655,490	1,890,317	2,913,560	368,973	589,811	331,691	287,735	83,741	635,610
Nondurable	6,696,709	726,411	1,982,996	1,227,572	443,065	1,063,224	368,665	372,443	81,178	431,155
Not specified	122,066	9,945	36,734	36,620	12,873	8,812	4,996	4,459	1,673	5,954
Transportation	4,368,302	231,810	1,016,475	923,303	442,475	511,394	238,496	391,499	167,446	445,404
Trade	10,547,563	652,037	2,281,734	2,170,834	1,035,860	1,294,180	589,553	1,007,686	350,713	1,164,966
Finance	1,916,220	140,470	551,848	361,019	162,134	199,615	76,533	143,710	49,819	231,052
Business services	1,411,397	86,582	319,523	288,030	142,441	151,821	73,327	125,296	52,084	172,293
Personal services	3,488,573	191,446	693,615	574,882	255,055	643,356	283,577	397,680	107,012	341,932
Entertainment services	554,032	28,704	122,439	105,574	45,541	61,442	25,575	47,471	22,344	91,942
Professional services	4,674,478	337,807	1,028,013	926,894	460,156	574,575	265,554	399,503	169,613	512,363
Public administration	2,488,778	156,586	496,522	418,066	197,615	468,213	122,721	209,575	102,926	316,554
Industry not reported	839,921	43,893	171,221	165,152	100,673	117,361	64,254	81,664	28,853	66,850

TABLE 58

POPULATION: EMPLOYMENT STATUS OF THE URBAN POPULATION 14 YEARS OLD AND OVER AND MAJOR OCCUPATION GROUP AND MAJOR INDUSTRY GROUP OF THE EMPLOYED URBAN POPULATION OF THE UNITED STATES, BY GEOGRAPHIC DIVISIONS: 1950

Employment Status, Occupation and Industry	United States	New England	Middle Atlantic	East North Central	West North Central	South Atlantic	East South Central	West South Central	Mountain	Pacific
EMPLOYMENT STATUS, ALL GROUPS										
14 years old and over	74,249,865	5,531,937	19,093,698	16,303,460	5,636,742	7,899,115	3,354,696	5,981,959	2,045,826	8,402,432
Total labor force	41,082,535	3,060,394	10,482,662	9,150,132	3,066,340	4,522,814	1,846,388	3,250,532	1,088,944	4,614,329
Civilian labor force	40,569,354	3,030,801	10,434,984	9,125,805	3,056,071	4,375,875	1,821,576	3,171,342	1,070,013	4,482,887
Employed	38,405,547	2,841,877	9,825,185	8,713,286	2,950,276	4,174,197	1,728,384	3,026,773	1,011,448	4,134,121
Unemployed	2,163,807	188,924	609,799	412,519	105,795	201,678	93,192	144,569	58,565	348,766
Not in the labor force	33,167,330	2,471,543	8,611,036	7,153,328	2,570,402	3,376,301	1,508,308	2,731,427	956,882	3,788,103
EMPLOYMENT STATUS, WHITE MALES										
14 years old and over	32,240,205	2,578,974	8,505,537	7,273,224	2,534,372	2,906,703	1,186,515	2,432,403	975,768	3,846,709
Total labor force	25,656,462	2,007,689	6,764,813	5,924,921	1,981,924	2,324,978	940,315	1,939,725	753,648	3,018,449
Civilian labor force	25,188,873	1,980,452	6,722,549	5,903,194	1,972,398	2,191,055	917,632	1,867,683	736,666	2,897,244
Employed	23,888,246	1,844,623	6,324,064	5,662,276	1,903,358	2,107,826	878,502	1,788,839	695,017	2,683,741
Unemployed	1,300,627	135,829	398,485	240,918	69,040	83,229	39,130	78,844	41,649	213,503
Not in the labor force	6,583,743	571,285	1,740,724	1,348,303	552,448	581,725	246,200	492,678	222,120	828,260
EMPLOYMENT STATUS, WHITE FEMALES										
14 years old and over	34,818,431	2,849,875	9,213,464	7,721,970	2,809,134	3,199,537	1,331,243	2,598,052	1,016,053	4,079,103
Total labor force	11,220,608	992,158	2,913,623	2,483,485	924,756	1,100,209	426,372	769,159	304,185	1,306,661
Civilian labor force	11,205,195	991,272	2,911,183	2,482,078	924,379	1,095,994	425,790	767,132	303,436	1,303,931
Employed	10,741,930	944,702	2,786,386	2,395,347	901,914	1,059,120	411,031	743,510	289,439	1,210,481
Unemployed	463,265	46,570	124,797	86,731	22,465	36,874	14,759	23,622	13,997	93,450
Not in the labor force	23,597,823	1,857,717	6,299,841	5,238,485	1,884,378	2,099,328	904,871	1,828,893	711,868	2,772,442
EMPLOYMENT STATUS, NONWHITE MALES										
14 years old and over	3,387,189	51,447	639,206	636,212	140,015	824,894	378,675	439,487	28,272	248,981
Total labor force	2,588,442	38,807	480,942	499,375	101,349	640,547	286,701	327,282	20,667	192,772
Civilian labor force	2,559,706	37,362	478,178	498,374	101,000	632,436	285,213	322,244	19,496	185,403
Employed	2,299,872	32,673	419,486	441,793	91,571	585,642	259,626	294,341	17,438	157,302
Unemployed	259,834	4,689	58,692	56,581	9,429	46,794	25,587	27,903	2,058	28,101
Not in the labor force	798,747	12,640	158,264	136,837	38,666	184,347	91,974	112,205	7,605	56,209
EMPLOYMENT STATUS, NONWHITE FEMALES										
14 years old and over	3,804,040	51,641	735,491	672,054	153,221	967,981	458,263	512,017	25,733	227,639
Total labor force	1,617,023	21,740	323,284	242,351	58,311	457,080	193,000	214,366	10,444	96,447
Civilian labor force	1,615,580	21,715	323,074	242,159	58,294	456,390	192,941	214,283	10,415	96,309
Employed	1,475,499	19,879	295,249	213,870	53,433	421,609	179,225	200,083	9,554	82,597
Unemployed	140,081	1,836	27,825	28,289	4,861	34,781	13,716	14,200	861	13,712
Not in the labor force	2,187,017	29,901	412,207	429,703	94,910	510,901	265,263	297,651	15,289	131,192
MAJOR OCCUPATION GROUP - MALE	26,188,118	1,877,296	6,743,550	6,104,069	1,994,929	2,693,468	1,138,128	2,083,180	712,455	2,841,043
Professional and technical workers	2,435,966	160,924	650,200	533,872	179,428	249,656	91,364	192,893	73,947	303,682
Farmers and farm managers	112,998	6,310	10,296	9,392	14,279	11,480	7,712	18,118	9,688	21,243
Managers, officials, and proprietors	3,406,188	222,861	894,134	687,351	274,459	356,921	143,299	303,891	106,519	416,753
Clerical and kindred workers	2,207,008	147,135	638,182	514,295	179,123	223,556	82,417	156,675	53,585	212,040
Sales workers	2,137,839	145,634	523,038	446,439	189,193	228,494	96,493	182,342	61,083	265,123
Craftsmen and foremen	5,552,570	412,589	1,377,095	1,373,889	419,337	539,876	230,845	420,935	152,516	625,488
Operatives	5,709,829	485,628	1,483,820	1,566,450	388,045	538,440	254,878	386,215	122,341	484,422
Private household workers	52,924	2,869	12,556	8,160	2,927	9,676	4,594	4,983	852	6,307
Service workers, exc. household	1,996,485	143,496	565,479	421,412	140,227	217,320	86,256	153,295	54,365	214,635
Farm laborers, unpaid family workers	6,735	418	687	1,170	943	726	520	834	617	820
Farm laborers, paid, incl. foremen	159,638	8,451	14,442	16,211	13,841	23,047	7,492	26,150	10,518	39,486
Laborers, except farm and mine	2,142,428	124,828	506,840	460,464	168,209	261,856	119,220	214,902	59,039	227,070
Occupation not reported	267,510	16,153	66,781	60,894	24,918	32,420	13,038	21,947	7,385	23,974
MAJOR OCCUPATION GROUP - FEMALE	12,217,429	964,581	3,081,635	2,609,217	955,347	1,480,729	590,256	943,593	298,993	1,293,078
Professional and technical workers	1,511,552	118,702	363,384	303,968	127,133	179,393	67,678	118,880	46,936	185,478
Farmers and farm managers	9,190	453	1,071	1,361	824	1,096	563	1,087	495	2,240
Managers, officials, and proprietors	518,584	29,893	116,398	101,133	41,477	57,185	23,609	51,332	18,288	79,267
Clerical and kindred workers	3,737,682	276,399	976,328	838,167	306,666	400,146	140,852	269,091	95,819	434,214
Sales workers	1,055,635	72,143	231,990	246,225	94,361	116,783	49,213	92,478	30,501	121,945
Craftsmen and foremen	198,193	18,394	55,854	49,591	15,521	17,256	7,764	11,366	3,705	18,777
Operatives	2,384,662	300,885	772,567	520,786	140,426	263,243	101,588	98,332	24,609	162,226
Private household workers	1,011,504	42,837	205,585	148,139	59,119	219,975	100,186	131,706	19,541	84,416
Service workers, exc. household	1,506,092	85,407	295,118	334,981	144,032	186,967	83,984	147,778	51,653	176,172
Farm laborers, unpaid family workers	2,926	128	439	409	263	300	149	235	173	830
Farm laborers, paid, incl. foremen	22,245	717	1,804	2,041	1,206	7,763	1,029	2,971	777	3,937
Laborers, except farm and mine	93,014	7,714	20,752	24,956	8,619	11,069	4,588	5,842	1,674	7,800
Occupation not reported	166,150	10,909	40,380	37,464	15,700	19,553	9,053	12,495	4,822	15,774
MAJOR INDUSTRY GROUP - BOTH SEXES	38,405,547	2,841,877	9,825,185	8,713,286	2,950,276	4,174,197	1,728,384	3,026,773	1,011,448	4,134,121
Agriculture	440,850	28,788	45,099	50,318	40,892	60,441	23,645	65,810	27,194	98,613
Mining	338,703	1,727	89,529	40,569	21,769	25,061	22,693	86,851	29,512	20,992
Construction	2,315,919	145,563	498,669	413,523	186,834	286,982	118,120	262,288	89,894	314,046
Manufacturing, total	11,304,078	1,129,474	3,323,267	3,406,029	671,272	919,581	412,672	467,768	115,522	858,493
Durable	5,946,044	527,759	1,562,472	2,373,001	299,872	302,210	174,013	175,993	53,104	477,620
Nondurable	5,263,966	593,487	1,728,209	1,007,812	361,083	612,050	235,687	288,519	61,157	375,962
Not specified	94,068	8,228	32,586	25,216	10,317	5,321	2,972	3,256	1,261	4,911
Transportation	3,469,484	190,968	887,334	748,941	327,749	365,731	159,928	300,719	115,942	372,172
Trade	8,425,322	551,868	2,027,115	1,760,619	743,255	915,491	397,814	779,087	255,572	994,501
Finance	1,689,965	120,677	514,836	317,838	133,327	164,599	60,824	125,133	41,409	211,322
Business services	1,047,429	65,597	269,624	217,559	90,173	94,527	41,468	90,135	35,513	143,133
Personal services	2,773,734	150,103	605,837	476,614	190,763	461,251	202,408	316,064	76,503	291,191
Entertainment services	464,684	24,078	111,249	87,812	34,188	49,566	19,328	38,527	16,959	82,977
Professional services	3,631,016	271,026	875,534	742,033	322,172	404,495	167,205	295,297	120,651	432,603
Public administration	2,000,995	130,619	438,525	344,158	142,144	368,364	78,237	159,345	72,558	267,045
Industry not reported	503,368	31,389	138,867	107,273	45,738	55,108	23,992	39,749	14,219	47,033

TABLE 59

POPULATION: EMPLOYMENT STATUS OF THE RURAL-NONFARM POPULATION 14 YEARS OLD AND OVER AND MAJOR OCCUPATION GROUP AND MAJOR INDUSTRY GROUP OF THE EMPLOYED RURAL-NONFARM POPULATION OF THE UNITED STATES, BY GEOGRAPHIC DIVISIONS: 1950

Employment Status, Occupation and Industry	United States	New England	Middle Atlantic	East North Central	West North Central	South Atlantic	East South Central	West South Central	Mountain	Pacific
						Geographic Division				
EMPLOYMENT STATUS, ALL GROUPS										
14 years old and over..............	22,219,813	1,335,782	3,331,114	3,972,744	2,254,982	4,232,841	2,009,335	2,261,113	975,694	1,846,208
Total labor force..................	10,847,706	677,973	1,615,650	1,906,713	1,057,484	2,176,653	923,864	1,045,249	493,190	950,930
Civilian labor force..............	10,386,689	657,937	1,584,222	1,873,776	1,042,747	2,028,046	887,216	997,783	464,626	850,336
Employed.........................	9,859,856	618,616	1,497,280	1,793,770	1,002,808	1,943,717	844,339	947,350	433,110	778,866
Unemployed.......................	526,883	39,321	86,942	80,006	39,939	84,329	42,877	50,433	31,516	71,470
Not in the labor force............	11,372,107	657,809	1,715,464	2,066,031	1,197,498	2,056,188	1,085,471	1,215,864	482,504	895,278
EMPLOYMENT STATUS, WHITE MALES										
14 years old and over..............	10,362,168	659,242	1,633,048	1,969,811	1,098,539	1,735,825	836,296	972,500	485,698	971,209
Total labor force..................	7,741,245	495,570	1,206,267	1,459,340	792,946	1,342,867	609,531	721,129	372,522	741,073
Civilian labor force..............	7,325,161	476,465	1,178,936	1,430,314	779,400	1,210,131	576,284	678,637	346,229	648,765
Employed.........................	6,950,054	446,615	1,111,364	1,367,946	747,964	1,163,337	548,538	645,889	322,257	596,144
Unemployed.......................	375,107	29,850	67,572	62,368	31,436	46,794	27,746	32,748	23,972	52,621
Not in the labor force............	2,620,923	163,672	426,781	510,471	305,593	392,958	226,765	251,371	113,176	230,136
EMPLOYMENT STATUS, WHITE FEMALES										
14 years old and over..............	10,043,719	666,355	1,619,246	1,935,838	1,117,844	1,665,226	842,184	945,189	432,778	819,059
Total labor force..................	2,226,953	177,326	375,384	424,853	250,546	396,173	156,305	171,420	94,642	180,304
Civilian labor force..............	2,218,239	177,062	374,600	423,731	250,168	392,238	156,031	170,966	94,207	179,236
Employed.........................	2,125,238	168,118	358,701	408,782	243,828	377,570	150,035	165,243	89,278	163,683
Unemployed.......................	93,001	8,944	15,899	14,949	6,340	14,668	5,996	5,723	4,929	15,553
Not in the labor force............	7,816,766	489,029	1,243,862	1,510,985	867,298	1,269,053	685,879	773,769	338,136	638,755
EMPLOYMENT STATUS, NONWHITE MALES										
14 years old and over..............	922,567	5,838	45,546	41,061	20,750	414,704	159,980	167,828	30,506	36,354
Total labor force..................	621,425	3,633	24,772	17,561	10,751	302,419	106,714	109,726	20,655	25,194
Civilian labor force..............	586,051	2,969	21,586	14,806	9,946	290,784	103,683	105,240	18,838	18,199
Employed.........................	545,730	2,559	19,183	12,655	8,183	276,992	97,481	96,517	16,591	15,569
Unemployed.......................	40,321	410	2,403	2,151	1,763	13,792	6,202	8,723	2,247	2,630
Not in the labor force............	301,142	2,205	20,774	23,500	9,999	112,285	53,266	58,102	9,851	11,160
EMPLOYMENT STATUS, NONWHITE FEMALES										
14 years old and over..............	891,359	4,347	33,274	26,034	17,849	417,086	170,875	175,596	26,712	19,586
Total labor force..................	258,083	1,444	9,227	4,959	3,241	135,194	51,314	42,974	5,371	4,359
Civilian labor force	257,238	1,441	9,100	4,925	3,233	134,893	51,218	42,940	5,352	4,136
Employed.........................	238,834	1,324	8,032	4,387	2,833	125,818	48,285	39,701	4,984	3,470
Unemployed.......................	18,404	117	1,068	538	400	9,075	2,933	3,239	368	666
Not in the labor force............	633,276	2,903	24,047	21,075	14,608	281,892	119,561	132,622	21,341	15,227
MAJOR OCCUPATION GROUP - MALE	7,495,784	449,174	1,130,547	1,380,601	756,147	1,440,329	646,019	742,406	338,848	611,713
Professional and technical workers...	453,989	35,992	77,691	83,692	52,348	66,409	33,635	40,992	23,614	39,616
Farmers and farm managers	227,570	6,313	16,490	32,833	40,070	38,724	28,830	31,253	17,800	15,257
Managers, officials, and proprietors.	800,942	52,758	111,294	147,401	117,585	126,057	60,688	78,176	38,526	68,457
Clerical and kindred workers........	323,976	21,692	54,615	68,750	37,108	54,774	23,983	27,222	13,557	22,275
Sales workers	383,495	26,790	53,982	71,112	47,883	72,174	33,308	34,345	14,297	29,604
Craftsmen and foremen	1,620,510	105,316	268,568	328,448	157,406	289,856	119,935	150,607	67,696	132,678
Operatives.........................	1,873,939	108,977	315,396	379,111	126,823	419,134	179,719	157,085	70,763	116,931
Private household workers..........	15,803	1,834	2,943	1,990	962	3,724	1,599	1,306	430	1,015
Service workers, exc. household.....	324,654	19,885	53,184	62,838	35,135	53,327	22,711	28,702	18,169	30,683
Farm laborers, unpaid family workers.	34,879	607	1,926	4,617	5,669	7,541	6,099	4,219	2,896	1,305
Farm laborers, paid, incl. foremen...	447,890	16,506	35,371	48,606	42,473	101,415	46,273	72,573	26,153	58,520
Laborers, except farm and mine.....	884,210	47,396	126,212	132,657	80,603	186,235	78,560	104,214	40,139	88,194
Occupation not reported...........	103,947	5,108	12,875	18,546	12,082	20,959	10,679	11,712	4,808	7,178
MAJOR OCCUPATION GROUP - FEMALE......	2,364,072	169,442	366,733	413,169	246,661	503,388	198,320	204,944	94,262	167,153
Professional and technical workers...	313,762	23,446	47,892	51,463	42,628	52,575	26,107	29,568	15,975	24,108
Farmers and farm managers	10,660	432	869	1,472	1,263	1,881	1,430	1,334	878	1,101
Managers, officials, and proprietors.	135,550	7,679	16,314	22,289	17,743	22,585	11,049	15,085	8,409	14,397
Clerical and kindred workers........	439,346	36,733	74,129	89,210	48,926	72,697	28,293	33,461	18,907	36,990
Sales workers	222,312	10,694	28,650	43,929	30,246	39,639	19,404	23,277	9,819	16,674
Craftsmen and foremen	29,922	2,718	5,778	6,857	3,149	4,975	1,913	1,868	797	1,867
Operatives.........................	484,287	49,292	103,603	82,566	24,477	141,644	38,739	19,494	6,775	17,697
Private household workers	242,551	14,253	28,185	28,184	18,132	74,593	32,145	29,369	6,973	10,717
Service workers, exc. household	341,023	18,097	46,092	66,587	46,881	50,939	24,641	35,674	20,136	31,976
Farm laborers, unpaid family workers.	12,144	171	722	1,682	1,872	2,804	1,450	1,586	999	858
Farm laborers, paid, incl. foremen...	47,122	786	2,264	2,093	1,306	22,355	5,557	6,658	1,072	5,031
Laborers, except farm and mine.......	26,504	1,824	4,666	5,560	2,387	5,568	1,779	2,065	665	2,050
Occupation not reported...........	58,889	3,317	7,649	11,277	7,651	11,133	5,813	5,505	2,857	3,687
MAJOR INDUSTRY GROUP - BOTH SEXES....	9,859,856	618,616	1,497,280	1,793,770	1,002,808	1,943,717	844,339	947,350	433,110	778,866
Agriculture........................	901,741	35,052	67,691	103,037	101,741	210,766	98,151	135,509	54,252	95,569
Mining............................	485,960	2,708	102,967	52,258	20,581	127,157	68,154	60,966	37,925	13,244
Construction	877,256	50,092	126,085	141,326	100,778	165,359	71,308	97,201	45,349	79,758
Manufacturing, total...............	2,524,615	232,455	493,645	588,324	115,452	546,117	188,533	144,593	41,903	173,593
Durable.........................	1,382,207	112,091	273,805	410,821	51,747	199,950	100,685	78,887	25,609	128,612
Nondurable......................	1,122,327	118,903	216,420	169,703	61,867	343,701	86,702	64,867	15,996	44,168
Not specified...................	20,081	1,461	3,420	7,800	1,838	2,466	1,146	839	298	813
Transportation	734,098	36,367	111,669	140,100	95,736	115,251	57,020	72,192	44,151	61,612
Trade..............................	1,775,603	91,160	225,105	343,387	255,944	305,615	143,168	183,722	83,174	144,328
Finance............................	187,674	18,091	32,781	34,485	24,075	28,554	11,802	14,580	7,036	16,270
Business services..................	301,996	18,917	43,697	57,838	44,720	46,305	23,872	27,777	14,427	24,443
Personal services..................	577,958	36,161	75,200	78,883	53,532	140,898	60,435	65,315	25,488	42,046
Entertainment services.............	78,068	4,257	10,023	15,245	10,176	12,983	5,220	7,583	4,787	7,794
Professional services..............	830,924	60,237	133,408	146,613	108,146	129,863	67,618	79,379	40,245	65,415
Public administration..............	393,195	22,995	50,789	58,547	45,765	79,657	30,609	37,765	25,418	41,650
Industry not reported.............	190,768	10,124	24,220	33,727	26,169	35,192	18,469	20,768	8,955	13,144

APPENDIX

TABLE 60

POPULATION: EMPLOYMENT STATUS OF THE RURAL-FARM POPULATION 14 YEARS OLD AND OVER AND MAJOR OCCUPATION GROUP AND MAJOR INDUSTRY GROUP OF THE EMPLOYED RURAL-FARM POPULATION OF THE UNITED STATES, BY GEOGRAPHIC DIVISIONS: 1950

Employment Status, Occupation and Industry	Geographic Division									
	United States	New England	Middle Atlantic	East North Central	West North Central	South Atlantic	East South Central	West South Central	Mountain	Pacific
EMPLOYMENT STATUS, ALL GROUPS										
14 years old and over	15,884,356	297,380	1,009,296	2,659,480	2,626,601	3,061,229	2,682,822	2,188,981	579,916	778,651
Total labor force	8,123,727	157,377	532,018	1,390,250	1,413,305	1,563,258	1,284,735	1,049,576	310,323	422,885
Civilian labor force...............	8,115,612	157,141	531,462	1,389,146	1,412,329	1,561,568	1,283,580	1,048,529	309,898	421,959
Employed	7,974,046	150,817	515,597	1,365,899	1,399,865	1,538,589	1,266,066	1,029,235	302,115	405,863
Unemployed	141,566	6,324	15,865	23,247	12,464	22,979	17,514	19,294	7,783	16,096
Not in the labor force	7,760,629	140,003	477,278	1,269,230	1,213,296	1,497,971	1,398,087	1,139,405	269,593	355,766
EMPLOYMENT STATUS, WHITE MALES										
14 years old and over..............	7,376,637	159,172	532,105	1,413,058	1,417,708	1,152,040	1,058,245	940,523	299,926	403,860
Total labor force	6,099,261	128,422	436,278	1,183,535	1,233,311	927,023	845,418	755,114	255,310	334,850
Civilian labor force...............	6,092,924	128,203	435,810	1,182,624	1,232,531	925,840	844,604	754,321	254,955	334,036
Employed	5,999,588	123,363	423,757	1,165,538	1,223,922	914,015	834,043	742,072	249,813	323,065
Unemployed	93,336	4,840	12,053	17,086	8,609	11,825	10,561	12,249	5,142	10,971
Not in the labor force	1,277,376	30,750	95,827	229,523	184,397	225,017	212,827	185,409	44,616	69,010
EMPLOYMENT STATUS, WHITE FEMALES										
14 years old and over..............	6,491,965	137,241	467,668	1,233,060	1,184,742	1,069,649	985,082	833,051	242,365	339,107
Total labor force	964,194	28,418	89,947	200,601	169,086	171,777	108,280	95,309	36,255	64,521
Civilian labor force...............	963,125	28,403	89,870	200,416	168,900	171,585	108,140	95,171	36,199	64,441
Employed	932,130	26,963	86,445	194,658	165,810	166,516	104,259	92,311	34,622	60,546
Unemployed	30,995	1,440	3,425	5,758	3,090	5,069	3,881	2,860	1,577	3,895
Not in the labor force	5,527,771	108,823	377,721	1,032,459	1,015,656	897,872	876,802	737,742	206,110	274,586
EMPLOYMENT STATUS, NONWHITE MALES										
14 years old and over..............	1,022,851	557	5,379	7,192	12,947	424,457	317,679	211,003	20,101	23,536
Total labor force	846,551	404	4,443	5,128	9,501	360,962	265,280	165,613	15,221	19,999
Civilian labor force...............	846,052	402	4,433	5,122	9,494	360,751	265,143	165,524	15,211	19,972
Employed	835,972	370	4,154	4,786	8,912	357,984	263,531	162,972	14,302	18,961
Unemployed	10,080	32	279	336	582	2,767	1,612	2,552	909	1,011
Not in the labor force	176,300	153	936	2,064	3,446	63,495	52,399	45,390	4,880	3,537
EMPLOYMENT STATUS, NONWHITE FEMALES										
14 years old and over..............	992,903	410	4,144	6,170	11,204	415,083	321,816	204,404	17,524	12,148
Total labor force	213,721	133	1,350	986	1,407	103,496	65,757	33,540	3,537	3,515
Civilian labor force...............	213,511	133	1,349	984	1,404	103,392	65,693	33,513	3,533	3,510
Employed	206,356	121	1,241	917	1,221	100,074	64,233	31,880	3,378	3,291
Unemployed	7,155	12	108	67	183	3,318	1,460	1,633	155	219
Not in the labor force	779,182	277	2,794	5,184	9,797	311,587	256,059	170,864	13,987	8,633
MAJOR OCCUPATION GROUP - MALE	6,835,560	123,733	427,911	1,170,324	1,232,834	1,271,999	1,097,574	905,044	264,115	342,026
Professional and technical workers ..	80,710	2,822	9,109	15,438	7,722	14,665	11,687	9,708	3,266	6,293
Farmers and farm managers	3,851,532	49,879	179,820	650,285	857,224	631,622	655,101	530,080	147,888	149,633
Managers, officials, and proprietors	133,549	4,607	12,831	23,898	12,391	28,044	19,221	17,052	4,625	10,880
Clerical and kindred workers	71,668	2,262	7,109	16,806	6,963	14,360	9,569	7,833	2,182	4,584
Sales workers	75,596	2,191	6,222	13,401	7,501	17,611	11,499	9,536	2,147	5,488
Craftsmen and foremen	373,814	11,229	41,540	84,654	33,161	76,048	47,146	43,398	10,409	26,229
Operatives.........................	536,545	14,970	57,127	120,338	35,450	134,770	84,299	52,244	11,111	26,236
Private household workers	4,517	259	645	637	269	1,118	566	463	174	386
Service workers, exc. household	51,338	1,751	5,419	10,733	3,952	10,820	6,282	5,670	2,232	4,479
Farm laborers, unpaid family workers	551,291	4,323	19,083	69,983	115,148	132,523	116,565	64,180	18,571	10,915
Farm laborers, paid, incl. foremen ..	750,632	18,299	57,097	109,599	118,169	126,794	81,389	117,054	49,957	72,274
Laborers, except farm and mine	276,568	9,800	27,366	41,678	21,738	68,944	41,620	35,914	8,443	21,065
Occupation not reported	77,800	1,341	4,543	12,874	13,146	14,680	12,630	12,130	3,110	3,564
MAJOR OCCUPATION GROUP - FEMALE	1,138,486	27,084	87,686	195,575	167,031	266,590	168,492	124,191	38,000	63,837
Professional and technical workers ..	114,229	3,349	9,456	19,701	19,874	21,600	16,845	11,932	4,484	6,988
Farmers and farm managers	96,585	1,917	5,206	13,192	12,159	17,911	22,132	13,716	3,266	7,086
Managers, officials, and proprietors	23,223	767	1,665	3,156	2,017	5,235	3,999	3,389	1,056	1,939
Clerical and kindred workers	115,643	4,751	12,988	28,963	13,039	19,494	11,560	10,352	4,497	9,999
Sales workers	51,939	1,130	3,948	9,525	5,293	11,935	8,135	6,673	1,839	3,461
Craftsmen and foremen	7,981	342	1,105	1,932	731	1,253	958	679	209	472
Operatives.........................	150,952	6,256	20,561	26,454	8,347	49,397	25,515	7,144	2,367	4,911
Private household workers	80,518	2,917	6,959	10,699	6,292	24,821	13,108	9,046	2,549	4,127
Service workers, exc. household	66,956	1,894	6,019	13,282	7,464	11,934	8,179	8,685	3,691	5,808
Farm laborers, unpaid family workers	302,383	1,732	12,506	51,848	72,321	68,300	39,825	34,274	10,072	11,505
Farm laborers, paid, incl. foremen	62,380	947	3,344	5,299	5,051	21,738	9,702	9,932	1,686	4,681
Laborers, except farm and mine	7,857	301	1,102	1,758	616	1,803	881	703	155	538
Occupation not reported	57,840	781	2,827	9,766	13,827	10,869	7,653	7,666	2,129	2,322
MAJOR INDUSTRY GROUP - BOTH SEXES ...	7,974,046	150,817	515,597	1,365,899	1,399,865	1,538,589	1,266,066	1,029,235	302,115	405,863
Agriculture	5,662,815	79,098	279,941	904,924	1,183,406	1,009,739	931,606	777,966	233,939	262,196
Mining.............................	104,489	388	13,274	15,310	5,522	28,711	24,321	12,689	2,663	1,611
Construction.......................	246,749	6,695	23,370	40,184	24,572	55,483	35,799	35,357	8,543	16,746
Manufacturing, total...............	747,010	29,917	93,135	183,399	38,187	196,149	104,147	52,276	9,167	40,633
Durable........................	428,677	15,640	54,040	129,738	17,354	87,651	56,993	32,855	5,028	29,378
Nondurable.....................	310,416	14,021	38,367	50,057	20,115	107,473	46,276	19,057	4,025	11,025
Not specified..................	7,917	256	728	3,604	718	1,025	878	364	114	230
Transportation.....................	164,720	4,475	17,472	34,262	18,990	30,412	21,548	18,588	7,353	11,620
Trade..............................	346,638	9,009	29,514	66,828	36,661	73,074	48,571	44,877	11,967	26,137
Finance............................	38,581	1,702	4,231	8,696	4,732	6,462	3,927	3,997	1,374	3,460
Business services..................	61,972	2,068	6,502	12,633	7,548	10,989	7,987	7,384	2,144	4,717
Personal services..................	136,881	5,200	12,578	19,385	10,760	38,207	20,754	16,301	5,021	8,695
Entertainment services.............	11,280	369	1,167	2,517	1,177	1,893	1,027	1,361	598	1,171
Professional services..............	212,538	6,544	19,071	38,248	29,838	40,217	30,731	24,827	8,717	14,345
Public administration..............	94,588	2,972	7,208	15,361	9,706	20,192	13,875	12,465	4,950	7,859
Industry not reported..............	145,785	2,380	8,134	24,152	28,766	27,061	21,793	21,147	5,679	6,673

APPENDIX

TABLE 61

POPULATION: EMPLOYMENT STATUS OF THE TOTAL POPULATION 14 YEARS OLD AND OVER AND MAJOR OCCUPATION GROUP AND MAJOR INDUSTRY GROUP OF THE EMPLOYED POPULATION OF THE UNITED STATES, BY GEOGRAPHIC DIVISIONS: 1940

Employment Status, Occupation and Industry	United States	Geographic Division								
		New England	Middle Atlantic	East North Central	West North Central	South Atlantic	East South Central	West South Central	Mountain	Pacific
EMPLOYMENT STATUS, ALL GROUPS										
14 years old and over..............	101,102,924	6,693,807	21,963,558	20,877,417	10,420,305	12,981,252	7,658,677	9,547,782	3,046,790	7,913,336
Civilian labor force..............	52,511,499	3,601,454	11,771,039	10,789,117	5,216,034	6,892,592	3,885,354	4,787,029	1,514,970	4,053,910
Employed	44,888,083	3,046,927	9,739,244	9,234,612	4,502,837	6,138,998	3,399,680	4,116,680	1,250,754	3,458,351
Unemployed, total...............	7,623,416	554,527	2,031,795	1,554,505	713,197	753,594	485,674	670,349	264,216	595,559
Seeking work	5,093,810	383,419	1,602,801	975,870	416,052	453,280	281,226	399,953	155,173	426,036
Not in the labor force.............	48,313,425	3,079,153	10,158,019	10,066,100	5,193,571	6,012,560	3,762,423	4,725,253	1,521,320	3,795,026
EMPLOYMENT STATUS, WHITE MALES										
14 years old and over..............	45,823,031	3,225,818	10,393,258	10,090,501	5,098,715	4,830,414	2,854,723	3,914,924	1,529,876	3,884,802
Civilian labor force..............	35,897,061	2,504,830	8,189,095	7,974,594	4,001,393	3,766,100	2,263,771	3,071,826	1,180,931	2,944,521
Employed......................	30,661,001	2,095,990	6,777,494	6,850,085	3,462,837	3,372,603	1,973,170	2,661,411	968,516	2,498,895
Unemployed, total..............	5,236,060	408,840	1,411,601	1,124,509	538,556	393,497	290,601	410,415	212,415	445,626
Seeking work	3,438,061	272,181	1,100,107	702,420	306,972	222,407	153,747	237,866	125,966	316,395
Not in the labor force.............	9,655,465	708,023	2,170,268	2,093,757	1,087,327	991,524	580,182	808,058	339,520	876,806
EMPLOYMENT STATUS, WHITE FEMALES										
14 years old and over..............	45,605,134	3,385,147	10,556,563	9,932,021	5,011,443	4,859,703	2,861,883	3,855,114	1,404,209	3,739,051
Civilian labor force..............	11,001,823	1,048,315	2,968,406	2,350,380	1,048,176	1,160,942	500,989	716,432	273,207	934,976
Employed......................	9,563,583	915,050	2,531,992	2,083,882	925,646	1,029,106	424,634	604,420	233,277	815,576
Unemployed, total..............	1,438,240	133,265	436,414	266,498	122,530	131,836	76,355	112,012	39,930	119,400
Seeking work	1,042,551	103,809	376,445	191,934	79,252	75,601	43,475	60,132	22,929	89,274
Not in the labor force.............	34,603,311	2,336,832	7,588,157	7,581,641	3,963,267	3,698,761	2,360,894	3,138,682	1,131,002	2,804,075
EMPLOYMENT STATUS, NONWHITE MALES										
14 years old and over..............	4,730,717	41,770	483,479	423,676	154,234	1,594,723	933,488	864,516	60,750	174,081
Civilian labor force..............	3,769,179	31,728	376,318	323,962	115,704	1,287,768	764,220	690,415	45,641	133,423
Employed......................	3,088,904	22,594	247,576	206,053	76,851	1,130,079	678,349	582,454	35,347	109,601
Unemployed, total...............	680,275	9,134	128,742	117,909	38,853	157,689	85,871	107,961	10,294	23,822
Seeking work	406,180	5,245	84,495	54,743	20,467	95,351	55,352	69,458	5,294	15,775
Not in the labor force.............	954,043	9,807	106,556	99,664	37,825	303,645	169,138	173,641	4,034	39,733
EMPLOYMENT STATUS, NONWHITE FEMALES										
14 years old and over..............	4,944,042	41,072	530,258	431,219	155,913	1,696,412	1,008,583	913,228	51,955	115,402
Civilian labor force..............	1,843,436	16,581	237,220	140,181	50,761	677,782	356,374	308,356	15,191	40,990
Employed......................	1,574,595	13,293	182,182	94,592	37,503	607,210	323,527	268,395	13,614	34,279
Unemployed, total..............	268,841	3,288	55,038	45,589	13,258	70,572	32,847	39,961	1,577	6,711
Seeking work.................	207,018	2,184	42,054	26,773	9,361	59,921	28,652	32,497	984	4,592
Not in the labor force.............	3,100,606	24,491	293,038	291,038	105,152	1,018,630	652,209	604,872	36,764	74,412
MAJOR OCCUPATION GROUP - MALE.......	33,749,905	2,118,584	7,025,070	7,056,138	3,539,688	4,502,682	2,651,519	3,243,865	1,003,863	2,608,496
Professional and technical workers..	2,075,311	146,149	546,856	453,952	185,359	214,219	93,286	158,833	64,854	211,803
Farmers and farm managers..........	4,991,715	75,215	246,761	807,917	989,213	797,230	861,045	830,328	195,581	188,425
Managers, officials, and proprietors	3,231,463	221,137	767,332	673,831	347,878	344,744	163,966	294,216	104,239	314,120
Clerical and kindred workers........	2,012,974	142,619	594,244	463,744	175,425	211,890	83,848	133,649	46,366	161,189
Sales workers......................	2,260,879	166,500	571,429	478,309	225,657	241,960	109,883	184,146	59,757	223,238
Craftsmen and foremen..............	5,029,971	414,501	1,255,417	1,259,938	400,898	547,369	241,006	338,183	130,050	442,609
Operatives	6,031,952	531,991	1,546,513	1,461,500	401,809	790,342	356,279	370,007	157,168	416,383
Private household workers..........	113,908	5,683	21,860	11,781	4,713	26,859	13,436	19,767	1,173	8,636
Service workers, exc. household....	1,962,098	144,424	560,589	444,424	157,557	219,864	93,340	149,122	51,112	181,906
Farm laborers, unpaid family workers	941,841	8,486	36,666	127,764	173,365	203,430	196,886	154,867	24,646	15,731
Farm laborers, paid, incl. foremen..	1,836,244	54,831	140,140	250,699	242,734	370,825	199,034	314,422	91,897	171,722
Laborers, except farm and mine......	3,016,815	189,405	676,371	610,695	212,019	502,515	223,954	277,861	69,851	254,144
Occupation not reported............	244,734	17,923	60,892	51,644	23,061	31,435	15,556	18,464	7,169	18,590
MAJOR OCCUPATION - FEMALE.........	11,138,178	928,343	2,714,174	2,178,474	963,149	1,636,316	748,161	872,815	246,891	849,855
Professional and technical workers..	1,490,836	120,297	350,192	289,281	169,415	177,997	81,777	119,041	47,847	134,989
Farmers and farm managers..........	151,899	2,810	7,086	15,801	17,214	32,955	37,243	25,136	4,880	8,774
Managers, officials, and proprietors	388,687	22,667	80,162	74,391	40,887	42,649	20,296	37,796	15,717	54,122
Clerical and kindred workers.......	2,357,844	205,717	668,859	541,864	211,389	240,472	86,469	137,732	52,278	213,064
Sales workers.....................	811,262	58,282	193,923	190,545	79,748	85,875	39,625	65,236	21,182	76,866
Craftsmen and foremen.............	122,204	13,799	38,068	29,237	8,759	11,924	5,097	4,973	1,732	8,615
Operatives	2,020,364	281,577	644,172	382,946	108,686	317,181	105,644	65,148	20,272	94,738
Private household workers..........	1,969,215	115,915	390,894	304,234	159,775	421,372	200,669	234,808	34,714	106,834
Service workers, exc. household.....	1,225,880	82,686	267,824	271,667	131,521	141,018	61,999	105,822	39,524	123,819
Farm laborers, unpaid family workers	223,279	638	3,460	11,200	8,987	72,794	77,120	41,343	2,107	5,630
Farm laborers, paid, incl. foremen..	97,929	791	2,746	2,968	2,093	51,030	15,612	17,327	925	4,437
Laborers, except farm and mine......	105,794	9,134	24,569	30,118	7,622	16,648	6,074	5,378	1,050	5,201
Occupation not reported............	172,985	14,030	42,219	34,242	17,053	24,401	10,536	13,075	4,663	12,766
MAJOR INDUSTRY GROUP - BOTH SEXES...	44,888,083	3,046,927	9,739,244	9,234,612	4,502,837	6,138,998	3,399,680	4,116,680	1,250,754	3,458,351
Agriculture.......................	8,496,147	162,044	458,693	1,244,130	1,452,544	1,589,368	1,403,719	1,419,497	330,817	435,335
Mining............................	913,600	4,633	237,401	113,488	46,407	152,726	107,038	117,192	80,441	54,274
Construction......................	2,075,274	143,148	468,684	385,242	184,055	291,988	132,260	191,119	66,872	211,906
Manufacturing, total..............	10,567,842	1,169,014	3,000,410	2,919,210	555,827	1,277,271	494,469	417,845	105,924	627,872
Durable	5,116,483	484,854	1,297,605	1,896,051	205,021	426,335	223,427	181,322	50,926	350,942
Nondurable	5,267,788	659,363	1,631,562	969,891	342,327	840,602	266,534	233,369	54,073	270,067
Not specified	183,571	24,797	71,243	53,268	8,479	10,334	4,508	3,154	925	6,863
Transportation...................	3,107,568	179,268	783,911	672,304	322,813	348,737	165,469	247,786	106,320	280,960
Trade............................	7,545,918	518,954	1,777,775	1,621,645	789,712	820,581	382,178	672,633	220,179	742,261
Finance	1,472,397	110,757	481,682	286,664	130,400	133,037	51,919	95,616	29,085	153,237
Business services.................	890,904	57,889	218,617	190,695	94,964	85,789	42,680	77,340	29,152	93,778
Personal services.................	3,974,717	255,629	865,245	670,044	331,802	697,828	320,917	429,499	92,691	311,062
Entertainment services............	419,527	23,322	102,483	79,525	35,718	43,536	15,711	32,487	12,835	73,910
Professional services.............	3,289,881	262,143	806,329	661,108	357,139	369,613	172,874	260,584	105,650	294,441
Public administration.............	1,406,472	103,462	324,392	256,884	134,709	238,056	69,260	100,315	50,377	129,017
Industry not reported.............	727,836	56,664	213,622	133,673	66,747	90,468	41,186	54,767	20,411	50,298

TABLE 62

POPULATION: EMPLOYMENT STATUS OF THE URBAN POPULATION 14 YEARS OLD AND OVER AND MAJOR OCCUPATION GROUP AND MAJOR INDUSTRY GROUP OF THE EMPLOYED URBAN POPULATION OF THE UNITED STATES, BY GEOGRAPHIC DIVISIONS: 1940

Employment Status, Occupation and Industry	United States	New England	Middle Atlantic	East North Central	West North Central	South Atlantic	East South Central	West South Central	Mountain	Pacific
EMPLOYMENT STATUS, ALL GROUPS										
14 years old and over	59,690,675	5,133,875	17,091,172	13,964,768	4,814,560	5,479,781	2,476,470	4,059,374	1,372,054	5,298,621
Civilian labor force	32,471,598	2,817,022	9,409,746	7,529,761	2,527,631	3,146,320	1,380,007	2,194,147	691,891	2,775,073
Employed	27,450,496	2,368,956	7,756,171	6,417,115	2,137,366	2,779,177	1,177,725	1,861,449	119,325	395,102
Unemployed, total	5,021,102	448,066	1,653,575	1,112,646	390,265	367,143	202,282	332,698	119,325	395,102
Seeking work	3,602,867	304,819	1,332,637	736,285	252,909	251,519	139,445	221,940	70,997	292,316
Not in the labor force	27,077,006	2,307,954	7,654,345	6,422,675	2,279,622	2,307,508	1,092,600	1,851,956	677,630	2,482,716
EMPLOYMENT STATUS, WHITE MALES										
14 years old and over	26,566,325	2,435,040	7,913,674	6,471,703	2,179,166	1,959,909	843,800	1,601,690	661,291	2,500,052
Civilian labor force	20,989,479	1,904,223	6,315,877	5,197,114	1,692,190	1,539,167	669,635	1,263,429	502,423	1,905,421
Employed	17,761,634	1,581,754	5,210,399	4,447,326	1,420,935	1,391,262	582,546	1,090,207	409,730	1,627,475
Unemployed, total	3,227,845	322,469	1,105,478	749,788	271,255	147,905	87,089	173,222	92,693	277,946
Seeking work	2,312,429	210,378	886,066	503,162	173,961	102,111	58,264	117,612	55,251	205,624
Not in the labor force	5,438,303	522,121	1,571,425	1,262,282	480,216	395,869	170,307	325,096	156,583	554,404
EMPLOYMENT STATUS, WHITE FEMALES										
14 years old and over	28,106,206	2,628,007	8,260,578	6,718,854	2,406,587	2,134,335	939,760	1,732,931	684,028	2,601,126
Civilian labor force	8,371,670	871,535	2,528,832	1,901,060	705,239	693,199	276,438	472,887	174,179	748,301
Employed	7,300,719	756,789	2,150,881	1,688,051	626,064	623,965	241,996	406,832	151,161	654,980
Unemployed, total	1,070,951	114,746	377,951	213,009	79,175	69,234	34,442	66,055	23,018	93,321
Seeking work	814,755	88,090	327,723	157,281	54,672	43,511	21,684	37,818	13,607	70,369
Not in the labor force	19,734,536	1,756,472	5,731,746	4,817,794	1,701,348	1,441,136	663,322	1,260,044	509,849	1,852,825
EMPLOYMENT STATUS, NONWHITE MALES										
14 years old and over	2,352,471	35,340	431,017	377,120	110,158	630,632	311,504	329,352	14,029	113,319
Civilian labor force	1,875,908	27,019	342,051	298,088	85,489	511,359	252,949	261,336	10,190	87,427
Employed	1,374,562	19,176	224,756	191,403	57,250	412,477	196,111	196,333	7,456	69,600
Unemployed, total	501,346	7,843	117,295	106,685	28,239	98,882	56,838	65,003	2,734	17,827
Seeking work	306,729	4,421	78,408	50,193	15,841	62,396	38,385	43,315	1,589	12,181
Not in the labor force	473,035	8,118	88,257	79,007	24,122	118,193	58,550	67,910	3,591	25,287
EMPLOYMENT STATUS, NONWHITE FEMALES										
14 years old and over	2,665,673	35,488	485,903	397,091	118,649	754,905	381,406	395,401	12,706	84,124
Civilian labor force	1,234,541	14,245	222,986	133,499	44,713	402,595	180,985	196,495	5,099	33,924
Employed	1,013,581	11,237	170,135	90,335	33,117	351,473	157,072	168,077	4,219	27,916
Unemployed, total	220,960	3,008	52,851	43,164	11,596	51,122	23,913	28,418	880	6,008
Seeking work	168,954	1,930	40,440	25,649	8,455	43,501	21,112	23,195	550	4,142
Not in the labor force	1,431,132	21,243	262,917	263,592	73,936	352,310	200,421	198,906	7,607	50,200
MAJOR OCCUPATION GROUP - MALE	19,136,196	1,600,930	5,435,155	4,638,729	1,478,185	1,803,739	778,657	1,286,450	417,186	1,697,075
Professional and technical workers	1,579,596	116,560	462,602	366,247	121,985	140,305	52,867	106,982	41,191	170,857
Farmers and farm managers	70,556	9,216	6,340	9,083	7,825	6,799	4,472	10,238	5,513	11,070
Managers, officials, and proprietors	2,346,481	175,767	640,799	515,447	212,313	213,115	91,789	194,097	63,927	241,227
Clerical and kindred workers	1,685,082	121,836	531,164	402,392	138,907	157,758	58,305	105,711	33,700	135,309
Sales workers	1,851,944	141,764	507,428	408,404	173,525	170,284	74,003	142,559	44,758	317,914
Craftsmen and foremen	3,652,825	329,141	1,017,379	985,531	275,574	309,006	136,427	205,969	75,884	317,914
Operatives	4,144,770	430,256	1,196,508	1,116,937	273,580	374,504	167,280	224,402	75,986	285,317
Private household workers	76,240	3,210	15,620	16,937	3,330	16,162	8,252	13,661	692	6,732
Service workers, exc. household	1,624,792	124,432	503,748	346,371	120,476	163,867	68,243	115,386	33,969	148,300
Farm laborers, unpaid family workers	4,835	1,048	665	675	421	—	342	251	246	684
Farm laborers, paid, incl. foremen	127,315	10,966	11,184	12,976	10,124	17,896	6,564	20,222	31,348	147,596
Laborers, except farm and mine	1,823,264	125,343	494,244	433,284	129,460	220,086	104,243	137,660	31,348	147,596
Occupation not reported	148,496	13,391	47,474	32,801	10,665	13,615	5,961	9,150	3,550	11,889
MAJOR OCCUPATION - FEMALE	8,314,300	768,026	2,321,016	1,778,386	659,181	975,438	399,068	574,909	155,380	682,896
Professional and technical workers	1,067,376	97,650	291,220	222,821	94,974	108,705	43,124	72,944	28,105	107,833
Farmers and farm managers	3,557	398	370	444	326	378	262	481	150	748
Managers, officials, and proprietors	279,307	16,894	66,627	56,934	25,600	26,093	10,661	24,781	9,107	42,610
Clerical and kindred workers	2,047,547	179,277	610,204	482,023	174,073	194,010	66,436	114,962	40,411	186,151
Sales workers	664,836	51,936	172,808	163,162	59,431	62,071	26,680	48,648	15,202	64,898
Craftsmen and foremen	103,927	12,150	34,166	25,429	7,028	8,716	3,892	4,002	1,250	7,294
Operatives	1,613,458	242,763	556,642	332,528	90,447	179,481	69,450	52,672	11,480	77,995
Private household workers	1,365,595	80,904	308,635	221,981	96,016	266,707	125,021	164,087	20,314	81,930
Service workers, exc. household	974,015	67,831	227,716	225,889	96,179	105,581	44,965	80,915	25,954	98,985
Farm laborers, unpaid family workers	2,279	129	231	292	188	263	126	204	42	804
Farm laborers, paid, incl. foremen	8,395	202	421	421	581	251	4,034	1,129	159	1,197
Laborers, except farm and mine	74,788	7,032	18,668	23,623	6,036	8,413	3,505	3,326	617	3,568
Occupation not reported	109,220	10,860	33,308	22,679	8,632	10,986	4,525	6,758	2,589	8,883
MAJOR INDUSTRY GROUP - BOTH SEXES	27,450,496	2,368,956	7,756,171	6,417,115	2,137,366	2,779,177	1,177,725	1,861,449	572,566	2,379,971
Agriculture	311,664	32,382	30,480	38,128	26,416	42,436	16,964	42,861	15,503	66,494
Mining	277,507	1,758	94,133	41,796	18,736	12,704	15,240	49,384	22,998	20,568
Construction	1,344,202	103,238	349,849	265,080	109,538	155,746	66,999	116,005	34,949	142,798
Manufacturing, total	8,053,686	957,361	2,516,942	2,418,674	448,995	659,634	283,911	258,719	63,569	445,881
Transportation	2,400,433	247,503	665,693	540,657	230,259	240,181	107,899	179,340	69,683	219,218
Trade	5,903,352	441,706	1,553,606	1,318,470	548,074	562,836	248,418	483,262	149,486	597,494
Finance	1,282,240	94,812	440,317	254,259	106,031	106,674	39,876	80,384	23,716	136,171
Business services	638,194	44,113	179,592	143,109	57,107	51,392	23,169	50,018	17,793	71,901
Personal services	2,968,055	191,078	716,539	531,412	225,218	468,850	211,847	315,329	59,875	247,907
Entertainment services	339,057	19,630	90,741	65,695	24,665	30,838	10,986	23,994	8,334	64,124
Professional services	2,360,934	208,054	659,941	502,641	215,413	227,971	92,602	162,962	63,037	226,313
Public administration	1,088,841	85,241	280,320	208,333	91,793	176,122	41,538	69,696	32,200	103,578
Industry not reported	482,331	42,080	178,018	88,861	35,121	43,793	17,996	29,495	11,443	35,524

APPENDIX

TABLE 63

POPULATION: EMPLOYMENT STATUS OF THE RURAL-NONFARM POPULATION 14 YEARS OLD AND OVER AND MAJOR OCCUPATION GROUP AND MAJOR INDUSTRY GROUP OF THE EMPLOYED RURAL-NONFARM POPULATION OF THE UNITED STATES, BY GEOGRAPHIC DIVISIONS: 1940

Employment Status, Occupation and Industry	United States	New England	Middle Atlantic	East North Central	West North Central	South Atlantic	East South Central	West South Central	Mountain	Pacific
EMPLOYMENT STATUS, ALL GROUPS										
14 years old and over..............	20,055,748	1,148,344	3,533,375	3,469,351	2,184,611	3,460,161	1,651,768	2,036,510	906,753	1,664,878
Civilian labor force...............	9,560,248	575,063	1,693,873	1,581,685	986,904	1,743,394	790,302	954,478	437,870	796,679
Employed..................	7,828,250	490,666	1,384,144	1,282,175	779,871	1,507,402	637,265	762,517	335,779	648,431
Unemployed, total..............	1,731,998	84,397	309,729	299,510	207,033	235,992	153,037	191,961	102,091	148,248
Seeking work..............	1,029,607	61,367	221,108	162,318	104,184	134,130	83,141	107,138	58,018	98,203
Not in the labor force..........	10,366,280	569,499	1,830,687	1,877,503	1,192,801	1,671,155	855,607	1,062,022	461,188	845,818
EMPLOYMENT STATUS, WHITE MALES										
14 years old and over..............	9,405,804	568,343	1,754,868	1,745,278	1,064,525	1,386,864	664,134	873,439	465,319	883,034
Civilian labor force...............	6,931,890	426,284	1,300,261	1,267,037	759,647	1,037,723	502,250	646,282	351,189	641,217
Employed..................	5,602,381	358,134	1,051,381	1,015,096	588,122	893,304	397,028	516,904	265,654	516,758
Unemployed, total..............	1,329,509	68,150	248,880	251,941	171,525	144,419	105,222	129,378	85,535	124,459
Seeking work..............	779,354	47,901	174,386	135,098	86,175	78,729	54,711	71,210	49,435	81,709
Not in the labor force..........	2,344,377	138,300	445,724	468,027	300,044	303,399	155,871	206,826	106,691	219,495
EMPLOYMENT STATUS, WHITE FEMALES										
14 years old and over..............	9,041,295	570,358	1,696,140	1,661,863	1,077,627	1,354,026	673,964	852,611	407,928	746,778
Civilian labor force...............	1,764,927	143,180	352,131	290,380	208,758	301,705	118,168	143,089	69,553	137,963
Employed..................	1,517,579	128,131	303,822	253,991	181,417	262,758	95,829	115,415	57,678	118,538
Unemployed, total..............	247,348	15,049	48,309	36,389	27,341	38,947	22,339	27,674	11,875	19,425
Seeking work..............	154,227	12,676	39,674	22,574	14,372	20,605	11,342	12,514	6,401	14,069
Not in the labor force..........	7,276,368	427,178	1,344,009	1,371,483	868,869	1,052,321	555,796	709,522	338,375	608,815
EMPLOYMENT STATUS, NONWHITE MALES										
14 years old and over..............	811,513	5,013	43,401	35,942	22,927	360,274	152,046	150,872	18,778	22,260
Civilian labor force...............	596,436	3,574	28,632	18,788	14,181	273,821	113,982	114,822	13,920	14,716
Employed..................	472,602	2,583	18,123	9,712	7,168	233,471	93,922	87,063	9,677	10,883
Unemployed, total..............	123,834	991	10,509	9,076	7,013	40,350	20,060	27,759	4,243	3,833
Seeking work..............	71,405	607	5,551	3,690	3,014	24,285	12,483	17,739	1,935	2,101
Not in the labor force..........	215,394	1,419	14,837	17,205	8,674	86,583	38,218	36,371	4,602	7,485
EMPLOYMENT STATUS, NONWHITE FEMALES										
14 years old and over..............	797,136	4,627	38,966	26,268	19,532	358,997	161,624	159,588	14,728	12,806
Civilian labor force...............	266,995	2,025	12,849	5,480	4,318	130,145	55,902	50,285	3,208	2,783
Employed..................	235,688	1,818	10,818	3,376	3,164	117,869	50,486	43,135	2,770	2,252
Unemployed, total..............	31,307	207	2,031	2,104	1,154	12,276	5,416	7,150	438	531
Seeking work..............	24,621	183	1,497	956	623	10,511	4,605	5,675	247	324
Not in the labor force..........	530,141	2,602	26,117	20,788	15,214	228,852	105,722	109,303	11,520	10,023
MAJOR OCCUPATION GROUP - MALE........	6,074,983	360,717	1,069,504	1,024,808	595,290	1,126,775	490,950	603,967	275,331	527,641
Professional and technical workers...	415,296	26,687	75,903	72,161	53,973	60,005	28,968	41,031	20,470	36,098
Farmers and farm managers....	126,276	2,922	9,717	17,002	17,508	21,621	16,282	21,691	12,045	7,488
Managers, officials, and proprietors.	750,128	41,552	114,544	135,043	120,740	105,170	52,854	81,579	35,589	63,057
Clerical and kindred workers.........	271,892	18,363	57,087	49,210	30,320	43,589	18,425	21,954	10,759	22,185
Sales workers......................	337,052	22,044	58,175	56,830	44,300	55,921	26,060	31,817	12,817	29,088
Draftsmen and foremen..............	1,092,243	72,962	205,136	209,720	100,301	179,747	71,939	101,288	45,863	105,287
Operatives........................	1,485,016	87,065	300,322	256,068	97,404	322,623	134,136	109,589	69,811	107,998
Private household workers...........	27,932	1,998	4,932	2,222	962	7,801	3,702	4,618	341	1,356
Service workers, exc. household.....	288,570	17,701	51,615	48,991	32,747	45,890	19,669	27,765	14,979	29,213
Farm laborers, unpaid family workers.	11,854	161	740	1,319	1,255	2,484	2,108	2,236	1,187	364
Farm laborers, paid, incl. foremen..	345,176	14,558	34,392	39,597	27,777	80,587	36,664	53,875	18,867	38,859
Laborers, except farm and mine.....	866,685	51,169	147,096	126,103	61,295	190,794	75,613	101,859	30,434	82,323
Occupation not reported............	56,863	3,535	9,845	10,542	6,708	10,543	4,530	4,666	2,169	4,325
MAJOR OCCUPATION GROUP - FEMALE........	1,753,267	129,949	314,640	257,367	184,581	380,627	146,315	158,550	60,448	120,790
Professional and technical workers...	286,216	18,329	47,318	43,789	43,048	45,690	21,687	30,569	14,568	21,218
Farmers and farm managers....	4,008	127	311	391	355	985	668	635	180	356
Managers, officials, and proprietors.	93,229	4,996	12,268	15,344	13,769	13,071	6,985	10,789	5,773	10,234
Clerical and kindred workers.........	247,335	22,824	51,405	43,853	29,601	36,749	14,625	17,476	9,324	21,478
Sales workers......................	117,538	5,605	18,626	21,372	16,952	17,805	9,303	12,745	4,977	10,153
Craftsmen and foremen..............	14,651	1,446	3,339	2,857	1,452	2,414	849	779	390	1,125
Operatives........................	314,964	33,785	73,342	36,363	13,655	107,329	23,622	9,513	3,644	13,711
Private household workers...........	391,752	25,955	61,617	46,808	30,700	104,816	48,793	48,088	8,659	16,316
Service workers, exc. household.....	204,571	12,472	34,191	35,802	29,574	27,731	12,772	20,074	11,079	20,876
Farm laborers, unpaid family workers.	2,485	19	138	148	106	803	531	464	62	214
Farm laborers, paid, incl. foremen..	19,135	237	974	492	233	10,288	2,441	2,961	207	1,302
Laborers, except farm and mine......	21,895	1,702	4,499	4,202	1,095	5,860	1,552	1,581	336	1,248
Occupation not reported............	35,488	2,452	6,612	6,126	4,041	7,086	2,487	2,876	1,249	2,559
MAJOR INDUSTRY GROUP - BOTH SEXES....	7,828,250	490,666	1,384,144	1,282,175	779,871	1,507,402	637,265	762,517	335,779	648,431
Agriculture........................	618,463	25,067	54,372	68,114	54,327	153,900	65,888	99,462	37,062	60,271
Mining............................	524,660	2,358	126,322	52,970	20,029	115,562	69,388	54,546	37,062	60,271
Construction......................	539,133	32,232	97,228	86,153	55,617	93,027	40,264	52,586	25,011	57,015
Manufacturing, total..............	1,939,054	182,390	410,196	371,927	81,235	456,448	139,772	118,961	30,567	147,558
Transportation....................	575,170	27,392	103,748	104,043	76,224	84,093	41,057	54,414	31,551	52,648
Trade.............................	1,361,871	67,585	199,848	248,974	209,420	201,344	98,169	151,026	61,302	124,203
Finance...........................	162,319	14,270	37,845	26,067	20,969	22,216	9,492	12,419	4,505	14,536
Business services.................	204,137	11,792	33,755	37,948	31,992	25,872	13,648	20,816	9,728	18,586
Personal services.................	727,954	51,048	119,441	92,901	67,966	164,081	74,821	83,772	24,618	49,306
Entertainment services............	69,625	3,237	10,680	11,422	9,688	10,893	3,931	7,048	3,993	8,733
Professional services.............	687,244	46,070	123,867	115,661	97,426	99,932	49,304	68,393	32,839	53,752
Public administration	254,522	15,154	38,226	37,869	35,190	49,506	18,602	23,515	14,861	21,599
Industry not reported.............	164,098	12,071	28,616	28,126	19,788	30,528	12,929	15,559	6,185	10,296

TABLE 64

POPULATION: EMPLOYMENT STATUS OF THE RURAL-FARM POPULATION 14 YEARS OLD AND OVER AND MAJOR OCCUPATION GROUP AND MAJOR INDUSTRY GROUP OF THE EMPLOYED RURAL-FARM POPULATION OF THE UNITED STATES, BY GEOGRAPHIC DIVISIONS: 1940

Employment Status, Occupation and Industry	United States	New England	Middle Atlantic	East North Central	West North Central	South Atlantic	East South Central	West South Central	Mountain	Pacific
EMPLOYMENT STATUS, ALL GROUPS										
14 years old and over	21,356,501	411,591	1,339,011	3,443,298	3,421,134	4,041,310	3,530,439	3,451,898	767,983	949,837
Civilian labor force	10,479,653	209,369	667,420	1,677,671	1,701,499	2,002,878	1,715,045	1,638,404	385,209	429,949
Employed	9,609,337	187,305	598,929	1,535,322	1,585,600	1,852,419	1,584,690	1,492,714	342,409	429,949
Unemployed, total	870,316	22,064	68,491	142,349	115,899	150,459	130,355	145,690	42,800	52,209
Seeking work	461,336	17,233	49,056	77,267	58,999	67,631	58,640	70,875	26,158	35,517
Not in the labor force	10,870,139	201,700	672,987	1,765,922	1,721,148	2,033,897	1,814,216	1,811,275	382,502	466,492
EMPLOYMENT STATUS, WHITE MALES										
14 years old and over	9,850,902	222,435	724,716	1,873,520	1,855,024	1,483,641	1,346,789	1,439,795	403,266	501,716
Civilian labor force	7,975,692	174,323	572,957	1,510,443	1,549,556	1,189,210	1,091,886	1,162,115	327,319	397,883
Employed	7,296,986	156,102	515,714	1,387,663	1,453,780	1,088,037	993,596	1,054,300	293,132	354,662
Unemployed, total	678,706	18,221	57,243	122,780	95,776	101,173	98,290	107,815	34,187	43,221
Seeking work	346,278	13,902	39,655	64,160	46,836	41,567	40,772	49,044	21,280	29,062
Not in the labor force	1,872,785	47,602	153,119	363,448	307,067	292,256	254,004	276,136	76,246	102,907
EMPLOYMENT STATUS, WHITE FEMALES										
14 years old and over	8,457,633	186,782	599,845	1,551,304	1,527,229	1,371,342	1,248,159	1,269,572	312,253	391,147
Civilian labor force	865,226	33,600	87,443	158,940	134,179	166,038	106,383	100,456	29,475	48,712
Employed	745,285	30,130	77,289	141,840	118,165	142,383	86,809	82,173	24,438	42,058
Unemployed, total	119,941	3,470	10,154	17,100	16,014	23,655	19,574	18,283	5,037	6,654
Seeking work	73,569	3,043	8,748	12,079	10,208	11,485	10,449	9,800	2,921	4,836
Not in the labor force	7,592,407	153,182	512,402	1,392,364	1,393,050	1,205,304	1,141,776	1,169,116	282,778	342,435
EMPLOYMENT STATUS, NONWHITE MALES										
14 years old and over	1,566,733	1,417	9,061	10,614	21,149	°603,817	469,938	384,292	27,943	38,502
Civilian labor force	1,296,835	1,135	5,635	7,086	16,034	502,588	397,289	314,257	21,531	31,280
Employed	1,241,740	835	4,697	4,938	12,433	484,131	388,316	299,058	18,214	29,118
Unemployed, total	55,095	300	938	2,148	3,601	18,457	8,973	15,199	3,317	2,162
Seeking work	28,046	217	536	860	1,612	8,670	4,484	8,404	1,770	1,493
Not in the labor force	265,614	270	3,462	3,452	5,029	98,869	72,370	69,360	5,841	6,961
EMPLOYMENT STATUS, NONWHITE FEMALES										
14 years old and over	1,481,233	957	5,389	7,860	17,732	582,510	465,553	358,239	24,521	18,472
Civilian labor force	341,900	311	1,385	1,202	1,730	145,042	119,487	61,576	6,884	4,283
Employed	325,326	238	1,229	881	1,222	137,868	115,969	57,183	6,625	4,111
Unemployed, total	16,574	73	156	321	508	7,174	3,518	4,393	259	172
Seeking work	13,443	71	117	168	303	5,909	2,935	3,627	187	126
Not in the labor force	1,139,333	646	4,004	6,658	16,002	437,468	346,066	296,663	17,637	14,189
MAJOR OCCUPATION GROUP - MALE	8,538,726	156,937	520,411	1,392,601	1,466,213	1,572,168	1,381,912	1,353,358	311,346	383,780
Professional and technical workers	80,419	2,880	8,185	15,441	9,485	13,993	11,498	10,867	3,233	4,837
Farmers and farm managers	4,794,883	63,077	230,704	781,832	963,880	768,810	840,291	798,399	178,023	169,867
Managers, officials, and proprietors	134,854	5,750	11,648	23,243	14,868	26,648	19,502	18,643	4,743	9,809
Clerical and kindred workers	56,000	2,405	5,968	12,140	6,200	10,548	7,130	5,997	1,908	3,704
Sales workers	71,883	2,662	5,778	13,095	7,803	15,772	9,854	9,804	2,172	4,943
Craftsmen and foremen	284,903	12,315	32,711	64,565	25,048	58,778	32,725	31,000	8,331	19,430
Operatives	402,166	14,902	50,472	88,758	30,757	92,583	54,462	35,818	11,301	23,113
Private household workers	9,736	476	1,308	977	421	2,896	1,481	1,488	140	549
Service workers, exc. household	48,736	2,022	5,115	9,043	4,337	10,166	5,468	6,006	2,174	4,405
Farm laborers, unpaid family workers	925,152	7,277	35,261	125,770	171,689	200,604	194,527	152,128	23,213	14,683
Farm laborers, paid, incl. foremen	1,363,753	29,282	94,603	198,134	204,773	272,495	155,837	240,225	66,584	101,820
Laborers, except farm and mine	326,866	12,892	35,085	51,302	21,264	91,598	44,072	38,335	8,074	24,244
Occupation not reported	39,375	997	3,573	8,301	5,688	7,277	5,065	4,648	1,450	2,376
MAJOR OCCUPATION - FEMALE	1,070,611	30,368	78,518	142,721	119,387	280,251	202,778	139,356	31,063	46,169
Professional and technical workers	137,244	4,283	11,533	22,623	31,471	23,659	17,012	15,565	5,193	5,905
Farmers and farm managers	144,334	2,285	6,405	14,966	16,533	31,592	36,313	24,020	4,550	7,670
Managers, officials, and proprietors	16,151	776	1,268	2,115	1,527	3,479	2,612	2,225	839	1,280
Clerical and kindred workers	62,962	3,636	7,292	15,973	7,705	9,700	5,381	5,278	2,538	5,459
Sales workers	28,888	743	2,495	5,983	3,374	5,992	3,635	3,841	1,006	1,819
Craftsmen and foremen	3,626	211	587	950	277	775	348	190	90	198
Operatives	91,942	5,006	14,137	14,021	4,529	30,516	12,613	2,965	5,140	3,015
Private household workers	211,868	9,056	20,651	35,521	33,069	49,758	26,832	22,635	5,737	8,609
Service workers, exc. household	47,294	2,381	5,902	9,984	5,763	7,715	4,270	4,835	2,491	3,953
Farm laborers, unpaid family workers	218,515	490	3,091	10,760	8,693	71,728	76,163	40,675	2,003	4,612
Farm laborers, paid, incl. foremen	70,399	350	1,346	1,892	1,610	36,709	12,763	13,244	559	384
Laborers, except farm and mine	9,111	399	1,402	2,482	492	2,369	1,018	395	96	1,339
Occupation not reported	28,277	752	2,409	5,451	4,344	6,259	3,818	3,488	821	1,926
MAJOR INDUSTRY GROUP - BOTH SEXES	9,609,337	187,305	598,929	1,535,322	1,585,600	1,852,419	1,584,690	1,492,714	342,409	429,949
Agriculture	7,566,020	104,568	373,972	1,137,616	1,371,738	1,393,447	1,320,951	1,276,980	278,324	308,424
Mining	111,433	517	16,946	18,791	7,642	21,460	22,130	22,513	6,910	12,116
Construction	191,939	7,695	21,673	34,015	18,895	43,165	24,957	39,890	11,638	34,374
Manufacturing, total	575,102	29,433	73,856	129,099	25,622	160,666	70,524	13,234	3,976	13,737
Transportation	131,965	4,400	14,703	27,650	16,291	24,339	16,412	13,987	5,061	9,113
Trade	280,695	9,517	23,446	53,839	32,239	56,740	35,844	38,835	9,462	20,773
Finance	27,838	1,680	3,501	6,316	3,409	4,158	2,561	2,819	864	2,530
Business services	48,573	1,965	5,162	9,621	5,885	8,587	5,917	6,539	1,634	3,263
Personal services	278,708	13,481	29,100	45,813	38,678	64,857	34,270	30,449	8,211	13,849
Entertainment services	10,845	458	1,090	2,413	1,350	1,787	788	1,437	453	1,069
Professional services	241,703	7,971	22,419	42,823	44,334	41,730	31,026	29,262	9,783	12,355
Public administration	63,109	3,049	5,735	10,637	7,767	12,500	9,134	7,123	3,322	3,842
Industry not reported	81,407	2,562	7,326	16,689	11,750	15,983	10,176	9,646	2,771	4,504

APPENDIX

TABLE 65

POPULATION: AGE, COLOR, AND SEX OF THE URBAN (OLD DEFINITION) POPULATION OF THE UNITED STATES, BY GEOGRAPHIC DIVISIONS: 1950

Age, Sex, and Color	United States	New England	Middle Atlantic	East North Central	West North Central	South Atlantic	East South Central	West South Central	Mountain	Pacific
					Geographic division					
AGE, ALL SEX-COLOR GROUPS										
All ages..........	88,927,464	6,922,733	22,643,772	19,982,717	7,018,000	8,997,310	4,079,879	7,700,860	2,476,628	9,105,565
Under 5 years......	8,801,128	659,196	2,029,470	1,988,528	706,794	917,861	447,538	881,069	283,431	887,241
5-9 years.........	6,797,718	529,074	1,633,912	1,521,035	527,200	704,172	337,102	668,217	215,387	661,619
10-14 years.......	5,530,262	427,362	1,352,030	1,245,901	433,992	575,997	280,537	531,055	177,017	506,371
15-19 years.......	5,697,347	453,722	1,399,476	1,234,645	468,952	614,754	296,640	516,759	172,764	509,585
20-24 years.......	7,150,601	530,545	1,725,128	1,582,695	584,448	800,799	370,585	681,794	205,571	669,036
25-29 years.......	7,699,677	565,283	1,900,410	1,725,296	583,047	839,948	369,220	705,758	212,823	797,892
30-34 years.......	7,135,866	539,621	1,832,559	1,608,644	516,658	757,619	319,389	609,860	193,415	758,101
35-39 years.......	6,940,191	512,885	1,826,648	1,538,466	497,179	733,970	314,413	594,090	181,350	741,190
40-44 years.......	6,362,934	471,603	1,705,600	1,412,447	471,131	649,449	283,508	537,268	162,878	669,050
45-49 years.......	5,727,775	432,648	1,551,177	1,294,906	434,525	561,625	246,292	467,072	139,589	599,941
50-54 years.......	5,282,156	423,579	1,482,671	1,203,502	411,528	488,954	211,134	389,221	125,499	546,068
55-59 years.......	4,579,191	385,815	1,268,002	1,079,884	375,055	393,790	170,729	315,901	111,493	478,522
60-64 years.......	3,804,407	323,490	1,045,148	890,727	322,989	316,565	137,604	251,855	96,446	419,583
65-69 years.......	3,064,066	262,166	806,122	688,557	265,598	271,606	124,327	216,720	79,887	349,083
70-74 years.......	2,660,484	185,992	530,071	456,782	187,300	179,421	81,065	142,767	55,670	241,416
75 years and older.......	2,293,661	219,752	555,348	510,652	231,604	190,780	89,796	161,454	63,408	270,867
WHITE MALE										
All ages..........	38,697,282	3,276,276	10,141,953	8,940,895	3,192,902	3,220,357	1,425,657	3,149,882	1,189,930	4,159,430
Under 5 years......	3,953,746	329,192	943,247	917,608	340,033	332,567	160,456	373,290	140,129	417,224
5-9 years.........	3,047,941	263,919	760,867	700,050	251,327	251,588	119,896	281,261	106,763	312,270
10-14 years.......	2,447,964	211,455	624,219	567,891	204,718	199,709	97,028	219,182	86,774	236,988
15-19 years.......	2,415,572	216,776	622,958	536,822	202,509	210,170	97,768	214,595	78,917	235,057
20-24 years.......	3,029,033	250,662	744,011	684,552	259,541	290,670	128,958	272,963	95,993	301,683
25-29 years.......	3,313,193	268,322	822,569	755,395	271,851	305,213	135,996	295,491	102,554	355,802
30-34 years.......	3,073,391	255,212	793,488	704,440	236,218	274,841	116,570	256,586	92,842	343,194
35-39 years.......	2,958,717	241,121	792,684	673,204	223,885	256,767	108,589	241,451	86,224	334,792
40-44 years.......	2,758,124	221,100	759,461	628,016	212,203	231,323	98,713	221,002	78,991	307,315
45-49 years.......	2,498,623	202,606	698,871	581,720	193,674	200,309	84,699	189,285	67,479	279,980
50-54 years.......	2,336,957	197,455	678,207	549,896	185,365	178,467	72,851	160,076	60,512	254,128
55-59 years.......	2,070,705	182,571	626,197	506,197	170,892	149,313	61,232	129,413	54,173	221,812
60-64 years.......	1,727,814	152,960	494,529	422,079	147,678	119,045	49,237	102,274	46,715	193,297
65-69 years.......	1,307,846	116,982	361,240	308,692	116,641	93,108	39,327	79,574	37,771	154,511
70-74 years.......	861,835	79,131	229,701	198,844	81,090	63,177	26,829	54,244	25,918	102,901
75 years and older.......	895,821	86,812	220,799	205,489	95,277	64,090	27,508	59,195	28,175	108,476
WHITE FEMALE										
All ages..........	40,970,582	3,509,761	10,738,930	9,336,616	3,444,383	3,472,664	1,555,467	3,310,176	1,224,925	4,377,660
Under 5 years......	3,804,253	314,781	903,033	882,339	327,316	319,639	156,615	360,151	136,307	404,072
5-9 years.........	2,963,211	254,012	734,892	681,215	244,964	245,992	117,596	274,300	103,672	306,568
10-14 years.......	2,404,302	205,688	605,152	558,290	201,328	198,393	114,141	217,229	85,968	234,935
15-19 years.......	2,636,679	227,554	660,944	588,642	240,874	232,872	114,141	241,069	89,432	241,151
20-24 years.......	3,524,718	267,271	827,206	748,981	294,905	310,332	150,015	305,054	103,862	317,092
25-29 years.......	3,498,981	282,669	893,189	793,916	278,715	321,545	143,601	305,208	104,215	375,923
30-34 years.......	3,272,904	272,589	875,110	749,047	251,410	289,355	122,863	260,532	95,144	356,854
35-39 years.......	3,182,107	261,252	871,970	714,706	242,993	276,981	117,686	254,756	90,169	351,594
40-44 years.......	2,925,749	242,045	807,482	658,207	230,977	252,557	107,879	228,726	79,796	318,080
45-49 years.......	2,628,235	222,209	731,200	598,960	214,991	218,263	92,459	197,497	68,516	284,140
50-54 years.......	2,463,377	219,153	707,517	562,025	203,769	196,994	80,503	165,940	61,958	265,518
55-59 years.......	2,170,726	197,766	609,499	509,128	186,540	167,121	68,295	138,905	54,906	238,566
60-64 years.......	1,829,632	166,246	505,280	424,216	161,859	140,345	57,629	114,409	47,788	211,860
65-69 years.......	1,522,671	141,431	409,440	342,931	136,012	121,002	50,821	97,782	40,367	182,885
70-74 years.......	1,073,587	104,466	280,685	238,368	98,958	85,759	35,998	68,657	28,674	132,022
75 years and older.......	1,269,450	130,629	316,331	285,645	128,772	95,514	42,047	79,961	34,151	156,400
NONWHITE MALE										
All ages..........	4,419,988	68,712	833,792	833,704	183,937	1,080,968	509,156	583,254	31,918	294,547
Under 5 years......	522,436	7,720	91,930	94,303	19,714	132,859	65,220	73,918	3,460	33,312
5-9 years.........	389,779	5,610	68,337	69,438	15,478	102,260	49,130	55,660	2,453	21,413
10-14 years.......	335,246	5,267	60,805	59,279	14,122	87,123	42,061	46,614	2,192	17,783
15-19 years.......	298,385	4,675	53,368	50,949	11,833	78,806	38,642	41,588	2,179	16,345
20-24 years.......	349,646	6,229	65,557	67,350	13,259	87,041	39,093	44,687	2,903	23,527
25-29 years.......	408,488	7,255	83,206	82,786	15,122	96,807	39,915	47,661	3,096	32,640
30-34 years.......	362,186	5,835	73,133	73,203	13,332	88,116	35,242	41,562	2,750	29,013
35-39 years.......	370,443	5,164	73,593	72,588	14,082	91,462	38,659	43,794	2,524	28,597
40-44 years.......	327,773	4,197	66,664	62,976	13,466	77,891	35,084	40,490	2,170	24,835
45-49 years.......	294,015	3,970	59,715	58,699	12,577	66,870	31,770	37,835	1,901	20,678
50-54 years.......	243,163	3,706	49,761	48,529	11,312	55,086	27,242	30,962	1,588	14,977
55-59 years.......	171,997	2,889	32,292	34,519	9,173	37,724	20,190	24,046	1,331	9,833
60-64 years.......	123,393	2,187	22,346	23,336	7,015	27,064	14,788	17,329	1,153	8,175
65-69 years.......	107,392	1,822	16,466	17,833	6,252	24,978	15,011	17,563	1,004	6,463
70-74 years.......	58,822	1,171	9,116	9,244	3,603	13,652	8,232	9,353	650	3,801
75 years and older.......	56,824	1,015	7,503	8,672	3,597	13,229	8,897	10,192	564	3,155
NONWHITE FEMALE										
All ages..........	4,839,612	67,984	929,097	871,502	196,778	1,223,321	589,599	657,548	29,855	273,928
Under 5 years......	520,693	7,503	91,260	94,278	19,731	132,796	65,247	73,710	3,535	32,633
5-9 years.........	396,787	5,533	69,816	70,332	15,431	104,332	50,480	56,996	2,499	21,368
10-14 years.......	342,750	4,952	61,854	60,441	13,824	90,772	44,129	48,030	2,083	16,665
15-19 years.......	346,711	4,717	62,206	58,282	13,736	92,906	46,089	49,507	2,236	17,032
20-24 years.......	447,204	6,383	88,354	81,812	16,743	112,756	52,519	59,090	2,813	26,734
25-29 years.......	479,015	7,037	101,446	93,199	17,359	116,383	49,708	57,398	2,958	33,527
30-34 years.......	427,385	5,985	90,828	81,954	15,698	105,307	44,714	51,180	2,679	29,040
35-39 years.......	428,924	5,348	88,401	77,968	16,219	108,760	49,499	54,089	2,433	26,207
40-44 years.......	351,288	4,261	71,993	63,248	14,485	87,678	41,832	47,050	1,921	18,820
45-49 years.......	306,902	3,863	61,391	55,527	13,283	76,183	37,364	42,455	1,693	15,143
50-54 years.......	238,699	3,265	47,186	43,052	11,082	58,407	30,538	32,243	1,441	11,445
55-59 years.......	165,763	2,589	31,109	30,040	8,450	39,632	21,012	23,537	1,083	8,311
60-64 years.......	123,568	2,097	22,993	21,096	6,437	30,111	15,950	17,843	790	6,251
65-69 years.......	126,157	1,931	18,976	19,101	6,693	32,518	19,168	21,801	745	5,224
70-74 years.......	66,240	1,224	10,569	10,326	3,649	16,833	10,006	10,513	428	2,692
75 years and older.......	71,566	1,296	10,715	10,846	3,958	17,947	11,344	12,106	518	2,836

TABLE 66

POPULATION: AGE, COLOR, AND SEX OF THE RURAL-NONFARM (OLD DEFINITION) POPULATION OF THE UNITED STATES, BY GEOGRAPHIC DIVISIONS: 1950

Age, Sex, and Color	United States	New England	Middle Atlantic	East North Central	West North Central	South Atlantic	East South Central	West South Central	Mountain	Pacific
AGE, ALL SEX-COLOR GROUPS										
All ages	38,693,358	2,012,474	6,122,780	6,705,228	3,313,075	7,546,338	3,347,120	3,620,000	1,735,851	4,290,492
Under 5 years	4,740,613	220,181	678,677	815,353	363,126	1,000,195	446,324	454,167	231,940	530,650
5-9 years	3,837,500	181,337	554,387	654,017	292,393	802,583	362,876	385,295	190,815	413,797
10-14 years	3,112,143	142,589	447,511	529,895	248,618	647,289	300,926	322,672	157,804	314,839
15-19 years	2,805,136	135,482	405,938	448,059	222,322	597,525	272,228	298,747	134,336	290,499
20-24 years	2,917,010	141,693	427,716	475,446	213,000	649,349	276,673	278,898	130,379	323,856
25-29 years	3,185,892	154,004	497,116	545,748	234,770	683,773	280,017	276,096	139,250	375,118
30-34 years	2,993,164	155,302	496,570	516,183	223,066	609,396	245,516	250,438	132,705	363,988
35-39 years	2,803,945	147,215	466,869	478,274	214,524	551,640	232,014	249,160	124,401	339,848
40-44 years	2,432,073	132,962	420,180	417,963	198,137	454,691	197,434	222,179	105,056	283,471
45-49 years	2,048,553	114,955	358,842	357,830	179,319	365,195	161,660	191,446	85,737	233,569
50-54 years	1,792,741	107,949	325,167	317,710	172,426	303,673	134,352	157,750	72,799	200,915
55-59 years	1,571,875	97,833	285,220	288,706	168,374	246,335	111,655	136,065	63,983	173,704
60-64 years	1,354,794	83,826	242,792	254,927	158,975	200,036	93,001	114,376	55,838	151,023
65-69 years	1,194,713	71,034	198,667	221,850	148,166	181,221	93,318	112,333	45,423	122,701
70-74 years	867,511	55,177	143,423	169,640	119,631	121,865	64,946	79,334	30,655	82,840
75 years and older	1,035,695	70,935	173,705	213,627	156,228	131,572	74,180	91,044	34,730	89,674
WHITE MALE										
All ages	18,028,680	998,402	2,999,728	3,332,258	1,622,033	3,107,533	1,401,666	1,548,627	848,722	2,169,711
Under 5 years	2,203,300	112,034	339,878	410,344	181,545	407,703	189,163	190,340	109,993	262,300
5-9 years	1,783,642	92,839	278,088	328,945	145,224	325,373	154,382	162,504	90,244	206,043
10-14 years	1,436,734	72,587	224,281	266,561	122,870	256,914	126,700	135,496	74,644	156,681
15-19 years	1,312,500	69,069	199,414	223,408	107,741	246,774	112,422	133,194	65,265	155,213
20-24 years	1,321,169	71,990	199,287	222,695	99,290	268,432	112,587	117,789	65,289	179,321
25-29 years	1,441,232	74,527	231,890	259,038	114,210	280,802	118,366	108,237	63,921	179,635
30-34 years	1,395,033	76,277	239,426	251,804	109,440	259,773	106,520	108,237	61,220	170,976
35-39 years	1,322,175	72,932	229,260	239,085	106,078	234,054	99,978	108,592	61,220	145,546
40-44 years	1,165,274	66,152	209,356	213,401	98,824	195,052	85,377	98,069	53,497	122,127
45-49 years	980,267	57,479	179,751	183,247	88,180	153,613	68,180	83,578	44,112	104,066
50-54 years	854,053	53,049	161,841	161,714	84,830	126,760	55,735	68,668	37,390	89,759
55-59 years	749,146	48,076	142,225	146,171	81,865	103,322	46,308	58,071	33,349	79,306
60-64 years	643,621	40,466	120,811	128,389	76,733	82,369	37,591	48,288	29,668	64,257
65-69 years	543,901	33,631	96,384	109,776	70,380	68,441	34,323	43,125	23,584	43,497
70-74 years	402,884	25,774	68,652	84,116	58,121	47,867	25,372	33,179	16,306	44,613
75 years and older	470,749	31,520	79,184	103,564	76,702	50,284	28,662	38,418	17,802	44,613
WHITE FEMALE										
All ages	17,505,535	998,669	2,973,754	3,241,652	1,624,876	3,019,104	1,400,895	1,484,566	780,911	1,981,108
Under 5 years	2,102,490	106,639	323,968	390,639	172,959	389,869	181,425	181,988	104,916	250,087
5-9 years	1,699,595	87,227	263,594	312,729	139,604	310,613	149,118	155,623	86,257	194,830
10-14 years	1,369,032	68,583	210,339	251,755	118,358	249,109	123,494	129,152	70,569	147,673
15-19 years	1,215,069	65,148	192,767	214,016	108,324	225,553	112,989	113,338	58,199	124,735
20-24 years	1,318,735	68,145	213,802	240,003	108,673	256,470	118,845	111,126	58,271	143,400
25-29 years	1,496,608	78,030	251,919	274,646	116,058	287,964	121,918	118,381	66,228	181,464
30-34 years	1,388,793	77,931	245,766	254,612	109,736	252,795	105,384	107,918	62,482	172,169
35-39 years	1,274,302	73,186	226,835	230,241	104,647	223,085	96,734	104,627	57,288	157,659
40-44 years	1,092,398	65,893	201,360	196,755	96,134	183,041	81,507	92,148	46,892	128,668
45-49 years	915,159	56,669	170,011	167,443	88,008	146,398	66,626	78,507	37,448	104,049
50-54 years	810,397	54,105	155,279	149,630	84,843	122,556	55,460	64,872	32,209	91,443
55-59 years	724,177	49,175	137,218	137,434	84,028	102,867	47,570	57,785	28,148	79,952
60-64 years	631,744	42,826	117,606	122,537	80,191	84,937	41,108	49,897	24,067	68,575
65-69 years	557,580	36,984	98,773	108,531	75,639	75,383	39,684	47,032	19,901	55,653
70-74 years	409,596	29,074	72,480	83,308	60,077	51,927	27,925	34,106	13,070	37,629
75 years and older	499,860	39,054	92,037	107,373	77,597	56,537	31,108	38,066	14,966	43,122
NONWHITE MALE										
All ages	1,593,592	8,406	80,027	73,922	34,701	705,998	266,072	289,316	55,532	79,618
Under 5 years	218,158	744	7,451	7,273	4,348	101,604	37,932	40,854	8,719	9,233
5-9 years	176,959	660	6,307	6,258	3,765	82,952	29,800	33,608	7,106	6,503
10-14 years	154,801	804	7,062	6,117	3,844	70,653	25,360	29,135	6,469	5,357
15-19 years	139,488	724	8,113	6,086	3,237	61,230	22,526	25,934	5,596	6,042
20-24 years	140,766	1,012	8,456	8,226	2,795	61,263	21,815	23,348	5,125	8,726
25-29 years	127,040	821	7,391	7,339	2,482	57,756	19,628	19,389	4,062	8,172
30-34 years	105,293	596	5,925	5,572	2,038	48,549	16,216	16,330	3,247	6,820
35-39 years	104,048	523	5,463	5,028	2,004	47,435	16,950	17,019	3,034	6,592
40-44 years	88,488	486	4,845	4,334	1,643	38,664	14,795	15,446	2,496	5,779
45-49 years	77,715	440	4,653	4,061	1,642	32,280	13,114	14,413	2,324	4,788
50-54 years	64,849	437	4,329	3,693	1,473	26,981	10,961	11,821	1,811	3,343
55-59 years	51,181	320	3,248	3,070	1,385	20,214	8,868	10,210	1,468	2,398
60-64 years	40,098	267	2,417	2,260	1,139	16,093	6,852	7,913	1,197	1,960
65-69 years	44,043	211	1,872	1,962	1,109	17,266	8,504	10,308	1,102	1,709
70-74 years	27,638	169	1,210	1,204	767	10,795	5,558	6,121	715	1,099
75 years and older	33,027	192	1,285	1,439	1,030	12,263	7,193	7,467	1,061	1,097
NONWHITE FEMALE										
All ages	1,565,551	6,997	69,271	57,396	31,465	713,703	278,487	297,491	50,686	60,055
Under 5 years	216,665	764	7,380	7,097	4,274	101,019	37,804	40,985	8,312	9,030
5-9 years	177,304	611	6,398	6,085	3,800	83,645	29,576	33,560	7,208	6,421
10-14 years	151,576	615	5,829	5,462	3,546	70,613	25,372	28,889	6,122	5,128
15-19 years	138,079	541	5,644	4,549	3,020	63,968	24,291	26,281	5,276	4,509
20-24 years	133,340	546	6,171	4,522	2,242	63,184	23,426	23,345	4,545	5,359
25-29 years	121,012	626	5,916	4,725	2,020	57,251	20,105	20,537	3,671	6,161
30-34 years	104,045	498	5,453	4,195	1,852	48,279	17,396	17,953	3,055	5,364
35-39 years	103,420	574	5,311	3,920	1,795	47,066	18,352	18,922	2,889	4,621
40-44 years	85,913	431	4,619	3,473	1,536	37,934	15,755	16,516	2,171	3,478
45-49 years	75,412	367	4,427	3,079	1,489	32,904	13,740	14,948	1,853	2,605
50-54 years	63,442	358	3,718	2,673	1,280	27,376	12,196	12,389	1,389	2,063
55-59 years	47,371	262	2,529	2,031	1,096	19,932	8,909	9,999	1,018	1,595
60-64 years	39,331	267	1,958	1,741	912	16,637	7,450	8,278	906	1,182
65-69 years	49,189	208	1,638	1,581	1,038	20,151	10,807	11,868	836	1,082
70-74 years	27,393	160	1,081	1,012	666	11,276	6,091	5,928	564	615
75 years and older	32,059	169	1,199	1,251	899	12,488	7,217	7,093	901	842

TABLE 67

POPULATION: AGE, SEX, AND COLOR OF THE RURAL-FARM (OLD DEFINITION) POPULATION OF THE UNITED STATES, BY GEOGRAPHIC DIVISION: 1950

Age, Sex, and Color	United States	New England	Middle Atlantic	East North Central	West North Central	South Atlantic	East South Central	West South Central	Mountain	Pacific
AGE, ALL SEX-COLOR GROUPS										
All ages...............	23,076,539	379,246	1,396,981	3,711,423	3,730,319	4,638,687	4,050,182	3,216,712	862,519	1,090,470
Under 5 years	2,621,830	36,969	141,925	383,637	419,372	560,837	495,419	369,240	105,969	108,462
5-9 years..	2,564,468	36,030	136,610	376,160	392,264	563,336	484,306	368,603	99,602	107,557
10-14 years	2,476,861	34,171	127,937	356,092	362,605	560,836	483,077	360,596	92,053	99,494
15-19 years	2,114,116	31,476	117,140	303,920	308,836	476,574	409,652	304,340	78,085	84,093
20-24 years	1,444,217	22,591	90,369	213,061	224,251	305,198	255,564	186,714	55,502	60,967
25-29 years	1,356,691	22,127	88,666	219,492	232,099	270,751	227,862	176,181	54,820	64,693
30-34 years	1,387,977	23,081	88,248	233,030	243,500	264,487	225,574	183,247	56,278	70,532
35-39 years	1,502,250	23,844	89,767	244,826	256,129	286,952	250,481	211,524	58,821	79,906
40-44 years	1,408,966	23,514	85,082	229,636	242,398	259,492	234,726	204,915	53,086	76,117
45-49 years	1,294,137	22,051	80,518	219,489	224,795	230,525	208,958	188,384	46,942	72,475
50-54 years	1,197,291	22,093	79,289	216,798	211,666	207,900	184,962	164,442	41,605	68,536
55-59 years	1,084,054	21,226	74,932	204,956	190,128	180,885	162,083	148,558	38,674	62,612
60-64 years	900,274	18,562	64,563	175,565	153,198	150,377	133,411	120,434	31,988	52,176
65-69 years	744,157	15,560	52,759	137,919	114,663	136,429	125,659	100,782	22,785	37,601
70-74 years	483,954	11,638	36,762	92,671	73,905	89,857	80,930	62,439	13,212	22,540
75 years and older........	525,296	14,313	42,414	104,171	80,510	94,251	87,518	66,313	13,097	22,709
WHITE MALE										
All ages.................	10,403,230	201,299	729,953	1,954,057	1,979,481	1,665,876	1,543,287	1,337,492	433,678	558,107
Under 5 years	1,087,165	18,967	72,020	196,356	212,690	176,364	169,715	138,951	49,525	52,577
5-9 years	1,083,547	18,664	69,608	193,382	200,014	184,606	173,334	143,305	47,051	53,583
10-14 years	1,059,837	17,952	65,949	185,054	185,678	190,014	177,814	143,054	44,315	50,007
15-19 years	957,753	17,425	63,547	166,619	169,594	170,420	159,084	127,275	39,488	44,301
20-24 years	649,580	12,628	49,053	117,149	124,750	109,129	97,963	78,993	27,836	32,079
25-29 years	595,282	11,532	44,671	110,277	118,911	94,710	85,834	72,400	26,106	30,841
30-34 years	612,186	11,650	44,244	116,054	123,321	94,894	86,405	75,029	27,075	33,514
35-39 years	675,049	12,271	45,771	125,297	133,049	105,036	96,586	88,820	29,468	38,751
40-44 years	650,131	12,289	43,822	119,641	127,925	99,662	93,130	88,152	27,494	38,016
45-49 years	601,284	11,782	42,162	114,711	120,195	88,652	81,670	80,333	24,536	37,243
50-54 years	565,115	11,674	41,235	113,747	114,278	81,274	73,377	71,792	22,197	35,541
55-59 years	531,037	11,369	39,954	109,744	105,555	74,093	67,661	67,087	21,317	34,257
60-64 years	457,964	10,245	35,148	97,131	87,741	63,645	57,998	57,267	18,811	29,978
65-69 years	371,267	8,653	29,525	78,012	66,824	55,779	51,295	45,648	13,497	22,034
70-74 years	248,589	6,605	20,746	53,268	43,634	38,540	35,165	29,777	7,802	13,052
75 years and older	257,444	7,593	22,498	57,615	45,322	39,058	36,256	29,609	7,160	12,333
WHITE FEMALE										
All ages	9,336,719	176,749	653,210	1,737,829	1,712,402	1,556,175	1,443,598	1,206,507	367,468	482,781
Under 5 years	1,033,550	17,895	68,358	185,290	201,210	168,673	162,462	132,393	47,056	50,213
5-9 years	1,018,636	17,273	65,645	180,690	187,341	174,947	163,718	135,121	44,235	49,666
10-14 years	976,660	16,079	60,591	168,726	172,134	176,492	164,766	131,698	40,429	45,745
15-19 years	792,947	13,951	52,395	135,651	135,350	144,891	136,646	105,565	32,291	36,207
20-24 years	532,952	9,873	40,143	94,832	96,798	91,206	86,723	65,475	22,518	25,384
25-29 years	579,508	10,500	42,883	108,325	111,080	93,578	87,436	71,237	24,455	30,014
30-34 years	614,024	11,356	43,028	116,054	118,203	98,353	90,199	77,310	25,824	33,717
35-39 years	646,123	11,515	43,023	118,386	121,055	105,206	96,868	86,412	26,158	37,500
40-44 years	598,614	11,156	40,399	108,818	112,542	97,164	89,836	81,613	26,971	34,115
45-49 years	545,786	10,196	37,589	103,507	102,747	86,456	79,738	74,276	22,971	31,460
50-54 years	505,540	10,337	37,374	101,864	95,707	78,345	70,287	64,440	19,817	29,980
55-59 years	449,941	9,787	34,433	94,095	83,153	68,291	61,114	57,286	17,206	26,191
60-64 years	361,831	8,269	28,963	77,512	64,268	56,161	50,206	44,463	15,591	20,330
65-69 years	282,321	6,865	22,879	59,153	46,755	47,931	43,229	33,575	11,659	14,044
70-74 years	185,084	5,008	15,812	38,918	29,618	32,609	28,592	21,378	4,567	8,582
75 years and older	213,202	6,689	19,695	46,028	34,441	35,872	31,778	24,265	4,801	9,633
NONWHITE MALE										
All ages	1,690,467	675	7,646	10,426	20,361	715,865	531,687	340,826	32,138	30,843
Under 5 years	251,359	49	801	1,005	2,789	108,189	81,931	48,916	4,748	2,931
5-9 years	232,688	47	710	1,073	2,560	102,344	74,152	45,427	4,165	2,210
10-14 years	225,815	90	756	1,267	2,511	99,670	71,705	44,044	3,786	1,986
15-19 years	187,645	50	641	880	1,976	83,354	58,445	37,182	3,174	1,943
20-24 years	113,099	59	668	636	1,443	51,478	33,737	20,459	2,667	1,952
25-29 years	86,843	59	612	474	1,075	39,905	25,233	15,122	2,232	2,131
30-34 years	76,634	37	518	417	992	34,481	22,442	14,175	1,700	1,872
35-39 years	87,112	31	529	558	1,004	37,313	26,356	17,038	1,642	2,641
40-44 years	80,479	35	469	591	1,002	31,603	24,956	17,247	1,388	3,188
45-49 years	74,462	34	444	656	991	27,400	23,358	17,239	1,422	2,918
50-54 years	64,511	45	388	651	956	24,061	20,552	14,577	1,215	2,066
55-59 years	55,980	47	332	624	837	20,611	17,933	13,314	983	1,299
60-64 years	44,948	31	296	556	714	16,676	13,787	10,618	933	1,337
65-69 years	50,112	26	227	459	662	17,772	16,853	12,079	865	1,169
70-74 years	29,061	13	131	279	392	10,660	9,803	6,548	534	701
75 years and older	29,719	22	124	300	457	10,348	10,444	6,841	684	499
NONWHITE FEMALE										
All ages	1,646,123	523	6,172	9,111	18,075	700,771	531,610	331,887	29,235	18,739
Under 5 years	249,756	58	746	986	2,683	107,611	81,311	48,980	4,640	2,741
5-9 years	229,597	46	647	1,015	2,349	101,439	73,102	44,750	4,151	2,098
10-14 years	214,549	50	641	1,045	2,282	94,660	68,792	41,800	3,523	1,756
15-19 years	175,771	50	557	770	1,916	77,909	55,477	34,318	3,132	1,642
20-24 years	118,586	31	505	444	1,260	53,385	37,141	21,787	2,481	1,552
25-29 years	95,058	36	500	416	1,033	42,558	29,359	17,422	2,027	1,707
30-34 years	85,133	38	458	525	984	36,759	26,528	16,733	1,679	1,429
35-39 years	93,966	27	444	585	1,021	39,397	30,671	19,254	1,553	1,014
40-44 years	79,742	34	392	586	929	31,063	26,804	17,903	1,233	798
45-49 years	72,605	39	323	615	862	28,017	24,192	16,536	1,167	854
50-54 years	62,125	37	292	536	725	24,220	20,746	13,633	987	949
55-59 years	47,096	23	213	493	583	17,890	15,375	10,871	783	865
60-64 years	35,531	17	156	366	475	13,895	11,420	8,086	585	531
65-69 years	40,457	16	128	295	422	14,947	14,282	9,480	533	354
70-74 years	21,220	12	73	206	261	8,048	7,370	4,736	309	205
75 years and older........	24,931	9	97	228	290	8,973	9,040	5,598	452	244

TABLE 68

POPULATION: AGE, COLOR, AND SEX OF THE TOTAL RURAL-FARM AND URBAN (OLD DEFINITION) POPULATION OF THE UNITED STATES, BY GEOGRAPHIC DIVISIONS: 1950

Age, Sex, and Color	United States	New England	Middle Atlantic	East North Central	West North Central	South Atlantic	East South Central	West South Central	Mountain	Pacific
AGE, ALL SEX-COLOR GROUPS										
All ages	112,004,003	7,301,979	24,040,753	23,694,140	10,748,319	13,635,997	8,130,061	10,917,572	3,339,147	10,196,035
Under 5 years	11,422,958	696,165	2,171,395	2,372,165	1,126,166	1,478,698	942,957	1,250,309	389,400	995,703
5-9 years	9,362,186	565,104	1,770,522	1,897,195	919,464	1,267,508	821,408	1,036,820	314,989	769,176
10-14 years	8,007,123	461,533	1,479,967	1,601,993	796,597	1,136,833	763,614	891,651	269,070	605,865
15-19 years	7,811,463	485,198	1,516,616	1,538,615	777,788	1,091,328	706,292	851,099	261,073	593,678
20-24 years	8,564,818	553,136	1,815,497	1,795,756	808,699	1,105,997	597,082	881,939	267,643	730,003
25-29 years	9,056,368	587,410	1,989,076	1,944,788	815,146	1,110,699	544,963	793,107	249,693	862,585
30-34 years	8,523,843	562,702	1,920,807	1,841,674	760,158	1,022,106	564,894	805,614	240,171	828,633
35-39 years	8,442,441	536,729	1,916,415	1,783,292	753,308	1,020,922	518,234	742,183	215,964	821,096
40-44 years	7,771,900	495,117	1,790,682	1,642,083	713,529	908,941	455,250	655,456	186,531	745,167
45-49 years	7,021,912	454,699	1,631,695	1,514,395	699,320	792,150	396,096	553,663	167,104	672,416
50-54 years	6,479,447	445,672	1,561,960	1,420,300	623,194	696,854	332,812	461,459	150,167	614,604
55-59 years	5,663,245	407,041	1,342,934	1,284,840	565,183	574,675	271,015	372,289	128,434	511,134
60-64 years	4,704,681	342,052	1,109,711	1,066,292	476,187	466,942	249,986	317,502	102,672	471,759
65-69 years	3,808,223	277,726	858,881	826,476	380,261	408,035	161,995	205,206	68,882	386,684
70-74 years	2,544,438	197,630	566,833	549,453	261,205	269,278	143,765	181,220	59,403	263,956
75 years and older	2,818,957	234,065	597,762	614,823	312,114	285,031	177,314	227,767	76,505	293,576
WHITE MALE										
All ages	49,100,512	3,477,575	10,871,906	10,894,952	5,172,383	4,886,233	2,968,944	4,487,374	1,623,608	4,717,537
Under 5 years	5,040,911	348,159	1,015,267	1,113,964	552,723	508,931	330,171	512,241	189,654	469,801
5-9 years	4,131,488	282,583	830,475	893,432	451,341	436,194	293,230	424,566	153,814	365,853
10-14 years	3,507,801	229,407	690,168	752,945	390,396	389,723	256,852	341,870	118,405	279,358
15-19 years	3,373,325	234,201	686,505	703,441	372,103	380,590	226,921	351,956	123,829	333,762
20-24 years	3,678,613	263,290	793,064	801,701	384,291	399,799	221,830	367,891	128,660	386,643
25-29 years	3,908,475	279,854	867,240	865,672	390,762	399,923	202,975	331,615	119,917	376,708
30-34 years	3,685,577	266,862	837,732	820,494	359,539	369,735	205,175	330,271	115,692	373,543
35-39 years	3,633,766	253,392	838,455	798,501	356,934	361,803	191,843	309,154	106,485	345,331
40-44 years	3,408,255	233,389	803,283	747,657	340,128	330,985	166,369	269,618	92,015	317,223
45-49 years	3,099,907	214,388	741,033	696,431	313,869	299,643	146,228	231,868	82,709	289,669
50-54 years	2,902,072	209,129	719,442	663,643	276,447	259,741	128,893	196,500	75,490	256,069
55-59 years	2,601,742	193,940	635,056	615,941	235,419	223,406	107,235	159,541	65,526	223,275
60-64 years	2,185,778	163,205	529,677	519,210	182,690	148,887	90,622	125,222	51,268	176,545
65-69 years	1,679,113	125,635	390,765	386,704	183,465	148,887	61,994	84,401	33,720	176,545
70-74 years	1,110,424	85,736	250,447	252,112	124,712	101,717	43,764	61,994	24,241	115,953
75 years and older	1,153,265	94,405	243,297	263,104	140,599	103,148	63,764	88,804	35,335	120,809
WHITE FEMALE										
All ages	50,307,301	3,686,510	11,392,140	11,074,445	5,156,785	5,028,839	2,999,065	4,516,683	1,592,393	4,860,441
Under 5 years	4,837,803	332,676	971,391	1,067,629	528,526	488,312	319,077	492,544	183,363	454,285
5-9 years	3,981,847	271,285	800,537	861,905	432,305	420,939	281,314	409,421	147,907	356,234
10-14 years	3,380,962	221,767	665,743	727,016	373,462	374,885	262,085	348,927	126,397	280,680
15-19 years	3,429,626	241,505	713,339	724,293	376,224	377,763	250,787	346,634	121,723	277,358
20-24 years	3,857,670	277,144	867,349	843,813	391,703	401,538	236,738	370,529	126,380	342,476
25-29 years	4,078,489	293,169	936,072	902,241	389,795	415,123	231,037	376,445	128,670	405,937
30-34 years	3,886,928	283,945	918,138	865,081	369,613	387,708	213,062	337,842	120,968	390,571
35-39 years	3,828,230	272,767	914,993	833,092	364,048	382,187	214,454	341,168	116,327	389,094
40-44 years	3,524,363	253,201	847,881	767,025	343,519	349,721	197,715	310,339	102,767	352,195
45-49 years	3,174,021	232,405	768,789	702,467	317,738	304,719	172,197	271,773	88,333	315,600
50-54 years	2,968,917	229,490	744,891	663,889	299,476	275,339	150,790	230,380	79,164	295,498
55-59 years	2,620,667	207,553	613,932	603,223	269,693	235,412	129,409	196,191	70,497	264,757
60-64 years	2,191,463	174,515	534,243	501,728	226,127	196,506	107,835	158,872	59,447	232,190
65-69 years	1,804,992	148,296	432,319	402,084	182,767	168,933	94,050	131,357	48,257	196,929
70-74 years	1,258,671	109,474	296,497	277,286	128,576	118,368	64,590	90,035	33,241	140,604
75 years and older	1,482,652	137,318	336,026	331,673	163,213	131,386	73,825	104,226	38,952	166,033
NONWHITE MALE										
All ages	6,110,455	69,387	841,438	844,130	204,298	1,796,833	1,040,843	924,080	64,056	325,390
Under 5 years	773,795	7,769	92,731	95,308	22,503	241,048	147,151	122,834	8,208	36,243
5-9 years	622,467	5,657	69,047	70,511	18,038	204,604	123,282	101,087	6,618	23,623
10-14 years	561,061	5,557	61,561	60,546	16,633	186,793	113,766	90,658	5,978	19,769
15-19 years	486,030	4,725	54,009	51,829	13,809	162,160	97,087	78,770	5,353	18,288
20-24 years	462,745	6,288	66,225	67,986	14,702	138,519	72,830	65,146	5,570	25,479
25-29 years	495,331	7,314	83,818	83,260	16,197	136,712	65,148	62,783	5,328	34,771
30-34 years	438,820	5,872	73,651	73,620	14,324	122,597	57,684	55,737	4,450	30,885
35-39 years	457,555	5,195	74,122	73,146	15,086	128,775	64,995	60,832	4,166	31,238
40-44 years	408,252	4,232	67,133	63,567	14,468	109,494	60,040	57,737	3,558	28,023
45-49 years	368,477	4,004	60,159	59,355	13,568	94,270	55,128	55,074	3,323	23,596
50-54 years	307,674	3,751	50,149	49,180	12,268	79,147	47,794	45,539	2,803	17,043
55-59 years	227,977	2,936	32,624	35,143	10,010	58,335	38,123	37,360	2,314	11,132
60-64 years	168,341	2,218	22,642	23,892	7,729	43,740	28,575	27,947	2,086	9,512
65-69 years	157,504	1,848	16,693	18,292	6,914	42,750	31,864	29,642	1,869	7,632
70-74 years	87,883	1,184	9,247	9,523	3,995	24,312	18,035	15,901	1,184	4,502
75 years and older	86,543	1,037	7,627	8,972	4,054	23,577	19,341	17,033	1,248	3,654
NONWHITE FEMALE										
All ages	6,485,735	68,507	935,269	880,613	214,853	1,924,092	1,121,209	989,435	59,090	292,667
Under 5 years	770,449	7,561	92,006	95,264	22,141	240,407	146,558	122,690	8,175	35,374
5-9 years	626,384	5,579	70,463	71,347	17,780	205,771	123,582	101,746	6,650	23,466
10-14 years	557,299	5,002	62,495	61,486	16,106	185,432	112,921	89,830	5,606	18,421
15-19 years	522,482	4,767	62,763	59,052	15,652	170,815	101,566	83,825	5,368	18,674
20-24 years	565,790	6,414	88,859	82,256	18,003	166,141	89,660	80,877	5,294	28,286
25-29 years	574,073	7,073	101,946	93,615	18,392	158,941	79,067	74,820	4,985	35,234
30-34 years	512,518	6,023	91,286	82,479	16,682	142,066	71,242	67,913	4,358	30,469
35-39 years	522,890	5,375	88,845	78,553	17,240	148,157	80,170	73,343	3,986	27,221
40-44 years	431,030	4,295	72,385	63,834	15,444	118,741	68,636	64,953	3,154	19,618
45-49 years	379,507	3,902	61,714	56,142	14,445	104,200	61,556	58,991	2,860	15,997
50-54 years	300,784	3,302	47,478	43,588	11,807	82,627	51,284	45,876	2,428	12,394
55-59 years	212,859	2,612	31,322	30,533	9,033	57,522	36,387	34,408	1,866	9,176
60-64 years	159,209	2,114	23,149	21,462	6,912	44,006	27,370	25,929	1,375	6,782
65-69 years	166,614	1,947	19,104	19,396	7,115	47,465	33,450	31,281	1,278	5,578
70-74 years	87,460	1,236	10,642	10,532	3,910	24,881	17,376	15,249	737	2,897
75 years and older	96,497	1,305	10,812	11,074	4,248	26,920	20,384	17,704	970	3,080

INDEX

D1482313